MACMILLAN
COMPENDIUM

AMERICAN HISTORY

AMERICAN HISTORY

SELECTIONS FROM THE
EIGHT-VOLUME

Dictionary of American History, Revised Edition and Supplements

MARK C. CARNES

Editor-in-Chief

MACMILLAN LIBRARY REFERENCE USA

Simon & Schuster Macmillan
New York

Prentice Hall International
London Mexico City New Delhi Singapore Sydney Toronto

Cover Photo Montage: Fireworks © Guy Motil/Westlight; statue of Lincoln © Galen Rowell/Corbis

Designed by Kevin Hanek

Macmillan Library Reference USA
Simon & Schuster Macmillan
1633 Broadway, 5th Floor
New York, NY 10019

Manufactured in the United States of America.

printing number
1 2 3 4 5 6 7 8 9 10

Library of Congress Cataloging-in-Publication Data

American history / Mark C. Carnes, editor-in-chief.
p. cm. — (Macmillan compendium)
"Selections from the eight-volume Dictionary of American History, revised edition and Supplements."
Includes bibliographical references and index.
ISBN 0-02-864978-8 (hardcover : alk. paper)
1. United States—History—Dictionaries. I. Carnes, Mark C. (Mark Christopher), 1950– . II. Series.
E174.A537 1998
973'.03—dc21 98-36732
CIP

This paper meets the requirements of ANSI/NISO Z39.48-1992 (Permanence of Paper).

American History

Table of Contents

N

O

Preface

ORIGINS

> *There has been an increasingly insistent demand for some one source to which an inquirer might go to find, and quickly, what he wished to know as to specific facts, events, trends or policies in our America's past. It is this need which the Dictionary of American History intends to fill.*
>
> From James Truslow Adams' Foreword to the first edition of the *Dictionary of American History* (January 2, 1940)

Since publication of the first edition in 1940 by Charles Scribner's Sons, the *Dictionary of American History* has been regarded as the most reliable and accessible reference source in the field of American history. In order to maintain this estimation, a major revision was undertaken in the 1970's and published by Scribners in 1976 to coincide with the Bicentennial of the American Revolution. A two-volume supplement was added in 1996 to reflect the many changes that have occurred in American life over the past twenty years.

Students, library patrons, and historians have indicated a need for a single-volume version of the prestigious *Dictionary of American History, Revised Edition,* especially one that incorporates material from the 1996 Supplement. *The Compendium of American History* is designed to fulfill that need.

The Compendium of American History retains the alphabetical structure and chronological sweep of the classic volumes from which it is derived. Mark C. Carnes of Barnard College selected articles that would best satisfy the needs of most students and researchers taking courses in American history and the social sciences. Nowadays American history is conceived far more broadly than in the past: the experiences of racial minorities, women, and workers, among other groups, figure prominently in historical scholarship, as do topics such as consumption, material and popular culture, and literature and language.

The need to distill the increasingly muddy complexity of American history into a single volume necessitated some compromises. This compendium provides detailed, unabridged entries on the major themes of American history, and on those signal events and developments that illuminate those themes. All of the nation's wars are included, but not the battles; all of the principal political, religious, and social movements, but not the incidents of specialized interest to scholars. There are proportionately fewer entries on topics such as academic psychology and literature whose relation to American history is commonly perceived as indirect. As in the original volumes, bibliographies and cross references appear at the end of each article. Certain articles in the 1996 Supplement were written to bring the original article up to date. In such cases, the Supplement article title is modified in this volume to include the language "Since the 1970s" or "in the Late Twentieth Century."

FEATURES

To add visual appeal and enhance the usefulness of the volume, the page format was designed to include the following helpful features.

- Call-out Quotations: These relevant, often provocative quotations are highlighted in order to promote exploration and add visual appeal to the page.
- Cross References: Appearing at the end of most articles, cross references will encourage further research.
- Photographs: Chosen to complement the text, the photo program is designed to further engage the reader.

There is also an extensive index at the end of the compendium which provides ample opportunities for further exploration.

ACKNOWLEDGMENTS

The *Compendium of American History* contains over one hundred illustrations. Acknowledgments of sources for illustrations can be found within in the illustration captions.

The articles herein, selected by Mark C. Carnes of Barnard College, were written for the *Dictionary of American History* and its 1996 Supplement by leading authorities at work in military history, science and technology, political science, economics, the arts, and general history.

This book would not have been possible without the hard work and creativity of the staff at Macmillan Library Reference. We are grateful to all who helped create this marvelous work.

Editorial Staff
Macmillan Library Reference

ABNAKI

Abnaki (from *Wabnaki*, "those of the sunrise"), a tribe of Algonkin-speaking Indians generally resident in western and central Maine. Although a population of 3,000 is estimated for them in 1600, some confusion arises because of the identification of the Abnaki with various adjacent Algonkins, such as the Malecite, Pennacook, Penobscot, Passamaquoddy, and Micmac. Possessing marked similarity in both language and culture, these groups tend to blend into one another, and all may be assigned to the Eastern Woodlands (Northeast) culture area. They were not drawn into the modified agricultural mode of life characteristic of some of the Algonkins to the south and of the intruded Iroquois but rather reflected a basic adaptation to the subarctic boreal forest. Hunting was the primary basis of subsistence of the Abnaki and their neighbors. Skill in hunting, together with its associated technology, permitted exploitation of available land and fauna, such as moose, beaver, deer, mink, and otter, and the development of extensive freshwater fishing. Wild foods were gathered, especially roots and berries; and wildfowl, taken in many ways, were important. Although village sites are listed for them in 17th-century sources, it was not the village but rather the hunting territory that identified both the Abnaki and their neighbors: the localized patrilineal family was identified with a specific hunting area that it owned and jealously guarded against trespass, and social units were thus made up of kindred people identified with a particular region. Birch bark canoes; wigwams and bark-covered houses; birch bark containers; snowshoes of rawhide; and a wide variety of traps and snares, again employing the subarctic rawhide, characterized the culture.

Although Abnaki political organization was family-centered, the strong political influences exerted by the intruded Iroquois made themselves felt early in the historic period. Political relations with other tribes began to be marked by the exchange of wampum, the tubular beads signifying ambassadorial status, as well as by the appearance of the calumet ("peace pipe"), suggesting increased emphasis in historic times on political and chiefly authority. Contacted in the 17th century and missionized by the French in the 18th century, the Abnaki identified with French interests. They were unsuccessful in hindering British expansion in 1724–25, and severe defeats reduced their numbers and forced their movement to the St. Francis River, in Quebec, along with many other Algonkin groups.

The Abnaki are best known through a dictionary compiled prior to their dispersion, by the missionary Sebastian Rasles.

BIBLIOGRAPHY

John R. Swanton, *The Indian Tribes of North America.*

— ROBERT F. SPENCER

ABORTION

From a medical standpoint abortion is intervention that knowingly or unknowingly terminates a pregnancy, but its cultural meaning and legal status have shifted dramatically over time, linked to changing ideas about sex and contraception and concerns about women's reproduction. There are few written records about the practice of abortion in colonial America, but historians have noted the absence of legal prohibition and moral censure in a society highly concerned with morality. Abortion certainly did occur, and with increasing frequency, in the republican era. A general loosening of sexual mores in the late eighteenth century, confirmed by a high level of premarital pregnancy, was accompanied by falling birth rates, indicating widespread use of contraception including abortion. Despite passage of restrictive laws early in the nineteenth century, abortion continued to be a widely used reproductive option, especially in urban areas. In 1871, for example, 200 full-time abortionists in addition to physicians practiced in New York City. Failure to enforce the early-nineteenth-century laws and the lack of public concern about the prevalence of abortion suggest a lackluster opposition to acceptance of abortion, even after some legal restrictions were enacted.

Beginning in the 1850s, physicians, through the American Medical Association (AMA), began well-organized and effective lobbying to restrict abortion, particularly when performed by midwives. At a time when physicians were striving to establish the credibility of medical science and their superiority to other health care practitioners, the AMA found an effective wedge in the abortion business, in which often dangerous abortifacients were widely advertised and sold through the mails, and any person, whether knowledgeable midwife or entrepreneurial quack, could set up a practice. The AMA also introduced moral and political arguments to appeal to opponents of women's equality. Physicians implied that access to abortion assisted women's independence and encouraged development of "unhealthy desires." They suggested that fear of pregnancy restrained women who might otherwise indulge in sexual pleasure while rejecting marriage and family.

The campaign to restrict abortion was primarily a professional lobbying effort with little popular dimension and almost no religious involvement except from some sectors of the Catholic church. Their influence was limited because of widespread anti-Catholic, anti-immigrant bias. Attempts to enlist the support of Protestant ministers by casting opposition to abortion as a moral crusade failed. Nevertheless, lobbying efforts resulted in passage of antiabortion laws in most states by 1900.

Beginning in the 1850s, physicians, through the American Medical Association, began well-organized lobbying to restrict abortion, particularly when performed by midwives.

Several factors contributed to the ultimate success of the AMA campaign. Lobbyists campaigned against women's rights, women's suffrage, and the presence of white, middle-income women in public life. Late-nineteenth-century women activists used the language of voluntary motherhood to argue for the right of women to govern their reproductive lives, because without birth control women from all walks of life resorted to abortions. Public advocacy of the right of women to control their own bodies, however, stirred deep resentment not only from proponents of women's domesticity but among Protestant nativists who framed the 1873 Comstock laws, which prevented dissemination of information on contraception and abortion and decreed that all sexually explicit material was lewd, indecent, and obscene. By eliminating birth control information, supporters of federal obscenity legislation and state statutes hoped to reverse the trend in birth rates and thus preserve Anglo-Saxon Protestants from committing "race suicide." Thus did Protestant ministers and their congregations begin to aid the AMA in its campaign against abortion. The Catholic church in the United States did not publicly join the anticontraception and antiabortion crusade until the late 1960s.

From 1900 through the 1950s access to safe abortions became extremely restricted except during the Great Depression. Increasingly a doctor performed an abortion only when there was a threat to the mother's life. Legal prohibition did not stop women from having abortions; it only made abortions more furtive and dangerous. The 1960s movement to legalize abortion developed from several sources. Physicians working in public clinics who treated women suffering complications from illegal abortions recognized the unfairness of psychiatrically based "therapeutic abortions" for wealthy women and the back-alley abortions available to poor women. They fought to expand reproductive services for women and deplored the previous AMA opposition to legal and safe abortions. More important, many feminists who had illegal abortions took up the cause of establishing women's right to control their bodies and reproductive decisions. The abortion debate was heightened when it was discovered that use of the drug thalidomide, marketed in Europe and elsewhere but not in the United States, had resulted in the birth of thousands of severely deformed children. The 1962 case of Sherri Finkbine of Arizona garnered public support for legalization of abortion after she took the drug—her husband had obtained it for her on a trip to Europe—and was denied her request for a legal abortion. Finkbine flew to Sweden for an abortion, and the publicity surrounding her case heightened public awareness about antiabortion legislation.

By 1970 Alaska, Hawaii, New York, Washington, and the District of Columbia had all legalized abortion. That same year in Texas a single, pregnant woman, Norma McCorvey, known as Jane Roe in order to protect her privacy, challenged the constitutionality of Texas law prohibiting abortion except in the case of saving the mother's life. McCorvey argued that this law violated the due process clause of the Fourteenth Amendment by denying her right to liberty. *Roe* v. *Wade* (1973) represented a dramatic shift when the Supreme Court affirmed a woman's fundamental right to privacy in reproductive choices. The Court decided by a seven-to-two margin that while women did not have an absolute right to abortion, a woman could legally terminate pregnancy in the first trimester (three months) of pregnancy. After the first trimester, however, states could impose regulations and restrictions.

Roe v. *Wade* led to statutory efforts to decrease access to abortion and to the growth of the antiabortion Right-to-Life movement. Restrictions on abortion imposed after the *Roe* decision decreased access, especially for rural and poor women. Only three years after *Roe*, Congress passed the Hyde Amendment, which allowed states to prohibit use of public Medicaid funds to pay for poor women's abortions except to save a woman's life. The Supreme Court upheld the amendment in *Harris* v. *McRae* (1980). Missouri legislators in 1986 passed a law further restricting women's access to abortion. This law was challenged in *Webster* v. *Reproductive Health Services.* On July 3, 1989, the Supreme Court handed down a five-to-four decision in *Webster*, declaring that *Roe* was not undermined by state restrictions on women's access to abortion. Five justices upheld three provisions of the restrictive 1986 Missouri statute: barring public employees from performing or assisting in abortion not necessary to save a woman's life; barring the use of public buildings for performing abortions even when there is no public funding; and requiring doctors to perform tests to determine fetal viability if the woman was at least twenty weeks pregnant. This splintered decision with its five separate opinions did not overturn *Roe* but eviscerated its meaning.

During the 1990s other Supreme Court rulings decreased access to abortions, especially for poor women. The Court affirmed the "gag rule" in *Rust* v. *Sullivan* (1991). According to this ruling pregnant women seeking abortions at any clinic receiving federal money through Title X could not receive abortion counseling, information, or referrals. President George Bush vetoed congressional legislation designed to overturn this decision, which obstructed the dialogue between pregnant women and medical care providers, raised free speech questions, and limited the reproductive choices of the nearly 4 million poor women seeking aid at the 4,500 federally funded clinics. Overturning the gag rule was one of the first actions taken by the Bill Clinton administration in 1993. Abortions were further limited by the Supreme Court decision in *Planned Parenthood of Southeastern Pennsylvania* v. *Casey* (1992). Among state restrictions on abortion upheld by this case were a twenty-four-hour waiting period for pregnant women seeking to obtain abortions and parental consent for women under eighteen. Women were required to prove "undue burden," that is, that state restrictions imposed "substantial obstacles" to their right to abortion. *Casey* did not find the increased expense to women imposed by a twenty-four-hour waiting period to be an undue burden.

In the 1970s, following *Roe*, the pro-choice movement also was challenged by poor women and women of color. Pointing out that high rates of sterilization and other obstacles to parenthood were as fundamentally obstructive as denial of the right to abortion, these women provoked a transformation in the pro-choice campaign. Feminists responded to these criticisms by expanding their movement into one for women's reproductive health and freedom. Thus, by the 1990s pro-choice activists opposed pending state and federal legislation that would deny increased benefits for women who have more children while receiving Aid to Families with Dependent Children (AFDC), the inadequacy of prenatal care for women of color, coercive use of the contraceptive Norplant against poor women, and continued sterilizations, especially of disadvantaged women.

According to the National Abortion Federation, between 1977 and 1987, 208 clinics reported bomb threats, 78 were either bombed or burned, and 60 clinic staff members received threats to their lives.

After *Roe*, antiabortion activists organized a grassroots movement that included an array of people and many organizations, the largest being the National Right to Life Committee. This movement held annual national marches and organized locally using networks with the Catholic church, fundamentalist Protestant groups, orthodox Judaism, and neoconservative organizations. Its members believed that human life begins with conception and that the fetus is a person under the law with civil rights separate from that of the pregnant woman. Thus, a woman's right to privacy and ability to control her reproductive life were pitted against the right of a fetus not viable outside the mother's body. Equating abortion with murder, many pro-life activists viewed as homicides most of the more than 1 million legal abortions performed each year since 1973. Such a position brooked no compromise. At the same time many opponents of abortion agreed that as a medical procedure abortion was permissible to save the mother's life. Under this principle, known as the doctrine of double effect, the fetus is not accorded exactly the same constitutional protection as a born individual. To say the least, those in the pro-life movement posed legal questions that may not be resolvable under traditional U.S. jurisprudence.

While most members of the pro-life movement remained committed to the goal of ending legal abortion through the courts or legislative channels, some attempted to overturn what remained of the *Roe* decision by direct actions, such as picketing abortion clinics, holding sit-ins at clinics, and engaging in harassment of clinic personnel and clients. Violence directed at clinics and personnel steadily increased. According to the National Abortion Federation, between 1977 and 1987 pickets surrounded 607 clinics, 208 clinics reported bomb threats, 78 clinics were either bombed or burned; and 60 clinic staff members received threats to their lives.

Beginning in 1987, Operation Rescue, founded by Randall Terry, became the major agent in the pro-life movement determined to close abortion clinics. Operation Rescue tactics included picketing, barricading, invading clinics, and using graphic visuals of allegedly mutilated fetuses. "Rescuers," as they referred to themselves, frequently harassed and verbally abused pregnant women clients and clinic personnel. Theoretically committed to nonviolence, some invoked the memory of Martin Luther King, Jr., but failed to condemn violence elsewhere in the movement. In response to the increase in harassment and the violence of clinic blockades, Congress in 1994 passed the Freedom of Access to Clinic Entrances Act. Harassment declined but death threats and acts of more brutal violence continued to rise. Pro-choice advocates attributed these developments to inflammatory pro-life materials such as those describing abortion clinics as "death camps." Pro-life advocates countered that this was protected free speech.

On Mar. 10, 1993, Dr. David Gunn was shot to death by Michael Frederick Griffin outside a clinic in Pensacola, Fla., the first physician to be killed during a demonstration. On Aug. 19, 1993, Dr. George Tiller was shot in both arms in Wichita, Kans. On July 29, 1994, Dr. John Bayard Britton and his escort, James H. Barrett, were shot and killed in Pensacola by the antiabortion crusader and ex-minister Paul Hill, who was convicted and sentenced to death. In December 1994 two doctors were assaulted by antiabortion protesters, one at his house in southern California, the other in Houston. On Dec. 30, 1994, two clinics in Brookline, Mass., were attacked by an armed antiabortionist, John C. Salvi III, who left five people wounded and took the lives of two clinic employees.

Abortion proponents called the spate of assaults and killings a watershed moment for the antiabortion moment. While most mainstream pro-life leaders condemned the violence, some in the pro-life movement declared their sympathy with the aims, if not the acts, of extremists, and still others continued to assert that murder of doctors and clinic employees was "justifiable homicide" in the struggle to end murder by abortion. The Clinton administration condemned the violence, and local and national authorities promised to step up clinic security. While antiabortion violence was expected to continue through the 1990s, many believed that science, in the form of the "morning-after" abortion pill RU 486 or other nonsurgical procedures, ultimately would diffuse abortion as a legal and political issue and that abortion would continue to be a private moral and religious dilemma for individual women.

[See also Contraception; Roe *v.* Wade*; Women's Movement.]*

BIBLIOGRAPHY

Ruth Colker, *Abortion and Dialogue: Pro-Choice, Pro-Life, and American Law* (Bloomington, Ind., 1992).

Barbara Hinkson Craig and David M. O'Brien, *Abortion and American Politics* (Chatham, N.J., 1993).

Mary Ann Glendon, *Abortion and Divorce in Western Law* (Cambridge, Mass., 1987).

Maureen Muldoon, *The Abortion Debate in the United States and Canada: A Source Book* (New York, 1991).

— NANCY B. PALMER

ACQUIRED IMMUNE DEFICIENCY SYNDROME

Acquired Immune Deficiency Syndrome (AIDS), an infectious disease that fatally depresses the human immune system, was recognized in the United States in 1980. By 1982 the disease had appeared in 24 states, 471 cases had been diagnosed, 184 people had died, and the Centers for Disease Control (CDC) in Atlanta had termed the outbreak an epidemic. AIDS has challenged the authority and integrity of respected medical institutions, strained the capacity of the health care system, forced the reevaluation of sexual mores, and tapped reservoirs of fear, prejudice, and compassion within individuals and communities.

On June 5, 1981, the CDC's *Morbidity and Mortality Weekly Report* published an article by Dr. Michael Gottlieb of the University of California at Los Angeles School of Medicine, describing five cases of *Pneumocystis carinii* pneumonia (PCP) in young homosexual men. A second *MMWR* article on July 4 documented ten additional cases of PCP, as well as twenty-six cases of Kaposi's sarcoma (KS), a rare skin cancer, in young homosexual males in New York City and San Francisco. PCP is normally seen only in patients with immune dysfunction and KS in elderly men. Under the direction of James Curran, the CDC began to investigate, hypothesizing that the young men were suffering from an immune-system deficiency related to their lifestyle. In early August, however, CDC staff identified the strange "gay plague" in heterosexual intravenous drug users in New York City.

In the first six months of 1982 cases were reported among hemophiliacs receiving blood components, Haitian refugees, and infants born to drug-using mothers. Transmission through blood transfusion was documented in June. Although physicians had named the outbreak GRID (gay-related immune deficiency), many suspected a viral infection transmissible through sexual contact or blood transfusion rather than a lifestyle-related disease; some proposed a multifactor etiology. At a meeting in July the CDC coined the term "AIDS," which became accepted usage for the several related disorders.

Many gays initially resisted involvement with the "gay plague," which threatened to deepen the stigma attached to homosexuality.

More than 1,000 Americans had been diagnosed with AIDS by early 1983; of those, 394 had died. Although the CDC had identified instances in which the infection had been transmitted through blood transfusion, the Red Cross and major blood banks refused to institute rigorous screening, which was costly and might discourage donors. In March the CDC and the Public Health Service, concerned about the risk of infection, issued a statement naming four "high-risk" groups of donors, advising them not to give blood and to avoid sexual contact. This warning, together with a May article in the *Journal of the American Medical Association* suggesting the possibility of infection through casual contact, heightened media and public awareness, intensified fears, and prompted ostracism of people with AIDS (PWAs). Some health care workers refused to treat PWAs. In many areas moral objections blocked inexpensive control measures, such as condom distribution and sterile-needle exchanges for drug users.

Researchers, including Robert Gallo at the National Cancer Institute in Bethesda, Md., and Luc Montagnier at the Pasteur Institute in Paris, attempted to identify and characterize the viral agent that caused AIDS. By January 1984 Gallo's laboratory had cultured twenty samples of a virus he named HTLV-III, believing it related to the human T-cell leukemia virus he had isolated in 1980. In February 1984 Montagnier's group reported their discovery of LAV (lymphadenopathy-associated virus), which they asserted was the AIDS virus. Their work was confirmed by Donald Francis at the CDC. Genetic testing established that LAV and HTLV-III were nearly identical. Gallo and Margaret Heckler, secretary of Health and Human Services, announced on Apr. 23, 1984, however, that the National Cancer Institute had found the AIDS virus and had developed an antibody test for blood screening, clinical testing, and diagnosis. An international committee renamed the virus HIV (human immunodeficiency virus) in late 1986. Shortly thereafter, President Ronald Reagan and France's President Jacques Chirac announced that the Pasteur Institute and the National Cancer Institute would share credit for the discovery and royalties from the patented blood test.

Isolation of the virus confirmed AIDS as an acute infectious disease, encouraging research into vaccines and therapeutic drugs. Lack of money hampered work, however. The Reagan administration was unwilling to initiate expensive programs to control a disease associated with homosexuality and drug use. Individual congressmen, including Phillip Burton of San Francisco and Henry A. Waxman of Los Angeles, together with Assistant Secretary for Health Edward Brandt, pushed for supplemental AIDS funding in 1983 and 1984, with limited success. Organizations such as the Gay Men's Health Crisis in New York and Mathilde Krim's AIDS Medical Foundation (AMF) provided funds but support for research remained inadequate.

The burden of care for AIDS patients, many without private insurance, fell on state and local governments and on volunteers largely drawn from the gay community. Many gays initially resisted involvement with the "gay plague," which threatened to deepen the stigma attached to homosexuality. Others resented public-health warnings to alter sexual practices. Gay organizations fought both universal antibody-screening and the closing of public bathhouses in New York and San Francisco, which authorities saw as reservoirs of infection. At the same time gay groups provided support, patient care, and money to PWAs, including nongays. Gays volunteered as research subjects in community-based drug trials organized by local physicians and developed patient networks that circulated experimental and imported drugs to treat PWAs suffering from opportunistic infections such as PCP and cytomegalovirus. Gay leaders lobbied for more money. A few risked community ostracism by becoming public advocates for safer sexual practices.

As of Dec. 31, 1984, 7,699 PWAs had been diagnosed and almost half of them were dead. Although the disease was taking a heavy toll among gay white males, more than half the cases now were nonwhites, including many women and children. The First International AIDS Conference, held in Atlanta in April 1985, made public much new clinical information. Participants debated screening programs advocated by the Reagan administration and public-health experts but opposed by gays and other potentially stigmatized groups. Conference reports contributed to increased fear and concern in 1985, which intensified when the country learned that the actor Rock Hudson was dying of AIDS. Shortly thereafter the news that Kokomo, Ind., had denied a young PWA named Ryan White the right to attend school with his classmates epitomized Americans' fear of and aversion to the disease. Attitudes were changing, however. Hudson's death in October shocked Hollywood, which was heavily affected by the disease. The American Foundation for Aids Research, supported by a Hudson bequest, merged with Krim's AMF to form AmFAR, which attracted support from such celebrities as Elizabeth Taylor. Ryan White was accepted by another Indiana school and became a national symbol of courage before his death in 1990. Health care workers, friends and families of PWAs, and others became AIDS advocates.

In October 1986 Surgeon General C. Everett Koop broke with the Reagan administration with a bluntly worded report on the epidemic, calling for sex education in schools, widespread use of condoms, and voluntary antibody testing. Koop's report followed statements from the Public Health Service and the National Academy of Sciences Institute of Medicine that described the administration's response to AIDS as inadequate. President Reagan in 1987 created the President's Commission on the Human Immunodeficiency Virus Epidemic and shortly afterward spoke at the Third International AIDS Conference in Washington, D.C. As the conference opened, 36,000 cases had been diagnosed and nearly 21,000 Americans had died.

In early 1985 Samuel Broder at the National Cancer Institute and other researchers confirmed that the compound AZT (azidothymidine), developed by the pharmaceutical firm Burroughs-Wellcome, appeared active against the AIDS virus in laboratory cultures. The Food and Drug Administration (FDA) quickly approved the manufacturer's plan for clinical trials and facilitated release to the market in 1987, although the efficacy trial lasted only seven months. The AIDS Clinical Trial Network, established by the National Institute for Allergy and Infectious Diseases (NIAID), developed protocols to test AZT in patient groups at hospitals across the country. Burroughs-Wellcome put AZT on the market in February 1987, at the price of $188 per 10,000 milligrams; the annual cost of the drug for some patients was reported to be $8,000 or higher. Although harshly criticized, the company waited until December before dropping the price 20 percent.

While NIAID pursued AZT trials, physicians and patients were trying other compounds to slow the disease or treat opportunistic infections. The FDA gave low priority to several compounds, such as AL721 and HPA23. In the case of others, such as the Syntex compound ganciclovir, PWAs received the drug at cost for several years under a compassionate use protocol. The FDA then required a blind comparison with a placebo before ganciclovir could be marketed, but few PWAs were willing to enroll in a placebo trial after they already had used an experimental compound or if they feared rapid progression of their disease. Investigators in the NIAID-endorsed AZT trials experienced difficulty recruiting subjects.

Gay AIDS activists sought access to more drugs, access to information about trials, trial protocols that recognized patient needs and risks, inclusion of minority PWAs in trials, and PWA participation in development and testing. ACT UP (AIDS Coalition to Unleash Power) captured media attention with demonstrations and street theater; the group soon acquired a radical image that alienated researchers, the public, and more conservative gay groups. The small group Treatment and Data Subcommittee (later the Treatment Action Group), led by Iris Long, James Eigo, and Mark Harrington, created a registry of clinical trials and gave testimony to the President's Commission and at congressional hearings. At the request of President George Bush, the clinical-trial authority Louis Lasagna held hearings in 1989 on new drug approval procedures. The hearings accentuated lack of progress by the FDA and NIAID and provided a forum for Eigo and Harrington to present their program. Anthony Fauci, director of NIAID and a target of ACT UP criticism, met with activists and backed a new parallel track for community-based, nonplacebo drug trials. The parallel track system was in operation by early 1990, but the concept remained controversial as it competed for money and trial subjects with conventional controlled trials. President Bush in 1990 appointed David Kessler as FDA commissioner, who quickly gained a reputation for activism and endorsed parallel track.

In 1986 Surgeon General C. Everett Koop broke with the Reagan administration in his bluntly worded report on the AIDS epidemic.

In 1991, after 200,000 reported cases and 140,000 deaths, the character of AIDS in the United States had changed again. Although incidence was increasing in all population groups, rates were most rapid among the poor, African Americans and Hispanic Americans, and women and children. Health care providers, researchers, and PWAs no longer defined the epidemic as an acute infectious disease responsive to early aggressive intervention. AIDS was recognized as a chronic disease characterized by a lengthy virus incubation (up to eleven years); onset of active infection possibly related to medical or lifestyle cofactors; an extended course involving multiple infectious episodes; and the need for flexible treatment with a variety of drugs as well as long-term supportive services. Public attitudes toward PWAs had gradually shifted from discrimination and fear to compassion and acceptance, but the burdensome costs of treatment and services were a challenge to the national will. In one example the Comprehensive AIDS Resource Emergency Act of 1990, often called the Ryan White Act, authorized $2.9 billion for areas of high incidence. It passed both houses of Congress with enthusiastic bipartisan support but a few months later budget negotiations reduced the money drastically.

Meanwhile the National Cancer Institute and its parent organization, the National Institutes of Health, faced a challenge to the integrity of one of NCI's most famous researchers. The remarkable similarity of LAV and HTLV-III (later HIV) prompted rumors that Gallo had allowed his laboratory cultures to become contaminated with a sample culture sent by Montagnier or had deliberately misappropriated the French virus, and that Montagnier was the discoverer of HIV. The Pasteur Institute filed suit against NCI in 1985, but the 1987 patent agreement had apparently settled the dispute. In November 1989, however, a long article in the *Chicago Tribune* launched a new series of investigations. The "Gallo probe" kept Gallo and his former laboratory assistant Mikulas Popovic under a cloud for three years. The investigation was complicated by the discovery that LAV had itself been contaminated by another French sample and that Popovic, attempting to develop a virus that would remain viable in the laboratory, had mixed together at least ten different viral samples. Investigators were unable to find any evidence of misappropriation but pursued Gallo and Popovic on minor charges until a federal appeals board overturned the Popovic case in November 1993. The case against Gallo was then dropped.

In late 1993 public concern for PWAs was reflected in critical acclaim for the film *Philadelphia* and the stage play *Angels in America*, both of which examined the personal and social consequences of AIDS. On Oct. 5, 1993, Congress approved an increase of $227 million in support, bringing the 1994 total to $1.3 billion. Fulfilling a campaign promise, President Bill Clinton created the position of national AIDS policy coordinator and appointed Kristine Gebbie to the post; in 1994, after lobbying by PWAs and researchers, he appointed NIAID immunobiologist William Paul to head the Office of AIDS Research, with full budgetary authority. As of January 1996 *The AmFAR HIV/AIDS Treatment Directory* listed 77 clinical trial protocols for HIV infection and 141 protocols for opportunistic infections and related disorders. Twenty-one drugs were available to patients through compassionate use or expanded access protocols. Researchers held out hope that the disease would prove susceptible to new agents used in combination with AZT and its relatives, ddl and ddo. Many trials, however, continued to have difficulty recruiting patients and some community-based trials were threatened by budget cuts. As of June 30, 1995, more than 476,000 AIDS cases had been diagnosed in the United States, and at least 6,000 new cases were being reported each month.

[See also Gay and Lesbian Movement; National Institutes of Health.]

BIBLIOGRAPHY

Dennis Altman, *AIDS in the Mind of America* (Garden City, N.Y., 1986)

Elizabeth Fee and Daniel M. Fox, eds., *AIDS: The Making of a Chronic Disease* (Berkeley, Calif., 1992).

Mirko D. Grmek, *History of AIDS: Emergence and Origin of a Modern Pandemic* (Princeton, N.J., 1990).

Randy Shilts, *And the Band Played On: Politics, People and the AIDS Epidemic* (New York, 1987).

— DANIEL M. FOX AND MARCIA L. MELDRUM

ADENA

The Adena culture was the first of a series of spectacular Early and Middle Woodland cultures in prehistoric eastern North America. Dating from about 1000 B.C. to A.D. 200, Adena sites are mainly concentrated in the central Ohio valley within 150 miles of Chillicothe, Ohio. The classic heartland includes sections of southern Ohio, eastern Indiana, northern Kentucky, northwestern West Virginia, and southwestern Pennsylvania. Even though the geographic extent of this prehistoric culture was severely restricted, the Adena experienced a cultural florescence that influenced the development of other Eastern Woodland cultures. The persistence of Adena art motifs, artifact forms, and ceremonial and burial rituals, particularly in the South and East, indicates the extent of this influence. For example, the raptorial bird, the hand-eye design, the death motif, and the circular eye remained dominant themes in Eastern Woodland art into the historic period.

Archaeologists have concentrated their excavations on the impressive burial and ceremonial centers of the Adena, which is why this aspect of their lifeway is known in greatest detail. The centers often contain both conical earthen burial mounds and large circular, square, and pentagonal earthworks. Open areas enclosed by the earthworks may have been the focus of ritual activities within the centers. Wooden palisades and round houses 20 to 80 feet in diameter are associated with some mounds and earthworks. The mounds vary widely in size and pattern of use. Some small mounds were built quickly to cover the body of a single individual. Other, larger, mounds were built up through successive interments over an extended period of time. Dozens of these burials were recovered in West Virginia from the 20-meter-high Grave Creek Mound. The famous Robbins Mounds site near Big Bone Lick, Ky., also has a large mound and more than fifty-two tombs. Graves ranged in Adena mounds from simple pits to clay-lined crematory basins and large log-lined cribs containing several extended skeletons. Important individuals were apparently buried in the larger tombs. Unlike later Hopewell mounds, Adena mounds did not usually contain grave goods.

The Adena people lived in clusters of small hamlets near these burial and ceremonial centers. Among the more unusual Adena artifacts are bowls made from human crania, rectangular stone tablets engraved with zoomorphic figures, stone chest ornaments in a variety of geometric shapes, shell beads, tubular pipes, and stone atlatl weights. Woodland cord-marked pottery and some southern check-stamped wares were used as containers. Evidence of the subsistence base that supported the construction of the impressive mounds and earthworks is still inconclusive. Varieties of pumpkin, gourd, sunflower, and goosefoot that may have been domesticated were found in association with Adena artifacts in Newt Kash Shelter, Ky. Small amounts of corn, a potentially more significant domesticate, were recovered in Kentucky from the Daines Mound 2, which has been dated by radiocarbon to 250 B.C. The basic subsistence pattern seems to have continued the broadly exploitive collecting emphasis characteristic of the Archaic. Although Mexican influence has been suggested as the source of the stimulus that led to the emergence of classic Adena, it seems more likely that the roots of the florescence will eventually be found in increased sedentism, population growth, and other indigenous Eastern Woodland processes. The Middle Woodland Hopewell cultures were in part a later elaboration of classic Adena.

BIBLIOGRAPHY

Don W. Dragoo, "Mounds for the Dead," *Annals of the Carnegie Museum*, vol. 37.

William S. Webb and Raymond S. Baby, *The Adena People.*

— GUY GIBBON

ADVERTISING

Advertising expenditures in the United States increased dramatically between 1976 and the early 1990s, rising from $36 billion to $126 billion. During that time, advertising followed the media in seeking narrower segments of the mass audience. This trend began in the 1950s. Although an audience would be smaller, it would be more attractive to an advertiser who had a specific product to sell. Acne medicine could be advertised on rock-and-roll radio stations that attracted teenage audiences, while hemorrhoid ointments could be sold on classical stations, which drew older listeners. Radio advertisers also responded to that medium's unique ability to reach captive consumers in transit via the automobile. The magazine industry responded in a similar manner. Such general interest magazines as *Life, Look,* and *Saturday Evening Post* lost advertising dollars and either went out of business or declined in circulation. Special-interest magazines increased from 759 in 1960 to 2,318 in the early 1990s. They appealed to smaller audiences that shared common interests—hobbies, sports, fashion, and music. By the 1970s running shoes could be advertised in *Runner's World,* rock albums in *Rolling Stone,* and vacation tour packages in *Travel and Leisure.* Magazine publishers were likely to use VALS (readers' values and life-styles) research. Also called psychographics, VALS research divides audiences into categories such as "achievers," "belongers," "narcissistics," and "societally conscious."

Cable television freed stations from the bounds of geography, released them from the interests of general audiences, and offered the opportunity to specialize.

In the 1970s the major television networks—ABC, NBC, and CBS—began to experience the same separations or distinctions in their advertising markets. The cable television boom began, a result of more satellites and cheaper satellite time. Cable freed television stations from the bounds of geography, released them from the interests of general audiences, and offered the opportunity to specialize. Between 1975 and 1992 the number of U.S. households with cable television jumped from 13 percent to more than 60 percent. The major networks' combined share of the prime-time audience shrank from 90 percent in the late 1970s to 60 percent in 1994. The result was a drop in the networks' share of advertising expenditures from 10 percent in 1980 to 7 percent in 1991. Special cable channels, such as MTV (Music Television, which went on the air in 1980), Nickelodeon (for children and teenagers), and CNN (Turner Network Television's Cable News Network, which also began in 1980), reached much smaller audiences but attracted advertisers seeking consumers who watched those networks. It no longer sufficed to know only the size of an audience or the circulation of a magazine. Researchers provided advertisers with information regarding audience age, income, education, marital status, location (urban or rural), spending habits, and political beliefs.

Newspapers that attracted retail advertising remained profitable, but advertisers increasingly advertised only with a city's circulation leader. This left only 2 percent of U.S. cities with two or more daily newspapers in 1991, compared with 60 percent many years ago. Readership remained stagnant between 1960 and 1990, with circulation at 63 million. Despite the many problems faced by newspapers in an increasingly electronic age, they still drew the largest slice of the advertising pie, garnering 23.1 percent of all U.S. advertising in 1993, as compared to television's 22.2 percent and radio's 6.8 percent.

One trend in advertising since the 1970s has been a proliferation of advertisements on virtually any medium that can accommodate them. Advertising and brand logos appear regularly on T-shirts, baseball caps, key chains, clothing, and plastic cups and mugs. Ads also can be seen on garbage cans, bicycle racks, parking meters, at the bottoms of golf cups, and in public restrooms. Advertisers place commercials on closed-circuit television screens above supermarket checkout counters and in airports (Turner Broadcasting's Airport and Checkout channels, and NBC's On-Site network, introduced in 1991), doctors' waiting rooms (Whittle Communications' Special Reports TV, introduced in 1990), and high school classrooms (Whittle's Channel One, launched in 1989). Star Broadcasting/Kidnews radio was introduced in 1993. Corporate sponsorship of sports events also increased dramatically, with PGA golf tournaments and college football games named after sponsors (for example, the Kmart Greater Greensboro Open and the Federal Express Orange Bowl). Corporate sponsorship became a major element of rock concerts, with Coca-Cola sponsoring an Elton John tour, Bacardi Rum sponsoring Gloria Estefan's 1991 tour, Pepsi-Cola allying with Michael Jackson in a variety of ventures, and AT&T sponsoring Harry Connick, Jr. Companies also sponsored cultural events.

As advertising proliferated, so did its guises. Movie producers began to charge for including products (product placement) in films. In exchange for money and tie-ins that plug both the film and product, producers display brands as props in films, excluding competing brands. One of the most successful product placements was the use of Reese's Pieces in the movie *E. T.* (1982), which resulted in a sales increase of 85 percent. In *Rocky III*, the moviegoer saw plugs for Coca-Cola, Sanyo, Nike, Wheaties, TWA, Marantz, and Wurlitzer. Critics viewed such advertising as subliminal and objected to its influence on the creative process. The Center for the Study of Commercialism described product placement as "one of the most deceitful forms of advertising." Product placement, however, was a way of rising above clutter, a way to ensure that a message would not be "zapped" in the age of the VCR and the remote control's mute button.

Although U.S. advertising agencies dominated the world in the mid-1970s, international agencies surpassed them during the 1980s by utilizing ads placed on television stations and in magazines in most countries. Many agencies have branch offices that adapt ad campaigns to local preferences. In 1995 only five of the top ten agencies in the world were based in the United States (four in New York and one in Chicago), while London had two, Tokyo two, and Paris one. The WWP Group in London was the world's largest agency in 1992 because of its acquisition of U.S. subsidiaries, Ogilvy and Mather and J. Walter Thompson. Companies that advertise outside the United States, some observers believe, prefer the British advertising style, which often uses understated humor. The change to international agencies resulted partly from U.S. antitrust regulations beginning in the late 1970s. Since the 1970s advertising also has had to deal with concern over international "cultural imperialism." Third World leaders have worried that the U.S. media, with the ability to reach remote countries, will destroy traditional cultures.

A notable trend in advertising since the 1970s has been a proliferation of advertisements on virtually any medium that can hold print, from T-shirts to key chains to plastic cups.

Since the 1970s advertising has provoked a variety of controversies, notably involving tobacco and alcohol advertising, which has been aimed increasingly at children and teenagers through such creations as the "Joe Camel" character featured in Camel cigarette ads. A 1991 study showed that six-year-old children were as familiar with the Joe Camel character as with Mickey Mouse, while another study showed a correlation between an increase in cigarette smoking by teenagers and the introduction of Joe Camel by R. J. Reynolds Company. The Federal Trade Commission in 1994 voted against restricting Joe Camel ads, but in 1995 President Bill Clinton announced stricter regulations concerning cigarette advertising and the sale of cigarettes to minors and demanded the cooperation of tobacco companies in educating children about the hazards of smoking.

Political campaign commercials began after the Republican candidate for president in 1952, Dwight D. Eisenhower, used television commercials in his campaign. Negative ads often have damaged the credibility of candidates. During the 1980s newspapers and television news programs began examining the need for responsibility and honesty in political advertising, but in the 1992 presidential and 1994 midterm elections, negative ads prevailed and showed no signs of abating for the remainder of the twentieth century. Concern also grew over the high cost of campaigning for national office, partly because of the necessity of television advertising, which handicaps less wealthy candidates and gives an advantage to incumbents.

As advertising pervaded American life, companies became concerned about effectiveness. Strong companies can buy all the time on a television program or all the ads in a magazine. In 1984 Apple Computer used "magazine-in-a-magazine" advertising to introduce the Macintosh, and in October 1991 Calvin Klein spent $1 million inserting a 128-page catalog-advertisement in *Vanity Fair* magazine, featuring photographs by Bruce Weber. It became increasingly difficult for advertisers with limited budgets to distinguish their products. Advertisers have sought to rise above the clutter with direct marketing, which includes telemarketing, direct-mail advertising, and catalogs. Direct marketing expanded to television with the Home Shopping Channel and QVC. While the established media—television, radio, magazines, newspapers—still held sway, direct marketing threatened to overtake them in the twenty-first century.

[See also Magazines; Music Television; Newspapers; Radio; Television; Tobacco Industry.]

BIBLIOGRAPHY

Stephen Fox, *The Mirror Makers: A History of American Advertising and Its Creators* (New York, 1990).

Roland Marchand, *Advertising the American Dream* (Berkeley, Calif., 1985).

— JEFFREY M. MERRON

AFFIRMATIVE ACTION

Affirmative action refers to federally sanctioned employment practices designed to protect women and minorities from discrimination and increase their representation in the workforce. Such practices resulted from a complex web of federal laws, presidential directives, administrative guidelines, and judicial decisions, beginning with passage of the landmark Civil Rights Act of 1964. Title VII of that act prohibited job discrimination and required employers to provide equal opportunities. It empowered individuals who believed they had suffered discrimination to sue in federal courts or file discrimination complaints with an agency created by the act, the Equal Employment Opportunity Commission (EEOC). The EEOC was commissioned to resolve complaints by arranging settlements between plaintiffs and defendants and to support plaintiff lawsuits. A year after the 1964 Civil Rights Act, President Lyndon B. Johnson signed Executive Order 11246, requiring federal contractors to "take affirmative action to ensure that applicants are employed, and that employees are treated . . . without regard to their race, color, religion, or national origin." Executive Order 11375, also signed by Johnson, added "sex" to this list. Both orders authorized the Department of Labor to establish procedures for such action.

The Department of Labor decided in 1968 that employers should hire and promote women and minorities in proportions roughly equal to their availability in qualified applicant pools.

The Department of Labor decided in 1968 that employers should hire and promote women and minorities in proportions roughly equal to their availability in qualified applicant pools. This decision assumed that failure to hire women and minorities indicated discrimination. Therefore, employers were instructed to conduct a "utilization analysis" to see whether women and minorities were underutilized (hired in proportions less than their presence in the particular applicant pool); if so, the department recommended actions to increase representation. The new policy reflected a shift in thinking about discrimination, generally assumed to result from the actions of individuals. Procedures thereafter assumed that discrimination can become systemic, independent of the intentions of prejudiced persons. In 1971 the Supreme Court ruled in *Griggs* v. *Duke Power Company* that "Title VII forbids not only practices adopted with a discriminatory motive, but also practices which, though adopted without discriminatory intent,

have a discriminatory effect on minorities and women." By setting a "disparate [unfavorable] impact" precedent in this decision, the Court let stand practices developed by the Department of Labor and by employers to diversify work forces. For example, targeting recruiting to increase the pool of female and minority applicants became widely accepted. Other practices, such as establishing numerical hiring goals and timetables (labeled "quotas" by critics) remained the subject of public debate.

Although some advocates deny that affirmative action involves preferential treatment, most observers acknowledge that many affirmative action practices are preferential. The center of controversy is whether the enabling legislation permits preference and whether preference ought to be allowed. Many critics believe that legislation permits only protective action, namely preventing and remedying discrimination by and against individuals. Such critics complain that class-action suits in particular discriminate against white men, calling such actions "reverse discrimination." Proponents of both individual and group affirmative action assert that results-oriented, preferential affirmative action, including practices that press employers to diversify workplaces, is a temporary, remedial effort to ensure that women and minorities receive equal consideration for jobs and promotion.

One effect is clear: affirmative action has eliminated many discriminatory hiring practices against women and minorities.

Between 1971 and 1989 several Supreme Court rulings established precedents restricting affirmative action. In *Bakke* v. *Regents of the University of California* (1978), the Court ruled that race (and presumably gender) "may" be a factor in university admission programs to increase minority enrollments. Other cases—*United Steelworkers of America* v. *Weber* (1979), *United States* v. *Paradise* (1987), *Johnson* v. *Santa Clara County Transportation Agency* (1987), *Watson* v. *Fort Worth Bank and Trust* (1988)—endorsed preferential plans but stipulated that remedies not involve quotas. In 1989 an increasingly conservative Court, including three appointees of President Ronald Reagan, made a series of rulings that suggested affirmative action might end. The most important was *Ward's Cove Packing Company, Inc.* v. *Atonio*, which reversed the eighteen-year disparate-impact precedent established by *Griggs*, making it more difficult for plaintiffs to obtain court-ordered programs. The decision reduced pressure on employers to adopt their own preferential affirmative action programs.

Many civil rights leaders, fearing wholesale repudiation of affirmative action, sought to overturn the Supreme Court rulings through acts of Congress. The effort was initially blocked by President George Bush, who called the Civil Rights Act of 1991 a "quota bill" and threatened to veto the act. The political climate changed after Republicans became vulnerable to charges of insensitivity toward gender bias and sexual harassment when, during testimony in confirmation hearings, Supreme Court nominee Clarence Thomas was accused of sexual harassment. Bush signed the Civil Rights Act of 1991 that essentially overturned several Supreme Court anti-affirmative action decisions, including *Griggs*. It restored a fragile base for antidiscrimination and affirmative action laws that urge employers to diversify workplaces. Uncertainty about the fate of these laws was underscored after Republicans, vowing to end affirmative action, gained control of Congress in 1994 and as the University of California's Regents repealed their affirmative action policies in 1995.

Critics of affirmative action argue that it exacerbates race- and gender-based hostility. Others assert that it psychologically harms individuals it purports to help. One effect is clear: affirmative action has eliminated many discriminatory hiring practices against women and minorities.

[See also Civil Rights Movement; Labor, Department of; Women's Movement.]

BIBLIOGRAPHY

Herman Belz, *Equality Transformed: A Quarter-Century of Affirmative Action* (New Brunswick, N.J., 1991).

Michael Rosenfeld, *Affirmative Action and Justice: A Philosophical and Constitutional Inquiry* (New Haven, Conn., 1991).

Bron R. Taylor, *Affirmative Action at Work: Law, Politics, and Ethics* (Pittsburgh, 1991).

— BRON R. TAYLOR

AFRICAN-AMERICAN RELIGIONS AND SECTS

The African experience in North America began with Spanish explorations in the fifteenth century, and some of the Africans who participated in those explorations were undoubtedly Christian, while others were Muslims or blackamoors. A distinctive African-American religious profile did not develop until after Africans were introduced into the English settlement at Jamestown in 1619. Of the original nineteen or twenty Africans exchanged in Jamestown by a Dutch sea captain for provisions, at least one was subsequently married in the local Episcopal church, but more than another century would pass before the Christian experience became generally available to Africans in America. Slavery was the principal impediment to a racially inclusive Christianity. Once African slavery had supplanted efforts at Indian slavery and European indenture as the principal sources of colonial labor, religion of any sort was generally discouraged among Africans in the interest of security and efficient slave management. The practice of dispersing slaves speaking the same language to discourage insurrection made the practice of African traditional religions based on a common set of beliefs and practices almost impossible. The drums used in ritual practices by various African tribes were forbidden. Soon a biblical justification of African slavery developed including the "curse of Ham," which allegedly forever condemned all blacks to do menial labor under white oversight. A similar religious and pseudoscientific convention held Africans to be a lower order of beings without souls, and therefore incapable of Christian commitment or salvation.

It was not until 1701, when the British Society for the Propagation of the Gospel in Foreign Parts sent forty missionaries to America to resuscitate the Anglicans (present-day Episcopalians) along the South Atlantic coast and to work among certain pacified Indian tribes, that any substantive effort was made to Christianize the African slaves. After protracted resistance from the planters, permission was obtained to proselytize some household slaves. In time, segregated auxiliary status was granted in some white churches. The vast majority of field slaves formed their own clandestine "invisible church" meetings, held secretly in remote areas, which eventually became stations on the abolitionist Underground Railroad escape routes to freedom. The first independent black church was probably a Baptist church founded at Silver Bluffs, S.C., around 1773. Soon there were other black Baptist churches all along the South Atlantic seaboard. These churches could hold worship services only if white persons were present and were usually prohibited by law from meeting at night. There were fewer black Methodist churches, because they lacked the autonomy enjoyed by the local Baptist congregations. By the beginning of the nineteenth century there were a handful of independent black Methodist churches in Pennsylvania, New York, Delaware, Maryland, and New Jersey that owed their existence to resistance to segregation in the white Methodist churches.

Elijah Mohammed, leader of the Black Muslims, at a prayer meeting at Griffith Stadium in Washington, D.C. on September 10, 1961. (UPI/Corbis-Bettmann)

In 1816 under the leadership of former slave Richard Allen, representatives of five of these congregations met at Bethel Church in Philadelphia to form the African Methodist Episcopal (AME) Church, the first African-American denomination. Allen had led the Bethel congregation out of Philadelphia's segregated St. George's Methodist Church in 1787 and was elected the first bishop of the new AME Church, which had a membership in 1993 of more than 2.5 million. A similar history of racial discord in John Street Methodist Church in New York City produced a second black denomination, the African Methodist Episcopal Zion Church in 1820. The AMEZ Church became famous as the "freedom church" because of the number of black abolitionists, such as Harriet Tubman and Frederick Douglass, who were once members. It was the first Methodist church to ordain women and in 1993 had a membership of 1.2 million. The Christian Methodist Episcopal (CME) Church is the third main body of black Methodism. Unlike its predecessor African Methodist denominations, the CME origins were linked with the Methodist Episcopal Church, South (MECS), which separated from the original Methodist church over the issue of slavery. After the Civil War however, many blacks wanted independence from segregation but also wanted to retain historic ties with MECS—that is, southern Methodism—and asked to form a separate body, the Colored Methodist Episcopal Church in America, organized in Jackson, Tenn., in 1870. In 1954 this body changed its name to Christian Methodist Episcopal Church to reflect its inclusiveness. In the early 1990s the CMEs had a membership of about 1 million.

Baptist churches reject complex hierarchical structures of governance and control, and they have accordingly been disproportionately favored by African Americans, who as slaves and freedmen were effectively shut out from founding or participating meaningfully in the life of many other congregations. At the beginning of the Civil War there were as many as thirty-five black Baptist churches in Virginia alone. The Baptist tradition of autonomous local congregations made denominational cohesion difficult, and a permanent denominational coalition among black Baptists did not emerge until 1895, when the National Baptist Convention, U.S.A., Inc. (NBC), was established in Atlanta. An internal schism in the NBC produced the National Baptist Convention in America (NBCA) in 1915 and the Progressive National Baptist Convention (PNBC) in 1961. The NBC is the largest African-American denomination, with 7.2 million members. NBCA has about 2.4 million members, and PNBC has 1.2 million.

Another major African-American denomination is the Church of God in Christ (COGIC), which was founded by Bishop Charles H. Mason in Lexington, Miss., in 1897. COGIC is a Pentecostal body with roots in the holiness movement of the nineteenth century. It is the only major black denomination with African-American origins and had a membership of 3.5 million in the 1990s. Together, these seven national denominations account for about 86 percent of all African-American Christians. The rest are scattered among the predominantly white Protestant and Catholic churches, and an undetermined number of small sects and cults. About 1 million African Americans identify with the religion of Islam.

Massive drops of membership that have corroded mainline white churches in recent years have barely touched the black church.

The black church is an inseparable part of the American cultural ethos and as such resonates to the issues and aspirations that define the general state of the nation. At the same time the black church retains a certain uniqueness born of its peculiar historical emergence and conformation, from which derives a distinctive sense of unity and direction. For example, the massive erosions that corroded the mainline white churches have barely touched the black church. Membership in the mid-1990s was not at its potential but neither has it plummeted. Issues of sexual preference, abortion, and gender relations have never been explosive in the black church. On the other hand, the hold the black church has on its youth is most precarious. Since the 1980s the black church has turned its attention to "economic empowerment." The results by the mid-1990s were not yet startling, but there were impressive demonstrations of the enormous potential the black church has for significant rescue of some of the millions of African Americans who need help to live with a modicum of Christian dignity.

[See also African Methodist Episcopal Church; Catholic Church; Protestantism.]

BIBLIOGRAPHY

Charles Edwin Jones, *Black Holiness: A Guide to the Study of Black Participation in Wesleyan Perfectionist and Glossolaic Pentecostal Movements* (Metuchen, N.J., 1987).

C. Eric Lincoln and Lawrence H. Mamiya, *The Black Church and the African American Experience* (Durham, N.C., 1990).

Benjamin Elijah Mays and Joseph William Nicholson, *The Negro's Church* (New York, 1933)

Gayroud S. Wilmore, ed., *African American Religious Studies* (Durham, N.C., 1989).

— C. ERIC LINCOLN

AFRICAN AMERICANS

The history of African Americans in the United States has been a continuous struggle against racism, segregation, and discrimination. Securing freedom as the Civil War closed in 1865, more than 400 years after the inception of the African slave trade, African Americans quickly realized that their fight was far from over and commenced a long battle for human rights. Despite many victories throughout the next hundred years, especially those secured by the civil rights movement of the 1950s and 1960s, African Americans continued to suffer setbacks. As the twentieth century drew to a close, persistent discrimination offset many of the gains achieved by African Americans.

A review of the demographic trends of the late twentieth century reveals the severity of the inequalities faced by African Americans. Between 1970 and 1990 the African-American population in the United States grew from 22.6 million to 30.3 million, between 12 and 13 percent of the total population. Civil rights legislation, educational opportunities, affirmative action programs, and residential desegregation allowed some African Americans upward mobility, but a vast majority remained entrapped by poverty and segregation. Unemployment rates ran disproportionately high. While 14 percent of the nation's population lived below the poverty line in the 1990s, the rate for African Americans was 33 percent. Poverty was especially prevalent among women and children. According to a 1993 Urban League study, at least half of African-American children were raised in poverty and single mothers headed nearly half of African-American households. Unemployment demonstrated similar patterns. African-American joblessness ran double the average rate. During the 1980s African-American unemployment reached almost 20 percent but dropped to 14.2 percent by 1991. The average income lagged well behind that of whites. In 1992 the estimated national median income was $27,325 but $21,609 for African Americans.

A 1993 National School Board survey showed that two-thirds of African-American youths attended schools populated predominantly by children of color.

The persistence of poverty and unemployment from the 1970s into the 1990s dramatically affected African-American life. Many African Americans were unable to afford basic health care. Heart disease and strokes remained the leading causes of death among African Americans but the spread of AIDS was an increasing threat. By the middle of the 1990s life expectancy was sixty-nine years, seven less than for other Americans. The difference in life expectancy between blacks and whites went beyond health care. Black neighborhoods were besieged by crime, gang violence, and drug abuse. A Senate hearing in 1991 revealed homicide as the principal cause of death for black males aged fifteen to nineteen.

The deterioration of urban centers precipitated by "white flight" to the suburbs; a decline in the tax base; a reduction of federal, state, and local funding; and the loss of job opportunities had severe consequences for African-American communities. Although African Americans began the twentieth century as primarily a rural population, by the end of the century most blacks lived in cities. Beginning in the late 1960s the African-American middle-income group began moving to the suburbs. Scholars have concluded that this resulted in a drain on the inner-city tax base and loss of leadership in urban African-American communities. Despite civil rights legislation, residential and educational segregation continued for the poor and many working blacks, perpetuated by the discrimination and poverty that confined African Americans to urban slums. A 1993 National School Board survey demonstrated that two-thirds of African-American youths attended schools populated predominantly by children of color. The decline of the average federal support for urban centers, which dropped from 11.5 percent in 1980 to 3.8 percent in 1990, contributed to the destitution of the black inner city and rise in crime. During the 1980s the numbers of African-American men incarcerated escalated, almost doubling from that of the 1970s. By the early 1990s one-quarter of African-American males were either in prison, on parole, or on probation.

Then there was the waning influence of the civil rights movement. With the assassination of Martin Luther King, Jr., in 1968, the movement lost its most powerful leader and shortly thereafter began to decline. Civil rights advocates found it increasingly difficult to influence lawmakers. Although President Richard M. Nixon (1969–1974) appointed African Americans to key positions and desegregated southern schools, many African Americans viewed his public opposition to busing as lack of support for civil rights in general. The Jimmy Carter administration (1977–1981) did not produce dramatic improvements in civil rights for blacks or other minorities.

The election of Ronald Reagan to the presidency in 1980 marked a philosophical shift in U.S. government. Reagan campaigned on a program designed to cut the size of and spending by the federal government. While Reagan and his successor, George Bush (1989–1993), actually drove up the federal debt with defense spending, they curtailed social welfare, and federal government support for civil and voting rights legislation gradually decreased. Contending that social welfare programs fostered dependence and hurt the communities they were designed to serve, the Reagan and Bush administrations reduced spending on job training, drug-abuse prevention, unemployment compensation, welfare benefits, and food stamps. Reagan attempted to block the extension of the Voting Rights Act and opposed the designation of King's birthday as a national holiday; his administration also opposed busing and affirmative action and relaxed enforcement of civil rights legislation. The Bush administration, one study suggests, did even more to undermine civil rights through budget cuts, legislative maneuvering, and appointment of conservatives to positions charged with enforcement of civil rights. In 1990 Bush vetoed a civil rights bill. Although the next year he signed the Civil Rights Act of 1991, critics charged he did so only to avoid a congressional override.

The election of Bill Clinton in 1992 raised the hopes of many supporters of civil rights. Committed to the civil rights movement, he spoke forcefully against racism and declared his intention to address problems plaguing African Americans. He proceeded to place them in influential positions in his administration and called for increased job training, inner-city revitalization, and health-care reform. By the middle of 1994 most of these proposals had failed. In addition, Clinton's cautious administrative style lessened his effectiveness. His withdrawal of the nomination of Lani Guinier as chief of the Justice Department's civil rights division, after conservatives questioned her position on minority voting, angered African-American leaders. President Clinton sought to reassure African Americans by continuing to voice support for equal rights, but the attack on affirmative action launched by the Republican-controlled 104th Congress appeared to be succeeding and spreading by 1995. Shortly after Congress successfully rejected the nomination of Dr. Henry Foster for surgeon-general, forces within the Republican party continued their campaign against equal opportunity, with California Governor Pete Wilson rolling back affirmative action laws and programs in his state.

Despite the federal government's uneven record on civil rights since passage of the Voting Rights Act of 1965, African Americans made advances in politics. Beginning with the 1967 election of Carl Stokes as mayor of Cleveland and Richard Hatcher as mayor of Gary, Ind., African Americans moved into local, state, and federal offices. African Americans served as mayors of such cities as Los Angeles, Atlanta, Washington, D.C., Chicago, and New York, among others. In 1988 L. Douglas Wilder was elected governor of Virginia, the first black governor in U.S. history. Although most African-American elected officials were males, African-American women were also elected. Shirley Chisholm of New York and Barbara Jordan of Texas served in the House of Representatives. Chisholm made an unsuccessful bid for the presidency in 1972. In 1992 Carol Moseley-Braun of Illinois became the first African American elected to the Senate since Reconstruction and the first African-American woman senator in U.S. history. During this period African Americans in Congress met together in the black caucus to further the cause of civil rights.

Despite the federal government's uneven record on civil rights since the Voting Rights Act passed in 1965, African Americans have advanced to high office as governors, presidential candidates, and to the U.S. Senate.

Tensions continued, however, and African-American liberal Democrats, who dominated elective offices, clashed with African-American conservatives, who secured appointments in the Reagan and Bush administrations. Black conservatives opposed affirmative action, social welfare, and occasionally civil rights, contending that support increased poverty and unemployment by undermining competition, individualism, and self-reliance. The philosophy of black conservatives received much attention during hearings for Supreme Court nominee Clarence Thomas. As head of the Equal Economic Opportunity Commission, Thomas received much criticism from Democrats and black activists who insisted he had not effectively pursued complaints of civil rights violations filed with his office. The Senate approved his nomination after heated controversy, most of which focused on allegations of sexual harassment by Anita Hill, a law professor at the University of Oklahoma.

One of the most important African-American political figures proved to be the Reverend Jesse Jackson, former aide to Martin Luther King, Jr., and founder of the Rainbow Coalition during the presidential election of 1984. As a candidate for president in 1984 and 1988, Jackson drew support from Native Americans, Latinos, Asian Americans, women, the poor, and working people. Advocating equal rights, he called for the federal government to support legislation and to increase opportunities for employment and education. Jackson made a good showing during the 1988 Democratic primaries. The coalition had difficulty maintaining its support into the 1990s.

In addition to gains made in the political arena, African Americans also made advances in the arts. Most notably, interest in African-American writers flourished in the last years of the twentieth century. Emerging to the forefront were Maya Angelou, selected to compose and deliver the Clinton administration's inaugural poem, and Toni Morrison, the recipient of the 1993 Nobel Prize for literature. Works by black authors exploring racial tension, the nature of the African-American experience, and the elements of black culture not only won accolades but also became best-sellers.

African Americans also gained recognition through their participation in entertainment and sports. Many African-American performers, such as comedian Bill Cosby, who originated the family sitcom *The Cosby Show*, and actor Denzel Washington, whose title role in *Malcolm X* received widespread praise, established positive images of African Americans and, along with many other African-American entertainers, joined the ranks of the nation's most popular stars. A similar situation occurred with many African-American athletes. The sports world offered an avenue of upward mobility to young African Americans and by the 1970s most of America's favorite sports heros were black. Sports fans of all races idolized Kareem Abdul Jabbar, Michael Jordan, Marcus Allen, and Jerry Rice, who led their teams to playoffs and championships. Tennis champion Arthur Ashe and Olympic skater Debbie Thomas made inroads into traditionally white-dominated sports. The long-term results, however, were mixed. While most black athletes offered positive role models for young African Americans, many in the black community worried about the media's focus on such achievements. They feared that the emphasis on sports led black youth to pursue unrealistic goals of fame and wealth through professional sports rather than careers in the sciences, business, and other professions where blacks remained severely underrepresented.

African American gifts to the arts include a flourishing of literary talent, as shown in the fiction and poetry of Toni Morrison, Alice Walker, and Maya Angelou.

During these years African Americans often turned inward to their communities to find strength and support. Black nationalism, which promoted pride in the distinctiveness of African and African-American culture, gained in popularity. Black nationalism assumed a variety of forms ranging from demand for neighborhood self-determination to calls for a separated African-American state. Its most notable advocate was Minister Louis Farrakhan, who in 1975 had assumed control of the Nation of Islam upon the death of its founder, Elijah Muhammad. An outspoken critic of the U.S. government, Farrakhan repeatedly called for compensation to African Americans for the centuries of slavery. During the 1980s his speeches included anti-Semitic comments and drew condemnation from both black and white leaders. He blamed the media for distorting his remarks. During the early 1990s anti-Jewish remarks were made by another minister in the Nation of Islam, Khalid Abdul Muhammad. A popular speaker on college campuses, he assailed Jews for draining money from the African-American community. Farrakhan's controversial reputation became even more problematic for black and white civil rights activists when he played a prominent role at NAACP meetings in 1994 at the invitation of the association's national executive director, Benjamin F. Chavis. Opinion within the black community was also divided when it was revealed in 1995 that Qubilah Shabazz, the daughter of Malcolm X, who witnessed her father's assassination in 1965, allegedly conspired to have Farrakhan killed. Farrakhan had long denied rumors he was involved in the assassination of Malcolm X. Farrakhan achieved some success with his organization of the October 1995 Million Man March, in which hundreds of thousands of African-American men converged on Washington, D.C., in a display of unity against the breakdown of black values.

The Los Angeles riot of 1992 drew national attention to the desperation felt by many African Americans. While the uprising did produce the appointment of an African American as chief of the Los Angeles Police Department, many of the community's grievances, especially the lack of economic opportunity, were not addressed. In general, the outlook for the twenty-first century was mixed as African Americans continued to struggle to realize the promises and goals of the civil rights movement. In June 1994 the National Association for the Advancement of Colored People (NAACP) organized a closed meeting of eighty of the nation's top African-American leaders, with the goal of eradicating joblessness, poverty, drug abuse, crime, and racism as the century came to an end.

[See also African-American; Affirmative Action; African-American Religions and Sects; Civil Rights Movement; Desegregation; Los Angeles Riots; National Association for the Advancement of Colored People.]

BIBLIOGRAPHY

Steven F. Lawson, *Running for Freedom: Civil Rights and Black Politics in America Since 1941* (New York, 1991).

Billy J. Tidwell, ed., *The State of Black America: 1994* (New York, 1994).
John White, *Black Leadership in America: From Booker T. Washington to Jesse Jackson* (New York, 1990).

— JILL WATTS

AFRICAN METHODIST EPISCOPAL CHURCH

African Methodist Episcopal Church, the oldest and largest denomination of Afro-American Methodists, organized in 1816 in Philadelphia with Richard Allen as its first bishop. The origins of the group lie in Allen's unsuccessful efforts to set up a separate place of worship for blacks soon after his arrival in Philadelphia in 1786. In this initial step he was opposed by blacks and whites. When friction developed around efforts to segregate blacks attending St. George's Methodist Episcopal Church, Allen, Absolom James, William White, and other blacks withdrew. Under Allen's leadership they organized the Free African Society, which developed into the Bethel African Methodist Episcopal church in 1794. Branches of the church were established in Baltimore, Md.; Wilmington, Del.; and several Pennsylvania and New Jersey cities; by 1816 a formal denominational organization was possible. Opposition to Afro-American organizations after Denmark Vesey's insurrection in 1822 checked the church's growth in the South. After several decades of slow growth the African Methodist Episcopal church grew rapidly during the latter half of the 19th century. In 1974 there were 1.1 million members and 6,000 churches. In doctrine that church is similar to the Methodist Episcopal, from which it separated.

BIBLIOGRAPHY

Harry A. Ploski and Ernest Kaiser, *Negro Almanac.*
J. Beverly F. Shaw, *The Negro in the History of Methodism.*
Charles H. Wesley, *Richard Allen, Apostle of Freedom.*

— HENRY N. DREWRY

AFRO-AMERICAN MIGRATION

In 1860, 95 percent of American blacks were rural dwellers and 92 percent lived in the South. In 1960, 14 percent were rural and approximately 60 percent lived in the South. Ten years later 28 percent were either suburban or rural dwellers and 52 percent still lived in the South. This movement from farms to cities of the South and from southern farms and cities to northern urban areas has been one of the major American population shifts. Although the shift of blacks to the urban North is part of the general urbanization of the American population, blacks became urbanized at a faster rate than others. Beginning after the Civil War, movement was at first within the South. By 1900 blacks outnumbered whites in Charleston, Vicksburg, Baton Rouge, Savannah, Montgomery, Jacksonville, Shreveport, and other cities. When white segregationists regained control of southern state governments following Reconstruction, the movement to northern cities began. Small at first, it continued throughout the 1880's and 1890's and significantly increased when wartime industrial needs boosted the demand for labor during World War I. The war almost completely cut off the flow of European immigrants who had supplied industrial labor, and the restrictive immigration policies of the 1920's prevented the return to the high prewar influx. The net black out-migration from the South was 454,000 between 1910 and 1920. The number rose to 969,000 in the following decade, declined to 348,000 in the 1930's, then spurted to 1,597,000 in the 1940's. It remained a high 1,457,000 during the 1950's, then declined slightly to 1,380,000 in the 1960's.

One of the major population shifts in U.S. history has been blacks' movement from the farms and towns of the South to northern cities and suburbs.

When migrating North, blacks tended to concentrate in large cities. New York's black population rose from 60,000 in 1910 to 1,660,000 in 1970. In Chicago the increase during this period was from 30,000 to 1,103,000; in Baltimore from 79,000 to 420,000; and in Washington, D.C., from 86,000 to 538,000. Even greater increases occurred in Detroit and Los Angeles, where the black population increased from 4,000 and 2,000, respectively, in 1910 to 660,000 and 523,000 in 1970. The 1970 census reported 72 percent of all blacks lived in cities, compared with 70 percent for the total population.

The causes of the migration were mainly but not entirely economic. The wage rate fell rapidly in the 1910's as a result of declining farm prices. In 1915 and 1916 a succession of floods and crop failures and increased destruction by the boll weevil drove many out of agriculture. Add to these the precarious economic condition of black tenant farmers and sharecroppers even in "good times" and the pressures to leave the South were clear. When war-stimulated industries offered opportunities for gainful employment at wages higher than those paid in the South, large numbers of blacks responded.

Also, less overt discrimination in day-to-day activities, better public school facilities, suffrage, possibilities for justice in the courts, and access to public places were available to a greater degree in the North. A contemporary effort to assess the cause and nature of the black migration, sponsored by the U.S. Department of Labor in 1917, pointed to the treatment blacks received at the hands of southern whites as an important factor.

While migration to the North allowed blacks to improve their condition, it was not without its problems. Northern life failed to fulfill the democratic expectations held by Afro-Americans. Crime, the shortage of housing, limitations on occupational advancement, and the breakdown of family and community under pressures of urban living became major concerns. In addition the increased numbers of blacks stimulated latent racism among white northerners. The creation of black ghettos, high unemployment among blacks, and a series of urban riots reflect the nature and intensity of white reactions.

— HENRY N. DREWRY

AGRARIAN MOVEMENT

Even before formation of the federal system, American agrarianism developed into one of the major forces shaping the policies of the new nation. The early agrarian movement was a mixture of philosophic idealism rooted in the 18th-century Enlightenment and in the hard, practical demands of colonial farmers, who were essentially a debtor class. As the nation evolved, agrarianism became a tradition of independence and self-reliance, of progress and scientific improvement, tinged with a sentimental romanticism that reached its height among American writers and artists of the 19th century.

Ten years before the Declaration of Independence, Thomas Jefferson expressed the classic ideal of agrarianism in his *Notes on Virginia*: "Those who labor in the earth are the chosen people of God, if He ever had a chosen people, whose breasts He has made His peculiar deposit for substantial and genuine virtue. It is the focus in which He keeps alive that sacred fire, which otherwise might escape from the face of the earth." Jefferson viewed the growth of industrialism and the concentration of population in cities as a menace to the fledgling republic, and he wanted to keep the Industrial Revolution confined to Europe. "It is better to carry provisions and materials to workmen there than bring them to the provisions and materials, and with them their manners and principles. . . . The mobs of great cities add just so much to the support of pure government, as sores do to the strength of the human body."

Although the population of the new nation at the end of the Revolution was mostly agricultural, the powerful merchant and trader class along the eastern seaboard attempted to dominate the debt-ridden farmers of the backcountry. This rivalry between agricultural and commercial interests was an important factor in the development of the two-party political system. The Federalists, led by Alexander Hamilton, advocated a strong central government favorable to commerce and opposed the rights of state governments, which agrarians sometimes controlled. The Jeffersonian Republicans, following the philosophy of their leader, represented the agrarians. After Jefferson was elected president in 1800, restrictive excise duties were repealed, and the purchase of the Louisiana Territory widened the land area for agrarian expansion and assured use of the Mississippi River as a market route to New Orleans for Jefferson's idealized "yeoman farmers."

Jefferson wanted the Industrial Revolution confined to Europe; he saw industrialism and burgeoning cities as a threat to the fledgling republic.

From these beginnings the agrarian movement continued to be closely involved with political movements. In the 1830's, when urban business interests gained power among National Republicans, the agrarians shifted to the Jacksonian Democrats. After slavery and the coming of the Civil War caused a split between plantation owners of the South and free-soil farmers of the North and West, the Republican party of President Abraham Lincoln won strong agrarian support with passage of the Homestead Act, creation of the U.S. Department of Agriculture, and passage of the Morrill Act establishing land grant colleges. During the agricultural depression of the 1890's many farmers turned to a third-party movement—the Populist—but they soon followed William J. Bryan to the Democratic party. In the 1920's other third-party movements had agrarian backing, but the New Deal measures of the Democrats in the 1930's won back a majority of the nation's farmers to that party.

Agrarianism was also a major force in the national expansionist movement that began with Jefferson's Louisiana Purchase (1803) and reached its zenith with the doctrine of Manifest Destiny (1845) and the conquest of Mexican and Indian lands. The expanding frontier, where there was always land for landless Americans, was regarded as a natural right, and the image of the farmer-settler became the national ideal. In 1858, Ralph Waldo Emerson was extolling the strength and dignity of the countryman, advising those poisoned by urban life and urban vices to go back to the land. By this time, however, the countrymen themselves were expressing skepticism about the traditional myths of rural life and its virtues as portrayed by poets, artists, and politicians, who never mentioned the endless toil, discomforts, and deprivations of farm life as compared with the social amenities, cultural opportunities, and higher standard of living of urban areas.

In the period after the Civil War, the contrasts between rural and urban life were so extreme that the agrarian movement became a movement of farmer organizations—such as the Grange and various alliances, unions, and bureaus—designed to improve the position of farmers in American society. These organizations forced passage of many laws favorable to agriculture, with the Department of Agriculture responsible for execution.

As an intellectual movement agrarianism again flowered briefly in the 1930's after a group of southern writers known as the Fugitives issued a statement of principles advocating rejection of industrialism and a national reacceptance of agrarianism. Instead of emancipating laborers, industry "evicts them," the Fugitives charged, and they expressed the belief "that the culture of the soil is the best and most sensitive of vocations and that therefore it should have the economic preference and enlist the maximum number of workers." With the deepening of the economic depression of the 1930's, which brought about a back-to-the-land movement among thousands of unemployed industrial workers, the theories of the Fugitives were widely debated. After World War II, however, the South—which the agrarians had viewed as the base for their movement—turned rapidly away from its agricultural tradition toward industrialization.

Technological changes, which had begun during the 19th century, accelerated after the war and revolutionized agriculture nationally. By 1960, two-thirds of all Americans lived in urban areas as compared with the extreme minority of Jefferson's time. Distinctions between urban and rural life vanished as the result of automobiles and paved highways, farm price supports, mechanized farming, standardized education, and a wide diffusion of information and entertainment through print and the electronic media. Cultural deprivations and social aridities were virtually eliminated from rural life, and farmers became businessmen with attitudes and values similar to those of their counterparts in cities. In the 20th century farm organizations adopted the methods of big business—some of them using the same pressure politics of industrial corporations—as well as extolling free enterprise and opposing excessive government regulation.

BIBLIOGRAPHY

Solon J. Buck, *The Agrarian Crusade.*

U.S. Department of Agriculture, *Farmers in a Changing World.*

— DEE BROWN

AGRICULTURE, DEPARTMENT OF

The functions of the U.S. Department of Agriculture (USDA) continued to expand after 1970 as farms and farming changed dramatically. The habits of food consumption in the United States also changed, and USDA became concerned that agriculture produce plentiful supplies of wholesome food and natural fibers, including cotton and wood. Further, USDA supervised the sharing of U.S. abundance with less fortunate countries. The department's work included food inspection and grading, monitoring of imports for health hazards, protecting genetic bases for research, and managing national forests. USDA increased research and education on soil erosion, agricultural water pollution, and conservation tillage. It expanded school breakfast and lunch programs, food stamps, and other assistance for lower-income Americans.

The USDA also provided food for lower-income countries through credit, donations, and the Export Enhancement Program, which reduces prices to foreign buyers. It helped sub-Saharan Africa through food crises. Export assistance programs in the 1990s helped the former Soviet Union and Eastern Europe shift from communism toward democracy; USDA programs helped such countries buy pork, poultry, vegetable oils, corn, wheat, sorghum, barley, soybeans, and soybean meal. Food assistance reinforced Middle East peace agreements. To promote agricultural exports and conduct diplomatic activities involving agriculture, USDA maintained agricultural counselors in most countries. The USDA provides statistical and economic information to help formulate agricultural policies, and this work increased beginning in the 1970s when U.S. agriculture encountered strong and volatile export demand. In 1973 USDA temporarily restricted agricultural exports because of limited domestic supplies. In the 1980s and early 1990s the government briefly instituted food export embargoes against the USSR, Iran, and Iraq to discourage hostile action against neighboring nations. The department was heavily involved in the U.S.-Canadian Free Trade Agreement, the North American Free Trade Agreement, and the General Agreement on Tariffs and Trade negotiations.

The USDA used its regional laboratories and the resources of land-grant universities to improve farming and marketing. Its Extension Service helped inform the public of this research. USDA researchers developed fruit varieties with reduced susceptibility to freezing, varieties of grain resistant to insects, and tomatoes that resist damage in handling and can ripen longer on the vine. They also developed improved methods of inspecting meat and preventing bacterial contamination during processing. Food safety became a key issue with two deaths and 400 cases of serious illness from meat contaminated with a deadly string of *Escherichia coli* bacteria in 1993. Approval in 1994 of bovine somatotropin (BST), which dramatically increases productivity of dairy cows, involved discussions over safety. USDA was reorganized in late 1994 and 1995. Field offices were consolidated and agencies combined, reducing the workforce by 7 percent and lowering costs $800 million per year. Reorganization was not expected to reduce the scope of USDA responsibilities.

BIBLIOGRAPHY

Wayne D. Rasmussen and G. L. Baker, *The Department of Agriculture* (New York, 1972).

U.S. Department of Agriculture, *An Overview of Federal Food Safety Research* (Washington, D.C., 1993), and *Report of the Secretary of Agriculture*, annual issues.

— ROBERT WISNER

AIR FORCE, UNITED STATES

Although the U.S. Air Force did not achieve independent status until 1947, the history of American military aviation reaches back to the Civil War, when civilian aeronauts and enlisted ground crews operated observation balloons for Union forces. The War Department became interested in heavier-than-air flight, funding the efforts of Samuel P. Langley in 1898, but was slow to exploit the work of the Wright brothers after their first powered flights in 1903. On Aug. 1, 1907, the U.S. Army created an aeronautical division within the Signal Corps, to take charge "of all matters pertaining to military ballooning, air machines, and all kindred subjects," and in 1909 it purchased its first airplane from the Wrights. Subsequent funding for aviation was tight, and weaknesses in this new military field were revealed in the 1916 Mexican border campaign. When the United States entered World War I, the American aviation arm possessed only thirty-five pilots and fifty-five mechanics.

The wartime Congress voted large sums for aviation, envisioning a decisive American air contribution. Results were disappointing, mainly because of American inexperience in aircraft design and production. Fewer than 200 planes of 740 in use by American squadrons at the close of hostilities were American built. The brief combat record was nevertheless creditable, over seventy American pilots qualifying as "aces" by destroying five or more enemy craft. In August 1918 certain French and all American frontline air units were placed under a single commander, Brig. Gen. William (Billy) Mitchell. Supported by other Allied units, Mitchell directed the war's heaviest concentration of air power in attacks against the German lines and rear areas about Saint-Mihiel. A similar, though smaller, air concentration was effected under Mitchell for the final Meuse-Argonne campaign.

When the U.S. entered the First World War, the American aviation arm had 35 pilots and 55 mechanics.

The air arm was separated from the Signal Corps in May 1918 and by legislation in 1920 became the Air Service, one of seven combatant arms of the army. The reform fell short of that recommended by air officers, and the energetic Mitchell promoted projects to increase awareness of the potential of aviation. A mass transcontinental flight in 1919, tests against battleships in 1921 and 1923, and a global circumnavigation advanced aviation, but failed to win further reform. Embittered, Mitchell invited the 1925 court-martial that ended his military career. Modest gains were detectable in the Air Corps Act of 1926, which changed the Air Service to the Air Corps, increased air representation on the General Staff, and authorized expansion. Funding remained tight, and when in 1934 the Air Corps undertook to fly the nation's airmail, a series of crashes ensued, revealing the arm's poor condition. Partial reorganization followed, establishing a single headquarters for control of most Air Corps combat units. In the 1930's aircraft and doctrine for "strategic" (or independent) air warfare emerged. The new heavy bomber, the XB-17, flew nonstop from Seattle to Dayton in August 1935. In contemplating employment of the new weapon, Air Corps officers avoided the idea of attacking civilian populations, but spoke of long-range coastal defense and, more circumspectly, of daylight, precision attacks against vulnerable joints of an enemy's economic system.

The collapse of France in 1940 shocked the United States into a massive air rearmament effort. The Army Air Forces (AAF) was created in June 1941, becoming coequal the following year with the army ground forces and the services of supply. The air arm thus attained a position of autonomy not far short of full independence.

World War II

The Japanese attackers on Dec. 7, 1941, badly surprised the AAF defenders of Hawaii. Later in the day, Japanese planes destroyed two B-17 squadrons on the ground in Luzon, soon thereafter establishing full command of the air over the Philippines. More psychological than strategic was the AAF reply—an attack on Tokyo on Apr. 18, 1942, by sixteen twin-engine bombers led by Lt. Col. James Doolittle and launched from the carrier *Hornet.* After building up forces in Australia, the AAF progressively regained command of the air over the southwest Pacific, attacking Japanese airfields, interdicting sea communications, and spearheading Gen. Douglas MacArthur's amphibious and airborne advance toward the Philippines. Seven days after the Oct. 20, 1944, landings at Leyte, P-38 fighters flew into a beachhead strip at Tacloban; after several weeks, Allied carrier- and land-based air units gained full dominance over Japanese air strength in the Philippines. Meanwhile, AAF transport aircraft based in India were sustaining Allied forces in difficult campaigns in Burma and were performing massive lifts of matériel into China, encouraging the Chinese to continue a war effort.

In the Mediterranean theater, AAF bombers contributed to late-1942 victories at both ends of North Africa. After assembling superior air forces and placing them under centralized control, the Allies asserted air supremacy over Tunisia, contributing massive tactical air support during the final ground offensive in April 1943. During the campaigns in Sicily and Italy, the AAF steadily pounded enemy communications (the extent of success is still controversial). Attacks against the Ploesti oil fields in Romania began with a historic raid on Aug. 1, 1943, carried out by more than 170 B-24's and costing 54 bombers. The Mediterranean air campaigns weakened Axis air power, but delayed both the campaign against the Luftwaffe over Germany, seen as an essential preliminary to the cross-channel assault, and the full buildup of the AAF in Britain.

The daylight air battle of Germany opened in 1943, although AAF heavy bombers regularly attacked France in 1942 and the RAF Bomber Command had long operated over Germany by night. The Americans were nearly defeated in their daylight air offensive, since escort fighters could accompany the bombers only as far as the German border. Over sixty four-engine heavies were lost on Aug. 17, 1943, in attacking ball-bearing factories at Schweinfurt and the fighter assembly plant at Regensburg, both deep inside Germany. A second Schweinfurt raid on Oct. 14 cost another sixty bombers. The tide turned in early 1944, when the Americans began using long-range P-47's (Thunderbolts) and P-51's (Mustangs), modified with external fuel tanks that eventually extended escort fighter radius beyond Berlin. These high-performance craft attacked the Luftwaffe in the air and on the ground, defeating an enemy already weakened by shortages of fuel and experienced pilots. In June 1944 the Normandy invasion proceeded without enemy air interference; the assault began with a two-division night parachute drop from AAF transports. Massive Allied tactical air forces supported the ensuing ground campaign. The heavy bombers, finally at full strength in mid-1944, returned to attacks against Germany, smashing the German economy by systematic efforts against transportation and synthetic oil targets. By April 1945 German oil production was 5 percent that of a year earlier. German jet interceptors, which in 1943 might have changed the course of the air war, appeared too late to impede the huge Allied fleets.

Strategic bombing of Japan by B-29 Superfortresses from bases in the Marianas began in November 1944, after logistics difficulties plagued an earlier effort from China. In early 1945, the AAF broke from its pattern in Europe, and the B-29's began night incendiary area attacks on Japanese cities. Ships flew at medium altitudes to increase bomb loads, engine life, and accuracy, without benefit of formation or close escort. Devastation was utter, over 600 B-29's bombing on certain nights. The atomic bombs, delivered accurately by a special B-29 unit, ended the resolution of Japan's leaders, confronted already with sea blockade, Russian war entry, and the prospect of continued bombing.

The wartime AAF was a citizen's air force, although its higher leadership was mainly from the few prewar professionals. Peak strength in 1944 was 2,400,000 persons. The immediate postwar demobilization was precipitate (as in 1919), strength declining to 485,000 by April 1946.

Postwar Years

The National Security Act of July 26, 1947, established a single Department of Defense, with three departments—the army, the navy (which retained naval and marine aviation), and the air force. Stuart Symington was sworn in as first secretary of the air force on Sept. 18, 1947; Gen. Carl Spaatz became the USAF's first chief of staff. Strategic and budget controversies quickly loomed, naval leaders challenging the usefulness of the new B-36 heavy bomber and the efficacy of strategic bombing itself.

The emergent cold war confirmed that the atomic bomb and the means to deliver it were militarily insufficient. After witnessing the subversion of non-

Communist governments in Eastern Europe, American leaders became resolute in the face of Soviet closure of surface routes to occupied Berlin in June 1948. The Berlin airlift kept the city supplied with coal, foodstuffs, and other necessities through the winter of 1948–49, presenting the USAF with its first major test. Pilots overcame difficult weather and crowded airspace, while innovation and tight organization made possible an enormous aircraft maintenance effort. During the 11-month period of the blockade, beginning on June 25, 1948, nearly 2 million tons were airlifted into Berlin, most of it in USAF C-54's. The single-day peak occurred on Apr. 16, 1949, when 1,398 transports delivered nearly 13,000 tons.

The National Security Act of 1947 established a single Department of Defense, with three departments—the army, navy, and air force.

Soviet detonation of an atomic device in 1949 emphasized that the USAF's first responsibility was the nation's nuclear deterrent. For nine years under the single-minded leadership of Gen. Curtis E. LeMay (1948–57), the Strategic Air Command (SAC) gained a reputation for the highest standards in professional airmanship and readiness. Jet-propelled B-47's entered SAC in early 1953, their limited range extended by a complex of overseas bases and a force of aerial tankers. For most SAC personnel, the frequent overseas deployments and the demanding alert requirements left little time for normal family life.

Korean War

The United States again reacted firmly when the North Koreans attacked South Korea on June 25, 1950. Two days later, USAF units in the Far East began munitions lifts into Korea, and commenced strikes against airfields, bridges, and targets of opportunity. A U.S. Army battalion was airlifted to Korea on the sixth day of the war. The Americans quickly won air superiority over the poorly equipped North Korean air force and persisted in attacks against the enemy's extended lines of communication, thus aiding the Allied defense of the southern tip of the peninsula and the return north. The USAF transports lifted forces into Seoul soon after the Inchon landings and made deliveries to units advancing up the mud-clogged North Korean roadways. During the late-year retreat from the Yalu River, air force and Marine Corps transports made resupply paradrops and landed at hastily prepared strips to evacuate over 4,000 wounded.

The entry of the Communist Chinese brought the latest Soviet-built MIG-15 fighters, far superior to the opposing USAF F-80 jets. The U.S. Fourth Fighter-Interceptor Wing was sent quickly to the Far East. Equipped with F-86A craft, the wing's pilots claimed their first MIG on Dec. 17, 1950. The MIG's and F-86's met regularly near the Yalu thereafter, the Americans claiming 792 MIG kills, with the loss of 78 F-86's in air-to-air combat. The jet battles served to preserve Allied command of the air over most of Korea. Through the protracted stalemate, USAF and navy jet and propeller fighters (including P-51's) attacked interdiction and close-support targets by day, while propeller bombers ranged by night. The Communists were resourceful—exploiting camouflage and darkness, and patiently making road repairs—but were unable to sustain another strong ground offensive. Allied difficulties in giving close support to ground troops grew out of poor radio equipment and divergent army and air force concepts, but were eased by use of airborne forward air controllers in light, Mosquito aircraft. For the air force, the Korean conflict was another citizen's war, involving many World War II veterans recalled from civilian reservist status.

From 1954 to 1965

The experience of the limited conflict in Korea stimulated reemphasis on tactical air forces during the next decade. The development of nuclear weapons small enough to be carried on fighter aircraft promised a means for deterring or overcoming future stalemates like the one in Korea. During the late 1950's, the Tactical Air Command remained ready to deploy nuclear-capable composite air task forces from the United States to overseas trouble spots. After 1960, interest in attaining greater flexibility produced expansion of air transport forces for hauling airborne troop units. By mid-1965, the Military Air Transport Service possessed 550 four-engine transports, including all-jet C-141 cargo carriers. Tactical fighter forces included twenty-three wings (over 1,000 aircraft) in the United States, with another eight wings overseas.

Task forces of fighter, reconnaissance, and airlift craft moved overseas in response to crises in Taiwan in 1958, in the Middle East in 1958, and in Laos in 1962. The USAF transports hauled extensively during emergencies in the Congo in 1960 and 1964, and moved 16,000 troops and equipment into the Dominican Republic in 1965. In 1962, photography by USAF pilots in U-2 reconnaissance craft permitted detection of missile construction in Cuba. During the ensuing crisis, tactical air forces moved to bases in Florida for possible operations against Cuba, and U.S. Army troop units moved to the southeast United States, in part by USAF airlift.

Most fundamentally, however, U.S. diplomacy continued to rest on the retaliatory capabilities of SAC. During the Cuban crisis, the command remained in highest alert status for four weeks, keeping some fifty thermonuclear-carrying B-52 bombers aloft around the clock. The B-52 had entered the inventory in 1956, replacing the B-36, as SAC moved toward an all-jet force. The SAC strength in bomber and tanker aircraft grew through 1957, and the command worked steadily to reduce SAC's vulnerability by dispersion, alert systems, and better communications. Transition into a mixed bomber-missile force began in 1957, upon activation of a unit equipped with Snark intercontinental cruise missiles. Overseas deployment of Thor and Jupiter intermediate-range ballistic missiles commenced in 1958; the first intercontinental ballistic missile unit, equipped with Atlas, approached operational status late in 1959. By mid-1965 the manned bomber force had declined to 900 aircraft, with over 800 intercontinental missiles (mostly solid-fuel Minutemen) on alert.

During the missile crisis, the Strategic Air Command remained on highest alert for four weeks, keeping some 50 nuclear bomb–carrying B-52s flying around the clock.

The Air Defense Command in the early 1950's consisted of fighter-interceptor squadrons and a net of radar and control units across the United States and Alaska. These were tied into radar lines crossing Canada, and in 1957 USAF completed construction of a 3,000-mile Distant Early Warning (DEW) line, entirely within the Arctic Circle. Airborne and sea-emplaced radar sites completed the net. The combined North American Air Defense Command (NORAD), with a USAF commander and a Canadian deputy, was created on Sept. 12, 1957. A large computerized control system became operative in 1958. Construction of huge antennae for the Ballistic Missile Early Warning System (BMEWS) was begun in 1959 in Greenland and Alaska; a third installation was built later in Britain. These were supplemented by "over-the-horizon" radar equipment, revealed in 1964. Fighter-interceptors carried air-to-air nuclear-tipped missiles, but the manned interceptors gradually relinquished their roles to ground-to-air missiles, including the Bomarc and Nike series.

Events in Southeast Asia claimed increasing attention. Reacting to what seemed an avowed Kremlin policy encouraging wars of national liberation, the air force in 1961 organized a sublimited warfare unit, equipped with low-performance aircraft and trained to operate in primitive environments. A detachment of twelve propeller-driven strike aircraft and four transports moved into Vietnam late in the year, soon joined by a line squadron of C-123 transports, several dozen U.S. Army helicopters, and a few aerial spray ships. The strike aircraft, painted with Vietnamese insignia, performed combat missions with combined American-Vietnamese crews. The American air package expanded modestly, but the basic objective remained that of vitalizing Vietnamese efforts, while various test projects sought ways of applying air power to problems of insurgency and nation building. Political instability in Saigon compromised the counterinsurgency program and compounded American frustration. Jet strike aircraft of USAF entered Vietnam following the Tonkin Gulf affair of August 1964 and they began attacks on Communist lines of communication in Laos that December. Communist actions in South Vietnam triggered further retaliation in early 1965, USAF planes for the first time joining navy jets against the North on Feb. 8. The first American ground units entered Vietnam in March, one marine battalion deploying by sea, a second by USAF C-130 lift from Okinawa.

From 1965 to 1973

The American air campaign against North Vietnam was designed to discourage and impede assistance to the Communist effort in the South. Air strikes were closely controlled from the White House, which gradually escalated pressure in hopes of gaining limited political objectives. Early missions were limited to military and transportation targets in the southern part of North Vietnam, with occasional forays against rail bridges farther north. In early 1966, petroleum targets near Hanoi were attacked, followed by systematic attacks on the rail lines from China. After several bombing pauses failed to start negotiations, targeting expanded in 1967 to include the North's only steel mill, electric power generating facilities, and transportation targets around Haiphong and Hanoi. North Vietnamese air defenses, initially weak, were strengthened by aid from the Soviet Union and China. MIG-17's and surface-to-air missiles appeared in 1965—the missiles were the more deadly, forcing the Americans to low levels where vulnerability to antiaircraft fire was high. By 1967 improved American electronic devices had reduced the effectiveness of the missiles, while recent attacks on airfields eased the MIG threat. Navy and air force fighter-bombers attacked the North almost daily, averaging more than 10,000 sorties per month during the summers of 1966 and 1967. Assisting the strike force were a variety of specialized aircraft, designed to provide air refueling, rescue, reconnaissance, electronic countermeasures, or radar-warning support, along with other fighters equipped to attack missile installations or engage enemy interceptors.

In South Vietnam, jet and propeller fighters provided heavy firepower for close support of ground troops, usually guided to targets by airborne controllers. B-52 heavy bombers pounded carefully selected areas with 30-ton loads of conventional bombs. Air force transports, including large numbers of four-engine C-130 turboprops, moved and resupplied brigade forces engaged in search-and-destroy operations, staging into forward airheads in remote regions. Some transports were modified as gunships, for night defense of friendly installations. Despite the enemy's use of Cambodian sanctuaries and its proven skill in camouflage and dispersion, the Allied air and ground steamroller in South Vietnam rendered hopeless the enemy's protracted strategy and prompted him to launch his 1968 Tet offensive. Allied air firepower and airlifts were instrumental in the recovery from the Tet attacks, as well as in the simultaneous defense of isolated Khe Sanh.

President Lyndon Johnson's 1968 decisions, to curtail and then suspend the bombing of the North, led to redirection of the Allied air effort toward the Laos panhandle. Acoustic and seismic sensors were placed along Communist infiltration routes, to detect movements and relay signals to a computerized ground center. American strike and gunship aircraft, many equipped with infrared and light-amplification devices for night target detection, became effective in destroying trucks despite improving antiaircraft and missile opposition. Elsewhere in Laos, USAF strike aircraft provided support for Laotian government forces. Interdiction operations by USAF helped the armed forces of Cambodia to retain control of key areas after 1970, and the Khmer regime was further bolstered by periodic C-130 airlifts of food and petroleum.

The USAF and Vietnamese air power was apparently a decisive factor in halting the North Vietnamese 1972 Easter offensive against the South. The USAF, which had severely reduced its strength in the Far East, brought back over 250 aircraft and 7,000 personnel from the United States during the crisis. Most dramatic were the air resupply and strikes about An Loc, sustaining an isolated and desperate garrison in the face of Communist surface-to-air missiles. The Communist invasion resulted in a modification of U.S. restraint, and determined air and mining campaigns helped produce terms of peace. Final Communist resistance to a settlement was eroded apparently by a twelve-day B-52 bombing campaign about Hanoi, in which fifteen of the giant planes were lost.

Most career personnel served one or more twelve-month tours in Southeast Asia; the air force avoided a major expansion. The conflict had painful aspects, including numerous covert programs leading to cases of deceptive strike reporting, and resulted in wide criticism of indiscriminate effects of air operations. The ending was not entirely bitter; the obvious courage and integrity of the returning prisoners of war (a majority of them USAF members) reminded the divided nation of its traditions.

The 660,000-man air force in early 1974 looked ahead to continued change. SAC maintained fewer than 450 manned bombers, along with over 1,000 intercontinental missiles in hardened silos, under limitations set in the 1972 strategic arms treaty with the Soviets. The worldwide tactical air forces anticipated a major role in post-Vietnam national strategy. Hostilities in the Middle East late the previous year called forth a major logistics effort, to marshal quantities of matériel and airlift them to Israel. Especially valuable in this effort were the load capacity and range of the huge C-5A's, their history stained by cost overruns and metal fatigue problems.

The history of the U.S. Air Force has mirrored the temper and aspirations of American society. The nation has found the promise of air power appealing, in hopes of avoiding heavy manpower losses in ground fighting. The military air arm, like the surface forces, was poorly prepared for combat in 1917, 1941, and 1950, but in each case underwent fast and substantial wartime expansion. Since the formal creation of USAF, roughly coinciding with American assumption of global responsibilities, air power and the air force have been keystones of the nation's military posture and diplomacy.

Research and Space Activities

From its birth, the air force's technical orientation was apparent in the emphasis given to research and development. Most effort has focused toward future air weaponry, such work drawing from and often contributing to general scientific knowledge. Meteorological research, aerial geodetic surveys, and various aeromedical research efforts have had wide application. Air force transports have provided essential airlift for scientific projects in the Arctic and Antarctic, including paradrops at the South Pole station.

Air force space activities have included numerous unmanned research, weather, detection, and communications satellite projects, as well as systematic surveillance and tracking of space objects. Upon cancellation of air force manned projects—a piloted space glider in 1963 and the Manned Orbital Laboratory in 1969—the USAF supported the manned ventures of the National Aeronautics and Space Administration. The air force contributed numerous technical personnel and astronauts for projects Mercury, Gemini, Apollo, and Skylab. Capt. Virgil I. Grissom in July 1961 became the second American in space, and Col. Edwin E. Aldrin with Neil A. Armstrong on July 20, 1969, became the first men on the moon. Air force ballistic missiles were transformed into reliable space-launch systems—Atlas and Titan boosters launched certain Mercury and all Gemini flights, respectively—and the early Thors propelled over 400 space launches, beginning in 1958. The United States adhered to a treaty signed by eighty-four nations in 1967, which provided against military exploitation of space.

Air Force Organizations

The basic USAF tactical unit has been the squadron, consisting of aircrews and enough ground crewmen for routine flight-line maintenance of the twelve to twenty-four assigned aircraft. The First Aero Squadron was organized in 1913, representing the only tactical air unit in the army prior to 1917. During World War II, tactical squadrons were combined into groups; later, they were placed under a wing headquarters, which also included heavy maintenance, supply, and sometimes base housekeeping units. A wing could occupy a single base, or its units could be dispersed at several locations.

Several wings could be organized into an air division, or be placed directly under the next echelon, the numbered air force. Several numbered air forces became famous in World War II, including the Eighth Air Force in Britain, the Fifteenth in the Mediterranean, and the Fifth in the South Pacific. The B-29 units in the Marianas were organized as XXI Bomber Command. The Fifth Air Force fought in Korea; the Seventh in Vietnam.

The First Aero Squadron, organized in 1913, was the only tactical air unit in the army until 1917.

Reorganizations after World War II brought into being the major air commands, including SAC, the Air Defense Command, and the Tactical Air Command. The Air Materiel Command and the Air Research and Development Command were reorganized in 1961 as the Air Force Logistics Command (responsible for maintenance, supply, and procurement) and the Air Force Systems Command (applied research and development). Overseas, air force component commands served in unified theater commands, parallel with army and navy component commands. Headquarters, USAF, headed by the chief of staff and under the office of the secretary of the air force, is located in Washington, D.C.

Air University

Formal professional education for air officers evolved from the Air Service Field Officers' School, created in 1920 at Langley Field, Va., to prepare officers for direction of air units in operations with other branches. Early classes were small, but included officers from first lieutenant through lieutenant colonel. The school was renamed Air Service Tactical School in 1922, and Air Corps Tactical School in 1926, moving to Maxwell Field, Ala., in 1931. Students from other arms and services were enrolled, and the school became an important breeding ground for ideas on the proper employment of the air weapon.

The Air University was established in September 1946 at Maxwell, with three main component schools. An Air Tactical School (later renamed Squadron Officer School) was designed for regular officers in their first five years, essentially to prepare them for squadron command or equivalent staff responsibility. The Air Command and Staff School (later College) was designed for selected officers prior to their twelfth year. At the apex was the ten-month Air War College, with annual classes selected from the best-qualified officers prior to their twentieth year of service; its first class, numbering fifty-five, graduated in June 1947. Despite temporary reductions during the Korean and Southeast Asian conflicts, all three schools have functioned continuously. Individuals could complete each of the three schools either in residence at Maxwell or by correspondence. Air force officers attended parallel institutions of the other services, as well as the National War College and the Industrial College of the Armed Forces, both located in Washington, D.C.

Air Reserve Forces

The Air National Guard and the Air Force Reserve constitute the air reserve forces of the United States. The first National Guard aviation unit was organized in New York in 1915. Although no such units were mustered into federal service in World War I, postwar National Guard regulations established air observation, balloon, and photo units. All twenty-nine observation squadrons were ordered to federal duty in September 1940. The Air National Guard separated from the National Guard upon USAF independence in 1947. Three-fourths of Air National Guard strength was brought to active duty in 1950–51; guard fighter squadrons mobilized and were deployed overseas during the 1961 Berlin crisis and after the *Pueblo* affair in early 1968. Guard squadrons began participating in the continental air defense system in 1954. Although the primary mission of the guard was to provide combat-ready units for the air force, the organization also afforded the individual states an organized military body, a role specified in the U.S. Constitution. The Air National Guard in 1974 included over 90,000 personnel and was principally equipped with Vietnam-vintage aircraft, including the F-100, F-102, F-105, and C-130.

The Air Force Reserve includes individuals assigned as augmentees for active duty units and members of reserve squadrons equipped with transport and other aircraft. Individuals (like certain guardsmen) receive pay for training and short active-duty periods. Organized reservists in 1949 numbered 42,000; another 60,000 were unpaid Volunteer Air Reservists. During the Korean War, all twenty-five reserve troop carrier and light bomber wings were recalled, although most personnel were redistributed among other units. Four squadrons were recalled in 1961, and eight during the Cuban missile crisis. Huge C-124's with Air Force Reserve crews proved vital during the 1965 Dominican intervention and routinely flew trans-Pacific hauls during the war in Southeast Asia. An "associate unit" system was begun in 1968, whereby reserve unit members helped fly and maintain aircraft belonging to an active unit. Under this plan the active unit's workload capacity could be raised instantly by calling the associate unit to active status. In early 1974, the Air Force Reserve numbered thirty-eight squadrons, mostly equipped with C-130's, as well as eighteen associate squadrons affiliated with active units of Military Airlift Command.

BIBLIOGRAPHY

Wesley F. Craven and James L. Cate, eds., *The Army Air Forces in World War II.*

Robert Frank Futrell, *The United States Air Force in Korea.*

Alfred Goldberg, ed., *A History of the United States Air Force, 1907–1957.*

John H. Scrivner, Jr., *A Quarter Century of Air Power.*

U. S. G. Sharp and William Westmoreland, *Report on the War in Vietnam.*

U.S. Department of Defense, *Annual Reports* (1948–68).

— RAY L. BOWERS

AIRCRAFT, DEVELOPMENT OF

On Dec. 17, 1903, after four and a half years of study and experiment, Orville and Wilbur Wright flew a biplane that achieved sustained, powered, and controlled flight. The Wright invention underwent rapid improvement. The aileron, a movable surface at the rear of the wing (sometimes between wings), supplanted the Wrights's method of controlling flight by a combination of wing warping and rudder movement. The yoke-and-wheel control column and the control stick replaced the body harness devised by the Wrights to coordinate the position of wings and rudder. Wheels proved superior to the launching rail and landing skid.

Before the outbreak of World War I, tests showed the military potential of airplanes. Glenn Curtiss experimented with aerial bombing as early as 1910; Eugene Ely performed shipboard takeoffs and landings (1910–11); James McCurdy demonstrated the feasibility of two-way radio contact between air and ground (1911); and Riley Scott invented a bombsight (1914). Monoplanes appeared in Europe, as did the elongated fuselage and the enclosed cabin. The first tailless, swept-wing biplane was designed in 1908 by J. W. Dunne, an Englishman, and built in 1913 by the Burgess Company of Massachusetts.

Glenn Curtiss pioneered in seaplane construction in 1911. One of his most successful craft, *America* (1914), was designed with the aid of J. C. Porte, a British naval officer, and manufactured in Britain for wartime use. With guidance from Rear Admiral David Taylor of the U.S. Navy, Curtiss built the postwar, four-engine navy Curtiss seaplane. In May 1919, one of these, the NC-4, completed a flight from St. John's, Newfoundland, to Plymouth, England, by way of the Azores and Portugal.

The U.S.'s principal technological achievement of WWI was the liquid-cooled, mass-produced Liberty engine developed in 1917 by Jesse F. Vincent.

America's principal technological accomplishment of World War I was the liquid-cooled, mass-produced Liberty engine, developed in 1917 under the direction of Jesse F. Vincent. A series of successful engines followed, including the liquid-cooled Curtiss, and the Pratt and Whitney and Wright air-cooled radials. Technological development of aircraft continued unabated after the war. The National Advisory Committee for Aeronautics (NACA), founded in 1915, opened a modern laboratory in 1920 and over the years made numerous discoveries, among them, a cowling to streamline radial engines and a variety of airfoils. The armed forces and industry called upon men like John Macready, Apollo and Zeus Soucek, and Wiley Post for experiments involving supercharged engines, oxygen equipment, and high-altitude clothing.

Wright engines powered two remarkable American planes, the Ryan Aeronautical *Spirit of St. Louis*, designed by Donald Hall for Charles Lindbergh's May 1927 nonstop flight from New York to Paris, and the Wright-Bellanca, designed by Giuseppe Bellanca. In June of that year, Clarence Chamberlain, accompanied by Charles Levine, flew a Wright-Bellanca nonstop from the United States to Germany. These two planes overshadowed such single-engine, Liberty-powered craft as the 1924 Douglas World Cruisers, in which army aviators circled the earth, and Grover Loening's amphibian, used on an aerial goodwill tour of Latin America in 1926–27.

The Lockheed Vega, a single-engine monoplane designed by Allan Loughead and John Northrop, was first flown in 1927 and later used by Wiley Post on two around-the-world flights. Of wooden monocoque construction, the Vega marked the successful revival of a building technique introduced in France before World War I. Post's second around-the-world flight was a 1933 solo effort made possible by an automatic pilot built by Sperry Gyroscope Company. Lawrence Sperry, a pioneer instrument maker, had tested a crude prototype as early as 1912.

The most significant American contribution to the development of the dirigible was the introduction of helium, a nonflammable lifting gas found only in the United States. A metalclad airship flew successfully, but loss of the navy's *Shenandoah, Akron*, and *Macon*—followed by the destruction in 1937 of Germany's hydrogen-filled *Hindenburg*—brought to an end the era of the great dirigibles.

First in a series of distinguished American commercial aircraft was the Ford trimotor transport of 1926. This all-metal plane, inspired by William Stout, was more famous for its rugged dependability than for aerodynamic innovation. More important in terms of technology was the highly streamlined, twin-engine Boeing 247 of 1933, credited to a team led by William E. Boeing and Robert Minshall. Donald Douglas, using a Northrop-designed wing, produced the bigger and faster DC-2, which with its successor, the DC-3, came to dominate the airways of the world. Lockheed introduced its own series of transports, one of which, Model 14 of 1937, boasted flaps designed by Harlan Fowler to increase wing area by deploying on rails from the trailing edge. In addition to these land planes, a number of successful seaplane transports were built by Igor Sikorsky, Glenn L. Martin, and Boeing.

The advance in transports accompanied similar achievements in bombers, as the twin-engine biplane gave way to the fast, all-metal, low-wing monoplane. The army also began acquiring the four-engine bombers that, after extensive modification, performed so effectively in World War II. Boeing's B-17 prototype flew in 1935 and the Consolidated B-24 in 1940. The latter featured a high aspect ratio wing, developed by David R. Davis, that reduced drag, thus increasing range.

In 1939, Hungarian-born Theodore von Kármán launched re-

The first motor-propelled flight by the Wright brothers (Orville at controls and Wilber on the ground) at Kitty Hawk, North Carolina, on December 17, 1903. (Corbis-Bettmann)

search into rocket-propelled airplanes, but progress in this area lagged; during World War II American aviation concentrated on piston-powered craft. Two transports, the Lockheed C-69 Constellation and the Douglas C-54 Skymaster, and two propeller-driven combat planes were noteworthy accomplishments. One of the latter was the North American P-51, built to fight at medium altitude, then fitted with a supercharged British-designed Merlin engine to become a successful escort for the high-altitude American bombers that were battering Germany by day. The other was the Boeing B-29, the largest bomber to see combat in the war—a plane that combined such innovations as remote-controlled gun turrets, four twin-row radial engines developing 2,200 horsepower each, and a pressurized cabin. Pressurization had worked well on the experimental Lockheed XC-35 and on the Boeing 307 transport, but never before on a heavy bomber.

The first practical helicopter appeared during World War II, but too late to see much service. Sikorsky introduced a craft that did not require twin main rotors turning in opposite directions. By installing a light, vertically mounted propeller at the rear of the fuselage to compensate for the torque of the blades rotating overhead, Sikorsky saved enough weight to enable the helicopter to carry a worthwhile payload.

German data on jet propulsion became available to American engineers as a result of the war. These data showed that a swept wing would delay the buildup of shock waves at extreme speeds. Building on the German foundation, Americans made further discoveries, such as Richard Whitcomb's area rule, which demonstrated that a wasp-waisted fuselage was the most efficient shape for supersonic flight.

In the postwar advance of aviation technology several experimental craft were trailblazers, such as the rocket-powered Bell X-1—suggested by John Stack of NACA and Robert Woods of Bell Aircraft—in which Charles Yeager exceeded the speed of sound in level flight. The Bell X-5 turbojet had a wing whose degree of sweep could be adjusted for various flight conditions. Most famous of the series was the North American X-15 rocket plane, in which Joseph Walker and Peter Knight exceeded 4,000 mph and both Walker and Robert White climbed above 300,000 feet.

C. L. Johnson of Lockheed Aircraft supervised the design of two famous reconnaissance planes: the U-2 and the SR-71. The U-2 resembled a jet-propelled sailplane and was able to take photographs from altitudes that interceptors could not reach. In contrast to the long, narrow U-2 wing was the small, modified delta wing of Johnson's SR-71. Powered by two engines in large nacelles on either side of the fuselage, this plane could attain a speed of 2,000 mph and an altitude of 80,000 feet.

American-designed transports continued to dominate the world's commercial airlines. First came the long-range, piston-powered types, culminating in the Lockheed Super Constellation and the Douglas DC-7C, a descendant of the wartime Skymaster. Britain in 1951 introduced the first practical jet transport, the Comet, but a series of tragic accidents caused its grounding and tarnished the reputation of a modified version. The expectation of military orders persuaded Boeing to build a prototype jet transport that was completed in 1954. When the U.S. Air Force purchased a tanker model, the KC-135, Boeing arranged to lease government-owned tools to build a commercial type, the successful 707. Along with the larger Douglas DC-8, the 707 fulfilled the promise shown by the Comet.

The U-2, resembling a jet-propelled sailplane, was able to take photographs from altitudes that interceptors could not reach.

Progress in general aviation, including business and personal planes, culminated in the production of William P. Lear's Learjet (1964), a jet-powered executive transport designed exclusively for the civilian market. Lockheed had already produced a business jet, but its 1959 JetStar was inspired by military needs. Other milestones in general aviation included the twin-engine Beechcraft Model 18 (1937), the Stinson Reliant (1936), and Cessna Airmaster (1934) single-engine monoplanes, and the Beechcraft Model 17 Staggerwing single-engine biplane (1932). The most popular of American light planes was the two-place, single-engine Cub, designed in 1932 by C. Gilbert Taylor. Piper Aircraft later took over Taylor's design, which remained in production for two decades.

In the early 1970's, the American aircraft industry concentrated on big transports such as the Boeing 747, McDonnell Douglas DC-10, and Lockheed L-1011 TriStar. They owed their success to powerful new turbofan engines that displace huge volumes of air, and to the ingenious use of wing slots, flaps, and other devices for increasing lift, especially at low speed.

After winning a federally supervised design competition with Lockheed Aircraft, Boeing began preliminary work on a supersonic transport (SST). Despite the investment of an estimated $900 million, the government in March 1971 ended its subsidy, in effect halting the development of an American SST to compete with those being built by an Anglo-French consortium and by the Soviet Union. Many of the same ecological and economic problems that led to termination of the Boeing project may prevent widespread acceptance of the foreign SST's.

BIBLIOGRAPHY

Charles H. Gibbs-Smith, *The Aeroplane: An Historical Summary.*
Alvin Josephy, ed., *The American Heritage Book of Flight.*
H. F. King and John W. R. Taylor, *Milestones of the Air: Jane's 100 Significant Aircraft.*
Robert Schlaifer and S. D. Heron, *Development of Aircraft Engines and Aviation Fuels.*

— BERNARD C. NALTY

ALAMO, SIEGE OF THE

Siege of the Alamo (Feb. 23–Mar. 6, 1836). When the revolting province of Texas swept its soil clear of weak Mexican garrisons in 1835 the commander-in-chief, Sam Houston, ordered a concentration on the theory that the Mexicans would return. He recommended the destruction and abandonment of the fortifications at San Antonio. For this cautious counsel Houston was deposed from command. A twenty-seven-year-old lawyer, Lt. Col. William Barret Travis, found himself in joint command, with James Bowie, of about 145 men at San Antonio when on Feb. 23 Antonio López de Santa Anna appeared with between 3,000 and 4,000 men.

Travis and Bowie could have retreated safely, but they moved into the stout-walled Alamo mission, answered a demand for surrender with cannon shot, and sent for reinforcements.

Travis and Bowie could have retreated safely. Instead they moved into the stout-walled Alamo mission, answered a demand for surrender with a cannon shot, and sent couriers for reinforcements. A message signed by Travis read: "I have sustained a continual Bombardment and a cannonade for 24 hours and have not lost a man. . . . Our flag still proudly waves from the wall. I shall never surrender or retreat. . . . VICTORY OR DEATH." On the eighth day of battle thirty-two recruits crept through the Mexican lines, the last reinforcements the garrison was to receive. This brought their number to about 187. Though suffering from want of sleep, and with ammunition running low, the Texans had lost the services of only one man, Bowie, ill and disabled by a fall.

At four in the morning of Mar. 6, the thirteenth day of battle, Santa Anna stormed the Alamo on all sides. The first and second assaults were broken up. At dawn the Mexicans attacked again. The Texans' guns were hot from heavy firing in the two assaults, their ammunition nearly out, and, though casualties had not been numerous, men were dropping from exhaustion. The walls were breached. The defenders fought throughout the mission compound, clubbing rifles and drawing knives. The last point taken was the church. There fell David Crockett and twelve volunteers who had followed him from Tennessee. By eight o'clock the last of the 187 defenders was dead, though the Mexicans spared about thirty noncombatants. Mexican losses were about 1,500 killed.

The fall of the Alamo sowed panic through Texas, precipitating a flight of the civilian population and of the government toward U.S. soil. Inwardly raging against Travis' disastrous stand, Houston gathered an army. Six weeks later, marching to meet Santa Anna, Houston paraded his men and in an impassioned address abjured them to "Remember the Alamo!" With that cry they vanquished the Mexicans at San Jacinto, establishing the independence of the Texas Republic.

BIBLIOGRAPHY

Marquis James, *The Raven.*

— MARQUIS JAMES

ALBANY CONGRESS

Albany Congress (1754), called by order of the British government for the purpose of conciliating the Iroquois and securing their support in the war against France, was more notable for the plans that it made than for its actual accomplishments. In June commissioners from New York, Massachusetts, Rhode Island, Connecticut, Pennsylvania, New Hampshire, and Maryland met with the chiefs of the Six Nations. Encroachment on their lands, the trading of Albany with Canada, and the removal of Johnson (later Sir William Johnson) from the management of their affairs had aroused a dangerous spirit of disaffection among the Indians. Gifts and promises were bestowed and the alliance renewed, but the Iroquois went away only half satisfied.

For the better defense of the colonies and control of Indian affairs it had long been felt that a closer union was needed than occasional meetings of governors or commissioners. Discussion of such a union now became one of the principal subjects of the congress. Massachusetts indeed had granted its delegates authority to "enter into articles of union . . . for the general defense of his majesty's subjects." The plan adopted was one proposed by Benjamin Franklin and frequently referred to at the time as the Albany Plan. It provided for a voluntary union of the colonies with "one general government," each colony to retain its own separate existence and government. The new government was to be administered by a president general appointed by the crown and a grand council of delegates from the several colonial assemblies, members of the council to hold office for three years. This federal government was given exclusive control of Indian affairs, including the power to make peace and declare war, regulate Indian trade, purchase Indian lands for the crown, raise and pay soldiers, build forts, equip vessels, levy taxes, and appropriate funds. The home government rejected this plan because it was felt that it encroached on the royal prerogative. The colonies disapproved of it because it did not allow them sufficient independence. Nevertheless this Albany Plan was to have far-reaching results. It paved the way for the Stamp Act Congress of 1765 and the Continental Congress of 1774, and when the need of a closer union was felt, it served as a guide in the deliberations of the representatives of the colonies.

BIBLIOGRAPHY

E. B. O'Callaghan. ed., *Documentary History of the State of New York.*

— A. C. FLICK

ALCATRAZ

Alcatraz, an island in San Francisco Bay, was discovered by Spanish explorers in the sixteenth century. The United States took possession of the island in 1850 and fortified it, using it first as a military prison and later as a federal prison, beginning in 1933. Because of the strong, cold currents surrounding the island, it was considered escape-proof. Of the twenty-six prisoners who attempted escapes, five remain unaccounted for. The prison was closed in 1963. In November 1969 Native American activists occupied the island for almost a year and a half. The island was opened to the public as part of the Golden Gate National Recreation Area in 1972.

[See also American Indian Movement; Native Americans.]

BIBLIOGRAPHY

John Godwin, *Alcatraz: 1868–1963* (Garden City, N.Y., 1963).

— PAUL S. VOAKES

ALGONQUIN

The Algonquin tribe, located with the Ottawa on the northern tributaries of the Ottawa River in southwestern Quebec, is to be contrasted with the extensive North American speech family, Algonkin (or Algonquian, or Algonquin), to which it has lent its name. The tribe itself was always small, a relatively isolated Eastern Woodlands (Northeastern) people. Like others in the woodlands pattern, the Algonquin were a nonagricultural hunting people, exploiting such faunal resources as moose, deer, beaver, otter, bear, fish, and wildfowl. Extensive use of birch bark for housing, canoes, and containers characterized their culture.

Most closely related in language to the Ojibwa (or Chippewa) of Ontario, Wisconsin, and Minnesota, the Algonquin, along with the neighboring Ottawa, appear to be a remnant of various Ojibwa bands that gradually shifted westward as a result of the pressures of European settlement. The tribe, perhaps 6,000 in 1600, was divided into various paternal groups associated with hunting territories. Originally lacking any political solidarity, the tribe was drawn gradually into the French orbit and patterned a series of political alliances with other tribes on the model of the Iroquois federation. But the group was never a potent military or political force, suffering decimation and dispersion at the hands of the hostile Iroquois. Members of the group surviving in the 20th century are identified only with difficulty.

The Algonquin tribe was drawn gradually into the French orbit and patterned a series of political alliances with other tribes on the model of the Iroquois federation.

The language phylum to which the Algonquin lent their name is, however, one of the most widely spread and important of the American continent. Careful philological analyses and comparisons demonstrate the language affiliation to an Algonkin family of such widely spread peoples as the Arapaho, Cheyenne, and Blackfoot in the Plains and the Yurok and Wiyot in California. There is also the suggestion that certain Gulf languages—for example, those formerly classified as Muskogean (or Muskhogean)—may have remote connections with the major Algonkin grouping. When to this is added the suggestion that some languages of Central America, such as Coahuiltecan, may derive from a proto-Algonkin, it seems clear that considerable antiq-

uity is implied. The source of the name of both the tribe and the language family is uncertain.

BIBLIOGRAPHY

John R. Swanton, *The Indian Tribes of North America.*

— ROBERT F. SPENCER

ALIEN AND SEDITION LAWS

In June and July, 1798, the Federalists, fearful of French invasion and certain they were only spelling out the details of the proper restraints on free speech and press implied by common law and American statute, introduced four bills designed to impede political opposition. Although they were debated as war measures, three of them were applicable in peacetime as well.

Skepticism of aliens and of their ability to be loyal to the nation permeated these laws. In place of the five-year residency requirement, the Naturalization Act of June 18, 1798, substituted fourteen years, five of which were to be spent in the state or territory in which the individual was being naturalized. The alien was required to declare an intention of becoming a citizen five years before the ultimate application. As a measure of control all aliens were to be registered with the clerk of their district court. This law was repealed in 1802. The Alien Friends Act (June 25, 1798) gave the president the power to deport aliens "dangerous to the peace and safety of the United States." Its terms were sweeping because it was passed in the context of an undeclared war with France. But it was limited to two years, and it was never enforced. On July 6, 1798, the Alien Enemies Act was passed—the only one of the group that gathered strong Republican support as a clearly defensive measure in time of declared war. It gave the president the power to restrain, arrest, and deport male citizens or subjects of a hostile nation.

The Act for the Punishment of Certain Crimes, signed into law on July 14, 1798, was the nation's first sedition act. It made it a high misdemeanor "unlawfully to combine and conspire" in order to oppose legal measures of the government, to interfere with an officer in the discharge of his duty, to engage in or abet "insurrection, riot, or unlawful assembly or combination, whether such conspiracy . . . shall have the proposed effect or not." The penalty was a fine of not more than $5,000 and imprisonment of up to five years. Moreover, the writing or printing of "any false, scandalous and malicious writing" with intent to bring the government, Congress, or the president "into contempt or disrepute, or to excite against them . . . the hatred of the good people of the United States," was punishable by a fine of up to $2,000 and imprisonment for up to two years. The Sedition Act carefully specified, however, that truth might be admitted as a defense, that malicious intent had to be proved, and that the jury had the right to judge whether the matter was libelous. Although President John Adams had not urged that the bills be enacted, he signed them into law without serious protest, and they were supported by most Federalists.

Enforcement against critics of the administration was pressed by Secretary of State Timothy Pickering. Ten Republicans were convicted; they included Congressman Matthew Lyon, political writer James T. Callender, the lawyer Thomas Cooper, and newspaper editors William Duane and John Daly Burk. Because Federalist judges frequently conducted the trials in a partisan manner, and because the trials demonstrated that the Sedition Act had failed to distinguish between malicious libel and the expression of political opinion, the laws were the catalyst in prompting a broader definition of freedom of the press.

The protest against these laws received its most significant formulation in the Kentucky and Virginia resolutions, drafted by Vice-President Thomas Jefferson and James Madison, which claimed for the states the right to nullify obnoxious federal legislation. The resolutions, however, did not seriously question the concept of seditious libel; they merely demanded that such prosecutions be undertaken in state courts, as indeed they were during Jefferson's own presidency.

BIBLIOGRAPHY

Leonard W. Levy, *Legacy of Suppression.*
James Morton Smith, *Freedom's Fetters: The Alien and Sedition Laws and American Civil Liberties.*

— LINDA K. KERBER

AMANA COMMUNITY

Born of religious enthusiasm, this unique community was founded in Germany in 1714 as the Community of True Inspiration in protest against the arbitrary rule of church and state. For mutual protection the Inspirationists congregated on several large estates, but high rents and unfriendly governments forced them to seek a new home in America.

Under the leadership of Christian Metz the Inspirationists crossed the Atlantic in the early 1840's and settled near Buffalo in Erie County, N.Y. Here they laid out six villages, called the settlement Ebenezer, built mills and factories, tilled the soil, and formally adopted communism as a way of life.

The rapid expansion of nearby Buffalo threatened that isolation which the Inspirationists had sought in the New World and in 1855 they moved to the frontier

state of Iowa. They located in Iowa County, incorporated as the Amana Society, and once more built houses, churches, schools, stores, and mills, and continued their community life of "brothers all." Consisting of approximately 1,500 people, living in seven villages and owning 26,000 acres of land in one of the garden spots of Iowa, the Amana community conducted for nearly a century the most successful experiment in communism recorded in the annals of American history.

The Amana community conducted for nearly a century the most successful experiment in communism recorded in the annals of American history.

Once the frontier disappeared, isolation became impossible, memories of the founding forefathers faded, the old idealism grew dim, and spiritual enthusiasm waned. In 1932 by unanimous vote the community reorganized on the basis of cooperative capitalism as a joint stock company where stockholders are both owners and employees.

BIBLIOGRAPHY

Bertha M. H. Shambaugh, *Amana, The Community of True Inspiration,* and *Amana That Was and Amana That Is.*

— BERTHA M. H. SHAMBAUGH

AMBASSADORS

Through the great-power Congress of Vienna (1815) and the Congress of Aix-la-Chapelle (1818) four standardized diplomatic grades were established: ambassadors were given the highest rank, followed, first, by ministers plenipotentiary and envoys extraordinary; second, by ministers resident; and third, by chargés d'affaires. Under the revised rules of the Vienna Convention on Diplomatic Relations of 1961, reducing the ranks to three by eliminating ministers resident, ambassadors remain senior. Ambassadors are accredited directly to the sovereign or the head of state, and they represent the highest authority of their own governments. Thus, American ambassadors represent the president of the United States even though they normally communicate with the president through the secretary of state. The ambassador longest accredited in a foreign capital is known as the dean, or doyen, of the international diplomatic corps, and as such represents it for certain purposes. The doyen may act to convey the corps's collective congratulations on occasions such as national holidays, thus simplifying the scale of protocol requirements. The doyen is likely to be the spokesman for any widespread diplomatic corps complaint. U.S. ambassadors rarely attain this distinction because of frequent rotation.

Until well into the 19th century only great powers exchanged ambassadors; other nations exchanged envoys of the rank of minister (plenipotentiary). Because the United States did not aspire to great-power rank, because it played only a small role in international affairs, and because ambassadors were associated with monarchy in the public mind, the United States did not exchange ambassadors until almost the close of the 19th century, sending ministers instead. The first U.S. ambassador, Thomas F. Bayard of Delaware, was commissioned to Great Britain on Mar. 30, 1893. In exchange, Sir Julian Pauncefote, minister plenipotentiary since 1889, presented his credentials as ambassador to President Grover Cleveland on Apr. 11, 1893.

The choice of Great Britain for the first U.S. ambassador reflected that nation's importance to America as well as Great Britain's determination to cultivate closer relations with the United States, in view of its increasingly difficult international position. By 1939 the United States was exchanging ambassadors with twenty nations. After World War II the number increased steadily, both because many new nations were coming into existence and because, as a matter of national pride, smaller nations were more and more demanding the equality of status signified by an exchange of ambassadors; the rank of minister came to be rarely used. In 1974 the United States exchanged ambassadors with 124 nations, sending ministers to none. Also, eight ambassadors were accredited to international organizations, such as the United Nations and North Atlantic Treaty Organization.

— FREDERICK H. HARTMANN

AMENDMENTS TO THE CONSTITUTION

Twenty-six amendments have been adopted since 1789. The first ten were drafted to meet the protests in numerous state ratifying conventions against the absence of a bill of rights in the Constitution. To fill this void, the First Congress, chiefly on the initiative of James Madison, submitted twelve amendments to the states; ten of these were ratified (1791) and constitute the Bill of Rights, which limits the powers of the federal government but not the powers of the states. These amendments—which guarantee the people's civil liberties—provide that Congress shall make no law infringing freedom of speech, the press, religion, assembly, or petition; reaffirm the right of trial by jury; protect against unreasonable searches or seizures; and assure that no individual shall be compelled to testify against himself in a criminal case or "be deprived of life, liberty, or property, without due process of law."

The Eleventh Amendment (1798) was designed to override the Supreme Court decision in the case of *Chisholm* v. *Georgia* (1793). It provides that the federal judiciary cannot accept jurisdiction of a suit against a state by a citizen of another state or by a citizen of a foreign state.

The Twelfth Amendment (1804) altered Article II, Section 1, of the Constitution, which had permitted presidential electors to vote for two persons without designating which was to be president and which vice-president, and instructed them to cast separate ballots for each of these executive officers. The election of 1796 and particularly the canvass of 1800, when Thomas Jefferson and Aaron Burr received an equal number of electoral votes, had demonstrated the inadequacy of the original presidential election machinery and stimulated interest in a reform to prevent such difficulties.

During Reconstruction following the Civil War, three amendments to the constitution abolished slavery, defined citizenship to include African Americans, and protected voting rights for former slaves.

Three amendments were ratified during the Reconstruction period following the Civil War. The Thirteenth Amendment (1865) abolished slavery and involuntary servitude. The Fourteenth Amendment (1868) for the first time defined citizenship, which included Afro-Americans. It stipulates that no state can deny individuals equal protection of the laws or deprive them of life, liberty, or property without due process of law, and provides for reduced representation in Congress for states that deny the right to vote in federal elections to adult male citizens. It also barred certain Confederate officers from holding state or federal offices unless pardoned by Congress and repudiated the Confederate debt. Disagreement over the meaning of this amendment continues to the present day, and it has been the subject of more Supreme Court cases than any other provision of the Constitution. The Fifteenth Amendment (1870), which secured the right to vote against denial or abridgment on the basis of race, color, or previous condition of servitude, was adopted when it was clear that the Fourteenth Amendment would not guarantee freedmen the right to the franchise.

Several amendments reflect the widespread desire for economic, political, and social reform during the early 20th century. The Sixteenth Amendment (1913), which overruled the Supreme Court decision in *Pollock* v. *Farmers' Loan and Trust Company* (1895), gives Congress the power to tax incomes from any source and without apportionment among the states according to population. The Seventeenth Amendment (1913) provides for direct, popular election of senators, revising Article I, Section 3, of the Constitution. It was thought that this method of election would make senators more responsive to the will of the people. Success for two other reform measures came at the conclusion of World War I. The Eighteenth Amendment (1919) prohibited the sale of intoxicating liquors and was the first amendment to specify a period of years (seven) within which it had to be ratified. Suffrage for women was guaranteed by the Nineteenth Amendment (1920), fulfilling a central demand of the women's rights movement.

The Twentieth, or "Lame Duck," Amendment (1933) set the dates for the beginning of presidential terms (Jan. 20) and congressional sessions (Jan. 3) and settled certain points with respect to presidential succession. The Twenty-first Amendment (1933) repealed the Eighteenth but gives the states power to regulate the use of intoxicating liquors; it is the only amendment to be ratified by special state conventions instead of state legislatures.

A two-term limit for presidents was established by the Twenty-second Amendment (1951), which was originally proposed by Republicans after the Democrat Franklin D. Roosevelt had been elected to a fourth term in office (1944) but was later endorsed by many who were wary of strong executive leadership.

The Twenty-third Amendment (1961) enables residents of the District of Columbia to vote for president and vice-president and gives the capital city three electoral votes, the number selected by each of the least populous states. State use of poll taxes in federal elections as a voting requirement, a device often employed to disfranchise Afro-Americans in the South, was banned by the Twenty-fourth Amendment (1964). Subsequently, the Supreme Court outlawed all poll taxes. Both amendments reflected the concern of the 1960's that all citizens should be guaranteed basic civil rights. One result of the assassination of President John F. Kennedy (1963) was the adoption of the Twenty-fifth Amendment (1967), which provides that whenever there is a vacancy in the office of the vice-president, the chief executive is authorized to nominate a successor who must be confirmed by a majority of both houses of Congress. It also empowers the vice-president to serve as acting president if the president is incapacitated. The Twenty-sixth Amendment (1971) lowered the voting age to eighteen, bypassing the traditional state control of that requirement.

A twenty-seventh amendment, known as the Equal Rights Amendment, was proposed by Congress on Mar. 22, 1972. It states that "Equality of rights under the law shall not be denied or abridged by the United States or by any State on account of sex." As of April 1975, thirty-four states had ratified the amendment; thirty-eight ratifications are needed by March 1979 for the amendment to succeed.

Three amendments proposed by Congress failed of ratification. The first, proposed to the states in May 1810, stated that any citizen accepting a title of nobility or honor from the head of a foreign nation would "cease to be a citizen of the United States." The Corwin amendment, proposed in March 1861, was an attempt to "freeze" the Constitution with regard to slavery by barring amendments that would give Congress "the power to abolish or interfere, within any State, with the domestic institutions thereof, including that of persons held to labor or service by the laws of said State." A child labor amendment, proposed in 1924, would have given Congress the power to regulate labor by persons under eighteen years of age, but the Fair Labor Standards Act was passed in 1938 before the necessary thirty-six ratifications had been achieved.

BIBLIOGRAPHY

Alfred H. Kelly and Winfred A. Harbison, *The American Constitution.*

— JOHN J. TURNER, JR.

AMERICA, DISCOVERY AND EARLY EXPLORATION OF

Norse Exploration

About the year A.D. 1000, roving Norsemen, starting from the Scandinavian colonies in Greenland, may have reached the coast of North America somewhere between Labrador and the Chesapeake. If they did, they left no undisputed archaeologic evidence of their visit. The legends of the voyages of Leif Ericson and Thorfinn Karlsefni depend upon three manuscripts of sagas written more than three hundred years after the possible discovery of that part of America which Leif called Vinland the Good. Admitting Leif to have been the discoverer of America, Edward Channing aptly said, "The history of America would have been precisely what it has been if Leif Ericsson had never been born and if no Northman had even steered his knorr west of Iceland."

Columbus landing in America, jumping from a barge to take possession of the new continent. Undated wood engraving. (Corbis-Bettmann)

Spanish Exploration

It is, however, undisputed historic fact that on Aug. 3, 1492, the Genoese Christopher Columbus, sailed from Palos, Spain, under the authority of the Spanish king and queen. On Oct. 12, 1492, Columbus saw some island in the Bahamas which the Indians called Guanahani, and which Co-

lumbus rechristened San Salvador. Its exact identity never has been conclusively established, but many scholars have accepted Watling Island as his first landfall. Following this, Columbus made three other voyages to the New World (1493, 1498, and 1502), during which he touched the coasts of South and Central America. But it must be remembered there is a documented story that one of the factors which induced Columbus to make his voyage was his actual meeting with, or knowledge of, a Spanish pilot who brought back news of having been wrecked on an island far west of the Madeiras as early as 1484.

In 1499, Alonso de Ojeda and Juan de la Cosa visited South America, and with them went Amerigo Vespucci who wrote such popular accounts of his own deeds that the German geographer Martin Waldseemüller coined the word "America" in a book published in 1507. The inevitability of the so-called discovery of America by Europeans is illustrated by the fact that the Portuguese Pedro Cabral, in 1500, tried to reach India by way of the African coast, and was accidentally blown to the west where unintentionally he reached the coast of Brazil.

Samuel de Champlain discovered much of the present-day U.S.; he found Maine in 1603, Cape Cod in 1605, and got as far as central New York State in 1615.

The island of Española (now Hispaniola) became the Spanish outpost from which further discoveries of the mainland were made. From there Vasco Núñez, de Balboa went to Central America, crossed the Isthmus of Panama, and discovered the Pacific Ocean, Sept. 25, 1513. The eastern coast of the mainland of North America had been seen and was cartographically traced by 1502. On Easter Sunday, 1513, Juan Ponce de León, from Española, found his way to the site of the present city of St. Augustine, Fla. Francisco Gordillo coasted as far north as Cape Fear (1521) and Lucas Vásquez de Ayllón followed and got as far as the James River in Virginia (1526). Meantime Hernando Cortés had landed in Mexico and conquered it in one of a series of the most amazing expeditions in all history (1519). Pánfilo de Narváez explored western Florida and possibly Georgia (1528) while his treasurer Álvar Núñez Cabeza de Vaca walked overland from Pensacola Bay, Fla., to the Gulf of California. In 1539 Hernando de Soto took an expedition from Tampa Bay, Fla., marched north to the Savannah River, turned west and proceeded overland until he reached the Mississippi River in 1541.

By this time Antonio de Mendoza had become viceroy of New Spain (Mexico, as opposed to Peru) and from his bailiwick, Franciscan friars were pushing up into what is now the Southwest of the United States. Fray Marcos de Niza (1539) brought back such reports of wealth in that region that Francisco Vásquez de Coronado started out in April 1540 on an expedition which took him as far north as central Kansas (1541).

French Exploration

Giovanni da Verrazano, acting under the favor of Francis I, came to North America in 1524 and possibly saw the Lower Bay of New York. Jacques Cartier coasted Labrador in 1534 and in the next year entered and explored the St. Lawrence River to the Lachine Rapids above Quebec. The discovery of much of the present area of the United States from the north was the work of Samuel de Champlain, who found Maine in 1603–04, and Cape Cod in 1605, and got as far as central New York State in 1615.

English Exploration.

Most effective of the discovering nations was England. In May 1497 John Cabot sailed from Bristol, England, under a patent from Henry VII, and some time in June probably discovered the continent of North America, first sighting land near Newfoundland. The Hawkinses—William, John, and James—explored the West Indies in the late 16th century. Sir Francis Drake doubled Cape Horn and reached the coast of California near, if not at, San Francisco Bay in June 1579. In 1602 Bartholomew Gosnold reached the coast of Maine near Cape Porpoise, skirted Cape Cod (which he named), and found Narragansett Bay. George Weymouth in 1605 sighted Nantucket and then headed north to find the coast of Maine in the neighborhood of Monhegan and Georges islands.

Other Exploration

Mention should be made of an alleged discovery of America by Swedes and Norwegians from Greenland in the 13th century, through Hudson Bay and the Red River of the North into the present state of Minnesota. This theory rests on an inscribed stone and certain artifacts which need further study. There are also stories of pre-Columbian discoveries of America by the Chinese, Welsh, Irish, Phoenicians, and others. These are all legendary.

BIBLIOGRAPHY

Edward Channing, *History of the United States*, vol. I.
Justin Winsor, *Narrative and Critical History of America*.

— RANDOLPH G. ADAMS

AMERICA FIRST COMMITTEE

Founded in 1940 to fight against U.S. participation in World War II, it was endorsed at the outset by Henry Ford and the historian Charles A. Beard. Isolationists in all parts of the United States were involved, but the committee was especially active in Chicago. By October 1941 the organization began to disintegrate.

— WAYNE ANDREWS

AMERICAN CIVIL LIBERTIES UNION

American Civil Liberties Union, founded in 1920 to defend constitutional freedoms, especially freedom of expression, due process, the right to privacy, and equal protection under the law. Supplemented by congressional lobbying, the ACLU's main activity consists of court litigation of test cases selected on the basis of constitutional principles involved. Counsel is provided without charge from a staff of about 5,000 volunteer lawyers, with expenses paid by contributions from the organization's 275,000 (1975) members. Policy is established by an elected board of directors.

During its early years the ACLU defended the right to teach evolution in public schools and the right of labor unions to organize; was defense counsel in the controversial Sacco-Vanzetti case; and won major Supreme Court cases in the 1930's protecting the right of public protest. More recently the ACLU has focused its efforts on such issues as amnesty for Vietnam War resisters, abortion and birth control, equal rights for women and children, sexual privacy, humane treatment of mental patients, and prison reform.

[See also Civil Rights and Liberties.]

BIBLIOGRAPHY

Charles L. Markmann, *The Noblest Cry: A History of the American Civil Liberties Union*.

— JOEL HONIG

AMERICAN COLONIZATION SOCIETY

Formed in 1817 to alleviate the plight of free Afro-Americans by removing them from the United States to Africa, the American Colonization Society also worked to aid the manumission of slaves and to suppress the African slave trade. Throughout its existence the society believed that the race question superseded the questions of slavery and discrimination, and was unable to visualize a biracial society. This led the society into conflicts with the abolitionists, the Radical Republicans, and most Afro-American leaders.

Various colonization schemes appeared in the late 18th century. These plans, increasingly centered in the upper South, emphasized what many felt to be the incompatibility of blacks and whites and proposed colonization as a solution to the problem created by the presence of free blacks as well as the evils of slavery. Following the War of 1812 the idea received impetus from the actions of Paul Cuffe, a black shipowner, who in 1815 transported thirty-eight American blacks to Africa at his own expense.

Colonization was taken up in 1816 by a New Jersey Presbyterian minister, Robert Finley, who convened a series of meetings that led to the formation of the society the following year. As one of the benevolent societies that appeared after the War of 1812, it gained the support of Congregational and Presbyterian clergy, along with that of most of the prominent politicians of the day. Among its early members were Supreme Court Justice Bushrod Washington, Henry Clay, and John Randolph. Official recognition was given to the society by several state legislatures, among them Virginia, Maryland, and Kentucky.

In 1822 the American Colonization Society established the colony of Liberia on the west coast of Africa. In the following decade the number of auxiliary societies increased yearly; receipts grew; and although a total of only 2,638 blacks migrated to Liberia, the number jumped every year. Yet during the decade efforts to secure federal support were rebuffed and the triumph of Jacksonian Democracy blocked the support necessary for a successful program. At the same time, opposition to the society from both abolitionists and proslavery forces combined with mounting debts and internal strife to undermine the organization.

The colony of Liberia on the west coast of Africa was founded in 1822 by the American Colonization Society; appeals for federal aid were rebuffed.

The independence of Liberia after 1846 lifted a great financial burden, and in the 1850's, under the leadership of William McLain, the fortunes of the society revived. Prominent politicians once again endorsed colonization, and for the first time there was some support for the idea from blacks. Although the Civil War might

have boosted the fortunes of the society further, it in fact had the opposite effect. Republicans reviled the society and most blacks—including Martin R. Delany, who had at times supported colonization—rejected it. Under the leadership of its secretary, William Coppinger, the society stressed its educational and missionary activities, sending fewer than 2,000 blacks to Liberia in the decade after 1870.

In the 1890's, when rising racial tensions gave voice to back-to-Africa sentiments among southern blacks, the society, which was constantly plagued by a lack of funds and in 1892 was deprived of the services of both the resourceful Coppinger and its longtime president J. H. B. Latrobe, found itself unequal to the task. After a brief period during which the society focused on an unsuccessful attempt to remodel the educational system of Liberia, the organization languished; by 1910, it had all but ceased to exist.

BIBLIOGRAPHY

Willis Dolmond Boyd, "Negro Colonization in the Reconstruction Era, 1865–1870," *Georgia Historical Quarterly*, vol. 40 (1956).

George M. Frederickson, *The Black Image in the White Mind.*

Edwin S. Redkey, *Black Exodus.*

P. J. Staudenraus, *The African Colonization Movement: 1816–1865.*

— WILLIAM G. SHADE

AMERICAN EXPEDITIONARY FORCES

This term was used to designate the American troops serving in Europe during World War I. The declaration of war found the United States without plans for organizing a force that would be capable of offensive action in modern warfare. On May 26, 1917, Maj. Gen. John J. Pershing, who had been selected by President Woodrow Wilson to command American land forces abroad, was directed to proceed with his staff to France. Shortly after his arrival, convinced that military assistance on a vast scale would be necessary to Allied success, Pershing cabled the War Department that its minimum undertaking should contemplate one million men in France by the following May, and that plans should be based on an ultimate force of three million. When the armistice came, approximately two million men had been transported to Europe, where they were trained, subsisted, and were equipped through their own supply system, and took a decisive part in bringing the war to a successful conclusion.

In the spring and early summer of 1918 a series of powerful German offensives threatened defeat of the Allies. In the crisis Pershing placed the entire resources of the American Expeditionary Forces at the disposal of the Allied High Command, postponing until July 24, 1918, the formation of the American First Army.

From France, General Pershing cabled the War Department that it should prepare for an ultimate force of three million men.

The assistance the United States gave the Allies in combat began in May with the capture of Cantigny by an American division in the first independent American offensive operation of the war. This was followed early in June by the entrance into battle of two divisions that stopped the German advance on Paris near Château-Thierry. In July two American divisions, with one Moroccan division, formed the spearhead of the counterattack against the Château-Thierry salient, which marked the turning point of the war. Approximately 300,000 American troops were engaged in this second Battle of the Marne. In the middle of September the American First Army of 550,000 men reduced the Saint-Mihiel salient. The Meuse-Argonne offensive began in the latter part of September. After forty-seven days of intense fighting, this great battle ended brilliantly for the First and Second armies on Nov. 11. More than 1,200,000 American soldiers had participated.

With the cessation of hostilities, attention was immediately turned to repatriating the troops. By the end of August 1919 the last American division had embarked, leaving only a small force in occupied Germany, and on Sept. 1, 1919, Pershing and his staff sailed for the United States.

— JOHN J. PERSHING

AMERICAN FEDERATION OF LABOR-CONGRESS OF INDUSTRIAL ORGANIZATIONS

The AFL and CIO were united in 1955 after almost twenty years of often intense and bitter rivalry. Forces leading to the merger were many and varied, including a hostile political environment (evident to labor leaders by the passage of the Taft-Hartley Act in 1947 and the election of a Republican president in 1952) and the conviction that the combined resources of the two organizations were required if the benefits of unionism were to be extended to burgeoning groups of white-collar workers, public employees, professionals, and others.

The merger did not change in any fundamental way the decentralized and essentially economic nature of the labor movement. The AFL-CIO does not itself engage in collective bargaining or issue strike calls (there are minor exceptions), this power residing, as it always has, with the autonomous national and international unions affiliated with the parent body. Power of the AFL-CIO over its affiliates did expand in important ways, however; this centralizing trend is best illustrated in the explicit constitutional authority given the AFL-CIO to expel unions for corruption or domination by Communist, Fascist, or other totalitarian forces. The AFL-CIO also adopted a vigorous antidiscrimination vow, created a single political arm (the Committee on Political Education), and moved with renewed spirit and a sizable bankroll into electioneering politics—officially on a nonpartisan basis but in reality in close alliance with the Democratic party.

In the late 1950's, the AFL-CIO's attention was focused on internal problems of corruption and racketeering. Televised hearings of Senator John L. McClellan's Select Committee on Improper Activities in the Labor or Management Field revealed dramatically the firm hold corrupt, and sometimes gangster-ridden, elements had taken of some AFL-CIO affiliates. Although President George Meany moved forthrightly against the racketeers and expelled several unions, including the huge International Brotherhood of Teamsters, the AFL-CIO could not prevent the passage of the Landrum-Griffin Act (1959). The act regulated internal union affairs and guaranteed democratic rights to union members.

In the 1960's, the AFL-CIO identified with the New Frontier and Great Society domestic programs of presidents John F. Kennedy and Lyndon Johnson. Its leadership and lobbying support contributed to legislative successes in such areas as civil rights, voting rights, housing, education, health and medical care, urban redevelopment, and poverty programs. Similar success did not follow its determined efforts to amend the Taft-Hartley Act (that is, repeal of section 14b).

The AFL-CIO found itself in opposition to much of the domestic legislation and policies of President Richard Nixon, particularly his anti-inflationary wage- and price-control program. Nevertheless, labor remained neutral in the 1972 presidential race, the first time in years that the Democratic candidate did not win the endorsement and heavy financial support of the AFL-CIO. After the 1972 election and the Watergate scandals, the AFL-CIO moved vigorously on two political fronts, reasserting its influence in the Democratic party and calling for the impeachment of President Nixon.

Approximately 13 million men and women were members of AFL-CIO unions in 1974. Some national and international unions have always remained independent of the AFL-CIO or have been expelled or suspended from it. Two of the biggest independent unions in the early 1970's were the International Brotherhood of Teamsters and the United Automobile Workers. The AFL-CIO has made some progress in organizing white-collar, public, and professional workers, but these groups are still among the largest potential sources for new union recruits.

American Federation of Labor

Launched in 1886, the AFL was in philosophy, structure, goals, and tactics the expression of a long process of evolution, its roots going as far back as the 1790's, when the first local unions emerged in the United States. Other streams of influence were European in origin, debts to the "new unionism" of the British labor movement and to "economic" Marxism being especially significant. Moreover, the philosophy, structure, and fundamental goals of the fledgling AFL have been remarkably successful and durable and continue to describe, in essence but with some important exceptions, the nature of the American labor movement today.

In technical language, the AFL was a trade union center, meaning that it was a "roof organization" under whose banner a large number and variety of other union organizations rallied in order to achieve greater economic and political strength and to pursue certain minimal, common objectives. The most powerful of these affiliates were the national and international unions (so called because they enrolled Canadian, as well as U.S., workers), such as the United Brotherhood of Carpenters and Joiners and the United Mine Workers. Initially their jurisdictions tended to cover a single trade or craft of skilled workers but—under pressures of technological change, changes in the skill mix of the labor force, and the emergence of the mass-production industries in the 20th century—they came to exercise jurisdiction over several trades or crafts, entire industries, and even related industries. Eventually well over a hundred national and international unions became affiliated with the AFL. They in turn were composed of local unions centered in towns, cities, or counties. Local unions from different national unions frequently formed city centrals to pursue common local political, educational, and community goals. Likewise, within each state, city centrals and local unions were the chief pillars upon which state federations of labor were erected, largely for political interaction with state governments.

Sovereign units within this structure were the national and international unions. They were the principal

Samuel Gompers, generally accepted as the father of the modern American labor movement, was the first president of the AFL. (Corbis-Bettmann)

founders of the AFL, and they carried primary responsibility for the achievement of labor's overwhelmingly economic goals of higher wages, shorter hours, and improved conditions of work. Their strategy was to organize enough of the trade or industry to gain control over the supply of labor, use that power position to force employers (via the strike or threat of it) to bargain collectively over the terms of their workers' employment, and sign a trade agreement embodying such terms. Unionism of this type has variously been called "business" unionism, "job control" unionism, or "pure and simple" unionism.

Within such a decentralized, essentially economic structure as described above, the AFL itself carried out limited functions of a service, political, and representative nature. For example, the AFL lobbied for or against legislation in the Congress, carried major responsibility for labor's international activities, helped organize the unorganized, and performed the role of labor's spokesman to the public. These functions were handled through an annual convention, an elected executive council, a president, a secretary-treasurer, and a growing number of service departments. Samuel Gompers, generally accepted as the father of the modern American labor movement, was the first president of the AFL (1886–94, 1895–1924). He was followed by William Green (1925–52) and George Meany (1953–55). The AFL merged with the Congress of Industrial Organizations in 1955 to form the current trade union center, the AFL-CIO.

Congress of Industrial Organizations

The CIO emerged as a strong rival and competitor of the AFL in the 1930's, although there had long before been dissatisfaction with AFL leadership and policies. From its earliest days, the AFL was challenged by Marxist organizations like the Socialist Labor party of Daniel DeLeon and the Socialist party of Eugene V. Debs. These leftist political groups believed that the primary battle facing American workers was on the political rather than the economic front and that major structural changes in the capitalist system were required in order to end exploitation and wage slavery. In addition, the Industrial Workers of the World, a militant but tiny anarchosyndicalist movement, sought to free workers through a cataclysmic general strike and the subsequent erection of a decentralized society run by the unions. Many of the AFL's own national unions were won over to the Socialist cause, yet none of these radical challenges ever succeeded in substituting its program for the procapitalist, job-control unionism of the AFL majority.

The CIO did not pretend to challenge the AFL on radical ideological or philosophical grounds, and it was therefore qualitatively a quite different movement from some of the AFL's earlier antagonists. The major quarrel CIO leaders had with the AFL concerned structure, organizing, and power. They wanted to organize the largely unorganized workers in the mass-production industries (auto, rubber, steel, glass, aluminum, chemical), which had grown explosively since the turn of the century. Moreover, they wanted to organize all of them, regardless of skills, into industrial unions rather than into the traditional craft unions of skilled workers. That the CIO was a successful movement is traceable both to the procapitalist philosophy it shared with the AFL and to the accuracy of its views on structure and organizing. Indeed, as the CIO began to leap forward in membership in the late 1930's, the AFL saw itself forced to abandon antiquated policies and compete vigorously with the CIO for members in the mass-production industries.

Lesser, but still very important, divergences of program between the rival AFL and CIO movements concerned the role of government and legislation, partisan politics, racial discrimination, corruption, and international affairs. The role of the federal government had changed from the laissez-faire concept to that of the general welfare state; unskilled workers in national market industries needed government protection more than skilled workers in local markets; finally, the victorious New Deal coalition of the Democratic party, resting in large part upon worker, black, and urban support, contained a clear message to politically minded union leaders, who wished to turn out huge metropolitan pluralities for friendly Democratic candidates—thus assuring favorable social and economic legislation and a friendly White House.

The CIO's success as a movement stemmed from its procapitalist philosophy—shared by the AFL—and from its accurate grasp of organizing and structure.

An effort to reform the AFL from within began in 1933 after recovery legislation had rekindled the union spirit. Failing to achieve the success they desired during 1933–35, the labor progressives set up the Committee for Industrial Organization in November 1935. Unions supporting the committee were suspended from the AFL the following year, and after spectacular organizing successes in the steel, automobile, rubber, and other industries, the committee became the Congress of Industrial Organizations in November 1938. Its first president and undoubtedly most dramatic and forceful leader was John L. Lewis (1938–40). He was succeeded by Philip Murray, who died in office in 1952, and by Walter P. Reuther (1952–55). The CIO merged with the AFL in 1955 to form the AFL-CIO.

BIBLIOGRAPHY

Irving Bernstein, *The Turbulent Years.*

Walter Galenson, *The CIO Challenge to the AFL.*

Arthur J. Goldberg, *AFL-CIO: Labor United.*

Samuel Gompers, *Seventy Years of Life and Labor.*

Joseph C. Goulden, *Meany: The Unchallenged Strong Man of American Labor.*

Edward Levinson, *Labor on the March.*

Lewis L. Lorwin, *The American Federation of Labor.*

James O. Morris, *Conflict Within the AFL.*

Philip Taft, *The AF of L in the Time of Gompers* and *The AF of L From the Death of Gompers to the Merger.*

— JAMES O. MORRIS

AMERICAN INDIAN MOVEMENT

American Indian Movement (AIM), a militant organization founded in Minneapolis in 1968 by Dennis Banks, George Mitchell, and Mary Jane Wilson that set out to alleviate poverty and disenfranchisement among nonreservation Native Americans, launching self-help projects and a "police the police" program in Minnesota. After 1971, with the recruitment of Russell Means, Carter Camp, and John Trudell and many other non-Minnesota natives, the organization became fully national in character and shifted its focus to agitation for recognition of American Indian treaty rights in reservation rather than urban settings. The locus of AIM's activity from late 1972 onward was the Pine Ridge Reservation in South Dakota. On June 26, 1975, in the midst of a counterinsurgency campaign coordinated by the Federal Bureau of Investigation (FBI), which by that point had cost more than forty activists their lives, a firefight near the reservation village of Oglala left another Indian and two federal agents dead. Three AIM members—Bob Robideau, Dino Butler, and Leonard Peltier—were charged with murdering the FBI men. Robideau and Butler were acquitted for having acted in self-defense. Peltier, however, was later convicted and sentenced to double life imprisonment. He remained incarcerated despite a federal appeals court having twice concluded that his trial was "fraught with government misconduct."

That same year a carrot was added to the stick. The Indian Self-Determination and Educational Assistance Act, proposed by President Richard Nixon and passed under President Gerald R. Ford, appeared to satisfy many Native American complaints and thereby eroded support for AIM-style confrontation. AIM never recovered from this combination of cooptation and violent repression. Although it mounted a few noteworthy efforts thereafter, such as the 1978 Longest Walk (from San Francisco to Washington, D.C.), the 1979 and 1980 Black Hills International Survival Gatherings, and the 1981–1984 Yellow Thunder Camp occupation in the Black Hills, AIM was largely a spent force. By the 1990s the movement had declined to such an extent that a small clique calling itself National AIM, Inc., chartered under the laws of Minnesota and existing on the basis of substantial federal and corporate subsidies, was able to appropriate even its name.

[See also Indian Affairs, Bureau of.]

BIBLIOGRAPHY

Ward Churchill and Jim Vander Wall, *Agents of Repression: The FBI's Secret Wars Against the Black Panther Party and the American Indian Movement* (Boston, 1988).

Peter Matthiessen, *In the Spirit of Crazy Horse,* 2nd ed. (New York, 1991).

— WARD CHURCHILL

AMERICAN LABOR PARTY

The ALP was formed in July 1936 as the New York State unit of the Nonpartisan League. Circumstances specific to New York dictated the creation of a separate party rather than a Committee for Industrial Organization campaign body allied to the Democratic party: a Tammany machine unsympathetic to President Franklin D. Roosevelt and the New Deal; a large ethnic bloc that was traditionally socialistic; and a state law permitting dual nominations. The successful campaigns of Fiorello H. La Guardia for New York City mayor in 1937 and Herbert H. Lehman for governor in 1938 demonstrated that the ALP held the balance of power between the two major parties. Nevertheless, this potent position, displayed in the elections of the next five years, eroded because of factional disputes and a loss of union support and voter allegiance—all the result primarily of Communist influence in the ALP. In 1944 the right wing split off to form the Liberal party, and subsequently the ALP lost its swing position in New York politics. Although it recorded its highest vote in the national election in 1948, as the New York unit of the Progressive party, the ALP thereafter declined rapidly and disbanded in 1954. The New York pattern of third-party pressure politics that it had pioneered continued, however, through the activities of the Liberal party and, from the opposite end of the political spectrum, of the Conservative party, founded in 1962.

BIBLIOGRAPHY

Warren Moscow, *Politics in the Empire State.*

— DAVID BRODY

AMERICAN LEGION

The American Legion is the largest U.S. veterans' organization, with membership open to any person, male or female, who has served honorably on active duty in the U.S. armed forces during the hostilities of World War I, World War II, the Korean conflict, or the war in Vietnam.

The Legion was founded in February 1919 by a group of Allied Expeditionary Forces staff officers at Paris. Led by Col. Theodore Roosevelt, Jr., the founders sought both to bolster soldier morale during the post-armistice period and to provide an alternative to veterans' groups being set up in the United States. They enunciated the organization's purposes at the Paris Caucus and saw them reaffirmed at the Continental Caucus, held three months later at St. Louis, Mo. The Legionnaires dedicated themselves to perpetuating the principles for which they had fought, to inculcating civic responsibility to the nation, to preserving the history of their participation in the war, and to binding together as comrades all those who had fought. Among other aims, they pledged themselves to defending law and order, to developing "a one hundred percent Americanism," and to working to help others.

The Legion soon assumed the role of spokesman for all former doughboys, although its 1920 membership of 840,000 represented only about 18.5 percent of eligible veterans. Over the next half-century the Legion's membership fluctuated from a low of 610,000 in 1925 to a high of 3,325,000 in 1946, followed by a general decline, leveling off by 1972 to 2,700,000.

Pursuit of its goals of Americanism, military preparedness, and extending veterans' benefits has led the Legion into many controversies. It has striven to rid school textbooks and public libraries' shelves of alien, Communist, syndicalist, or anarchist influences. During the "red scare" of 1919–20, four Legionnaires were killed in a shootout with Industrial Workers of the World organizers at Centralia, Wash. Its advocacy of preparedness during the late 1930's, when isolationism was dominant nationally, made the organization unpopular with many, as did its support of universal military training in the 1950's. Similarly its condemnation of U.S. participation in United Nations Economic and Social Council activities and its call for a total blockade of Communist Cuba during the 1960's sparked debates.

The American Legion's pursuit of its goals of Americanism, military preparedness, and extending veterans' benefits has led it into many controversies.

The Legion's strenuous efforts to obtain benefits for veterans earned for it the reputation by the late 1930's of being one of the nation's most effective interest groups. Its demand for a bonus for World War I veterans, finally met in 1936 over the objections of four successive presidents, and its promotion of the GI Bill of Rights for World War II veterans, achieved in 1944, testified to its highly publicized dedication to all veterans—not just its members. Other, less controversial activities of the Legion include support of programs for children's welfare and for physical and vocational rehabilitation; sponsorship of Cub Scouts, Boy Scouts, and Explorer Scout troops; and promotion of school oratorical and essay-writing contests on patriotic subjects.

The Legion has some 16,100 local posts throughout the world. These posts are bound together into departments at the state level, which send representatives to the annual national convention. The convention in turn sets policy for the organization and elects the national commander and national executive committee. The latter directs the organization from national headquarters at Indianapolis, Ind., between conventions. The Legion's charter forbids formal political activity by the organization or its elective officers. Nonetheless the Legion does maintain a liaison office in Washington, D.C., and publishes the monthly *American Legion Magazine* from its New York branch.

BIBLIOGRAPHY

Raymond Moley, Jr., *The American Legion Story.*

— DAVIS R. B. ROSS

AMERICAN PARTY

American Party, or the Know-Nothing party, enjoyed a meteoric career during the 1850's. It was founded in New York in 1849 as a secret patriotic society known as the Order of the Star Spangled Banner, but experienced little success until after 1852. Expansion from that time on was so rapid that by 1854 a national organization could be perfected.

This phenomenal growth was due partly to the charm of secrecy with which the party clothed itself. Members were initiated and sworn not to reveal its mysteries; their universal answer to questions was "I know nothing about it," thus giving their organization its popular name—the Know-Nothing party. All who joined were pledged to vote only for native Americans, to work for a twenty-one-year probationary period preceding naturalization, and to combat the Catholic church.

More important in accounting for the party's success was the period in which it thrived. Older party lines had been disrupted by the Kansas-Nebraska Act, and many voters, unwilling to cast their lot either with proslavery Democrats or antislavery Republicans, found refuge with the Know-Nothings. At this time, too, anti-Catholic sentiment, long fostered by churches, societies, and the press, was reaching its height. The American party attracted thousands of persons who sincerely believed that Catholicism and immigration menaced their land.

These factors account for the startling strength shown by the party. In the elections of 1854 and 1855 it was successful in a number of New England and border states, and its supporters fully expected to carry the country in 1856.

By this time, however, the slavery issue had caused a split in Know-Nothing ranks. A proslavery resolution, pushed through the 1855 convention by southern delegates, caused a lasting breach, and the American party entered the election of 1856 so hopelessly divided that its presidential candidate, Millard Fillmore, carried only the state of Maryland. This crushing defeat and the growing sectional antagonism over slavery brought about the party's rapid end.

BIBLIOGRAPHY

C. Beals, *Brass-Knuckle Crusade: The Great Know-Nothing Conspiracy.*
Ray Allen Billington, *The Protestant Crusade, 1800–1860.*
L. F. Schmeckebier, *History of the Know-Nothing Party in Maryland.*

— RAY ALLEN BILLINGTON

AMERICAN RAILWAY UNION

American Railway Union, started by Eugene V. Debs in June 1893 in an attempt to unite all railroad workers. In June 1894 it ordered its members not to handle Pullman cars in sympathy with the Pullman shop strikers. Violence resulting, President Grover Cleveland sent troops to stop interference with the mails. The union officers were jailed for violating an injunction secured by the railroads under the Sherman Antitrust Act. The strike was lost, and the union collapsed.

BIBLIOGRAPHY

McAlister Coleman, *Eugene V. Debs.*

— JAMES D. MAGEE

AMERICANS WITH DISABILITIES ACT

Americans with Disabilities Act (ADA) was passed in 1990 when Congress determined that the estimated 43 million disabled persons in the United States were a "minority . . . subjected to a history of purposeful and unequal treatment." The ADA prohibited private employers from disability-based discrimination if an individual could do a job's "essential functions" with or without "reasonable accommodations." The act also mandated accessibility and reasonable accommodations and prohibited disability-based discrimination in state and local government services, public transit, telecommunications, and public places (restaurants, stores, theaters, private schools, hospitals, and other entities offering the public goods and services). The ADA allowed exemptions if compliance would cause "undue hardship" because of excessive cost.

[See also Disability Rights Movement.]

BIBLIOGRAPHY

Stephen Percy, *Disability, Civil Rights, and Public Policy* (Tuscaloosa, Ala., 1989).

— PAUL K. LONGMORE

AMISTAD CASE

In 1839 fifty-four slaves on the Spanish schooner *Amistad* mutinied near Cuba, murdered part of the crew, and attempted to cause the remainder to sail to Africa. They landed on Long Island Sound in the jurisdiction of American courts. Piracy charges were quashed, it being held that it was not piracy for persons to rise up against those who illegally held them captive. Salvage claims, initially awarded by legal proceedings in Connecticut, were overturned by the Supreme Court in 1841 and the Africans were freed. Former President John Quincy Adams represented the Africans before the Supreme Court. Private charity provided their transportation back to Africa, and the organized support on their behalf played a part in the later establishment of the American Missionary Association. This case offers an interesting comparison with the *Creole* affair.

BIBLIOGRAPHY

J. W. Barber, *A History of the Amistad Captives.*

— HENRY N. DREWRY

AMNESTY

Amnesty, the decision of a government not to punish certain offenses, typically of a political nature. Amnesty is usually general, applies to certain groups or communities of people, and relates to a particular historical event. It overlooks both the offense and the offender. Amnesty is based upon the theory that forgiveness can be more in the interest of general welfare than prosecution. The U.S. Constitution gives the president the authority to grant pardon and, by interpretation, amnesty.

Amnesty was used by President George Washington to quell the Whiskey Rebellion of 1794. He offered amnesty to citizens of several Pennsylvania counties who refused to pay taxes levied upon the manufacture of alcohol. In 1807, President Thomas Jefferson pardoned army deserters outside the country if they turned themselves in within four months and resumed their duties. President James Madison issued three amnesty proclamations for deserters after the War of 1812. President Andrew Jackson issued an amnesty proclamation in 1830, but recipients were precluded from serving in the military.

Following the Civil War, no action was taken against southern deserters. Moreover, President Abraham Lincoln granted amnesty to all Union deserters; they were to return to their units within sixty days and serve out their enlistment or lose their citizenship. Although some Radical Republicans branded them traitors, the Confederates were entitled to the protection accorded participants in a recognized war. The establishment of the Confederacy was the deliberate act of an entire people through their organized state governments.

The executive branch of the government attempted, even during the Civil War, to provide genuine relief to those allied to the southern cause. Lincoln believed that through the use of his amnesty power he could facilitate reunion and ease sectional hatreds. He attempted—unsuccessfully—to establish a parole system for political prisoners and offered a pardon to southerners who would take an oath of allegiance to the federal government.

Following Lincoln's assassination, his successor, Andrew Johnson, a Tennessee Democrat, indicated he would be more reluctant to grant amnesty, especially to Confederate military and civilian leaders. However, during his three years in office he proclaimed three executive amnesties, each more liberal than the former. His final proclamation, on Christmas of 1868, was a universal amnesty that even included Jefferson Davis in its provisions.

Congress was at the opposite pole from the executive branch on the issue of clemency, both before and after the war. In addition to providing criminal and civil penalties for Confederates during the Civil War, Congress continued to press the southerners after the war by passing the Fourteenth Amendment (1868), the third section of which effectively precluded southerners who had previously served in federal or state offices from ever serving in a government position again. Another law passed by Congress denied all active supporters of the Confederacy the right to vote, even those who had been pardoned by the president. Although the Supreme Court declared this law invalid, a later act effectively denied the right to vote to those southerners who had been pardoned by the president.

One important reason why Congress was reluctant to grant amnesty was that the Radical Republicans believed that a lenient policy toward the South would ultimately undermine their numerical supremacy in Congress. Consequently, not until May 22, 1872, did Congress pass a limited amnesty law. Congress also enacted laws precluding Confederates from serving on juries and from receiving military commissions. Indeed, it was not until 1898 that the last political disability of southerners was removed by Congress, when it repealed the third section of the Fourteenth Amendment. The amnesty issue was a major reason for the impeachment and near removal of President Johnson. It created bitterness toward the Republicans that is still evident in the South and encouraged the founding of the Ku Klux Klan.

After World War I, there was no general amnesty for deserters, although President Woodrow Wilson did grant full amnesty to nearly 5,000 persons serving federal sentences for conscription violations. In 1924, President Calvin Coolidge restored citizenship to those who had deserted after the actual fighting in Europe stopped and before a final peace treaty was signed. Following World War II, President Harry S. Truman established an amnesty board, which recommended individual consideration of each amnesty request. Only 1,523 out of 15,000 persons were pardoned—most of them on religious grounds. No amnesty was granted to draft evaders or deserters following the Korean War.

In 1974 President Gerald R. Ford granted partial amnesty to those who had unlawfully avoided military service in the Vietnam War—provided they agree to some form of public service.

The Vietnam War was one of America's longest and most divisive wars. It was a cold war battleground in which the United States, as the military leader of the non-Communist world, was unable to wear down a Communist guerrilla army sheltered in dense Asian jungles. Eventually, the universities and the mass media within the United States began to ignite internal dissent, which adversely affected public opinion regarding the merits of pursuing the struggle. Over 500,000 men deserted the armed services during this increasingly unpopular war. An additional 8,000 men were convicted of draft violations. On Sept. 16, 1974, President Gerald R. Ford proclaimed a conditional form of clemency, providing for a method by which draft dodgers and military deserters would be forgiven following a prescribed time of public service. A presidential clemency board, with specific guidelines, was designated to carry out the task. On Mar. 31, 1975, the last day on which applications for clemency could be accepted, the clemency board had received approximately 25,000 applications (20 percent of the 125,000 persons eligible).

BIBLIOGRAPHY

Jonathan T. Dorris, *Pardon and Amnesty Under Lincoln and Johnson.*

— EDWARD M. BYRNE

ANARCHISTS

Anarchism is a political philosophy that rejects rule and particularly the rule of the state. To the anarchist, the modern state stands for everything he repudiates—centralization, harsh coercion, economic exploitation, and war. In the United States, anarchist views began to be expressed very early. The statement "That government is best which governs least," associated with Thomas Jefferson, while not anarchist, moves strongly in an anarchist direction. Josiah Warren (1798–1874), with his philosophy of the "sovereignty of the individual," was a good representative of early 19th-century anarchism.

Classical American anarchism—which evolved from the post–Civil War period to about World War I—developed two schools of thought about its goals and two about means. In terms of goals, some anarchists, like Benjamin E. Tucker (1854–1939), were "individualists." Their great fear was that the individual would be lost in the organized group. But other anarchists were "communists," tending to follow the teachings of men like Peter Kropotkin (1842–1921). Emma Goldman (1869–1940) and Alexander Berkman (1870–1936) were two of the best-known communist anarchists. Goldman was a pioneer in the birth-control movement and did much to advance the cause of freedom of expression. Many of her ideas were developed in her journal *Mother Earth* (1906–17). Berkman was an able advocate of communist anarchism in such books as *Now and After: The ABC of Communist Anarchism* (1929). In terms of means and strategies, there were "anarchists of the deed," who thought physical violence was permissible, and anarchists who stressed the importance of nonviolent methods. Leon Czolgosz, the assassin of President William McKinley, was an anarchist of the deed; and Berkman, in his 1892 attempt on the life of steel magnate Henry Clay Frick, seemed to espouse the same position. But many anarchists insisted on principles of nonviolence: thus, Tucker, in his magazine *Liberty* (1881–1908) and in books like *Instead of a Book* (1893), argued that the state must be abolished by education and nonviolent resistance; and in the latter part of his life Berkman emphasized nonviolent approaches. American anarchist followers of the Russian novelist Leo Tolstoy were, of course, radical pacifists. The Industrial Workers of the World (IWW), founded in 1905 and particularly active to the end of World War I, was often said to be anarchosyndicalist in its outlook: it distrusted the state and hoped to reorganize society along syndicalist (industrial union) lines.

While not exactly anarchist, the statement "That government is best which governs least," associated with Jefferson, moves strongly in an anarchist direction.

Anarchism left its imprint on American legislation and administrative practice. Thus, immigration legislation excluded anarchists, and so in 1919 Goldman and Berkman were deported to the Soviet Union. Legislators have often mistakenly assumed that all anarchists advocate overthrow of the government by force or violence.

Anarchist influence declined between World War I and World War II. After World War II, it was reflected in Dwight MacDonald's well-edited but short-lived journal *Politics*. Many in the so-called New Left movement of the 1960's, during their attacks on the largely Marxist Old Left, developed an outlook that, in its stress on decentralization and its distrust of organization, reminded some of certain classical anarchist positions.

BIBLIOGRAPHY

Paul Eltzbacher, *Anarchism*.
Emma Goldman, *Living My Life*.
Benjamin Tucker, *Individual Liberty*.
Robert Paul Wolff, *In Defense of Anarchism*.
George Woodcock, *Anarchism*.

— MULFORD Q. SIBLEY

ANDERSONVILLE PRISON

Andersonville Prison, established February 1864 in Georgia, was the largest and best known of Confederate military prisons. Hastily established because the number of prisoners constituted a military danger and a serious drain on the food supplies of Richmond, no adequate preparations were made for housing the captives. The poverty of the Confederacy, a defective transportation system, and the concentration of all resources on the army prevented the prison officials from supplying barracks, cooked food, clothing, or medical care to their charges. The prison consisted solely of a log stockade of sixteen and one-half acres (later enlarged to twenty-six acres) through which ran a stream of water. Rations to the prisoners generally consisted of cornmeal and beans, and seldom included meat. Bad sanitary conditions, lack of cooking facilities, poor food, crowding, and exposure soon produced respiratory diseases, diarrhea, and scurvy. The inadequate medical staff, without drugs, could not cope with the situation. During the summer the number of prisoners increased to 31,678. There are 12,912 graves in the national cemetery at Andersonville. Estimates place the total number of deaths at even higher figures. In September, the approach of Gen. W. T. Sherman's army caused the removal of all well prisoners to Charleston, S.C. Only enlisted men were confined at Andersonville; commissioned officers were held at Macon, Ga.

To the Union prisoners at Andersonville and their northern friends it appeared that the Confederates were deliberately murdering the captives through deprivation.

To the prisoners and to their friends in the North it appeared that the Confederates were deliberately murdering the captives. As a result of this belief, Capt. Henry Wirz, commander of the interior of the prison, was tried in August 1865 on charges of murder and conspiring with Jefferson Davis to murder. Although found guilty by a military commission and hanged, Nov. 10, 1865, subsequent investigation has revealed much in Wirz's favor. For many years Andersonville prison was a vital element in the "bloody shirt" issue in politics.

BIBLIOGRAPHY

W. B. Hesseltine, *Civil War Prisons: A Study in War Psychology*.

— W. B. HESSELTINE

ANIMAL PROTECTIVE SOCIETIES

Animal Protective Societies are incorporated under such headings as humane societies, anticruelty societies, animal rescue leagues, and societies for the prevention of cruelty to animals. They operate animal shelters either independently or in conjunction with local city governments. Many have animal hospitals and clinics. These protective societies work to secure and enforce laws that prevent cruelty to animals. Their workers may also become involved in investigating cases of cruelty to animals. They inspect facilities and monitor treatment where animals are housed and used. Much of their effort is devoted to promoting humane education to the general public.

The American Society for the Prevention of Cruelty to Animals, the first of its kind in the United States, was organized by Henry Bergh in New York City in 1866. Concerned over the mistreatment of animals and the squalor in which they were often kept, he also secured the first effective animal protective legislation that same year. Within ten years there were twenty-seven local humane organizations in operation from New Hampshire to California. In 1877 the American Humane Association was organized in Cleveland as a federation of animal protective societies. The following year the organization's declaration of organization was revised to include children. The humane movement has continued to grow, and the American Humane Association, headquartered in Denver, Colo., provides printed materials and services to more than 1,100 local humane groups. Incorporated in 1903, its charter purpose is the prevention of cruelty to children and animals and the distribution of humane education materials. In contrast to those groups opposed to the utilization of animals for man's benefit for specified purposes—antivivisectionists, antizoo groups, vegetarians—because some individuals may inflict suffering, the policy of the American Humane Association is to develop standards and controls applicable to individuals to prevent cruelty, rather than to seek to abolish any specific use of animals by mankind.

In recent years, animal protective agencies have worked closely with the packing and transportation industries to secure legislation for more humane treatment of animals in shipping and slaughtering. The protection of exotic pets and wildlife, particularly endangered species, has emerged as a major area of emphasis. Also, the current overpopulation of unwanted dogs and cats has led the humane movement to support research to find a suitable, inexpensive birth inhibitor, and education programs heavily stress the need for spaying or neutering pets.

Humane organizations are supported primarily by membership fees, contributions, and bequests. They are governed, at either local or national levels, by boards of directors.

BIBLIOGRAPHY

Eileen Schoen, *Early Years: A History of the American Humane Association.*

— DONALD M. HEGG

ANTIFEDERALISTS

The name Antifederalists was fixed upon the opponents of the adoption of the Constitution of the United States (1787–88) by the supporters of the Constitution, who appropriated the more attractive designation Federalists. Although Antifederalism thus came to be defined in relation to the Constitution, it originated as a political force during and after the American Revolution and represented those who favored the retention of power by state governments, in opposition to those who wanted a strong central government. The Federalists sought to assume the role of proponents of a federal form of government, but the Antifederalists were not opposed to such a system. Indeed, they in-

Patrick Henry, famous for his cry "Give me liberty or give me death!" was a leading Antifederalist. Here he addresses the First Continental Congress, in a painting by Clyde Osmen Deland. (Corbis-Bettmann)

sisted that in opposing the Constitution they were seeking to preserve the federal system created by the Articles of Confederation (1781–88), whereas the advocates of the new Constitution were attempting to replace federalism with nationalism and centralization. Some historians argue that a more appropriate name for the Federalists would be the nationalists, and for the Antifederalists, the federalists.

Philosophically, the Antifederalists suspected strong central governments and believed that the greatest gain of the Revolution was throwing off the central power of Great Britain and establishing the power of the states. They had no desire to see the power that had been centered in London transferred to Philadelphia or New York. Believing that freedom could be maintained only by governments close to the people, they supported the doctrine of lodging power in the legislative branch of government on the basis of its being more responsive to public opinion than the executive and the judicial branches. Antifederalist beliefs in the desirability of a weak central government and in the extension of democratic control were fundamental in their opposition to the Constitution. Nearly all Antifederalists were convinced that the Constitution established a national, not a federal, government and would produce a consolidation of previously independent states. They believed that concentrated power led to aristocracy and that power diffused led to democracy.

The Antifederalists published no group of papers comparable to *The Federalist*—authored by James Madison, Alexander Hamilton, and John Jay—but their political philosophy can be reconstructed from scattered articles in newspapers and pamphlets and from the debates in state ratifying conventions. These sources show a prevailing belief that republican government could exist only in a small geographical area and could not be extended successfully over a large territory with a numerous and heterogeneous population. Antifederalists believed that Americans were too diverse to be governed by a single national government and that the sheer size of the country was too great for one republican government. They favored a more rigid system of separation of powers and more extensive checks and balances than provided by the Constitution.

Antifederalists, including such leaders as George Mason, Patrick Henry, and George Clinton, decisively outnumbered Federalists in Rhode Island, New York, North Carolina, and South Carolina and were slightly more than a majority in Massachusetts and Virginia. In spite of the Antifederalist majority in at least six of the thirteen states—and the approval of nine states was required for ratification of the Constitution—the Antifederalists lost to the superior organization of the Federalists, who were aided also by the greater prestige of Federalist leaders, including George Washington and James Madison; by a pro-Constitution newspaper press; by the momentum of early ratification in certain states; by the promise of amendments to the new Constitution; and by the argument posed in some states in terms of union or no union.

The most extensive studies of the sources of strength of the two factions indicate that Antifederalism drew its greatest support from noncommercial interests isolated from the major paths of commerce and little dependent on the mercantile community or foreign markets, whereas the Federalists found their strongest support among the commercial elements, embracing merchants, townspeople, farmers dependent on major cities, and those who exported their surplus production.

With the ratification of the Constitution the Antifederalists did not persist as a group and did not form the basis for political party alignments in the new nation. Although Federalists in the 1790's frequently referred to their Republican opponents as Antifederalists, this usage reflected partisan tactics rather than evidence of historical continuity. Antifederalist ideas, however, did persist and can be seen in the growing concern over the centralized power of the national government that developed during the early decades under the Constitution and continued to some extent throughout American history.

BIBLIOGRAPHY

Noble E. Cunningham, Jr., *The Jeffersonian Republicans: The Formation of Party Organization 1789–1801.*

Cecelia M. Kenyon, ed., *The Antifederalists.*

Jackson Turner Main, *The Antifederalists: Critics of the Constitution, 1781–1788.*

Robert A. Rutland, *The Ordeal of the Constitution: The Antifederalists and the Ratification Struggle of 1787–1788.*

— NOBLE E. CUNNINGHAM, JR.

ANTI-IMPERIALISTS

Anti-imperialists, a term given to Americans who opposed U.S. colonial expansion after the Spanish-American War. Although a number of anti-imperialists had first opposed the acquisition of island territories during the administration of Ulysses Grant and others survived to proclaim the faith in the 1920's, anti-imperialism as a movement of political significance is limited to the years 1898–1900.

Many anti-imperialists rejected organizational activity, but a majority claimed membership in one of the branches of the Anti-Imperialist League that was founded in Boston in November 1898. By 1900 the league claimed to have 30,000 members and over half a million contributors. An organization whose primary goal was the education of public opinion, the league published hundreds of pamphlets denouncing the acquisition of an island empire and the abandonment of America's unique "mission" to hold before the nations of the world the model of the free and self-governing society. George S. Boutwell, Erving Winslow, Edwin Burritt Smith, David Starr Jordan, and Carl Schurz were prominent leaders of the league, and its chief financial contributor was Andrew Carnegie. The most important anti-imperialists working outside the league were William Jennings Bryan and George Frisbie Hoar.

By 1900 the Anti-Imperialist League, founded in Boston to oppose U.S. colonial expansion, claimed to have 30,000 members and over half a million contributors.

Although diverse in motives and party affiliation, the anti-imperialists shared common fears and beliefs. They were convinced that imperialism threatened the ideals and institutions of their own country, and they believed that it was unjust to dictate the political goals and institutions of foreign peoples. Although many anti-imperialists shared the racial bias of their imperialist opponents and some urged the expansion of foreign markets as a solution to domestic surplus, for most, racial "difference" did not require racial subordination nor did trade expansion demand gunboat diplomacy. The anti-imperialists insisted that it was as wrong for a republic to have colonies as it was for a representative government to have subject peoples. Tyranny abroad, they believed, could only undermine democracy at home. They also offered arguments against the constitutionality, economic wisdom, and strategic safety of a policy of insular imperialism. Colonial expansion not only denied the practice of the past, it would waste American resources, undermine the Monroe Doctrine, and embroil the United States in the rivalries of the European powers. Although hampered by having to preach a doctrine of abnegation to a nation of optimists and weakened by a failure to agree on a single policy alternative for the disposition of the Philippine Islands, the anti-imperialists were participants in one of the most intelligently reasoned debates in American history.

Even though they were important as a moral and educational force, the anti-imperalists must be classified among the political failures of American history. The heavy cost of the Philippine-American War and the labors of the anti-imperialists may have helped to check the territorial ambitions of the more zealous imperialists, but none of the immediate goals of the anti-imperialists was secured. The new island territories were officially annexed; President William McKinley easily won reelection in 1900, despite the opposition of the Anti-Imperialist League; and the Philippine Insurrection was mercilessly crushed.

BIBLIOGRAPHY

Robert L. Beisner, *Twelve Against Empire: The Anti-Imperialists, 1898–1900.*

E. Berkeley Tompkins, *Anti-Imperialism in the United States: The Great Debate, 1890–1920.*

— RICHARD E. WELCH, JR.

ANTI-MASONIC MOVEMENTS

Suspicion of secret societies was marked at an early date but the fact that George Washington and other patriots were Masons seemed proof that the order was not dangerous. In 1826, however, when William Morgan, a Freemason and author of a book revealing secrets of the order, disappeared, there was a widespread reaction in western New York, which assumed national importance with the organization of the Anti-Masonic party. Many Masons renounced their vows, membership in New York dwindling from 20,000 to 3,000 between 1826 and 1836. The number of lodges was reduced from 507 before 1826, to 48 in 1832. In Vermont the Grand Lodge voted down a proposal for dissolution, but agreed to receive charters from chapters desiring to surrender them and provided that funds of such lodges should go to the state public school fund. Many congregations were divided, especially Presbyterian, Baptist, Methodist, and Congregational. Masons were excluded from membership, and pastors were barred from their pulpits. In Pennsylvania, Anti-Masonry found favor among Quakers, Mennonites, Dunkers, Moravians, and some Lutheran and German Reformed groups. A Vermont law of 1833 forbade extrajudicial oaths; and elsewhere Masons were deprived of local office and dropped from jury rolls.

Anti-Masonic newspapers were an index of the rapid growth of the Anti-Masonic party. Charging intimidation of printers and suppression of facts of the Morgan trials, party leaders urged the establishment of "free presses." Thurlow Weed, who in 1828 had started the Rochester *Anti-Masonic Enquirer*, was given financial backing in 1830 for his *Albany Evening Journal*, the principal party organ. In 1832 there were forty-six Anti-Masonic papers in New York and fifty-five in Pennsylvania. In September 1831 a national Anti-Masonic convention was held at Baltimore, the first national nominating convention of any party, naming William Wirt of Maryland for president. This, the first third party, only drew support away from Henry Clay, and helped the sweep for Andrew Jackson in 1832. It received seven electoral votes from Vermont. The party also gained adherents in Pennsylvania, Ohio, New Jersey, Massachusetts, Connecticut, and Rhode Island; but only Pennsylvania, through the leadership of Thaddeus Stevens, and Vermont elected Anti-Masonic governors. In the late 1830's the excitement subsided, or was replaced by the antislavery agitation. By 1838 the party had merged with the Whigs.

After the Civil War there was another movement directed against secret societies. The National Christian Association was founded at Aurora, Ill., in 1868 to oppose secret orders, "Jesuitism, Mormonism, atheism, spiritualism and free love." It maintained a national organization and published a weekly, *The Christian Cynosure* (1867–71). This crusade was unsuccessful, and the 1880's and 1890's witnessed a great increase of fraternal orders.

BIBLIOGRAPHY

Charles McCarthy, *The Anti-Masonic Party* and *The Anti-Masonic Scrapbook*, 1883.

J. C. Palmer, *The Morgan Affair and Anti-Masonry*.

— MILTON W. HAMILTON

ANTINOMIAN CONTROVERSY

Antinomian Controversy, a theological dispute begun in Boston by Anne Hutchinson in the fall of 1636. She had been a parishioner and devout admirer of John Cotton in Boston, England, and with her husband followed him to the new Boston, where they were admitted to membership in the First Church. She was exceptionally intelligent, kind, learned, and eloquent and began innocently to repeat on weekdays to small gatherings the substance of Cotton's sermons, but soon commenced delivering opinions of her own. At the height of her influence, about eighty persons were attending lectures in her house.

She caused turmoil by putting a different conclusion from that maintained by the clergy upon the doctrine of the covenant of grace. The standard view held that the elect entered a covenant with God on the condition of their believing in Christ, in return for which God contracted to give them salvation, but that thereafter the justified saints devoted themselves to good works, not in order to merit redemption, but as evidence of their having been called. Mrs. Hutchinson declared that stating the matter thus put too much emphasis upon works and denied the fundamental Protestant tenet of salvation by faith alone. Consequently she preached that the believer received into his soul the very substance of the Holy Ghost and that no value whatsoever adhered to conduct as a sign of justification.

In 1637 Anne Hutchinson was examined by a synod of the ministers, found guilty of eighty erroneous opinions, and publicly repudiated by John Cotton, a minister she had once followed devoutly.

This conclusion made for a disregard of morality such as Protestant theologians had everywhere endeavored to resist, and it could clearly lead to disastrous social consequences; the New England clergy, recognizing in her teachings a form of "Antinomianism," that is, a discarding of the moral law, could not possibly have tolerated her. She made matters worse by accusing all the clergy except Cotton of preaching a covenant of works, so that Gov. John Winthrop stated it began to be as common in Massachusetts to distinguish the party of works and the party of grace "as in other countries between Protestants and papists." Thus she threatened to split the colony into factions, particularly when she was supported by her brother-in-law, the Rev. John Wheelwright, and the new young governor, Henry Vane. The other clergy and magistrates believed that the existence of the whole colony was at stake; led by Winthrop, and employing consummately clever tactics, they regained control of the government in May 1637, then proceeded to disarm Anne's partisans and suppress the movement. Anne was examined by a synod of the ministers, which found her guilty of eighty erroneous opinions; John Cotton publicly repudiated her. Wheelwright was banished to New Hampshire; Anne was arraigned before the general court, where she boasted of having received explicit revelations from the Holy Ghost, a possibility which no orthodox Protestant community could for a moment admit. She was excommunicated from the First Church in March 1638, John Cotton pronouncing sentence upon her, and banished from the colony by the court, whereupon she fled to Rhode Island.

BIBLIOGRAPHY

C. F. Adams, *Antinomianism in the Colony of Massachusetts Bay* and *Three Episodes of Massachusetts History*.

Emery Battis, *Saints and Sectaries: Anne Hutchinson and the Antinomian Controversy in the Massachusetts Bay Colony*.

Perry Miller, *Orthodoxy in Massachusetts*.

E. S. Morgan, "The Case Against Anne Hutchinson," *New England Quarterly*, vol. 10 (1937).

— PERRY MILLER

ANTI-SALOON LEAGUE

Anti-Saloon League, founded at Oberlin, Ohio, May 24, 1893. Creating this statewide organization was the idea of the Rev. H. H. Russell. This "Ohio plan" was copied by many states, and in 1895 a national organization, the Anti-Saloon League of America, was established at the Calvary Baptist Church, Washington, D.C. Soliciting and securing aid from the Protestant Evangelical churches, the league grew rapidly and came to regard itself as the "Church in Action Against the Saloon."

Prior to the Eighteenth Amendment the league centered its attention upon destroying the liquor traffic by legislation. To this end it sought and obtained local option, county option, state prohibition, regulation of interstate liquor shipments, and finally national prohibition. Following national prohibition the league sought by propaganda and pressure to achieve enforcement and the maintenance of this policy. For the first time in its history it was completely on the defensive. Accused of responsibility for the development of bootleg gangs, disrespect for law, and all of the undesirable social practices of the postwar period, the league slowly lost support. The depression of 1929 brought a diminution in the league's revenues. Faced by a public willing to try anything which might reestablish prosperity, and weakened internally, it lost ground rapidly. When in 1933 the Eighteenth Amendment was repealed, the league campaigned again for local option, but was no longer significant in national politics. In 1948 the league changed its name to the Temperance League of America; in 1950 it merged with the National Temperance Movement, forming the National Temperance League.

BIBLIOGRAPHY

E. H. Cherrington, *History of the Anti-Saloon League.*
Peter Odegard, *Pressure Politics.*
Justin Stewart, *Wayne Wheeler, Dry Boss.*

— DAYTON E. HECKMAN

ANTISLAVERY

Antislavery in the United States took several forms during its evolution from the quiet protest of the Germantown Quakers in 1688 through the tragic and violent Civil War, which spawned the Thirteenth Amendment in December 1865. Response to slavery varied from mild doubts concerning the wisdom of the institution to militant hostility toward what was viewed as a sinful and unjust practice. It was intimately connected to conceptions of the meaning of the American experience and intertwined with white racial attitudes, since slavery in the United States was almost exclusively black slavery. As a consequence, different elements within the society perceived the problem of slavery in radically different ways and proposed sometimes contradictory solutions.

In the United States, there existed not one antislavery impulse but rather several distinct movements whose makeup, organization, and objectives differed radically. Throughout the history of antislavery in the United States there were a small number of men and women who may with justice be called abolitionists. Their primary goals were the abolition of slavery throughout the country and the ultimate incorporation of the freed blacks into American society. In the 18th century, abolitionists generally supported plans for gradual emancipation, but a new generation of abolitionists who appeared in the 1830's demanded an immediate end to slavery and advocated the integration of American society. A much larger group among the opponents of slavery were those who feared that blacks neither could nor should be incorporated into American society as equals; it proposed instead the colonization of free blacks outside the United States. These colonizationists were centered in the states of the upper South and the Ohio Valley; increasingly they shifted away from their early opposition to slavery, to focus upon the removal of free blacks. What came to be the largest element in the antislavery crusade were the northern sectionalists, who opposed slavery as the basis of the social and political power of an aristocratic class that unfairly dominated the political process to the disadvantage of northern whites. The racial attitudes of this group covered a broad spectrum, and their main efforts centered upon restricting the expansion of slave territory.

Gradualism

Although the first antislavery tract in the colonies was written by a New England Puritan, Samuel Sewell, the early history of antislavery in America consisted primarily of the agitation of certain English and American Quakers. But even among the Friends, antislavery sentiments grew slowly. Many wealthy Quakers were slaveholders; and in the first half of the 18th century, they caused both Ralph Sandiford and Benjamin Lay to be repudiated by their coreligionists for their antislavery activities. Only at midcentury, when the Society of Friends faced a severe internal crisis brought on by the effects of the Great Awakening and the French and Indian War, did opposition to slavery increase measurably among Quakers. In 1758 the two foremost antislavery Quakers, John Woolman and Anthony Benezet, induced the Philadelphia Yearly Meeting of New Jersey and Pennsylvania Friends to report "an unanimous concern [over] the buying, selling and keeping of slaves." Their activities eventually led to similar actions by the New England and New York Quakers, but it was not until the 1780's that the major meetings could announce that none of their members held slaves.

By that time the opposition to slavery had spread beyond the Society of Friends to other men whose response to slavery was rooted in the secular thought of the Enlightenment. Because of its underlying republican ideology, emphasizing liberty and the rights of man, the American Revolution encouraged antislavery sentiments. James Otis, John Dickinson, and Thomas Paine equated the situation of the American colonists with the plight of their African bondsmen. Thomas Jefferson, although he excluded his attack on the African slave trade from the final draft of the Declaration of Independence, argued that abolition of slavery was a "great object" of the colonists. During these years all the states abolished the African slave trade and most moved toward the ultimate eradication of slavery.

Because of its underlying republican ideology, emphasizing liberty and the rights of man, the American Revolution encouraged antislavery sentiments.

This movement proceeded most rapidly in the states north of the Mason-Dixon line, where slavery was of minor economic importance. Vermont explicitly outlawed slavery in 1777; and the Massachusetts courts similarly interpreted that state's new constitution of 1780. In the same year, Pennsylvania freed, under certain restrictions, all future children of slaves; Rhode Island and Connecticut passed similar laws four years later. After a good deal of controversy, New York (1799) and New Jersey (1804) also accepted proposals for gradual emancipation. With the enactment of the Northwest Ordinance in 1787, slavery was confined to the area that increasingly became known as the South.

Gradual emancipation in the northern states was not achieved without opposition; and the newly formed antislavery societies, which by the 1790's could be found scattered from Massachusetts to North Carolina, played a crucial role in these early achievements. Pennsylvania Quakers established the first such society in 1775. In 1794 a national organization, the American Convention for Promoting the Abolition of Slavery and Improving the Condition of the African Race, held its first meeting. Aside from supporting gradual emancipation, these early antislavery societies attacked the Fugitive Slave Law and the African slave trade, distributed antislavery literature, and encouraged education of blacks. Although their membership included such prominent political figures as Benjamin Franklin, John Jay, Alexander Hamilton, and Benjamin Rush, these early organizations were generally dominated by Quakers. Because of this narrow sectarian base and the ideological limitations of early antislavery sentiment, the movement rapidly waned following its victories in the northern states.

Colonization

During the three decades following 1800, opposition to slavery entered a new phase. Efforts at gradual emancipation gave way to proposals for the colonization of free blacks, and the center of antislavery activity shifted to the upper South. By 1827 Benjamin Lundy could report that more than three-quarters of the members of active antislavery societies lived in the southern states. Although the most vocal opponents of slavery during these years—men such as David Rice, David Barrow, George Bourne, and John Rankin—were active in these states, true abolitionism never gained a foothold anywhere in the South. In the two decades following the Revolution all the southern states except Georgia and South Carolina moved toward emancipation by easing the process of private manumission, and between 1800 and 1815 societies devoted to gradual emancipation sprouted in all the states of the upper South. After 1800 the tide turned and flowed in the opposite direction. By 1830 nearly all the vocal abolitionists were forced to leave the South. Levi Coffin, James G. Birney, the Grimké sisters, Rankin, and even Lundy had to carry their antislavery activities north. As the crucial debate in the Virginia legislature in 1832 revealed, the only antislavery advocates remaining in the South by then were the rapidly dwindling supporters of the American Colonization Society (ACS).

The ACS had originated in response to fears that free blacks could not be successfully incorporated into American society. Its activities typified the conservative reform emanating from a period of fairly modest social and economic change, but its early membership included, along with some of the South's leading politicians, such abolitionists as Lundy, the Tappan brothers, Gerrit Smith, and the young William Lloyd Garrison. Abolitionists formed only a minor element in the ACS, however; although in the early years colonization was usually related to schemes for manumission and gradual emancipation, most advocates of these proposals cared little about the plight of the slave and hoped to rid the country of the troublesome presence of a race generally deemed inferior and degraded. The doctrine of gradualism based on a faith in the perfectibility of all men gave way to the racist perspectives that typified the 19th century. As the ACS became increasingly dominated by those whose main purpose was the deportation of free blacks and shed its antislavery character, the abolitionists turned against the organization.

Immediatism

The appearance of Garrison's *Thoughts on African Colonization* in 1832, and the debates held at Lane Seminary two years later under the direction of Theodore Dwight Weld, signaled a major shift in American antislavery and the emergence of the movement for immediate abolition. One can trace the roots of the doctrine of immediatism to the basic elements of 18th-century antislavery thought and relate its appearance in the United States in the 1830's to such causes as English influence, increasing black militancy, and the failure of gradual emancipation in the South. But the new intensity and enthusiasm that characterized the drive for immediate, uncompensated abolition came about primarily from evangelical perfectionism. Although abolitionists were often ambivalent about their precise programs, their new approach connoted a direct response to the recognition of the sinfulness of slavery and epitomized the abolitionist movement of this period. In rejecting the detached 18th-century perspective that had governed the psychology of gradual emancipation, the advocates of immediate abolition "made a personal commitment to make no compromise with sin."

In the 1830s, antislavery sentiments spread throughout the northern states and a new network of abolition societies began to form.

In the decade of the 1830's, antislavery sentiments spread throughout the northern states and a new network of abolition societies appeared. The New England Anti-Slavery Society was formed in 1831; two years later at a meeting in Philadelphia, delegates from Massachusetts, New York, and Pennsylvania established a national organization, the American Anti-Slavery Society (AAS). In rapid order, auxiliaries appeared in all the eastern states and an energetic effort was made to revive western abolitionism. Following the Lane debates, Weld served as an agent for the AAS, lecturing and organizing local groups throughout Ohio and the western portions of New York and Pennsylvania. His success prompted the AAS to extend the agency system, sending out a new host of agents, the "Seventy," to further expand the number of local societies and advance the idea of immediate abolition of slavery. Many of this group were former Lane students: "Their method was the evangelism of the Great Revival; their doctrine was a doctrine of sin; and their program was to convert congregations of the North to the duty of testimony against the slaveholders of the South."

As a result of such activities the number of state and local societies multiplied rapidly. By 1835 there were 225 auxiliaries of the AAS, a number that grew to 1,346 in the next three years; and by 1840 there were 1,650 such organizations, with a total of between 130,000 and 170,000 members. Little is known about the makeup of these societies except that they proliferated in rural Yankee areas "burned over" by the Great Revival and that a majority of their members were women. Abolitionist leaders were highly educated and moderately prosperous men of some importance in their communities. Their most significant characteristics were an intense religious commitment and Yankee origins. Nearly two-thirds were pastors, deacons, and elders of evangelical churches, and an even larger proportion of white abolitionist leaders traced their family origins to New England.

A distinctive group within the movement was made up of the free blacks who were prominent in the activities of the underground railroad and who provided a crucial element of abolitionist leadership. During the 1830's men such as James Forten, Theodore S. Wright, and Samuel Ringgold Ward cooperated with white abolitionists and held positions of power within the abolition societies. However, blacks were generally denied positions of power in these organizations and resented the racism and paternalism of the whites. During the 1830's and 1840's a series of all-black National Negro Conventions acted to focus the efforts of black abolitionists.

The major activity of the abolitionists in the 1830's consisted in the dissemination of antislavery arguments in the hope that moral suasion would effect the end of slavery in the United States. Birney estimated that in 1839 there were "upwards of a hundred" abolitionist newspapers, but most were short-lived and only a handful maintained continued existence during this period. The most famous of these were Garrison's *Liberator*, published in Boston from 1831 to 1865, and the *Emancipator*, which functioned as the major organ of the AAS. Aside from its newspaper, the AAS issued a quarterly, two monthlies, and a children's magazine. It also supported a yearly antislavery almanac and a series of pamphlets that included the classics of antislavery literature, such as Angelina Grimké's *Appeal to the Christian Women of the South* and James Throme and J. Horace Kimball's *Emancipation in the West Indies.* While it was not until the 1840's and 1850's that slave narratives, like that of Frederick Douglass, and sentimental antislavery novels, such as Harriet Beecher Stowe's *Uncle Tom's Cabin,* appeared, the appeal to sentiment was central to the most powerful of the abolitionist attacks on slavery published in the 1830's, Weld's *Slavery As It Is.* In this volume Weld chose to limit those characterizations of slavery that were "merely *horrid*" in order to "give place to those which are absolutely diabolical." Yet he drew most of these tales of cruelty directly from southern sources and insisted that they each could be thoroughly authenticated.

Denied positions of influence in the white abolitionist organizations, black abolitionists in the 1830's and 40's organized a series of all-black National Negro Conventions.

In 1835 the AAS launched its postal campaign under the direction of Lewis Tappan. The society hoped to inundate the South with publications and convince southerners to rid themselves of the wretched evils of slavery. In that year the AAS produced over a million copies of their publications and thousands of copies were mailed to whites in the South. Although the intention of the literature was to sway the minds and sentiments of the slaveholders, it was immediately viewed as incendiary. In July 1835, a mob attacked the Charleston, S.C., post office and burned a number of abolitionist newspapers. In the following year a law excluding antislavery literature from the mails, which Andrew Jackson strongly favored, failed in Congress by a narrow margin; but with the cooperation of the Jackson administration, local postmasters effectively eliminated the circulation of abolitionist material in the South.

When the postal campaign failed, the AAS shuffled its organizational structure and turned to a campaign to present Congress with petitions on a variety of subjects related to slavery. The petition was a traditional antislavery instrument, but in 1835 John C. Calhoun and his South Carolina colleague in the House, James Hammond, moved against hearing any antislavery pleas. In an effort to disassociate themselves from this attack on the civil rights of northern whites, northern Democrats accepted the more moderate gag rule that automatically tabled all antislavery petitions. Undaunted the AAS, using the numerous societies established by the Seventy, flooded Congress with petitions. Between January 1837 and March 1838, the AAS presented petitions signed by more than 400,000 people. The largest number of these opposed the annexation of Texas and called for the abolition of slavery in the District of Columbia. Yet by 1840, the gag rule had effectively stifled the petition campaign.

Political Antislavery

Although it had grown rapidly during the 1830's, at the end of the decade the abolition movement remained unpopular and generally weak. The abolitionists had encountered mob violence in the North; no major politician dared associate himself with their cause; and the leading religious denominations rejected their teachings. Factional bickering and financial reverses further undermined the movement. The theoretical Seventy agents had never reached full strength, and after 1838 their numbers dwindled drastically. Because the panic of 1837 and the subsequent depression dried up their sources of funds, the local societies were forced to curtail numerous activities. Then in 1840, after several years of bickering over the relation of abolitionism to the churches and to other reform movements, particularly women's rights, the AAS split into warring factions. In that year the radical followers of Garrison took over the AAS; the moderate element—led by Tappan, Birney, and Henry B. Stanton—formed a new organization, the American and Foreign Anti-Slavery Society (AFAS). By this time the Great Revival, which had fired the growth of abolitionism in the previous decade, had run its course, and neither of these organizations retained the vitality that had characterized the AAS in the first five years of its existence.

In 1839 the majority of American abolitionists, faced with the distinct possibility of failure and agreeing with Alvan Stewart that the tactics of the 1830's had "never . . . gained truth an advocate, or humanity a friend," decided to follow the urgings of those who advocated the establishment of a political party devoted to their cause. After an unsuccessful attempt to get New York gubernatorial candidates to respond publicly to their inquiries, Stewart, Gerrit Smith, and Myron Holley moved to form the Liberty, or Human Rights, party, which nominated Birney for president in 1840. At its inception the Liberty party was devoted to bringing the slavery question into politics and hoped to keep the doctrine of immediatism alive by offering individuals an opportunity to go on record against slavery. Through 1844 the new party retained its abolitionist character, attacking the immorality of slavery and demanding equal justice for free blacks. During these years its support grew among the moderate abolitionists associated with the AFAS; and in 1844 Birney, who was again the party's candidate, received 63,000 votes. While the Liberty party had clearly induced most abolitionists to join its ranks, it is doubtful that abolition sentiment grew in the North during these years. At the height of its popularity, the party's votes came mainly from men who had earlier converted to abolitionism but had voted Whig in 1840. It was strongest in the small, moderately prosperous Yankee farming communities that had earlier been touched by evangelical revivalism and had been centers of organized abolition activities. After 1844 the Liberty party split over the question of broadening the party's appeal, and the majority of its members drifted into the Free Soil party, which appeared in 1848.

The failure of both moral suasion and political activity led many blacks and a few whites to greater militancy. In 1843 Henry Highland Garnet's advocacy of self-defense and slave revolt was nearly adopted by the Buffalo National Convention; and within a decade, especially after the passage of the Fugitive Slave Law in 1850, numerous local conventions of blacks echoed his sentiments. In Christiana, Pa., Boston, and Syracuse, attempts by both blacks and whites to aid fugitive slaves became the focus of sporadic violence. However, it was not until 1859 that anyone connected with the abolition movement attempted to encourage rebellion among the slaves. After several years of planning, John Brown, with financial aid from white abolitionists and accompanied by sixteen whites and five blacks, launched his unsuccessful raid on Harpers Ferry.

Although individual abolitionists continued to agitate throughout the 1850's, organized abolitionism passed from the scene. As it emerged in the 1840's and 1850's political antislavery compromised abolitionist goals in order to present a program moderate and broad-gauged enough to attract voters in the North whose opposition to slavery arose from their desire to keep blacks out of the territories and slaveholders out of positions of power in the federal government. The final phase of antislavery activity in the United States was based primarily on hostility toward the slaveholder and the values of the society in which he lived. Antisouthernism provided a vehicle through which the Republican party could unite all forms of northern antislavery feeling by 1860.

The growth of popular antagonism toward the South in the northern states can be dated from the controversy over the gag rule. While the abolitionists had constantly attacked the slave power (the excessive political power wielded by slaveholders), Whig politicians in the early 1840's made the most use of the issue to define a moderate pro-northern position between the abolitionists and the Democrats. In numerous constituencies in the North this strategy forced Democratic candidates to oppose the gag rule and even, in a few cases, the annexation of Texas, to avoid depiction as "doughfaces," subservient to the interests of the southern slaveholders. The events associated with the Mexican War and actions of James Polk's administration caused a split in the Democratic party and the enunciation of the Wilmot Proviso, which would have excluded slavery from the territory gained by the war. The followers of Martin Van Buren in New York, increasingly enraged by the power of slaveholders within their party, joined with the so-called Conscience Whigs of Massachusetts and the majority of the Liberty party to form the Free Soil party. In 1848 Van Buren ran as the party's candidate for president and garnered nearly 300,000 votes. While its members included many true abolitionists, its platform represented both a broadening of the appeal of antislavery and a turning away from the earlier goals of the abolitionists. The party focused almost entirely on limiting the expansion of slavery to keep the territories free for the migration of whites. Its platform avoided traditional abolitionist demands, and its followers spanned the wide spectrum of contemporary racist opinion. Following the election, the party's largest faction, the New York Barnburners, returned to the Democratic fold; the Free Democratic party, as it was called in 1852, could manage only 150,000 votes for its presidential candidate, John P. Hale.

It was not until John Brown's raid of the Harpers Ferry arsenal in 1859 that anyone connected with the abolition movement attempted to encourage a slave rebellion.

During the years between 1850 and 1854 not only abolitionism but also antisouthernism seemed to fade. Northerners generally accepted the terms of the Compromise of 1850; and a leading southern paper noted "a calm comparatively in the political world." Yet at that very moment a surge of nativism and anti-Catholicism throughout the North shattered traditional party alignments. Then in 1854 and 1855 the fights over the

Kansas-Nebraska Act and the chaos in Kansas Territory revived antisouthernism and channeled it through the new Republican party, which ran John C. Frémont for president in 1856. Although it deserves credit for ending slavery in the United States, the Republican party was by no means an abolitionist party nor one devoted solely to antislavery. Its platform touched on a wide variety of economic and social questions and appealed to a diverse group of northerners.

The new party was made up primarily of ex-Whigs, with smaller but crucial groups of free-soil and nativist ex-Democrats, and the remnants of the Free Democratic party; consequently, it included both vicious racists and firm believers in racial justice. Although most Republicans had moderately liberal racial views for the day, many were attracted by colonization schemes and nearly all expressed reservations about the total integration of the society. The main focus of their antislavery sentiments was the southern slaveholder, and the only antislavery plank in their platform demanded the exclusion of slavery from the territories. In this limited form a majority of northerners could embrace antislavery, and in 1860 Abraham Lincoln received 54 percent of the section's vote. Yet the party shied away from any direct attack on slavery; when secession threatened, many Republicans were willing to guarantee the existence of slavery in the southern states through a constitutional amendment.

The needs of war, as much as the constant agitation of the small abolitionist element within the Republican party, propelled the country toward emancipation. Lincoln, who had long doubted the feasibility of social integration, prosecuted the war primarily to maintain the Union. Caught between the radical and conservative wings of his own party, the president moved cautiously toward the enunciation of the Emancipation Proclamation on Jan. 1, 1863, freeing the slaves in areas still in rebellion. Subsequently, with a good deal more forthrightness, he lent his support to the Thirteenth Amendment, which declared that "neither slavery nor involuntary servitude . . . shall exist within the United States, or any place subject to their jurisdiction."

BIBLIOGRAPHY

Gilbert Hobbs Barnes, *The Anti-Slavery Impulse.*
David B. Davis, *The Problem of Slavery in Western Culture.*
Martin Duberman, ed., *The Antislavery Vanguard.*
Dwight Lowell Dumond, *Antislavery.*
Louis Filler, *The Crusade Against Slavery, 1830–1860.*
Betty Fladeland, *James G. Birney.*
James McPherson, *The Struggle for Equality.*
Benjamin Quarles, *Black Abolitionists.*
Gerald Sorin, *New York Abolitionists.*
John L. Thomas, *The Liberator.*
Bertram Wyatt-Brown, *Lewis Tappan and the Evangelical War Against Slavery.*
Arthur Zilversmit, *The First Emancipation.*

— WILLIAM G. SHADE

ANTITRUST LAWS

The broad purpose of the federal antitrust laws is the maintenance of competitive conditions in the American private enterprise economy. The basic antitrust statutes are the Sherman Antitrust Act, the Clayton Act, and the Federal Trade Commission Act. This legislation, with its related body of case law, rests on the credo that competition is the most desirable regulator of economic activity and that restrictive trade practices and monopoly power are detrimental to the public interest and incompatible with the promotion of business opportunity in an open market. The origins of antitrust legislation lie in the post–Civil War era of industrial expansion and consolidation, with its accompanying wider use of the corporate form of organization, including the "trust." The rise of industrial trusts and monopolies brought a train of business abuses and political corruption that aroused the hostility of farmers, small proprietors, and consumers, all of whom feared economic and social domination by the large corporation. Some of the states enacted antitrust laws, which, however, proved inadequate for checking huge combinations doing business across state lines. Agricultural depression and rural opposition to monopoly sharpened a concern over the growing concentration of industrial and financial power.

The Sherman Antitrust Act, passed in 1890, was largely a response to public opinion—not least to the lively agitation of the trust issue by the Populist movement in the West and South. The act declared illegal every combination in restraint of interstate or foreign commerce and prohibited monopolization of any part of such trade. The U.S. attorney general was authorized to institute civil or criminal proceedings in the federal circuit courts, and injured private parties were allowed to bring civil suits for recovery of triple damages. Criminal violations were made punishable as a misdemeanor carrying a fine of up to $5,000 (increased in 1955 to $50,000) and/or imprisonment of up to one year. For the first decade or more of the Sherman Act, its enforcement against business combinations was generally feeble, save in cases of collusive price fixing, chiefly because of a negative attitude in the executive branch. The act was revitalized during the administrations of Theodore Roosevelt and William Howard Taft. A landmark in its judicial interpretation was the "rule of reason" applied in the Standard Oil and American Tobacco

cases in 1911, when the Supreme Court drew a distinction between reasonable and unreasonable restraints of trade that influenced subsequent decisions.

The legislative, administrative, and judicial history of the Sherman Act indicates an intent to preserve competition while reaping the material benefits of the large corporate enterprise. This ambivalence has left its stamp on the evolution of American antitrust policy in the 20th-century era of big business. The Sherman Act has been amended in important respects, notably by the Webb-Pomerene Export Trade Act of 1918, which with certain qualifications allows American exporters to enter into agreements in foreign commerce that would otherwise violate the statute, and by the Miller-Tydings Act of 1937 and the McGuire-Keogh Act of 1952, both of which give federal sanction to resale price maintenance, or so-called fair-trade laws, where these are authorized by the states. Official enforcement of the Sherman Act is the jurisdiction of the Antitrust Division, a unit of the Department of Justice dating from 1903.

Trust regulation was still a national issue in the election of 1912; it was evident that the Sherman Act had failed to halt the trend toward concentrated economic power. Dissatisfied with the vague and ambiguous language of the Sherman Act and with the uncertainty of judicial application of the rule of reason, Progressive reformers pressed for legislation prohibiting specific trade practices. The result was the Clayton Act of 1914, whose main provisions forbade price discrimination, exclusive dealing and tying contracts, stock acquisitions of other companies, and interlocking directorates in industry and banking, where the "effect may be to substantially lessen competition or to create a monopoly." The Clayton Act was amended by the Robinson-Patman Act of 1936, which outlawed unreasonably low prices tending to destroy competition, and the Celler-Kefauver Act of 1950, which strengthened the provision against anticompetitive mergers. The Federal Trade Commission Act of 1914 established a five-member independent regulatory agency, the Federal Trade Commission (FTC), which was empowered to investigate unfair methods of competition and to issue cease and desist orders, subject to judicial review, aimed at preventing unfair business practices. The scope of the FTC was broadened by the Wheeler-Lea Act of 1938, which banned "unfair or deceptive acts or practices in commerce."

In October 1974 a more vigorous enforcement policy was announced in the economic message sent to Congress by President Gerald R. Ford, who in the following December signed into law the Antitrust Procedures and Penalties Act. This legislation, the most significant reform of the federal antitrust laws in a quarter-century, changed some criminal violations, notably price-fixing, from misdemeanors to felonies; raised maximum allowable fines from $50,000 to $1,000,000 for corporations and from $50,000 to $500,000 for individuals; and increased the maximum prison sentence from one to three years. It also contained important provisions concerning the public disclosure and judicial affirmation of antitrust case settlements negotiated by the Department of Justice.

Opinion on the effectiveness of the antitrust laws is divided. Some contend that the very existence of an antitrust policy has discouraged excessive concentration of business power. Others, pointing to a post–World War II trend toward oligopoly and conglomeration, have proposed the establishment of explicit and statutory standards for the determination of monopoly power and for the structural deconcentration of giant enterprise through divestiture or dissolution. Such recommendations have not been enacted into law, and the federal government continues to adhere to its traditional approach. Some critics, maintaining that public acceptance of big business has muted the antitrust reform fervor of an earlier day, hold that antitrust policy is merely a ceremonial device that serves the purpose of appeasing the social consensus on free competition.

BIBLIOGRAPHY

Report of the Attorney General's National Committee to Study the Antitrust Laws.

J. M. Blair, *Economic Concentration.*

W. Letwin, *Law and Economic Policy in America.*

A. D. Neale, *The Antitrust Laws of the United States of America.*

H. B. Thorelli, *The Federal Antitrust Policy.*

— WILLIAM GREENLEAF

ANTITRUST LAWS SINCE THE 1960S

Federal antitrust laws date back to the Sherman Antitrust, Clayton, and Federal Trade Commission Acts. These late-nineteenth and early twentieth-century statutes, along with their interpretation by the courts, restrained monopoly and maintained free competition.

The hands-off approach to antitrust enforcement associated with the Reagan administration actually was already evident in the 1970s.

Responsibility for enforcement has resided in the Antitrust Division of the Justice Department and the Federal Trade Commission. Since the late 1960s antitrust policy has been based more on the economic effects of corporate behavior and less on purely legal objections to mergers and other monopolistic actions. The Antitrust Division and, to a lesser degree, the Federal Trade Commission have incorporated the views of certain conservative economists, who argue that free markets produce the most efficient results in price, supply, and allocation of resources. Even the largest corporations are presumed efficient and successful because of economies of scale. From this viewpoint, therefore, government regulation is generally suspect and should be limited to actions that produce a clear economic benefit and are not based on social or political theories about the dangers of the concentration of wealth.

This hands-off approach to antitrust enforcement is often linked to the presidency of Ronald Reagan (1981–1989), although it was already evident in the Antitrust Division during the 1970s. By 1978 the Economic Policy Office (later renamed Economic Analysis Group) within the division was responsible for deciding what cases to pursue. The Hart-Scott-Rodino Antitrust Improvements Act of 1976 provided for a premerger screening, whereby regulators advised corporations of their antitrust liabilities and helped arrange mergers acceptable to the government. The same trend was evident in *Continental TV, Inc.* v. *GTE Sylvania, Inc.* (1977), in which the Supreme Court ruled that vertical integration involving territorial and customer restraints, such as an agreement between a manufacturer and its dealers to restrict sales to certain locations, was not automatically illegal but would be judged according to a "rule of reason," meaning the extent of their anticompetitive effects.

By the 1980s the triumph of the competitive approach was complete in the executive branch, although Congress in 1986 resisted attempts to codify such policies in a set of rewritten antitrust laws. The Justice Department continued to prosecute cartel-like price fixing, a form of horizontal integration involving many participants, but it largely ignored mergers, acquisitions, and monopolization. From 1981 through 1987 the Antitrust Division challenged only 26 of more than 10,000 proposed mergers. In 1982 a case against the International Business Machines Corporation for anticompetitive practices in the computer industry was dropped despite more than a dozen years of investigation. That same year a long-standing case against American Telephone and Telegraph Company (AT&T) was settled out of court on a basis favorable to the company. In return for divesting itself of local telephone operating companies, AT&T was permitted to engage in various unregulated telecommunications fields. Proponents of reduced regulation stressed that government should not hinder firms engaged in fierce global competition. Critics pointed to the wave of corporate mergers and leveraged buyouts in the 1980s as evidence that these firms often preferred to engage in financial manipulation and the pursuit of short-term gains rather than in new investments in product development.

BIBLIOGRAPHY

Mark Allen Eisner, *Antitrust and the Triumph of Economics* (Chapel Hill, N.C., 1991).

U.S. Department of Justice, *Annual Report of the Attorney General of the United States* (Washington, D.C.).

— JOHN B. WEAVER

APACHE

With their linguistic relatives the Navaho, the Athapascan-speaking Apache pushed into New Mexico in prehistoric times, later fanning out into Arizona and western Texas and ranging over sections of northern Mexico. Unlike the Navaho, who were more strongly affected by Pueblo culture, the various groups of Apache became noted for the depredations they carried on against both their Indian neighbors and Spanish, Mexican, and U.S. settlers in the Southwest. Their very name apparently derives from the Zuni word for "enemy." Their war orientation reached a climax in the

Geronimo in 1944, last of the Apache raiders, whose war orientation was infamous. (UPI/Corbis-Bettmann)

19th century under the famous Chiricahua chiefs Cochise and Geronimo, and this somewhat sensational side of Apache life has made the group one of the best known of American Indians.

In the various sections of the Southwest in which the Apache settled, several distinct, closely related linguistic groupings appear. Moreover, some Apache adapted to a modified agriculture and others to hunting-gathering modes of subsistence. In the north of New Mexico the Jicarilla Apache took on Plains traits—the tipi and bison hunting. In central Arizona and New Mexico the San Carlos, White Mountain, Tonto, Mescalero, Chiricahua, and other groups, all divided in several bands. The Lipan Apache are a Mexican remnant. It has been suggested that the difficulties of living in a harsh desert environment led to the Apache "raiding economy."

Major Apache ceremonies involved the girls' rite and masked spirit impersonation, a probable borrowing from the Pueblo. Never effectively politically organized, the Apache had war chiefs only late in their history, and even they had only an ephemeral following.

[See also Apache Wars.]

BIBLIOGRAPHY

Robert F. Spencer, Jesse D. Jennings, and others, *The Native Americans.*

M. E. Opler, *An Apache Life-Way.*

— ROBERT F. SPENCER

APACHE WARS

The Apache of Arizona and New Mexico remained somewhat aloof from the Spaniards until after the Pueblo Revolt of 1680, when they intensified their raiding activities upon sedentary Indians and upon the Spanish towns along the Rio Grande, as well as raiding deep into Mexico, into Sonora and Chihuahua. By the 1690's the Apache were in control of a strip of territory 250 miles wide in which there were no Spanish settlements.

The Mexicans were no more successful in contending with the Apache menace than the Spaniards had been, despite an attempt to exterminate the predatory bands in the 1830's. By 1837 Mexican states were offering bounties for Apache scalps, but the Apache retaliated by stepping up their raids.

After the Mexican War (1846–48) the Anglo-Americans inherited the Apache problem. At first the Apache were more favorably disposed toward the Anglos, but Apache enmity was incurred when American authorities forbade raids into Mexico, the raids having become a vital part of Apache economy.

Among the famous Apache chiefs were Cochise of the central Chiricahua, who kept the peace until the Apache Pass expedition of 1861, and Mangas Coloradas, chief of the Mimbreño. Cochise and Mangas Coloradas joined forces to harass the whites.

The Mexicans were no more successful with the Apache menace than the Spanish had been, despite an attempt to exterminate the predatory bands in the 1830's.

War broke out also between the whites and the Tonto Apache when gold was discovered near Prescott, Ariz., in 1863. A ring of American forts was established, but it proved to be relatively ineffective either in protecting the settlers or in preventing Apache raids into Mexico. To many of the settlers and military men of the time, the only solution to the Apache problem was extermination.

Atrocities were committed by both sides, including the Camp Grant massacre in 1871. With the announcement of President Ulysses S. Grant's peace policy toward the Indians, Gen. George Crook was ordered into the Southwest with 3,000 soldiers to round up the Apache. This was a difficult directive to execute, but by 1875 some 5,000 Apache had been concentrated on the San Carlos Reservation in Arizona. Most of the Apache were willing to settle down by that time, but restless warriors repeatedly escaped from the reservation and resumed raiding under such leaders as Victorio of the Mimbreño and Geronimo of the southern Chiricahua. Victorio was killed in a fight with Mexican troops in 1880, but Geronimo eluded pursuit repeatedly, escaping to strongholds in the Sierra Madre in Mexico when hard-pressed. The Apache wars were finally ended with Geronimo's surrender in 1886.

BIBLIOGRAPHY

Odie B. Faulk, *The Geronimo Campaign.*

Ralph H. Ogle, *Federal Control of Western Apaches, 1848–1886.*

Dan L. Thrapp, *The Conquest of Apacheria.*

— KENNETH M. STEWART

APPALACHIA

Appalachia, a largely mountainous region in the eastern United States, extending generally from southwestern Pennsylvania southward through West Virginia and eastern Kentucky, and including western portions of Virginia, North Carolina, and South Carolina, eastern portions of Tennessee, and northern portions of Georgia and Alabama. It was settled in the 1790's and early 1800's—largely from the areas of eastern Pennsylvania, tidewater Virginia, and North Carolina—by people of English, Scotch-Irish, and German descent, joined by a scattering of other ethnic groups fleeing Western Europe during and after the Bonapartist disturbances. The settlers built their log cabins and clapboard houses on land lying generally between the Blue Ridge Mountains and the southern extension of the Allegheny Mountains. To the east of the Blue Ridge were landed estates and to the west were dense forests and hostile Indians. Many of the original settlers and their descendants remained in the area, engaging in logging, coal mining, small local industries, handicraft operations, and agricultural pursuits.

After many years of comparative isolation and neglect, Appalachia (since the 1930's) has come to the attention of the public and has gained government support for its efforts to improve its economy and living conditions. An aggressive and well-publicized attempt to control and curtail the strip mining of coal, principally in West Virginia and eastern Kentucky, and a return to the conventional method of shaft and drift mining, which leaves relatively few marks on the land surface and increases employment opportunities, have also fostered a new awareness of the region. Strip mining leaves physical surface scars marked by deep, bare gullies and ravines, treeless surface stretches, polluted waters, and destroyed home sites. In many cases in which there has been no restoration of the stripped surface, the environment is marred by destructive landslides, acid-polluted waters, and unsightly surface remains.

During the 1960's Appalachia became a *cause célèbre* for many former members of the Peace Corps, VISTA, and similar organizations, who went there to help improve living conditions, giving great impetus to the fight against strip mining and the allied environmental destruction and helping in other efforts to upgrade the region, particularly in efforts to improve the extent and quality of education.

BIBLIOGRAPHY

H. M. Candell, *My Land Is Dying.*

T. D. Clark, *Settlers on the Cumberland.*

E. C. Semple, *American History and Its Geographical Conditions.*

— THOMAS ROBSON HAY

APPOMATTOX

Appomattox, former courthouse (county seat) of the county of the same name in Virginia, 20 miles east southeast of Lynchburg, was the scene of the surrender of the Confederate Army of Northern Virginia to the Union Army of the Potomac, April 9, 1865. Gen. Robert E. Lee, commanding the Confederate forces which evacuated Petersburg and Richmond on the night of April 2–3, had planned to withdraw into North Carolina, via Danville, and to join Gen. Joseph E. Johnston; but on the third day of retreat, Lee found the federal troops across his front at Jetersville, on the Richmond and Danville Railroad. As he was dependent on the railways for supplies, he determined to move westward across country to the Southside Railroad at Farmville, where he hoped to procure rations for a march to Lynchburg. Thence he would turn south again toward Danville. En route to Farmville, Lee was attacked heavily on April 6, at Sayler's Creek, where he lost about 6,000 men. The next day at Farmville he was again assailed before he could victual all his troops. By that time, long marches without food had so depleted the Confederate ranks that Gen. Ulysses S. Grant addressed Lee a proposal for the surrender of the army. Lee did not consider the situation altogether hopeless and pushed on toward Lynchburg by the Richmond Stage Road. When the army bivouacked around Appomattox Courthouse on the evening of April 8, the reflection of federal campfires against the clouds showed that the surviving Confederates, now reduced to two small corps, were surrounded on three sides. Lee closed his column and prepared to cut his way out, but, when he found the next morning that the corps of John B. Gordon faced impossible odds on the Stage Road, he sent a flag of truce to Grant. A suggestion that the army break into small bands and attempt to slip through the enveloping lines was rejected by Lee on the ground that it would carry a hopeless struggle into country that had escaped the ravages of war. After some delay in communicating with Grant, who had made his dispositions with the greatest skill, Lee rode, on April 9 at about 1 P.M., into the village and, at the house of Maj. Wilmer McLean, formally arranged the surrender of all forces then under arms in Virginia. Grant's generous terms, which allowed officers to retain their side arms and provided for the parole of all surrendered troops, were exe-

Grant's terms, which allowed officers to retain their side arms and provided for the parole of all surrendered troops, were executed with the least humiliation to the defeated army.

cuted with the least humiliation to the defeated army. A full day's rations were issued the prisoners of war. When the troops marched into an open field to lay down their weapons and their flags (April 12), the federal guard presented arms. The number of Confederate infantrymen surrendered at Appomattox with arms in their hands was 7,892; the total number of troops paroled was about 28,000. In an interview with Lee on April 10, Grant sought to prevail on the Confederate commander to advise that all the remaining Confederate troops cease resistance, but Lee insisted that this was a question to be decided by the civil authorities.

Appomattox became a national historic site in 1954.

BIBLIOGRAPHY

D. S. Freeman, *R. E. Lee*, vol. 4.
U. S. Grant, *Personal Memoirs*, vol. 2.
R. U. Johnson and C. C. Buel, eds., *Battles and Leaders of the Civil War*, vol. 4.

— DOUGLAS SOUTHALL FREEMAN

APPRENTICESHIP

Apprenticeship, a system of occupational training for a specific period and under written contract whereby a young person learns a skill on the job, in a classroom, or in a combination of both. Apprentice training, based on ancient and medieval practice, was systematized in England under Elizabeth I by the Statute of Artificers (1563) and the Poor Law (1601), and transferred to the American colonies. In 1642, the Virginia legislature ordered that children of poor parents be apprenticed to learn "carding, knitting and spinning," while Massachusetts passed a similar law that became the prototype of legislation in the North. The binding out of such children and the voluntary contracts or indentures often included instruction in reading, writing, and religion, and later in language and arithmetic. Among the prominent Americans who underwent apprentice training were Benjamin Franklin and Andrew Johnson. The system even prevailed in the professions of law and journalism.

With the Industrial Revolution and the expansion of educational opportunity, the need for apprenticeship began to decline. It was not always certain that the provisions of indenture were carried out. Late in the 19th century, many masters were unwilling to teach their apprentices and the latter were often reluctant to spend long years to master a trade. Industrialists and educators felt increasingly that vocational and industrial training could do a better job of preparing skilled workers.

During the 20th century, apprenticeship was revived and refined, especially after the National Apprenticeship Act (1937), which established a Bureau of Apprenticeship and Training in the U.S. Department of Labor. The experiences of World War II also contributed to the retention of apprentice training. By the mid-1970's the system of formal training was widely recognized in many industries. Hundreds of skills were being taught to over 300,000 apprentices in such industries as printing, metalworking, and building and construction, and in such trades as baking, mechanics, and jewelry. Apprenticeship information centers in thirty large cities, union locals, and trade groups were providing information to prospective apprentices.

BIBLIOGRAPHY

H. F. Clark and H. S. Sloan, *Classrooms in the Factories*.
P. H. Douglas, *American Apprenticeship and Industrial Education*.
M. W. Jernegan, *Laboring and Dependent Classes in Colonial America, 1617–1783*.
U. S. Bureau of Apprenticeship and Training, *The National Apprenticeship Program*.

— WILLIAM W. BRICKMAN

ARAB AMERICANS

The 1990 census reported 870,000 Americans of Arab ancestry, although the figure is probably higher because of underreporting. The first arrivals in the late nineteenth century came mostly from Syria and Lebanon and established themselves as merchants. Since World War II immigrants frequently have been refugees fleeing wars and changes of leadership in the Middle East. Palestinians arrived after the creation of Israel in 1948, Egyptians left when the regime of Gamal Abdel Nasser came to power in 1952, Syrians fled revolutionary turmoil, and Iraqi royalists escaped republican regimes. The U.S. Immigration Act of 1965 ended a quota system favoring immigrants from Europe, thereby providing the means for increased Arab immigration. According to the 1990 census most Arab Americans lived in the states of New York, Michigan, and California and are concentrated in urban areas, notably New York City, Detroit, Los Angeles, and Long Beach, Calif. In general, they are better educated than most Americans, with 66 percent of adults possessing college and university educations, as compared with 45 percent of Americans in general. Most Arab Americans are relatively prosperous, with median household incomes in 1990 of $39,000 per annum, compared with a national average of $30,000. Distinguished Arab Americans include poet Kahlil Gibran, consumer advocate Ralph Nader, entertainers Danny Thomas and Marlo Thomas, astronaut and teacher Christa McAuliffe, Senator James Abourezk of South Dakota, and heart surgeon Michael DeBakey.

[See also Immigration; Middle East, Relations with.]

BIBLIOGRAPHY

Samia El-Badry, "The Arab American Market," *American Demographics* (January 1994), and *Fitting In* (Austin, Tex., 1987).

— SAMIA EL-BADRY AND SAMAR SAKAKINI

ARAPAHO

One of the more important of the bison-hunting Plains tribes, the Arapaho spoke an Algonkin language. They were closely connected with another Algonkin people, the Atsina, and appear to have been resident in the Red River Valley in early historic times. With the Atsina and followed by the Cheyenne, the Arapaho pushed into the Dakotas and northeastern Wyoming. There they adapted exclusively to bison hunting and assimilated the Plains war pattern, carrying on intermittent warfare with the Ute, Shoshone, and Pawnee, having also fought various of the Dakota and Comanche. A general peace was maintained with the Cheyenne. The tribe was generally dispersed following treaty and reservation allocation.

Like other Indians of the Plains, the Arapaho made capital of the horse, the tipi, and the general material inventory of the nomadic Plains. Theirs was a tightly knit societal organization, paralleling that of the Cheyenne. Five main subdivisions of the tribe were recognized, virtually autonomous tribelets, which met for the bison hunt and organized raiding parties. The Arapaho lost contact with their close relatives, the Atsina, when the latter, separated by the incursions of the Crow, became associated with the Assiniboine. The tribe offers a classic example of the interaction and movement of peoples in the Plains area.

BIBLIOGRAPHY

Alfred L. Kroeber, *The Arapaho.*

— ROBERT F. SPENCER

ARMISTICE OF NOV. 11, 1918

On Oct. 4, 1918, the German government appealed to President Woodrow Wilson for an armistice with a view to peace on the basis of the Fourteen Points. As a prerequisite, Wilson insisted on the practical democratization of the German government and hinted openly at the abdication of Kaiser William II. Gen. John Pershing, the American commander in France, wished to continue the war until Germany was thoroughly beaten, but the Allied commanders, including Marshal Ferdinand Foch, agreed to an armistice and Wilson accepted this view. On Nov. 5, the United States notified Germany that the Fourteen Points were accepted as the basis of peace, subject to two reservations: (1) the freedom of the seas was not to be discussed at that time; (2) Germany must make reparation for the damage done to the property of Allied nationals during the war. The terms of armistice were communicated to Germany on Nov. 8 and signed on Nov. 11 at 5 A.M., to take effect at 11 A.M. Germany had to evacuate all territory west of the Rhine, which was to be occupied by Allied troops; a neutral zone was established ten kilometers east of the Rhine. Germany surrendered large quantities of artillery, machine guns, airplanes, motor trucks, and railway rolling stock, as well as most of its navy: it was made impossible for Germany to resume fighting. It had also to renounce the treaties of Brest-Litovsk and Bucharest and to withdraw its troops from Russia, Rumania, and Turkey. The blockade was to continue until peace was made, and a blanket financial reservation was added that "any future claims and demands of the Allies and the United States of America remain unaffected." The armistice was for one month and was renewed from time to time until peace was signed in 1919.

As a prerequisite to armistice, President Woodrow Wilson insisted on the practical democratization of the German government, and hinted openly at the abdication of Kaiser Wilhelm II.

BIBLIOGRAPHY

Charles Seymour, *American Diplomacy During the World War.*

— BERNADOTTE E. SCHMITT

ARMS RACE WITH THE SOVIET UNION

The United States began a rapid postwar demobilization when Japan surrendered at the end of World War II. The 1945 war machine, with 12,123,444 men under arms, dropped in a year to 3,030,088—a number halved in 1947 to a norm of 1,583,000. Although there were U.S. government leaders who saw that Soviet-style totalitarianism was flourishing wherever Joseph Stalin's troops had advanced into Europe, the new threat was only slowly recognized by an American public sated with war, serene in sole possession of atomic bombs, and beguiled by the propaganda image of a kindly "Uncle Joe" Stalin. To many, President Harry Truman seemed alarmist in obtaining, in March 1947, legislation for aid to Greece and Turkey, which effectively stopped Communist takeovers. However, apologists for

Stalin were largely silenced by his June 1948 attempt to squeeze the United States, Britain, and France out of Berlin, foiled by the ingenuity of the Berlin airlift. An anti-Communist reaction began, intensified by the 1949 Communist victory in China and the explosion of the Soviet Union's first atomic bomb. Thenceforward a congressional majority was assured for passage of any major legislation intended to arrest the spread of Communism.

In January 1950 Truman funded research to develop hydrogen bombs, meeting success in November 1952, a bare nine months before the Russians—and against the backdrop of the Korean conflict. By his April 1951 dismissal of Gen. Douglas MacArthur, Truman plainly signaled the continuance of U.S. moderation; but Stalin was implacable. Truman therefore accepted a policy of "containment" and in February 1952 welcomed the foundation of the North Atlantic Treaty Organization, establishing a European army of fifty divisions. Uneasiness in the American electorate contributed to the 1952 election of Gen. Dwight D. Eisenhower to the presidency. Two months after his inauguration, however, hopes soared upon the sudden death of Stalin—and fell when Stalin's successors relentlessly continued the drive for military primacy.

During the period immediately after the Korean conflict U.S. defense rested on improving the air power of the strategic bomber force and aircraft-carrier navy developed during World War II, neither seriously rivaled by the Soviet Union, whose strength was in a huge, tank-centered army. Owing to the persistence of Rear Adm. Hyman C. Rickover, the U.S. Navy made a quantum jump in submarines by the harnessing of atomic energy, shown in the January 1954 unveiling of the *Nautilus.* But the Soviet Union took another road in the race for primacy. Having in 1945 overrun the Nazi rocket development center at Peenemünde, Soviets made good use of German engineering to astonish the world in August 1957 by demonstrating a 4,000-mile intercontinental ballistic missile (ICBM) as the follow-up to World War II V-2 rockets, realizing Hitler's dream of being able to bombard the U.S. mainland. This achievement was technologically dwarfed in October of the same year, when the Soviets sent into orbit the first artificial satellite, Sputnik.

A contest then began to perfect rockets for lofting nuclear warheads from one continent to another—across mountain, ocean, any barrier to any distance—at supersonic speeds, compressing into mere minutes the flight times between Moscow and Washington. In sheer size and payload of missiles, the Soviets maintained their early lead, while U.S. engineers used superior miniaturization to obtain greater sophistication and accuracy. For the United States the first advantage stemmed from the July 1960 launch of a missile from the submerged *George Washington,* the original Polaris nuclear-powered submarine.

In October 1962 the world teetered toward holocaust after U.S. aerial surveillance of Cuba uncovered the presence of Russian medium-range weapons that could reach northward as far as Detroit. President John F. Kennedy's firm stand and his naval quarantine of Cuba compelled the withdrawal of the missiles. Such triumph as there may have been for the United States in this encounter vanished in the subsequent steady buildup of a new Soviet navy, displaying the Kremlin's resolve never again to be faced down by a quarantine. The naval competition imposed yet another huge burden upon taxpayers, as the Soviets developed their own Polaris submarines and the requisite covering ships.

During these developments and despite the pre–World War II failures of all solemn treaties to limit arms, American presidents repeatedly tried to control the burgeoning atomic arms race. In November 1948 Truman tried for controls through the fledgling United Nations, only to be foiled by the Soviet Union. Soviet persistence in seeking atomic weapons was matched by U.S. efforts to control them. Eisenhower was apparently successful in October 1958, when the Soviet Union was finally persuaded to sit with the United States and Britain at Geneva to work out a treaty to outlaw nuclear testing. To display good will, Eisenhower suspended U.S. testing and Soviet Premier Nikita Khrushchev ostentatiously agreed to a moratorium. The talks, however, were futile because of Soviet intransigence over inspection methods to ensure future compliance. Khrushchev was buying time to gain secret momentum for a series of tests, in September 1961, of more than forty bombs, climaxed by the detonation in the polar sky of an unprecedented 50-megaton hydrogen bomb. Khrushchev gloated that a 100-megaton bomb was in the Soviet arsenal. Notwithstanding such bad faith, Kennedy persisted in trying to reach an agreement upon effective controls. His credibility attested by the Cuban missile crisis, Kennedy, in July 1963, brought about with the Soviet Union and Britain an agreement banning every type of test except underground tests.

This vital, if partial, success owed much to enormous advances in reconnaissance by orbiting satellites, which could substitute for on-site inspectors. For the Soviet Union, perhaps the dominant motive was to take a giant step toward nonproliferation of nuclear weapons, inasmuch as a hundred nations accepted the invitation to subscribe to the treaty. Communist China did not, however. In October 1964 China also had "the bomb," and the strange Sino-Soviet dispute suddenly had gen-

ocidal teeth. Ironically it was the Soviet Union that had set for China the precedent of refusal to guarantee mankind a future by making nuclear war impossible. China would agree to no limitation. In the Strategic Arms Limitation Talks (SALT) with the Soviet Union, the United States tacitly acknowledged the Soviet Union's worry over China—a worry that was rooted in the historic enslavement of Russia for 257 years by Batu Khan and the Mongols. The U.S.-Soviet SALT-1 treaty of May 26, 1972, found the United States agreeing to a five-year freeze on production of weapons, which superficially gave the Soviet Union some superiority—enough, it was hoped, to deter China while keeping a stand-off mutual deterrence with the United States. Then, in November 1974, President Gerald R. Ford and Leonid Brezhnev in furtherance of "détente" signed an agreement at Vladivostok. Ostensibly defining "nuclear parity," the agreement raised weapons levels. Some critics thought that the terms heavily favored the USSR, and alarm about the Soviet threat persisted.

BIBLIOGRAPHY

Ernest M. Eller, *The Soviet Sea Challenge.*

Raymond L. Garthoff, *Soviet Strategy in the Nuclear Age.*

Malcolm Mackintosh, *Juggernaut.*

Abdul A. Said, ed., *America's World Role in the 1970's.*

— R. W. DALY

DISARMAMENT SINCE SALT I

The arms control agreement concluded by the United States and the Soviet Union in January 1972—the Strategic Arms Limitation Treaty (known as SALT I)—seemed to promise progress toward nuclear disarmament, but in the years that followed the pace of technological innovation outstripped the efforts of arms negotiators. Proliferation of new and more capable weapons systems throughout the 1970s and 1980s fueled the arms race. Only the collapse in 1991 of the Soviet Union, exhausted and bankrupt, brought that race to a close. Far from releasing the world from the fear of nuclear devastation, however, the Soviet collapse exposed new dangers, for which technological and diplomatic solutions seemed elusive.

The SALT I treaty, signed by President Richard M. Nixon, restricted antiballistic missile (ABM) systems that either the United States or the Soviet Union might deploy and placed a ceiling on the total number of Soviet and U.S. delivery systems (land-based and sea-launched missiles but not long-range bombers). Those modest achievements were compromised by the treaty's failure to consider the capabilities offered by multiple, independently targeted reentry vehicles (MIRVs), miniaturized warheads incorporating their own propulsion and guidance systems. By fitting several MIRVs to one missile, a single delivery system could hit many targets. Throughout the 1970s, first the United States and then the Soviets added MIRVs to their missiles. As a result, although under SALT I the number of delivery systems did not increase, the effective size of the arsenals on both sides skyrocketed.

Far from freeing the world from the Cold War fear of nuclear devastation, the collapse of the Soviet Union has exposed new dangers in nuclear arms proliferation.

The architects of SALT I, especially Secretary of State Henry A. Kissinger, trumpeted the agreement as an important step toward arms control. Hopes of building on the success produced the SALT II negotiations, which began in November 1972. Progress toward a follow-on agreement proved to be tortuously slow. The negotiations triggered criticism in the United States from those unhappy with SALT I for not going far enough and from those who criticized it for conceding too much (and who disliked the Nixon-Kissinger policy of détente with the Soviets). Nixon's successor, Gerald R. Ford, and the Soviet leader, Leonid I. Brezhnev, signed the Vladivostok Accord in November 1974, placing a cap of 1,320 on MIRV missiles each superpower could possess and imposing on both the United States and the Soviet Union a ceiling of 2,400 delivery systems, including long-range bombers. By the time Ford left office in January 1977, several rounds of highly publicized negotiations had failed to produce a SALT II accord.

Technological innovation continued apace. Throughout the 1970s the Pentagon, supported by allies in Congress, pressed the case for updating the U.S. strategic triad (land, sea, and air weapons), arguing that existing systems were approaching obsolescence. Thus, the highly accurate MX missile was designed to supersede the Minuteman intercontinental ballistic missile (ICBM). The Trident submarine, with its longer-range missile, would replace earlier submarines with Polaris and Poseidon systems. The supersonic B-1 bomber replaced the B-52, which since the 1950s had been the workhorse of the U.S. Strategic Air Command. Cruise missiles—designed to evade radar detection by flying at low altitudes—promised to add a new group of weapons to the existing triad. Nor were technological advances limited to the range and accuracy of delivery systems. Advances in the design of radar and reconnaissance satellites greatly improved the prospects of receiving early warnings of attack. Virtually every effort at modernization undertaken by the United States was matched by the Soviets.

President Jimmy Carter in 1977 put forth a bold idea for ending the arms race. In his inaugural address, Carter vowed that his administration would seek to eliminate nuclear weapons. During the first year he canceled the B-1 and slowed development of the MX. In a speech at the United Nations he offered to cut the U.S. strategic arsenal in half if the Soviets would do likewise. Moscow promptly rejected this seemingly generous "deep cuts" proposal because it summarily invalidated the Vladivostok Accord. What led Carter to insist on SALT II terms more stringent than those agreed upon by Kissinger and Brezhnev was not simply his earnest "commitment to the goal of nuclear disarmament." It also appears to have been based on advice from Carter's national security adviser, Zbigniew Brzezinski, about a surprise Soviet breakthrough in ICBM guidance technology for the SS-18, which theoretically threatened the U.S. Minuteman ICBMs. Brzezinski reacted strongly to this Soviet breakthrough, fearing that "strategic superiority [of the Soviets] can influence political behavior." Secretary of State Cyrus R. Vance disagreed, but to no avail, as Carter followed Brzezinski's hard line in the SALT II talks. The Soviets made their own technological miscalculation by assuming that Carter's new offer meant that the United States had decided to rely more on cruise missiles than manned bombers.

Carter also appeared confused over whether he wanted to return to a policy of U.S. arms superiority over the Soviet Union or continue the policy of parity, equivalency, or sufficiency established by the Nixon administration. When canceling the B-1 not only failed to win Soviet concessions but also infuriated influential members of the Senate, notably Senator Henry M. Jackson of Washington, whose support would be essential to gain consent to any arms control agreement, the president appeared to waver. Jackson and others were highly skeptical of Carter's enthusiasm for arms control. They feared that the president was considering concessions to the Soviets in the category of ICBMs that would leave the United States in a position of strategic inferiority.

Key U.S. allies in the North Atlantic Treaty Organization (NATO), reacting to evidence of a Soviet military buildup in Eastern Europe, likewise worried that Carter's inexperience with disarmament issues might lead him to forget that their own security rested on the U.S. strategic deterrent. The president's decision not to go ahead with the neutron bomb—a weapon that killed people through radiation with minimal blast effects on buildings—reinforced those concerns. In the eyes of NATO military planners, adding the neutron bomb to the West's arsenal would reinforce deterrence. To the bomb's many critics, it seemed to invite nuclear war by portraying the use of nuclear weapons as less than horrifying. By first approving production of the neutron bomb and then reversing that decision Carter also raised more doubts within NATO about his understanding of and commitment to European security.

Negotiations over SALT II dragged on. In January 1979 revolution broke out in Iran, leading to the overthrow of the shah, Mohammad Reza Pahlavi, and the loss of several key U.S. intelligence facilities regarded as important for monitoring Soviet compliance with any future arms control agreements. This exacerbated doubts among SALT II's opponents as to whether any treaty would be verifiable. In the spring of 1979 Carter's determination to make a deal paid off when Soviet and U.S. negotiators initialed SALT II. In June the president and Brezhnev signed the treaty in Vienna. While the treaty marked a major step, it did not come close to the Carter-Brzezinski deep-cuts proposal that had stalled negotiations in 1977. SALT II placed both quantitative and qualitative restrictions on the strategic arsenals of the superpowers. It reaffirmed the ceilings on delivery systems and MIRVs contained in the Vladivostok Accord. It placed controls on the development of cruise missiles with a range greater than 600 kilometers. It created a variety of mechanisms intended to facilitate treaty verification.

President Carter attempted to dispel the impression that his administration was allowing the U.S. to slide into a position of nuclear inferiority.

Carter viewed all this simply as a step toward SALT III, which would move from merely limiting the growth of strategic arsenals to beginning the process of reducing their size. There could be no SALT III, however, unless the Senate first agreed to SALT II. From the moment of the treaty's signing, ratification was in doubt. Opposition to the treaty, even within the president's own Democratic party, was fierce. Critics argued that the treaty conceded military superiority to the Soviets; that under SALT II the Soviet "throw weight"—the cumulative destructive power of the warheads in the Soviet arsenal—would exceed that of the West; and that in tallying up Soviet nuclear capabilities the treaty ignored the new and highly capable Backfire bomber. They complained that the treaty was not verifiable—Soviet cheating would go undetected—and viewed the treaty as ill-advised and the president as naive.

Carter attempted to dispel the impression that his administration was allowing the United States to slide into a position of inferiority. He reversed his earlier decision to scrub full-scale production of the MX and opted for deployment of 200 new ICBMs in a mobile launch configuration, with each MX rotating randomly through a series of widely separated concrete shelters, an arrangement that would require 4,600 such shelters connected by 10,000 miles of road at a projected cost of $33 billion. The seemingly bizarre arrangement was designed to ensure the survivability of the MX against an attack by increasingly accurate Soviet ICBMs. Rather than reassuring conservatives worried about U.S. vulnerability to a Soviet first strike, the mobile MX plan angered liberals, who saw it as evidence that the Carter administration did not genuinely want to end the arms race. Efforts to reassure those who doubted Carter's commitment to European security likewise backfired. In December 1979 the president approved a NATO request to modernize the alliance's theater nuclear weapons—missiles with less than intercontinental reach—which, in practical terms, resulted in a decision to field in Europe 108 Pershing II intermediate-range ballistic missiles (IRBMS) and 464 Tomahawk cruise missiles. This, too, provoked controversy among peace activists in Europe and the United States, the net effect being not so much to reassure arms control skeptics as to alienate those who favored disarmament but who now increasingly saw Carter as vacillating and unreliable.

The Soviet Union dealt the decisive blow against SALT II. In late December 1979 the Soviets launched a massive military intervention in Afghanistan. With the Soviet-U.S. relationship at its chilliest in years, further bargaining with Moscow became politically unfeasible. A disappointed Carter asked that the Senate postpone indefinitely further consideration of SALT II. Carter's apparent ineffectiveness in national security affairs contributed to his failure to win reelection in the 1980 presidential race. His opponent, Ronald Reagan, promised to get tough with the Soviets and build up rather than negotiate away U.S. military strength. Reagan won by a landslide.

The new president committed the United States to a huge increase in military spending. He reversed Carter's decision to cancel the B-1 bomber, accelerated the deployment of the MX and the Trident submarine, and threw his support behind yet another new ICBM (Midgetman) and the long-range stealth bomber, designed to evade radar detection. He launched an ambitious, expensive, and highly controversial program to develop a comprehensive defense against ballistic missile attack known as the Strategic Defense Initiative (SDI) but widely—and often derisively—referred to as Star Wars. Reagan and his supporters justified these initiatives as essential to restore military parity with the Soviet Union. To his critics, however, Reagan's true goal was to achieve military superiority for the United States, a reckless undertaking that threatened to invite a nuclear showdown. As they saw it, the president was tampering with the concept of mutual assured destruction (MAD), the capacity of each superpower to absorb a first strike and still deliver a devastating blow against the other. Many observers viewed MAD as the essential condition for deterrence between nuclear-armed adversaries.

Although Reagan was not categorically opposed to arms control talks, he was in no hurry to renew talks with the Soviets. When negotiations related to long-range weapons resumed in 1982, they did so under a new name, Strategic Arms Reduction Talks (START), reflecting Reagan's belief that the only agreement worth signing was one that secured real reductions in nuclear arsenals. Meanwhile, Reagan followed through with the Carter-approved deployment of Pershing IIs and Tomahawks. With Soviet leaders and antinuclear activists in the United States and throughout Western Europe attacking the initiative as needlessly provocative, Reagan agreed to talks aimed ostensibly at reducing intermediate-range nuclear forces (INF) in Europe. The Reagan administration's approach to arms control negotiations was hard-nosed. One fruit of the INF talks became known as the "zero option." In exchange for a NATO

At the 1986 Reykjavík summit, Reagan and Gorbachev discussed arms reductions drastic enough to alarm U.S. allies and some members of the Reagan administration.

decision to cancel plans to deploy the Pershing IIs and Tomahawks, the United States wanted the Soviet Union to dismantle the substantially larger force of intermediate-range missiles already in Eastern Europe. Reagan's critics saw such demands as so extreme as to be nonnegotiable. They savaged the president's negotiating stance as cynical and hypocritical, intended not to reach agreements but to provide a fig leaf allowing him to continue his pursuit of superiority. Indeed, throughout Reagan's first term, progress toward agreement on either START or INF was negligible.

Only when Mikhail Gorbachev emerged as leader of the Soviet Union in 1985 did the stalemate end. Gorbachev brought to the negotiations a keen awareness of his country's crippling internal weaknesses. He understood that only in a military sense could the Soviet Union claim superpower status. The Soviet economy was backward and inefficient, and its technology was inferior to that of the West and falling farther behind. Its one-party political system was moribund and demoralization pervaded Soviet society. Addressing these problems was Gorbachev's overriding priority. Doing so required that he extricate the Soviet Union from the arms race, especially the expensive quest for ballistic-missile defense, which it simply could not afford. Thus, the need for reform within the Soviet Union created the conditions for arms control during Reagan's second term.

Gorbachev could not claim sole credit for what followed. Belying critics who dismissed his insistence on sweeping cuts in nuclear arsenals as a rhetorical ploy, Reagan demonstrated a surprising willingness to bargain with the Soviets. At the Reykjavík, Iceland, summit of October 1986, he and Gorbachev discussed reductions of long-range and intermediate-range weapons drastic enough to alarm U.S. allies and the more cautious quarters of Reagan's administration. Only the president's refusal to curb SDI development prevented agreement. The setbacks at Reykjavík did not slow the momentum in favor of arms control. The breakthrough came on INF the following year when the Soviets accepted the zero option formula. At the Washington summit meeting of December 1987, Reagan and Gorbachev signed a historic treaty that resulted for the first time in a whole class of nuclear weapons being dismantled and destroyed.

When George Bush succeeded Reagan as president in January 1989, the changes that were steadily transforming East-West relations made prospects for arms control propitious, but traditional approaches to disarmament became all but irrelevant, and new problems relating to weapons of mass destruction were exposed, when the Soviet empire disintegrated. Communist regimes ruling the Soviet client states in Eastern Europe were overthrown; the Warsaw Pact—the Soviet-led counterpart of NATO—unraveled; and the Berlin Wall came down, resulting in the reunification of Germany. By 1991 the Soviet Union itself ceased to exist, shattering into a collection of shaky successor republics. Among the emerging states, four inherited portions of the massive Soviet nuclear arsenal: Russia, Ukraine, Belarus, and Kazakhstan. The division of spoils was marred by disputes regarding ownership and control. Claimants vied for possession of components of the former Soviet military establishment, Russia and Ukraine both laying claim to the nuclear weapon-equipped Black Sea Fleet. A fundamental premise of disarmament—that securing bilateral agreements between co-equal superpowers could avert the threat of nuclear war—was demolished.

The new conditions contributed to a heightened sense of urgency to move forward before events in the former Soviet Union spun out of control. At least on paper, agreements reached during the Bush administration easily surpassed all the arms control achievements of the preceding forty years. Gorbachev's need to reduce the Soviet military presence in Eastern Europe brought success in negotiations regarding the Conventional Forces in Europe (CFE) Treaty. Signed in November 1990 by every member of both NATO and the Warsaw Pact, the CFE agreement provided massive cuts in non-nuclear arms on both sides of what had been the iron curtain. Of particular significance was the fact that the cuts were asymmetrical. The Soviet bloc accepted reductions ten times greater than those exacted of NATO. Gorbachev proved equally forthcoming with regard to strategic weapons. He dropped his insistence that the United States abandon SDI as the price for agreement to reduce long-range weapons, a concession that resulted in the START I treaty. Signed by Bush and Gorbachev in July 1991, START I reduced Soviet and U.S. ballistic missile warheads by half and one-third, respectively, cuts hitherto unthinkable.

The aftermath of the Gulf War showed that Iraq, a signatory to the nonproliferation treaty, had been well on its way to developing nuclear weapons.

Even the fall of the Soviet Union did not disrupt the succession of new treaties. In January 1993 Bush and Russian President Boris Yeltsin signed a START II agreement in which Russia and the United States agreed to reduce their strategic arsenals by two-thirds. START II provided for elimination of MIRVs from land-based ICBMs. Success had its drawbacks. As a result of these agreements, both countries faced the task of disposing of thousands of obsolete nuclear weapons. The costs of this complex and environmentally sensitive task were huge, far outstripping the capacity of the battered economies of the former Soviet republics. The United States promised hundreds of millions of dollars to help defray the expense of disassembling the weapons of its long time adversary.

As further indication of the new complexity in which arms control efforts proceeded, START II's bold provisions would not go into effect until Ukraine and Belarus agreed to START I and until those two nations and Kazahkstan joined the Nuclear Nonproliferation Treaty (NPT) negotiated in 1967. Indeed, in the new circumstances created by the end of the cold war and the collapse of the Soviet Union, proliferation superseded reduction of superpower arsenals as the centerpiece of the arms control agenda. By 1995, 179 nations had ratified the NPT, the premier instrument for limiting membership in the "nuclear club."

Problems were not over. The end of the cold war exposed gaps in the effectiveness of nonproliferation efforts. The aftermath of the Persian Gulf crises of 1990–1991 showed that Iraq—although a signatory of the NPT—had been well on its way to the covert development of nuclear weapons. By 1993 substantial evidence suggested that North Korea, another NPT signatory, had embarked upon a large-scale program to develop nuclear weapons and long-range ballistic missiles. North Korea seemed willing to sell its nuclear and missile technology to other states, such as Iran, that likewise sought to acquire nuclear capability. In October 1994, however, the United States and North Korea signed an agreement in which North Korea agreed to terminate all efforts to develop nuclear weapons in exchange for a multibillion dollar package of concessions.

Nonproliferation efforts received a welcome boost when the signatories to the NPT, meeting in New York, agreed in May 1995 to extend the treaty indefinitely. This was a major victory for the arms control advocates within the administration of President Bill Clinton. In return for agreeing to this extension, the nonnuclear powers extracted assurances from the United States and the other four declared nuclear powers that they would redouble their efforts to achieve real reductions in nuclear arms. The signatories also committed themselves to negotiating a comprehensive test ban treaty by 1996. With both China and France continuing to conduct nuclear tests, however, the prospects for the early negotiation of such an agreement did not appear promising.

[See also North Atlantic Treaty Organization; Strategic Arms Limitation Talks; Strategic Defense Initiative.]

BIBLIOGRAPHY

Richard Dean Burns, ed., *Encyclopedia of Arms Control and Disarmament*, 3 vols. (New York, 1993).

John Newhouse, *War and Peace in the Nuclear Age* (New York, 1989).

— ANDREW J. BACEVICH

ARMY, CONFEDERATE

Confederate Army, officially, the Army of the Confederate States of America, was the small regular force established by an act of the Confederate Provisional Congress on Mar. 6, 1861, to consist of one corps of engineers, one of artillery, six regiments of infantry, one of cavalry, and four staff departments (adjutant and inspector general's, quartermaster general's, subsistence, and medical). This force, incompletely organized when war began, was soon overshadowed by the volunteer forces known officially as the provisional army. Other acts of Feb. 28 and Mar. 6 authorized the president to assume control over military operations, to accept state forces and 100,000 volunteers for twelve months. By the end of April President Jefferson Davis had called for 82,000 men. On May 8 the Confederate congress authorized enlistments for the war and on Aug. 8, four more states having joined the Confederacy, 400,000 volunteers for one or three years' service. After the passage of the first conscription act in April 1862, men were taken into the provisional army directly without the necessary aid of the state authorities.

The highest office in the regular army was that of brigadier general until congress, May 16, 1861, estab-

Robert E. Lee, Commander in Chief of the Confederate Army. (Library of Congress)

lished the rank of general in order to give higher Confederate commanders control over major generals of state troops in the field. On Aug. 31 Davis nominated and the congress confirmed Samuel Cooper, Albert Sidney Johnston, Robert E. Lee, Joseph E. Johnston, and G.T. Beauregard as generals of the regular army. On April 12, 1862, Braxton Bragg became a general in that army, and in May 1864 E. Kirby Smith became a general in the provisional army. Major generals in the provisional army, under the act of Feb. 28, 1861, were first appointed in May of that year. In September 1862 the rank of lieutenant general in the provisional army was created.

Serious difficulties were encountered in arming, clothing, and feeding the troops. Most of the arms available in May 1861 were obsolete or inferior, and even these could not supply all the men. There was little powder. Only one foundry could cast cannon, and only one small powder mill was in operation. The chief reliance for improved arms was in purchases abroad, but getting them through the Union blockade was a slow, risky, and expensive process. The Confederate government made contracts with private firms for arms and set up its own arsenals and powder mills. Shoes, clothing, and blankets were hard to procure, for wool and leather were scarce and importations did not fill requirements. Food supplies, much more plentiful in the South, were often reduced by weak transportation facilities. By 1863 horses and mules had become scarce, thus reducing the mobility of the cavalry, artillery, and baggage trains. Although the Confederate soldier was often poorly armed, clothed, and fed, discipline in the larger armies was good and morale high until near the end.

Although the Confederate soldier was often poorly armed, clothed, and fed, discipline in the larger armies was good and morale high until near the end.

The Confederacy was divided into military departments, fluctuating in number and extent, under commanders responsible only to the war department and the president. Prompt coordination between these departments was often lacking. Other than President Davis himself, there was no commander in chief until Lee was appointed on Feb. 6, 1865, although Lee had been Davis' military adviser for a short time early in 1862 and Braxton Bragg from February to October in 1864.

Because of incomplete surviving records the number of enlistments in the Confederate armies has long been in dispute. Southern writers have estimated them at from 600,000 to 800,000 men, some northern students at from 1,100,000 to 1,500,000. This last figure is obviously too high for a white population of about 5,000,000. The U.S. census for 1860 indicates approximately 1,100,000 men of military age in the seceded states, but these figures are deceptive. Many sections where hostility to the Confederacy developed furnished few soldiers; other large areas were soon overrun by the Union armies. Apparently more men from the seceded states went into the Union army than came to the Confederate colors from the nonseceding slave states. Exemptions, details for industrial work, and other evasions of service cut down enlistments. Probably between 800,000 and 900,000 actually enrolled, but so many were never in service at any given date. Consolidated returns in the war department showed liberal allowances

	Total present and absent	*Total present*	*Total effective present for duty*
Dec. 31, 1862	449,439	304,015	253,208
Dec. 31, 1863	464,646	277,970	233,586
Dec. 31, 1864	400,787	196,016	154,910

for scattered commands not reported and for irregular organizations would not bring the total enrolled to more than 600,000 at any of these dates. The state militia, serving short terms, uncertain in number and of dubious value, probably fell short of 100,000 at any given date. Losses from battle, disease, capture, and desertion so reduced the numbers with the colors that only 174,223 surrendered in April and May of 1865.

BIBLIOGRAPHY

War of the Rebellion: Official Records of the Union and Confederate Armies

T.L. Livermore, *Numbers and Losses in the Civil War in America, 1861–65*

R.H. McKim, *The Numerical Strength of the Confederate Army*

— CHARLES W. RAMSDELL

ARNOLD'S TREASON

Brig. Gen. Benedict Arnold of the Continental Army had fought gallantly for the American cause from Ticonderoga (1775) to Saratoga (1777). But by the spring of 1779 several motives led him to open up a treasonable correspondence with the British headquarters in New York. These were (1) irritation at repeated slights by Congress, (2) resentment at the authorities of Pennsylvania who had court-martialed him, (3) need for money, and (4) opposition to the French alliance of

1778. Throughout the rest of 1779 and 1780 he transmitted military intelligence about the American army

Brig. Gen. Benedict Arnold of the Continental Army demanded from the British £20,000 in case he could betray West Point, and £10,000 in case he failed but turned his loyalties to the British.

to the British. On July 12, 1780, he "accepted the command at West Point as a post in which I can render the most essential services" (to the British). He demanded from the British £20,000 in case he could betray West Point and £10,000 in case he failed but himself went over to the British. Negotiations were carried on with Maj. John André, adjutant general of the British army. André visited Arnold at a point between the British and American lines Sept. 21, 1780. On Sept. 23, when returning from this meeting, André was captured by the Americans, and the incriminating documents found in his stocking were sent to Gen. George Washington. News of André's capture was also sent to Arnold, thus giving him time to escape down the Hudson River to the British before he could be arrested for treason. He became a brigadier general in the British army, went to England after the defeat of the British, and died there June 14, 1801.

BIBLIOGRAPHY

James Thomas Flexner, *The Traitor and the Spy.*

Carl Van Doren, *Secret History of the American Revolution.*

— RANDOLPH G. ADAMS

ARTICLES OF CONFEDERATION

The Continental Congress decided even before independence that it was necessary to set up a confederacy based upon a written instrument. Several plans appeared in the press, and the subject was embraced in R. H. Lee's motion of June 7, 1776, on independence. On June 11 Congress voted to appoint a committee. This body set to work at once and on July 12 reported through John Dickinson a set of articles of confederation, of which eighty copies were printed for the use of members. Congress was so engrossed in war problems, however, that debates on the scheme dragged through more than a year. The principal disputes raged over the questions whether taxes should be apportioned according to the gross number of inhabitants counting slaves or excluding them—the South of course wishing them excluded; whether large and small states should have equality in voting; whether Congress should be given the right to regulate Indian affairs; and whether Congress should be permitted to fix the western boundaries of those states which claimed to the Mississippi. On Nov. 15, 1777, Congress finally approved a draft and sent it to the states, on the understanding that all must ratify it before it went into effect. This draft, declared a circular letter of Congress, "is proposed as the best which could be adapted to the circumstances of all; and as that alone which affords any tolerable prospect of a general ratification."

The Articles did not become the law of the land until Mar. 1, 1781. Nine states ratified as early as July 1778, but several of the smaller ones held back because of the question of western lands. Maryland in particular had urged that these lands be regarded as a common possession of all the states and felt aggrieved when the Articles contained a clause declaring that no state should be deprived of territory for the benefit of the United States. Maryland first declared that it would not ratify until its powerful neighbor, Virginia, ceased to advance extravagant western claims. But when New York had yielded and Virginia seemed certain to do so, Maryland on Mar. 1, 1781, signed the Articles through its delegates and made them effective.

Although the Articles have been harshly criticized and the very shrewdest critics at the time saw their inadequacy, they were generally regarded in 1781 as offering a sound national constitution. They provided for a "perpetual union" or "firm league of friendship" between the states. Each remained sovereign and independent and retained every right not expressly ceded by the Articles to the general government. A single agency of government was established—a Congress; the states were to appoint from two to seven delegates annually to it, and each state was to have one vote. Rhode Island thus obtained a parity with New York or Virginia. The costs of government and defense were to be defrayed from a common treasury, to which the states were to contribute in proportion to the value of their surveyed land and improvements. The states were likewise to supply quotas of troops, in proportion to the white inhabitants of each, upon congressional requisitions. To Congress was entrusted the management of foreign affairs, of war, and of the postal service; it was empowered to borrow money, emit bills of credit, and determine the value of coin; it was to appoint naval officers and superior military officers, and control Indian affairs. But none of these powers was to be exercised save by vote of a majority of all states, and the more important could not be exercised save by the vote of nine. On paper, almost every important national authority was turned over to Congress save three: the authority to raise money directly, the authority to enlist troops directly, and the authority to regulate commerce. But the paper powers proved to be very different from actual power.

The Articles of Confederation provided that each state would remain sovereign and independent; states would retain every right not expressly ceded by the Articles to the general government.

It soon became evident that Congress was doomed to fail in its attempts to make the Articles workable. These attempts consisted chiefly in requests to the states for money that was never paid, pleas for troops which filled no army ranks, and petitions for special powers which the states never granted. At various points the powers of the states were supposedly limited. They were forbidden to enter into treaties, confederations, or alliances, to meddle with foreign affairs, or to wage war without congressional consent, unless invaded. Most important of all, they were to give to free inhabitants of other states all the privileges and immunities of their own citizens. A citizen of South Carolina, for example, who removed to Boston, at once became a citizen of Massachusetts. Interstate extradition of criminals was also provided. The states could impose duties, but not any which conflicted with the treaty stipulations of Congress. They were required to "abide by the determinations of Congress" on all subjects which the Articles left to that body. The states did respect each other's rights to a considerable extent (when two or more of them fell out, any one could submit the dispute to Congress). But they failed lamentably to respect the needs and requests of the national government. They refused to do what they should have done, especially in supplying money and men; they frequently did what they should have refrained from doing. A circular prepared by Congress not long after Maryland's ratification in 1781 declared: "The inattention of the States has almost endangered our very existence as a people."

Demands for amendment and invigoration of the Articles were made even before they became effective. New Jersey served notice on Congress Feb. 3, 1780, for example, that it was absolutely necessary to give the nation power to regulate commerce and to fix duties on imports. A committee which reported May 3, 1781, pointed to the chief defect of the Articles—the fact that they gave Congress no power to enforce its measures, and suggested a new article authorizing the employment of armed forces to compel recalcitrant states "to fulfill their Federal engagements." This would have led straight to civil war, and the plan failed. The years 1782–86 witnessed earnest efforts by Congress to obtain state consent to a federal impost, which would have furnished a stable revenue; earnest efforts also were made to obtain from the states a sufficient control over shipping to enable it to wage commercial warfare with nations discriminating against the United States. But some states, notably New York and Rhode Island, long proved stubborn; others were tardy; and when they did act, their laws were found to conflict. Again, while the states were bound to respect the treaties made by Congress, several of them indulged in gross violations of the Definitive Treaty of Peace. The close of the year 1786 found the Articles of Confederation in widespread discredit and many national leaders eager to find a wholly new basis for union. Yet the Articles, soon to give way to the Constitution, should not be regarded with contempt. They had served as a stepping stone to a new order; as John Marshall said later, they had preserved the idea of union until national wisdom could adopt a more efficient system. Had they not been agreed upon in time, the states might have fallen asunder after Yorktown.

BIBLIOGRAPHY

Merrill Jensen, *The New Nation.*
Forrest E. McDonald, *E Pluribus Unum.*
Edmund Morgan, *Birth of the Republic.*

— ALLAN NEVINS

ARTICLE X

Article X of the League of Nations Covenant was of wholly American origin and was regarded by President Woodrow Wilson as an extension of the Monroe Doctrine to the whole world. In Wilson's mind the undertaking "to preserve as against external aggression the territorial integrity and existing political independence of all Members of the League" was not a pledge to go to war in advance of congressional consideration and decision. He interpreted the obligations of the article as moral, not legal.

Opponents of the covenant in the Senate made Article X their principal target. They argued that it was not the proper business of the United States to guarantee either new boundaries or old empires or to intervene in cases of revolution against oppression. They contended that moral obligations would be found as binding as legal ones. Consequently the Senate adopted a ponderous reservation repudiating any obligation under the article except as the Congress should provide in any particular case. This was unacceptable to Wilson not for its legal effect but for its embodiment of an attitude destructive to the principle of international responsibility. He contemplated territorial change accomplished through the peaceful operation of Article XIX rather than the traditional resort to violence.

BIBLIOGRAPHY

D. F. Fleming, *The United States and the League of Nations, 1918–1920.*

— HAROLD S. QUIGLEY

ASIAN AMERICANS

The 1990 census showed Asian Americans to be the fastest-growing racial group in the United States, increasing from 3.8 million in 1980 to 6.9 million in 1989. That increase during a single decade was twice the increase among Latinos, six times that of Africans, and twenty times that of whites, and was driven by an immigration made possible by the 1965 Immigration (Hart-Celler) Act that ended the national-origins quota system. Between 1951 and 1960 Asians accounted for a mere 6 percent of immigrants to the United States, but between 1981 and 1989 they made up 42 percent of the total. Also assisting the increase were the Indochina Migration and Assistance Act of 1975, the Refugee Act of 1980, and the Amerasian Homecoming Act of 1987. Despite the fact that in 1990 Asian Americans were the largest group in Hawaii and the third largest in California (behind whites and Latinos), they represented only 2.8 percent of the population of the United States.

The term "Asian Americans" encompasses a range of people whose ancestries derive from countries in West, South, Southeast, and East Asia with widely different cultures and histories. Institutions and social relations define them as a whole, however, and Asian Americans during the 1960s sought a unifying designation while trying to preserve the cultural and historical integrity of their respective ethnic groups. Chinese are the largest group, followed by Filipinos, Japanese, Asian Indians, Koreans, Vietnamese, Laotians, Cambodians, Thais, and Hmongs.

Asian Americans have been widely touted as America's "model minority." The 1990 census showed the median income of Asian Americans to be $35,900, 3 percent higher than that of whites. Of Asian Americans aged twenty-five and older, 40 percent had four years of college education, compared with 23 percent of whites. With low crime and juvenile delinquency rates, low divorce rates, and cultural emphasis on the family, Asian Americans have been cited as indicators of successful adaptation to life in the United States and as proof that other minority groups, such as African and Hispanic Americans, can pull themselves up from poverty and discrimination. Others have pointed out, however, that median income is calculated per family unit, and Asian American families have more members and income-earners than whites. Despite higher levels of education, Asian Americans earn less than whites with comparable educational levels and occupy lower management positions in businesses. In addition, higher percentages of Asian Americans live in regions such as Hawaii, California, and New York and in urban areas, where a high cost of living prevails. Critics of the "model minority" image question the possible motives behind propagation of a stereotype that ignores problems among Asian Americans at a time of civil unrest among African and Hispanic Americans.

Asian Americans during the 1960s sought a unifying designation while trying to preserve the cultural and historical integrity of their various ethnic groups.

In 1980 a third of Vietnamese immigrants, half of Cambodians, and two-thirds of Laotians lived in poverty; among Asian Americans together poverty was more than twice that among whites in 1988. Asian Americans also faced racism and prejudice. A 1992 report of the Commission on Civil Rights showed Asian Americans to be 20 percent of Philadelphia's victims of hate crimes while constituting only 4 percent of Philadelphia's population. A Boston Police Department analysis of civil rights violations from 1983 through 1987 found Asian Americans suffered higher rates of racial violence than any other group in the city. In 1988 arsonists set fire to the Cambodian houses in Lynn, Mass.; in 1990 a Chinese church in Chandler, Ariz., and fifty-five Hindu temples nationwide were vandalized; during the 1980s Vietnamese fishermen were harassed by white fishermen in Florida and California and by the Ku Klux Klan in Texas. In 1987 Asian-American students at the University of Connecticut in Storrs were spat upon by fellow students on their way to a Christmas dance. Vincent Chin, a Chinese American, was killed by two white automobile factory workers in Detroit in 1982; Navroze Mody, an Asian Indian, was bludgeoned to death in 1987 by a gang of youths in Jersey City, N.J., where a group called the "Dotbusters" had vowed to drive out all of the city's Asian Indians; Hung Truong, a Vietnamese, was beaten to death in Houston in 1990 by two skinheads. Patrick Edward Purdy fired on and killed five Cambodian and Vietnamese children and wounded thirty others in 1989 in an elementary school yard in Stockton, Calif., using an AK47 assault rifle.

Contrary to popular opinion, Asian Americans are not recent immigrants. Some of the earliest Asian communities in the United States were formed with arrival of Filipinos in Louisiana, possibly as early as 1765, and with settlement of Asian Indians in Philadelphia and Boston during the 1790s. Asians arrived in the Hawaiian kingdom about a century before the islands were annexed in 1898, and sizable Chinese communities in California and New York City developed beginning in the 1850s, followed by Japanese in 1869 in California. Chinese were introduced by planters in the South during the 1870s, and many Koreans, Filipinos, and Asian Indians arrived in California after 1900.

Early communities were unlike the urban concentrations of the late twentieth century, called "ethnic enclaves." Filipinos formed distinctive fishing villages in Louisiana, but Mexicans and Spaniards lived within those communities. Asian Indians who arrived on the East Coast during the 1790s adopted English names and probably intermarried with African Americans. New York's Chinese lived among African and Irish Americans, and substantial numbers of Chinese men married Irish women. Chinese in California lived mainly in rural towns in mining and agricultural counties of the state before nativism drove them into San Francisco and Los Angeles. Asian Indians, mainly men, who arrived in California, married Mexican women and formed a Punjabi-Mexican-American community. Those porous borders of race and geography were made less permeable by anti-Asian laws and practices.

Asian Americans nonetheless have sought inclusion in the promise of equality for all citizens. In *Yick Wo* v. *Hopkins* (1886), a suit brought by Chinese Americans in San Francisco, the Supreme Court broadened equal protection under the Fourteenth Amendment by asking whether discrimination impinged the rights of a person or group. Because of this and other litigation brought by Asian Americans, the Court upheld the fight of Japanese-language schools in 1927, mandated bilingual education in public schools in 1974, and contributed to equal protection under the law, desegregation in schools and workplaces, and workers' and language rights.

[See also Asian Religions and Sects; Chinese Americans; Immigration; Japanese Americans; Korean Americans.]

BIBLIOGRAPHY

Sucheng Chan, *Asian Americans: An Interpretive History* (Boston, 1991).

Ronald T. Takaki, *Strangers from a Different Shore* (Boston, 1989).

U.S. Commission on Civil Rights, *Civil Rights Issues Facing Asian Americans in the 1990s* (Washington, D.C., 1992).

— GARY Y. OKIHIRO

ASIAN RELIGIONS AND SECTS

Asian religions, originating in India or the Far East, began flourishing in the United States after 1965, when earlier U.S. immigrant quota laws were superseded by a single allocation of a set number of immigrants from all countries outside the Western Hemisphere. Buddhism is the most widespread of all Asian religions in the United States, with Japanese forms having the largest following. The first Japanese Buddhist to come to the United States was a Rinzai Zen monk, Soyen Shaku, who addressed the World Parliament of Religions in 1893. In the 1960s and 1970s, after Daisetz Teitaro Suzuki's writings popularized Zen, Buddhist communities established monasteries in California, Hawaii, and New York State for intensive Zen meditation. Hsuan-hua, a Chinese Zen Buddhist, founded the Dharma Realm Buddhist Association in 1962. Eleven years later this organization, located in Talmage, Calif., set up the first Buddhist university in the West.

The first Hindu guru to arrive in the U.S., Protap Chunder Mozoomdar, was a guest of Mrs. Ralph Waldo Emerson, then a widow, in 1883.

The two largest Japanese Buddhist groups in the United States originally branch from Nichiren-shu, whose members follow the teachings of Nichiren, a thirteenth-century Japanese Buddhist leader, and believe that salvation results from chanting portions of the Lotus Sutra, and Pure Land (Jodo Shinshu), whose adherents believe that individual rebirth in the Western Paradise occurs through faith in Amida Buddha. The fastest growing branch of Buddhism in the United States is the Soka Gakkai International (which claimed 500,000 members in 1994, although actual membership was closer to 100,000–200,000), formerly the lay branch of Nichiren-shu whose members regard Nichiren as the Buddha of the age. One of the more popular Pure Land groups is the Buddhist Churches of America, with approximately 50,000 members in 1994.

Theravadan Buddhism, a form of Buddhism recognizing only the earliest Buddhist scriptures, predominates in Southeast Asia, and during the 1970s many adherents arrived from Southeast Asia, particularly Vietnam, with the result that there are more than 500,000 Theravada Buddhists in the United States, primarily on the West Coast and in large cities. Tibetan Buddhism came to the United States in 1945, under the auspices of the American Buddhist Society and Fellowship set up by Robert Ernest Dickhoff. The first Tibetans arrived in 1951 in Howell, N.J., and founded the Tibetan Buddhist Learning Center. Although all four Tibetan Buddhist lineages are represented in the United States, the largest group is Vajradhatu, representing the Kagyupa lineage. The sect's center, opened in Boulder, Colo., in 1973 by Rinpoche Chogyam Trungpa, includes the Naropa Institute, an accredited college. The Association of American Buddhists was founded in 1980 by Kevin R. O'Neill; its program stresses an American form of Buddhism, assuring non-Asians that one does not need Asian cultural forms to be a legitimate Buddhist.

The first Hindu guru to arrive in the United States, Protap Chunder Mozoomdar, was a guest of Ralph Waldo Emerson's widow in 1883. The charismatic Swami Vivekananda, the disciple of Sri Ramakrishna, brought Hinduism to prominence by founding the Vedanta Society in 1895. The society emphasizes universal philosophical principles instead of devotion to a guru. The Hindu community in the United States is remarkably diverse, although most worship one of three popular deities—Shiva, the Goddess, or Vishnu. The Vishwa Hindu Parishad serves the Indian-American community as an ecumenical group to bridge these manifold sectarian and linguistic Hindu communities. Swami Prabhupada established the International Society for Krishna Consciousness (ISKCON) in New York City in 1966, stressing a chanting exercise as an expression of devotion to Krishna, a manifestation of Vishnu. In 1995 there were, conservatively, 50,000 lay (congregation) and 1,000 monastic members in the United States, out of approximately 1 million lay members and 10,000 monastics worldwide. Another significant Vaishnava group, the Swami Narayan movement (60,000 members in 1991), started in the late 1960s and is largely composed of Gujarati Indian-Americans.

Sikhism, founded in India and which adopted elements from Hinduism and Islam, arose in the United States in 1905–1913, with the arrival of thousands of Sikhs, who opened their first gurdwara (house of worship) in Stockton, Calif. In 1969 Sikhs constructed the largest gurdwara in the world in Yuba City, Calif., one of the central places of worship for the roughly 350,000 Sikhs in the United States. During the 1970s Yogi Bhajan began converting non-Indian-Americans and established a national organization, the Sikh Dharma (10,000 members in 1992), headquartered in Los Angeles.

Many other religions originating in Asia are represented in the United States. Jainism, which stresses austere practices that avoid hurting any living creatures, has communities in Chicago and New York City. Taoism, based on the Chinese principles of yin-yang and ch'i (the flow of energy through the body), is taught at the Healing Tao Center founded by Mantak Chia and his wife, Maneewan Chia, in Huntington, N.Y., and at Hua-ching Ni's Shrine of the Eternal Breath of the Tao in Los Angeles. Shintoism, the indigenous religion of Japan, has many temples in Hawaii.

[See also Asian Americans.]

BIBLIOGRAPHY

Rick Fields, *How the Swans Came to the Lake*, 3rd ed. (Boston, 1992).

J. Gordon Melton, *Encyclopedia of American Religions*, 4th ed. (Detroit, 1993).

E. Allen Richardson, *East Comes West: Asian Religions and Cultures in North America* (New York, 1986).

— ARTHUR F. BUEHLER

ASSEMBLY, RIGHT OF

The right of assembly is protected by the federal and state constitutions. The First Amendment of the U.S. Constitution (1791) provides that Congress shall make no law abridging "the right of the people peaceably to assemble," and the Massachusetts constitution of 1780, to cite an early state document, declares that "the people have a right in an orderly and peaceable manner, to assemble to consult upon the common good." Although the right of peaceable assembly was once described by the Supreme Court as a by-product of the right of petition, Chief Justice Charles Evans Hughes declared in 1937 that it is "cognate to those of free speech and free press and is equally fundamental" (*De Jonge* v. *Oregon*, 299 U.S. 353, 364 [1937]). Indeed, it is regarded as so fundamental a right that its violation by a state is subject to review by the U.S. Supreme Court under the liberty guaranty of the due process clause of the Fourteenth Amendment (*Bates* v. *City of Little Rock*, 361 U.S. 516 [1960]).

Almost all constitutional clauses on the subject of assembly speak of "peaceful" or "orderly" assembly. Thus, like all other rights, the right of assembly is not unlimited. It is limited by the requirements of public order and public peace. In American law an unlawful assembly is usually defined as a gathering of three or more people, which has the common intent to attain a purpose, whether lawful or unlawful, that will interfere with the rights of others by committing acts in such fashion as to give firm and courageous people in the vicinity reasonable ground to apprehend a breach of the peace. To sustain a charge of unlawful assembly it must be proved that the defendants "assembled together" and intended to commit an unlawful act—such as intimidation, threats, boycott, or assault—or a lawful act in a violent, boisterous, or tumultuous manner. At the same time, it is clearly established in the law that a meeting cannot be prohibited merely because unpopular changes may be advocated. Thus the U.S. Supreme Court ruled in the famous case of *New York ex rel. Bryant* v. *Zimmerman*, 278 U.S. 63 (1928), that a terrorist organization such as the Ku Klux Klan may be required to submit a roster of its membership and a list of its officers to state authority, but that school teachers as a class (*Shelton* v. *Tucker*, 364 U.S. 479 [1960]), or an organization committed to lawful purposes, such as the National Association for the Advancement of Colored People (*Gibson* v. *Florida Legislative Investigation Committee*, 372 U.S. 539 [1963]), may not constitutionally be required to submit to any public authority a list of their associational ties or membership records. In *Henry* v. *City of Rock Hill*, 376 U.S 776 (1964), the Court ruled squarely that the Constitution does not permit a local government to make the peaceful expression of unpopular views in a public place a criminal act. Furthermore, in contrast to British courts, American courts do not usually accept the view that the police may forbid a public meeting merely because they have reasonable grounds to believe that public disorder may result if the meeting is held. Even so, police discretion under either system of law is very great, and is not subject to effective judicial review. Finally, the right to hold meetings in streets, parks, or other public places is well recognized, but it ends where traffic obstruction or unlawful assembly, riot, or other breach of the peace occurs.

To sustain a charge of unlawful assembly, it must be proved that the defendants "assembled together" and intended to commit an unlawful act—or a lawful act in a violent or tumultuous manner.

While an ordinance forbidding all processions on the streets is clearly unreasonable, the city may require a prior permit, providing that the administrative official is not given an undefined or uncontrolled discretion. A leading decision on this point of law is *Niemotko* v. *Maryland*, 340 U.S. 268 (1951), which expressed strong disapproval of conferring upon local officials a "limitless discretion" in granting or denying permits for the holding of meetings in public places.

BIBLIOGRAPHY

David Fellman, *The Constitutional Right of Association*, chaps. 1–2.

— DAVID FELLMAN

ATLANTIC CHARTER

The Atlantic Charter was signed Aug. 14, 1941, by President Franklin D. Roosevelt and Prime Minister Winston Churchill at a meeting in Argentia Bay off Newfoundland. The United States, still technically a neutral in World War II, already had taken a number of steps that brought it close to war. The charter, although less explicit, may be compared roughly to President Woodrow Wilson's Fourteen Points in that both declarations expressed idealistic objectives for a postwar world. The charter included the following points: the renunciation of territorial or other aggrandizement; opposition to territorial changes not approved by the people concerned; the right of people to choose their own form of government; equal access to trade and raw materials of the world; promotion of economic advancement, improved labor standards, and social security; freedom from fear and want; freedom of the seas; and disarmament of aggressor nations pending the establishment of a permanent system of peace.

Although only a press release as first issued, the charter was nonetheless well understood to be a pronouncement of considerable significance; and it soon acquired further authority when on Jan. 1, 1942, twenty-six countries (including the United States and Great Britain) signed the United Nations Declaration, which included among its provisions formal endorsement of the charter.

— CHARLES S. CAMPBELL

ATOMIC BOMB

Atomic bomb, a military weapon deriving its energy from the fission or splitting of the nuclei of certain isotopes of the heavy elements uranium or plutonium. A nuclear device using plutonium was tested by the United States at Alamogordo, N.Mex., on July 16, 1945; and a bomb of this type was dropped on Nagasaki, Japan, in military operations on Aug. 9, 1945. A bomb using uranium-235 was dropped on Hiroshima, Japan, on Aug. 6, 1945.

The theoretical possibility of developing an atomic bomb or fission weapon became apparent to scientists throughout the world in 1939 soon after the discovery of nuclear fission in Germany. Although both Germany and England investigated the possibility of a weapon early in World War II, only the United States had sufficient resources and scientific manpower to undertake the project during the war. In the United States, feasibility studies began in laboratories in 1942 under the direction of Vannevar Bush and James B. Conant of the Office of Scientific Research and Development. Before the end of the year, three isotope-separation processes for the production of uranium-235 were under investigation, and Enrico Fermi had succeeded in achieving the world's first sustained nuclear chain reaction in Chicago on Dec. 2. The nuclear reactor provided a means of producing plutonium and promised ultimately to be a new source of power.

The Manhattan District of the U.S. Army Corps of Engineers, under the command of Brig. Gen. Leslie R. Groves, was responsible for coordinating the design and construction of the full-scale plants at Oak Ridge, Tenn., and Hanford, Wash., for the production of uranium-235 and plutonium, as well as for the design, fabrication, and testing of the weapon itself at a special laboratory at Los Alamos, N.Mex. During the two years preceding the test of the first weapon device at Alamogordo in July 1945, J. Robert Oppenheimer and a group of other scientists struggled with the design of two types of atomic bombs. Although the availability of sufficient uranium-235 for the gun-type weapon and the feasibility of the implosion-type for the plutonium weapon were not established before July 1945, both types of bombs were successfully produced for use during the war.

The atomic bombs dropped on Hiroshima and Nagasaki each released energy equivalent to about 20,000 tons of high explosive. More than 105,000 people died and 94,000 were wounded in these two attacks. Thus the bomb introduced a new method of warfare that posed unprecedented threats to the security of national states and civilian populations. In the postwar period, after unsuccessful attempts to establish international control of atomic energy under the United Nations, the United States and other nations embarked on the further development and production of nuclear weapons. The U.S. Atomic Energy Commission began a series of expansions of production facilities for uranium and plutonium and for the mass production of fission weapons. Other nations soon succeeded in producing atomic bombs—the Soviet Union in 1949; the United Kingdom in 1952; France in 1960; China in 1964; and India in 1974. Research and testing in the United States resulted in the design of a wide variety of fission weapons suitable for mass production and ranging from very small tactical devices to large strategic weapons. Fission weapons were also developed to serve as "triggers" for much more powerful thermonuclear or hydrogen bombs.

The type of atomic bomb detonated over Nagasaki, Japan, in World War II. It is 60 inches in diameter and 128 inches long and weighs about 10,000 pounds. (UPI/Corbis-Bettmann)

BIBLIOGRAPHY

Leslie R. Groves, *Now It Can Be Told.*

Stephen Groueff, *Manhattan Project.*

Richard G. Hewlett and Oscar E. Anderson, Jr., *The New World, 1939–1946.*

Richard G. Hewlett and Francis Duncan, *Atomic Shield, 1947–1952.*

— RICHARD G. HEWLETT

ATTICA

The most violent prison riot in American history occurred at the Attica

State Correctional Facility, located forty miles east of Buffalo, New York. On Sept. 9, 1971, approximately 1,000 of the prison's 2,254 inmates (85 percent of whom were black) seized control of the southeast portion of the prison compound. More than thirty guards and civilian employees were taken as hostages. The convicts issued a list of demands for higher wages; religious and political freedom; dietary, medical, and recreational improvements; and total amnesty and freedom from reprisals upon the surrendering of the hostages. Negotiations began between the inmates and Russell G. Oswald, New York State commissioner of corrections.

At the convicts' request civilian observers, representing the government, several newspapers, the radical Young Lords and Black Muslims, and other social and professional groups, were admitted to the prison. This ad hoc observers committee served as a liaison between Oswald and the convicts during four days of tense negotiations. Oswald offered a list of twenty-eight reforms that he was willing to grant. He acceded to nearly all the inmates' major demands except the ouster of Attica Superintendent Vincent R. Mancusi and total amnesty. The inmates insisted upon full immunity from all criminal charges. Gov. Nelson Rockefeller also rejected the amnesty plea and despite requests by the observers committee refused to travel to Attica to participate in negotiations.

At 7:46 A.M. on Sept. 13, 1971, Oswald read an ultimatum to the prisoners that reviewed his concessions and demanded the release of all hostages. In response, the prisoners displayed several hostages with knives held to their throats. At 9:46 A.M., 1,500 heavily armed state troopers, sheriff's deputies, and prison guards began an assault upon cellblock D. Twenty-nine inmates and ten hostages died from wounds suffered during the assault. Three convicts and one guard had died prior to the attack.

A preliminary report stated that nine hostages died from slashed throats and were emasculated or otherwise mutilated. Autopsies revealed that although some hostages were beaten and cut, all died from gunshot wounds in the assault and none was mutilated. The inmates had no firearms and apparently the hostages, dressed like convicts, were mistakenly killed by their would-be rescuers. On Sept. 16, Rockefeller appointed a five-man supervisory panel to prevent reprisals against inmates and protect their constitutional rights during the restoration of order. Charges of brutality after the uprising made by the committee were denied by prison officials.

After conducting extensive public hearings, a subcommittee of the U.S. Congress filed a report in June 1973, which criticized the tactics that the police and prison officials had used, and deplored the beatings and inadequate medical treatment of wounded inmates following the attack. A nine-member citizens fact-finding committee, headed by Robert B. McKay, dean of the New York University Law School, also conducted interviews and hearings. Their final report, Sept. 12, 1972, criticized Rockefeller for failing to visit Attica, cited the chaotic quality of the assault, and stated that the riot was a spontaneous uprising stemming from legitimate inmate grievances. Rockefeller, Oswald, and the chairman of a state congressional investigatory commission argued that the revolt was planned in advance by highly organized revolutionaries.

The 1971 prison riot at Attica, the most violent in American history, was sparked by poor conditions, racial tension, and the inmates' increasingly radical politics.

The criminal investigation of the Attica uprising, originally conducted by Deputy Attorney General Robert Fischer, led to forty-two indictments by a Wyoming County grand jury against sixty-two inmates involved in the rebellion. In April 1975, one inmate was convicted of murdering a guard. Shortly thereafter Anthony G. Simonetti, Fischer's successor, was accused of covering up evidence of brutality and incompetence by state police officials during the riot. The matter was investigated as the trials continued.

Poor conditions, racial tension, and the inmates' increased radical political awareness were some elements that precipitated the riot. The Attica uprising compelled the nation to reexamine its prisons and prison policy. Commissions, study groups, a massive quantity of verbiage, and some reform legislation resulted. Controversy continued to rage over the extent and effectiveness of these reforms.

BIBLIOGRAPHY

Tom Wicker, *A Time to Die.*

— WILLIAM DUNKEL

AUBURN PRISON SYSTEM

The details of the separate or silent system were originally worked out in the prison being erected by New York at Auburn in the years following 1819. An act of that year and another of 1821 called for individual cells to displace the discredited congregate system. Rows of cells, 3½ by 7 by 7 feet in size, were erected in tiers, back to back, forming a cell block which was inclosed by the outer walls of the building. The plan differed strikingly from the Pennsylvania solitary pattern, but could trace a distant descent from the plans of the *maison de force* at Ghent. The cells provided separate sleeping quarters, from which the convicts marched in lockstep to the shops of contractors located in the prison yard. Strict rules of silence were enforced at all times. Religious services were conducted in chapels. The system was designed to isolate the convicts from each other and to encourage them to penitence without sacrificing the value of their labor. The fact that convict labor was thus available to the enterprising pioneers of the factory system in America helped to make Auburn the preferred pattern for state prisons during the next half-century.

BIBLIOGRAPHY

Blake McKelvey, *American Prisons.*

— BLAKE MCKELVEY

AUTOMOBILE

Widespread interest in the possibilities of individualized, long-distance highway transportation grew after introduction of the geared, low-wheeled "safety bicycle" in 1885 and after quantity production reduced the price of a bicycle to about $30. Bicycle organizations in the United States and abroad began to agitate for improved roads and gained a broad base of support in the 1890's. The crest of the bicycle movement in the United States coincided with the climax of several decades of agrarian discontent that had singled out as a prime target the abuse of monopoly power by the railroads. Perceiving highway transportation as an alternative, farmers began to complain about the scandalous lack of good "farm to market" roads; improved roads became a popular political issue.

This revival of interest in highway transportation provided a fertile climate for commercial exploitation of the great advances made in automotive technology during the 1860–90 period. More compact and efficient power units had been developed, and the idea of substituting a motor for the horse occurred independently to many inventors in several nations. American accomplishment was most notable in steam-powered and electric-powered cars, which were rapidly to become backwaters of automotive technology. German and French inventors were well ahead of their American counterparts by the 1890's in development of the gasoline-powered automobile. By 1885, in Germany, Gottlieb Daimler and his assistant William Maybach had perfected a four-cycle internal-combustion engine, introduced by Nicholas Otto in 1876, and between 1885 and 1889 Daimler and Maybach built four experimental motor vehicles to demonstrate their 1.5 horsepower, 600-rpm engine, which weighed 110 pounds. Karl Benz, another German manufacturer of stationary gas engines, built his first car in 1886 and by 1891 had developed the automobile to the stage of commercial feasibility. Émile Constant Levassor, who had acquired the French manufacturing rights for the Daimler motor, created the basic mechanical arrangement of the modern motorcar in 1891 by placing the engine in front of the chassis instead of under the seats or in the back, an arrangement that made possible the accommodation of larger, more powerful engines. By 1895 automobiles were already a common sight on the streets of Paris.

Levassor demonstrated that the eventual displacement of the horse by the internal-combustion engine was more than an idle dream by driving one of his cars over the 727-mile course of the 1895 Paris-Bordeaux-Paris race at the then incredible speed of 15 mph, with the longest stop for servicing being only 22 minutes. The event stimulated a flurry of automotive activity in the United States. E. P. Ingersoll launched the first American specialized automobile journal, *Horseless Age*; the first European automobiles were imported for sale; the U.S. Patent Office was deluged with over 500 patents relating to motor vehicles; and the Chicago *Times-Herald* sponsored the first American automobile race, run over snow-covered roads in freezing temperatures on Thanksgiving Day, 1895.

Credit for the first successful American gasoline automobile is generally given to the winners of the *Times-Herald* race—Charles E. Duryea and J. Frank Duryea of Springfield, Mass., bicycle mechanics who built their first car in 1893 after reading a description of the Benz car in *Scientific American* in 1889. It is now known that several American inventors built experimental gasoline automobiles prior to the Duryeas. However, these people made no lasting contribution to the implementation of the automotive idea in America. The Duryeas, in contrast, capitalized on the national publicity gained in winning the *Times-Herald* contest by initiating the manufacture of motor vehicles for a commercial market in the United States in 1896, when they made the first sale of an American gasoline-powered car and produced twelve more of the same design. Allowing for changes of name and early failures, thirty American automobile manufacturers produced an estimated 2,500 motor vehicles in 1899, the first year for which separate figures for the automobile industry were compiled in the *United States Census of Manufactures*. The most important of these early automobile manufacturers in volume of product was the Pope Manufacturing Company of Hartford, Conn., also the nation's leading bicycle manufacturer.

The market for motorcars expanded rapidly as numerous races, tours, and tests demonstrated that the automobile was superior to the horse. Three transcontinental crossings by automobile in 1903 inaugurated informal long-distance touring by the average driver. The most important organized reliability runs were the Glidden Tours, sponsored annually between 1905 and 1913 by the American Automobile Association. However, the central role played by motor vehicles in saving lives and property during the 1906 San Francisco earthquake capped the need for further reliability runs. Following the disaster, municipalities began to motorize emergency services, and the emphasis in formal tours shifted to gasoline economy runs. Speed tests and track and road races gave manufacturers publicity for their products and contributed much to the development of automotive technology. The clocking of a Stanley Steamer at near 128 mph at Daytona Beach, Fla., in 1906 was a spectacular demonstration of progress made since the turn of the century. Among the early competitions stressing speed, none excited the popular imagination more than the Vanderbilt Cup road races (1904–16).

Contrary to popular myth, there was great enthusiasm for the motorcar in the United States from its introduction. Municipal and state legislation intended to regulate motor vehicles developed slowly, reflected the thinking of the automobile clubs, and was typically far less restrictive than the uniform laws adopted by European nations. Years before Henry Ford conceived of his universal car for the masses, writers in popular periodicals confidently predicted the banishment of horses from cities and the ending of rural isolation and drudgery through the imminent arrival of the low-cost, reliable car. No one ever doubted that the automobile was cleaner and safer than the unsanitary, whimsical old gray mare. The automobile so excited the enthusiasm of the American people because no mechanical innovation in U.S. history has been so congruent with deeply ingrained traits of the American character. The automobile promised to revitalize the Jeffersonian agrarian myth in a new fusion of rural and urban advantages and to preserve and enhance the individualism and personal mobility threatened by the rise of an urban-industrial socioeconomic order. An absence of tariff barriers between the states and the higher per capita income and better income distribution relative to European countries were other factors encouraging Americanization of the automobile.

Some 458,500 motor vehicles were registered in the United States by 1910, making America the world's foremost automobile culture. Responding to an unprecedented seller's market for an expensive item, between 1900 and 1910 automobile manufacturing leaped from one hundred and fiftieth to twenty-first in value of product among American industries and became more important to the national economy than the wagon and carriage industry on all measurable economic criteria.

Automobile Manufacturing

Because the automobile was a combination of components already standardized and being produced for other uses—for example, stationary and marine gasoline engines, carriage bodies and wheels—the early automobile manufacturer was merely an assembler of major components and a supplier of finished cars. The small amount of capital and the slight technical and managerial expertise needed to enter automobile manufacturing were most commonly diverted from other closely related business activities—especially from the bicycle, carriage, and wagon trades, and from machine shops. Requirements for fixed and working capital were met mainly by shifting the burden to parts makers, distributors, and dealers. High demand for cars enabled the manufacturers to require advance cash deposits of 20 percent on all orders, with full payment upon delivery; and the process of assembling took much less time than the thirty- to ninety-day credit period the parts makers allowed. These propitious conditions for entry attracted some 515 separate companies into automobile manufacturing by 1908, the year in which Henry Ford introduced the Model T and William C. Durant founded General Motors.

The Association of Licensed Automobile Manufacturers (ALAM) attempted to restrict entry into, and severely limit competition within, the automobile industry. This trade association of thirty leading producers of gasoline-powered cars was formed in 1903 to enforce an 1895 patent on the gasoline automobile originally applied for in 1879 by George B. Selden. Litigation was begun against the Ford Motor Company and several other unlicensed "independents," who continued to make and sell cars without paying royalties to the association. A 1911 written decision sustained the validity of the Selden patent, while declaring that Ford and the others had not infringed upon it, because the patent did not cover cars using four-cycle engines. To avoid another divisive and costly patent controversy in the industry, the newly formed National Automobile Chamber of Commerce (which became the Automobile Manufacturers Association in 1932 and the Motor Vehicle Manufacturers Association in 1972) instituted a cross-licensing agreement among its members in 1914. This patent-sharing arrangement was probably the most effective antimonopoly measure to emerge from the Progressive Era, because it prevented use of the patent system to develop monopoly power in this vital industry.

The ALAM companies tended to emphasize higher-priced models that brought high unit profits, while Henry Ford and many other independents were more committed to the volume production of low-priced cars. Ransom E. Olds initiated volume production of a low-priced car, but the surrey-influenced design of his $650, one-cylinder, curved-dash Olds (1901–06) was soon outmoded. The $600, four-cylinder Ford Model N (1906–07) deserves credit as the first low-priced car with sufficient horsepower to be reliable. The rugged Ford Model T (1908–27) was even better adapted to the wretched rural roads of the day, and its immediate popularity skyrocketed Ford's share of the market for new cars to about 50 percent by the outbreak of World War I.

Mass production techniques perfected at the Ford Highland Park, Mich., plant in 1913–14—especially the moving-belt assembly line—progressively reduced the price of the Model T to a low of $290 for the touring car by 1927, making mass personal automobility a reality. Soon applied to the manufacture of many other items, Ford production methods resulted in a shift from an economy of scarcity to an economy of affluence; created a new class of semi-skilled industrial workers; and opened new opportunities for remunerative industrial employment to the immigrant, the black migrant to the northern city, the physically handicapped, and eventually women. The five-dollar, eight-hour day instituted at Ford in 1914—which roughly doubled wages for a shorter workday—recognized dramatically that mass production necessitated mass consumption and mass leisure.

To compete with the Model T's progressively lower prices, the makers of moderately priced cars innovated modern consumer installment credit with the creation of the Guaranty Securities Company in 1915 and the General Motors Acceptance Corporation in 1919. Over 110 automobile finance corporations were in existence by 1921. Time sales accounted for about three-fourths of all automobile sales by 1926; and the finance corporations, wishing to diversify their risks, played an active role in encouraging installment purchases of many other types of merchandise. By the late 1920's this kind of buying was eroding the values of hard work, thrift, and careful saving sanctified in the Protestant ethic and so central to the socioeconomic milieu of perennial scarcity predicted by the classical economists.

Effect of the Automobile

American life was transformed during the 1920's by the mass-produced car, combined with the development of long-distance trucking and the small farm tractor (exemplified by the Fordson) in response to the demands of World War I. Regional, sectional, and rural-urban differences diminished. With the dispersal of the population into outlying areas, the locations of industrial plants and retail stores became decentralized. Larger trading areas killed off the village general store, lessened deposits in small local banks, forced the mail-order houses to open retail stores, and meant large-scale reorganization of both retail and wholesale trade. The quality of rural life was greatly upgraded as city amenities, especially far better medical care, were extended by the Model T; as the school bus replaced the one-room school with the consolidated school; and as the tractor removed much of the drudgery from farm labor. Ironically, the displacement of horses by the Fordson and the Model T raised the farmer's fixed costs while leading to chronic overproduction of staple crops, making the small family farm an increasingly inefficient economic unit.

The advent of the automobile had a tremendous effect on the cities too. A suburban real estate and construction boom initiated in the 1920's, although interrupted by the 1930's depression, continued into the 1970's. So did its related problems: a proliferation of inefficient local governmental units, mounting expenditures for municipal governments incurred in extending essential services, and a declining tax base and loss of vitality for the central city. Public health benefited from the disappearance of horses from cities; but street play for city children became increasingly hazardous, and automobile accidents became a major cause of deaths and permanent disabilities. Modern city planning arose to meet growing traffic congestion and parking problems; and accommodation to the motorcar through longer blocks, wider streets, and narrower sidewalks combined with a widening of the individual's range of associations to threaten the urban neighborhood as a viable form of community. Parental authority was undercut by the automobile date, which moved courtship from the living room into the rumble seat and replaced home entertainment with attendance at the movies or sports events. Recreational opportunities were greatly expanded as the automobile vacation to the seashore or the mountains became institutionalized and as the Sunday golf game or drive became alternatives to church attendance, the family dinner, and a neighborhood stroll. The pace of everyday life was accelerated, while the cost of automobile ownership came to constitute a heavy drain on the average family's budget.

By the mid-1920's automobile manufacturing ranked first in value of product and third in value of exports among American industries. The automobile industry was the lifeblood of the petroleum industry; one of the chief customers of the steel industry; and the biggest consumer of many other industrial products, including plate glass, rubber, and lacquers. The technologies of these ancillary industries were revolutionized by the new demands of motorcar manufacturing. The motorcar was responsible also for the rise of many new small businesses, such as service stations and tourist accommodations. Construction of streets and highways was the second largest item of governmental expenditure during the 1920's. Thomas C. Cochran, social and economic historian, noted this central role of automobility and concluded: "No one has or perhaps can reliably estimate the vast size of capital invested in reshaping society to fit the automobile. Such a figure would have to include expenditures for consolidated schools, suburban and country homes, and changes in business location as well as the more direct investments mentioned above. This total capital investment was probably the major factor in the boom of the 1920's, and hence in the glorification of American business."

In 1929, the last year of the automobile-induced boom, the 26.7 million motor vehicles registered in the United States—one for every 4.5 persons—traveled an estimated 198 billion miles, and that year alone government spent over $2.2 billion on roads and collected $849 million in special motor vehicle taxes. After the turn of the century, the automobile clubs became the main force in the good-roads movement, with motorists consistently favoring higher use taxes as one means of securing better roads. The Lincoln Highway Association, formed in 1913 to create a coast-to-coast hard-surfaced road, was disbanded after the Federal Aid Road Act of 1916 appropriated $75 million for improving rural post roads over a five-year period. Phenomenal growth in motor vehicle registrations and demonstration of the value of long-distance trucking in World War I led to the Federal Highway Act of 1921, which provided federal aid to the states, through fifty-fifty matching grants, for building a federal highway system. In 1929 gasoline taxes, collected by then in all states, amounted to $431 million in revenue and were the main source of revenue for highway expenditures.

Improvements in Technology

Improved roads and advances in automotive technology ended the Model T era. As the 1920's wore on, consumers came to demand much more from a car than the low-cost basic transportation that the utilitarian Model T afforded. The self-starter, which obviated the onerous and dangerous method of using a hand crank to start the car, gained rapid acceptance after its introduction in the 1911 Cadillac. The basic open-car design of the Model T became obsolete as closed cars increased from 10.3 percent of production in 1919 to 82.8 percent in 1927, making the automobile a year-round, all-weather vehicle. Ethyl gasoline, the octane rating of fuels, and better crankshaft balancing to reduce vibrations were the most important breakthroughs that led to the introduction of the high-compression engine in the mid-1920's. By then four-wheel brakes, low-pressure "balloon" tires, and wishbone-type front-wheel suspension also had appeared—resulting in a smoother, safer ride. Syncromesh transmission and safety plate glass in all windows were features of the 1928 Cadillac. Mass-produced cars of all colors became possible after Duco lacquer made its debut in the "True Blue" of the 1924 Oakland (the Model T had come only in black after 1913 because only black enamel would dry fast enough). The trend too was toward annually restyled, larger, more powerful, and faster six-cylinder cars; by the mid-1920's a Chevrolet with these advantages cost only a few hundred dollars more than a Model T.

Thus, Henry Ford's market strategy of a single, static model at an ever-decreasing price became outmoded in the 1920's. Under the leadership of Alfred P. Sloan, Jr., General Motors parlayed into leadership in the automobile industry the counterstrategy of blanketing the market with cars in several price ranges, constant upgrading of product through systematic research and testing, and the annual model change and/or planned obsolescence of product. And while Henry Ford continued to run his giant company as an extension of his personality, without even an organizational chart, General Motors pioneered development of the decentralized, multidivisional structure of the modern industrial corporation and became the prototype, widely copied after World War II, of the rational, depersonalized business organization run by a technostructure.

Competition between automobile manufacturers sharpened with the onset of market saturation. Replacement demand first exceeded demand from initial owners and multiple-car owners combined in 1927, and the 1929 total production of over 5.3 million motor vehicles was not again equaled until 1949. Despite that, almost half of American families still did not have a car in 1927; the inadequate income distribution of Coolidge prosperity meant a growing backlog of used cars on dealers' lots; and only about a third of the automobile dealers were making money. A trend toward oligopoly in the automobile industry, observable since 1912, accelerated as economies of scale and the vertical integration of operations became more essential for survival. The number of active automobile manufacturers dropped from 108 to 44 between 1920 and 1929; and Ford, General Motors, and Chrysler came to be responsible for about 80 percent of the industry's total output. The 1930's depression shook out most of the remaining independents; despite mergers among the independents that survived into the post–World War II period, in the mid-1970's only American Motors (formed from Nash-Kelvinator and Hudson in 1954) continued to challenge Detroit's Big Three. Closure of entry into automobile manufacturing was underlined by the failure of new firms, such as Kaiser-Frazer, to succeed in the post-World War II industry.

The major innovations in modern automotive technology not yet incorporated by the late 1920's were the all-steel body, the infinitely variable automatic transmission, and drop-frame construction, which dropped the passenger compartment from its high perch upon the axles to its now familiar position down between the front and rear wheels, lowering the height and center of gravity of the car. Increasingly since the 1930's, emphasis has been on styling—the factor contributing most to the high cost of the contemporary car through its implications for stamping processes. Streamlined styling was pioneered in the Chrysler "Airflow" models of the 1930's and in the 1947 Studebaker. The automatic transmission was introduced in the 1939 Oldsmobile and by the 1970's became standard equipment along with power brakes, power steering, radios, and air conditioning. Development of the high-compression, overhead-cam, V-8 engine led to a horsepower race in the 1950's that culminated in the "muscle cars" of the late 1960's. But the industry trend toward larger, more powerful, and more expensive cars was reversed by mounting consumer demand throughout the 1960's for the economical Volkswagen, a number of Japanese-built compacts, and domestic models such as the Nash Rambler and the Ford Mustang. By the early 1970's Big Three production had shifted toward emphasis on smaller, sportier, more economical models.

State of the Industry

The post–World War II American automobile industry could be considered a technologically stagnant industry, despite its progressive refinement of product and automation of assembly lines. Neither motorcars nor the methods of manufacturing them changed fundamentally over the next generation. The most promising improvements during the 1970's in the internal-combustion engine—the Wankel, the stratified charge, and the split-cycle rotary engines—were being pioneered abroad; and Saab and Volvo were making the first significant attempts to depart from traditional patterns of assembly-line production. Common Market and Japanese producers also led in meeting consumer demand for economy and compact cars at lower unit profits. American automobile manufacturers in the main responded to increasingly stiffer foreign competition by trying to cut labor costs through heightened factory regimentation intended to increase the workers' productivity on domestic assembly lines and through accelerated expansion of overseas subsidiaries. Notable increases in absenteeism, alcoholism, drug use, and neuroses among automobile workers further threatened the quality of Detroit's product. And with the growth of the multinational corporation in automobile manufacturing, it became more and more difficult to determine what indeed constitutes an American-made car. Detroit's share of the world market for cars slipped from about three-fourths in the mid-1950's to little more than a third by the mid-1970's.

Federal legislation affecting the automobile industry proliferated from the New Deal era on. The National Labor Relations Act of 1935 encouraged the unionization of automobile workers; and with the capitulation of General Motors and Chrysler in 1937 and Ford in 1941, the United Automobile Workers became an institutionalized power in the automobile industry. The federal government stepped in to correct long-standing complaints about the retail selling of automobiles with passage of the so-called Automobile Dealer's Day in Court Act (Public Law 1026) in 1956. Automotive design came to be regulated by the federal government with passage of the Motor Vehicle Air Pollution Act of 1965 and the National Traffic and Motor Vehicle Safety Act of 1966. Prices for new cars, as well as the wages of automobile workers, were made subject to governmental approval with the establishment in 1971 of wage and price controls as a measure to curb inflation. Progressive governmental regulation of the post–World War II automobile industry, however, was accompanied by the massive, indirect subsidization of the Interstate Highway Act of 1956, which committed the federal government to pay, from a Highway Trust Fund, 90 percent of the construction costs for 41,000 miles of mostly toll-free express highways.

Up to the 1960's American enthusiasm for the automobile remained remarkably constant through peace and war, depression and prosperity. Although during the Great Depression motor vehicle registrations declined slightly and factory sales dwindled to a low of 1.3 million units in 1932, the number of miles of travel by motor vehicle continued to increase, and automobility was one of the few aspects of American life that escaped disillusioned questioning. Full recovery from the depression was coupled with conversion of the automobile industry to meet the needs of the war effort. Manufacture of motor vehicles for the civilian market ceased early in 1942, with tires and gasoline severely rationed for the duration of the war. The automobile industry converted its resources to the manufacture of some seventy-five essential military items, contributing immeasurably to the Allied victory. After the war, the pent-up demand for cars and general affluence insured banner sales for Detroit, lasting into the late 1950's, when widespread dissatisfaction with the outcome of the automobile revolution began to become apparent.

Increasingly in the 1960's the automobile came to be recognized as a major social problem. Critics focused on its contributions to environmental pollution, urban sprawl, the rising cost of living, and accidental deaths and injuries. Much of the earlier romance of motoring was lost to a generation of Americans, who, reared in an automobile culture, accepted the motorcar as a mundane part of the establishment. While the automobile industry provided directly one out of every six jobs in the United States, its hegemony in the economy and society had been severely undercut over the preceding decades by proliferation of the size, power, and importance of government, which provided one out of every five jobs by 1970. With increased international involvement on the part of the United States, the rise of a nuclear warfare state, and the exploration of outer space, new industries more closely associated with the military-industrial complex—especially aerospace—became, along with the federal government, more important forces for change than the mature automobile industry.

These considerations notwithstanding, the American automobile culture continued to flourish in the 1960's. Drive-in facilities were extended from motion picture theaters and restaurants to banks, grocery stores, and even churches; automobile races attracted enthusiastic crowds; the cults of the hot rod and the sports car gained devotees; interest in restoring antique automobiles grew by leaps and bounds; and a new mass market for recreational vehicles resulted in an avalanche of campers and trail bikes descending on the national parks. The best indication of the automobile culture's continuing vitality was that in 1972 motor vehicle factory sales exceeded 11.2 million; registrations surpassed 117 million; and 83 percent of American families owned cars. In 1972 production lagged behind demand for new cars, and record-breaking factory sales for the third straight year were anticipated. To the average man the automobile remained an important symbol of individualism, personal freedom, and mobility in an increasingly collectivized and bureaucratized American society.

This phenomenal post–World War II proliferation of the U.S. automobile culture was abruptly halted in 1973–74 by an alleged fuel shortage, associated with a worldwide energy crisis. Critics charged that the fuel shortage was a ploy by the major oil companies to justify raising gasoline prices to boost profit margins; to squeeze out the independent dealers; and to gain public support for an expansion of offshore drilling and completion of the trans-Alaska pipeline. Nevertheless, domestic oil reserves in mid-1973 were reported to be only 52 billion barrels, about a ten-year supply. Projections were that crude petroleum imports would increase from 27 percent in 1972 to over 50 percent by 1980 and that all known world reserves of petroleum would be exhausted within fifty to seventy years. An embargo by the Arab oil-producing nations resulted by Jan. 1, 1974, in a ban on Sunday gasoline sales, a national 55-mph speed limit, five- to ten-gallon maximum limitations on gasoline purchases, and significantly higher prices at the pump. Despite short-range easing of the fuel shortage with the lifting of the Arab embargo, dwindling oil reserves promised, at the very least, increasingly higher gasoline prices that would impose inevitable limits on the further expansion of mass personal automobility anywhere in the world.

The end of a two-decade trend toward cars that guzzled more and more gasoline was underlined as sales of small cars increased to 39 percent (60 percent in Los Angeles) of the American market for the first quarter of 1973. By December, for the first time in history, sales of compacts and subcompacts surpassed sales of standard-sized cars, and projections were that smaller cars would soon account for two-thirds of the U.S. market. Consumers were responding to the inroads on purchasing power of runaway inflation and mounting taxes as well as to the fuel shortage. The American auto industry was ill-prepared for this marked shift in consumer preference, and for the first quarter of 1974 Detroit's sales slipped drastically. Large cars piled up on storage lots and in dealers' showrooms, and massive layoffs of automobile workers accompanied the shifting of assembly lines to the production of smaller models. Only American Motors, which had emphasized the small car since the mid-1950's, increased its sales. Among the Big Three, Ford held a comfortable lead in the conversion to the small car, with five compact and subcompact models.

Independently of the fuel shortage, by 1974 the worldwide automobile revolution had reached its zenith of probable development, and most observers anticipated more balanced transportation systems in the foreseeable future. The American market for motorcars was saturated with one car for every 2.25 persons (more cars than people in the Los Angeles area); the auto markets in Japan and in the developed countries of Europe were saturated in ratio of cars to available land and paved roads; and the low per capita incomes and poor income distribution in underdeveloped countries prohibited the creation of new auto cultures. The year 1973 marked the beginning of diversion of the Highway Trust Fund into nonhighway transportation, and California's freeway-building program, the most ambitious in the nation, was near collapse. Both General Motors and Ford inaugurated mass-transit divisions and were moving toward becoming total transportation corporations, whose main business by the end of the century was anticipated to become the designing of modular transportation systems for metropolitan areas. While the motor vehicle was still expected to play a major role in these transportation systems of the future, and it seemed that Detroit could continue prosperous and powerful through diversification and adaptation to small urban cars, by the mid-1970's the end undoubtedly had come to the "age of the automobile"—over two generations of American historical development dominated by the automobile and the automobile industry.

Automobile Racing

Contests emphasizing speed were of minimal importance in popularizing the automobile in the United States because the specialized cars used seemed remotely related to the average man's transportation needs. As early as 1905 the automobile trade journals expressed doubt that participation in races even had much advertising value for automobile manufacturers. The main value of track and road racing, therefore, was in providing grueling tests for advances in automotive technology; and this value became increasingly questionable with the institutionalization of systematic testing over specially designed courses. Nevertheless, automobile manufacturers have continued to support racing—with varying degrees of eagerness and openness. Few spectator sports can match the thrills and excitement of automobile racing, which early became a popular form of mass entertainment.

Organized automobile racing and time trials were supervised by the American Automobile Association until taken over by the newly formed U.S. Automobile Club in 1955. The last important American road race was run in 1916 at Santa Monica, Calif., for the Vanderbilt Cup; road racing remained popular in Europe, with Europeans generally excelling over Americans at the sport. The most famous American closed-circuit track event remains the Indianapolis 500-mile race, run since 1911 at increasingly higher speeds annually—except during wartime—over a brick-surfaced track. Dirt-track racing always has been popular throughout the country; the cars raced have ranged from specially designed midgets to modified stock cars. Drag racing—the attempt to achieve maximum acceleration over a short distance—became popular after World War II, and an annual drag-racing competition was inaugurated on the Bonneville Salt Flats (Utah). Bonneville also became the site of continuing attempts to set new land speed records in jet-propelled vehicles that bear more similarity to spaceships than to automobiles.

Sports Cars

Americans have contributed little toward perfecting the sports car—a small, high-performance car designed for highway use rather than organized racing. Sparked initially by GI's returning from England after World War II, an American sports car cult developed. The most important of a number of sports car organizations formed is the Sports Car Club of America, which has sponsored many sports-car competitions. European-made sports cars—especially the Porsche—continued in the mid-1970's to be most popular among devotees. In the 1950's Detroit introduced the Ford Thunderbird and the Chevrolet Corvette to compete with European sports cars, but the Thunderbird quickly evolved into a full-size, conventional car. In response to the growing youth market for smaller, sportier-looking cars, Detroit brought out a number of other models—such as the Ford Mustang—that look like, but lack the superior performance capabilities of, the true sports car.

BIBLIOGRAPHY

James J. Flink, *America Adopts the Automobile, 1895–1910.*

John B. Rae, *The American Automobile*, and *The Road and the Car in American Life.*

Emma Rothschild, *Paradise Lost: The Decline of the Auto-Industrial Age.*

Lawrence J. White, *The Automobile Industry Since 1945.*

— JAMES J. FLINK

AUTOMOBILE INDUSTRY SINCE THE 1970S

Automobile industry in the United States underwent a marked change in the last quarter of the twentieth century. Defined in the 1970s as a mature industry with little prospect for growth, it suffered from and then responded to multiple challenges: oil price shocks, foreign competition, and new regulation, together with demands for world-class products and services. These developments damaged Ford Motor Company, hurt General Motors, pushed Chrysler to bankruptcy, and cost them an average of 34 percent of their home markets. Chrysler in 1979 was saved only by a last-minute

U.S. government loan guarantee. It managed, however, to launch the economy K-car line in 1980, invent the minivan in 1983, and repay its loan early. Chrysler also bought the American Motors Corporation from Renault in 1987, gaining the Jeep brand. Chrysler Chairman Lee A. Iacocca's television commercials helped revive the company. His best-selling autobiography, *Iacocca* (1984), championed a "level playing field" in import-export policy.

The oil embargo by the Organization of Petroleum Exporting Countries (OPEC) that followed the 1973 Arab-Israeli War raised gasoline prices, putting a premium on fuel efficiency, but the entrenched management of General Motors, Ford, and Chrysler (known as the Big Three) continued building large, fuel-inefficient cars and trucks, as the American public did not demand more fuel-efficient vehicles. After President Jimmy Carter embargoed Iranian oil in 1979, however, dealers were besieged by customers asking for 30 miles-per-gallon, front-wheel drive, economy cars—despite the fact that with demand high and supply short, many economy imports carried labels adding up to $2,000 to their list prices. Small cars from Japan and Europe of good (and improving) quality were available and carried the cachet of difference. Zero-to-sixty miles per hour figures became meaningless if not unpatriotic in the age of economy sparked by the embargo. Advertising began touting miles per gallon and four-speed transmissions.

Change in the automobile industry was also brought about by environmental and energy conservation legislation. The Clean Air Act of 1970 mandated a 90 percent reduction in carbon monoxide and hydrocarbon emissions by 1975 and a 90 percent drop in nitrogen oxide emissions by 1976. More than 110 countries, including the United States, began to phase out production of ozone-depleting chlorofluorocarbons (CFCs, also known by the trade name freon) by the end of 1995. The 1990 Clean Air Act banned release of CFCs during servicing and disposal of air-conditioning and refrigeration equipment. The Energy Policy and Conservation Act of 1975 applied Corporate Average Fuel Economy (CAFE) standards to all manufacturers in the U.S. market. The burden fell heaviest on domestic automakers, because their model mix was weighted toward larger, less fuel efficient cars and trucks. CAFE began with an 18 miles-per-gallon requirement in 1978, which was up to 20 miles by 1980 and 27.5 in 1994. The technological leap toward higher clean air standards was met by switching to unleaded gasoline, catalytic converters, computerized engine controllers to manage ignition timing, air-fuel ration, emissions control devices, and idle speed. Newly available compressed natural gas (COG) fuel systems produced fewer emissions and met or beat all applicable standards up to and including California's requirements for Ultra Low Emission Vehicles (ULEV).

Workers in an assembly line install an engine into a Ford Model T at a Highland Park, Michigan, factory in 1913. (Corbis-Bettmann)

Safety concerns also spurred governmental regulation. Ralph Nader attacked General Motors' rear-engine Corvair in his *Unsafe at Any*

Speed (1965), which began a critical review of automobile safety that greatly influenced the design of future cars. During the 1970s Big Three engineers worked overtime to modify cars for the new age of constraints, but they found that haste made waste. The 1971 Pinto met Ford's need for a sprightly economy car, but its ill-fated design had the gas tank wedged between the rear bumper and axle. When struck from behind, it was prone to gas leaks and fires. The resulting deaths led to widely publicized lawsuits, corporate denials, half-measures, and a "voluntary recall" in 1978—under threat of public hearing by the National Highway Traffic Safety Administration. The thrust for safety, once focused on the driver, had shifted to the vehicle. In the 1990s an automaker's prompt corrective recall was proof of commitment to owner satisfaction. Deaths from accidents dropped dramatically, as measured by fatalities per miles driven, from 7.6 deaths per 100 million miles in 1950 to 1.8 in 1992, a record low. The total of 40,000–50,000 highway deaths per year has remained constant and is not expected to drop before the year 2005. Alcohol factors into 10 percent of property damage by autos, 20 percent of injuries, and a striking 47 percent of accidents that lead to fatalities. In 1992 eliminating alcohol from accidents would have saved 18,400 lives and $9 billion in property damage. Seat belts saved an estimated 5,226 lives in 1992.

Ralph Nader's Unsafe at Any Speed *(1965), an attack on General Motors' rear-engine Corvair, initiated a critical review of automobile safety that greatly influenced automobile design.*

The number of franchised new car dealers in the United States dropped from a high of 49,000 in 1949 to 22,000 in 1994, with a shift to fewer but larger and better-financed outlets. Factory-mailed surveys question each buyer's satisfaction with the dealer's sales department, service, parts, facilities, and employee attitudes. Low scores cost the dealer incentive money and were grounds for loss of dealership. The average franchised dealer of the mid-1990s sold 550 new cars and trucks annually and had sales of $16 million, 50 employees, and a $1.5 million payroll. A typical dealership's pretax net profits were 1.5 percent of sales. During the 1980s dealers computerized bookkeeping, inventory control, sales, and service. The Big Three installed factory-dealer systems to speed warranty and parts and car ordering, and then added satellite links for on-line sales meetings, service training, billing, and sales data. Service departments installed test equipment for new models with onboard computers, easing problems for certified technicians. Mechanics began doing oil changes and underbody work.

Consumer confidence, disposable personal income, and available financing, along with the vehicle price, were the ingredients of a new car or truck sale in the 1990s. Car sales had a great economic impact because one in six U.S. jobs were linked to the automobile industry. Despite a rise in average car prices from $10,586 in 1984 to $18,294 in 1993, the actual cost based on weeks of disposable income changed little. Depending on the difference between the dollar and Japanese yen, the average work-week cost of an imported car reached 62 weeks; domestic-produced cars dropped to less than 50. This price difference, combined with improved press reports, largely accounted for sales increases by the Big Three. A popular no-haggle marketing idea, value pricing, was introduced in 1990 by GM's Saturn division. An indication of improved quality was that the average time of cars in service grew to eight years in 1992, as compared to six years in 1975. Most dealers offered customers the option of leasing instead of buying. Drivers benefited from guaranteed trade-in values, business write-offs, lower payments, and latest models. Lease credit requirements were stringent. Desirable low-mileage used cars were a growing offshoot of leasing.

The number of North American automakers grew from four in the 1970s to fifteen in 1994, including new plants built by BMW and Mercedes. The effect of these foreign-owned or joint ventures (known as "transplants") was enormous, accounting for 18.5 percent of U.S. sales in 1993. This transplant production, plus increased exports, was expected to lower the U.S. 1994 automotive trade deficit with Japan of $37.3 billion.

The "Big Three" of Detroit reinvented themselves as leaner, insistent on quality, innovative, staffed by empowered employees, environmentally aware, and profitable.

The Federal Highway Administration chart of miles traveled rose by one-third, to 2.293 trillion miles, in 1983–1993. The Big Three and the federal government began cooperating with one another. Antitrust laws were relaxed to allow joint research into emissions, alternative fuels, composite materials, battery development, and recycling, and the Department of Energy provided $260 million for electric car battery research.

A study within a sheet-stamping plant at Chrysler revealed how much the new "quality" culture depended on human relations. As stated in a 1994 article in *Automotive News*, "The automaker found that while it was important to study metal, listening to people was more fruitful." Body complaints dropped from 20.4 per 100 vehicles in 1993 to 9.8 in 1994. Chrysler's goal was to limit variations on body stampings and assemblies to two millimeters or less, about the thickness of a dime. The challenge was to get the assembly plant and stamping plant workers together and to push decision-making downward to workers. Although there were adjoining places of production, the communications systems were indirect and through channels. Until changes were made, workers had never met nor communicated directly with each other. Under the new procedure, when assembly plant workers find a problem, they call their counterparts in stamping; this shortcutting of channels saves three days. Welders were retrained to analyze measurements, make corrections, and gain a sense of responsibility regarding quality. The Chrysler plant achieved the two-millimeter goal in eighteen months, two years ahead of forecasts.

The Big Three reinvented themselves as leaner, cost-controlled, quality insistent, innovative, employee empowered, environmentally aware, export-minded, aggressive, and profitable. Quality improved, with problems per 100 cars dropping from 159 to 113 from 1989 to 1993. As efficiency soared, however, employment at GM, Ford, and Chrysler dropped from 717,000 in 1988 to 589,000 in 1994. It remains to be seen whether the North American Free Trade Agreement (NAFTA) of 1994 will create jobs and open new markets in the automobile industry, thus contributing to the domestic prosperity anticipated by American workers and consumers since the 1970s. The initial beneficiaries will be the Big Three because tariff barriers on import sales in Mexico were very high before NAFTA. Benefits may be derived by consolidating production of low-volume units into one plant in the United States, Canada, or Mexico, rather than operating up to three plants. Transplant makers in the United States will also enjoy the lowered barriers to sales in Mexico.

[See also Automobile; Consumer Protection; Environmental Protection Agency.]

BIBLIOGRAPHY

William R. Diem, *America at the Wheel: 100 Years of the Automobile in America* (n.p., 1993).

Joshua M. Harari, *Autos - Auto Parts*, Standard & Poors Industry Surveys (New York, 1994).

Daniel Roos et al., *The Future of the Automobile* (Cambridge, Mass., 1984).

— JAMES F. CAHILLANE

AVIATION INDUSTRY

Aviation industry, the industry concerned with the manufacture of aircraft, aircraft engines, propellers, and other components—excluding electrical and electronic equipment and weapons for military aircraft. The American aviation industry began in 1909, when the Wright brothers formed a company to build airplanes and conduct flying schools. They were followed by Glenn Curtiss (also 1909), W. Starling Burgess (1910), Glenn L. Martin (1912), William E. Boeing (1915), and Allan and Martin Loughead (1915). Growth was slow because of minimal support from the government ($500,000 from 1909 to 1914), and the aviation industry in the United States and elsewhere has existed largely on sales to governments.

World War I found the United States with totally inadequate resources for aircraft design and construction. Total output in 1914 was forty-nine planes. A massive building program was initiated by the government, but it came under much criticism because planes were not produced in any quantity before the war ended. There were charges of mismanagement and corruption, with some foundation; but the real difficulty was failure to realize the complexity of the problem. An easy assumption made by Americans in World War I and repeated in World War II was that existing industrial resources—especially the automobile industry—could be converted on short notice to aircraft construction.

The war terminated a patent controversy between the Wrights and Martin on one side and Curtiss and Burgess on the other. Among them they controlled most of the basic airplane patents and each was claiming infringement by the other. Governmental pressure brought about the creation of the Aircraft Manufacturers' Association in 1917, with the administering of a cross-licensing agreement as its principal initial function. In the process, Wright and Martin merged as the Wright-Martin Company and Curtiss and Burgess as the Curtiss Aeroplane and Motor Company.

The wartime program produced, up to Nov. 1, 1919, some 14,000 planes, 42,000 engines, and 41,000 balloons and airships at a cost of over $365 million. About 300 plants and 20,000 workers were involved. When the armistice came, war contracts were abruptly terminated and the aviation industry virtually collapsed within a year. Most of the wartime entrants disappeared.

The principal holdovers were the Wright Aeronautical Company, reorganized from Wright-Martin and now exclusively an engine manufacturer; Curtiss Aeroplane and Motor, briefly included in the Willys automotive empire; Boeing; and a reconstituted Glenn L. Martin Company. Two important new arrivals appeared in the early 1920's: Douglas, established in Los Angeles by Donald W. Douglas in 1920; and Consolidated, put together by Reuben Fleet from the remains of two wartime airplane companies, Dayton-Wright and Gallaudet, and located in Buffalo, N.Y.

The middle 1920's witnessed a steady, but still small-scale, growth of the industry, stimulated by the Kelly Air Mail Act of 1925, which put the carriage of airmail into private hands and therefore encouraged the development of more economical and efficient transport planes, and by the report of the Morrow Board in 1926, which provided a systematic five-year program of military and naval procurement. A number of new American airframe firms appeared, including Lockheed, a revival of the earlier Loughead company (the brothers changed the spelling of their name); Fairchild, originally a company engaged in aerial photography; and the companies founded by Igor Sikorsky, a brilliant Russian aeronautical engineer, and Anthony Fokker, the Dutchman who established a reputation as a designer of fighter planes for Germany in World War I. An outstanding entrant was William B. Stout's company, one of the first in the world to build all-metal aircraft. It was taken over by the Ford Motor Company in 1924 and produced the well-known Ford trimotor transport, the "tin goose." In addition, Wichita, Kans., emerged during the 1920's as the country's principal center for the manufacture of planes for general aviation—that is, planes that were neither military aircraft nor commercial transports.

Lindbergh's 1927 New York–Paris flight and the 1920's boom atmosphere stimulated optimism about the growth of aviation.

The greatest advance of this period came in the design and production of radial air-cooled engines. Because Adm. William A. Moffett, head of the U.S. Navy Bureau of Aeronautics, believed that this type of engine was ideally suited to the navy's needs, he encouraged its development by Wright Aeronautical (later Curtiss-Wright) and a new firm, Pratt and Whitney. The pioneering American work on the radial air-cooled engine was done by Charles L. Lawrance, whose company was acquired by Wright Aeronautical in 1923. By the end of the decade the United States had attained a clear leadership, both qualitative and quantitative, in radial air-cooled engines.

There was also an American effort to enter the lighter-than-air field, again because of naval interest. The dirigible *Shenandoah* was completed in 1923 by the Naval Aircraft Factory in Philadelphia. In 1924 the Goodyear Zeppelin Corporation was formed, with both German designs and German technicians. This company built the *Akron* (1931) and the *Macon* (1933), both designed as carriers for four small airplanes. All three of these airships were wrecked in storms, with the result that further development of large dirigibles was abandoned.

The enthusiasm generated by Charles A. Lindbergh's New York to Paris flight in 1927 and the boom atmosphere of the late 1920's stimulated optimistic hopes about the growth of aviation and led to several efforts at large-scale combinations of aircraft manufacturers and air-transport companies. The most important were United Aircraft and Transport, started in 1928 by William E. Boeing, North American Aviation, and the Aviation Corporation (later AVCO). Such combinations did not fulfill the expectations of their promoters. The stock-market crash temporarily shut off the flow of capital into aviation, and in 1934 a political controversy over the award of airmail contracts resulted in legislation requiring the separation of manufacturing and transport companies. In general, the aircraft manufacturers weathered the depression of 1929–32 with reasonable success. The main exception was Lockheed, which went into receivership and was bought in 1932 by a syndicate under the leadership of Robert and Courtlandt Gross.

This period of financial stress was the prelude to an era of phenomenal achievement. A number of aeronautical technologies were synthesized into the design that became virtually universal for military and commercial transport planes—the all-metal, monocoque, low-wing monoplane, with retractable landing gear, controllable pitch propeller, wing flaps, and wing slots. There were both military and economic incentives to improve design, and the first planes to incorporate these features in the early 1930's were the Martin B-10 and the Boeing B-9 bombers and the Boeing 247 transport; the B-9 and the 247 had, in fact, the same basic design. What gave the American industry a commanding lead in developing and producing such planes was the rivalry between airlines and between manufacturers. The desire for a competitor to the 247 led to the development of the Douglas DC series, with the result that by 1939 the

DC-3, introduced in 1935, dominated the world's airways. Commercial aviation also benefited from the introduction of long-range flying boats—the Sikorsky, Boeing, and Martin clippers—which made possible regular transoceanic service. As the decade ended, Boeing, Douglas, and Lockheed were all working on four-engined landplanes with pressurized cabins for high-altitude flight, but these did not go into regular commercial operation until after World War II. Simultaneously the American aviation industry became the leading producer of large bombers, beginning with the Boeing B-17 Flying Fortress in 1935.

There were also locational changes in the industry. In the mid-1930's the Pacific coast acquired the bulk of the country's airframe production when newcomers like North American (reconstituted from the holding company) and Northrop were added to the firms already in southern California and Consolidated moved from Buffalo to San Diego. Engine production was heavily concentrated in the Northeast. The industry was still small-scale. Its total output as late as 1939 was less than 6,000 planes for the year, and it ranked forty-first among American industries. On the world scene it led only in the production of transport aircraft; in military production the American industry was a minor factor. In the late 1930's five British aircraft firms and several German and Japanese firms exceeded any American company in volume of production and numbers employed.

World War II brought drastic changes. British and French orders began to stimulate expansion as early as 1938, and by 1940 American military demand was mushrooming; by 1943 the aviation industry was the country's largest producer and employer. This expansion was achieved partly by greater use of subcontracting and licensing but mainly by extensive construction of new facilities, government financed and located away from the supposedly vulnerable coastal areas. Most of these new plants were operated by airframe and aircraft engine companies, but some were run by automobile manufacturers. As in World War I, it became evident that automobile factories could not be converted to aircraft production, so that the automobile industry's contribution consisted of operating these wartime facilities plus making parts and components. Some of these plants, notably in Dallas and Fort Worth, Tex., remained permanent parts of the industry after the war.

Total output between 1939 and 1945 was approximately 300,000 aircraft, representing about 2 billion pounds of airframe weight. Peak employment in the aviation industry was 1,345,600 in 1943. The pressure to produce meant that there was much refinement and development of conventional aircraft types but little radical innovation. The American aviation industry, for instance, had very little to do with the development of jet propulsion. There was some experimental work; but the first American-built jets were based on British models, and none of them progressed far enough to be used in combat.

Total aircraft manufacture between 1939 and 1945 was 300,000; peak employment in the aviation industry was 1,345,600 in 1943.

When the war ended, the aviation industry faced major readjustments. Military demand dropped sharply, but that was expected. The novel, and at the time imponderable, factors were the future of jet propulsion and the prospective replacement of manned military aircraft by ballistic missiles. In addition, the helicopter had begun to demonstrate a variety of potential uses during the war. A substantial growth in helicopter manufacture took place, partly through existing companies (Bell, Sikorsky Division of United Aircraft) but also through several new and specialized firms.

Jet airplanes developed much faster than had been anticipated, largely because of intensive research and development by the military. At the time of the Korean conflict (1950–52) fighter planes were jet-propelled but bombers still relied on piston engines. Within a very few years jet engines attained the range and fuel consumption suitable for bombers and transports. The plans for the Boeing B-47 were actually laid out before the end of World War II, and the B-47 was soon followed by the B-52. The prototype 707 flew in 1954, based on the design of the KC-135 air force tanker; it went into regular airline service in 1958. Douglas followed a year later with the DC-8, after some years of brilliant success with the piston-engined DC-6 and DC-7. The only other serious competitors in the field of large jet planes were Convair (formed from a wartime merger of Consolidated and Vulte) and Lockheed, and neither attained the success of Boeing and Douglas.

The most striking readjustment of the industry after World War II was that the airframe manufacturers became the prime producers of missiles and, after 1957, of space vehicles. One major company, Martin, withdrew entirely from aircraft manufacture, but this was an exceptional case. The missile was not a substitute for civil aircraft, either commercial or general, and combat in Vietnam demonstrated that the manned military airplane was far from obsolete. Nevertheless, by 1960 the aviation industry had become the aerospace industry.

These changes affected the structure of the industry. It continued to be acutely dependent on the government, to which it made 80 percent of its sales. Because of the new technologies, research and development became the largest single item of cost and the unique situation was created in which this industry had more managerial and technical personnel than production workers. Organizational changes occurred also. Convair went through a corporate upheaval and was absorbed by General Dynamics in 1953. Martin and North American, seeking reduced dependence on government contracts, merged with nonaviation firms to become Martin-Marietta and North American Rockwell (later Rockwell International) in 1961 and 1967, respectively, and some of the lesser concerns also merged with companies in other industries.

At the beginning of the 1970's the American aerospace industry still led the world in the design and manufacture of transport aircraft. From the first jets of the 1950's had come a diversity of models for long and short hauls, heavy and light loads. However, support for a supersonic transport (SST) was cut back in 1970 and withdrawn completely in 1971, although it was clear that Soviet and Anglo-French plans for such a plane would continue. Declining military demand and curtailment of the space program were causing distress, reflecting again the industry's acute dependence on governmental orders.

BIBLIOGRAPHY

W. G. Cunningham, *The Aircraft Industry: A Study in Industrial Location.*

Lloyd Morris and Kendall Smith, *Ceiling Unlimited: The Story of American Aviation from Kitty Hawk to Supersonics.*

J. B. Rae, *Climb to Greatness: The American Aircraft Industry, 1920–1960.*

— JOHN B. RAE

B

BACON'S REBELLION

Bacon's Rebellion, a revolt in Virginia in 1676 led by Nathaniel Bacon, Jr., a young planter, against the aged royal governor, Sir William Berkeley. The revolt has, since the time of the American Revolution, usually been interpreted as an attempt at political reform directed against the allegedly oppressive rule of the governor. Recent scholarship has questioned this thesis and emphasized the controversy over Indian policy, over which Berkeley and Bacon disagreed, as a fundamental cause of, rather than a pretext for, the rebellion.

When Indian depredations occurred on the northern and western frontiers in the fall of 1675 and spring of 1676, Bacon demanded the right to lead volunteers against all Indians, even those living peacefully within the colony, in retaliation. Berkeley, fearing unjust dispossession and slaughter of the friendly Indians, refused. Bacon ignored the governor's restriction and led volunteers to the southern frontier in May 1676, where he slaughtered and plundered the friendly Occaneechee

> *When Berkeley attempted to raise forces to reestablish his own authority, Bacon turned on the governor with his volunteers, and civil war ensued.*

Indians. When the governor attempted to call him to account, Bacon marched to Jamestown and, at gunpoint, forced the assembly of June 1676 to grant him formal authority to fight the Indian war, which he then prosecuted against another friendly tribe, the Pamunkey. When Berkeley attempted to raise forces to reestablish his own authority, Bacon turned on the governor with his volunteers. Civil war ensued. Berkeley was driven to the eastern shore of Virginia. Jamestown, the capital, was burned. For a few months Bacon's word was law on the mainland. But suddenly, in October 1676, he died. Berkeley, having recruited forces on the eastern shore, returned to the mainland, defeated the remaining rebels, and, by February 1677, reestablished his authority. Soon thereafter 1,000 troops, sent by Charles II to suppress the rebellion, arrived, accompanied by commissioners to investigate its causes. Berkeley's strict policy toward the defeated rebels was severely censured by the commissioners who attempted to remove him from the governorship. Berkeley returned to England in May 1677 to justify himself but died on July 9, before seeing the king.

BIBLIOGRAPHY

Wilcomb E. Washburn, *Governor and the Rebel: A History of Bacon's Rebellion in Virginia.*

— WILCOMB E. WASHBURN

BAD LANDS

Bad Lands, a severely eroded area in South Dakota, created by precipitation of volcanic ash, sand, and Fuller's earth, perhaps borne by wind, from eruptions in the far Northwest that buried several hundred square miles more than 300 feet in depth. Water erosion carved this material into many fantastic forms. The precipitation engulfed vast herds of antediluvian monsters where they had been feeding in the swamps, the remains of which were later exposed by erosion. The federal government established the region as the Badlands National Monument in 1939 and built a system of highways into the more scenic regions of the park. The Bad Lands were discovered by fur traders early in the 19th century, and for more than 150 years scientific societies, museums, and educational institutions have engaged in unearthing the paleontological treasures, so long entombed. Included in these relics are fossil mammoths, elephants, Brontotheriums, Protoceras, camels, horses, and many of the Carnivora whose descendants are still extant. In these fastnesses the Sioux took refuge when pursued by the U.S. Army in the Messiah War of 1890. The term "badlands" is now used to describe any area with a similarly eroded topography, as in North Dakota.

BIBLIOGRAPHY

C. R. Swartzlow and R. F. Upton, *Badlands National Monument,* United States National Park Service Natural History Handbook.

— DOANE ROBINSON

BANK FAILURES

American financial history down to 1934 was characterized by an appalling number of bank failures, because the majority of banks were local enterprises, not regional or national institutions with numerous branches.

Lax state government regulations and inadequate examinations permitted many banks to pursue unsound practices. With most financial eggs in local economic baskets, it took only a serious crop failure or a business recession to precipitate dozens or even hundreds of bank failures. On the whole, state-chartered banks had a particularly poor record.

At the outset of the 19th century inability of a bank to redeem its notes in specie might cause it embarrassment, and later on states imposed penalties in those circumstances, but such an inability did not automatically signify failure. The first bank to fail was the Farmers' Exchange Bank of Glocester, R.I., in 1809. The statistics of bank failures between 1789 and 1863 are inadequate, but the losses were unquestionably large. John Jay Knox estimated that the losses to noteholders were 5 percent per annum, and bank notes were the chief money used by the general public. Not until after 1853 did banks' deposit liabilities exceed their note liabilities. During the three decades between 1830 and 1860 weekly newssheets called Bank Note Reporters gave the latest discount quoted on the notes of weak and closed banks. Worthless bank notes were a risk that all businesses had to allow for. Although some states—such as New York in 1829 and 1838, Louisiana in 1842, and Indiana in 1834—established sound banking systems, banking as a whole was characterized by many failures.

The establishment of the National Banking System in 1863 introduced needed regulations for national (nationally chartered) banks. These were more numerous than state banks, down to 1894, and were larger on the average. But even their record left much to be desired. There were 515 national bank suspensions during the fifty years 1864–1913, and only two years passed without at least one suspension. State banks suffered 2,491 failures during the same period. The nation had 1,532 banks in 1863 and 26,664 in 1913. The worst year was the panic year of 1893, with almost 500 bank failures. The establishment of the Federal Reserve System in 1913 did little to improve the record of national banks, all of which had to join it. They suffered 825 failures between 1914 and 1929 and an additional 1,947 failures by the end of 1933. During the same twenty years there were 12,714 state bank failures. By 1933 there were 14,771 banks in the United States, half as many as in 1920, and most of that half had disappeared by the failure route. During the 1920's Canada, employing a branch banking system, had only one failure. Half a dozen states had experimented with deposit insurance plans without success. Apparently the situation needed the attention of the federal government.

Depositors congregate outside the Union Bank of New York City, ordered closed by the state in 1931. (Corbis-Bettmann)

The bank holocaust of the early 1930's—9,106 bank failures in four years, 1,947 of them national banks—culminating in a nationwide bank moratorium in March 1933, at last produced the needed drastic reforms. In 1933 Congress forbade Federal Reserve member banks to pay interest on demand deposits and founded the Federal Deposit Insurance Corporation (FDIC). The FDIC raised its initial capital by selling two kinds of stock. Class A stock (paying dividends) came from assessing every insured bank 0.5 percent of its total deposits—half paid in full, half subject to call. All member banks of the Federal Reserve System had to be insured. Federal Reserve Banks had to buy Class B stock (paying no dividends) with 0.5 percent of their surplus—half payable immediately, half subject to call. In addition, any bank desiring to be insured had to pay 0.083 percent of its average deposits annually. The FDIC first insured each depositor in a bank up to $2,500; in mid-1934 Congress put the figure at $5,000; on Sept. 21, 1950, the maximum became $10,000; on Oct. 16, 1966, the limit went to $15,000; on Dec. 23, 1969, to $20,000; and on Nov. 27, 1974, to $40,000. At the end of 1971 the FDIC was insuring 98.6 percent of all commercial banks and fully protecting 99 percent of all depositors. But it was protecting only about 64 percent of all deposits, savings deposits being protected at a high percentage but business deposits at only about 55 percent. Considerable bank examining is called for, and the FDIC examines more than 50 percent of the banks in the nation, which account for about 20 percent of banking assets. It does not usually examine member banks of the Federal Reserve System, which tend to be the larger banks. There is a degree of rivalry between the large and small banks, the FDIC being looked upon as the friend of the smaller banks.

The bank holocaust of the early 30's—more than 9,000 failures in four years, including nearly 2,000 national banks—at last produced the needed drastic reforms.

Whereas in the 1920's banks were failing at an average rate of about 600 a year, during the first nine years of the FDIC (1934–42) there were altogether 487 bank closings because of financial difficulties, mostly of insured banks, and 387 of these received disbursements from the FDIC. During the years from 1943 to 1972, the average number of closings dropped to five per year. From 1934 to 1971 the corporation made disbursements in 496 cases involving 1.8 million accounts, representing $1.215 billion in total deposits, of which 97.5 percent has been paid. The FDIC in 1973 had $5.4 billion in assets. Through this protection people today are spared that traumatic experience of past generations, a "run on the bank" and the loss of a large part of their savings. For example, in 1974 the $5 billion Franklin National Bank of New York, twentieth in size in the nation, failed. It was the largest failure in American banking history. The FDIC, Federal Reserve, and comptroller of the currency arranged the sale of most of the bank's holdings, and no depositor lost a cent.

BIBLIOGRAPHY

Davis R. Dewey, *State Banking Before the Civil War.*

William H. Dillistin, *Bank Note Reporters and Counterfeit Detectors, 1826–1866.*

Oliver M. W. Sprague, *History of Crises Under the National Banking System.*

C. B. Upham and E. Lamke, *Closed and Distressed Banks.*

— DONALD L. KEMMERER

BANKING

The fundamental functions of a commercial bank during the past two centuries have been making loans, receiving deposits, and lending credit either in the form of bank notes or of "created" deposits. The banks in which people keep their checking accounts are commercial banks.

There were no commercial banks in colonial times, although there were loan offices or land banks, which made loans on real estate security with limited issues of legal tender notes. Robert Morris founded the first commercial bank in the United States, the Bank of North America, chartered Dec. 31, 1781. It greatly assisted the financing of the closing stages of the Revolution. The second bank was the Bank of Massachusetts, chartered Feb. 7, 1784; the third was the Bank of New York, which began without a charter June 9, 1784; and the fourth was the Bank of Maryland in 1790. By 1800 there were twenty-eight state-chartered banks and by 1811 there were eighty-eight.

Alexander Hamilton's financial program included a central bank to serve as a financial agent of the Treasury, provide a depository for public money, and be a regulator of the currency. Accordingly the first Bank of the United States—de facto the fifth—was founded Feb. 25, 1791, with a twenty-year charter. It was the nation's largest commercial bank. Its $10 million capital (huge for that day) and favored relationship with the government aroused much anxiety, especially among Jeffersonians. The bank's sound but unpopular policy of promptly returning bank notes for redemption in specie and refusing those of non-specie-paying banks, together with a political feud, were largely responsible for the narrow defeat of a bill to recharter it in 1811. Stephen Girard bought the bank and building. Between 1811 and 1816 both people and government were dependent on state banks, whose number increased to 246 and whose note circulation quadrupled. Nearly all but the New England banks suspended specie payments in September 1814 because of the War of 1812 and their own unregulated credit expansion.

The country soon recognized the need for a new central bank, and Congress established the second Bank of the United States on Apr. 10, 1816, also with a twenty-year charter. Its $35 million capitalization and favored relationship with the Treasury likewise aroused anxiety. Instead of repairing the overexpanded credit situation that it inherited, it aggravated it by generous lending policies. That precipitated the panic of 1819, in which it barely saved itself and incurred widespread ill will. Thereafter, under Nicholas Biddle, it was well run. As had its predecessor it required other banks to redeem their notes in specie, but most of the banks had come to accept that policy, for they appreciated the services and the stability provided by the second bank. The bank's downfall grew out of President Andrew Jackson's prejudice against banks and monopolies; the memory of the bank's role in the 1819 panic; and most of all, Biddle's decision to let rechartering be a main issue in the 1932 presidential election. Many persons otherwise friendly to the bank, faced with a choice of Jackson or the bank, chose Jackson. He vetoed the recharter. After Sept. 26, 1833, the government placed all its deposits with the "pet banks" (politically selected state banks) until it set up the Independent Treasury System in the 1840's. Between 1830 and 1837 the number of banks, bank note circulation, and bank loans all about tripled. Without the second bank to regulate them, the banks overextended themselves in lending to speculators in land. The panic of 1837 resulted—bringing with it a suspension of specie payments, many failures, and a depression that lasted until 1844.

For thirty years (1833–63) the country was without an adequate regulator of bank currency. In some states the laws were very strict or banking was forbidden, while in others the rules were lax. Banks made many long-term loans, especially on real estate, and they resorted to many subterfuges to avoid redeeming their notes in specie. Conditions were especially bad in parts of the Midwest and South, where there was some "wildcat" banking—the practice of lending notes at town branches but redeeming in specie only at a main office hidden away in a remote spot where only wildcats abounded. This practice probably began in Michigan. Almost everywhere bank tellers and merchants had to consult weekly publications known as Bank Note Reporters for the current discount on bank notes and turn to the latest Bank Note Detectors to distinguish the hundreds of counterfeits and notes of failed banks. This situation constituted an added business risk and necessitated somewhat higher markups on merchandise. In this bleak era of banking, however, there were some bright spots. These were the Suffolk Banking System of Massachusetts (1819–63), which kept New England notes at par; the moderately successful Safety Fund (1829–66) and Free Banking (1838–66) systems of New York, the latter copied, but achieving less success, in fourteen other states; the Indiana (1834–65), Ohio (1845–66), and Iowa (1858–65) systems; and the Louisiana Banking System (1842–62), which was the first to require a minimum percent of specie reserve behind liabilities and insisted also that loans be short term. Inefficient and corrupt as some of the banking was before the Civil War, the nation's expanding economy found it an improvement over the system of land banks, personal loans, and long-time borrowing from merchants on which the 18th-century economy had depended.

Secretary of the Treasury Salmon P. Chase began agitating for an improved banking system in 1861, one important motive for which was his desire to widen the market for government bonds. The National Banking Act creating the National Banking System was passed Feb. 25, 1863, and completely revised June 3, 1864. Its head officer was the comptroller of currency. It was based on several recent reforms, especially the Free Banking System's principle of bond-backed notes. But the reserve requirements for bank notes were high, and the law forbade real estate loans and branch banking, had stiff organization requirements, and imposed burdensome taxes. State banks at first saw little reason to join, but in 1865 Congress levied a prohibitive 10 percent tax on their bank notes, effective July 1, 1866, which drove most of these banks into the new system. There were 1,644 national banks by Oct. 1, 1866, and they were required to use the word "National" in their name. The use of checks had been increasing in popularity in the more settled regions long before the Civil War, and by 1853 the total of bank deposits exceeded that of bank notes. After 1865 the desire of all banks, both state and national, to avoid the various new restrictions on bank notes doubtless speeded up the shift to this more convenient form of bank credit. By the 1890's it was estimated that about 85 percent of all business transactions were settled by check payments. Since state banks were less restricted, their number increased again until it passed that of national banks in 1894. Most large banks were national, however. Improvements in state banking laws began about 1887.

The National Banking System constituted a substantial improvement over the pre–Civil War hodgepodge of banking systems. But it had three major faults and several minor ones. The first major fault was the perverse elasticity of the bond-secured bank notes, of which the supply did not vary in accordance with the needs of business. The second fault was the decentralization of bank deposit reserves, which operated in the following way. There were three classes of national banks. The lesser ones kept part of their reserves in their own vaults and deposited the rest at interest with the larger national banks, especially with the New York City banks; these in turn loaned a considerable part of the funds on the call money market to finance stock speculation. In times of uncertainty the lesser banks demanded their outside reserves; call money rates soared; security prices tobogganed; and some good as well as many weak banks were ruined by runs. The third major fault was that there was no central bank to take measures to forestall such crises or to lend to deserving banks in times of distress. Among the minor faults were a slow and cumbersome check collection system and inadequate use of commercial paper.

Four times—1873, 1884, 1893, and 1907—panics highlighted the faults of the National Banking System. Improvised use of clearinghouse certificates in interbank settlements somewhat relieved money shortages in the first three cases; "voluntary" bank assessments collected and loaned by a committee headed by J. P. Morgan gave relief in 1907. In 1908 Congress passed the Aldrich-Vreeland Act to investigate foreign central banking systems and suggest reforms and to permit emergency bank note issues. The nation used these emergency issues on only one occasion, when a panic occurred at the outbreak of World War I in August 1914. The Owen-Glass Act of 1913 superimposed a central banking system on the existing national banking system. It required all national banks to "join" the new system, which meant to buy stock in it immediately equal to 3 percent of their capital and surplus, thus providing the funds with which to set up the Federal Reserve System, which was accomplished in 1914. State banks might also join by meeting specified requirements, but by the end of 1916 only thirty-four had done so. A majority of the nation's banks have always remained outside the Federal Reserve System, although the larger banks have usually been members. The Federal Reserve System largely corrected the faults to which the National Banking System had been prey. Admittedly the Federal Reserve had its faults and did not live up to expectations, especially during 1919–20, 1927–29, after World War II, and 1965–75. Nevertheless the nation's commercial banks had a policy-directing head and a refuge in distress to a greater degree than they had ever had before. Thus ended the need for the Independent Treasury System, which finally wound up its affairs in 1921.

Between the opening of the Federal Reserve System on Nov. 16, 1914, and May 1974, the commercial banking system grew and changed, as might be expected in a nation whose population more than doubled and whose real national income septupled during that period. The number of banks declined from 27,864 in mid-1914 to 14,741 in 1974; the number of national banks, from 7,518 to 4,659. (Bank failures between 1920 and 1933 were the principal cause of these declines, mergers being a minor reason.) Demand deposits meanwhile grew from $10 billion to $237 billion; and time deposits, from $8.6 billion to $393 billion. Loans grew from $15.2 billion to $510 billion, a thirty-four-fold increase; investments, on the other hand, rose from $5.5 billion to $188 billion—30 percent in Treasury securities—a thirty-four-fold increase. Wholesale prices quadrupled in that same period. Every decade during the interval saw some further significant developments in commercial banking.

Only a few national banks gave up their charters for state ones to avoid having to join the Federal Reserve System, but during World War I many state banks became members of the system—there were 1,374 in it by 1920. All banks helped sell Liberty bonds and bought short-term Treasuries between bond drives, which was one reason for a more than doubling of the money supply (currency and demand deposits) and also of the price level from 1914 to 1920. A major contributing factor for these doublings was the sharp reduction in reserves required under the new Federal Reserve System as compared with the pre-1914 National Banking System.

By 1921 there were 31,076 banks, the all-time peak; many were small family-owned state banks. Every year local crop failures, other disasters, or simply bad management wiped out several hundred of them. By 1929 the number of banks had declined to 25,568. Admittedly mergers eliminated a few names, and the growth of branch, group, or chain banking provided stability in some areas, the Bank of America in California being an outstanding example. But the 1920's are most remembered for stock market speculation. Several large banks, such as New York's National City and Chase National, had a part in this speculation—chiefly through their investment affiliates, which were essentially investment banks. The role of investment adviser gave banks great prestige until the panic of 1929, when widespread disillusionment from losses and scandals brought them discredit.

The 1930's witnessed many reforms growing out of the more than 9,000 bank failures between 1930 and 1933 and capped by the nationwide bank moratorium of March 6–9, 1933. To reform the commercial and central banking systems as well as to restore confidence in them, Congress passed two major banking laws, one on June 16, 1933, and the other on Aug. 23, 1935. These laws gave the Federal Reserve System firmer control over the banking system, especially over the member banks. They also set up the Federal Deposit Insurance Corporation to insure bank deposits, and soon all but a few hundred small banks belonged to it. That move greatly reduced the number of bank failures. Other changes included banning investment affiliates, prohibiting banks to pay interest on demand deposits, loosening restrictions against national banks' having branches and making real estate loans, and giving the Federal Reserve Board the authority to raise (to as much as double) member bank legal reserve requirements against deposits. As a result of the depression the supply of commercial loans dwindled and interest rates fell sharply. Consequently, banks invested more in federal government obligations, built up excess reserves, and imposed service charges on checking accounts. The 1933–34 devaluation of the dollar, which stimulated large imports of gold, was another cause of those excess reserves.

During World War II the banks once again helped sell war bonds. They also converted their excess reserves into government obligations and increased their own holdings of these from $16 billion in 1940 to $84 billion in 1945. Demand deposits more than doubled. Owing to bank holdings of government obligations—virtually convertible into cash—and to Federal Reserve commitments to the Treasury, the Federal Reserve had lost its power to curb bank-credit expansion. Price levels nearly doubled during the 1940's.

By the Federal Reserve-Treasury "accord" of March 1951, the Federal Reserve System regained its freedom to curb credit expansion, and thereafter interest rates crept upward. That development improved bank profits and also led banks to reduce somewhat their holdings of federal government obligations. Term loans (five to ten years) to industry and real estate loans increased. Banks also encountered stiff competition from rapidly growing rivals, such as savings and loan associations and personal finance companies. On July 28, 1959, Congress eliminated the difference between reserve city banks and central reserve city banks for member banks. The new law kept the same reserve requirements against demand deposits (10–22 percent), but it permitted banks to count cash in their vaults as part of their legal reserves.

Interest rates rose spectacularly all during the 1960's, prime commercial paper reaching 9 percent in 1970, then dropped sharply in 1971, only to rise once more, hitting 12 percent in mid-1974. Whereas consumer prices had gone up 23 percent during the 1950's, mostly early in the decade, they rose 31 percent during the 1960's, especially toward the end of the decade as budget deficits mounted, and climbed another 24 percent by mid-1974. Money supply figures played a major role in determining Federal Reserve credit policy from 1960 on.

Money once consisted largely of hard coin. With the coming of commercial banks it came also to include bank notes and demand deposits. But the difference between these and various forms of "near money," such as time deposits, savings and loan association deposits, and federal government E and H bonds—all quickly convertible to cash—is slight. Credit cards, increasingly prevalent during the 1950's and particularly during the 1960's, carry the confusion a step further. How does one add up the buying power of money, near money, and credit cards? As new forms of credit become more like money, it becomes increasingly difficult for the Federal Reserve to regulate the supply of credit and prevent booms.

In more than 190 years commercial banks have come to serve the economy in several important ways. They provide a safe place in which to keep savings; they are an institution from which short-term borrowers, and to some extent long-term borrowers too, can borrow funds (with the result that savings do not lie idle and unproductive); and they supply the nation with most of its money.

[See also Banking and Finance Since 1970; Federal Reserve System.]

BIBLIOGRAPHY

Annual Reports of the Comptroller of the Currency.

Board of Governors of the Federal Reserve System, *The Federal Reserve System, Annual Reports,* and *Federal Reserve Bulletin.*

L. V. Chandler, *The Economics of Money and Banking.*

J. V. Fenstermaker, *The Development of Commercial Banking, 1782–1837.*

Milton Friedman and M. Schwartz, *A Monetary History of the United States, 1867–1960.*

B. Hammond, *Banks and Politics in America.*

J. T. Holdsworth, *The First Bank of the United States.*

E. W. Kemmerer and D. L. Kemmerer, *ABC of the Federal Reserve System.*

Paul A. Samuelson and H. E. Krooss, *Documentary History of Banking and Currency in the United States.*

W. B. Smith, *Economic Aspects of the Second Bank of the United States.*

Paul Trescott, *Financing American Enterprise.*

R. Westerfield, *Money, Credit and Banking.*

J. A. Wilborn, *Biddle's Bank: The Crucial Years* (esp. p. 133).

— DONALD L. KEMMERER

BANKING AND FINANCE SINCE 1970

Since 1970 banking and finance have undergone nothing less than a revolution. The structure of the industry in the mid-1990s bore little resemblance to that established in the 1930s in the aftermath of the Great Depression's bank failures. In the 1970s and 1980s, what had been a fractured system by design became a single market, domestically and internationally. New Deal banking legislation of the Depression era stemmed from the belief that integration of the banking system had allowed problems in one geographical area or part of the financial system to spread to the entire system. Regulators sought therefore to prevent money from flowing between different geographical areas (such as through intrastate and interstate branch-banking restrictions) and between different functional segments (for example, through separation of commercial and investment banking). These measures ruled out many of the traditional techniques of risk management through diversification and pooling. As a substitute, the government guaranteed bank deposits through the Federal Deposit Insurance Corporation and the Federal Savings and Loan Insurance Corporation.

In retrospect it is easy to see why the segmented system broke down. It was inevitable that the price of money would vary across different segments of the system, depending on the balance of supply and demand in each. It was also inevitable that borrowers in a high-interest area would seek access to a neighboring low-interest area, and vice versa for lenders. The only question is why it took so long for the pursuit of self-interest to break down regulatory barriers. Price divergence by itself perhaps was not a strong enough incentive. Rationing of credit during tight credit periods, such as the 1966 credit crunch, probably was the cause of most innovation. Necessity, not profit alone, seems to have been the cause of financial innovation.

Once communication between segments of the system opened, mere price divergence was sufficient to cause flows of funds. The microelectronics revolution, with its communication and computational technologies, enhanced flows, as it became easier to identify and exploit profit opportunities. Technological advances sped up the process of market unification by lowering transaction costs and widening opportunities. The most important consequence of the unification of segmented credit markets was a diminished role for banks. Premium borrowers found they could tap the national money market directly by issuing commercial paper, thus obtaining funds more cheaply than banks could provide. In 1972 money market mutual funds began offering shares in a pool of money market assets as a substitute for bank deposits. Thus, banks faced competition in both lending and deposit-taking, competition generally not subject to the myriad of regulatory controls facing banks.

Consolidation of banking became inevitable as its functions eroded. The crisis of the savings and loan industry was the most visible symptom of this erosion. Savings and loans institutions (S&Ls) had been created to funnel household savings to residential mortgages, which they did until the high interest rates of the inflationary 1970s caused massive capital losses on long-term mortgages, rendering many S&Ls insolvent by 1980. Attempts to regain solvency by lending, using cash from the sale of existing mortgages, to borrowers willing to pay high interest only worsened the crisis because high-yield loans turned out to be high risk. The mechanisms invented to facilitate mortgage sales, so-called "securitization," undermined S&Ls in the longer term as it became possible for specialized mortgage bankers to make mortgage loans and sell them without any need for the expensive deposit side of the traditional S&L business.

Throughout the 1970s and 1980s, regulators met each evasion of a regulatory obstacle with further relaxation of the rules, a practice that tended to generalize each innovation across the financial system as a whole. The Depository Institutions Deregulation and Monetary Control Act (1980) recognized the array of competitors for bank business by expanding the authority of the Federal Reserve System over the new entrants and relaxing regulation of banks. Pressed by a borrowers' lobby seeking access to low-cost funds and a depositors' lobby seeking access to high money-market returns, regulators saw little choice but capitulation. Mistakes were made, notably the provision in the 1980 act that extended deposit insurance coverage to $100,000, a provision that greatly increased the cost of the eventual S&L bailout. The provision found its justification in the need to attract money to banks. The mistake was in not recognizing that the world had changed, that the entire raison d'être of the industry had been undermined.

Throughout the 1970s and 1980s, regulators met each evasion of a regulatory obstacle with further relaxation of the rules.

Long-term corporate finance underwent a revolution comparable to that in banking. During the prosperous 1950s and 1960s, corporations shied away from debt, preferring to keep debt-equity ratios low and to rely on ample internal funds for investment. This preference, in part a legacy of Depression problems, was reinforced by the high cost of issuing bonds, a consequence of the uncompetitive system of investment banking. The bonds that corporations did issue were held largely by financial intermediaries, with insurance companies the most important. Corporate equities were mainly held by individual owners, not institutions. In the 1970s and 1980s, with increased competition and lower profits, corporations came to rely on external funds, so that debt-equity ratios rose substantially and interest payments absorbed a much greater part of earnings. The increased importance of external finance was itself a source of innovation, as corporations sought ways to reduce the cost of debt service. Equally important was increased resort to institutional investors—pension funds and insurance companies—as purchasers of securities. When private individuals were the main holders of equities, the brokerage business was uncompetitive and fees were high, but institutional investors used their clout to reduce the costs of buying and selling. Market forces became much more important in finance, just as in banking.

Institutional investors shifted portfolio strategies toward equities in part to enhance returns to meet pension liabilities after the Employment Retirement Income Security Act (1974) required full funding of future liabilities. Giving new attention to maximizing investment returns, the institutional investors became students of the new theories of rational investment decision championed by academic economists. The capital asset pricing model developed in the 1960s became the framework most used by institutional investors to make asset allocations.

The microelectronics revolution was even more important for finance than for banking. Indeed, it would have been impossible to implement the pricing model without high-speed, inexpensive computation to calculate optimal portfolio weightings across the thousands of traded equities. One may argue that computational technology did not really cause the transformation of finance, that increased attention of institutional investors was bound to cause a transformation in any event. Both the speed and extent of transformation would have been impossible, however, without advances in computational and communications technologies.

In the 1980s individual investors adopted the new investment strategies of the large institutional investors, with the help of an enormous expansion of the mutual fund industry. Assets under management in money, bond, and stock mutual funds increased tenfold.

[See also Banking; Savings and Loan Crisis; Wall Street.]

BIBLIOGRAPHY

James R. Barth, *The Great Savings and Loan Debacle* (Washington, D.C., 1991).

Peter Bernstein, *Capital Ideas; The Improbable Origins of Modern Wall Street* (New York, 1992).

Teresa Ghilarducci, *Labor's Capital: The Economics and Politics of Private Pensions* (Cambridge, Mass., 1992).

Raymond Goldsmith, *Financial Intermediaries in the American Economy Since 1900* (Princeton, N.J., 1958).

Martin Wolfson, *Financial Crises: Understanding the Postwar U.S. Experience* (Armonk, N.Y., 1986).

— PERRY G. MEHRLING

BANKRUPTCY LAWS

Bankruptcy laws existed in England in the 18th century but were limited to creditor-initiated proceedings against traders, bankers, brokers, factors, and underwriters. The subject of bankruptcy laws was not considered by the federal convention of 1787 until late in its proceedings. Charles Pinckney was the author of the first draft of the bankruptcy clause of the Constitution; it was adopted with practically no debate, with only one dissenting vote.

Congress did not immediately exercise the power "to establish . . . uniform laws on the subject of bankruptcies throughout the United States" (Article I, Section 8). The first American bankruptcy legislation on the federal level was enacted in 1800 as a result of the unsettled economic conditions arising out of widespread speculation in the shares of a multitude of newly incorporated companies dealing in land and in government scrip. The first legislation closely resembled the English statutes of the time. It applied only to traders, merchants, and brokers and provided only for involuntary bankruptcies, that is, creditor-initiated proceedings. It was essentially a liquidation provision—the assets of the bankrupt being seized and sold to satisfy the claims of creditors. A bankrupt was permitted to retain a certain percentage of his assets and could be discharged from any unsatisfied indebtedness by the consent of two-thirds of his creditors. The act of 1800 was a temporary measure, expressly limited to five years. The return to prosperity, coupled with growing public dissatisfaction with the workings of the act, resulted in its repeal in 1803.

The second national bankruptcy act was passed in 1841. It too was the product of hard times—the great panic of 1837 and the resulting depression. The second act was not limited to involuntary bankruptcies; debtor-initiated proceedings, that is, voluntary bankruptcies, were also permitted. Additionally, this second bankruptcy act eliminated creditor control of discharge: any debtor who surrendered his property and complied with the orders of the court could obtain a discharge. The act of 1841, like the act of 1800, was largely a product of financial stringency and was repealed after only eighteen months of operation, as economic conditions improved. Financial stress brought on by the Civil War resulted in the enactment of the third federal bankruptcy statute in 1867. The act of 1867 followed in many respects the patterns of its predecessors. It did, however, extend both voluntary and involuntary bankruptcy to moneyed and commercial corporations. The act of 1867 was repealed in 1878; the repeal was at least in part attributable to widespread abuses on the part of the courts in administering it.

Thus, during the first one hundred years of the nation's history, federal bankruptcy laws were in force for a total of only fifteen years. During the intervals between the repeal of one federal bankruptcy act and the passage of the next, state laws governed the debtor-creditor relationship. Such laws were not satisfactory. They were limited in scope because of the constitutional grant of power to Congress; they were not uniform; and they often discriminated against out-of-state creditors.

The panic of 1893 rekindled interest in national bankruptcy legislation, and in 1898 Congress enacted a bankruptcy bill drafted primarily by Colonel Torrey, a St. Louis attorney hired by various commercial interests. The act of 1898 has continued in force to the present day, the last serious attempts to repeal it having been in 1910. The act has been amended more than ninety times since its passage, most extensively in 1938 by the Chandler Act. As a result of amendments designed to combat the depression of 1929, the Bankruptcy Act contains not only liquidation provisions similar in nature to the earlier bankruptcy enactments but also a number of specialized rehabilitation provisions such as section 77, providing for the reorganization of railroads, and chapter X, regulating the reorganization of large publicly held corporations under the supervision of the Securities and Exchange Commission.

BIBLIOGRAPHY

Stefan Riesenfeld, *Creditors' Remedies and Debtor's Protection.*
Charles Warren, *Bankruptcy in United States History.*

— DAVID G. EPSTEIN

BARBARY WARS

Tripolitan War (1801–05)

After the Revolution the United States, following the example of European nations, made annual payments to the Barbary states (Morocco, Algiers, Tripoli, and Tunis) for unmolested passage along North Africa's Barbary Coast. Constant difficulties, however, ensued, such as the episode of the *George Washington,* and in 1801 Tripoli declared war and seized several Americans and their vessels. The war, entirely naval except for the Derna expedition, was feebly prosecuted by the commanders first dispatched, but in 1803 Commodore Edward Preble was sent out with the *Constitution, Philadelphia,* and several brigs and schooners. His arrival galvanized the entire force into vigorous action. Making a naval demonstration before Tangiers, which brought the Emperor of Morocco to make amends for treaty violations, Preble set up a strict blockade of Tripoli itself. Here on Oct. 31, 1803, the *Philadelphia* ran on a reef just outside the harbor and was captured by the Tripolitans, who a few days later floated it and anchored it under the guns of the citadel. But on Feb. 16, 1804, Lt. Stephen Decatur and eighty other officers and men recaptured and burned it in a daring night attack.

After the Revolution, the U.S. followed the European custom of making annual payments to Morocco, Algiers, Tripoli, and Tunis for unmolested passage along North Africa's Barbary Coast.

During August and September 1804, Preble, in addition to blockading, harassed the Tripolitan shipping and fortifications with frequent attacks in which the small gunboats fearlessly entered the harbor to enable the crews to board and capture piratical craft while the larger ships kept up a protective fire on batteries. Such activity reached a climax on Sept. 4, when the *Intrepid* with its cargo of gunpowder and explosive shells was maneuvered into the harbor at night. Apparently the explosion occurred prematurely, for all the participants were killed and little damage was done to the Tripolitan shipping.

When, soon after, Preble was relieved by Commodore Samuel Barron, and Barron was relieved in turn the next spring by Commodore John Rodgers, the Bey of Tripoli was ready to conclude peace. He was partly induced to this by the success of the Derna expedition, which had captured Derna and was threatening to march on Tripoli itself. The treaty, somewhat hastily concluded, June 4, 1805, abolished all annual payments, but provided for $60,000 ransom money for the officers and crew of the *Philadelphia.*

War with Algiers (1815)

Although payments were continued to the other Barbary states, the absence of American naval vessels in the years preceding the War of 1812 encouraged Algiers to seize American merchantmen such as the *Mary Ann*, for which $18,000 was paid Algiers, and to threaten others such as the *Allegheny*, where an increased payment was demanded and secured. Immediately after the determination of the war, Decatur, now a commodore, and William Bainbridge were ordered to the Mediterranean with an overwhelming force (*see* Decatur's Cruise to Algiers). By June 1815, within forty days after his departure from New York, Decatur, the first to arrive, had achieved his immediate mission. Capturing the Algerian flagship *Mashuda* in a running fight off Gat and appearing off Algiers, he demanded and secured a treaty humiliating to the once proud piratical state—no future payments, restoration of all American property, the emancipation of all Christian slaves escaping to American men-of-war, civilized treatment of prisoners of war, and $10,000 for a merchantman recently seized. As Tunis and Tripoli were forced to equally hard terms and an American squadron remained in the Mediterranean, the safety of American commerce was assured.

BIBLIOGRAPHY

G. W. Allen, *Our Navy and the Barbary Corsairs.*
Ray W. Irwin, *The Diplomatic Relations of the United States With the Barbary Powers, 1776–1816.*

— WALTER B. NORRIS

BARNUM'S MUSEUM

In December 1841, P. T. Barnum bought Scudder's American Museum at Broadway and Ann Street, New York. It was enlarged as Barnum's American Museum, opening weekdays at sunrise with a single fee of twenty-five cents. The museum had on exhibit not only thousands of curios and relics but also living curiosities and "transient novelties" (such as the midget Charles Stratton, billed as "Gen. Tom Thumb"). There was also a lecture room seating 3,000, in which plays were given. Fire destroyed building and contents, July 13, 1865. Barnum's less-famous New American Museum, opened Nov. 13, 1865, on Broadway between Spring and Prince streets, was also burned (1868).

BIBLIOGRAPHY

G. S. Bryan, ed., *Struggles and Triumphs*, Barnum's autobiography.

— G. S. BRYAN

BASEBALL

Baseball was born in obscurity, and its early history is a mishmash of mythology, unsubstantiated facts, and rampant sentimentality. Actually almost nothing is known of its origins. While some authorities have attempted to trace its ancestry back to various bat-and-ball games played by children even before George Washington became president, others insist with unconscious irony that the national pastime was derived from the English games of cricket and rounders. All experts agree, however, that a game in which a bat, ball, and bases were used was being played throughout the United States during the early years of the 19th century. In New England it was called town ball, which Oliver Wendell Holmes reported that he played as an undergraduate at Harvard College in the 1820's. In other parts of the country, it was apparently a team game that had evolved from one old cat. In both instances the playing field was a square rather than a diamond, and the batter stood midway between what are now home plate and first base.

One of baseball's most enduring myths is that the game was "invented" by Abner Doubleday in Cooperstown, N.Y., in 1839, and the National Baseball Hall of Fame and Museum was built in Cooperstown in 1939 to commemorate this legend. But baseball scholars—and there are many of them—have conclusively demonstrated that Doubleday had nothing to do with the game's beginnings or development and that in all likelihood the first games bearing some resemblance to modern baseball were played in New York City rather than in Cooperstown. In any event, in 1845, a group of New York sportsmen—several years later A. G. Spaulding, one of the most famous of the early professional ballplayers, called them "gentlemen to the manner born" and "men of high taste"—organized the Knickerbocker Baseball Club and drew up a set of rules, among which were several provisions that would be readily recognized by present-day fans. For the next few years baseball was played almost exclusively in and around New York City by the Knickerbockers and other teams composed of gentlemen sportsmen. If democracy in sports is equated with mass participation, baseball in its formative years was undeniably an aristocratic game. In this respect its history is similar to that of every other popular American sport except basketball.

During the decade preceding the Civil War several baseball clubs were organized in the larger cities of the Northeast. Many of these clubs, moreover, were composed of players from all walks of life, for interclub competition put a premium on skills that had nothing to do with an individual's social background. By 1860 more than fifty clubs belonged to the National Association of Baseball Players; several played regular schedules and charged admission; and one, the Excelsiors of Brooklyn, in 1860 toured from Buffalo to Baltimore taking on—and beating—all comers. The Civil War broke up the clubs and their schedules, but long before Appomattox baseball had become the most popular game among the troops (at least those in the northern armies) behind the lines. The demobilized soldiers took the game back with them to their home towns. A short time after the war baseball was being played in most towns in the North and many in the South, and a year after the end of the war more than 200 clubs were members of the National Association. In 1865, however, the fielders still did not wear gloves, the catcher still caught the ball on the first bounce, and the pitcher still used an underhand delivery. It would be at least another twenty-five years before the game was standardized into the form in which it is played today.

Baseball, like most other American sports, soon became a business enterprise. Although amateur clubs had occasionally paid some of their stars, the first all-professional team was the Cincinnati Red Stockings, which in 1869 toured the nation without losing a game. In the next few years other professional teams were formed, but from the outset the success of professional baseball was jeopardized by repeated instances of bribery, the widespread gambling that attended almost every game, and the lack of any overall organization. The clubowners, however, were businessmen, and like other entrepreneurs of the period they quickly recognized the advantages of monopoly over unregulated competition and of organization over chaos. Accordingly, in 1876, teams from eight cities established the National League of Professional Baseball Clubs. This organization, which is still in existence, gradually eliminated competition, introduced regularly scheduled games, and formulated and codified most of the rules under which baseball is played today.

During the half-century after the formation of the National League, professional baseball became a complex, ingeniously organized industry that was dominated by the major league clubowners. The pattern was set as early as 1882, when the American Association was organized under rules set down by the National League. In subsequent years minor leagues were established with National League approval in every section of the country. The structure was completed with the formation of the American League in 1901 and the establishment of the World Series in 1903. The result was an economic pyramid that has fittingly come to be called organized baseball. At the top of the pyramid were the major league team owners; at the bottom, the lowest minor league teams. All were held together by rules governing the exchange and contracts of players, who on at least one occasion banded together and complained that they were "bought, sold and exchanged like sheep." In that no team or league could be formed without the sanction of the organization, this was a monopoly. And like all monopolies it fought off interlopers, defeating the National Brotherhood of Baseball Players in the Brotherhood War in 1889–90 and a group of financiers who in 1914–15 attempted to operate the Federal League as a third major league.

Since World War I no two individuals have had a more profound effect on both the game and business of baseball than George Herman ("Babe") Ruth and Kenesaw Mountain Landis. Babe Ruth, an alumnus of a Baltimore orphanage, grew up to hit more home runs (60) in a season (1927) than any other player (a record not surpassed until 1961) and to receive a higher salary than the president of the United States. Ruth was almost singlehandedly responsible for changing baseball from a defensive game characterized by the bunt, squeeze, steal, and hit-and-run, into an offensive contest in which strategy was subordinated to sheer power as represented by the home run. Landis, a U.S. district judge, was named commissioner of baseball by the clubowners in 1921 as a result of the "Black Sox" scandal in which eight members of the Chicago White Sox accepted bribes to throw the 1919 World Series. Landis, who was to serve as "czar" of baseball until his death in 1944, barred from organized baseball the Chicago players who had accepted bribes and restored public confidence in the game by the strict discipline he imposed on the players and management. During his long reign the clubowners introduced many innovations, such as night baseball, ladies' days, radio broadcasts of the games, and farm systems.

Aside from practice games in spring training, the two major leagues have confined their rivalry to the World Series and All-Star games. At the end of the regular season in 1903 Pittsburgh, the pennant winner in the National League, challenged Boston to a series in which Boston won, five games to three. In the following year the New York Giants, leaders in the National League, refused to meet the American League winner, but in 1905 both leagues agreed to a set of rules that both regularized and institutionalized the World Series. Despite wars, depressions, and acts of nature, the World Series has been played every autumn since 1905 with the championship going to the winner of four games, except in the years 1919–21 when the title went to the team that won five games. The All-Star Game, which is played in midseason between teams of the outstanding representatives of both leagues, was the brainchild of a Chicago sportswriter who inaugurated it as a promotional stunt to take place during the 1933 Century of Progress Exposition in Chicago. At least one All-Star Game has been played in various major league cities since then, except for 1945, with the players being generally selected by their fellow players or the fans. The managers of the preceding year's pennant winners serve as the managers of the respective All-Star teams and are given some voice in the choice of players. Although some iconoclasts have suggested interleague games be held on a regular basis during the season, this proposal has never appealed to a majority of the clubowners in the two leagues.

In recent years professional baseball has not been altogether immune to the forces that have reshaped so many other aspects of American life. Almost a decade before the 1954 Supreme Court decision requiring racial integration in the schools, Jackie Robinson broke the color line in organized baseball, playing for the Montreal Royals in the International League in 1946 and the Brooklyn Dodgers in the National League in following years. By 1960 black players had become commonplace in organized baseball. Baseball was also markedly affected by new patterns of recreation and leisure. Television, while making new fans, did not necessarily create new customers, and it all but wrecked the minor leagues. The omnipresent automobile made a stadium's parking lot as important as its concession for the sale of hot dogs (which, incidentally, were "invented" at a big-league baseball park), while it succeeded in luring away many fans who formerly would have been in the bleachers.

Despite changes in popular tastes and customs, professional baseball has remained not only a business but also a monopoly. After the formation of a new league was announced in 1959, organized baseball responded by absorbing some of its potential competitors and expanding each league from eight to ten teams. Meanwhile the owners continued their pursuit of profits by establishing new teams and by shifting franchises to areas where it was hoped there were more paying customers, a larger television audience, and local officials willing to build new baseball parks. By 1973 each league consisted of twelve teams spread from the Atlantic to the Pacific and from Montreal to Texas and Georgia. At the same time the owners had to contend with a players' union, which in April 1972 conducted a thirteen-day strike that forced the postponement of the regular opening of the season. The players, moreover, continued to agitate for an alteration in the "reserve clause," which bound a player to his club until he retired or was traded, and in 1972 the Supreme Court in the Curt Flood case suggested that either the owners or Congress should modify the clause.

Baseball is a participant as well as a spectator sport, and for generations the game has been played by Americans from all social classes on teams representing colleges, schools, towns, factories, and clubs. All American boys may not play—or even like—baseball, but it is virtually impossible for any American boy to grow up without knowing a great deal about the game. He learns it at the playground or in physical education classes at school; he is urged—more often than not by his parents—to play on a local Little League team; and he is bombarded with news of professional baseball by his friends, by newspapers, and by radio and television announcers. In the 1970's, American girls began to take a greater interest in the game and, despite some opposition, joined a number of Little League teams. In 1974 President Gerald Ford signed a law making it illegal to bar girls from Little League teams. It is true that fishing and bowling are more popular participant sports than baseball and that horse racing is a more popular spectator sport, but it is also true that baseball, if not the national pastime, is a national cult. The only other nations in which baseball enjoys a comparable status are Japan and some Latin-American countries.

Baseball has always had certain features that set it off from other American sports. No other game combines team play and individual virtuosity with such felicity, and few other games provide both players and spectators with such sharp contrasts between the predictable and the unexpected. Baseball, moreover, is preeminently a game of statistics, for virtually every bit of action in a baseball game, season, and career can be reduced to figures, all of which eventually end up in the record books. These statistics are endlessly fascinating to many fans and also serve to give baseball a kind of continuity that is unique in the history of American team sports. Baseball, with its emphasis on statistics, may even have made a contribution to American education, for it is likely that many boys first learned about percentages, not in grade school, but from their own efforts to figure out batting averages or the standing of a favorite major league team.

BIBLIOGRAPHY

Allison Danzig, *The History of Baseball.*

Murray Olderman, *Nelson's 20th Century Encyclopedia of Baseball.*

Lawrence S. Ritter, *The Glory of Their Times.*

Harold Seymour, *Baseball: The Early Years,* and *Baseball: The Golden Age.*

— HAROLD C. SYRETT

BASEBALL SINCE 1970

Since the early 1970s the history of baseball has been dominated by divisive debate over its economic future, occasioned by legal decisions, labor strife, the infusion of massive amounts of revenue, and a redistribution of wealth from owners to players. It began with *Flood* v.

Kuhn (1972), a suit brought by outfielder Curt Flood. At issue was the reserve clause, a stipulation included in all player contracts that bound the player permanently to his team until management traded, released, or sold him to another franchise. The Supreme Court refused to void the reserve clause but did suggest it should be overturned either by legislation or collective bargaining. Over the next two decades, players won a series of labor-management disputes that left team owners complaining that the game was on the brink of ruin.

The person most responsible for the increased power and independence of the players was the executive director of the Major League Baseball Players Association (MLBPA), Marvin Miller, who came to baseball from the United Steelworkers of America. Miller's unification of the players and establishment of a grievance procedure and salary arbitration in the late 1960s and early 1970s set the stage for the most important developments for baseball in the second half of the twentieth century. Pitchers Andy Messersmith and Dave McNally played the 1975 season without contracts and then claimed to be free agents—in other words, that they were not bound to a team at management's discretion but rather free to negotiate a contract with any team. When arbitrator Peter Seitz cast the deciding vote upholding this claim the reserve clause was dead. Ownership failed in a court appeal and with a brief lockout of players from spring training. A new basic agreement in 1976 established free agency for six-year players and draft compensation for teams losing players. Draft compensation meant that a team losing a player via a free-agent signing would be compensated for the loss by being given an additional draft choice in the amateur draft of that year. Combined with salary arbitration after two years, upward pressures on salary became overwhelming and long-term contracts common. Average salaries went from $46,000 in 1975 to $135,000 in 1980.

Marvin Miller, who came to baseball from the United Steelworkers of America, was the person most responsible for the players' increased power and independence.

With failure to negotiate a new basic agreement in 1980, and no progress during the grace period of one year, the players struck on June 11, 1981. The issue was how to compensate teams for loss of a free agent. Ownership wanted a veteran player rather than a draft choice plus some sort of cap on salaries. The strike lasted fifty days, eliminating about one-third of the season. The new basic agreement established a player compensation pool for free-agent loss, which in the end pleased no one. There was no salary cap. To salvage the season Commissioner Bowie Kuhn devised the idea of a split season, with those in first place when the strike began declared first-half winners. They would have a playoff against second-half winners. This decision was roundly criticized. There was no incentive to win both halves of the season, and the team with the best overall record in baseball, the Cincinnati Reds, did not qualify for the playoffs.

In 1985, with no basic agreement in place, there was a two-day strike in August. Issues were salary arbitration, increased pension benefits, and a salary cap. The result was no cap, some increase in pensions, increase in eligibility for salary arbitration to three years, and an agreement to change the league championship series to a best-of-seven game format. Under Commissioner Peter Ueberroth the owners boycotted the free-agent market for three seasons, resulting in unfair labor suits being brought by the players. In three separate rulings the owners were found guilty of collusion and ordered to pay compensation totaling $280 million. After termination of the basic agreement in 1990, the owners tried another lockout at spring training. The new agreement signed in March extended the existing agreement for three years, with a slight change in arbitration eligibility.

The other major change on the labor front came with creation of the Major League Umpires Association in 1970. It made tremendous advances in salary, benefits, and working conditions for umpires, with one serious strike in 1979 lasting a little over a month and another during the 1984 playoffs. In the meantime, propelled by a combination of new revenues from television, free agency, and salary arbitration, players' salaries continued to rise. In 1984 the average salary was $330,000, in 1989 $858,000, and in 1992 $1 million. In the same period attendance increased steadily, with only an occasional dip; 1993 was a record year.

The three-year extension of the basic agreement in 1990 should have given owners and players adequate time to negotiate a new agreement, but the owners were no longer interested in a new agreement and were set on breaking the power of the MLBPA. The battle was no longer about money but about power that had flowed from players to owners over eight work stoppages. Despite claims to the contrary, profits were never higher and few teams were losing money. On Aug. 12, 1994, the players went out on strike, fearing that if they did not, the owners would declare an impasse and impose a new contract. The result was the end of the season, the cancellation of the playoffs and the World Series, and an alienation of the fans. As spring training approached for 1995, posturing by both owners and players led nowhere, and there were moves to open the season with replacement players. The season was saved when federal Judge Sonya Sotomayor of the Southern District of New York upheld the ruling of the National Labor Relations Board that the owners were in violation of federal labor law. The players ended their strike in early April 1995 and, fearing the courts, the owners declined to impose a lockout. As a result, the 1995 season, shortened by twenty games, was played to conclusion, but there were no winners and nothing had been settled. As the 1996 season approached there was no new agreement and no significant bargaining had taken place, and it appeared to some that permanent damage had been done to major league baseball.

During the 1970s national television revenues increased slowly when the ABC network joined NBC in covering baseball, while local television revenues doubled. The first big jump in revenues in the 1980s occurred in 1983, when NBC, seeking to drive ABC out of the market, offered $560 million for half of the television contract over six years. To NBC's surprise and baseball's benefit ABC matched the offer, resulting in a six-year network television package of $1.1 billion, or $4 million per team per year. In 1990 CBS took the package away from its two competitors by paying $1.08 billion for four years plus a $50 million radio package, and ESPN added another $400 million per year for cable television rights. The total package was worth $14.4 million per team per year. At the local level revenues also increased sharply but unevenly. Huge discrepancies between large- and small-market franchises raised the issue of revenue sharing.

The future of television revenues was in doubt entering the 1994 season. NBC and ABC in response to low ratings proposed to work with Major League Baseball to create a baseball network operating regionally. National television revenues were expected to drop by half, even with a new divisional lineup and an additional round of playoffs. Some experts predicted declining revenues bringing declining salaries and labor strife. Others, looking at an expected revolution in cable television, predicted an even brighter revenue picture. Revenues had been enhanced by increased attention to ticket marketing and to the selling of team logo merchandise. Most teams change uniform and cap design frequently and offer multiple styles and color combinations. At the marketing level attention had been given to the comfort of fans with the addition of amenities in the domes and the neoclassical ballparks.

The decision of major league owners to develop the Baseball Network with NBC and ABC was ill-fated. The players strike that started in August 1994 came just as the new television package went on the air. In 1995 the Baseball Network was tried again, with poor results. The decision to televise regionally deprived large areas of the country of key games in the race for playoff spots and the regionalization of both rounds of playoff games was greeted with disbelief. While trying to bring back the fans, the Baseball Network further alienated them. Before the end of the experiment it was declared dead. Shortly after the end of the 1995 World Series, a new five-year television contract, involving NBC, the Fox Network, and ESPN, was announced. Although it would not bring the extravagant sums of the 1990 CBS contract, it guaranteed each team $10 million per season for national television rights, a sum much greater than anticipated by most observers, and guaranteed fans access to all rounds of playoffs on a national basis.

The battle in 1994 was no longer about money but about power that had flowed from baseball players to owners over eight work stoppages.

After the move of the second version of the Washington Senators to Arlington, Texas, where they became the Texas Rangers, the franchise movement that began in the mid-1950s came to a close, although threats to move continued to be a way to secure local tax and stadium concessions. In 1977 the American League had one more round of expansion, adding franchises in Seattle and Toronto, but the National League resisted until it added the Florida Marlins in Miami and the Colorado Rockies in Denver for the 1993 season. These changes precipitated a reorganization of each league into three divisions, with another round of playoffs featuring divisional winners and the second-place team with the best record.

On the field the search for more offense led the American League in 1973 to adopt the "designated hitter." Most of organized baseball followed this lead with the exception of the National League. Other onfield changes included the lowering of the pitcher's mound and narrowing of the strike zone, designed to add offense. This was countered with increased use of relief specialists such as "set-up men" and "closers," with Rollie Fingers and Bruce Sutter establishing the closer as a key figure.

In the commissioner's office the period saw four distinct personalities and styles. Bowie Kuhn (1969–1984), while irritating nearly everyone at some time during his long tenure, brought increased revenues from television. Peter Ueberroth (1984–1989) brought greater awareness of marketing and led owners into the disastrous collusion policy. The short tenure of former Yale president A. Bartlett Giamatti was noted for declaring the Cincinnati Reds first baseman Pete Rose permanently ineligible for violating Rule 19, which prohibits gambling. Fay Vincent (1989–1992) slowly alienated the owners, who removed him and reduced the commissioner's powers and duties.

On the field of play several great players reached notable milestones. Hank Aaron surpassed Babe Ruth's career home-run record, Pete Rose surpassed Ty Cobb's career hit record, Lou Brock surpassed Ty Cobb's stolen base records, with Rickey Henderson in turn passing Brock, Nolan Ryan passed the 5,000 strikeout level and pitched his career record seventh no-hitter at the age of forty-four, and Cal Ripkin, Jr., surpassed Lou Gehrig's record of starting 2,130 consecutive games.

Despite the owners' claim that free agency would make the rich richer, team dynasties ended with the Oakland A's of 1972–1975. Free agency and payroll inflation for winning teams produced increased player movement. In addition, the 1980s were marked by a resurgence of minor-league baseball and the reemergence of college baseball as a source of major-league players. In the mid-1990s major league baseball's future was clouded by uncertain economic forces and uncertain leadership. Still, the game is more popular than ever and the most written-about professional sport in America.

BIBLIOGRAPHY

Lee Lowenfish and Tony Lupien, *The Imperfect Diamond* (New York, 1991).

James Miller, *The Baseball Business* (Chapel Hill, N.C., 1990).

John Thom and Pete Palmer, eds., *Total Baseball* (New York, 1993)

David Voigt, *American Baseball* (New York, 1993).

Andrew Zimbalist, *Baseball and Billions* (New York, 1992).

— RICHARD C. CREPEAU

BASKETBALL

Basketball has developed since its invention in 1891 by James Naismith into one of the most popular sports in the United States, both for playing and for viewing. Originally a game to be played indoors during winter months, amateurs now play it year-round, and the season of the National Basketball Association (NBA), the major U.S. professional league, lasts from November until June. One hundred years after the invention of the sport in Springfield, Massachusetts, basketball was being hailed as the "new national sport," instead of baseball, among young people in the United States. The stars of basketball teams became national celebrities and wealthy young men. Thousands of players have left their marks on both the amateur and professional levels. Perhaps the most remarkable achievement belongs to Wilt Chamberlain, who once scored one hundred points in a single NBA game in 1962. No NBA player has come close since. Chamberlain averaged an incredible fifty points per game for the entire season. Perhaps the most famous basketball team in history competes in neither the professional basketball league nor the college ranks; the Harlem Globetrotters, organized in 1927, have traveled the country and abroad, entertaining fans with performances that combine highly skilled basketball with humor.

The popularity and financial standing of the NBA suffered during the late 1970s, as players were caught using illegal drugs. During the 1980s, however, the addition of three stars—Larry Bird of the Boston Celtics, Earvin "Magic" Johnson of the Los Angeles Lakers, and Michael Jordan of the Chicago Bulls—prompted a remarkable revival, leading to league attendance records, large television contracts, and new teams through expansion of the league. In fact, potential team owners bid against each other in the late 1980s, offering millions of dollars for the rights to create new teams—this when the league expanded to include teams in Charlotte, Orlando, Minneapolis, and Miami. Outstanding basketball players developed lucrative side careers as spokesmen for company products, such as athletic wear. Jordan, for example, made millions of dollars annually as a spokesman for cereal, athletic shoes, and a fast-food restaurant chain, and his earnings from advertising far exceeded his earnings as a basketball player.

Originally an indoor game for the winter months, basketball is played year-round by amateurs, and the NBA season stretches from November to June.

The United States also exported basketball. NBA games were broadcast to nearly 100 other countries, and worldwide, basketball is second only to soccer in popularity. Basketball became an Olympic sport in 1936, and the United States dominated it until the 1970s, using college athletes. Professional players were prohibited from the games until 1992, and the NBA players on the dream team that represented the United States in the 1992 Summer Olympics in Spain were mobbed by international fans. The U.S. team dominated competition, winning by an average of more than forty points a game and won the gold medal.

Through the 1960s and early 1970s one college team dominated amateur basketball in the United States—Coach John Wooden's UCLA (University of California at Los Angeles) Bruins. In a span of twelve seasons (1963–1975) they captured ten national championships. When Wooden retired in 1975 the national college basketball scene changed. Since then, no team has won the National Collegiate Athletic Association (NCAA) Division I championship more than two years in a row. The competition in college basketball, beginning in the 1980s, sparked great interest among fans. Colleges recruit players and put intense pressure on these athletic teenagers. National publications report information about recruiting and the rankings and evaluations of each player. Coaches follow players' careers through high school, and some players report having received letters from colleges while they were in middle school, four or more years away from attending college. Violations of recruiting rules have led to the punishment of some teams by the NCAA. College basketball became a high-priced commodity in the late 1980s. CBS television paid a staggering $1 billion in 1990 for the rights to televise the NCAA men's tournament for seven years. The development in the 1980s of several all-sports cable television stations created an open market for programming; by the 1990s several hundred college basketball games were being telecast each season.

Significant on-court rules changes occurred from 1975 to 1995. The most dramatic change was the legalization of the dunk, perhaps the most exciting offensive play in the game, where a player soars above the rim and jams the basketball through the net. In addition, the NCAA approved a three-point shot, where players got three points for shots of longer distance, and instituted a shot clock, where the offense must shoot the basketball within a specific amount of time. The latter rule was designed to prevent teams from holding onto the ball, making for a dull game and drawing complaints from fans and television viewers.

Women's college basketball also showed great growth. Attendance at women's games has increased every year since 1985, and the women's NCAA tournament is now televised. Women's athletic programs fought for equal standing in the 1980s, under Title IX of the 1972 Education Amendments Act, which prohibits sex discrimination by educational institutions receiving federal aid. The most significant change in women's basketball during this era was NCAA authorization of the use of a smaller basketball than that used by men's teams.

Historically, athletics has provided opportunities for minority and underprivileged youths to attend college or earn money. Basketball has been an important factor in the integration of black and white athletes and in providing financial opportunities for the underprivileged. The focus in the 1990s was extended to opening coaching opportunities for minorities. Like their pro counterparts, the men's college basketball players became nationally known through widespread television exposure. Unlike the professionals, however, college players were barred from receiving outside financial benefits, besides scholarships and similar items allowed by the NCAA. There were no limits on coaches' benefits, however, and some well-known coaches received hundreds of thousands of dollars to wear—and to get their players to wear—a specific type of shoe. Nationally, critics argued that coaches were prostituting their universities and the players, and there were demands for limits to counter the influence of corporations upon college athletics. Responding to criticism about poor academic performances by athletes, the NCAA raised its minimum entrance standards for athletes at Division I schools. Critics cited this move as evidence of bias against minority athletes, saying that the entrance exams are racially biased. In addition, college presidents and the media began paying more attention to the graduation rates of athletic teams, which were low among some programs.

By 1995 the NBA was looking toward younger stars to continue the league's incredible resurgence in the 1980s behind the play of Jordan, Johnson, and Bird. All three all-stars retired during the early 1990s—Johnson in 1991, Bird in 1992, and Jordan in 1993. Johnson shocked the sports world when he announced that he was HIV-positive and would retire. One year later, he briefly returned to basketball before retiring again. Likewise, Jordan had second thoughts about retirement. He tried to become a professional baseball player and spent a year in the minor leagues for the Chicago White Sox, but when major league baseball players went on strike in spring 1995—and with a low batting average in his minor league career—Jordan returned to the NBA and the Chicago Bulls.

BIBLIOGRAPHY

Laura E. Bollig, ed., *NCAA Basketball's Finest* (Chicago, 1992).

John Feinstein, *A Season Inside: One Year in College Basketball* (New York, 1988).

Neil David Isaacs, *All the Moves: A History of College Basketball* (New York, 1984).

Jerry Krause and Stephen J. Brennan, *Basketball Resource Guide,* 2nd ed. (Champaign, Ill., 1990).

— BRADLEY J. HAMM

BAY OF PIGS INVASION

Bay of Pigs Invasion (Apr. 17, 1961), the abortive attempt by Cuban exiles—organized, financed, and led by the U.S. Central Intelligence Agency (CIA)—to overthrow the revolutionary regime of Premier Fidel Castro in Havana. The landing by the 1,453 men of Brigade 2506 on the swampy southwestern coast of Cuba turned within seventy-two hours into a complete disaster as the Castro forces captured 1, 179 of the invaders and killed the remaining 274. For the United States and for President John F. Kennedy, who had authorized the operation in his third month in the White House, the Bay of Pigs became a bitter political defeat as well as a monumental failure in a large-scale intelligence enterprise. The invasion is also believed to have inspired the Soviet Union to install missiles with nuclear warheads in Cuba the following year, leading to what constituted the most dangerous postwar crisis between Washington and Moscow.

The plans for the Bay of Pigs were conceived by the CIA during 1960, toward the end of the Eisenhower administration, on the theory—proved by events to have been totally erroneous—that a landing by the exiles' brigade would touch off a nationwide uprising against Castro. This was the essential intelligence miscalculation that most of the key participants subsequently acknowledged.

Besides being a monumental failure and a bitter political defeat, the Bay of Pigs fiasco is believed to have prompted the Soviets to install missiles in Cuba, which led to a more serious crisis.

To prepare for the invasion, the CIA trained the force in secret camps in Guatemala for nearly six months. But long before the landing, it was widely known in the Cuban community in Florida (and, presumably, the information was also available to Castro agents) that such a landing was in the offing. This was the second major intelligence failure: the inability to preserve secrecy. Finally, the invasion failed because Kennedy, as he had forewarned his aides, refused to provide U.S. air support for the brigade. Castro's aircraft easily disposed of the exiles' tiny air force and proceeded to sink the invasion ships and cut down the men holding the Bay of Pigs beachhead.

The final act came in December 1962, twenty months later, when Castro released the 1,179 Bay of Pigs prisoners in exchange for $53 million worth of medical supplies and other goods.

BIBLIOGRAPHY

Haynes Johnson, *The Bay of Pigs.*
Tad Szulc and Karl E. Meyer, *The Cuban Invasion.*

— TAD SZULC

BEIRUT BOMBING

Beirut Bombing (Oct. 23, 1983). Arguably the greatest foreign policy disaster of President Ronald Reagan's administration occurred when 241 U.S. marines and sailors were killed and 70 were wounded after a truck loaded with explosives crashed into U.S. marine barracks at Lebanon's Beirut international airport. When first deployed in September 1982, the mission of the multinational peacekeeping force, which included French, British, and Italian troops, was to facilitate the withdrawal of all foreign forces from Lebanon and to protect Palestinian refugees in and around Beirut. The task proved impossible. Eight years of sectarian strife, complicated by competing Syrian, Israeli, and Palestinian interests within Lebanon had transformed the country into a beleaguered armed camp. Four months of U.S.-brokered negotiations in 1983 failed to find a settlement and coincided with a suicide car bombing of the U.S. embassy in Beirut on April 18 that killed forty-six people. The sudden redeployment of Israeli forces south of Beirut on September 3 and 4 led to heavy fighting between Christian and Muslim forces and the sudden exposure of U.S. marines to enemy fire. The simultaneous suicide bombings by Muslim militants of U.S. and French peacekeeping headquarters on October 23 only renewed President Reagan's public determination to stay in Lebanon or risk a loss in credibility for the United States worldwide. The collapse of Lebanon's Christian-led coalition government on Feb. 5, 1984,

Even Reagan administration supporters admitted that the stationing of U.S. peacekeeping forces in Beirut failed to appreciate the intractable nature of Lebanon's bloody civil war.

and the routing of West Beirut's Christian militia two days later, forced Reagan to reconsider. By the time U.S. marines had been redeployed offshore on that date, 257 service personnel had been pointlessly killed, according to Reagan administration critics. Even administration supporters admitted that the well-meaning injection of U.S. peacekeeping forces in Beirut failed to appreciate the intractable character of Lebanon's bloody civil war. The evacuation of U.S. marines was quickly followed by the French, British, and Italians, and war-devastated Lebanon was left to the Lebanese.

[See also Middle East, Relations with.]

BIBLIOGRAPHY

A. Hourani and N. Shehadi, eds., *The Lebanese and the World* (New York, 1991).

Sandra Mackey, *Lebanon: The Death of a Nation* (Chicago, 1989).

Itamar Rabinovich, *The War for Lebanon, 1970–1983* (Ithaca, N.Y., 1984).

— BRUCE J. EVENSEN

BERLIN AIRLIFT

Berlin Airlift, history's largest exclusively aerial supply operation. For eleven months (1948–49) American and British planes sustained more than 2 million West Berliners and occupation troops after the Soviet Union blocked surface routes into Berlin in an effort to force withdrawal of the occupation forces of the West. Under World War II agreements the Soviet Union occupied eastern Berlin; the United States, Britain, and France occupied zones in western Berlin, with surface access presumably assured through the Soviet zone of Germany and air access assured along three twenty-mile-wide corridors. This four-power administration soon degenerated under such acts of Soviet intransigence as the flooding of the city with Soviet-printed currency. Starting in January 1948, the Soviets periodically closed access routes. After boycotting four-power occupation agencies, they halted all surface traffic into West Berlin on June 23 and denied coal and electricity from the Soviet zone.

Convinced the Soviets would stop short of war, the American commander, Gen. Lucius D. Clay, obtained U.S. government approval for an airlift requiring a minimum of 140,000 tons per month, an undertaking on a scale never before attempted. U.S. C-47 aircraft began flying into West Berlin's Tempelhof airfield on June 25, and British planes into Gatow airport on June 30. As larger U.S. Air Force C-54's, U.S. Navy R-5D's, and British Avro Yorks became available, tonnage reached a record 12,940 tons in one day on Apr. 16, 1949. One landing and takeoff occurred, on the average, every three minutes. The Soviets harassed some flights, but, as Clay predicted, stopped short of war. Hurt by reciprocal denial of imports from West Germany, they raised the blockade May 12, 1949, although the airlift continued into September.

The Berlin airlift of 1948 and 1949 brings supplies to the blockaded city of 2.5 million West Berliners. (Corbis-Bettmann)

The operation cost thirty-one American, thirty-nine British, and nine German lives. A total of 276,926 flights carried 2,323,067 tons. The U.S. cost alone was $234 million. Despite the success of the airlift, Soviet harassment of

Berlin continued at intervals over the years, although not again to the extent evidenced by the blockade.

BIBLIOGRAPHY

Frank Donovan, *Bridge in the Sky.*
Jean Edward Smith, *The Defense of Berlin.*

— CHARLES B. MACDONALD

BERLIN BLOCKADE

The Soviet blockade of Berlin, beginning on June 23, 1948, and the responding American-British airlift to keep West Berlin alive, was the most dramatic of the early cold war confrontations. Shortly after the defeat of Germany, the Soviet Union and the United States began to compete for the support of their former enemy. The United States and its allies, in control of most of Germany's population and industry, held the advantage. Initially seeking West Germany's economic recovery to promote the Marshall Plan's broader purpose—the economic reconstruction and growth of Western Europe—the United States in early 1948 imposed stringent German currency reforms and moved toward the creation of a West German constitution and government. These actions precipitated the Soviet blockade of the western half of Berlin, in an attempt to prevent the revival of West German power. Despite the stakes at issue, both powers were unwilling to risk war. Troops were not sent to reopen the Berlin corridor by challenging the Red Army, and the Soviets did not challenge the airlift. After 321 days of successful American and British sustenance of West Berlin's population with necessary supplies, the Soviets terminated the blockade.

[See also Berlin Airlift.]

BIBLIOGRAPHY

W. Phillips Davison, *The Berlin Blockade.*
Oran R. Young, *The Politics of Force.*

— JOHN W. SPANIER

BERMUDA CONFERENCE

Bermuda Conference (1957). After the deep Anglo-American rift caused by the Suez War in 1956, President Dwight D. Eisenhower and Harold Macmillan, the new British prime minister, met in Bermuda in March 1957 to bring the two allies closer together once again. European unity and the continued testing of nuclear weapons were stressed, and the two leaders announced an agreement whereby the United States would supply Britain with intermediate-range missiles.

— JOHN W. SPANIER

BICAMERAL LEGISLATURES

Bicameral legislatures in the United States have as their antecedents the British Parliament and colonial legislatures. They have been used by the national government and by almost all of the states since the adoption of the Constitution. After Vermont adopted the two-house legislature in 1836, the bicameral pattern prevailed in all states until Nebraska established a unicameral legislature in 1934. No other state has emulated this action. At the municipal level, nearly all cities use the single-chamber city council.

The bicameral legislature was developed as a device for resolving political conflict through compromise. For instance, the members of one house might be elected, and the members of the other house appointed. One house might be based on geographical subdivisions, while the other might simply represent population. Or differing political interests might be emphasized in each house: one might speak mainly for property owners and the economically powerful and the other might represent all the people. (However, a heterogeneous group of voters now selects the members of both houses in a bicameral legislature.) The length of term and the size of the district represented may differ for the two houses.

In a bicameral legislature, proponents claim, unwise and precipitous legislation is prevented: bills are reviewed more carefully; and checks and balances are promoted. These assertions remain essentially unproven. Moreover, the Nebraska experience has yielded mixed results and so has done little to resolve any controversy. Bicameral legislatures at the national and state levels are retained for several reasons. The constitutions creating them are difficult to amend, and few are willing to make the attempt. There is little public pressure for change. The superiority of the unicameral legislature has not been demonstrated conclusively. Those political interests who benefit from the existing organization of legislatures fear the uncertainties of change. Finally, the present pattern serves the purposes of many incumbent public officials.

BIBLIOGRAPHY

A. C. Breckenridge, *One House For Two.*
William J. Keefe and Morris S. Ogul, *The American Legislative Process.*

— MORRIS S. OGUL

BILL OF RIGHTS

The term "bill of rights" does not appear in the U.S. Constitution. It is, however, commonly used to designate the first ten amendments; and often it is used with latitude to include as well some later amendments affecting rights or liberties, such as the Nineteenth Amendment, granting the right of suffrage to women.

At the constitutional convention in 1787 George Mason proposed that the Constitution be "prefaced with a bill of rights." He argued that with the aid of state bills of rights already in existence, "a bill [of rights] might be prepared in a few hours." (Indeed, Mason was an old hand at the drafting of such documents, for he was the author of the Virginia Declaration of Rights, adopted in 1776 and the model for all later state bills of rights.) Elbridge Gerry moved the appointment of a committee to prepare a bill of rights, but the motion lost by a five-to-five vote. Accordingly, the Constitution as submitted for ratification contained no bill of rights. It did, however, include some important guarantees of personal rights and liberties: the privilege of the writ of habeas corpus was not to be suspended except in cases of rebellion or invasion (Article I, Section 9); no bill of attainder or ex post facto law was to be passed (Article I, Section 9); all crimes were to be tried by jury (Article III, Section 2); and no religious test could be required as a qualification to any office (Article VI).

The "Bill of Rights"—though the term does not appear as such in the Constitution—commonly refers to the first ten amendments.

When the Constitution came before the ratifying conventions, its opponents joined with advocates of a bill of rights in arguing that the Constitution was defective. They were answered by Federalists, in particular James Wilson and Alexander Hamilton, who argued that such personal guarantees were both unnecessary and dangerous because their inclusion in the Constitution might imply that the federal government had powers that in fact had not been conferred on it. "Why, for instance, should it be said," Hamilton asked rhetorically in *Federalist* 84, "that the liberty of the press shall not be restrained, when no power is given by which restrictions may be imposed?" James Madison tended to think along the same line, but in time he was won over to the side that favored a bill of rights. In a letter to Thomas Jefferson (Oct. 17, 1788), he wrote that notwithstanding the objections that he could see, he conceded that a bill of rights might nonetheless be useful in the following ways:

> 1. The political truths declared in that solemn manner acquire by degrees the character of fundamental maxims of free Government, and as they become incorporated with the national sentiment, counteract the impulses of interest and passion. 2. Although it be generally true . . . that the danger of oppression lies in the interested majorities of the people rather than in usurped acts of Government, yet there may be occasions on which the evil may spring from the latter source; and on such, a bill of rights will be a good ground for an appeal to the sense of the community.

The consequence of the debate over political philosophy and constitutional theory and interpretation was that some states sent along with their ratifications amendments that they wanted to see adopted by the new government (more than a hundred such amendments were proposed by the ratifying conventions).

On May 4, 1789, two months after the First Congress convened, Madison gave notice to the House of Representatives, where he sat as a member, that he intended to bring up the subject of amendments to the Constitution. On June 8 he proposed that the House resolve itself into a committee of the whole on the state of the Union to consider eight resolutions on amendments to the Constitution. Several members argued that there were more pressing matters; however, the House agreed that the matter would be referred to a committee of the whole. On July 21, Madison moved that the House become a committee of the whole to take up his amendments. The motion lost, and the amendments were then referred to a select committee of ten members, which included Madison. On Aug. 13 the House resolved itself into a committee of the whole to consider the select committee's report.

Madison spoke for incorporating the amendments into the body of the Constitution itself at appropriate places, so that then "they will stand upon as good a foundation as the original work." Furthermore, he said, the text of the Constitution would then be simpler than if the amendments were to consist of separate and distinct parts. The matter was debated, and at that point Madison's proposal won.

The select committee recommended fourteen amendments. The House, as a committee of the whole, considered and debated them for five days, and, with some changes, approved them all. On Aug. 19 the House took up the amendments as reported by the committee of the whole. Its first action was to decide that the amendments be appended as a supplement to the Constitution and not be distributed throughout the original document. But for this action, it would not be possible to speak of any one part of the Constitution as the Bill of Rights. On Aug. 20 and 21 the House considered the amendments and affirmed, except for some changes, the previous action it had taken as a committee of the whole; on Aug. 22 it referred the amendments to a committee of three "to arrange the said amendments." The committee submitted its report on Aug. 24, and the House voted a resolution proposing seventeen amendments to the states for ratification. The House then forwarded the amendments to the Senate.

Both the Bill of Rights and the French Declaration of the Rights of Man were modeled on bills of rights drafted by American states, notably Virginia and Massachusetts.

The record of the Senate proceedings is extremely meager. It shows that debate was taken up the following week, but it is doubtful that the Senate devoted more than two normal session days to the subject. It approved some articles and rejected others, and on Sept. 9 it reconsidered some of the actions it had previously taken. On Sept. 21 the Senate asked for a conference with the House to straighten out differences. As a result, the House reduced its original seventeen amendments to twelve, and these the Senate approved on Sept. 25. Thus, the Bill of Rights had been before Congress from June 8 to Sept. 25, 1789; but it is doubtful that more than a total of seven or eight session days had been devoted to consideration of the amendments.

On Nov. 20, 1789, New Jersey became the first state to ratify the amendments; Virginia, on Dec. 15, 1791, was the eleventh state to do so, completing the ratification process. On the latter date the Bill of Rights became effective. (Although Dec. 15 is not a legal or public holiday, by an act of Congress it is observed as Bill of Rights Day.) Two amendments failed of ratification, those related to the apportionment of representatives and the compensation of members of Congress—matters that were hardly germane to a bill of rights.

While Congress was trying to reach agreement on the amendments, in Paris on Aug. 26, 1789, the Constituent Assembly for the new French republic issued the Declaration of the Rights of Man and of the Citizen; and when the new French constitution came into force in 1791, the declaration was prefixed to it. In its generalities the declaration was modeled after the American Declaration of Independence. In their practical provisions, both the French declaration and the American Bill of Rights were modeled after the bills of rights of the American states—notably, the Virginia Declaration of Rights; the Massachusetts Bill of Rights (1780), drafted largely by John Adams; and the Virginia Statute for Establishing Religious Freedom (1786), drafted by Thomas Jefferson.

But both the Americans and the French had learned from the English models also: the Magna Charta (1215), the Petition of Right (1628), and the Bill of Rights (1689). Jefferson, Madison, and Mason had been influenced, directly or indirectly, by the writings of John Locke and John Milton, the pamphlets of Thomas Paine, the long tradition of natural law, the idea of a higher law implicit in the Hebrew Scriptures, Stoic philosophy, medieval political thought, and English revolutionary and constitutional theory.

In some four hundred words, the original Bill of Rights provides—in its more important articles—for freedom of religion, speech, press, and assembly and the right of petition (First Amendment); a guarantee against unreasonable searches and seizures (Fourth Amendment); a prohibition of double jeopardy, coerced testimony against oneself in any criminal case, and a prohibition against depriving any person of his life, liberty, or property without due process of law and against the taking of private property for public use without just compensation (Fifth Amendment); the right to a speedy and public trial, the right to be confronted by accusing witnesses, and the right to assistance of counsel (Sixth Amendment); the right to trial by jury (Seventh Amendment); a prohibition against excessive bail or fines and against cruel and unusual punishments (Eighth Amendment). The Ninth Amendment is a statement of the general principle that the provision of certain rights in the Constitution shall not imply the denial of other rights "retained by the people"; and so, too, the Tenth Amendment states that the powers not delegated to the federal government or prohibited to the states are reserved to the states or to the people.

The Supreme Court in 1833 in an opinion by Chief Justice John Marshall declared that the first ten amendments were adopted to guard against abuses by the federal government and not against encroachments by the states. This position, although repeatedly contested, was insistently reaffirmed by the Court. After adoption of the Fourteenth Amendment, it was contended that the procedural safeguards prescribed in the Bill of Rights are "fundamental principles of liberty and justice" and are therefore essential ingredients of due process of law applicable against the states; but the Court, except for Justice John M. Harlan (born 1833), rejected this argument. With respect to substantive provisions, Justice Harlan, in 1907, argued that the First Amendment freedoms of speech and press are "essential parts of every man's liberty" and are therefore protected by the Fourteenth Amendment's guarantee that no state may deprive a person of his "liberty" without due process of law. But this was in a dissenting opinion. Justice Louis D. Brandeis expressed the same view in 1920 but also in a dissenting opinion. The first constitutional breakthrough came in *Meyer* v. *Nebraska* (1923), in which the Court declared unconstitutional a state statute that prohibited any school, public or private, from teaching any subject in a language other than English. The Court's opinion by Justice James McReynolds broadly defined the "liberty" protected by the due process clause of the Fourteenth Amendment. And, two years later, in *Gitlow* v. *New York*, the Court said that it would "assume" that freedom of speech and press "are among the fundamental personal rights and 'liberties' protected by the due process clause of the Fourteenth Amendment from impairment by the states."

Chief Justice John Marshall declared in 1833 that the first ten amendments were to guard against abuses by the federal government, not encroachments by the states.

In subsequent cases decided in the 1930's the Court "assimilated" into the Fourteenth Amendment the First Amendment freedoms of religion and assembly; and in 1947, in *Everson* v. *Board of Education*, it held that the First Amendment ban on "establishment of religion" was applicable to the states by the Fourteenth Amendment. The Court has not, however, "incorporated" into the Fourteenth Amendment all the guarantees of the first eight amendments. The Court has proceeded slowly and on a case-by-case basis, and while there has been a definite line of progress, it has by no means been a straight line. It was not until 1963 that the Court, overruling a case it had decided in 1942, held that the Sixth Amendment right to counsel was applicable to the states under the due process clause of the Fourteenth Amendment. The chief proponent of the proposition that the framers of the Fourteenth Amendment intended that the entire Bill of Rights be applicable to the states was Justice Hugo Black, but his position was strongly challenged by Justice Felix Frankfurter and Justice John M. Harlan (born 1899). The intermediate position, which generally prevailed, was formulated by Justice Benjamin Cardozo in *Palko* v. *Connecticut* (1937). This position was that there is no total incorporation, but that only those guarantees in the Bill of Rights that are found to be "implicit in the concept of ordered liberty" become effective against the states. These must be rights found to be "of the very essence of ordered liberty"—such rights that "neither liberty nor justice would exist if they were sacrificed"—they must be principles of justice "so rooted in the traditions and conscience of our people as to be ranked as fundamental."

The constitutional guarantees are obviously not an exhaustive enumeration of basic human rights. From time to time other rights clamor for recognition. Accordingly, the Court has said that specific guarantees of the Bill of Rights "have penumbras, formed by emanations from those guarantees that help give them [i.e., the guarantees] life and substance" (Justice William O. Douglas in *Griswold* v. *Connecticut*, 1965). Among such rights recognized by the Court are the right to travel, the right of parents to send their children to a private school, the right to procreate, the right to privacy, and the right of association. This class of "peripheral" rights is, of course, not closed. One rationale for them is that without these rights, specifically enumerated rights would be less secure.

The Supreme Court under Chief Justice Earl Warren (1953–69) was especially vigilant and creative in the process of defining and implementing the Bill of Rights. It made the due process clause and the equal protection clause of the Fourteenth Amendment, especially when intertwined with the First Amendment, familiar terms to millions of citizens. Working closely with Chief Justice Warren were justices Black, Douglas, William J. Brennan, Arthur J. Goldberg, Abe Fortas, and Thurgood Marshall. Among their predecessors who made significant contributions to a recognition of the primacy of the Bill of Rights in American society and government were the first Justice Harlan; justices Oliver Wendell Holmes, Brandeis, Cardozo, Frank Murphy, Wiley B. Rutledge; and chief justices Harlan F. Stone and Charles E. Hughes.

[See also Amendments to the Constitution.]

BIBLIOGRAPHY

Z. Chafee, Jr., *Three Human Rights in the Constitution*, and *How Human Rights Got Into the Constitution*.
N. Dorsen, ed., *The Rights of Americans*.
M. R. Konvitz, *Bill of Rights Reader: Leading Constitutional Cases*, *Fundamental Liberties of a Free People*, and *Expanding Liberties*.
L. W. Levy, *Legacy of Suppression: Freedom of Speech and Press in Early American History*.
L. H. Pollock, ed., *The Constitution and the Supreme Court*, vol. II.
R. A. Rutland, *The Birth of the Bill of Rights, 1776–1791*.

— MILTON R. KONVITZ

BLACK CODES

The term "black codes" refers to legislation enacted in the former Confederate states in 1865 and 1866 for the purpose of limiting the freedom of recently freed blacks. It is sometimes considered to include southern antebellum legislation that restricted the action and movements of slaves, although such laws are more frequently referred to as slave codes. Persons using the term "black codes" to include all such laws see them as originating in the 17th century, continuing until the Civil War, and being reenacted in slightly modified form immediately after the war.

The laws passed in 1865–66 by the several states differed from one another, but their general concern was the same: they were intended to replace the social controls of slavery, which had been swept away by the Emancipation Proclamation and the Thirteenth Amendment, and to assure the South that free blacks would remain in a position subordinate to whites. Typical of the legislation were provisions for declaring blacks to be vagrants if they were unemployed and without permanent residence. As vagrants they were subject to being arrested, fined, and bound out for a term of labor if unable to pay the fine. Penalties existed for refusing to complete a term of labor as well as for breaking an agreement to work when it was entered into voluntarily; persons encouraging blacks to refuse to abide by these restrictive laws were themselves subject to penalties. In like manner, orphans could be apprenticed to work for a number of years. In many of these cases the whites to whom blacks were assigned turned out to be their former owners. Blacks could not testify in court cases involving whites and were often prohibited from bearing firearms. Intermarriage between the races was forbidden. Of the states with the most restrictive legislation, Mississippi limited the types of property blacks could own, and South Carolina excluded blacks from certain businesses and from the skilled trades.

Being strikingly similar to the antebellum slave codes, the black codes were, at the very least, not intended to protect the rights to which Afro-Americans were entitled as free men—and it is no overstatement to say that they aimed to reinstate the substance of the slave system without the legal form.

Enactment of black codes in the southern states was a factor in the conflict within the federal government, between the executive and legislative branches, for control of the process of Reconstruction. More than any other single factor it demonstrated what Afro-Americans could expect from state governments controlled by those who had actively supported the Confederate cause. Northern reaction to the codes helped to produce Radical Reconstruction and the Fourteenth and Fifteenth amendments, which temporarily removed such legislation from the books. Following Reconstruction, many of the provisions of the black codes were reenacted in the Jim Crow laws that continued in effect until the Civil Rights Act of 1964.

BIBLIOGRAPHY

John Hope Franklin, *From Slavery to Freedom.*
Theodore B. Wilson, *The Black Codes of the South.*
C. Vann Woodward, *The Origins of the New South.*

— HENRY N. DREWRY

BLACKFOOT

One of the most numerous and powerful of the tribes of the northwestern Plains, the Siksika ("black feet") were so named because their moccasins were black from the ash of prairie fires or were simply dyed black. While population figures are surmised with difficulty, especially because of the involvement of the Siksika with other and related Algonkin-speaking tribes, the Blackfoot nation at its peak, between 1700 and about 1870, may have had as many as 15,000 members. Spread from the North Saskatchewan River to the southern tributaries of the Missouri in Montana, the Blackfoot nation comprised several subtribes, which may all have had a common source in the area of Algonkin speech to the east. The Blackfoot proper; the Piegan and the Blood tribes, who were their close relatives; the Algonkin Atsina, who were an Arapaho offshoot; and the Athapascan Sarsi formed a military federation that was significant in the balance of power in the northwestern Plains in the 18th century.

The Blackfoot complex is one of classic Plains culture: bison hunting; the war and coup-counting patterns; movements of individual bands; and the great seasonal convocations for intensive hunting. The Blackfoot are also of interest in that they were in process of modifying their kinship organization at the time of their first contact with Europeans in the mid-16th century. Originally patrifocal, they began to model their institutions after those of the neighboring Crow and were developing matrilineal institutions. They had the best-developed system of military associations (divisions of warriors) based on age-grading.

BIBLIOGRAPHY

J. C. Ewers, *The Blackfeet,* and *The Horse in Blackfoot Indian Culture.*

— ROBERT F. SPENCER

BLACK FRIDAY

Black Friday (Sept. 24, 1869), the climactic day of an effort by Jay Gould, James Fisk, Jr., Abel Rathbone Corbin, and one or two associates to corner the ready gold supply of the United States. The nation then being on a paper-money basis, gold was dealt in as a speculative commodity on the New York exchange. Gould and Fisk first enlisted Corbin, who had married President Ulysses S. Grant's sister; they then drew the new head of the New York subtreasury, Daniel Butterfield, into the scheme and unsuccessfully tried to involve Grant's private secretary, Horace Porter. On June 15, 1869, they entertained Grant on Fisk's Bristol Line steamboat, attempted to learn the Treasury's gold policy, and argued that it was important to keep gold high in order to facilitate sales of American grain in Europe. Grant was noncommittal. A gold corner did not seem difficult if government nonintervention could be assured, for New York banks in the summer of 1869 held only about $14 million in gold, not more than a million was in local circulation, and time would be required to bring more from Europe. On Sept. 2 Gould began buying gold on a large scale; on the 15th Fisk began buying heavily and soon forced the price from 135 to 140. The movement excited much suspicion and fear, and the *New York Tribune* declared it the "clear and imperative duty" of the Treasury to sell gold and break up the conspiracy. Secretary of the Treasury George S. Boutwell visited New York but decided not to act; meanwhile Grant had gone to Washington, Pa., and was out of touch until he returned to Washington, D.C., on Sept. 22. On the 23rd, with gold at 144, the New York panic grew serious.

The Black Friday of 1869 caused heavy losses to businesses, besmirched the Grant administration, and left Fisk and Gould with $11 million in profits.

The climax of Black Friday found Fisk driving gold higher and higher, business profoundly disturbed throughout the nation, and the New York gold room a pandemonium as scores were ruined. As the price rose to 160 Boutwell in Washington urged the sale of three million dollars of the gold reserve, Grant suggested five, and the Secretary telegraphed an order to sell four. Gould, perhaps forewarned by Butterfield, had already begun selling, and gold sank rapidly to 135; Fisk immediately found means to repudiate his contracts. The episode caused heavy indirect losses to business and placed an ugly smirch on the Grant administration. Gould and Fisk made an $11 million profit.

BIBLIOGRAPHY

G. S. Boutwell, *Reminiscences of Sixty Years in Public Affairs.*

F. C. Hicks, ed., *High Finance in the Sixties.*

James Schouler, *History of the United States,* VII.

— ALLAN NEVINS

BLACK HAWK WAR

Black Hawk War (1832), a conflict between the United States and a faction of Sauk (or Sac) and Fox Indians, waged mainly in Illinois and Wisconsin. The leader of the Sauk and Fox was an aging chief named Black Hawk, who was the rival of another Sauk chief, Keokuk. Keokuk had been receptive to ceding land to the whites and with his faction of the Sauk and Fox had moved across the Mississippi River to Iowa in 1823. Black Hawk, who had fought on the side of the British in the War of 1812, declined to evacuate his village at Rock Island, Ill.

At issue was a treaty made at St. Louis in 1804, under the terms of which the Sauk and Fox supposedly agreed to cede all their lands on the eastern side of the Mississippi River in return for being allowed to remain undisturbed until the country should be opened to settlement. Black Hawk vehemently denied the validity of the treaty, maintaining that the party of Sauk and Fox who had signed the treaty had had no authority to do so and had been deceived while intoxicated. The issue became acute in 1831, when white settlers preempted the site of Black Hawk's village. Black Hawk was aroused and threatened resistance. Hostilities with the Indians were narrowly averted that year when an army of regulars and Illinois militiamen was assembled, but Black Hawk yielded to this threat of force and withdrew across the Mississippi.

Early in 1832, despite the opposition of Keokuk, Black Hawk, with 400 warriors and their families, crossed back into Illinois and moved toward Rock Island. Again the militia was called out, the settlers were alerted, and Gen. Henry Atkinson ordered Black Hawk to return to Iowa. Emissaries from Black Hawk were shot in cold blood. Black Hawk refused to comply with Atkinson's directive, and war erupted. Black Hawk retired up the Rock River, attacking and burning frontier settlements, with the soldiers in pursuit. The troops, poorly disciplined and inexperienced in Indian warfare, were at first unable to retaliate effectively. They were later strengthened, and Black Hawk, hard pressed, realized the futility of resistance and made offers of peace, which were ignored. On July 28 Black Hawk was overtaken by a force of volunteers under Gen. James D. Henry and was crushingly defeated; sixty-eight warriors were killed and many more wounded.

The remnant of Black Hawk's forces was pursued across southern Wisconsin to the mouth of the Bad Axe River, where on Aug. 3 they were massacred as they attempted to cross the Mississippi into Iowa. Black Hawk himself escaped but was later captured by the Winnebago, who turned him over to American troops for the reward. After imprisonment, he was taken to Washington, D.C., where, incongruously, he was honored. He was then allowed to return to the remnant of his tribe in Iowa, where he died in 1939.

Under the terms of the Black Hawk Purchase, signed on Sept. 21, 1832, the Sauk and Fox agreed to cede 6 million acres of land in eastern Iowa, a tract of 400 square miles being reserved along the western bank of the Mississippi for Keokuk and his followers, as a reward for having refrained from participation in the Black Hawk War.

BIBLIOGRAPHY

Cecil Eby, *"That Disgraceful Affair," The Black Hawk War.*
William T. Hagan, *The Sac and Fox Indians.*
Donald Jackson, ed., *Autobiography of Black Hawk.*

— KENNETH M. STEWART

BLACKLISTING

Blacklisting, a practice of employers to exclude from the job market individuals who are, or are believed to be, union men, labor agitators, or active in strike activities. Originating in the labor troubles of the 1830's, blacklisting, along with the use of agents provocateurs and injunctions, was one of the most widely used of anti-union weapons. Lists of suspects were usually available from an employer upon request, and on some occasions lists were circulated through employers associations. The use of the blacklist continued through the labor agitation following the Civil War, especially as violent conflicts between labor and business escalated in the late 19th century. The need for secrecy undoubtedly played a part in the formation in 1869 of the Knights of Labor, which did not fully cast off its status as a secret organization until 1881. Despite attempts to curb blacklisting, the ease with which employers could communicate with one another without surveillance made the use of the blacklist a fact of life for American labor until the advent of the New Deal. The passage of the National Labor Relations Act, or Wagner Act, in 1935 brought a measure of effective control. The establishment of the right to collective bargaining by the Wagner Act and the subsequent maturation of relations between business and labor significantly diminished the use of the blacklist in labor relations.

The need for secrecy undoubtedly played a part in the formation in 1869 of the Knights of Labor, which did not fully cast off its status as a secret organization until 1881.

A new dimension in blacklisting emerged following World War II with the development of the cold war. Investigations into Communist activities in America resulted in the expulsion of Communists from trade unions and of Communist-dominated unions from national labor organizations. The most glaring example of blacklisting resulted from congressional investigations of government employees and persons employed in the arts, particularly in the motion picture industry. The most celebrated such case of the postwar period was that of the so-called Hollywood Ten, who went to jail rather than answer questions concerning their political affiliations. With the rise of McCarthyism in the early 1950's, the House Un-American Activities Committee, under Chairman John S. Wood, made an exhaustive investigation into Communist influence in the entertainment world. Unlike the Hollywood Ten, the unfriendly witnesses in this probe used the Fifth Amendment, rather than the First Amendment, to defy the committee. Saved by this strategy from going to jail for contempt of Congress, they were consequently included in a show-business blacklist and barred from employment in motion pictures, television, and radio for the next decade. Although blacklisted writers managed to continue working under assumed names, most cinema actors either left the country or found other employment. Some were able to find employment in the theater because legitimate theater organizations, such as the Actor's Equity Association and the League of New York Theatres, were able to enforce a mutually agreed-upon antiblacklisting resolution.

BIBLIOGRAPHY

John R. Commons, *History of Labour in the United States.*
Robert Vaughn, *Only Victims.*

— JOSEPH A. DOWLING

BLACK PANTHERS

The Black Panther party was organized in Oakland, Calif., in 1966 by two young Afro-American militants,

Huey P. Newton and Bobby G. Seale, who in 1974 still dominated the party. Ideologically, the party represents a synthesis of black nationalism and Marxism: the Panthers believe in black liberation and sponsor programs to develop cohesiveness in the black community, but they also favor building coalitions with radical elements from other races.

In 1967, the Panthers organized the residents of Oakland's ghetto for purposes of self-defense against the city's police. On May 2, the party gained national publicity when thirty armed Panthers demonstrated on the steps of the California capitol to protest the passage of a bill that infringed on the Panthers' right to bear arms. The Panthers immediately became a symbol of black militancy to the entire nation; after this incident, party branches were established throughout the United States.

The Black Panthers achieved their greatest impact in 1968 when the party's minister of information, Eldridge Cleaver, published *Soul On Ice*, a bestselling defense of the black liberation movement. In addition, the Black Panthers merged with the Student Nonviolent Coordinating Committee (SNCC), whose principal leaders were named to prominent party positions. This merger quickly collapsed over the question of forming alliances with nonblacks, and Cleaver later left the party because of tactical disputes. In addition, the Panthers' notoriety and militancy triggered police harassment. Newton and Seale were arrested on numerous occasions and subjected to lengthy trials and imprisonment before their release. In the early 1970's, it appeared that the party was near extinction, but in a dramatic change of tactics, the Black Panthers turned to electoral politics, centering their attention on Oakland, where Seale unsuccessfully ran for mayor in 1973.

BIBLIOGRAPHY

Philip S. Foner, ed., *The Black Panthers Speak.*

Gene Marine, *The Black Panthers.*

Bobby Seale, *Seize the Time: The Story of the Black Panther Party and Huey P. Newton.*

— RICHARD P. YOUNG

BLACK POWER

Black power means the control by black people of the political, social, economic, and cultural institutions that affect their daily lives. The phrase came to prominence in the summer of 1966, when Stokely Carmichael and Willie Ricks of the Student Nonviolent Coordinating Committee (SNCC) proclaimed it upon the completion of the march through Mississippi begun by James Meredith. The term had been used earlier in a number of ways: *Black Power* (1954), Richard Wright's book on Ghana; in the conference held in Chicago during the summer of 1965 to establish an organization of black power; and in Adam Clayton Powell's speeches at Howard University and before Congress in the spring of 1966, when he urged that Afro-Americans seek black power. The term now embraces a wide variety of ideologies and specific strategies for the advancement of Afro-

Huey P. Newton, after being released on $50,000 bail from the Alameda County Courthouse on August 5, 1970, in Oakland, California. (UPI/Corbis-Bettmann)

Americans. Initially, as a result of the SNCC experience in registering black voters in the Deep South during the early 1960's, it meant that blacks should have political control of those areas in the South in which they constitute a majority of the population. This meaning was soon extended to the advocacy of black control of urban ghettos and of all the institutions that affect the lives and destinies of Afro-Americans. Black-power strategies cover the spectrum from black capitalism and electoral politics to armed struggle. Black-power goals range from pluralism (equal group status within American society) to separatism (an autonomous black city, county, state, or nation), to socialist revolution (replacing white American capitalism with black socialism). Most blacks tend to view black power as just another stratagem for uniting themselves as a group to enable them to achieve equality as individuals within American society.

BIBLIOGRAPHY

Joel D. Alberbach and Jack L. Walker, "The Meaning of Black Power: A Comparison of Black and White Interpretations of a Political Slogan," *American Political Science Review*, vol. 64 (1970).

Robert L. Scott and Wayne Brockriede, *The Rhetoric of Black Power.*

— JOHN H. BRACEY JR.

BLAND-ALLISON ACT

Bland-Allison Act, the first of several U.S. government subsidies to silver producers in depression periods. The five-year depression following the panic of 1873 caused cheap-money advocates (led by Representative R. P. Bland of Missouri) to join with silver-producing interests in urging return to bimetallism. The silver dollar had been omitted from the list of coins by a mint reform act, which lent itself to the political sobriquet of the "Crime of '73," and silver had depreciated with other commodities. The silver advocates demanded restoration of free coinage of silver at a ratio of 16 to 1, approximately $1.29 an ounce.

Free coinage, as the symbol of justice for the poor, was seized upon by greenbackers and others determined to prevent resumption of specie payments and to make government obligations payable in silver. When Bland's bill for free coinage, passed by the House (Nov. 5, 1877), jeopardized Secretary of the Treasury John Sherman's plans for resuming specie payments, Sherman substituted limited purchases for free coinage, through a Senate amendment sponsored by Sen. W. B. Allison of Iowa. The producers accepted the arrangement as likely to restore silver to $1.29.

The law, passed Feb. 28, 1878, over President Rutherford B. Hayes's veto, required government purchase, at market prices, of $2 million to $4 million worth of silver bullion monthly, and coinage into legal tender 16-to-1 dollars, exchangeable for $10 silver certificates receivable for public dues and reissuable. The president was directed to arrange an international bimetallic conference to meet within six months. These provisions signified victory for producers over inflationists, defeat of international bimetallists by national bimetallists, a drain on the Treasury through the customs in times of uncertainty, and failure for the conference.

BIBLIOGRAPHY

H. B. Russell, *International Monetary Conferences.*

— JEANNETTE P. NICHOLS

BONUS ARMY

Bonus Army, a spontaneous gathering of unemployed World War I veterans who, late in May 1932, began marching and hitchhiking to Washington, D.C., in small groups from all over the United States until about 15,000 were assembled there. The needy veterans, seeking some economic relief from Congress, eventually united in petitioning for immediate payment of the adjusted compensation, or "bonus," certificates approved by Congress in 1924 but not payable until 1945.

The problems of food, shelter, and sanitation for the impoverished veterans embarrassed Washington, and there was latent danger of disorder. But the leader, Walter W. Waters, maintained almost military discipline and expelled Communist agitators, while patriotism permeated the ranks. Although Washington's chief of police tried to provide quarters, most of the men built wretched hovels in which they lived.

The problems of food, shelter, and sanitation for the impoverished veterans embarrassed Washington, and there was latent danger of disorder.

In mid-June, Congress, by a narrow margin, defeated the bonus bill, but the disappointed "Bonus Expeditionary Force" stayed on, haunting the Capitol grounds. Late in July, the veterans were ordered to evacuate. Most of the veterans departed, but about 2,000 failed to do so. An attempt by police to remove the remaining veterans resulted in the death of two policemen and two veterans. On July 28, on instructions from the president, U.S. troops drove them from their quarters in public buildings and from their camps, using tanks, infantry, and cavalry.

BIBLIOGRAPHY

E. Francis Brown, "The Bonus Army Marches to Defeat," *Current History* (1932).

Walter W. Waters, *B.E.F., The Whole Story of the Bonus Army.*

— JOSEPH MILLS HANSON

BOOMTOWNS

Boomtowns, settlements that sprang up or rapidly increased in size as the result of some mineral or industrial development. Rochester, N.Y., was one of the earliest notable examples, its growth after 1825 as the result of the building of the Erie Canal and the development of the Genesee waterpower being phenomenal for the period. There were a few boomtowns in the Middle West, but the finest specimens began to be seen only with the discoveries of gold and silver in the Far West. San Francisco itself in 1849–51 was a remarkable example. Simultaneously, in the gold regions, before there were any sawmills, villages of tents, with an occasional log hut, sprang up and their occupants quickly formed city governments. By the time lumber began to be sawed county governments were being organized, and the crudest of small frame shacks became courthouses. Virginia City and other Nevada towns were mushroom growths from silver ore; meanwhile, in the 1860's, gold strikes contributed to the establishment of many others in Idaho, Montana, and Colorado, mostly ephemeral, though Helena, Mont., and Denver, Colo., proved to be permanent. Gold brought Deadwood, S.Dak., into being in 1876. Two cities built on silver evolved swiftly in 1878: Tombstone, Ariz., a new foundation; and Leadville, Colo., long a somnolent hamlet, but whose population leaped from 300 to 35,000 in two years. Oil City, Pa., in 1859 was the first of a long series of petroleum boomtowns, later continued in Ohio, Indiana, Oklahoma, and Texas. The opening of a portion of the Indian Territory to colonization in 1889 created Guthrie and Oklahoma City almost overnight. Immediately afterward, new gold discoveries in Colorado did the same for Cripple Creek and Creede. Hopewell, Va., was a typical creation of World War I munition plants, and other precocious towns arose in Florida during the land-speculation excitement of the 1920's. Similarly, beginning in 1956, Cape Canaveral, Fla., developed into a prosperous town, with over 35,000 inhabitants employed in the U.S. space program. However, cutbacks in federal appropriations for space flights and space research in the 1970's brought severe economic stress to the area. Construction of the Alaskan pipeline began in 1974, and boomtowns sprang up along the pipeline's route as work progressed.

BIBLIOGRAPHY

John M. Clampitt, *Echoes From the Rocky Mountains.*

Alvin F. Harlow, *Old Waybills.*

— ALVIN F. HARLOW

BOOTLEGGING

Bootlegging, a term derived from the early Indian traders' custom of carrying a bottle of liquor in the boot, especially applied to illicit deliveries of alcoholic beverages. The bootlegger is a peddler whose name differentiates his activities from those of the merchant who unlawfully purveys from a shop known variously as a blind tiger, blind pig, or speakeasy. The manufacture of illicit hard liquor is termed "moonshining," and the product, variously known, is often referred to as mountain dew.

Since the activity is illicit, no reliable estimates can be given as to its scope. In those times and places in which alcoholic beverages can be obtained lawfully at reasonable prices bootlegging has little reason for being; but heavy taxation or legal efforts to prevent the sale of liquor create a demand for an illicit supply. Between the effective date of the Eighteenth Amendment prohibiting manufacture of or traffic in liquor (Jan. 16, 1920) and its repeal (Dec. 3, 1933) the consumption of bootleg liquor in the United States was probably about 100 million gallons a year.

"Bootlegging," a term for illicit deliveries of alcoholic beverages, derives from the early Indian traders' custom of carrying a bottle of liquor in the boot.

The profits derived from bootlegging depend somewhat upon the source of the beverage and somewhat upon the methods of retailing. During Prohibition liquor was smuggled across the borders, brought in by boat, alcohol lawfully possessed for manufacturing purposes was sold for beverages, and a relatively small amount was distilled without license. In the larger cities powerful bootlegging organizations arose that arranged for a steady supply of hard liquor and beer, often themselves controlling illicit distilleries and breweries and smuggling operations, and set up a complete system of retailing, both through luxurious speakeasies that furnished a variety of entertainment as well as food and illicit drink and through the private calls of bootleggers upon regular customers. These organizations tried to create monopolies and were ready to murder competitors or their spies. The St. Valentine's Day massacre of 1929 in a populous section of Chicago's North Side was the slaughter of seven unarmed rivals by one of these bootlegging gangs.

To meet the rising tide of crime several steps were taken. The original National Prohibition Enforcement Act of 1919, the Volstead Act, was amended by the more much severe Jones Act of 1929. This law raised the maximum penalty for bootlegging to a fine of $10,000 plus five years in prison, but it carried a rider stipulating that it was the intent of Congress to apply this drastic punishment to major offenders only. A year later, a federal grand jury sitting at Chicago uncovered what was termed the largest liquor ring since the advent of Prohibition. The indictment of thirty-one corporations and 158 individuals cited violations in New York, Chicago, Detroit, Cleveland, Philadelphia, St. Louis, Minneapolis, St. Paul, Los Angeles, and North Bergen, N.J. This group was charged with the diversion of more than 7 million gallons of alcohol in the seven years preceding indictment and was alleged to have done a total business in excess of $50 million. The state of Michigan went so far as to declare bootlegging a felony and to provide that on a third conviction for felony the convict might be sentenced to life imprisonment.

Before the end of 1930 more than 200 persons had been killed in the process of enforcement of the Volstead Act, and moderates were beginning to question whether the enforcement of Prohibition was feasible. The public revealed this attitude in a *Literary Digest* poll, May 24, 1930, by returning 30.5 percent of their votes in favor of continuance and strict enforcement of the Prohibition amendment, 29.1 percent in favor of modification to permit light wines and beer, and 40.4 percent in favor of repeal of the Eighteenth Amendment.

A limited number of bootleggers has always operated and probably will continue, but since the quality of their merchandise and public support are both uncertain, their sales volume doubtless will remain relatively small. The federal Bureau of Alcohol, Tobacco, and Firearms reported seizing 15,000 stills in 1958. Only 1,300 were seized in 1974, but the bureau estimates that it confiscates one-third to one-half of all operating stills.

BIBLIOGRAPHY

Herbert Asbury, *Great Illusion.*

J. H. S. Bossard and Thorstein Sellin, eds., "Prohibition: A National Experiment," *Annals of American Association for the Promotion of Social Science*, vol. 158 (1932).

— ROBERT G. RAYMER

BORDER STATES

Border states, a designation applied to the tier of slave states bordering on the North, consisting of Delaware, Maryland, Virginia, Kentucky, and Missouri. They were largely southern in sentiment, though many of their economic ties were with the North. They owe their chief significance to their reaction toward secession and the Civil War. None seceded except Virginia, from which West Virginia separated. Kentucky set up and maintained for a few months in 1861 the unique policy of neutrality, and all except Delaware sent considerable numbers of soldiers to the Confederacy. Kentucky and Delaware were the only border states to cling to slavery until the Thirteenth Amendment abolished it.

BIBLIOGRAPHY

E. C. Smith, *The Borderland in the Civil War.*

— E. MERTON COULTER

BOSNIA-HERZEGOVINA

Bosnia-Herzegovina, former Yugoslavian republic that declared its independence in October 1991. Despite predictions that Yugoslavia would disintegrate following the collapse of communism, the United States did not object when its European allies recognized the independence of Yugoslavian republics Croatia and Slovenia in the summer of 1991. Serbia, another republic, in turn, invaded Croatia, proclaimed a new Federal Republic of Yugoslavia (including Montenegro) and incited Serbs living in the other Yugoslav republics—especially in Bosnia-Herzegovina—to take up arms. After Croatians living in Bosnia declared an independent state in April 1992, Serbs began to shell the cosmopolitan capital of Sarajevo. Bosnian Serbs seized territory and displaced Bosnia's Muslim population through "ethnic cleansing," wherein Serbian fighters brutalized Muslim women in "rape camps." As the United Nations imposed an arms embargo on both sides and tried to mediate, Serbian militia seized 70 percent of the Bosnian hinterland while systematically starving and bombarding the people of Sarajevo. France and Great Britain dispatched United Nations troops to safeguard relief supplies in Bosnia but recoiled from military intervention. Only belatedly did President George Bush back a UN flight ban over Bosnia. President Bill Clinton inherited the problem with his election to the presidency in 1992.

Clinton had criticized Bush's inaction, but most Americans, although appalled by the bloodshed in Bosnia, feared getting entangled in age-old ethnic rivalries impervious to outside influence. When Clinton asked for military options, the Pentagon cited the rugged terrain for not mounting an expeditionary force. During the spring of 1993 the pressure on the United States to act increased, coming from, among others, Nobel Laureate Elie Wiesel. Many officials urged air strikes to halt Serbian aggression, but polls indicated that only 30 percent of Americans favored air strikes, while 62 percent were opposed. Lacking foreign and domestic support for a major display of force, Clinton backed away. In August, when Serbs threatened to cut off Sarajevo and stop all relief supplies, Clinton pressed the North Atlantic Treaty Organization (NATO) for air strikes, but the Serbs retreated a few miles from the mountain heights surrounding the city, thus forestalling NATO bombs. The U.S. State Department desk officer for Bosnia thereupon resigned, protesting that the weak-kneed Department of State would "not act against genocide." Subsequently, more State Department specialists resigned over U.S. policy in Bosnia.

A Croatian offensive in August 1995, supported by NATO air strikes around Sarajevo, drove more than 180,000 Serbs from much of their previously held terrain.

In February 1994, when a mortar shell exploded amid a Saturday crowd in Sarajevo's open market, killing at least sixty-eight civilians, the carnage was captured on television, and the next day U.S. planes evacuated the wounded. After obtaining NATO approval, Clinton delivered an ultimatum—the Serbs must pull back their tanks and artillery beyond the 12.4-mile exclusion zone around Sarajevo or turn them over to UN peacekeepers. Clinton appealed directly to Russian President Boris Yeltsin to press the Serbs to comply. The Serbs met the deadline, barely. On February 28, NATO jets downed four Serbian planes violating the no-fly zone, the first combat action for NATO in its forty-five-year history. During the summer of 1994, Bosnian Serbs rejected a UN peace plan that would have given the Serbs 49 percent of Bosnia, with a Muslim-Croat coalition retaining the rest. With 200,000 already dead or missing, another winter of ethnic war followed. Former President Jimmy Carter brokered a four-month cease-fire agreement between the Bosnian government and the Bosnian Serbs on Dec. 31, 1994. While diplomats from the Contact Group of the United States, Great Britain, France, Germany, and Russia persevered in their attempts to find a permanent peace settlement, both sides built up their forces and the fighting spread beyond Bosnia to Zagreb, with Serbs and Croats renewing hostilities as well. A Croatian offensive in early August 1995, supported by North Atlantic Treaty Organization (NATO) air strikes around Sarajevo, eventually proved decisive, as more than 180,000 Serbs fled from much of their previously held terrain. Peace negotiations held in Dayton, Ohio, in November 1995 produced the following terms: a single Bosnian state divided into two parts, with 51 percent of the territory becoming a Muslim-Croat federation and 49 percent a Serb republic; a united multiethnic Sarajevo remaining as the capital; an elected collective presidency; a two-house parliament; a constitutional court; and a single currency. The agreement called for 60,000 NATO troops to act as peacekeepers, including 20,000 Americans, based in northeastern Bosnia. A great debate followed in the United States as to whether troop commitments to the peace process in Bosnia were in the national interest.

[See also North Atlantic Treaty Organization; United Nations.]

— J. GARRY CLIFFORD

BOSTON MASSACRE

British regulars arriving (Oct. 1, 1768) to maintain order in Boston produced soldier-civilian tensions that came to a head on the evening of Mar. 5, 1770. Seven grenadiers of the Twenty-ninth Regiment, led by Capt. Thomas Preston, marched to the relief of an eighth, on duty at the customshouse in King (now State) Street and beset by a taunting crowd of civilians. Preston, unable to disperse the crowd, loudly ordered his men, "Don't fire," while the mob was shouting "Fire and be damned!" The soldiers fired, killing three men instantly; two died later.

In October 1770 Preston, defended by John Adams and Robert Auchmuty, assisted by Josiah Quincy, Jr., was tried for murder and acquitted by a Boston jury. It has never been satisfactorily explained why the radicals Adams and Quincy undertook to represent Preston and, later, the soldiers; moreover, some surviving documents suggest that the jury in Preston's case was "packed." The soldiers—defended by Adams, Quincy, and Sampson Salter Blowers—won acquittals a month later, the jurors coming from towns outside Boston. Four civilians, accused of firing from the customshouse windows, were tried in December 1770; even though they lacked defense counsel, the evidence against them was so thin that the jurors peremptorily acquitted all.

BIBLIOGRAPHY

Hiller B. Zobel, *The Boston Massacre.*

— HILLER B. ZOBEL

BOSTON TEA PARTY

On the night of Dec. 16, 1773, 342 chests of tea belonging to the East India Company were thrown into Boston harbor by American patriots. This audacious destruction of British property was caused by the Boston Whigs' fear that if the tea were landed, its cheap price would prove an "invincible temptation" to the people. This, it was believed, would give the East India Company a monopoly of the American tea trade and establish the right of Parliament to raise a colonial revenue by means of port duties. Therefore, when it was learned at the town meeting of Dec. 16 that Gov. Thomas Hutchinson was determined to refuse the patriots' demand that the tea ships be permitted to return to England without paying the duty required by law, Samuel Adams exclaimed that the meeting could do nothing more to save the country. His words were the signal for a war whoop from the "Indians"—Sons of Liberty disguised with blankets and dusky complexions—waiting outside the meetinghouse. With the cry of "Boston harbor a tea-pot this night," the patriots streamed down to the waterfront, where, surrounded by an immense crowd of spectators, they made short work of the tea.

The Boston Tea Party was called "the boldest stroke which had yet been struck in America." It marked the beginning of violence in the dispute, hitherto waged chiefly with constitutional arguments, between mother country and colonies, and it put the most radical patriots in command throughout America. The efforts of the British government to single out Massachusetts for punishment served only to unite the colonies and hasten them into war with England.

BIBLIOGRAPHY

John C. Miller, *Sam Adams, Pioneer in Propaganda.*

C. H. Van Tyne, *The Causes of the War of Independence.*

— JOHN C. MILLER

BOXER REBELLION

Boxer Rebellion, an antiforeign uprising in China by members of a secret society known as Boxers, beginning in June 1900. A total of 231 foreigners and many Chinese Christians were murdered. On June 17 the Boxers began a siege of the legations in Peking. The United States joined Great Britain, Russia, Germany, France, and Japan in a military expedition for the relief of the legations, sending 5,000 troops for this purpose. The international relief expedition marched from Taku to Tientsin and thence to Peking, raising the siege on Aug. 14. The United States did not join in the punitive expedition under German Commander in Chief Count

The original caption to this undated engraving reads: Uncle Sam (to the obstreperous Boxer) "I occasionally do a little boxing myself." (Corbis-Bettmann)

von Waldersee. In July Secretary of State John Hay issued a circular note to "preserve Chinese territorial and administrative entity," and during the Peking Congress (Feb. 5–Sept. 7, 1901) the United States opposed the demand for a punitive indemnity, which might lead to the dismemberment of China. The Boxer protocol finally fixed the indemnity at $333 million, provided for the punishment of guilty Chinese officials, and permitted the major nations to maintain legation guards at Peking and between the capital and the sea. The U.S. share of the indemnity, originally set at $24.5 million but reduced to $12 million, was paid by 1924.

BIBLIOGRAPHY

Tyler Dennett, *Americans in Eastern Asia.*

H. B. Morse, *The International Relations of the Chinese Empire.*

— KENNETH COLEGROVE

BOYCOTTING

A boycott is a collective refusal to purchase commodities or services from a manufacturer or merchant whose employment or trade practices are regarded as unfair. Occasionally the economic boycott has been used by consumers against aggressor nations. Its chief use is by organized workers to secure better conditions of employment. Means for effecting a boycott include the distribution of cards, handbills, and lists of grievances and picketing.

In the United States the courts have made a distinction between primary and secondary boycotts. The former involves refusal of patronage by employees directly concerned in an industrial dispute; the latter involves attempts to persuade or coerce third parties to boycott an employer.

Considerable uncertainty and confusion characterize the law of boycotts in the United States, but a few general principles are fairly well established. In most jurisdictions it is not unlawful for an association of aggrieved workers to withhold patronage. Moreover, it does not appear to be unlawful in the several states for such workers to ask or persuade others to assist in their cause. It is illegal, however, to use physical violence, coercion, or intimidation. The behavior of pickets must be peaceful, and customers must be accorded complete freedom in entering and leaving the boycotted establishment.

The pivotal point in the law of boycotts is the use of pressure against third parties. Because most manufacturers do not distribute their goods directly but through wholesalers and retailers, organized labor can make a boycott effective only by bringing pressure upon such dealers. This is in essence a secondary boycott, which is regarded as unlawful in most jurisdictions. In Arizona, California, and Oklahoma all peacefully conducted boycotts have been held legal, and some of the lower courts of New York have sustained them. In Missouri and Montana the printing and distributing of circulars for purposes of boycott may not be directly enjoined by the courts.

The pivotal point in the law of boycotts is the use of pressure against third parties.

The boycott was held unlawful in the United States as early as 1886. In 1908 the Supreme Court in the Danbury hatters case decided that the secondary boycott constitutes a conspiracy in restraint of trade under the provisions of the Sherman Antitrust Act (1890). The Court held that treble damages might be recovered for losses sustained by the manufacturer through the interstate boycott. In the Buck Stove and Range Company case (1911), the same tribunal decided that all means employed to make effective an unlawful boycott are illegal, even though in themselves such means are innocent. Disregard of an injunction in this case by certain officials of the American Federation of Labor resulted in citation for contempt and jail sentence for one year. Although the sentence was subsequently set aside, the decision greatly discouraged the use of the boycott in labor disputes.

An attempt to escape from the restrictions of the Sherman act was made through section 20 of the Clayton Antitrust Act (1914), which prohibits the use of the injunction to restrain employees from picketing, boycotting, and advising others to withhold patronage from an employer when such activities are carried on by peaceful and lawful means. In the Duplex Printing Press Company case (1921), however, the Supreme Court ruled that all methods employed to make effective interstate boycotts involving third parties are unlawful.

Boycotts have also been used by unorganized groups appealed to through the press, mail, radio or television, or, in local instances, person to person. Informed by national news of a strike in California by the United Farm Workers, for example, some people across the nation stopped buying lettuce and other vegetables from that state. In the late 1960's, in protest against the policy of apartheid, U.S. college students carried on a campaign to force their institutions to rid their endowment funds of the securities of South African companies. On the local level consumer boycotts against anti-black discrimination on buses and in restaurants were successfully carried out in southern cities during the same decade.

Probably less successful, but still of some consequence, have been consumer boycotts in the 1970's against high meat prices. With national television networks, viewed daily by a large part of the total population, concerted boycotting action may be easier to achieve than ever before, and by means that make legal suppression difficult if not impossible.

BIBLIOGRAPHY

Francis B. Sayre, *Cases on Labor Law.*

— GORDON S. WATKINS

BRADDOCK'S EXPEDITION

On Apr. 14, 1755, Gen. Edward Braddock, appointed commander of all the British forces in America, was dispatched with two regiments for a campaign in the French and Indian War. The first objective was Fort Duquesne. The regulars and the colonial forces rendezvoused at Fort Cumberland, to start for Fort Duquesne by the route later called Braddock's Road. Wagons and horses were secured from Pennsylvania with Benjamin Franklin's aid; Indian allies came from Aughwick, but most of them deserted when Braddock ordered their families home.

The army, 2,200 strong, started west June 71 but had advanced only to Little Meadows (near Grantsville, Md.) by June 16. Then, on the advice of Lt. Col. George Washington, his aide-de-camp, Braddock pushed on rapidly with some 1,200 men and a minimum of artillery, leaving a command under Col. William Dunbar to bring up the heavier goods. On July 9 the expedition crossed and recrossed the Monongahela near Turtle Creek. Up to this point every precaution had been taken against surprise, but apparently the officers now grew overconfident. A hill commanding the route was left unoccupied, and the troops marched in an order too close for safety.

From Fort Duquesne Capt. Daniel Beaujeu led some 250 French and 600 Indians to oppose Braddock. He had not laid his ambush when the two parties unexpectedly met. The British opened fire, putting most of the French to flight and killing Beaujeu. His subordinate rallied the Indians to seize the hill that Braddock had neglected and to surround the British line. The van of the English, falling back, became entangled with the main body so that order was lost and maneuvering was impossible. For three hours the British stood under a galling fire; then Braddock ordered a retreat. The general was mortally wounded; many of the officers were killed; the retreat became a rout. Washington, sent to Dunbar by Braddock, reported the defeat and dispatched wagons for the wounded.

Dunbar, now in command, ordered quantities of stores destroyed, and retreated rapidly to Fort Cumberland. Refusing the request of Virginia and Pennsylvania that he build a fort at Raystown (Bedford, Pa.) and defend the frontier, he marched to Philadelphia in August and left the border to suffer Indian raids. Though Braddock's expedition failed, it demonstrated that an army could be marched over the Alleghenies, it taught the troops something of Indian fighting, and its very mistakes contributed to the success of the Forbes Expedition.

BIBLIOGRAPHY

Stanley Pargellis, "Braddock's Defeat," *American Historical Review* (1936).

Francis Parkman, *Montcalm and Wolfe.*

— SOLON J. BUCK

BRADY PHOTOGRAPHS

Brady Photographs, a collection of over 7,000 photographs (two negatives, in most cases) taken by Mathew B. Brady and his associates during the Civil War at an expenditure of over $100,000. They included portraits of officers and soldiers and scenes at the front and in the rear, along the battle lines from Washington to New Orleans.

The project bankrupted Brady, and the War Department acquired the plates and some negatives at public auction in 1874 for $2,840. Some copies of the photos are known to have passed into private hands. The largest collections are now in the National Archives and the Library of Congress.

BIBLIOGRAPHY

James D. Horan, *Mathew Brady: Historian With a Camera.*

F. T. Miller, *The Photographic History of the Civil War.*

— THOMAS ROBSON HAY

BROADWAY

Broadway, a street in New York City running the length of Manhattan. Most of the lower course of Broadway is said to follow the routes of old Indian trails. In New Amsterdam its first quarter mile was called the Heerewegh or Heere Straat. The name was anglicized to Broadway about 1668. Two public wells were dug in the middle of it in 1677 and abolished in 1806. The first paving, a ten-foot strip of cobblestones on each side of an earthen center, was done in 1707. The first sidewalks, four blocks on both sides, were laid in 1790. George Washington for a time during his presidency lived at 39 Broadway. In 1852 a franchise was granted for a cable-car line on Broadway, then the city's chief residential street. The line, which was fought in the courts for more than thirty years, was finally built in 1885, but long before that time the street had ceased to be residential and had become the main business thoroughfare of the city. As it progressed northward, it followed in general the line of the Bloomingdale Road to 207th Street. Beyond the Harlem River it becomes a part of the road to Albany. The first subway line under it was begun in 1900. In the latter 19th century theaters congregated along it, first below and then above Longacre (now Times) Square, until its name became a sym-

The first electric street lights in New York were placed on Broadway in 1880, and the brilliant lighting in the early 20th century brought it the nickname of the Great White Way.

bol for the American theater. The first arc electric street lights in New York were placed on Broadway in 1880 and the brilliant lighting in the early 20th century brought it the nickname of the Great White Way.

BIBLIOGRAPHY

Stephen Jenkins, *The Longest Street in the World.*

— ALVIN F. HARLOW

BROOKLYN BRIDGE

Brooklyn Bridge, the first bridge built across the East River between New York City and Brooklyn, and at the time the longest of all suspension bridges. There had been talk of bridging the river as early as 1840. The corporation to build the structure was organized in 1867, the city of Brooklyn subscribing for $3 million of the stock and New York for $1.5 million. John A. Roebling was chosen chief engineer, but he died in 1869, and his son Washington completed the task. The bridge was thirteen years in building, and cost $15.5 million. It was opened on May 24, 1883.

BIBLIOGRAPHY

David McCullough, *The Great Bridge.*

— ALVIN F. HARLOW

BROWN V. *BOARD OF EDUCATION OF TOPEKA*

Brown v. *Board of Education of Topeka*, two cases reaching the U.S. Supreme Court in 1954 and 1955 that were concerned with the legality of separation by race in public education. In the first case the Court held that segregation in public schools at all levels was illegal. In the second case it held that the pace of desegregation in schools was the responsibility of school authorities, would depend on the problems and conditions facing the individual community, and should be carried out "with all deliberate speed." After the 1955 decision, the case was returned to federal district courts for implementation. While *Brown* v. *Board of Education*, 347 U.S. 483 (1954), reversed *Plessy* v. *Ferguson* (1896), with its "separate but equal" ruling on railroad accommodations, the 1954 ruling came as a culmination of the legal debate on segregation in education before the courts since 1938. The earlier debate included the cases of *Gaines* v. *Canada* (1938), *Sipuel* v. *University of Oklahoma* (1948), *Sweatt* v. *Painter* (1950), *McLaurin* v. *Oklahoma State Regents* (1950), and *Byrd* v. *McCready* (1950). The *Brown* decision reflected no major shift of positions by the Court. The furor caused by the decision is more of a reflection on the opposition to the finding than on the novelty of the legal position.

Oliver Brown sued the Topeka, Kans., Board of Education when his daughter was denied admission to the school near her home because of her race. En route to the Supreme Court the case was combined with cases from three other states and one from the District of Columbia (*Davis* v. *County School Board of Prince Edward County, Harry Briggs, Jr.* v. *R. W. Elliot, Gebhart* v. *Bolton*, and *Bolling* v. *Sharpe*). In its 1954 decision the Court held that to separate Afro-American school children by race induces a sense of inferiority that retards educational and mental development, that "separate education facilities are inherently unequal," and that the plaintiffs were "by reason of the segregation complained of, deprived of the equal protection of the laws guaranteed by the Fourteenth Amendment." The decision limited its disapproval of the *Plessy* doctrine of "separate but equal" to education. Nevertheless it was construed to mean that racial segregation was not permissible in other public facilities; later Court action supported this view.

BIBLIOGRAPHY

Morroe Berger, *Equality by Statute.*
Loren Miller, *The Petitioner.*

— HENRY N. DREWRY

BUDGET, FEDERAL

The federal budget is submitted by the president to Congress every year in January, projects the expected revenues and the planned spending of the U.S. government for the fiscal year, which begins on October 1. The budget must be approved by Congress. The major sources of revenue for the federal government are personal income taxes and social security taxes, which in 1993 were 44 percent and 37 percent, respectively, of total revenues. The largest spending category is entitlements and other mandatory spending (such as social security and Medicare benefits), which in 1993 made up 54 percent of federal expenditures. Other major categories in that year were defense (21 percent), domestic discretionary spending (16 percent), and interest payments on the national debt (14 percent).

The budget is in deficit when expenditures exceed revenues. There has been a deficit every year since 1961 except 1969. Federal budget deficits are financed through the sale of government securities to the public. The deficit has been growing in absolute terms as well as relative to gross domestic product (GDP). During the 1960s the deficit averaged 0.85 percent of GDP, whereas during the 1970s it rose to 2.4 percent. During the 1980s it rose still further to 4.2 percent and by 1991–1993 the average was 4.6 percent of GDP. The sum total of all past deficits since the founding of the country (less debt repayment) is the national debt.

Public concern about budget deficits is based on three considerations. First, large budget deficits, if they occur at a time when the economy is at close to full employment, divert private savings from financing real capital formation (plant and equipment) to financing the deficit and thus retard the growth of both output and the standard of living. Second, under such circumstances large deficits may lead to accelerating inflation if the Federal Reserve, the nation's central bank, expands the money supply in an effort to keep interest rates from rising. Third, continuing large deficits may cause the national debt to grow more rapidly than GDP. As a result, taxes required to finance the interest costs of servicing the debt may pose growing burdens on future generations.

Several budget concepts are employed by economists and government officials. The standardized-employment deficit measures what would have resulted had the economy been operating at full employment. Because government tax revenues decline during a recession, this measure is preferable to recorded deficits for assessing the effect of the budget on the economy. Other concepts are the on-budget and primary budget deficits. The on-budget deficit excludes social security, and because the social security system has been running a surplus since 1985, the on-budget deficit is larger than the total deficit. The budget deficit exclusive of interest payments on the national debt is known as the primary budget deficit.

[See also Federal Reserve System.]

BIBLIOGRAPHY

B. Abel Andrew and Ben S. Bernanke, *Macroeconomics* (Reading, Mass., 1995).

Congressional Budget Office, *The Economic and Budget Outlook* (Washington, D.C., 1994).

— MICHAEL H. SPIRO

BULL MOOSE PARTY

Bull Moose Party, a popular nickname given to the Progressive party of 1912–16, which nominated Theodore Roosevelt for the presidency at a national convention in Chicago, Ill., in August 1912. The Progressives seceded from the Republican party following the renomination of President William H. Taft. The name itself was a tribute to Roosevelt, who often used the term "bull moose" to describe the strength and vigor of a person.

Thus he wrote, following his nomination for the vice-presidency on the Republican ticket in 1900, in a letter to Sen. Mark A. Hanna, "I am as strong as a bull moose and you can use me to the limit." Also, when shot by a would-be assassin in Milwaukee, Wis., on the evening of Oct. 14, 1912, he insisted on immediately filling an engagement to speak, saying to the audience, "It takes more than that to kill a bull moose."

The party was in large part reunited with and reabsorbed into the Republican party during the campaign of 1916, after the nomination of Charles Evans Hughes, who was acceptable to Roosevelt and the leading Progressives.

BIBLIOGRAPHY

J. B. Bishop, *Theodore Roosevelt and His Time.*

— WILLIAM STARR MYERS

BUNKER HILL

Bunker Hill (June 17, 1775). To force the British from Boston, on the night of June 16 the American militia besieging the town sent 1,200 men to seize Bunker Hill, on the peninsula of Charlestown. Instead, the detachment built a small redoubt on Breed's Hill, nearer Boston but easily flanked. Working silently, they were not discovered until daybreak, when British warships, anchored below, opened an ineffective fire. Col. William Prescott, commanding in the redoubt, strengthened his left flank, toward the Mystic River, by a breastwork, a rail fence stuffed with hay, and a slight defense of stones on the beach. The defenders of these were joined by perhaps 2,000 men, and were commanded by Maj. Gen. Israel Putnam, while in the redoubt Brig. Gen. Joseph Warren served as a volunteer. Meanwhile, under the command of Maj. Gen. Sir William Howe, 2,000 British infantry, with a few field guns, landed below the redoubt.

Dividing his men into two wings, early in the afternoon Howe attacked both the redoubt and the rail fence, expecting first to turn the fence by a column along the beach, which would make it easily possible to storm in front. The attack was bloodily repulsed by the provincials, chiefly New Hampshire men under John Stark, and the remainder of the British withdrew after being but briefly in touch with the Americans. At the second attack the British advanced on both wings with great courage; but the provincials, as before holding their fire until the regulars were close, cut them to pieces and forced their withdrawal. Still trusting to the desperate frontal attack, in the final attempt Howe merely feinted against the fence, and for the first time attacked the redoubt with the bayonet. For the first time, also, his fieldpieces got within effective range and drove the defenders from the breastwork. What would have happened had the Americans had enough powder cannot be known; but Prescott's men were out of ammunition and, after a first severe fire, on his order, quit the redoubt. In this assault fell Maj. John Pitcairn, British commander at Lexington, and Joseph Warren. The defenders of the fence covered the American retreat. After an engagement lasting less than two hours, the British were masters of the peninsula, but with heavy casualties of 1,054, while the Americans lost, in killed, wounded, and prisoners, but 441. At first regarded by the Americans as a defeat, Bunker Hill, because of the way in which militia resisted regulars, came to be regarded as a moral victory, leading to a dangerous overconfidence in unpreparedness.

BIBLIOGRAPHY

Allen French, *First Year of the American Revolution.*
Richard Frothingham, *History of the Siege of Boston.*
Don Higginbotham, *The War of American Independence.*

— ALLEN FRENCH

BURR CONSPIRACY

Burr Conspiracy, one of the most involved and mysterious episodes in early American history, and the climax of the dramatic struggle for power between President Thomas Jefferson and Aaron Burr, vice-president during Jefferson's first term. Essentially it was a compound of personal and political rivalry, discredited ambition, and land hunger.

Burr's exact intentions probably cannot ever be known. Following his duel with Alexander Hamilton in 1804, Burr became a creature of circumstances, hoping and scheming to regain something of his onetime popularity and power. To accomplish this he chose what he considered the most likely road to wealth and power—land conquest or seizure in Spanish territory west of the Mississippi.

Burr's first act was an attempt to attach England to his cause. Failing in this, he enlisted those who might be of help, yet never disclosed his exact intentions. Harman Blennerhassett, a trusting, visionary Irishman, who lived on an island in the Ohio River, was only one, though the most bizarre and reputedly the heaviest of the contributors to their venture. Burr went to the West, down the Mississippi River to New Orleans, and back overland, seeking friendly help and necessary funds. Returning to the East he sought successively to draw France and then Spain into his web of intrigue, but to no avail.

Before leaving Philadelphia in the summer of 1806, Burr wrote to his friend and co-conspirator Gen. James Wilkinson, who commanded the American army on the Mississippi, that the expedition would start for New Orleans before the end of the year. But Wilkinson, thoughtful for his own safety and uncertain as to Burr,

Following his duel with Alexander Hamilton in 1804, Aaron Burr became a creature of circumstances, scheming to regain something of his former power and popularity.

declined to be involved further. Instead, when Burr's advance flotilla reached the lower Mississippi, Wilkinson ordered its members arrested. As Burr came down he, too, was seized and then paroled. He attempted to escape to Spanish territory, but was again captured and taken East for trial. Burr was acquitted of treason and high misdemeanor, but the "conspiracy" had already collapsed.

BIBLIOGRAPHY

Thomas P. Abernethy, *The Burr Conspiracy.*
Herbert S. Parmet and M. B. Hecht, *Aaron Burr.*

— THOMAS ROBSON HAY

BURR-HAMILTON DUEL

The most famous duel in American history resulted in the mortal wounding of Alexander Hamilton at the hands of Aaron Burr, July 11, 1804. Burr issued his challenge ostensibly because Hamilton refused to disavow a "despicable opinion" of Burr, which he was reported to have expressed during Burr's unsuccessful New York governorship campaign in 1804. Actually, Burr vengefully blamed Hamilton for his defeat for the presidency of the United States in 1801. Hamilton had deflected Federalist votes to Jefferson, the Republican, rather than see his party elevate a man he deeply distrusted. Thus dashed—and snubbed as vice-president—Burr hoped to console himself as governor of New York. Hamilton feared that once in that office Burr would seek to head as dictator a secession, then brewing, of the New England and middle states from the Union.

Hamilton, morally opposed to dueling, doubted that his technical demurrer to Burr's charge would be accepted. Explaining his motives for meeting Burr, he admitted that he had been "extremely severe" in criticizing Burr's political and private character and said he believed that "the ability to be in future useful . . . in . . . public affairs" required him to conform to the prevailing code of honor. He rejected the plea of Rufus King, one of the few friends who knew of the threatened encounter, that he refuse to go to the field. He resolved, however, to throw away his first and perhaps even his second fire.

The duel took place beneath the Palisades at Weehawken, N.J. As Hamilton fell, he discharged his pistol wildly and, his second believed, involuntarily. After suffering excruciating pain from the ball lodged in his spine, Hamilton died the next day. Amid shocked mourning for Hamilton, Burr fled from the murder findings of coroners' juries. These charges were later quashed, but Burr's remaining years were doomed to discredit.

BIBLIOGRAPHY

Harold C. Syrett and Jean G. Cooke, *Interview at Weehawken: The Burr-Hamilton Duel as Told in Original Documents.*

— BROADUS MITCHELL

Drawing depicting the duel between Aaron Burr and Alexander Hamilton, 1804. (Corbis-Bettmann)

BURR TRIAL

The constitutional aspects of this trial have to do largely with the interpretation of the constitutional provision concerning treason. Aaron Burr was indicted for treason in 1807 and brought to trial in the U.S. Circuit Court at Richmond, Va., before Chief Justice John Marshall sitting as a circuit judge. The political passions of the times and the friction between President Thomas Jefferson and Marshall carried over into the trial and render appraisal difficult. An early incident of the trial was the Marshall opinion that a federal court might issue a subpoena *duces tecum* to the president of the United States. In guiding the jury as to the law of treason the chief justice gave an interpretation so restricting the meaning of the words "levying war" that in the case at hand only the assemblage at Blennerhassett Island could come within it. Burr, however much he may have counseled, advised, or planned that assemblage, was not present. Under the Marshall interpretation his absentee connection was not sufficient to render him guilty of treason. Marshall held that the broader definition asked by counsel for the prosecution would include the English doctrine of constructive treason, which the phrasing of the constitutional provision was intended to exclude. This statement of the law resulted in a verdict of acquittal. The chief justice was sharply criticized for inconsistency and bias, in that in a dictum in an earlier case in the Supreme Court involving two of Burr's messengers he had stated the law in a way which seemingly should have linked Burr with the treasonable assemblage.

BIBLIOGRAPHY

Reports of the Trials of Colonel Aaron Burr for Treason and for a Misdemeanor.

Thomas P. Abernethy, *The Burr Conspiracy.*

Herbert S. Parmet and M. B. Hecht, *Aaron Burr.*

— CARL BRENT SWISHER

C

CABEZA DE VACA, TRAVELS OF

In 1527, at the age of about thirty-seven, Álvar Núñez Cabeza de Vaca went to America as treasurer of the expedition led by Pánfilo de Narváez, which landed near the present city of Tampa, Fla., in April 1528. After a brief and disastrous exploration of the country the colonists built five horsehide boats and sailed for Cuba. A hurricane sank all but the one commanded by Cabeza de Vaca, and it soon was wrecked on the Texas coast. From the fall of 1528 to the spring of 1536 Cabeza de Vaca and his companions endured untold hardships, including imprisonment by Indians, in a 6,000-mile journey through the American Southwest and northern Mexico. After arriving safely in New Spain, Cabeza de Vaca returned to Old Spain to ask Charles V for the governorship of "La Florida." Instead he was given the governorship of Paraguay. His account of his travels was printed in 1555 at Valladolid, Spain, under the title *Relación y Comentarios.*

BIBLIOGRAPHY

Morris Bishop, *The Odyssey of Cabeza de Vaca.*

— A. CURTIS WILGUS

CABINET

This body, which has existed since the presidency of George Washington, rests on the authority of custom rather than the Constitution or statute. It is generally composed of the heads of the major federal administrative departments: State; Treasury; Defense; Justice; Interior; Agriculture; Commerce; Labor; Health, Education and Welfare; Housing and Urban Development; Transportation. In terms of money spent, number of persons employed, and scope of legal authority, these are the most significant units of the administration. The heads of these departments are presidential appointees, subject to confirmation by the Senate and serving at the pleasure of the president.

Although all presidents have, periodically, held formal cabinet meetings, the role of the cabinet in presidential decision making has generally been limited. The importance of the cabinet varies depending on the particular president (Dwight D. Eisenhower and Lyndon B. Johnson relied on the cabinet more than Franklin D. Roosevelt or John F. Kennedy did), but as a collective body it does not play a central role in any administration. Frequently cabinet meetings are largely symbolic; they are held because of the expectation that such meetings should take place. The cabinet collectively may lack significance; but individual members can have great influence in an administration because of their expertise, political skill, or special relationship to the president (for example, John Mitchell as attorney general under Richard M. Nixon; Secretary of Defense Robert McNamara under Kennedy and Johnson; and Attorney General Robert Kennedy under Kennedy). Frequently and increasingly, cabinet members are overshadowed by the expanding White House staff (personal assistants to the president). Also of considerable importance in any administration are informal advisers to and confidants of the president.

Cabinet members find that their survival and success generally do not depend on collegiality; often they must fend for themselves.

The cabinet in the United States, unlike that in most parliamentary systems, does not function as a collegial executive; the president clearly is the chief executive. Cabinet members in the course of their work find that their survival and success generally do not depend on their colleagues or on any sense of collegiality; rather, they must often fend for themselves. Particularly crucial are their own relationships to the president, the clientele of their agency, and Congress. Also, in contrast to parliamentary systems, U.S. cabinet members may not serve in the legislative body at the same time. If a person is a member of Congress when appointed to the cabinet, that person must resign the congressional seat.

BIBLIOGRAPHY

Richard F. Fenno, Jr., *The President's Cabinet.*
Louis Koenig, *The Chief Executive.*

— DALE VINYARD

CABOT VOYAGES

Early in 1496 a petition was placed before Henry VII of England in the name of John Cabot, an Italian navigator, and his three sons, Sebastian, Lewis, and Sanctius, for the privilege of making explorations in the New World. Letters patent dated Mar. 5, 1496, were granted to the Cabots, and in the spring of 1497 they sailed west from Bristol. Coasting southward they discovered, it is believed, Cape Breton Island and Nova Scotia. The following year letters patent were granted to John Cabot alone, authorizing him to make further explorations along the eastern coast of North America. The discoveries made on this voyage were supposedly recorded on a map and globe made by the explorer. Both are now lost. Because there is no firsthand data concerning the Cabot voyages, Sebastian Cabot has often been confused with his father, John. Important contributions to geographical knowledge were made by the Cabots, although the descriptions of the regions they explored apply to no portion of the United States.

BIBLIOGRAPHY

G. E. Nunn, *The La Cosa Map and the Cabot Voyages.*
J. A. Williamson, *Voyages of the Cabots and the English Discovery of North America Under Henry VII and Henry VIII.*

— LLOYD A. BROWN

CAHOKIA

Cahokia, the first permanent white settlement of consequence in Illinois, founded March 1699 by priests of the Seminary of Quebec who established the Mission of the Holy Family. Their chapel, which became the nucleus of the village, was located near the left bank of the Mississippi River, a short distance south of the present city of East Saint Louis. Cahokia took its name from the adjacent Indian village, which in 1699 contained about 2,000 Tamarca and Cahokia.

The mission at Cahokia quickly attracted French settlers, principally from Canada, occasionally from Louisiana. Their number, however, was never large. A census in 1723 enumerated only twelve white residents, while at Kaskaskia and Fort de Chartres, the other principal settlements, 196 and 126 were counted. In 1767, after many French had moved to Saint Louis because of the cession of the Illinois country to Great Britain, Cahokia contained 300 whites and 80 blacks—about half the population of Kaskaskia. By 1800 its population had increased to 719, while that of Kaskaskia had dropped to 467.

Throughout the 18th century Cahokia exemplified several of the features of a typical French village. There was a common pasture land and a large common field divided into strips for cultivation. The church was the center of village life and the priest the most influential resident. Most of the inhabitants were *coureurs de bois*, voyageurs, and traders who mingled freely with the Indians. English and American travelers usually criticized their squalor and lack of enterprise, but they noted also a carefree gaiety impervious to the hardships and uncertainties of their way of life.

Although Cahokia became the seat of Saint Clair County, the first county organized in Illinois, its growth was not commensurate with that of the territory. In 1927 the village was incorporated, and in 1970 had a population of more than 20,000.

BIBLIOGRAPHY

C. W. Alvord, *Cahokia Records, 1778–1790.*
Gilbert J. Garraghan, "New Light on Old Cahokia," *Illinois Catholic Historical Review* (1928).

— PAUL M. ANGLE

CALIFORNIA ALIEN LAND LAW

To check the increasing competition of Japanese immigrant farmers, the California legislature passed the Alien Land Law of 1913. The act was amended and extended by popular initiative in 1920 and by the legislature in 1923 and 1927. These laws expressly permitted aliens who were eligible for American citizenship to acquire, enjoy, and transfer real property in the state to the same extent as citizens of the United States. On the other hand, individual aliens who were not eligible for citizenship and corporations in which a majority of members were such aliens, or in which a majority of the capital stock was owned by them, were permitted to hold real property only as stipulated in existing treaties between the United States and their respective countries. The law was repealed in 1955 after it was ruled that the law violated the Fourteenth Amendment.

— P. ORMAN RAY

CAMPAIGNS, PRESIDENTIAL

Presidential campaigns have taken place in the United States every fourth year, beginning in 1788. They include both the process of candidate nomination and the subsequent campaign for election. Since the 1830's, nomination has centered on national party conventions called to choose individuals to run for president and vice-president and to adopt the party's platform. Delegate selection for these conventions was for a long time wholly extralegal and determined by local party traditions. Early in the 20th century some states set up presidential primaries to choose delegates and record voter preferences among the aspiring candidates. In the late 1960's a further reform movement began to broaden the ability of party members to participate in delegate selection and to reduce the influence of party organizations.

An incumbent president who desires renomination usually obtains it without a convention contest. If he does not want it or has already served two terms, the convention makes the final choice, sometimes only after a lengthy and bitter struggle. Since the late 1950's, rapid modes of transportation and ease of communication have often enabled one candidate to build up a strong lead prior to the convention and to win on the first ballot. Thus, the preconvention campaign has become the decisive part of the nominating process. Broadening public participation has reduced the role of state party leaders and hence has also reduced past practices of convention bargaining among politicians who control blocs of delegates.

Candidates for president were often chosen from among successful governors, especially the governors of key states like Ohio and New York, which have large blocs of electoral votes. Men who had made their reputations as military leaders were also frequent choices. After World War II the trend was away from governors in favor of U.S. senators because of greatly increased American concern with foreign relations and the greater national "visibility" senators can acquire.

Once chosen, the presidential candidate selects a new national party chairman and sets up his own campaign organization. In the 19th century the nominee himself did little stumping and conducted instead a "front porch" campaign, but the 20th century saw a tendency for increased candidate involvement, often reaching a frantic pace after the middle of the century. From the 1920's on, radio figured prominently in getting the candidates' messages disseminated; since the 1952 campaign, television has been the key medium. Generally the media increased in importance as grass-roots party organization declined in vigor and usefulness. Public relations experts and opinion pollsters also came to occupy crucial roles in campaign management.

Little has changed overall in the extent to which presidential campaigns emphasize general appeals and slogans rather than focus on clear-cut issues. With communications improvements, these appeals are more often carefully designed for national audiences instead of being tailored to each local group encountered on a campaign tour. Nevertheless, the New Deal era and the elections of 1964 and 1972 did see issues posed more sharply than is usual.

BIBLIOGRAPHY

Nelson Polsby and Aaron Wildavsky, *Presidential Elections.*
Gerald Pomper, *Nominating the President: The Politics of Convention Choice.*

— ELMER E. CORNWELL, JR.

Campaigns of 1788 and 1792

These first two campaigns had no formal nominations, only one presidential candidate, and little opposition to the second choice. The Constitution ratified, the Continental Congress delayed three months before fixing the first Wednesday in January 1789 for choosing electors, the first Wednesday in February for their voting, and the first Wednesday in March for starting the new government. Pennsylvania, Maryland, and Virginia elected electors; the Massachusetts legislature chose from elected electors; New Hampshire's election failed and its legislature appointed electors, as did those of the remaining states. Thirteen states could cast ninety-one votes; but two states had not ratified, and one (New York) failed to elect or appoint electors; four electors failed to vote. George Washington received sixty-nine votes, one of the two votes of every elector. John Adams received thirty-four of the second votes, and the other thirty-five were scattered among ten different candidates (John Jay, Robert Harrison, John Rutledge, John Hancock, George Clinton, Samuel Huntington, John Milton, James Armstrong, Edward Telfair, and Benjamin Lincoln).

In 1792 fifteen states could cast 132 electoral votes. Alexander Hamilton's financial measures and the consolidation of national power (*see* Federalist Party) roused an opposition (Jeffersonian Antifederalists), which centered its efforts on the defeat of Adams by the Antifederalist George Clinton, since to defeat Washington was seen to be futile. The attempt failed. Washington's vote was again unanimous, and Adams defeated Clinton by seventy-seven votes to fifty.

BIBLIOGRAPHY

Edward A. Stanwood, *A History of the Presidency.*

— JOHN C. FITZPATRICK

Campaign of 1796

For the first time, the national election was contested by political parties. The French Revolution, the Genêt affair, and the Jay Treaty resulted in bitter partisanship. Without the modern machinery of nomination, the Federalists informally agreed upon John Adams as Washington's successor; with him they chose Thomas Pinckney. With more enthusiasm the Democratic-

Republicans chose their leaders, Thomas Jefferson and Aaron Burr. Electors were chosen in sixteen states—in six by popular vote, in ten by the legislature. Of the total electoral votes Adams secured seventy-one, Jefferson sixty-eight, Pinckney fifty-nine, Burr thirty, and the remaining forty-eight were divided among nine others.

BIBLIOGRAPHY

Edward A. Stanwood, *A History of the Presidency.*

— FRANK MONAGHAN

Campaigns of 1800 and 1804

The election of 1800 marks a turning point in American political history. Its preliminaries were expressed in the Virginia and Kentucky Resolutions proffered by Thomas Jefferson and James Madison as a party platform. Its party machinery, still more essential to success, was directed by Aaron Burr with supplemental support in Pennsylvania and South Carolina.

Burr had already established the nucleus of a political machine that was later to develop into Tammany Hall. With this organization he swept New York City with an outstanding legislative ticket, gained control of the state assembly, and secured the electoral votes of New York for the Democratic-Republicans. He had already secured a pledge from the Democratic-Republican members of Congress to support him equally with Jefferson. Hence the tie vote (seventy-three each) that gave him a dubious chance for the presidency. The Federalist candidates were John Adams, sixty-five votes, and Charles Cotesworth Pinckney, sixty-four votes.

Publicly disclaiming any intent to secure the presidency, Burr was, nevertheless, put forward by the Federalists in order to defeat Jefferson and bring about another election. A slight majority in the House of Representatives enabled them to rally six states to Burr and divide the vote of two others, thus neutralizing the vote of the eight states that supported Jefferson. The contest was prolonged through thirty-five fruitless ballotings; on the thirty-sixth, by prearrangement, a sufficient number of Federalists cast blank ballots to give Jefferson ten states and the presidency.

This narrow escape from frustrating the popular will led the incoming administration to pass the Twelfth Amendment to the Constitution, separating the balloting for president and vice-president, in time for the 1804 election. Jefferson covertly helped eliminate Burr in New York, and the party caucus brought George Clinton forward as candidate for the vice-presidency. Burr, already divining his political ostracism, attempted to recover ground as an independent candidate for governor of New York. Representative Federalists of New England sought his support in their plans for disunion, but he refused to commit himself to such a program. The Federalists selected Pinckney as their presidential candidate, and chose Rufus King for the vice-presidency. Jefferson, preeminently successful in the more important measures of his administration, was triumphantly reelected in 1804 as president with Clinton as vice-president.

[See also Jefferson-Burr Electoral Dispute.]

BIBLIOGRAPHY

Edward A. Stanwood, *A History of the Presidency.*

— ISAAC J. COX

Campaigns of 1808 and 1812

Candidates for the Democratic-Republican nomination in 1808 were James Madison, the choice of Thomas Jefferson; James Monroe, somewhat tainted by affiliation with John Randolph and the Quids, who were anathema to the outgoing administration; and George Clinton, a New Yorker not favored by the Virginia dynasty. Jefferson's own refusal to consider a third term confirmed the two-term tradition for a president. At the party caucus Madison received eighty-three votes; his rivals, three each.

The Federalist opposition was led by Charles Pinckney and Rufus King, but the chief obstacle to the Madison slate came from his own party, notably in Virginia and Pennsylvania, where William Duane, a powerful journalist, was unreconcilable. The malcontents finally voted the party ticket, and in the electoral college Madison obtained 122 out of 176 votes. Clinton ran far behind on the presidential ticket, but became vice-president by a wide margin. Defeated for the presidency, the Federalists nevertheless made serious inroads upon the Republican majority in the House of Representatives.

In 1812 Madison secured his renomination by a tacit rather than a formal yielding to the demands of Henry Clay and the war hawks. Clinton having died in office, the vice-presidential nomination, tendered first to John Langdon of New Hampshire, went to Elbridge Gerry of Massachusetts. Opposition to the party slate was led by DeWitt Clinton of New York, who finally accepted nomination from the prowar Republicans, with the endorsement of the Federalists. Jared Ingersoll of Pennsylvania was nominated as his running mate. The electoral college gave Madison 128 votes, as against 89 for Clinton. Vermont and Pennsylvania stood by Madison, but New York was led by Martin Van Buren into the Clinton column. Gerry and the ticket could not carry the candidate's own state of Massachusetts, notwithstanding his recent election as governor. Thus, at the beginning of the War of 1812, the Republican party was seriously divided.

BIBLIOGRAPHY

K. C. Babcock, *The Rise of American Nationality.*
Edward Channing, *The Jeffersonian System.*

— LOUIS MARTIN SEARS

Campaigns of 1816 and 1820

There was no campaign by parties in 1816 worth the name, none at all in 1820. President James Madison's choice was James Monroe, old Jeffersonian protégé, secretary of state and war. Some Democratic-Republicans favored Gov. Daniel D. Tompkins of New York. Younger Republicans, interested in nationalist measures following the War of 1812, including a bank, protective tariffs, and internal improvements to speed the development of the West, preferred William H. Crawford, secretary of the treasury and citizen of Georgia. They gave him fifty-four votes in the congressional caucus to sixty-five for Monroe. In the electoral college Monroe overwhelmed Rufus King, signer of the Constitution and statesman of note, but a Federalist whose party now was thoroughly discredited by the Hartford Convention. Monroe was given 183 votes to 34 for King.

Newer sectional conflicts and rivalry among the younger leaders embittered the Era of Good Feelings, but President Monroe was secure. He was reelected in 1820, with only one dissenting electoral vote (cast by William Plummer of New Hampshire for John Quincy Adams). Federalists saw a greater menace to their propertied interests rising with the democracy of the West; it was to dethrone "King Caucus" (the congressional caucus nominating system) and the Virginia dynasty in the free-for-all campaign of 1824.

BIBLIOGRAPHY

Edward A. Stanwood, *A History of the Presidency.*

— ARTHUR B. DARLING

Campaign of 1824

With the second inauguration of James Monroe in 1820, preparations began for the next campaign, which was to mark the beginning of the transition from federalism to democracy with resulting voter realignment under new party emblems. The five candidates were prominent in national affairs and represented sections or factions rather than parties. In general, the politicians supported William H. Crawford; John Quincy Adams represented business; John C. Calhoun, the South and the rising slavocracy; Henry Clay, the expanding West; and Andrew Jackson, the people everywhere. The first three were cabinet members, Clay was speaker of the House, and Jackson was the country's most popular military figure.

Crawford was virtually eliminated by a paralytic stroke; Jackson was brought in late by his friends; Clay's support was never impressive; and Calhoun withdrew and became candidate for vice-president on both the Adams and Jackson tickets. No candidate received a majority electoral vote. Jackson secured the greatest number, 99; Adams, 84; Crawford, 41; and Clay, 37. Selection was made by the House of Representatives and Adams was chosen. Jackson's supporters charged that a "corrupt bargain" had been made when it was learned that Clay threw his support to Adams in exchange for the position of secretary of state.

BIBLIOGRAPHY

Bennett Champ Clark, *John Quincy Adams.*
Marquis James, *Andrew Jackson: Portrait of a President.*

— THOMAS ROBSON HAY

Campaigns of 1828 and 1832

In 1828 President John Quincy Adams stood for reelection on the National Republican ticket and Andrew Jackson of Tennessee made his second campaign for the presidency, his supporters now being called Democrats. Designated the people's candidate by the action of friends in the legislature of his own state, Jackson won and held the necessary support of influential leaders in New York, Pennsylvania, and South Carolina. The campaign was waged throughout the administration of Adams. It was not marked by any clear-cut declaration of political principle or program, and Jackson came to think of it as a personal vindication. Of the twenty-four states, Delaware and South Carolina still expressed their choice by vote of the legislature. In twenty-two states the elections were held in the period from late October to early December. There was a great increase in the popular vote cast, and both candidates shared in the increase: 647,286 being cast for Jackson and 508,064 for Adams. The electoral vote stood 178 for Jackson to 83 for Adams. John C. Calhoun of South Carolina was again elected vice-president. In many parts of the nation there was evidence of a more effective organization of the vote than in any previous contest, yet over and above all considerations in this election was the appeal that the frontier hero made to an increasing body of democratically minded voters. Jackson himself was the cause of an alignment of public opinion in the years that followed (*see* Jacksonian Democracy). Jackson men controlled the Congress, and platforms and programs were supported by leaders and sections and groups, but not by clearly defined political parties.

Naturally Jackson stood for reelection in 1832, although he had spoken in favor of a single term, and the campaign to renominate him began at once. After December of 1831, when Henry Clay returned to the Senate, he, rather than Adams, received the support of most of those who were opposed to Jackson. This did not include Calhoun, who in 1830 had broken with Jackson. Clay was formally presented by a national convention that met in December of 1831. He was endorsed by a national convention of young men, which prepared a platform in a meeting held in May of 1832. In that month a national convention of Jackson supporters nominated Martin Van Buren of New York for the vice-presidency. In this election the recently gathered Anti-Masonic party supported William Wirt of Maryland. The campaign not only witnessed the general use of the national party convention, but platforms were presented and cartoons freely used, and there was concentration of popular attention upon the pageantry of parades. Aside from the personal contest between Jackson and Clay the issue between the two centered on Jackson's attack on the Bank of the United States and particularly his veto of the bill for the recharter of the bank, a bill that had the backing of the supporters of Clay in both houses of Congress. Twenty-four states participated in this election, and all except South Carolina provided a popular vote. The electorate endorsed the administration of Jackson, for the distribution of the vote in twenty-three states gave Jackson 687,502, Clay 530,189, and Wirt 101,051. In the electoral college the vote stood Jackson 219, Clay 49, Wirt 7, with 11 votes representing the vote of South Carolina cast for John Floyd of Virginia.

BIBLIOGRAPHY

Claude G. Bowers, *Party Battles of the Jackson Period.*
S. R. Gammon, *The Presidential Campaign of 1832.*

— EDGAR EUGENE ROBINSON

Campaign of 1836

Made up chiefly of Anti-Masons, National Republicans, and anti-Jackson Democrats, the Whig party, formed in 1834, naturally lacked unity. Because of this, the Whig leaders decided to put forward several sectional candidates in the 1836 presidential campaign. Accordingly, Judge Hugh L. White was entered in the race through nomination by legislative caucuses in Tennessee and Alabama, held in January 1835. At about the same time, Judge John McLean was nominated by a legislative caucus in Ohio, but he withdrew from the race in the following August. Sen. Daniel Webster was nominated by a Massachusetts legislative caucus, also in January 1835. Still another candidate of the Whigs was Gen. William H. Harrison, who was formally nominated by both Anti-Masonic and Whig state conventions in Pennsylvania in December 1835.

Meanwhile, at the Democratic National Convention held in Baltimore on May 21–22, 1835, Martin Van Buren, who was President Andrew Jackson's personal choice, had been unanimously nominated for the presidency. No platform was adopted by the convention, but a committee was authorized to draw up an address. Published in the party organ, the Washington *Globe*, on Aug. 26, 1835, this address presented Van Buren as one who would, if elected, continue "that wise course of national policy pursued by Gen. Jackson." For all practical purposes, this address may be regarded as the first platform ever issued by the Democratic party.

When the election returns were finally in, Van Buren had won the presidency with 170 electoral votes and a popular vote of 765,483 to 739,795 for his opponents. White received 26 electoral votes, Webster 14, and Harrison 73, while South Carolina bestowed its 11 votes on W. P. Mangum. No candidate for the vice-presidency received a majority of the electoral vote, so on Feb. 8, 1837, the Senate chose the Democratic candidate, Richard M. Johnson, over his leading rival, Francis Granger.

BIBLIOGRAPHY

Edward A. Stanwood, *A History of the Presidency.*

— ERIK MCKINLEY ERIKSSON

Campaign of 1840

Distinctive in American history as the first national victory of the Whig party, the campaign of 1840 was unique for its popular and emotional appeal, organized on an unprecedented scale. To the Whigs belongs the credit of introducing into a presidential battle every political device calculated to sway the "common man."

The Whig convention, assembled at Harrisburg, Pa., Dec. 2, 1839, nominated Gen. William Henry Harrison of Indiana for president and John Tyler of Virginia for vice-president. No attempt was made to frame a platform; indeed, the only bond uniting the various groups under the Whig banner was a determination to defeat the Democrats. The Democratic convention held at Baltimore, May 5, 1840, was united on Martin Van Buren for president, but the choice of a vice-president was left to the state electors. A platform on strict construction lines was adopted.

The Whigs conducted their campaign at a rollicking pitch. Harrison was adroitly celebrated as the "Hard Cider and Log Cabin" candidate, a phrase which the Democrats had used in contempt. Popular meetings, "log cabin raisin's," oratory, invective against Van Buren the aristocrat, songs and slogans ("Tippecanoe and Tyler Too") swamped the country. In the election Harrison polled an electoral vote of 234, a popular vote of 1,274,624; Van Buren received 60 electoral votes and 1,127,781 popular votes. A minor feature in the campaign was the appearance of an abolition (the Liberty) party, whose candidate, James G. Birney, received 7,069 votes. Although the causes for Van Buren's defeat should be traced back to opposition to Jackson, the Panic of 1837, the unpopular Seminole War, and the campaign methods employed by the Whigs contributed largely to Harrison's success.

BIBLIOGRAPHY

D. B. Goebel, *William Henry Harrison.*
Edward A. Stanwood, *A History of the Presidency.*

— DOROTHY BURNE GOEBEL

Campaign of 1844

No outstanding Democratic candidate could muster the necessary two-thirds vote in the 1844 convention, so James K. Polk of Tennessee, the first "dark horse," was nominated, with George M. Dallas of Pennsylvania as running mate, on a platform demanding "the re-annexation of Texas and the re-occupation of Oregon" and in favor of tariff reform. The Whigs nominated Henry Clay of Kentucky and Theodore Frelinghuysen of New Jersey, on a platform favoring protective tariff and a national bank but quibbling on the Texas annexation issue, which alienated some of the Whigs. The Liberty party unanimously selected James G. Birney as its presidential candidate. Polk carried New York by a small popular majority and was elected, with 170 electoral votes to 105 for Clay. The popular vote was Polk, 1,338,464; Clay, 1,300,097; Birney, 62,300.

BIBLIOGRAPHY

Edward A. Stanwood, *A History of the Presidency.*

— WALTER PRICHARD

Campaign of 1848

The Whig nominee, Zachary Taylor, who sidestepped the burning issue of slavery extension, coasted to victory on his military reputation with Millard Fillmore as his vice-president. His Democratic opponent, Gen. Lewis Cass of Michigan, straddled the slavery extension question by advocating state sovereignty. The new Free Soil party, specifically opposed to extension and headed by Martin Van Buren, split the Democratic vote in New York and thus contributed materially to Taylor's triumph. (Gerrit Smith, the National Liberty party candidate and staunch abolitionist, advised those who would not vote for an abolitionist to vote for Van Buren, rather than Cass.) Taylor carried half the states, eight in the South and seven in the North. The popular vote was Taylor, 1,360,967; Cass, 1,222,342; Van Buren, 291,263; Smith 2,733. The electoral vote was Taylor, 163; Cass, 127.

BIBLIOGRAPHY

Edward A. Stanwood, *A History of the Presidency.*

— HOLMAN HAMILTON

Campaign of 1852

The Whig party in 1852 was apathetic and demoralized by the slavery issue. Democratic victory seemed almost certain, but the question of greatest interest was who would be the Democratic candidate. After many ballots, the leading Democrats, Lewis Cass, James Buchanan, and Stephen Douglas, were eliminated and a dark horse, Franklin Pierce of New Hampshire, was nominated with William R. King of Alabama. The Whigs nominated the military hero Gen. Winfield Scott; the Free-Soilers nominated the antislavery leader John P. Hale of New Hampshire. Both major parties endorsed the Compromise of 1850, so there were no issues and little contest. Pierce carried all states save Massachusetts, Vermont, Kentucky, and Tennessee. The popular vote was Pierce, 1,601,117; Scott, 1,385,453; Hale, 155,825. The electoral vote was Pierce, 254; Scott, 42.

BIBLIOGRAPHY

Roy F. Nichols, *Franklin Pierce.*

— ROY F. NICHOLS

Campaign of 1856

The Republican party in its first presidential campaign nominated John C. Frémont of California. Its platform opposed slavery expansion and condemned slavery and Mormonism as twin relics of barbarism. The American, or Know-Nothing, party nominated Millard Fillmore, who had succeeded to the presidency following the death of Zachary Taylor. The Democrats nominated James Buchanan. John C. Breckinridge was selected as his running mate. Their conservative platform stressed states' rights, opposed sectionalism, and favored a somewhat ambiguous plank, giving popular sovereignty to the territories. The electoral vote was Buchanan, 174; Frémont, 114; Fillmore, 8. The popular vote was Buchanan, 1,832,955; Frémont, 1,339,932; Fillmore, 871,731. The Republicans rejoiced in their showing, having won the votes of eleven free states, while the Democrats congratulated themselves upon having saved the Union.

— PHILIP G. AUCHAMPAUGH

Campaign of 1860

The Democratic National Convention met amid great excitement and bitterness over the slavery issue, at Charleston, S.C., April 23, 1860. The delegates from the eight states of the far South (Southern Democrats) demanded the inclusion of a plank in the platform providing that Congress should guarantee slave property in the territories. This was refused, and after several days of useless wrangling and failure to unite the convention upon a candidate, adjournment was taken to Baltimore on June 18 following. At this meeting the convention nominated Stephen A. Douglas of Illinois for president, and later the national committee nominated Herschel V. Johnson of Georgia for vice-president. The platform pledged the party to stand by the Dred Scott decision or any future Supreme Court decision that dealt with the rights of property in the various states and territories. Southern Democrat delegates met separately at Baltimore on June 28, and nominated John C. Breckinridge of Kentucky for president and Joseph Lane of Oregon for vice-president. The platform reaffirmed the extreme southern view with regard to slavery. Meanwhile, the remains of the old-line Whig and American (Know-Nothing) parties had met in a convention at Baltimore on May 9 and adopted the name of the Constitutional Union party, also the platform of "the Constitution of the country, the Union of the States and the enforcement of the laws." They nominated John Bell of Tennessee for president and Edward Everett of Massachusetts for vice-president and attempted to ignore the slavery and other sectional issues, with a plea for the preservation of the Union.

The Republican National Convention had met in Chicago on May 16. By means of the platform issues of nonextension of slavery and of a homestead law and by advocacy of a protective tariff, the agricultural elements of the northern and western parts of the country and the industrial elements of Pennsylvania, New England, and other northern and eastern sections of the country were united. At first it seemed that the convention would nominate either William H. Seward of New York or Salmon P. Chase of Ohio, but a deadlock between their respective supporters being threatened the convention nominated Abraham Lincoln of Illinois on the third ballot. Hannibal Hamlin of Maine was nominated for vice-president on the second ballot.

The split in the Democratic party made possible the election of Lincoln. He received 180 electoral votes as against 72 for Breckinridge who carried the extreme southern states, and 39 for Bell who carried the border states. Douglas received but 12 (9 from Missouri and 3 of the 7 from New Jersey). The popular vote totaled 1,865,593 for Lincoln, 1,382,713 for Douglas, 848,356 for Breckinridge, and 592,906 for Bell. The combined opponents thus received 958,382 votes over Lincoln, who was a minority president during his first administration.

BIBLIOGRAPHY

W. S. Myers, *The Republican Party, A History.*
Edward A. Stanwood, *A History of the Presidency.*

— WILLIAM STARR MYERS

Campaign of 1864

A national convention was called in the name of "the executive committee created by the national convention held in Chicago on the sixteenth day of May 1860." The use of the name Republican was carefully avoided. The convention met in Baltimore on June 7, 1864, and named itself the National Union Convention. The Republican leaders desired to appeal to Union sentiment and do away as far as possible with partisan influence. The platform, which was unanimously adopted, was a statement of "unconditional Union" principles and pledged the convention to put down rebellion by force of arms. Abraham Lincoln was nominated for a second term by the vote of every delegate except those from Missouri, who had been instructed to vote for Gen. Ulysses S. Grant. The nomination then was made unanimous. Andrew Johnson of Tennessee, a leading Southern Democrat who had been staunch in his loyalty to the Union, was nominated for vice-president.

The Democratic party met in convention on Aug. 29, at Chicago. Its platform declared the war a failure and advocated the immediate cessation of hostilities and the restoration of the Union by peaceable means. The convention nominated Gen. George B. McClellan for president and George H. Pendleton for vice-president. McClellan accepted the nomination but at the same time virtually repudiated the platform, for he was thoroughly loyal to the cause of the Union.

At first it appeared that the Democrats might defeat Lincoln, but the victories of the Union army in the field proved that the war was not a failure and rallied the people to the support of Lincoln and Johnson and the Union cause. The election took place on Nov. 8. For the first time in U.S. history certain states, those of the South, deliberately declined to choose electors for the choice of president. Lincoln carried every state that took part in the election but New Jersey, Delaware, and Kentucky. He received 212 electoral votes. McClellan received 21. Lincoln was given a popular majority of only 403,151 in a total of 4,010,725. This election was one of the most vital in the history of the country since upon its result might depend the perpetuation of the national Union.

BIBLIOGRAPHY

W. S. Myers, *General George B. McClellan.*
Edward A. Stanwood, *A History of the Presidency.*

— WILLIAM STARR MYERS

Campaigns of 1868 and 1872

The issues in 1868 were southern Reconstruction and the "Ohio Idea" (payment of the national debt in greenbacks). Horatio Seymour of New York and Frank Blair of Missouri, the Democratic nominees, ran on a platform calling for a restoration of the rights of the southern states and payment of the war bonds in greenbacks. Alarmed by Democratic victories in 1867, the Republicans nominated the war hero, Ulysses S. Grant, and Schuyler Colfax of Indiana. Their platform acclaimed the success of Reconstruction and denounced as repudiation the payment of the bonds in greenbacks.

Personal attacks on the candidates and Republican "waving the bloody shirt" featured the campaign. An effort to replace the Democratic nominees in October failed but foreshadowed defeat. Grant received 214 electoral votes to Seymour's 80, and nearly 53 percent of the popular vote, receiving 3,013,421 votes to 2,706,829 for Seymour. Seymour carried eight states. The result was a personal victory for Grant rather than for Republican policies.

Dissatisfaction with the Reconstruction policy and a desire for reform led to a Liberal Republican organization, supported by tariff and civil-service reformers, independent editors, and disgruntled politicians. The new party nominated Horace Greeley, with B. Gratz Brown of Missouri, to oppose Grant's reelection in 1872. (Grant's running mate in this campaign was Henry Wilson of Massachusetts.) Its platform demanded civil-service reform, universal amnesty, and specie payment. The tariff issue was straddled to please Greeley, a protectionist. The Democrats accepted the Liberal Republican platform and nominees. The Greeley campaign lacked enthusiasm, and he was mercilessly lampooned. Grant received 286 electoral votes to Greeley's 66 and over 55 percent of the popular vote, receiving 3,596,745 votes to 2,843,446 for Greeley. Greeley died shortly after the election and before the electoral college met. His electoral votes were scattered among four other candidates.

BIBLIOGRAPHY

C. H. Coleman, *The Election of 1868.*
E. D. Ross, *The Liberal Republican Movement.*

— CHARLES H. COLEMAN

Campaign of 1876

This campaign is especially notable because it resulted in the famous disputed presidential election. The leading aspirant for the Republican nomination was James G. Blaine of Maine. His name was presented to the national convention at Cincinnati by Robert G. Ingersoll in a striking speech in which he dubbed Blaine "the Plumed Knight." Among the other candidates were Benjamin H. Bristow of Kentucky, Roscoe Conkling of New York, Oliver P. Morton of Indiana, and Rutherford B. Hayes of Ohio. For six ballots Blaine led the field, but his involvement in a scandal brought to light a few weeks before the Republican convention caused a stampede to Hayes on the seventh ballot, resulting in his nomination. William A. Wheeler of New York was named as his running mate. The platform endorsed the Resumption Act and eulogized the Republican party for its work during the Civil War and Reconstruction.

Thomas F. Bayard of Delaware, Allen G. Thurman of Ohio, Winfield Scott Hancock of Pennsylvania, and Thomas A. Hendricks of Indiana sought the Democratic nomination, but the logical contender was Gov. Samuel J. Tilden of New York, who was named on the first ballot. Hendricks was then nominated for the vice-presidency. The scandals of the Grant administration were denounced in unsparing terms and "reform" was declared to be the paramount issue. Repeal of the clause of the act of 1875 providing for the resumption of specie payments was advocated, but Tilden personally was known to be a sound-money man rather than a Greenbacker. The platform also declared in favor of civil-service reform.

In the campaign the Democratic speakers dwelt heavily upon the scandals under Republican rule and contended that only through a change of men and parties could there be any real reform. Republican orators resorted to "bloody shirt" tactics (that is, revived the Civil War issues), questioned Tilden's loyalty during that conflict, and praised Hayes's military record—four honorable wounds and a brevet major generalcy. In the North the campaign was a quiet one, but in some of the southern states attempts to intimidate Afro-American voters produced violent disorders and considerable bloodshed.

Early returns on election night indicated the election of Tilden, but presently it appeared that the result would be in doubt. When the electoral college met and voted, Tilden received 184 unquestioned votes, Hayes 165. The 4 votes of Florida, the 8 votes of Louisiana, the 7 votes of South Carolina, and 1 vote of Oregon were claimed by both parties. After a protracted, bitter dispute, Congress created an electoral commission of five senators, five representatives, and five judges of the Supreme Court to help decide the result. Of the senators, three were to be Republicans and two Democrats; of the representatives, three were to be Democrats and two Republicans; four of the judges, two Republicans and two Democrats, were designated by their districts, and they were to choose the fifth judge. It was expected that the fifth judge would be David Davis, but his election to the Senate by the Democrats in the Illinois legislature gave him an excuse to decline the thankless task. The choice then fell upon Joseph P. Bradley, who had been appointed to the bench as a Republican, but some of whose decisions made him acceptable, temporarily, to the Democrats.

In case the two houses of Congress voting separately refused to accept any return, the dispute was to be referred to the commission, whose decision was to be final unless it was rejected by both houses. The two houses, voting separately on strict party lines, did disagree. Decision, therefore, rested with the commission, which, in all cases, by a vote of eight to seven (Bradley voting with the majority), refused to go against the election results as certified by the state authorities (in the case of Oregon by the secretary of state) and declared in favor of the Republican contenders. In each case the Senate accepted this decision, the House rejected it. All the disputed votes were therefore counted for Hayes and Wheeler and they were declared elected.

BIBLIOGRAPHY

J. H. Dougherty, *The Electoral System of the United States.*

P. L. Haworth, *The Hayes-Tilden Election.*

— PAUL L. HAWORTH

Campaign of 1880

Taking place during a business revival and with no definite issue before the country, the 1880 campaign was routine politics. The Republicans overcame a serious split between groups headed by James G. Blaine and Roscoe Conkling by nominating James A. Garfield, a member of neither faction, over former President Ulysses S. Grant, supported by the Conkling wing for a third term. The Conkling faction was appeased by the nomination of Chester A. Arthur for the vice-presidency. Against Garfield the Democrats nominated Winfield Scott Hancock, a nonpolitical Civil War general; but their party had no positive program, was discredited by its factious opposition to the Hayes administration, and was defeated by a close vote. The Republicans carried the "doubtful states" and regained control over Congress. The popular vote was Garfield, 4,453,295; Hancock, 4,414,082. The electoral vote was Garfield, 214; Hancock, 155.

BIBLIOGRAPHY

E. E. Oberholtzer, *United States Since the Civil War*, vol. IV.

T. C. Smith, *Life of James A. Garfield.*

— THEODORE CLARK SMITH

Campaign of 1884

Fought primarily between James G. Blaine, Republican, and Grover Cleveland, Democrat, the campaign of 1884 was one of the most vituperative in American history. There were several reasons why it became relentlessly personal in character. From the moment of Blaine's nomination at Chicago on June 6 he came under heavy fire from the reform element of all parties. He was believed to be allied with the spoils element in Republican politics; he had an unhappy record for baiting the South; he favored certain big business interests; and his railroad transactions had raised a suspicion that he had used his position as speaker of the House for personal profit. To divert attention from these attacks certain Republicans published evidence that Cleveland, nominated on July 10 at Chicago, was the father of an illegitimate son born in Buffalo some ten years earlier. There were virtually no serious issues between the two parties; both had good reason not to meddle seriously with the currency question or tariff, and international affairs attracted little attention. One leading feature of the campaign was the secession of a large body of Republicans who could not stomach Blaine and who became Cleveland Democrats, or Mugwumps. Another feature was the open enmity of Tammany Hall, under political boss John Kelly, for Cleveland, and the success of it and other malcontents in carrying many Irish voters over to Blaine or to the new Antimonopoly party headed by Benjamin F. Butler. After exchanges that one observer compared to the billingsgate of quarreling tenement dwellers, the two parties approached election day running neck and neck. Democratic victory was finally decided by the vote of New York state, in which the Rev. Samuel D. Burchard's "rum, Romanism and rebellion" speech at a reception for Blaine, the "Belshazzar's feast" of Republican millionaires and politicians at Delmonico's just before election, and Roscoe Conkling's knifing of Blaine all played a part. Cleveland and his running mate, Thomas A. Hendricks, obtained a popular vote of 4,879,507 against Blaine's 4,850,293, and an electoral vote of 219 against Blaine's 182. Butler's popular vote was just over 175,000, and that of John P. St. John, Prohibition candidate, was just over 150,000.

BIBLIOGRAPHY

Allan Nevins, *Grover Cleveland—A Study in Courage.*

— ALLAN NEVINS

Campaign of 1888

The tariff was the chief issue of this campaign, which resulted in the election of Republican candidate Benjamin Harrison over Grover Cleveland by a majority of the electoral college but not of the popular vote. The Republicans had approached the election with scant hope of victory, for Cleveland had proved an admirable president, when his annual message of 1887, devoted entirely to arguments for tariff reform, gave them new heart. The issue was one on which they could rally nearly all manufacturers, most general business, and perhaps a majority of workingmen. Benjamin Harrison, who represented extreme high-tariff demands, was nominated by the Republicans at Chicago on June 25, after James G. Blaine had withdrawn for reasons of health, and John Sherman and Walter Q. Gresham, whose tariff views were moderate, had failed to gain strength. Levi P. Morton was named for vice-president. Harrison, supported by Blaine, by manufacturing interests who were induced by the Republican chairman, Matthew S. Quay, to subscribe large campaign funds, and by Civil War veterans hungry for pension legislation, waged an aggressive campaign. His speechmaking abilities made a deep impression on the country. Cleveland, who was renominated by the Democrats at St. Louis early in June, felt that his presidential office made it improper for him to do active campaigning; his running mate, former Sen. Allen G. Thurman of Ohio, was too old and infirm to be anything but a liability to the party; and campaign funds were slender. Worst of all for the Democrats, their national chairman, Sen. Calvin S. Brice of Ohio, held high-tariff convictions, was allied with big business, and refused to put his heart into the battle. Two weeks before election day the Republicans published an indiscreet letter by Lord Sackville-West, the British minister, hinting to a supposed British subject that Cleveland would probably be more friendly to England than Harrison; and though Cleveland at once had Sackville-West recalled, the incident cost him many Irish-American votes. Cleveland received 5,537,857 popular votes, Harrison 5,447,129; but Cleveland had only 168 electors against Harrison's 233. Clinton B. Fisk of New Jersey, Prohibition candidate, polled 249,506 votes; Alson J. Streeter of Illinois, Union Labor nominee, 146,935.

BIBLIOGRAPHY

Edward A. Stanwood, *A History of the Presidency.*

— ALLAN NEVINS

Campaign of 1892

Grover Cleveland was reelected over Benjamin Harrison in 1892 by a majority the size of which surprised observers of both parties. Cleveland had been named on the first ballot at the Democratic convention in Chicago, although David B. Hill of New York had made a demagogic attempt to displace him. Adlai E. Stevenson was selected for the vice-presidency. Harrison, who had estranged the professional politicians of his party, who had quarreled with its most popular figure, James G. Blaine, and who had impressed the country as cold and unlikable, was reluctantly accepted by the Republicans at Minneapolis on June 10. It was impossible to repudiate his administration. However, the McKinley Tariff of 1890 had excited widespread discontent, the Sherman Silver Purchase Act of the same year had angered the conservative East, and heavy federal expenditures had caused general uneasiness. Cleveland's firm stand on behalf of the gold standard and low tariffs and his known strength of character commended him to large numbers of independent voters. One factor adverse to the Republicans was the great strength manifested by the Populists, who polled 1,040,000 votes for James B. Weaver of Iowa and James G. Field of Virginia, most of this coming from old Republican strongholds in the Middle West. Another factor was the labor war at Homestead, Pa., which showed that the highly protected steel industry did not properly pass on its tariff benefits to the worker. Cleveland, with a popular vote of 5,555,426, had 277 electors; Harrison, with a popular vote of 5,182,690, had 145; while Weaver won 22 electoral votes.

BIBLIOGRAPHY

Allan Nevins, *Grover Cleveland—A Study in Courage.*

— ALLAN NEVINS

Campaign of 1896

Following this campaign and election, a twenty-two-year period ended in which neither major party had been able to control the national government for more than the life of a single Congress; it ushered in a period of Republican domination which lasted until 1911.

Favored by Marcus A. Hanna's cannily managed campaign, William McKinley of Ohio was named on the first ballot by the Republican convention meeting at St. Louis. Garret A. Hobart was selected as the vice-presidential candidate. The traditional party platform was adopted with the exception of a declaration for the gold standard until bimetallism could be secured by international agreement. A bloc of western delegates bolted and organized the Silver Republican party.

There was no dominant candidate for the Democratic nomination. The important contest was over the platform. As presented to the delegates, it was an anti-administration document favoring free silver at the sixteen-to-one ratio, criticizing the use of injunctions in labor disputes, and denouncing the overthrow of the federal income tax. In its support William Jennings Bryan delivered his "Cross of Gold" oration and endeared himself to the silver delegates by his effective answers to the criticisms of the administration orators.

The enthusiasm growing out of that speech gave impetus to Bryan's candidacy for the presidential nomination. Back of this was also the long campaign he had waged by personal conferences, speeches, and correspondence with the inflationist delegates from the South and West. Another factor was the bolting Republicans and the Populists, who saw themselves being forced to support the Democratic nominee and demanded someone not too closely identified with the regular Democratic party platform. Bryan appealed to the delegates as the Democrat who could unite the silver and agrarian factions.

The Populists, Silver Republicans, and National Silver party members joined the Democrats in support of Bryan. The administration Democrats placed a National Democratic ticket in the field to hold conservative Democratic votes away from him, nominating John M. Palmer of Illinois as their presidential candidate.

The campaign was highly spectacular. The Democrats exploited Bryan's oratory by sending him on speaking tours back and forth across the country during which enormous crowds came out to hear him. In sharp contrast, the Republican management kept McKinley at his home in Canton, Ohio, where carefully selected delegations made formal calls and listened to "front porch" speeches by the candidate. More important were the flood of advertising, the funds for building local organizations, and the large group of speakers on the hustings, which were maintained by Hanna's organization. The metropolitan press, like the other business groups—except the silver miners—was essentially a unit in opposing Bryan. The results showed a sharp city-versus-rural division, with Bryan carrying the Solid South and most of the trans-Missouri states. The remainder, including California, Oregon, North Dakota, Kentucky, and Maryland, went to McKinley. With him were elected a Republican House and a Senate in which various minor party members held a nominal balance of power. The popular vote was unusually large, each candidate receiving larger totals than any previous candidate of his party, McKinley's vote being 7,102,246 and Bryan's 6,492,559. The electoral vote was 271 and 176, respectively.

BIBLIOGRAPHY

E. E. Robinson, *The Evolution of American Political Parties.*

— ELMER ELLIS

Campaign of 1900

The presidential candidates and most of the issues of the 1896 campaign were carried over to the 1900 campaign. With the trend of prices upward, the pressure for inflation had declined, and the expansion of American control over new territories had created the issue of imperialism.

At the Republican convention in Philadelphia a combination of circumstances forced Marcus A. Hanna and President William McKinley to accept Theodore Roosevelt as the vice-presidential candidate. The party's position on the new territories was defined as American retention with "the largest measure of self-government consistent with their welfare and our duties."

When the Democrats met at Kansas City they once again selected William Jennings Bryan as their presidential candidate, but they were unwilling to accept the conservatives' proposal to forget the last platform and make anti-imperialism the only issue. The 1896 platform was reindorsed, an antitrust plank added, and imperialism designated the "paramount issue."

The campaign lacked the fire of 1896. The Republicans emphasized the "full dinner pail" and the danger threatening it from the Democratic platform; the Democrats stressed the growth of monopolies under the McKinley administration and the danger of imperialistic government. The result was a more emphatic Republican victory than in 1896, one generally interpreted as an endorsement of both McKinley's domestic and foreign policies. The popular vote was McKinley, 7,218,491; Bryan, 6,356,734. McKinley obtained 292 electoral votes to 155 for Bryan. This election made Roosevelt's elevation to the presidency automatic upon McKinley's death in September 1901.

BIBLIOGRAPHY

E. E. Robinson, *The Evolution of American Political Parties.*
Edward A. Stanwood, *A History of the Presidency.*

— ELMER ELLIS

Campaign of 1904

Theodore Roosevelt, who succeeded to the presidency on the death of William McKinley in 1901, ardently hoped to be nominated and elected "in his own right." The death of Marcus A. Hanna of Ohio, whom the big business interests of the country would have preferred, made possible the president's nomination by acclamation when the Republican convention met in Chicago, June 21. Charles W. Fairbanks of Indiana was chosen for the vice-presidency.

The Democrats, meeting at St. Louis, July 6, pointedly turned their backs upon "Bryanism" by omitting from their platform all reference to the money question and by nominating for president Alton B. Parker, a conservative New York judge, who at once pledged himself to maintain the gold standard, and for vice-president, Henry Gassaway Davis, a wealthy West Virginia octogenarian. Business leaders, more afraid of the Democratic party than of Roosevelt, contributed so heavily to the Republican campaign chest that Parker rashly charged "blackmail." Corporations, he said, were being forced to contribute in return for the suppression of evidence that the government had against them. Roosevelt, indignantly denying the charge, won by a landslide that reclaimed Missouri from the Solid South and gave him 336 electoral votes to Parker's 140 and a popular plurality of 2,544,238. Prohibitionist, Populist, Socialist, and Socialist-Labor candidates received only negligible support.

BIBLIOGRAPHY

Edward A. Stanwood, *A History of the Presidency.*

— JOHN D. HICKS

Campaign of 1908

Theodore Roosevelt, though at the height of his popularity, refused to run for a second elective term in 1908, but swung his support in the Republican convention to William Howard Taft, who was nominated. James S. Sherman of New York was selected for the vice-presidency.

The Democratic convention was as completely dominated by William Jennings Bryan, who became its nominee. Party differences were not significant. After an apathetic campaign Bryan carried only the Solid South, Kansas, Colorado, and Nevada, though he received about 44 percent of the popular vote, securing 6,412,294 to Taft's 7,675,320. Taft's electoral vote was 321; Bryan's 162. The Republicans won the presidency and both houses of Congress.

BIBLIOGRAPHY

Samuel Eliot Morison and Henry Steele Commager, *The Growth of the American Republic.*

— CHESTER LLOYD JONES

Campaign of 1912

This campaign marked the culmination of the progressive movement in national politics and resulted in the return of the Democrats after sixteen years of Republican presidents.

The struggle for the Republican nomination became a sanguinary battle between the progressive and conservative wings, aided in each case by personal followings and some division of support from large interests. In the beginning it was the progressive Sen. Robert M. LaFollette of Wisconsin against the incumbent, William Howard Taft. But former President Theodore Roosevelt, who had been largely responsible for Taft's nomination in 1908, entered the race to rally behind him Republicans who believed Taft had been too friendly with the conservative Old Guard. The influence in Taft's hands was sufficient to return delegates pledged to him in most cases where they were named by conventions, but either Roosevelt or La Follette was successful in states where presidential primaries were held save one. The conservative-controlled national committee placed Taft delegates on the temporary roll in all contests, and the small majority resulting gave Taft the nomination. Roosevelt was later nominated by the newly organized Progressive (Bull Moose) party, consisting largely of Republican bolters.

The contest for the Democratic nomination was also hard fought with both of the leading candidates accepted as progressives. Beauchamp ("Champ") Clark of Wisconsin led from the beginning and had an actual majority in the convention for a time, but when William Jennings Bryan transferred his support to the second progressive, Woodrow Wilson, a shift began that resulted in the latter's nomination. The choice for vice-president was Thomas R. Marshall. All three party platforms were unusually favorable to progressive policies. Wilson, backed by a united party, won easily, and Roosevelt was second. There was an unusual amount of shifting of party loyalties, although most Democrats voted for Wilson and most Republicans for Roosevelt or Taft. Wilson's popular vote was 6,296,547, Roosevelt's was 4,118,571, and Taft's was 3,486,720. The electoral vote was, respectively, 435, 88, and 8. The Democrats won majorities in both branches of Congress. In spite of the three-way contest, a fourth candidate, Eugene V. Debs, Socialist, secured approximately 900,000 votes.

BIBLIOGRAPHY

E. E. Robinson, *The Evolution of American Political Parties.*
Edward A. Stanwood, *A History of the Presidency.*

— ELMER ELLIS

Campaign of 1916

This campaign reunited the Republican party and determined that American foreign policy should be left in Woodrow Wilson's hands. The Republicans reunited when, after the nomination of Charles Evans Hughes, Theodore Roosevelt, already nominated by the rapidly declining Progressive party, announced support of the ticket.

There was no opposition to the renomination of President Wilson and Vice-President Thomas R. Marshall. The Democrats defended the policies of the administration, especially the Underwood Tariff and the measures for the regulation of business. They also praised the foreign policy as one which had kept the United States out of war and preserved national honor. The Republicans attacked the policies of the administration, promised a stronger foreign policy, and were supported by the more extreme partisans of both alliances in the European war.

The results were in doubt for several days because of the close vote in several states. Wilson won the presidency, carrying Ohio, New Hampshire, the South, and most of the border and trans-Missouri states, including California, with an electoral vote of 277, against 254 for Hughes. The popular vote was Wilson, 9,127,695; Hughes, 8,533,507. Congress remained Democratic only because independent members of the House were friendly.

BIBLIOGRAPHY

E. E. Robinson, *The Evolution of American Political Parties.*

— ELMER ELLIS

Campaign of 1920

The debate on the League of Nations determined the alignment of political forces in the spring of 1920. The Republicans were confident: the wounds of the intraparty strife of 1912 had been healed; the mistaken strategy of 1916 admitted; and the conservative mood of the country was easily interpreted. They met in convention in Chicago, could not agree upon any one of the leading preconvention candidates, Frank O. Lowden, Hiram Johnson, or Leonard Wood, and nominated Warren G. Harding, senator from Ohio, on the tenth ballot. Calvin Coolidge, governor of Massachusetts, was nominated for the vice-presidency.

The Democrats met in San Francisco. None of the discussed candidates, William G. McAdoo, Alfred E. Smith, John W. Davis, A. Mitchell Palmer, or James M. Cox, commanded a great following. Cox, governor of Ohio, was nominated on the forty-fourth ballot, with Franklin D. Roosevelt, thirty-eight-year-old assistant secretary of the navy, as vice-presidential nominee. The Socialist party, meeting in May, nominated Eugene Debs for the fifth time. A Farmer-Labor ticket appeared also.

None of the platforms was unexpected or significant on domestic issues. The Republicans attacked the president and opposed American entrance into the League of Nations. The Democratic national committee supported Wilson's appeal for a "solemn referendum" on the covenant of the League; Cox waged a persistent and vigorous campaign. Harding, remaining at his home for the most part, contented himself with vague generalizations. Neither candidate had been nationally known at the outset of the contest, and no clear-cut issue developed and no real contest transpired. The total vote cast was 26,733,905. The Nineteenth Amendment had been proclaimed in August, and in every state women were entitled to vote. Harding won more than 60 percent of the total vote cast. Cox won the electoral vote in only eleven states, receiving 127 electoral votes to Harding's 404. The Socialist vote was 919,799, but the strength of all the third parties totaled only about 5.5 percent.

BIBLIOGRAPHY

E. E. Robinson, *The Presidential Vote, 1896–1932.*

— EDGAR EUGENE ROBINSON

Campaign of 1924

As in 1920, the candidates in 1924 were new in a presidential canvass. The Republican convention meeting in Cleveland, with a few scattering votes in dissent, nominated Calvin Coolidge, who as vice-president had succeeded to the presidency in August 1923 when President Warren Harding died. The vice-presidential nomination, refused by several, was accepted by Charles G. Dawes of Illinois. The platform was marked by extreme conservatism.

The Democrats met in New York and were in almost continuous session for two and a half weeks. Not only was there serious division upon the matter of American adherence to the League of Nations and upon the proposed denunciation of the Ku Klux Klan, but also upon the choice of the nominee. Each of the two leading candidates, Alfred E. Smith and William G. McAdoo, was sufficiently powerful to prevent the nomination of the other, and finally on the one hundred and third ballot the nomination went to John W. Davis of West Virginia. Gov. Charles W. Bryan of Nebraska was nominated for vice-president. The platform called for a popular referendum on the League of Nations.

The Conference for Progressive Political Action brought about a series of meetings and eventually a widespread support of Sen. Robert M. La Follette in his independent candidacy, with Burton K. Wheeler as his running mate. La Follette's platform, in which appeared most of the progressive proposals of the previous twenty years, was endorsed by the Socialist party and the officers of the American Federation of Labor. So real did the threat of the third party candidacy appear to be that much of the attack of the Republicans was on La Follette, who waged an aggressive campaign.

The total vote cast exceeded that of 1920 by 2.36 million, but because of the vote cast for La Follette (nearly 5 million), that cast for Republican and for Democratic tickets was less than four years earlier, Coolidge securing 15,718,211 votes, and Davis 8,385,283. La Follette carried Wisconsin (13 electoral votes). Coolidge topped the poll in thirty-five states, receiving 382 electoral votes, leaving the electoral vote for Davis in only twelve states, or 136 votes.

BIBLIOGRAPHY

E. E. Robinson, *The Presidential Vote, 1896–1932.*

— EDGAR EUGENE ROBINSON

Campaign of 1928

On Aug. 2, 1927, President Calvin Coolidge announced that he did not choose to run for president in 1928. The majority of the leaders of the Republican party were undecided with regard to the candidate they should support. A popular movement having its strength in the rank and file of the voters forced the nomination of Secretary of Commerce Herbert Hoover on the first ballot at the Republican National Convention, which met at Kansas City, Mo., in June. The platform contained strong support of the usual Republican policies such as a protective tariff and sound business administration. It advocated the observance and rigorous enforcement of the Eighteenth Amendment. Charles Curtis of Kansas was nominated for vice-president.

The Democrats met at Houston, Texas, and on June 28 nominated New York Gov. Alfred E. Smith, the first Catholic to be nominated for the presidency. They then nominated Arkansas Sen. Joseph T. Robinson for vice-president. The platform did not differ strikingly from that of the Republicans. The contest became one between rival personalities. Smith, an avowed "wet," took a stand in favor of a change in the Prohibition amendment, and advocated that the question of Prohibition and its enforcement be left to the determination of the individual states.

At the election on Nov. 6, Hoover was overwhelmingly successful. He carried forty states, including five from the Old South, with a total of 444 electoral votes. Smith carried eight states with an electoral vote of 87. The popular plurality of Hoover over Smith was 6,375,824 in a total vote of 36,879,414.

BIBLIOGRAPHY

W. S. Myers, *The Republican Party.*

— WILLIAM STARR MYERS

Campaigns of 1932 and 1936

The presidential campaign of 1932 began in earnest with the holding of the Republican National Convention at Chicago on June 14–16. President Herbert Hoover and Vice-President Charles Curtis were renominated on the first ballot. The platform praised the Hoover record, including his program for combating the depression. After a long debate a "wet-dry" plank on Prohibition was adopted which favored giving the people an opportunity to pass on a repeal amendment.

The Democratic National Convention was also held at Chicago, June 27-July 2, 1932. On the fourth ballot, Gov. Franklin Delano Roosevelt of New York was nominated for the presidency, defeating Alfred E. Smith and ten other candidates. John Nance Garner of Texas was selected as the vice-presidential candidate. The platform pledged economy, a sound currency, unemployment relief, old-age and unemployment insurance under state laws, the "restoration of agriculture," and repeal of the Eighteenth Amendment together with immediate legalization of beer.

After a campaign featured by Roosevelt's promise of "a new deal," the elections were held on Nov. 5. The popular vote for each party was as follows: Democratic, 22,809,638; Republican, 15,758,901; Socialist, 881,951; Socialist-Labor, 33,276; Communist, 102,785; Prohibition, 81,869; Liberty, 53,425; and Farmer-Labor, 7,309. The electoral vote was 472 for the Democrats and 59 for the Republicans.

In 1936 the Republican National Convention was held at Cleveland beginning on June 9. Gov. Alfred M. Landon of Kansas and Frank Knox, a Chicago publisher, were nominated for the presidency and vice-presidency, respectively. The platform strongly denounced the New Deal administration, from both constitutional and economic viewpoints. It pledged the Republicans "to maintain the American system of constitutional and local self-government" and "to preserve the American system of free enterprise."

The Democratic National Convention assembled at Philadelphia on June 25 for what proved to be a ratification meeting for the New Deal. President Roosevelt and Vice-President Garner were renominated without opposition. The platform vigorously defended the New Deal and pledged its continuance.

When the election was held on Nov. 3, the Democrats again won an overwhelming victory, carrying every state except Maine and Vermont. The popular vote for each party was as follows: Democratic, 27,752,869; Republican, 16,674,665; Union, 882,479; Socialist, 187,720; Communist, 80,159; Prohibition, 37,847; and Socialist-Labor, 12,777. The Democrats received 523 electoral votes while the Republicans received only 8.

— ERIK MCKINLEY ERIKSSON

Campaign of 1940

Although either Robert A. Taft, Arthur H. Vandenberg, or Thomas E. Dewey was expected to be the Republican candidate, the nomination was won by Wendell L. Willkie at Philadelphia, June 28, on the sixth ballot. As president of a large utilities corporation Willkie had fought the New Deal, but in foreign affairs he was an internationalist, and with Europe at war, this fact commended him to the liberal element of the party, which carried his nomination against the Old Guard. The nomination of a liberal by the Republicans, together with the international crisis, in turn made the nomination of Franklin D. Roosevelt by the Democrats (Chicago, July 16) a practical certainty, even though his running for a third term was unprecedented. Foreign affairs dominated the campaign. Both candidates promised aid to the Allies; both promised at the same time to keep the United States out of foreign wars. Roosevelt and Henry A. Wallace, secretary of agriculture, received 27,307,819 popular and 449 electoral votes against 22,321,018 popular and 82 electoral votes for Willkie and Charles L. McNary of Oregon.

— CHRISTOPHER LASCH

Campaign of 1944

Thomas E. Dewey, governor of New York, was nominated by the Republican convention in Chicago on June 26 with little opposition. John W. Bricker of Ohio was chosen as his running mate. President Franklin D. Roosevelt, running for a fourth term, encountered even less opposition at the Democratic convention in Chicago. The real struggle revolved around the choice of a vice-presidential candidate. With Roosevelt's support Vice-President Henry Wallace could probably have been nominated for another term, but the opposition to Wallace from within the party convinced the president that a compromise candidate had to be found. James F. Byrnes of South Carolina was acceptable to the White House and to the party conservatives, but not to labor, in particular not to Sidney Hillman of the Congress of Industrial Organizations. Accordingly Sen. Harry S. Truman of Missouri was nominated on the second ballot, July 20. In the November election Roosevelt received 25,606,585 popular and 432 electoral votes to Dewey's 22,014,745 popular and 99 electoral votes. The Democrats preserved their control of both houses of Congress.

— CHRISTOPHER LASCH

Campaign of 1948

The Republicans, having gained control of Congress in 1946, confidently expected to turn the apparently unpopular Truman administration out of power in the autumn elections, and for the first time in the party's history renominated a defeated candidate, Thomas E. Dewey, at the convention meeting in Philadelphia on June 21. The Democrats, on the other hand, suffered from severe internal conflicts. Truman's nomination at Philadelphia on July 15 caused no enthusiasm. Radicals left the party and, meeting in the same city on July 22, nominated Henry A. Wallace and Sen. Glen Taylor of Idaho as the candidates of the Progressive party. Southerners, offended by the civil rights planks of the Democratic platform, also seceded and at Birmingham, Ala., July 17, formed the States' Rights Democratic party, with Gov. J. Strom Thurmond of South Carolina and Gov. Fielding L. Wright of Mississippi as their candidates. Under these circumstances Truman's candidacy appeared to be hopeless. The president, however, proved to be a whistle-stop campaigner of unexpected ability. Moreover, he enjoyed the support not only of organized labor and of Afro-American voters but as it turned out, to the great surprise of prophets and pollsters, of midwestern farmers as well. The election was close—Truman retired for the evening on election night thinking he had lost. He and Alben W. Barkley of Kentucky polled 24,105,812 popular and 304 electoral votes against 21,970,065 popular and 189 electoral votes for Dewey and Gov. Earl Warren of California. Thurmond polled 1, 169,063 popular votes and the 38 electoral votes of South Carolina, Alabama, Mississippi, and Louisiana. Wallace won 1,157,172 popular votes. The Democrats regained control of Congress by small majorities.

BIBLIOGRAPHY

Samuel J. Lubell, *The Future of American Politics.*

— CHRISTOPHER LASCH

Campaign of 1952

After a long and bitter struggle, the internationalist wing of the Republican party succeeded on July 11 in bringing about the nomination of Gen. Dwight D. Eisenhower against the opposition of Sen. Robert A. Taft and his supporters. The Democrats, following the Republicans to Chicago ten days later, turned to Gov. Adlai E. Stevenson of Illinois, who consented to become a candidate only at the last moment. In the following campaign Stevenson suffered from revelations of corruption in the Truman administration, from the widespread dissatisfaction with the seemingly inconclusive results of the war in Korea, and from the vague feeling that it was "time for a change." Eisenhower's personal appeal, moreover, was immense. He and Sen. Richard M. Nixon of California polled 33,936,234 votes to 27,314,987 for Stevenson and Sen. John J. Sparkman of Alabama. The Republicans carried the electoral college, 442 to 89. They carried the House of Representatives by a narrow margin and tied the Democrats in the Senate.

BIBLIOGRAPHY

Samuel J. Lubell, *Revolt of the Moderates.*

— CHRISTOPHER LASCH

Campaign of 1956

Adlai E. Stevenson was renominated on the first ballot by the Democrats at Chicago, with Sen. Estes Kefauver of Tennessee as his running mate. President Dwight D. Eisenhower and Vice-President Richard M. Nixon were renominated by the Republicans at San Francisco with equal ease. The campaign, however, was far from being a rehash of 1952. Stevenson, having been advised that his serious discussions of issues in 1952 had been over the voters' heads, agreed to pitch his campaign at a somewhat lower level. The results disappointed his more ardent supporters without winning him any votes. The Suez crisis, occurring on the eve of the election, further strengthened the administration's position by creating a national emergency. In the election the president polled 35,590,472 popular and 457 electoral votes to Stevenson's 26,022,752 popular and 73 electoral votes. As in 1952, Eisenhower broke into the Solid South, carrying not only Florida, Virginia, and Tennessee, which he had carried in 1952, but Texas, Oklahoma, and Louisiana as well. In spite of his personal triumph, however, the Democrats carried both houses of Congress.

— CHRISTOPHER LASCH

Campaign of 1960

The Democrats nominated Sen. John F. Kennedy of Massachusetts at Los Angeles in July, with Sen. Lyndon B. Johnson of Texas as his running mate. The Republicans, meeting at Chicago two weeks later, nominated Vice-President Richard M. Nixon and Henry Cabot Lodge of Massachusetts. The most striking feature of the campaign was a series of televised debates, in which the candidates submitted to questioning by panels of reporters. By sharing a national audience with his lesser-known opponent, Nixon in this manner may have injured his own cause. Indeed, the debates, in view of the closeness of the result, may have been the decisive factor in Kennedy's victory. The final vote was not known until weeks after the election. Kennedy received 34,227,096, Nixon 34,108,546, and minor candidates 502,773. Despite the fact that Kennedy won by only 118,550 votes and had only 49.7 percent of the total vote as compared with 49.6 percent for Mr. Nixon, the President-elect won 303 electoral votes to Nixon's 219. At forty-three, Kennedy was the youngest man ever elected to the presidency (although not the youngest to occupy the office). He was also the first Roman Catholic ever to become president.

BIBLIOGRAPHY

Theodore White, *The Making of the President 1960.*

— CHRISTOPHER LASCH

Campaign of 1964

Upon assuming office following the assassination of President John F. Kennedy in November 1963, Vice-President Lyndon B. Johnson acted quickly to restore public calm and to achieve many of President Kennedy's legislative goals. Lyndon Johnson was subsequently nominated by acclamation by the Democrats, meeting in Atlantic City, N.J. The only uncertainty there was the choice of a vice-presidential nominee. After the earlier veto by Johnson of Attorney General Robert F. Kennedy, brother of the slain president, the choice of Johnson and the party fell to Minnesotan Hubert H. Humphrey, assistant majority leader of the Senate.

Conflict over the presidential nomination centered in the Republican party. New York's Gov. Nelson Rockefeller represented the moderate and liberal factions that had dominated the party since 1940. A new, conservative group was led by Arizona's Sen. Barry M.

Goldwater, who offered "a choice, not an echo." Presidential primaries indicated the limited appeal of both candidates, but no viable alternative emerged. Goldwater accumulated large numbers of delegates in the nonprimary states, particularly in the South and West, and sealed his first-ballot victory with a narrow win in the California primary. Rep. William E. Miller of New York was selected as his running mate.

The main issues of the 1964 campaign were presented by Goldwater, who challenged the previous party consensus on a limited welfare state and the emerging Democratic policy of accommodation with the Communist world. The Democrats defended their record as bringing peace and prosperity, while pledging new social legislation to achieve a "Great Society." The armed conflict in Vietnam also drew some attention. In response to an alleged attack on American warships in the Gulf of Tonkin, the president ordered retaliatory bombing of North Vietnam, at the same time pledging "no wider war."

In the balloting, Lyndon Johnson was overwhelmingly elected, gaining 43,129,484 popular votes (61.1 percent) and a majority in forty-four states and the District of Columbia—which was voting for president for the first time—for a total of 486 electoral votes. Goldwater won 27,178,188 votes (38.5 percent) and six states—all but Arizona in the Deep South—for a total of 52 electoral votes. There was a pronounced shift in voting patterns, with the South becoming the strongest Republican area, and the Northeast the firmest Democratic base.

BIBLIOGRAPHY

Philip E. Converse, Aage R. Clausen, and Warren E. Miller, "Electoral Myth and Reality: The 1964 Election," *American Political Science Review*, vol. 59 (1965).

John Kessel, *The Goldwater Coalition.*

Theodore H. White, *The Making of the President 1964.*

— GERALD M. POMPER

Campaign of 1968

The presidential election took place in an atmosphere of increasing American civil disorder, evidenced in protests over the Vietnam War, riots in black urban neighborhoods, and assassinations of political leaders. On Mar. 31, President Lyndon B. Johnson startled the nation by renouncing his candidacy for reelection. His withdrawal stimulated an intense contest for the Democratic nomination between Minnesota's Sen. Eugene McCarthy, New York's Sen. Robert F. Kennedy, and Vice-President Hubert H. Humphrey. Kennedy appeared to have the greatest popular support, his campaign culminating in a narrow victory over McCarthy in the California primary. On the night of this victory, Kennedy was assassinated. Humphrey abstained from the primaries but gathered support from party leaders and from the Johnson administration. At an emotional and contentious convention in Chicago, Humphrey was easily nominated on the first ballot. Maine's Sen. Edmund S. Muskie was selected as the vice-presidential candidate.

Former Vice-President Richard M. Nixon was the leading candidate for the Republican nomination. He withstood challenges from moderate Gov. Nelson Rockefeller of New York and conservative Gov. Ronald Reagan of California. Gaining a clear majority of delegates on the first ballot at the party's convention in Miami Beach, he then named Gov. Spiro T. Agnew of Maryland as his running mate. A new party, the American Independent party, was organized by Gov. George C. Wallace of Alabama and was able to win a ballot position in every state. Curtis LeMay, former air force general, was selected as the new party's vice-presidential candidate.

The campaign centered on the record of the Johnson administration. Nixon denounced the conduct of the war and promised both an "honorable peace" and ultimate withdrawal of American troops. He also pledged a vigorous effort to reduce urban crime and to restrict school desegregation. Wallace denounced both parties, calling for strong action against North Vietnam, criminals, and civil rights protesters. Humphrey largely defended the Democratic record, while also proposing an end to American bombing of North Vietnam.

The balloting brought Nixon a narrow victory. With 31,785,480 votes, he won 43.4 percent of the national total, thirty-two states, and 301 electoral votes. Humphrey won 31,275,166 votes, 42.7 percent of the total, thirteen states and the District of Columbia, and 191 electoral votes. Wallace gained the largest popular vote for a third-party candidate since 1924—9,906,473 votes and 13.5 percent of the popular total. The five southern states he captured, with 46 electoral votes, were too few to accomplish his strategic aim, a deadlock of the electoral college.

BIBLIOGRAPHY

Lewis Chester, Godfrey Hodgson, and Bruce Page, *An American Melodrama.*

Philip E. Converse et al., "Continuity and Changes in American Politics: Parties and Issues in the 1968 Election," *American Political Science Review*, vol. 63 (1969).

Richard Scammon and Ben Wattenberg, *The Real Majority.*

— GERALD M. POMPER

Campaign of 1972

The Nixon administration provided the campaign setting in 1972 by a series of American policy reversals, including the withdrawal of most American ground forces from Vietnam, the imposition of wage and price controls, and presidential missions to Communist China and the Soviet Union. President Richard M. Nixon's control of the Republican party was undisputed, resulting in a placid party convention in Miami, where he and Vice-President Spiro T. Agnew were renominated.

In the Democratic party, major party reform resulted in more open processes of delegate selection and increased representation at the convention of women, racial minorities, and persons under the age of thirty. At the same time, a spirited contest was conducted for the presidential nomination. The early favorite, Maine's Sen. Edmund S. Muskie, was eliminated after severe primary defeats. Alabama's Gov. George C. Wallace raised a serious challenge but was eliminated from active campaigning by an attempted assassination. The contest then became a two-man race between South Dakota's Sen. George S. McGovern and former Vice-President Hubert H. Humphrey, the 1968 candidate. A series of upset primary victories and effective organization in local party caucuses culminated in a direct victory for McGovern in the California primary and a first-ballot nomination in Miami, the convention city. The vice-presidential Democratic position was awarded to Missouri's Sen. Thomas Eagleton. After the convention adjourned, it was revealed that Eagleton had been hospitalized three times for mental depression. He was persuaded to resign, and the Democratic National Committee then, at McGovern's suggestion, named Sergeant Shriver as his running mate. With Wallace disabled, the American Independent party named Rep. John G. Schmitz of California as its presidential candidate.

The Democrats attempted to focus the campaign on the alleged defects of the administration, including the continuation of the war in Vietnam, electronic eavesdropping by the Republicans on the Democratic national headquarters at Washington's Watergate complex, and governmental favors for Republican party contributors. The full extent of these improprieties was not revealed, however, until the following year. Aside from defending the Nixon record, the Republicans attacked the Democratic candidate as advocating radical positions on such issues as amnesty for war resisters, marijuana usage, and abortion and as inconsistent on other questions. Much attention centered on 25 million newly eligible voters, including the eighteen-year-olds enfranchised by constitutional amendment.

The final result was an overwhelming personal victory for Nixon, who won the highest total and proportion of the popular vote in electoral history. Nixon won 47,169,905 popular votes (60.7 percent) and 521 electoral votes from forty-nine states. McGovern won 29,170,383 popular votes (37.5 percent), but only 17 electoral votes (from Massachusetts and the District of Columbia). Despite this landslide, the Republicans failed to gain control of the House and lost two seats in the Senate.

BIBLIOGRAPHY

Walter Dean Burnham, *Critical Elections and the Mainsprings of American Politics.*

Theodore H. White, *The Making of the President 1972.*

— GERALD M. POMPER

— ELMER E. CORNWELL, JR.

PRESIDENTIAL CAMPAIGNS SINCE THE 1970S

The five presidential campaigns between 1976 and 1992 represent a period of change in American politics, including new rules for campaigns, challenges to the two-party system, and altered electoral coalitions. The 1976 campaign was the first conducted under new rules for selecting convention delegates and new campaign finance regulations, and by 1992 these changes had been fully assimilated by both the Democratic and Republican parties. Extending the turmoil of the 1960s, these five campaigns witnessed regular challenges to the two-party system by divisive primaries and significant independent candidacies. In addition, the dissension associated with the Vietnam War protests and the Watergate scandal of 1972–1974 developed into a persistent "anti-Washington" theme in presidential campaigns. During this period there were significant changes in the major parties' electoral coalitions as well, with southerners and religious conservatives shifting from the Democratic to the Republican camp.

The dissension associated with the Vietnam War protests and the Watergate scandal developed into a persistent "anti-Washington" theme in presidential campaigns.

Campaign of 1976

The Democratic nomination attracted hopefuls from across the political spectrum. Former Georgia Governor James Earl (Jimmy) Carter, an unknown moderate, defeated better-known rivals in a classic campaign. Understanding the new delegate selection rules, Carter first attracted media attention by winning the Iowa caucus and the New Hampshire primary, and then defeated in turn each of his liberal and conservative rivals. The national convention displayed great unity, and Carter picked former Minnesota Senator Walter F. Mondale as his vice-presidential candidate. The Republican nomination contest was more divisive. Gerald R. Ford, the only president not to have been elected to the office, faced a conservative challenge from former California Governor Ronald Reagan. After a bitter campaign, Ford prevailed with slightly more than half the delegates, and at a divided national convention replaced Vice President Nelson A. Rockefeller (also appointed to office and not elected) with Kansas Senator Robert Dole. Ford ran on the record of his brief administration, emphasizing continued restraint on the federal government and détente with the Soviet Union. Carter offered a mix of conservative and liberal critiques of the Nixon-Ford record, including the poor economy and foreign policy controversies. His basic appeal was returning trust and morality to government, promising the voters, "I will never lie to you." Both candidates sought to avoid divisive social issues, such as abortion. On election day 54 percent of the electorate went to the polls and gave Carter a very narrow victory; he won 50 percent of the popular vote (40,828,929 ballots) and 23 states and the District of Columbia for 297 electoral votes. The key to Carter's success was victory in all but one of the southern states. Ford won 49 percent of the popular vote (39,148,940 ballots) and 27 states for 241 electoral votes. The independent campaign of former Senator Eugene McCarthy received one percent of the vote and influenced the outcome in several states.

Campaign of 1980

The 1980 presidential election occurred in an atmosphere of crisis. The taking of American hostages in Iran in 1978 and the invasion of Afghanistan by the Soviet Union in 1979 had produced popular indignation, while the scarcity of oil and a poor economy generated discontent. Tensions mounted with the founding of the Moral Majority, a religious interest group, and President Jimmy Carter declared the country suffered from a "malaise" and a "crisis of confidence." Under these circumstances, the Republican nomination attracted several candidates. Former California Governor Ronald Reagan was the early favorite but had to overcome spirited challenges from party moderates, including former Representatives George Bush of Texas and John Anderson of Illinois. At the national convention, Reagan chose Bush for vice president, but Reagan's conservatism led Anderson to run as an independent in the general election, stressing moderation. Meanwhile, President Carter faced serious divisions in the Democratic party. His principal challenger was Massachusetts Senator Edward Kennedy. Although popular with party liberals, questions about Kennedy's character and foreign policy crises undermined his campaign, allowing Carter to score early and decisive primary victories. Kennedy pursued his campaign into a divided convention, where he refused to endorse Carter. The fall campaign produced sharp ideological divisions. Carter ran a liberal campaign based on his comprehensive energy program, plans to manage the economy, the Equal Rights Amendment, and human rights in foreign policy. In contrast, Reagan ran a conservative campaign based on free enterprise, reduction of federal spending, traditional moral values, and an anticommunist foreign policy. The climax of the campaign came in the last televised presidential debate, when Reagan asked the voters "Are you better off than you were four years ago?" On election day, 54 percent of the electorate went to the polls and gave Reagan a decisive victory. He won 51 percent of the popular vote (43,899,248) and 44 states for 489 electoral votes; his victory extended to every region of the country, including the South. Carter won 41 percent of the popular vote (35,481,435) and 6 states and the District of Columbia for 49 electoral votes. Independent Anderson collected 7 percent of the vote but won no states.

Senator Kennedy pursued his campaign into a divided convention, where he refused to endorse Carter.

Campaign of 1984

The 1984 presidential campaign occurred in a climate of peace and prosperity. Anti-Soviet foreign policy produced a sense of security and a strong economy reduced discontent. While the nation faced many problems, the public was tranquil compared to previous elections. President Ronald Reagan enjoyed considerable personal popularity, even with voters who disagreed with him on issues, and was not challenged for the Republican nomination. Although there was some grumbling from the right-wing about Vice President George Bush, both he and Reagan were renominated by acclamation, giving the Republicans the luxury of a united party. They also enjoyed the support of a broad conservative coalition, including many southerners and religious conservatives, who came to be known as Reagan Democrats. Among the Democrats, former Vice President Walter Mondale was the front-runner, but he received a strong challenge from former Colorado Senator Gary Hart, who won the New Hampshire primary, and the Reverend Jesse Jackson, the first African-American candidate to make a serious presidential bid. A divided Democratic National Convention made history by nominating the first woman for the vice presidency, New York Representative Geraldine Ferraro. During the campaign Reagan ran on the theme of "It's morning in America," stressing national pride and optimism and his defense and economic policies. Mondale offered a liberal alternative, attacking Reagan's aggressive foreign policy and conservative economic program. Mondale received attention for his unpopular promise to raise taxes to reduce the federal budget deficit. The candidates also differed on women's rights and abortion, and a "gender gap" developed in favor of the Democrats. Reagan ran far ahead for most of the campaign, stumbling briefly when he showed apparent signs of age in a televised debate. On election day 53 percent of the electorate went to the polls and overwhelmingly reelected Reagan. He won 59 percent of the popular vote (54,281,858 ballots) and 49 states for a record high 525 electoral votes; indeed, he came within some 4,000 votes of being the first president to carry all fifty states. Mondale won 41 percent of the popular vote (37,457,215) and carried only the District of Columbia and his home state of Minnesota, for 13 electoral votes.

Campaign of 1988

The selection of candidates for the 1988 campaign began in an atmosphere of uncertainty. President Ronald Reagan could not run for reelection, and, although the economy was strong, some of the costs of Reagan's programs caused public concern. In addition, the Iran-Contra scandal had hurt Reagan's foreign policy, and tensions over social issues were increasing. The Democratic nomination attracted a crowded field. Because of his strong showing in 1984, former Colorado Senator Gary Hart was the favorite but a personal scandal ended his campaign early. Massachusetts Governor Michael Dukakis became the front-runner because of a well-financed and disciplined campaign. After winning the New Hampshire primary, Dukakis outlasted his rivals, including a strong surge for the Reverend Jesse Jackson, who finished second and hoped for the vice-presidential nomination. Instead, Texas Senator Lloyd Bentsen was chosen in an otherwise united national convention. Vice President George Bush, the Republican favorite, attracted numerous opponents and was upset in the Iowa caucus by Kansas Senator Robert Dole and televangelist Marion (Pat) Robertson and his "invisible army" of religious conservatives. Bush rallied to win in New Hampshire and the southern primaries that followed. The unity of the national convention was marred by a controversial vice-presidential choice, Indiana Senator J. Danforth (Dan) Quayle. The fall campaign began with Dukakis enjoying a big lead in the polls but it collapsed under Republican attacks on his record and liberal views, some of which had racial overtones. The Bush campaign stressed the Reagan record on foreign and economic policy and included the pledge, "Read my lips. No new taxes." Dukakis campaigned on his immigrant roots, fiscal conservatism, and the need for economic growth, calling for "good jobs at good wages." Fifty percent of the electorate went to the polls and gave Bush a solid victory—54 percent of the popular vote (48,881,221) and 40 states for 426 electoral votes. Dukakis won 46 percent of the popular vote (41,805,422 ballots) and 10 states and the District of Columbia for 112 electoral votes.

Campaign of 1992

The end of the cold war in 1990 left the United States in search of a "new world order," while major economic and social transformations suggested the need for a new domestic agenda, and the 1992 campaign occurred in a time of great change. These strains produced high levels of disaffection with politics and government. Republican President George Bush's popularity after the Persian Gulf War of 1991 reduced the number of contenders for the Democratic nomination. Arkansas Governor William J. (Bill) Clinton emerged early as the front-runner, and a unified national convention nominated another southerner, Tennessee Senator Albert Gore, for the vice presidency. Bush's early popularity also reduced the number of contenders for the Republican nomination, but a weak economy and his broken pledge not to raise taxes led commentator Patrick Buchanan to enter the race. Although Buchanan won no primaries, he embarrassed Bush and created dissension at the national convention, where Bush and Vice President Dan Quayle were renominated. The fall campaign began with Bush behind in the polls, but unlike in 1988 he never recovered. Bush campaigned on his foreign policy successes, free enterprise, and conservative social issues and sharply attacked his oppo-

Clinton ran a disciplined campaign, offering himself as a "new Democrat" with a moderate message of economic opportunity and personal responsibility.

nent's character. Clinton offered himself as a "new Democrat" with a moderate message of economic opportunity and personal responsibility and waged a disciplined campaign. The independent candidacy of Texas billionaire and political newcomer H. Ross Perot complicated the race. He launched his campaign from a television talk show in February but withdrew from the race in July, only to reenter in September. Drawing on voter discontent, Perot offered an attack on politics and government as usual. On election day 55 percent of the electorate went to the polls and gave Bill Clinton a narrow victory—43 percent of the popular vote (44,908,254 ballots) and 32 states and the District of Columbia for 370 electoral votes. At age forty-six, Clinton was the first baby boomer to win the White House. Bush won 38 percent of the popular vote (39,102,343 ballots) and 18 states for 168 electoral votes. Perot received 19 percent of the popular vote, for the second strongest performance by a twentieth-century independent candidate but won no states.

[See also Democratic Party; Presidency; Republican Party; Third Parties and Independents.]

BIBLIOGRAPHY

Gerald M. Pomper et al., *The Election of 1976: Reports and Interpretations* (New York, 1977), *The Election of 1980* (Chatham, N.J., 1981), *The Election of 1984* (Chatham, 1985), *The Election of 1988* (Chatham, 1989), and *The Election of 1992* (Chatham, 1993)

— JOHNS C. GREEN

CANADA, RELATIONS WITH

Canada remained within the U.S. strategic orbit in the last decades of the twentieth century, but relations soured amidst world economic instability provoked by the Arab oil embargo in 1973, a deepening U.S. trade deficit, and new cultural and environmental issues. Canadians complained about American films, television shows, and magazines flooding their country; acid rainfall generated by U.S. coal-burning power plants; and environmental damage expected from the U.S. oil industry's activities in the Arctic. After the U.S. tanker *Manhattan* scouted a route in 1968 to bring Alaska oil through the Canadian Arctic icepack to eastern U.S. cities, the Canadian parliament enacted legislation extending its jurisdiction over disputed passages in this region for pollution-control purposes. Subsequently, the oil companies decided to pump the oil across Alaska and ship it to U.S. West Coast ports from Valdez. Disputes over fisheries, a hardy perennial issue, broke out on both coasts. On the East coast, a treaty negotiated with Canada during the administration of President Jimmy Carter that resolved disputed fishing rights in the Gulf of Maine was rejected after protests by congressional representatives from Massachusetts and Maine. Ultimately, the issue was resolved by the World Court in the Hague. On the West Coast, the two countries argued over salmon quotas. Later, during the 1990s, when fish stocks had declined precipitously in both regions, the disputes broke out again with renewed intensity. In response to these issues, Prime Minister Pierre Trudeau's government (1968–1979, 1980–1984) struggled to lessen Canada's dependency. It screened U.S. investment dollars, sought new trading partners, challenged Hollywood's stranglehold on cultural products, canceled tax advantages enjoyed by U.S. magazines, and moved to reduce U.S. control over Canada's petroleum industry.

Relations improved notably in 1984 because of a startling convergence of personalities and policies. A new Canadian leader, Brian Mulroney (1984–1993), established affable relations with Presidents Ronald Reagan and George Bush. Scrapping Trudeau's nationalist agenda, Mulroney endorsed the U.S. presidents' hard line toward the Soviet bloc, joined the U.S.-dominated Organization of American States, and participated in the U.S.-led Persian Gulf War of 1991. Most important, Mulroney led Canada into a controversial, U.S.-initiated continental trade bloc via the Free Trade Agreement (1988) and the North American Free Trade Agreement (1992), between the United States, Canada, and Mexico and designed to eliminate all trade barriers between the countries. In trade, Canada and the United States depend more heavily on the other than on any other nation. Between one-quarter and one-third of all U.S. exports are purchased by Canadians, while about 80 percent of Canada's exports are sold to the United States. Similarly, each nation invests more capital across the border than in any other country, including Japan and Mexico.

[See also North American Free Trade Agreement.]

BIBLIOGRAPHY

Stephen Clarkson, *Canada and the Reagan Challenge: Crisis and Adjustment, 1981–1985* (Toronto, 1982).

J. L. Granatstein and Norman Hillmer, *For Better or for Worse: Canada and the United States to the 1990s* (Toronto, 1991).

John H. Thompson and Stephen J. Randall, *Canada and the United States: Ambivalent Allies* (Athens, Ga., 1994).

— ROBERT H. BABCOCK

CANALS

Since 1607, American river systems have provided an essential element in internal transportation. However, full-scale navigation ceased at the fall line. The earliest canals—such as the Patowmack Company's works at Great Falls, Md. (constructed 1786–1808), and the Western Inland Lock Navigation Company's canal at Little Falls, N.Y. (1795)—bypassed the fall line. Other early canals skirted mill dams and other river channel obstructions. The Middlesex Canal (1793–1804), connecting Boston with the Merrimac River, and the Santee and Cooper Canal (1790's), connecting these two rivers above Charleston, S.C., fully launched America into canal construction.

Lack of skilled engineers, compounded by the crude surveying equipment available, hampered canal construction efforts. Samuel Thompson erred over 30 feet in elevation (in 18 miles) in his Middlesex Canal survey. William Watson, his replacement, brought knowledge of English canals and more accurate surveying abilities to the project. The Erie Canal (1817–25) became the great school for American canal engineers and civil engineering in general. Benjamin Wright, its first chief engineer, derived his principal experience primarily from surveying the Erie route and working for the Western Inland Lock Navigation Company. Under his tutelage evolved the famed Erie school, including David Bates, James Geddes, John Jervis, Nathan Roberts, and Canvas White. Erie school engineers spread throughout the United States, working in all aspects of civil engineering, frequently moving from one job to another and field-training others in engineering disciplines. After leaving the Erie Canal, Roberts worked on the Pennsylvania Main Line Canal (1826–34) and the Chesapeake and Ohio (C & O) Canal (1828–50); built the bridge across the Potomac River at Harpers Ferry; and helped plan river navigation improvements at Muscle Shoals, Tenn. Some became engineers from necessity. Josiah White, a merchant, promoted the Lehigh Canal (1827–29), did his own engineering, and held several patents for canal lock construction.

Two main groups financed canals: states and private companies. When a canal would open up a large new territory and the canal's chances for financial success were limited, the state tended to provide the necessary capital. When a canal focused on a single natural resource (for example, coal) or was linked to a clearly established trade route, it usually was privately financed. Except for the Erie Canal, most state systems were financial disasters in spite of substantial land subsidies; for example, Indiana received 1,457,366 acres; Ohio, 1,100,361 acres; and Michigan, 1,250,000 acres. Indiana approached bankruptcy in the 1830's because of poor fiscal management and its commitment to canal construction. On the other hand, private companies—such as the Lehigh Coal and Navigation Company, the Delaware and Hudson (D & H) Company, and the Delaware and Raritan Company—prospered.

Private companies usually escaped the problems of poor construction based on contract favoritism, fiscal mismanagement, and pressures to locate in certain areas for political rather than sound engineering or business reasons. Not every private company was immune. On the C & O Canal, the lock tender's houses near the terminus are stone, further along brick, then frame, and finally log, demonstrating the declining condition of the company as construction progressed.

Financing took many forms. State systems received direct cash outlays or federal land subsidies. Both states and private companies issued stock. In several instances—for example, the Morris Canal (1825–31), the C & O Canal, and the Whitewater Canal (1836–43)—company script was issued. Lotteries helped finance construction of a canal in the District of Columbia and of the Amoskeag Falls Canal (1812–30), the Cumberland and Oxford Canal (1827–29), and the Union Canal (1821–27). The profits received from tolls on the Erie Canal helped to build the New York system of lateral canals. However, tolls rarely met expectations, and construction-recovery cost based upon projected revenue from tolls usually proved disastrous. Finally, some companies received outright grants from towns and villages in order to entice the canal into their area.

The principal engineering elements of a canal are the source of water supply, the canal bed, and locks to raise boats from one level to another. The main water supply for canals is a dam that feeds water either directly into the canal or into a feeder leading into the canal. Frequently, slack-water navigation is part of a canal system. The Lower Division of the Lehigh Canal, for instance, consisted of eight sections of canal and nine slack-water pools. The C & O Canal and the Schuylkill Canal (1816–25) also used slack-water navigation.

Canal beds were not uniform. A bed could have a shape varying from 45 to 60 feet at the top, with sloping side walls leading to a bottom between 30 and 45 feet wide. At first, canal depth was 4.5 to 5 feet, but most canals were deepened to 6 feet as boat drafts became larger.

Next to canalboats, locks varied most in size from one canal to another. Distance inside the chamber from gate to gate varied from 70 to 220 feet; width, from 9 to 24 feet. Lift ranged from 2 to 30 feet. Some locks were constructed of cut stone; others were composite locks consisting of loosely laid-up stone with board planking to hold the rubble in place. The completely wooden lock, number 1, on the Delaware and Raritan Canal (1831–34) at Bordentown, N.J., was a rarity. Balanced-beam miter gates ("V" gates with large wooden arms to help move them) were found both upstream and downstream. On the Delaware Canal (1827–30), Lehigh Canal, and portions of the C & O Canal, a drop or "fall" gate was used on the upstream end. Locks were named after the function they performed (for example, lift lock, guard lock, outlet lock, and tide lock). Almost all locks were lifting locks. Many canals had a weigh lock to determine the quantity of goods in a boat for toll purposes.

Other engineering elements were stop gates (to control water in long, open levels in case of a breach or during repairs), waste weirs, overflows (to maintain proper water level), culverts, and aqueducts. Many of these remains are engineering landmarks, such as the Monocacy Creek aqueduct and Paw Paw tunnel on the C & O Canal, the Roebling cable aqueduct across the Delaware River at Lackawaxen from the D & H Canal (1825–29), the Lockport flight (canal locks resembling a set of stairs) and Schoharie Creek aqueduct on the Erie Canal, the high lift locks of the Upper Division of the Lehigh Canal, and the floating towpath across Musconetcong Lake on the Morris Canal. Canal engineering also found unique answers to specific problems. Rather than large lock flights to overcome a rapid rise in elevation, as found on the Black River Canal (1838–55) in New York, the Morris Canal turned to a system of inclined planes that generated power for the plane cars with hydraulic Scotch turbines. The Allegheny Portage Railroad (Hollidaysburg to Johnstown, Pa.), part of the Pennsylvania Main Line Canal, utilized inclined planes powered by steam.

The most individual units on canals were the canalboats. Basically there were two types—packet (passenger) boats and freight boats. Packet boats, the fastest boats on a canal and usually pulled by horses, lasted only until railroads developed. Travelers' accounts from the middle of the 18th century (among them, Charles Dickens) picture both the joys and discomforts of the packet boat. Freight boats fall into two types—company boats and private boats. Company boats frequently were of one general style of construction for each canal, carried between 75 and 125 tons, and were identified by special colors and markings. Private boats were all shapes and sizes, with each owner trying to add his own touch of originality. In almost all cases, freight boats were pulled by mules. As canals declined, alternatives to mule power were sought, such as trolley cars, electric traction or mine cars, tractors, and self-propelled boats. All proved to be failures. In New York a group of boats called "line boats" carried both freight and passengers.

Finally, canal operation required personnel—lock tenders, maintenance men, ratters, level walkers, carpenters, and section bosses. A boat crew consisted of a minimum of a captain and driver, with a helper and second driver added when boating could be conducted 24 hours a day. Canal construction also drew heavily upon immigrant groups, especially the Irish and Germans.

Canals continue to play a key role in America. Both the Erie Barge Canal and the Chesapeake and Delaware Ship Canal are vital transportation links. Canal landmarks are becoming the basis for parks and other recreational development and, in several cases, are being restored to their 19th-century operating order. Canal museums are found in Syracuse, N.Y.; Canal Fulton, Ohio; and Easton, Pa. Canal societies have been formed in Maryland, Massachusetts, New York, Ohio, and Pennsylvania.

BIBLIOGRAPHY

Carter Goodrich, ed., *Canals and American Economic Development.*
Ralph D. Gray, *The National Waterway.*
Alvin C. Harlow, *Old Towpaths.*
Harry N. Scheiber, *Ohio Canal Era.*
Ronald E. Shaw, *Erie Water West.*

— HARRY L. RINKER

CAPITAL PUNISHMENT

Capital punishment refers to the imposition of the death penalty as an optional or mandatory punishment for the commission of certain types of crimes, thereby known as capital crimes. No definitive agreement has existed among the capital punishment jurisdictions of the United States as to what constitutes a capital offense. Furthermore, most jurisdictions adopted an optional procedure that granted judges or juries the authority to decide whether the death penalty or some other form of punishment would be imposed. Therefore, the death penalty has not been applied in a strictly uniform manner. There is sufficient similarity of application, however, to separate the types of capital crime into four categories. These are (1) crimes against the government, such as treason, espionage, and capital perjury; (2) crimes against property when life is threatened, such as arson, burglary, and train wrecking; (3) crimes against the person, which include murder, rape, and felony murders associated with kidnapping, assault, and robbery; and (4) miscellaneous crimes, a collection of assorted offenses created by panic legislation.

The principal arguments for capital punishment center upon a fundamental belief in retribution, retaliation, and deterrence. Proponents of the death penalty firmly believe it to be a just punishment that corresponds to the type of injury inflicted; a process to rid society of deviants; and, primarily, a device to inhibit people from committing capital crimes.

The advocates of abolition of the death penalty promote rehabilitation over death. They consider capital punishment both uncivilized and ineffective as a deterrent. Their position is supported by studies showing that, over time, the homicide rates in states with the death penalty and states without it are approximately the same; that changes in homicide rates are a result of societal and cultural differences; that emotional and prejudicial considerations on the part of judges and juries generally determine when the death penalty is used, turning it into a weapon of discrimination, primarily against the poor and against Afro-Americans; and, finally, that capital offenders rarely consider execution when they commit their crimes.

Capital punishment was adopted from the English system. The colonies, however, resisted the harsher characteristics of the English penal code and retreated from it during and after the American Revolution. Prompted by the growth of societies that advocated abolition of capital punishment, a major shift away from such punishment developed in the middle of the 19th century: Pennsylvania abolished public executions in 1834, and Michigan officially abolished the death penalty in 1847. These accomplishments were muted by the Civil War, when some states that had followed Michigan's example reinstated the death penalty. The opponents of capital punishment renewed their attack at the turn of the century. Their efforts, again impeded by war—the two world wars—were persistent; and a clear trend away from capital punishment became evident by the late 1960's.

In the 1960's and 1970's, opponents of the death penalty increasingly challenged the major principles of capital punishment in the courts. Their litigation resulted in a growing reluctance on the part of the states to execute capital offenders. Executions dropped from a high of 152 in 1947 to 7 in 1965, and none after 1967. In 1971, thirty-nine of the fifty-four U.S. jurisdictions (the fifty states, the District of Columbia, Puerto Rico, the Virgin Islands, and the federal criminal jurisdiction) provided for the death penalty as part of their system of criminal justice; fifteen jurisdictions had either abolished or restricted its use. In 1972, the Supreme Court ruled in *Furman* v. *Georgia* (408 U.S. 238) that the optional death penalty, as it applied in this and companion cases, was unconstitutional because it violated the Eighth (cruel and unusual punishment) and Fourteenth amendments of the Constitution.

The Court refrained from deciding whether the death penalty itself was cruel and unusual punishment; rather, it concentrated on the way in which judges and juries arbitrarily and infrequently imposed the death sentence. In essence, capital punishment as an optional sentence, which it was in the vast majority of cases, was abolished in the United States.

The *Furman* ruling may be viewed as a major achievement in the long struggle of the opponents of the death penalty. One immediate effect of the ruling was the commutation of the death sentence to life imprisonment for all 600 prisoners awaiting execution. This was followed by a series of appellate court rulings that state laws imposing the optional death penalty for certain kinds of capital offenses were unconstitutional.

The decision stimulated an intense national discussion on the merits of capital punishment. National surveys indicated that public opinion favored the use of the death penalty in certain types of cases. Legislation reinstating the death sentence for specific crimes was introduced in Congress and some state legislatures. The states acted quickly and began to pass new capital punishment laws featuring optional and mandatory death penalties for specific crimes. New York's optional death sentence was one of the first to be tested in the courts. The Supreme Court, in refusing to review the appellate court ruling that declared that new law unconstitutional, reaffirmed its decision in *Furman.*

BIBLIOGRAPHY

Hugo A. Bedau, ed., *The Death Penalty in America.*

Gerald Gunther, "The Supreme Court 1971 Term," *Harvard Law Review,* vol. 86 (1972).

Thorsten Sellen, ed., *Capital Punishment.*

— DONALD M. BOROCK

CAPITAL PUNISHMENT SINCE 1977

A decade-long moratorium on executions in the United States ended in 1977 when Gary Gilmore faced a firing squad in Utah. By the mid-1990s, nearly 3,000 prisoners in the United States sat on the death rows of thirty-five states (as of the fall of 1995, the death penalty was legal in thirty-eight states), and an average of three dozen inmates were executed each year. In sharp contrast, as a gradual worldwide trend toward abolition of the death penalty continued, the United States stood alone among Western democracies in retaining the death penalty. Increasingly, the main argument in favor of the death penalty has been retribution. Murderers have caused immense pain, and death penalty supporters hold that life imprisonment without parole, which was available in thirty-two states, is insufficient punishment. In addition, studies of imprisoned murderers have found that approximately 1 percent will repeat their crimes, which has led to a pro-death penalty argument called "incapacitation" that it is justifiable to execute 100 to ensure incapacitating the one who will kill again. Deterrence arguments are less central to modern death penalty debates than they were during the 1950s. While some politicians and prosecutors (but almost no scholars) in the 1990s based their support of capital punishment on deterrence, there is virtually no criminological research since the mid-1970s that claims to have found that executions have a greater deterrent effect than long imprisonment.

Increasingly, the main argument in favor of the death penalty has been retribution for the pain caused by murderers.

Opponents of the death penalty include the vast majority of U.S. religious groups (with the major exception of some fundamentalist Protestant denominations), civil rights groups, and human rights organizations (such as Amnesty International). The death penalty, they argue, has never been fairly applied, because those who kill whites are far more likely to be executed than those who kill blacks, that innocent people are occasionally executed, and that defendants able to afford high-quality attorneys are rarely sentenced to death. Death penalty abolitionists increasingly point out that each execution costs millions of dollars more than life imprisonment (because of the costs of trials for defendants who plead not guilty and their appeals), and that these funds could be better used to help families of homicide victims or finding more effective methods of reducing violent crime. Advocates of the death penalty agree that its liabilities are outweighed by its benefits. Opinion polls show that the public is divided on the issue, with approximately 75 percent of respondents favoring the death penalty in some circumstances, but only 50 percent or fewer favoring the death penalty if the alternative exists of life imprisonment without parole. While there were no signs in the 1990s of any state abolishing its death penalty, most states that have the death penalty sought to define the limits of its use by, for example, prohibiting the execution of juveniles (age seventeen or younger at the time of the crime) or the mentally retarded.

[See also Crime.]

BIBLIOGRAPHY

Raymond Paternoster, *Capital Punishment in America* (New York, 1991);

Michael Radelet and Margaret Vandiver, *Capital Punishment in America* (New York, 1988)

— MICHAEL L. RADELET

CAPITALISM

Capitalism, an economic system in which the ownership and control of land, natural resources, and capital; the production and marketing of goods; the employment of labor; and the organization and operation of the system as a whole are entrusted to private enterprise working under competitive conditions. The right to own property, the freedom to make contracts, and the freedom of entrepreneurs to make their own decisions, set prices, and make a profit are basic assumptions of the system, with acquisition of such consumers' goods as food and clothing as the goal. The accumulation, control, and use of capital (primarily by private enterprise) is the way that goal is most quickly reached.

Capital, which economists define as "produced goods intended for further production," includes such items as tools, machines, coal, oil, industrial supplies, and unfinished or unsold goods. Although cash and bank deposits are sometimes called "liquid capital" because they may be directed to any use the possessor wishes, they really are only titles to capital. Capital is man-made and can be created only through someone's saving. Interest is the rental price for its use. Generous use of capital, moreover, is the basis of mass production. The nations with the most capital per person have the highest standard of living.

Capital is produced in all types of economies—whether they be truly communistic; state socialistic, as the Soviet Union is; welfare; or fascistic—but methods of producing capital differ. In a capitalistic economy, capital creation is largely voluntary on the part of citizens and private firms because they are free to set prices and make a profit, subject always to the limitations of competition. In state socialism most capital is created by government decisions imposing forced savings (fewer consumer goods) on the people.

The percentage of the average individual's income drained off by government taxes and then presumably returned to him in the form of goods and services provided by the government can be a measure of the country's economic system. If taxes equal 1 or 2 percent, the system is anarchistic; 3 to 33 percent, capitalistic; 34 to 67 percent, socialistic; and over 67 percent, communistic. Some authorities use other percentages.

The first two English colonies in America were handicapped at the outset by lack of capital and lack of the profit motive. The Pilgrims did not bring a horse, cow, or plow. Their meager supplies soon gave out, and there was a period of starvation. Little incentive existed in either Virginia or Plymouth for the individual to work hard to build up a surplus, since the settlers were expected to put all their produce into a common fund from which all would be supported and out of which the companies financing the expeditions would receive repayment and profit—essentially a communistic system so far as the settlers were concerned. John Smith later remarked, "When our people were fed out of the common store and laboured jointly together . . . the most honest among them would hardly take so much true paines in a weeke as now for themselves they will doe in a day. . . . " When the settlers were permitted greater freedom of enterprise and allowed to accumulate private property, the colonies prospered and grew. Over a century and a half later, the Constitution in many ways reemphasized this way of life.

The right to own property and the freedom of entrepreneurs to make their own decisions and make a profit are basic assumptions of a capitalist economy.

The Industrial Revolution in the capitalistic United States, just as in England earlier, was a spontaneous development, arriving when technology was sufficiently advanced and the rate of saving was about double the rate of capital depreciation. In a socialistic state, in contrast, development is not spontaneous, and the government decides when it will build a factory or a railroad.

In a truly capitalistic economy neither giant private monopolies nor government regulatory bodies should interfere with the operation of the free market system. Even under laissez-faire no such free market system has ever actually existed. But abuses by trusts in the late 19th century and after provided good reason for increasing government regulation of big business. Later on wars and major depressions provided others. After the mid-1960's, chronic inflation supplied excuses for still more regulation, including a growing amount of price fixing by government. Thus, by the early 1970's the federal government was regulating virtually every business in some way. Many big ones (steel, auto, oil, public transportation) either had to get government permission to raise prices or were very limited in how much they could freely raise them. And whereas tax collectors of federal, state, and local governments in 1902 took only 10 percent of the national income, by 1969 they drew off 42 percent. If the United States could any longer be said to have a capitalistic economy, it is only in comparison with the state socialistic economies of Eastern European nations or with the somewhat less socialistic economies of Sweden, Britain, and a few others. The kind of capitalism under which the United States had made its material advances in the 19th century no longer exists.

BIBLIOGRAPHY

R. Blodgett, *Comparative Economic Systems.*

R. Blodgett and D. L. Kemmerer, *Comparative Economic Development.*

T. C. Cochran and T. B. Brewer, *Views of American Economic Growth.*

M. I. Goldman, *Comparative Economic Systems.*

D. L. Kemmerer and C. C. Jones, *American Economic History.*

C. Nettels, *The Roots of American Civilization.*

W. W. Rostow, *The Stages of Economic Growth.*

C. Snyder, *Capitalism the Creator.*

— DONALD L. KEMMERER

CARPETBAGGERS

Carpetbaggers were northerners who went to the South just after the end of the Civil War and, sooner or later, became active in politics as Republicans. The term was a derogatory epithet utilized by their political opponents to stigmatize them as settlers who were so transitory and propertyless that their entire goods could be carried in carpetbags, a then common kind of valise covered with carpeting material. Some individuals may have fitted this stereotype, but no single term—certainly not one devised by their partisan foes—can accurately describe the diverse group of northerners who participated in southern politics as Republicans during Reconstruction. Few of the carpetbaggers were wealthy or prominent when they came to the South, but few, on the other hand, were penniless vagabonds. Primarily they were aspiring young men who, like earlier frontiersmen, moved from their homes to improve their personal lives and status. Many had gained wartime experience in the South while serving as soldiers in the Union army or as agents of the Treasury Department and the Freedmen's Bureau. Others had been sent as missionaries from the North to minister to the educational and religious needs of former slaves.

Whatever drew them to the South, most of the so-called carpetbaggers arrived before the Reconstruction Act of 1867 offered them political opportunities by enfranchising black southerners and disqualifying many former Confederate officeholders. In the constitutional conventions elected in 1867–68, they took an active part in shaping the new state constitutions. When the new governments were established, hundreds of northerners served as Republican state and local officials. At least forty-five sat in the U.S. House of Representatives and seventeen in the Senate; ten were state governors. As is true with any group of political leaders, their conduct and influence varied from state to state and from county to county. Some were corrupt; others were honest. Some were capable; others were inept. Their attitudes toward black southern Republicans varied from close, dedicated alliance to open, hostile opposition. Whenever their Democratic opponents gained control of a state in the 1870's—whether by election or by violence—the role of the carpetbaggers declined rapidly. Many returned to the North or continued their migration toward the West; others remained in the South for the rest of their lives. They disappeared almost completely as a distinguishable class in southern politics after the federal government in 1877 abandoned the enforcement of various Reconstruction measures.

BIBLIOGRAPHY

Richard N. Current, *Three Carpetbag Governors.*

Jonathan Daniels, *Prince of Carpetbaggers: M. S. Littlefield.*

Otto Olson, *Carpetbagger's Crusade: The Life of Albion Winegar Tourgée.*

— JOSEPH LOGSDON

CATHOLIC CHURCH

The Roman Catholic Church grew rapidly in the United States through the nineteenth and early twentieth centuries, from a tiny "Old Catholic" elite with English roots dating to the colonial era and centered in Maryland to a vast congregation of immigrants and their descendants from Ireland, southern Germany, Italy, Poland, and the Slavic countries. The church became important politically at the beginning of the twentieth century; Catholic voters and politicians came to dominate Boston, New York, Philadelphia, Chicago, and Milwaukee, Catholic cathedrals, housing lordly bishops, made a dramatic statement on the urban landscape. Despite the church's growth in the first half of the century, Catholics seemed outsiders. The coincidence of a Catholic president, John F. Kennedy (1961–1963) and the Second Vatican Council (Vatican II, 1962–1965) accelerated the assimilation of the Catholic community, diminishing its sense of being apart and encouraging it to play fuller and often more flexible roles in every aspect of American life.

For a time after Vatican II, religious experiments flourished, including new vernacular liturgies, folk music during services, political radicalism as a form of religious activism, and protests against building churches rather than feeding the poor. Hundreds of priests and nuns, urged to examine their consciences in the light of new intellectual movements as well as Catholic traditions, decided to abandon their vocations. Some religious orders seemed fated to collapse. The number of new vocations each year finally stabilized by 1980, but at a level far lower than in the 1950s. By the time of Pope Paul VI's death in 1978, many Catholics feared that the era of experiment and "updating" had gone too far. They welcomed the forceful leadership of Pope John Paul II, the first Polish pope, who tried to restore a strong central au-

A priest conducts Catholic services for soldiers in a Union Army camp, probably the 69th New York State Militia, during the Civil War. Photograph dated circa 1861-1865. (The National Archives/Corbis)

thority along with a greater emphasis on doctrinal and moral uniformity throughout the Catholic world.

Moral issues continued to beset the American Catholic Church. The 1980s saw a succession of acutely embarrassing sexual scandals, with priests being accused and often convicted of molesting children in their care. Other priests were shown to have buried evidence by moving malefactors to different parishes rather than delivering them from temptation. Even Cardinal Joseph Bernardin of Chicago was accused, in 1993, although he was fully exonerated. Critics of clerical celibacy in the church used these cases to press their argument, but there was no sign in the early 1990s that celibacy would soon be abandoned, despite the practical advantages such a course seemed to offer.

After Vatican II bishops were encouraged to assemble and discuss the affairs of their particular countries. Bishops in the United States welcomed this initiative and created the National Conference of Catholic Bishops (NCCB). In the early 1980s, under the vigorous leadership of Cardinal Bernardin, the NCCB decided to make statements on important political issues, including nuclear weapons, the economy, and the condition of women. The statements were debated in open sessions, each going through several drafts, and often were issued in the form of pastoral letters that became the focus of heated controversy. On nuclear weapons the bishops were strongly influenced by Father Bryan Hehir, who argued that it was intolerable for Christians to threaten the mass annihilation of Soviet citizens as a way of safeguarding the United States and Western Europe. As a result, the letter *The Challenge of Peace* (1983) invoked the Catholic "just war" tradition to condemn a deterrence-based foreign policy. Arguing against Hehir, combative neoconservative Catholics, notably Michael Novak and George Weigel, upheld the principle of deterrence by stressing its practicality and reliance on the weaponry not being used.

Inner-city parochial schools were a popular choice among educationally ambitious African-American families who feared the laxity and physical hazards of public schools.

Novak and U.S. Secretary of the Treasury William Simon led the opposition to the bishops' letter on the economy, *Economic Justice for All* (1986), on grounds that it argued for far-reaching economic rights and wealth equalization in a way they considered utopian. Press commentators took *Economic Justice for All* as a rebuke to President Ronald Reagan's policies. The debate over women as priests also caused controversy, with most bishops upholding the traditional ban on women priests and denying that the church was a sexist institution. This time opposition came from the left, with Rosemary Ruether, Mary Segers, and others, nuns and laity, reproaching the hierarchy for holding to outmoded gender notions.

One issue on which most vocal Catholics agreed was abortion. Church teaching had always opposed it, and church bishops had added their voices to the general condemnation in the late nineteenth century, but the Supreme Court's decision in *Roe* v. *Wade* (1973) gave abortion legal protection. In the 1970s the church encouraged Catholic activists to ally with evangelical Protestants. Since then, Catholics have played a prominent role in the antiabortion and anticontraception movements, including the militant Operation Rescue, which has obstructed access to abortion clinics and, in the tradition of the African-American leader Martin Luther King, Jr., in confronting injustice, has cited loyalty to a higher law. One Catholic antiabortion activist, Joan Andrews, faced repeated arrest and imprisonment, including eighteen months of solitary confinement in a Florida prison, for her part in "rescues" and destruction of abortion clinics. Catholic bishops condemned abortion but they had to be careful not to breach the line of church-state separation. Cardinal Bernardin noted that by favoring economic liberalism and opposing abortion, the bishops placed themselves in an anomalous position, both left and right on the political spectrum, but, he said, on both issues Catholics venerated human life and dignity, so their argument created a "seamless garment" (a reference to Jesus's cloak). In 1994 the National Conference of Catholic Bishops announced it would oppose any national health plan that financed abortions.

The abortion issue caused Catholic politicians great anxiety, since favoring either side could cost them many votes. A few were willing to accept the consequences of antiabortion advocacy, notably Robert P. Casey, pro-life Democratic governor of Pennsylvania from 1986 to 1994, whose career showed that his views on the issue did not prevent electoral success (he retired undefeated after a heart transplant). More common was the compromise position proposed by New York Governor Mario Cuomo (1982–1994), who said he was personally opposed to abortion but would uphold the law and accept its consequences until it could be changed by the legislature. Geraldine Ferraro, the Democratic candidate for vice president in 1984 and a Catholic, favored the Cuomo compromise.

In the late nineteenth and early twentieth centuries American Catholics built a large educational system, which enabled families to have their children schooled in the faith from kindergarten to graduate school. Some Catholic universities, notably Notre Dame and Georgetown, achieved academic distinction. John Tracy Ellis, professor of history at Catholic University of America, wrote in 1955 that Catholic intellectual life lagged woefully behind its secular rival. After a lengthy, heated debate, Catholic colleges in the following decades raised their standards. A bitter faculty strike at New York's St. John's University (1965–1966) over salaries and lack of academic freedom, prompted the Vincentian order to place the university in the hands of a lay board of trustees. Lay boards became the norm in the 1970s and 1980s, and Catholic colleges and universities began to stress quality education more strongly than Catholic distinctiveness. An important Supreme Court decision, *Tilton* v. *Richardson* (1971), assured the schools and their students of access to federal funds as long as the buildings being financed were for educational rather than religious activities. Even so, no Catholic educational institution was on any national list of best colleges and universities in the early 1990s. Meanwhile, parochial schools enjoyed a recovery for their willingness to uphold strict disciplinary standards and emphasize educational basics (reading, writing, arithmetic, and religion). Inner-city parochial schools were a popular choice among educationally ambitious African-American families that feared the laxity and physical hazards of public schools.

Catholic commentators such as Andrew Greeley have noted a residual anti-Catholicism in the media, evidenced in pejorative remarks that would be intolerable if spoken about other groups.

Just as the character of the church changed in the nineteenth century with mass immigration, it changed again between 1960 and 1990 as increasing numbers of Latin American immigrants came to the United States. Their loyalty to different saints and traditions, notably St. Rose of Lima and Our Lady of Guadalupe, meant that church and liturgy took on a rather different appearance in Los Angeles and Tucson than in Boston and Detroit. Hispanic priests rose to senior positions in the church, notably Patricio Flores, the son of migrant farm workers who became bishop of San Antonio in 1970. There was little enthusiasm among their congregations for liberation theology, which linked political liberation for persecuted Latin American peoples in, for example, El Salvador and Nicaragua, to the promise of the Gospel. Some of the new Catholics, especially exiles from Cuba and South Vietnam, had every reason to dread the linkage of their faith with left-wing political movements.

Catholic commentators, such as the prolific sociologist and novelist Andrew Greeley, noted that in the 1980s there was a residual anti-Catholicism in America, especially in the media and among intellectuals, and that it was common to hear pejorative remarks about Catholics that would have been intolerable if made about Jews or African Americans. Even Greeley had to admit, however, that anti-Catholicism was less intense than thirty years earlier. Another sociologist, Robert Wuthnow, noted a large-scale restructuring of American religion, whereby conservative Catholics, Jews, and Protestants found themselves allied on political questions against liberal Catholics, Jews, and Protestants.

[See also Abortion.]

BIBLIOGRAPHY

Patrick Allitt, *Catholic Intellectuals and Conservative Politics in America, 1950–1985* (Ithaca, N.Y., 1993).

Timothy Byrnes and Mary Segers, eds., *The Catholic Church and the Politics of Abortion* (Boulder, Colo., 1992).

Jay P. Dolan, *The American Catholic Experience* (Garden City, N.Y., 1985).

James Hennessy, *American Catholics* (New York, 1981).

Robert Wuthnow, *The Restructuring of American Religion* (Princeton, N.J., 1988).

— PATRICK ALLITT

CATTLE DRIVES

Contrary to popular conception, long-distance cattle driving was traditional not only in Texas but elsewhere in America long before the Chisholm Trail was dreamed of. The Spaniards, the establishers of the ranching industry in the New World, drove herds northward from Mexico as far back as 1540. In the 18th century and on into the 19th the Spanish settlements in Texas derived most of their meager revenue from horses and cattle driven into Louisiana, though such trade was usually contraband. Meantime in the United States, herds were sometimes driven long distances. In 1790 the boy Davy Crockett helped drive "a large stock of cattle" 400 miles from Tennessee into Virginia; twenty years later he took a drove of horses from the Tennessee River into southern North Carolina. In 1815 Timothy Flint "encountered a drove of more than 1,000 cattle and swine" being driven from the interior of Ohio to Philadelphia. The stock in the states was gentle, often managed on foot. The history of trail driving involves horses as well as cattle.

Notwithstanding antecedent examples, Texans established trail driving as a regular occupation. Before they revolted from Mexico in 1836, they had a "Beef Trail" to New Orleans. In the 1840s they extended their markets northward into Missouri—Sedalia, Baxter Springs, Springfield, and Saint Louis becoming the principal markets. During the 1850's emigration and freighting from the Missouri River westward demanded great numbers of oxen, the firm of Russell, Majors and Waddell in 1858 utilizing 40,000 oxen. Texas longhorn steers by the thousands were broken for work oxen. Herds of longhorns were driven to Chicago, and one herd at least to New York.

Under Spanish-Mexican ownership, California as well as Texas developed ranching, and during the 1830's and 1840's a limited number of cattle were trailed from there to Oregon. But the discovery of gold in California arrested for a while all development there of the cattle industry and created a high demand for outside beef. During the 1850's, although cattle were occasionally driven to California from Missouri, Arkansas, and perhaps other states, the big drives were from Texas. Steers worth $15 in Texas were selling in San Francisco for as high as $150. One Texas rancher in 1854 hired for $1,500 a famous Indian fighter to captain his herd of 1,000 steers to California; thirty-five armed men accompanied it. These drives were fraught with great danger from both Indians and desert thirst.

During the Civil War, Texas drove cattle throughout the states for the Confederate forces. At the close of the war Texas had probably 5 million cattle—and no market. Late in 1865 a few cowmen tried to find a market. In 1866 there were many drives northward without a definite destination and without much financial success; also to the old but limited New Orleans market, following mostly well-established trails to the wharves of Shreveport and Jefferson (Texas). In 1867 Joseph G. McCoy opened a regular market at Abilene, Kans. The great cattle trails, moving successively westward, were established and trail driving boomed. In 1867 the Goodnight-Loving Trail opened up New Mexico and Colorado to Texas cattle. By the tens of thousands they were soon driven into Arizona. In Texas itself cattle raising was expanding like wildfire. Caldwell, Dodge City, Ogallala, Cheyenne, and other towns became famous because of trail-driver patronage.

During the 1870's the buffaloes were virtually exterminated and the Indians of the Plains and Rockies were at the same time subjugated, penned up, and put on beef rations. An empire was left vacant. It was first occupied by Texas longhorns, driven by Texas cowboys. The course of empire in America has been west, but over much of Oklahoma, Kansas, Nebraska, the Dakotas, Wyoming, Montana, and parts of Nevada and Idaho the precursors of this movement were trail men from the South. The Long Trail extended into Canada. In the 1890's herds were still driven from the Panhandle of Texas to Montana, but trail driving virtually ended in 1895. Barbed wire, railroads, and nesters ended it. During three swift decades it had moved over ten million cattle and one million range horses, stamped the entire West with its character, given economic and personality prestige to Texas, made the longhorn the most historic brute in bovine history, glorified the cowboy over the globe, and endowed America with its most romantic tradition relating to any occupation—a peer to England's tradition of the sea.

BIBLIOGRAPHY

Andy Adams, *The Log of a Cowboy.*
J. H. Cook, *Fifty Years on the Old Frontier.*
E. E. Dale, *The Range Cattle Industry.*
J. Evetts Haley, *Charles Goodnight.*
J. M. Hunter, *The Trail Drivers of Texas.*
E. S. Osgood, *The Day of the Cattleman.*
W. M. Raine and Will C. Barnes, *Cattle.*
Walter P. Webb, *The Great Plains.*

— J. FRANK DOBIE

CAVALRY, HORSE

Horse Cavalry, a branch of the U.S. Army, used with varying effectiveness from the American Revolution through the Indian wars in the West. In 1775 and 1776 the Continental army fought with a few mounted militia commands as its only cavalry. In December 1776 the Congress authorized 3,000 light horse and the army organized four regiments of cavalry. Because these regiments were never even at half strength, George Washington recommended that they be converted to legions in 1780. The four legions and various partisan mounted units were used mainly for raiding; they were seldom employed in pitched battles. At the end of the war, all cavalry commands were discharged. During the next fifty years when regular cavalry units did exist, they were organized for short periods of time and comprised only a minute part of the army. Most states, however, possessed organized mounted militias, and these commands were employed by the army under the terms of the Militia Act of 1792.

Indian trouble along the western frontier revived the need for federal horse soldiers. In 1832 Congress passed

"An Act to Authorize the President to Raise Mounted Volunteers for the Defense of the Frontier." Organized along the lines of emergency state militia, the six Mounted Volunteer Ranger companies showed the value of using mounted government troops in the West but also proved that a more efficient, less expensive force was needed. With little or no training or discipline, the volunteers had cost the government almost $154,000 more than a regiment of dragoons; the army needed a more permanent organization. On Mar. 2, 1833, Congress replaced the Mounted Rangers with the Regiment of United States Dragoons, a ten-company force mounted for speed but trained to fight both mounted and dismounted. In May 1836 the Second Regiment of Dragoons was formed to fight in the Seminole War.

Ten years later, after the commencement of the Mexican War, Congress augmented the two dragoon regiments with the Regiment of Mounted Riflemen; a third dragoon regiment; and several voluntary commands. The only new organization to escape the standard army reductions at the conclusion of hostilities was the Mounted Riflemen. In 1855 the government enlarged the mounted wing by two additional regiments—the First Cavalry and the Second Cavalry. According to the general orders, these new regiments were to be a distinct, separate arm of the army. Mounted forces from 1855 until 1861 were divided into dragoons, mounted riflemen, and cavalrymen.

Not until the Confederate cavalry corps demonstrated the efficiency of mass tactics and reconnaissances did the Union cavalry begin to imitate the southern horse soldiers.

During the Civil War the U.S. Cavalry evolved into an efficient organization. In August 1861 the army redesignated the regular horse regiments as cavalry, renumbering them one through six according to each organization's seniority. The First Dragoons thereupon became the First Cavalry. Not until the Confederate cavalry corps demonstrated the efficiency of mass tactics and reconnaissances, however, did the Union cavalry begin to imitate the southern horse soldiers. By the end of the war, the cavalry corps had demonstrated devastating effectiveness. After the Civil War, the six regiments were not able to perform all duties assigned. Consequently, in July 1866 Congress authorized four additional regiments—the Seventh, Eighth, Ninth, and Tenth. The new regiments increased the number of cavalry troops from 448 to 630 and the total manpower from 39,273 to 54,302. The Ninth and Tenth Cavalry represented a departure from past traditions. These regiments were manned by black enlisted men and noncommissioned officers commanded by white officers. During the western Indian wars, the cavalry performed adequately under adverse conditions. Much of the time there were too few troops for so vast a region and such determined foes; a cost-conscious Congress rarely provided adequate support.

After the conclusion of the Indian wars in the early 1890s, the horse cavalry declined in importance. Some troops served as infantry during the Spanish-American War, and the cavalry was revived briefly during Gen. John Pershing's punitive expedition into Mexico. But during World War I only four regiments were sent to France, after which the mechanization of armies made the horse cavalry obsolete.

BIBLIOGRAPHY

James M. Merrill, *Spurs to Glory: The Story of the United States Cavalry.*

Francis Paul Prucha, *The Sword of the Republic: The United States Army on the Frontier, 1783–1846.*

Robert M. Utley, *Frontiersmen in Blue: The United States Army and the Indian, 1848–1865,* and *Frontier Regulars: The United States Army and the Indian, 1866–1891.*

— EMMETT M. ESSIN III

CENTENNIAL EXPOSITION

Centennial Exposition, celebrating the one hundredth anniversary of the Declaration of Independence, held in Philadelphia in 1876, was the first great international exposition held in America. It was ten years in the planning and building; it covered more than 450 acres in Fairmount Park; its total cost was more than $11 million. Thirty-seven foreign nations constructed pavilions, many in their native architectural styles. The 167 buildings of the exposition housed more than 30,000 exhibitors from 50 nations. The gates were opened on May 10, and during the 159 days that followed there were 8,004,274 cash admissions. There were seven principal divisions in the exposition: mining and metallurgy, manufactured products, science and education, fine arts, machinery, agriculture, and horticulture. The Woman's Building, an innovation in expositions, demonstrated the relative emancipation of women in America.

There was no midway or similar amusement, for nothing could have competed with the intense public interest in the working models of many new machines and processes. The architecture was confused, but impressive. The influence of various foreign exhibits evoked a new interest in interior decoration in America. In this exposition the world, for the first time, saw industrial America on display. Americans realized that the machine age had arrived and that their country was, in many ways, at last coming of age. The centennial exposition was honest, homely, and revealing; it provided an immense stimulus to the growing aesthetic, social, and industrial consciousness of America.

BIBLIOGRAPHY

Dee Brown, *The Year of the Century: 1876.*

— FRANK MONAGHAN

CENTRAL INTELLIGENCE AGENCY

Central Intelligence Agency (CIA), described as both the most famous and least-known U.S. agency, exists to provide the knowledge of the world beyond the United States that U.S. policymakers need for decision and action. The failure of U.S. intelligence to warn of the Japanese attack on Pearl Harbor in 1941 and the role of the Office of Strategic Services (OSS) in World War II led President Harry S. Truman in early 1946 to establish a small interdepartmental Central Intelligence Group (CIG) to coordinate and summarize intelligence from existing organizations. Headed by a director of central intelligence (DCI), the CIG soon collected and produced intelligence independently and carried out clandestine operations overseas. As the Soviet Union emerged as the principal potential enemy, the United States organized a new national security structure. The 1947 National Security Act gave the president leadership of the new system, the centerpiece of which was the National Security Council (NSC). The Joint Chiefs of Staff (JCS) and a new Central Intelligence Agency (to replace the CIG) were to provide the NSC with coordinated military and intelligence advice. Independent of any department and with no policymaking role, the CIA was to gather information otherwise unobtainable and assess the world situation from a national perspective. The CIA chief kept the title of director of central intelligence, and since none of the existing departmental intelligence organizations was dissolved, the director's role was to coordinate—not to command or control—what was soon called the U.S. intelligence community.

Soon after the outbreak of the Korean War in 1950, President Truman appointed a new DCI, Lieutenant General Walter Bedell Smith, to reorganize, reform, and expand the CIA. When Smith left in January 1953, the CIA had acquired a central administration, large functional directorates, and a mechanism for producing national intelligence estimates—authoritative intelligence community appraisals of future developments—for the president and NSC. Smith also formed a single clandestine service by merging the Office of Policy Coordination, which the NSC had created in 1948 to carry out anticommunist covert action programs, with the CIA's more traditional espionage units. While supporting the war in Korea, the CIA played a larger role in preparations abroad for the global conflict U.S. policymakers feared was imminent.

U.S. intelligence's failure to anticipate the Japanese attack on Pearl Harbor and the Office of Strategic Services' work in WWII led Truman in 1946 to establish a centralized intelligence bureau.

As DCI from 1953 to 1961, Allen Dulles developed the CIA's covert action capabilities to orchestrate worldwide propaganda, influence foreign elections, and if necessary mount coups against unfriendly governments, as in Iran in 1953 and Guatemala in 1954. Although the Soviet Union remained the principal espionage target, the CIA increasingly worked against communist takeovers in developing countries. This led to deep involvement in Southeast Asia and to a disastrous attempt to overthrow Cuba's Premier Fidel Castro in the Bay of Pigs invasion of 1961. As Soviet weaponry developed, the CIA's high-altitude U-2 aircraft and new satellite reconnaissance systems vastly increased the quantity and reliability of intelligence on the USSR. In the early 1960s these systems demonstrated that fears of a growing Soviet lead in missile development were groundless and that there was no "missile gap" between the Soviet Union and the United States, as some critics had argued.

From 1961 to 1965 DCI John McCone built up the CIA's reconnaissance satellite capabilities, fought the air force for control of them, and formed an effective new Directorate of Science and Technology. The agency's success in spotting Soviet intermediate-range missiles in Cuba in the October 1962 crisis compensated for its failure to warn that the crisis was coming. Vietnam loomed over the entire 1960s as the CIA played out its assigned role in pacification, nation-building, and the massive U.S. military intervention. The CIA's generally pessimistic estimates on Vietnam were sound, but by the late 1960s Richard Helms, DCI under both Presidents Lyndon B. Johnson and Richard M. Nixon, faced increasing public criticism of the CIA's role in two decades of covert action that had supported anti-Soviet forces (especially of the noncommunist left) in Western Europe's trade unions, political parties, student movements, and intellectual circles.

The CIA's time of trial came in the 1970s and resulted in a new accountability to Congress as well as to the president. After Helms rebuffed White House efforts to use the CIA for the Watergate cover-up, President Nixon dismissed him and appointed James R. Schlesinger in early 1973. In five months as DCI, Schlesinger revamped the agency's management, reduced secrecy, and consolidated the agency's technological base. His forced reduction of personnel left the agency shaken. His successor, William Colby, brought changes in producing national intelligence estimates, managing priorities and resources, and bringing daily intelligence to the president. By early 1975, however, sensational press disclosures of past domestic operations and assassination attempts abroad enmeshed the CIA in investigations by a presidential commission and by a select committee in each house of Congress, one chaired by Representative Otis Pike and the other by Senator Frank Church. These exhaustive and exhausting investigations led to formation of a permanent intelligence oversight committee in the Senate in 1976 and in the House in 1977. Succeeding Colby in 1976, DCI George Bush worked to restore public confidence in the CIA and to reassure the agency that it had top-level political support. Admiral Stansfield Turner, President Jimmy Carter's DCI, made further personnel reductions, reduced covert actions, emphasized technical collection, and sought good relations with the new congressional oversight committees. From late 1979 the U.S. government, including the CIA, had to cope with the Iranian hostage crisis and the Soviet army's invasion of Afghanistan.

In the early 1980s the CIA's funds, personnel, and roles expanded rapidly as President Ronald Reagan's administration renewed the cold war with words, covert activities, and greatly increased defense spending. Under DCI William J. Casey the intelligence directorate (which prepares analyses for the president and other top policymakers) was reorganized by geographical regions and the production of estimates increased. After Casey intensified covert action support—begun under Turner—for the Afghan rebels, Soviet forces withdrew in 1989. Support for the contras in Central America, however, proved politically sensitive, and only Casey's death in May 1987 cut off inquiry into his role in the Iran-Contra affair. Casey's successor, DCI William Webster, sought to rebuild public and congressional trust in the CIA and led the agency through the Gulf War of 1991, the collapse of the Soviet Union, and the end of the cold war.

The breakup of the Soviet empire brought the demise of the CIA's principal target for more than four decades. Succeeding Webster as DCI in late 1991, Robert M. Gates recognized the large and diverse new problems the CIA faced, from nuclear proliferation and high-technology transfer to regional and ethnic conflicts, international terrorism, and drug trafficking. Forming a host of task forces, Gates made important changes in the CIA's structure and policies. In early 1992 he began, and his successors continued, an unprecedented openness policy to make the CIA more accountable to the public, providing greater access to the CIA, including a program to declassify the CIA's records.

After Richard Helms rebuffed White House efforts to use the CIA for the Watergate cover-up, Nixon dismissed him and appointed James Schlesinger.

R. James Woolsey, appointed DCI by President Bill Clinton in 1993, pressed Congress to avoid rapid budget cuts and permit an orderly reduction in the size, cost, and capabilities of the CIA and intelligence community. Congressional criticism of the CIA intensified, however, after the revelation in 1994 that a midlevel operations officer, Aldrich Ames, had been selling the agency's secrets to the Soviet KGB and its successor Russian intelligence service since 1985. Ames's treason had betrayed—some to their deaths—most of the remarkable array of Soviet and East European spies that the CIA recruited in the 1980s. Using the CIA inspector general's 450-page classified report, both House and Senate intelligence oversight committees castigated the agency, which, in the words of the Senate report, was "unwilling and unable to face, assess, and investigate the catastrophic blow Ames had dealt to the core of its operations."

After strengthening counterintelligence and security, especially in its Directorate of Operations, DCI Woolsey resigned in 1995, reportedly persuaded that he lacked the president's support in dealing with both the Ames case and wider issues of restructuring the CIA and intelligence community. In early 1995 President Clinton formed a new commission to study the intelligence community's post–cold war roles and capabilities and to report back to the president and Congress by March 1996. When former Deputy Secretary of Defense John Deutch took office as DCI in May 1995, the president gave him both cabinet rank and a mandate to assemble a new leadership team for the CIA and the intelligence community.

[See also Cold War; Federal Bureau of Investigation; Gulf War of 1991; Iran-Contra Affair.]

BIBLIOGRAPHY

Christopher M. Andrew, *For the President's Eyes Only: Secret Intelligence and the American Presidency from Washington to Bush* (New York, 1995).

William M. Leary, ed., *The Central Intelligence Agency: History and Documents* (University, Ala., 1984).

G. J. A. O'Toole, *The Encyclopedia of American Intelligence and Espionage* (New York, 1988).

Thomas Powers, *The Man Who Kept the Secrets: Richard Helms and the CIA* (New York, 1979).

John Ranelagh, *The Agency: The Rise and Decline of the CIA* (New York, 1987).

— J. KENNETH MCDONALD

CENTRAL PACIFIC–UNION PACIFIC RACE

Central Pacific–Union Pacific Race, a construction contest between the two companies bidding for government subsidies, land grants, and public favor. The original Pacific Railway Act (1862) authorized the Central Pacific to build eastward from the California line and the Union Pacific to build westward to the western Nevada boundary. This legislation was unpopular with the railroad companies, and they planned to build beyond the designated boundaries. Their attitude led to amendments to the Pacific Railway Act (1865–66), which authorized the roads to continue construction until they met. The amendments precipitated a historic race, 1867–69, because the company building the most track would receive the larger subsidy.

The competing companies projected their lines 300 miles in advance of actual construction, which was technically within the law. But when surveys crossed and recrossed, the railroad officials got into legal battles and the crews into personal ones. When the two roads were about 100 miles apart, Congress passed a law compelling the companies to join their tracks at Promontory Point, Utah, some 50 miles from the end of each completed line. The final, and most spectacular, lap of the race was made toward this point in the winter and spring of 1869, the tracks being joined on May 10. Neither company won the race because there was no definite goal on Promontory Point that had to be reached. The race was a dead heat if anything because both tracks reached the immediate vicinity at about the same time.

BIBLIOGRAPHY

Gen. G. M. Dodge, *The Dodge Records.*

— J. R. PERKINS

CHALLENGER DISASTER

Challenger disaster (Jan. 28, 1986). Perhaps no tragedy since the assassination of President John F. Kennedy in 1963 so riveted the American public as the explosion of the space shuttle *Challenger,* which killed its seven-member crew. The horrific moment came 73 seconds after liftoff from Cape Canaveral and was captured on television and rebroadcast to a stunned and grieving nation. Nearly nineteen years to the day that three Apollo astronauts were killed by a fire during a launch rehearsal, the *Challenger* crew prepared for the nation's twenty-fifth space shuttle mission. Successes of the National Aeronautics and Space Administration (NASA) in shuttle missions had made Americans almost immune to the dangers of space flight. If not for the fact that a New Hampshire schoolteacher, Sharon Christa McAuliffe, had been chosen to be the first private citizen to fly in the shuttle, the launch might have received little attention in the nation's media. The temperature

Perhaps no tragedy since the JFK assassination so riveted the U.S. public as the televised explosion of the space shuttle Challenger.

on the morning of the launch was thirty-eight degrees, following an overnight low of twenty-four degrees, the coldest for any shuttle launch. Liftoff occurred sixteen days after the space shuttle *Columbia* was launched, the shortest interval ever between shuttle flights. Sixty seconds after the launch NASA scientists observed an "unusual plume" from *Challenger*'s right booster engine. A burn-through of the rocket seal caused an external fuel tank to rupture and led to an unforgettable flash and then the sickeningly slow fall of flaming debris into the Atlantic Ocean. In addition to McAuliffe the dead included *Challenger* pilot Michael J. Smith, a decorated Vietnam War veteran; flight commander Francis R. Scobee; laser physicist Ronald E. McNair, the second African American in space; aerospace engineer Ellison S. Onizuka, the first Japanese-American in space; payload specialist Gregory B. Jarvis; and electrical engineer Judith A. Resnick, the second U.S. woman in space. The diversity of the crew, reflecting that of the American people, made the tragedy an occasion for national mourning.

A commission led by former Secretary of State William P. Rogers and astronaut Neil Armstrong concluded that NASA, its Marshall Space Flight Center, and the contractor Morton Thiokol, the booster's manufacturer, were guilty of faulty management and poor engineering. NASA's ambitious launch schedule, it was found, had outstripped its resources and overridden warnings from safety engineers. The successful launch of the space shuttle *Discovery* on Sept. 29, 1988, marked the nation's return to manned space flight. The *Challenger* disaster had sobered the space agency, prompting hundreds of design and procedural changes costing $2.4 billion. The shuttle was now tied almost exclusively to delivering defense and scientific payloads, and the space program, long a symbol of U.S. exceptionalism, continued to receive substantial if less enthusiastic support from the public.

[See also Space Program.]

BIBLIOGRAPHY

Sue L. Hamilton, *Space Shuttle Challenger* (Bloomington, Minn., 1988).

Diane Vaughn, *The Challenger Launch Decision* (Chicago, 1996).

— BRUCE J. EVENSEN

CHARTERED COMPANIES

Chartered companies, British trading companies that played an important part in colonization in the New World, though they did not originate for that purpose. The joint-stock company was already in existence in many countries in the 16th century as an effective means of carrying on foreign trade, and when the New World attracted the interest of merchants, companies were formed for purposes of trade in that direction. Since production of certain desired articles required the transportation of laborers, colonization became a by-product of the trading company. The first English company to undertake successful colonization was the Virginia Company, first chartered in 1606 and, through two subcompanies, authorized to operate on the Atlantic coast between thirty-four and forty-five degrees north latitude. The original project was somewhat enlarged and developed more in detail by later charters in 1609 and 1612 to the London branch of the Virginia Company, and in 1620 to the Council for New England, the successor to the Plymouth branch. Down to the Puritan Revolution this method of sponsoring colonization predominated. The Newfoundland Company of 1610, the Bermuda Company of 1615, an enlargement of an earlier project under the auspices of the Virginia Company, the Massachusetts Bay Company of 1629, and the Providence Island Company of 1630 represent the most important attempts at trade and colonization. After the Puritan Revolution, the lord proprietor superseded the trading company as preferred sponsor of colonization, both king and colonists becoming increasingly distrustful of corporations. Massachusetts and Bermuda, the last of the companies in control of colonization, lost their charters in 1684, but the former had long since ceased to be commercial in character.

BIBLIOGRAPHY

C. M. Andrews, *The Colonial Period of American History*, vol. I.

H. L. Osgood, *The American Colonies in the Seventeenth Century*.

— VIOLA F. BARNES

CHECKS AND BALANCES

Checks and balances is the term used to denote the separation of powers of government that was the underlying principle upon which the government of the United States was created by the Convention of 1787. This theory became popular in America in large part because of the writings of Montesquieu and William Blackstone. It consists in setting off legislative and executive departments from each other and the courts against both. Each department of government is supposed to operate as far as possible within a separate sphere of administration, but the cooperation of all three is necessary for the conduct of the government.

The makers of the Constitution were aware of the weakness of the Continental government under the Articles of Confederation. This consisted in the complete conduct of the government by the Continental Congress with practically no executive or judicial departments. For this reason the office of president of the United States was created and largely modeled upon the kingship of Great Britain. In order to prevent executive aggression, such as had caused the misgovernment of George III, the system of checks and balances was introduced and also provision was made for a federal judiciary. Furthermore it was provided that the Senate and House of Representatives should act as checks upon each other in the national Congress.

BIBLIOGRAPHY

W. Wilson, *Constitutional Government in the United States*.

— WILLIAM STARR MYERS

CHEROKEE TRAIL

Cherokee Trail, also known as the Trappers' Trail, was laid out and marked in the summer of 1848 by Lt.

Abraham Buford in command of Company H of the First Dragoons. It had previously been followed by trappers en route to the Rocky Mountains. It extended from the vicinity of Fort Gibson up the Arkansas River to the mouth of the Cimarron and up the latter stream to a point in the northwestern part of what is now Oklahoma. From here it ran west to the Sante Fe Trail, which it joined at Middle Cimarron Spring. It was followed by many Cherokee and whites from northeastern Arkansas on their way to the gold fields of California.

BIBLIOGRAPHY

Ralph P. Bieber, ed., *Southern Trails to California*, Southwest Historical Series, vol. V.

— EDWARD EVERETT DALE

CHEROKEE WARS

Cherokee Wars (1776–81). The Cherokee Indians had generally sided with the English in their wars against the French, but friendly relations with the British colonists were endangered by the steady encroachment of the latter upon Cherokee lands. In 1760 the Cherokee were provoked into a war of two years' duration with Carolina colonists. Agreements were subsequently approved by some Cherokee chiefs, but not by others, to cede lands not only to the Carolinas but also to Georgia and Virginia.

During the Revolution, the Cherokee sided with the British, despite the fact that in 1776 commissioners of the Continental Congress held a conference with the Cherokee for the purpose of conciliating them. Restless because of the continued encroachment upon their lands by the colonists, encouraged and supplied with ammunition by British agents, and incited by Shawnee and other northern Indians, the Cherokee were soon engaged in a general war on the frontiers of the Carolinas, Virginia, and Georgia. In the summer of 1776 the Cherokee, joined by some Tories, began attacking frontier settlements along the Watauga and Holston rivers in eastern Tennessee, but they were beaten off. The raids brought punitive expeditions of militiamen converging upon the Cherokee from Georgia, the Carolinas, and Virginia. Dispirited because of the refusal of the Creek Indians to come to their assistance and receiving little of the anticipated aid from the British, the Cherokee offered inadequate resistance and were soon decisively defeated. Nearly all the Cherokee towns were plundered and burned. Several hundred Cherokee fled to British protection in Florida. Cherokee elder leaders sued for peace with the colonies in June and July 1777, at the price of further cessions of Cherokee lands.

Not all the Cherokee were willing to settle for peace, and a tribal schism resulted. The dissident and more warlike faction, under the leadership of Dragging Canoe, separated from the rest of the tribe, pushing down the Tennessee River and establishing new settlements on Chickamauga Creek. They became known as the Chickamauga, and during the next four years they intermittently raided the frontier communities. In 1779 the Overhill Cherokee also reverted to hostility, joining the Chickamauga and some Creek in cooperating with

During the Revolution, the Cherokee sided with the British, even though commissioners of the Continental Congress had met with the Cherokee in 1776 in an attempt to conciliate them.

Gen. Charles Cornwallis and Maj. Patrick Ferguson in attacking some colonial frontier settlements. Again a joint Virginia and North Carolina expedition devastated the Cherokee towns. In the spring of 1781 a peace treaty was made with the Cherokee that confirmed the land cessions of 1777. The treaty was thereafter strictly observed by all the Cherokee except the Chickamauga, against whom John Sevier led expeditions in 1781 and 1782. The Chickamauga moved farther down the Tennessee River and built the Five Lower Towns, continuing their hostility to the whites.

BIBLIOGRAPHY

R. S. Cotterill, *The Southern Indians: The Story of the Civilized Tribes Before Removal.*

Fred Gearing, *Priests and Warriors: Social Structures for Cherokee Politics in the Eighteenth Century.*

Grace S. Woodward, *The Cherokees.*

— KENNETH M. STEWART

CHEYENNE

One of the better known and perhaps more dramatic of the Plains tribes, the Cheyenne ranged, in the 17th century, through western South Dakota, eastern Montana, and much of northern Wyoming; a branch of the tribe pushed well into Colorado. From the 18th century onward, the Cheyenne were continually on the move. They are of special interest because their historical migrations are well authenticated. An Algonkin-speaking group, the Cheyenne appeared on the Minnesota River before 1700, while some of the tribe are known to have visited the fort of Robert Cavelier, Sieur de La Salle, in

Illinois in 1680. Yielding to population pressures and to incursions against them by other tribes, notably the Ojibwa (or Chippewa), the Cheyenne pushed into the Missouri River valley by 1800. In the setting of the high Plains, they abandoned a way of life connected with farming and pottery making and, becoming superior horsemen, threw themselves into the Plains pattern. They took over the classic Plains encampment organization, the general social and political patterns, the military societies, and ritual and ceremonial life. Never too numerous a group—one estimate gives 3,500 as the population in 1780—the Cheyenne nevertheless became a power in the area, making and breaking alliances with other tribes.

Between 1832 and 1851 some of the Cheyenne settled on the upper Arkansas River at Bent's Fort; others remained near the headwaters of the Platte and Yellowstone. The split is reflected in the division between the Northern and Southern Cheyenne. The southern groups fought the Kiowa but later allied with them, while the northern segment was involved with the Dakota, participating in part in the wars against Gen. George Armstrong Custer in the 1870's. The separation demonstrates the primacy of the local band in the Plains.

BIBLIOGRAPHY

G. B. Grinnell, *The Cheyenne Indians.*
E. A. Hoebel, *The Cheyennes, Indians of the Great Plains.*

ROBERT F. SPENCER

CHICAGO FIRE

Modern Chicago began its growth in 1833; by 1871 it had a population of 300,000. Across the broad plain that skirts the Chicago River's mouth buildings by the thousand extended, constructed with no thought of resistance to fire. Even the sidewalks were built of resinous pine and the single pumping station which supplied the mains with water was covered with a wooden roof. The season was one of excessive dryness. A scorching wind blew up from the plains of the far Southwest week after week and withered the growing crops and made the structures of pine-built Chicago dry as tinder. A conflagration of appalling proportions awaited only the starting spark.

It began on Sunday evening, Oct. 8, 1871. Where it started is clear; how it started no one knows. Living in a small shingled cottage at the corner of Jefferson and DeKoven streets was a poor Irish family by the name of O'Leary. The traditional story is that Mrs. O'Leary went out to the barn with a lamp to milk her cow; the lamp was upset and cow, stable, and Chicago were engulfed in one common ruin. But Mrs. O'Leary testified under oath that she was safe abed and knew nothing about the fire until she was called by a friend of the family.

Once started, the fire moved onward resistlessly to the north and east until there was nothing more to burn. Between nine o'clock on Sunday evening and ten-thirty the following night an area of five square miles, including the central business district of the city, was burned, over 17,500 buildings were destroyed, and 100,000 people were rendered

A view of the corner of Lake Street and Wacker Drive after the 1871 Chicago fire. A pine-board structure was erected temporarily in the corner. (UPI/Corbis-Bettmann)

homeless. From Taylor Street to Lincoln Park, from the river to the lake, the city lay in ruins. The direct property loss was about $200 million. The loss of human lives, while never known, is commonly estimated at between 200 and 300. The mass of misery and the indirect material losses entailed by the fire were never measured.

BIBLIOGRAPHY

Robert Cromie, *The Great Chicago Fire.*

— M. M. QUAIFE

CHICKASAW TREATY

Chickasaw Treaty (1783), negotiated by Virginia's commissioners with the Chickasaw, under the great Piomingo and other chiefs, at Nashborough (Nashville). This treaty removed the claim of that tribe to the territory between the Cumberland River and the ridge that divided the waters of that river from those of the Tennessee, to the south of Nashborough. The primary purpose of the Virginia government was to obtain a cession of western Kentucky, between the Tennessee and the Mississippi. That failed, and the remarkable result was that, at Virginia's expense, her commissioners, treating on North Carolina soil, cleared for North Carolinians the Indian title from one of the most fertile stretches of land in the West. Another result was the cementing of a firm friendship between the Cumberland settlers and the Chickasaw, a tribe ever noted for its fidelity.

BIBLIOGRAPHY

T. P. Abernethy, *Western Lands and the American Revolution.*

— SAMUEL C. WILLIAMS

CHILD LABOR

Child labor, once thought to have been virtually eliminated except in agriculture, again became a social issue in the 1970's. Although the enactment of the Fair Labor Standards Act in 1938 was believed to be the beginning of the end of the widespread practice of child labor in the United States in most areas, in 1974 there was still no federal law that regulated the employment of children in nonhazardous agricultural work outside of school hours. After more than thirty-five years of restrictive child labor laws, the incidence of violation of those laws, both in agricultural and nonagricultural jobs, was believed to be considerable and probably growing. Unlike the conditions up to 1938—when children were indiscriminately employed in steel mills, spinning mills, and mines—most child employment in the 1970's was in such activities as short-order restaurants, motels, food stores, and small businesses. In the 1970's more than 800,000 children under the age of fourteen made up one-third of the seasonal agricultural work force. Also, there was growing pressure from some parents, social planners, and educators to liberalize the existing child labor laws to allow for more, not less, work. Most of the serious and informed advocates of liberalized child labor laws saw this as essential to the correction of the problems encountered in a highly industrialized society that keeps its youth in school and isolated from most work experiences well into late adolescence or beyond.

Just as in an earlier period compulsory school-attendance laws were considered a necessary corollary to child labor laws, the new advocates of liberalized policies generally wished to create patterns of school attendance that would allow for a flexible and coordinated pattern of study and work under the joint supervision of school and employer. Opponents of liberalizing existing child labor laws believed that stricter enforcement was necessary to avoid the exploitation of children who frequently work at less than a minimum wage. Opponents also urged strict compliance with laws because the records of the U.S. Department of Labor indicated that occupational injuries were especially numerous and serious for young workers as a group. One Department of Labor study showed the rate to be 1.5 times that for adult workers. Others favored keeping young workers in school and out of the labor market as long as possible because the job market in the 1970's simply did not provide enough jobs for everyone. Hundreds of thousands of young workers seeking jobs would greatly increase the unemployment figures and deprive some adult heads of households of needed employment in those jobs requiring marginal skills.

Opponents of liberalizing existing child labor laws believed stricter enforcement was necessary to prevent the exploitation of children at less than minimum wage.

The controversy over child labor laws must be seen against more than a century of the most oppressive forms of child labor in the United States. The first evidence that such oppressive work had begun to decline was noted in the 1920 census, although major abuses did not come to an end until the successful passage of the Fair Labor Standards Act in 1938. This act and two others presently regulate the employment of children.

The Fair Labor Standards Act sets the minimum working age at fourteen for employment outside of school hours in nonmanufacturing, at sixteen for employment during school hours in interstate commerce, and at eighteen for occupations called hazardous by the secretary of labor. The Public Contracts Act (1936) sets the minimum age at sixteen years for boys and at eighteen for girls employed in firms that supply goods under federal contract. The Sugar Act (1937) sets the minimum age at fourteen for employment in cultivating and harvesting sugar beets and cane. State laws vary greatly both as to standards and coverage; they govern the ages, hours, and conditions of employment and prohibit certain occupations for minors.

Most of this important legislation, which succeeded in radically curbing the social evil of child labor, came about as the result of aggressive campaigns early in the 20th century. Before the early 1900's, child labor was rampant. Knowledge of its extent prior to 1870 is fragmentary because child labor statistics were not available, but juvenile employment probably existed in the spinning schools established early in the colonies. Textile mills founded after the Revolution are known to have employed children for excessively long hours, but there is no indication of an acute problem. As the 19th century advanced, child labor became more widespread. Two-fifths of the factory workers in New England in 1832 were reported to be children. Agitation for compulsory school-attendance legislation had appeared in the previous decade. In the 1840's Connecticut, Massachusetts, and Pennsylvania passed laws limiting the hours of employment of minors in textile factories.

The child labor problem had grown to the point of national significance by the time of the census of 1870, which reported the employment of three-quarters of a million children between ten and fifteen years of age. From 1870 to 1910, the number of children reported as gainfully employed increased steadily. Aroused to action, the Knights of Labor projected a campaign for child labor legislation in the 1870's and 1880's that resulted in the enactment of many state laws. Conditions in the canning industry, the glass industry, anthracite mining, and other industries began to attract considerable attention at the turn of the century. In the South, the threefold rise in numbers of child laborers in the decade ending in 1900 aroused public sentiment for child labor laws. In the North, insistence on improved standards of legislation and their adequate enforcement led to the formation of the National Child Labor Committee in 1904. This committee, chartered by Congress in 1907 to promote the welfare of America's working children, investigated conditions in various states and industries and spearheaded the push for state legislation with conspicuous success. By 1920, census reports began to reflect a decline in child labor that continued in the 1930's.

The backwardness of certain states and the lack of uniformity of state laws after 1910 led to demands for federal regulation. The U.S. Supreme Court set aside attempts at congressional regulation in 1918 and 1922 (*Hammer* v. *Dagenhart; Bailey* v. *Drexel Furniture Company*). Child labor reformers, nevertheless, began to push for a child labor amendment to the Constitution. In 1924, the amendment was submitted to the states, but by 1950 only 24 states had ratified it.

Since the passage of the Fair Labor Standards Act in 1938 and passage of a major amendment in 1948 (prohibiting children from farm work during the hours school is in session in the district in which they reside while employed), almost no modification has been made in the federal law. From 1960 to 1974, bills submitted to Congress each year to amend the child labor provisions of the Fair Labor Standards Act to extend coverage of the act to children in agriculture outside of school hours failed to be enacted into law. In May 1974 the first major amendments covering children who work in agriculture became law. This new coverage prohibited work by any child under age twelve on a farm that was covered by minimum-wage regulations (farms using at least 500 man-days of work in a calendar quarter). Twelve- and thirteen-year-olds would be permitted to work on such farms only with written permission of their parents.

Almost immediately efforts were begun both in Congress and in federal court to void the new amendments. Because of vigorous opposition of senators from states that used child labor the law was not enforced in 1974. However, the court found the amendment constitutional in September 1974.

Despite the existence of prohibiting legislation, considerable child labor continues to exist, primarily in agriculture. The workers, for the most part, are children of migrant farm workers and the rural poor. Child labor and school-attendance laws are least likely to be enforced in behalf of these children. A study of migrant children in the early 1970's revealed that school-attendance officers in some places continue to ignore the absence of older children of poor families when it is known they are working. This practice contributes, no doubt, to the fact that the educational attainment of migrant children is still half that of the rest of the population.

BIBLIOGRAPHY

Martin Hamburger, "Children and Work: Protection and Opportunity," *New Generation*, vol. 53.

National Child Labor Committee and American Friends Service Committee, *Child Labor in Agriculture, Summer 1970.*

— CASSANDRA STOCKBURGER

CHILDREN'S RIGHTS

Children are those persons who have not reached the age of majority (usually eighteen or twenty-one) as defined by state and federal law. Children's rights are the moral and legal obligations shared by a child, its parents, and the state. Tension exists between the rights of parents to raise their children as they wish, the state's interest in how children are raised, and children's own rights. The concept of children's rights arose from two outlooks, one being that of the "child savers," who believe children should have a legal right to intervention to protect their welfare, and the "kiddie libbers," who think that children should have more power to make decisions that affect their lives and that children should have many of the constitutional rights granted to adults.

The child savers first appeared in the nineteenth century with the movement to enact child labor laws, compulsory school attendance laws, and child welfare laws and to establish juvenile courts to handle children in a more humane way than the criminal justice system. Prior to that time children were the chattel of their parents, and parents were responsible for providing for their children. When parents failed to meet this responsibility, the church and, to a limited extent, the state intervened by placing the children in orphanages. The kiddie libbers emerged in the 1960s and were instrumental in the granting of constitutional rights to children. *In re Gault*, which was heard before the Supreme Court in 1967, granted children due process rights, including the right to counsel, to notice of charges, to freedom from self-incrimination, and to examine and cross-examine witnesses. By the mid-1990s, however, children still did not have the federal right to bail, to a speedy trial, or to a jury trial and could be arrested for acts that would not be considered crimes if the child were an adult. *Gault* led the way to extending due process rights to neglect cases, to divorce proceedings where children sometimes have their own independent counsel, and to due process rights in schools.

Children gained the constitutional right to peaceful protest in 1969, but in 1988 the Supreme Court upheld the right of school authorities to censor student publications. With the ratification of the Twenty-sixth Amendment in 1971, eighteen-year-olds were granted the right to vote. While children gained privacy rights regarding abortion (*Planned Parenthood* v. *Danforth*, 1976) and contraception (*Carey* v. *Population Services*, 1977), many states required parental notification when children exercised these rights. Other health care decisions remained the choice of a child's parents. While adults could not be committed involuntarily to a mental health facility unless it was proven that they were dangerous to themselves or others, parents could commit their children to such facilities without any sort of judicial review. Similarly, although adults increasingly chose not to secure medical treatment when such treatment would do no more than prolong life, children could rarely make such choices, even when they had reached an age when they can be determined to know the consequences of their decisions. Illegitimate children gained rights similar to those of legitimate children (*Weber* v. *Aetna Casualty and Surety Company*, 1972). Prior to this time illegitimate children did not necessarily have the right to be supported by their parents or the right to inherit property from their parents.

Children gained the constitutional right to peaceful protest in 1969, but in 1988 the Supreme Court upheld the right of school authorities to censor school publications.

Congress also became active on behalf of children in the 1970s. While much congressional attention focused on education, federal legislation also addressed child welfare—laws for adoption assistance, child abuse and neglect prevention and treatment, child support enforcement, education for handicapped children, protection of children against sexual exploitation, Native American child welfare, juvenile justice and delinquency prevention, missing children, parental kidnapping prevention, family support, better child care, victims of child abuse, and the family and parental leave. Through expansion of the Medicaid program during the 1980s, children became eligible for more health care. Congress addressed the nutritional needs of poor children through the National School Lunch Program (1962), and the Women's Infant and Children Program (1972) provided food for pregnant women and their preschool children.

[See also Family.]

BIBLIOGRAPHY

Kathleen A. Hempelman, *Teen Legal Rights: A Guide for the '90s* (Westport, Conn., 1994).

Robert H. Mnookin and D. Kelly Weisberg, *Child, Family and State* (Boston, 1988).

Alan Sussman, *The Basic ACLU Guide to the Rights of Parents* (New York, 1980).

— DORIS-JEAN BURTON

CHINA, U.S. RELATIONS WITH

Over the last two centuries American attitudes toward China have ranged from attitudes of profound respect, avuncular concern, and affection in the early 19th century all the way to uncompromising hostility during the first two decades of the Communist regime on the mainland.

In 1789, the year George Washington was inaugurated as president of the United States, fifteen American vessels were carrying on trade with China. American images of China at that time were deeply colored by the Marco Polo story. When the *Empress of China* sailed into Canton Harbor (1784), Cathay was seen by Americans as a great, ancient, and exotic culture devoted to the arts and sciences. Early American writings about China are permeated with a feeling of profound respect and admiration. That the Chinese had invented such things as paper, gunpowder, and the compass and had great sages and philosophers was known to the founders of the American republic. Symbolic of the thinking of this period was the American conception of Confucius as a venerable Chinese sage who had developed a profound ethical system centuries before the West had become civilized.

Once the seafaring Yankees of the Canton trade had established actual contact with China and the Chinese, American attitudes changed drastically. Most of the Americans who came to China in these early days were interested in making a profit, making converts, or both. Merchants and missionaries now began to see China as a backward nation, and the exotic acquired a tinge of the inferior. In almost all the early American travelogues there are stories about pigtails, bound feet, ancestor worship, female infanticide, and a host of other practices considered to be sinister. Life in China was no longer described as superior but as upside down. The respected Chinese became "Chinamen"; the bearers of a superior civilization became "teeming faceless millions"; and the originators of a profound ethical system became godless heathens to be converted by determined and well-meaning missionaries. The attitude of superiority of Chinese officials toward Americans was perceived as grotesque arrogance. In Harold R. Isaacs' telling phrase, the Age of Respect was giving way to the Age of Contempt.

The first American emissary to China was Caleb Cushing, a lawyer from Newburyport, Mass., who in 1844 arrived with a naval squadron of four vessels to formalize the first Sino-American treaty, signed at Wanghia. Under the terms of this treaty, China granted the United States commercial privileges equal to those that had been granted to Britain. Thus, Americans received most-favored-nation privileges by virtue of the British victory over China in the Opium War (1839–42).

In 1899 Secretary of State John Hay dispatched a circular memorandum to London, St. Petersburg, Berlin, Paris, Rome, and Tokyo in which the United States asked the six powers in these capitals not to interfere in each others' treaty ports and spheres of influence and to observe trade equality for everyone. These were the famous Open Door notes. Most Americans hailed this initiative as a triumph of American diplomacy and as a commendable effort by an idealistic United States to disassociate itself from the predatory European powers. Actually the Open Door notes were quickly overtaken by events when, in June 1900, the Boxers laid siege to Peking. By August 1900 an international relief expedition, including 2,500 American troops, was on its way to Peking to break the siege. Most Americans generally perceived the Boxers as ruffians, and most contemporary American diplomats tended to regard the Boxer Protocol of 1901 as a lenient settlement for China. This ended the American policy of the Open Door in China.

During the 19th century, then, the attitude of the United States toward the Chinese Empire was one of moral superiority. Although the Americans had not waged war against China, they had received the same privileges as the European powers. Nevertheless, they wished to draw a clear distinction between themselves and the "imperialists." This the American government attempted to do through the Open Door notes. The Americans saw the Chinese as their wards and themselves as superior to the petty power politics of the Europeans. To America, the Open Door was a democratic policy guaranteeing equal opportunity to all while at the same time protecting the integrity of China. To China, the Americans had arrived late at the Western holdup, but just in time to share in the spoils. The door of China had never opened voluntarily; it had been forced open.

The Age of Contempt gave way to the Age of Alliance during the tenure of the Nationalist government of Sun Yat-sen and Gen. Chiang Kai-shek on the mainland of China. After the Nationalist revolution of 1911 and up until World War II, most Americans perceived the two Nationalist leaders in a very favorable light. Sun Yat-sen was seen as a Christian with high ideals and the determination to make of China a democratic nation. Chiang Kai-shek was seen virtually as a soldier saint with a brave wife by his side. Designated as man and wife of the year in 1938 by *Time* magazine, they were known as Christians, allies in the war against Japan, and later allies in the struggle against world communism. Only during the civil war between 1945 and 1949, when Chiang Kai-shek's mandate began to slip, did American disillusionment begin to set in. A mission headed by Gen. George C. Marshall and sent to mediate between Mao Tse-tung and Chiang Kai-shek ended in failure.

When the Communist government of Mao Tse-tung took over the mainland in 1949 and drove Chiang Kai-shek to Formosa, most Americans perceived this event as a victory of evil over good. This was reflected in the determination of the American government during the next twenty-three years not to recognize the Communist regime, to oppose its entry into the United Nations, and to form and maintain a military alliance with the Chiang Kai-shek regime on Formosa. In late 1950 Chinese Communist soldiers intervened in the war in Korea and encountered American troops on the field of battle. This military encounter lasted for almost two years and ended in a stalemate. For an entire generation most Americans regarded Chiang Kai-shek as the leader of "free China" and Mao Tse-tung, together with Joseph Stalin, as the Communist menace. This policy was retained throughout the presidencies of Harry Truman, Dwight Eisenhower, John Kennedy, and Lyndon Johnson.

President Richard Nixon reversed U.S. policy with his historic trip to Peking in 1972. Thereafter, American attitudes toward mainland China began to mellow once again. Exchanges between athletes, scholars, journalists, and commercial interests began to develop. (In October 1971 the People's Republic of China had been seated in the United Nations and the Taiwan regime ousted.) In 1973 the United States established a liaison office in Peking that stopped just short of diplomatic recognition, with David K. Bruce as its first "ambassador" to Peking. In the meantime the American defense treaty with Taiwan remained intact, although the alliance was no longer widely proclaimed to the American public. In short, by the mid-1970's, most Americans had moved beyond ideological rigidity and had begun to form their attitudes to the two Chinas on a more pragmatic and realistic basis.

BIBLIOGRAPHY

John K. Fairbank, *The United States and China.*

Klaus Mehnert, *China Returns.*

John G. Stoessinger, *Nations in Darkness: China, Russia and America.*

Barbara W. Tuchman, *Stilwell and the American Experience in China, 1911–1945.*

— JOHN G. STOESSINGER

CHINESE RELATIONS SINCE THE 1970S

The most significant development in U.S.-China relations since the early 1970s has been the "second opening" of China to the outside world, culminating in the hesitant but irrevocable incorporation of China into the global economy. During this period relations between the two nations developed rapidly, although not without frictions.

Between 1949 and 1969 the U.S. government had refused to recognize the People's Republic of China (or PRC, the communist government of mainland China), lending support instead to the Republic of China (ROC) on the island of Taiwan, where Nationalist forces had fled in defeat at the hands of Mao Zedong's communist revolutionaries in 1949. In the early 1970s, however, the administration of President Richard M. Nixon began to explore ways to effect a rapprochement with the PRC. Although Nixon had always been known as a hardline anticommunist, he and his advisers hoped to take advantage of the schism that had developed between China and the Soviet Union, America's cold war nemesis. Both U.S. and Chinese leaders saw the strategic advantages closer ties would bring in curbing the power of their mutual foe. As a first step the United States in 1971 approved the admission of the PRC into the United Nations, although U.S. efforts to prevent expulsion of the ROC by pressing for dual representation were unsuccessful.

China has been repeatedly criticized for human rights abuses in Tibet; the Dalai Lama, Tibet's spiritual leader, went into exile following China's 1951 invasion.

In February 1972 President Nixon made his historic visit to Beijing that culminated in the Shanghai Communiqué. This document acknowledged differences between the two nations, especially over the issue of Taiwan, but established a basis for continued and open diplomatic relations. The following year liaison offices were established in Washington and Beijing. Trade between the two countries, which had been another motive for closer ties along with strategic considerations, began to flourish. Progress toward establishing full diplomatic relations, however, was slowed by internal political turmoil in both countries—the Watergate scandal and resignation of President Nixon in the United States, and in China the deaths of leaders Mao Zedong and

Zhou Enlai. It was not until 1978 that the Jimmy Carter administration began to engage in secret talks with the Chinese government, now led by Deng Xiaoping, with a view toward normalizing relations.

On Dec. 15, 1978, President Carter announced an agreement stating that full diplomatic relations would be opened with the PRC as of Jan. 1, 1979. The agreement called for an end of official relations with Taiwan, abrogation of the treaty the United States had signed in 1954 pledging defense of Taiwan, withdrawal of U.S. forces from the island, and acknowledgment of Beijing's long-held position that there was only one China and that Taiwan was part of it. Carter assured Taiwan that informal and cultural ties would continue, as would arms sales after a one-year moratorium. There was no doubt, however, that this loss of U.S. support would mean increased international isolation for the ROC as well as the end of Nationalist hopes for an independent Taiwan.

Many members of Congress resented the administration's secret diplomatic initiative and objected to the agreement as a breach of loyalty toward a longtime cold war ally. A bipartisan majority in 1979 passed the Taiwan Relations Act, which extended to Taiwan many of the rights accorded states with full diplomatic recognition and provided that arms sales would continue with or without the sanction of the PRC. Further, fifteen members of Congress led by Republican Senator Barry Goldwater filed a federal suit to overturn Carter's abrogation of the U.S.-Taiwan mutual defense treaty. The courts dismissed the suit, ruling that the president possessed the constitutional right both to recognize and withdraw recognition from foreign governments. The issue did not end there, however, especially among conservative Republicans, and during the 1980 presidential campaign Ronald Reagan promised to restore relations with Taiwan.

Once in office, Reagan never acted on this pledge, largely because his administration was too heavily invested in cold war confrontation with the Soviet Union to risk destroying the relationship with Beijing. Nonetheless, there were differences, primary among them the continuing dispute over U.S. arms sales to Taiwan. The Chinese leadership also was distanced both by Reagan's anticommunist rhetorical style and by such matters as his administration's policy of reducing U.S. financial contributions to the United Nations Fund for Population Activities, based on claims that China forced its women citizens to undergo abortions. (China's "one-child" policy, initiated in an effort to stop the growth of a population that had topped a billion by the 1980s, had in practice resulted in the abortion or abandonment of daughters, traditionally considered less valuable than sons.) Another subject of continuing U.S. criticism was human rights abuses in Tibet, which the Chinese had invaded in 1951, eventually forcing the Tibetan leader, the Dalai Lama, into exile. For all these ideological conflicts, however, the Reagan administration continued along the lines of the previous two administrations in strengthening political, cultural, and economic relations with China. The same policies continued under President George Bush, although with a greater sense of amity because of Bush's personal relationship to the country and especially to Deng, dating back to Bush's sojourn in China in the 1970s as the U.S. emissary.

During the 1980s the U.S. public delighted in news stories of the Chinese people's embrace of Coca-Cola, McDonald's, high fashion, and rock and roll and interpreted these as signs that China was progressing toward capitalism and Western values, including Western-style democracy. In reality, the picture was somewhat different. While economic reforms had brought positive results, they also generated inflation, unemployment, and corruption. Several times during the decade Chinese leaders carried out purges, arresting dissidents in an attempt to quell the spread of Western ideas. Prevented by a repressive government from addressing their problems through political reform, many Chinese were frustrated and dissatisfied.

In the spring of 1989 students staged a demonstration in Tiananmen Square in Beijing to bring attention to these issues, calling for greater freedom of speech and press and an end to corruption. At the same time, Soviet president Mikhail Gorbachev was in the country for a historic meeting with Chinese leaders. This resulted in international television coverage of the demonstration as well as of the meeting between Gorbachev and Deng. Western observers and journalists began to characterize the demonstration not as a call for political reforms but as the dawn of a national democratic revolution. The international coverage was an embarrassment to China's aged leaders, who in the early hours of June 4 sent in troops and tanks, massacring the demonstrators, and then instigated a wave of arrests throughout China.

Horrified Americans demanded a hard-line U.S. policy to "punish" the Chinese. Economic sanctions as well as ostracism by the international community were brought to bear on the Chinese leadership. Concerns were raised about the future of Hong Kong, as observers worried that China might no longer be willing to abide by its agreement, signed in the Sino-British Joint Declaration of 1984, to grant Hong Kong fifty years of autonomy after its reversion to China in 1997. The Bush administration did its best to contain the animosity. Although President Bush called off high-level talks with Beijing following the Tiananmen massacre, he secretly resumed diplomatic relations that July, a move that was widely criticized when knowledge of these visits became public later that year. In any event, Tiananmen Square put an end to Americans' growing, if somewhat misapprehended, amiability toward China. The relationship was further eroded by the collapse of the Soviet Union soon thereafter, which took away the strategic rationale for U.S.-Chinese friendship.

During the 1990s differences between the United States and China centered on human rights and economics, issues that became increasingly intertwined as the use of prison labor in Chinese manufacturing became widely publicized. Outside estimates of the numbers of Chinese in prisons and labor camps ran from one million to the tens of millions. These prisoners, many of them not criminals, were put to work under harrowing conditions to produce toys and other products that then were sold to U.S. markets. By purchasing these products, Americans not only were supporting a slave-labor system but were undercutting their own home industries. Of particular concern were the fates of political dissidents imprisoned after Tiananmen Square. The Chinese government in 1994 claimed that 3,317 people had been sentenced as "counterrevolutionaries," but outside observers estimated the number to be far larger. In response, the Chinese position was that such criticism constituted unwarranted intrusion into its internal affairs, and that in any case the United States, with its record of crime, violence, and racial tension, had no right to lecture China on human rights.

The connection between human rights and economic policy became explicit as U.S. leaders proposed that China's most-favored-nation trading status be linked to improvements in its human rights record. Further, as a presidential candidate in 1992, Bill Clinton pledged to impose trading sanctions against China toward the same end. Ultimately, however, the Clinton administration backed off rather than jeopardize the relationship with China. In 1994, on the eve of renewal of most-favored-nation status for China, Secretary of State Warren Christopher was dispatched to Beijing to discuss human rights with the Chinese leadership as a condition of renewal. Not only did the leadership rebuff Christopher but, in an indication of changing times, the secretary came under criticism from U.S. businesses with interests in China. Unable to link most-favored-nation status and human rights, the Clinton administration initiated a policy of "intensive engagement" that would serve as a framework for negotiations with the Chinese on a range of issues.

A persistent problem for the United States was its trade deficit with China, which had reached $30 billion by 1994. Foreign investment, including investment by U.S. companies, played a part in China's rapid economic development. Relocation of U.S. production in China to take advantage of lower wages and a controlled labor force contributed both to loss of domestic jobs and the trade deficit. Another aspect of the problem was that the Chinese government turned a blind eye to the widespread copyright infringement practiced by its manufacturers, who flooded the Asian market with pirated CDs, videotapes, and other U.S. intellectual property in violation of international copyright law. Early in February 1995 this issue seemed to come to a crisis when the United States imposed a 100 percent tariff on more than $1 billion worth of Chinese goods in an attempt to force the Chinese government to crack down on its manufacturers. A planned sale of U.S. wheat and other transactions went forward, however, signaling the administration's unwillingness to initiate an all-out trade war, and negotiations with the Chinese over the piracy issue resumed almost immediately.

As students demonstrated for democracy in Tiananmen Square in the spring of 1989, Soviet President Gorbachev was in Beijing for a historic meeting with Chinese leaders.

Taiwan, too, remained a source of friction. Although relations between Taiwan and the mainland were less antagonistic and trade and tourism flourished, Beijing continued to look with suspicion upon any U.S. actions that treated Taiwan as a separate entity, such as facilitating its entry into the General Agreement on Tariffs and Trade (GATT). Tensions came to a head in 1995 when Congress passed a resolution calling for an "unofficial visit" to the United States by ROC President Lee Teng-hui. PRC leaders denounced the visit as interference in its internal affairs and recalled its ambassador from Washington until the affair was smoothed over two months later.

Almost immediately thereafter, U.S.-Chinese frictions once again erupted into controversy as China hosted the United Nations Fourth World Conference on Women. First Lady Hillary Rodham Clinton, who led the U.S. delegation, was criticized by U.S. conservatives for attending the conference in light of China's record of human rights abuses. Such criticism was quelled when, in a speech to the delegates assembled in Beijing, she spoke more forcefully on human rights issues than any American ever had within China, taking its leaders to task for attempting to limit free and open discussion of women's issues, which, she said, were inseparable from human rights issues. The Chinese government rebuked her for her speech. During the conference Western officials accused China of obstructing a meeting of 20,000 women in Huairou, an hour away from Beijing, charging disorganization, surveillance of visitors, ejection of accredited journalists, and disruption of transportation links to Beijing.

At the end of the twentieth century the United States and China found themselves locked into an uneasy relationship marked by economic interdependence and ideological difference. The Chinese resented U.S. efforts to remake China in its own image and insisted that the two countries tend to their economic relations without dragging in other issues. The United States sought to balance idealism against self-interest. Both sides were culpable, if in different degrees, in using human rights for political and economic purposes. Without the strategic threat of the Soviet Union to act as a motivating factor, disputes were more difficult to resolve, and relations were continually undermined by criticism, misperception, and suspicion. As the integration of the global economy continued, however, both countries seemed well aware that the contact they had initiated so tentatively back in the early 1970s now constituted a relationship from which there was no turning back.

BIBLIOGRAPHY

Warren I. Cohen, *America's Response to China*, 3rd ed. (New York, 1990).

Harry Harding, *A Fragile Relationship: The United States and China Since 1972* (Washington, D.C., 1992).

Michael H. Hunt, *The Making of a Special Relationship* (New York, 1983).

Michael Schaller, *The United States and China in the Twentieth Century*, rev. ed. (New York, 1990).

David Shambaugh, *Beautiful Imperialist* (Princeton, N.J., 1991).

CHINESE AMERICANS

According to the 1990 U.S. census, Chinese Americans were the largest ethnic group among Asian Americans, numbering 1,645,472 or one-fourth of the total, representing a 104 percent increase among Chinese Americans between 1980 and 1990. Although present in every state of the union, the heaviest concentrations of Chinese Americans were in California and New York, followed by Hawaii, Texas, New Jersey, and Massachusetts. Like the category "Asian Americans," Chinese Americans are a diverse group with linguistic, cultural, and historical differences that complicate the more commonly known distinctions between Cantonese and Mandarin speakers, the regional variations of mainland China, and Chinese from the mainland, Hong Kong, and Taiwan. In the United States, Chinese from Southeast Asia, including Vietnam, Indonesia, and the Philippines, mingle with Chinese from Africa, Central America, South America, and the Caribbean.

Chinese Americans have been central figures in the stereotype of Asian Americans as the "model minority." Indeed, in 1980, 90 and 87 percent of Chinese-American men and women respectively between the ages of twenty-five and twenty-nine completed high school, as compared with 87 percent of the same general American age cohort. Occupational figures show that 15 percent of all Chinese Americans were among the managerial class in 1980 as compared with 14 percent among whites, and 24 percent of Chinese Americans were professionals, whereas only 12 percent of whites were professionals. A closer look at those figures reveals that among Chinese-American women age forty-five to fifty-four, only 58 percent completed high school, as compared with 70 percent of white women, and 22 percent of all Chinese Americans were employed in the service sector, in contrast to 8 percent of whites. Similarly, 11 percent of Chinese-American families lived in poverty in 1980, while 7 percent of white families lived below the poverty line.

Chinese Americans continued to face racial discrimination late in the twentieth century. In 1990 vandals spray-painted "No Chinks, Go Home to China" on a Chinese-American church in Arizona and fired five rounds of ammunition through its door. Two Chinese Americans, a father and son, were attacked the same year in Castro Valley, Calif., and severely beaten by several youths who also hurled racial epithets, and Chinese Americans Vincent Chin in Detroit in 1982 and Jim Ming Hai Loo in Raleigh, N.C., in 1989 were beaten and killed by white men who said, according to witnesses, they hated "Japs," "gooks," and "chinks." A study of Asian Americans in California's Bay Area, based on the 1980 U.S. census, suggests that Chinese Americans suffered from discrimination in the labor market. Chinese Americans, according to the study, clustered in occupations with limited upward mobility, and Chinese-American men earned less than other Americans.

That pattern of racial discrimination was established when the first Chinese migrated to the United States. Long before Europeans arrived in China, Chinese sailors plied trade routes to Southeast Asia, India, the Arabian peninsula, and the East African coast. China's maritime commerce was centered in south China, in the provinces of Fujian and Guangdong, at the port cities of Canton and Quanzhou from the seventh to eighteenth centuries, and it was from those provinces and particularly from Canton that Chinese emigrated to Southeast Asia, Hawaii, and North America. The Portuguese established a trading post near Canton in 1515 and held a monopoly of trade until the British established a factory there in 1684. The arrival in Canton of the *Empress of China* from the United States in 1785 marked the beginning of a trade that rivaled that of the British. Yankee clippers left port cities in the Northeast, traded rum and beads for furs in the Pacific Northwest, watered and picked up sandalwood in Hawaii, and traded these in China for teas, silks, porcelain, and furniture, which were imported into the United States at handsome profits.

After the end of the Atlantic slave trade in about the mid-nineteenth century, new sources of labor were sought by Europeans for their plantations and mines in Southeast Asia, Africa, and the Americas. The established precedent of Chinese migrant workers transported by Chinese shippers to the plantations of Malaysia was replaced in the 1840s by British, French, Spanish, Portuguese, and U.S. shippers who took the workers, called coolies, to Southeast Asia and other parts of the world. Between 1848 and 1874, about 125,000 Chinese were shipped to Cuba and about an equal number to Peru. In 1862 Congress prohibited U.S. involvement in the coolie trade, but shippers of ostensibly free laborers to California appear to have carried on the same practices of the coolie trade. Overcrowding on board ships was common, fresh meat and vegetables were rare, and sometimes even water was rationed. In 1854 the *Libertad* left Hong Kong with 560 passengers when its legal limit was 297, and six days before reaching San Francisco the Chinese were given no more water and 100 died.

Chinese communities developed around 1850 in Hawaii, California, and New York, largely as a consequence of U.S. trade with China and a need for labor in the American West. Before the first American sugar plantation was established in Hawaii, Chinese migrants established their own processing mills, perhaps as early as 1802. Chinese contract workers arrived in 1852 and continued to immigrate as Hawaiian sugar production grew and as the indigenous Hawaiian population declined. By 1900 more than 46,000 Chinese laborers had been brought into Hawaii, but only 25,767 remained in the islands at the time of annexation by the United States in 1898. A majority were single men and did not establish families, but many married Hawaiian women, as many as 1,500 before 1900 according to one estimate, and most of them became a part of the Hawaiian community.

Chinese settlements developed in California and the American West after the discovery of gold in 1848. In 1852 more than 20,000 Chinese arrived in San Francisco, seeking what the migrants called "Gold Mountain." Nearly all of the Chinese in the United States were in California in 1860, fully 78 percent, and 84 percent of those lived and worked in the state's mining counties. Those figures declined until 1900, when half of Chinese Americans lived in California and 12 percent were in mining counties. The trend reflected the wider pattern of opportunities and restrictions, particularly in employment, for Chinese Americans. They lived and worked in places and industries that were desirable and open to them. Mining taxes, depletion of surface gold deposits, and expulsions from mining counties drove the Chinese into other occupations, such as railroad construction, land reclamation, and agriculture. Chinese merchants established businesses in the mining camps, along railroad lines, and in farming clusters and rose to become the most prosperous and prominent members of communities.

Chinese communities developed around 1850 in Hawaii, California, and New York as a consequence of U.S. trade with China and a need for labor in the American West.

Perhaps the first Chinese in New York City arrived as early as 1785 as sailors, cooks, and stewards on board European and U.S. ships that sailed the Pacific lanes but also the Indian and Atlantic oceans. Many adopted English names—John Huston, William Longford, Lesing Newman; they married Irish women and started such businesses as sailors' boardinghouses, cigar and candy peddling, and laundries. Some who arrived after 1850 came by way of the notorious Peruvian guano pits or from Cuba, where they learned cigar grading and wrapping. A few managed to gain citizenship through naturalization, and one Chinese American may have voted in the 1880 presidential election. Some Chinese ventured eastward after completion of the transcontinental railroad in 1869, while other Chinese were recruited by employers.

From the vantage point of the 1990s, San Francisco's Chinatown seemed to typify the Chinese-American experience, but the nineteenth-century landscape, like contemporary times, was populated by a range of communities, from Hawaii to the Pacific Northwest to California's central valleys to the American Southwest to the Rocky Mountains and Midwest to the American South and the Atlantic seaboard. Those unique groups were made to seem homogeneous by undifferentiated representations of Chinese Americans, by laws and practices that restricted and excluded them as a group, and by the sweep of national and international forces that victimized and galvanized them. Chinese Americans were variously seen as cheap coolie labor and model minorities, workers were prevented from entering by the Chinese Exclusion Act of 1882, and children were forced to attend segregated schools from California to Mississippi.

Chinese Americans served in the U.S. armed forces during World War II, and with China an ally of the United States in the war, they gained a measure of opportunities, such as employment in wartime industries, but the exclusion law was replaced in 1943 by a quota of 105 per year, and immigration was closed when China turned communist with Mao Zedong's triumph in 1949. The most significant event in transforming Chinese-American communities after World War II was the 1965 Immigration and Nationality Act, which allowed a fivefold increase among Chinese Americans between 1965 and 1990, accompanied by an increase in Chinese-American women and greater geographical dispersion.

[See also Asian Americans; Chinese Exclusion Acts.]

BIBLIOGRAPHY

Clarence E. Glick, *Sojourners and Settlers: Chinese Migrants in Hawaii* (Honolulu, 1980).

Peter Kwong, *The New Chinatown* (New York, 1987).

Shih-shan Henry Tsai, *The Chinese Experience in America* (Bloomington, Ind., 1986).

— GARY Y. OKIHIRO

CHINESE EXCLUSION ACT

After the discovery of gold in California in 1848, workers were scarce, and the immigration of Chinese laborers was welcomed. The Burlingame Treaty of 1868 facilitated this immigration. But the completion of the transcontinental railways brought more white laborers to the West, and they complained of Oriental competition. In 1877, in a San Francisco riot, twenty-one Chinese were killed. The agitation for exclusion was led by Denis Kearney, president of the Workingmen's party. In 1877 a committee of the U.S. Senate reported in favor of modification of the Burlingame Treaty, and in 1879 Congress passed the Fifteen Passenger Act, restricting Chinese immigration, which was vetoed by President Rutherford B. Hayes as a violation of the treaty. On

The fear of miscegenation, which motivated the Asiatic Exclusion League and other organizations to support anti-Chinese legislation during the 1870s and 1880s, finds sympathetic expression in a racist 1877 cartoon. (Corbis-Bettmann)

Nov. 17, 1880, a commission headed by James B. Angell signed a treaty with China permitting restrictions upon the immigration of laborers but exempting teachers, students, merchants, and travelers. This was followed by the Chinese Exclusion Act in 1882, which suspended Chinese immigration for ten years. The Scott Act of 1888 and the Geary Act of 1892 contained flagrant violations of the treaty of 1880, partly induced by the failure of China to ratify the Bayard Treaty of 1888, sanctioning a prohibition of immigration of laborers for twenty years. A new treaty with China, in 1894, permitted for ten years the absolute prohibition of the entrance of Chinese laborers into the United States. The act of 1902 enforced this severe prohibition. In the following years, many Chinese laborers entered the United States (and after 1898 the Philippines) on fraudulent certificates issued by Chinese officials. In 1904 the Chinese government refused to renew the treaty of 1894, while harsh enforcement of the immigration laws in the United States led in 1905 to a boycott of American goods in China. Nevertheless, the laws excluding Chinese laborers remained on the statute book. Chinese resentment of this treatment was more than offset by the goodwill resulting from American friendly relations in the events following the Boxer Rebellion in 1900 and the establishment of the republic in 1911, and friction over the exclusion policy soon disappeared.

BIBLIOGRAPHY

Mary R. Coolidge, *Chinese Immigration.*
R. D. McKenzie, *Oriental Exclusion.*
Elmer C. Sandmeyer, *The Anti-Chinese Movement in California.*

— KENNETH COLEGROVE

CHIPPEWA

Chippewa (or Ojibwa, a variation of the name). Like many other native peoples of the Eastern Woodlands of North America, or Northeastern culture area, the Chippewa lacked any sense of tribal or national solidarity. Yet a strong linguistic identity continues to exist, since the Chippewa form one of the main Algonkin-speaking groups of the Great Lakes or northeastern area. Scattered today on what were formerly reservations in Minnesota, Wisconsin, and Ontario, with remnants in other areas, such as Oklahoma and the Dakotas, the Chippewa constitute the second largest tribe in North America; with a population in excess of 50,000, they fall only slightly behind the Navaho of the American Southwest. Demographic figures are obtained with difficulty, because many still keep an orientation to traditional culture in a rural woodland setting, while others have adapted to life in such urban centers as Milwaukee, Minneapolis, Chicago, and Los Angeles. Some occupy an intermediate position, shifting residence seasonally from rural to urban life, as economic opportunities arise.

The Chippewa, as classic Woodland Algonkins, were first encountered by Europeans in the middle Great Lakes regions, generally in the area of Sault Sainte Marie. Although their traditional culture was like that of other Algonkin-speaking peoples of the Northeast, resembling that of the Abnaki, Penobscot, and Micmac, they were touched as early as the 16th century by the French fur trade. As a result, the Chippewa became middlemen on the French trade routes. While one branch, known generally as the Saulteaux, moved into northwestern Ontario, the remainder filed gradually into the upper Midwest, settling there by the mid-18th century and beginning a series of conflicts with the Dakota tribes. Indeed, a cultural as well as a natural boundary is established at the confluence of the Minnesota and Mississippi rivers, where the Woodlands shade into the Plains and where two different native ecological systems came into contact and conflict.

The Chippewa were thus recipients of trade goods from abroad early in their historic past. Originally hunters, divided into small bands with informal headmen, dependent on birch bark for the making of houses, containers, and canoes, the Chippewa adopted metal tools and firearms at an early date. The result was an accelerated series of changes in the native culture patterns. Chiefs became more important as a result of European contact, the paternal-patrilineal tie became stronger, and certain religious ideas, such as the notion of the "Happy Hunting Ground" and the "Great Spirit," may have evolved as a result of missionization. Although not farmers, the tribe made a special adaptation to the Minnesota-Wisconsin lakes in developing the wild rice (*Zinzania aquatica*) resource. While not cultivated, wild rice was sowed broadcast in the lakes and marshes. It remains an important economic resource of the group. The Chippewa also evolved the Midewiwin, or Grand Medicine Lodge, a form of secret society for both curing and prestige. It was this Midewiwin complex, with its involvements of initiation, secrecy, age grading, and symbolism, that underlay much of Chippewa society and created a sense of ethnic solidarity.

Because of their large population and their strategic position, the Chippewa became well known to Europeans and Euro-Americans. To some degree glamorized by the scholarly Indianist Henry R. Schoolcraft in the 1850's, the Chippewa caught the attention of Henry Wadsworth Longfellow. Although the *Song of Hiawatha* bears an Iroquois name, its legends and tales are distinctively Algonkin.

BIBLIOGRAPHY

F. Densmore, *Chippewa Customs.*
M. I. Hilger, *Chippewa Child Life and Its Cultural Background.*
R. Landes, "Ojibwa Sociology," *Columbia University Contributions to Anthropology*, vol. 29.

— ROBERT F. SPENCER

CHISHOLM TRAIL

Chisholm Trail, a cattle trail leading north from Texas, across Oklahoma to Abilene, Kans. Much controversy has existed as to the origin of its name and even as to its exact location. It was apparently named for Jesse Chisholm, a mixed-blood Cherokee, who followed a part of this route in freighting supplies and may have guided a detachment of soldiers over it soon after the close of the Civil War. The southern extension of the Chisholm Trail originated near San Antonio, Tex., though there is considerable doubt as to whether or not the Texas portion of it was ever known by that name. From here it ran north and a little east to the Red River which it crossed a few miles from the site of the present town of Ringgold, Tex. It continued north across Oklahoma, passing near the sites of the present towns of Waurika, Duncan, Marlow, Chickasha, El Reno, and Enid to Caldwell, Kans. It therefore ran not far from the line of the ninety-eighth meridian. From Caldwell it ran north and a little east past the site of Wichita to Abilene, Kans. At the close of the Civil War the low price of cattle in Texas and the much higher prices in the North and East caused many Texas ranchmen to drive large herds north to market. The establishment of a cattle depot and shipping point at Abilene, Kans., in 1867 brought many herds to that point to be shipped to market over the southern branch of the Union Pacific Railway. Many of these were driven over the Chisholm Trail, which in a few years became the most popular route for driving cattle from Texas to the North.

The Chisholm Trail decreased in importance after 1871, when Abilene lost its preeminence as a shipping point for Texas cattle, as a result of the westward advance of settlement. Dodge City, Kans., became the chief shipping point and another trail farther west, crossing the Red River near Doan's Store, Tex., became of paramount importance. The extension of the Atchison, Topeka and Santa Fe Railway to Caldwell, Kans., in 1880, however, again made the Chisholm Trail a most important route for driving Texas cattle to the North, and it retained this position until the building of additional trunk lines of railway south into Texas caused rail shipments to take the place of the former trail driving of Texas cattle north to market.

[See Cattle Drives.]

BIBLIOGRAPHY

Evan G. Barnard, *A Rider of the Cherokee Strip.*
E. E. Dale, *The Range Cattle Industry.*
Sam P. Ridings, *The Chisholm Trail.*

— EDWARD EVERETT DALE

CHISHOLM V. *GEORGIA*

Chisholm v. *Georgia*, 2 Dallas 419 (1793). The heirs of Alexander Chisholm, citizens of South Carolina, sued the state of Georgia to enforce payment of claims against that state. Georgia refused to defend the suit, and the Supreme Court, upholding the right of citizens of one state to sue another state, under Article III, Section 2, of the U.S. Constitution, ordered judgment by default against Georgia. No writ of execution was attempted because of threats by the lower house of the Georgia legislature. The Eleventh Amendment ended such actions.

[See also States' Rights.]

BIBLIOGRAPHY

U. B. Phillips, *Georgia and State Rights.*

— E. MERTON COULTER

CHRISTINA, FORT

Fort Christina, established by Peter Minuit and a group of Swedish settlers on Mar. 29, 1638. It was the capital of New Sweden until 1643 and was made the seat of authority again in 1654. The following year it was surrendered to the Dutch, who in turn surrendered it to the English in 1664. The town that grew around the fort was the first permanent white settlement in Delaware and the whole Delaware River valley. Quakers settled here in the 1730's and the town developed into a prosperous port. Thomas Penn, the proprietor, renamed the town Wilmington.

[See also New Netherland.]

BIBLIOGRAPHY

Amandus Johnson, *The Swedish Settlements on the Delaware 1638–1664.*
Anna T. Lincoln, *Three Centuries Under Four Flags.*

— LEON DE VALINGER, JR.

CHURCH OF ENGLAND IN THE COLONIES

The first successful English settlement in America was made by members of the established church at Jamestown in 1607. The church was provided for in the earliest plans for Virginia, and as soon as the colony was strong enough, it was legally established. All the other southern colonies, except Maryland, were founded under the leadership of churchmen, and, in time, the Church of England was established in all of them, though this did not occur in North Carolina until 1765. Maryland was founded by a Roman Catholic proprietor, but the Protestant settlers there obtained control in the Revolution of 1689 and by 1702 had secured the establishment of the Church of England. In New York the church was established in the four leading counties, but not elsewhere. In the other northern colonies it enjoyed no establishment and depended for support largely upon the English Society for the Propagation of the Gospel in Foreign Parts, founded in 1701.

During the 18th century the Church of England advanced in the colonies where it was not established and lost ground in those where it was—a phenomenon which corresponded with the general breakdown of colonial religious barriers that marked that century. The American Revolution deprived the church of its establishments in the South and of the aid of the Society for the Propagation of the Gospel in the North, exposed it to some popular opposition, and confronted it with the problem of forming a national organization and obtaining a native episcopate.

BIBLIOGRAPHY

W. W. Manross, *History of the American Episcopal Church.*
W. S. Perry, *History of the American Episcopal Church.*

— W. W. MANROSS

CITIZENSHIP

Citizenship is generally defined as membership in a political community attended by certain privileges and responsibilities. In the United States, under its federal system most persons live under two governments with the result that they have a dual citizenship of a special sort, federal and state. Since it is by the terms of the Fourteenth Amendment of the Constitution that a U.S. citizen is automatically made a citizen of the state in which he is a legal resident, U.S. citizenship is primary and state citizenship derivative; by the ratification of that amendment in 1868, it became impossible for a person to be a citizen of a state who is not a U.S. citizen.

Under the federal system, most persons in the U.S. live under two governments, with the result that they have a dual citizenship of a sort—federal and state.

Under the Fourteenth Amendment, U.S. citizenship can be acquired either by birth or by naturalization. Two basic rules govern citizenship by birth: the principle of *jus soli* bases citizenship on place of birth, whereas the principle of *jus sanguinis* bases citizenship on parentage. The former is the principal rule under the Fourteenth Amendment. The only qualification to this rule is that persons must be born under U.S. jurisdiction as well as in U.S. territory. As interpreted by the Supreme Court in *United States* v. *Wong Kim Ark* (169 U.S. 228 [1898]) this qualification affects only four categories of persons: children of U.S. diplomats (but not consuls); those born on foreign public ships in U.S. territorial waters; those born of enemies during hostilities on American soil; and children of American Indians living in tribal relations. This last group was removed from the list in 1924, when by act of Congress citizenship was conferred upon all noncitizen American Indians born within the territorial limits of the United States. Also by statute *jus sanguinis* has been applied to children of American parents resident in foreign countries, provided there has been a period of residence in the United States by at least one of the parents. The details of the application of these rules are set forth in the Immigration and Nationality Act of 1952, title III. This statutory arrangement is necessary so as to ensure citizenship to those born to U.S. citizens outside the territorial limits of the United States and at the same time to avoid the possibility of statelessness resulting from birth in a country whose government might fail to recognize *jus soli* under such conditions.

The process of acquiring citizenship by naturalization is completely set forth in federal statutes. It may involve either collective or individual naturalization. The former is a conferring of citizenship on a group as a whole either by statute or by treaty, treaties having been used for inhabitants of Florida, Louisiana, and Alaska and statutes having been used for inhabitants of Texas, Hawaii, Puerto Rico, and the Virgin Islands. As noted, noncitizen American Indians were also the beneficiaries of collective naturalization by statute. Individual naturalization involves a detailed process in which the alien himself seeks citizenship.

Loss of citizenship is possible for a U.S. citizen by the acquisition of citizenship in another country. By statute Congress has specified a variety of actions by citizens that are regarded as evidence of implicit renunciation of U.S. citizenship. These include such matters as service in the armed forces of another country. It must be noted, however, that the Supreme Court has voided a number of these as violative of the constitutional rights of the persons involved. Citizenship secured illegally or fraudulently may be revoked.

BIBLIOGRAPHY

L. Gettys, *The Law of Citizenship in the United States.*
U.S. Government Printing Office, *Becoming A Citizen.*

— PAUL C. BARTHOLOMEW

CIVIL DISOBEDIENCE

The Civil Rights Movement of the 1960's went beyond the traditional legal challenges to racial discrimination to embrace the tactics of direct action, including civil disobedience. The historical roots of these strategies lie in the ideas of Henry David Thoreau and Mohandas Gandhi and are undoubtedly related also to the tactics used by union organizers in the 1930's and by conscientious objectors during World War II. Direct action, as expounded by its major contemporary proponent, Martin Luther King, Jr., attempts to dramatize issues in such a way as to force negotiations on the law or institution considered unjust. For example, persons denied service in a public facility, such as a restaurant, may simply enter, sit down, and refuse to leave—a practice known as a sit-in. Civil disobedience may also involve not only deliberate violation of the "unjust" law but also, on occasion, resistance to other laws. For example, groups concerned with racial injustice may block traffic by stalling cars on thruways or sitting down in streets, in a general way attempting to cause enough disruption to attract attention to the injustice. The latter approach, generally advanced by the more radical segments of the Civil Rights Movement, has broadened at times into a general attack on government, corporations, universities, and other institutions as racist, sexist, and so on.

The moral and legal questions involved in civil disobedience are difficult and complex. Most of its advocates avow it to be a strategy for overturning state and local laws and institutions that violate the Constitution and federal statutes and, so, claim to be, in a sense, supporting the law rather than resisting it. In 1968 the American Civil Liberties Union attempted to clarify its position on civil disobedience by disavowing at least two types of action. The organization declared it would not defend the deliberate violation of a constitutional law by an individual who believed it unjust, nor would it defend the violation of one law to call attention to the evils of some other law. The Supreme Court, prior to the enactment of the Civil Rights Act of 1964, decided most sit-in cases on narrow technical grounds rather than by establishing any broad constitutional rule (*Garner* v. *Louisiana*, 1961; *Brown* v. *Louisiana*, 1966). The Court's dilemma was most clearly revealed in *Bell* v. *Maryland* (1964), in which six justices took the opportunity to present conflicting interpretations of the constitutionality of sit-ins. Fortunately for the Court, the Civil Rights Act of 1964 settled the question of discrimination in establishments serving the public, and judicial consensus on sit-ins was restored.

BIBLIOGRAPHY

Charles L. Black, Jr., "Problems of the Compatibility of Civil Disobedience With American Institutions of Government," *Texas Law Review*, vol. 43 (1965).

C. Herman Pritchett, *The American Constitution*.

— JOSEPH A. DOWLING

Morning line-up in a Civilian Conservation Corps camp in Shasta National Forest, California, July 1933. (USDA-Forest Service/Corbis)

CIVILIAN CONSERVATION CORPS

Created in March 1933, the Civilian Conservation Corps (CCC) was the first New Deal agency specifically charged with providing relief for unemployed young people. Through it, the federal government placed nearly 3 million single men from seventeen to twenty-five years of age, including 250,000 veterans of World War I and 90,000 American Indians, on a large variety of conservation tasks throughout the country, during the period between 1933 and 1942. Reforestation was the most important of these tasks—indeed, more than half of all the public and private tree-planting ever done in the United States was performed by the CCC—but enrollees were also engaged in significant numbers in erosion control, fire prevention, drought relief, land reclamation, and pest eradication. Enrollees, who normally lived in camps or companies of 200 men each, were paid $30 monthly for their work, $25 of which was sent home to their families.

Between 1933 and 1942, the federal government placed nearly 3 million single men, from 17 to 25, on a large variety of conservation tasks throughout the country.

Under the supervision of a national director, the operation of the CCC involved four federal departments. The Department of Labor, working through state and local relief agencies, selected the men to be enrolled; the Department of War administered the work camps or companies, each of which had an army officer in command; the departments of Agriculture and the Interior were responsible for organizing and supervising the work projects. The director of the CCC formed policy and generally coordinated the activities of the federal departments. From 1933 until his death in 1939, Robert Fechner, a member of the International Association of Machinists and a vice-president of the American Federation of Labor, directed the agency. His successor was James J. McEntee, also of the machinists' association.

Although uneasiness was sometimes expressed at the important role played by the army in the CCC's organization and although the organization admittedly never provided much in the way of long-term vocational training for its enrollees, the CCC was probably the most widely accepted of all the New Deal agencies, even among those sections of the population generally opposed to the Franklin D. Roosevelt administration. The benefits it brought, both to the national domain and to its enrollees, were easily perceivable and noncontroversial. Certainly Roosevelt believed it to be among his most important achievements, and there was no other agency in which he took more pride or personal interest. It was abolished in 1942, not because of unpopularity, but because burgeoning reemployment caused by World War II rendered its continued existence unnecessary.

BIBLIOGRAPHY

John A. Salmond, *The Civilian Conservation Corps, 1933–1942.*

— JOHN A. SALMOND

CIVIL RIGHTS AND LIBERTIES

Civil rights and liberties refer to the various spheres of individual and group freedoms that are deemed to be so fundamental as not to tolerate governmental infringement. These include the fundamental political fights, especially the franchise, that offer the citizen the opportunity to participate in the administration of governmental affairs. Since these individual and group freedoms may also be abridged by the action or inaction of private institutions, demand has increased for positive governmental action to promote and encourage their preservation.

Constitutional provisions, statutes, and court decisions have been the principal means of acknowledging the civil rights and liberties of individuals; for those rights to be maximized, their acknowledgment must be accompanied by supportive action. Any conception of individual rights that does not include this action component may actually be instrumental in limiting the exercise of such rights.

The U.S. Constitution drawn up in the summer of 1787 included guarantees of the following civil rights and liberties: habeas corpus (Article I, Section 9), bill of attainder and ex post facto law (Article I, Sections 9 and 10), jury trial (Article III, Sections 2 and 3), privileges and immunities (Article IV, Section 2), and no religious test for public office (Article VI, Paragraph 3). Four years later ten amendments (Bill of Rights) were added to the Constitution in response to demands for more specific restrictions on the national government. The Bill of Rights guarantees certain substantive rights (notably freedom of speech, of the press, of assembly, and of religious worship) and certain procedural rights in both civil and criminal actions (notably a speedy and public trial by an impartial jury). In 1833 (*Barron* v. *Baltimore*, 7 Peters 243) the Supreme Court ruled that these amendments were designed to serve as protections against federal encroachment alone and did not apply to state and local governments. The Supreme Court's position in this case, as stated by Chief Justice John Marshall, was to prevail throughout the 19th and early 20th centuries, despite efforts of attorneys arguing that the intent of the framers of the Fourteenth Amendment's due process clause (1868) was to extend the protection of the Bill of Rights to the actions of states and localities. From 1925 (*Gitlow* v. *New York*, 268 U.S. 652) through 1969 (*Benton* v. *Maryland*, 395 U.S. 784), Supreme Court rulings had the effect of incorporating most of the major provisions of the Bill of

Rights into the due process clause of the Fourteenth Amendment, thereby making them applicable to states and localities as well as to the federal government.

Prior to the adoption of the Civil War amendments there had been little effort to invoke federal authority to preserve individual rights. Furthermore, revisionist historians have shown that the generation that framed the first state declarations of rights and the federal Bill of Rights was not as libertarian as is traditionally assumed—the Alien and Sedition Acts of 1798 being a case in point. The Thirteenth, Fourteenth, and Fifteenth amendments and the five general civil rights acts spanning the years 1866–75 established the bases for a vast expansion of federal authority. Although the Thirteenth abolished slavery and involuntary servitude and the Fifteenth prohibited the abridgment of a citizen's fight to vote because of race, color, or previous condition of servitude, the Fourteenth proved to be of greatest import to the subsequent development of individual rights.

The first sentence of Section 1 of the Fourteenth Amendment defines U.S. citizenship: "All persons born or naturalized in the United States, and subject to the jurisdiction thereof, are citizens of the United States." This provision overturned the Supreme Court's 1857 decision in the *Dred Scott* case (19 Howard 393) and recognized the primacy of national citizenship. (Citizenship was later described by Chief Justice Earl Warren [*Perez* v. *Brownell*, 356 U.S. 44, 64] as "man's basic right, for it is nothing less than the right to have rights.") The remainder of the first section of the amendment prohibited the states from abridging the privileges and immunities of citizens of the United States (which received judicial short shrift); depriving any person of life, liberty, or property without due process of law; and denying any person within its jurisdiction the equal protection of the laws.

The five general civil rights acts of the post–Civil War period were efforts to implement the Civil War amendments. Although Congress was primarily motivated by a concern for the newly freed blacks, these statutes, which provided federal protection of individual rights against interference either by public officials or private individuals, never made specific references to the Afro-American as such. The last of these 19th-century civil rights statutes, the Civil Rights Act of Mar. 1, 1875, was designed to guarantee to blacks equal accommodations with white citizens in all inns, public conveyances, theaters, and other public places. In 1883 the U.S. Supreme Court (*Civil Rights Cases*, 109 U.S. 3) concluded that the framers of the Fourteenth Amendment had not intended to enable Congress to prohibit private persons from discriminating against blacks. The Fourteenth Amendment was interpreted as prohibiting discriminatory acts by the states only, and consequently the act was declared void.

The major test of state legislation designed to support the segregation and suppression of blacks came in 1896. In *Plessy* v. *Ferguson* (163 U.S. 537) the Supreme Court upheld a Louisiana statute requiring separate accommodations for blacks and whites on public carriers, as long as the accommodations were equal. In the years that followed segregation of the races on the basis of the separate-but-equal doctrine became commonplace throughout the South, and segregation resulting from Jim Crow legislation continued to be pervasive into mid-century; in 1947 President Harry S. Truman's Committee on Civil Rights reported that the separate-but-equal doctrine was "one of the outstanding myths of American history, for it is almost always true that while indeed separate, . . . facilities are far from equal."

The separate-but-equal doctrine became deeply entrenched in the field of public education in the South, and it was not until 1938 (*Missouri ex rel. Gaines* v. *Canada*, 305 U.S. 337) that the Supreme Court began to examine the equality requirement. From 1938 until 1950 the Court, in a series of cases involving graduate school education, held that the separate facilities provided black students were not equal educationally, but in granting relief to black plaintiffs, the Court did not publicly reexamine the separate-but-equal doctrine. Nevertheless, these decisions paved the way for the Supreme Court's landmark decision of May 17, 1954 (*Brown* v. *Board of Education of Topeka*, 347 U.S. 483) overturning the *Plessy* v. *Ferguson* precedent and unanimously holding that the separate-but-equal doctrine had no place in the field of public education. The Court based its decision on the equal protection clause of the Fourteenth Amendment, which prohibited states from denying any person within their jurisdiction the equal protection of the laws. A companion case (*Bolling* v. *Sharpe*, 347 U.S. 497) prohibited segregation in the public schools of the District of Columbia.

In *Brown* the Court relied heavily on social science evidence that segregation itself meant inequality. A year later, in its implementation decree in the *Brown* case, the Court ordered the desegregation process to be carried out "with all deliberate speed," thereby apparently rejecting social science evidence that suggested the desirability of avoiding any gradualism or ambiguity that might encourage massive resistance. Massive resistance occurred, most notably in Arkansas and Virginia, and in 1964 (*Griffin* v. *County School Board of Prince Edward County*, 377 U.S. 218) the Court held that the time for mere "deliberate speed" had run out. Subsequent implementation decrees emphasized the obligation of school districts to terminate dual school systems at once and to operate only unitary schools thereafter. When confronted in 1971 with the question of the scope of a federal district court's ability to order school busing to correct state-enforced racial school segregation, the Supreme Court was unanimous in finding that the district court had not transcended the limits of "reasonableness" in its remedial order concerning busing (*Swann* v. *Charlotte-Mecklenburg Board of Education*, 402 U.S. 1).

It was not until 1974 (*Bradley* v. *Milliken*, 41 Lawyers' Edition 2d 1069) that the Supreme Court appeared to be deviating from the *Brown* holding and its constitutional underpinnings. Although as late as 1971 in the *Swann* decision the Court had unanimously upheld court-order busing within a single school district, in *Bradley* the Court by a five-to-four margin refused to permit a federal court to impose a multidistrict, areawide plan (including interdistrict busing) to remedy state-enforced segregation in a single district, in the absence of any finding that the other included districts had also failed to operate unitary school systems. Justice Thurgood Marshall, who had been the principal lawyer for the National Association for the Advancement of Colored People in the *Brown* case in 1954, responded in his dissent that "after twenty years of small, often difficult steps toward that great end, the Court today takes a giant step backwards." Although the majority did not entirely rule out the possibility of remedial plans in which district lines might be crossed—if, for example, the discriminatory acts of the state or a local district were the substantial cause of interdistrict segregation—it was generally agreed that the majority's standards for proving such causation would be difficult to meet. Somewhat ironically, the Supreme Court eliminated the dual-school systems that were prevalent in the South in the mid-20th century, while apparently finding that the courts are without power to remedy—at least through the use of metropolitan, areawide plans—segregation resulting from residential housing patterns in the major urban areas of the country, most of which are in the North and West.

The nonviolent Civil Rights Movement, which had its beginning in 1955–56 in the Montgomery, Ala., bus boycott led by Martin Luther King, Jr., received increasing national attention during the sit-ins and "freedom rides" of the early 1960's. Mass demonstrations in Birmingham, Ala., also led by King, further heightened the urgency of Afro-American demands and helped precipitate President John F. Kennedy's civil rights legislative proposals of June 19, 1963. This legislation, including provisions regarding access to public accommodations, use of federal funds without discrimination, and equal employment opportunity, was signed into law (July 2, 1964) during the early months of President Lyndon B. Johnson's administration. It was the most far-reaching civil rights legislation since 1875.

The public accommodations title of the 1964 act, title II, was similar in substance to the 1875 provisions struck down in the *Civil Rights Cases*; this time the legislation rested upon both the commerce clause and the equal protection clause of the Fourteenth Amendment. The Supreme Court in 1964 found the commerce clause fully adequate to sustain the public accommodations title (*Heart of Atlanta Motel* v. *U.S.*, 379 U.S. 241, and *Katzenbach* v. *McClung*, 379 U.S. 294).

Title VI, which prohibited discrimination in any federally assisted programs, was to prove instrumental in accelerating school desegregation during the Johnson administration. In particular, the passage of the Elementary and Secondary Education Act of 1965 provided funds of sufficient magnitude to place most school districts at a serious disadvantage by the termination of federal assistance. Finally, title VII created the Equal Employment Opportunity Commission, which struggled for seven years before it was to be granted enforcement powers—that is, the ability to institute suits in federal courts to enforce U.S. laws against job discrimination.

The nonviolent Civil Rights Movement received increasing national attention during the sit-ins and "freedom rides" of the early 1960's.

The Voting Rights Act of 1965 was passed in the aftermath of black demonstrations, especially in Selma, Ala., against discriminatory practices in voter registration in the South. This was the most sweeping voting rights legislation of the century, even though there had been antecedents in the civil rights acts of 1957, 1960, and 1964. The Voting Rights Act of 1970, in addition to being a five-year extension of the 1965 act, included provision for the eighteen-year-old vote in all elections. Before the year was over the original jurisdiction of the Supreme Court was invoked to test the constitutionality of the new minimum voting age provisions. Although the Court sustained the provisions insofar as they pertained to federal elections, it held that the Fourteenth Amendment's equal protection clause and enforcement clause did not authorize Congress to impose such a requirement in state and local elections. This latter action necessitated the adoption of the Twenty-sixth Amendment, which lowered the minimum voting age to eighteen in all elections.

Of the major civil rights problems confronting the country, housing was the last to be dealt with by Congress. It was not until 1968, shortly after the assassination of King, that Congress passed comprehensive legislation that prohibited discrimination in the sale or rental of about 80 percent of the nation's housing, the major exceptions being owner-occupied dwellings with no more than four units and the sale or rental of private homes without the services of a real estate agent.

As the nation's largest minority, blacks have been in the vanguard of efforts to secure individual civil rights; but the other large minority groups—Indians, Mexican-Americans, Puerto Ricans, and Asians—have also been victims of the same types of discrimination. Unquestionably, the black revolution has had a salutary effect on the struggles of these minorities for the effectuation of the civil rights guaranteed them by the Constitution. One tangible example is the so-called Indian Civil Rights Act, a rider to the Civil Rights Act of 1968. In view of the anomalous position of the tribal governments of American Indians, the legislation was designed to ensure that tribal governments would be bound by the same limitations imposed by the Constitution on the federal and state governments. Since the enumeration of these restraints was not a complete catalog of those included in the Constitution, it falls to the federal courts to interpret the legislation in a manner consistent with the tribes' cultural autonomy.

By the beginning of the 1970's a whole spectrum of constitutional provisions, laws, executive orders, and judicial decisions acknowledged the need for protection against discrimination in virtually every aspect of life—education, public accommodations, employment, voting, and housing—but a wide discrepancy existed between promise and performance. In the face of the militancy within the black community and the impact of the Vietnam War on domestic priorities, the national commitment to the effective establishment of civil rights and liberties of blacks, Indians, Spanish-speaking Americans, and other minorities was on the wane.

BIBLIOGRAPHY

Henry J. Abraham, *Freedom and the Court: Civil Rights and Liberties in the United States.*

Thomas I. Emerson et al., *Political and Civil Rights in the United States.*

Leon Friedman, ed., *Argument: The Complete Oral Argument Before the Supreme Court in* Brown v. *Board of Education of Topeka, 1952–1955.*

Alfred H. Kelly and Winfred A. Harbison, *The American Constitution: Its Origins and Development.*

C. Herman Pritchett, *The American Constitution.*

U.S. Commission on Civil Rights, *Federal Civil Rights Enforcement Effort,* and *Twenty Years After Brown: The Shadows of the Past.*

— HOWARD WHITCOMB

CIVIL RIGHTS MOVEMENT

The civil rights movement is generally dated from the Supreme Court's decision of 1954 in *Brown* v. *Board of Education of Topeka* to the passage in 1965 of the Voting Rights Act. Reformist in nature and based in the South, the movement was a sustained and massive nonviolent, direct-action campaign by black organizations and individuals and their white allies to achieve the full integration of Afro-Americans into every sphere of American life. Similar to other social movements in American history, the civil rights crusade had deep antecedents in the past, being rooted in a 300-year-old tradition of protest and resistance. The protracted struggle for freedom and equality waged previously by rebellious slaves, black abolitionists, and militant protest leaders formed the historical background out of which the modern black liberation movement was born.

Although an extension of past struggles, the civil fights movement was the direct outgrowth of liberalized racial views in America and important victories won by increased black agitation for equal fights during and after World War II. The original March on Washington movement, organized by black labor leader A. Philip Randolph (1941); the subsequent issuance of an executive order by President Franklin D. Roosevelt prohibiting discriminatory employment practices in defense plants (1941); Roosevelt's establishment of the Fair Employment Practices Committee (1941); the positive impact on racial attitudes of Gunnar Myrdal's classic study, *An American Dilemma* (1944); and a Supreme Court decision (*Smith* v. *Allwright*) abolishing the all-white primary (1944) were all important wartime developments. Joined with President Harry S. Truman's endorsement in 1947 of civil rights recommendations contained in a report prepared by his Committee on Civil Rights, the inclusion of a strong civil rights plank in the 1948 Democratic party platform, and Truman's decision in 1948 to desegregate the military and civil service, these postwar advancements contributed greatly to the social climate that produced the Supreme Court ruling of 1954 and the Montgomery, Ala., bus boycott of 1955–56.

Prior to the great demonstrations of the 1960's, litigation in the courts primarily by lawyers of the National Association for the Advancement of Colored People (NAACP) was the governing strategy of the civil rights movement. Reliance upon the U.S. judiciary as a means to racial justice was an extremely slow process, but it was not without positive results. In a gradual reversal of previous opinions upholding the legality of racial segregation, the Supreme Court had begun in the New Deal era to strike down Jim Crow practices in voting, interstate travel, housing, and education. This liberal trend continued during the administrations of President Truman and President Dwight D. Eisenhower, culminating in 1954 with the monumental *Brown* decision. Given precedents in *Sipuel v. University of Oklahoma* (1948), *Sweatt* v. *Painter* (1950), and *McLaurin* v. *Oklahoma State Regents* (1950) and given psychological evidence of the harmful effect of segregated education on black children, the U.S. Supreme Court issued on May 17, 1954, a unanimous opinion, written by Chief Justice Earl Warren, ruling that separate educational facilities for blacks and whites were inherently unequal and therefore a violation of the equal protection clause of the Fourteenth Amendment. By repudiating in *Brown* v. *Board of Education* the separate-but-equal doctrine of *Plessy* v. *Ferguson*, which had stood since 1896, the Supreme Court had set into motion a new era in the black freedom movement.

Despite the hope that the *Brown* ruling engendered among blacks and whites favoring school desegregation, implementation of the decision proceeded at a sluggish pace. The action of the Supreme Court in May 1955 to grant local school boards time to prepare desegregation procedures and its directive ordering the admission of black children to all-white public schools "with all deliberate speed" may have been intended to bring about integration with orderly dispatch, but they actually gave segregationists the opportunity to pass statutes and resolutions delaying compliance with the law. Nevertheless, the *Brown* judgment unleashed forces that were to cause major social and political upheavals in the United States over the next twenty years.

The expectations of Afro-Americans, particularly those of an expanding black middle class, were significantly heightened by the Warren court's decision. As black expectations quickened, many Afro-Americans, frequently immobilized in the past by self-doubt and fear, derived inspiration and newfound courage from the ruling. The first dramatic sign of a changed attitude appeared in December 1955, when Rosa Parks, a black seamstress, boarded a municipal bus in Montgomery, Ala., and took a seat in the section reserved for whites. Because she refused to surrender her place to a white passenger, Mrs. Parks was arrested and jailed, an event that was to have profound consequences for the future course of American history.

Aroused by Mrs. Parks's arrest, black community leaders organized the Montgomery Improvement Association, which under the guidance of Martin Luther King, Jr., conducted a successful year-long boycott of the city bus system that resulted in its desegregation. International and national attention given to the Montgomery bus boycott not only publicized the deep-seated nature of American racism but significantly raised black consciousness in the United States, established King as the leader of the civil rights movement, and popularized among Afro-Americans the philosophy of nonviolence and civil disobedience.

The black people of Montgomery had effectively altered the style of black protest in 20th-century America and had given added impetus to the battle for civil rights. However, no coordinated and frontal attack against southern racism ensued. The Southern Christian Leadership Conference (SCLC) had been founded in Atlanta, Ga., in 1957 to galvanize the support of black Christians, but conditions were not yet right for a massive civil rights campaign in the South. Between 1956 and 1960, the direction of the civil rights movement remained largely in the hands of the moderate and legalistic NAACP. During these years, black activity was more evident in the courthouses of the country than on the streets of the nation's cities. Southern white resistance to desegregation was, on the other hand, often more visible.

After marking time for approximately a year, during which limited progress was made in the border states and upper South toward school integration, segregationists began actively in early 1956 to obstruct implementation of the *Brown* decision. The unanticipated action of lower courts in upholding the Supreme Court's ruling bred widespread panic among many southern whites and gave rise in the region to a pervasive mood of defiance. Politicians in Virginia urged massive resistance to the Court's orders and invoked the doctrine of interposition, claiming that the state had a right to interpose its authority against an alleged violation of the Supreme Court. One hundred Congressmen issued a southern manifesto in March 1956, censuring the Supreme Court and praising state efforts to resist forced integration by lawful means. White citizens' councils sprang up in numerous southern communities, ostensibly to protect the constitutional rights of whites, but actually to prevent the free access of blacks to public schools. Given a new lease on life by the mood of resistance sweeping the South, a revived Ku Klux Klan found considerable support among hardcore segregationists ready to commit or condone any act, no matter how heinous, to preserve white supremacy in America.

In this reactionary atmosphere progress toward school integration came almost to a halt. President Eisenhower was compelled in September 1957 by the magnitude of white mob violence to use federal marshals and troops to ensure the right of black children to attend the previously all-white Central High School in Little Rock, Ark. Generally, however, enforcement of the *Brown* decision was not vigorously pursued by the conservative Eisenhower administration. To avoid "another Little Rock," some states outside of the Deep South began in the fall of 1959 to relax their resistance to school integration, and yet by the end of the Eisenhower presidency in 1960, token integration at best had been achieved in southern school districts.

The first phase of the civil rights movement, with its heavy emphasis on court action, ended in 1960 when black youths, impatient with the slow pace of desegregation and disappointed by the cautiousness exhibited by King after the Montgomery boycott, took the initiative and launched a massive drive for equal rights unprecedented in scope and intensity. On Feb. 1, 1960, four students from North Carolina Agricultural and Technical University in Greensboro sat down at a segregated lunch counter and ordered coffee. When refused service, they continued to sit in silent protest until the store closed. News of their courageous stand spread rapidly throughout the country, stimulating black youths and occasionally white sympathizers in other cities to similar demonstrations. Soon a wave of student-led sit-ins, wade-ins, and sleep-ins directed against segregated public facilities had engulfed the nation. Under the mounting black offensive, public places, especially in the cities of the upper South, were desegregated with relative ease.

To maintain the momentum gathered by the sit-ins and to ensure cooperation between the various student groups, the Student Nonviolent Coordinating Committee (SNCC) was formed in Raleigh, N.C., in April 1960 on the advice of King. The idealistic white and black youths who joined SNCC were to endure severe verbal and physical abuse, even death, as they conducted over the next several years scores of demonstrations, sponsored numerous voter registration drives, and organized community projects in the South. In May 1961, members of the Congress of Racial Equality (CORE), founded originally in 1942, began a series of "freedom rides" through the Deep South to test a Supreme Court decision banning segregation in interstate bus terminals. After a bombing of one of CORE's integrated buses and the mobbing of another, SNCC volunteers joined the riders to continue the push southward. Massive arrests in Jackson, Miss., prevented the riders from proceeding further, but the publicity given their efforts produced a new order from the Interstate Commerce Commission desegregating all facilities used in interstate transportation.

By the end of 1961, SNCC and CORE, along with SCLC, were clearly in the vanguard of the movement. The staid NAACP and National Urban League, for years leading spokesmen for the black American, had been eclipsed by the younger advocates of direct action. In 1962 and 1963 the direct-actionists, often backed with legal support provided by the NAACP, stepped up their attack. A coalition of SNCC, CORE, SCLC, and the NAACP called the Council of Federated Organizations (COFO) was organized to register black votes in the South. Preaching salvation through the ballot, COFO conducted in the summer of 1962 a voter education program in Mississippi, where the ballot had been effectively denied to blacks. The following year, in April and May, King led large demonstrations to desegregate Birmingham, Ala., a city well known for its racism. The brutal force used by the Birmingham police to break up the demonstrations and the slaying of Medgar Evers, NAACP field secretary in Mississippi, a month later moved President John F. Kennedy in June 1963 to ask Congress to enact a comprehensive civil rights law to protect the rights of black Americans.

By sending federal troops to the University of Mississippi in September 1962 to ensure the admission of black student James Meredith and by its general support of civil rights, the Kennedy administration had established itself in the eyes of most Afro-Americans as a friend and protector of their rights. President Kennedy, however, was not successful in gaining congressional passage of his proposed civil rights legislation. Congress did not enact any new measures until after the civil rights movement peaked on Aug. 28, 1963, when some 200,000 persons, one-quarter of them white, participated in a march on Washington to demonstrate their support for the civil rights bill then pending before Congress.

After further black agitation and white violence, including the death of four black girls in the bombing of a black church in Birmingham, and the assassination in November 1963 of John F. Kennedy, the bill was successfully maneuvered through Congress by President Lyndon B. Johnson and made law in July 1964. With its sweeping prohibitions of racial segregation and discrimination in public accommodations, voting, and education, the bill was hailed as the Afro-American's Magna Charta. Black unrest, however, did not cease with the passage of the law. Inadequacies in the law concerning voting rights and the murder of three civil rights workers in the summer of 1964 led to additional civil rights demonstrations. To dramatize the urgency of further legislation and to focus attention on Alabama, where only 2 percent of voting-age blacks were registered, King planned a march in Alabama from Selma to Montgomery, the state capital, in March 1965. It was the vicious beatings and murder of some of the marchers followed by an impassioned plea of President Johnson for racial accord that in the end prompted Congress to pass the Voting Rights Act of August 1965.

Passage of the 1965 Voting Rights Act represented the culmination of the civil rights movement and marked the end of a decade of large-scale demonstrations to desegregate American society. Full integration, of course, had not been achieved in the South or, for that matter, in the North, where racist practices were beginning to come under attack, but the future looked bright. Then, in the middle and late sixties, there occurred an ideological shift in black America that drastically changed the focus of the black freedom movement. A white backlash in northern communities to black progress; urban riots during the long, hot summers of 1964–67; the continued frustrations of black ghetto dwellers, whose objective conditions had not been improved by the civil rights movement; the influence upon blacks of the radicals Malcolm X and Stokely Carmichael and of revolutionary voices from Africa and the Third World; and the assassination of King in April 1968 led many Afro-Americans to reject the assimilationist and middle-class aims of the civil rights movement as illusory and to turn toward the nationalist goals of "black power" and self-determination. Since the late 1960's, the nationalist philosophy, encompassing various shades of conservative, moderate, and radical politics, has dominated the thrust of the black liberation struggle.

BIBLIOGRAPHY

Lerone Bennett, Jr., *What Manner of Man: A Biography of Martin Luther King, Jr.*

John Hope Franklin, *From Slavery to Freedom.*

Vincent Harding, "Black Radicalism: The Road From Montgomery," in Alfred F. Young, ed., *Dissent: Explorations in the History of American Radicalism.*

Martin Luther King, Jr., *Stride Toward Freedom, Why We Can't Wait,* and *Where Do We Go From Here.*

David Lewis, *King: A Critical Biography.*

Rayford W. Logan and Michael R. Winston, *The Negro in the United States.*

James M. McPherson et al., eds., *Blacks in America: Bibliographical Essays.*

Allen J. Matusow, "From Civil Rights to Black Power: The Case of SNCC, 1960–1966," in Barton J. Berstein and Allen J. Matusow, eds., *Twentieth-Century America: Recent Interpretations.*

Benjamin Muse, *Ten Years of Prelude,* and *The American Negro Revolution.*

John A. Williams, *The King God Didn't Save.*

C. Vann Woodward, *The Strange Career of Jim Crow.*

Robert L. Zangrando, "Black Protest: From the Politics of Entree to the Politics of Liberation," *Journal of Afro-American Studies* (1970).

Harold Zinn, *SNCC: The New Abolitionists.*

— WILLIAM R. SCOTT

CIVIL RIGHTS MOVEMENT SINCE THE 1960S

In the years since passage of the 1965 Voting Rights Act, generally considered the culmination of the Civil Rights Movement, the struggle among African Americans to achieve full political, social, and economic justice has been marked by significant progress in some areas and frustration in others. In the South, the immediate results of the Voting Rights Act and the 1964 Civil Rights Act were breathtaking given the context of a century of institutionalized segregation. Public accommodations immediately and with little protest from whites opened their doors to black customers on an equal basis. Voting rolls bulged with new black voters. Prior to 1965 less than 20 percent of the eligible black electorate was registered to vote. Within three years more than two-thirds of eligible African Americans had registered to vote. Perhaps most important, the movement and its successes had imparted a sense of personhood, identity, and destiny to the South's blacks, a people told by both words and actions that they had counted for little in the region's development. No longer did black citizens endure the daily sense of humiliation and inferiority imparted by the words "white" and "colored," and the denial of the basic tenet of U.S. citizenship embodied in the right to vote. The South stood poised for an economic takeoff, with the historic partnership between two ancient and unequal cohabitants.

The movement liberated southern whites as well. Most whites had acquiesced in maintaining a segregated society. Once blacks had demonstrated both the folly and tragedy of racial separation, many whites felt relieved to have the burden of justifying the unjustifiable lifted from themselves and their region. Blacks and whites had lived in the South together for centuries and had shared the same soil, the same work, the same history, and the same blood, but they had been strangers to one another. Through the Civil Rights Movement blacks had demonstrated to their white neighbors that it was possible to be both southern and integrated. Using the language of evangelical Protestantism, of suffering and redemption, blacks spoke to whites in a familiar language. Through their dignity and their appeals to a higher moral ground, black southerners spoke to the better instincts of southern whites. The Civil Rights Movement as a piece of southern vernacular accounts, in part, for the difficulties Martin Luther King, Jr., and his colleagues experienced in trying to translate the movement to the ghettos of the urban North. There, amid family and institutional breakdown, the message of hope, redemption, and interracial harmony had much less resonance.

The forces that propelled the Civil Rights Movement to its greatest legislative victories in 1964 and 1965 disintegrated shortly after the passage of the 1965 Voting Rights Act. The coalition of civil rights organizations, never cohesive to begin with, split over differences in strategies, white involvement, and personalities. The riot in the Watts section of Los Angeles less than a week after President Lyndon B. Johnson signed the Voting Rights Act in August 1965 inaugurated a series of long hot summers in the black ghettos of the North. The violence and accompanying calls for "black power" evaporated the reservoir of white northern goodwill toward black demands for civil and social equality. The Vietnam War diverted energy, attention, and funds from civil rights. The assassinations of King and Robert F. Kennedy in 1968 removed from the national scene two of the most articulate advocates for equality. When the Kerner Commission, appointed by President Lyndon B. Johnson to investigate the disturbances in the nation's cities, argued in 1968 that "the nation is rapidly moving toward two increasingly separate Americas . . . a white society principally located in suburbs . . . and a Negro society largely concentrated within large central cities," few challenged the conclusion.

Still, the Civil Rights Movement generated important changes for the better, particularly in the South. Title VI of the 1964 Civil Rights Act prohibited job discrimination and southern blacks benefited immediately. More than 100,000 black workers entered the textile industry. While the provisions of the act outlawing segregation in public accommodations did not result in a totally integrated society, many public facilities, such as parks, playgrounds, theaters, hotels, and restaurants, now opened to the black community. Southern blacks benefited more from the 1965 Voting Rights Act. The sudden injection of blacks into southern politics moderated race-baiting, initiated an era of two-party politics, and resulted in the election of many black officeholders. By the 1980s the South led the nation with 4,000 African-American elected officials, including the mayors of such cities as Atlanta, Charlotte, Richmond, New Orleans, Birmingham, and Little Rock.

As a result of the *Swann* v. *Charlotte-Mecklenburg Board of Education* case in 1971, the federal government forced cities across the South to achieve racial desegregation in public schools, sometimes by using the controversial method of busing. By the 1980s the South had the most integrated public school system in the nation. With policies such as affirmative action (initially part of the 1964 Civil Rights Act, but strengthened during Richard Nixon's administration and by the federal courts) and the booming Sun Belt economy, the numbers of middle-income blacks in the South rapidly increased. One estimate held that between 1975 and 1990 the black urban middle class in the South grew from 12 percent of the black population to nearly half.

Nationally, results after 1968 were less promising. The transformation from a manufacturing to a service-

Martin Luther King, Jr., leads thousands of civil rights demonstrators in Montgomery, Alabama, in the last leg of their 50-mile march from Selma to Montgomery. (UPI/Corbis-Bettmann)

oriented economy heavily affected the mainly semiskilled and unskilled black labor force. While the northern black middle class grew in size and affluence, a bifurcation emerged in black society with expansion of the black underclass. Affirmative action, especially in education and employment, boosted the black middle class, but for those mired in poverty, it proved irrelevant or elusive. The decline in federal funding for poverty programs during the Ronald Reagan and George Bush administrations exacerbated the socioeconomic split in the black community. Immigration from Latin America and Asia during the 1980s and 1990s added ethnic conflicts and competition to an already inauspicious future for the black poor. In the South the political transformation wrought by the entrance of blacks into the electoral process gave rise to a predominantly white, conservative Republican party. Also, given changes in the U.S. economy and the decline of federal funding, black officeholders were unable to offer much surcease for their poorest constituents. In addition, urban school districts became increasingly black or, as in the cases of Norfolk and Little Rock, voluntarily resegregated to maintain racial balance in the rest of the system.

The forces that propelled the civil rights movement to its greatest legislative victories in 1964 and 1965 disintegrated shortly after the passage of the 1965 Voting Rights Act.

If the 1960s were years of civil rights confrontation, when southern blacks confronted whites with their consciences and their past, and the 1970s and 1980s were decades of consolidation, when blacks, especially in the urban South, built on the gains of the 1960s, then the 1990s were the decade of confusion and contradiction—an era of incomparable black middle class affluence and unprecedented numbers of impoverished blacks. The old interracial coalition of the 1960s disintegrated into numerous competing groups and interracial and religious antagonisms. Even the major purpose of the old movement—integration—appeared anachronistic in an era that promoted diversity and multiculturalism. Some black leaders reminisced about the era of segregation and the strength and identity blacks derived from building and maintaining their own communities and institutions.

Polls in the 1990s indicated that black and white Americans had sharply different understandings of the role of government in solving social problems, and affirmative action guidelines and set-aside programs came under national attack after the election of a conservative Republican Congress in 1994. The targets for civil rights activism were more elusive and ambiguous than ever before. Experts offered up economic explanations, genetics, and cultural theories to explain the persistent dilemma of race. Racism alone no longer seemed the clear-cut explication of race relations that it was in the 1960s, nor did the solutions seem obvious in terms of legislation and court rulings. Although venerable civil rights organizations, such as the National Association for the Advancement of Colored People, the Congress of Racial Equality, the Urban League, and Southern Christian Leadership Conference, persisted into the 1990s, their influence among rank-and-file blacks had diminished. The Reverend Jesse Jackson's Rainbow Coalition, an antipoverty organization, achieved some success, beginning in the mid-1980s, and Nation of Islam leader Louis Farrakhan's message of self-help and race pride won him a growing following, as evidenced by the Million Man March on Washington, D.C., in October 1995. Farrakhan's rhetorical attacks on other races and religious groups, however, often divided rather than united blacks. The true spirit of the Civil Rights Movement lies with hundred of local organizations that sponsor day-care facilities, lunch programs, after-school activities, and other grassroots efforts.

The Civil Rights Movement of the 1960s, one may conclude, reflected the best in U.S. society, the struggle to live up to the ideals of the Declaration of Independence and the Constitution. If that struggle fell short in certain areas, it succeeded in others. Perhaps the greatest legacy of the movement is that it serves as a reminder that Americans can overcome racial problems given the willingness of whites to change behavior and of the federal government to encourage change.

[See also Affirmative Action; African Americans; Civil Rights Movement; Desegregation; National Association for the Advancement of Colored People.]

BIBLIOGRAPHY

David J. Garrow, *Bearing the Cross: Martin Luther King, Jr., and the Southern Christian Leadership Conference* (New York, 1986).

David Goldfield, *Black, White, and Southern: Race Relations and Southern Culture, 1940 to the Present* (Baton Rouge, La., 1990).

Hugh Davis Graham, *The Civil Rights Era: Origins and Development of National Policy* (New York, 1990).

Richard Kluger, *Simple Justice: The History of* Brown *v.* Board of Education *and Black America's Struggle for Equality* (New York, 1977).

Steven F. Lawson, *Black Ballots: Voting Rights in the South, 1944–1969* (New York, 1976), and *In Pursuit of Power: Southern Blacks and Electoral Politics* (New York, 1985).

Aldon D. Morris, *The Origins of the Civil Rights Movement: Black Communities Organizing for Change* (New York, 1984).
Robert J. Norrell, *Reaping the Whirlwind: The Civil Rights Movement in Tuskegee* (New York, 1985).
Howell Raines, *My Soul Is Rested: Movement Days in the Deep South Remembered* (New York, 1983).

— DAVID GOLDFIELD

CIVIL SERVICE

Civil service, the term applied to the appointed civilian employees of a governmental unit, as distinct from elected officials and military personnel. Increasingly, most civil service systems in the United States are characterized by a merit system of employment based on technical expertise, as determined by competitive examinations, and on permanent tenure and nonpartisanship. A few positions in the federal civil service and many more in state and local governments are filled by employees who owe their appointments primarily to political considerations. Such employees and the offices that they fill are known as the patronage, and the appointment mechanism is known as the spoils system. Much of the history of the U.S. civil service has had to do with its transformation from a spoils system to a predominantly merit system—a struggle spanning more than a hundred years and still going on in some state and local jurisdictions.

Under President George Washington and his successors through John Quincy Adams, the federal civil service was stable and characterized by relative competence and efficiency. However, the increasingly strong pressures of Jacksonian egalitarian democracy after 1829 rudely adjusted the civil service of the Founding Fathers, and for more than a half-century the federal, state, and local services were largely governed by a spoils system that gave little or no consideration to competence.

The unprecedented corruption and scandals of the post–Civil War era generated the beginnings of modern civil service reform. An act of 1871 authorized the president to utilize examinations in the appointing process, and President Ulysses S. Grant appointed the first U.S. Civil Service Commission in that year. But Congress refused appropriations; full statutory support for reform waited until 1883 and the passage of the Pendleton Act, still the federal government's central civil service law. This act reestablished the Civil Service Commission, created a modern merit system for many offices, and authorized the president to expand this system. Behind the reforms of the late 19th century lay the efforts of the National Civil Service League, supported by public reaction against the corruption of the times. Successive presidents, requiring more and more professional expertise to carry out congressional mandates, continued and consolidated the reform—notably Grover Cleveland, Theodore Roosevelt, and Herbert Hoover. By 1900 the proportion of the federal civil service under the merit system reached nearly 60 percent; by 1930 it had exceeded 80 percent.

The depression period of the 1930's saw both a near doubling of the federal civil service and some renaissance of patronage politics, especially in the administration of work relief. With public and congressional support during his second term, President Franklin D. Roosevelt was empowered to, and did, expand the competitive system to most positions in the new agencies. Moreover, Congress extended a version of the merit system to first-, second-, and third-class postmasters; federal agencies were all required to have personnel offices; the Tennessee Valley Authority, under a special merit system statute, commenced to pioneer in government-employee labor relations; and pay- and position-classification systems were improved.

After World War II, federal personnel management, which had formerly consisted mainly of administering examinations and policing the patronage, further expanded its functions. The operation of personnel management was largely delegated to well-staffed personnel offices of agencies. Improved pay and fringe benefits, training and executive development, a positive search for first-rate talent, new approaches to performance rating, equal employment opportunity, improved ethical standards, loyalty and security procedures, incentive systems, and special programs for the handicapped were major developments. These developments and a full-scale labor relations system based on a precedent-shattering executive order by President John F. Kennedy in 1962 have characterized the transformation of 19th-century merit system notions into public personnel management as advanced as that anywhere in the world. In a federal civil service of 3 million, there are fewer than 15,000 patronage posts of any consequence.

Beginning in the late 19th century, civil service reform came also to many state and local governments, although relatively more slowly and less completely. In 1883 New York State adopted the first state civil service act and was followed almost immediately by Massachusetts. By 1940 one-third of the states had comprehensive merit systems; by 1970 two-thirds had them. The reform spread, from the East, through cities as well, after several New York and Massachusetts cities set up civil service commissions in the 1880's. Chicago followed in 1895. Most metropolitan centers and many of the smaller cities have modern merit systems. A few have systems for police and fire departments only. Most cities act under their own statutes, but in New York, Ohio, and New Jersey there is general coverage of local jurisdictions by state constitutional or other state legal provision. In one-quarter of the states—notable among which is California—the state personnel agencies may perform technical services for localities on a reimbursement basis. Whereas a bipartisan civil service commission provides administrative leadership in most jurisdictions, the single personnel director is becoming more popular.

The most important 20th-century developments in civil service have to do with federal-state cooperative personnel arrangements. In part, such arrangements stem from a 1939 amendment to the Social Security Act of 1935, which required the federal government to apply merit system procedures to certain state and local employees paid in whole or in part through grants-in-aid. A considerable number of similar statutes followed, so that by the 1970's perhaps a million state and local positions fell within personnel systems closely monitored by the federal government. Federal supervision was for many years managed by a bureau of the Social Security Administration and later by a division of the Department of Health, Education, and Welfare. The Intergovernment Personnel Act of 1970, signed by President Richard M. Nixon on Jan. 5, 1971, relocated the supervision of grant-in-aid employees within the U.S. Civil Service Commission. But, equally important, this act authorized federal grants-in-aid to state and local governments in support of modern personnel systems within these jurisdictions. The function of handling these grants-in-aid is also with the U.S. Civil Service Commission. Thus, it has become the central personnel agency not only of the federal government but also, in many respects, of the entire intergovernmental system.

The most important 20th-century developments in civil service concern federal-state cooperative personnel arrangements.

In size, the federal civil service has grown from an institution of a few hundred employees in 1789 to nearly 3 million. During major wars the federal civil service has doubled and even quadrupled; its peak occurred in 1945 when civil service employees numbered nearly 4 million. There has been a similar growth in state and local services, employment in the former totaling more than 3 million persons by 1975 and in the latter, more than 8 million. One out of six persons in the employed civilian labor force worked for a unit of American government in the middle 1970's. The federal civil service saw its greatest continuing expansion between 1930 and 1950; progressive expansion of state and local civil service rosters began in the late 1940's, when state and local goverments started on the road to becoming the fastest growing segment of American enterprise, public or private. By the 1970's federal civil employees functioned almost entirely under merit system procedures, as did some 75 percent of those in state and local governments. Civil service reform is therefore nearly an accomplished fact in the United States.

Civil service reform in the United States has produced a uniquely open system, in contrast to the closed career system common to other nations—which one enters only at a relatively early age and remains within for a lifetime, in the manner associated in the United States mainly with a military career. The Pendleton Act of 1883 established this original approach, providing that the federal service would be open to persons of any age who could pass job-oriented examinations. Persons may move in and out of the public service, from government to private industry and back again, through a process known as lateral entry. It is this openness to anyone who can pass an examination, this constant availability of lateral entry, that has set the tone and character of public service in the United States at all levels. One consequence of U.S. civil service policy has been to provide a notable route for upward mobility, especially for women and blacks. Thus, the U.S. civil service has reflected the open, mobile nature of American society and, in turn, has done much to support it.

BIBLIOGRAPHY

H. Eliot Kaplan, *The Law of Civil Service.*
Frederick C. Mosher, *Democracy and the Public Service.*
O. Glenn Stahl, *Public Personnel Administration.*
Paul P. Van Riper, *History of the United States Civil Service.*

— PAUL P. VAN RIPER

CIVIL WAR

Civil War (1861–65). In understanding the background of the Civil War it is essential to distinguish such broad factors as southernism in terms of culture types, economic and political motives of the planter aristocracy, southern defense reaction to northern criticism, the whipping up of excitement by agitators on both sides, economic sectionalism (agrarian versus industrial tendencies), northern thought patterns as to democracy and slavery, Republican party strategy, and the highly overemphasized issue of slavery in the territories. Sectional tension grew ominously in the 1850's and a major southern crisis, accompanied by intense popular excitement, followed the election of President Abraham Lincoln in November 1860. By early February 1861, the seven states of the Lower South (South Carolina, Mississippi, Florida, Alabama, Georgia, Louisiana, and Texas) had withdrawn from the Union and had begun the establishment of the southern Confederacy. After a period of inaction, the sending of an expedition by Lincoln to relieve the federal garrison at Fort Sumter in Charleston harbor precipitated a southern attack upon that fort, which was surrendered on April 13. This specifically was the opening of the war. Each side claimed that the other began it. Southerners argued that Lincoln's expedition was an invasion of a sovereign state; the federal government maintained that it meant no aggression in holding its own fort and that the first shot had been fired by the South.

Within three months of Lincoln's 1860 election, seven southern states had withdrawn from the Union and had begun establishing a southern Confederacy.

Lincoln's inaugural address of Mar. 4, 1861, had been conciliatory in tone; nevertheless his decision to retain Sumter, which necessitated sending food to the garrison, placed the opening incident in precisely that area where peace was most unstable and where emotion had been roused to greatest sensitivity. Fort Pickens in Florida, though similar in status to Sumter, presented no such menace of emotional outbreak. Lincoln's Sumter policy involved two main points: the sending of the provisioning expedition, and, after the fort had been fired upon, the call for 75,000 militia to be furnished by the states. This policy, while it produced a united North, served equally to unite the South; it was not until after Lincoln's call for militia that the four important states of the Upper South (Virginia, Arkansas, Tennessee, and North Carolina) withdrew from the Union and joined the Confederacy. In this sense Lincoln's April policy, interpreted in the South as coercion, played into the hands of the secessionists while former President James Buchanan's avoidance of an outbreak had supplied the setting for compromise efforts.

On the side of the Union there were twenty-three states with 22 million people as against eleven states and 9 million people (including 3.5 million slaves) within the Confederacy. In wealth and population as well as in industrial, commercial, and financial strength the Union was definitely superior to the Confederacy. On the other hand the South had the advantage of bold leadership, gallant tradition, martial spirit, unopposed seizure of many federal forts and arsenals, interior military lines, and unusual ability among its generals. Its military problem was that of defense, which required far fewer men than offensive campaigns and widely extended hostile occupation. Between the two sections was a populous middle region (the Union slave states of Delaware, Maryland, Kentucky, and Missouri; the area that became West Virginia; and the southern portions of Ohio, Indiana, and Illinois) within which the choice of the people was for the Union while on the other hand there was cultural sympathy for the South and spirited opposition to the Lincoln administration.

Legally the war began with Lincoln's proclamations: the proclamation of Apr. 15, 1861, which summoned the militia to suppress "combinations" in the seven states of the Lower South; and the proclamations of Apr. 19 and Apr. 27, 1861, which launched a blockade of southern ports. Internationally the Confederacy achieved recognition of belligerency, as in the British queen's proclamation of neutrality (May 13, 1861), but never achieved full standing in the sense of a recognition of independence by any foreign power. Nor did any foreign nation intervene in the struggle, although the British government seemed at times to be seriously contemplating it and the government of Napoleon III did offer mediation which was indignantly rejected by the United States (February-March 1863).

Before Lincoln's first Congress met in July 1861, the president had taken those measures that gave to Union war policy its controlling character. Besides proclaiming an insurrection, declaring a blockade, and summoning the militia (definite war measures), he had suspended the habeas corpus privilege, expanded the regular army, directed emergency expenditures, and in general had assumed executive functions beyond existing law. A tardy ratification of his acts was passed by Congress on Aug. 6, 1861, and in 1863 these strongly contested executive measures were given sanction by the Supreme Court in a five-to-four decision sustained chiefly by Lincoln's own judicial appointees. In general, Lincoln's method of meeting the emergency and suppressing disloyal tendencies was not to proceed within the pattern of regular statutes, but to grasp arbitrary power by executive orders or proclamations, as in the Emancipation Proclamation (in which the president exercised a power which he insisted Congress did not have even in time of war), and his extensive program of arbitrary arrests, wherein thousands of citizens were thrust into prison on suspicion of disloyal or dangerous activity. These arrests were quite irregular. Prisoners were given no trial (usually not even military trial); they were deprived of civil guarantees and were subjected to no regular accusations under the law. Such measures led to severe and widespread opposition to the Lincoln administration. In their denial of the habeas corpus privilege these measures were denounced as unconstitutional in a hearing before Chief Justice Roger B. Taney (*Ex parte Merryman*, May 1861), but in the Vallandigham case (1864) the Supreme Court, to which the Merryman case had not been brought, declined to interpose any obstacle to arbitrary arrest, thus in a negative way sustaining the president. (In 1866, however, in the Milligan case, the Court did overrule a wartime military commission.) Yet it cannot be said that Lincoln became a "dictator" in the 20th-century sense of the word. He allowed freedom of speech and of the press, contrary examples being exceptional, not typical. He tolerated widespread newspaper criticism of himself and of the government, interposed no party uniformity, permitted free assembly, avoided partisan violence, recognized opponents in appointments, and above all submitted himself, even during war, to the test of popular election. This testing resulted in a marked Republican loss in the congressional election of 1862, while in 1864, although the situation looked very dark for the Republicans in August, the election in November brought in a considerable electoral majority.

In the military sense both sides were unprepared; had any conceivable policy of prewar preparedness been promoted (under the southern secretaries of war of the 1850's) it could hardly have given the Union side that advantage which military writers often assume. The first Battle of Bull Run (July 21) was the only large-scale engagement in 1861. Although a Union defeat, it was, like most of the battles, an indecisive struggle. Except during the generalship of Union officers George B. McClellan, George G . Meade, and Ulysses S. Grant, the southerners had the undoubted advantage of military leadership on the main eastern front; Robert E. Lee's notable, though indecisive, victories of second Bull Run, Fredericksburg, and Chancellorsville were won against John Pope, A. E. Burnside, and Joseph Hooker. At Antietam, however, McClellan stopped Lee's northern invasion of September 1862, while the ambitious Confederate offensive of 1963 was checked at Gettysburg. In the West most of the operations were favorable to the Union side. This was especially true of the "river war" (resulting in the capture of Columbus, forts Henry and Donelson, Nashville, Corinth, and Memphis); the Union half-victory of Shiloh; and more especially the important Union victories of 1863 at Vicksburg and in the Chattanooga area. Later campaigns involved Confederate Gen. J. E. Johnston's unsuccessful operations against William Tecumseh Sherman in upper Georgia, Sherman's capture of Atlanta and his famous raid through Georgia and the Carolinas, Union Gen. Philip H. Sheridan's devastating operations in the Valley of Virginia, the Grant-Meade operations against Lee in Virginia (involving the costly battles of the Wilderness, Spotsylvania, and Cold Harbor), the J. B. Hood–G. H. Thomas campaign in Tennessee, and final operations in the Petersburg and Appomattox areas, which culminated in the fall of Richmond and the close of the war. In the naval aspects Union superiority was impressively shown in the blockade of southern ports, which were eventually closed to the Confederacy's own warships, the capture and occupation of coastal positions, the cooperation of western flotillas with the armies, the seizure of New Orleans in April 1862, the complete control of the Mississippi River after the fall of Vicksburg and Port Hudson in July 1863, and the defeat and sinking of the Confederacy's proudest ship, the *Alabama*, by the *Kearsarge* (June 19, 1864). On the other hand, Confederate cruisers and privateers did considerable damage to Union commerce, the Union Navy failed in the operations against Richmond, and several ports (Wilmington, Charleston, Mobile) remained in southern hands until late in the war. Galveston did not yield until after the war was over, June 1865. Privateering was authorized by both sides but practiced only by the Confederacy, and that chiefly in the first year of the war. The military decision in favor of the United States was registered in the surrender of Lee to Grant at Appomattox, Apr. 9, 1865, and the surrender of Johnston to Sherman near Durham, N.C., on Apr. 26.

Both sides were militarily unprepared; had any conceivable policy of prewar preparedness been promoted, it could hardly have given the Union the advantage commonly ascribed by military writers.

Methods of military recruiting and administration were amateurish, haphazard, and inefficient. Conscription was used on both sides but by neither side with real effectiveness. The Union system of army administration was marred by such factors as commutation money, bounties, bargaining in substitutes, draft riots, irregular popular recruiting, undue multiplication of military units, lack of a general staff, and inadequate use of the very small regular army. Somewhat similar difficulties existed also in the South. Guerrilla warfare, though never a decisive factor nor a part of major strategy, was extensively practiced. The administration of the U.S. War Department under Secretary Simon Cameron (to January 1862) was marred by fraud and corruption; under Secretary Edwin M. Stanton the system was improved, but profiteering and military blundering existed to a marked degree throughout the war. In addition, the Union cause was weakened by state control of national military processes, congressional interference, anti-McClellanism (involving the unwise abandonment of McClellan's peninsular campaign in the summer of 1862), confusion and circumlocution among diverse army boards, councils, and advisers, undue control of army matters by such men as Gen. Henry W. Halleck and Stanton, extensive desertion, and atrocious inadequacy in the care of hundreds of thousands of prisoners, the last-named abuse being chiefly due to utter breakdown in the exchange or cartel system. Black troops were extensively used in the Union armies. The Confederate government, late in the war, authorized their enrollment, but this was never put into practice.

What happened behind the lines would constitute a very elaborate story. Civilian relief for the North was supplied by the U.S. Sanitary Commission (similar to the later Red Cross) and war propaganda was spread by the Union League and the Loyal Publication Society; in the South anti-Union efforts were promoted by the Sons of Liberty and Knights of the Golden Circle. Financial instability and monetary abnormality carried prices to fantastic heights in the South; in the North the disturbance was far less, but specie payments were suspended and treasury notes (greenbacks) depreciated to such an extent that the paper price of gold reached $2.84 in July 1864. Taxation was heavy, yet a federal debt of approximately $3 billion was accumulated. Federal bonds were marketed by the semiofficial efforts of Jay Cooke and Company. Currency and banking regulations were drastically modified by the establishment of the national banking system. Labor obtained from the war far less advantage than business entrepreneurs. Immigration was encouraged and the wartime increase of wages was not commensurate with the depreciation of the money system. Greed was widespread, stock speculation was rife, lobbying was rampant, contractors cheated the government, and large numbers of men became unjustifiably rich. High wartime tariff laws gave ample protection to manufacturers. Various reforms and progressive schemes were delayed or wrecked by the war, but laws were passed for assigning free homesteads to settlers, for encouraging western railroad building, and for federal aid in the establishment of land grant colleges.

To a people once united but split asunder by the tragedy of war there came the inevitable horrors of war psychosis; this took manifold forms including un-Christian sputterings of hatred in the churches. One of the most savage of the wartime fanatics was "Parson" W. G. Brownlow of Tennessee. Yet Quakers and other honest religious objectors to war were given, by administrative procedure and later by law, the alternative of noncombatant service when drafted. Efforts of peace groups to end the war in 1864 received notable support from Horace Greeley, but, being associated with partisan politics, they met failure in every case; even the official efforts of highly placed statesmen met failure in the Hampton Roads Conference of February 1865. War aims changed as the conflict progressed; the declaration of Congress on July 22, 1861, that the war was waged merely for the restoration of the Union was belied by the Radical Republicans who by 1864 had determined in the event of victory to treat the South as a subordinate section upon which drastic modifications would be imposed. One of the striking examples of wartime Radical policy was seen in the second confiscation act (July 17, 1862), which, against Lincoln's better judgment, decreed the forfeiture to the United States of the property of all adherents to the "rebellion." The relation of the war to the slavery question appeared in various emancipating measures passed by Congress, in Lincoln's Emancipation Proclamation as well as his abortive compensated emancipation scheme, in state measures of abolition, and finally in the antislavery amendment to the Constitution. The distinction of Lincoln was discernible not in the enactment of laws through his advocacy, nor in the adoption of his ideals as a continuing postwar policy, nor even in the persuasion of his own party to follow his lead. Rather, the qualities which marked him as leader were personal tact (shown notably in a cabinet crisis of December 1862), fairness toward opponents, popular appeal, dignity and effectiveness in state papers, absence of vindictiveness, and withal a personality that was remembered for its own uniqueness while it was almost canonized as a symbol of the Union cause. Military success, though long delayed, and the dramatic martyrdom of his assassination must also be reckoned as factors in Lincoln's fame. On the other side southern memory of a cherished lost cause has been equally identified with the lofty perfection of Lee's personality.

To measure the war in terms of manpower and casualties is a highly controversial task made doubly difficult by sectional pride, popular tradition, amateur history writing, and inadequate statistics. Gen. Marcus J. Wright, a Confederate officer attached to the War Department after the war, estimated Confederate manpower at 600,000 to 700,000. Others, including T. L. Livermore and J. F. Rhodes, have put it much higher. Col. W. F. Fox, a military statistician, considered that the Union forces did not exceed 2 million separate individuals. Comprehensive records are especially lacking on the Confederate side, while the better statistics on the Union side are in terms of enlistments and have been only conjecturally corrected to allow for numerous cases of reenlistment. Comparable units of military measurement have been hard to obtain in determining the totals involved in particular campaigns or battles, and inadequate attention has been given to the precise meaning of such terms as "effectives," men "present for duty," and forces "actually engaged." Grand totals include men in home guards, thousands who were missing, and many other thousands who enlisted in the final weeks or were otherwise distant from fighting areas. On the Union side in April 1865, there were approximately 1 million men in the field, with 2 million of the "national forces" not yet called out. The number of those subject to military call in the North was actually greater at the end of the war than at the beginning. Confederate dead have been estimated at 258,000, Union dead at 360,000. The stupendous economic and material loss has never been more than roughly estimated.

Among Lincoln's principal leadership qualities were his personal tact and dignity, popular appeal, fairness toward opponents, and an absence of vindictiveness.

Aside from the obvious consequences of slaughter and destruction, the results of the war (or concomitants of the war and postwar period) involved suppression of the "heresy" of secession, legal fixation of an "indestructible" Union, national abolition of slavery, overthrow of the southern planter class, rise of middle-class power in the South, decline of the merchant marine, ascendancy of the Republican party, inauguration of a continuing high-tariff policy, far-reaching developments in terms of capitalistic growth associated with centralization of government functions, and adoption of the Fourteenth Amendment (intended to consolidate party control by the protection of Afro-American civil rights but later applied as a shield to corporations). But with the mention of these factors the enumeration of long-time results is only begun. A full enumeration would also include postwar intolerance, partisanship associated with the "bloody shirt" tradition, immense pension claims with their many abuses, a deplorable complex of reconstruction evils and excesses, carpetbag and scalawag corruption, and, as the continuing result of all this, the "solid South."

— J. G. RANDALL

Civil War Diplomacy

The basic diplomatic policy of the United States during the Civil War was twofold: to prevent foreign intervention in behalf of the southern Confederacy; and to gain the acquiescence of the great maritime powers, England and France, in the vast extension of maritime belligerent rights which was considered necessary in order to crush the South. The chief diplomatic figures in northern diplomacy were Secretary of State William H. Seward, supported and advised by President Lincoln; Charles Francis Adams, minister to England; William Dayton, minister to France; John Bigelow, consul general in France and, after Dayton's death in 1864, minister in his stead; and Thomas Corwin, minister to the Juárez government of Mexico. The United States had its diplomatic representatives in all the other principal nations. But since France and England were great maritime powers and none too friendly toward the United States at the time, they seemed to offer the only serious danger of foreign intervention. At the same time they were the nations that had to be appeased because of aggression against their commerce in prosecution of the war against Confederate trade. Federal diplomacy, therefore, was largely concerned with these two nations as far as it related to the Civil War.

In the very beginning, Seward deliberately gave the British government the impression that he was willing if not anxious for the United States to fight Great Britain should that country show undue sympathy for the Confederacy. The recognition of Confederate belligerency before war had really begun—except the firing on Fort Sumter—gave Seward and Adams a tangible and even bitter grievance against both England and France. It resulted in Seward's issuing an ultimatum to England, threatening to break off diplomatic relations should England receive, even unofficially, the Confederate diplomatic agents. This grievance was constantly held up by Adams and Seward; and the launching of the Confederate cruisers and the building of the Confederate rams in England—and France—gave other even stronger grounds upon which the American diplomats could complain. The sale of munitions and the colossal blockade-running business carried on with the Confederacy furnished further and constant complaints, particularly against England. French intervention in Mexico was an added score against France. The piling up of grievances by the United States against France and England, particularly the latter, cannot be overlooked as a powerful factor in making these two Western European powers extremely cautious with reference to even friendly intervention in the Civil War. It helped create the very definite belief that intervention meant a declaration of war by the United States. As for war, neither France nor England cared to pay such a price to see the United States permanently divided. These grievances of the United States were used to counteract the grievances of England and France in the blockade of their West Indian ports and the seizure of their merchant vessels, under the doctrine of ultimate destination, hundreds of miles from the Confederate coast when apparently destined to neutral ports. England, of course, was glad to see the reestablishing of the paper blockade and the doctrine of ultimate destination; but the methods employed in the seizure and search of scores of vessels, including the *Trent,* created a deep resentment in England, and Adams and Seward cleverly used the Alabama claims and other similar grievances as counter-irritants.

A list of U.S. grievances against England and France made the Europeans hesitant to consider intervention on the South's behalf.

The objective of Confederate diplomacy was to obtain foreign assistance in gaining independence. The Confederate government based its plans, first, upon European dependence upon southern cotton and, second, upon the well-known desire of England to see a powerful commercial rival weakened, and of Napoleon III to see the champion of the Monroe Doctrine rendered impotent to frustrate his attempted annexation of Mexico. The Confederacy first sent William L. Yancey, Pierre A. Rost, and A. Dudley Mann as joint commissioners to obtain European aid and recognition. Later Yancey resigned, the commission was dissolved, Mann was sent to Belgium as permanent commissioner, and Rost to Spain. James M. Mason and John Slidell—taken prisoner by Charles Wilkes and later released by the federal government on the demand of Great Britain—were sent to Great Britain and France respectively as Confederate diplomatic agents. The Confederacy sent John T. Pickett to the Juárez government in Mexico and Juan Quintero to the government of Santiago Vadaurri, governor-dictator of Nuevo León and virtual ruler of several of the neighboring border states of Mexico. The Confederate diplomats were ably supported by propagandist agents in both England and France. Edwin DeLeon and Henry Hotze were the chief propagandist agents. The Confederate diplomatic agents were informally received in May 1861 in England; but after that Lord Russell refused even that much recognition under the pressure of Seward's ultimatum. However, the British government did continue to deal with the Confederate agents by means of correspondence. In Belgium, Spain, France, Mexico, and even at the Vatican, Confederate diplomatic agents were received informally but freely. In fact, Slidell in France was on such good terms with Napoleon that the latter made a practice of intercepting messages to Dayton for him.

The Confederacy failed to obtain foreign intervention because the things to be gained by war on the part of England and France would not offset war losses. Europe had a surplus of cotton during the first year of the war; and after this surplus gave out, war profits, particularly in England, from cotton speculation, linen and woolen industries, munitions, blockade running, and the destruction or transfer of the American merchant marine to British registry, dwarfed the losses among the cotton-mill operatives and removed the chief economic motives for intervention. It is also contended that the wheat famine in England made that country dependent upon the United States for its bread supply, and that this operated as an important factor in preserving the neutrality of the British.

— FRANK L. OWSLEY

Union Financing Problems

When Salmon P. Chase reluctantly resigned from the Senate to become secretary of the treasury in March 1861, the state of the federal finances was not encouraging, especially in view of the impending war. During the preceding four years of the Buchanan administration the Treasury had financed deficits annually through the flotation of government obligations, a factor that had shaken the confidence of investors in these securities. Chase himself, at first, could only float additional loans to meet the essential expenditures of government.

Shortly, faced with the problem of financing the war, Secretary Chase decided on a tax program to cover the regular expenses of government, while the extraordinary expenses resulting from the war were to be financed by the sale of bonds and notes. During the fiscal year 1861, 64.3 percent of total net receipts came from taxes and only 35.7 percent from loans.

The situation changed radically in the next fiscal year. The customs law which had been enacted on Chase's recommendation did not yield sufficient revenue to cover even the ordinary expenses, and war expenditures, of course, increased rapidly. Moreover, the sale of government securities was not easy as it was usually required by law that such securities could not be put on the market below par, while the interest authorized was not sufficient to attract investors at par or above.

It was under these circumstances that Thaddeus Stevens and Elbridge G. Spaulding of the House Ways and Means Committee were able to secure the passage of the first legal tender act (authorizing the issuance of $150 million of greenbacks) on Feb. 25, 1862. Passage of this act was procured under the plea of dire necessity, although the opposition showed that by selling government obligations on the market for what they would bring the issuance of greenbacks could have been avoided. In the fiscal year 1862 only 10.7 percent of total net receipts was obtained from taxes, whereas, of the remaining 89.3 percent, over one-third came from non-interest-bearing obligations, mainly U.S. notes (greenbacks).

A second legal tender act was passed on July 11, 1862, and a third on Mar. 3, 1863, each authorizing $150 million of greenbacks. Further issues were avoided as a result of increased revenues from taxation with a concurrent and consequent improvement in the government's credit. Thus, in the fiscal years 1863–66 the proportion of net receipts coming from taxes increased successively from 15.8 to 25.9 to 26.9 to 83 percent.

The reasons for the failure to tax more heavily in the earlier years of the war are easily explained. Chase was not experienced in finance and also contemplated a relatively short struggle. The Republican party was new and lacked solidarity. Internal taxes had not been levied for many years, and the Republicans did not dare to risk the unpopularity that a heavy internal tax probably would have called forth. Accordingly, although heavier taxes early in the war would have been sounder financially, they were obviously not politically feasible until a later period.

— FREDERICK A. BRADFORD

Propaganda and Undercover Activities

The abolition crusade and the proslavery reaction laid the psychological bases for the war. Upon the outbreak of the conflict, press and pulpit, North and South, further stirred the emotions of the people. In the South, propagandists devoted their efforts to asserting the right to secede and to proving that the aggressive North was invading southern territory. In the North, the preservation of the Union, patriotism, and the crusade against slavery were the major themes. On both sides, atrocity stories—largely concerned with the brutal treatment of the wounded, military prisoners, and political dissenters—abounded. Southern efforts in propaganda lacked coordination, but in the North the radical Committee on the Conduct of the War gave official direction to the gathering and dissemination of atrocity stories that professed to reveal rebel depravity and to show the felonious and savage nature of the southerners. The Sanitary Commission and the Union Leagues were the chief unofficial agencies in this work. Both sides attempted to influence European opinion, and President Lincoln sent journalists and ecclesiastics to England and the Continent to create favorable sentiment.

Despite these efforts, many on both sides remained unconvinced. The prosouthern Knights of the Golden Circle in the North were paralleled by numerous secret pronorthern "peace" societies in the South. These organizations encouraged desertion; aided fugitive slaves, refugees, and escaping prisoners; and occasionally attempted direct sabotage.

— W. B. HESSELTINE

Munitions

The standard equipment of the Union army was muzzle-loading Springfield or Enfield rifles and the type of cannon now so often found cluttering up courthouse lawns. Many early regiments, however, went to the front with nondescript arms of their own procuring. Other hundreds of thousands of rifles were furnished by contractors who took all the antiquated, castoff weapons of European armies. A large proportion of these, sold to the War Department at extravagant prices, had to be scrapped immediately. Others, which were issued to the soldiers, proved more dangerous to the man behind the breech than to the enemy before the muzzle. Before 1861 various American companies had been making breech-loading repeating rifles, which, by repeated testimony of experts, would fire fifteen times as rapidly as the best of muzzle-loaders, with equal accuracy and force, and with greater ease of manipulation. But the backwardness of the War Department and its staff prevented the use of such improved weapons. All sorts of excuses, none of them valid, were conjured up against them. In the closing months of the war a new chief of ordnance, Alexander B. Dyer, equipped a few companies in the Southwest with repeating rifles, and with these weapons in their hands the men proved invincible. When the war was over, the same arms were adopted for the regular army.

Throughout the war those persons responsible for its conduct preferred to set up huge armies with inferior guns to form a larger target for the enemy, rather than equip a smaller and more compact force with weapons of multiple effectiveness. Even Gatling guns, firing 250 shots a minute with frightful precision, were dismissed in cavalier fashion. A dozen of them were supplied to Gen. B. F. Butler, whose men proved their merits. But again, the weapon was not adopted for general use until after the war. Following a few initial blunders there was not much difficulty in procuring a plentiful supply of good muzzle-loading guns or of powder and shot.

The munitions of the Confederacy were inferior to those of the North. Battlefield captures, raiding expeditions, imports from Europe, and an increasing production from southern munitions plants kept the troops armed. Largely cut off by the blockade from European supplies, and with little industrial development, manufacturing plants had to be built and manned, and materials had to be obtained and prepared. While saltpeter and sulfur in the raw state were plentiful in the Confederacy, machinery and labor for conversion were generally lacking. Yet, in 1864, lead-smelting works, bronze foundries, a cannon foundry, rifle, carbine, and pistol factories were operating. The big problem of supply was the lack of adequate transportation.

— FRED A. SHANNON

Freedom of the Seas

The blockade of the Confederacy set up by the federal government was far from satisfying the stringent requirements of international law set down in the Declaration of Paris (not ratified by the United States) and of previous diplomatic practice of the United States. Further, the Supreme Court on appeal from prize courts developed the doctrine of continuous voyage one step beyond British practice during the Napoleonic Wars: it applied the doctrine to confiscate neutral property, contraband or no contraband, in transit between Great Britain and the British West Indies, when that property was ultimately destined, by a subsequent maritime leg of an essentially continuous voyage, to a blockaded Confederate port. When the property was ultimately destined by a subsequent land journey (for example, in the case of the *Peterhoff* via the neutral port of Matamoros) continuously to the Confederacy, the Court did not construe the blockade to exist on land between the neutral country (Mexico) and the Confederacy, but it did confiscate the absolute contraband found on board.

Great Britain cheerfully acquiesced in the loose blockade and in the new interpretation of the doctrine of continuous voyage, which later gave it a valuable precedent with which to enforce, as against the United States, an imperfect blockade of Germany in 1914–17.

In the *Trent* case the United States acknowledged the force, if not the justice, of a British protest, accompanied by an ultimatum, against forcibly taking rebellious American citizens off a British merchant ship on the high seas, an act analogous to British impressment of disobedient subjects (some of them naturalized American citizens) from American neutral vessels on the high seas during the Napoleonic Wars.

— SAMUEL FLAGG BEMIS

Union Cotton Trade

At the beginning of the war the U.S. government decided to permit a restricted trade in cotton in cotton-growing areas held by the Union forces. This was done partly because of the foreign demand for cotton and partly to enable destitute southerners to buy necessities. The trade was authorized by acts of Congress passed July 13, 1861, and July 2, 1864. In accordance with these laws, regulations were issued at various times, notably on Sept. 11, 1863, and on July 29, 1864, to control the trade. By them the commerce was restricted to treasury agents; private individuals and members of the military and naval forces were not allowed to participate in the traffic, and there was to be no commercial intercourse with the Confederates. These rules covered the subject thoroughly, but owing to the profits involved they could not be enforced. Cotton at Boston was worth ten times as much as at the front and consequently Memphis and New Orleans, the principal trade centers, were infested with unscrupulous cotton buyers who proffered bribes for connivance in their illicit trade. Traders were thus able to purchase cotton from the Confederates in exchange for military supplies and to engage in private trade with them. Military expeditions, even, were sent out to get cotton for the traders: the Confederates would be warned of impending raids—in which they parted with cotton and in return received supplies that enabled them to maintain their forces.

In 1864 enough cotton went north to supply the factories, while each week $500,000 worth of goods was going south through Memphis.

The trade, legal and illegal, attained immense size. In the spring and summer of 1864 enough cotton went North to supply the factories, while each week $500,000 worth of goods was going South through Memphis. The results of the trade were harmful to the Union cause. According to Gen. Ulysses S. Grant and other officers it prolonged the war at least a year.

— A. SELLEW ROBERTS

War Supply Contracts

In the first year of the war, the federal government and a score of states were bidding against each other for war supplies, with disgraceful consequences. Too often the rule was to award the contract to the highest bidder, that is, to the one who would give the biggest kickback to the officials and inspectors. Simon Cameron himself, as secretary of war, apparently was not guiltless. It is a notorious fact that several of the great personal fortunes had their origins in Civil War contracts. Colt's revolvers, which sold at $14.50 on the market, brought $25 by army contracts, or $35 when bought by John Frémont. Furthermore, goods of inferior quality often found readier sales than first-class products. Shoddy for clothing, sand for sugar, parched grain for coffee, brown paper for sole leather, and worthless foreign guns for weapons were among the things foisted on the soldiers. After a year of this sort of profiteering the War Department began serious efforts at reform, but the contract business remained slightly malodorous until the end of the war. The situation seems to have been not much better in the Confederacy. At any rate, there was much grumbling against contractors and blockade runners.

— FRED A. SHANNON

Surrender of the Confederate Armies

The most important surrender after Appomattox (Apr. 9, 1865) was that of Confederate Gen. Joseph E. Johnston to William T. Sherman at the Bennett house near Durham Station, N.C., April 26. Parole was granted to 37,047 prisoners on the same terms Ulysses S. Grant had given Robert E. Lee. Previously Sherman had joined Gen. J. M. Schofield at Goldsboro, N.C., on March 23, their combined force being about 80,000. Johnston, stationed before the town of Raleigh, had about 33,000 effective troops. On April 10, two days before the news of Appomattox arrived, Sherman advanced to Raleigh and Johnston retreated toward Greensboro, where he convinced President Jefferson Davis that further resistance, though possible, would merely entail prolonged suffering with ultimate subjection. The result was a conference between Sherman and Johnston on April 17–18, resulting in a memorandum to be submitted to Davis and the government at Washington. The proposed surrender included President Lincoln's principles of reconstruction, which, though far more reasonable than the ultimate congressional plan, were outside Sherman's authority to offer. The refusal of Secretary of War Edwin M. Stanton to accept these terms led Johnston, from motives of humanity, to agree to unconditional surrender. Not content with this outcome, Stanton published an embellished account of Sherman's action, made unjust accusations, and created a national scandal.

The capitulation of the rest of the Confederate forces followed as a matter of course. On May 4, Gen. Richard Taylor surrendered to Gen. Edward R. S. Canby at Citronelle, Ala., thus ending Confederate forces east of the Mississippi. Six days later Jefferson Davis was captured by James H. Wilson's cavalry near Irwinville, Ga., and was imprisoned at Fortress Monroe. The final act was the surrender of Kirby-Smith and the trans-Mississippi troops to Canby at New Orleans on May 26. The total number surrendered and paroled from April 9 to May 26 was 174,223.

— FRED A. SHANNON

Economic Consequences in the North

Destructive as it was of material as well as of human values, the Civil War proved to be a great stimulus to the economic life of the North. Government contracts, paper-money inflation, and a new protective tariff system brought a rapid expansion of capital and a new prosperity to northern industry, with large-scale industry increasingly common. Cotton manufacturing declined because of a shortage of raw material, but woolen manufacturing and the munitions and war supplies industries in general experienced sharp gains. The young petroleum industry was given an important place in the rapid growth of American capitalism. The telegraphs and railways led the way to a new era of corporate consolidation. The later years of the war brought a new national banking system which promised a check upon the paper issues of the existing state banks. Out of these developments and, in addition, a frenzied stock-market speculation, came new fortunes that were often summed up as constituting a "shoddy aristocracy."

While the war meant devastation and economic suffering for the South, it brought a rapid expansion of capital and prosperity to the North.

To the common man this prosperity was not an unmixed boon. Agriculture experienced new gains with an expanded area and an increased use of farm machinery; this was often, however, at the price of overexpansion and debt. With wages lagging far behind a price rise that more than doubled the cost of living, labor found even less in which to rejoice; it therefore turned new energies toward organizing its forces in national craft unions. The burden of taxation was borne with little complaint. Excise taxes were levied upon as many articles as possible; tariff schedules reached in 1864 an average rate of 47 percent, partly offset by the internal revenue levies; income taxes came to be assessed upon all incomes in excess of $600 a year, although less than a half-million persons were affected. Thus was secured one-fifth of the wartime needs of the government. The rest was borrowed directly or indirectly; the war ended with a federal debt of over $2.6 billion. Yet the national wealth had been greatly increased and a new era of American capitalism was ahead.

— ARTHUR C. COLE

Economic Consequences in the South

The Civil War brought economic suffering, devastation, and ruin to the South. As a result of the blockade, the interruption of intercourse with the North, and the strain of supporting the armed forces, the people were subjected to extreme privation. Large land areas were laid waste by military operations. Accumulated capital resources were dissipated. Railroads were either destroyed or allowed to deteriorate to the point of worthlessness. Livestock was reduced by almost two-thirds. Slave property valued at about $2 billion was wiped out. Approximately one-fourth of the productive white male population was killed or incapacitated. Land values were undermined; agricultural production was greatly retarded; trade was disrupted; banks and mercantile houses were forced into bankruptcy; the credit system was disorganized; and commercial ties with foreign nations were broken.

The war also brought sweeping changes in the economy of the South. The destruction of slavery together with the devastation wrought by the conflict forced the plantation system to give way to a sharecropper, tenancy, and small farm system. A central feature of this transition was the rise of the crop lien, which tended to make necessary continued concentration on cotton cultivation. With the breakup of the plantations there occurred a great increase in the number and economic importance of the small towns and their inhabitants—merchants, bankers, lawyers, and doctors.

The war also brought a diminution in the part the South played in the determination of national economic policies. During the postwar period, tariff, monetary, railroad, banking, and other such matters were generally decided without any consideration for the wishes and needs of the South. The result was economic exploitation of the South by other sections of the nation.

— HAYWOOD J. PEARCE, JR.

[See also Army, Confederate; Reconstruction.]

BIBLIOGRAPHY

Official Records of the Union and Confederate Armies.
Official Records of the Union and Confederate Navies.
E. D. Adams, *Great Britain and the American Civil War.*
M. M. Boatner, *The Civil War Dictionary.*
E. M. Callahan, *Diplomatic History of the Southern Confederacy.*
Bruce Catton, *The Centennial History of the Civil War.*
J. A. C. Chandler et al., eds., *The South in the Building of the Nation.*
Hamilton Cochran, *Blockade Runners of the Confederacy.*
David L. Cohn, *The Life and Times of King Cotton.*
D. R. Dewey, *Financial History of the United States.*
Charles B. Dew, *Ironmaker to the Confederacy.*
William B. Edwards, *Civil War Guns.*
E. D. Fite, *Social and Industrial Conditions in the North During the Civil War.*
W. L. Fleming, *Documentary History of Reconstruction.*
D. S. Freeman, *R. E. Lee,* and *Lee's Lieutenants.*
W. B. Hesseltine, *Civil War Prisons,* and *The Tragic Conflict.*
R. U. Johnson and C. C. Buel, eds., *Battles and Leaders of the Civil War.*
W. C. Mitchell, *A History of the Greenbacks.*
Allan Nevins, *War for the Union.*
F. L. Owsley, *King Cotton Diplomacy.*
Benjamin Quarles, *The Negro in the Civil War.*
J. G. Randall, *The Civil War and Reconstruction.*
T. J. Scharf, *History of the Confederate States Navy.*
Fred A. Shannon, *Organization and Administration of the Union Army.*
Robert P. Sharkey, *Money, Class and Party: An Economic Study of the Civil War and Reconstruction.*
G. Tatum, *Disloyalty in the Confederacy.*
F. E. Vandiver, *Basic History of the Confederacy,* and *Ploughshares Into Swords.*
R. S. West, *Mr. Lincoln's Navy.*
B. I. Wiley, *Embattled Confederates.*
Kenneth P. Williams, *Lincoln Finds a General: A Military Study of the Civil War.*
T. Harry Williams, *Lincoln and His Generals.*

CLASS CONFLICT

Compared with European nations, the United States has been relatively free from the convulsions of class conflict. From the early days of colonization, tensions between classes were diffused by the absence of abject poverty, expansion of civil liberties, political rights, economic opportunity, and a juridical emphasis on individual rights rather than class interests—at least for free white males. Immigration mitigated class conflict because the colonies attracted neither the very rich nor the very poor, but drew the "middling sorts," settlers who had some resources, skills, or family support. Even indentured servants obtained independent status, although female servants usually had to marry to improve their socioeconomic condition. The pattern of including "middling sorts" in new economic and political developments continued after the creation of the federal government, symbolized by Thomas Jefferson's ideal of the yeoman republic. In the Jacksonian era (1829–1837) white male suffrage became the norm and—at the expense of Native American lands and the destruction of the Bank of the United States—land ownership, speculation, and economic development continued apace, despite the panic of 1837 and the depression that followed and lasted until 1843.

After the Civil War the country experienced both increased industrialization and immigration, which gave rise to labor unions among skilled workers, but American trade unionism was never characterized by strong socialist views about class struggle as in Europe, except briefly during World War I. While unions grew stronger among all types of workers during the Great Depression and immediately following World War II, they represented vehicles for entering the middle class rather than socialist or communist visions about a nonmaterialistic society. Like small businessmen, laborers enjoyed the postwar prosperity of the 1950s and 1960s, and the Civil Rights Movement promised to expand political and economic opportunities to minorities and women. In the 1970s, however, the U.S. economy began to decline, trade unions began losing their bargaining power, conditions for racial minorities living in inner cities deteriorated, women realized that a "glass ceiling" prevented them from rising to top positions, angry white males began to blame affirmative action and other social policies for their economic problems, and U.S. corporations started downsizing—a practice that tended to demoralize workers at all levels.

A 1995 World Bank report cited the U.S. as "the most economically stratified of industrial nations" because one in five households received 48% of all income.

A 1995 World Bank report cited the United States as "the most economically stratified of industrial nations" because one in five households received 48 percent of all income, while a columnist for the *Wall Street Journal* predicted that the "prospect of a class war is genuine among the very people who have been the strongest supporters of the American system," referring to white, lower-income groups. In 1970 families with an annual income between $15,000 and $50,000 were 65 percent of the population. Twenty-five years later, when adjusted for inflation, fewer than 50 percent fell within that range. Faced with unusual competition in a global economy, large U.S. economic interests began to look after themselves without giving traditional consideration to including small producers and workers in their economic and political plans. This caused increasing class anxiety among middle management and workers, who feared being left behind in the global economy. Alienation from and fear of government and business interests was reflected in the growth of paranoid, supernationalist fundamentalist cults and paramilitary groups.

By 1992 evidence abounded that the country was fragmenting. A wave of immigrants since 1965, largely Hispanics and Asians, was not as desirous of becoming assimilated. Many of these newcomers pressured the government to recognize their diversity through identity politics and such group rights as bilingual education. Fragmentation also existed among prosperous, old stock, Protestant Americans, who found themselves challenged not only from the bottom by increased crime and random violence but also from the top by a new technological aristrocracy who controlled access to and distribution of information and technology. As evidence of their newly found class consciousness, the most affluent one-eighth of the U.S. population by 1992 had begun to live in guarded suburban enclaves with security guards. By 1995 it was estimated that 4 million Americans lived in closed-off gated communities and about another 28 million lived in areas governed by private community associations, including condominiums and cooperatives, all with their own covenants, codes, and restrictions on the behavior and life styles of their inhabitants. That number was expected to double by the year 2005.

By the mid-1990s socioeconomic fragmentation took many forms. Ethnic, racial, religious, and educational differences, as well as increased economic disparities between rich and poor, made many question whether the U.S. economy would continue to provide living wages for a majority of its workers. Further, as "globocorps" of the twenty-first century extend their economic power, nation-states will be subsumed, leaving workers and small producers without democratic processes with which to seek redress of economic inequality.

[See also Civil Rights Movement; Fundamentalism; Immigration; Labor Unions.]

BIBLIOGRAPHY

Robert H. Frank and Philip J. Cook, *Winner-Take-All Society* (New York, 1995).

William Knoke, *Bold New World* (New York, 1996).

Lester C. Thurow, *The Future of Capitalism* (New York, 1996).

— MARIAN YEATES

CLAYTON ANTITRUST ACT

Clayton Antitrust Act was one of the leading pieces of reform legislation in the New Freedom program of President Woodrow Wilson, who in 1912 waged his election campaign largely on a pledge to check monopoly and restore free competition.

The "rule of reason" promulgated by the Supreme Court in the Standard Oil case of 1911 had created uncertainty about explicit standards of "reasonable" and "unreasonable" trade restraints and had left to the courts sweeping powers of interpretation in applying the rule. Accordingly, businessmen favoring suppression of unfair control of trade joined with Progressive advocates of stronger antitrust legislation in supporting a clarifying measure to outlaw certain monopolistic or restrictive trade practices not specifically covered by the Sherman Antitrust Act (1890). The omnibus bill introduced in 1914 by Rep. Henry D. Clayton, chairman of the House Judiciary Committee, was in its final, compromise version linked to companion legislation creating the Federal Trade Commission.

The Clayton Antitrust Act prohibited discrimination in prices among purchasers; exclusive dealing and contracts tying a purchaser to a single supplier; acquisition of competing companies; interlocking directorates in industrial corporations capitalized at $1 million or more and in banks with assets of more than $5 million; and interlocking shareholdings through the purchase of stock in competing firms, where the effect of all such practices might be "to substantially lessen competition or tend to create a monopoly." Among the remedies provided by the act for such violations were cease-and-desist orders issued by the Federal Trade Commission, court injunctions, and triple-damage suits. Under pressure from labor and agricultural interests, the act stipulated that neither trade unions nor farm organizations lawfully seeking to attain legitimate objectives should be construed as illegal combinations in restraint of trade. A declaratory passage stating that "the labor of human beings is not a commodity or article of commerce" was acclaimed by Samuel Gompers, president of the American Federation of Labor, as "labor's Magna Charta"; but it proved to be merely an expression of opinion with no standing in law. Supreme Court rulings in the decade after 1914 (notably *Duplex Printing Press Co.* v. *Deering,* 1921) demonstrated that this declaration, as well as other labor provisions of the act, had not conferred upon trade unions broad immunity from antitrust prosecution.

In the 1920's the Supreme Court's interpretation of the business sections of the statute substantially weakened its potential value as a public policy tool for preventing the buildup of monopoly power through merger. The most important amendments of the Clayton Antitrust Act were the Robinson-Patman Act of 1936, dealing with price discrimination, and the Celler-Kefauver Act of 1950, which outlawed corporate mergers "in any line of commerce in any section of the country" whose effect tended to stifle competition or to promote monopoly.

For some two decades after 1945 the government made a concerted effort to challenge giant mergers and to check anticompetitive practices; but the effectiveness of the Clayton Antitrust Act in this effort was largely undercut by congressional exemption of various industries from the reach of the statute, the tendency of the executive branch to equate large firms with technological efficiency and economies of production, and the failure to evolve an antitrust doctrine aimed at curbing conglomerates.

BIBLIOGRAPHY

C. Kaysen and D. F. Turner, *Antitrust Policy.*
M. W. Watkins, *Public Regulation of Competitive Practices.*
S. N. Whitney, *Antitrust Policies.*

— WILLIAM GREENLEAF

CLOVIS CULTURE

Clovis culture, or Llano culture, is the earliest and most famous of the Late Lithic big-game hunting cultures, located in the North American High Plains and the Southwest. An extensive array of radiocarbon dates demonstrates that this hunting culture existed in late Pleistocene environments with now extinct animal species 11,250 years ago. The Clovis people are known from the archaeological excavation of a small number of their base camps and from at least a dozen kill sites. The settlements of these hunters are identified archaeologically by the presence of bones of mammoths and Clovis fluted projectile points. Although kill sites always

The Clovis people are known from archaeological excavations of a small number of base camps and from at least a dozen kill sites.

contain remains of mammoths, other animals, including bison, horse, and tapir, were also hunted. The fluting at the base of the lanceolate projectile points, which range from three to six inches in length, is believed to be a New World innovation, for earlier counterparts have not been found in adjacent Old World centers (for example, northeastern Asia). These points were attached to the ends of lances or darts and atlatls (throwing sticks). Other artifacts used by the Clovis hunters include prismatic blades and the stone cutting and scraping tools typical of a hunter's tool kit. Famous Clovis sites include Blackwater Draw, N.Mex.; Lindenmeier, Colo.; Naco, Ariz.; and Domebo, Okla. The latter site is a mammoth kill that marks the eastern boundary of the culture.

Clovis fluted points are also found scattered across the rest of the continent. Apparently contemporary with the Clovis culture in the Plains and Southwest, these points are associated with the earliest cultures known in the East. Thousands of these points have been discovered in the Midwest and East, whereas only a few dozen have been found in the Plains and Southwest. Earlier cultures may have existed west of the Rockies, although their presence is still only weakly documented. The relationship between the Clovis culture and these contemporary cultures to the east and west is an unsolved puzzle. The origin of the culture also remains a debated mystery. In the 1970's available evidence indicated that the Clovis culture derives from Mousteroid cultures that entered the New World between 26,000 and 23,000 years ago or from more recent arrivals who spread southward from the Bering Strait near the close of the Ice Age about 13,000 years ago.

BIBLIOGRAPHY

Jesse D. Jennings, *Prehistory of North America.*
Richard S. MacNeish, ed., *Early Man in America.*

— GUY GIBBON

COAL MINING AND ORGANIZED LABOR

Anthracite mining is concentrated in five counties of east central Pennsylvania; various bituminous coals are mined in Pennsylvania, Ohio, the Virginias, Indiana, Illinois, Kentucky, Alabama, and, to a lesser extent, Maryland, Missouri, Tennessee, Colorado, Utah, and Alaska. From the Civil War to 1940 coal was the nation's chief source of fuel. After World War I, coal suffered a relative decline in importance as compared with other fuels and an absolute decline in its production and the manpower involved. Following World War II, rapid substitution of competing fuels, swift mechanization of underground mining, and massive strip mining accelerated these declines. Contributing more than 90 percent of the country's thermal energy in 1880 and 53 percent in 1940, coal furnished barely 20 percent in 1970. Similarly, employment in bituminous mines fell from the 1923 peak of 704,000 men to less than 140,000 in 1970. Anthracite employment fell from its peak of 179,000 in 1914 to fewer than 7,000 in 1970. Obviously these contractions profoundly affected the industry and its workingmen.

Always dirty and exceedingly dangerous, coal mining has been historically an industry plagued by instabilities of production, consumption, and price. Moreover, a gamut of dispersed production units, ranging from a

A coal miner waiting his turn to go underground, near Pittsburgh, Pennsylvania, in November 1942. (Library of Congress/Corbis)

host of small marginal mines to the great captive mines (those owned by, and producing coal for, the steel and railroad companies), have either engendered or threatened cutthroat competition and have made private, as well as governmental, supervision, inspection, and regulation extremely difficult, although from the industry's earliest days operators and workers alike have generally conceded the necessity of many types of regulation.

Unionization of mine labor began in the 1840's. It was variously a response to fraternal impulses among workers, to unhealthy and dangerous working conditions, to unsatisfactory wages, to truck payments (payment in goods), to abuses by company towns and privatized police, to the introduction of scab labor, to blacklisting and yellow dog contracts, and to seasonal and chronic unemployment. Unionization was complicated by the presence of thousands of immigrant workers in the pits; by ethnic, cultural, racial, and linguistic barriers among and between foreign and native-born workers and the general public; by the isolation of miners from one another; by their relative immobility; and by dual unionism and organizational mistakes.

Employer reactions to mine unionism varied. Sometimes, as in the anthracite fields in the mid-1870's, unions were invidiously associated with Molly Maguires or, as in the efforts to unionize southern fields in the 1930's and 1940's, with communism. Sometimes employers have resorted to armed repression, although evictions, lockouts, and strike-breaking have been more common reactions. Yet employers have often recognized the conservative influences of mine unions and tacitly accepted and often cooperated with them to help stabilize the industry and discipline labor.

Governments have also responded to unions variously: the use of local police, state militias, or federal troops against unions was common in the 19th century, becoming rarer after the militia violence against miners in 1913 at Ludlow, Colo. The Wilson administration invoked the aid of the courts to forestall a coal strike in 1919; injunctions against union activities were frequent in the 1920's; and during the first Truman administration, Federal District Judge T. Alan Goldsborough heavily fined both the United Mine Workers of America (UMWA) and its president, John L. Lewis, for noncompliance with federal policy. Since the 1930's, despite President Franklin D. Roosevelt's legal bouts with the UMWA and his threat to use troops to mine coal during World War II, government generally has moved positively to regulate the industry and its labor through the Norris-LaGuardia Act of 1932, the National Industrial Recovery Act of 1933, the Guffey Coal Acts of 1935 and 1940, wage stabilization measures, the Taft-Hartley Act of 1947, and supervision of union elections.

Unionization in the mid-1800's was complicated by the ethnic, linguistic, and cultural barriers among thousands of immigrant workers.

Since January 1890, miners have been chiefly represented by the UMWA, an industrial union that was founded by bituminous miners from Pennsylvania, Ohio, Indiana, and Michigan but quickly encompassed anthracite miners also. Creation of the UMWA was preceded by half a century of abortive unionization: prominent among the early unions were the Bates Union of 1848; the American Miners' Association, formed by Illinois and Missouri miners in 1861; John Siney's famed Workingmens' Benevolent Association, which in the 1870's sustained the Long Strike and battled the Reading Railroad; the Miners' and Laborers' Benevolent Association of the 1870's, also led by Siney; and the Knights of Labor, which, in company with the National Federation of Miners and Mine Laborers, carried unionism into the 1880's. Of these early unions, nearly all were led by English, Irish, Scottish, Welsh, and occasionally Polish or Hungarian immigrants; nearly all, contrary to myth, were moderate and conciliatory, favoring arbitration over strikes. Although all of these unions were short-lived, all contributed to educating mine workers about their condition and their rights.

The UMWA, in this tradition, was founded in 1890 and rose to power under two of the most famous and conservative unionists of their generations: John Mitchell, who led the union through the great coal strike of 1902, winning national notoriety for his 150,000 followers, as well as shorter hours and better wages; and John L. Lewis, who watched his 500,000-man union dwindle during the 1920's to 150,000 and then revived its membership. As a result of various public regulations applied to coal mining and long years of union negotiating, labor's circumstances in the coal-mining industry, if unsatisfactory in some regards, have been vastly improved in certain important respects (working conditions, wages, pensions, medical benefits, and other welfare programs) over those prevalent until World War II, despite the diminished importance of the coal industry and the reduced mine payrolls.

BIBLIOGRAPHY

Ralph E. McCoy, *History of Labor and Labor Unionism in the U.S.: A Selected Bibliography.*

Joseph G. Rayback, *History of American Labor.*

— C. K. YEARLEY

COERCION ACTS

Coercion Acts, also known as the Restraining Acts and, in part, as the Intolerable Acts, were a series of four measures passed by the English Parliament in the spring and summer of 1774, partly in retaliation for such incidents as the *Gaspée* affair and the Boston Tea Party, but also partly as the enunciation of a more vigorous colonial policy. First, the Boston Port Act, designed as a direct reply to the Tea Party, closed the harbor to all shipping until the town had indemnified the East India Company for the destruction of its tea and assured the king of its future loyalty, pending which Marblehead was made the port of entry. The second measure, the Massachusetts Government Act, deprived Massachusetts of its charter and the right to choose its own magistrates, reducing it to the status of a crown colony. Third, the Act for the Impartial Administration of Justice provided that judges, soldiers, and revenue officers indicted for murder in Massachusetts should be taken to England for trial. The fourth was the Quartering Act, which removed all obstacles to the billeting of troops in any town in Massachusetts.

BIBLIOGRAPHY

G. E. Howard, *The Preliminaries of the Revolution.*

C. H. Van Tyne, *The Causes of the War of Independence.*

— FRANK J. KLINGBERG

COLD WAR

Cold War, the struggle for world supremacy between the United States and the Soviet Union following World War II and continuing into the 1960's. It was a struggle waged by diplomatic means, propaganda, and threats of force, rather than by outright military force—except in limited, local wars fought largely by proxies of the great powers—because the strains imposed by World War II and the threat of nuclear devastation deterred recourse to a "hot war." The cold war was a product of the polarization of power after World War II, when the United States and the Soviet Union overshadowed all other powers and thoroughly dominated their respective alliance systems. But the 1960's were destined to bring the emergence of substantial concentrations of political, economic, and sometimes military power independent of the two superpowers, in China, Western Europe, and Japan. This development made diplomatic alignments far more complex and helped bring a gradual dissipation of the cold war.

Meanwhile, American historians have been among those reacting to the strains of this conflict. Disappointed that World War II was followed, not by a reasonably stable peace, but by a contest between the superpowers, sensitive to the danger that the cold war might have erupted into a nuclear holocaust, and disillusioned by one of the most recent war episodes—the localized hot war in Vietnam—American historians have made the cold war one of the most searchingly debated events of the recent past. They have sought variously to fix not only causes but blame for a trying and perilous period.

The cold war had begun developing before World War II ended, as conflicting Soviet and Anglo-American designs for Eastern Europe strained President Franklin D. Roosevelt's efforts to maintain global harmony at the Yalta Conference (February 1945). Old suspicions were reawakened between the Communist and the non-Communist members of the wartime Grand Alliance. By the time of Harry S. Truman's accession to the presidency and the Potsdam Conference (July 17–Aug. 2, 1945), the American and Soviet governments were freezing into postures of mutual hostility. While the proposition of some historians—that the atomic bomb was used less to defeat Japan than to threaten the Soviets—is dubious, Truman and some of his advisers evidently regarded the bomb as a useful bargaining tool in Soviet-American diplomacy. However, foreign ministers' conferences showed signs of progress toward settling war issues, and the Soviets seemed conciliatory in Eastern Europe—especially in their withdrawal from Iran in 1946—with the result that the full cold war did not begin until 1947.

At that time British retrenchment caused withdrawal of active British support from anti-Communist governments in Greece and Turkey, which prompted the United States to announce the Truman Doctrine of aid to such governments, while American arms and economic support were hurried into Greece and Turkey to head off Communist takeovers. The Truman Doctrine expressed the newly formulated American policy of "containment" of Communist power. Quickly intensifying the cold war came the Marshall Plan for economic restoration of Europe and the Soviet refusal to participate in the plan. A consequence was further division of Europe into eastern and western blocs. This division was aggravated by the Communist coup in Czechoslovakia in February 1948; disagreement over Germany and the Soviet blockade of Berlin (June 1948–May 1949); and completion of the Communist conquest of China. In Europe, these events led to the hardening of military lines between the two power blocs, following formation of the North Atlantic Treaty Organization in April 1949; in Asia, they reached a climax in the Korean War.

The U.S. government, as well as official and otherwise sympathetic historians, have seen the hostility between the American and Soviet blocs and the American containment policy as the necessary results of a Soviet intention to impose Communist power wherever non-Communist weakness permitted. The United States, according to this view, thus was moved to respond to an expansionist Soviet empire by building positions of military and economic strength all around the borders of the Communist world.

But "revisionist" cold war historians—appearing in increasing numbers as the tensions and dangers of cold war rivalry became prolonged—have argued that Washington administrations misperceived the Soviet desire for security against invasion as aggressiveness and compounded the misperception, aggravating Soviet insecurity, by seeking after World War II a global open door to opportunities for American capitalism. In this view, an aggressive America must bear primary responsibility for the cold war.

Still another group of historians has come to view the cold war as the virtually inevitable outcome of the sharing of world power between two superpowers whose vastly different traditions, values, and goals were bound to generate distrust between them.

The threat of massive nuclear retaliation may well have been indispensable to keeping the contest merely cold as the superpowers confronted each other through the Korean War and a series of Berlin, Middle Eastern, and Eastern European crises in the 1950's. In the 1960's, however, not only did the end of the polarization of world power help force both superpowers into new diplomatic postures, but each of the superpowers found habitual cold war policies leading it into frustration—the Soviet Union in the Cuban missile crisis of 1962 and the United States in Vietnam. As a result, more flexible policies and a Soviet-American détente could more readily recommend themselves. By the end of the decade, the détente was in prospect, however hesitantly approached, and by 1974 the cold war seemed to be becoming history.

BIBLIOGRAPHY

John Lewis Gaddis, *The United States and the Origins of the Cold War, 1941–1947.*

Joyce and Gabriel Kolko, *The Limits of Power: The World and United States Foreign Policy, 1945–1954.*

John W. Spanier, *American Foreign Policy Since World War II.*

Adam B. Ulam, *The Rivals: America and Russia Since World War II.*

— JEANNETTE P. NICHOLS

COLD WAR SINCE THE 1960S

By the end of the 1960s, the cold war—the bitter and protracted competition between the communist Soviet bloc and a group of noncommunist nations led by the United States—was entering its third decade and seemed to be an immutable feature of the international landscape. Since its inception in the immediate aftermath of World War II, the confrontation had divided much of the developed world into two heavily armed and hostile camps. It had spawned a series of harrowing crises in which all-out nuclear war was avoided by the narrowest of margins. It had given birth to proxy wars in such places as Indochina and Korea. In addition, it had fostered a climate of pervasive mistrust and fear, sustained on both sides by a relentless stream of apocalyptic rhetoric, that seemed to broach no compromise.

The early 1970s saw the first break in the cold war, a change captured in the word "détente." Détente was the creation of Richard M. Nixon, who became president in 1969, and of Henry A. Kissinger, Nixon's national security adviser and, later, his secretary of state. Although elected president largely on the basis of his promise to terminate the Vietnam War, Nixon brought into office a far more ambitious diplomatic agenda. A self-described realist, Nixon did not entertain any expectations of ending the cold war. Through skillful statecraft, however, he hoped to make competition between the great powers less dangerous and even to encourage some limited cooperation within an environment of continuing rivalry. The key to Nixon's grand design was China, estranged from the United States since 1949, when the communist regime had seized power in Beijing. By normalizing relations with China, Nixon and Kissinger hoped to place the United States in a position to play China and the Soviet Union off against each other to its own advantage. The two rival communist powers would contain one another, with the United States able to influence each of them. Competition between the superpowers would be muted, thereby reducing the risk of a nuclear war. The resultant equilibrium would permit the expansion of economic ties and improve the prospects for disarmament, and improved relations with China and the Soviet Union might help the United States disengage from the Vietnam War on something near acceptable terms.

Efforts to arrange an "opening to China" culminated in February 1972 with Nixon's trip to Beijing. This achievement was crucial to the administration's overall strategy. Absent any rapprochement with China, there would be no détente. Parallel initiatives to Moscow were of comparable importance. Washington and Moscow agreed to cooperate on space exploration ventures and to serious arms control negotiations. Although this latter effort proved to be slow and paid few immediate dividends, in May 1972 the Strategic Arms Limitations Talks (SALT) achieved a breakthrough, producing a major arms control agreement that heralded a series of even more ambitious agreements. In July Nixon approved massive grain sales to the Soviet Union, protecting the communist regime from the consequences of its failing agricultural system. The administration also encouraged increased trade and investment with the Soviets, helping to prop up their flagging economy.

By normalizing relations with China, Nixon and Kissinger hoped to play China and the Soviet Union off against each other to the U.S.'s advantage.

Détente did not produce anything remotely resembling peace between the major cold war antagonists. In this sense, it disappointed critics who yearned to dispel the atmosphere of animosity that had marred the postwar era. Indeed, under the umbrella of détente, the U.S.-Soviet rivalry continued, often carried out through proxies but no less vicious and hardly less dangerous for that fact. Thus, regional conflicts, such as the Arab-Israeli War of October 1973, the Indo-Pakistani War of 1971, and the civil war in Angola beginning in the mid-1970s, found the United States and the Soviet Union arrayed on opposite sides.

Détente survived Nixon's resignation from the presidency in August 1974. Kissinger remained secretary of state for Nixon's successor, Gerald R. Ford, thereby ensuring a basic continuity of U.S. policy. During Ford's brief term, however, distaste for the power politics that Nixon and Kissinger had brought to Washington became increasingly widespread. Realpolitik now seemed amoral and even cynical. A scathing report issued in 1975 by a congressional committee headed by Senator Frank Church of Idaho detailed U.S. efforts in the early 1970s to destabilize the regime of Chile's Marxist president, Salvador Allende, and became an indictment of the U.S. approach to diplomacy—a reliance on dirty tricks by the Central Intelligence Agency (CIA), a willingness to make common cause with unsavory militarists and dictators, and the assumption that the ends of U.S. policy justified the use of any means. The 1975 Conference on Security and Cooperation in Europe, held in Helsinki, brought together the nations of the West and those of the Soviet bloc and produced an agreement endorsing a list of human rights. Surprising even the agreement's signatories, the human rights agreement rapidly established itself at the very forefront of the international agenda. A U.S. administration preoccupied with considerations of power and grand strategy now seemed singularly out of step. In the eyes of many, Ford's refusal—lest he offend the Kremlin—to receive the exiled Russian author and dissident Alexandr Solzhenitsyn at the White House affirmed the extent to which U.S. cold war policy by the mid-1970s had become loosed from its moral underpinnings.

When Democrat Jimmy Carter succeeded Ford as president in January 1977, he vowed to restore the moral stature of the United States and promised to make concern for human rights the centerpiece of his foreign policy. Carter pledged to spurn the dictators with whom his predecessors had become cozy, redeeming the U.S. image in the Third World. He promised to cut military spending, reduce U.S. arms sales abroad, and make nuclear disarmament a reality. Although Carter appreciated the importance of managing the U.S. relationship with the Soviet Union, his administration assumed that the cold war was virtually a thing of the past. In one speech Carter chided the American people for their "inordinate fear of communism," challenging them to move on to other things, but the cold war soon entered a new and chillier phase.

The revived U.S. emphasis on human rights contributed to that chill. In chastising other nations for failing to respect human rights, Carter did not spare the Soviet Union. He roundly criticized the Kremlin for its refusal to allow Soviet Jews to emigrate to Israel and for its treatment of Soviet dissidents, who had become increasingly numerous and vocal in the aftermath of the Helsinki Accords. Offended, Soviet leaders saw Carter's policy as a premeditated violation of the unwritten rules of détente. The president's determination to reduce further a U.S. military establishment already weakened by its long, failed involvement in Vietnam contrasted sharply with evidence that the Soviet Union was embarked upon a major military buildup. The Soviets modernized and expanded their forces; they also evinced a willingness to use their power with a new boldness, particularly in support of leftist regimes or movements in Africa and Central America.

Influential U.S. policymakers came to believe that the Soviets were engaged in a concerted effort to exploit the vulnerability of a United States crippled by its defeat in Vietnam. According to this view—held even by key members of the president's party—a failure to rebuild U.S. military might and to reassert U.S. leadership of the West would invite further Soviet expansionism and perhaps even permanent Soviet domination. This resurgence of hawkish public opinion generated enormous political pressure on Carter and undercut his hope of making progress toward nuclear disarmament. Any wisp of a concession to the Soviets was immediately denounced as tantamount to appeasement. Although Carter and Leonid Brezhnev, chairman of the Soviet Communist party, signed the SALT II agreement in Vienna in June 1979, skepticism of the Soviet Union had by then become so pronounced that Senate ratification of the treaty seemed highly doubtful.

In fact, the treaty did not even come up for a vote. In December 1979 the Soviet military launched a massive intervention into neighboring Afghanistan, seeming to confirm the views of those who had insisted that the Kremlin could not be trusted. This invasion swept away the surviving remnants of détente, and Carter acted swiftly to punish the Soviets. He terminated grain shipments, withdrew the SALT II treaty from the Senate, and announced that the United States would boycott the Olympic Games scheduled to be held in Moscow in summer 1980. More significant, Carter proposed a substantial increase in the level of U.S. military spending and ordered the CIA to undertake a large-scale covert operation to support the Afghan rebels. Although he had slowly, albeit reluctantly, become something of a hawk, Carter could not escape responsibility for the revival of cold war tensions in the late 1970s. To his critics, Carter had allowed the United States to appear weak in the eyes of its adversaries. This perceived weakness had supposedly encouraged the Kremlin to devise new expansionist designs. Worse was to come. In late 1979 Iranian revolutionaries seized U.S. diplomats in Tehran and held them hostage for more than a year in defiance of U.S. protests, sanctions, and military action. Carter's helplessness in the face of this humiliation seemed to confirm his responsibility for having allowed the United States to become a paper tiger. Foreign policy failures and a stagnating domestic economy combined to demolish Carter's hopes of reelection in 1980. In the November elections Carter was trounced by California Governor Ronald Reagan, who had tapped wellsprings of popular discontent by insisting that the time had come for the United States once again to "stand tall."

Far from lamenting the demise of détente and the revival of cold war tensions, President Reagan and the conservative ideologues who filled key positions in his administration all but welcomed the prospect of confrontation with Soviet communism. They viewed the cold war in stark moral terms, and Reagan himself called the Soviet Union an "evil empire." He believed it imperative that the United States operate from a position of strength and immediately began the largest sustained peacetime military buildup in U.S. history. The most spectacular—and most controversial—component was Reagan's plan to create a vast system of antiballistic missile defense. Officially known as the Strategic Defense Initiative (SDI), the plan was popularly (and often derisively) known as Star Wars, after the science fiction movie of that name. Reagan believed that the communists were on the march, even in the Western Hemisphere. In accordance with the so-called Reagan Doctrine, the president committed the United States actively to support anticommunists who opposed the Soviets or Soviet clients. The administration expanded U.S. support to the Afghan rebels and provided similar assistance to anticommunist insurgents in Nicaragua, Angola, and Cambodia. In El Salvador the fear that a leftist insurgency might topple the government persuaded the Reagan administration to offer assistance on a massive scale, despite the Salvadoran military's reputation for brutality and its disregard for human rights. In October 1983 Reagan ordered U.S. military forces to intervene in Grenada, ousting the leftist regime governing that tiny Caribbean country. Relations with the Soviet Union, meanwhile, became icy. Peace movements in the United States and throughout the West enlisted legions of new recruits fearful that U.S. contentiousness would provoke a showdown leading to World War III.

With U.S.-Soviet relations recalling the worst of the early days of the cold war, developments inside the Soviet Union were laying the basis for changes of far-reaching importance. In 1985 Mikhail Gorbachev emerged as the new Soviet leader, ending a period during which the Kremlin had been under the control of a succession of geriatric party hacks. Gorbachev faced up to what his predecessors had either denied or studiously ignored—the Soviet empire was vastly overextended. Only in a military sense could the Soviet Union claim true superpower status. By almost any measure, Soviet domestic institutions were in steep decline; absent comprehensive reforms, the Soviet Union was likely headed toward collapse. Nothing would do more to undermine reform within the Soviet Union than to continue the wasteful arms race. Saving the Soviet Union required that its new leader avoid overheated competition with the United States on such issues as Star Wars. Gorbachev needed to extricate the Soviet Union from the cold war.

Beginning in 1987 Gorbachev began to present an initially wary Reagan with a series of dramatic initiatives aimed at transforming relations between the United States and the Soviet Union. The first breakthrough came in December 1987, with the Intermediate Range Nuclear Forces (INF) Treaty, which dismantled a major category of weapons on terms demanded by the United States. In April 1988 the Soviets accepted a United Nations–brokered plan to withdraw their forces from Afghanistan. In December Gorbachev announced that he would reduce the Soviet military by 500,000—without any corresponding action by the West. Reagan, for his part, concluded that Gorbachev's initiatives represented a fundamental reorientation of Soviet policy.

All of these events were nothing compared to those of 1989. That summer Gorbachev let it be known that the Soviet Union henceforth would not intervene to suppress uprisings against its client regimes. Within months Eastern Europe erupted in revolution. One after another, communist governments toppled—Poland, Hungary, East Germany, Czechoslovakia, and Romania. The Warsaw Pact ceased to exist as a meaningful alliance. In November the Berlin Wall fell, paving the way for the reunification of Germany. In 1990 the Baltic republics of Lithuania, Latvia, and Estonia—constituent parts of the Soviet Union since their annexation in 1940—declared their independence. The response of the once-feared Soviet giant to this upheaval was one of tacit acceptance. Gorbachev complied when he was told by the successor states of Eastern Europe to begin withdrawing the Soviet garrisons that had occupied their soil since 1945.

While this climactic chapter of the cold war played itself out, George Bush became president in January 1989. Possessing neither Reagan's ideological zealotry nor Nixon's geopolitical insight, Bush was a prudent if unimaginative diplomatist fated to confront the most profound changes the world had seen since the close of World War II. Bush presided over the denouement of the cold war, a process that far outstripped his or Gorbachev's capacity to control. Coming around to the notion that Gorbachev's words and actions did not represent some clever trick, Bush responded favorably to Soviet proposals for the reduction of nuclear and conventional arms. He helped set in motion the process of bringing the Soviet Union into the world economy, a step desperately sought by Gorbachev. Washington played a key role in persuading the Soviets to accept German unification on a basis that would keep Germany within the European Community and within the North Atlantic Treaty Organization.

In 1989 Gorbachev let it be known that the USSR would no longer intervene to suppress uprisings against its client regimes; within months, Eastern Europe erupted in revolution.

Bush was less successful at the daunting task of envisioning what sort of order might reasonably replace the bipolar structure that had defined international politics since the late 1940s. The United States had barely begun to contemplate the end of the cold war when beginning in 1991 a host of new crises arose: war in the Persian Gulf, the collapse of states unable to survive once the coercive presence of communism had been removed, fears that weapons from the vast nuclear arsenals accumulated during the preceding four decades might fall into irresponsible hands, and unrest in Moscow itself, which led in short order to the disintegration of the Soviet Union. The cold war was over, but it was soon painfully evident that its detritus would remain to haunt the world for many years to come.

[See also Arms Race and Disarmament; Arms Race with the Soviet Union; China, Relations with; Gulf War of 1991; Human Rights; Soviet Union; Strategic Arms Limitation Talks; Strategic Defense Initiative.]

BIBLIOGRAPHY

Warren I. Cohen, *America in the Age of Soviet Power, 1945–1991* (New York, 1993).

Walter LaFeber, *America, Russia, and the Cold War, 1945–1990,* 6th ed. (New York, 1991).

Thomas G. Paterson, *On Every Front: The Making and Unmaking of the Cold War,* rev. ed. (New York, 1992).

— ANDREW J. BACEVICH

COLLECTIVE BARGAINING

Collective bargaining is a two-party, rule-making process important in relationships between employers, or their associations, and workers represented by their unions. It is institutionalized in the United States, where it is widely practiced and highly sophisticated, as an alternative to rulemaking by employers alone or by government through legislation, compulsory arbitration, or edict. Although this two-party process is private rather than governmental, government does exert an influence.

Collective bargaining in the United States arose out of the need felt by workers for a voice in, and some control of, the determination of wages, hours, and conditions of employment. In the United States such a role was originally denied to workers or was beyond their reach. As individuals they had no power, and the burgeoning power of employers was favored by the one-sidedness of the contracts of employment and by court rulings that were unfriendly to concerted action by workers.

The practice of collective bargaining is older than the name. Sidney and Beatrice Webb, writing on the subject within the context of the British scene during the early 1890's, created the name, and it was adopted in the United States. Previously, in both England and the United States, the word "arbitration" had been used. Arbitration originally had a broader meaning than it has in current usage, where it implies a decision by a third party to settle a dispute. Historians, uninformed or unwary, could be confused or misled about the history of collective bargaining in its early years.

The free pursuit of economic self-interest—the hallmark of capitalistic, enterprise society and the basis of the prima facie theory of torts, upon which enterprise is legally grounded—also became a legal basis for unionism and collective bargaining. In the background of this is the early landmark decision in *Commonwealth of Massachusetts* v. *Hunt* (1842), which practically freed unions from the crime of conspiracy. Thereafter, in civil actions the courts looked to "ends" and "means," yet judges with prejudiced views about unions had little difficulty in finding illegality in objectives and actions of unions. But a more effective later deterrent was deliberate use of injunctions to block organizing or other concerted efforts of unions. Easily obtained, they were widely used because they were effective and made long actions in court unnecessary. Concurrently, unions also suffered from inclusion under the Sherman Antitrust Act (1890) and did not escape, as they intended, with enactment of the Clayton Act (1914)—which Samuel Gompers, president of the American Federation of Labor (AFL), heralded as "labor's Magna Charta"—because courts quickly denied what unions thought they had gained. Yet the principle of free pursuit of self-interest was more and more affirmed by liberal judges, particularly in opinions—dissenting ones at first—of Oliver Wendell Holmes (for example, in *Vegelahn* v. *Guntner*, Massachusetts, 1896) and of Louis D. Brandeis (for example, in *Duplex* v. *Deering*, U.S. Supreme Court, 1921).

The free pursuit of economic self-interest became a legal basis for unionism and collective bargaining.

The principle that civil harm is actionable unless it occurs incidental to the lawful pursuit of economic self-interest is worth further comment if one would understand the place of collective bargaining in American society. Free pursuit of economic self-interest is the essence of competition, which is considered worth what it costs, a view espoused by Holmes. He argued that the conduct and objectives of unions should be judged on this principle and saw "combination" (possibly meaning "association") as inevitable. He was willing to accept on the part of unions a degree of monopoly already accepted among businesses. Legalization of unions as associations of workers calls to mind historical parallels in which corporations, or associations of capital, were accommodated under the law. As all businessmen strive for monopolistic advantages, so leaders of unions seek controls in the labor market to strengthen the union and protect or advance interests of members. While legalization of unions and establishment of collective bargaining relationships arose slowly, when included under the rule of law permitting and justifying free pursuit of economic self-interest, lawful conduct of labor was placed alongside business conduct, under the same legal principle. Thus, unionism and collective bargaining are integral to a free enterprise society; in fact, collective bargaining is not to be found in authoritarian or totalitarian regimes, where different forms of rulemaking for the workplace prevail.

Very important in the recent history of legalization of collective bargaining, however, is a series of laws. In 1932 the Norris–La Guardia Act (Anti-injunction Act) was passed: it was basically laissez-faire in labor disputes, because government support of employers was removed by denying federal courts the power to issue injunctions in labor disputes. Yet neutrality by government was short-lived—although the Norris–La Guardia Act remained—because the National Industrial Recovery Act (1933) and the National Labor Relations Act (1935) gave direct support to the practice of collective bargaining. It is to be noted, though, that support of unions was modified and the role of government broadened by the Taft-Hartley Act (1947) and the Landrum-Griffin Act (1959).

During the long history of common-law and legislative developments, unions struggled to function. With the formation of the AFL in the 1880's, a continuous labor movement developed, primarily concerned with collective bargaining. Its slow growth, however, was occasionally punctuated with spectacular growth, as it was during World War I and in the middle and late 1930's. Its development was uneven, taking place mostly in the northern industrial areas and more strongly in certain industries and in transportation. It developed very little in the South, in agriculture, or in the service and white-collar trades. It was in the mass production industries that the spurt to unionization in the New Deal period took place, marking the beginning of extensive collective bargaining. But a bitter struggle between unions over structure of organization developed, with the AFL adhering to the craft principle and a group that split off in 1935 and formed the Congress of Industrial Organizations (CIO) adhering to the industrial principle. The CIO, however, was equally committed to collective bargaining, and after twenty years of bitter conflict, the two federations merged, taking the combined name AFL-CIO.

Unions practice collective bargaining mainly as an alternative to political action and mutual insurance, although the latter two practices sometimes complement collective bargaining. Unions have sought legislation to protect or enhance the right to organize and engage in bargaining, and they support protective social legislation. In pursuit of both goals, they engage in "nonpartisan" politics to elect "friends" and punish "enemies." On a continuum reaching from collective bargaining, or action on the economic front, to political action, unions in the United States stand at, or near, the collective bargaining end. Essentially they are bargaining institutions and only to a much less degree interested in political action.

Collective bargaining takes place within an identifiable context of postulates, for there is a mutuality of interest between labor and management, which is both ideological and pecuniary. Both parties accept the system and each other (at least after initial conflict), and each wants the enterprise to be successful. But there is a concurrent conflict of pecuniary interest; the parties do have diverse views about the division of the proceeds from the enterprise and about the conditions governing employment and work. They are also subject to external and internal restraints. The external restraints arise from, or inhere in, the laws or legal system and in the range of economic, political, and social conditions that influence or control them to varying degrees. All set limits. The internal restraints have to do with the conditions existing within unions and companies (or employer associations), arising from their purposes, structures, functions, and rules—informal as well as formal—and internal politics.

Each party is concerned with its power, especially vis-à-vis the power of the other party. Bargaining structures are an important outgrowth of the need to achieve a balance of power in order to make negotiations feasible. The balance is necessary to avoid the imposition of terms by the stronger party. Hence, the structure of the bargaining relationship is always important to the power quotient and is a problem until a structure satisfactory to both is achieved. Collective bargaining is basically a power process, not an exercise in economic problem-solving.

Collective bargaining structures are varied, because of a number of determinative factors. They range from very small to huge ones, numbering in excess of 150,000 as reflected in the total number of collective agreements in existence. From one point of view, collective bargaining in the United States is decentralized, with small bargaining structures being most common. From another point of view, a relatively few huge bargaining structures exert a central influence. Of the 20 million workers covered by collective agreements in 1970, the average number of workers per agreement was only 130. Only 252 agreements covered 5,000 or more workers, but they accounted for 20 percent of the work force covered. About 3 percent of the agreements covered 1,000 or more workers, but they accounted for nearly half of all workers covered. The pattern-setting influence of these huge bargaining structures can hardly be denied, but small bargaining structures do have bargaining power in their own right. Some are strategically powerful by virtue of their economic position.

Bargaining structures are determined by (1) market structures, with product markets (local or national, as the case may be) and labor markets playing critical roles; (2) issues at the bargaining table, some, such as seniority, tending to be highly local and others, such as wages and pensions, tending to be marketwide; (3) representational factors, stemming from the goals of the parties and reflecting individual or group interests; (4) government policies, as administered by the National Labor Relations Board (NLRB), which has played an important role in determining "appropriate" bargaining units; and (5) power tactics of the parties. All these factors, plus the institutional needs and requirements of the parties, impinge on the power factor. Unions, in particular, have varied interests, depending upon their constituencies. These have to be kept in focus, for they influence the structure of bargaining as well as the process; but, then, managements too are confronted with internal differences and forces.

Consequently, bargaining structures are as varied as the industries in which they arise. Some are local; others national. Some are highly centralized; others decentralized. Some are small, others large. Some are multiunit, comprising several companies (ranging from formal to informal associations) or unions. Partly as a result of company mergers and the development of conglomerates but also for strategic and tactical reasons, some unions, in addition to desiring to achieve companywide agreements, have been pushing to achieve either coordinated or coalition bargaining, where several unions join forces to present a united front to employers or a single bargaining approach.

At the beginning of a negotiating situation, neither party knows what terms the other is willing to settle for. To understand what goes on in negotiations, one must appreciate that what takes place in the process is contrived and used to find out the settlement position of the other party without prematurely revealing one's own position. A certain amount of ritualism takes place, but those who see collective bargaining negotiations only as a ritual overlook the basic fact that negotiations are going on for the purpose of ascertaining where the other party will settle. Also, it is not just a battle—and never a battle for extermination once recognition of collective bargaining has been achieved. Exorbitant demands, numerous meetings, deadlines, marathon sessions prior to the deadline, eleventh-hour and "corridor" settlements rather than settlements at the bargaining table—these are the typical observable manifestations of collective bargaining.

What takes place in collective bargaining negotiations is contrived to find out the settlement position of the other party without prematurely revealing one's own.

Settlements are commonly reached without resorting to overt power—strikes, for example—although the ever-present possibility of a strike is an important factor and the strike that does not take place may play as great a role as the one that does. What needs to be stressed, understood, and appreciated is that the parties are trying to find out each other's settlement positions. They do this by constant recognition and evaluation of messages or signals given, both unintentional and intentional, as the negotiations proceed. Central to the process, also, is that it is essential to achieve consent—that is, to have the respective constituencies accept the bargain that is finally struck. Frequently the internal bargaining within each side is more difficult than the bargaining between sides. If, when the agreement—within the two sides and across the board—is achieved, the majority of the constituents of each side accepts the results, it is the mark of a good agreement; the parties will abide by it. This aspect of collective bargaining makes it valuable because of its salutary effect. It even helps to achieve peaceful relations, since at least the majorities on each side will abide by it.

The agreement is not self-administering. Analytically, collective bargaining can be viewed not only as a contract-making or agreement-making process but also as a contract-administering or agreement-administering process. Of course it is both, and each complements the other. The agreement is often called a contract, but it does not satisfactorily fit the requirements governing contracts. The Constitution does not recognize groups or associations, and the courts have found it comfortable to recognize, on the one hand, individuals, who make contracts, and on the other, government, which enacts legislation. But the courts have not yet developed a clear law of associations. What the association or group does falls somewhere between contract and legislation and, in some respects, partakes of each, but never fully. The relationship of the union and the employer that is covered by the agreement is never-ending (at least some parts of it are), despite the fact that it usually contains a termination date. It is understood that the terms of the agreement will continue unless modified after the agreement is opened for negotiation of issues raised.

The agreement does not serve without continuous attention by the parties. Problems are resolved within the context or terms of the agreement, including procedures commonly provided. A measure of continuous negotiating with respect to some issues that arise remains, for no agreement could possibly be specific about every eventuality. The terms of agreements range from the very specific to the very general. Even the former sometimes need interpretation or application, and the latter obviously leave room for, or require, future clarification. Almost universally, agreements provide machinery for grievance or dispute settlement, often providing for arbitration (rather than a work stoppage or a resort to force) if agreements or settlements cannot be reached in the steps of the grievance machinery.

Collective bargaining fits the values and needs of an enterprise society, and contrary to appearances under some circumstances and the use of the work stoppage to help effectuate agreements, it is a very sane, rational process. It is to be evaluated against the alternative rule-making possibilities—unilateral decision by management or action by government through legislation, compulsory arbitration, or edict. Historically, employers have not refrained from abusing workers when they did not have power, through their unions, to resist. Government, in turn, has been notoriously inept whenever it has intervened in the labor and management world, and it is doubtful whether legislators can develop the expertise required to be effective in making rules for the workplace and setting remuneration. Compulsory arbitration requires a "judiciary" and an entirely different forum, which, some conclude, denigrates freedom and undercuts negotiations. Hence, collective bargaining is the most viable and useful procedure for making rules for the workplace in a free enterprise society.

BIBLIOGRAPHY

Irving Bernstein, *A History of the American Worker.*

Derek C. Bok and John T. Dunlop, *Labor and the American Community.*

Charles O. Gregory, *Labor and the Law.*

Harry A. Millis and Emily C. Brown, *From the Wagner Act to Taft-Hartley.*

Harry A. Millis and Royal E. Montgomery, *Organized Labor*, vol. III.

Sumner H. Slichter, James J. Healy, and E. Robert Livernash, *The Impact of Collective Bargaining on Management.*

Lloyd Ulman, ed., *Challenges to Collective Bargaining.*

— VERNON H. JENSEN

COLONIAL POLICY, BRITISH

British colonial policy is technically the policy that was laid down or was evolved after the union of England and Scotland in 1707. This policy was based largely on the earlier English policy, which envisaged the promotion of domestic industry, foreign trade, the fisheries and shipping, and the planting of crown lands in the New World with the establishment of colonial settlements, or the exploitation of the resources of America through such commercial companies as the Hudson's Bay Company and the South Sea Company. It also included the policy of encouraging the utilization of the vast labor resources of Africa in the establishment and maintenance of plantations for the production of so-called colonial staples.

The earliest manifestations of English colonial policy are embodied in the 16th-century patents to Sir Humphrey Gilbert and Sir Walter Raleigh; then in 1606 patents were granted to the London and Plymouth companies of Virginia in connection with which a settlement policy was laid down. The settlement policy, among other features, embodied the idea of direct crown control; but in 1609 this was modified in the charter of that year issued in favor of the Virginia Company substituting indirect for direct control and providing for a definite and extensive grant of land. This new policy also found expression in the creation of the Council for New England in 1620. Direct control made its reappearance in 1624, when with the withdrawal of the political powers of the Virginia Company, Virginia took its place as the first of the so-called royal colonies under a system of government that permitted the survival of the colonial assembly. Nevertheless, this new policy was not to become basic until the beginning of the new century, for the year 1629 saw the appearance of the corporate colony of Massachusetts Bay with a charter that was sufficiently broad to permit the transfer of the government of the company to the New World, and 1632 that of the proprietaryship of Maryland with the granting to the Baltimore family of very wide powers. Thus three types of colonial government appeared as the result of the formulation of colonial policy—or perhaps one might suggest more accurately as the result of the failure of the government to formulate a policy—royal, proprietary, and charter.

Up to the Interregnum, colonial policy emanated from the crown and was directed by it. Then with the outbreak of the English Civil War the Long Parliament assumed control, acting mainly through a special commission or council provided for by the Ordinance of 1643, which gave to its president, the Earl of Warwick, the title of governor-in-chief and lord high admiral of all the English colonies in America. Moreover, between the years 1645 and 1651 Parliament laid down various regulations that looked to a strict control of colonial commerce in favor of English shipping and manufactures. Nor did this parliamentary interference with the colonies cease with the Restoration, which not only gave validity to these restrictions but added to them in a series of measures beginning with the so-called Navigation Act of 1660 and culminating in the very comprehensive Act of 1696. During the Commonwealth period Oliver Cromwell introduced a striking but temporary departure in colonial policy in 1654 with his ambitious plan known as the Western Design, which had a twofold purpose: the acquisition of the Spanish empire in the New World and in this connection the removal of northern English colonists to the warmer climes.

The growth in importance of the colonies led, moreover, to various experiments in their supervision such as the Laud Commission appointed by Charles I, and the various councils of Charles II ending with the transference in 1675 of this function to the Lords of Trade, a committee of the Privy Council, which continued to function after a manner until in 1696 William III brought into existence the Lords Commissioners for Trade and Plantations, a body that survived until after the American Revolution and that in the main fully justified its existence.

Colonial policy in the 18th century was characterized not only by efforts to reduce the colonies to a uniform type—that of the royal colony—which met with considerable success, but also by increased restrictions upon colonial enterprise with such acts as the Woolen Act of 1699, the White Pine Acts, the Hat Act of 1732, the Sugar Acts of 1733 and 1764, and the Iron Act of 1750. By the middle of the 18th century an important modification of policy may be noted with the growing menace of French competition. Side by side with mercantilism (with the emphasis upon immediate economic gain), modern imperialism (with the emphasis upon power politics, territorial aggrandizement, centralization of authority, and a unified Indian policy) made its appearance. With the collapse of the French empire in North America, Parliament turned its attention to securing a direct revenue from the colonies, passing for this purpose the Stamp Act of 1765 and the Townshend Acts of 1767. Reliance upon these new policies helped to bring on a crisis in colonial affairs that led to the Revolution.

[See Paris, Treaty of.]

BIBLIOGRAPHY

Cambridge History of the British Empire, vol. I.

L. H. Gipson. *The British Empire Before the American Revolution.*

— LAWRENCE HENRY GIPSON

COLONIAL SETTLEMENTS

Various colonies were planted along the coastal ribbon of the Atlantic for different reasons. Governments encouraged them to serve the economic needs of their nations, capitalists hoped for profit, and people sought better opportunities. Tragedy stalked the efforts to colonize. Ships, abundant capital, and many people were demanded to found a prosperous colony. The loss of life and money was tragic. Some ventures were stillborn, others were nursed through a puling infancy to maturity, a few grew lustily from birth.

Sir Humphrey Gilbert landed with his company on Newfoundland's shores in 1584. A few months saw them sail away. Sir Walter Raleigh in 1585 settled a few colonists on Roanoke Island (Carolina coast), but sustained effort failed to keep the venture alive. The time was not ripe and the cost was too heavy for private purses. The close of the war with Spain in 1604 freed England to turn to America. Joint-stock companies, combining capital and credit, entered into colonization. In 1607 the Plymouth Company tried a settlement on the Kennebec River (Maine), the London Company on the James River (Virginia). A rigorous winter and the death of the chief promoter soon sent the Kennebec settlers away. The Council for New England (1620) proved to be only a land company whose subgrants resulted in a few fishing, trading, and lumbering camps on New England's shores. Against heavy odds the London Company persisted. During its existence about 5,500 emigrants left England for Virginia; in 1625 a few over a thousand were living in the colony. The distress on a long voyage, disease, starvation, and Indians in the colony took a deadly toll. Virginia lived to be the first permanent English colony, with a population of 5,000 in 1634, rising to 50,000 in 1690.

In 1624 the Dutch West India Company sent over thirty families that founded New Amsterdam and Fort Orange (Albany). Forty years of effort showed a population of only about 8,000. The Dutch were not a migrating people, and a grasping company attracted few settlers. In 1638 the New Sweden Company began Fort Christina on the Delaware with a few people, but New Sweden never contained over a few hundred Swedes and Finns. Sweden's wars in Europe left it inadequate sources for colonial ventures. New Sweden ceased to be when captured by the Dutch in 1655.

The economic motive was not the only factor in colonial enterprise. Abundant land meant little without people. At first no urgent expulsive forces drove people away. Settlers were hard to secure until intolerable conditions sent them to the new land. This stream began in 1620 when the Pilgrims found their weary way to plant the colony of Plymouth. Villagers from northern England, denied freedom of worship, went to Holland for refuge, but finding Dutch life uncomfortable, they came to New England. The stream widened with the exodus of over 16,000 to New England during 1630–40. Various motives explain the migration, but primary was the purpose to establish in Massachusetts a city of God along Puritan lines. Unable to reform the Anglican Church, visited with harsh royal authority, the Puritan leaders found the answer in Massachusetts. Villagers from Massachusetts Bay, in 1635, founded the colony of Connecticut, where better land was available and a milder brand of Puritanism was practiced. A small band of devoted Puritans began the colony of New Haven in 1638. In 1662 New Haven was merged with Connecticut and thirty years later the greater colony numbered about 18,000 people. Intolerable conditions in Massachusetts peopled Rhode Island. The Bay colony dealt severely with dissent. The radical views of Roger Williams drove him to find refuge in the settlement of Providence in 1636. The strange ideas of Anne Hutchinson and her followers brought exile, some settling at Portsmouth, others at Newport. Rhode Island contained about 4,000 people by 1690. Massachusetts added Maine by purchase and secured Plymouth colony by merger and before 1700 the Bay province had over 50,000 people. New Hampshire was a slender little colony that harbored a few people under the proprietorship of Capt. John Mason. Maryland owed its genesis to Lord Baltimore, who under a royal charter in 1632 desired to find a refuge for Catholics and to build up a great landed estate. From small beginnings its population rose to 30,000 within sixty years.

Villagers from Massachusetts Bay founded the colony of Connecticut (1635), where better land was available and a milder brand of Puritanism was practiced.

After 1660 colonial expansion took on a renewed life. Again promoters sought profit and people better opportunities. The circle of English colonies was completed by the conquest of New Netherland in 1664, renamed New York and granted to the Duke of York. He subgranted New Jersey to Sir George Carteret and Lord John Berkeley. Carolina, granted to eight men by charter in 1663, divided into two colonies, North Carolina peopled from Virginia and South Carolina settled by discontented planters from Barbados and persecuted Protestants from France and England. After thirty years of effort neither colony had over 3,000 people. Quakerism, with its democratic and mystical principles, came into tragic collision with orthodoxy in both Old and New England. The Quakers found a welcome in Rhode Island and established their own colonies on the Delaware. In 1674 Berkeley sold West Jersey, which finally came into the hands of the Quakers who settled along the Delaware River at Burlington and other places. East Jersey, purchased from the Carteret estate in 1680, soon fell under the control of a large board in which the Quakers were prominent. Before the century closed East Jersey counted less than 10,000 people, West Jersey about 4,000. In 1681 William Penn received a charter for Pennsylvania where he tried a "Holy Experiment" in Quaker principles. The province became a haven of refuge for the persecuted, welcoming English, Welsh, and Irish Quakers, and Germans. It grew lustily, having a population, inclusive of Delaware, of over 12,000 within a decade. Delaware, granted to William Penn by the Duke of York, governed at first as part of Pennsylvania, in 1704 became a province with Penn as proprietor. Georgia came into existence in 1732 in response to humanitarian motives. Georgia harbored debtors from English jails and Lutheran exiles from Germany.

[See Great Migration.]

BIBLIOGRAPHY

Charles E. Clark, *The Eastern Frontier.*

Wesley Frank Craven, "The Southern Colonies in the Seventeenth Century, 1607–1689," in *A History of the South.*

E. J. Eccles, *France in America.*

Charles Gibson, *Spain in America.*

John Pomfret and Floyd M. Shumway, *Founding the American Colonies.*

— WINFRED T. ROOT

COLONIAL WARS

Although English, French, and Spanish colonies in North America were repeatedly plunged into war by the outbreak of hostilities in Europe involving their parent states, the colonial wars, from the outset, were much more than mere New World phases of Old World conflicts. America's natural resources and the supposed advantages of controlling American markets led Europeans to seek vast holdings here, and economic rivalries among the colonials themselves were intensified by racial and religious antagonisms. Louis XIV, concentrating on aggressions in Europe, gave little practical support to offensives in America; thus in King William's War (1689–97) Louis de Buade, Comte de Frontenac, resorted to the employment of Indian allies in ruthless border raids. Similar raids were utilized, chiefly by the French, in the subsequent conflicts: Queen Anne's War (1702–13), King George's War (1744–48), and the French and Indian War (1754–63).

At the outset of hostilities, and in 1711, English colonials and English regulars tried, futilely, to capture Quebec, the ultimate conquest of which by James Wolfe, in 1759, is the best known of many dramatic episodes of these wars. English forces, chiefly colonial, captured Port Royal in 1690 and again in 1710, although not until the Treaty of Utrecht (1713) was Acadia confirmed to the English, becoming their outpost, Nova Scotia. At Utrecht France also yielded Newfoundland and its claims to the Hudson Bay territory. During the "long peace" following 1713 (actually marred by hostilities in America and the West Indies) France established Louisbourg on Cape Breton Island, a base of operations against English participation in North Atlantic fisheries and trade routes. The restoration of Louisbourg to France (1748) after its capture by New Englanders (1745) embittered many colonials, already indignant at England's tragic mismanagement of colonial volunteers in an expedition against Cartagena (1740). Other friction between England and its colonies was caused by the former's attempts to dominate military operations and the latter's failure to meet, fully or promptly, English requisitions for men, money, and supplies, as well as by the colonies' persistence in trading with the enemy. Spain entered the conflict in Queen Anne's War, exchanging blows with the English in Florida and South Carolina. When King George's War began Spain and England already were engaged in the War of Jenkins' Ear. Spain, a late entrant in the French and Indian War, lost Florida to England. This conflict was precipitated by English expansion westward and French advances into the Ohio Valley, the link between New France (Canada) and French Illinois and Louisiana. Edward Braddock's defeat (1755) near Fort Duquesne was followed by English disappointments and defeats at Crown Point, Niagara, Oswego, Ticonderoga, and elsewhere, until the turning of the tide in 1758, usually accredited to England's new war minister, William Pitt. By the Treaty of Paris (1763) France retained most of its West Indian Islands and some fishing bases off Canada; its other North American possessions east of the Mississippi, except the neighborhood of New Orleans, were ceded to England.

BIBLIOGRAPHY

S. M. Pargellis, ed., *Military Affairs in North America, 1748–1765.*

F. Parkman, *A Half-Century of Conflict,* and *Montcalm and Wolfe.*

T. C. Pease, *Anglo-French Boundary Disputes in the West, 1749–1763.*

W. Wood and R. H. Gabriel, *The Winning of Freedom.*

G. M. Wrong, *The Conquest of New France.*

— LOUISE B. DUNBAR

COLT SIX-SHOOTER

Colt six-shooter, the invention of Samuel Colt, the first practical firearm of its kind. With the rifle, it had its place in revolutionizing methods of warfare and was an important link in the development of arms from the muzzle-loading musket to the magazine rifles and machine guns of today.

Its manufacture began at Paterson, N.J., in 1836. Colt's patent, secured Feb. 25, 1836, covered the revolution and locking of the cylinder firmly in place, so that the chambers of the cylinder came in line with the barrel by simply pulling the hammer back to full cock. From the first, all the barrels were expertly rifled to give the greatest possible accuracy to the bullet. Although various models were produced at Paterson, the arms did not at first receive the endorsement of government officials, and the company failed in 1842.

A few Colt arms, used by army officers in the Seminole Wars and by Texas Rangers during the border troubles, proved the worth of the "revolving pistol," and a supply was ordered by the government in January 1847. As Colt had no factory at that time, the first two or three thousand were made for him at the plant of Eli Whitney, son of the inventor, in New Haven, Conn. These were heavy revolvers of .44 caliber and soon became the standard of the U.S. Army and the Texas Rangers. Colt resumed the manufacture of revolvers at Hartford, Conn., in 1848. From 1856 to 1865 there were 554,283 of the powder-and-ball revolvers manufactured at the Hartford factory. Large quantities of these arms were used during the Civil War by both Union and Confederate troops. All Colt revolvers, up to the early 1870's, were made to shoot loose powder and lead bullets, the powder being ignited by a percussion cap. From that period, envelope cartridges, enclosing powder and bullet, were used until the advent of metallic ammunition.

Colt six-shooters played a prominent part in the development of the West. When first used in Indian fighting the six-shooter was a surprise weapon, as the Indians did not look for more than one shot, and when opposed by a single-shot arm it was their custom to draw fire and then rush the settler while he was reloading.

The six-shooter won its popularity in the West because it was easily carried, accurate, and of high capacity. Sheriffs, cowboys, and plainsmen quickly became expert marksmen. It was an ideal weapon for mounted rangers and cattlemen and was used for hunting as well as for defense.

— SAMUEL M. STONE

COLUMBIA RIVER EXPLORATION AND SETTLEMENT

The estuary of the Columbia River in the northwest United States was first seen, described, and mapped in 1775 by Capt. Bruno Hezeta, who named it Bahía de la Asumpción, though Spanish maps showed it as Ensenada de Hezeta. In 1792 Capt. Robert Gray of Boston sailed ten miles up the river proper and six miles up Gray's Bay, naming it Columbia's River after his ship. The same year W. R. Broughton of Capt. George Vancouver's party surveyed and charted to Cottonwood Point, 119 statute miles from the Pacific Ocean.

The Lewis and Clark expedition, in 1805, explored from the mouth of the Yakima to Cottonwood Point, 214 miles. In 1807 David Thompson explored for 111 miles, from the mouth to the Columbia River's source in Columbia Lake; and in 1811 Finan McDonald navigated from Kettle Falls to Death Rapids, 255 miles. In the same year Thompson navigated the entire river.

Prior to the great wagon train of 1843, settlements had been started along the river in over forty localities. The posts of the fur traders included those of the North West Company, the Astoria posts, and those of independent traders. Among the earliest were Fort Clatsop (1805) and Francis G. Chouteau's post (1807). Other settlements were Fort Colville (1825); Willamette Valley, an agricultural settlement (1829); Benjamin Louis de Bonneville's cantonment (1832); Whitman Mission (1836); and Coeur d'Alene (1842). After 1843 the wagon train rapidly opened the country, and subsequently the steamboat, railroads, and highways transformed the wilderness into a prosperous and populous region.

BIBLIOGRAPHY

H. H. Bancroft, *History of the North West Coast* and *History of Oregon.*

— J. NEILSON BARRY

COLUMBUS QUINCENTENARY

Columbus Quincentenary (1992), marking the 500th anniversary of the landing of Christopher Columbus (properly, Cristóbal Colón) on the shores of what came to be called the Americas, was an unexpectedly restrained celebration in the United States and elsewhere. Major events took place, including a summer Olympics dedicated to Columbus in Barcelona, Spain; a $5 billion world's fair in Seville, Spain, with exhibits from 110 nations; the opening of the world's largest Columbian monument, a 390-foot-high lighthouse, in the Dominican Republic; and the largest flower show ever in the Western Hemisphere, the $50 million AmeriFlora exposition in Columbus, Ohio. Nevertheless, the numbers of visitors to these events were fewer than expected, media attention was scanty, and financial goals were not met. A quincentenary encyclopedia was published in the United States, but several planned public events and scholarly meetings were either curtailed or canceled. Several factors explain the quincentenary's failure to evoke enthusiasm. One frequently cited reason was lack of money, public and private, because of the worldwide recession. Another was a sense that the Spanish admiral could not have "discovered" a world where 200 million people lived. The central reason was probably opposition raised by indigenous peoples in both North and South America to the idea of celebrating a man they believed had brought conquest and colonization to the Americas, accompanied by the transmission of diseases

Christopher Columbus. Oil painting attributed to Ridolfo del Ghirlandaio. (The Granger Collection, New York)

that killed 90 percent of the original inhabitants, and introduced environmental exploitation and despoliation. Most of the quincentenary festivities and exhibits combined celebration and protest, and coverage of the occasion, popular and scholarly, was similarly mixed. One benefit was that previously uncritical treatments of Columbus and his achievement—such as at the World's Columbian Exhibition of 1893 in Chicago—gave way to more understanding of the explorer's purposes and goals.

BIBLIOGRAPHY

Kirkpatrick Sale, *The Conquest of Paradise: Christopher Columbus and the Columbia Legacy* (New York, 1990).

— KIRKPATRICK SALE

COMANCHE

Comanche, the most famous Indian tribe of the Plains, dominated southwestern Texas and southwestern Oklahoma from the time of their acquisition of the horse in the early 18th century until their reservation confinement in 1875. It was, in fact, against their depredations that the Texas Rangers were organized. Like many of the Indians of the Plains, the Comanche pushed into their historic habitat from another area, being attracted to the Plains in their quest for horses. The tribe speaks a language of the Shoshonean branch of the Uto-Aztecan family, thus relating to the Shoshonean Basin pattern. The Comanche have been traced to Montana and seem to have resided originally in the general Basin-Plateau area. They carried with them into the Plains the essentially simple social organization of their home area.

It is known that by 1719 the Comanche, not as a single tribe or nation but rather as independent bands, occupied a section of southwestern Kansas on the northern bank of the Arkansas River. Pushing farther to the south, they successfully expelled the Jicarilla and Lipan Apache, driving the latter across the Mexican border. Fully adapted to the Plains Indian war pattern, the Comanche thereafter regarded the various Apache as their enemies. At the same time, they carried on attacks against the Spanish settlers and, later, against the American. They were gradually subdued and located with the Kiowa on two Texas reservations in 1854, ceding these in 1867 in favor of an Oklahoma parcel. Not until after uprisings in 1874–75 did they adapt to reservation life.

The historic role played by the Comanche was essentially a negative one, in that they hindered European expansion into northwestern Texas. No prominent leaders stand out; rather the tribe is distinguished by the collective spirit of its warriors and their pursuit of military advantage. The Comanche represent the epitome of Plains Indian culture in their extreme development of a highly mobile, maximally streamlined fighting force. While other Plains tribes elaborated an art or gave attention to certain other material and technological aspects of their culture, the Comanche remained content with a bare minimum of goods. They sought booty in trade items, such as guns, cloth, iron tools, and blankets. For these, along with horses, they were willing to carry on extensive and vigorous raids. Like other Plains tribes, the Comanche hunted the bison, emulating war patterns in hunting.

More, perhaps, than any other Plains people, the Comanche aimed in war at killing an enemy; although the custom of coup counting was adhered to, it was the slayer of an enemy who was accorded highest status.

BIBLIOGRAPHY

Ralph Linton, "The Comanche," in A. Kardiner, ed., *Psychological Frontiers of Society.*

E. Wallace and E. A. Hoebel, *The Comanches.*

— ROBERT F. SPENCER

COMMERCE, DEPARTMENT OF

The Department of Commerce was designated as such by an act of Congress on Mar. 4, 1913. This legislation reorganized the Department of Commerce and Labor, which had been created on Feb. 14, 1903, by transferring labor activities into a separate department. The secretary of commerce, who heads the department of that name, is appointed by the president with the advice and consent of the Senate and is a member of the president's cabinet. Among those who have served as secretary are such well-known personalities as Herbert Hoover, Harry Hopkins, Henry Wallace, and Averell Harriman.

The original mission of the Department of Commerce was "to foster, promote, and develop the foreign and domestic commerce" of the United States. As a result of legislative and administrative additions, the present mission is much broader in scope. Now the department seeks to "foster, serve and promote the Nation's economic and technological advancement" by participating with other governmental agencies in the creation of national policy; promoting progressive business policies and growth; assisting states, communities, and individuals toward economic progress; strengthening the international economic position of the United States; improving man's comprehension and uses of the physical environment and its oceanic life; assuring effective use and growth of the nation's scientific and technical resources; and acquiring, analyzing, and disseminating information concerning the nation and the economy to help achieve increased social and economic benefit.

Upon the creation of the Department of Labor in 1913, the Commerce Department retained responsibility for the bureaus of the Census, Corporations, Fisheries, Foreign and Domestic Commerce, Lighthouses, and Standards, as well as for the Coast and Geodetic Survey and the Steamboat Inspection Services. Many of these functions assigned to the department had been performed by various agencies since early in the nation's history. For example, the first census was taken in 1790; coast and geodetic surveys were authorized as early as 1807; and the Bureau of Navigation was established in 1884.

The transferring of functions, the addition of responsibilities, and internal reorganizations and name changes of constituent units have been commonplace with respect to the department. Of the original units in the department, only the Bureau of Standards is recognizable today from a departmental organizational chart. The functions of the Coast and Geodetic Survey and the Census Bureau remain within the department but under unfamiliar names: the former has been incorporated in the National Oceanic and Atmospheric Administration, and the latter, in the Social and Economic Statistics Administration. The remaining original units have been transferred to other departments, abolished, or had their functions dispersed among other units in the Commerce Department.

Additional bureaus have also come and gone, with logic and politics each contributing to the changes. For example, the Bureau of Mines was transferred from the Interior to the Commerce Department in 1925 and then back to Interior in 1934. The Patent Bureau was transferred to Commerce in 1925 from Interior and has remained there. The Weather Bureau was brought in from the Department of Agriculture in 1940, lost for five years to an independent agency, and reunited with Commerce in 1970 as a part of the National Oceanic and Atmospheric Administration. The Bureau of Public Roads was gained from the General Services Administration in 1949 but went to the new Department of Transportation in 1966.

A brief examination of other units within the department shows that while the business community is well served, other constituencies are also given assistance. The Maritime Administration, for instance, administers programs to aid in the development of the U.S. Merchant Marine. The U.S. Travel Service was established in 1961. The Economic Development Administration was established in 1965 to plan long-range economic development of areas characterized by severe unemployment and low family incomes. The Office of Minority Business Enterprise was created in 1969. The National Technical Information Service came into being in 1970, as did the Office of Telecommunications. Other units in the department are the Bureau of Domestic Commerce, the Bureau of International Commerce, and the Office of Foreign Direct Investments.

BIBLIOGRAPHY

Annual Reports of the secretaries of commerce.

— GUY B. HATHORN

THE DOC SINCE 1970

The role of the Department of Commerce (DOC) to promote trade and U.S. economic and technological advancement has evolved and grown as the needs of the national economy changed. The DOC took on the role of promoting tourism starting in the 1960s and in 1981 elevated that priority with the creation of the U.S. Travel and Tourism Administration. It has in recent years drastically improved its statistical information on the economy as a resource for commerce, reflecting the increasingly complicated and sophisticated needs of a global economy. With the increasing emphasis on diversity and issues pertaining to women and minorities, the DOC stepped up its activities on behalf of those groups, especially through the Minority Business Development Agency. It also greatly increased its role in promoting foreign trade. In 1961 the first overseas trade center was opened in London, the first in a long series of steps to promote U.S. products abroad. Nonetheless, by the late 1970s the U.S. trade deficit had soared, and in 1980 Congress passed the Trade Reorganization Act, which established a new national export policy and created the International Trade Administration.

During the tenure of Secretary of Commerce Malcolm Baldrige (1981–1987), the DOC became a major force in national policymaking. The DOC took a lead role in the Export Trading Act of 1982 to provide new export-related jobs by allowing smaller businesses to enter export markets. In 1987 the Bureau of Export Administration was created to handle licensing and export enforcement. The DOC became increasingly active in the promotion of U.S. goods and businesses abroad. For example, in one six-day stretch in 1985, Baldrige held trade conferences with leaders of the Soviet Union, India, and China. In the 1990s Secretary of Commerce Ronald H. Brown went on numerous trips to such countries as India, Saudi Arabia, South Africa, and China with business leaders of the nation's airline, manufacturing, utility, and other industries to support business on their behalf.

Since the early 1970s the DOC has accelerated efforts to spur the technological development of the U.S. economy. The National Telecommunications and Information Administration was created in 1978 in response to the explosive growth in communications technology and has played a prominent role in public discussions and investments in the nation's technological resources. In addition, in 1988 the National Bureau of Standards (founded in 1901) was renamed the National Institute of Standards and Technology, which strengthened and advanced the application of science and technology in the national interest and for the benefit of the public.

The National Oceanic and Atmospheric Administration (NOAA), the largest agency in the Department of Commerce, was created in 1970 to unify the oceanic and atmospheric programs of the nation. NOAA consists of the National Ocean Service, which surveys U.S. coastlines and the ocean floor and oversees aeronautical charting; the National Weather Service, which underwent a massive modernization in the early 1990s to improve forecasting capabilities; the National Marine Fisheries Service, which promotes the fishing industry, preserves fishing resources, and protects endangered marine species; the National Environmental Satellite, Data, and Information Service; and the Office of Oceanic and Atmospheric Research.

Despite shifting priorities to the apparent demands of the general public, the DOC came under attack in the 1990s. The election of a Republican majority to Congress in 1994 endangered the existence of the DOC as a cabinet-level agency. Citing the need for downsizing government, an increasing number of prominent national leaders cited the department as an unnecessary expense (31,000 employees and a $3 billion annual budget in the mid-1990s), but most plans for dismantling the DOC called for the dissemination of most of its functions to other government departments, as when the Maritime Administration was transferred in 1987 to the Department of Transportation.

BIBLIOGRAPHY

U.S. Department of Commerce, *From Lighthouses to Laserbeams: A History of U.S. Department of Commerce* (Washington, D.C., 1988).

— ERIK BRUUN

COMMITTEES OF CORRESPONDENCE

Committees of Correspondence, organized by the colonies as part of the transitional revolutionary machinery to facilitate the spread of propaganda and coordinate the patriot party. Samuel Adams was the promoter of the first local committees, persuading Boston to establish a standing committee of correspondence (Nov. 2, 1772) to send a statement of rights and grievances to other towns in the colony. Within three months Gov. Thomas Hutchinson reported that there were more than eighty such committees in Massachusetts. On Mar. 12, 1773, Virginia organized another type, the colony committees that were in reality standing committees of the legislature. A third type and the most important was the county committee that was chosen by the local units and acted as the agent of the central colonial committees. The importance of these committees as channels for the creation and direction of public opinion during the preliminaries of the Revolution can hardly be overemphasized. They exercised at times judicial, legislative, and executive functions and, containing the germ of government, gave rise to the later committee system.

BIBLIOGRAPHY

H. M. Flick, "The Rise of the Revolutionary Committee System," *New York History*, vol. III.

— A. C. FLICK

COMMON SENSE

Common Sense, a tract by Thomas Paine, was published in Philadelphia, January 1776. In contrast to writers who denounced British tyranny but insisted on colonial loyalty, Paine described reconciliation as only "an agreeable dream." He maintained that, being of age, the colonies were qualified for independence and that their future interest demanded it. While many men had similar beliefs, none had so graphically stated the case. With its circulation of 120,000 in the first three months, the tract greatly fertilized the independence spirit that flowered so brilliantly in July 1776.

BIBLIOGRAPHY

M. D. Conway, ed., *The Writings of Thomas Paine.*

— CHARLES F. MULLETT

COMMUNIST PARTY, UNITED STATES OF AMERICA

Communist Party, United States of America, had its beginning in Chicago in 1919, when a schism split the Socialist party (SP), then headed by Eugene V. Debs, and advocates of Bolshevik doctrinary positions more radical than the progressive gradualism of the SP ethic broke away. The left wing that emerged from the SP was split into two factions, each claiming revolutionary legitimacy—the Communist party (CP) and the Communist Labor party (CLP). The first was dominated by the Russian-language federation, and the second was somewhat more oriented toward American realities, although just as revolutionary. When the U.S. Department of Labor and the attorney general of the United States launched extensive antisubversive programs in 1919 and 1920—in which thousands of radical aliens were rounded up and deported—the two new revolutionary factions went underground, continuing their intense factional rivalry. In 1920 an effort was made at a convention in Bridgman, Mich., to resolve the factional splits between the CP and the CLP, and the United Communist party (UCP) was created. But the new party was, in the main, the old CLP with a handful of CP members. The CP maintained a separate organization, and the split persisted, except that the factions were slightly modified as the UCP and the CP.

Unity was imposed on the fighting factions by the Communist International (Comintern) in 1921, when it told the Americans that they would either unite by themselves or the Communist movement in the United States would be reorganized from without. The CP and the UCP then came together and created a new organization known as the Communist Party of America.

During this period the Comintern urged the American Communist movement to operate in the open and to participate in electoral and other parliamentary activities, since there had not occurred the expected collapse of bourgeois society in the aftermath of the war and of the Bolshevik revolution. The ideological line of the party was not to be weakened, but its public activities were to be less doctrinally rigid and hostile. Accordingly, in December 1921, the Workers Party of America was created to serve as the public voice of American communism. The Communist Party of America formally dissolved itself in 1923, and until 1925 it was the Workers Party of America that spoke and acted for the Communist movement. In 1925 the name of the party was changed to Workers (Communist) Party of America, and in 1929 it became the Communist Party, United States of America (CPUSA).

With the Stalinization of the American party in 1929, the party waged unremitting struggle against liberal reformers, centrists, and socialists—in short, against all other groups of leftist tendency.

The change in the party in 1929, however, was more than a change in name. After the death of Nikolai Lenin in Russia in 1924, Joseph Stalin emerged as the chief of state, following a series of actions against rivals of left and right in the Russian party. The first action was an alliance with Nikolai Ivanovich Bukharin against the left represented by Leon Trotsky, who was driven into exile and later murdered in Mexico. The suppression of the left was followed by the suppression of the right when Stalin defeated Bukharin and reigned alone as leader of the Soviet Union. The pattern was paralleled in America. In the American party a leftist tendency appeared with the creation of a Trotskyist faction under the leadership of James P. Cannon. There was also a rightist faction, under the leadership of Jay Lovestone, which argued for what came to be known as American exceptionalism—that is, the existence in the United States of conditions different enough from European experiences to justify modification for the United States of the full rigor of Communist international policy. Both factions were expelled from the CPUSA in 1928–29 (the Cannon group first), and the Stalinist element came to prevail under the leadership of William Z. Foster. The climax came in May 1929, when an "American commission" of the Comintern rejected the theory of

American exceptionalism, and Lovestone, Benjamin Gitlow, Bertram Wolfe, and Max Bedacht were ordered to support the decision of Moscow. All but Bedacht refused to do so and were expelled from the party.

With the Stalinization of the American party in 1929, what may be called a strategy of alienation was undertaken, by which the party sought to combat the traditional unions of the American labor movement by creating rival organizations; the party also waged unremitting struggle against liberal reformers, centrists, and socialists (called "social fascists")—in short, against all other groups of leftist tendency. The strategy of alienation was based on the assumption that all other parties had to be opposed and presumably eventually liquidated in order to prepare the CPUSA to assume its historically prescribed duty upon the collapse of capitalism—which had been declared to be at hand by Stalin and Bukharin at the Sixth World Congress in Moscow in 1928.

The hard line of rigid alienation continued until 1935 and coincided with the Comintern line in European countries. Franklin D. Roosevelt was depicted as a leader serving the interests of finance capital and moving toward the suppression of the workers. The *Daily Worker*, the newspaper of the CPUSA, declared that a "fascist slave program" had been instituted by the National Industrial Recovery Act (1933) and an "antistrike" law passed as the National Labor Relations Act (1935), under which the trade union movement finally became a vigorous and important element of American political and economic life.

Because of the growing menace of Germany's Nazi regime, which Stalin had grossly underestimated, the international party line was changed, and directions were reversed. At the Seventh World Congress of the Communist International in Moscow in 1935, it was laid down that "at the present historical stage, it is the main and immediate task of the international labor movement to establish the united fighting front of the working class": the new policy was to make common cause with liberal elements everywhere. Socialists who had been recently reviled as social fascists became brothers. Unity was to be achieved even with liberal capitalist elements, and it was to be proper for American Communists to support their own government. The Popular Front ushered in a period of what may be called the "strategy of enticement." To signal the change, William Z. Foster, who had been the general secretary of the American party during the period of alienation, was moved to one side; his place was taken by Earl Browder, who wrote that "Communism is the Americanism of the twentieth century." Recriminations against the New Deal were stopped, and friendly words were said of George Washington, Abraham Lincoln, Thomas Jefferson, and, of course, Stalin as fighters for the people.

The period of the Popular Front, which lasted from 1935 to 1939, was the period of the party's greatest vogue. Hundreds of organizations were formed to promote the agitational goals of the party. Although the power goals of the party were carefully concealed, Communist leaders were successful in great measure in managing and manipulating the front organizations they had created. Instead of fighting the trade-union movement, the Communists joined it, and they established strong centers of influence, notably in the fur workers', automobile, rubber, steel, electrical, communications, and longshoremen's unions. Because the agitational goals of the CPUSA seemed to coincide with the aspirations of the millions of Americans who supported the liberal reformism of the New Deal, the front organizations were strongly supported by hundreds of thousands who had no ideological connection with the CPUSA at all. Anti–New Deal and antilabor politicians later often attempted to characterize liberals of the 1930's as "fellow travelers" of the Communist party; the fact was that the Communist party was a fellow traveler of the liberals.

The Popular Front period came to an end when the power goals of the Soviet Union changed. In 1939 the Soviet Union negotiated a nonaggression pact with Nazi Germany, freeing Adolf Hitler of immediate concern for a second front in the East and opening the way for the invasion of Poland, which promptly followed. The shock of the nonaggression pact in the Communist movement in the United States was seismic. Thousands of members of the party and of the front organizations who had supported the agitational goals of the party during the period of the Popular Front immediately left the party. All had been taught for years that Hitler was the enemy of the working class, and it could not be easily comprehended why he was no longer. But the party had an answer: with the outbreak of war in Europe, English imperialism had become "the chief enemy of the working class." Since the Soviet Union was, temporarily, a passive partner in the spread of war, it became the duty of its supporters to oppose intervention by the United States. The energies of the CPUSA were therefore applied to the organization of a "peace" movement, with slogans like "The Yanks Are Not Coming"—a movement that had a remarkably short life. On June 21, 1941, the German armies invaded the Soviet Union, and what had been, on June 20, an imperialist war that America should stay out of became, on June 22, a peoples' war that America should enter.

From 1941 to 1945 the CPUSA was in the forefront of patriotic striving because the military aims of the

United States and the Soviet Union coincided with respect to the defeat of the German armies. Whereas strikes and other forms of labor agitation had been normal, even traditional, methods for the advancement of the class struggle, Communist policy now opposed strikes or any other disruption of wartime production. Communist party leaders even favored incentive pay, formerly regarded as a device of capitalist bosses for splitting the workers and harassing the poor. One of the party's showcase blacks, Benjamin Davis, a member of the City Council of New York City, put the interests of the Soviet Union before those of the black community when he opposed certain antiracist measures in employment. In 1943 the Soviet Union, in a gesture of amity, abolished the Comintern; and in May 1944, Earl Browder abolished the CPUSA as a legal and corporate entity and created instead the Communist Political Association.

Browder believed that the Teheran Conference of 1943 meant that the postwar period would be a period of class collaboration and that the goals of communism would be achieved without class warfare. But with the end of World War II in 1945 the international Communist line changed again and the period of the cold war began. Browder was attacked abroad by the French Communist Jacques Duclos for promoting serious heresies, the chief of which was his departure from the Marxist fundamentalism of class warfare. As a consequence, he was deposed by his American colleagues; the Communist Political Association was abolished; the CPUSA was reestablished under the leadership of William Z. Foster; and Browder was driven out of the party.

By 1957 the party was brought to the point of collapse by three developments. First, Foster's ultra-leftism fastened on the party a conception of the future that was as much out of phase as that of the Sixth World Congress had been in 1928. It was his view that the years immediately ahead would be years of war, fascism, and American imperialism and that the party should therefore be prepared to resume a hard line. But a hard line had not succeeded from 1929 to 1935 in bringing the Communists to power or even in establishing a mass base, and the prospect for doing so was even more dim under Foster's new leadership, because in 1947 there had been a strong reaction against Communist influences in the Congress of Industrial Organizations (CIO), some unions being expelled and Communists removed from positions of influence in others.

Second, the CPUSA was put under strong pressure by government authorities. Loyalty programs in the federal government were inaugurated by President Harry S. Truman in 1947, continued by President Dwight D. Eisenhower, and established in many states. The House Committee on Un-American Activities and the Internal Security Subcommittee of the Senate Committee on the Judiciary held extensive hearings on Communists in the government service and in other areas of American life, that were adversary in nature. But the most effective action against the Communist party was the prosecution of its leaders under the Smith Act of 1940, which made it a crime to advocate or teach the necessity of the violent overthrow of government or to conspire to do so. After a nine-month trial the eleven top leaders of the CPUSA were convicted in October 1949 of advocating violent overthrow of the government, and the Supreme Court of the United States upheld the convictions in *Dennis* v. *United States* in 1951. Other prosecutions followed. The most immediate effect of these actions on the party as a whole was a decision to go underground. A skeletal public organization was maintained, but some of the convicted leaders went into hiding to escape imprisonment, as did those who had been indicted in other prosecutions but had disappeared before trial and some who might expect to be indicted. An effort was made also to protect some members of the party, not necessarily prominent, who were possible future leaders; and many of these were sent abroad and ordered to change their lives completely.

Communist party leaders were prosecuted under the Smith Act of 1940, which made it a crime to advocate the violent overthrow of government, or to conspire to do so.

Third, it was the denunciation of Stalin by Nikita Khrushchev at the Twentieth Congress of the Soviet Communist Party in 1956 that traumatized many American party members and finally brought the CPUSA to the point of collapse. Stalin was condemned by Khrushchev for having promoted a "cult of personality," which was alien to Marxist-Leninist principles, and for having established a personal tyranny. Contrary to the dogma of the past, it was also said that war with the capitalist states was not inevitable and that peaceful coexistence could obtain between them and the Communist countries. The shock of these pronouncements shattered the American party. To make catastrophe complete, in October 1956 the revolt of Hungarians against the Communist regime was crushed by Soviet armed forces, and another fiction of the international brotherhood of the working class was destroyed. The *Daily Worker* stopped publication in 1958 because of disagreements over the Hungarian intervention by Soviet forces and was out of circulation until 1968, when it was revived under the name *Daily World.*

For the twenty-five years between 1930 and 1955, a conservative estimate places Communist party membership at 7,500 at the start and at about 22,600 at the end of the period, with peaks of 55,000 in 1938 and 65,000 in 1945. One estimate for 1973 puts the figure at 15,000 dues-paying members. The precise figures are less important, however, than the trends they reflect. First, despite its pretensions, the CPUSA has never been a mass party. Second, although hundreds of thousands of people have passed through the CPUSA since its founding, it has never managed to retain either the loyalty or the interest of most of them. Third, the party's greatest prosperity occurred when the party was most American and least Russian. It was up when its agitational goals supported American aspirations, as in the years of the New Deal and World War II; it was down when its policies were most obviously in service of the power goals of the Soviet Union, as at the time of the Nazi-Soviet pact in 1939 and the suppression of the Hungarian Revolution in 1956. In national politics, the party's greatest success was the campaign of 1948, when it supported the Progressive party of Henry A. Wallace and dominated its management. Although Wallace received no electoral college votes, he did win more than one million popular votes, over half of which came from New York City and California. He was thoroughly disaffected before the campaign was over, however, and thought that if the Communists had left the campaign he might have lost 100,000 Communist votes but would have gained three or four million others. When Wallace broke with the Progressive party in 1950, he said that he had never realized the extent to which the Communists had controlled things.

In the 1960's a New Left movement had considerable vogue among young people in America, especially on college campuses, but it had little in common with the Communist party, which represented the Old Left. From the Communist point of view, the New Left was undisciplined, anarchic, negative, self-indulgent, untheoretical, anti-intellectual, and disorganized. From the New Left point of view, the CPUSA was old, rigid, bureaucratic, and not relevant. The CPUSA survived the New Left, but it was nevertheless as impotent an agency for social revolution in America in the 1970's as it had been fifty years before, and for at least two of the same reasons: an incurable tendency to split into factions and an infatuation with the Soviet Union.

BIBLIOGRAPHY

Gabriel Almond, *The Appeals of Communism.*

Theodore Draper, *The Roots of American Communism* and *American Communism and Soviet Russia.*

Morris Ernst and David Loth, *Report on the American Communist.*

Nathan Glazer, *The Social Basis of American Communism.*

Irving Howe and Lewis Coser, *The American Communist Party: A Critical History (1919–1957).*

Earl Latham, *The Communist Controversy in Washington.*

David A. Shannon, *The Decline of American Communism.*

Joseph R. Starobin, *American Communism in Crisis, 1943–57.*

— EARL LATHAM

COMPROMISE OF 1850

Compromise of 1850, a designation commonly given to five statutes enacted in September 1850, following a bitter controversy between the representatives of the North and South. The controversy reached a fever pitch during the weeks following the assembling of Congress in December 1849, when the election of a speaker under the customary majority rule was prevented by the unwillingness of the Free Soil members, who held the balance of power, to be drawn into an arrangement with either of the two major parties. In the course of the prolonged balloting criminations and recriminations passed between the hotheaded spokesmen of the two sections. Pointing to indications that the principle of the Wilmot Proviso might be enacted into law and receive the signature of President Zachary Taylor, southerners insisted as a matter of right upon the recognition of the Calhoun doctrine, which stated that under the Constitution all the territories should be deemed open to slavery. There was talk of secession unless this principle was recognized in fact or as a basis for some adjustment. Plans were underway for the discussion of a satisfactory southern program at a southern convention called to meet at Nashville in June.

In the face of increasing sectional strife Henry Clay returned to the U.S. Senate in 1849 and on Jan. 29, 1850, suggested a series of resolutions intended to provide the basis for the prompt adjustment of the main questions at issue between the two sections. His resolutions were shortly referred to a select committee of thirteen, of which he was made chairman. Its report (May 8), which covered the ground of Clay's resolutions, recommended an "omnibus bill" providing for the admission of California under its free state constitution, for territorial governments for Utah and New Mexico silent on slavery, and for the settlement of the boundary dispute between Texas and the United States. It also recommended a bill for the abolition of the slave trade in the District of Columbia and an amendment to the fugitive slave law.

The hope of compromise was tied up with the fate of the omnibus bill. Clay rallied to his support the outstanding Union men, including Daniel Webster, Lewis Cass, Henry S. Foote, and Stephen A. Douglas; the latter became the active force in the promotion of the necessary legislation. President Taylor wanted the admission of California but no action on New Mexico and Utah until they should be ready to become states; he was, therefore, a formidable obstacle to the plans of the compromisers until his death on July 9. Even the active support of the bill by his successor, Franklin Pierce, did not offset the fact that the idea of compromise "united the opponents instead of securing the friends" of each proposition.

In the North there was widespread denunciation of the iniquities of the Fugitive Slave Act and deliberate declaration that its enforcement would never be tolerated.

Compromise as such had clearly failed; the ground that it had contemplated was covered in five statutes each formerly included as sections of the proposed omnibus bill. The act establishing a territorial government for Utah (Sept. 9) contained the important popular sovereignty clause providing that any state or states formed out of this territory should be admitted with or without slavery as their constitutions should prescribe. An identical clause was appended to the New Mexico territorial act (Sept. 9), which also resolved the conflict between Texas and the federal government over the Santa Fe region by a cession, with compensation to Texas, to the newly created territory. On the same date the act admitting California under its constitution prohibiting slavery in the new state was approved. The Fugitive Slave Act of Sept. 18, 1850, which amended the original statute of Feb. 12, 1793, provided for the appointment of special commissioners to supplement the regular courts empowered after a summary hearing to issue a certificate of arrest of a fugitive "from labor," which authorized the claimant to seize and return the fugitive (with a fee of ten dollars when the certificate was issued and of only five dollars when denied); in no trial or hearing was the testimony of the alleged fugitive to be admitted as evidence nor was a fugitive claiming to be a freeman to have the right of trial by jury; federal marshals and deputy marshals were made liable for the full value of fugitives who escaped their custody and were empowered to call to their aid any bystanders, or *posse comitatus*; and any person willfully hindering the arrest of a fugitive or aiding in his rescue or escape was subject to heavy fine and imprisonment, as well as to heavy civil damages. The Act Abolishing the Slave Trade in the District of Columbia was approved on Sept. 20.

These statutes were presented to the country as a series of compromise measures. They did not, however, magically calm the sectional storm. In the North, there was widespread denunciation of the iniquitous features of the Fugitive Slave Act and deliberate declaration that its enforcement would never be tolerated. At the same time the conservative forces organized a series of Union meetings and pleaded the obligations of the North to pacify the South. In the latter section the other four enactments precipitated the most serious disunion crisis that the country had ever faced. In Georgia, Mississippi, and South Carolina the Southern Rights, or secession, forces were checkmated only by the most strenuous efforts of the Union or Constitutional Union elements. Both sides foreswore old party labels and fought under their new banners to win control over the official state conventions that were ordered. The Southern Rights forces lost in the first test fight in Georgia and had to carry this moral handicap in the remaining contests. It was not until 1852 that the country at large made clear its acquiescence in what at length became known by the oversimple label the Compromise of 1850.

BIBLIOGRAPHY

J. B. McMaster, *History of the People of the United States*, vol. VIII.

J. F. Rhodes, *History of the United States Since the Compromise of 1850*, vol. I.

— ARTHUR C. COLE

COMPUTERS

The electronic computer is clearly one of the most exciting, as well as one of the most important, technological developments of the modern age. From the vantage point of the present, it is difficult to realize that the world's first electronic computer, the Electronic Numerical Integrator and Computer (ENIAC), was not publicly unveiled until February 1946. In 1946 the word "computer" still referred to a person (that is, "one who computes").

Computers can be broken down into three main types: analog, digital, and hybrid. However, as with all attempts at classification, it is clear that these categories are artificial. There are digital devices that make use of analog techniques and analog devices that digitize some portion of information. Hybrid machines are those that use both analog and digital techniques; therefore, this article will deal only with analog and digital computers. In a true hybrid system, digital and analog computers play equal roles.

Analog Computers

An analog device is one in which physical magnitudes—such as the rotation of a shaft, the voltage of a circuit, or the motion of a slide—are used to represent quantities of a given problem. In a computational sense, an analog calculation, then, is one in which one looks at some physical process that happens to have the same mathematical equations as the process that one is interested in. A slide rule and a speedometer are examples of such devices. The earliest analog computers were special-purpose devices such as James Thomson's ball and disc integrators (about 1870), his brother Lord Kelvin's (William Thomson) harmonic synthesizer (1872), Kelvin's tide predictor (1876), and A. A. Michelson and S. W. Stratton's harmonic analyzer (about 1897).

A harmonic analyzer is essentially an integrating machine that determines the components of a curve representing a periodic function. A harmonic synthesizer deals with the opposite problem, that of finding a curve when its components are known. Michelson used his machine as both an analyzer and a synthesizer in the optical studies he was making. As a synthesizer, the machine added the interference fringes represented by simple harmonic curves; as an analyzer, it decomposed a visibility curve into components representing the distribution of light in the source.

One of the milestones in the development of analog devices was the invention of the differential analyzer by Vannevar Bush in the 1930's, a device used extensively during World War II and on into the 1950's. An outgrowth of Bush's interest in solving the differential equations related to the electric circuitry problems connected with failures and blackouts in power networks, this first differential analyzer was entirely mechanical, with the exception of the electric motors. All of the required changes in connections between shafts were performed manually. In 1935 Bush built a machine on which all the connections could be made electrically, significantly reducing the number of operations required.

One of the milestones in the development of analog computers was Vannevar Bush's invention of the differential analyzer in the 1930's, a device used during World War II and into the 1950's.

In 1932, the U.S. Army Ordnance had begun investigating possible use of the differential analyzer for ballistics calculation, and one was put into operation for this purpose in 1935. Shortly before American entry into World War II, a larger Bush differential analyzer was constructed by the Moore School of Electrical Engineering, with the cooperation of Aberdeen Proving Ground. This collaboration not only gave the army the capability to perform needed wartime ballistics calculations, it also established the links of cooperation that resulted in the creation of ENIAC.

Preelectronic Calculating Devices

The first person to envision what is now described as a card-programmed general-purpose automatic calculator was Charles Babbage (1835). Although never completed, Babbage's analytic engine, as conceived, was surprisingly similar to the modern computer. It contained a memory ("store") in which numbers were stored; an arithmetic unit ("mill") that performed all four arithmetic operations; punched card data and program input; and a punched card or printed output. With hindsight, it is easy to look at a Jacquard loom and see how naturally Babbage's ideas evolved. Nevertheless, it is almost a century after Babbage's analytic engine before major thrusts in the direction of increasing man's computational ability through the use of physical devices are seen. In addition to Bush's work, two independent activities stood out in the latter half of the 1930's: the work of Howard Aiken at Harvard University and that of George Stibitz at the Bell Telephone Laboratories. Not only was their work independent and highly original, but both took full advantage of the then available technology. To both men, reliability and accuracy were important; and these criteria were reflected in their accomplishments.

Although never completed, Charles Babbage's analytic engine, as conceived in the 1830's, was surprisingly similar to the modern computer.

Related Technical Developments

Before discussing digital computation, it is necessary to digress for a moment to the developing technology of the first half of the 20th century. The development of high-speed computers required electronic means of storing information ("flip-flops"), electronic means of controlling the flow of information ("gates"), and electronic amplification—as well as the ability to accept input from users and to provide readable output. The electronic flip-flop was developed by W. H. Eccles and F. W. Jordan in 1919. The development of radar, first in England and later in the United States during World War II, made available the necessary pulse technology and electronic switching elements. Relay technology had achieved a high level of reliability, primarily in the telephone industry. In addition, punched cards for handling data, as well as teletype and electric typewriters, became available for output as well as input. The 1930's also saw the beginnings of a systematical formulation by Harold Hazen, of the Massachusetts Institute of Technology, of control theory, or the theory of servomechanisms. A servomechanism is any device that guides or controls other apparatus, and Hazen recognized that the variety of processes involved could be reduced to a set of fundamental principles independent of any particular process. Thus, by 1940, most of the required elements were present to make the building of an electronic computer feasible. What was lacking, primarily, was pressure from the scientific and commercial communities for improving the data-processing and information capability of computers.

Digital Computers: The Beginning

Digital computation is essentially descended from the abacus, which itself is a mechanical extension of counting by the use of one's fingers. Digital devices are discrete because they recognize only discrete values such as zero, one, and two and can represent these discrete values in the form of physical objects like the teeth of a gear or the on-off states of a circuit.

The first large-scale digital computer that was actually operational was the Automatic Sequence Control Calculator (Mark I) at Harvard University. In 1937, Howard Aiken circulated a memorandum that gave a detailed description of the characteristics of a calculating device based on the then conventional punched card machines. In 1939, Harvard entered into a contract with the International Business Machines Corporation (IBM) to build this massive device; it was completed by IBM in 1944 and presented to Harvard, where it went into immediate operation on war-related calculations. The Mark I was built by IBM engineers C. D. Lake, B. M. Durfee, and F. E. Hamilton using available technology. Numerical data were introduced on punched paper tape, on punched cards, or by manually set dial switches. The computer had four tape readers, three for interpolation and one for sequence control. With the installation of Mark I and the establishment of the Harvard Computation Laboratory, Aiken and his staff were able to encourage people with a variety of interests to become exposed to an information-processing environment. After the war Aiken went on to build successively the Mark II (a relay machine), and the Marks III and IV, which were electronic.

George Stibitz's beginnings were much more modest than Aiken's. One evening at home in 1937, Stibitz constructed a simple relay device capable of adding two one-digit numbers. Whereas Aiken's first machine operated in the decimal system, Stibitz's research on relay calculation led him to operate in the binary mode. His first relay-calculating device was the Complex Calculator, completed in 1939. This machine, capable of performing the four arithmetic operations on complex numbers, was demonstrated at a meeting of the American Mathematical Society at Dartmouth College in August 1940, using a remote teletype terminal that was linked to the calculator in New York City. In 1939, Stibitz had proposed that a large-scale calculator be constructed, but his proposal was rejected. When the United States entered World War II, however, the proposal was realized with a succession of large-scale relay calculators (these were later named the Bell Models IV, V, and VI) built at Bell Laboratories for Aberdeen Proving Ground and Langley Field under Stibitz's guidance and employing the engineering of E. G. Andrews, Thornton Fry, and Sam Williams. These machines were characterized—like those of Aiken—by their high level of reliability and dependability. They could run for hours without attendance and still produce error-free results. This latter ability resulted from building in checking codes, failure-detection devices, and even error-detection codes.

There were other attempts to build calculating devices during this period. At Iowa State College, John Atanasoff, with the assistance of Clifford Berry, designed and built a portion of an electronic device to solve a system of twenty-eight simultaneous equations. When the war broke out, the input-output and decimal-binary convertors were incomplete and the machine was abandoned. At the National Cash Register Company (NCR), in 1940, Joseph Desch and his associates made their own thyrotron tubes for use in a machine that could perform addition, subtraction, and multiplication electronically. This machine was still working in the mid-1970's, but it appears to have had no impact on later developments. The same statement can probably hold for a pair of mechanical computational devices built by Konrad Zuse in Germany in 1936 and 1940, respectively, and a binary calculating device demonstrated by E. W. Phillips in 1936 at a meeting of the Institute of Actuaries in England. Despite the lack of direct impact of these events, they were indicative of a change in attitude about how computation is performed.

At least two other events in the 1930's had a critical ultimate impact on the development of computers. The first was the publication by Alan Turing in 1936 of his paper "On Computable Numbers . . . " (*Proceedings of the London Mathematical Society*, vol. 42), which introduced the concept of a theoretical machine that could do any calculation a human being is capable of performing. This theoretical machine is now commonly referred to as the Turing universal computer. The second was the publication in 1938 of Claude Shannon's paper, "A Symbolic Analysis of Relay and Switching Circuits" (*Transactions of the Institute of Electrical and Electronic Engineers*, vol. 57). Shannon's work showed how symbolic logic could be applied to the design of circuits.

The First Electronic Computer: ENIAC

Two themes stand out in connection with ENIAC that have been prevalent in the computer scene ever since—obsolescence and serendipity. The first is made obvious by the rapid development of computer technology, which almost guarantees the obsolescence of a computer by the time it is operative. The second is obvious too when one looks at the background leading up to the introduction of any new hardware or software. Both factors were at play in 1941, when John Mauchly joined the faculty of the Moore School of Engineering at the University of Pennsylvania after having been a professor of physics at Ursinus College. (It was at the Moore School that Mauchly met a young graduate student, J. Presper Eckert, an engineer who became his collaborator on ENIAC and remained a close associate for many years.) While at Ursinus, Mauchly had built a harmonic analyzer and experimented with other computational devices. When he joined the Moore School, he was involved in computational projects under the auspices of Aberdeen Proving Ground, and in August 1942 he submitted an informal memorandum outlining a high-speed electronic device to increase the calculating ability of their war-related effort. This memo was rejected and lost. (It was only rediscovered about 1969.)

In 1943, the original memo was reconstructed at the encouragement of Herman Goldstine, then a lieutenant in army ordnance, who had been assigned to assist in increasing the production of needed ballistics computations. On Apr. 9, 1943, with Mauchly and Eckert still writing a more detailed proposal, Goldstine presented the project for funding to a group at Aberdeen that included the mathematician Oswald Veblen and the director of the Ballistic Research Laboratory, Col. Leslie Simon. The project was approved and two years and a half million dollars later, in the fall of 1945, ENIAC (the first acronym of the computer age) was working on ballistics tables, atomic energy problems, and assorted mathematical problems.

The first electronic computer, ENIAC, at the University of Pennsylvania's Moore School of Electrical Engineering, in 1946. The two men in the foreground are the co-inventors, J. Presper Eckert and John Mauchly. (UPI/Corbis-Bettmann)

ENIAC was a massive machine (30 tons compared to Mark I's 5 tons) that occupied 1,800 square feet of floor and had about 18,000 vacuum tubes, 70,000 resistors, and 10,000 capacitors. Its speed was 1,000 times that of Mark I.

Before ENIAC was completed, Eckert and

Mauchly were already thinking ahead to the next machine. John von Neumann had established contact with the ENIAC project starting in mid-1944. This collaboration resulted in the issuance by von Neumann (June 30, 1945) of a draft report that contained the first logical design of an electronic computer in which the program could be stored and modified electronically. As described, EDVAC would take another quantum jump beyond ENIAC—it was to be what is now called an internally stored program, general-purpose computer.

The First Generation of Electronic Computers

The first generation of machines was plagued by many difficulties involving reliability and dependability, and the foremost problem was with the memory unit. ENIAC had a memory of only twenty words using the vacuum tube, which at the time of design was the only reliable high-speed storage device available. This limitation was overcome with Eckert's development of an acoustic delay-line memory. Mercury delay lines had been used to delay pulses in wartime radar equipment, and Eckert conceived of the idea of feeding the output of a delay line through an amplifier and pulse reshaper back into its input, thereby storing a large number of pulses in the circulating memory. This enabled the designers to think in terms of building a memory of, say, 512 or 1,024 words with only a few tubes, in contrast to the large tube requirement for ENIAC's small memory capacity. The first internally stored program computer, the EDSAC, was designed and built at Cambridge University by Maurice Wilkes. BINAC, a computer built by the Eckert-Mauchly Corporation (formed in the fall of 1946) for Northrop Aircraft Corporation, had its first successful run in Philadelphia sometime during 1949.

Two themes stand out in connection with ENIAC that have been prevalent in computer science ever since: obsolescence and serendipity.

Two other forms of memory commonly used by first-generation computers were electrostatic tubes and magnetic drums. The electrostatic-tube memory was developed in England by F. C. Williams of Manchester University. The Williams tube used a conventional television cathode-ray tube, in which information was stored in the form of charges on the inside surface of the tube. In the magnetic-drum memory, the information is recorded by magnetizing (or not magnetizing) fixed positions on a rotating cylinder that has been coated with magnetizable material.

Most of the computers conceived and developed in the decade after World War II were one-of-a-kind machines. Some were dead ends in terms of immediate impact, while others had clearly spawned offspring. All, however, had an important impact on the development of needed technology and confidence. One of the most prolific computers was the machine built at the Institute for Advanced Study (IAS) under the conceptual leadership of von Neumann, Goldstine, and Arthur Burks and under the engineering direction of Julian Bigelow. Its progeny included MANIAC, ILLIAC, JOHNNIAC, ORDVAC, AVIDAC, SILLIAC, and WEIZAC. Von Neumann originally planned to have the IAS machine use for its memory a selectron tube that was being developed by Jan Rajchmann at RCA. However, when the selectron tube failed to perform properly in time, a Williams tube memory was installed.

Another major computer of this period was Whirlwind, built at the Massachusetts Institute of Technology. The Whirlwind project began in 1944 when Gordon Brown was asked to build an aircraft simulator for the navy in his M.I.T. Servomechanism Laboratory. The original plan was to build an analog device. The real-time simulation required, however, proved to be too slow; and in 1946, under the leadership of Jay Forrester, the project evolved into a design for what eventually became the digital computer Whirlwind I, which went into operation in about 1951. While on the Whirlwind project Forrester developed the first effective magnetic-core memory. With this development, memory went from being the most unreliable element of a computer to the most reliable. Among its other major accomplishments, the Whirlwind computer was the first to operate in real time. This led to its becoming the prototype of the SAGE Air Defense system, which became fully operational in 1958.

With the delivery of UNIVAC I in 1951 to the Bureau of the Census by the Eckert-Mauchly Corporation, computers lost their individual uniqueness. They also began to be recognized as having a variety of practical applications in addition to scientific and military uses. IBM's entry into the electronic digital computer field came with the development, beginning in 1951, of the Defense Calculator. Delivery, under the series number 701, occurred in 1953. Nineteen IBM 701's were built, the majority for use in the aircraft industry on the West Coast. Other milestones of this era include the developmental work at the National Bureau of Standards (SEAC and SWAC) and the construction of computers such as Raytheon Corporation's RAYDAC, the Bendix G-15, Librascope's LGP-30, the IBM 650, the Burroughs 220, and a number of computers built in England (Pilot Ace, MADM, LEO, EDSAC).

The American Federation of Information Processing Societies estimates that if one defines computer power as the number of additions that all computers installed in the United States could perform in one second, between 1955 and 1960 that power had increased 20 times, and between 1960 and 1965 it increased 800 times. In the 1970's, the proliferation of computational devices makes that figure impossible even to estimate.

The years 1955–65 saw a number of new accomplishments. One of the most significant was the development of computer languages. The first of these was FORTRAN, developed by a team headed by John Backus at IBM. In 1959 the first automated computerized process control system was installed (at Texaco's Port Arthur refinery); the banking industry adopted MICR (Magnetic Ink Character Recognition); and transistors began to replace vacuum tubes. By 1964, a new generation of machines utilizing integrated circuits had come on the scene. Then came miniaturized circuits, which can contain approximately 1,500 elements on chips an eighth of an inch square. The 1960's saw a dramatic reduction in the cost of calculation; they also saw an equally rapid rise in the productivity of programs and ease of use.

As in the first-generation machines, electronic information processing devices of the mid-1970's were still largely limited in performance by the speed, capacity, and reliability of their memory registers. The fastest and most flexible memory systems consist of either tiny ring-shaped ferrite cores strung on a mesh of fine wires or transistor circuits laid down on tiny silicon chips. Despite these dramatic technological breakthroughs, a good deal of research is currently going on in an attempt to improve these factors and at the same time reduce both cost and size. One promising area of research revolves around what are called magnetic bubbles (actually, a cylindrical magnetic domain embedded in a thin magnetic film of opposite polarity).

BIBLIOGRAPHY

Charles Eames and Ray Eames, *A Computer Perspective.*

Herman H. Goldstine, *The Computer: From Pascal to von Neumann.*

Brian Randell, ed., *The Origin of the Digital Computers. Selected Works.*

— HENRY S. TROPP

COMSTOCK LODE

Comstock Lode, one of the richest deposits of precious ores ever discovered, located in Virginia City, Nev. From its discovery in 1859 to its decline in 1879, it held the spotlight of the world. During this period more than $500 million in silver and gold were taken from these mines.

Great hoisting machines, giant pumps, heavy stamps, drills, cables, and hundreds of other things were manufactured to mine this ore. To drain hot water from underground reservoirs, Adolph Sutro completed a five-mile tunnel from the floor of the Carson River to the Comstock mines in 1878. To extract the silver from the rock, the old Mexican patio method was first used; later, the amalgamating process was employed for the reduction of the ore.

Water for the 40,000 inhabitants of Virginia City and vicinity was brought from Marlette, an artificial lake, thirty miles away in the Sierra Nevada Mountains, through pipes, tunnels, flumes, and a large inverted siphon. The pipe and siphon were made, piece by piece, in San Francisco, to fit around mountains, to cross Washoe Valley, and to extend up the Virginia Mountains.

The discovery of the Big Bonanza in the California Consolidated Mine, 1873, made multimillionaires of John W. Mackay, James G. Fair, James C. Flood, William S. O'Brien, William Sharon, and William C. Ralston.

San Francisco was the residuary legatee of the Comstock wealth. With this money palatial homes were built, and the San Francisco Stock Exchange, banks, and dozens of other businesses were established.

BIBLIOGRAPHY

Eliot Lord, *Comstock Mining and Miners.*

George D. Lyman, *The Saga of Comstock Lode.*

— EFFIE MONA MACK

CONFISCATION ACTS

Confiscation Acts (1861–64). During the Civil War the Confederate and Union governments punished the opposing civilian and military populations by confiscations of private property. The federal law of Aug. 6, 1861, authorized Union seizure and condemnation through federal courts of property put to hostile use, and declared forfeited all claims to the labor of slaves who bore arms or worked in military or naval service with permission of Confederate masters. When generals John Frémont and David Hunter exceeded this statute and proclaimed emancipation, President Abraham Lincoln repudiated their action. The second act, of July 17, 1862, embodied their principles in modified form. It also designated local, state, and Confederate officials, both civil and military, as classes of citizens whose property was subject to seizure. Other individuals aiding the

South were given sixty days in which to reassume their allegiance. The Confederate Congress had retaliated on Aug. 30, 1861, by providing for the sequestration of property and credits of Union adherents. The federal Captured and Abandoned Property acts of Mar. 12, 1863, and July 2, 1864, were, in principle, confiscatory, although the proceeds from seizure were recoverable within two years after the cessation of war. Property was defined as abandoned when the owner was absent and aiding the southern cause. The amount of abandoned land controlled, both during and after the war, comprised less than one-five-hundredth of southern territory. Cotton formed about 95 percent of the possessions seized under the Captured Property acts; and this seizure acted as a retarding factor in southern economic reconstruction.

BIBLIOGRAPHY

J. G. Randall, *Constitutional Problems Under Lincoln.*

— JOHN C. ENGELSMAN

CONGRESS, UNITED STATES

The U.S. Congress is a unique institution, one deliberately conceived by the makers of the Constitution to achieve maximum individual liberty in conjunction with social order. In its deliberations the 1787 Constitutional Convention first chose to argue the form of the legislative branch: Article I of the Constitution thus deals with the legislature. The formulation of this article presented more difficulties for the drafters than all other parts of the document together. The basis for representation in the legislative branch in particular caused prolonged and angry debate, primarily between the large and small states. The convention was saved from collapse by the Connecticut, or "Great," Compromise, which proposed a Congress of two houses—a Senate in which each state would have equal representation regardless of population and a House of Representatives in which states would be represented according to population.

The Constitution created a legislative branch coequal in stature and authority with the executive and judicial branches; its powers, and limits thereon, were spelled out in writing. The distinct division of power between the three branches—designed to enhance individual freedom—insured friction, particularly between the legislative and executive branches. Clashes between Congress and the president began in George Washington's administration and are foreordained for the future. Operations of Congress in modern times are shaped not only by the Constitution but also by custom and by an ever-growing body of precedents in both House and Senate. Most important, perhaps, are precedents set by the First and Second congresses (1789–93), which are ranked as second only to the Constitutional Convention among influences shaping modern American government.

Functions and Powers

One can view the basic functions of Congress as follows: (1) Through the passage of bills that become law, Congress determines national policies to be carried out by the executive branch. (2) Congress raises and appropriates the money required for the executive branch to carry out these policies. (3) Congress has the duty, as well as the authority, to oversee the executive branch to determine whether such national policies are being carried out, and whether such appropriations are being spent in accordance with congressional intent. (4) Through investigations, public hearings and reports, debates on the floor, public speeches, newsletters, press conferences, and other methods, congressmen perform a vital educational function, enhancing public understanding of a wide variety of national issues. (5) By serving as the bridge between the individual citizen and an enormous federal bureaucracy, congressmen perform an attorney or "errand boy" function, seeking to bring justice out of conflicts between citizens and their government. (6) Congress is a great national forum—the one arena in which 535 freely elected representatives of more than 200 million Americans, mirroring an enormous variety of economic, political, ethnic, and social interests, can seek solutions, however temporary, to the great passionate issues that often divide the nation.

The powers of Congress are defined in the Constitution, but phrases such as "provide for the common Defence and general Welfare" have received such broadening judicial interpretations that congressional power has expanded steadily since the First Congress. The basic powers are to tax, spend, and borrow; to regulate foreign and interstate commerce; to maintain a defense establishment; to declare war; to admit new states; and to propose constitutional amendments. Congress also has an almost unlimited power of investigation to obtain information on which to base future legislation or to expose alleged wrongdoing. The Constitution also limits congressional power: it may not tax exports, grant titles of nobility, or pass ex post facto laws. The Bill of Rights prohibits Congress from abridging freedom of speech, the press, the free exercise of religion, the right of peaceful assembly, the right of petition, and other freedoms.

Since it has the constitutional power to ratify treaties and confirm cabinet and ambassadorial nominees, the Senate jealously regards itself as the president's chief foreign policy adviser. Not all presidents have agreed to such a role for the Senate. The imprecise division of powers between Congress and the president in the field of foreign policy and in the making of war is a source of frequent friction. The Constitution provides that "Congress shall have Power . . . To Declare War," but presidents frequently have involved American troops in foreign military undertakings without congressional consent, including two major wars in the 20th century. Since World War II, the foreign policy role of the House, previously modest, has increased because foreign undertakings usually require money, and on appropriations the House has power equal to the Senate.

Congress has other nonlegislative powers in connection with the presidency. If no candidate receives a majority of the electoral votes, the House of Representatives determines the president and the Senate determines the vice-president. If the vice-presidency becomes vacant, the House and Senate both must confirm the president's nominee to fill the vacancy. In the case of presidential disability, Congress has grave, complicated duties under the Twenty-fifth Amendment, including in certain circumstances the decision as to who shall discharge the powers and duties of the presidency. Finally, Congress alone has the power to impeach and remove from office the president and all federal civil officers.

Membership

Congress has grown with the nation. The First Congress (1789–91) consisted of 26 senators and 65 representatives; the Ninety-fourth (1975–77) had 100 senators and 435 representatives. The Constitution provides that representation in the House be kept up-to-date through a federal census every ten years. Sentiment is strong against enlargement of the House in the future; many believe that even 435 members (the number fixed by Congress since 1929) makes the House unwieldy.

States originally had a free hand in drawing congressional district boundaries, but as gross inequities in representation arose, particularly between over-represented rural areas and underrepresented urban areas, the Supreme Court in a landmark decision, *Wesberry* v. *Sanders* (1964), laid down the one man, one vote doctrine, ruling that congressional districts must be substantially equal in population. Regardless of its population, each state is guaranteed one House member by the Constitution. Senate vacancies are filled by governors or at special elections according to state laws, but no House member may ever be appointed—vacancies can be filled only by special elections.

Representatives have two-year terms; senators, six. All House members thus face reelection every two years. Minimum age for House members is twenty-five; for senators, thirty. All must be citizens, and at the time of election must reside in the state from which elected.

The Constitution provides that members "shall, in all Cases except Treason, Felony and Breach of the Peace, be privileged from Arrest during their Attendance at the Session of the respective Houses, and in going to and returning from the same." Maximum freedom of debate is encouraged by the constitutional provision that "for any Speech or Debate in either House, they shall not be questioned in any other Place," which generally bars libel and criminal suits.

All expenses of Congress are paid from the federal treasury. Members of the First Congress were paid $6 per day; those in the Ninety-fourth Congress, $42,500 a year. Members receive free office space in Washington and in their home district; large staffs; allowances for mail, travel, telephone, and office supplies; valuable retirement and insurance benefits; and other financial assistance. For decades service in Congress was a part-time occupation. Salaries were small; Washington housing was scarce; members had to have an outside income; and federal activities were limited. The First Congress received 268 proposals; the Seventy-eighth Congress (1943–45), 7,845; and the Ninety-first (1969–71), 29,040. By the 1960's Congress had become a demanding year-round occupation.

Rules and Procedures

Under the Constitution, the Congress must meet every January; the president may call special sessions of either body. In contrast to royal tradition, the president cannot prevent Congress from meeting or dismiss it except when the two houses cannot agree on an adjournment date. The Constitution provides also that the vice-president shall preside over the Senate without a vote except in case of a tie. The House chooses its own presiding officer, the speaker of the House, from its membership. The role and power of the speaker of the House and of party leaders are particularly crucial, for their constant unofficial communication and bargaining lie at the very heart of the complex congressional operation.

Both houses have great power over their internal operations and procedures and disciplining of members. Each judges its members' qualifications; decides election contests; and, by a two-thirds vote, may expel members. Any member may introduce a bill or resolution on any subject, except that all bills for raising revenue must originate in the House—but may be amended freely by the Senate.

The House and Senate must keep—and make public—a journal of their proceedings except for secret matters. Recent procedural reforms have made voting, both on the floor and in committee, more a matter of public record than before. Of great historical importance is the *Congressional Record*, a relatively verbatim account of debate with much additional material. It remains the most reliable contemporary mirror of the American nation.

Over the past century the Democratic and Republican parties have developed elaborate extralegal machinery to improve the legislative process in both the House and Senate. Majority and minority leaders and whips and a battery of regional whips (in the House), plus paid staffs and offices, go unmentioned in the formal rules, but they are indispensable in making Congress operate. Although not created by law, this party machinery is financed out of the federal treasury.

Committee System

"Congress in session is Congress on public exhibition, whilst Congress in its committee rooms is Congress at work," wrote Woodrow Wilson. Not envisioned by the makers of the Constitution, the committee system, evolved through trial and error, is still evolving; old committees are abolished or consolidated and new ones created as new problems arise. The committees have specific, written jurisdictions. Working usually through hundreds of subcommittees, committees choose which bills to consider and which to ignore; they amend, rewrite, kill, or recommend passage for bills—with or without public hearings. They dominate investigations of any subject within their jurisdiction.

The House committee system is more powerful than that of the Senate. Great in size, the House performs most technical work through committees; committee recommendations have an excellent chance of being adopted by the entire House, usually without major amendments. The smaller Senate, with historic pride in its freedom of debate, more often makes major changes in committee recommendations. But in both houses, committees, subcommittees, and their chairmen usually exercise extraordinary power over legislation within their jurisdiction.

Since 1789 committee vacancies have been filled in various ways—sometimes through election by the entire chamber, more often through appointment by the presiding officers. Eventually the parties developed devices such as caucuses and committees on committees to make these choices. Thus the seniority system came into being; in essence, a member, once appointed to a committee, moving up the ladder in power and seniority as members with more committee service leave. The seniority system became highly controversial in the mid-20th century, its critics insisting that it gave disproportionate power to elderly, ultraconservative members, usually those from the South.

House and Senate

One of the most notable differences in House and Senate operating methods is debate. For decades senators regarded themselves as ambassadors from their sovereign states and therefore answerable to no one save their states. This created the tradition of unlimited debate, still very strong. As it rapidly grew in numbers, the House soon found it necessary to put rigid limits on the length and privileges of debate.

Senators normally hold membership on far more committees and subcommittees than House members, thus necessitating larger staffs. Because it is smaller and its proceedings are easier to follow, the Senate receives more attention from the media than the House, and senators find it easier to gain national attention. Thus senators are often mentioned as presidential contenders; House members seldom are.

Despite frequent references to the Senate as the upper house, the Constitution clearly created two equal, coordinate bodies, neither superior to the other. No bill can be sent to the president until it passes both houses in identical form: neither house can adjourn for more than three days without permission of the other; and senators and representatives receive identical salaries.

Congress has lived under constant criticisms as being unrepresentative, incapable of meeting national challenges, lacking in expertise, too responsive to greedy pressure groups, and lax in morality. As an institution its popularity has never been great. Yet few members are defeated for reelection. While voters may damn Congress as an institution, they register high approval of their own congressional representative.

For almost two centuries Congress has shaped laws to govern a nation growing from 4 million to more than 200 million people as it expanded from a narrow Atlantic beachhead to world primacy, from an era of frontier simplicity to one of scientific, sociological, and technological revolution. Legislative bodies of almost every major nation have undergone drastic, often violent, changes during this same period; the U.S. Congress has been modified by only two major alterations: the direct election of senators (Seventeenth Amendment) and the court-ordered correction of apportionment injustices (1964).

By common scholarly judgment, the U.S. Congress is the most powerful legislative body in the world.

BIBLIOGRAPHY

Charles L. Clapp, *The Congressman: His Work as He Sees It.*

Congressional Quarterly, *Guide to the Congress of the United States.*

Richard F. Fenno, Jr., *Congressmen in Committees.*
Richard F. Fenno, Jr., *The Power of the Purse.*
George Goodwin, Jr., *The Little Legislatures: Committees of Congress.*
George H. Haynes, *The Senate of the United States.*
Stephen Horn, *Unused Power: The Work of the Senate Committee on Appropriations.*
Charles O. Jones, *Minority Party Leadership in Congress.*
Neil MacNeil, *Forge of Democracy: The House of Representatives.*
John F. Manley, *The Politics of Finance: The House Committee on Ways and Means.*
Floyd M. Riddick, *The United States Congress: Organization and Procedure.*
Randall B. Ripley, *Congress—Process and Policy.*
Randall B. Ripley, *Majority Party Leadership in Congress.*
Donald G. Tacheron and Morris K. Udall, *The Job of a Congressman: An Introduction to Service in the House of Representatives.*

— D. B. HARDEMAN

CONGRESS SINCE THE 1970S

United States Congress, an institution of many contradictions, seeks to balance local interests with national needs. While members work for consensus legislation, their success depends as much upon maintaining their relations with voters in their districts and states as upon accomplishments in Washington. The conflicting demands of lawmaking and representation have resulted in a low public opinion of the legislative branch as a whole, but a high reelection rate of individual members. In addition, Congress has grown to be a large body—100 senators, 435 representatives, and five delegates—divided not only between the Senate and House of Representatives, but by parties and by factions within the parties. The divisions make it difficult for Congress to operate swiftly or efficiently, often creating gridlock.

Post-Watergate Reforms

Public approval of Congress rose in the wake of the Vietnam War and the Watergate scandal. Congress reasserted its authority against presidential power and instituted reforms to democratize its own operations. In 1973, over President Richard M. Nixon's veto, it passed the War Powers Resolution, requiring presidents to notify Congress whenever troops were sent into combat and to seek congressional approval to keep troops in combat for protracted periods. In 1974 Congress enacted the Congressional Budget and Impoundment Control Act, to prevent presidents from impounding (not spending) appropriations and to gain greater legislative control over the federal budget.

Congress established internal reforms to democratize and streamline its proceedings, although some observers believed these reforms fragmented leadership and weakened Congress as a body. After Watergate, a large group of younger, more liberal members was elected. They pressed reforms to curtail committee chairmen, who lost authority to hire staff, appoint subcommittees, and determine agendas. A proliferation of subcommittees gave their chairs and ranking members independent budgets and authority to hire and direct staff, and a forum for attracting public attention and promoting legislation.

Liberal Democrats in the House worked through their party caucus, rather than attempting to change rules on the House floor, where conservative Democrats and Republicans could vote together. Caucus reforms established secret-ballot elections of committee chairs at the beginning of each Congress. Committee chairs had to respond to sentiments within the caucus or face being deposed. The House Democratic Caucus removed elderly chairmen and elevated younger members. The Speaker of the House gained power to appoint the House Rules Committee, which schedules bills and sets rules under which they will be debated and voted upon. Through the Democratic Steering Committee the Speaker gained authority over committee assignments previously exercised by the Ways and Means Committee. Despite augmented powers, Democratic Speakers acted as party facilitators, seeking to promote the majority's legislative agenda rather than dominate House proceedings.

While members of Congress work for consensus legislation, their success depends as much on maintaining ties with voters "back home" as upon accomplishments in Washington.

Senate party conferences adopted similar rules, but refrained from actions that might dismantle the seniority system. (Republican Speaker Newt Gingrich, who took the post in 1994, employed the powers of the office more aggressively.) In 1977 the Senate reorganized its committee structure; abolished most joint, select, and special committees; and cut the numbers of standing committees. Jurisdictional lines between committees were clarified, and senators were limited in the number of committees and subcommittees on which they could serve. The House adopted a less sweeping committee reorganization in 1979. "Sunshine" reforms adopted in the 1970s opened most congressional committee hearings to the public, including sessions in which bills are "marked up" before being reported to the floor. Open sessions were intended to make members more accountable, but attendance of lobbyists at mark-up sessions made it harder for members to make concessions necessary to reach compromise.

The staffs of Congress became larger than those of any other national legislature. During the 1970s House and Senate committee staffs more than doubled. The personal staffs of members increased, particularly those working in members' home states. Growth in staff reflected the need to handle increasingly complex legislation, as well as congressional distrust of the executive branch as a source of information. Staff members won recognition as experts in policy analysis, causing critics to charge that large staffs complicated the legislative process, generating too many bills and amendments and giving too much power to "unelected representatives." By the 1990s the size of staffs stabilized because of government retrenchment, widespread use of computers, and limited office space. In 1995 Republican majorities further reduced the size of committee staffs.

Post-Watergate congressional reforms produced a more decentralized institution. Diffusion of power shifted lawmaking from committee rooms to the House and Senate chambers through a virtual explosion in floor amendments. The congressional workload (numbers of bills, hearings, hours in session, and votes) expanded. After reaching a peak in the 1970s, the workload declined as Congress passed longer and more complex bills. The trend toward consolidation helped move legislation, but longer bills reflected a tendency to micromanage the executive branch in far greater detail—a further reflection of distrust between Congress and the White House.

Congress and the Presidents

After several presidents had seized the initiative in policymaking and raised fears of an "imperial presidency," Congress attempted to restore its constitutional authority in both foreign and domestic matters. As a reaction to having written the president a blank check with passage of the Gulf of Tonkin Resolution in 1964, which may have led the nation into the Vietnam War, Congress moved away from bipartisan support for cold war foreign policy. Passage of the War Powers Resolution of 1973 was followed by increased congressional supervision of U.S. intelligence. During the 1980s Congress passed legislation to prevent intervention against the left-wing government of Nicaragua. To circumvent this proscription, high-level members of President Ronald Reagan's administration (1981–1989) attempted to underwrite the Nicaraguan Contra rebel forces with proceeds from arms sales to Iran. The administration's actions led to a congressional investigation and the Iran-Contra scandal in 1986. Congress did not, however, invoke the War Powers Act during the Persian Gulf War of 1990–1991, giving President George Bush a free hand to send troops into combat in the Middle East.

Congress intensified its oversight of the executive branch through the legislative veto, a statutory arrangement by which a presidential action would stand unless either the House or Senate voted against it. In 1983 the Supreme Court, in *Immigration and Naturalization Service* v. *Chadha*, found the legislative veto unconstitutional, a violation of the doctrine of separation of powers. This ruling affected more than 200 statutes containing legislative-veto provisions enacted over fifty years, on issues ranging from consumer matters to war powers. In 1985 the Supreme Court specifically voided the impoundment control provision of the 1974 act, but Congress continued to employ its appropriation power to inquire into the affairs of the executive branch by investigating, by requesting studies from the General Accounting Office, and by using data from its own budget office to counter budgets submitted by the executive branch.

Presidential nominations encountered mounting resistance from the Senate. In 1987 the Senate rejected President Reagan's nomination of Robert Bork to the Supreme Court, believing him too ideological. In 1989 former Senator John Tower was rejected as secretary of defense when doubt surfaced regarding his personal character. Despite a Democratic majority, in 1993–1994, President Bill Clinton's nominees encountered many delays, and he was forced to withdraw several nominations.

In reaction to having written the president a blank check with the Gulf of Tonkin Resolution in 1964—widely viewed as the U.S.'s ticket into the Vietnam War—Congress retreated from bipartisan support for Cold War foreign policy.

Periods of divided government, when the White House was held by Republicans and when Democrats retained majorities in Congress, brought legislative gridlock. While the rules of the House favor the majority, in the Senate political and ideological minorities made use of filibusters to block or modify legislation. Even though the numbers of senators needed to invoke cloture were reduced from two-thirds to three-fifths in 1975, filibusters increased, and those resorting to filibusters devised such tactics as the post-cloture filibuster, in which opponents of a bill proposed amendments that had to be debated after cloture was adopted. Although President Gerald R. Ford (1974–1977) vetoed much legislation, Democratic majorities in Congress regularly overrode his vetoes. By contrast, when the Republican minority in the Senate voted together, President Bush (1989–1993) had assurance that his party could block any vote to override his vetoes. Gridlock on such occasions proved highly unpopular and contributed to the defeat of both Ford and Bush, as well as to public dissatisfaction with Congress. Another form of gridlock occurs when liberal or conservative members of Congress break party ranks and vote together.

Party Politics

In 1955 the House of Representatives entered the longest period of one-party majority in its history. Democrats retained control for forty-one years despite election of Republican presidents. By contrast, majorities in the Senate shifted when Republicans won control in 1980 and lost it in 1986. As for factionalism that crossed party lines, in the 1970s only one-third of all roll call votes produced straight party divisions. By the 1980s they sometimes accounted for nearly two-thirds. Party unity became notable on roll call votes, fostered in the House by introduction of electronic voting in 1973. Divided government accounted for much of the partisanship, but even during the administrations of Presidents Jimmy Carter (1977–1981) and Clinton (1993–1997), congressional Democrats—after years of opposing Republican presidents—were not about to follow presidents of their own party. When President Reagan enacted his program of tax reductions and increased defense spending, he had the support of a Republican majority in the Senate as well as bipartisan conservative support in the House. Faced with Democratic majorities, President Bush won the lowest percentage of roll call votes on measures he endorsed of any first-term president in modern times.

During the Reagan and Bush administrations, conservatives charged that Congress had departed from its constitutionally prescribed path. Through the perquisites of office and the advantage of incumbents in raising campaign funds, members enjoyed an unusually high rate of reelection. In particular, campaign financing reforms of the 1970s led to uncontrolled spending by political action committees (PACs) in the 1980s and 1990s—usually on behalf of incumbents. Despite odds favoring incumbents, both houses have seen an increasing diversity of membership since the 1970s, with election of more women, African Americans, Hispanic Americans, and Asian Americans, in addition to conversion of the South from solidly Democratic to two-party competition. Critics also blamed pork barrel budgeting—projects that would benefit members' constituents—for higher federal deficits and taxes. They proposed constitutional amendments to curb the "imperial Congress," including a balanced-budget amendment and a line-item veto—by which the president could veto portions of a bill without voiding the entire piece of legislation. Opponents objected that these measures would transfer the power of the purse from Congress to the president. In 1995 Congress enacted an accountability measure that subjected Congress to the same laws—particularly for employee protection—that applied to private enterprise.

Congressional Scandals

A series of scandals plagued Congress in the post-Watergate era. During the 1970s an influence-peddling scandal known as Korea-gate accused prominent members of the House of taking expensive gifts from a Korean lobbyist. In the so-called Abscam sting of the 1980s, a Federal Bureau of Investigation agent dressed as an Arab lobbyist offered bribes in return for votes and influence in Congress, leading to the indictment and resignation of a senator and several representatives. Five senators accused of attempting to influence an executive agency on behalf of an unscrupulous savings and loan executive, Charles Keating, were tagged the Keating Five. In 1989 House Speaker Jim Wright resigned over accusations that he had violated House ethics rules. An investigation of the House post office led to indictments, including, in 1994, the powerful chairman of the Ways and Means Committee, Dan Rostenkowski. Exposure of habitual check bouncing in the House bank caused a record number of members of Congress to retire from office rather than face defeat. Television broadcasts exposed junkets abroad and other benefits. Radio talk shows vented anger over salary raises. Polls showed a belief that members had lost touch with the people back home. Several states enacted term limits, seeking to restrict senators to two six-year terms and House members to six two-year terms. At the same time, large numbers of members of Congress chose not to run for reelection, causing a high turnover even without formal term limits. In 1992 the states revived and ratified the Twenty-seventh Amendment to the Constitution, which had been introduced 200 years before. It prevented congressional salary increases from taking effect until after the next election. In 1994 public dissatisfaction with Congress resulted in the election of Republican majorities in both the House and Senate.

Congress and the Media

Some of the greatest changes in Congress were associated with media coverage. Television covered Senate hearings as early as the 1940s, but cameras were not permitted into House hearings until the 1970s. In 1979 the House allowed televised floor proceedings, followed by the Senate in 1986. Proceedings were carried live nationally over the Cable Satellite Public Affairs Network (C-SPAN). Television promoted the careers of younger, attractive members who could master speaking in short, quotable "sound bites." It encouraged members to speak out on a range of issues, rather than concentrate on bills reported by their own committees. Congressional party organizations developed sophisticated means for members to provide audio and visual materials for the media in their home states. Television, word processors, and electronic mail also increased congressional mail exponentially. Lobbyists, special interests, PACs, and the president could easily stimulate public reaction to congressional actions, increasing pressure on members. Media concentration on Congress's faults has further caused members to set themselves apart from the institution and run against it, complicating the ability of Congress to enact consensus legislation.

Media concentration on congressional faults has inspired members to campaign against the institution to which they seek reelection—further weakening Congress's ability to enact consensus legislation.

[See also Congressional Caucuses; Corruption, Political; Democratic Party; Iran-Contra Affair; Political Action Committees; Republican Party; War Powers Act; Watergate, Aftermath of.]

BIBLIOGRAPHY

Roger H. Davidson and Walter J. Oleszek, *Congress and Its Members,* 4th ed. (Washington, D.C., 1994).

Louis Fisher, *Constitutional Conflicts Between Congress and the President,* 3rd rev. ed. (Lawrence, Kans., 1991).

Walter J. Oleszek, *Congressional Procedures and the Policy Process,* 3rd ed. (Washington, D.C., 1989).

Norman J. Ornstein, Thomas E. Mann, and Michael J. Malbin, *Vital Statistics on Congress* (Washington, D.C., 1994).

Ronald M. Peters, Jr., *The American Speakership: The Office in Historical Perspective* (Baltimore, 1990).

Mark A. Peterson, *Legislating Together: The White House and Capitol Hill from Eisenhower to Reagan* (Cambridge, Mass., 1990).

James L. Sundquist, *The Decline and Resurgence of Congress* (Washington, D.C., 1981).

George F. Will, *Restoration: Congress, Term Limits, and the Recovery of Deliberative Democracy* (New York, 1992).

— DONALD A. RITCHIE

CONGRESSIONAL CAUCUSES

Congressional caucuses, informal groups of members of the U.S. House of Representatives. Although their history dates back to the late nineteenth century, congressional caucuses proliferated after World War II and have increased significantly in number since the early 1970s. Caucuses are created by groups of representatives who decide they have enough in common to meet and communicate regularly; they expire when members no longer find it in their interest to sustain them. The objectives of caucus members are to exercise influence in Congress, determine public policy, or simply share social and professional concerns. Members create caucuses because their constituents share common economic concerns (Steel Caucus, Textile Caucus, Arts Caucus); regional interests (Northeast-Midwest Coalition, Sunbelt Caucus); ethnic or racial ties (Hispanic Caucus, Black Caucus); ideological orientation (Conservative Opportunity Society, Main Street Forum, Progressive Caucus); or partisan and policy ties (Chowder and Marching Society, Wednesday Group, Democratic Study Group). One of the fastest growing of these groups was the Congressional Caucus for Women's Issues, which admitted men in 1981. Caucuses range in size from a dozen members to, in a few instances, more than 150. Caucuses vary as to whether they have a paid staff, a formal leadership structure, division of labor among members, and a formal communications network. The larger groups have all of these characteristics. Those that impose dues for paid staff are regulated by House rules.

[See also Congress, United States.]

BIBLIOGRAPHY

William Clay, *Just Permanent Interests: Black Americans in Congress, 1870–1992* (New York, 1992).

Irwin N. Gertzog, *Congressional Women: Their Recruitment, Integration, and Behavior* (Westport, Conn., 1995).

— IRWIN N. GERTZOG

CONQUISTADORES

Conquistadores (conquerors), the name properly given leaders of the Spanish conquest of the Americas—though their followers are also included in the term. Juan Ponce de León, in search of the fabled fountain of youth, had landed on the shores of Florida (1513) before the great Hernando Cortes took Mexico in 1519. Immediately thereafter, other *conquistadores* began exploring and subduing lands northward. Notable among them were Pánfilo de Narváez, whose shipwreck on the Texas coast (1528) resulted in the seven years' walk of Álvar Núñez Cabeza de Vaca, a survivor, across the continent to Sinaloa in western Mexico; Hernando de Soto, who in 1839, with 550 men, 200 horses, and a herd of hogs, marched north from Tampa Bay, reached Tennessee, wandered across Oklahoma and Arkansas, and was buried in the Mississippi River he had discovered before the wretched remnant of his men found succor in Mexico four years after their *entrada* began; Francisco Vásquez de Coronado, whose fantastic search (1540–42) for the mythical Seven Cities of Cibola took him into New Mexico, across the Staked Plains, and perhaps into Kansas; Antonio de Espejo, who, looking for a lake of gold, discovered rich ores in Arizona (1583); Juan de Oñate, who in 1598 began the settlement of New Mexico; and Alonso de León, who (1688) penetrated Texas to prevent French occupation of that territory and founded a colony. *Conquistadores* explored California thoroughly, seeking a passage to the Atlantic.

No plungers into unknown oceans ever surpassed the *conquistadores* in daring and intrepidity. Their explorations, generally well detailed in diaries and official reports, made known to the civilized world the fauna, flora, aboriginal tribes, and geography of much of America. Through their indomitability, Spanish architecture, land laws, language, folklore, and techniques in ranching, mining, and irrigation remain indelibly stamped on the great Southwest. Their horses gave the Plains Indians a new culture that was conveyed to the Anglo-Americans who rode these Indians down.

BIBLIOGRAPHY

H. E. Bolton, *Spanish Exploration in the Southwest.*

C. E. Chapman, *Colonial Hispanic America.*

C. F. Lummis, *Flowers of Our Lost Romance.*

— J. FRANK DOBIE

CONSCIENTIOUS OBJECTORS

Conscientious objectors, originally persons of various religious and social sects who opposed war as being contrary to the tenets of their faiths and creeds. Since the Civil War the U.S. government has broadened the definition to include persons objecting to participation in, and support of, all wars on moral and intellectual grounds. From the colonial wars onward, conscientious objectors have presented unique problems for governments during times of military crisis. As early as 1661 the colony of Massachusetts made provisions for exempting "nonresisters" from military service, and William Penn made similar allowances in 1701 for Quakers in Pennsylvania.

The American Revolution produced the first major conflicts between religious objectors (particularly Quakers, Mennonites, and Dunkards) and governmental demands for militia service. The Continental Congress of 1775 took a sympathetic position toward conscientious objectors in stating it "intended no Violence to their Consciencies." The Congress hoped that such persons would make noncombatant contributions to the struggle for independence. Patriotic fervor in Pennsylvania, Maryland, and Virginia did lead to passage of legislation discriminating against the major nonresistant religious sects by levying fines; and in some instances such believers were labeled Tory sympathizers. Nevertheless, the revolutionary governments usually treated conscientious objectors sympathetically.

The major peace churches maintained theological pacifistic stances after the revolutionary war, but problems of conscientious objection did not appear again until the Civil War. Although the Confederacy enacted conscription legislation in October 1862 that provided military exemptions to religious objectors who would furnish substitutes or pay a tax of $500, the South generally treated conscientious objectors as pro-Union sympathizers. The Union government was less hostile in its treatment of objectors. The first federal Conscription Act was passed in March 1863 and provided exemptions if an individual obtained a substitute or paid $300 to the War Department. No specific provisions were made for northern conscientious objectors until February 1864, when Congress provided noncombatant alternative service for religious objectors. A few Union military commanders failed to recognize the noncombatant status of Quakers, Mennonites, and others and severely harassed them. More representative of the Union attitude toward objectors was President Abraham Lincoln's opinion that "people who do not believe in war make poor soldiers" and should be left "at home where they will make their contributions better than they would with a gun."

The Vietnam War sparked the most dramatic confrontations in U.S. history between government demands for military service and citizens' objections to warfare.

World War I marked the initiation of new governmental policies for conscientious objectors by eliminating commutation and substitution provisions from the Selective Service Act of May 1917. Congress recognized the sanctity of conscience in not requiring objectors to bear arms, but President Woodrow Wilson was authorized to induct all draft-eligible objectors for noncombatant service. Almost 4,000 soldiers were inducted as conscientious objectors; many others refused noncombatant status and 450 objectors were court-martialed and sentenced to prison terms of up to 25 years. With the exception of those convicted for disloyalty, sedition, and dissemination of propaganda, President Wilson granted amnesty to all objectors by 1919. World War I introduced the concept in the United States that military service was "personal, universal, and absolute" for those liable to the draft, with provision allowing conscientious objectors alternative noncombatant military or civilian duties.

The United States experienced limited problems with objectors during World War II and the Korean conflict. Once again provisions were made for noncombatant status and the classification of objectors was broadened to include not only members of peace churches but also anyone basing his claim on religious principles. Claims made for objector status on social, political, and intellectual grounds were disallowed in federal courts (*United States* v. *Kauten*, 1943; *Berman* v. *United States*, 1946).

The Vietnam War in the 1960's became the seedbed for the most dramatic confrontations in the history of the United States between government demands for military service and citizens objecting to warfare. While traditional conscientious objectors took religious stands opposed to active participation, thousands of others objected to the war on moral grounds and refused military service by going to Canada and Europe; still others publicly burned draft cards as a symbol of protest.

[See also Amnesty.]

BIBLIOGRAPHY

Peter Brock, *Pacifism in the United States.*
Mulford Q. Sibley and Philip E. Jacob, *Conscription of Conscience.*
Edward N. Wright, *Conscientious Objectors in the Civil War.*

— ROGER G. DAVIS

CONSERVATION

Conservation has become increasingly more difficult to define formally because of oversimplification, limited focus, and conflicting interests and philosophies. Defined succinctly, conservation means the wise use of resources, which would include not only land, the basic resource, but also the people living on it. Other principal resources that need conserving are water, wildlife, and minerals. Historically, two different philosophies have evolved concerning conservation. One group of conservationists has promoted natural resource development or use, and another group has promoted preservation or nonuse.

During the 17th century several significant attempts were made in America to regulate the use of resources. In 1626 the Plymouth colony passed an ordinance regulating the cutting and sale of timber on colony lands. Newport, R.I., initiated an ordinance in 1639 that promoted deer hunting for only six months of the year. William Penn decreed in 1681 that one acre in five be left in forest on the lands that had been allotted to him and distributed to the settlers. In 1691 British government policy provided for the conservation of large trees that were to be used by its navy and merchant marine.

Conservation is the wise use of resources, including land (and the people living on it) as well as water, wildlife, and minerals.

The first Americans to focus attention on the man-nature relationship were the transcendentalist writers, especially Ralph Waldo Emerson and Henry David Thoreau. Their influence on both the ethical and aesthetic schools of conservation thought has been pervasive. Another influential writer was George Perkins Marsh, considered the principal forerunner of the modern conservationist in the United States. Marsh, who had observed man's relationship with nature in both Europe and the Middle East, contended that the abuses that were prevalent in those areas would soon prevail in America if some attempts were not made to study the relationship between man and nature. Writing in 1864, Marsh declared that man disrupts the fundamental harmony or balance of nature. This thesis has led to the eventual rise of the ecological approach to conservation.

Very little was done with respect to conservation by the U.S. government during the 18th century, and not until 1828 did another series of events concentrate on it. In that year President John Quincy Adams withdrew 30,000 acres of live-oak forests on Santa Rosa Peninsula, Fla., for later use in building navy ships. In 1849 the U.S. Department of the Interior was established, and Carl Schurz, secretary of the interior from 1877 to 1881, recommended the scientific care of forests and the establishment of federal forest reservations. The Forest Reserve Act was signed in 1891, permitting President Benjamin Harrison to set aside 13 million acres as forest reservations; and in the next administration, Grover Cleveland withdrew an additional 21 million acres and placed them in reserve. In 1872, Apr. 10 was designated as Arbor Day as a result of the efforts of J. Sterling Morton. Yosemite Valley, Calif., was reserved as a state park in 1864, the same year that Marsh published his *Man and Nature*. Yellowstone National Park was established in 1872, and Yosemite became a national park in 1891. Several societies and clubs emphasizing conservation were created during the latter half of the 19th century and early 20th century, beginning with the American Forestry Association in 1875, the Appalachian Mountain Club in 1876, the Sierra Club in 1892, and the National Audubon Society in 1905.

Conservation as a social movement was not initiated until the administration of Theodore Roosevelt, who was an active outdoorsman. Gifford Pinchot, a professional forester who was named head of the Division of Forestry in 1898, became the primary influence on Roosevelt. He chose the term "conservation" in 1907 to describe his program. Some of the lasting achievements of the Roosevelt-Pinchot era were the Reclamation Act of 1902, which fostered western development; the Antiquities Act of 1906, which set aside federal land for the preservation of natural monuments; the establishment of the Inland Waterways Commission in 1907; the White House Conference of 1908, called to discuss the status of U.S. resources; the establishment of the National Conservation Commission in 1908, appointed to inventory resources; and the North American Conservation Conference of 1909, where delegates from the United States, Canada, Mexico, and Newfoundland met to analyze resources of the three countries. Also during the Roosevelt administration 234 million acres of forest land were set aside for future use.

After Roosevelt left office few public conservation acts were passed until the 1930's, but more organizations emerged to increase interest in the use of resources. The American Game Protective and Propagation Association was founded in 1911, the Save-the-Redwoods League in 1918, and the Izaak Walton League in 1 922. Although legislation was limited, the National Park Service Act was passed in 1916; the Migratory Bird Treaty Act with Canada, which restricted hunting of migratory species, became law in 1918; and the Mineral Leasing Act, regulating mining on federal lands, and the Federal Water Power Act, giving the Federal Power Commission authority to issue licenses for hydropower development on public lands, were both passed in 1920.

The period 1933–39 has been called the "golden age of conservation." The primary conservation emphasis during the administration of Franklin D. Roosevelt was on land planning, with a special focus on soil-improvement programs. This period was also characterized by the passage of considerable legislation and the creation of numerous bureaus and agencies to examine the resource supply of the country, including people as one of the greatest resources. Some of the more far-reaching acts allowed for the establishment of the Soil Erosion Service, Civilian Conservation Corps, and Tennessee Valley Authority in 1933, and the Soil Conservation Service and the Resettlement Administration in 1935. With the outbreak of war in Europe, the nation's interest turned from the domestic scene to the international scene, and the conservation movement had to wait for the postwar era.

As the nation grew even more urbanized in the 1950's, private organizations increased their participation in the area of conservation. The Conservation Foundation and Resources for the Future, dating from 1948 and 1952, respectively, were particularly active in promoting conservation research and education. Mission 66, a ten-year improvement program for the National Park Service, was launched in 1956. Congress appointed the Outdoor Recreation Resources Review Commission in 1958 to study and report on the nation's future needs.

With the inauguration of John F. Kennedy as president, renewed attention was focused on conservation. One of his first acts in the realm of conservation was to request the National Academy of Sciences to evaluate the research that had been conducted concerning conservation and the development of America's natural resources. In the spirit of Theodore Roosevelt, President Kennedy called a White House conference on conservation in May 1962; 500 conservationists convened in Washington to draw up plans that would aid in facilitating the elimination of resource problems. The following year saw two significant achievements pertaining to conservation: the Clean Air Act, which appropriated federal funds for a cooperative attack on air pollution; and the establishment of the Bureau of Outdoor Recreation within the Department of the Interior to coordinate federal efforts in that area. President Lyndon B. Johnson and his wife, Lady Bird, continued the Kennedy emphasis on conservation. During his administration the Wilderness Act of 1964 was passed, establishing the National Wilderness Preservation System; a White House Conference on Natural Beauty was held in 1965; and the National Historic Preservation Act was passed in 1966. The interest in conservation of the Kennedy-Johnson years was translated in the 1970's into an interest in the actual and potential quality of life that is possible in the United States. The primary focus of the conservation movement became the issue of environmental quality. The National Environmental Policy Act of 1969 has been described as a "bill of rights" for the environment. It established the Council of Environmental Quality to oversee the nation's efforts in dealing with pollution and to make environmental policy recommendations to the president. The federal government has grouped its environmental efforts under the Environmental Protection Agency (EPA), which has proposed several national quality standards pursuant to the mandates of such legislation as the Clean Air Act of 1967 and the Water Quality Improvement Act of 1970. As attempts to resolve problems of environmental quality promote greater cooperation between the ecological and the economic-technological schools of thought, a greater general interest appears to be evolving in investigating and developing a general systems approach as a means of evaluating the entire complex of resources.

BIBLIOGRAPHY

Shirley Walter Allen and Justin Wilkinson Leonard, *Conserving Natural Resources: Principles and Practices in a Democracy.*

Roderick Nash, *The American Environment: Readings in the History of Conservation.*

Guy-Harold Smith, *Conservation of Natural Resources.*

Richard H. Wagner, *Environment and Man.*

— GEORGE CARNEY

CONSERVATISM

American conservatism, it is generally agreed, has not been as strong a force as American liberalism. Clinton Rossiter, historian of conservatism, has called it "the thankless persuasion." Yet there is undoubtedly a conservative tradition in American life and thought, one that since World War II has enjoyed a vigorous, self-conscious revival among many intellectuals.

Described as "the thankless persuasion," conservatism has never been as strong a force in American society as liberalism.

Although a colonial America that included slaveholders and Puritans was in part a conservative society, the American Revolution and the Declaration of Independence were plainly at odds with the standing order. Even so, the Constitution and organization of a strong national government under George Washington blunted the edge of this revolutionary radicalism. There was, it is true, little popular backing for Alexander Hamilton's notion of an American monarchy; but John Adams' concept of a balanced republic recognized the desirability of having a mixed type of government that combined elements of monarchy, aristocracy, and democracy. Conservative Federalists like Adams also took alarm in 1789 at the news of the French Revolution, and in England, Edmund Burke published his important *Reflections on the Revolution in France* (1790). Burke, who had sympathized with American protests against British rule, became a symbol of Anglo-American conservatism. But Burke's emphasis on the historic institutions of church and state and his opposition to the natural rights philosophy limited his appeal in the United States. Conservatism itself was hard pressed after Thomas Jefferson defeated the Federalists in 1800. John Marshall, chief justice of the Supreme Court, and the famous senatorial triumvirate of Henry Clay, John C. Calhoun, and Daniel Webster later furnished dramatic leadership for the conservative minority's hostility to Jacksonian democracy. But none of these statesmen was able to gain the presidency, and only Calhoun, who attacked majoritarian democracy in his defense of the slave system of the Old South, won recognition as an original political theorist.

After the Civil War certain values identified with the antebellum agrarian society of Jefferson and Jackson, such as democracy and individualism, were taken over by the Republican party and adapted to the needs of the rising business community. Conservatives also buttressed their individualistic economic philosophy with the evolutionary theories of Charles Darwin and Herbert Spencer, utilizing the concepts of natural selection and survival of the fittest to justify business leadership. William Graham Sumner, Spencer's foremost American disciple, vigorously opposed all state intervention. Few businessmen, however, were as consistent in their laissez-faire ideas as Sumner, and one may question too whether individuals as innovative as Andrew Carnegie or John D. Rockefeller were true conservatives. But both the Republican party and big business were indeed conservative in their resistance to social reforms and to government regulation of the economy.

In the early 20th century, modern mass society provoked a reconsideration of conservatism. The aristocratic philosophy that had characterized some of America's outstanding men of letters, including Irving Babbitt and Paul Elmer More, was made explicit in the 1920's by H L. Mencken, Albert Jay Nock, and such informal literary groups as the New Humanists and the Southern Agrarians. In national politics, however, Herbert Hoover's defeat in 1932 ended an era of generally conservative Republican control. Henceforth conservatives were forced to react defensively to the policies of Franklin D. Roosevelt and the New Deal.

Even the revival of the Republican party under President Dwight D. Eisenhower after World War II made no fundamental change in the New Deal pattern of social and economic planning. Conservative politics accordingly came to be identified with the military ethos, exemplified by Gen. Douglas MacArthur, or with such figures on the radical right as the Republican senator from Wisconsin Joseph R. McCarthy and the southern Democratic governor George C. Wallace of Alabama. An old-fashioned conservative type like Sen. Robert A. Taft was denied the Republican presidential nomination in 1948 and 1952, but Sen. Barry Goldwater, a right-wing laissez-faire Republican from Arizona, was chosen (and badly defeated) in 1964. Like Goldwater in politics, the writers who have played important roles in the post-World War II revival of a conservative philosophy—Peter Viereck, Russell Kirk, and William F. Buckley, Jr., for example—have been unable to attract widespread mass support.

By the 1960's the most interesting phenomenon in American conservatism was the ideological rapprochement between right-wing libertarians and those young radicals from the New Left who were really more anarchistic than socialistic. What united the components of this strange amalgam was its opposition to the modern big-business, big-government establishment forged by the cold war. The new libertarians also rejected the formal conservatism of the Richard M. Nixon administration.

By the 1960's the most interesting phenomenon in American conservatism was the ideological rapprochement between right-wing libertarians and New Left radicals who were really more anarchist than socialist.

Conservatism, it is clear, has seldom been a simple ideological persuasion. Even the Burkean's traditional opposition to sudden change has been contradicted by those unconventional conservatives who would restore a preindustrial society in America. Meanwhile, conservatives face the challenge of a world disrupted by modern space technology and the expanding range of human expectations. Conservatism in America, therefore, although still an important literary and philosophical credo, may be an anachronism in terms of its long-range political future and popular appeal.

BIBLIOGRAPHY

Allen Guttmann, *The Conservative Tradition in America.*
Ronald Lora, *Conservative Minds in America.*
Clinton Rossiter, *Conservatism in America.*

— ARTHUR A. EKIRCH, JR.

CONSTITUTION

Constitution, an American 44-gun frigate authorized by Congress on Mar. 27, 1794. It was designed by Joshua Humphreys, built in Edmund Hartt's shipyard, Boston, and launched Oct. 21, 1797. In the naval war with France it served as Commodore Silas Talbot's flagship, and in the Tripolitan War as the flagship of Commodore Edward Preble, participating in five different attacks on Tripoli from July 25 to Sept. 4, 1804. The *Constitution* was victorious in several notable single-ship engagements in the War of 1812. During the fight with the *Guerrière*, a seaman gave it the nickname "Old Ironsides" when, seeing a shot rebound from its hull, he shouted, "Huzza, her sides are made of iron." Ordered broken up in 1830 by the Department of the Navy, it was retained in deference to public opinion aroused by Oliver Wendell Holmes's poem "Old Ironsides." It was rebuilt in 1833, served as a training ship at Portsmouth, Va., from 1860 to 1865, was partially rebuilt in 1877 and again in 1925, and, except for one cruise, has been docked at the Boston navy yard since 1897.

BIBLIOGRAPHY

Ira N. Hollis, *The Frigate Constitution.*

— LOUIS H. BOLLANDER

CONSTITUTION OF THE UNITED STATES

The Constitution, which has served since 1789 as the basic frame of government of the republic of the United States, was the work of a constitutional convention that sat at Philadelphia from late May 1787 until mid-September of that year. The convention had been called into being as the culminating event of a lengthy campaign for constitutional reform staged by a number of nationalistic political leaders, above all James Madison and Alexander Hamilton, both of whom had long been convinced that the Articles of Confederation were hopelessly deficient as a frame of government. By 1786, the growing somnolence of the Confederation Congress, the manifest incompetence of the Confederation government in foreign affairs, and the obvious state of national bankruptcy, together with the sense of panic and dismay occasioned by Shays's Rebellion in Massachusetts, had at long last spurred the states into concerted action.

In the immediate background of the gathering at Philadelphia were the Alexandria and Annapolis conventions. In November 1785, delegates from Virginia and Maryland met in convention at Alexandria, Va., to reconcile certain boundary and commercial disputes between them. So successful was this meeting that the two states then issued a call to all the states for a convention to assemble at Annapolis in September 1786 to develop a common interstate commercial policy. In the immediate sense, the Annapolis convention was a failure, delegates from only five states putting in an appearance. But Madison and Hamilton seized upon the occasion to call for another and more comprehensive convention. The Virginia legislature thereupon issued an invitation of its own to its sister states to meet in convention in Philadelphia the following May. As one after another of the other states responded, the Confederation Congress reluctantly joined in the call.

Drafting the Constitution.

Twelve states in all sent delegates to the convention at Philadelphia. Rhode Island alone, then in the grip of a paper-money faction fearful of federal monetary reform, boycotted the meeting. In all, the twelve participating states appointed seventy-four delegates, of whom fifty-five actually put in an appearance. Of these, some fifteen or twenty men were responsible for virtually all of the convention's work; the contribution of the others was inconsequential.

Dominating the convention's proceedings from the beginning was a group of delegates intent upon the creation of a genuinely national government possessed of powers adequate to promote the security, financial stability, commercial prosperity, and general well-being of all of the states. Prominent among them were George Washington, whom the delegates chose as their presiding officer; James Madison, whose leadership in the convention would one day earn him the well-deserved title of "Father of the Constitution"; James Wilson, congressman and legal scholar from Pennsylvania; Gouverneur Morris, a brilliant and conservative aristocrat of New York background, also present as a Pennsylvania delegate; Rufus King, a highly respected veteran congressman from Massachusetts; and Charles Cotesworth Pinckney and John Rutledge of South Carolina, representatives of that state's rice-planter aristocracy. In the nationalist camp also were the aged, garrulous, but vastly prestigious Benjamin Franklin of Pennsylvania; the pretentious but somewhat lightweight Edmund Randolph of Virginia; and Alexander Hamilton, whose extremist beliefs in centralized aristocratic government together with his inability to control the states' rights majority in the New York delegation cast a shadow on his convention role.

The nationalists also could command on most occasions the support of a group of moderate delegates who accepted the necessity for strong central government but were willing to compromise substantially with the convention's states' rights bloc when that proved necessary. Prominent among these men were Elbridge Gerry of Massachusetts, Oliver Ellsworth and Roger Sherman of Connecticut, and Abraham Baldwin of Georgia.

A small, but significant, bloc of states' rights delegates was firmly opposed to the creation of a sovereign national government. Its leaders included William Paterson of New Jersey, the author of the New Jersey Plan; John Dickinson from Delaware; Gunning Bedford of Maryland; and John Lansing and Robert Yates of New York. These men recognized the necessity for constitutional reform but believed strongly that a confederation type of government ought to be retained and that by granting the Congress certain additional powers—above all the power to tax and to regulate commerce—the Articles of Confederation could be converted into an adequate frame of government.

Voting in the convention was by states, each state having one vote. On most occasions, the nationalist bloc controlled the votes of Massachusetts, Pennsylvania, Virginia, and the two Carolinas; on several critical decisions they proved able to muster the votes of Connecticut and Georgia as well. The states' rights party, by contrast, could count upon the votes of New York, New Jersey, Maryland, and Delaware, and occasionally Connecticut and Georgia. (New Hampshire was not yet represented in the convention.) Thus, the nationalist bloc in general controlled the convention. However, the states' rights delegates held one trump card—their implicit threat to break up the convention if they did not obtain certain concessions deemed by them to be fundamental to their cause.

The nationalist faction demonstrated its power at the very outset of the proceedings. Following organization for business, Edmund Randolph rose and in the name of his state presented what has since become known as the Virginia Plan—a proposal for a thoroughly nationalistic frame of government. Without debate the convention accepted the fifteen resolutions of the Virginia Plan as the basis for its further deliberations. The outstanding characteristic of this plan was its provision for a government that would exercise its authority directly upon individuals, in contrast to the Confederation government's dependence upon the states as agents to effect its will. The plan thus called for a genuinely national government rather than one based upon state sovereignty. The Virginia Plan's nationalism was also apparent in the broad sweep of legislative power it granted to Congress: to legislate in all cases in which the states were severally "incompetent." It also proposed to endow Congress with the power to disallow state laws "contravening" the articles of Union—in effect a proposal to lodge "the ultimate power" of judging the respective spheres of sovereignty of the national government and the states with an agency of the national government. An ill-conceived provision would have empowered Congress to use force against any state derelict in its obligations to the Union, a procedure the nationalists soon recognized as unwise and unnecessary in a genuinely national government that would no longer use the states as agents to effect its will.

For the rest, the Virginia Plan provided for a two-house legislature, the lower house to be elected by the people of the several states and the upper to be elected by the lower out of nominations submitted by the state legislatures. A separately constituted executive officer was to be elected by Congress for an unspecified term and to be ineligible for reelection. There was also provision for a national judiciary, a portion of which, sitting with the executive, was to constitute a "council of revision," with an absolute veto over all legislation.

All this added up to a proposal to junk the Articles of Confederation outright, and to erect a powerful new national government, federal only in that it would still leave to the states a separate if unspecified area of sovereignty. To make this point overwhelmingly clear, the nationalists at the outset of debate put forward a resolution submitted by Randolph and Morris declaring that "no Union of States merely federal" would be sufficient; instead, "a national government ought to be established, consisting of a supreme legislative, executive, and judiciary." Although several states' rights–oriented delegates objected that this would commit the convention to the establishment of an all-powerful central government, the Randolph-Morris resolution carried almost unanimously, Connecticut alone voting opposition.

The most serious conflict between the nationalist and states' rights factions came over the composition of the legislature. Here the nationalists, after intermittent debate lasting some seven weeks, were eventually forced to compromise, although without vital damage to the principle of nationalism. Madison, Wilson, Morris, and their fellow nationalists began the debate with the demand that both houses of Congress be apportioned according to representation and that the lower house, at least, be elected directly by the people of the several states. Only on the mode of election of the upper house did they show a disposition to compromise: here the convention early accepted unanimously a recommendation by Dickinson that senators be elected by state legislatures. But the states' rights faction, with some support from the moderates, early made it clear that they would accept nothing less than state equality in at least one house. In mid-June, to emphasize their point, they introduced the so-called New Jersey Plan, which called for a one-chamber legislature based upon state equality—that is, a continuation of the Confederation Congress. The New Jersey Plan met prompt defeat, but the impasse remained. The ultimate solution was found in the so-called Great Compromise, reported early in July by a special Committee of Eleven, one delegate from each state. This provided that the lower house of Congress be apportioned according to population, that each state have one vote in the upper house, but that all bills for raising revenue originate in the lower house. A further resolution, offered by Elbridge Gerry, provided that senators were to vote as individuals and not as state delegations. After two weeks of further debate, the nationalists yielded and accepted the compromise.

The most serious conflict between the nationalist and states' rights factions came over the composition of the legislature.

At the time, the nationalist faction looked upon the Great Compromise as a serious defeat for their principles. In actual practice, it was to prove otherwise. On most occasions since 1789, the Senate has been more nationalist-minded than the House of Representatives. Furthermore, the divisions of American politics have not, generally speaking, been between large and small states, as both nationalists and states' rights delegates feared; rather they have been drawn along sectional, economic, and partisan lines. The Great Compromise, in short, was of more significance in saving the convention from dissolution than it was in its subsequent impact on the "living Constitution."

The debate on the executive proved to be protracted and difficult, but it too yielded what amounted ultimately to a victory for a strong national government. The nationalists were determined to have a powerful, independently constituted executive, and to this end they soon decided that the provision in the Virginia Plan for election of the president by Congress was altogether unsatisfactory. But for a long time no adequate alternative appeared. Direct popular election, early proposed by Wilson, was rejected as too democratic; choice of the president by state legislatures conceded too much to states' rights.

At length, after protracted debate marked by vacillation and uncertainty rather than bitter dispute, the delegates accepted another idea originally advanced by Wilson: choice of the president by electors chosen by the several states. In early September, a second Committee of Eleven brought in a plan to allot to each state a number of electors equal to its whole number of senators and representatives. Each state was to be allowed to choose its representatives as it wished—thus reserving a role for the states but opening the door for eventual choice of electors by popular vote. The electors, assembled in their separate states, were to vote by ballot for two candidates for president. The candidate receiving the highest total vote among all the states, if this were a majority of the electors, was to be declared elected president, while that candidate receiving the second highest number of votes, if that were also a majority of the electors, was to be declared elected vice-president. If no candidate received a majority, the Senate was to elect the president from the five leading candidates. The convention altered the committee proposal only to provide for election of the president by the House of Representatives, voting by states, instead of by the Senate, should no candidate receive an electoral majority. The Senate, in the amended plan, was to elect the vice-president.

In practice, the convention's solution to the problem of electing the president was to prove a victory for the proponents of a strong president, for nationalism, and—in the long run—for democracy. The rise of political parties resulted in a situation in which the electoral college rather than the Congress commonly chose the president—only one election, that of 1824, being settled in the House of Representatives for want of an electoral college majority for any candidate. The requirement for an electoral college majority also was to prove a powerful factor in encouraging intersectional political parties and the reconciliation of sectional differences, again an important element in the development of American nationalism. Finally, the fact that the finished Constitution allowed the states to choose their electors in any manner they wished opened the way, after 1789, for the selection of electors by direct popular election—a mode of election every state in the Union except South Carolina was to adopt by 1832. Adaptability of the Constitution to the growth of political democracy was to be a major factor in the new charter's remarkable durability.

Equally nationalistic in its long-range implications was the convention's resort to the judiciary to solve the difficult problem of guaranteeing federal sovereignty and national supremacy against incursion by the states. The convention early rejected coercion of derelict states as inconsistent with the prospective government's sovereign character. State coercion, the nationalists had come to realize, implied state sovereignty. A little later the delegates abandoned congressional disallowance of state legislation as also involving a wrong principle; exercise of a veto over unconstitutional legislation, they had concluded, was properly a judicial, rather than a legislative, function.

Quite surprisingly, the states' rights–oriented New Jersey Plan supplied the final solution. This plan carried a clause declaring the Constitution, treaties, and laws of the national government to be the "supreme law of the respective states" and binding the state courts to enforce them as such, anything in their own constitutions and laws to the contrary notwithstanding. Following rejection of the congressional veto, the convention adopted the supremacy clause from the New Jersey Plan, at the same time altering its language to make the federal Constitution, treaties, and acts of Congress "the supreme law of the land."

Incorporation of the supremacy clause in the new Constitution was a tremendous victory in disguise for the nationalist cause. On the surface the clause made an agency of the states—the state courts—the final judge of the limits of both federal and state sovereignty, which explains why the states' rights faction acceded so readily to its adoption. But the convention, meanwhile, had also provided for the establishment of a national judiciary, with a Supreme Court and such lower courts as Congress should determine upon, and had vested in the federal courts jurisdiction over all cases arising under the Constitution, treaties, and laws of the United States. By implication, as the nationalists were shortly to realize, this gave the federal judiciary appellate power to review state court decisions involving federal constitutional questions. This in turn meant that the Supreme Court of the United States would possess the ultimate power to settle questions involving the respective spheres of state and federal sovereignty. The Judiciary Act of 1789, virtually an extension of the Constitution itself, was to write into federal law this system of appeals from state to federal courts on constitutional questions. And the Supreme Court in *Martin* v. *Hunter's Lessee* (1816) and *Cohens* v. *Virginia* (1821) was to confirm the constitutionality of the Supreme Court's role as the final arbiter of the constitutional system.

The convention early rejected coercion of derelict states as inconsistent with the prospective government's sovereign character.

Meanwhile, in a concession to the states' rights party, the convention had quietly dropped the sweeping delegation to Congress of power to legislate in all cases in which the states were severally "incompetent" and had resorted instead to a specific enumeration of the powers of Congress, as the Articles of Confederation provided. The new Constitution's enumeration, however, was far more impressive than that in the articles. In addition to the familiar authority to legislate upon matters of war, foreign affairs, the post office, currency, Indian affairs, and the like, Congress was also to possess the all-important powers of taxation and regulation of foreign and interstate commerce, as well as authority to enact naturalization, bankruptcy, and patent and copyright laws. Further, the convention in its final draft incorporated an important clause giving Congress the power to enact "necessary and proper" legislation in fulfillment of its delegated powers, and it accepted a vaguely drafted "general welfare clause" that, with the "necessary and proper" provisions, was to serve in the 20th century as the basis for a tremendous expansion of federal power.

Ratification

In mid-September 1787 the convention put its various resolutions and decisions into a finished draft and submitted the Constitution to the states for approval. The convention had provided for ratification of the Constitution by conventions in the several states, stipulating that ratification by any nine states would be sufficient to put the Constitution into effect. This mode of ratification gravely violated the provision in the Articles of Confederation for ratification of constitutional amendments by unanimous action of the several state legislatures; but it also gave the Constitution a reasonable chance for adoption, which it otherwise would not have had.

In fact, the Federalists, as the proponents of ratification of the Constitution soon became known, in the next ten months carried every state but two, failing only in Rhode Island and North Carolina. There were several reasons behind their impressive victory. Most important, the Federalists had a positive and imaginative remedy to offer for the country's grave constitutional ills. Their opponents, the Antifederalists, although they opposed the Constitution as a dangerous instrument of potential tyranny, could offer no constructive proposal of their own.

Very influential was the fact that most of the young republic's illustrious public figures—Washington, Franklin, Hamilton, Madison, Jay, Rutledge, King, Pinckney, and Wilson among them—favored ratification. It was a galaxy that quite outshone Antifederalists Patrick Henry, Richard Henry Lee, George Mason, and the vacillating Sam Adams. Such was his immense prestige that Washington's voice alone may well have been decisive in the ratification debate.

The distribution of delegates in the state ratifying conventions also helped the Federalist cause. Delegates to these bodies were in every instance elected from the existing districts of the various state legislatures, most of which had for many years been gerrymandered in favor of the tidewater regions. But it was precisely in these districts that the people generally were most keenly aware of the deficiencies of the Confederation government and that support for ratification was strongest.

The Federalists also won impressive early victories in several less populous states, where public sentiment was heavily influenced by the Constitution's provision for state equality in the Senate. Delaware and New Jersey, which ratified in December; Georgia and Connecticut, which ratified in January; and Maryland, which ratified in April, fell into this category. This initial ratification surge proved to be very favorable psychologically to the Federalist cause.

The Federalists' political strategy also was far superior to that of their opponents. In Pennsylvania, where public sentiment strongly favored ratification, the Federalists first defeated an attempt in the legislature to block the quorum necessary for a convention call. Under Wilson's masterful leadership, the Federalists in December then drove the Constitution through to ratification in the state convention. In South Carolina, the Federalists effectively thwarted an Antifederalist attempt to defeat a convention call. They controlled the subsequent convention without difficulty.

Federalist strategy was most impressive in Massachusetts, Virginia, and New York. In each instance initial prospects for ratification had been dubious. In Massachusetts, where Antifederalist feeling was exacerbated by bitter memories of Shays's Rebellion, the Federalists first won over John Hancock and Sam Adams with hints of high national office. They then converted a number of marginal Antifederalists by freely accepting a variety of proposals for a federal bill of rights. Ratification followed in February by the narrow vote of 187 to 168. The Virginia convention, which assembled in June, witnessed a spectacular debate between Patrick Henry and Madison, in which the quiet and scholarly Madison used carefully reasoned analysis of the Constitution to refute Henry's impassioned assault. Again, ready Federalist acceptance of proposals for a bill of rights helped carry the day. The Federalists triumphed on the ratification vote (89 to 79). In New York, over two-thirds of the delegates to the June convention were declared Antifederalists, and the state's powerful landed aristocracy also opposed ratification, mainly because of the

Constitution's potential impact on New York's revenue system. But the Constitution's supporters earlier had softened public opinion somewhat with a series of newspaper articles by Hamilton, Madison, and Jay, published eventually under the title of *The Federalist*, which still stands as one of the most brilliant analyses of the Constitution ever written. News that both New Hampshire and Virginia, the ninth and tenth states to ratify, had lately acted favorably and that the Constitution would in any event go into operation badly damaged Antifederalist morale. Again, conciliatory Federalist acceptance of proposed amendments, together with their support for a meaningless resolution calling for a second federal convention, proved decisive. On the final vote the Constitution was ratified (30 to 27).

The Rhode Island legislature, still controlled by hostile paper-money advocates, had refused even to call a convention. In the essentially frontier state of North Carolina, where public sentiment heavily opposed ratification, the state convention, meeting in July, was dominated by Antifederalists. This body finally adjourned without any formal vote on ratification. At length, in November 1789, a second North Carolina convention, convening several months after the new government had gone into operation, ratified the Constitution without incident. In Rhode Island, a Federalist faction captured control of the state legislature in the spring of 1790. The new assembly promptly called a convention, which ratified the Constitution in May (34 to 32).

Nature of the Constitution

Both the drafting and ratification of the Constitution were triumphs for the framers' Enlightenment philosophy: faith in the essentially rational character of man and society, and belief in man's ability to define and solve social and political problems adequately. Indeed the Constitution itself is perhaps best understood as an Enlightenment document, embodying as it does in its preamble the objectives of justice, order, liberty, and the general welfare, and with its explicit and implicit commitments to the ideals of limited government, civil liberties, separation of church and state, the confinement of military power, and an open society.

The Constitution has sometimes been interpreted either as an antidemocratic document—as contrasted with the Declaration of Independence with its profession of faith in universal human equality—or as no more than an instrument of selfish class interests. Both views are superficial and essentially erroneous. The Constitution was adopted by a process far more democratic than was the Declaration of Independence, which was promulgated without any popular validation or consent whatever. At the time of its adoption, the Constitution also was by far the most popular and democratically oriented frame of national government in the world. It provided for a republican government when all others, with a few minor exceptions, were monarchical. Furthermore, in its provisions for a popularly based legislative house and for a president and Senate indirectly subject to democratic processes, in its sharp limitation upon the power of government to punish for treason, and in its general concern for limited government and civil liberties, it went a great deal farther in the direction of modern democracy than any other national government then in existence. Moreover, the Constitution's open-ended character, which later made it possible to adapt its provisions to the steady growth of political democracy, was no accident. It expressed instead the self-conscious belief of the framers in the idea of flexibility and growth in government, rather than stifling rigidity.

Nor was the Constitution, viewed in the large, a product of selfish and exclusive class interests. In 1913 the historian Charles A. Beard published *An Economic Interpretation of the Constitution of the United States*, in which he asserted that the Constitution was the work of an economic elite whose wealth was concentrated in paper: land speculators, bondholders, moneyed merchants and lawyers, and the like. The Constitution, Beard asserted, reflected the interests of this class. In support of his argument, he pointed to the Constitution's provisions banning states from issuing paper money or impairing the obligations of contracts, guaranteeing the national government control over money and credit, and guaranteeing the national debt. But careful research in the 1950's and 1960's has shown that the framers as a group were not especially involved in bondholding and speculative operations and that they were drawn as much from planter, agrarian, and nonspeculative mercantile and legal interests as from any moneyed elite. The Constitution did indeed reflect the special concern of men of property, learning, position, and community standing for stable, well-ordered government. This was hardly narrow selfishness; rather it constituted enlightened patriotism.

The Constitution's amendable, open-ended character expressed the framers' belief in flexibility and growth in government, rather than stifling rigidity.

It remains only to be observed that constitutional growth since 1789 has made the present-day "living Constitution" a very different thing from the charter drafted at Philadelphia in the late 18th century. The doctrine of broad construction—first set forth in Hamilton's Bank Message in 1791 and later elucidated by John Marshall in *McCullough* v. *Maryland* (1819) and *Gibbons* v. *Ogden* (1824)—has led since 1880 to a vast increase in federal powers, as the national government has adapted itself to modern urbanization and industrialization. The changes wrought by the adoption of the Civil War amendments—abolishing slavery and imposing extensive guarantees of civil rights and civil liberties upon the states—have been equally profound. Yet the fundamental ordering of power in government that the framers decreed, their pervasive provisions for limited government, and their profound concern for individual liberty still lie at the very heart of the American constitutional system.

[See also Amendments to the Constitution.]

BIBLIOGRAPHY

Charles A. Beard, *An Economic Interpretation of the Constitution of the United States.*

Max Ferrand, ed., *Records of the Federal Convention.*

Alfred H. Kelly and Winfred A. Harbison, *The American Constitution: Its Origins and Development.*

Cecelia Kenyon, *The Anti-Federalists.*

Forrest McDonald, *We the People: The Economic Origins of the Constitution.*

Andrew McLaughlin, *A Constitutional History of the United States.*

J. T. Main, *The Anti-Federalists: Critics of the Constitution, 1781–1788.*

Clinton Rossiter, *The Grand Convention.*

— ALFRED H. KELLY

Constitution of the United States

PREAMBLE. WE THE PEOPLE of the United States, in Order to form a more perfect Union, establish Justice, insure domestic Tranquility, provide for the common defence, promote the general Welfare, and secure the Blessings of Liberty to ourselves and our Posterity, do ordain and establish this Constitution for the United States of America.

ARTICLE I. *Section 1.* All legislative Powers herein granted shall be vested in a Congress of the United States, which shall consist of a Senate and House of Representatives.

Section 2. The House of Representatives shall be composed of Members chosen every second Year by the People of the several States, and the Electors in each State shall have the Qualifications requisite for Electors of the most numerous Branch of the State Legislature.

No Person shall be a Representative who shall not have attained to the age of twenty five Years, and been seven Years a Citizen of the United States, and who shall not, when elected, be an Inhabitant of that State in which he shall be chosen.

Representatives and direct Taxes shall be apportioned among the several States which may be included within this Union, according to their respective Numbers, which shall be determined by adding to the whole Number of free Persons, including those bound to Service for a Term of Years, and excluding Indians not taxed, three fifths of all other Persons. The actual Enumeration shall be made within three Years after the first Meeting of the Congress of the United States, and within every subsequent Term of ten Years, in such Manner as they shall by Law direct. The Number of Representatives shall not exceed one for every thirty Thousand, but each State shall have at Least one Representative; and until such enumeration shall be made, the State of New Hampshire shall be entitled to chuse three, Massachusetts eight, Rhode-Island and Providence Plantations one, Connecticut five, New-York six, New Jersey four, Pennsylvania eight, Delaware one, Maryland six, Virginia ten, North Carolina five, South Carolina five, and Georgia three.

> *". . . in Order to form a more perfect Union, establish Justice, insure domestic Tranquility, provide for the common defence, promote the general Welfare, and secure the Blessings of Liberty . . ."*

When vacancies happen in the Representation from any State, the Executive Authority thereof shall issue Writs of Election to fill such Vacancies.

The House of Representatives shall chuse their Speaker and other Officers; and shall have the sole Power of Impeachment.

Section 3. The Senate of the United States shall be composed of two Senators from each State, chosen by the Legislature thereof, for six Years; and each Senator shall have one Vote.

Immediately after they shall be assembled in Consequence of the first Election, they shall be divided as equally as may be into three Classes. The Seats of the Senators of the first Class shall be vacated at the Expiration of the second Year, of the second Class at the Expiration of the fourth Year, and of the third Class at the Expiration of the sixth Year, so that one third may be chosen every second Year; and if Vacancies happen by Resignation, or otherwise, during the Recess of the Legislature of any State, the Executive thereof may make temporary Appointments until the next Meeting of the Legislature, which shall then fill such Vacancies.

No Person shall be a Senator who shall not have attained to the Age of thirty Years, and been nine Years a Citizen of the United States, and who shall not, when elected, be an Inhabitant of that State for which he shall be chosen.

The Vice-President of the United States shall be President of the Senate, but shall have no Vote, unless they be equally divided.

The Senate shall chuse their other Officers, and also a President pro tempore, in the Absence of the Vice-President, or when he shall exercise the Office of President of the United States.

The Senate shall have the sole Power to try all Impeachments. When sitting for that Purpose, they shall be on Oath or Affirmation. When the President of the United States is tried, the Chief Justice shall preside: And no Person shall be convicted without the Concurrence of two thirds of the Members present.

Judgment in Cases of Impeachment shall not extend further than to removal from Office, and disqualification to hold and enjoy any Office of honor, Trust or Profit under the United States: but the Party convicted shall nevertheless be liable and subject to Indictment, Trial, Judgment and Punishment, according to Law.

Section 4. The Times, Places and Manner of holding Elections for Senators and Representatives, shall be prescribed in each State by the Legislature thereof; but the Congress may at any time by Law make or alter such Regulations, except as to the Places of chusing Senators.

The Congress shall assemble at least once in every Year, and such Meeting shall be on the first Monday in December, unless they shall by Law appoint a different Day.

Section 5. Each House shall be the Judge of the Elections, Returns and Qualifications of its own Members, and a Majority of each shall constitute a Quorum to do Business; but a smaller Number may adjourn from day to day and may be authorized to compel the Attendance of absent Members, in such Manner, and under such Penalties as each House may provide.

Each House may determine the Rules of its Proceedings, punish its Members for disorderly Behaviour, and, with the Concurrence of two thirds, expel a Member.

Each House shall keep a Journal of its Proceedings, and from time to time publish the same, excepting such Parts as may in their Judgment require Secrecy; and the Yeas and Nays of the Members of either House on any question shall, at the Desire of one fifth of those Present, be entered on the Journal.

Neither House, during the Session of Congress, shall, without the Consent of the other, adjourn for more than three days, nor to any other Place than that in which the two Houses shall be sitting.

Section 6. The Senators and Representatives shall receive a Compensation for their Services, to be ascertained by Law, and paid out of the Treasury of the United States. They shall in all Cases, except Treason, Felony and Breach of the Peace, be privileged from Arrest during their Attendance at the Session of their respective Houses, and in going to and returning from the same; and for any Speech or Debate in either House, they shall not be questioned in any other Place.

No Senator or Representative shall, during the Time for which he was elected, be appointed to any civil Office under the Authority of the United States, which shall have been created, or the Emoluments whereof shall have been encreased during such time; and no Person holding any Office under the United States, shall be a Member of either House during his Continuance in Office.

Section 7. All Bills for raising Revenue shall originate in the House of Representatives; but the Senate may propose or concur with Amendments as on other Bills.

Every Bill which shall have passed the House of Representatives and the Senate, shall, before it become a Law, be presented to the President of the United States; If he approve he shall sign it, but if not he shall return it, with his Objections to that House in which it shall have originated, who shall enter the Objections at large on their Journal, and proceed to reconsider it. If after such Reconsideration two thirds of that House shall agree to pass the Bill, it shall be sent, together with the Objections, to the other House, by which it shall likewise be reconsidered, and if approved by two thirds of that House, it shall become a Law. But in all such Cases the Votes of both Houses shall be determined by yeas and Nays, and the Names of the Persons voting for and against the Bill shall be entered on the Journal of each House respectively. If any Bill shall not be returned by the President within ten Days (Sundays excepted) after it shall have been presented to him, the Same shall be a Law, in like Manner as if he had signed it, unless the Congress by their Adjournment prevent its Return, in which Case it shall not be a Law.

"Every Bill which shall have passed the House of Representatives and Senate, shall, before it become a Law, be presented to the President of the United States."

Every Order, Resolution, or Vote to which the Concurrence of the Senate and House of Representatives may be necessary (except on a question of Adjournment) shall be presented to the President of the United States; and before the Same shall take Effect, shall be approved by him, or being disapproved by him, shall be repassed by two thirds of the Senate and House of Representatives, according to the Rules and Limitations prescribed in the Case of a Bill.

Section 8. The Congress shall have Power To lay and collect Taxes, Duties, Imposts and Excises, to pay the Debts and provide for the common Defence and general Welfare of the United States; but all Duties, Imposts and Excises shall be uniform throughout the United States;

To borrow Money on the credit of the United States;

To regulate Commerce with foreign Nations, and among the several States, and with the Indian Tribes;

To establish an uniform Rule of Naturalization, and uniform Laws on the subject of Bankruptcies throughout the United States;

To coin Money, regulate the Value thereof, and of foreign Coin, and fix the Standard of Weights and Measures;

To provide for the Punishment of counterfeiting the Securities and current Coin of the United States;

To establish Post Offices and post Roads;

To promote the Progress of Science and useful Arts, by securing for limited Times to Authors and Inventors the exclusive Right to their respective Writings and Discoveries;

To constitute Tribunals inferior to the supreme Court;

To define and punish Piracies and Felonies committed on the high Seas, and Offences against the Law of Nations;

To declare War, grant Letters of Marque and Reprisal, and make Rules concerning Captures on Land and Water;

To raise and support Armies, but no Appropriation of Money to that Use shall be for a longer Term than two Years;

To provide and maintain a Navy;

To make Rules for the Government and Regulation of the land and naval Forces;

To provide for calling for the Militia to execute the Laws of the Union, suppress Insurrections and repel Invasions;

To provide for organizing, arming, and disciplining, the Militia, and for governing such Part of them as may be employed in the Service of the United States, reserving to the States respectively, the Appointment of the Officers, and the Authority of training the Militia according to the discipline prescribed by Congress;

To exercise exclusive Legislation in all Cases whatsoever, over such District (not exceeding ten Miles square) as may, by Cession of particular States, and the Acceptance of Congress, become the Seat of the Government of the United States, and to exercise like Authority over all Places purchased by the Consent of the Legislature of the State in which the Same shall be, for the Erection of Forts, Magazines, Arsenals, dock-Yards, and other needful Buildings;—And

To make all Laws which shall be necessary and proper for carrying into Execution the foregoing Powers, and all other Powers vested by this Constitution in the Government of the United States, or in any Department or Officer thereof.

Section 9. The Migration or Importation of such Persons as any of the States now existing shall think proper to admit, shall not be prohibited by the Congress prior to the Year one thousand eight hundred and eight, but a Tax or duty may be imposed on such Importation, not exceeding ten dollars for each Person.

"No Money shall be drawn from the Treasury, but in Consequence of Appropriations made by Law."

The Privilege of the Writ of Habeas Corpus shall not be suspended, unless when in Cases of Rebellion or Invasion the public Safety may require it.

No Bill of Attainder or ex post facto Law shall be passed.

No Capitation, or other direct, Tax shall be laid, unless in Proportion to the Census or Enumeration herein before directed to be taken.

No Tax or Duty shall be laid on Articles exported from any State.

No Preference shall be given by any Regulation of Commerce or Revenue to the Ports of one State over those of another: nor shall Vessels bound to, or from, one State, be obliged to enter, clear or pay Duties in another.

No Money shall be drawn from the Treasury, but in Consequence of Appropriations made by Law; and a regular Statement and Account of the Receipts and Expenditures of all public Money shall be published from time to time.

No Title of Nobility shall be granted by the United States: And no Person holding any Office of Profit or Trust under them, shall, without the Consent of the Congress, accept of any present, Emolument, Office, or Title, of any kind whatever, from any King, Prince, or foreign State.

Section 10. No State shall enter into any Treaty, Alliance, or Confederation; grant Letters of Marque and Reprisal; coin Money; emit Bills of Credit; make any Thing but gold and silver Coin a Tender in Payment of Debts; pass any Bill of Attainder, ex post facto Law, or Law impairing the Obligation of Contracts, or grant any Title of Nobility.

No State shall, without the Consent of the Congress, lay any Imposts or Duties on Imports or Exports, except what may be absolutely necessary for executing its inspection Laws: and the net Produce of all Duties and Imposts, laid by any State on Imports or Exports, shall be for the Use of the Treasury of the United States; and all such Laws shall be subject to the Revision and Controul of the Congress.

No State shall, without the Consent of Congress, lay any Duty of Tonnage, keep Troops, or Ships of War in time of Peace, enter into any Agreement or Compact with another state, or with a foreign Power, or engage in War, unless actually invaded, or in such imminent Danger as will not admit of delay.

ARTICLE II. *Section 1.* The executive Power shall be vested in a President of the United States of America. He shall hold his Office during the Term of four Years, and, together with the Vice-President, chosen for the same Term, be elected, as follows.

Each State shall appoint, in such Manner as the Legislature thereof may direct, a Number of Electors, equal to the whole Number of Senators and Representatives to which the State may be entitled in the Congress: but no Senator or Representative, or Person holding an Office of Trust or Profit under the United States, shall be appointed an Elector.

The Electors shall meet in their respective States, and vote by Ballot for two Persons, of whom one at least shall not be an Inhabitant of the same State with themselves. And they shall make a List of all the Persons voted for, and of the Number of Votes for each; which List they shall sign and certify, and transmit sealed to the Seat of the Government of the United States, directed to the President of the Senate. The President of the Senate shall, in the Presence of the Senate and House of Representatives, open all the Certificates, and the Votes shall then be counted. The Person having the greatest Number of Votes shall be the President, if such Number be a Majority of the whole Number of Electors appointed; and if there be more than one who have such Majority, and have an equal Number of Votes, then the House of Representatives shall immediately chuse by Ballot one of them for President; and if no Person have a Majority, then from the five highest on the List the said House shall in like Manner chuse the President. But in chusing the President, the Votes shall be taken by States, the Representation from each State having one Vote; A quorum for this Purpose shall consist of a Member or Members from two thirds of the States, and a Majority of all the States shall be necessary to a Choice. In every Case, after the Choice of the President, the Person having the greatest Number of Votes of the Electors shall be the Vice-President. But if there should remain two or more who have equal Votes, the Senate shall chuse from them by Ballot the Vice-President.

The Congress may determine the Time of chusing the Electors, and the Day on which they shall give their Votes; which Day shall be the same throughout the United States.

No Person except a natural born Citizen, or a Citizen of the United States, at the time of the Adoption of this Constitution, shall be eligible to the Office of President; neither shall any Person be eligible to that Office who shall not have attained to the Age of thirty five Years, and been fourteen Years a Resident within the United States.

In Case of the Removal of the President from Office, or of his Death, Resignation, or Inability to discharge the Powers and Duties of the said Office, the Same shall devolve on the Vice-President, and the Congress may by Law provide for the Case of Removal, Death, Resignation or Inability, both of the President and Vice-President, declaring what Officer shall then act as President, and such Officer shall act accordingly, until the Disability be removed, or a President shall be elected.

The President shall, at stated Times, receive for his Services, a Compensation, which shall neither be encreased nor diminished during the Period for which he shall have been elected, and he shall not receive within that Period any other Emolument from the United States, or any of them.

"No Person except a natural born Citizen, or a Citizen of the United States, at the time of the Adoption of this Constitution, shall be eligible to the Office of President."

Before he enter on the Execution of his Office, he shall take the following Oath or Affirmation:—"I do solemnly swear (or affirm) that I will faithfully execute the Office of President of the United States, and will to the best of my Ability, preserve, protect and defend the Constitution of the United States."

Section 2. The President shall be Commander in Chief of the Army and Navy of the United States, and of the Militia of the several States, when called into the actual Service of the United States; he may require the Opinion, in writing, of the principal Officer in each of the executive Departments, upon any Subject relating to the Duties of their respective Offices, and he shall have Power to grant Reprieves and Pardons for Offences against the United States, except in Cases of Impeachment.

He shall have Power, by and with the Advice and Consent of the Senate, to make Treaties, provided two thirds of the Senators present concur; and he shall nominate, and by and with the Advice and Consent of the Senate, shall appoint Ambassadors, other public Ministers and Consuls, Judges of the supreme Court, and all other Officers of the United States, whose Appointments are not herein otherwise provided for, and which shall be established by Law: but the Congress may by Law vest the Appointment of such inferior Officers, as they think proper, in the President alone, in the Courts of Law, or in the Heads of Departments.

The President shall have Power to fill up all Vacancies that may happen during the Recess of the Senate, by granting Commissions which shall expire at the End of their next Session.

Section 3. He shall from time to time give to the Congress Information of the State of the Union, and recommend to their Consideration such Measures as he shall judge necessary and expedient; he may, on extraordinary Occasions, convene both Houses, or either of them, and in Case of Disagreement between them, with Respect to the Time of Adjournment, he may adjourn them to such Time as he shall think proper; he shall receive Ambassadors and other public Ministers; he shall take Care that the Laws be faithfully executed, and shall Commission all the Officers of the United States.

Section 4. The President, Vice-President and all civil Officers of the United States, shall be removed from Office on Impeachment for, and Conviction of, Treason, Bribery, or other high Crimes and Misdemeanors.

ARTICLE III. *Section 1.* The judicial Power of the United States, shall be vested in one supreme Court, and in such inferior Courts as the Congress may from time to time ordain and establish. The Judges, both of the supreme and inferior Courts, shall hold their Offices during good Behaviour, and shall, at stated Times, receive for their Services, a Compensation, which shall not be diminished during their Continuance in Office.

Section 2. The judicial Power shall extend to all Cases, in Law and Equity, arising under this Constitution, the Laws of the United States, and Treaties made, or which shall be made, under their Authority;—to all Cases affecting Ambassadors, other public Ministers and Consuls;—to all Cases of admiralty and maritime Jurisdiction;—to Controversies to which the United States shall be a party;—to Controversies between two or more States;—between a State and Citizens of another State;—between Citizens of different States;—between Citizens of the same State claiming Lands under Grants of different States, and between a State, or the Citizens thereof, and foreign States, Citizens or Subjects.

In all Cases affecting Ambassadors, other public Ministers and Consuls, and those in which a State shall be Party, the supreme Court shall have original Jurisdiction. In all the other Cases before mentioned, the supreme Court shall have appellate Jurisdiction, both as to Law and Fact, with such Exceptions, and under such Regulations as the Congress shall make.

The Trial of all Crimes, except in Cases of Impeachment, shall be by Jury; and such Trial shall be held in the State where the said Crimes shall have been committed; but when not committed within any State, the Trial shall be at such Place or Places as the Congress may by Law have directed.

Section 3. Treason against the United States, shall consist only in levying War against them, or in adhering to their Enemies, giving them Aid and Comfort. No Person shall be convicted of Treason unless on the Testimony of two Witnesses to the same overt Act, or on Confession in open Court.

The Congress shall have Power to declare the Punishment of Treason, but no Attainder of Treason shall work Corruption of Blood, or Forfeiture except during the Life of the Person attainted.

ARTICLE IV. *Section 1.* Full Faith and Credit shall be given in each State to the public Acts, Records, and judicial Proceedings of every other State. And the Congress may by general Laws prescribe the Manner in which such Acts, Records and Proceedings shall be proved, and the Effect thereof.

Section 2. The Citizens of each State shall be entitled to all Privileges and Immunities of Citizens in the several States.

A Person charged in any State with Treason, Felony, or other Crime, who shall flee from Justice, and be found in another State, shall on Demand of the executive Authority of the State from which he fled, be delivered up, to be removed to the State having Jurisdiction of the Crime.

No Person held to Service or Labour in one State, under the Laws thereof, escaping into another, shall, in Consequence of any Law or Regulation therein, be discharged from such Service or Labour, but shall be delivered up on Claim of the Party to whom such Service or Labour may be due.

Section 3. New States may be admitted by the Congress into this Union; but no new States shall be formed or erected within the Jurisdiction of any other State; nor any State be formed by the Junction of two or more States, or Parts of States, without the Consent of the Legislatures of the States concerned as well as of the Congress.

The Congress shall have Power to dispose of and make all needful Rules and Regulations respecting the Territory or other Property belonging to the United States; and nothing in this Constitution shall be so construed as to Prejudice any Claims of the United States, or of any particular State.

Section 4. The United States shall guarantee to every State in this Union a Republican Form of Government, and shall protect each of them against Invasion; and on Application of the Legislature, or of the Executive (when the Legislature cannot be convened) against domestic Violence.

ARTICLE V. The Congress, whenever two thirds of both Houses shall deem it necessary, shall propose Amendments to this Constitution, or, on the Application of the Legislatures of two thirds of the several States, shall call a Convention for proposing Amendments, which, in either Case, shall be valid to all Intents and Purposes, as Part of this Constitution, when ratified by the Legislatures of three fourths of the several States, or by Conventions in three fourths thereof, as the one or the other Mode of Ratification may be proposed by the Congress; Provided that no Amendment which may be made prior to the Year One thousand eight hundred and eight shall in any Manner affect the first and fourth Clauses in the Ninth Section of the first Article; and that no State, without its Consent, shall be deprived of its equal Suffrage in the Senate.

ARTICLE VI. All Debts contracted and Engagements entered into, before the Adoption of this Constitution, shall be as valid against the United States under this Constitution, as under the Confederation.

This Constitution, and the Laws of the United States which shall be made in Pursuance thereof; and all Treaties made, or which shall be made, under the Authority of the United States, shall be the supreme Law of the Land; and the Judges in every State shall be bound thereby, any Thing in the Constitution or Laws of any State to the Contrary notwithstanding.

The Senators and Representatives before mentioned, and the Members of the several State Legislatures, and all executive and judicial Officers, both of the United States and of the several States, shall be bound by Oath or Affirmation, to support this Constitution; but no religious Test shall ever be required as a Qualification to any Office or public Trust under the United States.

ARTICLE VII. The Ratification of the Conventions of nine States, shall be sufficient for the Establishment of this Constitution between the States so ratifying the Same.

done in Convention by the Unanimous Consent of the States present the Seventeenth Day of September in the Year of our Lord one thousand seven hundred and Eighty seven and of the Independence of the United States of America the Twelfth

In witness whereof We have hereunto subscribed our Names,

George Washington—President and deputy from Virginia

New Hampshire—John Langdon, Nicholas Gilman

Massachusetts—Nathaniel Gorham, Rufus King

Connecticut—William Samuel Johnson, Roger Sherman

New York—Alexander Hamilton

New Jersey—Wil: Livingston, David Brearley, William Paterson, Jona: Dayton

Pennsylvania—B Franklin, Thomas Mifflin, Robt Morris, Geo. Clymer, Thomas FitzSimons, Jared Ingersoll, James Wilson, Gouv Morris

Delaware—Geo: Read, Gunning Bedford jun, John Dickinson, Richard Bassett, Jaco: Broom

Maryland—James McHenry, Dan of St. Thomas Jenifer, Daniel Carroll

Virginia—John Blair, James Madison Jr.

North Carolina—William Blount, Richard Dobbs Spaight, Hu Williamson

South Carolina—J. Rutledge, Charles Cotesworth Pinckney, Charles Pinckney, Pierce Butler.

Georgia—William Few, Abr Baldwin

Amendments to the Constitution

Resolved by the Senate and House of Representatives of the United States of America, in Congress assembled, two thirds of both Houses concurring, that the following Articles be proposed to the Legislatures of the several States, as Amendments to the Constitution of the United States, all, or any of which Articles, when ratified by three fourths of the said Legislatures, to be valid to all intents and purposes, as part of the said Constitution, viz.

ARTICLE I. Congress shall make no law respecting an establishment of religion, or prohibiting the free exercise thereof; or abridging the freedom of speech, or of the press; or the right of the people peaceably to assemble, and to petition the Government for a redress of grievances.

ARTICLE II. A well regulated Militia, being necessary to the security of a free State, the right of the people to keep and bear Arms, shall not be infringed.

ARTICLE III. No Soldier shall, in time of peace be quartered in any house, without the consent of the Owner, nor in time of war, but in a manner to be prescribed by law.

"Congress shall make no law respecting an establishment of religion, or prohibiting the free exercise thereof; or abridging the freedom of speech, or of the press . . ."

ARTICLE IV. The right of the people to be secure in their persons, houses, papers, and effects, against unreasonable searches and seizures, shall not be violated, and no Warrants shall issue, but upon probable cause, supported by Oath or affirmation, and particularly describing the place to be searched, and the persons or things to be seized.

ARTICLE V. No person shall be held to answer for a capital, or otherwise infamous crime, unless on a presentment or indictment of a Grand Jury, except in cases arising in the land or naval forces, or in the Militia, when in actual service in time of War or public danger; nor shall any person be subject for the same offence to be twice put in jeopardy of life or limb; nor shall be compelled in any criminal case to be a witness against himself, nor be deprived of life, liberty, or property, without due process of law; nor shall private property be taken for public use, without just compensation.

ARTICLE VI. In all criminal prosecutions, the accused shall enjoy the right to a speedy and public trial, by an impartial jury of the State and district wherein the crime shall have been committed, which district shall have been previously ascertained by law, and to be informed of the nature and cause of the accusation; to be confronted with the witnesses against him; to have compulsory process for obtaining witnesses in his favor, and to have the Assistance of Counsel for his defence.

ARTICLE VII. In Suits at common law, where the value in controversy shall exceed twenty dollars, the right of trial by jury shall be preserved, and no fact tried by a jury, shall be otherwise re-examined in any Court of the United States, than according to the rules of the common law.

ARTICLE VIII. Excessive bail shall not be required, nor excessive fines imposed, nor cruel and unusual punishments inflicted.

ARTICLE IX. The enumeration in the Constitution, of certain rights, shall not be construed to deny or disparage others retained by the people.

ARTICLE X. The powers not delegated to the United States by the Constitution, nor prohibited by it to the States, are reserved to the States respectively, or to the people.

ARTICLE XI. The Judicial power of the United States shall not be construed to extend to any suit in law or equity, commenced or prosecuted against one of the United States by Citizens of another State, or by Citizens or Subjects of any Foreign State.

ARTICLE XII. The Electors shall meet in their respective states and vote by ballot for President and Vice-President, one of whom, at least, shall not be an inhabitant of the same state with themselves; they shall name in their ballots the person voted for as President, and in distinct ballots the person voted for as Vice-President, and they shall make distinct lists of all persons voted for as President, and of all persons voted for as Vice-President, and of the number of votes for each, which lists they shall sign and certify, and transmit sealed to the seat of the government of the United States, directed to the President of the Senate;—The President of the Senate shall, in the presence of the Senate and House of Representatives, open all the certificates and the votes shall then be counted;—The person having the greatest number of votes for President, shall be the President, if such number be a majority of the whole number of Electors appointed; and if no person have such majority, then from the persons having the highest numbers not exceeding three on the list of those voted for as President, the House of Representatives shall choose immediately, by ballot, the President. But in choosing the President, the votes shall be taken by states, the representation from each state having one vote; a quorum for this purpose shall consist of a member or members from two-thirds of the states, and a majority of all the states shall be necessary to a choice. And if the House of Representatives shall not choose a President whenever the right of choice shall devolve upon them, before the fourth day of March next following, then the Vice-President shall act as President, as in the case of the death or other constitutional disability of the President.—The person having the greatest number of votes as Vice-President, shall be the Vice-President, if such number be a majority of the whole number of Electors appointed, and if no person have a majority, then from the two highest numbers on the list, the Senate shall choose the Vice-President; a quorum for the purpose shall consist of two-thirds of the whole number of Senators, and a majority of the whole number shall be necessary to a choice. But no person constitutionally ineligible to the office of President shall be eligible to that of Vice-President of the United States.

ARTICLE XIII. *Section 1.* Neither slavery nor involuntary servitude, except as a punishment for crime whereof the party shall have been duly convicted, shall exist within the United States, or any place subject to their jurisdiction.

Section 2. Congress shall have power to enforce this article by appropriate legislation.

ARTICLE XIV. *Section 1.* All persons born or naturalized in the United States, and subject to the jurisdiction thereof, are citizens of the United States and of the State wherein they reside. No State shall make or enforce any law which shall abridge the privileges or immunities of citizens of the United States; nor shall any State deprive any person of life, liberty, or property, without due process of law; nor deny to any person within its jurisdiction the equal protection of the laws.

"Neither slavery nor involuntary servitude, except as a punishment for crime whereof the party shall have been duly convicted, shall exist within the United States."

Section 2. Representatives shall be apportioned among the several States according to their respective numbers, counting the whole number of persons in each State, excluding Indians not taxed. But when the right to vote at any election for the choice of electors for President and Vice-President of the United States, Representatives in Congress, the Executive and Judicial officers of a State, or the members of the Legislature thereof, is denied to any of the male inhabitants of such State, being twenty-one years of age, and citizens of the United States, or in any way abridged, except for participation in rebellion, or other crime, the basis of representation therein shall be reduced in the proportion which the number of such male citizens shall bear to the whole number of male citizens twenty-one years of age in such State.

Section 3. No person shall be a Senator or Representative in Congress, or elector of President and Vice-President, or hold any office, civil or military, under the United States, or under any State, who, having previously taken an oath, as a member of Congress, or as an officer of the United States, or as a member of any State legislature, or as an executive or judicial officer of any State, to support the Constitution of the United States, shall have engaged in insurrection or rebellion against the same, or given aid or comfort to the enemies thereof. But Congress may by a vote of two-thirds of each House, remove such disability.

Section 4. The validity of the public debt of the United States, authorized by law, including debts incurred for payment of pensions and bounties for services in suppressing insurrection or rebellion, shall not be questioned. But neither the United States nor any State shall assume or pay any debt or obligation incurred in aid of insurrection or rebellion against the United States, or any claim for the loss or emancipation of any slave; but all such debts, obligations and claims shall be held illegal and void.

Section 5. The Congress shall have power to enforce, by appropriate legislation, the provisions of this article.

ARTICLE XV. *Section 1.* The right of citizens of the United States to vote shall not be denied or abridged by the United States or by any State on account of race, color, or previous condition of servitude.

Section 2. The Congress shall have power to enforce this article by appropriate legislation.

ARTICLE XVI. The Congress shall have power to lay and collect taxes on incomes, from whatever source derived, without apportionment among the several States, and without regard to any census or enumeration.

ARTICLE XVII. *Section 1.* The Senate of the United States shall be composed of two Senators from each State, elected by the people thereof, for six years; and each Senator shall have one vote. The electors in each State shall have the qualifications requisite for electors of the most numerous branch of the State legislatures.

Section 2. When vacancies happen in the representation of any State in the Senate, the executive authority of such State shall issue writs of election to fill such vacancies: Provided, That the legislature of any State may empower the executive thereof to make temporary appointments until the people fill the vacancies by election as the legislature may direct.

Section 3. This amendment shall not be so construed as to affect the election or term of any Senator chosen before it becomes valid as part of the Constitution.

ARTICLE XVIII. *Section 1.* After one year from the ratification of this article the manufacture, sale, or transportation of intoxicating liquors within, the importation thereof into, or the exportation thereof from the United States and all territory subject to the jurisdiction thereof for beverage purposes is hereby prohibited.

Section 2. The Congress and the several States shall have concurrent power to enforce this article by appropriate legislation.

Section 3. This article shall be inoperative unless it shall have been ratified as an amendment to the Constitution by the legislatures of the several States, as provided in the Constitution, within seven years from the date of the submission hereof to the States by the Congress.

ARTICLE XIX. *Section 1.* The right of citizens of the United States to vote shall not be denied or abridged by the United States or by any State on account of sex.

Section 2. Congress shall have power to enforce this article by appropriate legislation.

ARTICLE XX. *Section 1.* The terms of the President and Vice-President shall end at noon on the 20th day of January, and the terms of Senators and Representatives at noon on the 3d day of January, of the years in which such terms would have ended if this article had not been ratified; and the terms of their successors shall then begin.

Section 2. The Congress shall assemble at least once in every year, and such meeting shall begin at noon on the 3d day of January, unless they shall by law appoint a different day.

"The right of citizens of the United States to vote shall not be denied or abridged by the United States or by any State on account of sex."

Section 3. If, at the time fixed for the beginning of the term of the President, the President elect shall have died, the Vice-President elect shall become President. If a President shall not have been chosen before the time fixed for the beginning of his term, or if the President elect shall have failed to qualify, then the Vice-President elect shall act as President until a President shall have qualified; and the Congress may by law provide for the case wherein neither a President elect nor a Vice-President elect shall have qualified, declaring who shall then act as President, or the manner in which one who is to act shall be selected, and such person shall act accordingly until a President or Vice-President shall have qualified.

Section 4. The Congress may by law provide for the case of the death of any of the persons from whom the House of Representatives may choose a President whenever the right of choice shall have devolved upon them, and for the case of the death of any of the persons from whom the Senate may choose a Vice-President whenever the right of choice shall have devolved upon them.

Section 5. Sections 1 and 2 shall take effect on the 15th day of October following the ratification of this article.

Section 6. This article shall be inoperative unless it shall have been ratified as an amendment to the Constitution by the legislatures of three-fourths of the several States within seven years from the date of its submission.

ARTICLE XXI. *Section 1.* The Eighteenth Article of amendment to the Constitution of the United States is hereby repealed.

Section 2. The transportation or importation into any State, Territory, or possession of the United States for delivery or use therein of intoxicating liquors, in violation of the laws thereof, is hereby prohibited.

Section 3. This article shall be inoperative unless it shall have been ratified as an amendment to the Constitution by conventions in the several States, as provided in the Constitution, within seven years from the date of the submission hereof to the States by the Congress.

ARTICLE XXII. *Section 1.* No person shall be elected to the office of the President more than twice, and no person who has held the office of President, or acted as President, for more than two years of a term to which some other person was elected President shall be elected to the office of the President more than once. But this Article shall not apply to any person holding the office of President when this Article was proposed by the Congress, and shall not prevent any person who may be holding the office of President, or acting as President, during the term within which this Article becomes operative from holding the office of President or acting as President during the remainder of such term.

Section 2. This article shall be inoperative unless it shall have been ratified as an amendment to the Constitution by the legislatures of three-fourths of the several States within seven years from the date of its submission to the States by the Congress.

ARTICLE XXIII. *Section 1.* The District constituting the seat of government of the United States shall appoint in such manner as the Congress may direct:

A number of electors of President and Vice-President equal to the whole number of Senators and Representatives in Congress to which the District would be entitled if it were a State, but in no event more than the least populous State; they shall be in addition to those appointed by the States, but they shall be considered, for the purposes of the election of President and Vice-President, to be electors appointed by a State; and they shall meet in the District and perform such duties as provided by the twelfth article of amendment.

Section 2. The Congress shall have power to enforce this article by appropriate legislation.

ARTICLE XXIV. *Section 1.* The right of citizens of the United States to vote in any primary or other election for President or Vice-President, for electors for President or Vice-President, or for Senator or Representative in Congress, shall not be denied or abridged by the United States or any State by reason of failure to pay any poll tax or other tax.

Section 2. The Congress shall have power to enforce this article by appropriate legislation.

ARTICLE XXV. *Section 1.* In case of the removal of the President from office or of his death or resignation, the Vice-President shall become President.

Section 2. Whenever there is a vacancy in the office of the Vice-President, the President shall nominate a Vice-President who shall take office upon confirmation by a majority vote of both Houses of Congress.

Section 3. Whenever the President transmits to the President pro tempore of the Senate and the Speaker of the House of Representatives his written declaration that he is unable to discharge the powers and duties of his office, and until he transmits to them a written declaration to the contrary, such powers and duties shall be discharged by the Vice-President as Acting President.

Section 4. Whenever the Vice-President and a majority of either the principal officers of the executive departments or of such other body as Congress may by law provide, transmit to the President pro tempore of the Senate and the Speaker of the House of Representatives their written declaration that the President is unable to discharge the powers and duties of his office, the Vice-President shall immediately assume the powers and duties of the office as Acting President.

Thereafter, when the President transmits to the President pro tempore of the Senate and the Speaker of the House of Representatives his written declaration that no inability exists, he shall resume the powers and duties of his office unless the Vice-President and a majority of either the principal officers of the executive department or of such other body as Congress may by law provide, transmit within four days to the President pro tempore of the Senate and the Speaker of the House of Representatives their written declaration that the President is unable to discharge the powers and duties of his office. Thereupon Congress shall decide the issue, assembling within forty-eight hours for that purpose if not in session. If the Congress, within twenty-one days after receipt of the latter written declaration, or, if Congress is not in session, within twenty-one days after Congress is required to assemble, determines by two-thirds vote of both Houses that the President is unable to discharge the powers and duties of his office, the Vice-President shall continue to discharge the same as Acting President; otherwise, the President shall resume the powers and duties of his office.

ARTICLE XXVI. *Section 1.* The right of citizens of the United States, who are 18 years of age or older, to vote shall not be denied or abridged by the United States or any State on account of age.

Section 2. The Congress shall have the power to enforce this article by appropriate legislation.

— ALFRED H. KELLY

CONSUMER PROTECTION

Legislative protection of the consumer dates back to the codes of antiquity. In the United States the imposition of standards of coinage and of weights and measures in commercial transactions constituted an essential prelude to national economic development. Congressional power in this field is embedded in Article I, Section 8, of the U.S. Constitution, which provides that Congress shall have the power to "coin Money, regulate the Value thereof, . . . and fix the Standard of Weights and Measures."

In early American agrarian communities the buyer was effectively shielded by his knowledge of products and often by strong community sanctions against fraudulent practices. With the rise of specialization and of division of labor, the modern corporation became a distant and frequently anonymous market force. The growing power of product advertising allowed sellers to make exaggerated claims concerning the values alleged to be lodged in articles offered for sale. A growing consumer skepticism ensued from such overexuberant practices, followed by the enactment of legislation designed to afford the consumer protection from exaggerated claims, especially where product safety was involved. Among early protective laws was that banning the use of the mails for perpetration of fraud, passed in 1872. State and local governments also early provided "sealers" to inspect the accuracy of weights and measures and inspectors to check on sanitation standards. By 1906 the Pure Food and Drug Act was passed, following journalistic exposés of the sale of unsanitary meats and the peddling of worthless patent medicines. In 1914 the Federal Trade Commission was created to monitor false and misleading advertising.

Much of this early consumer legislation was ineffective because of narrow court interpretations and inadequate enforcement. Self-policing attempts by the advertising industry, as reflected in the rise of Better Business Bureaus, eliminated some superlatives but generally left consumers bewildered by rival product claims and cheated by dubious practices. In fact, a commercial advantage could be obtained by deception. Since the strongest promotion efforts were often applied on behalf of the most dubious products, self-policing of advertising was prone to be ineffective.

The demand of the American consumer for more legislative protection took shape in the 1920's with the appearance of the "guinea pig" books, which warned against product quackery. This agitation brought in 1928 the appearance of Consumers Research, a private nonprofit organization designed to substitute the publication of laboratory test results for partisan advertising claims. Consumers Research was soon to be overshadowed by a rival nonprofit testing organization, Consumers Union, formed in 1936. The latter had a subscription roster of 2,250,000 for its magazine *Consumer Reports* by 1974.

These consumer testing efforts greatly accelerated the growth of consumer legislation, including strengthening amendments to the Food and Drug Act and the Federal Trade Commission law, and also provided increased support for the consumer protective efforts of the Department of Agriculture, the Department of Transportation, and a host of other federal, state, and local governmental agencies. In 1961 President John F. Kennedy formed the Consumer Advisory Council, and during the administration of Lyndon B. Johnson the position of special assistant on consumer affairs and the President's Committee on Consumer Interests were established. Much of the emphasis on "consumerism" in the 1970's placed a new accent on product safety, environmental concerns, and reliance on product standards rather than advertising in product choice. National, state, and local consumer organizations were formed in the 1960's and 1970's under the aegis of the Consumer Federation of America to assist in the handling of buyers' complaints, to lobby for legislation, and to introduce consumer education into the schools. Similar consumer testing organizations have emerged abroad and have become federated in an International Organization of Consumers Unions founded in The Hague in 1960 to afford an international technical interchange.

The consumer protective movement has by no means eradicated fraud and misrepresentation from the marketplace. It has, however, compelled greater truth in labeling, encouraged a more substantial approximation to truth in advertising, and brought an increasing recognition by regulatory agencies that their mission is not centrally that of assisting business but of helping to provide honesty and fair dealing in the marketplace. Although consumers still speak with muted voices before regulatory commissions, a better balance of power between the consumer and the business interests was beginning to characterize the economy.

BIBLIOGRAPHY

Leland J. Gordon and Stewart Lee, *Economics for Consumers.*

Dexter W. Masters, *An Intelligent Buyer's Guide to Sellers.*

Ruby Turner Morris, *Consumers Union: Methods, Implications, Weaknesses and Strengths.*

— COLSTON E. WARNE

CONSUMER PROTECTION SINCE THE 1970S

As the modern consumer movement matured during the late 1970s and into the 1980s and 1990s, it found itself both enjoying the successes of trying to improve product safety and consumer awareness but also battling strong political and business attempts to curb or eliminate the movement's power. The consumer movement's successes included such important safety measures as the standard use of seat belts and air bags in cars and trucks sold in the United States. Consumers could also learn about the nutritional level of the packaged foods they bought, once the federal government, under prodding of the consumer movement, forced foodmakers to include such labeling on products. The movement also showed success on the antismoking front, with many public and private places across the country banning smoking. To others, however, the movement's maturity strangled the nation and business with regulations, increased costs for consumers, employed too many nonproductive lawyers, and added to the individual and collective sense of aggrievement that permeated much of American society during the late twentieth century.

The career of the man most responsible for the modern consumer movement—Ralph Nader—typifies the ups and downs of the movement. Nader, who during the late 1960s and early 1970s could claim credit for some of the nation's most important federal consumer protection laws, including the National Traffic and Motor Vehicle Safety Act (1966), the Freedom of Information Act (1966), and the Consumer Product Safety Act (1972), used the almost half-million dollars he received from General Motors to settle an invasion of privacy lawsuit to fund a network of dozens of consumer groups during the 1970s. Perhaps Nader's greatest success was improved auto safety. His 1965 book, *Unsafe at Any Speed*, exposed the safety mishaps and design flaws of U.S. automobiles and spurred safety and design changes in the auto industry leading to such innovations as seat belts, air bags, and antilock brakes. Traffic deaths in the United States fell from roughly 55,000 in the early 1970s to 47,000 in 1990. Nader could claim some credit for this decrease, together with such other factors as the raising of the drinking age to twenty-one in most states. During the late 1980s and 1990s Nader appeared to fall out of the public's favor and conservative commentators often criticized him. Nader, however, turned more political, by opposing the 1992 North American Free Trade Act and the 1993 revisions to the General Agreement on Tariffs and Trade. Nader said the agreements would undermine U.S. sovereignty and allow unsafe goods into the country. Passage of these acts may have blunted his public influence.

Other groups, both private and governmental, contributed to the consumer movement as well. Private groups included the Consumer Federation of America, the Center for Science in the Public Interest, and Consumers Union, which published the highly successful *Consumers Reports,* a monthly magazine with articles evaluating products and detailing political and business issues of importance to consumers. The movement also brought a consumerist bent to government agencies, with the Food and Drug Administration, the Federal Trade Commission, and the Environmental Protection Agency, among others, showing an understanding of consumer issues.

When some of Nader's Raiders went into private practice they found that their idealism on behalf of injured consumers could also mean ample monetary reward for themselves.

The movement for consumer protection and rights, however, led to many lawsuits, with debatable results. Many of Nader's Raiders were law students or young lawyers just out of law school; when some of them went into private practice they found that their idealism on behalf of injured consumers and workers could also mean ample monetary reward for them. Lawsuits proliferated in the 1970s, 1980s, and 1990s, as lawyers sued not just large corporations but small businesses, doctors, and other individuals over a multitude of real and imagined injuries. Many lawsuits addressed real wrongs. Thousands of women were part of the class-action suits brought against the manufacturers of tampons causing toxic shock syndrome, a form of poisoning that killed or permanently injured the women. The lawsuits brought millions of dollars in damages and forced tampon manufacturers to alter their products. Lawsuits also recovered damages for victims of the Ford Pinto, an automobile that, because of a design flaw, tended to explode and burn when struck from behind. Many lawsuits, however, were filed on much less justifiable grounds, clogging the courts and leading to outlandish jury verdicts, particularly when juries awarded punitive damages designed to punish defendants for their actions rather than compensate plaintiffs. In the 1980s and 1990s many state legislatures, as well as Congress, moved to restrict punitive damages.

As conservatives reasserted their power—first with Ronald Reagan's two terms as president during the 1980s, then with the Republican sweep of the 1994 congressional elections—many of the political and bureaucratic gains of the consumer movement came under attack and repeal. Taking their cue from the 1994 campaign document known as the "Contract with America," congressional Republicans introduced legislation the following year to curb or repeal such legislation as the Clean Water (1967) and Clean Air (1970) acts, which they deemed harmful to business. They also wanted to severely restrict the ability of stockholders to sue a company while also making it more difficult to sue a company for product liability. In addition, they moved to repeal some of the nation's banking laws that benefited consumers.

[See also Automobile Industry; Freedom of Information Act.]

BIBLIOGRAPHY

Ralph de Toledano, *Hit & Run: The Rise—and Fall?—of Ralph Nader* (New Rochelle, N.Y., 1975).

Jeffrey A. Hollender, *How to Make the World a Better Place: A Guide to Doing Good* (New York, 1990).

Robert N. Mayer, *The Consumer Movement: Guardians of the Marketplace* (Boston, 1989).

Richard Zimmerman, *What Can I Do to Make a Difference?: A Positive Action Sourcebook* (New York, 1991).

— THOMAS G. GRESS

CONTINENTAL CONGRESS

Continental Congress, the body of delegates of the American colonies first assembled in September 1774 and again in May 1775 as an advisory council of the colonies. It eventually became the central government of the union, serving as such until it was superseded on Mar. 4, 1789, by the new government under the Constitution.

The First Continental Congress, which sat at Philadelphia from Sept. 5 to Oct. 26, 1774 (the title officially adopted was simply "The Congress," although in popular usage the word "Continental" came to be prefixed to distinguish it from various provincial congresses), consisted of fifty-six delegates from twelve colonies

(Georgia did not elect or send delegates). It was called together to concert measures for the recovery of colonial rights and liberties held to have been violated by a succession of acts of the British government, culminating in a series of repressive measures primarily directed against Massachusetts but believed to involve threats to all the colonies. The principal measures taken by this Congress were the adoption of a Declaration of Rights (Oct. 14), of an Association (Oct. 20) whereby the colonies bound themselves in a nonimportation, a nonconsumption, and a nonexportation agreement, and of a resolution voicing the opinion that, unless the grievances had meanwhile been redressed, another congress should be assembled on May 10, 1775.

The grievances were not redressed, and the Second Continental Congress met in Philadelphia the following May. Meanwhile something close to war had broken out between Massachusetts and the British military forces, whereupon Congress resolved to give aid to Massachusetts, took over the provincial army at Boston, and appointed George Washington commander in chief "of all the continental forces, raised, or to be raised, for the defence of American liberty" (June 15, 1775). With these steps Congress definitely advanced from a mere clearinghouse of colonial opinion toward the superintending power over the unified colonial cause. For nearly six years thereafter, with little authority other than a general acquiescence, Congress not only took general direction of the war with Great Britain, but became the collective voice of the colonies, soon to become states, for a multitude of their other common activities as well.

In the early months of the Congress of 1775 the objective was still the recovery of rights, though not less the restoration of union and harmony between Great Britain and the colonies; but before another year had passed, as the conviction gathered strength that only by the force of arms could the prized liberties be preserved, the idea of independence had laid its grip upon the public mind. The result was that, on July 2, 1776, Congress adopted a resolution "that these United Colonies are, and of right ought to be, free and independent States"; two days later it adopted the Declaration of Independence.

Prior to the Declaration of Independence colonial jealousies had led Congress to draw back from every suggestion of a permanent union; but now the necessity for an effective organization of the states for the promotion of the common cause became evident; while some minds even glimpsed national unity as a goal to be sought for its own sake. Accordingly, Congress at once set about to frame an instrument of union. The task was exceedingly difficult, particularly reconciling the antagonistic views and interests of the small and large states, and it was not until after nearly a year and a half of effort, accompanied by numerous hot controversies, that Congress was able to come to an agreement upon that framework of government known as the Articles of Confederation (Nov. 15, 1777).

Ratification of the Articles by the several states was still necessary, and it was only on Mar. 1, 1781, that the last of the thirteen ratifications, that of Maryland, was obtained. From then on Congress was on a constitutional basis, a distinction sometimes emphasized by employing for this period the title "Congress

George Washington is appointed Commander in Chief in the Continental Congress, June 15, 1775. An 1876 lithograph by Currier and Ives. (The Granger Collection, New York)

of the Confederation." Passing from an unwritten to a written constitution made no great difference in the conduct of affairs by Congress. The principal change was that some things theretofore done in a more or less irregular manner were now regularized, such as the election of delegates, all phases of which formerly had been entirely at the discretion of the states, whether it was the number chosen or the times and terms of their election.

That the Articles of Confederation were defective in several particulars, none knew better than the very men who had framed them. For one thing, the method of voting by states, each state having one vote, adopted in the beginning as a concession to the small states, was perpetuated, with many unfortunate results. For another, no provision was made for the support of the central government other than through contributions by the states upon the requisition of Congress. This deficiency was not so clearly sensed at the outset, because Congress undertook to finance the war by means of its own bills of credit, and, so long as those bills were good as well as plentiful, Congress could speak and the states would listen. But when Continental money depreciated and Congress began to call on the states for help, there was grumbling and worse. A third serious defect of the Articles was the requirement of unanimous consent of the states to any amendment; every effort to obtain amendments was defeated by a single state. Still another defect was in the constitution of Congress itself. The sole embodiment of the government—legislative, executive, judicial—Congress was not fit to conduct a war or the administrative business of a government. Long hesitant to part with even the semblance of power—largely restrained by the fear of a strong executive that would pervade the states—Congress did little toward developing its administrative arm until the war was nearly over.

With the war and its impelling power for unity at an end, the states lost in great measure their concern for the Congress of their union and even drifted toward a dissolution of that union; while Congress, for its part, advanced not from strength to strength but from weakness to weakness. Only the determination of a small group to save the union led, through the Annapolis Convention, to the Convention of 1787, and finally to the newly framed Constitution. Congress was not wholly hostile to a constitutional convention; that plan had been broached in Congress several times and more than once was almost adopted. Nor was the government that was inaugurated under the Constitution the antithesis of the old Congress. On the contrary, the new government adopted much of the essential machinery and also a considerable body of substantive law from the old Congress.

[See Lexington and Concord.]

BIBLIOGRAPHY

Edmund C. Burnett, *Letters of Members of the Continental Congress.*
Edward Channing, *History of the United States.*
F. N. Thorpe, *Constitutional History of the United States.*

— EDMUND C. BURNETT

CONTRACEPTION

The contraceptive revolution began in the 1960s with the introduction of two highly effective methods of birth control—the oral contraceptive ("the pill") and the intrauterine device (IUD)—both of which separated the act of contraception from the act of sexual intercourse in time and space. Barrier methods of contraception (condom, diaphragm) must be applied at the time of intercourse and involve the genitals. The IUD is inserted by a physician and requires no further action from either the female or male partner. A woman takes the pill (orally) at any time of day, an action not related to the time of intercourse. The pill was approved as a prescription drug by the Food and Drug Administration (FDA) in 1960. By 1965 it became the most popular contraceptive in the United States, used by more than one out of four married women. By the end of the decade, however, the safety of oral contraceptives had been called into question by both medical experts and lay observers. A Senate committee conducted hearings to determine whether women were receiving adequate information about the health risks associated with the pill. The FDA subsequently required manufacturers to include an information pamphlet for patients within every pill package. After more than thirty years of experience with the pill, public health officials in the early 1990s began to consider the possibility of changing the status of oral contraceptives from prescription to over-the-counter drugs.

The contraceptive revolution began in the 1960's with the introduction of the oral contraceptive ("the pill") and the intrauterine device (IUD).

The IUD was never as popular as the pill in the United States. In the 1970s hundreds of lawsuits were filed against A. H. Robins, the manufacturer of the Dalkon Shield, because of the serious, even fatal, side effects of the device. This episode cast a shadow over all types of IUDs, and by the mid-1980s two other manufacturers had joined Robins in discontinuing sales in the United States. Use in this country dropped by two-thirds, although IUD use continued to be widespread elsewhere in the world, particularly in developing nations.

According to the National Survey of Family Growth, the leading method of birth control in 1988 was the pill, followed closely by female sterilization. Male and female sterilization taken together, comprised the most popular means of contraception among married couples. The condom gained acceptance, particularly among unmarried women, as the only method of contraception also effective in preventing the spread of AIDS and other sexually transmitted diseases. In the early 1990s two new contraceptive methods were introduced in the United States. Norplant, a subdermal implant that continuously releases a synthetic hormone into the blood over a five-year period, has been embroiled in social controversy because of legislative proposals offering incentives to welfare mothers who use it and judicial decisions mandating its use in sentencing of abusive mothers. Depo-Provera, a hormone injection with a contraceptive effect of three month's duration, was developed in the 1960s but did not receive FDA approval until 1992 because of concern about its carcinogenicity. Feminist groups object to Norplant and Depo-Provera because these long-lasting contraceptives may facilitate introduction of voluntary or mandatory birth-control programs and because reliance on such hormonal methods may curtail the use of condoms, increasing the risk of exposure to sexually transmitted diseases.

By the late 1980s all but one of the major pharmaceutical companies in the United States had withdrawn from contraceptive research and development, perhaps because of the increasingly litigious nature of U.S. society. As a result innovative methods of contraception, such as a male pill or an antifertility vaccine, were unlikely to be realized before the turn of the century.

BIBLIOGRAPHY

Linda Gordon, *Woman's Body, Woman's Right* (New York, 1990).
Nicole J. Grant, *The Selling of Contraception* (Columbus, Ohio, 1992).
James Reed, *The Birth Control Movement and American Society* (Princeton, N.J., 1984).

— ELIZABETH WATKINS

COOKERY

The preparation of food in the United States has come a long way since the first cookbook, *American Cookery* by Amelia Simmons, appeared in 1796. It was written in folksy language and described the dishes consumed by New England farmers. Over the next two hundred years, cooking methods, equipment, and utensils changed from the open-hearth to the wood stove and coal range to electrical and gas units and then to the microwave oven. While U.S. cookery includes fast food and health food, including vegetarian items, it is traditionally divided into seven regional areas in each of which can be found traces of its history.

The cookery of New England's Native American, English, Irish, and Canadian inhabitants had a heavy emphasis on fish, such as lobster, cod, salmon, and clams; stews such as chowders and mulligan stew; other mixed foods, including baked beans, succotash, and hash; and the ever-present cranberries for dessert. The Northeast's cuisine is traceable to the groaning tables of the Pennsylvania Dutch, Quakers, Scotch-Irish, and Germans, whose influences can be found in Philadelphia pepper pot soup, noodles, shad roe, crab cakes, hot dogs, dumplings, hamburgers, and the dessert shoo-fly pie. The influx of immigrants to urban areas created a medley of cuisines in cities such as New York, where in 1995 there were more than 6,000 restaurants serving the food of such ethnic groups as Italians, Jews, Chinese, Japanese, Koreans, Thais, Vietnamese, Greeks, Armenians, Turks, Pakistanis, Indians, Puerto Ricans and other Spanish-American people, and African Americans.

The first American cookbook, Amelia Simmons's American Cookery *(1796), described the dishes favored by New England farmers.*

Southern cookery owes a debt to its Anglo-Saxon and African heritage. The former contributed the soup known as mulligatawny, Virginia ham, baking-powder biscuits, hush puppies, and pecan pie, while the plantation slaves who were permitted to keep only chickens, cornmeal, and "all the black catfish caught" gave us soul food, including fried chicken, hominy grits, hog jowls, black-eyed peas, red beans and rice, catfish, chitterlings, and spoon bread. Gulf Coast cookery, called Creole or Cajun, is a mixture of French and Spanish cooking with a touch of African and Native American. A native seasoning called filé, made from dried and powdered sassafras leaves was added to okra, crayfish, shrimp, rice, and corn to create jambalaya and gumbo.

The cuisine of the Midwest owes its origins to the pioneers and Middle European immigrants who brought kielbasa, sauerkraut, and matzoon (yogurt soup) to America, as well as to the Scandinavians who settled in Wisconsin and Minnesota, which became famous dairy regions. The word "Danish" became synonymous with coffeecake and Wisconsin became noted for its cheeses. Because of the early cattle trail history of the area, during which Chicago became the meat-packing center of the United States, the primary element in Midwestern cooking is still steak. The Southwest's fiery dishes and salsas pay tribute to the Mexican-Indian beginnings of this area, where meat, chicken, beans, corn, and pepper are the bases of such recipes as chili con carne, enchiladas, tacos, refried beans, and mole. The Spanish-Mexican custom of roasting an animal *barba a cola*, from beard to tail, was the origin of the outdoor American barbecue. The cookery of the Northwest, including the Alaskan frontier, emphasizes fish and game, such as salmon, crab, and venison, all served with sourdough bread, so named from the yeast or sourdough starters that were valuable to the early pioneers; the settlers of Nome and Anchorage were themselves called "Sourdoughs."

Modern technologies, such as canned and frozen foods and the refrigerated trucks that transport them and fresh foods all over the United States, have diminished regional differences in cookery, while modem advertising has created demands for new concoctions, such as frozen pizza bagels, which can only be described as a distinctly American product.

BIBLIOGRAPHY

Evan Jones, *American Food: The Gastronomic Story*, 2nd ed. (New York, 1981).

Harvey A. Levenstein, *Paradox of Plenty: A Social History of Eating in Modern America* (New York, 1993), and *Revolution at the Table: The Transformation of the American Diet* (New York, 1988).

Waverly Root and Richard de Rochemont, *Eating in America* (New York, 1976).

Sallie Y. Williams, *American Feasts: The Best of American Regional Cooking* (New York, 1985).

— JOHN J. BYRNE

COOPERATIVES, FARMERS'

Farmers' cooperatives have been of continuing importance in American agriculture. Farmers use these associations for marketing products, purchasing farm supplies, and providing themselves with such services as insurance, credit, electricity, and irrigation. In general they function as democratic self-help organizations on a cost-of-service basis. Farmers' cooperatives in the United States go back to the early 19th century. They began to develop rapidly after the Civil War with promotion by the Granger movement. Their intensive development started about 1900, and they have expanded steadily. One of the major cooperative marketing organizations of the 1970's, Sunkist Grower's, Inc., began operations before the turn of the century. For many years it has served as a model in the cooperative field. By 1920 farmers' marketing and purchasing associations were doing an annual business of about $1 billion and were serving nearly one million farmers. By the end of World War II their annual volume had increased to approximately $5 billion and they were serving over 3 million farmers.

The years 1920–45 saw all forms of cooperative enterprise in the United States advance, with the active encouragement of the federal and state governments. During this period the legal status of cooperative organizations was clarified by acts of Congress and court decisions. Farmers' cooperatives gained further stature under the New Deal, which brought about the establishment of the cooperative Farm Credit Administration to help with farmers' financial problems and the Rural Electrification Administration to help provide electricity through cooperative associations. During World War II, farmers' cooperatives demonstrated their usefulness in mobilizing agricultural resources for the war effort. Since 1946 they have played an important role in modernizing American agriculture. Many farmers' cooperatives are now large, integrated organizations serving tens of thousands of farmers. Several are included in *Fortune* magazine's list of 500 major industrial corporations. Many large cooperatives are federations of local cooperatives; others are centralized associations that the farmers join directly.

Farmers' cooperatives benefited from the New Deal, which brought about the cooperative Farm Credit Administration and the Rural Electrification Administration.

Government statistics for 1969–70 recorded a total of 7,719 farmers' cooperatives representing a total membership of about 6 million farmers. However, many farmers belong to more than one cooperative. The total net business done by farmers' marketing and purchasing cooperatives in 1969–70 amounted to $19 billion, and the total investment of farmers in these associations in 1971 amounted to $3.7 billion, as compared with $330 million in 1940. Farmers' cooperatives are well established in all parts of the United States.

While Minnesota leads all states in number of memberships, California leads in volume of business done by such associations.

BIBLIOGRAPHY

Joseph G. Knapp, *The Rise of American Cooperative Enterprise, 1620–1920,* and *The Advance of American Cooperative Enterprise, 1920–1945.*

Edwin G. Nourse, *The Legal Status of Agricultural Cooperation.*

Ewell Paul Roy, *Cooperatives—Today and Tomorrow.*

— JOSEPH G. KNAPP

COPPERHEADS

Copperheads, originally, a term used to designate the Democratic followers of Andrew Beaumont in Luzerne County, Pa., about 1840, who were opposed to the Democratic faction led by Hendrick B. Wright. It was revived during the Civil War to describe the Democrats opposed to the war policy of President Abraham Lincoln. The term "Copperhead" appeared in the *New York Tribune* on July 20, 1861, and within a year was common. Strongest in Ohio, Indiana, and Illinois, the Copperheads, sometimes known as Butternuts or Peace Democrats, were encouraged by Democratic successes in the elections of 1862.

Generally described as treasonable, the Copperheads advocated a union restored by negotiation rather than war. They denounced military arrests, conscription, emancipation, and other war measures. C. L. Vallandigham of Ohio was their chief spokesman. His arrest in May 1863 for alleged disloyal statements embarrassed the Lincoln administration. Other leaders were Alexander Long of Cincinnati, Fernando Wood of New York, and B. G. Harris of Maryland. Prominent newspapers supporting the Copperheads were the *Columbus* (Ohio) *Crisis*, the *Cincinnati Enquirer*, and the *Chicago Times*.

Their lack of sympathy for the Confederates was shown by the Copperheads in July 1863, when they joined unionists in defending Indiana and Ohio during Col. John H. Morgan's raid. Persecuted by the military and the Union League, the Copperheads in 1862 organized the Knights of the Golden Circle, borrowing the name and ritual of a southern rights organization of the 1850's. The organization was known as the Order of American Knights in 1863, and the Sons of Liberty in 1864, when Vallandigham became supreme commander. He counseled them against treason and violence. In 1864 extremists of the order were charged with plotting the formation of a "Northwestern Confederacy" and planning the release of Confederate prisoners at Camp Douglas near Chicago, and elsewhere. The plot was uncovered before any overt acts took place. In the fall of 1864 six members of the Sons of Liberty were tried for treason before a military court in Indiana, and three were condemned to death, including L. P. Milligan.

In 1864 the Copperhead element in the Democratic party was able to control the party platform, which included a plank written by Vallandigham pronouncing the war a failure and demanding peace on the basis of a restored federal union. The successful termination of the war discredited the Copperheads, and the Democratic party was handicapped for some years because of its wartime Copperhead affiliates.

BIBLIOGRAPHY

E. J. Benton, *The Movement for Peace Without a Victory During the Civil War.*

— CHARLES H. COLEMAN

CORONADO'S EXPEDITION

Coronado's Expedition (1540–42). Inspired by the reports of Marcos de Niza about the incredibly wealthy Seven Cities of Cibola, the expedition of the Spanish nobleman Francisco Vásquez de Coronado, accompanied by de Niza, started north from Mexico City on Feb. 22, 1540. The army consisted of 300 mounted and armored Spaniards and 800 Mexican Indian footmen. Coronado followed the route previously traversed by de Niza and Esteban through Arizona and New Mexico. On July 7 he entered and captured the Zuni pueblo of Hawikuh but was bitterly disappointed to find no treasures there. Meanwhile, a maritime branch of the expedition under Hernando de Alarcón had sailed up the west coast of Mexico and had ascended the Colorado River in small boats for some distance while a land party under Melchior Diaz had crossed the desert in Sonora, Mexico, and in southern Arizona to attempt to join Alarcón.

During the summer and winter, Coronado sent out exploring parties to the northeast, where other towns had been reported. Pedro de Tovar entered the villages of the Hopi, while a detachment under García López de Cárdenas discovered the Grand Canyon. Capt. Hernando de Alvarado went east to the country of the Rio Grande Pueblo, moving as far north as Taos and east to the grassy plains of the Llano Estacado ("staked plains").

Proceeding east, Coronado himself set up headquarters at Tiguex, a large Tiwa pueblo on the Rio Grande in New Mexico. A subsequent revolt of the Indians at Tiguex was put down with great severity.

Lured on by tales of gold related by a Plains Indian captive living at the pueblo of Pecos, Coronado in 1541 pushed east into the Plains in quest of the allegedly fabulously wealthy country of Quivira. Early in July 1541 his expedition came to the grass huts of the villages of the Quivirans, who were Wichita, in what is now Kansas. They had no treasures. The disillusioned Coronado returned to spend another winter on the Rio Grande and then went back to Mexico in 1542. Although he had discovered no cities of gold, his journey was an important one of exploration, for it acquainted the Spaniards with the Pueblo and opened the Southwest to future exploration and settlement.

BIBLIOGRAPHY

Herbert E. Bolton, *Coronado, Knight of Pueblos and Plains*, and *Coronado on the Turquoise Trail.*

George P. Hammond and Agapito Rey, *Narratives of the Coronado Expedition.*

George P. Winship, *The Journey of Coronado.*

— KENNETH M. STEWART

CORPORATIONS

The great trading companies chartered in the 16th and 17th centuries by the English monarchs were the first corporations in American history. The London and Plymouth companies, the Massachusetts Bay Company, and the Hudson's Bay Company played a large part in the establishment and support of European colonies in North America. The royal charter of such companies made legitimate a wide range of essentially governmental functions, including local government, control of customs and the terms of trade, and even the formulation of foreign policy in the geographical areas in which their charters gave them jurisdiction.

By the 18th century the governmental functions of corporations had receded and they had become primarily trading companies. Furthermore, their monopoly in trade was held by judges to exclude competition only from other chartered companies; unincorporated companies could lawfully compete with them. Indeed, the greater part of economic activity in the colonies came to be organized by single proprietors or partnerships under the common law of contract and property. Royal governors and colonial legislatures did, however, charter a few business corporations.

From the Revolution until about the late 1880's, business corporations were created by state legislatures for well-defined, limited purposes, and their charters fixed in great detail their internal structure. The burden of proof was on the businessman to show the legislature that a public purpose would be served by a state grant of special privilege. The charter granted both status as a legal entity and franchise rights to use assets in ways not open to men generally. Unlike most other associations of businessmen in joint ventures, the corporation was given the right to hold title to property and to make contracts as if it were a natural person without obligating the individual members of the group beyond their commitment of capital. A charter thus created an organization whose governing rules for conflict resolution had the force of law and whose life could survive the withdrawal or the death of its members.

By the 18th century the governmental functions of corporations had receded and they had become primarily trading companies.

From 1780 to 1801, U.S. state legislatures chartered 317 business corporations. Almost all of these were created for such public purposes as supplying water, transport, insurance, or banking services. During the 19th century, as mining and manufacturing grew relative to agriculture in the U.S. economy, corporations came to be used more and more for general business purposes. As early as 1811, New York had enacted a general incorporating statute, but it was of limited application. The Connecticut incorporating act of 1837 was much broader and more flexible, while the New Jersey incorporating act of 1875 embodied many provisions long sought by business and gained in individual instances by particular companies only through special enactment. In the 1870's, however, the privileges granted by corporate charters remained insufficient to facilitate as much centralization of control of manufacturing as some businessmen desired. As the U.S. transportation network grew and markets became interstate in character, multistate business entities arose in the form of trusts. In several industries, trustees exercised control by holding the stock of a number of corporations operating throughout the country.

In 1890 Congress enacted the Sherman Antitrust Act, declaring combinations in restraint of trade to be illegal. But between 1887 and 1893 the New Jersey legislature enacted a series of statutes greatly liberalizing its 1875 law and making resort to the trust device unnecessary for the achievement of centralization of control of an industry through a New Jersey corporation, whether the corporation operated directly or through subsidiaries in other states, or even in foreign nations. Whereas earlier general incorporation had typically delimited the geographical region in which the corporation could hold property and carry on business, New Jersey in 1887 amended its law to allow foreign corporations to own real estate in New Jersey and in 1892 removed all restrictions on its own corporations doing business outside the state. The earlier laws had also restricted corporate growth in other ways. Expansion had required either the slow process of accumulation of surpluses from earnings or charter amendment to raise funds through increased capitalization. Corporate growth and mergers were greatly facilitated by several other changes in the New Jersey law about 1890. These changes included blanket grants of power to previously chartered, as well as new, corporations to merge; to increase the amount of capital stock; to exchange newly issued stock for property; and to purchase stock in any other corporations with cash or newly issued stock.

Although the U.S. Constitution makes no reference to corporations, it gives Congress the power to regulate commerce between the several states and with foreign nations. Congress used this power in chartering national banks and transcontinental railroads in the 19th century. Federal incorporation as a prerequisite to engaging in interstate commerce has been proposed and debated over the years, but Congress has chosen to carry out its corporate responsibility by regulation of state-chartered corporations, and since 1890 the federal government has played the major role in constraining the power of state-chartered corporations to centralize control of economic activity throughout the nation and the world. In addition to specifically regulating such industries as transportation, radio broadcasting, and atomic energy, the federal government regulates corporations engaged in interstate and foreign commerce through antitrust laws.

A revolutionary change in the structure of control of the mining and manufacturing industries occurred around the turn of the century, a change that the Sherman act failed to prevent. In 1895, in the E C. Knight case, the Supreme Court held that the commerce clause of the Constitution did not grant the federal government power to prevent a state-chartered corporation from acquiring control of plants producing 98 percent of the refined sugar in the nation. That decision, coupled with the liberal New Jersey incorporation laws, made combinations legal that otherwise would have been held in restraint of trade. Between 1896 and 1904 the remaining trusts were converted into New Jersey holding companies; and most other manufacturing industries were brought under centralized control through the great merger movement that took place at that time. The oligopoly structure, in which a few corporations control the bulk of the capacity of an industry, has been typical since that time.

In 1903 Congress reacted to the merger movement by creating the Antitrust Division in the Department of Justice, by enacting the Expediting Act to get antitrust cases quickly before the Supreme Court, and by creating the Bureau of Corporations. The bureau's function was to investigate and publicize the state of control of industries by corporations. In 1904 the Supreme Court put some life back into the Sherman act by ordering dissolved the Northern Securities Company, a New Jersey corporation chartered for the purpose of combining control of two transcontinental railroads. In 1911, largely through the work of the Bureau of Corporations, both the Standard Oil Company and the American Tobacco Company were also ordered dissolved by the Supreme Court under the Sherman act.

Although the U.S. Constitution makes no reference to corporations, it gives Congress the power to regulate commerce between the states and with foreign nations.

In 1914 the Bureau of Corporations was removed from the Department of Commerce and converted into an independent agency by the Federal Trade Commission Act, which also made unfair methods of competition illegal under federal law. The Clayton Antitrust Act, passed also in 1914, supplemented the Sherman act with specific provisions on tying contracts, interlocking directorates, intercorporate stockholding, and price discrimination. But in 1920, in the United States Steel case, the Court sanctioned a corporate structure in which one company controlled about half of the industry, U.S. Steel having been created in 1901 by a consolidation of about 180 formerly independent corporations. In 1950, the Celler-Kefauver Act strengthened the law on corporate mergers and acquisitions; but the role of the corporation has continued to grow.

Fortune magazine reported that its list of the 500 largest American industrial corporations in 1971 accounted for 66 percent of the sales of all industrial companies in the United States, 75 percent of their total profits, and 75 percent of all their employees. A 1969 Federal Trade Commission staff report showed that in 1968 the largest 100 corporations held 49.3 percent of all assets held by industrial corporations; the largest 100 in 1968 held a larger share than the largest 200 had held in 1947. Concentration of control of industry in the hands of a relatively few very large corporations, along with the relative decline of agriculture, has changed the American economy from one organized primarily by small businesses buying and selling in competitive markets into a bureaucratically administered "new industrial state."

Response in the 20th century to the growth of power in the hands of state-chartered corporations controlled by a relatively small number of persons has been to create, through federal action, countervailing power. Beginning in the 1930's, national policy encouraged labor unions and collective bargaining by workers. In the 1960's and 1970's the power of corporations over the lives of consumers began to elicit a similar response in the growth of public interest law firms, class-action suits, and organized political and educational activities by groups of consumers and environmentalists. Federal control of product quality to protect the public health and safety is not new: as early as the 1830's federal safety rules were enforced for steamboat engines on navigable waterways. Public pressure for such regulation of corporations grew steadily in the 1960's, however, as confidence waned in the corporation as an adequate protector of the public interest.

A new chapter in the history of the corporation in America may be emerging in the last quarter of the 20th century. The transformation of commerce from state to interstate scope gave rise to a shift from state to federal government as the arena of public policy. A similar transformation from national to multinational scope has also taken place. Almost all of the hundred or so very large American corporations operate directly or through subsidiary corporations in world markets. Their power in the economies of other nations has in some nations given rise to governmental responses that create conflict between governments as well. Indeed, America's great multinational corporations may come to play a role in the world not unlike that of the great English trading companies that played such a major role in the founding of America.

BIBLIOGRAPHY

Paul A. Baran and Paul M. Sweezy, *Monopoly Capital: An Essay on the American Economic and Social Order.*

Adolph A. Berle, Jr., and Gardner C. Means, *The Modern Corporation and Private Property.*

John M. Blair, *Economic Concentration.*

Joseph S. Davis, *Essays in the Earlier History of American Corporations.*

Edwin Merrick Dodd, *American Business Corporations Until 1860.*

James Willard Hurst, *The Legitimacy of the Business Corporation.*

Ferdinand Lundberg, *The Rich and the Super-Rich.*

Morton Mintz and Jerry Cohen, *America, Inc.*

Willard F. Mueller, *A Primer on Monopoly and Competition.*

— DAVID DALE MARTIN

CORRUPTION, POLITICAL

Political corruption has four principal meanings. The first is patently illegal behavior in the sphere of politics; bribery is a prime example. The second relates to governmental practices that, while legal, may be improper or unethical. To some people, patronage is such a practice—although, it should be noted, patronage can also serve democratic ends and can even be used to combat corruption. A third meaning involves conflicts of interest on the part of public officials—for example, the vote of a legislator who owns oil stock and casts his vote in favor of oil depletion allowances. James Madison made this point eloquently in *Federalist* No. 10: "No man is allowed to be a judge in his own cause, because his interest would certainly bias his judgment, and, not improbably, corrupt his integrity." The fourth meaning also has an ethical, rather than a legal, basis. It relates to political behavior that is nonresponsive to the public interest. The Watergate scandals provide vivid examples of such corrupt behavior, but the classic formulation of this view remains the one given by John E. E. Dalberg-Acton (Lord Acton): "Power tends to corrupt and absolute power corrupts absolutely."

Charges of corruption have been a constant feature of American politics since the birth of the Republic. During the Revolution, George Washington spoke of the "stock-jobbing and fertility in all the low arts to obtain advantage of one kind or another," as well as the "want of virtue" and the "dirty, mercenary spirit" prevailing in the realm of politics.

The 19th century witnessed corruption on a grand scale, generally in connection with the workings of the spoils system. Among the most prominent instances of corruption were: (1) the Indian land frauds of the 1850's (and for several decades thereafter), (2) the scandals of Ulysses S. Grant's administration, especially the Crédit Mobilier affair, and (3) the murky bargaining after the 1876 presidential election, resulting in the "election" of Rutherford B. Hayes.

Congress was a major center of corruption during the 19th and early 20th centuries. Between 1863 and 1883, for example, every speaker of the House of Representatives who was in office for at least one full term was charged with corruption. The Senate, too, was rife with corruption and scandal, especially before 1913, when members of that body were selected by state legislatures. Bribery and "influence peddling" among state legislators were so widespread, people quipped "We have the best senators that money can buy."

Charges of corruption are nothing new: George Washington spoke of the "want of virtue" and the "dirty, mercenary spirit" prevailing in politics.

The Teapot Dome affair was probably the most significant episode of political corruption to occur during the first half of the 20th century. In the 1960's, Bobby Baker, secretary of the Senate majority, engaged in "influence peddling," utilizing his political position and influence to enrich himself. (He ultimately was convicted of grand larceny.) The Watergate scandal of the Richard M. Nixon era involved corruption on a vaster scale. It included illegal political contributions, the "laundering" of campaign funds, the "sale" of ambassadorships, and the use of government agencies by the administration for personal and political gain. The president was charged, in the articles of impeachment drawn up by the House Judiciary Committee, with "obstruction of justice," "abuse of his powers," and "contempt of Congress."

Instances of corruption at state and local governmental levels have also been numerous and varied. They have included illicit or improper dealings in contracts, franchises, prostitution, drugs, and countless other goods and services, and a range of other crimes limited only by participants' opportunities and ingenuity. Perhaps the most famous network of corrupt local officials—and certainly one of the most successful—was the Boss Tweed (William Marcy Tweed) ring. Between 1865 and 1871 (when Tweed went to prison), the ring stole approximately $100 million from New York City.

In the face of the prevalence of current political corruption, there is a tendency to evoke a golden past in which officials were untainted. Historical data suggest the opposite. Ethical standards have improved. If, for example, today's standards had been applied in John Marshall's time, the great chief justice would have been unable to take part in the case of *Marbury* v. *Madison* (1803), much less write the majority opinion. It was Marshall who, as secretary of state, failed to deliver the signed and sealed commission appointing William Marbury as justice of the peace, and Marbury was contesting the withholding of the commission. Today, any member of the Court who had been so intimately involved in the early stages of a case would disqualify himself from taking part in the decision. Also, while serving both as a member of Congress and as counsel for the Bank of the United States, Daniel Webster received $47,000 from a group of businessmen when the bank's charter came up for renewal. Supposedly, there were no strings attached. The facts caused little excitement at the time, although the circumstances were well known. Today, a great furor would take place over such an action.

Controls over political corruption take three forms: (1) conflict and competition among the different branches of government, political parties, interest groups, and the mass media, (2) laws defining certain acts as illegal and prescribing appropriate punishments, and (3) regulations limiting the excesses of the spoils system, governing financial matters, and controlling lobbying. The Pendleton Act of 1883, establishing the civil service, was the first of these. Statutes adopted in 1907, 1910, and 1925 have served to regulate campaign funding, and the Federal Regulation of Lobbying Act of 1946 sets limits on the activities of paid lobbyists. These and other laws have been amended, and still others have been enacted, in an effort to close loopholes in the system of controls. The effort has not been entirely successful; some old loopholes have remained, and a number of new ones have been developed.

The continued existence of corruption is testimony to the imperfections of the American political system. Continuing spotlighting of such corruption is testimony to two interrelated aspects of the system: its self-correcting and adjusting nature and the close connection between political and societal practices, values, and institutions.

BIBLIOGRAPHY

Arnold A. Rogow and Harold D. Lasswell, *Power, Corruption, and Rectitude.*

— NORMAN JOHN POWELL

COTTON

Although grown in the South since the founding of Jamestown in 1607, cotton did not become a cash crop during the colonial period. Most was consumed locally in domestic manufacture. By the late 18th century, revolutionary inventions in the English textile industry began the process that would transform the American South into the "cotton kingdom." John Kay's flying shuttle (patented 1733) and James Hargreaves' spinning jenny (patented 1770) speeded up weaving and spinning processes, and when these innovations were adapted first to water and then to steam power, English textile production soared. Cotton imports increased fiftyfold in the second half of the 18th century, but rising prices indicated that the cotton supply was failing to meet the spiraling demand of Lancashire's mills. When trade with England reopened after the Revolution (1783), planters in the coastal areas of South Carolina and Georgia found a lucrative market for their long-staple, black-seed cotton. Further inland, only the short-staple (or uplands) variety would grow; and because its green seeds stick so tenaciously to the staple, they had to be picked out by hand, a time-consuming process that even prevailing high prices could not support.

When in 1793 Eli Whitney invented his cotton gin, a device that quickly and cheaply separated the seeds from the staple, Georgia and South Carolina planters expanded production of the new cash crop. Exports increased from 500,000 pounds in 1793 to 18 million pounds by 1800 and more than 90 million pounds a decade later. The cotton belt in Georgia and South Carolina rapidly expanded westward as farmers and planters pushed into the virgin lands in south-central Alabama; into the rich delta lands in Mississippi, northern Louisiana, Arkansas, and Tennessee; and into western Texas. In 1860, the United States produced more than 2 billion pounds (4.5 million bales) of cotton, almost 80 percent of which came from the states of Georgia, Alabama, Mississippi, and Louisiana. About 75 percent of this crop was exported, mainly to England where American cotton enjoyed a near monopoly.

Southerners proclaimed that "cotton was king," and indeed the evidence seemed to support this view. Cotton attracted millions of settlers into the Southwest; southern demand for foodstuffs helped bring population into the Old Northwest; eastern merchants found some of their best customers in the cotton belt; New England textile manufacturers and workers relied for their well-being on the South's chief product; and in the last three antebellum decades, cotton provided well over half the nation's exports.

Cotton was grown by small farmers, but the most efficient and extensive production was by planters with gangs of slave labor. Planting began in early spring; the long hot days of summer were spent thinning the plants and chopping out menacing weeds; picking started in late August and continued for several months. The cotton was ginned, pressed, and baled on the plantation and then shipped to market—usually New Orleans, Charleston, Savannah, or Mobile—and consigned to factors who sold it to representatives of American and European mills. Factors purchased supplies and other goods for their clients and then, after deducting expenses and commissions, remitted the net proceeds of the crop to the planter.

The Civil War proved that cotton was not king. The Union blockade separated the South from its markets and sources of supply; and the British, despite the so-called cotton famine, neither recognized the South nor attempted to break the blockade. The war left most cotton farmers destitute, their fields and equipment in neglect or ruin, and their black labor force now free. Gradually the South returned to cotton but under a much altered system of production and marketing. Land was rented out in small parcels, usually under the sharecropping system by which the tenant, in return for the right to use the land and some equipment, shared his crop with the landlord. For his supplies, food, and clothing, the sharecropper turned to a local storekeeper (called the "furnishing merchant"), who furnished goods on credit in return for a crop lien that gave him first call on the sharecropper's proceeds from the growing crop. At first most of the tenants were recently freed slaves but in time more and more farmers themselves lost their land and became tenants. In 1880, 36 percent of cotton farmers were tenants; in 1920 this figure had risen to almost 50 percent; and in 1935 it had risen to over 60 percent. By the turn of the century, more whites than blacks were tenants.

Planting began in early spring; the long hot days of summer were spent thinning and weeding the plants; picking started in late August and continued for several months.

Meanwhile, cotton production increased. Within a decade after the end of the Civil War, the prewar high of 4.5 million bales was equaled, and the output continued to grow, reaching 10 million bales by 1900 and 16 million bales on the eve of World War I. Acreage devoted to cotton increased from fewer than 8 million acres in 1869 to 25 million in 1900 and more than 35 million in 1914.

By this time there were signs of serious trouble in the southern cotton belt. Declining prices and production inefficiencies brought poverty and hardship to millions of cotton growers, a condition worsened by the boll weevil infestation that entered Texas in 1892 and gradually spread north and east, reaching Georgia and South Carolina in 1922. The United States lost its domination of the raw cotton markets as countries such as India, China, the Soviet Union, and Brazil increased production. Rich, irrigated lands in the western states of California, Arizona, and New Mexico were shifted to cotton production; and these areas—free from the uncertainties of weather, the boll weevil, and weed infestation—offered disastrous competition to the older cotton areas. With the Great Depression, cotton prices dropped still lower and conditions reached crisis proportions.

Once again change came to the cotton belt. Cotton acreage, which had reached a high of almost 45 million in 1925, dropped to half that total in the immediate post–World War II years and continued to drop, reaching about 11 million in 1971. Production also declined but at a much slower rate. While acreage devoted to cotton dropped 75 percent from the mid-1920's to 1972, production decreased only about 30 percent, from 16 million to 11 million bales. As marginal lands were taken out of cotton, production on better lands became mechanized with the introduction of tractors, plows, weeders, and automatic pickers. Sharecroppers fled the cotton fields or were driven away by the introduction of machinery; output per man-hour on the mechanized cotton farms increased nine times between 1940 and 1973. The eastern cotton states became minor producers as the cotton belt shifted west. In 1970, Texas was the largest producer, followed by Mississippi, California, and Arkansas; and Arizona grew more cotton than did Alabama, Georgia, and the Carolinas.

Although the United States remained the world's leading cotton producer, its onetime near monopoly was gone. By the early 1960's its share of world production had dropped to less than 30 percent, and by 1971, to 19 percent. Moreover, cotton growers, despite increasing efficiency and ample government price supports, apprehensively faced a new threat in the increasing popularity of man-made fibers. Per capita consumption of cotton in the United States fell from 30 pounds in 1950 to less than 19 pounds in 1970, while per capita consumption of artificial fibers rose from 10 pounds to 32 pounds during the same period.

— HAROLD D. WOODMAN

Cotton Manufacturing

The processing of raw cotton begins with the breaking of compressed bales (average weight 478 pounds). Bale breakers, openers, and pickers loosen and blend the tufts of cotton and remove impurities. Carding engines complete the cleaning process, eliminate short and broken fibers, and separate and align those remaining into soft, ropelike "slivers." To obtain high-quality yarn, combers process fine (thin) cotton into slivers, removing as much as 20 percent of the shorter fibers. Drawing frames begin the process of attenuating and twisting the slivers and enhance their regularity by drawing them between rollers and arranging them in parallel rows. A series of machines collectively known as "speed frames" conclude the preparation of cotton for the spinning frames, principally by further drawing out and twisting the material into a rope called "roving" and adding strength to the fibers by making them cling to each other more closely. In the spinning stage, frames equipped with ring spindles draw and twist the fibers into yarn while winding them on a bobbin. The process is continuous, with drawing, twisting, and winding taking place simultaneously. During the preparatory and spinning processes cotton suffers a loss in weight of 9–12 percent. In comparison, man-made filament fibers spun into yarn on cotton textile machinery incur a negligible loss. Approximately two-thirds of man-made fibers come from chemical producers already processed as filament yarn.

Cotton yarns are processed into fabrics by knitting, tufting, and weaving. Knitting consists essentially of interlacing a single strand of yarn into a series of interlocking loops. Hundreds of items of cotton and cotton-blended apparel are produced in knitting mills. Considerable quantities of cotton yarn are also converted into a variety of tufted products on tufting machines and consumed in various nonwoven constructions, in which fibers are bonded together with adhesives. The greatest proportion of cotton yarn continues to be channeled into broadloom weaving, where additional preparation is required depending on whether it is destined to be warp (longitudinal) or weft (transverse) yarn. Weaving, conducted on high-speed automatic looms, involves the interlacing of yarn at right angles so as to form a fabric.

Upon leaving the weave shed, most unbleached gray goods are subject to finishing treatments. Initially, the fabric passes in succession through a series of scouring, washing, and bleaching units. It is then dyed and printed. A wide range of mechanical and chemical processes have been developed to render the fabric more useful and fashionable. Mechanical processes can stiffen, glaze, and improve the texture of the cloth. Chemistry can provide additional strength, such as fire retardance and abrasion and wind resistance, or it can impart various qualities desirable in apparel, such as permanent press, crease resistance, and shrinkage control, as well as a silklike sheen and the puckering quality of seersucker.

Industry Changes

The eroding role of cotton in the American textile industry is reflected in the breakdown of major end-uses for all fibers. Between 1968 and 1973, cotton's percentage of total poundage in apparel dropped from 45 to 33 percent; in home furnishings, from 45 to 29 percent; in other consumer-type products, from 45 to 29 percent; and in industrial uses, from 32 to 21 percent.

Aggregate cotton consumption by U.S. mills in 1973 amounted to 3,641,700,000 pounds (29.2 percent of total fiber consumption) compared to 3,773,600,000 pounds consumed in 1970 (39.5 percent of total fiber consumption).

The new textile technology has flourished in the Southeast, where large pools of white and black female labor are readily available in hundreds of small towns.

During the 1960's the American textile industry became increasingly multifiber. The versatility of modern textile technology has permitted the processing of cotton, cotton-synthetic blends, and various man-made fibers without requiring a change in machinery layout. In addition, both capital and labor requirements have been lowered as faster and larger-capacity equipment has reduced both the number of machines and the number of operatives and maintenance workers needed for a given output. A small number of large, multiplant firms accounts for a high proportion of capital expenditures for plant and equipment as well as for most textile research. During the 1958–70 period, capital expenditures for the textile industry as a whole increased at an 11.3 percent annual rate. For knit fabric mills the annual rate was 23 percent; for cotton broadloom weaving establishments, on the other hand, the rate was only 3.7 percent per annum.

The new textile technology has flourished in the sprawling, single-story structures dotting the southeastern United States, where large pools of white and black female labor are readily available in hundreds of small communities. At the same time, the trend toward technological modernization has hastened the obsolescence of the aged, multistory mills that predominated in New England. By 1970 three-fourths of cotton textile employment was concentrated in the Southeast. Blue-collar occupations—primarily semi-skilled machine tending—constituted 85 percent of textile employment, a smaller share of jobs going to professional, research, clerical, and sales personnel than in most manufacturing industries. Women workers made up more than 65 percent of the employees in knitting mills but only 25 percent of the employees in textile-finishing establishments.

Although cotton manufacturing remains more fragmented and highly competitive than most industries, a trend toward fewer and larger firms is taking place; numerous mergers and acquisitions were effected during the 1960's, and many small mills shut down. By 1970, the four largest establishments making cotton broadwoven fabric accounted for 33 percent of total industry value of shipments (compared with 13 percent in 1947), while the eight largest firms accounted for 50 percent of the value of broadwoven shipments (compared to 22 percent in 1947).

BIBLIOGRAPHY

Stuart Bruchey, *Cotton and the Growth of the American Economy, 1790–1860.*

L. C. Gray, *History of Agriculture in the Southern United States to 1860.*

M. B. Hammond, *The Cotton Industry.*

J. H. Street, *The New Revolution in the Cotton Industry.*

H. D. Woodman, *King Cotton and His Retainers.*

— JACK BLICKSILVER

COWBOYS

Although considered an American institution, the cowboy has his roots in antiquity and belongs equally to the biblical era, the fierce Arab tribesmen, and all the modern tenders of cattle from Canada and Mexico nearly to the tip of South America and over to Australia. As a folk hero, the American cowboy was discovered in the western United States after the Civil War, and a folk hero he has remained ever since. Indeed, what is legend and what is a unique occupational type are not always distinguishable.

The cowboy began his career when the first cattle were unloaded on the Caribbean coast of Mexico during the conquest by Hernando Cortes in 1519. As generations passed, the cattle ate their way northward and sometimes, as they were by Father Eusebio Kino in Arizona, were brought into the future United States by soldiers and missionaries. Along the way, methods for tending cattle without fences were evolved, and when settlers began moving into Texas in the 1820's, they adopted the methods of the local Mexican vaqueros for herding and handling cattle.

Although the range cattle industry and its superintendent, the cowboy, were of some importance in Texas before the Civil War, the heyday for the cowboy began in the quarter-century following 1867. In that year Joseph G. McCoy, a twenty-six-year-old Illinois commission merchant, convinced railroad management, town promoters, and Texas cattlemen that a cow town should be built in Kansas west of settlement. The founding of this first real cow town, Abilene, Kans., enabled the Texas cattle, several million strong after years of neglect because of the Civil War, to be trailed to a railhead without encountering enraged farmers whose crops had been destroyed by previous herds or quarantine laws designed to protect local cattle from contracting Spanish (or Texas) fever, to which Texas cattle were immune. In that first year 250,000 cattle were taken up the Chisholm Trail to Abilene, where their owners found a ready market and the cowboys themselves found an opportunity for frolic that was to make them notorious. Over the next quarter-century more than 10 million cattle were trailed from Texas into Kansas, Nebraska, New Mexico, Colorado, Wyoming, and Montana. As the trails moved westward, other cow towns had their day in the sun, but the pattern was set at Abilene.

Gradually the country was fenced in, free range became scarcer, and the number of cattle taken north began to diminish. The cowboy became a victim of his own success, for the advertising of his accomplishment persuaded people that this hitherto forbidding land of the Great Plains was livable. The rise of the range cattle industry in Texas at the end of the Civil War meant that this westernmost Confederate state never felt the impact of Reconstruction, so that Texas became as much a western state as a southern one.

One reason the cowboy so captured the popular imagination was his unique working gear, most of it borrowed from the Mexican vaquero. His high-crowned sombrero, high-heeled boots, leather chaps, yellow slicker, lariat, and spurs all served to mark him as a man of interest. To the cowboy his gear was functional and necessary, but to the man who read about him and later saw him in the movies, he was picturesque in the extreme. Furthermore, the cowboy represented courage and devotion to duty, for he tended cattle wherever he had to go, whether in bogs of quicksand; swift, flooding rivers; or seemingly inaccessible brush. He rode with lightning and blizzard, ate hot summer sand, and was burned by the sun.

The discovery of the cowboy by the "penny dreadfuls" (popular novels of violent adventure that originally sold for a penny) gave the nation a hero who was neither ex-Union nor ex-Confederate. He represented an ideal of physical prowess and courage that accorded well with the mores of the day. In fact, so dangerous was the life that seven years was the average limit of the cowboy's riding life. He gave simple answers to complex questions, was respectful, observed a rigid code of justice, and was a fascinating storyteller. But most of all, he could be judged on performance rather than by breeding or social position and thus represented the ultimate frontier ideal of democracy.

The 20th-century cowboy still fascinates, although he is generally just another outdoor employee, as he tends his cattle from a truck, eats hot food delivered in insulated containers from the ranch-house galley, and sleeps every night in a bed. On some spreads he even tends cattle by helicopter at a far remove from the epic hired man on horseback.

An undated group portrait of American cowboys. (Corbis-Bettman)

BIBLIOGRAPHY

Andy Adams, *Log of a Cowboy.*

Joe B. Frantz and J. W. Choate, *The American Cowboy: Myth and Reality.*

Philip A. Rollins, *The Cowboy.*

— JOE B. FRANTZ

COXEY'S ARMY

Jacob Sechler Coxey, of Massillon, Ohio, was a successful self-made businessman and a reformer with a special interest in fiat money.

During the depression following the panic of 1893 he worked out a plan to save the country. He wanted two bills enacted that would provide for large issues of legal-tender currency to be spent for good roads and other public improvements, thus furnishing work to the unemployed. His device to arouse public and congressional interest in these bills—the march of a "living petition" of the unemployed to Washington, D.C.—was attributed to his picturesque California associate, Carl Browne. As a result of Browne's curious religious notions the organization was called the Commonweal of Christ. The Commonweal marched out of Massillon on Easter Sunday 1894, with about a hundred men, followed by half as many reporters, who gave the "army" plenty of free publicity. Instead of the 100,000 he had predicted, Coxey had about 500 men when he arrived in Washington in time for a great demonstration on May Day. His parade was cheered by an enormous crowd, but when he tried to speak from the Capitol steps he was arrested, fined, and sent to jail for carrying banners and walking on the grass in the Capitol grounds.

Meanwhile, "industrial armies" larger than Coxey's had been formed by the unemployed on the Pacific coast and elsewhere, the largest and best organized being from Los Angeles and from San Francisco. They decided to join Coxey in Washington. When the railroads refused to give them free rides on freight trains they stole trains and ran them themselves. Sometimes, when local authorities were unable or unwilling to suppress them, federal judges enjoined Coxeyites from stealing trains. The injunctions were enforced by U.S. marshals or the army, setting precedents for the government's action against the Pullman strikers in July. Armies that crossed the Mississippi found the population and the railroads more hostile, and they disintegrated before reaching Washington, although remnants straggled in until about 1,200 were encamped there. The District of Columbia finally paid their way home.

The Coxeyites, Commonwealers, or Industrials, as they were called indiscriminately, demanded measures that were mainly Populist, and were generally supported by the Populists and organized labor. Although they failed in their objectives, they were significant as symptoms of the economic unrest of the period and as an unusual type of Populist propaganda.

BIBLIOGRAPHY

D. L. McMurry, *Coxey's Army.*

— DONALD L. MCMURRY

CREEK WAR

Creek War (1813–14), the only serious revolt of the Creek Indians of Alabama and Georgia against the Americans, was a consequence of many factors, emanating principally from the forced acculturation of the Indians. The Creeks were feeling increased pressure from the white landseekers of the expanding American nation, and during the half-century preceding the war they had split into two factions, because of disagreements over how best to cope with the intrusions. Benjamin Hawkins, agent to the Creek just before the turn of the 19th century, had sponsored a program of "civilization" that appealed to one faction but aroused the opposition of the more traditional group. A strong opposition to the proposed changes developed among the Upper Creek of central Alabama, influenced in 1813 by a visit from the Shawnee chief Tecumseh, who preached nativism, anti-Americanism, and resistance to further encroachments by the whites. The Upper Creek, known as the Red Sticks, were hostile, while the Lower Creek, or White Sticks, remained loyal to the United States. Numerous prophets arose among the Red Sticks, inciting them to war.

On Aug. 30, 1813, the Red Sticks sacked and burned an American stockade, Fort Mims, on the Alabama River, killing more than 350 Americans and prowhite Indians. Soon retaliatory forces were assembled in Tennessee, Georgia, and Mississippi, but the principal attack was made by Tennessee militiamen under Gen. Andrew Jackson, aided by White Stick Creek and prowhite Cherokee. Jackson vigorously pursued a campaign against the Red Sticks, sacking the Indian village of Talishatchee on Nov. 3 and on Nov. 9 crushing a Creek force at Talladega. With a force of Georgians and White Stick Creek, Gen. John Floyd on Nov. 29 attacked the Creek village of Auttosee on the Tallapoosa River, burning the village and killing 200 Creek. At the battle of Econochaca in northern Alabama on Dec. 23 Mississippi volunteers burned the village of the Red Stick leader William Weatherford (Red Eagle).

On Mar. 27, 1814, Jackson almost wiped out the Red Stick forces at the Horseshoe Bend of the Tallapoosa River in eastern Alabama, killing an estimated 850 or 900 warriors and making prisoners of 500 women and children. This defeat effectively broke the power of the Red Sticks, many of whom fled to join the Seminole in Florida, while others went into hiding. Ironically, the White Sticks, despite having aided Jackson in the war, were compelled to sign the Treaty of Fort Jackson (Aug. 9, 1814), under the terms of which they were forced to cede to the United States more than 20 million acres in the present states of Georgia and Alabama.

BIBLIOGRAPHY

Angie Debo, *The Road to Disappearance.*
H. S. Halbert and T. H. Ball, *The Creek War of 1813 and 1814.*

Theron A. Nunez, Jr., "Creek Nativism and the Creek War of 1813–14," *Ethnohistory*, vol. 5.
John R. Swanton, *Early History of the Creek Indians and Their Neighbors.*

— KENNETH M. STEWART

CREOLES

Creoles, people of European ancestry born in the Western Hemisphere. Derived from the Spanish *Criollo*, the term "Creole" was originally employed to distinguish Europeans born in the American colonies from their fellow nationals born in the mother countries; but in later times it has been restricted to individuals of French, Spanish, or Portuguese ancestry born in the Americas.

In parts of the South, Afro-Americans of French or Spanish ancestry and retaining some of the European culture are also known as Creoles.

The Creoles of Spanish America led the movement for independence early in the 19th century and have played the dominant role in the subsequent history of the republics to the south of the United States. The French Creoles of Louisiana have markedly influenced the development of that state, and the French and Spanish Creoles have left their impress on other sections of the United States formerly held by France or Spain. The Canadians of pure French blood, whose culture and influence are still predominant in certain sections of that country, are Creoles, scientifically speaking, although not commonly so called.

BIBLIOGRAPHY

George W. Cable, *The Creoles of Louisiana.*
Grace Elizabeth King, *Creole Families of New Orleans.*

— WALTER PRICHARD

CRIME

Criminal proscriptions in colonial New England derived from the English common law and the ascetic Christianity of the Puritans. Intoxication, sexual irregularities, irreverence, and other departures from biblical strictures were the commonest crimes; heresy and witchcraft were the ultimate offenses. Punishment was swift and relied heavily for its effect upon the infliction of corporal pain and public humiliation. Adding to the problem of crime committed by ordinary citizens was the introduction of the criminogenic lower-class culture of England. The courts in England transported to the southern colonies convicts who had been offered the alternative of indentured servitude on plantations to punishment in England. The increase of maritime traffic between the Old World and the New encouraged the spread of piracy on the high seas, which was transformed into the respectable enterprise of privateering during the Revolution.

Post-Revolution national development proceeded far more rapidly than institutions of social control. Violent gangs in New York, Boston, Baltimore, and Philadelphia carried on their predations with little interference from the law; river pirates terrorized inland waterways; large numbers of runaway youths and vagrants supported themselves by theft. The high tide of lawlessness was reached in the Draft Riots of 1863 in New York City, which developed into a criminal insurrection supported both by anti-Civil War factions and by criminal gangs that exploited the breakdown of controls to loot riot-torn sections of the city.

The expansion of the western frontier in the 19th century provided the setting for the exploits of notorious outlaws and resolute law officers, giving rise to sagas that constitute one of the best-known elements of the American heritage. Prostitution, gambling, and predacious crime flourished in the absence of effective law enforcement. The custom of carrying arms for self-protection increased the risk of violent crime. Interpersonal conflict boiled over into assault with a deadly weapon, manslaughter, or murder; armed robbery thrived. Countermeasures were severe: lynch law, perfunctory trials, and harsh punishments were dispensed by peace officers who were as remorseless as their criminal adversaries.

The massive immigration during the century of Irish and, later, of eastern and southern Europeans set the stage for gangster-controlled organized crime. By the 1880's, violent and predatory urban crime increasingly involved Irish immigrants, whose criminality—like that of previous and later depressed immigrant groups—subsided as they were assimilated into the dominant social structure. By the end of the 19th century, patterns of criminal behavior indigenous to southern Italy and Sicily had been adapted to meet the demand for goods and services proscribed by puritanical American laws. This criminal activity took the form, principally, of illicit trade in alcoholic beverages during Prohibition; regional and national networks of prostitution rings, which declined in the 1940's; gambling syndicates, whose leadership continues to amass immense power and wealth; and, more recently, international coordination of the production and distribution of narcotics. As late as the 1950's, intergang rivalries were still frequently erupting into vendetta slayings and mass killings like the infamous Saint Valentine's Day Massacre in Chicago in 1929. The gang leadership, predominantly of recent European immigrant origin, consisted of such highly publicized racketeers as Al Capone, Lepke Buchalter, Frank Nitti, Arnold Rothstein, "Legs" Diamond, Jake Guzik, Tony Accardo, and "Lucky" Luciano, who achieved success at the cost of the corruption of law enforcement at all levels. There have been increasing indications since the 1960's of the displacement of white racketeers by blacks in the control of gambling and narcotics operations in the urban ghetto. Continuing change in the character of organized crime was noted as early as 1951 by the U.S. Senate Committee to Investigate Organized Crime, which produced extensive evidence of the infiltration of more than seventy separate kinds of legitimate business by organized crime seeking to invest its enormous profits from illicit enterprises.

The relatively infrequent crime of kidnapping wealthy persons for purposes of ransom achieved its highest incidence in the 1930's. The kidnapping of the infant son of the celebrated aviator Charles A. Lindbergh and the writer Anne Morrow Lindbergh by Bruno Hauptmann in 1932 constitutes one of the most sensationally reported criminal episodes in American history. Receiving perhaps equal coverage in the news media in 1974, the abduction of Patricia Hearst, granddaughter of publisher William Randolph Hearst, by the revolutionary Symbionese Liberation Army, followed by her apparent renunciation of former ties and affiliation with her captors, seemed to be motivated by revolutionary ideology rather than simply pecuniary gain. In this case the Hearst family met the kidnappers' demand to distribute food to the needy.

The common varieties of property and assaultive crimes have had their highest incidence in the United States in settings of low socioeconomic status, characterized by family instability, unemployment, low educational attainment, and migrant population. Official crime statistics published annually since 1930 in *Uniform Crime Reports* indicate a striking increase generally in rates of serious crime. Between 1960 and 1973 the number of serious crimes known to the police per 100,000 of population increased almost fourfold, from 1,038 to 4,116, making "law and order" a key issue in political elections of the late 1960's and early 1970's. Historical studies of police records of major urban centers, however, contest the popular view that the actual current crime rate is higher than it was in the 19th century. Rates of serious crimes in cities whose police departments have maintained reliable records since the first half of the 19th century—notably Boston and Buffalo—exhibit a downward trend between the third quarter of the 19th century and the middle of the 20th. Federal Bureau of Investigation statistics show a decline in criminal homicide rates from 9.7 per 100,000 of population in 1933 to 4.5 in 1958, followed by a gradual rise to 7 in 1973. It is true that changes in technology and social organization have affected the incidence of old patterns of criminal behavior and have created new patterns. Car theft, for example, has replaced horse theft. The civil rights movement of the 1960's, although on the whole peaceable, touched off bloody, costly riots in communities such as Watts in Los Angeles (1965), Detroit (1967), and Newark (1967). The vulnerability of air transportation to political and economic extortion has posed fresh challenges to law enforcement and pointed up the desirability of international cooperation to cope with air piracy. White-collar crime—violations committed in the course of performing business and professional duties—has become more common as the social class structure has broadened at the middle and upper levels. Because of its low detectability and indirect cost, such crime does not provoke nearly so great a public outcry as the more overt forms of criminal behavior. The extensiveness and costliness of one of the more covert forms of white-collar crime, the violation of antimonopoly laws, were brought to light in 1960 when the major American manufacturers of electrical equipment were indicted by the federal court in Philadelphia for price fixing in violation of the Sherman Antitrust Act. In the disposition of the case seven high-ranking corporate executives were jailed; twenty-three were put on probation; and fines totaling more than $80 million were imposed upon twenty-nine corporations. Far more shocking to the national consciousness were the revelations in the Watergate case in 1973 and 1974, resulting in the convictions of high governmental officials and close presidential advisers for their roles in the conspiracy to effect the burglary of the national headquarters of the Democratic party and the efforts to cover up the crime.

There is a current trend in criminal legislation to remove from the books certain victimless crimes or to reduce their gravity as offenses. The most successful instance of this trend has occurred in laws governing pornography. Many citizens' groups and law enforcement officers also support the decriminalization of public intoxication, possession of marijuana, vagrancy, prostitution, and gambling, offenses that in 1973 accounted for about 30 percent of all arrests.

BIBLIOGRAPHY

Daniel Bell, "Crime as an American Way of Life," *Antioch Review*, vol. 12 (1953).

Mabel Elliott, *Crime in Modern Society*.

Theodore N. Ferdinand, "The Criminal Patterns of Boston Since 1849," *American Journal of Sociology*, vol. 72 (1967).

Philip D. Jordan, *Frontier Law and Order*.

Elwin H. Powell, "Crime as a Function of Anomie," *Journal of Criminal Law, Criminology, and Police Science*, vol. 57 (1966).

— EDWARD GREEN

CRIME SINCE THE 1970S

Crime in the mid-1990s continued to be one of the foremost social, political, and legal issues facing the United States, both in terms of statistics and public understanding. Since 1965 crime rates have reached all-time highs, making crime control and criminal justice central to debate at all levels of government. Criminal activity has been postulated as both the source and product of other social problems, and as a result radically divergent solutions have been proposed and implemented. The trend since the 1980s toward stricter enforcement and stiffer punishment has inundated the legal and penal systems. Public concern for the seriousness of crime has intensified, partly from actual experience but also from media coverage, particularly of certain egregious and infamous crimes.

In a nation of more than 250 million people policed by several different levels of law enforcement agencies, it is difficult to gauge exactly the pervasiveness of criminal activity. The two primary government sources of crime statistics, the National Crime Victimization Survey (NCVS) and the Uniform Crime Reports (UCR), which are based on different sources, provide inconsistent information about crime rates. Although crime had become more prevalent since the 1960s, the NCVS and UCR agreed that the mid-1990s crime rate for the general population, while considerable, was lower than in previous years. For certain segments of society, however particularly teenagers, violent crime was increasing at an alarming rate.

Public concern over the seriousness of crime has intensified, partly from actual experience but also from media coverage, particularly of sensational and egregious crimes.

According to the NCVS, compiled annually since 1973 by the Bureau of Justice Statistics based on interviews with 100,000 Americans age twelve and older, crime rates dropped considerably since 1975. Violent crime (not including homicide) reached a peak in 1981 at 35.3 per 1,000 persons, but by 1992 the rate had dropped to 32.1 per 1,000 persons. The rate was virtually the same in 1992 as in 1973. When all personal crimes were taken into account (including both violent crimes and crimes of personal larceny), the NCVS found that in 1992 the rate of personal crimes had dropped 24.3 percent, from 120.5 per 1,000 persons in 1981. The rates for aggravated assault and robbery each dropped more than 11 percent between 1973 and 1992, and the rate for rape dropped almost 30 percent. Household crimes (burglary, larceny, and motor vehicle theft) peaked at 236.5 per 1,000 persons in 1975. By 1992 the rate had receded 35.6 percent to 152.2 per 1,000 persons. Burglary was down 47 percent, and personal larceny (classified as a personal crime) was down 35 percent from 1973 rates. In 1975 almost one in three households was touched by crime of some sort; by 1992 the rate had dropped to fewer than one in four.

Statistics compiled annually since 1929 by the Federal Bureau of Investigation in the UCR, based on incidents known to law enforcement officials at all levels of government, told a slightly different story. That rates reported by the UCR are lower than those compiled in the NCVS indicates that many crimes are never reported. According to the UCR, the total crime index (including murder and nonnegligent manslaughter, forcible rape, robbery, aggravated assault, burglary, larceny theft, and motor vehicle theft) reached a peak of 5,950 crimes per 100,000 persons in 1980, a staggering 215 percent increase over the rate in 1960. By 1993 the rate had dropped to 5,482.9 offenses per 100,000 persons.

The murder rate of 10.2 per 100,000 persons peaked in 1980, which was double the rate from 1960 and 6.9 percent higher than the 1993 rate of 9.5 per 100,000 persons. Even at the decreased 1993 rate, the United States continued to be the most violent country in the industrial world, with a homicide rate seventeen times that of Japan, fifteen times that of England, ten times that of Germany and France, and five times that of Canada. According to the UCR, the only exception to the general trend of crime rates peaking in the early 1980s was the rate of violent crime (murder and nonnegligent manslaughter, forcible rape, robbery, and aggravated assault), which peaked in 1991 at 758.1 offenses per 100,000 persons, 371 percent higher than the rate in 1960. The rate in 1993 remained stable at 746.1 offenses per 100,000 people.

While these statistics indicate that the crime rate might have been declining, they mask an increase in violent crime among segments of the population, particularly teenaged African-American males. In 1990 the homicide rate for nonwhite (mostly African-American) males aged fifteen to nineteen was 92 murders per 100,000 persons, more than nine times the rate for the general population. This rate had doubled from 1985, an increase believed attributable to poverty, drugs, the ready availability of firearms, and an increase in cases of neglect and abuse. According to the NCVS, African-American males ages sixteen to nineteen were victimized by violent crimes at a rate of 158.1 crimes per 1,000 persons in 1992, 392 percent higher than the rate for the general population. Teens, white and black, carried out a disproportionate percentage of violent crimes in 1992; 22 percent of all violent crimes were by fifteen- to nineteen-year-old males, the highest percentage of any age group.

Statistics indicated that residents of the nation's cities were disproportionately affected by crime. In 1993 the UCR measured the rate of violent crime in large cities at 975 per 100,000 persons, compared with 461 per 100,000 in suburban counties and 233 in rural counties. According to the 1994 independent study *Homicide in the United States: Who's at Risk?* by the Population Reference Bureau, the District of Columbia was by far the most violent area in the country, with 66.5 murders per 100,000 persons. Louisiana, with 18.5 murders per 100,000, had the highest rate for any state, and seven of the ten states with the highest rates were in the South. Iowa and North Dakota had the lowest rates, at 2.0 murders per 100,000 persons.

The Federal Sentencing Guidelines enacted in 1984 disavowed rehabilitation as a goal and supported retribution, education, deterrence, and incarceration.

These trends were not lost on the American public, which continued to be apprehensive about crime, particularly violent crime. A 1990 poll showed that 84 percent of individuals surveyed felt that there was more crime in the United States than in the previous year, while a 1994 poll indicated that 88 percent of those surveyed thought that violent crime was at an all-time high. In another 1994 poll, 52 percent of men and 68 percent of women said they personally were fearful of becoming victims of violence. While not necessarily borne out by statistics, the public's fear of crime clearly influenced efforts to combat crime.

Since 1965 two major schools of thought emerged about the causes and cures of crime. By one account, blame for crime should be placed solely on the perpetrator who is unwilling to abide by society's rules. Advocates of this approach argue that the best way to eliminate crime is to emphasize enforcement and imprisonment with an eye toward punishment and retribution, in the hope that deterrence will follow. This approach gained popularity in the 1980s as politicians moved to appease voters clamoring for a quick solution to the highest crime rates in the country's history. It was manifest in President Ronald Reagan's administration's war on drugs, in which prevention and rehabilitation took a backseat to increased funding for enforcement and stiff sentences. As a result, drug-related prosecutions and convictions skyrocketed, filling prisons and necessitating more correctional facilities. By 1994 more than 60 percent of inmates in federal prisons had been sentenced for drug crimes.

The Federal Sentencing Guidelines, which were enacted in 1984 and took effect in 1987, disavowed rehabilitation as a goal of imprisonment, and supported retribution, education, deterrence, and incarceration. The guidelines remove discretion in sentencing from federal judges and employ a mathematical procedure to calculate a sentence based on the defendant's criminal history, severity of the crime, and the defendant's role in the crime. Perhaps most important, the federal sentencing guidelines contemplate no role for parole; with the exception of the possibility of earning fifty-four days for each year (after the first year) served with good behavior, offenders serve the terms reached through application of the guidelines. A more recent phenomenon is the "three strikes and you're out" approach to sentencing, in which any person convicted of three serious felonies receives life in prison without possibility of parole. The 1994 Crime Bill embraced this approach, and more than half the states have enacted or are considering similar proposals. Consistent with this approach is use of the death penalty for an expanding number of offenses. Between reinstatement of capital punishment in 1977 and the end of 1994, 257 people were executed. In 1995 fifty-six people were put to death in the thirty-eight states that allowed for capital punishment, the highest number of executions since 1957. More than 3,000 prisoners were on death row at the end of 1995.

This "tough on crime" approach has not been without cost. According to a 1995 Justice Department report, at the end of 1994, 1.5 million inmates were in federal and state prisons and local jails, and another 3.5 million convicted criminals were on probation or on parole. A nongovernmental group placed the incarceration rate in mid-1995 at 565 per 100,000 people, the highest rate in the world. The economic ramifications of this approach are profound. In 1990 expenditures for the justice system at all levels of government totaled $74.5 billion, a 600 percent increase since 1971. Some $25 billion was spent on corrections in 1990, nearly eleven times the total spent in 1971.

The second school of thought about the causes of and cures for crime dominant in the 1960s and 1970s saw crime as the result of underlying social problems, namely poverty and lack of job opportunities. This school of thought was waning in popularity by the early 1980s. Proponents of this philosophy argue that enforcement and incarceration are not long-term cures for the crime problem; rather, it is necessary to solve underlying problems that cause people to turn to crime. They advocate spending for education and job training, community recreation, and rehabilitation of prisoners. The two approaches to crime are not exclusive; efforts to curb crime often involve both. The 1994 Crime Bill aimed $13 billion at law enforcement, including $9 billion to hire new police officers, and also directed $7 billion at prevention programs.

Gun control laws are also a controversial attempt to combat crime and have produced much contention. Statistics released by the American Medical Association in 1993 indicated that firearm violence accounted for one-fifth of all injury deaths in the United States, second only to motor vehicles as a cause of fatal injury. In 1993 there were 200 million handguns, rifles, and assault weapons in possession of private citizens in the United States, and a firearm of some type was used in 68 percent of violent crimes committed that year. Proponents of gun control have argued that reducing the number of guns will lead to a decrease in violent crimes by removing guns from the hands of criminals. Opponents argue that gun control will deprive individuals of ability to protect themselves and leave guns in the hands of criminals; they cite the Second Amendment's "right of the people to keep and bear Arms," although courts have not taken this position. Gun control proponents won two small but symbolic victories in the early 1990s: the Brady Bill, which mandated a five-day waiting period to allow background checks before a gun may be purchased; and a provision of the 1994 Crime Bill that banned the sale of certain types of assault weapons. The assault weapons ban, however, faced possible repeal in the mid-1990s, after opponents of gun control gained power when Republicans won control of Congress in 1994.

According to a Justice Department report, at the end of 1994 there were 1.5 million inmates behind bars and another 3.5 million convicted criminals on probation or on parole.

One reason for the fear of crime among Americans that exceeds statistical evidence of its occurrence may be media coverage of certain egregious or infamous crimes. While such crimes constituted only a small percentage of crimes committed in the United States, they received a disproportionate amount of coverage. Live television coverage of the trial of football star O. J. Simpson for the murder of his wife, Nicole Brown Simpson, and Ron Goldman, put the criminal justice system in the spotlight throughout 1994 and 1995; Simpson was ultimately acquitted of the charges. Also prominent was the coverage given to serial killers, individuals who murder several people over an extended period of time. Serial killers whose names became embedded in the American consciousness included John Wayne Gacy, convicted of murdering thirty-three young men and boys and burying them underneath his house from 1972 through 1978 (executed in 1994); David Berkowitz ("Son of Sam"), who panicked New York City by murdering five women and one man in 1976 and 1977; Ted Bundy, convicted of killing three Florida women and suspected in thirty-six other killings in the Northwest (executed in 1989); Wayne Williams, convicted in 1982 for killing two black men and suspected in the deaths of twenty-nine black children in Atlanta; Richard Ramirez (the "Night Stalker"), convicted of killing thirteen people in southern California during house break-ins in 1984 and 1985; and Jeffrey Dahmer, convicted in 1992 of killing and dismembering fifteen people in Milwaukee (beaten to death in prison in 1994, allegedly by another inmate).

Several mass murders, killings of four or more people in a single instance, gained notoriety. In 1991 a lone gunman killed twenty-two people in a Texas cafeteria, the worst mass murder in U.S. history. Such events were not infrequent through the 1980s and 1990s. In 1984 a gunman killed twenty-one people in a California fast-food restaurant; in 1986 an employee of the U.S. Postal Service killed fourteen co-workers in Oklahoma; in 1989 a gunman with an AK-47 killed five students and wounded twenty-nine others at an elementary school in California; in 1991 nine people, including seven Buddhist monks, were murdered in an Arizona temple; and in 1993 a man killed eight people at a Los Angeles law firm. Criminologists estimate that mass murders occur at the rate of two per month in the United States.

Other crimes or criminal prosecutions were prominent because of the identity of the victim or perpetrator or the nature of the crime. The rape trial and conviction of world heavyweight boxing champion Mike Tyson was covered extensively during 1990, as was the prosecution of William Kennedy Smith, tried and acquitted for rape in 1991. The murder of popular musician John Lennon in 1980, as well as the attempted assassinations of Presidents Gerald Ford in 1975 and Ronald Reagan in 1981, brought public outrage against handgun violence. The brutal sexual assault of a jogger in New York's Central Park by a group of "wilding" teens, the murder of several foreign tourists in Florida in 1992 and 1993, and a spate of violent carjackings in the early 1990s drew worldwide attention to violent crime.

Captivating national attention—and conjuring visions of the race riots of the 1960s—was rioting in 1992 in the aftermath of a racially charged trial in Los Angeles. The rioting had its genesis in an incident involving a Los Angeles resident named Rodney King, an African American stopped by Los Angeles police officers after a high-speed chase. As an onlooker recorded the incident on videotape, white officers severely beat King while he crawled on the ground. The officers were brought to trial on state charges, but when they were acquitted by an all-white jury, rioting broke out in Los Angeles and other communities throughout the country. In all, fifty-three people were killed, with an estimated $1 billion in property damage. Two of the officers were later convicted on federal charges. Two events during the early 1990s made Americans aware that the United States was not immune from the terrorist attacks that had plagued much of the rest of the world throughout the 1970s and 1980s. In 1993, 6 people were killed and 1,000 injured when a bomb exploded in the basement parking lot of New York City's World Trade Center, two of the world's tallest buildings. Four Muslim extremists were found guilty of carrying out the attack, and in a separate trial ten others were found guilty of conspiring to wage a war of urban terrorism by planning to bomb other New York landmarks and assassinate political leaders. In April 1995 a bomb exploded at a federal building in Oklahoma City, killing 169 people and injuring scores of others. Although early speculation was that foreign terrorists had carried out the attack, the two men charged with the crime were American members of an antigovernment militia movement.

[See also Capital Punishment; Crime; Gun Control; Oklahoma City Bombing; Riots; Terrorism; Urban Living.]

BIBLIOGRAPHY

Bureau of Justice Statistics, *National Crime Victimization Survey* (Washington, D.C., various years), and *Sourcebook of Criminal Justice Statistics—1993* (Washington, D.C., 1994).

Federal Bureau of Investigation, *Uniform Crime Reports: Crime in the United States* (Washington, D.C., various years).

Lawrence M. Friedman, *Crime and Punishment in American History* (New York, 1993).

Victor E. Kappeler, Mark Blumberg, and Gary W. Potter, *The Mythology of Crime and Criminal Justice* (Prospect Heights, Ill., 1993).

— SCOTT T. SCHUTTE

CRIME, ORGANIZED

Organized crime is a term often used to describe entrepreneurial activities that provide customers with illegal goods or services, including prostitution, gambling, bootlegging, and the sale of narcotics. During the colonial period, the seacoast cities, like port cities around the world, offered groggeries, prostitutes, and gambling for a transient population of sailors, dockworkers, and travelers. In the same cities there developed a handful of elite houses of prostitution and elite gambling houses to serve a more select clientele of well-to-do residents.

After the Revolution, as population spread rapidly westward, the burgeoning commercial cities of the Midwest also provided prostitution and gambling. Transportation lines, as well, became centers for entertainment, and so, the colorful Mississippi riverboat gambler entered into American folklore. In the Far West, after the gold rush of 1849, San Francisco became a "city of sin," attracting prostitutes from Paris, Latin America, and China and also attracting gamblers who saw a greater chance for profits in running gambling houses than in mining gold. In the years that followed, the mining towns of the West attracted itinerant gamblers and prostitutes, who formed an important and accepted part of the social life of a raw, frontier society.

Red-light districts in the larger cities usually covered an extensive area on the periphery of the central business district, as in San Francisco's Barbary Coast, Chicago's Levee, New Orleans's Storyville, and New York's Tenderloin.

Before the Civil War, gambling and prostitution were generally not coordinated operations. In the decades after Appomattox, a number of factors led to the increasing coordination, especially in populous urban centers.

Entertainment, or red-light, districts developed in the larger cities, usually covering an extensive area on the periphery of the central business district—notably San Francisco's Barbary Coast, Chicago's Levee, New Orleans' Storyville, and New York's Tenderloin. The entertainment districts served a variety of functions. Con men, pickpockets, burglars, and other professional thieves hung out in their saloons and gambling halls. A variety of deviant subcultures carried on their social life within their confines. Addiction to opiates and cocaine was widespread; and in the red-light districts were con-

Al Capone was the king of organized crime in Chicago during the late 1920s and early 1930s. (Corbis-Bettman)

centrated the Chinese opium dens and drugstores that sold morphine or cocaine. Red-light districts also offered a variety of commercial entertainment: gaudy dancehalls, burlesque theaters, pornography shops, and cabarets.

Most important, perhaps, the districts featured prostitution in a wide variety of forms. Each district had a few expensive parlor houses boasting excellent cuisine, fine wines, a small band, and charming hostesses. Other houses, with ordinary drinks and a "perfessor" playing the piano, specialized in speed rather than quality of service. For sailors, hobos, and other lower-class clients, there were "cribs," in which aging prostitutes often worked on an assembly-line basis in small, filthy rooms. Other prostitutes solicited customers on the streets or in saloons. Because of the heavy concentration of prostitution and entertainment in restricted districts, local police and politicians generally coordinated the activities by taking money in return for the privilege of operating.

While red-light districts were thriving after the Civil War, changes in gambling brought increasing syndication. Horse racing, long a favorite American sport, became an important urban leisure activity. Around major cities, racetracks sprang up, and soon northern and western cities had racing meets from spring to fall, while southern cities had winter racing as well. By the 1880's, bookmakers, unknown before the Civil War, were paying the tracks $100 daily for the privilege of managing betting between the many fans. (Indeed, many of the tracks were promoted and controlled by bookmakers.) Away from the tracks, gamblers also developed offtrack bookmaking syndicates for fans who could not attend the races or wished to bet on races run in other cities.

One factor that led to coordination of offtrack bookmaking was the system of communication. Offtrack bookmakers required up-to-the-minute information from the tracks. This was offered for a fee by telegraph companies, chief among them Western Union. By the late 1890's, by means of telephone switchboards, some bookmakers were able to receive racing information by telegraph and then to telephone the information to numerous subordinate bookmakers in saloons, barber shops, cigar stores, and other local outlets. The bookmaking was coordinated by a number of syndicates having informal monopolies in various parts of each city.

Policy gambling also became a syndicate activity after the Civil War. As early as the 18th century, policy (in which a bettor chose a number or numbers that would appear in a drawing) had been run as a sideline to the legal lotteries used to raise money for local governments or private charitable institutions. With the beginning in the 1830's of the progressive banning of lotteries by the states, policy shops—independent of lotteries—sprang up. Feeding upon many small bets, policy became the special gambling game of the poor, particularly blacks. Even before the Civil War, dream books were sold in New York to assist the players in choosing lucky numbers. Both policy syndicates and bookmaking syndicates were closely tied to politics. Syndicate leaders supported politicians with money, while in many neighborhoods local political organizations and gambling syndicates had overlapping memberships.

The Irish were instrumental in putting together the system of organized crime. Arriving in America as lovers of racing and gambling, they dominated gambling outside the southern cities by 1900. As sportsmen, they invested money in racehorses and promoted racetracks. They were also disproportionately represented in urban political machines and police departments. A sense of Irish identity, then, often tied together the gamblers, sportsmen, politicians, and policemen. In the period from 1890 to 1905, organized crime may have reached its high point in the United States in terms of the proportion of the population that constituted customers and in terms of the impact upon local police and politicians.

In the decade preceding World War I, local reform crusades significantly affected organized crime. A movement to enforce gambling laws closed racetracks in all but five states (Kentucky, Maryland, Louisiana, Colorado, and Nevada) and thus virtually eliminated ontrack bookmaking. The movement also forced gambling houses, policy operations, and offtrack bookmaking to operate in a more clandestine manner. Furthermore, Western Union, under pressure from reformers, abandoned direct management of the race wire in May 1904. This was only a temporary setback, for gamblers were soon operating their own nationwide service.

Perhaps more important, a movement against prostitution, particularly after 1907, eliminated the open red-light districts in city after city. By World War I only two major cities, New Orleans and Philadelphia, still had open red-light districts; and these were closed during the war under pressure from military authorities. Obviously, elimination of open red-light districts did not end prostitution. But the generally more clandestine operations made transactions more difficult and thus decreased the extent and profitability of prostitution. Passage of the Harrison Act (1914), which controlled interstate shipments of opiates and cocaine, rapidly reduced the illegal sale of such narcotics at the same time.

The moral crusades that brought decline to gambling, prostitution, and narcotics in the early part of the 20th century were climaxed by passage of the Eighteenth (Prohibition) Amendment to the U.S. Constitution (1919). With sale of alcoholic beverages illegal, a market for illicit enterprise opened up. In many ways, bootlegging was a more complex operation than gambling or prostitution. At the bottom were the numerous retail outlets: speakeasies, roadhouses, bellhops, and janitors, for example. At the next level were the distributors, who stored the liquor and trucked it to the retail outlets. Finally, there were the original suppliers: importers from Canada, Europe, or the West Indies; owners of distilleries and breweries, who oversaw manufacture; experts at fraud, who diverted legal industrial alcohol into illegal channels; and even individuals who supplied local distributors from home stills.

Those who rose to prominence as bootleggers were primarily distributors. As such, they attempted to carve out and expand districts in which they would have monopolies of distribution; and, to assure a steady supply, they often opened their own distilleries and breweries and operated their own import services, thereby minimizing their reliance on independent suppliers. Because of the rapid rise of bootlegging gangs and their efforts to expand, disputes often occurred, and they were sometimes settled by assassinations. Although organized crime before 1920 was seldom characterized by resort to murder, the 1920's ushered in a level of violence that persisted well beyond the decade, especially by groups that in the 1920's became accustomed to violence as a means of dispute settlement.

By World War I, among the major cities only New Orleans and Philadelphia still had open red-light districts, but these were closed during the war under pressure from military authorities.

Bootlegging had other effects. One was the rapid success of a new generation of criminals: men who had been born between 1896 and 1902 and were in their late teens and early twenties as national Prohibition began. They were still relatively young men when Prohibition ended in the winter of 1933–34, and many continued careers in gambling, labor racketeering, and other illicit activities. As a result of their prominence as bootleggers and their active criminal careers afterward, there developed the myth that the 1920's had created organized crime in America.

The rapid success of young bootleggers also brought new ethnic groups into prominence in organized crime. Although Jews and Italians had made important inroads into the operation of red-light districts in many cities before World War I, bootlegging greatly accelerated their rise. By the end of the 1920's, Italians (for example, Al and Ralph Capone in Chicago, Alfred Polizzi in Cleveland, and Charles "Lucky" Luciano in New York) and Jews (Max "Boo Boo" Hoff in Philadelphia, Moe Dalitz in Cleveland, and Ben "Bugsy" Siegel and Meyer Lansky in New York) were prominent in bootlegging.

Publicity given to bootleggers obscured other important developments in organized crime in the 1920's. Although blacks did not become important as bootleggers, black entrepreneurs—in New York's Harlem, Chicago's South Side, and elsewhere—opened cabarets and provided jazz music and bootleg liquor for white and black customers. More important, perhaps, the creation of black ghettos in northern cities during World War I allowed the formation of black-controlled policy operations (as well as the closely related numbers rackets). Soon the wealthy black policy and numbers kings became crucial economic and political influences in black neighborhoods. Their importance continued, even though in the 1940's some black operators began paying a portion of their profits to Italian or Jewish crime figures in return for political protection and the right to continue operations.

Other forms of gambling, too, expanded in the 1920's and 1930's. Horse racing, for instance, made a comeback. Because the comeback was often under state regulation, combined with the use of pari-mutuel betting at the tracks, bookmakers were largely barred from the tracks. But gambling houses and offtrack bookmaking throve. Although gambling on sports events had long been practiced, betting on baseball and football rapidly expanded in the 1920's and began to rival betting on horse races in popularity. Slot machines, in existence since at least the 1890's, also flourished in the 1920's. Many gambling operations continued under the control of old-time gamblers, who had little contact with the bootleggers. At the same time, from the mid-1920's into the 1940's, the *nouveau riche* among the bootleggers established their own gambling operations or else moved into the operations of others.

After the repeal of Prohibition in 1933, many bootleggers continued to cooperate locally and regionally in a variety of other enterprises. Leaders from New York and Cleveland, for instance, jointly invested in the operation of legal beverage companies. Along with associates in labor unions, several became involved in labor racketeering. Perhaps the most notorious example was the takeover of the International Alliance of Theatrical Stage Employees, with jurisdiction over movie projectionists, and the use of the union to shake down both the owners of movie theater chains and the Hollywood producers themselves, until the federal government secured convictions in 1941. From 1945 through the early 1950's Meyer Lansky led a group of largely Jewish investors from New York, Miami, Cleveland, and elsewhere in the development of Las Vegas as a legal gambling center. He also developed gambling centers in Miami, Havana, and London.

Although foreshadowed in earlier years, two expanding areas of criminal opportunity became important after World War II. One was the sale of heroin. By the 1950's there was a fairly stable system by which poppies were harvested in Turkey and the Near East, processed into heroin in clandestine laboratories near Marseilles, and then shipped to the United States, often through agreements with Italian-dominated crime groups in New York or Miami. The second area was the loan-sharking racket, made possible when many states tightened their laws with regard to maximum interest rates and strengthened enforcement. These restrictions created a substantial illicit market for loans at high interest, and crime groups in many large cities found loan-sharking a profitable way to invest money earned in gambling or in other activities.

A final development from 1930 to 1960 was the emergence of some Italians to a crucial position in organized crime in a number of cities. Partly this was the result of the fact that the old-time Irish and Jewish crime leaders who retired were not always replaced by young men from their own ethnic groups, while certain young Italian-Americans continued to seek out the opportunities provided by illegal enterprises. During the 1930's and 1940's, Italian criminals in the New York–New Jersey region coalesced into some five or six major "families." By the mid-1930's, Lucky Luciano was perhaps the most respected among the Italian crime leaders in the region; by the post–World War II period, Frank Costello played a similar role. Although the families consisted of informal and shifting business partnerships during time of peace, they often took on a paramilitary form of governance during periodic hostilities between groups. In cities outside the New York–New Jersey region—among them Providence, Buffalo, Detroit, Chicago, New Orleans, and Kansas City—coalitions that were primarily Italian achieved important, or even predominant, positions within organized crime by the 1940's and 1950's. Leaders from the various cities often met socially in Miami or Las Vegas, carried on joint business activities, and, like any other businessmen, occasionally held informal conventions to discuss common business problems.

Two expanding kinds of criminal opportunity after World War II were the sale of heroin and the loan-sharking racket.

As a result of U.S. Senate hearings under Estes Kefauver (Special Committee to Investigate Organized Crime in Interstate Commerce) in 1950–51; the meeting of large numbers of Italian criminals at Apalachin, N.Y., in November 1957; and the testimony by Joseph Valachi before the McClellan committee in 1963, political leaders, law enforcement officials, and the communications media discovered the strong Italian influence in organized crime, leading to the creation of a popular and scholarly myth that a Mafia or Cosa Nostra controlled crime throughout the nation. In the 1960's, therefore, local and national law enforcement agencies focused upon Italian criminals and began campaigns of joint investigations and prosecutions. Books, newspaper stories, and movies gave wide publicity to the role of Italians in organized crime and to the Mafia or Cosa Nostra myth.

Even without the law enforcement campaigns against it, a number of factors in the 1960's would have threatened Italian importance in organized crime and created a transition period. The rapid expansion of heroin use in the 1960's, especially in black ghettos, meant that new groups began importing and distributing drugs. Latin-Americans, including Cuban refugees, were among the groups that seized the new opportunities. Perhaps even more important, the use of marijuana and of LSD and other psychedelic drugs spread rapidly among college students and younger teenagers. Large numbers of entrepreneurs—often young persons in their twenties who were college dropouts and involved on the fringes of the counterculture—became importers, manufacturers, distributors, and pushers of drugs. Their operations were largely independent of traditional, organized criminal groups. Finally, changes in black and Puerto Rican ghetto culture led to the growth of independently operated indigenous drug distribution and numbers gambling operations in the ghettos. The 1960's therefore may well turn out to be a watershed period in organized crime, marking not only the end of the importance of criminal organizations originally developed by the Prohibition generation of Italians and Jews but also the rise of new coalitions.

By the late 1960's there were movements to modify or repeal some of the laws making certain goods or services illegal and thus creating the markets for organized crime. As a result of a series of U.S. Supreme Court decisions, the possibility of successful prosecution of pornography sellers became so difficult that "adult book" stores multiplied in American cities and operated on the fringes of legality. As a result of legislative changes in a few states, but especially as a result of Supreme Court decisions, abortion ceased to be illegal under most circumstances, if performed under medical supervision. Similarly, a concerted effort began to persuade legislators to modify or eliminate the laws against marijuana and to convince the courts that such laws be found unconstitutional. Although the campaign has had only limited success, in many urban areas the police and district attorneys no longer make arrests or undertake prosecutions except in cases of major dealers. Finally, a number of states established lotteries, and New York established a government-run offtrack betting (OTB) system. Proponents argue that state-run gambling helps the states to raise much-needed revenue and will also reduce the profits of illegal gambling. Thus far, state-run gambling has not raised the expected revenue, nor has it interfered with illegal gambling. The illegal gambler can offer his customers personal relationships, convenient locations, flexible credit arrangements, winnings that will be kept secret from the Internal Revenue Service, and, in many cases, better odds than the state.

BIBLIOGRAPHY

Joseph L. Albini, *The American Mafia: Genesis of a Legend.*

Herbert Asbury, *Sucker's Progress: An Informal History of Gambling in America From the Colonies to Canfield.*

Francis A. J. Ianni, *Black Mafia: Ethnic Succession in Organized Crime.*

John Landesco, *Organized Crime in Chicago.*

Hank Messick, *Lansky.*

David F. Musto, *The American Disease: Origins of Narcotic Control.*

William H. P. Robertson, *The History of Thoroughbred Racing in America.*

Dwight C. Smith, *The Mafia Mystique.*

Gus Tyler, ed., *Organized Crime in America.*

Howard B. Woolston, *Prostitution in the United States, Prior to the Entrance of the United States Into the World War.*

— MARK H. HALLER

CRITTENDEN COMPROMISE

Crittenden Compromise, the most important proposal made in 1860–61 in the attempt to resolve the conflict between North and South by peaceful measures. The plan, presented to the U.S. Senate on Dec. 18, 1860, by Sen. J. J. Crittenden of Kentucky, included six articles proposed as amendments to the Constitution and four resolutions. The heart of the compromise was in the first article, which provided that north of 36°30′, the line of the Missouri Compromise, in all territory then held or thereafter acquired, slavery would be prohibited and that south of the line slavery would be protected as property. Crittenden's proposal referred only to territory then held, but the phrase "or hereafter acquired" was added. Other articles prohibited Congress from abolishing slavery in places under federal jurisdiction in the slave states or in the District of Columbia without compensation and consent of Virginia and Maryland. The sixth article provided that there should be no constitutional amendment to alter the other five articles of the compromise and that Congress should have no power to interfere with slavery where it then existed.

This plan was the chief subject of consideration by the Senate Committee of Thirteen, the House Committee of Thirty-three, and the Peace Convention in Washington. It was defeated by vote on Dec. 22, 1860, in the crucial Committee of Thirteen, chiefly because the Republicans, in consultation with Abraham Lincoln, then president-elect, refused to yield on prohibition of slavery in the territories. The resolution for an amendment to prohibit interference with slavery in the states passed Congress in February and March 1861, but it was never ratified by the states.

BIBLIOGRAPHY

James Ford Rhodes, *History of the United States, 1850–1877,* vol. III.

— C. MILDRED THOMPSON

"CROSS OF GOLD" SPEECH

"Cross of Gold" Speech, "You shall not press down upon the brow of labor this crown of thorns, you shall not crucify mankind upon a cross of gold." So William Jennings Bryan, a delegate from Nebraska, concluded his attack upon the single gold standard before the Democratic national nomination convention at Chicago on July 8, 1896. Bryan's speech was not so notable for the cogency of its reasoning as for the distinction of its rhetoric and the perfection of its delivery; all of which, in spite of the appearance of spontaneity, was carefully planned in advance. The free-silver delegates, recognizing in Bryan the leader they had sought, made him the convention nominee.

BIBLIOGRAPHY

W. J. Bryan, *The First Battle.*
Mark Sullivan, *Our Times: The Turn of the Century.*

— JOHN D. HICKS

CUBA, RELATIONS WITH

The warming of relations between Cuba and the United States begun by President Gerald R. Ford in 1975 continued during the administration of President Jimmy Carter (1977–1981), a result of Carter's desire to be at least a better neighbor, if not a good one. Cuba and the United States agreed in 1977 to exchange diplomatic representatives, a step that fell short of formal recognition but resulted in regulation of offshore fishing. A dialogue began between the exile community in Miami and the Cuban government, bringing the release of 3,500 political prisoners as well as resumption of charter flights between the two countries. Beginning in 1980 the thaw in relations ended. Concerned with the Sandinista triumph in Nicaragua, as well as the arrival of Cuban military forces in Africa, the United States once again looked upon Cuba as a threat. In the same year, the Mariel boatlift brought 125,000 refugees to the United States in boats supplied by Cuban exiles in Florida. The exodus proved to be a policy and public relations disaster for both countries. The administration of President Ronald Reagan (1981–1989) demonstrated little interest in improved relations. In 1985 it began sponsoring Radio Marti, broadcasting to anti-Castro Cubans.

By 1992, however, Cuba had ceased to be a threat in the minds of many people throughout Latin America. The United States stood nearly alone in its lack of formal relations with Cuba. The administration of President George Bush (1989–1993) negotiated an agreement that called for admission of 20,000 Cubans each year, in return for Cuba's taking back 2,500 of the criminals jailed after the Mariel boatlift. By this time the collapse of the Soviet Union had brought an end to massive Russian support of Cuba's economy, and it appeared that Cuba would collapse economically if not politically. In 1994 Cuban President Fidel Castro announced a streamlining of government that abolished state committee and economic agencies, notably the central planning board that supervised Cuba's imports from the former Soviet Union. New measures included price increases as well as taxes on alcohol and cigarettes. As gloomy as the economic forecasts were, predictions that Castro's regime would be a casualty of the collapse of the Soviet Union proved premature. Cuba by the mid-1990s had renewed relations with most of the American, European, and Asian countries. These nations did not seem to care that they were exchanging relations with a Latin American dictator who at the outset of his career had supervised executions of opponents after trials in baseball stadiums and who had imprisoned opponents mercilessly. As he had done earlier, in 1994 Castro again extended a hand to Cuban exiles, the majority of whom were in the United States. Castro went on television to excoriate U.S. President Bill Clinton, who gave the impression that Castro was little more than a nuisance. After a new exodus of Cubans by boat in the summer of 1994, however, Clinton found himself forced to send the refugees not to Florida, a state that did not want them, but to camps on Guantánamo, the small enclave in Cuba controlled by the United States since the Spanish-American War of 1898.

[See also Cuban Americans; Grenada Invasion; Latin America, Relations with.]

BIBLIOGRAPHY

Fidel Castro, *Nothing Can Stop the Course of History* (New York, 1986).
Jorge I. Dominguez, *To Make a World Safe for Revolution: Cuba's Foreign Policy* (Cambridge, Mass., 1989).
Franklin W. Knight and Colin A. Palmer, *The Modern Caribbean* (Chapel Hill, N.C., 1989).
Tad Szulc, *Fidel: A Critical Portrait* (New York, 1986).
Howard J. Wiarda et al., eds., *The Communist Challenge in the Caribbean and Central America* (Washington, D.C., 1987).

— MARY COMMAGER

CUBAN AMERICANS

Cuban Americans who came to the United States during the mid-nineteenth century to work in the cigar industry and as political exiles first formed communities in New York City and Key West and Tampa, Florida. Migration continued with changing political and economic conditions in Cuba and increased dramatically in 1959, when Fidel Castro ousted dictator Fulgencio Batista. During the first wave of Cuban immigration in 1959–1962, more than 215,000 persons migrated to the United States. These exiles hoped to overthrow Castro and return to Cuba. Supported by the Central Intelligence Agency, some 1,300 of them invaded Cuba at the Bay of Pigs in 1961. The landing failed. Furthermore, the U.S. pledge in 1962 not to intervene militarily in Cuba in exchange for the Soviet removal of its missiles there dashed hopes for a quick return. Meanwhile, a Cuban refugee program provided basic necessities, health services, job placement, and educational assistance; financed resettlement in areas outside Miami; and retrained professionals. Legislation passed in 1966 eased citizenship requirements. Such refugee assistance was unprecedented and reflected the significance of anticommunism in U.S. foreign and domestic policies.

Emigration from Cuba rose dramatically after Fidel Castro ousted dictator Fulgencio Batista in 1959; many of the exiles expected to return soon to overthrow Castro.

During the second wave of Cuban immigration from 1965 to 1973, more than 300,000 Cubans came to the United States. Those with relatives in the United States were permitted by Cuba to emigrate, coming by boat until the U.S. and Cuban governments arranged air transportation. Fewer migrants came during the third wave in 1980, but the migration was rapid and dramatic. The Cuban government opened the port of Mariel, and Cubans rushed there by boat from Miami to retrieve relatives and friends. In five months, 125,000 Cubans joined those already in the United States. Between waves and since 1980, some Cubans have migrated through third countries, by boat, or as released political prisoners. In 1994 immigration increased as more than 24,000 immigrants left Cuba on boats and rafts and were intercepted and detained by U.S. authorities. The migration ceased when the United States agreed to increase visas for legal immigration and Cuba agreed to halt the exodus.

Each wave of migrants became more diverse and more representative of Cuban society. The first-wave migrants had higher skill and educational levels than the Cuban population as a whole. The second-wave migrants were less educated and less skilled than first-wave migrants. The 1980 migrants were comparable in skills and education, but they were younger, more were males, and more were mulattoes and blacks. Prisoners and mental patients, deported by the Cuban government, and male homosexuals were among the migrants. Half of the 1980 migrants were released to sponsors in Miami, while others were held in military camps. The U.S. media focused on the camp population and portrayed the migrants as criminals. An estimated 16 percent of the camp population had been jailed in Cuba. Although some were convicted felons, many had been imprisoned for participating in the black market or for refusing military service.

The 1990 census reported 1,053,197 Cubans in the United States, with 54 percent living in the Miami-Hialeah area of Florida. Sizable communities also emerged in Union City and West New York, New Jersey; New York City; and San Juan, Puerto Rico. Settlement was shaped by economic opportunities, networks of family and friends, and the U.S. government's resettlement program. While some migrants regained their status as professionals, others turned to business. The earliest exiles brought skills and resources, secured federal and private loans, and gained footholds in textiles and other manufacturing. These businesses employed later arrivals. Cuban women entered the labor force in unprecedented numbers, with many working in the Miami garment industry. The refugee program and migrants' education and skills prior to migration improved their socioeconomic status.

Increasingly, many Cubans, especially the generation that became adults after emigration, viewed their stay in the United States as permanent. During the 1970s more Cubans became naturalized citizens and registered to vote. They became a force in local politics, electing members of their community to the Miami board of education and to city offices in Miami and Hialeah; Xavier L. Suarez was elected mayor of Miami in 1985. They made their voices heard in national politics through such organizations as the Cu-ban American National Foundation, founded in 1981 and based in Washington, D.C. The vehemently anti-Castro views that had once unified the Cuban community gave way to greater diversity by the 1970s. Some advocated a dialogue with Cuba to promote the release of political prisoners, family reunification, and family visits. Debates arose over the U.S. trade embargo of Cuba. Although some observers viewed naturalization and socioeconomic gains as signs of assimilation, others saw Cuban Americans as following a path of biculturalism that emphasized both adaptation to life in the United States and retention of Cuban cultural heritage. The Cuban-American community continued to be shaped by experiences in the United States and by cultural ties to Cuba.

[See also Cuba, Relations with; Hispanic Americans.]

BIBLIOGRAPHY

Thomas Boswell and James Curtis, *The Cuban-American Experience* (Totowa, N.J., 1983).

Center for Latin American Studies, "The Cuban Exodus: A Symposium," *Cuban Studies/Estudios Cubanos* 11 and 12 (July 1981 and January 1982).

— CARMEN TERESA WHALEN

CUBAN MISSILE CRISIS

By August 1962 it was common knowledge that the Soviet Union was engaged in a large-scale military buildup in Cuba, greatly heightening American anxiety. Throughout the summer and early fall President John F. Kennedy was under heavy pressure to launch an invasion of Cuba, to impose a blockade, or to take any one of a number of suggested actions to topple Cuba's Premier Fidel Castro, but these pressures were more than offset by the caution of those who feared that direct action might lead to an atomic war or, at the least, might alienate Latin Americans, traditionally wary of U.S. power in the hemisphere.

The Kennedy administration tried to meet the Cuban challenge with political and economic measures. An effort was made to solidify hemispheric isolation of Cuba; and Europeans were urged to cease supplying Cuba with the sinews of war. Many Latin Americans, however, opposed new restrictions against Cuba, and non-Communist shippers were reluctant to drop the lucrative Cuban trade.

As Soviet arms and men piled up in Cuba, the public clamor for Kennedy to "do something" increased in volume, but he continued to handle the problem circumspectly. Early in September he said that there was no "evidence of . . . significant offensive capability" in Cuba, but he added that "were it to be otherwise, the gravest issues would arise." On Sept. 26 Congress adopted a resolution that was a compromise between the Republican proposal to give the president the authority to use troops to invade Cuba and the president's request for standby authority to call up military reserves in case of need. Kennedy chose to interpret the resolution as a demand for action if, and only if, the Cubans threatened violence to the rest of the hemisphere.

By Oct. 21, tension had increased. That evening the president went on television to announce that "unmistakable evidence has established the fact that a series of offensive missile sites is now in preparation on that imprisoned island" and that "to halt this offensive buildup a strict quarantine of all offensive military equipment under shipment to Cuba is being initiated." The president did not say that the United States was imposing a blockade, for under international law a blockade is an act of war; but it was obvious that the United States was doing so, for the navy was directed to order ships carrying offensive weapons to Cuba to turn back or to face sinking. The quarantine, Kennedy emphasized, would not be lifted until the administration was assured that the missiles had been withdrawn and the bases dismantled. The president announced, ominously, that he had ordered stepped-up surveillance of Cuba and had directed the armed forces "to prepare for any eventualities."

On Oct. 24 the deadline for the imposition of the quarantine came and passed without incident. The Soviet bluff, if it was that, had been called. Soviet ships that were approaching Cuba changed course, indicating the Soviet Union's unwillingness to face an immediate showdown. Even more encouragingly, Soviet Premier Nikita Khrushchev, in a letter to the British pacifist Lord Bertrand Russell, castigated the United States but also suggested a summit meeting to avert war. On Oct. 28 Khrushchev formally capitulated. In a message to Kennedy he said that the Soviet missiles in Cuba would be dismantled and shipped back to the Soviet Union under the supervision of the United Nations and asked that the United States, in turn, commit itself not to invade Cuba. Kennedy agreed to this quid pro quo, although he made it clear that the withdrawal of the quarantine and the pledge not to invade Cuba hinged on "effective international verification" of the removal of the offensive weapons and the cessation of any additional missile shipments to Cuba. The chief stumbling block to a definite conclusion was Castro. His prestige badly damaged, he attempted to salve his wounded pride by refusing to accept any form of UN inspection. Castro's stubbornness gave the United States a good reason to continue its reconnaissance flights and, perhaps, to modify its pledge not to invade Cuba. Despite a number of diplomatic loose ends that remained to be tied, the Cuban crisis was over by the end of November.

BIBLIOGRAPHY

Robert A. Divine, ed., *The Cuban Missile Crisis* (1971).

Andrés Suárez, ed., *Cuba: Castroism and Communism* (1967).

— JACOB E. COOKE

CUMBERLAND ROAD

Cumberland Road, also known as the United States Road, National Road (especially along its western portions), or National Turnpike, was the first national road in the United States. Its influence upon the development of the Ohio and upper Mississippi valleys was incalculable. Prior to the construction of this highway the only route through southwestern Pennsylvania to the West had been Braddock's Road. The latter for many years had deteriorated, and travelers had come to prefer the more northerly Forbes Road. In April 1802 Congress passed an enabling act for Ohio preparatory to its admission into the Union. One of the provisions of this law set aside 5 percent of the net proceeds of the public lands sold by Congress within Ohio for the building of a national road from the waters flowing into the Atlantic, to and through the state of Ohio. A second act passed in March 1803 allocated 3 of the 5 percent for the construction of roads within Ohio and the remaining 2 percent for the road from the navigable waters draining into the Atlantic to the Ohio River. Congress in March 1806 provided for the marketing and construction of the road from Cumberland, Md., as the eastern terminus, to the Ohio.

The construction of the road began in 1811, and by 1818 the U.S. mail was running over it to Wheeling, now in West Virginia. In general the route followed older roads or trails, especially Braddock's Road. Immediately the popularity of the road was tremendous.

Although Maryland, Pennsylvania, and Ohio each gave permission (in 1806, 1807, and 1824, respectively) for the building of the road within their boundaries, constitutional difficulties arose. In 1822 Congress passed a bill for the establishment of tollgates along the highway to permit the collection of revenues for the repair of the road. President James Monroe, however, saw danger in the enforcement of such legislation and vetoed the bill. Penalties to be inflicted upon those who violated the requirements of the law, in his opinion, would involve an unconstitutional assumption of the police power of the states by the federal government. Congress, nevertheless, soon voted money for repairs and, in March 1825, appropriated funds for extending the road from Wheeling to Zanesville, Ohio. Over this route the highway followed the first road built in Ohio, Zane's Trace, which at Zanesville turned southwestward to Lancaster, Chillicothe, and the Ohio River. Parts of the Cumberland Road were later turned over to Maryland, Pennsylvania, Ohio, and Virginia (1831–34), tollgates in some cases being erected by the state authorities. From time to time Congress voted additional funds for the continuance of the road through Ohio, Indiana, and Illinois. The highway, however, was completed in Indiana and Illinois only after the federal government had relinquished its control. The last important federal appropriation for it was made in 1838, an additional small item on the account of the survey to Jefferson City, Mo., being voted in 1844.

The road to Vandalia, Ill., its western terminus, was 591 miles in length, built at a cost of

A Currier and Ives lithograph depicts a championship baseball game between the Athletic Baseball Club of Philadelphia and the Atlantics of Brooklyn on October 22, 1866 in Philadelphia. (Corbis-Bettman)

almost $7 million to the federal government. The Cumberland Road has since been modernized and is now U.S. Route 40.

BIBLIOGRAPHY

A. B, Hulbert, *The Paths of Inland Commerce.*

Jeremiah S. Young, *A Political and Constitutional Study of the Cumberland Road.*

— FRANCIS PHELPS WEISENBURGER

CURRIER & IVES

Nathaniel Currier, a lithographer, began issuing original colored prints in New York City in 1835. James M. Ives joined the firm in 1850, and from 1857, as a partner, Ives's name appeared on the prints with that of Currier. The firm's prints—sentimental, journalistic, sporting, humorous, and historical—became tremendously popular. Currier retired in 1880 and his son Edward succeeded him. When Ives died in 1895 his interests in the firm were inherited by his son Chauncey. The sons continued the firm until 1902 when Chauncey Ives bought out Currier. In 1907 Ives sold the firm to Daniel Logan, who went out of business a few years later.

When James Ives died, the photograph was displacing the lithograph, and the partners' outmoded pictures, with their slight artistic value, seemed destined for oblivion. But by 1915 they were eagerly sought for, and their prices rose enormously. In November 1973 one Currier & Ives print, *The American National Game of Base Ball*, sold for $7,000 at auction.

BIBLIOGRAPHY

Harry T. Peters, *Currier & Ives: Printmakers to the American People.*

— ALVIN F. HARLOW

D

DAKOTA

The Dakota Indians are represented in western Minnesota, North Dakota, South Dakota, and eastern Montana and Wyoming by no fewer than seven main tribes and a number of lesser tribal or band groupings. These are groups sometimes categorized as Sioux, primarily a linguistic reference, since the Dakota, along with several other major peoples in the Great Lakes and Woodlands region, speak languages classified as Siouan, Hokan-Siouan, or Siouan-Yuchi. The Wisconsin Winnebago, for example, spoke a Siouan language, while Yuchian, an apparent branch, was spoken in Tennessee and North Carolina. The Siouan-speaking peoples—including, in the Plains, the Hidatsa and Assiniboine (Assiniboin), as well as the linguistically more remote Mandan—appear to have come out of the Woodlands into the Plains in late prehistoric or early historic times. The various Dakota tribes, closely related to each other in language, made an early adjustment to life in the northern Plains.

Like other Plains tribes, the Dakota gave primary allegiance to the band, the broadly spread local group, rather than to the tribe as such. Convocations of several bands for bison hunting or war gave rise to a tribal sense. Although the Dakota tribes have been classified as eastern and western, such a division oversimplifies the picture: the eastern Dakota are more properly called Santee Dakota, consisting, in turn, of the Mdewankanton, Wahpeton, Wahpekute, and Sisseton (sometimes described as the forest Dakota); the central and western branches, those of the high Plains and prairie, include the Yankton, Yanktonai (from whom the Assiniboine are said to have separated), and Teton. Such a division, however, does not take account of the many bands associated with these major tribal elements, many of which are tribes in their own right, functioning as units in hunting and war. Thus, the complex Teton Dakota embrace the upper and lower Brulé, the Hunkpapa, Miniconjou, Oglala, Oohenonpa (Two Kettle), Sans Arcs, and Sihasapa. Well-known Indian personalities came from such subdivisions: Crazy Horse and Red Cloud, for example, from the Oglala and Sitting Bull from the Hunkpapa. The Dakota language had begun to assume some dialectic diversity by the 19th century, the eastern peoples using the term for themselves as *Dakota*, while the Teton modified the word to *Lakota* and the Yankton-Yanktonai to *Nakota*.

Taken together, the Dakota peoples formed one of the larger Plains Indian groups, numbering about 25,000 in 1780. The year is significant, since it was by this time that the equestrian mode of life was fully integrated in the Plains; by then horticulture, which had probably been practiced by the Dakota for about a century, had been abandoned in favor of the classic Plains hunting pattern. With the horse, the Dakota moved as bands across their vast territory, exploiting the bison in the grasslands and engaging in warfare against the Arikara, Mandan, Hidatsa, and any other peoples whom they encountered, particularly the Crow and Cheyenne. As elsewhere in the Plains, war enhanced individual prestige and provided a source of horses, although the northern Plains were poor in horses as compared with Mexico, into which the southern Comanche sent raiding parties. Given their basic Plains orientation, the various Dakota took on all the material, social, and ceremonial trappings associated with the area: the tipi, the use of buckskin, beadwork, skin painting, extremely strong social ties, and the ritual and religious features of vision quest, Sun Dance, and medicine bundles or fetish objects.

The Dakota peoples formed one of the larger Plains Indian groups, numbering about 25,000 in 1780.

The various western Dakota are believed to have reached the Black Hills before 1765, having passed through Minnesota, probably coming from the Southeast. Some Dakota, resentful of governmental insistence that they farm, fought expansion by Euro-Americans during the Civil War, resulting, after the suppression of the New Ulm uprising of 1862, in the expulsion of the eastern groups from Minnesota into the Dakotas. The gold rush of the 1870's into the Black Hills, with its consequent encroachment on Indian lands, created for the first time some solidarity among the Dakota peoples. Their alliance, fanned by the spread of the Ghost Dance, brought the Dakota, notably the Teton, together with the Cheyenne and culminated in the 1876 battle with Gen. George Armstrong Custer and his men at the Little Bighorn. A second Ghost Dance movement resulted in the Battle of Wounded Knee in December 1890, the last Dakota military action. Dakota are currently to be found on former Indian land reserves in North Dakota and South Dakota.

BIBLIOGRAPHY

Elden Johnson, "The Teton Dakota," in R. F. Spencer and J. D. Jennings, *The Native Americans.*
Robert H. Lowie, *Indians of the Plains.*
N. H. Winchell, *Indians of Minnesota.*

— ROBERT F. SPENCER

DAKOTA TERRITORY

Dakota Territory, created by act of Congress, Mar. 2, 1861. It corresponded to the present states of North Dakota, South Dakota, and much of Wyoming and Montana. The greater part of this immense region was included in the Louisiana Purchase of 1803; an indefinite part, from the forty-ninth parallel southward, was confirmed as belonging to the United States by the Convention of 1818 with England. All of it fell within the vast Missouri Territory created in 1812. That part of the Missouri Territory east of the Missouri and White Earth rivers was added to Michigan Territory in 1834. In 1836 Dakota became part of Wisconsin Territory; in 1838, part of Iowa Territory; and in 1849, part of Minnesota Territory. From 1834 to 1854 the western part of the later Dakota Territory was known as Indian Country, and in 1854 was included in Nebraska Territory. Dakota Territory, as created in 1861, included all of Minnesota Territory west of the present boundary of that state and all of Nebraska Territory north of the forty-third parallel to the Missouri River, with the exception of a small strip west of that river that was annexed to the State of Nebraska in 1882. Montana Territory, with the present state limits, was cut off from Dakota Territory in 1864. This reduced Dakota Territory to the area included within the present states of Wyoming, North Dakota, and South Dakota. When Wyoming Territory was created, in 1868, Dakota Territory was reduced to the region comprising the two Dakotas of today.

So far as is known, this region was first visited by white men in 1738. The first trading post was built by Jean Baptiste Truteau in Charles Mix County, S.Dak., in 1794. The Lewis and Clark expedition wintered at the Five Villages in 1804–05. The most famous trading post on the Missouri River was Fort Union, built at the mouth of the Yellowstone River in 1829.

The first legislative assembly of the territory convened at Yankton on Mar. 17, 1862. Yankton was the capital until 1883, when it was moved to Bismarck. Legislative sessions were held at Yankton in 1862–83 and at Bismarck in 1885–89.

The discovery of gold in the Black Hills in 1874 resulted in the opening, two years later, of that section to white settlement. In 1889 the territory was divided into the existing states of North Dakota and South Dakota.

BIBLIOGRAPHY

G. W. Kingsbury, *History of Dakota Territory.*

— O. G. LIBBY

DALE'S LAWS OF VIRGINIA

Dale's Laws of Virginia, a criminal code issued by Sir Thomas Dale for colonial Virginia (1611–16). When Dale arrived in Jamestown, he found the colonists rebellious and disinclined to work. He placed them under martial law and issued a code notable for its pitiless severity even in an age of barbarous punishments.

BIBLIOGRAPHY

W. F. Prince, "The First Criminal Code in Virginia," *Report of the American Historical Association,* vol. I (1899).

— FRED B. JOYNER

DAWES GENERAL ALLOTMENT ACT

The white solution of the Indian problem long remained that of conquest and removal westward, followed by confinement on reservations, education, and assimilation. The reservations were slowly divided into allotments of land to families or individual Indians, on which, it was hoped, the Indians would live and practice the white man's skills of cultivation and grazing. From the colonial period to the late 19th century, allotments and small individual reservations were granted to chiefs and headmen and were increasingly used to win approval from them for the cession of parts of their tribal reserves.

Between 1850 and 1887, fifty treaties or agreements with various tribes provided for allotments of 80 to 320 acres. In the latter year a combination of greedy westerners, who were anxious to hasten the process of breaking up the remaining reservations through allotments, whether or not the Indians wished to take them (many did not), and misguided, but well-meaning humanitarians, put the Dawes General Allotment Act through Congress. With later amendments the act applied to all tribes with reservations in the public land states. It provided for the breakup of the Indian tribal relationship and the abandonment of the domestic nation theory. Reservations were to be surveyed and allotments of 40 to 160 acres assigned to heads of families, orphans, and children; the surplus lands were to be opened to white settlement. That the assignment of allotments to the Indians had wholly failed to convert them to the acquisitive society of the whites based on private ownership was well known but disregarded by Congress. Although the allotments were inalienable for twenty-five years, they quickly fell into the hands of whites, who thus acquired the best lands within the reservations, leaving in diminished reserves the least useful tracts.

Allotment proved a tragic blunder. In 1934, the allotment policy was halted by the Indian Reorganization Act, and efforts were made to restore tribal organization and to recover some of the lost land. For a time reconstitution of tribal organization progressed, but in the early 1950's another shift of policy took place. A series of termination acts was passed to break up the tribes and to effect their assimilation, despite the fact that past history had shown the futility of such a policy. Termination was as disastrous as the Dawes Act and was soon ended.

BIBLIOGRAPHY

Angie Debo, *A History of the Indians of the United States.*

— PAUL W. GATES

DECLARATION OF INDEPENDENCE

There were two declarations of independence—the first a decision by the Continental Congress made on July 2, 1776, and the second a paper written by Thomas Jefferson that Congress entitled "The Unanimous Declaration of the Thirteen United States of America" and released to the world on July 4. Both sprang from a resolution introduced in Congress on June 7 by Richard Henry Lee, who, speaking for Virginia, asked his colleagues to resolve that "these United Colonies are, and of right ought to be, free and independent States . . . and that all political connection between them and the State of Great Britain is, and ought to be, totally dissolved." In the debate that followed, those for the resolution argued that necessity demanded it; that independence would improve the chances for treaties of commerce and for foreign loans; that it would animate the people; that the coming summer military campaign required it; and, finally, that "the people wait for us to lead the way." Those opposed, a vocal and defiant minority, held that the colonies were not yet ripe for independence and that "to take any capital step till the voice of the people drove us into it" would be to court disaster. Obviously, the thirteen "clocks," to use John Adams' metaphor, were not yet ready to strike as one; and on June 10 it was agreed that Lee's resolution be postponed for three weeks and that in the meantime a committee should be appointed to "prepare a Declaration to the effect of the said . . . resolution." The committee chosen consisted of Thomas Jefferson, John Adams, Benjamin Franklin, Roger Sherman, and Robert R. Livingston. Jefferson, elected with the most votes, by custom automatically became chairman of the committee and thus the assignment of preparing a declaration of independence fell to him.

As Jefferson saw it, "An appeal to the tribunal of the world . . . for our justification . . . was the object of the Declaration." This meant that to catch the ear of European leaders he had to destroy the British contention that the colonies were rebelling against lawful authority. He also had to discard the argument used during the preceding decade—that Americans sought only to preserve their rights as Englishmen—for one with a broader appeal. Thus, in the opening paragraph of the Declaration, Jefferson stated that it was necessary for Americans not to revolt from, but to dissolve their ties with, the mother country. They were entitled to "the separate and equal station" they would assume in the world of nations by the "Laws of Nature," not by the rights of Englishmen. Jefferson went on in the second paragraph of his draft to summarize the doctrine of natural rights as it was then understood throughout Western Europe. All men are endowed with certain "inherent & inalienable rights," he said, and "to secure these rights governments are instituted among men, deriving their just powers from the consent of the governed." When a government tramples upon these natural rights, "it is the right of the people to alter or to abolish that government." The phrase "consent of the governed," essential to Jefferson's argument, advanced a political theory unwelcome among the crowned heads of Europe; but Jefferson diluted its revolutionary implications by presenting it as an abstract concept. In promoting the right of a people to revolt, he had traveled deftly over treacherous ground, condemning no particular form of government but only despotic rulers.

Jefferson understood that the colonies must be seen by the European powers not as rebelling against lawful authority, but as dissolving outworn ties and taking their rightful place among the world of nations.

Thus, the opening paragraphs of the Declaration laid the theoretical basis for America to separate from Great

Britain. In the next step of the argument, Jefferson declared that "facts" must now be submitted to "a candid world" to show that Americans had endured "a long train of abuses" designed "to reduce them under absolute Despotism." It was necessary to attribute these abuses to George III. Americans had begun their quarrel with the British government by arguing that Parliament had the right to legislate for the colonies, but only in certain instances. By 1774 Thomas Jefferson, John Adams, James Wilson, and others were holding that Parliament "has no right to exercise authority over us." The effort to work out a scheme that permitted the colonies to exist within the framework of the British empire without being tied to Parliament led to the theory that the colonies owed allegiance only to the king, that they were equals within the empire and could make their own laws and levy their own taxes, as Englishmen in Britain did through Parliament. The king, then, remained the last link between England and the colonies. To break that link the king had to be shown to have acted tyrannically. In the seventeen brief paragraphs of charges that Jefferson directed at the king in his early draft, Parliament enters into only one charge, cloaked in the phrase "he has combined with others." The skillfully chosen catalog of transgressions, several of them more hypothetical than real, touched upon every part of the American continent. Few citizens could read the list without feeling that somewhere along the line they had been injured by the king. Only the last of the draft's charges—that dealing with slavery—could give awkward pause. The king, said Jefferson, has "determined to keep open a market where men should be bought & sold, he has prostituted his negative for suppressing every legislative attempt to prohibit or to restrain this execrable commerce. . . . "

Having "proved" his case against the king, Jefferson turned to censuring "our British Brethren," whom, he said, Americans must now hold "as we hold the rest of mankind, enemies in war, in peace friends." That done, he made a formal renouncement of all ties with Great Britain and then, with a pledge of "our lives, our fortunes, & our sacred honour," ended his paper.

From the time Jefferson completed his draft until he laid it before Congress, some thirty-one changes were made in the Declaration—either by Jefferson; by his committee, which he certainly called into session after he had finished; or, more likely, by both the committee and Jefferson. Except for the addition of three new charges against the king, probably suggested by the committee, most of the changes were relatively minor and mainly stylistic. Franklin, abed with gout, received the revised version by messenger and made five more changes, all of them minor. Jefferson then drew up a fair copy of the Declaration and placed it on the desk of the secretary of the Continental Congress on June 28.

Congress assembled on July 1 prepared to vote on Lee's resolution. But first John Dickinson of Pennsylvania, "alarm'd at this Declaration on being so vehemently presented," appalled that America dared "to brave the storm in a skiff made of paper," felt impelled to speak. "It is our interest," ran the theme of his long oration, "to keep Great Britain in the opinion that we mean reconciliation as long as possible." John Adams' reply rehearsed all the arguments for independence made in Congress during the past six months. Neither speech changed delegates' minds. An unofficial vote taken later in the day while Congress sat as a committee of the whole showed nine colonies for independence and four—Pennsylvania, South Carolina, Delaware, and New York—either against, split, or forced to abstain for lack of instructions from the home government. A formal vote was postponed until the next day in the hope that recalcitrant delegates could be brought around. The delay worked. On July 2, by a unanimous vote (New York abstaining), Congress resolved "that these United Colonies are, and, of right, ought to be Free and Independent States; that they are absolved from all allegiance to the British crown, and that all political connexion between them and the state of Great Britain is, and ought to be, totally dissolved."

Immediately after the vote for independence, Congress turned to editing Jefferson's paper, upon which it worked for more than two days. The first half of the Declaration escaped almost untouched. Congress made only a few stylistic changes in the early paragraphs. "Inherent & inalienable rights," for example, became "certain unalienable Rights." Only minor alterations were worked into the list of charges against the king, until Congress came to the one dealing with slavery. It was struck out, said Jefferson, "in complaisance to South Carolina & Georgia, who had never attempted to restrain the importation of slaves and who on the contrary still wished to continue it. Our Northern brethren also I believe felt a little tender under those censures; for tho' their people have very few slaves themselves yet they had been pretty considerable carriers of them to others."

The deletions from this point on were heavy. Out went several lines censuring George III; they were judged "too personal." Out went Jefferson's inaccurate statement that "submission to their Parliament was no part of our constitution, nor ever in idea, if history may be credited." Out went the last half of the penultimate paragraph, which dealt with "these unfeeling brethren," the English people. Swept away in the excision were some of Jefferson's happiest phrases—"the road to happiness & to glory is open to us too; we will climb it apart from them"—but the cuts were sound. It was not the British people but their oppressive monarch who had caused the break with England. The last paragraph was reworked to include the original wording of Lee's resolution; and the final sentence, which as Jefferson wrote it has been called "perfection itself," was amended to include the italicized phrase: "And for the support of this Declaration, *with a firm reliance on the protection of divine Providence,* we mutually pledge to each other our Lives, our Fortunes and our sacred Honor."

In spite of some forty additions and extensive cuts that reduced the paper by one-quarter, Congress had left Jefferson's document pretty much intact, and in most instances its editing improved his handiwork. Thirteen colonies whose representatives only two years earlier had first met in Philadelphia and been appalled at the diversity of customs, laws, and traditions among themselves, and who only three weeks earlier had been at loggerheads over the practical aspects of independence, had with little difficulty been able to agree on a set of fundamental political beliefs for the United States of America they had brought into being.

Congress completed its revision of the Declaration in the early evening of July 4. The finished document was turned over to a Philadelphia printer, who placed July 4 at the top of his broadside of the Declaration. Thus did that day come to be celebrated with the pomp and ceremony John Adams had expected to be given over to July 2, the day Congress actually declared America's independence.

Signing of the Declaration

Few facts are known about the signing of the Declaration of Independence. The Declaration was printed July 4 bearing only the names of John Hancock, as president, and Charles Thomson, as secretary of Congress. On July 19, after learning New York had approved the Declaration, Congress voted that the document "be fairly engrossed . . . on parchment with the title and style of 'The unanimous Declaration of the thirteen united States of America.' " On Aug. 2, the *Journal* of the Continental Congress notes, "The Declaration of Independence being engrossed and compared at the table was signed by the members." A number of those who signed—among them, Richard Henry Lee, George Wythe, Samuel Chase, Charles Carroll, and Oliver Wolcott—had not been present to vote for independence. At least two who signed—George Read and Robert Morris—had opposed and still opposed independence. Others—such as Matthew Thornton, Elbridge Gerry, and Thomas McKean—were not present for the Aug. 2 ceremony but signed later. The names of the signers were kept secret until Jan. 19, 1777, when they were released to the world.

"We must be unanimous," said John Hancock; "we must all hang together." Replied Benjamin Franklin, "Yes, we must all hang together, or most assuredly we shall all hang separately."

Although facts about the signing are few, anecdotes about it abound. Hancock, after centering his name below the text of the Declaration, is supposed to have said, "There! John Bull can read my name without spectacles, and may now double his reward of £500 for my head. That is my defiance." He is also supposed to have said, "We must be unanimous. There must be no pulling different ways; we must all hang together." Benjamin Franklin is said to have answered, "Yes, we must all hang together, or most assuredly we shall all hang separately." Carroll, a newly appointed delegate from Maryland and reputedly the richest man in America, was asked if he would sign. "Most willingly," he is said to have replied, which prompted another delegate to remark, "There goes a few million." Stephen Hopkins, aged sixty-nine, is supposed to have said as he placed his shaky signature, "My hand trembles, but my heart does not!" Benjamin Harrison, a large, heavy man, is reported to have turned to Gerry while they waited to sign and said, "I shall have a great advantage over you, Mr. Gerry, when we are all hung for what we are now doing. From the size and weight of my body I shall die in a few minutes, but from the lightness of your body you will dance in the air an hour or two before you are dead." These tales may be true, but none has been verified by contemporary evidence and all came into circulation long after the signing. The Harrison-Gerry anecdote, for instance, was told by Benjamin Rush in 1811. Rush was present for the signing on Aug. 2, but Gerry was not. If Harrison spoke as he did, it must have been to another delegate.

BIBLIOGRAPHY

Carl Becker, *The Declaration of Independence: A Study in Political Ideas.*

Julian P. Boyd, *The Declaration of Independence: The Evolution of the Text.*

Edward Dumbauld, *The Declaration and What It Means Today.*

Herbert Friedenwald, *The Declaration of Independence.*

David Hawke, *A Transaction of Free Men: The Birth and Course of the Declaration of Independence.*

J. H. Hazelton, *The Declaration of Independence: Its History.*

— DAVID FREEMAN HAWKE

DECLARATION OF INDEPENDENCE

In Congress, July 4, 1776

The unanimous Declaration of the thirteen united States of America

When in the Course of human Events, it becomes necessary for one people to dissolve the political bands which have connected them with another, and to assume among the powers of the earth, the separate and equal station to which the Laws of Nature and of Nature's God entitle them, a decent respect to the opinions of mankind requires that they should declare the causes which impel them to the separation.—We hold these truths to be self-evident, that all men are created equal, that they are endowed by their Creator with certain unalienable Rights, that among these are Life, Liberty and the pursuit of Happiness.—That to secure these rights, Governments are instituted among Men, deriving their just powers from the consent of the governed,—That whenever any Form of Government becomes destructive of these ends, it is the Right of the People to alter or to abolish it, and to institute new Government, laying its foundation on such principles and organizing its powers in such form, as to them shall seem most likely to effect their Safety and Happiness. Prudence, indeed, will dictate that Governments long established should not be changed for light and transient causes; and accordingly all experience hath shewn, that mankind are more disposed to suffer, while evils are sufferable, than to right themselves by abolishing the forms to which they are accustomed. But when a long train of abuses and usurpations, pursuing invariably the same Object, evinces a design to reduce them under absolute Despotism, it is their right, it is their duty, to throw off such Government, and to provide new Guards for their future security.—Such has been the patient sufferance of these Colonies; and such is now the necessity which constrains them to alter their former Systems of Government. The history of the present King of Great Britain is a history of repeated injuries and usurpations, all having in direct object the establishment of an absolute Tyranny over these States. To prove this, let Facts be submitted to a candid world.—He has refused his Assent to Laws, the most wholesome and necessary for the public good.—He has forbidden his Governors to pass Laws of immediate and pressing importance, unless suspended in their operation till his Assent should be obtained; and when so suspended, he has utterly neglected to attend to them.—He has refused to pass other laws for the accommodation of large districts of people, unless those people would relinquish the right of Representation in the Legislature, a right inestimable to them and formidable to tyrants only.—He has called together legislative bodies at places unusual, uncomfortable, and distant from the depository of their public Records, for the sole purpose of fatiguing them into compliance with his measures.—He has dissolved Representative Houses repeatedly, for opposing with manly firmness his invasions on the rights of the people.—He has refused for a long time, after such dissolutions, to cause others to be elected; whereby the Legislative powers, incapable of Annihilation, have returned to the People at large for their exercise; the State remaining in the mean time exposed to all the dangers of invasion from without, and convulsions within.—He has endeavoured to prevent the population of these States; for that purpose obstructing the Laws for Naturalization of Foreigners; refusing to pass others to encourage their migrations hither, and raising the conditions of new Appropriations of Lands.—He has obstructed the Administration of Justice, by refusing his Assent to Laws for establishing Judiciary powers.—He has made Judges dependent on his Will alone, for the tenure of their offices, and the amount and payment of their salaries.—He has erected a multitude of new offices, and sent hither swarms of Officers to harass our people and eat out their substance.—He has kept among us, in times of peace, Standing Armies without the Consent of our legislatures.—He has affected to render the Military independent of and superior to the Civil power.—He has combined with others to subject us to a jurisdiction foreign to our constitution, and unacknowledged by our laws; giving his Assent to their Acts of pretended Legislation:—For quartering large bodies of armed troops among us:—For protecting them, by a mock Trial, from punishment for any Murders which they should commit on the Inhabitants of these States:—For cutting off our Trade with all parts of the world:—For imposing Taxes on us without our Consent:—For depriving us in many cases, of the benefits of Trial by Jury:—For transporting us beyond Seas to be tried for pretended offences:—For abolishing the free System of English Laws in a neighbouring Province, establishing therein an Arbitrary government, and enlarging its Boundaries, so as to render it at once an example and fit instrument for introducing the same absolute rule into these Colonies:—For taking away our Charters, abolishing our most valuable Laws, and altering fundamentally the Forms of our Governments:—For suspending our own Legislatures and declaring themselves invested with power to legislate for us in all cases whatsoever.—He has abdicated Government here, by declaring us out of his Protection and waging War against us.—He has plundered our seas, ravaged our Coasts, burnt our towns, and destroyed the lives of our people.—He is at this time, transporting large Armies of foreign Mercenaries to compleat the works of death, desolation and tyranny, already begun with circumstances of cruelty & perfidy scarcely paralleled in the most barbarous ages, and totally unworthy the Head of a civilized nation.—He has constrained our fellow Citizens taken Captive on the high Seas to bear Arms against their Country, to become the executioners of their friends and Brethren, or to fall themselves by their Hands.—He has excited domestic insurrections amongst us, and has endeavoured to bring on the inhabitants of our frontiers, the merciless Indian Savages, whose known rule of warfare, is an undistinguished destruction, of all ages, sexes and conditions. In every stage of these Oppressions We have Petitioned for Redress in the most humble terms: Our repeated Petitions have been answered only by repeated injury. A Prince, whose character is thus marked by every act which may define a Tyrant, is unfit to be the ruler of a free people. Nor have we been wanting in Attentions to our Brittish brethren. We have warned them from time to time of Attempts by their legislature to extend an unwarrantable jurisdiction over us. We have reminded them of the circumstances of our emigration and settlement here. We have appealed to their native justice and magnanimity, and we have conjured them by the ties of our common kindred to disavow these usurpations, which, would inevitably interrupt our connections and correspondence. They too have been deaf to the voice of justice and of consanguinity. We must, therefore, acquiesce in the necessity, which denounces our Separation, and hold them, as we hold the rest of mankind, Enemies in War, in Peace Friends.

"That these United Colonies are, and of Right ought to be Free and Independent States; that they are absolved from all Allegiance to the British Crown."

We, therefore, the Representatives of the UNITED STATES OF AMERICA, in General Congress, Assembled, appealing to the Supreme Judge of the world for the rectitude of our intentions, do, in the Name, and by Authority of the good People of these Colonies, solemnly publish and declare, That these United Colonies are, and of Right ought to be FREE AND INDEPENDENT STATES; that they are absolved from all Allegiance to the British Crown, and that all political connection between them and the State of Great Britain, is and ought to be totally dissolved; and that as Free and Independent States, they have full Power to levy War, conclude Peace, contract Alliances, establish Commerce, and to do all other Acts and Things which Independent States may of right do.—And for the support of this Declaration, with a firm reliance on the protection of divine Providence, we mutually pledge to each other our Lives, our Fortunes and our sacred Honor.

John Hancock

New Hampshire—Josiah Bartlett, Wm Whipple, Matthew Thornton

Massachusetts—Saml Adams, John Adams, Robt Treat Paine, Elbridge Gerry

Rhode Island—Step. Hopkins, William Ellery

Connecticut—Roger Sherman, Saml Huntington, Wm Williams, Oliver Wolcott

New York—Wm Floyd, Phil. Livingston, Frans. Lewis, Lewis Morris

New Jersey—Richd Stockton, Jno Witherspoon, Fras Hopkinson, John Hart, Abra. Clark

North Carolina—Wm Hooper, Joseph Hewes, John Penn

Georgia—Button Gwinnett, Lyman Hall, Geo Walton

Pennsylvania— Robt Morris, Benjamin Rush, Benja Franklin, John Morton, Geo. Clymer, Jas. Smith, Geo. Taylor, James Wilson, Geo. Ross

Delaware—Caesar Rodney, Geo Read, Tho M:Kean

Maryland—Samuel Chase, Wm Paca, Thos Stone, Charles Carroll of Carrollton

Virginia—George Wythe, Richard Henry Lee, Th Jefferson, Benja Harrison, Thos Nelson, jr., Francis Lightfoot Lee, Carter Braxton

South Carolina—Edward Rutledge, Thos Heyward, Junr., Thomas Lynch, Junr., Arthur Middleton

DEFENSE, DEPARTMENT OF

The Department of Defense (DOD), established by the National Security Act (1947), was initially named the National Military Establishment (NME). Including cabinet departments of the army, navy, and air force, the Joint Chiefs of Staff, and several other defense agencies, the NME replaced the War and Navy departments. President Harry S. Truman, understanding the need for interservice coordination and the security threats posed by the Soviet Union, had urged creation of the new national security system, which included the Central Intelligence Agency and the National Security Council.

James V. Forrestal, the first secretary of defense (1947–1949), had a difficult task—molding a workable organization, dealing with squabbling among the services over roles and missions, and developing a viable defense budget. In addition, he had to deal with the Soviet takeover of Czechoslovakia, the Berlin blockade and airlift, and the Sinai War between Arabs and Israelis. Creation of the Marshall Plan (1948) and the North Atlantic Treaty Organization (NATO, 1949) also challenged the DOD. In 1949, based on Forrestal's proposals, the NME became the Department of Defense; the army, navy, and air force became departments without cabinet status; and the secretary of defense's control over these departments was broadened.

Forrestal's successor, Louis A. Johnson (1949–1950), took some of the blame for initial U.S. military reverses in the Korean War, which began in June 1950. He also had trouble with the services over roles and missions and military funding. In September 1950 General George C. Marshall replaced him as secretary. By this time the United States had begun to carry out NSC-68, a document emphasizing Soviet aggressiveness and urging increased production of atomic weapons, enlargement of the military budget, expansion of the services, and broadened military and economic assistance to allies. War costs caused the defense budget to increase from $13.5 billion to $48 billion for the fiscal year (which then began in July) 1951. Marshall supported Truman's 1951 decision to dismiss General Douglas MacArthur, the Far East commander who challenged the president's policy against expanding the Korean military action into Communist China. His successor, Robert A. Lovett (1951–1953), carried on his policies.

President Dwight D. Eisenhower (1953–1961) gave personal attention to defense, and three men served as secretary of defense under him—Charles E. Wilson (1953–1957), Neil H. McElroy (1957–1959), and Thomas S. Gates, Jr. (1959–1961). Eisenhower's New Look policy assumed that any major war would be nuclear, with weapons to be delivered by strategic air forces (massive retaliation), expanded continental defense, modernization of reserve units, and thereby smaller conventional forces. This approach, Eisenhower believed, would make possible defense budget cuts. Secretary Wilson carried out this policy in the face of severe criticism within the army and the public. To some observers the New Look ruled out limited or nonnuclear war. McElroy and Gates promoted deployment in Europe of intermediate-range ballistic missiles to offset the intercontinental-range missiles (ICBMs) deployed by the Soviet Union. The United States began development of the Minuteman ICBM in underground silos in the United States as a deterrent and for use after an attack. Charges against Eisenhower that the Soviet Union was ahead of the United States in missile development played a role in the 1960 presidential campaign but turned out to be unfounded.

President John F. Kennedy appointed Robert S. McNamara, president of the Ford Motor Company and an advocate of systems analysis in defense decision-making, as secretary of defense in 1961. McNamara's civilian "whiz kids" played an important role in his controversial decisions on weapon systems by which he cancelled the B-70 bomber but carried forward the F-111 aircraft. McNamara supported Kennedy's flexible response policy, including maintaining strategic arms to deter nuclear attacks against the United States. Kennedy disavowed massive retaliation, which he thought narrowed U.S. choices to "inglorious retreat or unlimited retaliation." Conventional forces again became important—and this along with the military buildup necessitated by involvement in Vietnam after 1964 led to a significant force expansion. McNamara's relations with the services gradually deteriorated, both because of this effort to centralize authority in the Office of the Secretary of Defense and decisions the services considered detrimental to their interests. In addition to two crises involving Cuba—the Bay of Pigs invasion (1961) and the missile crisis (1962)—there was the war in Vietnam, McNamara's biggest problem. The secretary supported President Lyndon B. Johnson's increased military personnel in Vietnam (from 17,000 in 1963 to 550,000 in 1968). Gradually, however, McNamara changed his mind, as the dollar and human cost of the conflict rose. When he and his department became targets of a massive antiwar movement, the disillusioned secretary resigned in February 1968. His successor, Clark M. Clifford (1968–1969), persuaded Johnson to halt troop increases and stop the bombing in North Vietnam. By the time Johnson left office in January 1969, the United States had begun to negotiate with North Vietnam.

Melvin R. Laird (1969–1973), President Richard M. Nixon's first secretary of defense, developed the policy of Vietnamization, shifting the military burden to South Vietnam. U.S. forces in Vietnam declined from a peak of 543,400 under Johnson to 24,200 at the end of 1972. Secret negotiations by Nixon and Henry Kissinger led to a belated settlement of the Vietnam War in January 1973. In September 1971 Laird also ended the controversial military draft. He retired in January 1973. His successor, Elliot L. Richardson, served only four months before becoming attorney general. Secretary of Defense James R. Schlesinger (1973–1975) believed it necessary to maintain a strategic nuclear capacity essentially equivalent to that of the Soviet Union. He adopted a partial counterforce policy—attack only military targets and avoid cities in the hope that the Soviet Union would follow suit. Schlesinger vociferously argued for larger defense budgets, and President Gerald R. Ford disagreed and dismissed him in late 1975, but his successor, Donald H. Rumsfeld (1975–1977), continued Schlesinger's policies, including advocacy of increased budgets.

The Democrats, the party of President Jimmy Carter (1977–1981), argued for decreased defense spending, and Carter did cut the defense budget for fiscal year 1978. Heavy criticism from Republicans, combined with crises in Afghanistan (the Soviet invasion in 1979), Iran (the fall of the shah and the taking of American hostages in 1979), caused Carter to begin a defense buildup. Secretary of Defense Harold Brown (1977–1981) pursued a policy of essential equivalence in nuclear capacity with the Soviet Union. He worked to upgrade the strategic triad of long-range bombers, ICBMs, and submarine-launched ballistic missiles (SLBMs). He pushed members of the North Atlantic Treaty Organization to increase defense spending and emphasized arms control, which moved ahead with the Strategic Arms Limitation Treaty of 1979 (SALT II).

Under President Ronald Reagan (1981–1989) and Secretary of Defense Caspar W. Weinberger (1981–1987), the DOD's budget increased to $300 billion, strengthening the U.S. strategic position, which Reagan believed had fallen behind the Soviet Union. Strategic bomber modernization (B-1B bombers), production of the MX ICBM, and development of a new SLBM (Trident II) and a stealth (radar-evading) aircraft were central to Reagan's defense program. Weinberger obtained large budget increases, but gradually Congress became less willing to approve increases. Secretary of Defense Frank C. Carlucci (1987–1989) was less pressing on the budget but carried on the Reagan policies. The president used force to achieve U.S. objectives—he expelled a Marxist dictator from Grenada (1983) and arranged for the bombing of Libya (1986), suspected of international terrorism. He also warmed to arms control, however, agreeing to the 1987 Intermediate-range Nuclear Forces Treaty with the Soviet Union and talks on limiting longer-range weapons.

Reagan's successor, George Bush, and his secretary of defense, Richard B. Cheney (1989–1993), also used force. The United States invaded Panama in 1989 to oust a leader hostile to the United States, and after Iraq's dictator, Saddam Hussein, invaded neighboring Kuwait in August 1990, Bush sent 500,000 troops to Saudi Arabia. In the Gulf War of 1991 the United States and its United Nations allies drove Iraqi forces from Kuwait. Meanwhile, pressure increased to cut defense spending, stimulated in part by a serious national budget deficit, by the end of the cold war, and the dissolution of the Soviet Union. Bush and his successor, President Bill Clinton, had to devise a new policy to respond to the collapse of the nation's main adversary. The DOD decided to close many military bases, slow or cancel production of some weapon systems, and reduce troops stationed overseas, especially in Europe. The military services began to decline from a total of more than 2 million service personnel in the 1980s to a stated goal of about 1.4 million in the late 1990s. President Clinton pledged a military force large enough to protect the nation's interests. He and Secretaries of Defense Les Aspin (1993–1994) and William J. Perry (1994–1996) proceeded with a process of downsizing the military services and their budgets.

[See also Arms Race and Disarmament.]

BIBLIOGRAPHY

Alice C. Cole et al., eds., *The Department of Defense: Documents on Establishment and Organization, 1944–1978* (Washington, 1978).

John Lewis Gaddis, *Strategies of Containment: A Critical Appraisal of Postwar American National Security Policy* (New York, 1982).

Paul Y. Hammond, *Organizing for Defense: The American Military Establishment in the Twentieth Century* (Princeton, N.J., 1961).

Steven L. Rearden, *History of the Office of the Secretary of Defense*, vol. 1, *The Formative Years, 1947–1950* (Washington, 1984).

Roger R. Trask, *The Secretaries of Defense: A Brief History, 1947–1985* (Washington, 1985).

— ROGER R. TRASK

DEFICIT, FEDERAL

Since the federal government's annual receipts and expenditures never balance exactly, a surplus or deficit must result. All wars and most major depressions have caused a deficit. There were eighty-one annual deficits during the period 1791–1973. Minor ones, financed by bank loans or bond issues, have been paid off by higher taxes or greater tax receipts in better times. Major ones have been financed by one or more of three fundamental methods—inflation, borrowing, and taxation.

The American Revolution was financed largely by domestic loans and issues by the Continental Congress and by state congresses of paper money, most of which was later repudiated or redeemed at very low rates. The War of 1812 caused a four-year deficit of $68 million, which was financed two-thirds by internal loans and one-third by circulating treasury notes. The Mexican War produced a three-year deficit of $53 million that was easily taken care of by government borrowing. The Civil War was accompanied by a four-year deficit of $2.619 billion, which was financed largely by borrowing on long-term bonds and interest-bearing notes.

Greenback issues took care of about one-sixth the amount. The Spanish-American War caused a two-year deficit of $127 million, and was financed by a "popular loan" and increased internal taxes. World War I produced a three-year deficit of $24.9 billion. The government met immediate needs by selling the banks short-term treasury notes. These were soon retired with the proceeds of the next Liberty Loan. There were five such loans. Banks cooperated by lending to people who wanted to buy the bonds and accepting the bonds as security. The government then drew checks on the deposits thus created. A deposit currency inflation resulted, accentuated by the lower reserve requirements that had been set by the Federal Reserve Act of 1913. Consumer prices approximately doubled between 1916 and 1920.

Not until after 1929 did a depression constitute a major emergency comparable to a war. From 1931 through 1941 the federal government had an annual deficit averaging almost $3 billion a year, 54 percent over receipts. The economic thinking of the Franklin D. Roosevelt administration was that deficit spending was necessary to bring about economic recovery. The deficits were financed by the sale of government obligations to the public and to banks. At the end of 1941, as the United States entered World War II, member banks and Federal Reserve banks held $22 billion worth of government obligations, roughly 44 percent of the federal debt. There was also fear of inflation in the latter 1930's, but the continued depression and unemployment kept price rises modest.

Not until after 1929 did a depression constitute a major emergency comparable to a war; from 1931 to 1941 the federal government had an annual deficit averaging 54 percent over receipts.

World War II produced the greatest deficit of all, $183 billion during 1942–46, and precipitated a price inflation fed not only by its own enormous spending but also by the government spending of the 1930's. A complex policy of "maintaining a pattern of rates" so anyone could redeem his government securities at any time at par meant that the Federal Reserve System, in the final analysis, had to "support" the government security market. That in turn meant monetizing a portion of the public debt somewhat as in World War I. The worst of the price inflation occurred after the war. Consumer prices almost doubled from 1939 to 1952.

The Korean War, the cold war, and foreign aid to nations devastated by World War II were largely responsible for the next deficit, $16.6 billion, in 1952–54. The inflationary effects of this deficit were quite mild.

The second largest federal deficit began in 1961 and may be attributed to the costs of the war in Vietnam; extensive social welfare reforms, especially since 1962; the cold war with the Soviet Union; and explorations of outer space. The sum of all deficits in the 1961–73 period, less the 1969 surplus, totaled almost $150 billion at the end of fiscal 1973 (June 30). This deficit, moreover, had over half its growth in the last three years of the period. To a degree, incurring annual deficits has become a way of life for the federal government. Various justifications have been given. One is that this course of action stimulates economic growth; another is that reversing the trend would increase unemployment and bring on a depression. Unfortunately banks have absorbed a considerable portion of this mounting debt, thereby increasing the money supply. Federal deficits are the most basic cause of price inflation. Between 1965 and mid-1973, consumer prices rose about 56 percent and the government twice had to devalue the dollar.

BIBLIOGRAPHY

Federal Reserve Board, *Federal Reserve Bulletin.*

A. D. Noyes, *War Period of American Finance.*

P. Studenski and H. Krooss, *Financial History of the United States.*

Tax Foundation, Inc., *Facts and Figures on Government Finance.*

U.S. Bureau of the Census, *Historical Statistics of the United States, Colonial Times to 1957.*

— DONALD L. KEMMERER

DELAWARE

The history of the Delaware tribe, located as it was in New Jersey, western Long Island, and Staten and Manhattan islands, mirrors the fate of many Atlantic seaboard American Indians. Theirs is a story of many contacts with Europeans and a gradual movement westward until their final settlement in Oklahoma. It was this tribe that was first contacted by the Dutch in 1609 and that is alleged, probably apocryphally, to have sold Manhattan Island in 1626. Gradually the Delaware gave up their coastal villages. In 1682 they attended a council with William Penn at Germantown, Pa.; by 1751, dominated by the Iroquois, they had pushed on into Ohio. They settled in Indiana, and then they pushed into Missouri, Arkansas, and Texas, where they resided, along with a band of Shawnee, in 1820; in

1835 they were living on a reservation in Kansas; and by 1867 they had allied with the Cherokee nation in Oklahoma. In the course of this long odyssey, they were involved with the French and Spanish, fought the British, became converted to Moravian Christianity, and so generally lost their earlier cultural associations.

Considering that change had come to the Delaware as early as the 17th century, it is difficult to give a precise description of the native culture. It is clear that they were Algonkin-speakers of the Atlantic Coast, and they were often identified with the Abnaki. A mixed aboriginal dependence on hunting and basic maize agriculture can be supposed. Similarly, bark houses and containers, village autonomy with village chiefs, and political alliances with others of the same language grouping might be expected given the area. An early chief's name survives, Tamenend, lending itself to the famous Tammany political organization.

BIBLIOGRAPHY

W. W. Newcomb, *The Culture and Acculturation of the Delaware Indians.*

— ROBERT F. SPENCER

DEMOCRACY

Democracy is a system of government in which the authority to govern is exercised by public officials who are responsible to a broad electorate that periodically chooses from among competing candidates for office in free elections. For democracy to be meaningful, at least most adults must be eligible to vote and hold office, and they must be at liberty to organize and to discuss or to listen to the expression of different or competing points of view. Thus, democracy may be said to exist where most adults have the right to stand for office and to vote, where freedom of association in competing political parties is recognized and protected, and where public opinion is informed through an unfettered press, freedom of speech, and general education. While democracy insists that all persons are equal under the law and have equal rights and responsibilities, it does not assume that individuals are equal in all respects—for example, in intelligence, physical strength, or attractiveness. Thus, democracy is an amalgam of concepts of equality and liberty. It is a tribute to the compelling strength of the democratic idea that in the 20th century many authoritarian, one-party Communist states call themselves "people's democracies" and thus assert a claim to democracy even though they are profoundly antidemocratic.

Democracy developed gradually in the course of American history. In the early colonial period, government was not democratic. Indeed, the Puritan leaders in New England were committed to an authoritarian tradition that rejected democracy as a desirable form of government. The middle and southern colonies were governed for the most part by landed aristocracies. Even so, as the colonial period progressed, there were democratic developments, notably the rise of locally elected popular branches of the legislatures to positions of self-confidence and power. Since these legislative assemblies were elected by a fairly substantial body of voters—although qualifications for the suffrage were far from democratic—they represented a wide spectrum of colonial opinion. In resisting the assertion of British authority in the New World, they reflected ideas the colonists had brought with them from their mother country, for by the end of the 17th century Britain had made giant strides in the direction of what later became democratic institutions. By the end of the 18th century the British people had long since abandoned feudalism and had developed representative government: one king had been beheaded and another summarily driven from the land in a bloodless revolution; Parliament had become the center of political authority; an independent judiciary and an elaborate system of common law committed to fundamental personal liberties had matured—and all these developments formed the stock of ideas that determined the body of political thought so eloquently stated by John Locke following the Glorious Revolution of 1688 and carried to the colonies by emigrants. By the end of the long colonial period, the colonists had come a great distance down the difficult road to democracy.

Government was not democratic in the early colonial period; the Puritan leaders in New England held to an authoritarian tradition, while the middle and southern colonies were governed by landed aristocracies.

The American Revolution advanced the cause of democracy by eliminating the monarchy and a hereditary titled aristocracy from the American scene and by broadening the base of social, economic, and political power. The party line of the American Revolution was that all men are endowed by their Creator with equal natural, inalienable rights and that government rests upon the consent of the governed. The battle cry "No taxation without representation" embraced and nurtured the fundamentally democratic concept of government by consent, central to the American theory of democracy.

Following the achievement of independence and the adoption of the Constitution in 1789, the American people gradually committed themselves to one of two political parties, and out of their confrontation the terms of democratic development were defined and developed. On the one side were the Federalists, with George Washington, John Adams, and Alexander Hamilton as their leaders, favoring centralized government and a highly stratified social system. On the other side the followers of Thomas Jefferson espoused maximum states' rights—that is, local control—and a more fluid social system. Thus, the election of Thomas Jefferson to the presidency in 1800 marked an important step toward a democratic society, since the effect of the so-called Jeffersonian revolution was to arrest the growth of the sort of centralized government and class system so ardently desired by the Hamiltonian Federalists. Political power was more widely distributed on the basis of Jeffersonian assumptions regarding the natural rationality and goodness of ordinary people and their ability to learn through education.

The right to vote and hold office without regard to property qualifications was greatly expanded during the following Jacksonian period, with the result that by the middle of the 19th century most adult males were eligible to vote and hold public office. The right to vote was extended to free blacks by state action in only six states in 1860. The Fifteenth Amendment to the Constitution in 1870 forbade the denial of the right to vote because of race or color and gave Congress the power to enforce this concept by appropriate legislation. The struggle to translate this commitment into reality continued, however, all during the following century, culminating in the enactment by Congress of the Voting Rights Act of 1965. By 1920, fifteen states had extended the suffrage to women, beginning in the last quarter of the 19th century, and the right of women to vote was nationalized with the addition of the Nineteenth Amendment to the Constitution in 1920. Finally, the voting age was reduced in 1971 to eighteen, with the ratification of the Twenty-sixth Amendment. Thus, a completely democratic suffrage was finally achieved.

There were many factors in America that created a milieu favorable to the development of a democratic governmental system. The total absence of an established national church, which in the Old World had invariably been an arm and ally of authoritarian institutions, encouraged the growth of freedom of thought, and thus political freedom, and created a climate favorable to social experimentation. The firm constitutional guarantee of freedom of religion led to the development of a large number of churches operating independently of one another, thus encouraging the pluralism in American society that has played a significant role in expanding the right to differ and disagree, which is the hallmark of democracy. Furthermore, the absence of a feudal property system and a monarchy buttressed by a hereditary land-owning aristocracy encouraged the dispersal of economic power and the growth of a property system that could serve as the foundation for a large and self-confident middle class. An abundance of natural resources and a sense of national security nurtured by the protection of two great oceans insulating Americans from the ancient tensions of both Europe and the Far East contributed to the release of the American mind from bondage to traditional and historically authoritarian authority. A frontier that moved steadily westward to the very end of the 19th century provided a safety valve for population pressure building up in the more heavily settled, older sections of the country and re-created for successive waves of immigrants the basic conditions of equality that characterized life on the frontier. Although the frontier cannot accurately be accounted the sole—or even principal—source of American democracy, it assuredly exerted a powerful influence in shaping the American destiny.

In addition, a firm commitment to public education at all levels of learning for all segments of the population strengthened and informed an expanding electorate. Thus, with fluid class lines, with conditions that facilitated social mobility, and with freedom from traditional restraints of ancient, Old World vintage, American democracy could grow and flourish. Having survived a terrible Civil War, several international wars, and periodic recessions and depressions, American democracy approached the 200th anniversary of its independence in 1976 as the world's oldest and most powerful democratic nation. Granted the United States had serious problems to resolve in the fourth quarter of the 20th century, but it confronted them with institutions and doctrines that had generated the resolution of social and economic problems through 200 years in conformity with the principles and usages of a body of constitutional law resting upon the twin foundations of equality and freedom.

BIBLIOGRAPHY

A. J. Beitzinger, *A History of American Political Thought.*
Ralph H. Gabriel, *The Course of American Democratic Thought.*
Reinhold Niebuhr, *Children of Light; Children of Darkness.*
Vernon Louis Parrington, *Main Currents in American Thought.*

— DAVID FELLMAN

DEMOCRATIC PARTY

Conventional historical investigations of the origins of American political parties trace the beginnings of the Democratic party to the formative decade immediately following the ratification of the Constitution in 1789. Indeed, the Antifederalists of that seminal period were, as often as not, individuals who had opposed ratification. The policies proposed as alternatives to those of the completely dominant Federalist party were based principally on constitutional interpretations, and they were as diverse as their proponents—intellectual leaders of the caliber of Thomas Jefferson and the multitude of irreverent newspaper critics of the Federalist administrations. The Jay Treaty (1794) became the focal point of opposition to foreign policy, while Alexander Hamilton's fiscal plans aroused domestic criticism.

Despite policy debates, the American party system emerged not so much because of them as because of the deep divisions engendered by the dominant Federalists' frequent rejection of the legitimacy of organized partisan opposition. In the words of Paul Goodman ("The First Party System," in Chambers and Burnham, *The American Party Systems*), they "mistook parties for factions, assuming that those with whom they differed were disloyal to the nation and its ideals." Indeed, it was in the debates on the Alien and Sedition Acts (1798) in the House of Representatives that Democratic-Republican Albert Gallatin made the vital distinction between the total constitutional system and the national officials currently governing under the authority of the Constitution, thus anticipating by nearly two centuries the educator David Easton's adoption of the phrase "regime support."

In contrast, the American party system that emerged during the first two decades of the 19th century was characterized by a general acceptance of the legitimacy of a party in opposition to a regime in power and by the fuller development of a national (in contrast to a largely regional) arena for political conflict and development. The Democratic party, or its predecessor the Democratic-Republican party, while not yet fully developed, played a critical role in the establishment of legitimate two-party competition as the mode of political succession and change. Its early positions included narrow construction of federal power to make internal improvements and to impose the embargo of 1807–09. Although the Democratic-Republicans were originally identified as the party of strict or narrow construction of the Constitution, the party position in each state was often determined by political expediency, and when the party assumed power, its leaders often found it expedient to apply a broad constructionist interpretation. President Jefferson's manner of handling the Louisiana Purchase (1803) provides a classic example of the resolution of an issue, not on the basis of principle but on the basis of immediate political or territorial interest. The party not only adapted its constructionist position to the circumstances of constitutional interpretation but also embraced a diversity of positions, notably on the tariff and the embargo, and sometimes contradictory coalitions. Although it remained in ascendancy into the third decade of the 19th century, it disintegrated into competing factions, and in 1824 a viable opposition party, successor to the Federalist party, emerged—first designated National Republican and later Whig. Its founders were Henry Clay and John Quincy Adams, elected president in that year, as Andrew Jackson became the dominant figure in the Democratic party, to be elected president in 1828. While both parties were national in scope and no region could be considered a fiefdom of one or the other during the following three decades of their preeminence, it would be inaccurate to assume a full-blown party structure and organization. The Democratic party in the Jacksonian era was substantially consistent in its opposition to a national bank, to the tariff, and, on the whole, to federal internal improvements. Subsequently the failure of the Whig party and the Democratic party to resolve the slavery issue resulted in the former's disintegration and replacement by the Republican party (1856) and the latter's massive defeat in national politics (1860). While the post-Civil War era brought a long period of presidential losses to the Democratic party, it also saw the beginning of the sectional party divisions that gave the Democrats almost unchallenged control of the South until the mid-20th century. The Southern Democratic constituency brought with it a generally conservative ideology, and the impact of the candidacies of William Jennings Bryan also gave the Democratic party a rural and anticorporate policy orientation. By 1896 the party had lost the bulk of its urban voters, and only through the circumstance of the William H. Taft-Theodore Roosevelt split of 1912 did the party achieve victory in that year. After Woodrow Wilson's presidency (1913–21) the Democratic party appeared once again to sink into the role of a minority party, characterized by regional attributes and by successive defeat. The impact of the Great Depression provided the basis for Franklin D. Roosevelt's landslide victory of 1932. His coalition-building skills brought urban labor into the ranks of the Democratic party and laid the foundation for successive victories until 1952.

The inability of both major parties to hold mass membership against the inroads of strong radical movements such as the Know-Nothing party of the mid-19th century and the George C. Wallace movement of 1968 has stimulated serious scholarly reappraisal (for example, Walter Dean Burnham) of the generally held assumption that the long-established Democratic and Republican parties secure national politics against extremism.

BIBLIOGRAPHY

Walter Dean Burnham, "Political Immunization and Political Confessionalism: The United States and Weimar Germany," *Journal of Interdisciplinary History* (1972).

William Nisbet Chambers and Walter Dean Burnham, *The American Party Systems: Stages of Political Development.*

Noble E. Cunningham, Jr., *The Jeffersonian Republicans: The Formation of Party Organization, 1789–1801.*

Arthur N. Holcombe, *The New Party Politics.*

Richard P. McCormick, *The Second American Party System.*

— JOHN R. SCHMIDHAUSER

THE DEMOCRATIC PARTY SINCE THE 1960S

After the election of President Franklin D. Roosevelt in 1932, the Democratic party came to dominate American politics for the next thirty-two years, winning all presidential elections except for the two terms of war hero Dwight D. Eisenhower (1953–1961). By 1964, when Lyndon B. Johnson won 61.1 percent of the national vote, Democrats outnumbered Republicans by more than two to one. The Democratic dominance was based on a voter coalition that included white Southern Democrats; the urban working class, union members, and the rising middle class; and ethnic and religious minorities, such as Roman Catholics, African Americans, and Jews. Geographically, the party was strongest in the Northeast, the industrial Midwest, and the South, as well as parts of the Pacific coast. It gained support from such programmatic achievements as the New Deal, the subsequent extensions of social welfare programs, and U.S. international leadership, as well as from strong party organizations in the major cities.

Even as it came to dominance, however, the Democratic majority began to weaken. Suburbanization, the decline of union membership, population movement away from the industrial heartland, and individual social mobility eroded the demographic foundations of party support. The advent of television and individualist techniques of campaigning undermined the party organizations that had provided strong support for Democratic candidates. These social trends added to the fragility and internal conflicts of the party coalition. As blacks came to demand full equality, from public school integration to better job opportunities, the party lost support among segregationists in the South and working-class whites in the North. Democrats also became divided on issues of foreign policy, as conflicts over U.S. involvement in Vietnam fractured party support of the anticommunist programs of the cold war. Political rifts also developed on issues of lifestyle and personal morality, including civil rights, control of crime, ecology, and abortion. These divisive issues replaced the unifying party program, familiar since the New Deal, of government management of the economy and income redistribution.

The effects of these conflicts became evident in the national party's organization and character. In 1968 civil disturbances and protests against the war in Vietnam culminated in the withdrawal of President Johnson from his reelection campaign. The assassinations of Reverend Martin Luther King, Jr., and Senator Robert Kennedy caused further disarray among rank-and-file Democrats and their leaders. The party's national convention in Chicago was marred by street demonstrations, police violence, and disruptive convention sessions. The fractious nomination of Vice President Hubert H. Humphrey, who had not campaigned in the primaries, was seen as an undemocratic manifestation of "boss rule."

In an effort to heal party wounds, the Democrats appointed the first of a series of reform commissions, chaired by South Dakota Senator George McGovern, then by Minnesota Representative Donald Fraser. The new rules put forth by the commissions before the 1972 election attempted to give "all Democratic voters . . . a full, meaningful, and timely opportunity" to participate in selecting the party's presidential candidate. Over the next two decades, the commissions fundamentally changed the party's internal government and its presidential selection process. The national party, once powerless, developed permanent centralized institutions and assumed the authority, upheld by the courts (as in *Democratic Party* v. *La Follette*, 1981), to prescribe rules for state parties. These changes included a charter commission to restructure the party, a judicial council to enforce national rules, midterm national conventions to develop party programs, and a compliance review commission to monitor the selection of convention delegates.

The most significant changes were in the selection of delegates to the national convention and, consequently, in the presidential nominating process. Most of the delegates came to be chosen in direct primary contests among presidential aspirants, even though this change was not mandated by the reform commissions. Furthermore, delegates were apportioned among the candidates, in rough proportion to their share of the primary vote, preventing unity among state delegations and eliminating traditional favorite-son candidacies.

Without intervention by the state organizations, presidential nominations were transformed from a bargained decision among party leaders to a plebiscitary contest among aspirants. Nominations passed out of the hands of the traditional brokers of smoke-filled rooms. Influence shifted toward the mass media and campaign specialists, such as pollsters and advertising consultants. The influence of the states on the nominations also changed, as a consequence of the focus on mass media and direct elections. Because Iowa and New Hampshire chose their delegates early in a presidential election year, candidates focused on those states first and then on the southern primaries. The industrial states, previously the core of the Democratic coalition but voting later in the year, drew less attention and exerted less influence.

The immediate result of these changes was to shift power within the party. State control over the selection of convention delegates was replaced by national rules. Demographic goals or quotas were established, so that half the delegates would be women and that ethnic minorities and other groups would be represented in proportion to their numbers among Democratic voters. Union leaders and established figures holding party or public office lost power to leaders of ideological and demographic factions. By 1972, encouraged by the new rules, new and more ideological activists had entered the party, making convention delegates far more liberal than rank-and-file Democratic voters. These new party activists accomplished the nomination of Senator McGovern, only to witness his landslide defeat by incumbent President Richard M. Nixon.

The Democrats then tried various means to restructure the party and restore their electoral position. The new party rules were modified to provide convention representation for "superdelegates"—designated party leaders, such as members of Congress and the national committee. Special-interest factions were no longer given official recognition within the party, and quotas (except for women) were replaced by general guidelines. Midterm conventions and efforts toward a binding party platform were abandoned. In place of structural change the Democrats turned in the 1980s toward making the party more effective electorally. Actions included the training of party candidates; coordinating campaigns with state organizations; establishing a large staff for polling, issue research, and television production; and building a permanent Washington, D.C., headquarters for the Democratic National Committee. Particularly important was the growth of financial resources. By 1992 the three national party campaign committees (for president, the Senate, and the House) were raising more than $100 million annually.

Nevertheless, the electoral fortunes of the Democrats remained uncertain. From 1968 until 1992 the party won only the presidential election of 1976, and even that victory by Jimmy Carter, in the aftermath of the Watergate scandal, was razor-thin. The party suffered defeat when it nominated a southern moderate (Carter's reelection bid in 1980), a Midwest liberal with a female vice presidential running mate (Walter Mondale and Geraldine Ferraro in 1984), or an eastern progressive (Michael Dukakis in 1988). Republican Ronald Reagan's victory in 1980 ushered in a period of conservative public policy, reversing established Democratic programs of government intervention in the economy, special assistance for racial minorities, and women's rights. The administrations of Reagan and Republican George Bush (1989–1993) also undermined the partisan base of the Democrats. After the 1988 election, the two parties were virtually equal in self-identified partisans, while nearly a third of the electorate declared itself independent.

By 1972, new and more ideological activists had entered the Democratic party, making convention delegates far more liberal than rank-and-file Democratic voters—thus the nomination of George McGovern.

Although the party weakened in presidential elections, it remained strong in other arenas. The Democrats retained control of the House of Representatives and dominance in the Senate for all but six years (1981–1987), as well as a majority of governorships and state legislatures. In Congress, particularly the House, the authority of party leaders grew, overcoming the dispersion of power in the 1970s. In contrast to seniority rules, the party caucus now demanded party loyalty from committee chairs, and an extensive whip organization mobilized the membership on critical decisions. As a result, party unity on roll-call votes rose until after 1980, reaching the highest levels recorded since World War II.

With the election of Arkansas Governor William Jefferson Clinton as president in 1992, the Democrats returned to power in Washington. Clinton came to prominence as a leader of the Democratic Leadership Council, an organization of moderate Democratic officeholders who sought to develop programs more appealing to centrist and former Democratic voters. Clinton attempted to merge past party commitments to the disadvantaged, blacks, and women with new appeals to the middle class, including welfare reform, control of crime, health care, and budget deficit reduction. He succeeded in winning almost all the states in the Northeast, Midwest and Pacific coast, as well as four southern states, while attracting pluralities among white voters in all regions but the South. Elected with only 43 percent of the popular vote in a three-way contest (against Republican incumbent Bush and independent candidate Ross Perot), Clinton lacked a clear popular mandate, limiting his influence over senators and representatives. Although often forced to compromise, Clinton still achieved much of his early agenda, including increased taxation on the wealthy, mandatory family leave (without pay), and educational reform, and the extension of health care. In the 1994 elections, however, Republicans returned to power in the Congress, winning their first Senate majority in eight years and their first House majority since 1954. By the end of 1995 the Democratic president and Republican-controlled Congress were at odds over issues ranging from Medicare to a mandated balanced budget.

[See also Congress, United States; Congressional Caucuses; Presidency; Republican Party]

BIBLIOGRAPHY

Norman H. Nie, Sidney Verba, and John R. Petrocik, *The Changing American Voter* (Cambridge, Mass., 1976).

David E. Price, *Bringing Back the Parties* (Washington, D.C., 1984).

— GERALD M. POMPER

DEMOGRAPHY

Demography, the quantitative and statistical analysis of populations that focuses upon the vital events of birth, marriage, and death and upon the phenomenon of geographical mobility. Until as recently as the early 1960's, historians paid little attention to the study of American population history. Ignoring the extensive collections of information accumulated since the mid-19th century by genealogists and relying heavily upon literary sources supplemented by intuition, historians rarely hesitated to make bold assumptions and to offer broad generalizations about the conditions of life in the past that influenced both individuals and the population as a whole. As a result, the illusion of knowledge was maintained despite the profound ignorance of the realities of demographic experience in the past. Despite the accomplishments of some pioneering scholars who collected census data, analyzed changes in sex composition in early America, and studied epidemiology and public health, there was little investigation of 17th-, 18th-, or 19th-century American population history. The increased interest in, and use of, quantitative techniques; the introduction of new methods of investigation; and the awareness of new sources of information resulted in the emergence of historical demography as a highly promising field of research in the 1960's. Historians began to probe the complex development of American population from the colonial period to the present, adding a new dimension to the understanding of the past.

Shortly after World War II, the invention of the techniques of family reconstitution by Louis Henry and the advancements in methodology achieved by the group of historical demographers working with Henry at the Institut National d'Études Démographiques in Paris demonstrated to other historians in Europe and particularly in England (where the influential Cambridge Group for the History of Population and Social Structure was formed) the immense promise of historical demography for the recovery of essential data about human experience in the past. Subsequently, two basic methods of analysis have been employed by historical demographers on both sides of the Atlantic: aggregative analysis, which involves the collection of vital data for a whole population by month and year, accumulated for substantial periods of time, thus providing graphic evidence for long-term trends in births, marriages, and deaths for specific communities; and family reconstitution, which involves the detailed recovery of vital events for each individual and family in specific communities, thus providing a remarkably complete collection of data on many of the most intimate aspects of human experience, including the spacing of children, sizes of families, practice of birth control, fertility, marriage ages, and longevity.

Aggregative analysis is relatively simple and rapid for most preindustrial communities, but family reconstitution is exceedingly time-consuming. With the advent of the computer, a number of historians in England, the United States, and Canada have been attempting to perfect computer programs for nominal record linkages that would permit the rapid transformation of raw vital information from parish and town records into reconstituted families, thus making possible the sort of extensive analysis of populations that hand methods of reconstitution in the early 1970's rendered virtually impossible, and providing a major breakthrough in the techniques of historical demography. At the same time, increasingly sophisticated statistical methods of analysis by historians help to insure the validity of the results of demographic research and to provide the solid basis of data needed by other historians for their own studies of the past.

The first serious American contributions in the field of demography were made by historians of early America whose work began to appear during the mid-1960's. Focusing upon specific communities (such as Andover, Dedham, Hingham, Ipswich, and Salem in Massachusetts; Bristol in Rhode Island), colonies (Plymouth and Barbados), or groups (Quakers, the Albany Dutch), a number of historians began to make use of the methods of European historical demographers and to demonstrate for the first time what actually happened to people living in 17th- and 18th-century American communities. The results of these studies often proved surprising: the ages of marriage for men, for instance, were much higher in some communities than anyone had anticipated, resembling European patterns of marriage ages far more than 19th-century American patterns; longevity was much greater than most people expected, at least among New Englanders; birth control was used much earlier among selected populations than had been thought likely; population growth was far more variable in magnitude and marked by more fluctuation than anticipated; mobility often was far less in New England towns at certain periods than imagined.

It is clear that these studies represent only a tiny fraction of the total population even of New England and neglect the populations of most regions outside of New England. Works in progress on the middle and southern colonies should supplement the New England studies. In the 1970's historians began to probe the demographic history of the United States during the 19th century, especially in terms of geographic mobility, family size, and household composition. The analysis of census listings in particular was providing new information and insights into the demographic experience of both white and black populations in urban and rural settings. Given the intensive investigations under way and the excitement generated among many young historians by historical demography in the 1970's, significant advances both in the data revealing fundamental dimensions of human experience and in the understanding of the dynamics of population growth and movement were anticipated.

BIBLIOGRAPHY

John Demos, "Notes on Life in Plymouth Colony," *William and Mary Quarterly*, vol. 22.

Richard A. Easterlin, "The American Population," in *American Economic Growth.*

Philip J. Greven, Jr., *Four Generations: Population, Land, and Family in Colonial Andover, Mass.*

Kenneth Lockridge, "The Population of Dedham, Mass.," *Economic History Review*, vol. 19.

Susan Norton, "Population Growth in Colonial America: A Study of Ipswich, Mass.," *Population Studies*, vol. 25.

Daniel Smith, "The Demographic History of Colonial New England," *Journal of Economic History*, vol. 32.

Robert V. Wells, "Family Size and Fertility Control in 18th-Century America: A Study of Quaker Families," *Population Studies*, vol. 25.

— PHILIP J. GREVEN, JR.

DEMOGRAPHIC CHANGES

Demographic changes in the United States since 1975 reflect prior trends in fertility, patterns of internal population redistribution, and trends in immigration and refugee migration. The population increased between 1970 and 1990, although at declining rates of growth. According to decennial censuses, the national population increased by 11.5 percent between 1970 and 1980 and by 9.8 percent between 1980 and 1990. During the early 1990s average growth per year was estimated at 1.1 percent. The Census Bureau estimated that the population reached 250 million between July 1 and Aug. 1, 1994. Despite a relatively low growth rate, the United States ranked fourth in population in the world, following China, India, and former Soviet Union.

Fertility among U.S. women continued its decline, from the postwar baby boom until the late 1970s, when increases in the crude birth rate (births per 1,000 population) were observed, due largely to women born during the baby boom reaching childbearing ages. Crude birthrates increased from 14.6 per 1,000 in 1975 to 16.7 in 1990, decreasing slightly in 1991 to 16.2. Shifts in age patterns of fertility also occurred from 1970 to 1990. Increased fertility among older women was apparent as women continued to enter the labor force and delay childbearing. Between 1980 and 1990 fertility rates of women ages thirty-five to thirty-nine increased by 60 percent and among women forty to forty-four by 41 percent. There were also increases in fertility among women under the age of twenty. Rates for women fifteen to nineteen years increased by 13 percent during 1980–1990 and among girls under fifteen by 27 percent. Differences in levels of childbearing continued to exist among racial and ethnic groups. Crude birthrates among whites, African Americans, and Latinos were 15.5, 22.4, and 26.7, respectively, in 1990.

Overall levels of mortality continued to decline. The crude death rate (deaths per 1,000 people) declined from 8.9 in 1975 to 8.6 in 1990. A better measure of mortality differentials among population groups is life expectancy at birth, which, unlike the crude death rate, is not influenced by age structure. Life expectancy among men increased from 70 years in 1980 to 71.8 in 1990, and for women from 77.4 to 78.8; the differential between men and women thus narrowed during the period, from 7.4 to 7.0 years. Mortality levels for African Americans also declined since 1975 but remained persistently higher than for the white population. Gender differences in mortality are also greater for African Americans than for whites. In 1990 life expectancy for African-American men was 64.5 years and for African-American women 73.6, a difference of 9.1 years.

Heart disease, cancer, and stroke continued to account for the largest proportion of annual deaths in the United States, 64 percent in 1990. A new cause of death, Acquired Immune Deficiency Syndrome, or AIDS, was recognized in 1981. Deaths from AIDS account for about 1.2 percent of total deaths in the United States, and in 1993 AIDS became the leading cause of death for persons twenty-five to forty-four years of age.

The legacy of trends in fertility and mortality is the current age structure of the population. Interruption of the secular decline in fertility by the postwar baby boom has had dramatic effects on the age structure of the population since the 1970s, as people born during the 1950s and 1960s entered middle age. Since 1970 decline of the proportion of people in early working years was reversed. Between 1970 and 1980 the proportion of the population in the twenty to forty-four age bracket increased from 31.7 percent to 37.1, and in 1990 it increased again, to 40.1 percent. The aging of the population continued, a trend begun at the end of the nineteenth century. Between 1970 and 1980 the proportion of the population sixty-five years and older increased from 9.9 percent to 11.3 percent of the population; in 1990 the proportion in this age group increased to 12.5 percent. Anticipation of baby boomers entering retirement years raised concerns about social security and health care and about the decline in the population of working age.

Because of the low levels of fertility and mortality in the United States, demographic change for regions, metropolitan areas, and rural places is most significantly influenced by migration. Since 1975 important shifts in population redistribution occurred as a result of both patterns of internal migration and increases in immigration. Between 1970 and 1980 a reversal appeared in the increasing concentration of population in metropolitan areas. Nonmetropolitan counties increased in population by 11.4 percent, while metropolitan areas increased by 10.2 percent. Moreover, significant growth occurred in nonmetropolitan areas that were not adjacent to cities, provoking the term "rural renaissance." Rural population growth reflected increased levels of retirement migration associated with changes in age structure, migration to rural areas, and shifts in location of industries and companies to areas with lower population densities and lower levels of unionization. The trend shifted again in the 1980s, when metropolitan areas grew at a greater rate than rural areas. In contrast to these general trends, migration patterns among African Americans during the 1970s and 1980s were, on balance, toward U.S. metropolitan areas, and, in particular, toward central cities.

Because of low levels of fertility and mortality in the U.S., demographic change is mostly influenced by immigration and internal migration.

Patterns of migration continued from states in the Northeast and Midwest to the South and West. Between 1970 and 1990 states in the South increased their share of the population from 30.9 percent to 34.4 percent, and states in the western region from 17.1 percent to 21 percent. In contrast, the proportion of the population residing in northeastern states declined during the period from 24.1 percent to 20.4 percent, and for the Midwest, from 27.8 percent to 24.0 percent. Shifts in the regional distribution of the population reflect levels of internal migration and patterns of settlement of immigrants. During 1990–1991 more migrants left states in the Northeast than entered; net outmigration for the region was 585,000. Consistent with continued patterns of migration to the Sunbelt, more than 80 percent of migrants from the Northeast moved to states in the South and West. States in the western region received more migrants, a net of 167,000 between 1990–1991; for states in the South, net migration was 433,000.

International migration had important consequences for demographic changes in regions and in the nation as a whole. Since the 1970s immigration to the United States increased as a result of changes in immigration law in 1965 and 1990; the admission of refugees from Indochina, Central America, and Eastern Europe; and the legalization of undocumented aliens qualified under the 1986 amnesty program. According to the Immigration and Naturalization Service, 4.49 million alien immigrants were admitted to the United States for permanent residence between 1971 and 1980; 7.34 million immigrants were admitted between 1981 and 1990. Immigrant admissions increased sharply during the 1980s as a result of the legalization of undocumented aliens under the Immigration Reform and Control Act of 1986. A significant proportion of U.S. immigration since the 1970s also reflects refugee admissions. During the 1970s refugees composed approximately 12 percent of total immigration, and in the 1980s the proportion grew to 14 percent. Estimates suggest that one-third of alien immigrants admitted to the United States eventually depart.

National origins of immigrants also shifted as a result of changes in policy and in the demand for immigration among sending countries. Amendments to immigration law in 1965 resulted in large increases in immigration from Asia, from 13 percent of annual immigration during 1961–1970 to 29 percent for 1990–1993, and decreases in European immigration, 34 percent in the 1960s to 11 percent since 1990. Immigration from North America (Canada, Mexico, the Caribbean, and Central America) also increased, from 43 percent of total immigration during the 1960s to 55 percent since 1990. In 1993 the leading sources of immigration were Mexico, the former Soviet Union, the Philippines, the Dominican Republic, and India.

The foreign-born proportion of the U.S. population reversed its downward trend since 1910 and increased from 4.7 percent to 6.2 percent between 1970 and 1980, and to 7.9 percent in 1990. The regional effects of immigration were pronounced. Nearly two-thirds of immigrants settled in six states: California, New York, Texas, Florida, New Jersey, and Illinois. The foreign-born proportion of California's population increased from 8.8 percent in 1970 to 15.1 percent in 1980; according to the 1990 census, this proportion was 21.7 percent. The foreign-born population of New York also continued to increase, from 11.6 percent in 1970 to 13.6 percent in 1980 to 15.9 percent in 1990.

[See also Acquired Immune Deficiency Syndrome; African Americans; Asian Americans; Cuban Americans; Hispanic Americans; Immigration; Mexican Americans; Urban Living.]

BIBLIOGRAPHY

Richard T. Gill, Nathan Glazer, and Stephan A. Thernstrom, *Our Changing Population* (Englewood Cliffs, N.J., 1992).

David Plane and Peter Rogerson, *The Geographical Analysis of Population* (New York, 1994).

John Weeks, *Population* (Belmont, Calif., 1994).

— ELLEN PERCY KRALY

DESEGREGATION

Modern desegregation efforts began with attempts to integrate public education. In the 1930s and 1940s the Legal Defense Fund of the National Association for the Advancement of Colored People (NAACP) first waged its attack on institutions of higher learning. In a series of court cases against law and graduate schools—*Missouri ex rel. Gaines* v. *Canada* (1938), *Sipuel* v. *Oklahoma State Board of Regents* (1948), and *Sweatt* v. *Painter* (1950)—NAACP attorneys, led by future Supreme Court Justice Thurgood Marshall, eventually won for African Americans the right to free and equal access to these institutions. They struck their biggest blow against segregation when they won the 1954 case *Brown* v. *Board of Education of Topeka, Kansas,* which overturned the infamous "separate but equal" doctrine in the 1896 Supreme Court ruling in *Plessy* v. *Ferguson.* The Court declared in *Brown* that "separate but equal is inherently unequal." Unfortunately, they added the corollary that desegregation should proceed with "all deliberate speed," which was vague enough for southern whites to delay its implementation. African Americans, however, demanded immediate action. In Little Rock, Ark., in 1957, the confrontation between blacks and intransigent whites forced a reluctant President Dwight D. Eisenhower to send federal troops to protect students who sought admission to Central High School. Whites remained defiant throughout much of the South, with Atlanta's relatively smooth process of integration in 1961 proving to be an exception.

The next phase of the desegregation struggle attacked segregation on conveyances and in public accommodations. In December 1955 Rosa Parks was arrested for refusing to bow to the law that required blacks to sit in the back of the bus if whites filled the front seats in Montgomery, Ala. Led by Rev. Dr. Martin Luther King, Jr., and a number of other local black leaders, the African-American community of Montgomery mounted a successful 382-day boycott against the local bus system. Their struggle sparked a similar protest in Tallahassee, Fla. The Supreme Court eventually sided with the protestors.

The freedom rides and other major events in 1963 forced the federal government's hand as the civil rights struggle began to command international attention.

In February 1960 four black students in Greensboro, N.C., targeted segregated lunch counters at Woolworth's department stores. Their stand inspired hundreds of other students throughout the nation to engage in "freedom rides." Trained in tactics of nonviolent direct action and sustained spiritually by the "freedom songs," members of the Congress of Racial Equality (CORE) and the Student Nonviolent Coordinating Committee (SNCC) tested segregation by traveling south under the protection of federal interstate commerce laws. In this effort, as in most others, the federal government was often disinterested, if not hostile.

The freedom rides and a series of other major events in 1963 forced the national government's hand as the civil rights struggle began to command international attention. In May 1963 police in Birmingham, Ala., used dogs and fire hoses to repress civil rights protestors. On Aug. 28, 1963, 200,000 demonstrators participated in the March on Washington, during which King gave his renowned "I Have a Dream" speech. U.S. leaders became increasingly embarrassed about the treatment of African Americans as they competed in international circles to gain allies in Asia and Latin America and among newly independent African nations. As a result, Congress finally passed the Civil Rights Act of 1964, which gave African Americans basic rights of citizenship. The legislation outlawed segregation in education and public accommodations, established the Equal Employment Opportunity Commission, and authorized the withdrawal of funding to federally funded programs that refused to desegregate.

The civil rights movement brought down many of the barriers of segregation, but the struggle continued through the 1970s. The major battlegrounds in those years were urban public schools in the North and Midwest, where, because of residential segregation patterns, neighborhood schools manifested de facto forms of segregation. Court-ordered busing, which was upheld in *Swann* v. *Charlotte-Mecklenburg Board of Education* (1970), was initiated in Cleveland, Detroit, Denver, Kansas City, and other cities across the country. Busing spurred protests in many cities, notably Boston, where angry whites in 1975 hurled rocks at buses carrying black children to white schools and more than 10,000 students left the Boston public school system.

Rosa Parks sits in the front of a bus in Montgomery, Alabama, on December 21, 1956 after the Supreme Court ruling banning segregation on public transit vehicles. Parks's arrest a year earlier for sitting in a bus forward of white passengers touched off the Montgomery bus boycott. (UPI/Corbis-Bettmann)

One method of addressing the segregated housing patterns that resulted in school segregation was to incorporate suburban schools into city busing programs or to create so-called magnet schools—inner-city schools with special curricula or facilities that would attract white students. *Milliken* v. *Bradley* (1973) limited the scope of this solution by requiring proof that suburbs used racial discrimination to create segregation problems, but it has been used successfully to desegregate schools in such cities as Louisville, Ky., and Indianapolis, Ind.

In the 1980s, however, reaction against

busing and other forms of school desegregation gained momentum as federal courts relaxed enforcement of desegregation orders. The result was a pronounced trend toward the return of segregation. In 1995 two-thirds of African-American students and three-fourths of Hispanic-American students attended schools that were predominantly minority, with a third attending schools that were 90 percent minority. School districts such as those of Norfolk, Va., sought and were granted "unitary status," that is, being freed from court-ordered desegregation by showing the courts that the district had eliminated racial discrimination, but "elimination of discrimination" was not synonymous with "integration." In Denver, for example, relative numbers of minority and white students did not significantly change between 1974, when court-ordered busing began, and 1995, when the order was abandoned. In a dramatic reversal of the principles of *Brown,* advocates calling for an end to busing—who in many cities crossed racial and ethnic lines—rejected the idea that separate inherently means "unequal" in quality of education and called for a change in focus from resegregation to improvement of neighborhood schools.

In *Missouri* v. *Jenkins* (1995) the Supreme Court handed down a ruling that was widely believed to presage the end of court-ordered desegregation. At issue was the order of a Kansas City district judge for the State of Missouri to pay $1.4 billion for the creation of magnet schools to attract white suburban students to Kansas City public schools, which were 70 percent black. Chief Justice William H. Rehnquist, writing for the majority, held that the judge had exceeded his authority and that "the proper response to an intradistrict violation is an intradistrict remedy," in effect saying that urban districts could not look to the greater resources of the suburbs for solutions to their problems. The ruling was expected to affect hundreds of school districts across the country still under desegregation decrees. Observers feared that, as far as the public schools were concerned, the nation had moved once again toward the "separate but equal" principle articulated a century earlier in *Plessy* v. *Ferguson.*

[See also Affirmative Action; African Americans; Brown v. *Board of Education of Topeka; Civil Rights Movement; Freedom Riders; Plessy* v. *Ferguson.]*

BIBLIOGRAPHY

Steven F. Lawson, *Running for Freedom: Civil Rights and Black Politics in America Since 1941* (New York, 1991).

J. Anthony Lukas, *Common Ground* (New York, 1985).

Billy J. Tidwell, ed., *The State of Black America: 1994* (New York, 1994).

J. Harvie Wilkinson III, *From Brown to Bakke: The Supreme Court and School Integration, 1954–1978* (New York, 1979).

— ALTON B. HORNSBY, JR.

DISABILITY RIGHTS MOVEMENT

Disability Rights Movement comprises a number of related but distinct social movements advocating civil rights for an estimated 43 million U.S. citizens with physical, sensory, psychological, or cognitive disabilities that affect their daily activities. Emerging after World War II, these movements replaced a medical model of disability with a minority-group model. The medical model defined disability as physical, psychosocial, and vocational limitation resulting from illness or injury. Locating the problem within individuals, it prescribed the solution as treatment to cure or at least correct individual functioning. The minority model asserted that limitations in social and vocational functioning were not the exclusive and inevitable result of bodily impairment but were also a product of the inadequacies in the architectural and social environment. Thus, for example, paralyzed legs did not inevitably cause limitations in mobility, but the absence of ramps did. The new model saw devaluation of disabled persons as producing socioeconomic discrimination.

The disability rights movements arose in response to a historic legacy of discrimination and segregation. In the late nineteenth and early twentieth centuries, most professionals in medicine, social services, and education increasingly attributed a lack of moral and emotional self-control to the "defective classes," which included virtually anyone with a disability, blaming them for the poverty, vice, crime, and dislocations of the new industrial order. People with mental retardation, epilepsy, or cerebral palsy were often permanently institutionalized as a danger to society. Others with physical disabilities were at times segregated by such ordinances as Chicago's "ugly" law, which prohibited "diseased, maimed, mutilated, or . . . deformed" persons from appearing in public. Reacting to an emerging deaf subculture, an "oralist" movement began in the 1880s to oppose sign language and insist that deaf people learn speech and speechreading. Led by Alexander Graham Bell, it took over much of deaf education and sought to disperse the deaf community. Eugenicists pressed for the sterilization of people with various disabilities, and by 1931 more than half the states had adopted sterilization laws, and thousands of people were sterilized. Meanwhile, contemporary welfare policy defined disability as the incapacity for productive labor and, in effect, incompetency to manage one's life, and thus brought many disabled people under permanent medical and social-service supervision and relegated them to a stigmatized and segregated economic dependency.

Beginning during World War I some professionals avowed continuing faith in treatment and training. Special education of disabled children and medical-vocational rehabilitation of disabled adults sought to correct the functional limitations that allegedly prevented social integration. People with physical and sensory disabilities were imbued with an ethos of individualistic striving known as "overcoming," with President Franklin D. Roosevelt as the prime example during the 1930s and early 1940s. Mentally handicapped people, however, were still often institutionalized or subjected to social control in the community. After 1945 the disability rights movements developed in opposition to these ideologies and practices. Parents' groups lobbied in state legislatures and in Congress for the right of disabled children to a "free and appropriate" public education in "the least restrictive environment"—integration to the maximum extent. These principles were embodied in the Education for All Handicapped Children Act of 1975. Other parents' groups and reform-minded professionals promoted deinstitutionalization and community-based group homes for developmentally disabled persons.

The disability rights movement demanded federal protection against discrimination in education, jobs, public accommodations, and government-funded activities.

Beginning in the late 1960s deaf advocates redefined deafness as a linguistic difference and demanded their rights to sign language and cultural self-determination. Their efforts culminated in the March 1988 "Deaf President Now" campaign at Gallaudet University, when a student strike at that university for deaf people, supported by the deaf community, won its demand for selection of a deaf educator to head the university. Meanwhile, physically disabled activists launched an independent-living movement for self-directed, community-based living. They also claimed the right of equal access to public transit and public accommodations. Through lobbying and demonstrations they won passage and increasing enforcement of accessibility statutes. The organized blind movement, long the most politically effective disability movement, lobbied successfully for both access (the right to use white canes and guide dogs in public places) and policies to advance economic well-being (through tax exemptions, for example).

All these efforts reflected an emerging minority consciousness documented in a 1986 opinion survey of disabled adults: 54 percent of those aged eighteen to forty-four identified disabled people as a minority group that faced discrimination. The movement thus demanded federal protection against discrimination in education, jobs, public accommodations, and government-funded activities. Antidiscrimination and the right of equal access were the basis of fifty federal laws that began with the Architectural Barriers Act of 1968 and culminated in the Americans with Disabilities Act of 1990. These statutes adopted the disability rights movements' major contribution to U.S. civil rights theory—the concept of equal access. Adaptive devices, assistive services, and architectural modifications (for example, Braille markings, sign-language interpreters, and ramps) had been considered special benefits to those who were fundamentally dependent. Equal access moved beyond such social welfare notions by viewing these provisions as reasonable accommodations for different ways of functioning. Traditional civil rights theory sometimes allowed differential treatment of a minority as a temporary remedy to achieve equality. Disability rights ideology argued that for persons with disabilities, permanent differential treatment in the form of accessibility and reasonable accommodations was legitimate because it was necessary to achieve and maintain equal access and thus equal opportunity for full participation in society.

[See also Americans with Disabilities Act.]

BIBLIOGRAPHY

Richard K. Scotch, *From Good Will to Civil Rights: Transforming Federal Disability Policy* (Philadelphia, 1984).

Joseph P. Shapiro, *No More Pity: People with Disabilities Forging a New Civil Rights Movement* (New York, 1993).

Peter L. Tyor and Leland V. Bell, *Caring for the Retarded in America: A History* (Westport, Conn., 1984).

— PAUL K. LONGMORE

DOLLAR DIPLOMACY

Dollar diplomacy is the policy of promoting a nation's economic interests abroad and strengthening its power to effect its policy objectives by using its economic resources. In the United States it received its most explicit expression by President William Howard Taft, who described his policy as "substituting dollars for bullets." He sought, unsuccessfully, to persuade U.S. bankers to share in an international consortium to finance railroad building in China and to refinance the foreign debt of Nicaragua. Taft stated that his policy was "frankly directed to the increase of American trade upon the axiomatic principle that the Government of the United States shall extend all proper support to every legitimate and beneficial American enterprise abroad." This policy was actually as old as the nation, but its statement at this time set off a bitter debate over the merits of dollar diplomacy that culminated in the anti-imperialist and antimilitarist writing of the interwar years. William Jennings Bryan and President Woodrow Wilson were among the severe critics of this orientation of Taft's and Theodore Roosevelt's policy; yet they also practiced dollar diplomacy in the negotiation of the Bryan-Chamorro Treaty with Nicaragua (1914) and in the occupation of Haiti and the Dominican Republic.

Pejorative use of the term declined in later years. Some scholars pointed out that U.S. intervention in the Caribbean was motivated less by the objective of advancing business interests than by the desire to secure the collaboration of those interests in advancing U.S. power and strategic objectives. The administration of Franklin D. Roosevelt endeavored to revive international trade and to confront the German trade drive in the 1930's through reciprocal trade agreements to lower trade barriers and through the financing of international trade by means of the newly established Export-Import Bank. As the international crisis of the 1930's evolved into World War II, military and economic aid was given to extend the U.S. defense perimeter to include South America.

Post–World War II foreign economic and military aid programs, including U.S. participation in the Alliance for Progress, constituted a revival and extension of dollar diplomacy on a broad scale. The policy emphasis had shifted, however, from that of the Taft days. The Export-Import Bank increased the use of public credit to expand trade; in more direct ways the use of public credit to aid reconstruction and development also increased. At the same time, the foreign investment of private capital was encouraged. As in earlier days, critics of foreign aid raised the cry of "dollar diplomacy" in a pejorative sense. U.S. opposition to the Cuban revolution was castigated as a policy in support of U.S. sugar, landowning, and mining interests. Critics of President Richard M. Nixon's administration charged that in its relations with developing countries the U.S. policy, including congressional restrictions on economic and military aid, supported regimes friendly to multinational corporations in which U.S. capital was invested and opposed, or even collaborated in, the overthrow of regimes hostile to them.

BIBLIOGRAPHY

Simon G. Hansen, *Dollar Diplomacy, Modern Style.*

F. C. Howe, "Dollar Diplomacy and Imperialism," *Proceedings of the American Academy of Political Science* (1917–18).

Scott Nearing and Joseph Freeman, *Dollar Diplomacy.*

— HAROLD EUGENE DAVIS

DOUGHBOY

The word "doughboy" was universally used in the U.S. Army to mean an infantryman, and specifically an American infantryman, up until World War II when it was replaced with "GI." When it was first used is uncertain, but it can be traced as far back as 1854, when it was already in use on the Texas border. The explanation then was that the infantrymen wore white belts and had to clean them with "dough" made of pipe clay. Originally a term of opprobrium used by the mounted service, it was adopted by the infantry itself and used with great pride.

BIBLIOGRAPHY

Mitford M. Mathews, ed., *A Dictionary of Americanisms on Historical Principles.*

— OLIVER LYMAN SPAULDING

DRAFT

Draft, a process of selection of some of the male population for compulsory military service. It is a peculiarly American concept distinct from the European practice of conscription, which involves the regularized training of the entire male population, generation after generation.

The concepts of universal military training and of compulsory military service in time of emergency were established in the United States under the legal systems of all the colonial powers. They were rigorously applied in Puritan Massachusetts but not applied at all in Quaker Pennsylvania. Even in Massachusetts the Minutemen were a body selected from the mass of the universal, or "common," militia. The compulsory militia laws were used sporadically during the Revolution both for local defense and for support of the Continental army. Service in the Continental force could be avoided by hiring a substitute or by direct payment of a fee. Selection of eligibles was conducted by the states, often by use of a lottery. Compulsory universal-militia service was written into the constitutions of the states and remains in force in the majority of state codes to the present day. The U.S. Constitution provides for the training of state militias under standards to be prescribed by Congress. The Militia Act of May 8, 1792, provided a broad organizational structure for the militia but contained no means of enforcing a program of training. The inadequacies of that legislation and the disappearance of any continuing military threat in the more populous eastern states led to disintegration of the old universal-militia concept.

From the end of the Revolution until 1863, American military manpower procurement for the regular services was based entirely on volunteers. Although the able-bodied manpower of the states was still enrolled in the militia and reported more or less regularly, the only viable units of the militia were also composed entirely of volunteers. The armies of both the Union and the Confederacy were organized on the same basis (that is, a mass of state volunteer militia units organized around a nucleus of regulars from the prewar U.S. Army). The initial surge of enthusiasm on both sides wore off in the bloody campaigns of 1861 and 1862. The states sought to keep their original regiments up to strength and to create new units by resorting to the revolutionary war formula of bounties and compulsion. Once again those selected in the state lotteries were permitted to hire a substitute or to avoid service by payment of a fee.

When neither voluntary enlistment nor the erratic pattern of state compulsory service produced the manpower needed, both the North and the South resorted to a federal draft. The implementing legislation in the North was the Enrollment Act of 1863. Hiring substitutes or paying fees in lieu of service continued to be authorized under the federal system. Resentment against the gross economic discrimination of the state system flared into open violence when those inequities were continued and expanded under the federal draft. Bitter opposition to the draft continued throughout the remainder of the war. The Civil War draft was administered directly by the army through presidential quotas assigned to each congressional district. Voluntary enlistments were credited against the district quotas, with selection of the remainder by lot. Ultimately only about 6 percent of the total strength of the Union army could be identified as a direct product of the draft. The indirect pressures, notably through operation of the substitution and bounty systems, produced a substantially larger total.

From the end of the Civil War until 1903, military manpower procurement reverted to the prewar voluntary system. During both the Mexican and the Spanish-American wars the army met its manpower needs by individual voluntary enlistments and by accepting entire units from the state volunteer militias as "U.S. Volunteers." During this same period American military policy was reexamined by a group of theoreticians led by Brig. Gen. Emory Upton (*The Military Policy of the United States*), Lt. Col. Matthew Forney Steele (*American Campaigns*), and Homer Lea (The Valor of Ignorance). The work of these theoreticians manifested itself in a series of legislative acts between 1903 and 1916.

The state volunteer militia—by now known as the National Guard—was brought under greater federal control. A federal military reserve was created under the direct control of the War and Navy departments. The foundation was laid for an army that, once mobilized, could be supported only by a federal draft. Over a prolonged period of mobilization the infusion of draft-produced replacements and the products of the then newly established Reserve Officer Training Corps would gradually eliminate the distinctions between units originally identified with the regular army, the National Guard, and the "national army" formed subsequent to mobilization. This would be a much different force from the aggregation of state militias envisaged by the framers of the Constitution.

Organization of an effective army general staff as part of the pre-World War I reforms helped to make possible a thorough review of the mistakes of the Civil War draft and the development of plans for a more efficient and a more equitable system. These plans had scarcely been formulated when they were ordered into effect by the Selective Service Act of 1917. Under this act the hiring of substitutes and the payment of bounties were outlawed. In place of the army of soldiers required to administer the Civil War draft, enrollment and selection were to be done by local civilian boards organized under federally appointed state directors and operating under uniform federal regulations. Civilians established the categories of deferment and acted on appeals. Manpower requirements were developed by the army general staff and apportioned as state quotas. The order of induction was determined by lottery.

Despite the relatively short duration of American participation in World War I, the diffusion of drafted men throughout all units of the army was well under way at the time of the armistice. Of approximately 4 million men under arms, over half were draftees. The World War I draft was challenged in the courts and was found by the Supreme Court to be constitutional (*Arver* v. *United States*, 245 U.S. 366 [1918]). In general, the new Selective Service program was accepted by the public as fair and reasonable. Opposition to any continuing program of compulsory service in peacetime continued to be overwhelming and the several proposals to continue the program got nowhere.

The fall of France and the worsening of U.S. relations with Japan led to the enactment of the nation's first peacetime draft with the passage of the Selective Training and Service Act of 1940. The act was the product of continuing studies by the army general staff of the successful World War I model, and it incorporated all the principal features of that experience. The impact of the World War II draft was pervasive. Over 10 million men were inducted, representing the most extensive mobilization of the nation's manpower in its history. Draftees were assigned to all the armed services, including the U.S. Navy and Marine Corps—services that had previously maintained themselves by voluntary recruitment even in time of war. By 1946 the armed forces were a homogeneous instrument of federal power. That power represented a blend of all the traditional elements of American military strength, both state and federal, but the influence of the federal draft was at once dominant and indispensable.

With the exception of one year (March 1947 to March 1948), the draft was in continuous operation from 1940 to Jan. 27, 1973. The administrative machinery established during World War II had been modified but never dismantled. From 1940 until 1967 the Selective Service System was geared to the requirements of total war and total mobilization. Therein lay the seeds of political turmoil. The system's reputation for fairness had been built upon the near total use of the nation's manpower during the two world wars. The military manpower requirements of the Korean and Vietnam conflicts were much smaller. Requirements during the intervals of international tension between those wars were even more limited. Successive administrations chose to deal with this problem by liberalizing deferments, thereby reducing the pool of eligibles to the size needed.

By offering deferment from active service to young men who chose to enlist in the National Guard or in one of the federal reserve forces, a direct link was established for the first time between the draft and the civilian reserves. By the end of the 1960's this link had become as dominant a factor in the National Guard and reserve forces as it had been for some time previous in the active forces. The remaining pool of draft eligibles came to consist largely of young men who had not chosen to marry and to father a child in their teens, who were not successfully enrolled in a college or university, and who upon graduation from college had not taken jobs in teaching or in one of the other exempted occupations. So long as this system resulted only in a period of active service with little or no personal risk, its obvious inequities were tolerated or ignored. As the manpower requirements of the Vietnam War and the personal risks of service increased, the consequences of the deferment policies could no longer be accepted.

The initial response by the successive administrations of presidents Lyndon B. Johnson and Richard M. Nixon was a return to the lottery as a substitute for some of the most obviously discriminatory deferments. Early in 1973 the Nixon administration ended the draft, returning to a reliance on volunteers, but with maintenance of the Selective Service System in a standby, or "zero draft," status. The manpower requirements of the active and reserve forces were met by large increases in pay and related incentives.

Critics in Congress and elsewhere charged that reliance on economic incentives was the old Civil War substitution system in a new and vastly more expensive form. An outbreak of violence and sabotage aboard ships of the U.S. Navy in 1972 was alleged by other critics to reflect a reduction in moral and mental standards in order to meet recruiting goals. Still others alleged that in order to create an appearance of success the authorized manpower of the army was being adjusted steadily downward to conform to the number of recruits available.

Beginning with the decline in inductions in 1972, the National Guard and reserve forces experienced great difficulty in maintaining strength. Even when total authorizations were met, imbalances existed between units and the quality of the recruits was subject to frequent criticism. Unit performance was further weakened by diversion of cadres from training to recruiting duties.

The reduction of active forces during the period 1970–72 had been based to a considerable extent on increased reliance on the guard and reserve. If the civilian components could not maintain their strength, the national leadership would be confronted with some difficult decisions.

The return to a volunteer system produced more private and public studies of the draft and its alternatives than at any previous time in American history. Several of these studies concluded that the attempt to meet continuing large military manpower requirements from volunteers alone was but one more stopgap in a long search for a reliable and equitable program. In the view of these critics it would be necessary to convert the traditional concept of an emergency military draft to a broader permanent program of national service.

In general, the draft as it operated from the end of World War II until 1967 had been deemed unsatisfactory. Whether reliance on volunteers would be a workable substitute would depend in part on the international situation and in part on the country's willingness to pay the high costs of attracting recruits. An international crisis that required expansion of the armed forces at the high pay rates of the volunteer system would be likely to produce a new national debate over manpower procurement policy.

BIBLIOGRAPHY

James M. Gerhardt, *The Draft and Public Policy.*
M. M. Stoddard, *American Conscription: A Policy Evaluation.*

— WILLIAM V. KENNEDY

THE DRAFT SINCE THE 1970S

The all-volunteer force (AVF) replaced selective service in 1973 as the method for raising U.S. military forces. Local draft boards were dismantled, although National Selective Service Headquarters remained as a cadre for future reactivation. With the AVF plagued by inadequate numbers and disproportionate representation of minorities, the administration of President Jimmy Carter reinstituted compulsory draft registration for eighteen-year-old males in 1980, partly as a political response to the Soviet invasion of Afghanistan. About 9 percent of those men required to do so failed to register. President Ronald Reagan, who had campaigned against the draft as an unnecessary infringement on individual liberty, nonetheless continued compulsory registration and prosecuted those who refused to register. In *Rostker* v. *Goldberg* (1981) the Supreme Court affirmed the action and held that the registration of only men and not women was constitutional because women could not be assigned to combat duty. Congress subsequently tied registration to federal education benefits.

President Reagan, who had campaigned against the draft as an infringement on individual liberty, nonetheless continued compulsory registration and prosecuted those who refused to register.

Reagan relied on higher pay, not the draft, to increase enlistments. Some observers, however, urged a return to the draft to ensure that the armed forces were socially representative and to overcome the isolation of the military from society. Opponents continued to characterize the draft as undemocratic, expensive, and unprofessional. The General Accounting Office reported that the AVF cost much less than conscript forces. The end of the cold war temporarily muted the debate. The spectacular success of the AVF in the Gulf War of 1991 did not necessarily settle the question of how armed forces should be raised in a post–cold war era.

[See also Gulf War of 1991.]

BIBLIOGRAPHY

Eliot A. Cohen, *Citizens and Soldiers: The Dilemmas of Military Service* (Ithaca, N.Y., 1985).
James F. Dunnigan and Raymond Macedonia, *Getting It Right: American Military Reforms After Vietnam to the Gulf War* (New York, 1993).
G. Q. Flynn, *The Draft 1940–1973* (Lawrence, Kans., 1993).

— J. GARRY CLIFFORD

DRAFT RIOTS

Although there had been minor disturbances connected with personal enrollments, or conscription, under the Civil War act of Mar. 3, 1863, actual violence awaited the draft itself. Minor riots occurred in Rutland, Vt.; Wooster, Ohio; Boston, Mass.; and Portsmouth, N.H.; but none equaled in length or destructiveness those in New York City. Fanned by Democratic opposition to the war, indiscreet remarks by Gov. Horatio Seymour, and arguments alleging violation of constitutional liberties, objection to the draft in New York rested chiefly on the provision for money payments in lieu of service, which distinguished between rich men's money and poor men's blood. Shortly after the drawing of lots commenced on July 13 at the Ninth Congressional District draft headquarters, a mob, mostly of foreign-born laborers, stormed the building; overpowered attendants, police, firemen, and militia; attacked residences, other draft district headquarters, saloons, hotels, restaurants, and even railway tracks. For four days the city was a welter of conflagrations, assaults, and defiances, resulting in a thousand casualties and $1.5 million in property loss. On July 15 militia regiments sent toward Gettysburg began to return, and order was restored. Picked troops from the Army of the Potomac were brought in, and on Aug. 19 drawings proceeded peaceably.

BIBLIOGRAPHY

J. F. Rhodes, *History of the United States*, vol. IV.

— ELBRIDGE COLBY

DRED SCOTT CASE

Dred Scott Case (*Dred Scott* v. *John F. A. Sanford*, 19 Howard 393) was decided by the Supreme Court on Mar. 6, 1857. The basic judgment was that Scott, because he was a slave, was neither a citizen of Missouri nor a citizen of the United States and had no constitutional right to sue in the federal courts. In reaching this decision, the Court discussed several highly controversial slavery issues over which sectional hostility had long seethed. Rather than settle these issues, the decision accelerated the polarization that resulted in the Civil War.

Dred Scott began his litigation in 1846 in the state courts of Missouri, in a bona fide freedom suit based

Dred Scott. Painting after a photograph, around 1858. (The Granger Collection, New York)

on Missouri law and his earlier residence in free territory. The lower court declared him free. But the Missouri Supreme Court, openly propounding partisan proslavery doctrines and overthrowing long-standing legal precedents, reversed the decision. A new suit was then instituted, in the federal courts, seeking not only Scott's freedom but also a broader Supreme Court decision that might settle the divisive political disputes over slavery in the territories. At first the Court tried to avoid these controversial issues, but strong political pressures and deep-rooted partisanship ultimately prevailed. When the decision finally was rendered, each judge wrote a separate opinion. Chief Justice Roger B. Taney's was considered the opinion of the Court. Six other judges presented concurring opinions; two dissented. But because the former differed in their reasoning, controversy has always existed over what principles the Court actually adjudicated by majority concurrence, what was asserted by a minority, and what was obiter dictum.

The only judgment rendered by an undeniable majority was that a slave could not be a citizen. Other principles laid down whose legality was disputed were that (1) blacks could not be citizens; (2) black slaves were a species of property protected by the Constitution and, hence, Congress had no authority to abolish slavery in the territories and the Missouri Compromise was unconstitutional; and (3) a black slave, even though freed by residence in a free state or territory, was remanded to slavery when he returned to a slave state. Apparently giving judicial endorsement to the proslavery point of view, the decision stirred inflammatory reactions that aggravated already serious sectional hostility and helped precipitate the Civil War. After the war, the Thirteenth and Fourteenth amendments superseded the Dred Scott decision.

Apart from its role in pre–Civil War sectionalism, the case is important in American constitutional history for other reasons. It was the first instance since *Marbury* v. *Madison* (1803) in which the Supreme Court held an act of Congress unconstitutional. Also, by his analysis of Fifth Amendment protections guaranteeing that no citizen could be deprived of property without due process of law, Taney laid the foundation for broader substantive due process interpretations by later Courts.

BIBLIOGRAPHY

Walter Ehrlich, "Was the Dred Scott Case Valid?," *Journal of American History*, vol. 55, and "The Origins of the Dred Scott Case," *Journal of Negro History*, vol. 59.

Vincent C. Hopkins, *Dred Scott's Case.*

Stanley I. Kutler, *The Dred Scott Decision: Law or Politics?*

— WALTER EHRLICH

DUE PROCESS OF LAW

Due Process of Law, which has come to be perhaps the most important provision of the Constitution of the United States, appears in both the Fifth and Fourteenth amendments. The provision is that neither the federal nor any state government may "deprive any person of life, liberty, or property, without due process of law." The phrase comes from a British statute, 28 Edw. 3, ch. 3, which provided that "no man . . . shall be put out of his lands or tenements nor taken, nor disinherited, nor put to death, without he be brought to answer by due process of law." This statute in turn had its foundation in Magna Charta (1215, 1225), in which the king promised that "no freeman (*liber homo*) shall be taken or imprisoned or dispossessed or outlawed or exiled or in any way ruined, nor will we go or send against him, except by the lawful judgment of his peers or by the law of the land (*per legem terrae*)." In 1855 the Supreme Court held that the words "due process of law" were "undoubtedly intended to convey the same meaning as the words 'by the law of the land' in Magna Charta" (*Murray* v. *Hoboken Land and Improvement Company*, 18 Howard 272). The first part of the due process clause has its analogue in the phrase that Thomas Jefferson wrote into the Declaration of Independence (1776), "life, liberty, and the pursuit of happiness," which in turn may have harked back to the thought of John Locke that man has the power "by nature" to preserve "his life, liberty, and estate" (*Second Treatise of Civil Government*, 1690).

Although the due process clause first operated to preserve the right to certain procedures, in time the emphasis shifted from procedural to substantive due process. The Supreme Court in effect divided the constitutional provision into two different guarantees. One was the guarantee of substantive rights to life, liberty, and property, of which a person may not be deprived, no matter how fair the procedure might be when considered by itself; the other was a guarantee of fair procedures by the judicial or administrative bodies.

The first part of the due process clause has its analogue in the phrase Jefferson wrote into the Declaration, "life, liberty, and the pursuit of happiness."

The earliest American precedents for the recognition of substantive due process were three cases. The first was *Bank of Columbia* v. *Okely*, 4 Wheaton 235 (1819), in which Justice William Johnson of the Supreme Court said in an obiter dictum that the words of Magna Charta about the law of the land "were intended to secure the individual from the arbitrary exercise of the powers of government, unrestrained by the established principles of private right and distributive justice." The second precedent was established in 1856 when the New York Court of Appeals, in *Wynehamer* v. *People*, 13 New York 378, had before it a state prohibition law that had the effect, with respect to liquors in existence, of destroying property. But a state, the court held, has no power to destroy property "even by the forms of due process of law." In the very next year, this line of thought received the approval of the U.S. Supreme Court when it decided, in the case of *Dred Scott* v. *Sanford*, 19 Howard 393 (1857)—the third precedent case—that the section of the Missouri Compromise that excluded slavery from the territories was unconstitutional under the Fifth Amendment, for Congress had no power to forbid people to take their property (slaves) to places that were held in common by the American people, regardless of the procedures provided by Congress for putting the prohibition into effect.

The original Bill of Rights, including the Fifth Amendment, was held to be a limit only on the federal government (*Barron* v. *Baltimore*, 7 Peters 243 [1833]). The Fourteenth Amendment, with its due process clause, was expressly intended as a limit on the states. For the first thirty years after ratification of the latter in 1868, the Supreme Court was reluctant to use its powers to enforce the amendment, believing that the original federal equilibrium ought to be maintained. In the *Slaughterhouse Cases*, 16 Wallace 36 (1873), however, Justice Joseph P. Bradley argued in his dissent that the Louisiana statute that vested exclusively in a corporation the right to engage in the slaughterhouse business deprived people of both "liberty" and "property." The right of choice in adopting lawful employments is, he said, "a portion of their liberty: their occupation is their property." Justice Noah H. Swayne agreed with this position and said that liberty in the Fourteenth Amendment "is freedom from all restraints but such as are justly imposed by law. . . . Property is everything which has an exchangeable value. . . . Labor is property. . . . The right to make it available is next in importance to the rights of life and liberty." Leading state courts followed the line of these dissenters by stressing the substantive, rather than the procedural, aspects of the due process clauses of their own state constitutions. The result was the doctrine of freedom of contract, which read a laissez-faire ideology of private enterprise into the due process clauses of the Fifth and Fourteenth amendments as interpreted by the Supreme Court from 1897 to 1937 (*Allgeyer* v. *Louisiana*, 165 U.S. 578 [1897]; *Lochner* v. *New York*, 198 U.S. 45 [1905]).

Under the impact of New Deal legislation and its underlying liberal philosophy, the Supreme Court in 1937 said that it would no longer substitute its own social and economic beliefs for the judgment of the legislatures (*National Labor Relations Board* v. *Jones and Laughlin Steel Corporation*, 301 U.S. 1 [1937]). This meant the end of substantive due process with respect to economic and social legislation affecting property rights and relations. In 1963, Justice Hugo L. Black, in an opinion for the Court (*Ferguson* v. *Skrupa*, 372 U.S. 726), said that "we emphatically refuse to go back to the time when courts used the Due Process Clause 'to strike down state laws, regulatory of business and industrial conditions, because they may be unwise, improvident, or out of harmony with a particular school of thought.' . . . Whether the legislature takes for its textbook Adam Smith, Herbert Spencer, Lord Keynes, or some other is no concern of ours."

But substantive due process did not end; it only shifted its locus from property to life and liberty. The rationale for this new version of the doctrine was given by the second Justice John Marshall Harlan (*Poe* v. *Ullman*, 367 U.S. 497) in 1961: "Were due process merely a procedural safeguard it would fail to reach those situations where the deprivation of life, liberty or property was accomplished by legislation which . . . could, given even the fairest possible procedure in application to individuals, nevertheless destroy the enjoyment of all three."

An intimation of this view may be found in a decision of the Supreme Court in 1891, *Union Pacific Railroad Company* v. *Botsford*, 141 U.S. 250, and a more explicit version in *Meyer* v. *Nebraska*, 262 U.S. 390 (1923), in which the concept of liberty as used in the due process clause is by itself held to be a restriction upon arbitrary state action. In 1925 the Court held that "liberty" in the Fourteenth Amendment puts the same restraints on the states that the First Amendment does on the federal government (*Gitlow* v. *New York*, 268 U.S. 652). Since then, substantive due process in its new meaning and thrust has had a continuing life and has constituted—along with equal protection—the most creative development in constitutional law. It accounts for the priority won for fundamental liberties in the meaning and reach of the Constitution.

A parallel development has taken place with respect to procedural due process. While substantive due process with respect to property and freedom of contract was flourishing, the Supreme Court was reluctant to apply the due process clause to correct injustices in state criminal trials; but beginning in the early 1930's the Court began to apply the clause to set aside state criminal convictions and, moving on a case-by-case basis, the Court applied to state criminal procedures most of the procedural requirements spelled out in the Bill of Rights as requirements for federal cases. The Court agreed with Justice Felix Frankfurter (*Joint Anti-Fascist Refugee Committee* v. *McGrath*, 341 U.S. 123 [1951]) that achievements of our civilization, "as precious as they were hard won[,] were summarized by Justice Brandeis when he wrote that 'in the development of our liberty insistence upon procedural regularity has been a large factor.' . . . It is noteworthy that procedural safeguards constitute the major portion of our Bill of Rights."

Whether the due process clause of the Fourteenth Amendment incorporates all the provisions of the Bill of Rights (Justice Black's view) or incorporates its provisions only selectively, whether it is limited to the specifics of the first eight amendments (again, the view of Justice Black) or may reach beyond the specifics to the broad concept of liberty to embrace those rights that are "fundamental" and should belong to the citizens of any free government—for example, the right of privacy (see opinion of Justice Lewis F. Powell, Jr., for the Court and concurring opinion of Justice Potter Stewart in *Roe* v. *Wade*, 93 Supreme Court 705 [1973])—the result has been a flowering of emergent rights and liberties, both substantive and procedural, under the shelter of the constitutional due process clauses.

BIBLIOGRAPHY

C. W. Collins, *The Fourteenth Amendment and the States.*
H. E. Flack, *The Adoption of the Fourteenth Amendment.*
L. P. McGehee, *Due Process of Law Under the Federal Constitution.*
R. L. Mott, *Due Process of Law.*
B. Schwartz, ed., *The Fourteenth Amendment: Centennial Volume.*
H. Taylor, *Due Process of Law.*
J. tenBroek, *The Antislavery Origins of the Fourteenth Amendment.*

— MILTON R. KONVITZ

DUMBARTON OAKS CONFERENCE

Dumbarton Oaks Conference (Aug. 21–Oct. 7, 1944). Held at an estate in Georgetown, Washington, D.C., the Dumbarton Oaks Conference was called to prepare a charter for a "general international organization," as stipulated in the Declaration of Four Nations at Moscow in November 1943. Because the Soviet Union was not engaged in the Far Eastern conflict, the meetings were conducted in two phases: until Sept. 28 with representatives of the United States, Great Britain, and the Soviet Union; from Sept. 29 to Oct. 7 the Republic of China replaced the Soviet Union. Preliminary negotiations had established some guidelines, including the creation of a Security Council and a General Assembly.

The Dumbarton Oaks Conference of 1944 was called to prepare a charter for a "general international organization" to follow the world war.

Discussion encompassed areas of jurisdiction of the proposed organization, namely, economic and social as well as security matters; membership in the two bodies; voting procedure; veto privileges; provision for sanctions, economic and military; and a multitude of technical details. Among the unresolved issues were the Soviet demand for sixteen seats in the General Assembly and the question of great-power veto in the Security Council, as well as arrangements for a full United Nations conference to agree on the final charter. The proposals emanating from this conference were published by the four governments on Oct. 9, 1944.

BIBLIOGRAPHY

Thomas M. Campbell, *Masquerade Peace: America's UN Policy, 1944–1945.*

Harley A. Notter, *Postwar Foreign Policy Preparation, 1939–1944.*

— RAYMOND G. O'CONNOR

DUST BOWL

Dust Bowl, a name given to an area within the Great Plains during the climatic storms that spread dust across the nation during the drought of the 1930's. The dust clouds were the product of a severe dry spell lasting several years, during which the vegetative cover became so depleted that the fields were directly exposed to wind action. The exposed soil particles were set in motion by the wind, and the lighter ones became airborne. The so-called bowl was centered within a group of counties lying in the adjoining corners of New Mexico, Texas, Oklahoma, Kansas, and Colorado. Within its perimeters lay the cities of Amarillo, Tex.; Pueblo, Colo.; and Dodge City, Kans. The drought and the wind temporarily, but seriously, scarred the land as well as its occupants. Many families were forced to leave. Fortunately, the land area was restored by the application of scientific principles of land use and is again productively occupied.

BIBLIOGRAPHY

Elmer Starch, "Better Life on the Plains," *Yearbook of Agriculture* (1970).

Lawrence Svobida, *An Empire of Dust.*

— ELMER STARCH

DUTCH-INDIAN WAR

Dutch-Indian War (1643–45), which brought such desolation and distress to the struggling colony of New Netherland, was caused by the brutal and unwise Indian policy of William Kieft, the director-general of the colony. In February 1643, without warning the outlying and unprotected settlements of his intention, Kieft attacked an encampment of Indians at Pavonia and murdered about eighty men, women, and children in their sleep. The tribes rose in fury. Kieft, terrified, asked the colonists to elect a board to advise with him, and "the Eight" were chosen. With the director they armed the colonists and company servants and hired as soldiers a number of English settlers under the command of John Underhill of Stamford. Conditions in the province were desperate. Long Island, Westchester, and Manhattan itself were laid waste. With the exception of distant Fort Orange and Rensselaerswyck, safety was to be found only in the immediate vicinity of Fort Amsterdam on Manhattan Island. The fort itself, described as "utterly defenseless," offered but a poor refuge. The frightened colonists faced starvation. Hostile bands of Indians, 1,500 strong, threatened attack. Fortunately, the Indians had no common or sustained plan of attack, and raiding parties sent out from the fort met with some success. June 1644 brought reinforcements, but over a year dragged by before a general peace was signed on Aug. 29, 1645.

BIBLIOGRAPHY

A. C. Flick, ed., *History of the State of New York.*

— A. C. FLICK

DUTCH WEST INDIA COMPANY

Dutch West India Company, organized by a group of Dutch merchants in imitation of the Dutch East India Company and chartered by the States General on June 3, 1621. Under this charter the company was given enormous powers, both political and commercial, which included the exclusive right to trade on the west coast of Africa, in the West Indies, on the east and west coasts of America, and in Australia. In addition, the company was empowered to make alliances with the natives, to build forts, and to plant colonies. Nineteen directors administered the general affairs of the company. In 1624 the company planted a settlement at Fort Orange and, in 1625, on Manhattan Island, forming the colony of New Netherland. Strict obedience to the orders of the company was imposed on all colonists. The director and council acted under instruction from the company. Although later important matters affecting New Netherland often came before the States General, the continued despotic control of the company and its interest in trade rather than colonization was detrimental to the welfare of the colony.

BIBLIOGRAPHY

J. R. Brodhead, *History of the State of New York.*

— A. C. FLICK

E

EDUCATION

The roots of education in the United States are to be found in the ideas and practices of the schools of ancient Judea, Greece, Rome, and early Christendom. The American secondary school is a direct descendant of the grammar school of the Renaissance. The origins of the American college can be traced to the medieval university of western Europe.

The more immediate antecedents of education in the United States are to be located in the Protestant Reformation and the Catholic Counter-Reformation, as well as in the scientific and commercial revolutions of the 17th and 18th centuries. The schools of colonial New England, New Netherland, New Jersey, and North Carolina drew their religious teachings from the Calvinism of the Old World: English Puritanism, Scotch Presbyterianism, and the Dutch Reformed Church. The educational work carried on in the peripheral regions—the West, Southeast, and Southwest—took place within the framework of Roman Catholic theology. The growing impact of experimental science and of international trade brought about profound changes in education during the later colonial period with respect to aims, courses of study, and school organization. These forces operated also to modify the structure, functions, curriculum, and administration of American colleges.

England's contributions to colonial education included many ideas and practices, such as providing by law for vocational training for the poor; ecclesiastical control of education; textbooks; teaching practices; and patterns of curriculum and organization for all schools from the elementary through the collegiate. Scotland—via Ireland—was a source of inspiration for the idea of universal education, an objective also common to other Calvinists and to Lutherans. According to some educational historians, 17th-century Netherlands—small in size but vast in culture, education, and learning—may have exerted a potent influence on early American education.

Colonial Period

The earliest educational efforts in the New World took place in the home. Those children whose parents could not afford to pay for schooling or who had no parents were enabled, through apprenticeship laws passed by the various colonial legislatures, to obtain vocational training and instruction in the fundamentals of reading and religion; for example, a law passed by the General Court, or legislative body, of Massachusetts in 1642 required town authorities to make certain that children were trained "to read and understand the principles of religion and the capitall lawes of this country" and imposed fines for neglect. Apparently success was not achieved by this plan, and the General Court therefore passed in 1647 the Old Deluder Satan Act, which required that each township of fifty families engage a teacher to instruct children in reading and writing and that each township of one hundred families establish a "grammar schoole" capable of fitting youth for the university, again under the penalty of a fine. In this law may be found three principles typical of the public school system at the present time: the obligation of the community to establish schools, local school administration, and the distinction between secondary and elementary schools.

Laws similar to the Massachusetts act of 1647 were enacted in all the New England colonies except Rhode Island, where education was considered a private matter. Although there were private schools in the colonies, such as the dame schools, the most important educational work was accomplished in the town schools; the teachers were paid through local taxes and supervised by the town authorities or by the education committee (later known as the school board). These town schools were publicly supported and publicly controlled, but they were sectarian in purpose and content, as well as in control, since for much of the colonial period there was cooperation between church and government. As the population grew, new schools were opened to meet new needs. In the 18th century the "moving school" arose, a teacher being located for a few months at a time in each of the villages surrounding a town. The moving school was replaced by the district school, which served sparsely settled areas with limited numbers of children. The district school system continued to serve rural settlements all over the country into the 20th century.

Probably the most widely circulated elementary textbook in the colonial era was *The New England Primer* (Boston, 1690), which was reputed to have "taught millions to read and not one to sin." A total of 3 million copies is said to have come off the presses, many of these carrying differing titles but including much of the content of the original colonial edition. The primer, which came to the colonies from England, where it had been used for several centuries, taught reading, spelling, and catechism and contained other religious matter. The alphabet was presented through the medium of rhymed couplets—for example, "In Adam's Fall/We sinned all" and "A Dog will bite/A Thief at Night"—together with crude woodcut illustrations. *The New England Primer* was used in schools until the 1840's, when it gave way to other textbooks, including Noah Webster's very popular *The American Spelling Book*, first published in 1783 and known as "the blue-backed spelling book."

Secondary education in New England began with the establishment of the Boston Latin School in 1635. Graduates of this and other Latin grammar schools were qualified for admission to Harvard College, once it was established. These schools featured the teaching of the Latin language and literature and of Greek by men whose scholarship and ability were immeasurably above those of the teachers in the elementary schools, among the best known being Ezekiel Cheever in Boston, educated at Cambridge University. During the mid-18th century, the academy, a new kind of school that offered nonclassical and practical subjects, became increasingly attended; it foreshadowed the decline of the Latin grammar school.

Higher education in New England was inaugurated in 1636, when the Massachusetts General Court decided to allot £400 "towards a schoole or colledge," later named Harvard College after a clergyman who donated £780 and his library of 400 books to the new institution. The aim of Harvard, as stated in the charter of 1650, was to educate colonial and Indian young people "in knowledge and godliness" and "in good literature, Artes and Sciences." Three more colleges were opened in colonial New England: Yale in 1701, partially because of orthodox Calvinists' belief that Harvard was too liberal in theology; Brown in 1764, a Baptist institution whose charter rejected religious tests for admission and provided that faculty and students should "forever enjoy full free Absolute and uninterrupted Liberty of Conscience"; and Dartmouth in 1769, a Congregationalist college for the training of students of the ministry and Indians.

Education in the middle colonies varied from area to area, because of the differences of origin of the settlers. The Dutch in New Netherland set up public elementary schools in which reading, writing, religion, and sometimes arithmetic were taught; many of these schools continued to teach the Dutch language even after the English took over the colony in 1664. Under the English in the 18th century, the poor were taught in schools of the Society for the Propagation of the Gospel in Foreign Parts, an Anglican association founded in 1701 and primarily dedicated to missionary work among the Indians in the North American colonies. Grammar schools were founded in New York, including one that prepared students for King's College. This college, now Columbia University, was chartered in 1754 under Anglican auspices and intended, in the words of its first president, Rev. Samuel Johnson, "to set up a Course of Tuition in the learned Languages, and in the liberal Arts and Sciences," as well as in religious knowledge and piety.

The principle of religious toleration prevailed in New York, Pennsylvania, New Jersey, Rhode Island, Maryland, and Delaware, with the result that the various religious sects—Congregationalists, Baptists, Quakers, Lutherans, Dutch Reformed, Anglicans, Presbyterians, Roman Catholics, and Jews (with the exception at times of Catholics in New Jersey)—were enabled to establish elementary schools of their own. Of special interest was the first work on teaching published in colonial America, a German book, *Schul-Ordnung* (1770), by Christoph Dock, "the pious schoolmaster on the Skippack" (Pennsylvania). In secondary education Pennsylvania led the other middle colonies with the founding in 1689 of the Friends' Public School of Philadelphia (now called the William Penn Charter School); with the establishment of secondary schools organized by religious groups to train ministers; and especially with the founding of the Academy in Philadelphia, proposed by Benjamin Franklin in 1743 and opened in 1751. Franklin's Academy was organized into Latin, English, and mathematics departments, with the Latin department developing into the University of Pennsylvania. This school offered such subjects as languages, science, history, and geography, and it also intended "that a number of the poorer Sort will be hereby qualified to act as Schoolmasters in the Country." By an act of the Maryland General Assembly, King William's Secondary School, a free public school, was founded at Annapolis in 1696. A century later, the school became Saint John's College.

In addition to King's College in New York City, higher education in the middle colonies comprised the College of New Jersey (Princeton University), founded in 1746 by Scotch-Irish Presbyterians to maintain orthodox religion in the spirit of the Great Awakening; the College of Philadelphia (University of Pennsylvania), the new name for Franklin's Academy by the rechartering of 1755, and devoted to the teaching of the sciences and other modern subjects, in line with the principles underlying the Enlightenment; and Queen's College (Rutgers University), chartered in 1766 and designed by leaders of the Dutch Reformed Church to provide for "the education of youth in the learned languages, liberal and useful arts and sciences, and especially in divinity, preparing them for the ministry and other good offices."

Whereas New England school policy may be described as that of compulsory public maintenance and that of the middle colonies as parochial education, the southern colonial policy may be characterized as laissez-faire and pauper education. The geographical, social, and economic conditions in the South resulted in a system of colonial laws for apprentice training of poor and orphaned children; charity schools for the poor; private schools and tutorial training for the children of wealthy parents; and so-called Old Field Schools, which were elementary schools established on abandoned wasteland. A particularly significant type of elementary school in the South was the school with an endowment derived from a will or bequest. Notable among these was the Syms-Eaton School in Virginia, which originated with the will of Benjamin Syms in 1634 and was enlarged with funds from Thomas Eaton's will of 1659; this school, probably the first endowed lower-educational institution in the colonies, lasted into the 20th century. There were instances of educational provisions for black children, mainly because plantation owners were interested in teaching them Christianity. However, there was no serious, systematic, and successful attempt in the colonies in the South to legislate in behalf of public schools until the time of the Revolution.

The only college in the South during the colonial period was the College of William and Mary, which, although chartered in 1693, was only a grammar school in reality and did not confer degrees until 1700. The original objective of the college—training young men for the ministry—was modified in 1779 by Thomas Jefferson, who reorganized the institution, providing a modern curriculum of languages, law, the social sciences, and the physical and natural sciences. From William and Mary, "alma mater of statesmen," were graduated Jefferson, James Monroe, John Tyler, and John Marshall.

The Early American Republic

The Revolution, which disrupted education on all levels in many areas, led to a greater awareness on the part of Americans that new educational forms and policies were necessary for the new society. Proposals were made for a national school system based on democratic principles, and the creation of a national university was urged; George Washington bequeathed his shares in the Potomac Company toward the establishment of such an institution. Most of the early state constitutions included some provisions for education, mainly directed toward adding to the already existing facilities and providing for the children of the poor. Some states—such as Georgia in 1785, North Carolina in 1789, Vermont in 1791, and Tennessee in 1794—granted charters for state universities; but the only state university to grant degrees in the 18th century was North Carolina.

The U.S. Constitution makes no reference to education, and therefore, under the provisions of the Tenth Amendment to the Constitution, educational control is reserved to the several states. However, by virtue of the principle of "general welfare" in the Preamble and the doctrine of implied powers, the federal government has spent billions of dollars all through its history to provide instruction in agriculture and vocational subjects; to maintain schools for Indians; to fund the U.S. Office of Education and Library of Congress; to support the U.S. Military Academy, the U.S. Naval Academy, and the other service academies; and to finance a large variety of other educational projects.

In the Land Ordinance of 1785, Congress reserved a lot, known as Section Sixteen, in every township in the Western Territory "for the maintenance of public schools." The Northwest Ordinance, July 13, 1787, expressed a remarkable policy in its third article: "Religion, morality, and knowledge, being necessary to good government and the happiness of mankind, schools and the means of education shall forever be encouraged." On July 23, 1787, a congressional ordinance concerning the sale of the Western Territory confirmed the reservation of Section Sixteen for public education and stated that lot number 29 was "to be given perpetually for the purposes of religion," with "not more than two complete townships to be given perpetually for the purpose of a university." By means of the land grant policy the federal government was able to furnish the basic aid necessary for the promotion of a public school system, especially in the Middle West and the Far West.

Washington, with his interest in a national university, was but one of many American statesmen who showed a concern for educational matters in the early years of the new Republic. Jefferson submitted bills to the Virginia legislature for the organization of a public school system in which intellectual ability would be stressed so as to enable the best minds to be developed to provide public leadership. Among the other educational activities of Jefferson, in addition to his curriculum reforms at the College of William and Mary, were the founding of the University of Virginia, various writings on education, and a plan to transplant the University of Geneva to the United States. John Adams, James Madison, and Benjamin Rush were also notable among the public figures who devoted much attention to the need for educational reform; Rush and several other educators submitted plans for a national system of education on the occasion of a competition organized by the American Philosophical Society.

Until the early 19th century, New England was the only region that could lay claim to anything resembling a public school system. Only eight of the first sixteen states inserted provisions regarding education into their constitutions. As a general rule, except for Connecticut and Massachusetts, schools were few and standards low. Various political, industrial, and social changes brought about a decline in apprenticeship education, with the result that the only formal education available to most of the poor was in charity schools supported by religious groups.

A Massachusetts law of 1789 legally established the district school system—leading to lower standards in both primary and secondary education—and in 1827 the district school system was made compulsory. While democratic control by local government was established under these two laws, educational efficiency was severely hampered by a lack of sophisticated centralized direction, as Horace Mann was to point out in later years. The frontier conditions that were in force had, thus, a dual influence on the development of education in early national history.

New York State was active in setting up a statewide school system during this period. In 1784 it organized, and in 1787 it reorganized, the University of the State of New York, a centralized school system according to the French pattern. In 1812 the state set up a system of administration, with Gideon Hawley as the first state superintendent of schools. The leadership of governors George Clinton and DeWitt Clinton in particular made possible the early establishment of an educational system with provisions for teacher training and secondary schools.

Considerable effort was expended all over the young nation to create educational systems in the several states. Many conscientious persons saw the defects of the charity or pauper schools and were determined to do what they could to remedy conditions. Voluntary groups came into being, such as the Free (later the Public) School Society of New York City, which offered free educational opportunities from 1805 until its merger with the city's board of education in 1852. Typical of similar societies all over the country outside New York was the Society for the Promotion of Public Schools of Philadelphia, which was founded in 1827.

Funds for education were sometimes raised by means of lotteries, which fell into disfavor with changes in moral attitudes; permanent school funds derived from license fees, direct state appropriations, fines, sales of public lands, and other sources of revenue; rate bills (tuition fees) in accordance with the number of children of the family attending school; and local taxes, such as required by the Massachusetts law of 1827. The struggle for free public schools in the first half of the 19th century involved the abolition of the rate bill and the enactment of state laws for a free school system. In this campaign for free and universal education a number of educational statesmen played a decisive role—notably Horace Mann and James Gordon Carter of Massachusetts, Henry Barnard of Connecticut, John D. Pierce of Michigan, and Calvin H. Wiley of North Carolina. To their efforts must be added those of workers' organizations, the clergy, and the press. The combined campaign in behalf of a democratic school system was won over substantial obstacles, such as objections based on fear of governmental power, opposition of property owners to school taxes, indifference of many public figures, and competition for pupils with long-established private schools.

Teaching procedures in the early national era consisted largely of memorization, repetition, and individual recitation, the textbook being the principal source of pupils' knowledge. Important new textbooks, many of them compiled with the purpose of fostering patriotism in pupils, were written by Noah Webster, Jedediah Morse, and Samuel G. Goodrich (Peter Parley). Later, textbooks were prepared in accordance with the pedagogical principles of Johann Heinrich Pestalozzi, the Swiss educational reformer whose ideas on the adaptation of instruction to interests and needs of pupils were brought to America by leading American educators in the 19th century; among the writers of these were Warren Colburn (arithmetic), William C. Woodbridge (geography), and Lowell Mason (music). The subjects included in the new elementary curriculum were grammar, spelling, geography, drawing, physiology, and history. Moral training was promoted, often in a religious context—so much so that Catholics, Jews, and various Protestant minorities found themselves forced to open their own schools to escape sectarian instruction in the public schools. Overall, the American elementary school in the early decades of the 19th century granted more freedom to the child than previously given, reduced or abolished corporal punishment, broadened the concept of education, and began to take into consideration the abilities and interests of the individual child. This generalization did not apply, of course, to the district school; to the infant school, which was transplanted from England after 1810; or to the Lancastrian (or monitorial) schools, likewise of English origin, in which one teacher instructed hundreds of young children under the supervision of pupil teachers or monitors.

In secondary education the Latin grammar school of colonial times gave ground to the English grammar school, to the academy, and finally to the high school. Such schools as the Phillips Andover Academy and the Phillips Exeter Academy, founded in 1778 and 1781, respectively, exist to this day, although with altered aims. The academy was characterized by a curriculum of many subjects, including astronomy, geology, and other theoretical and practical sciences; various foreign languages; philosophy, art, and music; rhetoric and oratory; and English language and literature. The high school—a term borrowed from Edinburgh, Scotland—was first introduced into Boston in 1821 as the English classical school, renamed the English high school in 1824. A high school for girls was opened in 1826, also in Boston. In 1827 the Massachusetts legislature recognized the value of the new type of school by passing a law under which each town or district having 500 families was required to maintain a tax-supported school offering American history, geometry, bookkeeping, and other subjects; and every town having a population of 4,000 was obliged to teach Latin, Greek, and general history as well. By the end of the century the high school had become established as an integral part of the public school system.

The American college, recovering from the adverse effects of the Revolution, inaugurated a broader curriculum in response to social demands. The natural and physical sciences, modern foreign languages, law, and the social sciences made their appearance at a number of colleges, including Harvard and William and Mary. Studies for the profession of medicine were promoted as well. An effort was made for a while to discourage American youth from studying abroad, but it failed; and Americans flocked all through the 19th century to foreign universities, especially in Germany.

A number of significant changes took place in the administration and control of higher education. Gradually the religious influence was replaced by the secular. Professional schools were opened for the training of engineers, physicians, clergymen, and lawyers. The Dartmouth College decision handed down by the U.S. Supreme Court in 1819 prevented state control of a chartered private college. The ultimate impact of this important decision was such that, on the one hand, private and denominational schools were founded in large numbers, and, on the other, state legislatures established their own colleges and universities. Although the state university had had its beginnings toward the end of the 18th century, it did not develop to any great extent until the mid-19th century.

One of the major arguments in American higher education was beginning to emerge before 1830. The influence of Jefferson at the University of Virginia and that of George Ticknor at Harvard led to experimentation with allowing students to choose to some extent their courses. The elective system, which later entered higher education on a large scale, was favored in principle in the Amherst College faculty report of 1826, but it was repudiated by the Yale College faculty report of 1828, which upheld the traditional classical curriculum.

Teacher training received an impetus before 1830 through the publication of several treatises on pedagogy, such as Joseph Neef's "Sketch of a Plan and Method of Education" (1808) and Samuel Read Hall's "Lectures on School-Keeping" (1829); the opening of private teachers' seminaries by Hall in 1823 and by James Gordon Carter in 1826; and the publication of teachers' journals—*The Academician* (1818–20) and William Russell's *American Journal of Education* (1826–31). The press and the pulpit also joined in the clamor for better teachers, in line with the widely quoted maxim "As is the teacher, so is the school."

Educational Development Until 1900

The growth of the nation in population, territory, and wealth was not accomplished without educational pains. Among the factors leading to educational progress were the demands of labor groups for a public school system; the reports by American educators of school methods and progress in Europe; the pressures exerted by governmental, cultural, and educational leaders; and humanitarian efforts to aid the poor, the immigrant, and the handicapped.

Through the efforts of James Carter and Horace Mann, Massachusetts set up a state board of education in 1837; under the direction of Mann as secretary, it extended school facilities, increased teachers' salaries, instituted supervision and in-service training of teachers, and introduced other reforms. In 1852, Massachusetts pioneered nationally in enacting legislation to make school attendance compulsory. Significantly, Mann's crusading zeal in promoting educational change and giving public expression to his satisfaction with European practices he had observed resulted in a controversy with the educators of Boston. His insistence that no religion should be taught in the public schools but that the Bible should be read without comment in the class also involved him in controversy. In spite of such criticism Mann became recognized as the most influential American educator of the century and one whose ideas affected education in such far-off countries as Argentina and Uruguay.

Another highly effective educator was Henry Barnard, who did for Connecticut and Rhode Island what Mann did for Massachusetts. Barnard edited a new

American Journal of Education (1855–82) and served as the first U.S. commissioner of education (1867–70). Virtually every state had an educational leader of comparable, if not identical, stature.

Elementary education underwent changes during the second half of the 19th century. The kindergarten, based on the ideas of the German educator Friedrich Froebel, was first established on American soil in 1856 by Mrs. Carl Schurz, as a German-speaking school in Watertown, Wis. A private English-language kindergarten was opened in 1860 by Elizabeth Palmer Peabody in Boston, and the first public school kindergarten was set up in 1873 by Susan Blow in Saint Louis, Mo., under the supervision of the prominent educator and philosopher William Torrey Harris.

The Pestalozzian ideas were revived, but in a more formal teaching method through close examination of objects, by Supt. Edward A. Sheldon of the Oswego, N.Y., schools after he had observed an exhibit in 1859 in a museum in Toronto. Toward the end of the century the theory and the practice of Johann Friedrich Herbart were introduced, especially in connection with the teaching of social studies and character. Also contributing to character training were the widely used readers of William Holmes McGuffey. New ideas stressing a curriculum and a methodology based on child growth, development, and interest were first put into operation by Francis Wayland Parker in Quincy, Mass., and later in Chicago. The elementary school founded by John Dewey at the University of Chicago (1896–1904) experimented with these ideas and served as a model for the progressive school education that has dominated much of elementary education in the 20th century. The testing movement, which was to become a significant educational force, began in the 1890's. And the entire curriculum of the elementary school came under scrutiny in the *Report of the Committee of Fifteen on Elementary Education*, prepared in 1895 under the chairmanship of William H. Maxwell for the National Education Association (NEA).

The high school grew in prestige throughout the 19th century, taking the place of the academy as the favored form of secondary education. It received legal recognition in 1874, insofar as support by public taxes was concerned, by the Kalamazoo Case decision (1874) in the Michigan Supreme Court. Thereafter, it became the typically American school of the people—free, public, universal, comprehensive in curriculum, and both academic and vocational. Problems of secondary education were reviewed in two significant reports: one in 1893 by the NEA Committee of Ten on Secondary School Studies, with President Charles William Eliot of Harvard as chairman; and the other in 1899 by the Committee on College Entrance Requirements. As the high school became increasingly popular among the American people it became evident that it had developed into what some educators called "the American road to culture."

Higher education in the 19th century showed several new tendencies: emergence of new subjects, such as agriculture, sociology, anthropology, and education; secularization of colleges and universities, in part under the influence of Darwinian ideas; a steady increase in the number of private and public institutions of higher learning; and greater emphasis given to creative scholarship, following the example of the German universities. The subject of science received considerable emphasis during the century, first in the theoretical courses offered by the established colleges and then in the applied science and engineering courses taught at the U.S. Military Academy at West Point, N.Y. (1802), the Rensselaer Polytechnic Institute at Troy, N.Y. (1824), the U.S. Naval Academy at Annapolis, Md. (1845), the Sheffield Scientific School at Yale and the Lawrence Scientific School at Harvard (both 1847), and the Chandler School at Dartmouth (1851).

The passing of the first Morrill Act by Congress in 1862 made land grants available to the states for the establishment of colleges in which "agriculture and the mechanic arts" would be taught. The act made a special point of including military science and "other scientific and classical studies" and of stating that the aim of these colleges was "to promote the liberal and practical education of the industrial classes in the several pursuits and professions in life." This law, as well as the Morrill Act of 1890, brought about an expansion of state universities in the Middle West and Far West, especially in agriculture and engineering education.

Women's higher education was provided in parts of the country before the Civil War on a private, denominational basis. The earliest graduates were given the degree of *Domina Scientiarum.* High academic standards were characteristic of Elmira Female College (date of first instruction, 1855) and of Vassar Female College (1865), both in New York State. Coeducation began with Oberlin Collegiate Institute (1833) and Antioch College (1853), both in Ohio, and at the state universities of Utah (1850), Iowa (1855), and Washington (1861). Other important developments in the century were the granting of the earned Ph.D. degree in 1861 by Yale, the introduction of the elective system at Harvard by President Charles Eliot in 1869, and the founding of the Johns Hopkins University in 1876 as the first graduate school in the United States.

Teacher education was characterized by the raising of standards of training in the normal schools and the admission of educational psychology, history of education, and other courses in education into the university curriculum. With the appearance of textbooks in education, periodicals, and teachers' organizations, it was evident that education was on the way toward becoming a profession.

Professional education flourished with the opening of the Massachusetts Institute of Technology (incorporating charter, 1861), the establishment of the American Medical Association (1847) and the Association of American Medical Colleges (1890), and the founding of the Association of American Law Schools (1900). Adult education was promoted by the lyceum, a lecture movement organized in 1821 by Josiah Holbrook, and the Chautauqua forum movement, inaugurated in 1874 by John H. Vincent.

Religious education was given in parochial schools by Episcopalians, Presbyterians, Lutherans, Catholics, and Jews. The Roman Catholic Bishops' Third Plenary Council in Baltimore (1884) decreed that all Catholic parents must send their children to the parochial schools to be erected in every parish. All through the century there was a debate concerning the role of religion in public education and the question of providing public funds for religious schools.

For Afro-Americans opportunities for education were limited, although indeed some colleges were opened for them before the Civil War. After the Civil War, from the establishment of the Freedmen's Bureau in 1865, schooling of all kinds—most of it racially segregated—was made available to blacks. The legal precedent for segregated schools, "separate but equal" education, was set by the decision of the U.S. Supreme Court in 1896 in the case of *Plessy* v. *Ferguson*, and the pattern of Afro-American education, all over the South and in several states in the North, was determined for the next six decades.

The 20th Century

The elementary school grew at a rapid pace after 1900, with the expansion of the population. One of the problems that had to be faced until about 1920 was the continually increasing enrollment of new pupils of immigrant parents. The kindergarten became more accepted and was instituted in many public school systems across the country. The nursery school was introduced about 1920 for children who were less than four years of age, and preschool education was later supported by the federal government, especially during the depression years and World War II, to free mothers to work. In the late 1920's and early 1930's, the activity plan, which gave elementary school children a more flexible learning program, came into vogue. In time very few elementary schools made use of formal class teaching procedures in fixed seats. Curriculum changes in the 1950's involved an emphasis on science and the inclusion of foreign languages.

Tests of intelligence and achievement and diagnosis and prognosis came to be frequently used in elementary education. The doctrines and practices of John Dewey, Edward Lee Thorndike, and William H. Kilpatrick exerted a deep influence on teachers, parents, and school administrators. The parent-teacher association, which was promoted by the progressive educators who followed the lead of Dewey and Kilpatrick, became an outstanding feature of the American elementary school in the 20th century. The impact of the federal government on elementary education was, of necessity, indirect—for example, through the National School Lunch Act of 1946 and other temporary, supportive measures; the White House Conferences on Children and Youth in 1940, 1950, 1960, and 1970–71; and the White House Conferences on Education in 1955 and 1965. During the century the Supreme Court handed down a number of influential decisions concerning education: declaring invalid a Nebraska law against teaching foreign languages in private elementary schools (1923); upholding the constitutionality of religious and other private schools (1925); allowing states to furnish bus transportation for pupils in parochial schools (1947); permitting released time for religious instruction, but only outside the public school (1948, 1952); requiring public schools to discontinue the segregation of black pupils (1954, 1955); ordering immediate desegregation of public schools (1969); supporting the constitutionality of pupil busing to bring about desegregation (1962); upholding the ban on public school prayers (1962) and Bible reading in public schools (1963); and upholding the supplying of free secular textbooks to parochial school students (1968) and the prohibiting of public financial aid to parochial school teachers (1971).

The junior high school first appeared in Berkeley, Calif., about 1910. Many large cities reorganized their secondary education in terms of the new type of school. In the 1960's, the middle school appeared, a four- or three-year school following grade five or six. The secondary school curriculum was the subject of many investigations—particularly by NEA (1918), American Mathematical Association (1923), American Classical League (1924), Modern Language Association (1929), and Progressive Education Association (1941). In addition, the federal government sponsored the National Survey of Secondary Education (1933) and the Commission on Life Adjustment Education for Youth (1949). The Regents' Inquiry into the Character and Cost of Public Education in New York State (1938) received widespread attention. During the 1950's and 1960's, reforms were instituted in curriculum structure, content, and methodology of many secondary school subjects.

The report by NEA in 1918 set down the Seven Cardinal Principles of Secondary Education, which have exerted an influence on the curriculum of the American high school: health, vocation, command of fundamental processes, worthy home membership, worthy use of leisure, citizenship, and ethical character. Vocational education was promoted by the Smith-Hughes Act passed by Congress in 1917, the Vocational Education Act of 1963, and the federal campaign for career education beginning in 1970. In the 1950's secondary education applied the principle of tying two or more courses together in the "core curriculum." The report on the American high school in 1959 by James B. Conant, former president of Harvard University, made some specific recommendations toward improvement but essentially endorsed the system of secondary education in the United States. Conant's report in 1960 on the junior high school stressed learning of academic subject matter. Since the 1950's the leading issues in secondary education have been the position of academic studies vis-à-vis the vocational or life adjustment program, provisions for the talented student, and the enrichment of programs for students not preparing for college.

In 1900 the Association of American Universities was formed to promote high standards among the institutions of higher education. The public junior college movement had its start in 1902 at Joliet, Ill. The junior college attained considerable popularity, especially in Texas and California, and in the period after World War II it began to multiply under the name of community college. The number of such institutions rose from 521 in 1960 to 891 in 1970, while enrollment increased 261 percent.

The early 20th-century college curriculum was diversified and practical, so much so that professors, administrators, and other critics of the contemporary college began to express their opinions in journals and in numerous books. Among these proponents of the liberal arts and the scholarly status of higher education were Albert Jay Nock, Irving Babbitt, Norman Foerster, and Robert Maynard Hutchins. Perhaps the most widely read critique of undergraduate and graduate instruction was Abraham Flexner's *Universities: American, English, German* (1930). One of the most devastating attacks on the American college was the report on *American College Athletics*, issued in 1929 by the Carnegie Foundation for the Advancement of Teaching. Adverse criticism and the reevaluation of curriculums by college officials led to the founding of experimental colleges and teaching programs, as well as to the spread of the general education movement, with its emphasis on the liberal arts.

Among the other significant developments in 20th-century higher education have been the Harvard University faculty report *General Education in a Free Society* (1945); the report of the President's Commission on Higher Education (1949); the founding of the Southern Regional Education Program (1949); the establishment of the State University of New York (1949), a pioneer in statewide higher education; the report by the President's Committee on Education Beyond High School (1958); and the numerous reports published by the Carnegie Commission on Higher Education in the 1970's. Another development of outstanding importance was that of federal government activity in higher education. The government aided higher education through the GI Bill of Rights for the veterans of World War II (1943, 1944), the Korean War (1952), and the Vietnam War (1966); the Fulbright (1946), the Smith-Mundt (1948), and the Fulbright-Hays (1961) acts for the exchange of students, faculty, and research workers with foreign countries; the National Defense Education Act of 1958, which promoted the teaching of sciences, modern foreign languages, and mathematics and other aspects of education in the colleges and universities; the Higher Education Act of 1965, which aided teacher education and library services; and the Education Professions Development Act of 1967.

In the field of teacher education, the normal schools of the 19th and the early 20th century became teachers colleges that granted degrees, and in the period after World War II many of them were transformed into state colleges with liberal arts programs added to professional teacher training. Teachers College at Columbia University, the University of Chicago, the George Peabody College for Teachers, and New York University were among the most influential. During 1958–60 professors of academic subjects and professors of education made a national effort to arrive at a common policy on the education and certification of teachers.

The standards of medical education were raised suddenly and sharply with the publication in 1910 of a report by Flexner for the Carnegie Foundation for the Advancement of Teaching. The other professions also concerned themselves with the modification of curriculum and the upgrading of standards. The fields of law, engineering, journalism, and business administration were particularly active in providing an adequate general education as a basis for professional study.

From the 1920's on, adult education flourished through Americanization programs for immigrants, through the "Great Books" discussion programs, and the activities of organized bodies, such as the Adult Education Association of the U.S.A., the Fund for Adult Education, and the American Library Association. Universities, public schools, churches, labor unions, governmental agencies, various voluntary organizations, and the mass media of communications offered different programs of study, recreation, and aesthetic enjoyment to adults. The Adult Education Act of 1966 was a move by Congress to improve educational opportunities for mature citizens.

The education of Afro-Americans, which had been encouraged by the philanthropy of George Peabody (1867) and John F. Slater (1882), was further benefited by funds set up in the names of John D. Rockefeller in 1903, Anna T. Jeanes in 1905, Phelps-Stokes in 1909, and Julius Rosenwald in 1911. Although opportunities increased for Afro-Americans at all levels of public and private education, the South and part of the North continue to practice racial segregation in education. Of principal importance for the racial integration of higher education were the U.S. Supreme Court decisions in the cases of Gaines (1938), Sipuel (1948), Sweatt (1950), and McLaurin (1950). The case of *Alston* v. *Norfolk School Board*, decided by a federal circuit court of appeals in 1940, was the precedent for the practice of paying equal salaries to white and to black teachers in the public schools. But the most fundamental civil rights events in education were the U.S. Supreme Court decisions of 1954 and 1955, which declared segregation in public schools contrary to the doctrine of equality as guaranteed by the Constitution and ordered desegregation to be carried out "with all deliberate speed." Although public schools were integrated in several southern and northern states as a result of these decisions, resistance in Alabama, Tennessee, Arkansas, and Louisiana slowed down the process. In 1960 only 6 percent of the Afro-American pupil population attended classes with white children; full segregation on all levels of education was still maintained in 1960 in Alabama, Georgia, Mississippi, and South Carolina. However, during the 1960's, developments in race relations and human rights changed the entire situation rapidly. Racial integration of the public schools and various actions to equalize the educational opportunities of Afro-Americans were accelerated by the Civil Rights Act of 1964, which provided for the withholding of federal funds from public school districts in which racial segregation was practiced. State and federal court decisions, including those by the U.S. Supreme Court in 1970 and 1971, required speedier desegregation and confirmed the constitutionality of crosstown conveyance of children by buses to achieve integration in public schools. During the early 1970's the campaign in behalf of racial equality in education was fully under way on both the *de jure* and *de facto* fronts, in the South and in the North.

Trends and Problems

According to an estimate by the U.S. Office of Education, the statistics of public and private school enrollment for 1972–73 were as follows: 35.9 million in elementary education, from kindergarten through the eighth grade; 15.5 million in secondary education, grades nine through twelve; and 9 million in institutions of higher education. The grand total of 60.4 million students in the fifty states and in the District of Columbia constituted a record figure in the history of American education. On the other hand, the elementary enrollment declined for three years in a row (1970–72), primarily because of the lower birthrate of the 1960's. During 1971–72 a record number of 144,708 students from a large number of foreign countries were enrolled in colleges and universities all over the country.

The problems, issues, and controversies that face American education are manifold. Outstanding among these have been how much, relatively, to emphasize general, as opposed to professional or vocational, subjects in the curriculum; the procurement of an adequate number of qualified teachers, scientists, and engineers, and, later, a surplus; the selection and education of the gifted child and adolescent; the low salaries and frequently unsatisfactory teaching conditions in schools and colleges; the continuing shortage of funds for school facilities and new school buildings; and the effect on education of the persistent growth of juvenile delinquency and crime.

The specific concerns of the 1960's and early 1970's included variations of these problems, plus certain "innovations." Educational administration and policy brought forth the concepts of differentiated staffing, performance contracting, accountability, and national assessment of educational improvement. The civil rights movement helped to effect community control by decentralization; equalization of school finance to eliminate the gap between affluent and poor school districts; equalization of opportunity of racial-ethnic (Afro-American, Puerto Rican, Mexican-American, and American Indian) and economically disadvantaged groups; and crosstown and intercounty school busing to achieve racial-ethnic integration. Flexible or modular scheduling, mini-courses, and schools without walls were introduced, as well as demands for the "deschooling" of society. The numerical decline of the Catholic parochial schools occurred during this period, as did the assertion of power by students, parents, and teachers through violence and strikes, and the withering away of standards of dress, grooming, behavior, and speech. Other important developments were the unionization of teachers and professors; the enthusiasm for systems analysis; the growth of the three- to four-year middle school; the introduction of preschool projects (Head Start, Follow Through, Sesame Street) on the basis of the researches of European and American psychologist-educators; and the importation of the English infant school with the aid of Ford Foundation financing.

In the area of curriculum and instruction, developments included innovation and change in various subjects (mathematics, the sciences), the Right to Read Program of the federal government, the growth on a wide scale of new courses and programs (black studies, ethnic studies, sex education, women's studies, environmental or ecological studies, drug abuse education, career education), and the growing attention to special education (the physically, mentally, and emotionally handicapped). The use of microteaching and team teaching aroused much interest, as did the application of behavioral objectives to the teaching process. Among the newer approaches involving the teacher were performance-based teacher education, teacher centers, utilization of teacher aides, and the TTT (Training of Teachers of Teachers) program for the in-service improvement of professors of education and academic professors. In higher education the innovations included the open-admissions plan for the disadvantaged, the proliferation of free universities and counteruniversities, the importing of the open university from England, the formation of "universities without walls," the recognition of the external degree in New York State and elsewhere, and the adoption of the new degrees of master of philosophy and the doctor of arts as consolation prizes in lieu of the Ph.D. degree.

BIBLIOGRAPHY

William W. Brickman, *Educational Systems in the United States.*

John S. Brubacher and Willis Rudy, *Higher Education in Transition: A History of American Colleges and Universities, 1636–1968.*

Daniel Calhoun, ed., *The Educating of Americans: A Documentary History.*

Lawrence A. Cremin, *American Education: The Colonial Experience, 1607–1783.*

Merle Curti, *The Social Ideas of American Educators.*

Newton Edwards and Herman G. Richey, *The School in the American Social Order.*

Edgar Fuller and Jim B. Pearson, eds., *Education in the States.*

Robert J. Havighurst, ed., *Leaders in American Education.*

Richard Hofstadter and Wilson Smith, eds., *American Higher Education: A Documentary History.*

I. L. Kandel, *American Education in the Twentieth Century.*

Clarence J. Karier, *Man, Society, and Education: A History of American Educational Ideas.*

Edgar W. Knight, *Fifty Years of American Education,* and *A Documentary History of Education in the South Before 1860.*

Edward A. Krug, *The Shaping of the American High School.*

Robert E. Potter, *The Stream of American Education.*

S. Alexander Rippa, ed., *Educational Ideas in America: A Documentary History.*

Frederick Rudolph, ed., *Essays on Education in the Early Republic.*

Rush Welter, ed., *American Writings on Popular Education: The Nineteenth Century.*

— WILLIAM W. BRICKMAN

EDUCATION IN THE 1970S, 1980S, AND 1990S

Since the earliest home-based efforts of the colonial period Americans have sought to develop a system that gave most citizens a basic education. By World War II public schools were open to all, from first grade through high school, although many were segregated; most school systems also included a kindergarten. As education became compulsory across the nation, most districts mandated schooling from ages six to sixteen. The *Brown* v. *Board of Education of Topeka* decision in 1954 declared segregation in public schools contrary to the Constitution and ordered desegregation to be carried out "with all deliberate speed." The Civil Rights Act of 1964 allowed the withholding of federal funds from school districts practicing racial segregation. The federal government enlarged its role in education in the 1960s and 1970s with compensatory programs, notably Head Start, designed to prepare disadvantaged preschoolers. Educational opportunities for handicapped children sought to end discrimination based on mental and physical disabilities. In addition, the American quest for egalitarianism and the growing number of state-subsidized and financial aid programs fostered the notion of universal access to college or university education.

Although public and private education flourished after World War II, many observers raised concerns about quality. The launching by the Soviet Union of *Sputnik 1*, the first artificial satellite, in 1957, provoked the fear that American education was deteriorating, especially in mathematics and science; a flurry of efforts to improve school curricula followed. In the 1960s and 1970s critics began describing curricula as old-fashioned and unresponsive, and students demanded curriculum reform, along with civil rights and an end to the Vietnam War. In 1975 the College Board disclosed that the average score on the Scholastic Aptitude Test (SAT, now renamed the Scholastic Achievement Test), used for admissions by institutions of higher education, had been declining for the previous eleven years. Businesses complained about the difficulty of finding competent workers and the need to set up remedial programs in the workplace. In 1979 the federal government acknowledged the significance of education by separating education from the Department of Health, Education, and Welfare and establishing the cabinet-level Department of Education. Despite President Ronald Reagan's election pledge in 1980 to dismantle the new department, it remained in existence but came under attack after the Republican victory in the 1994 midterm elections.

In April 1983 the National Commission of Excellence in Education presented a report on the condition of the education system, *A Nation at Risk: The Imperative for Educational Reform,* claiming that the average graduate of public schools and of colleges and universities was not as well educated as graduates of twenty-five to thirty-five years earlier. Dozens of similarly negative reports on education emerged, notably "High School: A Report on Secondary Education in America" (Carnegie Foundation for the Advancement of Teaching) and "Making the Grade" (Twentieth Century Fund). They asserted the need to stress basics, to provide more intensive education, and for better-trained teachers. "Excellence" became the watchword.

Defining excellence and the role of the school both for the individual and the community were central to the debate that ensued and continued into the mid-1990s, although agreement on the most appropriate schooling for a democratic society proved difficult. Describing public schools as a nineteenth-century factory-type institution, many educators called for a recognition that changes in society and population required realignment of schools. Other educators pointed to the short school day and a plethora of subjects in the curriculum other than basics, such as sex and drug education. Comparisons were made to education in other countries, notably Japan, where students spend 8 hours a day in school for 240 days versus 6.5 hours and 180 days in the United States.

In the 1980s "back to basics" characterized educational reform. The National Commission on Excellence urged higher requirements for all in what they termed the five new basics—four years of English, three of mathematics, three of science, three of social studies, and a half-year of computer science. They insisted that the curriculum in the eight grades leading to high school should provide a sound foundation for study in those basics. Conservative educators argued that a proper education would offer few electives and focus on academic subjects, art and music, Socratic discussion, and Western literature. Others maintained that curricula must meet the needs of children from different backgrounds. Although both groups concurred on a common curriculum for elementary school children, liberals believed that the high school curriculum should satisfy different interests and talents.

Defining "excellence" and the role of the school were central to a debate on educational quality that continued well into the 1990s.

The quest for excellence resulted in reform in several areas. Between 1980 and 1990 forty-five states set higher standards for graduation, through achievement tests, academic course requirements, and performance expectations for promotion. Competency tests for new teachers (most commonly the National Teachers' Examination) became a requirement in forty-four states, in contrast to ten states in 1980. Teacher training programs, long criticized for their emphasis on pedagogy over academic content, attempted improvement by elevating liberal arts requirements, increasing efforts to attract better teacher candidates, and creating alternative pathways to teacher certification. Rising levels of teacher pay became an incentive for prospective educators. The average teacher's salary doubled in the 1980s, with the real rate of increase 27 percent. Merit pay for teachers, based on student achievement, was introduced over the objection of teachers' unions, which cited the difficulty of determining fair assessment standards and the potential for destroying collegiality.

Curriculum revision became the most contentious area for reform. During the 1960s and 1970s a laissez-faire attitude prevailed, exemplified by A. S. Neill's Summerhill, where students learned what they wanted, when they wanted, if they wanted. Student choice of subjects and diminished adult authority, particularly in high school, became increasingly common. High school curricula were driven by a philosophy of consumerism resulting in electives; student preferences based on "relevance" replaced intrinsic value as the guiding principle. Enrollments in science, mathematics, and foreign languages dropped. Concurrently, colleges lowered requirements for admission.

Along with excellence, equity became a theme of the 1980s; both the federal government and educators increased the emphasis on children with special needs. The Education for All Handicapped Children Act of 1975 mandated education for handicapped children and promoted mainstreaming rather than special programs. The Bilingual Education Act of 1968, designed as a transitional program to help low-income children learn English, grew into a program to offer all children instruction in their native languages and cultures as well as English. The Supreme Court unanimously affirmed in *Lau* v. *Nichols* (1974) that federally funded schools must "rectify the language deficiencies in order to open instruction to students who had 'linguistic deficiencies.'" Amendments to the act greatly increased the number of possible participants, and the number of language groups receiving bilingual education grew from 23 in 1974 to 145 by 1990.

The equity movement created debate over the practice of tracking, the assignment of pupils to courses and programs on the basis of ability or career plans. Opponents of tracking said it was biased toward minority groups by disproportionate placement of blacks and Hispanics in lower, that is, vocational and general rather than academic, groups, leading to lower expectations and performance. In the 1990s, however, there was a resurgence of vocational programs on high school campuses.

Money played an important role in educational reform. Inequity in funding resulting from appropriations based primarily on local property taxes prompted lawsuits in which children and school districts sued states for more money and fairer financing. Census data for 1986–1987 showed that the ten richest school districts spent three times as much per elementary pupil as the ten poorest and twice as much at the high school level. Since 1989 five state supreme courts have ruled that their school systems cannot violate the equal opportunity provisions of state constitutions. The advent of computers and telecommunications, and the concomitant cost of equipment for educating students in these technologies, added to the disparity of opportunity in rich and poor school districts.

Enrollment in private elementary and secondary schools (including church-related and nondenominational schools) grew from 7,350,000 in 1975 to 8,206,000 in 1990, a period during which the public school population declined by 1.5 million students. Parents concerned about disciplinary problems, violence, and large class sizes opted for private schools; racial tensions and busing, especially in larger cities, contributed to this increase. President Reagan favored tuition tax credits for private school tuition. In *Mueller* v. *Allen* (1983) the Supreme Court upheld a Minnesota law that provided tax deductions for educational expenses.

Businesses became more involved in schools as they found it difficult to relocate people in communities with poor schools. The National Center for Education Statistics reported more than 140,000 partnerships with industry and private foundations; more than 40 percent of the nation's elementary and high schools participated in at least one cooperative program. Corporate donations to precollege education totaled approximately $200 million in 1987. Industrialist Eugene M. Lang's I Have A Dream Foundation offered college scholarships to students at a New York inner-city high school, inspiring other philanthropists to aid at-risk students. Universities formed alliances with schools to improve education, notably the contract between Boston University and the school system of Chelsea, Mass. Since the late 1980s business entrepreneurs with plans to operate schools-for-profit at no greater cost to taxpayers have been hired by various cities, including Baltimore, Milwaukee, and Miami. Several states permit the establishment of charter schools.

The role of schools was constantly challenged and expanded in the last quarter of the twentieth century but the result was mixed. By 1994 SAT math scores had risen, since reaching a nadir in 1980–1981. Verbal scores remained problematic because of a decline in composition and grammar courses. Black and Hispanic students scored below Orthodox Jewish, Asian American, and. Caucasian students. There was a narrowing of score differences between college-bound males and females. Attempts were made to establish comprehensive schools, with before- and after-school programs for children and parents. More than thirty states offered prekindergarten classes. About 15 percent of the nation's 15,000-plus school districts either provided some form of child care or allowed community groups to use their buildings for that purpose. The growing demand for higher education among all socioeconomic and ethnic groups fostered open-admission programs and expansion of two-year community colleges. Colleges offered remedial courses for freshmen. By the mid-l990s government officials, teachers, and parents, however, debated multiculturalism in the curriculum, grade inflation, violence in the schools, accountability, school prayer, and the role of standardized testing. At the college level, charges of political correctness, increasing racial divisiveness, and self-segregation also caused concern.

BIBLIOGRAPHY

Ernest L. Boyer, *College: The Undergraduate Experience in America* (New York, 1987).

Chester E. Finn, Jr., *Our Schools and Our Future* (New York, 1991).

Beatrice and Ronald Gross, eds., *The Great School Debate* (New York, 1985).

Myron Lieberman, *Public Education, An Autopsy* (Cambridge, Mass., 1993), and *Privatization and Educational Choice* (New York, 1989).

Robert Emmet Long, ed., *American Education* (New York, 1984).

— MYRNA W. MERRON

EDWARDSEAN THEOLOGY

Edwardsean Theology, the evangelical philosophy of Jonathan Edwards, preacher of the Great Awakening—a religious revival in the 1730's. Edwards, in his fiery sermons, preached that he had absolute divine authority to confer salvation and damnation. To his contemporaries a conventional though brilliant Calvinist, Edwards appeared to later generations a radical theologian who had endeavored to bring contemporary thought (primarily British) and Christian orthodoxy to terms in his posthumous writings on metaphysics and ethics. For the rest, he interpreted Christian theology within the framework of the Westminster Confession. Obscurities in the latter's chapter on "Assurance" prompted Edwards to an empirical study of varieties of religious experience (*The Nature of the Religious Affections*) for which the Great Awakening supplied ample case material. He had already helped initiate the revival by his solution to the Calvinistic dilemma of divine sovereignty and human initiative. The principles set forth in sermons at that time (1735), directed against the passivism that is the nemesis of Calvinism, later found full-fledged expression in his most famous dissertation, *Freedom of the Will.*

— A C. MCGIFFERT, JR.

Jonathan Edwards (1703-1758), a Congregational clergyman, is considered the greatest theologian of American Puritanism. (Library of Congress/Corbis)

EIGHTEENTH AMENDMENT

Eighteenth Amendment, also known as the Prohibition Amendment (1919–33). This amendment to the Constitution prohibited the manufacture, sale, transportation, import, or export of intoxicating liquors for beverage purposes and authorized Congress and the several states to enforce this prohibition by appropriate legislation.

The Anti-Saloon League, founded in 1893, launched its campaign for national prohibition in November 1913. A joint resolution of Congress failed to get the necessary two-thirds vote in the House on Dec. 22, 1914. Three years later both houses of Congress voted to submit the proposed amendment to the states. Neither major political party cared to sponsor the movement, and it remained strictly nonpartisan. Nebraska, the thirty-sixth state to ratify, acted on Jan. 13, 1919, making the amendment effective; nine others soon followed, leaving only Connecticut, New Jersey, and Rhode Island as nonratifiers. In the meantime, Prohibition had been voted as a war measure for the duration of World War I. On Oct. 27, 1919, the Volstead Act was passed to enforce the Eighteenth Amendment.

Cessation of the normal channels of supply of alcoholic beverages created thousands of bootleggers and gave rise to numerous speakeasies. The National Commission on Law Observance and Enforcement, also known as the Wickersham Commission on Prohibition, filed a five-volume report with the U.S. Senate in 1931. This document stated that in 1929 Prohibition agents had seized 15,730 distilleries, 11,416 stills, 7,982 still worms, and 1,140,063 gallons of spirits. Demand for grapes to be used for private winemaking was four times as great in 1925 as in 1917. The volume of production of hops, a universal ingredient of beer, indicated consumption of illegal beer at possibly 543 million gallons in 1927. In 1930 the federal director of Prohibition made public an estimate that in the year ending June 30, 1930, 118,476,200 gallons of wine, 684,476,800 gallons of beer, and 73,386,718 gallons of spirits were manufactured.

In the first ten years of enforcement effort, 71 officers and 181 civilians were killed. By 1933 the federal courts had received 595,104 criminal cases under the Volstead Act; for the fiscal year 1932–33 the federal budget allotted $11,369,500 for enforcement.

By 1932 public sentiment in support of the amendment was definitely waning. Juries were refusing to convict and states were withdrawing their support. Both the American Legion and the American Federation of Labor demanded repeal. The Republican platform demanded return to state option; the Democratic platform favored repeal. A better than two-thirds vote in Congress started a repealing amendment to the states

The Eighteenth Amendment (1919–33) prohibited the manufacture, sale, transportation, import, or export of intoxicating liquors.

in February 1933, providing for the first time in American history that ratification should be by special convention rather than legislative action. On Dec. 5, 1933, the Eighteenth Amendment was repealed.

[See also Bootlegging; Twenty-first Amendment.]

BIBLIOGRAPHY

Herbert Asbury, *Great Illusion: Prohibition.*
E H. Cherington, *Evolution of Prohibition.*
John A. Krout, *The Origins of Prohibition.*
James H. Timberlake, *Prohibition and the Progressive Movement.*

— ROBERT G. RAYMER

EISENHOWER DOCTRINE

In an address to Congress, Jan. 5, 1957, President Dwight D. Eisenhower declared that the United States would use its military and economic power to protect the Middle East against the danger of Communist aggression. The doctrine was designed to reassure Western allies that the United States regarded the Middle East as vital to its security. At the president's insistence the doctrine took the form of a congressional resolution, which was signed into law on Mar. 9.

— JACOB E. COOKE

ELECTION OF THE PRESIDENT

Election of the President of the United States, perhaps the most dramatic, regular political event in the world, derives directly from the structure of the U.S. Constitution and from the nature of the two-party system the Constitution helped create.

After prolonged discussion of various proposals, the drafters of the Constitution provided that the president would be chosen by electors, especially selected for that purpose in such manner as the legislature of each state should prescribe. Each state was to be entitled to "a number of electors equal to the whole number of Senators and Representatives to which the State may be entitled in the Congress." (In 1962 the Twenty-third Amendment added three electoral votes for the District of Columbia.) Each elector was to cast two votes; the candidate who received the largest number was to become president and the runner-up was to become vice-president, provided the largest number of votes constituted a majority. Should no candidate receive a majority, selection was to fall to the House of Representatives, where each state would be entitled to one vote.

The framers assumed that the electors would be men of high station and independent judgment and that they would exercise their choices accordingly. For that reason some leaders—and James Madison in particular—thought the electors would normally cast their votes for so many different persons that the required electoral majority would be rare, thus forcing the election ordinarily into the House of Representatives.

The early development of a two-party system in the United States produced notable changes in the projections of the framers of the Constitution. In the election of 1800 each Democratic-Republican elector cast his two votes for the two candidates of his party, creating a tie for the presidency between Thomas Jefferson and Aaron Burr, a result not foreseen by the party organizers. Consequently the Twelfth Amendment was passed in 1804, requiring electors to vote once for president and once for vice-president. In still another way the development of the party system has invalidated the expectations of at least some of the framers of the Constitution, by virtually guaranteeing one presidential candidate a majority of the electoral vote; since its maturation after 1824 the House of Representatives has never had to elect a president. Finally, the two-party system has democratized the presidential selection process, again contrary to the plans of the Founding Fathers.

During the first decades of the Republic the state legislatures selected the electors. By 1828 the present practice of selecting electors by popular, partisan vote was nearly universal, and since that time the voting of the electoral college has been regarded as simply an official recording of "the people's choice." The presidential candidates still campaign, technically, for the election of their electors, because all states now provide that the electors shall be chosen by the people at the general election.

All the electoral votes of each state go to the candidate receiving the most votes in the state. This winner-take-all practice allows the designation of a president who has received fewer popular votes than his opponent, and the electoral college has twice elected such presidents: Rutherford B. Hayes in 1876 and Benjamin

Harrison in 1888. To avoid such results in the future a variety of constitutional amendments has been proposed, ranging from direct election of the president to modifications in the operation of the electoral college.

Political parties occupy major roles in presidential elections. Nominations for president and vice-president are made at national conventions whose delegates have been selected through party primaries, by state party conventions, or by state party central committees. The national committees of each party—buttressed by independent, nonparty campaign committees—raise campaign funds, develop organizations to influence the voter, and assist in research and public relations.

BIBLIOGRAPHY

Nelson Polsby and Aaron Wildavsky, *Presidential Elections.*

— ARTHUR L. PETERSON

ELECTIONS

An election is an act of individuals duly qualified to vote who indicate individually and select collectively their choices among candidates for office—or, occasionally, indicate that they elect to remove an officeholder from office. Often public votes upon referenda are improperly referred to as elections; proposed constitutional amendments, new state constitutions, city charters and amendments, and certain laws passed by legislatures do not involve selection of candidates for office.

The presence or absence of free choice from among a number of candidates for public office by the general population is the principal factor that distinguishes democracies from dictatorships. In addition to being the principal vehicle for effecting a democratic system of government, free expression of individual will by citizens in elections acts as a safety valve, reducing the possibilities of insurrection and revolution, by providing a means to release tension and frustration.

The four major purposes of elections are (1) to obtain a sounding of the main opinions existing within the public; (2) to ensure majority rule; (3) to elect leaders and representatives; and (4) to reinforce the stability of the organization or government. The three types of elections are primary, general, and recall. A primary election precedes a general, or final, election; its purpose is the nominating of candidates for office. The purpose of a general election is to make a final selection among candidates, who may have been chosen in a primary or nominated by some other system. A recall is an election providing for removal of an elected official, usually requiring a substantial number of signatures before it can be held.

The U.S. Constitution requires a congressional election every two years to elect all 435 members of the House of Representatives for two-year terms and one-third of the members of the Senate for six-year terms. Every four years a president must be elected. Each state constitution contains provisions for what officers are to be elected, the requirement of the secret ballot, times of elections, and qualifications of voters. Other election details are left to statutory law.

Only duly qualified voters may vote in an election. Voting is still considered a privilege, given to the electorate by the government, and not a right. The Fifteenth and Nineteenth amendments to the Constitution prohibit exclusion of people from voting because of "race, color, or previous condition of servitude" and because of sex. The equal protection clause of the Fourteenth Amendment is further protection against exclusion. Except for federal elections, the states have jurisdiction over the qualifications required of each citizen to vote. The doctrine of exclusion and inclusion is specifically detailed in the election laws of each state.

In early American history, such voting requirements as social status and ownership of land existed. Today, freehold and other economic qualifications have disappeared; in 1962, the last vestige, the poll tax, was outlawed by the Twenty-fourth Amendment, for national elections. The "one man, one vote" doctrine laid down by the Supreme Court in *Baker* v. *Carr* (1962) continues to receive widespread support, and current practice in reapportionment and redistricting according to that principle is evidence of a changing concern for giving every individual an equal say and for proportional representation.

The states do not have uniform voting requirements, but the types of qualifications are similar, such as (1) U.S. citizenship; (2) a minimum period of residency in the state; (3) age (eighteen years); (4) requirement to register before given deadlines.

To prevent fraud, registration of voters is mandatory. This requires a personal appearance and the filling out of forms. In some areas periodic registration is necessary, calling for a repetition of the process before each election. Permanent registration requires that the voter appear only once if he remains in a voting district or continues to vote there. Various registration plans are now before Congress to make the process of registration and voting simpler and thus allow as many people as possible to vote. In practice, however, of registered voters, only approximately 65 percent or less vote in presidential elections, and less than 50 percent vote in local general elections.

Elections, by definition, produce opposing groups, allied because of a common allegiance to a particular person or to certain policies or political philosophies—and these soon organize themselves into political parties. Antecedents of the Republican and Democratic parties formed in George Washington's cabinet. Although having no constitutional basis, political parties perform a vital role in the functioning of American government. They help organize the citizens and consolidate the expression of their views along philosophical, economic, and other lines. Party organizations, formed at national, state, and local levels, perform several major functions in the election process: (1) assist in the selection and nomination of candidates for various offices; (2) create or highlight issues meaningful to the electorate; (3) help administer the conduct of elections; (4) develop cohesiveness within the party to win elections; (5) provide ideological outlets for the electorate; (6) perform campaign activities for candidates, such as fund raising, speaking, arranging schedules, and carrying out publicity and public relations programs; (7) serve as an auxiliary to the government in promoting programs, issues, and ideas.

There is not a month in the year when some kind of election is not being held in the U.S.

On election day, the polls are held in each precinct or neighborhood and are kept open for voting from early morning until early evening. Usually, two judges of election representing the two major parties, one inspector, and several clerks are required to administer the election in each precinct. The clerks check the voter's name against the registration list to be sure he or she is eligible to vote. The voter is given a blank ballot, goes to a booth, votes, and deposits the ballot in the ballot box; or he casts his vote through a voting machine.

Absentee voting is allowed both for civilians and for military personnel. It accounts for at least 2 percent of the total vote—and in presidential elections can amount to several million votes. Although varying in particulars, the absentee voting procedure is essentially the same in all states: the absent qualified voter must apply for an absentee ballot within a prescribed period preceding the election; a ballot, with a return envelope, is sent to the voter by an election official; and, after a notary public or other official signs the ballot envelope, the voted ballot is returned to the official with an affidavit that the voter has complied with the election laws.

After the polls close, the clerks and judges count the votes, put the poll book and tally sheets in the ballot box, seal it, and return it to the city or county clerk, board of election, or canvassing board. The secretary of state is responsible for collection of all state and national returns in his state and issues certificates of election to the winners, permitting them to assume office at a designated time.

There is not a month in the year when some kind of election is not being held in the United States. However, most state and county elections are held in the fall of even-numbered years at the same time as presidential and congressional elections. Most township, school district, and municipal elections are held in the spring of odd-numbered years. But there is no universal rule about the time for holding state and local elections. Federal general elections are held at a definite time set by law, which is the first Tuesday after the first Monday in November of even-numbered years. Usually state and county elections are held at the same time to save administrative costs and to gain the benefit of a larger voter turnout.

The cost of elections is borne by both the government and the private sector. The government role lies in paying for the administration of elections and keeping election records. Money spent by the private sector—individuals and special-interest groups and organizations of various sorts—amounts to hundreds of millions of dollars each year. The cost of the presidential campaign is fast approaching $100 million; in the 1970's an average Senate campaign cost $500,000; and the cost of a congressional campaign ranged between $75,000 and $300,000.

While election laws, improved administration, and increased use of voting machines have reduced election fraud almost to zero, the most serious threat to honesty and fairness in elections is in the area of financing campaigns. Despite passage by Congress of the 1972 campaign financing law, which limits amounts that can be spent on certain methods of campaigning, as in the mass media, there is still no ceiling on the total amount that can be spent. The implications of giving money to candidates for the purpose of gaining control and influence over government are still being studied.

BIBLIOGRAPHY

V. O. Key, Jr., *Politics, Parties, and Pressure Groups.*

— RONALD F. STINNETT

ELECTORAL COLLEGE

The concept of the electoral college emerged at the Constitutional Convention as a compromise among diverse plans for selecting the chief executive, ranging from election by direct vote of the people to selection by the national legislature. The plan adopted provided instead for indirect election, selection of the president and vice-president by electors from each state. Each state was to be entitled to the same number of electors as it had senators and representatives in Congress.

Originally the electors were selected by state legislatures. But with the development of a party system, which was firmly established by the late 1820's, voters were asked to choose among slates of electors put forth by the parties and generally pledged to particular candidates. Although at first some electors were selected by districts (usually congressional districts), a statewide system of electors has generally prevailed since the 1830's.

Under the present system, voters designate their presidential choice by voting for a slate of electors pledged by law or custom to a party's candidates for president and vice-president. Under the prevailing winner-take-all principle the party ticket receiving the most popular votes in a state receives all the electoral votes of that state. The winning slate of electors of each state convenes in its state capital in December, and the electors cast their votes. In a sense, a series of electoral colleges exists, not a single electoral college. In early January the electoral votes, having been delivered to the president of the Senate, are counted before a joint session of Congress. The Constitution requires that the votes be cast separately for president and vice-president (Twelfth Amendment), and each must receive an absolute majority (in 1976, 270 votes) for election. If such a majority does not exist, which is likely if there are more than two candidates, there is provision for a contingency election of the president by the House of Representatives, where the members choose among the three candidates having the greatest number of votes. Each state delegation has only one vote. If a contingency election is required for the office of vice-president, it is carried out by the Senate, each member having one vote.

In most instances the electoral college simply ratifies the results of the popular vote. It has failed, however, in three instances to select a president (1800, 1824, 1876). In the first two instances, the decision was made in the House because no candidate had the necessary electoral majority. In 1876, Congress established an electoral commission to rule on disputed sets of electoral returns from several states. In a number of other cases the shift of relatively few popular votes in several states having large blocs of votes would have thrown the election into Congress (1916, 1948, 1960, 1968). In two cases the candidate selected in the electoral college had fewer popular votes than his opponent (1876, 1888), producing a "minority president"; in a number of other elections the shift of a few votes in several states would have produced others.

The institution of the electoral college has been subject to continual criticism, and numerous proposals for change have been put forward. Critics have attacked the actual results, the possibilities inherent in the process for mischief and breakdown, and its differential impact on groups and interests in the nation. For example, the electoral college, particularly under the winner-take-all tradition, enhances the power of large, urbanized, industrialized states—such as New York, California, and Illinois—and especially well-organized groups concentrated in such pivotal states. As a result, attempts to alter or reform the college involve questions of power and ideology. While there is general agreement on the need for change, it is difficult to achieve consensus on the exact form or type of change.

BIBLIOGRAPHY

Lawrence Longley, *Politics of Electoral College Reform.*
Neal Pierce, *The People's President.*

— DALE VINYARD

ELEVENTH AMENDMENT

After the decision of the Supreme Court in *Chisholm* v. *Georgia* (1793), a surge of states' rights sentiment developed throughout the country and in Congress. This resulted in the submission of the Eleventh Amendment on Mar. 5, 1794, proclaimed by the president, Jan. 8, 1798. Whereas the Court had held that a state could be sued by a citizen of another state in case of an alleged breach of contract, the amendment declared that "the judicial power of the United States shall not be construed to extend to any suit in law or equity, commenced or prosecuted against one of the United States by citizens of another state, or by citizens or subjects of any foreign state." In actual practice, the amendment does not have any great significance, for while a state may not be sued by an individual without its consent, all the states have given such consent, and have established conditions and procedures under which such suits may be brought. The amendment does not affect the jurisdiction of the Supreme Court in suits between states, nor does it prohibit a suit by an individual against the officers of a state to enjoin them from enforcing legislation alleged to be in violation of the federal Constitution.

BIBLIOGRAPHY

Charles K. Burdick, *The Law of the American Constitution.*
W. W. Willoughby, *Constitutional Law of the United States.*

— W. BROOKE GRAVES

ELLIS ISLAND

In 1890 the U.S. government assumed complete responsibility for screening immigrant arrivals at the Port of New York. The state of New York had acted as its local agent under congressional legislation of 1882. But the state's reception facilities on Manhattan Island (the Battery) were viewed as unsatisfactory by Congress, which selected Ellis Island as more suitable for handling massive numbers of immigrants. Owned by the federal government since 1808, this island one mile southwest of Manhattan received its first immigrants in 1892. The island's original three acres were ultimately extended by landfill, providing space for facilities in which to determine the admissibility of 5,000 or more persons daily. The island also housed any arrival who was detained. More than 16 million immigrants passed through Ellis Island, almost three-fourths of all immigrants to the United States having landed there.

Both World War I and restrictive immigration legislation in the 1920's reduced the importance of Ellis Island. Immigrant admissions fell drastically below the prewar level because of the restrictive quotas. Since the reduced numbers of immigrants could be processed on their vessels of entry, the island lost its importance as an inspection center in the 1930's. By World War II, the island handled only new arrivals being detained and aliens being deported. In 1954 its facilities were closed. Eleven years later the Statue of Liberty National Monument assumed control of Ellis Island.

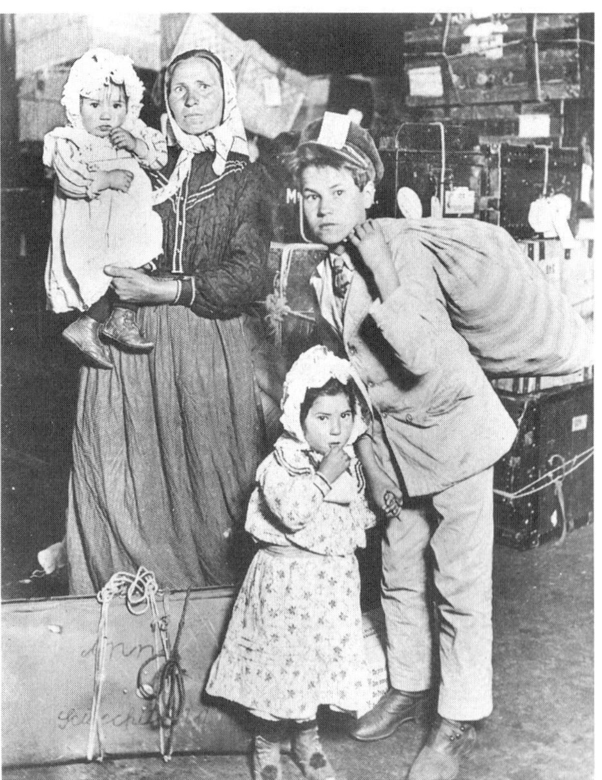

Italian mother with her three children after arrival on Ellis Island, New York. (Corbis-Bettman)

BIBLIOGRAPHY

Willard A. Heaps, *The Story of Ellis Island*

Thomas M. Pitkin, "High Tide at Ellis Island," *New-York Historical Society Quarterly* (1968).

— A. WILLIAM HOGLUND

EMANCIPATION PROCLAMATION

Emancipation Proclamation, Abraham Lincoln's grant of freedom on Jan. 1, 1863, to slaves in states then in rebellion. In conformity with the preliminary proclamation of Sept. 22, 1862, it declared that all persons held as slaves within the insurgent states—with the exception of Tennessee, southern Louisiana, and parts of Virginia, then within Union lines—"are and henceforth shall be, free." The proclamation was a war measure based on the president's prerogatives as commander in chief in times of armed rebellion. Admonishing the freedmen to abstain from violence, it invited them to join the armed forces of the United States and pledged the government to uphold their new status. Unlike the preliminary proclamation, it contained no references to colonization of the freed slaves "on this continent or elsewhere."

Enshrined in American folklore as the central fact of Lincoln's administration, the actual proclamation was a prosaic document. On the day it was issued, it ended slavery legally and effectively only in limited areas, chiefly along the coast of South Carolina. Eventually, as Union forces captured more and more southern territory, it automatically extended freedom to the slaves in the newly conquered regions. Moreover, the mere fact of its promulgation ensured the death of slavery in the event of a northern victory. The Emancipation Proclamation may thus be regarded as a milestone on the road to final freedom as expressed in the Thirteenth Amendment, declared in force on Dec. 18, 1865.

Although Lincoln had always detested the institution of slavery, during the first year of the war he repeatedly emphasized that the purpose of the conflict was the maintenance of the Union rather than the emancipation of the slaves. Fully conscious of the necessity to retain the support of both the border states and the northern Democrats, he wisely refrained from pressing the antislavery issue prematurely. Thus, he countermanded Gen. John C. Frémont's emancipation order in Missouri and Gen. David Hunter's proclamation in the Department of the South. But he signed confiscation bills, by which the private property of southerners was subject to forfeiture, as well as measures freeing the slaves in the District of Columbia and in the federal territories. In addition, he urged loyal slave states to accept proposals for compensated emancipation.

These piecemeal measures did not satisfy the radical Republicans. Tirelessly advocating a war for human freedom, they sought to induce the president to implement their program. As it was evident that a war for emancipation would make it difficult for foreign powers to recognize the slaveholding Confederacy, Lincoln was confronted with the task of not alienating the border states and their allies while at the same time satisfying his radical Republican supporters and reaping the diplomatic rewards of an antislavery policy. The peculiar wording of the Emancipation Proclamation was his answer to this problem.

The Emancipation Proclamation of 1863 declared that all persons held as slaves within the insurgent states "are and henceforth shall be, free."

The president wrote the first draft of the preliminary proclamation during June 1862 in the telegraph office of the War Department. On July 13, 1862, while riding in a carriage to attend the funeral of one of the secretary of war's children, he revealed his purpose to Secretary of State William H. Seward and Secretary of the Navy Gideon Welles. Nine days later he read the document to the cabinet but, upon Seward's advice, postponed its publication. To promulgate the proclamation so shortly after Gen. George B. McClellan's early summer failure before Richmond would have been impolitic. It is also possible that Salmon P. Chase, secretary of the treasury, desiring piecemeal emancipation, caused Lincoln to wait a bit longer.

During the following weeks various groups sought to influence Lincoln to adopt an emancipation policy; even though he had already decided to comply with their request, he refused to commit himself and remained silent about the document then in preparation. Even in his celebrated reply to Horace Greeley's Prayer of Twenty Millions (Aug. 22, 1862), he emphasized that his paramount object in the war was to save the Union, not to destroy slavery. Although he conceded that his personal wish had always been that all men everywhere could be free, it was not until after the Battle of Antietam (Sept. 17, 1862) that he believed the time had come for the proclamation. Informing his cabinet that his mind was made up, he accepted a few minor alterations and published the document on Sept. 22, promising freedom to all persons held as slaves in territories still in rebellion within the period of 100 days.

The reaction to the preliminary proclamation was varied. Denounced in the South as the work of a veritable fiend, in the North it was generally acclaimed by radicals and moderates. Conservatives and Democrats condemned it, while all blacks enthusiastically hailed it as a herald of freedom.

During the 100 days' interval between the two proclamations some observers questioned Lincoln's firmness of purpose. Republican reversals in the election of 1862, the president's proposal in December for gradual compensated emancipation, and the revolutionary nature of the scheme led many to believe that he might yet reconsider. But in spite of the conservatives' entreaties, Lincoln remained steadfast. After entertaining some editorial suggestions from his cabinet, especially Chase's concluding sentence invoking the blessings of Almighty God, in the afternoon of Jan. 1, 1863, he issued the proclamation.

The appearance of the Emancipation Proclamation clearly indicated the changed nature of the Civil War. It was evident that the conflict was no longer merely a campaign for the restoration of the Union but also a crusade for the eradication of slavery. In the remaining period of his life, Lincoln never altered his fixed purpose. Having already said that he would rather die than retract the proclamation, he insisted on its inclusion in all plans of reunion and amnesty. His administration became ever more radical, and he actively furthered the adoption of the Thirteenth Amendment. It is therefore with considerable justice that he has been called the Great Emancipator.

The president's calculations proved correct. In spite of the cotton famine in Europe, following the issuance of the Emancipation Proclamation and increased evidence of federal military prowess, neither Great Britain nor any other power recognized the Confederacy; nor did any border states desert the Union. The document thus stands as a monument to Lincoln's sense of timing, his skill in maneuvering, and his ability to compromise. The freedom of some 4 million human beings and their descendants was the result.

BIBLIOGRAPHY

F. B. Carpenter, *The Inner Life of Abraham Lincoln: Six Months at the White House.*

Charles Eberstadt, *Lincoln's Emancipation Proclamation.*

John Hope Franklin, *The Emancipation Proclamation.*

Benjamin Quarles, *Lincoln and the Negro.*
Hans L. Trefousse, *Lincoln's Decision to Emancipate.*

— HANS L. TREFOUSSE

EMBARGO ACT

Embargo Act, a measure taken by Thomas Jefferson to deal with abuses to U.S. shipping by England and France. The act was a high point in the American quest for the formula of pacifism. Passed by Congress on Dec. 22, 1807, it was the practical application of a Jeffersonian principle that had been long maturing.

The underlying cause for an American embargo was a series of restrictions on U.S. commerce imposed by the European belligerents. In the early stages of the Napoleonic wars, the United States had grown wealthy as the chief of neutral carriers at a time when British shipping was dedicated to war purposes. This era of prosperity endured from about 1793 to 1805, to the great enrichment of New Englanders, and to some extent of merchants in the Middle States, and to the corresponding enlargement of the American merchant marine. Commercial restrictions then cut in on these profits, although in 1806 the blockade, which excluded Americans and other neutrals from the Seine to Ostend only, was relaxed somewhat. Subsequently, the Orders in Council of Jan. 7 and Nov. 11, 1807, and the Berlin and Milan decrees of Nov. 21, 1806, and Dec. 17, 1807, respectively, threatened direst penalties to any neutral venturing into a port of the enemy of either belligerent.

Americans, as leading carriers, had cause for grievance. There was the added goad of a distressing national humiliation—the *Chesapeake* incident of June 22, 1807, in which the British, searching for deserters, boarded an American ship and impressed into service four sailors on the plea that they were British. War would have been a logical reaction, but the United States was not prepared for war. Instead, Jefferson was determined to withhold the raw materials and finished products from the United States. The embargo aimed to secure a submission that could not be achieved by armed forces through economic pressure.

The embargo was effective to a degree. Exports experienced a 75 percent decline against a 50 percent decline in imports. New England suffered most from the embargo, but it found some compensation in the stimulus given to manufacturers. In the Middle States commercial losses were less extreme. The South suffered in its staples almost equally with New England in its commerce. But it hoped to share in the anticipated profits from growing manufactures. When the hope was not realized the South was disappointed, but it continued to support the embargo, leaving New England as the most articulate spokesman for the opposition.

Jefferson proved himself in the execution of this favorite project an administrator of uncommon energy. At the Treasury, moreover, where the brunt of administration naturally fell, he enjoyed the aid and brilliant counsel of Albert Gallatin. The embargo, like the Napoleonic decrees for that matter, provided certain loopholes that were taken advantage of, notoriously by Gov. James Sullivan of Massachusetts. There was much direct evasion, chiefly on the borders of Maine and Florida, but close study of the period reveals surprising efficiency in keeping the embargo.

Throughout 1808 it became increasingly apparent that the U.S. lacked the unity and energy to press the Embargo Act to its ultimate conclusion.

But the embargo did not last. Throughout 1808 it became increasingly apparent that America lacked the unity and energy to press the embargo to its ultimate conclusion. Opposition to the embargo grew steadily. Josiah Quincy and Timothy Pickering, both of Massachusetts, led the fight in Congress and John Randolph of Roanoke, Va., bored from within the Republican ranks to undermine party unity. Debate in Congress even led to a duel—George W. Campbell of Tennessee fought to vindicate the administration against Barent Gardenier of New York. John Adams, in retirement, lent moral support to the embargo.

During the closing months of his second term it became a point of honor with Jefferson for the embargo to survive his term of office. But the act was repealed three days before his term expired in March 1809. James Madison was left with the less stringent Non-Intercourse Act substituted by Congress.

BIBLIOGRAPHY

Louis Martin Sears, *Jefferson and the Embargo.*

— LOUIS MARTIN SEARS

EMINENT DOMAIN

Eminent domain is the inherent right of a sovereign power to take private property for public use without the owner's consent. The Fifth Amendment of the U.S. Constitution implicitly acknowledges this right of the national government by providing that private property shall not "be taken for public use, without just compensation." By Supreme Court interpretation of the due process clause of the Fourteenth Amendment, the same right and limitation have been attributed to state governments (*Chicago, Burlington Railroad* v. *Chicago*, 166 U.S. 226 [1897]).

The right of eminent domain is an ancient one, and the American colonies readily utilized the concept. A 1639 statute in Massachusetts allowed governmental acquisition of private property for the purpose of building roads, but it also provided for compensation to the deprived owners. Numerous early colonial statutes, along with English common law, carried the philosophy of eminent domain over into U.S. jurisprudence with such firm tradition and authority that the basic right has never been seriously challenged. However, the scope of eminent domain is still unsettled, and many authorities insist that the problems are, by their very nature, insoluble. Most of the historic conceptual debates focus upon one of two questions: (1) What amounts to a "taking," in which compensation to the owner is mandated by the Constitution? (2) What amounts to a "public use," in which the sovereign power may exercise its right to eminent domain?

A taking has been described as "any limitation on the free use and enjoyment of property," but this broad definition, taken alone, would encompass many ordinarily noncompensable government activities, such as zoning. Certain sovereign actions to protect public health, morals, safety, or even to "promote the general welfare" are performed within the government's inherent police power and, as such, are not takings within the eminent domain power. Courts are still left the task of determining what is a taking and what is a regulation within the exercise of the police power.

A sovereign may not take property except for a public use. Until recently courts held the narrow view that public use meant literally "use by the public": taken property could not be turned over to private owners, even if the public would be benefited thereby. The modern, broader view is that "public use" means "public advantage" or "public purpose" and permits takings even when the property is subsequently conveyed to new private owners (*Berman* v. *Parker*, 348 U.S. 26 [1954]). Also, courts now usually consider it a strong presumption that the taking has been for a public purpose if a legislature has so stated, even when the public purpose is aesthetic.

What is "just compensation" must be determined by an impartial body, not necessarily a court or a jury. Nor does the determination in the case of land have to be in advance of the taking. But the owner must have an opportunity to be heard on the question of value. In theory, just compensation requires the equivalent money value of the property taken; the measure is the owner's loss and not the government's gain. The basis of judgment is generally market value—what a willing buyer would pay in cash to a willing seller.

BIBLIOGRAPHY

Harold W. Chase and Craig R. Ducat, *Corwin's The Constitution and What It Means Today.*

Julius Sackman, *Nichols' The Law of Eminent Domain.*

Joseph L. Sax, "Takings and the Police Power," *Yale Law Journal*, vol. 74 (1964).

— HAROLD W. CHASE AND ERIC L. CHASE

ENGLISH SETTLEMENT

English Settlement, a colony for English artisans and laborers established by Morris Birkbeck and George Flower, and located in Edwards County, Ill. The location was selected in 1817; the first immigrants arrived the following year. Thereafter, for nearly thirty-five years, groups from England came periodically, enabling the settlement to retain its original homogeneity for half a century. Although the settlement was predominantly rural, two towns were established: Wanborough, which soon died, and Albion, a town that in 1970 had a population of 1,791. Because of the extensive literature it inspired, the English settlement attracted much attention to Illinois, and its members constituted a valuable intellectual leaven in the new state.

BIBLIOGRAPHY

George Flower, *History of the English Settlement in Edwards County, Illinois.*

— PAUL M. ANGLE

ENVIRONMENTAL MOVEMENT

The publication in 1962 of Rachel Carson's *Silent Spring* is one of the markers of the beginning of the environmental movement in the United States. The best-selling book sounded this tocsin to the world: "As man proceeds toward his announced goal of the conquest of nature, he has written a depressing record of destruction, directed not only against the earth he inhabits but against the life that shares it with him." Carson established beyond a doubt that chemicals in the air and water, especially DDT, were killing "birds, mammals, fishes, and indeed practically every form of wildlife." Out of the shock engendered by Carson's book grew a new sensibility about and a dedication to saving and protecting the environment. An older form of environmentalism, usually called conservationism, had existed for decades and was associated with John

Muir, Aldo Leopold, William O. Douglas, Howard Zahnister, and David Brower, among others, but the effort that emerged in the 1960s was the first concerted, populous, vocal, active, and influential movement, and several new organizations were established, such as the Environmental Defense Fund, the Natural Resources Defense Council, Environmental Action, Friends of the Earth, and the Clearwater Project. The decade ended with Earth Day 1970, an outpouring of environmental sentiment involving an estimated 20 million people that, according to its chief organizer, Senator Gaylord Nelson of Wisconsin, sent "a big message to the politicians—a message to tell them to wake up and do something."

In the 1970s pollution became a major concern for the American public. Congress passed three amendments to the Clean Air Act of 1970—the Water Quality Act, the Solid Waste Disposal Act, and the Wilderness Act—the last to keep 9 million acres of public land pristine. The most significant act, the National Environmental Protection Act of 1970, was given its impetus and power by public enthusiasm and created the Environmental Protection Agency. The EPA became the largest regulatory body ever established in the federal government. The act also created the environmental impact statement, which requires federal agencies to assess the environmental consequences of all projects and transformed the way the United States built, planned, moved, and thought.

The growing acceptance of the nation's environmental crisis—and of the human as an endangered species—became evident in the 1970s in an array of popular works with titles like *The Last Days of Mankind, The Death of Tomorrow, Terracide, The Doomsday Syndrome, This Endangered Planet,* and *The Limits to Growth.* There was widespread media coverage of such events as the North Sea oil blowout in 1977, the revelation in 1978 that the houses along Love Canal in Buffalo, N.Y., were built on contaminated soil, the accident at the Three Mile Island nuclear power plant in Pennsylvania in 1979, and the EPA disclosure in 1979 that 50,000 sites in the United States were dangerously toxic. Membership in environmental groups increased dramatically; the National Audubon Society (founded 1905) tripled its membership in the 1970s to 400,000, the National Wildlife Federation (1936) membership reached 818,000, and that of the Sierra Club (1892) rose to 165,000. New groups appeared everywhere: Greenpeace (1971), the Trust for Public Land (1972), the Cousteau Society (1973), Worldwatch Institute (1975), and Sea Shepherd (1977). Environmental organizations began to exercise their political influence in Washington, where many of them established their headquarters, moving with increasingly sophisticated tactics to get Congress to pass no fewer than eighteen far-ranging environmental laws, from the Pesticide Control Act of 1972 and the Endangered Species Act of 1973 to the Federal Land Policy Act of 1976 and the Ocean Dumping Act of 1977.

The election of Ronald Reagan as president in 1980 and the effect of the conservative agenda he supported temporarily checked the momentum of the environmental movement. The real strength of the movement became apparent when it resisted the administration and continued to operate effectively. The national environmental groups, most headquartered in Washington, expanded memberships and staffs; the National Wildlife Federation, the Sierra Club, and the Wilderness Society were sufficiently influential to earn designation by the *National Journal* as three of the most effective lobbying groups in Washington. At the same time, local grass-roots organizations mushroomed, and by 1987 there were an estimated 25 million environmental activists across the country. A Harris poll reported in 1985 that 80 percent of the U.S. public supported environmental laws and regulations.

A more radical strain of environmentalism developed in the 1980s, one that scorned the environmental lobbying organizations and was committed to direct action, sometimes even illegal action. Earth First!, established in 1980 by people frustrated with the failures and compromises of the mainstream groups, was the most prominent of these new groups, with seventy-five chapters and half a million members. The group engaged in demonstrations, guerilla theater, media stunts, and, most notorious, "ecotage," the sabotage of equipment used for clearcutting, roadbuilding, and dam construction. Other radical groups developed around such new ideas as bioregionalism, ecofeminism, and deep ecology (a philosophy espousing the equality and the right of all species to life and denouncing the anthropocentrism of most of the traditional environmental movement).

A more radical strain of environmentalism that developed in the 1980s scorned mainstream environmental lobbying efforts and concentrated instead on direct—and sometimes illegal—action.

By the 1990s the effect and importance of environmentalism was a fact of life in the United States. Congressional action included the passage of amendments to the Clean Water Act, first passed in 1960, Resource Conservation and Recovery Act of 1976, the Safe

Drinking Water Act of 1974, and the Coastal Zone Management Act of 1972 and appropriating enough funds to allow the EPA to implement all its regulations. On the electoral front, environmentalists selected and supported candidates at all levels; both the League of Conservation Voters, formed in 1980, and a variety of environmental political action committees disbursed funds, organized campaigns, canvassed membership lists, and advised candidates. The election in 1992 of Vice President Al Gore, an avowed and committed environmentalist, seemed to signal the effectiveness of this strategy.

By 1992, thirty years after it had begun, the environmental movement constituted the most powerful and successful social change movement since the nineteenth-century abolitionists. Membership in the largest national organizations was about 20 million (the largest, the National Wildlife Federation, had 5.6 million), and three-fourths of the American public described themselves as environmentalists. Spending on environmental causes was estimated at $2.5 billion in 1991, and the budgets of the leading organizations were $600 million. Earth Day 1990 was celebrated by an estimated 100 million people in 140 countries, including 25 million in the United States, with a fervor that led the *New York Times* to call environmentalism "a modern secular religion." An array of laws at the federal level ensured that environmental causes would remain embedded in national public policy, with the government's regulatory tasks estimated to cost society $125 billion each year. Despite this apparent success, however, the environment in the United States and around the world had not improved substantially and had declined in many areas. The WorldWatch Institute reported in 1993 that there was not a single life-support system on the planet that was not strained and threatened. In 1992 more than half the U.S. population lived in counties with polluted air. Five tons of carbon per person were poured into the air, more than 170,000 lakes and millions of acres of forests were acidified, 90 percent of the garbage went unrecycled, 95 percent of the worst toxic waste sites were untreated, topsoil was lost at a rate of 3 billion tons a year, and water was depleted and polluted annually at the rate of 10 billion gallons. The biosphere itself was an endangered species, and all the considerable efforts at saving it were failing.

[See also Conservation; Ecology; Environmental Protection Agency; Wildlife Preservation.]

BIBLIOGRAPHY

Peter Borrelli, *Crossroads* (Washington, D.C., 1988).

Stephen Dunlap, Riley E. Mertig, and Angela G. Mertig, *American Environmentalism: The U.S. Environmental Movement, 1970–1990* (Washington, D.C., 1992).

Stephen Fox, *John Muir and His Legacy: The American Conservation Movement* (Boston, 1981).

Samuel P. Hays, *Beauty, Health, and Permanence: Environmental Politics in the U.S., 1955–1985* (New York, 1987).

John McCormick, *Reclaiming Paradise: The Global Environmental Movement* (Bloomington, Ind., 1989).

Kirkpatrick Sale, *The Green Revolution: The American Environmental Movement 1962–1992* (New York, 1993).

— KIRKPATRICK SALE

ENVIRONMENTAL PROTECTION AGENCY

Environmental Protection Agency (EPA), federal agency established in 1970 that combined a number of earlier federal entities within the present Departments of Health and Human Services, then Health, Education, and Welfare; Agriculture; and Interior. President Richard M. Nixon announced plans to organize a viable process within the EPA to prevent or eliminate damage to the environment. In the glow from the 1970 Earth Day, leading environmentalists foresaw the possibility of genuine accomplishments. William D. Ruckelshaus became the initial administrator and labored diligently to organize this gigantic task with its diverse functions. He brought with him lawyers from the Department of Justice and reorganized EPA into areas of planning and management, standards and compliance, and research and monitoring.

EPA's task was awesome. Common objectives and goals were difficult to formulate within the agency. Congress and the White House were at cross-purposes, and the courts became a haven for delay and stalling by business and special-interest groups. From the beginning, it was impossible to weigh cost against the effects on humans. Only estimates are available. Nevertheless, by 1975, 70 percent of the air quality regions met federal standards, but utilities and steel mills, major polluters that accounted for 20 percent of all industry, failed to meet state directives. Pollution from new cars lagged behind the goal of 90 percent reduction in 1977, while fully 10 percent of water polluters did not use effective reduction equipment. Adding to its difficult burden, the EPA by 1977 had to meet congressional mandates to include economic factors in all studies and subsequent rules, a requisite later flaunted by opponents of strict rules as "jobs versus environment."

The chemical DDT was banned in 1972. Many uses of asbestos faced bans by 1993 and all others by 1997. PCBs (polychlorinated biphenyls) were banned or, in some types, phased out. When EPA lawyers in the 1970s went after industrial violators, however, they soon became enmeshed in a legal thicket, facing suits and complaints. Sometimes the Department of Justice annoyed the EPA with its slow and selective prosecutions. A battle ensued toward the end of President

Jimmy Carter's administration in 1980, with the EPA pitting the cost-effective standards against known environmental pollution. Fines were levied against violators. A rather hypocritical arrangement, known as the Superfund, appeared in 1980 legislation. Violators could purchase shares or permits enabling them to continue polluting and even to pass off polluting rights to other companies. The Superfund limited EPA controls over pollution.

Douglas M. Costle, Carter's head of EPA, was a former assistant director of the Congressional Budget Office. Environmentalists expected highly positive results as he used the impetus of the Love Canal case to seek stronger legislative curbs on hazardous dump sites, but they were disappointed by Costle's actions and Congress's efforts to do more. Meanwhile, the public was not properly educated about the limits of environmental protection. For example, zero discharge of pollutants is virtually impossible because some are produced unintentionally, as when fossil fuels are burned and waste is incinerated. DDT is still being found in lakes, probably carried in the atmosphere from Central America and South America. Annually, cows burp millions of tons of hydrocarbons into the air.

EPA and the White House generated controversies, largely beginning with the administration of President Ronald Reagan in 1981. He picked Anne Gorsuch Burford, a corporate lawyer and conservative state politician from Colorado, to head EPA. Burford attempted an internal reorganization that threatened the emphasis on enforcement and shifted more responsibilities to the states. The National Audubon Society vigorously opposed both moves, fearing weakened control. She hired business lawyers for EPA from many of the corporations under scrutiny as polluters. By early 1983 dozens of congressional Republicans had joined the Democrats in resolutions calling for her ouster. Despite high praise from Reagan, she resigned in March 1983. Ruckelshaus returned as head of EPA to restore its tarnished image, which he did by stepping up the agency's enforcement. When Ruckelshaus left again in 1985, Lee M. Thomas, assistant administrator, succeeded him. A career civil servant, he had been at the Federal Emergency Management Administration before coming to EPA. He had led the federal investigation of the dioxin contamination at Times Beach, Mo., during the winter of 1982–1983 and as EPA administrator did not hesitate to close contaminated oceanside beaches and tackle the growing problem of ozone depletion. Having raised the hopes of environmentalists, Thomas then disappointed them in 1986 by describing acid rain as a problem, not an emergency. He toyed with the idea of stronger rules as his term expired.

George Bush campaigned in 1988 as a supporter of strong environmental policies. His EPA administrator, William K. Reilly, appeared to espouse the environmentalist cause, insisting that economic growth is consistent with strong environmental protection, calling for cooperation and consensus, and expressing disappointment at the pace of toxic waste dump cleanups. White House and business pressure, however, led him to apply best available control technology in the case of a trash-burning incinerator emitting sulfur dioxide in Spokane, Wash., and to promote "market incentives" and continuation of the Superfund. EPA Region 10 advised the separation of trash before incineration, but Reilly denied the request, citing costs. Reilly initiated the asbestos bans and continued the wetlands project, promising no net loss in the acreage of swamps, bogs, and marshes to developers or farmers. A major disappointment involving EPA came with the Earth Summit of 1992 at Rio de Janeiro. Reilly was originally enthusiastic about the U.S. role, setting forth his views in an internal EPA memorandum. He chided the United States for not joining other nations in signing the treaty on species protection or to favor strict controls over emissions and pollutants identified with global warming. The White House, however, ordered Reilly to adopt the administration's views or leave. He remained.

President Reagan's first choice for EPA chief was a conservative corporate lawyer who attempted an internal reorganization that threatened the agency's emphasis on enforcement.

President Bill Clinton promised a vigorous approach to the environment as his new appointment, Carol M. Browner, took over the reigns at EPA in 1993. A former chief of the Florida Department of Environmental Regulation, she had also been legislative aide to Senator Al Gore and associate director of Citizen Action in the mid-1980s. She undertook vigorous reappraisal of EPA duties and policies. In her first year, tougher auto emission standards were proposed, new rules were issued for refrigerators and air conditioners regarding the use of freon, and unsafe levels of lead were investigated in numerous municipal water systems. Meanwhile, a battle raged over purer gasoline mixed with ethanol extracted from corn or the controversial methyl tertiary butyl ether (MTBE), supported by the oil industry but allegedly constituting a cancer agent. Du Pont reached a $4.25 million settlement with four growers over use of the pesticide Benlate, a fungicide supposedly causing crop damage.

An accurate assessment of EPA's first twenty-five years is difficult. Some environmentalists call the record a complete failure, claiming that despite its huge costs, changing the methods of technology is the only effective means of lasting protection. They cite redesigning automotive engines, turning to new ways of crop fertilization, reformulating (breaking down or rendering harmless) military explosives and radioactive wastes, and revamping the electric power industry as some of the things that must be done. They observe that EPA controls begin only after the pollutants have contaminated the environment and that the agency has not taken the lead in prevention. Conversely, conservatives claim that nearly all of EPA's efforts are useless, that science cannot prove the adverse effects of dioxin, radon, PCBs, DDT, asbestos, acid rain, or global warming. The picture regarding EPA effectiveness is mixed. Certainly, politics played too much of a role in EPA, with business winning too many times, but the EPA has exacted numerous heavy fines against violators and identified many polluters. The degradation of Lake Erie has been slowed, and both Canada and the United States are working to improve the entire Great Lakes region. In addition, the air is cleaner but much else remained undone.

[See also Conservation; Environmental Movement; Global Warming.]

BIBLIOGRAPHY

Barry Commoner, *Making Peace with the Planet* (New York, 1990).

Marc K. Landy, Marc J. Roberts, and Stephen R. Thomas, *The Environmental Protection Agency: Asking the Wrong Questions* (New York, 1990).

Dixy Ray Lee and Lou Guzzo, *Trashing the Planet* (Washington, D.C., 1990).

Alfred A. Marcus, "Environmental Protection Agency," in *Government Agencies*, edited by Donald R. Whitnah (Westport, Conn., 1983).

— DONALD R. WHITNAH

EQUAL RIGHTS AMENDMENT

First proposed as an addition to the U.S. Constitution in 1923, the Equal Rights Amendment (ERA) stated that "equality of rights under the law shall not be denied or abridged by the United States or by any state on account of sex." Supporters argued that the Constitution must include the principle of equality of rights for women and that such an amendment would remove sex-based discrimination. Opponents of women's rights objected, as did some women's rights advocates who feared it would jeopardize recent legislation providing female industrial workers minimum protection against exploitative working conditions. The Supreme Court had upheld protective legislation for women in *Muller v. Oregon* (1908) but not for men, claiming the need to protect citizens able to bear children. Convinced that Congress would not extend protection to men and that the Court would therefore deny it to women if the amendment passed, organized labor opposed the ERA. It remained in the House Judiciary Committee for forty-seven years despite efforts to secure passage.

Legislators opposed to the ERA argued that the amendment would mean an intrusion of federal power that would diminish their ability to govern and the right of individuals to live as they choose.

The 1960s brought renewed attention to the amendment. Hopes had faded that the Supreme Court would use the equal protection clause of the Fourteenth Amendment to subject laws that discriminated on the basis of sex to the same strict scrutiny applied to laws discriminating on the basis of race. When protective legislation was revealed to have harmed the very group it was intended to protect, liberal feminists had an additional reason for urging passage of the ERA. After massive lobbying Congress in March 1972 voted overwhelmingly to submit the Twenty-seventh Amendment to the states. Twenty-two states rushed to ratify; by 1975, however, momentum had slowed. Even after the original period for ratification was extended to 1982 supporters could secure favorable votes from only thirty-five of the thirty-eight states needed for passage. Five states meanwhile rescinded their endorsements. In December 1981 a federal judge ruled that those rescissions were legal and that Congress had acted illegally in extending the ratification deadline. Before ERA supporters could appeal the ruling to the Supreme Court the deadline for ratification, July 30, 1982, expired, leaving opponents of the amendment victorious.

Opposition in the 1970s and 1980s differed in important ways from that encountered in previous decades. Conservative legislators in mostly southern and western states voted against the amendment. They believed it would mean an intrusion of federal power that would diminish their ability to govern as well as the right of individuals to live as they chose. Such politicians could vote their apprehensions and still claim to be responsive to the wishes of female constituents who opposed the amendment. Another factor was the skill with which far-right activists transformed popular perceptions of the amendment. By equating ERA and feminism, especially radical feminism, and making it appear dangerous to women, opponents succeeded in eroding the national consensus for the amendment. Although some states passed equal rights amendments to their own constitutions in the 1970s, efforts to secure congressional passage of a new federal amendment failed.

[See also Women's Movement.]

BIBLIOGRAPHY

Susan D. Becker, *Origins of the Equal Rights Amendment* (Westport, Conn., 1981)

Sharon Whitney, *The Equal Rights Amendments* (New York, 1984).

— JANE SHERRON DE HART

ERIE CANAL

After the Revolution the rapid settlement of upstate New York intensified the demand for an artificial waterway to the Great Lakes through the Mohawk Gateway. The New York legislature in 1808 authorized a survey and in 1810 set up a canal commission that selected Lake Erie for the western terminus. DeWitt Clinton, canal commissioner and later governor (1817–22, 1824–28), proposed the undertaking and was responsible for its execution. His speeches and memorial of 1815, giving details as to route, costs, and benefits, prodded the legislature in 1817 to authorize construction.

Untrained but able men such as Benjamin Wright overcame construction problems by developing new mortar, by inventing machines to cut roots and uproot stumps, and by building aqueducts such as one across the Genesee River. The 4-foot-deep ditch was 363 miles long, with eighty-three locks lifting boats a total of over 600 feet; it cost over $7 million. Farmers did most of the work, but they were reinforced by Irish laborers in difficult places. By 1823 boats from Albany could reach Rochester or Lake Champlain over the Champlain Canal. Two years later Clinton led a procession of canal boats from Buffalo to New York City.

The success of the Erie Canal in cutting transportation charges, raising land values, stimulating the growth of cities, and capturing for New York City most of the western trade led to a canal "mania." The legislature constructed branches in Oswego, Chenango, Genesee Valley, Black River, Cayuga, and Seneca. During the 1850's railroads began to capture freight; by the 1870's canal tonnage had fallen substantially. The abolition of tolls in 1882 did not check the Erie's decline.

The Erie Canal became part of the New York State Barge Canal system, which was built between 1909 and 1918. It is the most important link in the barge canal, extending from Lake Erie near Tonawanda, N.Y., to the Hudson River near Waterford, N.Y. This branch is 340 miles long, 150 feet wide, and 12 feet deep, and contains thirty-four locks. Although the railroads have taken over much of the freight, the canal, especially during World War II, has relieved railroads of many of their bulky loads.

BIBLIOGRAPHY

David M. Ellis, *A Short History of New York State*, and "Rivalry Between the New York Central and the Erie Canal," *New York History*, vol. 29.

Nathan Miller, "Private Enterprise in Inland Navigation: The Mohawk Route Prior to the Erie Canal," *New York History*, vol. 31.

— DAVID M. ELLIS

ESKIMO

The Eskimo (or Inuit) were the first native Americans to be contacted by Europeans. Groups of Eskimo had spread gradually across the American Arctic from a western source and reached Greenland a century or so

An Eskimo mother and child photographed in Alaska in 1903. (The Granger Collection, New York)

before the first Norse discoveries. Gunnbjörn Ulfsson, it is thought, reached Greenland by A.D. 875, while a century later, in 982 or 983, Eric the Red opened the five-century contact between Scandinavia and Greenland-Labrador. Sagas describe the "Skraelings," apparently Eskimo with whom the Vikings came into uneasy contact from time to time. The Norse abandoned their Greenland colonies by the mid-15th century. Later, stimulated by the successful exploitation of Arctic regions by the Russians in their expansion into Siberia, the Danes returned to Greenland and began in 1721, with the missionary Hans Egede, processes of modernization that carry on to the present, imposing European education and developing natural resources and industries.

Although the Russians claimed all of Alaska, their contacts with native peoples, both Eskimo and Aleut, were limited to the southwest and the Aleutian archipelago. The Eskimo of north Alaska, both of the tundra interior and of the coasts north and east of the Bering Straits, did not have iron tools until the 1820's or 1830's, at which time such tools, along with tobacco, began to be traded by Eskimo and Indian middlemen northward from Russian colonies. Meanwhile, the central Eskimo, those from the mouth of the Mackenzie River to Hudson Bay and including the island populations to the north, remained generally out of contact with Europeans until late in the 19th century.

The Eskimo are one of the most widely distributed peoples of the world. The territory they inhabit runs from southeastern Alaska around the Arctic coasts to Angmassalik in eastern Greenland. They are found at various points from fifty-eight to eighty-two degrees north latitude. Yet a mode of life based on hunting has tended to limit population growth. At no point does the Eskimo population appear to have exceeded 60,000, excluding perhaps 16,000 Aleut, a linguistically related people. The numbers of most groups declined sharply after contact with Europeans; 20th-century public health measures have overcome the earlier susceptibility to introduced diseases, and the Eskimo population appears to be increasing.

The Eskimo are the one people in the world whose physical type, language, and basic culture are common to the entire population. The uniqueness of the Eskimo as against other native Americans is manifested in certain genetic traits, such as an increased body surface as an adaptation to cold; the presence of the language phylum, Eskaleut, appearing nowhere else in the world; and a mode of subsistence and social organization based on the hunting of sea and land mammals.

As an Arctic people the Eskimo are remarkable in their environmental adaptation. To effect this, they have made use of every hunting resource available to them. Whaling, for example, was practiced in north Alaska, the groups there feeling no trepidation at pursuing in fragile skin-covered boats the world's largest mammal. Where no other game was available, the ubiquitous seal served as the economic mainstay. Some Eskimo, especially those to the west of Hudson Bay, pushed inland to make capital of the caribou. In line with the demands of the environment the Eskimo were highly inventive, much drawn to the material side of their culture. The central Eskimo—not the Alaskan or Greenland groups—invented the domed ice lodge, the iglu, used both for quasi-permanent residence and for temporary shelter on the hunt. The harpoon with detachable shaft, the saucerlike stone lamp, tailored clothing, special footgear, boats, sleds and sledges, dog traction, and the use of driftwood are all elements in the complex technology and material culture of the Eskimo. Yet the stress on the material tended to limit the growth of their society. There might be hunt leaders, but no chiefs. Even the community lacked corporate reality because the stress on lines of kinship was primary. The picture that emerges of Eskimo life is one based on familial networks. The result was that tribes as such were lacking among the Eskimo.

Eskimo life was based primarily on familial networks; as a result, tribes as such were lacking among the Eskimo.

In the course of their contact with Europeans, whether in Greenland, Alaska, or northern Canada, the Eskimo have generally adjusted well. This is especially true of their acceptance of items of technology from the outside, such as guns, outboard motors, and, especially, the snowmobile. A problem faced by any administrative unit concerned with the Eskimo is that of drawing them into a cash economy. While some groups, especially in Canada, are able to retain their hunting patterns, others, especially in Alaska, are drawn into European-American organizational patterns. The presence in Alaska of considerable petroleum deposits on the north slope will unquestionably have a continuing and changing effect.

BIBLIOGRAPHY

Kaj Birket-Smith, *The Eskimos.*

E. W. Weyer, *The Eskimos: Their Environment and Folkways.*

— ROBERT F. SPENCER

ESPIONAGE ACT

Espionage Act (June 15, 1917) authorized severe punishments, in time of peace or war, for any person transmitting, communicating, or delivering information, or attempting to do so, regarding the national defense; or for interfering with the national forces in any way. Material urging insurrection, treason, or forcible resistance to U.S. laws was declared to be nonmailable. Provisions were also included to punish attempted interference with shipping, passport frauds, counterfeiting of the government seal, and violations of American neutrality.

On May 16, 1918, important amendments, generally referred to as the Sedition Act, were added by Congress. Chief of the new provisions was the one that provided heavy punishment for anyone who should, during a period of war, "utter, print, write, or publish any disloyal, profane, scurrilous, or abusive language" about the flag, the armed forces or their uniforms, the Constitution, or the form of the government of the United States.

BIBLIOGRAPHY

Zechariah Chafee, Jr., *Freedom of Speech.*

— ERIK MCKINLEY ERIKSSON

EUTHANASIA

Euthanasia means mercy killing and most often refers to painless termination of the life of a person suffering from a painful and incurable medical condition. The word derives from Greek and literally means a good or easy death. In almost every country, euthanasia is homicide under the law; regardless of motive, purposeful taking of human life is considered to demean its sanctity. Uruguay alone explicitly exempts mercy killing from all criminal sanctions. In the Netherlands euthanasia is formally prohibited but openly tolerated. In the United States euthanasia is and has always been illegal, at least insofar as it involves actively putting to death a living person. Physicians consider themselves unable to participate because of the Hippocratic oath commanding them to do no harm, but it has not always been easy to discern the borderline between euthanasia and acceptable behavior. A patient has a right to refuse medical treatment—a right respected in common law and more recently deemed protected in the U.S. Constitution. Withdrawal by a physician, at a patient's request, of the feeding tube necessary to sustain life could be considered euthanasia, because the physician commits an act knowing that the patient will thereby die. The act, however, also respects the patient's refusal to consent to the treatment; both law and medical ethics forbid treatment without the patient's informed consent.

Since at least the 1970s, there has been much public debate about the scope of the right to refuse treatment. Partly responsible are advances in medical technology and fear of forcing persons to spend their terminal years connected to elaborate medical equipment considered costly to the patient's dignity as well as to the health care system, society, and the patient's family. By the 1990s a broad right to refuse treatment was recognized. Advocates of expanding individual choice concerning the circumstances of dying have argued for a constitutional "right to die," relying upon the same right to choose on the grounds of privacy involved in the constitutional debate over abortion. In addition, the due process clause of the U.S. Constitution has been held to give individuals the right to make fundamental decisions free from unreasonable restrictions by government. Examples are the rights to marry and to have children or to choose not to. Under the rubric of the right to die, the right to refuse unwanted medical treatment has been added to the list. Moreover, all states, in the name of individual choice, allow competent persons to choose in advance, through such procedures as a living will or power of attorney, to refuse specified treatments if and when they become incapacitated.

The right to refuse treatment is not the same as a legal or constitutional right to commit suicide, and the recognized right to die does not encompass any right to assisted suicide, as with a physician-administered lethal injection or a prescription for medication to bring about death. Assistance of this sort by physicians is considered forbidden euthanasia. In the 1990s, however, debate raged about whether a person wishing to die should be entitled to seek a physician's help in accomplishing the task with dignity and whether physicians should be permitted to assist those wishing to end their lives. Administering a lethal injection seems far more humane than leaving a person to starve without a feeding tube. Advocates of assisted suicide, at least when the person choosing to die is terminally ill and in severe pain, include Dr. Jack Kevorkian, a Michigan pathologist who assisted in many deaths and was the target of a 1993 Michigan law forbidding assisted suicide. With the help of the American Civil Liberties Union, Kevorkian challenged the law in court, claiming that the right to choose how to die should extend to a right to assistance in dying.

Opponents fear that accepting assisted suicide in some situations would open a Pandora's box of issues. It is unclear whether the right would be limited to persons physically unable to kill themselves or would extend to persons who could do it on their own. It is also uncertain whether the right should be limited to persons in terminal conditions and incurable pain (however those conditions come to be defined) or whether either alone is sufficient. Some believe that rather than facilitating death, physicians should concentrate on ameliorating the pain and depression that make a patient want to die. At the other extreme, however, the right, as one of personal autonomy, might not be limited to persons in any particular condition but available to anyone of sound mind who chooses to exercise the right. Opponents fear making physicians the dispensers of death as well as life would both change the attitudes of physicians and erode patients' confidence. They fear that this initial inroad into respect for the sanctity of human life will lead to others. Eventually, it may extend to termination of life when useful to society and the patient's family, even without the request of the individual to be terminated.

An equally important and difficult area for euthanasia involves not individuals choosing to terminate their lives but individuals making choices for others. Only legally competent persons make their own medical choices. Persons not allowed to do so include children, comatose persons, some persons with mental illness or mental retardation, and some elderly persons. In the case of children older than newborns, their legal inability to decide for themselves most likely forecloses a choice of death, by either child or parent, but in some of the other categories, individuals make choices to forgo treatment on behalf of others. Some characterize such decisions to let other persons die as euthanasia, but others see them as necessary protection of the incompetent individual's "right to choose," even though the choice is made for, not by, the individual who will die.

States vary regarding when they permit family members to make these decisions for incapacitated persons who did not leave instructions when they were competent. The Supreme Court held in *Cruzan* v. *Missouri Department of Health* (1990) that a state could forbid termination of treatment in the absence of "clear and convincing evidence" of the patient's own wishes. Many states have chosen less stringent standards, permitting surrogates to make decisions based upon a probability of the patient's own wishes or upon the best interests of the patient. Commonly such decisions are limited to forgoing treatment and not active assistance in dying. Even if suicide and assisted suicide were recognized as rights for competent persons, they might be considered nondelegable rights that, like the right to vote, cannot be exercised on a person's behalf.

BIBLIOGRAPHY

Baruch A. Brody, ed., *Suicide and Euthanasia* (Norwall, Mass., 1989).

Martha A. Field, "Killing 'the Handicapped'—Before and After Birth," *Harvard Women's Law Journal* 16 (1993).

President's Commission for the Study of Ethical Problems in Medicine and Biomedical and Behavioral Research, *Deciding to Forgo Life-Sustaining Treatment* (Washington, D.C., 1983).

— MARTHA A. FIELD

EXECUTIVE AND CONGRESS

The makers of the Constitution created a strong executive and a strong Congress, endowed each branch with independent power, and provided a minimum of structuring of the relations between them. Some key functions—such as appointments, lawmaking, and treaties—are shared, an arrangement that facilitates the encroachment of the branches upon each other. Few of those functions that were not deliberately designed to be shared are the exclusive province of one branch. Thus, although Congress declares war, the president also initiates it. And although treaties require action by both the president and the Senate, the president can often gain the same ends by making executive agreements independently of the Senate and Congress. Not surprisingly, the history of relations between these two branches has been one of struggle, with the courts playing little part in the outcome, having chosen not to intervene as arbiters. Although the fortunes of Congress and the executive have fluctuated, the predominant share of successes, and therefore of enlarging power, has accrued to the executive.

The history of relations between the executive and legislative branches has been one of struggle, with the courts playing little part in arbitration.

Several patterns of executive-congressional relations are discernible. In one, the executive achieves clear ascendance, if not dominance. A president in a speedy, successful war, such as either of the two world wars, or even in a prolonged conflict, such as the cold war, initiates and maintains combat and forms alliances with ample congressional support and without sustaining any significant legislative rebuff. The most sweeping assertion of presidential power occurred in the Civil War, when President Abraham Lincoln, under what he termed the "war power," expanded the armed forces, drew unappropriated funds from the Treasury, closed the Post Office to "treasonable correspondence," suspended the writ of habeas corpus, and committed other acts that in effect claimed for the executive a virtually unlimited power to legislate.

In an opposite pattern, Congress is ascendant. American entry into the Spanish-American War was more the work of Congress than of the reluctant President William McKinley. For all of President Woodrow Wilson's world leadership and commitment to the League of Nations, it was the Senate that decided that the United States was not to join.

In a further pattern, Congress and the executive may be drawn together in consensus and cooperation. Wilson's New Freedom program of social legislation, Franklin Roosevelt's New Deal program, and Lyndon Johnson's Great Society program each comprised a flow of legislation that made striking innovations in domestic policy. Typically, these efforts involved highly effective presidential leadership that rallied public sentiment and evoked congressional support through manipulation of patronage and other executive largess and through deft bargaining. In these cooperative successes, members of Congress also played leading parts. Senator George W. Norris long championed what eventually became the Tennessee Valley Authority, and Senator Robert F. Wagner's pioneering in labor legislation prodded the executive to act in that area. Congress may also enlarge upon presidential proposals, as it did with the Voting Rights Act of 1965.

Finally, as a common pattern, legislative-executive relations may repose in deadlock. In his 1960 campaign, John F. Kennedy advocated an ambitious program to move the country forward again. Most of his campaign pledges required legislative fulfillment, but only a minor part bore fruit during his lifetime. Much of the transformation heralded in the campaign became stalled in deadlocked executive-legislative relations. Likewise, Richard Nixon, fulfilling a campaign pledge, championed welfare reform promptly upon attaining the presidency; but nothing happened in his first term, and the topic remained on the agenda of his second term.

No one of these patterns of executive-legislative relations lastingly prevails. Rather, forces of war and diplomacy, fluctuating economy and social expectations, and uneven skills of passing leaders move the pendulum first toward one pattern and then toward another. The continued empowerment of both the executive and Congress assures that their relationships will always be volatile.

BIBLIOGRAPHY

Wilfred E. Binkley, *President and Congress.*

James MacGregor Burns, *The Deadlock of Democracy.*

— LOUIS W. KOENIG

EXECUTIVE ORDERS

Executive orders of the president are based on his constitutional powers or derive from statutory authority. Congress often delegates to the president the responsibility of filling in the details of some legislative policy that is set forth generally in statute. Executive orders deal with a wide variety of internal administrative matters of the executive branch, such as departmental reorganization and the promulgation of civil service rules and regulations. Executive orders also affect private individuals, as in orders requiring the registration of aliens. Through executive orders, Franklin Roosevelt and his presidential successors have prohibited racial discrimination in the employment of workers in defense industries and government. President John Kennedy, unable to secure civil rights legislation from Congress, advanced many civil rights policies through executive orders.

The courts have regularly ruled that executive orders have the same force of law as if they were included in an act of Congress. The courts have also ruled as unconstitutional executive orders that lack a basis in constitutional or statutory law. Thus, President Harry Truman's seizure of steel mills during the Korean War, implemented through executive orders, was held unconstitutional, a violation of Congress' power to legislate (343 U.S. 579). Similarly, in the 1935 "Hot Oil" decision (*Panama Refining Company* v. *Ryan*, 293 U.S. 388), the Supreme Court struck down, as excessive and comprising policy determinations properly made only by Congress, a congressional delegation of power to the president (on which executive orders had been based) to prohibit the interstate transportation of oil products in excess of state allowances. The Court concluded that Congress provided inadequate guidelines and standards for executive action.

Congress too may object to executive orders. President Richard Nixon's Philadelphia Plan, which required contractors on federally assisted projects to set specific goals for hiring members of minority groups, was assailed by a Senate subcommittee in 1971 as a "blatant case of usurpation of the legislative function by the executive branch." Administration spokesmen contended that these critics overlooked the executive order "as an independent source of law." A federal court upheld the legality of the Philadelphia Plan and the executive order that promulgated it. The unfolding debate in the 1970's over the question of excessive presidential power embraced the power to issue executive orders.

Until 1907, executive orders were unnumbered. Since then, they have been numbered chronologically. Orders are published in the *Federal Register* and are incorporated annually in the *Code of Federal Regulations.*

BIBLIOGRAPHY

Louis Fisher, *President and Congress: Power and Policy.*

James Hart, *The Ordinance Making Power of the President.*

— LOUIS W. KOENIG

EXPANSION

Expansion in the form of territorial acquisition was the predominant theme of American diplomatic history during the 19th century. Although that theme was subjected to variation and interruption, there was a close association between the increase of American power and resources and the extension of the nation's territorial boundaries. In the 20th century, the continued growth of American power and influence has taken other forms, and the nation's geographic boundaries have experienced no significant expansion.

Although historians have long quarreled over the dominant inspiration for American expansion, few subscribe to a single explanatory cause. Among the more important causes have been fear of powerful neighbors, geographic determinism (the destined acquisition of contiguous areas forming a natural geographic unit with the United States), missionary zeal (religious and secular), strategic necessity (real and imagined), and economic ambition (agrarian and commercial). Although all of these motives were usually present, their relative influence varied in different regions and at various times. A fear of the power of Napoleonic France was the primary motive for the Louisiana Purchase (1803) and the expansion of the country from the Appalachians to the Missouri Valley. A belief in geographic determinism was the primary motive for the prolonged effort to annex Florida (1810–19). Missionary zeal, in its secular manifestation as Manifest Destiny, was particularly important in the territorial acquisitions of the 1840's, while strategic necessity was probably the dominant consideration in the annexation of Puerto Rico (1898) and the Panama Canal Zone (1903). In the form of land hunger, economic ambition was a major motive in the unsuccessful effort to conquer Canada in the War of 1812 and, translated as a desire for industrial markets and expanding foreign commerce, was probably the chief impetus in the decision to retain the Philippine Islands after the Spanish-American War.

The physical expansion of the United States in the 19th century occurred in discernible waves. Advocates of expansion enjoyed majority support only at intervals, usually as a result of external and fortuitous circumstances. The difficulties and divisions of the European powers periodically served to give reality to the ambitions of the expansionists in the United States. This was particularly true during the first wave of expansion (1803–19), when the United States acquired the Louisiana Territory and the Floridas; confirmed a portion of its northern border; and negotiated with Britain the first treaty for joint occupation of the Oregon Country.

The most dramatic increase in the nation's geographic boundaries came with the second wave of expansion in the 1840's, when the western boundary of the United States reached the Pacific Ocean. If the continental ambitions of the extreme advocates of Manifest Destiny were frustrated by the Oregon partition treaty (1846), the years 1845–48 saw the annexation of Texas, the acquisition of the Oregon Territory up to the forty-ninth parallel, and the cession of California and the New Mexico Territory following the Mexican War. Through these acquisitions the national domain was increased by 1,204,000 square miles. Except for the acquisition of southern Arizona with the Gadsden Purchase (1853) and the purchase of Alaska (1867), the continental boundaries of the United States were completed with the Treaty of Guadalupe Hidalgo in 1848.

The most dramatic increase in the nation's geographic boundaries came with the second wave of expansion in the 1840's, when the western limits of the U.S. reached the Pacific Ocean.

After the Civil War, Secretary of State William Seward sought to initiate a third wave of expansionist growth. His ambitions embraced Santo Domingo, the Danish West Indies, Hawaii, and Alaska, but with the exception of the last his efforts were abortive. The quarter-century following the Civil War was a time of industrial growth and internal consolidation, and although the expansionist urge did not disappear, it found neither opportunity nor public sympathy.

The next wave of expansionism came in the 1890's. It was supported by a more self-conscious ideology—

one that combined the earlier convictions of Manifest Destiny with social Darwinism, false doctrines of race, and an accentuated concern for the markets of the Far East. The expansionism of the 1890's was imperial in tone, colonial in method, and insular in direction. In part the product of the needs of industrial capitalism, it was more imitative of Europe and more economic in motive than earlier waves of expansionist activity. It culminated in the establishment of a protectorate over Cuba and the annexation of Puerto Rico and a chain of islands across the Pacific—Hawaii, Guam, Wake, American Samoa, and the Philippines.

Except for the acquisition of the Panama Canal Zone and the Virgin Islands, those annexations concluded the expansion of U.S. territorial boundaries. The 20th century would see periodic increase in the diplomatic and economic influence of the United States in Latin America, as exemplified by the Roosevelt Corollary to the Monroe Doctrine and the "dollar diplomacy" of the William Howard Taft era, but no further territorial acquisition. Similarly, although cold war competition in the quarter-century after World War II inspired the establishment of U.S. bases and military and economic aid programs throughout the globe, the national boundaries were not enlarged. The sense of mission—the belief that America has a destiny to demonstrate to the world the superior virtues of its democratic ideals and republican institutions—persists, but in the 20th century the United States has seemingly rejected the association of mission with territorial conquest.

BIBLIOGRAPHY

Frederick Merk, *Manifest Destiny and Mission in American History: A Reinterpretation.*

R. W. Van Alstyne, *The Rising American Empire.*

— RICHARD E. WELCH, JR.

EXTRADITION

Extradition, the surrender by one sovereign government to another of a fugitive from justice. In the United States the term has two different applications. First, it is used to denote the process by which the national government of the United States requests the return of a person who is accused of violating a national or state law from some foreign country in which he has been found. Such requests are made only under definite treaty arrangements that usually establish reciprocity in such matters. Thus, the return of Samuel Insull from Greece in 1932 to stand trial in Illinois was retarded by the absence of an adequate extradition treaty between the United States and Greece.

The second meaning of extradition in the United States refers to Article IV, Section 2, of the Constitution, which states, "A Person charged in any State with Treason, Felony or other Crime, who shall flee from Justice, and be found in another State, shall, on Demand of the executive Authority of the State from which he fled, be delivered up, to be removed to the State having jurisdiction of the crime." This provision, although apparently mandatory, has been held by the U.S. Supreme Court to be discretionary. The duty of the governor of the state of refuge is moral, not legal.

A request for extradition, or interstate rendition, is made by the governor of the state in which the crime was committed. A copy of the indictment or information is attached to the extradition papers. The governor of the state of refuge may grant the request at once, or he may hold a hearing to examine the facts. After the hearing he may grant or deny the request. The usual grounds for denial are that the act complained of is not a crime in the state of refuge, that the accused will not receive a fair trial if returned, or that the person sought to be extradited has become an upright citizen. No reason need be given.

BIBLIOGRAPHY

J. M. Mathews, *The American Constitutional System.*

J. B. Moore, *A Treatise on Extradition and Interstate Rendition.*

— HARVEY WALKER

EXXON VALDEZ

Just after midnight on Mar. 24, 1989, the *Exxon Valdez,* an oil tanker transporting Prudhoe Bay crude oil from the terminus of the pipeline at Valdez, Alaska, to refineries in the lower forty-eight states, struck a reef and grounded in Prince William Sound. The tanker's holding tanks were breached, and over the next few days 258,000 barrels of crude oil—11 million gallons—spilled into the sound and the Gulf of Alaska. It was the largest oil spill in history up to that time. The effect was extensive. Ten percent of the shoreline of Prince William Sound and the Gulf of Alaska—approximately 1,100 miles—received deposits of floating crude. Some 36,000 birds of an estimated local population of 10 million died, as did more than 1,000 sea otters of an estimated local population varying between 14,000 and 30,000 and 153 bald eagles out of an estimated local population of 5,000. By 1990 the Exxon Corporation had spent some $2 billion on cleanup, mandated under the Comprehensive Environmental Response, Compensation, and Liability Act of 1980. Treatment consisted of skimming and recapturing floating oil, spraying the beaches with high-pressure water heated to 140 degrees Fahrenheit, and spreading high-nitrogen fertilizers on the beaches to speed microbial biodegration of the oil. Of the spilled oil, 8 percent was removed by skimmers, 6 percent recovered from the sand and gravel on the beaches, 20 percent evaporated, 50 percent biodegraded on the beaches, and the remaining 15 percent persisted either sunken below the surface or as tar on intertidal shores. Subsequent assessment indicated that both animal and plant species on the shores had largely recovered by 1993. Exxon settled with government agencies in 1991 by payment of $1 billion; of this sum $100 million constituted a fine and the remaining $900 million formed a fund to finance restoration of the environment. In September 1994 a jury awarded 34,000 Alaskan residents $5 billion in punitive damages.

BIBLIOGRAPHY

Alan W. Maki, "The *Exxon Valdez* Oil Spill: Initial Environmental Impact Assessment," *Environmental Science and Technology* 25 (1991).

National Research Council Commission on Engineering and Technical Systems, Marine Board Committee on Tank Vessel Design, *Tanker Spills: Prevention by Design* (Washington, D.C., 1991).

— NANCY M. GORDON

F

FAIR DEAL

Fair Deal, the phrase adopted by President Harry S. Truman to characterize the program of domestic legislation he sought to have enacted into law during his years in the presidency. The term did not become common until the president used it in his State of the Union message of Jan. 5, 1949. In a rudimentary way the Fair Deal existed from the time he took office on Apr. 12, 1945. In September of that year he sent a lengthy message to Congress in which he proposed twenty-one points to be considered by that body as subject matter for legislation. In his opinion these proposals fulfilled the promises made in the Democratic platform of 1944, and he regarded them as continuing and extending the policies of his predecessor, Franklin D. Roosevelt.

Among these points was a request for a full-employment law. The national government was to see to it that conditions were such that every man who was willing and able to work would have a worthwhile position. As Truman put it in 1953, "full employment means maximum opportunity under the American system of responsible freedom." He also requested that the wartime Fair Employment Practices Committee be put on a permanent basis. In other messages that followed he requested legislation on housing, health insurance, aid to education, atomic energy, and the development of the Saint Lawrence Seaway. In general Congress did not respond to these requests, though the Employment Act of 1946 was passed in accordance with his wishes and under it the Council of Economic Advisers was set up to assist the president in the preparation of the annual economic report to Congress.

In the campaign of 1948 Truman succeeded in defeating the Republican candidate, Gov. Thomas E. Dewey of New York, despite the defection from Democratic ranks of numerous Southerners, particularly those who shifted their allegiance to the States' Rights, or Dixiecrat, party, and of numbers of northerners, particularly those who supported Henry Wallace and the Progressive party of that year. After his surprising victory the president gathered together many of the proposals he had made in previous years in his annual message to Congress in January 1949. He asked for laws on housing, full employment, higher minimum wages, better price supports for farmers, more organizations like the Tennessee Valley Authority, the extension of social security, and fair employment practices. Although filibusters prevented the passage of an anti-poll-tax law and a fair employment practices bill, the Housing Act of 1949 facilitated slum clearance throughout the country; the minimum wage level was lifted from 40 to 75 cents an hour by an amendment to the Fair Labor Standards Act of 1938; and the Social Security Act of 1950 extended the benefits of that law to about 10 million more people. The coming of the Korean War in June 1950, the increasing complexity of foreign affairs, and a general prosperity lessened interest in the Fair Deal program, but many of Truman's social welfare proposals—as well as his proposals for the development of atomic energy and the Saint Lawrence Seaway, for example—were legislated in subsequent administrations.

— VINCENT C. HOPKINS

FAIR LABOR STANDARDS ACT

Fair Labor Standards Act, popularly known as the Wages and Hours Bill, was enacted on June 25, 1938, culminating several years of endeavor by proponents of federal regulation of hours and wages. The Black-Connery bill represented the first attempt to reduce the hours of labor in interstate commerce and in industries affecting such commerce. Although this bill passed the Senate in April 1933, it was never voted on in the House. The National Industrial Recovery Act of 1933 established the National Recovery Administration (NRA) to regulate the operation of industries under industrial codes, which included the regulation of prices, trade practices, wages, hours, collective bargaining, and labor conditions. However, in 1935, the Supreme Court invalidated the entire program (*Schechter* v. *United States*). Congress responded by enacting the Bituminous Coal Conservation Act of 1935, which sought to create a "Little NRA" to formulate a bituminous coal code fixing the price of soft coal, and regulating wage and hour standards in the industry. In 1936, the Supreme Court invalidated the act while avoiding a direct ruling on the power of Congress to regulate wages (*Carter* v. *Carter Coal Company*). The result of these decisions was increased agitation for a general federal law regulating wages, hours, and conditions of labor.

Encouraged by the Supreme Court's later liberal rulings, President Franklin D. Roosevelt in 1937 urged a federal wage-and-hour law. The proposal precipitated opposition from industrial interests, which sparked controversies among industries seeking recognition of geographical differentials in the act. The culmination of this effort was the Fair Labor Standards Act of 1938, an omnibus bill that regulated hours of labor, wages, and child labor. The act, which created a Wage and Hour Division in the Department of Labor, headed by an administrator, applies in industries affecting or producing goods for interstate commerce. For the first year a minimum wage of 25 cents an hour was established; thereafter, increases to 40 cents an hour were included in the bill. Child labor under the age of sixteen was prohibited, with certain exceptions, and specific hazardous occupations were forbidden to youths under eighteen. Time-and-a-half pay was required for employment above a 44-hour week the first year; above 42 hours for the second; and above 40 hours thereafter. In addition to prescribing criminal penalties for its violation, the act provided for the exclusion from interstate commerce of such goods as were not produced in accordance with its standards. The Supreme Court upheld the validity of the act (*United States* v. *Darby Lumber Company*) in 1941.

Owing to the numerous exemptions within the act and the many exceptions from its rules, as promulgated under subsequent administrative rulings and regulations, the act has remained the source of substantial litigation. Since its inception, similar legislation has been enacted within the various states, primarily for the protection of employees not covered by the federal law.

BIBLIOGRAPHY

John H. Leek, *Government and Labor in the United States.*

— DAVID MANDEL AND ALFRED J. PETIT-CLAIR, JR.

FAIR-TRADE LAWS

Fair trade is a euphemism for resale price maintenance, or the control by a supplier of the selling prices of his branded goods at subsequent stages of distribution by means of contractual agreement under state and federal laws.

Statutes legalizing such price fixing were introduced originally in state legislatures primarily as a result of efforts on the part of independent druggists and other small retailers. California first enacted a fair-trade law in 1931. Thereafter, all states except Missouri, Texas, and Vermont and the District of Columbia passed similar legislation.

These highly controversial laws were frequently subjected to judicial or other tests. In 1936 the U.S. Supreme Court ruled in *Old Dearborn Distributing Company* v. *Seagram Distillers Corporation* that state fair-trade laws were legitimate means of protecting a manufacturer's goodwill as symbolized by his trademark. Legislation later introduced at the federal level resulted in the passage in 1937 of the Miller-Tydings Amendment to the Sherman Antitrust Act of 1890, thereby exempting interstate fair-trade agreements from the antitrust laws.

"Fair trade" is a euphemism for resale price maintenance, or the control by a supplier of the selling prices of branded goods at subsequent stages of distribution.

The Miller-Tydings Amendment made no reference to nonsigners' clauses incorporated in many of the state laws, whereby the manufacturer by making a contract with one retailer (or wholesaler) in a fair-trade state could legally bind all other retailers (or wholesalers) in that state to maintain his stipulated resale prices. Businessmen and the courts assumed that the Miller-Tydings Amendment sanctioned all details of state laws for purposes of interstate commerce. Nevertheless, violations of fair-trade agreements were not uncommon, and enforcement became especially difficult where the nonsigners' clause was involved.

In April 1950 the General Electric Company initiated a suit against R. H. Macy and Company in New York for selling small appliances manufactured by General Electric at less than the established fair-trade prices. General Electric won an injunction in the New York Supreme Court conditioned on the continuation by General Electric of vigorous enforcement activities. However, in May 1951 the U.S. Supreme Court rendered an unexpected judgment in *Schwegmann Brothers* v. *Calvert Distillers Corporation*, invalidating all fair-trade price structures in interstate commerce that were based on the use of nonsigners' clauses. The *Schwegmann* decision also started a highly publicized price war in New York in the summer of 1951. In 1951 and 1952 the Sunbeam Corporation, which had revised its system of fair-trade agreements after the *Schwegmann* decision by making individual resale price maintenance agreements with each of its wholesalers and its dealers, was involved first as plaintiff and then as defendant in cases involving fair-trade pricing practices. Before these cases were settled federal law had again been changed. The Fair Trade Enabling Act (commonly called the McGuire

Act) was passed into law as an amendment to the Federal Trade Commission Act in July 1952. This statute ended much of the uncertainty about the legal status of resale price maintenance by specifically restoring to manufacturers the power to require retailers and wholesalers to adhere to fixed minimum price schedules whether they had signed fair-trade contracts or not.

But fair trade again became caught up in a crossfire of court action at the state level. By August 1956, eight state supreme courts had handed down adverse decisions on fair trade, rendering it virtually inoperative in some areas. Courts in several states ruled that nonsigners' clauses violated state constitutions. This greatly weakened a manufacturer's ability to enforce resale price maintenance agreements effectively.

In 1957 the U.S. Court of Appeals in New York, interpreting the McGuire Act, held that Masters, Inc., a New York discount house that had been enjoined from selling below fair-trade prices in New York, could nevertheless service its New York customers by mail through a subsidiary selling in the District of Columbia (a non-fair-trade area) at discount prices. This decision dealt a near mortal blow to fair-trade laws as more states declared them unconstitutional.

Proponents of resale price maintenance realized that tougher legislation would be needed if fair trade were to survive. Believing it politically premature to plump for federal laws to strengthen resale price maintenance during the late 1950's, they again worked aggressively in support of fair-trade legislation at state levels. By 1964 a quiet campaign to put through a new federal resale price maintenance law, called a "quality stabilization" bill, had gathered so much momentum that its backers then saw little likelihood that it would fail to become law. If it had, a manufacturer's power to enjoin price cutting would have applied everywhere except in states that had adopted laws to prohibit it within their borders. Despite widespread contrary predictions, the quality stabilization bill failed of passage in Congress in 1964.

Meanwhile, critics of fair trade continued to fight against it at the state level. By early February 1975, the District of Columbia and fourteen states had become non-fair-trade areas, twenty-two states had fair-trade laws for signers only, and only fourteen others still retained nonsigners' clauses. By mid-1975 only twenty-five states still had fair-trade laws of any kind on the books, and the federal government seemed on the verge of wiping out the two federal laws (the Miller-Tydings Amendment and the McGuire Act) that still made surviving state fair-trade laws viable in interstate commerce. Subcommittees in both houses of Congress had approved bills repealing fair trade, and President Gerald R. Ford backed the moves. Thus, the legislative remains of the 1930's appeared to be dying out.

Throughout their history the fair-trade laws served to polarize disparate streams of American political and economic thought on the recurring debates over such things as states' rights, balance of payment problems, trade protectionism, inflation, consumer protection, business failures, corporate marketing strategy, equity positions in advertised brands, and small business versus big business ideology. But, because of difficulties inherent in their enforcement, fair-trade laws were widely flouted. As a result, the potentially significant effects of fair-trade practices became muted.

— THOMAS LEROY BERG

FAMILY

Family, universally, a small kinship-structured group with the key function of nurturant socialization of the newborn. Kinship structure refers to social, not biological, descent (that is, the feeling of being derived from someone in a social sense). The person (or persons) who emotionally cares for an infant during the infant's first five or ten years of life is the person that infant will feel it has descended from. This feeling of descent is the essence of kinship. In most societies the person giving nurturance (that is, emotional response and support, and not necessarily physical care) to the newborn is the mother of the child, but that is not essential in this definition. The essential family quality is the feeling of descent that derives from nurturance.

Related to the family institution are the courtship institution, which has the key function of mate selection, and the marital institution, which legitimizes parenthood. The courtship, marital, and family institutions are closely interrelated. Viewed collectively, they may be called the "family system." Every known society has such a family system. Although the family system is universal, a tremendous diversity in other features exists in specific cultures.

In America the family system has varied according to region. In New England, for instance, the family system made use of civil marriages. The clergy and the populace often clashed over certain aspects of courtship, such as the popular winter custom of bundling. The situation in the South was different, with more church influence present in Virginia and other southern states. And on the frontier, common-law marriages became established, owing to the difficulty of locating a minister. To this day, in the law a common-law marriage implies the intent of eventual legal marriage. Despite this diversity, 18th- and 19th-century European visitors gave rather similar accounts of the overall U.S. family system.

Among other things, historians were surprised by the high degree of equality of the sexes, by the freedom given young people in their courtship, and by the climbing divorce rates.

The 19th-century books on the family spoke of marriage becoming purely a civil contract for the happiness of the husband and wife; they also mentioned the frequent employment of wives in diverse industries and the rising tide of divorce. From the time of the Civil War to World War I, divorce rates increased fourfold. Between 1915 and 1920 the rate doubled again. From 1920 to the early 1960's the divorce rate fluctuated up and down, but by only about 25 percent. From 1968 to 1973, divorce rates started rising rapidly again, at the rate of about 10 percent a year. One fundamental reason for high divorce rates in the United States is the American type of open courtship system, with marriages based on a love choice. The more emphasis there is on love choice, the more likely is divorce, because of the feeling that one may have made the wrong choice. During the 20th century, as the European countries increasingly adopted the American type of courtship, their divorce rates rose and began to approach the American rates. The same trend was also beginning in the Soviet Union.

All three institutions that make up the family system showed radical changes in America during two key periods of the 20th century: the first was approximately 1915–20, and the second, roughly 1965–70. The values of individual choice, personal happiness, and equality have long been present in America, but these two periods stressed and actualized such values more than before. Such periods also existed in earlier centuries. The 19th century saw the feminist movement, the experimental family forms illustrated by the Oneida experiment (1848–81), and the increasing employment of women so that by 1900, 5 million women were working.

Changes in family-related attitudes and behavior during these two periods in the 20th century clearly illustrate the nature of the changes American society was undergoing. In the 1915–20 period, which was also the time of World War I, the proportion of women entering marriage nonvirginally doubled from 25 to 50 percent; the divorce rate also doubled. The major public debate on divorce of this time was being resolved with more emphasis on personal choice than on divorce per se. From this time until the early 1960's the social changes that had occurred in the family seemed to be consolidating, and were becoming more accepted and rationalized. For example, no rapid changes in female nonvirginity rates and only small fluctuations in the divorce rate were evident.

In the late 1960's rapid social change in the family reoccurred. The premarital intercourse rates rose again; the divorce rate doubled between 1963 and 1973; and the United States was again involved in a world war. In addition, a feminist movement for equality between the sexes in and out of marriage arose—the first such powerful movement since 1920. The long-term downward trend in the birthrates that had been interrupted in most of the 1940's and 1950's began to reassert itself. By 1973 the United States had reached the lowest birthrate in its history—a rate that if continued for a generation would put the country at zero population growth. Over 40 percent of married women were working as of 1971. Married women made up over 60 percent of all working women—a great increase over a generation earlier. Almost 30 percent of the married women with children under six were working in 1971 and this too was a notable change; twenty years earlier only about 10 percent of such women were working. New family experiments began to occur, as they had in the 19th century. Communes of all types multiplied across the country. Many saw these changes as part of an overall change of American society from the industrial society created around World War I to a postindustrial society more concerned with equitable distribution of goods and services than before.

In many ways these changes show a search for the basic values the early settlers brought with them—values such as individualism, freedom, equality, happiness, and love. People are less willing to tolerate an unhappy marriage; they are less willing to have children, or a certain number of children, just to conform to group norms; they are even less willing to marry, and the age at first marriage began to rise in the 1960's for the first time since the precipitous drop that occurred in the 1940's.

Overall, Americans now have a greater variety of family alternatives from which people can choose. The universal functions of the family system, such as nurturance of the newborn, mate selection, and legitimation of parenthood, have continued and will probably remain, for they seem crucial to the development of the next generation in any society. But the ways in which these universal functions are achieved have multiplied. The range of choice and the legitimation of such choices are at an all-time high. It is likely that choices will become socially ranked as to general preference, but the range of choice will surely remain greater than it was before. Based on the experience of the family as it was following the rapid changes of 1915–20, one could expect American society to stabilize and start to consolidate these changes before the end of the 1970's.

BIBLIOGRAPHY

Arthur W. Calhoun, *A Social History of the American Family From Colonial Times to the Present.*

Sidney Ditzion, *Marriage, Morals and Sex in America.*

Abbott L. Ferriss, *Indicators of Trends in the Status of American Women.*

William O'Neill, *Divorce in the Progressive Era.*

Ira L. Reiss, *The Family System in America.*

— IRA L. REISS

RECENT CHALLENGES FOR THE FAMILY

Changes since the 1950s in the composition of the American family have raised questions about whether the American family is evolving or dissolving. Many Americans see the family as being synonymous with the nuclear household of a mother, father, and children, while others hold a less delineated view about whether two or more people who share resources, values, goals, and an obligation toward one another are a family. In the 1950s more than half of American families consisted of husbands who worked and wives who stayed at home with their children. It was an unprecedented time. Marriage rates were high, divorce rates were low, and couples married at an earlier age than before or after. In contrast, the 1990s produced the highest rate of marriage-divorce-remarriage in the world. The head of one out of three U.S. households was fifty years old or older. Men were marrying for the first time on average at age twenty-six and women at about twenty-four. Many couples were living together before marrying, perhaps in part because cohabitation was no longer taboo. Marriages were also delayed because of financial advantages; two unmarried people with similar incomes paid less in taxes than a married couple. Nevertheless, by age forty-four only 9 percent of Americans had never married. Married couples made up 83 percent of white family households in 1990, 50 percent in black households, and 70 percent in Hispanic households.

Once married, both partners in the 1990s tended to continue working. In 1947 only 20 percent of married women worked; in 1991 the figure was 59 percent; by the year 2000, it was estimated that 75 percent of women with children would be working outside the home. The two-paycheck family altered family patterns. In the 1990s the traditional roles of men as financial providers and women as caretakers of the home and children had blurred, with more women working and many men no longer functioning as sole providers. This change was not restricted to middle-income white families. Women's incomes in African-American families were critical to survival, because the median income of African-American men was 23 percent less than that of white men. Technically, not being the sole provider should have freed men to assume more household and child-care duties. Instead, two-income families created extra work for women who continued to do most of the shopping, cooking, cleaning, and child care. With more time spent working or traveling between home and work, parents had less time to spend with their children. In 1965 parents averaged thirty hours per week in direct or indirect contact with their children. In 1985 the figure was down to seventeen hours. The working family created the need for child care centers in U.S. communities. About 60,000 day-care centers were in operation in the late 1980s, and seven out of ten mothers used day care. Day-care costs in the 1990s sometimes exceeded $500 a month per child, forcing many families to rely on grandparents or friends or one parent to work at a different time of day from his or her spouse in order to watch their children.

School-age children posed a different problem for families incapable of providing after-school care. The 5 million to 10 million children who returned each day to empty houses came to be called "latch-key kids." Almost half of all children under eighteen often cared for themselves at times. Parents, concerned for their children's security, often required them to stay indoors, making television their baby-sitter, and older children left alone sometimes became involved with drugs and alcohol. Even parents who could afford day care debated whether it was good or bad for children. Research revealed that children might be better off at home from birth to two years of age. At the same time, understaffing plagued day-care centers. Day-care workers rank in the lowest tenth of all wage earners and typically receive no benefits. A high worker-to-child ratio causes hygienic problems and creates an environment that does not promote learning. Still, a preschool project of Ypsilanti, Mich., observed 123 black children for twenty years and found that these children stayed in school longer and committed fewer crimes. Research also showed that children in day care were six to nine months ahead of those who stayed at home.

Children in the last quarter of the twentieth century were raised in households quite different from the *Ozzie and Harriet* television family of the 1950s. While seven out of ten households consisted of two parents, only one out of four was a nuclear family in which the woman stayed home. Many two-parent households were stepfamilies in which one or both parents combined children from previous marriages. One out of every six children in the 1990s was a stepchild, and family difficulties often arose as stepchildren had to adapt to new parents and siblings. The single-parent family became a much-discussed phenomenon. In past centuries war and disease left single parents to raise children, but in the 1990s most single-parent families resulted from divorce or separation. The number of single-parent families has soared since the early 1970s. In 1980, 20 percent of all households were single-parent families, with 90 percent of them headed by women. Two out of ten of these women had never married, and more than half of these single mothers were under seventeen years of age. By 1992 the greatest increase in single mothers was among white women over twenty. Teenage pregnancies accounted for half of all out-of-wedlock births in 1973 but dropped to 30 percent in 1992 because of increased availability of contraceptives and the use of abortion. More than half of all teenage pregnancies ended in abortion. Only 10 percent of teenage mothers married. The debate over teen pregnancies centered around beliefs that welfare benefits tempted teenagers to get pregnant. Political leaders in the early 1990s called for slashing benefits and putting teenage mothers in group homes, providing safety for children from parental neglect and adult instruction in parenting and child rearing.

In past centuries, war and disease left single parents to raise children, but in the 1990's most single-parent families resulted from divorce or separation.

Since the 1960s growing numbers of single, young adults were returning to the family household. Between 1960 and 1990 unmarried adult children living at home, known as "nesters," rose from 43 percent to 53 percent—the highest ever. Two-thirds of those eighteen to twenty-four lived with their parents, as did one-third of those aged twenty-five to twenty-nine. Many returned home because of divorce or unemployment. In addition to sheltering grown children, U.S. households increasingly contained elderly grandparents. The parents in the middle became a "sandwich generation." To some extent this development marked a return to an earlier household pattern in which extended families were more common. While extended families often helped to preserve cultural heritage, adoptive families joined people of different races and cultures in the same household, as did the 900,000 interracial families in the United States in the 1990s. Each year Americans accepted into their homes 150,000 unrelated children, many of them from abroad. The reasons for adoption ranged from infertility to overpopulation, and many states began to allow adopted children to know and visit biological parents.

In 1989 a court in New York ruled that gay couples constituted a family with rights to rent-controlled housing. Among homosexuals in the United States, half of the men and 70 percent of the women were in long-term relationships. Most of the children came from previous heterosexual marriages, but 5,000 to 10,000 lesbians had children after openly declaring their sexual orientation. By 1990 there were 2 million gay mothers and fathers in the United States. For infertile heterosexual couples and for homosexual couples wanting children, artificial reproduction was widely used. In July 1978 Lesley Brown, a thirty-year-old Englishwoman, gave birth to the world's first test-tube baby. Forms of artificial reproduction included AID (artificial insemination by a donor), IVF (in vitro fertilization), and SET (surrogate embryo transfer). If artificial reproduction helped counter the decline in the fertility rates, it also raised ethical and moral questions and challenged the traditional definitions of mother and father.

The United States had more homeless families in the 1990s than ever before. Mothers and their children constituted the fastest growing portion of the homeless. One hundred thousand children were homeless. The Department of Health and Human Services found that 265 federally funded shelters could house only 20 percent of those in need.

Divorces resulted in children living with the mother nine times out of ten. After the divorce less than half of fathers saw their children weekly. After three years half of the fathers did not visit at all. In 1988 the Federal Office of Child Support Enforcement collected only $5 billion of the $25 billion that fathers owed that year in child support. Divorce left half of African-American mothers and one-third of white mothers in poverty, in part because of gender bias resulting from the application of no-fault divorce laws.

Violence in the family received increasing attention in the 1990s. In the late 1980s the Federal Bureau of Investigation stated that on average a woman was beaten by her husband every eighteen seconds. The National Committee for Prevention of Child Abuse reported that 1 million children were abused each year.

Debate flared on whether employers could do more to address family needs. Some offered flextime or allowed two employees to share one job. On-line computers created opportunities for employees to work at home. In 1987 there were 6 million employers in the United States, but only 3,000 provided day care. In the early 1990s there was a shift in responsibility for the American family from the federal to state and local governments. Congress battled over legislation for social programs and for promoting the family through tax relief and enforcing child support. In 1990 national legislation was passed to strengthen the Internal Revenue Service's ability to help custodial parents collect overdue child support payments. In 1991 Congress approved $18.3 billion in tax credits and $4.25 billion for new grant programs over five years to help low and moderate income families pay for child care as well as help states improve the quality of their child care. This was the first major child-care program since 1971. In 1993 the passage of the Family and Medical Leave Act allowed workers to take up to twelve weeks of unpaid leave because of the birth or adoption of a child or the care of any family members with a health condition. This act forced employers to support an employee's need to maintain both family and job.

[See also Abortion; Marriage and Divorce; Poverty.]

BIBLIOGRAPHY

Stephanie Coontz, *The Way We Never Were* (New York, 1992).

Amitai Etzioni et al., "Who Cares About the Kids?," *Utne Reader* (May-June 1993).

Joseph M. Hawes and Elizabeth I. Nybakken, *American Families* (New York, 1991).

Sam Roberts, *Who We Are* (New York, 1993).

Karen Bornemann Spies, *The American Family* (New York, 1993).

Viqi Wagner and Karin Swisher, eds., *The Family in America* (San Diego, Calif., 1992).

— HOWARD EGGER-BOVET

FARMERS' ALLIANCE

Farmers' Alliance, the name commonly given to either or both of two powerful agricultural organizations of the 1880's and 1890's.

The National Farmers' Alliance, also known as the Northern, or the Northwestern, Alliance, was a nonsecret organization founded in 1880 by Milton George, editor of the *Western Rural*, a Chicago farm journal, as a means of combating the unfair discrimination of the railroads against the rural classes. Under George's leadership the organization developed into a loose federation of powerful state alliances, with numerous locals in Kansas, Nebraska, the Dakotas, Minnesota, and other northwestern states. Its most active growth took place in the later 1880's, when the hard-pressed farmers of the "middle border" joined it by the hundreds of thousands with the hope that through it they could somehow curb the railroads and the trusts and bring about a lowering of interest rates and an easing of the mortgage burden. When pressure on the established political parties failed to bring satisfactory results, the alliance began to go into politics, and by 1890 third-party tickets for state and local offices were general throughout the Northwest.

The National Farmers' Alliance and Industrial Union originated about 1874 in Lampasas County, Tex., when a group of frontier farmers united in a secret, ritualistic alliance against the local cattle kings and land sharks. The order soon spread into neighboring counties, but it died out during the later 1870's owing to dissension over the greenback issue. In 1879 it took new root in Parker County, Tex., and, as the Farmers' State Alliance, again began to grow. After 1886, with an aggressive new president, C. W. Macune, in control, it succeeded in absorbing the Louisiana Farmers' Union, the Arkansas Agricultural Wheel, and local farmers' clubs all over the South into what remained, under various names, a strongly centralized organization. Macune and his agents promised, among other things, to arrest through cooperative buying and selling the alarming decline in southern prosperity that had followed the downward trend of cotton prices. A number of business exchanges were founded; when most of them failed, the Southern Alliance went into politics, as had its northern prototype. Third-party action was carefully avoided, for most southerners feared that a split in white solidarity might pave the way for black participation in politics. Instead, the alliance set out to capture the Democratic party of the South, and by 1890 it was well on the way to success. Meantime, a subordinate and well-disciplined Colored Farmers' Alliance and Cooperative Union had been founded to look after the welfare of the Afro-Americans.

The National Farmers' Alliance originated about 1874 in Lampasas County, Texas, when a group of frontier farmers united in a secret, ritualistic alliance against the local cattle kings and land sharks.

From time to time unavailing efforts were made to unite the two great sectional alliances into one order. The divergent economic interests of northwestern and southern farmers account in part for the failure of these efforts, but an even more effective obstacle was the formation, mainly under the auspices of the Northwestern Alliance, of the People's, or Populist, party in 1892. This development proved to be disastrous to both alliances. Northwestern Alliance members forgot the old farm order in their enthusiasm for the new political party, while those of the Southern Alliance deserted by the tens of thousands at the mere threat of party division. Thus, by the middle 1890's, the vitality had gone out of both alliances.

[See also Granger Movement.]

BIBLIOGRAPHY

John D. Hicks, *The Populist Revolt.*

— JOHN D. HICKS

FEDERAL-AID HIGHWAY PROGRAM

Although the development and maintenance of public roads in the United States have been historically within the authority of the state and local governments, the period from 1920 to the mid-1970's has seen a steadily mounting participation by the federal government in highway construction and management. About 43,000 miles of interstate and defense highways have been built, largely at federal expense, the states having contributed only 10 percent of total cost of construction. In addition, more than 900,000 miles of primary and secondary roads are maintained on a 50–50 basis by the federal and state governments acting jointly. The Federal Highway Administration, one of several operating administrations in the Department of Transportation, is charged with the administration of the Federal-Aid Highway Construction Program. The National Highway Traffic Safety Administration, also within the department, is responsible for promoting safe and efficient travel on the nation's highways.

The Bureau of Public Roads, from which the Federal Highway Administration evolved, had its origin in the Office of Road Inquiry, established within the Department of Agriculture in 1893. Following the passage of the Federal-Aid Highway acts of 1916 and 1921, the bureau became the chief agency for promoting a national network of highways. Successive administrative changes placed the bureau in the Federal Works Agency; in the Department of Commerce; and finally, in 1967, in the newly created Department of Transportation. In 1970 the bureau was reorganized and its duties assigned to the Federal Highway Administration.

The Federal Highway Administration, in cooperation with the states, administers the financial aid given the states for highway construction. It works closely with state highway departments in correcting dangerous stretches on existing roads, in promoting safe highway construction by a vigorous inspection program, and in improving the efficiency of inter- and intraurban road systems as well as in preserving the natural beauty along the roadways. The Highway Beautification Program comes within its purview. Planning in the critical field of urban transportation has been made its responsibility by the Highway Act of 1962, as amended.

BIBLIOGRAPHY

C. Borth, *Mankind on the Move.*

U.S. Department of Transportation, *Highway Statistics* (1970).

— PAUL DOLAN

FEDERAL BUREAU OF INVESTIGATION

Federal Bureau of Investigation (FBI), the investigative arm of the U.S. Department of Justice, which has as its mandate law enforcement in the United States and domestic intelligence. The FBI has been controversial in both areas, particularly during the directorship of J. Edgar Hoover (1924–1972), when critics claimed the bureau was denying the existence of organized crime and spying on law-abiding American citizens. Dossiers were compiled not only on U.S. Communist party functionaries but even on presidents of the United States. The FBI had little to do initially because crime control remained largely the prerogative of state and local governments. Exceptions included the White Slave Traffic

J. Edgar Hoover (1895–1972) served with the FBI from 1921 until his death. He became its director in 1924, revamping the bureau to improve its efficiency and focusing efforts to combat organized crime. A controversial figure, he was accused of using his office to pursue his own anti-liberal vendettas and enforce racist policies around the country. (Library of Congress/Corbis)

(Mann) Act of 1910 and the Motor Vehicles (Dyer) Act of 1919. During World War I the bureau investigated socialists and other critics of the war. Hoover joined the Justice Department in 1917 as a clerk and made his mark by organizing the postwar raids by Attorney General A. Mitchell Palmer against alien subversives and leading the government's action against Marcus Garvey and the Universal Negro Improvement Association. As FBI director he transformed the bureau from an agency riddled with corruption and rocked by involvement in the administration scandals of President Warren G. Harding into an efficient police agency. He labored in obscurity until the New Deal era, when Franklin D. Roosevelt's administration submitted anticrime legislation that dramatically expanded bureau jurisdiction. By the late 1930s Hoover and his "G-men" (government men) had become celebrities through their capture or killing of Depression-era criminals John Dillinger, Kate "Ma" Barker, and "Baby Face" Nelson. FBI domestic intelligence activity increased dramatically during World War II and especially the cold war. Hoover emerged as perhaps the federal government's most respected anticommunist, and his agents were seen as providing the first line of defense against a growing communist menace, but the director resisted further expansion on other fronts in the 1960s. He fought with some success against Attorney General Robert F. Kennedy's attempts to force more aggressive bureau investigations of organized crime and violations of federal civil rights laws.

J. Edgar Hoover impressed his superiors by organizing the Palmer Raids against alien subversives and leading the government's action against Marcus Garvey and the Universal Negro Improvement Association.

After Hoover's death in 1972, many of the FBI's files were opened under the Freedom of Information Act. They revealed that the bureau had done much more than compile intelligence on such "dissidents" as civil rights leader Martin Luther King, Jr. Special agents committed thousands of burglaries to gather information and ran counterintelligence programs to "neutralize" communists and anti–Vietnam War protestors. In so doing, the agency engaged in what a Justice Department task force described in 1977 as felonious conduct. The FBI kept a high and controversial profile thereafter. SWAT and hostage-rescue teams, first formed in 1973 and 1983 respectively, combated domestic terrorism, and the Behavioral Science Unit played a role in tracking down several of the nation's most infamous serial killers, including Wayne B. Williams, convicted in the Atlanta child murders case. Bureau agents entered President Ronald Reagan's war on drugs in 1982, finally overturning the Hoover dictum that drug cases should be avoided because the large amounts of cash involved would tempt and inevitably corrupt agents. The proposed merger of the Drug Enforcement Administration (DEA) into the FBI, however, never took place because it was opposed by both agencies. An interim proposal for the DEA administration to report to the attorney general through the FBI was also never implemented.

Solid police work and an occasional spectacular accomplishment were balanced by negative publicity. Critics pointed to the FBI's role in the 1993 siege and tragic storming of the Branch Davidian compound in Waco, Texas. Nor did they like its efforts to investigate opponents of the Reagan administration's Latin American policy. During the development of the Aldrich H. Ames affair within the Central Intelligence Agency in the late 1980s and early 1990s—the most serious infiltration of the CIA in its entire history, with the possible exception of the work of H. A. R. "Kim" Philby in the late 1940s—the CIA failed to call in the FBI. Therefore, Ames's successes as a Soviet mole, revealed in 1994 and involving the death of at least ten Russian officials who had been spying for the United States within the USSR, had nothing to do with any FBI failure. In fact, because of the Ames case, Congress passed legislation in 1994 putting the FBI in charge of all counterespionage efforts.

[See also Central Intelligence Agency; Waco Siege.]

BIBLIOGRAPHY

Curt Gentry, *J. Edgar Hoover: The Man and the Secrets* (New York, 1991).

Diarmuid Jeffreys, *The Bureau: Inside the Modern FBI* (Boston, 1995).

Ronald Kessler, *The FBI* (New York, 1993).

Kenneth O'Reilly, *Racial Matters: The FBI's Secret File on Black America, 1960–1972* (New York, 1989).

Sanford J. Ungar, *FBI* (Boston, 1975).

— KENNETH O'REILLY

FEDERAL COMMUNICATIONS COMMISSION

Federal Communications Commission, created by the Communications Act of 1934, superseded the Federal Radio Commission of 1927 and was given powers that had been scattered among the Interstate Commerce Commission and the Commerce and Post Office departments. The Federal Communications Commission (FCC) is an independent agency charged with regulating interstate and foreign communications by radio, television, telegraph, wire, and cable. It is responsible for the orderly development and operation—but not censorship—of broadcast services and for rapid and efficient nationwide and worldwide telephone and telegraph service at reasonable rates. It also coordinates licensed communications services into the national defense effort through the Emergency Broadcast System.

The commission consists of seven members appointed for seven-year terms by the president with the advice and consent of the Senate. The chairman, aided by the executive director, is responsible for general administration of the agency. He is designated by the president and serves at the president's pleasure. The principal operating sections are the Cable Television Bureau, which has regulated 3,000 CATV systems since 1970; the Common Carrier Bureau, which regulates foreign and interstate communications services and rates; the Broadcast Bureau, which licenses and regulates radio and television broadcast stations; and the Safety and Special Radio Services Bureau, which licenses and regulates, in particular, aviation, police and fire, taxicab, National Guard, and amateur facilities. Through nearly fifty field offices and many mobile units, the Field Engineering Bureau performs monitoring, inspection, operator examination, and investigative functions. The commission's jurisdiction covers the fifty states, Guam, Puerto Rico, and the Virgin Islands.

In 1934 the FCC was established with a budget of $1,146,885 and a staff of 442. In the early 1970's the agency had a budget of $27 million and nearly 1,600 employees. By the 1970's it was returning to the U.S. Treasury an amount in fees nearly equal to its budget. In the FCC's first four decades the number of broadcast stations increased more than ten times, to nearly 8,000 (commercial and educational, AM and FM, radio and television); the number of special broadcast stations jumped thirty-five times, from 51,000 to almost 1.8 million; and common-carrier telephone and telegraph revenues increased by billions.

Since the 1940's the commission has had to deal with one communications advance after another. Commercial television was approved in 1941 and very high frequency (VHF) channels assigned in 1945. Controversy over competing color television systems was resolved in 1951. Ultra high frequency (UHF) channels were assigned in 1952, and since 1963, new sets have been required to be capable of receiving VHF and UHF. Pay-TV was approved in 1969, and cable television expanded enormously during the 1960's and 1970's. Technical areas such as computer and satellite communications, land mobile frequency requirements, and telephone attachments are also matters of FCC concern, as well as organizational problems, such as the structure of the television industry and conglomerate ownership of broadcasting facilities. The regulation of broadcast time for political candidates continues to be a small, but important and vexatious, function of the FCC.

The decisions of the FCC may be appealed to the courts. While the power to regulate communications in the public interest, convenience, or necessity has occasionally involved the FCC in charges of censorship, the commission has been able to respond effectively to an extraordinary range of technical and administrative problems.

BIBLIOGRAPHY

Federal Communications Commission, *Annual Reports.*
C. Wilcox, *Public Policies Toward Business.*

— PAUL P. VAN RIPER

FEDERAL GOVERNMENT

Outwardly the U.S. federal government still resembles the political system created by the founding fathers at the Constitutional Convention of 1787. In many respects it accords with the original outline: the institutions of government (Congress, the presidency, and the Supreme Court); the basic roles and powers assigned to each of the three branches; the federal system, which, to prevent a concentration of authority, divides power on a territorial basis between national and state governments; the principle of separation of powers, which, again to prevent a concentration of authority, provides for an allocation of power to each of the three branches; and the checks-and-balances system, designed to protect the jurisdiction of each branch against encroachment by either of the other two. The Congress is still a bicameral body, endowed with the legislative authority and reflecting the two principles of representation originally prescribed: population in the House and state equality in the Senate. The president is still designated as the chief executive officer of the nation and is charged with the faithful execution of the laws. And the Supreme Court, and all other federal courts created by Congress under constitutional authority, still exercise such judicial power as is vested in them by the Constitution and by legislation.

Although all these likenesses can be found, the resemblance of today's federal government to that instituted by the Constitutional Convention is faint indeed. Massive changes have taken place with respect to (1) the scope of the powers of the federal government; (2) the character of the relationships between the branches of the federal government; and (3) the relationships between the government of the United States and the states. Because of these great changes it is not possible to understand the federal government solely by reference to the Constitution, nor may these changes be attributed to the amending process described in Article V.

As time and experience have demonstrated, federalism has not produced a lasting, inflexible division of powers between the two levels of government. Some matters—such as foreign relations, war and peace, a uniform monetary system, and control over foreign and interstate commerce—are obviously of such nature that a single national policy is required. Therefore these matters have been since the nation's inception exclusively within the jurisdiction of the federal government. But other matters that were once thought to be solely within the private realm or under state jurisdiction have come to be national concerns by reason of their nature and impact. Industrialization and urbanization have been principal contributing factors in this development, for the social problems they have created have demanded national solutions rather than the piecemeal answers sought by the states. For example, the federal Pure Food and Drug Act, by bringing the power of the federal government to bear, could accomplish what many different states could not. In addition, the failure of the states to provide equality of protection to all citizens under the law has led the federal government to extend its concern into this realm, and through legislative, administrative, and judicial actions it has been able to move the nation closer to honoring the principles set forth in the Constitution than was possible in the absence of federal involvement. Another contributing factor has been the transformation of the United States from a nation playing a largely isolated role in international politics to one of the wealthiest, most industrialized, and militarily strongest world powers.

Industrialization and urbanization have contributed to a need for federal problem-solving, for the social problems they have created have demanded nationwide solutions rather than the piecemeal responses sought by the states.

Equally important, these massive changes were not brought about by constitutional amendments. The twenty-six amendments made to the Constitution in nearly 190 years are not great in number; neither are they the principal reasons for the structural and policy changes that have occurred. These amendments are not inconsequential, for in securing the rights of the people, in seeking the destruction of both the institution and heritage of slavery, and in promoting new democratic goals (as in extending the voting privilege to Afro-Americans, women, and the young), they have been indeed important. Nevertheless, the most significant changes in the federal government have been produced by informal means, by constitutional interpretation, and by the use of precedent.

Each branch of the federal government shares equally in the power to interpret the Constitution. Congress has interpreted its power under the commerce clause to reach goals that relate only distantly to interstate commerce in its establishment of the "headless fourth branch" of government, the more than forty independent regulatory agencies—among them the Interstate Commerce Commission, the Federal Communications Commission, and the National Labor Relations Board—that claim either the commerce clause or some other as their constitutional base. These agencies exercise powers that are legislative, administrative, and judicial in character. Yet, unlike the three main branches, their existence and powers are ordained by ordinary legislation rather than by constitutional provision. Similarly, Congress has used its implied powers, an authority derived from the "necessary and proper" clause (Article I, Section 8, Clause 18), to reach special goals through legislation on such matters as minimum wages, maximum hours, social security, welfare, and medicare; to prohibit racial discrimination in employment, public accommodations, and housing; and to define as federal offenses certain criminal activities carried on across state lines, which, incidentally, benefits states by assisting them in enforcing their own criminal laws.

The president interprets the Constitution in claiming authority to deal directly with internal and international situations. He has become, in a sense, the chief legislator through his State of the Union message and his veto power and through the virtual renunciation by Congress of its control over the purse by vesting in the executive branch the responsibility for preparing the annual budget. And the president's role as chief executive officer has been broadened to make him chief peace officer of the nation as well: claiming constitutional authority, presidents have used U.S. troops, federal marshals, or state National Guardsmen to cope with industrial and racial disputes—to act when it has appeared that law and order have broken down at the state level.

Although the Supreme Court has the power of judicial review—that is, the power to declare unconstitutional an act or action of one of the political branches—the Court is likely to be significantly influenced in its interpretation of the meaning of the Constitution by the interpretations of those branches themselves. Although the Court has used this power in more than 120 instances to protect property or other rights against national laws, it has also repudiated its earlier decisions on occasion as a consequence of the justices' accepting an interpretation previously rendered by Congress or the president.

Custom and usage are the other informal means of change, providing authority for a similar course of action later. The frequent reuse of precedents leads to their becoming institutionalized features of the political system, even though devoid of constitutional sanction. Among the principal examples are the cabinet (introduced by George Washington), political parties, the two-party system, national nominating conventions, and the presidents' use of executive agreements in lieu of treaties (avoiding constitutional requirement of senatorial consent). Prominent among institutionalized precedents is the power of the president to commit U.S. troops to hostilities without a congressional declaration of war. (The Vietnam War has served as a catalyst to increase demands that the president's warmaking power be curtailed.)

Because of two factors—increased national involvement in internal affairs and America's emergence as a world power—the authority, roles, and responsibilities of the federal government have grown tremendously. Internally this growth is reflected in the increased number of federal civil service employees (roughly 2.5 million in 1974) and the addition of new federal departments and agencies (for example, the Department of Health, Education, and Welfare and the Department of Housing and Urban Development). The international situation has led to an armed forces of approximately 2.5 million in 1974. Even more apparent as an outgrowth of the expanded role of the federal government have been the enlargement and expansion of the powers, roles, and responsibilities of the presidency—a powerful executive office, not contemplated by the founding fathers and in fact abhorred by them. Although the evolution of the original constitutional structure permits the characterization of the federal government as a strong presidential system, events since 1970, and principally the forced resignation of President Richard Nixon, have shown that the chief executive is subject to external restraints.

BIBLIOGRAPHY

P. A. Dionisopoulos, *The Government of the United States.*

— P. ALLAN DIONISOPOULOS

FEDERALIST PARTY

The first Federalists were men whose experiences during the Revolution predisposed them to seek national solutions for the major issues of their time. Beginning as a cluster of nationalists within the Continental Congress, including Robert Morris, James Madison, George Washington, and John Jay, they were instrumental in calling the Constitutional Convention in 1787. Although they probably represented only a bare majority—if that—of public opinion in 1788, they were able to wage a sophisticated and successful political campaign that resulted in the ratification of the federal constitution.

Virtually all members of the First Congress counted themselves Federalists; so did the president and all the members of the cabinet. Initially Federalism was compatible with a wide range of opinion. Federalists were slow in acknowledging their partisanship. So long as they remained in power, staffing the cabinet and the agencies of federal government, Federalists could think of themselves as the government, not as a party. But the First Congress quickly developed pro- and antiadministration alignments; most noticeably on financial policy as outlined by Secretary of the Treasury Alexander Hamilton, on foreign policy as managed by President Washington and Secretary of Foreign Affairs Jay, on the location of the capital city, and on the breadth of executive discretionary power. The policies of the successive Federalist administrations emphasized neutrality in foreign affairs while increasing trade with England, vigorous action against Indians on the frontier, and a national revenue system, backed by a funded national debt and a national bank. Washington had been elected president by a unanimous electoral college, but there was less enthusiasm for John Adams in the 1796 election. A shift of three electoral votes would have placed Thomas Jefferson, the Democratic-Republican candidate, in office. Adams was faced with increasing opposition from within his own party. By the end of Adams' term, Hamilton had openly published a virulent attack against the leader of his own party. By 1800 there were two Federalist factions in Congress: one group of Federalists, like Robert Goodloe Harper, who reacted to the French challenge far more sharply than Adams thought wise and who initiated the Alien and Sedition Acts, a large army, and new loans, and those who, like John

Marshall, supported Adams' management of the Quasi-War with France.

Federalists seem to have included a disproportionate number of gentry. In all areas except Virginia the established elites were Federalist. There were vigorous Federalist parties in commercial cities also, but they faced strong opposition. Federalism was least likely to be opposed in areas that were isolated and whose growth was static. The party also attracted strong and continuing support from less prosperous groups: frontier farmers in New York, who were pleased with the maintenance of stable relations with Indians, and farmers in western Virginia, who were skeptical of the tidewater planters. Nevertheless, throughout the 1790's what had once been overwhelming public support for the Federalists eroded as supporters became alienated by a fiscal policy apparently keyed to the interests of northern merchants and commercial farmers and a foreign policy that could be interpreted as unduly dependent on the maintenance of good relations with England. By 1795 it was clear that an opposition party had been mobilized by former allies, notably Madison and Jefferson; by 1800 the vote of the electoral college for the presidency resulted in a tie between two members of the opposition, Jefferson and Aaron Burr.

Throughout the 1790's, public favor for the Federalists dwindled as supporters became disenchanted with a fiscal policy keyed to the interests of northern merchants.

The election of 1800 was thrown into the Federalist-controlled House of Representatives, where the Federalists, in part on Hamilton's urging, eventually backed Jefferson rather than Burr. Theirs became the first modern political party to accept peaceably a fall from power. After 1800 they did not again win a national election, but they continued to offer substantial challenge to their opponents for local and national office. In defeat they were forced to broaden their appeal and rationalize their organization; particularly in Massachusetts and New Jersey they developed a very complicated network of local conventions and county committees through which popular support could be absorbed. In their dissent to the Jefferson and Madison administrations the Federalists were joined by disaffected Republicans, like John Randolph of Virginia, and after 1807 they attracted more supporters by their opposition to Jefferson's embargo (1807–08) and to Republican foreign policy. But despite the vigor of their opposition and their modest success in local politics, they continued to be outvoted in Congress on major national issues: the reform of the judiciary, the purchase of Louisiana, the embargo, and finally the War of 1812.

In 1804 a small cluster of impatient Federalists, without mass support, toyed with schemes of disunion. Thereafter Federalists expressed antiembargo and antiwar sentiments by mobilizing public dissent in corresponding committees and state conventions. The Hartford Convention, held in 1815, was the best organized and the most important of these. An attempt by the opposition to get its way without resorting to nullification of the Constitution, the convention petitioned for constitutional amendments that might make it impossible for a war similar to the War of 1812 to occur. These amendments would have prohibited embargoes of more than sixty days, required a two-thirds vote of Congress to declare war or admit new states, and limited the presidency to one term. The convention also attacked the three-fifths compromise (by which three-fifths of the slave population was to be counted in the apportionment of representation) as an arrangement that gave undue political influence to slave states.

Although many Federalists drifted into the Republican party during the war years, as did Oliver Wolcott, Jr., of Connecticut, Federalists retained their partisan identity well into the so-called Era of Good Feeling (1817–25), during President James Monroe's two terms. They continued to control the state governments of Maryland, Delaware, Connecticut, and Massachusetts and to represent large popular minorities in other states. But the party disintegrated during the 1820's, as a political perspective forged in the years of the Revolution came to seem increasingly inappropriate and outdated.

BIBLIOGRAPHY

John C. Miller, *The Federalist Era.*

David Hackett Fischer, *The Revolution of American Conservatism.*

James M. Banner, Jr., *To the Hartford Convention.*

Linda K. Kerber, *Federalists in Dissent.*

— LINDA K. KERBER

FEDERAL RESERVE SYSTEM

Federal Reserve System, the central bank of the United States, was founded by the Owen-Glass Act of Dec. 23, 1913. It is unique in that it is not one bank but twelve regional banks coordinated by a central board in Washington, D.C. A central bank is a bank for banks: it does for them what they do for individuals and business firms. It holds their deposits (their legal reserves) for safekeeping; it makes them loans; and it creates its own credit in the form of created deposits (additional legal reserves) or bank notes (Federal Reserve notes). It lends to them only if they appear strong enough to repay the loan. It also has the responsibility of promoting economic stability insofar as that is possible by control of credit.

The nation's first bank, the Bank of North America, founded in 1781, was possibly its first central bank. Certainly the first Bank of the United States (1791–1811), serving as fiscal agent and regulator of the currency as well as doing a commercial banking business, was a central bank in its day. So likewise was the second Bank of the United States (1816–36), although it performed that function badly in 1817–20 but well in 1825–26. The Independent Treasury System (1840–41, 1846–1921) was in no sense a central bank. A great fault of the National Banking System (1863–1913) was its lack of a central bank. The idea, and even the name, was politically taboo, which helps explain the form and name taken by the Federal Reserve System.

The faults of the National Banking System—perversely elastic bank notes, the paradox of dispersed legal reserves that were unhappily drawn as if by a magnet to finance stock speculation in New York, and the lack of a central bank to deal with the panics of 1873, 1884, 1893, and 1907—pointed out the need for reform. After the 1907 panic a foreign central banker called the United States "a great financial nuisance." J. P. Morgan was the hero of the panic, saving the nation as if he were a one-man central bank, but in doing this he also showed that he had more financial power than it seemed safe for one man to possess in a democracy. The 1912 Pujo Money Trust investigation further underlined his control over all kinds of banks. Meanwhile the Aldrich-Vreeland Currency Act of May 30, 1908, provided machinery to handle any near-term crisis and created the National Monetary Commission to investigate foreign banking systems and suggest reforms. Republican Sen. Nelson Aldrich proposed a National Reserve Association in 1911 consisting of a central bank, fifteen branches, and a top board controlled by the nation's leading bankers (in turn dominated by J. P. Morgan, critics said). It never passed, and the Democrats won the 1912 election. They accepted the groundwork done by Aldrich and others, but President Woodrow Wilson insisted that the nation's president choose the top board of this quasi-public institution. Democratic Rep. Carter Glass pushed the bill through Congress.

All national banks had to subscribe immediately 3 percent of their capital and surplus for stock in the Federal Reserve System to provide it capital to begin. State banks might also become "members" (that is, share in the ownership and privileges of the system). The Federal Reserve System was superimposed on the National Banking System, the new law correcting the major and minor shortcomings of the old one. In addition to providing a central bank, it supplied an elastic note issue of Federal Reserve notes based on commercial paper whose supply rose and fell with the needs of business; it required member banks to keep half their legal reserves (after mid-1917 all of them) in their district Federal Reserve banks; and it improved the check-clearing system. The seven-man board took office Aug. 10, 1914, and the banks opened for business Nov. 16. World War I having just begun, the new system was already much needed. But parts of the law that had been controversial were so vaguely written that only practice could provide an interpretation of them. For that to be achieved, the system needed wise and able leadership. This did not come from the board in Washington, chaired by the secretary of the treasury and often in disagreement about how much to cooperate with the Treasury, but from Benjamin Strong, head of the system's biggest bank, that of New York. He was largely responsible for persuading bankers to accept the Federal Reserve System and for enlarging its influence.

At first the Federal Reserve's chief responsibilities were to create enough credit to carry on the nation's part of World War I and to process Liberty Bond sales. The system's lower reserve requirements for deposits in member banks contributed also to a sharp credit expansion by 1920, accompanied by a doubling of the price level. In 1919, out of deference to the Treasury's needs, the Federal Reserve delayed unduly long in raising discount rates, a step needed to discourage commodity speculation. That was a major mistake. In 1922 the system's leaders became aware of the value of open-market buying operations to promote recovery and open-market selling operations to choke off speculative booms. Strong worked in the 1920's with Montagu Norman, head of the Bank of England, to help bring other nations back to the gold standard. To assist them, he employed open-market buying operations and lowered discount rates so that Americans would not draw off their precious funds at the crucial moment of resumption. But plentiful U.S. funds and other reasons promoted stock market speculation here. Strong's admirers feel he might have controlled the situation had he lived, but he fell sick in February 1928 and died Oct. 16. As in 1919 the Federal Reserve did too little too late to stop the speculative boom that culminated in the October 1929 crash. In the years 1930–32 more than 5,000 banks failed, and 4,000 more failed in 1933. Whether the Federal Reserve should have made credit easier than it did is still a debated point. Businessmen were not in a borrowing mood, and banks gave loans close scrutiny. The bank holocaust, with a $1 billion loss to depositors, brought on congressional investigations and revelations in 1931–33, and demands for reforms and for measures to promote recovery. Congress overhauled the Federal Reserve System.

By the act of Feb. 27, 1932, Congress temporarily permitted the Federal Reserve to use federal government obligations as well as gold and commercial paper to back Federal Reserve notes and deposits. A dearth of commercial paper in the depression and bank failures that stimulated hoarding were creating a currency shortage, and a new backing for the bank notes was essential. However much justified at the moment, the law soon became permanent and made inflation in the future easier.

Four other measures about this time were very important. These were the Banking Act of June 16, 1933; parts of the Securities Act of May 27, 1933, and of the Securities Exchange Act of June 19, 1934; and the Banking Act of Aug. 23, 1935. Taken together, the acts attempted to do four basic things: (1) restore confidence in the banks, (2) strengthen the banks, (3) remove temptations to speculate, and (4) increase the powers of the Federal Reserve System, notably of the board. To restore confidence, the 1933 and 1935 banking acts set up the Federal Deposit Insurance Corporation, which first sharply reduced, and after 1945 virtually eliminated, bank failures. To strengthen the banks, the acts softened restrictions on branch banking and on real estate loans and admitted mutual savings banks and some others. It was felt that the Federal Reserve could do more to control banks if they were brought into the system. To remove temptations to speculate, the banks were forbidden to pay interest on demand deposits, forbidden to use Federal Reserve credit for speculative purposes, and obliged to dispose of their investment affiliates. To increase the system's powers, the board was reorganized, without the secretary of treasury, and given more control over member banks; the Federal Reserve bank boards were assigned a more subordinate role; and the board gained more control over open-market operations and got important new credit regulating powers. These last included the authority to raise or lower margin requirements and also to raise member bank legal reserve requirements to as much as double the previous figures.

The board in 1936–37 doubled reserve requirements; for reduced borrowings during the depression, huge gold inflows (caused by the dollar devaluation in January 1934) and the growing threat of war in Europe were causing the member banks to have large excess reserves. Banks with excess reserves are not dependent on the Federal Reserve and so cannot be controlled by it. This probably helped to bring on the 1937 recession.

During the Great Depression, World War II, and even afterward, the Federal Reserve, with Marriner Eccles as board chairman (1936–48), kept interest rates low and encouraged member banks to buy government obligations. The new economic (Keynesian) philosophy stressed the importance of low interest rates to promote investment, employment, and recovery, with the result that for about a decade it became almost the duty of the Federal Reserve to keep the nation on what was sometimes called a "low interest rate standard." In World War II, as in World War I, the Federal Reserve assisted with bond drives and saw to it that the federal government and member banks had ample funds for the war effort. Demand deposits tripled between 1940 and 1945, and the price level doubled during the 1940's; there was somewhat less inflation with somewhat more provocation than during World War I. The Federal Reserve's regulation limiting consumer credit, price controls, and the depression before the war were mainly responsible. Regulation W was in effect from Sept. 1, 1941, to Nov. 1, 1947, and twice briefly again before 1952. The board also kept margin requirements high, but it was unable to use its open-market or discount tools to limit credit expansion. On the contrary, it had to maintain a "pattern of rates" on federal government obligations, ranging from three-eighths of 1 percent for Treasury bills to 2.5 percent for long-term bonds. That amounted often to open-market buying operations, which promoted inflation. Admittedly, it also encouraged war-bond buying by keeping bond prices at par or better. Securities support purchases (1941–45), executed for the system by the New York Federal Reserve Bank, raised the system's holdings of Treasury obligations from about $2 billion to about $24 billion. The rationale for the Federal Reserve's continuing these purchases after the war was the Treasury's wish to hold down interest charges on the $250 billion public debt and the fear of a postwar depression—based on Keynesian economics and memory of the 1921 depression—by the administration of Harry Truman. The Federal Reserve was not fully relieved of the duty to support federal government security prices until it concluded its "accord" with the Treasury, reported on Mar. 4, 1951. Thereafter interest rates moved more freely, and the Federal Reserve could again use open-market selling operations and be freer to raise discount rates. At times bond prices fell sharply and there were complaints of "tight money." Board Chairman William McChesney Martin, who succeeded Thomas McCabe (1948–51) on Apr. 2, 1951, pursued a middle-of-the-road policy during the 1950's, letting interest rates find their natural level whenever possible, but using credit controls to curb speculative booms in 1953, 1956–57, and 1959–60 and to reduce recession and unemployment in 1954, 1958, and late 1960. After the Full Employment Act of 1946 the Federal Reserve, along with many other federal agencies, was expected to play its part in promoting full employment.

For many years the thirty member banks in New York and Chicago complained of the unfairness of legal reserve requirements that were higher for them than for other banks, and bankers generally felt they should be permitted to count cash held in the banks as part of their legal reserves. A law of July 28, 1959, reduced member banks to two classifications: 295 reserve city banks in fifty-one cities, and about 6,000 "country" banks, starting not later than July 28, 1962. According to this law, member banks might count their vault cash as legal reserves. Thereafter the requirement for legal reserves against demand deposits ranged between 10 and 22 percent for member city banks and between 7 and 14 percent for member country banks.

During the period between 1961 and 1972 stimulating economic growth, enacting social welfare reforms, and waging war in Vietnam were major activities of the federal government that raised annual expenditures from $97 billion in fiscal 1960 to $268 billion in fiscal 1974; saw a budget deficit in all but three years of that period; raised the public debt by almost 70 percent; and increased the money supply (currency and demand deposits) from $144 billion on Dec. 31, 1960, to $281 billion on Oct. 30, 1974. As early as 1958 the nation's international balance of payments situation was draining off its gold reserves (reflected in the Federal Reserve's gold certificate holdings). These fell from $23 billion on Dec. 31, 1957, to $15.5 billion on Dec. 31, 1964. With only $1.4 billion free (without penalties to the Federal Reserve) for payments to foreign creditors, Congress on Feb. 18, 1965, repealed the 25 percent gold certificate requirement against deposits in Federal Reserve banks on the theory that this action would increase confidence in the dollar by making $3.5 billion additional gold available to foreign central banks or for credit expansion at home. But the situation worsened. On Mar. 18, 1968, Congress removed a similar 25 percent reserve requirement against Federal Reserve notes, thereby freeing up all the nation's gold. Nevertheless the gold drain became so alarming that on Aug. 15, 1971, President Richard M. Nixon announced that the United States would no longer redeem its dollars in gold.

All these developments affected, and were affected by, Federal Reserve policies. During much of the 1960's, government economists thought they had the fiscal and monetary tools to "fine tune" the economy (that is, to dampen booms and to soften depressions), but the recession of 1966 damaged that belief. During the late 1960's the monetarist school of economists, led by Milton Friedman of the University of Chicago—seeking to increase the money supply at a modest but steady rate—had considerable influence. In general, Chairman Martin advocated a moderate rate of credit expansion, and in late May 1965 he commented on the "disquieting similarities between our present prosperity and the fabulous '20's." But Congress and President Lyndon B. Johnson continued their heavy spending policies. And the president reappointed Martin as chairman in March 1967: his departure might have alarmed European central bankers and precipitated a monetary crisis. With Martin's retirement early in 1970 and Arthur F. Burns's appointment as board chairman, credit became somewhat easier again.

Throughout this era, restraining inflation, a vital concern of the Federal Reserve, was increasingly difficult. What did the money supply consist of? If demand deposits are money, why not readily convertible time deposits? And if time deposits are money (as monetarists contended), then why not savings and loan association "deposits" or U.S. government E and H bonds? And what of the quite unregulated Eurodollar supply? As a result of such uncontrolled increases in the money supply, consumer prices rose 66 percent in the period 1960–74, most of it after 1965.

As of Nov. 27, 1974, members of the Federal Reserve System included 5,767 banks of 14,384 in the United States, and they held 77 percent of all bank deposits in the nation.

BIBLIOGRAPHY

G. L. Bach, *Federal Reserve Policy Making.*

L. Chandler, *Benjamin Strong: Central Banker.*

Federal Reserve Board, *The Federal Reserve System, All Bank Statistics, 1896–1955,* and *The Federal Reserve Bulletin.*

Milton Friedman and A. Schwartz, *A Monetary History of the United States.*

E. W. Kemmerer and D. L. Kemmerer, *ABC of the Federal Reserve System.*

P. A. Samuelson and H. Krooss, *Documentary History of Banking and Currency in the United States.*

P. M. Warburg, *The Federal Reserve System.*

— DONALD L. KEMMERER

THE FEDERAL RESERVE SYSTEM SINCE THE 1970S

Federal Reserve System, usually referred to as "the Fed," has changed markedly in structure, scope, and procedures since the 1970s. In the middle of that decade, the Fed confronted what came to be known as "the attrition problem," a drop-off in the number of banks participating in the Federal Reserve System. The decrease resulted from the prevalence of unusually high interest rates that, because of the Fed's so-called reserve requirement, made membership in the system unattractive to banks. In the United States, bank charters are issued by the federal government (to national banks) or by states (to state banks). All national banks were required by statute to join the Federal Reserve; membership was optional for state banks. The Fed provided many privileges to its members but required them to hold reserves in non-interest-earning accounts at one of the twelve district Federal Reserve banks or as vault cash. While many states assessed reserve requirements for nonmember banks, the amounts were usually lower than the federal reserves, and the funds could be held in an interest-earning form. As interest rates rose to historical highs in the mid-1970s, the cost of membership in the Fed began to outweigh the benefits for many banks, because their profits were reduced by the reserve requirement. State banks began to withdraw from the Federal Reserve, and some national banks took up state charters in order to be able to drop their memberships. Federal Reserve officials feared they were losing control of the national banking system as a result of the attrition in membership.

The Depository Institutions Deregulation and Monetary Control Act of 1980 addressed the attrition problem by requiring reserves for all banks and thrift institutions offering accounts on which checks could be drawn. The act phased out most ceilings on deposit interest and allowed institutions subject to Federal Reserve requirements (whether members or not) to have access to the so-called discount window (that is, to borrow from the Federal Reserve) and to use other services, such as check processing and electronic funds transfer on a fee-for-service basis.

In the same decade a period of dramatic growth began in international banking, with foreign banks setting up branches and subsidiaries within the United States. Some U.S. banks claimed to be at a competitive disadvantage because foreign banks escaped the regulations and restrictions placed on domestic banks, such as those affecting branching of banks and nonbanking activities. In addition, foreign banks were free of the reserve requirement. The International Banking Act of 1978 gave regulatory and supervisory authority over foreign banks to the Federal Reserve. Together with the Depository Institutions Act of 1980, it helped "level the playing field" for domestic banks.

Unlike most other countries where the central bank is closely controlled by the government, the Federal Reserve System enjoys a fair amount of independence in pursuing its principal function—the control of the nation's money supply. Since passage of the Full Employment and Balanced Growth (Humphrey-Hawkins) Act of 1978, the Federal Reserve has been required to report to Congress twice each year, in February and July, on "objectives and plans . . . with respect to the ranges of growth or diminution of the monetary and credit aggregates." The Federal Reserve System must "include an explanation of the reason for any revisions to or deviations from such objectives and plans." These reports enable Congress to monitor monetary policy and performance and to improve coordination of monetary and government fiscal policies. The independence of the Federal Reserve System and its accountability continued to be controversial issues into the 1990s.

[See also Banking and Finance.]

BIBLIOGRAPHY

Board of Governors of the Federal Reserve System, *The Federal Reserve System: Purposes and Functions* (Washington D.C., 1994).

— EARL W. ADAMS

FIFTEENTH AMENDMENT

Fifteenth Amendment, proclaimed Mar. 30, 1870, forbids federal and state governments to deny or abridge the right to vote "on account of race, color, or previous condition of servitude" and empowers the Congress "to enforce this article by appropriate legislation." Earlier attempts by Radical Republicans to guarantee the franchise to the newly emancipated slaves had failed. The Fifteenth Amendment proved for many years to be equally ineffective.

The endless countermeasures the amendment evoked in the southern states fell into two categories: those that purported to be legal and those that frankly defied the law, relying upon violence, intimidation, and fraud. As popular attitudes and public authorities combined to keep Afro-Americans from the polls, such discrimination was not significantly countered until the late 1950's. Thereafter, the Civil Rights acts of 1957, 1960, and 1964, in small measure, and more especially the Voting Rights Act of 1965 drastically diminished the force of discriminatory tactics.

Chief among the so-called legal modes of disfranchisement were enactments that imposed, or authorized political parties and local election officials to impose, various qualifications with which the mass of Afro-Americans might be shown to be unable to comply. Without mentioning race, the requirements, often very intricate, were so framed that they could be construed to disqualify most blacks, and they were selectively enforced to exempt whites. Among the chief "legal" subterfuges were literacy tests, poll taxes, grandfather clauses, and white primaries, all of them effectually disposed of by the late 1960's by laws and court decisions grounded upon the Fifteenth Amendment itself or upon the equal protection clause of the Fourteenth Amendment.

Federal legislation of the 1960's to enforce the Fifteenth Amendment weakened literacy tests, and then the federal courts struck them down, even though impartially applied, because older patterns of unequal educational opportunities still produced disproportionately high rates of illiteracy among Afro-Americans. State grandfather clauses were declared unconstitutional as early as 1915 by the Supreme Court as direct affronts to the Fifteenth Amendment. The white primary, confining participation in Democratic primaries to whites, was also overthrown by the Court as offensive to the equal protection clause. When it was later revived in more "judge-proof" form, it was disposed of in *Smith* v. *Allwright* (1944), strictly on Fifteenth Amendment principles. The poll tax was swept from state practice, as far as federal elections were concerned, in 1964 by the Twenty-fourth Amendment, and two years later the prohibition was judicially extended to state and local elections purely on Fifteenth Amendment grounds.

The eventual effectuation of the amendment by legislation, litigation, and executive enforcement on federal and state levels had, by 1972, eliminated the major obstacles encountered by blacks in their attempts to vote. In 1940 a mere 5 percent of voting-age southern blacks were registered, but in 1972 the figure approached 60 percent and was still rising. Meanwhile, growing compliance, especially after 1960, also resulted in the election of numerous blacks to public office. In 1969 there were in the United States some 1,200 black elected officials, 385 of them in the South. At the close of 1972 there were approximately 1,200 in the South alone, including members of Congress from Georgia and Texas.

BIBLIOGRAPHY

Richard Bardolph, *The Civil Rights Record: Black Americans and the Law, 1849–1970.*

Jack Greenberg, *Race Relations and American Law.*

Donald R. Matthews and James W. Prothro, *Negroes and the New Southern Politics.*

— RICHARD BARDOLPH

FILIBUSTER, CONGRESSIONAL

Congressional filibuster, the practice in the U.S. Senate of prolonging debate and using other delaying tactics to prevent action, or the possibility of action, by forcing the body to end its consideration of a proposal. Although it has been supported as a means to promote full and open debate on issues, the filibuster has been used more frequently simply to frustrate attempts to pass legislation.

The filibuster was used intermittently in the Senate from 1806 to 1917, an era when no general rule limited debate. In the House of Representatives, its use has been minimized by the early adoption of strict limits on debate.

The modern history of the filibuster began in 1917 when the Senate amended Rule 22 by adopting cloture provisions for limiting debate. Since then more than fifty major filibusters have been recorded on such measures as civil rights bills (the most conspicuous usage), the communications satellite bill, and reform of the military draft system. The longest filibuster ranged over seventy-five days in 1964. The individual record belongs to Sen. J. Strom Thurmond, who in 1957 held the floor for over twenty-four hours.

According to the amended Rule 22 the Senate may, upon the petition of sixteen senators and after two days' delay, act to end a filibuster or any other debate by a three-fifths vote of the senators duly chosen and sworn (normally sixty votes) except on a measure or motion to amend the Senate rules, in which case a vote by two-thirds of those present and voting is required. If a petition for cloture is approved, each senator may still speak for one hour before debate automatically ends. From 1917 to 1975 some 100 cloture petitions have been voted on; on only 21 of these was the filibuster ended. Cloture has been used successfully on a variety of issues, such as the Versailles Treaty (1917), the World Court (1925), branch banking (1927), Prohibition (1927), communications satellites (1962), civil rights (1964), voting rights (1965), open housing (1968), and the military draft system (1971).

The longest filibuster ranged over 75 days in 1964; the individual record belongs to Sen. Strom Thurmond, who in 1957 held the floor for over 24 hours.

Many proposals have been introduced to make it easier to close off debate; few have been adopted. Resistance to reforming the cloture rule is based on such motives as a genuine desire to air issues, a sensitivity to minority rights, and the latent fear of many senators that they themselves might want to filibuster some day, as well as the apparent complexity of changing the Senate rules. In addition, filibusters are not attempted so frequently as to regularly impede the work of the Senate. Thus, most senators seemingly do not view the obstructive capacity of the filibuster as excessive.

The importance of the filibuster lies in the ability of a few senators, or even one senator, to prevent issues from coming to a vote. The potential power of the filibuster is enhanced in the last few days of a session when there is usually a large backlog of significant legislation waiting to be considered. Since a filibuster brings almost all organized Senate activity to a halt, there is substantial pressure to drop the filibustered item from consideration so as to proceed to the rest of the agenda.

On the whole, while filibusters usually add little either to the knowledge of senators or to public awareness, they may provide some restraint on precipitous majority action. In the last analysis the filibuster remains a potentially powerful weapon only in especially emotion-laden situations when opinion in the Senate is strongly divided. It is used successfully only to the extent that a large number of senators permit such usage. A large, determined majority in the Senate, as evidenced in 1964 in the debates on the Civil Rights Bill and in 1965 on the Voting Rights Bill, can end a filibuster whatever the issue. But in the diverse American society, it is frequently difficult to create such a majority. The filibuster benefits minorities and is most harmful to weak and transient majorities.

BIBLIOGRAPHY

Congressional Quarterly, *Guide to the Congress of the United States.*

L. A. Froman, Jr., *The Congressional Process.*

William J. Keefe and Morris S. Ogul, *The American Legislative Process.*

— MORRIS S. OGUL

FINNEY REVIVALS

Finney Revivals began under the preaching of the evangelist Charles G. Finney in central New York about 1825. The period of their greatest intensity was from 1827 to 1835, during which meetings were held in most of the large cities of the country and resulted in thousands of conversions. Although supported by such wealthy philanthropists as Lewis and Arthur Tappan and Anson G. Phelps, the revivals aroused much opposition because of Finney's "new measures," especially his introduction of the "anxious bench," where awakened sinners sat in public view. His converts furnished a large proportion of the leadership for the many reform movements of the three decades preceding the Civil War.

BIBLIOGRAPHY

Charles G. Finney, *Memoirs of Rev. Charles G. Finney, Written by Himself.*

W. G. McLoughlin, *Modern Revivalism.*

— WILLIAM W. SWEET

FIRST LADY

First lady, the wife of the president of the United States or a woman designated by him to be the hostess in the White House. Without a constitutional assignment or an appointed office, the wives of the presidents have occupied a strategic political position. Beginning with Abigail Adams in 1800, when the White House was completed, the first lady has represented the cultural and social aspects of the presidency as the nation competed with European courts. Dolley Madison exerted unusual influence during James Madison's presidency (1809–1817) because of her ability to use social occasions to her husband's advantage. In many ways the position has reflected American's expectations for upper-class women. By the time of the Progressive Era, good works, charities, and goodwill described the role and spheres of interest of the first lady. Eleanor Roosevelt demonstrated admirably in twelve years (1933–1945) what the first lady could accomplish for the nation's poor, women, and children. Jacqueline Kennedy set the social standard for the remainder of the twentieth century during John F. Kennedy's brief term (1961–1963).

Congress and the press often objected when the first lady became outspoken or appeared publicly to have a political partnership with her husband and her own political power. In the nineteenth century controversies arose when Abigail Adams voiced her political opinions and suggested government appointments, and when Sarah Polk served as her husband's secretary (1845–1849). In the twentieth century the exercise of such derivative political power stirred controversy when Edith Wilson, for example, controlled information and access to Woodrow Wilson during his illnesses in 1919, and when Eleanor Roosevelt urged the nation's citizens to write her and acted like a vice president by traveling widely to represent her disabled husband. Objections also arose when Rosalynn Carter attended President Jimmy Carter's cabinet meetings (1977–1981) and when Nancy Reagan publicly corrected her husband's statements during his presidency (1981–1989) and determined some of his public appearances by consulting an astrologer. When Hillary Rodham Clinton headed a major national task force on health, she came to symbolize the dilemma of all assertive first ladies: Should power derived from their husbands be made accountable to Congress or the public? The actions of the first ladies have always been publicly observed, evaluated, and criticized. With expanded mass media in the post–World War II era and the newsworthiness of the first lady, it became impossible for these women to hide within the White House, even when they were ill, as did Carolina Harrison (1840) and Ida McKinley (1897–1905). Someone like Elizabeth "Bess" Truman (1945–1953), although a reticent woman, received more coverage in the *New York Times* than the more socially active Lou Henry Hoover (1929–1933). The position of first lady reflects American womanhood and is constantly evolving. As more and more women hold careers independent of their husbands, this unpaid but staffed position may be less compelling. The role of hostess at the White House may be turned over to protocol appointments and her social causes may be assigned to administrative departments. Indeed, it is probable that a woman may one day be elected president of the United States and her spouse independently pursue a career, as did the husbands of British Prime Minister Margaret Thatcher and Irish President Mary Robinson during their tenure in office.

BIBLIOGRAPHY

Carl Sferrazza Anthony, *First Ladies: The Saga of the Presidents' Wives and Their Power, 1789–1961* (New York, 1993).

Betty Boyd Caroli, *First Ladies* (New York, 1987).

Myra G. Gutin, *The President's Partner: The First Lady in the Twentieth Century* (New York, 1989).

Betty Houchin Winfield, "Anna Eleanor Roosevelt's White House Legacy: The Public First Lady," *Presidential Studies Quarterly* 18 (1988).

— BETTY HOUCHIN WINFIELD

FIVE-POWER NAVAL TREATY

Five-Power Naval Treaty, one of seven treaties negotiated at the Washington Conference on Limitation of Armaments. Settlement of Far Eastern questions, principally through the Four-Power and Nine-Power treaties, made possible the Naval Treaty of Washington, signed on Feb. 6, 1922, placing limitations upon capital ships, aircraft carriers, and Far Eastern naval bases. Aggregate battleship tonnage was restricted to 525,000 for the United States and Great Britain, 315,000 for Japan, and 175,000 for France and Italy. This quota required the United States to scrap twenty-eight capital ships then under construction or completed. Competitive building of cruisers, destroyers, and submarines continued until the 1930 London Treaty.

— DUDLEY W. KNOX

President Franklin D. Roosevelt and Mrs. Eleanor Roosevelt at the Inaugural Parade in Washington, D. C. (F. D. R. Library)

FOLK ART

Between the 1970s and 1990s there was a surge of interest in folk art, particularly contemporary folk art that was also identified as "self-taught" and "outsider" art. This work assumed a high profile in the marketplace and in the art media, with increasing numbers of exhibitions and published catalogs and monographs. The level of attention was reminiscent of the first wave of interest in the 1910s and 1920s, when a group of modernist artists including Robert Laurent, Yasuo Kuniyoshi, Elie Nadelman, Charles Sheeler, Marsden Hartley, the curator Holger Cahill, and the gallery owner Edith Gregor Halpert began to collect and study artworks by self-taught creators. In effect, they invented the genre now called American folk art, which encompasses a wide variety of works, including paintings, ink drawings, sculpture, carvings, fiber art, and "visionary environments," a term describing highly personalized creations, usually handmade with materials easy to come by, that often are the result of many years of the creator's concentrated efforts.

The connection between schooled and unschooled artists continued in subsequent decades. Charles Shannon befriended Bill Traylor after the two met in downtown Montgomery, Ala., in 1939. Sterling and Dorothy Strauser, Pennsylvania artists, became patrons of Victor Joseph Gatto in the 1940s and of Justin McCarthy and Jack Savitsky in the 1960s. Whitney Halstead, an art historian on the faculty of the Chicago Institute of Art, met Joseph Yoakum in 1957 and introduced the artist and his watercolor drawings to the artists Jim Nutt and his wife, Gladys Nilsson. Nutt discovered the drawings of Martin Ramirez in 1968 while the former was working as a visiting instructor at Sacramento State College. The sculptor Michael Hall and his wife, Julie Hall, recognized the artistry of Kentucky carver Edgar Tolson in the 1960s. Phyllis Kind, owner of a contemporary art gallery, showed the art of Yoakum and Ramirez in the early 1970s and added to her roster that of Tolson, Eddie Arning, Steve Ashby, Peter "Charlie" Attie Besharo, Mary K. Borkowski, Miles Carpenter, Henry Darger, Minnie Evans, Howard Finster, Elijah Pierce, Drossos P. Skyllas, P. M. Wentworth, and Malcah Zeldis.

Between the 1970s and the 1990s folk art assumed a high profile in the marketplace and in the art media—a resurgence of interest reminiscent of the first wave in the 1910s and 1920s.

A confluence of circumstances in the 1970s brought new attention to contemporary folk art. The 1976 Bicentennial triggered a reification of the cultural heritage of the United States, reflected in the increased collecting, study, connoisseurship, exhibition, and interpretation of American paintings, sculpture, and decorative objects that transcended their original purposes or were created for more personal reasons. Works were studied in a new cultural context. The civil rights movement, feminism, and heightened sensitivity to the nation's cultural diversity began to influence both what was seen and how it was seen. Herbert Walde Hemphill, Jr., a founder and early curator of the Museum of American Folk Art, expanded the meaning of contemporary folk art by mounting such innovative shows as *Contemporary Self-Taught Artists* (1970), which included a vast range of two- and three-dimensional objects; *Tattoo* (1971); and *The Occult* (1973). Hemphill's book *Twentieth-Century American Folk Art and Artists* (1974), written with Julia Weissman, included painting, sculpture, and textiles as well as road signs, toys, decoys, storefront art, graveyard art, scarecrows, fantasy gardens, and visionary environments.

Transmitters: The Isolate Artist in America in 1981, a landmark exhibition at the Philadelphia College of Art, presented nonacademic artworks as full-blown "pure" art objects and underscored the strong personal/psychological component in the work. Some strong followers of the field are proponents of the European *art brut* (that is, "raw art") definition, which emphasizes personal aspects and deemphasizes the folk elements of creators and their works. Another seminal exhibition, *Black Folk Art in America 1930–1980*, opened at the Corcoran Gallery of Art in Washington, D.C., in 1982 and featured paintings, drawings, and sculpture. Such exhibitions as *Dream Singers, Story Tellers: An African-American Presence* (organized by the New Jersey Department of State and the prefecture of Fukui, Japan, 1992) and *Parallel Visions: Outsider Art and the Mainstream* (Los Angeles County Museum, 1992) featured work by both academically trained and self-taught artists, thus crossing the segregationist boundaries of traditional art history and presentation and expanding the scope of folk art with a look at comparative European material.

The acquisition of folk art for permanent museum collections demonstrated the interest of the mainstream art world in folk art. In 1986 the National Museum of American Art purchased some 400 works from the Herbert Walde Hemphill, Jr., Collection of American Art. In 1989 the Milwaukee Art Museum acquired the core collection of Michael and Julie Hall. Subsequent acquisitions by the Philadelphia Museum of Art, the Akron Museum of Art, the High Museum of Art, and the New York State Historical Association showed a commitment to building collections of significant works by self-taught artists.

Earlier notions that authentic folk artists must be elderly and/or living in rural environments were challenged in the late 1980s and 1990s as contemporary folk art scholars identified younger and urban artists, among them Lonnie Holley, Ronald Lockett, Purvis Young, Ray Materson, and Anne Grgich. This broadening of folk art "categories" reflected the diversity of perspectives from which contemporary folk art was viewed at the end of the twentieth century, ranging from the aesthetic standards of the more formal contemporary art world to the contextual focus of the folklorist or cultural anthropologist. Neither monolithic nor narrowly circumscribed, this robust, authentic art form remained resistant to a single definition.

BIBLIOGRAPHY

Herbert W. Hemphill, Jr., and Julia Weissman, *Twentieth-Century American Folk Art and Artists* (New York, 1974).

Chuck Rosenak and Jan Rosenak, *Museum of American Folk Art Encyclopedia of Twentieth-Century American Folk Art and Artists* (New York, 1990).

Betty-Carol Sellan with Cynthia J. Johanson, *Twentieth Century American Folk, Self-Taught, and Outsider Art* (New York, 1993).

— LEE KOGAN

FOLSOM CULTURE COMPLEX

Folsom Culture Complex, one variety of Paleo-Indian culture, named from the initial discovery at a kill site near Folsom, in northeastern New Mexico, in 1926. Subsequent to the initial find, several other kill sites and camping places of the Folsom hunters were found in an area extending from Saskatchewan, Canada, south to northern Mexico. Evidences of Folsom man include distinctive fluted lance points, scrapers, knives, gravers, and other tools. Folsom remains are almost always found with bison, especially *Bison taylori*, an animal typical of the Late Wisconsin period. The Folsom complex dates later than the Sandia (25–23,000 B.C.) and the Clovis (about 9,000 B.C.). The Folsom hunters roamed the high plains from 9,000 to 8,000 B.C.

— FRANK C. HIBBEN

FOOD AND DRUG ADMINISTRATION

Congress placed the responsibility for enforcing the Pure Food and Drug Act of 1906 in the Bureau of Chemistry of the Department of Agriculture, which continued its previously existing research functions. When the increased cost of regulation led to a shrinkage of funds for research, the secretary of agriculture decided that both functions might receive larger appropriations from Congress if structurally separate. In 1927 Congress yielded to his request; in an appropriation act, the Food, Drug, and Insecticide Administration was created to enforce the 1906 law, the Insecticide Act of 1910, and several minor statutes. In 1930 Congress shortened the name to Food and Drug Administration (FDA) without changing the agency's duties.

The Food, Drug, and Cosmetic Act of 1938—the fundamental law that, with subsequent amendments, is still controlling these areas—became finally effective in all its provisions on July 1, 1940. By coincidence, on the day before, the FDA had been transferred from the Department of Agriculture to the Federal Security Agency, in accordance with President Franklin D. Roosevelt's Reorganization Plan No. 4 to rationalize bureaucratic function and structure. In 1953, as a result of President Dwight D. Eisenhower's Reorganization Plan No. 1, Congress converted and elevated the loosely knit Federal Security Agency units into the Department of Health, Education, and Welfare. The FDA became a part of that department, the FDA commissioner being responsible directly to its secretary.

In 1968 the secretary of the Department of Health, Education, and Welfare fused the FDA with two other agencies to form the Consumer Protection and Environmental Health Service (CPEHS). The next year that step was reversed because the FDA's consumer-protection responsibilities precluded it from conducting broader chemical-environmental research and because the FDA issues diverted CPEHS efforts from environmental problems.

Under the 1938 law and other statutes, the FDA has immense regulatory responsibility: the safety of foods and their appropriate labeling, with additives and special dietary products matters of special concern; the safety, efficacy, and labeling of prescription and nonprescription drugs and the accuracy of prescription drug advertising; the certification of antibiotics and insulin; the safety of veterinary drugs and animal feed; the safety of cosmetics, health devices, and man-made sources of radiation. In 1972 Congress transferred to the FDA from the National Institutes of Health control over serums, vaccines, and other biological products and removed from the FDA to the new Consumer Product Safety Commission authority over such hazardous wares as fireworks, flammable fabrics, and unsafe toys. Legal weapons employed by the FDA through the federal courts are seizure actions, injunctions, and criminal prosecutions; the agency also wields informal controls, like pressure on a manufacturer to withdraw voluntarily from the market an offending product. From 1954 to 1974 the FDA budget soared from $5.5 million to $198 million.

BIBLIOGRAPHY

Food and Drug Administration, *Annual Reports.*

Wallace F. Janssen, "FDA Since 1962," Lyndon Baines Johnson Presidential Library.

Rufus E. Miles, Jr., *The Department of Health, Education, and Welfare.*

Gustavus A. Weber, *The Food, Drug, and Insecticide Administration.*

— JAMES HARVEY YOUNG

FOOD AND DRUG ADMINISTRATION

Food and Drug Administration (FDA), an agency of the Public Health Service of the Department of Health and Human Services, charged with ensuring that food is safe and pure, drugs and medical devices are safe and effective, cosmetics are safe, and products are labeled truthfully and informatively. Six bureaus within the FDA carry out these responsibilities: Foods, Drugs, Medical Devices, Veterinary Medicine, Radiological Health, and Biologics. Enforcement includes factory inspections, testing food and drugs for purity and potency, approval of premarket clinical trials on the safety and efficacy of drugs, informing industries of legislation and working to establish procedures that will prevent violations, publicizing irresponsible industry activities, and taking action against violators that includes seizure of substandard products, injunction suits, and criminal prosecutions.

Public concern over consumer protection issues remained strong throughout the twentieth century, reflected in legislation ranging from the landmark Pure Food and Drug Act of 1906 to regulations governing food labeling in the 1990s. In the 1970s, however, free-market advocates initiated a strong countermovement against consumer-protection forces. Where consumer groups favored more stringent regulation and stressed safety considerations, conservative proponents of the free market pointed to increased research and development costs and a slower pace of product innovation as liabilities associated with federal drug regulations. A stalemate developed. In 1974 and 1976 the Senate passed bills that would have increased FDA authority but they died without House action. On the other hand, in 1976 a House investigations subcommittee concluded that nine major U.S. government agencies, including the FDA, were biased in favor of regulated industry. Also in 1976 the FDA was granted greater authority to regulate medical devices, such as heart valves and kidney dialysis machines.

By the early 1980s the FDA was taking a less aggressive stance toward the drug industry. President Ronald Reagan's administration promoted voluntary compliance with federal regulations and in 1984 relaxed approval for generic versions of drugs in an effort to increase price competition. The result was a decrease in inspections, seizures, and legal actions. Several FDA officials were convicted of taking bribes from generic drugmakers. In 1989 FDA Commissioner Frank E. Young was demoted amid criticism of laxity toward the drug industry. David A. Kessler was named as his replacement and continued as head of the FDA under the Bill Clinton administration. Kessler pursued a more active role for the FDA, broadened by passage of the omnibus health package in 1988 that included the first rules for coping with the AIDS epidemic. In 1990 further legislation provided for consolidation of the twenty-three Washington offices of the FDA, an automated system for processing drug applications, and higher salaries for biomedical scientists. In 1994 Commissioner Kessler took his most controversial action by declaring that tobacco should be declared an addictive substance and regulated by the federal government.

The FDA has found itself in other highly politicized controversies. In the early 1970s these included the use of diethylstilbestrol (DES) as a growth stimulant in livestock and in a morning-after contraceptive pill. In the early 1990s controversy erupted over approval of genetically engineered recombinant bovine somatotropin (BST) to stimulate milk production in dairy cows. The debates were complicated by concerns among environmental and religious groups over genetically altered products (as in the case of BST) and the growing intensity of the abortion debate. In the 1980s women's health and family-planning organizations, along with several drug companies, became interested in the possibility of introducing the morning-after pill RU-486 into the United States. The drug was widely used in France as a safe and effective alternative to early abortions. Religious and antiabortion groups sprang into opposition because RU-486 would make abortion clinics and traditional abortion procedures obsolete. In 1993 President Bill Clinton authorized research in the United States on the French abortion pill, making its availability to U.S. women possible before the end of the twentieth century.

One of the major controversies of the 1980s and 1990s was over the government's response to the AIDS crisis. When AIDS emerged in the 1980s, gays and lesbians were already a well-organized political force. Their experiences had often led them to be skeptical of the medical and scientific communities. AIDS activist groups, such as the New York–based ACT UP (AIDS Coalition to Unleash Power) and the San Francisco–based Project Inform, pressured the FDA to provide promising but still experimental drugs to people with AIDS on a parallel track with the standard clinical trials required before FDA approval of drugs. Despite resistance the FDA moved toward such a policy and established accelerated approval procedures in 1992. Accelerated approval is intended to get promising but still unproven drugs for life-threatening diseases to patients as quickly as possible. The drugs must still be shown to be safe but the usual standards of efficacy are relaxed. While drug companies have long resisted increasing regulation, this particular case did not meet with resistance. Unlike other consumer groups, AIDS activists had an interest in less stringent regulations, and by the late 1980s prominent researchers became convinced that there was a moral obligation to provide promising therapies as early as possible.

Accelerated approval is intended to get promising but still unproven drugs for life-threatening diseases to patients as quickly as possible.

Another FDA concern has been the reform of food labeling. Responding to reports of nutritional deficiencies, the FDA in 1973 adopted voluntary labeling that emphasized vitamins, minerals, and proteins. While nutritional deficiencies are now uncommon, problems with labeling became apparent. As consumers became concerned about the link between diet and disease, the food industry began adding phrases such as "light" and "healthy" or "low fat" to labels. What these phrases meant was unclear. The Nutrition Labeling and Education Act of 1990 required food labels and the FDA set standard serving sizes. In 1994 requirements for a standardized food label took effect, making it easier for consumers to check the nutritional content of packaged foods.

[See also Acquired Immune Deficiency Syndrome; Consumer Protection; Health Care; Tobacco Industry.]

BIBLIOGRAPHY

Henry G. Grabowski and John M. Vernon, *The Regulation of Pharmaceuticals: Balancing the Benefits and Risks* (Washington, D.C., 1983).

Kathi E. Hanna, ed., *Biomedical Politics* (Washington, D.C., 1991).

Peter Temin, *Taking Your Medicine* (Cambridge, Mass., 1980).

U.S. Food and Drug Administration, *Annual Reports* (Washington, D.C.).

James Harvey Young, *Pure Food* (Princeton, N.J., 1989).

— M. SEAN DONNELLY

FOOD STAMP PROGRAM

The United States has steadily expanded and improved its program for better nutrition among low-income families since the 1930's, when food assistance began with the distribution of foods acquired under price-support and surplus-removal activities. Later, a new approach—the food stamp program—was introduced. In this form of assistance, food coupons are used to increase the family's existing purchasing power. Families taking part in the program purchase food coupons according to a scale of purchase requirements based on the size of the family and its income. Additional "bonus" food coupons are provided free of charge by the U.S. Department of Agriculture, to give the family the buying power for an economy-level diet. Participating families shop for food in any authorized food store. They may buy all foods for human consumption, including seeds and plants for use in gardening to produce food for the personal consumption of the eligible household. Retailers are first trained, and then authorized, to accept coupons. They redeem the coupons—just like checks—through banks or authorized food dealers; in turn, local banks send the coupons to Federal Reserve banks.

After the food stamp program proved to be an effective means of expanding farm markets and providing better nutrition for needy families, the Food Stamp Act was signed into law on Aug. 31, 1964.

In the early 1970's the program was sharply expanded as increased resources were made available. Purchase requirements for stamps were reduced, and benefits available through the program were increased. As a result, participation in the program increased sharply. By December 1974, the program was in operation virtually everywhere in the country and 17.1 million people were taking part.

The food stamp program is a cooperative activity of local, state, and federal governments. It is administered nationally by the Department of Agriculture's Food and Nutrition Service and locally by the welfare departments in states and counties. Families with low incomes are encouraged to check at their local welfare departments to find out if they are eligible for the program.

— EDWARD J. HEKMAN

FOOTBALL

The American sport of football was dominated by the intercollegiate game, the first played in 1869, for almost a century. Professional football was much less important from its beginning in the 1890s until its popularization in the 1950s and 1960s. The 1958 nationwide telecast of the National Football League (NFL) championship, won in overtime by the Baltimore Colts over the New York Giants, added greater interest to the professional game. Professional football was more innovative than the game of the collegians, who were steeped in such conservative traditions as homecomings, marching bands, cheerleaders, and tailgating.

Professional Football

By the 1970s professional football was more popular than the college game. Football was well suited to television. The Sports Broadcasting Act of 1961 freed the NFL from possible antitrust action and allowed equal distribution of television monies to teams through a single network plan. The Super Bowl championship, begun in 1967, contributed to professional football's popularity. It followed the 1966 merger agreement of the American Football League (AFL) with the older and more prestigious NFL, formed in the 1920s. Founded in 1960, the AFL had survived competition with the NFL, partly thanks to television money. The AFL-NFL merger, made official in 1970 under the NFL name, resulted in an expanded league of twenty-six teams. By then the Super Bowl had become the highest-rated program on television, easily surpassing baseball's World Series. Television's impact on professional football was evident in the introduction of *Monday Night Football.* Created in 1970 by football commissioner Pete Rozelle in conjunction with the innovative Roone Arledge of ABC, it introduced football to prime-time evening television. For two decades, *Monday Night Football* outstripped all other regular sportscasts in popularity, including the regular Sunday afternoon NFL telecasts that brought in millions of dollars per team.

Professional football differed from other big businesses in the United States in that Congress had granted it certain antitrust exemptions. The players formed the National Football League Players Association in 1956, a union not recognized by the NFL owners until 1968. Growing television revenues resulted in substantial team profits and increasing player demands for a larger share of the income. Several NFL player strikes occurred from 1968 to the mid-1980s. Owners battled back to maintain profits for themselves and to increase the value of their franchises, some of which were worth more than $100 million.

The popularity and wealth of the NFL produced team dynasties and interlopers who formed new, competing leagues. The Green Bay Packers, the dominant team of the 1960s, gave way to the Miami Dolphins and Pittsburgh Steelers in the 1970s. In that decade the upstart World Football League could not compete successfully against the expanded NFL and died during its second season in 1975. The San Francisco 49ers dominated the 1980s with its four Super Bowl victories. In 1983 a new United States Football League (USFL) began as a spring sport. The March to July schedule did not conflict with the stronger NFL for television viewership, but the new league signed star college players desired by the NFL. As a result, player salaries rose considerably. The USFL could not survive financially, and after winning an antitrust suit in 1986 against the NFL that resulted in a triple-damage award of only $3, the new league collapsed. Three years later the NFL established the World League of American Football (WLAF) with teams in Europe and North America. The WLAF acted as a farm system, expanding the college football feeder arrangement that had existed for much of the century. The NFL expanded slowly, adding the Seattle and Tampa Bay teams in 1976 and the Carolina and Jacksonville teams in 1995.

Like baseball and basketball, pro football desegregated following World War II; by the 1990's, about 60 percent of professional football players were African American.

Like baseball and basketball, professional football desegregated following World War II. Football led the way in 1946, although its action was less visible than Jackie Robinson's entry into major league baseball in 1947. Increasing numbers of African Americans were signed to play in the NFL, and in the 1990s they comprised about 60 percent of the players, but few were kickers, centers, or quarterbacks, and fewer still were coaches and executives.

College Football

While the professional game became dominant, the college game remained the major sport in most institutions of higher education. Colleges fed the professional game with quality players through a draft system going back to the 1930s, just as the colleges were nourished by high school athletes. Most of the best high school players attended a group of about one hundred "big-time" institutions that dominated the collegiate game. These institutions had major stadiums, some holding more than 70,000 spectators. To control college football, institutions looked to the national governing body, the National Collegiate Athletic Association (NCAA), created out of the brutality and ethical turmoil of the 1905 football season. Members of the NCAA divided unofficially into two groups, the large and small colleges. Following World War II the NCAA received legislative and enforcement powers, which often meant that the NCAA controlled football at the national rather than conference or institutional level. Major football powers came into conflict with smaller colleges over rules and regulations. By the 1970s the NCAA had recognized the dichotomy between small and large colleges by creating three divisions. Big-time football institutions called for greater distinctions and further reorganization of the NCAA. When this did not occur quickly, a group of the football powers, including five major conferences and independents, created the College Football Association (CFA) in 1976. Similar to a lobbying group within the NCAA, the CFA threatened to withdraw its members and form a rival administrative unit if the NCAA did not agree to the demands of the football powers.

Television became the focus of a power struggle between big-time, Division I football institutions and those in Division II and Division III. Institutions without successful commercial football programs wanted a larger portion of television monies from the NCAA-controlled monopoly established in 1951. Big-time schools had witnessed a funneling of television revenues from football into the funding of Divisions II and III championship events in all sports. For more than a decade, the football powers threatened to withdraw from the NCAA rather than share their wealth. While the withdrawal did not occur, the Universities of Oklahoma and Georgia won a lawsuit against the NCAA to end the latter's football television monopoly. Backed by the CFA, the suit culminated in a 1984 Supreme Court decision that found the NCAA in violation of antitrust laws. Individual institutions, conferences, and the CFA were free to create their own television networks. Notre Dame, the leading football school since the 1920s, benefited most with an NBC television contract in 1990 worth more than $7 million a year. College football conferences have since expanded to accommodate television monies, following the professional-commercial model.

One anomaly in college football is the absence of a championship for Division I institutions to determine the best teams or individuals. Every sport in each division of the NCAA, except big-time football, has a championship. Football has concluded its season with bowl games since the Rose Bowl became an annual event in 1916. A myriad of bowl games developed following the 1930s when the Cotton, Sugar, and Orange bowls were instituted to promote business, primarily in southern climes. Because bowl games generated revenue and promoted institutions, they were favored over a structured play-off. At the time that the first NFL Super Bowl was being promoted and the four-division play-off system of the professionals was being planned, the colleges discussed the need to counter the luster of professional football with a play-off for the national championship, but it never materialized.

For well over a century, football in America has developed differently than in most countries in the world, where association football, or soccer, as it is known in the United States, has come to dominate. The game first thrived in the colleges, where it was believed to promote manliness. In its early years, play was often brutal. It has remained a game principally for boys and men, while basketball is a popular women's game in schools and colleges and baseball had a professional women's league in 1943–1954. As the twenty-first century approached, football remained more popular than either baseball or basketball in schools and colleges and at the professional level.

BIBLIOGRAPHY

Richard O. Davies, *America's Obsession: Sports and Society Since 1945* (Fort Worth, Tex., 1994).

Jack Falla, *NCAA* (Mission, Kans., 1981).

David S. Neft, Richard M. Cohen, and Rick Korch, *The Sports Encyclopedia: Pro Football* (New York, 1992).

Ronald A. Smith, *Sports and Freedom: The Rise of Big-Time College Athletics* (New York, 1988).

Paul D. Staudohar, *The Sports Industry and Collective Bargaining* (Ithaca, N.Y., 1986).

— RONALD A. SMITH

FORCE ACTS

Force Acts, the general name popularly applied to various federal statutes passed to enforce certain national laws and constitutional amendments, particularly in the South. The act of Mar. 2, 1833, authorizing President Andrew Jackson to use the army and navy, if necessary, to collect customs duties, was a reply to South Carolina's vigorous defiance of the tariffs of 1828 and 1832 in its ordinance of nullification, Nov. 24, 1832. With the Force Bill went moderation, however. Jackson had conferred with South Carolina Unionists, including Joel Poinsett, and Henry Clay had composed a compromise tariff that substantially met southern objections. The Force Act, signed on the same day as this new tariff, was therefore only a gesture of national authority to enforce a law already in effect repealed. On Mar. 18, 1833, South Carolina maintained its theoretical sovereignty by nullifying the Force Act itself.

In order to maintain the political power of the Republican party and of the northern industrial class against "white supremacy" aims in the South, as supported by the Ku Klux Klan and other similar organizations, Congress, between 1870 and 1875, passed four acts to enforce recognition of the freedmen's civil and political rights as guaranteed by the Fourteenth and Fifteenth amendments. (1) The act of May 31, 1870, reenacted the Civil Rights Act of Apr. 9, 1866; reaffirmed the political rights of Afro-Americans as guaranteed by constitutional amendment; authorized federal courts, marshals, and district attorneys to enforce penalties on states, groups, and individuals who interfered with registrations or voting in congressional elections; and empowered the president to use the land and naval forces to enforce the act. (2) The federal election law of Feb. 28, 1871, prompted by Republican reverses in the election of 1870 and passed after a Senate investigation, provided for federally appointed election supervisors. (3) The act to enforce the Fourteenth Amendment, Apr. 20, 1871, was aimed particularly at the Ku Klux Klan and other groups that were preventing the registration, voting, officeholding, and jury service of Afro-Americans. It extended the earlier acts, provided additional federal penalties for violations, and authorized the president to make summary arrests. Under this act nine counties in South Carolina were placed under martial law in October 1871. Eventually over 5,000 indictments and about 1,250 convictions resulted throughout the South under this and the earlier statutes. (4) The Supplementary Civil Rights Act of Mar. 1, 1875, passed as a memorial to Charles Sumner, just before the Republicans lost control of Congress, gave Afro-Americans social equality of treatment in theaters, public conveyances, hotels, and places of amusement. Meanwhile, the Supreme Court had maintained discreet silence on these acts, but between 1876 and 1883, in four decisions the Court declared the severest of the measures unconstitutional. The Court maintained that the Fourteenth and Fifteenth amendments permitted federal protection against discrimination only by states and not by individuals or groups; that such protection was limited only to discrimination because of race and color, and limited only to civil rather than social discrimination; and that the Fifteenth Amendment did not contain a positive grant of the franchise. In 1894 Congress repealed most of the provisions of the force acts, after an unsuccessful attempt in 1890 to pass a new force bill.

[See Grandfather Clause.]

BIBLIOGRAPHY

C. S. Boucher, *The Nullification Controversy in South Carolina.*

D. F. Houston, *A Critical Study of Nullification in South Carolina.*

J. G. Van Deusen, *Economic Bases of Disunion in South Carolina.*

— MARTIN P. CLAUSSEN

FOREIGN AID

Foreign aid, the transfer of resources from one nation to another for the purpose of attaining the donor nation's diplomatic objectives, has been a prominent instrument of U.S. foreign policy since the beginning of World War II, although some aid had been made available before then in special situations in the form of loans, credits, and gifts.

The Lend-Lease Act of March 1941 authorized the president of the United States to "lend, lease, or otherwise dispose of" arms, equipment, and supplies to any country whose defense he deemed vital to the security of the United States. Designed to provide a way for the United States to support the British war effort without creating the international debts problem that had plagued diplomats after World War I, the Lend-Lease Act set a precedent for postwar foreign-aid programs. A total of approximately $50 billion worth of resources was transferred to America's allies between 1941 and 1945 to aid in the struggle against Germany and Japan. Some of this material was returned, some of it was paid for, and some recipient nations made reverse lend-lease available to the United States in the form of goods or services. The great bulk of lend-lease aid was given without expectation of repayment.

U.S. officials recognized that there would be a tremendous need for economic assistance to war-devastated areas after World War II, but they hoped to establish institutions for handling this problem on a multilateral rather than a unilateral basis. Three organizations were created during the war to assist postwar reconstruction: the United Nations Relief and Rehabilitation Agency (UNRRA), set up to provide immediate relief to devastated areas; the International Bank for Reconstruction and Development (IBRD), intended to encourage private investment and to provide long-term capital for projects that did not interest private investors; and the International Monetary Fund (IMF), designed to help resolve international payments difficulties. The United States put up most of the capital for each of these multilateral agencies and therefore to a large extent enjoyed a controlling voice in their administration.

Events surrounding the end of World War II quickly made it clear that multilateral aid programs would not suffice to meet the objectives of U.S. foreign policy. UNRRA had only limited funds available to it, and Congress balked at making additional appropriations for an organization whose dispersal of funds the United States could not wholly control. The IBRD and IMF had not yet gone into operation; revival of the international economic system required immediate, large-scale aid far beyond the resources of these organizations. Moreover, the onset of the cold war had made aid very much an instrument of diplomatic policy, a tendency that encouraged unilateralism.

Highly conscious of American economic strength at the end of World War II, Washington officials, despite their endorsement of the principles of multilateralism, did not hesitate to employ U.S. economic power to gain political objectives. Thus, aid to Great Britain in the form of a $3.75 billion loan in 1946 was made conditional upon Britain's willingness to dismantle the imperial preference system. A proposed loan of between $1 billion and $6 billion to the Soviet Union was never made because the Soviets refused to accept the political conditions Washington attached to it. In early 1947 President Harry S. Truman asked for, and Congress approved, $400 million in military and economic aid to Greece and Turkey for the purpose of resisting the expanding influence of the Soviet Union in that part of the world.

Conscious of American economic strength at the end of World War II, in the giving of foreign aid, Washington officials did not hesitate to employ U.S. economic power to gain political objectives.

Truman justified aid to Greece and Turkey with the argument that "it must be the policy of the United States to support free peoples who are resisting attempted subjugation by armed minorities or outside pressures," a statement that quickly became known as the Truman Doctrine. Read literally, this statement seemed to commit the United States to a global policy of extending aid to contain communism, but in fact the administration's attention in the 1947–49 period was directed toward Europe. In June 1947, Secretary of State George C. Marshall announced the willingness of the United States to support the reconstruction and rehabilitation of Europe to make that continent less vulnerable to Communist subversion and increase the volume of international trade.

The Marshall Plan let the Europeans themselves determine how aid was to be used, and aid was even offered to the Soviet Union and its East European satellites, although without any serious expectation that they would accept it. After some initial hesitation, the Soviets rejected participation in the European Recovery Program (ERP), probably because this would have meant too great an interference by Western officials in the still-secret economies of the USSR and Eastern Europe. In the end, Congress approved extending some $17 billion in aid over a four-year period to Great Britain, France, the Benelux countries, the Republic of Ireland, Austria, Denmark, Greece, Turkey, Iceland, Italy, Norway, Portugal, Sweden, Switzerland, and West Germany. These nations created the Organization for European Economic Cooperation (OEEC) to supervise the distribution of ERP aid.

U.S. aid policies took on a new shape between 1949 and 1951. Early in 1949, President Truman broadened the geographical scope of foreign aid by proposing Point Four (so named because this was the fourth point in his inaugural address), a program of technical assistance to underdeveloped countries. Little of importance was accomplished at the time under this plan, because the increasing belligerence of the Soviet Union, the Soviet atomic bomb, the victory of communism in China, and the onset of the Korean War forced a new emphasis on military, at the expense of economic, aid.

Both the Marshall Plan and Point Four had been based on the assumption that economic distress led to international violence, and that reconstruction, rehabilitation, and development would bring about an orderly world. The events of 1949–50 challenged this assumption; from that time on, military aid constituted the largest share of U.S. foreign aid programs.

Late in 1949, the United States began making military assistance available to the members of the North Atlantic Treaty Organization to create a Western European army capable of resisting a Soviet attack. In 1950, aid to the French in Indochina and to the Nationalist Chinese on Formosa was stepped up (aid had been given to Chiang Kai-shek during 1947–49, but the amounts involved had been small and the intent had been more to pacify congressional critics of the administration's China policy than to establish a viable center of resistance to communism in China). During the remainder of the 1950's, the preponderance of U.S. expenditures for foreign aid would be devoted to providing military assistance to nations along the periphery of the Soviet Union and Communist China.

The increasing interest of the Soviet Union in expanding its influence in the underdeveloped world after the death of Joseph Stalin led to a growing awareness on the part of American officials of the importance of supporting economic development in those areas. The administration of President Dwight D. Eisenhower, reluctant to approve outright grants or loans repayable in nonconvertible currencies (soft loans), placed primary emphasis on attracting private capital for investment, a difficult task given the political instability that existed in those countries. Not until 1957 did the administration commit itself, through creation of the Development Loan Fund, to the use of soft loans as a technique for stimulating economic development. In 1954 Congress did approve the Agricultural Trade Development and Assistance Act, which allowed the government to sell surplus agricultural commodities in return for nonconvertible currencies, but it could be argued that the savings to the United States in storage costs on these items at least equaled the benefits recipient nations derived from this program.

The chief focus of American concern for economic development in the 1950's was directed toward Asia and the Middle East, but by the time John F. Kennedy took office in 1961, the proliferation of newly independent states in Africa and the growth of anti-Americanism in Latin America had forced U.S. policymakers to broaden the scope of their aid program. The Kennedy administration's aid policy had two main thrusts: the Peace Corps, an elaboration of Truman's Point Four program that involved sending young American volunteers to underdeveloped parts of the world to furnish technical aid; and the Alliance for Progress, a plan to spend $20 billion over a ten-year period for economic development in Latin America. The Alliance for Progress failed to achieve its objectives. The United States found it difficult to bring about the social and economic reforms in Latin America upon which success of the program depended, and continued instability in that part of the world inhibited private investment, which the administration of President Lyndon B. Johnson supported with increasing emphasis after coming to power in 1963. The achievements of the Peace Corps are more difficult to assess. There can be no doubt that the enthusiasm of dedicated young volunteers did win the United States a considerable amount of goodwill abroad, but the extent to which the Peace Corps achieved significant economic development is questionable.

By the end of the 1960's, the U.S. foreign-aid program was coming under increasing criticism from many of its former supporters. The Vietnam War was partly responsible for this; both domestic critics and overseas recipients of aid worried that economic assistance programs might lead, as they had in Vietnam, to military involvement. But there were two other reasons for the declining support of foreign aid. First, defenders of the program found it difficult to explain with any precision what tangible contribution the approximately $125 billion in aid the United States had extended since World War II had made to American security. Second, the relaxation of tension between the United States and both the Soviet Union and Communist China removed the major reason for the program's existence—its use as an instrument of diplomacy in the cold war.

The need for assistance in the underdeveloped world had not diminished; indeed, the gap between the world's richest and poorest nations was widening. But by the end of Richard M. Nixon's first administration it had become clear that traditional techniques of extending foreign aid no longer commanded support as the best means of meeting this challenge.

BIBLIOGRAPHY

David A. Baldwin, *Economic Development and American Foreign Policy, 1943–62.*

David A. Baldwin, ed., *Foreign Aid and American Foreign Policy.*

William A. Brown and Redvers Opie, *American Foreign Assistance.*

Merle Curti and Kendall Birr, *Prelude to Point Four.*

Jacob J. Kaplan, *The Challenge of Foreign Aid.*

Harry B. Price, *The Marshall Plan and Its Meaning.*

— JOHN LEWIS GADDIS

FORTY-NINERS

On Jan. 24, 1848, James Wilson Marshall discovered gold in the tailrace of a sawmill that he and John A. Sutter were erecting on the South Fork of the American River, about 50 miles northeast of the present city of Sacramento, Calif. The news, first published on Mar. 15 in the *San Francisco Californian,* eventually spread throughout the world. The earliest account reached "the states" about Aug. 1, when a courier brought it to Saint Joseph, Mo., but the first printed news in the East did not appear until Aug. 19 in the *New York Herald.* A nationwide trek to California soon began.

The news of the discovery of gold at Sutter's Mill near Sacramento, first published in March 1848 in the San Francisco Californian, *soon spread throughout the world.*

Some traveled by sea, but most proceeded overland. Leaving eastern and southern ports, thousands boarded clipper ships or other sailing vessels; their routes, wholly or partly by water, were via Cape Horn, Panama, Nicaragua, or Mexico; poor food and short rations were common, and their sufferings included seasickness, scurvy, and yellow fever. Most emigrants went by land, traveling either northern or southern trails. Those who took the former started from Missouri or Iowa early in 1849 and journeyed west via the Platte River, South

Pass, and Humboldt River. Those who chose the latter started from Texas, Arkansas, or Missouri, crossed the Great Plains to the eastern slope of the Rocky Mountains, and proceeded across northern Mexico or via Cooke's wagon road, the Old Spanish Trail, or the route through Salt Lake City. The overlanders organized themselves into companies before venturing upon the Plains, using prairie schooners or pack animals for transportation. Of the hardships endured, cholera, scurvy, and dysentery were the most fatal. Other sufferings were caused by heat, dust, mud, deep sand, and a scarcity of water and provisions; some of the latecomers encountered snow, ice, and severe cold in the mountains. One company suffered such heavy losses crossing a desert in southern California that the area was named Death Valley.

BIBLIOGRAPHY

R. P. Bieber, *Southern Trails to California in 1849.*
O. C. Coy, *The Great Trek.*

— RALPH P. BIEBER

FOURTEEN POINTS

In order to counteract the negative effects of the publication by the Soviet government in late 1917 of secret treaties among the Allies, President Woodrow Wilson addressed Congress on Jan. 8, 1918, and stated in fourteen points America's terms of peace. Briefly, they were (1) "open covenants of peace openly arrived at"; (2) freedom of the seas; (3) removal of economic barriers and equality of trade conditions; (4) reduction of armaments to the lowest point consistent with domestic safety; (5) impartial adjustment of colonial claims; (6) evacuation of Russian territory and Russian self-determination; (7) evacuation and restoration of Belgium; (8) evacuation of France and restoration of Alsace-Lorraine to France; (9) readjustment of Italian frontiers; (10) autonomous development for the peoples of Austria-Hungary; (11) readjustments in the Balkans; (12) autonomous development for the non-Turkish nationalities of the Ottoman Empire and the opening of the Dardanelles; (13) restoration of an independent Poland with access to the sea; (14) establishment of a general association of nations. No attempt was made to secure Allied acceptance of the points until the German government in October 1918 applied for an armistice and peace on the basis of the fourteen points. After an official interpretation had been communicated to the Supreme War Council, and Col. Edward M. House, the American representative, had threatened that the United States might make a separate peace with Germany, the fourteen points were accepted by the Allies on Nov. 4, 1918—with the reservation that they reserved to themselves "complete freedom" on the subject of freedom of the seas and with the further understanding that "compensation will be made by Germany for all damage done to the civilian population of the Allies and their property by the aggression of Germany by land, by sea and from the air." With these limitations, the fourteen points became the legal basis for the ensuing treaty of peace.

BIBLIOGRAPHY

C. Seymour, *The Intimate Papers of Colonel House.*

— BERNADOTTE E. SCHMITT

FOURTEENTH AMENDMENT

Added to the Constitution in 1868, the Fourteenth Amendment is one of three Civil War amendments, including the Thirteenth and Fifteenth, designed primarily to restrain the states from abridging the civil rights and liberties of individual citizens, especially those of emancipated slaves.

Section 1 is the most important part of the Fourteenth Amendment. It is composed of four primary clauses: the citizenship clause; the privileges and immunities clause; the due process clause; and the equal protection clause. Federal and state citizenship was provided for almost all emancipated slaves by Section 1, granting both federal and state citizenship to " . . . all persons born or naturalized in the United States." The citizenship clause has also been the basis for Supreme Court decisions on congressional power to expatriate citizens (*Afroyim* v. *Rusk*, 387 U.S. 253 [1967] and *Rogers* v. *Bellei*, 401 U.S. 815 [1971]).

The Fourteenth Amendment, adopted in 1868, was intended to restrain states from abridging the civil rights and liberties of citizens—former slaves in particular.

The *Slaughterhouse Cases*, 16 Wallace 36 (1874), interpreted the privileges and immunities clause in such a restrictive manner that its potential significance has never been realized. The *Slaughterhouse* Court held that civil rights were primarily derivatives of state citizenship and that only rights of U.S. citizenship were protected by the privileges and immunities clause from state abridgment. Consequently, the clause was not a limit upon the states in dealing with its own citizens on matters of state concern, an interpretation that has never been explicitly overruled.

The due process clause states: " . . . nor shall any State deprive any person of life, liberty, or property without due process of law." Most significant in terms of free speech and criminal procedure, the due process clause is a reiteration of the same guarantee in the Fifth Amendment, raising the question whether the Fourteenth Amendment was intended to "incorporate" the Bill of Rights. Incorporation would have made the Bill of Rights applicable to the states, thereby overruling *Barron* v. *Baltimore*, 7 Peters 243 (1833), which had held that the Fifth Amendment as well as the entire Bill of Rights applied only to the national government and did not constrain state power in any way. Debate on the incorporation issue has sharply divided constitutional scholars and jurists. While the Supreme Court has never held that the due process clause automatically incorporated the entire Bill of Rights, it has made almost all of its provisions applicable to the states through incorporation, on a selective basis (*Palko* v. *Connecticut*, 302 U.S. 319 [1937]).

The equal protection clause is the basis for virtually all of the racial discrimination decisions. *Brown* v. *Board of Education*, 347 U.S. 483 (1954), declared segregated public schools to be "inherently unequal" and therefore in violation of the equal protection clause. *Brown* overruled *Plessy* v. *Ferguson*, 63 U.S. 537 (1896), which had held that "separate but equal" facilities did not violate equal protection requirements. Since *Brown* a major question has been what constitutes "state action" because the Fourteenth Amendment prohibits denial of equal protection only by states, not by private individuals (for example, *Moose Lodge #107* v. *Irvis*, 401 U.S. 992 [1972]).

In *Reynolds* v. *Sims*, 377 U.S. 533 (1964), the Supreme Court held that apportionment of representation in both houses of bicameral state legislatures must be based upon the criterion of "one man, one vote" in order to satisfy the equal protection clause. Geographic representation (as well as any other apportionment criteria not based upon population equality) was thereby prohibited. Decisions since 1964 have extended the *Reynolds* rule (for example, *Avery* v. *Midland County*, 390 U.S. 474 [1968]).

Sections 2, 3, and 4 of the Fourteenth Amendment pertain to issues arising directly from the Civil War and the fact of emancipation, such as the basis for determining state populations for purposes of apportioning congressional representation and the status of war debts. Section 5 is an enabling clause, permitting Congress to enforce the provisions of the amendment by appropriate legislation.

BIBLIOGRAPHY

Henry J. Abraham, *Freedom and the Court.*

Edward S. Corwin, *The Constitution and What It Means Today.*

William Lockhart, Yale Kamisar, and Jesse Choper, *Constitutional Rights and Liberties.*

— STEFAN J. KAPSCH

FOX

Historic references to the Fox Indians place them on the central Wisconsin coast of Lake Michigan. There as many as 2,000 were encountered by the French in 1670. The Fox were traditionally allied with the Sauk tribe (with whom they shared a common Algonkin language) and with the Kickapoo. All three are believed to have moved into Wisconsin from Michigan in the early 17th century. Like so many other Algonkin tribes in the Eastern Woodlands, the Fox and their neighbors were caught in the westward movement attendant on both the fur trade and the dispossession of the Atlantic coastal Indians. The relatively small Fox tribe found itself in conflict both with the French and with the Chippewa. Displacing the Illinois, the Fox moved southward and were caught in Iowa with the Sauk in the Black Hawk War in 1832. Moving to Kansas, they separated from the Sauk and returned to a reservation in Iowa on land they purchased themselves.

Although originally possessing a Woodland culture, the many wars in which they engaged, as well as their frequent change of habitat, modified their original culture considerably, drawing it into the Plains sphere and into western modes as well.

BIBLIOGRAPHY

Frederick O. Gearing, *The Face of the Fox.*

— ROBERT F. SPENCER

FRANCHISE

In the broadest sense a franchise is a special privilege of any sort granted to an individual or a group of individuals (for example, the right to establish a corporation and to exercise corporate powers). More specifically, in the constitutional or statutory sense, the term denotes the right of suffrage. Persons upon whom this privilege is conferred are voters or electors; collectively, they make up the electorate, which may be defined as that part of the people of a state who are legally qualified to declare their will authoritatively—in direct primaries and general elections, on initiative and referendum measures, and in recall elections—in the choice of public officials or with respect to other political matters.

Idealistic statements of qualifications for the privilege of suffrage may include loyalty to the Constitution, political comprehension, and willingness to use the vote according to one's conscience for the general good of the commonwealth. However desirable loyalty, comprehension, and conscientiousness may be in the abstract, it is evident that it would be a very complicated and, perhaps, controversial undertaking to establish tests of their existence among potential voters. It is not strange, therefore, that actual qualifications for voting laid down by federal and state constitutions and laws deal with more tangible matters, such as age, sex, race, nationality, literacy, property holding, payment of taxes, and periods of residence.

The history of the suffrage in the United States has had three distinct lines of development: (1) the movement toward universal suffrage beginning in 1789; (2) efforts to establish suffrage for black Americans, from the Civil War to the present; and (3) the movement to remove the suffrage from state to national control, beginning in the second half of the 20th century.

Universalizing the Suffrage

During colonial days property and tax-paying qualifications for voting were high, and as a result, only about 75 percent of the adult white males in the North and somewhat less than 50 percent in the South were qualified. Immediately prior to the Revolution, religious tests were still in effect in Rhode Island, New York, Virginia, and Maryland, but all that were of a sectarian character had disappeared by 1810. The enormous subsequent extension of the suffrage throughout the nation is revealed by estimates that the proportion of the total population that possessed the franchise increased from only 6 percent in 1789 to 66 percent in 1972.

Prior to the adoption of the Constitution the nearest approach in the new nation to inclusive suffrage for all white males was made in Vermont, which in its constitution of 1777 provided that "every freeman . . . who [had] a sufficient interest in the community" might vote. It was the newly formed western states—offering poor settlers not only land and opportunity but also the right to vote—that put pressure on the eastern seaboard states to alter suffrage requirements. White manhood suffrage was practically established in the constitutions of Kentucky and Tennessee when they became states in 1792 and 1796. Early in the 19th century the new states formed out of the Northwest and Southwest territories followed suit. Under such pressures, Massachusetts in 1820 established a poll tax and admitted to suffrage all male citizens who paid it. New York abolished property qualifications for white male citizens in 1826. Thereafter white male suffrage was more or less taken for granted as new states entered the Union.

At the outbreak of the Civil War free black males were admitted to suffrage in only four states: Maine, Massachusetts, New Hampshire, and Vermont. It was not until the adoption of the Fifteenth Amendment in 1870 that universal male suffrage, in theory, was established—by the provision that "the right of citizens of the United States to vote shall not be denied or abridged by the United States or by any State on account of race, color, or previous condition of servitude."

On another front, the first organized push for universal suffrage began with the 1848 convention for equal rights for women called by Elizabeth Cady Stanton at Seneca Falls, N.Y. It led to the formation in the same year of the Equal Rights Association, made up of both women and men, concerned with equal rights for black Americans as well as for women. Worcester, Mass., was the site of the first national convention, 1850, aimed at securing suffrage for women. Through the Civil War the push for women's suffrage was enmeshed with antislavery efforts, and after the war women agitated particularly for their enfranchisement in the South, arguing that it would counterbalance the new black vote. When suffrage was not extended to women, the women activists felt betrayed by the Radical Republican congressmen whom they had vigorously supported.

The first organized push for universal suffrage began with the 1848 convention for equal rights for women called by Elizabeth Cady Stanton at Seneca Falls, New York.

In 1869 the Equal Rights Association split over goals and tactics—the East versus the Midwest and Far West—but re-formed as the National American Woman Suffrage Association (NAWSA) in 1890, under the leadership of Mrs. Stanton and Susan B. Anthony. Shortly after the breakup, the territorial legislatures of Wyoming (1869) and Utah (1870) granted women suffrage. The real advance came when the Progressive party, a strong proponent, won a series of state referenda—in Washington (1910); California (1911); and Arizona, Kansas, and Oregon (1912)—and a territorial referendum in Alaska (1913). At the same time, the Progressives were instrumental in Woodrow Wilson's presidential victory in 1912. With the establishment of women's colleges (as distinguished from finishing schools) in the second half of the 19th century and the matriculation of women at some previously male universities, education for women came to be taken seriously. At the turn of the century, further, women entered the professions and also unionized themselves in factories—outside the American Federation of Labor (AFL). Suffrage for women was firmly backed by Samuel Gompers and his AFL, if for no reason other than to try politically to eliminate the potentially damaging wage-rate differential between the male and female work forces. During World War I women also gained respect for their wartime industrial productivity.

To focus national and political attention on their cause, members of the NAWSA under their new leader, Carrie Chapman Catt, led a march on Washington, D.C., during Wilson's 1913 inauguration; the march ended in a brawl. The Progressives pressured Wilson, who needed their continued support for reelection; congressmen, who had come to respect the women, felt threatened in their reelection bids. The upshot of the situation was passage of the Nineteenth Amendment in 1920, which took the text of the Fifteenth Amendment and substituted "sex" for "race, color, or previous condition of servitude."

Following the passage of the somewhat particularistic Twenty-third Amendment in 1961—giving the vote to citizens of Washington, D.C., in presidential elections—the last federal extension of the suffrage came in 1971—lowering the voting age to eighteen. The franchise had already been granted to eighteen-year-olds by Georgia in 1944, on the ground that a person old enough to wage war is old enough to vote, and by Kentucky in 1955. There was no ground swell of support or well-organized movement for lowering the voting age; rather, the passage of the amendment was the result of a quiet revolution stemming from a 1970 congressional amendment to the Voting Rights Act of 1965. After passage of this amendment the Department of Justice sued Arizona and Idaho for noncompliance, while Oregon and Texas brought suit against the federal government; the Supreme Court upheld the lower voting age in federal elections only (*Oregon* v. *Mitchell, Attorney General,* 400 U.S. 112 [1970]). The states were left with the administrative problems of dual records and separate ballots for federal and for state and local offices. Congress acted by proposing the Twenty-sixth Amendment (1971), which was adopted by the states in a record three months.

Implementing Suffrage for Black Americans

Suffrage for black Americans came under attack shortly after it was granted by the adoption of the Fifteenth Amendment. The ruling Radical Republican–black coalition was weakened by the withdrawal of federal troops from the South with the end of Reconstruction and was struck a fatal blow when native white southerners organized to assume political control, by force if necessary. Threatened with violence, many blacks did not exercise their recently acquired right to vote and Radical Republicans moved north. Again at the helm of state governments, white southerners established constitutional means to disfranchise black Americans. The principal techniques were invented in Louisiana, Mississippi, and South Carolina—the states having black majorities in 1890. The constitutional convention that Mississippi held in 1890 initiated the following widely imitated provisions: (1) a residency requirement of two years in the state and one year in the locality, based on the notion that blacks were nomadic; (2) a two-year cumulative poll tax and evidence of payment of all legally required taxes; (3) literacy at the level of being "able to read any section of the Constitution of this State; or . . . to understand the same when read to him, or give a reasonable interpretation thereof"; (4) registration four months before election; and (5) disqualification for petty crimes, which were thought to be committed principally by blacks. In order not to disfranchise illiterate whites, South Carolina (1895) allowed, as a substitute for literacy, the ownership of property and the payment of taxes for the previous year on property assessed at a minimum of $300. Louisiana (1898) concocted the " grandfather clause," which enfranchised illiterates who were sons or grandsons of persons who were bona fide voters prior to 1867.

Between 1890 and 1904, poll taxes were adopted by all the former Confederate states except Georgia, which had such a tax since 1789. However, in 1904, Georgia adopted one of the most burdensome taxes in American history by requiring the payment of the poll tax and all other taxes due for each year since 1877 as a prerequisite to voting. Alabama (1902) also had a restrictive poll tax that cumulated for all years between ages twenty-one and forty-five for a maximum of $36, while the Georgia poll tax alone, cumulated for all years between ages twenty-one and sixty, amounted to a maximum of $47.47. Seven of these states—the Deep South plus North Carolina and Virginia—also adopted literacy tests. While voter participation declined 7.6 percent in the southern and border states between 1876 and 1880, political scientists Jerrold Rusk and John Stucker have found that intimidation, poll taxes, and literacy tests took a heavy toll on voter turnout between 1890 and 1918. From an average turnout in the border states of 72.1 percent of the eligible voters, it decreased to 57.2 percent in the states having literacy tests, to 40.2 percent in those having poll taxes, and to 24.2 percent in the southern states having both literacy tests and poll taxes.

Although the Supreme Court disallowed the grandfather clause in 1915 (*Quinn* v. *United States*, 238 U.S. 347), it reiterated its traditional doctrine that fairly administered and fairly authorized literacy tests need not be unconstitutional. At the same time, the Court ruled that poll-tax payment as a voting prerequisite was legal (*Breedlove* v. *Suttles*, 302 U.S. 27 [1937]). What did come under persistent attack by the Court was a variation of the direct primary. With the South dominated by the Democratic party after Reconstruction and conventions replaced by a system of primary elections to facilitate competition for office by the turn of the century, white primaries were instituted to disfranchise black American citizens. One Texas law passed for that purpose was declared unconstitutional in 1927 (*Nixon* v. *Herndon*, 273 U.S. 536); but the landmark and controlling decision by the Court on this matter was *Smith* v. *Allwright*, 321 U.S. 649 (1944), which recognized the primary as an integral part of the electoral process and thus subject to federal regulation. The capstone came in 1953 when the Court ruled unconstitutional a Texas three-tiered system of elections in effect since 1899, a system whereby the Jaybird Association, a private club composed of registered white voters, held preprimary elections among its membership, the winner of which the local Democratic party subsequently adopted as its official primary and general election candidate (*Terry* v. *Adams*, 345 U.S. 461).

Nationalizing the Suffrage

The assumption of responsibility by the national government for suffrage requirements began in the 1960's, when Congress, backed by the Supreme Court, moved on the traditional state authority over elections assumed from the U.S. Constitution, Article I, Section 5. After twenty years of legislative attempts and over the opposition of a southern filibuster, Congress enacted an anti–poll-tax amendment for federal elections, the Twenty-fourth Amendment, ratified in 1964. The most comprehensive voting rights legislation to pass Congress in ninety-five years, the Voting Rights Act of 1965, provided (1) for the suspension of literacy tests as a qualification to vote in state and local elections; (2) for the appointment by the U.S. attorney general of federal examiners to supervise voter registration in states and subdivisions where literacy tests were in force Nov. 1, 1964, "and where fewer than 50% of voting age residents were registered to vote on that date or actually voted in the 1964 Presidential election"; (3) for the authorization of federal courts to suspend tests used "with the effect" of discriminating, in voting rights suits brought by the U.S. attorney general; (4) for the guarantee of a citizen's right to vote in spite of an inability to read or write English if he had completed a sixth-grade education conducted in another language in a school under the American flag; (5) for approval by the U.S. attorney general of new voting laws enacted in states or subdivisions where voter qualification laws had been nullified; (6) for a prohibition "against the lifting of a suspension of tests and devices for five years after the entry of a federal court finding that a state or political subdivision had discriminated against voters"; (7) for review by a three-judge federal district court in Washington, D.C., to determine registration compliance and an ending of the federal examiners' role in a locality; (8) for subsequent lawsuits to enjoin a new law in an area whose voter qualification laws had been nullified; (9) for the end of poll taxes in state and local elections; and (10) for criminal penalties for "officials who denied any qualified voter the right to vote," including participation in party primaries, caucuses, and conventions.

As a result of the 1965 Voting Rights Act, black voter registration by 1968 had increased from 43.3 percent to 62 percent in the South, and from 6.7 percent to 59.4 percent in Mississippi alone.

The major provisions of the Voting Rights Act were upheld by the Supreme Court (*Harper* v. *Virginia Board of Elections*, 383 U.S. 663 [1966]; *South Carolina* v. *Katzenbach*, 383 U.S. 301 [1966]; *Katzenbach* v. *Morgan*, 384 U.S. 641 [1966]; *Bond* v. *Floyd*, 385 U.S. 116 [1966]; *Allen* v. *Virginia State Board of Elections*, 393 U.S. 544 [1969]; *Gaston County* v. *United States*, 395 U.S. 285 [1969]; and *Hadnott* v. *Amos*, 394 U.S. 358 [1969]; as well as others). As a result of the act, black voter registration by 1968 had increased from 43.3 percent to 62.0 percent in the South and from 6.7 percent to 59.4 percent in Mississippi alone.

The Voting Rights Act was extended by Congress for five years in 1970 and amended to include (1) an extension from five to ten years of the period during which an affected area must abstain from using literacy or other qualifying tests; (2) the basing of the automatic "trigger formula" (where fewer than 50 percent of the eligible residents were registered to vote) on 1968 presidential voting; (3) the suspension of literacy tests until Aug. 6, 1975; (4) a thirty-day residency requirement for voting in presidential elections (applied to state and local elections but subsequently amended by the Court to allow a fifty-day period, *Marston* v. *Lewis*, 410 U.S. 679 [1973]); and (5) a voting age of eighteen for all elections (ruled valid by the Court for federal elections only but subsequently made effective by the Twenty-sixth Amendment).

The Court even ventured into the legality of property qualifications—ruled legal for special-purpose districts in *Salyer Land Company* v. *Tulare Lake Basin Water Storage District*, 410 U.S. 719 (1973)—and into the value of the vote, via the representativeness of election districts—in its reapportionment decisions.

The franchise, then, was extended legally from propertied white males to black American males, to women, and to eighteen-year-olds. Later, it was made meaningful for blacks by further legislation. Backed by the Supreme Court, Congress effectively nationalized franchise regulations. Moreover, beginning in the 1960's, by persistently broadening the franchise, Congress assumed a duty formerly left to state governments.

BIBLIOGRAPHY

Richard Claude, *The Supreme Court and the Electoral Process.*
Congressional Quarterly, Inc., *Congressional Quarterly Almanac.*
V. O. Key, Jr., *Southern Politics.*
Penn Kimball, *The Disconnected.*
David Morgan, *Suffragists and Democrats.*
Frederick D. Ogden, *The Poll Tax in the South.*
Nelson W. Polsby, ed., *Reapportionment in the 1970's.*

— CHARLES D. HADLEY

FREE BLACKS

Free blacks were among the first North American settlers in the 16th century, but by midcentury a slave system restricted to people of African ancestry threatened the future status of black people. The 1790 census counted approximately 60,000 free blacks in the United States, and by 1860, approximately 500,000. Some of the free blacks were descendants of those who had never been slaves; the remainder had been freed under a variety of circumstances. All the northern states abolished slavery shortly after the Revolution, thus supplying the base for the northern free black population. In the slave states of the South the transition from slave to free was difficult. Some slaves purchased their freedom; others ran away to the North. The free blacks who remained in the South were those freed by their masters, a practice that was discouraged and sometimes specifically prohibited by slave states in the 19th century. Therefore, in both North and South the free black population grew primarily because of the excess of births over deaths.

The lower-class status of the free blacks was identified in the white mind with the African's visible racial differences, and class and race combined to contain most free blacks in a servile position. Differences in northern and southern treatment of free blacks and in opportunities available to them in each section were not so great as has been believed, although there were some important exceptions. In general, opportunities for free blacks were most restricted in the South, were only slightly better in the newly opened West, and were most promising in the older northeastern and Middle Atlantic states.

In the West and Old Northwest, blacks were never allowed to vote. In the northeastern and Middle Atlantic states black disfranchisement resulted from the increased political activities of lower-class white workers and the new immigrants who swelled their numbers in the 1830's and 1840's. These urban white workingmen, who perceived free blacks as the closest challengers to their precarious economic and social status, insisted that politics be conducted on a white-only basis. Thus, by the 1840's free blacks were virtually disfranchised everywhere in the United States. In the

A free black is kidnapped and returned to slavery. (Corbis-Bettmann)

South laws regulating the life of free blacks varied in severity and were more or less strictly enforced, depending upon real or imagined threats to the slave system. In the North, blacks found their lives carefully circumscribed by social custom and public hostility where laws were lacking. In public accommodations, schooling, housing, employment, hospital care, and even interment in cemeteries, the place of blacks was carefully prescribed.

Economic opportunities for free blacks were generally bleak. A few black entrepreneurs and skilled tradesmen were able to make a comfortable living, but the majority of free blacks were restricted to the most undesirable occupations and lived in abject poverty. Ironically, as economic opportunities expanded dramatically in the 1830's and 1840's, the limited opportunities open to free blacks were further restricted as a result of the competition and hostility of the new immigrants.

The 1790 census counted approximately 60,000 free blacks in the U.S., and, by 1860, about 500,000.

An important distinction between southern and northern free blacks was that the latter could organize, speak out, and petition, although admittedly with difficulty and always with the threat of physical violence. Despite these obstacles northern free blacks formed their own church groups and mutual aid societies; initiated a convention movement led by the most skilled and articulate of their members to aid and support others; and, when allowed to do so, participated in the abolitionist movement.

The participation of free blacks in the abolitionist movement reveals most clearly the mood of northern whites as they confronted the problem of redefining the black's place in American society. Northern blacks were relegated to minor roles in the movement. Abolitionists reasoned that keeping black participation to a minimum would attract more northern white support. While blacks were often on display, sometimes to inform their listeners of harrowing escapes from "slavocracy," they rarely shared in the decisionmaking process of the movement.

Changes began to take place in the 1830's that vitally influenced American thoughts on slavery and race and profoundly affected the free black's place in society. The expansion of democratic ideals and equality for white Americans was accompanied by a marked increase in racial prejudice and the emergence of a doctrinaire belief that the black is biologically inferior to the white. A few resisted these racial theories, but most found them acceptable, and the free black became a pawn in the controversy. Northern blacks were exhorted by abolitionists to disprove allegations of racial inferiority through self-improvement and individualism at the very time that other northern whites were insisting upon black servitude. The apparent inability of the free black to function successfully in northern society buttressed the arguments of those who defended slavery as the only realistic solution to the presence of the black man in America.

Although the Civil War ended the peculiar legal status of the free black, it did not eliminate the fundamental issue of equal rights for blacks in American life.

BIBLIOGRAPHY

George Fredrickson, *The Black Image in the White Mind.*
August Meier and Elliott Rudwick, *From Plantation to Ghetto.*

— JOHN M. MCFAUL

FREEDMEN'S BUREAU

Freedmen's Bureau, a federal agency created to assist black Americans in their transition from slavery to freedom at the end of the Civil War. On Mar. 3, 1865, Congress established the Bureau of Refugees, Freedmen, and Abandoned Lands. The bureau provided emergency food and shelter to people dislocated by the war and was expected to define how former slaves would provide for their own subsistence. It established schools, conducted military courts to hear complaints of both former slaves and former masters, and supervised the post-Emancipation arrangements for work made by the freedmen.

The black southerners encountered the men of the invading Union army both as marauders and deliverers. As many of the freedmen were destitute, the army gained jurisdiction over abandoned lands and arranged for former slaves to farm them. The bureau was assigned to the War Department and Maj. Gen. O. O. Howard of Maine was named commissioner. Assistant commissioners were appointed in the seceded states to direct the work of other officials, known generally as Freedmen's Bureau agents, who were sent into the field. The bureau was dependent on the army payroll and, with few exceptions, the agents were young army officers. A few of them were black officers, but resentment by some powerful white people caused most of these agents to be either discharged or moved into relatively uncontroversial posts in the education division. In 1868 bureau officials numbered 900.

Howard, a Bowdoin and West Point graduate known as the "Christian General," had a charitable attitute toward the freedmen. He had commanded an army in Gen. William Tecumseh Sherman's march to the sea and had visited the South Carolina coastal islands seized in 1861 from fleeing planters. Plantations there had been divided into small holdings and farmed successfully by former slaves. With this example in mind, Congress directed the bureau to divide similarly abandoned lands across the South into forty-acre units and award them to the freedmen. Shortly thereafter President Andrew Johnson abrogated this important precedent for land redistribution by using presidential pardons to return to white former owners virtually all the land that was to have been divided.

The most important continuing contribution of the Freedmen's Bureau was in the establishment of such educational institutions as Howard University, Hampton Institute, and Fisk University.

With the restoration of the lands to white owners, Howard tried to convince the freedmen to accept a contract labor system. Under the contracts, former slaves worked, often in field gangs, for their former masters in return for food, shelter, and wages. The freedmen resisted this mode of labor, so similar to slavery. In some cases bureau agents forced compliance with the contracts; in others they sought to gain it with moral suasion, appealing to the freedmen to work and to the landowners to treat the workers fairly. Dissatisfaction with this system led to share-cropping arrangements.

The most important continuing contribution of the Freedmen's Bureau was in the area of education. Private freedmen's aid societies supplied teachers and their salaries; the bureau supplied buildings and transportation. Howard participated enthusiastically in fund raising for the schools, particularly after the early efforts at land reform had been aborted. By 1871 eleven colleges and universities and sixty-one normal schools had been founded. Among the most important were Hampton Institute in Hampton, Va.; Atlanta University; Talladega College in Talladega, Ala.; Straight College (later Dillard University) in New Orleans; Fisk University in Nashville; and Howard University in Washington, D.C. The bureau spent over $6 million for its schools and educational work. In its seven years of existence, the bureau also appropriated more than $15 million for food and other aid to the freedmen. These funds were distributed throughout the southern and border states in which most of the nation's 4 million black citizens lived.

The Freedmen's Bureau lost the support of Radical Republicans in Congress when it failed to protect the lives of freedmen in riots in Memphis and New Orleans in 1866. Bureau agents played one more highly important role when they registered black voters under the Congress's radical reconstruction plan, which transferred the direction of racial policy from the executive branch of the government to the reconstructed state governments. The Freedmen's Bureau was closed in 1872. Its legacies were the colleges begun under its auspices and the aspirations engendered among Afro-Americans.

BIBLIOGRAPHY

George R. Bentley, *A History of the Freedmen's Bureau.*

William S. McFeely, *Yankee Stepfather: General O. O. Howard and the Freedmen.*

— WILLIAM S. MCFEELY

FREEDOM OF INFORMATION ACT

Passed by Congress in 1966, the Freedom of Information Act (FOIA) became effective on July 4, 1967. Amended in 1974 in light of the Watergate scandal and by the Freedom of Information Reform Act of 1986, FOIA provides citizen access to documents held by agencies in the federal government's executive branch, including government and government-controlled corporations. The law does not apply to elected officials or the federal judiciary. FOIA requests may be denied only if they fall under one of nine exemptions: classified national security materials, matters relating to internal personnel rules and practices, information exempt under other laws, confidential business information obtained from private sector sources, internal communications regarding the formation of policy, personnel and medical files of individuals, law enforcement investigatory records, information about government-regulated financial institutions, and geological and geophysical data on oil and natural-gas wells. A requester may file an administrative appeal for access to withheld documents and if denied may file a judicial appeal in U.S. District Court, where the burden of justifying withholding of information lies with the government.

Freedom of information evolved in the twentieth century into a political issue symbolic of the perennial struggle between Congress and the presidency. With the rise in the 1930s of the modern administrative state and its proliferating agencies and bureaucracies, executive responsibility expanded in an often bewildering manner. The security interests of the cold war compounded matters. A minor freedom-of-information movement in Congress culminated in the 1966 legislation, but the law lacked forcefulness until Vietnam- and Watergate-era events discredited claims of executive privilege based on national-security or separation-of-powers rationales. The 1974 amendments allowed courts to review contested materials to determine whether they were being properly withheld.

During the 1980s the administration of President Ronald Reagan sought to reduce the use of FOIA. The result was a reduction of personnel responsible for reviewing documents. Executive Order 12356 in 1982 required reviewers to weigh security needs more heavily than the public's right to know. Congressional amendments in 1986 further narrowed the scope of releasable information. In 1994 President Bill Clinton reversed the policy of nine previous presidents and declared that because the National Security Council, which advises the president on security matters, is not an agency of the federal government, its records must be considered strictly as presidential papers not subject to the FOIA and other records laws. No matter how flawed or otherwise deferential to the White House, or the fact that it is used extensively by convicted felons to obtain appeals and corporate executives to gather data on their competitors, FOIA has led to greater access to government information. When used by journalists covering current events and scholars probing the origins and workings of laws and administrations, it has brought the nation closer to its founders' ideals. "A popular Government without popular information or the means of acquiring it," wrote James Madison in 1822, "is but a Prologue to a Farce or a Tragedy or perhaps both."

BIBLIOGRAPHY

Justin D. Franklin and Robert F. Bouchard, eds., *Guidebook to the Freedom of Information and Privacy Acts* (New York, 1986).

Peter Hemon and Charles R. McClure, *Federal Information Policies in the 1980s: Conflicts and Issues* (Norwood, N.J., 1987).

— KENNETH O'REILLY

FREEDOM OF THE PRESS

Freedom of the Press is a constitutional restraint on government that, in the language of the Supreme Court, "was fashioned to assure unfettered interchange of ideas for the bringing about of political and social changes desired by the people" (*Roth* v. *United States*, 1957). It implements a "profound national commitment to the principle that debate on public issues should be uninhibited, robust, and wide-open" (*New York Times Company* v. *Sullivan*, 1964).

British tradition had afflicted the colonial press with official printing monopolies, licensing, secrecy, hazards of seditious libel, and discriminatory taxation; anxieties generated by experience helped inspire adoption of the American Bill of Rights. Colonial governments—particularly the Massachusetts theocracy—had also interfered with the press: in Boston the first colonial newspaper (1690) had been suppressed at once, and licensing had been imposed, but unevenly enforced, on other publications into the 1730's. The trial of John Peter Zenger for seditious libel in New York in 1735 became a celebrated symbol of resistance to executive interference with the press when the jury, disregarding the judge's instructions, acquitted the defendant.

The federal sedition acts of 1798–1801 authorized the defense of truth; however, antigovernment editors were, upon conviction, fined and committed to prison. In the 19th century antislavery publications were suppressed under state criminal laws in the South, and some unpopular Copperhead newspapers in the North were harassed during episodes of martial law. During World War I the federal Espionage Act of 1917 and similar state laws were used in a two-year frenzy of prosecution during which freedom of the press temporarily disappeared. The extent of such prosecutions is now obscured by the homage paid to justices Oliver W. Holmes, Jr., and Louis D. Brandeis for development of the clear-and-present-danger test, which, for the most part, they could use only in futile protest against opinions with which they did not agree. The test later was used to reach many decisions favorable to free speech and press. The Espionage Act, originally applicable only in wartime, was restated in 1948 as Section 2388 of Title 18, Crimes and Criminal Procedures, and continues in active use.

Although the First Amendment has never been held to be absolute, state prepublication censorship (*Near* v. *Minnesota* [1931]) and guilt by association (*De Jonge* v. *Oregon* [1937]) were denounced by the Supreme Court under Chief Justice Charles Evans Hughes. The *Near* case decision began forty years of steady expansion of First Amendment freedoms under court protection.

A major First Amendment opinion by Justice Hugo Black for the Court (*Bridges* v. *California* [1941]) came in the same cycle and stopped state and federal judges from punishing their journalistic critics in criminal contempt trials without a jury. Congress had limited punishment for contempt in 1831 to disobedience in the presence of the Court or so near thereto as to obstruct the administration of justice; but widespread reaction set in after the Civil War.

During President Franklin D. Roosevelt's second term, justices Black, William O. Douglas, Stanley Reed, Frank Murphy, and Robert Jackson, among others, came to the Court, and Justice Harlan Stone was advanced to chief justice. Although far from agreed on law and issues, these judges frequently used the First Amendment against the states, and they increased the scope and number of cases taken for review. During the 1950's and 1960's the desegregation issue provoked important cases that, when decided by the Court under Chief Justice Earl Warren, also expanded freedom of the press. In one racial protest incident in 1964, the Court, in an opinion by Justice William Brennan, denied damages to Alabama officials suing the *New York Times* for libel and, stating a new rule, singled out and required public officials suing thereafter to prove either that the newspaper or broadcasting station knew its words were false or that it showed reckless disregard of whether they were false or not. This rule was extended the same year to criminal libel and in 1967 to persons in public life. Ordinary citizens caught up in official action were required briefly to offer the same proof in 1971, but a new coalition of judges completed a major rewriting of the libel laws by reversing this part of the rule in 1974.

A grievance of trial courts as old as the Republic against press reporting of criminal incidents before and during trial was resolved in principle when the court authorized trial judges to make and enforce rules for release of information by law enforcement officials to the press (*Sheppard* v. *Maxwell* [1966]). Jailing of some journalists who published information obtained in violation of rules of court and of others who refused to identify their news sources to grand juries (*Branzburg* v. *Hayes* [1972]) revived contempt-of-court tensions and the Supreme Court, this time, gave the press no relief. Television cameras were barred, by constitutional rule, from hearings and trials in state and federal courts (*Estes* v. *Texas* [1965]).

From the *Near* case in 1931 until 1971, no other newspaper was enjoined to prevent publication. In 1971, however, the *New York Times* and the *Washington Post* began printing serially a Defense Department document—the Pentagon Papers—about the Vietnam War that had been classified as secret. After two lower courts enjoined further publication, the Supreme Court set aside the injunctions on the principal ground that the government had not shown sufficient reason to warrant breach of the First Amendment. The Court, again, did not declare the First Amendment absolute.

With respect to censorship of sexual materials, state and federal courts followed the British courts until the 1930's, testing for obscenity by judging the effect of communication on "those whose minds are susceptible to immoral influences, that is, particularly those who are young, ignorant, or lacking in control of sexual impulses and who would be likely to come into contact with such presentations." This rule began to erode in 1933, and in 1957 new and permissive standards were set forth: "All ideas having even the slightest redeeming social importance, unorthodox ideas, controversial ideas, even ideas hateful to the prevailing climate of opinion—have the full protection of the guaranties, unless excludable because they encroach on the limited area of more important interests." Work had to be judged in its entirety, by "whether to the average person, applying contemporary community standards, the dominant theme of the material taken as a whole appeals to prurient interest." The Supreme Court began to apply its definition of obscenity nationally in 1964, but under Chief Justice Warren Burger the Court gave state legislatures and local juries more discretion but still held them to a national definition of hard-core pornography (*Marvin Miller* v. *California* [1973]; *Jenkins* v. *Georgia* [1974]).

The Court has stated that the First Amendment protects broadcasting but "where there are substantially more individuals who want to broadcast than there are frequencies to allocate it is idle to posit an unabridgable First Amendment right to broadcast comparable to the right of every individual to speak, write or publish" (*Red Lion Broadcasting Company* v. *Federal Communications Commission* [1969]). As a consequence of this definition, broadcasters seem consigned to endless litigation before regulatory agencies. Rules of the Federal Communications Commission (FCC), upheld by the courts, abjure censorship while condoning influence on content. Other FCC rules limit the use of station time by networks in order to stimulate local programming. The FCC, to encourage diversity, places somewhat flexible limits on single ownership in one city of more than one station or joint ownership of stations and newspapers.

Finally, distribution of political and religious literature may not be subjected to discretionary licensing or taxed so as to burden distribution. Publishers and broadcasters are subject to normal business taxation, but a discriminatory rate or levy falls under the First Amendment ban.

BIBLIOGRAPHY

Thomas I. Emerson, *The System of Freedom of Expression.*

Donald A. Gillmor and Jerome A. Barron, *Mass Communication Law.*

Harold L. Nelson and Dwight L. Teeter, Jr., *Law of Mass Communications.*

— J. EDWARD GERALD

RECENT DEVELOPMENTS REGARDING FREEDOM OF THE PRESS

Freedom of the Press, protected under the First Amendment to the U.S. Constitution, offers citizens access to the widest range of information while restraining the government from interfering with this exchange. Thomas Jefferson urged James Madison to include such protection in the Constitution because he believed a free press was critical in maintaining democracy, and the First Amendment was the result. It has sometimes seemed as if Supreme Court rulings have diminished the effect of the First Amendment. For example, in a five-to-four decision the Court ruled in 1972 that reporters cannot refuse to testify if they have discovered activities of interest to a grand jury (*Branzburg* v. *Hayes*), and in 1992 the Court ruled that if a reporter breaks a vow of confidentiality the defendant can collect damages (*Cohen* v. *Cowles Media Company*). Many states have so-called shield laws that protect reporters from revealing their sources. Nonetheless M. A. Faber, a *New York Times* reporter, was convicted by a New Jersey lower court in 1978 for contempt because he refused to turn over notes pertaining to a local murder trial.

Two Supreme Court rulings have given the press access to courtroom hearings. The Court ruled that blanket gag orders were unconstitutional (*Nebraska Press Association* v. *Stuart*, 1976). Another ruling permitted television cameras in courtrooms and avowed that their presence would not prejudice a jury (*Chandler* v. *Florida*, 1981). In 1972 the *Washington Post* and the *New York Times* published secret documents (the Pentagon Papers) belonging to the Department of Defense. A lower court stopped publication, but the Supreme Court sided with the newspapers, ruling that the government had a "heavy burden" of proof if it hoped to prevent publication. Justice William O. Douglas stated that while it was a crime to publish defense information, such as secret codes during wartime, there was no law that prevented publication, by which he seemingly meant the requirement of a specific law. Wartime censorship of the press remained a problem. For example, acting in the name of national security in the 1980s, the administrations of Presidents Ronald Reagan and George Bush did not inform the press about the planned invasions of Grenada or Panama; the Bush administration also restricted coverage of the Gulf War of 1991. Vigorous press complaints about this new level of prior restraint in violation of the First Amendment resulted in less censorship of the press when U.S. troops were dispatched to Somalia, Haiti, and Kuwait in the first half of the 1990s.

Some legal scholars in the 1990s believed that a new tort was forming—the right to publicity. Since 1970 the courts have generally decided in favor of the individual but upheld cases involving parody or satire. The California Appellate Court ruled in favor of singer-actress Bette Midler when a car company used a sound-alike singer in an advertisement. Television personality Johnny Carson won a sizable settlement from the manufacturer of bathroom commodes that named one "Here's Johnny!" and advertised it using the *Tonight Show* theme song. The Reverend Jerry Falwell, however, lost a Supreme Court case against *Hustler*, an adult magazine that parodied his first sexual experience in the guise of a liquor advertisement.

Vigorous press complaints about restricted coverage of the 1991 Gulf War resulted in less censorship of the press several years later when U.S. troops were dispatched to Somalia, Haiti, and Kuwait.

In some instances the First Amendment has shielded individuals or activities that many found distasteful. Beginning in 1957 the Supreme Court began ruling that only obscene or pornographic materials found by a nationally established standard to be "utterly without redeeming social importance" were not protected. Sixteen years later the Court under Chief Justice Warren Burger loosened this definition and granted state legislatures and local juries the freedom to incorporate local community beliefs of the "average person" in determining where material was wholly without importance (*Miller* v. *California*, 1973). In *Pope* v. *Illinois* (1987) "reasonable person" was substituted for "average person." This decision weakened community standards for determining what constituted obscene material and gave most pornographic representations First Amendment protection.

Since 1970 the Supreme Court also has added new levels to libel cases, branching out to establish the difference between a public versus a private individual in terms of defamation; allowing an individual to "explore" a journalist's state of mind to determine actual malice; and considering whether a journalist in the act of "cleaning up" quotes may apply creativity (*Masson* v. *New Yorker Magazine, Inc.*, 1993).

[See also Freedom of Speech.]

BIBLIOGRAPHY

Jonathan Bartlett, ed., *The First Amendment in a Free Society* (New York, 1979).

Jethro K. Lieberman, *Free Speech, Free Press, and the Law* (New York, 1980).

Lucas A. Powe, *The Fourth Estate and the Constitution: Freedom of the Press in America* (Berkeley, Calif., 1991).

Melvyn Bernard Zerman, *Taking on the Press* (New York, 1986).

— HEIDI KELLEY ZUHL

FREEDOM OF RELIGION

The framers of the U.S. Constitution drafted the religious liberty clauses to protect the freedom of conscience for all Americans from the actions of the federal government. By guarding the principles of free exercise and nonestablishment, the authors of the Constitution believed that freedom of religion could be ensured. The Constitution is still intact, but the United States is no longer predominantly Protestant; virtually all religions of the world practice their faiths here. Furthermore, an increasing number of Americans choose not to make religion a part of their lives. Since the 1970s the way people understand themselves religiously has greatly affected how the courts and the nation as a whole understand religious liberty.

Debates over religion arose during the Vietnam War era when the Supreme Court heard a series of conscientious objector (CO) cases called the Selective Draft Law Cases (*United States* v. *Seeger* [1965], *Welsh* v. *United States* [1970], *Gillette* v. *United States* [1971]). The Court determined that one need not come from a pacifist religious background (for example, Quakers and Mennonites) to become a CO. It ruled that because one's relationship with God was a private, personal matter, those applying for CO status could be nonreligious. This ruling represented a marked shift from the traditional Judeo-Christian understanding of religion, in which God transcends humankind.

Since 1970 the role of religion in education and in the public schools has shaped much of the debate over what kind of institutions the nation should have and what kind of country the United States should become. Public schools were once a place where children learned the beliefs of the predominant Protestant culture, but with many religions observed today, educators, parents, and government officials alike debate how the traditional learning should be replaced. In 1984 Congress passed the Equal Access Act, which permitted student-run prayer groups in public schools and universities, a law upheld by the Supreme Court in *Board of Education of the Westside Community Schools* v. *Mergens* (1990). Many critics of the decision said religion was a personal commitment that belonged in the home. They believed that religion had correctly been eliminated from the schools in the 1960s because it would divide, not unify, students. Yet in an age that stresses the importance of diversity, little is mentioned about religious diversity. It seems that public school administrators prefer that people learn religion elsewhere rather than educate them about the importance of religion in a representative democracy.

Religious cults gained notoriety in the mid- to late 1970s and challenged the previously held interpretations of religion. Some cults had nontraditional methods of recruiting members, which the courts would later identify as kidnapping. Because of the Supreme Court's interpretation of religion from the Selective Draft Law Cases, however, the courts initially tended to side with the cults because they stressed the individual personal relationship with a supreme being. Cult control laws were established in the late 1970s, but the courts had difficulty arriving at a definition of the term "cult." Those that made the attempt viewed cults as simply another variety of religious belief.

During the Vietnam War, the Supreme Court ruled that because one's relationship with God is a private, personal matter, those applying for conscientious objector status could be nonreligious.

The case law that emerged from the Supreme Court during the 1970s and 1980s had a common, yet largely unstated, theme—equality. Both the draft law cases and those dealing with the issue of student-initiated prayer in public schools were resolved by the Court's application of principles requiring equal treatment of both religious speech and of all the religious traditions that are conscientiously opposed to all war. This trend continued as the twentieth century drew to a close. The Court held that state officials may not deny services to children with disabilities simply because the child is enrolled in a religiously affiliated school (*Zobrest* v. *Catalina Hills School District*); that a school district that allows community groups to use its auditorium after school hours may not deny religious groups the same opportunity (*Lamb's Chapel* v. *Center Moriches District*); and that government may not discriminate either in favor of or against religious speech on the basis of its content (*Rosenberg* v. *Rector and Visitors of the University of Virginia, Texas Monthly* v. *Bullock, Capitol Square Review and Advisory Board* v. *Pinette*).

Debates over the proper role of religion in a pluralistic society, and over the propriety of governmental policies involving religion and religious believers, have been with the nation since before its founding. There is no doubt that these debates will continue as the United States approaches the twenty-first century. Under the U.S. Constitution the power to protect liberties is shared by Congress and the states. That division of responsibility gives the law governing religious liberty and civil rights in the United States a fluid, adaptable nature, which is unique among the Western democracies. It permits jurists and policymakers on the national, state, and local levels ample room to adjust past practice and precedent to the needs of an increasingly diverse society.

[See also Catholic Church; Judaism; Protestantism; Religious Liberty.]

BIBLIOGRAPHY

Michael S. Ariens and Robert A. Destro, *Religious Liberty in a Democratic Society* (Durham, N.C., 1996).

James Davison Hunter, *Culture Wars: The Struggle to Define America* (New York, 1991).

John T. Noonan, Jr., *The Believer and the Powers that Are* (New York, 1987).

— ROBERT A. DESTRO AND CHARLES HAYNES

FREEDOM OF SPEECH

Freedom of speech is, by virtue of the First Amendment, protected from abridgment by Congress. This provision in the Constitution has neither clear analogue nor predecessor in English and colonial common law. The absence of substantive debate on its adoption makes it possible to argue plausibly that the intent was either merely to restate the common law; to expand radically the degree of freedom, particularly as a response to efforts to suppress religious freedom; or simply to guarantee federalism, totally excluding national intervention but retaining older standards at the state levels.

It was the great debate after passage of the Alien and Sedition Acts of 1798 (and the reciprocal failure of Jeffersonian efforts on the state level to suppress Federalist expression) that "first crystallized a national awareness of the central meaning of the First Amendment" (*New York Times Company* v. *Sullivan*, 376 U.S. 254, 273 [1964]). A growing tolerant, libertarian interpretation was sporadically invoked during such debates as those over rights of abolitionists in the 1850's or anarchists in the last quarter of the 19th century. But it took real shape only with World War I and the prosecutions arising from opposition to it. Justice Oliver Wendell Holmes then formulated the clear-and-present-danger rule as a proposed boundary line, first in the majority decision in *Schenck* v. *United States* (1919) and later in dissent. It was destined to reemerge as the dominant rule for more than two decades, from the 1930's until the decision in *Dennis* v. *United States* (1951), which exposed inadequacies in the approach.

More significant, the Court in *Gitlow* v. *New York* (1925) extended the protection of the First Amendment to state action, through what was to become its usual route of incorporation of provisions of the Bill of Rights into the due process clause of the Fourteenth Amendment. While justices still argue the position of Robert Jackson, Felix Frankfurter, and John M. Harlan that states are freer to regulate speech than the national government, in fact, equal (arguably more stringent) supervision by the Court has prevailed.

Since the *Dennis* case the Court has avoided a single overarching rule. It has retained clear-and-present danger as a test for crowd situations. It has not overtly embraced Justice Hugo Black's view that the Constitution totally prohibits any regulation of content of communication, only permitting control of times, manner, and place. But it has accepted a similar and generous view of expression as "political freedom" seminal to the very being of a reflective republic and regulatable only in the presence of an overriding public need that cannot be met by any means other than regulation. (Since this test is applied to both content of communications and their means of transmission, the majority view is in many ways more protective than Black's "absolutist" view.) Similarly, while rejecting the view that "symbolic speech" involving action is exempt from normal regulation as action, the Court has noted that acts may also be part of communication. In such instances the Court "balances" the gains and losses without the virtually absolute presumptions attached to "pure" speech.

In short, the justices have developed a multiplicity of tests in various types of situations that underscore "the principle that debate on public issues should be uninhibited, robust, and wide-open" (*New York Times Company* v. *Sullivan*).

BIBLIOGRAPHY

Harry Kalven, *The Negro and the First Amendment.*

Leonard W. Levy, *Freedom of Speech and Press in Early American History: Legacy of Suppression.*

Martin Shapiro, *Freedom of Speech: The Supreme Court and Judicial Review.*

— SAMUEL KRISLOV

FREEDOM OF SPEECH SINCE THE 1970S

Freedom of speech was quietly transformed during the last quarter of the twentieth century. While conservative attempts to outlaw flag burning provoked an intense controversy, feminist and civil rights advocates became the most prominent proponents of censorship. The leading free speech issues also changed. Federal courts from the 1970 to the mid-1990s were more concerned with campaign finance reform than with state efforts to interfere with freedom of speech. The Supreme Court ignited the most intense free speech controversy of the 1980s by ruling in *Texas* v. *Johnson* (1989) that persons had a constitutional right to burn the American flag as a symbol of political protest. Public response to that decision was overwhelmingly hostile. Warding off calls for a constitutional amendment, Congress passed the Flag Protection Act of 1989. Although that measure was declared an unconstitutional "content based limitation" on speech in *United States* v. *Eichman* (1990), public interest in flag burning soon abated and efforts to amend the Bill of Rights were abandoned.

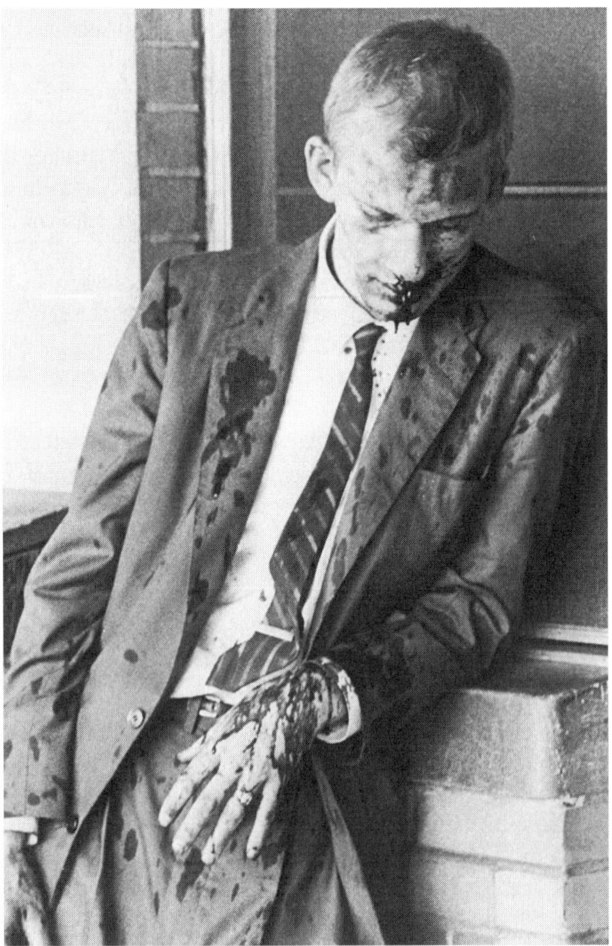

Freedom Rider James Zwerg stands bleeding after an attack by white pro-segregationists at the Greyhound bus terminal in Montgomery, Alabama, May 20, 1961. Zwerg remained in the streets over an hour after the beating, since "white" ambulances refused to treat him. (UPI/Corbis-Bettmann)

Political controversies over pornography and hate speech proved more enduring. In the wake of an attempted Nazi demonstration in Skokie, Ill., in 1977, increased racial incidents on college campuses, and feminist attacks on pornography, many previous defenders of First Amendment freedoms called for limits on racist and sexist expression. Such measures were vigorously opposed by other feminists and civil rights advocates, as well as by an increasingly conservative federal judiciary. A lower federal court declared Indianapolis's ban on pornography unconstitutional, and the Supreme Court in *R.A.V.* v. *City of St. Paul* (1992) struck down a local ordinance that forbade the placing "on public or private property" of objects that might "arouse anger, alarm, or resentment in others on the basis of race, color, creed, religion, or gender." The justices did, however, rule that states could impose higher sentences on criminals who used race to select their victims.

Despite the publicity given to "political correctness," which raised the issue of free speech, campaign finance reform was the most important constitutional issue in the post-Vietnam era. Disturbed by the increased costs of political campaigns, Congress passed the Federal Elections Campaign Finance Act Amendments of 1974, the first comprehensive national effort to control electoral costs. The law had a mixed judicial reception. *Buckley* v. *Valeo* (1976) sustained the congressional power to regulate individual contributions to campaigns, but the justices declared unconstitutional all limits on the sums candidates spent or on "independent" expenditures on behalf of candidates. "The concept that government may restrict the speech of some elements of our society in order to enhance the relative voice of others," the Court ruled, "is wholly foreign to the First Amendment."

The hate speech and campaign finance cases suggested that the Supreme Court under Chief Justices Warren Burger and William Rehnquist was hostile to all speech regulation, whether the censorship of certain doctrines or promotion of greater equality in the marketplace of ideas. For many U.S. citizens the central issue that freedom of expression presents is no longer whether they will have the right to speak but whether they will have the resources necessary to be heard.

BIBLIOGRAPHY

Donald Alexander Downs, *The New Politics of Pornography* (Chicago, 1989).

Mark A. Graber, *Transforming Free Speech* (Berkeley, Calif., 1991).

— MARK A. GRABER

FREEDOM RIDERS

Freedom Riders were blacks and whites, many associated with the Congress of Racial Equality (CORE), who traveled in buses from Atlanta to Alabama in the spring of 1961 and to Mississippi in November 1961 in protest against segregation at bus terminals in the South. Their ride took place fourteen years after CORE had organized the first bus ride by blacks and whites to test discrimination in interstate travel.

The Alabama and Mississippi Freedom Riders received violent receptions. Riders on the first bus were assaulted when they arrived in Birmingham and Anniston, Ala.; riders on the second bus were assaulted at Montgomery, Ala.; and riders protesting the continuation of segregation in Mississippi were attacked at McComb, Miss.

The violence precipitated federal action to protect the Freedom Riders and to prohibit segregation in interstate travel, and it also solidified public support of federal action. More than 400 federal marshals were sent to Montgomery. Upon petition, the attorney general received a ruling from the Interstate Commerce Commission outlawing segregation in all trains, buses, and terminals. The Justice Department also moved successfully to end segregation in airports. Within the next two years, systematic segregation in interstate travel was ended by government rulings and lawsuits. The 1964 and 1968 Civil Rights acts both contained prohibitions against segregation in public facilities for interstate travel.

— SHEILAH R. KOEPPEN

FREE SOIL PARTY

Free Soil Party, a political party, organized at Buffalo, N.Y., on Aug. 9, 1848, that opposed the extension of slavery into the western territories. As antislavery-extension sentiment developed and found expression in the Wilmot Proviso formula, which prohibited slavery in the territory acquired from Mexico, considerable northern dissatisfaction with the evasive policy of the old parties appeared. The New York Democratic Barnburners not only broke away from the regular organization but, meeting on June 22 and 23, 1848, undertook the nomination of their leader, Martin Van Buren, for the presidency. Simultaneously a convention at Columbus, Ohio, dominated by Conscience Whigs, proclaimed dissatisfaction with the regular parties and called a national convention to meet at Buffalo on Aug. 9. These elements, together with the members of the Liberty party and a group of land reformers, now cooperated in the broader movement that nominated a ticket of Martin Van Buren and Charles Francis Adams. Their platform announced a policy of "no more slave states and no more slave territory" and of free homesteads to actual settlers. Van Buren polled 291,263 votes, largely in New York State and in the Northwest; by running second in New York he prevented the election of Lewis Cass. The election of a dozen members of Congress, who later held the balance of power in the House, and a considerable number of state legislators indicated a fair success for the movement. The campaign of 1852 in support of the candidacy of John P. Hale saw the Free Soil vote fall to 155,825. Two years later its disorganized remnants became absorbed in the newly forming Republican party.

BIBLIOGRAPHY

J. B. McMaster, *History of the People of the United States*, vol. VII.

T. C. Smith, *The Liberty and Free-Soil Parties in the Northwest.*

— ARTHUR C. COLE

FREE TRADE

The economic rationale for free trade lies in the principle that if trade is free, certain goods and services can be obtained at lower cost abroad than if domestic substitutes are produced in their place. The concept has each country producing for export those goods in which production is relatively efficient, thereby financing the import of goods that would be inefficiently produced at home. This comparative advantage in production between nations is expected to shift over time with changes in such factors as resource endowments and rates of technological advance. Free trade is therefore thought to facilitate the optimal use of economic resources: each country commands a higher level of consumption for a given level of resource use than would be otherwise possible. Advocates of tariff protection take exception to the doctrine on two fundamental bases: (1) at times national goals other than maximized consumption must be served (for example, national defense), and (2) the interests of specific groups do not parallel those of the nation as a whole. Thus, the history of tariffs and other barriers to free trade is a chronicle of shifting economic interests between industries and geographic areas.

Until 1808 the export of American farm and forest products to foreign markets was so profitable and imports were so cheap that there was little incentive to engage in manufacturing. Existing duties were low and designed for revenue rather than protection. War and embargo in the years 1808–15 stimulated manufacturing (wool, cotton, iron); restoration of peace caused a flood of imports. Free trade then became a sectional issue, a strong protectionist movement developing in the middle and western states. Depression in 1819–20 convinced workers that protection was necessary to save jobs from foreign competition, while farmers felt that building strong American industry would create higher demand and prices for farm goods. New England was divided between the manufacturing and the commercial interests, while the South solidly favored free trade because of its desire for cheap imports and fear of English retaliation against raw cotton imported from the United States.

The history of tariffs and other barriers to free trade is a chronicle of shifting economic interests between industries and geographic areas.

By 1833 free-trade sentiment revived, as northern farmers, believing that young industries no longer needed protection, joined forces with John C. Calhoun and the South in an alliance that kept tariffs low until 1860. After the Civil War the protectionists controlled tariff policy for many years. Continued southern devotion to free trade and persistent, although wavering, low-tariff sentiment in the West produced only the short-lived horizontal duty reduction of 1872 and a few haphazard reductions in 1883. In the campaign of 1888 free-traders rallied around Grover Cleveland as the tariff for the first time became strictly a party issue. But the protectionists won again and passed the Tariff Act of 1890.

Popular hatred of monopoly—evidenced in the Sherman Antitrust Act of 1890—came to the support of free trade by implicating the tariff as "the mother of trusts." Cleveland won election in 1892 against the high-tariff Republicans, but the Democrats were torn over free silver and lost the opportunity to liberalize tariffs. However, continued antitrust feeling had bred such hostility to extreme protectionism that even the Republicans promised tariff reduction in the election of 1908. Sectional interests continued to thin the ranks of free-traders; the West and South demanded lower tariffs in general but supported the particular agricultural tariffs that served their interests in the Tariff Act of 1909.

Recurring economic crises, particularly the depressions of 1893–97 and 1907–08, further shook public confidence in the virtues of the "American system." Only the large industrial interests appeared to be consistently served by the cyclical pattern of economic growth (for example, Standard Oil's combining of small companies during depression, as indicated in the Sherman antitrust case of 1911). The height of tariffs, identified closely by the public with large industry, became a major political issue in 1912. The victorious Democrats promised reduction but held that no "legitimate" industry would be sacrificed. Although a considerable number of items were placed on the free list, rates were reduced, on an average, 10 percent only.

After World War I, with the Republicans in power, extreme protection held sway. Agriculture accepted any tariffs on farm products—although still grumbling about industrial tariffs—and the South found its former solid free-trade front broken by districts with a stake in tariffs on products of farm and factory. In the campaign of 1928 the tariff positions of the two major parties were scarcely distinguishable. Following a full year of debate in Congress, the Hawley-Smoot Tariff Act became law in 1930; the act constructed the highest tariff wall in the nation's history, and its contribution to the shrinkage of world trade and the severity of worldwide depression was considerable. Revulsion from the indiscriminate protectionism, distress with the worsening depression, and the leadership of Cordell Hull, an old-fashioned southern tariff liberal, again turned the country toward trade liberalization.

The Trade Agreements Act of 1934 and its twelve extensions through 1962 beat a steady retreat from the high-water mark of protection reached in 1930. Reacting to the severe decline in the volume of U.S. exports after 1930, the administration of Franklin D. Roosevelt conceived reciprocal trade concessions as an antidepression measure to generate recovery in export-related industries. Following World War II a political impetus was added; by opening its markets, the United States could assist the war-ravaged European economies in reconstruction and could similarly aid the process of development in poor nations. The economic implications of the Trade Agreements Act and its extensions were conflicting: there was a steady trend of tariff reduction, expedited after 1945 through the General Agreements on Tariffs and Trade (GATT) and application of the unconditional most-favored-nation concept; but the reductions were tempered by a "no-injury" philosophy, adopted to minimize injury to domestic industry. Escape clauses, peril points, and national security regulations have hedged the U.S. commitment to agreed tariff reductions. The 1958 extension was notable in firmly establishing these concepts and the necessary enforcement machinery. Under the peril-point provision the U.S. tariff commission was to determine before negotiations the level to which a tariff rate could fall before seriously damaging the domestic industry; this estimate was to provide an effective limit to the authority extended negotiators. An industry experiencing severe injury from a tariff already reduced could petition for relief under the escape clause, which had appeared in U.S. trade agreements since 1943; if the U.S. Tariff

Commission found sufficient injury, the concession could be withdrawn.

The Trade Expansion Act of 1962 made a significant departure from the reciprocal agreements in providing programs for alleviating injury caused by trade liberalization. Benefits and retraining for labor and special loans and tax treatment for industry were extended on the rationale of reallocating resources into more efficient uses. The reciprocal trade legislation had avoided this process by rescinding the tariff reduction when injury was inflicted. Administration of the provisions of the 1962 act has been difficult, however, in that distinguishing losses owing to increased imports from losses owing to the domestic industry's inefficiency is not easily accomplished. The 1962 act extended authority for sizable tariff reductions, to be negotiated through the offices of GATT during the five years following. Tariff reductions on items not excepted from this Kennedy Round of negotiations amounted to about 35 percent. As the U.S. trade balance worsened in the late 1960's, culminating in a trade deficit in 1971—the first in the 20th century—the forces of protection threatened to reverse the forty-year trend of trade liberalization.

BIBLIOGRAPHY

M. E. Kreinin, *International Economics.*
F. W. Taussig, *The Tariff History of the United States.*

— THOMAS L. EDWARDS

FRÉMONT'S EXPLORATIONS

John Charles Frémont led five expeditions into the Far West. In the first three, he explored the Southwest—which belonged to Mexico at the time—with the expert assistance of Christopher "Kit" Carson and others. From June to October 1842, he investigated the Oregon Trail, crossing the plains and mountains to southern Wyoming and ascending Frémont's Peak. The next expedition was his most important. In May 1843 and July 1844 he explored the region immediately north of the Great Salt Lake, the Snake and Columbia river valleys, the Klamath Lake country, and eastern Nevada, going through Kit Carson Pass to Sutter's Fort, and returning east by way of the San Joaquin Valley and the Old Spanish Trail. In July 1845, crossing again to California, he went through the Sacramento Valley to Oregon and returned by way of that same valley to California, where the last official expedition was terminated when Frémont became involved in the conquest of California in June 1846. His fourth and fifth expeditions (October 1848 to February 1849, and September 1853 to February 1854) were organized to explore a route for a railroad across the Rocky Mountains in the vicinity of thirty-seven and thirty-eight degrees north latitude. They were privately financed, added nothing to Frémont's fame, and contributed no practical information for prospective railroads to the Pacific coast.

BIBLIOGRAPHY

F. S. Dellenbaugh, *Frémont and '49.*
John Charles Frémont, *Memoirs of My Life.*
Cardinal Goodwin, *John Charles Frémont.*
Allan Nevins, *Frémont.*

— CARDINAL GOODWIN

FRENCH AND INDIAN WAR

French and Indian War (1754–63), the final struggle between the French government and its colonies in America and the English government and its colonies in America for control of the North American continent. It was part of, and overshadowed by, the Seven Years' War that embroiled Europe from 1756 to 1763.

The English settlements were confined to the region along the Atlantic seaboard from Maine to Florida, extending as far west as the Appalachian Mountains, although some of the English colonies by their charters had claims to lands west of the mountains. The French settlements, developing from fur-trading posts, extended from the mouth of the Saint Lawrence River up its course to the Great Lakes, southward to Lake Champlain, along the Great Lakes, and southward along the Mississippi River to Saint Louis and New Orleans. By encirclement the French hoped and threatened to restrict English settlements to the relatively small area east of the mountains. From 1689 to 1748, throughout three wars, both the French and the British colonists struggled for control of the lucrative fur trade of the hinterland and for the land itself, primarily for speculative purposes, because there were as yet too few settlers to occupy the land. Rivalry for fishing privileges along the Atlantic seaboard off the Grand Banks also contributed to the outbreak of the French and Indian War.

Both the 70,000 French and 1.5 million British colonists attempted to project their control into the Ohio region between 1748 and 1753 by peaceful penetration. The area was dominated by the powerful Iroquois League, consisting originally of Mohawk, Oneida, Onondaga, Seneca, and Cayuga, augmented about 1712 by the Tuscarora to form the Six Nations. Thanks to the diplomacy of the British superintendent of Indian affairs, Sir William Johnson, the Six Nations favored the British, to whom they ceded the upper Ohio Valley. The French found allies among the Delaware, Shawnee, Wyandot, and smaller tribes, such as the Mingo and

Abnaki: they entered the hostilities more actively than the Iroquois.

The war originated in the plan of the governor of Canada, Roland Michel Barrin, Marquis de La Galissonière, to construct some nine forts, including Sandusky and Machault, on the Great Lakes, the Ohio and its tributaries, and the Mississippi to New Orleans, which was garrisoned by 1,400 regulars. He put some 1,500 troops into the Ohio venture and only a few score in each of the other forts. His move south of his new fort at Presque Isle on Lake Erie encroached on territory claimed by Virginia, whose governor, Robert Dinwiddie, in November 1753, sent George Washington on a mission to Fort Le Boeuf to warn the French that they were trespassing. Dinwiddie also ordered Washington to find a site suitable for a fort to counter the French, and in 1754 construction was begun near present-day Pittsburgh. Overwhelming French forces pushed Washington back and into a capitulation at Great Meadows, which compelled him to return to Virginia.

The French and Indian War resulted from the governor of Canada's plan to establish nine French forts at points on the Great Lakes, the Ohio River and tributaries, and along the Mississippi River down to New Orleans.

London, and especially Prime Minister Thomas Pellam-Holles, Duke of Newcastle, were shaken by the news, for peace had barely been established after the arduous fighting of the confusing War of the Austrian Succession ended in 1748. Since there were scarcely 800 British troops in the American colonies, Newcastle called upon the Royal Navy to stop any reinforcements for Canada, in order to give diplomacy a chance to keep the peace. Unfortunately, the orders to Adm. Edward Boscawen were equivocal, and when in June 1755 his fleet captured two French ships near Louisburg, on Cape Breton Island, the bulk of the Brest fleet was carrying Gen. Ludwig August Dieskau and 3,171 French regulars up the Saint Lawrence to Quebec. For his trifling gain, Boscawen inflamed France. Eleven months passed in maneuvers for allies, Britain and Prussia ranging against France, Austria, and Russia. War was formally declared in May 1756.

Well before that time there had been action in America, and long-range plans were in progress. As of June 1754, anxious to secure the help of the powerful Iroquois or at least secure their neutrality, Newcastle had their leaders invited to the Albany Congress in the hope of making a treaty with them. The British were also planning to exploit a weakness of the French, who, in zealous quest of fur, had spurned agriculture to the extent that Canadian farms could not support many troops; even for a small French army food would have to come from France, across an ocean cruised by the British navy. At the same time, Newcastle clearly did not comprehend the realities of war in the forests of America, particularly that the French had the great advantage of river and lake passages to the battlefields and that the British would have to make roads. He dispatched, under Gen. Edward Braddock, only 800 regulars, who were to be guided from Fort Cumberland by some 600 Virginians under Washington to the scene of the 1753 humiliation. Braddock's expedition cut a way toward Fort Duquesne, only to be surprised on the Monongahela River just below the fort and badly defeated by an inferior force of French and Indians. Meanwhile, Johnson, with 3,000 militia and 300 Iroquois, marched north from Albany to Lake George. Dieskau had 1,700 regulars, Canadians, and Indians in Crown Point and Ticonderoga to hold Lake George and Lake Champlain. As a springboard, Johnson established Fort Edward on the Hudson. At Lake George, in a well-selected defensive position, Johnson, in hard fighting, including the Battle of Bloody Pond, won a victory that was not pursued.

In 1756, Newcastle's government abstained from any operations in America except for building a few frontier forts, including Fort Augusta on the Susquehanna. The colonists' concentration of 7,000 at Albany fumed in exasperation. Sickness slew some 3,000, which was blamed on the dilatory commander in chief, John Campbell, Earl of Loudoun, who divided his time between developing a supply system and a plan. In April the Royal Navy failed to intercept the French commander, Marquis Louis Joseph de Montcalm, who reached Quebec and started a drive to sweep the British from their foothold on Lake Ontario. The surprised garrison at Oswego held out until their colonel was killed by a cannonball, whereupon his 1,600 troops surrendered, many to be massacred.

Although Gov. William Shirley of Massachusetts militantly urged attack upon strategic Fort Niagara, the Oswego disaster had convinced Lord Loudoun that it would be best to avoid the forests and to utilize the navy to strike directly up the Saint Lawrence to Quebec. In 1757, ordering only three regular battalions to help the militia stand on the defensive on the frontier, he began massing at New York City, planning a June capture of Louisburg, the strongest French fortress and guardian of the Saint Lawrence. Loudoun was frustrated by the slowness of the navy and impatiently jumped without escort to Halifax. By the time his battle fleet arrived there in July, the French had a superior one protecting Louisburg, and so Loudoun abandoned the attack. He was excoriated by the colonists, who demanded his relief, for during his absence Montcalm had seized the forward post of Fort William Henry at Lake George, hard won by Johnson in 1755. Loudoun deserved better. He had created a rational supply system for finishing the war, convinced London that the French could be conquered via Quebec, and coaxed the forwarding of 15,000 scarce regulars for his field force.

Regulars were doubled for 1758 by William Pitt (the elder), who had come firmly to power in Britain and was determined to drive the French from the American continent. Gen. James Abercromby replaced Loudoun and was ordered with a main body to take Crown Point and Ticonderoga and to deploy smaller columns against Fort Frontenac, commanding the entrance of the Saint Lawrence into Lake Ontario, and Fort Duquesne, commanding the Ohio. These operations were intended to distract the French from the principal blow against Louisburg by an expedition straight from England, led by Gen. Jeffrey Amherst. In July, Abercromby, with 6,367 regulars and 9,034 colonials, made a rash frontal attack against Montcalm at Ticonderoga. The 3,600 French inflicted 1,944 casualties upon Abercromby—which seriously undermined the year's plan by requiring the diversion of replacement troops from Amherst's force and thus preventing him from pursuing the Quebec phase of the Saint Lawrence campaign. In August, Fort Frontenac fell to Col. John Bradstreet's expedition. As Gen. John Forbes's expedition approached Fort Duquesne, the French withdrew; subsequently they caught and made casualties of nearly half a careless British detachment at Grant's Hill but were themselves repulsed in a reckless attack on the British encampment at Loyalhanna. More important than the military operations of the year was the shrewdness of Gov. William Denny of Pennsylvania in pacifying the Delaware and Shawnee by the Treaty of Easton, which detached most of them from the French and made the turning point in the wilderness war.

For 1759, Pitt prescribed a four-element campaign. The capture of Quebec by Gen. James Wolfe was to be the main effort: his Louisburg force, assisted by the navy, was to be joined at Quebec by Amherst's, coming via Lake Champlain, while Gen. John Prideaux and Johnson were to take Niagara and thence endeavor to reach the rear of Montreal. A small column under Gen. John Stanwix was to mop up isolated forts on the Great Lakes. The juncture of Wolfe and Amherst was frustrated by the excellent delaying strategy of Gen. François de Bourlamaque and his 3,600 troops, pitted against Amherst's 12,000. After inducing Amherst into the labor of siege preparations at Ticonderoga in July, Bourlamaque abandoned the fort and went into Crown Point, which he also abandoned when Amherst was ready to assault. Bourlamaque retired to the Isle aux Noix in the Richelieu River north of Lake Champlain and suddenly disclosed a small naval force that Amherst would have to overcome in order to advance. Harassment by hovering Abnaki and a drenching by October storms at last stopped Amherst for the winter, but he sent Rogers' Rangers on their famous long-range retaliatory strike at the Saint Francis Abnaki. Concurrently, besieging Niagara, Prideaux was accidentally killed on July 20 by a bursting mortar. The able Johnson assumed command, and his 900 Iroquois friends helped mightily to defeat 1,700 French and Indians from the lake forts, who were vainly trying to relieve the 600 in Niagara. The fort was surrendered on July 25—a victory that cut French water communication to Louisiana as well as opening the back door to Montreal. By necessitating the detachment of troops for the protection of Montreal it had the additional effect of weakening Montcalm at Quebec.

Wolfe's victory on the Plains of Abraham on Sept. 13, 1759, did not guarantee a British hold on Quebec, much less Canada, and his death in the battle was itself a serious loss to the British. Some 10,000 French combatants still held Montreal under the governor, Pierre François de Rigaud, Marquis de Vaudreuil-Cavagnal, who had succeeded to the French command after Montcalm's death at Quebec, and the outcome for 1760 depended upon whose navy would first reach the Saint Lawrence. Indeed, Montcalm's protracted 1759 defense against Wolfe had been made possible by failure of the British navy to catch a convoy of supply ships to Quebec. In the winter of 1759–60 the 7,000 troops of Gen. James Murray, icebound in Quebec, became victims of Wolfe's previous destruction of neighboring farms. Lack of fresh provisions caused scurvy, and by April 1760, Murray had barely 3,000 men on their feet when Gen. François Gaston de Lévis marched with 9,000 from Montreal to try to recapture Quebec. This time, however, the British navy did intercept the supply ships from France, and on May 9, it was a British frigate that hove first into straining view of besieged and besiegers. The French then retreated upon Montreal to await the summer campaigning. Vaudreuil was resolved, if necessary, to abandon Montreal and go deeper inland in order to maintain a fighting presence that could influence the inevitable peace agreements. Amherst presciently planned to forestall any such withdrawal. He shifted his main body for an advance from Ontario onto

Montreal, leaving Col. William Haviland to finish the Lake Champlain–Richelieu River approach, while the resuscitated troops of Murray closed in from Quebec. The three columns converged smoothly, and on Sept. 8 Vaudreuil surrendered without useless bloodshed.

Canada was won by the British, but anxious times remained. On Aug. 7, 1760, the Cherokee, incited by French agents, attacked Fort Loudoun, built by South Carolinians on the Little Tennessee River, and burned the fort and massacred some thirty persons. Amherst detached a punitive force of 1,300 under Archibald Montgomery, but he failed to subdue the Cherokee. It was not until 1761 that their uprising was quelled by a punitive force of 1,200 under Gen. James Grant.

With the removal of the French forces after 1763, British colonists began seriously to question the billeting of twenty regiments of British regulars on the American continent.

Of more significance in 1761, Amherst received orders at his new headquarters in New York City to dispatch his veterans to West Indian operations, 2,000 to Dominica and 7,000 to Martinique, even as British replacement of French authority in the interior was unsettling the Indians, notably the Shawnee and Oneida. Johnson, as superintendent of Indian affairs, at a council at Detroit temporarily mollified most, but unwittingly antagonized the Ottawa, particularly Pontiac, one of their leaders. Upon Spain's declaration of war against Britain in 1762, Amherst had to part with 4,000 more troops to participate in the British seizure of rich Havana. So it was that West Indian fevers were winnowing Amherst's army when a small French squadron of 1,500 troops from Brest audaciously in late June pounced upon the fishery town of Saint John's, Newfoundland, and destroyed 500 vessels. Because of the stripping of his army, Amherst had to collect the garrisons of Nova Scotia for the recapture, led by his younger brother William, in September.

Britain, France, and Spain moved toward the Treaty of Paris, and it was signed on Feb. 10, 1763. The British had only 8,000 weary troops in America when Pontiac convoked the Ecorse River Council on Apr. 27 and then took to open warfare.

With the removal of the French, British colonists began seriously to question the billeting of twenty regiments of British regulars on the American continent.

[See also King George's War.]

BIBLIOGRAPHY

Julian S. Corbett, *England in the Seven Years War.*
John Fortescue, *The History of the British Army.*
Lawrence H. Gipson, *The Coming of the Revolution.*
Edward P. Hamilton, *The French and Indian Wars.*
George T. Hunt, *The Wars of the Iroquois.*
Francis Parkman, *Montcalm and Wolfe.*
William Wood, *The Fight for Canada.*

— R. J. FERGUSON AND R. W. DALY

FRONTIER

As most commonly conceived in North America, the frontier was the line separating at any moment the settled regions from those as yet unoccupied; or it was the region on either side of that line (sometimes defined as having from two to six inhabitants to the square mile) whose few inhabitants had as their chief concern the pioneer labor of breaking land and building homes. Its existence as an interesting phenomenon was noted long before American independence. The narrow life and the crude behavior of its people aroused comment, not always favorable, from most of the visitors who journeyed through the English colonies or the United States. Most often used to describe the zone along the western edge of agricultural occupation, the word "frontier" was often applied to margins other than that of farming. There was a frontier of the discoverer, of the priest or soldier, of the trapper, and, in later days, of the turnpike or the railroad. But the usual meaning of the word recognized the fact that wherever the farmer appeared, his necessary operations changed the face of the land and destroyed forever its virgin character.

The frontier acquired a third meaning—that of process—when in 1893 a young professor at the University of Wisconsin, Frederick Jackson Turner, produced a brief paper on "The Significance of the Frontier in American History." Born in a region just ceasing to be a frontier, schooled in a state possessing the greatest of manuscript collections relating to frontier experience, and trained at a time when the results of economic forces were commanding study, Turner inquired why the United States was as it was. He noted that the solvent population of the United States, the whites, came only from the races that had built the civilizations of western Europe. Yet in America the children of the immigrants had begun by the 18th century to play the part of changelings: they were not Europeans, but Americans. He looked for causes for the transformation, finding no single variation of great consequence in the environment except in the fact that in the North American settlements of England the children of Europeans had come into contact with relatively unlimited quantities of cheap arable land.

Accepting the notion that the open frontier with its cheap land might have been a causal factor, Turner had a new perspective on America. From the earliest settlements at Atlantic tidewater until the latest on the western edge of the high plains, Americans had lived within easy reach of cheap land. In their old homes the dirt farmer was a dependent person, with something less than freedom. In America independence was there for the taking; freedom at a low level to be sure, but freedom. Turner suggested that in the process of occupying the continent, forces were created or released that built the mental structure of Americans, shaped their ideas of government, and contributed to the development of their institutions.

Turner's 1893 essay did little more than suggest the theme. For the rest of his life he and his students tested its applications in many places and many periods, while no important voices challenged the validity of his hypothesis until after his death. From his continuing studies came the meaning of frontier as process. As a social process he conceived of frontier as a state of society in which ancient life and old ideas undergo continuous adaptation to the requirements of new communities, unusually freed from the dead hand of the past. For 300 years the process continued without check, as young men created farms, farmers created local governments, states succeeded territories, and national government smoothed the processes of home rule. Throughout it all ran evidence suggesting that from the cheap land came influences to break down the definitions of conservative society, to encourage the initiative of the individual citizen, to build up a spirit for home rule, to encourage political democracy as a teammate with economic egalitarianism, and to advance the federal structure of the government of the United States and the exercise of national authority by that government.

From the frontier in its three meanings Turner derived an hypothesis whose compelling plausibility shaped most of the writing on United States history for a generation after 1893. Like any other historical generalization, the hypothesis stood upon its reasonableness rather than upon proof and upon the absence of verified facts to challenge its soundness. When he launched the hypothesis Turner took pains to point out that the open frontier had already become an environment of the past. When the frontier closed, the United States of necessity passed into a different chapter of its history.

BIBLIOGRAPHY

F. J. Turner, *The Frontier in American History,* and *The Significance of Sections in American History.*

— FREDERIC L. PAXSON

FUGITIVE SLAVE ACTS

Fugitive Slave Acts, a series of local, state, and federal acts intended to discourage runaways among slaves, to punish those who harbored such persons, and to make possible the recovery by slaveowners of their slave property. Such laws existed in colonial America and had predecessors in acts requiring magistrates to recover runaway indentured servants by armed force and increasing the time a fugitive was required to serve. The development of the American slave system is reflected in the evolution of these laws.

In 1672 legislation in Virginia authorized killing a runaway who resisted arrest and public payment of his value. A similar law existed in Maryland. In North Carolina by an act of 1715 a person swearing he had killed a fugitive in self-defense while apprehending him was not held accountable. Persons harboring fugitives were required to make payments to owners. An act of 1741 rewarded persons who captured a runaway and increased the fine on harborers.

Emancipation in the northern colonies and the Northwest Ordinance of 1787 rendered the status of fugitive slaves in free territory a problem. The ordinance did recognize the right of owners to reclaim slaves, and the Constitution provided similar support for slaveowners.

Under the Constitution, Congress passed two major pieces of legislation concerning runaway slaves—the Fugitive Slave acts of 1793 and 1850. The act of 1793 authorized the claimant or his agent to arrest runaways in any state or territory and to prove orally or by affidavit before a magistrate that the fugitive owed service. Thereupon the magistrate issued a certificate to the applicant for removing the fugitive to the state or territory from which he had fled. Any person knowingly harboring a fugitive or obstructing his arrest was liable to a $500 fine for each offense.

Emancipation in the northern colonies and the Northwest Ordinance of 1787 rendered the status of fugitive slaves in free territory a problem.

The Fugitive Slave Act of 1850 was part of the Compromise of 1850. It was intended to supplant the law of 1793, which had proved to be ineffective in halting runaways or suppressing aid given to them. The new law added U.S. commissioners to the usual courts to issue warrants for the arrest of fugitives and certificates for their removal from the state. The claimant's affidavit was all that was necessary to establish ownership, making the enslavement of free blacks possible and likely. Once arrested, an alleged fugitive was taken before a commissioner, who determined the matter summarily. Citizens were required to assist in carrying out the law. Anyone harboring, concealing, or rescuing a fugitive was liable to a fine of $1,000, six months' imprisonment, and civil damages of $1,000 for each runaway with whom he was involved. A U.S. marshal or any of his deputies refusing to execute a warrant for the arrest of an alleged fugitive was subject to a $1,000 fine and civil damages. A commissioner received $10 for issuing a warrant but only $5 for discharging a person of being a runaway; thus, it was financially beneficial to find in favor of a person claiming to be an owner.

The result of the 1850 law was a period of slave hunting and kidnapping of free men and women, movement of blacks from free states to Canada, and increased activity by the underground railroad. The situation regarding fugitives was one of the slave-related issues that increased tensions throughout the 1850's and helped to bring on the Civil War.

BIBLIOGRAPHY

Stanley W. Campbell, *The Slave Catchers.*

— HENRY N. DREWRY

FUNDAMENTALISM

Fundamentalism, a movement within U.S. Protestantism marked by twin commitments to revivalistic evangelism and to militant defense of traditional Protestant doctrines. By the end of World War I a loose coalition of conservative Protestants had coalesced into a movement united in defending its evangelistic and missionary endeavors against theological, scientific, and philosophical "modernism." The threatened doctrines had recently been identified in a collaborative twelve-volume series entitled *The Fundamentals* (1910–1915). Battles over issues—most frequently biblical inerrancy, the virgin birth of Jesus, substitutionary atonement, bodily resurrection, and miracles—soon erupted within several leading denominations, principally among northern Baptists and Presbyterians. Many members separated from their churches to form new denominations committed to defending the fundamentals. Fundamentalists took their campaign into public education, where such organizations as the Anti-Evolution League lobbied state legislatures to prohibit the teaching of evolution in public schools. The former Democratic presidential candidate William Jennings Bryan led this effort, which culminated in his prosecution of the Dayton, Tenn., teacher John T. Scopes for teaching evolution. The "monkey trial" of 1925 attracted national attention, and the ridicule of Bryan's views during the trial by the defense lawyer, Clarence Darrow, helped to discredit fundamentalism.

Over the next three decades the fundamentalists' twin commitments to evangelism and doctrinal purity produced a flurry of activity that escaped much public notice but laid the groundwork for a resurgence in the late 1970s. Evangelists and missionaries began supplementing earlier revival methods with radio programs. Thousands of independent churches formed, many loosely linked in such umbrella organizations as the Independent Fundamental Churches of America. These churches sent missionaries abroad through independent mission boards. Bible colleges and seminaries trained the missionaries. Internecine squabbles over doctrine marked this period. The dispensational premillennialism outlined in the Scofield Reference Bible began to take on the status of another fundamental. Others formalized a doctrine of separation from the world's corruption. Such developments prompted some leaders to forge a new evangelical movement that differed little from fundamentalism in doctrine but sought broader ecclesiastical alliances and new social and intellectual engagement with the modern world. By the late 1960s a set of institutions supported a movement centered in Baptist splinter groups and independent churches. Listener-supported Christian FM radio stations began proliferating across the country. Evangelists began television ministries. This burgeoning network reached an audience far broader than the fundamentalist core, allowing fundamentalists, evangelicals, and pentecostals to identify a set of concerns that drew them together.

By the early 1970s fundamentalists came to believe that an array of social, judicial, and political forces threatened their beliefs. They began battling this "secular humanism" on several fronts, advocating restoration of prayer and the teaching of creationism in public schools and swelling the ranks of the prolife movement after *Roe* v. *Wade* (1973). In the late 1970s fundamentalists within the Southern Baptist Convention mounted a struggle, ultimately successful, for control of the denomination's seminaries and missions. At the same time the fundamentalist Baptist preacher Jerry Falwell mobilized a conservative religious coalition that would promote moral reform by supporting conservative candidates for public office. Many political analysts credited Ronald Reagan's presidential victory in 1980 to the support of Falwell's Moral Majority.

Falwell disbanded his organization in 1988 but activists continued to exert influence into the mid-1990s. Journalists as well as some students tended to label this post-Falwell coalition as "fundamentalist" and applied the term to antimodernist movements within other religions. Sharp differences, however, continued to distinguish fundamentalists from evangelicals and pentecostals. Indeed, fundamentalists themselves remained divided—separationists denounced efforts to form common cause with other religious groups, and political moderates criticized alliances of groups such as the Christian Coalition with the Republican Party. Despite this factiousness the movement displayed great resourcefulness in adapting modern communications technology to defend its fundamentals against the modern world's ideas.

[See also Abortion; Presbyterianism; Scopes Trial; Terrorism.]

BIBLIOGRAPHY

Nancy T. Ammerman, *Bible Believers: Fundamentalists in the Modern World* (New Brunswick, N.J., 1987).

George Marsden, *Fundamentalism and American Culture* (New York, 1980).

Martin E. Marty and R. Scott Appleby, eds., *Accounting for Fundamentalisms* (Chicago, 1994).

— TIMOTHY D. HALL

FUR TRADE

The traffic in furs and skins began with the first contacts between European explorers and the Indians along the shores of North America, and has continued without interruption. Scarcely any part of the continent has not at one time or another been the scene of the trader's activities. The area involved has naturally become more and more restricted with advancing settlement, although in northern Canada the fur trade is still conducted along lines that are in some respects reminiscent of methods that originated in the 17th century. The industry represents a transitional stage in the development of any particular region, to such a degree that it is customary to refer to the "fur trader's frontier."

Furs always commanded a ready market in Europe, and they were almost the only New World commodity that afforded immediate returns. Furs were fairly compact in relation to their value and could be easily transported, while the aid of the Indians could be enlisted in procuring them. Many circumstances determined the subsequent development of the trade, including the variety and abundance of fur-bearing animals, the conditions of the European market, facilities for transportation, especially by water, and the attitude of the various Indian tribes. Competition between individual traders as well as national groups was also an important factor.

The fur trade tended to subdivide into regional areas, depending upon the nationality of settlers and political jurisdiction, but especially upon transportation routes. While these areas constantly shifted, the following may be fairly clearly distinguished: the Saint Lawrence–Great Lakes region and the upper Mississippi; New England; the southern Atlantic colonies, with the hinterland converging upon the Ohio Valley; the lower Mississippi and its tributaries, dependent upon New Orleans; and, as the tide of settlement rolled westward, the Missouri River and Rocky Mountain areas and the Pacific coast. To the north there is the vast area continuously exploited by the Hudson's Bay Company since 1670.

As regards the greater part of the continent, the fur trade has not been a permanent phenomenon, but it has not been without historical significance. Trade and exploration have proceeded hand in hand and it was long an axiom that Indian trade and Indian diplomacy were synonymous terms. In

A fur trader in the council tepee. Original by Frederick Remington. (Corbis-Bettmann)

the rivalry among English, Dutch, Spanish, French, and Americans, the fur trade played a major role. The difficult task of regulating the trade, moreover, engaged the attention of government agencies from the beginning. The traders themselves have left a vast body of letters, journals, and diaries that constitute a valuable literary heritage in which one of the most picturesque aspects of American history has been recorded.

— WAYNE E. STEVENS

G

GABRIEL'S INSURRECTION

Gabriel's Insurrection (1800), a conspiracy of Gabriel and other slaves near Richmond, Va., to seek freedom. The plot was revealed and the conspirators arrested before they could strike. Fear spurred the state to begin negotiations to the end of acquiring lands "whither persons obnoxious to the laws or dangerous to the peace of Society may be removed." Although unsuccessful in this early attempt, Virginia later supported the American Colonization Society generously.

BIBLIOGRAPHY

T. M. Whitfield, *Slavery Agitation in Virginia, 1829–32.*

— THEODORE M. WHITFIELD

GADSDEN PURCHASE

The Treaty of Guadalupe Hidalgo (1848) did not settle the so-called Mexican question. The United States was soon charged with not enforcing Article XI, which promised Mexico protection from inroads of American Indians. A boundary-line dispute also arose involving territory held necessary by some Americans for a southern railroad route to the Pacific Ocean. Diplomatic tension was increased by activities of American speculators in Mexico. In 1849 P. A. Hargous of New York City purchased the Garay grant, made in 1842 by the Mexican government to open a transit concession across the Isthmus of Tehuantepec. This concession was nullified in 1851 by Mexico, but in 1853 A. G. Sloo was given an almost identical grant. Both Hargous and Sloo demanded American protection for their concessions.

In July 1853, James Gadsden, minister to Mexico, was instructed by President Franklin Pierce to make a treaty not only settling the issues involved but also securing enough territory for the proposed southern railroad route. Financial needs of the administration of Antonio López de Santa Anna aided negotiation of a treaty whereby territory in northern Mexico was sold to the United States. Article XI of the Treaty of Guadalupe Hidalgo was abrogated, but the United States was to aid in suppressing Indian depredations. For these concessions the United States was to pay Mexico $15 million and assume all claims of its citizens against Mexico, including the Hargous claim. The United States promised to cooperate in suppressing filibustering expeditions.

The treaty met strong opposition in the Senate. Antislavery senators opposed further acquisition of slave territory. Lobbying by speculators gave the treaty a bad reputation. Some senators objected to furnishing Santa Anna financial assistance. The Senate, by a narrow margin, ratified the treaty on Apr. 25, 1854, but only after reducing the territory to be acquired to that considered essential for the railroad route. All mention of private claims and filibustering expeditions was deleted. The payment to Mexico was lowered to $10 million, and an article was inserted promising American protection to the Sloo grantees. A combination of the advocates of the southern railroad route and the friends of the Sloo grant made ratification possible.

By the Gadsden Treaty the United States secured 45,535 square miles of territory. This tract became known as the Gadsden Purchase and comprises the southern part of Arizona and New Mexico.

BIBLIOGRAPHY

Paul Neff Garber, *The Gadsden Treaty.*

— PAUL NEFF GARBER

GAG RULE, ANTISLAVERY

On May 26, 1836, the House of Representatives adopted a gag rule to hold back the flood of antislavery petitions that rushed in following the growth of antislavery sentiment and the formation of the American Antislavery Society in 1833. The gag rules, variously phrased, prevented discussion of antislavery proposals. Originally adopted by southerners with the aid of northern Democrats, the gag rule was rescinded on Dec. 3, 1844, after the northern Democratic support had fallen away. The gag rule strengthened the antislavery movement by adding the issue of deprivation of the right of petition to the ordinary antislavery arguments.

BIBLIOGRAPHY

G. H. Barnes, *The Antislavery Impulse, 1830–1844.*

— ROBERT P. LUDLUM

GAMBLING

Called "gaming" by proponents, legalized gambling is one of the fastest-growing industries in the United

States, taking in $300 billion per year in 1993 with profits of $30 billion. State lotteries alone bring in between $25 billion and $30 billion and illegal numbers operations may harvest double that amount. In 1924 gambling was illegal everywhere in the United States, but by 1994 only Utah and Hawaii permitted no wagering of any kind, and the array of legal wagering opportunities was constantly expanding. Depending upon location, it is possible to bet legally on lotteries, bingo, casino games, horse or dog races, slot machines of various kinds, jai alai, sports, or "Las Vegas night" charity events.

Legal lotteries in the United States date to colonial times. The first were operated privately by such individuals as Thomas Jefferson, George Washington, and Benjamin Franklin. The United States Lottery was established in 1776 to raise money to support the Revolution, lending it a patriotic air that is still exploited by state lotteries. The first state lottery was established in New Hampshire in the mid-1960s and soon was emulated in New Jersey and New York. By the 1990s thirty-seven states operated lotteries. Although casino gambling was legalized in Nevada in 1931, the first casino, the Flamingo, did not open until 1946. New Jersey passed a law permitting casino gambling in Atlantic City in 1976 and the first casino opened there in 1978. South Dakota legalized casino gambling in 1990 and Iowa was the first state to legalize riverboat gambling. The first riverboat casino opened in Bettendorf, Iowa, on Apr. 1, 1991.

Many politicians saw lotteries as a way to fill state coffers while avoiding the politically perilous action of raising taxes.

Native-American tribes have been able to cash in on the gambling boom. In 1987 the Supreme Court ruled that because of their sovereign status Native American reservations could host any form of gambling that was permitted by the states in which the reservations are located. High-stakes bingo parlors quickly opened followed by casinos, the first being in Minnesota. Foxwoods High Stakes Bingo and Casino, near Mystic, Conn., is owned by the Mashantucket Pequot Tribe and is the most successful casino in the world, currently taking in $1 million in profit per day. In 1994 Native Americans owned eighty-eight casinos. In 1995 gambling in some form organized by Native Americans existed in twenty-two states and has allowed some tribes to escape the poverty common in reservation life. The majority of Native Americans, however, have yet to share in the benefits of gaming and it is likely that many never will.

The phenomenal rise in legal gambling since the late 1970s is due to both economics and ideology. In the early 1980s state economies were mired in a deep and lingering recession. At the same time, the federal government reduced federal assistance to state and local governments and trumpeted an antitax philosophy. Many political leaders saw lotteries as a means to fill state coffers while avoiding the politically perilous action of raising taxes. Indeed, states often advertise their lotteries in ways that suggest it is the patriotic duty of citizens to participate because the profits go to worthy causes, such as education or support of the elderly. Casino gambling, including riverboat casinos, were seen as a way to provide jobs and bring business through tourism and to support local governments by taxing such establishments. Organized religion meanwhile has dissipated much of its moral authority to oppose gambling as many churches have often sponsored it themselves in the form of bingo or Las Vegas nights. Legal gambling has raised many questions, especially with respect to social costs. It must be asked whether gambling accomplishes the tasks of increasing revenues without raising taxes and whether it creates jobs. Gambling in general and lotteries in particular are extremely regressive forms of revenue enhancement. Lotteries tend to attract individuals from the lower end of the economic spectrum who hope that a small investment will bring a huge gain. The odds are overwhelmingly against winning, usually being between 12 million and 14 million to 1. Although gambling is advertised as a form of amusement, social critics see it eating away at the moral fiber and work ethic that has provided the foundation for the rise to world power of the United States. Another concern is that gambling attracts the criminal element. Indeed the first casino, the Flamingo, was opened by mob figure Bugsy Siegel. Other Las Vegas, and later Atlantic City, casinos allegedly had ties to organized crime as well. After seeing the potential for huge profits, however, interested corporations pressured lawmakers to get organized crime out of legalized gambling. In addition, the huge capital investments necessary to finance casino construction and operation have been a deterrent to illegal interests. There is currently little evidence that organized crime has been involved in the recent boom in legal casino gambling. Official corruption, however, is another matter. State officials in South Carolina and Kentucky have been convicted of accepting bribes from gambling interests. Finally, legal gambling creates a paradoxical situation wherein for government to realize a profit its citizens must lose.

[See also Native Americans.]

BIBLIOGRAPHY

David Johnston, *Temples of Chance* (New York, 1992).

— GARRY E. CHICK

GAY AND LESBIAN MOVEMENT

Gay and Lesbian Movement in the United States refers to organized efforts to fight prejudice, discrimination, and persecution resulting from the classification of homosexuality as sin, crime, or illness. While its proponents disagree about the origins of homosexuality (whether inborn or acquired), they are united around the concept of homosexuality as a component of personal and political identity. Although historians often date the movement's origin from the June 1969 riot at the Stonewall Inn, a gay bar in New York City where patrons fought with police, the movement's origins can be traced to World War II and earlier. Gay and lesbian subcultures were present in American cities for most of the twentieth century. During World War II, however, military deployment offered homosexuals greater opportunities to meet each other, increasing the size and visibility of these subcultures and reinforcing the concept of homosexual community. Both abroad and at home lesbians benefited from the greater freedom women in general were experiencing (mobility, different work, wearing slacks), as new standards for acceptable female behavior more closely matched their own. Nonetheless, the greater visibility of homosexuals coincided with use of psychiatry in the military services to define gay people as unfit for service and encouraged the belief that homosexuality is a mental illness.

In the 1950s anticommunists associated homosexuality with political danger, arguing that gay people were mentally or emotionally unstable and therefore security risks; others simply equated homosexuality with communism. Many persons seen as gay lost their jobs, some were imprisoned, and others were subjected to "therapies" ranging from shock treatment to castration. In this atmosphere arose the homophile movement embodied in the Mattachine Society, founded in 1950–1951, and the Daughters of Bilitis, founded in 1955, the first sustained homosexual organizations in the United States. (The earliest known group, the Chicago Society for Human Rights, lasted only a few months in 1924–1925.) Both groups sought to unite homosexuals around social and political goals and by the late 1950s emphasized accommodation to heterosexual (straight) society while seeking support from the legal and medical professions. At the same time, other gay men and lesbians continued to develop roles by which to define themselves in relation to each other and to straight society. Butch-femme roles became prominent among working-class lesbians, and many gay men continued to dress in drag (female attire).

Gays and lesbians rally for equality on November 2, 1974. (Hulton-Deutsch Colletion/Corbis)

Homosexual organizations experienced the same tensions that characterized other movements. Coalitions such as the East Coast Homophile Organizations (ECHO) and the North

American Conference of Homophile Organizations (NACHO) broadened the movement by the mid-1960s, while such groups as the Society for Individual Rights (SIR) and dissenters within older organizations advocated a more assertive stance. In the wake of the Stonewall riot, "gay liberation" built upon the growing sense of identity within the general climate of revolution. From civil rights and the New Left came tactics and ideas, while feminism and sexual liberation shared many goals and strategies with gay liberationists. The phrases "gay power" and "gay pride" emerged, and political organizing was revitalized. According to historian John D'Emilio, the two features of gay liberation were "coming out" (publicly declaring oneself a homosexual) and the development of lesbian feminism and a lesbian liberation movement. The Gay Liberation Front (GLF) represented a rejection of what liberationists saw as the homophile movement's over-reliance on experts and assimilation. Out of the GLF came the Gay Activists Alliance, a less radical group devoted to reform within, which produced the National Gay Task Force (later the National Gay and Lesbian Task Force).

In the 1970s the new activism reached into higher education in the form of the Gay Academic Union, caucuses within academic organizations, student groups, and the first gay and lesbian studies courses. The concept of a gay community became important socially and politically. Bars continued as the primary locus of the movement, while symbols, styles of dress, newspapers, fiction, and even music and humor arose as part of an open gay-lesbian movement. Gay-pride parades were opportunities to unite publicly. Gay and lesbian activists scored several victories. The American Psychiatric Association removed homosexuality from its diagnostic manual and a few communities adopted antidiscrimination laws. Harvey Milk, an openly gay San Francisco supervisor, was murdered in 1978 along with Mayor George Moscone, and the light sentence given the man convicted of both shootings galvanized gay communities.

In the 1980s two factors brought setbacks for the movement, the AIDS epidemic and the hostility of conservative Christian groups, but visibility continued as the main strategy of gays and lesbians. A few entertainment and sports figures came out (movie star Rock Hudson, who died of AIDS, tennis champion Martina Navratilova, country singer K. D. Lang). Gay advocates such as the Gay and Lesbian Alliance Against Defamation (GLAAD) monitored the media for tone and content, while others formed direct-action groups, such as ACT UP (AIDS Coalition to Unleash Power) and Queer Nation. After 1990 the movement focused increasingly on fighting the ban on homosexuals in the military, continuing the struggle for equal legal treatment, and promoting the idea of gay people as an economic as well as political force. In 1987 and 1993 gay people participated in marches on Washington to protest government support of discrimination in such areas as employment, housing, health care and insurance, parental rights, and adoption.

[See also Acquired Immune Deficiency Syndrome.]

BIBLIOGRAPHY

Barry D. Adam, *The Rise of a Gay and Lesbian Movement*, rev. ed. (New York, 1995).
Bruce Bawer, *A Place at the Table* (New York, 1994).
Margaret Cruikshank, *The Gay and Lesbian Liberation Movement* (New York, 1992).
John D'Emilio, *Sexual Politics, Sexual Communities* (Chicago, 1983).
John D'Emilio and Estelle B. Freedman, *Intimate Matters* (New York, 1988).
Martin Duberman, *Stonewall* (New York, 1993).
Lillian Faderman, *Odd Girls and Twilight Lovers* (New York, 1991).
Jonathan Ned Katz, *Gay American History* (New York, 1992).

— VICKI L. EAKLOR

GENERAL AGREEMENT ON TARIFFS AND TRADE

The world's major multinational trade agreement and the international secretariat that oversees its operations are both referred to as the General Agreement on Tariffs and Trade (GATT). More than 100 nations are signatories and many others pattern their trade policies on its provisions. Although cold war tensions excluded some nations, including the Soviet Union and the Chinese governments in Taipei and Beijing, GATT served as the major international trade agreement, affecting the vast majority of world trade. The concept for such an approach to international trade policy originated in bilateral Anglo-American discussions during World War II and sought to alleviate postwar economic problems. In the original plan the International Monetary Fund and the World Bank were to be joined by the International Trade Organization (ITO), which would regulate commerce. The general agreement that emerged from the Havana Conference in 1947 was drafted only as a temporary measure to stabilize world trade until the ITO took over. When the U.S. Senate refused to consent to the ITO charter, President Harry S. Truman decided to join GATT through an executive order. Another twenty-two nations joined the United States in endorsing the new arrangement. The agreement incorporated many provisions in the ITO's charter but lacked envisioned enforcement powers. GATT has managed to survive and remain effective primarily because of the goodwill of member nations, the benefits they enjoy from expanded trade, and their desire to avoid retaliation from other nations that support it. Despite absence of a rigid structure and enforcement authority, GATT has played a major role in reduction or elimination of high trade barriers among Western industrialized nations, contributing factors to the Great Depression of the 1930s and the onset of World War II.

The agreement's goal is to encourage member nations to lower tariffs and eliminate import or other regulatory quotas. Nondiscrimination is a key principle in all of its many subagreements. That principle is carried out primarily through most-favored-nation provisions in tariff treaties, which require that no signatory shall impose greater burdens on one trading partner than another. A second principle is that a GATT member may not rescind any tariff concession without compensation for trading partners adversely affected. The agreement also urges all parties to rely on negotiations and consultation to resolve trade conflicts. The arrangement is not without problems. Exceptions to its rules are permitted to accommodate the special needs of developing nations that may wish to continue relations with former colonial powers. Perhaps the most important exception to the most-favored-nation approach is one that furthers GATT's goal of reducing trade barriers. If a group of nations decides to create a free-trade zone, such as the European Community or the North American Free Trade Agreement, it can do so without retaliation or sanction from other GATT members.

GATT has helped reduce or eliminate high trade barriers among Western industrialized nations; such barriers were contributing factors to the Great Depression and World War II.

A series of negotiating periods or "rounds" took place after the initial agreement in 1947: Geneva, Switzerland (1947); Annecy, France (1949); Torquay, England (1950–1951); Geneva (1955–1956); and the Dillon Round, named for U.S. Secretary of the Treasury Douglas Dillon, in Geneva (1961–1962). These first five rounds followed the pattern that had characterized negotiations under the U.S. Reciprocal Trade Agreements Act of 1934. Representatives of the primary supplier of a commodity or product would engage in talks with a major consumer, each party seeking reductions in rates. Once a bilateral bargain was struck and added to the multinational agreement, the most-favored-nation principle extended rates to all parties. In this way world tariffs on industrial products fell to 13 percent.

The sixth round was named for President John F. Kennedy and took place in Geneva from 1964 to 1967. The United States brought in a new strategy when it offered broad, across-the-board reductions. Negotiators focused on deciding what commodities or items to exclude. The Tokyo Round (1973–1979) continued tariff reduction, leading to a general overall rate of 4 percent on industrial commodities. GATT succeeded in reducing tariffs but did not deal nearly as effectively with nontariff barriers (NTBs). The Kennedy Round was the first at which they were given serious attention, and they dominated discussions at the Tokyo Round. Negotiations led to a series of codes of conduct directed at NTBs. These attempted to lessen or eliminate such practices as dumping, government subsidized exports, exclusionary government procurement policies, and arbitrary customs valuations. Most industrial nations agreed to abide by these codes but developing nations did not. The Uruguay Round concluded seven years of negotiations on Dec. 15, 1993, having pursued a most ambitious agenda. In addition to further tariff reductions, it fashioned partial agreements on agricultural products, services, and intellectual property rights that earlier rounds had failed to address. As with all previous GATT negotiations, special interests in many nations were critical of the round, but prospects for international acceptance appeared positive.

[See also North American Free Trade Agreement; Tariff.]

BIBLIOGRAPHY

Robert E. Baldwin and Anne O. Krueger, eds., *The Structure and Evolution of Recent U.S. Trade Policy* (Chicago, 1984).

John W. Evans, *The Kennedy Round in American Trade Policy* (Cambridge, Mass., 1971).

— JOHN M. DOBSON

GENEVA ACCORDS OF 1954

Geneva Accords of 1954, a series of agreements reached at a conference held at Geneva, Switzerland, between May 8 and July 21, 1954, intended to settle the first Indochina War (1946–54) between France and the Vietnamese Communist forces led by Ho Chi Minh. Participants in the conference, which had been called by the Soviet Union, Great Britain, the United States, and France, included, in addition to those nations, the People's Republic of China, the Democratic Republic of Vietnam (Vietminh), and the Associated States of Vietnam, Laos, and Cambodia, which, at that time, were still within the French Union. Great Britain and the Soviet Union served as cochairmen of the conference.

The Geneva accords actually consisted of four separate documents: cease-fire agreements between the French and Vietminh for Vietnam, Laos, and Cambodia, and a "final declaration" issued by all participants in the conference. This declaration was not signed, but all participants except the State of Vietnam (South Vietnam) and the United States expressed either tacit or verbal assent. The U.S. representative "took note" of the provisions of the final declaration and promised that the United States would "refrain from the threat or the use of force to disturb them" but refused to associate the United States formally with the terms of that document.

The cease-fire agreement for Vietnam temporarily divided that country into two zones, with a provisional demarcation line, bordered on either side by a demilitarized area, at approximately the seventeenth parallel. Within 300 days French Union forces were to withdraw to the south of this line and the Vietminh were to regroup to the north of it. In each zone civil administration, "pending the general elections which [were to] bring about the unification of Viet Nam," was to be "in the hands of the party whose forces [were] regrouped there." Until movements of troops were completed, civilians in either zone were to be free to move permanently to the other zone. Aside from normal rotation and replacement, no new foreign military personnel or weapons were to be introduced into either zone. No new military bases could be constructed, and neither zone was to be allowed to participate in military alliances with foreign governments. The International Control Commission, made up of representatives from India, Canada, and Poland, was to supervise implementation of the cease-fire.

The cease-fire agreements for Laos and Cambodia provided for the withdrawal of French Union and Vietminh forces from both of these countries, although the French were to be allowed to maintain a small force in Laos for the purpose of training the Laotian national army. The Khmer Issarak, Cambodian allies of the Vietminh, were to be demobilized and reintegrated, without reprisals, into the "national community." The Pathet Lao, Laotian allies of the Vietminh, were not to be demobilized; they were to regroup in the provinces of Phong Saly and Sam Neua, in northern and northwestern Laos. The International Control Commission was to supervise implementation of the cease-fire in both countries. The governments of Laos and Cambodia also pledged themselves not to join any military alliances inconsistent with the cease-fire agreements or the United Nations Charter and not to accept foreign military aid "except for the purpose of the effective defence of the territory."

The agreements reached at Geneva left the precise obligations of the conference participants unclear. Although the French had indicated that they planned to give full sovereignty to the State of Vietnam under the Emperor Bao Dai, the Saigon government was not asked to sign the Vietnamese cease-fire agreement and refused to be bound by the final declaration of the conference. The United States, which had dissociated itself from the terms of the final declaration, began furnishing economic and military aid directly to South Vietnam almost immediately after the conclusion of the conference. Encouraged by Washington, the Saigon regime, by 1956 an independent republic led by Ngo Dinh Diem, refused to hold the nationwide elections that the Geneva Conference had scheduled for that year. There followed a renewal of the struggle for control of Vietnam that, within a decade, spilled over into Laos and Cambodia and provoked massive U.S. intervention in support of South Vietnam.

The Geneva accords were so hastily drafted and ambiguously worded that, from the standpoint of international law, it makes little sense to speak of violations of them by either side. At the same time, it is clear that the intent of the participants at Geneva, with the possible exception of the Americans and the South Vietnamese, was to establish a single, unified Vietnamese state and that the division of that country between two hostile regimes—neither acknowledging the legitimacy of the other and each dependent upon support from outside—was contrary to the spirit of those agreements.

BIBLIOGRAPHY

Phillippe Devillers and Jean Lacoutre, *End of a War: Indochina, 1954.*

George M. Kahin and John W. Lewis, *The United States and Vietnam.*

Robert W. Randle, *Geneva 1954: The Settlement of the Indochina War.*

— JOHN LEWIS GADDIS

GERRYMANDER

The word "gerrymander" was first used during Elbridge Gerry's second term as governor of Massachusetts, when a bill was passed (Feb. 11, 1812) redistricting the state in order to give the Jeffersonian Republicans an advantage in the election of state senators. It was derived from a caricature representing a strangely shaped three-member Republican district in Essex County as a salamander, which quickly became "gerrymander."

Gerrymandering, the advantage obtained by some group through discretionary districting, has applied to congressional, state legislative, and local districts. The purpose of partisan gerrymandering is to strengthen one party by concentrating the opposing party's voters into only a few districts. The purpose of racial gerrymandering is to limit, perhaps to none, the number of districts in which the unfavored group is dominant.

Although the United States Supreme Court since 1964 has mandated that districts must be essentially equal in population, eliminating the "silent gerrymander" that left urban areas underrepresented as population shifted, and has outlawed racial gerrymandering, it has yet to limit partisan gerrymandering. Although criteria for districting, such as contiguity, compactness, and respect for subdivision boundaries, are often required, substantial leeway exists for legislators to safeguard majority party candidates or incumbents of any party. Even districts drawn by neutral commissions or judges will have differential effects. Redistricting by computer usually follows a program set to give advantage to one party.

BIBLIOGRAPHY

R. G. Dixon, *Democratic Representation,* and *Reapportionment in Law and Politics.*

E. C. Griffith, *Rise and Development of the Gerrymander.*

N. W. Polsby, *Reapportionment in the 1970's.*

— CHARLES H. BACKSTROM AND LEONARD ROBBINS

GETTYSBURG ADDRESS

Gettysburg Address, delivered by President Abraham Lincoln at the dedication of the national cemetery at Gettysburg, Pa., on Nov. 19, 1863. The address was not written while Lincoln was traveling by train, as readers of *The Perfect Tribute* have been led to believe, but was completed in Washington, although Lincoln made minor changes at Gettysburg. At the dedication the president read slowly from manuscript. Tired by the two-hour oration of Edward Everett, the crowd applauded without enthusiasm. Contrary to the general belief, some American critics recognized the literary merit of the address almost at once; others, for partisan reasons, belittled or denounced it.

BIBLIOGRAPHY

W. E. Barton, *Lincoln at Gettysburg.*

— PAUL M. ANGLE

GHENT, TREATY OF

Negotiations leading to the Treaty of Ghent, which effected the end of the War of 1812 in February 1815, were begun only shortly after the start of the war. On June 26, 1812, the American government made preliminary overtures for peace, although on terms unlikely of acceptance. On Sept. 21, 1812, the Russian chancellor proffered a mediation, accepted at Washington, D.C., Mar. 11, 1813, but rejected at London. The British foreign secretary, Robert Stewart, Viscount Castlereagh, on Nov. 4, 1813, offered a direct negotiation, which was accepted on Jan. 15, 1814. Henry Clay and Jonathan Russell joined James Bayard, Albert Gallatin, and John Quincy Adams, who had already been named in response to the czar's preliminary offer of mediation. The British representatives were Adm. James Gambier, Henry Goulburn, and William Adams. Negotiations took place at Ghent, Belgium.

America's chief demand, abandonment of impressment, was relinquished on June 27 as unattainable. Castlereagh had returned from Paris with what Alfred T. Mahan calls a "consciousness of mastery." Far from making concessions on impressment, England was making demands—for a buffer state to protect its Indian allies, along with other territorial readjustments, and for military control over the Great Lakes. A position so advanced was unwarranted by the military situation and proved untenable. When the United States rejected these proposals, Great Britain fell back on a proposal to restore to the Indians their treaty rights as of 1811. The United States denied that the Indians were a subject for direct negotiation, but agreed that Indian rights should be respected.

On Sept. 27, 1814, news reached London of the capture and burning of Washington, D.C., but, out of deference to Czar Alexander I, a conciliatory tone was not abandoned. Lord Henry Bathurst, British secretary for war and colonies, did, on Oct. 18 and 20, contend for *uti possidetis,* or the principle that each party should retain existing holdings. On Oct. 21 news reached London of Commodore Thomas Macdonough's victory on Lake Champlain, thereby diminishing the importance of the capture of Washington, and on Oct. 24 the Americans rejected *uti possidetis,* insisting on complete mutual restitution. A temporary deadlock ensued.

But larger forces worked for peace. The continental situation grew increasingly involved. British finances labored under an unprecedented strain. The Duke of Wellington, Arthur Wellesley, refused an American command with a warning, Nov. 9, that a decisive victory in North America was hopeless without British supremacy on the Great Lakes. The opinion of Wellington fortified the ministry in withdrawing some of its extreme demands. *Uti possidetis* gave way on Nov. 13 to *status quo ante bellum,* which was mutually acceptable.

While continental dangers hastened British acquiescence, the United States abandoned not only its demands regarding impressment but also demands for commercial losses incurred in the war between France and England. American rights in the Newfoundland fisheries were acknowledged. Both parties agreed to employ their best efforts to abolish the slave trade. Boundary commissions were provided for subsequent negotiations.

A treaty was signed by the eight negotiators on Dec. 24, 1814. It reached the United States on Feb. 11, 1815, and was formally ratified on Feb. 17.

BIBLIOGRAPHY

Henry Adams, *History of the United States, 1801–1817.*

A. T. Mahan, "The Negotiations at Ghent in 1814," *American Historical Review*, vol. 11.

— LOUIS MARTIN SEARS

GHOST DANCE

The name Ghost Dance applies to two waves of a nativistic or messianic movement that originated among the Paiute Indians of Nevada in the 19th century.

In 1869 a prophet named Wodziwob began to prophesy supernatural events, claiming that the worn-out world would end, thus eliminating white men, after which all dead Indians would return to rebuild the world. Wodziwob professed to be in communication with the dead, and he instructed his followers to dance a circle dance and sing certain divinely revealed songs. The movement spread to the Indians of southern Oregon and northern California, but it gradually subsided when the promised supernatural events did not occur.

In 1889 there was a resurgence of the Ghost Dance led by another Paiute messiah named Wovoka, or Jack Wilson. Wovoka claimed to have visited the spirit world while in a trance and to have seen God, who directed him to announce to the Indians that they should love one another and live peacefully, returning to the old Indian ways. They were to hasten the millennium by dancing and singing certain songs, and these rites were to result in the disappearance of the whites, the restoration to the Indians of their hunting grounds, and reunion with departed friends.

The revitalized Ghost Dance gained its principal strength among tribes to the east, and beyond the Rockies it was received with enthusiasm by some Plains tribes, including the Sioux, Cheyenne, Arapaho, and Comanche. It became a militant movement among former warriors who were discontented and confined to reservations. The Sioux began to hold all-night dances and to wear "ghost shirts," which had magic symbols on them and were thought to be impervious to bullets. In 1890 nearly 300 Sioux were massacred by U.S. troops at Wounded Knee, S.D., where they had assembled to perform the rituals of the Ghost Dance.

The Arapaho assemble to perform a ghost dance in this painting attributed to Mary Irvin Wright, circa 1900. (The National Archives/Corbis)

BIBLIOGRAPHY

Anthropological Records of the University of California, vol. III, no. 1.

Cora A. DuBois, *The 1870 Ghost Dance.*

James Mooney, *The Ghost Dance and the Sioux Outbreak of 1890.*

— KENNETH M. STEWART

GI BILL OF RIGHTS

The initials "GI" originally stood for anything of government issue; eventually they came in army slang to designate an enlisted man in the U.S. armed forces. Congress in 1944 passed the Servicemen's Readjustment Act, the so-called GI Bill of Rights, which provided government aid for veterans' hospitals and vocational rehabilitation; for the purchase by veterans of houses, farms, and businesses; and for four years of college education for veterans—$500 a year for tuition and

The GI Bill of Rights provided government aid for veterans' hospitals and vocational rehabilitation; for purchases of houses, farms, and businesses; and for four years of college education.

books and a monthly allowance of $50, which was later progressively raised. The act was extended to veterans of the Korean War. The Readjustment Benefits Act of 1966 gave similar rights to all veterans of service in the U.S. armed forces, whether during wartime or peacetime, and subsequent acts provided for additional benefits.

— CHRISTOPHER LASCH

GILDED AGE

Gilded Age, the period of currency inflation, widespread speculation, overexpansion of industry, loud booming of dubious enterprises, loose business and political morals, and flashy manners that extended from the end of the Civil War in 1865 to the Panic of 1873. It was the result of two main forces. One was the business boom produced by paper money, large government expenditures, high tariffs, such new inventions as Bessemer steel, the rapid development of the Middle West and Far West, and the exuberant confidence of the victorious North. The other was the moral laxity produced by wartime strain, easy money, the pressure of rich corporations on the government, and frontier influences. The title "Gilded Age" was attached to the period by the novel of that name that Mark Twain and Charles Dudley Warner published in 1873.

BIBLIOGRAPHY

Allan Nevins, *The Emergence of Modern America.*

— ALLAN NEVINS

GLOBAL WARMING

The burning of fossil fuels emits carbon dioxide gas into the atmosphere in amounts comparable to what circulates through natural processes. Because of the "greenhouse effect" (absorption of heat rays by the earth's surface and their reradiation into the atmosphere, where they are then partly reradiated to earth by carbon dioxide molecules), the additional gas raises the planet's average temperature. The likelihood of warming was noticed in 1896 by Svante Arrhenius of Sweden. A few other scientists, notably Thomas C. Chamberlain in the United States, called for research on the matter, but the greenhouse effect seemed only one of many speculations about climate change, which scientists of the day had no way to sort out. When a long-term warming trend in the United States was reported in the 1930s, scientists believed it to be a phase of some natural cycle with an unknown cause. Interest in global warming increased in the 1950s as scientists found ways to study climate. Scientists reconstructed past temperatures by studying ancient pollens and ocean shells and found ways to make computer models of future climates. Gilbert N. Plass attracted attention by insisting that carbon dioxide released by humans would warm the atmosphere by a degree or more over the next few centuries.

Many scientists supposed that warming would be delayed because carbon dioxide added to the atmosphere would be absorbed by the oceans. Roger Revelle and Hans Suess, however, showed that this absorption was insufficient. The message was driven home when Charles Keeling measured an actual rise, year after year, in atmospheric carbon dioxide. Reports by the National Science Foundation in 1963 and by the President's Science Advisory Committee in 1965 drew attention to the need for additional research on global warming. In 1967 a computer model by Syukoro Manabe and his colleagues suggested that average temperatures might rise by a few degrees within the next century; subsequent computer studies tended to confirm this hypothesis. Meanwhile, other scientists pointed out that human activity increases atmospheric dust, smog particles, and other contaminants that can block sunlight and cool the world. Indeed, a cooling trend that began around 1940 was detected in the 1960s.

In the 1970s public and media concerns about the global climate increased markedly. Scientists warned that steps should be taken to safeguard agriculture against changes in rainfall and temperature. Studies by scientists around the world showed that the climate system is influenced by a great many forces. It became clear that climate is so delicately balanced and so subject to feedback that change in any one force can lead to major alterations in other aspects of climate. When West European and Soviet teams extracted cores from deep within the Greenland and Antarctic ice sheets, they found evidence of disconcertingly large and swift temperature changes in the past, accompanied by changes in the level of carbon dioxide. Scientists also discovered that industrial and agricultural expansion was rapidly adding other gases, such as methane and chlorofluorocarbons, to the atmosphere. These gases not only contribute to global warming but affect the atmosphere's ozone layer.

In 1985 the World Meteorological Organization came out for active policy changes to prepare for possible global warming. Under United Nations auspices and with substantial U.S. funding, a major research program, the International Geosphere Biosphere Program, was launched. Nevertheless, when a 1989 world conference proposed future policy steps to limit carbon dioxide production, the U.S. government blocked any practical action. For many decades scientists have suggested that variations in the sun's output of energy, along with gases emitted by volcanoes and other natural changes, are powerful enough to defy any control measures undertaken by humans. Some scientists have argued that the climate system is so complex and unstable that it goes through chaotic variation entirely of its own accord. Activists reply that scientists generally agree that the greenhouse effect will produce global warming, with severe consequences for many regions. They urge that action to retard damage begin as soon as possible, especially policy changes that would be desirable for their beneficial effects on the environment.

[See also Environmental Movement.]

— SPENCER R. WEART

GOLD STANDARD

Gold Standard, a monetary system in which gold is the standard or, in other words, in which the unit of value—be it the dollar, the pound, franc, or some other unit in which prices and wages are customarily expressed and debts are usually contracted—consists of the value of a fixed quantity of gold in a free gold market.

U.S. experience with the gold standard began in the 1870's. From 1792 until the Civil War the United States, with a few lapses during brief periods of suspended specie payments, was on a bimetallic standard. This broke down in the early days of the Civil War, and from Dec. 30, 1861, to Jan. 2, 1879, the country was on a depreciated paper money standard. In 1873 the currency laws of the federal government were revised and codified, and in the process the standard silver dollar was dropped from the list of coins whose minting was authorized by law. The law of 1873 continued the free and unlimited coinage of gold and unlimited legal tender quality for all gold coins and declared the gold dollar to be the unit of value. There was a free market in the United States for gold, and gold could be exported and imported without restriction. Nonetheless the United States for six more years continued on a *de facto* greenback standard, the greenback and national bank notes that constituted the principal currency of the country, circulating at a smaller and smaller discount from gold parity. In accordance with the provisions of the Resumption Act of 1875, paper dollars became officially redeemable in gold on Jan. 2, 1879, but many banks had begun redemption by Dec. 17, 1878.

Under the gold standard as it then operated in the United States, the unit of value was the gold dollar, which contained 23.22 grains of pure gold. Inasmuch as a troy ounce contains 480 grains, an ounce of gold could be coined into \$20.67 (480/23.22 = \$20.67). Under free coinage, therefore, anyone could take pure gold bullion in any quantity to an American mint and have it minted into gold coins, receiving \$20.67 (less certain petty charges for assaying and refining) for each ounce, while anyone melting down American gold coins of full weight would get an ounce of gold out of every \$20.67. This was called the "mint price" of gold, although saying that an ounce of gold was worth \$20.67 was like saying that a yard is 3 feet long. Clearly mint price is not a market price that fluctuates with the changing demand and supply of gold.

The Gold Standard Act of 1900, following the monetary difficulties associated with the bimetallic controversy and the silver legislation of 1878, 1890, and 1893, made legally definitive a gold-standard system that had existed *de facto* since 1879. This act declared that the gold dollar "shall be the standard unit of value, and all forms of money issued or coined by the United States shall be maintained at a parity of value with this standard and it shall be the duty of the Secretary of the Treasury to maintain such parity." That meant that the value of every dollar of paper money and of silver, nickel, and copper coins and of every dollar payable by bank check (with which hundreds of billions of dollars of business annually were effected) was equal to the value of a gold dollar—namely, equal to the value of 23.22 grains of pure gold coined into money. Anything therefore that affected the value of gold in the world's markets affected the value of the gold dollar in terms of which this tremendous amount of business was being done and in terms of which all American debt obligations were expressed. If the supply of gold thrown on the world's markets relative to the demand increased, gold depreciated and commodity prices in the United States, as in all other gold-standard countries, tended upward. If the world's demand for gold increased more rapidly than the supply of gold, gold appreciated and commodity prices in all gold-standard countries tended downward.

It is highly desirable that the value of the monetary unit—that is, its purchasing power over goods and services—be stable; but owing to the widespread variations in the world's supply of gold and in the world's demand for gold, the value of gold, when viewed over any considerable period of time, has usually shown substantial fluctuations. If one thinks of the gold dollar as a yardstick of value and represents the purchasing power of this dollar over commodities at wholesale in the year 1926 in the United States by a length of 36 inches, the length of this yardstick would have been as follows for the dates specified: 1913, 52 inches; 1920, 23 inches; 1921, 37 inches; 1929, 37 inches; 1932, 57 inches.

The goal of stable money has been the great monetary problem of the ages.

When the yardstick shrinks, there is inflation, a rising cost of living, and excesses in speculation; and when the yardstick expands, there is deflation and depression. Inflation usually helps the debtor at the expense of the creditor, the exporter at the expense of the importer, the speculator at the expense of the man with a fixed income, and the capitalist at the expense of the laborer. Deflation does substantially the opposite.

Until the Great Depression there was general agreement among economists that neither deflation nor inflation is desirable and that a stable unit of value is best. Since then some economists have held that stable prices can be achieved only at the expense of some unemployment and that a mild inflation is preferable to such unemployment. The goal of stable money has been the great monetary problem of the ages. While gold as a monetary standard during the half-century 1879–1933 was far from stable in value, it was more stable than silver, the only competing monetary metal, and its historical record was much better than that of paper money. Furthermore, its principal instability was usually felt during great wars or shortly thereafter, and at such times all other monetary standards were highly unstable.

The appearance of Keynes's *General Theory of Employment, Interest and Money* in 1936 and his influence on the policies of the Roosevelt administration caused a revolution in economic thinking. The new economics deplored oversaving and the evils of deflation and made controlling the business cycle to achieve full employment the major goal of public policy. It advocated a more managed economy. In contrast, the classical economists had stressed capital accumulation as a key to prosperity, deplored the evils of inflation, and relied on the forces of competition to provide a self-adjusting, relatively unmanaged economy. The need to do something about the Great Depression, World War II, the Korean War, and the cold war all served to strengthen the hands of those who wanted a strong central government and disliked the trammels of a domestically convertible gold-coin standard. The rising generation of economists and politicians held such a view. After 1940 the Republican platform ceased to advocate a return to domestic convertibility in gold. Labor leaders, formerly defenders of a stable dollar when wages clearly lagged behind prices, began to feel that a little inflation helped them. Some economists and politicians frankly urged an annual depreciation of the dollar by 2, 3, or 5 percent, allegedly to prevent depressions and to promote economic growth; at a depreciation rate of 5 percent a year the dollar would lose half its buying power in 13 years (as in 1939–52), and at a rate of 2 percent a year, in 34 years. Such attitudes reflected a shift in economic priorities because capital seemed more plentiful than formerly and thus required less encouragement and protection.

After World War II a new international institution complemented the gold standard of the United States. The International Monetary Fund (IMF)—agreed to at a United Nations monetary and financial conference held at Bretton Woods, N.H., July 1–22, 1944, by delegates from forty-four nations—went into effect in 1947. Each member nation was assigned a quota of gold and of its own currency to pay to the IMF and might, over a period of years, borrow up to double its quota from the IMF. The purpose of the IMF was to provide stability among national currencies, all valued in gold, and at the same time to give devastated or debt-ridden nations the credit and, hence, time to reorganize their economies without sacrificing their meager reserves. Depending on the policy a nation adopted, losing reserves could produce either a chronic inflation or deflation, unemployment, and stagnation. Commenting on the IMF, the Federal Reserve's top economist, E. A. Goldenweiser, said: "Under the gold standard as under the Fund, each country ultimately must find means of paying for its foreign purchases by the sale of its goods and services. Under both arrangements temporary deficits can be met by gold shipments and by credit, and under neither of the arrangements can these methods offer permanent solutions." Admittedly, under the IMF a nation might devalue its currency more easily than before. But a greater hazard lay in the fact that many nations kept part of their central bank reserves in dollars, which, being redeemable in gold, were regarded as being as good as gold. For about a decade dollars were much sought after. But as almost annual U.S. deficits produced a growing supply of dollars and increasing short-term liabilities in foreign banks, general concern mounted. Some of these dollars were the reserve base on which foreign nations expanded their own credit.

Supporters of the gold standard distrust inconvertible paper money because of governments' temptation to increase the money supply too fast and thus to cause a rise in prices.

The world had again, but on a grander scale, the equivalent of the parasitic gold-exchange standard it had had in the 1920's. Foreign central bankers repeatedly told U.S. Treasury officials that the dollar's being a reserve currency imposed a heavy responsibility on the United States; they complained that by running deficits and increasing its money supply, the United States was enlarging its reserves and, in effect, "exporting" U.S. inflation. But Asian wars, foreign aid, welfare, and space programs produced deficits and rising prices year after year. At the same time, American industries invested heavily in Common Market nations to get behind their tariff walls and, in doing so, transmitted more dollars to those nations.

Opponents of the gold standard insist that the monetary gold in the world ($45 billion at the $42.22-an-ounce valuation current in early 1975) is insufficient to serve both as a reserve and as a basis for settling large balances between nations, given the rapid expansion of world trade. They also contend that a gold standard would increase unemployment and hamper the achievement of costly social welfare programs. Supporters of the gold standard distrust inconvertible paper money because of a strong tendency by governments, when unrestrained by the necessity to redeem paper money in gold on demand, to increase the money supply too fast and thus to cause a rise in price levels. Whereas opponents of the gold standard allege there is insufficient monetary gold to carry on today's huge international trade—they speak of there being insufficient "liquidity"—supporters stress that national reserves do not have to be large for this purpose, since nations settle only their net balances in gold and not continually in the same direction. Supporters also emphasize that even at a price of $35 an ounce, $1.4 billion in gold was produced annually between 1962 and 1971, and they suggest that if the mint price were set substantially higher, the output would rise sharply, as it did in the 1930's.

BIBLIOGRAPHY

D. C. Barrett, *The Greenbacks and Resumption of Specie Payments, 1862–1879.*
W. A. Brown, Jr., *The Gold Standard Reinterpreted, 1914–34.*
Federal Reserve Board, *Bulletins.*
D. L. Kemmerer and C. C. Jones, *American Economic History.*
E. W. Kemmerer, *Gold and the Gold Standard.*
M. Palyi, *The Twilight of Gold, 1914–36.*
J. D. Paris, *Monetary Policies of the United States, 1932–38.*
P. Samuelson and H. Krooss, *Documentary History of Banking and Currency in the United States.*
W. E. Spahr, *The Case for the Gold Standard.*
P. Studenski and H. Krooss, *Financial History of the United States.*

— DONALD L. KEMMERER

GOLDEN GATE BRIDGE

Golden Gate Bridge, erected across the entrance of the harbor at San Francisco, Calif., at a cost of approximately $35 million, by the Golden Gate Bridge and Highway District, created by the California legislature (1923, 1928). The bridge links San Francisco peninsula with counties along the Redwood highway to the north. The central span is 4,200 feet long; and the total length, including approaching viaducts, is 13/4 miles. Six lanes are provided for motor traffic, and sidewalks for pedestrians. Actual construction work began Jan. 5, 1933, and the bridge was opened to traffic, May 28, 1937.

BIBLIOGRAPHY

H. J. Hopkins, *A Span of Bridges: An Illustrated History.*
Shirley Smith Hubert, *The World's Great Bridges.*

— P. ORMAN RAY

GOOD NEIGHBOR POLICY

The aspiration to be a good neighbor to other countries of the Western Hemisphere has been voiced by more than one U.S. politician since the last quarter of the 19th century, but the elevation of intent to policy was accomplished in the decade of the 1930's by President Franklin D. Roosevelt, Secretary of State Cordell Hull, and Undersecretary of State Sumner Welles.

In his first inaugural address Roosevelt stated: "In the field of world policy I would dedicate this nation to the policy of the good neighbor—the neighbor who resolutely respects himself and, because he does so, respects the rights of others." The commitment of the United States to this policy and the spelling out of its practical meaning—both for the United States and for its neighbors—were tested and established through experience, and ratified both in public treaties and in private directives. The first action required was the cessation by the United States of a well-established practice of sending armed forces to Latin-American countries to maintain political stability or to protect the lives of U.S. citizens. The administration of President Calvin Coolidge, for example, had landed marines in Nicaragua in 1927, a military venture that lasted six years and turned out to be ineffective, expensive, and embarrassing. President Roosevelt was determined to avoid another Nicaragua, and he did so, if barely, when challenged by the civil strife in Cuba in the summer of 1933. The lesson of that experience was expressed in the U.S. acceptance of the protocol on nonintervention at the 1936 Buenos Aires Conference of American States, which declared intervention "inadmissible . . . for whatever reason, in the internal or external affairs of any other of the Parties." By "intervention" Roosevelt meant the landing of U.S. armed forces, and neither he nor any succeeding president violated the pledge made at Buenos Aires until the intervention in the Dominican Republic in 1965.

Renouncing intervention, however, was not enough, either for Latin Americans or for the Roosevelt administration. A further renunciation was therefore made, that of refusing to interpose or offer "advice" about domestic political developments in Latin-American and Caribbean countries. Such advice, wrote Secretary Hull, "rapidly came to be considered as intervention and, in fact, sometimes terminated in actual intervention." Thus the principle of noninterference was incorporated into the policy of nonintervention as an essential part of the Good Neighbor policy.

In 1938, when disputes erupted between U.S.-chartered oil companies and the governments of Bolivia, Mexico, and Venezuela, the Roosevelt administration decided that it would follow principles of protection of such corporations that would be not only wholly pacific but would also be political rather than legal in character. The disputes were settled amicably on the principle that the national interests of the United States were more important than those of the oil companies.

This full implementation of the Good Neighbor policy aided the United States in securing the strong support of nearly all Latin-American countries during World War II. Following the war, successors of the Roosevelt administration followed different principles, notably in efforts to prevent the election of Juan Perón in Argentina in 1946 and to assist Cuban exiles to overthrow Fidel Castro in the Bay of Pigs invasion in 1961. New officials and a changing international situation brought about other modifications and innovations, so that the term of the Good Neighbor policy may best be regarded as spanning the years from 1933 to 1946.

BIBLIOGRAPHY

Gordon Connell-Smith, *The Inter-American System.*
Dana G. Munro, *Intervention and Dollar Diplomacy in the Caribbean, 1900–1921.*
Bryce Wood, *The Making of the Good Neighbor Policy.*

— BRYCE WOOD

GRAND ARMY OF THE REPUBLIC

Grand Army of the Republic, founded by Benjamin F. Stephenson, a physician of Springfield, Ill., who had served as surgeon of the Fourteenth Illinois Infantry, as an association for Union veterans of the Civil War. Stephenson and a small group of friends formed the nucleus of an organization at Springfield in the spring of 1866. On Apr. 6, 1866, the first post was established at Decatur, Ill. By July 12, 1866, when a state convention was held to form the Department of Illinois, thirty-nine posts had been chartered. At the first national encampment, held at Indianapolis on Nov. 20, 1866, ten states and the District of Columbia were represented.

The first commander in chief was Gen. Stephen A. Hurlbut of Illinois. Hurlbut was succeeded by Gen. John A. Logan, also of Illinois, who served three successive terms. Logan's successor was Gen. A. E. Burnside.

The Grand Army of the Republic (GAR) quickly attained a preeminent place among the veterans organizations formed at the close of the Civil War, but its membership grew slowly. Between 1881 and 1882, however, membership rose from 87,718 to 131,900, and during the next eight years the increase was rapid. The peak was reached in 1890, when 409,489 members were reported. Membership thereafter dropped. At the last encampment in 1949 only six members attended and it was decided to disband the organization when the last of the six died. The last member, Albert Woolman, died Aug. 6, 1956.

One of the purposes of the GAR, as set forth in its constitution, was the "defense of the late soldiery of the United States, morally, socially and politically." At an early date in its history partisan purposes were forbidden, but for many years the organization was a powerful political force. Its unremitting efforts for pension increases and other benefits for veterans and their dependents led both major political parties to bid for its support by favoring such measures, and its members were generally disposed to vote for the higher bidder. By 1900 the GAR had ceased to be a dominant force in politics.

The GAR also gave rise to or attracted auxiliary societies—the Woman's Relief Corps (organized on a national basis in 1883), the Ladies of the Grand Army of the Republic (1886), and the Sons of Union Veterans of the Civil War (1881). These three organizations and the Daughters of Union Veterans of the Civil War and the Auxiliary to the Sons of Union Veterans of the Civil War carry on the work begun by the GAR in the establishment and improvement of veterans facilities.

BIBLIOGRAPHY

Robert M. Beath, *History of the Grand Army of the Republic.*

Donald L. McMurry, "The Political Significance of the Pension Question, 1885–1897," *Mississippi Valley Historical Review* (1922).

— PAUL M. ANGLE

GRANDFATHER CLAUSE

Grandfather Clause, a device in southern state constitutions to circumvent the suffrage requirements of the Fifteenth Amendment. Exemption from property-owning, tax-paying, or educational requirements in state suffrage laws was granted to those who had had the right to vote on Jan. 1, 1867, and to their lineal descendants. Since blacks in the South could not vote at that time, they were excluded from the privilege granted to impoverished or illiterate whites. The clause, applicable for a limited time, was adopted in South Carolina, 1895; Louisiana, 1898; North Carolina, 1900; Alabama, 1901; Virginia, 1902; Georgia, 1908; and Oklahoma, 1910. In 1915 the Supreme Court declared the grandfather clause unconstitutional.

BIBLIOGRAPHY

G. T. Stephenson, *Race Distinctions in American Law.*

— C. MILDRED THOMPSON

GRANGER MOVEMENT

Granger Movement grew out of a farmers lodge, the Patrons of Husbandry, founded in 1867 by Oliver Hudson Kelley, a clerk in the Post Office Department at Washington, D.C. The preceding year, Kelley, then in the employ of the Department of Agriculture, had made a tour of the South and had been struck by the enslavement of southern farmers to outworn and traditional methods of agriculture. This situation, he believed, could best be remedied by an organization that would bring farmers together in groups for the study and discussion of their problems. Accordingly, with the help of a few interested friends, he devised a secret ritualistic order, equally open to women and to men, and became its first organizer. Each local unit, or Grange, was admonished to select among its officers a "lecturer," whose duty should be to provide some educational diversion, such as a lecture or a paper, for every meeting.

Early in 1868 Kelley started west to his home in Minnesota, hoping to organize Granges as he went. He had little success until he reached his destination and began work among his former neighbors. There his organization won adherents, less for its social and educational advantages than for the opportunity it presented for farmers to unite against the monopolistic practices of railroads and elevators and to institute for themselves cooperative methods of buying and selling. By the end of 1869 there were thirty-seven active Granges in Minnesota; a year later the order had expanded into nine widely separated states; and when the panic of 1873 broke, there were Granges in every state of the Union but four. Membership claims, always hard to substantiate, reached a maximum during the mid-1870's of about 800,000, the total number of Granges being estimated at about 20,000. The center of Granger activity remained during the entire period in the grain-growing region of the upper Mississippi Valley.

The grievances that drove the northwestern farmers into organized revolt grew out of their almost complete dependence on outside markets for the disposal of their produce and on corporation-owned elevators and railroads for its handling. The high prices that accompanied the Civil War in the United States and the Bismarckian wars in Europe enabled the farmers, during those wars, to pay the high charges the corporations exacted, but afterward, when prices began to drop, the grain growers found themselves in acute distress. In 1869 they paid at the rate of 52.5 cents a bushel to send grain from the Mississippi River to the Atlantic seaboard and nearly half as much to send it from an Iowa or Minnesota farm to Chicago. Elevators, often themselves owned by the railroads, charged high prices for their services, weighed and graded grain without supervision, and used their influence with the railroads to ensure that cars were not available to farmers who sought to evade elevator service.

Rumblings of revolt were heard throughout the later 1860's, and in 1869 the legislature of Illinois passed an act that required the railroads to charge only "just, reasonable, and uniform rates"; but because the act provided no adequate means of enforcement, nothing came of it. The next year, Illinois adopted a new constitution in which the legislature was definitely authorized to legislate to correct railway abuses and extortions. Acting on this authority, the legislature of 1871 set maximum freight and passenger rates and established a board of railroad and warehouse commissioners to enforce them. These laws the railroads flatly refused to obey, a position in which they were sustained by the state supreme court. But in 1873 a more carefully drawn law ran the gauntlet of a revised supreme court, for in the meantime at a judicial election the angered farmers had replaced one of the offending judges with a judge more Granger-minded.

By that time the Grange had become far more political than educational in nature and, ably assisted by a host of unaffiliated farmers clubs, was in the thick of the fight for state regulation of railroads and elevators. At Granger lodge meetings and picnics the farmers exhorted one another to nominate and elect to office only those who shared their views and, in case corporation control over the Republican and Democratic parties could not be overthrown, to form independent, reform, or antimonopoly parties through which to carry on the fight. So many farmers made Independence Day 1873 an occasion for airing these views that the celebration was long remembered as the Farmers' Fourth of July. On that day many rural audiences listened with approval to the reading of a "Farmers' Declaration of Independence," which recited grievances and asserted their determination to use the power of the state to free themselves from the tyranny of monopoly. Victories at the polls led to the passage of a series of so-called Granger laws for the regulation of railroads and warehouses, not only in Illinois but also in several other northwestern states. These measures were not always well drawn, and for the most part they were soon repealed or drastically modified. Nevertheless, the U.S. Supreme Court, in *Munn* v. *Illinois* and a number of other cases, all decided in 1877, sustained the Granger contention that businesses of a public nature could, in accordance with the federal Constitution, be subjected to state regulation—a precedent of far-reaching consequence.

So many farmers made Independence Day 1873 an occasion for airing antimonopolist views that the celebration was long remembered as the Farmers' Fourth of July.

Hardly less important than the political activities of the various Granges were their business ventures. Under Granger auspices numerous cooperative elevators, creameries, and general stores were founded, although most of these establishments failed to survive the ruthless competition of private business. The Granges tried many other experiments also, such as buying through purchasing agents or through dealers who quoted special prices to Grangers, patronizing mail-order houses, and manufacturing farm machinery. The last-mentioned undertaking, ill conceived and overdone, resulted in serious financial reverses and had much to do with the sudden decline in Granger popularity that, beginning about 1876, brought the movement to an untimely end.

Despite its short span of life the Granger movement had taught farmers many things. They had learned that their political power, when they chose to use it, was great; that business cooperatives, although hazardous, might, if properly managed, limit the toll paid to middlemen; and that such social and educational activities as the Grange had fostered could greatly brighten rural life. The Patrons of Husbandry as a lodge survived the Granger movement, won new eastern adherents to replace the western deserters, and in the 20th century even recovered some of its influence in politics.

BIBLIOGRAPHY

Solon J. Buck, *The Granger Movement*, and *The Agrarian Crusade*.

— JOHN D. HICKS

GREAT AWAKENING

Great Awakening, the period of religious fervor that began with the arrival in Philadelphia of English evangelist George Whitefield in December 1739. It spread as Whitefield traveled through the American colonies preaching, and inspiring some American ministers to preach, a revivalistic message and ended roughly in 1744 as ministerial and popular enthusiasm gave way to reinvigorated institutionalized religion. Antecedents of the Awakening can be found in isolated and sporadic outbursts provoked by individual ministers—Solomon Stoddard in western Massachusetts in the late 17th century, Theodorus Frelinghuysen and Gilbert Tennent in the Delaware River valley in the 1720's, and Jonathan Edwards in Northampton, Mass., in 1734. Such outbreaks are sometimes included in consideration of the Great Awakening per se, as are subsequent outbreaks in the southern backcountry, particularly the Methodist revival of 1775–85. It seems better, however, to consider the Great Awakening in the more limited context of 1739–44, foreshadowed by earlier, and establishing a pattern for successive, incidents of revivalism.

The process of the Great Awakening can be discerned as a call for conversion and reformation issued by ministers and a response on the part of the laity. The call by some ministers probably stemmed from their awareness of a growing religious complacency among their parishioners and a tendency among leading laymen—and even among some ministers—to divorce God's immediate hand from human affairs and reduce religion either to a pro forma affair or to the exercise of polite moralisms (for example, deism). The ministerial call, consequently, stressed an absolute dependence on God and the individual's innate sinfulness in God's eyes, the inevitability and justice of divine punishment, and the ecstatic joy of joining with God, accepting His ordinances, and partaking of His pardon. The sheer oratorical force of the movement's preachers—Whitefield in particular—can account for some of their success. But in larger part success had its origin in the condition of their listeners. Demographic and social pressures in colonial society—a disjunction of felt needs and expectations, on the one hand, and of acceptable avenues for achievement, on the other—left men and women vulnerable to the preachers' call. In this sense the Great Awakening cannot be separated from the broad social history of Anglo-America.

Whitefield was at first welcomed by most regular religious figures, for the complacency of the laity was generally discerned. But as he provoked ever more enthusiastic outbursts, particularly in New England and the middle colonies, the ministers split: some adopted extreme enthusiasm and by their preaching further intensified the Great Awakening and spread it geographically, but others hardened against enthusiasm. Single churches, even whole denominations, split between "new light" (the Awakeners) and "old light," "new side" and "old side." In the subsequent quarreling among ministers and between specific ministers and their congregations, ministerial authority was inevitably weakened and, as some have argued, the entire authority structure of Anglo-America shaken, making easier the resistance to authority inherent in the American Revolution. The larger effect was to accentuate denominational differences; to fragment American religion still further; and, ironically, by accentuating the concern of religious institutions for the purity of their particular doctrines, to divorce American religion even more from the totality of everyday life.

BIBLIOGRAPHY

Richard L. Bushman, ed., *The Great Awakening: Documents on the Revival of Religion: 1740–1745.*

Darrett B. Rutman, ed., *The Great Awakening: Event and Exegesis.*

— DARRETT B. RUTMAN

GREAT MIGRATION

During the "personal government" of Charles I (1625–40) discontent in England and prospects for better things abroad grew to such proportions that approximately 60,000 persons emigrated. About one-third of them went to New England, founding the colonies of Massachusetts Bay, Connecticut, and Rhode Island. Others settled in Old Providence, on the coast of Honduras, other Caribbean isles, and elsewhere.

The great majority of these emigrants were religious or political Puritans, chiefly of the nonseparating Congregationalist persuasion, who found Bishop William Laud's Anglicanism or the Stuart government intolerable. Puritans were exasperated by the Stuarts' failure materially to assist the defeated Protestants on the continent and dismayed when their efforts failed to "purify" the Anglican church of vestigial popery and to limit the Stuarts to constitutional procedures. As Laud rose to power, he applied the screws of conformity until Puritans had no choice but to conform or emigrate. Already, the Puritan clergyman John White of Dorchester and Robert Rich, Earl of Warwick, as well as others, had pointed the way by organizing companies chartered for New World trade and colonization. Between 1627 and 1635 several such companies were organized under Puritan auspices. Of these, the Massachusetts Bay Company was most successful. With White's West Country enterprise, the New England Company, as nucleus, the Massachusetts Company was dominated by East Country Puritans. By the Cambridge Agreement, the latter bound themselves to go to Massachusetts provided the company and the charter were legally transported there by Sept. 1, 1630. Thus, the 140 West Country people who sailed from Plymouth in March 1630 and founded Dorchester, Mass., were greatly outnumbered by East Country Anglicans who had sent fourteen ships by June. The Great Migration had begun. During the next decade, about 20,000 people emigrated to the Bay Colony.

The basic cause for the Great Migration was Puritan discontent; the migration eased off when life in England became more hopeful after the Long Parliament assembled.

Of course, not all these emigrants were Puritans. Depression in agriculture and the cloth trade led many to emigrate for economic betterment—persons often discontented and troublesome in the Bible commonwealth. Nor was there complete unity among Puritans themselves. Differences between the West Country group and the East Country majority precipitated disputes in the general court, and were perhaps a factor in the former's wholesale migration to Connecticut. But the basic cause for the Great Migration was Puritan discontent, as evidenced by its cessation when the English scene became more hopeful after the Long Parliament assembled. Meantime, Puritans had enlarged English Caribbean trade, garnered bullion from the Spanish Main, established fisheries in New England, laid the basis for shipbuilding and the West Indies trade, and founded permanent, populous colonies in New England.

BIBLIOGRAPHY

The Cambridge History of the British Empire.

A. P. Newton, *The Colonising Activities of the English Puritans.*

— RAYMOND P. STEARNS

GREAT PLAINS

Historically the Great Plains may be roughly defined as the region lying between the ninety-eighth meridian and the Rocky Mountains. With some exceptions, the area has a relatively level surface sloping gradually upward to the foothills of the mountains. It is almost treeless and it is subhumid or semiarid, with little rainfall. In these two respects it presented an environment strikingly different from that to which American settlers had been accustomed in their westward march. Before white occupation the Great Plains were the grazing area of huge herds of buffalo and the home of such Indian tribes as the Sioux, Cheyenne, Arapaho, Pawnee, Comanche, and Apache.

The Great Plains first appear in recorded history in the reports of early Spanish explorations, especially that of Francisco Vásquez de Coronado between 1540 and 1542. During the next two centuries the Spanish established themselves in what are now New Mexico and Texas, and extended their knowledge of the country northward at least as far as Nebraska or Wyoming. During the first half of the 18th century, French explorers and traders saw many portions of the Great Plains area, as did other traders working out of Saint Louis after 1763, while the whole region was in Spanish possession. However, Americans in general knew very little of the region when the northern portion was transferred to the United States by the Louisiana Purchase.

Discouraging reports concerning the habitability of the Great Plains were given by the explorers Meriwether Lewis and William Clark (1804–06), Zebulon M. Pike (1806–07), and Stephen H. Long (1820). As a result, the region came to be known as the Great American Desert—a barrier to the further westward expansion of American settlements. This belief, in part at least, led to the Indian removal policy, formulated by John C. Calhoun and James Monroe in 1825 and carried into effect during the administration of Andrew Jackson. By 1840 the Great Plains were included in what was confidently designated as the permanent Indian country.

Even before 1840 the observations of traders going to and from Santa Fe began to modify the general belief in the desertlike character of the Great Plains. Then, during the 1840's, the region was crossed by emigrants to Oregon, by military and exploring expeditions, by the Mormons on their way to Utah, and by thousands of gold seekers rushing to California. During this decade, also, the territorial jurisdiction of the United States was greatly expanded by the annexation of Texas, the acquisition of Oregon, and the Mexican cession. Not only did the entire Great Plains region now belong to the United States, but it was no longer thinkable that an inviolable Indian country should bar the way to the free movement of Americans to the new and desirable possessions.

During the 1850's the Great Plains region was alive with activity. Commissioners and Indian agents were busy making treaties with the Indians by which the tribesmen ceded territory, agreed to move, or gave permission for laying out roads and establishing military posts. Emigrants continued to pour over the trails to California and Oregon, and in 1859 there was a stampede to the Colorado gold fields. After the congressional act of 1853 the region was crossed by parties surveying routes for a railroad to the Pacific. Stagecoaches carrying mail and passengers to California began running early in the decade, and by 1858 John Butterfield's famous overland mail was operating over a southern route.

The discoveries of gold in the entire Rocky Mountain area during the early 1860's greatly stimulated transportation and communication across the Plains. Not only were stagecoach lines expanded, but a vast wagon-freighting business was developed, and the famous pony express greatly expedited mail service. By the close of the Civil War the Great Plains area was aflame with Indian wars, which continued until the end of the decade, with frequent outbreaks still later. During this same period the Union Pacific Railroad was built westward, to be followed soon by other transcontinental railroads.

Thus far the Great Plains had been regarded mainly as an unattractive country to be crossed in order to reach more desirable localities. Beginning late in the 1860's and during the ensuing two decades the region was the scene of the rise and decline of the great range cattle industry, with its succession of cow towns, its long drives from Texas to the northern ranges or to shipping points on the railroads, its roundups, and its huge areas of illegally fenced public land. The decline of this colorful activity was due chiefly to the relentless pressure of the settlers who, after the Civil War, launched themselves onto the Great Plains and year by year steadily narrowed the open range, until it finally disappeared before the end of the century. The later history of the last American frontier is largely concerned with problems of agricultural adjustment to an unfavorable environment, particularly during the 1930's when terrific dust storms devastated many sections of the Great Plains. Between 1930 and 1970 the rural population of the Plains area in the United States decreased by more than 30 percent, while urban population increased by 166 percent. Many farmers lived in towns and commuted to work as farms became fewer but larger.

[See also Pikes Peak Gold Rush; Sioux Wars.]

BIBLIOGRAPHY

Dan E. Clark, *The West in American History.*
Frederic L. Paxson, *History of the American Frontier.*
Walter P. Webb, *The Great Plains.*

— DAN E. CLARK

GREAT SOCIETY

Great Society, the theme of President Lyndon B. Johnson's presidential campaign of 1964, announced on May 22 at Ann Arbor, Mich. By the phrase, the president meant a society in which poverty would be abolished, education would be available for all, peace would prevail, and every man would be free to develop his potential.

— JACOB E. COOKE

GREENBACK MOVEMENT

Greenback Movement was a reaction against the tendency to reestablish specie payments in place of the greenback standard of exchange that had prevailed since 1862. It made its strongest appeal to debtor farmers. It included the "Ohio idea" of retiring at least the five-twenties among the federal government bonds by issuing new greenbacks and thus ending the government's large interest payments as well as the tax-free character of a particular type of investment. Its most essential demand was that greenbacks be given complete legal-tender status and be issued freely. Besides the debtor character of the movement, it united opposition to national banks and their currency with resentment against the handsome profits that holders of Civil War bonds were to take out of the funds raised by taxes.

Although these ideas had strong support in both major parties in rural areas and received partial endorsement in the national Democratic convention in 1868, the greenback movement thereafter became chiefly one for minor parties. The campaign of 1872 found the only organized support of greenback policies in the new National Labor Reform party. The independent state Granger parties that sprang up following the panic of 1873 were inflationist in only a few instances, but two of them, in Indiana and Illinois, furnished the leadership to create a new national party committed to greenback policies. The Indiana party issued a call for a conference at Indianapolis in November 1874. It was attended by representatives of several states, including representatives from the National Labor Reform party. A permanent organization was established, and a national nominating convention met at Indianapolis on May 17, 1876. This party, variously called Independent National, National, and Greenback Labor, is commonly referred to as the Greenback party and represents the most important political phase of the movement. Within the party the more extreme members organized the Greenback clubs, which agitated extensively, and in party conventions protested against local fusion with the major parties. For its first national campaign the party nominated Peter Cooper, the New York philanthropist, for president. Its platform demanded the repeal of the recently enacted Resumption Act and enactment of the greenback plans for a national currency. This first platform failed to go outside currency for an issue, and the party did not conduct an aggressive campaign. It was handicapped by the fact that in most districts in which the party's ideas were popular they were supported by candidates of the two major parties, with the result that the Greenback party received only slightly more than 80,000 votes, most of them coming from midwestern farm states.

The most evident results of the campaign were the election to the Illinois legislature of a number of Greenback party members and their combination with Democrats to elect Justice David Davis of the U.S. Supreme Court to the Senate, a move that in the judgment of some historians kept Samuel J. Tilden from becoming president.

The labor difficulties the next year made that part of the movement more active, and the Greenback party showed notable increases in state elections. A broader orientation was evident in a party conference at Toledo in 1878, when to the older Greenback planks were added a denunciation of the demonetization of silver and endorsements of legal restrictions on the hours of labor, of the abolition of Chinese immigration, and of the reservation of public lands for the use of settlers. In the congressional elections of that year the Greenback party scored the most notable victory in its history by sending to the House of Representatives a large number of congressmen. Of these, fourteen or fifteen chose to act as party-conscious Greenbackers, the remainder staying with the major party that had supported them.

Historians credit the party with over I million votes in the 1878 election, including votes received by some candidates through the support of one of the major parties. This striking success for the young party created a bloc in the House, which, under the leadership of Rep. James B. Weaver of Iowa, gave direction to the organization. The national character of its support is indicated by the fact that the bloc included representatives from every section of the country except the Pacific coast.

This success raised high hopes among party leaders of a steady march toward major-party status. The successful resumption of specie payment in 1879 destroyed the most distinctive plank in the party's platform, and the convention of 1880 broadened its appeal by adding planks favoring a graduated income tax, woman suffrage, government regulation of interstate commerce, and social-welfare legislation. Weaver was named the candidate for president, and high hopes were held for attracting a large vote. The disappointing result was a vote of 300,000, less than 4 percent of the total. The bloc in the House was reduced to ten members. This decline continued, and in 1882, while at least five congressmen were elected with Greenback support, only one of them could be called a party-conscious Greenbacker.

The decline of the party was steady. Although it nominated the peripatetic Benjamin F. Butler for president in 1884, it was impossible to revive the enthusiasm of 1878 and 1880. The earlier farmer support seemed to be passing away entirely, and Butler's vote was less than 200,000. A convention was hopefully called in 1888, but it contented itself with a declaration of principles. Faithful Greenbackers supported the candidate of the Union Labor party, Alson J. Streeter, and its greenback platform, making a bridge between the Greenback and the Populist parties.

Despite its surprising success in 1878 the party had failed to maintain its strength. The achievement of the resumption of specie payments had undermined the appeal of its program; the growing disparity of values between silver and gold made free coinage of silver a far more feasible political goal than greenback inflation. But although its political success was limited the Greenback movement was a significant predecessor of subsequent agrarian and labor political movements and educated a group of voters toward political independence. It also trained leaders who were to play an active part in the Populist crusade.

BIBLIOGRAPHY

S. J. Buck, *The Agrarian Crusade.*

F. E. Haynes, *Third Party Movements Since the Civil War.*

— ELMER ELLIS

GREEN MOUNTAIN BOYS

In 1749 Gov. Benning Wentworth of New Hampshire began to grant lands in the region west of the Connecticut River that is today Vermont, even though New York put in a strong claim to the area. In 1764 the king decided that the jurisdiction belonged to New York, and in 1770 the New York Supreme Court held that all Hampshire patents were invalid. This meant that persons who had settled under New Hampshire had to rebuy their lands.

The people of the New Hampshire grants west of the Green Mountains promptly resolved to keep their lands by force if necessary, formed military companies, and elected Ethan Allen colonel commandant of the Green Mountain Boys. Settlers under New York jurisdiction were terrorized. The "birch seal" was cut into naked Yorker backs; fences were torn down; cattle disappeared; and cabins were burned or had their roofs taken off and replaced, to symbolize "conversion" to the Yankee cause. The Green Mountaineers built rude fortresses on Otter Creek and Onion, or Winooski, River. New York proclamations and laws of outlawry were disregarded, and New York sheriffs were driven off. The British government refused to use military force to put down the Green Mountain men and forbade New York to grant more land until the dispute could be settled.

With the coming of the revolutionary war, the Green Mountain Boys espoused the patriot cause, took Ticonderoga, raised a separate regiment under Col. Seth Warner, fought at Hubbardton, and were a potent factor in the British defeat at the Battle of Bennington. Led by Ira Allen, Thomas Chittenden, and Jonas Fay, they declared an independent republic of Vermont in 1777 and set about securing support from the New England delegates in the Continental Congress. In 1790 New York relinquished its claim, and in 1791 the Green Mountain state was admitted into the Union.

BIBLIOGRAPHY

E. P. Alexander, *A Conservative Revolutionary: James Duane of New York.*

John Pell, *Ethan Allen.*

— EDWARD P. ALEXANDER

GRENADA INVASION

Grenada Invasion (1983). The Caribbean island of Grenada was under British rule from 1763 until independence in 1974. The country's first prime minister, Sir Eric Gairy, ruled until 1979, when his government was overthrown in a coup led by Maurice Bishop. By late summer 1983 Bishop's New Jewel Movement had split into two factions. On 19 October the more left-wing element, under Deputy Prime Minister Bernard Coard and General Hudson Austin, which favored closer ties to communist states, arrested and subsequently executed Bishop and some of his ministers. Two days later leaders of six of the seven island nations comprising the Organization of Eastern Caribbean States (OECS) met and voted to intervene militarily to restore order (Grenada did not vote). Lacking adequate forces, they appealed to nonmember states Jamaica, Barbados, and the United States. An October 23 meeting of British and U.S. diplomats with Grenadian officials proved unproductive. Amid growing concern in Washington for the safety of U.S. nationals in Grenada, President Ronald Reagan authorized the commitment of U.S. forces. A combined force of 6,000 troops from the United States and 1,000 troops from Jamaica, Barbados, and the OECS states landed on Grenada on October 25. U.S. forces deployed in Operation Urgent Fury included airborne, army Ranger, special operations, and marines. They were opposed by 750 Grenadian troops and 600 Cuban construction workers building a new international airport at Point Salines. U.S. ground units were supported by a carrier battle group and massive logistical support. U.S. casualties were 19 killed and 115 wounded; Cuban casualties were 24 killed, 59 wounded; Grenadian casualties (military and civilian) were 45 killed and 337 wounded. By October 28 the island was secured. The operation was a military success, although not free from error. U.S. public opinion narrowly supported the intervention, the first in the Caribbean since that in the Dominican Republic in 1965, but the United Nations Security Council and later the General Assembly voted to deplore the action as a flagrant violation of international law. Depending on one's viewpoint, Operation Urgent Fury either destroyed a democratic regime or it ended a growing threat to regional and U.S. security interests.

BIBLIOGRAPHY

Anthony Payne et al., *Grenada: Revolution and Invasion* (New York, 1984).

— RICHARD W. TURK

GUADALCANAL

Guadalcanal (August 1942–February 1943). To check the Japanese advance, protect the United States-Australia line of communications, and open the way for a strategic offensive against Rabaul, the Allies planned to seize bases in the southern Solomon Islands. When the Japanese began building an airfield on Guadalcanal in July 1942, Allied preparations were hurried to send an invasion force, under Rear Adm. Richmond K. Turner, carrying Maj. Gen. Alexander A. Vandegrift's First Marine Division (19,000 men) and supported by a three-carrier task force under Rear Adm. Frank J. Fletcher. On Aug. 7, the marines landed on Guadalcanal and nearby Tulagi, scattering small Japanese forces on both islands.

Japanese reaction was swift and violent. First, Japanese aircraft struck at the beachhead and amphibious forces. Then, in a surprise night attack against Allied naval forces early on

American soldiers display a Japanese flag captured in action in Guadalcanal, Solomon Islands. (Corbis-Bettmann)

Aug. 9 (Battle of Savo Island), seven Japanese cruisers and a destroyer sank three American cruisers, an Australian cruiser, and an American destroyer at negligible cost to themselves. These developments forced Turner and Fletcher to withdraw their naval units from the area. Left unsupported, Vandegrift could only request reinforcements and dig in to defend the airfield, Henderson Field.

Marine planes quickly flew into the airfield, while the Japanese landed about, 1,000 ground troops. A second Japanese reinforcement effort was defeated in the naval battle of the Eastern Solomons (Aug. 23–25), but the Japanese continued to bring in small elements in nightly destroyer runs ("Tokyo Express"). On the ground, American and Japanese patrols clashed frequently, while the marines dug in deeply for protection against shelling by Japanese warships. In mid-September, the Japanese, now about a division strong, made a major effort to crush the marine positions (Battle of Bloody Ridge), only to be repulsed with heavy losses.

For the next month, heavy air and sea battles took place in the Guadalcanal area. By mid-October, Vandegrift had more than 23,000 troops ashore, but the Japanese, under Maj. Gen. Haruyoshi Hyakutaku, had almost as many. Attacks by Hyakutaku at the end of the month were sharply repulsed, and Vandegrift began expanding the marine perimeter. Further Japanese efforts to reinforce their troops were frustrated in a series of naval actions. The marines, however, were soon replaced by more than 50,000 army troops under Maj. Gen. Alexander Patch. The Japanese, now short on supplies and weakened by disease, fell back before heavy American attacks. During the first week of February 1943, the 13,000 Japanese survivors were evacuated in night operations, leaving Guadalcanal in American hands.

BIBLIOGRAPHY

Samuel B. Griffith II, *The Battle for Guadalcanal.*

— STANLEY L. FALK

GUADALUPE HIDALGO, TREATY OF

The Treaty of Guadalupe Hidalgo, signed at the village of Guadalupe Hidalgo near Mexico City, Feb. 2, 1848, specified the terms of peace at the close of the Mexican War. It was negotiated by Nicholas P. Trist, the chief clerk of the Department of State under Secretary of State James Buchanan.

In April 1847 President James K. Polk decided to send Trist secretly as a peace commissioner to Gen. Winfield Scott's army headquarters, with a treaty prepared by Buchanan. Trist was given authority to receive expected Mexican peace proposals and to suspend hostilities. In late August Scott arranged an armistice to facilitate a conference for peace negotiations, which, however, proved futile.

Polk then ordered (Oct. 1) Trist's recall, in order to discourage false Mexican views of American anxiety for peace. Trist delayed his departure and eventually (Dec. 3) decided to remain and to assume the responsibility of negotiating a treaty substantially on the basis of the territorial demands of his original instructions. On Jan. 24 he was able to secure the completed draft of the treaty, signed Feb. 2.

The treaty provided for the establishment of the American-Mexican boundary at the middle of the Rio Grande from the Gulf of Mexico to a point where that river met the southern boundary of New Mexico (which southern boundary was then identical with the present southern boundary east of the Rio Grande); thence west on this southern boundary of New Mexico to the western line of New Mexico (identical at that point with the present western line); thence north along that western line until it intersected the first branch of the Gila River; thence down that branch and the middle of the Gila to the Colorado River; thence direct to the Pacific at a point one marine league south of the southernmost point of the port of San Diego. The treaty also provided for the cession to the United States by Mexico of the territory of New Mexico and Upper California for a payment of $15 million. It was promptly accepted by Polk and ratified, with amendments, by the Senate, Mar. 10, 1848.

Because of the inaccuracies of Disturnell's map, used by the negotiators of the treaty, and the difficulties that prevented the surveyors from agreement on the identity of the first branch of the Gila, the line between the Rio Grande and the Gila was never marked, and the dispute remained unsettled until its international importance was ended during the administration of President Franklin Pierce by the negotiation of the Gadsden Purchase of 1853.

BIBLIOGRAPHY

J. M. Callahan, *American Foreign Policy in Mexican Relations.*
C. E. Hill, *Leading American Treaties.*
J. S. Reeves, *American Diplomacy Under Tyler and Polk.*

— J. M. CALLAHAN

GUERRILLAS

Guerrillas, a term originally applied to quasi-military and irregular groups of Spanish partisans who fought against Napoleon (1808), but the type of warfare im-

A portrait of Dr. Hale and "Tinker Dan" Beatty, Union guerrillas during the Civil War. Photograph circa 1861–1865. (U.S. Army Military History Institute/Corbis)

plied by the term is found everywhere in history, from the most ancient times to the present. The spectrum of guerrilla activity runs from conventional military operations by organized groups to uncoordinated, spontaneous, individual acts of sabotage, subversion, or terrorism carried out against an enemy. Guerrillas normally operate outside of constituted authority.

American guerrilla warfare during colonial times, the Revolution, and the War of 1812 was based to a large degree on knowledge of the Indian tactics of hit-and-run raids, ambush, and cover and concealment. During the revolutionary war, for example, the exploits of Francis Marion, the "Swamp Fox" of the southern campaign, used these techniques against the more traditionally organized British forces. In the war with Mexico (1846–48) enemy guerrillas caused the American army much trouble. The 1850's saw the rise of partisan bands, on both sides of the border-state issue, that carried on guerrilla, or bushwhacking, activity that was more often banditry than support for a cause. This activity continued through the Civil War period and was enlarged by deserters on both sides who raided for profit. Many of these groups—the James and Younger gangs were the most notorious—continued their brigandage well after the war ended.

Until 1917 American troops were engaged in guerrilla and partisan activities fighting Indians in the West and aiding those fighting for independence in Cuba. They also fought Boxers in China, insurrectionists in the Philippines, and bandits on the Mexican border. Not until World War II were Americans again involved in guerrilla warfare. In the Philippines especially, many American soldiers and civilians, finding themselves cut off, fought with Filipino guerrillas against the Japanese. In all theaters, assistance was given to partisans fighting their homeland's invaders. Most often this aid was carried out by members of the Office of Strategic Services.

In the Korean War, Americans participated in a number of activities either directed at the enemy's guerrilla campaign in the south or in support of South Korean guerrilla operations in the north. In the Vietnam War a major part of the pacification effort was directed at the elimination of Communist guerrilla activities in the countryside. Major elements of both U.S. and South Vietnamese military forces were effectively tied down by much smaller numbers of insurgents, who operated in every province and district in the country. The ability of the insurgents to blend into the populace and the terror tactics used to insure their security made their dislodgement and elimination extremely difficult.

BIBLIOGRAPHY

Roy E. Appleman, *South to the Naktong, North to the Yalu.*
Louis Morton, *The Fall of the Philippines.*
David H. Zook and Robin Higham, *A Short History of Warfare.*

— JOHN E. JESSUP, JR.

GULF WAR OF 1991

The invasion of Kuwait by 140,000 Iraqi troops and 1,800 tanks on Aug. 2, 1990, eventually led to U.S. involvement in war in the Persian Gulf region. Instead of repaying billions of dollars of loans received from Kuwait during the eight-year war between Iran and Iraq (1980–1988), Iraqi dictator Saddam Hussein resurrected old territorial claims and annexed Kuwait as his country's nineteenth province. President George Bush feared that Saddam might next invade Saudi Arabia and thus control 40 percent of the world's oil. Bush organized an international coalition of forty-three nations, thirty of which sent military or medical units to liberate Kuwait, and he personally lobbied United Nations Security Council members. By November the UN had imposed economic sanctions and passed twelve separate resolutions demanding that the Iraqis withdraw. Bush initially sent 200,000 U.S. troops as part of a multinational peacekeeping force to defend Saudi Arabia (Operation Desert Shield), describing the mission as "defensive." On November 8, Bush expanded the U.S. expeditionary force to more than 500,000 to "ensure that the coalition has an adequate offensive military option." Contingents from other allied countries brought the troop level to 675,000. UN Security Council Resolution 678 commanded Iraq to evacuate Kuwait by Jan. 15, 1991, or else face military attack.

Off-the-books U.S. arms transfers to Iraq were kept from Congress from 1982 to 1987, in violation of the law.

What Saddam Hussein had hoped to contain as an isolated regional quarrel provoked an unprecedented alliance that included not only the United States and most members of the North Atlantic Treaty Organization (NATO) but also Iraq's former military patron, the Soviet Union, and several Arab states, including Egypt and Syria. The Iraqi dictator must have found Washington's outraged reaction especially puzzling in view of recent efforts by the administrations of Presidents Ronald Reagan and Bush to befriend Iraq. Off-the-books U.S. arms transfers to Iraq were kept from Congress from 1982 to 1987, in violation of the law. Washington had supplied intelligence data to Baghdad during the Iran-Iraq war, and Bush had blocked congressional attempts to deny agricultural credits to Iraq because of human rights abuses. The Bush administration had also winked at secret and illegal bank loans that Iraq had used to purchase $5 billion in Western technology for its burgeoning nuclear and chemical weapons programs. Assistant Secretary of State John H. Kelly told Congress in early 1990 that Saddam Hussein acted as "a force of moderation" in the Middle East. Only a week before the invasion Ambassador April Glaspie informed Saddam Hussein that Washington had no "opinion on inter-Arab disputes such as your border dispute with Kuwait."

Bush and his advisers, without informing Congress or the American people, apparently decided early in August to use military force to expel Saddam Hussein from Kuwait. "It must be done as massively and decisively as possible," advised General Colin Powell, chairman of the Joint Chiefs of Staff. "Choose your target, decide on your objective, and try to crush it." The president, however, described the initial deployments as defensive, even after General H. Norman Schwarzkopf had begun to plan offensive operations. Bush did not announce the offensive buildup until after the November midterm elections, all the while expanding U.S. goals from defending Saudi Arabia, to liberating Kuwait, to crippling Iraq's war economy, even to stopping Saddam Hussein from acquiring nuclear weapons. UN sanctions cut off 90 percent of Iraq's imports and 97 percent of its exports. Secretary of State James Baker did meet with Iraqi Foreign Minister Tariq Azziz in early January 1991, but Iraq refused to consider withdrawal from Kuwait unless the United States forced Israel to relinquish its occupied territories. Bush and Baker vetoed this linkage, as well as any Arab solution whereby Iraq would retain parts of Kuwait. Iraq's aggression, which the president likened to Adolf Hitler's, should gain no reward.

Although Bush claimed he had the constitutional authority to order U.S. troops into combat under the UN resolution, he reluctantly requested congressional authorization, which was followed by a four-day debate. Senator Joseph R. Biden of Delaware declared that "none [of Iraq's] actions justify the deaths of our sons and daughters." Senator George Mitchell of Maine cited the risks: "An unknown number of casualties and deaths, billions of dollars spent, a greatly disrupted oil supply and oil price increases, a war possibly widened to Israel, Turkey or other allies, the possible long-term American occupation of Iraq, increased instability in the Persian Gulf region, long-lasting Arab enmity against the United States, a possible return to isolationism at home." Senator Robert Dole of Kansas scorned the critics, saying that Saddam Hussein "may think he's going to be rescued, maybe by Congress." On January 12, after Congress defeated a resolution to continue sanctions, a majority in both houses approved Bush's request to use force under UN auspices. Virtually every Republican voted for war; two-thirds of House Democrats and forty-five of fifty-six Democratic senators cast negative votes. Those few Democratic senators voting for war (among them Tennessee's Al Gore and Joseph Lieberman of Connecticut) provided the necessary margin.

Operation Desert Storm began with a spectacular aerial bombardment of Iraq and Kuwait on Jan. 16, 1991. For five weeks satellite television coverage via Cable News Network enabled Americans to watch "smart" bombs hitting Iraqi targets and U.S. Patriot missiles intercepting Iraqi Scud missiles. President Bush and

Secretary Baker kept the coalition intact, persuading Israel not to retaliate after Iraqi Scud attacks on its territory and keeping Soviet Premier Mikhail Gorbachev advised as allied bombs devastated Russia's erstwhile client. On Feb. 24 General Schwarzkopf sent hundreds of thousands of allied troops into Kuwait and eastern Iraq. Notwithstanding Saddam's warning that Americans would sustain thousands of casualties in the "mother of all battles," Iraq's largely conscript army put up little resistance. By February 26 Iraqi forces had retreated from Kuwait, blowing up as many as 800 oil wells as they did so. Allied aircraft flew hundreds of sorties against what became known as the "highway of death," from Kuwait City to Basra. After only 100 hours of fighting on the ground, Iraq accepted a UN-imposed cease-fire. Iraq's military casualties numbered more than 25,000 dead and 300,000 wounded; U.S. forces suffered only 148 battle deaths (35 from friendly fire), 145 nonbattle deaths, and 467 wounded (out of a coalition total of 240 dead and 776 wounded). An exultant President Bush proclaimed, "By God, we've kicked the Vietnam syndrome."

The war itself initially cost $1 million per day for the first three months, not including the ongoing expense of keeping an encampment of 300,000 allied troops in Saudi Arabia, Iraq, and Kuwait. The overall cost of the war was estimated to be $54 billion; $7.3 billion paid by the United States, with another $11 billion from Germany and $13 billion from Japan, and the remainder ($23 billion) from Arab nations. For the first time in the twentieth century, the United States could not afford to finance its own participation in a war.

Bush chose not to send U.S. forces to Baghdad to capture Saddam Hussein, despite his earlier designation of the Iraqi leader as public enemy number one. Attempts during the fighting to target Saddam had failed, and Bush undoubtedly hoped that the Iraqi military or disgruntled associates in the Ba'ath party would oust the Iraqi leader. When Kurds in northern Iraq and Shi'ites in the south rebelled, Bush did little to help. As General Powell stated: "If you want to go in and stop the killing of Shi'ites, that's a mission I understand. But to what purpose? If the Shi'ites continue to rise up, do we then support them for the overthrow of Baghdad and the partition of the country?" Powell opposed "trying to sort out two thousand years of Mesopotamian history." Bush, ever wary of a Mideast quagmire, backed away: "We are not going to permit this to drag on in terms of significant U.S. presence à la Korea." Saddam used his remaining tanks and helicopters to crush these domestic rebellions, sending streams of Kurdish refugees fleeing toward the Turkish border. Public pressure persuaded President Bush to send thousands of U.S. troops to northern Iraq, where the UN designated a security zone and set up makeshift tent cities. Saddam's survival left a sour taste in Washington, and created a situation that Lawrence Freedman and Efraim Karsh have compared to "an exasperating endgame in chess, when the winning player never seems to trap the other's king even though the final result is inevitable."

For the first time in the twentieth century, the U.S. could not afford to finance its own participation in a war.

Under Security Council Resolution 687, Iraq had to accept the inviolability of the boundary with Kuwait (to be demarcated by an international commission), accept the presence of UN peacekeepers on its borders, disclose all chemical, biological, and nuclear weapons including missiles, and cooperate in their destruction. What allied bombs had missed, UN inspectors did not. Saddam Hussein's scientists and engineers had built more than twenty nuclear facilities linked to a large-scale Iraqi Manhattan Project. Air attacks had only inconvenienced efforts to build a bomb. Inspectors also found and destroyed more than a hundred Scud missiles, seventy tons of nerve gas, and 400 tons of mustard gas. By the fall of 1992 the head of the UN inspection team rated Iraq's capacity for mass destruction "at zero."

Results from the war included the restoration of Kuwait, lower oil prices, resumption of peace negotiations between Israel and the Arabs, and at least a temporary revival of faith in the United Nations. Improved relations with Iran and Syria brought an end to Western hostage-taking in Beirut. Firefighters extinguished the last of the blazing oil wells ignited by the retreating Iraqis in November 1991, but only after the suffocating smoke had spread across an area twice the size of Alaska and caused long-term environmental damage. An estimated 200,000 civilians died, largely from disease and malnutrition. Millions of barrels of oil befouled the Persian Gulf, killing more than 30,000 sea birds.

[See also Middle East, Relations with; Oil Crises; United Nations.]

BIBLIOGRAPHY

Rick Atkinson, *Crusade* (Boston, 1993).

Lawrence Freedman and Efraim Karsh, *The Gulf Conflict, 1990–1991* (Princeton, N.J., 1993).

Bruce Jentleson, *With Friends Like These: Reagan, Bush, and Saddam, 1982–1992* (New York, 1994).

Jeffrey Record, *Hollow Victory* (New York, 1993).
Bob Woodward, *The Commanders* (New York, 1991).

— J. GARRY CLIFFORD

GUN CONTROL

Gun Control broadly refers to laws regulating firearms or anything related to firearms. The term therefore covers everything from registration of privately owned guns to mandatory prison sentences for anyone who uses a gun during the commission of a crime to outright bans on the manufacture, sale, or possession of certain types of firearms. Among the estimated 20,000 gun control laws in force in the United States are ones that regulate manufacturers, importers, wholesalers, retailers, and purchasers of guns. Some laws attempt to control firearms, while others regulate ammunition or control the uses of guns, such as when and where people may hunt. Other laws focus on the purchase, carrying, or possession of guns.

Federal gun control laws, such as the Gun Control Act (GCA) of 1968, the Firearm Owner's Protection Act of 1986, the Brady Handgun Violence Prevention Act of 1993, and the federal Crime Bill of 1994 are in force in all states. The GCA prohibits gun purchases by minors, persons with a felony conviction, and persons with a history of mental illness or substance abuse. The Brady Act mandates a five-day waiting period for new handgun purchases. The 1994 Crime Bill prohibits the sale of certain assault weapons. Most gun control laws, however, are state and local ordinances. Advocates of stricter gun control argue that inconsistent state and local laws are inadequate and that more and stricter federal laws are needed. Public opinion polls have shown that most people favor many commonly urged measures, such as requiring a police permit to obtain a gun and an outright ban on assault weapons, as enacted in 1994. At the same time, others oppose bans on the ownership of all guns and large majorities believe they have a constitutional right to keep and bear arms. Most gun control laws are neither more nor less stringent than measures taken to safeguard against abuses of other potentially dangerous commodities, such as automobiles, notably requiring permits to carry concealed weapons or to own automatic weapons and bans on gun acquisition by felons, drug addicts, and alcoholics. Mandatory registration of new handgun purchases and screening of new gun buyers are other widely adopted state measures.

It is unclear whether more stringent gun controls would reduce crime and violence. Most firearms used by criminals are obtained in off-the-record transactions that fall outside the many gun control laws. Some studies show that stricter gun laws reduce violence but these studies are very controversial; other studies show no effect resulting from stricter gun laws. Advocates for stricter controls counter that in the absence of strict federal laws, gun control has not received a fair test, although the effects of gun control measures enacted in the 1994 Crime Bill may resolve this issue.

[See also National Rifle Association.]

BIBLIOGRAPHY

Nigel Hawkes, *Gun Control* (New York, 1988).
Gary Kleck, *Point Blank* (New York, 1991).
Robert E. Long, *Gun Control* (New York, 1989).

— JAMES D. WRIGHT

GUNBOATS

Gunboats, in the simplest sense, have generally been tiny men-of-war extremely overgunned in proportion to size. They significantly entered U.S. history in the 1776 Battle of Valcour Island on Lake Champlain, when Benedict Arnold with 700 men in fifteen green-timber boats with cannon halted a British invasion from Canada. (The *Philadelphia*, which was sunk during the battle, has been raised and restored and is exhibited in the Smithsonian Institution.)

In America's first Barbary War, there proved to be a need for gunboats, fourteen of which were hastily bought from the Italians; Congress in 1803 authorized the building of fifteen others, one typically carrying twenty to twenty-three men and two 24- or 32-pounders (cannon) in a hull 70 feet long, 18 feet broad, and nearly 5 feet deep. Eight of the new boats reached Tripoli; a ninth was lost without a trace en route. The boats were effective only along a coast, since for them to be stable on the open sea, their crews had to stow the cannon along the keel, making the vessels defenseless against an enemy. To Thomas Jefferson, anxious to keep the fledgling United States from entanglement in the Napoleonic Wars, such a severe limitation seemed a virtue because pacific intentions would be proved by almost complete investment of naval funds in craft only able to fight in U.S. territorial waters.

Congress authorized another 25 gunboats in 1805 and 75 more the next year, making a total of 278 for the U.S. Navy, of which 176 were at hand for the War of 1812. The gunboats were worthless except for Joshua Barney's squadron on the Potomac. This squadron was of some value simply because Barney burned it and with his seamen and guns made a battery that helped delay the British army's march on Washington for a precious few hours. Since the token two dozen U.S. blue-water frigates and sloops won many glories at sea, the U.S.

Navy early learned the perils of imbalance by overinvestment in any single type of man-of-war.

Gunboats were useful in the suppression of West Indian piracy and in the Seminole Wars. In the Civil War, with Union blue-water vessels mostly on blockade or out hunting raiders, improvised gunboats were found on embattled rivers everywhere. Often their heavy guns, up to a normal 11 inches and even an abnormal 15 inches, inhibited Confederate movement or prevented such Union disasters as those at Shiloh and Malvern Hill. The innovative ironclads, especially the unseaworthy monitors, were basically of use against forts rather than against other ships.

The innovative ironclads, especially the unseaworthy monitors, were basically for use against forts rather than against other ships.

In the decades before the Spanish-American War, European neocolonialism introduced "gunboat diplomacy," calling for larger, hybrid craft that could safely cross oceans; assume a year-round anchorage on a foreign strand; possess sufficient shallow draft to go up a river; and, of course, carry heavy armament. The 1892 U.S.S. *Castine*, for example—in which Chester W. Nimitz, who in World War II served as U.S. commander of the Pacific Fleet, served as a lieutenant—was 204 feet overall, weighed 1,177 tons, and had eight 4-inch rifles, making it a far stronger man-of-war than the famous destroyer type then emerging. Of the score of American gunboats before World War II, the half dozen of the Chinese Yangtze River patrol were immortalized in the novel *Sand Pebbles* by Richard McKenna. In real life, the *Panay* was sunk without provocation on Dec. 12, 1937, by Japanese bombers. The others in the Far East were destroyed early in World War II.

The 1936 *Erie*, fated with its sister ship, the *Asheville*, to be sunk by German torpedocs, had a very successful rough-weather design and was adopted by the Coast Guard for the Campbell class, outstanding in the Battle of the Atlantic. The *Erie* at 2,000 tons was between a destroyer and a light cruiser in size, and was armed with four of the latter's 6-inch rifles.

The inshore fighting of World War II found 41 small gunboats (patrol gunboat, or PG) and 23 still smaller motor gunboats (patrol gunboat motor, or PGM) being built, with the emphasis on a multiplicity of automatic weapons and on rocket launchers for shore bombardment. The gunboat concept of relatively enormous firepower in a small vessel had a new impetus from rocket weaponry. The Soviet Union became particularly interested and by 1972 had at least 200 gunboats with two to four 20-mile-range missiles on hulls displacing up to 200 tons and reaching speeds of 35 knots. In the Baltic, the most impressive boats competing with those of the Soviet Union were larger, faster, West German types.

The U.S. Navy had no interest in modernizing gunboats until the Vietnam War spawned a variety of tiny types used in swarms either to police the shoreline or to penetrate the riverways. The heaviest types revived the name of "monitor." As for countering Soviet types, the U.S. Navy had not by 1972 become committed to this goal, but it was testing designs seeking great speeds, such as the patrol gunboat hydrofoil *Tucumcari* (PGH 2), reported to reach 70 knots, and "surface effect" vessels theoretically expected to weigh 5,000 tons and to attain speeds of 100 knots.

BIBLIOGRAPHY

Office of Naval History, *Dictionary of American Fighting Ships*.

— R. W. DALY

H

HABEAS CORPUS, WRIT OF

Writ of habeas corpus is a legal process through which someone who alleges that he is being detained illegally may secure a quick judicial inquiry into the lawfulness of his detention. Detention takes many forms: incarceration in a penitentiary pursuant to court judgment; detention in a police station following arrest; commitment to a mental institution; service in the armed forces; detention through quarantine regulations; and restraint through private authority, as in the custody of children. Whatever form restraint of liberty may take, habeas corpus is available so that a judge may inquire into its legality. The writ is addressed to the person responsible for the detention and requires him to produce the petitioner quickly so that the court may decide upon the lawfulness of the detention. There is no statute of limitations, or time limit, with respect to the writ of habeas corpus, because the right to personal freedom from illegal restraint never lapses. One failure to secure the writ does not bar a later application, and unlike other legal actions the writ may be petitioned for by a relative or friend if the concerned individual is unable to apply on his own. Called "the most important human right in the Constitution," the great writ was once described by Chief Justice Salmon P. Chase as "the best and only sufficient defense of personal freedom" (*Ex parte Yerger*, 8 Wallace U.S. 85, 95 [1868]).

There is no time limit with respect to the writ of habeas corpus because the right to personal freedom from illegal restraint never lapses.

Although the roots of habeas corpus are not clear, the writ is traceable to Section 39 of Magna Charta (1215). It had various uses during the Middle Ages, but its availability as a remedy against the crown dates from the end of the 15th century. The Habeas Corpus Act adopted by the British Parliament in 1679, as amended by various later statutes, spells out the essential elements of the writ as it is now commonly used. In the American colonies the writ was available as part of the common law. After independence was declared, it was guaranteed in most of the revolutionary state constitutions, and the U.S. Constitution in Article 1, Section 9, Clause 2, forbade its suspension "unless when in Cases of Rebellion or Invasion the public Safety may require it." The Judiciary Act of 1789, the very first statute adopted by the First Congress dealing with the courts, empowered all federal courts "to grant writs of habeas corpus for the purpose of an inquiry into the cause of commitment." All states have similar habeas corpus acts.

The writ is purely procedural. Habeas corpus statutes do not attempt to describe which detentions are illegal; all they provide for is a procedure by which a court may look into the matter. If the court concludes that the detention is illegal, the petitioner is freed by the judge at once. While historically the writ was mainly concerned with jurisdictional questions, the courts and legislative bodies have expanded the uses of the writ through a broadening of the concept of jurisdiction. In 1867 Congress adopted a statute making federal habeas corpus available to state, as well as federal, prisoners and authorizing the writ wherever any person is restrained of his liberty in violation of any federal law (Constitution, acts of Congress, treaties), such as, above all, the Fourteenth Amendment's due process right to a fair hearing. A state prisoner is not eligible to apply to a federal judge for habeas corpus until he has first exhausted whatever remedies are available to him under state law, including litigation of his federal claim. Similarly, a member of the armed forces is not entitled to bring a habeas corpus proceeding in a federal district court until he has exhausted the remedies provided for him in the military court system.

In England, the writ of habeas corpus can be suspended only by act of Parliament; this has happened several times, as during the Napoleonic Wars. President Abraham Lincoln suspended the writ at the beginning of the Civil War; but Chief Justice Roger B. Taney protested that only Congress may do that, and soon afterward Congress validated the suspension after the fact by statute. The limited suspensions of the writ in 1871 and 1905 were announced by the president pursuant to statute, and a suspension in 1941, in Hawaii, without statutory authorization, was held by the Supreme Court to be without legal authority (*Duncan* v. *Kahanamoku*, 327 U.S. 304 [1946]).

BIBLIOGRAPHY

David Fellman, *The Defendant's Rights.*

— DAVID FELLMAN

HALF MOON

Half Moon, the ship the Dutch East India Company provided for the voyage of exploration made by Henry Hudson in 1609, in the course of which the Hudson River was discovered. A vessel of 80 tons, it was a flat-bottomed two-master, of a type designed to navigate the difficult approaches to the Zuider Zee in the Netherlands. Called by the Dutch a *vlieboot*, a term derived from the island of Vlieland, it has been translated into English, without reference to its derivations, as "fly-boat." Later employed in the East India trade, the *Half Moon* was wrecked in 1615 on the shore of the island of Mauritius, then owned by the Dutch.

— A. C. FLICK

HALFWAY COVENANT

If, as they reached adulthood, children of the founders of Massachusetts and Connecticut gave no acceptable proof of that spiritual experience called regeneration, should they be granted full church membership? In June 1657, an intercolonial ministerial conference at Boston attempted to answer through the Halfway Covenant, whereby membership was granted to the children whose parents had experienced regeneration but, pending regeneration of their own, participation in the Lord's Supper and voting in the church were withheld. Liberals objected, and although a Massachusetts synod proclaimed it for all Massachusetts churches (1662), controversy continued for more than a century.

BIBLIOGRAPHY

Williston Walker, *The Creeds and Platforms of Congregationalism*.

— RAYMOND P. STEARNS

HAMILTON'S FISCAL POLICIES

When Alexander Hamilton was appointed the first secretary of the treasury on Sept. 11, 1789, he was confronted with a chaotic economic situation. The fiscal legacy resulting from the desperate financial necessities of the Revolution and the inept economic measures of the Confederation included disrupted commercial and revenue systems, inadequate currency, a host of unsettled claims, and what was for the 18th century a very considerable foreign and domestic debt. A strong proponent of economic nationalism, Hamilton intended to correct these fiscal and commercial problems with an integrated plan for a national economy that would serve the additional purpose of binding the states and their citizens closer to the new central government. Among the measures he considered essential were the revival of confidence in public credit at home and abroad, a sound currency, an integrated system of manufactures, the revival of foreign trade, and the establishment of a national bank and a mint. Fortunately for Hamilton's plans, the congressional act establishing the treasury gave the secretary considerable authority in drawing up plans for public credit, revenue, and expenditures and in reporting proposed measures directly to Congress. In spite of some reluctance on the part of Congress to relinquish control of fiscal matters, the exigencies of the nation's finances compelled it to do so. It was probably this peculiar relationship between the Treasury Department and Congress as much as his reliance on Hamilton's judgment that caused President George Washington to give him such a free hand in financial matters.

The nation's liquidated debt in 1789 amounted to \$40,414,085.94, and the foreign debt contracted during the Revolution to \$11,710,378.62. Arrears of interest on both approached \$15,000,000. Continental bills of credit outstanding amounted to \$2,000,000, and an estimation of state debts placed them at over \$18,000,000. The total debt clearly surpassed \$70,000,000. The fundamental problem facing the new nation, Hamilton believed, was the restoration of its credit, and on Jan. 14, 1790, he presented to Congress the first of his plans for fiscal reforms. A properly funded national debt, he pointed out, would reestablish confidence and form the foundation for most of the country's fiscal necessities. It would provide the basis for loans, and readier access to capital would facilitate agricultural and commercial expansion. An orderly arrangement of the debt would remove the temptation to invest capital in the type of speculation that had plagued the Confederation government. The national debt, he believed, should be discharged according to the terms of the original contract. Arrears of interest, as well as the original debt, should be paid eventually. The state debts contracted during the Revolution should be assumed along with the national debt.

Hamilton formed an integrated plan for a national economy that would serve the additional purpose of binding the states and their citizens closer to the new central government.

Hamilton's plan for providing for the public debt included a reorganized and orderly system of collecting duties on imports and tonnage, implemented by a duty on imported wines, spirits, coffee, and teas and an excise on domestically distilled spirits. These revenues would provide for the interest on the debt and for the current expenses of government. The payments of principal due on the foreign debt could be provided for by floating new loans abroad; interest would be paid out of the excise. He pointed out as a fundamental maxim that "the creation of debt should always be accompanied with the means of extinguishing it." Provision for the payment of the debt itself would be carried out through the establishment of a sinking fund, under the administration of a board of commissioners who would make judicious purchases of the debt when the purchase price was below par, resulting in the double benefit of retiring the debt and raising the price of stock. Hamilton preferred excise taxes to taxes on land and houses, thinking these sources of revenue should be kept in reserve for times of national crisis. Duties on imported articles should be raised but not beyond certain limits, since it was vital not to disrupt foreign trade. Virtually all Hamilton's proposals were enacted, although they led to the first great debate in Congress, most of the opposition centering on Hamilton's refusal to discriminate between the original holders of certificates and later purchasers and on the assumption of the debts of the states by the federal government.

One of Hamilton's first fiscal measures was to deal with the pressing foreign debt contracted during the Revolution. When the new government went into operation, the principal of the foreign debt stood at $6,296,296 due to France, $174,011 due to Spain, and $3,000,000 due to Holland, plus over $1,500,000 in arrearages of interest. Unlike the domestic debt, about which there was room for compromise between debtor and creditor, the foreign debt—principal and interest—had to be paid promptly according to the schedule of the original contracts. Acting under two congressional acts, of Aug. 4 and Aug. 12, 1790, which authorized the borrowing of $14,000,000 to support public credit, Hamilton and his European agent, William Short, proceeded to negotiate a series of European loans. Hamilton and Short, acting primarily through the Dutch banking house of Willink, Van Staphorst, and Hubbard, were able to secure funds to establish a schedule of punctual payments of principal and interest due abroad. In spite of the success of these maneuvers, Hamilton's administration of these loans led to the Giles Resolutions of 1793, which accused the secretary of violating the law in the disposition of funds borrowed under the August 1790 acts. A similar attack on Hamilton's foreign loan policies occurred in 1794. In both cases he was exonerated by Congress, although his critics remained unconvinced.

A crucial aspect of Hamilton's plans for economic development was the creation of a national bank. Advocating a money bank rather than a land bank, Hamilton emphasized that such an institution would act as a means of increasing capital, discouraging speculation, and supplying through its bank notes a ready medium of exchange. The constitutionality of the bill to establish the first Bank of the United States was challenged almost at once by such able opponents as James Madison, Thomas Jefferson, and Edmund Randolph. Hamilton's arguments in favor of the bank's constitutionality were embodied in his cabinet opinion to the president, in which he reiterated the doctrine of implied powers in the Constitution, arguing that that document must be flexible enough to meet the future needs of the nation.

The bill establishing the bank was enacted into law on Feb. 25, 1791, and by July of that year all shares were oversubscribed. The bank, with a charter of twenty years, was capitalized at $10,000,000, consisting of 25,000 shares to be sold at $400 each, payable one-fourth in specie and three-fourths in the percent funded debt. Bank notes, which could be exchanged for gold or silver on demand, were receivable for all payments due the United States. The government subscribed to $2,000,000 of the stock, borrowing an equal sum to be used for various necessities of government. Eventually branches for discount and deposit were established in a number of major cities. During Hamilton's tenure the bank was a useful agent of the treasury, helping to regulate the currency, facilitate the collection of taxes, prevent the proliferation of state banks, and provide a ready source of loans for the federal government. The mint, another institution that Hamilton advocated, was established in 1792, but to his disappointment, it was placed under the State Department rather than the Treasury Department.

Although not strictly a fiscal matter, Hamilton's plans for the future of American manufacturing were an integral part of his economic program. His plan for the development of manufacturing was the only one of his proposals to be ignored by Congress, largely because his plan for providing tariff protection and bounties for infant industries was regarded as inimical to the interests of agriculture and as providing special favor to a small economic class. Hamilton did not conceive of manufacturing as replacing agriculture; rather, he thought it would increase immigration, provide work for the indigent, and stimulate a ready home market for agricultural surplus, thus contributing to national self-sufficiency. Although he advocated protective duties, he preferred premiums and bounties to stimulate the production of manufactured goods and the invention of machinery. Federally sponsored internal improvements, such as roads and canals, were to facilitate the movement of raw materials and stimulate the distribution of manufactured goods.

The success of Hamilton's fiscal policies depended greatly on the quality of their administration, carried out by a small army of subordinates who required and received constant advice and supervision. Collectors of the customs in every major port were given detailed instructions for enforcing the revenue laws and reported directly to the secretary. He guided the activities of the Coast Guard, negotiated contracts for the construction and repair of lighthouses, maintained a close control over the operation of the excise laws, and was the most active of the commissioners of the sinking fund instituted in 1790 to superintend purchases of the public debt. In many ways he functioned more as a prime minister than as a member of the cabinet. His fiscal activities spilled over into other departments, and his passion for accuracy and efficiency, as well as his ambition, laid him open to the charge of interdepartmental meddling.

Hamilton's economic philosophy was fundamentally pragmatic and relevant to the needs of the emerging nation. He was not by any means an advocate of laissez-faire but rather of a managed economy with government bounties for business and industry and with a government-supported system of internal improvements. Although he was branded a conservative, his economic program was truly radical, and he succeeded in impressing it upon the American economy for generations to come. Politically his measures were less successful. He did indeed rally the business community behind the new government, but his fiscal program had little appeal to the small farmer and shopkeeper, and by 1800 the majority of that class was firmly in the Republican camp. Once he set up his fiscal program, he made little effort to mollify his opposition—particularly on the questions of discrimination and the assumption of state debts—and he probably cost the Federalists the grass-roots support necessary to build a viable political party. He was more concerned with a sound economic foundation for the new nation than with the ideals of political democracy, but his fiscal system provided the economic stability that made political development possible.

BIBLIOGRAPHY

John C. Miller, *Alexander Hamilton: Portrait in Paradox.*

Broadus Mitchell, *Alexander Hamilton, the National Adventure, 1788–1804.*

Curtis P. Nettels. *The Emergence of a National Economy, 1775–1815.*

Donald F. Swanson, *The Origins of Hamilton's Fiscal Policies.*

Harold C. Syrett et al., eds., *The Papers of Alexander Hamilton.*

Leonard D. White, *The Federalists.*

— DOROTHY TWOHIG

HANDSOME LAKE CULT

Handsome Lake Cult, a nativistic movement among the Iroquois, was founded by a Seneca prophet named Handsome Lake in 1799. It spread rapidly to the other tribes of the Six Nations, although not to non-Iroquoian-speaking tribes. The prophet began to speak the "Good Message," which prescribed the way the Seneca should follow to escape the evils of white civilization and to attain the heavenly path. The doctrine combined native Iroquois beliefs with those of the Quakers, among whom Handsome Lake had been reared, and it stressed both ethical prescriptions and ritual purification. The religion held a strong appeal for the Iroquois,

Handsome Lake preached that he had been visited in dreams by three supernatural beings, sent to him by the Master of Life.

most of whom had lost their lands as a result of siding with the English in the Revolution and whose numbers had been diminished by disease, war, and alcoholism. Handsome Lake preached that he had been visited in dreams by three supernatural beings, sent to him by the Master of Life, who instructed him to tell his people to purge their lives of all that was worldly and profane, to live in peace with the whites, and to revive their ancient ceremonies. The religion, which provides for congregational worship in the longhouse, still survives among the Iroquois in an altered form.

BIBLIOGRAPHY

Merle H. Deardorff, *The Religion of Handsome Lake: Its Origin and Development,* in William N. Fenton, ed., *Symposium on Local Diversity in Iroquois Culture.*

Arthur C. Parker, *The Code of Handsome Lake, the Seneca Prophet.*

Anthony F. C. Wallace and Raymond Fogelson, *The Death and Rebirth of the Seneca.*

— KENNETH M. STEWART

HARTFORD CONVENTION

Hartford Convention (Dec. 15, 1814–Jan. 5, 1815), called at the invitation of the Massachusetts legislature, was a meeting of twenty-six New England Federalists. They were backed by New England mercantile interests, the Essex Junto, and Federalists generally, who opposed Jeffersonian-Republican policies and the War of 1812. Delegates, elected by the legislatures, were sent from Massachusetts, Connecticut, and Rhode Island. Vermont and New Hampshire failed to cooperate, although two counties in the former and one in the latter sent delegates. The convention was held in secret sessions at Hartford, Conn., for the declared purpose of considering the advisability of calling a general convention to revise the Constitution. It was a distinguished group, and, with one or two exceptions, was not drawn from the radical Federalist element. The most prominent figure was Harrison Gray Otis, who looked on the convention as a safety valve for pent-up Federalist feeling.

Resentment in New England against commercial restrictions and westward expansion had been augmented by the unpopular war with England, which raised vexatious problems as to the control of state militia and the protection of the New England coast. The resolutions adopted for the consideration of New England legislatures recommended interstate cooperation in repelling British attacks, the use of federal revenues in state defense, and the protection of citizens against unconstitutional military acts. The New England states were also urged to support constitutional amendments that would limit southern political power, commercial embargoes and trade restrictions, declarations of war, admission of new states into the Union, and office-holding by naturalized citizens.

Having made tentative plans for calling another meeting in six months, the convention adjourned. Both because of its secrecy and because of the immediate end of the war it was laid open to ridicule and charges of treasonable intent, and the doctrines of state and sectional rights it advocated were temporarily discredited throughout the nation.

BIBLIOGRAPHY

Theodore Dwight, *History of the Hartford Convention.*

Samuel Eliot Morison, *The Life and Letters of Harrison Gray Otis, 1765–1848.*

— ROBERT A. EAST

HARVARD UNIVERSITY

Founded at Cambridge, Mass., in 1636 with a grant of £400 from the Massachusetts General Court, Harvard is the oldest college in the United States; its first classes were held in 1638. It owes its name to John Harvard, a graduate of Emmanuel College in Cambridge, England, who left the institution half his property and his entire library. The first head, Nathaniel Eaton, was dismissed at the end of a year. He was succeeded by Henry Dunster, president of Harvard from 1640 to 1654, who in 1650 secured the charter under which Harvard has continued to operate. According to this charter, college affairs are administered by the Corporation (consisting of the president and five fellows, given perpetual succession) and by a second governing committee known as the Board of Overseers. The most distinguished president in the early days was Increase Mather (1685–1701), but he treated the office as a part-time job.

In 1780 Harvard became a university; in 1782 a medical school was established; and in 1817 a law school was added. Under John T. Kirkland, president from 1810 to 1828, the college acquired professors with European training. George Ticknor, who taught French and Spanish after studying at Göttingen and meeting Johann von Goethe and Madame de Staël, was a Kirkland appointee. When Ticknor resigned after eighteen years as chairman of the modern languages department, his place was taken by Henry Wadsworth Longfellow and later by James Russell Lowell. Another Kirkland appointee was Edward Everett, who taught Greek after his stay in Göttingen. When Everett himself became president (1846–49), he made Louis Agassiz professor of zoology and geology.

Harvard's greatest advances were made under Charles William Eliot, president from 1869 to 1909, who turned the school from a provincial college into a great national university.

The greatest advances were made under Charles William Eliot, president from 1869 to 1909, who turned Harvard from a provincial college into a great national university. Eliot laid the foundations of the graduate school in 1872, revived the law school by appointing Christopher Columbus Langdell dean, and reformed the medical school. He also secured the most brilliant faculty in the history of any American university. When Henry Adams declared that he knew nothing about medieval history, Eliot was adamant. "If you will point out anyone who knows more, Mr. Adams, I will appoint him," he said. Henry Adams and Edward Channing lent a sudden new distinction to the history department; and William James, Josiah Royce, Charles Sanders Peirce, and George Santayana gave the philosophy department an unrivaled reputation. Charles Eliot Norton, who inaugurated the fine arts department in 1874, was not so wise a choice: Norton, a loyal disciple of John Ruskin, decided that the fine arts had come to an end in 1600. But Norton was one of the rare mistakes of the Eliot administration. Believing that students should not be forced to study subjects in which they had absolutely no interest, Eliot introduced the elective system, challenging Harvard men to cultivate their particular interests.

Abbott Lawrence Lowell, president from 1909 to 1933, was also an exceptional administrator. "The teaching by the professor in his class-room on the subjects within the scope of his chair ought to be absolutely free," he maintained. When German-born Hugo Münsterberg of the psychology department was harried for expressing his sympathy for Germany in World War I, the Corporation refused to dismiss him, and he died a Harvard professor in 1916. When Harold Laski, an instructor in political science, was criticized for addressing the wives of the Boston policemen on the right to strike in 1919, Lowell told the Corporation and the Board of Overseers that if Laski were forced to leave, he would resign. The overseers acquiesced, but Laski left shortly afterward for the University of London.

Tempering Eliot's emphasis on the elective system, Lowell asked undergraduates to concentrate in one discipline and introduced the tutorial system. One of his major achievements was the founding of the Society of Fellows. Under this plan twenty-four junior fellows, the graduates of any college, were freed from taking courses or studying for a degree and given the opportunity to engage in any approved writing or research. But the great blessing of the Lowell years was the house plan, financed by about $12 million from Edward S. Harkness, an 1897 Yale graduate. In this plan the three upper classes were lodged with their tutors in residential units, virtually eliminating the social influence of the Harvard clubs.

Lowell was followed by James Bryant Conant, a chemistry professor, who served until 1953. Under Conant, the historic connection between the president and the college was weakened to a considerable degree. As he himself commented on the reorganization of 1945, "The president becomes actively acquainted with a faculty and its problems only when a new dean is to be appointed." The president from 1953 to 1971 was Nathan M. Pusey, under whom the operating budget rose from $39 million to nearly $200 million and the student population from less than 20,000 to more than 40,000. Pusey was succeeded by Derek Curtis Bok, former dean of the law school.

Among the architects who have contributed to the distinction of Harvard Yard and its environs, Charles Bulfinch of the class of 1781 must be mentioned for his design of University Hall. Henry Hobson Richardson of the class of 1859 planned Seaver Hall and Austin Hall for the law school. The firm of McKim, Mead and White was responsible for the gates of Harvard Yard.

Five graduates of Harvard have become presidents of the United States: John Adams, John Quincy Adams, Theodore Roosevelt, Franklin D. Roosevelt, and John F. Kennedy. A sixth president, Rutherford B. Hayes, attended Harvard law school for a year and a half.

By June 30, 1973, the Harvard endowment had risen to $1.357 billion, testifying to the loyalty of the alumni to the standards set by President Eliot.

— WAYNE ANDREWS

An engraving depicts a patrol wagon attacked by a mob of 12,000 rioters at the anarchist Haymarket riot in Chicago, Illinois, May 4, 1886. (Corbis-Bettmann)

HAYMARKET RIOT

Haymarket riot (May 4, 1886) arose as an incident of the militant movement in 1886 in

Chicago for an eight-hour working day. The movement was frequently accompanied by conflicts between strikers and police. In protest against the shooting of several workmen, August Spies, editor of the semianarchist *Arbeiter-Zeitung*, issued circulars demanding revenge and announcing a mass meeting at the Haymarket. Amidst general anticipation of violence, large police reserves were concentrated nearby. Mayor Carter H. Harrison attended the meeting but he soon left, judging the speeches to be innocuous. Despite Harrison's advice, 180 police advanced on the meeting and ordered the crowd to disperse. At this point, a bomb, thrown by an unknown hand, fell among the police, resulting in 7 deaths and 70 injured. Popular fears of a general anarchist plot made impartial investigation impossible; eight alleged anarchists were convicted on a conspiracy charge and four were hanged. The eight-hour movement collapsed beneath the stigma of radicalism. Gov. John P. Altgeld pardoned the three surviving prisoners in 1893, declaring that the trial had been a farce—an opinion severely condemned by the conservative press, but highly praised by organized labor.

BIBLIOGRAPHY

Henry David, *The History of the Haymarket Affair.*

Joseph G. Rayback, *A History of American Labor.*

— HARVEY WISH

HEALTH CARE

Health Care refers to the system of medical care to prevent and treat disease and to promote physical well-being. Since 1970 Americans have been the recipients of a broad range of advances in medical technology and care. Life expectancy has increased, deaths from many cancers have declined (with the important exception of lung cancer), and infant mortality rates have decreased. The breadth as well as the quality of health care has improved. Since the late 1960s, Medicaid and Medicare have expanded coverage dramatically, allowing the indigent and elderly greater access to medical facilities. Since 1970 federal and private funding for scientific research has grown, leading to expanded medical technology. Laser and computer technology, heart-lung machines, transcutaneous medication patches, and automated chemistry analyzers were only a few of the devices widely used in the 1990s. Many of these improvements made possible earlier detection of disease and provided for substantially improved health.

These improvements were accompanied by fundamental changes in American society—political, economic, and ethical—and the U.S. health care system in the mid-1990s, despite gains, appeared to be in a state of crisis. Both health care providers and outsiders recognized the problems arousing this sense of crisis. There was a feeling that medical science and practice may have reached their limits. While some diseases were declining, others, especially AIDS, had emerged as new and deadly. By the mid-1980s AIDS itself had been defined as a public health crisis. The United States spends more per capita on health care than any other Western nation, but in most measures of health status—such as infant mortality and life expectancy—it ranks from tenth to twentieth. In the mid-1990s, 37 million Americans had no health insurance, even though spending on health care had increased from $27 billion in 1960 to $838 billion in 1992, or 14 percent of the gross domestic product. Violence and homelessness were increasing in the 1990s, bringing with them various morbidities, particularly in poor urban neighborhoods and rural areas. Differences in mortality and disease rates between whites and blacks and between rich and poor had not diminished since the early 1970s and in some cases had increased. Some leaders of the medical establishment were slipping into pessimism. The 1989 medical publication *Unnatural Causes* asks whether medical science has met its "medical nemesis." Some of this pessimism sprang from criticism of medical technology. The explosive pace of technological change raised new problems, identified and examined by ethicists, social scientists, medical personnel, theologians, policymakers, and consumers themselves. A large share of health care expenditures went toward applying and, some argued, overusing such technical procedures as computerized tomography, nuclear magnetic resonance imaging, coronary angioplasty, mammography, and hip replacements.

In the mid-1990's, 37 million Americans had no health insurance, even though spending on health care had increased from $27 billion in 1960 to $838 billion in 1992.

Beginning in the 1970s the expanded use of technology promoted the establishment of presidential commissions and hospital review boards to study research protocols, life-sustaining therapies, patient autonomy, and informed consent procedures. Policies became necessary for human subjects in experimental trials. In 1966 the surgeon general, responding to revelations of abuse, required that institutional review boards evaluate risks and procedures. Later, Congress established the National Commission for the Protection of Human Subjects of Biomedical and Behavioral Research Collection, and the White House subsequently created the President's Commission for the Study of Ethical Problems in Medicine and Biomedical and Behavioral Research. Both identified ethical guidelines for institutional review boards and developed more standardized guidelines for research. Technology also raised issues concerning the end of life. In 1976 the New Jersey Supreme Court granted Karen Ann Quinlan's father guardianship status for the purpose of removing the respirator keeping his comatose daughter alive. Her case generated tremendous media coverage and debate. Since then the courts have been called on increasingly to adjudicate such cases, and the federal government has established regulations. By 1984 about one out of four hospitals had ethics committees to develop policy concerning the right of patients to determine their final care.

Life expectancy for elderly persons, especially women, has increased since the 1960s, creating additional health care needs. The burden falls on women family members, leaving many women caught between mothering and caring for aging or infirm parents. Much of the health care dollar of the 1990s was being spent on the last six months of life. Poverty among the elderly is closely associated with health. Compared to those above the poverty line, elderly poor women have worse health and more limitations on daily activities; they also more commonly report themselves as unwell. The place where the elderly receive their health care has shifted since the 1960s. Largely to cut labor and technical costs, home health care for the elderly became increasingly popular. The turn to home health care initiated for-profit and hospital-affiliated home health-care agencies. Before 1980 home health care was administered by visiting nurse associations and public health agencies, but with allowances in Medicare policy starting in 1980, home health care agencies proliferated, earning nearly $30 billion in 1983. Home health technology, including electronic infusion pumps, ventilators, and intravenous drug mechanisms, became a boom industry, with annual sales in the billions of dollars.

Until the early 1980s home health care involved relatively low-level technical procedures. Care was geared toward stable cardiac and diabetic patients, wound care, and impacted bowels; patients had close contact with nurses and aides. New reimbursement policies developed largely in the 1970s and 1980s covered highly technical procedures for sicker patients in the home, including many procedures once performed only in hospitals, such as intravenous antibiotic administration and chemotherapy and parenteral and enteral nutrition. By the early 1990s registered nurses were treating dying cancer and AIDS patients. Moreover, home care had become the most common discharge disposition for Medicare-Medicaid patients—although 82.5 percent of such patients received no post-hospital care, and of those who did only 14.6 percent got home care, leaving the others at risk for higher morbidity and mortality.

The so-called new reproductive technologies constitute another area of technological change and development. Since scientists documented the first successful in vitro fertilization (IVF) in 1978, numerous reproductive technologies have been developed, such as superovulation with fertility drugs, GIFT (ga-mete intrafallopian transfer), surrogacy, fetal tissue transplants, genetic screening, and embryo and egg freezing. Some women have had success with these technologies and argue that they provide important flexibility in making parenting decisions, such as delaying childbearing. Many feminist and women's health activists challenge the idea that these technologies liberate women, arguing that techniques such as IVF subject women to arduous, expensive, and often dangerous medical procedures with success rates not well established. In the area of birth control, the development of the synthetic hormone progestin in the form of Norplant and Depo-Provera has been identified by many women's health advocates as potentially dangerous. They have also objected to attempts to promote with financial incentives the use of these devices among largely poor racial minorities.

Technology has not been the only issue propelling reform since 1970. Cost and access are additional matters of concern. Medicaid and Medicare were established in 1965 by President Lyndon B. Johnson and later expanded dramatically. By 1980 those receiving federal aid through medical assistance numbered 43.5 million people. The programs were designed to pay most of the medical bills for 25 million elderly; 3.5 million disabled people; 10 million poor children; and 5 million unmarried, low-income parents. In the 1980s the rising costs of medical assistance systems were defined as problematic, and under the administration of President Ronald Reagan, Medicare eligibility was tightened, entitlement programs were reduced, and states assumed many of the health-related responsibilities previously covered by the federal government. Supplemental social security income grants for disability were cut, reducing the enrollment by 200,000, although the nutrition program for pregnant women, infants, and children (WIC) grew by 4 percent. Diagnostic-related groups and health maintenance organizations were introduced to control costs, and such companies as Kaiser Permanente became leaders in managed costs.

Since the 1970s gaps in insurance coverage and inequities in access, spiraling health care costs in both the private and public sectors, the AIDS epidemic, the emphasis on highly specialized and expensive medical treatment, and the growing gaps in health status between rich and poor have led to widespread criticism of the health system. In the 1990s these developments converged to create a renewed public debate on the right to medical care. President Bill Clinton's 1993 health security bill offered universal coverage, guaranteed benefits, and increased preventive care to be funded through a "managed competition" model, but it failed to pass Congress.

Pressure on the health care system has increasingly come from outside the health establishment. Women's health activists, AIDS activists, the hospice movement, midwifery programs, and the National Breast Cancer Coalition are only some of the groups that have become important catalysts for change. For example, in 1985 only 13 percent of people died at home, a great decrease from 1950. In light of this trend, the hospice movement sought to provide a more humane, less technological environment for dying. The movement believes that technology should be used to give more choice to patients by allowing them to leave the hospital and go to their homes, to nursing homes, or to hospices. The AIDS crisis added impetus to the movement. Women's health activists became more influential, and since the 1960s their ranks have grown to include medical practitioners, academics, grass-roots activists, midwives, policy-makers, alternative providers, and hundreds of national organizations and thousands of local health centers. They have no single goal, but among the objectives many hold in common are preventive care, access to safe and legal abortion, expanded research into pharmaceutical and technological devices, and inclusion of domestic abuse and violence screening in health assessments. The Clinton administration increased funding for women's health. HIV and AIDS activists have persistently—and by many accounts successfully—demanded changes in Food and Drug Administration (FDA) regulations, the establishment of hospice care centers, and legal protections for people with AIDS. In the 1980s, especially when AIDS was still closely associated with gay men, activism was also directed at eliminating the stigmas attached to the disease.

[See also Acquired Immune Deficiency Syndrome; Contraception; Euthanasia; Health Maintenance Organizations; Medicare and Medicaid; Medicine.]

BIBLIOGRAPHY

Nona Glazer, *Women's Paid and Unpaid Labor* (Philadelphia, 1993).

Russell C. Maulitz, ed., *Unnatural Causes: The Three Leading Killer Diseases in America* (New Brunswick, N.J., 1989).

David Mechanic, *Painful Choices: Research and Essays on Health Care* (New Brunswick, N.J., 1989).

Janice G. Raymond, *Women as Wombs: Reproductive Technologies and the Battle Over Women's Freedom* (San Francisco, 1993).

Duncan Yaggy, ed., *Health Care for the Poor and Elderly* (Durham, N.C., 1984).

— JACQUELYN S. LITT

HEALTH, EDUCATION, AND WELFARE, DEPARTMENT OF

Established on Apr. 11, 1953, the Department of Health, Education, and Welfare (HEW) was created under the president's Reorganization Plan No. 1 of 1953, which abolished its predecessor organization, the Federal Security Agency, and transferred all components and functions of that agency to the new cabinet-status department. President Dwight D. Eisenhower selected Oveta Culp Hobby to be the first secretary; she was succeeded by Marion B. Folsom, Arthur S. Flemming, Abraham A. Ribicoff, Anthony J. Celebrezze, John W. Gardner, Wilbur J. Cohen, Robert H. Finch, Elliot L. Richardson, and, in 1972, Caspar W. Weinberger.

Although HEW is one of the younger federal departments, many of its services can be traced to responsibilities that were assumed by the federal government at an earlier date. To provide treatment for disabled American merchant seamen, President John Adams, in 1798, signed an act establishing the Marine Hospital Service, the forerunner of the Public Health Service. In 1867, Congress established the Office of Education. In order to cope with the problems of sanitation in food handling and the complexities arising from the manufacturing processes for foods and medicines, the Food and Drug Administration was created in 1907. The Children's Bureau was organized in 1912; the Office of Vocational Rehabilitation was formed in 1920; and the Social Security Administration was established in 1935. In 1939, Congress created the Federal Security Agency, which included all these and other agencies and remained in existence until 1953.

The broad range of health, education, and welfare concerns of HEW reaches every American in one way or another. The services are carried out by four operating agencies: the Office of Education; the Social Security Administration; the Social and Rehabilitation Service; and the Public Health Service. This last consists of the National Institutes of Health; the Food and Drug Administration; the Alcohol, Drug Abuse and Mental Health Administration; the Center for Disease Control; the Health Resources Administration; and the Health Services Administration. The department also has certain responsibilities for three unique educational institutions: Howard University, established in 1867 to provide higher education for Afro-Americans; Gallaudet

College, the only institution in the world specifically for the higher education of the deaf; and the American Printing House for the Blind, which produces materials for teaching blind children.

The growth of HEW during its first two decades is reflected in budget and employment statistics. In the fiscal year 1954 the total budget of the department was about $6,978,648,000; its fiscal year 1973 budget was $89.2 billion. In 1953 the total number of paid employees of the department was 35,408; in 1971 it was 112,104. And whereas in 1955 HEW managed about 80 programs, by 1972 the number had grown to an estimated 280 programs. The department conducts its work through an extensive network of national, state, and local agencies, both public and private. Approximately 90 cents of every dollar appropriated is returned to the states, to cities, to universities, to private research groups, and to many other nonfederal agencies.

— MANFRED WASERMAN

HEALTH AND HUMAN SERVICE, DEPARTMENT OF

The Department of Health and Human Services (HHS) was created in 1979 and assumed control of all but the education functions of the former Department of Health, Education, and Welfare. The HHS controls a massive budget, amounting to $208.9 billion in 1995. Its divisions include the Public Health Service, which incorporates the Food and Drug Administration, the National Institutes of Health, the Centers for Disease Control, the Alcohol, Drug Abuse, and Mental Health Administration, and the Health Resources and Services Administration; the Health Care Financing Administration; the Office of Child Support Enforcement; the Social Security Administration; and the Office of Community Services. HHS has been at the center of many controversial national concerns: AIDS, arthritis, birth control and abortion, child care and child abuse, Medicare and Medicaid, nursing homes, Alzheimer's disease, smoking, food and drug testing, steroids, breast implants, proposals for health care rationing in Oregon, use of dioxin (Agent Orange), and policies toward the disabled. Some of these concerns originated within HHS, while others resulted from actions by other agencies of the federal government.

The department suffered many vicissitudes during its first fifteen years. It had to deal with such difficult problems as medical malpractice, the overcharging of Medicare by physicians, overcharging by universities awarded research grants, the improper manufacturing of generic drugs by pharmaceutical companies, and the disciplining of hospitals with high death rates. Moreover, HHS had internal problems. Some employees were cited for malfeasance and misuse of funds, political favoritism, or racial insensitivity. The department suffered budget cuts, especially under President Ronald Reagan's administration (1981–1989), which refused to spend funds appropriated by Congress. In the mid-1990s, disagreement over abortion, comprehensive health care, and social security kept the department at the center of domestic political controversy.

[See also Food and Drug Administration; Health Care; Health, Education, and Welfare, Department of; Medicare and Medicaid; National Institutes of Health; Social Security.]

BIBLIOGRAPHY

Edward D. Berkowitz, *America's Welfare State: From Roosevelt to Reagan* (Baltimore, 1991).

Edward D. Berkowitz and Mark Leff, eds., *Social Security After Fifty Years* (Westport, Conn., 1987).

— DONALD R. WHITNAH

HEALTH MAINTENANCE ORGANIZATIONS

Health Maintenance Organizations (HMOs), prepaid plans that provide medical services, usually including physical examinations, treatment, education, and preventive programs, for a fixed monthly premium. Among the first HMOs, and historically the most significant, was the prepaid health plan of the Kaiser Steel Corporation, begun in 1933 and covering union employees at plants in California. The Kaiser plan opened its rolls to the public in 1945. In the 1990s, long independent of its parent, it operated under the name Kaiser Permanente and was a major health care player in the United States, particularly in the West. There are basically two types of HMO: the staff HMO, modeled after Kaiser Permanente, and the individual practice association (IPA). The staff HMO has its own physicians. IPAs contract with physicians in the community who see HMO members in their own offices and are paid for their services by the HMO on an agreed basis. IPA physicians treat patients other than HMO members. An HMO member's primary doctor is the primary care physician (PCP), or gatekeeper. PCPs are family doctors who make referrals to specialists and services as needed.

Strictly speaking, HMOs are not insurance. Patients covered by traditional insurance policies submit their hospital, doctor, and related bills to their insurance company, which pays them on the basis of services rendered. Insurance policies commonly require that the insured pay a stated amount (a deductible) out of pocket before the insurance company becomes responsible for payment, and that after the amount is surpassed the insured pay a substantial portion (a copayment) of the amount charged for each service. Policyholders are free to choose their medical care providers without restriction. HMOs, on the other hand, do not generally impose deductibles and require members to make only a token copayment, but HMO members can use non-HMO providers only in medical emergencies. An HMO may be an independent company, such as Blue Cross and Blue Shield, or may be maintained by an employer, hospital, union, government agency, or, for that matter, an insurance company. An HMO may be for profit or not for profit. HMOs should be distinguished from preferred provider organizations (PPOs), a form of insurance in which the insurance company offers an employer a contract with providers who agree to furnish fee-for-service care at a reduced price.

Advocates for HMOs argue that they are an effective approach to health care cost-saving and point to HMOs' emphasis on education and prevention.

HMOs have grown in popularity. In 1976, 6 million people in the United States were covered by HMOs; in 1992, 37 million. More than one-fifth of those whose medical bills are paid by nongovernmental sources such as Medicaid and Medicare are enrolled in HMOs. Detractors say that HMOs limit their members in selecting health care providers and tend to be bureaucratic. Advocates for HMOs argue that they are an effective approach to health care cost-saving and point to the fact that HMOs emphasize education and prevention. Supporters also contend that because HMOs are not paid on a fee-for-service basis, they do not render more complicated service than necessary.

[See also Health Care; Medicare and Medicaid.]

BIBLIOGRAPHY

Daniel K. Freeborn and Clyde R. Pope, *Promise and Performance in Managed Care: The Prepaid Group Practice Model* (Baltimore, 1994).

Howard L. Smith and Richard A. Reid, *Competitive Hospitals* (Rockville, Md., 1986).

— JACK HANDLER

HISPANIC AMERICANS

The Hispanic population of the United States includes a diverse array of ethnic groups—at least twenty—connected by language. Among the groups are persons from Mexico, Puerto Rico, Cuba, the Dominican Republic, Spanish-speaking countries in South America and Central America, and those with other Spanish, Hispanic, or Latino origins. From 1960 to 1990 the Hispanic population increased significantly in size and as a proportion of the U.S. population, from 6.9 million to 22.4 million, from 3.9 percent of the U.S. population to 9.0 percent. Those figures include 13.5 million Mexicans, more than 60 percent of the Hispanic population; 2.7 million Puerto Ricans; 1 million Cubans; and 5.1 million persons of other Hispanic origins. Because Puerto Ricans are U.S. citizens, migration between Puerto Rico and the U.S. mainland is not regulated by immigration law. Migration from Puerto Rico increased sharply after World War II. Between 1960 and 1993 more than 650,000 Cubans were admitted as immigrants to the United States, four-fifths of whom were refugees. During the same period, approximately 930,000 immigrants from Central America and 1.2 million immigrants from South America were admitted. Immigration from Mexico was the largest among Hispanic groups. Since 1960 more than 4 million immigrants from Mexico have been admitted. A large proportion were undocumented Mexican aliens who were legalized under the Immigration Reform and Control Act of 1986, which among other provisions established an amnesty program for long-term undocumented aliens. Mexicans constituted three-quarters of the aliens receiving legal status under this act.

Given differences among Hispanic groups, it is not surprising that unified political organization of Hispanic populations has yet to emerge in the U.S.

During the first half of the twentieth century, Hispanic migration was largely of Mexican origin and concentrated in the Southwest, where much of the population continues to reside. In 1990 more than 80 percent of Mexicans in the United States lived in California, Arizona, New Mexico, Colorado, and Texas. After World War II Puerto Rican communities developed in the New York-New Jersey metropolitan area. Cuban refugees entered the United States beginning in 1960, settling in Florida and northeastern metropolitan areas; in 1990, 80 percent of Cuban Americans resided in Florida, New York, and New Jersey. Central and South American populations resided primarily in metropolitan areas and were in large degree residentially segregated from the non-Hispanic white population. According to the 1990 census, the percentage of the U.S.

population age twenty-five and older having completed a high school degree or higher was 75.2 percent. Among Hispanics this percentage was much lower, 49.8 percent; 44.2 percent of Mexicans had completed at least a high school degree, 53.4 percent of Puerto Ricans, and 56.2 percent of Cubans.

Fertility among Hispanics is higher than among the U.S. population but, as among all U.S. women, has been declining. In 1990 the average number of children born per married woman was 2.1; for Hispanic women this average was 2.7 children. Average fertility among Mexican women was 3 children, the highest among Hispanic groups; among Puerto Ricans, 2.5; and among Cuban women, 1.9, lower than the average for all U.S. women.

Given differences among Hispanic groups, it is not surprising that unified political organization of Hispanic populations has yet to emerge in the United States. There are significant differences among Hispanic groups in rates of naturalization. Among immigrants admitted since 1982, 24 percent of Cubans have become U.S. citizens, while only 11 percent of Mexicans have been naturalized. Hispanic groups also vary in levels of voting and political affiliation. The political importance of the growth in Hispanic populations, however, has been dramatic. As a result of population growth during the 1980s, California, Texas, and Arizona, states with the largest Hispanic populations, gained eleven congressional seats.

[See also Cuban Americans; Demographic Changes; Immigration; Mexican Americans; Puerto Rican Americans.]

BIBLIOGRAPHY

Lawrence A. Clayton, ed., *The Hispanic Experience in North America* (Columbus, Ohio, 1992).

Alejandro Portes and Ruben G. Rumbaut, *Immigrant America* (Berkeley, Calif., 1990).

Frank L. Schick and Renee Schick, *Statistical Handbook on U.S. Hispanics* (Phoenix, 1991).

— ELLEN PERCY KRALY

HISS CASE

Alger Hiss, an adviser to the State Department on economic and political affairs, had also served as secretary-general of the San Francisco conference for the organization of the United Nations and had been appointed president of the Carnegie Endowment for International Peace. In August 1948, Whittaker Chambers, a self-professed member of a Communist spy ring, testified before the House Un-American Activities Committee, stating that he knew Hiss to be a member of the same spy ring in the 1930's and that Hiss had passed secret State Department documents to him in 1938. Hiss denied under oath that he had passed the documents and stated that he had not seen Chambers after Jan. 1, 1937. Hiss was indicted in December 1948 on two counts of perjury (the statute of limitation for espionage charges had run out). The first trial ended in July 1949 in a hung jury. On Jan. 21, 1950, at a second trial, Hiss was found guilty and sentenced to five years in prison. After serving three years, he was released and returned to private life.

Committee on Un-American Activities on August 25, 1948. Hiss was accused of being a member of a pre-World War II Communist underground in Washington, D. C. (UPI/Corbis-Bettmann)

BIBLIOGRAPHY

Whittaker Chambers, *Witness.*

W. A. Jowitt, *The Strange Case of Alger Hiss.*

Ralph De Toledano and Victor Laskey, *Seeds of Treason.*

HOME RULE

Home Rule is a term usually used to describe the policy that permits cities and counties to draft their own charters, to establish their own governmental structures, and to control matters that are local in nature. The policy may be established by state legislation alone, by the state constitution supplemented by enabling legislation, or by self-executing constitutional provisions. The strong American tradition of local self-government has supported the campaign for municipal home rule for most of the nation's history, but this campaign did not become organized and clearly identifiable as a movement until the 20th century.

The primary impact of home rule in those cities in which it has been adopted has been to permit variations in governmental structure. The long-standing domination by the states of general governmental functions and the increasing complexity of modern urban problems have led to the definition of very few policy areas as purely local and amenable to local control. This limitation on home rule is not widely recognized, and municipal interests continue to press for state constitutional revisions to permit the establishment of home rule charters.

BIBLIOGRAPHY

George S. Blair, *American Local Government.*

Joseph McGoldrick, *The Law and Practice of Municipal Home Rule, 1916–1930.*

— JOHN H. BAKER

HOMESTEAD MOVEMENT

It is difficult to fix a date for the beginning of the movement that culminated in 1862 in the passage of the Homestead Law. Free land was ingrained in the thoughts and desires of westward-moving settlers from early colonial days, but until the West became politically powerful the demand passed unheeded. The revenue motive was basic in determining the public land policy of the new nation, and more than three quarters of a century were to elapse after the great land ordinance of 1785 before the advocates of free land to settlers were victorious.

Nevertheless, Congress began very early to receive petitions asking that land in certain regions be given without price to settlers. In 1797 such a petition came from the Ohio River area, and two years later one came from Mississippi Territory. In 1812 Rep. Jeremiah Morrow of Ohio presented a request from the True American Society, whose members considered "every man entitled by nature to a portion of the soil of the country." Other instances could be cited to show that some pioneers insisted that their services in making farms in the wilderness entitled them to land free of price. In 1825 Thomas Hart Benton moved that an inquiry be made into the expediency of donating lands to settlers. The House committee on public lands reported in favor of such a policy in 1828. In his message of Dec. 4, 1832, President Andrew Jackson expressed the opinion that "the public lands should cease as soon as practicable to be a source of revenue." Thus the basic doctrines of homestead legislation were steadily attracting adherents.

During the 1830's the westerners gained an ally in organized labor. The National Trades Union Convention in 1834 and in 1836 adopted resolutions favoring giving land to settlers. Perhaps the most active leader in the movement was George Henry Evans, who became the editor of *The Working Men's Advocate*, established in 1844. About the same time the National Reform Association was organized. It gave much of its attention to agitation for free land by means of public meetings, petitions, and circulars. Horace Greeley also espoused the cause and brought it the powerful aid of his *New York Tribune.* In 1852 he presented a lengthy statement of the views of the "land reformers," the central idea being that the public land system should "be so modified that every person needing Land may take possession of any quarter-section not previously located, and that none other than a person needing land shall be allowed to acquire it at all."

The increasing public agitation was reflected in Congress by resolutions and petitions; and in 1846, by the introduction of homestead bills by Felix G. McConnell of Alabama and Andrew Johnson of Tennessee. The latter continued to be an ardent promoter of the homestead movement until success was achieved in 1862. A general bill for free land actually came to a vote in Congress in 1852, but it was defeated in the Senate. Special laws donating land to settlers in Florida and Oregon under certain conditions were passed in 1842 and 1850, respectively.

The homestead movement first became a definite political issue in 1848, when the Free Soil party declared in favor of free land to actual settlers "in consideration of the expenses they incur in making settlements in the wilderness . . . and of the public benefits resulting therefrom." Four years later the same party gave its support even more vigorously, but on different grounds. Now they asserted that "all men have a natural right to a portion of the soil; and that, as the use of the soil is indispensable to life, the right of all men to the soil is as sacred as their right to life itself." Therefore, they contended, "the public lands of the United States belong to the people, and should not be sold to individuals nor granted to corporations, but should be held as a sacred trust for the benefit of the people, and should be granted in limited quantities, free of cost, to landless settlers." These two platforms contained the main arguments used from first to last by the advocates of free land, namely, reward for public service in developing the country and natural right.

No major political party came to the support of a homestead policy until 1860, but the adherents of the idea were far more numerous than the small votes polled by the Free Soil candidates indicated. In Congress the defeat of the bill of 1852 did not discourage the introduction of similar measures in both houses in the succeeding sessions. Until 1860, however, the formidable opposition to free land made it impossible to get a law through both houses.

Most southerners were opposed to homestead legislation, mainly because they believed it would result in the peopling of the territories by antislavery settlers. Many easterners disapproved of the movement because of their fear of the effect of its success on the economic situation in eastern states. They contended that it would accelerate the westward movement, lower the value of land in the East, and deprive the federal government of an important source of revenue. Besides these sectional antagonisms to a measure so eagerly desired by westerners, there was the opposition of the Know-Nothing party and other antialien groups to any proposal to give free land to foreign immigrants.

Most southerners opposed homestead legislation, mainly because they believed it would result in the peopling of the territories by antislavery settlers.

The forces of opposition were strong enough until 1860 to prevent the passage of a homestead law. That year a bill, introduced by Galusha A. Grow of Pennsylvania, and amended in the process of debate and conference, passed both houses. Although this law as finally passed retained a price of 25 cents an acre, it was vetoed by President James Buchanan, who used most of the arguments that had hitherto been advanced against free land, including unconstitutionality. The effort to override the veto failed by a small margin, and the defeat was a bitter disappointment to the homestead advocates.

But victory was approaching. The very sectional conflict that had raised the most formidable obstacle to homestead legislation soon led to a situation that left the road to success entirely open. The new Republican party in 1860 declared that "we demand the passage by Congress of the complete and satisfactory Homestead measure." The victory of the Republicans and the secession of the South left the triumphant party free to carry out its program. On May 20, 1862, President Abraham Lincoln attached his signature to the Homestead Law, and free land—the goal sought by generations of westerners since the inception of the public-land policy—was attained.

The Homestead Law gave to "any person who is the head of a family, or who has arrived at the age of twenty-one years, and is a citizen of the United States, or who shall have filed his declaration of intention to become such," the privilege of obtaining a quarter-section of land free of charge, except for a small filing fee, by living on the land for five years and meeting certain conditions with respect to cultivation.

BIBLIOGRAPHY

Gilbert C. Fite, *The Farmers' Frontier, 1865–1900.*
Benjamin H. Hibbard, *A History of the Public Land Policies.*
Fred Shannon, *The Farmer's Last Frontier, 1860–1897.*

— DAN E. CLARK

HOMESTEAD STRIKE OF 1892

Homestead Strike of 1892 is regarded as a landmark in the development of labor organization in the steel industry and in the general history of organized labor in America. The Amalgamated Association of Iron, Steel and Tin Workers at this time was a powerful labor organization, which had established working relations with the Carnegie Steel Company at Homestead, Pa. In 1892 Henry Clay Frick, the chairman of the company, was determined to break the power of the union and demanded that its members accept a decrease in wages. When the union refused, Frick brought in nonunion labor. Violence and disorder involving pitched battles between workers and a force of detectives hired by the company ensued. The militia was then called in to check the strikers. The strike was lost. Thus, organized labor's first struggle with large-scale capital ended in failure.

BIBLIOGRAPHY

Daniel Aaron, ed., *America in Crisis.*
J. G. Rayback, *A History of American Labor.*

— HERBERT MAYNARD DIAMOND

HOOKWORM

Hookworm, an intestinal parasite prevalent in the sandy soils of warm climates, is spread by soil pollution. It inhibits growth and development in children and is generally debilitating in adults, weakening their resistance to other diseases. Known as "miner's anemia" in Italy, the disease was diagnosed in 1838 and reached epidemic proportions in Europe during the late 19th century. Bailey Ashford was the first to note the presence of hookworm in Puerto Rico in 1899, while Charles Stiles, helminthologist for the U.S. Natural History Museum, described in 1900 the differences between European hookworm and the new variety, which he named American killer. Stiles then studied the disease in the southern United States and tried to generate interest in a campaign against it. Government sources proved fruitless, so Stiles turned to private groups and convinced John D. Rockefeller, Sr., to fund the Rockefeller Sanitary Commission for the Eradication of Hookworm Disease in 1909.

The commission, whose efforts were concentrated in the South, was an experiment in public health, a joint venture of the medical profession, public health officials, a variety of civic groups, and private philanthropy. Its goals were to eradicate the disease itself, to strengthen public health administration, and to work for education of the public in health and hygiene. The venture resulted in the stimulation of state boards of health to greater activity, the establishment of county health officers in some participating states, and the alerting of the general medical profession and the public not only to hookworm but also to various related diseases. At another level the commission drew attention to hookworm in social and economic terms. Boards of education were major campaign supporters because students progressed more rapidly in school after treatment, while industrial interests supported the effort for the sake of increased production from healthy employees.

When the commission was dissolved in 1914, many of its activities were taken up by individual public health agencies. The local hookworm campaigns enabled these agencies, the medical profession, and the general public to consider a specific disease—its causes and effects—and jointly to take practical steps to control it and at the same time to improve sanitary conditions.

BIBLIOGRAPHY

Mary Boccaccio, "Ground Itch and Dew Poison: The Rockefeller Sanitary Commission 1909–14," *Journal of the History of Medicine and Allied Sciences*, vol. 27.

— MARY BOCCACCIO

HOPEWELL

Hopewell, the name given to the first great cultural climax in prehistoric North America, between 300 B.C. and A.D. 250. Apparently less a culture than an exchange system or cult, the Hopewell complex probably developed in Illinois, but it soon spread to southern Ohio, where impressive earthworks were eventually constructed. The regional cultures that participated in this exchange system or cult shared design motifs and ornamental or ceremonial objects. Artisans manufactured clay figurines, platform pipes, carved stone tablets, copper head and chest ornaments, earspools, panpipes, and flat celts, as well as other finely made status items. Raw materials, including mica, copper, shell, pipestone, meteoric iron, shark and alligator teeth, bear teeth, obsidian, and tortoiseshell, flowed throughout the network that connected the regional cultures. High quality stone projectile points, knives, atlatl weights, axes, adzes, and ceramics were among the wide array of other items made by Hopewell artisans. Each of the regional traditions also maintained distinctive local styles in their artifacts. The Hopewell burial-mound-and-log-tomb complex was often built in two stages and frequently accompanied by elaborate grave offerings; about three-fourths of the bodies were first cremated. The rectangular, circular, and octagonal Ohio ceremonial earthworks were larger and more complex than those built earlier in the same region by the Adena. Notable examples in Ohio are those at Mound City and Great Serpent parks.

Although corn became widespread in the Middle Woodland period, during which the Hopewell complex flourished, it apparently never became a staple in the economic systems of the Hopewell regional cultures. The harvesting of a wide variety of wild plants and animals probably sustained the Illinois Hopewell populations.

The Hopewell exchange system or cult strongly influenced other regional cultures throughout the Eastern Woodlands. The Marksville complex in the lower Mississippi Valley and the Santa Rosa complex in Florida are examples of Hopewell derivatives.

BIBLIOGRAPHY

Joseph R. Caldwell and Robert L. Hall, eds., *Hopewellian Studies*, Illinois State Museum Scientific Papers, vol. 12.

Thorne Deuel, *Hopewellian Communities in Illinois*, Illinois State Museum Scientific Papers, vol. 5.

— GUY GIBBON

HOPI

Hopi, classic representatives of Pueblo culture, occupy three mesas (tablelands) at the edge of the Painted Desert in northeastern Arizona. Seven major towns—among them Walpi, Oraibi, and Mishongnovi—and some dependent settlements mark the habitat of the Hopi, a group numbering about 4,000 in the mid-1970's. Each town forms a basic social unit; there is thus no tribe as such, although administrative organization and a commonality of language, culture, and associations create a sense of unity. The Hopi speak a Shoshonean language, a branch of the major Uto-Aztecan (or Aztec-Tanoan) linguistic phylum that has affinities both in Mexico and in the Great Basin. Although the Shoshonean of the Hopi is remotely related to the Tanoan languages spoken by the people of the Rio Grande pueblos to the east, there is no mutual intelligibility, despite a basic cultural similarity. It is suggested that the Hopi are deeply rooted in time in their present location.

Hopi, along with the linguistically unrelated town of Zuni in western New Mexico, forms the cultural province of the western Pueblo. Both stress a complex societal organization based on matrilineal institutions. Variant social patterns with patrilineal descent are found among the Pueblo to the east. The Hopi, on the other hand, are divided into maternal units, or clans: the individual takes his group affiliation from his mother, and ownership of house, farmland, and the important ceremonial paraphernalia pass from mother to daughter. Political authority, vested in groups and special clan offices, passes to men through the female line of descent. Elaboration of ceremonial activity—seen especially in priestly associations and involving initiation and the impersonation of spirits or gods with masked dancing—aims at agricultural fertility, world renewal, and societal stability. Although the Hopi fought defensive wars, especially against the intrusive Navaho (on whose culture they left a strong imprint), the primary orientations of their society were—and are still—directed toward peace. Although an association of warriors existed, its functions were more ritual than practical.

The Hopi and their neighbors offer a striking example of cultural integrity, having maintained their native culture against pressures and inroads from outsiders.

Like the other Pueblo, the Hopi have adopted the pattern of intensive agriculture. Their complete dependence on farm products (particularly maize and associated food plants), tobacco, and an aboriginal cotton is remarkable, considering the desert conditions under which they live. Water is carefully controlled; crops are planted at the base of a mesa to catch even the morning dew; and rainmaking rituals form a vital part of Hopi religious observances. The so-called Snake Dance, carried on by priests of the Snake society in alternate years, is a popularly known element in a symbolism that identifies the snake, lightning, and rain.

The Hopi and their neighbors offer a striking example of cultural integrity. They have successfully maintained their native culture against pressures and inroads from outsiders, including the expedition of Francisco Vásquez de Coronado in 1540, Franciscan missionization begun in 1629, and the effects of the Pueblo Revolt of 1680, which forced the movement of some of the Hopi. In 1700 a group of Tewa-speaking Tanoans, the Hano, moved into Hopi country from the Rio Grande, still retaining a linguistic identity but being assimilated by the Hopi. Despite these and the contacts that followed, both Mexican and American, the Hopi retain a pattern of culture in which traditional ideals survive.

BIBLIOGRAPHY

Fred Eggan, *Social Organization of the Western Pueblos.*
Mischa Titiev, *Old Oraibi.*

— ROBERT F. SPENCER

HOSTAGE CRISES

In the 1970s and 1980s the age-old and widespread practice of hostage-taking became identified chiefly with the Middle East, where radical groups took hostages for leverage over state opponents too powerful to face on the field of battle. Beginning in the late 1960s rival Palestinian factions, often acting in defiance of the Palestine Liberation Organization (PLO), hijacked airliners to draw attention to their cause. In one of the most dramatic hostage incidents the terrorist group Black September seized eleven Israeli athletes at the 1972 Olympic Games in Munich. Caught in a German police ambush, all the hostages and five of the eight guerrillas died. As the decade progressed, bringing greater international support and recognition, Palestinian groups gradually abandoned as counterproductive the taking of hostages.

More spectacular were the hostage incidents that followed the success of the 1979 Iranian revolution. When the United States admitted the deposed shah, Muhammad Reza Pahlavi, for medical treatment, Iranians suspected a conspiracy to restore him to the throne. On

Nov. 4, 1979, militant students seized the U.S. embassy in Tehran, taking hostage its sixty-three occupants. They demanded return of the shah and all his wealth. The Iranian government supported the students. Seizure of the embassy served many purposes, not the least of which was to direct attention away from internal problems and toward the "Great Satan," the United States. The hostage crisis lasted more than a year. President Jimmy Carter's administration attempted to free its diplomats by every conceivable method, including an abortive rescue mission, all to no avail. President Carter lost the 1980 election to Ronald Reagan, who made much of Carter's alleged softness toward the Iranians. Eventually Algeria worked out an agreement, including the return of $8 billion in Iranian assets held in the United States, ending the crisis. The beleaguered hostages left Iran on Jan. 20, 1981, only hours after Reagan was sworn in as president, constituting a final humiliation of President Carter on this matter.

President Reagan, however, was to have his own hostage problems with Shiite Iran. The success of militant Islam in Iran galvanized the discontented throughout the Middle East. Shortly after the June 1982 Israeli invasion of Lebanon extremist Shiite groups, some closely allied with Iran, others with no apparent connection, began to seize Western hostages in retaliation for real and imagined wrongs. In the throes of civil war the city of Beirut became the center of this activity. U.S. citizens became prime targets, in part because of Washington's continuing support for Israel, and by early 1985 seven people had been taken hostage. President Reagan was in a vulnerable position because of his earlier taunting of his predecessor. National Security Council officials suggested that the United States take advantage of the fact that Iran, then engaged in a bloody war with Iraq, was in desperate need of arms. Presuming that Iran controlled the hostage-takers in Beirut, the officials recommended selling arms for hostages and negotiating with Iranian moderates. Soon quantities of U.S. arms began to arrive in Tehran via a complicated process of questionable constitutionality involving dealings with Israel and Nicaraguan rebels (Contras), but the United States got little in return. Only three hostages were released and three others took their places. The arrangement came to an abrupt end in November 1986 when news of the secret transactions leaked and became part of the Iran-Contra congressional investigation. The last of the U.S. hostages, the journalist Terry Anderson, regained his freedom in December 1991.

[See also Beirut Bombing; Iran-Contra Affair; Middle East, Relations with; Terrorism.]

BIBLIOGRAPHY

Terry A. Anderson, *Den of Lions: Memoirs of Seven Years* (New York, 1993).

Warren Christopher et al., *American Hostages in Iran: The Conduct of a Crisis* (New Haven, 1985).

Theodore Draper, *A Very Thin Line: The Iran-Contra Affair* (New York, 1991).

— JAMES F. GOODE

HOUSE COMMITTEE ON UN-AMERICAN ACTIVITIES

In 1938 a resolution of the House of Representatives authorized appointment of a special committee to investigate "un-American propaganda activities in the United States," whether "instigated from foreign countries or of a domestic origin," that attacked the nation's government "as guaranteed by the Constitution." The committee's findings were to aid Congress "in any necessary remedial legislation." Pursuant to the resolution the Special Committee on Un-American Activities (HUAC) was established in the same year under the chairmanship of Democratic Rep. Martin Dies, Jr., of Texas.

The committee was not the first to conduct a congressional inquiry into subversion. Earlier inquiries aimed at communism and other "isms" had been undertaken in 1919, 1930, and 1934. But Dies's committee was to be the most strident, controversial, and lasting. It won five renewals by overwhelming votes, and in 1945 it was made a standing committee of the House of Representatives.

Chief sponsor of the move to set up the committee was Democratic Rep. Samuel Dickstein of New York, who expected it to concentrate on ferreting out foreign agents, notably those from Nazi Germany and the Soviet Union. But under Dies and his successors the committee, although giving due attention to Communists and Fascists, directed much of its fire at New Deal liberals, intellectuals, artists, labor leaders, and immigrants. Bias against Jews and blacks bubbled close to the surface of many of the committee's inquiries.

HUAC Chairman Martin Dies, Jr., accused eleven-year-old actress Shirley Temple of being a "Red."

The Committee on Un-American Activities, rechristened the Internal Security Committee in 1969, reached its apogee in the years between the end of World War II and the early 1950's, when a parade of turncoat radicals and publicity-seekers came before it to testify against alleged subversives in government, labor unions, the press, religious organizations, and Hollywood. Committee hearings were characterized by the badgering of unfriendly witnesses and by scant regard for due process. Frequently they had their zanier moments, as when Chairman Dies accused eleven-year-old actress Shirley Temple of being a "Red." Not a few ambitious members of the House, among them Richard M. Nixon, achieved national publicity through the committee. In 1948–49 Nixon starred in the investigation of Alger Hiss, a high-ranking State Department official subsequently convicted of perjury. One zealous committee chairman, J. Parnell Thomas of New Jersey, was sent to a federal penitentiary for defrauding the government during the early 1940's by padding his office's payroll with the names of persons who did not work for him and then pocketing their salaries.

HUAC declined in prominence with the rise in the early 1950's of the flamboyant Sen. Joseph R. McCarthy of Wisconsin, whose Senate investigations drove HUAC's own hearings from the national headlines. Indirectly a victim of the public reaction against McCarthyism, the committee was relatively quiescent from the late 1950's on. In January 1975 the House abolished the committee.

BIBLIOGRAPHY

Alvah Bessie, *Inquisition in Eden.*
W. F. Buckley, *The Committee and Its Critics.*
R. K. Carr, *The House Committee on Un-American Activities, 1945–1950.*
Walter Goodman, *The Committee.*
A. R. Ogden, *The Dies Committee.*

— HOWARD H. QUINT

HOUSING

American housing has been shaped by two quite different historic influences. One stems from traditional values of American individualism: self-reliance, family independence, and private enterprise. The other, an older and more universal tradition, reflects civic values: community pride, and public responsibility for the collective welfare.

One obvious heritage from pioneering days is the desire for home ownership. On each successive frontier settlers built themselves primitive shelters, which were gradually replaced by better structures as family resources expanded. The freestanding house, individually owned even if produced by a commercial builder, is still the dominant and favored building type wherever land prices and convenience permit.

But civic requirements have also influenced American homes from the start. The colonial towns of the eastern seaboard apparently exercised a relatively high degree of community responsibility for the period, in terms of elementary municipal services and regulations with respect to roads,

Screen star Gary Cooper tells the House Committee on Un-American Activities that he had rejected a number of movie roles because the scripts were "tinged with Communist ideas," though he could not recall the names of the scripts. October 23, 1947. (UPI/Corbis-Bettmann)

fire safety, and minimal sanitation. In the higher density centers, wooden structures were outlawed in favor of a European dwelling form, the brick row house. Piped water systems were beginning to reach homes in several communities before the Revolution. As the frontier moved westward, civic initiative was weaker, and the homestead ideal had a stronger influence on urban patterns. Later, the midwestern bungalow and the western ranch house flooded eastern suburbs.

But economic progress, modern science, and technology steadily increased the burden of collective problems and responsibilities with respect to living conditions. In the early stages, industrialization and the immigrant flood led to factory enclaves with company-built housing, but the major result was big cities where poverty, crowding, and land prices created slums that neither individual nor commercial enterprise has been able to remedy. Meanwhile, the great public health revolution created a new concept of "minimum standards," essential to the welfare of both rich and poor. And municipalities slowly began to develop the vast present-day network of sanitary services and housing regulations.

The modern bathroom and kitchen were great achievements in which America led the world. But they also raised both the direct and indirect costs of minimal housing, and helped to put lower-income families outside the market for acceptable accommodations. Rising central densities, with stricter regulation of new construction, also increased costs. The slums remained, in many cases more crowded than ever.

Transportation technology started a new chapter in housing history. The automobile, following the railroad and trolley car, opened up vast areas of cheap suburban land for middle- and upper-class home ownership, inaugurating a period of chaotic metropolitan expansion. The old slums still accommodated the latest waves of low-income immigrants, and there were ever-widening rings of blight, decay, and overcrowding in once-adequate residential districts.

A demand for more positive measures to improve urban housing conditions began to take shape even before World War I, stimulated by European examples, but it was a series of national emergencies that sparked direct public action. In 1917 the federal government built housing projects for war workers. In the postwar shortage, several state and local governments took various tentative steps. Some civic-minded private experiments had considerable influence on later housing and community design practice.

With the depression of 1929 came disaster in the housing market, critical unemployment in the building industry, and many kinds of federal measures, including overall credit controls, mortgage insurance for private builders, and subsidies for low-rent public housing. World War II and its aftermath again brought emergency shortages, with a big federal program for war workers, then special aids for veterans. But the decay in central districts continued. Federal grants for redevelopment were inaugurated in 1949, with added incentives since 1954 for rehabilitation, conservation, broader physical planning, and private housing. Federal mortgage insurance and other credit aids stimulated millions of suburban tract houses, sporadic rental construction, some cooperatives, and some housing initiative for the elderly, but the erosion of adequate housing continued, particularly for families of minority race. Several states provided additional housing aids, and most residential development became subject to public guidance through local planning and zoning as well as building regulations, but little effective planning or housing responsibility was shown at the metropolitan level. Suburbia became a "problem area" along with blighted central districts.

In 1965 the cabinet-level Department of Housing and Urban Development (HUD) was established by Congress to alleviate some of these problems. In 1968, under the Housing and Urban Development Act, HUD was able to provide financing for homes and rental housing for low- and middle-income families. One of the major functions of HUD is to eliminate discrimination in construction projects in which it is involved, and it has favored cities with records of nondiscrimination.

BIBLIOGRAPHY

Edith Elmer Wood, *The Housing of the Unskilled Wage Earner*, and *Recent Trends in American Housing.*

— CATHERINE BAUER WURSTER

HOUSING IN THE LATE TWENTIETH CENTURY

The most common types of housing in the late twentieth century included single-family, detached suburban houses; suburban low-rise apartment buildings; high-rise, inner-city apartments; condominium or cooperative apartments; and mobile homes. The 1990 census counted 102 million year-round housing units in the United States. Of these, 59 million (72 percent) were in single-unit structures; 9.6 percent of housing structures contained from two to four units; 17.7 percent had five or more; and 7.2 percent were mobile homes. Southern states had the greatest number of single units and mobile homes, while the heavily urbanized northern states were the most frequent sites of structures of ten or more units.

Housing is affected by economic, social, political, and demographic factors. Economics plays an inexorable role in individual choice. The cost for a one-family house in the United States has been a prominent indicator of inflation since the mid-1970s. The average sale price of newly constructed houses jumped from $39,300 in 1975 to $120,000 in 1991. The Northeast, at $155,400 per average house, and the West, at $142,300, were the most expensive areas for housing, while the South, at $100,000, was the cheapest. Honolulu was the most expensive metropolitan area for one-family houses at $349,000; the lowest-price homes were in Louisville, Kentucky, and Tulsa, Oklahoma, at $65,400. These figures are well-known in the highly cyclical housing industry. Construction of privately owned housing units, a major indicator of economic growth, slumped from 2.02 million in 1978 to 1.062 million in 1982, recovered for several years, and then fell to a twenty-year low of 1.014 million in 1991. The hardest-hit region was the Northeast, which dropped from 278,000 starts in 1973 to 113,000 in 1991, compared to 414,000 starts in the South in 1991. In 1993 the total number of new privately owned housing units was up to 1.241 million, with an increase to 124,000 in the Northeast and a much larger increase to 554,000 in the South.

Actions of federal and state governments to reverse past racism by implementing the housing provisions of 1960s civil rights legislation have caused political controversy. While whites, blacks, Hispanics, and Asians all own modest-value property, nonwhite residents are rarely found in expensive neighborhoods, since racially biased practices block their way. These practices include redlining (bank loan discrimination), steering (directing nonwhites away from white neighborhoods), and terrorism by white homeowners. Moreover, blacks were far more likely to live in rental apartments in the crowded Northeast than whites. The region where it was easiest for blacks to buy a single-unit suburban house was in the West.

Other social factors affecting housing markets included the rising numbers of post-1960 divorces, which caused rapid housing turnover that in turn created a shortage of affordable rental units for single and recently divorced persons. As the baby-boom generation aged, divorce rates went down, and by the early 1980s the family housing market lacked new and used units at prices and monthly payments that couples and young families could afford. A corollary issue was the rising number of single people; by 1980 more than 11 million women lived alone. Problems in the 1980s and 1990s also included housing for senior citizens and housing in low-income urban neighborhoods. Rural America, the sector with the poorest plumbing and highest citings of water leakage, remained a problem area for housing.

Houses of the prosperous increasingly adapted architecture to the tastes of owners. Americans with large disposable incomes built luxurious theaters for television screens and sound equipment, arranged athletic courts, and installed complex computer systems. Their houses sometimes resembled castles, with activities focused within the moat and walls. With upper-income Americans feeling threatened physically by less well-off fellow citizens, they installed security systems. At the beginning of the 1990s, one-eighth of the wealthiest in the United States lived in guarded compounds.

[See also Housing and Urban Development, Department of.]

BIBLIOGRAPHY

John S. Adams, *Housing America in the 1980s* (New York, 1987).

David C. Shapiro et al., *A New Housing Policy for America* (Philadelphia, 1988).

— GRAHAM RUSSELL HODGES

HOUSING AND URBAN DEVELOPMENT, DEPARTMENT OF

The Department of Housing and Urban Development (HUD), cabinet-level department established on Sept. 9, 1965, by President Lyndon B. Johnson. The fundamental argument of proponents of the new department centered on the tremendous urbanization that had transformed twentieth-century America. The predominantly urban character of American society prompted Democratic Representative Dante B. Fascell of Florida to sponsor the bill establishing the department, with the Housing and Home Finance Agency as its nucleus. With passage of the Housing and Urban Development Acts of 1965 and 1968 and the model cities legislation of 1966, HUD received programs that went beyond traditional public housing, urban renewal, and Federal Housing Administration insurance, including a rent supplement program for low-income families, an inner-city rebuilding program (model cities), and an interest-subsidy program for both multifamily dwellers and home buyers. As of the mid-1990s no president had shown as much faith in such funding as Johnson, but President Richard Nixon thought the model cities program "one of the worst boondoggles left over from Johnson's Great Society." His HUD secretary, George Romney, announced a moratorium on all federal housing programs in early 1973. Two separate White House task forces evaluated the programs and both concluded they should be continued. Faced with these reports and opposition from his own cabinet members, Nixon approved $2.3 billion to fund model cities from 1969 to 1973. In 1974 the program was made a part of special revenue-sharing for community development, and funding continued at a rate that was consistent with the target figures the Johnson administration had originally given to Congress. Nonetheless, the president installed Secretary James T. Lynn at the end of 1972 with instructions to dismantle the department. Congressional Democrats, however, were able to extract a small housing program within the Section 8 rental assistance clause of subsequent legislation.

President Jimmy Carter wanted to revive federal housing without significant increase in expenditures. Officials under HUD Secretary Patricia Roberts Harris approached the housing problem with serious intentions, but instead of advancing initiatives in the administration decided to try to make the small Nixon program work. During the Carter years 100,000 units were built annually for low-income families, but this was 400,000 to 500,000 units short of the annual number built earlier. During President Ronald Reagan's administration, budget cutters found a target in the Section 8 program, leaving only 50,000 units in the budget. The duty of imposing austerity fell to HUD Secretary Samuel Pierce, Jr., whose aides later were imprisoned for taking bribes. President George Bush's HUD secretary, Jack Kemp, canceled HUD's moderate rehabilitation program, its coinsurance plan with private mortgage companies, and its retirement center program. In an overreaction to abuses of his predecessor, Kemp instituted a series of draconian penalties against erring developers and managers of HUD-assisted housing. On the positive side, he championed his theme of "empowerment" by persuading Congress to approve purchase of public housing units by tenants.

Because of concern for national economic recovery and growth, President Bill Clinton appointed a vigorous personality as HUD secretary in 1993, the former mayor of San Antonio, Henry Cisneros. Budget restraints prevented Cisneros from increasing housing, and he focused on such issues as discrimination and homelessness, bringing attention to them by using such public incidents as those in Vidor, Texas, where the Ku Klux Klan intimidated African Americans in public housing, and in Washington, D.C., where a homeless woman died in front of the HUD building. As a result of Republican victories in the 1994 congressional elections, Secretary Cisneros promulgated a radical downsizing of HUD, consolidating its various programs into four basic ones, all in the name of "reinventing HUD."

[See also Housing.]

BIBLIOGRAPHY

Tom Forrester Lord, *Decent Housing: A Promise to Keep* (Cambridge, Mass., 1977).

M. Carter McFarland, *Federal Government and Urban Problems* (Westview, Colo., 1978).

— TOM FORRESTER LORD

HUDSON RIVER

Giovanni da Verrazano, an Italian explorer in French employ, was, so far as is known, the first white man to have seen the Hudson River. In 1524, after entering New York Harbor, he wrote of "a very large river, deep at its mouth," which he had ascended for about half a league. The Portuguese Esteban Gómez noticed the Hudson in 1525. French traders traversed it, mostly from Canada, during the 16th century, trading with the Mohawk Indians, and founded a small fort near the site of Albany in 1540, but this was later abandoned. Henry Hudson, exploring for the Dutch West India Company, ascended the river in 1609 as far as the neighborhood of Albany and sent some of his men to explore it some twenty-five miles farther, past the mouth of the Mohawk. It thereupon became an artery for Dutch colonization, with Albany founded as a fur-trading station in 1614. Other settlements along the river soon followed. A party of Walloons suffering persecution in the Flemish Netherlands emigrated to what is now Ulster County in 1660, founding Kingston and other villages, while Germans from the Palatinate settled in the valley in 1710. After the British took over the Dutch possessions in 1664 the English population increased rapidly.

The Hudson River was perhaps the greatest single factor in making New York City the American metropolis, yet its depth and breadth long kept trains from entering the city from the west.

For more than a century after settlement began the Hudson was almost the only avenue of travel and transportation between what is now upper New York State and New York City or the coast, and for more than two centuries it remained the chief avenue. During these two centuries, freight and passengers were carried up and down almost entirely in sloops. After the Erie Canal was completed in 1825, all its great through traffic to and from New York State, the Great Lakes region, and the Middle West used the Hudson between Albany and New York, the Champlain Canal adding more business to and from northern New York, Vermont, and Canada. Robert Fulton's *Clermont* was tested on the Hudson in 1807, and thereafter steamboats began to displace the sloops. Tugs or towboats drew great fleets of loaded Erie Canal boats from Albany down to New York, bringing them back sometimes loaded, sometimes empty. Large and elegant passenger steamboats plied the river in the mid-19th century, and were the pawns in traffic wars between Cornelius Vanderbilt, Daniel Drew, and others. The completion in 1851 of the Hudson River Railroad along its eastern bank brought about a steady diminution of the river's freight traffic. The fine steamboats, because of their greater comfort and luxury, held a considerable share of the through passenger traffic for decades afterward.

The Hudson was perhaps the greatest single factor in making New York City the American metropolis; yet it handicapped the city, too. It is so vast that all railroads from the west (save the New York Central, coming via Albany and the east bank) had to stop on the New Jersey shore and transfer passengers and freight across by ferry. Only one railroad entered from the west—the Pennsylvania, which completed a tunnel connection under the river in 1910. The river is so wide and deep, its banks for the most part so rugged, that below Albany, nearly 150 miles from its mouth, it was not bridged until 1889, when a cantilever railroad structure was completed at Poughkeepsie. Thirty-six years elapsed before the next bridging, that at Bear Mountain in 1925; and the first bridge to cross at New York City was the George Washington suspension bridge, in 1931. (The Holland Tunnel, connecting Manhattan and New Jersey, was completed in 1927.) Because of its size and the fact that for the most part it is an estuary rather than a river, the Hudson has never been subject to serious floods.

BIBLIOGRAPHY

H. Robert Boyle, *The Hudson River: A Natural and Unnatural History.*

Carl Carmer, *The Hudson.*

John Reed, *The Hudson River Valley.*

— ALVIN F. HARLOW

HUDSON'S BAY COMPANY

Hudson's Bay Company came into being as a result of the western explorations of Pierre Esprit Radisson and Médard Chouart, Sieur de Groseilliers, in the middle of the 17th century. On trips into the Wisconsin and Minnesota country they learned from the Indians of a great fur country northwest of Lake Superior that might be reached via Hudson Bay. This idea, linked with one of a probable Northwest Passage through Hudson Bay, led the Frenchmen to England in the middle 1660's. There a sort of syndicate of wealthy and influential men was formed to try out their ideas. Out of this grew the Hudson's Bay Company, which received its charter on May 2, 1670, as the Governor and Company of Adventurers of England Trading into Hudson's Bay. Under that charter and supplemental charters the company still operates, although it has now lost its monopoly of trade, its territory, and its administrative rights in the West that were granted by the first document. It is thus one of the oldest commercial corporations in existence.

During the heyday of the fur trade, the company had posts in most parts of what is now Canada. It also had a few forts on U.S. soil. These were mostly along the boundary line west from Grand Portage, in the area where the chief impact of the company on U.S. history was felt. Some of that impact came with the bitter struggle carried on between the Hudson's Bay Company and the North West Company, which resulted largely from the establishment by Thomas Douglas, Lord Selkirk, of a colony on company lands near the Red River of the North (now Manitoba) in 1811. Selkirk was one of the largest owners of stock in the English company. Just before the differences were settled by a union of the two companies in 1821, Selkirk died, and for some years his colony was administered by the company. The colony's founding and struggles had a bearing on the founding of Fort Saint Anthony (now Fort Snelling) in 1819; the misfortunes of the colonists led many of them to emigrate to Fort Snelling to be Minnesota's earliest settlers. The need of a market for the colony led to the development of the Red River cart traffic with Minnesota settlements; and proximity to U.S. soil and discontent of the colonists under company rule led to annexation hopes and schemes on both the part of the colonists and the United States between 1849 and the surrender of the company's territories in 1869.

Other effects of the company on Minnesota and North Dakota history are those resulting from the sending of missionaries to the Indians and half-breeds under the aegis of the company. Missionaries also played an important part in the company's relations to the history of the Oregon country, where company men appeared after the union of 1821 to carry on the fur trade begun years earlier by the North West Company, and where a joint occupation agreement between the United States and Great Britain was in force between 1818 and 1846. By welcoming American traders, explorers, missionaries, and settlers, Dr. John McLoughlin, the company's chief factor, helped Oregon to become American, though the decline of the fur trade is probably the basic reason for Great Britain's consent in 1846 to abandon its claims south of the forty-ninth parallel and thus avert a threatened war.

BIBLIOGRAPHY

George Bryce, *The Remarkable History of the Hudson's Bay Company.*
Douglas MacKay, *The Honourable Company.*
Beckles Willson, *The Great Company.*

— GRACE LEE NUTE

HUGUENOTS

The term Huguenot, of unknown origin, was first applied to French Protestants during the religious struggles of the 16th century. Henry IV had granted religious toleration to his Protestant subjects by the Edict of Nantes (1598), but this was revoked by Louis XIV in 1685. Approximately 300,000 persecuted French Huguenots fled to Prussia, Switzerland, Holland, England, and America. Attempted settlements in Florida and South Carolina (1562 and l564) failed. In 1623 Huguenots, largely French-speaking Walloons, settled New Amsterdam. Peter Minuit was a Walloon, and Jean Vigne, first white child born on Manhattan Island, was French and probably Huguenot. Fort Orange (Albany), Kingston, and New Paltz in New York were Huguenot settlements. Some 200 or 300 Huguenot families came to Boston after the Dragonades.

After 1685 increasing numbers of Huguenots came to America, settling in Rhode Island, in Hartford and Milford in Connecticut, and in New Rochelle, N.Y. They mingled with other settlers in Delaware, Maryland, and Pennsylvania, where they were called Dutchmen and confused with German settlers. In Virginia the first of the "French Protestant Refugees," as the name appears officially in the Virginia records, was Nicholas Martiau. He arrived before 1620 and is the earliest known Virginia ancestor of George Washington. The shipload coming to Manakintowne on July 23, 1700, and two more shiploads in the same year, made up the largest single settlements of Huguenots in America. This group with its local church and pastor was absorbed into the Church of England. King William Parish was set aside for them, but their blood soon mingled with the English people of the colony.

In South Carolina Huguenots began coming in 1670, played a large part in the settlement of Charleston in 1680, and by 1687 had established four settlements largely or wholly French: Jamestown on the Santee River, the "Orange Quarter" on the Cooper River, Saint John's Berkeley, and Charleston. In 1732, 360 French-Swiss Protestants settled Purysburg on the Savannah River, and in 1764 the last French colony was founded, New Bordeaux in Abbeville County. Huguenots preserved their identity in South Carolina more completely than in other colonies. The only Huguenot church in America is in Charleston, preserving its service, doctrine, and organization unchanged. The Huguenot religion was Calvinistic in theology, ritual in form, Presbyterian in government, and tolerant in principle. Until well within the 20th century one service each year was conducted in French in the Charleston Huguenot church, and the same continuity of tradition is true of the people.

BIBLIOGRAPHY

Donald Douglas, *The Huguenot: Emigrations, Particularly to New England.*

— JAMES ELLIOTT WALMSLEY

HUMAN RIGHTS

Conceptions of human rights found expression as early as 1639 in the "Act for the liberties of the people" approved by the Maryland General Assembly a hundred and fifty years before Congress adopted the Bill of Rights of the U.S. Constitution. This colonial enactment provided that all freemen should "have and enjoy all such rights liberties immunities privileges and free customs . . . as any natural born subject of England hath or ought to have or enjoy." The idea that certain rights and liberties are inseparable from the citizen as a free man was rooted in the biblical conceptions of covenant, of man made in the image of God, of freedom of the will to choose good or evil, and of right law being ultimately founded on the righteousness of God and not on the will of the king. It was rooted in the classical tradition of natural law and the teachings of Stoic philosophy regarding the inviolability of human dignity. It found support in the natural law philosophy of John Locke; the Glorious Revolution of 1688; the natural rights teachings of Baruch Spinoza, John Milton, Hugo Grotius, and Samuel von Pufendorf; and, in the late 18th century, the writings of the French Enlightenment. The emphasis on the right of the individual conscience that was associated with the Protestant and Puritan reformations and the stress on the inherent dignity of man that can be found in the great Renaissance writers like Desiderius Erasmus and Giovanni Pico della Mirandola left their mark. The culmination was the idea that certain rights and liberties are so natural to man that every man has them in fact or ought to have them by right. They are rights and liberties that are not dependent upon any government; they are inherent in the very nature of man and so are beyond the power of any government to give or to take away.

No catalog of human rights provides more than broad ideals or particular illustrations. The Declaration of Independence names life, liberty, and the pursuit of happiness. Locke mentions rights to life, liberty, and estates or property; freedom of religious conscience; the right to marry and have children; and the right of parents to teach their children. In 1789, when the U.S. Constitution was ratified, Congress at once undertook to fulfill the wish of the American people to add a bill of rights, and this was accomplished by the first ten amendments, which were ratified in 1791. While the amendments enumerated specific guarantees, the Ninth Amendment was designed to foreclose the argument that rights that were not named were necessarily excluded. The Supreme Court has, in fact, recognized rights and liberties that have not been expressly enumerated—the right of parents to educate their children; the right of privacy, specifically in terms of the right to use contraceptives; the right to study a foreign language; and freedom to associate and the right of privacy in one's associations. In addition the Court has recognized "peripheral rights" that help secure the guaranteed rights. Thus, human rights have been—and continue to be—in a process of evolution and differentiation. Some expressly enumerated guarantees (such as the right to bear arms) receive recognition only because they are provided for in a written constitution, while others, whether written or unwritten, have come to receive a high priority because they are considered indispensable for life in a free and just society; and it is the latter that have come to be known as human rights and have received international recognition or sanction, as in the Nuremberg trials of the Nazi war criminals and in the declarations of human rights adopted by the United Nations and the Council of Europe.

BIBLIOGRAPHY

Irving Brant, *The Bill of Rights.*

Zachariah Chafee, Jr., *Documents on Fundamental Human Rights.*

Milton R. Konvitz, *Fundamental Liberties of a Free People.*

Roscoe Pound, *The Development of Constitutional Guarantees of Liberty.*

— MILTON R. KONVITZ

HUMAN RIGHTS DURING THE LATE TWENTIETH CENTURY

The atrocities committed during World War II provided the catalyst for the developments in human rights law that characterized the second half of the twentieth century. Although there is no precise agreement on the content of human rights, three substantive areas have been recognized—individual rights, economic and social rights, and collective rights. A major innovation of the approach to human rights has been the recognition that rights are interdependent and that all persons are entitled not only to traditional civil and political rights but to economic, social, and cultural rights. The international community has also recognized that the observance of human rights by countries for their own nationals is a matter of international concern.

Human rights were central in the planning and drafting of the United Nations Charter (1945), which reaffirms the faith of the world's peoples in "fundamental human rights, in the dignity and worth of the human person, in the equal rights of men and women and of nations large and small." Chapter I, article I, specifies that one of the purposes of the United Nations is to "achieve international co-operation in . . . promoting and encouraging respect for human rights and for fundamental freedoms for all without distinction as to race, sex, language or religion." Through the charter, the United Nations is required to promote the observance of human rights, and all member states are pledged to cooperate in the achievement of this goal. Despite strong human rights provisions, the charter includes no codification or enumeration of rights. The Commission on Human Rights was created to draft such a list. As chair of the first Human Rights Committee, Eleanor Roosevelt was instrumental in securing the Universal Declaration of Human Rights, adopted without dissent by the General Assembly in 1948. The declaration was not intended to be a legally binding document but was, as stated in its preamble, a "common standard of achievement for all people and all nations." Its importance, however, cannot be overestimated. It has been characterized as similar to the Magna Carta, its provisions have been incorporated in the constitutions of many countries, and many of its articles have been accepted as international law. As a statement of goals and principles the declaration was a major step. Its thirty articles spell out basic civil, political, economic, social, and cultural rights: freedom of religion, expression, and assembly; freedom from arbitrary arrests or ex post facto laws; and equal protection under the law. It also recognizes a right to work, to education, and to a standard of living adequate to health and well-being.

The atrocities committed during World War II spurred the developments in human rights law in the second half of the twentieth century.

To achieve the rights contained in the Universal Declaration, two multilateral conventions, one on civil and political rights, the other on social and economic rights, were drafted by the Human Rights Committee in 1954 and approved by the General Assembly in 1966. These conventions are legally binding on the nations that ratify them and subject those nations to the enforcement procedures set forth. The International Covenant on Civil and Political Rights, ratified by the United States in 1992 and by 114 other countries, not only encompasses most of the rights contained in the U.S. Bill of Rights but provides for the right to self-determination, the right to dispose of property, the right to nationality at birth, the right to move freely within a country, and the right to leave a country. It prohibits slavery; forced or compulsory labor; unlawful interference with privacy, family, or honor and reputation; propaganda for war; and advocacy of national, racial, or religious hatred that constitutes incitement to discrimination, hostility, or violence. The International Covenant on Economic, Social and Cultural Rights, ratified by more than 118 states, excluding the United States, protects the right to work and just and favorable conditions of work, including fair wages and equal remuneration for work of equal value; the right to social security and an adequate standard of living; the right to the highest attainable standard of physical and mental health; the right to education; and the right to take part in cultural life and to enjoy the benefits of scientific progress.

Numerous human rights conventions have been widely ratified, including the Convention on the Prevention and Punishment of the Crime of Genocide, the Convention on the Elimination of All Forms of Racial Discrimination, the Convention on the Elimination of All Forms of Discrimination Against Women, the Convention on the Elimination of Torture, and the Convention on Rights of the Child. Despite the proliferation of instruments and conventions that define and seek to protect human rights, a fundamental weakness of the system is a lack of effective enforcement mechanisms. Typically, nations that have ratified the conventions are required to report on their progress toward fulfilling their commitments. Unless a state, through a separate agreement, allows an individual to bring a complaint against the state, the individual has no recourse for relief from human rights abuses in an international forum. Nevertheless, respect for human rights is espoused by virtually all nations, has become an important foreign policy issue, and influences the activities of such organizations as the International Monetary Fund and the World Bank.

In the second half of the twentieth century, human rights of specific groups, such as women, minorities, indigenous peoples, and children, were addressed by the international community. Human rights of women are particularly and systematically abused through gender-based violence, sexual exploitation, harassment, and international trafficking in women. As a group, women are particularly vulnerable to religious extremism and to certain traditional and customary practices, such as dowry and genital mutilation. In addition, during armed conflicts, women are often systematically subjected to rape and prostitution. In 1994 the United Nations took a significant step toward addressing this serious human rights violation by adopting the Declaration on the Elimination of Violence Against Women, which urges nations to combat violence perpetrated against women not only by the state but by individuals (including domestic violence).

In 1993 the World Conference on Human Rights sponsored by the United Nations was held in Vienna. Nearly every country sent an official delegation to the conference. The Vienna Declaration reaffirmed the universality of human rights despite the efforts of some countries, notably China, to assert that human rights are not universal but culturally based. It affirmed that all human rights are interdependent and that civil and political rights must be linked with economic and social rights. An important result of the conference was the recognition of women's rights as human rights and the emphasis on rights of minority and indigenous peoples. The Vienna Declaration affirmed that the human rights of women and girls are an inalienable, integral, and indivisible part of universal human rights and urged full and equal participation of women; the eradication of all forms of discrimination on grounds of sex became a priority objective of the international community.

A significant development in the late twentieth century was the emphasis on democracy as a human right. After the demise of the Soviet Union and the political upheavals accompanied by the overthrow of dictators, there were greater freedoms and choices for many oppressed peoples. Democracy based on the freely expressed will and choice of peoples to determine their political, economic, social, and cultural systems was recognized as an important aspect of human rights law. The Vienna Declaration of 1993 and other human rights instruments affirm that democracy, development and respect for human rights, and fundamental freedoms are interdependent and reinforce each other.

The U.S. position on human rights is ambiguous. The Constitution and the Bill of Rights are based on the liberal tradition articulated by the philosopher John Locke and recognize that the individual possesses certain inalienable rights that the government may not trample on. They protect civil and political rights but not economic and social rights. Individual rights are protected from government infringement and increase individual liberty. They do not allow an individual to make claims upon the government for economic or social rights, such as subsistence and housing. Attempts through litigation to secure constitutional protection for economic and social rights, such as the right to an education or to a minimum standard of living, have failed. In practice, however, free education is provided to all, and government entitlement programs, such as social security and welfare, have been a part of U.S. law for several decades.

Despite its relatively good record with respect to observance and protection of human rights, until 1986 the United States was not a party to any of the major human rights conventions. Objections were generally based on legal grounds related to, for example, federalism. The ratification in 1992 by the United States of the Covenant on Civil and Political Rights indicated a change in U.S. policy in this area. The United States continued to monitor human rights abuses throughout the world, by linking a nation's observance of human rights to the granting of some economic or strategic benefit or to most-favored-nation trade status. For example, the former Soviet Union was subjected to economic pressure because of its policy on emigration.

Despite the advances in the development and acceptance of human rights as an integral part of international law, abuses of human rights continued. Amnesty International, a leading organization in monitoring human rights abuses, reported a lack of consistent commitment to human rights among 161 governments surveyed, although no nation was prepared to admit abuses of the rights of its own nationals. The international community, through the United Nations, has been effective in setting human rights norms and securing their acceptance. The challenge for the future is to achieve these norms worldwide.

[See also Women's Movement.]

BIBLIOGRAPHY

Louis Henkin, *The Age of Rights* (New York, 1990).

Ellen L. Lutz, Hurst Hannum, and Kathryn J. Burke, eds., *New Directions in Human Rights* (Philadelphia, 1989).

— ELIZABETH F. DEFEIS

HYDROGEN BOMB

Hydrogen Bomb, a type of military weapon that derives its energy from the fusion of the nuclei of one or more light elements, particularly the deuterium and tritium isotopes of hydrogen. Nuclear physicists recognized the fusion, or thermonuclear, reaction as the source of the sun's energy as early as 1938. J. Robert Oppenheimer and other theoretical physicists in the United States saw the possibility of designing a thermonuclear weapon early in World War II but set the idea aside because its success appeared to depend on the prior development of a fission weapon (atomic bomb) to achieve the extremely high temperatures (hundreds of millions of degrees) required for fusion.

Although the United States had developed and used the atomic bomb by 1945, only modest theoretical research on fusion was done until the Soviet Union first detonated an atomic bomb in September 1949. During the next six months a largely secret, but wide-ranging, debate took place at the highest levels in the administration of Harry S. Truman over whether to develop the hydrogen bomb. Most of the members of the U.S. Atomic Energy Commission and its General Advisory Committee opposed the idea on practical and moral grounds. The military services and the Joint Congressional Committee on Atomic Energy favored development as vital to national defense. President Truman, on Jan. 31, 1950, announced his decision to accelerate work on the hydrogen bomb, thereby ending the debate and launching the commission's scientists into an emergency effort to design and test a thermonuclear weapon.

A long series of complex theoretical studies at the commission's Los Alamos, N.Mex., weapons laboratory failed to produce a feasible design, but in February 1951, Stanislaw M. Ulam and Edward Teller devised a new design principle that was incorporated in the first test device detonated at Eniwetok Atoll in the Pacific Ocean on Oct. 31, 1952. This event ushered the world into the thermonuclear age. Other nations tested thermonuclear devices—the Soviet Union in 1953, the United Kingdom in 1957, China in 1967, and France in 1968.

Meanwhile, the U.S. Atomic Energy Commission developed better materials and improved the design of thermonuclear weapons. A series of large-scale weapons tests in the Pacific during the 1950's made possible the production of fusion weapons that contained the energy of millions of tons of high explosives yet were small enough to be carried in a single missile warhead. This new weapon became the backbone of the American strategy of deterrence against Soviet nuclear attack during the cold war of the 1960's. The ultimate threat of such weapons to national security and to civilization itself was matched only by the potential benefits of the thermonuclear reaction as a source of controlled energy for peaceful purposes.

BIBLIOGRAPHY

Richard G. Hewlett and Oscar E. Anderson, Jr., *The New World, 1939–1946.*

Richard G. Hewlett and Francis Duncan, *Atomic Shield, 1947–1952.*

Henry Kissinger, *Nuclear Weapons and Foreign Policy.*

— RICHARD G. HEWLETT

I

IMMIGRATION

Immigrants are persons who have voluntarily and permanently carried themselves and their goods from their native environment to the United States for the purpose of settling and establishing a new life: they are aliens, other than returning resident aliens, who are admitted into the United States for permanent residence. The flow of migrants to the central regions of the North American continent—which came on the heels of the European voyages of discovery—constitutes the greatest movement of peoples in Western history.

In the years between 1820 and 1971—for which the most reliable and detailed figures are available—the total of persons who emigrated to the United States is 45,533,000; they came at an average annual rate of 3.7 newcomers per 1,000 of population. All regions and countries of the world figure in the massive movement of peoples that took place during that 150-year span, but the country of Germany alone sent 15.2 percent of the total, and Italy, 11.4 percent. Other nations, principally of Europe, ranked relatively high: Great Britain, 10.5 percent; Ireland, 10.3 percent; Austria-Hungary, 9.4 percent; Canada, 8.8 percent; Russia and the Soviet Union, 7.4 percent; Mexico, 3.6 percent; and Sweden, 2.8 percent. France, Greece, Norway, Poland, China, and the West Indies each sent from 1 percent to 1.99 percent of the total.

The account of American immigration may be divided into three periods: (1) the colonial, from 1607 to 1776; (2) the "old" immigration, from 1776 to 1890; and (3) the "new" immigration, of the 1890's and the 20th century. Immigrants from northern and western Europe predominated until the close of the second period, about 85 percent of immigrants arriving before 1883 having come from these areas.

Some idea of the magnitude of this migration is conveyed by the fact that included in the total population of 76 million in the continental United States in 1900 were 10.5 million born in Europe and 26 million more with at least one foreign-born parent. According to the census of 1940, in a total white population of about 132 million, the foreign-born and persons with at least one foreign-born parent amounted to 34.5 million, or 26 percent of the total. The foreign stock (that is, the number of foreign-born plus those of foreign or mixed foreign and native parentage) decreased slowly in absolute figures after World War II, but the percentage of persons in this category fell markedly from near 31 percent in 1930 to 22.3 percent in 1950; 18 percent in 1960; and 15.5 percent in 1970. The relative decline in the foreign stock reflects in a graphic way the changes in policy expressed in the restriction laws of 1921, 1924, 1952, and 1965.

Immigration Laws

The first sweeping restriction of immigration into the United States was not effected until the passage of the Immigration Act of 1921. And then soon thereafter the Immigration Act of 1924, commonly known as the Johnson Bill, was passed by Congress by overwhelming majorities and signed by President Calvin Coolidge on May 26, 1924, and remained essentially in force to 1952. It provided a more drastic limitation on numbers of immigrants than had the act of 1921 by reducing the quota from 3 percent, on the basis of the number of foreign-born of various nationalities as recorded in the 1910 census, to 2 percent, on the basis of the 1890 census. Until 1920 there had been only a qualitative limitation on immigration, the exclusion of an individual being based on a judgment that he was unfit in health or character or because of a criminal record.

The act of 1924 provided for an annual quota of 164,667 until July 1, 1927; at that time the quota was to be fixed at 150,000 and the admission of persons of any national group eligible for naturalization was to be limited to the percentage of that base figure that that national group had constituted in the total population in 1920.

The immigration acts of 1921 and after are exclusionary with respect to certain areas of Europe, the Orient, Africa, and Oceania. They omit consideration of the Western Hemisphere, and thus it happens that the actual immigration since the 1920's has always far exceeded the stated quota totals. Immigration from Canada and Mexico, under restriction or limitation in these years, accounts for the bulk of the immigration outside the framework of the quota allowances. In addition, a number of Europeans in special situations, but outside the quota allowances, have been admitted in every year by special acts of Congress.

The Immigration and Nationality Act of 1952, the McCarran-Walter Act, simplified the national-origins formula of 1924 by basing the annual quotas of national groups on a flat one-sixth of 1 percent of the population by the 1920 census. New quotas, effective Jan. 1, 1953, were established in a series of presidential proclamations for each country or quota area, and these were put in force at a level of approximately 160,000 per annum.

In addition a number of special acts were passed between 1948 and 1960 to authorize the entry of certain groups of displaced persons and refugees from Communist-dominated countries, victims of natural calamities, and orphan children, all outside the ceilings and quotas otherwise established.

The Act of 1965 (Public Law 89-236), effective Dec. 1 of that year and still in force in the mid-1970's, set aside the system of quota by national origin. With respect to the Eastern Hemisphere it set up instead an overall limit of 170,000 for quota immigrants and an annual limit of 20,000 for natives of any single foreign state. (For a transition period, to June 1968, it provided that unused quotas might be reassigned.) In the categories of "immediate relative" and "special immigrant" were placed parents, spouses, and children under twenty-one years of age whose parents were U.S. citizens; persons in those categories were to be admitted without regard to quota limitations. The issuance of entry visas for other applicants was made subject to a new preference system: high priority to persons who desired reunification with their families and relatives; second priority to persons who brought special abilities, whether artistic, scientific, or professional; next, skilled workers; then, unskilled labor; and finally, displaced persons or refugees from political, racial, or religious discrimination.

Effective Dec. 1, 1965, provision was made for the entry of persons called special immigrants, who were exempt from numerical ceilings. This category included parents, spouses, and children of U.S. citizens; returning resident aliens; certain former citizens; and natives of Western Hemisphere countries and their spouses and children. Effective July 1, 1968, a ceiling figure of 120,000 with respect to the total of Western Hemisphere natives was set, but this placed no limitation on the number admissible from any single country, and it exempted immediate relatives and other special immigrants.

With respect to natives of the Western Hemisphere the figure of 120,000 was set, effective July 1, 1968, but without limitation on the number from any single country and with the exemption of immediate relatives and special immigrants from the ceiling. In regard to all applicants in the categories of skilled and unskilled laborers, the new law required that the U.S. Department of Labor certify that their entry would not adversely affect the wages and working conditions of U.S. workers in similar employment.

Colonial Immigration

The colonial, the old, and the new immigrations had their own characteristic forms and causes; they involved different groups within their respective countries of origin. The Dutch colony of New Netherland for fifty years separated the English colonies of New England and those of the South. Throughout the English settlements American blood was already decidedly mixed by 1776, although early American institutions remained basically Anglo-Saxon. There were large settlements of Scotch-Irish on the frontier; Huguenot French in the larger cities as far south as the Carolinas; small Jewish groups from Spain and Portugal in Rhode Island; Welsh in Pennsylvania; Germans in Pennsylvania and in scattered settlements throughout the South; Swedes in present-day Delaware; and Danes, Scotch, Irish, and Finns in the highly cosmopolitan Philadelphia of the 18th century. In Pennsylvania, for example, the Germans were so numerous that it was feared that the colony was in danger of losing its "American" character. Proprietors and speculators especially encouraged the flow of immigration as an adjunct to direct colonization. Thousands of true immigrants originating in countries other than England came as indentured servants and redemptioners, apart from the thousands of slaves from Africa. The influence of non-English immigrants on the social, economic, and cultural developments of colonial America was significant. The diversity of religions in the colonies—to take one example—made religious toleration a necessity, and the final separation of church and state, apart from its being a matter of democratic theory, became an inescapable necessity under colonial circumstances.

The Scotch-Irish and the Germans are numerically the most prominent of colonial immigrant groups. To assess the exact dimensions of Scotch-Irish immigration before 1820 is difficult. Statistics are lacking for the colonial era and even after 1820 the figures are unreliable, since large numbers of Irish persons sailed from Scottish and English ports or migrated from other British lands into America. In the 17th century there was a small number of arrivals as servants or migrants from the West Indies. There were more than 350,000 Scotch-Irish and Irish in the colonies in 1776, settled predominantly in Pennsylvania and the Appalachian frontier. Bishop John Carroll reported to Rome in 1785 that there were over 18,000 Roman Catholics in the United States and that all but 2,000 of them resided in Maryland. The total of immigrants from 1783 to 1820 is conventionally put at 250,000, of which it is doubtful more than 20 percent were Irish Catholics. As late as 1820 there were less than 4,000 Irish arrivals, and not for fifteen years was the United States more popular than British America with its official encouragement and cheaper fares, at least as a temporary resting place; nor did the Celtic surpass in numbers the Scotch-Irish division of the Irish people. Although the Scotch-Irish entered through all the ports up and down the length of the colonies, and rapidly spread inland and westward to the frontier in all sections, the real mecca of the Scotch-Irish was Pennsylvania. By 1750 this element constituted approximately 25 percent of the total population of the colony; by 1776 Benjamin Franklin estimated it at one-third of the total.

German immigration came on the heels of the settlements of peoples from the British Isles and the Netherlands. The German stream carried with it a great diversity of types. At the time of the Declaration of Independence, it is estimated, there were about 225,000 people of German blood in the United States, constituting a little more than 10 percent of the total population. Of these, 33 percent resided in Pennsylvania. This colonial migration was the product of religious, political, and economic persecution and distress. The great majority of immigrants came from the Rhine country, especially from the Palatinate and Württemberg, where humble people were the victims of political and religious persecution and of economic disorders that accompanied and followed the Thirty Years' War and the wars of Louis XIV. In the first half of the 18th century, but especially from 1720 to 1750, Mennonites, Dunkards, Lutherans, and members of the Moravian and German Reformed churches settled in large numbers in the middle and southern colonies.

The Old Immigration

While the American stock in the Republic from 1790 to 1820 multiplied vigorously from roughly 4 to 10 million, the influx of immigration was relatively slow during those years. With the close of the War of 1812 and the Napoleonic Wars, the constant stream of immigration took its inception. It was at that point that the rapid modern growth of population in Europe suddenly made itself felt; it had roughly doubled between 1700 and 1800. This old immigration was stimulated by the rapid development of steamship and railroad transport and encouraged with vigor by the governments of the new states of the Midwest, whose primary need in those years was to build up a population. Thus, after the decade of the 1830's, wave after wave of immigration set down on American shores newcomers from almost every country of Europe and, later in the century, newcomers from China and Japan.

European peasants, artisans, and intellectuals became expatriates out of dissatisfaction with conditions in Europe and a belief that they would be favorable in the United States. The ultimate force that caused the individual to uproot himself and strike out on the adventure of transplantation was most often, although not always, the expectation of economic betterment. Population pressure, land hunger, the Poor Law in England, and economic dislocation in continental Europe attendant on the rapid increase in agrarian population; the enclosure of the common lands; the rise of early industrial civilization in which many could not find their place—these forces made for hopelessness and frustration. Indeed, the emigration movement is part of the broad agrarian development that revolutionized the European countryside and made obsolete the traditional village economy. Whole sections of the rural and lower middle classes in one locality after another fell victim to a class movement—popularly known as America fever—that spread from parish to parish. This fever was transmitted most effectively by hundreds of thousands of "America letters" written by enthusiastic immigrants to relatives and friends in their native lands. The immigrants' longings for all the good things awaiting them in the rich and fertile "dollar land" could not have been satisfied without cheap and rapid means of transportation. The steamship and the railroad, together with inventions that revolutionized agriculture and manufacturing, not only brought tremendous adjustments in the lives of workers and laborers in Europe and America but also shortened the traversing of the Atlantic Ocean from eight weeks in the days of sail to eight days in the era of the steam engine and the screw propeller.

The Irish Wave

Irish immigration increased rapidly in the decades after 1820, rising from 54,338 during 1821–30 to 207,381 during 1831–40. Given the inordinate labor supply in industrial England and Scotland, whence unemployed Irishmen were being deported back to Ireland, and given the slow development of Canada, the United States was popular for emigrants—with its wages of two dollars a day for artisans and a dollar for laborers in the busy season; its demand for labor attendant on the growth of factories and on the coastal migration to the frontier; and its political and religious freedom. In general the Irish came as individuals and sent for their families and friends; they were of the artisan, small-farmer class, of sturdy physique, and in the prime years of life; many were the victims of land clearances and consolidations. They settled largely in coastal cities or in growing towns along the road, canal, and railroad construction projects on which they worked, and they accounted for the rapid growth of cities and provided the cheap labor necessary for incipient industries.

In the two decades 1841–60, official figures account for 1,694,838 Irish immigrants, exclusive of those entering via Newfoundland and Canada, of returning immigrants, and of those from the large Irish colonies in London and in the industrialized sections of north England and Scotland. The pressure upon peasants and laborers to emigrate was aggravated by a number of circumstances: Ireland had an excessive population of 8 million; Great Britain was burdened with continuing economic difficulties and a wretched agrarian system; potato famines occurred in the late 1840's; the small farms were consolidated in the interest of landlords' economy; and there was a shift from tillage to grazing, caused partly by the competition of American agriculture. Despite the Civil War, during which agents of the U.S. northern states in Ireland sought labor and, no doubt, potential volunteers, there was a heavy emigration, so that the decade 1861–70 saw 435,778 Irishmen enter the United States.

Until 1890 the influx continued to hold steadily at about 500,000 Irish per decade. In the century and a half after 1820 over 4.7 million Irishmen entered the United States, a number exceeding by some 200,000 the entire population of the home island in the 1970's. After 1890, Irish immigration declined as the Irish laborers in America came into competition with continental immigrants and as conditions in Ireland improved as a result of new land legislation, rising wages, and a stabilization of the population at lower levels. The rise of a new nationalism in Ireland in the early decades of the 20th century brought the number of immigrants down to 146,181 for the decade 1911–20. In 1921–30 admissions stood at 221,000; in 1931–40, at 13,167; in 1951–60, at 57,332; and in 1961–70, at 36,461.

The German Wave

After the collapse of the Confederacy the stream of immigration assumed such great volume as to open a new phase, without bringing about, however, any significant change in patterns of origin. The seventh decade of the 19th century deposited on American shores more than 5 million immigrants—a figure exceeded only in the two decades 1900–19, when the respective arrivals were 8,795,386 and 5,735,811. In 1905, for the first time, the number arriving within a single year reached the million mark; and in 1907 the total was 1,285,349, the peak for all years before and since.

In the three decades from 1860 to 1890, Germany ranked highest in American immigration statistics; and in three decades, 1840–60 and 1890–1900, it held second place. From 1820 to 1959 the total of immigrants from Germany to the United States was 6,696,842, and if German-speaking immigrants were to be included, the number would be considerably augmented. Prior to 1860, emigration from Ireland had exceeded that from Germany; in the last decade of the century emigration from Italy forced Germany from first to second place.

Between the signing of the Declaration of Independence and 1820, when German immigration was temporarily ebbing low, the existing German-American population had made rapid progress in assimilation. Thereupon, at the close of the Napoleonic Wars, the second wave began to gather momentum. It brought two distinct cultural groups. From eastern and northern Germany came peasants who were conservative in politics and religious belief. From southwestern Germany and the Rhineland came a liberal sprinkling of political exiles and agnostics, university-trained men and intellectuals who became prominent in various walks of life in their adopted country. They were called *Dreissiger*, or Grays, and Forty-eighters, or Greens, the former having emigrated after the political disturbances of 1830 and the latter within a few years after the revolutions of 1848. The more impatient and radical Greens were the more implacably revolutionary in theory and spirit, in their journalistic agitation, and in a sweeping program for reforming America.

The great bulk of immigrants of the period before the Civil War were fairly well-to-do farmers, mechanics, laborers, and small tradesmen who were hungry for land rather than thirsty for release from persecution. It is significant, however, that a strong contingent of "Old Lutherans," whose attachment to confessional Lutheranism made the union of Lutheran and Calvinist churches odious to them, left Saxony and laid the foundations of the powerful Missouri Synod, in the decade of the 1840's. After the Civil War, political and religious considerations were overshadowed by the economic motive. Agricultural America had a special appeal for rural Germans whose homeland was in the process of industrial development; the Homestead Act remained the star of hope, although an increasing number of immigrants gravitated to cities.

The German immigrants distributed themselves more uniformly throughout the United States than did any other immigrant stock, although certain sections and cities were more favored by them than others: the northern Mississippi Valley; Milwaukee; Saint Paul; Saint Louis; Chicago; Cincinnati; Cleveland; and Davenport, Iowa. According to the census of 1880, Wisconsin had a larger percentage of German-born residents than any other state.

In spite of a vociferous utopian element that had sought in the 1860's to realize separate German statehood and preserve a massive German-speaking enclave in the United States, German immigrants tended to assimilate and Americanize as readily as did the members of other immigrant groups. Their farm communities radiated thrift and efficiency, and their vast numbers of German societies, such as the Männerchor and the Turnverein, fostered love for music and manly sports.

The Swiss immigration amounted to 278,187 between 1820 and 1924. Before 1881, the peak year was 1854, when nearly 8,000 arrived, but the greatest influx was in 1881–83, with more than 10,000 arrivals. A number of group settlements were carried out by the Swiss, notably a colony in Switzerland County, Ind., shortly after 1800, and the farming community of New Glarus, in Green County, Wis., in 1845.

Quotas for Germany fell from 68,059 under the act of 1921 to 51,227 under the act of 1924 and to 25,957 with the national-origin ratio effective in 1929. Under the 1952 act it remained at 25,814. Figures for German immigration show that 477,765 were admitted in the decade of 1951–60 and 190,796 in 1961–70, with a marked decrease in the last four years.

The Scandinavians

Patterns of immigration from Sweden and Norway coincide with those of the German wave of the 19th century. In the years from 1820 to 1971, immigration from Sweden accounted for 2.8 percent of the total, or 1,267,574 individuals. That of Norway amounted to 1.9 percent, or 853,783 individuals. For Norway the peak decade was 1901–10, with 190,505 arrivals, while Sweden at the same time sent 249,534. For the decade of the 1850's, by contrast, the figures are as follows: Norway, 22,935 and Sweden, 21,697; for the 1860's, Norway, 15,484 and Sweden, 17,116. Figures for Denmark and Finland run parallel with those for the two larger countries. Overall, Denmark accounts for 0.8 percent of all immigration since 1820 and Finland for 0.1 percent.

The New Immigration

The new immigration, which began in the 1890's, had as its principal source the crowded and relatively backward agricultural communities of eastern and southern Europe. Once upon American shores, these immigrants settled in the industrial centers and became factory wage-earners or laboring hands in the mining camps. In crowded city surroundings the new immigrants often remained segregated from the mainstream of American life and institutions. Since the 1890's agitation for restriction on immigration was directed in large part against the alleged characteristics of this group. The objection was a protest of descendants of older settlers against the rapid increase of south European, Slavic, and Oriental peoples; a religious protest against the large Catholic infusion that they represented; and finally, an economic protest from American labor against the competition of those who were willing to accept a lower standard of living than the American norm.

Strikingly new patterns of immigration may be observed between 1931 and 1971, particularly in the fluctuations in rank of certain northern European, as contrasted with southern and eastern European, countries, and in the dramatic rise in the rates and absolute numbers of arrivals from nations of the Western Hemisphere. In the decade of 1931–40 the grand total of immigration from all countries fell from 4.1 million to slightly over a half million. The figure for Europe was a mere 347,289, as compared with 2,477,853 in the previous decade; for Asia, only 15,344, as compared with 97,400. In 1931–40 the countries of the world were ranked as follows, counting immigrants by country of origin: Germany-Austria (117,000), Canada (109,000), Italy (68,000), Mexico (22,000), England (22,000), Poland (17,000), Czechoslovakia (14,000), Ireland (13,000), and France (13,000). In 1961–70 these countries were ranked by place of last permanent residence as follows: Germany-Austria (211,000), fourth; Canada (413,000), second; Italy (214,000), third; Mexico (453,000), first; Great Britain (210,000), fifth; Poland (54,000), fourteenth; Czechoslovakia (3,000), thirty-ninth; Ireland (37,000), nineteenth; and France (45,000), sixteenth. In addition to those cited above, by 1961–70 the following moved high in the ranking: Cuba (208,000), sixth; the West Indies (134,000), seventh; the Philippines (98,000), eighth; the Dominican Republic (93,000), ninth; Greece (86,000), tenth; Portugal (76,000), eleventh; Hong Kong (75,000), twelfth; Colombia (72,000), thirteenth; and Argentina (49,000), fifteenth. Germany-Austria ranked first from 1931 through 1960 but stood fourth in 1961–70. Italy ranked second in 1931–40 and third in 1961–70 as well as in the years between. Poland ranked sixth in 1931–40, seventh in 1941–60, but fell to fourteenth place in 1961–70. Mexico moved from fourth place in 1931–40 and 1941–50 to third in 1951–60 and first in 1961–70.

The Italians

In 1930 New York City had more people of Italian stock than Rome—1,070,355 persons of Italian birth or parentage—according to the U.S. census of that year, out of a total of 4,651,195 of Italian stock living in the United States. During 1907, the peak year of Italian immigration, more Italians were admitted than the

1960 population of Venice. From 1820 to 1930, over 4,628,000 Italian immigrants arrived, and of this number over 3,500,000 came in the 20th century. Before 1860, at the time when emigration from northern and western Europe was getting under way in earnest, only about 14,000 Italians, mainly from the northern provinces, migrated to the United States—"fantastic vanguard of the brawny army to follow." Among these early arrivals there were a few political refugees, of whom Giuseppe Garibaldi was the most famous, and a few goldseekers who early founded the Italian colony in California. Since 1890 more than one-half of the Italian population has resided in New Jersey, New York, and Pennsylvania; about 15 percent in New England; and slightly less than 15 percent in Illinois, Indiana, and Ohio.

Coming from a country with a rapidly increasing population, extensive tracts of unproductive soil, obsolete methods of agriculture, meager mineral resources, excessive subdivision of land, poor means of communication, heavy taxes, and, especially in the south, a high percentage of illiteracy, the Italian immigrants found inviting opportunities for employment on railroad construction gangs, on streets, in mines, in the clothing industry, and as fruit vendors, shoe-makers, stonecutters, barbers, bootblacks, and truck farmers.

The Mexicans

The records of immigration show an average annual influx of Chicanos of well under 100 until 1900. However, the record since then displays a rapid rise in rate and in absolute numbers: 1901–10, 49,642; 1911–20, 219,004; 1921–30, 459,287; 1931–40, 22,319; 1941–50, 61,000; 1951–60, 299,000; 1961–70, 453,000. In 1961–70, Mexico accounted for 13.7 percent of all immigration and thereby came to head the list of all nations. The total recorded for the entire period from 1820–1971 is 1,642,916.

The Canadians and French Canadians

In the decade 1961–70, Canada was ranked second among all nations sending immigrants to the United States. Statistics on the immigration of French Canadians are incomplete and unreliable, chiefly because of lax immigration laws in the past and loose inspection conducted along the international boundary, but according to U.S. Census reports, French Canadians residing in the United States in 1890, 1910, and 1930 numbered 302,496; 385,083; and 370,852, respectively. French Canadians are estimated to have made up about 33 percent of the total of 3,991,417 persons who emigrated to the United States from Canada and Newfoundland after the passage of the act of 1921.

Most French Canadians settled in highly industrialized regions of New England and found employment in factories, particularly in the textile industry. Some settled in the northern areas on abandoned farms—a profitable undertaking in view of the cheap land and the growing markets in industrial centers. The French Canadians and their children have adhered tenaciously to the Roman Catholicism and the language and customs of their native provinces.

The Ibero-Americans

Although immigrants from Portugal began to arrive in the United States in relatively large numbers in the 1870's—and to become known to coastal New Englanders as resourceful fishermen and skilled artisans—the peak of influx of Spanish laborers and skilled workmen was not reached until 1911–20, when 68,000 were counted. Spanish immigration was, however, appreciably smaller than the Portuguese. Portuguese numbering 76,000 constituted 2.3 percent of the total number of immigrants in 1961–70.

The Peoples of Eastern Europe

To the year 1900, immigration from the Balkan states and eastern Europe, exclusive of Russia, was ascribed in official U.S. reports either to Poland, European Turkey, or Austria-Hungary. The latter designation embraced, of course, a number of distinct nationalities and ethnic groups, which differed from one another in language, history, and culture. Accurate data on the immigration of these several Austro-Hungarian peoples as they are now grouped and associated in the new states that arose from the fragments of the Hapsburg empire at the close of World War I are not easily obtained.

The U.S. Immigration and Naturalization Service and the Bureau of the Census have published figures presenting their best estimates of Czech, Hungarian, Austrian, and Yugoslavian immigration between 1820 and 1973. Unfortunately, these figures, tabulated according to nationality and applied to the present political units of Eastern Europe, are incomplete and not mutually comparable. They suggest a certain picture and provide clues as to 19th-century conditions, but in themselves they fail to give specific coverage to particular areas such as Poland, Hungary, or Czechoslovakia. On the other hand, the counts of the foreign-born white population of the United States for 1940 and 1950, by country of birth, while in themselves fully reliable and useful, deal primarily with persons who emigrated in the 1920's and 1930's and thus add little to one's knowledge of the latter 19th and early 20th centuries.

The following table brings together the available data on immigration from Eastern European countries and

Country	Population 1970 (millions)	Immigrants by Country of Last Permanent Residence, 1820–1970	Immigrants by National Composition, 1820–1951	Immigrants by Country of Birth, 1951–60	Foreign-born Population in U.S. by Country of Birth, 1940
Poland (except 1899–1919)	33	495,684	422,424	128,000	993,479
Czechoslovakia	14.47	135,347	128,448[a]	28,800	319,971
Yugoslavia	20.9	98,214	58,817[b]	58,700	161,093
Hungary	10.4	not available	484,758[c]	64,500	290,228
Austria-Hungary	7.4	4,309,625	4,181,927[d]	29,700	479,906
Russia (USSR)—Europe and Asia—including parts of Poland 1938–45	250	3,348,392	3,343,905	46,500	1,040,884

[a] Since 1920 only.
[b] Since 1922 only.
[c] Since 1905 only.
[d] From 1861 on, except 1938–45.

on East European nationalities in the general population.

While 4 million immigrants in the class Austro-Hungarians were admitted since 1820, the peak years of migration were the decade 1901–10, when a total of 2,145,261 from this single country were recorded. The national affiliation or province of origin of these peoples cannot be specified. However, one indication of the distribution of these nominally Austrian persons among the nationalities is afforded by a report that has survived and that identifies the land of origin of a total of 205,961 émigrés of a twelve-month period in 1902–03.

These figures, compiled in Vienna, show the following distributions of the national, linguistic, and ethnic groups of Austria-Hungary in that year:

German-Austrians	23,597	
Hungarians	27,113	
Poles	37,499	
Jews	18,759	
Rumanians	4,173	
Italians	2,170	
Slovakians	34,412	Total "proto-Czechoslovakians," 53,808
Ruthenians	9,819	
Czechs	9,577	
Croations and Slovenians	32,892	Total "proto-Yugoslavians," 38,842
Bulgars, Serbs, and Montenegrins	4,227	
Dalmatians, Bosnians, and Herzegovinians	1,723	

These figures would suggest—if they are at all representative of long-term trends—that the relatively smaller groups of proto-Czechoslovakians were sending a somewhat disproportionally large number of immigrants to the United States when compared with the later Yugoslavian lands. However, in the overall picture of migrations, it would appear that the still smaller land of Hungary has in the longest time span alone sent more immigrants than either of these new lands. In any event, the southern areas lagged behind the more centrally located regions of Hungary, Bohemia, Slovakia, and Moravia.

REFUGEES AND DISPLACED PERSONS. The Displaced Persons Act of 1948 was the first of eight special acts passed between 1948 and 1960 that provided for the admission of refugees from Communist-dominated countries, victims of natural calamities, and orphan children. Specifically under the Refugee Relief Act of 1953 and the acts of July 25, 1958, of July 14, 1960, and of Oct. 3, 1965, a total of 554,523 refugees were admitted from East Europe between 1954 and 1973, as follows: from Poland, 17,532; from Czechoslovakia, 10,742; from Yugoslavia, 46,213; from Hungary, 50,357; and from the Soviet Union, 7,624.

REPRESENTATION IN THE FOREIGN-BORN WHITE POPULATION (1940). The East European countries ranked relatively high in the 1940 census count of the foreign-born in the United States. Five countries exceeded a million in this count at that time: Italy, Germany, Canada, Great Britain, and the Soviet Union. Poland ranked sixth, with 993,479; Austria, eighth, with 479,906; Czechoslovakia, eleventh, with 319,971; Hungary, twelfth, with 290,228; and Yugoslavia, sixteenth, with 161,093. Only Ireland, Sweden, Mexico, Norway, Lithuania, and Greece ranked higher than Yugoslavia between the sixth and fifteenth positions.

THE POLISH. Some half million persons have been counted as immigrants from Poland between 1820 and 1973. These figures are known to be low, for they omit the two full decades from 1899 to 1919. In addition, the numerous boundary changes in the 19th century led to discrepancies in the counts of persons who belonged ethnically and culturally to the Polish nation. The annual quota has been set at a relatively high level of 4.2 percent, and after midcentury the United States admitted near to a quarter million: 1951–60, 128,000; 1961–70, 73,300; 1970, 3,600; and 1973, 4,900. The Bureau of the Census computed the Polish component in the foreign white stock in the United States in 1930 as 3,342,000, or 8.5 percent of the total, and in 1950 as 2,786,000, or 8.4 percent. The area of residence of the foreign-born Polish people is predominantly the Middle Atlantic, the East North Central, and the Northeast regions.

THE CZECHOSLOVAKIANS. Czechoslovakia, homeland of the Czechs, Slovakians, and Ruthenians, was fashioned into a new nation out of the principalities of the former Bohemia, Moravia, and Slovakia, to name only the most important. Census data show the modern Czechoslovak component in the foreign-born white population at the level of 319,972 (2.8 percent) in 1940 and 278,268 (2.7 percent) in 1950; and of the total foreign white stock in the United States in 1930, 3.5 percent, or 1,382,000, were counted as Czechoslovakian. Immigration since the 1950's has been moderate: 21,400 persons of Czechoslovakian birth entered in the decade 1961–70, and in the single year 1973 just 1,600 entered. The Czechoslovak peoples in the United States are concentrated most heavily in the Middle Atlantic and East North Central regions.

THE YUGOSLAVIANS. The Immigration Act of 1924 set a small quota of 671 persons (0.6 percent) for the country of Yugoslavia, and it has remained extremely low ever since. Immigrants from Yugoslavia, counted by country of last permanent residence, from 1820 to 1971, numbered 90,234; the figure published for the entrance of Yugoslav nationals between 1922 and 1951 was 58,817 persons. The 1950 census counted 143,956 Yugoslavians (1.4 percent) among the foreign-born white population and calculated a total of 384,000 (1.1 percent) for the Yugoslavian element in the foreign white stock. By far the greater part of the immigration of nearly 105,000 persons since 1951 has been in the categories of displaced persons and refugees. In America the Yugoslavs have settled in the industrial centers of the East North Central, Middle Atlantic, and Pacific regions.

THE HUNGARIANS. Since immigrants from Hungary were counted with the large Austro-Hungarian block until 1905, it is difficult to arrive at an estimate of their numbers for the 19th century. The total of Austrians and Hungarians emigrating to America from Austria-Hungary between 1861 and 1951, counting by nationality composition, was 4,181,927; the figure of 4,309,625 is cited for the span from 1820 to 1973, counting by country of last permanent residence. Since 1905 the total arriving from Hungary alone is listed at 484,758, and in 1911–20, the decade of peak immigration, 422,693 emigrants from Hungary were counted. The census of 1940 listed 290,228 persons of Hungarian birth, and that of 1950 listed 268,022. Except for the decade of the 1950's, with its large influx of refugees, the flow of Hungarian migration remained at a low level, averaging fewer than a thousand per year from 1921 to 1973. Hungarians settled in the urban industrial centers of the East and Midwest and sought employment as factory hands and laborers in heavy industry.

THE RUSSIANS. In 1940 and 1950 the Russian component in the foreign-born white population of the United States was 1,040,884 (9.1 percent) and 894,844 (8.8 percent), respectively. Of the total foreign white stock in the United States in 1930 and 1950, the Russian component was estimated at 2,670,000 (7.0 percent) and 2,542,000 (7.5 percent), respectively. These figures for the areas of European and Asiatic Russia include the large eastern Jewish element, which is culturally and ethnically distinct from other Russian nationals. Immigration from the Soviet Union, tallied according to country of birth, was at the level of 15,700 in the decade 1961–70; 900 in 1970; and 1,200 in 1973. The Bureau of the Census reports the largest concentration of Russian-born immigrants, Jewish and non-Jewish, as having settled in the Middle Atlantic region.

Asia

Of a grand total of 39.5 million immigrants to the United States counted by nationality composition in the period 1820–1951, less than 1 million—954,230 in exact numbers—have been ascribed to Asiatic countries: China, 399,217; India, 11,743; Japan (since 1861), 279,407; Asian Turkey (since 1869), 205,584; other, 58,279.

The figures for total immigration from Asia when counted by country of last permanent residence appear in the following table. This is the cumulative figure covering the entire period from 1820 through 1973, as published by the Immigration Service.

All Asia	2,018,673 (4.3% of all)
China (including Taiwan since 1957)	468,564
Hong Kong (since 1951)	119,710
India	81,416
Iran	21,730
Israel	63,260
Japan	63,260

Jordan	24,307
Korea	94,886
Lebanon	28,031
Philippines	204,309
Turkey	379,820
Other Asia	151,466

The figures for all countries except China and Turkey cover the years 1951–73 only. Prior to 1951 these countries were included with the category "Other Asia." According to this list, only China contributed as much as 1 percent of the total number of immigrants within the given period. Japan and Turkey stand next highest, with 0.8 percent each.

As is well known, the immigration acts of 1921, 1924, and later had the direct effect of suppressing the opportunity for migration to the United States from Asiatic lands. As a result, the quotas for Asia as a whole have been extremely low: 1,699 in 1921; 1,400 in 1924; 1,549 in 1929; and 3,215 since 1952.

A count of the foreign-born white population as reported by the censuses for 1940 and 1950 cited 39,424, or 0.3 percent of the total population in 1940, as having been born in Asia and 180,024 (1.8 percent) in 1950. A count of the foreign stocks in the United States in 1930 and 1950 was reported by the Census Bureau as follows:

	1930	1950
Asia, white	310,000 (0.8%)	420,000 (1.2%)
Chinese	75,000	118,000
Japanese	139,000	142,000
Filipinos	45,000	
Hindus	3,000	
Koreans	2,000	
All others, non-white		110,000
Total	574,000	790,000

In the years 1954–73 refugees admitted from Asia by provision of the special refugee acts of 1948–60, by country of birth, show a total of 56,727 from Asia, well over half of these coming from China (inclusive of Taiwan) and Indonesia.

Foreign-born immigrants from Asia are located principally in the following areas: the Middle Atlantic, the Pacific coast, the East North Central, and the New England regions.

Trends of the 1960's and 1970's

In 1973 the effects of the Immigration Act of 1965 were beginning to be evident. The work regulations specified in the act tended to curtail the flow of laborers from northern Europe and South America; and the high priority given relatives in the new law had increased the influx from southern Europe, Mexico, Canada, and Asia. For the year ending June 30, 1971, the countries of origin ranked as follows: Mexico (50,103); Philippines (28,417); Italy (22,137); Cuba (21,611); Greece (15,939); Jamaica (14,571); China, inclusive of Taiwan (14,417); India (14,310); Korea (14,297); Canada (13,128); Dominican Republic (12,624); Portugal (11,692); the United Kingdom (10,787). The following regions or countries sent from 2,000 to 8,000: all Africa, France, Germany, Poland, Spain, Yugoslavia, Hong Kong, Japan, Jordan, Colombia, Ecuador. All other countries sent fewer than 2,000 in the year.

Also notable was an overall decline in immigration from Europe. Whereas in 1931–40 Europe as a whole sent 348,000 persons as compared with 160,000 for all the Western Hemisphere, the proportions by 1961–70 were altered in favor of the Americas. In 1961–70 Europe sent 1,123,363 persons, or 33.8 percent of the total of all immigrants, but the countries of the American continents from Canada to Chile sent 1,716,374, or 51.7 percent of the total. The figures for the continent of Asia rose from under 3 percent of the total in 1931–40 to 427,771, or 12.8 percent in 1961–70. What was once clearly a westward expansion of European peoples toward America as a frontier had changed to a complex intermingling of peoples from all directions—prominently from Latin America, Canada, and the Far East.

BIBLIOGRAPHY

Rowland Berthoff, *British Immigrants in Industrial America, 1790–1950.*

Oscar Handlin, *Boston's Immigrants, 1790–1865,* and *The Newcomers.*

Marcus Lee Hansen, *The Atlantic Migration, 1607–1860,* and *The Immigrant in American History.*

Maldwyn A. Jones, *American Immigration.*

James G. Leyburn, *The Scotch-Irish.*

Carl F. Wittke, *The Irish in America, Refugees of Revolution,* and *We Who Built America: The Saga of the Immigrant.*

— ARTHUR R. SCHULTZ

RECENT TRENDS IN IMMIGRATION

During and immediately after World War II, Congress began to liberalize the immigration restrictions enacted in the 1920s. Legislators repealed the Chinese exclusion acts in 1943 and between 1946 and 1952 removed all racial barriers to immigration and naturalization. Beginning with the Displaced Persons Act of 1948, Congress passed special legislation to admit European refugees. These acts were necessary because of limits imposed by the national-origins quotas of the 1920s, which remained at the time of the McCarran-Walter Act of 1952. President Dwight D. Eisenhower established a precedent when he used the parole power to admit thousands of Hungarians following the failed Hungarian revolution of 1956.

Important as all of these modifications were, the major change in immigration policy came in 1965 when Congress passed the far-reaching Hart-Celler Act. Fully effective in 1968, it marked a departure in twentieth-century immigration policy. It repealed the national-origins quotas and gave each Eastern Hemisphere nation an annual quota of 20,000, excluding immediate family members of U.S. citizens. The Eastern Hemisphere received altogether 170,000 places and the Western Hemisphere 120,000. Congress in 1978 created a worldwide immigration system by combining the two hemispheres. Within uniform national quotas of 20,000 the new system reserved most of the visas for family unification and the remainder for those with skills needed in the United States or for refugees, who were defined as persons fleeing communism. Because the number of refugees was limited, presidents used the parole power to admit refugees above the quota numbers, and Congress enacted legislation to grant refugee status to the parolees. A new refugee law, the Refugee Act of 1980, established a "normal" annual flow of 50,000 and changed the definition of "refugee." Instead of persons escaping communism, refugees were people fleeing a "well founded fear of persecution" based on national origin or membership in a political organization. In reality, for many years the executive branch, which had the power to admit refugees by determining who faced persecution, continued to admit persons primarily from communist nations.

The major change in U.S. immigration policy came in 1965 when Congress passed the far-reaching Hart-Celler Act, which repealed the national-origins quotas.

Legislators worried about undocumented immigrants, that is, persons entering or staying illegally. After years of debate the Immigration Reform and Control Act of 1986 (IRCA) provided amnesty to undocumented immigrants who had entered before 1982 or engaged in agricultural work for ninety days during 1985–1986. The measure outlawed the knowing employment of undocumented immigrants.

Proponents of groups using the family-unification arrangements did not want to see family preferences reduced in favor of more visas for individuals possessing labor skills. Congress hence increased the number of places both for family unification and for labor skills. The Immigration Act of 1990 provided for a 35 percent increase in immigration. For a three-year period immigration was to be 700,000; after that the figure was set at 675,000, but this did not include the annual influx of 100,000 refugees. Thus, 800,000 new immigrants annually were expected when the 1990 law was operative. These figures did not include the estimated 100,000 to 300,000 undocumented aliens entering the United States each year in the early 1990s. Some immigrants intended to stay for only a short time and in traditional fashion returned home with their earnings. The federal government did not keep return data after 1957, but scholars estimate that at least one out of five immigrants went back to his or her native land. Return rates were high for Caribbean countries and Mexico.

All these changes led to dramatic shifts in immigration after 1968. During the 1960s, 3.3 million immigrants arrived; the number grew to 4.4 million in the next decade and 7.3 million during the 1980s. IRCA amnesties yielded 3 million claiming eligibility for immigrant status. In 1991, 1.8 million immigrants were recorded, the highest annual number ever. IRCA applicants, together with increases provided by the 1990 act, promised to make the 1990s the largest era of immigration in U.S. history. Proportionally, the foreign-born population was increasing faster than the native-born; in 1990 the Bureau of the Census reported 20 million of the nation's population born abroad, 7.9 percent of the total population. Immigration was accounting for one-third of population growth. The backlog of individuals awaiting immigrant visas grew steadily, to 3 million in 1993.

Europe no longer dominated immigration as it had for most years since the United States began gathering statistics in 1820. While the Hart-Celler Act made it possible for greater numbers of Greeks, Italians, and other peoples from Europe to enter the United States, by the early 1970s backlogs in noncommunist European nations eased. During the late 1970s the Soviet Union permitted tens of thousands of Jews to emigrate. With the collapse of communism Russia again allowed many citizens to leave, most of them Jews but also Armenians and Pentecostals. During the late 1980s immigration from Ireland picked up, partly because of IRCA and the 1990 immigration act.

When Congress enacted the Hart-Celler Act, Asian immigrants amounted to 20,000, or 5 percent of the total. By the 1980s Asian countries were sending ten times that figure and accounting for 40 percent of the total, although Asian Americans still made up only 2.9 percent of the U.S. population in the mid-1990s. Indochinese refugees explain part of this increase. When the U.S.-backed South Vietnamese government in Saigon fell in 1975, 130,000 desperate refugees fled to the United States. They were soon joined by escaping "boat people" and by Vietnamese who crossed the border to refugee camps in Thailand. When the United States and Vietnam during the 1980s reached an agreement on immigration policy, additional Vietnamese arrived. Thousands of Cambodians fleeing the terror of the Khmer Rouge regime, as well as many Laotians who did not wish to live under communism, added to the flow.

The largest Asian group came from the Philippines. It at first included families of U.S. citizens and many medical professionals. Poor economic conditions and political oppression explained much of this migration, as did the fact that Filipinos had direct knowledge of the United States because of their nation's history as a U.S. colony (1898–1946) and because of U.S. military bases there. Annually, as many as 40,000 Filipinos were heading for the United States despite a long waiting period to obtain a visa.

Chinese from Hong Kong, Taiwan, and China accounted for many of the new Asian immigrants. Taiwanese often came as students and became immigrants. Some from Hong Kong were refugees from China. After 1981, when the United States established a quota for Taiwan and China, the Chinese government permitted citizens to emigrate directly to the United States. Korea sent few immigrants before the 1950s. The Korean War and the 1965 immigration act changed that. Between 1952 and 1965 Korean women married to U.S. servicemen arrived, followed by immigrants using the 1965 law. The number of Asian Indians sharply increased after 1965, rising to 20,000 annually by the 1980s. Most early Indians were highly educated professionals, such as physicians and engineers; family members followed. Immigration from Pakistan, Thailand, and other South and East Asian nations, although less than that of the above-mentioned groups, increased during the 1980s.

Changes in the law permitted increasing numbers of Middle Easterners to emigrate. The poverty of the region as well as turmoil between Israel and its Arab neighbors provided incentives. Israelis increased, as did Palestinians, but numbers of the latter were unknown because many arrived with Jordanian passports. In the 1970s the civil war in Lebanon prompted departures. Immigrants from Iran came after the 1979 revolution overthrew the U.S.-supported shah and an Islamic state was proclaimed. Following the Soviet invasion of Afghanistan the United States opened its doors to a few Afghan refugees. The number of immigrants from Africa did not increase significantly. Egyptians accounted for the largest single group, while others came from Ethiopia fleeing a Marxist revolution, a few came from South Africa, and an increasing number came from West African countries such as Nigeria. Nigerians were among the most highly skilled and educated immigrants to arrive. In the Western Hemisphere, Mexican immigrants dominated, and in many years its nationals were the largest group to enter the United States. Other Hispanics include Colombians, Dominicans, and Cubans. French- or Creole-speakers from Haiti migrated as did English-speakers from the West Indies.

Post-1970 immigrants, like so many newcomers before them, tended to settle in the same cities, suburbs, and towns as had others from their countries. In the case of Indochinese refugees the federal government made special efforts to scatter them, but many moved after initial settlement, heading for California, home for one-third of such immigrants. Indochinese refugees were not the only newcomers attracted to California. For much of U.S. history immigrants had poured into the United States through Ellis Island at the tip of Manhattan in New York City. After the 1965 immigration reform, however, California displaced New York as the gateway to the United States. It became home for Mexicans, Central Americans, Koreans, Chinese, Middle Easterners, and Filipinos. By the 1980s one-quarter of all immigrants were settling in that state.

New York's main immigrant groups included Asian Indians, Chinese, Koreans, and peoples from the Caribbean. Half the nation's Jamaicans and most of the Dominicans settled in the New York area. Other states drawing such immigrants were Florida, Texas, Illinois, New Jersey, Arizona, and Pennsylvania. Mexicans settled in Texas and Arizona, while Miami became the center of Cuban-American life. Miami also housed many Haitians and Nicaraguans. Chicago and Philadelphia attracted many foreign born. While congregated in these cities and states, immigrant communities could be found in every state by the 1990s. Lawrence, Mass., had a community of Cambodians; Minneapolis of Hmong; Newark, N.J., of Portuguese; the Washington, D.C., area of Indochinese and Africans; and New Orleans of Indochinese refugees and Central Americans. In Garden City, Kans., packing plants drew Mexican, Vietnamese, Salvadoran, Cambodian, and Laotian workers.

Like immigrants of past generations, newcomers came to the United States for economic reasons. Many fled political or religious persecution but the line between political and economic migrants often blurred. Soon after passage of the 1965 act observers noted that a "brain drain" was bringing highly educated Third World professionals who were seeking a better life than they could find at home. Although professionals continued to arrive in the 1980s and 1990s and were encouraged by the 1990 act, only a minority of the immigrants of this period represented a brain drain. Chinese with few skills arrived. Mexicans were not as well educated as Asian Indians, and many Haitians arrived with little money and few skills. While the first wave of Cuban refugees in the 1960s represented the elite of Cuban society, a large influx in early 1980 leaving from the port of Mariel in Cuba was mainly manual workers.

Like immigrants of past generations, newcomers came to the U.S. for economic reasons; many fled political or religious persecution, but the line between political and economic migrants often blurred.

Beginning in the 1930s women constituted a majority of immigrants, a pattern that continued into the 1980s, but the gender ratios were not highly skewed and varied by country. The bulk of Mexicans were young males as was the majority of Asian Indians and Africans. Often one person arrived, established himself or herself, and sent for family members who could qualify under the immigration regulations.

The effect of new immigration was readily apparent by the 1980s, especially in the eight states where most of the immigrants congregated. Foreign-born medical professionals staffed many urban hospitals; Asian Indians ran newsstands and operated motels; Koreans opened fruit and vegetable stores; Mexicans worked in motels, restaurants, and garment shops; Dominicans owned small stores called bodegas in New York City; Chinese opened and worked in garment shops in New York City and San Francisco. The presence of diverse peoples soon became noticeable in U.S. social and cultural life. In 1970 Spanish replaced Italian as the nation's second language. The 1990 census revealed English as a second language for 32 million Americans. The mix of languages in some school districts was amazing. In both New York City and Los Angeles more than one hundred languages could be heard. New festivals, parades, and religious organizations appeared. The vast majority of Americans remained Protestant or Catholic but in the quarter century after the 1965 immigration act, Hindu, Sikh, and Buddhist temples were organized and mosques opened to accommodate the Islamic population. In 1993, for the first time, the U.S. Army enrolled a Muslim chaplain.

Native-born citizens did not always view the new wave of immigration as beneficial. Some complained that immigrants took jobs from them or that newcomers used social services such as hospitals and schools without paying their share. Others worried about the effect of so many people on the environment. Polls after 1970 demonstrated concern about immigration and some incidents of violence were recorded, but while scholars differed about the effect of immigration, most believed that the nation benefited from this new wave of immigrants. Congress agreed, and on the whole was considerably more liberal than were critics of immigration.

The general public and political leaders worried most about undocumented aliens and those seeking asylum. Most refugees were admitted from leftover quotas of other nations, but if an individual entered, even illegally, he or she could claim asylum. If the applicant could prove a well-founded fear of persecution if returned home, he or she could receive asylum. The Refugee Act of 1980 contained 5,000 places for asylum. Tens of thousands of applications were being made annually by the late 1980s, 150,000 alone in 1993. There were so many that some observers believed asylum was being abused and breaking down as lists became longer. Undocumented aliens caused even greater apprehension. IRCA had not stopped people from entering illegally. The numbers of people caught along the Mexican border dropped briefly but rose in the 1990s. It would have required draconian measures and considerable funds to seal this border, and Congress was unwilling to take such steps. Following the 1994 congressional elections, however, the legislators were willing to consider cuts in immigration and increase the border patrol. Congress was following the strong reactions in several states in illegal immigration. In November 1994 California voters approved Proposition 187 that made illegal immigrants ineligible for state benefits such as education and regular medical care in public hospitals. The courts postponed making the proposition law, however, pending a decision on its constitutionality. Nonetheless, several other states began to consider similar proposals and instituted lawsuits to force the federal government to pay for the costs of public services utilized by illegal immigrants. This growing opposition to undocumented immigration did not deter persons from trying to enter the United States illegally. They and the large numbers entering legally would continue the country's heritage as a nation of immigrants.

[See also Arab Americans; Asian Americans; Chinese Americans; Cuban Americans; Hispanic Americans; Irish Americans; Italian Americans; Japanese Americans; Korean Americans; Mexican Americans; Polish Americans.]

BIBLIOGRAPHY

Alejandro Portes and Ruben G. Rumbaut, *Immigrant America: A Portrait* (Berkeley, Calif., 1990).

David M. Reimers, *Still the Golden Door* (New York, 1992).

Reed Ueda, *Postwar Immigrant America: A Social History* (New York, 1994).

— DAVID M. REIMERS

IMMIGRATION RESTRICTION

Immigration Restriction, as a movement, emerged in the 1870's, stemming from the enormous social and economic changes that were producing a more visibly stratified society, class tensions, and labor conflicts. Particularly disturbed by the increasing number of newcomers from the less familiar lands of Asia and southeastern Europe—and finding them poorer, less literate, more radical, and generally more disorderly than their predecessors—restrictionists urged a program of more selective immigration. They argued that limitations on immigration were necessary to protect the vaunted American values of democracy, stability, and progress.

Restrictionism originated in several quarters that tended to coalesce about the time of World War I in a drive to limit "new" immigrants, particularly the "less American" Asians, Slavs, Italians, and Jews.

The earliest opponents of unlimited immigration were labor spokesmen, for economic and possibly racial reasons. After the Supreme Court ruled in 1876 that the federal government had responsibility for immigration regulation, western leaders—notably Denis Kearney of the California Workingmen's party—urged Congress to bar Chinese, claiming that they undercut American wages. A Chinese Exclusion Act prohibiting the immigration of Chinese for ten years was passed in 1882 and, after being extended, was made permanent in 1902. Also, the Knights of Labor lobbied to bar the recruitment of "pauper labor" overseas, the result being an 1885 law prohibiting the importing of workers under contract. The influx of Japanese labor that began in the 1890's led the United States to exchange a series of notes with Japan, in 1907–08, whereby the Asian country agreed to stop emigration of some of its unskilled workmen. Down to the 1920's the American Federation of Labor continually supported restriction to protect the American workingman.

Another source of restrictionist sentiment was the anti-Catholicism that erupted at the turn of the century. Directed at specific nationalities, it aroused massive support under the leadership of the American Protective Association in the 1890's and the Ku Klux Klan in the 1920's.

The third group advocating immigration restriction was made up of American intellectuals, mainly from New England. Affected by a loss of status in the new social order, they regarded themselves as the particular guardians of American principles, directing their efforts specifically against new immigrants. Accepting the principles of Darwinian selection, they advocated so-called Anglo-Saxon superiority as the basis of American achievements. They argued that the new immigrant groups must be barred because they appeared uninterested in assimilating American civic virtues, concentrating themselves in their separate urban ghettoes. President Francis Walker of the Massachusetts Institute of Technology, for example, warned of Anglo-Saxon "race suicide" if unlimited immigration continued, while historian John Burgess of Columbia University endeavored to justify a superior Anglo-Saxon culture in his writings. Biologists and eugenicists fostered popular notions of qualitative racial differences by showing the determining power of heredity; one well-known racial theory was that of Madison Grant, propounded in his *Passing of the Great Race* (1916).

Restrictive legislation after World War I reflected a view that conformity to Anglo-Saxon attitudes and mores was patriotic; further, the Bolshevik Revolution had tainted all eastern Europeans as radicals in the American mind.

An early practical attempt to preserve Anglo-Saxon America was the bill proposing a literacy test for admission introduced in Congress by Sen. Henry Cabot Lodge of Massachusetts. Vetoed by presidents Grover Cleveland, William H. Taft, and Woodrow Wilson, it became law in 1917, but the test was abandoned in the next decade. Just after World War I a major change in policy—a restrictionist legislative victory—occurred because of new developments: the public now regarded conformity to Anglo-Saxon attitudes and mores as a patriotic virtue, the Bolshevik Revolution tainted all eastern Europeans as radicals in the American mind, and restrictionist Albert Johnson assumed the chairmanship of the House of Representatives' immigration committee. The first quota law was passed in 1921, limiting immigration substantially and, more important, selecting arrivals by national-origin quotas, which favored northwestern Europeans. It reduced arrivals in one year from 805,228 to 309,556 in 1922. A more basic law was the Johnson-Reed Act of 1924 which further reduced total immigration from Europe and Asia and maintained the national-origins idea, although it did not restrict arrivals from the Western Hemisphere and repealed the Chinese and Japanese exclusion laws.

The national-origins philosophy continued to underlie federal policy until the mid-1960's, although the professed rationale became, not race, but economic and national security. The McCarran-Walter Act of 1952 made immigration even more difficult, adding further occupational and security limitations. Congress finally discarded the discriminatory principle in 1965. This law, effective Dec. 1 and still operative in 1975, set aside the national-origins basis but kept the occupational priorities, now applying them to all Eastern and Western hemispheric sources. Since then a new nativist movement has appeared asking for new restrictions. Advocates of population limitation, critics of Vietnam War refugee resettlement, and complainants of the economic recession of the 1970's have revived demands for further immigration restriction.

BIBLIOGRAPHY

Robert A. Divine, *American Immigration Policy.*
Mark Haller, *Eugenics.*
John Higham, *Strangers in the Land.*
Alexander Saxton, *The Indispensable Enemy.*
Barbara Solomon, *Ancestors and Immigrants.*

— VICTOR GREENE

IMPEACHMENT

The Constitution of the United States provides that "The President, Vice-President, and all civil Officers of the United States, shall be removed from Office on Impeachment for, and Conviction of, Treason, Bribery, or other high Crimes and Misdemeanors" (Article II, Section 4). The importance of the power to impeach in the considerations of the framers of the Constitution was underscored by the special attention placed on the trial itself and by the detailed discussion of the nature of the penalty. Interestingly enough there are no specific instructions concerning the manner in which impeachment proceedings shall originate other than the section granting the House of Representatives "the sole Power of Impeachment" (Article I, Section 2, Paragraph 5). In contrast, Section 3, Paragraph 6, of the same article provides that "The Senate . . . shall have the sole Power to try all Impeachments." It then states that "When sitting for that Purpose, they [the Senators] shall be on Oath or Affirmation. When the President of the United States is tried, the Chief Justice shall preside: and no Person shall be convicted without the Concurrence of two thirds of the Members present." Article I, Section 2, Paragraph 7, also holds that "Judgment in Cases of Impeachment shall not extend further than to removal from Office, and disqualification to hold and enjoy any Office of Honor, Trust or Profit under the United States: but the Party convicted shall nevertheless be liable and subject to Indictment, Trial, Judgment and Punishment, according to Law."

Impeachment and conviction as a method of removal from public office was introduced from England into the state constitutions created during the American Revolution. It had been claimed in behalf of the colonial assemblies, but was denied except in the proprietary government of Pennsylvania. After the adoption of the federal Constitution in 1789, the impeachment provisions of that document became the model emulated in the constitutions of the states. Controversy, from time to time, has centered on the definition of high crimes and misdemeanors. Impeachable offenses were not defined in England, and the framers of the Constitution did not attempt to enumerate the crimes or offenses for which a person can be impeached. Consequently, issues regarding the historic antecedents of the American constitutional provisions are considered significant in specific impeachment contests. Legal historian Raoul Berger contended that the major purpose of the impeachment power has been overlooked in modern times: "Once employed to topple giants—Strafford, Clarendon, Hastings—impeachment has sunk in this country to the ouster of dreary little judges for squalid misconduct." Thus, according to Berger, this preoccupation with judicial impeachment has tended to obscure the major objective of the framers of the Constitution to curb executive power. The model for the framers was not the 18th-century development of parliamentary power, but the direct conflicts between king and Parliament in 17th-century England. Berger's historical and legal analysis focused on several important issues concerning the evolution of the impeachment clause. First, the historic evidence supported the broad constructionist interpretation. Thus, an impeachable offense in English constitutional history was not limited to indictable common-law crimes but to offenses determined by Parliament. These offenses generally involved matters directly related to what Parliament considered excessive executive influence and were also related to the ultimately successful attempt by Parliament to make ministers accountable to it rather than to the king. Despite the fact that the constitutional framers rather explicitly chose not to limit impeachment to indictable offenses, it was not until 1913 that the interpretation consistent with antecedent English practice and the framers' intentions was applied. Indeed, the framers' exemption of impeachment from jury "Trial of all Crimes" (Article III, Section 2, Paragraph 3) also supported the broad interpretation and, inferentially, so did the exclusion of the Sixth Amendment's requirements for a "speedy and public trial by an impartial jury," as a factor interfering with the impeachment process itself.

Impeachments have been voted by the House of Representatives and tried by the Senate of the United States on a number of occasions, primarily involving judges. In a few cases, the proceedings were abandoned. The two-thirds vote of the Senate necessary for conviction has been obtained in only three cases. The first important use of impeachment was the case of Associate Justice Samuel Chase of the U.S. Supreme Court in 1805. In obtaining an acquittal, counsel for Chase insisted that indictable offenses alone were comprehended within the impeachment power. The closely contested impeachment trial in 1868 of President Andrew Johnson, while very dramatic, not only did not result in removal, but did not add substantially to the precedents surrounding the use of the impeachment power. In fact, it was not until the impeachment trial of Associate Judge Robert W. Archbald of the U.S. Commerce Court in 1913 that a broad constructionist interpretation of the power was applied. The charges against Archbald, set forth in thirteen articles of impeachment, presented no indictable offenses. In all cases, they alleged instances of misconduct in office that, if true, constituted breaches of the good behavior tenure granted federal judicial officers. The conviction of Archbald was a clearcut recognition of the broad constructionist interpretation of the impeachment power.

Within the states the impeachment power has not been used extensively, because the short terms attached to public offices make enforced removals unnecessary. Where impeachments have been undertaken they have usually been instruments of party warfare. The impeachment of judges from partisan motives was carried out in several instances in Pennsylvania and Ohio at the beginning of the 19th century. More than 100 years later (1913), Gov. William Sulzer of New York was impeached and removed from office, the charges resting on broad grounds of unfitness and involving offenses committed by Sulzer prior to his election. Subsequently, governors in Texas and Oklahoma were removed from office after impeachment and conviction. Although partisanship was the motivating force in these impeachments, they have served to give broader scope to the power of impeachment.

Impeachment proceedings against Nixon were begun in October 1973, shortly after his firing of Special Prosecutor Archibald Cox.

The most significant developments relating to the impeachment power occurred at the federal level. Indeed, the most direct 20th-century invocation of the power as a curb on a president was made in the early 1970's, against President Richard M. Nixon. Impeachment proceedings against Nixon were begun in October 1973, shortly after his firing of Special Prosecutor Archibald Cox. The responsibility for making an inquiry into Nixon's conduct was given to the House Judiciary Committee, chaired by Rep. Peter W. Rodino of New Jersey. The inquiry was authorized by a vote of 410 to 4 (House Resolution 803) by the House of Representatives on Feb. 6, 1974. The committee utilized a staff of nearly 100 under the direction of John M. Doar, former assistant attorney general. Information was gathered and analyzed from February to May, while Doar and Albert Jenner, chief minority counsel, also negotiated with the White House for relevant material. Among the highlights of the months-long controversy over the availability of material were (1) a decision on Mar. 18 by federal district Judge John J. Sirica to turn over to the Judiciary Committee "a sealed envelope and fat briefcase" containing evidence and the findings of the original Watergate grand jury, (2) the announcement on Apr. 3 by the White House that the president would pay about $465,000 in back taxes and interest, (3) the Judiciary Committee vote of 33 to 3 to subpoena Nixon for the tapes and records of more than forty conversations held in the White House Oval Office, and (4) the release on Apr. 30 by Nixon of edited transcripts of forty-six conversations. The committee's action set a precedent as the first time in American history that a president was subpoenaed for purposes related to impeachment. On May 15 two more subpoenas for additional materials were issued to the president. On May 22 Nixon refused to comply. Subsequently the reaction to his refusal came on May 30, when the Judiciary

Committee issued another subpoena (by a vote of 28 to 10), indicating that noncompliance might be considered grounds for impeachment. The lengthy proceeding reached a climax in late July when open formal Judiciary Committee debate began. The conclusion of these actions was the adoption of articles of impeachment on several counts and rejection on others. Specifically, article I—obstruction of justice—was adopted on July 27 by a vote of 27 to 11; article II—abuse of presidential power—was adopted on July 29, by a vote of 28 to 10; and article III—contempt of Congress—was adopted on July 30, by a vote of 21 to 17. Two proposed articles relating to income taxes and the bombing of Cambodia were rejected on July 30, by identical votes of 12 to 26. Debate by the House of Representatives on the articles adopted was scheduled for Aug. 19. But on Aug. 5 Nixon released additional tapes, the contents of which brought a flood of additional commitments for impeachment from most of his ardent congressional supporters. Many of them appealed for his resignation. Finally, on Aug. 8, in a televised speech, Nixon resigned. The impeachment power was not fully invoked but the purposes of the impeachment process were perhaps partially fulfilled. Vice-President Gerald R. Ford became president automatically when Nixon's letter of resignation reached Secretary of State Henry Kissinger at 11:30 A.M. on Aug. 9. The final major act in the near impeachment drama was finished on Sept. 8, when President Ford granted Nixon a "full, free and absolute pardon . . . for all offenses against the United States which he . . . has committed or may have committed" during his terms as president."

[See also Impeachment Trial of Andrew Johnson; Nixon, Resignation of.]

BIBLIOGRAPHY

Raoul Berger, *Impeachment: The Constitutional Problems.*
William S. Carpenter, *Judicial Tenure in the United States.*

— JOHN R. SCHMIDHAUSER

IMPEACHMENT TRIAL OF ANDREW JOHNSON

The greatest state trial in the United States followed the impeachment of President Andrew Johnson in 1868. Johnson was the first and only American president to suffer this ordeal. (Although in July 1974 the House Judiciary Committee recommended three articles of impeachment to the House of Representatives, President Richard M. Nixon resigned before a full House vote could be taken on the matter.)

After an eventful career in both houses of Congress, Johnson was elected vice-president in 1864 as President Abraham Lincoln's running mate. On Lincoln's death he became president and promptly took his stand for Lincoln's plan of Reconstruction. The Radical Republicans began at once maneuvering to thwart him. Above all else they wanted the continuance of Edwin M. Stanton as the secretary of war, which was the object of the Tenure of Office Act passed on Mar. 2, 1867, over Johnson's veto. It provided generally that all civil officers in whose appointment the Senate had participated could be removed only with the advice and consent of that body and made removal contrary to the act a "high misdemeanor." In August 1867 Johnson found it impossible to tolerate Stanton any longer and when Stanton refused to resign, Johnson suspended him and appointed Gen. Ulysses S. Grant as secretary of war ad interim.

Admission ticket to the impeachment trial of President Andrew Johnson, 1868. (Corbis-Bettmann)

On Feb. 21, 1868, Johnson removed Stanton from office, and three days later the House of Representatives, by a vote of 126 to 47, impeached the president for removing Stanton in defiance of the Tenure of Office Act.

The Constitution provides that the House has the sole power to prefer charges against a president, that is, articles of impeachment, and that the Senate sits as a court for the trial of the charges and is presided over by the chief justice of the Supreme Court. A two-thirds vote of the senators present is necessary for a conviction.

On Mar. 13, 1868, the trial began. Sen. Benjamin F. Butler, a virulent partisan, opened for the prosecution with a vitriolic tirade, going far outside the charges. The evidence for the prosecution consisted largely in establishing that Johnson had in fact removed Stanton. The defense was that under the Constitution the president had the right to do so and that the Tenure of Office Act, in seeking to deprive him of that right, was unconstitutional. Johnson himself did not attend the trial.

The scene in the Senate on May 16, 1868, when the vote was taken, was a dramatic one. For days the Radicals had been working feverishly in and out of Congress to bring pressure to bear upon the senators to vote for conviction. The roll was called first on the eleventh article of the thirteen to be voted on. Sen. James W. Grimes of Iowa, suffering from a stroke of paralysis, was borne into the Senate chamber at the last moment to vote for an acquittal. In dead silence the galleries waited for the tally. At last it was announced that thirty-five senators had voted guilty and nineteen not guilty. Two-thirds not having pronounced guilty, the chief justice thereupon declared that the president was "acquitted on this article." He had been saved by one vote. But there were twelve articles that had not yet been voted on. The court thereupon adjourned to permit the representatives and senators to attend the National Republican Convention. It was hoped that on their return to Washington some of the wavering senators might change their minds in favor of conviction. On May 28 the Senate reconvened to vote on the second and third articles. Again the roll was called, and again thirty-five senators voted for conviction and nineteen for acquittal; once more Johnson was saved by one vote. The remaining articles were never voted on.

BIBLIOGRAPHY

Lloyd Paul Stryker, *Andrew Johnson, A Study in Courage.*

— LLOYD PAUL STRYKER

IMPERIALISM

Imperialism, in its most precise usage, means the forcible extension of governmental control over foreign areas not destined for incorporation as integral parts of the nation. The term is often used more broadly to signify any important degree of national influence, public or private, over other societies, while to some it refers principally to foreign economic exploitation with or without other actions. In the case of the United States its application is further complicated by the nation's early contiguous expansion over such areas as the Florida, Louisiana, and Oregon territories and the Mexican cession. All of these were destined to be populated mainly by immigrants from the preexisting states and territories, and to be incorporated into the Union as equal self-governing units; however, to the extent that their acquisition involved the conquest of indigenous Indian, Mexican, or other peoples, elements of imperialism may be said to exist. In any case, the purchase of Alaska in 1867 ended the period when all new territory was assumed to be on the path to eventual statehood, and thereafter U.S. expansionism took forms more properly labeled "imperialistic."

During the last third of the 19th century the sharp rise in U.S. power and productivity coincided with the flood tide of European colonialism, ultimately creating in Americans a spirit of emulation and mission and an interest in the economic and domestic problem-solving aspects of overseas expansion. Early and abortive post-Civil War moves to annex or control the Dominican Republic, the Danish West Indies (Virgin Islands), Samoa, and Hawaii were followed by the beginnings of a modern navy and a quickening quest for new overseas markets beyond traditional trade ties to western Europe. One result by the 1890's was enhanced American interest and activity in Latin America and the Far East, marked in the latter case by a strong Protestant missionary movement, as well as by diplomatic and economic activity.

The emotions and disruptions caused by a Cuban revolt against Spanish rule simultaneously mobilized these growing interests and embroiled the United States in war with Spain. After a brief conflict in 1898 the victorious United States assumed responsibility for most of the remaining Spanish empire. Puerto Rico, Guam, and the Philippine Islands became outright colonies, while Cuba was made a self-governing protectorate after two years of U.S. occupation. Hawaii, which later gained old-style territorial status in 1900, was also annexed during the war. These developments occasioned a national debate over imperialism from 1898 to 1900 and became a leading issue in the presidential campaign of 1900. The annexation of the Philippines, a distant oriental archipelago already populated by an alien society and clearly outside the mystic confines of the Monroe Doctrine, set off the hottest battle. The decision to annex was defended on the grounds that the Filipinos needed enlightened U.S. rule and that the islands' possession would aid greatly in American penetration of a supposedly vast and growing China market. The main actual result was a Filipino rebellion against the United States, which was crushed only after three years of warfare, a circumstance that helped to end the vogue of colonial annexations of the traditional type.

Annexation of the Philippines was defended on the grounds that the Filipinos needed enlightened U.S. rule and that the islands' possession would greatly aid market penetration in China.

While no more territorial annexations occurred, the United States continued to spread its influence through the use of various types of protectorates. The early 20th century saw this trend focused on the Caribbean, where concern for the Panama Canal and fear of European influence were guiding considerations. The establishment of a protectorate in Cuba (1901) was followed by similar actions in Panama (1903), the Dominican Republic (1905, 1916), Nicaragua (1912), and Haiti (1915). These acts to spread U.S. influence, along with the annexation of Puerto Rico (1899) and the purchase of the Virgin Islands (1917), caused the Caribbean to be regarded as an "American lake." In China also, the United States attempted to gain influence, although less successfully. The Open Door notes (1899, 1900) marked a U.S. attempt to impose its own commercial and diplomatic guidelines upon the great-power rivalry in China, while the administration of William Howard Taft (1909–13) strove to gain financial influence in that country. The situation was different from that in the Caribbean area, however, for the United States was only one of a number of powers involved in the Far East and its effectiveness in China was accordingly limited.

After World War I a period of retrenchment seemed to mark the end of U.S. imperialism. Caribbean military occupations were liquidated, and the Good Neighbor policy of the 1930's involved a general abandonment of formal protectorates. In 1934 Congress provided for eventual Philippine independence via a transitional period ending in 1946. Some scholars nevertheless argue that U.S. imperialism merely took new forms, since the nation's policy-makers after World War I intended to use the country's newly gained financial and economic supremacy to achieve greater overseas economic expansion and to enforce policies that would maintain the world status quo while insuring free entry everywhere to U.S. money and products.

The unique position of power and wealth into which the United States emerged after World War II enabled it to reach unprecedented levels of global influence, while the cold-war rivalry with the Soviet Union became the justification for a proliferation of alliances, military commitments, and client states. Those who define imperialism broadly argue that the postwar complex of U.S. overseas military bases, foreign aid, multinational corporations, intervention, and limited wars can best be described by that term. Others hold that intimate economic ties, military self-defense, and unequal power relationships do not in themselves constitute imperialism unless the term is to become too all-embracing to be meaningful. Such events as the wars in Korea (1950–53) and Vietnam (1963–73) or the interventions in Guatemala (1954), Lebanon (1958), and the Dominican Republic (1965) thus do or do not illustrate U.S. imperialism, according to the ways in which these events are viewed and imperialism is defined.

BIBLIOGRAPHY

Walter La Feber, *The New Empire: An Interpretation of American Expansion, 1860–1898.*
Ernest May, *Imperial Democracy: The Emergence of America As a World Power.*
Ronald Steel, *Pax Americana.*
Richard Van Alstyne, *The Rising American Empire.*

— DAVID HEALY

IMPRESSMENT OF SEAMEN

Impressment of seamen was one of the chief causes of bad relations between Great Britain and the United States during the early years of the Republic. Recruits for the Royal Navy were forcibly mustered in the 18th century by the press gang. While neutral vessels appear to have been so victimized prior to 1790, the problem became acute between that date and 1815. Under cover of the belligerent right of search British boarding parties removed from the decks of foreign neutrals any seamen "deemed" British. The practice was steadfastly regarded in England as indispensable to sea power in the war with France. Improvement of the naval service to induce voluntary enlistment was not then conceived of.

Although American seamen, in common with those of a few of other nations, were the occasional victims of the press gang in England, and although persons allegedly British subjects were removed from American ships in British ports, the real issue concerned the impressment of seamen on the high seas. The American merchant marine, prospering and expanding under wartime conditions, offered unexcelled opportunities to British seamen. It is estimated that between 1790 and 1815 about 20,000 of them—including deserters from the Royal Navy—signed up on American ships. The conflict between the traditional doctrine of inalienable allegiance, held to by England, and the new, revolutionary American doctrine of the right of the individual to change his allegiance made an insuperable difficulty. As British Foreign Secretary George Canning put it, "when [British] mariners . . . are employed in the private service of foreigners, they enter into engagements inconsistent with the duty of subjects. In such cases, the species of redress which the practice of all times has . . . sanctioned is that of taking those subjects at sea out of the service of such foreign individuals. . . . " In no circumstances was naturalization as an American citizen a protection to the seaman.

The British left the matter of determining nationality to the discretion of the press gangs and boarding officers—and it is not recorded that they were careful in making distinctions. Use of the English language appears to have been the main test applied. Of the 10,000 persons estimated to have been impressed from American ships, only one-tenth proved to be British subjects.

The British returned native-born American seamen to the United States, without indemnity, if their citizenship could be established. But the British authorities themselves took little responsibility to determine citizenship, and each separate case had to be handled by the American government. In the meantime the impressed person had to remain in service and go wherever he was commanded. As early as 1796 the United States issued certificates of citizenship to its mariners in an effort to protect them, but these "protections" were soon abused. They were easily lost or were sold to British subjects. An American sailor could buy a protection from a notary public for one dollar and sell it to a Britisher for ten. The British consequently refused to honor the certificates.

American protest against impressment dates from 1787, and in 1792 President Thomas Jefferson tried to proceed on the simple rule "that the vessel being American shall be evidence that the seamen on board of her are such." But legally this doctrine was defensible only for the high seas. It had no pertinency to American vessels in British ports. On the other hand, Great Britain refused any concessions whatever to the principle. Three times the United States tried to negotiate a treaty in which each party would deny itself the right to impress persons from the other's ships, and offered various concessions. Although linked with other issues of neutral trade, impressment came to assume first place in American diplomacy. The climax occurred in 1807 when four men were removed from the American frigate *Chesapeake.* In 1812 Congress alleged impressment to be the principal cause of the declaration of war against Great Britain, but in view of the ambitions of the western war hawks this allegation can be discounted.

Impressment of seamen has been, since 1815, nothing but a historical curiosity. But there have been several modern derivatives: (1) On the basis of inalienable allegiance naturalized American citizens have been impressed into the armed services of the country of their birth upon returning there. (2) During the Civil War two Confederate commissioners en route to England were seized from the British steamer *Trent* by the captain of a U.S. vessel. (3) In World War I the Allies removed enemy aliens, particularly military reservists, from American vessels.

BIBLIOGRAPHY

Reginald Horsman, *The Causes of the War of 1812.*

Bradford Perkins, *Prologue to War: England and the United States, 1805–1812.*

— RICHARD W. VAN ALSTYNE

INCOME TAX CASES

Income Tax Cases (1895). The judicial overthrow of the federal income tax of 1894 ranks among the most celebrated episodes in Supreme Court history. Confronted with a sharp conflict of social and political forces, the Court chose to vitiate a hundred years of precedent and void the tax (*Pollock* v. *Farmers' Loan and Trust Company,* 157 U.S. 429; *Rehearing,* 158 U.S. 601). Not until 1913, after adoption of the Sixteenth Amendment, could a federal income tax be levied.

The 1894 tax of 2 percent on incomes over $4,000 was designed by southern and western congressmen to rectify the federal government's regressive revenue system (the tariff and excise taxes) and commence the taxation of large incomes. Conservative opponents of the tax, alarmed by the social tensions of the times—the agitation against the trusts, the rise of populism, and the Pullman strike, for example—saw the tax as the first step in a majoritarian attack on the upper classes.

Constitutionally the tax seemed secure. The Court had unanimously upheld the Civil War income tax in 1891 (*Springer* v. *United States,* 102 U.S. 586), declaring that an income tax was not a "direct tax" within the meaning of the Constitution and thus did not require apportionment among the states according to population. The Court had based its decision on a 1796 precedent (*Hylton* v. *United States,* 3 Dallas 171) that had established the rule of feasibility to determine whether a tax was direct: If a tax could not be levied practicably by apportionment, then it was not direct. And the Court had strongly intimated in *Hylton* that the only direct taxes were poll taxes and taxes on land. This rule had been carefully followed.

Confronted with a sharp conflict of social and political forces, the Supreme Court decided in 1895 to void the income tax.

Prominent counsel opposing the 1894 tax appealed to the Supreme Court to overthrow or bypass the *Hylton* and *Springer* precedents. The oral arguments also featured widely publicized declamations against populistic majorities and class legislation. Defenders of the tax, including Attorney General Richard Olney, warned the Court not to interfere in a divisive political issue.

On Apr. 8 the Court delivered a partial decision, holding by six to two (one justice was ill) that the tax on income from real property was a direct tax and had to be apportioned. Since a tax on land was direct, said Chief Justice Melville W. Fuller for the Court, so was a tax on the income from land. On other important issues the Court was announced as divided, four to four.

A rehearing was held, with the ailing Justice Howell E. Jackson sitting, and on May 20 the entire tax was found unconstitutional, five to four. Personal property was not constitutionally different from real property, the chief justice argued, and taxation of income from either was direct; the rest of the tax, because inseparable from the unconstitutional parts, was also invalid. The *Springer* precedent, specifically involving personal property, was not mentioned.

The four dissenting justices gave forceful opinions attacking the decision. Most surprising, Justice Jackson was among the dissenters; apparently, one of the majority justices had changed his vote between the first and second opinions. Public and professional criticism was intense, and the Democratic party platform of 1896 hinted at Court-packing to gain a reversal.

The income tax cases were later described by Charles Evans Hughes as one of the Court's "self-inflicted wounds." From the perspective of the judicial role in the 1890's, the *Pollock* decisions, together with other leading cases of the period—such as the *E. C. Knight* case and the *Debs* injunction case—marked the triumph of a conservative judicial revolution, with far-reaching consequences.

BIBLIOGRAPHY

E. S. Corwin, *Court Over Constitution.*
W. L. King, *Melville Weston Fuller.*
A. M. Paul, *Conservative Crisis and the Rule of Law.*
Sidney Ratner, *American Taxation.*
E. R. A. Seligman, *The Income Tax.*

— ARNOLD M. PAUL

INDENTURED SERVANTS

Indentured servants in colonial America were for the most part adult white persons who were bound to labor for a period of years. There were three well-known classes: the free-willers, or redemptioners; those who were kidnapped or forced to leave their home country because of poverty or for political or religious reasons; and convicts. The first class represented those who chose to bind themselves to labor for a definite time, usually three or five years, to secure passage to America. The best known of these were the Germans, but a great many English and Scottish came in the same way. The second class, those who were kidnapped or deviously enticed, was numerous because of the scarcity of labor in the colonies. Their services were very profitably sold to plantation owners or farmers and the victims indentured for a period of years. The third class, the convicts and paupers, were sentenced to deportation and on arrival in America were indentured unless they had personal funds to maintain themselves. Seven years was a common term of such service. The West Indies and Maryland appear to have received the largest numbers of this third class.

Most of the colonies regulated the treatment of indentured servants, and it was commonly required that they be provided with clothing, a gun, and a small tract of land upon which to establish themselves after their term of service. These requirements applied especially to those who were unwilling servants. There was no permanent stigma attached to indentured service, and the families of such persons merged readily with the total population. Children born to persons while serving their indenture were free. Indentured servants outnumbered slaves in the southern colonies during the 17th century and always far outnumbered the slaves in the other colonies. In the 18th century they were most numerous in the middle colonies. Terms of an indenture were enforceable in the courts, and runaway servants could be compelled to return to their masters and serve out their terms, additional periods being added for the time they had been absent.

The treatment of indentured servants varied. Some were mistreated; others lived as members of the family. The presence of so many redemptioners in the later years of the colonial period indicates that the hardships were not considered excessive. Although indentured service of the colonial genre ceased after the American Revolution, various similar kinds of contract labor were widespread in the United States during periods of labor shortage until the passage of the Contract Labor Law of 1885.

BIBLIOGRAPHY

Edward Channing, *A History of the United States*, vol. II.

— O. M. DICKERSON

INDIAN AFFAIRS, BUREAU OF

Bureau of Indian Affairs, the principal federal agency responsible for Indian programs. Referred to at times as the Office of Indian Affairs, the Indian Department, and the Indian Service, it has been known as the Bureau of Indian Affairs since the 1950's. Established by order of Secretary of War John C. Calhoun in 1824, the bureau received congressional blessing ten years later in an act that provided for the organization of a "department of Indian Affairs." The use of the word "department" in this legislation was incorrect, however, since the bureau was one of various agencies within the War Department, where it remained until 1849 when it was transferred to the newly created Home Department, later the Department of the Interior. The head of the bureau has always been called the commissioner of Indian Affairs, a designation confirmed by Congress in 1832.

The forerunner of the bureau was the Office of the Superintendent of Indian Trade, established in 1806 and abolished in 1822. While regulation of trade with the Indians, including the licensing of traders on the reservations, has continued to be a function of the bureau, other responsibilities have surpassed it in importance: land and resource management and development, education, vocational training and placement, law and order, and social welfare. Until 1954, when the Indian Health Service was established within the Department of Health, Education, and Welfare, the bureau also provided health care for reservation Indians.

During the late 1860's, when many Indian tribes throughout the West and Southwest were making war on the white settlers, considerable sentiment emerged to return the Bureau of Indian Affairs to the War Department. Local bureau officials were accused of maladministration and of defending Indians at the expense of the whites. Influential missionary groups, strongly opposed to placing the bureau back in the War Department, helped to defeat legislation introduced for that purpose; the bureau remained in the Interior Department, although in the late 1960's some Indians advocated making it an independent agency or placing it directly under the jurisdiction of the Executive Office of the President.

Because of strong criticism of the bureau, Congress in 1869 set up a Board of Indian Commissioners to exercise joint control with the secretary of the Interior Department over Indian appropriations. The board was highly influential in Indian affairs until the early 1900's. President Franklin D. Roosevelt abolished it by executive order in 1933.

Since the 1950's the Bureau of Indian Affairs has had three principal levels of administrative responsibility: (1) a national headquarters with a small policy staff in Washington, D.C.; (2) area offices composed of both technical and supervisory personnel at strategic locations throughout the country; and (3) local offices, usually known as agencies, serving the reservations directly and staffed primarily with technicians. In a few locations such as the area around Puget Sound in Washington where a single agency serves many small, widely scattered reservations the bureau has set up subagencies to provide immediate technical services in such fields as forestry and fisheries management.

Complaints by Indian leaders that bureau employees at local levels were being stifled by area and Washington office supervisors led to efforts in the mid-1970's to reduce the size of staffs at these upper levels and provide for greater delegations of authority to agency heads.

A major feature of Indian policy in the 1970's was the transfer of authority and responsibility for various programs from the Bureau of Indian Affairs to the individual tribes. This approach will eventually reduce the bureau to a granting and contracting agency having relatively few direct program responsibilities.

Throughout much of its history the bureau has ministered principally to Indians living on or near established reservations. Supreme Court decisions in the mid-1970's suggested, however, that the government's responsibilities, at least in certain instances, may extend to Indians who have left these areas. Other Supreme Court decisions of the mid-1970's established that Indian job preference within the Bureau of Indian Affairs (conferred by the Indian Reorganization Act of 1934) extends to promotion as well as to hiring. Already heavily Indian in character (all U.S. Indian commissioners since 1966 have been Indians), the bureau could, as a result of these decisions, become an all-Indian agency.

BIBLIOGRAPHY

William T. Hagan, *American Indians.*
Jay P. Kinney, *A Continent Lost—A Civilization Won.*

D'Arcy McNickle, *Native American Tribalism.*
U.S. Department of the Interior, *Federal Indian Law.*

— JAMES E. OFFICER

INDIAN LAND CESSIONS

The policies and procedures involved in the extinguishment of American Indians' rights to lands constitute an important chapter in American history and present interesting comparisons with the practices of other nations in dealing with native peoples inhabiting countries over which these nations have claimed and maintained jurisdiction. At the outset it should be stated that, with a few possible exceptions, the Indians themselves had little or no concept of either individual or tribal ownership of land. To them land was like air or water—something that was necessary to life, but not capable of being bought or sold. Thus it was difficult for them to understand the meaning of treaties in which they relinquished their rights. In some instances it was held by the Indians that no single tribe had the power to alienate land unless all the tribes living in a given territory were in agreement.

The English based their territorial claims upon discovery, exploration, or settlement, as did the other European nations colonizing North America. Fundamentally they ignored the rights of the Indians. That the newly discovered lands were inhabited by native peoples was no barrier, in their view, to the making of grants to individuals and companies or the planting of colonies. In fact, it was not until near the close of the colonial period that the English home government formulated any definite policy in regard to the possessory rights of the Indians. The proprietors and other colonial authorities were left to deal with the Indians largely in their own way.

The Indians had little or no concept of either individual or tribal ownership of land; to them, land was like air or water: essential to life, but not capable of being bought or sold.

Policies and practices differed from colony to colony, though, having a different perspective from that of the home government, most settlers, almost from the beginning, conceded that the Indians possessed rights of occupancy of their lands that must be extinguished by purchase or treaty before such lands could be occupied by white men. While in many instances individuals purchased land directly from the Indians on their own responsibility, it early became the practice to prohibit such dealings without the permission of the colonial authorities. Indeed, it soon became customary to require that treaties of any kind with the Indians be negotiated only by agents of the colonial government.

It would be difficult, if not impossible, to determine the date or terms of the first Indian land cession within the present boundaries of the United States. Furthermore, it would be an almost hopeless task to attempt to unravel the tangled and ambiguous accounts of Indian land cessions during the early colonial period. Boundaries were often exceedingly vague and indefinite. For instance, there were numerous "walking treaties," in which land areas were described in terms of distances a man could walk in a day or a given number of days; and similarly, there were "riding treaties," in which the distances a man could cover on horseback in given periods of time were used as measurements. Other treaties were even less specific in the matter of boundaries. There was also much overlapping, even in the land cessions of a single tribe to a single colony, to say nothing of the cessions by different tribes.

A few illustrations will serve to indicate the character of the Indian land cessions made during the colonial period. William Penn was notably successful in his dealings with the Indians, and one of his early acts was the holding of a council at Shackamaxon in 1682, at which the Indians deeded to him a vaguely defined area in return for a considerable amount of merchandise that was itemized in the treaty. In the succeeding years several other treaties were made with the Indians of Pennsylvania, including the Walking Treaty of 1686. In 1744 representatives of Pennsylvania, Virginia, and Maryland concluded a treaty with the Six Nations, or Iroquois, at Lancaster, Pa., in which these important tribes ceded their rights to land between the frontier of Virginia and the Ohio River. After the close of the French and Indian War in 1763 a so-called Indian boundary line was established in a series of treaties, among which three are outstanding. First was the Treaty of Fort Stanwix in 1768 with the Iroquois, in which they agreed to relinquish their claims to lands east and south of a line running roughly from the vicinity of Fort Stanwix in New York southward to the Delaware, then southwestward to the Allegheny, and down that river and the Ohio to the mouth of the Tennessee. By the Treaty of Hard Labor the same year and by the Treaty of Lochaber in 1770 the Cherokee ceded their claims to lands in the present state of West Virginia. Mention should also be made of the Treaty of Sycamore Shoals, privately negotiated in 1775 between the Transylvania Company and the Cherokee, who ceded to the company approximately 20 million acres of land lying between the Cumberland and Kentucky rivers.

When the United States came into existence, the government followed the policy adopted during the colonial period with respect to the rights of Indians to their land. It was held that the ultimate title to the soil resided in the federal government, although the Indians had a right to the use and occupancy of the lands they claimed that could be extinguished only by their consent. Negotiations for Indian land cessions were to be conducted only by agents of the federal government except in certain cases in which the original states were permitted to act. Article IX of the Articles of Confederation gave Congress the power to regulate the trade and manage all affairs with the Indians. A proclamation of Sept. 22, 1783, prohibited any person from "purchasing or receiving any gift or cession of such lands or claim without the express authority and direction of the United States in Congress assembled." The Constitution made no specific reference to dealings with Indians except to give Congress power to regulate commerce with them. In practice negotiations with Indians were based upon the treaty-making power.

For nearly a century after the founding of the United States Indian land cessions were accomplished by means of treaties couched in the formal language of an international covenant. These treaties were negotiated with Indian chieftains and leaders by appointees of the executive branch of the federal government, signed by both parties, and ratified by the U.S. Senate. In 1871 the fiction of regarding the Indian tribes as independent nations was abandoned, and thereafter simple agreements were made with them. This change of practice seems to have been dictated mainly by the determination of the House of Representatives to have a voice in the making of commitments entailing appropriations of money, for the agreements required the approval of both houses of Congress.

Although the first treaty made by the United States with any Indian tribe was that made with the Delaware in 1778, the first Indian land cession to the new nation was that made by the Six Nations, or Iroquois, by the second Treaty of Fort Stanwix, in 1784, by which land in northwestern Pennsylvania and in the extreme western part of New York was ceded. The following are brief summaries of selections from the long list of Indian land cessions made between 1784 and 1871. They furnish some indication of the rapidity with which the Indian title was extinguished as the tide of American settlers swept westward.

Treaty of Hopewell, 1785, with the Cherokee, ceding land in North Carolina west of the Blue Ridge and in Tennessee and Kentucky south of the Cumberland River.

Treaty of New York City, 1790, with the Creek, ceding a large tract of land in eastern Georgia.

Treaty of the Holston River, 1791, with the Cherokee, ceding land in western North Carolina and northeastern Tennessee.

Treaty of Greenville, 1795, with the Wyandot, Delaware, Shawnee, Ottawa, Chippewa, Potawatomi, Miami, Eel River, Wea, Kickapoo, Piankashaw, and Kaskaskia, ceding large areas in southern and eastern Ohio comprising nearly two-thirds of the present state, some land in southeastern Indiana, and small tracts around Michilimackinac in Michigan.

Treaty of Tellico, 1798, with the Cherokee, ceding three tracts of land mostly in eastern Tennessee.

Treaty of Buffalo Creek, 1802, with the Seneca, ceding lands in western New York involved in the purchase of the Holland Land Company (an unusual treaty in that the land was ceded directly to the company).

Treaty of Vincennes, 1803, with the Kaskaskia, ceding a large area in central and southeastern Illinois comprising about one-half of the present state—other tribes ceding their claims to this area in the Treaties of Edwardsville, 1818 and 1819.

Treaty of Fort Clark, 1808, with the Osage, ceding land between the Arkansas and Missouri rivers, comprising nearly one-half of Arkansas and two-thirds of Missouri.

Treaty of Fort Jackson, 1814, with the Creek, ceding large areas of land in southern Georgia and in central and southern Alabama.

Treaty of Saint Louis, 1816, with the Ottawa, Chippewa, and Potawatomi, ceding land between the Illinois and Mississippi rivers in Illinois, as well as some land in southwestern Wisconsin.

Treaty of Old Town, 1818, with the Chickasaw, ceding land between the Tennessee and Mississippi rivers in Tennessee and Kentucky.

Treaty of Saginaw, 1819, with the Chippewa, ceding a large area surrounding Saginaw Bay and numerous other scattered tracts in the present state of Michigan.

Treaty of Doak's Stand, 1820, with the Choctaw, ceding land in west-central Mississippi.

Treaty of Chicago, 1821, with the Ottawa, Chippewa, and Potawatomi, ceding land in southern Michigan and northern Indiana.

Treaties of Saint Louis, 1823, with the Osage and Kansa, ceding extensive areas of land in the present states of Missouri, Kansas, and Oklahoma.

Treaty of Prairie du Chien, 1830, with the Sauk and Fox, Sioux, and other tribes, ceding land in western

Iowa, southwestern Minnesota, and northwestern Missouri.

Treaty of Fort Armstrong, 1832, with the Sauk and Fox, ceding a 50-mile strip of land along the west bank of the Mississippi in Iowa (known as the Black Hawk Purchase).

Treaty of Sauk and Fox Agency, 1842, with the Sauk and Fox, ceding all of south-central Iowa.

Treaty of Traverse des Sioux, 1851, with the Sisseton and Wahpeton bands of the Sioux, ceding claims to lands in southern Minnesota, comprising more than one-third of the present state, and in northern Iowa.

Treaty of Fort Laramie, 1851, with the Sioux, Cheyenne, Arapaho, and other tribes, ceding land in North Dakota, Montana, and Wyoming (the provisions being altered by the Senate and never ratified by the Indians).

Treaty of Table Rock, 1853, with the Rogue River Indians, ceding land in southern Oregon.

During this period of the signing of such a multiplicity of treaties, groups of treaties were also negotiated in the light of particular national developments. In 1854, in order to make way for the organization of Kansas and Nebraska territories, there were signed a number of treaties in which land was ceded by Indian tribes that, for the most part, had been located along the eastern border of the so-called Indian Country, in accordance with the government's Indian removal policy. After the discovery of gold in California and the rush of settlement toward the Far West, the center of interest shifted there, and especially to the region of the Great Plains, where the powerful tribes were becoming increasingly restless. In 1861, for instance, the Arapaho and Cheyenne ceded their claims to enormous tracts of land in the present states of Nebraska, Kansas, Colorado, and Wyoming. Before the end of the 1860's the old Indian Country on the Great Plains was reduced to the area known as the Indian Territory, which later became the state of Oklahoma. During the same period the extinguishment of Indian titles was proceeding rapidly from the Rocky Mountain region to the Pacific coast.

By 1871, when the making of formal treaties with the Indians was abandoned, there was little left to be done to complete federal control of the land from coast to coast, and by 1890 the process was practically complete. Of the reservations on which Indians resided at the turn of the century, either in accordance with treaty provisions or under authority conferred by the federal government, many have since been abandoned, consolidated, or reduced in area.

A total of 720 Indian land cessions is indicated by Charles C. Royce on the maps accompanying his digest of *Indian Land Cessions in the United States,* which covers the period from 1784 to 1894. It must be remembered, however, that it often required treaties or agreements with several tribes to clear the Indian title of a given area of land. Also, many treaties dealt with the ceding of relatively small reservations set aside previously when a much larger area had been relinquished.

Compensation to the Indians for the land ceded by them consisted of livestock, various kinds of merchandise (often including guns and ammunition), and annuities. A government report of 1883 indicates that up to 1880 the federal government had expended more than $187 million for the extinguishment of Indian land titles. How much of this sum actually reached the Indians, either in goods or in money, would be impossible to determine. In numerous instances traders gobbled up the annuities as fast as they were paid, on the ground that the Indians were indebted to them. If government figures are accepted at their face value, however, it may be contended that the United States has dealt quite liberally with the native inhabitants, since the total sum paid to Spain, Mexico, and Texas for the territory acquired from them was less than $75 million.

Compensation to the Indians for the lands ceded consisted of livestock, various kinds of merchandise (often including guns and ammunition), and annuities.

It has sometimes been asserted that the United States has never dispossessed the Indians of their right in the land without their consent. Literally speaking, with a few exceptions, this statement is true. If, however, the term "willing consent" is substituted, the case is quite different. A survey of the history of Indian land cessions reveals that they fall into three large general groups when considered in the light of the conditions or causes that produced them. In the first place, many of the cessions were made at the close of wars. In this group are the cessions made at the Treaty of Greenville, following Gen. Anthony Wayne's campaign; the Treaty of Fort Jackson, following Gen. Andrew Jackson's campaign in the South; and the Black Hawk Purchase, or Treaty of Fort Armstrong, following the Black Hawk War. To be sure, the Indians signed these treaties, but scarcely voluntarily. In the second place, there are the land cessions made after the government had exercised pressure in order to accomplish particular purposes. Illustrations are to be found in the treaties with both eastern and western tribes when the Indian removal policy was being put into effect following the passage of the Indian Removal Act of 1830 and the treaties secured when the policy of maintaining the Indian Country was being abandoned after 1853. Finally, numerous treaties ceding land were clearly brought about by the demand for more land for settlement, for instance, the treaties negotiated by William Henry Harrison opening up land in Indiana. It would be difficult, indeed, to find a land cession made by the Indians entirely of their own volition.

[See also Indian Policy, Colonial; Indian Policy, National.]

BIBLIOGRAPHY

Dan E. Clark, *The West in American History.*
Charles J. Kappler, *Indian Affairs: Laws and Treaties,* vol. II.
Charles C. Royce, *Indian Land Cessions in the United States.*

— DAN E. CLARK

INDIAN POLICY, COLONIAL

From the earliest colonial times Indian title to the soil was construed by the British to be one of occupancy, with the ultimate fee in the crown and colony.

Before 1755 Indian affairs were largely controlled by the individual colonies. Policies were initiated by the colonial governors; the assemblies appropriated the money to pay the expenses involved and passed laws to regulate Indian trade and to compel traders to secure licenses. Colonial control resulted in the native Americans' being robbed of their lands and cheated in trade. Many tribes, therefore, allied themselves with the French during the French and Indian War, 1754–63. To win Indian support, the British inaugurated a system of imperial management in 1755 and 1756 by creating two separate Indian departments and appointing a superintendent for each. Sir William Johnson was appointed, in 1755, superintendent of Indian affairs for the northern department; he continued to serve in that capacity until his death in 1774, when his nephew, Guy Johnson, succeeded him. Edmund Atkin was appointed superintendent of the southern department and held the office until 1762, when he was succeeded by John Stuart, who continued to serve until his death in 1779.

By 1761 the right to buy Indian lands had been denied the American colonies and was directed by the home government. The Proclamation of 1763 guaranteed to the Indians "for the present" the lands between the Appalachian Mountains and the Mississippi River. No colonial official could make land grants within that territory until the king's further pleasure was known, and no settlements therein were allowed. No trader was permitted within the reservation without a license obtained from the colony in which he resided.

This administrative system subordinated the Indian superintendents to the military authorities, and so in 1764 they presented a plan designed to give them more independence. The proposal provided that they be permitted to regulate such Indian affairs as treaties, trade, land purchases, and matters pertaining to peace or war without political or military interference; that all Indian traders were to be placed under the control of the superintendent; that civil cases were to be tried by the Indian agents and appeals taken to the superintendent; and that all provincial laws relating to Indian affairs were to be repealed. Although Parliament never sanctioned the plan, the superintendents proceeded to administer Indian affairs according to it.

In 1767 Sir William Petty, Earl of Shelburne, British secretary of state, recommended the abolition of home control of Indian affairs and reversion to the earlier practice of colonial regulation. His proposal to abolish the Indian departments was rejected because it was felt that such matters as land purchases, treaties, boundaries, and conferences should be in the hands of British officials. It was agreed, nevertheless, that the regulation of Indian trade should be transferred to the colonies and a definite Indian boundary surveyed. If ever permitted, westward colonization was to be under imperial control. Thus the compromise between imperial and colonial control was effected. Boundary agreements were accordingly negotiated, and the surveys were made.

The real problem then was to prevent encroachments upon the frontier lands. The desired prevention was most difficult because the powers of the superintendents had been weakened. Despite the efforts of Stuart and Guy Johnson to prevent Indian land cessions to individuals and to companies, these continued until the Revolution. The British, nevertheless, succeeded in retaining the friendship of the major tribes throughout the revolutionary war.

The Indians were paid very little for land cessions, and permanent annuities were never granted during the colonial period. The Revolution prevented the formulation of a permanent Indian policy; the Indian policy of the United States was largely derived from British policy and the policies pursued by the colonies.

BIBLIOGRAPHY

C. W. Alvord, *The Mississippi Valley in British Politics.*
W. H. Mohr, *Federal Indian Relations, 1774–1788.*
Helen L. Shaw, *British Administration of the Southern Indians, 1756–1783.*

— GEORGE D. HARMON

INDIAN POLICY, NATIONAL

American Indian policy was modeled on that of the British, and many concepts underlying this policy have endured to the present day. Two basic elements have been especially important. The first of these is legal recognition of the fact that Indians have ownership interests in the lands they traditionally used and occupied, even though they lacked formal title documents. The second is the notion that Indians require government assistance and protection because they are not sophisticated in the ways of European society.

After experimenting with other approaches, the British concluded about the middle of the 18th century that the administration of Indian affairs should be placed in the hands of crown officials rather than entrusted to colonial administrators who seldom accorded Indians treatment equal to that accorded colonists. Being familiar with the British experience, those who drafted the Articles of Confederation insisted upon placing full authority over Indian affairs in the hands of the federal government. The Constitution is much less specific in this regard, although, in Article I, Section 8, it does endow Congress with the power to "regulate Commerce with foreign Nations, and among the several States, and with the Indian Tribes." Powers deriving from other portions of the Constitution have also been used to develop legislation for the implementation of federal Indian policy. Among these are the powers to make expenditures for the general welfare, to control the property of the United States, and to make treaties. Important too are the powers of Congress to admit new states and prescribe the terms of their admission, to make war, to establish post roads, to create tribunals inferior to the Supreme Court, and to promulgate a "uniform Rule of Naturalization." As a result of the use of all those powers, Indians have a much more profound and direct relationship with the federal government than do other inhabitants of the United States.

Before the War of 1812, U.S. Indian policy had two principal objectives: to keep Indians pacified and to gain control of Indian trade. Both the British and the French, who retained interests in areas near the borders of the United States following the American Revolution, tried to incite the Indians against the Americans and to persuade the Indians to trade furs and other items to them rather than to the Americans. When Congress established the War Department in 1789, it made the new department responsible for administering Indian affairs. Between 1798 and 1822 the department operated trading houses where Indians were guaranteed fair prices for the goods they had to sell and those they wished to buy. This operation was known as the factory system. The first federal official within the department to have primary responsibilities in Indian administration was the superintendent of Indian trade, whose office was established in 1806. The threat from the French ceased with the Louisiana Purchase of 1803, and the British threat ended with the conclusion of the War of 1812. While Indian trade continued to be important, it fell increasingly into the hands of private citizens after 1820, and the Office of the Superintendent of Indian Trade was eliminated two years later.

Before the War of 1812, U.S. Indian policy had two main objectives: to keep Indians pacified and to gain control of Indian trade.

Emerging as major objectives in Indian policy after the War of 1812 were the twin goals of territorial acquisition and Indian isolation, usually referred to as Indian removal. The roots of the new policy can be found in some of the treaties negotiated before 1800, but its real foundation was laid in 1802 when Georgia ceded certain lands to the United States with the understanding that the federal government would thereafter "peaceably obtain, on reasonable terms," the Indian title to some of the lands in the ceded area and to all the land inside Georgia itself. President Thomas Jefferson regarded the territory obtained through the Louisiana Purchase as ideal for a new Indian homeland. Legislation for Indian removal was introduced in Congress before the War of 1812, but no general law for this purpose was enacted until 1830, during the administration of President Andrew Jackson. However, at least as early as 1817, when John C. Calhoun became secretary of war, it was evident that a removal program would be undertaken, and in fact, most of the treaties negotiated after 1817 included provisions for land cessions and Indian resettlement. With the passage of the Indian Removal Act in 1830, the process of resettling the eastern Indians was greatly accelerated. Administering the program was the Bureau of Indian Affairs, which had been established within the War Department in 1824 and confirmed by Congress ten years later. Best known of all the removal actions was that forced upon the Cherokee, which produced in 1838–39 the infamous incident in American history known as the Trail of Tears. By midcentury removal was an accomplished fact, the United States having acquired more than 450 million acres of Indian land at a cost of approximately 20 cents per acre. When the Home Department (later the Department of the Interior) was created in 1849, the Bureau of Indian Affairs was transferred there.

As the Civil War neared, new features of Indian policy were developed. Important among them was land allotment. The treaty of 1854 with the Omaha contained the first comprehensive provision for the division of Indian land into individual holdings and provided a model both for other treaties and for the general allotment act that followed thirty-three years later.

Although the federal government helped finance Indian education beginning about 1820, the administration of Indian schools was left to the missionaries. With the establishment of Carlisle Indian School in Carlisle, Pa., in 1879, the Bureau of Indian Affairs adopted the policy of operating, as well as financing, Indian schools.

The major thrust of federal policy following the Civil War was toward subduing the still-hostile western tribes and placing their members on reservations. Congress, in an 1871 appropriations bill, decreed that the federal government would not enter into any further treaties with Indian tribes, thereby setting aside a policy that had prevailed since the days of British rule. Also in the 1870's many missionary groups began to advocate policies aimed at Indian assimilation. Foremost among these was land allotment designed to break up the communal holdings of each tribe and distribute the land among its members. Many serious-minded persons were convinced that an allotment program would make yeoman farmers of the Indians, thereby placing them on the road to assimilation. In 1887 the Dawes General Allotment Act was passed, providing for the breakup of the reservations.

Another element of the forced assimilation policy prevailing after the 1880's was the off-reservation boarding school. It was widely believed that if Indian youngsters could be removed from their families and educated in the ways of the white men, the Indian "problem" would be solved within one or two generations.

Far from having the expected results, the assimilation program, which moved ahead at full steam until about 1920, resulted in the alienation of millions of acres of Indian land, destroyed the security that Indians had gained both from their land base and from their tribal institutions, and produced an acute state of social disorganization among them. The 1920's, as had been the decade following the Civil War, were years of confusion as new policy proposals were made and considered. One notable accomplishment of the period was the passage in 1924 of an Indian citizenship act.

A major study of Indian administration undertaken by Lewis Meriam and associates for the Institute for Government Research produced in 1928 the so-called Meriam Report, which recommended the abandonment of the allotment program, the continuance of federal trusteeship over lands already allotted, and the construction of schools near the homes of Indian youngsters (with consequent abandonment of the off-reservation boarding schools). These recommendations and others from the report were incorporated by Commissioner John Collier into the Indian Reorganization Act of 1934, which is still the basic legislation in Indian affairs. The act also provided for the establishment of democratic local government on the reservations; most tribal organizations are based on models developed during the years just after its passage. In addition to ending the federal allotment program, continuing federal stewardship over Indian land, and providing for local government, the act established the policy of Indian preference with respect to employment in the Bureau of Indian Affairs.

In 1946, Congress enacted the Indian Claims Act, which made it possible for tribes to bring suit against the U.S. government before a special tribunal known as the Indian Claims Commission, whereas previously Indians had been able to sue the government in the Court of Claims only through special acts of Congress. By 1974 the Indian Claims Commission had entered judgments favorable to Indians in an amount exceeding $500 million, and many suits remained to be settled.

In the field of Indian education the major policy objective by the 1930's was to enroll Indian youngsters in public schools. Major impetus toward public school enrollment was provided by passage of the Johnson-O'Malley Act of 1934, which provided the federal government authority to contract with states and their subdivisions for Indian education and other purposes. By 1960 Indian youngsters were enrolled in public schools in most parts of the United States, though the Bureau of Indian Affairs continued to operate schools for tribes of the Southwest and Alaska, as well as in a few other locales. Missionary influence in Indian education during most of the 20th century has been slight, owing to the fact that government subsidies to sectarian schools were discontinued in the 1890's.

The dominant policy theme during much of the period of the 1950's was that of withdrawing special federal services from Indians and elevating them to a status of equality with other citizens. The institution of this policy, known to the Indians as "termination," produced an outcry of protest from nearly all the reservations, and Indian defense organizations united in their effort to have it overturned. Some lingering sentiment for "termination" remained among members of the Senate through the 1960's, but it ceased to be a major policy thrust after about 1958.

Beginning in the 1960's and continuing throughout the early 1970's, the principal federal policy direction in regard to Indian affairs was toward placement of administrative responsibility for reservation services in the hands of Indians, while the federal government continued to finance these services. Special legislation to permit the Bureau of Indian Affairs to contract with Indian tribes and make grants to them was passed by Congress in January 1975. The Indian preference policy enunciated in the Indian Reorganization Act was strengthened in 1974 by a Supreme Court decision that extended this policy to promotions as well as to hiring in the Bureau of Indian Affairs and that incorporated the ruling that the basic policy does not violate civil rights acts prohibiting discrimination on the basis of race.

The bureau's long-standing policy of providing services only for Indians living on or near reservations was threatened in some measure by a Supreme Court decision in the mid-1970's that declared a Papago family living in Ajo, Ariz., to be eligible for social welfare assistance from the bureau. The issue involved was a relatively narrow one, and the overall effect is likely to be a refinement of the traditional policy rather than its reversal.

BIBLIOGRAPHY

D'Arcy McNickle, *Native American Tribalism.*

Roger L. Nichols and George R. Adams, eds., *The American Indian: Past and Present.*

James E. Officer, "The American Indian and Federal Policy," in Jack O. Waddell and O. Michael Watson, eds., *The American Indian in Urban Society.*

Edward H. Spicer, *A Short History of the Indians of the United States.*

U.S. Department of the Interior, *Federal Indian Law.*

— JAMES E. OFFICER

INDIAN REMOVAL

The predominant theme in U.S. government Indian policy between the War of 1812 and the middle of the 19th century was that of transferring to lands in the West all those Indians east of the Mississippi River who wished to continue their tribal status. This so-called removal program had the support not only of speculators who coveted Indian lands but also of uneasy settlers in frontier areas who feared Indian attacks and of missionary groups who felt that relocation would save the Indians from degrading white influences and permit them to continue their traditional ways.

The seeds of a removal program were sown in the series of negotiations with southeastern tribes that began with the first Treaty of Hopewell in 1785. The citizens of Georgia in particular felt that these negotiations, which were conducted by the federal government, provided too many concessions to powerful, well-organized tribes, such as the Creek and Cherokee. In 1802 when Georgia was asked to cede the lands from which the states of Alabama and Mississippi were later created, its officials insisted that, in return, the federal government promise to "peaceable obtain, on reasonable terms," the Indian title to all lands inside the state.

In 1803 President Thomas Jefferson saw an opportunity to appease Georgia and, at the same time, to legitimize his controversial Louisiana Purchase through a constitutional amendment authorizing Congress to exchange lands west of the Mississippi River for lands possessed by the Indians to the east. Such an amendment was drafted, but it was never submitted for ratification. The following year Congress enacted legislation authorizing the president to work out an exchange of eastern lands for those in the West, providing the Indians would continue their allegiance to the United States.

During the next several years attempts were made to persuade the Cherokee, one of Georgia's principal tribes, to move westward. Some of the Indians favored escaping white harassment through resettlement, but many more opposed the idea. By 1809, when James Madison became president, substantial opposition to removal had developed among the eastern tribes, motivated in part by the unhappy experiences of small groups of Cherokee, Delaware, and Shawnee who had voluntarily gone westward in the years between 1785 and 1800.

Successful conclusion of the War of 1812 was followed by renewed interest in Indian removal, which became a basic item in a majority of the Indian treaties negotiated thereafter. In 1817 John C. Calhoun, a strong advocate of Indian removal, was named secretary of the War Department in President James Monroe's cabinet. He joined forces with war hero Gen. Andrew Jackson and Lewis Cass, governor of Michigan Territory, in urging formal adoption of a removal policy.

The first major removal treat was that signed by the Delaware in 1818. Having been progressively shoved westward, the Delaware were living in Indiana at that time. The following year the Kickapoo of Illinois agreed to resettle on lands in Missouri formerly occupied by the Osage. Throughout the area northwest of the Ohio River, Cass pushed vigorously for treaties of cession and removal. In the Southeast, also, federal negotiators were at work seeking removal. Treaties aimed at achieving this end were signed by the Choctaw in 1820 and the Creek in 1821.

Monroe gave his full support to a removal policy in January 1825 when he delivered a special message to Congress describing it as the only means of solving "the

Indian problem." Immediately thereafter, Calhoun issued a report calling for the resettlement of nearly 100,000 eastern Indians. He recommended an appropriation of $95,000 for this purpose. Within a month after Calhoun's report was made public, the Creek signed a treaty agreeing to resettle on lands in the West by Sept. 1, 1826, but many Creek leaders and some whites (including John Crowell, Indian agent to the Cherokee) protested the manner in which the treaty had been negotiated. Crowell also recommended special federal protection for William McIntosh, the Creek chief who was the principal treaty signer. The requested protection was not forthcoming, and a short time later McIntosh was assassinated by fellow tribesmen. In 1826 the Creek were successful in having the treaty set aside, but another was immediately negotiated and signed.

The end of the War of 1812 was followed by renewed interest in Indian removal, which became a basic item in a majority of the Indian treaties negotiated thereafter.

The Cherokee in 1827 adopted a written constitution, thereby adding new fuel to the flames of their controversy with Georgia. The Georgia legislature, fearful that this action might result in the establishment of a separate Indian nation (with subsequent removal of Cherokee lands from within the boundaries of the state), enacted a resolution declaring that the Cherokee had no real title to their lands and should be evicted. Eager to see the controversy resolved, Congress the following year appropriated $50,000 to carry into effect the agreement of 1802. The Cherokee refused to sign a removal treaty, whereupon Georgia began passing legislation extending its jurisdiction over them.

Jackson entered the White House in January 1829 and quickly let it be known that he would espouse a national policy of Indian removal. He defended his stand by stating that removal was the only course that could save the Indians from extinction. The following year, after much debate, Congress passed the national Indian Removal Act, which authorized the president to set up districts within the so-called Indian Territory for the reception of tribes agreeing to land exchanges. The act also provided for payment of indemnities to the Indians, for assistance in accomplishing their resettlement, for protection in their new locations, and for a continuance of the "superintendency and care" previously accorded them. The sum of $500,000 was authorized to carry out the act. The pace of removal was greatly accelerated with the passage of the 1830 act. Treaty negotiators set to work both east and west of the Mississippi to secure the permission of the indigenous tribes in Indian Territory who were being asked to accept strangers onto their lands and to obtain the approval of those tribes to be removed.

Treaties negotiated in the aftermath of the War of 1812 had reduced the Indian population of Ohio, Indiana, and Illinois, but this remained a critical area of activity for federal officials carrying out the provisions of the removal act. The Shawnee gave up their last lands in Ohio in 1831 in exchange for 100,000 acres in the Indian Territory. In the same year, the Ottawa ceded Ohio lands for a promise of 30,000 acres on the Kansas River. The Wyandot sold their Ohio acreage in 1832, thus effectively ending Indian settlement in that state. Illinois and Indiana were similarly cleared of Indians in the early 1830's. The remaining Kickapoo of Illinois, under the prophet Kanakuk, held out until 1832, when they agreed peacefully to relocate to lands in Kansas.

Among the other tribes moved to new homes at that time were the Chippewa, who were pushed into Wisconsin and Minnesota; the Sauk and Fox, Winnebago and Potawatomi, who were resettled in what is now Iowa; and the Ottawa, Kaskaskia, Peoria, Miami, and some New York Indians, all of whom were assigned tracts in the Indian Territory along the western border of Missouri.

As might have been expected, the greatest amount of resistance to removal came from the Indians of the Southeast. Even the small Seminole tribe chose to fight rather than consent to removal. The most tragic story, however, is that of the Cherokee, who were by white standards of the day a highly "civilized" tribe. For five years following the passage of the Indian Removal Act the Cherokee resisted signing a removal treaty. Finally, in 1835, they capitulated, signing the Treaty of New Echota. However, a deep split had developed between those who favored removal and those who did not. Despite the treaty many Indians stayed on their lands, a decision that prompted the War Department in 1838 to send Gen. Winfield Scott with a contingent of troops into Georgia to force the Cherokee to go to their designated lands in Indian Territory. The removal took place during the winter of 1838–39, producing the Trail of Tears, one of the most infamous incidents in the history of U.S. Indian administration. Nearly one-fourth of the Indians who began the journey from Georgia and nearby areas beyond the Mississippi did not live to finish it.

Life in the West was not easy for the relocated tribes. They quickly came into conflict with the indigenous groups, and the lands set aside for them often became the haven of criminals escaping prosecution. By 1850 the period of Indian removal was essentially over, but white settlement having by that time pushed across the Mississippi River, the Indian Territory was no longer a place where Indians could be isolated and left to their own devices. The 1850's and 1860's saw the holdings of the relocated Indians further reduced as new states were created out of the lands that had once been regarded as permanently set aside for Indian use and occupancy.

Small pockets of Indians remained in many eastern states; some had been given special grants of land, while others had chosen to disavow tribal ways.

By no means all the Indians east of the Mississippi River moved westward. Small pockets remained in many eastern states. In some cases the Indians who remained behind were treaty-signers who had been given special grants of lands within ceded areas; in other instances they were persons who had chosen to disavow tribal ways and to take up the "habits and arts of civilization" as these were practiced by the whites. In still other cases they were individuals who had simply refused to leave and who had managed to hide out until the storm blew over, by which time their numbers were so insignificant that they were not considered threats to the surrounding whites.

Among the Indians escaping removal was a small band of several hundred fugitive Cherokee who fled to the mountains on the border between North Carolina and Tennessee, where they lived as refugees until 1842. In that year, through the efforts of an influential trader named William H. Thomas, they received federal permission to remain on lands set apart for their use in western North Carolina. These lands make up the Qualla Reservation, one of the largest Indian areas under federal supervision in the eastern United States.

By 1850 the federal government had concluded 245 separate Indian treaties, by means of which it had acquired more than 450 million acres of Indian land at a total estimated cost of $90 million.

BIBLIOGRAPHY

George Dewey Harmon, *Sixty Years of Indian Affairs.*

J. P. Kinney, *A Continent Lost—A Civilization Won.*

Roger L. Nichols and George R. Adams, eds., *The American Indian: Past and Present.*

Francis Paul Prucha, ed., *The Indian in American History.*

— JAMES E. OFFICER

INDIAN TERRITORY

Indian Territory, so-called, original included all the present state of Oklahoma except the panhandle. It was never an organized territory, but was set aside as a home for the Five Civilized Tribes, who were removed to it in the period 1820–42. In 1866 they ceded the western part of this region to the United States as a home for other tribes. A part of this ceded area was opened to white settlement in 1899, and the following year it was formed into the Territory of Oklahoma, which eventually came to include all the lands ceded in 1866. The reduced land of the Five Civilized Tribes, then called Indian Territory, had an area about equal to that of Indiana; it was occupied by more than 75,000 Indians. Lands were held in common, and each tribe had its own government. In 1907 the two territories were again united and admitted to the Union as the state of Oklahoma.

BIBLIOGRAPHY

Thomas Donaldson, *The Public Domain.*

Roy Gittinger, *The Formation of the State of Oklahoma.*

— EDWARD EVERETT DALE

INDUSTRIAL REVOLUTION

Industrial Revolution, the period during which mechanical devices were generally substituted for human skills and inanimate power or energy was substituted for animate power, with consequent changes in transportation and the use of raw materials. Implied by the term is generation of an ongoing process leading to more and more production. But the period referred to as a "revolution" varies greatly in length: some scholars apply the term only to the initial development of steam-powered iron or steel machinery, and others to the whole process of industrial growth that is still continuing. In America it is popularly confined to the time when the economy was based on coal, steam, and iron, a period that reached its apogee around 1900. It was to be superseded by a stage in the 20th century, sometimes called the "second industrial revolution," when more oil, electricity, and automotive power were used. Since examination of the periods covered by such broad definitions amounts to an encapsulated survey of much of modern economic history, the interpretation presented here is that the "revolution" involved only the secure establishment of the coal, steam, and iron phase.

Establishing this new phase of technology, however, depended on a favorable business environment and a demand for more goods. Both occurred in England during the course of the 18th century. Great increases in trade, particularly with the empire, inspired merchants and master workers to seek greater productivity through more specialized business and manufacturing facilities and better inland transportation. Business specialization took the form of banking, insurance, specialized middlemen, and transportation companies. In manufacturing, simple labor-saving machines were introduced and greater division of labor was achieved by distributing the various steps of a process once done by a single worker among a number of workers. By about 1800 machinery for textile and some other types of manufacturing was becoming more complex, and in a few factories steam engines were taking the place of waterwheels.

Besides expanding trade and a business system capable of rapid adjustment, England had social and geographic advantages for industrial development not enjoyed by any other nation. No area was far from water transportation, agriculture was highly productive, climate was mild, iron and coal were in close proximity, and the social structure was fluid enough to reward financial success. Regardless of their technical knowledge, other European nations lacking many of these advantages found it difficult to imitate the British system.

The chief retarding factors in Europe as a whole were rugged terrain, a lack of proximity of known resources of coal and iron, and a social structure not conducive to business expansion. In addition, the Continent was ravaged by war from 1793 to 1815 and consequently lagged behind both Britain and the United States until about 1840.

Meanwhile, independence, a financially sound national government, and capital from foreign trade led to a truly revolutionary development of business and a spread of factory industry in the United States. In contrast to the nations of Europe, America readily chartered business corporations and frequently subscribed to their stock. The result was that improvements in business, transportation, and technology that had taken a century to mature in Britain were copied and occasionally improved upon in the United States within one or two decades.

An entrepreneurial climate was generated in which many men were looking for new devices and in which one innovation led to others. Interruption of British imports and general ocean trade by Thomas Jefferson's embargo of 1807–09 and by the War of 1812 led a group of rich Massachusetts merchants to try wholly mechanized production of coarse cotton cloth. The factory, using inexact copies of English machinery, was opened at Waltham in 1814; it is said to have been the first textile factory in the world to take in raw cotton and turn out finished cloth.

One high-pressure steam engine, perfected early in the century almost simultaneously by Oliver Evans in Pennsylvania and Richard Trevithick in Wales, opened the way for powerful river steamboats and railroad locomotives. Whereas river-steamboat development quickly became indigenous to the United States, railroad technology was largely borrowed from Britain in the 1820's. These two new forms of transportation, together with the completion of important canals, such as the Erie in New York State in 1825, opened a broader market for manufactures.

Continental Europe was ravaged by war from 1793 to 1815; consequently, in its industrial expansion it lagged behind both Britain and the U.S. until about 1840.

Each major northeastern seaport strove to connect itself with the rapidly growing interior market. The result was a virtual frenzy of state-aided canal and railroad building that often exceeded local financial resources but had, by 1851, produced an accessible national market stretching to the frontiers of settlement on the edges of the great western plains.

At the beginning of this transportation revolution the United States still lacked the combination of good veins of coal for making coke and nearby ore deposits, necessary for cheap iron. American iron was still smelted and refined by the use of charcoal from wood and could not compete in the industrial regions of the East with British imports. Then Pennsylvanians discovered that anthracite coal, abundant in the eastern part of the state, could be used in its natural form for all the operations involved in making iron. Use of this knowledge proceeded rapidly from 1830 to 1845, at the same time that the French were shifting from wood to coke. By 1845, therefore, potentially competitive iron industries existed outside Britain and iron machinery run by steam could displace wood machinery and waterpower.

As usual with major innovations, the results were not immediate. The lag in time between new inventions in British technology—such as the hot-blast furnace in 1828—and their adoption in the United States was often a decade or more. In a partial survey of U.S. industry in 1832 only 106 factories reported more than $100,000 in assets, and of those, 88 were textile mills. Of the 36 having more than 250 employees, 31 were in textiles and only 3 in iron. Except in the Pittsburgh region, only a negligible number used steam.

By 1840, with major canal systems and hundreds of river and lake steamboats in operation, trunk-line railroads under construction, domestic production of machine tools, and cheap coal-smelted iron available, the United States was ready to move ahead. Econometrists estimate that the decade from 1839 to 1849 showed the most rapid expansion of manufacturing in American history. By the time the British held their Crystal Palace Exposition in 1851, industrial products from the United States were so striking that parliamentary commissions were sent to the United States in 1854 and 1855 to examine the "American system of manufacturing." The commissioners reported that the United States had an "advanced industrial economy." Small shops and mills had in many cases become factories employing from 500 to 700 workers and managed according to specialized functions. In the process of growth, industry had moved increasingly to cities served by railroads.

The rapid industrial progress in the United States as compared with that in Great Britain or western Europe in the first half of the 19th century inevitably raises questions of causation. In addition to a highly favorable business system, two things must be given considerable weight: the supply of anthracite coal in the United States and the possession of a common language with Great Britain. British mechanics emigrating to the United States could communicate fully with their employers, and English technical journals could be read by Americans.

A complex of geographic factors was also of major importance. The East Coast had good natural water transportation—not as good as that of Britain, but better than that of either France or Germany. Beyond the Appalachian Mountains, level land made for cheap canal construction, while the Great Lakes and the vast Mississippi River system opened the continent east of the Rockies to barges and steamboats. These level north-central lands also lent themselves to cultivation of farms by machinery and hence to the production of great surpluses to feed industrial workers.

A rapidly growing population and a high rate of migration to new farms, towns, and cities led to an unprecedented demand for cheap home and farm implements that might be mass-produced by machinery. Even when the whole process could not be mechanized, this large-scale demand led to a greater division of labor in the production of farm tools, for example, than was the practice in Europe.

Finally, and perhaps most important of all, American society was suited to the needs of industrial business. In the United States the remnants of feudalism were insignificant, money was the common measure of success, and all occupations that made large profits were prestigious. It may be said that whereas Europe fitted industrialism to the Procrustean bed of its existing social structure, the United States shaped its customs to fit industrialism. The factors already mentioned all contributed to an unusual optimism among American businessmen. Confident of the support of state and national governments and unafraid of foreign invasions, they did not hesitate to take long-term risks in economic development. Meanwhile, valid expectations of high rates of profit encouraged saving for productive purposes and drew the ablest young men into entrepreneurial careers.

BIBLIOGRAPHY

Stuart Bruchey, *The Roots of American Economic Growth, 1607–1861.*

Alfred D. Chandler, Jr., "Anthracite Coal and the Beginnings of the Industrial Revolution," *Business History Review*, vol. 46 (1971).

Thomas C. Cochran, "The Business Revolution," *American Historical Review*, vol. 79 (1974).

David S. Landes, *The Unbound Prometheus: Technological Change and Industrial Development in Western Europe to the Present.*

— THOMAS C. COCHRAN

INDUSTRIAL WORKERS OF THE WORLD

Industrial Workers of the World, a radical labor organization founded in Chicago in June 1905 as an alternative to the more moderate and exclusive American Federation of Labor. Among the more prominent founders of the IWW were Eugene V. Debs, William D. Haywood, and Daniel DeLeon. Best by political and personal splits during its first years, the IWW barely survived its birth, but from 1909 to 1918 the IWW achieved success and notoriety as the most militant and dangerous institution on the American Left.

Under the leadership of Vincent St. John (1908–15) and Haywood (1915–18) the IWW appealed to all workers regardless of skill, nationality, race, or sex. It sought to organize them into vast industrial unions that would use direct economic action to seize control of industry and abolish capitalism. Antipathetic to political action and dedicated to the destruction of state power, the IWW was the American version of the syndicalist movement that stirred European labor in the pre-World War I years. At its peak in 1917 the IWW had no more than 150,000 members, but more than 3 million workers had passed through its ranks and many more had come under its influence. During World War I, federal and state governments feared the IWW as a threat to national security and arrested, indicted, and convicted over 200 IWW officials on sedition and espionage charges.

Never fully able to recover from wartime persecution, after 1919 the IWW fell victim to state antisyndicalist laws, competition from Communists, and the successful organization of mass-production workers in the 1930's by the Congress of Industrial Organizations. The IWW survives today as a skeletal organization on the fringes of U.S. radicalism.

BIBLIOGRAPHY

Joseph R. Conlin, *Bread and Roses Too.*
Melvyn Dubofsky, *We Shall Be All: A History of the Industrial Workers of the World.*
Patrick Renshaw, *The Wobblies.*

— MELVYN DUBOFSKY

INFLATION

There is no generally accepted definition of inflation, but from the standpoint of the public, inflation means rapidly rising prices of commodities and services. According to traditional analysis, such price rises are caused by an increase in the quantity of money that is not paralleled by a corresponding increase in the quantity of goods and services coming on the market. The increased money demand for goods, without a corresponding increase in the amount of goods offered for sale, causes prices to rise and constitutes inflation.

In the 1950's a new analysis of inflation, which may be termed the "wage-cost push" theory, received substantial support. According to this theory, higher money wages in excess of increased labor productivity engender higher operating costs and thus force producers to raise their selling prices to consumers, the result being an upward thrust in prices. The cause of inflation is thus transferred from the demand to the cost side of the picture.

Whether the initial force bringing about a rise in prices is excessive money demand or an increase in the money costs of producers resulting from higher wages, inflation cannot be maintained without an increase in the quantity of money in excess of the increase in the flow of goods to market. And in the end, money demand is the determining factor, since producers will not grant wage increases that necessitate higher prices for their products unless they feel sure that consumers will have the necessary money to buy those products at increased prices.

Inflation resulting from the wage-cost push is of the creeping variety; that is, it consists of relatively small, but regular, increases in the price level extending over a long period, as opposed to the more violent type of inflation that has occurred chiefly as a result of war and its aftermath.

The evils attending a violent inflation—the impairment, or even destruction, of savings and insurance policies; the near pauperization of those living on fixed or slowly changing incomes; hyperspeculative activity; and so on—are well known and univer-

The police drive the International Workers of the World off of the sidewalk at Union Square in New York City, April 14, 1914. (UPI/Corbis-Bettmann)

sally deplored. Creeping inflation, on the other hand, prevents the attainment of equilibrium in the economy. It discourages saving and encourages investment, with resulting misallocation of capital and wrong investment and managerial decisions. It tends to foster uneconomic speculation, and it injures the country's position in international trade. Finally, it eventually engenders all the evils of violent inflation as well, but stretched over a longer period.

In some respects creeping inflation is the more dangerous sort, chiefly because its evils are not readily recognized by the public. This circumstance is aggravated by the fact that some professional economists condone creeping inflation as essential to continued economic growth, although sound growth is impeded rather than furthered by inflation of this sort.

"Creeping inflation" prevents economic equilibrium by discouraging saving and encouraging investment, with resulting misallocation of capital and wrong investment and managerial decisions.

Prior to the Revolution, inflation occurred in many of the colonies where bills of credit were issued by the government and made legal tender. The issue of such bills was prohibited by Parliament by acts passed in 1751 and 1764. With the outbreak of the revolutionary war, bills of credit were put into circulation on a large scale by both the states and the Continental Congress. Between 1775 and 1779, the Continental Congress authorized the issuance of $241,552,780 in such bills, and the various states issued an additional $209,524,776. As there was no corresponding increase in goods and services, the purchasing power of these bills decreased rapidly. By January 1781, this currency was valued at 100 to 1 in relation to specie, and by May it had lost its value almost completely. The Continental Congress and the various states attempted to fix prices by law, but without success.

After the collapse of the Continental currency and the establishment of the Union, prices remained moderate until the War of 1812, when another inflation occurred. This was caused by the overissuance of bank notes rather than the issuance of bills by the government. Prices peaked in 1814–15; thereafter the price level receded sharply until 1821, after which a fairly long period of relatively stable prices ensued.

The next major inflation in the United States occurred at the time of the Civil War. In order to help finance the war, Congress authorized three issues of greenbacks of $150 million each. The currency was thus inflated, and prices rose rapidly, reaching a peak in 1864–65. At the same time, an even more intense inflation was occurring in the Confederacy. The price level dropped rapidly after 1865 until 1880.

Following the resumption of specie payments by the government on Jan. 1, 1879, the United States had no major inflation until the outbreak of World War I in 1914. Prices soon began to rise rapidly, and they continued to mount after the United States entered the war in 1917. The peak was not reached until the spring of 1920, when the wholesale price index stood at 244 percent of the prewar level. People with fixed incomes and those receiving salaries and fees more or less fixed by custom suffered severely from the great increase in the cost of living.

The inflation during and after World War I differed from that of the Civil War period in that it was caused by an overexpansion of check currency and bank notes rather than by the issuance of fiat money by the government. The government sold bonds to the banks and the people, and many of the people borrowed from the banks in order to buy the bonds. Thus, monetary purchasing power was expanded much more rapidly than production, and prices rose accordingly.

The period from 1922 to 1929 was one of comparatively stable prices, but it was argued by many economists that prices should have fallen because of the vast increase in the production of goods and that some inflation therefore existed. In any event, there is no doubt that stock prices were severely inflated between 1924 and 1929.

From the autumn of 1929 to the spring of 1933 a severe deflation occurred, and the administration of Franklin D. Roosevelt decided on what was popularly termed a policy of reflation—that is, raising the prices of commodities to the predepression level. Through the sale of government obligations to the banks, check currency was greatly expanded. Business did not respond to the increase in monetary purchasing power for a number of reasons, and the commodity price level remained below that of the predepression period until the country's entry into World War II in December 1941.

Because of the introduction of price, wage, and other direct controls in 1942, official price indexes rose only moderately (10 to 15 percent) until the middle of 1946, when controls were removed, although the actual price rise was greater than that indicated by the indexes, which could take no account of prices obtained in black-market transactions. With the removal of controls in mid-1946, the unleashing of monetary purchasing power built up during the war period drove prices up again. They reached their highest level in the fall of 1948, rising to an inflationary peak approximately equaling that of World War I.

Beginning in the late 1950's the United States and the prospering nations of Western Europe all suffered from disturbingly high annual rates of inflation. The conventionally accepted factors appeared to operate to some degree: wage increases in excess of growth in productivity pushed up costs; domestic markets with only limited competition encouraged more than compensatory price increases; trade and service were forced eventually to follow the wage trends in the more unionized sectors of manufacturing and transportation; and governments anxious to promote prosperity hesitated to tax or drastically to limit the available supply of money. Up to 1967 the United States held back inflation somewhat better than the leading nations of Europe, other than Germany, but as of that year the unusual demands of the Vietnam War and a series of extremely unbalanced federal budgets raised the annual rate of inflation in the United States above the "creeping" 2 percent level to an economically upsetting range above 5 percent. Perhaps most disturbing of all was the fact that a mild depression induced by a tight money policy in 1969 did not substantially check the upward movement of prices. From 1971 to 1974 the Republican administration of Richard Nixon entered with extreme reluctance into price control by administrative decrees and commissions. As the mandates were changed frequently and inadequately enforced, their net effect is a matter of dispute among economists. Obscuring any conclusion is the major inflationary effect of the Arab oil embargo of 1973–74. This raised energy and petrochemical costs to heights that disrupted the entire price structure. The crisis, occurring simultaneously with the Watergate hearings, was not met by any effective federal action beyond decreeing a ceiling on oil prices and a fifty-five mile an hour national speed limit.

The market forces set in motion by the energy squeeze produced both recession and a 14 percent rate of inflation during 1974 and early 1975. At first the administration of President Gerald Ford viewed inflation as the primary problem and urged a tight money policy and a more balanced budget, but as depression deepened at the end of 1974 and the early months of 1975, the president hesitantly joined with congressional leaders in planning for the largest deficit budget in peacetime history. While the rate of inflation was lessening because of poor business conditions in the spring of 1975, tax reductions and the federal deficit made the future rate highly uncertain.

— THOMAS C. COCHRAN

INFLUENZA

Influenza, commonly called the "flu," reached America early in colonial history, and its periodic visitations have continued to the present. The first epidemic struck in 1647 and was described by John Eliot as "a very depe cold, with some tincture of a feaver and full of malignity . . . " In the succeeding years a series of outbreaks, described in such terms as "a general catarrh," "winter feavers," "epidemical colds," and "putrid pleurisies" swept through the colonies, bringing sickness and death on a large scale. The precise etiology of these epidemics cannot be determined, but from accounts of the symptoms and the pandemic nature of the outbreaks, some strain of influenza is a logical suspect. Colonial records show a great many local outbreaks, and some form of respiratory disease reached major epidemic proportions in 1675, 1688, 1732–33, 1737, 1747–50, 1761, and 1789–91.

The 19th century saw a similar pattern of influenza epidemics—major pandemics interspersed with local or regional outbreaks. The disease was widespread in Europe and America in 1830, 1837, and 1847; eased up for a long period; and then broke out on a worldwide scale from 1889 to 1893. Two minor outbreaks involving an unusual number of pneumonic complications were experienced in 1916 and 1917. In the summer of 1918, a deceptively mild wave of influenza swept through army camps in Europe and America and was immediately followed by the second and third waves of the greatest recorded pandemic of influenza in history. In America the heaviest toll was exacted by a major wave lasting from September to November of 1918. One can only guess at the worldwide impact of this pandemic, but it is estimated to have killed 15 million individuals. In the United States, approximately 28 percent of the population was attacked by the disease, and the death toll amounted to 450,000. To make matters worse, half of the deaths occurred among young adults between the ages of twenty and forty. Pneumonia was a frequent sequela, and the effect of the disastrous pestilence was compounded by a concurrent outbreak of some form of encephalitis (*encephalitis lethargica*).

Several outbreaks occurred in the 1920's, but the morbidity and mortality from influenza gradually declined in the succeeding years. Nonetheless, a study by the Metropolitan Life Insurance Company showed that the combination of influenza and pneumonia consistently remained the third ranking cause of death among its policyholders as late as 1935.

Influenza in one form or another is still present and rarely do as many as three years go by without a fairly serious outbreak. Between 1918 and 1951 no less than twenty epidemics occurred and the pattern has continued since that date. Most are minor but once or twice every decade the disease flares up. The introduction of new therapeutics in the 1940's led to a steady drop in the overall influenza mortality rate until the outbreaks of Asiatic influenza in 1957, 1958, and 1960. The influenza death rate per 100,000 reached 4.4 in the latter year, the last time this figure exceeded 4. In three epidemic years since 1960 (1963, 1968, and 1969) the annual death rate for influenza was successively 3.8, 3.5, and 3.4 per 100,000.

In 1933, the influenza virus now known as influenza virus A was identified, and subsequently other strains were recovered. Influenza vaccines had had only limited value by the mid-1970's, but the introduction of sulfonamides, penicillin, and antibiotics in the World War II era greatly improved the treatment for pneumonia and thus helped to reduce the cast fatality rate from influenza. At the same time, it is possible that higher living and sanitary standards have helped to reduce the number and virulence of influenza outbreaks.

BIBLIOGRAPHY

Walter R. Bett, *The History and Conquest of Common Diseases.*

John Duffy, *Epidemics in Colonial America.*

W. H. Frost, "The Epidemiology of Influenza," *Journal of the American Medical Association*, vol. 73 (1919).

— JOHN DUFFY

INTERIOR, DEPARTMENT OF THE

Whereas during the nineteenth century the Department of the Interior was primarily occupied with efforts to dispose of lands and resources, in the twentieth century its main responsibilities were the supervision of public lands and Indian affairs. As new bureaus, such as forestry (1897–1905), reclamation (1903), mines (1910), the National Park Service (1916), and the Fish and Wildlife Service (1939) were added, the resource management component of the Interior Department's task of public lands management shifted its focus from land disposal to resource conservation. After unsuccessful attempts to transfer public lands to the states, Congress enacted the Taylor Grazing Act of 1934 to manage the large areas of arid grazing land west of the hundredth meridian. During President Harry Truman's administration (1945–1951) this policy shift continued as the Grazing Service, and the General Land Office merged into the Bureau of Land Management in 1946. The Federal Land Policy and Management Act of 1976 put an end to the era of public land sales.

Conflicts between aesthetic environmentalists and utilitarian conservationists in the 1980s and 1990s occasionally embroiled the department in controversy. The 1980s saw the growth of lobbying on the part of environmental groups because aesthetic environmentalism conflicted with the budget cuts and decreased emphasis on wilderness and research instituted during the administrations of Presidents Ronald Reagan and George Bush. Alle-

Children of families stricken by the influenza epidemic wait in line for food from volunteers, in Cincinnati, Ohio. (Corbis-Bettmann)

gations that some concessionaires in national parks were receiving special and unfair favorable treatment led to revisions of policies regarding such businesses, such as allowing greater review of the business practices of concessionaires. The National Park Service also came under attack in the summer of 1988, when huge forest fires consumed large areas of Yellowstone National Park. An emotional debate later ensued over the reintroduction of wolves to Yellowstone. The administration of President Bill Clinton became embroiled in controversy in 1993 and 1994, when it aligned itself with environmentalists emphasizing research and improving land management, reauthorizing the U.S. Biological Survey, and trying to raise grazing fees.

The federal government's decision in the 1950's to end its traditional special relationship with Indian tribes proved disastrous to thousands of Indians and enormously expensive for the government.

From the middle of the nineteenth century, the federal government forced Indian tribes onto reservations where the department assumed responsibility for services under treaties and grants. During the 1950s the federal government tried to terminate its special relationship with Indian tribes. This relationship, based on a long-standing tradition derived from treaties and customs, assumed a limited sovereignty status of Indian tribes differing from that of the states. The termination policy, however, proved enormously expensive to the federal government and economically and culturally disastrous to thousands of Indians. The policy of terminating special services and programs waned after 1958, and the Interior Department moved toward policies that encouraged self-determination. Indian militancy in the early 1970s brought public attention to the desperate conditions common on reservations. In response, the government allowed tribes to negotiate contracts with the Bureau of Indian Affairs that allowed them to administer public safety, education, and social services programs for themselves. As tribes moved toward self-determination, other programs, such as the Indian Gaming Regulatory Act of 1988 and the Indian self-governance program, generated controversy, especially as the Interior Department became involved with issues related to gambling on Indian reservations, an activity in which the Interior Department, with its emphasis on land and resource management, had little experience.

In addition to the bureaus and services mentioned, in 1994 the Department of Interior also oversaw the activities of the Geological Survey, Minerals Management Service, Office of Surface Mining Reclamation and Enforcement, Office of Small and Disadvantaged Business Utilization, and Office of Territories and International Affairs.

[See also Gambling; Indian Affairs, Bureau of; Native Americans.]

BIBLIOGRAPHY

Thomas G. Alexander, *Clash of Interests: Interior Department and Mountain West 1863–1890* (Provo, Utah, 1977).

Eugene P. Trani, *The Secretaries of the Department of the Interior* (Washington, D.C., 1975).

— THOMAS G. ALEXANDER AND DAVID R. WILSON

INTERSTATE COMMERCE COMMISSION

Interstate Commerce Commission, the first of the independent regulatory commissions, was devised to apply technical expertise and a semijudicial and less partisan approach to the regulation of complex economic affairs. The Interstate Commerce Act of 1887, which created the Interstate Commerce Commission (ICC), derived from a highly charged political controversy over railroad rates, during which the Supreme Court had ruled (*Wabash, Saint Louis and Pacific Railroad Company* v. *Illinois*, 118 U.S. 557) that the states had no power to regulate interstate shipments. Congress responded, under its constitutional power to regulate interstate commerce, with its first broad regulatory statute aimed at major private enterprise, in this case primarily the railroads and any water carriers they might own.

The act provided for a five-person commission—later increased to seven and then to eleven—appointed by the president and confirmed by the Senate, for staggered terms of seven years. In 1970 an annually rotating chairman, primarily responsible for the internal management of the agency, was replaced by one who is presidentially appointed. By the early 1970's the agency had 1,700 employees, mostly in Washington, D.C., but 500 or so of whom were in nearly eighty field offices. The annual budget of the commission was over $30 million.

Throughout its history the principal task of the ICC has been the regulation of the railroads and, since 1935, the motor carriers. The initial law was aimed at "just and reasonable" rates of an antimonopolistic character. But increasing complaints brought about legislation that greatly broadened the commission's powers. The supervision of safety was added by the Railroad Safety Appliance Act of 1893 and remained with the ICC until transferred to the new Department of Transportation in 1967. The Elkins Act of 1903 and the Mann-Elkins Act of 1910 were aimed at discriminatory practices among shippers. The Hepburn Act of 1906 strengthened the rate-making authority of the ICC, made its orders binding without a court order, and extended its jurisdiction to pipelines and express companies. The Esch-Cummins Railway Act of 1920 gave the ICC broad powers to prescribe minimum as well as maximum rates for railroads and to encourage reorganization of the companies into more efficient economic units. Authority over telephone, telegraph, and cable service, granted in 1888, was transferred to the Federal Communications Commission in 1934.

Through the Motor Carrier Act of 1935, ICC authority was extended over the railroads' principal competitor. The Transportation Act of 1940 gave the commission power over certain interstate common carriers by water. The Rail Passenger Act of 1970, which established Amtrak, a government corporation operating an integrated passenger rail service, also authorized the ICC to assist Amtrak, establish standards of service, and report on its operations.

BIBLIOGRAPHY

R. C. Fellmuth, *The Interstate Commerce Omission: The Public Interest and the ICC.*

I. L. Sharfman, *The Interstate Commerce Commission.*

— PAUL P. VAN RIPER

INTERSTATE COMMERCE LAWS

The scope of interstate commerce laws in the United States is much broader than the jurisdiction of the Interstate Commerce Commission, which covers only some forms of transportation. However, at its formation in 1887, constitutional doctrine largely confined federal powers in the regulation of interstate commerce to transportation and communications. Much of the history of interstate commerce in the United States has to do with this expansion of federal powers over interstate commerce during the 20th century. The Constitution specifically grants the federal government power "to regulate Commerce . . . among the several States." Chief Justice John Marshall stated in *Gibbons* v. *Ogden* (1824) that federal legislation was supreme over a state law that might affect interstate or foreign commerce. But for a century there was little federal regulation of interstate commerce other than transportation and communications, for with regard to the reserved powers of the states in the absence of federal legislation, the Supreme Court has tended to be generous to the states. The states have regulated grade crossings and public utilities, controlled practices in food production and sanitation, and limited the loads of trucks on their highways. Indeed, the main body of commercial law in the United States is state law.

It was not until the post-Civil War period, when the growth and power of the modern corporation became clearly evident through corrupt, arbitrary, and discriminatory practices that the national political environment began to change. The Interstate Commerce Act of 1887 was only the first major example of a long series of important and complex federal statutes regulating business under the authority of the commerce clause, only a few of which can be noted here.

The Sherman Antitrust Act of 1890, aimed at curbing monopolies, was supported in 1914 by the Clayton Antitrust Act (which in addition exempted labor organizations from the antitrust laws) and by the creation of the Federal Trade Commission in 1914 to regulate "unfair methods in restraint of trade." The food and drug acts of 1906 and 1938 as amended—plus a series of related laws, such as the Meat Inspection Act of 1906—have been aimed at preventing adulteration and mislabeling. Additional powers given to the Federal Trade Commission in 1938 forbid false advertising. The Truth-in-Packaging Act of 1966 and the Consumer Credit Protection (Truth-in-Lending) Act of 1969 have brought further protection to consumers. The publicity acts of 1903 and 1909 were forerunners of the Securities and Exchange Act of 1934, all of which were aimed at the sale of fraudulent securities.

The Sherman Antitrust Act of 1890 was supported in 1914 by the Clayton Antitrust Act and the creation of the Federal Trade Commission to regulate "unfair methods in restraint of trade."

Controls over additional modes of transport came with the Shipping Act of 1916, which established the U.S. Shipping Board, whose authority was reestablished in 1936 under the Maritime Commission. Federal regulation of utilities came with the creation in 1920 of the Federal Power Commission. The Federal Radio Commission of 1927 was broadened into the Federal Communications Commission in 1934. Government regulation of the labor relations of industries engaged in interstate commerce culminated in the formation of the National Labor Relations Board in 1935, whose powers and duties were revised by the Taft-Hartley Act of 1947 and several amendments to it. The Civil Aeronautics

Act of 1938, setting up the Civil Aeronautics Authority (later Civil Aeronautics Board), concluded formation of the series of agencies known as the independent regulatory commissions. Moreover, some regulatory authority derived from the interstate commerce clause lies in the hands of the traditional departments and other agencies, such as the Atomic Energy Commission.

Interstate commerce laws are not limited to regulative and punitive measures. Subsidies are available, for example, to maritime shipping and to large segments of agriculture. Many federal agencies engage in, and disseminate the results of, research of interest to business and commercial organizations of all kinds. The Tennessee Valley Authority (TVA) was created in 1933 to help in the total development of an entire economic area. Moreover, the federal government has from its beginning stimulated commerce through statutes implementing its additional powers over coinage and money, the mails, weights and measures, and copyrights and patents.

As the political environment changed and a network of federal laws evolved, the views of the Supreme Court on federal powers under the interstate commerce clause gradually broadened. Thus, for some decades the implementation of certain statutes was modified or negated by the Court's opinions on what constituted interstate commerce. Not until the late 1930's did the Court include manufacturing plants and processes, for example, within the scope of regulation under the commerce clause: child-labor laws were struck down in 1918 (*Hammer* v. *Dagenhart*) and in 1922 (*Bailey* v. *Drexel Furniture Company*), and it was frequently difficult to apply the Sherman Antitrust Act to some corporate combinations. By 1946, in the case of the *American Power and Light Company* v. *Securities and Exchange Commission*, the Court concluded that "the Federal commerce power is as broad as the economic needs of the nation." The determination of what is interstate commerce and what shall be done in support or regulation of it is now essentially in the political arena.

BIBLIOGRAPHY

A. S. Miller, *The Supreme Court and American Capitalism.*

E. S. Redford, *American Government and the Economy.*

C. Wilcox, *Public Policies Toward Business.*

— PAUL P. VAN RIPER

INTOLERABLE ACTS

Intolerable Acts, in part also known as the Coercion Acts, were five acts of Parliament directly related to the American colonies, all of which became effective between March and June of 1774: the Boston Port Act, the Massachusetts Bay Regulating Act, the Act for the Impartial Administration of Justice, the Quartering Act, and the Quebec Act. The first four acts were designed to punish Boston for the Tea Party and to reinforce royal authority at the expense of popular liberty by alterations in the Massachussets charter; the Quebec Act, although lumped by Americans with the Coercion Acts, was not a punitive measure, but in the hands of colonial propagandists it was made to appear a menace to the religious as well as the civil liberties of the colonists. To the consternation of the British prime minister, Lord Frederick North, these acts, intended to restore peace and order in America and to isolate Massachusetts, threw the colonies into ferment and became the justification for calling the first Continental Congress in September 1774.

BIBLIOGRAPHY

J. T. Adams, *Revolutionary New England.*

— JOHN C. MILLER

IRAN-CONTRA AFFAIR

On July 8, 1985, President Ronald Reagan addressed the American Bar Association and described Iran as part of a "confederation of terrorist states . . . a new, international version of Murder, Inc." Ironically, that same month members of the Reagan administration were initiating a clandestine policy through which the federal government helped supply arms to Iran in its war with Iraq, the nation supported by the United States. Millions of dollars in profits from the secret arms sales were laundered through Israel and then routed to Central America in support of rebel forces known as the contras, whose professed aim was to overthrow the duly elected government in Nicaragua. Both Secretary of State George P. Shultz and Secretary of Defense Caspar Weinberger opposed the policy but lost the debate to members of the National Security Council. The Iran-Contra affair, arguably the crisis that did most to erode public confidence in the Reagan presidency, occupied the nation's attention through much of the next two years.

Reagan's staunch opposition to communism and his commitment to the safety of U.S. citizens throughout the world fostered the crisis. In 1979 a communist Sandinista government assumed power in Nicaragua. Soon after Reagan assumed office in 1981 his administration began to back the contra rebel forces with overt assistance. Congress terminated funding for the contras when evidence of illegal covert actions surfaced and public opinion turned against administration policy. At the same time, the public shared the president's disillusion with events in the Middle East because of the

October 1983 bombing of a U.S. marines barracks in Beirut, Lebanon, that killed 241 Americans and the contemporaneous abduction in Lebanon of several U.S. citizens as hostages. Events in both hemispheres came together in the late summer of 1985. From then until 1986 the United States provided Iran with TOW antitank missiles and parts for ground-launched Hawk antiaircraft missiles. The actions violated both the government's embargo on weapons sales to Iran and its avowed policy of not arming terrorists, because the Iranian government apparently was sponsoring Lebanese terrorism. The administration's rationale for its actions was the benefits promised for the contras. Private arms dealers, acting with the knowledge and approval of President Reagan's National Security Council staff, overcharged Iran for the weapons and channeled the money to the rebels.

During a White House ceremony early in November 1986 reporters asked the president to comment on rumors that the United States had exchanged arms for hostages. He repudiated the stories, then appeared on national television one week later to explain the administration's case, a case grounded in denial of any wrongdoing. "We did not," he declared in his conclusion, "repeat—did not trade weapons or anything else for hostages, nor will we." Just six days later, however, on November 19, Reagan opened a press conference by announcing that he had based his earlier claims on a false chronology constructed by the National Security Council and the White House staff. He announced formation of the President's Special Review Board, known as the Tower Commission. Headed by former Senator John Tower, the board included former Secretary of State Edmund Muskie and former national security adviser Brent Scowcroft. In late February 1987 the board concluded that the president was guilty of no crime but found that Reagan's lax management allowed subordinates the freedom to shape policy.

During a White House ceremony in November 1986, reporters asked President Reagan to comment on rumors that the U.S. had exhanged arms for hostages.

Concurrent executive branch and congressional investigations of Iran-Contra proceeded into 1987. As independent counsel, a position created by the Ethics in Government Act of 1978, former federal Judge Lawrence E. Walsh explored allegations of wrongdoing. In May 1987 a joint Senate and House committee hastily convened for what became four months of televised hearings that included 250 hours of open testimony by thirty-two public officials. In its report on November 17 the committee held President Reagan accountable for his administration's actions because his inattention to detail created an environment in which his subordinates exceeded their authority. In the spring of 1988 former national security adviser Robert C. McFarlane pleaded guilty to withholding information from Congress and later attempted suicide. Criminal indictments were returned against Rear Admiral John M. Poindexter, the president's national security adviser; arms dealers Richard V. Secord and Albert A. Hakim; and Lieutenant Colonel Oliver L. North of the National Security Council staff. The convictions of North and Poindexter were ultimately dismissed because evidence against them was compromised by their congressional testimony. In December 1992, just before leaving office, President George Bush pardoned six others indicted or convicted in the Iran-Contra affair, including Weinberger, whose diaries allegedly would have shown that both Reagan and Bush knew of the arms-for-hostages deal.

[See also Beirut Bombing; Corruption, Political; Hostage Crises; Middle East, Relations with; Terrorism.]

BIBLIOGRAPHY

Lou Cannon, *President Reagan: The Role of a Lifetime* (New York, 1991).

William S. Cohen and George M. Mitchell, *Men of Zeal: A Candid Inside Story of the Iran-Contra Hearings* (New York, 1988).

President's Special Review Board, *The Tower Commission Report* (New York, 1987).

Ronald Reagan, *An American Life* (New York, 1990).

Report of the Congressional Committees Investigating the Iran-Contra Affair, with Supplemental, Minority, and Additional Views (Washington, D.C., 1987).

— DAVID HENRY

IRISH AMERICANS

In the 1990 census 44 million Americans claimed some Irish ancestry. Since 1820 more than 4.5 million Irish emigrants have come to the United States. The vast majority arrived during the great Irish potato famine of 1845–1921. By the middle of the twentieth century Irish ethnics were migrating out of urban neighborhoods to the suburbs in search of better housing, jobs, and educations for their families. By the 1970s the Irish were perhaps the best educated and had the highest incomes among white ethnic Catholics in the United States. Known for their political skill, the Irish were also well-represented in business, theater, film, the Roman

Catholic church, and the professions. In their struggle for success they left the tight immigrant communities that initially had molded and maintained their Irish-American identity and culture.

Economic growth and improved social welfare in Ireland, coupled with a 1965 change in U.S. immigration laws, slowed Irish immigration by the 1960s and 1970s. By the end of the 1970s, however, growing interest in the nation's immigrant past and the escalation of violence surrounding the presence of British troops in Northern Ireland contributed to a revival of ethnic identity. The renewal coincided with a steady increase in immigration from Ireland after the 1979–1980 recession. Throughout the 1980s young immigrants streamed into the United States, describing themselves as the New Irish. They differed in several ways from the previous generations of immigrants. For one thing, they were better educated. Most significantly, they entered the country as illegal aliens. The 1965 law made family reunification the criterion for immigration, and the New Irish lacked the family sponsors they needed to enter the country legally. Most of them arrived as tourists, overstayed their visas, and went to work without documentation. At one time estimates of the number of illegal Irish ranged from 40,000 to 150,000. The New Irish concentrated in urban areas with Irish-American populations, such as New York City and Boston. Activists in New York created the Irish Immigration Reform Movement. The group tapped the established Irish-American power in government, business, and the Catholic church to lobby for change in the immigration laws. Because of superior organization and grass-roots efforts, the Irish won nearly half of the pool of nonpreference visas made available by Congress through lotteries in the late 1980s. The New Irish revitalized interest among Irish and non-Irish Americans in Irish pubs, sports, music, dance, film, and drama. They also revived the ethnic communities where they settled, but their long-range effect on Irish-American culture is difficult to predict because they are a transient population. Modern transportation and communication make it possible for immigrants to maintain contact with Ireland and travel regularly between both countries. Prominent Irish Americans in the late twentieth century included Senators Edward M. Kennedy and Daniel Patrick Moynihan, executives Anthony O'Reilly and Mary Lou Quinlan, novelists Mary Higgins Clark and Anna Quindlen, the Reverend Andrew Greeley, and Cardinal John O'Connor.

Nuns from the Loreto Convent surrounded President John F. Kennedy when he visited Wexford, Ireland on June 27, 1963. A third cousin of the president, Mother Clement (formerly Florence Ward), lived at the convent. (UPI/Corbis-Bettmann)

BIBLIOGRAPHY

Andrew Greeley, *The American Catholic: A Social Portrait* (New York, 1977).

Kerby Miller, *Emigrants and Exiles: Ireland and the Irish Exodus to North America* (New York, 1985).

— LINDA DOWLING ALMEIDA

IRONCLAD WARSHIPS

Thickening a ship's sides against penetration by shot was common practice in the sailing-ship era—of which early American frigates afford examples—but with the perfection of the rifled cannon in the first half of the 19th century there was a sharp upsurge in the development of armored warships. The first ironclad undertaken in the United States was the *Stevens Battery*, of 4,683 tons and 6¾-inch side armor, begun in 1842 but never completed. In the Civil War inadequate shipbuilding facilities forced the Confederates to fit armor on existing hulls; the captured Union steam frigate *Merrimack* (renamed *Virginia*) was the first so converted, with a waterline belt and an armored central casemate having inclined sides. Although similar conversions were made by both sides on the Mississippi River, the Union generally relied on newly constructed iron or wooden vessels designed to carry metal armor. The *Monitor* was the first completed, and its success against the *Virginia* on Mar. 9, 1862, led to the construction of many others of the same type—characterized by a very low freeboard, vertically armored sides, and armored revolving gun turrets. Vessels of other types, designed for and fitted with armor, were also built simultaneously; the large, unturreted, and very seaworthy *New Ironsides* was most successful.

BIBLIOGRAPHY

J. P. Baxter, *The Introduction of the Ironclad Warship.*

— DUDLEY W. KNOX

IROQUOIS

The Iroquoian-speaking tribes were intrusive into the Northeast, having moved up from the South before contact with Europeans. Although the Erie and Huron (the so-called neutrals) and several other tribes may originally have been part of this migration, it is to the Five Nations that primary historic attention is given. Settling in the lake region and Mohawk Valley in north central New York, on a line extending from the Hudson River to the Genesee River, the Seneca, Cayuga, Oneida, Onondaga, and Mohawk formed a political union and a military machine that for two centuries dominated the Algonkin peoples round about. The famous League of the Iroquois held at times a key to the balance of power in the North American struggles of the British and French and played a significant role in pre-Revolution history.

Whether the formation of what is regarded as the most elaborate political system of native North America north of Mexico is pre-Columbian in origin remains an open question. Probably it is, to the extent that political alliances characterized the southeastern and Gulf peoples before contact. Legend ascribes the formation of the league to the heroes Dekanawida and Hiawatha, and it was said that the confederation aimed at peace—although, clearly, it was peace in Iroquois terms. Joined after 1712 by the linguistically related Tuscarora, whose conflicts with European settlers in North Carolina resulted in their alliance with the Oneida, the league became known as the Six Tribes. Even so, like other groups given protective status by the original five—other Iroquoian tribes allegedly choosing not to join—the Tuscarora never achieved equal standing. The confederacy was fully integrated by 1700, and political reciprocities between the original five were so well defined that the beginnings of the union can probably be dated early in the 16th century, although 1570 is an often quoted date. It is known that the Dutch at Albany were supplying guns to the Iroquois after 1624, a factor in the domination by the five tribes of a wide area surrounding them.

The famous League of the Iroquois held a key to the North American power struggles between the British and French, and influenced pre-Revolution American history.

It is probably not true, although the claim has been made, that elements of the political organization of the League of the Iroquois found their way into the Constitution of the United States. The concepts of federation and representation suggest parallels, but it is doubtful that the authors of the Constitution were sufficiently aware of the Iroquois political structure to have used it as a model. Each tribe had a council to regulate its own local affairs, and a great council, consisting of fifty peace chiefs, or sachems, met once yearly at Onondaga, N.Y. Judicial, legislative, and military questions were resolved first within the individual tribes and then passed on to the representative body, where unanimous consensus was required, there being no concept of majority voting. The number of sachems for each tribe was fixed by a developing tradition in the representative council. In addition to local classes of sachems the Seneca were represented on the council by eight, and the Onondaga, by fourteen. Ambassadors, usually of titular rank within the local tribe, traveled to advise of decisions, questions, and times of meeting; they carried the tubular beads of accreditation, the wampum. Both councils, tribal and intertribal, were highly susceptible to public opinion. The unanimous decisions were reached only after discussion, all opinions being heard in an atmosphere of dignified oratory.

The various ranks of chieftainship, together with such rights and privileges as might accrue to sachem status, as with the Onondaga "Keeper of the Wampum," passed on matrilineally through the clans that made up the society of the five tribes. A sachem received political office by virtue of its matrilineal inheritance by the clan and his designation to it by the women of the clan. Through their power to appoint, the women of the clan had a vital political role; but in addition, the women of a chief's clan in the generation of his mother had the power to warn and depose him. Although they held no political office as such, women were free to speak, to initiate political issues, and by the pressures they were able to exert, to direct events. It has been said that the Iroquois come as close as any other people in the world to having a matriarchal system.

Iroquois culture, thus probably derived from a southeastern source, differed sharply from that of the Great Lakes—New England Algonkins. The development of stockaded villages with communal dwellings for clan segments (the so-called long houses), elaboration of maize cultivation, and matrilineal descent suggest the southeastern peoples. The Iroquoian languages also have affinities with the speech of southern native Americans, relating to Cherokee, and are related ultimately to a Siouan or Hokan-Siouan phylum. Public festivals, plus elaborate myths and the important role of dreams, characterized Iroquois religion. These too, with their emphasis on fertility, suggest southern origins. Distinctive, however, are the Iroquois curing groups, the "false face" curers, related to secret lodges, a tradition suggestive of northeastern, or Algonkin, origins.

The league ceased to be effective after the American Revolution, and the tribes, in part at least, were forced to disperse. A flurry of messianism, reflecting a cultural revival, began in 1799 with the advent of the prophet Handsome Lake, founder of a syncretistic pagan-Christian movement among the Seneca.

No consideration of the Iroquois is complete without reference to their role in the intellectual history of Marxism. The league was described in detail by the Rochester, N.Y., barrister, Lewis H. Morgan, in 1851, in one of the first detailed accounts of an exotic people, *The League of the Ho-dé-no-sau-nee, or Iroquois.* It was, however, Morgan's *Ancient Society* (1871) that exerted an influence on the theories of Karl Marx and on those of Friedrich Engels as well. German trade unionists of the period before World War I could discuss learnedly the communalism in politics, property, and kinship that characterized the Iroquois. The conservative Morgan would never have supported Marxism, yet his evolutionary theories about the nature of society as gleaned from his analysis of the Iroquois continue to play a role in Marxist thought.

BIBLIOGRAPHY

William N. Fenton, *The Iroquois Eagle Dance.*
Anthony F. C. Wallace, *The Death and Rebirth of the Seneca.*

— ROBERT F. SPENCER

IROQUOIS TREATY

At Albany on July 13, 1684, Gov. Thomas Dongan of New York; Lord Howard of Effingham, governor of Virginia; delegates from both colonies; and Col. Stephen Cortland, one of the Council of New York, representing Massachusetts Bay, met in council with seventeen sachems of the Mohawk, Onondaga, Oneida, and Cayuga nations. Gov. Howard rebuked the Indians for breaking treaties and allowing their warriors to attack the settlers and Indians of Virginia.

On the following day, the Mohawk denied that they had broken faith and rebuked the Cayuga, Oneida, and Onondaga, demanding that they keep the peace. They thanked Howard for having interceded with the governor of Maryland, advocated peace for all nations, and asked that the Duke of York's arms be placed upon their castles. The other nations, with ceremony, agreed to live at peace with the English. On August 2, the Onondaga and Cayuga declared themselves and their lands under the sovereignty of the Duke of York. On Aug. 5, the Seneca arrived and confirmed the action of the other nations.

BIBLIOGRAPHY

Cadwallader Colden, *The History of the Five Nations of Canada.*

— ROBERT W. BINGHAM

ISLAM

As of 1994, 5 million Muslims had constructed more than 600 mosques and other Islamic centers throughout the United States, especially on the East Coast, in the Midwest, and in California, and including one on a Navajo reservation. To coordinate activities of this rapidly growing American Muslim community, Cedar Rapids, Iowa, hosted the first national Islamic Conference in North America in 1952, and successive conferences were coordinated by the Islamic Society of North America beginning in 1982. By the 1990s there were Muslim chaplains in the U.S. armed forces, and Muslims had offered the opening prayers before Congress. It was estimated that by 2015 the American Muslim community will be the nation's largest non-Christian religious group.

As many as 20 percent of West African slaves brought to the United States in the eighteenth and nineteenth centuries were Muslims before their conversion to Christianity. By the end of the nineteenth century, large numbers of Muslim immigrants began to arrive. Most were male migrant workers who lived in small ethnic communities. The latest wave of Muslim immigration occurred after 1965. Coming from a variety of countries, they were usually highly educated and Westernized. African Americans who converted to Islam since the 1920s make up one-third of the Muslim community. In 1913 Noble Drew Ali founded the Moorish Science Temple of America, with current headquarters in Baltimore. Following Drew Ali's death in 1929, Wallace D. Fard began a group in Detroit called the Lost-Found Nation of Islam in the Wilderness of North America (1930). He claimed that African Americans were really Muslims and had been denied their heritage.

Muslims in the U.S. have been faced with a media-supported anti-Islamic bias that contradicts the religious tolerance that is supposed to exist in a secular state.

Designated by Fard as the "messenger of God," Elijah Muhammed became the leader of the Nation of Islam in 1934. Whites were excluded from membership. Members stressed education and black-owned businesses, with the goal of creating a separate black nation. When Elijah died in 1975 there were about seventy temples and 100,000 members in the United States. Most members of the Muslim community did not recognize Elijah's group as Muslims. The larger community considered the racist stance and the other practices unique to the Nation of Islam to be contrary to the egalitarian nature of Islam. Malcolm X, the best-known disciple of Elijah, left the Nation of Islam in 1964, after experiencing the lack of racial and color distinctions during his pilgrimage to Mecca. The issue of joining Islam or of maintaining a separate African-American community greatly complicated leadership struggles after 1975. Warith Deen Muhammed, Elijah's son, succeeded his father as leader of the Nation of Islam. He proceeded to integrate the nation with orthodox Islam, merging the nation into the larger U.S. Muslim community in 1985. Breaking with Warith Deen in 1978, Louis Farrakhan continued the agenda of Elijah along with the organizational structure, racist ideology, and goal of a separate nation. Although both Farrakhan and Warith Deen were committed to the spiritual and material advance of their people, each attempted to represent the African-American community. The merger of Warith Deen's community into mainstream Islam did not affect the sixty Clara Muhammad schools, which provide high quality secular and religious education to elementary and high school students.

Ahmadiyya Muslims, who believe in the prophethood of the northern Indian Mirza Ghulam Ahmad (1835–1908), began to proselytize in the United States in 1921. They achieved considerable success in the African-American community and have headquarters in Washington, D.C. As of 1992 they had 10,000 members, with active centers in thirty-seven cities. Shia Muslims, who look to a descendant of the prophet Muhammad for personal religious leadership, formed their own national organizations, Shia Association of North America and the Ismaili Council for the U.S.A. They usually worship in mosques separate from the mainstream Muslim community. Caucasian Muslim converts in the United States often come to Islam through small groups of mystics, commonly called Sufi groups. Inayat Khan (1882–1927) of the Indian Chishti Order came to the United States in 1910 and set up the Sufi Order, whose leadership was continued by his son, Vilayat Khan. One of the largest Sufi groups in the United States was that of Bawa Muhaiyaddeen, who came to Philadelphia from Sri Lanka in 1971 and was buried there after his death in 1982.

Despite the size of the Muslim community in the United States, individual Muslims experience many incongruities between the norms of American society and the practices of Islam, including conflicts between U.S. civil law and Islamic law, social pressures while fasting during the month of Ramadan, the inability to attend obligatory Friday midday prayers. The most pervasive and blatant discrepancy encountered by Muslims in the United States involved a media-supported anti-Muslim prejudice that contradicted the message of religious tolerance that is supposed to exist in a secular state. This unfortunate situation carried over to foreign Muslim students, who often return to their own countries as anti-American Islamic revivalist leaders.

[See also Arab Americans; Middle East, Relations with.]

BIBLIOGRAPHY

Yvonne Haddad, ed., *The Muslims of America* (New York, 1991).

— ARTHUR F. BUEHLER

ISOLATIONISM

Isolationism refers to American noninterventionist and unilateralist attitudes and to concomitant opposition to involvement in European alliances and wars. Although isolationism developed early in American history, the term itself gained prominence only in the 20th century as critics attacked the view.

Isolationists did not want to cut the United States off from the rest of the world. They did not oppose foreign trade and did not necessarily oppose American expansion. They were not pacifists; they favored maintaining military forces to guard American interests and security in the Western Hemisphere. They distrusted Europe and England in particular. They believed the United States could do more for the world by building prosperity and freedom in America than it could through diplomatic and military involvement in Europe.

Isolationism evolved from the beginnings of American colonial history when settlers fled from difficulties in Europe and expected a better life in America. Isolationists often cited President George Washington's farewell address of 1796, in which he urged America "to steer clear of permanent Alliances." The efforts by President John Adams (1797–1801) to avoid war with France were part of the isolationist tradition. In his first inaugural address in 1801, President Thomas Jefferson advised against "entangling alliances." Even the War of 1812 against England was not waged in alliance with any European belligerents and the United States did not send troops to fight in Europe. The Monroe Doctrine of 1823 advised America "not to interfere in the internal concerns" of Europe. Continental territorial expansion from 1803 to 1867 was accomplished within the isolationist framework. Even the extensive U.S. acquisition of territories in the Caribbean and the Pacific in the 19th and early 20th centuries was accomplished through unilateral actions, not joint actions with European states.

The efforts of the United States to stay out of World War I from 1914 to 1917 and its rejection of membership in the League of Nations afterward were consistent with isolationism. In the 1920's and 1930's isolationists led by senators William E. Borah, Hiram W. Johnson, Gerald P. Nye, and Arthur H. Vandenberg vigorously opposed involvement in European controversies. The Senate Munitions Investigating Committee under Nye (1934–36) was part of that noninterventionist effort, as was the enactment of neutrality laws from 1935 to 1937. When World War II erupted, isolationists fought a last-ditch battle against involvement abroad. Winning some followers in all parts of the country, they gained their greatest support in the Middle West, among rural and small-town people, among German-Americans and Irish-Americans, and within the Republican party. In 1940–41 many of them worked through the America First Committee, the leading noninterventionist pressure group before the attack on Pearl Harbor. Gen. Robert E. Wood was its national chairman, and Col. Charles A. Lindbergh became its most famous speaker.

With the Japanese attack on Pearl Harbor on Dec. 7, 1941, and American entry into World War II, isolationism lost the strong position it had had in American thought. In the second half of the 20th century it became an enfeebled and discredited legacy of America's past, although nostalgia for that view did not completely disappear, and controversies that surrounded U.S. involvement in the Vietnam War gave renewed currency to some of the arguments advanced by isolationists a generation before.

BIBLIOGRAPHY

Selig Adler, *The Isolationist Impulse.*

Wayne S. Cole, *Senator Gerald P. Nye and American Foreign Relations,* and *America First.*

Manfred Jonas, *Isolationism in America.*

— WAYNE S. COLE

ISRAEL-PALESTINE PEACE ACCORD

Israel-Palestine Peace Accord (Aug. 20, 1993). After one of international diplomacy's best-kept secret negotiations, the State of Israel and the Palestine Liberation Organization (PLO) initialed a peace accord (Declaration of Principles) aimed at bringing to an end four and a half decades of rivalry and hostility. The accords, which outlined major principles to be settled in subsequent negotiations, were reached after arduous bargaining in Oslo, Norway, where Norwegian Foreign Minister Johan Jürgen Holst and his aides acted in secret as intermediaries between the parties to the conflict. The official signing ceremony took place at the White House in Washington, D.C., on September 13, where Israeli Prime Minister Yitzhak Rabin and PLO Chairman Yasir Arafat exchanged handshakes before U.S. President Bill Clinton. Israel's foreign minister, Shimon Peres, and the foreign policy aide for the PLO, Mahmoud Abbas, signed the accords, which granted self-government to Palestinians in the Israeli-occupied Gaza Strip and on the occupied West Bank. The most significant aspect of the accord was that Israel acknowledged that the Palestinians are a distinct people entitled to negotiate their own destiny and that the Palestinians accepted Israel's right to exist. The handshake between Rabin and Arafat symbolized a reconciliation that transformed their conflict from an ideological struggle into a practical one—how to share the land formerly known as Palestine.

The Declaration of Principles called for a five-year period of limited self-rule for Palestinians in the occupied territories, and the two sides were to begin negotiating the final status of the territories in 1996. Within three months of signing the declaration, Israel withdrew its troops from the Gaza Strip and the West Bank town of Jericho. The extent of the troop withdrawal and the areas of control to be granted to the Palestinians had been left vague, pending further negotiations, but within nine months of signing the accord, Palestinians held elections for a municipal council to oversee taxation, education, economic development, and social services. In addition, the PLO formed a police force, but its size and responsibilities and its relationship to Israeli troops remained imprecise. The accord also left unresolved the question of how best to protect Israeli settlers living in the West Bank and the Gaza Strip. Moreover, the difficult issue of the future of Jerusalem (claimed by both sides) was postponed until the final negotiations. A joint Israeli-Palestinian economic cooperation committee was established to carry out economic development programs in the West Bank and Gaza Strip.

In many ways the Israel-Palestine Accord was a byproduct of the Camp David Accords of 1978, which called for a five-year interim stage of Palestinian autonomy. The 1993 agreement went beyond Camp David, however, by accepting the principle of Israeli withdrawal from specific territory as a way to make the terms of the agreement more credible to the Palestinians. The accord also recognized the PLO—an organization long reviled by Israel as a murderous terrorist group—as the representative of the Palestinian people. Threatening all attempts to carry out the accord was the fierce opposition by militants on both sides, whose violent activities were aimed at torpedoing the agreement. In February 1994 an Israeli settler killed at least twenty-nine Palestinians at the mosque at the Cave of the Patriarchs in Hebron, which touched off riots throughout the territories and caused a temporary suspension of the talks. More tragically, an Israeli law student assassinated Rabin in November 1995, but both the Israeli and the PLO leadership remained committed to peace, as did the leaders of other Arab nations that had begun peace negotiations with Israel.

[See also Middle East, Relations with.]

BIBLIOGRAPHY

Jane Corbin, *The Norway Channel: The Secret Talks that Led to the Middle East Peace Accord* (New York, 1994).

Shimon Peres, *The New Middle East* (New York, 1993).

— ISAAC ALTERAS

ITALIAN AMERICANS

In the decade between 1971 and 1980 a total of 129,400 Italians emigrated to the United States; between 1981 and 1990 that number dropped to 12,300. This was a far cry from the mass migration concentrated in the years 1876–1924, when 4.5 million arrived. The migration of the past took place for reasons that are easy to set out. Most immigrants were petty landowners and sharecroppers (*contadini*) or farm laborers (*giornalieri*) from southern Italy, the most impoverished region of the country. They left a homeland beset by problems of over-population, agricultural crisis, and social unrest to seek unskilled, manual labor in America's expanding industrial economy. The great exodus initially consisted of temporary migrants, men who desired immediate employment, maximum savings, and quick repatriation. Using kin- and village-based networks they crowded into urban "Little Italys" concentrated in the Northeast and Midwest. After 1900 women and families began to migrate, creating permanent settlements and a vibrant cultural life. Italian-language theaters, newspapers, mutual aid societies, and churches flourished in ethnic communities, providing comity and support. Immigrants clustered because of discrimination in housing, employment, and social access. Nativist stereotypes centered on the immigrants' Catholicism, poverty, clannishness, illiteracy, low rates of naturalization, and alleged proclivity toward crime.

Italian Americans are prominent in every walk of life, from Supreme Court Justice Scalia and filmmakers Coppola and Scorsese to pop star Madonna.

Immigration restrictions in the 1920s put an end to massive Italian emigration to the United States. Italian Americans, however, continued to make economic gains and played an increasingly prominent role in U.S. mainstream culture. In 1990, 14.7 million Americans claimed Italian ancestry and constituted 5.9 percent of the national population. They were moving to different parts of the country. Half had been born in the Northeast and were still there, while others concentrated in Florida, California, and other parts of the Sunbelt. In the big cities Italian enclaves largely disappeared; the few that remained tended to become tourist attractions. Little Italy in New York City, the North End of Boston, and South Philadelphia were known for their restaurants, outdoor food markets, and religious festivals. Some observers contended that Italian Americans had become so assimilated they were in danger of disappearing as an ethnic group. Fewer than a million had been born abroad. In 1980, the census year for which a careful study of Italian Americans was made, only 1.5 million spoke Italian. That year the once-popular New York newspaper *Il Progresso* ceased publication. Only half of Italian Americans claimed Italian origin for both parents and intermarriage was changing the nature of families. Gone were families of ten or twelve children. The birth rate was declining to the 1980 "typical" U.S. family size of 1.5 children, and divorces were increasing, especially among those of one-parent Italian ancestry.

Economically, Italian Americans flourished. Their distribution by occupation did not differ from that of Americans in general. Their incomes in 1980 were 25 percent higher than the national average. Their economic success was symbolized by the rise to prominence of Lido (Lee) Anthony Iacocca, a top executive of the Ford Motor Company and then president of the Chrysler Corporation, which he nearly singlehandedly saved from bankruptcy. In the 1990s Italian Americans were prominent in virtually every walk of life. In politics they claimed such figures as the three-term governor of New York, Mario M. Cuomo; Governor James Florio of New Jersey; Senators Alfonse M. D'Amato of New York, Dennis DeConcini of Arizona, and Pete V. Domenici of New Mexico; and the mayor of New York City, Rudolph Giuliani. Among women political leaders was Geraldine Ferraro, Democratic candidate for the U.S. vice presidency in 1984. Antonin Scalia was an associate justice of the Supreme Court. Italian-American athletes included Joe Montana, one of football's all-time greatest quarterbacks; one of the best-known U.S. writers was John Ciardi, author of forty books of poetry and criticism and translator of Dante. Italian-American filmmakers were Francis Ford Coppola and Martin Scorsese; actors included Robert De Niro, Al Pacino, and Sylvester Stallone; and in a class by herself was the pop star Madonna (Madonna Louise Ciccone).

BIBLIOGRAPHY

Richard D. Alba, *Italian Americans: Into the Twilight of Ethnicity* (Englewood Cliffs, N.J., 1985).

Graziano Battistella, ed., *Italian Americans in the '80s* (New York, 1989).

Jerre Mangione and Ben Morreale, *La Storia: Five Centuries of the Italian American Experience* (New York, 1992).

— GEORGE E. POZZETTA

J

JACKSONIAN DEMOCRACY

The association of the Democratic party with the rise and triumph of democracy during Andrew Jackson's presidency, from 1829 to 1837, was a dominant theme in American historical writing from the late 19th century through the 1950's. The term "Jacksonian Democracy" is of unknown origin. Contemporaries of President Jackson did not use it, although Jackson's supporters frequently did make claims that the president represented the will of the people. The major 19th-century biographers of Jackson, James Parton and William Graham Sumner, made no reference to Jacksonian Democracy; to them Jackson was a demagogue who had corrupted American life by introducing the spoils system. During the last quarter of the 19th century the term "Jacksonian Democracy" does appear in the writings of several historians, but it was used in a narrow sense to refer to the programs and policies embraced by the Democratic party under Jackson's leadership.

The historian most responsible for broadening the concept of Jacksonian Democracy to signify a general democratic upheaval was Frederick Jackson Turner. The presentation of his famous paper on "The Significance of the Frontier in American History," in 1893, signaled the beginning of the dominance of a democratic-agrarian school in the writing of Jacksonian history for the next forty years. Where Turner had led, 20th-century historians soon followed—notably William McDonald, John Spencer Bassett, Vernon Parrington, and Claude Bowers. By the 1920's the standard textbook interpretation of the Jacksonian era went something like this: Jackson's election to the presidency over John Quincy Adams in 1828 marked a great victory of the common people over the privileged; it was also a triumph of West over East, democracy over conservatism, equal opportunity over special privilege, agrarianism over capitalism, and honest labor over aristocratic leisure. Historians wrote in clear terms of a political movement they called Jacksonian Democracy and the emergence from it of the Age of the Common Man. They saw Jackson's introduction of the spoils system as a democratic advance because it eliminated entrenched officeholders and, presumably, made all areas of government responsive to the popular will. Similarly they interpreted Jackson's successful war on the second Bank of the United States as the beneficial destruction of a major bastion of aristocratic privilege. Other developments cited as characteristic of Jacksonian Democracy include the substitution of party conventions for the caucus system to choose candidates and draw up party platforms, the adoption by most states of universal white adult male suffrage, and the emergence of widespread humanitarian reform movements.

As interpreted by Turner and his followers, Jacksonian Democracy sprang primarily from sectional conflict—the egalitarian West gaining supremacy over the elitist East. But by the 1920's their emphasis on the frontier West as the source of the Jacksonian movement was being modified. Arthur Schlesinger, Sr., in a 1922 essay, suggested that the wellsprings of Jacksonian Democracy were to be found not only in the agrarian West

Andrew Jackson with the Tennessee forces on the Hickory Grounds, Alabama in 1814. Historians considered Jackson's election to the presidency over John Quincy Adams in 1828 a victory of the common man over the privileged. (Library of Congress)

but also in the laboring classes of the industrializing Northeast. According to his interpretation newly enfranchised eastern laborers, suffering from deteriorating economic conditions and insecurities of status, spearheaded the Jacksonian drive to control the exploitative power of capitalist groups. This thesis—that class conflict was the mainspring of Jacksonian Democracy—found its strongest exponent in Schlesinger's son, Arthur Schlesinger, Jr., whose *Age of Jackson* appeared in 1945.

In the decade after 1945 Schlesinger's class-conflict explanation of Jacksonian Democracy came under sharp attack. The most popular thesis to emerge during the post-Schlesinger debates was the entrepreneurial interpretation advanced by Joseph Dorfman, Richard Hofstadter, and Bray Hammond. According to these historians Jacksonian Democracy could best be understood as a movement of expectant capitalists eager to overthrow the previously established economic elite in order to initiate equal opportunities for themselves under the reign of laissez-faire capitalism.

Although historians have not always agreed about the sources of Jacksonian Democracy, they were united from the turn of the century until after World War II in seeing the Jacksonian movement as advancing democracy. Since the 1950's, however, that consensus has broken down. Notable among the historians who have challenged nearly every aspect of the traditional interpretation are Marvin Meyers, Lee Benson, Richard H. Brown, Douglas Miller, and Edward Pessen. As early as 1953 Meyers suggested that the Whigs were more optimistic and progressive in outlook than Jackson's Democrats. Benson, in his 1961 book *The Concept of Jacksonian Democracy,* analyzed political behavior in New York State and concluded that none of the assumptions implicit in the term "Jacksonian Democracy" were valid. During the next decade Brown pointed out the proslavery position of the Jacksonian Democrats, and both Miller and Pessen argued that democratic trends of the age had been overemphasized and that the stress of Jacksonian Democrats on political, social, and economic equality was more rhetorical than real. Not only do these scholars challenge the idea that the common man was dominant in the Jacksonian era, they also claim that the economic developments of the time created sharper social stratifications.

Debate over the validity of the concept of Jacksonian Democracy undoubtedly will continue. But it seems unlikely that in the future historians will rely so heavily and unquestioningly on this generalizing phrase. Although some scholars continue to stress the democratic aspects of the years of Jackson's presidency—and especially the emergence of a modern two-party system—few continue to use the term "Jacksonian Democracy" with such certainty as earlier authors displayed. Perhaps historians will return to the original limited and factual use of the term merely to refer to the policies and programs of the political party led by Jackson.

BIBLIOGRAPHY

Lee Benson, *The Concept of Jacksonian Democracy.*
Alfred A. Cave, *Jacksonian Democracy and the Historians.*
Richard Hofstadter, *The American Political Tradition.*
Douglas T. Miller, *Jacksonian Aristocracy, The Birth of Modern America.*
Edward Pessen, *Jacksonian America.*
Arthur M. Schlesinger, Jr., *The Age of Jackson.*
Charles Grier Sellers, Jr., "Andrew Jackson Versus the Historians," *Mississippi Valley Historical Review,* vol. 44 (March 1958).
Frederick Jackson Turner, *The United States, 1830–1850.*

— DOUGLAS T. MILLER

JAMESTOWN

When James I granted a charter to the Virginia Company of London, or London Company, in the spring of 1606, Jamestown had its start. The London Company, modeled after other English joint-stock trading companies, sent three vessels in late 1606 under Capt. Christopher Newport to create a colony in Virginia, find gold, and discover a route to the Pacific Ocean. In May 1607 the settlers landed on a marshy island in the James River estuary and by mid-June had built a triangular fort and planted grain.

In choosing this site, the settlers violated their instructions to locate in a defensible and healthy place. Jamestown was defensible, but it was unhealthy, being low and marshy and lacking a ready source of fresh water. Disease appeared quickly, probably malaria and dysentery, and many settlers died during the first summer. Friendly Indians, who supplied corn and wild meat, enabled the colonists to survive the first winter, although the number of colonists dropped from over 100 to about 40 by December, when Newport brought in 120 more settlers.

From the beginning the settlers quarreled among themselves. Of the original leaders, Capt. Bartholomew Gosnold died of illness, George Kendall was shot for treachery, Edward Maria Wingfield was deposed as president of the council, and Capt. John Smith and John Robinson successfully sued Wingfield for slander. All these events occurred within the first three months of settlement. Despite the arrival of additional supply vessels with more settlers in 1608, the colony teetered on the edge of disaster.

In 1608 Smith took firm control of the settlement and prescribed a regimen of from four to six hours' work per day per man. The conundrum of such a light work load in the face of omnipresent disaster can only be explained by the settlers' debility from disease, by the fact that too many of them were gentlemen and adventurers, by inflated English expectations of the New World based upon Spanish successes in South America, and by English attitudes toward work.

When Smith returned to England in the fall of 1609, even his limited efforts stopped, and the colony almost collapsed in the winter of 1609–10. During that "starving time" 90 percent of the settlers died. As governor, Sir Thomas Dale brought about a revival of the colony in the summer of 1610 by introducing a more stringent legal code and by abandoning the colony's communal system of production. Although the colony exported shipmasts and lumber, it never turned a profit for the London Company. John Rolfe in 1612 experimented with tobacco, highly prized in England but previously secured from the Spanish colonies, and tobacco cultivation soon dominated the colony. By 1614 its economic outlook had brightened. However, the number of inhabitants remained at only some 350. Jamestown boasted two rows of framed timber houses, each three stories tall; three storehouses; and a reinforced palisade. Several houses were also situated outside the fortifications.

The year 1619 saw the beginning of prosperity in Jamestown and the arrival of the first blacks in Virginia; in the same year, the town became the seat of the first legislative assembly in the New World. In March 1622, Virginia shuddered under an Indian attack, and Jamestown became a refuge for the survivors. By 1625, 124 persons resided in Jamestown, which had twenty-two houses, three stores, and a church. As the colony prospered and expanded, however, Jamestown lost its preeminence; Virginia's life centered about the tobacco farms scattered along the many navigable rivers. Hopes continued for the town's development, and in 1631 an effort was made to make it the colony's exclusive port; but not even the government could contradict the edicts of geography. In 1676 the town was burned during Bacon's Rebellion, and it never regained its limited vitality. In 1698 another fire ravaged Jamestown, and the government was moved to Williamsburg in 1699, allowing the remains of the original capitol to molder. Of the original site, only the excavated foundations of buildings and the ruined tower of the brick church built about 1680 are preserved.

In 1930 the Colonial National Historical Park was established, including most of Jamestown Island. The upper end of the island, site of the first representative legislative government on the continent, was declared a national historic site in 1940.

BIBLIOGRAPHY

Wesley Frank Craven, *The Southern Colonies in the Seventeenth Century, 1607–1689.*

Edmund S. Morgan, "The Labor Problem at Jamestown, 1607–18," *The American Historical Review*, vol. 76.

— LAWRENCE H. LEDER

JAPANESE AMERICANS

Japanese Americans, the largest Asian-American group within the total U.S. population in 1970, slipped to third largest (behind Chinese and Filipinos) in 1980 and 1990, numbering in the latter year 847,562 or 12 percent of all Asian Americans. Japanese Americans increased the least among Asian Americans by immigration, comprising a mere 1 percent, 41,739, of the total Asian immigration between 1980 and 1989. Several factors accounted for the small number of immigrants. Foremost was the economic boom in Japan, which made emigration less desirable or necessary. In addition, Japanese Americans did not experience a huge gender imbalance like other Asian-American groups, and in fact Japanese Americans were the only group before 1965 in which women outnumbered men. Family reunification, a key feature of the post-1965 Asian-American immigration, was not a pressing concern for Japanese Americans. The largest concentrations of Japanese Americans by far were in California and Hawaii, with the states of New York and Washington a distant third and fourth. Japanese Americans, like all Asian Americans, are a diverse group, the major distinction being between those from Japan and those from Okinawa, which was the independent kingdom of Ryukyu until incorporated as a prefecture by Japan in 1879.

Because of high educational levels and family incomes and especially because their rise from the poverty caused by World War II detention appeared so spectacular, Japanese Americans were widely praised as a "model minority." That achievement was accomplished, wrote commentators, through their determined effort but also because of cultural values that resembled dominant American values, including centrality of the family, regard for schooling, a premium placed on the future, and belief in the virtues of hard work. As early as 1960 Japanese Americans had a greater percentage of high school and college graduates than other Americans, and ten years later median family incomes were higher by nearly $3,000. By 1980 employment for Japanese Americans paralleled closely that of Americans in general. Observers noted, however, that Japanese Americans have greater numbers of workers per household, accounting in part for higher median incomes. According to a study of Asian Americans in California's San Francisco Bay area, based on the 1980 U.S. census, Japanese-American individuals worked more hours.

The history of Japanese Americans reaches back to the nineteenth-century U.S. policy of Manifest Destiny in the Pacific, which involved trade with China, the opening of Japan in 1854, and eventual annexation of Hawaii in 1898. Hawaiian sugar planters, mainly U.S. citizens, recruited Japanese contract workers. The first Japanese settlers on the mainland arrived in San Francisco in 1869. The group established the Wakamatsu Tea and Silk Farm Colony on 600 acres near Sacramento. The mulberry shoots and tea seeds they brought from Japan withered in the dry California soil, the colony failed, and people drifted away. After passage of the Chinese Exclusion Act of 1882, labor recruiters from the mainland visited Hawaii to lure Japanese workers with promises of higher wages and better working conditions. Their appeal was attractive compared with the rigors of sugar plantation life. Between 1902 and 1906, 34,000 Japanese left Hawaii for the West Coast. President Theodore Roosevelt stopped that flow in 1907 by executive order and the 1908 Gentlemen's Agreement between Japan and the United States, whereby Japan agreed not to issue passports to Japanese workers planning to migrate to the United States, and passage of the 1924 Immigration Act effectively closed off Japanese immigration. Meanwhile, migration of Japanese women, mainly as "picture brides" from 1908 to 1920, helped even the mainland gender ratio. Japanese Americans who did reach the United States labored in occupations open to them. While exclusion ended immigration, segregation reduced opportunities in education, housing, and employment, and alien land laws enacted in several western states thwarted their advancement in agriculture.

The first Japanese settlers on the mainland arrived in San Francisco in 1869 and founded the Wakamatsu Tea and Silk Farm Colony on 600 acres near Sacramento.

Japan's attack on Pearl Harbor in 1941 and World War II brought martial law in Hawaii, which contained Hawaii's Japanese, and on the mainland the army removed all Japanese Americans from the West Coast following President Franklin D. Roosevelt's Executive Order 9066 of Feb. 19, 1942. Although Japanese Americans had nothing to do with Japan's attack on Pearl Harbor and did not pose an internal threat to the nation, in Hawaii 1,466 were placed in detention facilities and 1,875 were taken to and confined in mainland detention camps; in all, more than 120,000 Japanese Americans were held in camps. During the war Gordon Hirabayashi, Minoru Yasui, and Fred Korematsu tested the constitutionality of these actions, and dozens refused to be drafted from the camps into the military as a way of protesting the loss of civil liberties. Others claimed conscientious objector status, but still many other young men and women served in the U.S. military. The Supreme Court in *Ex Parte Endo* (1944) ruled that a loyal citizen could not be deprived of his or her freedom. The numbers of Japanese Americans in the camps steadily declined as students were released to attend college and workers received temporary permits. By January 1945 the camps still held 80,000 people. In Hawaii martial law had been lifted in October 1944.

Like other World War II veterans, Japanese Americans used the GI Bill to gain college educations. In Hawaii veterans entered politics, organized the Japanese-American vote, and reshaped the Democratic party in the islands, ushering in the "revolution of 1954," which ended nearly fifty years of Republican party rule. In the Civil Rights Restoration Act of 1987, the U.S. government apologized for wrongs to Japanese Americans during the war and authorized monetary redress.

[See also Japanese-American Relocation; Japanese Exclusion Acts; Asian Americans; Hawaii.]

BIBLIOGRAPHY

Dorothy Ochiai Hazama and Jane Okamoto Komeiji, *Okage Sama De: The Japanese in Hawai'i, 1885–1985* (Honolulu, 1986).
Brian Niiya, ed., *Japanese American History* (New York, 1993).
David J. O'Brien and Stephen S. Fugita, *The Japanese American Experience* (Bloomington, Ind., 1991).

— GARY Y. OKIHIRO

JAPANESE EXCLUSION ACTS

In the later part of the 19th century there was increasing immigration of Asians to the United States. Opposition to these immigrants developed principally in the West Coast states, because of a widespread belief that the Asians' lower standard of living was detrimental to the interests of American labor and agriculture. After demands for legislation to restrict Asian immigration had produced the Chinese Exclusion Act of 1882, repeated efforts were made to extend the restrictions to the Japanese.

In order to head off the demands for restrictive legislation aimed at the Japanese, President Theodore Roosevelt in 1901 negotiated an agreement with Japan whereby the latter vowed to limit severely the issuance of passports to Japanese laborers, but it was ineffective. In 1907 negotiations were reopened and led to the conclusion of the so-called Gentlemen's Agreement with Japan. Its text has never been published, but it unquestionably provided that in consideration of the U.S. government's refraining from passage of an exclusion law, the Japanese government would not issue passports to Japanese laborers who intended to migrate to the United States. In any event the successful implementation of this agreement temporarily satisfied the advocates of restriction, and no restrictive legislation aimed at the Japanese was then adopted.

In 1924 Congress considered, and ultimately enacted, a law imposing numerical restrictions on immigration from all countries outside the Western Hemisphere. One provision of this law, known as the Johnson Act, completely barred the immigration of aliens who were ineligible for citizenship, a provision unquestionably designed to exclude Japanese, who were, in common with other Asians, statutorily barred from naturalization at that time. While the bill was under consideration, the Japanese ambassador sent a note warning of "grave consequences" if the exclusion of Japanese were enacted. This note aroused strong hostility in Congress, which abruptly rejected all attempts at reconciliation and overwhelmingly adopted the act of exclusion. The enactment of this legislation was strongly resented in Japan and continued for many years to be a hindrance to good relations between the two countries. Some believe that the resentments generated by the Immigration Act of 1924 were one of the causes of the hostilities between the United States and Japan in World War II.

A complete change in public sentiment after World War II resulted in the elimination of the immigration restrictions directed against Asians. The Chinese Exclusion Act was repealed in 1943. The more general provision excluding aliens ineligible for citizenship, to which the Japanese had objected in 1924, was repealed by the McCarran-Walter Act of 1952. In the mid-1970's there was no provision in the laws of the United States sanctioning the exclusion of Japanese or other Asians solely because of their race or national origin.

BIBLIOGRAPHY

Charles Gordon and Harry N. Rosenfield, *Immigration Law and Procedure.*

— CHARLES GORDON

JAY'S TREATY

Jay's Treaty, signed Nov. 19, 1794, adjusted a group of serious Anglo-American diplomatic issues arising out of the Definitive Treaty of Peace of 1783, subsequent commercial difficulties, and issues over neutral rights.

The principal issues arising out of the treaty of peace were Great Britain's deliberate refusal to evacuate six controlling frontier forts in American territory along the northern river-and-lake boundary established by the treaty; obstacles of state courts to the collection of prewar debts by British creditors, despite the guarantees of the treaty of peace; alleged confiscation by states of property of returning Loyalists in violation of treaty protection against any such acts after the peace; and unsettled boundary gaps. To these grievances were added Britain's refusal to admit American ships into the ports of its remaining colonies in North America and the West Indies; its refusal to make a treaty of commerce, or even to exchange diplomatic representatives, during the period of the Confederation, 1783–89; and Britain's active intrigue with the western Indian tribes that had been its allies during the Revolution but were left within the boundaries of the United States. It was the hope of the British government to establish north of the Ohio River a "neutral Indian barrier state" as the price of any settlement with the United States, or even to put off any settlement at all in expectation of the ultimate breakup of the feeble American Confederation.

The new Constitution of the United States of 1787 and the evolution of the national government of President George Washington established in 1789 checked these expectations. New national navigation laws, championed by James Madison in Congress, and supported by Secretary of State Thomas Jefferson, leader of the crystallizing Republican party (Jeffersonian), revealed the possibility of serious discrimination against British trade by its best foreign customer, and it induced the government of British Prime Minister William Pitt (the younger) to send a minister, George Hammond, to the United States in 1791, empowered to discuss issues. The discussions had produced nothing by the time war broke out between France and Great Britain on Feb. 1, 1793, largely because Alexander Hamilton, secretary of the treasury, assured Hammond that he would try to block any commercial discrimination against Great Britain. Hamilton had just restored American credit by a fiscal system that depended for its revenues on import duties, and nine-tenths of that revenue came from taxes on imports from Great Britain. A commercial war might thus mean the collapse of American credit and with it of the newly established American nation.

Arbitrary British naval orders in 1793 and the consequent capture of hundreds of American neutral ships, combined with a bellicose speech of Sir Guy Carleton, Baron Dorchester, the governor-general of Canada, to the western Indians, precipitated the war crisis of 1794. Hamilton and the Federalist leaders pressed Washington to stop short of commercial reprisals (Congress did vote an embargo for two months), and Chief Justice John Jay was sent to London as minister plenipotentiary and envoy extraordinary on a special peace mission. In the negotiations with William Wyndham Grenville, British secretary for foreign affairs, Jay could have made more of the American cause. On Hamilton's secret advice (Jefferson had been succeeded by Edmund Randolph as secretary of state), Jay acquiesced in British maritime measures for the duration of the war, in return for the creation of a mixed commission to adjudicate American spoliation claims ($10,345,200 paid by 1802) for damages made "under color" of British Orders in Council (not in themselves repudiated); Great Britain agreed to evacuate the frontier posts by June 1, 1796 (executed substantially on time); the United States guaranteed the payment of British private prewar debts, the total amount to be worked out by another mixed commission (£600,000 *en bloc* settlement made in 1802); and two mixed boundary commissions were set up to establish correctly the line in the northwest (this one never met) and in the northeast (agreed on identity of the Saint Croix River).

Arbitrary British naval orders in 1793 and the consequent capture of hundreds of American neutral ships precipitated the war crisis of 1794.

Washington got the treaty through the Senate and the House (where the Jeffersonian Republicans tried to block the necessary appropriations) only with great difficulty. The temporary acquiescence in British maritime measures was the price the Federalists paid for (1) redemption of American territorial integrity in the Northwest, and (2) peace with Great Britain when peace was necessary for the perpetuation of American nationality. On its part Great Britain was anxious for a treaty (1) to keep its best foreign customer, and (2) to keep the United States as a neutral during the European war then raging.

BIBLIOGRAPHY

Samuel Flagg Bemis, *Jay's Treaty, A Study in Commerce and Diplomacy.*

— SAMUEL FLAGG BEMIS

JEFFERSON-BURR ELECTORAL DISPUTE

Thomas Jefferson and Aaron Burr were the Democratic-Republican candidates for the presidency and vice-presidency, respectively, in the acrimonious campaign of 1800. Because of the growing effectiveness of the two-party system the Democratic-Republican candidates each received seventy-three votes in the electoral college, and the Federalist vote split sixty-five for John Adams, sixty-four for Charles Cotesworth Pinckney, and one for John Jay. Thus, the election went to the Democratic-Republicans. But since the votes for Jefferson and Burr were exactly equal, the opportunity for a quibble was presented. The Constitution as it then stood read as follows: "The Person having the greatest Number of Votes shall be the President, if such Number be a Majority of the whole Number of Electors appointed; and if there be more than one who have such Majority, and have an equal Number of Votes, then the House of Representatives shall immediately chuse by Ballot one of them for President." Accordingly, the election was thrown into the House. But, again by the wording of the Constitution, "in chusing the President, the Votes shall be taken by States, the Representation from each State having one Vote; A quorum for this Purpose shall consist of a Member or Members from two thirds of the States, and a Majority of all the States shall be necessary to a Choice." The Federalists, still in control from the elections of 1798—despite the opposition of Alexander Hamilton and other reputable leaders and in cynical disregard of popular interest—schemed to put Burr into the presidency. Jefferson received the vote of eight states and Burr of six; the representatives of Maryland and Vermont were equally divided. Thus, there was no majority among the sixteen states then belonging to the Union. For weeks intrigue went on amid rumors of forcible resistance should the scheme succeed. On Feb. 17, on the thirty-sixth ballot, the Federalist members from Maryland and Vermont declined to vote, with the result that Jefferson had the votes of ten states and was declared elected. The Twelfth Amendment, correcting the procedure of the electoral college, became effective before the next election, but the constitutional provisions allowing for a "lame duck" Congress, an important factor in this episode, remained unreformed until 1933.

BIBLIOGRAPHY

Jonathan Daniels, *Ordeal of Ambition: Jefferson, Hamilton, Burr.*
Dumas Malone, *Jefferson the President: First Term, 1801–1805.*
Arthur M. Schlesinger et al., eds., *History of American Presidential Elections, 1789–1968.*

— W. A. ROBINSON

JEFFERSONIAN DEMOCRACY

To understand Jeffersonian Democracy it is necessary to consider Thomas Jefferson's generalizations, his more specific attitude toward democracy, and his theory of the functions of government.

The most resounding and influential of the first are to be found in the Declaration of Independence, where he states that "all men are created equal" and endowed with certain inalienable rights. The interest and faith of Jefferson in the common man run through all his writings and his life. It is this strain that gives the peculiar flavor to Jeffersonian, as contrasted with Hamiltonian, political philosophy and has made him one of the revered leaders of world democracy.

It is easy to misunderstand Jefferson unless one considers carefully his more specific attitude. The America of his day was 90 percent agricultural, and the Virginia county in which he was brought up, Albemarle, was a sample of frontier life at its very best. The common man, as Jefferson envisioned him in his democratic ideology, was essentially an independent farmer. Although in later years Jefferson somewhat altered his views about manufactures, he always feared the influence of them and of cities. He wrote that he believed Americans would remain virtuous, politically, as long as there was free land to be taken up; but "when they get piled upon one another in large cities, as in Europe, they will become corrupt as in Europe." He believed that, with limited immigration, the country would not be filled for 1,000 years. He did not foresee the Industrial Revolution and the age of steam and electricity.

Thomas Jefferson, author of the Declaration of Independence and second president of the United States. His view of the rights of the common man established him as a revered champion of democracy. (Library of Congress)

An extremely able political organizer, he was the first to have the combined support of the common men of his day, the farmers, and the city workers, but it must be recalled that the American cities of the period had none of the proletarian cast of London or Paris. Even so, he feared such a development, and all the measures he advocated sprang from a coherent and close-knit philosophy, that of a democracy that could be based safely only on agriculture, as carried on by a citizenry of small, educated, independent freeholders.

Thus his fight against both primogeniture and entail arose from his fear that the small freeholder, even in ample America, might be squeezed out if families could keep large landholdings permanently in their own hands. Although a firm believer in the right of private property, he did not believe in its maldistribution or tying it up permanently, but in its wide distribution among the capable, energetic, and thrifty.

His theory of state education is particularly illuminating for his doctrine of democracy. He considered an educated citizenry essential; he believed that society would benefit by utilizing all the talent available by paying to educate those who could not afford to educate themselves, up to the limit of their ability to benefit, but not beyond. In his plan—the foundation for the modern French system, but not the American—all children were to receive an education in the lower grades, above which a steady sifting process was to go on, leading certain selected students through higher grades and college. Thus, taxes for education would pay social dividends but not be squandered. His carefully worked out system for state education is a most important gloss on his generalization that all men are created equal.

To his essentials for democracy, the independence of free ownership of land and an education, he added freedom of religion, speech, and the press. In spite of the fact that few presidents have been more bitterly assailed, he never gave up his belief in, and defense of, these last three. Without them he believed democracy impossible. He did not believe it possible everywhere and under all circumstances, or in the Europe of his time. All his writings and acts indicate fear of democracy except in a nation of small country free-holders, with few city wage earners.

His theory of government is succinctly and best expressed in his first inaugural address. He believed in limiting governmental functions to the minimum; in a strict construction of the Constitution and in reserving to the states as much power as possible; in majority rule as a working compromise that could not be rightful unless it recognized the equal rights of minorities; in "the honest payment of our debts and sacred preservation of the public faith"; in economy on the part of government so that "labor may be lightly burthened"; in freedom of trade; and in as small a debt as possible. He was bitterly against inflation, from which he had deeply suffered.

Essentially an aristocrat in taste, character, and private life, he was the greatest American advocate of the democratic doctrine and of the common man (as he saw the common man—and the potential common man—of his day). America has changed so much since he lived and served that it is impossible to know what views he might hold about contemporary conditions and policies. It may be suggested, however, that many who claim to be Jeffersonian democrats are far from his specific doctrines. The appeal made by the invocation of his name is chiefly the appeal for interest in the common man—but the 20th-century "common man" is different from any Jefferson knew. He is not the small freeholder, in whom Jefferson solely believed, nor is he the peasant or the city proletarian whom Jefferson knew in France. In light of Jefferson's theory about government functions and his specific attitudes it is difficult for any later political party properly to call itself Jeffersonian, but the generalizations remain, often without the limitations that Jefferson himself, in writings and acts, laid upon them.

BIBLIOGRAPHY

J. T. Adams, *The Living Jefferson.*
G. Chinard, *Thomas Jefferson.*
W. A. Robinson, *Jeffersonian Democracy in New England.*

— JAMES TRUSLOW ADAMS

JEHOVAH'S WITNESSES

Jehovah's Witnesses are one of the most important Adventist and apocalyptic sects to have emerged in America. Founded by Charles Taze Russell in 1872, they were known as Millennial Dawnists, Russellites, and International Bible Students until 1931, when the current name was adopted. Since 1879 the principal means of spreading the Witnesses' message has been the *Watchtower,* a publication that gives the Witnesses' views on life. In 1884 the movement was incorporated as the Watchtower Bible and Tract Society. After the death of Russell in 1916, leadership passed to Joseph Franklin Rutherford, popularly known as "Judge," and, at his death in 1942, to Nathan Homer Knorr. Jehovah's Witnesses believe in an Arian Christology—the nontrinitarian belief that Christ was an archangel—and in the imminence of the millennium. In that golden age, they believe, 144,000 will share in the kingly rule of Christ; others may escape destruction, but only if they work with the Witnesses in the present. The movement is tightly organized and engages in widespread evangelistic activities.

According to Jehovah's Witnesses, in a golden age to come, 144,000 will share in the kingly rule of Christ; others may escape destruction, if they work with the Witnesses in the present.

Jehovah's Witnesses have been at the center of a number of court cases because of their claim to exemption from military service and their proselytizing activities; beginning in the 1940's legal controversy arose from their refusal to join in the pledge of allegiance to the flag because Jehovah alone should be obeyed. Despite popular animosity their right to dissent has been consistently affirmed by the courts. In 1974 the membership of the movement in the United States was 498,177. U.S. headquarters are located in Brooklyn, N.Y.

BIBLIOGRAPHY

Marty Cole, *Triumphant Kingdom.*
Herbert H. Stroup, *The Jehovah's Witnesses.*
William Whalen, *Armageddon Around the Corner: A Report on Jehovah's Witnesses.*
Timothy White, *A People for His Name: A History of Jehovah's Witnesses and an Evaluation.*

— GLENN T. MILLER

JESUITS

Jesuits, the conventional designation for members of the Society of Jesus, a religious order of men founded by Saint Ignatius Loyola (1491–1556) and formally approved by the Holy See Sept. 27, 1540. The Jesuits were an influence in the development of colonial America, particularly through their explorations and missions. They were associated with the Calverts in the founding of Maryland, 1634; they inaugurated the Catholic ministry in the Middle Atlantic states, the upper Great

Lakes region, and the Mississippi Valley, making at the same time contributions to the economic and cultural beginnings of the territory in which they worked.

Jesuit activities in post-colonial America date from the organization of the Maryland Mission of the order in 1805. From Maryland the order spread to the Middle West, opening in 1823 at Florissant, in Missouri, what proved to be a starting point of subsequent far-flung expansion. In 1841 it became established in the Pacific Northwest and in 1849 in California. Meantime, Jesuit houses had been opened in Kentucky, 1832; Louisiana, 1837; and New York, 1846. The activities of the American Jesuits have been, and continue to be, highly diversified. They range from the foreign missions to the parochial ministry; the pastoral care of Indian reservations; the direction of retreats built about the *Spiritual Exercises* of Saint Ignatius Loyola; chaplaincies in the armed forces, prisons, and hospitals; and inner-city programs. But the major interest of the Jesuits is education. The first American Jesuit college, Georgetown University, in Washington, D.C., dates from 1789. Saint Louis University, in Missouri, the oldest school of university grade west of the Mississippi, has been conducted by the Jesuits since 1829. There are seventy-six educational institutions, parochial schools apart, under their management in the United States, including eighteen universities, ten colleges, and forty-eight high schools. The American Jesuits, organized into ten provinces or administrative units, numbered 6,458 in 1974, the worldwide membership of the order being 29,436.

BIBLIOGRAPHY

W. V. Bangert, *A History of the Society of Jesus.*
F. X. Curran, *The Return of the Jesuits.*
G. J. Garraghan, *The Jesuits of the Middle United States.*
W. J. McGucken, *The Jesuits and Education.*

— W. V. BANGERT

JEWS, AMERICAN

The most prominent experience of America's Jews in the post-World War II era was their rapid social and economic mobility. Prior to 1945 a large majority of American Jews lived in the major cities of the Northeast and Midwest and were employed as workers, craftsmen, and small shopkeepers. By 1990 most adult Jews were college graduates, working in white-collar jobs and the professions. Within a few decades America's Jews thus had become the nation's most affluent and best-educated religious and ethnic group. The economist Thomas Sowell termed this transformation the greatest collective success story in U.S. history. As Jews moved up the economic and social ladder they took on the characteristics of their Gentile counterparts—smaller families, more divorces, and an emphasis on individual autonomy and cultural modernism. This resulted in the shrinkage of the Jewish population. Jews had comprised 3.8 percent of the American population in the late 1930s, but made up no more than 2.5 percent in 1990. By then it was common for sociologists to talk about the crisis of the American Jewish family. One cause of the upward economic and social mobility of American Jews was the rapid receding of anti-Semitism. The question that Barbra Streisand asked as Fanny Brice in the movie *Funny Girl* (1968)—"Is a nose with a deviation a crime against the nation?"—was answered in the negative. Neighborhoods and resorts previously restricted to Gentiles lowered their barriers against Jews, and there were new employment opportunities in banking, insurance, and automobile manufacturing. Jews became part of America's economic and cultural elite. In 1974 Irving Shapiro, the son of a pants-presser from St. Paul, Minn., became president and CEO of the Du Pont Corporation, America's oldest corporation. Anti-Semitism had not disappeared but it was now important only to groups on the fringes of the American social and political life, such as the Liberty Lobby and the Nation of Islam, which embraced bizarre conspiratorial theories of history.

To many Jews, the most worrisome indicator of the faith's condition in recent years has been a soaring intermarriage rate: by 1990 the number of Jews marrying Gentiles had passed 40 percent.

Impelled by the impulses that inspired other Americans, Jews moved to suburbia. The hitherto vibrant and dense Jewish neighborhoods of Brownsville, East New York, and the South and East Bronx in New York City; West Chicago; and Dorchester-Roxbury-Mattapan in Boston disappeared. Prior to World War II, Jews had not been welcome in Newton, an affluent suburb of Boston. By the 1970s there were so many Jews in Newton that its sobriquet, the Garden City, was said to come from the fact that there was a Rosenbloom on every corner. Jews also migrated to the Sunbelt. In 1945 more than two-thirds of America's Jews lived in New England and the mid-Atlantic states. By 1990 just under one-half (48.6 percent) lived in the Northeast. There were more Jews in Los Angeles than in all of Latin America, more in the San Francisco Bay Area than in Baltimore,

more in Phoenix than in Pittsburgh, and more in the Miami area than in Philadelphia.

This social and economic mobility was not without its price. A growing number of Jews chose not to identify with the Jewish community, to provide their children with a Jewish education, or to observe Jewish rituals and customs. The most worrisome barometer of the Jewish condition was a soaring intermarriage rate. By 1990 the number of Jews marrying Gentiles had passed 40 percent. The Jewish situation was not universally bleak. Perhaps a third of the Jewish population remained involved in Jewish affairs. They supported Jewish philanthropies, sent their children to Jewish schools, read Jewish magazines and books, and regularly attended synagogue. The most important question facing American Jewry at the end of the twentieth century was whether this saving remnant would be large enough to preserve the institutional vigor and influence of the American Jewish community.

BIBLIOGRAPHY

Edward S. Shapiro, *A Time for Healing: American Jewry Since 1945* (Baltimore, 1992).
Charles E. Silberman, *A Certain People: American Jews and Their Lives Today* (New York, 1985).
Marshall Sklare, *America's Jews* (New York, 1971).
Chaim I. Waxman, *America's Jews in Transition* (Philadelphia, 1983).

— EDWARD S. SHAPIRO

JIM CROW LAWS

Jim Crow Laws, first enacted by some southern legislatures in 1865 to separate the races in public conveyances, came to embrace racial segregation in all areas of southern life from the cradle to the grave. Origins of the term "Jim Crow" are obscure; it was used before the Civil War in reference to racial separation on the railroads in Massachusetts. Continuing fears of black power raised in white minds by Reconstruction, together with the U.S. Supreme Court emasculation in 1883 of the federal Civil Rights Act of 1875, prompted southern legislatures to embark systematically on legal separation, beginning in the 1880's. Following action by Tennessee in 1881, southern states led off by passing laws requiring segregation on railroads. Southern legislatures then passed laws requiring separation in schools, hospitals, asylums, theaters, hotels, streetcars, cemeteries, and residences. Theoretically, as sanctioned by the Supreme Court in such cases as *Plessy* v. *Ferguson* (1896), facilities were to be equal; in practice those facilities made available to blacks were always inferior.

The basic intent of the laws, which gave legal sanction to custom, was to solidify the color-caste system by impressing further upon Afro-Americans their permanent subordination. Most states defined "a person of color" as one having a small fraction of Afro-American blood, and they forbade by law intermarriage between blacks and whites. In the South, the Jim Crow system was completed with the passage of laws that effectively disfranchised the black population in spite of the Fifteenth Amendment.

Caste had hardly become systematized in law before it was under attack. Founded in 1909, the National Association for the Advancement of Colored People began a forty-five-year campaign to end racial segregation, culminating in *Brown* v. *Board of Education of Topeka* (1954), in which the Supreme Court ruled that segregation in education was unconstitutional. Between the end of World War II and the end of the Korean War, the United States desegregated its armed services. These breaches in the color line resulted from a host of social and political factors: the growing political and organizational power of Afro-Americans; the expansion of federal power; the evolution of a more liberal racial ideology; and the exigencies of America's moral leadership in international affairs. In the 1960's black self-assertion in the form of nonviolent, direct action combined with federal civil rights acts and court decisions to topple segregation in transportation and public accommodations and to curb opposition to voter registration in the South. The Jim Crow laws were rendered nugatory, but old attitudes and practices died hard.

BIBLIOGRAPHY

H. A. Bullock, *A History of Negro Education in the South.*
C. S. Mangum, Jr., *The Legal Status of the Negro.*
G. T. Stephenson, *Race Distinctions in American Law.*
C. V. Woodward, *The Strange Career of Jim Crow.*

— OTEY M. SCRUGGS

JINGOISM

Jingoism, in American usage, a term for the blatant demand for an aggressive foreign policy. The word is probably derived from the "by jingo" of a music-hall song popularized by Gilbert Hastings Macdermott in England during a crisis with Russia in 1877–78:

> We don't want to fight, but, by jingo, if we do,
> We've got the ships, we've got the men and got the money too.

By March 1878, "jingo" was a term of political reproach. In the United States those who have advocated the annexation of Canada, the seizure of Mexico, expansion in the Caribbean or Pacific, or a bellicose interpretation of the Monroe Doctrine have been charged with jingoism.

— STANLEY R. PILLSBURY

JOHN BIRCH SOCIETY

John Birch Society, an ultraconservative organization, founded in 1958 by Robert H. W. Welch, Jr., a retired Massachusetts businessman. It was named after John Birch, a Fundamentalist Baptist missionary from Georgia. Welch never knew Birch, who, while serving as a U.S. intelligence officer, was killed by Chinese Communists ten days after V-J Day, 1945, thereby making him the first hero of the cold war, according to the society. The declared aim of the society is to fight communism on a so-called intellectual basis apparently by adopting some of communism's own most vicious and ruthless tactics. Among other ancillary elements of its program are its advocacy of a return to minimum federal government and the abandonment of the Federal Reserve System, the Commodity Credit Corporation, and the veterans' hospitals. Violence is not advocated, but a number of public men and others have been charged by the society with being "dedicated agents" of "the Communist conspiracy." The organization is composed of a semisecret network of cells of "Americanists" throughout the country. The society publishes a journal, *American Opinion*, eleven times a year. Its main headquarters are in Belmont, Mass.

— THOMAS ROBSON HAY

A sheet of right-wing political bumper stickers from the John Birch Society hangs on display in Seattle, Washington, on May 19, 1966. (Seattle Post-Intelligencer Collection; Museum of History & Industry/Corbis)

JOHNSON DOCTRINE

Johnson Doctrine, an expansion of the Roosevelt Corollary to the Monroe Doctrine enunciated on May 2, 1965, by President Lyndon B. Johnson in justification of his dispatch of U.S. Marines in April of that year to quell civil disorders in the Dominican Republic. It stated that "the American nations . . . will not permit the establishment of another Communist government in the Western Hemisphere." The doctrine was amplified by a resolution of the House of Representatives on Sept. 20, 1965.

— JACOB E. COOKE

JOINT-STOCK LAND BANKS

Joint-Stock Land Banks were chartered under the authority of the Federal Farm Loan Act, approved July 17, 1916. These banks were financed with private capital and were permitted to make loans in the states in which they were chartered and one contiguous state. About eighty-seven charters were granted, but not all of the banks opened for business. The joint-stock banks had their largest growth both in number and volume of business in the better agricultural areas—Iowa, Illinois, Minnesota, Missouri, Texas, and California. At first the law did not limit the size of loans, but the act was amended in 1923 limiting the size of loans to one borrower to $50,000. All loans were required to be made for agricultural purposes. Land was appraised by federal government appraisers, and the amount of a loan was limited to a percentage of the value of the appraised land and buildings. They were permitted to issue tax-exempt bonds up to twenty times their capital. These banks did a thriving business during the World War I land booms but declined rapidly with the less profitable conditions of agriculture in the late 1920's. Many of the banks failed. Accusations of mismanagement sprang up, and many of the banks reorganized or liquidated. The Emergency Farm Mortgage Act of 1933 ordered the joint-stock land banks liquidated. To aid in carrying out the liquidation of these banks the Farm Credit Act of 1933 provided the Land Bank Commission with $100 million for two years, and renewed the provision for two more years in 1935.

BIBLIOGRAPHY

Farm Credit Administration, *Annual Reports* (since 1933).

Federal Farm Loan Board, *Annual Reports* (1916–1933).

Ivan Wright, *Farm Mortgage Financing.*

— IVAN WRIGHT

JOLLIET AND MARQUETTE DISCOVERY

Louis Jolliet was a native of New France who, after being educated at the Jesuit schools of Quebec, embarked on a career of exploration in the far western country of the 17th century. On one of his voyages to Lake Superior in 1669 he met the Jesuit missionary Jacques Marquette, then at the mission of Sault Sainte Marie. Three years later the authorities of New France commissioned Jolliet to undertake the discovery of the great central river of the continent, which the Indians had described and spoken of as the Missisippi. Jolliet requested that Marquette be appointed chaplain of the expedition, and late in the autumn of 1672 set out for the Northwest to prepare for the voyage. Jolliet found Marquette at the mission of Saint Ignace on the north shore of Mackinac Strait. Together they prepared maps and planned for the discovery during the ensuing winter; the map Marquette then drew still exists, showing the route of his discovery that he traced on it.

On May 17, 1673, the two explorers left Saint Ignace in two canoes with five voyageurs, "fully resolved to do and to suffer everything for so glorious an undertaking." They went by way of Lake Michigan, Green Bay, and the Fox River, a route that was well known as far as the upper villages on the Fox. At the Mascouten, village guides were obtained to lead them to the portage. Friendly Indians tried to dissuade the explorers, enlarging on the difficulties of the voyage; but the travelers pressed on, and a month from the time of departure their canoes shot out from the Wisconsin into a great river, which they instantly recognized as the one they sought. Marquette wished to name the river the Conception for the Immaculate Conception of the Virgin Mary; Jolliet called it first the Buade, after Louis de Buade, Comte de Frontenac, governor of New France. Ultimately he christened it the Colbert, for the prime minister of France; but the Indian name persisted.

On May 17, 1673, Jolliet and Marquette set off in two canoes with five voyageurs, "fully resolved to do and to suffer everything for so glorious an undertaking."

The two explorers in their canoes drifted down the river as far as the Arkansas; they met few Indians, and these for the most part friendly. They saw no monsters except painted ones on the cliffs high above the stream. They encountered no falls or whirlpools, and the voyage, while memorable, was not dangerous. From the Arkansas they turned back upstream, fearing to encounter Spaniards on the lower river. Acting on Indian advice, they did not return to the Fox-Wisconsin waterway, but ascended the Illinois and the Des Plaines, portaging at Chicago to Lake Michigan. They were thus the first white men to stand on the site of that city.

Returning by Lake Michigan and Green Bay to the mission at De Pere, Marquette remained there to regain his health. Jolliet, after a winter of exploring around the lake, went in 1674 to Canada to report his discovery. Just before he reached Montreal, his canoe overturned in the rapids, and he lost all his journals, notes, and maps and saved his life only with difficulty. Thus Marquette's journal has become the official account of the voyage, and Jolliet's share has been somewhat minimized. Jolliet was an expert mapmaker, later the official hydrographer of New France; his maps of the expedition, however, were drawn from memory, and the Jesuit maps superseded his. The discovery was widely heralded in France and formed the basis for the exploration and exploitation of the Mississippi Valley by Robert Cavelier, Sieur de La Salle, and other French voyagers in the late 17th century.

BIBLIOGRAPHY

Louise Phelps Kellogg, *French Régime in Wisconsin and the Northwest.*

— LOUISE PHELPS KELLOGG

JONESTOWN MASSACRE

Jonestown Massacre (Nov. 18, 1978), the mass suicide of 913 members of the People's Temple cult led by the Reverend Jim Jones. After moving his People's Temple to California in 1965, Jones persuaded his followers to relocate to Jonestown, Guyana, in 1977 following allegations of financial misconduct. Friends and relatives of cult members warned U.S. officials that Jones was using physical and psychological torture to prevent defections from Jonestown. On Nov. 14, 1978, U.S. Congressman Leo Ryan of California flew to Guyana with a group of journalists and relatives of cult members to investigate the charges. Ryan and four members of his party were murdered by cultists. On November 18, Jones presided over an enforced suicide ceremony during which his followers drank cyanide-laced punch. Jones died later that day from a gunshot wound, possibly self-inflicted.

BIBLIOGRAPHY

Judith Mary Weightman, *Making Sense of the Jonestown Suicides* (New York, 1984).

— CAROLYN BRONSTEIN

JUDICIAL REVIEW

Judicial Review is the power of courts to hold that legislative enactments or executive decisions violate a written constitution. The world's oldest and leading practitioners of judicial review are the courts of the United States, all of whom have the power to refuse to enforce statutes or executive orders that they find to be contrary to the Constitution. Although the U.S. Constitution makes no direct statement on the subject, it has always been assumed that American courts, when confronted with conflicting rules of law, must prefer the law of superior obligation to a rule of inferior standing. For the Supreme Court this thesis was first spelled out by Chief Justice John Marshall, in 1803, in the celebrated case of *Marbury* v. *Madison* (1 Cranch 137). In holding a portion of an act of Congress unconstitutional, he reasoned that either the Constitution is the "superior paramount law, unchangeable by ordinary means, or it is on a level with ordinary legislative acts" and that there is no middle ground between these alternatives. If the Constitution is the superior paramount law, then a statute contrary to it cannot be law. If, however, the Constitution is alterable at the will of the legislature, then it must be regarded as an absurd attempt to limit power that is by its nature illimitable. "It is emphatically the province and duty of the judicial department," Marshall reasoned, "to say what the law is." If the Constitution is superior to legislation, then the Constitution, and not an ordinary statute, must supply the rule of decision when the Constitution and a statute conflict with each other. He added that since judges must take an oath to support the Constitution, they are obliged to invalidate any statute that conflicts with it.

Since most countries that have written constitutions do not practice judicial review, the proposition that a written constitution necessitates judicial review is clearly the embodiment of certain political theories not universally accepted. While it is agreed that a written constitution takes precedence over a conflicting statute, it does not follow necessarily that judges must have the power so to declare. Furthermore, members of Congress and the chief executive also take oaths to support the Constitution, and since constitutional interpretation is neither a mechanical nor an automatic process, there is no a priori reason that legislators and executive officials cannot make their own readings of the fundamental law. But historically the seeds of judicial review are deeply implanted in American experience. As Justice Oliver Wendell Holmes observed in 1927, "Research has shown and practice has established the futility of the charge that it was a usurpation when this court undertook to declare an act of Congress unconstitutional" (*Blodgett* v. *Holden*, 275 U.S. 142, 147). In fact, the American doctrine of judicial review was the natural result of practices and ideas that were well known when the Constitution was written: during the colonial period many colonial statutes were disallowed by the Board of Trade in the name of the crown, and the Privy Council had the authority to annul colonial statutes in the course of ordinary litigation, often doing so when sitting as an appellate court. Above all, during the revolutionary period the American colonies appealed to doctrines of natural rights inherent in a body of natural law that was regarded as superior in obligation to acts of Parliament. Furthermore, at the time the government was being formed, there was widespread distrust of legislative power and a deep conviction that security from the abuse of such power would be found in such contrivances as written constitutions, the separation of powers, and checks and balances. Most of the leading members of the Constitutional Convention of 1787 and many members of the early congresses indicated in one way or another that they accepted the propriety of judicial review. In addition, many state appellate courts rendered decisions prior to 1803 holding state statutes invalid on constitutional grounds.

Judicial review has often been criticized as being undemocratic because it gives appointed, life-tenure judges the power to frustrate the popular will. It has been characterized as dangerous because it tends to minimize the responsibility of legislative bodies and to discourage popular interest in public affairs. It has also been described as ineffective, since many judicial decisions can be ignored, evaded, or circumvented by new legislative formulas. Many jurists in other countries take the view that judicial review violates the theory of the separation of powers; that it unwisely establishes the supremacy, not of the Constitution, but of the judiciary; and that it has the unfortunate consequence of involving the courts in politics. They question the wisdom of permitting judges to exercise so much power over the elected legislature through the manipulation of phraseology that is general and open to a variety of interpretations. Even so, while the exercise of judicial review in particular cases is often the subject of lively and even bitter controversy, the institution itself is accepted as a normal part of the governmental scene in the United States. This acceptance is based in substantial measure on the requirements of the U.S. government as a federal system, for there are bound to be conflicts of jurisdiction between central and local governments and it has been found desirable to authorize the highest court of the land to serve as an umpire to settle these disputes in a rational and peaceful manner.

That the U.S. Supreme Court has recognized the extraordinary character of judicial review is reflected in the fact that in its entire history it has invalidated only about 100 acts or parts of acts of Congress. It has also ruled unconstitutional about 750 state statutes and state constitutional provisions, and this is but a tiny fraction of the enormous body of constitutional and statute law in the fifty states. Clearly—and this is equally true for the state supreme courts and the lower federal courts—the power of judicial review has been exercised sparingly, in accordance with a well-developed philosophy of judicial self-restraint through which the judges have imposed limitations upon their own powers.

The Court has frequently called attention to the "great gravity and delicacy" of its function in ruling on the validity of acts of Congress. Thus, since the jurisdiction of the Court is limited to actual cases involving real controversies between adversary parties, it declines to give advisory opinions. Nor will the Court anticipate a question of constitutional law before it is essential to do so, and it will not formulate a rule of constitutional law broader than is required by the precise requirements of the case. In addition, the Court will not rule on a constitutional issue, even though properly presented in the record, if the case may be disposed of on some other ground, since it prefers statutory construction to constitutional interpretation. Nor will the Court rule on the validity of a statute on the complaint of one who fails to show that he is injured by its operation or who has taken benefits under it, such as sums of money from the public purse.

The Court insists that the constitutional issue raised must be specific and live; it will not entertain an abstract general issue, such as an invocation of the Constitution as a whole. The issue must be substantial, and not trivial, and must be of central significance in the case. If the constitutional question is political in character—for example, whether a state government is "republican" in form—the Court defers to the judgment of the legislative and executive branches of the government and thus considers the issue nonjusticiable. In addition, the Court will not usually inquire into—much less evaluate—the motives of the legislators who voted for a challenged statute. Nor will the Court rule a statute invalid on vague grounds—as being, for example, unwise, unfair, undemocratic, contrary to the spirit of the Constitution, or in violation of principles of natural law. Finally, there is a presumption in favor of the validity of challenged legislation: since it is assumed that the legislative body did not intend to violate the Constitution, the burden of proof rests upon those who challenge the constitutionality of statutes.

The history of judicial review of the U.S. Supreme Court indicates that this power has been exercised unevenly. The Marshall Court considered the validity of many federal statutes, but the net effect of its decisions was to uphold a broad exercise of powers by the national government; Marshall and his colleagues were Federalists in politics and nationalists in spirit, and through a vigorous assertion of the doctrine of implied powers, they created the juristic foundations of a governmental system that endured. It was not until more than fifty years after the *Marbury* decision that the Court held an act of Congress invalid, in the controversial *Dred Scott* case (1857), in a vain effort to dampen the fierce quarrels that soon led to the Civil War.

Because it is assumed that the legislative body did not intend to violate the Constitution, the burden of proof rests upon those who challenge the constitutionality of statutes.

During Reconstruction the Supreme Court used its judicial powers frequently and vigorously to reduce the possible bite of the Civil War amendments to the Constitution—the Thirteenth, Fourteenth, and Fifteenth—in order to preserve the traditional federal system. The Court insisted that those amendments were not intended to enlarge the powers of the national government to the point at which the states would be "fettered and degraded." Accordingly, the Court invalidated a large body of federal legislation through highly technical and rather literal interpretation of relevant constitutional provisions.

A handful of state statutes were held unconstitutional during the pre-Civil War years, but most such decisions came later. Of the roughly 750 state laws and constitutional provisions held unconstitutional by the Supreme Court, about 650 involved cases decided after 1870.

The second great period of the Court's activism was during the years that Chief Justice Melville W. Fuller presided over the deliberations, 1888–1910, when its principal constituency was the conservative business community. The Court read laissez-faire economics into the Constitution as a limitation upon both federal and state legislative power. The high-water mark of conservative activism was reached in the years 1934–36, when the Court held thirteen New Deal statutes—most of them of major significance—to be unconstitutional.

The Court's determined frustration of the will of the president and Congress led to a tremendous public controversy and to an attempt to pack the Court by increasing its membership. Although the attempt failed, the Court changed course abruptly in the spring of 1937 and relieved the pressure that had been generated, by sustaining the constitutionality of various state and federal laws dealing with such subjects as the relief of farm debtors, minimum wages, the right of labor to collective bargaining, and a national social security system. The important decisions of 1937 launched what has often been described as a judicial revolution, for since then the invalidation of federal statutes of a reform character relating to the economy has practically come to a halt. Only a few acts of Congress have been ruled invalid since 1937.

Under the leadership of Chief Justice Harlan F. Stone (1941–46), the Court began, albeit hesitantly, to be particularly concerned with the protection of basic civil liberties. Owing to the pressure of the cold war the Court, under Chief Justice Fred M. Vinson (1946–53), yielded to the government in respect to issues involving loyalty. Under Chief Justice Earl Warren (1953–69) the Court committed itself wholeheartedly to a strong civil liberties position. The meaning of the due process clause of the Fourteenth Amendment as a limitation upon the states was expanded, especially in the area of the rights of the accused in criminal cases: for example, the right to counsel, freedom from compulsory self-incrimination and unreasonable searches and seizures, and trial by jury—which the federal Bill of Rights had secured against the national government since its adoption in 1791—were absorbed into the due process clause as limitations upon the states. In addition, notable decisions were rendered in the field of free speech, freedom of the press, the right of association, and freedom of religion. The Court also gave new life to the equal protection clause of the Fourteenth Amendment by striking out against racial segregation, malrepresentation in legislative bodies, and the denial of rights to indigent defendants because of their poverty, such as the right to take an appeal from a conviction. With the appointment by President Richard M. Nixon, during his first three years in office, of a new chief justice, Warren E. Burger, and three new associate justices, the Court began gradually to shift ground, and it was noticeable by the end of the 1971–72 term that the civil-libertarian ardor of the Warren Court had begun to cool.

Clearly the power of judicial review is exercised within the context of society's political, social, and cultural setting. The principle of *stare decisis*, the following of precedents in the interest of legal stability, sets limits to discretion. Similarly judges are inclined to show considerable deference to legislative bodies and are by no means indifferent to the prevailing facts of political life. In considerable measure they are confined by the demands of well-articulated legal procedures and by the techniques and thought patterns of their calling. They are subject to a continuous stream of informed criticism from the learned profession to which they belong. Judges are also under pressure to treat problems and persons in a uniform way, so that the demands of equality guide the processes of judicial decisionmaking in significant measure. Furthermore, each judge is influenced by his own sense of judicial integrity—that is to say, by the image he has concerning his expected role in society.

Court decisions are often set aside by later statutes or constitutional amendments, and even overturned by the Court itself. And judges realize that compliance with their decisions is neither automatic nor always substantial. Lower courts have a way of modifying decisions of higher appellate courts through the construction of ambiguous language, and many decisions, such as those of the Supreme Court relating to prayer and Bible-reading in the public schools, are simply ignored in many places. Certainly implementation of the 1954 decision against racial segregation in the public schools has been slow and spotty and has encountered great resistance all the way from the White House and Congress to the lowliest of local school boards. There are, accordingly, many good reasons why judges should heed Justice Felix Frankfurter's admonition in a 1958 decision that the Court "must observe a fastidious regard for limitations on its own power, and this precludes the Court's giving effect to its own notions of what is wise or politic" (*Trop* v. *Dulles*, 356 U.S. 86, 120). But there have always been judges who actively promote those objectives they regard as necessary and desirable. The tension between those who take an activist position and those who practice judicial self-restraint is at the very core of the exercise by courts of the power of judicial review.

BIBLIOGRAPHY

Charles L. Black, *The People and the Court: Judicial Review in a Democracy.*

Leonard W. Levy, ed., *Judicial Review and the Supreme Court.*

— DAVID FELLMAN

JUDICIARY

Judiciary of the United States has its historical background in the legal and political institutions of England. The tribunals set up in the colonies were similar to those of the mother country, and acts of Parliament and the principles of the common law and equity were enforced in the new country as in the old, with the added responsibility on colonial courts of enforcing the enactments of colonial assemblies. The judiciary in the colonies was inadequate in significant respects.

For the large part, these inadequacies did not result from the inherent characteristics of the judiciary as an institution, but rather because of the subjection of judicial institutions, procedures, and rulings to the will and purposes of England. Several of these inadequacies are outlined in the Declaration of Independence as complaints against the king.

Colonial and Constitutional Origins

At the base of the colonial judiciary was the office of justice of the peace, for dealing with minor civil and criminal matters. Above that office was the court usually known as the county court, having original jurisdiction in more important matters. A right of appeal to the colonial assembly existed in some colonies, analogous to appeal to the House of Lords in England. There was in some cases a right of appeal from colonial courts to the judicial committee of the Privy Council in England.

After the colonies became independent states, their court systems remained fundamentally the same, except for the development of courts of appeals with full-time professional judges.

Whereas no provision for an adequate federal judiciary had been included in the Articles of Confederation, all the proposed plans of government submitted to the Constitutional Convention of 1787 provided for a national judiciary distinct from the judicial systems of the states. The adoption of the federal Constitution introduced two major breaks with the past: state judiciaries were subordinated to the federal judiciary in that the Constitution and federal laws and treaties were made the supreme law of the land, and an independent judiciary was explicitly created under the doctrine of the separation of powers. The early establishment of the principle of judicial review in 1803 emphasized the prestige and authority of the judiciary as an independent branch of government.

The first three articles of the Constitution, which were drafted to provide for a high degree of separation of powers, provided respectively for the establishment of the legislative, executive, and judicial branches of the government. Section 1 of Article III provided that the judicial power of the United States should be vested in a Supreme Court and such inferior courts as Congress might establish. It provided also that all federal judges were to hold office during good behavior and that their salaries were not to be diminished during their service in office. By Article II, dealing with the executive, the president was authorized to nominate, and, by and with the advice and consent of the Senate, to appoint Supreme Court judges. Section 2 of Article III prescribed the content of federal judicial power. Within the limits of that power the original jurisdiction of the Supreme Court was defined, while the jurisdiction of particular federal courts was left to congressional determination. Six articles in *The Federalist*, all written by Alexander Hamilton, analyzed and defended the judiciary provisions, and the proposed Constitution was adopted. The first ten amendments (Bill of Rights), added in 1791 to meet criticisms voiced in the ratifying conventions, included additional prescriptions with respect to the courts and the protection of individual rights.

The first three articles of the Constitution provided respectively for the establishment of the legislative, executive, and judicial branches of government.

The judiciary provisions of the Constitution were given effect in the Judiciary Act of 1789, enacted after eleven states had ratified the Constitution. The judicial system was headed by a Supreme Court consisting of a chief justice and five associate justices. Below the Supreme Court were three circuit courts, which had no judges of their own but were conducted by two Supreme Court judges and a district judge. Below the circuit courts were thirteen district courts, for each of which a district judge was to be appointed by the president in the same manner in which the Supreme Court judges were appointed. The districts established were coterminous with state lines except that two states were each divided into two districts.

The Supreme Court was given the jurisdiction allotted to it by the Constitution and appellate jurisdiction in certain cases from decisions of the circuit courts and the highest state courts. The circuit courts had original jurisdiction in cases involving large sums of money and serious offenses and in some instances appellate jurisdiction over cases originating in the district courts. In the early years the major portion of the work of the circuit courts was with cases involving state laws, in which federal jurisdiction depended on the fact that the parties were citizens of different states. The district courts were given original jurisdiction in minor offenses against federal laws and in a wide range of admiralty cases, the latter making up the burden of their work in early years.

The Federal Judiciary

The federal judiciary has seen a steady expansion of business—stemming from increases in territory, population, and legislation; the development of an increasingly complex society; and a growing inclination toward litigation. The district courts have undergone drastic jurisdictional changes, assuming in 1891 all the trial court responsibility originally allocated to both them and the circuit courts. Such change naturally resulted in their proliferation, and by 1973 the district courts in the United States numbered ninety-four as compared with thirteen in 1789; thirty-five times as many district judges (both active and retired but active) were required to conduct them. The circuit court system was modified repeatedly from 1801 until the early part of the 20th century, particularly as the jurisdiction of the district courts expanded. With the abolishment of circuit trial court jurisdiction in 1891, the circuit courts assumed increased appellate jurisdiction, and permanent judges were provided for the new circuit courts of appeals. In the interim the membership of the Supreme Court was altered several times, being increased to an all-time high of ten in 1863 and established at nine in 1869. It was not until 1891, however, that Supreme Court justices were relieved of obligations to ride circuit and much of their appellate jurisdiction.

To enable the Supreme Court to keep up with the growing stream of important cases, it was necessary to make further jurisdictional reductions from time to time, particularly by limiting the classes of cases that might be taken to the Supreme Court as a matter of right, in contrast with those that might be accepted or rejected by the Court after a preliminary scrutiny to determine their public importance. Provisions with respect to appellate jurisdiction are exceedingly complex. For example, some cases are taken directly from the district courts to the Supreme Court. Some go from the district courts to the circuit courts of appeals and then to the Supreme Court. Some cannot go beyond the circuit courts of appeals. Some go directly to the Supreme Court from special courts of three district judges made up for the trial of particular cases. Some cases from territorial courts go to circuit courts of appeals. With the exception of a few agencies that have special procedures, orders of independent regulatory commissions, such as the Civil Service Commission, the Atomic Energy Commission, the Federal Trade Commission, and the National Labor Relations Board, are reviewable by circuit courts of appeals. Cases involving federal questions go to the Supreme Court from the highest state courts having jurisdiction over them. The purpose of Congress in prescribing the appellate jurisdiction of the several courts is to provide for the expeditious appeal to the highest court of cases of greatest public importance, while moving those of less importance at a slower pace and limiting the right of appeal with respect to them or cutting it off altogether. In the mid-20th century concern emerged that judicial decisions have maximum finality at early stages, that appellate workloads be reduced, and that the process of bringing appeals be less complex; there was substantial pressure for reform.

Although the federal judiciary, in a narrow sense, consists only of the several courts created pursuant to the provisions of Article III of the Constitution, the exercise of certain powers requires Congress to create other tribunals to exercise judicial functions—for example, the powers to govern territories, to grant patents, and to appropriate money to pay claims against the United States. These tribunals are known as legislative courts, in contrast with the so-called constitutional courts organized under Article III. These courts include those established in the territories of the United States, the Court of Claims, the Court of Customs and Patent Appeals, and the Tax Court of the United States. (The courts of the District of Columbia were once regarded as legislative, but are now considered constitutional courts.) Bearing some resemblance to legislative courts are numerous independent agencies, such as the Interstate Commerce Commission, the Federal Trade Commission, and the National Labor Relations Board, which exercise functions seemingly judicial in character (commonly called quasi-judicial) although they are usually not classified as judicial tribunals.

The appointment of federal judges by the president with the consent of the Senate has been criticized from time to time, but there has been no serious movement for popular elections, such as the movement that took place in connection with state judges. The provision for lifelong tenure during good behavior has been regarded by many as a serious defect in the judicial system. Many judges have proved unwilling to resign from the bench even after reaching the stage of senility. In 1869 and 1919 Congress authorized various procedures for federal judges, other than members of the Supreme Court, to continue to receive full pay if they resigned after reaching seventy years of age with ten years on the bench—but this promise of continued compensation did not bring about resignations. The second of these acts authorized the president to appoint an additional judge for each judge eligible for retirement who did not resign or retire, if he had suffered permanent mental or physical disability for the performance of his duties. A proposal to make such appointments automatic rather than dependent on findings of disability, and to include the Supreme Court along with other federal courts, was much debated in connection with a bill submitted to Congress by President Franklin D. Roosevelt in 1937. The bill proposed that for each Supreme Court justice who failed to retire at age seventy, the president could appoint an additional justice until the total membership of the Court reached fifteen. The proposal failed, but during the period of debate a measure was enacted providing for the retirement of Supreme Court judges according to the procedure already prescribed for the judges of the lower courts. A constitutional amendment authorizing compulsory retirement of judges at a fixed age has been much discussed and has attracted widespread support but has never been implemented in regard to federal judges, except that chief judges of circuit and district courts are required to step down from their administrative duties at the age of seventy.

A barrier to efficiency in the federal courts has been the technicality and diversity in rules of practice. In 1792 Congress empowered the Supreme Court to adopt uniform rules of practice for the federal courts in equity and admiralty cases, and in 1898 the same power was given with respect to bankruptcy cases. Concerning actions at law, however, it was provided in the Conformity Act of 1872 that the federal courts should conform "as near as may be" to the practice currently in effect in the state courts. State practice varied widely. Federal practice, therefore, varied from state to state and was often archaic and cumbersome. After many years of agitation Congress in 1934 authorized the Supreme Court to adopt and promulgate uniform rules of civil procedure for the federal courts—which rules became effective in 1938, marking an outstanding achievement in judicial reform. These rules have undergone revision and similar rules of criminal and appellate procedure have been adopted. In 1973 new federal rules pertaining to evidence were adopted.

The expansion of the work of the federal courts and the increase in the number of courts and judges created a need for central coordination of the judiciary. An act of Congress in 1922 provided for a Judicial Conference of the senior circuit judges, to be presided over by the chief justice of the United States. Later representative district and special judges were added to the council's membership. Pursuant to the act, the conference met annually, and it was charged with making policy related to all aspects of the administration of the federal courts.

The Administrative Office Act of 1939 fundamentally changed the federal judicial system. The Judicial Conference was given a central administrative arm, the Administrative Office of the United States Courts. (Formerly the Justice Department had served in the housekeeping role for the U.S. judiciary.) Circuit councils were also created as regional administrative structures. Although manned by all the U.S. circuit appellate judges, the circuit councils never assumed the vast administrative power conferred on them. In 1971 Congress allocated each circuit a circuit court executive as staff. Previously (1967) Congress had also established the Federal Judicial Center as a research and development center for the U.S. courts.

State, County, and Municipal Courts

The state judicial systems differ greatly among themselves and from the federal system in matters of appointment, tenure, jurisdiction, organization, and procedure. Until the Jacksonian era the selection of state judges was made almost entirely by state legislatures or by some system in which they had indirect control; as late as 1974, in a little over half of the states, including a number of the original thirteen and other older states, judges of appellate courts and courts of general jurisdiction were selected by legislatures or governors or by cooperation between governors and legislatures or senates. The Jacksonian movement toward popular election of judges had prevailed in other states. Both methods are generally regarded as defective in that they involve the judiciary in politics in some measure and often fail in selecting the best personnel; a nonpartisan appointive-elective method (Missouri or Kales plan) was thus evolved and found favor in many states in the last half of this century. Tenure of judicial service varies greatly from state to state and from court to court; some states provide for lifetime appointment, as is true of the federal system, but some have provided means for removing judges before the expiration of their terms. In slightly over half of the states judicial qualification commissions were operative in the 1970's. The machinery of impeachment, although increasingly available in those states, remained cumbersome to use. In other jurisdictions removal was even more difficult. Thirty-three states provided maximum age limits (generally seventy, but up to seventy-five, depending on the state and the level of the court) for mandatory retirement of judges. In all but eleven states provisions existed for calling judges for service after retirement.

The highest state appellate courts rarely have original jurisdiction. Moreover, in order to relieve the highest courts of excessive burdens, almost half of the states have added intermediate appellate courts between them and the courts of original and general jurisdiction.

The expansion of court work and the increase in the number of tribunals created a need for centralized control of the judiciaries of the states. In the 1920's and 1930's a number of states, some in advance of the federal government and some later, organized judicial councils to aid in bringing order from the confusion. The judicial councils, although a great improvement, have generally proven to be a weak administrative model hindered by infrequent meetings, a lack of staff, and an inability to act authoritatively. The replacement of justice-of-peace courts with municipal courts within cities, beginning in the 1920's, was, however, a step toward increased efficiency and consistency. In the 1960's and 1970's court structure was being modified by the establishment of unified state court systems, with central administrative responsibility vested in the state's chief justice and supreme court—including the provision of centralized administrative staffs to assist the supreme courts in exercising their responsibilities. Efforts were being made to eliminate overlapping jurisdictions and the need for trial *de novo* and to simplify and solidify the administrative structure. Although state constitutional amendments have usually been required, over half of the states had adopted the unified state court model by 1973, and it was expected that the remainder would follow.

The state judicial systems differ greatly among themselves and from the federal system in matters of appointment, tenure, jurisdiction, organization, and procedure.

The geographical jurisdiction of general trial courts over criminal cases and civil disputes is usually organized on a county or multicounty basis, while municipal courts are organized on the basis of the city or borough. General trial courts have subject matter jurisdiction over felony criminal cases, all juvenile, domestic relations, and probate cases, and civil actions involving claims in excess of $5,000. Municipal courts generally have jurisdiction over the remainder of state cases, including criminal misdemeanors, local ordinances, and minor civil cases. The municipal court jurisdiction is similar to that originally assigned to the lay justice of the peace, who still survives with minor dissatisfaction in rural areas and in a few urban centers. One increasingly popular way of simplifying this complex web of geographical and subject matter jurisdictional responsibility is the consolidation of all state trial courts into a single-level trial court to be organized in a county or multicounty area with separate internal divisions to deal with specialized subject matter areas. In the 1960's and 1970's this approach to unifying state court systems was increasingly adopted. In addition, professional managers are increasingly employed by courts, and only six did not have professional state court administrative staff by 1973. Almost every trial court of ten or more judges employed a professional manager.

Complexities of procedure have embarrassed the states as well as the federal government. In the middle of the 19th century a movement was started for the codification of procedure with some elimination of unnecessary technicalities. An attempt at broad simplification was made in the 1920's and 1930's, led by the American Law Institute. After World War II significant progress occurred in the form of model codes promulgated by the American Bar Association and with groups of lawyers. In 1973 all but three states operated under Modern Rules of Criminal and/or Civil Procedure; some states lacked either civil or criminal improvement but had reformed the practice in the remaining area. The problem was more apparent with respect to modern rules of criminal procedure: thirteen states lacked modern criminal rules.

The Status Quo and Reform

Although there is no complete separation of powers in any state or in the federal government, the several judiciaries have maintained their strength against legislative and executive departments. There have been popular outbursts against particular courts at particular times but rarely against the courts as institutions. Nevertheless, there is great concern about the courts' ability to keep pace with the acute increase in litigation.

Increasingly efforts at reform are directed toward diverting case flow away from the courts: examples include no-fault insurance to cut down on the numerous tort cases that result from automobile accidents, efforts to deal with so-called victimless criminal cases with nonadjudicatory procedures, and efforts to simplify the issues of proof and liability in domestic relations litigation. Courts are attempting to increase their administrative and management capacities through the employment of skilled managers, improved judicial structure, and the application of modern management technology and procedures. Although the prestige and power of the courts are often strained because of both the volume of work and the explosiveness of the issues that must be resolved (particularly at the U.S. Supreme Court and other appellate courts), their pivotal position within government seems assured. In general courts have continued to maintain their integrity, ensure the protection of fundamental individual rights against the excesses of the executive and legislature, and preserve the tradition of government by law rather than men.

BIBLIOGRAPHY

American Law Institute, *A Study of the Business of the Federal Courts.*

Peter Graham Fish, "The Circuit Councils; Rusty Hinges of Federal Judicial Administration," *The University of Chicago Law Review,* vol. 37 (1968).

E. Friesen, E. Gallas, and N. Gallas, *Managing the Courts.*

S. Goldman and T. Jahnige, *The Federal Courts as a Political System.*

National Conference on the Judiciary, *Justice in the States.*

Roscoe Pound, "Principles and Outline of a Modern Unified Court Organization," *Judicature,* vol. 23 (1940).

— GEOFFREY S. GALLAS

JURY TRIAL

Jury Trial is the characteristic mode of determining issues of fact at common law. It developed by a process of evolution that dates far back into the Middle Ages. It came to be so highly regarded as a procedure devised for the protection of the rights and liberties of the people that the eminent English legal historian Sir William Blackstone characterized it as "the glory of the English law." It was transplanted from England to the American colonies and became an integral part of their legal system in both civil and criminal common law cases, with the exception that a more summary procedure was allowed in petty cases. The Constitution of the United States as proposed in 1787 contained, in Article III, Section 2, the provision that "The Trial of all Crimes, except in cases of Impeachment, shall be by Jury." No mention was made of jury trial in civil cases. The omission was much criticized, and it was argued by some that the failure to include the requirement of jury trial in civil cases was in effect to abolish it. In No. 83 of *The Federalist* Alexander Hamilton refuted this argument and attempted to show that the subject was one much better left to legislation than to constitutional statement. The Constitution was adopted without any provision for jury trial in civil cases, but in the articles of amendment adopted soon afterward to quell the fears of those concerned about the omission of a bill of rights a provision was included to the effect that in common law suits involving more than twenty dollars the right of trial by jury should be preserved. The Sixth Amendment elaborated on the subject of jury trial in criminal cases by providing that "the accused shall enjoy the right to a speedy and public trial, by an impartial jury of the State and district wherein the crime shall have been committed. . . . "

In the several states the procedure of jury trial has continued to evolve since the date of the establishment of the federal government. Some states, for instance, have not adhered rigidly to the old common law requirement that the jury be composed of not more or less than twelve persons and the requirement that the verdict be unanimous. For the federal government, on the other hand, these changes are held to be forbidden by the Constitution. The courts have held that the constitutional phrases mean now what they meant when they were adopted, to the extent that juries must be of twelve persons and verdicts must be unanimous.

Jury trial has not been required in cases involving petty offenses, and in all cases, including cases involving serious crimes, the right of

The grand jury of the Scopes "Monkey" trial stands for a photograph on July 12, 1925. Fearing for the floor of the courthouse because of the number of spectators, the judge had moved the trial out onto the lawn. Note that the jury is composed of only white men. (UPI/Corbis-Bettmann)

trial by jury may be waived by the parties. The constitutional requirement does not extend to equity cases or to civil cases arising out of statutes. The jury system has undergone serious criticism in the 20th century, partly because of the clogging of court calendars and the inadequacy of juries in dealing with complex questions beyond the limits of their experience. There has therefore been some tendency to avoid jury procedure wherever possible.

BIBLIOGRAPHY

William Anderson, *American Government.*
John M. Mathews, *The American Constitutional System.*

— CARL BRENT SWISHER

JUSTICE, DEPARTMENT OF

The Department of Justice was established June 22, 1870, by act of Congress. However, the office of attorney general had been created by Congress at the birth of the Republic in the Judiciary Act of 1789. It reached cabinet rank when the first attorney general, Edmund Randolph, attended his initial cabinet meeting on Mar. 31, 1792.

For many years the attorney general served almost solely as the legal counsel to the president and had no department as such. The other cabinet departments had their own solicitors who handled their legal affairs and argued their cases. In the country's various district courts, the U.S. district attorneys who tried federal cases were completely independent of the attorney general. His staff was so small that special counsel had to be retained in trying important cases. He had no official established office of his own; he was permitted to continue his outside law practice; and he was often absent from Washington in pursuit of that practice for long periods of time. Such a situation worked against the development of a unified legal policy for the United States and against any effort to evoke from the courts the consistent body of interpretive law needed by the young nation.

The proliferation of federal offenses proscribed by statute and the growth of civil litigation between private parties and the government transformed the office of attorney general. By the Civil War he was conducting most federal cases, both civil and criminal. He had an office and a growing staff and was devoting all his time to the task. Direction of U.S. attorneys and U.S. marshals had been transferred from the courts to his office. This trend was formalized by the act of Congress of June 22, 1870, that created the Department of Justice under the attorney general; put him in charge of substantially all federal prosecution and litigation; and established a solicitor general to argue government cases, especially before the Supreme Court.

Thus the president was given a legal arm responsible for enforcing federal laws and protecting federal legal interests and at the same time capable of seeking consistent lines of interpretation from the courts. Thus also an organization came into being that could be charged with additional legal duties as they might arise from future legislation—and as early as 1871 the federal prison system was placed under the department's jurisdiction. The growth of laws specifying federal criminal offenses necessitated a Criminal Division, established in 1909. Increased federal interest in developing the public lands brought creation of the Lands Division (later the Land and Natural Resources Division) in 1910. Other legislation, such as the antitrust laws of the late 19th and early 20th centuries, created the need for special offices. In the extensive departmental reorganization of 1933, several of these offices were made into divisions, including the Antitrust Division, the Tax Division, and the Claims Division (later the Civil Division). The process of elevating working groups to formal status continued; the Internal Security Division was created in 1954 and the Civil Rights Division in 1957. As legislation for the protection of the public continued to increase, further special offices were created—the Pollution Control Section in the Land and Natural Resources Division (1970), the Consumer Affairs Section in the Antitrust Division (1971), and the Economic Stabilization Section in the Civil Division (1971).

Meanwhile, enforcement duties were added to the department's litigative work. An investigative arm, the Bureau of Investigation (later the Federal Bureau of Investigation) was created in 1908. The Immigration and Naturalization Service was transferred from the Department of Labor to the Department of Justice in 1940. Antinarcotics enforcement was concentrated in the Department of Justice with the creation of the Bureau of Narcotics and Dangerous Drugs in 1968. In 1972 the president stepped up the federal effort against illegal drugs by creating within the Department of Justice the Office for Drug Abuse Law Enforcement, to coordinate all such federal and state efforts, and the Office of National Narcotics Intelligence, to be a clearinghouse for information on the drug traffic.

In the 1960's the department was assigned service functions beyond its traditional litigative and enforcement duties. The Office of Criminal Justice, charged with examining and proposing improvements in the entire criminal justice process, was created in 1964. Providing federal financial aid to help states and localities upgrade their criminal justice systems was the task given in 1965 to the Office of Law Enforcement Assistance (a program greatly enlarged under the Law Enforcement Assistance Administration in 1968). The Community Relations Service, created by the Civil Rights Act of 1964 and charged with assisting minority groups in a variety of community problems, was transferred from the Department of Commerce to the Department of Justice in 1966.

Thus the expansion of the Department of Justice flowed directly from the American public's continually expanding use of federal legislation to solve economic and social problems. By the mid-1970's the Department of Justice had become by far the largest law office in the world, with a staff of more than 30,000 persons in the United States and its territories.

BIBLIOGRAPHY

Homer Stille Cummings and Carl McFarland, *Federal Justice.*
Luther A. Huston, *The Department of Justice.*
Albert George Langeluttig, *The Department of Justice of the United States.*
U.S. Department of Justice, *Annual Report of the Attorney General* (1970).

— RICHARD KLEINDIENST

JUSTICE, DEPARTMENT OF

Since the mid-1970s, Department of Justice attorneys and officials have remained on the cutting edge of the major issues facing the United States. During the Gerald Ford presidency (1974–1977), Attorney General Edward H. Levi issued guidelines to govern the domestic security investigations of the Federal Bureau of Investigation, which resulted from a congressional inquiry revealing harassment of Martin Luther King, Jr., and other individuals. The Justice Department was involved in the sometimes violent debate in Boston and elsewhere about court-ordered busing of school children to achieve racial integration. Under the Jimmy Carter administration (1977–1981) and Attorney General Griffin Bell, affirmative action emerged as the most tendentious issue facing the department. This was due in large part to the highly publicized Supreme Court case *Regents of the University of California* v. *Bakke* (1978), which addressed the issue of reverse discrimination against white males.

During the presidencies of Ronald Reagan (1981–1989) and George Bush (1989–1993), the Justice Department launched two major crusades. The first, against illegal drugs (notably crack cocaine), was noncontroversial in theory but quite controversial in method. The second crusade challenged many of the civil rights achievements of the previous three decades, including the premise underlying *Brown* v. *Board of Education* (1954), the Civil Rights Act of 1964, and the Voting Rights Act of 1965. William Bradford Reynolds, assistant attorney general for civil rights, led the charge, and the most publicized case involved the department's effort to secure tax exemptions for Bob Jones University and other private religious schools regardless of whether they practiced racial or gender discrimination. Other efforts included unenergetic investigations into the Iran-Contra and savings and loan scandals. The department was much more aggressive, however, in pursuing federal civil rights charges against the Los Angeles police officers who were videotaped beating Rodney King in 1991.

Among the controversial Clinton-era events was Attorney General Reno's decision to storm the Waco, Texas, compound of the Branch Davidian sect—a move that resulted in a fiery mass suicide.

During President Bill Clinton's administration, which began in 1993, the Justice Department confronted the so-called Whitewater affair, a relatively minor episode in the savings and loan scandal that forced the resignation and eventual plea bargain of the department's third highest ranking official, Webster Hubbell. Whitewater also cast a cloud over the president himself, as Hubbell and first lady Hillary Rodham Clinton had been members of the same law firm in Little Rock, Ark. Another controversial Clinton-era event involved Attorney General Janet Reno's decision to lay siege to and eventually storm the Waco, Tex., compound of the Branch Davidian religious sect. That decision resulted in a fiery mass suicide. On a more programmatic level, the department has given increasing attention to the issue of illegal immigration, the result of a movement that gained momentum in the 1994 elections with the success of a ballot proposition in California to deny the children of illegal immigrants access to the state's public schools.

[See also Antitrust Laws; Federal Bureau of Investigation; Iran-Contra Affair; Savings and Loan Crisis; Waco Siege.]

BIBLIOGRAPHY

Paul Anderson, *Janet Reno: Doing the Right Thing* (New York, 1994).
Griffin B. Bell and Ronald J. Ostrow, *Taking Care of the Law* (New York, 1982).
William French Smith, *Law and Justice in the Reagan Administration* (Stanford, Calif., 1991).

— KENNETH O'REILLY

K

KANSAS-NEBRASKA ACT

Three important areas of concern are reflected in the enactment of the Kansas-Nebraska bill in 1854 and the repeal of the Missouri Compromise of 1820: (1) the basis of the struggle surrounding the bill, that is, why it was being proposed; (2) the political complexities involved in its enactment; and (3) the ensuing ramifications.

The historical context of the bill is complex, but frontier expansion was a major factor. With the Compromise of 1850 settling the slavery issue in New Mexico and Utah, it had been hoped that further controversy over slavery would be avoided. But it soon arose again, largely because of schemes for building a transcontinental railroad to the Pacific coast.

Four cities vied to become the terminus of the railroad: Chicago, Saint Louis, Memphis, and New Orleans. The argument in favor of the latter two cities was that lines extending from either of them would go through already settled territory, Texas and the Southwest. To justify building the railroad from a northern city, the "Great American Desert" would have to be settled.

Northern, antislave forces were traditionally more favorable to such programs as homesteading and internal improvements than were southerners. Moreover, expanding in the area west of Missouri and Iowa would benefit the northern economy, particularly because the Great Plains territory was suitable for farming. Further, the building of a northern transcontinental railroad through the Kansas-Nebraska region would present a tempting prospect for lucrative investment of capital, more abundant in the North than in the South.

The actual enactment of a Kansas-Nebraska bill illustrates the fact that the issue of frontier expansion permeated many issues of the day, dictating political alignments and policies on many questions. The bill was introduced by Sen. Stephen A. Douglas of Illinois, a Chicago resident who wanted his region to be the eastern terminus of the proposed railroad to the Pacific. (There is no clear evidence that Douglas had any personal interests in a Chicago-based line.) Although Douglas is usually regarded as the bill's author, there is significant evidence that the political reason for the bill's introduction lay more in the infighting taking place in the Democratic party in Missouri in 1853–54 than in Douglas' interests, which happened to coincide with territorial expansion into Kansas and Nebraska.

Missouri's influential Sen. David R. Atchison was seeking reelection in 1854, and his chief opponent was former Sen. Thomas Hart Benton, currently a member of the House of Representatives. Benton was a leader of slavery restrictionists, with support mostly in the eastern part of Missouri. Atchison, from the western area, had a much stronger proslavery constituency. Both men supported territorial expansion into Kansas and Nebraska, and both favored building a railroad to the Pacific through the region. Atchison also wanted to repeal the Missouri Compromise, which prohibited slavery north of 36°30′ north latitude, for repeal would allow his slaveholding constituents to move into the new Kansas and Nebraska territories with their human property.

For repeal of the Missouri Compromise, the support of President Franklin Pierce was essential—and with Pierce's support enactment of the Kansas-Nebraska bill was likely. The president was in a difficult political situation: the Senate support that he needed for the confirmation of his appointments and ratification of his treaties was in jeopardy because some of his political appointments had angered southern partisans, and many of them felt the president had free-soil leanings—a notion far from the facts. Pierce could ill afford defections in the Senate in this tenuous situation, and Atchison, as president pro tempore of the Senate, was in a position of power and not unwilling to take advantage of the president's predicament. Unlucky Pierce decided he had little choice but to support the Kansas-Nebraska bill—and once he gave his support, he worked hard for its approval, for he did not want to risk the loss of prestige that would accompany the defeat of his first administration measure.

Here Douglas, chairman of the Senate Committee on Territories, entered the picture directly and importantly. He reported the bill for territorial organization of Kansas and Nebraska out of his committee in January 1854, including a provision that, by indirection, repealed the Missouri Compromise. The bill asserted that the Compromise of 1850 had superseded the 1820 principle that 36°30′ north latitude was the northern demarcation line for slave states; the bill also stated that the question of slavery in the territories should be settled by the people living in them.

This language conveniently favored Atchison in his senatorial campaign and faced Benton with a difficult dilemma. If Benton voted for the bill, he would betray his antislavery sympathies; but if he voted against it, he would be defaulting on his promise to work for expansion into Kansas and Nebraska. He voted against the bill and suffered defeat in the race with Atchison. The final bill explicitly repealed the Missouri Compromise, and the possibility of slavery in the new territories was made real.

The political ramifications of the enactment of the Kansas-Nebraska bill reached deeply into the general political climate in which it was passed. Support for it from southern members of Congress was nearly unanimous. Northern Democrats were seriously split, half of their votes in the House going for the measure and half against it. Nearly all northern Whigs opposed the bill.

This severe political division fractured the structure of the political party system. The Whig party was essentially destroyed in the South. The Democrats were so seriously divided that their tenuous congressional majority became highly vulnerable. A coalition of anti-Nebraska Democrats, northern Whigs, Know-Nothings, and nativist groups joined the newly organized Republican party, making it a viable political force. By 1856 the Whigs had all but disappeared, and the Republican party was able to confront the weakened Democrats with strong opposition.

In addition to these basic political changes, the Kansas-Nebraska Act had direct ramifications. Kansas and Nebraska were promptly opened for settlement in 1854. Although Nebraska remained relatively quiet, Kansas, the destination of most of the new settlers, became a political hotbed. Settlers came to Kansas not only to develop the frontier but also—and perhaps more importantly—to lend their weight in the determination of whether Kansas would be free or slave.

The administration of the new territory further complicated Pierce's political difficulties. Immediately, the first governor he appointed for Kansas, Andrew H. Reeder, a Pennsylvania Democrat with southern sympathies, was the source of an endless series of problems for Pierce. Reeder became deeply involved in speculation in Kansas lands. His personal interests led to charges that he cheated Indians, and, worse still, he was unable to satisfy either proslavery or antislavery groups because both suspected his motives.

Thus, from the outset, political stability was lacking in Kansas. The absence of effective, overall, political control of the territory spawned bitter conflict. From the South, proslavery Missourians traveled into Kansas to vote in favor of slavery—and they sometimes came in armed bands. Groups in the North and East, such as the Emigrant Aid Company, helped so large a number of antislavery settlers into the territory that it was generally thought that an honest referendum of actual settlers would not permit slavery in Kansas. But Missouri raiders entering the territory in great numbers made an honest count impossible. In these circumstances a proslavery legislature was elected in 1855, and slavery was legalized. The weight of influence of the roving Missourians on the final tally is uncertain, but the antislavery forces repudiated the vote, wrote their own constitution banning slavery, and then chose a governor and legislature, centered in the town of Lawrence. The stage was thus set for violent confrontation. Proslavery posses, consisting mostly of Missourians, were formed and arrested the free-state leaders. The town of Lawrence was sacked, and some lives were lost. Revenge was taken, and the conflict escalated until some 200 people were killed.

Settlers came to Kansas not only to develop the frontier but also to lend their weight in determining whether Kansas would be a free or a slave state.

The situation was a difficult one for Pierce to handle. He found he could only give his lawful support to the duly elected proslavery legislature, not to the free-state insurgents. At the same time he wanted to avoid direct intervention because he felt that the people of Kansas themselves should be responsible for maintaining order. Accordingly, he condemned the free-state faction, but also attacked the Missouri invaders. He ordered a halt to civil disorders and urged Kansans to bring peace to the territory through their own efforts. His attempt to end the crisis without intervention failed, and federal troops were brought in to restore order. Not until September 1856, near the end of Pierce's term, did the Kansas situation begin to stabilize.

In every respect the Kansas-Nebraska Act, incorporating the repeal of the Missouri Compromise, stands as a far-reaching piece of legislation. The basis of its proposal exemplifies the serious problems posed by frontier expansion. The complexities of its enactment illustrate the depth of political division in the country at the time and show, through Pierce's predicament, the difficulties of leading the nation and avoiding civil conflict during that period. Finally, the ramifications of the act not only drew the battle lines in the settlement of Kansas but also had an immeasurable effect on American party structure.

BIBLIOGRAPHY

James C. Malin, *The Nebraska Question, 1852–1854.*

R. F. Nichols, *Disruption of the Democracy.*

Robert R. Russel, "Kansas-Nebraska Bill, 1854," *Journal of Southern History,* vol. 29.

— JEANNETTE P. NICHOLS

KELLOGG-BRIAND PACT

Kellogg-Briand Pact, also known as the Pact of Paris, an agreement signed in Paris by fifteen nations on Aug. 27, 1928. Eventually nearly all other governments adhered to the treaty. It grew out of negotiations that were begun between the United States, represented by Secretary of State Frank B. Kellogg, and France, represented by the foreign minister Aristide Briand. Article I provides that the parties renounce war as an instrument of national policy in their relations with one another. Article II provides that the settlement of disputes between the parties shall never be sought except by pacific means. Connected with the text of the pact are certain interpretations by Kellogg which were included as a part of the negotiations and which made clear that the treaty did not prevent wars of self-defense, that it was not inconsistent with the Covenant of the League of Nations, and that it did not interfere with the rendering of aid under the Locarno treaties and the so-called treaties of neutrality.

BIBLIOGRAPHY

D. H. Miller, *The Peace Pact of Paris: A Study of the Briand-Kellogg Treaty.*

J. T. Shotwell, *War as an Instrument of National Policy and Its Renunciation in the Pact of Paris.*

— BENJAMIN H. WILLIAMS

KENNEDY, JOHN F., ASSASSINATION

On Nov. 22, 1963, at 12:30 P.M. (central standard time), President John F. Kennedy was assassinated while riding in a motorcade in Dallas, Tex. Also in the motorcade were Texas Gov. John B. Connally, Vice-President Lyndon B. Johnson, and Mrs. Kennedy. Kennedy's car was approaching a triple underpass beneath three streets—Elm, Commerce, and Main—and heading for the Stemmons Freeway when three shots rang out from the sixth floor of the Texas Public School Book Depository on Elm Street. The president was shot twice, in the lower neck and, fatally, in the head. Gov. Connally, in the same car, was also hit and seriously, though not fatally, wounded. Kennedy was killed instantly, though he was rushed to Parkland Hospital where extraordinary efforts were made to revive him; he was pronounced dead at 1 P.M. Within an hour Lee Harvey Oswald, a twenty-four-year-old Dallas resident, was arrested as a suspect in the murder of a Dallas policeman; before midnight Oswald was charged with Kennedy's murder. Oswald worked at the depository building and was located at the scene of the crime; he was also the purchaser and owner of the murder weapon. The assassin was never brought to trial; within forty-eight hours of his capture he was fatally shot by Jack Ruby of Dallas. A presidential commission under Chief Justice Earl Warren concluded that Oswald was the assassin and that he had acted alone.

BIBLIOGRAPHY

Report of the President's Commission on the Assassination of President Kennedy.

William Manchester, *Death of a President.*

— AIDA DIPACE DONALD

KENT STATE PROTEST

In April 1970 Kent State University (21,000 students) in Kent, Ohio (28,000 population), was markedly less radical than comparable institutions across the United States. In 1968 it had experienced some disturbances under pressure from Students for a Democratic Society, and in 1969 there had been some mass disturbances resulting in arrests. But by 1970 the campus was quiet and even lethargic.

Opinions differ sharply about what triggered trouble on the night of Friday, May 1, 1970. Activists insist that students were outraged by President Richard M. Nixon's invasion of Cambodia. The average student argues that it was a case of traditional spring fever. That night students and many casual hangers-on gathered at a string of bars on North Water Street, far from the campus, and proceeded to create a minor disturbance. City police responded late and inexpertly. A real riot developed, in which damage estimated at either $10,000 or $100,000 was done. A curfew was imposed.

On Saturday night students convened in mass on the campus and burned down the Reserve Officers' Training Corps (ROTC) building, an outdated, frame relic of World War II, whose value was stated by authorities to be $100,000; by real estate men, less than $5,000. Students refused to allow city firemen to fight the blaze. During the fire a detachment of more than 400 Ohio National Guardsmen rode into town to restore order.

On Sunday a picnic atmosphere prevailed, and most observers judged the crisis to be over. That night some students broke curfew to create a minor disturbance at the main gate to the campus. In general, however, both students and Guardsmen conducted themselves well and tensions relaxed.

On Monday, May 4, the legal position governing the campus was confused. No one knew precisely who was in charge, how far the authority of the National Guard ran, or what edicts were in effect. About 2,000 students gathered casually, but Gen. Robert Canterbury, commanding the Guardsmen, believed that an order of his had outlawed such assembly. The riot act was read, repeatedly and in all areas, but the students ignored it. Canterbury thereupon gave the order for his troops to clear the campus.

At 11:59 A.M. 113 Guardsmen wearing gas masks, carrying M-79 tear-gas launchers, and armed with M-1 high-powered rifles (deadly at two miles) set forth. With bad luck they marched into a cul-de-sac at the football field. Hemmed in by a high wire fence, they fell into confusion while students threw rocks at them, lobbed back their own gas cannisters, and subjected them to strident and obscene verbal abuse. Distances were so great that no Guardsmen were hurt.

The Guardsmen had no option but to retreat. Students interpreted the retreat as victory, and some pursued the soldiers. Canterbury claimed that rampaging students "threatened the lives of my men," but numerous photographs taken at the time by journalism students fail to confirm his statement. At 12:24, with an escape route open before them, the Guardsmen suddenly wheeled, turned back to the area where they had been humiliated, and fired for thirteen seconds, discharging fifty-five M-1 bullets, five pistol shots, and one blast from a shotgun. At this moment the student nearest the Guardsmen was twenty yards distant.

A major consequence of the Kent State shootings was the "sympathy shut-down" of some 700 colleges and universities—probably the largest nationwide protest in American history.

Thirteen students were struck by bullets, eleven men and two women. Four were killed—Allison Krause, Sandra Scheuer, William Schroeder, and Jeff Miller. The closest was 265 feet away, the farthest, 390 feet. Of the thirteen students hit, the majority had had no possible connection with the disturbances; they had been passing to their next class.

A state grand jury was convoked. It quickly exonerated the Guardsmen, then brought in thirty-one indictments covering forty-three different offenses allegedly committed by twenty-five young people. The jury then added a long, intemperate obiter dictum, castigating the university and its professors. A federal court of review ordered the obiter dictum to be deleted but allowed the indictments to stand. Belatedly, the trials started, but after one young man was found guilty of obstructing firemen, public opinion found the judicial process so offensive that the state wisely decided to drop all charges. In 1974 a federal judge in Cleveland dismissed a criminal trial of seven selected Guardsmen accused of firing on the students.

A major consequence of the Kent State tragedy was the closing down, in sympathy, of some 700 colleges and universities. Many did not reopen during the spring term. This was probably the largest nationwide protest in American history.

BIBLIOGRAPHY

James A. Michener, *Kent State.*

— JAMES A. MICHENER

KING, MARTIN LUTHER, ASSASSINATION

On Apr. 4, 1968, in Memphis, Tenn., the Rev. Dr. Martin Luther King, Jr., a clergyman and an outstanding leader of the nonviolent movement for civil rights in the United States, was assassinated. He had gone to Memphis on Apr. 3 to prepare the community for a march on Apr. 8 in support of the striking Sanitation Worker's Union. An earlier march on Feb. 28 had been broken up by police, and another, led by King on Mar. 28, had ended in violence. Preparing to leave the Lorraine Motel on the evening of Apr. 4, King went out on the second-floor balcony and was hit by a bullet fired from a rooming house across from the motel. He died one hour later (7:05 P.M.) at Saint Joseph's Hospital.

President Lyndon B. Johnson, addressing the nation over television, proclaimed Apr. 7 a national day of mourning. The U.S. flag was ordered to be flown at half-staff at all federal facilities until King's interment. Many public schools, libraries, and businesses were closed as memorial services and marches were held throughout the nation.

King's body was flown to Atlanta, Ga., where he was born, and there lay in state at Sister's Chapel of Spelman College and later at Ebenezer Baptist Church, of which he was minister. On Apr. 9, after funeral services at the church, the casket was placed on a crude flatbed faded green farm wagon and pulled three and a half miles through the streets of Atlanta by two mules. The funeral cortege consisted of between 50,000 and 150,000 per-

sons, including national leaders. It ended at Morehouse College, from which King had received his bachelor's degree, and there a final eulogy was given prior to temporary interment at Southview Cemetery.

Preparing to leave the Lorraine Motel on the evening of April 4, 1968, Dr. King went out on the second-floor balcony and was hit by a bullet fired from a nearby rooming house.

The assassination, the second but not the last for the violence-filled 1960's, was followed by an outbreak of rioting, looting, and arson in black districts of more than a hundred cities across the nation. Thousands were injured and forty-six people were killed in the wave of violence that followed the King assassination. In the nation's capital the outbreak of racial violence, one of the worst in the city's history, devastated several blocks and brought about the death of ten people and the injury of more than a thousand others.

The search for the alleged assassin, one of the most extensive in police history, ended on June 8 when James Earl Ray was arrested at Heathrow Airport, London. After extradition to the United States, Ray pleaded guilty on Mar. 10, 1969, to the charge of murder and was sentenced to ninety-nine years in prison. Several appeals by Ray for a new trial were refused, but on Oct. 21, 1974, he was granted a review based on his claim that his lawyers coerced him to plead guilty.

BIBLIOGRAPHY

Gerold Frank, *An American Death.*
Coretta Scott King, *My Life With Martin Luther King Jr.*
William Miller, *Martin Luther King, Jr.*

— JOYCE A. SWEEN

KING GEORGE'S WAR

King George's War (1744–48). Nominally at peace from 1713 to 1744, France and England developed irreconcilable colonial conflicts over boundaries of Acadia in Canada and northern New England and possession of the Ohio Valley. When England's commercial war with Spain (1739) merged into the continental War of Austrian Succession (1740–48), England and France, first fighting as "auxiliaries" on opposite sides, threw off the mask and declared war (Mar. 15, 1744). The French at Louisburg (Cape Breton Island) first learned of the war on May 5, 1744, surprised and captured Canso on May 13 but failed to take Annapolis (Port Royal). In retaliation New Englanders captured Louisburg (June 15, 1745), in the most daring and decisive victory in the colonial war, and planned, with English aid, to attack Quebec and Montreal simultaneously. Seven colonies cooperated to raise forces, ready in 1746, but promised English help did not arrive and the colonials finally disbanded the next year. Meanwhile, France had sent a great fleet in June 1746 to recapture Louisburg and devastate English colonial seaports, but storms, disease, and the death of the fleet's commander frustrated the attempt. A second fleet, sent May 1747, was defeated on the open sea by combined British squadrons. Gruesome raids along the New England–New York borders by both conflicting parties and their Indian allies characterized the remainder of the war, with no result except a temporary check on frontier settlement. Weary of futile, costly conflict, the warring parties signed the Peace of Aix-la-Chapelle in October 1748, granting mutual restoration of conquests (Louisburg for Madras, India), but leaving colonial questions unsolved.

BIBLIOGRAPHY

H. L. Osgood, *The American Colonies in the Eighteenth Century.*
Francis Parkman, *A Half-Century of Conflict.*

— RAYMOND P. STEARNS

KING PHILIP'S WAR

King Philip's War (1675–76). No longer of value to New Englanders, who, by 1660, produced their own food and valued fishing and commerce above fur trade, Indians played little part in New England economy. Their lands were coveted and their presence denounced, as New Englanders pushed the frontier forward. Conversely, Indians suspected English motives, chafed under English laws, and resented missionary efforts. When Massasoit died (1662), new Indian leaders rejected friendship with the English, ignored the fate of the Pequot, and were suspected of conspiring against New Englanders.

Chief conspirator was Massasoit's second son, Metacom, or Philip, sachem of the Wampanoag after his elder brother Alexander died (1662). Philip renewed the peace covenant with Plymouth Colony, but repeated reports of plots with the Narragansett, the French, and others led Plymouth (1671) to demand an account. Philip haughtily protested peaceful intentions, and agreed to surrender firearms. Sullen peace followed, but the Wampanoag surrendered suspiciously few arms. When three Wampanoag were executed for the murder of John Sassamon, a Christian Indian informer, the warriors attacked and plundered nearby farms. Philip's alliances were not concluded, but the English were unprepared and widely scattered. On June 18, 1675, Wampanoag marauders provoked Swansea settlers to begin hostilities. Swift, devastating raids on Swansea and neighboring towns threw the colonists into panic, intensified when the militia found no Indians to fight—for the Indians never made a stand. The war was a series of Indian raids with retaliatory expeditions by the English.

The English counterattack was ill planned and indecisive and antagonized other tribes. Jealous colonial commanders and troops cooperated badly, the soldiers were poorly equipped and ignorant of Indian warfare, and the troops lacked scouts to track the enemy and refused at first to employ friendly Indians. When combined Plymouth and Massachusetts forces drove Philip from Mount Hope into Pocasset swamps (June 30), he easily slipped into central Massachusetts. Then, suspicious of the Narragansett, colonial forces raided their country and compelled a few lingerers to sign a treaty of neutrality on July 15, but the warriors, led by Canonchet, had joined in Philip's War. The English sale of captives into West Indian slavery and the slaughter of innocent Christian Indians drove Nipmuck, Abnaki, and even some converted Indians into opposition—though they never united under one leader.

Before the end of 1675, disaster overtook New England on all sides. Mendon, Brookfield, Deerfield, Northfield, and other towns were devastated, abandoned, or both; two colonial forces were ambushed and destroyed (Sawmill Brook, Sept. 3; Muddy Brook, Sept. 18). Similar raids devastated New Hampshire and Maine settlements. The English in turn destroyed the Narragansett in the Great Swamp Fight. As winter came on, the Indians encamped at Quabaug and Wachusett. Philip and a small band wintered at Scaticook, near Albany, in hopes of gaining aid from the Mohawk and the French.

In 1676 the war turned temporarily against the English. Planning to attack the eastern settlements in order to concentrate English forces there while they planted crops in the Connecticut Valley, the Indians (Feb. 9) fell on Lancaster—where Mary Rowlandson was captured—and threatened Plymouth, Providence, and towns near Boston. Meanwhile, the colonies reorganized their forces, destroyed Narragansett food supplies (December–January, 1675–76), and, though they temporarily fell into the Indian strategic trap, captured and executed Canonchet on Apr. 3. The Mohawk threatened to attack the valley Indians from the west, thereby helping the English; and (May 18–19) Capt. William Turner with 180 men surprised and massacred the Indians at Deerfield and broke their resistance in the valley. By the end of May the tide had turned in the west. Capt. Benjamin Church, assisted by able scouts, harried Philip and his followers in swamps near Taunton and Bridgewater. They captured his wife and son on Aug. 1, surrounded his camp, and shot and killed Philip as he tried to escape on Aug. 12.

Philip's death marked the end of the war, though hostilities continued in New Hampshire and Maine, where the Abnaki and others, supplied with French arms and encouragement, wreaked havoc on settlement after settlement. On Apr. 12, 1678, articles of peace were signed at Casco, Maine, with mutual restoration of captives and property. Since June 1675, sixteen towns in Massachusetts and four in Rhode Island had been destroyed, no English colonist was left in Kennebec County (Maine), and all along New England frontiers, expansion had been retarded. But the Indians no longer posed a threat to the colonists in southern New England. Thereafter their struggle was confined to the northeast and northwest, where it merged with the struggle be-

Colonists and Native Americans face off with weapons (muskets and bayonets versus bows and arrows) during the 1675 King Philip's War. An 1801 engraving. (Library of Congress/Corbis-Bettmann)

tween the colonists and France for control of the continent.

BIBLIOGRAPHY

James Truslow Adams, *The Founding of New England.*
George W. Ellis and John E. Morris, *King Philip's War.*

— RAYMOND P. STEARNS

KING WILLIAM'S WAR

King William's War (1689–97). This first of the French and Indian wars was already smoldering on the New England frontier when England declared war with France in May 1689. Angry at the plundering of Saint Castin's Trading House, the French had incited the Abnaki tribes of Maine to destroy the rival English post of Pemaquid and to attack the frontier settlements. The revolution in England, which forced James II from his throne, was followed by revolt against his representatives in the northern English colonies. The Dominion of New England split into ten or twelve independent parts, each jealous of its own frontiers. In New York, the civil and military officers of Albany, the key point for Indian relations, were at odds with Jacob Leisler, who had usurped control of the southern part of the province.

In Canada conditions were little better. When Louis de Buade, Comte de Frontenac, arrived in 1689 to begin his second term as governor, he found the colony terror-stricken by Iroquoian raids. To revive the courage of the French and to regain the allegiance of his Indian allies, he sent out during the winter of 1690 three war parties: the first destroyed Schenectady, the second attacked and burned the little settlement of Salmon Falls on the New Hampshire border, and the third forced the surrender of Fort Loyal, an outpost at the site of the present city of Portland, Maine.

Terror spread throughout the English colonies, and Massachusetts raised a fleet of seven ships, under the command of Sir William Phips, who captured and plundered Port Royal, Nova Scotia. In May 1690, at the invitation of Leisler, representatives of Massachusetts, Plymouth, Connecticut, and New York met in New York City. A united attack by land on Montreal was planned with the promised cooperation of the Iroquois; Massachusetts and the other New England colonies undertook to attack Quebec at the same time by sea. Both expeditions were failures. Although a small number of New York and Connecticut troops under the command of Fitz-John Winthrop set out from Albany, they were unable to advance farther than the foot of Lake Champlain. Phips, who commanded the New England fleet, fared no better. Realizing that neither their financial resources nor their military organization was equal to the task, the leaders of the northern English colonies made repeated appeals to the English government for help. In response, in 1693, a fleet was dispatched under the command of Sir Francis Wheeler. This fleet, after operating in the West Indies, reached Boston with fever-stricken crews, and as no preparations had been made to cooperate with it, nothing was accomplished. Frontenac, also, made urgent appeals for help, with no better luck. The French squadron sent to capture Boston was delayed by head winds, ran short of provisions, and could do nothing.

With both the French and English colonies thus thrown back on their own resources, the results were altogether favorable to the French. Their numerous Indian allies were always available for raids on the English frontier. Pemaquid, which had been rebuilt, was again captured by the French, and the New England frontier suffered cruelly. New York suffered less, but the Iroquois, frightened by French attacks, were with difficulty held to their alliance. The Treaty of Ryswick (1697) ended the fighting, but did little to settle the questions under dispute.

BIBLIOGRAPHY

Herbert L. Osgood, *American Colonies in the 18th Century.*

— A. C. FLICK

KINSEY REPORT

In 1948 Alfred C. Kinsey, professor of zoology at Indiana University, and his associates published the results of their interviews with more than 5,000 American males concerning sexual behavior (*Sexual Behavior in the Human Male*). In 1953 a comparable book on almost 6,000 females (*Sexual Behavior in the Human Female*) was published. Both books, constituting what was popularly known as the Kinsey Report, created a sensation. Many hundreds of articles and books discussed the research and the findings. Because Kinsey's in-depth interviews were so numerous, his statements carried far more weight than earlier and similar studies based on small samples. The lesson the public learned was that in the 1940's astonishingly high numbers of deviations

The Kinsey Report alerted the American public to astonishingly high numbers of deviations from conventional norms of sexual conduct.

from conventional norms of sexual conduct occurred in the United States. If the Kinsey sample was at all representative (which some doubted), premarital, extramarital, animal, homosexual, oral-genital, and other types of sex "outlets" (Kinsey's term) had been practiced by large segments of the population. Dramatic class differences in behavior patterns also appeared. The reports engendered much opposition from critics who said that reporting a high incidence of deviation from monogamous-marriage missionary-position intercourse would encourage more deviation. Those commentators who claimed that great changes in sexual standards occurred after the appearance of the books looked back to them as both cause and symptom. Others felt the reports simply led to more openness about common, but formerly hidden, sexual practices.

BIBLIOGRAPHY

Wardell B. Pomeroy, *Dr. Kinsey and the Institute for Sex Research.*

— JOHN C. BURNHAM

KLONDIKE RUSH

On Aug. 16, 1896, gold was discovered on Bonanza Creek of the Klondike (Ton-Dac) River, a tributary of the Yukon River in Canada's Yukon Territory, by George Carmack and his two Indian brothers-in-law, allegedly on a tip from Robert Henderson. Carmack made his discovery known at the town of Forty Mile, and the miners from there and other settlements came up and staked claims. At the confluence of the two streams, which was fifty miles east of the Alaskan border, Joseph Ladue laid out Dawson City.

News of the discovery reached the United States in January 1897, and in the spring of that year a number of persons made preparations to depart by boat by way of Saint Michael up the Yukon or up the Inside Passage to Lynn Canal and over the Chilcoot and White passes and from there down the upper tributaries of the Yukon. On July 14, 1897, the steamer *Excelsior* arrived at San Francisco with $750,000 in gold; on July 17, the *Portland* arrived at Seattle with $800,000. No other compelling news event was before the country when the ships arrived, and the press played up the gold strike. Thousands of inquiries were received by chambers of commerce, railroads, steamship lines, and outfitting houses, and these agencies, seeing the commercial possibilities, began a well-financed propaganda campaign that precipitated the rush.

The peak of the rush occurred during 1897–99, when some 100,000 persons left for Alaska. The passage to the Klondike was facilitated by the progressive construction of the White Pass and Yukon Railroad from Skagway to White Horse. The miners worked their claims for the coarse gold and then sold them—principally to the Guggenheim Exploration Company, which sent up dredges and introduced scientific methods of gold recovery. By 1900, $27 million in gold per year was being taken from the region, but it declined thereafter as the richer deposits were exhausted.

The Klondike Rush had far-reaching economic results, particularly for Alaska. Those who were unable to secure claims on the Klondike spread over Alaska, finding gold at Nome, Fairbanks, and at numerous lesser places. Many turned to other pursuits. Taken together, the participants in the rush were the principal factor in the diffuse settlement of Alaska and the economic development of the territory.

BIBLIOGRAPHY

Tappan Adney, *Klondike Stampede.*
Jeannette P. Nichols, "Advertising the Klondike," *Washington Historical Quarterly* (1922).
Clarence L. Andrews, *The Story of Alaska.*

— V. J. FARRAR

KNIGHTS OF LABOR

Knights of Labor, a secret league founded by Uriah Stevens and other garment workers in Philadelphia in December 1869. For a time the order grew slowly, but during the early 1880's it became an open organization and its membership increased in spectacular fashion. In 1886 it included between 600,000 and 700,000 persons. Organized into mixed local and district assemblies, its aim was to weld the whole labor movement into a single disciplined army. All gainfully employed persons except lawyers, bankers, professional gamblers or stockbrokers, saloon keepers, and (prior to 1881) physicians were eligible.

The natural consequence of this all-inclusive membership and of the structural arrangements of the order was a bent in the direction of political action and broad social reform. The underlying premise was that of an abundance of opportunity to be shared among all workers of hand and brain, and the mission of the producing classes was conceived to be to regain for themselves and to protect this opportunity.

Several factors contributed to the rapid decline of the Knights of Labor after 1886. Of immediate and circumstantial character were the unsuccessful outcome of the strike policy, the internal friction, and the depletion of union finances resulting from the failure of the producers' cooperatives supported by the Knights. Of more basic importance were the structural characteristics of the order and the fallacies in assumption. The centralized control and the mixed character of local and district assemblies inevitably invited difficulties with the job-conscious trade unions affiliated in the Federation of Organized Trades and Labor Unions (called American Federation of Labor after 1886). These unions had evolved a program of worker control of jobs that attracted and held the mass of skilled craftsmen, and by 1890 their federated organization overshadowed the Knights of Labor.

BIBLIOGRAPHY

Gerard N. Grob, *Workers and Utopia: A Study of Ideological Conflict in the American Labor Movement, 1865–1900.*

Terence Powderly, *The Path I Trod.*

— ROYAL E. MONTGOMERY

KOREAN AMERICANS

Korean Americans, according to the 1990 U.S. Census, were the fifth largest Asian-American ethnic group, behind Chinese, Filipino, Japanese, and Asian-Indian Americans, totaling 798,849 persons or nearly 12 percent of all Asian Americans. The number of Korean Americans increased dramatically after passage of the Immigration Act of 1965, in which year there were 45,000 Korean Americans. That number grew to 69,510 in 1970, or 5 percent of the Asian American population. By 1980 Korean Americans totaled 357,393 or 10 percent of all Asian Americans. By 1980 four-fifths of Korean Americans were foreign-born, a figure second only to the then-developing Vietnamese-American refugee community. Several factors influenced the pattern of immigration. The Korean War (1950–1953) had crippled South Korea's economy and reconstruction was slow and difficult, while during the 1960s and 1970s South Koreans experienced harsh repression in a dictatorial state. A sizable number emigrated as occupational migrants. Later immigrants came increasingly under the family reunification category. In 1980 there were 72.3 men to 100 women among Korean Americans; more women than men have emigrated to the United States since 1965. Family reunification and women married to U.S. servicemen partially explain the gender imbalance among Korean immigrants, but other factors, such as the decline of patriarchy and employment opportunities for women in the United States influenced the choices of women immigrants.

Korean Americans have settled throughout the United States, and, unlike Chinese, Filipino, Japanese, and Vietnamese Americans, less than half (44 percent) live in the West, whereas 23 percent live in the Northeast, 19 percent in the South (where few Asian Americans have chosen to live), and 14 percent in the Midwest. Still, California has the largest number by far, followed by New York, Illinois, New Jersey, Texas, Maryland, and Virginia. Among Korean Americans residing in New York and Illinois, most are concentrated in New York City and Chicago. The achievements of Korean Americans in education, business, and the arts are well known. In 1980, 94 percent of Korean-American men aged twenty-five to twenty-nine had completed high school, compared with 87 percent of American males of that age group; 15 percent of Korean Americans held managerial positions while 14 percent of the general U.S. population held such positions; and 19 percent of Korean Americans were listed as professionals as compared with 12 percent of the populace. For the same year, however, only 79 percent of Korean-American women aged twenty-five to twenty-nine had high school educations, compared with 87 percent nationally, and the median income for a full-time Korean-American worker was $14,224, with 13 percent of Korean-American families living in poverty, whereas the median income of U.S. workers was $15,572, with 7 percent of families among the poor.

There has been discrimination against Korean Americans. The Los Angeles riots of 1992 saw Latino, African, and Anglo Americans loot and burn businesses and residences within south-central Los Angeles and Koreatown; one Korean American was killed and perhaps fifty Korean-American merchants were injured; and the damage to 2,000 Korean-American stores topped $400 million.

[See also Asian Americans.]

BIBLIOGRAPHY

Illsoo Kim, *New Urban Immigrants* (Princeton, N.J., 1981).

Mary Paik Lee, *Quiet Odyssey: A Pioneer Korean Woman in America* (Seattle, 1990).

Ivan Hubert Light and Edna Bonacich, *Immigrant Entrepreneurs: Koreans in Los Angeles, 1965–1982* (Berkeley, Calif., 1988).

— GARY Y. OKIHIRO

KOREAN WAR

Korean War (1950–53). The Soviet land grab of Japanese Manchuria during the last week of World War II was halted in Korea by the American occupation northward to the thirty-eighth parallel of the Korean peninsula. The parallel became the divider between zones of trusteeship scheduled to end within five years by the establishment of an independent, united Korea. By late 1947, because of the cold war that had begun, the United States despaired of forming a provisional government and invoked the jurisdiction of the United Nations, which in November sought to arrange Korea-wide free elections. The North Koreans, refusing to participate, established in February 1948 a Soviet-satellite form of government called the Democratic People's Republic (DPR) of Korea. The following July UN-sponsored measures resulted in the creation of the Republic of Korea (ROK), with Syngman Rhee as president.

Shortly afterward U.S. military government formally ended, but left forces at Rhee's UN-endorsed request to maintain order pending the development of a ROK army. To the majority of the UN General Assembly, Rhee's government had the legal status for ruling all Korea; the Soviet bloc claimed the same for the DPR. The views were irreconcilable. Through revolts, sabotage, and the inexperience of his administration Rhee found his political power waning in the May 1950 elections. The North Koreans, ostensibly seizing an opportunity to win by legitimate methods, in early June masked plans for military action by asking the UN to supervise elections for an all-Korea government. Then, on June 25, 1950, the North Korean army, trained and armed by the Russians, suddenly attacked across the parallel with 100,000 troops plentifully supplied with tanks, artillery, and modern equipment.

By then U.S. military commitments had been reduced to 500 advisers training the 95,000 recruits of the new ROK army, which was neither fully trained nor well equipped. The North Koreans advanced irresistibly, ignoring a UN cease-fire order. President Harry S. Truman accepted a mandate to intervene and authorized Gen. Douglas MacArthur to commit U.S. occupation forces in Japan. Other disputes had caused the Soviet delegate to boycott the UN Security Council, which on June 27 appealed for military units from the fifty-three member nations who had condemned the North Koreans as aggressors. The ROK and U.S. forces were joined by substantial or token contingents from Australia, Belgium, Canada, Colombia, Ethiopia, France, Great Britain, Greece, Luxembourg, the Netherlands, New Zealand, the Philippines, South Africa, Thailand, and Turkey.

At the outset, except for U.S. Air Force sorties from Japan and U.S. Navy carrier strikes, the ROK army fought desperately alone. Seoul, the capital, fell on June 28. On July 7, 700 men, constituting the first UN aid in ground action, spearheaded the understrength U.S. Twenty-fourth Infantry Division being airlifted from Japan to Pusan. The U.S. First Cavalry Division landed on July 18, a U.S. Marine brigade on Aug. 2, and the U.S. Second Infantry Division and Fifth Regimental Combat Team on Aug. 3. These sufficed to stiffen the battered ROK formations and to check North Korean momentum. A perimeter was established enclosing a meager 500 square miles hinged on Pusan.

MacArthur, commanding the UN forces as of July 8, exploited UN sea and air supremacy to plan a bold "end run" around the victorious North Koreans, which would cut their communications by striking amphibiously at Inchon, the port of Seoul, and the invaders' logistic base. On Sept. 15, 1950, U.S. Marines took Inchon and estab-

U.S. marines launch rockets against Communist positions along the Korean battle line. The U. S. committed 1.6 million servicemen to Korean "police action" of 1950–53. (UPI/Corbis-Bettmann)

lished a firm beachhead. On Sept. 17 American forces captured Seoul. Almost simultaneously the UN forces at Pusan commanded by U.S. Gen. W. H. Walker broke out of the perimeter and advanced northward toward Seoul, meeting a southward drive of the marines on Sept. 26. The North Koreans, fatally overextended and hit in rear and front, became disorganized and fragmented. As they retreated, MacArthur was authorized by a large majority of the UN membership to pursue across the thirty-eighth parallel into North Korea and to demilitarize the aggressors. Pyongyang, the DPR capital, fell on Oct. 19. Terrain features and overconfidence began to divide the advancing, road-bound UN troops into eastern and western segments. Between these, a gap of 80 miles opened as they neared the Yalu River, which formed the border with Red China.

Since the Korean War was dominated by the possibility of a third world war, Red China observed the letter of neutrality but freed large numbers of "volunteers" in organic formations that suddenly and skillfully struck between the UN columns. In turn caught overextended, the UN forces were compelled to retreat. Pyongyang was given up on Dec. 5 and Seoul on Jan. 4, 1951, before the Red Chinese attack was checked. The retreat was brightened by the famous march-to-sea evacuation at Hungnam by the U.S. Marines: against great odds, the marines brought out their casualties and equipment and remained battle-ready.

MacArthur was forbidden to strike across the Yalu, and nuclear armament, still a U.S. monopoly, was withheld. Under these conditions, the war could not be concluded on satisfactory military terms, especially after increasing numbers of Soviet-built jet fighters based on trans-Yalu fields began to contest command of the air. MacArthur's objective became the destruction of Communist forces actually in Korea. This was to be achieved by Operation Killer, wherein control of territory was subordinated to the purpose of creating tactical situations in which maximum losses could be inflicted. In two months Operation Killer restored a defensible battle line slightly north of the parallel. But the trans-Yalu area remained a secure staging and regroupment area for the Communists. MacArthur's publicized conviction that the war could not be won without decisive measures against Red China itself led President Truman to replace him with Gen. M. B. Ridgway on Apr. 11, 1951.

A few trials of strength failed to restore decisive movement to the war of attrition. Peace negotiations commenced at Kaesong in July 1951, were resumed at Panmunjom in October 1951, and dragged out to an armistice signed on July 27, 1953.

In general, except for a slightly rectified frontier, the *status quo ante bellum* was restored and the basic problem of Korean unity left unsolved. Both sides claimed victory. On balance, if strategic and tactical victory remained out of the grasp of the military on either side, the war was a political success for the UN, which had undeniably (1) fielded an international fighting force to oppose aggression, (2) held the aggressors back from their objective, and (3) confined the conflict to limited and nonnuclear bounds. Some students of the Soviet scene contend that there was an even greater long-range victory, insofar as the solidarity of the Communist bloc might be undermined by Communist yielding on the fundamental issue of prisoner-of-war exchange, which was the main cause for delay in reaching an armistice. In the course of World War II, Western powers had conceded the Soviet demand of forced repatriation of Soviet nationals wherever and however found. At Panmunjom UN representatives established the principle of voluntary repatriation of prisoners of war. It was underscored by the decision of 114,500 Chinese and 34,000 North Korean prisoners not to return to their homelands, while only 22 Americans elected to stay with their captors.

The United States put 1.6 million servicemen into the war zones. Losses were 54,246 killed, 4,675 captured, and 103,284 wounded. The war cost the United States about $20 billion. After the first few months the American public became almost apathetic toward the war, in strong contrast to the national patriotism that burned through World War II. President Truman set the tone with his description of it as a "police action."

BIBLIOGRAPHY

R. E. Appleman, W. G. Hermes, and J. F. Schnabel, *The United States Army in the Korean War.*
Carl Berger, *The Korea Knot.*
M. W. Cagle and M. E. Wolfe, *The Sea War in Korea.*
Mark W. Clark, *From the Danube to the Yalu.*
R. F. Futrell, *United States Air Force in Korea, 1950–53.*
L. M. Goodrich, *Korea.*
S. L. A. Marshall, *Porkchop Hill.*
John Miller and others, *Korea, 1951–1953.*
Lynn Montross and N. A. Canzona, *U.S. Marine Operations in Korea.*
J. W. Spanier, *The Truman-MacArthur Controversy and the Korean War.*

— R. W. DALY

KU KLUX KLAN

19th Century

As a movement, the Ku Klux Klan was relied upon by southern whites to recoup their prestige, destroyed by the Civil War and Radical Reconstruction. Spontaneously organized in May 1866 in Pulaski, Tenn., by a group of young veterans, it had a potential for intimidating freedmen that was soon discovered. Its quick flowering over the South was encouraged by unprecedented economic, political, and social conditions.

At least one design of Radical Reconstruction was to abolish the once dominant political power of the agrarian South by attaching the recently enfranchised freedmen to the Republican party. With leading southern whites disfranchised and with elections conducted by federal troops, state and local governments were soon in the inexperienced and unscrupulous hands of ex-slaves, carpetbaggers, and scalawags. As a group, the blacks had new powers they did not always use wisely, and they often fell into wanton indiscretions. Long used to sharp social distinctions and to a semblance of honest government, southern whites turned to secret means to rectify the new order of things, which was protected by federal bayonets.

At Nashville, in 1867, the Ku Klux Klan was organized into the "Invisible Empire of the South" ruled by a Grand Wizard; the Realms (states) were ruled by Grand Dragons; the Provinces (counties) were headed by Grand Titans; the individual Dens were under the authority of a Grand Cyclops. The Dens had couriers known as Night Hawks. Secret, the organization wanted to protect the white people from what they felt was humiliation by freedmen and to open the way for the reassertion of the supremacy of the whites politically and socially.

Most of the Klan's work was directed against blacks who, according to the Klan, were behaving obstreperously. To intimidate the superstitious and to escape being identified by federal troops, the Klansmen covered their bodies in white robes, masked their faces, wore high, cardboard hats, and rode robed horses with muffled feet. One of their favorite practices was to ride out of woods, surprising blacks walking home in the darkness from meetings of the Union League, an organization that sought to direct their votes into the proper Republican channels. The Klan invariably rode at night.

The Klan also intimidated carpetbaggers and scalawags and played unseen influential roles in many trials in the South. It was responsible for floggings, lynchings, and other acts of violence and lawlessness. It was formally disbanded in the spring of 1869, but it did not die.

In April 1871, a joint select committee of seven senators and fourteen representatives was selected "to inquire into the Conditions of Affairs in the late Insurrectionary States. . . . " In 1871 the Ku Klux Act was passed, empowering the president to use federal troops and to suspend the writ of habeas corpus in an effort to abolish the "conspiracy" against the federal government in the South. The gradual resumption of political power by whites saw the activities of the Klan decline.

— HAYWOOD J. PEARCE, JR.

20th Century

As was its predecessor, the reborn Klan has been a secret, fraternal, and vigilante organization for native-born, white, Protestant Americans. In 1915, prompted by southern negrophobia and D. W. Griffith's epic movie version ("The Birth of a Nation") of Thomas Dixon's *The Clansman* (1905), an Alabama fraternalist, "Col." William J. Simmons, recreated the Klan at a Stone Mountain, Ga., ceremony.

After World War I, two supersalesmen, Edward Y. Clarke and Elizabeth Tyler, began hard-sell merchandising. To everyone's amazement, the Klan spread nationwide. At its mid-1920's peak, it had perhaps 3 million members. It marched, elected, and sometimes terrorized from Maine to California. It helped choose at least sixteen U.S. senators and eleven governors, although few high officeholders were actual members. It was strongest in Georgia, Alabama, Louisiana, Texas, Indiana, Ohio, Pennsylvania, and New York.

The Klan was the great fraternal lodge for the old-stock Americans of the 1920's, sworn to protect small-town values from foreigners, immorality, and change. The enemy was the outsider-alien, symbolized by Roman Catholicism. Although the Klan did well in inland and western cities, its violence was primarily restricted to the South and Southwest and mainly directed against fellow white, natural-born, Protestants in the name of threatened morality. The Klan was a major issue and force at the Democratic Convention and in the election of 1924. Nevertheless, poor leadership and internal conflict, combined with violence, community disruptiveness, corruption, and immorality, soon destroyed its power.

At its peak in the mid-1920's, the Klan had nearly 3 million members nationwide; its greatest strength was in Georgia, Alabama, Louisiana, Texas, Indiana, Ohio, Pennsylvania, and New York.

The depression-era Klan discovered communism, the Jews, and the Congress of Industrial Organizations, but its ranks were thin, and its influence outside of the

Southeast was gone. The Dallas dentist Hiram W. Evans, who wrested the Klan away from Simmons in 1922, sold it to a Terre Haute, Ind., veterinarian, James A. Colescott, in 1939. Back taxes, bad publicity over German-American Bund connections, and World War II temporarily retired the Klan.

When its postwar resuscitator, Atlanta obstetrician Samuel Green, died in 1949, the Klan fragmented chaotically until a Tuscaloosa rubber worker, Robert M. Shelton, Jr., brought some order and unity in the 1960's and 1970's. Despite occasional violence and friends in office in Alabama and Georgia, the Klan offered little resistance to integration. Violence, particularly the murders of three civil rights workers (1964) and Viola Liuzzo (1965), helped bring civil rights laws, surveillance by the Federal Bureau of Investigation, some convictions, thinned ranks, and community rejection.

BIBLIOGRAPHY

David M. Chalmers, *Hooded Americanism, The History of the Ku Klux Klan.*

— DAVID M. CHALMERS

L

LA SALLE, EXPLORATIONS OF

Until New France became a royal colony in 1663, its development was slow. Following this change, a period of marked progress set in. The Iroquois were subdued, industry and commerce were fostered, and geographical expansion was vigorously prosecuted.

Foremost in promoting this renaissance of New France were Intendant Jean Talon and Gov. Louis de Buade, Comte de Frontenac. Among the great explorers of the period, the most notable was Robert Cavelier, Sieur de La Salle, who came to Canada in 1666 and began near Montreal the development of a seigniory. Soon, however, his active mind became absorbed in the possibilities inherent in the Indian trade, and the coming of Frontenac as governor in 1672 offered him an opportunity to exploit them.

Frontenac was an imperialist, and the fur trade offered the prospect of recouping his ruined fortune. In 1673 he founded Fort Frontenac on the site of present-day Kingston, Ontario, in the Iroquois country, and the next year sent La Salle to France to enlighten Louis XIV concerning his expansionist designs. The king approved his plans, and La Salle returned with a patent of nobility for himself and the grant of Fort Frontenac as a seigniory.

In 1677 La Salle again went to France to seek royal approval of a far greater design: he desired to establish a colony in the country south of the Great Lakes and to this end desired a trade monopoly of the region to be developed and authority to build forts and govern it. The king was willing to approve all but the idea of colonizing, and in 1678 La Salle was back in New France making preparations for the actual invasion of the West, to be launched the following season. A small vessel, the *Griffon*, was built above Niagara, and in August 1679, La Salle set sail for Green Bay. From there the *Griffon* was sent back to Niagara, laden with furs, while La Salle himself journeyed southward by canoe around Lake Michigan to the mouth of the Saint Joseph River.

There he tarried until December, building Fort Miami and awaiting the return of the *Griffon*, which had vanished. At length he ascended the Saint Joseph to South Bend, Ind., where he crossed to the Kankakee and descended that stream and the Illinois to Lake Peoria, where he built Fort Crèvecoeur and a vessel in which to descend the Mississippi. He also dispatched Franciscan missionary Louis Hennepin and two companions to explore the upper Mississippi, while he himself set out in midwinter for distant Fort Frontenac to procure badly needed supplies.

Iroquois raids and other obstacles were encountered, but La Salle doggedly fought on, and the close of 1681 found him again at Fort Miami ready to renew his push for the sea. Descending the Illinois, he reached the Mississippi on Feb. 2, 1682, and on Apr. 9 was at the Gulf of Mexico, where with fitting ceremony he formally claimed the entire Mississippi Valley for his king and named it Louisiana.

The way to Mexico was open, and the realization of his plans seemed assured, when Frontenac was replaced by a new governor who proved a bitter enemy of La Salle. Facing utter ruin, he again went to France to appeal to his monarch in person. His requests were approved, and in 1684 he sailed for the Gulf of Mexico, equipped with men and means to establish a post on the lower Mississippi to serve as the southern outlet of his colony. He was unable to find the river's mouth, however, and the colonists were landed on the coast of Texas, where most of them eventually perished. La Salle himself was murdered by mutineers in 1687 while still trying to find the Mississippi and establish contact with his post in Illinois. Although his life closed in seeming failure, his dream survived, and in the following century Louisiana became the fairest portion of New France.

BIBLIOGRAPHY

Pierre Margry, *Découvertes et Établissements des Français dans l'ouest et dans le sud de l'Amérique Septentrionale.*

Francis Parkman, *The Discovery of the Great West.*

— M. M. QUAIFE

LABOR, DEPARTMENT OF

Responding to the broad class mandate inherent in its creation in 1913, the U.S. Department of Labor has sought to defend workers' rights and mediate labor-management relations. As a result, the department has been one of the federal government's more controversial agencies. Given the volatile combination of class interests and partisan political conflict that it embodies, the department has seen its mission continuously modified by succeeding presidential administrations and each new secretary of labor. The installation of University of Texas economist Ray Marshall as secretary of labor by Democratic President Jimmy Carter in 1977 produced another such change. Under Marshall's direction the Department of Labor became a much more activist agency than it had been during the previous several years. A recognized authority on national manpower policy, Marshall devoted much attention to the employment and training problems that accompanied the stagnant economy of the 1970s. He revised and strengthened the Job Corps, created in 1964, and the department's employment and training programs, which had been reorganized in 1973 under the revenue-sharing provisions of the Comprehensive Employment and Training Act (CETA). The Department of Labor also created a substantial array of new programs to provide job training for veterans, retraining for displaced workers, and skills instruction and development to reduce the persistently high rate of youth unemployment.

Established in 1913, the Department of Labor is charged with defending workers' rights and mediating labor-management relations.

Meanwhile, with some success, business critics urged executive and legislative leaders to limit the mandate of one of the department's most important but controversial agencies, the Occupational Safety and Health Administration (OSHA). Established in 1970 and charged with assuring safe working conditions for everyone in the United States, OSHA aroused the ire of employers who resented such federal intervention in the workplace. With Marshall's encouragement and support, OSHA Director Eula Bingham reorganized the agency and streamlined its rules and procedures, leaving it in a stronger position to protect worker health and safety and to withstand the Republican assaults on the department's budget during the 1980s.

Regulatory relief became the predominant theme of the Republican administrations of Presidents Ronald Reagan (1981–1989) and George Bush (1989–1993). Reflecting the changing political agenda to "less government," the Department of Labor devoted increased attention to reforming or eliminating regulations that employers found cumbersome and coercive. It also devoted more time and energy to developing cooperative programs between government and business to address the problems of unemployment, occupational training and retraining, and U.S. industrial competitiveness. Reflecting this new emphasis, Congress passed the Job Training Partnership Act in 1982, which replaced CETA and encouraged employers to help design new programs to train the unemployed. In similar fashion, where Democratic administrations had supported and encouraged trade unionism and collective bargaining, Republicans considered the adversarial relationship inherent in such negotiations costly and inefficient. The new emphasis on industrial harmony was institutionalized in the department's renamed Bureau of Labor-Management Relations and Cooperative Programs. New appointments to the Office of Secretary of Labor also reflected the department's changing mandate. Rather than people who considered themselves working-class spokespeople, the Republican appointees tended to be either businesspeople (Raymond Donovan, 1981–1985, and Ann Dore McLaughlin, 1987–1989) or professional politicians (William E. Brock, 1985–1987; Elizabeth H. Dole, 1989–1991; and Lynn Martin, 1991–1993). Democrat Bill Clinton's election in 1992 and his choice in 1993 of Richard Reich to head the Department of Labor once again produced a significant shift in the agency's policies and procedures. Like Marshall, Reich, an academic economist, embraced the role of working-class advocate in the federal government.

[See also Affirmative Action; Labor Unions.]

BIBLIOGRAPHY

Gary M. Fink, "F. Ray Marshall: Jimmy Carter's Ambassador to Organized Labor," *Labor History* (1996).

Jonathan P. Grossman, *The Department of Labor* (New York, 1973).

Judson E. MacLaury, *U.S. Department of Labor: The First Seventy-Five Years* (Washington, D.C., 1989).

— GARY M. FINK

LABOR PARTIES

The policy of support for independent parties representing specifically working-class interests, pursued by organized labor in most industrialized nations, has been eschewed by the national spokesmen of American labor during the 20th century. Nevertheless, on several occasions since the early 19th century, city and state labor organizations have initiated and supported labor parties, and even at a national level the "labor party question" has been a live issue from time to time.

The world's first labor parties appeared in a number of American cities after 1828, usually on the initiative of newly founded city labor organizations. They supported a variety of causes important to working men but failed to develop into a national force and did not survive the depression that began in 1837. Since then the city labor party has been a recurring phenomenon. The movement in New York between 1886 and 1888, for instance, attracted national interest by supporting the candidacy of Henry George for mayor. Similar labor parties appeared at the same time in Chicago and other cities and occasionally grew to state level organizations. In 1900 organized labor in San Francisco promoted a Union Labor party.

The first labor organization of national scope, the National Labor Union, formed a short-lived political party between 1870 and 1872. As well as supporting demands of labor such as the eight-hour day, its platform reflected the then-current greenback agitation, demonstrating the connection with farmers' movements that characterized most labor politics in the late 19th century. Thus, the Greenback Labor party, founded nationally in 1878, received the support of the Knights of Labor, whose division into district and local assemblies was admirably suited to political activity. T. V. Powderly, the best-known leader of the Knights, was elected mayor of Scranton, Pa., on a Greenback Labor ticket in 1878 and was later active in the founding of the Populist party in 1889. By then, the American Federation of Labor (AFL) was replacing the Knights as the chief national labor organization. Although an important minority of the members of the new organization advocated support of the labor populists, the AFL convention of 1894 rejected this policy, partly owing to the parliamentary tactics of its president, Samuel Gompers.

Meanwhile, some Socialist trade unionists, chiefly of German origin, had founded the Socialist Labor party in 1877. Their party sometimes participated in the various movements already discussed, but Socialist doctrines often caused dissension, which contributed to the demise of "united labor" parties. After the foundation of the more moderate Socialist Party of America in 1901, its members within the AFL constantly argued for endorsement of the Socialist party, but they never succeeded. Had the AFL followed the example of the British Trade Union Council in forming a labor party in 1906, as seemed a possibility after several adverse court decisions, many Socialists would probably have supported it.

After World War I a labor party finally did emerge. Initiated by several state federations of labor and city centrals, the National Labor party was formed in 1919, and it renewed the earlier policy of alliance with farmers' groups by organizing the Farmer-Labor party the following year. The AFL remained aloof. Only in 1924 did it join a coalition of farmers, labor groups, and Socialists in support of Robert M. La Follette's presidential candidacy under the banner of the Conference for Progressive Political Action (CPPA). Disappointing hopes for a new national party, the CPPA disintegrated after the election. The Farmer-Labor party survived in Minnesota, and small minorities of trade unionists continued to support the Socialist Party of America, the Socialist Labor party, and the Communist party (under different names). The American Labor party (now the Liberal party) was a means by which mainly old-guard Socialists of the garment trades could support Franklin D. Roosevelt and still retain a separate identity from the Democratic party. In general, the state of the American Left since 1924 has made the traditional "nonpartisan" policy of the AFL seem all the sounder. Adopted in 1906, this policy has aimed at "rewarding friends and punishing enemies" irrespective of party. In practice it has usually involved close alliance with the Democratic party.

Explanations usually offered for the failure of labor parties stress American sociocultural patterns inimical to class-based parties and a political system that is flexible enough to absorb all third-party movements. Less optimistic explanations might include the ethnic and racial divisions within the working class and the minority status of labor within American society. The role played by leaders of the AFL during its formative period should not be overlooked in explaining American developments.

BIBLIOGRAPHY

C. M. Destler, *American Radicalism, 1865–1901.*

W. M. Dick, *Labor and Socialism in America.*

Nathan Fine, *Labor and Farmer Parties in the United States, 1828–1928.*

— W. M. DICK

LABOR UNIONS

Labor unions are groups of employees who band together to negotiate with their employers for better wages and working conditions. The first permanent labor union in the United States was founded by Philadelphia shoemakers in 1792, and several decades later all eastern urban areas had unions in various crafts. A principal difficulty confronting labor in the nineteenth and first third of the twentieth centuries was that of effectively organizing unskilled and semiskilled workers, given the hostile attitude of employers and the wide-open immigration policies. By the 1930s labor unions had become national, enrolling locals under umbrella organizations to deal with large-scale industrial employers. A flagship organization, the American Federation of Labor (AFL), represented unionists for political and legislative purposes. Unions expanded significantly from the

1930s to the 1950s. The Great Depression led to a government policy encouraging unionization through the 1935 National Labor Relations (Wagner) Act. The Congress of Industrial Organizations (CIO), a new national federation, took up the challenge of organizing the millions of unskilled industrial workers in the mass-production industries. World War II brought tacit management acceptance of unions, and competition between the AFL and the CIO increased union growth. By 1954 membership reached one-third of the labor force. In 1955 the AFL and CIO merged, but, except for public employee unionization during the 1960s and 1970s, union membership has declined consistently.

The decline of membership accelerated in the late 1970s during the Democratic presidency of Jimmy Carter. Revival of world competition led highly unionized manufacturers to lose markets. Nonunion employers backed by local governments attempted to ensure "union free" workplaces and flaunted the Wagner Act's protection of the right to organize. The failure of labor's efforts to pass a labor law reform bill in 1977–1978 served as a harbinger of more employer antiunionism. Government moves to deregulate oligopolistic industries, also begun during the Carter administration, similarly put tremendous competitive market pressure on such highly unionized businesses as trucking. While manufacturing and other unionized blue-collar jobs declined precipitously through the early 1990s, service sector and other nonunionized white-collar jobs expanded significantly.

Events of the 1980s under the Republican presidencies of Ronald Reagan and George Bush buffeted U.S. unions. President Reagan seemed to display a "get tough" attitude toward unions when he dismissed thousands of air-traffic controllers who struck illegally in 1981. General Motors and Ford Motor Company pressed the United Auto Workers into agreeing to concessionary ("give back") contracts and began experimenting with labor-management efforts to improve productivity and halt job losses. Government budget cuts and rising public objections to tax increases placed public employee unions on the defensive, as unrestrained foreign competition continued to affect employment levels. The AFL-CIO attempted to elect its longtime supporter, former Democratic Vice President Walter Mondale, to the presidency in 1984. It failed because even its own members generally supported Mondale's opponent, Reagan. Increasingly, hard-fought and sometimes violent strikes erupted, such as those of Greyhound Bus Lines (1983) and Hormel Meatpacking (1985–1986). Employers stepped up their willingness to use "permanent replacements" (called "scabs" by unionists) and even provoked strikes to rid themselves of unions.

> *The AFL–CIO attempted to elect its longtime supporter, Walter Mondale, to the presidency in 1984, though a majority of its members supported Mondale's opponent.*

By the late 1980s and early 1990s union leaders showed a rising reluctance to accept concessions and permanent replacements. To their way of thinking, employers had reneged on the postwar accord unions had established with business. A strike at the Pittston mines in Virginia in 1989 involved broad civil disobedience, and the dispute became a cause célèbre, resulting in a truce. Successful strikes in the telephone and newspaper industries and union-sponsored passage of the Worker Adjustment and Retraining Notification Act of 1988 showed new strength among union members. With the 1992 election of President Bill Clinton, a centrist Democrat, unions had a closer friend in the White House. The quick passage of the union-supported Family and Medical Leave Act and formation of the president's Commission on the Future of Worker-Management Relations brought hope, but union-backed legislation to prevent the use of worker replacements during strikes failed to pass the Democrat-dominated Congress in 1994.

Nevertheless, membership continued to decline and approached pre-Great Depression levels. Statistics for 1993 put membership at 15.8 percent of the labor force, which in absolute figures translated to 16.6 million workers, of whom only 9.9 million (11.9 percent) are in the private sector. Union leaders began a process of self-analysis and suggestions abounded for a "new unionism" or alternative modes of employee representation. It was hoped that the country's unions, historically the primary method of industrial citizenship, would find a way to renew their appeal to the workforce of the future, which will contain large numbers of women, minorities, and semiprofessional and professional white-collar workers.

[See also Labor, Department of; National Labor Relations Act.]

BIBLIOGRAPHY

David Brody, *Workers in Industrial America,* 2nd ed. (New York, 1993).

Charles C. Heckscher, *The New Unionism* (New York, 1988).

Robert H. Zieger, *American Workers, American Unions*, 2nd ed. (Baltimore, 1994).

— GILBERT J. GALL

LAISSEZ-FAIRE

Laissez-faire, a term originated by the disciples of the 18th-century school of economists in France known as the Physiocrats and given added meaning and widespread influence in the last quarter of the century by the Scottish economist Adam Smith. Translated literally as "let (people) do (as they choose)," and freely as "let things alone," the term designates a doctrine that was a reaction against restrictions imposed on trade by the medieval guilds and the mercantilism of the 16th and 17th centuries. The theory rests upon the assumption that the economic well-being and progress of society are assured when individuals are free to apply their capital and their labor without hindrance by the state. In obedience to his own self-interest the individual, it is believed, will always do what conduces to his own best advantage and the general well-being of the community. State intervention through such agencies as protective social legislation and restrictions on freedom of trade is condemned as socially injurious. The doctrine of laissez-faire involves not only a negative social policy of nonintervention but also a positive philosophy that recognizes a natural order in which harmony of individual and social interests is the rule.

In the United States there has never been an undivided allegiance to this doctrine, either theoretically or practically. The tariff, which has been an established policy almost from the foundation of American sovereignty, is a contravention of the principle of individualism expressed in the doctrine of laissez-faire. The same can be said concerning the antitrust legislation represented in the Sherman Antitrust Act (1890) and the Clayton Act (1914). Numerous examples of protective labor legislation, such as minimum-wage laws, workmen's compensation statutes, hours legislation, and social security laws, belied professed allegiance to the principle of laissez-faire during the first half of the 20th century, and after World War II it was espoused by only a small minority of Americans.

BIBLIOGRAPHY

Henry C. Adams, *Relation of the State to Industrial Action.*
O. F. Boucke, *Laissez-Faire and After.*
John Dewey, *Individualism Old and New.*

— GORDON S. WATKINS

LAND POLICY

Because the new government of the United States needed revenue, the Land Ordinance of 1785 was passed, decreeing that the public lands should be sold for what was then a high price, $1.00 an acre—raised to $2.00 an acre in 1796 and lowered to $1.25 after 1820. Not until 1811 did the revenue from land sales amount to as much as $1 million, but thereafter it increased, until in 1836 the public lands produced 48 percent of the revenue of the federal government. As late as 1855 the income from this source was 17 percent of the total federal income. Western settlers insisted it was unfair to require them to pay $1.25 an acre for raw land, a price that added heavily to the capital cost of making a farm. Supported by Horace Greeley and his powerful *New York Tribune* and by eastern workingmen, the demand for free land gradually won converts. In 1862 they won their objective with the adoption of the Homestead Act. This act was just one of the many steps Congress had taken, and was to take, to make pioneering on the public lands of the West attractive.

Congress, responsive to western interests, had previously aided the building of canals, roads, and railroads in the public land states by generous grants of land. It had also made grants of land for public schools and for the construction of public buildings, state universities, agricultural colleges, and other public institutions, on the assumption that such grants enhanced the value of the remaining lands and encouraged their sale and settlement. All such institutions were expected to sell their lands to produce the greatest possible revenue at the same time that the United States was giving land to settlers. Through these lavish donations, free grants to settlers, and huge purchases by speculators, the public lands were rapidly alienated. Although much land was still publicly owned in 1890, it was a poor remnant of a once-proud heritage, and the superintendent of the census could say, "The Frontier is gone."

Little thought was given to the consequences of this speedy transfer of lands to private ownership until the threatened exhaustion of the forest resources of the Great Lakes states and the rising price of timber raised fundamental questions about the wisdom of past disposal policies. By the turn of the century, conservation of the remaining resources under federal ownership was being vigorously advocated by John Muir, Gifford Pinchot, and Theodore Roosevelt. National forests were set aside as permanent reservations under controlled management. Places of special scenic beauty were created national parks; Yellowstone was the first, in 1872. In 1934 the remaining rangelands in public ownership were organized into management districts under the Taylor Grazing Act, thereby virtually ending the era of free land. The United States thus entered a new era, in which it cherished, and indeed largely added to, national parks and monuments, recreational areas, forests, and wilderness areas by purchasing lands that had previously passed into private ownership.

BIBLIOGRAPHY

Paul W. Gates, *History of Public Land Law Development.*

— PAUL W. GATES

LATIN AMERICA, RELATIONS WITH

With the beginning of the Latin-American wars for independence in 1810, leaders of the newly formed governments sought U.S. recognition and support. President James Madison issued a neutrality proclamation on Sept. 1, 1815, that had the effect of conceding belligerency rights to the rebellious colonies, with whom many in the United States strongly sympathized; but the American government withheld diplomatic recognition from any of the new countries until after a treaty with Spain for U.S. annexation of Florida had been ratified and the trend of military events in South America pointed clearly to victory for the independence forces. The first new nation accorded diplomatic recognition by the United States was Colombia in June 1822, and similar action was soon taken with respect to Mexico, the Federation of Central America, Brazil, Chile, the United Provinces of La Plata, and Peru. United States opposition to any effort on the part of European powers to reestablish colonial rule was articulated in the Monroe Doctrine in 1823, and the concept was gradually extended to signify that the American government viewed the entire Western Hemisphere as an area of special concern in its foreign policy.

Early efforts to initiate general discourse between the American republics in the interest of mutual assistance and support came to naught. Simón Bolívar convened a conference at Panama in 1826, but U.S. delegates did not arrive and resolutions adopted by delegates of the four participating states were never ratified. With final defeat of the Spanish army in Upper Peru (now Bolivia), threat of further European impositions subsided. Soon U.S. relationships with Latin America focused on issues deriving from national expansion across the North American continent and establishment of American economic and military hegemony in the Caribbean region. War with Mexico in 1846–48 ended with that country ceding its extensive northern territories to the United States, and various gestures were made toward the possible annexation of Cuba and the Dominican Republic. A diplomatic conflict with Great Britain over control of a canal route across the Central American isthmus resulted in eventual British withdrawal from a dominant role in the Caribbean and cleared the way for the United States to construct a canal at Panama after efforts by a French company to do so under a concession from the Colombian government failed. The preeminence of the United States in the Caribbean area was firmly established by the Spanish-American War in 1898–99, which concluded with the annexation of Puerto Rico and the creation of a protectorate status over a nominally independent Cuba.

North American investments and trade became important in Mexico and Cuba in the latter part of the 19th century, but commercial relationships with the rest of Latin America remained of minor importance. European capital and trade were predominant in South America, and commercial and intellectual leaders of the southern continent continued to look to Europe and to travel there for business and study.

The first important step toward closer relations with the Latin-American republics as a group was initiated by Secretary of State James G. Blaine. In 1889, at the beginning of Benjamin Harrison's administration, Blaine presided over the First International Conference of American States convened in Washington, D.C., by invitation of the United States. Blaine's chief purpose in calling the conference was to promote trade, but the Latin-American delegates came with political objectives in mind, such as the mutual guarantee of the sovereignty of small and weak states. An adopted resolution supporting compulsory arbitration of pecuniary claims was never ratified, and about the only lasting result of the conference was the creation in Washington of a Commercial Bureau of American Republics, which later became the Pan American Union.

Subsequent inter-American conferences at Mexico City in 1901–02, Rio de Janeiro in 1906, and Buenos Aires in 1910 accomplished little apart from the adoption of resolutions of commercial significance, many of which were never ratified by the signatory governments. A growing hostility toward the American government was manifest as early as the second conference, reflecting in part a strong resentment of its increasingly interventionist role in the affairs of neighboring republics in the Caribbean area. Argentine statesmen were the most articulate spokesmen for Latin-American opposition to U.S. policies and actions. Although the Pan American Union was created by resolution of the Buenos Aires meeting in 1910, the location of its headquarters in Washington and the chairing of its governing board by the U.S. secretary of state suggested all too obviously that Pan-Americanism was largely an invention of the United States designed to further American commercial and political interests.

The United States began to show an increased interest in the internal affairs of the Caribbean and Central American republics soon after the Spanish-American

War. Once the American government decided to build the Panama Canal, security of the waterway and its approaches made it imperative that states in the vicinity not be permitted to fall under the domination of a potentially hostile power. In accordance with Theodore Roosevelt's corollary to the Monroe Doctrine, the United States undertook to eliminate political disorder and financial mismanagement in several states whose internal difficulties exposed them repeatedly to European intervention. To restore order and assure that governments met their international obligations, the American government sent military forces into Cuba frequently, into Haiti in 1915, into the Dominican Republic in 1916, and into Nicaragua in 1912 and repeatedly in 1926–27. In 1914 and in 1916, during Mexico's turbulent revolution, the United States intervened militarily in that country. These actions, coming on the heels of Roosevelt's forceful separation of Panama and its canal route from Colombia, created fear and distrust of American intentions.

World War I for a time distracted attention from Latin-American differences with the United States and brought about improved political relationships as well as a marked increase in commercial activity. North American capital discovered new opportunities in Central and South American mines, railroads, and public utilities, and the pace of investment quickened during the 1920's. A number of governments borrowed heavily from American banks to undertake public improvements. Opposition to the interventionist policy of the United States continued to be expressed at the fifth and sixth inter-American conferences, however. The sixth meeting, held at Havana in 1928, unleashed a wave of acrimonious attack on American policies, particularly its intervention in Nicaragua. American quarantine of Argentine beef because of hoof-and-mouth disease caused further complaint.

U.S. policy began to change during the administration of President Herbert Hoover, and he withdrew the remaining marines from Nicaragua just before the end of his term in 1933. He also took steps to end the American military presence in Haiti, which had continued since the 1915 intervention. President Franklin D. Roosevelt specifically repudiated intervention, announcing instead the Good Neighbor policy in his inaugural address. Secretary of State Cordell Hull, at the seventh inter-American conference in Montevideo in 1933, signed a convention that specifically forbade intervention by any state in the external or internal affairs of another. Subsequently, the United States terminated its military protectorates over Cuba and Panama.

Latin-American relations with the United States rapidly improved, and at a special conference at Buenos Aires in 1936 and the eighth inter-American conference at Lima in 1938 a far more cordial atmosphere prevailed. Both conferences, the first of which was attended by Roosevelt, were used to strengthen peacekeeping machinery in the hemisphere. Steps to lower trade barriers through reciprocal agreements were proposed by the United States and welcomed by the other countries, but implementation proved a slow process.

When World War II broke out in Europe, the foreign ministers of the American republics held meetings to formulate hemispheric defense policy and forestall the spread of Axis influence in the Americas. After Japan's attack on Pearl Harbor, a meeting at Rio de Janeiro in January 1942 recommended that the American governments break off diplomatic relations with the Axis powers. All did so promptly except Chile and Argentina. Eventually, both countries took the recommended step, but Argentina was ruled by a pro-Axis government until the end of the war and the rupture of relations constituted a meaningless gesture that only masked continued Argentine sympathy for the German Nazi regime. In contrast, Brazil sent an expeditionary force to join in the Italian campaign, where it saw active combat, and Mexico sent an air squadron to the Pacific theater.

Plans for strengthening the inter-American system were formulated at a conference held at Mexico City in 1945. These resulted in the Inter-American Treaty of Reciprocal Assistance signed at a conference at Rio de Janeiro in 1947 and in the creation of the Organization of American States (OAS) at the ninth inter-American conference at Bogotá in 1948. The 1947 treaty pledged the signatory countries to aid any American state that became the victim of attack in the Western Hemisphere, and the charter of the OAS created a regional organization within the framework of the newly created United Nations system to promote political, economic, and cultural cooperation among the member states. The "supreme organ" of the OAS was to be the inter-American conference, to meet every five years. Between conferences, major problems were to be dealt with by meetings of the ministers of foreign affairs or by the council of the organization, sitting in Washington with a representative from each state. A number of technical organizations and specialized agencies were to function under the supervision of the OAS, and the Pan American Union became its secretariat. After 1948, the peacekeeping machinery of both the Rio treaty and the council was called upon repeatedly to settle disputes that threatened or had caused armed strife between member states, principally in the Caribbean area.

At the Bogotá conference in 1948, U.S. alarm over the threat of Communist subversion was already manifest. With a left-leaning government in power in Guatemala, the tenth inter-American conference at Caracas in 1954 devoted much of its attention to the efforts of the American government to secure approval of a resolution supporting collective action against any Communist threat. Secretary of State John Foster Dulles was successful, but only after bitter exchanges with the Guatemalan representative, with whom many sympathized, and the conference adjourned under a cloud of renewed resentment against the United States. No subsequent inter-American conference was held. One scheduled for Quito in 1960 was postponed indefinitely. In 1967 an extraordinary conference of the OAS in Buenos Aires approved a reform protocol, which, among other innovations, modified the charter to substitute an annual general assembly for the inter-American conference. The assembly's membership is composed of representatives of the member states.

The leftist Guatemalan government was shortly overthrown by revolution, but with the emergence of a Communist regime in Cuba after Fidel Castro's overthrow of Fulgencio Batista in 1959 and the Soviet Union's subsequent support of the Castro government, the Communist threat became a reality few could question. The United States sought to mobilize support against Castro in meetings of the foreign ministers but encountered widespread opposition. Having broken diplomatic and commercial relations with Cuba, the American government supported an abortive invasion by counterrevolutionary forces in April 1961, but both the effort and its failure further undercut Latin-American sympathy for the U.S. position. Secretary of State Dean Rusk obtained a vote to exclude the Cuban government from participation in the inter-American system in January 1962, but only during and after the Soviet effort to install long-range nuclear missiles in Cuba in October of that year was anything approaching a united front achieved. Before ordering the successful interdiction of weapons delivery on Oct. 23, President John F. Kennedy obtained from the OAS council a resolution demanding Soviet withdrawal from Cuba of all weapons with offensive capability. Subsequently, all Latin-American countries with the exception of Mexico broke diplomatic and commercial relations with the Castro regime.

The United States intervened militarily in the Dominican Republic in April 1965 to prevent what it feared would be a Communist takeover, and OAS support for the action was sought and obtained only after initiation of the invasion. Adverse reaction throughout Latin America was eased by the subsequent arrival of Brazilian military forces, as well as token troops from Costa Rica, Nicaragua, and Honduras, and the placing of a Brazilian general in charge of the "peacekeeping" force. Withdrawal took place after a new election in 1966.

In 1970 a Socialist-Communist government of Marxist ideology was elected in Chile, and it moved rapidly to expropriate the properties of American mining companies and other enterprises. A new Cuba-type crisis was avoided by the Chilean government's continued adherence to constitutional form and by moderation on the part of the United States. The almost complete solidarity in the isolation of Cuba was soon broken by Chile's reestablishment of full diplomatic and commercial relations with Castro's government, and in mid-1972 Peru followed Chile's example. By early 1973 even the American position appeared to be softening when, after President Richard M. Nixon embarked on a policy of détente with the People's Republic of China and the Soviet Union, an agreement between Cuba and the United States to curtail aircraft hijacking was arranged through intermediaries. By early 1975 the effort to maintain Cuba's isolation was virtually dead as country after country reopened embassies in Havana.

In September 1973 the Chilean armed forces overthrew the Marxist government of President Salvador Allende, who committed suicide rather than surrender. Congressional inquiries in the United States subsequently brought to light U.S. Central Intelligence Agency involvement in financing anti-Communist groups in Chile both prior to and during Allende's rule. Although few Latin-American governments had openly sympathized with the Chilean Marxist regime, this revelation did little to improve the U.S. image in the region.

Both the Nixon administration and that of President Gerald Ford, who succeeded Nixon in the summer of 1974, were criticized by many Latin-American leaders as neglectful of their countries' interests, particularly their economic and development needs. A new American trade law became a lightning rod for attacks upon U.S. policy, and in spite of Secretary of State Henry A. Kissinger's talk of "opening a new dialog" little progress had been made by mid-1975. Furthermore, a seeming impasse in negotiations with Panama over a new canal treaty posed the possibility of new difficulties over that explosive issue.

The American government's program to extend technical aid and economic assistance to the less-developed countries of the world after World War II aroused hopes in Latin America of rapid economic and social progress. Technical and military assistance was provided, but the administration of Dwight D. Eisenhower made clear to Latin-American governments that they would have to look to private American capital to finance their industrialization programs. Loans from the World Bank or the Export-Import Bank might be obtained for suitable projects. This policy proved highly unpopular because Latin-American leaders saw government grants and loans flow from the United States to Asian and Middle Eastern countries more immediately threatened by Communist blandishments and subversion. Even the relatively modest aid program the United States did offer to Latin America seemed to favor pro-American dictatorships rather than countries seeking to couple economic and social development with structural reforms and popular democracy.

In the face of mounting unpopularity throughout Latin America, the American government accepted a proposal from President Juscelino Kubitschek of Brazil for a new effort at closer cooperation, and following a meeting of the foreign ministers of the American republics in Washington in 1958, the Inter-American Development Bank was launched in 1959, with the United States contributing a significant part of the capital. This move was followed in March 1961 by President Kennedy's proposal for the Alliance for Progress, the charter of which was approved at Punta del Este, Uruguay, in August of the same year. The alliance involved a massive effort to combine national development planning with basic social, educational, land-tenure, and taxation reforms, all of which were to be financed by a strong infusion of public and private capital from abroad and a major effort to stimulate domestic investment in development programs. A special committee of nine was set up under OAS auspices to approve development programs and set loan and other assistance priorities.

In spite of an auspicious beginning and some significant successes, the goals of the alliance proved far more difficult to achieve than its creators had anticipated. Government instability, resistance to social and economic reforms, financing below promised levels by the United States, and vacillation in American aid policy all served to impede progress and to create gradual disillusionment in both the United States and Latin America. A meeting of presidents of the participating countries at Punta del Este in 1967 sought to revive waning enthusiasm; but President Lyndon B. Johnson spoke without the support of Congress, and his colleagues knew it. American attention was focused on other parts of the world. The incoming Nixon administration in 1969 showed no inclination to revive the moribund Alliance for Progress.

The Good Neighbor policy, the emergence of the United States as a world power second to none after World War II, and the Alliance for Progress each contributed to a gradual, but increasingly significant, political, economic, and cultural orientation of Latin America toward the United States. Thousands of Latin-American students choose to pursue their education in the United States rather than Europe, and business and commercial ties have grown steadily closer. On the other hand, opposition to the American government's policies has also increased, stemming in part from a fear of American economic power and military interventionism and, rather paradoxically, from a sense of neglect and the relatively low priority accorded Latin America in American international concerns. A growing sense of national power and cultural autonomy has come to infuse the outlook of such countries as Brazil, Mexico, and Argentina. The sudden and dramatic increase in the price of oil dictated by the Organization of Petroleum Exporting Countries after the Arab-Israeli War of 1973 poured unexpected riches into the coffers of both Venezuela and Ecuador. New discoveries in Mexico gave promise of sharp income increases for that country also, while exploration for new petroleum resources was intensified throughout the hemisphere. By mid-1975 it seemed clear that new centers of power were emerging that could not fail to alter old relationships permanently and affect the American role in the region. The form that the new relationships might take, however, remained obscure.

BIBLIOGRAPHY

Norman A. Bailey, *Latin America in World Politics.*

Howard F. Cline, *The United States and Mexico.*

John C. Dreier, *The Organization of American States.*

Yale H. Ferguson, ed., *Contemporary Inter-American Relations.*

Federico G. Gil, *Latin American-United States Relations.*

Lincoln A. Gordon, *A New Deal for Latin America: The Alliance for Progress.*

Simon G. Hanson, *Dollar Diplomacy Modern Style.*

George C. Lodge, *Engines of Change: United States Interests and Revolution in Latin America.*

William Manger, ed., *The Alliance for Progress—A Critical Appraisal.*

J. Lloyd Mechan, *A Survey of United States-Latin American Relations,* and *The United States and Inter-American Security, 1889–1960.*

James Petras et al., "The United States and Latin America," in James Petras, ed., *Latin America: From Dependence to Revolution.*

Robert F. Smith, *The United States and Cuba: Business and Diplomacy, 1917–1960.*

Víctor L. Urquidi, *The Challenge of Development in Latin America.*

U.S. Department of State, *The Story of Inter-American Cooperation: Our Southern Partners.*

— WENDELL G. SCHAEFFER

LATIN AMERICAN POLICY SINCE 1970

United States policy toward Latin America since the mid-1970s continued to exhibit the previous era's curious, often confusing, mingling of imperialist actions, good intentions, and colossal ignorance of the differences between the countries that are lumped together as "Latin America." At the same time, Latin American attitudes and actions showed a certain consistency as area leaders continued to condemn one week, and court the next, U.S. support for national and international purposes and to complain alternately of neglect and of unceasing meddling in their affairs. This situation remained especially true in the Caribbean basin, or circum-Caribbean area, including Mexico and Central America, the traditional setting for U.S. interest and intervention for strategic, political, and economic reasons. Indeed, many of the most dramatic events during this period—the covert war in Nicaragua, the invasion of Panama, the effort to restore deposed Haitian president Jean-Bertrand Aristide, and the prolonged battle to win congressional approval of the North American Free Trade Agreement with Mexico—involved countries traditionally "plagued in the name of liberty," to use Simon Bolívar's phrase, by the United States.

Although much seemed the same in Latin American relations, many changes had occurred between 1965, when U.S. troops landed in the Dominican Republic, and 1983, when President Ronald Reagan sent them to Grenada. Politically the Caribbean had redefined itself. In 1965 there were five independent nations; in 1983 there were sixteen, most of them former colonies of Great Britain. Such dramatic changes were not restricted to the Caribbean basin. Beginning in 1964, when Brazilian generals ousted the civilian government, a wave of military-dominated authoritarian governments hit Latin America. By 1975 few civilian governments remained. Even some of the region's most stable democracies, such as Chile and Uruguay, were swept away. Dictatorship, not democracy, appeared to be the inescapable legacy in Latin America. The Cassandras, however, were proved wrong. When President Bill Clinton initially called the Summit of the Americas for December 1994, with invitations to all "democratically elected governments," only Haiti and Cuba were omitted from the guest list. Once Aristide was restored to power, Haiti also attended.

The United States, long a supporter and protector of democracy in the hemisphere, could take little credit for democracy's return. Scholars and political observers, foreign and domestic, argued that without covert, in some cases overt, support from the United States, the military could not have been triumphant or have held on to power so tenaciously. The United States, locked in mortal combat with the other post-World War II superpower, the Soviet Union, was often more concerned with containing communism than preserving democracy. Washington under President Richard Nixon (1969–1974) aligned with military regimes and even encouraged them, as in Chile. The generals might be dictators, but they were anti-communist. Ironically, the "stability" achieved in the hemisphere provided a backdrop for rapprochement with the two largest communist countries. Nixon established relations with China in 1972 and that same year became the first U.S. president to visit the Kremlin in Moscow.

The U.S., locked in mortal Cold War combat with the Soviet Union, was often more concerned with containing communism than with preserving democracy.

The lessened communist threat made it possible for President Jimmy Carter to focus hemispheric relations on human rights and to accept political pluralism, as exemplified by his initial acceptance of the Sandinistas in Nicaragua and the New Jewel Movement under Maurice Bishop in Grenada. He was able to negotiate with Panama and navigate through Congress treaties that provided a symbolic and practical end to "imperialism" in that country. All U.S. troops were to vacate Panama by the end of 1995, and the canal would be turned over to Panama in December 1999. Under Carter Latin American generals like Augusto Pinochet in Chile and despotic civilian dictators like Anastasio Somoza Debayle found that they had lost their U.S. ally. The guarantee of human rights, however, proved to be a difficult objective. Although withdrawal of U.S. support contributed to the ouster of Somoza, threats to withhold economic aid and military assistance did little to deter Pinochet or the military in Brazil and Guatemala. Supporters praised the Carter administration for concentrating more on north-south issues than casting Latin American policy in terms of the east-west conflict. Critics charged that the tolerance of the Carter administration emboldened antidemocratic, communist forces.

The election of Ronald Reagan in 1980 brought a return to the earlier policy, defended as necessary to wage and win the cold war. For the eight years of the Reagan administration, the United States again assumed that its priority was to defend the hemisphere against foreign ideology and intervention, much as in the days of President James Monroe's administration (1817–1825). Once again the menace was the Russian Empire, recast as the Evil Empire of the Soviet Union. The covert war in Nicaragua, lasting from 1981 to 1989, exposed how far the Reagan administration was willing to go to win in Central America. Its efforts included the secret mining of Nicaragua's harbors in 1984. The refusal of the United States to accept the World Court's jurisdiction in the matter intensified the alarm. Many Americans were stunned to learn of secret arms deals that provided weapons to Iran, an avowed enemy of the United States since the hostage crisis in 1979, in exchange for money to support the Contras fighting the Sandinista government.

The most direct assault on communism, the invasion of Grenada in 1983, was arguably justified, even if scholars debate its legality. Most people in the United States, reeling from the deaths of 241 marines in Lebanon two days earlier, reacted passively to the news that the United States had invaded a country few had heard of and most had difficulty locating on a map. Those knowledgeable enough to condemn the invasion had hardly sharpened their pencils before the troops returned home. Supporters argued that the invasion was undertaken at the request of the Organization of Eastern Caribbean States and was intended to rescue American medical students threatened by political upheaval. The capture of 700 Cuban workers also provided evidence of the need to intervene.

Six years later President George Bush sent troops to Panama. By then a shift had occurred in U.S. policy, and the president had returned to speaking in terms of north-south relations rather than east-west. The intervention was undertaken to remove Panamanian strongman Manuel Noriega, who had been indicted in the United States for his connections to drug traffickers. Changes internationally as well as nationally had altered the rhetoric of policymakers. Foremost among the changes was the end of the cold war and the dismantling of the Soviet Union. In 1989 came the symbolic end to hostilities as East and West Germans breached and tore down the Berlin Wall. In 1991 the Soviet Union itself collapsed. Of equal importance, if less dramatic, was the growing concern for the economic position of the United States. Gone were the days when the United States led the world as an economic power. The Reagan years had provided prosperity for some Americans, but by the president's second term the rosy economic picture had darkened. The stock market crashed in October 1987, dropping a staggering 508 points in a single day. By 1988 the federal deficit stood at $3.2 trillion, and the effects of international competition were apparent in the growing trade imbalance with Japan.

"Trade, not aid," became the policy of Presidents Bush and Clinton. In 1989 Bush promoted the inclusion of Mexico in the North American Free Trade Agreement (NAFTA) with Canada, and the following year he announced the Enterprise for the Americas, which would embrace all American countries in a free trade zone, and emphasized trade, debt reduction, and investment. Clinton negotiated NAFTA through Congress in the fall of 1993. The Enterprise for the Americas was greeted with enthusiasm throughout the hemisphere. Latin Americans had long been troubled with economic issues, and economic decline through the 1980s heightened concern. Indeed, it was largely the military's inability to halt the economic decline that brought the return to civilian rule in Argentina (1983) and Brazil (1985). Falling oil prices hurt Mexico and Venezuela, and falling agricultural prices hampered Brazil and Argentina in their quest for economic self-sufficiency, political stability, and social welfare. In 1982 Mexico almost defaulted on its external debt. By 1984 the debts of all Latin American countries had reached the unmanageable sum of $400 billion dollars. By the end of the decade, however, most countries had restructured their debts and agreed to the demands of lending institutions to implement austerity programs, control inflation, and privatize state-run industries.

Economic concerns of the United States promoted a renewal of Pan-Americanism. In 1983, the year of the Grenada invasion, Colombia, Mexico, Panama, and Venezuela met on the island of Contadora to discuss prospects for peace in Central America. The Contadora Support Group, composed of Argentina, Brazil, Peru, and Uruguay, soon formed to encourage the initiative. In August 1987 five Central American leaders met to sign a peace accord arranged by Costa Rican president Oscar Arias. The year before, the Contadora and Contadora Support Groups met in Rio de Janeiro, emerging as the Rio Group to support the peace process announced by Arias. Since then, Latin American leaders have continued to meet formally. The Organization of American States, which includes the United States, serves as a hemispheric forum for discourse and debate, but as the Rio Group expanded to thirteen members, many Latin American leaders came to see that their interests did not always align with those of the United States.

Challenges to U.S. hemispheric hegemony began to mount in the economic as well as political arena, with Latin Americans forming their own economic alliances, such as Mercosur (Argentina, Brazil, Paraguay, and Uruguay) and the Group of Three (Mexico, Colombia, and Venezuela). Nevertheless they remained open to discussion and attended the Summit of the Americas in December 1994, which passed a resolution calling for completion of negotiations on the "Free Trade Area of the Americas" by the year 2005.

[See also Cuba, Relations with; Grenada Invasion; Iran-Contra Affair; North American Free Trade Agreement; Panama Invasion.]

BIBLIOGRAPHY

G. Pope Atkins, ed., *South America into the 1990s* (Boulder, Colo., 1990).

John J. Johnson, *A Hemisphere Apart* (Baltimore, 1990).

Abraham Lowenthal, ed., *Exporting Democracy* (Baltimore, 1991).

— MARY COMMAGER

LATTER-DAY SAINTS, CHURCH OF JESUS CHRIST OF

The Church of Jesus Christ of Latter-day Saints, more commonly known as Mormons. The Mormons are members of an American religious movement that originated in the "burned-over" district of western New York during the Second Great Awakening. The church was founded in 1830 by Joseph Smith, who claimed to have discovered and translated the Book of Mormon on the basis of visions from heaven. After his work was finished, Smith maintained that the golden plates on which the message had been written were taken away into heaven. The Book of Mormon purports to be the history of certain of the lost tribes of Israel that fled to America after the conquest of their homeland. After Christ's Resurrection, these tribes were visited by Him and lived as Christians until, after a series of disasters and wars, they either lost the faith or were destroyed. Within the framework of the history, many of the burning questions of 19th-century evangelicalism, such as the nature of holiness, were raised and settled. The early success of the movement is partially attributable to its ability to provide authoritative solutions to the issues of the day.

After the publication of Smith's initial revelation, the Mormons moved in 1831 to Kirtland, Ohio, where Smith hoped to found an ideal community. Unfortunately, the movement rested its fortunes on a shaky, and possibly illegal, bank that collapsed during the panic of 1837. Some Mormons fled to Missouri, where they quickly became unpopular with the "gentile" (non-Mormon) population. In part, this antagonism was deserved, as the Mormons had boasted that they would soon be in complete political control of the state.

The Mormons next attempted to establish their ideal community in the town of Nauvoo, Ill., a new city said to have been planned by Smith. By 1843, it was the largest town in the state. The Nauvoo period was crucial in the development of Mormon doctrine. It was during this time that Smith received the revelations that separated Mormonism from other frontier evangelical movements. The most important of these modifications was Smith's vision of the Temple and his elaboration of its sacerdotal system, which bears some relationship to Masonic rites. Smith also came to teach that there was more than one God, that Christ was a separate deity, that the goods and relationships of this life would continue in the next, and that polygamy conformed to the will of God. The rumor that the community was ready to begin to implement this latter revelation, plus gentile resentment of the community's political power, provoked the attack that carried Smith prisoner to Carthage, Ill. He was murdered there by a band of masked gunmen on June 27, 1844.

The death of the community's prophet caused a crisis within the movement, but Brigham Young (1801–77), who had been Smith's second in command and *de facto* leader of the group, was able to reorganize those who remained. He led the survivors on a march across the Great Plains to form the state of Deseret in the valley of the Great Salt Lake. Here, isolated from outside influences, the Mormons were able to build their Zion. Tightly organized by Young, they built an island of prosperity that virtually became an independent nation. After the Mexican War, the Mormons were forced to abjure the practice of polygamy and admit non-Mormons to the territory.

In the 1970's the Mormons were one of the fastest-growing religious groups in the United States, with every Mormon male being obligated to spend at least two years as a missionary. Their influence remains worldwide, and they have churches throughout Europe. Although the Temple at Salt Lake City is still the center of the faith, several new temples are being planned. There were four Mormon denominations in the mid-1970's: Church of Jesus Christ of Latter-Day Saints, the main body, with a membership of approximately 3.3 million; Reorganized Church of Jesus Christ of Latter-Day Saints, 179,763 members; Church of Latter-Day Saints (Bickertonites), 2,439 members; and Church of Christ, 2,000 members.

BIBLIOGRAPHY

Nels Anderson, *Desert Saints: The Mormon Frontier in Utah.*

Leonard J. Arrington, *Great Basin Kingdom: An Economic History of the Latter-Day Saints.*

William Muelder, *The Mormons in American History.*

Brigham Roberts, *A Comprehensive History of the Church of Jesus Christ of Latter-Day Saints.*

Richard Vetterli, *Mormonism, Americanism and Politics.*

— GLENN T. MILLER

MORMONISM SINCE WORLD WAR II

The Church of Jesus Christ of Latter-day Saints, commonly known as Mormonism, is the largest religious group tracing its heritage to founder Joseph Smith, Jr., in the nineteenth century. In the twentieth century, the Latter-day Saints (LDS) were accepted as a somewhat authoritarian sect with an aggressive missionary program. Since World War II Mormonism has moved far beyond the American West to open missions throughout the world. Membership rose to 3.3 million by the 1970s and by the early 1990s there were 4.4 million members in the United States and 8 million members worldwide. This growth was made possible in part by the 1978 decision to ordain blacks to the priesthood, something the church had withheld for historical and scriptural reasons. The church nonetheless has many issues of modernity with which to deal; portions of its North American membership urge it to accept gender and racial equality, differences over sexual preference, and more accommodating social concerns. At the end of the twentieth century its members were generally viewed as politically conservative, socially responsible, and obedient. Its temples are prominent in many major metropolitan areas.

Some of the church leadership's resistance to change were the result of its struggle with success. Two closely related concerns—rapid growth and development as an international church—dominated the LDS leadership in the second half of the twentieth century. Historians James B. Allen and Glen M. Leonard contended that while the years since World War II were "marked by" attempts to deal with internal problems and changes and to work with new social and political concerns, "all this seemed transitory compared with the continuing challenge of administering a rapidly growing organization, accommodating programs to suit diverse cultures, and carrying out a determination to expand even further." In fact, however, all of these issues were interrelated. Exceptional growth necessitated that the church develop a bureaucracy that itself fostered internal strife; the development of an international church forced the institution to interact with other cultures; and growth meant more visibility, in order for members and nonmembers to be aware of the church's stand on social and political concerns.

Mormonism was started by a young man with a vision, and those who joined the early church were viewed as radicals.

Because of its success the LDS church became one of the richest nonprofit institutions in the United States. (Information on the church is difficult to obtain, however, because it has not published its financial statements since 1958.) In 1982 the church reduced its assessment on local congregations for new construction projects to 4 percent of costs; the church later absorbed all construction costs. In 1990 church leaders announced that all ward and branch operating costs would come from tithes and offerings, which eliminated the need for church members to pay "budget," an allotment in addition to tithing that paid for the upkeep of meetinghouses and the congregation's activities.

Mormonism was started by a young man with a vision, and those who joined the early church were viewed as radicals. Near the end of the twentieth century the Mormon church was run by leaders who matched the Victorian ideal more than the Mormons who lived in the nineteenth century. Despite the fact that the LDS church seemed out of step with the postmodern world, it continued to grow not despite but because of its conservatism, but the large growth throughout the world, with the accompanying bureaucracy necessary to maintain it, represent both the great success and overarching challenge facing the leadership of the Mormon church in the twenty-first century.

BIBLIOGRAPHY

James B. Allen and Glen M. Leonard, *The Story of the Latter-day Saints*, 2nd rev. ed. (Salt Lake City, 1992).

Leonard J. Arrington and Davis Bitton, *The Mormon Experience: A History of the Latter-day Saints* (New York, 1979).

Robert Gottlieb and Peter Wiley, *America's Saints: The Rise of Mormon Power* (New York, 1984).

Klaus J. Hansen, *Mormonism and the American Experience* (Chicago, 1981).

Daniel H. Ludlow, ed., *Encyclopedia of Mormonism*, 5 vols. (New York, 1992).

Jan Shipps, *Mormonism: The Story of a New Religious Tradition* (Urbana, Ill., 1985).

— ROGER D. LAUNIUS

LEAGUE OF NATIONS

League of Nations, formed on the basis of the first twenty-six articles of the Treaty of Versailles, which ended World War I. The idea of a world government or association of nations was not new—ancient Greece had its Amphictyonic League, and in modern times numerous proposals for a parliament of man had been advanced—but the idea remained inchoate until the ravages of a world war persuaded the nations to take formal steps to create such an organization.

In the United States the most active wartime proponents of the league idea belonged to a group known as the League to Enforce Peace. Numbering among its members such prominent figures as former President

American cartoon, around 1919, satirizing President Woodrow Wilson's deep commitment to the League of Nations. Congress failed to approve the Treaty of Versailles that ended World War I, and the U. S. did not join the League. (The Granger Collection, New York)

William Howard Taft, the League to Enforce Peace favored a postwar association of nations that would guarantee peace through economic and military sanctions. In 1916, President Woodrow Wilson spoke before this group and set forth his own developing ideas on the subject. The president included self-determination and freedom from wars of aggression as fundamental prerequisites of a stable peace. Most important, he wanted to see the United States take the lead in a "universal association of the nations to maintain the inviolate security of the highway of the seas for the common and unhindered use of all the nations of the world, and to prevent any war begun either contrary to treaty covenants or without warning and full submission of the causes to the opinion of the world—a virtual guarantee of territorial integrity and political independence." In subsequent speeches both before and after the United States entered the war in April 1917, Wilson elaborated on these themes. He called for "a peace without victory," a peace based on open diplomacy, arms reduction, removal of economic barriers between nations, and impartial settlement of colonial claims. Such a peace, he said, must be maintained not by entangling alliances or a balance-of-power system but by a concert of power in which the Monroe Doctrine would become "the doctrine of the world."

Not all Americans shared the vision of Wilson or the League to Enforce Peace. Some people believed in the general concept of a league but opposed giving a league any physical power over its members. Others rejected outright any league that would transform the Monroe Doctrine from its original character or violate the nation's tradition of isolationism except when directly threatened. Questions of physical force versus the power of public opinion, national sovereignty versus possible world government, and moral versus legal obligations to other nations underlay the great debate.

By autumn of 1918, as the war drew to an end, debate over a peace settlement intensified. The off-year congressional elections assumed added importance because of the Senate's constitutional power to approve or reject treaties. Fearful that the Democrats would lose their slim majorities in both houses of Congress, Wilson appealed to the voters to elect Democrats to office. Republicans called the appeal gross partisanship and cited Wilson's earlier pledge to adjourn politics until the war was over. When the votes were counted, Republicans had won both the Senate and the House. Significantly, the new majority leader in the Senate and chairman of the Foreign Relations Committee was Henry Cabot Lodge, a man whose ideology and personality clashed with the president's.

Relations between Wilson and his critics, both within Congress and outside, deteriorated further when the president announced that he would attend the peace conference and would not take either a senator or a prominent Republican to serve with him on the American commission. Such actions, following closely upon the election results, were regarded as unwise and partisan even by some of Wilson's closest advisers.

At the peace conference, Wilson revealed skills as a courageous negotiator in the face of Old World opposition to his ideas. Battling those who wanted to postpone discussion of a league until the spoils of war had been divided, Wilson succeeded in getting the League of Nations tentatively adopted. The heart of the League of Nations Covenant was Article X, which stated that the signatory nations agreed "to respect and preserve as against external aggression the territorial integrity and existing political independence" of all members. Other key articles were Article VIII, calling for the reduction of national armaments; Article XI, making "any war or threat of war . . . a matter of concern" to the league; Article XII, proposing arbitration or submission to the executive council of disputes between members; Article XVI, providing for economic and, if necessary, military sanctions against members violating Article XI; Article XVIII, entrusting the league with supervision of the arms trade when necessary for the common good; and

Article XXII, establishing a mandate system over formerly German colonies.

The league structure consisted of a nine-member executive council, an assembly of all the members, the Permanent Court of International Justice, and a secretariat. In addition, various commissions were established to oversee particular areas of concern. When the final Treaty of Versailles was signed with Germany in June 1919, the Covenant of the League of Nations made up the first section of the treaty. By thus integrating the league with the general peace settlement, Wilson believed that any mistakes could be rectified later through the league.

Wilson's attempt to persuade the Senate to approve the treaty and thereby bring the United States into the league became one of the classic executive-legislative struggles in American history. Lodge united the Republican senators and a few Democrats behind a series of reservations to the treaty, the most important of which disavowed U.S. obligations to uphold the peacekeeping articles of the league unless Congress should so provide. Wilson rejected these reservations, contending that they were unnecessary and contrary to the spirit of the league and that because they made substantive changes in the treaty, they would necessitate reopening the peace conference. He agreed to accept a few "interpretations" to the treaty that would not change its substance. This impasse over reservations reflected real or perceived ideological differences over the future direction of American foreign policy as well as senatorial jealousy of its prerogatives and the partisanship of Republicans and Democrats.

Had Wilson been willing to accept the Lodge-backed reservations, the Senate would have approved the treaty, the reservations probably would have been accepted by the other powers, and the United States would have joined the League of Nations. Wilson, however, believed that to enter the league under such circumstances would be both dishonorable and possibly fatal to the league's success, depending as it would on an attitude of trust and cooperation. In March 1920, the Senate failed to give the Treaty of Versailles the necessary two-thirds approval.

The United States maintained informal relations with the league in the 1920's and 1930's and, at times, acted jointly with the world body. Whether its membership in the organization, either as Wilson wished or with reservations, would have strengthened the league sufficiently to allow it to cope with the problems that led to World War II is an unanswerable question. Most historians have been dubious, given the enormity of the problems and the lack of commitment to universal collective security. Nevertheless, the league served as an example—both negatively and positively—for those who founded the United Nations after World War II. The league had ceased to function politically early in 1940, and its physical assets were turned over to the United Nations in April 1946.

BIBLIOGRAPHY

Thomas A. Bailey, *Woodrow Wilson and the Great Betrayal.*

D. F. Fleming, *The United States and the League of Nations.*

Warren F. Kuehl, *Seeking World Order.*

N. Gordon Levin, *Woodrow Wilson and World Politics.*

Arthur Link, *Wilson the Diplomatist.*

Ralph Stone, *The Irreconcilables and the Fight Against the League of Nations.*

J. Chalmers Vinson, *Referendum for Isolation.*

— RALPH A. STONE

LEAGUE OF WOMEN VOTERS OF THE UNITED STATES

League of Women Voters of the United States, founded in 1920 to help the newly enfranchised women make intelligent use of voting privileges, has become an outstanding agency for nonpartisan political education and a sponsor for legislation and policies judged by the league to be desirable for public welfare. The league strongly supported the Equal Rights Amendment, presented to the states for ratification in 1972.

— LOUISE B. DUNBAR

LECOMPTON CONSTITUTION

From Sept. 7 to Nov. 8, 1857, during the dispute over the admission of Kansas to the Union as a free or slave state, a convention of proslavery Kansans met at Lecompton and framed a state constitution. Antislavery men had abstained from voting at an election of delegates on the preceding June 15. The constitution that was framed provided for the usual forms and functions of a state government, but an article covering slavery declared slave property inviolable, denied the power of the legislature to prohibit immigrants from bringing in slaves or to emancipate them without compensation and the owner's consent, and empowered the legislature to protect slaves against inhuman treatment. The schedule provided for a vote on the alternatives, a "constitution with slavery" or a "constitution with no slavery," the latter actually meaning no interference with slavery. Other provisions prevented amendment before 1865 and placed responsibility for canvassing returns upon the presiding officer.

On Dec. 21 the slavery clause was approved, 6,226 to 569 (although it was later learned that 2,720 of the votes were fraudulent), antislavery men declining to vote. The antislavery legislature (there being two legislatures—one proslavery and one antislavery—operating in Kansas at the time) called an election for Jan. 4, 1858, at which time the Lecompton Constitution was rejected, 10,226 to 162.

Against the advice of some of his friends, President James Buchanan recommended on Feb. 2 that Kansas be admitted to the Union under the Lecompton Constitution. The constitution was approved by the U.S. Senate, but Republicans, Democratic allies of Sen. Stephen A. Douglas, and others united to defeat it in the House. A compromise bill was suggested by Rep. William H. English of Indiana. It provided for a referendum in which Kansans would vote on the acceptance of a government land grant to Kansas, rather than on the constitution. If the Kansans accepted the land grant (5 million acres of land), Kansas would become a state under the proslavery Lecompton Constitution. If rejected, statehood would be postponed until the territory had a larger population. On Aug. 2 the Kansans rejected the land grant, 11,300 to 1,788, thereby expressing their opposition to the Lecompton Constitution.

BIBLIOGRAPHY

W. E. Connelley, *A Standard History of Kansas and Kansans.*
D. W. Wilder, *Annals of Kansas.*

— WENDELL H. STEPHENSON

LEGAL TENDER

Legal tender is anything that, by law, a debtor may require his creditor to receive in payment of a debt, in the absence of the appearance in the contract itself of an agreement for payment in some other manner. The tender is an admission of the debt and in some jurisdictions, if refused, discharges the debt.

There were two periods of American history when the question of legal tender was an important political issue. The first was in the period between 1776 and 1789; the second was in the years just after the Civil War. In the first period the question was whether the states should be permitted to print currency and require its acceptance by creditors regardless of its severe depreciation in value. In the second period the question was whether Congress had power, under the Constitution, to cause the issuance of paper money (greenbacks) that would be legal tender in payment of private debts.

The amount of circulating medium in the newborn states was insufficient to finance a costly war. Nearly every state early had recourse to the printing presses in order to meet its own expenses and the quota levies made by the Continental Congress. At first these issues were small and notes passed at their face value. Soon, however, they began to depreciate, and the state legislatures resorted to laws requiring the acceptance of state bank notes at par. In Connecticut, for example, in 1776, the legislature made both Continental and state notes legal tender and ordered that anyone who tried to depreciate them should forfeit not only the full value of the money he received but also the property he offered for sale. Attempts were also made at price regulation. The South particularly went to excess in the abuse of public credit. Virginia, for example, practically repudiated its paper issues at the close of the Revolution.

When the Constitutional Convention met in 1787 there was general agreement on the desirability of providing for a single national system of currency.

The leaders in business and finance in the states were not slow to see the undesirability of a repetition of this financial orgy. Therefore when the Constitutional Convention met in 1787 there was general agreement upon the desirability of providing for a single national system of currency and of prohibiting note issues by the states. Accordingly Article I, Section 10, of the Constitution contains the following prohibitions upon the states, "No state shall . . . coin Money; emit Bills of Credit; make any Thing but gold and silver Coin a Tender in Payment of Debts; pass any . . . ex post facto Law or Law impairing the obligation of Contracts."

The question raised after the Civil War related to the constitutionality of the Legal Tender Act passed by Congress in 1862. It was alleged that Congress, in requiring the acceptance of greenbacks at face value was violating the Fifth Amendment, which forbade the deprivation of property without due process of law. But the Supreme Court had the power to make paper money legal tender, since the Constitution itself clearly denies such powers to the states.

BIBLIOGRAPHY

Allan Nevins, *The American States During and After the Revolution.*
Charles Warren, *The Supreme Court in United States History.*

— HARVEY WALKER

LEGAL TENDER ACT

Legal Tender Act (1862). To provide funds to carry on the Civil War, Congress issued fiat money. By the act of Feb. 25, 1862, and by successive acts, the government put into circulation about $450 million of paper money dubbed "greenbacks." No specific gold reserve was set aside, nor was any date announced for their redemption. To insure their negotiability, Congress declared these notes legal tender in "payment of all taxes, internal duties, excises, debts, and demands of every kind due to the United States, except duties on imports, and of all claims and demands against the United States . . . and shall also be lawful money and legal tender in payment of all debts, public and private, within the United States." Wall Street and the metropolitan press opposed this measure. On the Pacific coast the law was frequently evaded through the passage of acts allowing exceptions on the basis of specific contracts. In 1870 the Supreme Court declared the Legal Tender Act unconstitutional and void in respect to debts contracted prior to its passage, but after two vacancies were filled the Court reversed its decision.

BIBLIOGRAPHY

Joseph Ellison, "The Currency Question on the Pacific Coast During the Civil War," *Mississippi Valley Historical Review* (June 1929).

W. C. Mitchell, *A History of the Greenbacks With Special Reference to the Consequences of Their Issue, 1862–1865.*

— J. W. ELLISON

LEGISLATURE

Central to democracy, the legislature serves as a link between the desires and needs of the people and the performance of their government. This very centrality frequently makes it the most criticized government organ. Legislative bodies on the national, state, and local levels have shown infinite variety in detail, but great similarity in broad outline. The U.S. Congress has provided the norm. It operates under a constitutional system of separation of powers in which the chief executive is popularly elected, rather than being chosen by and from the legislature. As a result, the president and others of the administration are excluded from direct participation in Congress. The legislature is bicameral, with a Senate that gives equal representation to each state and a House of Representatives that has members apportioned on the basis of each state's population. The two major political parties, Democratic and Republican, elect the overwhelming majority of the members of both houses. Their parliamentary members choose their own leaders, and the party with a majority organizes each house. More than in most systems, in which the executive is part of the legislature, the party leaders have to share their power with the leaders of the standing committees of the two houses.

All state constitutions provide for separation of powers. Nearly all have bicameral legislatures. Georgia, Pennsylvania, and Vermont experimented with unicameralism in their early history. Nebraska has been operating with a single chamber since 1934. Various bases of representation have been used, with population and units of local government the most common. The U.S. Supreme Court, in *Baker* v. *Carr* (1962) and *Reynolds* v. *Simms* (1964), insisted on a population base for state representation and acted to ensure that legislative districts are frequently redrawn to comply with the principle of one man, one vote. Some have party organizations that are more powerful than those of Congress; others, especially where the two national parties do not approach equality, are less party oriented. Minnesota and Nebraska have abandoned partisan legislative elections.

Local governments have departed furthest from the traditional pattern. In the 20th century a number of local governments, especially those of middle-sized cities, have experimented with unification of powers. The manager form of government provides for a chief executive chosen by, but not from, the legislature, much as superintendents are chosen by school boards. The great majority of local governments have abandoned bicameralism. They have also frequently departed from the pattern of electing legislators from single-member districts, in many cases choosing them citywide. Less likely to have two-party competition, many local governments have organized their elections on a nonpartisan basis.

BIBLIOGRAPHY

William J. Keefe and Morris S. Ogul, *The American Legislative Process: Congress and the States.*

— GEORGE GOODWIN, JR.

LEND-LEASE

Put in its simplest terms, lend-lease was a subsidy for America's allies that provided the economic and military aid they needed in order to fight effectively during World War II. Its primary purpose was to provide the sinews of war for Great Britain, the Soviet Union, China, and various members of the British Commonwealth of Nations, although many smaller participants also received lend-lease goods. By the close of the war a total of $47.9 billion of lend-lease aid had been extended by the United States to thirty-eight different countries—most of it in the form of military supplies, although a substantial amount of agricultural goods, raw materials, and manufactured goods also was distributed. Even exchanges of certain scientific information, particularly between Britain and the United States, fell under the provisions of the Lend-Lease Act of 1941.

Domestic politics and the reluctance of the administration of President Franklin D. Roosevelt to force the aid issue with the so-called isolationists made the subterfuge of lend-lease necessary. After the fall of France in June 1940, the new British prime minister, Winston S. Churchill, warned the American government that Britain could not pay cash for war materials much longer. Unfortunately for England, American law (the Johnson Debt-Default Act of 1934) required any nation at war to pay cash for goods purchased in the United States. This law, a reaction to American intervention in World War I as well as a slap at those nations who had refused to pay their debts from that war, had widespread support in the Congress, and the Roosevelt administration chose not to attempt a repeal. Suspicion that Great Britain and its empire possessed vast amounts of hidden wealth, plus the upcoming presidential election of November 1940, combined to delay any action designed to relieve Britain's financial crisis. Not until after the election, when the British made both public and private pleas for aid, did Roosevelt instruct the Treasury Department and Secretary Henry Morgenthau, Jr., to draw up legislation that would provide Britain and any other nation fighting Germany with the goods to do the job. Knowing that Germany planned to attack the Soviet Union, Roosevelt asked for a bill to provide a broad grant of power that would permit the president to designate the recipients of aid. The highly successful campaign for public support began with Roosevelt's famous analogy of lending one's garden hose to a neighbor to enable him to put out a fire in his house—told at his press conference of Dec. 17, 1940.

Roosevelt's full motives are difficult to determine. He and his advisers were fully convinced that Britain's survival was essential to American national security and that that alone justified their action. In addition, it is clear that he saw the Lend-Lease Act as a key extension of presidential powers—a grant he needed in order to carry out his policies without constant congressional interference. There is also some evidence that Roosevelt hoped that lend-lease would make full military intervention by the United States unnecessary, although few of his cabinet and military advisers believed that. If he did see lend-lease as a sly means of involving America in the European war, as the isolationists claimed, he never said so either publicly or privately.

Roosevelt's sense of timing was perfect. After full and heated debate in Congress, the bill received overwhelming support, with most of the opposition coming from Republicans who voted against anything Roosevelt proposed. The legislation gave the president the authority to "lease, lend, or otherwise dispose of" anything to any country he specifically designated as assisting in the war effort. Repayment terms were left up to the president, and although the inference was that goods were being lent or leased, the reality was that the bulk of the debts was written off with nominal repayment, since Roosevelt and his successor, Harry S. Truman, considered the military efforts of recipients as a fair exchange.

Roosevelt and his advisers were fully convinced that U.S. national security depended on Britain's survival, and that that alone justified the Lend-Lease Act.

In essence the lend-lease program was the precursor of America's postwar foreign aid. The United States frequently used it to prop up unstable governments against internal subversion or to bribe smaller nations into joining the alliance against the Axis countries. The long-term effect of lend-lease was extensive. Not only did it constitute a declaration of economic warfare against Germany and lead inevitably to convoying and a naval confrontation with Germany, but it also eliminated the nasty problem of war debts that had clouded the international scene in the interwar years. Logistically it proved to be essential to the development of effective aid programs to America's allies, since it brought virtually all military and economic assistance during the war into a single organization. It was also a major step in the growth of presidential war powers, for Congress retained only a financial veto and a requirement for regular reports. All attempts to limit the scope of the act were labeled as isolationist during the congressional debates and were easily defeated or emasculated. The only loose end left by lend-lease was the failure to negotiate a settlement with the Soviet Union. That settlement was a casualty of the cold war and was not resolved until 1972, as part of an overall Soviet-American trade package.

BIBLIOGRAPHY

George Herring, *Aid to Russia, 1941–1946.*

Warren F. Kimball, *The Most Unsordid Act: Lend-Lease, 1939–1941.*

Edward Stettinius, *Lend-Lease: Weapon for Victory.*

— WARREN F. KIMBALL

LEWIS AND CLARK EXPEDITION

Lewis and Clark Expedition (1804–06). The problem that Meriwether Lewis and William Clark undertook to solve in 1804 had originated with the dawn of American history. Christopher Columbus had been intent on finding a new way to the Orient, and the accidental discovery of America had been for him a great tragedy. As soon as contemporaries perceived that America barred the way to the Indies, they took up the task of finding a way around or through the troublesome continent, and for centuries this goal afforded one of the chief incitements to further American exploration. President Thomas Jefferson was deeply interested in scientific discoveries, and the Louisiana Purchase in 1803 afforded him a pretext for sending an expedition to explore the western country.

Lewis, Jefferson's private secretary, was appointed to command the expedition, and he associated his friend, William Clark, younger brother of Gen. George Rogers Clark, in the leadership. The party was assembled near Saint Louis late in 1803 in readiness to start up the Missouri River the following spring. In the spring of 1804 it ascended the river by flatboat and keelboat to the group of Mandan and Arikara towns in west central North Dakota.

There the winter was passed, and on Apr. 7, 1805, while the flatboat returned to Saint Louis, the explorers, in six canoes and two keelboats, set their faces toward the unknown West. Besides the two leaders, the party included twenty-six soldiers; George Drouillard and Toussaint Charbonneau, interpreters; Clark's servant, York; and Charbonneau's Indian slave companion, Sacajawea, and her infant son.

On Nov. 7, 1805, the explorers gazed upon the Pacific Ocean. They had ascended the Missouri and its Jefferson fork to the mountains, which, by a rare combination of skill, perseverance, and luck they had crossed to the Snake; thence down the Snake and the Columbia to the sea. The winter was passed in a shelter (named Fort Clatsop) near present-day Astoria, Oreg., and in March 1806 the return journey was begun. After crossing the Rockies the explorers separated into three groups to make a more extensive examination of the country than a single party could accomplish. Thus both the Missouri and the Yellowstone rivers were descended, near whose junction the groups reunited. From here the party passed rapidly downriver to Saint Louis, on Sept. 23, 1806, where the expedition ended.

A great epic in human achievement had been written. Thousands of miles of wilderness had been traversed; an important impulse to the further extension of American trade and settlement had been supplied; and important additions to the existing body of geographical and scientific knowledge had been made.

BIBLIOGRAPHY

Bernard DeVoto, *The Course of Empire.*

Donald Jackson, ed., *Letters of the Lewis and Clark Expedition With Related Documents, 1783–1854.*

Ernest S. Osgood, *The Field Notes of Captain William Clark.*

— M. M. QUAIFE

LEXINGTON AND CONCORD

On the evening of Apr. 18, 1775, the British military governor of Massachusetts sent out from Boston a detachment of about 700 regular troops to destroy military stores collected by the colonists at Concord. Detecting the plan, the Whigs in Boston sent out Paul Revere and William Dawes with warnings. The detachment consequently found at Lexington, at sunrise on Apr. 19, a part of the minuteman company already assembled on the green. At the command of British Maj. John Pitcairn, the regulars fired and cleared the ground. Eight of the Americans were killed and ten were wounded. The regulars marched for Concord after but a short delay.

At Concord the Americans, outnumbered, retired over the North Bridge and waited for reinforcements. The British occupied the town, held the North Bridge with about a hundred regulars, and searched for stores. Of these they found few; but the smoke of those they burned in the town alarmed the watching Americans, and, reinforced to the number of about 450, they marched down to the bridge, led by Maj. John Buttrick. The regulars, seeing them, hastily formed on the farther side to receive them and began to take up the planks of the bridge. Buttrick shouted to them to desist. The front ranks of the regulars fired, killing two Americans and wounding more. Buttrick gave the famous order, "Fire, fellow soldiers, for God's sake, fire!" The response of his men and their continued advance were too much for the British, who (with two killed and several wounded) broke and fled. The Americans did not follow up their success, and after a dangerous delay the British marched for Boston about noon.

At Meriam's Corner their rear guard was fired upon by the men of Reading, and from there to Lexington a skirmish fire was poured upon the British from all available cover. By the time they reached that town the regulars were almost out of ammunition and completely demoralized. They were saved from slaughter or surrender only by the arrival of a column from Boston, under Sir Hugh Percy, with two fieldpieces that overawed the militia and gave the regulars time to rest. When they marched on again, the militia closed in once more and dogged them all the way to Charlestown, where before sundown the regulars reached safety under the guns of the fleet.

The casualties of the day bear no relation to its importance. Forty-nine Americans and seventy-three British were killed; the total of those killed and wounded of both sides was 366. But the fighting proved to the Americans that by their own method they could defeat the British. In that belief they stopped the land approaches to Boston before night, thus beginning the siege of Boston.

BIBLIOGRAPHY

Major John R. Galvin, *The Minute Men: A Compact History of the Defenders of the American Colonies, 1645–1775.*

John Shy, *Toward Lexington: The Role of the British Army in the Coming of the American Revolution.*

— ALLEN FRENCH

LIBERAL REPUBLICAN PARTY

The Liberal Republican Party was the result of revolt of the reform element in the Republican party during President Ulysses S. Grant's first administration (1869–73). It advocated a conciliatory policy toward the South and civil service reform and condemned political corruption. Some members of the party favored tariff revision. The movement was led by B. Gratz Brown, Carl Schurz, Charles Sumner, Charles Francis Adams, and Horace Greeley. Greeley was named for president and Brown for vice-president in 1872, and both candidates were later endorsed by the Democrats. In the ensuing campaign Greeley was overwhelmingly defeated by Grant.

[See Reconstruction.]

BIBLIOGRAPHY

Edward Stanwood, *A History of the Presidency From 1788 to 1897.*

— GLENN H. BENTON

LIBERALISM

The specific objectives of liberals vary from one generation to the next and are sometimes subject to vigorous debate even within a generation, but their basic philosophy has been constant throughout American history. Believing in the rationality of man and the dignity of the individual, committed to freedom, equal justice, and equal opportunity, liberals have always been reformers with little reverence for tradition and great faith in the power of human intelligence to establish a more just society. They have distrusted power and privilege, felt sympathy for the exploited and deprived, and relied upon rational and enlightened social and economic policies to rehabilitate even the lowest elements of society.

The Anglo-American liberalism of the 18th and 19th centuries, traceable to John Locke and Adam Smith, was a reaction against powerful monarchies that oppressed the masses and dispensed special privileges to a favored few. It espoused a strictly limited, decentralized government. The natural rights of the individual—most frequently identified as rights to life, liberty, property, and the pursuit of happiness—had to be protected from the state. This supposition underlay the American Revolution, the Bill of Rights, Jeffersonian Democracy, Jacksonian Democracy, and the antislavery movement. The liberal conviction that all men have basic rights and are entitled to basic opportunities led liberal reform to be identified with popular, democratic movements; on the other side of the coin was the necessity to protect natural rights even against the will of the majority. Overall, the liberalism of the antebellum American republic was a persuasion well suited to an individualistic agrarian society hardly touched by the forces of industrial capitalism.

In the late 19th century liberalism began to find new definitions in response to the rapid growth of monopolistic corporate power. As private power structures appeared to be the greatest threats to the natural rights of the individual, the state emerged as a protector. Laissez-faire no longer seemed a viable formula for a newly complex society with increasingly visible injustices. Workers, farmers, and intellectuals all began to develop the ideal of a strong activist government affirmatively promoting the welfare of its citizens.

The Populist movement, primarily the vehicle of depressed southern and midwestern farmers, advocated a wide range of reforms. The multifaceted Progressive movement of the early 20th century, more urban and middle class in its constituency, indicated the maturation of the new liberalism. The Progressives struggled for a variety of measures designed to bring government closer to the people. They sought to curb corporate power through either trust-busting (the New Freedom) or trust regulation (the New Nationalism). They formulated the beginnings of a social welfare state that would work for the goals of human dignity and equal opportunity through active government programs in behalf of the underprivileged.

The New Deal was based squarely upon the intellectual heritage of progressivism. Its most important achievements were the adoption of a vast body of reform legislation and the building of a durable liberal political coalition. Its failures involved problems the Progressives had been unable to solve—most notably corporate concentration—or had not faced—for example, mass unemployment. The New Deal erected a rudimentary social welfare state, recognized struggling minorities, and established a rough system of countervailing power that strengthened agriculture and labor in what had been a corporate-dominated society. Perhaps most important, it brought forth a political coalition, based on labor and the urban lower classes, that would provide the sustenance for successor liberal movements—the Fair Deal, the New Frontier, and the Great Society.

In its approach to diplomacy American liberalism has faced the dilemma inherent in the use of liberal idealism as the guideline for dealing with an illiberal world. Not prone to think in terms of national self-interest or power politics, most liberals have been able to accept war only if it could be justified as essential to a quest for the near-total fulfillment of an international liberal vision. Those who supported the two great world wars of the 20th century, for example, did so in the belief that the outcome of each would be a planet safe for democracy and free from oppression. In both cases the imperfect results disillusioned many. After World War I most liberals turned to isolationism, but after World War II, impressed by the horrors of Stalinist communism and by the surface idealism of U.S. foreign policy, they reluctantly supported the cold war.

By the last third of the 20th century liberalism was in some measure in disrepute. Large, expensive neo-New Deal social welfare programs appeared to have achieved scant success in resolving the discontent of the underprivileged. The unhappy American venture in Vietnam, brought to its peak by a liberal president, had divided the liberal movement and left it without a solid foreign policy orientation. Liberal reformers faced the task of redefining their objectives at home and abroad.

BIBLIOGRAPHY

E. F. Goldman, *Rendezvous With Destiny.*
L. Hartz, *The Liberal Tradition in America.*
R. Hofstadter, *The Age of Reform.*

— ALONZO L. HAMBY

LIBERALISM SINCE THE NEW DEAL

As a political philosophy, liberalism has at its core a general distrust of authority and a concern with the protection of the rights, liberties, and integrity of individuals against governmental excesses. It never has been altogether coherent, however, either as a set of principles or as a set of policies. Since the days of the New Deal, liberals in the United States have looked to government for remedies of social and political ills and especially for the provision of welfare benefits. In the last quarter of the twentieth century liberalism was on the defensive and in disarray, more often defined by what its critics said about it than by its own claims and accomplishments. As a theory, liberalism was attacked by communitarians, libertarians, and advocates of virtue-based politics. The communitarian attack contended that the individualist perspective of liberalism is antagonistic to the achievement of equality and destructive of shared values. The libertarian criticism faulted liberalism for placing too much faith in the reallocative functions of government and other regulatory institutions and undermining individual rights and liberty. The appeal to virtue criticized liberalism for its failure to provide for the development of a viable "civil society" in which familial, religious, and moral values are the proper concerns of the public. Although these attacks often confused theoretical objectives with policy proposals, they also pointed to shortcomings in the doctrines.

Policies associated with liberalism were severely damaged by the failures of Jimmy Carter's presidency (1977–1981) and the election of Ronald Reagan in 1980. Cardinal items of the Democratic party's liberal platforms were severely undercut, including the large-scale social welfare programs begun under President Lyndon B. Johnson in the mid-1960s, concentration of power in the central government in Washington, support of constitutionally protected abortion rights, and social and environmental restrictions on business and industry. The term "liberalism" became a political epithet—the "L" word, as it was called in the presidential campaign of 1988. The election of Bill Clinton on a moderately liberal platform in 1992 suggested a partial rebirth of liberal politics, but once in office President Clinton embraced many of the policies of his conservative opponents as his popularity declined early in his term. In the midterm elections of 1994 Republicans ran on an outspokenly antiliberal, populist, and often avowedly Christian "Contract with America," the sentiments of which echoed many of the theoretical complaints about liberalism. Capturing majorities in both houses of Congress, conservatives continued to dismantle liberal programs.

[See also Conservatism; Liberalism.]

BIBLIOGRAPHY

Richard E. Flathman, *Willful Liberalism: Voluntarism and Individuality in Political Theory and Practice* (Ithaca, N.Y., 1992).
Theodore J. Lowi, *The End of Liberalism: The Second Republic of the United States*, 2nd ed. (New York, 1979).

— GORDON SCHOCHET

LIBERTY LOANS

Upon the entry of the United States into World War I in April 1917, it at once became apparent that large sums in excess of tax receipts would be needed both to provide funds for European allies and to conduct the war activities of the nation. To obtain the necessary funds, the Treasury resorted to borrowing through a series of bond issues. The first four issues were known as liberty loans; the fifth and last was called the victory loan.

The issues were brought out between May 14, 1917, and Apr. 21, 1919, in the total amount of $21,478,356,250. The separate issues were as follows: first liberty loan, $2 billion; second liberty loan, $3,808,766,150; third liberty loan, $4,176,516,850; fourth liberty loan, $6,993,073,250; and victory loan, $4.5 billion. The liberty loans were long-term bonds bearing from 3.5 to 4.25 percent interest, and the victory loan consisted of two series of three- and four-year notes bearing interest at 3.75 and 4.75 percent. The issues were all oversubscribed.

The disposal of this vast amount of obligations was accomplished by direct sales to the people on an unprecedented scale. Liberty loan committees were organized in all sections of the country, and almost the entire population was canvassed. Four-minute speakers gave high-powered sales talks in theaters, motion picture houses, hotels, and restaurants. The clergymen of the country made pleas for the purchase of bonds from their pulpits. Mass meetings were held upon occasion, and the banks assisted by lending money, at a rate no higher than the interest on the bonds, to those who could not afford to purchase the bonds outright. In this way it was possible to secure the funds wanted and to obtain oversubscriptions on each issue.

BIBLIOGRAPHY

D. R. Dewey, *Financial History of the United States.*
A. D. Noyes, *The War Period of American Finance.*

— FREDERICK A. BRADFORD

LIBERTY PARTY

Liberty Party, the first antislavery political party, was formed by opponents of William Lloyd Garrison's abolitionists in 1839. James G. Birney, the party's candidate for president in 1840, won about 7,000 votes in the election. In 1844 he won more than 62,000, drawing enough votes from Henry Clay to give New York and the election to James K. Polk. In 1848 the party nominated John P. Hale, but he withdrew and the party merged with the Free Soil organization. The leaders of the Liberty party included Salmon P. Chase, Gerrit Smith, Myron Holley, and Charles Torrey.

BIBLIOGRAPHY

T. C. Smith, *History of the Liberty and Free Soil Parties in the Northwest.*

— THEODORE W. COUSENS

LIBRARIES

From their beginnings libraries in the United States have been characterized by diversity of size, type, and resources. Although sharing the basic functions of acquiring, organizing, preserving, and disseminating recorded knowledge, they have served a variety of clienteles and thus have had different focuses.

After the founding of the Harvard College Library in 1638 libraries developed sporadically until well into the 18th century. Capt. Robert Keayne willed a sum to the city of Boston in 1655 for various public purposes, including a town library, and the city met the conditions of his bequest by erecting a public building in which a room was set aside for a library. This library was destroyed by fire in 1747. Some years later a number of church-related libraries were established along the Atlantic seaboard by Thomas Bray, a clergyman who spent a few months in the colonies under the sponsorship of the Anglican church in 1689; the largest of these libraries was in Annapolis, Md. At the turn of the century libraries were established with the founding of William and Mary College and Yale College in 1693 and 1701, respectively. A few New England towns inherited small collections, as had Boston from Keayne, but no provision was made for their expansion or upkeep and they passed out of existence.

Not until 1731 did the next significant library development occur, with the founding of the first subscription library by Benjamin Franklin. Having organized the Junto, a social club for intellectual discussion and debate, he soon realized that a library was necessary to support the club's activities and astutely arranged for the members to pool their personal book collections to form the Library Company of Philadelphia. Other social libraries were soon founded in Durham and Lebanon, Conn., and in 1750 the Redwood Library, which is the oldest library in the United States, was erected in Newport, R.I.

As the country turned increasingly from agriculture to manufacturing and mercantile pursuits the need for greater access to educational materials in population centers found expression in social libraries. The social library was the basis for the first library movement in the United States and was to dominate the library scene for well over a hundred years. It was of two basic types: proprietary and subscription. The proprietary library was, in effect, a joint-stock company, whereas the subscription library was a corporation to which a member paid an annual fee for service. Proprietary libraries levied assessments on shareholders and in some cases permitted others to use the library for an annual fee. Between 1733 and 1850 more than 1,000 social libraries were established, mostly in New England, but also in Ohio, Kentucky, and Indiana as the population moved westward. Although these collections were small and members few, the fees were low enough to make the organizations attractive to many classes of society. There were, for example, social libraries for mechanics, clerks, juveniles, and factory workers. The major weaknesses, lack of continuity beyond the founding group and uncertain financial support—common to all voluntary associations—contributed to the decline of the social library and its replacement by the free, public, tax-supported library in the mid-19th century.

Free public libraries for juveniles had been founded in Salisbury, Conn., in 1803 and in Lexington, Mass., in 1827. But it was Peterborough, N.H., that first took advantage of state education funds to found a free public town library, opened in 1833 and supported by annual appropriations; as of the mid-1970's it was still in operation. The primacy of Peterborough in introducing a new library organization concept was overshadowed in 1852 when the Boston Public Library came into being. The report of its trustees issued in July of that year is still recognized as the most comprehensive statement of purpose, functions, and objectives for the modern American public library. It was nearly half a century later before the endowment trusts of John Jacob Astor, James Lenox, and Samuel J. Tilden were combined in 1895 to make possible the New York Public Library.

Encouraged by a commitment to free, popular education and permissive state legislation, public libraries quickly began to spread out, absorbing or supplanting social libraries. Several of the states followed the pattern set by New York in permitting school districts to levy a tax to establish and support public libraries. As the Civil War approached, the concept of the public library had just been established, and although the nation boasted more than 500 libraries only those at Harvard and Yale could count as many as 50,000 volumes. Literary societies were still important in campus life, providing for the library needs of their members with collections often rivaling those of the college libraries.

Several developments significant in modern library history occurred in the pivotal year 1876. At a meeting held during the Centennial Exposition in Philadelphia, Oct. 4–6, a group of librarians voted on the third day of the conference to form the American Library Association. Among them was Melvil Dewey, then not yet twenty-five years of age and only recently graduated from Amherst College, who was to be a dominant force in the library world for the next thirty years. In the same year the U.S. Office of Education issued its first report on libraries, *Public Libraries in the United States of America: Their History, Condition and Management*, in two parts. The first part contained the results of a survey of over 3,800 public libraries. The second part comprised Rules for a Printed Dictionary Catalogue by Charles Ammi Cutter, librarian of the Boston Athenaeum. These rules were quickly adopted by libraries for both printed and card catalogs. The first library periodical, *Library Journal*, was founded in 1876 and Dewey's famous decimal classification scheme, the most widely used library classification system in the world, first appeared in the same year.

In 1900 the library school at Columbia College had produced its first graduates, and Herbert Putnam had moved from the Boston Public Library to begin his impressive forty-year career as Librarian of Congress. Within a few years every major type of library was represented in the United States and most were well established, headed by the Library of Congress. Under Putnam it assumed a dual role, serving the U.S. Congress and functioning as a national library. From 1850 to 1876 the Library of Congress collection grew from 50,000 volumes to about 300,000 volumes; by 1974 its collections held nearly 74 million items, including books and pamphlets, as well as slides, films, prints, sheet music, manuscripts, and art reproductions. The Library of Congress defines its scope as universal, but the growth of other major federal libraries, including the National Library of Medicine and the National Agricultural Library, has tended to diminish the significance of that claim.

Closely related to the Library of Congress by their support for research, but separate in development, are the many research libraries in the United States. University libraries dominate this category, although a few research libraries—such as the Newberry Library in Chicago, the Henry E. Huntington Library in San Marino, Cal., and the Library Company of Philadelphia—remain private and independent. Still others, although independently controlled, have become associated with universities, for example, the John Carter Brown Library at Brown University and the William L. Clements Library at the University of Michigan. The university research library developed in response to an increased emphasis on research and graduate work, as exemplified by Johns Hopkins University under Daniel Coit Gilman. The growing demands of scholarly research are reflected in the fact that in 1876 only two libraries—Harvard and Yale—held more than 100,000 volumes, whereas by 1891 the number had grown from two to five; by the early 1970's more than fifty university libraries contained over 1 million volumes.

From their beginnings in the late 19th century through the first half of the 20th century, school libraries had minimal educational influence, primarily because elementary and secondary education remained textbook oriented until the 1940's. With the passage of the National Defense Education Act in 1958 massive financial assistance became available to school libraries, and in 1965 the Elementary and Secondary Education Act augmented that assistance. With those new sources of funds—and guided by standards and the concept of the school media center—such libraries soon came to constitute the largest category of libraries and continue a growing, vital force in American education.

More than 10,000 U.S. libraries are devoted to special subject matter or a specialized clientele. Among these are libraries of private companies—banking, insurance, research, manufacturing—and those associated with public institutions, including government agencies.

The urban public library is the prototype library in the United States. It serves, or has served, all the clientele served by other libraries. It has pioneered in the development of most of the significant concepts of American librarianship, for example, the open shelf, by the Cleveland Public Library, and subject divisional organization, by the Providence Public Library. In the latter part of the 20th century, however, costs and diminishing income, combined with ambiguity of purpose, reduced the capability of public libraries to respond quickly to changing public needs.

After 1956 the federal government began to play an increasingly influential role in library development. Federal funds supported extended service to rural areas, construction of new facilities, training of new librarians, and extensive research into library problems. By the mid-1970's the sharing of responsibility for library service by federal, state, and local government brought U.S. libraries of all types to the verge of launching a national library system capable of equalizing library resources and services to all Americans.

BIBLIOGRAPHY

Jean Key Gates, *Introduction to Librarianship.*

Douglas M. Knight and Nourse Shepley, eds., *Libraries at Large.*

Jesse H. Shera, *Foundations of the Public Library: The Origins of the Public Library Movement in New England, 1629–1855.*

— ROBERT WEDGEWORTH

LIBRARIES IN THE LATE TWENTIETH CENTURY

Beginning in the 1970s enormous changes, both positive and negative, swept the fields of library and information sciences. Libraries grew at an unprecedented rate. State and local support combined with federal largesse encouraged libraries to expand in numbers and size. Public libraries added branches, campuses developed subject-related libraries, and even businesses and law firms developed substantial in-house collections. Librarians increasingly turned to computerization in the 1980s to control their burgeoning collections. Libraries began using on-line systems for interlibrary loans, circulation, and acquisition. National databases of cataloged books were developed, which led to replacement of card catalogs. Machine-readable cataloging allowed the Library of Congress, for example, to share its national cataloging responsibility across the country through on-line computer services and to store some of its materials on CD-ROMs. Databases provided indexes to journals and technical and legal publications, and by the mid-1990s the full texts of some books and journals had become available on-line. There have been problems, however. Federal financial support began to decline just at the time when specialization was leading to rapid growth in numbers of books published and numbers of journal titles and when costs of books and especially journals were climbing precipitously, notably in the fields of science and technology. Widespread cuts both in staff and in purchases of materials, especially periodicals, became commonplace. Equally daunting is the problem of "acid paper." Books and periodicals made from paper with a high acid content, especially since the 1940s, were literally disintegrating in the 1990s in their own chemicals as librarians, archivists, government agencies, and paper manufacturers continued to search for a solution that is both economically feasible and environmentally sound.

Federal financial support began to decline just as the numbers and the costs of books and journals were starting to escalate.

[See also Library of Congress.]

BIBLIOGRAPHY

Arthur T. Hamlin, *The University Library in the United States* (Philadelphia, 1981).

Robert Wedgeworth, ed., *ALA World Encyclopedia of Library and Information Services*, 2nd ed. (Chicago, 1986).

Wayne A. Wiegand, *The Politics of an Emerging Profession: The American Library Association, 1876–1917* (Westport, Conn., 1986).

Patrick Williams, *The American Public Library and the Problem of Purpose* (New York, 1988).

— R. DAVID MYERS

LIBRARY OF CONGRESS

Library of Congress, established by the same act of Congress, approved Apr. 24, 1800, that made provision for the removal of the government of the United States to the new federal city, Washington, D.C. It provided for "the purchase of such books as may be necessary for the use of Congress" and for "fitting up a suitable apartment" in the Capitol to house them. The original collections of the library, obtained from London, consisted of 152 works in 740 volumes and a few maps. To administer them, Congress, in an act of Jan. 26, 1802, provided that a librarian be appointed, and three days later President Thomas Jefferson named John James Beckley, clerk of the House of Representatives, who held both posts until his death.

When British troops burned the Capitol in 1814, the library of some 3,000 volumes was lost. To replace it, Congress purchased Jefferson's personal library, consisting of an estimated 6,487 books, for $23,950. This fine collection, far-ranging in subject matter, was "admirably calculated for the substratum of a great national library," proponents of its purchase contended. In 1851 a Christmas Eve fire destroyed some 35,000 volumes, including two-thirds of the Jefferson library. By the end of 1864, the collections had grown to some 82,000 volumes, but they were far from distinguished, and national only in the sense that the government owned them. Then Congress, in less than three years, passed four laws that cast the library in the mold of greatness: an act of Mar. 3, 1865, requiring the deposit in the library of a copy of all books and other materials on which copyright was claimed, with loss of copyright for failure to deposit; an act of Apr. 5, 1866, transferring to the Library of Congress the Smithsonian Institution's unique collection (40,000 volumes plus future increments) of scientific materials and transactions of learned societies, gathered from all over the world; an act of Mar. 2, 1867, strengthening international exchange of official publications and making the library the beneficiary; and an appropriations act of Mar. 2, 1867, providing $100,000 for the purchase of the Peter Force collection of Americana—the first major purchase since the Jefferson library and the library's first distinguished research collection. The 19th century also saw the creation (1832) of the Law Library in the Library of Congress, the assignment (1870) to the library of responsibility for the administration of the copyright law, and the first substantial gift to the library by a private citizen—Dr. Joseph Meredith Toner's collection of medical literature and of materials for the study of American history and biography, which was accepted by Congress in 1882.

In 1897 the library, which had grown to nearly a million volumes, moved from the Capitol to its own building. In preparation, Congress, in an appropriations act of Feb. 19, 1897—the nearest to an organic act the library has—provided for the appointment of the librarian by the president, by and with the advice and consent of the Senate, and vested in the librarian the authority to make regulations for the government of the library and to appoint members of the staff "solely with reference to their fitness for their particular duties."

The collections are housed in the "old" or main building; in the annex, which was occupied in 1939; and in rental space. Some moved to the Library of Congress James Madison Memorial Building, authorized by Congress in 1965 for construction on a Capitol Hill site adjacent to the main building and to the Cannon House Office Building.

The functions of the library were extended by Congress until it became, in effect, the national library, serving the Congress, federal agencies, other libraries, and the public. It provides research and reference services to the Congress; for example, 210,893 requests were directed in 1974 to the Congressional Research Service, one of the six departments of the library, by members and committees of Congress. The library's comprehensive collections are open to adults for reference use, and some reference service is provided by mail. The use of the book collections is extended through interlibrary loan for persons unable to locate the research materials they need in libraries in their own regions, and is further extended through the Photoduplication Service, from which various types of photocopies of unrestricted materials can be purchased.

The library contains the national Copyright Office for the registration of claims to copyright, and its collections are enriched from the copyright deposits. It is the United States partner in the official, intergovernmental exchange of publications and has thousands of exchange agreements with private research institutions throughout the world. It also purchases materials, obtains them through official transfer, and receives gifts to the nation in the form of personal papers, rare books, and other valuable materials.

During the 20th century, the Library of Congress emerged as a library "universal in scope, national in service," as Librarian Herbert Putnam termed it. By June 30, 1974, the collections totaled almost 74 million items and constituted unparalleled resources for research. They included more than 16 million books and pamphlets on every subject and in a multitude of languages. Among them are the most comprehensive collections of Chinese, Japanese, and Russian materials outside the Orient and the Soviet Union; over 2 million volumes relating to science and technology and nearly as many legal materials, outstanding for foreign as well as American law; the world's largest collection of aeronautical literature; and the most extensive collection of incunabula in the Western Hemisphere, including a perfect copy of the Gutenberg Bible printed on vellum.

The manuscript collections totaled more than 31 million items relating to American history and civilization and included the personal papers of twenty-three presidents. The music collections, from classical to modern, contained more than 3.4 million volumes and pieces, in manuscript form and published. Other materials included more than 3 million maps and views; 8.4 million photographic items, from the Civil War photographs of Mathew B. Brady to date; 428,000 recordings, including folk-songs and other music, speeches, and poetry readings; 174,000 fine prints and reproductions; newspapers and periodicals from all over the world; and motion pictures, microfilms, and many other kinds of materials.

The library plays a central role in a national program for the preservation of library materials, working with other libraries, library associations, and technical agencies and associations. It is also taking the lead in the automation of library processes.

Thousands of libraries throughout the world use the subject-classification system and cataloging codes developed by the library. Since 1901 the library has made its printed cards available to other libraries, and more recently it has offered bibliographic information in book form as well, including by 1975, 350 volumes of *National Union Catalog, Pre-1956 Imprints.* Since 1966 cataloging data in machine-readable form also have been distributed to libraries and library networks through the MARC (MAchine-Readable Cataloging) Distribution Service; and the MARC format has been accepted as a national and international standard. A program started in 1971, Cataloging in Publication, is providing publishers with cataloging data that can be printed in the published book; in 1975 such information was available in most of the trade books issued by American publishers.

Both acquisitions and cataloging for the Library of Congress and other U.S. libraries have benefited from two special programs authorized by Congress. In the 1960's, under Public Law 480, as amended, the Library of Congress acquired for itself and some 350 other U.S. libraries, through the use of surplus U.S.-owned foreign currencies, over 16 million books and serial pieces published abroad. Through the National Program for Acquisitions and Cataloging, begun under the Higher Education Act of 1965, the library promptly acquires other foreign materials and speeds up its cataloging service by utilizing the cataloging done in the countries of origin for their own national bibliographies.

The Pratt-Smoot Act in 1931 authorized the library to establish a free, nationwide library service for adult blind readers; in 1952 the act was amended to permit service to blind children as well; and in 1966 the service was extended to all persons unable to read conventional printed materials because of physical or visual limitations. The library in the mid-1970's served over 300,000 readers through fifty-three cooperating regional libraries.

The Library of Congress Trust Fund Board, created by an act of Congress on Mar. 3, 1925, accepts—with the approval of the Joint Committee on the Library—and administers gifts and bequests that enable the library to develop tools for research, to enrich its collections, to issue special publications, and to present cultural programs in the fields of music and literature. Concerts and literary programs presented in the library's Coolidge Auditorium are made available to a national radio audience through such gifts, and exhibits of items from the collections, shown first in the library's own exhibit halls, are circulated to libraries and museums throughout the country with the help of a fund established by a gift.

There had been eleven librarians of Congress by the mid-1970's: John J. Beckley, 1802–07, and Patrick Magruder, 1807–15, both of whom served as clerk of the House of Representatives; George Watterston, 1815–29, the first to hold the separate post of librarian; John Sylva Meehan, 1829–61; John G. Stephenson, 1861–64; Ainsworth Rand Spofford, 1864–97; John Russell Young, 1897–99; Herbert Putnam, 1899–1939; Archibald MacLeish, 1939–44; Luther Harris Evans, 1945–53; and L. Quincy Mumford, 1954–74.

— ELIZABETH HAMER KEGAN

LIBRARY OF CONGRESS SINCE 1976

Striking changes have occurred at the Library of Congress since 1976, primarily the expansion in 1980 into the James Madison Memorial Building, the library's third major structure on Capitol Hill; the "closing" of the card catalog at the end of 1980, when the computer terminal became the preferred means of access to current catalog information; and the development in the late 1980s and 1990s of electronic information systems that enable the library to share bibliographic data and many of its collections with readers around the world. The library's bibliographic records became available on the Internet in 1993; two years later more than 40 million computerized records of books, legislation, and copyright registrations could be accessed. In 1995 the library announced a plan to digitize 5 million items from its core American history collections by the year 2000, the institution's bicentennial. This new National Digital Library was being developed through partnerships with other research institutions, the U.S. Congress, and the private sector, which by mid-1995 had pledged $15 million to the effort. The recognition of the crucial importance of private funds in building and sustaining national outreach efforts led the library to create a Development Office in 1988; two years later the James Madison Council, a private-sector support body, was established.

The Quarterly Journal of the Library of Congress, established in 1943, ceased publication in 1983. In late 1994 a new general interest, commercial publication was launched, entitled *Civilization: The Magazine of the Library of Congress.* Under the leadership of historian Daniel J. Boorstin, who served as librarian of Congress from 1975 to 1987, and historian James H. Billington, who took office in 1987, the library's annual appropriation and the size of its collections have continued to grow. Key acquisitions have included the Alexander Graham Bell papers, the NBC Radio Collection, the Charles and Ray Eames Collection of Design, the George and Ira Gershwin Collection, and the Leonard Bernstein Archives. The Library of Congress collects research materials in 450 languages and in most media. It is the largest library in the world and its collections of more than 110 million items (including 22 million books) fill 530 miles of shelf space. By simultaneously serving government, the public, and scholarship, it occupies a unique place in the culture and civilization of the United States.

BIBLIOGRAPHY

John Y. Cole, *Jefferson's Legacy: A Brief History of the Library of Congress* (Washington, D.C., 1993).

Charles A. Goodrum, *Treasures of the Library of Congress,* rev. ed. (New York, 1991).

Jane Aiken Rosenberg, *The Nation's Great Library: Herbert Putnam and the Library of Congress, 1899–1939* (Urbana, Ill., 1993).

— JOHN Y. COLE

LINCOLN, ASSASSINATION OF

On Apr. 14, 1865, at 10:15 P.M., while attending a performance of "Our American Cousin" at Ford's Theatre in Washington, D.C., President Abraham Lincoln was shot in the back of the head by John Wilkes Booth. As soon as the fatal nature of the wound was apparent, Lincoln was carried to a lodging house opposite the theater. There, without regaining consciousness, he died at 7:22 on the following morning.

Despite the fact that Booth broke his leg in jumping from the presidential box to the stage, he made his way from the theater, and, with David E. Herold, escaped from Washington in the direction of Virginia before midnight. They first went to the house of Dr. Samuel A. Mudd, who set Booth's leg, and then to the Potomac River, where they hid in a pine thicket waiting their chance to cross to Virginia. During their wait, a farmer, Thomas A. Jones, brought them food. All the forces of the government were directed toward his capture, but hysteria, greed for the reward, and incompetence hindered the pursuit to such an extent that it was not until Apr. 26 that Booth and Herold were surrounded in a tobacco shed on the farm belonging to Richard H. Garrett, near Port Royal, Va. There Herold surrendered, but Booth defied his captors and was shot—possibly by Boston Corbett, possibly by his own hand.

Abraham Lincoln, Sixteenth President of the United States. His assassination on April 14, 1865 was a national tragedy that spurred a bitter Reconstruction of the South after the Civil War. (Library of Congress)

Before the death of Booth the government had implicated nine persons in the assassination—George A. Atzerodt, Lewis Payne, Herold, Mary E. Surratt and her son John H. Surratt, Edward Spangler, Samuel Arnold Mudd, Michael O'Laughlin, and Booth. All except John H. Surratt were tried before a military commission, May 9-June 30, 1865. All were found guilty, although the verdict in the case of Mary Surratt was certainly a miscarriage of justice. Atzerodt, Payne, Herold, and Mary Surratt were hanged on July 7. Arnold, Mudd, and O'Laughlin were sentenced to life imprisonment while Spangler was given six years; the four were imprisoned in Fort Jefferson, Dry Tortugas, in the Florida Keys. Jones and Garrett were not indicted. John H. Surratt was brought to trial in 1867, but the jury failed to agree, and his case was later dismissed. By Mar. 4, 1869, President Andrew Johnson had pardoned all the imprisoned men, except for O'Laughlin, who had died in 1867.

The assassination of Lincoln was a national tragedy in the broadest sense. It removed a president who was averse to vindictive measures, and by transforming widespread northern inclination to leniency into a passion for retribution, it gave Reconstruction its popular sanction.

BIBLIOGRAPHY

D. M. DeWitt, *The Assassination of Abraham Lincoln and Its Expiation.*
Otto Eisenschiml, *Why Was Lincoln Murdered.*
Lloyd Lewis, *Myths After Lincoln.*

— PAUL M. ANGLE

LINCOLN-DOUGLAS DEBATES

Lincoln-Douglas debates took place between Republican Abraham Lincoln and the Democratic incumbent, Stephen A. Douglas, during the senatorial campaign in Illinois in 1858. Douglas' opening speeches in his reelection drive, with their effective frontal attack on Lincoln's "house divided" doctrine, alarmed Lincoln's managers and led him to issue a formal challenge to Douglas: "Will it be agreeable to you to make an arrangement for you and myself to divide time, and address the same audiences during the present canvass?" Douglas' speaking dates were already set through October, but he agreed to one debate in each of seven congressional districts.

About 12,000 gathered at Ottawa, Aug. 21, for the first debate, which was preceded and followed by parades and punctuated by shouts and cheers. Douglas was well dressed, with a ruffled shirt, a dark blue coat with shiny buttons, and a wide-brimmed soft hat. Lincoln wore a rusty, high-topped hat, an ill-fitting coat, and baggy trousers so short as to show his rusty boots. Their speaking manners likewise contrasted. Douglas talked fast and steadily, in a heavy voice. He would shake his long, black hair and walk back and forth across the platform with great effectiveness. Lincoln's voice was light, almost nasal, and at the start had an unpleasant timbre, but carried well. Both gave a sense of profound earnestness.

Douglas' theme at Ottawa was the sectional bias, the strife-fomenting nature, of Republican doctrine. He read a series of resolutions he mistakenly believed had been adopted when the party was formed in Illinois in 1854 and pressed Lincoln to deny his endorsement of them. Douglas likewise assailed Lincoln's own position on the slavery issue, and Lincoln seemed troubled by his questions.

Lincoln went to Freeport for the second debate on Aug. 27 determined to impale Douglas on the horns of a dilemma. There he asked the famous Freeport questions, related to the Supreme Court's ruling in the Dred Scott case. Either Douglas must accept the Supreme Court's decision, which would mean that slavery could go anywhere, or he must cease urging the sanctity of Supreme Court decisions. It was not a new issue for Douglas, who was more realist than dialectician. "Slavery cannot exist a day," he answered, "or an hour, anywhere, unless it is supported by local police regulations." This was an effective counter in the debate.

The other debates were hard fought and colorful, but Ottawa and Freeport had set the tone for the rest of them. The third took place on Sept. 15 at Jonesboro, a little town deep in "Egypt," the southernmost region of the state, where neither antagonist had many partisans. At Charleston, three days later, the crowd was fairly evenly divided. Lincoln, smarting under Douglas' charges that he favored equality for blacks, toned down his earlier statements. Thereupon Douglas said his opponent's views were "jet black" in the North, "a decent mulatto" in the center, and "almost white" in Egypt.

On Oct. 7 the fifth debate took place at Galesburg, an abolitionist stronghold. On Oct. 13 the two men grappled at Quincy, and the last debate was two days later at Alton. There Lincoln and Douglas epitomized again their points of view. Lincoln repeated the charge that Douglas looked to "no end of the institution of slavery." But Douglas said: "I care more for the great principle of self-government, the right of the people to rule, than I do for all the Negroes in Christendom. I would not endanger the perpetuity of this Union."

Lincoln lost the election, but the debates brought his name to the attention of people outside Illinois. His defeat cannot necessarily be attributed to the debates, since at that time congressional senators were not elected by popular vote, but by a joint ballot of the state legislatures. Lincoln and Douglas were, therefore, actually campaigning for the election of state legislators from their own parties. There were some Republican victories in the 1858 election, but one-half of the state legislature had been elected in 1856, a year when the Democrats were strongly in power.

BIBLIOGRAPHY

Paul Angle, ed., *Created Equal—The Complete Lincoln-Douglas Debates of 1858.*
Robert W. Johannsen, *Stephen A. Douglas.*
Allan Nevins, *The Emergence of Lincoln.*

— GEORGE FORT MILTON

LINDBERGH KIDNAPPING CASE

On the night of Mar. 1, 1932, the eighteen-month-old son of Col. Charles A. Lindbergh was abducted from his parents' country home near Hopewell, N.J. The kidnapper climbed to the window of the second-story nursery by a ladder brought with him. He left a note demanding $50,000 ransom. After some futile attempts at closer contact with him, John F. Condon, a retired New York teacher, acting as intermediary, succeeded in having two night interviews with the man in a cemetery. On the second occasion, Apr. 8, the money was paid the kidnapper upon his promise to deliver the child—a false promise, as the child had been slain immediately after the abduction. Its body was found on May 12 near the Lindbergh home. The serial number of every note of the ransom money was made public. On Sept. 15, 1934, a carpenter named Bruno Hauptmann passed one of the bills at a New York filling station and was arrested. More than $14,000 of the ransom money was found concealed about his house. At his trial at Flemington, N.J., in January-February 1935 the ladder was identified as having been made with plank taken from his attic. He was convicted, and executed on Apr. 3, 1936.

BIBLIOGRAPHY

Anne Morrow Lindbergh, *Hour of Gold, Hour of Lead.*
Sidney B. Whipple, *The Lindbergh Crime.*

— ALVIN F. HARLOW

LINDBERGH'S ATLANTIC FLIGHT

The first nonstop flight between New York and Paris, and the first one-man crossing of the Atlantic by air, was made by Charles A. Lindbergh, May 20–21, 1927. Previously, several attempts had been made to win the prize of $25,000 offered by Raymond Orteig in 1919 for the first continuous flight between New York and Paris over the Atlantic. In 1926 René Fonck had crashed when taking off from Roosevelt Field, Long Island, N.Y.; two American naval officers had been killed on a trial flight; and two French aviators had been lost over the Atlantic while attempting the difficult east-to-west crossing.

Charles Lindbergh standing in front of the Spirit of St. Louis, *the monoplane with which he completed history's first transatlantic flight, from New York City to Paris, on May 20–21, 1927. His achievement made him a symbol of daring, courage, and international brotherhood. (Corbis-Bettmann)*

Backed by a group of Saint Louis businessmen, Lindbergh supervised the construction of a Ryan monoplane, christened the *Spirit of St. Louis.* It had a wing spread of 46 feet and a chord of 7 feet, weighed 5,135 pounds, and was propelled by a 225-horsepower Wright Whirlwind motor. On the morning of May 20, 1927, taking advantage of an area of high pressure reported over the Atlantic, Lindbergh took off from Roosevelt Field with a load of 425 gallons of gasoline. Encountering fog and sleet, the aviator was compelled to fly blind part of the way at an altitude of 1,500 feet. Later he dropped closer to the water, flying at times ten feet above the waves. Sighting the coast of Ireland, he turned his course toward France. After flying over England, he crossed the English Channel and at ten o'clock in the evening saw the lights of Paris. After circling the Eiffel Tower, he made for the Le Bourget airfield, where he landed, after having flown 3,605 miles in thirty-three hours and thirty minutes.

The reception of the young aviator in the capital of France was enthusiastic and demonstrative. Under the guidance of Myron T. Herrick, the American ambassador at Paris, Lindbergh made a favorable impression on the French public. A round of fetes in his honor failed to mar his attractive modesty, and he became a symbol of daring, courage, and international fraternity. In Brussels, Berlin, and London he was received with equal enthusiasm. He returned to the United States from Cherbourg on the U.S.S. *Memphis*, sent by command of President Calvin Coolidge.

BIBLIOGRAPHY

Charles E. Lindbergh, *The Spirit of St. Louis.*

— KENNETH COLEGROVE

LITERACY TEST

Literacy test has been used by the federal government as an adjunct to its immigration and naturalization laws and by many states as a device to determine qualifications for voting. The federal government's use of the literacy test has not been a matter of major controversy, and the passage of immigration reform legislation in 1965, which abolished the national origins system, removed one of the primary objections raised when the literacy test act was passed in 1917.

As used by the states, the literacy test gained notoriety as a means for denying the franchise to blacks. Adopted by a number of southern states, the literacy test was generally combined with civic understanding tests (usually the interpretation of a portion of a state's constitution), and registration officials often applied it in a discriminatory manner against black potential voters. Effective federal action to counter this discrimination did not occur until the 1960's. In 1964, the Civil Rights Act provided that literacy tests used as a qualification for voting in federal elections be administered wholly in writing and only to persons who had not completed six years of formal education. The 1965 Voting Rights Act suspended the use of literacy tests in all states or political subdivisions in which fewer than 50 percent of the voting-age residents were registered as of Nov. 1, 1964, or had voted in the 1964 presidential election. In a series of cases, the Supreme Court upheld the legislation and restricted the use of literacy tests for non-English-speaking citizens. Under the 1970 extension of the Voting Rights Act, the use of the literacy test was suspended in all states and their political subdivisions until Aug. 6, 1975. The suspension of the literacy test has been accompanied by significant increases in black registration in the seven southern states covered by the 1965 law, and the registration problems faced by non-English-speaking citizens have been eased by subsequent judicial and legislative actions.

— DENNIS IPPOLITO

LITERATURE

If the definition of American literature is confined to belles lettres, literary art in the United States can be said to begin with the random appearance of occasional poetry in the 17th century, broaden into a general acceptance of the patterns of British imaginative writing in the 18th century, and come to fruition only after the Republic was well established. But if American literature includes the literature of knowledge as well as that of power, it begins in the bosom of the Renaissance, speaks maturely from its beginnings, and continues to be full and rich until the present time.

On the first line of development a beginning was made by two minor figures—Anne Bradstreet (*The Tenth Muse Lately Sprung Up in America*, 1650) and Edward Taylor (although his *Poetical Works* were not printed until 1937). The literary magazine was not effectively established until 1741, when Andrew Bradford printed the *American Magazine* and Benjamin Franklin established his *General Magazine and Historical Chronicle*, both emanating from Philadelphia. American fiction begins even later with *The Power of Sympathy*, by William Hill Brown, in 1789 and *Charlotte Temple*, by Susanna Haswell Rowson, in 1791. The great body of imaginative writing in the United States came after the Revolution.

The American mind has its truer beginnings in the great literature of discovery, exploration, and settlement from Richard Hakluyt's *Principal Navigations, Voyages, Traffiques and Discoveries* (1589) onward. A library of narratives by Capt. John Smith, Gov. William Bradford, Gov. John Winthrop, Edward Johnson, Thomas Morton, George Alsop, Mary Rowlandson, and others vigorously describes and thoughtfully interprets the first ventures of the English people into the New World. These books have the vitality of English prose of the 17th century. The writing shares the intellectual excitement of the eras of John Milton and Francis Bacon; it develops theories of history, of salvation, and of the relation of church and state that had a profound influence on American thought. The highest expression of the New England mind came in the next century in the work of Jonathan Edwards: *A Faithful Narrative of the Surprising Work of God* (1737) and *Enquiry Into the Modern Prevailing Notions of Freedom of the Will* (1754). Virginia, which has never lacked a literary culture, neatly counter-pointed the metaphysics of Edwards with the secularity of William Byrd, whose *History of the Dividing Line* (1738, first printed 1841 in *The Westover Manuscripts*) remains a humorous minor masterpiece; whose secret journals, not published until 1941 and 1942, reveal an American Samuel Pepys; and whose career is a blend of the Renaissance and the Enlightenment. Byrd carried his considerable learning lightly, like a flower; Cotton Mather—whose *Magnalia Christi Americana* (1702) ends the New England 17th century and brings the New England mind face to face with the Enlightenment—boasts of erudition. More widely read than any of these, the first American to have worldwide influence was Benjamin Franklin, whose adroit *Autobiography* is a classic of Western literature and whose letters, satires, bagatelles, almanacs, and scientific writings are the work of a citizen of the world.

The intellectual brilliance of American thought between the end of the Seven Years' War (1763) and the creation of the federal government (1789) is among the wonders of the history of ideas. The constitutional issues of the 18th century could not have been more ably debated, as Edmund Burke, William Pitt, and other British statesmen testified. Franklin participated, but so did Samuel Adams, John Adams, Thomas Paine, Thomas Jefferson, and a company of others. Of this group Paine, the propagandist, whose *Common Sense* (1776) and *The Crisis* (1776–83) awakened American enthusiasm, and Jefferson, the principal author of the Declaration of Independence and the author of an unrivaled collection of letters and papers that reveal an encyclopedic mind, are best remembered today. The obsession of modern literary theory with problems of symbolism, depth psychology, and the like has turned attention away from this body of great argument, albeit many are willing to grant with the American historian Carl Becker that Jefferson's prose has a haunting felicity.

The Revolution, the Peace of Paris, and the adoption of the federal Constitution created a drive toward cultural independence. The satires of Philip Freneau, Francis Hopkinson, and John Trumbull are mainly of interest to scholars, but Freneau, in lyric poetry and in an exercise in Gothic romanticism, *The House of Night* (1779), marks the transition from the Enlightenment to romanticism. Trumbull was one of the Connecticut Wits, a group conscientiously endeavoring to create a national literature. The romances of Charles Brockden Brown have more vitality; *Wieland* (1798), *Arthur Mervyn* (1799), and *Edgar Huntley* (1799), compounded of Gothicism, romantic "science," propaganda, realism, and rodomontade, attracted Percy Bysshe Shelley by their power.

Maturer years began with the appearance in literature of three writers associated with New York. William Cullen Bryant—whose "Thanatopsis" (1817) was the product of a wunderkind, and whose philosophical poems, such as "The Prairies," have intellectual dignity—edited the *New York Evening Post* from 1829 to 1878, giving space in its columns to advocates of liberal and radical movements. More popular was Washington Irving, whose *History of New York by Diedrich Knickerbocker* (1809) gave that city a symbolic figure, whose *Sketch Book* (1819–20) created Rip Van Winkle and Ichabod Crane, and whose *Alhambra* (1832), an exercise in the sentimental exotic, scarcely prophesied his *Tour of the Prairies* (1835) and his substantial biographies. The third was James Fenimore Cooper, of worldwide fame, whose Leatherstocking series (*The Pioneers*, 1823; *The Last of the Mohicans*, 1826; *The Prairie*, 1827; *The Pathfinder*, 1840; *The Deerslayer*, 1841) has been called an American prose epic. Cooper's sea novels, of which *The Pilot* (1823) is most often read, were the best in the language before those of Joseph Conrad. Widely misjudged as a critic of American society, Cooper in later books endeavored to stem the tide of Jacksonian Democracy by plumping for a doctrine of *noblesse oblige* among a governing elite.

Of those who sought a cosmopolitan solution to the question of what literary culture should be, the Cambridge poets—James Russell Lowell, Oliver Wendell Holmes, and Henry Wadsworth Longfellow—are characteristic. The most influential was Longfellow, who appealed to religious, patriotic, and cultural desires, in translations (his version of Dante Alighieri, 1865–69, is notable), short lyrics, remarkable sonnets, and narrative poems of special interest to the American of the 19th century—*Evangeline* (1847), *The Song of Hiawatha* (1855), *The Courtship of Miles Standish* (1858), and *Tales of a Wayside Inn* (1863, 1872, 1873). Holmes, in verse and prose, sought to liberate Americans from the tyranny of theology, and Lowell, from cultural provincialism. Associated with this group is the Quaker abolitionist John Greenleaf Whittier, whose *Snow-Bound* (1866) is an unforgettable vignette of rural America.

Moderns find the Concord group—Ralph Waldo Emerson, Henry David Thoreau, Nathaniel Hawthorne, and, a little apart from them, Herman Melville—more exciting. Emerson was, par excellence, the mover and shaker in 19th-century American idealism, with *Nature* (1836), "The American Scholar" (1837), "The Divinity School Address" (1838), and the Essays (1841, 1844). His crisp Yankee accent penetrated where metaphysics could not reach. Industrial society pays more attention to Thoreau, whose *Walden* (1854) is more widely read and whose vigorous essays on what Americans of the late 20th century call civil rights are applicable to present problems. The modern appeal of Hawthorne in such books as *The Scarlet Letter* (1850), *The House of the Seven Gables* (1851), and *The Marble Faun* (1860), as well as in his short stories, was heightened in the 20th century with a spurt of interest in neo-Calvinist theories of human nature. A later, drastic revolution in literary values has placed Melville among the literary giants for much the same reason; and *Mardi* (1849), *Moby-Dick* (1851), *Pierre* (1852), and *Billy Budd* (not available until 1924) are studied for their symbolism of good and evil.

The South and the West had been developing writers of their own, but only one antebellum author rose to the importance of the writers just discussed—Edgar Allan Poe, if he can be called southern. Although the present tendency is to derogate his genius, his influence as critic, short-story writer (*Tales of the Grotesque and Arabesque*, 1840), and poet has been worldwide. The reputations of fictionists John Pendleton Kennedy and William Gilmore Simms are local in comparison, and the West did not speak with unmistakable authority until Mark Twain's *Roughing It* (1872).

The age of radio and television may not believe that oratory was ever a branch of literature, but in the second quarter of the 19th century the speeches of Daniel Webster and of his great rivals John C. Calhoun and Henry Clay approached Roman dignity in discussing the constitutional issues that led to the Civil War. Abolitionism lacked a similar great forum; yet Harriet Beecher Stowe's *Uncle Tom's Cabin* (1852), partisan, sentimental, and melodramatic, went around the world. After a great deal of unsuccessful hack writing, Walt Whitman produced the first version of *Leaves of Grass* (1855), a work he continued to rewrite and expand until 1892. Famous as metrical experimentation, this gospel was part of the 19th-century religion of humanity. In *Calamus* (1860), *Drum Taps* (1865), *Democratic Vistas* (1871), and *Specimen Days and Collect* (1882), Whitman caught the epic quality of the Civil War, as Abraham Lincoln caught its mystic quality in the Gettysburg Address (1863); or denounced political corruption as Mark Twain and Charles Dudley Warner did in the uneven novel they wrote together, *The Gilded Age* (1873), which gave its name to the postwar period.

The Civil War is a historical watershed dividing the culture of agrarian America from that of industrial America. But one of the results of that conflict was curiosity about the far-flung nation; and the increasing effectiveness of literary periodicals, notable in the creation of the *Atlantic Monthly* in 1857, gave rise to a varied literature of local color. The South found comfort in glamorous or sentimental pictures of its antebellum culture, as in George Washington Cable's *Old Creole Days* (1879); Joel Chandler Harris' *Uncle Remus: His Songs and Sayings* (1880), now dismissed as Uncle Tomism but a treasury of folklore; F. Hopkinson Smith's *Colonel Carter of Cartersville* (1891), a sentimental picture of the Confederate colonel; and Thomas Nelson Page's *Red Rock* (1898), an equally sentimental version of life in old Virginia, which the novels of Ellen Glasgow in the 20th century were to correct.

New England salved its hurts during its "decline" in the charming and occasionally powerful genre stories of such writers as Sarah Ome Jewett, Mary Eleanor Wilkins Freeman, and Alice Brown. California produced Bret Harte's *The Luck of Roaring Camp* (1870), and partially through Harte the influence of Charles Dickens was filtered into the school of regional literature. Tennessee was pictured by Mary Nouailles Murfree ("Charles Egbert Craddock"), whose *In the Tennessee Mountains* (1884) preludes the exploitation of the mountaineer as subject, and New York State produced *David Harum* (1898), by Edward N. Westcott. Local color verse by John Hay, Joaquin Miller, Will Carleton, and James Whitcomb Riley, sometimes in dialect, accompanied the vogue.

After the Civil War the vigorous philosophic idealism of Concord deliquesced into the cultural propriety of the genteel tradition. The moderns find it difficult to be fair to the work of this tradition, exemplified by the poetic theories of Edmund Clarence Stedman (*The Nature and Elements of Poetry*, 1892), the aesthetic teachings of Charles Eliot Norton, and the criticism of W. C. Brownell. But the disciplinary quality of genteel criticism (for example, that of Brander Matthews) in curbing the excesses of romantic self-expression was an important contribution; and the postwar years also saw the rise of a mature literature of biography, history, and expository prose. Biography was of moment to the Puritans, but American biography really struck its stride with James Parton's *Life and Times of Benjamin Franklin* (1864) and has continued to produce masterly works ever since. American achievement in historical writing begins early and matures in such books as William Hickling Prescott's *History of the Conquest of Mexico* (1843) and Francis Parkman's distinguished series *France and England in North America* (1851–92)—

these two, together with John Lothrop Motley, being classed as "romantic" historians. The influence of European scholarship is more directly evident after the Civil War in the work of Henry Harrisse, Justin Winsor, James Schouler, John Bach McMaster, and James Ford Rhodes. Stylistic craftsmanship is most evident in the work of Henry Adams, whose *History of the United States During the Administrations of Jefferson and Madison* (1889–91) challenges the literary supremacy of Parkman. All the world knows Adams' *Mont-Saint-Michel and Chartres* (1904) and *The Education of Henry Adams* (1904).

Historians had no monopoly on expository scholarship or propaganda. The *Personal Memoirs* of Ulysses S. Grant (1885) have the clarity and simplicity of Julius Caesar's *De bello Gallico*; Henry George's *Progress and Poverty* (1877–79) and Edward Bellamy's *Looking Backward* (1888) were as influential in their way as Paine's books had been in theirs; and a varied literature of science, philosophy, and theology developed as the country discovered Charles Darwin. Andrew Dickson White's powerful, if uneven, *History of the Warfare of Science With Theology in Christendom* (1896) is perhaps the single best monument of this debate, although writers as excellent as Asa Gray, John Fiske, and Josiah Royce participated. All this is the background for William James's classic *Principles of Psychology* (1890), the prelude to pragmatism; *The Will to Believe and Other Essays* appeared in 1897.

American fiction came of age in the late 19th century, however great the contributions of Hawthorne's generation. In *The Adventures of Huckleberry Finn* (1884), Mark Twain created a classic work; and if his collected writings are uneven, he moved steadily from the "oral" manner of *The Innocents Abroad* (1869) to the Voltairean irony of *The Mysterious Stranger* (1916) as hilarity gave way to pessimism. But the gathering forces of realism—evident, for example, in the work of John William De Forest and Albion W. Tourgée—found their spokesman in William Dean Howells. His *Criticism and Fiction* (1891) summed up realistic, but not naturalistic, theory; in *A Modern Instance* (1881), *The Rise of Silas Lapham* (1884), and *A Hazard of New Fortunes* (1890), he showed that the business of literature was with the here and now, not with trumpet-and-drum romances and sentimental tales. Beneath the serene surface of his prose there is a sardonic feeling, an ironic vision. Realists and naturalists (none of them consistent) were grouped around him—Hamlin Garland, Stephen Crane, Frank Norris, and others; and out of the excitement emerged the slow, awkward genius of Theodore Dreiser, whose *Sister Carrie* (1900) marks the transition in fiction between the realism of the 19th century and that of the 20th.

While realists and sentimentalists and naturalists and idealists argued, Henry James, self-exiled, opened the modern manner in fiction by concentrating on the subjective world. His progress from *The American* (1877) through *The Portrait of a Lady* (1881) to *The Wings of the Dove* (1902), *The Golden Bowl* (1904), and *The Sense of the Past* (1917) is for admirers a march toward subtlety of insight and of craftsmanship. For others he becomes so difficult that the game is not worth the candle. He was a theorist of literary art (for example, *Notes on Novelists*, 1914); and his example has profoundly influenced contemporaries and successors of the rank of Edith Wharton (*The House of Mirth*, 1905), Willa Cather (*A Lost Lady*, 1923), and Ellen Glasgow (*The Sheltered Life*, 1932). Indeed, the way leads from Henry James through William James to the stylistic experimentation of Gertrude Stein.

The end of the 19th century and the opening of the 20th saw a pause in the rhythm of American literature, as if the country awaited the coming of World War I and, so far as writing is concerned, the scarcely less powerful impact of Sigmund Freud and his successors on the literary imagination. Poetry seemed to recapture the great audiences it had lost since Longfellow, when Vachel Lindsay, Edgar Lee Masters, Edwin Arlington Robinson, Carl Sandburg, and Robert Frost achieved vast reading publics. But foreign influences from France and Italy and the impact of the war, summed up in T. S. Eliot's *The Waste Land* (1922) and in the energetic propaganda of Ezra Pound, diverted poetry into the more difficult styles of Conrad Aiken, Wallace Stevens, Hart Crane, and Marianne Moore.

Reacting against the canons of the 19th century, critical theory, whether it concerned literature or culture, took on new importance about 1910. Preluded by Joel Spingarn, Randolph Bourne, John Macy, and their elder fellow, George Santayana, critics turned to a reexamination of the American present and a reevaluation of the American past. Van Wyck Brooks, in *America's Coming of Age* (1915), campaigned for a "usable past," which he created in later volumes; H. L. Mencken demanded "sophistication" in various books of *Prejudices* (1919–27); and Walter Lippmann in *A Preface to Morals* (1929) and Joseph Wood Krutch in *The Modern Temper* (1929) declined to accept traditional canons of the dignity of man. In vain the neohumanists—Irving Babbitt, Paul Elmer More, Stuart P. Sherman, and others—asserted that long-run sagacity lay with tradition. The distinguished prose of Lewis Mumford, in such books as *Sticks and Stones* (1924) and *The Brown Decades* (1931), demonstrated that the modern spirit was not identical with iconoclasm.

In retrospect the 1920's resemble the 1850's—a great creative decade beginning with the smashing success of Sinclair Lewis' *Main Street* (1920) and closing with the troubled rhetoric of Thomas Wolfe's *Look Homeward, Angel* (1929), a singular specimen of the confessional literature associated with the European romantics. A brilliant ten years included F. Scott Fitzgerald's *The Great Gatsby* (1925) and the works of Ernest Hemingway; James Boyd's *Drums* (1925), which was a historical novel; and a spate of "sophisticated" writers, including James Branch Cabell, Joseph Hergesheimer, and Carl Van Vechten. Cabell's *Beyond Life* (1919) set forth a theory of sophistication that governed the whole movement of literary smartness. Possibly the soundest products of the self-conscious school were Thornton Wilder's philosophical contes, such as *The Bridge of San Luis Rey* (1927).

The cry was for "freedom," although no one quite knew what kind of freedom was meant; and the angry thirties, as they have been called, took revenge by nourishing proletarian fiction that included the *Studs Lonigan* trilogy (1932–35) of James T. Farrell, the three-volume national canvas of John Dos Passos' *U.S.A.* (1937), and the struggles of "the little man" in John Steinbeck's *In Dubious Battle* (1936) and *The Grapes of Wrath* (1939). The neonaturalistic novel also emphasized environment as the shaper of lives, especially in the social protest of Nelson Algren and the exposés of the black's plight in the work of Richard Wright, Erskine Caldwell, and Lillian Smith. The emerging genius of the 1930's was William Faulkner, an experimentalist in fictional forms who used his native Mississippi, as James Joyce had used Dublin, for a background to his criticism of the hollowness of modern society. A somber view of human failure and of race relations, *The Sound and the Fury* (1929), was followed, but not superseded in brilliance, by *Light in August* (1932), *Absalom, Absalom!* (1936), and twelve other novels. It more and more appeared that America was not promises; and foreign reporting of unexampled penetration by John Gunther, Edgar Snow, Vincent Sheean, and others not only pictured the death of Europe but also prepared Americans for a second world war. The spate of novels concerning World War I—John Dos Passos' *Three Soldiers* (1921), E. E. Cummings' *The Enormous Room* (1922), and Hemingway's *The Sun Also Rises* (1926) and *A Farewell to Arms* (1929) are examples—were at once the result of shock and of a return to European literary techniques. The novels of World War II lacked the shock techniques, but were frequently disturbing indictments and even previsions of future problems, notably James Gould Cozzens' *Guard of Honor* (1948), Norman Mailer's massive *The Naked and the Dead* (1948), and Joseph Heller's surreal *Catch-22* (1961).

The first three decades after World War II saw powerful pressures on the literary arts. The apocalyptic vision of total destruction in John Hersey's report *Hiroshima* (1946) not only heralded the postwar era's chief concern—survival—but also illustrated the difficulty creative writers experienced in matching the vitality and the violence in the world around them. As the American dream turned into a nightmare, the novelist and the poet have had to compete with an increasing public interest in theology and philosophy, history and sociology, and the phenomenon known as "the new journalism." David Riesman's study of human behavior, *The Lonely Crowd* (1950); Paul Tillich's argument for religious existentialism, *The Courage To Be* (1952); Erik H. Erikson's *Childhood and Society* (1950); the historical studies of C. Vann Woodward; the psychoanalytic critiques of Norman O. Brown; and revivals of Oriental mysticism have had wide currency. Even more popular are the essays of certain journalists who combine autobiography with polemic, historical facts with anecdote: such black writers as James Baldwin and Eldridge Cleaver; such novelists turned journalists as Mailer, Truman Capote, Wright Morris, and Gore Vidal; and such cultural observers as Tom Wolfe and John Cage—all of whom have reached an audience that might have chosen fiction over nonfiction in the decades before the war.

But to say that the traditional genres—fiction, poetry, and drama—have diminished beyond expectation since midcentury will not do. Philip Roth, author of the popular *Goodbye, Columbus* (1959), believes the postwar novelist "has his hands full in trying to understand, and then describe, and then make *credible* much of the American reality," but attempt it the novelist does in various guises. The hero is frequently an antihero, a rebel-victim, an outsider; yet he is not without vitality and diversity. Deriving from the works of Nathanael West and Henry Roth in the 1930's, the contemporary Jewish novel flourishes in the fiction of Saul Bellow, Bernard Malamud, and J. D. Salinger. The southern novel retains older traditions and more diverse talents, notably Eudora Welty, Carson McCullers, and Flannery O'Connor. Many novelists have recorded the black experience in America, but none more graphically than Ralph Ellison in his only novel, *Invisible Man* (1952). The fantasists express their subjectivism in satire, parody, and absurdist humor (John Barth, Donald Barthelme, John Hawkes, Thomas Pynchon) or in the prophetic visions of science fiction (Ray Bradbury, Robert A. Heinlein, Isaac Asimov). Virtuoso novelists who are difficult to classify—Vladimir Nabokov (*Lolita*, 1955) and John Updike (*Rabbit Redux*, 1971)—keep the genre alive by sheer linguistic agility.

The postwar poets have had a more difficult time. The Pound-Eliot tradition is waning as the reputations of Wallace Stevens and William Carlos Williams rise. The younger poets have had to begin afresh, seeking their own private faiths, and have focused on individualized and subjective experience. Chief among them is Robert Lowell, who admitted in 1961 that it was "hard to think of a young poet who has the validity of Salinger or Saul Bellow," but ten years later found himself with an international reputation, while Salinger was strangely silent. Lowell's early Catholic visions in clotted, elliptical verse forms gave way to intensely personal confessions (*Life Studies*, 1959) and public utterances on civil issues (*For the Union Dead*, 1964; *Notebook, 1967–1968*, 1969) that mark a major talent, a poet who has found his right métier. Had they lived past middle age, Theodore Roethke, a romantic lyricist and mystic; John Berryman, a learned, idiosyncratic original, the inventor of "dream songs"; and Randall Jarrell, the witty poet-critic-teacher, might have achieved Lowell's eminence. Had they not dissolved almost as quickly as they assembled, several groups of poets—namely, the Black Mountain poets (Charles Olson, Robert Creeley), the beat generation (Allen Ginsberg, Gregory Corso), the San Francisco group (Lawrence Ferlinghetti, Gary Snyder), the New York school (John Ashbery, Frank O'Hara, Kenneth Koch)—might have left a deeper impress upon American literary history.

The impress made by contemporary playwrights is probably even slighter, and Eugene O'Neill continues to be the leading dramatist of this century. Except for the meteoric careers of Arthur Miller and Tennessee Williams during the later 1940's and 1950's and the brief promise of Edward Albee in the 1960's, American writing for the theater declined, partly because of the high cost of producing plays, partly because of the competition of television.

Literary criticism seems also to have weakened. The death of Edmund Wilson in 1972 (*Axel's Castle*, 1931; *To the Finland Station*, 1940; *Memoirs of Hecate County*, 1946) removed from the scene America's one unquestioned man of letters, albeit Alfred Kazin (*On Native Grounds*, 1942; *The Inmost Leaf*, 1955) and Lionel Trilling (d. 1976) (*The Liberal Imagination*, 1950; *Beyond Culture*, 1965) maintain an intellectual tradition. Writers such as Leslie Fiedler and Richard Poirer breathe life into literary polemics, and E. B. White has kept the essay form alive. But belles lettres no longer hold the position of eminence they held in the 19th century.

BIBLIOGRAPHY

Jacob Blanck, *Bibliography of American Literature.*

James D. Hart, *The Oxford Companion to American Literature.*

Howard Mumford Jones and Richard M. Ludwig, *Guide to American Literature and Its Backgrounds.*

Robert E. Spiller, Willard Thorp, Thomas H. Johnson, Henry Seidel Canby, Richard M. Ludwig, and William M. Gibson, eds., *Literary History of the United States.*

William Peterfield Trent, John Erskine, Stuart P. Sherman, and Carl Van Doren, eds., *The Cambridge History of American Literature.*

Moses Coit Tyler, *A History of American Literature, 1607–1765*, and *The Literary History of the American Revolution.*

— HOWARD MUMFORD JONES

LITERATURE SINCE 1970

American literature, the thousands of books of poetry, fiction, and criticism that appear annually, has varied remarkably in subject and method since 1970. The decline of critical consensus about national identity and the powerful intrusion of contemporary life on the artistic consciousness have produced a multicultural literature. Since the end of the Vietnam War in 1973, violence, drug addiction, and despair have become prosaic themes in serious and popular fiction. Inspired by the civil rights and women's movements of the 1960s, the rise of ethnic nationalism in the 1970s, and the emergence of gays and lesbians in the 1980s, authors have redefined the American tradition. Publishers have promoted these new themes. Well-known publishers were the surest vehicles for success, as judged by sales and critical attention. In popular literature, espionage writer Tom Clancy, suspense novelist Lawrence Sanders, and romance novelist Danielle Steel produced frequent best-sellers, augmented by lucrative subsidiary profits for television, cinema, and accessory rights. Perhaps the most financially successful author is horror writer Stephen King. Beginning with *Carrie* (1975) and *The Stand* (1978), through twenty more novels, short-story collections, and screenplays, King racked up unprecedented sales and a $50 million five-book contract. Meanwhile, the rise of such mass-market bookstore chains as B. Dalton, Barnes and Noble, Borders, and Crown greatly affected print runs.

Allen Ginsberg, whose poetry thrilled and scandalized the nation in the 1950's, won popular admiration through his combination of a Whitmanesque vision with antiwar and gay politics.

Huge profits for publishers also came from anonymous authors of romance novels, which in the 1990s accounted for approximately 40 percent of all book sales. A highly traditional genre, Harlequins, present social issues to vie with matters of the heart. Romances are also age-specific. Teen romances include historical novels with characters from several racial and ethnic groups. Other innovations since the 1980s are the Odyssey line, which focuses on African-American characters, and Naiad Press, which specializes in lesbian writings. Another popular genre was the crime novel. Writers depicting society's violent confrontations with psychopathic criminals have included Elmore Leonard, who presents the fierce and ugly vernacular of policemen and drug dealers in Miami and Detroit; James Ellroy, who offers violent, historical panoramas of Los Angeles; and Walter Mosley, who revived Chester Himes's tradition of folksy, black detectives. Prolific science-fiction writers like Ursula Le Guin and Samuel Delany introduced contemporary gender politics into the fiction of the future. Small presses published authors of innovative works and emerging ethnic and sexual genres. Vastly divergent in politics, quality of production, and aesthetics, small publishers benefited from such technological advances as desktop publishing and electronic dissemination of texts.

Another novelty was the professionalization of writers in the late 1970s. Universities began to offer graduate degrees in the writing of fiction and poetry. Scholarly attention to contemporary literature made an academic imprimatur helpful for the life of a book and the career of its author. To some critics, highly academic poetry and fiction became so overtheorized as to lose touch with ordinary readers. In response, critics divided literary audiences between "real" consumers of serious literature and "pseudo-literates" who read only popular writing.

For a few writers, primarily male, the late twentieth century marked the culmination of their careers. Saul Bellow received the Nobel Prize for Literature in 1976 after publication of *Humboldt's Gift* (1975). John Updike completed his series about Rabbit Angstrom, a small-town car salesman. Norman Mailer, enfant terrible of the 1950s, capped his career with the award-winning *The Executioner's Song* (1979), then experimented with crime novels, historical novels about Egypt, and filmmaking. Philip Roth used satire on Jewish-American culture to comment on the larger society. Kurt Vonnegut's satires on modern life became staples of every college dormitory.

Authors once considered radical were accepted into the canon. Jack Kerouac's *On the Road* (1957), dismissed as trivial after publication, became a greatly loved rite of passage. Allen Ginsberg, whose poetry scandalized Dwight D. Eisenhower's America in the 1950s, combined a Whitmanesque vision with antiwar and gay politics to gain popular adulation. William S. Burroughs, whose novel *Naked Lunch* (1959) was banned as pornographic, was elected to the American Society of Arts and Letters and his writings were regularly reviewed in the *New York Times.*

Women expanded their presence among novelists, poets, essayists, and literary critics. Cynthia Ozick, novelist and short-story writer, chronicled Jewish ethical questions. Joyce Carol Oates, a prodigious author working in genres from poetry to boxing criticism, published more than seventy-five books, including nineteen novels; Oates identified with feminism and regarded the artist as socially committed and influential. Susan Sontag became a deeply influential critic, novelist, playwright, essayist, and ethical presence.

Minimalism appeared as a radical alternative in the early 1980s and became widely accepted. Known as "Kmart realists," minimalists shared a common, populist concern with the silenced majority of America whose lives were burdened by poverty, drug and alcohol dependency, and a malaise that crossed the boundaries of class. Using slight plots and local vernacular, minimalists Raymond Carver, Ann Beattie, Marilyn Robinson, and Richard Ford probed the scattered lives of divergent Americans, from trailer-park residents to disaffected New York intellectuals. They differed sharply from social realists of previous decades by eschewing social solutions.

Another alternative to traditional narrative was magical realism. Latin American writers Gabriel García Márquez, Carlos Fuentes, Manuel Puig, and Isabel Allende and Russian philosopher Mikhail Bakhtin influenced a wide spectrum of American writers known as postmodernists. Avoiding traditional narrative, consensus politics, and modernity, these writers mix time, labyrinthine plots, and stereotypical characters to induce a radical instability in their fiction: vulgarisms are appended to classical references; quotations allude to consumer products, minor news stories, and television programs; and lists catalog arcane scientific information. These methods are evident in Thomas Pynchon's *Gravity's Rainbow* (1973) and *Vineland* (1990), Robert Coover's *The Public Burning* (1977), and Don DeLillo's *Ratner's Star* (1976). The postmodern approach abetted by the new critical method of deconstructionism destabilized traditional ideas of culture. Such right-wing political critics as William Bennett, Hilton Kramer, and Allan Bloom contended that literature was being diminished by neglect of "established masterpieces."

The postmodernist approach deeply affected literary performance. In the early 1980s the Conversations with Writers series in New York City offered racially integrated poetry and fiction readings combined with music performances. Later in the decade the Nuyorican Cafe virtually reinvented the art of poetry and dramatic readings, using oral contests known as "slams" to attract audiences. Performance art, combining autobiography, poetry, and drama, was the most radical device. Karen Finley's scatological reminiscences of her parents performed at Public School 122, a forum for performance poetry, in New York City in the mid-1980s raised the ire of some critics. Undaunted, Finley became a cause célèbre and appeared at Lincoln Center.

The postmodern approach to literary interpretation, abetted by the critical method of deconstruction, destabilized traditional ideas of culture and meaning.

Writers bounded by race and gender are more receptive to postmodernism and magic realism. Throughout the twentieth century black writers such as Richard Wright, Ralph Ellison, Gwendolyn Brooks, and James Baldwin received recognition. Conservative and racially exclusive critics scorned black writers as overly political or aesthetically inadequate. Black male writers made two interlocking responses. Amiri Baraka (LeRoi Jones) in poetry, drama, autobiography, and political pamphlets fused black nationalism and left-wing politics. Never shy about the use of popular genres, Baraka organized street theater and sung poetry with rhythm-and-blues bands. The postmodernist novels of Ishmael Reed were another response. As much as Pynchon and Coover, Reed's novels, plays, and poetry regard American life as a conspiracy, managed by technological control over race mixed with puritanical sexual oppression. One of his projects created a huge multicultural booking agency, another a literary magazine crossing ethnic boundaries.

Female writers also became better recognized in the 1980s and 1990s. Using multiple postmodern styles, employing structural principles from jazz and gospel, and fusing myth with realistic drama, the work of Toni Morrison is especially noteworthy, and in 1993 Morrison received the Nobel Prize. Alice Walker's epistolary novel *The Color Purple* (1982) became required reading and an award-winning movie. Maya Angelou, poet and autobiographer, read at President Bill Clinton's inaugural in 1993; her books of poetry spent three consecutive years on best-seller lists. Audre Lorde gained acclaim for her poetry and lesbian activism. Jayne Cortez's powerful synthesis of Third World and African-American mythologies, revolutionary ideologies, and popular music created a bridge between older radicals and younger rap poets.

Black writers revived the tradition of the public intellectual. Critics and essayists such as Henry Louis Gates, Jr., Cornel West, bell hooks, Manning Marable, and Stanley Crouch insisted on consideration of race as a necessity for understanding American society. There was little unanimity among these writers; indeed, the late 1980s also saw the emergence of conservative black writers, such as Shelby Steele, Thomas Sowell, and Glenn Loury.

Inspired by the struggles of farmworkers led by Cesar Chavez and the Teatro Campesino, which used political theater to raise money for the struggle, Latino writers in California viewed literature as an instrument of social activism. Beat poet Allen Ginsberg enhanced the mainstream popularity of Latino writing. Infused by the rhythm and energies of Latino literature, poets created a virtual oral harmony with their audiences. In the 1970s Latino publishing houses sprouted throughout California. In southern California, nurtured by cultural centers at colleges and universities and inspired by the poet Alurista's recreation of the myth of Aztlán, writers promoted bilingualism, homage to the barrio, brotherhood, and commitment to bettering the conditions of the people. On the East Coast, Puerto Rican writer Piri Thomas (*Down These Mean Streets*, 1967) and Nicholasa Mohr (*Nilda*, 1973) marked the resurgence of Latino writers. This writing also was political and bilingual, directed toward elimination of the colonial status of Puerto Rican society and language. It was enhanced by Latin American writers from many countries who clustered around the Institute of Latin American Writers in New York City. Influenced by the feminist movement of the 1970s and intent upon challenging the powerful male bias of their culture, Latina writers in the early 1980s introduced themes of intracultural resistance. Small presses issued direct challenges in multicultural anthologies. First was the 1978 anthology *Ordinary Women*, edited by Sara Miles et al., followed in 1981 by *This Bridge Called My Back: Writings by Radical Women of Color*, edited by Cherrie Moraga and Gloria Anzaldua, and *Chicana Lesbians: The Girls Our Mothers Warned Us About* (1991), edited by Carla Mari Trujillo.

Asian-American literature has seen the commercial success of such works as Maxine Hong Kingston's *The Woman Warrior* (1976), Amy Tan's *The Joy Luck Club* (1989) and *The Kitchen God's Wife* (1991), and David Henry Hwang's *M. Butterfly* (1988). Their ascendancy sparked controversy among Asian-American writers about the goals of literature. Frank Chin's introduction to the 1974 collection *Aiiieeeee: An Anthology of Asian-*

American Writers, argued that a true Asian-American literature was non-Christian, nonfeminine, nonimmigrant, and limited to three subgroups—Chinese, Japanese, and Filipino—each with its own ethos. Critics argued over distinctions between "real" and "fake" Asian-American literature, an approach taken in J. Chan's *The Big Aiiieeeee! An Anthology of Chinese American and Japanese American Literature* (1991). Countering this practice were anthologies, particularly by women, that broadened the definition of "Asian American" and avoided groupings. Examples include Shirley Lim et al., eds., *The Forbidden Stitch: An Asian American Women's Anthology* (1989); Sylvia Watanabe and Carol Bruchac, eds., *Home to Stay: Asian American Women's Fiction* (1990), which included first-generation Korean and Asian-Indian writers; and the Asian Women United of California's 1989 collection *Making Waves*, with selections by Vietnamese women. Language was ideological with one critic, Elaine Kim, who insisted that the meaning of Asian-American literature called for expressions in English by Asian Americans. As the critic Sau-ling Cynthia Wong argued, this choice between tracing Asian roots and demonstrating the American historical experience may have stemmed partly from the recent arrival of many Asians in America and from the white society's racial perception of Asians as exotics. Wong contended that Asian-American critics should avoid discussion of the exotic.

Native American authors are part of a large world of alternative voices often printed by small presses. Louise Erdrich's novels *Love Medicine* (1984) and *The Beet Queen* (1986), James Welch's *Winter in the Blood* (1974) and *The Death of Jim Loney* (1979), and the works of Leslie Silko and N. Scott Momaday received national recognition and distribution. Together with the poets Simon Ortiz and Joy Harjo and the anthologist Joseph Bruchac, they focused on recreating, within discrete Native American experiences, the non-Western, nonempirical traditions of native cultures while presenting the harsh, often dismal reality of reservation life.

Postmodernism brought a reevaluation of gender in literature. Lesbian writers flourished. In the early l970s lesbian novels created three prominent and pervasive lesbian myths: the self, the couple, and the nation. Best known was Rita Mae Brown's *Rubyfruit Jungle* (1973), which emphasized the quest for a lesbian self and concluded by creating a lesbian hero. Much lesbian writing of the l970s was explicitly political, centering on self-discovery, but culturally narrow. This changed in 1981 after publication of *This Bridge Called My Back*, which decried racism in the lesbian community and introduced talented new writers for whom race was as central to their identity as was sexuality. Political controversies over sexual issues dominated lesbian writing in the 1980s, particularly over AIDS, pornography, sadomasochism, and separatism from men. Judith Barrington's 1991 anthology *An Intimate Wilderness: Lesbian Writers on Sexuality* celebrated the breadth of lesbian sensuality. Lesbian consciousness also entered other genres, including ethnic literature, nature writing, and health literature. By the late 1980s lesbian literature blossomed in a torrent of books and independent publishers issuing lesbian mysteries, humor books, self-help manuals, and voluminous autobiographical works.

Gay men moved beyond the realism of despair epitomized by John Rechy's *City of Night* (1963), and gay novelists sought to create a self-identity. The experience of coming out, or identifying oneself as gay, was the concern of Edmund White's *A Boy's Own Story* (1982), John Fox's *The Boys on the Rock* (1984), and David Leavitt's *The Lost Language of Cranes* (1986). Gay dramatists became highly prominent in what was sometimes called "queer theater." The Ridiculous Theater Company of the late 1960s produced three important gay playwrights: Ronald Tavel, who used comedy to satirize sexual role-playing; Charles Ludlam, who used transvestites and multiple sexual puns to parody mainstream drama; and Kenneth Bernard, whose theater of cruelty makes desire a universal tragedy. Gay drama received an enormous boost in 1978–1979, when Harvey Fierstein's *Torch Song Trilogy* had a lengthy run on Broadway. The AIDS epidemic became a powerful metaphor for gay essayists and dramatists. Paul Monette chronicled the advance of the disease in *Borrowed Time: An AIDS Memoir* (1988), *Afterlife* (1990), and *Becoming a Man: Half a Life Story* (1992). The activist and playwright Larry Kramer shocked Broadway with *The Lonely Heart* in 1985. Tony Kushner received a Pulitzer Prize in 1993 for his meditation on AIDS, *Angels in America* (1992).

Dual approaches of narrative and postmodernism coexisted uneasily in American literature of the 1990s. The most commercially successful writers adhered to traditional story-telling, but multicultural literature, abetted by technological advances and tight-knit organizations, survived within niche markets. African Americans seemed to have bridged this gap with an audience that was both ethnic and national.

BIBLIOGRAPHY

Judith Barrington, ed., *An Intimate Wilderness: Lesbian Writers on Sexuality* (Portland, Oreg., 1991).

Cathy Davidson et al., eds., *The Oxford Companion to Women's Writing in the United States* (New York, 1995).

Emory Elliott and Cathy Davidson, eds., *The Columbia History of the American Novel* (New York, 1991).

Roberta Fernandez and Jean Franco, eds., *In Other Words: Literature by Latinas of the United States* (Houston, Tex., 1994).
Sau-ling Cynthia Wong, *Reading Asian American Literature* (Princeton, N.J., 1993).
Bonnie Zimmerman, *The Safe Sea of Women: Lesbian Fiction, 1969–1989* (Boston, 1990).

— GRAHAM RUSSELL HODGES

LOBBIES

Lobbies, groups of individuals acting for themselves or others who seek to influence the decisions of government officials primarily by informal off-the-record communications and exchanges. Their tactics range from such high-pressure techniques as bribery, threats of electoral retaliation, and mass mailings to such low-pressure methods as supplying research and information in support of their views. Intermediate forms of influence include campaign contributions and persuasion.

The objects and tactics of lobbying have shifted sharply in American history. In the 19th and early 20th centuries the typical lobbyist focused on the legislative arena and used high-pressure methods, including bribery, to influence legislators. By the 1950's many lobbyists had enlarged their focus to include the executive branch and shifted to soft-sell tactics. This shift in technique was a response to exposure of lobbying scandals at both state and national levels.

Congress began investigating lobbies in 1913 with a study of the National Association of Manufacturers (NAM). Since that time there has been at least one major investigation in every decade. The investigations were followed first by piecemeal legislation and then, in Title III of the Legislative Reorganization Act of 1946, by general legislation to regulate lobbies. These acts and subsequent legislation aim at control primarily through publicity, but many loopholes remain that permit lobbies such as the NAM and Washington, D.C., law firms to avoid registration and others to avoid full disclosure of their activities. While not eliminating lobbies, the investigations and legislation have encouraged lobbies to seek a lower profile by moving away from high-pressure methods.

Since Congress began scrutinizing lobbies in 1913, there has been at least one major investigation in every decade.

With the rise of the executive branch as initiator of legislation and the growth of the administrative bureaucracy, the focus of lobbyists began to shift from legislative bodies to executive offices. As a corollary, the growing proportion of lobbying that occurs outside the legislative limelight reduces its overall visibility. Increasingly, chief executives and bureaucratic agencies lobby for legislative passage of bills they have initiated. They often appear to be the sole influence on legislation, even though it is not uncommon for regulatory agencies to be lobbying in the interests of the clientele they are supposed to be regulating. These changes have led critical observers to question the validity of distinguishing between private and public lobbies.

In the 1970's most lobbyists were still acting for associations with an economic interest—business, farm, labor, and the professions. Over half of all registered lobbyists in Washington, D.C., are specialized business associations such as the American Petroleum Institute and Aerospace Industries Association. Although multi-interest peak associations such as the AFL-CIO, the Farm Bureau Federation, and the NAM continue to lobby on a variety of congressional issues, critics of lobbying have moved on to new targets—for example, the "military-industrial complex" and the impact of corporate campaign contributions on executive policymaking. In addition to primarily economic lobbies, the 20th century has seen major lobbying efforts by prohibition groups like the Anti-Saloon League, civil rights groups like the National Association for the Advancement of Colored People (NAACP), reform groups like Common Cause, and peace groups like the National Peace Action Committee.

BIBLIOGRAPHY

Grant McConnell, *Private Power and American Democracy.*
Lester Milbrath, *The Washington Lobbyists.*
Karl Schriftgiesser, *The Lobbyists.*

— EDWARD S. MALECKI

LOCAL GOVERNMENT

Local government is the designation given to all units of government in the United States below the state level. The number of such units is constantly changing, but the most reliable enumeration is that contained in the census of governments conducted every five years by the U.S. Bureau of the Census. The 1967 tabulation was as follows:

Unit	*Number*
Counties	3,049
Municipalities	18,048
Townships	17,105
School districts	21,782
Special districts	21,264
Total	81,248

In the original colonial settlements on the Atlantic coast, towns and counties played the most significant local governmental role. In New England the town was of central importance; but as one looked farther south, counties became increasingly important, and they formed the dominant pattern in the South. Local patterns were carried west by migrants, with few modifications. Increasing urbanization in the 19th century shifted the emphasis gradually from counties and towns to municipalities. By the mid-20th century, 70 percent of the population lived in incorporated urban places and received local government services through them to a much greater degree than through counties, towns, and townships.

The functions of local government have remained relatively constant throughout American history, even though the responsible local unit often has changed with increasing urbanization. These functions include law enforcement, fire protection, welfare, public health, public schools, construction and maintenance of roads, election administration, and assessment and collection of the property tax. Although local governments continue to perform these functions, increased federal and state activity in these areas has altered the political environment significantly.

The New England town that developed in the colonial period as a small unit devoted to direct democracy continues to be an important general purpose unit of government in rural New England. Increased population and governmental complexity have forced many towns to abandon direct democracy in favor of representative government, but the primary functions remain unaltered except in heavily urbanized areas in which municipalities have replaced towns as the prime general purpose unit.

In other regions the county has followed much the same pattern as the New England town—maintaining its significance as a general purpose government primarily in rural areas. But even in highly urbanized areas, the county frequently plays an important role in welfare, public health, tax assessment and collection, and election administration. Furthermore, as urban problems have outgrown the boundaries of municipal governments, more and more urban counties have begun to assume major general governmental responsibilities. The structures that counties utilize to perform these functions appear almost infinitely variable from state to state and frequently within states. The most common structural problem has been the absence of a single executive officer to administer the unit. A few counties have elected chief executives, and an increasing number have hired managers; the vast majority of counties have no executive leadership.

City governments in the United States initially followed the English model, with a mayor and a council. In the late 18th and early 19th centuries, fear of strong executives and a desire to copy the U.S. Constitution led to institutionally weak mayors and to bicameral councils. The bicameral council proved unworkable and was gradually abandoned. The weakness of the mayor and the corruption of political machines led to other reforms in city government, but these reforms were adopted unevenly across the country. Most major cities did provide for some strengthening of the office of mayor in the late 19th and early 20th centuries. The move to short ballots and nonpartisanship was more pronounced in middle-sized cities than in large, metropolitan centers. Other reforms of city government were attempted as well. In the first half of the 20th century several hundred cities experimented with a commission structure in which legislative and executive functions were combined in one body. This experiment proved to be unsatisfactory in all but a few communities, and only 111 cities still use this form of government.

Council-manager government has been much more popular, particularly in those medium-sized cities that are relatively homogeneous socially and economically. This type of structure began in Staunton, Va., in 1908 and spread rapidly, until by 1975 nearly one-half of all cities used it. Its major feature is a strong, centralized, professional executive branch under a city manager who is hired by the city council. Council-manager government has less of an impact in large, complex cities in which at-large, nonpartisan elections and an appointed chief executive are unpopular and in very small cities that are unable to afford the services of a professional manager and staff.

Widespread consolidations have reduced drastically the number of school districts in the United States. In the 1930's the U.S. Census Bureau reported over 128,000 such governmental units. By 1967, the number had been reduced by 100,000. Some school systems are administered by counties, towns, or municipalities, but most have separate governmental structures designed to insulate them from the normal political arena and to provide them with a separate tax base. Traditionally these districts are operated by elected boards of education that hire a professional superintendent as administrator.

Other special districts have proliferated, particularly in the mid-20th century. The majority of these local governments are established to provide a single service or to perform a single function. The functions include fire protection, water, sewerage, mosquito abatement, parks and recreation, airports, and a variety of other activities. In a few instances, special districts have been created for multiple purposes such as water and sewerage, but all are limited in scope. The governing boards of special districts are often appointed rather than elected, and this gives rise to some concern over the degree of popular control possible in these governments. Two major reasons exist for the rapid growth of special districts. First, many potential service areas do not coincide with the boundaries of existing local governments, and special districts can be created to fit these service areas. Second, many local governments have exhausted the taxing and bonding authority granted to them by the state legislatures, and each special district can begin with a new grant of authority to tax and to borrow.

As the density of population in urban areas increased, particularly in the 20th century, local governments increased as well and began to overlap both functionally and geographically. This led reformers to suggest a rationalization of governmental structures, particularly in metropolitan areas. The most far-reaching of these suggestions would have merged counties and cities into a single unit of metropolitan government. This suggestion was followed with some modification in Nashville, Tenn.; Jacksonville, Fla.; and Indianapolis, Ind. Other reform efforts attempted to reallocate local governmental functions among counties and municipalities on an areawide rather than a local basis. The outstanding example of this latter approach is Miami–Dade County in Florida.

Local governments and their citizens have generally resisted sweeping reforms that would alter the basic structure of government in metropolitan areas. Instead, many local governments have sought other means to avoid duplication and inefficiency in the provision of services. One increasingly popular device is the intergovernmental agreement. By utilizing contractual agreements, existing governments can band together to provide services that single units are unable to afford. In other cases, as in California's Lakewood Plan, cities can contract for services with an urban county that can provide services across most of the local government spectrum. Such agreements are popular because they permit existing governments to continue operation and allow local citizens to maintain mechanisms for local control of policy.

Another way to address the problem of the proliferation of local governments is through the metropolitan council of governments or the regional planning agency. Although this coordinative mechanism was initially adopted in metropolitan areas, it has spread to more sparsely populated areas as well. Such agencies consist of representatives of local governments in the area. They have no formal governmental powers or status, but requirements in federal grant-in-aid legislation since 1960 have increased their importance. Most grant proposals from local governments to the federal government must now be endorsed by such a regional body before they can be considered by federal agencies. These councils and agencies do not address the fundamental problem of proliferation of local governments but they do provide a mechanism through which some of the more serious intergovernmental conflicts can be resolved if federal funds are to be forthcoming.

Local governments and their citizens have generally resisted sweeping reforms that would alter the basic structure of government in metropolitan areas.

In the late 1960's another movement began that was designed to make a fundamental change in the structure of local government. This movement focused its attention on large cities and proposed neighborhood governments within existing municipalities. Such efforts are diametrically opposed to the metropolitan consolidation movement. The values of local control of policymaking that have long sustained small-town and suburban governments have been recommended for units of comparable size within the big cities. The structure and functions of such local governments have not yet been clearly delineated. Experiments with limited neighborhood participatory mechanisms occurred under the Office of Economic Opportunity programs in the 1960's. After the passage of the Demonstration Cities and Metropolitan Development Act of 1966, broader participatory mechanisms were developed in the model neighborhoods of the designated model cities. These mechanisms have varied widely in form, and the pattern of social services to which they direct their attention also changes from city to city, with some general emphasis on health, welfare, and housing. Some large cities, particularly New York, have also experienced pressures for neighborhood control of the schools. Because of continuing requirements by the federal government, neighborhood participatory mechanisms will continue to develop. By the mid-1970's, none of these mechanisms had yet developed into a full-fledged local government, although because of the backing of the federal government, they sometimes possessed a veto over local governmental policy decisions.

BIBLIOGRAPHY

George S. Blair, *Local Government in America.*

— JOHN H. BAKER

LOG CABIN

It has been asserted that log construction was introduced into the New World by the Swedes who settled on the lower Delaware in 1638. But a log blockhouse, the McIntyre Garrison at York, Maine, far distant from the Delaware, built about 1640–45, is cited by others as evidence that the New England colonists, somewhere between 1620 and 1640, had learned log construction for themselves—though some one among them might have seen one of the log buildings that had long been in use in Scandinavia and northern Germany. Such construction increased rapidly in the 17th century, and the one-room or two-room log cabin became the typical American pioneer home, being supplemented by outbuildings also of log construction. For the dwelling, the sides of the logs facing each other were adzed flat, and the chinks between were luted with flat stones or chips of wood embedded in clay. In stables, the crevices were usually left unfilled. As the frontier was pushed westward across the continent, small log buildings became the first churches and schools, the first mills, stores, and hotels, and the first seats of town and county government and of the courts. In the South tall tobacco barns were built of long logs with wide, unfilled chinks between, so that the wind might blow through and dry the leaf tobacco racked inside. Many a solitary pioneer had to build his little log hut singlehanded or with the aid of his wife and children; but where there was a settlement, a houseraising became a pioneer social function, as neighbors gathered and completed the essential structure in one day. More prosperous farmers or villagers might erect two-story log houses of several rooms, which were shingled on the outside in New England or often weather-boarded farther west, though in Pennsylvania they were occasionally stuccoed.

BIBLIOGRAPHY

Carl W. Condit, *American Building: Materials and Techniques From the Beginning of the Colonial Settlements to the Present.*

— ALVIN F. HARLOW

LONG DRIVE

At the close of the Civil War cattle were plentiful and cheap in Texas. High prices in the North led cattlemen to seek a market. The building of the railroads to the Pacific opened the way. Beginning in 1866 cowboys drove herds of cattle, numbering on an average 2,500 head, overland to rail points on the northern Plains. Gradually homestead settlement pushed the trails westward, extinguishing them at the base of the Rocky Mountains about 1890. The average time consumed in driving a herd these hundreds of miles was from six weeks to two months.

BIBLIOGRAPHY

Edward E. Dale, *The Range Cattle Industry.*

— EVERETT DICK

LONG, HUEY, ASSASSINATION

On Sept. 8, 1935, Sen. Huey Pierce Long was shot at the state capitol at Baton Rouge, La., by Carl A. Weiss, the son-in-law of Judge B. H. Pavy, leader of an anti-Long faction. Weiss was shot dead on the capitol steps by Long's bodyguards; Long died two days later.

Nicknamed "Kingfish," Long exercised dictatorial control as governor (1928–31) through his political machine. He was also noted for organizing the Share-the-Wealth program, promising a homestead allowance of $6,000 and a minimum annual income of $2,500 for every American family.

BIBLIOGRAPHY

T. Harry Williams, *Huey Long.*

LOS ANGELES RIOTS

Los Angeles riots (May 1992), an uprising following the acquittal of four white police officers in the 1991 beating of Rodney King, a black man who had led Los Angeles police on a high-speed automobile chase. The beating was videotaped by a bystander and broadcast repeatedly by news organizations. Most observers were shocked when the jury did not convict the officers, who had been shown savagely beating King as he lay on the ground. Their attorney argued that they had used only the force necessary to restrain King. The riots ravaged inner-city Los Angeles. At least 53 people were killed and 2,400 injured. More than 8,000 people were arrested, and cost estimates climbed to more than $1 billion. Rioters burned and looted stores, leaving 1,200 businesses destroyed. Reginald Denny became a national symbol of the riots. A white truck driver, he was pulled from his vehicle as he drove through south-central Los Angeles and severely beaten by a group of young black men, leaving him unconscious and critically injured. That beating was caught on videotape as well and for a while dominated national news. Another group of black residents came to Denny's rescue and took him to a hospital, where he recovered. In 1993 two of the acquitted officers were convicted on federal civil rights charges of assault with a deadly weapon and brutality. A commission investigating the riots partly blamed the Los Angeles Police Department and its former chief, Daryl Gates, for the extent of the damage, concluding that the force was inadequately prepared for violence. Rampant poverty, a dearth of jobs, and social decay were also blamed for igniting the uprising.

BIBLIOGRAPHY

Robert Gooding-Williams, ed., *Reading Rodney King, Reading Urban Uprising* (New York, 1993).

Don Hazen, ed., *Inside the L.A. Riots* (New York, 1992).

— KATHLEEN B. CULVER

LOST GENERATION

Lost generation, a term used to designate a group of American writers, notably Hart Crane, e. e. cummings, John Dos Passos, William Faulkner, F. Scott Fitzgerald, Ernest Hemingway, Thornton Wilder, and Thomas Wolfe, most of whom were born in the last decade of the 19th century. These writers had in common the fact that their early adult years were framed not so much by their American cultural heritage as by World War I. Their psyches and their talents were shaped by the war and by self-imposed exile from the mainstream of American life, whether in Europe or in Greenwich Village in New York City—or, in Faulkner's case, in the small Mississippi town of his birth. Although the origin of the phrase is disputed, it probably derives from a remark made in the presence of Gertrude Stein by a hotel owner in Paris shortly after the end of World War I. Whether the characterization "You are all a lost generation" was originally addressed only to the French artisan class (specifically to a young mechanic) or to the whole international generation who had given the war their educable years—those in which they would probably have learned a culture or the skills of a trade—is moot. In 1926 Hemingway used it as the epigraph to *The Sun Also Rises* and thereby guaranteed its passage into literary history.

F. Scott Fitzgerald reads at his desk. Fitzgerald was one of the foremost writers of the post-World War I "Lost Generation." He authored The Great Gatsby, Tender Is the Night, *and other influential novels and short stories. (Minnesota Historical Society/Corbis)*

Malcolm Cowley, a chronicler of the era, has suggested that a distaste for the grandiose and sentimental language of the patriotic manifestos of the war gave them a common standpoint, though they are widely different in their techniques and responses to life. Salvation of the language was made doctrine by Dos Passos, who fulminated against the politicians and generals who, as he wrote, "have turned our language inside out . . . and have taken the clean words our fathers spoke and made them slimy and foul," and by Hemingway, who was the emblem of the movement. The influence of T. S. Eliot, James Joyce, and Stein and the encouragement of the editors and publishers of such little magazines as *Dial, Little Review, transition*, and *Broom* were significant in their development.

BIBLIOGRAPHY

Malcolm Cowley, *Exile's Return*, and *A Second Flowering*.

Ernest Hemingway, *A Moveable Feast*.

— SARAH FERRELL

LOUISIANA PURCHASE

In 1803 the French province of Louisiana embraced the Isle of Orleans on the east bank of the Mississippi and the vast area between that river, the Rocky Mountains, and the Spanish possessions in the Southwest. The purchase of the colony from France by the United States in that year ended forever France's dream of controlling the Mississippi Valley and began a program of expansion destined to carry the American flag to the Pacific.

For a generation Louisiana had been a pawn in European diplomacy. France ceded it to Spain in 1762. The first French minister to the United States, Edmond

Charles Genêt, planned to attack it from the United States in 1793, but France turned to diplomacy as a means of recovering it between 1795 and 1799. By the Treaty of San Ildefonso, Oct. 1, 1800, and the Convention of Aranjuez, Mar. 21, 1801, Napoleon Bonaparte acquired Louisiana for France in return for placing the son-in-law of the Spanish king on the newly erected throne of Etruria.

The acquisition of Louisiana was part of an ambitious plan by which Napoleon and his minister of foreign affairs, Charles Maurice de Talleyrand-Périgord, hoped to build a colonial empire in the West Indies and the heart of North America. The mainland colony would be a source of supplies for the sugar islands, a market for France, and a vast territory for settlement. Two million francs were spent on an expedition for Louisiana assembled in Holland, at Helvoët Sluys, in the winter of 1802–03. Fortunately for the United States the ships were icebound in February, just as they were ready to sail.

The Louisiana Purchase ended forever France's dream of controlling the Mississippi Valley, and allowed an expansion of "manifest destiny" that pushed the American borders to the Pacific.

By the Treaty of San Lorenzo, Spain, in 1795, had granted American citizens the privilege of depositing their goods at New Orleans for reshipment on ocean-going vessels. The United States was deeply aroused when Juan Ventura Morales, the acting intendant of Louisiana, revoked this right of deposit on Oct. 16, 1802, and failed to provide another site, as the treaty required. It was assumed at the time that France was responsible for the revocation, but all available documentary evidence indicates that the action was taken by Spain alone, and for commercial reasons.

President Thomas Jefferson handled the crisis in masterly fashion by appointing James Monroe as special envoy to assist Robert R. Livingston, the minister at Paris, in securing American rights. Monroe's instructions authorized an offer of $10 million for the Isle of Orleans, on which New Orleans stood, and the Floridas, erroneously thought to be French. If France refused this proposition, the ministers were to seek a commercial site on the Mississippi, or at least permanent establishment of the right of deposit at New Orleans.

In the meantime Livingston had pursued his country's interests with a zeal deserving even better results. He proposed the cession of New Orleans and the Floridas, belittled the economic value of Louisiana for France, and, after the closing of New Orleans, urged the cession to the United States of the Isle of Orleans and all the trans-Mississippi country above the Arkansas River. This was the first hint by anyone that France surrender any part of the right bank of the Mississippi.

By the spring of 1803 Napoleon's plans for his American empire had all gone astray. Spain refused to round out his possessions by ceding the Floridas. The resistance of resident blacks and yellow fever thwarted the attempt to subjugate Santo Domingo. War with Great Britain was imminent. In the United States there was growing hostility to France and talk of an Anglo-American alliance. Particularly disturbed at such a prospect, Napoleon decided to reap a nice profit and placate the Americans by selling them all of Louisiana.

When Monroe arrived in Paris on Apr. 12, the first consul had already appointed François de Barbé-Marbois, minister of the public treasury, to conduct the negotiations. On Apr. 11 Talleyrand had amazed Livingston by asking what the United States would give for the entire colony. Barbé-Marbois conferred with Livingston on the evening of Apr. 13, thereby initiating the negotiations before the formal presentation of Monroe. Some jealousy arose between the American negotiators, but it did not handicap their work. Monroe was at first less inclined than Livingston to exceed their instructions and purchase all of Louisiana. By a treaty and two conventions, all dated Apr. 30, the United States paid $11.25 million for Louisiana, set aside $3.75 million to pay the claims of its own citizens against France, and placed France and Spain on an equal commercial basis with the United States in the colony for a period of twelve years.

Serious barriers to American ownership of Louisiana yet remained. Napoleon's action required the confirmation of the French legislature, and the sale was a violation of his solemn pledge to Spain never to alienate the colony to a third power. There was also grave doubt regarding the constitutionality of such a purchase by the United States. None of these dangers materialized. Napoleon ignored the legislature; Spain did nothing more than protest; and Jefferson put his constitutional scruples conveniently aside. On Nov. 30, 1803, Spain formally delivered the colony to Pierre-Clément Laussat, the French colonial prefect, who on Dec. 20 transferred the territory to William C. C. Claiborne and Gen. James Wilkinson, the American commissioners.

BIBLIOGRAPHY

E. Wilson Lyon, *Louisiana in French Diplomacy, 1759–1804.*

Dumas Malone, *Jefferson the President: First Term, 1801–1805.*

Francis S. Philbrick, *The Rise of the West, 1754–1830.*
Marshall Smelser, *The Democratic Republic, 1801–1815.*

— E. WILSON LYON

LOYALISTS

Loyalists, or Tories, those who were loyal to Great Britain during the American Revolution, comprised about one-third of the population of the thirteen revolting colonies. In Georgia and South Carolina they were a majority; in New England and Virginia, a minority; elsewhere they were more or less evenly matched by the patriots. Included in their ranks were all classes: great landowners such as the De Lanceys, Jessups, and Philipses of New York; rich merchants, such as the Whartons and Pembertons of Philadelphia and the Higginses and Chandlers of Boston; large numbers of professional men—lawyers, physicians, and teachers; prosperous farmers; crown officials and Anglican clergy and laity; and dependents of Loyalist merchants and landlords. While a few of the more conservative stood for the rigid execution of imperial law, the majority opposed the objectionable acts of the British Parliament, served on the early extralegal committees, and were not hostile to the calling of the first Continental Congress in 1774, working hard to elect delegates of their own convictions to it. Although anxious to maintain their rights by means of petition and legal protest, and in some cases not even averse to a show of force, they were strongly opposed to separation from the British empire. The Declaration of Independence gave finality to their position.

Before April 1775 few efforts were made to arrest or suppress the Loyalists, but after the Battle of Lexington the war fervor rapidly grew more intense. Great numbers of Loyalists flocked to the royal colors or, in a few instances, organized militia companies of their own under commissions from the crown. Although they probably contributed 60,000 soldiers, their military service was not commensurate with their numerical strength: their only outstanding exploits were an expedition against the coast towns of Connecticut; frontier raids; and a savage guerrilla warfare against patriots in the South.

As the struggle progressed, the patriots resorted to more and more drastic measures against the Loyalists. All who refused to take an oath of allegiance to the new governments were denied the rights of citizenship and could not vote, hold office, or enjoy court protection. In many cases they were forbidden to pursue professions or to acquire or dispose of property. Free speech was denied them, and they were not allowed to communicate with the British. When these laws failed to accomplish their purpose, the more ardent Loyalists were jailed, put on parole, sent to detention camps, or tarred and feathered. Nearly all the new state governments eventually enacted legislation banishing those who refused to swear allegiance. It is probable that before the war was over 200,000 Loyalists died, were exiled, or became voluntary refugees to other parts of the British empire—a large number of citizens for struggling frontier communities to lose.

To banishment was added confiscation of property. In the early days of the Revolution Thomas Paine advised confiscation of Loyalist property to defray the expenses of the war, and several states followed his suggestion. The definition of treason by Congress supplied a legal basis for action, and late in 1777 Congress advised the states to confiscate and sell the real and personal property of those who had forfeited "the right of protection" and to invest the proceeds in Continental certificates. Although some of the more conservative patriots protested that confiscation was "contrary to the principles of civil liberty," statutes of condemnation and forfeiture were enacted in all the states before the end of the war.

Many persons were the victims of private grudges and persecution. Evidence abounds that the execution of the sequestration laws was frequently attended by scandal and corruption. The amount of property seized is uncertain. Claims totaling £10 million were filed with the commission established by the British Parliament in 1783, and the claims for less than £1 million were disallowed.

On the whole, throughout the conflict, the Loyalists lacked organization and good leadership. They were conservatives who were suspicious of the innovations demanded by a crisis. The triumph of the patriots accentuated their hesitancy. They had placed implicit trust in the invincibility of the British army, and the unexpected development of the conflict dazed them.

All things taken into consideration, the treatment of the Loyalists was moderate. The period was one in which the most bitter and most harsh human emotions were aroused—a civil war within a state. Although the laws of banishment and sequestration were severe, there was no such slaughter and terrorism as prevailed later during the French Revolution, and surprising care was taken to make sure that punishment of Loyalists was carried out only in accordance with law.

BIBLIOGRAPHY

Wallace Brown, *The Good Americans: The Loyalist in the American Revolution.*
North Callahan, *Flight From the Republic: The Tories of the American Revolution.*

— A. C. FLICK

LOYALTY OATHS

Loyalty oaths are statements of allegiance to a cause, a concept, an institution, a community, a party, a group, a political or religious association, a leader, or even a symbol, as in the pledge of allegiance to the flag. Historically the loyalty oath has been intended to increase the security of authority from real or fancied refusals to accord it legitimacy; to mark nonjurors for ostracism, expulsion, or punishment; and to bind the compliant to obligation. It is also a ceremony of faith and submission. In 1086, for example, William the Conqueror at Salisbury imposed an oath on the most prominent lords of the land that they would be faithful to him. After his break with Rome, Henry VIII—and later Elizabeth I—enforced oaths to secure the new religious establishment. They were employed by James I after the Gunpowder Plot as a measure to secure the realm against religious subversion. In the earliest colonial charters all those immigrating to the New World were required to take oaths of loyalty to the crown. The Massachusetts Bay Colony and other colonies enforced oaths of loyalty to the colonial regime.

During the American Revolution, loyalty oaths were used by radicals to enforce boycotts against the Tories, and both rebel and royal loyalty oaths were freely employed to maintain the security of the conflicting forces. Perhaps because colonial-state loyalties were so strong, no provision for oaths of loyalty to the new central government was made in the Articles of Confederation in 1781. But in the federal Constitution of 1787, a specified oath is required of the president in Article II, Section 1, Clause 8, that he will faithfully execute his office and, to the best of his ability, "preserve, protect, and defend the Constitution of the United States." And Article VI does require an oath of all federal and state officers to "support this Constitution."

Tensions over loyalty led to the adoption of the Alien and Sedition Acts of 1798, but it was through prosecutions rather than oaths that the Federalists sought to silence critics. Tensions over nullification in South Carolina in 1833 led to the widespread enforcement of oaths of loyalty to the state in its conflict with the federal authority. During the Civil War, test oaths were enforced in both the North and the South. The center of Abraham Lincoln's program for reconstruction in 1863 was a pledge of future loyalty to the Union, unlike the test oath enacted by Congress in 1862, which required pledges of past loyalty. The Supreme Court in *Cummings* v. *Missouri* (1866) held unconstitutional a state oath requiring voters, teachers, candidates for public office, and others to swear that they had not participated in rebellion against the United States. On the same day, in *Ex Parte Garland*, the Court held unconstitutional a congressional statute requiring a similar oath of attorneys practicing in the courts of the United States.

In the postwar agitation over communism, loyalty testing became commonplace, from the executive and legislative branches to municipal employees and public school teachers.

Although loyalty testing was carried to excessive lengths in World War I, it (like the actions of 1798) was carried on primarily in the courts, under the Espionage and Sedition Acts of 1917 and 1918, and through private groups operating under the doubtful auspices of the Department of Justice and the Department of War. Oaths did not play a primary role in either of the two world wars, although both these conflicts contributed to a new kind of concern about loyalty as an aftermath. Issues of property and social structure were not absent from questions of loyalty during the Revolution, the nullification controversy, and the Civil War, but the primary conflict in all three was political difference over the relations between the central and local governments in two kinds of confederation, imperial and national. Out of the two world wars, concern grew for what was perceived to be a threat by social radicals to the security of all political authority and the prevailing distribution of property. The Hatch Act of 1938 required as a condition of federal employment that the applicant swear that he did not belong to an organization advocating the violent overthrow of the government.

Loyalty testing programs were conducted by federal officials during World War II as a minor routine. But in the agitation over Communists in the postwar period, loyalty testing became a prominent activity in the executive establishment. It was also a principal feature of the work of congressional committees in both the House of Representatives and the Senate and punishments for contempt or perjury were meted out to many who refused to make exculpatory statements or who swore falsely. Many state legislatures and municipal bodies required loyalty oaths of teachers, public and private, and governmental employees, most of which were upheld by the Supreme Court, especially in the 1950's. Although the Court later showed some tendency to decide such cases in favor of defendants, as late as 1972 the Supreme Court upheld a Massachusetts statute that required a public employee to swear "to support and defend" the Constitution and to oppose the overthrow of government by violent means.

Although loyalty oaths have an Anglo-American history of a thousand years, it is doubtful that they contribute much to the security of authority; more likely, they reflect its anxiety rather than its strength.

BIBLIOGRAPHY

Eleanor Bontecou, *The Federal Loyalty-Security Program.*
Morton Grodzins, *The Loyal and the Disloyal.*
Harold M. Hyman, *To Try Men's Souls.*
John H. Schaar, *Loyalty in America.*

— EARL LATHAM

LUSITANIA, SINKING OF THE

The Cunard liner *Lusitania* was sunk without warning by the German submarine U-20 off Old Head of Kinsale, Ireland, on May 7, 1915. Of the 1,959 passengers and crew, 1,198 perished, including 128 (out of 197) Americans. Since on May 1, the day of sailing, the German embassy in Washington, D.C., had published an advertisement in American papers warning Atlantic travelers that they sailed in British or Allied ships at their own risk, it was widely believed that the sinking was premeditated. The log of the U-20, published years later, shows, however, that the submarine had sunk other ships, met the *Lusitania* by chance, and sank it from fear of being rammed. The ship carried 4,200 cases of small-arms ammunition and 1,250 shrapnel cases, allowed by American law; this cargo, stored well forward, about 150 feet from the spot where the torpedo struck, may have exploded and contributed to the rapid (eighteen minutes) sinking of the ship. A thorough examination prior to sailing revealed no evidence that the liner was armed. Why the captain of the ship had reduced speed, failed to follow a zig-zag course, and kept close to shore, in violation of orders from the British admiralty, was not satisfactorily explained.

The catastrophe created intense indignation in the United States, especially since, on Feb. 10, 1915, the American government had denied the legality of submarine warfare (as practiced by Germany) and had warned that it would hold the German government to "a strict accountability" for the observance of American rights on the high seas. In May, President Woodrow Wilson resisted considerable popular clamor for war (chiefly in the East), and in three successive notes (May 13, June 9, and July 21, 1915) demanded that Germany make reparation for and disavow the sinking; the last note concluded with the statement that a repetition of the act "must be regarded by the Government of the United States, when they affect American citizens, as deliberately unfriendly." Secretary of State William Jennings Bryan thought the American demands too severe and likely to lead to war, and resigned on June 8. The German government agreed to make reparation and eventually gave a promise (after the sinking of the *Arabic*) that liners would not be sunk without warning and without safety of the lives of noncombatants; but it steadfastly refused to disavow the sinking of the *Lusitania.* No settlement of this question was reached before the United States entered World War I.

BIBLIOGRAPHY

T. A. Bailey, "The Sinking of the Lusitania," *American Historical Review*, vol. 61.
Adolph A. Hoehling and Mary Hoehling, *The Last Voyage of the Lusitania.*
Charles Seymour, *American Diplomacy and the World War.*

— BERNADOTTE E. SCHMITT

LYNCHING

Lynching, whereby a mob without any authority at law inflicts injury or death upon a victim, has its roots deeply embedded in American life. The term derives from a Virginian, Col. Charles Lynch, who presided over the flogging of local criminals and Tory sympathizers during the revolutionary war. Since then, mob justice has taken many other forms: lynchings of alleged desperadoes along America's expanding southern and western frontiers throughout the 19th century; of blacks from the Reconstruction era to mid-20th century; and occasionally of unpopular immigrants and of outspoken labor, radical, or antiwar figures. Since 1882 (the earliest year for which there is reliable data) lynch mobs have killed over 4,730 persons; at least 3,341 of these were blacks. The sustained lynching of blacks in southern and border states coincided with the disfranchisement and Jim Crow prohibitions inflicted upon the Afro-American community at the turn of the century. From 1886 through 1916 alone, lynch mobs murdered 2,605 black men and women. Despite assertions about "protecting" white womanhood, less than 30 percent of black victims were accused—let alone tried and convicted—of rape or attempted rape.

Given the diversities of time, place, and victims, generalizations about American lynchings are difficult to establish. Certainly the search for quick solutions, an enthusiasm for force as an instrument of public conduct, a strong sense of conformity to local or regional mores, a determination to impose majority rule upon a

Two men lean out of a barn loft above an African-American man tied for lynching. On the ground below, men stand around the victim and hay is piled at the victim's feet to be set afire. (Library of Congress/Corbis)

vulnerable minority, and support for a mechanism of control in a biracial environment have all applied.

Lynching did not go unchallenged. Founded in 1909, the National Association for the Advancement of Colored People (NAACP) conducted a national drive against mob violence for over four decades. The Atlanta-based Association of Southern Women for the Prevention of Lynching campaigned diligently throughout the 1930's. The numbers of reported lynchings declined after 1935. The long years of antilynching work, the growing political power of Afro-American voters in northern and western urban centers, concerns about America's international cold-war image, and the widely publicized recommendations of President Harry S. Truman's Committee on Civil Rights (1947) all contributed to that decline. For the first time ever, no reported lynchings occurred in a three-year period (1952–54). Lynchers did kill three black persons in 1955 and at least one in 1959, and the murders and beatings of civil rights workers during the 1960's reaffirmed that certain segments of the United States had not fully disavowed a lynching mentality.

Lynching Legislation

Legislation to deal with anticipated lynchings, lynchers, or delinquent officials—or to indemnify survivors—was enacted in several states during the 1890's (Georgia, North Carolina, South Carolina, Kentucky, Texas, Tennessee, Ohio, and Indiana among them). Public attitudes and fears of political reprisals impeded corrective action; when black victims were involved, 99 percent of mob members escaped prosecution and punishment. From 1918 to 1950, the NAACP tried, unsuccessfully, to secure a federal antilynching statute. Its first effort in Congress resulted from a bill introduced by Rep. L. C. Dyer of Missouri. The measure passed the House of Representatives in 1922, as did other bills in 1937 and 1940, but none made it through the Senate. Notwithstanding the 1947 recommendations of Truman's Committee on Civil Rights, Congress still refused to enact an antilynching law. Belatedly, the 1968 Civil Rights Act authorized federal action if two or more persons should conspire to intimidate a citizen in the free exercise of constitutional rights, whether or not death ensued. Formerly, civil rights advocates relied on Title 18, Sections 241 and 242, of the U.S. Code. Derived from Reconstruction statutes and difficult to implement, these sections were central in two U.S. Supreme Court rulings in 1966 (one involved three slain civil rights workers). On three earlier occasions (1923, 1936, 1940), the Court had invoked the due process clause of the Fourteenth Amendment to undercut "legal lynchings" by reversing convictions based on "evidence" and "confessions" obtained through torture.

BIBLIOGRAPHY

Richard Bardolph, ed., *The Civil Rights Record: Black Americans and the Law, 1849–1970.*

James H. Chadbourn, *Lynching and the Law,* and *To Secure These Rights: The Report of the President's Committee on Civil Rights.*

Richard Hofstadter and Michael Wallace, eds., *American Violence: A Documentary History.*

Arthur F. Raper, *The Tragedy of Lynching.*

Walter White, *Rope and Faggot: A Biography of Judge Lynch.*

— ROBERT L. ZANGRANDO

M

MAGAZINES

Magazine publishing in America began with the almost simultaneous appearance in 1741 of Andrew Bradford's *American Magazine, or Monthly View* and Benjamin Franklin's *General Magazine and Historical Chronicle.* Franklin indignantly alleged he had already begun to plan his publication when Bradford stole his idea; but it was not really a very serious matter, since neither magazine lasted a year. Bradford was able to bring out three issues, Franklin six, before both ceased publication. Since then, magazine publishing has remained a perilous venture, and it is no wonder Noah Webster remarked in 1788 that "the expectation of failure [was] connected with the very nature of a Magazine."

Conditions for magazine publishing at first made success nearly impossible. Such reading public as existed habitually read newspapers and books, very largely theology and the English classics, with some Greek and Latin. Mails were few and slow, and circulation by mail was thus difficult; newsstand circulation was so limited as to be nearly useless. Promotion was nearly impossible. National advertising, with its large profits, for all practical purposes did not exist. There were practically no writers or editors able to capture and hold the attention of a fairly wide public. Woodcuts or expensive metal engravings were the only possible illustrations.

In spite of difficulties, stubborn printers continued to undertake what proved to be short-lived ventures; and it was natural, since writers were few, that the reprint magazines, based mainly on clippings from British reviews, became fairly abundant. There seems to have been no difficulty about copyright, although a copyright statute had been on the books since the reign of Queen Anne. Reprint magazines, although fewer in number, continued far into modern times. *Littell's Living Age,* founded in 1844, was published for nearly a century. The *Literary Digest* lasted until its unfortunate prediction of President Franklin D. Roosevelt's defeat at the polls in 1936. *Reader's Digest,* originally a reprint magazine, still contains some reprinted material.

A change came as education became more widespread, enlarging the reading public; as printing processes, photography, and photoengraving improved; as the development of industry made national advertising, and thus financial profit, possible; and as improved postal organization and generous second-class mailing privileges for periodicals made distribution cheap and easy. Advertising, at first unimportant, became the main source of revenue for both magazines and newspapers as a huge advertising industry sprang up and became a major influence in American life. *Reader's Digest,* nevertheless, proved highly profitable for many years, even without advertising, which it began including in April 1955. Advertising was for a time regarded as faintly discreditable to a publication. As late as 1864, *Harper's Magazine* refused to carry any advertising except its own announcements of Harper books. The publishers felt seriously insulted when offered an $18,000 contract for sewing-machine advertising.

Among early magazine successes were *Godey's Lady's Book,* Robert Bonner's *New York Ledger,* and later "quality" magazines, such as *Century, Harper's, Scribner's, Atlantic,* and *Forum.* During the latter part of the 19th century, these were important influences in American literature and life, but they began to disappear fairly early in the 20th century as a mass culture arose, rigorous educational standards slackened, and many new distractions began to interest and amuse the mass public. *Atlantic* and *Harper's* still remain, although much changed.

As the reading public became vastly larger and much less thoroughly educated, a group of elaborately illustrated popular magazines, with very large circulations justifying much profitable advertising, developed. The *Saturday Evening Post,* which traced a somewhat tenuous ancestry to one of Benjamin Franklin's 18th-century periodicals, developed into a successful and highly profitable "mass" magazine. *Liberty, Look, Life,* and *Collier's* developed enormous circulations.

The rise of radio and television has drawn off great numbers of possible readers and has provided an enormous market for advertising. The huge mass magazines have succumbed one by one to this competition, especially when a formidable rise in mailing and other costs developed in the early 1970's.

Successful news magazines, such as *Time* and *Newsweek,* continued; various university reviews more or less replaced the "serious" quality magazines; the *New Yorker* took the place of the older humorous magazines, making an especial point of avoiding their somewhat monotonous "he-she" jokes; and *Playboy* ventured into daring illustrations and text that would have been quite impossible even one generation earlier. Innumerable smaller magazines still represented the special interests of special groups.

BIBLIOGRAPHY

John Bakeless, *Magazine Making.*
Frank Luther Mott, *History of American Magazines.*
Lyon N. Richardson, *History of Early American Magazines.*
Roland E. Wolseley, *The Magazine World.*
James Playsted Wood, *Magazines in the United States.*

— JOHN BAKELESS

MAGAZINES SINCE WORLD WAR II

Following World War II specialization became the route to success, or at least survival, for magazines. In the 1990s general interest weeklies such as the *Saturday Evening Post* were gone, but magazine racks groaned beneath the weight of new ventures, most of which quickly sank. Weeklies such as *Sports Illustrated* and *Money* attracted upscale readers that advertisers wanted to reach, as did such monthlies as *Bride's* and *Yachting. Time* and other giants changed ads and copy on selected pages in each weekly edition, and thus delivered issues customized geographically and according to readers' interests. For example, a college student's issue could differ from the one delivered that same week to his or her parents.

A few regional magazines prospered, notably *Sunset,* a home magazine for readers in the West, and *Southern Living.* Although most city magazines concentrated on listing restaurants and entertainment, a few, such as *Philadelphia Magazine,* won national reporting awards. Many specialized publications, such as *Engineering News-Record,* boasted large but controlled circulations, that is, they were mailed free to every individual in the defined field but others could not even buy a copy. Again, this served the advertisers who want to reach only their best prospects. Magazines for African Americans multiplied and also specialized. *Ebony* prospered as a general monthly, while other publications targeted black young women (*Essence*), businessmen (*Black Enterprise*), and scholars (*Black Scholar*).

As the number of newsstands began to diminish after World War II, retail stores, especially supermarkets, became major magazine outlets. Although supermarket tabloids look like newspapers, the Audit Bureau of Circulations classified them as magazines. In 1994 the six largest sold a total of 10 million copies a week, with the *National Enquirer* having the largest circulation. Comic books, many intended for adults, made a comeback in the 1980s. Illustration and text became more diverse in men's magazines. *Playboy*'s pages contained not only pictures of nude women and cartoons but also works by leading authors. Another showplace for writing was *Esquire,* whose contributors were at the center of the so-called "new journalism," in which writers immersed themselves in topics to convey the "true essence" to readers, even if it required invented dialogue and composite characters. Literary magazines, mostly quarterlies affiliated with universities, continued to publish fiction and poetry.

In 1994 the six largest magazines sold a total of 10 million copies a week, with the National Enquirer *having the largest circulation.*

Reader's Digest continued to lead all general magazines in circulation, with a paid circulation in 1993 of more than 16 million copies. Although *Modern Maturity* had a larger circulation, it is tied to a membership organization, the American Association of Retired Persons. At the same time, *TV Guide* was the leading weekly. Women's magazines (*Better Homes and Gardens, Family Circle, Good Housekeeping*) were among the top ten magazines in 1993. *Time* continued to outsell other newsmagazines by more than 1 million copies, and its 1993 circulation of 4.1 million was followed on the list of leading magazines by *People,* with 3.4 million copies. Magazines in the 1990s were increasingly being published on CD-ROM for access by computers.

BIBLIOGRAPHY

Michael Emery and Edwin Emery, *The Press and America* (Englewood Cliffs, N.J., 1988).

— JOHN D. STEVENS

MAINE, DESTRUCTION OF THE

Destruction of the *Maine* (Feb. 15, 1898). In January 1898, the second-class battleship *Maine,* under the command of Capt. Charles D. Sigsbee, was ordered from Key West, Fla., to Havana, Cuba, during that island's revolt against Spanish rule, as an "act of friendly courtesy." Spanish authorities in Havana objected to the arrival of the *Maine.* For three weeks the ship lay moored to a buoy 500 yards off the Havana arsenal. There was considerable ill feeling against the United States among the Spaniards, but no untoward incident took place until 9:40 P.M. on Feb. 15, when two explosions threw parts of the *Maine* 200 feet in the air and illuminated the whole harbor. A first dull explosion had been followed by one much more powerful, probably that of the forward magazines. The forward half of the ship was reduced to a mass of twisted steel; the after section slowly sank. Two officers and 258 of the crew were killed or died soon afterward. Most of these were buried in Colón Cemetery, Havana.

Separate investigations were soon made by the American and Spanish authorities. Their conclusions differed: the Spaniards reported that an internal explosion, perhaps spontaneous combustion in the coal bunkers, had been the cause; the Americans, that the original cause had been an external explosion that in turn had set off the forward magazines.

The explosion of the Maine *in Havana harbor stirred up nationalist fervor and was a major factor in the U.S.'s declaration of war against Spain on April 25, 1898.*

News of the disaster produced great excitement in the United States, and accusations against the Spaniards were freely expressed by certain newspapers, including the *New York Journal.* Without doubt the catastrophe stirred up national feeling over the difficulties in Cuba, crystallized in the slogan "Remember the *Maine,*" and was a major factor in bringing the United States to a declaration of war against Spain on Apr. 25 (retroactive to Apr. 21).

The wreck remained in Havana harbor until 1911, when U.S. Army engineers built a cofferdam about the wreck, sealed the aft hull of the ship, the only part still intact, and floated it out to sea. There, on Mar. 16, 1912, appropriate minute guns boomed as the *Maine* sank with its flag flying. The remains of sixty-six of the crew found during the raising were buried in Arlington National Cemetery, Va. During the removal of the wreck, a board of officers of the navy made a further investigation. Their report, published in 1912, stated that a low form of explosive exterior to the ship caused the first explosion. "This resulted in igniting and exploding the contents of the 6-inch reserve magazine, A–14–M, said contents including a large quantity of black powder. The more or less complete explosion of the contents of the remaining forward magazine followed." The chief evidence for this was that the bottom of the ship had been bent upward and folded over toward the stern. European experts, perhaps influenced by several internal explosions in warships in the intervening years, still maintained the theory of an internal explosion. No further evidence has ever been found to solve the mystery.

BIBLIOGRAPHY

F. E. Chadwick, *The Relations of the United States and Spain: Diplomacy.*

Charles D. Sigsbee, *The Maine.*

— WALTER B. NORRIS

MAJORITY RULE

A fundamental American concept, evolved from the principle of the sovereignty of the people, is that when two candidates are running for an office, the one who receives more than half of the total votes cast shall be elected and his policies shall be entitled to a fair trial. If three or more candidates are seeking the same office, the concept holds that an absolute majority is not required but that the one who receives a mere plurality, or more votes than any other candidate, shall be elected.

The operation of majority rule was well illustrated when the election of Thomas Jefferson to the presidency was accepted as sufficient warrant for refusing to approve Federalist changes in the judiciary. President Andrew Jackson interpreted his reelection in 1832 as approval of his hostility to the second Bank of the United States. During the Reconstruction period, the Radical Republicans believed their 1866 election victories justified them in imposing a harsh program of military reconstruction on the South. In 1933 President Franklin D. Roosevelt and the public generally interpreted his overwhelming victory at the polls as authority for inaugurating his far-reaching New Deal.

Majority rule is limited somewhat by the Constitution. Civil liberties are specifically protected by the fundamental law and cannot be suppressed by a temporary majority. The Constitution itself cannot be amended without the consent of three-fourths (thirty-eight) of the states. Because of constitutional guarantees of freedom of speech and of the press and other liberties, minority groups in the United States are able to oppose the majority. Minority criticism and the ever-present possibility that the minority will become the majority have operated to make majority rule work well.

BIBLIOGRAPHY

James Bryce, *The American Commonwealth,* vol. II

Alexis de Tocqueville, *Democracy in America.*

— ERIK MCKINLEY ERIKSSON

MALARIA

Malaria is a disease characterized by chills and fever that recur at regular intervals, anemia, and an enlarged spleen; it is caused in man by four species of *Plasmodium*, a protozoan. Long prevalent in Europe and Africa, malaria was probably brought to the Americas by European colonists and black slaves. By 1700 it had become established from South Carolina to New England. The ague, chills and fever, and intermittents of 18th- and early 19th-century medical literature were commonly malaria, as were many of the autumnal bilious remittent fevers. Malaria spread into the Mississippi Valley with the American settlers, where it became a commonly accepted part of life. Generally chronic and debilitating to all ages and often fatal, it placed a heavy burden of ill health on settlers, especially along the waterways that formed the chief routes of commerce. Its effects are portrayed in the sallow countenances and listless, emaciated forms described by travelers.

Malaria was at its height in New England in the 18th century and after 1800 appeared only sporadically. In the Midwest it reached its peak about 1875, declining thereafter quite rapidly in the North. Associated since antiquity with marshes, malaria in the United States tended to rise with the initial clearing of land and to fall with cultivation and drainage, as Benjamin Rush noted in 1785. Better housing, an increase in dairy cattle (which the mosquito may prefer to man), and the development of railroads, moving settlement out of the river bottoms, were other factors in the decline of malaria.

Cinchona bark, a specific for malaria, was brought to Europe in the 1630's from Peru, and by the 18th century it was widely used, although often incorrectly. Well into the 19th century, many American doctors also relied on bloodletting and cathartics. The isolation of quinine by French chemists in 1820 made rational therapeutics more practicable, and from the 1850's there was a great upsurge in the use of quinine not only to cure or suppress malaria but also to prevent its appearance. While prophylactic use of quinine cannot eradicate malaria, its enormous use in the 1880's and 1890's no doubt helped directly by abating sickness and indirectly by enabling people to make the improvements that led to the virtual disappearance of malaria in the North by about 1900 without specific antimosquito measures.

In 1880 a French army surgeon, Alphonse Laveran, demonstrated the parasitic cause of the disease in the blood of man. Dr. A. F. A. King of Washington, D.C., speculated on mosquito transmission in 1882, and William George MacCollum added significantly to knowledge of the complex life history of the plasmodium in 1897 by elucidating the significance of the extramammalian flagellated form. A British physician, Ronald Ross, made the crucial demonstration of mosquito transmission in avian malaria in 1898; others soon confirmed this for man. Using antimosquito measures and prophylactic quinine, William C. Gorgas in 1901 initiated a campaign that reduced the malaria rate in Havana from 909 per 1,000 in 1899 to 19 per 1,000 in 1908. Later he obtained comparable results in the Canal Zone and made possible the building of the Panama Canal.

After World War II the Public Health Service used the newly developed insecticide DDT in its program to eradicate malaria in the U.S.

Extended campaigns began in the United States in 1912, when the U.S. Public Health Service instituted malaria surveys in cooperation with several southern states and the Rockefeller Foundation. A decline in antimalaria programs in the 1920's, followed by the depression, led in the early 1930's to a resurgence of the disease, which was attacked by drainage and other measures under New Deal relief programs. During World War II both the Public Health Service and the army increased antimalaria programs in the United States, while overseas actions brought home the global importance of the disease. With quinine supplies cut off, new and more effective drugs were developed. After the war the Public Health Service, using the newly developed insecticide DDT, inaugurated a program to eradicate malaria in the United States. In 1935 there were about 4,000 malaria deaths in the country, in 1945 about 400, and by 1952 only 25. In the 1970's the United States was free of significant indigenous malaria, although the possibility of importation in troops from Korea in the 1950's and Vietnam in the 1960's had been a continuing threat. Since World War II the United States has also participated in antimalaria campaigns in other countries, through various bilateral and international agencies. Although these efforts have greatly reduced the incidence of malaria, it remains a major health problem in many of the less developed countries.

BIBLIOGRAPHY

Erwin H. Ackerknecht, "Malaria in the Upper Mississippi Valley 1760–1900," *Bulletin of the History of Medicine*, Supplements, no. 4 (1945).

Paul F. Russell, *Man's Mastery of Malaria.*

— JOHN B. BLAKE

MANDAN, HIDATSA, AND ARIKARA

The northern Plains of America, in which most Indian tribes depended on bison hunting, were the home of three peoples that practiced river-bottom agriculture along the Missouri River in the general area of North Dakota. This is the northernmost point of the aboriginal spread of maize cultivation. The three tribes, the Mandan, Hidatsa, and Arikara, although sharing this common economic mode, were from different geographic areas and spoke mutually unintelligible languages. The Arikara appear to have branched off from the Skidi Pawnee, a Caddoan-speaking tribe, before the arrival of Europeans. Both the Mandan and the Hidatsa spoke Siouan languages, but those of subbranches long separated from each other. The Hidatsa language is closest to the Crow of Montana, while the Mandan language, in its structure, seems most closely allied to the East, to Winnebago. The Arikara are believed to have brought knowledge of farming up the Missouri, and the Hidatsa and Mandan are said to have been introduced to agriculture by contact with the Arikara.

Although farming appeared in the eastern Plains, among such sedentary peoples as the Omaha, Osage, and Oto, it is somewhat out of place so far north and east, but the Mandan, Hidatsa, and Arikara tended toward residential stability. Although they used the tipi and shared other distinctive elements of the culture of the nomadic bison hunters of the Plains, their use of a complex earth lodge, possibly Pawnee and thus southeastern in origin, suggests a trend toward permanent villages. Even so, bundles, the vision quest, ranked clubs or fraternities, the Sun Dance, and the war complex were as much a part of the life of these groups as they were of the life of such other nonagricultural peoples of the area as the Crow, Cheyenne, Assiniboine, and the various Dakota.

The three Missouri River tribes were first known from the account of Pierre Gaultier de Varennes, Sieur de La Vérendrye, who visited the area in 1738. He and his contemporaries created some confusion in the designation of local tribes, identifying the Hidatsa as "Gros Ventres"; this is a misnomer, the designation "Gros Ventre" probably being more properly applied to the Algonkin-speaking Atsina, a group related to the Arapaho and culturally identified with the hunters of the Plains. Meriwether Lewis and William Clark mention in some detail their encounters with the Mandan, Hidatsa, and Arikara in 1805, and there are accounts and depictions of them from the 1830's by the German naturalist Prince Maximilian zu Wied and the American painter George Catlin.

Never large groups, the three tribes suffered greatly from smallpox, which reduced their population in the mid-19th century. At times hostile to European incursion, their effectiveness was curtailed by both geographic location and epidemics.

BIBLIOGRAPHY

Robert F. Spencer, "Introduction" to Washington Matthews, *Ethnography and Philology of the Hidatsa Indians.*

— ROBERT F. SPENCER

MANHATTAN PROJECT

After the discovery of nuclear fission in Germany in late 1938, physicists the world over recognized the possibility of utilizing the enormous energy released in this reaction. From 1939 on, experiments were performed to determine whether neutrons were released during fission and, if so, how to utilize them to achieve a sustained process, called a chain reaction, in which at least one neutron produced in fission of a uranium nucleus strikes another uranium atom, causing it to break apart. If the chain reaction could be controlled at a suitable rate, a power source, or reactor, was envisaged. Alternatively, if the reaction proceeded unchecked, an instant release of energy—of a magnitude greater than that obtainable from any chemical explosive—was likely.

Frustrated by the leisurely pace of progress in America and fearful that Germany might produce a bomb first, Leo Szilard and some other refugees from Nazi persecution convinced Albert Einstein to use his influence to urge government support from President Franklin D. Roosevelt. This tactic was successful, and after the fall of 1939 funding was at a significantly higher level, allowing theoretical and experimental research to move faster. With the entry of the United States into World War II, British and French scientists joined the efforts in the Western Hemisphere.

By mid-1942, it was obvious that pilot plants—and eventually full-sized factories—would have to be built, and that the scientists were ill prepared for this sort of activity. Because the work was now being done in secrecy and considerable construction was foreseen, Gen. Leslie R. Groves of the U.S. Army Corps of Engineers was given controlling authority. Scientific direction was retained by the National Defense Committee and subsequently by the Office of Scientific Research and Development, both under Vannevar Bush. Because much early research was performed at Columbia University in New York, the Engineers' Manhattan District headquarters was initially assigned management of such work, from which came the name "Manhattan Project" for the nationwide efforts.

Groves, possessed of great energy and willing to use his authority, soon had most research consolidated at the University of Chicago, under Arthur H. Compton. Groves purchased the Oak Ridge, Tenn., site for separation of the fissionable uranium-235 isotope, found to the extent of only 0.7 percent in uranium ores, and began bringing industrial giants, such as the contracting company of Stone and Webster and the Dupont Chemical Company, into the project. Funds, totaling an enormous and unforeseen $2 billion by the war's end, came from a special account that Congress voted the president for secret purposes. With such backing and under pressure to produce a weapon for use in the current war, Groves proceeded simultaneously on as many fronts as possible. No approach could be disregarded until proven unsatisfactory. Hence, liquid thermal diffusion, centrifuge, gaseous diffusion, and electromagnetic separation processes were all tried to extract U-235 from U-238. The last two techniques, developed in huge plants at Oak Ridge, ultimately proved to be the most successful.

In December 1942, Enrico Fermi succeeded in producing and controlling a chain reaction in the pile, or reactor, he built at the University of Chicago. This reactor not only provided necessary information for construction of a weapon but also furnished the means for a second path to the bomb. Uranium-238, while it does not fission in a reactor, can capture neutrons and ultimately be transformed into a new element, plutonium, not found in nature but highly fissionable. Plutonium, moreover, was seen to have the advantage of possessing different chemical properties, which would permit its extraction from uranium in processes simpler than the physical means required to separate the uranium isotopes. Five gigantic reactors were constructed on the banks of the Columbia River, near Hanford, Wash., to produce plutonium.

Appreciable quantities of U-235 from Oak Ridge and plutonium from Hanford were not produced until 1945, although means to employ these materials in a bomb were studied earlier. In late 1942, Groves placed J. Robert Oppenheimer in charge of a newly created weapons laboratory on an isolated mesa at Los Alamos, N. Mex. Oppenheimer's stature as a leading theoretical physicist encouraged many scientists to "drop out of sight" and work on the project for the duration of the war. Relatively little difficulty was encountered in designing a uranium weapon. Ballistics was a well-developed subject; one piece of U-235 could, with confidence, be fired at another in a gun barrel, with the knowledge that together they would form a critical (explosive) mass. The atomic bomb dropped on Hiroshima, Japan, on Aug. 6, 1945, was of this construction. The technique was unsuitable for plutonium, because an isotope that fissioned spontaneously was discovered and it was feared that the neutrons released might cause predetonation. Therefore, a new approach called implosion was conceived. A small sphere of plutonium is surrounded by a chemical high explosive; and when this outer covering is ignited the pressure wave compresses the plutonium core into a mass dense enough to reach criticality (enough neutrons strike plutonium nuclei to maintain the chain reaction). Since this process was entirely novel, a test was held at Alamogordo, N.Mex., on July 16, 1945, before the weapon was used against Nagasaki, Japan, on Aug. 9, 1945.

The Manhattan Project was unique in the size and cost of the effort, the employment of large numbers of scientists for military purposes, the standards of purity and performance required of materials, the one-step scaling-up of several microscopic laboratory processes to full-size industrial production facilities, and the skill and speed with which basic science was brought to application. Numerous confounding technical problems ultimately were overcome—for example, production of a suitable porous membrane for the gaseous diffusion process and discovery of a means of canning uranium cylinders in aluminum jackets.

Leo Szilard and James Franck, among other scientists, feared a postwar arms race and questioned the planned use of nuclear weapons against a nearly defeated Japan.

The nontechnical problems were less tractable: scientists chafed under military supervision, particularly the security regulations that permitted them knowledge only of their own specific topic. More significantly, some scientists, Szilard and James Franck prominent among them, feared a postwar arms race and questioned the planned use of nuclear weapons against a nearly defeated Japan. Because the public knew nothing of the project and could not debate the issue, they felt their own insights should be accorded more weight by those in government. The wisdom and necessity of the Hiroshima and Nagasaki bombings are, of course, still being debated. After the war scientists, and nuclear physicists in particular, were regarded with considerable public awe and veneration and were able to capitalize on this in several ways; but the effect of science on society and the question of morality in science were to become increasingly important issues. Finally, the Manhattan Project may be seen as the starting point for a qualitative change in weaponry that figured large in the postwar arms race.

BIBLIOGRAPHY

Richard G. Hewlett and Oscar O. Anderson, *The New World, 1939/1946.*

— LAWRENCE BADASH

"MANIFEST DESTINY"

"Manifest destiny," a phrase in common use in the 1840's and 1850's, suggesting the supposed inevitability of the continued territorial expansion of the United States. The phrase first appeared in the *Democratic Review* for July-August 1845, in an article in which the editor, John L. O'Sullivan, spoke of "our manifest destiny to overspread the continent allotted by Providence for the free development of our yearly multiplying millions." Although this article referred specifically to the annexation of Texas, the phrase was quickly caught up by the expansionists of the period and utilized in the controversy with Great Britain over Oregon and in the demand for annexations of territory as a result of the war with Mexico in 1846–48. It was also used, in the next decade, in connection with the desire to annex Cuba.

Believers in "manifest destiny" derived their faith in part from the phenomenal rate of population growth in the United States, in part from a conviction of the superiority of American talents and political institutions over those of neighboring countries. Although at first a tenet chiefly of the Democratic party, "manifest destiny" also had its devotees among Whigs and, later, Republicans—notably William H. Seward, who as secretary of state purchased Alaska and sought vainly to annex sundry Caribbean and Pacific islands. "Manifest destiny" was revived as a Republican doctrine in the 1890's and was in evidence in connection with the annexation of Hawaii and the islands taken from Spain in 1898 in the Spanish-American War.

[See also Westward Movement.]

BIBLIOGRAPHY

Julius W. Pratt, "The Origin of 'Manifest Destiny,'" *American Historical Review*, vol. 32.

A. K. Weinberg, *Manifest Destiny.*

— JULIUS W. PRATT

MANN ACT

In 1910 Congress enacted the so-called Mann Act, the title of which was "An Act Further to Regulate Interstate and Foreign Commerce by Prohibiting the Transportation therein for Immoral Purposes of Women and Girls, and for Other Purposes." The object of the legislation was the suppression of the white-slave traffic. The law is an example of federal police legislation for the protection of public morals, based constitutionally upon the commerce power. Although attacked as denying to American citizens the privilege of free access in interstate commerce, as invading the legislative domain of the states, and as exceeding the proper scope of the commerce power, the law was declared constitutional. The Supreme Court held that no person has any constitutional right to use the channels of interstate commerce to promote objectionable or immoral transactions, that the act is a proper exercise of the power to regulate commerce, and, as such, that its effect on the normal scope of state police power is irrelevant. The act was further upheld in the sections forbidding the interstate transportation of women for immoral purposes without any pecuniary element; "the mere fact of transportation" was sufficient. The act is significant in the extension of congressional control over a social and economic problem for the general welfare of the country. The Mann Act was reinforced by anti-racketeering laws passed by Congress in 1961 that made interstate travel or transportation for illegal purposes—such as prostitution—illegal.

BIBLIOGRAPHY

R. E. Cushman, "National Police Power," *Minnesota Law Review*, vol. 3 (1918–19).

— THOMAS S. BARCLAY

MANUFACTURING

Colonial Period to the Civil War

Most manufacturing in the United States was still in the handicraft stage when George Washington became president. The only power-using plants were mills for making flour, lumber, paper, and gunpowder and for grinding plaster. Establishments in the fuel-using industries were limited to charcoal furnaces and forges for working iron; kilns for making lime, tar, and potash; distilleries; brickyards; and a few small glassworks and potteries.

During the next quarter of a century, ending with the War of 1812, such enterprises increased in size and number. More significant were the introduction of machine spinning and weaving, the erection of nearly 200 cotton mills in New England and the middle states, and the use of steam to move machinery. Meanwhile, a manufacturing interest, which had been vocal in a small way when the first federal revenue laws were drafted in 1789, had acquired sufficient influence by 1816 to give a protectionist color to subsequent customs legislation.

Between the War of 1812 and the Civil War American manufacturing acquired its characteristic pattern. Faced by a scarcity of accumulated funds and entrepreneurial experience, its leaders adopted corporate organization as a device for assembling capital and economizing management. This was particularly true in New England. Funds came at first from the accumulations of merchants engaged in trade with Europe and the Far

East. Later the investment reserves of insurance companies and other financial institutions were a source of capital. The mercantile origin of many factories accounted for the early appearance of the agency or factor system and through it of larger corporation groups.

During this period the growth of manufacturing was encouraged by a rapidly expanding market protected to some degree by tariffs and held together by canals and steam transportation on land and water. Factories specialized in the quantity production of standardized goods to supply the multiplying demands of middle-class consumers. Native ingenuity and scarcity of labor stimulated the use of power devices. Yankee inventors designed textile machinery that enabled relatively inexperienced operatives to make plain fabrics for common use cheaply and efficiently. Americans developed interchangeable mechanisms and their correlative, automatic machinery, for working wood and metals, in order to produce tools, agricultural implements, household utensils, firearms, shelf clocks, and vehicles on a large scale and at low cost. These goods were demanded in ever larger quantities by the expanding population of the older settlements and the rapidly growing West. At the same time, imperative tariff demands led to the establishment of shops and foundries to build steamboat machinery and locomotives, and improved transportation hastened the urbanization of industry.

During these fifty years the advent of factory goods in place of household and homespun manufactures revolutionized consumption. Although in 1860 plain fabrics, hats, footwear, axes and nails, plowshares, and hoes still dominated manufacturing output, refinements and modifications of these staples as well as new inventions and novelties already held a conspicuous position in the market. The production of machine-knit goods, collars and cuffs, garment accessories, and silks had become important industries. Manufactures of rubber were familiar. Pressed glass and porcelain, plated metalwares, lamps, and numerous minor conveniences turned out in quantities by machinery had ceased to be luxuries. Changing fashions increasingly determined consumer demand and the industries that served it.

Quantitative evidence of progress was even more imposing. Between 1810 and 1860, or within the memory of people still alive at the latter date, the number of factory cotton spindles in the country increased from a few hundred thousand to over 5 million, each doing far more work than its predecessors. Output of pig iron rose from less than 60,000 tons to nearly 1 million tons. The factory system extended from textiles to the production of clocks and watches, firearms, sewing machines, and other metal manufactures. In 1853 American methods of making interchangeable mechanisms with automatic machinery had aroused European attention and were studied by special commissioners from Great Britain.

Meanwhile a division of labor developed along sectional lines, so that by 1860 the northeastern states were engaged chiefly in mechanical production, the South in growing staple crops such as cotton, and the West in producing and processing other raw materials and provisions.

Reconstruction to World War I

The outcome of the Civil War gave the industrial states control over federal policies and inaugurated a period of high protection during which new branches of manufacture were brought to America from Europe. The discovery of petroleum, the introduction of Bessemer steel, the opening of new mines on Lake Superior and in the South, the growth of inland cities, and a great influx of immigrants from Europe combined to turn the nation's energy increasingly toward manufacturing and to move industries from older sites to centers near new sources of raw material and recently created markets. This phase of American manufacturing development was passing at the close of the century and ended by World War I.

Inventions and scientific discoveries multiplied at an accelerated rate as the industrial organism grew more complex. Some of these, suggested at first by an immediate need, later created new industries. In the 1840's, ten years after the advent of railways, the electric telegraph arrived to facilitate their operation. But a major electric industry did not arise until forty years later, when the incandescent lamp and alternating current changed illumination and power distribution and substituted electric power for shaft and belt transmission in large plants. In 1851 William Kelly, a Kentucky ironmaster, invented a rudimentary Bessemer-type process for steel that enabled him to make better boiler plates for steamboats. The perfected process did not come to America until nearly twenty years later, after heavier traffic made steel rails and bridges a necessity. Petroleum appeared at the opportune moment to provide lubricants for millions of machine-age bearings and subsequently suggested the development of internal combustion engines, which made oil an indispensable source of power.

Public enthusiasm for industrial development was increased by a series of international expositions. Two years after the Crystal Palace Exhibition at London in 1851, where American manufacturers first exhibited their skill to Europe, a similar though smaller exhibition in New York testified to a national awakening on the subject. America was officially represented at the Paris

Exposition of 1867 and at subsequent international fairs in Europe and learned much from this participation. At home the Centennial Exhibition at Philadelphia in 1876 for the first time enabled the public to compare foreign and domestic manufacturing attainments in a systematic way.

Inventions and scientific discoveries multiplied at an accelerated rate as industrial development grew more complex.

The economy continued the rapid rate of expansion of the pre-Civil War decades. By 1890 the United States had surpassed its nearest rivals, England and Germany, in the production of iron and steel and was by almost any method of reckoning the leading industrial nation. Between 1869 and 1914 the number of wage earners engaged in manufacturing more than trebled. Meanwhile, the horsepower employed in factories increased nearly tenfold and the gross value of manufactured products rose from $3.4 billion to $24.2 billion.

Before the turn of the century important manufacturing enterprises had begun to assemble all operations, from extracting raw materials to marketing finished products, under unified control. Along with this vertical integration a horizontal grouping of plants engaged in similar processes of production but situated in different parts of the country occurred under the ownership and direction of giant companies such as the United States Steel Corporation, formed in 1901. This movement necessitated large-scale financing from a center such as New York City and caused control over many large companies to pass from the major stockholders to investment bankers. Simultaneously, management was increasingly entrusted to professional salaried administrators rather than to the chief owners. Although proprietary establishments and moderate-size corporations continued to grow in number, large companies dominated the highly capitalized industries and made big business a characteristic of American manufacturing.

During the 19th century most manufacturing consisted of processing or shaping materials with hand tools or power machinery. The development of new substances was a relatively minor part of industrial activity. The factory overshadowed the laboratory. Only in the 20th century was organized research, made possible in part by the concentration of industrial capital in great corporations, directed consciously and continuously to the discovery of processes and products hitherto unknown. As early as the Civil War, when Abram S. Hewitt watched his furnace assays and introduced gunmetal from Great Britain, research into the structure and qualities of metals and alloys began slowly to emancipate American metallurgy from rule-of-thumb limitations. A line of advance indicated by the requirements of the Bessemer process in the 1870's and of high-test armor plate in the 1880's as well as the development of electrolytic processes and the commercial production of aluminum in the same decade eventually gave industry the metals that made airplanes and automobiles possible. Plastics such as celluloid film led to motion pictures, and the development of synthetic fibers such as rayon greatly changed the textile industry. While the domestic dye industry was largely the result of interrupted trade with Germany in World War I, chemical processes in general were gaining in importance.

Post-World War II

Up to 1940 continuously pursued research was largely confined to the electrical, chemical, rubber, and power machinery industries; in other lines innovation came from outside or by chance more than by design. World War II added aircraft and scientific instruments, over 60 percent supported by government orders or grants, to the research-oriented industries.

Research directed toward the perfection of existing processes inevitably spawned ideas for new ones, and firms engaged in research tended to diversify their products. Large corporations also saw added security in product diversification, while high corporate taxes added an incentive to absorb companies with "carry-over" tax losses regardless of the type of product. Thus rubber companies came to produce moving pictures, and chemical companies made scores of unrelated items. By the second quarter of the 20th century the control of production was so well understood that companies did not fear the problems of managing plants making strange products; the difficulties arose in marketing. Here there were several failures by very large concerns that found that their dealer organizations, educated for a particular purpose, could not efficiently take on radically different tasks.

The unusual needs and taxes of World War II increased the pace of diversification. In World War I, the United States had been chiefly a supplier of raw materials and semifinished goods; in World War II it became the chief source of finished military supplies. And these supplies took on a complexity never dreamed of before. The automobile industry, converted to military products, was the great mass supplier of motors and various assemblies. Wartime needs expanded small electronics operations into the manufacture of radar, computers, and other devices that had continuing postwar importance. Meanwhile, government-financed research penetrated some of the secrets of atomic fission and fusion and laid the base for atomic power in future decades. The development of rockets, confined in the United States to hand and traditional artillery weapons, also led quickly to navigation in outer space. The war also raised real wages and thereby created a permanently larger consumer demand.

Outwardly, the most striking change in United States industry between 1940 and 1960 was its relocation. The breakup of large urban industrial complexes with their high land values and congestion of population had always been inherent in the use of electricity and motor transportation, but it accelerated only after 1940, when massive government and private investments led to the construction of new plants and the underwriting of new housing. Electric power that could make the small plant as efficient as the large one, and automobiles and trucks that could carry small shipments more cheaply than the railroads, opened the whole countryside to factory location. Typically, the movement of factories was from central cities to urban fringe areas, and plants that used highly skilled or middle-income employees moved before those requiring large numbers of unskilled workers.

Outwardly, the most striking change in U.S. industry between 1940 and 1960 was its relocation from large urban plants to the countryside.

The most spectacular industrial developments of the mid-20th century were in electronics and the many new products made by airplane companies. In the electronics field the total value added by manufacture was not great, but the digital computer promised wide future effects on all types of technology. By the late 1960's jets, missiles, and aerospace equipment made the "airplane" census subdivision of the manufacturing list second only to motor vehicles in value added.

By the early 1970's the largest aggregate industrial groups, based on value added, were transportation equipment, machinery other than electrical, food, electrical supplies, and chemical products. Machinery other than electrical, electrical supplies, transportation equipment, and food were also the major employers, each utilizing about 2 million workers.

BIBLIOGRAPHY

Victor S. Clark, *History of Manufactures in the United States.*
Thomas C. Cochran, *American Business in the Twentieth Century.*

— THOMAS C. COCHRAN

MARBURY V. MADISON

Marbury v. *Madison*, 1 Cranch 137 (1803), was decided by the U.S. Supreme Court on Feb. 24, 1803. The importance of the decision in American constitutional history lies chiefly in the position taken that the Court would declare unconstitutional and void acts of Congress in conflict with the Constitution. By this decision the doctrine of judicial review was firmly entrenched in the governmental system, and the position of the judiciary was strengthened in the balance of powers among the legislative, executive, and judicial branches of the government.

The case grew out of the attempt of William Marbury to compel James Madison, secretary of state, to turn over to Marbury a commission as justice of the peace that had been made out to Marbury by Madison's predecessor in office. The Supreme Court had to decide whether it could and should issue a mandamus to compel the secretary of state to act. Intimately involved were issues of contemporary politics. The appointments of Marbury and other Federalists to newly created offices had been made as the Federalist administration under John Adams was retired, to be succeeded by Republicans under the leadership of Thomas Jefferson. At the head of the Supreme Court was Chief Justice John Marshall, a staunch Federalist. Granting the writ of mandamus would therefore be regarded as an exertion not merely of judicial power on the executive, but of Federalist power on Democratic-Republican party leadership as well. The customs of the Constitution were not yet well established, and it was not known whether the writ would be obeyed even if issued.

The opinion of the Supreme Court, written by the chief justice, began not with the constitutional question, the existence of which was not generally recognized, but with the question of Marbury's right to the commission. He found that Marbury had such a right. Reasoning from accepted principles of government, he concluded that the laws of the country must provide a remedy for the violation of a vested legal right, and that the writ of mandamus was the proper form of remedy. The remaining question was whether the Supreme Court could issue the writ. The power was not included among the grants of original jurisdiction made to the Supreme Court in the Constitution, but it was given by a section in the Judiciary Act of 1789, which had the effect of expanding the original jurisdiction of the Court beyond the group of powers enumerated in the Constitution. The chief justice argued that Congress could not expand the original jurisdiction of the Court. The act was therefore in conflict with the Constitution, and it became necessary to decide whether an act repugnant to the Constitution could become the law of the land. The Court answered in the negative. It held the statutory provision unconstitutional, and decided that the writ of mandamus could not be issued by the Supreme Court.

Contemporary interest lay less in the doctrine of judicial review than in the political aspects of the case. The chief justice succeeded in condemning the acts of the Jefferson administration, and then, by a step that appeared superficially to be an act of judicial self-restraint, avoided a resulting decision that might have terminated in mutiny when it came to enforcement. Only gradually did emphasis in appraisal of the case shift to the topic of the power of the courts to invalidate federal legislation deemed by them to be in conflict with the Constitution.

[See also Midnight Judges.]

BIBLIOGRAPHY

A. J. Beveridge, *The Life of John Marshall.*

Charles Warren, *The Supreme Court in United States History.*

— CARL BRENT SWISHER

MARRIAGE AND DIVORCE

Twentieth-century family trends in the United States, as in other industrialized countries, have been on a seesaw. In the nineteenth century and the first third of the twentieth century, average age at marriage increased, family size declined, and divorce became easier to obtain. After the Depression of the 1930s, however, all three of these trends turned around—the median marriage age for women dropped to near twenty, there was a "baby boom" in which the birth rate increased by 60 percent, and the divorce rate fell. By the late 1960s the seesaw reverted to its former position as the habits of previous decades reemerged. The baby boom now looked like an aberration, a reaction to the deprivations and disruptions of the Great Depression and World War II, when many could not plan on a stable future. The abrupt return to an older age at marriage, a decline in fertility, and rise in the divorce rate created a "crisis" atmosphere, leading many to fear the "end" of the family.

This decline in the centrality of marriage in adult lives reflected socioeconomic and demographic changes in American society beginning in the late 1960s, but the causal relationship between those changes and the decline was difficult to pinpoint. It may have been that many adults in the United States did in fact celebrate romance but at the same time placed a high value on personal freedom, particularly as the U.S. economy made that freedom possible. It was no longer necessary to find oneself trapped in an unhappy marriage. Another possibility was that the necessity for both partners to work to support themselves and their children in a way they deemed satisfactory, and the emphasis on commitment that characterized many occupations, led women and men to have little time for family life. The growth of organized leisure, sports, and other recreation provided many adults with absorbing alternatives to family life as well.

The decline in the centrality of marriage in adult lives reflects socioeconomic and demographic changes beginning in the 1960's, but causal relationships are difficult to pinpoint.

Perhaps two more phenomena account for the reduced importance of marriage in the lives of adults. First, changes in gender roles made marriages difficult to negotiate and maintain. In the nineteenth century industrialization took men away from the family to work, which deprived them of involvement with children and left the tasks and reward of child rearing to women. The result was that men were far less likely than women to see children either as a source of personal meaning, happiness, stability, or as a source of adult status in the community. As more and more women entered the workforce, people became confused about what the division of labor inside marriage should be. Some opted to form other relationships, cohabiting with others (of the same or opposite sex) or living alone.

The growth in the number of people living alone was another force influencing change in family life. The living arrangements of unmarried adults changed dramatically after World War II, with the result that in 1990 more than one-quarter of U.S. households contained only one person, compared with only 10 percent in 1940. Much of this increase reflected a decline in family extension among the unmarried, as those who once lived with available family members (parents, adult children, or other kin) were able to afford homes of their own. This change, however, meant that young adults no longer had to marry to leave their parents, and those contemplating ending a marriage had alternatives that preserved their privacy, autonomy, and adult status.

One result of the increase in the divorce rate has been the impoverishment of women. Professional women suffered inequalities of divorce settlements to be sure, but poor women suffered more, especially after the introduction of no-fault divorce in the late 1960s. The reason for impoverishment was in part visible in a statistic of the 1980s, namely, that less than 4 percent of divorced women received alimony, and only half of all women awarded child support received the full amount, with women receiving $2,500 annually on average.

The decline in marriage and remarriage has also meant that many children are raised by and often born into one-parent families. In 1991 the median family income of female-headed households with children was only 30 percent the level of income of households where both parents were living with children. In other industrialized countries, child poverty rates were a third or less than in the United States, because either the divorce rate was still low, as in Japan and southern Europe, or welfare programs supporting children were substantial. Children in the poorest U.S. communities have disproportionately suffered from these trends in poverty and family dislocation. Marriage declined dramatically in African-American communities. By 1990 more than half of all black children lived in one-parent families, compared with less than one-quarter of white or Hispanic children. About one-third of white children living with one parent were poor, while this was the case for nearly two-thirds of minority children.

By the 1990s many novelties accompanied the return of the marriage-trend seesaw. As divorces increased to nearly one of every two marriages so did remarriages. Although more than 70 percent of divorced men and women remarried, it was predicted 60 percent of those remarriages would fail, resulting in 1 million remarriages every year and leading to the practice known as "serial monogamy." Remarried couples suffer from more stress than those couples marrying for the first time, including greater financial problems, stepparenting, and dealing with former spouses. About 40 percent of remarriages in the 1990s involved stepchildren, and those couples experienced a higher divorce rate than childless remarried couples.

Another novel aspect of the post-baby boom era has been the increasing frequency of detailed contracts along with the general contract of marriage itself. Beginning in the colonial period, wealthy women tried to protect themselves with prenuptial agreements. These contracts fell into disuse, only to reappear and became quite common in the 1980s, as couples attempted to transform a relationship of love, or perhaps reinforce it, by resorting to economics. An economic agreement, it was believed, would protect both sides of a marriage. By 1995 all fifty states permitted such contracts, although only thirty recognized them as legal instruments.

Conservative commentators often urge that a return to the family patterns and gender roles of the 1950s, that is, yet another swing of the seesaw, is needed to preserve the family. Others argue that marriage and family life will need to continue to change to reflect the new realities of men's and women's lives. An altogether new equilibrium, centered on a family-friendly workplace in which men and women build long-term relationships around children, home, and community, is theoretically possible, although the complexities of the late twentieth century made the likelihood of its achievement uncertain.

[See also Family.]

BIBLIOGRAPHY

Andrew J. Cherlin, *Marriage, Divorce and Remarriage*, rev. ed. (Cambridge, Mass., 1992).

Frances K. Goldscheider and Linda Waite, *New Families, No Families? The Transformation of the American Home* (Berkeley, Calif., 1991).

David Popenoe, *Disturbing the Nest: Family Change and Decline in Modern Societies* (New York, 1988).

Lenore J. Weitzman, *The Divorce Revolution: The Unexpected Social and Economic Consequences for Women and Children in America* (New York, 1985).

— FRANCES K. GOLDSCHEIDER

MARSHALL PLAN

Marshall Plan, the popular name of the European Recovery Program (1948–52), which grew out of a proposal by Secretary of State George C. Marshall in a speech at Harvard University on June 5, 1947. Designed to revive the European economy in order to provide political and social conditions under which free institutions could survive, the plan proposed that European countries take the initiative in assessing their resources and requirements to show what they could do to give effect to American economic aid.

Sixteen countries, led by Great Britain and France, established the Committee of European Economic Cooperation to outline a four-year recovery program. This was later replaced by the permanent Organization of European Economic Cooperation (OEEC), to which West Germany was also ultimately admitted. The U.S. Congress in April 1948 enacted legislation for a recovery program that was placed under the control of the

Economic Cooperation Administration (ECA), headed by Paul J. Hoffman. In an effort to restore agricultural and industrial production to prewar levels, create financial stability, promote economic cooperation, and expand exports, the United States in a four-year period appropriated some $12 billion (plus $1.5 million for assistance on credit terms). This period saw great efforts made toward European reconstruction; the gross national product of Western Europe rose 25 percent, or 15 percent over prewar levels. The Soviet Union and its satellites refused to participate in the program.

BIBLIOGRAPHY

Harry Bayard Price, *The Marshall Plan and Its Meaning.*

— FORREST C. POGUE

MARTIAL LAW

Martial law is the use of military forces to control part or all of an area in which the civil authorities are losing or have lost control or in which their continued functioning would be dangerous. In practice in the United States, martial law may exist side by side with civil courts, and military commanders may find themselves subject to judicial review for actions that, judged against the pressures, apparent facts, and necessities of the moment, appear unreasonable. Martial law must be declared by the president in federal cases; this is a power he cannot delegate. Governors may declare martial law within their states.

Martial law in the United States is directly descended from English practice of the 17th and 18th centuries. President George Washington set the precedent when he dispatched troops to quell the Whiskey Rebellion of 1794 by ordering all rebels to be delivered to civil courts for trial. Thereafter, martial law was rarely invoked until World War II, even though troops have been called to assist civil authorities. Andrew Jackson declared martial law in New Orleans in the face of imminent British attack in 1814. It was also declared in Indiana in 1864 in the face of Copperhead threats and led to the important Supreme Court decision in *Ex parte Milligan* (1866) protecting civilians from being arbitrarily tried by the military authorities when civil courts are still functioning. Troops were called out during the railroad strikes of 1877, in Idaho in 1899, and again during the coal strikes in Colorado in 1893–94, 1896–97, 1902–03, and 1927–28.

Murry D. Van Wagoner at a German railroad station near the Czech border during ceremonies marking the delivery, under the Marshall Plan, of 75 freight cars for West Germany. (UPI/Corbis-Bettmann)

Martial law was not actually declared in all cases. In a few instances the declaration did not come from the president or *eo nomine* ("in his name") as the law requires. The state governments involved have often hesitated to invoke martial law, and the reasons have sometimes been more political than legal, as can well be seen in the exchanges between President Lyndon Baines Johnson and his potential Republican opponent in the 1968 elections, Gov. George Romney of Michigan, at the time of the July 1967 Detroit riots. Martial law has also been used on occasion after natural disasters, as in Wilkes-Barre, Pa., when the Susquehanna River flooded following Hurricane Agnes in June 1972.

Martial law has been declared within the United States thirty times during the period 1789–1975. The pattern apparent by 1972 was the use of martial law to bolster civil authority rather than to replace it, with lawmen making arrests and taking the prisoners before civil rather than military courts. This suits the military, who are rarely happy in the legal morass of a civilian situation, especially since 1932, when the Supreme Court modified the 1909 *Moyer* v. *Peabody* decision by a ruling in *Sterling* v. *Constantin* that placed martial law under judicial review. Later court decisions upholding the rights of individuals rather than those of society in criminal cases have made even such matters as preventing looting more difficult.

For a short period right after World War I, martial law was declared and the War Department made illegal use of troops because the National Guard had not yet been reorganized. Regulations that were in other respects quite clear were not violated, except that the president's approval was not obtained (Woodrow Wilson was unavailable). Much more patent abuses of martial law were its invocation by the governors of Oklahoma (1935), South Carolina (1935), Arizona (1935), Tennessee (1939), and Georgia (1940) for political purposes. In Arizona the state attempted to interfere with a federal project on federal land. Rhode Island also employed martial law against horse racing (1937).

Martial law was used in June 1943 to stop a race riot in Detroit. It was also used in Hawaii in the aftermath of the attack on Pearl Harbor. There for the first time the federal government was involved in the consequences. Faced with the apparent threat of invasion and concerned over the possibility that the Japanese population in the islands would prove to be fifth columnists, the governor called upon the military authorities to take over. He acted in violation of the Hawaiian Organic (Territorial) Act and invoked the concept of military government, which was only proper in an invaded enemy territory. What was required was a declaration of martial law. The proper procedure would have been for the military to have supported, rather than supplanted, the local police forces. A much more serious mistake was the closing of the civil courts and the trial of civilians in military courts. The cases of White, an embezzling stockbroker, and of Duncan, a civilian who scuffled with a marine guard, reached the Supreme Court (*Duncan* v. *Kahanamoku*, 327 U.S. 304 [1946]). In *Duncan* the Supreme Court went beyond judicial review in declaring military trials of nonmilitary personnel unlawful. Further cases may arise, since army manuals in 1969 still envisaged military trials of civilians.

After the milestone Supreme Court decision in *Brown* v. *Board of Education of Topeka* (1954), the use of martial law accelerated. Incidents at Little Rock, Ark., in 1957; Oxford, Miss., in 1962; and Selma, Ala., in 1965 recalled the old doctrine that the entire force of the nation could be used to uphold the Constitution and the Court, revived the use of the anti-Ku Klux Klan legislation of 1871, and saw the federalization of the state National Guard after U.S. troops appeared and the employment of U.S. marshals supported by troops. In April 1968, after the death of Martin Luther King, Jr., the Riot Act of 1792 was read to the crowds in Washington, D.C., and troops were then employed. Of the ten declarations of martial law from 1945 to 1969, five were to support the federal government, four were to aid the states, and one was to disperse "Resurrection City" in Washington, D.C., in June 1968.

BIBLIOGRAPHY

Robin Higham, ed., *Bayonets in the Streets.*

Frederick Bernays Wiener, "Martial Law Today," *American Bar Association Journal*, vol. 55 (1969).

— ROBIN HIGHAM

MASON-DIXON LINE

Mason-Dixon line is the southern boundary line of Pennsylvania, and thereby the northern boundary line of Delaware, Maryland, and West Virginia, formerly part of Virginia. It is best known historically as the dividing line between slavery and free soil in the period of history before the Civil War, but to some extent it has remained the symbolic border line between North and South, both politically and socially.

The present Mason and Dixon line was the final result of several highly involved colonial and state boundary disputes, at the bottom of which was the Maryland Charter of 1632, granting to the Calvert family lands lying "under the fortieth degree of Northerly Latitude." Acute trouble arose with the grant and charter to William Penn in 1681 that contained indefinite and even impossible clauses with regard to boundaries. The terms of the two charters were inconsistent and contradictory. A full century of dispute with regard to the southern boundary of Pennsylvania was the result. At first the trouble was between Pennsylvania and Maryland. Had all Pennsylvania claims been substantiated, Baltimore would have been included in Pennsylvania, and Maryland reduced to a narrow strip. Had all Maryland claims been established, Philadelphia would have been within Maryland. There were conferences, appeals to the Privy Council, much correspondence, attempted occupation, temporary agreements, all without permanent solution. The Maryland and Pennsylvania proprietors continued the quarrel until 1760, when an agreement was finally made. Under its terms, two English surveyors, Charles Mason and Jeremiah Dixon, began the survey of the boundary line in 1763. Completed after four years' work, the boundary line between Maryland and Pennsylvania was set at 39°43′17.6″ north latitude. The results were ratified by the crown in 1769. In the meantime, Virginia contested the boundary west of Maryland in a dispute that lasted for many years and ended with the extension of the Mason and Dixon line westward, a settlement not completed until 1784. Historically the line embodies a Pennsylvania boundary triumph.

BIBLIOGRAPHY

John E. Potter, "Pennsylvania and Virginia Boundary Controversy," *Pennsylvania Magazine of History and Biography*, vol. 38.

James Veech, *Mason and Dixon's Line: A History*.

— ALFRED P. JAMES

MASSACHUSETTS BAY COMPANY

The history of the Massachusetts Bay Company is in reality not the history of a trading company, but of a theocracy, one of the most interesting of the early American experiments in utopias. The royal charter of 1629 confirmed to a group of merchants and others land already granted to them, presumably, by the Council for New England in 1628, with power to trade and colonize in New England between the Merrimack and the Charles rivers. Under the council's patent the Massachusetts group had local powers of self-government, subject to the general government to be established by the council over all New England. The royal charter removed Massachusetts from its position of dependence on the council's general government and allowed the company to establish whatever government it chose for its colony, subject to no superior authority except that of the king. The company in its beginnings closely resembled other trading companies operating in the New World, but almost immediately after receiving its charter, it changed the emphasis of its interest from trade to religion. Puritan stockholders who considered prospects for religious and political reforms in England increasingly hopeless under Charles I decided to migrate to New England with their families, possessions, and the company charter. Some compromises concerning the business administration were made with the merchants remaining behind, but control of the enterprise for the future lay with those who left England in the Great Migration of 1630, and the government designed for the trading company in England became that of the colony of New England.

Almost immediately after receiving its charter, the Massachusetts Bay Company changed the emphasis of its interest from trade to religion.

The charter of 1629 provided for the usual organs of government—governor, assistants, and general court of the stockholders—but omitted the clause requiring the company to hold its business sessions in England. This omission made it possible for Puritan leaders among the stockholders to transfer the company with its charter to the colony in New England and to superimpose upon the colony the government designed for the company. By so doing they could use the power of the general court to admit new members as a means of limiting the suffrage in the colony to those of their own religious faith and in a few years to transform the enterprise from a trading company existing for profit into a theocracy practically free from outside control. As a further safeguard, the assistants tried to govern the colony without the share of the general court except in annual elections, but when this breach of charter terms was objected to, the general court received back its legitimate authority. With the expansion of settlement, representative government evolved and the general court came to be composed of deputies from the towns who sat with the governor and assistants, until a bicameral court was established in 1644. Dissent within the theocracy resulted in the voluntary exile of the group that founded Connecticut, and the forced exile of Roger Williams and Anne Hutchinson, founders of Rhode Island towns.

The Council for New England under the leadership of its president, Sir Ferdinando Gorges, almost immediately charged that the charter had been surreptitiously obtained, and, aided by leading officials of government, including Archbishop William Laud, began a campaign to have it annulled. In 1635 the council surrendered its own charter and asked the king to regrant the land in eight charters to eight members of the council, a process that would give the new patentees an opportunity to inspect all previous grants for purposes of confirmation. It was expected that the Massachusetts charter would be caught in this net. The plan failed because only one of the eight patents, that for Maine, passed the seals before the outbreak of the Puritan Revolution.

Massachusetts Bay Company remained neutral during the Puritan Revolution in England, but joined with Plymouth, Connecticut, and New Haven in a defensive confederation in 1643, perhaps partly as a protection against being drawn into the struggle. The Massachusetts government considered itself an independent commonwealth after 1649. Nevertheless, when the monarchy was restored in 1660, the company recognized the relationship to the mother country that the charter defined. After the Navigation Acts were passed, the leaders in the theocracy found it extremely difficult to be reconciled to the dependent position of the colony. Because they refused to accept many features of England's new colonial policy, they gradually incurred the displeasure of the crown. The commission sent over in 1664 to conquer New Netherland was instructed also to visit the New England colonies and investigate conditions. The commission and others reported Massachusetts at error in many respects: coining money without authority, extending government over the region of Maine and New Hampshire at the north, restricting the suffrage to church members, denying freedom of worship to dissenters, and, most important of all, refusing to obey the Navigation Acts or to recognize Parliament's authority over them. The company avoided trouble for a while by a policy of procrastination and evasion, but in 1676 Edward Randolph was dispatched on another mission of investigation. His report was even more damning than that of the 1664 commission. At the king's demand the company sent over agents to negotiate some sort of compromise, but thereafter failed to fulfill the promises made by the agents. The Lords of Trade, exasperated by the long delays and the failure to get results, recommended annulling the charter on the ground that the company had not lived up to its terms. Formal charges were made against the company and the charter withdrawn by *scire facias* proceedings in 1684, after which the company as a corporation ceased to exist. Its government, however, continued to function without legal status until the establishment of the Dominion of New England in 1686.

Although the company very early lost its character as a trading company and became a theocracy, the charter itself was necessary to the maintenance of that theocracy because of the almost complete governmental control it gave to the company's general court. Under that outer shell the colony developed a very close union of church and state, a theocracy more or less on the Calvinist pattern. To maintain the purity of the religious ideals of the leaders, the very limited suffrage was necessary, as was the weeding out of dissenters, the control of the school system, and the refusal to recognize the power of Parliament over it. Yet the colony was too weak to resist the authority of the mother country by force; it had to resort to strategy. The faith of the leaders in God's protection of them led them to believe that in a crisis He would come to their aid. This faith allowed them to dare to procrastinate and at times even to defy the mother country. If they had been more conciliatory they might have preserved the charter. As it was, their actions and attitude made England believe that no policy of colonial administration could ever be successful as long as the Massachusetts Bay theocracy existed. The only way to destroy it was to destroy the company through its charter.

BIBLIOGRAPHY

C. M. Andrews, *The Colonial Period in American History*, vol. I.

H. L. Osgood, *The American Colonies in the Seventeenth Century*, vol. I.

— VIOLA F. BARNES

MAYFLOWER

Mayflower, a three-masted, double-decked, bark-rigged merchant ship of 180 tons, with a normal speed of 2.5 miles per hour. Christopher Jones became its master in

Engraving of the Mayflower, published by John A. Lowell, 1905, after a painting by Marshall Johnson. (Corbis-Bettmann)

1608 and its quarter owner in 1620. The *Mayflower* was chartered in London to take the Pilgrims to America. They left Leiden, Holland, on July 31, 1620 (all dates are new style), for Delfthaven, and the next day they sailed for Southampton, England, aboard the *Speedwell*, a smaller but older craft that they had outfitted for the voyage to America. There they met the *Mayflower* and took on supplies for the voyage. The two ships sailed on Aug. 15, but put back into Dartmouth harbor about Aug. 23 because of the leaky condition of the *Speedwell*. They sailed again about Sept. 2, but the *Speedwell* continued unseaworthy and they were again forced to return, this time to Plymouth harbor, where the smaller ship was abandoned. Some of the passengers returned to shore and 102 passengers and crew finally sailed on the *Mayflower* on Sept. 16, sighted Cape Cod on Nov. 19, and arrived in what is now the harbor of Provincetown, Cape Cod, Mass., on Nov. 21. Some time was spent in taking on wood and water, in mending their shallop, and in exploring the bay and land, so that they did not reach the site of Plymouth, Mass., until Dec. 21, 1620. The *Mayflower* followed the land-exploring party and sailed into Plymouth harbor on Dec. 26, where it remained until houses could be built for the new settlement. It sailed for England on Apr. 5, 1621, reaching London safely. It was in the port of London again in 1624, after which its history is uncertain because of confusion with several other contemporary ships of the same name.

BIBLIOGRAPHY

William Bradford, *History of the Plymouth Plantation.*
W. S. Nickerson, *Land Ho!—1620.*

— R. W. G. VAIL

MAYFLOWER COMPACT

Mayflower Compact, the agreement signed on Nov. 11, 1620, by the male passengers on the *Mayflower*, before coming ashore, that they would form a body politic and submit to the will of the majority in whatever regulations of government were agreed upon. Its purpose, according to William Bradford, was to hold in check the restless spirits on board who had threatened to strike out for themselves when the Pilgrim leaders decided to land in New England instead of Virginia. The Pilgrims held a patent from the Virginia Company granting rights to the soil and to local self-government, but this patent was of no use after they settled in New England. The compact appears therefore to have been a voluntary agreement to establish a local government that, although having no legal status until a patent could be obtained from the Council for New England, would at least have the strength of common consent. Its significance lies rather in its similarity to later ideas of democratic government than in any new philosophy of popular government in the minds of its authors. Plymouth Colony, though never so completely theocratic as Massachusetts, nevertheless leaned more toward theocracy than toward democracy.

BIBLIOGRAPHY

H. L. Osgood, *The American Colonies in the Seventeenth Century.*

— VIOLA F. BARNES

MAYSVILLE VETO

Maysville Veto, an episode in the long struggle over internal improvements. In 1830 Congress passed a bill authorizing a subscription of stock in the Maysville, Washington, Paris and Lexington Turnpike Road Company. In vetoing the bill President Andrew Jackson pointed out that the project lay entirely within one state (Kentucky), that it had no connection with any established system of improvement, and that it therefore violated the principle that such works, to receive federal aid, had to be national and not local in character. The attitude of Jackson was in accord with prevailing Democratic principles but he was perhaps not unmindful of its political effect. "The veto," wrote Martin Van Buren, "was the wedge which split the party of internal improvements, a party which was wielded by a triumvirate of active and able young statesmen as a means through which to achieve for themselves the glittering prize of the Presidency."

BIBLIOGRAPHY

Archer Butler Hulbert, *Historic Highways of America.*

— J. HARLEY NICHOLS

MCCARRAN-WALTER ACT

McCarran-Walter Act of June 27, 1952, was the basic United States immigration law from 1952 until passage of the Immigration and Nationality Act, which went into effect Dec. 1, 1965. The McCarran-Walter Act revised all previous laws and regulations regarding immigration, naturalization, and nationality, and brought them together into one comprehensive statute. The law retained the national-origin system of the Immigration Act of 1924, under which the United Kingdom, Germany, and Ireland were allotted more than two-thirds of the annual maximum quota of 154,657 persons (380 more than the previous maximum). The most significant changes effected by the McCarran-Walter Act were: (1) It removed race as a bar to immigration and naturalization; thus, countries whose citizens were previously ineligible for naturalization were assigned annual quotas of not fewer than 100 persons. (Far Eastern countries, particularly, had bitterly resented the exclusion policy.) (2) It removed discrimination between sexes. (3) It gave preference to aliens with special skills needed in the United States. (4) It provided for more rigorous screening of aliens in order to eliminate security risks and subversives, and for broader grounds for the deportation of criminal aliens.

The law aroused much opposition, mainly on the grounds that it discriminated in favor of northern and western European nations, and that its provisions for eliminating undesirable aliens were unduly harsh. It was passed over President Harry S. Truman's veto.

— CHARLES S. CAMPBELL, JR.

MCCARTHY-ARMY HEARINGS

In 1954 the Permanent Investigations Subcommittee of the Senate Committee on Government Operations, commonly known as the "McCarthy Committee," conducted hearings on the charges and countercharges arising out of its investigation (beginning October 1953) of alleged spying at the army base at Fort Monmouth, N.J. These hearings proved to be a crucial turning point in the career of Sen. Joseph R. McCarthy of Wisconsin. Although "McCarthyism" (a term that came to mean unsubstantiated charges of communism) continued to flourish, the hearings dealt his reputation a blow from which it never recovered.

The hearings were the outgrowth of McCarthy's charges that the army was lax in ferreting out Communist spies. He claimed it was protecting those responsible for granting a left-wing dentist at Fort Monmouth a promotion and honorable discharge following the discovery of his political sympathies.

After some unsuccessful attempts to mollify McCarthy and have him call off his investigation, Robert T. Stevens, the secretary of the army, charged that McCarthy and his subcommittee's chief counsel, Roy M. Cohn, had intervened to obtain special treatment for Private G. David Schine, the recently drafted son of a millionaire hotel chain owner who, as a good friend of Cohn, had acted as a sometime subcommittee "expert" on communism. The army charged that, having failed to obtain an officer's commission for Schine, McCarthy and his staff were using the Fort Monmouth hearings to harass the army into granting Schine an assignment to the subcommittee in New York rather than the overseas tour he could normally expect. McCarthy and Cohn then charged that the army was, in effect, holding Schine "hostage" in an effort to force them to abandon their investigation of subversion.

McCarthy temporarily gave up his seat on his own subcommittee to allow it to investigate the charges, insisting, however, on the right to cross-examine witnesses at any length. In return, the army was granted the same privilege. This privilege proved disastrous to McCarthy, for the hearings soon turned into a seemingly interminable shambles. The tone was set on the very first day (Apr. 22) when, during the reading of the army's charges against him, McCarthy repeatedly interrupted with "points of order" that merely presaged rambling, seemingly irrelevant speeches. Characteristically, he also challenged the testimony of the army's first witness, a high-ranking officer, with the apparently irrelevant (and false) charge that the officer's brother had been forced to resign from the State Department as a "security risk."

The hearings were shown daily on national television. As they dragged on, McCarthy's "points of order" and rambling, bulldogged, monotonic interjections became the object of widespread exasperation and (worse for his reputation as a serious enemy of dangerous Communists) standard fare of television and nightclub comedians. His vicious attacks on Maj. Gen. Ralph Zwicker, the highly decorated war hero who was the commanding officer at Fort Monmouth, shocked many Americans, raising questions about the nature of McCarthy's own vaunted "patriotism." Meanwhile, Cohn looked like McCarthy's *éminence grise*, whispering in McCarthy's ear and scowling at adversaries. Only too late, halfway through the hearings, did McCarthy and Cohn realize what was happening and begin an effort to project a new image.

McCarthy's "points of order" and rambling interjections became the object of widespread exasperation and standard fare for television and nightclub comedians.

Just as they seemed to be making headway in establishing a new, less sinister look, McCarthy made his major blunder. Angered by the cross-examination of Cohn by the army's wily old Boston counsel, Joseph N. Welch, McCarthy blurted out that he had information that one of the junior members of Welch's law firm had belonged to a left-wing lawyers' organization. Welch was prepared for the attack. Tears welling in his eyes, he said that until this moment, when McCarthy had tried to wreck the promising career of a brilliant young lawyer, he had not realized how cruel and reckless he could be. In a short statement redolent of sadness and bitterness, he lashed out at McCarthy and his methods, making him appear like a vicious bully. McCarthy himself was taken aback by Welch's emotional attack. Moreover, for the first time many Americans gained an insight into the kind of human tragedy McCarthy's "investigations" had caused. From then on, despite the efforts of McCarthy and Cohn to be on their best behavior, they were discredited in the eyes of a majority of the television viewers, if not in the eyes of a majority of the subcommittee.

After the subcommittee ended its thirty-six days of hearings, it issued four separate reports. The Republican-dominated majority report cleared both McCarthy and the army of most of the charges against them but agreed that Cohn had intervened inordinately to obtain special treatment for Schine. The army was at fault for not reporting his intervention, they said, and McCarthy was negligent in not controlling the actions of the subcommittee staff. Cohn was thereupon forced to resign (July 20) his position as chief counsel.

With McCarthy's prestige and public support greatly damaged by the hearings, his opponents in the Senate initiated hearings to censure McCarthy for contempt of the Senate Privileges and Elections Committee and for unwarranted abuse of Zwicker. The Zwicker charge was eventually dropped, but, by a vote of sixty-seven to twenty-two on Dec. 2, the Senate "condemned," but did not "censure," McCarthy.

BIBLIOGRAPHY

Richard H. Rovere, *Senator Joe McCarthy.*

— HARVEY LEVENSTEIN

MCCORMICK REAPER

The machine with which the name of Cyrus Hall McCormick has always been associated had many inventors, notably Obed Hussey, who patented his machine in 1833, a year before the first McCormick patent, and whose machine was the only practicable one on the market before 1840. It was the McCormick reaper, however, that invaded the Middle West, where the prairie farmer was ready for an efficient harvester that would make extensive wheat growing possible. In 1847 McCormick moved from the Shenandoah Valley in Virginia, where the first machine was built, to Chicago.

Perhaps, as his biographer contends, McCormick, or his father, Robert McCormick, did most effectively combine the parts essential to a mechanical grain cutter. Other improvements came in the 1950's and 1860's—the self-raker, which dispensed with the job of raking the cut grain off the platform, and then the binder, first using wire to bind the sheaves and later twine. The first self-raker was sold in 1854, seven years before McCormick produced such a machine. The first wire binder was put on the market in 1873, two years before the McCormick binder. Through effective organization the McCormick reaper came to dominate the field.

BIBLIOGRAPHY

H. N. Casson, *The Romance of the Reaper.*
Victor S. Clark, *History of Manufactures in the United States.*
W. T. Hutchinson, *Cyrus Hall McCormick.*

— ERNEST S. OSGOOD

MCCULLOCH V. MARYLAND

McCulloch v. *Maryland* (4 Wheaton 316) was decided by the Supreme Court of the United States on Mar. 6, 1819. Congress had incorporated the second Bank of the United States, a branch of which was established in Baltimore. The state of Maryland required all banks not chartered by the state to pay a tax on each issuance of bank notes. When James W. McCulloch, the cashier of the Baltimore branch of the bank, issued notes without paying the tax, Maryland brought suit. Two questions were involved in the case: first, whether Congress had power under the Constitution to establish a bank and, second, whether Maryland could impose a tax on this bank.

Chief Justice John Marshall wrote the opinion for a unanimous court upholding the power of Congress to charter a bank as a government agency and denying the power of a state to tax the agency. Marshall's discussion broadly interpreting the powers of Congress is still a classic statement of the implied powers of the federal government. Congress has been granted the power "to make all laws which shall be necessary and proper for carrying into execution" the expressed powers in the Constitution. Since the Constitution empowers the government to tax, borrow, and engage in war, Congress by incorporating a bank was creating the means to attain the goals of these powers. The chief justice phrased the basic point as follows: "Let the end be legitimate, let it be within the scope of the Constitution, and all means which are appropriate, which are plainly adapted to that end, which are not prohibited, but consist with the letter and spirit of the Constitution, are constitutional." Along with this principle Marshall expounded the notion of federal supremacy, noting that the national government "though limited in its powers, is supreme within its sphere of action."

This led to the second question in the case, the power of the state of Maryland to tax a branch of the U.S. bank located in that state. The answer of the Court was the sum total of several propositions. The power of the federal government to incorporate a bank had been established; the supremacy of the federal government in legal conflicts with state authority had likewise been set forth; and there was agreement that "the power to tax involves the power to destroy." It followed from all of this that an admittedly legal function of the federal government could not be subjected to possible destruction by an inferior government through taxation. The state tax was void.

BIBLIOGRAPHY

A. J. Beveridge, *The Life of John Marshall.*

Charles Warren, *The Supreme Court in United States History.*

— PAUL C. BARTHOLOMEW

MCGUFFEY'S READERS

McGuffey's Readers formed a series of textbooks that molded American literary taste and morality, particularly in the Middle West, from 1840 until the early 20th century. The total sales reached 122 million copies by 1920. Only the Bible and *Webster's Spelling Book* have enjoyed equal acceptance in the United States. William Holmes McGuffey undertook the preparation of the Eclectic Series of school readers at the request of Winthrop B. Smith, a Cincinnati publisher interested in books adapted to the western schools. The *First Reader* (1836) followed the conventional pattern of readers, as indeed did its successors. Its fifty-five lessons with accompanying pictures taught principles of religion, morality, and patriotism. The *Second Reader* (1836) contained eighty-five lessons and sixteen pictures. It included considerable lore about nature, games and sports, manners, and attitudes toward God, relatives, teachers, companions, unfortunates, and animals. Here the pioneer youth found a code of social behavior to carry him safely through any experience. This book plagiarized *Worcester's Readers;* in 1838 damages were paid and the offending pages changed. In 1837 the *Third Reader* and *Fourth Reader,* for older pupils, completed the series. The *Third,* with only three pictures, contained many rules for oral reading. The *Fourth,* an introduction to standard British and American literature, elaborated the objectives of the whole series, the ability to read aloud with sense, clearness, and appreciation. Several revisions were made. In 1844 a *Fifth Reader* was added; in 1857 the material was regraded and a *Sixth Reader* (by Alexander H. McGuffey, a brother) and a *High School Reader* were added; in 1879 the books were completely remade; and in 1901 and 1920 the series was recopyrighted with slight changes.

The popularity of the McGuffey Readers arose partly from the happy adaptation of the substance to frontier interests. The lessons enforced proverbial wisdom, advising accuracy, honesty, truthfulness, obedience, kindness, industry, thrift, freedom, and patriotism. The problems of the world were simplified, so that in the end right always conquered and sin or wrong was always punished. In defense of the many religious selections McGuffey wrote: "In a Christian country that man is to be pitied who at this day can honestly object to imbuing the minds of youth with the language and spirit of the word of God."

BIBLIOGRAPHY

H. C. Minnich, *William Holmes McGuffey and His Readers.*

— HARRY R. WARFEL

MEAT INSPECTION LAWS

Meat inspection laws in the United States originated with the campaign for pure food legislation. After 1887 the publications of the Department of Agriculture, under the supervision of H. W. Wiley, did much to stimulate national and state interest. Spurred to action by the "embalmed beef" scandal at the time of the Spanish-American War, Congress passed in 1906 the Meat Inspection Act, a comprehensive meat inspection statute. This act gave the secretary of agriculture, under the interstate commerce clause, power to inspect all meat and condemn such products as are "unsound, unhealthful, unwholesome, or otherwise unfit for human food." Although modified and amended, this enactment has remained the basis of activity by the federal government.

BIBLIOGRAPHY

C. W. Dunn, ed., *Food and Drug Laws, Federal and State.*

Gustavus Weber, *The Food, Drug and Insecticide Administration.*

— BENJAMIN F. SHAMBAUGH

MEDICARE AND MEDICAID

In most industrialized countries, virtually everyone is covered by governmentally insured health care. The uniquely expensive U.S. medical system, however, consigns most citizens to private health insurance or to none at all. Medicare (government health insurance for the elderly and seriously disabled) and Medicaid (health coverage for the poor under welfare) stand as notable exceptions, accounting for almost one of every three dollars spent on health care in the early 1990s. Since the 1910s major government reform of the U.S. health care system has often seemed to be just around the corner, but, despite overwhelming public support, it has usually foundered on pressures from the medical establishment, crippling charges of socialized medicine, and predictions of greater expense and intrusive, impersonal bureaucracy. President Franklin D. Roosevelt thus omitted health insurance from his Social Security proposals in the 1930s, and President Harry S. Truman's plan in 1945 for national health insurance succumbed to conservative partisanship and an attack from the American Medical Association. With the vast expansion of private health insurance, particularly union-negotiated medical plans, in the 1940s, government plans seemed doomed, but in the 1950s key officials in the Social Security Administration, a group commonly at the core of U.S. welfare state expansion, shifted strategy. To make government health insurance more politically marketable, they proposed that it be confined to the elderly and tied to the increasingly popular old-age insurance program. After all, older Americans, who had to stretch incomes half the national average to cover medical expenses three times as great, could not easily be cast as unworthy welfare cheats. By the late 1950s Medicare was backed by organized labor and many Democrats, including candidate and future president John F. Kennedy. Kennedy never was able to push the program through either house of Congress, and even the legendary legislative skills of his successor, Lyndon B. Johnson, at first could only secure Senate passage. In 1965, however, Kennedy's martyred legacy combined with a strong economy and the overwhelming Democratic congressional majority elected on the coattails of Johnson's 1964 landslide to allow passage of the Social Security Act Amendments of 1965, which established both Medicaid and Medicare as part of Johnson's Great Society.

The uniquely expensive U.S. medical system consigns most citizens to private health insurance or to none at all.

Medicaid's success came less controversially. Medical interests saw some virtue in the government picking up the tab for hospital or doctor bills of "charity cases," and confining government-funded health care to the poor was a common fall-back position for opponents of more wide-ranging plans. As early as 1950 states had been allowed to make payments under federally subsidized welfare programs directly to hospitals, nursing homes, and doctors. An amendment to the Social Security Act in 1960 (the Kerr-Mills program) beefed up these so-called "vendor payments" for the elderly poor while adding coverage of the "medically indigent" elderly, whose health care expenses would otherwise leave them impoverished. In 1965 a new medical assistance program (Medicaid) extended this coverage of the elderly poor's medical costs to low-income people of all ages who qualified under any federally subsidized, state-administered welfare program.

The Medicaid program had a marked impact. It allowed the poor to receive much more care from doctors and hospitals than previously, when they had often postponed treatment until they required emergency-room care. While two-thirds of its recipients by the mid-1990s were low-income women and children, half of its outlays went to nursing home and other long-term institutional services for the elderly, the disabled, and AIDS patients. It became, in short, a safety net for the American medical system, assisting in coverage ranging from the elderly poor's Medicare premiums and copayments to long-term institutional services for the developmentally disabled and AIDS patients. Medicaid, however, carried the stigma of welfare, and wide disparities among state programs assured that many who needed medical treatment would receive inadequate coverage or none at all. Medicare, by contrast, was a federally administered, contributory, social insurance program, provided to almost all Americans aged sixty-five and over as a right that they had purportedly earned through previous payments. Medicare opponents sought to limit government's role by proposing the alternative of government-subsidized voluntary private insurance that, they noted, would cover a wider range of medical services, including doctor bills, than the original Medicare plan. Wilbur Mills, chairman of the House Ways and Means Committee, cannily adapted this alternative into a new Part B of Medicare. Thus, Medicare Part A, financed by payroll taxes on employers and employees, reimbursed recipients for hospital and limited post-hospitalization home health care and nursing-home costs, while Part B offered older Americans cut-rate insurance policies (made possible by a 75 percent subsidy taken from government general-revenue funds) covering doctor bills, ambulance charges, and certain lab tests.

Despite, or perhaps because of, the gap between the perception of Medicare as an earned benefit and the reality that most of its costs had not been paid by the elderly themselves, the program became very popular, but it was also much more expensive than advocates had anticipated, even though the Social Security

Administration's overhead to administer the program was gratifyingly low. To gain the acquiescence of medical interests, Medicare had no cost-control provisions to speak of. Guaranteed reimbursement of all customary or reasonable fees, hospitals and doctors cashed in, pushing up medical prices far faster than general inflation, and provided medical services, lab tests, and technologies that a more cost-conscious system might have precluded. Medicaid reimbursement rates soon became less generous, enough so that many doctors refused to participate. Even so, Medicaid expenditures also rocketed, fueled less by sensational cases of provider fraud than by a combination of greater use of medical services and a 700 percent increase in the number of recipients over the program's first fifteen years—a boon, to be sure, for the health of the poor, but an increasingly resented bust for state budgets. Facing mounting costs, Medicare kept increasing payroll taxes, deductibles, and copayments, and in 1983 and 1992 established systems to limit allowable charges by hospitals and doctors. By the mid-1990s Medicare, Medicaid, and medical costs in general approached financial crisis, assuring further reform.

To gain the acquiescence of medical interests, Medicare had no cost-control provisions to speak of.

[See also Health Care; Social Security; Welfare.]

BIBLIOGRAPHY

Edward D. Berkowitz, *America's Welfare State* (Baltimore, 1991).

Sheri I. David, *With Dignity: The Search for Medicare and Medicaid* (Westport, Conn., 1985).

— MARK H. LEFF

MEDICINE AND SURGERY

The early settlers of the American colonies faced the hardships of the frontier and most of the same infectious illnesses they had encountered in their European homelands. Malnutrition and a "starving time" were also common. Few physicians were among the early migrants, and so medical care fell to the traditional sources of comfort and wisdom—grandmothers, clergymen, and other sympathetic souls. When the United States came into being, there were only about 400 physicians with an earned M.D. degree in the nation. The many others who called themselves doctors were trained locally by apprenticeship, but in most cases they were no less successful in coping with the prevalent malaria or the outbreaks of smallpox, diphtheria, and yellow fever than were their European-trained medical colleagues.

Also lacking in the English colonies was the professional focus for medicine. Books were in short supply, and medical schools nonexistent. An occasional ordinance regulating practitioners was passed, but no regular licensing boards, medical societies, or hospitals existed until the late 18th century.

Life expectancy around 1750 was about thirty to thirty-five years, although precise figures are difficult to obtain. Sickness rates were high and malnutrition still rife. Fevers (including malaria), tuberculosis, diphtheria, and measles all continued to abound. Smallpox was a particular scourge. Unlike their European counterparts who were exposed to the disease in infancy, North American children often escaped exposure and thus failed to build up immunity; in times of epidemics of smallpox, American adults often succumbed because they had not met the disease earlier in life.

Medical developments in the colonies during the 18th century were sparse. In 1721, Cotton Mather, a clergyman, and Zabdiel Boylston, a physician, both of Boston, were among the first to try the new procedure of variolation to immunize against smallpox, and they also added significantly to the store of proven medical knowledge. Using simple statistics, they clearly demonstrated that of those who had been immunized, only about 2 percent were likely to succumb to the epidemic form of the disease, whereas in the rest of the population mortality was about 15 percent. From its opening in 1752, the Pennsylvania Hospital in Philadelphia played an important role in medical teaching and in care of patients, and in 1765 the first American medical school opened its doors in the same city. By the end of the century three additional schools had been founded. These developments were strikingly meager in comparison to those in the more settled countries of Europe. Even as late as 1800 only a bare beginning had been made in developing a profession of medicine in the United States with requisite educational institutions, such as schools and hospitals, and collegial bodies, such as medical societies and licensing authorities.

As Americans moved westward, disease continued to burden the early settlers, even after they established themselves permanently. Malaria, scurvy, dysentery, and the respiratory diseases of winter were prevalent in New England as well as in the South and the West. Many Americans of the 18th and 19th centuries, especially those living on the frontier, had little understanding of medical education and cared less about their doctors' training. As the regular doctors began to dose more and more vigorously and yet became no more effective in curing, their patients began to look toward others professing medical knowledge, especially the homeopaths and the botanical practitioners. The high disease rate in all parts of the country continued to create a great demand for the doctor's craft. Tuberculosis was, throughout most of the 19th century, the leading cause of death. All physicians were powerless in its wake, although sanatoriums built in many healthful mountain retreats were of some help. Against the repeated outbreaks of cholera and yellow fever, physicians were no more effective, but these epidemics did spur local and national public health legislation that led to sanitary improvements.

In view of the great number of widespread settlements and the dearth of physicians, especially in the rural areas, it is not surprising that home medical advisers sold well. Such books as *Every Man His Own Doctor;* or *The Poor Planter's Physician*, in the 18th century, and John C. Gunn's *Domestic Medicine*, in the 19th century, were found in many homes. Some of these were written by laymen, such as John Wesley's *Primitive Physic*, very popular after its initial appearance in England in 1747. Others were written by physicians—notably Gunn—and like similar volumes written in the 20th century, contained enough information about regulating the family diet, tending to fevers, and treating the injured to enable most families to manage quite well.

By 1837 there were about 2,500 medical students enrolled in thirty-seven schools. Many more schools were founded as the century progressed, reaching a total of 457 by 1910. Although more and more schools existed, teaching did not improve much. Medical instruction could, after all, be only as good as the state of medical knowledge would allow. Not until the advent of the research-oriented, laboratory-based medical schools of the late 19th century did they add appreciably to the store of medical knowledge and to the understanding of disease processes.

Most American medical schools prior to 1900 were of the proprietary type, meaning that fees paid by students went into the pockets of their professors. Failing a student resulted in an economic loss for the faculty, as did stringent entrance requirements. By the 1880's there were some three-year schools teaching a graded course, but most still awarded the M.D. degree after two years. In most cases the "year" included only four months of didactic lectures, the second year being a repeat of the first. Limitation of books, equipment, and—in some schools—professors led to the need for repeating everything to assure each student's exposure to the necessary fundamentals of medicine. Many students attended lectures in two schools so as to avoid complete duplication. This nongraded curriculum was less expensive for both teachers and students.

As late as 1892 philanthropic aid to medical schools amounted to only about $600,000, whereas schools of theology received over $17 million. Medical students were generally ill prepared and often rowdy and boisterous. Better students usually went into schools of theology or law; the course work relied mainly on lectures, there being only a few demonstrations. Anatomical dissection was often slighted; rarely did students help with surgical operations, and rarely did they see, much less assist in, the delivery of a baby until they were faced with the realities of practice. Yet for all this the results often seemed better than the system.

Even though Jacksonian notions of democracy had led to the suspension of license requirements in many states in the 1830's, a man was expected to fulfill several requirements before he could call himself a doctor. He was to have attended two courses of lectures at a medical school; he was to have studied medicine for at least three years (as an apprentice); he must have reached the age of twenty-one; and, finally, he was expected to possess "proper morals." Often the apprenticeship was the most important part of these requirements, since the medical school term lasted only sixteen weeks and since the second course might be a mere repetition of the first. With the advent of the American Medical Association (AMA) in 1847, there was increasing talk of reform in medical education, but the apprenticeship was still an important means by which a young man learned about disease and how to treat it. Apprenticeship continued to be a major means of medical education until the latter years of the 19th century. It was an efficient method of practical instruction. Not until medical science developed sufficiently to require the student to learn the contents of a theoretical body of knowledge did the medical school almost completely replace the preceptorship. The preceptor usually took the apprentice into his practice as a junior assistant. The student, in return for the privilege of observing his teacher and reading what books the older man might possess, was expected to help mix potions and pills, bleed patients, clean the office, and do other general chores; in addition he paid a fee to the preceptor. Often the apprentice was taken into the family home of his teacher. The chief virtue of the preceptorial system was that it gave the student a practical clinical experience and prevented him from becoming a mere theorist. The most apparent weakness of the system was that everything depended on the training and conscientiousness of the preceptor. If he had few books or little interest in passing on what meager knowledge he himself had acquired, the preceptor did not aid much in the development of the fledgling physician.

Several factors were basic to the problems and concerns facing medical men and the public in the mid-19th century. The gravest issue was the limited effectiveness of the physician to cure patients. There were purges and sedatives, sudorifics and anodynes, but physicians had to rely most heavily upon nature for cures. In the 1840's more physicians began to appreciate this fact, and their understanding culminated in a call for a "rational medicine" in the 1850's. Because Americans were activists, they demanded some form of "dosing," even though effective therapy did not always exist. This was still a problem in the late 20th century. The American physician Worthington Hooker typified the thought of the 1850's when he wrote, "Perhaps the disposition to demand of the physician an active medication in all cases exists to a greater degree in this than other countries. We are preeminently an energetic and enterprising people, and therefore the bold 'heroic' practitioner is apt to meet with favor from the public." (From "Nature of Evidence in Practical Medicine," *New Englander*, vol. II.)

A major problem that the regular medical profession had to face was the increasing popularity of the irregulars, and so the AMA, immediately after its founding, concerned itself with sectarianism. The medical journals repeatedly strove to disprove the claims and charges made by homeopaths, botanics, and others. But this was no easy task. The public was not readily convinced that the practice of calomel-prescribing physicians was better than that of homeopaths who prescribed in minute doses; and, of course, the regulars often achieved no better results. Much of the public realized this full well. It was not merely the uneducated who consulted the sectarians, as was so often the case in the 20th century. George T. Strong, a well-educated New York lawyer and diarist, wrote that he would renounce allopathy and become a zealous convert to homeopathy if the latter were to give relief to his headaches: "Certainly if there be any substitute for the old system, that dispenses with emetics and cathartics and blistering and bleeding and all the horrors anticipation of which makes 'the doctor's' entry give me such a sinking of spirit, it's worth trying."

The regular physicians frequently argued the question of nature versus art. Following the 1835 essay on "Self-Limited Diseases" by Jacob Bigelow, a degree of skepticism regarding therapeutics was engendered. Nature's healing powers had been recognized since antiquity, but in the heyday of heroic medicine as favored by Benjamin Rush during the 1810's and 1820's, nature had been forced to take a back seat to vigorous dosing with drugs and bleeding with the lancet and by leeches. To have been a patient with a febrile disease before the late 19th century must have been an exceedingly unpleasant experience. To the patient already weakened by fever, further insult was brought by blood loss, followed by calomel or castor oil to induce copious diarrhea. The theory was that the disease was caused by a maldistribution of the basic humors of the body—blood, phlegm, yellow bile, and black bile. Purging and bleeding, or perhaps counterirritation by means of blisters, would serve to redistribute the humors to their proper place and normal balance.

Moreover, the practice of medicine in the 19th century was generally not the lucrative business it has become. Where local medical societies existed, they usually published a fee bill stating the standard charges for house calls, bleeding, and other medical services, but payment often went uncollected. The situation was aggravated by the fact that there was an excess of physicians in many urban locales. Many doctors turned to nonmedical activities—such as farming, running drug stores, and other business ventures—simply because of economic necessity.

It would be misleading to assume that the work of the profession was entirely futile. In the first place, as has continued to be the case, many of the physician's therapeutic abilities rested not merely on the use of drugs but also on his skill and art. Second, there were some effective drugs—such agents as cinchona, opium, and digitalis. But American medical advances appeared slowly in the 19th century. Medicine, as was true of American culture in general, still looked to Europe for its lead. By the 1830's the profession had established enough permanent institutions to be able to withstand the continuing encroachment by the sectarians. A number of important discoveries stemming from the work of Americans also began to appear. The physiological studies of digestion carried out by William Beaumont, using the gastric fistula of Alexis Saint Martin, a French-Canadian trapper who had been wounded by a musket shot, captured European interest as well as praise. Beaumont published his findings as a monograph in 1833. Four years later William W. Gerhard of Philadelphia clearly differentiated typhus from typhoid; these two distinct diseases, with different epidemiological characteristics, had been lumped together as one. In 1846, after several false starts and some unreported success, ether anesthesia was announced to the world with immediate acclaim. "Anesthetics constitute our chief claim in the eyes of the civilized world," wrote Oliver Wendell Holmes, Sr., who had witnessed its successful use on Oct. 16, 1846, during a surgical operation at the Massachusetts General Hospital. The surgical work of J. Marion Sims, who devised an effective repair for vesicovaginal fistula in 1849, using several very patient slave women with this troublesome disorder; the abdominal operations for gall bladder disease and for appendicitis; and the work in cardiac surgery in the 20th century, are but a few examples of American surgical innovations.

American medical education was of decidedly uneven quality, and often poor, throughout the 19th century, but many young American physicians spent from a few months to several years studying medicine and doing research in the leading medical centers of Europe, returning with substantial competence. Late in the colonial period they went to Leiden and to Edinburgh. In the Jacksonian period Paris was the favorite, and in the decades after the Civil War the German clinics and laboratories were especially popular.

From the Paris hospitals, these Americans returned with a zeal for clinical observation and correlation of premortern with postmortem findings. An example of the fruitfulness of this approach may be seen in Gerhard's work on typhus. Others returned with knowledge and enthusiasm for using new diagnostic instruments, such as the stethoscope and the ophthalmoscope as well as the microscope.

Toward the end of the 19th century the laboratories of Germany, as well as that country's elaborate postgraduate clinical training systems, became the basis for the "new medicine," which combined the laboratory and the clinic. Among the first medical schools to adopt the German pattern were those of Harvard and Michigan universities, and especially the Johns Hopkins Medical School after its opening in 1893; they exposed their students to four years of rigorous study. William S. Halsted and William Osler, professors of surgery and of medicine respectively at Johns Hopkins, introduced the residency system into postdoctoral training, taken from the German model. They also took the medical student out of the lecture room and put him in the laboratory, in the clinic, and on the hospital wards. Abraham Flexner's well-known report about American medical schools in 1910 pointed to Johns Hopkins and a few other schools as exemplary. Already during the previous decade proprietary schools had begun closing, and stimulated by Flexner's work, this trend continued. With the advent of an increasingly scientific basis for medicine, the proprietary schools simply could not keep up because medical education became an increasingly expensive proposition.

American scientific medicine came into its own in the 1890's with such work as that of William H. Welch and his co-workers at Johns Hopkins, where numerous young men received excellent training in basic research methods. Although Welch himself discovered the gas-gangrene bacillus, it was of minor significance: the climate for research he created was of much greater importance. One group of his students, headed by Walter Reed and Jesse W. Lazear, clearly demonstrated the mosquito spread of yellow fever. This was a monumental piece of work carried out in Cuba and reported in 1900. Its impact on public health was immediate and widespread. Of equal scientific importance was the earlier work of Theobald Smith, who about 1890 determined the causative parasite of Texas cattle fever and clearly showed that it was spread by ticks, thus establishing the model for a vector-borne disease.

The growing importance of U.S. medicine and surgery in the 20th century may be demonstrated by a variety of yardsticks. Increasingly, discoveries were made in the leading centers of research. Some of those centers were in the medical schools; others were in privately endowed institutes, such as Rockefeller, Sloan-Kettering, and McCormick. The numbers of Nobel prizes awarded to Americans also began to increase as more and more of the influential medical literature in the form of monographs, texts, and journals stemmed from the western side of the Atlantic. Accompanying this rise in American medical literature in the mid-20th century was the reversal of the flow of students. Europeans, as well as students from other continents, began to make the medical pilgrimage to the United States.

As one attempts to account for the American rise to the top of the scientific ladder of medicine, neither men alone nor the creation of educational and research institutions will furnish a satisfactory explanation. Again and again one must return to economic reasons. A high standard of living available to a nation with a highly industrialized economy allows money to be spent on basic and applied research, and the result is greater scientific and technological advance.

Closely related to the striking scientific developments in medicine and surgery during the 20th century have been the increasing specialization of practitioners and the pronounced increase in hospitals and their use. An 1873 survey showed that there were only 149 hospitals for the care of the sick in the entire country, of which only six had been established prior to 1800; by 1973 there were more than 7,000 hospitals with 1.65 million beds. In the 19th century, only the poorer classes generally used hospitals. The upper classes not only delivered their babies at home, as was generally custom but also nursed their sick in the home and submitted to surgery on the kitchen table. Postoperative infection rates were actually lower under these circumstances than in the large, urban hospitals. Not until the acceptance of Lister's principles of antisepsis in the 1870's, which Americans were quite slow to adopt, and the advent of heat sterilization of operating-room equipment in the 1890's did surgery of the cavities of the body become feasible and safe. It is primarily the rapid strides in surgery that account for the changing locus of medical practice from the home to the hospital in the 20th century.

Along with changing patterns of medical care have gone changing patterns of disease and a slowly rising life expectancy. In 1900 the commonest causes of death were infections, such as tuberculosis, influenza, and dysenteries. By midcentury heart disease, cancer, stroke, and accidents accounted for the majority of mortality. The age distribution of the population had changed as well, as the elderly and the very young came to constitute larger percentages. This demographic pattern had implications for medical care because it is precisely these two age groups that require the most physician visits and hospital beds.

The overall drop in mortality rates from 17.2 per 1,000 in 1900 to about 9.4 per 1,000 in 1972 is a reflection of both medical and nonmedical factors. Specific preventive measures for some infectious diseases (notably smallpox, tetanus, and diphtheria), antibiotic therapy for many infectious illnesses, hormone therapy, and surgical advances account for some of the change. Improved housing and nutrition and a higher level of education have also been significant. Improved prenatal and postnatal care has been extremely important in helping to lower infant mortality, probably the most significant factor in increasing life expectancy from about fifty years in 1900 to seventy years in the 1970's. Diarrheas, malnutrition, and respiratory disorders no longer threaten young children as they once did. By the mid-20th century most families could expect all their children to grow to maturity—which was not the case during the 19th century when between 25 and 50 percent of children died before reaching the age of five.

In the latter part of the 20th century, as advances in scientific medicine continued apace, a paradox continued to puzzle the medical profession, the public, and health planners. The more effective medical services have become, the greater has been the demand for them; at the same time, they have become more expensive and so more difficult of access for many. Two conflicting concepts of medical care have always existed in American medicine—as a public service and as private enterprise.

BIBLIOGRAPHY

G. H. Brieger, *Medical America in the Nineteenth Century.*

Joseph Kett, *The Formation of the American Medical Profession.*

W. F. Norwood, *Medical Education in the United States Before the Civil War.*

W. Rothstein, *American Physicians in the Nineteenth Century.*

R. H. Shryock, *American Medical Research: Past and Present, and Medicine and Society in America, 1660–1860.*

— GERT H. BRIEGER

MEDICINE IN THE LATE TWENTIETH CENTURY

In the United States as elsewhere, scientific medicine came of age in the twentieth century. Since its improvised colonial beginnings, medicine in America has evolved into an imposing system of skills and technology capable of delivering strikingly successful therapies, but its successes are increasingly powered by a large and complex scientific, commercial, and governmental establishment that many observers criticize as bureaucratic, depersonalizing, and unaffordable. Not coincidentally, the final decades of the twentieth century witnessed important transformations in the way in which medical care was delivered, who delivered it, and how it was financed.

Equally significant changes occurred in the nature of the diseases that affect us and the rate at which they occur. Some of these changes are also the paradoxical legacy of contemporary medicine's successes. As people live longer, the resulting increase in the number of aging Americans has led to a dramatic increase in the degenerative diseases of old age—cancer, heart and kidney disease, dementia, and stroke. Changing social realities have required that matters not previously considered medical, such as the use of tobacco products, become public health issues. A rapidly increasing alcohol- and drug-addicted population became a major public health concern, as did the shocking escalation in the number of injuries and deaths from firearms.

Acquired immune deficiency syndrome (AIDS), a disease first reported in 1981, quickly assumed epidemic proportions, particularly among gay men and intravenous drug users, but fifteen years later AIDS was spreading more rapidly among heterosexual women. By 1995 more than a quarter of a million people with AIDS had died in the United States, and about a million more were infected with the lethal virus, for which no immunization or cure has been discovered. Despite an impressive rate of improvement through use of new antipsychotic and antidepressant drugs, many people required care for mental illness.

Perhaps the most significant advance in medicine in the last quarter of the twentieth century was the burgeoning ability to study human genetic diseases, a breakthrough made possible by the development of recombinant DNA technology. The investigation of a number of devastating genetic diseases, including sickle-cell anemia, Down's syndrome, Huntington's disease, cystic fibrosis, and muscular dystrophy, was made possible by this technology. Historically, disease was dealt with by treating its overt symptoms. It appeared likely that the next advance would be the revolutionary ability to treat disease at its molecular level by introducing normal copies of defective genes into the existing, abnormal genetic structure. In the mid-1990s clinical trials were under way employing gene therapy in the treatment of rheumatoid arthritis, hemophilia, and some types of cancer, as well as sickle-cell anemia, cystic fibrosis, muscular dystrophy, and other conditions.

Important developments also took place in neurology and psychoneuroimmunology, with the discovery that the normal release of chemicals in the brain has an extremely far-reaching effect that influences most of the body's systems, nerve functioning, and emotional behavior. The development of medications that enhance or inhibit the production of serotonin, dopamine, and other neurotransmitters mitigated the debilitating neurological and psychological symptoms of disorders such as Parkinson's disease, Huntington's disease, and depression.

Other major advances occurred at the juncture of recombinant gene therapy, immunology, and virology. In 1994 vaccines were licensed for chicken pox and hepatitis A. A hepatitis B vaccine was licensed a decade earlier. The rapidly mutating influenza virus has defeated all efforts to bring it under effective control, but a global network of laboratories, led by the World Health Organization, began collaborating to identify new strains of influenza as they appear, saving many lives by minimizing the time between the beginning of epidemics and the production and distribution of appropriate vaccines. Although neither immunization nor a cure had been found for AIDS, the duration and quality of the lives of HIV and AIDS patients improved dramatically with the development of a number of drugs that inhibit reproduction of the virus at various stages of the disease.

Prevention was one totally nontechnological approach that came to the fore as an important part of medical intercession.

A substantial number of the major breakthroughs in contemporary medicine were technological. Extremely sophisticated diagnostic techniques were developed, including nuclear medicine scanning tests and imaging devices such as magnetic resonance imaging (MRI) and computerized axial tomography (CAT scans), which provide images of the brain, heart, gastrointestinal tract, and other soft tissues. Advances in Doppler echo and other ultrasound technology provided a noninvasive technique for determining blood flow velocity in various locations in the body. This technology affords the opportunity for noninvasive anatomical evaluation in many fields, including obstetrics, gastroenterology, and urology. DNA science now permits replication of human genes and their transfer to products that can be used for therapeutic purposes. Furthermore, its diagnostic, predictive, and forensic uses have become increasingly refined. Equally sophisticated therapeutic and surgical procedures also rely on complex, advanced technology, such as organ transplantation.

One totally nontechnological field that came to the fore as an important part of medical intercession was prevention. Since the 1970s much emphasis is placed on educational programs designed to teach people proper nutrition and exercise in order to avoid illness. Nutrition and exercise were recognized as important in the prevention and control of heart disease, hypertension, diabetes, and other chronic diseases and in promoting health generally. Nonetheless, technology is central to contemporary medicine and is very costly. Reliance upon elaborate equipment and procedures resulted in a growing number of people receiving outpatient examination, testing, and treatment in hospitals rather than in doctors' offices or at home. The greatest increase in the cost of medical care since the 1960s was in hospital care. The enormous medical establishment that evolved in the last third of the twentieth century included pharmaceutical and medical equipment manufacturers, insurance carriers, and an abundantly supported research community, as well as federal, state, and local government.

The federal government is involved in important ways in the furnishing of health care. On the civilian side, through the Department of Veterans Affairs, it operates approximately 900 hospitals, nursing homes, ambulatory care clinics, and veterans counseling centers. It also directs the Indian Health Service, which provides comprehensive health care services to Native Americans. Through the Public Health Service, the federal government administers the Centers for Disease Control and Prevention (CDC) and the National Institutes of Health (NIH). The CDC is the federal agency charged with providing leadership and direction in the prevention and control of diseases and responding to public health emergencies. The NIH is the principal biomedical research agency of the federal government. Both were intimately involved in virtually all of the significant advances since the mid-1960s. The medical contributions of the military are not limited to the health services commands of the armed forces. Ultrasound technology, adapted from military sonar, is an example of an important military contribution to the health of the population as a whole.

Beginning in the 1970s, the trend among physicians toward specialization was reversed and more family practitioners, general pediatricians, and internists entered practice. Increasingly, too, physician assistants, nurse-practitioners, and nurse-midwives—often referred to as physician extenders—performed many procedures traditionally reserved to physicians.

Ethical issues have always been critical in medicine because they deal with matters of life and death, but the medical technology developed in the late twentieth century gave new urgency to ethical questions. The ability to prolong life for months and even years after a person's heart or lungs have failed recasts the question of what life is and when death occurs. Organ transplantation and human medical experiments generate great debate, and DNA science has raised a new world of ethical concerns.

[See also Acquired Immune Deficiency Syndrome; Euthanasia; Health and Human Services, Department of; Health Care; Health Maintenance Organizations; Medicare and Medicaid; National Institutes of Health.]

BIBLIOGRAPHY

James H. Cassedy, *Medicine in America: A Short History* (Baltimore, 1991).
Lester S. King, *Transformations in American Medicine* (Baltimore, 1991).
Jeff Lyon and Peter Gorner, *Altered Fates: Gene Therapy and the Retooling of Human Life* (New York, 1995).
Paul Starr, *The Social Transformation of American Medicine* (New York, 1982).

— JACK HANDLER

MENNONITES

Mennonites are descendants of an Anabaptist group that received its distinctive form from the teachings of Menno Simons, first propounded in the 1530's and 1540's. Mennonites are generally pacifists who maintain a high degree of community discipline through moderate use of the ban—a disciplinary power of the congregation over the believer, for public and private sins—and who practice adult baptism. The Amish, a conservative body of Mennonites founded by Jacob Amman in the 1690's, are particularly notable because they maintain strict customs of dress and advocate separation from the world.

The first Mennonite settlers to come to the New World settled in Pennsylvania in 1683, coming to be known as the Pennsylvania Dutch. Renewed persecutions of Mennonites in Russia in the 1870's led to a second wave of immigrants, who settled primarily in the American and Canadian Midwest.

The principal Mennonite denominations and their 1974 membership figures are Beachy Amish Mennonite Churches, 4,069 members; Church of God in Christ (Mennonite), 6,204 members; Evangelical Mennonite Brethren, 3,784 members; General Conference of Mennonite Brethren Churches, 13,000 members; Hutterian Brethren, 3,405 members; General Conference of the Mennonite Church, 36,129 members; Old Order Amish Church, 14,720 members; Old Order (Wisler) Mennonite Church, 8,000 members; Reformed Mennonite Church, 500 members.

BIBLIOGRAPHY

Harold S. Bender, *Two Centuries of American Mennonite Literature . . . 1727–1928.*
Cornelius Dyck, *An Introduction to Mennonite History: A Popular History of the Anabaptists and the Mennonites.*
John A. Hostetler, *Amish Society,* and *Annotated Bibliography on the Amish.*
Charles Henry Smith, *The Story of the Mennonites.*
John C. Wenger, *The Mennonite Church in America, Sometimes Called Old Mennonites.*

— GLENN T. MILLER

MENTAL ILLNESS, TREATMENT OF

The line between so-called mental illness and mental health has always been tenuous, and so definitions of mental illness have always been varied and ambiguous. Many persons who would not be considered mentally ill by currently accepted definitions were institutionalized in mental hospitals, as for example, epileptics, severe retardates, and homeless senile men and women. This article deals primarily with the treatment afforded persons previously called insane and today termed psychotic.

Early in the nineteenth century, moral treatment emphasized care for the emotional needs of patients through the creation of a total therapeutic, benevolent environment.

With some exceptions, American approaches to the care of the mentally ill have been derived from European models, and even periodic reform movements that have had uniquely American characteristics can be related to similar developments abroad. Thus, as in Europe, prevailing ideas and practices have tended to run a cyclical course: times of pessimism and custodial care have alternated with periods of optimism and active treatment, and commitment to physical and pharmacological therapies has alternated with belief in psychological, environmental treatment.

By the early 18th century the ancient idea of mental disorder as divine retribution or satanic possession had given way among physicians and sophisticated laymen to the view that it was a physical disease of the brain, amenable to treatment by physicians in institutions established for the purpose.

In British North America, as elsewhere, the vast majority of mentally disordered persons did not receive such treatment. Instead, friends, relatives, or town authorities supplied care for "madmen" or "lunatics," often secreted and physically restrained in attics, outhouses, cellars, or shacks. If the town assumed responsibility and the "lunatic" was not considered dangerous, he might be auctioned off to anyone who would care for him at the least public cost. Sometimes he might be surreptitiously abandoned far away so that another community would be burdened with his support, or he would be left free to wander about begging for food and lodging. At the close of the colonial period, the newly constructed workhouses and jails frequently also housed the insane, where on rare occasions a physician might visit them.

The opening in 1752 of the first general hospital in the British colonies, the Pennsylvania Hospital at Philadelphia, marked what was more a portent of better care than an achievement of it, but conducted on somewhat more humane principles was the first hospital in the colonies devoted exclusively to mental patients, now the Eastern State Hospital at Williamsburg, Va., opened in 1773 by a family of physicians and keepers, the Galts. Lay keepers administered the small asylum with the advice of a physician, who came weekly to see patients and prescribed the conventional contemporary medical therapy—cathartics, emetics, bloodletting, cold and warm showers, and special diets and tonics. More famous were the reforms introduced at the Pennsylvania Hospital by Dr. Benjamin Rush, often called the father of American psychiatry, after he took charge of the mental patients in 1783. Although Rush adhered dogmatically to the traditional belief in bloodletting, as well as dosing with mercury, as a cure for all ills, he took an innovative stance, endeavoring to deal with the emotional condition of the mental patients under his care. He tried to establish a kindly, albeit authoritarian, relationship with them and initiated improvements in their living conditions, including opportunity for some sort of occupation.

More thoroughgoing reforms were proposed in France, England, and Italy, where physicians and lay activists originated a new system called moral treatment;

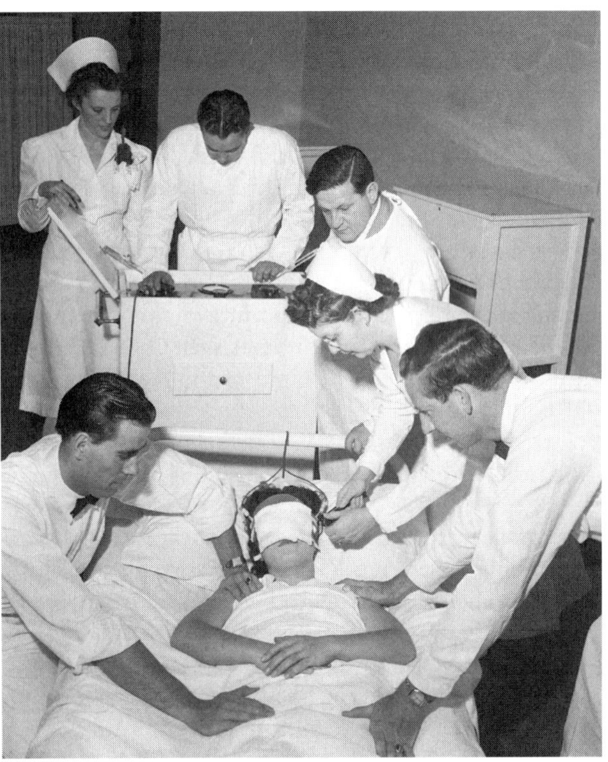

Doctors demonstrate the use of electric shock therapy for patients with "manic-depressive psychoses" in San Bernardino, California, on May 5, 1942. Doctors believed that the electric jolts could remedy short circuits in the brain's switchboard. (UPI/Corbis-Bettmann)

transplanted to the United States, it flourished during the first half of the 19th century. A precursor of what were considered innovative theories of treatment in the mid-20th century, moral treatment emphasized the emotional needs of patients through the creation of a total therapeutic, benevolent environment. Although initially conventional medical therapy was not rejected in moral treatment asylums, it did not predominate, and by 1850 bloodletting was virtually abandoned, depletive drugs and low diets infrequently prescribed, and most mechanical restraints eliminated. The stress was on kindness and activity: occupational therapy (especially farming and gardening) was encouraged, and there were recreational programs, such as lectures, lantern-slide showings, scientific demonstrations, and musical concerts. Open hospital practices were variously adopted in the form of open wards, freedom of the grounds, the right of patients to visit the neighboring town, and group activities.

From 1817 to 1824 four new hospitals on the moral treatment model opened, all of them nonprofit corporate institutions under private management; they tended to cater mainly to middle-class and upper-class patients. Later, in the 1830's and 1840's, several state hospitals established during the wave of antebellum social reform also practiced moral treatment, the best known being the asylum at Worcester, Mass., under Dr. Samuel Woodward. The most original American practitioner of moral treatment was Woodward's mentor, Dr. Eli Todd, first superintendent of the Hartford Retreat (later the Institute of Living), which opened in 1824. The founding of a professional organization, the Association of Medical Superintendents of American Institutions for the Insane (later the American Psychiatric Association) in 1844 and of the *American Journal of Insanity* (predecessor of the *American Journal of Psychiatry*) during that same year by Dr. Amariah Brigham, the chief of the new state hospital at Utica, N.Y., helped to spread the idea of moral treatment and fostered the acceptance of institutionalized medical care for the insane. The latter trend was accelerated by the philanthropist and reformer Dorothea Lynde Dix's success in persuading state legislatures to establish some twenty mental hospitals. In all, there were approximately 26 mental hospitals in the United States by 1849, over 60 by 1866, and 200 by 1900. In 1844 approximately 3.1 percent of the persons estimated to be insane (probably no more than half are so recognized at any time) were in mental hospitals, and by 1900, 24 percent; not until 1940 did the figure rise to 60 percent, most of the patients living in giant state hospitals.

Institutional care changed after the Civil War, often for the worse, and especially at the state hospitals, which had to cope with inadequate funding and too many patients. Moral treatment declined, as did reported therapeutic successes—from 20 to 30 percent of yearly admissions as compared with from 40 to 60 percent during the 1830's and 1840's. Social resentment against the large immigrant population of the latter 19th century brought with it a revival of theories of the hereditary and incurable nature of insanity. Concomitantly new scientific discoveries, most notably the germ theory of disease, encouraged a reversion to a physiological approach to mental illness. Such drugs as opium compounds, bromides, belladonna, and cannabis were used to subdue agitated patients, but most hospitals became primarily custodial.

There were some bright spots at the turn of the 20th century as a result of research into disorders that cause mental abnormalities. In 1891 G. R. Murray's work led to the prevention of goitrous cretinism, and in 1914 J. Goldberger described his method of preventing and treating pellagra by diet. Interest in the psychological and administrative aspects of the care of the mentally ill also revived at this time, partly under the influence of physicians' work with noninstitutionalized patients. Significant in this respect was the new medical specialty neurology, which expanded to include "nervous diseases" that had no visible physical basis as well as those that did and whose practitioners came to dominate psychiatry; leading mental hospitals had as their chiefs men trained in neurology. A large proportion of the neurologists' patients seemed to be suffering from a supposedly newly discovered disorder; named neurasthenia in 1868 by the neurologist Charles A. Beard, it actually resembled the hysteria and hypochondria of old and the conditions called neuroses in the 20th century. The preferred treatment for neurasthenia, which was characterized by weakness, lassitude, tension, and anxiety, was that prescribed by the famous neurologist and novelist Silas Weir Mitchell—bed rest, nourishing food, and isolation, with a dose of moralizing about self-control. Although some neurasthenics were hospitalized, most were treated by neurologists in their private offices, and thereby was initiated a dual system of dealing with emotional disorders: psychotics within hospitals and neurasthenics (neurotics) in private practice.

Psychoanalysis, another influential therapeutic system, was first applied to nonpsychotic patients and then tried with psychotics in some hospitals. Sigmund Freud introduced his theories to Americans at Clark University in 1909, and his work was brought to the attention of the psychiatric profession by prominent psychiatrists like Abraham A. Brill (his American translator) and William Alanson White.

An institutional trend that began at about the same time was the establishment of the psychopathic hospital as a teaching and research center associated with a general hospital, where the latest therapeutic methods were employed. The prototype was the Phipps Psychiatric Clinic at Johns Hopkins, which opened in 1913 with Adolf Meyer as chief. Another new idea was the training of social workers to serve in mental hospitals.

A new reform movement was launched in 1909 with the founding of an organization designed to improve hospital conditions, the National Committee for Mental Hygiene. It was founded by Clifford W. Beers, a former mental patient whose description of his unhappy experiences in mental hospitals in *A Mind That Found Itself* created a sensation when published in 1908. The committee's call for nonrestraint and emphasis on prevention encouraged improvements in the leading mental institutions and the establishment of child guidance clinics; but for the vast majority of institutionalized patients there was little change.

During World War I the high incidence of "shell shock" made the mental health of servicemen a national concern. Dr. Thomas W. Salmon, medical director of the National Committee for Mental Hygiene, developed an effective program of prompt psychiatric treatment of soldiers in the field that consisted mainly of reassurance and return to active duty. Hospitalization of "shell-shocked" men had proven counterproductive, leading to chronic invalidism or disability, a lesson quickly forgotten and relearned only during World War II.

The first effective treatment for what had always been an intractable mental illness was the fever therapy first tried in Vienna in 1917 by J. Wagner-Jauregg for general paresis, the final stage of syphilis (by then known to be caused by the spirochete). It was not until 1943, however, when J. F. Mahoney and co-workers suggested the use of penicillin and the National Research Council furnished the expensive new drug to a few psychiatrists, that physicians thought it possible to all but eradicate paresis.

During the 1930's somatic treatments developed in Europe became popular in American mental hospitals, most notably the shock therapies, which seemed to be helpful in cases of depression—insulin shock, metrazol, and then electroshock. Because electroshock had fewer side effects, it became in the 1940's the method of choice among nonpsychoanalytically oriented psychiatrists. Another "new" treatment, psychosurgery, came into widespread use, commonly in the form of lobotomy, the removal of white tissue from the frontal lobe of the brain, advocated by W. Freeman to modify the behavior of chronic psychotics. Condemned later as mutilation of helpless patients, lobotomy declined by the 1960's as more effective drugs came into use. At the same time that shock therapy and psychosurgery became fashionable, a number of psychiatrists in the United States—including Harry Stack Sullivan, Frieda Fromm-Reichman, Fritz Redlich, and Silvano Arieti—practiced psychoanalysis on schizophrenic patients in private hospitals. During World War II some American psychiatrists also turned to hypnotherapy; the Society for Clinical and Experimental Hypnosis was formed in 1949.

One of the most significant developments in the history of psychopharmacology occurred in 1950 when the Swiss chemist Paul Charpentier synthesized the tranquilizer chlorpromazine. Thereafter the number of psychopharmacological compounds used in the treatment of mental illness proliferated; tranquilizing drugs dramatically decreased patients' excitement and thereby the "need" for violent wards, and antidepressant drugs seemed to relieve the anxiety of depressed patients. Both kinds made it possible for many patients to live outside the hospital. The success of these drugs also stimulated scientific searches for biochemical and genetic features of mental illness.

Concomitant with the appearance of the new drugs and to some extent made possible by the relative calm they produced in patients, new psychologically and sociologically oriented approaches to patient care gained popularity, especially milieu therapy, which, unknown to its originators, resembled the moral treatment of a century before. Also gaining ground during the 1950's and 1960's was the application of behaviorist theories, especially B. F. Skinner's work in operant conditioning, whose popularity among psychotherapists can be related to disillusionment with psychoanalysis.

Some reformers wanted to deinstitutionalize patients altogether. In recognition of the observation that long-term hospitalization not only failed to help but frequently harmed patients, the first American hospital where patients not needing constant supervision could come only at night to sleep was established, on the model of similar institutions inaugurated in Moscow and Montreal. This approach received recognition and funds in 1963 from the federal government, through the National Institute for Mental Health, by then the major research and funding agency for mental health programs in the United States. The goal set by community mental health advocates was the return of the majority of mental patients to their original communities, to live at home or in specially supervised residences (halfway houses), with therapeutic support from local mental health centers.

Former mental patients formed organizations to change hospital conditions, and legal steps were taken to prevent persons from being institutionalized against their will.

In the 1960's, under the influence of radical and humanist critics within the professions of psychiatry and psychology and coinciding with the growth of sociopolitical movements in behalf of oppressed minorities, a new wave of questioning and change seemed to be upon psychiatry. Former mental patients began to form organizations to change hospital conditions; psychosurgery was being challenged in the courts; and legal steps were being taken to prevent involuntary commitment of persons in mental hospitals and to require adequate treatment of patients in state hospitals. The question whether mental illness was illness or an understandable response to a disturbed familial and social environment was raised, as well as the propriety and usefulness of conventional institutions for persons deemed mentally ill.

Whatever power the various reform movements gained began to erode in the late 1960's with the federal government's retrenchment of social and health programs. By the mid-1970's this decline, intensified by economic recession, had reached a level that threatened the collapse of reforms in the mental hospitals as well as of the community health programs designed as alternatives to hospital care and as agencies of prevention of serious mental illness.

BIBLIOGRAPHY

Clifford W. Beers, *A Mind That Found Itself: An Autobiography.*

Norman Dain, *Concepts of Insanity in the United States, 1789–1865*, and *Disordered Minds: The First Century of Eastern State Hospital in Williamsburg, Virginia, 1766–1866.*

Albert Deutsch, *The Mentally Ill in America: A History of Their Care and Treatment From Colonial Times.*

Gerald N. Grob, *The State and the Mentally Ill: A History of the Worcester State Hospital in Massachusetts, 1830–1920.*

Nathan G. Hale, *Freud and the Americans: The Beginnings of Psychoanalysis in the United States, 1876–1917.*

David J. Rothman, *The Discovery of the Asylum: Social Order and Disorder in the New Republic.*

— NORMAN DAIN

MERCANTILISM

Mercantilism, as applied to the British colonies, did not follow the general theories of that doctrine very closely. It was always tempered by the fact that the colonies were self-governing subdivisions of the British Empire, inhabited by Englishmen. The mercantilist trading company was used to initiate the first colonies, but was soon abandoned for direct imperial control. This control took the form of many measures intended to regulate the trade, production, and manufacture of both England and the colonies with the object of promoting the prosperity of all. These included the Navigation Acts, by which the trade within the empire was confined to English seamen and English ships. The word English in these and subsequent acts referred to nationality and not to residence. Thus, a merchant from Boston was just as English as a resident of London.

Other phases of the Navigation Acts required that certain colonial products be shipped from their place of production to England, or to another British or colonial port, and not directly to a foreign country. Asian goods and European manufactured goods were in turn required to reach the colonies only by way of England. This program permitted the profits from colonial trade and commerce to center in England, promoted English shipping, and enabled the British government to support itself by taxing this trade as it flowed through England.

The colonies were chiefly producers of raw materials, homes for surplus British population, and markets for goods produced in the home country. Colonial manufacture for an export trade that competed with that of the home country was discouraged by prohibitive legislation: wool in 1699, hats in 1732, and wrought iron and steel in 1750. On the other hand, colonial production of articles needed within the empire was encouraged. The sugar islands were given a practical monopoly of the colonial market for molasses (1733). Virginia and its neighbors were given a monopoly of the tobacco market in England by acts forbidding the growing of tobacco in England and by prohibitive tariffs on competing Spanish tobacco. Direct bounties, paid from the British treasury, were used to promote the colonial production of hemp, tar, pitch, and other naval stores, and very large sums were paid out for this purpose between 1705 and 1774. Other colonial products that benefited from bounties were raw silk, masts, lumber, and indigo. Payments from the British treasury on this account averaged more than £15,000 a year in the decade preceding the Revolution. Preferential tariffs gave colonial products favored treatment in the British markets. Colonial products like sugar and tobacco that were not needed for the British market were, on exportation, assisted by drawbacks of the import duties so that they reached their European markets burdened by a minimum of British taxes. Drawbacks also were used to promote American colonial use of such goods from the British colonies in Asia as tea after 1767. The total export drawbacks paid out by Great Britain in an average year—for example, 1772—amounted to £2,214,508 in a total export trade valued at £16,159,412, nearly one-third of its exports to America. Exports from Scotland show a similar relationship. Thus colonial and foreign goods flowed through Great Britain to the colonies without too much burden.

The colonial markets were developed by favors instead of compulsion. The usual inducement was export bounties, especially in the case of British manufactures that had foreign competition. The chief articles so aided were cordage, gunpowder, linen, sailcloth, silk manufactures, and refined sugar. The total payments by England alone averaged about £40,000 a year at the close of the colonial period, but had amounted to more than £61,000 in 1771, according to treasury reports. In this way the British market was made attractive to colonial purchasers. Both England and the colonies profited from this 18th-century policy of enlightened mercantilism.

The opposition to mercantilism in its later stages came from free traders like Adam Smith, who admitted that the system worked, but insisted it was wrong in theory. It is difficult to find opposition to the system among revolutionary Americans, so long as measures were purely regulatory and did not levy a tax on the colonists. The system was specifically approved by the First Continental Congress in the Declaration of Rights of Oct. 14, 1774.

[See also Colonial Policy, British.]

BIBLIOGRAPHY

Lawrence A. Harper, *English Navigation Laws.*

— O. M. DICKERSON

METHODISTS

The Methodist church was founded as a separate entity by John Wesley in 1744 in England. He had initially hoped to reawaken the Church of England to the demands of vital piety. Wesley's theology was a warm-hearted evangelicalism that stressed the experience of Christ within the heart, man's capacity to accept Christ's offer of redemption, and the need for a disciplined life. In his later years Wesley came to believe in the possibility of entire sanctification or holiness (a state of perfection) and taught that it should be the goal of every Christian. This latter doctrine has contributed to many of the divisions within Methodism.

Methodist ideas entered the American colonies informally at first, notably through the efforts of Robert Strawbridge and Philip Embury, and their success prompted Wesley to send Richard Broadman and Joseph Pilmoor to America in 1769. Two years later he sent Francis Asbury, who was to become the great apostle of early Methodism in America. At first, Methodism was an extremely small movement that existed on the fringes of the Anglican church, but after the revolutionary war, the Methodists completely separated from that body. The Christmas Conference, held in Baltimore in 1784, marks the beginning of the Methodist church in America. At that meeting sixty preachers joined with Richard Vassey, Richard Whitcoat, and Thomas Coke, delegates from Wesley, in ordaining Francis Asbury and establishing an order for the church. The conference decided on a form of government by deacons, elders, and superintendents (later bishops); adopted the Book of Discipline, which regulated the life of the church and its members; and elected Coke and Asbury as its first superintendents.

Almost immediately after the Christmas Conference, Methodism entered a period of rapid expansion. The system of circuit riders, which Wesley had experimented with in England, met the need for clergymen in outlying regions and allowed relatively uneducated men to enter the ministry. Wherever the circuit rider could gather a crowd, he would stop, preach a sermon, and organize a Methodist class to continue the work until he was able to return. Methodist theology was also easy for the average man to understand, and the Methodist emphasis on discipline was invaluable to communities that were far from the ordinary restraints of civilization. The Methodist combination of simplicity, organization, and lay participation not only made it the largest Protestant denomination but also decisively influenced the other frontier churches. Other denominations, even those of Calvinist background, were forced to accept elements of Methodist theory and practice in order to survive.

The 19th century was a period in which the Methodists, like many other American denominations, experienced internal division. The question of slavery, an important issue for churches located in both the North and the South, led to the formation of three separate ecclesiastical bodies: the Methodist Episcopal church (1844); the Methodist Episcopal church, South (1844); and the Wesleyan Methodist Connection, a small antislavery church founded in 1843. After the Civil War most black Methodists formed their own denominations. In the same period, the increasingly middle-class nature of the church contributed to disputes over the issue of entire sanctification, and the lower-class membership largely withdrew into the "Holiness" or "Pentecostal" movement.

After the Civil War, the Methodist church's lower-class membership withdrew into the "Holiness" or "Pentecostal" movement.

In the 20th century, Methodism has been involved in both the ecumenical movement and the Social Gospel. The Methodist Social Creed was adopted by the Federal Council of Churches in 1908 as its own statement of social principles. Methodism has also begun to heal the divisions within its own ranks. In 1939 the Methodist Episcopal church; the Methodist Episcopal church, South; and the Methodist Protestant church merged. In 1968 this church merged with the Evangelical United Brethren to form the United Methodist church.

The principal Methodist groups and their 1974 membership figures are United Methodist church,

10,192,265 members; African Methodist Episcopal church, 1,500,000 members; African Methodist Episcopal Zion church, 1,024,974 members; African Union First Colored Methodist Protestant church, 8,000 members; Christian Methodist Episcopal church, 466,718 members; Evangelical Methodist church, 10,519 members; Free Methodist church of North America, 65,066 members; Fundamental Methodist church, 722 members; Primitive Methodist church, U.S.A., 11,945 members; Reformed Methodist Union Episcopal church, 5,000 members; Reformed Zion Union Apostolic church, 16,000 members; Southern Methodist church, 9,917 members; Union American Methodist Episcopal church, 28,000 members.

BIBLIOGRAPHY

Emory Stevens Bucke and others, eds., *History of American Methodism.*

Hunter Dickinson Farish, *The Circuit Rider Dismounts: A Social History of Southern Methodism.*

Gerald K. Kennedy, *The Methodist Way of Life.*

Ralph Ernst Morrow, *Northern Methodism and Reconstruction.*

Warren William Sweet, *Methodism in American History.*

— GLENN T. MILLER

MEXICAN AMERICANS

Mexican Americans represent both an old and a new ethnic group in the United States. Some can trace their backgrounds to the early Spanish-Indian encounters in both Mexico and the U.S. Southwest. Others migrated to the United States from Mexico in the twentieth century. It is this combination of old and new, past and present, that gives the history of Mexican Americans its character. Spain's conquest of Mexico and the Aztec empire in 1521 led to development of a mixed or mestizo people consisting of Indians and Spaniards. This encounter became the basis for the colonial missions and settlements that stretched from Texas to California. A Spanish-Mexican cultural presence was implanted that is visible today in the names of southwestern locations. These Spanish-Mexican settlements, however, were coveted by the United States following independence from Great Britain. The United States undertook an expansionist drive after the Louisiana Purchase (1803) from France placed the young nation in direct proximity to Spain's northern frontier. After Mexico's own independence from Spain in 1821, it came under increased U.S. pressure to cede its inherited northern borderlands. In 1836 Texas, under control of U.S. immigrants, established its independence, and in 1845 it was annexed by the United States. Coveting additional Mexican territory, the United States successfully waged war against Mexico in 1846–1848. The subsequent Treaty of Guadalupe Hidalgo provided for transfer of the balance of Mexico's northern lands, which included the present-day states of Colorado, Nevada, Utah, California, and most of Arizona and New Mexico. The resident Mexican population became U.S. citizens.

The period following the Mexican War marked a dark era in Mexican-American history. U.S. rule led to pressures on Mexican-American landowners resulting in loss of property to squatters, litigation, taxes, and market pressures. In addition, Mexican Americans were treated like second-class citizens. Mexican Americans might have become a footnote in U.S. history had it not been for a subsequent mass migration from Mexico. Pushed out of their own country by both poverty and the Mexican Revolution that began in 1910, immigrants were drawn into the United States because of the need for labor for U.S. railroads, mines, and farms. More than a million crossed the border between 1900 and 1930. They expanded older settlements in the Southwest, established new barrios, and renewed the Mexican-American cultural presence in the United States. The Great Depression stopped this migration and generated pressure to deport immigrants. In response, U.S.-born Mexicans launched a civil rights movement focusing on discrimination in education, jobs, wages, housing, political representation, and racial and cultural stereotyping. They sought integration in U.S. society. The move was vastly assisted by the involvement of thousands of Mexican Americans in World War II, in which many were awarded citations for bravery, including the Medal of Honor.

A new generation, that of Chicano Americans, appeared in the 1960s. Composed of children or grandchildren of immigrants, this generation of activists defiantly called themselves Chicanos (a working-class barrio term) and advocated cultural pride. Influenced by the struggle of farm workers led by Cesar Chavez, they brought pressure on schools to institute Chicano studies and bilingual education. They instituted a cultural and artistic resurgence centered on Chicano identity. There was a Chicano anti-Vietnam War movement and the beginning of a Chicano feminist movement. They established a Chicano political party (La Raza Unida). The most widespread Mexican-American protest movement in history, the Chicano movement brought the plight and aspirations of Mexican Americans to national and international attention. The Chicano movement of the 1960s and 1970s defeated some but by no means all forms of discrimination. The emergence of a more conservative U.S. political climate in the 1980s and 1990s made civil rights struggles more difficult. Still, Mexican Americans continued to integrate into U.S. society while asserting their identity in a pluralistic nation, partly because of their and other Hispanics' growing numbers in the United States. By 1990 Mexican Americans constituted three-fifths of the twenty-two million Hispanics in the United States.

While Mexican Americans have constituted a permanent and settled part of the U.S. population for some time, immigration from Mexico has continued to reinforce this population and remains a key factor in Mexican-American life. During World War II, for example, thousands of braceros (contract workers) were imported into the United States from Mexico to work, especially in agriculture. The Bracero Program was maintained from 1942 to 1964. Many braceros did not return to Mexico at the prescribed time and remained in the United States without proper documentation. Moreover, the Bracero Program helped stimulate an increase in undocumented immigration; many who did not qualify for the program crossed the border illegally and undocumented immigration continued to escalate after the program ended. To deal with the impact of illegal immigration, Congress in 1986 passed the Immigration Reform and Control Act, which provided amnesty for those who could prove they had been working in the United States for a number of years.

[See also Guadalupe Hidalgo, Treaty of; Immigration; Mexican War; Mexico, Relations with.]

BIBLIOGRAPHY

Mario T. Garcia, *Desert Immigrants: The Mexicans of El Paso, 1880–1920* (New Haven, Conn., 1981), and *Mexican Americans: Leadership, Ideology, and Identity, 1930–1960* (New Haven, Conn., 1989).

Peter Skerry, *Mexican Americans: The Ambivalent Minority* (New York, 1993).

— MARIO T. GARCIA

MEXICAN WAR

Mexican War (1846–48) had remote or indirect causes in the increasing distrust arising from diplomatic indiscretions, quibblings, and misunderstandings of the first decade of American-Mexican diplomatic relations. Its more immediate cause was the annexation of Texas, which the Mexican government regarded as equivalent to a declaration of war and which was followed by withdrawal of the Mexican minister from Washington, D.C., in March 1845 and the severance of diplomatic relations. Another cause was the American claims against Mexico arising from injuries to and property losses of American citizens in the Mexican revolutions.

The American government strove to preserve peace. It adopted a conciliatory policy and made the first advances toward renewal of diplomatic relations. Recognizing that the chief aim of American foreign policy was the annexation of California, President James K. Polk planned to connect with that policy the adjustment of all difficulties with Mexico, including the dispute over jurisdiction in the territory between the Nueces River and the Rio Grande.

In September 1845, assured through a confidential agent that the new Mexican government of José Joaquín Herrera would welcome an American minister, and acting on the suggestion of James Buchanan, secretary of state, Polk appointed John Slidell as envoy-minister on a secret peaceful mission to secure California and New Mexico for $15 million to $20 million if possible, or for $40 million if necessary—terms later changed by secret instructions to $5 million for New Mexico and $25 million for California. In October, before Slidell's departure, Buchanan sent to American consul Thomas O. Larkin at Monterey, Calif., a confidential statement of the American "goodwill" policy to acquire California without war and with the spontaneous cooperation of the Californians.

Mexico refused to reopen diplomatic relations. In January 1846, after the first news that the Mexican government under various pretexts had refused to receive Slidell, partly on the ground that questions of boundary and claims should be separated, Polk ordered Gen. Zachary Taylor to advance from Corpus Christi, Tex., to the Rio Grande, resulting shortly in conflicts with Mexican troops.

On May 11, after arrival of news of the Mexican advance across the Rio Grande and the skirmish with Taylor's troops, Polk submitted to Congress a skillful war message, stating that war existed and that it was begun by Mexico on American soil. He obtained prompt action authorizing a declaration of war, apparently on the ground that such action was justified by the delinquencies, obstinacy, and hostilities of the Mexican government; and he proceeded to formulate plans for military and naval operations to advance his purpose to obtain Mexican acceptance of his overtures for peace negotiations.

The military plans included an expedition under Col. Stephen W. Kearny to New Mexico and from there to California, supplemented by an expedition to Chihuahua; an advance across the Rio Grande into Mexico by troops under Taylor to occupy the neighboring provinces; and a possible later campaign of invasion of the Mexican interior from Veracruz.

In these plans Polk was largely influenced by assurances received in February from Col. A. J. Atocha, a friend of Antonio López de Santa Anna, then in exile from Mexico, to the effect that the latter, if aided in plans to return from Havana, Cuba, to Mexico, would recover his Mexican leadership and cooperate in a peaceful arrangement to cede Mexican territory to the United States. In June, Polk entered into negotiations with Santa Anna through a brother of Slidell, receiving verification of Atocha's assurances. Polk had already sent a confidential order to Commodore David Conner, who on Aug. 16 permitted Santa Anna to pass through the coast blockade to Veracruz. Having arrived in Mexico, Santa Anna promptly began his program, which resulted in his own quick restoration to power, but he gave no evidences whatever of his professed pacific intentions.

On July 3, 1846, the small expedition under Kearny received orders to go via the Santa Fe Trail from Fort Leavenworth, Kans., to occupy New Mexico. It reached Santa Fe on Aug. 18, and a part of the force (300 men) led by Kearny marched to the Pacific at San Diego. From there it arrived (Jan. 10, 1847) at Los Angeles to complete the work begun at Sonoma by insurgents under John Charles Frémont, and at Monterrey and San Francisco Bay by Commodore John Drake Sloat, shortly succeeded by Robert Field Stockton.

The expedition of Taylor into northern Mexico, which was organized to carry out the plan for an advance southward into the interior of Mexico, began to cross the Rio Grande to Matamoros on May 18, 1846, and advanced to the strongly fortified city of Monterrey, which after an attack was evacuated by Mexican forces on Sept. 28. Later, in February 1847, at Buena Vista, Taylor stubbornly resisted and defeated the attack of Santa Anna's Mexican relief expedition.

The chief problem for the U.S. was to find a government with enough power to negotiate a peace treaty to prevent American annexation of all Mexico.

Soon thereafter the theater of war shifted to Veracruz, from which the direct route to the Mexican capital seemed to present less difficulty than the northern route. In deciding on the campaign from Veracruz to Mexico City, Polk probably was influenced by the news of Sloat's occupation of California, which reached him on Sept. 1, 1846. In November 1846, Polk offered the command of the Mexico City expedition to Gen. Winfield Scott, who promptly accepted. After the capture of the fortress of Veracruz on Mar. 29, 1847, Scott led the army of invasion westward via Jalapa to Pueblo, which he entered on May 15, and from which he began (Aug. 7) his advance to the mountain pass of Cerro Gordo.

Coincident with Scott's operations against Veracruz, Polk began new peace negotiations with Mexico through a "profoundly secret mission." On Apr. 15 Buchanan had sent Nicholas P. Trist as a confidential peace agent to accompany Scott's army. In August, after the battles of Contreras and Churubusco, Trist arranged an armistice through Scott as a preliminary step for a diplomatic conference to discuss peace terms—a conference that began on Aug. 27 and closed on Sept. 7 by Mexican rejection of the terms offered. Scott promptly resumed his advance. After hard fighting (Sept. 7–11) at the battles of Molino del Rey and Chapultepec, he captured Mexico City on Sept. 14 and with his staff entered the palace, over which he hoisted the American flag.

Practically, the war was ended. Santa Anna, after resigning his presidential office, made an unsuccessful attempt to strike at the American garrison Scott had left at Pueblo, but he was driven off and obliged to flee from Mexico.

The chief remaining American problem was to find a government with enough power to negotiate a treaty of peace to prevent the danger of American annexation of all Mexico. Fortunately, Trist was still with the army and in close touch with the situation at the captured capital. Although recalled, he determined (Dec. 3–4) to assume the responsibility of remaining to renew efforts to conclude a treaty of peace even at the risk of disavowal by his government. After some delay, he was able to conclude with the Mexican commissioners a treaty in accord with the instructions that had been annulled by his recall. The chief negotiations were conducted at Mexico City, but the treaty was completed and signed on Feb. 2, 1848, at the neighboring town of Guadalupe Hidalgo. By its terms, which provided for cessation of hostilities, the United States agreed to pay $15 million for New Mexico and California. Polk received the treaty on Feb. 19 and promptly decided to submit it to the Senate, which approved it on Mar. 10 by a vote of thirty-eight to fourteen. Ratifications were exchanged on May 30, 1848.

Among the chief results of the war were expansion of American territory; increased American interest in the problems of the Caribbean and the Pacific and in the opening and control of isthmian interoceanic transit routes at Panama, Nicaragua, and Tehuantepec; and ebullitions of "manifest destiny" in the period of "young America" from 1848 to 1860. In domestic affairs the large acquisition of territory was reflected in political controversies relating to the slavery problem.

[See also Compromise of 1850.]

BIBLIOGRAPHY

Seymour V. Connor and Odre B. Faulk, *North America Divided: The Mexican War, 1846–1848.*

Otis A. Singleton, *The Mexican War.*

George Winston Smith and Charles Judah, eds., *Chronicles of the Gringos: The United States Army in the Mexican War, 1846–1848.*

— J. M. CALLAHAN

MEXICO, GULF OF

Gulf of Mexico, which by its form and position has had a profound influence on the climate of the southeastern part of the United States and all the eastern coast, has also had a large influence in American national history, especially on American foreign policy. Its early importance was determined by the Spanish search for a possible water passage through the continental barrier, the Spanish settlement at Havana, Cuba, in 1519, the expedition of Hernando Cortes into the interior from Veracruz, Mexico, and the subsequent discovery of gold in Mexico. Later it was also influenced by several settlements along the northern coast, a Spanish permanent settlement at Pensacola in 1696, and French settlements at Mobile in 1702 and New Orleans in 1718.

Its subsequent increased importance was especially due to its relations as the receiver of the Mississippi drainage and as the natural commercial outlet of the trans-Allegheny West. Its strategic geographic importance was recognized by the British seizure of Havana in 1762 and by the British colonial opposition to the surrender of Havana in 1763, by the American hope to secure the Floridas from England in the Revolution, by Napoleon's dreams of a circum-Gulf colonial empire before 1803, by the American acquisition of Louisiana by purchase in 1803 in order to secure for the increasing American trans-Allegheny settlements free access to the Gulf via the mouth of the Mississippi, and by the consequent American claim to the entire Gulf coast from the Perdido on the east to the Rio Grande on the west.

In 1819, influenced in part by the British use of Spanish harbors on the Gulf in the War of 1812, the American government obtained a cession of all the Floridas in order to secure the safety of a logical American abutment on the Gulf and the complete control of the American rivers that reached the Gulf through this territory. The United States also wanted to prevent the danger of a transfer of the strategic territory by Spain to some other European power. In the decade of 1825–35, the United States unsuccessfully negotiated to extend the Gulf frontage west of the Sabine River; in 1845 it was able to extend it to the Rio Grande by annexation of the independent state of Texas.

As a result of increasing interest in the Gulf after it obtained control of the mouth of the Mississippi, the American government had a vital interest in the political condition and destiny of Cuba, which guarded the commercial portal water between the Gulf and the Atlantic and which was regarded as the strategic key to the Gulf, and therefore to the Mississippi.

After the Mexican War and the subsequent opening of practical transit routes across Panama and Central America, American interest in the Gulf was extended by the increasing use of the Yucatán Channel, the natural line of communication between the mouth of the Mississippi and the new interoceanic transits. In the 1850's such prominent southern quixotic leaders as Robert Toombs and Judah P. Benjamin urged the acquisition of Cuba as a means of making the Gulf a *mare clausum*, on the ground that the Gulf was the reservoir of the Mississippi and must be practically an American lake for purposes of American security.

The commercial and political interests and relations that were influenced or determined by geographic conditions of the Gulf region reached a logical consequence in the expulsion of Spain (1898) from its last foothold in the Western Hemisphere, in the later significant advance of American influence and control and ascendancy in the Caribbean and in Panama and Central America, and in the subsequent growing commercial importance of the American southern seaboard. The Gulf of Mexico continues to be of great economic significance. In addition to its geographical importance there are vast oil and gas reserves and great supplies of fish and sulfur. During the 1970's approximately 1 million barrels of oil were being taken from the Gulf daily, and several million tons of sulfur were taken annually. By the mid-1970's, however, the Gulf was becoming increasingly polluted with wastes, especially pesticides and other pollutants from the Mississippi River.

[See also Spanish-American War.]

BIBLIOGRAPHY

J. M. Callahan, *Cuba and International Relations.*

Ellen C. Semple, *American History and Its Geographic Conditions.*

— J. M. CALLAHAN

MEXICO, PUNITIVE EXPEDITION INTO

Punitive expedition into Mexico (1916–17). On Mar. 9, 1916, Francisco (Pancho) Villa, with 485 men, crossed the border from Mexico and raided Columbus, N.Mex., killing 18 people; the raid was the culmination of a series of border troubles involving murder and robbery of Americans by Mexican bandits. In hopes of stopping it, Brig. Gen. John J. Pershing was ordered into the state of Chihuahua in northern Mexico with a force that eventually numbered over 11,000. At the start the United States concluded an agreement with Mexico, giving each country the right to cross the boundary in pursuit of bandits. Mexico understood the agreement to take effect in the event of future raids, whereas the United States interpreted it retroactively, to authorize the Pershing expedition after Villa, which it actually did not. A long series of diplomatic correspondences ensued. Venustiano Carranza's government rightly considered the uninvited Pershing force an infringement of its sovereignty, and the United States rightly considered that something must be done to protect American life and property in the face of chaotic conditions in northern Mexico, since Carranza's government seemed helpless to do so. Mexicans generally were hostile to the expedition, and on two occasions, at Parral on Apr. 12 and at Carrizal on June 21, armed clashes occurred between American and Mexican troops. For a time war seemed imminent. President Woodrow Wilson called out the National Guard of three border states on May 9 and that of the whole United States on June 18. Negotiations between the governments took place from September 1916 to January 1917 but ended without a settlement. The United States ordered Pershing's force withdrawn in February 1917. Although Villa had not been caught, a number of his chieftains had been killed or wounded and his band was generally broken up. The expedition provided valuable training for the national guardsmen on the border and the regular army in Mexico, served as a testing ground for equipment, and demonstrated the command capacity of Pershing, as a result of which he was appointed to head the American Expeditionary Forces in World War I.

BIBLIOGRAPHY

Haldeen Braddy, *Pershing's Mission in Mexico.*
Clarence C. Clendenen, *Blood on the Border.*
Herbert M. Mason, Jr., *The Great Pursuit.*

— DONALD SMYTHE

MEXICO, RELATIONS WITH

Relations between the United States and Mexico have been marked variously by suspicion, hostility, and friendly cooperation. Contentions have centered on territorial boundaries, claims, trade regulations, and the status of American investments in Mexico. Less frequent periods of harmony have reflected mutual desires for economic advantage and solidarity in resisting extrahemispheric threats.

Boundary problems predominated for thirty years after the United States recognized Mexican independence in 1822. By 1830 some 20,000 Americans had settled in Texas. When Mexico tried to restrict immigration and impose tighter control the Texans rebelled; they won independence in 1836. U.S. annexation of Texas in 1845 led to war the next year. By the Treaty of Guadalupe Hidalgo (1848), Mexico acknowledged the loss of Texas and ceded over a half million square miles to the United States for a consideration of $18,250,000. In 1853 the United States bought 54,000 square miles of the Mesilla Valley (Gadsden Purchase) for use as a railroad route to California.

The seizure of power by Mexican liberals in 1855 triggered internal strife and foreign intervention. The defeated conservatives appealed to France for aid, and in 1862 Napoleon III dispatched an army to place Archduke Maximilian of Austria on the Mexican throne. The United States, engulfed in the Civil War, was unable to counter France's violation of the Monroe Doctrine until after Appomattox. Then the United States sent troops to the border, and Napoleon, already disillusioned with his imperial adventure, withdrew from Mexico.

During the long rule of Porfirio Diaz (1876–1911) official relations became increasingly cordial. Diaz welcomed foreign capital, and U.S. investments in mining, land, and manufacturing rose to over a billion dollars, earning huge profits but also arousing resentment among Mexican opponents of the dictatorship.

The revolution that began in Mexico in 1910 produced a generation of conflict between the two nations. The U.S. government recognized the moderate Francisco I. Madero, but Woodrow Wilson's antipathy toward Victoriano Huerta, who overthrew Madero in 1913, culminated in the American occupation of Veracruz in 1914. U.S. forces invaded again in 1916 in response to Francisco (Pancho) Villa's raid on Columbus, N.Mex. Although Washington accredited an ambassador to Venustiano Carranza's government in 1917, the promulgation that year of a revolutionary constitution containing severe restrictions on foreign economic activities aroused new animosities in the United States. In 1923 President Álvaro Obregón agreed to moderate the application of the objectionable regulations and to arbitrate U.S. claims through mixed commissions, but the intractable policies of his successor, Plutarco Elías Calles, nullified the attempt at conciliation. Ambassador Dwight W. Morrow's success in persuading Calles to soften his anti-United States stand and to end a serious church-state conflict reduced American hostility to the revolutionary regime and paved the way for better relations. A 1934 accord provided for partial payment of U.S. claims for damage suffered during the revolution. Lázaro Cárdenas' expropriation of major U.S. petroleum holdings in 1938 created a crisis, but Franklin D. Roosevelt, committed to his Good Neighbor policy and anxious to secure Mexican benevolence at a time when war threatened in Europe, arranged a peaceful solution. A Mexican-American general agreement signed in 1941 settled most outstanding issues. Mexico joined the war against the Axis powers and became a charter member of the United Nations.

After World War II, relations were harmonious despite periodic Mexican dissatisfaction over American trade policy. The presidents of both countries regularly exchanged visits. Government personnel cooperated to eliminate the aphthous fever epidemic and to combat the illicit narcotics trade. Diplomacy assuaged Mexico's ire over treatment of its migrant laborers in the United States and settled the century-old dispute over ownership of the Chamizal district in El Paso. Mexico asserted its autonomy in foreign affairs by maintaining relations with Fidel Castro but aligned itself with the United States in other cold war conflicts.

BIBLIOGRAPHY

J. M. Callahan, *American Foreign Policy in Mexican Relations.*
H. F. Cline, *The United States and Mexico.*

— DAVID C. BAILEY

MEXICAN RELATIONS IN THE LATE TWENTIETH CENTURY

U.S. relations with Mexico in the second half of the twentieth century were complicated, principally because the two nations, despite strikingly different cultures and often conflicting political agendas in the international arena, nonetheless created economic bonds of lasting importance. The modern relationship between Mexico and the United States took form during and after World War II, when Washington's need for strategic resources and cheap Mexican labor coincided with Mexican determination to achieve U.S. approval of its revolutionary agenda and to modernize its economy. The half century after World War II witnessed volatile political exchanges between Washington and Mexico City over cold war issues (such as the Cuban and Nicaraguan revolutions), immigration, trade, U.S. business in Mexico, debts, drugs, and political corruption—but the intertwining of the two economies continued. The approval of the North American Free Trade Agreement (NAFTA) in 1993 merely formalized this unequal economic union, particularly along the 2,000-mile border. By the year 2000, some observers believe, the 100-mile-wide swath on either side of the legal demarcation may be the most populated region in North America and will be filled with factories. Unlike its Canadian-U.S. counterpart, however, the Mexican-U.S. border embodies the anticipated social, cultural, and political dysfunctions that accompany the meshing of a postindustrial with a putative Third World economy.

Some observers expect that by the year 2000, the 100-mile-wide swath on either side of the U.S.-Mexico border will be the most populated region in North America, and filled with factories.

Since the early 1970s the border industrialization program, which was designed to create jobs in Mexico and thus retard the flow of illegal entries into the United States, has instead exacerbated the problem. Confronting a financial crisis brought on by overspending and a $100 billion foreign debt, Mexican President José López Portillo nationalized his country's banks. The Mexican standard of living, particularly for the middle class, fell sharply. After more than a decade of debate, in 1986 the U.S. Congress passed the Immigration Reform and Control Act, establishing sanctions against U.S. employers who knowingly employ undocumented workers. Two years later, after a bitterly fought campaign laced with charges of fraud, Harvard-educated Carlos Salinas de Gortari, candidate of the ruling Institutional Revolutionary Party, became president of Mexico. Salinas committed his administration to a revival of the Mexican economy through strengthened economic ties with the United States. A decade earlier, a more bombastic Mexican leader had defied the United States, condemning its intervention in Central America and proclaiming Mexico as a leader in the Third World. Weathering the inevitable charges hurled at him by nationalists, Salinas endorsed an economic union with the United States and Canada.

President George Bush pushed hard for NAFTA and President Bill Clinton expended considerable political energy getting the measure through the U.S. Congress, despite opposition from environmentalists and organized labor. Unlike the European Economic Community, now the Economic Union of Nations, NAFTA does not erase national boundaries or create a common currency; rather, it represents the formalization of the symbiotic economic relationship that began during World War II. Continued charges of political corruption and socioeconomic injustice on the part of the Mexican government, which was unable to put down a revolt of Indians in the state of Chiapas in 1994, belie the positive image projected of Mexico during the NAFTA debates.

[See also Mexican Americans; North American Free Trade Agreement.]

BIBLIOGRAPHY

Lester D. Langley, *Mexico and the United States* (Boston, 1991).

Robert A. Pastor, *Integration with Mexico* (New York, 1993).

— LESTER D. LANGLEY

MIDDLE EAST, RELATIONS WITH

Prior to World War I the United States had few diplomatic relations with the Middle East. Only in major capitals such as Istanbul, Cairo, and Tehran was there a continuous U.S. diplomatic presence. Private citizens, archaeologists, a few businessmen, and, most important, Protestant missionaries and educators acted as unofficial representatives of the United States. Although few in number the latter exerted influence through their educational institutions, such as the American University of Beirut, Robert College in Istanbul, and Damavand College in Tehran, where they trained many future Mideast leaders. These U.S. citizens had political contacts in Washington and when occasion demanded could call upon the assistance of their government. In the early 1880s the missionary community of Iran prevailed upon President Chester A. Arthur to send a permanent diplomatic representative to Tehran. As in East Asia, missionaries often served as consuls in cities where there was no permanent U.S. representative in residence. In the years following World War I, U.S. oil companies became interested in regional resources. European companies had discovered oil in Iraq and neighboring Iran and arranged to keep control for themselves. Successive Republican administrations helped to open the door for U.S. capital, but the heyday of the nation's economic penetration would come after World War II, with the discovery that much of the region adjacent to the Persian Gulf was floating on a sea of oil.

The heyday of U.S. economic penetration of the Middle East came with the discovery that much of the region around the Persian Gulf was floating on a sea of oil.

World War II served as a catalyst for U.S. involvement in the Middle East. The administration of President Franklin D. Roosevelt helped to maintain a bridge to victory for the Allies from 1942, channeling military supplies through Iran to the Soviet Union. In 1943 important Allied meetings took place at Casablanca, Cairo, and Tehran, where leaders worked out strategies for defeating the Axis powers. As a sign of changing times Roosevelt met with King Abd al-Aziz Ibn Saud of oil-rich Saudi Arabia on his way back from the Yalta Conference in 1945. After the war the U.S. government would have been content to let Great Britain and France continue to represent Western diplomatic interests in the Middle East. Faced with the rising force of nationalism and demands for independence, however, the European colonial powers had neither the resources nor the energy to reimpose their domination. Great Britain withdrew from Palestine (now Israel, the West Bank, and Gaza) in 1948, Egypt in 1954, Aden (later the People's Republic of Yemen and now part of Yemen) in 1967, and the Persian Gulf in 1971. France withdrew from Lebanon in 1943, Syria in 1946, Morocco and Tunisia in 1956, and finally Algeria after a bloody struggle that raged from 1954 to 1962.

As the cold war with the Soviet Union intensified, only the United States had the power to oppose communist penetration of the region. Until the end of this struggle in the late 1980s, the two principles of U.S. Middle East policy were to contain the Soviets and guarantee regional oil supplies for the West. Many historians believe the cold war began in the Middle East, where the two superpowers openly disagreed over the issue of Soviet troop withdrawals from postwar Iran in 1945–1946. Then Great Britain, plagued by deficits, withdrew from Greece, where a civil war raged. President Harry S. Truman, believing that the Russians had instigated the turmoil there and that they also threatened neighboring Turkey, in 1947 announced the Truman Doctrine of economic and military assistance for the two states. In 1952 Greece and Turkey became members of the North Atlantic Treaty Organization (NATO), anchoring the eastern flank of the alliance.

Step by step the United States entered more deeply into regional affairs. No undertaking would be more decisive than Truman's support in 1948 of an independent Jewish state in the former British mandate of Palestine. A combination of factors inspired the president: sympathy for survivors of the Holocaust, lobbying by Zionists (supporters of a Jewish state) in the United States, a desire to thwart Soviet moves to befriend the Jewish settlers in Palestine, and a wish to nurture a stable, democratic, pro-Western state in the region. Although historians differ on the importance of these factors, they agree that the issue divided the Truman administration. Officials who opposed recognition feared it would antagonize the Arabs and push them into closer contact with the Soviets.

Since 1948, Arab hostility toward the United States, Israel's staunchest ally, has at times become intense and threatened to undermine U.S. goals in the region. Egyptian president Gamal Abdul Nasser tried to buy arms from Washington after an Israeli attack into the Egyptian-controlled Gaza Strip in February 1955. When President Dwight D. Eisenhower refused, Nasser purchased them instead from Soviet-controlled Czechoslovakia, inaugurating years of Soviet-Egyptian collaboration. Secretary of State John Foster Dulles decided to teach Nasser a lesson and withdrew U.S. support for the project to build a higher dam at Aswan on the Nile River. Nasser in turn nationalized the Suez Canal and contracted with the Soviet Union to complete the dam project. Great Britain, France, and Israel joined in a war against Nasser in October 1956. Eisenhower pressed them to withdraw. His action produced a surge of pro-U.S. sentiment throughout the Middle East but worsened relations with Washington's two European allies and Israel.

Many historians believe the cold war began in the Middle East, where the two superpowers openly disagreed over the issue of Soviet troop withdrawals from postwar Iran in 1945–46.

When the United States supported Israel in its June 1967 preemptive war against Egypt and Syria, many Arab states broke diplomatic relations. In the October 1973 Yom Kippur War, Nasser's successor, Anwar as-Sadat, sent Egyptian forces across the Suez Canal, taking Israeli defenders by surprise. Sadat wanted to regain the Sinai Peninsula, occupied by Israel since 1967. Arab states criticized President Richard M. Nixon's decisions in the middle of the war to release military supplies to Israel and to announce a large loan for Tel Aviv. This time the Arab states, led by Saudi Arabia, imposed an oil boycott on the United States, sending gasoline prices skyrocketing.

The United States tried repeatedly to work out a compromise that would reconcile the Arabs to the existence of Israel but the barriers were formidable and each initiative fell short of its goal. Democratic administrations, especially those of Truman, John F. Kennedy, and Lyndon B. Johnson, tended to look more favorably on the Jewish state than did Republican ones, in particular those of Eisenhower, Gerald R. Ford, and George Bush. Whenever the United States attempted negotiations the fate of the Palestinian Arabs proved the hardest issue to resolve. Displaced in the 1948 and 1967 wars, they had become part of a great diaspora; many lived in primitive refugee camps in states bordering Israel. In 1968 they selected the activist Yasir Arafat, founder of the guerrilla group Fatah, to lead the Palestine Liberation Organization (PLO). Rival Palestinian factions began to target Israeli and U.S. citizens in an effort to draw attention to their cause. Airliners and airports came under terrorist attack. For years the U.S. government refused all contact with the PLO, even after members of the League of Arab States recognized the organization as the sole legitimate representative of the Palestinian people. Washington was bound by a 1975 agreement with Israel not to negotiate with the PLO as long as the latter refused to recognize the existence of Israel. Secretary of State Henry Kissinger, renowned for his shuttle (airport-to-airport) diplomacy after the October War, had agreed to this demand to secure a partial Israeli withdrawal from the Sinai.

Only in 1988, as the Palestinian Intifada (uprising) raged in the Israeli-occupied West Bank and Gaza Strip, did the United States open talks with Arafat. Initiated by the Ronald Reagan administration and continued by President Bush and his secretary of state, James Baker, the talks resulted in a peace conference in Madrid and the September 1993 signing of an interim Palestinian-Israeli peace accord at a ceremony in Washington hosted by President Bill Clinton. Despite early optimism in the United States, however, Israelis and Palestinians were far from a just and lasting peace. Much earlier the United States had achieved an important breakthrough with the Camp David Accords. In September 1978 President Jimmy Carter helped negotiate a treaty establishing peace and diplomatic relations between Egypt and Israel. Egypt thus became the first Arab state to recognize Israel. The agreement came at a high price for the United States, which consented to increase dramatically its economic and military assistance to the two signees. Thereafter they received more than half of all U.S. foreign aid. The Arab world ostracized Egypt for breaking ranks and Cairo consequently moved closer to Washington.

From the early post-World War II years the United States looked for friends in the region. As elsewhere in the world, it often found them in the ranks of conservative nations headed by hereditary rulers, such as Iran, Libya, and Saudi Arabia. This policy, which incidentally guaranteed access to vast oil reserves, often placed the United States in the position of supporting the status quo. Critics accused Washington of ignoring regional problems in pursuit of a global strategy of winning the cold war. The pro-Western king of Libya was overthrown in September 1969. Colonel Mu'ammar al-Gadhafi, a young, militant Arab nationalist, replaced him as leader of the oil-rich state and immediately pressed the United States to evacuate its Wheelus Air Force Base. The crisis in U.S.-Libyan relations, however, came much later, during the Reagan administration. Gadhafi supported liberation movements around the world and reportedly had ties to the terrorist bombing of a West Berlin disco in April 1986 at which two U.S. soldiers were killed and many others were injured. Reagan, pursuing a tough policy on terrorism, ordered a massive retaliatory raid on Gadhafi's compound in Tripoli. The Libyan leader narrowly escaped, but U.S. bombs killed an adopted daughter and wounded two of his sons. After this attack, which received strong support in the United States but considerable criticism from U.S. allies in Europe and the Middle East, both nations pulled back from the brink of open hostilities.

In 1951 a crisis developed in Iran over the rights of the Anglo-Iranian Oil Company to monopolize production and sale of petroleum. An elderly nationalist leader, Mohammad Mosaddeq, ignited popular enthusiasm for nationalizing the company's holdings. Becoming prime minister in May of that year, he waged a two-year struggle to force the British, who had initiated a worldwide blockade of Iranian oil, to accept the takeover. At first the United States sympathized with Mosaddeq and urged Great Britain to compromise, but as the prime minister's internal support weakened and the local communist party, the Tudeh, seemed to gain ground, the new Eisenhower administration turned against him. The Central Intelligence Agency (CIA) plotted with groups of dissident Iranians to undermine the regime and restore Shah Mohammad Reza Pahlavi to power. After a coup d'état in August 1953, the United States consistently supported the increasingly dictatorial shah.

Many Iranians came to view the shah as Washington's puppet—which he decidedly was not—and their disillusionment with him and the United States increased. Opposition to the shah passed into the hands of the religious class, many of whom rejected the increasing secularization of the Pahlavi state. Ayatollah Ruholla Khomeini, an exile since 1964, organized his forces from afar to destroy the shah's regime. Suffering secretly from a terminal illness, the shah vacillated and the opposition took heart. After a series of blunders and with mixed signals from the Carter administration, which was divided on the issue, the shah fled the country in January 1979. Khomeini returned to establish an Islamic republic with himself as final arbiter. The U.S. government had few ties with the new Iranian leadership and officials in Washington were again divided over whether to adopt a hard-line or a conciliatory approach. When President Carter allowed the ailing shah to enter the United States in October 1979 for medical treatment, Iranians, remembering the events of 1953, feared a conspiracy to restore the ousted monarch. On Nov. 4, 1979, militant students seized the U.S. embassy in Tehran and took its occupants hostage. The ensuing crisis lasted until the end of Carter's term, helping to deny him reelection.

After 1981 the United States had several brushes with the prickly revolutionaries in Tehran. Diplomatic relations languished. U.S. officials feared the spread of militant Islam to neighboring states. Their concern brought closer ties with Iran's only Arab neighbor, Iraq. U.S.-Iraq relations have resembled the dips and rises of a roller coaster. Washington worked closely with the monarchy to establish the anti-Soviet Baghdad Pact in 1955 (Iraq, Iran, Turkey, Pakistan, and Great Britain), but three years later revolutionary forces overwhelmed the conservative, pro-Western regime of King Faisal II and Premier Nuri al-Said. At the same time Jordan's King Hussein faced increasing challenges. It seemed the royal dominoes were falling. Acting under the Eisenhower Doctrine announced in 1957 to block communist aggression in the region, the United States sent marines into Lebanon to strengthen its pro-Western president, who had come under attack. This also served as a gesture of support to other friendly regimes in the region. The crisis passed quickly and the marines soon went home but the U.S. action (and similar British steps in Jordan) left many Arabs bitter. Ostensibly the move was to thwart communists but the real threat, as Eisenhower knew, came from supporters of Egypt's Nasser, who preached a pan-Arab union, which they believed would restore past glories.

In November 1979, Iranian students seized the U.S. embassy in Tehran and took its occupants hostage; the ensuing crisis lasted over a year—until the inauguration of President Reagan.

Ties with Iraq were never again as cordial as they had been prior to 1958. Baghdad broke relations in 1967 and they were only restored in 1984 during the Iran-Iraq War. Washington saw the Iraqi leader, Saddam Hussein, as a barrier to the spread of revolutionary ideas from Iran. The Reagan and Bush administrations overlooked the brutal, authoritarian character of the regime, seeing it as the cork in the Iranian bottle. Iraq also offered a lucrative market for U.S. business. The 1989 collapse of the Soviet Union, a longtime ally of Iraq, removed a restraining influence on Saddam Hussein. The United States seemed to offer no opposition to his hints of annexing tiny neighboring Kuwait, over which he had long claimed sovereignty. The U.S. message had been ambiguous, but once Iraq's army poured into Kuwait in August 1990, President Bush left no doubt about his policy. He condemned Iraq and rushed to organize an international coalition to force its withdrawal. In the ensuing Gulf War of 1991 the Iraqi army suffered near-total defeat. Kuwait was restored and Iraq was forced to accept a series of United Nations resolutions. President Bush stopped short of removing Saddam Hussein; he restricted U.S. ground forces to a zone in southern Iraq far from Baghdad. He did this because his Arab coalition partners disagreed and because of fears that removal might trigger a power struggle during which surrounding states, including Iran, would seek territorial gains at Iraq's expense. The success of the Gulf War gave impulse to plans to resolve the Palestinian-Israeli conflict. With the end of the cold war, Israel lost some of its leverage as a bastion of anticommunism in the region. One reason the United States moved with such speed against Iraq was the threat it posed to the oil-rich Gulf states adjacent to Kuwait. Despite attempts in the 1970s to lower imports of foreign oil and to develop energy alternatives, the 1980s saw increasing consumption of Middle Eastern petroleum. The United States had a vested interest in maintaining stability in the Persian Gulf.

After the cold war, President Bush and his successor, Bill Clinton, spoke of a new world order, but no one knew what was envisioned for the United States in this part of the world. As pressures for change built throughout the region, it was unclear how conservative regimes like Saudi Arabia would adjust. In states such as Egypt and Algeria the United States aligned itself with the status quo against Islamic activists. Some observers questioned whether these corrupt and inefficient regimes would be able to introduce much-needed reform. The United States risked being identified with governments that many believed served the interests of only a minority of their citizens.

[See also Arab Americans; Beirut Bombing; Foreign Aid; Gulf War of 1991; Hostage Crisis; Iran-Contra Affair; Israel-Palestine Peace Accords; Oil Crises.]

BIBLIOGRAPHY

James A. Bill, *The Eagle and the Lion* (New Haven, Conn., 1988).
John A. DeNovo, *American Interests and Policies in the Middle East, 1900–1939* (Minneapolis, 1963).
George Lenczowski, *American Presidents and the Middle East* (Durham, N.C., 1990).
William B. Quandt, *Decade of Decisions: American Policy Toward the Arab-Israeli Conflict, 1967–1976* (Berkeley, Calif., 1977).
Barry M. Rubin, *Paved With Good Intentions: The American Experience and Iran* (New York, 1980).
Steven L. Spiegel, *The Other Arab-Israeli Conflict* (Chicago, 1985).
Robert W. Stookey, *America and the Arab States* (New York, 1975).
Seth P. Tillman, *The United States in the Middle East* (Bloomington, Ind., 1982).

— JAMES F. GOODE

MIDDLE PASSAGE

Middle Passage, the term applied to the trip from Africa to the West Indies, the second leg of the triangular voyage of a slave ship. During the passage the slaves, packed in holds 18 inches to 5 feet deep, and allowed above only for air, food, and exercise, died in large numbers.

[See also Triangular Trade.]

BIBLIOGRAPHY

U. B. Phillips, *American Negro Slavery.*
J. R. Spears, *The American Slave Trade.*

— FLETCHER M. GREEN

MIDNIGHT JUDGES

Midnight judges refers to the judicial appointments made by John Adams just before he was succeeded in the presidency by Thomas Jefferson. The action of Adams was assailed as an attempt "to make permanent provision for such of the Federalists and Tories as cannot hope to continue in office under the new administration." Congress, dominated in the next session by the partisans of Jefferson, reconstructed the inferior courts and legislated most of the midnight judges out of their commissions. In the case of a justice of the peace for the District of Columbia the delivery of his commission was refused. This act led to the famous Supreme Court case of *Marbury* v. *Madison.*

BIBLIOGRAPHY

W. S. Carpenter, *Judicial Tenure in the United States.*

— WILLIAM S. CARPENTER

MIDWAY ISLANDS

Midway Islands, located 1,200 miles northwest of Honolulu, are part of a coral atoll containing two islands (Sand and Eastern), with a total area of about two square miles. Discovered in 1859 by Capt. N. C. Brooks, they were annexed by the United States in 1867. The U.S. Navy was given administrative responsibility over the islands in 1903, and they became a station link in the transpacific cable in 1905. Attacked by the Japanese in World War II, Midway was the scene of a naval aircraft battle (June 1942) that resulted in a severe defeat for Japan. By checking the Japanese advance toward Hawaii, the battle proved to be one of the decisive American victories of the war. Since World War II the islands have served as a naval and air base and as a stopover point for commercial transpacific flights.

— SEDDIE COGSWELL

A group of U. S. fighter planes in formation over the reefs of Midway Island, November 14, 1942. Several months earlier, on June 4–6, U. S. forces had decisively defeated the Japanese at the Battle of Midway. (UPI/Corbis-Bettmann)

MIGRATION, GROUP

The single family was the typical unit in the westward movement that resulted in the settlement of America. Nevertheless, a large number of communities in the West were settled by groups of people previously associated with each other who migrated in one body to a new home. Usually, although not always, the destination of these groups was predetermined by agents sent out in advance to select favorable locations, and often even to purchase land before the movement was undertaken.

These group migrations fall into two classes. The first class was made up of groups of people who were governed by the same motives that in general impelled settlers westward, but who decided to move and settle in a body for mutual aid and protection, or in order to make sure of having friendly neighbors in the new home, or for other reasons. The second class was composed of religious groups or experimental colonies seeking more favorable environments in which to carry out their particular purposes. In both classes were to be found not only groups migrating westward from eastern communities, but also groups that came directly from Europe.

From earliest colonial times the westward advance presented examples of groups of the first class moving into the interior. The first settlements in the Connecticut Valley were made by the groups that followed Roger Ludlow from the Massachusetts Bay Colony. In fact, community migration into new lands previously surveyed was quite typical of the method of early frontier expansion in the New England colonies. The original settlement of Germans and their subsequent migrations in New York were of this type, as were many of the German and Scotch-Irish movements to Pennsylvania. In the early 1770's there was mention of a group of adventurers from Connecticut who settled on a tract of land on the Mississippi in West Florida.

Frequent examples of the same phenomena were found throughout the years when the country west of the Alleghenies was being occupied by settlers. One authority states that Rev. Lewis Craig's congregation moved in a body from Virginia to Kentucky in 1781. In 1788 the Ohio Associates from New England founded Marietta in Ohio. Two decades later *Niles' Weekly Register* commented on the tendency of the people of Connecticut to move in groups, after previous investigation, to new homes in the Western Reserve in northern Ohio. About the same time a New York editor described "a cavalcade of upwards of twenty waggons containing one company of 116 persons, on their way to Indiana, and all from one town in the district of Maine." In 1819 a party of 120 persons was seen on its way to Illinois. In Michigan in 1822 there were said to be numerous individuals spying out lands for groups of settlers who were to follow. A colony of Quakers on the River Rouge was mentioned the following year.

In 1839 an Iowa editor reported that "whole neighborhoods in Illinois, Indiana and Ohio are 'organizing' for emigration." To one locality in Wisconsin a few years later came a group of more than 100 persons from Rochester, N.Y., of whom 62 were members of one family. During the 1850's the rush to the newly opened Kansas-Nebraska country contained many groups, such as the one made up of friends and acquaintances from Outagamie County, Wis., which founded Fremont, Nebr., in 1856. Illustrations of this nature might be multiplied indefinitely to show the part played by groups in the westward movement.

In the second class of group migrations, various experimental colonies and religious groups migrated westward. The Harmony Society, led by George Rapp and made up of a sect from southern Germany, established a settlement in western Pennsylvania in 1805 and moved to Indiana ten years later. The Zoarites came to Ohio in 1817 from Württemberg, Germany. In the 1830's a group of ministers in New York's Mohawk Valley drew up a plan for a religious and educational community in the West. An exploring committee sent out in 1835 selected land in Illinois and the result was the founding of Galesburg and Knox College. The establishment of Oberlin, Ohio, and Oberlin College was accomplished in a similar manner a few years earlier. The Mennonites nearly always moved in groups, after previous investigations of localities, when they established their various communities throughout the country, whether they came directly from Europe or moved from their earlier centers of settlement in America. Another instance of group migration may be found in the history of the Iowa community known as Amana—a religious colony that for almost a century was communistic in organization.

The final illustration of this type of group migration may be in many respects the most notable of all. The Mormon church had its origin about 1830 in western New York. In that year a temporary domicile was selected at Kirtland, Ohio, but at the same time Independence, Mo., was chosen as a permanent location, and by 1831 more than 1,000 members of the sect had moved there. Two years later the Mormons were forced to move to the Far West, north of the Missouri River. In 1839 the hostility of the neighboring settlers caused another move, this time to Nauvoo, on the eastern bank of the Mississippi River in Illinois. After seven years at Nauvoo, the leaders decided to seek an asylum in the Rocky Mountains, and the result was the historic hegira of the Mormons to Utah, which began in 1846.

BIBLIOGRAPHY

Earnest E. Calkins, *They Broke the Prairie.*
William A. Linn, *The Story of the Mormons.*

— DAN E. CLARK

MINIMUM-WAGE LEGISLATION

The concept of a minimum wage may be said to go back to pre-Christian times, in the sense that a slaveowner was required to provide minimum subsistence for his bondsmen lest they perish. In many other societies wages were set at a "just" level (the medieval period) or, as with England's 16th-century legislation, at fixed maximums. Legal recognition of the idea of a minimum wage as a humanistic, as well as economic, desideratum is found first in a New Zealand law of 1894. In the United States the first such law was passed in 1906 in California; it provided for a minimum wage of $2 a day for almost all public employees. In 1912 Massachusetts enacted the first minimum-wage law that applied to private enterprise, but it affected only women and children. Fourteen other states and the District of Columbia and Puerto Rico had similar laws on their books within the next ten years. But the apogee of the minimum-wage movement had already been passed. In

1919 and 1921 Nebraska and Texas repealed their enactments. In 1923, in the case of *Adkins* v. *Children's Hospital*, the Supreme Court declared a District of Columbia minimum-wage statute to be unconstitutional on the ground that it violated the due process clause of the Fifth Amendment. The majority reasoned that in arbitrarily fixing a wage on the basis of the employee's minimum cost of living, the law might be requiring the employer to pay more than the services were worth and thus taking the employer's property. Within the next few years the Supreme Court invalidated several other state laws on the basis of similar reasoning but based its ruling on the Fourteenth Amendment. Kansan and Puerto Rican courts declared their own laws unconstitutional, and the Minnesota attorney general's opinion excepted only girls under eighteen from such a judicial ban.

In pre-Christian times, a slaveholder was required to provide minimum subsistence for his bondsmen lest they perish.

Not until the effects of the Great Depression were felt in the early 1930's did the states revive their efforts in the area of minimum-wage legislation. In 1933, Connecticut, Illinois, New Hampshire, New Jersey, New York, Ohio, and Utah enacted such laws, followed by Massachusetts in 1934 and Rhode Island in 1936, but they sought to avoid the judicially rejected cost-of-living base by adopting a new approach. The states did not now attempt to regulate or fix wages directly but, through an investigation of any occupation in which women and minors received less than a living wage, set wages on the supposed judicially approved standard of what is "fairly and reasonably commensurate with the value of services rendered" and yet sufficient for the minimum necessary for health and well-being. This new attempt also failed at first, but only because of a procedural technicality. In a 1936 decision (*Morehead* v. *Tipaldo*) it was only a bare majority that ruled against the New York State minimum-wage law, and it rested its determination on the fact that "no application [had] been made for reconsideration of the constitutional question" decided in the *Adkins* case. Within ten months such an application was made in a Washington State case, *West Coast Hotel Company* v. *Parrish* (1937), and a new five-to-four majority upheld the law because of "the economic conditions which [had] supervened [since the *Adkins* decision] and in the light of the reasonableness of the exercise of the protective [police] power of the state." Thus, as long as a reasonable procedure is utilized that takes into account all economic views and factors, such as the relation of the type, hours, and conditions of the work to the employer's required payment, so that no judicially unreasonable wage determination eventuates, then such minimum-wage laws are constitutional.

After 1937 numerous state and federal laws involving or affecting minimum wages were quickly enacted. By 1974 forty-one states had such laws on the books, the exceptions being Alabama, Georgia, Iowa, Mississippi, Nebraska, South Carolina, Tennessee, Texas, and Virginia. Most of these laws cover only women over eighteen, but others also cover minors, with a few including men. In most states a general minimum wage is set by the legislature and in the others machinery is provided for administrative determinations. There are also state and federal laws relating to particular minimum-wage considerations—for example, setting minimums for apprentices and minors, affecting farm laborers, and establishing minimum overtime payments.

The principal federal law affecting wages is the Fair Labor Standards Act of 1938, commonly called the Wages and Hours Law, the enforcement of which is supervised by an administrator and ultimately enforced by the courts. (Where a state fixes a higher minimum, it, rather than the federal one, applies; furthermore, since the Fair Labor Standards Act is limited to industries in or affecting interstate commerce and therefore does not cover all employees and since it also contains several exemptions, state laws are a necessary adjunct to it.) The Fair Labor Standards Act was amended in 1947 by the Portal-to-Portal Act, which overturned a Supreme Court decision permitting extra pay for preparation and cleaning up work, so that only such work as is an integral and indispensable part of the employee's principal activities is today compensable. In 1963 another amendment, the Federal Equal Pay Act, provided equal pay for equal work in industries engaged in commerce. In addition, legislation has been passed specifically relating to the federal government as an employer and as a purchaser of goods and services, requiring it to pay set (minimum) wages to its employees and requiring the payment of minimum wages by parties that hold government contracts—the Davis-Bacon Act of 1931 and the Walsh-Healey Public Contracts Act of 1936.

Originally the Fair Labor Standards Act was aimed at establishing a 40 cents per hour minimum wage—raised to 75 cents per hour in 1949 and $1.00 per hour in 1956. By 1975 the federally established minimum wage had reached $2.10 per hour for nonfarm workers and $1.80 for farm workers, first covered in 1966.

BIBLIOGRAPHY

Barbara N. Armstrong, *Insuring the Essentials.*
Bureau of National Affairs, *Wage and Hour Manual.*
J. R. Commons and J. B. Andrews, *Principles of Labor Legislation.*
Morris D. Forkosch, *A Treatise on Labor Law.*

— MORRIS D. FORKOSCH

MINORITY RIGHTS

Doctrines of natural rights, under whose aegis the Declaration of Independence was issued, enunciate the view that while governments must indeed make certain binding decisions for society, there are rights of human beings that must not be impaired by those decisions. Thus, while governments may have to restrict liberty in controlling crime, they should do so only under fixed procedures ("due process of law"); and certain rights such as freedom of speech, association, and the press are particularly sacrosanct. Basic rights of minorities are to be respected, according to many thinkers, for a number of reasons. First, human beings should be valued as ends in themselves and not merely as means to other ends. Second, the idea of majority rule itself requires that respect be given the rights of minorities: thus if freedom of speech is suppressed by today's majority, present minorities will not be able to become tomorrow's majority through peaceful discussion and persuasion. Federal and state checks and balances and constitutional bills of rights were thus designed to protect minorities against established governments. James Madison argued (*Federalist Papers*, No. 10) that protection against the pressures of a potentially monolithic public opinion may be undergirded by diversity of interests, parties, factions, and sects, or what has since been termed social, economic, and cultural pluralism.

American history suggests that minority rights are always in peril and that their protection depends not only on the courts but also on the attainment of economic and political power by the minorities themselves.

American history has been characterized by an almost constant struggle to protect minority rights against various kinds of encroachments. In 1798, for instance, the Alien and Sedition Acts imposed restrictions on freedom of speech and the press; and the acts were vigorously opposed. Before the Civil War, proponents of slavery attempted to limit antislavery agitation through gag rules involving petitions to Congress and other measures, but they were overcome by the war itself.

After the Civil War increasing social and economic complexity, expanded use of government regulatory power, and several wars posed new problems and dramatized old ones. Workers, particularly industrial workers, seeking to form unions, were restricted in their attempts to organize labor unions throughout the 19th century, and only in the 1930's were these restrictions somewhat abated. Alleged abrogations of the rights of religious minorities have been the occasion for Supreme Court decisions, as when the Court upheld the right of the children of Jehovah's Witnesses not to salute the U.S. flag in *West Virginia State Board of Education* v. *Barnette*, 319 U.S. 624 (1943). Political minorities have often found it difficult to express themselves freely: they were jailed during World War I for circulating anticonscription pamphlets; investigated by constitutionally and morally questionable methods, particularly in the 1920's and 1950's; often confronted by state statutes making it difficult for minority parties to be listed on the ballot; and punished, not for overt acts, but for allegedly conspiring to organize the Communist party and to teach and advocate the forcible overthrow of the government, as in *Dennis et al.* v. *United States*, 341 U.S. 494 (1951). During World War II, without trial and solely on the grounds of race, the U.S. government forced thousands of Japanese-Americans to leave their homes and to reside in camps. Afro-Americans were long relegated to racially segregated and inferior schools until in *Brown* v. *Board of Education of Topeka*, 347 U.S. 483 (1954), the Supreme Court held that racially segregated schools were inherently unequal; and the civil rights movement of the 1960's sought to secure the rights of racial minorities in public accommodations and other areas. Also in the 1960's and 1970's efforts were made to buttress the rights of the poor and the aged, of prisoners, and of Indians.

The American experience suggests that minority rights are always in peril and that their protection depends not only on law and the courts but also on the development of economic and organizational power by the minorities themselves. Minorities, many have argued, must struggle for their own rights through such activities as public agitation, strikes, and, on occasion, civil disobedience.

BIBLIOGRAPHY

Robert E. Cushman, *Civil Liberties in the United States.*
Robert B. Downs, ed., *The First Freedom.*
Paul L. Murphy, *The Meaning of Freedom of Speech.*

— MULFORD Q. SIBLEY

MINT, FEDERAL

Robert Morris, secretary of finance, urged the Continental Congress in 1782 to establish a mint. In 1786 Congress ordered the Board of the Treasury to study the subject, but not until Apr. 2, 1792, three years after the birth of the new government, was the creation of a mint authorized. It was set up in Philadelphia, then the national capital, in 1793, and remained there permanently after other government agencies had been moved to Washington, D.C. Silver coinage began in 1794 and gold coinage in 1795. The staff at first consisted of eleven officers and clerks, nineteen workmen in the coining department, and seven men at the furnaces. The total coinage produced in 1794–95 was less than $500,000. By 1807 the output exceeded $1 million; in 1851 nearly $63.5 million was struck, all of it gold save about $800,000. In the earlier years the mint often lacked gold and silver with which to work. In 1820 it operated only part of the time because of this scarcity and the small demand for copper coins. In 1835 Congress established three branch mints—one at New Orleans and two in the new goldfields, at Charlotte, N.C., and Dahlonega, Ga. The one at New Orleans was taken over by the Confederates at the beginning of the Civil War and operated by them from Jan. 26 to May 31, 1861, when operations were suspended. It did not resume work until 1879; in 1909 it ceased to coin and became an assay office. The mint at Dahlonega closed in 1861; that at Charlotte was used as barracks by Confederate soldiers and never operated after that. A branch mint was installed at San Francisco in 1854 and operated until 1955. Another was legally established at Denver in 1862, but no coins had yet been made there when in 1870 it was turned into an assay office. In 1895 it was again authorized to coin, but no money was made there until 1906. A sixth branch mint began work at Carson City, Nev., in 1870, but its production was not great, and it closed in 1893. Another, authorized in 1864 at the Dalles, Oreg., was in process of construction in 1871 when it was destroyed by fire and the project was abandoned. A mint authorized in 1902 at Manila, in the Philippines, had a comparatively small output. By acts of 1846 and later, the various mints were made public depositories. The Bureau of the Mint was created by Congress on Feb. 12, 1873, as a division of the Treasury Department, and supervises the two remaining coinage mints—Denver and Philadelphia; the two assay offices—San Francisco and New York City; and the two bullion depositories—Fort Knox, Ky. (gold), and West Point, N.Y. (silver). The minting of gold coins ceased in 1934.

BIBLIOGRAPHY

Jesse P. Watson, *The Bureau of the Mint.*

— ALVIN F. HARLOW

Minutemen on the march in a Currier and Ives print, 1876. The first minutemen were a regiment of the 1774 Massachusetts militia who were ready for any emergency "at a minute's warning." (Corbis-Bettmann)

MINUTEMEN

While the term "minuteman" goes back at least to 1756, the famous body developed under that name first appeared in the reorganization of the Massachusetts militia by the Worcester convention and the Provincial Congress in 1774. To rid the older militia of Tories, resignations of officers were called for in September in the three Worcester regiments, which were broken into seven. New officers were elected. These officers were to enlist a third of the men in new regiments, which were specifically called (Sept. 21) regiments of minutemen, who were to elect their officers. The Provincial Congress, meeting in October, found the same process voluntarily going on in the militia of other counties, and directed its completion (Oct. 26). Thus a double system of regiments was established in the province, the minutemen to be ready for any emergency "at a minute's warning."

The formation of the minuteman regiments proceeded slowly. On Feb. 14, 1775, as returns that had been called for were not forthcoming, the Provincial Congress set May 10 for a complete return. None was ever made, and only scattered records show that while Marblehead organized its company on Nov. 7, 1774, Woburn, though close to Boston, did not vote to establish its minutemen until Apr. 17, 1775, two days before the outbreak of war. No complete list of minuteman companies and regiments was possible, and only from town records, a few lists, and the "Lexington alarm lists" of minutemen and militia can a fragmentary roster be patched together of an organization that never was completed.

On Apr. 19 militia and minutemen turned out together to resist the British expedition to Concord, Mass. The men whom the British killed on Lexington green were minutemen, and minutemen led the march down to Concord bridge. But militia were also in the column, and men of both kinds harried the British back to Boston. The minuteman organization was then abandoned by the Provincial Congress in organizing the Eight Months Army. As this was formed, it drew men from both minutemen and militia; those who could not join went back into the militia, and the minutemen thenceforth disappeared in Massachusetts.

Other colonies organized their minutemen on the recommendation of the Continental Congress (July 18, 1775) to use them for rounds of service on special brief enlistments. Maryland (August), New Hampshire (September), and Connecticut (December) are on record as accepting this plan, and Connecticut minutemen are credited with resisting William Tryon's expedition against Danbury. There are statues commemorating the minutemen in Concord and Lexington, Mass., and Westport, Conn.

BIBLIOGRAPHY

Allen French, *First Year of the American Revolution.*

— ALLEN FRENCH

MIRANDA V. *ARIZONA*

Miranda v. *Arizona*, 384 U.S. 436 (1966). Up to the 1960's the admissibility of confessions in state cases was governed by the "voluntariness" test. By the 1950's the voluntariness test had come to mean not only that a confession must be free of influences that made it untrustworthy or "probably untrue" but also that it must not be the product of police methods offensive to a "sense of fair play and decency"—such as "relay" interrogation or "incommunicado" detention. Even as expanded, the voluntariness test had serious shortcomings. Because it developed on a case-by-case basis and depended upon the totality of circumstances of each particular case (for example, the particular defendant's intelligence, age, education, and powers of resistance), it seemed unlikely to furnish much guidance to the police. The courts also found it extremely difficult to reconstruct the tenor, atmosphere, and conditions of police questioning behind closed doors.

In *Miranda* v. *Arizona*, a five-to-four majority of the Supreme Court scrapped the voluntariness-totality-of-circumstances test in favor of what the dissenters called a "constitutional code of rules for confessions." The so-called *Miranda* rules provide that the prosecution may not use statements obtained by "custodial interrogation" (questioning initiated by law enforcement officers after a person has been taken into custody) unless the person is warned prior to any questioning that "he has a right to remain silent, that any statement he does make may be used as evidence against him, and that he has a right to the presence of an attorney, either retained or appointed." Moreover, if the defendant "indicates . . . at any stage of the process that he wishes to consult with an attorney before speaking [or continuing to speak] there can be no questioning."

The *Miranda* case was bitterly criticized by many law enforcement officials and politicians for unduly restricting police interrogation during a national crime crisis, and in 1968 Congress passed the Crime Control Act, which purports to "repeal" the decision. The validity of the statute had not been tested by the Supreme Court by the mid-1970's.

BIBLIOGRAPHY

Fred Graham, *The Self-Inflicted Wound.*

Yale Kamisar, "A Dissent From the Miranda Dissents," *Michigan Law Review*, vol. 65 (1966).

Yale Kamisar, Fred Inbau, and Thurman Arnold, *Criminal Justice in Our Times.*

— YALE KAMISAR

MISCEGENATION

The idea of a prohibition against interracial marriage originated in America, for at the time the colonies were settled, England had no ban on miscegenation. Among the colonists marriage between black slaves and whites (especially white women who were indentured servants) caused great moral concern and concern about potential economic loss, for the children of a marriage between a slave and a free person were free.

The first antimiscegenation statutes were enacted in Maryland (1661) and Virginia (1691); Massachusetts, North Carolina, and Pennsylvania soon followed suit. When the nation moved west, similar laws were passed in many of the frontier states. It was argued that such laws were designed to preserve racial integrity, but they generally prohibited only interracial marriages involving a white person and a person of another color, not, for example, those between an Indian and a black. As late as 1950 some thirty states still had such laws on their books.

Between 1950 and 1967 the widespread attention given a 1948 decision of the California Supreme Court holding its state antimiscegenation law unconstitutional and the momentum of the general movement for legal and political racial equality led fourteen states to repeal their statutory bans on miscegenation. In 1967, in the case of *Loving* v. *Virginia* (388 U.S. 1), a unanimous U.S. Supreme Court declared such laws unconstitutional. Restricting the individual's "fundamental freedom" to marry solely on the basis of race, ruled the Court, violated both the equal protection clause and the due process clause of the Fourteenth Amendment. If racial classifications are ever to be upheld, observed the Court, "they must be shown to be necessary to the accomplishment of some permissible state objectives independent of the racial discrimination which it was the object of the Fourteenth Amendment to eliminate." The Court could find no such legitimate independent purpose.

The *Loving* ruling was expected, for, on a related question, in *McLaughlin* v. *Florida* (1964), the U.S. Supreme Court had held it a denial of equal protection of the laws for a state to prohibit cohabitation by a white and black not married to each other while not restricting cohabitation by unmarried couples generally.

BIBLIOGRAPHY

Harvey Applebaum, "Miscegenation Statutes: A Constitutional and Social Problem," *Georgetown Law Journal*, vol. 53 (1964).

Alfred Avins, "Anti-Miscegenation Laws and the Fourteenth Amendment: The Original Intent," *Virginia Law Review*, vol. 52 (1966).

— YALE KAMISAR

MISSIONS, FOREIGN

Foreign missions constitute a phase of the expansion of Christianity. More specifically, they represent a modern movement since the early 18th century analogous to the rise in earlier times of the orders of preaching friars. Protestant missions followed, at first, Dutch, English, and Danish conquests and colonization, whether in India, the East Indies, or North America. The German Moravians were the first Protestants to undertake (in 1732) foreign missions apart from colonial expansion. The American movement received its initial impulse from England, where William Carey, the first great missionary herald, founded (1792) the Baptist Missionary Society, and himself undertook service in 1793 in India. In England Protestant churches began the formation of missionary societies, which were organized to spread the gospel to the "uttermost parts" of the world, and to convert all non-Christian peoples. There was at the time little critical reckoning with certain substantial elements in the non-Christian cultures and religions.

American participation began in 1810 with the organization of the American Board of Commissioners for Foreign Missions, a society that served the interests of Congregational, Presbyterian, and Reformed churches. Thereafter, separate societies were formed by Baptists (1813), Methodist Episcopalians (1819), Protestant Episcopalians (1820), Presbyterians (1836–37), Lutherans (1839), and others, in turn. Bible societies, such as the American Bible Society, undertook the translation of Holy Scripture into the tongues of mission lands. The development of the foreign-missions enterprise was most notable between 1850 and 1930. In 1920, 236 American Protestant societies were operating through about 9,000 missionaries, on an income of about $30 million. Reduction in income, unrest in mission lands, opposition from foreign cultures and religions, and a reappraisal by the churches themselves of the gospel in relation to non-Christian faiths have caused a cutback in foreign missions, although many continue to be active.

BIBLIOGRAPHY

Wade C. Barclay, *History of Methodist Missions.*

Robert F. Berkhofer, Jr., *Salvation and the Savage: An Analysis of Protestant Missions and the American Indian Response, 1787–1862.*

Joseph L. Grabill, *Protestant Diplomacy and the Near East: Missionary Influence on American Policy, 1810–1927.*

— JOHN CLARK ARCHER

MISSIONS, FRONTIER

Frontier missions grew out of the feeling among Christians in the older parts of the United States that it was their duty to send the gospel to the new settlements in the West. The frontier was usually regarded in the East as a region of crudeness, lawlessness, and low moral standards. In religion it was thought to be characterized paradoxically both by irreligion and by excessive emotionalism; unorthodox creeds, such as Mormonism, were thought to flourish there. But as the new territories increased in population and were admitted to the Union it became evident that the West would sometime hold the balance of power in the nation; hence it was important that "sound principles" be established in the frontier communities. Another powerful motive was the rivalry between the various denominations to win adherents and to hold their own constituents in the new settlements; the spread of Roman Catholicism especially was an incentive for Protestant missionary activity. Disinterested Christian benevolence, however, is the chief explanation of home missions.

Folks back East regarded the frontier as a lawless, immoral region; in religion, the West was seen as prone to godlessness, excessive emotionalism, and unorthodox creeds.

Missions to the frontiers began early in the 18th century. By the opening of the 19th century the rapidly expanding field led to the organization of many local home missionary societies in New England and New York. These in turn generally grew into or merged with national denominational societies between 1820 and 1835. Preachers and churches were the chief agencies employed, but academies and colleges were useful adjuncts. Among the more important Protestant denominations it appears that a majority of their congregations west of the Alleghenies have at some time received missionary assistance. Indian missions, since they normally operated beyond the frontier of settlement, were regarded as foreign missions.

BIBLIOGRAPHY

O. W. Elsbree, *The Rise of the Missionary Spirit in America.*
Colin B. Goodykoontz, *Home Missions on the American Frontier.*
P. G. Mode, *The Frontier Spirit in American Christianity.*
W. W. Sweet, *The Rise of Methodism in the West.*

— COLIN B. GOODYKOONTZ

MISSISSIPPIAN CULTURES

The prehistoric Mississippian cultures dominated the lower and middle Mississippi Valley from about A.D. 700 to the historic period. Some of the most famous archaeological sites in eastern North America are Mississippian settlements. Cahokia, Ill.; Moundville, Ala.; Aztalan, Wis.; Etowah, Ga.; and Spiro, Okla., are among the many sites of this culture that are visited yearly by tourists. Settlements ranged in size from small villages to the city of Cahokia, with an estimated population of 30,000 inhabitants. Characteristic traits of the cultures are centralized political organization; social stratification; the platform mound-and-plaza complex; intensive cultivation of corn, beans, and squash; and pottery with crushed-shell temper. A highly religious cult referred to as the Southern Cult or the Southeastern Ceremonial Complex was an important social institution within most Mississippian cultures. The cult is characterized by monolithic stone axes, macelike batons, ceremonial flint knives, and a wide variety of iconographic symbols and other objects. Monks Mound at Cahokia is the third largest temple mound in the New World, measuring 200 by 300 meters (650 by 967 feet) at the base and 30 meters (97 feet) in height. A chiefdom has been suggested as the level of political organization reached by many of these cultures, and a state-level society may have existed at Cahokia. Many features of these Mississippian cultures—including the mound-and-plaza complex, religious symbolism, and elements in shapes and decorations of pottery vessels—indicate a Middle American stimulus, or at least extensive borrowing from that center. But the main impetus leading to the emergence of these prehistoric Mississippian cultures apparently came from indigenous developments, such as population growth and the adoption of an economic system sustained by domesticated plant foods.

BIBLIOGRAPHY

Jesse D. Jennings, *Prehistory of North America.*
Gordon R. Willey, *Introduction to American Archaeology*, vol. I.

— GUY GIBBON

MISSISSIPPI VALLEY

Until it came into the possession of the United States the Mississippi Valley was the prize sought by the leading nations of Europe. Spaniards—Hernando de Soto and Francisco Vásquez de Coronado (1541)—discovered the lower valley, but Spain did not follow up the discoveries and more than two centuries elapsed before that country became really interested in the region. It was far different with the French. Their explorers and *coureurs de bois*—Jean Nicolet (1634); Pierre Esprit Raddison and Médard Chouart, Sieur de Grosseilliers (1654–60); Louis Jolliet and Father Jacques Marquette (1673); Robert Cavelier, Sieur de La Salle (1669–84); and many others—penetrated far and wide into the valley. When in 1699 Pierre Lemoyne, Sieur d'Iberville, and Jean Baptiste Le Moyne, Sieur de Bienville, established a colony near the mouth of the Mississippi River, the French were in almost undisputed control of the great valley—a control they maintained for half a century. Although claiming the region on the basis of their sea-to-sea charters, the English colonists were slow in finding their way to the "western waters." But when English traders and land companies became actively interested in the Ohio Valley, about the middle of the 18th century, the great struggle between the French and English, known as the French and Indian War, was precipitated.

At the close of the war in 1763 France lost its possessions in America, relinquishing its claims west of the Mississippi to Spain and the region east of that river to the English. In the Definitive Treaty of Peace, 1783, the new United States received jurisdiction westward to the Mississippi and north of Spanish Florida. Twenty years later the Louisiana Purchase gave the United States the entire valley, after Spain had ceded Louisiana back to France in 1800. Even before the revolutionary war there were American settlements in Kentucky and Tennessee. After 1783 the floodgates were opened and Americans poured across the mountains in ever-increasing numbers to take possession of their new domain.

The influences and problems arising out of the settlement of the Mississippi Valley made the United States a strong nation. In meeting the demands of the westerners for protection against the Indians, for autonomous local governments, for roads and river improvements, for mail service, and for liberal land legislation, the powers of the federal government were vastly extended and strengthened. It was in the Mississippi Valley that the frontier had its most characteristic influence on American life and institutions. At the same time, in the Mississippi Valley the sectionalism that culminated in the Civil War developed its greatest bitterness.

BIBLIOGRAPHY

Dan E. Clark, *The West in American History.*

James K. Hosmer, *A Short History of the Mississippi Valley.*

— DAN E. CLARK

MISSOURI COMPROMISE

The Missouri Territory comprised that part of the Louisiana Purchase not organized as the state of Louisiana in 1812. Ever since it had been a French province, slavery had existed in the territory. From 1817 to 1819 the Missouri Territorial Assembly petitioned Congress for statehood, with boundaries limited to approximately those of the present state. In 1819 there was an equal number of slave and free states. When the House of Representatives reported a bill authorizing Missouri to frame a constitution, James Tallmadge of New York proposed an amendment prohibiting the further introduction of slaves into Missouri and providing that all children born of slaves should be free at the age of twenty-five. The amendment was passed by the House on Feb. 16–17, 1819, but rejected by the Senate. Congress adjourned without further action but the South was stricken with fear.

When Congress reconvened in December 1819, Maine had formed a constitution and was requesting admission as a free state. The House passed an act admitting Maine. The Senate joined this measure to the one admitting Missouri without mention of slavery. Sen. J. B. Thomas of Illinois offered an amendment to the Senate bill for the admission of Missouri as a slave state, but with the provision that, in the remainder of the Louisiana Purchase, slavery should be prohibited north of 36°30′ north latitude. A debate followed that startled the nation. It came, said Thomas Jefferson, "like a fire bell in the night." A sectional alignment threatened the Union.

The House passed a bill, Mar. 1, 1820, admitting Missouri as a free state. The Senate took up the measure, struck out the antislavery provision, and added the Thomas amendment. A compromise was effected by admitting Maine as a free state, Mar. 3, 1820 (effective Mar. 15), and by authorizing Missouri to form a constitution with no restriction on slavery, Mar. 6, 1820. The region of the Louisiana Purchase north of 36°30′, except for the state of Missouri, was thus dedicated to freedom.

The Missouri debate startled the nation with the threat of sectional division. It came, said Thomas Jefferson, "like a fire bell in the night."

Missouri called a constitutional convention to meet at Saint Louis on June 12, 1820. The constitution empowered the legislature to exclude free blacks and mulattoes from the state. This restriction caused another bitter debate in Congress. A second compromise was, therefore, effected on Mar. 2, 1821. This stipulated that Missouri would not be admitted until it agreed that nothing in its constitution should be interpreted to abridge the privileges and immunities of citizens of the United States. The pledge was secured. On Aug. 10, 1821, Missouri became a state.

The compromise was respected and regarded as almost sacred until the Mexican War, when the power of Congress to exclude slavery from the territories was again questioned, by the Wilmot Proviso. In 1848 Congress passed the Oregon Territory bill prohibiting slavery. President James K. Polk signed it on the ground that the territory was north of the Missouri Compromise line. Soon afterward proposals were made to extend the compromise line of 1820 through the Mexican cession to the Pacific. These efforts failed to secure the extension of the 36°30′ line across the continent. Instead, the principle of popular sovereignty prevailed in the Compromise of 1850. The admission of California in 1850 gave the free states a majority of one. In 1854 the Missouri Compromise was repealed.

[See also Kansas-Nebraska Act.]

BIBLIOGRAPHY

George Dangerfield, *The Awakening of American Nationalism, 1815–1828.*

Glover Moore, *The Missouri Controversy.*

— GEORGE D. HARMON

MOBILIZATION

Mobilization is the process of assembling and organizing troops and matériel for the defense of a nation in time of war or national emergency. It has become a central factor in warfare since the French Revolution and the rise of nationalism. Whereas 18th-century powers most often hired mercenaries to fight limited wars, 19th-century nations increasingly demanded that every able-bodied citizen respond to mobilization calls. American attitudes toward war further reinforced the concept of total war because threats to public tranquility were interpreted as being illegal and immoral and thus as calling for nothing short of total war to reestablish the peace. In 20th-century wars it has been necessary to mobilize not only men and matériel but also psychological support, as illustrated by President Woodrow Wilson's vow to "make the world safe for democracy" and President Franklin D. Roosevelt's call for Germany's "unconditional surrender."

While embracing the notion of total war, the United States, until the 20th century, was notoriously inept at mobilizing troops and retaining them for the duration of the wars it fought. Congress was ever suspicious of standing armies and of all efficient means that would enable the executive to mobilize the state militia forces, feeling that these instruments might serve partisan causes.

The mobilization problems experienced in the War of 1812 and the Mexican War (1846–48) continued to plague U.S. military efforts throughout the 19th century. For instance, the militia system was never workable. This fact, together with the unreliability of the volunteers and the vices of the bounty system, demonstrated the necessity for conscription in any extended war in which the United States was involved. Furthermore, the tendency to mobilize manpower before mobilizing matériel was to create confusion down to World War I.

In the Mexican War, mobilization was based largely upon an expansible standing army and the calling of volunteers, because the militia's poor performance in the War of 1812 had demonstrated that the militia system was irredeemable. There were traces of preplanning in this first foreign war, as arms and supplies were provided by the federal government based on the needs of the whole mobilized army.

The Civil War was a total war and thus a modern conflict, even though many of the mobilization mistakes of previous wars were repeated. At the outset, few were able to perceive the conflict's full dimensions, and thus mobilization proceeded sporadically. Initially President Abraham Lincoln called 75,000 state militia troops. But since this element had not been called since 1836 at the outset of the second Seminole War, the 2,471,377 troops on its rolls represented only a paper force in 1861. Next, a call was issued for volunteers; with no effective mobilization plan, the War Department was unable to process the overwhelming number of recruits. Later, when the ardor of volunteering cooled, other methods of raising troops were resorted to, such as the draft, implemented by the Conscription Act of 1863. Although the act netted few draftees, it forced many to volunteer who otherwise would not have. Other extraordinary measures employed to mobilize manpower included accepting blacks for army service and organizing special service units to receive invalid volunteers for noncombatant duty.

The Japanese attack on Pearl Harbor in 1941 catapulted the U.S. into the most massive mobilization effort in history.

All the old nightmares of poor mobilization were present in the Spanish-American War (1898), plus some new ones. With no plan of mobilization there was no integration of manpower with matériel and no training in combined naval and military operations. Only the fact that the war was short and successful helped to ameliorate some of the potentially disastrous problems. A series of postwar reforms was instituted to remedy the worst mobilization shortcomings, among which was the founding of the Army War College in 1901 to study the mobilization process.

U.S. participation in World War I (1917–18) and World War II (1941–45) introduced speed into the warmaking equation. Although the urgency of mobilization was slightly cushioned by the prior entry of America's allies into both wars, the gigantic scale of mobilization, the increased importance of technology, the total absorption of a sophisticated industrial economy into the war effort, and the huge number of troops all raised mobilization planning to the highest councils of war.

By the National Defense Act of 1916 the United States avoided some of the desperate measures used to raise manpower in previous wars: uncertain calls for militiamen and volunteers were no longer to be relied on, and draftees were not to make substitutions, purchase exemptions, or receive bounties. Whereas in earlier American wars estimates of manpower requirements had been based largely on guesses of what public sentiment would allow, in World War I the calls for manpower were limited only by the manpower requirements for industry. Therefore, the great mobilization problems of World War I were not those of recruiting, but of equipping, training, organizing, and transporting the army to the front.

The Japanese attack on Pearl Harbor in 1941 catapulted the United States into the most massive mobilization effort in history. As in World War I the armed forces and the war industries were in competition for manpower. In addition, there were the requirements of not one but five theaters of war, the need of maintaining lines of communication to each theater, and the need to dovetail efforts with coalition partners. The squeeze upon American manpower extended the search for able hands to the enlisting of women, indigenous personnel, prisoners of war, and the physically handicapped.

The leading role of the United States in the cold war significantly altered its traditional mobilization techniques. Although never implemented, universal military training, authorized in principle by the Universal Military Training and Service Act of 1951, was supposed to provide a peacetime pool of manpower that could be drafted in time of national emergency. Until the Korean War (1950–53) the emphasis on air power and nuclear arms allowed the army's strength to slip.

Selective-service legislation passed in 1955 assured that reserve units would be manned by trained men; but instead of the reserves being called for the Vietnam War, as had been done in the Korean War, forces were raised through increased draft calls. The decision to do so was prompted by problems experienced in the reserve call-up during the Berlin crisis in 1961 and by political exigencies. But not calling the reserves was generally considered to have been a mistake, for it gravely weakened the army's strategic reserve.

BIBLIOGRAPHY

M. G. Henry and M. A. Kreidberg, *History of Military Mobilization in the United States Army 1775–1945.*

M. Matloff, *American Military History.*

— DON E. MCLEOD

MODOC WAR

Modoc War (1872–73), last of the Indian wars to affect northern California and southern Oregon, had complex causes. The war was a final desperate resistance to the impact of the white man's culture on an Indian way of life, as well as a reaction to mistreatment of the Indians by the settlers. The removal of the Modoc to the Klamath reservation in Oregon in 1864 antagonized them for several reasons: no cognizance was taken of a rivalry between a Modoc chief named Sconchin and a younger chief, Captain Jack (Kintpuash), which had resulted in a physical division of the tribe; the Modoc were dissatisfied with reservation life; and they were not welcome among their hereditary enemies, the Klamath.

In 1872 Captain Jack led the more aggressive elements among the Modoc back to their former habitat in the vicinity of the Lost River in northern California and refused to return to the reservation, although Sconchin's faction remained quietly on the reservation. An attempt by a detachment of cavalry to return Captain Jack's Modoc to the reservation failed after a skirmish in which there were casualties. The situation was aggravated when fourteen settlers were killed by the Modoc. Captain Jack and his band then retreated south of Tule Lake to the lava beds, which constituted an impregnable natural stronghold. The Modoc band consisted of only 75 warriors and about 150 women and children, but they held out in the lava beds for six months against all attempts by troops to dislodge them. The first attack on the lava beds, on Jan. 17, 1873, in a dense fog, was an utter failure; sixteen U.S. soldiers were killed and fifty-three were wounded, while not a single Modoc died in the battle. On Apr. 11, Gen. Edward R. S. Canby and another member of a peace commission that had entered the lava beds to negotiate were killed by the Modoc. The Modoc were finally dislodged only after military operations involving more than 1,000 U.S. soldiers and after dissension had developed among the Modoc themselves. In June 1873 the Modoc left the lava beds and scattered. They were pursued by soldiers and captured, thus ending the war. Captain Jack and three others were tried by a court-martial for murder, found guilty, and hanged, while the rest of the band was exiled to Indian Territory.

BIBLIOGRAPHY

Keith A. Murray, *The Modocs and Their War.*
Erwin N. Thompson, *Modoc War: Its Military History and Topography.*

— KENNETH M. STEWART

MOHAVE

The so-called River Yumans, including such native American tribes as the Halchidhoma, Yuma, and Cocopa, as well as the Mohave, were unique in their adaptation to their native terrain and in their cultural development. All four, the Mohave being the northernmost, settled along the lower reaches of the Colorado River at the present-day Arizona-California border. The Maricopa, historic residents of the middle Gila drainage, were earlier associated with the Colorado River groups. The largest tribe, however, was the Mohave, having a population of about 3,000 in 1680. All spoke Yuman languages, Yuman being a subgrouping of a conceptual Hokan or Hokan-Siouan macrophylum.

The ethnographic problem posed by the River Yumans is one of cultural affinities. They appear to be a California Basin archetype, over which have been laid Southwestern elements. An original gathering mode of life was enriched by the addition of knowledge of maize cultivation. In the rich alluvial soils of the Colorado the Mohave raised corn but at the same time gathered mesquite beans. The absence of regulated land ownership suggests a late, yet still prehistoric, integration of agriculture. Unlike other Californian tribes, the Mohave abandoned basketry in favor of pottery making, a Southwestern trait.

The distinctiveness of aboriginal Mohave culture lies in several features not seen among other Indian tribes. With the other Yumans they shared a strong nationalist sense even though formal political officials were lacking. The exception was the war chief, who organized formalized battles, virtual games that the tribes of the area carried on among themselves. It is in religion, however, that the Mohave and their related neighbors were most distinctive. Among them, ceremonials of a group nature were subordinated to dream cycles that formed an integral part of Mohave life: individual dream experiences, either of tribal history and lore or of individual fantasy life were recounted in association with a ritual that suggests a view of reality different from that general among native North Americans.

Contacts of the Mohave with Europeans may have taken place as early as 1540, and it is certain that Juan de Oñate visited them in 1604. But the Mohave and their neighbors remained essentially free of contact with outsiders, and although relegated to the Colorado River Reservation by 1876 by executive order, they entered into no treaty with the United States.

BIBLIOGRAPHY

A. L. Kroeber, *Handbook of the Indians of California*, Bureau of American Ethnology, Bulletin 78 (1925).
William J. Wallace, "The Mohave Indians of the Lower Colorado River," in R. F. Spencer, J. D. Jennings, and others, eds., *The Native Americans.*

— ROBERT F. SPENCER

MOLASSES ACT

Molasses Act, passed in 1733, laid a prohibitive duty of ninepence on every gallon of rum, sixpence a gallon on molasses, and five shillings a hundredweight on sugar imported from foreign colonies into Great Britain's American colonies, to be paid before landing.

The act originated in the conflicting economic interests of continental and island colonies. Barbados, which was suffering from the effects of a recent hurricane, the exhaustion of its soil, the restraints of the Navigation Acts, and a burdensome export tax, led the other British sugar colonies in petitioning Parliament to prohibit the "Bread Colonies" from selling provisions to, or buying sugar products from, the more fertile foreign West Indies. The continental colonies had a sound economic answer, that the British West Indies could not consume all their provisions nor satisfy their demand for molasses; but the sugar colonies had the better political connections in Parliament.

Colonial smuggling minimized the act's effects. Although one cannot measure the exact extent of the illicit trade, it is clear that New England distilled considerably more rum than could have been produced from legally imported molasses. Yet it was expensive to evade officials or to procure their connivance, and the act probably served as a mildly protective tariff in favor of the British West Indies until its repeal in 1764 by the Sugar Act.

BIBLIOGRAPHY

G. L. Beer, *British Colonial Policy.*
C. W. Taussig, *Rum, Romance and Rebellion.*

— LAWRENCE A. HARPER

MOLLY MAGUIRES

Molly Maguires, a secret and eventually criminal society, also known as the Buckshots, White Boys, and Sleepers, that terrorized the anthracite region of Pennsylvania from about 1865 until it was broken up in a series of sensational murder trials between 1875 and 1877. The name of the society was taken from a group of anti-landlord agitators in the 1840's led by a widow named Molly Maguire. Most members of both groups were of Irish origin.

The Molly Maguires used their power in labor disputes for the benefit of their members and intimidated or murdered recalcitrant mine bosses and colliery superintendents. In 1874, at the height of their power, Franklin B. Gowen, president of the Philadelphia Coal and Iron Company and the Philadelphia and Reading Railroad Company, determined to suppress them. A Pinkerton detective, James McParlan, posing as a counterfeiter and killer, established himself in the coal regions, joined the organization, and rose to be secretary of his division.

After a particularly outrageous murder in 1875, one assassin was condemned to death, the first capital conviction of a Molly. In view of evidence brought out at the trial, suspicion arose that a detective was at work and quickly centered on McParlan. Evading one plot to murder him, he continued his pose for some time and then quietly withdrew. The murder prosecutions that followed were based largely on his evidence and shattered the organization forever.

Illustration entitled "The March to Death" depicting Molly Maguire members on the way to the gallows in Pottsville, Pennsylvania following the sensational murder trials of 1875–77. Undated engraving. (Corbis-Bettmann)

BIBLIOGRAPHY

Anthony Bimba, *Molly Maguires.*
F. P. Dewees, *The Molly Maguires.*
Allan Pinkerton, *The Molly Maguires and the Detectives.*

— JOHN BAKELESS

MONEY

Money is any generally accepted medium of exchange, standard of value, or store of value. Although this definition is universally accepted, there has always been some disagreement about what the term "money" includes.

In the 19th and early 20th centuries some authorities insisted that only specie (gold and silver) should be considered money, but most defined money to include currency—that is, coin and paper money—as well as specie. The definition of money was gradually broadened, so that by the mid-1920's, money was considered to include demand deposits in commercial banks. Later, authorities came to include commercial bank time deposits and other assets that could be quickly turned into cash (U.S. Treasury bills and deposits in savings banks and savings and loan associations) as "near money." The money supply, or stock of money, differs from money in that it does not include currency and deposits owned by commercial banks and by the federal government; it includes only currency and demand deposits owned by the public.

The Monetary Standard

The monetary standard of the United States is the commodity that the U.S. Congress designates as the basis of the monetary system. It is the commodity for which all other kinds of money can be exchanged at a fixed ratio. Money that is not redeemable in a specific commodity at a specific rate is fiat money—that is, money backed only by the credit of the issuer.

During the colonial period there was no specific monetary standard: colonists used many commodities as money—wampum in New England, beaver skins in the Middle Colonies, and tobacco and many kinds of foodstuffs in the South. During the 18th century individual colonies issued paper currency.

Soon after the United States became an independent republic, Congress in 1791 established a bimetallic standard at a ratio of 15 ounces of silver to 1 ounce of gold. The mint was authorized to accept silver and gold and to issue in exchange silver dollars of 371.25 grains and gold pieces containing 24.75 grains of gold per dollar. In 1834 the administration of President Andrew Jackson devalued the gold dollar, but it retained the bimetallic standard. The ratio of silver to gold was changed to approximately 16 to 1, by reducing the gold content of the dollar to 23.2 grains (23.22 in 1837). Soon thereafter, silver ceased to circulate, because it was undervalued at the mint; consequently, the country, although legally on a bimetallic standard, was actually on a monometallic gold standard. During the Civil War the monetary standard ceased to have any real significance, because the right to redeem paper money in specie was suspended. Gold became a commodity that could be bought and sold in a free market, and its value in paper money was no longer fixed but fluctuated from day to day. To be sure, this suspension of specie payments had occurred in every previous depression, but each previous suspension had been short-lived. The suspension that began in the Civil War lasted for eighteen years, until Jan. 1, 1879.

Although the United States continued on a bimetallic standard *de jure* until the turn of the century, Congress in 1873 stopped the minting of silver dollars, but in 1878 it adopted a limping standard by authorizing the coinage of a debased silver dollar. Bimetallism officially came to an end when the Coinage Act of 1900 established a monometallic gold standard. A series of presidential executive orders and acts of Congress in 1933 severely compromised the gold standard by abrogating the right to redeem paper money in gold. The last vestiges of a metallic standard disappeared in the acts of Mar. 3, 1965, and Mar. 18, 1968, which eliminated the gold reserve against Federal Reserve deposits, and the act of July 23, 1965, which ended the coining of silver dollars. Thereupon, all money in the United States came to be fiat money, although U.S. dollars were still accepted internationally on a severely modified gold bullion standard.

Purchasing Power of Money

The value of money, or its purchasing power, is the reciprocal of the price level. Its relative rise and fall can, therefore, be measured by a price index. Such an index of wholesale prices dates from 1720 (it is discussed here with the 1957–59 value of $1.00 as the basis).

In most of the colonies, prices rose sharply and the purchasing power of money dropped under the pressure of large infusions of paper money. A similar experience occurred in the revolutionary war. The dollar's value fell from $3.79 at the start of the war to 28 cents in 1780. From there it sprang back to $3.15 in 1789 and then receded to about $2.00 in 1801, where it remained for the next decade. With the War of 1812, prices again rose, and the dollar's purchasing power fell to about $1.60 in 1814.

After the War of 1812, prices declined significantly until 1821. From $2.80 in 1821, the dollar's value declined to $2.40 in 1836 but resurged to $3.90 in 1843. The late 1840's and 1850's produced little change, but the Civil War brought money's purchasing power down to $1.30. There followed a long period of declining prices, so that the dollar's purchasing power had risen to $3.90 by 1896. In the first years of the 20th century, prices rose more than in any previous time of peace. By 1915 the dollar's purchasing power had declined to $2.70.

Prices soared during World War I, and the dollar's value dropped to $1.30 by 1920. It quickly recovered to $1.90 in 1921—around which level it fluctuated narrowly for the rest of the decade. The depression of the 1930's brought the price level almost back to where it had been in the 1840's and 1890's. At its highest point in 1932, the dollar's value was again close to $3.00.

From 1934 on, the price level rose—slowly at first, but at a greatly accelerated pace during World War II. By 1948 the dollar was worth $1.14 in 1958 prices. By 1970 it was worth 85 cents and still going down at a rate of between 4 and 7 percent a year.

Currency

During much of American history gold and silver coins issued first by the crown and then by the federal government have not circulated. Instead Americans have used many different kinds of currency.

In the colonial period most transactions were handled through barter or open-book accounts. Although the money of account was the same as in England, only a small amount of pounds, shillings, and pence circulated. Most of the money that the colonists used consisted of commodities, non-English coins, and paper money. The coins were of two types: foreign coins, especially Spanish dollars, and occasional colonial coin issues, such as the Pine Tree shilling of 1652. The paper money was of four types: bills of credit or government notes; paper certificates representing deposited coin, bullion, or other commodities; bank notes issued by land banks; and fractional currency (that is, notes in denominations of a shilling or less). Each colony set its own legal value for current coin, and gradually nominal and arbitrary valuations for the current Spanish coins were established, giving rise to an extraordinary confusion of values. A New Yorker accustomed to a shilling value for the Spanish real had to adjust himself to a nine-pence value in Boston and an eleven-pence value in Philadelphia. The confusion was rendered worse by a multitude of paper-money issues. When the first issue (or "first tenor") depreciated, it was replaced by a "second tenor" and then a "third tenor." The first issue by Massachusetts in 1690 was the first authentic government paper money in history, although the 1685 "playing-card money" issued to French troops in Canada somewhat resembled government paper.

In the colonial period most transactions were handled through barter or open-book accounts.

The issuance of colonial money ended in New England in 1751 and in other colonies in 1764 when it was proscribed by the crown. During the Revolution the colonists embarked on a new money splurge. To assist in financing the war, the Continental Congress authorized $241,552,780 of bills of credit between June 22, 1775, and Nov. 29, 1779. In addition, the individual states issued $209,524,776, and there were doubtless other batches of unauthorized issues. Much of this paper money was fractional currency. In an effort to make it conform to the differing valuations of Spanish coins, which circulated widely, the individual states issued denominations ranging from 1 penny to 10 pence and from 1/16 to 3/4 of $1. The paper money depreciated, slowly at first and then more rapidly. Only a negligible quantity of the fractional currency was ever redeemed, although the Funding Act of 1790 provided for the redemption of the higher values of paper money at a rate of $1 of specie for $100 of Continental currency. In 1779 the depreciation, in relation to specie, rose from 8 to 1 on Jan. 14, to 38 1/2 to 1 on Nov. 17. In spite of partial redemption and retirement after 1779, the old Continental currency depreciated more rapidly than ever. By January 1781 it was valued at 100 to 1 and by May had practically lost its value. The phrase "not worth a Continental" comes from this period.

The currency history of the United States under the Constitution began with the Mint Act of Apr. 2, 1792. Based on the suggestions and proposals of Alexander Hamilton, Thomas Jefferson, and Robert Morris, the act authorized the establishment of a mint to coin gold eagles ($10 gold pieces), containing 247.50 grains of pure gold, half eagles, and quarter eagles; dollars, containing 371.25 grains of pure silver, half dollars, quarter dollars, dismes, and half dismes; and cents, containing 11 pennyweight of copper, and half cents. The weight of the cent was changed to 208 grains of copper in 1793. Although the Mint Act demonstrated an impressive familiarity with monetary principles, the system it created did not work. Gold was vastly undervalued at the mint, and consequently by the early 1800's, gold coins ceased to circulate. The silver coins disappeared because they were accepted at face value in Spanish America even though they contained less silver than the Spanish dollar. The circulation of cents also ran into sporadic difficulties, for the market value of the copper in a cent was often higher than 1 cent. Immediately, bills were introduced in Congress to abolish the mint, but none was adopted; in 1806, President Jefferson, by executive order, stopped the minting of silver dollars.

Even if mint ratios had been the same as market ratios, gold pieces and silver dollars would not have circulated in everyday transactions. They were too cumbersome. What Americans actually used for currency, in addition to foreign coins, consisted of a hodgepodge of paper money issued by state-chartered commercial banks, by the two United States banks (1791–1811 and 1816–36), and, occasionally, by nonbank corporations. Although the absence of large-denomination coins was not a hardship, the absence of fractional coins (halves, quarters, dimes) was. To some extent, paper fractional currency, so-called "shinplasters," filled the need for currency in denominations of less than $1, but it was never completely satisfactory.

The devaluation of the gold dollar in 1834 increased the circulation of gold coins. Congress further encouraged gold circulation by authorizing the minting of $1 and $20 gold pieces. But whatever was done for gold made the circulation of silver even more remote, because the metal in the subsidiary silver coins was worth more as bullion in the open market than its face value as money. In 1851, Congress tackled the problem of providing a fractional currency by creating a 3-cent piece composed of silver and copper. But no halves, quarters, or dimes circulated. Then, in 1853, Congress brought subsidiary coinage back by reducing the silver content of the half dollar from 206.25 grains to 192 grains, 9/10 fine. The other fractional silver coins were reduced proportionately. Because of the 1853 reform it was no longer necessary to use foreign coins, and Congress removed their status as legal tender in 1857. At the same time, the half cent was eliminated and the composition of the cent was changed to 72 grains, 88 percent copper and 12 percent nickel. From then until the Civil War the money and currency used by the public consisted of state bank notes in various denominations upward from a few cents, gold coins, and subsidiary silver coins and copper cents.

The Civil War revolutionized the American money system. To help pay for the war, Congress authorized $450 million in paper money, officially known as United States notes but more popularly called greenbacks or legal tender notes. This was the first paper money printed by the federal government, and eventually the U.S. Treasury issued $431 million in paper money. (After the war some greenbacks were retired, but in 1878 Congress fixed their circulation at the amount then outstanding, $346,681,016.)

Early in the war the banks stopped redeeming paper money in specie. The government also stopped paying its obligations in specie. Gold became a commodity, and its value climbed in terms of paper money, $100 in gold eventually commanding $250 in paper. In March 1863, Congress authorized the issue of gold certificates, which were really warehouse receipts, because they were issued in denominations of $20 or more in exchange for gold coin and bullion deposited with the U.S. Treasury. These certificates were temporarily discontinued between January 1879 and July 1882 and permanently ended by executive order in April 1933; the Gold Reserve Act of January 1934 created a new gold certificate that could be held only by Federal Reserve banks.

The Civil War also drove subsidiary silver coins out of circulation, because the wartime increase in the demand for silver pushed its price above the face value of the coins. After an unhappy experience with the use of postage stamps, Secretary of the Treasury Salmon P. Chase authorized the issue of fractional notes, commonly called postage currency. Congress legalized Chase's action in July 1862. In March 1863, Congress authorized $50 million in fractional paper currency. To further alleviate the currency shortage, Congress, in April 1864, changed the weight of the cent to 48 grains, 95 percent copper and 5 percent tin and zinc. It also provided for a 2-cent piece. Then, in 1865, it authorized the coinage of a 3-cent piece of 30 grains, 75 percent copper and 25 percent nickel.

The federal government also effected a major change in bank currency. The National Bank (or Currency) Act of February 1863, amended in June 1864, established a federally chartered banking system; each national bank was authorized to issue bank notes against federal bonds. Subsequently, in July 1866, Congress imposed a 10 percent tax on nonnational bank notes, driving them out of circulation.

Controversies over money characterized the last quarter of the 19th century. Farmers, silver-mine owners, and some businessmen called for the reinstatement of bimetallism, which had been effectively ended with the so-called Crime of 1873. Bankers and other sound-money adherents resisted, and much legislation was passed attempting to reconcile the two opposing views. Whereas the Crime of 1873 had eliminated the silver dollar and also provided for a trade dollar of 420 grains of silver, 9/10 fine, the Bland-Allison Act of February 1878 authorized the purchase of between $2 million and $4 million of silver per month to be coined into silver dollars containing 412.50 grains of silver, 9/10 fine. The latter act also provided for silver certificates in denominations of $10 or more to be issued against deposits of silver coin. In 1886 the denominations were changed to include $1, $2, and $5. The Sherman Silver Purchase Act of 1890 replaced the Bland-Allison Act by providing for the purchase of 4.5 million ounces of silver a month. The Treasury was to pay for these purchases with Treasury notes, redeemable in coin. After considerable struggle, sound-money adherents succeeded in repealing the Sherman Silver Purchase Act in November 1893. The Gold Standard Act of Mar. 14, 1900, ended the silver controversy by adopting a monometallic gold standard.

Minor coinage laws in the late 19th century included the authorization in May 1866 of a 5-cent piece of 77.16 grains, 75 percent copper and 25 percent nickel; the authorization in March 1875 of a 20-cent piece, which was discontinued in May 1878; and the discontinuance of the $1 and $3 gold pieces and the 3-cent nickel. The Federal Reserve Act of December 1913 made additional basic changes in the currency by providing for a Federal Reserve note secured by gold and commercial paper and a Federal Reserve bank note secured by government bonds.

Although few currency changes occurred in the two decades after 1913, the depression of the 1930's created a new flurry in currency and banking. In April 1933, President Franklin D. Roosevelt issued a proclamation recalling gold coin, gold bullion, and gold certificates, in effect taking the country off the gold standard. In January 1934 the dollar was devalued from 23.22 grains pure to 13.714 grains. The price of gold was raised from $20.67 to $35 per ounce. Further changes in the currency were made in July and August 1935 by retiring the last of the bonds with the circulation privilege, thus ending the issuance of national bank notes.

The American money system has evolved from a gold-and-silver bimetallism through a monometallic gold standard to what has been called "managed money."

The depression made silver a controversial issue again. The Thomas amendment to the Agricultural Adjustment Act of May 1933 authorized the president to accept $200 million in silver in payment of international debts. Further congressional acts during the New Deal ordered the Treasury to buy all newly mined domestic silver and to issue silver dollars or silver certificates against the purchases.

Since the 1930's the gold cover has been removed from Federal Reserve notes and deposits. In July 1965 the minting of standard silver dollars came to an end, and the silver certificate was also discontinued. In the mid-1970's the currency system consisted of fractional, subsidiary silver and copper currency ($7 billion), a few silver dollars, and $60 billion of paper money issued by Federal Reserve banks. By far the largest part of the money supply was the $200 billion in demand deposits in commercial banks.

The evolution of the American money system has been from bimetallism through a monometallic gold standard to what has been called "managed money." The payments mechanism has evolved from a hodgepodge of currencies in the 19th century to a standard fiat money. Checks drawn against demand deposits constitute 75 percent of the money supply and cover well over 90 percent of the dollar volume of transactions. Indications are that in the mid-19th century they covered about 60 percent. By 1837 checks were more important than cash in the cities; by 1850, for the country as a whole; and in 1890, in the rural areas.

BIBLIOGRAPHY

Milton Friedman and Anna Jacobson Schwartz, *A Monetary History of the United States.*

Herman E. Krooss, *A Documentary History of Banking and Currency.*

Paul Studenski and Herman E. Krooss, *Financial History of the United States.*

— HERMAN E. KROOSS

MONOPOLY

Monopoly in its most elementary form is the exclusive control of the output of a good or a service by a single seller. The significance of monopolistic control lies in the power to restrict output in order to increase the price of the commodity or service above the competitive level and, therefore, above the necessary economic costs of production.

Monopolistic power may exist in markets of more than one seller, and in fact few markets are so monopolized as to contain but a single supplier. In the medieval guild system local craftsmen were able to monopolize their markets by exercising control over entry into their trades; while a town might have several artisans in each craft, this control over entry and guild discipline served to keep the prices of goods or services above the competitive level. As the guild system declined in the face of technological change and the expanding geographical dimensions of economic markets, other forms of monopolization developed. The most important of these was the English patent system, utilized by the crown to grant to its favored subjects the exclusive right to manufacture or to distribute a commodity in domestic or foreign markets. Popular pressures against this system culminated in Parliament's enactment of the Statute of Monopolies in 1623, limiting patents to important inventions.

American public policy against monopoly derives in part from early English laws against engrossing, forestalling, and regrating—practices that were also illegal under ancient Roman law: they involve the purchase of essential commodities in order to influence their prices and to reap considerable profits from resale. The Anglo-American tradition has also frowned on formal or informal agreements to limit output or to raise prices, although the common law that prevailed until the late 19th century did not make the practice illegal: public disapproval was manifested in the fact that the parties to the agreement could not enlist the court's assistance in enforcing its terms. The pervasive price-fixing and market-sharing agreements of numerous American enterprises in the 19th century—notably trunk-line railroads, cast-iron pipe manufacturers, pig-iron producers, and whiskey distillers—eventually brought about statutory restraint of such practices through the Sherman Antitrust Act of 1890. These overt price-fixing and market-sharing agreements have been ruled to be per se violations of the Sherman Act, and more direct attempts to monopolize through acquisitions and mergers have been found unlawful under the Clayton Antitrust Act of 1914 (as amended in 1950).

A more direct route to monopoly lies in the acquisition of competing firms. J. P. Morgan built the United States Steel Corporation in this manner, acquiring companies that produced more than one-half of all finished steel in the United States in 1901. Similarly, John D.

Rockefeller acquired a large number of competing refiners to gain control of nearly 90 percent of the U.S. market for refined petroleum products by the end of the 19th century. Rockefeller also utilized the trust form of organization through which the control of ostensibly independent refiners was vested in a single board of trustees, but this form of control was adjudged a violation of the Sherman Act in 1906. The acquisition of monopoly power through merger has since been sharply curtailed by the Clayton Act and the subsequent amendment in 1950.

American public policy against monopoly derives in part from early English laws against engrossing, forestalling, and regrating—practices also illegal under ancient Roman law.

The growth of markets in the United States and throughout the world has greatly reduced the incidence of pure monopoly in the production and distribution of goods and services. The Aluminum Company of America held one of the closest approximations to a pure monopoly in the United States, but its monopolistic position ended in 1945. Nevertheless, sellers of such products as computers, flat glass, office equipment, automobiles, and office copiers continue to enjoy some monopolistic power because either patents, large capital requirements, or both limit competitive enterprise in these areas.

BIBLIOGRAPHY

F. Machlup, *The Political Economy of Monopoly.*
H. Thorelli, *The Federal Antitrust Policy.*

— ROBERT W. CRANDALL

MONROE DOCTRINE

Since the adoption of the U.S. Constitution there has been a strong tendency to differentiate America from Europe and to assume that as little political connection should exist between the two as possible. Expressions of this viewpoint can be found in President George Washington's farewell address and in President Thomas Jefferson's first inaugural. President James Monroe's message to Congress of Dec. 2, 1823, supplemented this previous formula by seeking to exclude European intervention from the Western Hemisphere. The message was the result of two different sets of circumstances. The pretensions of the Russian government to exclude all but Russian vessels from the Northwest coast of the United States north of fifty-one degrees precipitated a diplomatic controversy in the course of which Monroe's secretary of state, John Quincy Adams, laid down the principle that European governments could establish no new colonies in the Western Hemisphere, every portion thereof having been already occupied. In his message of 1823 Monroe repeated Adams' formula virtually in Adams' own words, declaring that "the American continents, by the free and independent condition which they have assumed and maintained, are henceforth not to be considered as subjects for future colonization by any European powers." A second reason for the message lay in the fear that the continental European powers were planning the reconquest of the Spanish American republics that had declared their independence of Spain. Suggestions of such a purpose came to Monroe and his cabinet from Richard Rush, U.S. minister in London, who got them from George Canning, the British foreign secretary, and more directly from the language of Czar Alexander I in a memorandum addressed to the U.S. government in October 1823. After long cabinet discussions, the president fixed upon a pronouncement that warned against intervention, and, with regard to the Spanish colonies, declared that "we could not view any interposition with the view of oppressing them or controlling in any other manner their destiny by any European power, in any other light than as the manifestation of an unfriendly disposition toward the United States."

While the message was enthusiastically received in the United States, it had little practical influence at the time. The European powers never intended intervention on any considerable scale and viewed the message with irritation and contempt.

The United States itself, on four separate occasions in the years immediately following 1823, refused to make any commitments looking to the carrying out of the policy outlined by Monroe, and the debates on the Panama Congress in 1826 showed that, beyond the shadow of a doubt, U.S. opinion was hostile to any alliance with the new states in the hemisphere. They themselves, as a matter of fact, became economically and financially, if not politically, more dependent on Great Britain than on the republic to the north.

For some time after 1826 Monroe's message remained virtually unnoticed, and minor violations of it occurred in the British encroachments in Central America and in the acquisition by Great Britain of the Falkland Islands.

The first great revival of interest in the doctrine came in 1845. This was produced by the intrigues of Great

Britain and France to prevent the annexation of Texas to the United States, by the difference of opinion over Oregon between Britain and the United States, and by fear of British purposes in California. On Dec. 2, 1845, President James K. Polk reiterated the principles of Monroe, condemning not only intervention but also the application of the principle of the balance of power to the Western Hemisphere. He emphasized particularly the significance of this principle with regard to North America. Again, as in 1823, the immediate results were not important, but the principle had begun to sink into the American mind, and Polk gave it new expression. On Apr. 29, 1848, in a message in which he declared that an English or Spanish protectorate over Yucatán would be a violation of the principles of 1823, Polk declared that the threat of such action might compel the United States itself to assume control over the region in question. In this message, for the first time, the Monroe principle was made the basis for measures of expansion. No action was taken, however.

In the 1850's, the message figured again and again in connection with the dispute over the Central-American question and attained increasing popularity. From a partisan or democratic dogma, it began to rise to the rank of a national principle. It was cited in international correspondence and its significance was recognized (although its validity was denied) by more than one European statesman.

The Civil War offered to the powers of Europe an excellent opportunity to challenge Monroe's principles. Taking advantage of the situation, Spain intervened in Santo Domingo, and France sought to establish in Mexico an empire under the rule of the Austrian Archduke Maximilian. When, at the outbreak of the war, Secretary of State William H. Seward attempted to invoke the Monroe Doctrine against the first of these powers, he received a sharp rebuff, but learning from experience, he waited before challenging the French in Mexico until the success of American arms made it possible for him to assert the doctrine with increasing vigor. While other circumstances contributed to the collapse of Maximilian's empire, there can be no question that the diplomatic pressure exerted by the U.S. government in 1865 was keenly felt in Paris, and that fear of the United States was a factor in the French decision to withdraw its troops from Mexico. The doctrine, in the meantime, had attained immense popularity at home.

The events of the 1870's and the 1880's are less dramatic, but a steady tendency developed to expand the scope of the doctrine. The principle that no territory might be transferred in the New World from one European power to another, not altogether unknown in the previous epoch, became more and more closely linked with Monroe's principles, especially through the efforts of President Ulysses S. Grant and his secretary of state, Hamilton Fish. The doctrine was cited even less in consonance with its original terms, or with Polk's interpretation of it, as forbidding the construction by Europeans of a transisthmian canal, and still more as implying that such a canal must be under the exclusive guarantee of the United States. This point of view, the cause of acute diplomatic controversy in the 1880's, was accepted by Great Britain in the first Hay-Pauncefote Treaty (Feb. 5, 1900).

One of the most dramatic extensions of the doctrine was President Grover Cleveland's assertion that its principles compelled Great Britain to arbitrate a boundary dispute with Venezuela over the limitations of British Guiana. Cleveland's position produced a serious diplomatic crisis, but the moderation displayed by the British government permitted a peaceful solution of the difficulty.

The growing nationalism of the United States toward the end of the 19th and the beginning of the 20th century was not without its effect upon the doctrine. The joint intervention of Great Britain, Germany, and Italy against Venezuela, looking to the satisfaction of pecuniary claims, concealed no ulterior purpose, but it produced widespread irritation in the United States. The story of German designs of conquest is pure legend, but it is certainly true that the administration of Theodore Roosevelt, which began with an attitude of great moderation, was gradually rendered more and more nervous by the intervention and was considering diplomatic measures to bring it to an end. On Roosevelt himself the effect of the intervention was important. He moved toward the position that the United States must assume a measure of control of the more unruly of the Latin-American states in order to prevent European action against them, and in 1905 a treaty for American control of customs in Santo Domingo was negotiated. While it met with opposition in the Senate, it was ratified in 1907. In the meantime the president, in his annual message to Congress in 1904, had definitely laid down the doctrine (later called the Roosevelt Corollary to the Monroe Doctrine) that chronic wrongdoing by a Latin-American state might compel American action. The precedent that he established was applied or attempted more than once, especially in the Caribbean area. And, in general, the doctrine has figured as justification in the not infrequent interventions in the affairs of Caribbean states.

During the two decades following World War I, a change took place. Increasing resentment against American interference in the affairs of the republics of Latin America has been reflected in actual policy. The interventions of the United States in Haiti and Santo Domingo in 1915 and 1916, during the administration of President Woodrow Wilson, were liquidated, respectively, in 1934 and 1924. The intervention in Nicaragua during the administration of Calvin Coolidge was short-lived. Under President Franklin D. Roosevelt pledges against armed intervention were given, and at the seventh Pan-American Conference (Montevideo, Dec. 3–26, 1933) a definite treaty was signed, pledging the signatories not to intervene in the internal and external affairs of one another. At Buenos Aires in 1936 the practice of collecting pecuniary obligations by armed force was declared illegal.

The Monroe Doctrine has proven useful as a justification of U.S. interventions in the affairs of Caribbean states.

The Monroe Doctrine has never obtained a true international status. At the World War I peace conference in 1919, in order to placate domestic opposition to the covenant of the League of Nations, Wilson was obliged to incorporate in that document an article declaring that nothing therein contained should affect the legal validity of a regional understanding such as the Monroe Doctrine. The exact interpretation of such a phrase must remain doubtful, and it is difficult to maintain that it implies complete European recognition of the American dogma. It was certainly far from acceptable to the more nationalistic supporters of Monroe's principles in the United States.

In the United States, as the evolution of the American attitude toward intervention shows, there has been somewhat of a reaction against extreme interpretations of the principles of 1823. Secretary of State Charles E. Hughes attempted to dissociate various U.S. interventions in the Caribbean area from the Monroe Doctrine. In 1929 the Committee on Foreign Relations of the Senate of the United States, in transmitting the Kellogg-Briand Pact, added a separate report in which the Monroe Doctrine was conservatively interpreted and based on the principle of self-defense. The Roosevelt Corollary of 1904 was definitely excluded.

But Argentina's policy of neutrality during World War II was a major obstacle to hemispheric unity against the Axis powers. The Inter-American Conference on Problems of War and Peace, called to strengthen arrangements for collective security in the Western Hemisphere during the war and to discuss problems in Argentina, was assembled in February 1945, and on Mar. 6 adopted the Act of Chapultepec, which broadened the Monroe Doctrine by incorporating the principle that an attack on one country of the hemisphere was to be considered an act of aggression against all the countries of the hemisphere. The act also contained a provision for the negotiation of a defense treaty among the American states after the war. Meeting at Petrópolis, outside Rio de Janeiro, Aug. 15–Sept. 2, 1947, the United States and nineteen Latin-American republics drew up the Rio Pact (Inter-American Treaty of Reciprocal Assistance), a permanent defensive military alliance that legally sanctioned the principle that an attack on one is an attack on all. The following year the Organization of American States was established, its charter going into effect in December 1951, through which the principles of the Monroe Doctrine could be effected by a system of Pan-Americanism. Despite this emphasis on hemispheric unity, the U.S. fear of Communist infiltration in Latin America led it to take action unilaterally in Guatemala (1954), Cuba (1960–61), and the Dominican Republic (1965) without prior approval or with only very tardy approval by inter-American consultative bodies. But, in general, the United States has maintained an active interest in the Organization of American States and continued to support Pan-Americanism.

[See also Latin America, Relations with; Manifest Destiny; Polk Doctrine.]

BIBLIOGRAPHY

A. Alvarez, *The Monroe Doctrine.*

Samuel Flagg Bemis, *The Latin American Policy of the United States.*

Phillips Bradley, *A Bibliography of the Monroe Doctrine, 1919–1929.*

Worthington C. Ford, "Genesis of the Monroe Doctrine," *Proceedings of the Massachusetts Historical Society*, vol. 15, series 2.

C. H. Haring, *South America Looks at the United States.*

Charles Evans Hughes, *The Pathway of Peace.*

C. C. Hyde, *International Law Chiefly as Interpreted and Applied by the United States.*

J. B. Moore, *A Digest of International Law.*

Dexter Perkins, *A History of the Monroe Doctrine.*

David Y. Thomas, *One Hundred Years of the Monroe Doctrine, 1823–1923.*

— DEXTER PERKINS

MONTGOMERY CONVENTION

Montgomery Convention assembled at Montgomery, Ala., Feb. 4, 1861, to organize the Confederate States of America. Representatives were present from six states of the lower South (South Carolina, Georgia, Alabama, Mississippi, Florida, and Louisiana). The convention drafted a provisional constitution for the Confederate states. It then declared itself a provisional legislature and set up a government without waiting for the ratification of the constitution. The next important step in setting up this government was the selection of the president and vice-president. For president, the convention selected Jefferson Davis of Mississippi, a conservative who had not actively supported secession. For vice-president, Alexander H. Stephens of Georgia, who had actively opposed secession, was chosen.

The convention continued to sit in Montgomery until May 20, 1861, when it adjourned to meet in Richmond on July 20. It added new members as other states seceded and acted interchangeably as a constitutional convention and a provisional legislature. It completed a permanent constitution (adopted Mar. 11, 1861), and supervised its ratification. It directed the election in November 1861 at which a congress and a president and vice-president were elected; it also passed all laws necessary to adapt the existing laws and machinery of the government of the United States to the needs of the new government. With the inauguration of the permanent government (Feb. 22, 1862) it adjourned.

BIBLIOGRAPHY

J. G. Randall, *The Civil War and Reconstruction.*

— HALLIE FARMER

MONTICELLO

Monticello was the home of Thomas Jefferson, on a "little mountain," near Charlottesville, Va. The spot came into Jefferson's possession by inheritance from his father. Excavation and the preparation of lumber were started in 1767–68. The following summer the summit was leveled and brickmaking begun. A small brick house, still standing, was constructed, into which Jefferson moved in 1770. For a decade the big house was under construction. Jefferson, as his own architect, built in Italian style, on the model of Andrea Palladio. But after five years in Europe and examination of many buildings, Jefferson greatly altered Monticello. The result was an Italian villa with a Greek portico, a Roman dome, and many colonial features. The home of Jefferson for fifty-six years, Monticello was the mecca of tourists and visitors, the entertainment of whom impoverished Jefferson. On his death the estate passed from his heirs to Uriah Levy, who willed it to the people of the United States, but the will was overthrown. Eventually the estate came under the control of the Thomas Jefferson Memorial Foundation. Jefferson is buried on the grounds.

The front portico of Thomas Jefferson's Monticello at Charlottesville, Virginia. Jefferson, as his own architect, built and remodeled the house over several decades.(G. E. Kidder/© Corbis)

BIBLIOGRAPHY

Paul Wilstack, "Jefferson's Little Mountain," *National Geographic Magazine* (April 1929).

— ALFRED P. JAMES

MONTREAL, CAPTURE OF

Capture of Montreal (1760). British Gen. James Wolfe's victory over the French at Quebec in 1759 was followed on Sept. 8, 1760, by the surrender of Montreal. The spirits of the French had been raised by the success of François Gaston de Lévis at Sainte Foy on Apr. 28, but not for long. Everything depended on whether the French or the English fleet would first come to the rescue. On May 15 the vanguard of the English ships appeared below Quebec. Lévis, abandoning hope of help from France, raised the siege and retreated up the river. The English, knowing that Montreal was doomed, prepared at their leisure for the final stroke. The plan of campaign had been carefully prepared. While Gen. Geoffrey Amherst moved north from New York to Lake Ontario and descended the Saint Lawrence River, Gen. James Murray with another army and the fleet moved up the river, and Col. William Haviland approached by way of Lake Champlain. On Sept. 8, 1760, the governor, Pierre François de Rigaud, Marquis de Vaudreuil-Cavagnal, at Amherst's demand, surrendered Montreal, and with it Canada.

BIBLIOGRAPHY

William Wood, *The Fight for Canada.*

George M. Wrong, *The Fall of Canada, 1759–1760.*

— LAWRENCE J. BURPEE

MOON LANDING

On Wednesday, July 16, 1969, half a million people gathered near Cape Canaveral (then Cape Kennedy), Fla. Their attention was focused on three astronauts—Neil A. Armstrong, Edwin E. Aldrin, Jr., and Michael Collins—who lay in the couches of an Apollo spacecraft bolted atop a Saturn V launch vehicle, awaiting ignition of five clustered rocket engines to boost them toward the first lunar landing. This event took place eight years after President John F. Kennedy, in the wake of Soviet Sputnik and Vostok successes, issued a challenge to land men on the moon before 1970 and thus give the United States preeminence in space exploration. After twenty manned missions—two to the vicinity of the moon itself—the United States was ready to achieve that goal.

On July 20, 1969, half a billion people watched on television as the two astronauts moved about on the lunar surface with its gravity one-sixth that of earth's.

At 9:32 A.M., eastern daylight time, the historic voyage, watched by millions via television, began without incident. After less than two revolutions of the earth to check out their spacecraft, the Apollo 11 crew fired the 200,000-pound-thrust Saturn S-IVB stage to escape earth's gravitational field. The flight path was so nearly perfect that only one of four planned trajectory corrections had to be made. On their way to the moon, the astronauts monitored systems, ate, and slept. Several times via television they showed scenes of the receding earth and their own cabin activities.

Early Saturday afternoon (July 19), seventy-six hours after launch, the crew slowed their ship while on the back side of the moon to enter lunar orbit. Following this maneuver, Aldrin slid through a passageway into the lunar module, called Eagle, to test its systems and then returned to the command module Columbia so that he and the other crew members could sleep before the descent to the lunar surface.

On Sunday (July 20) Armstrong and Aldrin in the lunar module told Collins, "The Eagle has wings," as they cut loose from the command module and headed toward the surface of the moon. Dodging a boulder-strewn area the size of a football field, Armstrong set the craft down at 4:17 P.M. (EDT), reporting: "Houston, Tranquility Base here. The Eagle has landed." Six and one-half hours later, after donning a protective suit and life-sustaining backpack, Armstrong climbed down and set foot on lunar soil, saying: "That's one small step for [a] man, one giant leap for mankind." Aldrin soon followed. From the first step through the ensuing walk, half a billion people watched on television as the two astronauts moved about on the lunar surface with its gravity one-sixth that of earth's.

While on the Sea of Tranquility, Armstrong and Aldrin deployed a television camera, raised the American flag, collected about 47 pounds of samples, talked with President Richard M. Nixon, set up scientific equipment that would remain on the moon, and gave millions of listeners a description of their experiences. After two hours of exploring, they returned to the lunar module, rested for eight hours, and then started the engine of the ascent stage to rejoin Collins, who was orbiting the moon in Columbia, late Monday afternoon (July 21). Discarding the Eagle, the astronauts fired the service module engine shortly after noon the next day to escape the lunar gravitational field for the return to earth. During the return flight, they tended their ship, conducted television transmissions to earth, and told their fellow men what going to the moon had meant to each of them.

Apollo 11 splashed down in the Pacific Ocean on Thursday (July 24), a week and a day (195 hours) after departing the Florida launch site. The astronauts, greeted by Nixon aboard the U.S.S. *Hornet*, were kept in quarantine for sixteen days, because scientists feared the introduction of pathogens from outer space. None was found. Thus ended man's first visit to a celestial body.

BIBLIOGRAPHY

James Byrne, ed., *10:56:20 PM EDT, 7/20/69: The Historic Conquest of the Moon as Reported to the American People by CBS News Over the CBS Television Network.*

Michael Collins, *Carrying the Fire.*

Richard S. Lewis, *Appointment on the Moon.*

— JAMES M. GRIMWOOD

MORMON TRAIL

The Mormons, after their expulsion from Nauvoo, Ill., in February 1846, took a westerly route along a well-beaten trail, through what is now Iowa, to the Missouri River. By permission of the Omaha Indians, they crossed the Missouri River into Nebraska Territory, and established winter quarters, where they remained during the winter of 1846–47. In April 1847 the first company, consisting of 143 men, 3 women, and 2 children, started west, under the leadership of Brigham Young. They followed the north bank of the Platte River to Fort Laramie, Wyo. At this point they continued their journey over the old Oregon Trail, until they reached Fort Bridger in Wyoming. Traveling to the southwest through Echo Canyon to the Weber River, they ascended East Canyon, crossed the Big and Little mountains of the Wasatch Range, and entered the valley of the Great Salt Lake in Utah through Emigration Canyon on July 24, 1847.

BIBLIOGRAPHY

Orson F. Whitney, *History of Utah.*

— L. E. YOUNG

MORRILL ACT

Long agitation by agricultural societies, farm journals, and other advocates—especially Jonathan Baldwin Turner of Illinois—of vocational training for farmers and mechanics influenced Sen. Justin S. Morrill of Vermont to introduce into Congress a bill to aid in the establishment of agricultural and mechanical arts colleges in every state in the Union. The measure passed Congress in 1858, but constitutional objections induced President James Buchanan to veto it. A similar measure, since called the Morrill Act, was signed by President Abraham Lincoln in 1862. States were offered 30,000 acres of land for each representative and senator they were entitled to in the national legislature as an endowment for the proposed schools. In some states the lands were given to existing institutions, as in Wisconsin, where the state university was the beneficiary; elsewhere they were conveyed to newly established agricultural and technical colleges, such as Purdue University and the Illinois Industrial University, now the University of Illinois. Morrill was henceforth called the "father of the agricultural colleges."

BIBLIOGRAPHY

Paul W. Gates, *Agriculture and the Civil War.*

Fred A. Shannon, *The Farmer's Last Frontier, 1860–1897.*

John Y. Simon, "The Politics of the Morrill Act," *Agricultural History,* vol. 37 (1963).

— PAUL W. GATES

MOST-FAVORED-NATION PRINCIPLE

One of the fundamental objects of American foreign policy from the beginning has been to break through the dikes of colonial trade monopoly and the barriers of discriminatory national tariffs. The first expression of this was the so-called conditional most-favored-nation article, which was inserted into the Treaty of Amity and Commerce with France of 1778, by which "The most Christian King, and the United States engage mutually not to grant any particular Favour to other Nations in respect of Commerce and Navigation, which shall not immediately become common to the other Party, who shall enjoy the same Favour freely, if the Concession was freely made, or on allowing the same Compensation if the Concession was Conditional." The conditional feature was inserted at the initiative of the French negotiators. The conditional most-favored-nation formula became a standard article of treaties of commerce of the United States whenever it could be secured, until 1923, when the Department of State changed over to the unconditional formula.

Before World War I it had become the tendency of European powers to accept the unconditional formula in their treaties, and American theorists argued in favor of this practice as more liberal, and, if universally pursued, more efficacious in lowering tariff walls everywhere. But by the time the reform of American policy had taken place, the European nations, following World War I, in a wave of neomercantilism, had gone back to the old conditional most-favored-nation formula. As a result a network of such treaties was erected, known as compensation trade treaties.

BIBLIOGRAPHY

Samuel Flagg Bemis, *A Diplomatic History of the United States.*

— SAMUEL FLAGG BEMIS

MOUNDS AND MOUND BUILDERS

Mounds and mound builders, terms used to designate, respectively, the numerous ancient artificial structures of earth and stone widely scattered over the eastern United States and the primitive peoples responsible for their construction.

What may be termed the General Mound Area corresponds approximately to the basins of the Mississippi and its tributaries, particularly those to the east, and the Gulf and southeastern seaboard regions. There are few major remains east of the Appalachians, from the Carolinas northward through New England.

In its broader interpretation the word "mounds" comprises all major remains of prehistoric man within the area: conical mounds, truncated temple mounds, effigy and linear mounds, defensive earthworks, geometric enclosures, and shell heaps. Conical mounds are artificial hillocks of earth, earth and stone, and, occasionally, stone only, and more or less conical in form; in height they range from almost imperceptible elevation to 70 feet. They occur generally throughout the mound area and were intended mainly as places of interment and as monuments to the dead. Two striking examples of conical mounds are the Grave Creek Mound in Marshall County, W.Va., and the Miamisburg Mound in Montgomery County, Ohio, each of which is a trifle short of 70 feet in height.

Truncated mounds occur mostly in the lower Mississippi Valley. Most are quadrangular flat-topped pyramids, which served as bases or platforms for sacred and domiciliary structures. Surprisingly, the greatest of the truncated mounds lies near the northern limit of their occurrence—the great Monks Mound, the third largest mound in the New World, near East Saint Louis, Ill. This tumulus, one of more than eighty comprising the Cahokia group, is 100 feet high and covers 16 acres of ground.

The effigy mounds (so called because they are built in the images of animals, birds, and men) and the associated linear mounds center in southern Wisconsin and adjacent parts of Iowa, Minnesota, and Illinois. Within this area are numerous examples, occurring both singly and in groups, particularly in and adjacent to the city of Madison, Wis. The greatest of the effigy mounds, however, is the Serpent Mound, in Adams County, Ohio. This effigy, following the sinuous coils of the serpent, measures 1,330 feet in length. It is supposed that the effigy mounds were adjuncts of the religious observances of their builders.

The defensive earthworks, or fortifications, usually occupy the more or less level tops of isolated hills and consist of walls of earth and stone following the outer circumferences of such areas, supplementing the natural barriers against intrusion. The walls were usually fortified by means of pointed upright stakes or pickets. They are of general occurrence, having their greatest development in southern Ohio, where Fort Ancient, in Warren County, is the most striking example.

The greatest of the effigy mounds is the Serpent Mound in Adams County, Ohio; the serpent's sinuous coils measure 1,330 feet long.

Geometric enclosures, as contrasted to the defensive works, invariably occur in level valley situations, without consideration of defensive factors, and are strictly adjuncts of the Hopewell culture of southern Ohio and adjacent regions. They are usually low walls of earth, in the form of circles, squares, octagons, and parallel walls, occurring singly or in combination. Their function apparently was social and ceremonial, rather than defensive. Examples are the Hopewell, Mound City, and Seip groups, in Ross County, Ohio; and the Newark Works, at Newark, Ohio.

Shell mounds are accumulations of shells of both marine and fresh-water mollusks, and are incidental to the use of these as food. They occur to some extent adjacent to inland streams, but mainly along the Atlantic tidewater, particularly in Florida, and often are of great extent. Other major fixed remains of aboriginal occupancy are village sites, cemeteries, and flint quarries, occurring generally throughout the area.

Builders of the ancient mounds were once thought to have been a separate and distinct race of people, but archaeological investigations have demonstrated that they were members of the single great race to which the Aztec, Maya, and Inca and others of the native stocks pertained. While some of the cultures of mound-building peoples cannot be directly identified with historic tribes and nations, it is probable that for the most part they were the ancestors of Indian nations living in the same general area at the time of the discovery of America. It is further probable that the Creek, Choctaw, and Natchez to the south, the Cherokee and Shawnee in the Ohio Valley, and the Winnebago and some others of the Siouan family, at some time and to some extent, were builders of mounds. Hernando de Soto and other explorers of the 16th century found certain tribes in the South using, if not actually building, mounds. The occasional occurrence of objects of European manufacture as original inclusions in mounds toward the southeast and to the west of the Great Lakes indicates a limited survival of the trait in early Columbian times, but mound building had for the most part disappeared by that time.

Since mounds and their builders antedate the historic period of America, their age must be established by the radiocarbon dating technique and other techniques independent of the historical record. The shell mounds in general date to the Archaic period—in particular the middle and late Archaic period, between 5000 B.C. and 1000 B.C. Earthworks and burial mounds were both constructed from shortly before 1000 B.C. to the historic period. Temple mounds were built beginning about A.D. 700. While the mound-building peoples were still in the Stone Age era, certain of them had achieved a considerable degree of advancement. Copper was hammered into implements and ornaments; very creditable potteryware was made; and woven fabric of several types was produced. In the lower Mississippi Valley and to an even greater extent in the Ohio Valley, a surprising artistic development, in the form of conventional design and small sculptures in the round, probably was not surpassed by any people in a similar stage of development.

BIBLIOGRAPHY

Henry Clyde Shetrone, *The Mound Builders.*

— HENRY C. SHETRONE

MOUNTAIN MEN

Mountain men, the pioneers of the Rocky Mountain West, came first as fur trappers, lured to the West by beaver as these animals were lured to traps by castor bait. With virgin streams producing the prize catches, trail blazing was rewarded, and the trappers thus became the explorers of the Far West. Frenchmen, the most experienced fur gatherers, mingled with Americans and Spaniards at Saint Louis in the first decades of the 19th century and made this the great western emporium of the fur trade. Trapping parties and trading company caravans laden with supplies and Indian goods for the mountain trade left from Saint Louis. A season or two of trapping and the adventurer boasted the sobriquet of "mountain man."

Trapper life held an irresistible appeal to a variety of men—to the restless and daring it offered adventure; to the homeless, a home; to the lawless, an asylum. Wedded to the wilds and usually to the Indian, the mountain man became a recognizable type. The mixed racial strains produced a polyglot jargon, spiced with metaphor and figure, and known as mountain talk. Mingling with the Indian, he adopted the aborigine's manner of life, his food, shelter, morals, and frequently his superstitions. He took on the Indian love of adornment, bedecking himself in moccasins and fringed buckskin suit, adorned with dyed porcupine quills or colored glass beads. An Indian buffalo skin lodge provided winter shelter. His rifle, steel traps, skinning knife, and horse made him independent and free. Jim Bridger, Christopher ("Kit") Carson, Thomas Fitzpatrick, and Bill Williams were examples of the fraternity. There were three classes: the hired trapper, paid annual wages by a fur company; the skin trapper who dealt with one company only; and the free trapper, who trapped and disposed of his furs when and where he pleased.

The summer rendezvous at Green River, Wyo., or other appointed mountain valley, became the most interesting and typical institution of fur trade days. White trappers and Indians gathered there. Fur companies from Missouri brought out their supplies and trade goods, and barter flourished. With drinking, gambling, racing, and contests of skill the mountain man had a holiday. His regular meat diet was now varied by limited supplies of flour, coffee, and similar luxuries from the "states." In a few days of prodigal living he frequently spent his year's earnings.

With the introduction of the silk hat and the consequent decline in beaver skin prices, from six or eight dollars apiece to two dollars or less, the mountain man forsook his traps and began to trade with the Indian. Buffalo robes replaced beaver pelts, and the trading post supplanted the rendezvous. With the coming of emigrant homeseekers and government exploring and military expeditions, the trapper-trader became scout and guide to lead newcomers over the paths he broke. Advancing civilization "rubbed out" the mountain man.

BIBLIOGRAPHY

LeRoy R. Hafen, *The Mountain Men and the Fur Trade of the Far West.*

Carl P. Russell, *Firearms, Traps, and Tools of the Mountain Men.*

— LEROY R. HAFEN

MOVIES

Historians place the beginning of projected images in the mid-seventeenth century, when two Germans, Athanasius Kirschner and Johannes Zahn, first mounted figures on glass slides inside a rotating cylinder. Such "magic lanterns," lacking as they were in pliable celluloid film, electromotive force, and, not unimportantly, urban crowds large enough to support this machine-driven form of communication, could hardly be called motion pictures in any contemporary sense, but the optical principles that made Kirschner and Zahn's work possible pointed toward a future that included commercial movies made for mass audiences. Tinkerers and inventors of several European nations, along with several Americans, carried on their experiments. In 1877

Leland Stanford, the American railroad entrepreneur, commissioned an eccentric researcher, Eadweard Muybridge, to settle a bet on the question of whether or not the hooves of a galloping horse ever simultaneously left the ground; the issue was resolved in the affirmative when Muybridge caught the horse at full gallop by means of a row of cameras linked to trip wires over which the horse raced. By 1890 George Eastman had patented a reel of flexible celluloid that made possible exposing film in sequential frames, and beginning in 1896 movies were projected onto screens for audiences at Koster and Bial's Music Hall in New York City.

The new theaters, called Nickel Odeons, helped establish movies as a medium distinct from performance theater, such as vaudeville.

Inventor Thomas Edison managed to synthesize much research by engaging the scientist William Kennedy Laurie Dickson and by buying up patents for ancillary inventions filed by Thomas Armat, Woodville Latham, and others. At first Edison's firm focused only on his Kinetoscope, a hand-cranked device through which a single viewer peered at a few moments of motion—Annie Oakley firing a rifle, shots of the daily lives of Western Indians, and other fleeting vignettes. Patented in 1891, demonstrated at the Columbian Exposition of 1893 in Chicago, shown to a paying public in the spring of 1894 in New York City, the Kinetoscope peep shows quickly gave way to projected images, again invented by Edison, only two years later at Koster and Bial's. In 1902 Thomas L. Tally opened his Electric Theatre in Los Angeles, a debut soon followed by theater owners in McKeesport and New Castle, Pa., and eventually in every major city. These new theaters—Nickel Odeons, as they were called—helped establish movies as a medium distinct from performance theater, such as vaudeville. Movies soon began to appear in a complex national network of chain theaters supplied by distribution centers called "exchanges." Studios anticipated the Hollywood system of vertically integrated, script-to-screen enterprise.

To a great extent the early system of making and distributing movies was held in place by a patent pool, the Motion Picture Patents Company, led by Edison and other patent holders who used licensing fees as a means of restraining competition. Oddly, these inventive entrepreneurs were aesthetically conservative to the point that few of them thought audiences could tolerate feature-length movies. By 1913 the rivals of the pool had begun to make inroads into its market. Carl Laemmle moved his studio from the Midwest to southern California, where he could get 200 sunny shooting days per year, cheap real estate, and a haven remote from lawyers of the Patents Company. The pioneers included Samuel Goldwyn, Jesse L. Lasky, and Cecil B. DeMille, who together made one of the first features in Hollywood, *The Squaw Man* (1914). Parallel to this westward movement, other movie innovators, such as George Kleine and Adolph Zukor, imported lengthier and more prestigious films, with Zukor bringing in *Queen Elizabeth* (1912) with Sarah Bernhardt. The campaign against the patents trust was also assisted by the success of D. W. Griffith, J. Stuart Blackton, and others. They synthesized an emerging canon of cinematic techniques—narrative editing, expressive closeups, and mobile cameras—into an aesthetic that made possible the evolution of feature-length films. Moviemaking by 1915 had been transformed into the Hollywood system by circumstances seemingly unrelated. Griffith completed *The Birth of a Nation* (1915), his famous (and racist) jeremiad against Reconstruction, which demonstrated the political power of the medium and expanded its capacity for advertisement. Gradually the rebels against the mainly Anglo-Saxon patents trust evolved into a Jewish elite whose recent arrival in the United States inspired a broad synthesis of America that harmonized old and new, immigrant and settler, working class and middle class.

World War I stifled European moviemaking so much that American studios, by filling the void, assumed a dominant place in the international marketplace. By the time the United States entered the war in 1917, movies dominated popular culture and movie "stars" were engaged to sell millions of dollars worth of war bonds. By war's end the Hollywood system had become institutionalized, with power in the hands of such producers as Irving Thalberg of Metro-Goldwyn-Mayer. The movie business eventually generated 600 movies each year (some of which grossed millions of dollars), built 5,000 new theaters, raised capital totaling $2 billion, and dominated the world's markets. "The film is to America what the flag was once to Britain," warned the *London Post* in 1925. "By its means, Uncle Sam may hope some day . . . to Americanize the world." "Movies in the age of innocence" described the era when Hollywood's reach seemed limitless and its style universal. Westerns grew into vast epics, such as *The Iron Horse* (1924) and *Covered Wagon* (1923). *The Thief of Baghdad* (1924), *The Phantom of the Opera* (1925), and *The Hunchback of Notre Dame* (1923) filled screens with exotically romantic eras and places. The demimonde appeared in *Broken Blossoms* (1919) and *Beggars of Life* (1928). Racial tensions strained the fabric of *Showboat* (1929) and *Uncle Tom's Cabin* (1927). Social dramas played out in *Manslaughter* (1922) and *Male and Female* (1919). The Judeo-Christian Bible came vividly to life in *The King of Kings* (1927) and other spectacles. The system gradually stifled the artistic impulses of directors—Erich von Stroheim's movies were edited into miniatures and Griffith made his last film in 1931—all this in the name of profitability.

The coming into theaters of sound-on-films is more accurately explained by studio connections with brokers and bankers than by the old legend of a fiscally shaky Warner Brothers gambling everything on sound films as if on a last throw of the dice. Sound film had existed for years but proved usable only when accompanied by the wherewithal to wire thousands of theaters. Between 1926 and 1929, sound film came in the form of *Don Juan* (1926); Al Jolson in *The Jazz Singer* (1927); the first all-talkie, *Lights of New York* (1928), and the first attempts at depicting African-American life on film, all in 1929—*Hallelujah!, Hearts in Dixie*, and Bessie Smith's short film by Dudley Murphy, *The St. Louis Blues*. The quick success of sound film encouraged studios to try Herbert Kalmus's long-simmering Technicolor process. From the first Technicolor short, *La Cucaracha* (1934), to David O. Selznick's epochal *Gone with the Wind* (1939), color changed from a costly adventure in research and development into an increasingly common element in movie aesthetics. Here is another innovation best explained by a symbiosis between scientists and investors rather than by a romantic legend of bold moguls saving their studios.

With the coming of the Great Depression, Hollywood studios sought to move against the tide, and some actually made a profit. Only Paramount, overextended in theatrical realty, brushed against bankruptcy. Indeed, as sound film became conventional the studios extended their range into whole new genres. As the American theatrical stage became more naturalistic, its best works, such as Eugene O'Neill's *Anna Christie* and Sidney Kingsley's *Dead End*, came to the screen in 1930 and 1937, respectively, along with movie versions of such American novels as Sinclair Lewis's *Dodsworth* in 1936, Ernest Hemingway's *A Farewell to Arms* in 1932, and John Steinbeck's *The Grapes of Wrath* in 1940. At the same time, DeMille and other makers of movie epics adapted their silent movie styles to sound film in such works as *Cleopatra* (1934), *The Crusades* (1935), and *Union Pacific* (1939). Biographies from Abraham Lincoln to Lillian Russell emerged from every studio, especially Twentieth Century-Fox. The "star system" flourished, again particularly at Fox, in such Shirley Temple films as *The Little Colonel* (1934), *The Littlest Rebel* (1936), *Wee Willie Winkie* (1937), and a score of others. Will Rogers had his own genre of local color in such movies as *David Harum* (1934), *Judge Priest* (1934), and *The County Chairman* (1935). Crime dramas that portrayed a dark underside of urban culture—*Scarface* (1932), *Bullets or Ballots* (1936), and *Public Enemy* (1931), to name but a few—became vehicles by which moviemakers addressed social dysfunctions brought about by the Great Depression. Even such musicals as *The Gold Diggers of 1933* (1933) served not only as escapist fare but as ideologically optimistic responses to the economic crisis. The Hollywood system reached an apogee of sorts in 1939, the year of *Gone with the Wind, The Wizard of Oz, Stagecoach, Wuthering Heights, Juarez*, and *Goodbye Mr. Chips*.

During this heady era, Hollywood studios reached a complex level of corporate structure. Each maintained a close affiliation with bankers and brokers on both the East and West coasts, a system of producer units on each lot, sales departments that presented their products to the world, stables of contractual stars and directors, adversarial links to many craft guilds, and influential links to movie fan magazines. Most compelling in defining the Hollywood product, however, was the Hays Office of the Motion Picture Producers and Distributors of America (MPPDA) (after 1945 known as the Motion Picture Association of America, or MPAA). Hollywood created the MPPDA in 1922 in response to scandals involving movie stars. Will H. Hays became its first president. When critics continued to charge that moviegoing caused moral and social decay, the movie industry adopted a production code in 1930. Heavily moral in emphasis but also politically conservative, the code was largely the work of a Jesuit priest, Daniel A. Lord. The ability of Hays and the MPPDA to enforce the code was strengthened in 1934 with the creation of the Production Code Administration (an arm of the Hays Office) and the Roman Catholic Legion of Decency (independent of Hays), which could organize some 8 million Catholics to boycott offensive movies. Thenceforth, evildoers met bad ends and virtue was rewarded on theater screens.

The movie industry entered World War II with considerable concern, generated by the prospect of federal interference. A newly minted Office of War Information (OWI) sought to prescribe Hollywood's contribution to the war effort. Even before the war, a Senate committee had investigated Hollywood's alleged "warmongering," and a House committee had probed a presumed infiltration of the movie industry by the Communist party. As it turned out, the OWI proved an accommodating monitor, and the congressional committees put aside their curiosity for the duration of the war. Furthermore, Hollywood's craft guilds, like most other trade unions, deferred strikes. Within their familiar formulas the studios produced simply phrased war movies, and satisfied audiences provided studios with their greatest profits ever. War movies typically ranged over a wide field to influence Anglophobes, draftees in search of war aims, African Americans in need of a reason to fight despite their oppression at home, and civilians who felt the loss of their men under arms. These movies also sometimes served the country simply by offering diversions from the stresses imposed by war. *Sergeant York* (1941) defined the notion of a "just war" in folkish terms; *Sundown* (1941) contained an implicit promise that a victorious Britain would find a way out of colonialism; *Sahara* (1943) and *Lifeboat* (1944) dramatized the virtues of allying against fascism; *Mrs. Miniver* (1942) and *In Which We Serve* (1942) revealed a Britain unified across class lines; *Bataan* (1943) and *Crashdive* (1943) placed black Americans in the military ranks; *Casablanca* (1943) traced the conversion of an American in Morocco from isolationism to action against the Germans; and *Since You Went Away* (1944) and *Gangway for Tomorrow* (1943) brought the war to civilians. At the same time, outside the circle of Hollywood studios the war stimulated a movement of documentary filmmakers toward a cinema of social advocacy. Responding to requirements of the Signal Corps, OWI, and other agencies, filmmakers turned out a sweeping range of propaganda movies, such as *The Negro Soldier* (1944), *The Battle of Midway* (1942), *With the Marines at Tarawa* (1943), and *The Memphis Belle* (1944). After the war these same filmmakers brought their training to bear on U.S. political and social issues in such films as *The Quiet One* (1947) and a generation of television documentaries such as *The Twentieth Century* (1957–1966).

Unfortunately for the Hollywood that America had come to know, the era of peace brought an irresistible assault of pent-up social forces. Simmering labor disputes produced strife at the studio gates, resulting in soaring labor costs; wartime savings led consumers on a binge of leisure-time spending, seemingly on everything but moviegoing, that brought a period of inflation, which meant another boost in moviemaking costs; Congress, freed from wartime pressures for unity, revived its inquiry into communism in Hollywood, this time with a vengeance that trampled on the civil rights of its victims; the Supreme Court, which had muted its opposition to trusts, handed down the 1948 *Paramount* decision that obliged studios to dismantle the vertical integration of the system that had brought each movie from script to screen; and finally, the shaken system was first threatened, then dominated by the new medium of network television. Such innovations as stereophonic sound and widescreen processes, like CinemaScope, only momentarily gave movies an edge in the face of TV's popularity. In the twenty-five years after World War II, Hollywood lost hundreds of millions of dollars. Hollywood recovered, but at the price of transforming its very nature. Its will to survive drove it into the arms of television, first selling off its vast libraries of feature films and, second, becoming the principal producer of the thousands of hours of broadcast time that television required. The made-for-television movie and the miniseries became staples of the old studios, while hour-length serial dramas and "sitcoms" assumed the role of older, cheaply made B-movies.

The mainstream fare, with its undemanding embrace of middle American values, was challenged during the 1960s by theatrical movies that brought to the screen occasionally revolutionary ideas and images that could find no place on the TV schedule. *Bonnie and Clyde* (1967) celebrated the lives of two murderous bank robbers of the Depression era. *Easy Rider* (1969) sympathetically portrayed the romantic rebels known as "flower children." *Sweet Sweetback's Baadasssss Song* (1971) offered a violent depiction of a black assault on white oppressors personified in a sadistically brutal Los Angeles police force.

Congress, freed from wartime pressures for unity, revived its inquiry into communism in Hollywood, this time with a vengeance.

Accompanying this sectoring of the audience into interest groups of television viewers and newly selective and politically aware audiences, was an opening of the nation's screens to foreign films, often played in "art houses" set apart from the increasingly unused downtown "picture palaces." At their best they included psychologically and socially sophisticated fare from Europe, some of them—such as Jules Dassin's *Never on Sunday* (1960)—running for more than a year in a single art house. Some, like *La Chinoise* (1967), were highly charged leftist films, while others paid homage to older American forms, much as *Tirez sur le Pianiste* (1960) echoed American gangster movies and the bleak postwar detective movies that came to be known as film noir. Still other imports, such as *Rashomon* (1950) and *Pather Panchali* (1955), came from Japan and India, respectively. Each in its way undercut the market for

American movies and all but drove Hollywood into other areas of entertainment, as in the case of MGM's hotels and casinos. In the 1970s a few studios recovered by reaching for a newly discovered audience, a disaffected, urban, black youth that embraced the violence of so-called "blaxploitation" movies, such as Gordon Parks's *Shaft* (1971), which simultaneously recast the private detective into black terms and saved MGM from closure.

In the Hollywood that survived, several trends marked off the new generation from the old. Directors and writers such as Martin Scorsese and Steven Spielberg came to Hollywood from university film schools rather than up through the studio hierarchies. Some came willing to take risks, as in the case of George Lucas, who used computer-generated techniques in *Star Wars* (1977). Both in television and movies, the makers embraced a strategy of betting resources on hoped-for "blockbusters"—impressively expensive theatrical films that earned hundreds of millions—or television miniseries during "sweeps weeks," when audience-sampling firms provided the networks with data on the nation's viewing habits upon which advertising rates were based. Because audiences were ever younger, the movie year took on a rhythm grounded in the hiatuses of the academic year. Prospective blockbusters opened in summer and at Christmas, while offbeat movies such as Spike Lee's *She's Gotta Have It* (1986) opened in the new off-seasons of fall and spring. By the 1990s Hollywood had taken on the traits of conglomeration, an international trend in corporate enterprise, so that studios often came to be owned by foreign firms such as Sony, energy firms such as Gulf and Western, and soft-drink companies such as Coca-Cola. Accompanying this trend toward conglomeration, however, there was also a small growth of independent cinema that offered hope for ethnic minorities and cinematic innovators.

[See also Television.]

BIBLIOGRAPHY

Robert C. Allen and Douglas Gomery, *Film History* (New York, 1985).

David Bordwell, Janet Staiger, and Kristin Thompson, *The Classical Hollywood Cinema* (New York, 1985).

Thomas Cripps, *Slow Fade to Black: The Negro in American Film* (New York, 1977).

Douglas Gomery, *Movie History* (Belmont, Calif., 1991).

Garth Jowett, *Film: The Democratic Art* (Boston, 1976).

Robert Sklar, *Movie-Made America* (New York, 1975).

— THOMAS CRIPPS

MUCKRAKERS

Muckrakers, a group of young reformers who, through novels and popular magazine articles, laid bare the abuses that had crept into American political, social, and economic life. The era of the muckrakers began in 1903 with the publication of Lincoln Steffens' "The Shame of the Cities" and Ida M. Tarbell's "History of the Standard Oil Company" in *McClure's Magazine*. These were followed by numerous other articles, delving into every phase of American life—the most important of which were Ray Stannard Baker's "The Railroads on Trial" (*McClure's*, 1905–06), Thomas W. Lawson's "Frenzied Finance" (*Everybody's*, 1905–06), and David Graham Phillips' "The Treason of the Senate" (*Cosmopolitan*, 1906–07). *Collier's* exposed food adulteration, traffic in women and children, and fraudulent advertising of patent medicines. Of the novelists, the most important was Upton Sinclair who, in *The Jungle* (1906), revealed the unsavory conditions in the packing plants of Chicago. Although the authors were specific in their charges, no major suit was ever entered.

An irresponsible host of sensation mongers was soon attracted and a reaction threatened that would have hindered reform. President Theodore Roosevelt, thoroughly annoyed, in two addresses (Mar. 17 and Apr. 14, 1906), likened the authors of the exposure literature to the man with the rake in John Bunyan's *Pilgrim's Progress*, who was more interested in the filth on the floor than in a celestial crown, and referred to them as "muckrakers." He declared that the time had come to cease exposure for its own sake and to turn to constructive reform. In 1909 muckraking attached itself to the Progressive movement. The muckrakers, primarily responsible for most of the progressive legislation of the period, passed into oblivion after 1912.

BIBLIOGRAPHY

Roy Stannard Baker, *An American Chronicle.*

David Mark Chalmers, *The Social and Political Ideas of the Muckrakers.*

— RAYMOND C. WERNER

MUGWUMPS

Mugwumps, one of many derisive terms applied to those liberal, or independent, Republicans who bolted the party ticket in the presidential campaign of 1884 to support actively the candidacy of Grover Cleveland. They held one national and many regional meetings and were credited with being a strong factor in the defeat of James G. Blaine.

BIBLIOGRAPHY

E. E. Sparks, *National Development.*

— ASA E. MARTIN

MULTICULTURALISM

In the 1990s multiculturalism dominated interpretive and curricular debates about history in schools and universities. The idea responds in part to the diversity of students, especially in urban areas, increasingly from African-, Hispanic-, and Asian-American backgrounds. Taken together, minority groups are nearing a majority in such major cities as New York and Los Angeles and in states including California, Texas, Florida, and New York. By the year 2000 non-European ethnic minorities are expected to make up one-fourth of the nation's population. State and federal education officials, test designers, and educational publishers are concerned by these changes. Since demonstrations at Stanford University in 1988, educators on campuses across the country have debated the extent to which a history curriculum should be Eurocentric, that is, be based on classical Western texts, take a triumphal view of national settlement or expansion by Europeans, or emphasize the history of U.S. political and economic elites. Some multiculturalists claim that white Americans of European heritage have unjustly tried to impose ethnocentric values on nonwhite Americans. They hold that the school-based imposition of Western history, literature, ideas, institutions, and values on children of non-European backgrounds is unjust and culturally biased. Other scholars assert that the nation's political institutions, language, cultural ideals, and economic system derive mainly from Europe, notably from England.

Multiculturalism emphasizes the recognition and study of national diversity, especially along lines of ethnicity and gender. Both pluralists and group separatists claim its philosophical foundations: Multiculturalism may acknowledge qualities of U.S. culture and politics that transcend group differences, or it may contend that racial, ethnic, sexual, religious, and other human characteristics create "separate realities" and "multiple cultural perspectives" of learning. Many multiculturalists reject the idea of a common culture, including older ethnic melting-pot ideals and the idea of pluralism. The multicultural concept is often linked to self-esteem training used to advance the self-image of minorities and women. Some educators envision multiculturalism as a tool to change the educational environment so that students from various groups and social classes will experience equal educational opportunity. According to a 1991 New York City Board of Education declaration, "Multicultural education is an interdisciplinary approach to education designed to foster intergroup knowledge and understanding, to engender greater self-esteem within the entire school community, and to equip students to function effectively in a global society." Some philosophers distinguish between multiculturalism and pluralism in that the former "repudiates the idea of national identity and the emotion of national pride." They worry that such a repudiation, if standard in history and government, invites social fragmentation and civil disorder, whereby students will identify with groups rather than through bonds of citizenship, language, and law.

Multiculturalism emphasizes the recognition and study of national diversity, especially along lines of ethnicity and gender.

— GILBERT T. SEWALL

MUNICIPAL REFORM

Municipal reform is a movement in American local government that has traditionally focused on achieving the goals of honesty in public officials and efficiency and economy in government. The movement has attempted to realize these goals by working for changes in local electoral systems and in the structure of municipal governments. No clear date can be established for the beginning of the campaign for municipal reform; the first efforts in this area probably occurred with the creation of formal municipal governments in the colonial period. Such governmental reform efforts have been tied closely to an ever-present dissatisfaction with policy decisions on the part of a dissident group in the community.

The municipal reform movement became clearly identifiable on a large scale at the close of the 19th century, when the corruption of machine-dominated big cities received publicity in the popular press. Reforms of the electoral system that involved nonpartisan elections and the at-large election of councilmen were designed to destroy the power of party machines. Most of the structural reform emphasized the introduction of professional management personnel in the executive branch of municipal government. The main thrust of this reform has been embodied in the campaign for council-manager government that was first suggested by Haven Mason in 1899 and was fully articulated by Richard Childs in the form adopted by Sumter, S.C., in 1912.

The council-manager plan continues to be the main focus of the municipal reform movement in the United States. This reform effort has been most successful in middle-sized cities, which are homogeneous enough to support nonpartisan and at-large electoral reforms but large enough to afford professional executives. Reform had touched large cities as well.

The council-manager type of government has led to the concentration of greater power in the executive. Large cities have also tended to reduce the number of executive offices and to concentrate power in the office of the mayor. In addition, the complexities of big city government have increased the need for professional managers in the executive branch, and these professionals have been hired as deputies or assistants to the elected mayor.

BIBLIOGRAPHY

Charles R. Adrian, *State and Local Governments.*
John H. Baker, *Urban Politics in America.*
Hugh L. LeBlanc and D. Trudeau Allensworth, *The Politics of States and Urban Communities.*

— JOHN H. BAKER

MUSEUMS

Museums exist principally to care for significant objects that, having outlasted their original function, would otherwise be in danger of loss or destruction. Since they do for objects what libraries do for books, it is not surprising that the earliest learned and historical societies in the United States maintained "cabinets," as museums were often called in the 18th century. The 1769 by-laws of the American Philosophical Society provided for curators "to take charge of, and preserve, all *Specimens of natural Productions*, whether of the *Animal, Vegetable* or *Fossil* Kingdom; all Models of Machines and Instruments, and all other matters and things belonging to the Society, which shall be committed to them; to class and arrange them in their proper order." An 18th-century cabinet might also include coins, medals, paintings, prints, and sculpture; almost anything that was rare, curious, or from distant parts, whether natural or man-made, was grist for such a mill.

The Massachusetts Historical Society, the first of its kind (having been founded in 1791), included among its purposes "the collection and preservation of materials for a political and natural history of the United States," but almost from the start, the physical difficulties of preserving birds, fishes, and animals were recognized. Books, manuscripts, and maps predominated in the earliest accessions. Some indication of the relative values of the society's interests is indicated by its vote of Oct. 25, 1796, which authorized the cabinet keeper "to exchange some of the shells belonging to the Society for Governor Hutchinson's picture." As specialized scientific organizations were created during the 19th century, the older societies devoted less attention to their undifferentiated collections of objects. The founding of the Boston Society of Natural History in 1830, for example, permitted the Massachusetts Historical Society to relinquish any obligations that it had originally assumed in that field. By 1897 the American Philosophical Society had deposited practically all its museum holdings that had any scientific or educational value with other institutions.

The federal government established the Smithsonian Institution in 1846. An early director of the Smithsonian, George Brown Goode, defined "an efficient educational museum as a collection of instructive labels each illustrated by a well-selected specimen." (G. E. Kidder/© Corbis)

The Peabody Museum of Salem, Mass., is the oldest museum in continuous operation in the United States, by virtue of perpetuating the collections of the East India Marine Society, founded in 1799. This group of shipmasters, whose requirements for admission were as exacting as those for a club restricted to astronauts would be today, had, in addition to sociable and benevolent purposes, the following objectives: "to collect such facts and observations as may tend to the improvement and security of navigation" and "to form a Museum of natural and artificial curiosities, particularly such as are to be found beyond the Cape of Good Hope and Cape Horn." While some of the objects brought back to the museum by members were mere curiosities, some—particularly those from the Pacific islands—provide continuingly important evidence of indigenous methods of hunting, fishing, and agriculture. Although Nathaniel Hawthorne's 1842 story entitled "A Virtuoso's Collection" satirized the contents of East India Marine Hall, this shipmasters' cabinet of "natural and artificial curiosities" has evolved into an important modern museum, specializing in maritime history, the ethnology of the Pacific islands and Japan, and the natural history of Essex County, Mass.

Private individuals also created early museums. The painter Charles Willson Peale in 1794 rented part of the American Philosophical Society's hall in Philadelphia for his natural-history museum, begun in his home in 1786, but the association lasted only until 1811. By the time its founder died in 1827, Peale's museum had become a commercial venture. The explorer William Clark created a museum devoted to the American Indian in Saint Louis in 1816; its collections were dispersed shortly before his death in 1838. The Western Museum of Cincinnati, founded in 1820 with high scientific purpose, lapsed into commercialism within three years; until its disappearance in 1867 it offered chiefly entertainment in the manner of an amusement park.

In the second third of the 19th century the word "museum" often connoted entertainment for the commercial advantage of the proprietor. A British visitor of the period, Edward P. Hingston, observed:

> A "Museum" in the American sense of the word means a place of amusement, wherein there shall be a theatre, some wax figures, a giant and a dwarf or two, a jumble of pictures, and a few live snakes. In order that there may be some excuse for the word, there is in most instances a collection of stuffed birds, a few preserved animals, and a stock of oddly assorted and very dubitable curiosities; but the mainstay of the "Museum" is the "live art," that is, the theatrical performance, the precocious mannikins, or the intellectual dogs and monkeys.

A Boston showman, Moses Kimball, a friend and collaborator of P. T. Barnum, built a theater in 1845 that he called the Boston Museum. To justify the use of the name he exhibited the gigantic painting by Thomas Sully of George Washington crossing the Delaware, as well as Chinese curiosities, two stuffed elephants and a giraffe, live Indians, and similar attractions. But the theater was the heart of the place; Kimball's motive, like Barnum's, was personal profit, based on attracting and amusing a crowd.

The federal government's involvement with museums dates from the 1846 act creating the Smithsonian Institution and providing for the formation of a museum of natural history and a gallery of art under its auspices. With the establishment of the American Museum of Natural History (1869) and the Metropolitan Museum of Art (1870) in New York City and of the Museum of Fine Arts (1870) in Boston, the word "museum" ceased to suggest a sideshow. Like the U.S. National Museum, these were institutions concerned with the preservation of objects for the highest of motives. During the 20th century establishment of museums of art, history, and science in all parts of the United States accelerated rapidly; in some cases buildings were constructed before objects worthy of preservation were collected. The 1975 edition of the *Official Museum Directory* of the American Association of Museums listed 5,225 museums in the United States and Canada and stated that since 1965 six new museums had been founded every seven days; the 1974 edition of the *Encyclopedia Britannica* gives a lower, but still disquieting, estimate of the rate of creation of new museums—one every 3.3 days.

Late 19th-century museums tended to exhibit objects of the same kind together, whether they were stuffed bears or silver teapots. In the 20th century an attempt was made to place objects in an approximation of their natural setting. While "habitat groups" in natural history museums required work by artists and modelmakers, art museums cannibalized ancient buildings to procure structural elements for their "period rooms." The American Wing of the Metropolitan Museum in 1924 brought together architectural elements from widely scattered sources to provide a background for examples of American decorative arts, as did the Henry Francis du Pont Winterthur Museum in 1951 in Winterthur, Del. The restoration of Williamsburg, Va., substantially completed between 1926 and 1941, turned an entire 18th-century town into a museum. Its popularity inspired the foundation of several historical museums in rural areas where, with space available, the re-creation of an image of the American past was attempted, following the precedent of the open-air museums of Scandinavia, where buildings were moved to new locations for preservation. Typical examples are a New England village synthetically re-created in Sturbridge, Mass., and a seaport at Mystic, Conn. In contrast to such general evocations of the past are such institutions as the Hagley Museum in Greenville, Del., and the Merrimack Valley Textile Museum in North Andover, Mass., which specialize in local economic and industrial history.

Although a museum is actually a mausoleum, in the sense that it preserves objects that have passed out of current use, the didactic urge has long led museum directors and curators to evoke the educational usefulness of their institutions. George Brown Goode, assistant director in charge of the Smithsonian Institution from 1887 until his death in 1896, defined "an efficient educational museum as a collection of instructive labels each illustrated by a well-selected specimen." His notion called for a museum that was essentially a vast "dictionary," illustrated by original, three-dimensional objects. But such an institution, although like the dictionary, admirable for specific reference and for desultory browsing, could not be counted on to provide systematic knowledge of any subject; moreover, it would be vast and necessarily incomplete, for not even the U.S. National Museum could illustrate everything in three-dimensional form. In the 20th century the dictionary-type collection of the American Museum of Natural History was transformed, through the efforts of Henry Fairfield Osborn and Roy Chapman Andrews, into a "textbook," wherein exhibits were designed to aid self-instruction in a great variety of subjects. Theoretically the visitor could educate himself by a careful study of the exhibits. The idea, although elevated and appealing, had the disadvantage of requiring an immense amount of space; moreover, as scientific discoveries proliferated, exhibits constantly became obsolete. The Museum of Science in Boston, under the leadership of Henry Bradford Washburn, Jr., who became its director in 1939, abandoned the notion that a museum could be an all-inclusive organization, providing the possibility of self-instruction in science and technology through its exhibits and lectures. Washburn's policies were directed at exciting the visitor's imagination and inspiring him to pursue the study of a subject in school or college, or by independent study.

BIBLIOGRAPHY

Whitfield J. Bell, Jr., Clifford K. Shipton, John C. Ewers, Louis L. Tucker, and Wilcomb E. Washburn, *A Cabinet of Curiosities: 5 Episodes in the Evolution of American Museums.*

Walter Muir Whitehill, *Independent Historical Societies, Museum of Fine Arts, Boston: A Centennial History,* and *The Salem East India Marine Society and the Peabody Museum of Salem.*

— WALTER MUIR WHITEHILL

MUSIC, CLASSICAL

Classical music encompasses instrumental and vocal music written by trained composers. It expresses more fully the artistic values of composers than music of an essentially commercial nature (popular) or music that develops anonymously and is transmitted aurally (folk). In the United States classical music has appealed to fewer people than popular or folk music. In the eighteenth century, classical music could be heard in Boston, Philadelphia, New York, Williamsburg, Charleston, and New Orleans and elsewhere in the houses of the well-to-do. Composers such as William Billings, Francis Hopkinson, and Alexander Reinagle produced hymns, songs, instrumental music, and opera similar in style to that of European contemporaries but noteworthy for a degree of originality. None of these composers could make a living from compositions; Billings died penniless. Much of their best music went unpublished in their lifetimes, as was the case with a Reinagle piano sonata that was not published until 1978. The music of such Europeans as George Handel, Antonio Vivaldi, Arcangelo Corelli, Luigi Boccherini, Jean-Philippe Rameau, and Joseph Haydn was probably better known and more often played in these coastal cities and in the houses of talented amateur musicians, such as Robert Carter and Thomas Jefferson, both of Virginia.

Composition of American classical music in the nineteenth century was dominated by a group of people eager to emulate the European masters, particularly those in the Germanic tradition. Many studied with teachers in Germany and did not deviate from what they learned. John Knowles Paine, the first musician to hold a professorship in a university (Harvard), became the prototype of the academic composer and, along with Dudley Buck, Edward MacDowell, Horatio Parker, Amy Cheney Beach, and George Whitefield Chadwick, wrote symphonies, concertos, songs, and choral music in the style of European contemporaries. Some African-American composers, beginning with Harry Thacker Burleigh, practiced more compositional diversity in an effort to express their African-American heritage. A significant result of this endeavor was William Grant Still's "Afro-American Symphony" of 1930.

Audiences, performing venues, and important musical organizations emerged in the nineteenth century. The predecessor of the New York Philharmonic, the Philharmonic Society, gave its first concert in 1842. Orchestras were established in Boston (1881), Chicago (1891), St. Louis (1893), and Cincinnati (1895). As early as the 1790s operas were performed in New Orleans and Philadelphia. In New York City opera was performed in theaters and the Academy of Music. The Metropolitan Opera House opened in 1883 and in 1910 transmitted a radio broadcast. Performers went on tour, the most famous being the Swedish singer Jenny Lind, promoted by the greatest of all entertainment entrepreneurs of the century, Phineas T. Barnum. Very little music, however, by native composers was performed.

In the twentieth century, opera flourished in the United States. An early work, *Treemonisha*, by composer and popularizer of ragtime Scott Joplin, received a limited production in 1915, and George Gershwin's *Porgy and Bess* was first heard in 1935. A new Metropolitan Opera House opened in 1966 with a production of *Antony and Cleopatra*, written by Samuel Barber in the tradition of European grand opera. In 1957 Barber had composed *Vanessa*, which was performed at the Metropolitan and elsewhere. Other composers of opera were Marc Blitzstein (*Regina*, 1949), Leonard Bernstein (*Trouble in Tahiti*, 1952), Douglas Moore (*The Ballad of Baby Doe*, 1956), Gian Carlo Menotti (*The Medium*, 1945; *The Consul*, 1949; *Amahl and the Night Visitors*, composed for television in 1951), Virgil Thomson (*Four Saints in Three Acts*, 1934), Philip Glass (*Einstein on the Beach*, 1975; *Satyagraha*, 1981; *The Voyage*, 1992), John Adams (*Nixon in China*, 1987; *Death of Klinghofer*, 1991), John Corigliano (*The Ghosts of Versailles*, 1991), and Hugo Weisgall (*Six Characters in Search of an Author*, 1956; *Esther*, 1987).

American composers produced a wealth of instrumental music over the course of the twentieth century. Some sought to innovate; others enriched European tradition. Most taught at universities or such conservatories as Juilliard (established 1905), the Eastman School of Music (1919), and the New England Conservatory (1867). The giant of American innovative composers was Charles Ives, whose music had to wait until after his death in 1951 for full recognition, as did that of Charles Tomlinson Griffes, who died in 1920, and Carl Ruggles, who died in 1971. French-born Edgar Varèse took up residence in the United States in 1915 and influenced native composers, notably Henry Cowell and Harry Partch, to write music to unsettle, shock, disturb. Two other innovators were John Cage and Milton Babbitt, whose 1989 work "Transfigured Notes" was unplayable because of limited rehearsal time by the Philadelphia Orchestra. Leonard Bernstein and Aaron Copland, who many have characterized as the deans of American composers, stand out because of the quantity and variety of their compositions and because of their roles as performers and advocates of music.

Among the best representatives of postromantic and expressionist music are Roger Sessions, called the greatest of American symphonists; Roy Harris; Howard Hanson; Peter Mennin; Walter Piston; and David Diamond. Leslie Bassett and Elliott Carter might also be placed in the expressionist tradition. Harris, composer of fourteen symphonies, and Robert Palmer wrote music showing the influence of central European nationalism. Barber and Hanson, who for forty years headed the Eastman School of Music, sustained an Italian, Scandinavian, and Russian romanticism. The career of George Rochberg encompassed experiments with atonality, but most of his output is expressionistic and romantic.

American composers—some in the European tradition and others breaking new ground—produced a wealth of instrumental music over the course of the twentieth century.

Much American classical music found audiences because of the large numbers of American symphony orchestras—1,400 by the late twentieth century. Radio and television disseminated music, as illustrated by the Metropolitan Opera's Saturday afternoon radio broadcasts beginning in 1940 and such public television series as *Great Performances* and *Live from Lincoln Center*. New halls and cultural centers opened in New York, Washington, Atlanta, San Francisco, Los Angeles, Dallas, and other cities; older halls, including former movie theaters, were renovated and restored in Detroit, Pittsburgh, Oakland, and St. Louis.

Despite observations suggesting trouble in the world of classical music (the recital and symphony orchestra dead or dying, for example), enrollment in conservatories and music schools and attendance at a growing number of summer music festivals increased. Many orchestras expanded seasons, encouraged new music through composer-in-residence programs, and showed a remarkable ability to innovate in programming and format. Classical music at the end of the twentieth century remained a vital part of the musical culture of the United States.

BIBLIOGRAPHY

Gilbert Chase, *America's Music: From the Pilgrims to the Present*, 3rd rev. ed. (Chicago, 1992).

Richard Crawford, *The American Musical Landscape* (Berkeley, Calif., 1993).

John Dizikes, *Opera in America: A Cultural History* (New Haven, Conn., 1993).

Monroe Levin, *Clues to American Music* (Washington, D.C., 1992).

Stanley Sadie and H. Wiley Hitchcock, eds., *The New Grove Dictionary of American Music*, 4 vols. (New York, 1986).

— CHARLES A. WEEKS

MUSIC, COUNTRY AND WESTERN

Country and western music, often referred to just as country music, eludes precise definition because of its many sources and varieties. It can best be understood as a style of popular music that originated in the folk culture of the rural South, a culture of European and African origin. Fiddlers, banjo players, string bands, balladeers, and gospel singers drew upon existing music to develop materials suitable for performance at family and community events. As southerners migrated to northern cities in the early twentieth century, their music went with them; and, beginning in the 1920s, radio and recordings did much to popularize and diversify this music. Musicians from Texas, Louisiana, and Oklahoma were especially innovative with regard to developing and promoting this essentially rural form of entertainment. In 1934, when a radio hillbilly singer from Texas named Orvon Gene Autry went to Hollywood, the era of the great cowboy singer in the movies began. The Grand Ole Opry in Nashville, beginning in the 1940s, made that city a mecca for country music fans, many of whom listened religiously to its performances on the radio. The popularity of rock and roll through the revolution in popular music begun by Elvis Presley in the mid-1950s posed a challenge to country music, but it was countered in part by development of a new style known as country pop or the Nashville Sound. By the 1990s country and western music had an international following.

[See also Music, Rock and Roll.]

BIBLIOGRAPHY

Bill C. Malone, *Country Music, U.S.A.: A Fifty-Year History*, rev. ed. (New York, 1985).

— CHARLES A. WEEKS

MUSIC, JAZZ

Jazz music is characterized by improvisation, bent pitches or blues notes, syncopation, and polyrhythms. It first appeared in the southern part of the United States during the late nineteenth century, blossomed in New Orleans at the turn of the century, and spread to other cities between 1890 and 1920, as dance halls, cabarets, restaurants, and theaters proliferated to satisfy a growing demand by Americans for pleasure and self-expression. The first jazz recording was made in New Orleans by the Original Dixieland Jazz Band in 1917, and during the 1920s jazz and jazz-influenced dance music became the popular music of the United States. F. Scott Fitzgerald entitled a collection of his short stories *Tales of the Jazz Age* (1922), and the phrase became part of the lexicon of the decade. In the next two decades the success of jazz was assured by the big swing bands. By the end of World War II, bebop, which originated in the practice of vocalizing or singing instrumental lines and was played by small groups of three to six members, was becoming popular among musicians who disliked the size and formality of the swing bands. Another style, cool jazz, emerged at the same time. By the 1960s rock and rock-based styles had displaced jazz as the popular music of the United States. Since the 1970s many styles have flourished, including modal jazz, an avant-garde free jazz, and jazz rock or fusion. Beginning in the 1980s a movement emerged to preserve a purer or classical jazz against attempts to fuse it with rock or rhythm and blues.

Charles Mingus (1922–79), jazz bass player, in a 1960 photograph. Mingus was known for extending the frontiers of jazz composition, and for his distinctive and innovative sound. (UPI/Corbis-Bettmann)

BIBLIOGRAPHY

Frank Tirro, *Jazz: A History*, 2nd ed. (New York, 1993).

— JOSHUA L. COX AND CHARLES A. WEEKS

MUSIC, ROCK AND ROLL

Rock and roll music reflected youth and social change in post-World War II America. It integrated musically blacks and whites in the mid-1950s, was pivotal in the youth counterculture and protest movements of the mid-1960s through the early 1970s, and reflected societal divisions from the 1970s through the 1990s. Elvis Presley helped create rock and roll with "That's Alright Mama" (1954), "Mystery Train" (1955), and other recordings for Memphis-based Sun Records, which also produced the Jerry Lee Lewis classics "Whole Lot of Shakin' Going On" (1957) and "Great Balls of Fire" (1957). Presley's blend of blues and country smashed the color barrier between black and white musical styles, triggering a musical revolution that was amplified by Chuck Berry, a black guitarist who drew heavily from white country music when writing such enduring standards as "Johnny B. Goode" (1958). White youths increasingly embraced black music, from the smooth harmonies of the Drifters to the hyperkinetic screams of Little Richard (Richard Penniman), whose "Tutti Frutti" (1965) stunned unprepared listeners. By 1956, when Presley began to enjoy massive national popularity, black and white music were achieving an integration rare in the larger society.

The early 1960s heard the Beach Boys harmonizing about a mythic California; Phil Spector's "wall of sound," which exploded with the Crystals epic "Then He Kissed Me" (1963); the Ventures' influential instrumental rock, and the emergence of such Motown Records stars as Smokey Robinson and Marvin Gaye. It was the Beatles, however, who defined rock and roll in a way no act has before or since. They not only dominated the American popular music charts (beginning with their 1964 hit "I Want to Hold Your Hand") but also helped lead the music's expansion from simple adolescent love songs to complex aggressions that could reflect the social and political changes sweeping the United States. Bob Dylan's stunning *Highway 61 Revisited* (1965) and *Blonde on Blonde* (1966) were pivotal albums in this transformation, which was accelerated by other albums, such as the Beatles' *Rubber Soul* (1965) and *Sgt. Pepper's Lonely Hearts Club Band* (1967) and the Rolling Stones' *Aftermath* (1966) and *Let It Bleed* (1969). Despite growing diversity, rock and roll did not seem fragmented at the end of the 1960s. The Woodstock music festival (1969) was able to encompass Jimi Hendrix's guitar explosions, the Grateful Dead's folk-rock, Sly Stone's eclectic funk, Credence Clearwater Revival's straightforward rock, Janis Joplin's anguished blues, the Who's furious intellectualism, and much more.

By the 1970s, however, rock's fault lines grew. The disco music of Donna Summer and others was reviled by the heavy metal fans of Led Zeppelin, while devotees of such introspective singer-songwriters as Paul Simon or Joni Mitchell were at best puzzled by the Sex Pistols, Patti Smith, Television, and other pioneering punk rockers. New-wave bands, such as the Talking Heads, expanded rock's musical vocabulary, but they too spoke to one part of what had once seemed a unified audience.

In the 1980s Madonna (Madonna Louise Ciccone) combined sexual provocation and steely business acumen to win huge commercial success, while rap music restored distinctly black music to a central place in rock. Although such rappers as Run-DMC developed an interracial appeal, other hip hop artists seemed to encourage an animosity toward whites that was unknown to such earlier black music exemplars as Aretha Franklin and James Brown, and many whites remained hostile to rap. Rock artistry thrived in the 1990s, from Prince's (Prince Rogers Nelson) infectious fusion of musical styles to Nirvana's incendiary mix of punk and heavy metal, but no one could rejoin the splintered rock audience. Such top acts as Michael Jackson and REM spoke to different musical worlds, while Bruce Springsteen, one of the most popular and important artists of the 1980s, sang only to that fraction of listeners eager to hear him. The music that had grown out of the integration power of Elvis and had reached its mythic unifying peak at Woodstock was deeply divided as the United States faced a new millennium.

BIBLIOGRAPHY

Greil Marcus, *Mystery Train: Images of America in Rock 'n' Roll Music*, rev. ed. (New York, 1982).

Ed Ward et al., eds., *Rock of Ages: The "Rolling Stone" History of Rock & Roll* (New York, 1986).

— ANDREW L. AOKI

MUSIC TELEVISION

Music Television (MTV), the first all-music television network, began broadcasting on Aug. 1, 1981, and targeted an audience aged twelve to thirty-four. The network's programming comprised back-to-back videos created by record companies to promote their artists. MTV was troubled in its early years by accusations of racism, concerning failure to broadcast videos by black artists. The founders, among them Robert Pittman, prescribed a policy of "narrow-casting" drawn from radio, which aired only a restricted range of music. British "new pop" acts such as Duran Duran and the Thompson Twins were so heavily programmed that observers credited MTV with launching a second "British invasion" (the first being the Beatles in the 1960s) of the U.S. music marketplace. Because music videos are primarily advertisements for recording artists, MTV has been frequently criticized for commercialism. It was also criticized by women's groups for sexism. Following the

MTV has been frequently criticized for commercialism—since music videos are primarily advertisements for recording artists—as well as for sexist depictions of women.

sale of MTV from Warner-Amex to Viacom International in 1986, the network diversified its output, expanding into nonmusic programming and encompassing a broader range of music. Heavy metal was for some years the staple, and following the success of *Yo! MTV Raps* in 1989 (for some time the most popular show on the network), many rap artists concluded that MTV was responsible for introducing this form to Middle America. In 1987 MTV launched MTV Europe and began a period of world expansion. By 1994 it was available in fifty-eight countries to a potential audience of 240 million households. It continued to expand nonmusic programming (notably with its highest-rated show, the controversial cartoon *Beavis and Butt-head*) and was credited with mainstreaming the "grunge" rock of Nirvana, Pearl Jam, and Soundgarden. News coverage on MTV stressed social and political issues relevant to young people. In 1992 MTV's "Rock the Vote" campaign was credited by President Bill Clinton with helping increase the youth vote.

[See also Music, Rock and Roll; Television.]

BIBLIOGRAPHY

Andrew Goodwin, *Dancing in the Distraction Factory* (Minneapolis, 1992).

— ANDREW GOODWIN

MUTINY

An examination of various military authorities leads to a welter of contradiction in defining mutiny. From actual conditions a working definition may be evolved and stated as "concerted insubordination, or concerted opposition or resistance to or defiance of lawful military authority, by two or more persons subject to such authority, with the intent to usurp, subvert, or override such authority, or to neutralize it for the time being." When examples of mutiny are sought, difficulty is encountered in that the larger number of cases that might possibly be so designated are tried for lesser charges, such as insubordination or refusal to obey orders. This gives rise to many borderline cases. U.S. history does afford some definite examples. The most striking is that of the entire Pennsylvania Line, six regiments, which mutinied at Morristown, N.J., on Jan. 2, 1781, and started for Philadelphia to lay their grievances directly before Congress.

A year before, on May 25, 1780, two regiments of the Connecticut Line paraded without their officers in a spirit of mutiny. They were brought back under authority by a Pennsylvania brigade. On Jan. 20, 1781, three New Jersey regiments sought to imitate the Pennsylvania Line. George Washington ordered Gen. Robert Howe to handle the situation. He surrounded the mutineers with infantry and artillery at Ringwood and gave them five minutes to come to time. They yielded; the ringleaders were immediately tried and two of them hung, whereupon the regiments returned to duty. In June 1783, recruits of the Pennsylvania regiments marched on Congress at Philadelphia. When Congress fled to Princeton, N.J., Gen. Howe again stepped in and settled matters.

In the War of 1812, the Twenty-third Infantry mutinied at Manlius, N.Y.; the Fifth Infantry at Utica; a company of volunteers at Buffalo; and, in 1814, a regiment of Tennessee militia, part of Gen. Andrew Jackson's forces, had a sergeant and five privates condemned to death for inciting mutiny.

A conspicuous maritime case was that on the U.S. brig *Somers* in 1842 when Midshipman Phillip Spencer (son of the then Secretary of War Ambrose Spencer) was one of three prisoners hanged on shipboard as a mutineer. As of the mid-1970's no later case of mutiny on a U.S. Navy vessel had occurred.

BIBLIOGRAPHY

William Hough, *Precedents in Military Law.*
Oliver L. Spaulding, *The United States Army in War and Peace.*
James Thacher, *Military Journal During the American Revolution.*
William Winthrop, *Military Law and Precedents.*

— ROBERT S. THOMAS

N

NATIONAL ADVISORY COMMISSION ON CIVIL DISORDERS

The wave of urban ghetto riots that began in New York City and Rochester, N.Y., in 1964 and in the Watts section of Los Angeles in 1965 reached its peak in the summer of 1967 when a total of sixty-six people were killed in Newark, N.J., and Detroit, Mich. Only days after these two riots, President Lyndon B. Johnson created the National Advisory Commission on Civil Disorders, headed by Judge Otto Kerner of Illinois. On the basis of formal hearings and a series of studies by a large number of distinguished social scientists, the commission issued a widely circulated report in March 1968. This report concluded that America's tradition of white racism was responsible for the riots. The commission deplored the polarization of the nation into two societies, one black and one white, and recommended a massive program of federal spending to correct the inequities produced by centuries of racial discrimination. Shortly after the report was issued, the assassination of Martin Luther King, Jr., produced a new wave of riots. Thereafter civil disorders quickly subsided, and at least partly for that reason, only a few of the commission's recommendations were carried out. But its widely read report, which gave official sanction to the view that the blame and the remedy for racial inequalities lay with white America, had appreciable impact upon public opinion and governmental actions.

— ELLIOTT RUDWICK

NATIONAL AERONAUTICS AND SPACE ADMINISTRATION

During the decade of the 1960's the United States became a space-faring nation, primarily as a result of intense international rivalry with the Soviet Union. The establishment of the National Aeronautics and Space Administration (NASA) was the foremost legislative manifestation of a mood of national anxiety—often approaching hysteria—that followed the orbiting of the earth by the first two artificial satellites, belonging to the Soviet Union, in the fall of 1957. The Soviet Sputniks were immediately associated in the thinking of government officials, military strategists, and the general public with the Soviet news agency's announcement late the previous summer that the Soviet Union had successfully tested an intercontinental ballistic missile (ICBM) capable of carrying a nuclear warhead to targets in the United States. In the winter of 1957–58 the conviction that the "space lag" and the alleged "missile gap" constituted a severe national security crisis became even more pronounced as the Vanguard rocket (which was to orbit a small scientific payload as part of the U.S. contribution to the International Geophysical Year) exploded on its launch stand and as a Senate subcommittee investigation revealed delays, duplication, and rampant interservice rivalry in the nation's missile programs.

In early 1958, two U.S. satellites—Explorer and Vanguard—were sent into orbit, and within a few years, the United States had deployed several times as many intercontinental nuclear-tipped missiles as had the Soviet Union. Eventually it became apparent that the missile gap had never been more than a cold war nightmare.

Although he remained convinced of the adequacy of the American nuclear deterrent, President Dwight D. Eisenhower moved to coordinate and accelerate missile development, especially work on the Atlas ICBM. Eisenhower also sought a design for an overall national space effort. He was determined that any American program for the exploration of space would be controlled by civilian officials and that its objectives would be essentially nonmilitary. From this "Space for Peace" orientation stemmed the basic decision to organize a national space program around the National Advisory Committee for Aeronautics (NACA), which had been created in 1915.

On Apr. 2, 1958, the president proposed the establishment of a "National Aeronautical and Space Agency" to absorb NACA and assume responsibility for all "space activities . . . except . . . those projects primarily associated with military requirements." The new agency's executive authority would be exercised by a single director, who would be advised by a seventeen-member space board. The proposed organization would not only conduct research but would have developmental, managerial, and flight operational responsibilities as well as extensive authority for contracting research and development projects. On July 29, 1958, the National Aeronautics and Space Act, creating NASA, was signed into law. Among the major changes incorporated in the final legislation were the upgrading of the original "agency" and "director" to "administration" and "administrator"; the transformation of the space board into a smaller space council charged with advising the president, who was to be its chairman; and the creation of a civilian-military liaison committee to ensure full exchange of information acquired in NASA and Defense Department programs. Space activities of a strictly military nature were to remain under the aegis of the Defense Department.

Eisenhower's choice for NASA administrator was T. Keith Glennan, president of Case Institute of Technology and a former member of the Atomic Energy Commission. Hugh L. Dryden, director of NACA since 1947, became deputy administrator. The new organization acquired NACA's full personnel complement, facilities, and appropriation, as well as the Vanguard project from the Naval Research Laboratory, the Explorer project from the Army Ballistic Missile Agency, the services of the Jet Propulsion Laboratory (previously an army contractor), various air force engine projects and satellite study contracts, and $117 million in appropriations for space activities from the Defense Department. In August Eisenhower assigned NASA specific responsibility for developing and carrying out the mission of manned spaceflight, thereby quashing the hopes of the military services.

From this varied and complex organizational base, NASA formally began business on Oct. 1, 1958. Its first year was full of uncertainties. The Eisenhower administration, struggling to balance the federal budget, was reluctant to commit heavy funding to space ventures; congressional support was unpredictable; and additional organizational transfers had to be worked out, most notably the transfer of the famed rocket design team led by Wernher von Braun from the army together with its million-pound-thrust Saturn booster project. But by the end of 1960 NASA was on firm ground, having established two new spaceflight centers (Goddard at Greenbelt, Md., and Marshall at Huntsville, Ala.) and secured a sizable 1961 budget increase.

Beginning in September 1959, when it carried out its first successful satellite launching (Vanguard III, which gathered data on earth's magnetic field and the radiation belts first revealed by Explorer I), NASA launched hundreds of instrumented satellites and space probes, the cumulative effect of which was to transform the state of man's knowledge of earth's atmosphere, near space, and the moon and nearby planets. During the 1960's a network of satellites launched by NASA for the private Communications Satellite Corporation established a worldwide system of visual and telephonic communication.

Overshadowing all other NASA undertakings was the manned spaceflight program, which became the dramatic focus of U.S.-Soviet space rivalry. In Project Mercury, established in November 1958, NASA undertook to place a series of one-man ballistic capsules in earth orbit. Between May 1961 and June 1963, Mercury astronauts successfully flew two sub-orbital and four orbital missions, extending from three to twenty-two circuits of earth. Late in May 1961, in the aftermath of the Soviet Union's launch of the first manned satellite and a comparatively modest American suborbital launch, President John F. Kennedy set as a national goal manned landing on the moon "before this decade is out."

For the next few years NASA's budgets continued to grow—to a peak of $5.25 billion for fiscal year 1965. NASA Administrator James E. Webb, Kennedy's appointee, oversaw an enormous expansion of the space administration's research and development operations. To carry out Project Gemini, which was to perfect the rendezvous and docking procedures essential to the lunar-orbit mode chosen for the moon mission, and Project Apollo, the moonflight program itself, as well as to carry to completion Project Mercury, NASA moved to create a huge space development aggregation, consisting of the rocket launch facilities at Cape Canaveral, Fla.; the Marshall Space Flight Center in Alabama; a rocket assembly and test plant in southeastern Mississippi; and a new management, crew training, and flight control installation called the Manned Spacecraft Center, near Houston, Tex. By the mid-1960's, NASA employed some 36,000 persons at its Washington, D.C., headquarters, five research centers, four development centers, and various other offices and installations across the country.

The Gemini program sent twenty astronauts into orbit in two-man spacecraft during 1964–66. Project Apollo, although set back a year by the deaths of three crewmen in a spacecraft fire on the launch pad in January 1967, continued its buildup through earth-orbital and lunar-orbital missions until the Apollo XI mission in July 1969, when two Americans set foot on the moon's surface. By this time Thomas O. Paine had succeeded Webb as NASA administrator. Moreover, the Soviets had dropped out of the "moon race" (if they had ever been in it), although the Soviet Union continued to launch not only the full panoply of instrumented satellites and space probes but also a series of long-duration manned spacecraft that made clear the Soviet intention to construct an orbiting space station.

By the early 1970's, NASA, under Administrator James C. Fletcher (who succeeded Paine in 1971), faced its most uncertain period since 1959. After a succession of budget cuts beginning in the late 1960's, accompanied by the discharge of almost 10,000 employees and the closing of its Electronics Research Center at Boston, Mass., the NASA budgets seemed to have leveled off at about $3.3 billion. As the manned lunar exploration program ended with the Apollo XVII mission in December 1972, it became obvious that, as Fletcher said, "Moon exploration, for a time, will be left completely to the Soviets." More and more the space program was equated with the increasingly powerful military-industrial complex, with the protracted war in Indochina, and with the generally destructive effects of modern technology. Lunar missions after Apollo XI, while they returned steadily increasing quantities of data about the moon's geological, geophysical, and meteorological characteristics, attracted steadily diminishing public attention.

Yet Project Skylab established an American-manned orbital space station in 1973; the development and deployment of a space shuttle system were approved in 1972 to make "the space frontier of the 1970's . . . easily accessible for human endeavor in the 1980's and 1990's"; and a joint U.S.-Soviet undertaking to rendezvous and dock an American Apollo and a Russian Soyuz spacecraft was successfully concluded in 1975. It appeared that space exploration, born in cold war conflict in the 1950's, might become the means of promoting international harmony, as its most visionary advocates had always foreseen.

[See also Space Program.]

BIBLIOGRAPHY

Jay Holmes, *America on the Moon: The Enterprise of the Sixties.*

John M. Logsdon, *The Decision to Go to the Moon: Project Apollo and the National Interest.*

Robert L. Rosholt, *An Administrative History of NASA, 1958–1963.*

Loyd S. Swenson, James M. Grimwood, and Charles C. Alexander, *This New Ocean: A History of Project Mercury.*

Vernon Van Dyke, *Pride and Power: The Rationale of the Space Program.*

— CHARLES C. ALEXANDER

NATIONAL ASSOCIATION FOR THE ADVANCEMENT OF COLORED PEOPLE

The NAACP was founded in 1909–10 by white progressives and black militants belonging to the Niagara Movement in response to the Springfield, Ill., race riot of August 1908. Shocked by the violence, a distinguished biracial gathering that included the journalist William English Walling, social worker Mary White Ovington, newspaper editor Oswald Garrison Villard, and scholar W. E. B. Du Bois issued a call on Feb. 12, 1909, the centennial of Abraham Lincoln's birth, for a national conference on black rights. Held in New York City on May 30–June 1, the conference formed the National Negro Committee, out of which the NAACP emerged in May 1910.

Except for Du Bois, who became the association's director of publicity and editor of *Crisis*, its official publication, all of the organization's first national officers were white. At its formation the NAACP adopted a militant program of action based on the platform of its radical forerunner, the Niagara Movement, demanding equal educational, political, and civil rights for blacks and the enforcement of the Fourteenth and Fifteenth amendments.

Relying on an integrated and middle-class approach to reform, the NAACP stressed corrective education, legislation, and litigation. Under the leadership of Arthur B. Spingarn, chairman of its legal committee, white and black attorneys for the NAACP won important victories before the U.S. Supreme Court in 1915 (*Guinn* v. *United States*) and 1917 (*Buchanan* v. *Warley*), which struck down the grandfather clause as unconstitutional and nullified Jim Crow housing ordinances in Louisville, Ky. During the postwar period, the organization, spearheaded by James Weldon Johnson, its black executive secretary, focused its attention on antilynching legislation. Although no federal antilynching bill was passed by Congress, the NAACP's aggressive campaign heightened public awareness of and opposition to mob violence against blacks and established the organization as the national spokesman for Afro-Americans.

Over the next three decades the NAACP directed its attention to voting rights, housing, and the desegregation of public education. With Thurgood Marshall as its special legal counsel, the NAACP figured prominently in a series of Supreme Court decisions that banned the all-white primary (*Smith* v. *Allwright*, 1944); outlawed residential covenants against black home buyers (*Shelley* v. *Kraemer*, 1948); ordered the integration of the University of Missouri Law School (*Missouri ex rel. Gaines* v. *Canada*, 1938), the University of Oklahoma (*Sipuel* v. *University of Oklahoma*, 1948), and the University of Texas (*Sweatt* v. *Painter*, 1950); and, in the landmark case *Brown* v. *Board of Education of Topeka* (May 1954), declared segregated schools unequal and unconstitutional.

Under its executive secretary, Roy Wilkins, the NAACP was a leading participant in the civil rights movement of the 1960's. Direct actionists, such as the Student Nonviolent Coordinating Committee (SNCC), ended the organization's hegemony as the country's major civil rights group, but with a 1975 membership of 433,118 and 1,555 branches in all fifty states, the NAACP entered the fourth quarter of the 20th century as an active force among black Americans committed to racial integration.

BIBLIOGRAPHY

Jack Abramowitz, "Origins of the NAACP," *Social Education*, vol. 15 (1951).

Langston Hughes, *Fight for Freedom: The Story of the NAACP.*

Charles Flint Kellogg, *NAACP: A History of the National Association for the Advancement of Colored People, 1909–1920*, vol. I.

Robert L. Zangrando, "The 'Organized Negro': The National Association for the Advancement of Colored People and Civil Rights," in James C. Curtis and Lewis L. Gould, eds., *The Black Experience in America.*

— WILLIAM R. SCOTT

NAACP SINCE 1975

National Association for the Advancement of Colored People (NAACP). Since 1975 the NAACP has continued to fight for equal rights for African Americans but internal divisions and lack of funding have stifled its progress. Although the NAACP's victories historically came through litigation in the courts, the organization found it increasingly difficult to sustain such activity in the 1970s and 1980s. Much of this resulted from a rift between the NAACP and the independent NAACP Legal Defense and Educational Fund (LDF). Disagreement became so intense that in May 1982 the NAACP sued the LDF in an effort to control the LDF's activities. The split shifted the NAACP's focus from legal action to lobbying against federal policies that threatened existing civil rights legislation and affirmative action programs.

In 1993 the NAACP's longtime executive director, Benjamin Hooks, retired and was succeeded by Benjamin F. Chavis. An aggressive civil rights activist and head of the United Church of Christ's Commission for Racial Justice, Chavis in 1982 coined the term "environmental racism," to describe the tendency of manufacturing and other companies to dump toxic waste in or near areas where racial minorities resided. Chavis promised to revamp the NAACP by developing a marketing plan targeted at the younger generation through music videos, by promoting health care reform, and by embracing issues of global human rights. When Chavis took office the NAACP had shown little growth since the 1970s and had only 500,000 members with about 2,000 chapters nationwide. He was determined to recruit not only more African Americans, but Latinos, Asian Americans, and people of color around the world.

Chavis immediately ran into criticism for embracing Louis Farrakhan, minister of the Nation of Islam; for producing a deficit of $3 million; and for his lobbying efforts on behalf of corporations attempting to avoid paying for toxic waste cleanup. He was fired in 1994 for not informing the NAACP board of directors that he had agreed to pay more than $300,000 in NAACP funds to a former female employee who had charged him with sexual harassment. William F. Gibson, chair of the NAACP board of directors since 1985, supported Chavis until his ouster, only to find himself under investigation for excessive spending. With the future of the NAACP in doubt, Myrlie Evers-Williams, civil rights activist and widow of Medgar Evers, unseated Gibson as chair by one vote in February 1995. She faced the challenge of a $4.5 million deficit, falling contributions because of the perceived state of disarray within the organization, and the task of finding a new executive director. In February 1996 Democratic Congressman Kweisi Mfume of Maryland resigned his seat in the House to take over the executive directorship of the NAACP. Mfume, former leader of the congressional black caucus, promised to rehabilitate the NAACP and unite it for aggressive action and embarked immediately on a voter registration drive.

[See also Affirmative Action; African Americans; Civil Rights Movement.]

BIBLIOGRAPHY

Lynne Duke, "What Is Happening to the NAACP?," *Washington Post National Weekly Edition* (Jan. 16–22, 1995).

Kenneth Goings, *The NAACP Comes of Age* (Bloomington, Ind., 1990).

Matthew S. Scott, "Chavis to Lead NAACP into New Era," *Black Enterprise* (July 1993).

Hanes Walton, Jr., *When the Marching Stopped: The Politics of Civil Rights Regulatory Agencies* (Albany, N.Y., 1988).

— JILL WATTS

NATIONAL INSTITUTES OF HEALTH

National Institutes of Health originated as the Laboratory of Hygiene and was established at the Marine Hospital, Staten Island, N.Y., in 1887 for research on cholera and other infectious diseases. In 1891 it was renamed the Hygienic Laboratory and moved to Washington, D.C., and in 1930, as a result of the Ransdell Act, it became the National Institute of Health. In 1937 the National Cancer Institute was added, and the following year Congress authorized the construction of new, larger laboratory facilities and the transfer of the National Institute of Health (NIH) to Bethesda, Md. Legislation in 1948 established a National Heart Institute and changed the name of the National Institute of Health to National Institutes of Health.

An agency of the Department of Health, Education and Welfare since that department's establishment in 1953, NIH has the mission of improving the health of all Americans. To achieve this goal it conducts biomedical research; provides grants to individuals, organizations, and institutions for research, training, and medical education; assists in the improvement and construction of library facilities and resources; and supports programs in biomedical communications. From its beginnings in a one-room laboratory, NIH has developed into a great research center consisting of ten institutes (Cancer; Heart and Lung; Allergy and Infectious Diseases; Dental Research; Arthritis, Metabolism, and Digestive Diseases; Neurological Diseases and Stroke; Child Health and Human Development; General Medical Sciences; Eye; and Environmental Health Sciences); four divisions (Computer Research and Technology; Research Grants; Research Resources; and Research Services); the National Library of Medicine; and two centers, the research hospital Clinical Center and the John E. Fogarty International Center.

The NIH campus consists of over 300 acres and includes laboratories, libraries, and clinical facilities for highly sophisticated research into the biomedical sciences. NIH also has annual lectures, honors, exhibits, and symposia. Among its scientists are three Nobel laureates, and since 1938 NIH has supported the work of another fifty-six Nobel Prize winners, thirty-nine of whom received grant support for research conducted prior to their awards and were thus directly assisted by NIH in making their discoveries.

BIBLIOGRAPHY

U.S. Department of Health, Education and Welfare, Public Health Service, National Institutes of Health, *NIH Almanac* (1975).

Ralph Chester Williams, *The United States Public Health Service, 1798–1950.*

— MANFRED WASERMAN

NIH IN THE 1970S, 1980S, AND 1990S

National Institutes of Health (NIH) has changed since the mid-1970s, although its objective has remained constant—to recruit high-quality biomedical researchers in the service of health for Americans—and two new funding programs were created to achieve this objective. The intramural program supports research in NIH laboratories on the Bethesda, Md., campus, and the extramural program distributes grants to university investigators across the United States and makes collaborative arrangements with researchers in other countries. The NIH annual budget in the early 1990s was more than $8 billion, and personnel on the Bethesda campus numbered more than 16,000. In 1993 Congress directed the NIH to include more women in research designs and analysis instead of continuing to concentrate on studies involving only men. Other changes since the mid-1970s include organizational shifts of the different institutes, centers, divisions, and offices that comprise the NIH. In 1994 the NIH consisted of seventeen institutes (Aging; Alcohol Abuse and Alcoholism; Allergy and Infectious Diseases; Arthritis and Musculoskeletal and Skin Diseases; Cancer; Child Health and Human Development; Deafness and Other Communication Disorders; Dental Research; Diabetes and Digestive and Kidney Diseases; Drug Abuse; Environmental Health Sciences; Eye; General Medical Sciences; Heart, Lung, and Blood; Mental Health; Neurological Disorders and Stroke; and Nursing Research); two divisions (Computer Research and Technology and Research Grants); four centers (Center for Research Resources; John E. Fogarty International Center; National Center for Human Genome Research; and Warren Grant Magnuson Clinical Center); three offices (Women's Health; Alternative Medicine; and Minority Health); the National Library of Medicine; and the Children's Inn at NIH. The NIH also funds three field units (the Gerontology Research Center in Baltimore, Md.; the Rocky Mountain Laboratories in Hamilton, Mont.; and the NIH Animal Center in Poolesville, Md.). NIH has joined with other agencies to advance biomedical research. In one of the larger projects, NIH and the Howard Hughes Medical Institute launched a multimillion-dollar cooperative program to encourage physicians to enter research.

In addition to bench research, the NIH supports patient studies and experimental treatments.

As of 1995 there had been four Nobel Prize laureates among NIH researchers who were intramural scientists as well as seventy-one laureates whose projects were supported by NIH grants. Much intramural research includes bench research, which takes place in laboratories on campus. Such research has resulted in prominent scientific advances. In 1984 National Cancer Institute scientists headed by Dr. Robert Gallo, Jr., uncovered evidence that variants of a human cancer virus (called HTLV-III) are the primary cause of acquired immunodeficiency syndrome (AIDS). Beyond bench research NIH supports clinical research, including patient studies and experimental treatments. A landmark treatment took place in 1991, when cancer patients were treated with the first human-gene therapy. Much clinical research takes place in the Warren Grant Magnuson Clinical Center involving surgery, outpatient clinics, diagnostic radiology, clinical pathology, and nuclear medicine.

[See also Acquired Immune Deficiency Syndrome; Health and Human Services, Department of.]

BIBLIOGRAPHY

Edward H. Ahrens, Jr., *The Crisis in Clinical Research* (New York, 1992).

William N. Kelley et al., *Emerging Policies for Biomedical Research* (Washington, D.C., 1993).

U.S. Department of Health, Education, and Welfare, Public Health Service, National Institutes of Health, *NIH Almanac* (Washington, D.C., 1992).

— CHERI L. WIGGS

NATIONAL LABOR RELATIONS ACT

Enacted in 1935, the National Labor Relations Act (NLRA) is the cornerstone of national labor policy. Known initially as the Wagner Act, it guarantees the rights of workers to organize and to bargain collectively with their employers. It encourages collective bargaining and provides governmental processes for the selection of employee bargaining representatives. It provided for the establishment of the National Labor Relations Board (NLRB) to administer its provisions.

As originally enacted, the NLRA prohibited unfair labor practices by employers but not by labor organizations. Employers were prohibited from interfering with, restraining, or coercing employees in the exercise of their rights to form unions, to bargain collectively, and to engage in other concerted activities. The right to strike thus was protected for employees subject to the law. The act outlawed company unions or employer-assisted unions. It prohibited discrimination in employment to encourage or discourage membership in a labor organization but permitted "closed shops" established by collective-bargaining agreements between employers and unions with exclusive bargaining rights. It prohibited employers from discharging or otherwise discriminating against employees who file charges or give testimony under the act. It also made it unlawful for an employer to refuse to bargain collectively with the representative chosen by a majority of employees in a group appropriate for collective bargaining.

The NLRA was amended in 1947 by the Labor Management Relations Act, commonly known as the Taft-Hartley Act. The most important 1947 amendments were those that made it unlawful for unions to engage in certain unfair labor practices. Among other things, unions were prohibited from restraining or coercing employees in exercising their rights under the law, refusing to bargain in good faith with an employer when the union is the representative of employees, and engaging in secondary boycotts and certain types of strikes and picketing. Closed shops were outlawed by the Taft-Hartley amendments, but a proviso permitted an employer and a union to agree to a "union shop," requiring employee membership thirty days after date of hire to the extent of tendering the uniformly required dues and initiation fees. Another proviso stated that union-shop agreements could not be authorized in states where they were forbidden by state law; in all other respects the NLRA preempted state laws. The 1947 amendments also reorganized the NLRB, providing for the president to appoint the general counsel, who was assigned statutory responsibility for the investigation of charges of unfair labor practice, the issuance of complaints, and the prosecution of complaints before the board.

The NLRA was amended again in 1959 by the Labor-Management Reporting and Disclosure Act, commonly known as the Landrum-Griffin Act. By the more important 1959 amendments, unions were precluded from picketing or threatening to picket to force recognition by the employer or to force the employees to accept the union as their representative if the union was not certified to represent the employees. Unions and employers were barred from entering into "hot cargo" contracts; that is, with certain exceptions the law declared void and unenforceable any contract by which a company agreed to cease handling, using, selling, transporting, or otherwise dealing in the products of any other company.

The NLRA generally applies to all employers engaged in interstate commerce. It does not apply to railroads and airlines, which are covered by the Railway Labor Act, or to governmental agencies. As a matter of policy the board has not exercised its legal jurisdiction to the fullest extent so as to take cases in all businesses or industries that affect interstate commerce. Some groups of employees—such as agricultural laborers, domestic employees, and supervisors—are excluded from coverage.

The board is composed of five members appointed by the president subject to approval by the Senate, with each member having a term of five years. The general counsel, whose appointment also must be approved by the Senate, has a term of four years. Headquartered in Washington, D.C., the agency has thirty-one regional offices and eleven smaller field offices throughout the country. Total Washington and field staffs numbered approximately 2,400 in 1972. Between 1935 and 1972 the agency processed more than 300,000 cases in which unfair labor practices were alleged and it conducted more than 190,000 secret-ballot employee self-determination elections. Millions of employees have cast ballots in these elections; 25 million voters entered the polling place by 1967.

The board members act primarily as a quasijudicial body in deciding cases on formal records, generally upon review of findings of fact and decisions by its administrative law judges (formerly called trial examiners) in cases of unfair labor practice or upon review of regional director decisions in representation cases. The NLRB has no independent statutory power of enforcement of its orders, but it may seek enforcement in the U.S. courts of appeals; parties aggrieved by board orders also may seek judicial review.

BIBLIOGRAPHY

H. A. Millis and E. C. Brown, *From the Wagner Act to Taft-Hartley.*
National Labor Relations Board, *Summary of the National Labor Relations Act,* and *Annual Reports.*
Louis G. Silverberg, *How to Take a Case Before the NLRB.*

— FRANK M. KLEILER

NATIONAL RECOVERY ADMINISTRATION

The National Industrial Recovery Act (NIRA), a New Deal emergency measure, became law on June 16, 1933. It included provisions to give the nation temporary economic stimulation and provisions intended to lay the ground for permanent business-government partnership and planning. The act provided for codes of fair competition, for exemption from antitrust laws, and for the government licensing of business; in section 7a it guaranteed the right of collective bargaining and stipulated that the codes should set minimum wages and maximum hours.

The National Recovery Administration (NRA) was created under Administrator Hugh S. Johnson after the NIRA went into effect. From its inception through March 1934 the NRA was chiefly engaged in code-making. Industrial councils were authorized to draw up codes of fair competition. Administered by a code authority in each industry, the codes were supposed to stop wasteful competition, effect more orderly pricing and selling policies, and establish better working conditions. Every code had to guarantee freedom of workers to join their own unions and provide for maximum hours and minimum wages; a group offering a code had to be truly representative of the trade or industry involved; and no code could be designed to promote monopoly or oppress or eliminate small enterprises. Within a year nearly all American industry was codified.

In the fall of 1934 Johnson was replaced by Donald R. Richberg as administrator. On Feb. 20, 1935, the president recommended to Congress the extension of the NIRA for two years beyond its expiration date of June 1935. On June 14, Congress voted to extend the recovery legislation until Apr. 1, 1936, but repealed the provisions authorizing the president to approve or prescribe codes of fair competiton. (On May 27, 1935, in *Schechter Poultry Corporation* v. *United States,* the Supreme Court had invalidated the code-making provisions of the act.) The NRA was terminated on Jan. 1, 1936.

The chief purpose of the NRA was recovery—to increase purchasing power by the net reduction of unemployment, the spreading of work through shorter hours, and the increase of wages. In 1933 it helped to generate employment. Beyond that, it established the principle of maximum hours and minimum wages on a national basis, abolished child labor, and made collective bargaining a national policy, transforming the position of organized labor.

BIBLIOGRAPHY

Broadus Mitchell, *Depression Decade.*
Basil Rauch, *The History of the New Deal.*
Arthur M. Schlesinger, Jr., *The Coming of the New Deal.*

— MORTON J. FRISCH

NATIONAL REPUBLICAN PARTY

All the presidential electors chosen in 1824 were Jeffersonian Republicans, but the party failed to unite on a candidate and the electors divided their votes among four Republican leaders who sought the presidency. Election by the House of Representatives followed in 1825 and resulted in the choice of John Quincy Adams on the first ballot. Because Adams won partly through the support of Henry Clay and his friends and then placed the Kentuckian in the Cabinet as secretary of state, opposing elements drew together in support of Andrew Jackson. Thus the Jeffersonian Republicans became divided into two parties. Leaders and members of both wings continued to call themselves Republicans, but often those who adhered to the administration were called Clay-Adams men, while those who rallied to the standard of Jackson were called Jackson men. As the years passed, members of the Clay-Adams party were referred to as National Republicans and those of the Jackson faction as Democratic-Republicans. Most of the Federalists remaining on the scene in 1825 gravitated to the National Republicans, though many of them joined the Jackson party. Accurately speaking, there were no Whigs and no Democrats until 1834. Then the National Republican party was absorbed by the new and larger Whig party, and Democratic-Republicans took on the name Democrats during the next few years.

BIBLIOGRAPHY

William O. Lynch, *Fifty Years of Party Warfare.*

— WILLIAM O. LYNCH

NATIONAL RIFLE ASSOCIATION

National Rifle Association (NRA) was founded in 1871 to encourage marksmanship and is the largest organization in the United States opposed to gun control. The NRA lobbies to protect the rights of gun owners and to oppose more stringent gun controls through its Institute for Legislative Action and its literal interpretation of the Second Amendment to the U.S. Constitution ("the right of the people to keep and bear Arms, shall not be infringed"), contrary to the Supreme Court interpretation of the amendment. The organization has its largest following in small town and rural areas. For many years the NRA was considered one of the most powerful lobbying groups in Washington, but its failure to prevent passage of the Brady Handgun Violence Prevention Act (Brady Bill) in 1993 and the federal Crime Bill in 1994 was seen by many observers as evidence that the NRA's influence had diminished, while public concerns about crime had increased.

The NRA lobbies to protect the rights of gun owners and to oppose limits to gun ownership.

[See also Gun Control.]

BIBLIOGRAPHY

Osha Gray Davidson, *Under Fire: The NRA and the Battle for Gun Control* (New York, 1993).
Gary Kleck, *Point Blank: Guns and Violence in America* (Hawthorne, N.Y., 1991).
James D. Wright, Peter H. Rossi, and Kathleen Daly, *Under the Gun* (Hawthorne, N.Y., 1983).

— JAMES D. WRIGHT

NATIONAL ROAD

National Road, the name often given to the section of the Cumberland Road extending from Wheeling (in present-day West Virginia) to its western terminus in Ohio. This western portion was probably not so significant as was the section built from Cumberland, Md., to Wheeling (1815–18), for much of the traffic in the West was diverted to steamboats on the Ohio River. As the interior of Ohio was developed, the National Road through that state became a crowded highway; as many as a hundred teams might be encountered in a journey of twenty miles.

For some years construction west of Wheeling was uncertain because of constitutional questions, raised especially by old-school Republicans. The work was begun from Wheeling toward Zanesville, Ohio, in 1825, following (Ebenezer) Zane's Trace. By 1833 the road was opened to Columbus. The last appropriation for the road—in Ohio, Indiana, and Illinois—was made by Congress in 1838. Parts of the road had been surrendered to the states following President James Monroe's veto of a bill for the collection of tolls by the federal government in 1822. The states undertook repairs and erected tollgates to ensure the financing of such operations. The road through Indiana was completed only in 1850 by a state corporation. When Illinois received the custody of its portion, it was unfinished, although graded and bridged as far west as Vandalia, then the state capital.

The road meant less to Indiana and Illinois than to Ohio, and after 1850 the canal, the railroad, and the telegraph contributed generally to the decline of its importance. With the advent of the automobile the National Road became U.S. Route 40, a primary route for motor travel in the United States.

BIBLIOGRAPHY

Philip D. Jordan, *The National Road.*

— FRANCIS PHELPS WEISENBURGER

NATIONAL URBAN LEAGUE

Founded in New York in 1911 through the consolidation of the Committee for Improving the Industrial Condition of Negroes in New York (1906), the National League for the Protection of Colored Women (1906), and the Committee on Urban Conditions Among Negroes (1910), the National Urban League quickly established itself as the principal agency dealing with the problems of blacks in American cities. An interracial organization committed to integration, it relied on tools of negotiation, persuasion, education, and investigation to accomplish its economic and social goals. Concerned chiefly with gaining jobs for blacks, it has placed workers in the private sector, attacked the color line in organized labor, sponsored programs of vocational guidance and job training, and striven for the establishment of governmental policies of equal employment opportunity. During the Great Depression it lobbied for the inclusion of Afro-Americans in federal relief and recovery programs; in the 1940's it pressed for an end to discrimination in defense industries and for the desegregation of the armed forces.

In the 1960's the Urban League supplemented its traditional social service approach with a more activist commitment to civil rights.

As much concerned with social welfare as with employment, the Urban League has conducted scientific investigations of conditions among urban blacks as a basis for practical reform. It trained the first corps of professional black social workers and placed them in community service positions. It works for decent housing, recreational facilities, and health and welfare services, and it has counseled Afro-Americans new to the cities on behavior, dress, sanitation, health, and homemaking.

In the 1960's the Urban League supplemented its traditional social service approach with a more activist commitment to civil rights: it embraced direct action and community organization, sponsored leadership training and voter-education projects, helped organize massive popular demonstrations in support of the enforcement of civil rights and economic justice (the March on Washington of 1963 and the Poor People's Campaign of 1968), called for a domestic Marshall Plan, and began to concentrate on building ghetto power among Afro-Americans as a means to social change.

BIBLIOGRAPHY

Guichard Parris and Lester Brooks, *Blacks in the City: A History of the National Urban League.*

Nancy J. Weiss, *The National Urban League, 1910–1940.*

— NANCY J. WEISS

NATIVE AMERICANS

The U.S. census of 1990 enumerated some 2 million Native Americans, a more than 40 percent increase over 1980, making them one of the fastest-growing ethnic groups in the country, although they constitute less than 1 percent of the total U.S. population. The Cherokee (308,000) and Navajo (219,000) are the largest tribal groups. More than 60 percent of Native Americans live in such cities as Los Angeles, Chicago, and New York. The urban environment fosters contacts and cultural exchange through such institutions as the American Indian Community House in New York City. Native Americans generally return home to reservations each year, and some attempt to relocate to home reservations at some time in their lives.

Reservation environments, always fragile, have felt the impact of industrialization. Oil wells, coal mines, and the extraction of natural gas and uranium have disrupted environments from the Navajo and Hopi reservations in the Southwest to Inuit communities at the edge of the Arctic Sea. Hydroelectric projects have decimated fish populations in the Northwest, and pollution has had a deleterious effect on reservation ecologies. The expanding U.S. population in the Southwest has placed severe constrictions on water use, and Indians have had to sue for their water rights, sometimes successfully. The Clean Air Act of 1977 made it possible for the Northern Cheyenne to shut down or alter the operations of factories polluting their territories. The Exxon Corporation agreed to pay $20 million when the Exxon *Valdez* oil spill in 1989 ruined Alaskan hunting and fishing grounds at least in the short run. In some communities people were contaminated by nuclear radiation as a result of mining operations, particularly the Navajo. Others, such as the Chickasaw, offered to store nuclear waste to make money from government contracts, much to the dismay of local environmentalists and some tribal members.

Since the 1970s the past generation of Native Americans has attempted to revive such religious rituals as pipe ceremonies, spirit dances, sweats, and vision quests. Programs have sprung up to record and pass down tribal languages. Nonetheless, various forms of Christianity have become "traditional" in virtually every community, and perhaps only 100 of the 300 or so aboriginal languages are still spoken, many only by a handful of elders. At most, one of three Native Americans speaks a native language. Traditions are always in danger, especially when half of marriages are to non-Indians.

In 1977 the American Indian Policy Review Commission recommended that the United States recognize greater Native American sovereignty. The next two decades witnessed a marked growth in Indian sovereignty, despite congressional reluctance to accept the commission's report. Tribes possess the right to determine membership; 147 tribal courts have power not only over members but nonmembers in their territories. Tribal governments possess a right to tax their members. Reservation businesses have an exemption from state sales taxes. By 1995 federally recognized tribes had increased to 547, an increase of 22 since the federal acknowledgment process began in 1978. In the mid-1990s more than 100 other groups were seeking recognition. In 1994 President Bill Clinton issued a directive to federal agencies to treat the tribes with the same deference given to state governments.

Based on the Indian Claims Commission (ICC) Act (1946), tribes have pressed suits against the United States and individual states for recompense or return of lands taken illegally. In 1978 the ICC expired, after hearing 670 cases, with another 80 cases appealed. It had awarded $774 million to claimants. In the next decade the courts awarded another $487 million. From the Penobscot in Maine to the Puyallup in Washington, tribes have received substantial payments. Some tribes, such as the Sioux in South Dakota, have refused cash settlements, holding out for return of lands. Award money has helped tribes establish investment schemes and social service systems. Titles to lands have increased, so that 4 percent of U.S. land in 1995 was held by tribes on 267 reservations. Some 140 of the total 287 reservations in the United States are entirely tribally owned.

The Indian Gaming Regulatory Act of 1988 encouraged Indian nations to establish gambling casinos, with the approval of and regulation by individual states. By 1995 seventy-four tribes had opened casinos, none more successful than the 300-member Mashantucket Pequot, who earned $600 million in profits in 1993 alone and who provide $80 million from these earnings each year as a "gift" (technically not a tax) to the state of Connecticut. Their $10 million bequest to the Smithsonian Institution (to help create the National Museum of the American Indian) was the largest donation ever received by the Smithsonian. By the mid-1990s Native American gaming was a $6 billion industry. Gambling is not the only form of economic enterprise on reservations. The Mescalero Apache maintain resorts; the Ak-Chin Pima and Maricopa grow cotton; the Choctaw assemble wire devices for automobiles; the Skagit make decorative boxes and sell salmon; and the Turtle Mountain Chippewa build house trailers. The Passamaquoddy hired investment bankers who helped boost the tribe's portfolio to $100 million. The Cherokee produce parts for military contractors. Native American art earns $500 million a year, protected from forgeries by the 1990 Indian Arts and Crafts Act.

Since the mid-1970s public and governmental sympathy for Native American culture has been growing, and the American Indian Religious Freedom Act (1978) attempted to direct governmental agencies to protect Indian spiritual interests, such as sacred sites. In 1992 the Columbus Quincentenary was marked by a debunking of Columbus's accomplishments, as tribes asserted the value of their ways of life. When the film *Dances with Wolves* played to packed movie houses in 1990, audiences applauded the deaths of white soldiers at the hands of the noble Lakota Sioux. Not everyone applauds Indian commerce. The Interstate Congress for Equal Rights and Responsibilities has attempted many times since its founding in 1976 to abrogate Native American treaties and hence destroy the underpinnings of recognition and sovereignty. The landmark decision in *United States* v. *Washington* (1979) gave half of the salmon catch in the state of Washington to Native Americans based upon treaty rights, which not only helped Northwest Indian economies but aroused the fury of non-Native American fishermen from Washington to Wisconsin.

In 1990, the median annual per capita income on Indian reservations was $5,000, and unemployment ran as high as 80 percent.

Since the 1970s there has sometimes been violence within Indian communities, such as among the Mohawk at Akwesasne, N.Y. Several times in the 1970s and 1990s fighting broke out, and violence occurred in 1990 over the issue of gambling. Alcoholism continued to plague Native American communities throughout North America, with rates three times those in U.S. society as a whole. Suicides, accidental deaths, and arrest rates are connected to alcohol, and fetal-alcohol-syndrome births were distressingly high, as many as one-fourth of all births on some reservations.

Indians are the poorest population group in the United States, with 31 percent living in poverty in 1990. On reservations the median household income per annum was $13,000, per capita income was under $5,000, and unemployment was as high as 80 percent. The poorest county in the United States (Shannon, S.Dak.) was that of the Pine Ridge Lakota Sioux Reservation, where two-thirds of the population lived below the poverty line and per capita income was $3,000. In 1978 Congress passed the Tribally Controlled Community College Assistance Act; in 1995 there were twenty-six Native American-run colleges or junior colleges from the state of Washington to Michigan, most of them on the northern Great Plains. Only three are four-year institutions, including Sinte Gleska University in Rosebud, S.Dak. About 13,000 students attend these colleges. Tribal colleges emphasize Native American values and traditions, as well as training Indians for jobs in the modern world.

[See also Exxon Valdez*; Gambling; Poverty.]*

BIBLIOGRAPHY

Mary B. Davis, ed., *Native America in the Twentieth Century: An Encyclopedia* (New York, 1994).

Marlita A. Reddy, ed., *Statistical Record of Native North Americans* (Detroit, 1993).

— CHRISTOPHER VECSEY

NATIVISM

Nativism, the policy of favoring native inhabitants of a country as against immigrants, has through the course of American history fostered antagonism toward the Roman Catholic church and its communicants rather than toward any particular alien group. Until well into the 20th century many Americans consistently held to the belief that this church endangered both the traditional Protestantism and the democratic institutions of the United States and viewed immigrants with alarm because many were Catholics rather than because of their alien birth.

This antipapal sentiment, brought to America by the first English colonists, was fostered in the new country by the 18th-century wars with Catholic France and Spain. Colonial laws and colonial writing both reflected this intolerance. The Revolution abruptly changed the American attitude toward Roman Catholicism, for the liberal spirit of the Declaration of Independence and the French alliance of 1778 both contributed toward a more tolerant spirit. It endured until the 1820's, despite the efforts of New England Federalists, who were largely responsible for the antialien sections of the Alien and Sedition Acts and the proposals of the Hartford Convention.

Anti-Catholic sentiment reappeared in the late 1820's, inspired by a mounting Catholic immigration and by the English propaganda that accompanied the passage of the Catholic Emancipation Act of 1829. Protestants, under the influence of the revivalism of Charles G. Finney, quickly rushed to the defense of their religion. *The Protestant* was founded in 1830, and a year later the New York Protestant Association began holding public discussions to "illustrate the history and character of Popery." By 1834 intolerance had grown to a point at which the mob destruction of an Ursuline convent at Charlestown, Mass., was condoned rather than condemned by the mass of the people. This sign of popular favor resulted in the launching of two new anti-Catholic papers, the *Downfall of Babylon* and the *American Protestant Vindicator*; the release of a flood of anti-Catholic books and pamphlets; and the formation of a national organization, the Protestant Reformation Society in 1836.

The sensational propaganda spread by the Protestant Reformation Society probably turned many Protestants against Catholicism, but it remained for the New York school controversy of the early 1840's to win over the churchgoing middle class. In this controversy Catholic protests against the reading of the King James version of the Scriptures in the public schools were immediately misrepresented by propagandists, who convinced Protestants that Catholics were opposed to all reading of the Bible. Alarmed, the churches took up the cry against Rome, giving nativists sufficient strength to organize the American Republican party with an anti-Catholic, antiforeign platform. Before more than local political success could be gained, a series of riots between natives and immigrants in Philadelphia in 1844 turned popular sentiment against the anti-Catholic crusade. For the remainder of the decade the Mexican War and the slavery controversy absorbed national attention.

Nativistic leaders, recognizing that the stigma of past sensationalism could be wiped out only by a new organization, formed the American Protestant Society in 1844 to take the place of the Protestant Reformation Society. This new body, by promising a labor of "light and love . . . for the salvation of Romanists," won the endorsement of nearly all Protestant sects and influenced hundreds of clergymen to deliver anti-Catholic sermons. Its methods proved so successful that in 1849 a merger was effected with two lesser anti-Catholic organizations, the Foreign Evangelical Society and the Christian Alliance, to form the most important of the pre-Civil War societies, the American and Foreign Christian Union, pledged to win both the United States and Europe to Protestantism.

The propaganda machinery created by these organized efforts, combined with the heavy immigration from famine-stricken Ireland and Germany, so alarmed Americans that political nativism seemed again feasible. The Compromise of 1850, apparently settling the slavery question for all time, opened the way for the Know-Nothing, or American, party, which enjoyed remarkable success in 1854 and 1855, carrying a number of states and threatening to sweep the nation in the presidential election of 1856. Its brief career was abruptly halted by the passage of the Kansas-Nebraska Act, for as Americans became absorbed in the slavery conflict, they forgot their fears of Rome. The Civil War doomed both the Know-Nothing party and the American and Foreign Christian Union to speedy extinction.

After the war the nation's attention was so centered on the problems of reconstruction and economic rehabilitation that nativistic sentiments remained dormant until the 1880's. By that time mounting foreign immigration and unsettled industrial conditions had created a state of mind receptive to antialien propaganda, but instead of being directed against immigrants, this propaganda was again aimed almost exclusively at the Roman Catholic church. A "committee of one hundred" from Boston flooded the country with anti-Catholic documents; newspapers bent on exposing the "errors of Rome" were founded; and a fraudulent document alleged to be a papal bull calling for the massacre of all Protestants "on or about the feast of St. Ignatius in the Year of our Lord, 1893" was widely circulated and given credence. The American Protective Association, formed in 1887 to crystallize these prejudices, although pledging its members neither to vote for nor employ Catholics, scarcely mentioned Protestant aliens, indicating that religion and not birthplace was the point of objection.

In the period following World War I, an intense nationalism in the U.S. bred antagonism toward all groups that were not conservative, Protestant Americans.

The political failure of the American Protective Association combined with the interest aroused by the free silver campaign of 1896 to check nativistic agitation. In the years after 1898 there was another brief flurry occasioned by the continuing immigration and two events that centered attention on the Roman Catholic church: the celebration of the centenary of the erection of the diocese of Baltimore into a metropolitan see and the meeting in Chicago of the first American Catholic Missionary Conference. New anti-Catholic organizations were formed, the most prominent being the Guardians of Liberty, the Knights of Luther, the Covenanters, and the American Pathfinders. Anti-Catholic newspapers, led by the *Menace*, began to appear, but before this phase of the movement could be translated into politics World War I intervened.

The next burst of nativistic excitement occurred during the 1920's. The United States, in the restless period that followed World War I, developed an intense nationalism that bred antagonism toward immigrants, Communists, and Catholics—toward all groups that were not conservative, Protestant Americans. During the early part of the decade the Ku Klux Klan shaped and fostered this prejudice. The Klan's excesses and political corruption brought about its decline, but intolerance did not abate—a fact clearly shown by the presidential campaign of 1928. The presence of Alfred E. Smith, a Catholic, as the Democratic candidate aroused a bitter nativistic propaganda that was important in causing his defeat.

The depression of the 1930's and World War II focused attention away from nativism, and the election of a Roman Catholic, John F. Kennedy, to the presidency in 1960 seemed to declare that it was substantially a dead issue.

BIBLIOGRAPHY

John Higham, *Strangers in the Land.*

Ira M. Leonard and Robert Parmet, *American Nativism, 1830–1860.*

Seymour Lipset and Earl Raab, *The Politics of Unreason.*

— RAY ALLEN BILLINGTON

NAT TURNER'S REBELLION

Nat Turner's Rebellion (1831) was the most significant of a number of slave revolts that occurred in the United States. Under the leadership of Nat Turner, a group of Southampton County, Va., slaves conspired to revolt against the slave system.

Nat Turner was a thirty-one-year-old religious mystic who considered it God's work that he strike against slavery. He was literate and had, from time to time, served as a preacher. He had been owned by several different whites and on one occasion had run away from his owner after a change in overseers.

Southampton County, in which the uprising took place, is located in the tidewater section of Virginia near the North Carolina border. It was entirely agricultural and rural. In 1830 its population included 9,501 blacks and 6,574 whites.

On Aug. 21, 1831, Turner and six other slaves attacked and killed Turner's owner and the owner's family, gathered arms and ammunition as they could find it, and set out to gain support from other slaves. Turner's force grew to about seventy-five slaves, and they killed approximately sixty whites. On Aug. 23, while en route to the county seat at Jerusalem, the blacks encountered a large force of white volunteers and trained militia and were defeated. Turner escaped and attempted unsuccessfully to gather other supporters. He was captured on Oct. 30, sentenced to death by hanging on Nov. 5 after a brief trial, and executed on Nov. 11. Several of his followers had been hanged earlier.

The immediate effect of the rebellion on the actions of whites was the institution of a reign of terror resulting in the murder of a number of innocent blacks, the passage of more stringent slave laws, and the more vigorous enforcement of existing statutes. The immediate effect of the rebellion on the attitudes of blacks toward slavery and toward themselves is difficult if not impossible to document, but there is evidence that Turner was highly thought of. The long-range effect was to add to the conflict over slavery that led to the Civil War.

BIBLIOGRAPHY

Herbert Aptheker, *Nat Turner's Slave Rebellion.*

Henry Irving Tragle, *The Southampton Slave Revolt of 1831.*

— HENRY N. DREWRY

NATURALIZATION

Citizenship in the United States is acquired by birth—either in the United States or abroad to American citizen parents—or by naturalization. Naturalization is the formal and legal adoption of an alien into the membership of a political community. Under English practice, as late as the 19th century, naturalization was granted only through special acts of Parliament. But the American colonial assemblies, subject to frequent interference from Parliament, exercised a limited right to naturalize certain individuals and classes of persons. Upon achieving independence, the states were free to determine their own conditions for citizenship, but diversity in state legislation resulted. Therefore, the Constitution (Article I, Section 8, Clause 4) provided that Congress shall have power "to establish an uniform Rule of Naturalization." Since then it has been clear that the authority to grant naturalization rests exclusively with Congress.

Naturalization can occur in several ways. The principal methods of granting citizenship to aliens are through collective naturalization, judicial naturalization, and derivative naturalization. Collective naturalization entails the simultaneous grant of citizenship to groups of aliens, ordinarily following the acquisition of territory in which they reside, and it is usually accomplished by treaty or by statute. In the acquisition of several territories—for example, Louisiana, Florida, the Mexican cessions, and Alaska—such provisions were incorporated into the treaties of acquisition. The Texans received American citizenship through a joint resolution of Congress (1845). By statutes, citizenship was thereafter bestowed on the Hawaiians (1900), the Puerto Ricans (1917), the American Indians (1924), the U.S. Virgin Islanders (1927), and the Guamanians (1950).

Whereas these methods of collective naturalization do not necessarily require any individual applications or the issuance of formal citizenship papers, judicial naturalization, which is the most widely used and recognized form, is authorized by general legislation and entails an individual application by each alien seeking naturalization. Provisions for judicial naturalization have been on the statute books since the First Congress enacted a naturalization law in 1790. A major revision of the naturalization laws occurred in 1906 and instituted procedural reforms to eliminate widespread frauds in the naturalization process, particularly on the eve of elections. Other major revisions and recodifications of the naturalization laws occurred in 1940 and 1952.

Since the First Congress the process of individual naturalization has been entrusted to the courts. Brief deviations from this consistent practice occurred during World War I and during World War II, when administrative officers were authorized to grant naturalization to aliens serving overseas in the armed forces of the United States. The present statute authorizes the grant of naturalization by specified naturalization courts, which include all federal district courts and designated state courts. Since 1906 administrative officers, now in the Department of Justice, have been entrusted with important responsibilities in supervising the naturalization process and in assisting the courts.

In order to qualify for naturalization an alien must satisfy several preliminary requirements. First, he or she must have been lawfully admitted to the United States for permanent residence and have resided continuously thereafter in the country for five years. The requisite period of residence is reduced for certain special classes, including spouses of American citizens. In addition, the applicant for naturalization must establish that during the prescribed period of residence he has been of good moral character and attached to the principles of the Constitution of the United States. For many years the naturalization laws limited eligibility to "free white persons" and thus excluded blacks and Orientals. These racial disqualifications were gradually modified, and they were completely eliminated by the McCarran-Walter Act of 1952, which provides that the right to naturalization shall not be denied or abridged on the basis of race or sex.

The procedure is relatively simple. At one time a preliminary declaration of intention ("first papers") was required, but this requirement was eliminated in 1952. Now a person who believes himself or herself qualified for naturalization, after completing the requisite lawful residence, obtains a naturalization application from the Immigration and Naturalization Service and files it with that service, which processes the application and then notifies the applicant to appear in court with two witnesses in order to file a formal petition for naturalization. The applicant and the witnesses are questioned by a naturalization examiner, who conducts any necessary inquiries and investigations and makes a recommendation to the naturalization court. The next step is the final court hearing. In most instances this is a formality, since a favorable recommendation by the naturalization examiner is usually approved by the court without further inquiry. In exceptional cases the court conducts its own inquiry. The final step in the naturalization process is the court order, usually admitting the applicant to citizenship and directing that he or she take the oath of allegiance. Thereupon the applicant becomes a citizen of the United States, and the court issues a certificate of naturalization as evidence of his or her citizenship status.

Derivative naturalization is an automatic process and, like collective naturalization, does not depend upon the beneficiary's application. In appropriate cases, it results from the naturalization of another person, usually a spouse or parent.

Until 1922 an alien woman acquired derivative U.S. citizenship upon marriage to an American or upon the naturalization of her alien husband. As one aspect of the political emancipation of women the Cable Act of Sept. 22, 1922, provided that a married woman would thereafter retain and determine her own citizenship. Since then an alien woman who is married to a citizen of the United States does not automatically acquire U.S. citizenship. She may make her own application for naturalization, after her lawful admission for permanent residence, and her required period of residence is reduced to three years.

The naturalization laws have always provided for automatic acquisition of derivative citizenship by alien minor children upon the naturalization of their parents, although the conditions for such acquisition have varied. Under the present law, effective since 1952, an alien child generally acquires U.S. citizenship upon the naturalization of his parents if such naturalization and the child's acquisition of lawful permanent residence in the United States occur while the child is under the age of sixteen years.

BIBLIOGRAPHY

C. Gordon and B. Rosenfield, *Immigration Law and Procedure.*

— CHARLES GORDON

NAVAHO

Navaho, or "Navajo" according to tribal preference, is a southwestern American Indian tribe paradoxical in several ways. Their culture, despite changes in their location and their subsistence patterns, remains remarkably intact. Further, even though they reside in the inhospitable San Juan plateau of northern Arizona and New Mexico, spilling over into the extreme south of Utah and Colorado, they constitute the largest contemporary American Indian tribe. In 1937 a report of the Bureau of Indian Affairs estimated the Navaho population at 45,000, and it had more than doubled by 1970.

The Athapascan language, spoken by the Navaho and Apache, is not indigenous to the area, and archaeologists continue to debate the question of precisely when the migration of these two tribes into the American Southwest occurred. It was probably late pre-Columbian times, about 1375–1475. The Athapascan incursions may have been a factor in the abandonment by the Pueblo of their great sites of Mesa Verde, Colo., and Chaco Canyon, N. Mex., and their general spread eastward, although the great drought of the end of the 13th century may also have played a role. Since the Athapascan languages are mainly focused in northwest Canada and central Alaska, it has been assumed that it is from this area that the Navaho and the Apache gradually made their way. An original hunting culture may be assumed, which changed as accommodation was made to desert conditions. Whereas the Apache retain some remnants of their northern origins, notably in their stress on the rituals surrounding girls' puberty, the Navaho were so heavily influenced by their Pueblo neighbors that much of their culture is clearly of Pueblo, and especially Hopi, origin. It must be stressed that the resemblance is superficial; to the extent that the Navaho adopted Pueblo culture, they so modified it that they created a mode of life distinctively their own.

The Navaho were drawn into the southwestern farming complex. But whereas the Pueblo chose to build permanent towns and to farm the lands adjacent, the Navaho spread out over a vast area, preferring to develop small, isolated family plots and moving to new fields as water and wood were available. From the Spanish the Navaho acquired domesticated sheep and, as a result, assumed a mixed farming-pastoral mode. The Navaho are the only American Indians who depend on livestock (exclusive of the horse), and they were successful in adapting their culture to this new economic base even though the problems associated with sheep raising, water supply, overgrazing, and soil conservation posed serious difficulties for so populous a group. Even in derivative cultural elements the stamp of the Navaho is distinctive. For weaving, they adopted a loom of European type, but the designs they employ are distinctive variations of basic southwestern artistic elements. Their clothing is Pueblo in origin, but again with a Navaho accent, at least for men; women's dress suggests 18th-century Mexico. A brush shelter, reminiscent of the Great Basin, was the rule among them but gave way to the hogan, a rounded, often octagonal dwelling, in the construction of which they relied on brush. Their corn cultivation is Pueblo; their sheep husbandry is Spanish;

and their hunting and gathering techniques are suggestive of the Basin.

The names and structure of the matrilineal units on which Navaho social organization is based suggest the Hopi and Zuni. And the very existence of the Navaho as a tribe is based not on any political structure but rather on language and this network of maternal clans, some sixty in all, which are diffused through the group. Men live until marriage with the mother's clan. At marriage, men go to live in the grouping of the wife. Divorce is not unusual, the father leaving and the children remaining with the mother as members of her clan. Although a man may act as a leader of a local group, any authority he has is wholly informal. It was not until 1923 that the Navaho organized a tribal council.

It is in religion that the Navaho penchant for realigning borrowed cultural elements comes most to the fore. The paraphernalia of their religion is clearly Pueblo: corn pollen, rain symbolism, ritual curing, altars made of multicolored sands (the so-called "dry" paintings), masks, and so through a host of parallels. But while Pueblo religion aimed primarily at fertility and rain, Navaho ritual was directed toward curing. The Navaho developed a series of chants, rituals associated with the creation of a balance beween man and nature, and through these chants they sought the establishment of communal good through the restoration of the health of the ill. The various chants, or "ways," are extremely complex, highly ritualized, and reflective of a uniquely Navaho development.

Apart from the contacts that brought sheep into Navaho life, the group remained fairly aloof from Spanish contact. Always at war with their Pueblo neighbors, the Navaho extended their depredations to white settlers. Treaties of 1846 and 1849 failed to keep the Navaho at peace, and in 1863 Col. Christopher ("Kit") Carson led a punitive expedition against them, destroying their crops and rounding up their sheep; they were carried off into captivity at Bosque Redondo, N. Mex., on the Pecos River, supervised by a garrison at Fort Sumner. Continued resistance by the Navaho—and the great cost to the War Department of enforcing their confinement—led the federal government in 1868 to sign a treaty with the Navaho whereby a reservation of nearly 4 million acres was set aside for their use in New Mexico and Arizona. Since then they have increased remarkably in population but have generally maintained their composite yet vital culture.

Perhaps no other native American tribe has so influenced surrounding peoples as have the Navaho. They have created a special tone in developing their widely disseminated art forms. Their rugs, woven by women from wool and fibers, continue to be popular, although they do not reach the high standards of the beginning of the 20th century. Their silver necklaces, bracelets, rings, and other jewelry—made originally of Mexican coin silver by processes learned from Mexicans sometime in the 1850's—now incorporate locally mined turquoise, reaching the level of a fine art; it is now being copied by various of the Pueblo, notably the Zuni, as a source of cash.

A Navaho man and woman survey the reservation land by carriage in 1939. An 1868 treaty established the reservation of nearly 4 million acres in New Mexico and Arizona. (UPI/Corbis-Bettmann)

BIBLIOGRAPHY

Clyde Kluckhohn, *The Navaho.*
Dorothea Leighton and Clyde Kluckhohn, *The Children of the People.*
E. Z. Vogt, *Peoples of Rimrock.*

— ROBERT F. SPENCER

NAVIGATION ACTS

Navigation Acts had their origin in Britain's regulation of its coastwise trade, which was extended to the colonies as they developed. The first formal legislation affecting the colonies was enacted by Parliament in 1649 and in 1651. This legislation was modified, consolidated, and reenacted in 1660 and became the basic Navigation Act. This law and others were revised in the final act of 1696. The object was to protect British shipping against competition from Dutch and other foreign seamen. Under these acts no goods could be imported into or exported from any British colony in Asia, Africa, or America except in English vessels, English-owned, and manned by crews three-fourths English. Other clauses limited the importation of any products of Asia, Africa, or America into England to English vessels and provided that goods from foreign countries could be imported into England only in vessels of the exporting countries or in English ships.

Wherever the word "English" was used in these and subsequent acts it referred to the nationality of individuals and not to their place of residence. Thus American colonists were just as much English as their compatriots who resided in London. The net effect of these basic laws was to give Englishmen and English ships a legal monopoly of all trade between various colonial ports and between colonial ports and England. Even the trade between colonial ports and foreign countries was limited to English vessels. Thus foreign vessels were excluded entirely from colonial ports and could trade only at ports in the British Isles.

Another field of legislation related to commodities. Certain important colonial products were enumerated and could be exported from the place of production only to another British colony or to England. At first the list included tobacco, sugar, indigo, cotton, wool, ginger, and fustic and other dyewoods. Later, the list was extended to include naval stores, hemp, rice, molasses, beaver skins, furs, copper ore, iron, and lumber.

Asian goods and European manufactures could be imported into the colonies only from England—though an exception was made in the case of salt or wine from the Azores or the Madeira Islands and food products from Ireland or Scotland.

The clauses of the Navigation Acts in which these commodities were enumerated were enforced by a system of bonds that required the master of the vessel to comply with the provisions of the acts. These operated in such a way as to give American shipowners a practical monopoly of the trade between the continental and West Indian colonies. Residents of Great Britain in turn had a general monopoly of the carrying of the heavy enumerated goods from the colonies to the British Isles.

Closely related to the Navigation Acts was another series of measures called Trade Acts, and usually confused with the Navigation Acts proper. Most of these were enacted after 1700, and they gradually developed into a complicated system of trade control and encouragement. The general plan was to make the entire British Empire prosperous and the trade of one section complementary to that of other sections.

Colonists were largely limited to buying British manufactures. This was not necessarily a disadvantage, because an elaborate system of export bounties was provided so that British goods were actually cheaper in the colonies than similar foreign goods. These bounties averaged more than £38,000 per year for the ten years preceding the Revolution. From 1757 to 1770 the bounties on British linens exported to the colonies totaled £346,232 according to British treasury reports. In addition to bounties there was a series of rebates, or drawbacks, of duties on European goods exported to the colonies. These, too, ran into formidable sums. Those to the West Indies alone amounted to £34,000 in 1774. The average payments from the British treasury in bounties and drawbacks on exports to the colonies in 1764 amounted to about £250,000 sterling per year.

The general plan of the Navigation and Trade Acts was to make the entire British Empire prosperous and the trade of each section complementary to that of the others.

Colonial production of articles desired in the British markets was encouraged by a variety of measures. Colonial tobacco was given a complete monopoly of the home market by the prohibition of its growth in England and the imposition of heavy import duties on the competing Spanish tobacco. Other colonial products were encouraged by tariff duties, so levied as to discriminate sharply in favor of the colonial product and against the competing foreign product. Some colonial commodities that were produced in greater volume than English demand called for were given rebates on reexportation so as to facilitate their flow through British markets to their foreign destinations. In other cases surplus colonial products, such as rice, were permitted to be exported directly to foreign colonies and to southern Europe without passing through England. In still other cases direct cash bounties were paid on such colonial products as hemp, indigo, lumber, and silk on their arrival in England. These alone totaled more than £82,000 from 1771 to 1775. Naval stores also received liberal bounties, totaling £1,438,762 from 1706 to 1774, and at the time of the Revolution were averaging £25,000 annually.

In the main the navigation system was mutually profitable to colonies and mother country. Occasionally colonial industry was discouraged by parliamentary prohibition if it threatened to develop into serious competition with an important home industry: notable are the laws forbidding the intercolonial export of hats made in the colonies and wool grown or manufactured in the colonies and the act forbidding the setting up of new mills for the production of wrought iron and steel. These laws produced some local complaint, although they evidently affected few people.

So long as the trade and navigation laws were limited to the regulation of trade and the promotion of the total commerce of the empire, they were generally popular in America; at least that was true after 1700. The attempt to use them as taxation measures was resisted. The enumerated products came largely from the colonies that remained loyal. The bounties went largely to the colonies that revolted. The New England shipping industry rested directly on the protection of the Navigation Acts. Consequently the First Continental Congress in its resolutions approved the navigation system, and Benjamin Franklin offered to have the acts reenacted by every colonial legislature in America and to guarantee them for a hundred years if taxation of America were abandoned.

BIBLIOGRAPHY

George E. Howard, *Preliminaries of the Revolution.*

— O. M. DICKERSON

NAVY, UNITED STATES

This article discusses the U.S. Navy under the following headings: The Revolution to the Mexican War; The Civil War to World War I; World War II to Vietnam; Peacetime Work; Training and Education; Fleets; Ships; Armament; Facilities; Naval Reserve.

The Revolution to the Mexican War

As colonials, Americans had served in the British navy and aboard merchantmen and had been expert privateers against Britain's foes. In seeking independence, it was natural for them to carry the struggle to sea. Such efforts were spontaneous and opportunistic, the most consequential resulting from the issuance of some 2,000 letters of marque.

The Continental navy was founded by the Continental Congress on Oct. 13, 1775, to perform duties that privateers shunned. Of twenty-seven small men-of-war at sea, only three survived hard fighting and cruising. Continental captains, including John Paul Jones, John Barry, Lambert Wickes, and Nicholas Biddle, were distinguished from privateers by eagerness to engage warships: Capt. Biddle blew up with the 32-gun frigate *Randolph* against the 64-gun ship-of-the-line *Yarmouth* on Mar. 7, 1778, while Jones gave the navy its battle cry of "I have not yet begun to fight!" in conquering the 44-gun frigate *Serapis* with the 42-gun merchantman *Bonhomme Richard* on Sept. 23, 1779. Eleven colonies also had navies that, when totaled, exceeded Continental numbers; Pennsylvania's was particularly aggressive under leaders like Capt. Joshua Barney.

During the Revolution, all maritime branches brought in about 800 prizes, whose cargoes were indispensable to the cause, especially before 1779 when the French alliance and sea power became effective. The British were further humiliated by the capture of 102 minor men-of-war mounting 2,322 guns, besides 16 privateers with 226 guns. It was the French navy that was decisive, by keeping the Royal Navy from relieving besieged Gen. Charles Cornwallis in the Yorktown campaign.

American navies vanished in peacetime. Nevertheless, independence brought problems. Barbary pirates and then warring British and French preyed on U.S. commerce. Consequently, the Navy Department was founded on Apr. 30, 1798. Benjamin Stoddert, as first secretary of the navy, directed twelve frigates and sloops commissioned to protect trade in the West Indies against French freebooters. Appropriately, the first man-of-war afloat was the 44-gun frigate *United States.*

In the Quasi-War with France (1798–1800), the U.S. Navy was expanded to forty-nine vessels through the conversion of merchantmen. Three French warships and eighty-one privateers were captured. Thomas Truxtun was the outstanding captain. In the 36-gun *Constellation,* he took the 40-gun *Insurgente* and shattered in night battle the 40-gun *Vengeance.* More enduringly, as a squadron commander Truxtun infused a professional order and attitude. Similarly, the Tripolitan War (1801–05) was most important for the example and training provided by Commodore Edward Preble.

By 1805, the officer cadre was firmly established. President Thomas Jefferson, alarmed by the implications of having fought offensively overseas, turned to gunboat construction to manifest intent to fight only defensively. Construction was halted on eight 74-gun ships that Stoddert had started. The 176 gunboats that were built proved useless in the War of 1812, while 22 seagoing vessels won glory. The *United States* and its sister *Constitution* under captains Stephen Decatur, Isaac Hull, and William Bainbridge won dazzling victories before preponderant British power closed American ports. Losing 12, the navy captured 15 minor warships and 165 merchantmen. The ubiquitous privateers took an additional 991 merchantmen and 5 small men-of-war. Significant as such successes were in hurting British trade and shortening the war, more significant were the victories of "pygmy fleets" on inland waters. Capt. Oliver Hazard Perry's victory on Lake Erie (Sept. 10, 1813), buttressed by Capt. Thomas Macdonough's on Lake Champlain (Sept. 11, 1814), settled much of the Canadian boundary. Daniel Todd Patterson's handful of ships was essential to the defense of New Orleans. The war stabilized the U.S. Navy, which was rewarded by a few 74-gun ships of the line. The *Independence*, commanded by William Crane and flying the commodore's pendant of William Bainbridge, was the first to go to sea, during the second war with Barbary pirates.

The Algerian War (1815), suppression of West Indian pirates (1816–29), and antislavery patrols (1820–50) provided training for the Mexican War. Then unchallenged, the navy of sixty-three vessels conducted blockade and amphibious operations, the latter destined to become a U.S. specialty. Captains John Sloat and Robert Stockton helped secure California. Captains David Conner and Matthew Perry had the bulk of the fleet in the Gulf of Mexico, making possible the transportation to, and landing at, Veracruz (Mar. 13, 1847) and maintenance of the lifeline for Gen. Winfield Scott's triumphal march to Mexico City.

The Civil War to World War I

When the Civil War began, Gideon Welles, the Union secretary of the navy, had only 8,800 personnel and forty-two of seventy-six vessels ready to close 185 registered harbors in 12,000 miles of indented coastline, exclusive of rivers. Stephen Russell Mallory, the Confederate secretary of the navy, began with 3,000 personnel and twelve sequestered vessels. By war's end, the Union navy had mushroomed to 58,000 sailors in 671 vessels. After Confederate confiscation of some federal ships, the Union lost 109 more. In action, thirty-four warships were sunk conventionally and fourteen by mines, while sixteen were captured. The rigors of blockade were witnessed by thirty-eight men-of-war lost to the sea, including the famous *Monitor*. Seven more burned accidentally. Confederate figures can only be approximated. Extant official records indicate that Mallory approximately doubled manpower and commissioned 209 vessels, always too little and too late.

The Union navy had three main missions: blockade, army cooperation, and commerce protection. Blockade was mounted through capturing a coaling base at Port Royal, S.C. (Nov. 7, 1861), between Charleston and Savannah, and was completed by the amphibious capture of the seaport of Wilmington, Del. (Jan. 15, 1865). Altogether, 1,504 blockade runners were captured or destroyed. Cooperating with the army, the navy helped take the Mississippi River, notably by seizing New Orleans (Apr. 25, 1862) and by providing assistance at Vicksburg (Mar. 13–July 4, 1863). Even more decisive was naval support along the rivers feeding into the Chesapeake Bay. Only on the high seas did the Confederate navy conspicuously succeed; the *Alabama* and 11 other ships took or sank 250 merchantmen. Prudently, one-third to one-half of northern shipowners sought foreign registry. Such shipping did not return to the flag. Since then, government subsidy of the merchant marine has been increasingly necessary.

The Union navy had three main missions: blockade, army cooperation, and commerce protection.

The U.S. Navy withered in peace until given rationale by the historian Alfred Thayer Mahan, whose writings on sea power (1890–1914) became classics. A small "new navy" of only twenty-one modern warcraft was far readier than the Spaniards for the War of 1898, which was distinguished by the easy victories won by Commodore George Dewey at Manila (May 1) and by Commodore William Sampson at Santiago (July 3). The navy won national support and began its expansion to a position of supremacy. Unpleasant duty in helping to suppress insurrection in the newly acquired Philippines was followed by the world cruise of the "great white fleet" of sixteen new battleships (1907–09), which demonstrated the maturity of American engineering as well as the substance for the "big stick" policy then popular.

Through World War I, the navy had 497,030 personnel to man 37 battleships and 1,926 lesser vessels. Contracts for 949 others, including 32 battleships and battle cruisers, would have made the navy almost equal to all others combined, if completed. Operations were unglamorous. Since the British after the Battle of Jutland (1916) contained the German navy, the prime mission of the United States became the establishment of a bridge to France for 2,079,880 troops and their supplies. The submarine was the foe, combated defensively by convoy and escort and offensively by minefield and airplane. The U.S. Navy was brilliantly successful. Although primitive submarines sank nearly 13 million tons of shipping, including 124 American merchantmen, no American soldier was lost in a France-bound convoy. Only 1 of 178 submarines sunk fell to an American destroyer, but the stupendous North Sea mine barrage, 80 percent laid by the United States, sank or damaged about 17 more and reputedly broke the morale of German submariners. War losses were minimal for the navy, which lost 1,142 lives in forty-five miscellaneous men-of-war: thirteen were sunk by U-boats, three by mines, and twenty-nine by collision or mischance. The heaviest combat loss was the Coast Guard cutter *Tampa*, which went down with 111 men. (The Treasury Department's "navy" has been under naval control in all wars except those with Barbary pirates.)

Besides the portents of the submarine and airplane, the war had unveiled the amphibious potential that the navy had in the combat readiness and excellence of the marines. Quintupled from prewar strength to 67,000 men, the U.S. Marine Corps won immortality in France and a firm place in naval plans. In 1933 the Fleet Marine Force was created, a heavy-infantry organization dedicated to amphibious assault at a time when the perfecting of the aircraft carrier and naval gunfire promised to revolutionize war at sea.

World War II to Vietnam

When the storm of World War II broke, the U.S. Navy had the concepts, if not the numbers, for bold, flexible operations. Rebounding from the surprise attack on Pearl Harbor, the navy expanded to 3 million men and women serving on 8 battleships, 48 cruisers, 104 aircraft carriers, 349 destroyers, 203 submarines, 2,236 convoy-escort craft, 886 minesweepers, 4,149 large and 79,418 small amphibious craft, 1,531 auxiliaries, and 22,045 other types. American combat losses to Oct. 1, 1945, were 2 battleships, 5 heavy and 7 escort aircraft carriers, 10 cruisers, 79 destroyers, 52 submarines, 36 minesweepers, 69 PT boats, 172 large amphibious craft, and 254 other types. Casualties of the navy, marines, and Coast Guard totaled 56,206 dead, 8,967 missing, and 80,259 wounded. The U.S. Navy destroyed 132 German and 8 Italian submarines in supplementing air and British naval operations, but as the major combatant in the Pacific theater of war, the navy annihilated the initially triumphant Japanese, sinking 11 battleships, 15 fleet and 5 escort aircraft carriers, 33 cruisers, 119 destroyers, and countless lesser craft.

Fleet Adm. Ernest J. King, who commanded from 1941 to 1945, in his *U.S. Navy at War* divided the Pacific war into four stages. Phase one, from Dec. 7, 1941, to June 1942, was defensive. The period had ten naval engagements capped by the Battle of the Coral Sea (May 7–8, 1942), when Rear Adm. Frank J. Fletcher with the *Yorktown* and *Lexington* carrier task forces stopped a superior Japanese thrust at southeast New Guinea. Superb intelligence procedures detected Japanese intentions to take Midway Island. The ensuing battle (June 3–6, 1942) was the turning point of the war. Outnumbered American carriers decisively decimated their opposites in the first sea fight by fleets whose ships never sighted each other.

The defensive-offensive period of Midway was a brief phase two, merging with phase three, the offensive-defensive period that committed the marines to the long fight for Guadalcanal (Aug. 7, 1942–Feb. 9, 1943) and produced a dozen night battles amid shallows and islands, as well as supporting carrier engagements in the open sea. Together they exacted battle losses exceeding those at Jutland. The Japanese, rebuilding carrier strength after Midway, improvidently fed idle naval aviation into the fray, thus undermining their carrier potential in trying to stop the marine drive up the Solomons to join pressure with Gen. Douglas MacArthur's combined forces outflanking the Japanese naval and air bastion of Rabaul on New Britain. About this time, American submarines hit their stride with a deadliness that sank two-thirds of Japanese shipping, an attrition in itself sufficient to have produced eventual victory through the starvation of Japan.

The pure offensive, phase four, opened with the navy thrusting westward into the Marshall Islands. The Battle of the Philippine Sea, nicknamed the "Marianas Turkey Shoot" (June 19–20, 1944), disclosed the fatal deterioration of Japanese carrier aviation when 402 Japanese planes were downed with an American loss of only 17 planes. Saipan, Guam, Tinian, Peleliu, and Ulithi were milestones in the drive, forging a logistic line for naval juncture with the successful forces of MacArthur in a campaign for recapture of the Philippines. On Oct. 20, 1944, MacArthur landed at Leyte Island. The Japanese naval counterattack produced a complex of farflung actions (Oct. 23–26) that crushed Japan as a naval power and left the home islands completely vulnerable. Japan itself became the objective. To add fullest weight of air power to the assault on Japanese home industry and to supplement the mounting submarine blockade, marines took Iwo Jima at heavy cost (Feb. 19–Mar. 16, 1945), but the island thereafter provided essential fighter cover for long-range bombers. On Apr. 1, marines and army landed on Okinawa, within easy reach of southern Kyushu. Desperate kamikaze attacks failed to dislodge the supporting fleet, which sustained 5,000 fatalities, 368 damaged ships, and 36 minor vessels lost. When atomic attacks on Hiroshima and Nagasaki ended the war, the navy was preparing for the invasion of Kyushu and a drive on Tokyo itself. Strangulation by sea and air had produced the first unconditional surrender of a major nation without invasion.

In the war with Germany, the U.S. Navy was preoccupied anew with defense of sea communications and began as a junior partner to the British navy, which was mastering effective antisubmarine warfare in the period before U.S. belligerency. Concurrently, the Germans were perfecting submarine tactics, making the Battle of the Atlantic bitter and too often close. In the summer of 1943 the advent of American escort-carrier groups ("hunter-killers") gave defense the decisive edge. Allied forces destroyed 753 of a phenomenal 1,170 U-boats (the figures given by German Adm. Karl Doenitz), which sank 197 warships and 2,828 merchantmen totaling 14,687,231 tons (according to the historian Samuel Eliot Morison).

The liberation of Europe was predicated on reentry onto the Continent, which American amphibious techniques made possible. Beginning with a meager 102 vessels for landings in French Morocco (Nov. 8, 1942), the U.S. Navy multiplied amazingly to 2,489 amphibious craft for the Normandy invasion (June 6, 1944) and loaned an equal number to the British. The liberality of such lend-lease is the most convincing evidence that America had noncompetitively overtaken England in naval superiority. England was the recipient not only of amphibious craft but also of an impressive navy in the form of 38 escort-carriers, 189 blue-water convoy-escorts, 9 submarines, 187 minesweepers, and 415 specialized craft. The Soviet Union was second, receiving some 615 naval and military vessels and 90 merchantmen. France was third, with 145 minor men-of-war.

In the uncertainties of the nuclear age, the navy continued to perfect the potentials of carriers, submarines, and amphibians. Gradually budgeted down to 238 major combat craft, 393,893 personnel, and 74,396 marines, the navy was professionally keen in 1950 when the Korean War broke out. Besides vital close air support from carriers and amphibious outflanking as at the port of Inchon, naval gunfire proved invaluable in preventing free Communist use of the coasts. The 16-inch guns of the battleships were unexpectedly useful in firing across Communist territory from the seaward rear to knock out positions on reverse slopes of mountains, where Communist forces were otherwise safe from front-line fire. By the time of the armistice of July 27, 1953, the navy operated 408 major and 720 minor vessels, with reserves swelling manpower to 800,000 personnel and 248,612 marines. The navy lost 5 ships and had 87 damaged, while 564 downed aircraft added heavily to the 458 killed or missing and 1,576 wounded.

The U.S. Navy first became involved in Vietnam after the collapse of the French there in 1954. In August of that year the vanguard of an ultimate 100 amphibious and auxiliary vessels under Rear Adm. L. S. Sabin began evacuating more than 300,000 refugees from the new Communist government to the south from Haiphong. In 1955 a small group of advisers, rising to 60 by 1960 and to 742 by 1964, helped train South Vietnam's neophyte navy. The presence of American warships began in December 1961, with minesweepers assuming radar watch near the seventeenth parallel to assist Vietnamese patrols in finding possible infiltrators among the thousands of coastal fishing craft. A few months later, destroyer escorts briefly made the same surveillance in the Gulf of Thailand. By the end of 1964, when 23,000 U.S. troops were engaged in military operations in South Vietnam, naval commitment soon followed. In March 1965 the destroyers *Black* and *Higbee* started an anti-infiltration patrol-and-search operation code-named Market Time. This coast-surveillance force shortly became Task Force 115, using conventional warships to maintain radar coverage for directing scores of high-speed miniwarships appropriately named "Swift" boats and 26 U.S. Coast Guard small cutters, together with U.S. airplanes and the units of the Vietnamese navy. Broadened to include shore bombardment, this inshore blockade continued until the U.S. withdrawal in 1973.

The U.S. Navy first became involved in Vietnam in 1954 after the collapse of French efforts against the Viet Cong.

In April 1966, another kind of naval operation began with Task Force 116, code-named Game Warden, which consisted of 120 boats designed to patrol within the numerous outlets of the Mekong River. Task Force 117, activated in June 1967, was the Riverine Assault Force, whose boats bore heavy weapons and were armored against small-arms fire. The pygmy capital-ship types with turrets were "monitors."

Training and expansion of the Vietnamese progressed so that the U.S. Navy could initiate transfer of its miniature men-of-war in February 1969, completed by 1971, releasing all but advisers, who left in 1972.

The major operation was inaugurated on Aug. 5, 1964, when airplanes from the *Constitution* and *Ticonderoga* of the Seventh Fleet struck targets in North Vietnam. Subsequently, the nuclear *Enterprise* and the fossil-fuel *America, Constitution, Coral Sea, Forrestal, Hancock, Kitty Hawk, Midway, Oriskany, Franklin D. Roosevelt,* and *Saratoga* rotated into duty. In May 1972, a concentration of six ships conducted the aerial mining of Haiphong and other North Vietnamese harbors in order to halt delivery by sea of munitions from Russia, China, and other Communist-bloc countries. Carrier operations caused the heaviest U.S. naval losses of personnel during the hostilities.

Peacetime Work

Although the U.S. Navy's primary occupation in peacetime is to prepare for hostilities, it has a rich history in diplomacy, humanitarianism, and exploration.

Throughout the 1900's, officers often acted on their own initiative to maintain or to advance U.S. foreign policy. Thus, in 1818, Capt. James Biddle and the *Ontario* began effective protection of Americans overseas by securing the freedom of some U.S. citizens imprisoned by the Spanish authorities in Valparaiso, Chile, during a revolution. In 1822, judicious conduct by Comdr. Robert Field Stockton of the *Alligator* helped to establish the country of Liberia. Lt. Charles Wilkes in 1842 negotiated a treaty with the Sultan of Sulu. The circumspect conduct of Capt. Lawrence Kearny and his squadron at Canton during Britain's first Opium War was crucial in bringing about the first U.S. treaty with China in 1844 on a "most-favored-nation" basis. Peacekeeping in the Caribbean dates from 1853 when Comdr. George N. Hollins and the *Cyane* brought disciplinary measures to Honduras, at a time when Comdr. Duncan Ingraham in the Mediterranean Sea at Izmir (Smyrna), Turkey, underscored the U.S. concept of *jus domus* by compelling an Austrian warship to release a naturalized American. Commodore Matthew Perry's spectacular "opening of Japan" in 1854 overshone the firm security simultaneously afforded by John Kelly and the *Plymouth* to Americans and foreigners beset by the Chinese in Shanghai. In 1859, a squadron under William B. Shubrick sailed down the Paraná River to quiet a bellicose Paraguay. Similarly, in 1873 a show of naval force off Cuba soothed the aftermath of the *Virginius* affair. In the same year in the Pacific, Capt. Richard Meade and the *Narragansett* laid effective claim to part of Samoa. The first treaty that Korea made with any Western power was negotiated in 1882 by Comdr. Robert W. Shufeldt on the *Swatara.*

The complete initiative of naval officers ended with the establishment of direct control from Washington, D.C., first made possible by underwater cable. By World War I, radio made such control almost instantaneous; this control was strikingly present in the 1962 Cuban missile crisis, when President John F. Kennedy personally gave orders over radiotelephone to the bridge of the commander whose destroyer was within hailing distance of the first Soviet merchantman sighted.

In foreign affairs, the post-World War II naval role was to show force in readiness to friends and possible foes. The permanent stationing of the Sixth Fleet helped avert Communist takeovers in Greece and Lebanon, dampened the Suez crisis, and limited the Six-Day War between Israel and the Arab states. The Seventh Fleet shielded Taiwan from Red China.

The Navy routinely charted U.S. shores, but in the late 1830's, interest shifted to the exploration of foreign lands.

Apart from numerous rescues of persons innocently trapped in shooting situations, the navy has often sped food, clothing, and medical aid to victims of major natural disasters, as the 1902 eruption of Mount Pelée that killed 40,000 on Martinique; the 1906 San Francisco earthquake; the 1908 earthquake in Sicily that killed 80,000; and the 1923 earthquake in Tokyo and Yokohama that killed 100,000. The development of long-range aviation made possible a swift response when earthquakes afflicted Ecuador in 1949, Chile in 1960, Yugoslavia in 1963, and Peru in 1970. Floods found navy and marine helicopter crews ready to sacrifice themselves to save others, as during the January 1969 rains on southern California. The outstanding example of aid to women and children victimized by war was by the cruiser-destroyer force of Rear Adm. Mark L. Bristol, which in 1919 entered the Black Sea to assist in the distribution of food and other supplies for relief. In 1920 the ships evacuated many persons fleeing the victorious Red Army in the Crimea. During the turbulence of 1920–22 in the Near East the navy covered the single-day embarkation of 30,000 Greeks from Izmir.

Navy hydrographers use ships' logs and observations for continual updating of charts and notices to mariners. The navy routinely charted U.S. shores until the formation of the Coast and Geodetic Survey. In the late 1830's, interest shifted to the exploration of foreign lands. Lt. Edwin J. De Haven with two vessels tried to find the British explorer Sir John Franklin and his companions, lost in the Arctic. Comdr. William Lynch charted the Jordan River and the Dead Sea in 1848 and the west coast of Africa in 1853. The Ringgold-Rodgers squadron in 1853–54 amplified the findings in the Pacific made by the earlier exploring expedition of Charles Wilkes (1838–42). Other officers surveyed the Isthmus of Panama for canal routes. Lt. Thomas Page charted southern South American rivers and thereby nearly caused a war with Paraguay. The possibilities of laying a transatlantic cable from Newfoundland to Ireland were inspired by the work of O. H. Berryman and given a sound basis by the work of Lt. Matthew Fontaine Maury.

Training and Education

In sailing ships, the ratings for noncommissioned officers or "mates" were the gunners, boatswains, quartermasters, carpenters, yeomen, storekeepers, and surgeon's mates. Ships powered by steam first needed the engineman, boilerman, and machinist and then the electrician, metalsmith, pipe fitter, molder, patternmaker, steelworker, and damage controlman. Aviation required its special varieties of ordnanceman. The development of radio and electronics created the radioman, fire controlman, sonarman, radarman, and electronics technician. By 1973 there were twelve categories with sixty-nine ratings, including the ocean-systems technician, missile technician, and data-systems technician, required by modern naval technology.

Until the time of the Civil War, experienced seamen came directly into the navy from civilian vessels. The withering of the merchant marine largely brought about by the *Alabama* and other Confederate ships shrank the ready supply of seamen. In 1875, Capt. Stephen B. Luce hit upon the notion of recruiting boys and training them as naval apprentices, completely solving the problem.

By the mid-1970's there were hundreds of special schools for recruits. Entry to the first of the six grades of petty officer is usually accomplished by completing a basic school. After various periods of experience depending upon the rating and after passing examinations for promotion, a petty officer is able to advance higher by success at a second school and sometimes a third. The skills acquired in the rating, except for such outright military skills as that of gunner's mate, usually carry directly into a civilian counterpart.

Beyond training that is essentially military, the navy vigorously urges high school dropouts to volunteer for off-duty programs in order to win diplomas or certificates of equivalency. As for college-level opportunities conferring credit toward a degree, by the mid-1970's more than 6,000 correspondence courses, from language study to nuclear fission, were available. The special college-credit program begun aboard Polaris submarines to help ease the monotony of sixty-day submerged patrols has become available for all ships. Harvard University is one of the sponsoring institutions.

Stationed ashore and close to a college or university, navy personnel may have duties arranged to allow for part-time attendance at a school, a substantial part of the cost for the studies paid by the navy. A petty officer may attend a junior college full-time for an associate degree in arts, engineering, or science, and the whole cost is paid in exchange for a period of additional service. If a person has the requisite ability and volunteers for a scientific major desired by the navy, the navy pays for the whole four years and grants a commission. As of the 1970's every class entering the Naval Academy had eighty-five openings for young men from the fleet and another eighty-five for reservists.

By the mid-1970's young women had all the same opportunities as men plus the opportunities offered by the Bureau of Medicine for full-time attendance at a college studying for a degree in nursing or medical dietetics, with a commission upon graduation.

Also in the mid-1970's, members of minority groups were able to take advantage of Project BOOST (Broadened Opportunity for Officer Selection and Training), which provided them a maximum of two years in a preparatory school at San Diego, Calif., before competing in the examinations for entry to the Naval Academy or college with a Naval Reserve Officers' Training Corps (NROTC).

As for officers, by 1975 the greater number came from Officer Candidate School after having completed a bachelor's or higher degree in any accredited subject at a college or university (*see* Naval Reserve). After some years of duty, graduates from Officer Candidate School were able to qualify for regular commissions.

The traditional regular officer still comes from the Naval Academy, founded at Annapolis, Md., in 1845. The brigade of midshipmen at the academy is kept at a strength of approximately 4,200 by a dozen methods of entry, in which congressional appointment predominates.

Career officers gain professional depth at the Naval War College, conceived and established in 1884 at Newport, R.I., by Stephen B. Luce. The college had its purpose and value crystallized in the publications of its most illustrious faculty member, Alfred Thayer Mahan. By 1975 there were about 360 students, primarily from the navy but also including members of other services, government civilians, and foreign officers, enrolled at the college. On two-year assignment, officers explore and reflect upon strategy, tactics, logistics, and the philosophy of war, testing theories in war games, assisted by electronic displays and computers. The Naval War College has had a wide influence, notably in the adoption of all U.S. services of its "estimate of the situation" and "completed staff study" concepts.

Postgraduate education of officers in military "hardware" began modestly in 1904 with a handful of men taking courses in marine engineering given in the appropriate bureau. Success encouraged transfer to the

Naval Academy, which in 1912 established a postgraduate department. Well received, the department flourished and was finally housed in the academy's erstwhile marine barracks. Capt. Ernest J. King was the first head of the newly named "PG School" after World War I. Congress in 1945 authorized the school to confer the master's degree and the doctorate in technical fields, although by then a substantial number of students were primarily interested in refresher courses to enable them to enter civilian universities in pursuit of the same degrees. Relocated at Monterey, Calif., in 1954, the school was serving some 2,000 officers with an increasingly distinguished faculty by the mid-1970's.

The navy also strongly encouraged study at universities, not just in engineering but also in a considerable range of subjects from law to international relations. The latter subject, for instance, has about twelve officers a year entering the Fletcher School at Tufts University in Massachusetts. In exchange for full support, an officer must agree to an appropriately extended period of active service.

Many military installations have after-hours educational programs for which the navy pays part of the cost. An example is the master's in personnel administration conducted by George Washington University in Naval Academy classrooms for the officer-faculty.

Fleets

The squadron concept that began in the Quasi-War with France was the basic tactical organization until 1907, when the Atlantic, Pacific, and Asiatic fleets were formed. Within this structure the force concept grew into the now-familiar task force. In World War II there were eleven fleets with specific geographic areas of operations, except for the Tenth Fleet, which was charged with antisubmarine warfare. At that time, odd-numbered fleets were located in the Pacific, and even-numbered in the Atlantic. The most famous fleets in wartime were the Third, Fifth, and Seventh fleets, the latter with MacArthur. The Third and Fifth were in the Central Pacific and consisted largely of the same ships, designated Third when under Adm. William F. Halsey and Fifth when under Adm. Raymond A. Spruance.

Students reading World War II naval history may encounter numeral designations such as Task Element 38.4.6.2. In this designation, subdivision is indicated by italics:

3–.–.–.–. = *Third Fleet*
38.–.–.–. = *Task Force 8* of Third Fleet
38.4.–.–. = *Task Group 4* of Task Force 38
38.4.6.–. = *Task Unit 6* of Task Group 38.4
38.4.6.2. = *Task Element 2* of Task Unit 38.4.6

For purposes of administration, ships are also organized into type commands: for example, submarines, Atlantic (SUBLANT); submarines, Pacific (SUBPAC); and destroyers, Atlantic (DESLANT). Basic tactical organizations are division (two or more vessels of the same type); squadron (generally two or more divisions); and flotilla (generally two or more similar squadrons).

By 1971 the Atlantic Fleet maintained the Second and Sixth fleets, the latter in the Mediterranean, while the Pacific Fleet had the First and Seventh fleets, the latter in Southeast Asian waters. Each great fleet has force subdivisions, such as amphibious, antisubmarine warfare, cruiser-destroyer, hunter-killer, mine, naval air, and submarine. There are five sea frontier commands for Alaska, Hawaii, the continental western and eastern coasts, and the Caribbean. Naval forces are assigned to Antarctica, the eastern Atlantic, Europe, Japan, Key West, Korea, the Middle East, the South Atlantic, and until 1973 to Vietnam. Such ships include the ships committed to the North Atlantic Treaty Organization (NATO). In 1973 some consolidation commenced, the First Fleet and the Pacific Antisubmarine Force merging into a new Second Fleet headquartered at Pearl Harbor.

Ships

The increasing power of cannon about the year 1700 required ships to have a defensive thickness of hull that gradually eliminated the adaptation of merchant vessels for war, except for their use as privateers. The principal types in the sail era were the ship of the line and the frigate. The Civil War witnessed the conversion of civilian vessels, even ferryboats, by the hundreds into gunboats and cruisers, a situation forced upon both the North and the South by the small prewar size of the U.S. Navy. Even so, the actual construction during the war was principally of ironclads. Later technology in steel brought into being the familiar battleships, aircraft carriers, cruisers, submarines, and destroyers, obviously built only for combat. Merchantmen continue to be valuable for wartime expansion of fleet auxiliaries, as for supply carriers and tankers.

Although the system of type designations of warships (such as CAG-2) reflects the considerable complexity of many specialized types of ships and may seem cryptic, this system is a form of shorthand describing a vessel's main mission and equipment.

The first letter in the designation identifies certain broad categories:

A = auxiliary vessel
B = capital gunship
C = cruiser or aircraft carrier
D = destroyer types
L = landing craft

M = mine warfare types
P = patrol types
S = submarines
Y = yard vessels

Some of the above letters may be doubled; they then mean:

BB = battleship
DD = destroyer
MM = fleet minelayer
SS = fleet submarine

The primary meaning does not necessarily carry over into a secondary position, as in

CA = heavy cruiser (8-inch guns)
CL = light cruiser (5-inch or 6-inch)
DL = frigate
MS = minesweeper

In the secondary position, most of the alphabet is used: for instance, AH for hospital auxiliary; AK for cargo ship; and AO for oiler auxiliary. The V in CV denotes an aircraft carrier.

Among letters used in the third and fourth positions, the most notable are B for ballistic missile; G for guided missile; H for helicopter; and N for nuclear-powered. Thus, SSBN is a nuclear-powered submarine armed with ballistic missiles, commonly called a Polaris sub; DDG is a destroyer with guided missiles; and CVH is a helicopter carrier.

A CAG-2 designation would thus signify: C (cruiser), A (heavy), G (guided missile). The number 2 indicates the place in the sequence in a type. The CAG-1 is the *Boston*, and the CAG-2, the *Canberra* (named for an Australian cruiser lost at the Battle of Savo Sound).

Traditionally battleships were named after states, carriers after battles or historic ships, cruisers after cities, submarines after sea creatures, and destroyers after naval heroes. There has been some modification of this practice. Names of fleet ballistic-missile submarines may honor outstanding Americans (*Patrick Henry*, SSBN-599), as have some carriers since 1955 (*James V. Forrestal*, CVA-59, A standing for "attack"). The torpedo-armed SSN's continue bearing the names of sea creatures, but the 688 begun in 1972 was named the *Los Angeles*, borrowing from the cruiser tradition. Increasingly, larger frigates that would once have been called destroyer flotilla leaders fittingly honor famous battle admirals (*George Dewey*, DLG-14), but the even larger DLGN-37 was laid down in 1972 as the *South Carolina*, hinting at the role of the future battleship.

From a 1969 peak of 932 commissioned vessels, of which 481 were combatants, the navy had been shrinking during the 1970's from the combined pressures of soaring costs and federal economizing. The 1974 plan was for 523 vessels in commission, of which 311 were combatants: 15 attack carriers, 7 cruisers, 29 frigates, 128 destroyer types, 12 diesel and 108 nuclear submarines, 15 amphibians, and 15 patrol types. Strength dropped to 502 in 1975. It is noteworthy that nuclear submarines constitute a substantial third, with the planned replacement of some of the 16-missile Polaris submarines with the colossal 24-missile Trident type.

Traditionally, battleships were named after states, carriers after battles or historic ships, cruisers after cities, and submarines after sea creatures.

Armament

For several centuries the main battery of line-of-battle warships was artillery, rivaled in World War II by aircraft and in the 1970's by rocketry.

The primary cannon of the Continental and U.S. navies were muzzle-loading smoothbore pieces known by weight of shot, from 24-pounders down through 18-, 12-, 9-, 6-, and 3-pounders. The largest could take up to three minutes to load, depending upon the efficiency of a crew. All were extremely inaccurate, with effective ranges of 1,200 yards at most, making for tactics of close combat, victory often gained by grappling and boarding. The main projectiles were solid spheres slightly less than the diameter of a bore and aimed to pierce a hull. Antipersonnel projectiles were grapeshot—small shot sewn into canvas—and canister, a can filled with musket balls, both kinds breaking open after firing to create giant shotgun effects. Antirigging langrage consisted of jagged-edged metal or even broken glass. Contrary to much fiction, very few exploding shells were fired from long guns until reliable, safe fuses appeared in the 1820's. Only privateers gambled with the early wooden fuses in long guns. The "bombs bursting in air" over Fort McHenry were fired from mortars. For incendiarism, a shot of lesser caliber could be heated white-hot and loaded against a green-wood core protecting the powder charge. The carcass was made by suspending a bag of gunpowder within a spherical framework of metal hoops, which was dipped into warmed tar to be shaped into rounded smoothness. Ignited by discharge, a carcass would burn until the gunpowder exploded to spew blazing tar.

As improving technology produced better tackle for handling weights, guns steadily grew in size. In the 1850's there was a whole new generation of cannon whose bores were measured in inches; these were scientifically perfected by John Dahlgren and others. The pair of XI-inch Dahlgrens of the *Monitor* fired 168-pound projectiles, the double-turreted *Miantonomoh* had XV-inch, but none was fitted with his monstrous XX-inch, if only because its projectiles weighed more than half a ton. These were the ultimate smoothbores, because technology concurrently mastered the rifling of iron and the ramming of a projectile to produce the muzzle-loading Parrott gun whose 30-pound shot flew more than two miles.

By the 1880's the revolution in steel made possible huge masses that could be easily machined; electric motors replaced muscles; and the modern, breech-loading rifle was born, doubling and redoubling in size until it reached the standard 16-inch gun of the battleships. The *New Jersey* hurled one-ton shells twenty miles onto coastal targets in Vietnam.

Cannon could be made even larger, as attested by the 18-inch guns of the Japanese *Yamato*, but the boundaries of prohibitive cost were well in view when airplanes came to offer a far cheaper means of accurately delivering ordance at comparatively vast ranges far beyond cannon possibilities. The challenge of the airplane arose during World War I, but the battleship was believed to have met the supposed deadliness of the torpedo plane, which had to attack on a straight course at suicidally slow speed to drop its delicate weapon. Level bombing had been inconclusive in the protracted tests by Gen. William ("Billy") Mitchell's airmen against the helplessly anchored *Ostfriedsland*, and although in 1936 during the Spanish Civil War the antiquated Republican battleship *Jaime I* was sunk by German level bombers, all major navies continued launching battleships. Late in the 1920's, accurate dive-bombing techniques were being pioneered by the U.S. Marines and U.S. Navy, techniques that would dominate during World War II in the Pacific. The new era dawned at the 1942 battles in the Coral Sea and at Midway, which were decided without any of the surface foes sighting each other.

In practical terms, the dive-bomber extended battle ranges to hundreds of miles. The 1944 advent of German rocketry simply spurred postwar development of airborne varieties into the 1972 "smart bombs" used against North Vietnam. Late in World War II, ground-scanning radar made high-level bombing somewhat more accurate, but carpet-bombing—a formation of airplanes salvoing together—remained the best means of hitting a desired target.

Those who expected gigantic missiles to supersede the aircraft carrier, just as the carrier had superseded the battleship, were given pause by the 1945 atomic bombs. Total destruction is implicit both in the fitting of nuclear warheads in an aircraft's air-to-ground missiles for stand-off firing and in the placing of nuclear warheads on ballistic missiles. Indeed, there is a saying among Polaris submarine crews that "if we have to shoot, it means we've failed," pointing up the belief that the chief value of modern missiles is as a deterrent. As for critics of the aircraft carrier who claim it is fatally vulnerable to nonnuclear-warhead missiles, advocates point to the Japanese kamikazes as virtual missiles that were unable to drive the U.S. Navy away from the conquest of Okinawa.

Secondary batteries during the American Revolution were formed by cannon lighter than the main battery and generally mounted on fore and after castles. The Quasi-War with France found the new navy adopting the British carronade, which created an extremely unusual armament situation, insofar as this secondary weapon was usually more powerful than the main battery. Being about a third of the weight of its equivalent long gun and served by a fourth as many men, a stubby carronade within 300 yards intensified a broadside. Because of its lightness, it was ideal for mounting on the highest decking. A frigate such as the *Constitution* with a 24-pounder main battery could have 32-pounder or even 42-pounder carronades, sizes not in the U.S. Navy long-gun inventory until after the War of 1812. Carronades account for some discrepancies in accounts of sea battles; the *Constitution* might have had a dozen carronades to make a total of fifty-six muzzles, but it was still officially rated a forty-four, the number of its long guns.

The principle of using smaller guns to complement a main battery continued into the 20th century. The steel revolution and the development of breech-loading weapons vastly increased rates of fire, while improvements in mounting brought in the dual-purpose quick-firing gun that could be aimed at the horizon and upward to directly overhead. The 5-inch/38 was the most famous in World War II; it was a very effective antiaircraft weapon when fired with the VT, or proximity fuse. The common antiaircraft weapon in the 1970's was the radar-controlled 3-inch/70.

The machine guns introduced in the 1880's, such as the 1-pounder Hotchkiss, were comparatively heavy, being intended to sink torpedo boats. Antiaircraft was the primary mission of the .50 Browning, 20-mm Oerlikon, and 40-mm Bofors used in World War II.

The self-propelled torpedoes, first carried aboard tiny speedboats, never fulfilled their threat because they had to be launched at a few hundred yards, necessitating a run-in that afforded an alert man-of-war ample time. By 1900 the speedboat had been replaced by the larger vessel with greater speed originally known as the torpedo-boat destroyer, which carried the torpedoes in World War I and down to the mid-1970's. The ideal torpedo carrier turned out to be the submarine. As a result, one of a surface ship's best defenses is an anti-submarine torpedo.

Mines, known as "torpedoes" during the Civil War, made a deadly quantum jump from explosion by direct contact to explosion by detonator when the antenna mine was perfected by the Bureau of Ordnance during World War I. It made possible in World War I the laying of the stupendous North Sea mine barrage that diminished the zest of German submarine crews for trying to enter the North Atlantic. World War II brought the magnetic and acoustic types of mines, the sophisticated versions of which were air-dropped during 1972 in the approaches to Haiphong harbor in North Vietnam.

Facilities

The thirteen colonies had a very strong maritime tradition, and easily produced men-of-war for fighting in the Revolution. Construction of naval vessels by private companies has been done ever since. The naval base is centered on a navy yard, which is primarily devoted to the upkeep of ships and, in some cases, to the construction of ships as well. The first navy yard began operations in 1799 within the boundaries of the young nation's new capital, Washington, D.C. Initially engaged in the construction of small gunboats, the Washington Yard soon turned to the production of cannon to such an extent that it became known as the Naval Gun Factory. (It is now a naval museum.) In 1800, yards were established at Portsmouth, N.H., Boston, Mass., and Norfolk, Va.; in 1801 at Philadelphia, Pa., and Brooklyn, N.Y.; in 1825 at Pensacola, Fla.; in 1854 at Mare Island, Calif.; in 1901 at Charleston, S.C.; and in 1902 at Bremerton, Wash. A dozen more followed. Later some bases phased out shipbuilding. Pensacola, for example, concentrated on training naval aviators. By World War I, navy yards were generally kept free for the repairing of war-damaged units, letting private contractors build the new vessels needed, a procedure resumed during World War II. The Great Depression had shown the value of federal spending in priming the economy. After the peace of 1945, the government's desire to fend off a depression kept many private yards in business, enabling some, such as the Electric Boat Company of Groton, Conn. (a submarine contractor), to become giants. Not one of the fifty-seven major units on the ways in 1973—including two aircraft carriers, nineteen submarines, and sixteen destroyers—was built in a navy dock.

The thirteen colonies had a very strong maritime tradition, and easily produced men-of-war for fighting in the Revolution.

During World War II, the navy had some 7,200 shore facilities, a figure that was cut back to 800 by 1949 and that has been dwindling ever since in recurrent budget squeezing by the government, compelling the navy to undergo sacrifices that would maximize forces at sea and underwrite research. The transfer of ownership of the tremendous Brooklyn Navy Yard to New York City in 1969 was a forecast of the wholesale shutdown in 1973 of 200 facilities. Ten shipyards, including historic Boston and San Francisco, were closed. Key West, the bulk of Newport, R.I., and Long Beach, Calif., closed down. Air bases were discontinued at famous Quonset Point, R.I.; Lakehurst, N.J.; Albany, Ga.; Imperial Beach, Calif.; and elsewhere. No less stunning were the closure of New York's Saint Alban's Naval Hospital and the decommissioning of the hospital ship *Repose.*

Since 1830 the navy has led in research and development with the opening in Washington, D.C., of the Naval Observatory and the Hydrographic Office, where Maury found world renown. The gun-testing station built in 1848 on the Potomac River moved its scientific personnel to the present Indian Head, Md., Naval Proving Ground in the 1890's. The Naval Torpedo Station (1869) at Newport developed the torpedo. The David Taylor Model Basin (1900) at Carderock, Md., is a leader in ship design. The naval aircraft factory begun at Philadelphia in 1917 completely relinquished production in the 1920's to civilian firms and went on in aerodynamic experimentation, notably in guided bombs before World War II. The Mine Laboratory (renamed the Naval Ordnance Laboratory), established in 1918 at White Oak, Md., developed the antenna mine. The Naval Research Laboratory (1923) at Anacostia in Washington, D.C., has evolved into one of the largest centers of applied and pure research, originally paying its way by the 1937 introduction of a practical, seagoing radar. In 1939 its scientists laid the foundation of what became the Manhattan Project for making the atomic bomb. By 1946 the complex of naval research centers required coordination, so the present Office of Naval Research began a systematic study of the basic sciences, including medicine. By the 1970's, there was little in science and technology that remained untouched by the navy.

Naval Reserve

During the years the American merchant marine was expanding, its seamen constituted a virtual reserve, epitomized by the volunteers who filled the ships during the Civil War. The ensuing decline of American shipping created a need for formal organization and recruiting. Massachusetts led the way on Mar. 18, 1890, by founding a naval militia, soon adopted by other seaboard states. Development paralleled the National Guard until militias were brought under federal control on Feb. 16, 1914. The National Naval Volunteers Act of Aug. 29, 1916, created the naval reserve as such, which absorbed the militias. Thereafter the naval reserve proliferated in conformance with technological advances to a complexity that in World War II provided about 90 percent of naval personnel.

The Act of July 9, 1952, created the present ready, standby, and retired categories, primarily differentiated by liability to recall to active duty. Normally, a reservist passes from the ready reserve through standby to retired status. Qualifications are maintained through drills in a broad program of some forty different types of pay and nonpay units, through two-week active-duty-for-training periods, officer schools, correspondence courses, and other ways approved by the chief of naval personnel. The success of the 1946 "weekend warrior" program for aviation units resulted in a selected reserve program for small ships, principally antisubmarine warfare types, which are kept ready by a small, permanent crew to be manned in a matter of hours by reserves who train afloat throughout the year, one weekend a month.

To supplement the traditional appointment of qualified officers from the merchant marine or from civilians with applicable specialties, the Student Navy Training Corps was established in 1917 at ninety colleges and universities. This became the basis for normal peacetime procurement and evolved into the present Naval Reserve Officers Training Corps (NROTC) at fifty colleges (1975 figure). Selected appointees receive pay throughout the four years of college work in fields of individual choice and concurrently take six hours a week of naval training plus appropriate summer cruises. After graduation and commissioning, they serve a stipulated time on active duty and then have the option, if recommended, of transferring into the regular navy for a career. The same NROTC units also have contract candidates who, after satisfactory grades and aptitude for the first two years, are paid during the last two. For non-NROTC collegiate institutions, there is the Reserve Officer Candidate (ROC) program, in which a college student may earn a commission by satisfactory completion of two six-week training courses during the summer. The Naval Aviation Cadet program is another means of entry. The major means for obtaining the number of junior officers needed annually is the Officer Candidate School at Newport, R.I. Every six weeks a class of college graduates starts the "ninety-day wonder" course. The navy and naval reserve have through such programs the largest percentage of college graduates in the armed services.

During the Vietnam War, service in the naval reserve was very popular, and every unit had long lists of waiting applicants. In the aftermath of the war, the navy commenced an augmentation policy demanding swifter readiness for call-up and more time on active duty, which, in the climate of the hoped for "zero draft," eroded the former popularity of the naval reserve.

BIBLIOGRAPHY

American State Papers, Naval Affairs.
Civil War Naval Chronology.
Dictionary of American Naval Fighting Ships.
F. M. Bennett, *The Steam Navy of the United States.*
W. R. Carter, *Beans, Bullets, and Black Oil.*
F. E. Chadwick, *The Spanish-American War.*
H. I. Chapelle, *History of the American Sailing Navy.*
W. B. Clark, ed., *Naval Documents of the American Revolution.*
E. J. King, *The U.S. Navy at War.*
D. W. Knox, *The History of the U.S. Navy,* and *Barbary Wars.*
D. W. Knox, ed., *Naval Documents of the Quasi-War With France.*
A. T. Mahan, *The War of 1812.*
S. E. Morison, *United States Naval Operations in World War II.*
Secretary of the Navy, *Annual Reports* (since 1836).
W. S. Sims, *Victory at Sea.*

— ROBERT W. DALY

NEUTRALITY

The concept of neutrality has two aspects: it is a legal status and a political policy. Both have figured prominently in American history from 1776 to 1941, but both have declined in importance since World War II.

The legal aspect of neutrality guided the relations between belligerents engaged in a recognized war and all other states not parties to the conflict. The purpose of neutrality was to reconcile the conflicting military necessities of belligerents that adversely affected neutrals with the neutrals' insistence that hostilities be limited to the territories, armies, navies, and civilian populations of the belligerent states.

Under traditional international law, a neutral state has the following duties toward belligerents: (1) impartiality; (2) abstention from assistance to belligerents; (3) prevention of the use of neutral territory as a base for belligerent operations; and (4) acquiescence in belligerent interference with neutral commerce to the extent permitted by international law. The belligerents had corresponding duties toward the neutral: (1) abstention from violations of neutral territory (including territorial waters and air space); (2) respect for the neutral's impartiality; and (3) abstention from interference with neutral commerce except under the guidelines of international law.

Historically, the principal area of application of neutral rights and duties was on the high seas. Neutrality was always a reflection of the legal status and material characteristics of war. The traditional law of neutrality developed in a period when recourse to war was a sovereign prerogative of all states. International law and diplomacy did not impose conditions on the decision of a state to go to war. The law was confined to the role of registering the fact of formal armed conflict and specifying the legal consequences of that fact.

This international law of neutrality developed in a period of limited wars, in the 17th and 18th centuries. The trend toward "total" wars, beginning as early as the Napoleonic Wars (1799–1815), was at odds with the traditional concept of neutrality. The intensity of the stakes, the technological changes in warfare, and the increased mobility of belligerents tended to make wars more bitter, destructive, and widespread in their effects. All of these factors mitigated against the traditional notion of neutrality as the international equivalent of forming a circle around two men engaged in a fist fight. By World War I the contradictions between the assumptions of traditional neutrality and the realities of modern total war were evident. They were not adequately recognized, however, until World War II.

The foregoing overview of the concept of neutrality as a legal status explains in part the troubled history of American neutrality. The United States came into existence just before such developments as the French Revolution and the Industrial Revolution unleashed the human and material forces that combined to make total war the central problem of the international community. Accordingly, the struggling American republic was obliged to seek neutral rights in an environment hostile to those rights.

For the United States, neutrality was a wise policy as well as a legal status. George Washington's administration rejected alliance with the new French republic and, indeed, with any foreign power. But the desire to avoid foreign entanglements did not preclude foreign trade. The United States wanted to avoid participation in foreign wars while profiting from them by trade with the belligerents. Under the circumstances, even the traditional 18th-century neutrality proved precarious. Violations of neutral rights, which had plagued European neutrals, were also inflicted on the United States. There were recurring threats of war with Great Britain and the undeclared war with France over neutral rights (1798–1800), all before the more comprehensive phase of European Napoleonic Wars.

George Washington's administration rejected alliance with the new French republic and, indeed, with any foreign power.

Thomas Jefferson anticipated modern aspirations for alternatives to armed force in his attempts to protect American neutral rights through embargoes against belligerents who consistently violated those rights (1807–09). These embargoes apparently failed, although appraisal is difficult. It appears that the domestic American constituencies most adversely affected by British and French violations of their rights (mainly in the Northeast) preferred to take their chances with those belligerents rather than punish both the belligerents and themselves by embargoing trade. The Hawks of the period, not themselves the principal target of belligerent violations of U.S. neutral rights, wanted to fight for those rights, *inter alia*, because of their expansionist aspirations in the South and West.

Although the War of 1812 was supposedly fought with the protection of U.S. neutral rights as a major objective, the results were inconclusive. The end of the Napoleonic Wars in 1815 left a legacy of generally successful violation of neutral rights by the great maritime powers, Britain and France. The principal change in the law of neutrality of the 19th century came with the Declaration of Paris in 1856. This agreement abolished privateering—that is, commissioning of private ships so as to give them belligerent status to raid enemy shipping.

The United States did not adhere to the Declaration of Paris, because of the declaration's inadequate recognition of the rights of private neutral property on ships subject to search and seizure. However, the American posture as a leading proponent of neutral rights was altered considerably during the Civil War. Enforcement of the blockade of the Confederacy led to adoption of many of the same practices earlier objected to by the United States. As a belligerent rather than a neutral, the United States adopted the doctrine of continuous voyage, in order to deal with the problems of transshipment of supplies destined for the Confederacy through British and French possessions and Mexico. These departures from traditional neutral positions were later invoked against the United States when it was once again a neutral in the early years of World War I.

A major issue was raised in the wake of the Civil War in the Alabama Claims Arbitration (1871). The United States sought compensation from Great Britain for losses inflicted on U.S. shipping by Confederate raiders outfitted and based in British territory. The final settlement was more of a political compromise than a legal decision. In a precedent of continuing importance, Great Britain did agree that neutral territory henceforth should not be permitted to provide bases for belligerent operations. This precedent remains relevant even after the decline of the forms of maritime warfare that gave rise to it. Thus, connivance or acquiescence in the use of a state's territory as a base for civil war, terrorism, subversion, or other kinds of indirect aggression is contrary to contemporary international law.

The general U.S. policy of neutrality was potentially at variance with the Monroe Doctrine (1823), although the special interest claimed by the principle of European nonintervention in the Western Hemisphere was never brought to a major test. By the end of the 19th century the United States was adding a further special interest to its claims, this time in insistence on the Open Door policy for China. This policy, plus U.S. expansion in the Pacific, meant that the logic and integrity of a general posture of isolation and neutrality were questionable.

Efforts to codify the law of war and neutrality at sea at the Hague conferences of 1899 and 1907 were unsuccessful. A final attempt in the Declaration of London (1909) was never ratified. The greatest stumbling block was disagreement over the definition of "contraband of war," a term that came to include virtually all commerce with belligerents. World War I began with the law of neutrality in disarray. The United States attempted to maintain a policy of neutrality in this war and to protect its neutral rights. Both efforts were in vain.

World War I, the first modern total war, involved the continuous mobilization of the whole societies of the belligerents. Whatever distinctions had been previously possible between combatants and noncombatants, public and private property, free goods and contraband, were destroyed. The conduct of the war was incompatible with such distinctions and rights. Moreover, the heavy dependence of the Allies on U.S. trade and financial support made U.S. policies inherently unneutral and critically injurious from the German–Central Powers viewpoint.

Other factors affected the U.S. policy of neutrality and insistence on neutral rights: majority popular sentiment for the Allies over the Central Powers, effective Allied propaganda, heavy-handed Central Powers diplomacy, and attempts at subversion. But the essential element was Allied dependence on U.S. economic support—given at enormous profit—and the conviction of the Central Powers that this support must be interrupted. In a growing record of infringement of U.S. neutral rights the character of German violations arising out of submarine attacks overcame the substantial reaction against Allied practices. The United States went to war with neutral rights once again foremost among its war aims, although given the performance of the United States in the Civil War, it was not surprising that Allied total-war practices were immediately adopted and neutral rights virtually ceased.

American reaction against war, power politics, foreign entanglements, and allies who did not repay their war debts contributed to a return to an isolationist policy and to insistence on neutral rights in the interwar period. This trend was further encouraged by broad revulsion against the munitions industries, which, according to congressional investigations (1934–36), were greatly responsible for war and U.S. involvement therein. In the context of the failure of attempts at disarmament (for example, at the Geneva Conference, 1931–33), the failure of economic and other sanctions against Japan after its Manchurian takeover (1931–32) and Italy during its Ethiopian conquest (1935–37), and growing evidence of Nazi aggressive intentions, the United States continued to proclaim political and legal neutrality in preference to support for collective security.

The complicated development of U.S. neutrality laws in the late 1930's reflected the division between strong isolationist sentiment in Congress and increasing determination in the executive branch to resist aggression. Neutrality acts passed by Congress in 1935, 1936, 1937, and 1939 reflected these differences, as did the uneven record of their enforcement by the administration of Franklin D. Roosevelt.

These differences erupted in the debate over American neutrality from the outbreak of World War II (September 1939) until the Pearl Harbor attack (Dec. 7, 1941). Roosevelt consistently sought liberalization of the U.S. neutrality laws, beginning with "cash-and-carry" armament sales by private concerns and proceeding to the "destroyer deal," whereby the U.S. government directly supplied navy vessels, field artillery, half a million rifles, and other arms and munitions to Britain in exchange for leases on Caribbean bases. Meanwhile, Roosevelt and Prime Minister Winston Churchill planned all manner of increased U.S. involvement, including participation in British convoys and consequent loss of U.S. naval vessels in combat. The concept of neutral impartiality was replaced with that of the arsenal of democracy.

The duty to cooperate with collective security or collective defense measures—as with NATO, for example—generally overrides the presumption of neutral impartiality.

U.S. interventions on behalf of Great Britain and its allies were clearly unneutral and would have justified a German declaration of war in defense of traditional neutral rights. Adolf Hitler's disinclination to take this course does not alter the lesson that the concept of neutrality cannot survive the conviction of a powerful neutral that one party to a conflict is an evil aggressor and the other a victim to be saved. This point is demonstrated in the case of the Declaration of Panama of October 1939, which sought to ban belligerent action within an enormous security zone enveloping the Western Hemisphere south of Canada. In addition to the practical impossibility of enforcing the declaration against German submarines, manifest nonapplication of the ban to Great Britain reflected U.S. unneutral policies.

Thus, technological advances in warfare, total-war attacks in an economically interdependent world, and aspirations for collective security against aggressors destroyed the foundations of neutrality as a policy and as a legal status. Since World War II these forces have continued to preclude a return to traditional neutrality. Although true collective security under the United Nations has not been feasible, nations such as the United States still distinguish illegal aggressors from their victims, as in the Korean conflict (1950–53). The duty to cooperate with collective security or collective defense measures—for example, under the North Atlantic Treaty Organization or the Organization of American States—generally overrides the presumption of neutral impartiality.

Ideological East-West rifts have produced a new concept of neutralism or nonalignment. Nations in the developing Third World have proclaimed their neutrality in the cold war's recurring conflicts and competitions. Additionally, some states such as Austria have become "neutralized," somewhat following the model of Switzerland. During the 1950's, Secretary of State John Foster Dulles and other U.S. statesmen denounced neutralism and sought unity in the non-Communist "Free World." By the 1970's the United States had become reconciled to neutralism and had moved cooperatively with the Soviet Union, the People's Republic of China, and other Communist states to soften the edges of ideological conflict. Nevertheless, a return to the international system in which neutrality developed appears remote.

BIBLIOGRAPHY

William W. Bishop, *International Law: Cases and Materials.*
Edwin Borchard and William Potter Lage, *Neutrality for the United States.*
Cecil V. Crabb, Jr., *The Elephants and the Grass: A Study in Nonalignment.*
Charles G. Fenwick, *International Law.*
Charles Cheney Hyde, *International Law.*
Myres S. McDougal and Florentino P. Feliciano, *Law and Minimum World Public Order.*
Roderick Ogley, *The Theory and Practice of Neutrality in the Twentieth Century.*
Robert W. Tucker, *The Law of War and Neutrality at Sea.*
Marjorie M. Whiteman, *Digest of International Law,* vols. 10 and 11.

— WILLIAM V. O'BRIEN

NEW AMSTERDAM

New Amsterdam was founded in July 1625, when the little settlement planted by the Dutch West India Company on Nut (now Governors) Island was transferred to the lower end of Manhattan Island. In accordance with the instructions of the company directors, a fort, pentagonal in shape, was built, and a street connecting the two gates was laid out, with a marketplace in the center; houses built around it were to be used as offices for the company and homes for the director and members of his council. In 1626, because of troubles with the Indians of the area, the families settled at Fort Orange, now Albany, were moved to New Amsterdam. Two roads (now Whitehall and Pearl streets) and two canals (now covered by the pavements of Broad and Beaver streets) formed the limits of the settlement. A wagon road led from the fort along present-day Broadway, Park Row, and Fourth Avenue up to about East 14th Street, east of which lay the five company farms and that of the director of the province.

The inhabitants of New Amsterdam had no voice in the government of the settlement, which was administered by the director of the province and his council, appointed by the directors of the company. Obedience to the orders and laws of the company was expected. Life in New Amsterdam in the early years of the settlement was far from pleasant. The directors were autocratic, and members of the council quarreled with the director and with each other. Jonas Michaelius, the first ordained minister to New Netherland, who arrived in 1628, was sharply critical of conditions. He declared the people oppressed, the food supply scarce, and many of the inhabitants loafers who needed to be replaced by competent farmers and industrious laborers. Housing conditions were little better than at the beginning of the settlement. Although the population then numbered 270 men, women, and children, the majority of the people were still lodged in primitive huts of bark, huddled near the protecting ramparts of the fort. Religious services were held in the loft of the horse mill.

Despite difficulties the town grew and made progress. A new fort, girded with stone, was built. A barracks for the soldiers, a bakery, and more houses for company servants were constructed. A wooden church was begun, and shortly afterward a house for the minister was built.

In 1637 the brutal and unwise Indian policy of Director Willem Kieft resulted in a war that threatened to wipe out the settlement. Peace was made in 1645, but when Peter Stuyvesant arrived in 1647 to succeed Kieft, he found New Amsterdam in a state of complete demoralization. New ordinances were passed to curb drunkenness in the town, which boasted seventeen taphouses; three street surveyors were appointed to remedy the deplorable conditions of the houses, streets, and fences; and steps were taken to raise money to repair the fort, finish the church, and build a school.

In 1652, as a result of much popular agitation, Stuyvesant was instructed to give New Amsterdam a burgher government. Accordingly, in February of the following year, a schout, two burgomasters, and five schepens were appointed. These officials together constituted a court with both civil and criminal jurisdiction; it met once a week—and continued to function until merged in the supreme court of the state of New York in 1895. The magistrates met in the Stadt Huis, which had originally been built by Kieft as a tavern. In 1654 the magistrates received the power, if permitted by the council, to levy taxes and to convey lands. A painted coat of arms, a seal, and a silver signet were delivered to them with impressive ceremonies. In 1658 they were allowed to nominate their successors. Two years later the company granted additional prestige to the office of city schout, by removing from the schout his previous duties as sheriff, prosecutor, and president of the magistrates. In 1657 burgher rights were granted, and from that time on no merchant could do business, or craftsman ply his trade, without admission to the freedom of the city by the magistrates.

In 1655 a war with neighboring Indians was again threatened, but after some show of force a truce was patched up. A census taken in 1656 showed 120 houses and 1,000 inhabitants in the city. From the earliest days New Amsterdam had a cosmopolitan character: in 1644 the Jesuit missionary Isaac Joques reported that eighteen different languages were spoken in or about the town. New Amsterdam passed into the hands of the English, becoming New York City, with the fall of New Netherland in 1664. After the recapture of the colony by the Dutch in 1673, it was called New Orange, and then renamed New York after the restoration of the colony to England in 1674.

BIBLIOGRAPHY

Thomas J. Condon, *New York Beginnings: The Commercial Origins of New Netherland.*

Allen W. Trelease, *Indian Affairs in Colonial New York, The Seventeenth Century.*

— A. C. FLICK

NEW DEAL

New Deal is a term used to describe the various measures proposed or approved by President Franklin D. Roosevelt from his inauguration in 1933 to 1939 when, as he put it in 1943, "Dr. New Deal" had to make way for "Dr. Win-the-War." He first used the expression "New Deal" on July 2, 1932, when he addressed the Democratic convention in Chicago that had nominated him.

These measures fall into three general categories—relief, recovery, and reform—although there were some overlappings. Some of these measures were aimed at relieving the hardships caused by the economic depression that had started in October 1929. Others had as their chief purpose the recovery of the national economy. Still others were intended to reform certain practices that the president and his advisers regarded as harmful to the common good or were measures that they thought would further the general welfare. In many ways these laws curtailed traditional American individualism, and through them the government regulated aspects of its citizens' lives hitherto regarded as beyond its competence. The New Deal has been distinguished into two phases, the first New Deal, which lasted from 1933 to the beginning of 1935 and had recovery as its primary aim, and the second New Deal, running from 1935 to 1939, during which the chief objective was reform.

In implementing his program Roosevelt had the assistance of the members of his cabinet and numerous other advisers who were called the "New Dealers." Not all of those so termed agreed on principles or practices. There was much variety of opinion among them. As secretary of state, the president chose Cordell Hull of Tennessee, a Wilsonian Democrat with long congressional experience who was interested in free trade. William H. Woodin, a Pennsylvania industrialist, was made secretary of the Treasury but, due to ill health, was succeeded after a few months by Henry Morgenthau, Jr., of New York, a Dutchess County neighbor of the president. Henry A. Wallace, a progressive Republican from Iowa, an agricultural expert and the son of the secretary of agriculture under President Warren G. Harding, was named to the same post as his father. As secretary of the interior, Roosevelt appointed another progressive Republican, Harold L. Ickes of Illinois. Frances Perkins, a New York social worker, became secretary of labor and the first woman to hold a cabinet post. James A. Farley of New York, who had done so much as chairman of the Democratic National Committee to bring about Roosevelt's victory, became postmaster general. As secretary of commerce, the president chose Daniel C. Roper of South Carolina, a former commissioner of internal revenue who practiced law in Washington, D.C. Roosevelt appointed George H. Dern, a former governor of Utah, and Claude A. Swanson, a senator from Virginia, chiefs of the War and Navy departments, respectively. Homer S. Cummings of Connecticut was named attorney general. Those on whom Roosevelt leaned for advice who were not members of his official family became known as the "Brain Trust." Membership in this group shifted rather frequently. It included professors, social workers, lawyers, labor leaders, and financiers. Leading members of the group at one time or another were Raymond Moley, a Columbia professor who had worked under Roosevelt when he was governor of New York on ways to improve the administration of justice in the state; Rexford G. Tugwell—at one time a member of the faculties of the universities of Pennsylvania and Washington and Columbia University—who was concerned about the plight of the small farmers; and Adolph A. Berle, Jr., a lawyer and an authority on corporations who was also on the Columbia faculty. Iowa-born Harry L. Hopkins, a social worker who headed the New York State Temporary Relief Administration under Roosevelt, remained close to the president as director of relief agencies, secretary of commerce, and a roving diplomat.

On Mar. 6, 1933, in order to keep the banking system of the country from collapsing, Roosevelt availed himself of the powers given by the Trading With the Enemy Act of 1917 and suspended all transactions in the Federal Reserve and other banks and financial associations. He also embargoed the export of gold, silver, and currency until Mar. 9 when Congress met in special session. On that day the Emergency Banking Relief Act was passed and signed. This gave the president the power to reorganize all insolvent banks and provided the means by which sound banks could reopen their doors without long delay. On Mar. 12 Roosevelt delivered the first of many "fireside chats" to reassure the country and win support for his policies. The Civilian Conservation Corps (CCC) was established on Mar. 31 to provide work for young men in reclamation projects and in the national parks and forests. About 250,000 youths were so employed at a wage of $30 a week, $25 of which was sent to their families. The Federal Emergency Relief Administration (FERA) was set up on May 12 and placed under the direction of Hopkins. This agency had an appropriation of $500 million, and it was authorized to match the sums allotted for the relief of the unemployed by state and local governments with federal funds. In 1933 there were nearly 13 million people out of work. By the Home Owners' Loan Act of June 13 the Home Owners' Loan Corporation (HOLC) was authorized to issue bonds to the amount of $3 billion to refinance the mortgages of owners who were about to lose their homes through foreclosure.

Members of Roosevelt's "Brain Trust" included professors, social workers, lawyers, labor leaders, and financiers.

The first major recovery measure of the administration was the Agricultural Adjustment Act, which created the Agricultural Adjustment Administration (AAA). Passed on May 12, the act empowered the AAA to control the production of wheat, cotton, corn, rice, tobacco, hogs, and certain other commodities by paying cash subsidies to farmers who voluntarily restricted the acreage planted with such crops or who reduced the number of livestock. These cash subsidies were to be paid out of the proceeds of a tax levied on the processors of farm products. The act also authorized the federal government to make loans on crops to farmers so that they could hold them for better prices, and to buy surpluses outright. By these means it was hoped that demand would catch up with supply and that farm prices would rise. Those who favored inflation as the remedy for the country's ills succeeded in adding an omnibus amendment to the Agricultural Adjustment Act, proposed by Sen. Elmer Thomas of Oklahoma, which gave the president the power to inflate the currency by the coinage of silver at a ratio of his own choice, by printing paper money, or by devaluating the gold content of the dollar. Secretary Wallace and George N. Peek, a former associate of Bernard Baruch on the War Industries Board during World War I and of Gen. Hugh S. Johnson in the Moline Plow Company and the first administrator of the AAA, undertook the job of persuading the farmers to curtail production.

Having tried to assist the farmer in recovery, the administration turned its attention to industry and labor. The National Industrial Recovery Act (NIRA), passed on June 16, set up the National Recovery Administration (NRA). Under governmental direction employers, employees, and consumers were to draft codes by which the various industries would be controlled. The employers were assured that these regulatory codes, which were similar to those drawn up by a number of trade associations in the 1920's, would be exempt from prosecution under the antitrust laws and that production would be limited to raise prices. Under section 7a the employee was promised collective bargaining and that minimum wages and maximum hours would be established. The NRA was placed under the direction of Gen. Hugh S. Johnson, a West Point graduate who had drafted and applied the Draft Act of 1917. Johnson threw himself into the work of codemaking with great energy and considerable showmanship. A great many codes were drawn up and the subscribing companies were allowed to stamp their product with the "Blue Eagle," the symbol indicating that they had conformed to the code of their industry and were helping the country to recover. The second section of this act set up the Public Works Administration (PWA). Charge of this was given to Secretary Ickes, to the disappointment of Johnson, who did not think the NRA would be effective unless one office controlled both the regulation of industry and the disbursement of funds. The PWA was an extension of the policy of President Herbert Hoover to provide employment by the construction of public works. Under Ickes it was administered honestly but too slowly to be of assistance in recovery.

Three measures that were passed during the "hundred days" of this special session of the Seventy-third Congress belong more to the reform category than to relief or recovery. One was the Tennessee Valley Authority Act of May 18, which set up the Tennessee Valley Authority (TVA). This agency was to develop the economic and social well-being of an area that embraced parts of seven states. A corporation was organized and given the right of eminent domain in the valley. It was authorized, among other things, to erect dams and power plants, to improve navigation and methods of flood control, to undertake soil conservation and reforestation projects, and to sell electric power and fertilizers. Arthur E. Morgan, president of Antioch College, was named chairman of the TVA and David E. Lilienthal was made counsel. Lilienthal soon became the driving force in the authority.

Another reform was the Federal Securities Act of May 27. New issues of securities were to be registered with the Federal Trade Commission along with a statement of the financial condition of the company of issue. This statement was also to be made available to all prospective purchasers of the securities. The bill contained no provision for the regulation of stock exchanges. It was revised in 1934, and such regulatory power was entrusted to the Securities and Exchange Commission (SEC). The Glass-Steagall Banking Act, passed on June 16, separated investment from commercial banking so that there could no longer be speculation with the depositors' money. Another provision gave the Federal Reserve Board power over interest rates to prevent speculation with borrowed money. It also set up the Federal Deposit Insurance Corporation, by which the government guaranteed bank deposits below $5,000, later increased to $10,000 (by 1974, $40,000).

By Dec. 5, 1933, three-fourths of the state legislatures had ratified the Twenty-first Amendment to the Constitution, which repealed the Eighteenth Amendment. The states were henceforth to decide whether they would allow the sale of alcoholic beverages or not. As a national experiment, the "dry era" ended. Revenue from liquor taxes helped finance state and federal expenditures.

Despite all this legislation and activity, farm prices, industrial employment, and payrolls declined, and there was dissatisfaction with the recovery program. In an effort to raise prices the president experimented with an inflationary devaluation of the dollar by reducing its gold content, the third of the methods allowed him by the Thomas Amendment to the Agricultural Adjustment Act. This move in the direction of economic nationalism, based on the "commodity dollar" theory of George F. Warren of Cornell University, nullified the work of the International Monetary and Economic Conference then meeting in London. The resulting cheapening of American goods in foreign markets convinced European manufacturers that the United States was seeking an unfair advantage in world trade. It was also a blow to the more conservative advisers of the president, such as Lewis Douglas, the director of the budget, and the banker James Warburg, who wished to maintain the gold standard. The dollar was eventually stabilized by an executive order of Jan. 31, 1934, which fixed the gold content of the dollar at 59.06 percent of its former value. Title to all gold in the Federal Reserve banks was transferred to the government, which was also buying gold in the world market above the current price. By the Gold Clause Act of 1935 no one has the right to sue the government because of gold-clause contracts or claims arising out of changes in the gold value of the dollar. The president also set up the Civil Works Administration (CWA) to "prime the pump" of recovery by increasing the purchasing power of the people at large. This was not intended to be a permanent solution to the problem of unemployment and was ended on Apr. 1, 1934.

While the president's policy of a managed currency was nationalistic in the sense that it was aimed at raising prices at home, it did not mean American isolation from world commerce. Partly to increase American foreign trade Roosevelt, after securing certain guarantees for American citizens from Maksim Litvinov, commissar for foreign affairs of the USSR, recognized the Soviet Union Nov. 16, 1933, and diplomatic representatives were exchanged. The Reciprocal Trade Agreement Act, which was passed on June 12, 1934, was also aimed at stimulating foreign commerce. After a long struggle between Hull and Peek, whom Roosevelt had made foreign trade adviser after he left the AAA, over the interpretation of the act, Hull's more international policy won out over Peek's idea that the act did not intend a general tariff reduction but merely provided a means for drawing up bilateral agreements with various countries. By the end of 1935 reciprocal trade agreements had been negotiated with fourteen countries and the process continued. Such treaties fitted in with the Good Neighbor policy of the administration, which brought an end to U.S. intervention in the internal affairs of Latin America and created a mutual security system for both continents.

During 1934 attempts were made to control the monopolistic tendencies of the larger companies under the NRA codes. During June the Railway Retirement Act was passed and the president appointed a committee to prepare plans for a general program of social security. In the same month the Frazier-Lemke Farm Bankruptcy Act became law. This made it possible for farmers to reacquire lost farms on reasonable terms and to stay bankruptcy proceedings for five years if creditors were unreasonable.

In his message to Congress of Jan. 4, 1935, Roosevelt emphasized the idea that reform was essential to recovery. He called for legislation that would provide assistance for the unemployed, the aged, destitute children, and the physically handicapped. He asked for laws concerning housing, strengthening the NRA, reforming public utilities holding companies, and improving the methods of taxation. Recovery was to be achieved by placing purchasing power in the hands of the many rather than by encouraging price rises in the hope that the benefits would seep down to the employees in the form of higher wages. This marks the opening of the second New Deal.

A 1934 cartoon by Otto Soglow on the bubbling "alphabet soup" of boards, bureaus, codes, and corporations. (The Granger Collection)

The Social Security Bill was introduced on Jan. 17, 1935. A federal tax on employers' payrolls was to be used to build up funds for unemployment insurance. A state that had approved insurance systems could administer up to 90 percent of the payments made within its borders. A tax of 1 percent, which would reach 3 percent by 1949, was levied on the wages of employees and the payrolls of employers to provide funds for old-age pension insurance. The bill was opposed by various groups. Among them were Dr. Francis E. Townsend's Old Age Revolving Pension movement, the American Federation of Labor (which was against the tax on wages), the National Association of Manufacturers, and the Communist party. It became law in August. On May 6, 1935, the Works Progress Administration (WPA) was established with Hopkins as director. Many projects were organized to spread employment and increase purchasing power. Critics of the administration considered many of them to be trivial and called them "boondoggling," as they had termed the jobs provided by the CWA. Among the agencies it established was the Resettlement Administration (RA), under Tugwell in the Department of Agriculture, the purpose of which was to remove farmers from submarginal to better land and to provide poorly paid workers with "Greenbelt towns" outside cities where they could supplement their salaries by part-time farming. An enthusiastic supporter of these ideas was Eleanor Roosevelt, the president's wife, whose political and social interests ranged widely. Another was the Rural Electrification Administration (REA), established May 11, which offered low interest loans to farmers' cooperatives to build power lines with WPA labor in localities where private companies thought investment unjustified. A third was the National Youth Administration (NYA), formed June 26, which aimed at keeping young people at school and out of the labor market. Money was turned over to school administrators who paid it out to students for various types of work about the school. The Federal Theatre Project provided work for many actors, directors, and stage crews; the Federal Writers' Project turned out a series of state guides; the Historical Records Survey brought to light many documents in local archives. The wages paid WPA workers were higher than relief payments but lower than those paid by private enterprise. In 1936, after considerable pressure from the workers, the government raised wages on WPA projects to the prevailing level but reduced the number of hours worked a month so that wage totals remained at security level. The government wished the workers to return to private enterprise as soon as possible.

In June 1935 the president sent a special message to Congress on tax revision. Tax burdens, he said, should be redistributed according to ability to pay. Higher taxes on large individual incomes, inheritances, and gifts would lead to a wider distribution of wealth. The principle of ability to pay should also be extended to corporations. The Wealth Tax Act, which embodied these proposals, was opposed by Sen. Huey P. Long of Louisiana and his "Share Our Wealth" movement as too moderate, but it was passed on Aug. 30. Taxes on large individual incomes were steeply scaled to 75 percent on those over $5 million. Taxes on estates were increased. Excess profits taxes on corporations ranged from 6 percent on profits above 10 percent to 12 percent on profits above 15 percent. Income taxes on corporations were graduated from 12.5 percent to 15 percent. The act was regarded by many as a soak-the-rich scheme and as a punitive measure on the part of the administration, which had parted company with big business by this time.

The president submitted the Public Utility Holding Company Act to Congress, which was designed to prevent abuses in that field, especially those made possible by the pyramiding of such companies. The bill did not require the abolition of utility holding companies but imposed a "death sentence" on those that could not prove their usefulness in five years. The act as finally passed on Aug. 28, 1935, permitted two levels of holding companies but otherwise retained the "death sentence" clause.

In June 1935, FDR sent a message to Congress that tax burdens should be redistributed according to ability to pay, and should lead to a wider distribution of wealth.

Roosevelt requested the extension of the much criticized NRA for two more years. The Senate voted to extend it for ten months. At the same time it was considering the Wagner-Connery National Labor Relations Act, which was designed to strengthen section 7a of the NIRA. The bill proposed to outlaw employer-dominated unions and assure labor of its right to collective bargaining through representatives chosen by itself. While a number of the senators thought that this bill and section 7a overlapped, it passed on May 16. The bill, which did not become an administration measure until the NIRA was declared unconstitutional, became law on July 5, 1935. By it the National Labor Relations Board (NLRB) was set up to determine suitable units for collective bargaining, to conduct elections for the choice of labor's representatives, and to prevent interference with such elections.

The constitutionality of this controversial legislation became a central issue in 1935. Of the nine justices who then sat on the bench of the Supreme Court four were considered to be conservatives: Willis Van Devanter, George Sutherland, James Clark McReynolds, and Pierce Butler; three to be liberal: Louis Brandeis, Benjamin N. Cardozo, and Harlan F. Stone; while Chief Justice Charles Evans Hughes and Justice Owen J. Roberts were thought to occupy an intermediate position. On Jan. 7 the court decided that section 9c of the NIRA was an unconstitutional delegation of legislative authority by Congress to the executive. This led to doubts about the constitutionality of the whole act. On May 6 the court invalidated the Railroad Retirement Act, which raised the question of the constitutionality of the Social Security Act that was before Congress. On May 27 the Frazier-Lemke Farm Bankruptcy Act was declared unconstitutional because under it private property was taken without compensation. On the same day a unanimous court declared, in *Schechter Poultry Corporation* v. *United States*, that the legislature's delegation of the codemaking power to the president in the NIRA was an unconstitutional surrender of its own proper function. The court also found that the Schechter Corporation's activities, the sale of chickens in Brooklyn, N.Y., had only an indirect effect on interstate commerce. Roosevelt termed this a "horse-and-buggy" interpretation of the commerce clause.

A way out of this impasse was found in part by rewriting some of this legislation so as to meet the objections of the court. The Frazier-Lemke Farm Mortgage Moratorium Act of 1935 and the Wagner-Crosser Railroad Retirement Act replaced those found unconstitutional. The Guffey-Snyder Bituminous Coal Stabilization Act, passed on Aug. 30, practically reenacted the whole bituminous coal code of the NRA. The Wagner National Labor Relations Act replaced section 7a of the NIRA. When the court found the AAA unconstitutional in January 1936, because the tax on food processors was an unjust expropriation of money and because the powers of the states were invaded, it was replaced by the Soil Conservation and Domestic Allotment Act of Feb. 29, 1936, and later by the second Agricultural Adjustment Act of 1938. Rewriting did not save all this legislation. On May 18, 1936, the Guffey-Snyder Act was invalidated. When, on June 1, a New York minimum wage law was declared unconstitutional because it violated freedom of contract, the president said that the court had created a "no man's land" where neither a state nor the federal government could act.

At the Democratic convention held in Philadelphia in June 1936, Roosevelt and Vice-President John Nance Garner were nominated practically without opposition. Alfred E. Smith and a number of conservative Democrats, who had joined with others to form the Liberty League, attempted to lead "Jeffersonian Democrats" out of the party but without much success. The convention also repealed the two-thirds rule with which Democratic conventions had been so long saddled. In his acceptance speech Roosevelt defended the measures of his administration and attacked his opponents, whom he termed "economic royalists." The Republicans nominated Gov. Alfred M. Landon of Kansas, who was strongly supported by publisher William R. Hearst, for president and Frank Knox of Illinois for vice-president. A third party was formed out of the followers of the Rev. Gerald L. K. Smith, who had taken over Long's "Share Our Wealth" movement after the senator was assassinated in 1935, of Dr. Francis Townsend, and of the Rev. Charles E. Coughlin of the Social Justice movement who had become strongly anti-Roosevelt. It was called the Union party and it nominated Rep. William F. Lemke of North Dakota for president. The Socialists nominated Norman Thomas and the Communists, Earl Browder. Labor took a very active part in the campaign and the new industrial labor organization, the Committee on Industrial Organization (CIO), under the leadership of John L. Lewis and Sidney Hillman, set up Labor's Nonpartisan League and raised a million dollars for the support of Roosevelt and other prolabor candidates of either party. After a stormy campaign the popular vote was 27,752,869 for Roosevelt and 16,674,665 for Landon. The electoral vote was 523 to 8. Only Maine and Vermont cast their votes for the Republican candidate.

After this resounding victory at the polls the president sent a proposal to Congress to reorganize the federal judiciary on Feb. 5, 1937. In his message he pointed out Congress' power over the federal judiciary and the difficulties arising from insufficient personnel, crowded dockets, and aged judges. He suggested that the number of federal judges be increased when the incumbent judges did not retire at seventy. He asked that cases involving the constitutionality of legislation be removed from the lowest court to the Supreme Court immediately and that such cases should have precedence there. This proposal shocked a great many people and Roosevelt was accused of trying to "pack" the court with judges who favored his legislation. During the debate over this bill the Democrats in Congress and throughout the country split. The situation was helped at this point by certain decisions of the Supreme Court. On Mar. 27 it upheld, by a vote of five to four, both the Washington State Minimum Wage Act, which was similar to the invalidated New York law, and the Frazier-Lemke Farm Mortgage Act. Justice Roberts joined Chief Justice Hughes and justices Brandeis, Cardozo, and Stone in these decisions. On Apr. 12 it found the Wagner Act, which had been declared unconstitutional by the circuit court of appeals in San Francisco, valid. On May 24 it declared the Social Security Act constitutional. Despite this change on the part of the Court and the fact that his party was divided on the matter, Roosevelt continued to press his judiciary reorganization bill. A substitute was proposed and the Judicial Procedure Reform Act was passed on Aug. 24. No mention of the appointment of new judges was made in the bill. This was the president's first important defeat at the hands of Congress.

During the summer of 1937 an economic recession started that lasted through 1938. Many attributed it to the administration's hostility to business and capital. High taxes, it was said, discouraged business expansion and personal initiative. Roosevelt again resorted to pump priming and expanded bank credits.

On Feb. 16, 1938, Congress passed a second Agricultural Adjustment Act. Like the first, it aimed at controlling surpluses but used different means. Whenever a surplus in an export crop that would cause a fall in prices appeared likely, the AAA would fix a marketable quota and the farmers who agreed not to market more than the product of the acreage allotted to them could store their surpluses under government seal until a shortage developed. In the interim they could receive loans on them. The AAA would also fix a parity price that represented the purchasing power of a unit of the crop concerned during the years 1909 to 1914. The farmer was to sell his surplus when the price was at parity or above. Thus, the "ever normal granary," a favorite project of Wallace, would be established. The act also had provisions taking care of the special problems raised by conditions in the Dust Bowl, the area of the semi-arid high Plains, and for soil conservation.

On June 25 the Fair Labor Standards Act was passed. The law sought an eventual minimum wage of 40 cents an hour and a maximum work week of 40 hours. Time-and-a-half was to be paid for overtime, and labor by children under sixteen was forbidden. Exceptions were made for various localities. The National Housing Act of Sept. 1, 1937, made low-rent housing available in many cities. The second New Deal was written into law.

The Fair Labor Standards Act (1937) sought a minimum wage of 40 cents an hour and a maximum work week of 40 hours; overtime would be paid at time-and-a-half.

These measures had not gone unopposed. In addition an executive reorganization bill, which had been proposed by Roosevelt, like many of its predecessors was defeated largely because it was regarded as connected with his judiciary reorganization bill. The legislature also repealed the graduated tax on the undistributed profits of corporations of 1936. The president personally entered the congressional campaigns of 1938 and urged the voters not to reelect certain Democratic members of Congress who had not supported his program in recent sessions. Leading targets were Sen. Walter George of Georgia, Sen. Ellison DuRant ("Cotton Ed") Smith of South Carolina, Sen. Millard E. Tydings of Maryland, and Rep. John O'Connor of New York. Except for O'Connor the president was unsuccessful in his attempt to "purge" the party, and for the first time since 1928 the number of Republicans in Congress increased.

By 1938 the world situation had become very tense. Japan, Italy, and Germany were threatening international peace. The Democratic party was divided on foreign policy. The South, although not enthusiastic about all of Roosevelt's domestic policies, supported his program of resistance to aggression, while the Middle West and West were in favor of his domestic reforms but tended to isolationism. The Northeast alone supported him in both. In the face of world conditions, especially after the Munich crisis of September 1938, Roosevelt felt compelled to subordinate his domestic reforms to keep southern support for his foreign policy. His failure actively to support an antilynching bill indicated a new outlook. Henceforth, he would strive chiefly for party and domestic unity as the nations prepared for war.

BIBLIOGRAPHY

Irving Bernstein, *Turbulent Years: A History of the American Worker, 1933–1941.*

James McGregor Burns, *Roosevelt: The Lion and the Fox.*

William Leuchtenberg, *Franklin D. Roosevelt and the New Deal, 1932–1940.*

Raymond Moley, *The First New Deal.*

Dexter Perkins, *The New Age of Franklin D. Roosevelt.*

Arthur M. Schlesinger, Jr., *The Age of Roosevelt: The Crisis of the Old Order, 1919–1933.*

— VINCENT C. HOPKINS

NEW ENGLAND

New England, embracing the six states of Maine, New Hampshire, Vermont, Massachusetts, Rhode Island, and Connecticut, formed a distinct section with a character of its own from the beginning of European settlement in North America. It is significant that New England first developed the idea of a complete separation of the colonies from Great Britain, that it opposed westward expansion of the country, and that it was first to suggest secession from the Union. Its sectionalism, separatism, and local character have many causes.

Geographically, the section is largely cut off from the rest of the continent by the northern spurs of the Appalachian mountain range, and it has no river system, such as the Mohawk-Hudson, giving it access to the hinterland. Although the Puritan outlook was widespread in the period of early English settlement in all the colonies, New England was settled by the strictest of the Puritans. In Massachusetts the government set up was a theocracy, which, owing to the transfer of the charter, was practically independent of England for a half-century. Connecticut and Rhode Island colonies never had royal governors. Owing to altered conditions in the home country, immigration almost ceased for two centuries after 1640. The early establishment of Harvard in 1636, though it was scarcely more than a grammar school, increased parochialism, for potential leaders who might have been broadened by going to Britain for their education remained in the narrow atmosphere of the colony. The poor soil and broken terrain prevented the development of large estates or staple crops, as well as of slavery. The section became a land of small farms and independent farmers as stubborn as their soil, of fishermen along the coast, and of traders overseas who, lacking furs and staple crops, had to be ingenious in finding ways of making money.

There were local differences, such as the religious intolerance of Massachusetts and the freedom of Rhode Island, but in the period from 1630 to 1830, roughly, the New England, or Yankee, character was becoming set in the section as a whole. The lack of immigrants and of outside contacts and control by the clerical oligarchy were factors of importance. Moreover, even when New Englanders migrated, they usually did so in groups of families or entire congregations; everywhere group solidarity helped to maintain customs and character.

The typical institutions of New England were thus developed almost in isolation—schools, the Congregational church, the town system of government, and the "New England conscience"—as was the New Englander's preoccupation with religious and spiritual matters. The opening of the Erie Canal in 1825, linking Lake Erie to New York City, isolated the section yet more, and for long, owing to characteristic insistence on short local lines, even its railroads did not link it to the nation. But training in mind, self-reliance, and ingenuity had developed the most skilled workmen in America, and New England developed manufactures, especially those calling for a high degree of individual skill, to an extent that no other section did. The growth of manufactures appeared to call for an increase in cheap labor, and after 1840 foreign immigration was so great as largely to change the population and character. For example, Puritan Massachusetts came to be an overwhelmingly Roman Catholic state.

The New England strain of character, set through its centuries of struggle and separatism, persisted, and contributed much to other sections by migration. Among the earliest movements were those to eastern Long Island and New Jersey—and even to South Carolina. Later there were settlements in Pennsylvania, the Mohawk Valley, Ohio, Illinois, Michigan, Wisconsin, and Oregon. There are towns and districts all across the northern United States that seem like transplanted bits of New England, and wherever groups of settlers went, they carried New England ideas of education, the Congregational church, the township and town meeting, and the peculiar flavor of the New England character and attitude. Sectional as it has been, the influence of New England on the rest of the United States has been out of all proportion to its size and population.

[See also Hartford Convention.]

BIBLIOGRAPHY

J. T. Adams, *History of New England.*

L. K. Mathews, *The Expansion of New England.*

— JAMES TRUSLOW ADAMS

"NEW ENGLAND WAY"

"New England Way," a phrase used to refer to the ecclesiastical polity, its relation to the civil powers, and the practices of the Massachusetts Bay Colony churches, and sometimes, indiscriminately, to those of Connecticut or Rhode Island. Intended to prove that "Discipline out of the Word" enforced by godly magistrates was possible, Massachusetts considered its churches examples for Puritan reconstruction of the Church of England. English reformers inquired into the system (1637), and after the Long Parliament began ecclesiastical "reform" (1641), interest in Massachusetts polity led John Cotton to expound its principles in *The Way of the Churches of Christ in New England . . .* (1645); the short title of his work, *The New England Way,* made permanent an expression already common.

Massachusetts considered its churches examples for Puritan reconstruction of the Church of England.

Originally a platform of opposition to English prelacy, based upon teachings of Henry Jacob, William Ames, and others, the "New England Way," immature in the 1640's, developed into New England Congregationalism. The church, originating neither in princes nor parliaments but in God's Word, was a body of professed regenerates (the "elect") who subscribed to a "covenant" (or creed), selected officers, chose and ordained its minister, and was subject to no interchurch organizations save "consociations" for counsel and advice. Being "visible saints," they admitted only persons who approved the covenant and whose piety and deportment recommended them to the congregation. They denied separation from the Anglican church; they separated only from its "corruptions," considered themselves true "primitive churches of Christ," and were supremely intolerant of others. Magistrates, "nursing fathers of the churches," were limited in civil authority by the Word (in practice, as interpreted by ministers) and compelled both to conform and to purge churches and state of heterodoxy. Citizenship depended on church membership. Church and state were indissolubly united. The "New England Way" did not appeal to English Separatists, whose multiple sects required embracing toleration, or to Presbyterians, whose synods held great interchurch authority, or to parliamentarians, who required the church to be subject to parliamentary prerogative. Thus, in many particulars, the "New England Way" was impracticable as an English model, and New England Congregationalists parted company with their English brethren.

BIBLIOGRAPHY

Benjamin Hanbury, ed., *Historical Memorials Relating to the Independents and Congregationalists From Their Rise to the Restoration.*
Perry Miller, *Orthodoxy in Massachusetts.*

— RAYMOND P. STEARNS

NEW FRANCE

For a century after the discovery of America the kings of France, preoccupied with dynastic and civil wars, devoted little attention to New World enterprises. In 1524 Francis I sent out Giovanni da Verrazano, whose expedition provided a paper claim to much of North America, while the three expeditions of Jacques Cartier (1534–42) served to fix French attention on the region adjoining the Gulf of Saint Lawrence. The short peace with England between 1598 and 1610 made possible the first permanent French establishment in America, at Quebec in 1608. For over half a century the government followed the policy of making grants to various companies to exploit the colony, and despite the devotion of Samuel de Champlain, its growth was painfully slow.

In 1661 Louis XIV assumed direct control of the colony, and a notable renaissance ensued. Soldiers were sent out to defend it and families to establish homes. Numerous measures looking to its economic betterment were instituted, and the Iroquois, who had previously been dangerous enemies, were subdued. These things prepared the way for a remarkable geographical expansion, whereby the boundaries of New France were extended along the Great Lakes and the entire Mississippi Valley—notably by Simon François Daumont, Sieur de Saint Lusson; Louis Jolliet; Robert Cavelier, Sieur de La Salle; Louis Hennepin; and Daniel Greysolon, Sieur Duluth.

The revolution of 1688, which placed William III on the English throne, initiated the second Hundred Years' War between France and England. To Old World rivalries the colonies added their own, and the period 1689–1763 witnessed four international wars, in each of which the American colonies participated. The long conflict ended with the surrender of Canada to England (Sept. 8, 1760), while the remainder of New France was divided between England and Spain. New France as a political entity thus ceased to exist, although the French people and culture remained permanently seated in the valley of the Saint Lawrence.

[See also Paris, Treaty of.]

BIBLIOGRAPHY

Adam Shortt and Arthur G. Doughty, eds., *Canada and Its Provinces: A History of the Canadian People and Their Institutions by One Hundred Associates.*
G. M. Wrong and H. H. Langton, eds., *Chronicles of Canada.*

— M. M. QUAIFE

NEW FREEDOM

New Freedom, a term generally accepted as descriptive of the political and economic philosophy underlying the domestic policies of President Woodrow Wilson at the opening of his first administration in 1913. Wilson's more significant utterances in the campaign of 1912 were published under the title *The New Freedom* early the following year. They constituted an earnest plea for a more humanitarian spirit in government and business and political reforms that would restore government to the people and break the power of selfish and privileged minorities. The growth of corporate power, he argued, had rendered obsolete many traditional concepts of American democracy. Wilson felt that government must have not a negative, but a positive, program in that regard and use its power "to cheer and inspirit our people with the sure prospects of social justice and due reward, with the vision of the open gates of opportunity for all."

BIBLIOGRAPHY

R. S. Baker, *Life and Letters of Woodrow Wilson.*

— W. A. ROBINSON

NEW FRONTIER

New Frontier, the term used to describe the economic and social programs of the presidency of John F. Kennedy (Jan. 20, 1961, to Nov. 22, 1963). The young, vigorous, articulate president inspired a new élan in the nation's political culture. His administration made innovations at home in economic and defense policies, a manned-flight moon program, and civil rights bills. Abroad, Kennedy supported the Bay of Pigs invasion of Cuba and the commitment of troops to Vietnam; he also formed the Peace Corps, favored reciprocal trade and the Alliance for Progress, protected Berlin, forced the Soviet Union to take its missiles out of Cuba, neutralized Laos, and signed the nuclear test ban treaty.

BIBLIOGRAPHY

Aida DiPace Donald, *John F. Kennedy and the New Frontier.*
Arthur M. Schlesinger, Jr., *A Thousand Days.*
Theodore C. Sorensen, *Kennedy.*

— AIDA DIPACE DONALD

NEW HARMONY SETTLEMENT

New Harmony Settlement, in Posey County, Ind., was founded in 1825 by Robert Owen, the English philanthropist and industrialist, on the site previously occupied by the Harmony Society of Pennsylvania. Owen attempted to put into practice the theories of socialism and human betterment that he had evolved. By December 1825 New Harmony had attracted a heterogeneous population of about 1,000 men, women, and children of all sorts and conditions. Following a preliminary organization the constitution of the New Harmony Community of Equality was adopted, Feb. 5, 1826. It provided for absolute equality of property, labor, and opportunity, together with freedom of speech and action. The absence of any real authority in the community government resulted in virtual anarchy, and after several abortive attempts to better conditions, Owen admitted the failure of the experiment on May 26, 1827. A number of communities modeled on New Harmony sprang up in other states at that time and were equally short-lived.

BIBLIOGRAPHY

G. B. Lockwood, *The New Harmony Communities,* and *The New Harmony Movement.*

— EDGAR B. NIXON

NEW NATIONALISM

New Nationalism, the term used to describe the political philosophy of Theodore Roosevelt that the nation is the best instrument for advancing progressive democracy. In more detail, the phrase implied emphasis on the need for political, social, and industrial reforms, such as government regulation and control of corporations, better working conditions for labor, conservation of natural resources, and a concentration of more power directly in the people. Implied also were the ineffectiveness of the states in dealing with these problems and the consequent necessity of using the powers of the national government and of increasing those powers to the extent necessary.

[See also New Deal; New Freedom.]

BIBLIOGRAPHY

Joseph Bucklin Bishop, *Theodore Roosevelt and His Time.*

— CLARENCE A. BERDAHL

NEW NETHERLAND

No serious attempt was made to plant a colony in New Netherland before the organization of the Dutch West India Company in 1621. In the spring of 1624 a group of thirty families, most of whom were Walloons, were sent in the ship *New Netherland.* A few of the emigrants remained at the mouth of the Hudson River but the greater part were settled up the river at Fort Orange, where the city of Albany now stands. A fort was also built on Nut (now Governors) Island. Shortly afterward Willem Verhulst was appointed *commies* and sailed for New Netherland. Three months after Verhulst's arrival in 1625 the thinly settled colony was reinforced by the coming of forty-two new emigrants. In addition one of the directors of the company sent 103 head of livestock, including horses, cows, hogs, and sheep. In July 1625 the settlement was moved from Nut Island to Manhattan Island and called New Amsterdam. A new fort was built.

Verhulst did not remain long in New Amsterdam. His own council found him guilty of mismanagement. He was dismissed, and Peter Minuit was appointed in his place as the first director general. Minuit negotiated the purchase of Manhattan from the Indians, paying the value of sixty guilders ($24) in trinkets, thus legalizing the occupation already in effect. In 1626, because of trouble with the Indians, Minuit moved the families at Fort Orange to Manhattan, leaving only a small garrison behind under Sebastian Crol.

Members of the settlement had no voice in its administration. Power was centered in the hands of the director and his council, who were appointed by and represented the company. The colonists for the most part were not free agents, but were bound by contracts to the company. Although farmers were allotted free land, they were obliged to stay in the colony for six years. The company had right of first purchase of the produce from their fields, and they could sell their farms only to one of the other colonists. Indentured husbandmen, under still more rigid restrictions, worked the company farms. Instructions in considerable detail were sent to the director by the company, and only in cases of urgent necessity was he allowed to modify his orders. New legislation was submitted to the executive committee of the company, as were appeals in judicial cases. The Reform Church was supported, though freedom of conscience was granted.

Peter Minuit negotiated the purchase of the island from the Manhattan Indians, paying the value of sixty guilders ($24) in trinkets, thus legalizing the occupation already in effect.

The first few years showed a moderate profit to the company from trade, but the efforts at colonization proved a loss. Among the directors of the company two parties appeared, one favoring active colonization of the province, the other desirous of restricting the company to its trading function. The former group was successful in 1629 in the passage of the Charter of Freedoms and Exemptions, which provided for the grant of great estates, called patroonships, to such members of the company as should found settlements of fifty persons within four years. The effect of patroonships under the charter has been overemphasized: with the single exception of Rensselaerswyck, they were unsuccessful. Another type of landholding provided for in the charter was destined to be of far greater importance: "private persons" were allowed to take possession of as much land as they could cultivate properly. In 1638, further to encourage colonization, trade restrictions in the colony were reduced, better provision was offered for transportation of settlers and their goods, and the fur-trade monopoly was discontinued. The revised charter of 1640 reduced the size of future patroonships and held out promises of local self-government.

In 1631 Minuit was recalled, and Wouter Van Twiller was named his successor. The administration of Van Twiller was marked by violent quarrels with his council and prominent colonists. In 1637 his failure to send reports to the company resulted in his recall and the appointment of Willem Kieft as director general. An adventurer with a bad record, Kieft did nothing to improve it during his administration. By the summer of 1641 his brutal and unwise Indian policy had created so dangerous a situation that he was constrained to ask the colonists to elect a board to advise with him, and the Twelve Men were chosen. Although they had been called only to give advice on Indian affairs, to Kieft's annoyance they drew up a petition asking for much-needed reforms. The Indian difficulties died down temporarily, but in September 1643 an unprovoked night attack on an Indian encampment, instigated by Kieft, caused the Indians to rise in fury. Safety was to be found only in the immediate vicinity of the fort. Distant Fort Orange alone was not molested. Kieft once more called for an election of representatives, and the Eight Men were chosen. In October 1643 and again in the following year they petitioned the company for aid, bitterly criticizing Kieft's management of Indian relations. Conditions in the province were desperate. The frightened settlers huddling in or near the fort faced starvation. Hostile bands of Indians, estimated as totaling 15,000, threatened attack, but they had no common and concerted plan. June brought reinforcements, but hostilities dragged on, and it was not until August 1645 that a general peace was signed. The Indian war had not extended to Fort Orange and the patroon's colony of Rensselaerswyck, although trade had suffered. Despite the restrictions imposed by the company this little settlement had grown by 1645 into a sizable colony.

The complaints of the Eight Men and similar protests from private persons resulted in the recall of Kieft, and on May 11, 1647, Peter Stuyvesant, his successor, arrived in New Amsterdam. The new director was honorable, active, and conscientious, but his autocratic disposition and his hostility to popular demands led to continual friction. Conditions in the province were bad; trade was in a state of confusion; morals were low; and money was urgently needed. In September 1647, as a means of raising revenue, Stuyvesant called for an election of representatives. The Nine Men were chosen. They met the requests of the director general fairly and expressed themselves as willing to tax themselves to help finish the church and reorganize the school. Then, despite protests from Stuyvesant, they drew up and sent to Holland two documents known as the Petition and the Remonstrance of New Netherland. The Petition was a concise statement of the unsatisfactory condition of the province with suggested remedies; the Remonstrance, a longer document, furnished in detail the facts on which the appeal was based. In April 1652 the company, inclined to grant some of the concessions asked, instructed Stuyvesant to give New Amsterdam a burgher government.

Although Stuyvesant made a sincere attempt to maintain friendly relations with the Indians, he had to fight three Indian wars. The first broke out in 1655 in New Amsterdam and extended to the Esopus settle-

Peter Stuyvesant, Director-General of New Netherland, 1646-1664. This 17th-century painting now belongs to the New York Historical Society. (Corbis-Bettmann)

ment, near Kingston, and to Long Island. Five years later there was a serious outbreak at Esopus, which was aggravated when Stuyvesant sent some of the Indian captives to Curaçao as slaves. This incident rankled, and the Indians rose again; so it was not until May 1664 that a general peace was signed.

The gradual encroachment of settlers from New England on territory claimed by the Dutch had been a source of trouble since the beginning of the colony. Rivalry over the fur trade and complaint from the English traders against the tariffs levied at New Amsterdam increased the ill feeling. Stuyvesant took up the quarrel vigorously. No decision was reached over the tariff and Indian trade disputes, but the question of boundaries was finally settled by the Treaty of Hartford in 1650. The last year of the Dutch regime in New Netherland was fraught with grave fear of Indian wars, rebellion, and British invasion. Stuyvesant tried vainly to put the province in a state of defense, but on Aug. 29, 1664, he was forced to surrender to an English fleet, which came to claim the province in the name of James, Duke of York.

BIBLIOGRAPHY

A. C. Flick, ed., *History of the State of New York*, vols. I, II.

— A. C. FLICK

NEW PLYMOUTH COLONY

New Plymouth Colony was founded by a group of about a hundred English emigrants who came to New England in the *Mayflower* in 1620. The dominant element in this group consisted of religious dissenters who had separated from the Anglican church because of their dissatisfaction with its doctrines and practices. Some of these Separatists had come from Leiden in the Netherlands, where they had been living for more than a decade since leaving their original homes in northern England to escape persecution and association with their Anglican neighbors. After a brief sojourn in Amsterdam, they had settled in Leiden, where they had organized a flourishing church. Although they enjoyed religious freedom, they became dissatisfied in their new home. They were unwilling to give up the language and customs of England for those of Holland, had difficulty in making a comfortable living in a foreign land, and were disturbed about the enticements to worldliness and immorality to which their children were subjected. Accordingly, some of them (thirty-five in number) decided to join others of their religious persuasion in England and go to the New World. Both groups sailed on the *Mayflower* from Plymouth, England, Sept. 16, 1620. On Dec. 26, after five weeks spent in exploring Cape Cod, the *Mayflower* anchored in the harbor of what came to be Plymouth, Mass. The task of erecting suitable houses was rendered difficult by the lateness of the season, although the winter was a comparatively mild one. Nearly all the Indians in the vicinity had been destroyed by pestilence, and the few survivors gave no trouble. On the contrary, their deserted cornfields afforded the settlers quite an advantage. Partly because of poor housing, but more because of the run-down condition of the emigrants as a result of a lack of proper food on the voyage, there was great suffering the first winter and nearly half of them died. By spring there had come a turn for the better, and in a few years the menace of a food shortage was permanently removed.

The capital for the undertaking was furnished by a group of London merchants. An agreement was entered into between them and the settlers whereby a sort of joint-stock company was formed. The arrangement proved unsatisfactory to both the planters and their backers, and in 1627 the merchants sold their interests to the settlers and thus withdrew from the venture. From that time on the planters were the sole stockholders of the corporation, which had become a colony.

During the first decade of its existence Plymouth was the only settlement in the area, but gradually other villages were established; so the town of Plymouth widened into the colony of New Plymouth.

Before embarking for America the Pilgrims had received assurances from James I that they would not be molested in the practice of their religion. A patent was also received from the Virginia Company authorizing them to settle on its grant and enjoy the right of self-government. But because they had landed outside the limits of the Virginia Company this patent was of no avail. The settlers, therefore, had no title to their lands and no legal authority to establish a government. It was not long, however, before a valid title to the land was obtained in the form of patents issued in 1621 and 1630 by the Council for New England—but the power to form a government was not conferred by these patents. Nevertheless a liberal government was founded for the colony, for the Pilgrims had, before landing, organized themselves into a body politic by entering into a solemn covenant that they would make just and equal laws and would yield obedience to the same. This agreement, known as the Mayflower Compact, had been signed by all the adult male settlers except eight, who were probably ill at the time. Laws were made by the General Court, at first a primary assembly and later a representative assembly of one house, the members of which were chosen annually by popular election. Administrative and certain important judicial functions were performed by the governor and the assistants, who were elected each year by the freemen, or qualified voters. On the death of the first governor, John Carver, in April 1621, William Bradford was chosen his successor. He was continued in office by reelection for more than thirty years.

New Plymouth was not well adapted to agriculture, since there was a scarcity of cultivable land in the colony. Nor was the location of the settlement so favorable for a profitable business in fishing and fur trading as were the locations of the other Puritan colonies. Consequently, the Pilgrims did not play a leading role in the history of colonial New England, although it was largely because of their initiative that the Congregational form of church government was adopted in that section. New Plymouth was quite overshadowed by its neighbors, Connecticut and Massachusetts Bay, and was absorbed by the latter in 1691.

BIBLIOGRAPHY

W. T. Davis, ed., *Bradford's History of Plymouth Plantation.*

R. G. Usher, *The Pilgrims and Their History.*

— O. P. CHITWOOD

NEW SOUTH

New South, a phrase originally used to designate the post-Reconstruction economic development of the South, particularly the expansion of industry, which has come to be applied to the post-Civil War South generally, with particular reference to the fundamental changes that have occurred. In the years immediately following Reconstruction, many southerners came to look upon the agrarian economy of the antebellum South as no longer viable and to believe that their region's future lay in the development of industry. F. W. Dawson, editor of the *Charleston* (S.C.) *News and Courier,* was an early prophet of this New South concept. He preached the South's need for more industry, arguing that the great significance of the Civil War was the white man's emancipation from slavery and cotton. Also influential and well known among those who advocated the growth of industry in the South was Henry W. Grady, longtime editor of the *Atlanta Constitution.* Grady orated to northern audiences as well as southern ones in his pursuit of an industrial economy for his native region, and his editorials in the late 19th century espoused this theme with vigor. Grady popularized the phrase "New South" in a famous address in New York in December 1886.

Southern politicians joined the South's opinion makers and economic leaders to turn the southern economy upside down; all these groups actively pursued the moneyed interests of the North and Europe. Northerners poured investments into the South at an amazing rate, especially after 1879, at the end of an economic depression, when both northern and foreign capital were seeking investment opportunities. Northern money meant northern control, and the South soon became an economic appendage of the North. This colonial status of the southern economy was well established in several industries before the end of the 19th century, and it continued to exist and to expand in the years following. Activities in regard to the public domain in the South illustrated the exploitative aspects of northern economic policy. Northern speculators acquired millions of acres of virgin timberlands from the national and southern state governments, making hundreds of millions of dollars as they denuded the land. Southern railroad development proved to be even more attractive to northern and foreign capital than southern real estate. Southern railroad mileage increased from 16,605 miles in 1880 to 39,108 in 1890, a 135.5 percent increase, in comparison with an 86.5 percent increase for the nation as a whole. In the 1880's more than 180 new railroad companies instituted activities in the region. Consolidations then took place, putting more economic power in the hands of northern bankers and financiers. The southern iron and steel industries followed the railroading pattern as the South felt the impact of great quantities of northern and English capital. Alabama's iron production in 1889 amounted to ten times the state's output a decade earlier. In the final quarter of the 19th century the South's pig iron production increased seventeenfold, more than twice the national rate. Great iron deposits, their proximity to coal and limestone, the rapidly developing transportation system, and northern investment capital all combined to increase the South's iron and steel output. Northern companies continued to control these industries in the 20th century.

The most important southern industry before the Civil War had been cotton textile manufacturing, and this industry expanded rapidly in the postwar years. Between 1860 and 1880 several southern states more than doubled their prewar production. In the following decades growth and production were so great that many people inaccurately assumed that 1880 marked the beginning of the industry in the South. In a dizzying period of expansion, the number of mills in the South rose from 161 in 1880 to 400 in 1900. The rate of growth in the 1890's was 67.4 percent, compared with the national increase of 7.5 percent. Capital investment in southern cotton mills increased by 131.4 percent between 1880 and 1900, while investments in New England mills increased by only 12.1 percent. World War I caused boom years for southern textile production and throughout the 1920's mill promoters continued their crusade for regional economic salvation through the textile industry. In the 20th century many New England mills with southern branches moved their major operations to the South, causing much social and economic distress for some areas of the Northeast.

The South led in tobacco manufacturing before the Civil War, and it resumed the lead early in the postwar period. The enlarged tobacco industry resulted mainly from mechanization and the increased demand for cigarettes. By the middle of the 20th century Americans were consuming more and more tobacco products per capita, despite cancer scares, and southern tobacco companies continued to expand and increase their output.

In addition to lumbering, railroading, and tobacco and textile manufacturing, the 20th-century South produced large quantities of furniture, paper, and aluminum. Also related to the South's natural resources, oil and its by-products, gas, and sulfur came to transform the western edge of the South. Petrochemicals became big business. World War II further stimulated southern industrial and economic development. Industries related to warfare, atomic energy, and the space age changed the southern landscape and gave southerners increased income and purchasing power. Billions of dollars worth of government contracts were awarded to companies in the southern states during the war years, and many army posts and camps were established or enlarged. Military research and the advent of space exploration altered Oak Ridge, Tenn.; Paducah, Ky.; Houston, Tex.; and Cape Canaveral, Fla. Thousands of related or lesser industries added to the South's drive toward industrialization.

While some white backlash has been apparent, white southerners on the whole have tolerated (if not entirely accepted) the growing influence of African Americans.

Although the term "New South" was first used (and continues to be used) to describe the industrialized South, it is also commonly applied generally to the South since 1865, just as the term "Old South" describes the antebellum South. Used in this way, the phrase "New South" refers to a South that is changing not only economically but also politically, demographically, agriculturally, educationally, socially, racially, and intellectually. The so-called Solid South is disappearing slowly as the Republican party grows in the region. The face of the South is changing as rural dwellers move to the towns, as towns become cities, and as metropolitan sprawl characterizes such cities as Atlanta; Birmingham, Ala.; New Orleans; and Houston. Both blacks and whites have moved to the population centers seeking economic advancement and have added to urban problems. Even though the South remains an agricultural region, farming methods have changed; mechanization has taken the drudgery out of farm work; and hard-surfaced, farm-to-market roads have permitted farmers to live in towns and cities. The South's state educational systems have been upgraded as the states have increased expenditures for the education of their youth. As biracial school systems have declined, southern states have spent their money more wisely. The relationship of the races has been altered as blacks have pressed for and obtained better economic conditions, equal access to public accommodations, and more nearly equal education. While some white backlash has been apparent, white southerners on the whole have tolerated (if not entirely accepted) the new position of the Afro-American. In the 1970's the continued presence of the Ku Klux Klan, white citizens' councils, "segregation academies," and opposition to busing to achieve equal educational opportunities for all races were reminders that the New South was not yet all new, but the forces of change were overcoming these obstacles.

BIBLIOGRAPHY

Monroe Billington, *The American South: A Brief History.*

Thomas D. Clark, *The Emerging South.*

Paul Gaston, *The New South Creed: A Study in Southern Mythmaking.*

George Brown Tindall, *The Emergence of the New South, 1913–1945.*

C. Vann Woodward, *Origins of the New South, 1877–1913.*

— MONROE BILLINGTON

NEWSPAPERS

From the first New World printers with their toilsome, awkward handpresses to the specialized managers of the multifaceted journalistic enterprises nearly three centuries later; from the rabidly partisan sheets of the early 1800's by way of the literary grace of William Cullen Bryant's *New York Evening Post* (1829–78) and the Illinois martyrdom of Elijah Parish Lovejoy in defense of his weekly *Observer's* right to speak out for abolition; from the robust paragraphs signed Mark Twain but contributed by a young newshawk named Samuel Langhorne Clemens in Virginia City, Nev., in 1862, to cartoonist Bill Mauldin's dog-tired foot soldiers, Willie and Joe, in the *Stars and Stripes* of World War II; from the small-town Main Street, shirt-sleeve reporting of William Allen White in his *Emporia* (Kans.) *Gazette*, beginning in 1895, to the sensation-filled mass-circulation tabloids of the big cities and the encyclopedic *New York Times*, the *Wall Street Journal*, and the *Christian Science Monitor* with their national distributions in the 1970's—the history of American newspapers has been a record of infinite variety in editorial leadership and outlook, in effort and application. It is a record of countless dissimilarities that are part and parcel of an individualized people's pattern of continuous innovation and change, in the press as everywhere else.

Publick Occurrences

The earliest colonial newspaper was *Publick Occurrences Both Forreign and Domestick*, which made its first and only appearance in Boston, Mass., on Sept. 25, 1690. It was immediately suppressed. Publisher Benjamin Harris, exiled London bookseller and printer of the *New England Primer*, and his printer, Richard Pierce, offended the colonial authorities by not obtaining official permission to publish. Moreover, portions of the contents were found objectionable, including "the passage referring to the French King and to the Maquas [Mohawk Indians]" that caused the governor and the council "much distaste." Arranged in double columns on three handbill-sized pages, it reported, in a news style anticipating those of modern newspapers, the Thanksgiving plans of "Plimouth" Indians, a suicide, the disappearance of two children, a decline in smallpox, a fire, and other events. Harris planned to issue it "once a month (or if any Glut of Occurrences happen, oftener). . . ." But after the authorities declared their "high resentment and Disallowance," there was no similar publication, so far as is known, for fourteen years. The only copy preserved was found in 1845 in the London Public Record Office.

Boston News-Letter

The next recorded attempt to establish a publication in the colonies was made by the *Boston News-Letter.* Successful in that it was not interrupted by the authorities, it or its successors continued to appear down to the Revolution. Issue No. 1 covered the week of Apr. 17, 1704. Boston Postmaster John Campbell was the original publisher and Bartholomew Green was the printer. They introduced their first illustration in the issue of Jan. 19, 1708. When Green became the owner and publisher in 1723, he renamed it the *Weekly News-Letter* and so it remained until 1763, when the name was changed to the *Boston Weekly News-Letter and New England Chronicle.* That was still the name when the British troops withdrew from Boston in 1776, whereupon publication ended. Campbell and those who followed him joined newspaper publication with job printing, the issuance of pamphlets and books, and the general retailing of printed matter and stationery.

Pennsylvania Gazette

The colonial *Pennsylvania Gazette*, made famous by Benjamin Franklin, was founded at Philadelphia on Dec. 24, 1728, by Samuel Keimer. Its original name was the *Universal Instructor in All Arts and Sciences: and Pennsylvania Gazette.* Although only the second newspaper in the Middle Colonies, it did not prosper, and on Oct. 2, 1729, it was purchased by Franklin, who had helped publish the *New England Courant* (1721) in Boston, and Hugh Meredith, who shortened the name to the *Pennsylvania Gazette.* After Meredith's retirement in 1732, Franklin used his ownership to turn it into the "most successful colonial newspaper." Franklin's innovations included the first weather report, an editorial column, the first cartoon, and humor. Essays and poetry had their place, but Franklin did not introduce them. David Hall joined in a partnership in 1748 that lasted until Franklin's retirement in 1766. The newspaper was published in York, Pa., for six months, beginning in December 1777, because of the British occupation of Philadelphia. The last issue was dated Oct. 11, 1815.

Zenger Case

The outstanding colonial case involving freedom of the press centered around John Peter Zenger and his *New-York Weekly Journal*, the first newspaper to be the organ of a political faction. In the early 1730's, New York became the focus of opposition to colonial policies on the part of merchants, lawyers, and other influential groups. Backed by this protest movement, Zenger, former printer for William Bradford's *New York Gazette*, first issued his paper on Nov. 5, 1733. Many articles were contributed, but Zenger, as publisher, was held responsible for them, and he produced his share of the criticism of colonial rule. Late in 1734 the Common Council ordered four numbers of the *Weekly Journal* to be burned. Zenger was arraigned and jailed for about ten months. In 1735 he was tried for seditious libel. Andrew Hamilton, who defended him, won acquittal with the plea that the jury had a right to inquire into the truth or falsity of the printed words. The paper, which appeared regularly because of the persistence of Zenger's wife, printed his report of the court proceedings and then issued separately in 1736 *A Brief Narrative of the Case and Tryal of John Peter Zenger*. The latter publication went through a series of printings and was widely circulated in the colonies and in England. Zenger was rewarded by being made New York public printer in 1737. The case set a precedent against judicial tyranny in libel suits.

Later Colonial Period

Following the success of the *Boston News-Letter*, by 1750 other colonial newspapers had been set up in Boston; New York; Philadelphia; Charleston, S.C.; Annapolis, Md.; Williamsburg, Va.; and Newport, R.I. By 1775, on the eve of the Revolution, there were thirty-seven papers in the seaboard colonies; the number would have increased rapidly but for the stringencies of the war for independence. The usual plan of the four-page weekly gazette was to devote the first page to foreign intelligence, the second page to domestic news, the third to local matters, and the back page to advertisements. Since there was no other form of communication except by word of mouth, this was the means by which the colonists learned about deliberations in the councils, the actions of their governors, and other official matters. As a consequence the newssheets began to join the colonial peoples in common interests and eventual resistance to the crown. Other than the Bible and the almanac, the local gazette undoubtedly was the only printed material that entered most colonial homes.

Massachusetts Spy

Outstanding among patriotic gazettes in the years leading to the Revolution, the *Massachusetts Spy* won Isaiah Thomas a place of honor in preindependence journalism. Thomas, a Boston printer and publisher, became the partner of Zechariah Fowle in 1770 and in the same year founded the *Spy* in Boston to advance colonial interests. His devotion to the rank and file was widely known and appreciated, except by the royal governors. When the British troops took over Boston in 1773, Thomas moved his printing press to Worcester. En route he joined Paul Revere in the historic warning of Apr. 18, 1775, and he himself was a minuteman in the engagements at Lexington and Concord. The May 3, 1775, issue reported the news of those early clashes at arms. In Worcester he was also the official printer for the patriots. The *Spy* became the *Worcester Gazette* in 1781. Thomas' long association with the *Spy* and early journalism led him into such related fields as printing almanacs, music, and magazines; writing a history of printing; and, in 1812, founding the American Antiquarian Society, of which he was the first president.

Editors as Political Leaders

With the development of political factions, the early editors became in effect spokesmen for opposing groups. After the Revolution and in the first years of the new nation one journal after another enlisted in and led the public debate over political issues. Thus, the Federalist mouthpiece, the *Gazette of the United States*, later known (1804–18) as the *United States Gazette*, edited by John Fenno, espoused the principles of George Washington and John Adams so vigorously that Secretary of State Thomas Jefferson subsidized a competing *National Gazette*, begun Oct. 31, 1791, at Philadelphia, by appointing its editor, Philip Freneau, translator in the State Department. Freneau's criticisms of Alexander Hamilton brought on complaints from Washington, who held Jefferson responsible. The *National Gazette* ceased publication in 1793, soon after Jefferson's resignation from the secretaryship. In the meantime William Coleman and the *New York Evening Post* became linked to Hamilton, as Noah Webster and the *American Minerva* became associated with John Jay and Rufus King. Frequently political editors wrote so vitriolically and at such length that their articles were reprinted and circulated as partisan pamphlets.

Sedition Act Victims

Concern late in the 18th century over possible war with France brought on a suspicion of aliens, with the result that the Federalists put through Congress the Alien and Sedition Acts of 1798. Almost immediately the enforcement of these laws was directed against supporters of Jefferson, among them Democratic-Republican newspaper editors. Ten journalists were found guilty and fined and in several instances jailed for alleged seditious utterances. One of the first to feel the whip was William Duane, a New Yorker who, after serving as a printer in Ireland, Calcutta, and London, settled in Philadelphia, where he made the *Aurora* the foremost newspaper backing Jefferson. He opposed the restrictions of the Alien and Sedition Acts and in 1799 was arrested. Soon acquitted, he continued his criticism and again was arrested. Following Jefferson's election in 1800 the charges were dropped and Duane worked for repeal of the offensive statutes. Anthony Haswell, editor of the *Vermont Gazette or Freeman's Depository*, issued at Bennington, was among those jailed. Haswell, who was born in England, was both a soldier and editor during the Revolution, having edited the *Massachusetts Spy* in 1777. His Bennington gazette, the only publication in Vermont at the time, led to his indictment and trial for sedition in 1800. Haswell's imprisonment for two months amounted to political persecution. The $200 fine that he was required to pay was returned to his heir by act of Congress in 1844. There were to be other periods with civil liberties under restraint but no time when freedom of the press was so restricted.

Expansion Westward

Independence was followed by a veritable explosion of new journals. In the seven decades of colonial rule some 100 gazettes had been started, and during the conflict perhaps as many as 50 more were undertaken. Between the peace treaty in 1783 and the year 1800, at least 500 were begun in the original thirteen states. A careful historian of the early press, Douglas C. McMurtrie, concluded that inasmuch as about 200 more newspapers were launched in the new states from 1800 to 1820, some 1,200 newspapers were begun in less than forty years of independence as against about 150 in the eighty years prior to separation from the English crown. Venturesome printers soon moved west from the seaboard. The first newspaper beyond the Appalachians was the *Pittsburgh Gazette*, issued July 29, 1786, by Joseph Hall and John Scull. After seeing the promising site of Pittsburgh, Hugh Henry Brackenridge, a lawyer and veteran of the Revolution, urged the two young Philadelphia printers to move there and help develop the area. Even more daring was Kentuckian John Bradford, a surveyor, who transported a press through the wilderness and on Aug. 11, 1787, while the Constitutional Convention was deliberating in Philadelphia, founded the *Kentucke Gazette* in Lexington.

Along the Great Rivers

New territories meant new governments, with laws and proclamations, and for these as well as for frontier journals printing presses were a necessity. By Nov. 5, 1791, Robert Ferguson and George Roulstone had left North Carolina to begin publication of the *Knoxville Gazette* in Tennessee. William Maxwell set up the *Centinel of the North-Western Territory* in Cincinnati, Nov. 9, 1793; and Elihu Stout moved from Kentucky to Vincennes, where he was both public printer for Indiana Territory and publisher of the *Indiana Gazette*, beginning July 31, 1804. Meriwether Lewis and William Clark were hardly back from their expedition to the Pacific Northwest when Joseph Charless started the *Missouri Gazette*, July 12, 1808, in Saint Louis. Still another pioneer printer was Matthew Duncan, one-time Kentuckian who began the *Illinois Herald* in May 1814, at Kaskaskia, the first Illinois capital. Other newspapers in the new West included the *Mississippi Gazette* of Benjamin M. Stokes at Natchez, in 1799 or 1800; the *Mobile Centinel* of Samuel Miller and John B. Hood, May 23, 1811; and the *Detroit Gazette* of New Yorkers John P. Sheldon and Ebenezer Reed, July 25, 1817. By 1821 some 250 papers had come into being in the new West. Many were short-lived; most were struggles against odds, but as a whole they helped open up and tame the wilderness.

Assassination of Lovejoy

What doubtless was the most tragic occurrence in American journalism has been relatively little cited—the murder of Elijah Parish Lovejoy in Alton, Ill., in the struggle over slavery. Lovejoy, a native of Maine and a graduate of Waterville (now Colby) College, edited a Whig newspaper in Saint Louis in the late 1820's. After being licensed to preach, he published the Presbyterian weekly for the West, the *Saint Louis Observer*. Soon he was deep in the abolition movement, and rather than moderate his views to suit the Missouri critics, Lovejoy moved across and up the Mississippi River to Alton. There two of his presses were pushed into the river by his opponents. When he sought to protect a third press from attack by a mob, he was shot and killed on the night of Nov. 7, 1837. The fearless editor was not yet thirty-five years old. Lovejoy was the first editor to give his life in defense of freedom of the press in the United States, and his martyrdom fired the abolitionists all the way to New England. After blood had stained his press, there was no turning back in the antislavery crusade.

Coming of the Daily

The first gazettes did well to fare forth once a week, but in the larger communities semiweeklies and triweeklies made their appearance before independence was won. Philadelphia was the scene of Benjamin Towne's *Pennsylvania Evening Post and Daily Advertiser* in May 1783. The next year John Dunlap and David C. Claypoole brought out the *Pennsylvania Packet and Daily Advertiser*, while the *South-Carolina Gazette* was launched in Charleston. Then in 1785 two dailies were begun in New York City. Francis Childs' *New York Daily Advertiser* was the first daily that had not been published previously on a less frequent basis. By 1790 the total number of dailies had reached eight. The Sunday newspaper came slowly. The *Weekly Museum* with a Sunday date was started in Baltimore in 1797, but it lasted for only a few weeks. The Sunday *Observer* appeared in New York in 1809 and survived for some two years. The prevailing strictures against work on the Sabbath prevented early acceptance of newspapers for Sunday circulation and reading.

Penny Press

Newspapers left their gazette era behind with the coming of the "penny press." The first one-cent-a-copy venture to succeed was Benjamin H. Day's *New York Sun*, begun in 1833, and its success was immediate. Within two years it boasted the largest daily circulation in the world. At the time the older, well-established, generally dignified dailies sold for six cents, and they were quick to denounce the cut-price upstart as catering to the lower public tastes. Without question the penny press was directed at the common people, but also without question the interests of the common people had gone largely unrecognized in news reporting. Unfortunately, the *Sun* promoted sensationalism to the point of outright faking. James Gordon Bennett's *New York Morning Herald*, launched in 1835, began competing for news scoops and stressed writing that caught the reader's eye. Bennett also developed financial coverage and used steamships for transmitting foreign news on a regular basis. But Horace Greeley's *New York Weekly Tribune*, denouncing the "degrading police reports" of the penny papers, in 1841 undertook to raise standards by reporting new ideas by distinguished writers. The one-cent papers capitalized on street sales, giving rise to the newsboy who ran about the city with a bundle of newssheets, calling out the top headlines. The press was closer to ordinary people than ever before. And "yellow journalism" was on its way.

Civil War Coverage

By 1860 roving editors and correspondents had made Washington, D.C., a regular "beat," had written up the excitements of the West and the local color of the South, and had described European scenes and peoples in leisurely newsletters. Experimental war reporting, undertaken in the Mexican War, became a major news activity in the Civil War. Sharing the soldiers' hardships and eluding censors, a network of news gatherers relayed eyewitness dispatches from the battlefronts. Outstanding among the war correspondents was Dublin-born Joseph B. McCullagh, who won a national reputation for his reports in the *Cincinnati Commercial* that stood the tests of reliability and fairness. When McCullagh's first Cincinnati newspaper, the *Gazette*, refused to print his account of the early fighting at Shiloh, which discredited the Union performance, "Little Mack" forthwith quit the *Gazette* and joined the *Commercial*. Meantime cameraman Mathew B. Brady compiled his monumental photographic record of the war and its participants. As interest in the conflict mounted, circulations rose rapidly and "extras" became commonplace. News columns held ascendancy over editorial commentary, with the readers seeking eagerly to learn the latest military developments and the conduct of the government in Washington, D.C. The southern press supported the Confederacy, and although northern editors generally upheld the Union cause, not a few were opposed to President Abraham Lincoln and some were openly Copperhead.

Yellow Journalism

After the Civil War the *New York Sun*, bought by Charles A. Dana in 1868, exalted artistic writing, while Henry Villard's *New York Evening Post* (1881), especially after Edwin L. Godkin became editor in chief in 1883, combined literary grace with Tammany exposures, and Joseph Pulitzer's *New York World* (1883) carried on its crusades for the working classes. But the sensationalism introduced to the press by Bennett's *Herald* in the 1830's was revived and extended by the new reliance on advertising. For by 1880 advertising met a major part of the costs of publishing a daily—and advertising rates were based on circulation. A consequence was hard-fought competition for both subscribers and street sales. To capture weekend readers, Pulitzer promoted the *New York Sunday World*, with special articles and features including a comic section, first produced in November 1894. Prominent among the comic strips was Richard F. Outcault's "Yellow Kid," a harum-scarum boy in long yellow garb. In less than a year, William Randolph Hearst, publisher of the *San Francisco Examiner*, entered the New York scene by purchasing the *Morning Journal* and going into headlong conflict with the *World* for circulation. The Cuban problem, the sinking of the *Maine*, and the Spanish-American War were exploited with banner headlines and irresponsible claims and charges. Coupled with detailed accounts of scandals and sob-sister stories, the total result became known as yellow journalism. Not all editors succumbed, but the malaise characterized an era.

Comic Strips and Funny Papers

A natural extension of the hearty humor of the 1870's and 1880's, the funny paper, as it was first called, abetted an expanding newspaperdom, bent on circulation and experimenting with color printing. James Swinnerton drew comic bear pictures for the *San Francisco Examiner* in 1892, and the *New York Daily News* printed an isolated comic strip as early as 1884. But the forerunner of the comic pages was Outcault's "Origin of a New Species," Sunday, Nov. 18, 1894, in the *New York World.* The bad-boy character featured in the comics, known as the Yellow Kid, proved exceedingly popular, and Hearst, then a newcomer to New York, bid him away from Pulitzer's *World* to the *New York Journal* in 1896. For a time both papers had Yellow Kids, and from the excessive competition with its shameless exploitations came the term "yellow journalism." Rudolph Dirks' Katzenjammer Kids, who first appeared in the *Journal* in 1897, set a pattern, also shaped by H. C. ("Bud") Fisher's six-days-a-week "A. Mutt," in the *San Francisco Chronicle* beginning in 1907.

Early comic characters such as Happy Hooligan, Buster Brown, Foxy Grandpa, Little Jimmy, Hans and Fritz, and Nemo, if not elevating, were relatively harmless. Yet critics denounced the funny paper's influence, and in 1937 the International Kindergarten Union asked parents to protect their children from it. The power of the comics over circulation was demonstrated when they set styles, gave turns to speech, and affected advertising. Arthur Brisbane rated the comics as second only to news in the newspapers, while surveys showed how attached readers were to their favorites. So important were the strips that two Washington, D.C., newspapers took to the Supreme Court their dispute over the right to print "Andy Gump." Syndicates grew up around the leading comics and bought them away from one another as fortune-making businesses developed from "Jiggs and Maggie," "Mutt and Jeff," "Toonerville Folks," and their contemporaries. As many as 2,500 newspapers used some 250 strips and single panels from some seventy-five agencies. At its peak *Hearst's Comic Weekly: Puck*, distributed by seventeen newspapers, with a total circulation of 5.5 million, ran fifty comics in its thirty-two pages. One syndicate claimed a circulation of more than 50 million. Comic section advertising skyrocketed from $360,000 in 1931 to more than $16.5 million in half a dozen years, cost per page reaching some $20,000.

After World War II the strips generally changed from comics to serial picture stories presenting everything from domestic affairs, ethnic life, military routine, the medical profession, and the conservation of natural resources to high adventure, international intrigue, crime and its detection, and the space age. A few educators found the new strips more degrading than ever, but experts in child care and development served as advisers for some, and the award-winning television program "Sesame Street" received high marks for beneficial influence. Syndicates employed translators to prepare the picture serials for demand all over the world. The leading characters became real in that they were a part of their readers' daily lives. When Orphan Annie's dog, Sandy, was lost, Henry Ford telegraphed her creator to do all he could to find it. Whether or not juveniles were harmfully affected by the worst of the strips, they continued to be popular, as Popeye supplanted Paul Bunyan, Clare Briggs' "Days of Real Sport" provided a genuine contribution to humor, and Gaar Williams recorded a nostalgic and precious past in "Among the Folks in History." By the mid-1970's some strips or panels were narrowly focused intellectual exercises, but Charles Schulz, with his "Peanuts" small-fry troupe (Charlie Brown, Linus, Lucy, Schroeder, Violet, Snoopy, Woodstock, and associates), produced a company so widely captivating that they turned up literally everywhere—on television, on the stage, in magazines, on stationery, on greeting cards, on clothing, and as art objects. These characters popularized the phrase "Happiness is . . . ," as their comic page neighbors helped shape the speech of the times. A "dagwood" was a tremendous, all-inclusive sandwich named after its creator, Dagwood Bumstead, the husband in "Blondie." "Grin and Bear It" often had the most incisive editorial comment of the day, much as Frank McKinney ("Kin") Hubbard's Hoosier philosopher, Abe Martin, had a generation earlier. Nor did the comic strips stop short of politics. Sen. Joseph R. McCarthy was readily recognizable in Walt Kelly's "Pogo," and "Doonesbury" used the White House as a backdrop and referred by name to the Watergate figures, including President Richard M. Nixon, and even went to Vietnam. Although appearing in comic strip format, Gary Trudeau's "Doonesbury" received a Pulitzer Prize for distinguished editorial cartooning in 1975.

Political Cartooning

The predecessor of 19th-century political cartoons appeared in early colonial times. Franklin's *Pennsylvania Gazette* in 1754 carried a drawing of a snake in eight disconnected pieces, each labeled for a colony. The caption, "Join, or Die," became a rallying cry for united action. Another influential colonial drawing was that of a snake warning the British, "Don't Tread on Me." The first cartoonist of national note, Thomas Nast, a native of Germany, devised the elephant and donkey symbols for the Republican and Democratic parties, respectively. After starting at fifteen as staff artist for *Frank Leslie's Illustrated Newspaper*, Nast became famous on *Harper's Weekly*, where he drew for a quarter century (1862–86). Lincoln called him the Union's "best recruiting sergeant." An uncompromising foe of the Tweed Ring, Nast portrayed Tammany as a predatory tiger. Walter H. McDougall appears to have been New York's first daily political cartoonist. The *New York World's* Rollin Kirby identified the Prohibition Amendment with a sour-visaged, long-nosed antisaloon character wearing a tall hat and carrying an umbrella. Oscar E. Cesare, born in Sweden, drew powerfully for peace in the *New York Evening Post* in the World War I period and then sketched world notables for the *New York Times*.

Chicago presented widely admired cartoonists in John T. McCutcheon and Carey Orr of the *Tribune*, Vaughan Shoemaker of the *Daily News*, and Jacob Burck of the *Sun-Times*. The national syndication of Jay N. Darling, known as Ding, a pioneer conservationist, embraced both world wars, while the wide distribution of William Henry (Bill) Mauldin followed his creation of Willie and Joe, battle-weary infantrymen, for the *Stars and Stripes* during World War II. The blunt, uninhibited conceptions of Daniel R. Fitzpatrick covered most of a half century, beginning in 1913, in the *Saint Louis Post-Dispatch*. The *Washington Post's* fearless Herbert L. Block—"Herblock"—hit so tellingly day after day that presidents Dwight D. Eisenhower and Richard M. Nixon would not look at his cartoons. Patrick B. Oliphant of the *Denver Post*, also syndicated, was merciless on the Watergate scandals. Don Hesse of the *Saint Louis Globe-Democrat* was representative of the syndicated conservative while Walt Partymiller of the *York* (Pa.) *Gazette and Daily* stood out among small-city cartoonists. Two of the most talented political cartoonists in the 20th century, Robert Minor and Arthur Henry (Art) Young, were highly esteemed, even though most of their work appeared in the radical press.

Era of Outstanding Editors

Beginning with William Cullen Bryant (*Evening Post*) and Benjamin H. Day (*Sun*), rivals in New York, the 19th century developed a galaxy of editor-publishers who not only became community and regional leaders but also in notable instances national figures. Among these, James Gordon Bennett (*Morning Herald*), Horace Greeley (*Tribune*), Henry J. Raymond (*Daily Times*), Charles A. Dana (*Sun*), Edwin L. Godkin (*Evening Post*), Joseph Pulitzer (*World*), William Randolph Hearst (*Evening Journal*), and Adolph S. Ochs (*Times*) were situated in New York. Others of distinction issued newspapers over the country. They included Samuel Bowles (*Springfield* [Mass.] *Republican*), Joseph Medill (*Chicago Daily Tribune*), Henry Watterson (*Louisville Courier-Journal*), William B. McCullagh (*Saint Louis Globe-Democrat*), William Rockhill Nelson (*Kansas City Evening Star*), Clark Howell (*Atlanta Constitution*), James King (*San Francisco Bulletin*), and Harrison Gray Otis (*Los Angeles Times*). All these stamped journalism with their personalities, while such an extremist as Frederick G. Bonfils of the *Denver Post* became widely known for his gaudy excesses. King was so unrestrained in his attack on the corrupt elements in San Francisco's political and business life (1855–56) that he was shot and killed on May 14, 1856, by an enemy—a tragedy that led to the revival of the San Francisco Vigilance Committee.

In the 20th century editors of reputation included the McCormicks and the family of Marshall Field in Chicago and the Binghams in Louisville; Oswald Garrison Villard (*New York Evening Post*), Frank I. Cobb (*New York World*), Gardner Cowles (*Des Moines Register and Tribune*), Victor F. Lawson (*Chicago Daily News*), Lucius W. Nieman (*Milwaukee Journal*), Ernest Greuning (*Portland* [Maine] *Evening News*), Clark McAdams and Oliver K. Bovard (*Saint Louis Post-Dispatch*), John S. Knight (*Miami Herald*), Eugene C. Pulliam (*Arizona Republic*), William T. Evjue (*Madison* [Wis.] *Capital Times*), John N. Heiskell (*Arkansas Gazette*), Palmer Hoyt (*Portland Oregonian* and *Denver Post*), Douglas Southall Freeman (*Richmond News Leader*), Josephus and Jonathan Worth Daniels (*Raleigh News and Observer*), Thomas M. Storke (*Santa Barbara* [Calif.] *News-Press*), Ralph McGill (*Atlanta Constitution*), Virginius Dabney (*Richmond Times-Dispatch*), and George B. Dealey (*Dallas Morning News*). Kansas afforded the nation a remarkable pair of small-city editors with broad outlook in William Allen White of the *Emporia Gazette* and Edgar Watson Howe of the *Atchison Daily Globe*.

The World Wars and Indochina

Although the Hearst-Pulitzer rivalry helped bring on the Spanish-American War, the war itself was so short that the press could do little more than sensationalize developments. Reporter Richard Harding Davis and illustrator Frederic Remington were journalists who rose to national notice. World War I saw the press under heavy censorship on the one hand and acting largely as a propaganda machine on the other. George Creel's wartime Committee on Public Information produced more than 6,000 anti-German patriotic news releases, widely and dutifully printed in the press. Censorship at first was voluntary, but acts of Congress against espionage in 1917 and sedition in 1918 put newspapers under severe restraint. Editors and publishers generally fell in with the wishes of Washington, while the force of law bore against German-language and radical papers. Wartime controls barred two pacifistic Socialist dailies, the *New York Call* and the *Milwaukee Leader*, from the mails. Among the correspondents who made it the most closely covered war to that time were Floyd Gibbons, Irvin S. Cobb, William H. (Will) Irwin, Frank H. Simonds, Wythe Williams, Paul Scott Mowrer, Edgar Ansel, Raymond Gram Swing, Karl H. von Wiegand, Sigrid Schultz, Westbrook Pegler, Frazier Hunt, Edward Price Bell, and Walter Duranty.

World War II censorship began with the bombing at Pearl Harbor, and Congress quickly passed the first War Powers Act with the legislative basis for the Office of Censorship, of which Byron Price, executive news editor of the Associated Press, became director. Although war zone dispatches had to be cleared with military censors, most of the censorship was voluntary, self-applied as set out in a "Code of Wartime Practices for the American Press," issued Jan. 15, 1942. Several pro-Nazi and Fascist papers were ordered closed. A vast net of war correspondents spread around the globe. In a category by himself was Ernest T. (Ernie) Pyle, Hoosier reporter, who described in simple, homely, yet graphic, terms the battlefront existence of GI Joe in Africa, Europe, and the Pacific, where Pyle himself was killed. His colleagues included Herbert L. Matthews, Quentin Reynolds, George Fielding Eliot, Hal Boyle, Joseph Barnes, Richard L. Stokes, Raymond Clapper, Webb Miller, A. T. Steele, Joseph Driscoll, Drew Middleton, Edward W. Beattie, Wallace R. Deuel, and C. L. Sulzberger.

Censorship plus outright misstatement continued in the cold war years, as evidenced by the slow issuance of full facts from officialdom concerning the U-2 spy plane episode in 1960, the Bay of Pigs fiasco in 1961, and the Cuban missile crisis in 1962. In the Korean and Indochinese conflicts adverse news was not only frowned on officially but occasionally forbidden. Since the war in Indochina was never formally declared, actual censorship was difficult to apply. Manipulation took its place. Correspondents learned that too often the facts were not as presented in military briefings, as, for example, shortly before the Tet offensive. Thus, the newswriters began to dig for the truth for their publications. One was David Halberstam, whose *New York Times* reports led President John F. Kennedy to recommend his removal. The Associated Press's Malcolm Browne, United Press International's Neil Sheehan, and *Time's* Charles Mohr joined in informing American readers that U.S. forces were indeed in combat when the official line was to the contrary.

The conclusion was inescapable that many of the untruths were deliberate, intended to deceive and, in so doing, to protect diplomatic and military mistakes. Inescapable too was the fact that the press played along far too frequently. When the My Lai massacre was brought to light, Seymour Hersch, then a freelance reporter, found it almost impossible to get newspapers to take his disclosures seriously. Hanoi's broad-scale operation, which finally brought Saigon's collapse and the end of the war, took the press, along with the military intelligence network, by surprise. The seizure of the cargo ship *Mayaguez* in 1975 by Cambodians retaught the press that the full information can be slow to emerge from the government in an embarrassing situation.

Tabloids

The post–World War I tabloid-sized newspaper had a forerunner in the diminutive *New York Daily Graphic*, 1873–89, which specialized in sensational pictures. Three decades passed before Joseph M. Patterson brought out his *New York Illustrated Daily News*. Launched on June 26, 1919, it was patterned on Alfred C. W. Harmsworth, Lord Northcliffe's successful London tabloid, the *Daily Mail*, half regular size for the convenience of riders of crowded subways. A largely uncultivated audience was quickly reached by the *News*. In two years "this unholy blot against the Fourth Estate," as one critic called it, had the largest circulation in New York, and twenty years later its distribution was nearly 2 million daily and more than 3 million on Sunday. Enticed by this mass welcome of the *Daily News*, Hearst produced the *New York Daily Mirror* in 1924 and Bernarr Macfadden attempted to build a daily circulation on cheap entertainment in the *Evening Graphic* (1924–32). Cornelius Vanderbilt, Jr., undertook a chain of "clean" tabloids, only to see it collapse in 1926–27. Crime, sex, sports, and comics were the main fare of tabloids; but some, including the *Chicago Sun-Times*, became popular pleaders for policies favorable to masses of city and suburban dwellers. In the 1950's and 1960's the tabloid-shaped *York* (Pa.) *Gazette and Daily*, published by Josiah W. Gitt, was as uninhibited a voice as the free press knew. In the 1970's the *New York Daily News* still enjoyed the nation's record circulation. Meanwhile it, like many other tabloids, had improved itself to serve its readers better.

Columnists

As the strong editors declined in number and the editorial pages tended toward a more common denominator, a new form of journalistic expression emerged—the signed column. Previously there had been well-heeded individual voices; before making up their own minds on the day's issues countless mid-19th-century citizens awaited the weekly *New York Tribune* to learn Greeley's views. The byline columnist, with regular offerings of opinion, came decades later with the syndication of Arthur Brisbane and Heywood Broun. Brisbane, who appeared on page 1 of the Hearst press, dealt briefly but positively with almost everything under the sun. Broun, whose far more literary essays decorated the *New York World*'s "opposite editorial page," discussed such heated problems as the Sacco-Vanzetti case, even to the point of being let go by his employers, the second generation of Pulitzers.

Although not the most widely read, former *World* editor Walter Lippmann was perhaps most highly esteemed for his thoughtful views, particularly on foreign affairs. Ranging from strongly liberal to equally strongly conservative were a spectrum of opinion shapers, among them Raymond Clapper, Dorothy Thompson, Arthur Krock, Thomas L. Stokes, Marquis W. Childs, Roscoe Drummond, George E. Sokolsky, James J. Kilpatrick, William S. White, Max Lerner, Mike Royko, William F. Buckley, and Carl T. Rowan. By the 1970's the *New York Times* shared its editorial columnists, via its wire service, to the extent that James Reston, Tom Wicker, William Safire, Anthony Lewis, C. L. Sulzberger, and William V. Shannon regularly spoke out far more vigorously than the local editors in whose pages they appeared. Some specialized. Drew Pearson, Robert S. Allen, and Jack Anderson engaged in disclosure reporting, often in the muckrakers' style. Even the humorists Franklin P. Adams, Don Marquis, O. O. McIntyre, Will Rogers, Kin Hubbard, Russell Baker, and Art Buchwald entered the public arena, the latter most irreverently. Sylvia Porter won an appreciative readership for her columns on business, economic, and consumer concerns. Other specialists centered on the military, the family, religion, movies, nature, gardening, sports, recreation, and a variety of other interests.

Ethnic Press

Newspapers in languages other than English and devoted to diverse social groups appeared in colonial times. Franklin's *Philadelphische Zeitung*, started in 1732 for German immigrants to Pennsylvania, was short-lived, but Christopher Sower's German-language paper, *Zeitung*, launched in 1739, caught on in Germantown, Pa. As Germans settled in Cincinnati, Saint Louis, Milwaukee, and other river and lake communities, a press in their language followed them. A Santo Domingoan, taking refuge in Louisiana, opened a French-language press as early as 1794. In Saint Louis the *Westliche Post* of Carl Schurz and Emil Preetorius provided immigrant Joseph Pulitzer with his first newspaper job in 1868. In the late 1800's papers in Italian, Polish, Spanish, Yiddish, and other tongues were published in the larger cities, where differing immigrant populations kept their customs and traditions alive in part through papers in their native languages. It was much the same for the agricultural Scandinavians who spread across the upper Mississippi Valley and onto the Plains.

The foreign-language press encouraged the characteristics of the ethnic groups being served. Differences to the point of antagonisms continued for decades; thus, papers in languages other than English tended to accent nationalistic concerns and religious rivalries. Refugees, many of whom reflected the revolutionary spirit of the 1840's, frequently brought radical ideas about government. A foremost outlet was the Jewish *Voice*, begun in New York in 1872 and emulated in Yiddish in other centers of Jewish population. The German-language press, which held to a generally high level, reached its peak in numbers in the mid-1890's. But as a whole the foreign-language press expanded until about 1914, when there were more than 1,300 such publications. World War I put the German press at a heavy disadvantage as only a few, led by the *New York Staats-Zeitung*, had sought to be "an American newspaper published in German." In World War II the Japanese-language press was looked upon by many as a disloyal force. Assimilation of later generations, along with wars and economic tribulations, undercut foreign-language newspapers until in 1970 only some 230 had survived. The largest circulation, about 76,000, was that of the New York daily *El Diario*, a tabloid in Spanish primarily for emigrants from Puerto Rico.

The story of the black press in the United States is an almost unknown chapter in American journalism. Rev. Samuel Cornish and John B. Russwurm brought out *Freedom's Journal* in 1827 in New York as the first paper written for black people. They began it, so they declared, because "too long others have spoken for us." Frederick Douglass, a former slave, issued the *North Star* in 1847 and sounded a continuing rallying cry for abolition in the years leading to the Civil War. W. E. B. Du Bois established *The Crisis* in 1910 as the voice of the National Association for the Advancement of Colored People, the crisis being, in his words, the idea that "mentally the Negro is inferior to the white."

By the mid-1970's, some 3,000 black-owned and black-conducted papers had been started, but the average life-span was only nine years. Thus, survivors in 1972 numbered fewer than 100. The largest black papers and their founding dates are the *New York Amsterdam News*, 1909; *Baltimore Afro-American*, 1892; *Chicago Defender*, 1905; *Pittsburgh Courier*, 1910; *Philadelphia Tribune*, 1884; and the Norfolk *Journal and Guide*, 1911. Once-high circulations fell after World War II; for example, the *Pittsburgh Courier's* asserted 250,000 in 1945 dropped to 60,000. Others underwent similar losses.

In 1972 *Muhammad Speaks*, a leader in the black revolution, listed its circulation as 400,000. Unquestionably the new publications that espoused black power were outdistancing the older, essentially conservative black papers. Change also came in the field of integration. Robert S. Abbott of Chicago earned a national reputation as publisher of the oldest surviving black daily, and his nephew, John H. Sengstacke, in 1970 became the first black journalist elevated to the board of directors of the American Society of Newspaper Editors.

The American Indian press had to hoe a hard row. Efforts to produce a national paper met with language and distribution difficulties. In the mid-1970's *Wassaja*, with both news and comment, issued monthly from San Francisco's Indian Historical Press. Scattered sheets serving tribes and reservations, some begun in the early 1800's, survived for varying periods. New interest in the native Indian as a minority raised interest in Indian publications.

Ownerships, Chains, and Syndicates

The oneman editor-publisher practice of journalism, although persisting in rural areas, followed business trends into partnerships, companies, and corporations with many owners who held shares of stock. Chain ownership and management developed near the end of the 19th century. The Scripps brothers, Edward W., James E., and George H., with Milton A. McRae, began the first chain in the mid-1890's by establishing newspapers in medium-sized cities. By 1914 the Scripps-McRae League of Newspapers controlled some thirteen daily publications. In the 1920's the organization became the Scripps-Howard chain, after its new driving force, Roy W. Howard, who extended the enterprise from coast to coast and into New York City.

William Randolph Hearst was a close second in chain operation. After taking over the *San Francisco Examiner*, he bought the *New York Journal* in 1895 and soon moved into Chicago. By 1951 he owned seventeen dailies and two Sunday papers, to which he supplied national news, editorials, and features. Subsequently the Hearst organization retrenched, and its numbers declined while chain ownership generally expanded. In the mid-1970's the Gannett chain consisted of fifty-one newspapers, the largest number in one ownership. The Knight and Ridder chains merged in 1974 to form Knight-Ridder Newspapers with a national coverage of thirty-five newspapers in sixteen states and a combined circulation of 27 million. Important chains included Chicago Tribune, Cowles, Copley, Lee, Newhouse, and Thomson. Some of the newspapers with the largest circulations were chain owned, among them the *New York Daily News*, *Philadelphia Inquirer*, *Detroit Free Press*, *Chicago Tribune*, and *Los Angeles Times*. Approximately half the dailies were owned by companies or persons that owned other dailies. In nearly half the states more than 50 percent of the newspapers were chain owned and in Florida the total in chains was 83 percent. Chain newspapers accounted for nearly half of the total circulation in 1960, a proportion stepped up to about two-thirds in less than two decades. A continuation of these trends would place almost all dailies in chain ownership by 1990.

Another trend diversified even major newspaper companies. In 1975 the *New York Times*, the outstanding daily of record as well as the only standard-sized paper of general circulation in New York City, had many other business enterprises. These included daily and weekly newspapers in North Carolina and Florida; magazines for the family, golfers, tennis players, and medical circles; television and radio properties; book and music publishing; news and feature services; and teaching materials, filmstrips, a microfilm edition, a large-type weekly, an index service, and newsprint interests. Similarly the Dow Jones Company, publisher of the *Wall Street Journal*, owned and operated *Barron's*, the *National Observer*, the Ottway group of newspapers, a news service, a computerized news retrieval system, and ten daily printing plants nationwide.

Syndication began before the coming of chains, but the syndicate and chain operation went hand in hand. Hearst, for example, circulated feature material to syndicate subscribers who were not in his chain. The syndicate business grew to vast proportions, providing columnists and comics, religion and recipes, fashions and family counseling, and more in prepackaged daily installments.

Improvements in Production: Unions and Contracts

Newspaper production changed greatly as mechanical methods supplanted typesetting by hand and hand-fed presses. The steam-powered press was used in 1822, but a decade passed before it was common. The cylinder press, imported in 1824, took a larger sheet of paper. Although the stereotype was developed in the 1830's, its adoption awaited the coming in 1861 of the curve-shaped form that could be clamped on rotary-press cylinders. By 1863 newsprint was delivered in rolls instead of cut sheets; in another decade roll-fed presses were common. By 1876 these presses were equipped with folders so that a newspaper of several sections could be printed on as many presses, folded, and assembled for transportation and delivery. The outstanding contributors to printing-press development and manufacture in the 1800's were Robert Hoe, a native of England and founder of R. Hoe and Company, and his son Richard M. Hoe, holder of important patents for inventions and adaptations in press design.

Paper continued to be of the expensive rag manufacture until 1870, when wood-pulp paper began to take its place. From the mid-1840's the telegraph was employed in transmitting news, and it was a notable factor in reporting the Civil War. The *New York Daily Graphic* is credited with printing the first line engraving in March 1873, thus launching the photoengraving process. The *Daily Graphic* pioneered again in 1880 with the halftone reproduction from a photograph.

Although few occupations were as laborious as setting type by hand, the hand method was slow to yield to machine methods. James O. Clephane, a Washington stenographer, failed in his effort in 1876 to apply the typewriter principle, but his work inspired Ottmar Mergenthaler, a Baltimore machinist, who worked for a decade on a series of machines, each better than its predecessor. Finally Mergenthaler produced one that cast lines from molten metal, automatically spaced, by means of individual matrices assembled via a hand-operated keyboard and returned to a magazine after each use. Mergenthaler's first patent was issued in 1884, and on July 3, 1886, a "linotype" was successfully operated at the *New York Tribune.* Use of the machine spread quickly: 60 were in use in eighteen months, and by 1895 there were 3,100 speeding up typesetting across the country. The speedup proved a boon to afternoon newspapers. The tramp printer's days were numbered, and a new era had come to printing.

The linotype fell prey to progress, and by the mid-1970's many newspaper composing rooms had removed their last "linos," as offset printing and other new techniques took over. Notable developments came, too, in color printing and rotogravure for feature sections, and some newspapers used color in their news and advertising columns. The wire services meantime developed the means by which a single impulse at the starting point caused a step in type production to be taken in the plants of many member newspapers.

As newspapers became mechanized, labor unions were formed to bargain collectively with employers. Although this movement began with typographers, pressmen, mailers, and related workers, unionization spread to reporters and other staff members with the formation of the American Newspaper Guild in the 1930's. Since about 1950, newspaper shutdowns occurred in many cities as contract disputes dragged on, sometimes for many weeks.

Elevation of Professional Standards

The press, which criticized the practices and morals of other social institutions, for decades ignored criticism raised by readers against its own performance. Protests grew until in 1922, under the impetus of Casper S. Yost, *Saint Louis Globe-Democrat* editorial page editor, a small group of journalists formed the American Society of Newspaper Editors. One of their early acts was to draw up a code of ethics with a strong emphasis on raising journalistic standards. Other organizations that sought to advance professional quality included the National Conference of Editorial Writers, the International Society of Weekly Newspaper Editors, and the Society of Professional Journalists: Sigma Delta Chi. The latter maintained a committee that called attention to infringements on freedom of the press and speech and issued annual reports on gains and losses.

Professional as well as public opinion continued to call for greater accountability, with the result that in 1972 a task force of the Twentieth Century Fund proposed the establishment of the National News Council to provide readers with a forum in which they might have their complaints heard on their merits. This council was incorporated on May 2, 1973, with nine professional and six public members and a professional staff in New York. It was charged with the investigation of complaints brought against national news associations or newspapers with national distribution—"the principal national suppliers of news." Many leading newspapers supported the idea, but others, including the *New York Times*, opposed it as a possible hindrance to press freedom. The council, with a grievance committee and one on freedom of the press, made a sustained but unsuccessful effort to obtain from President Nixon documentation for his charge that the reporting, after his dismissal of Special Watergate Prosecutor Archibald Cox and the resignation of Attorney General Elliott Richardson, was, in Nixon's words, the "most outrageous, vicious, and distorted" that he had ever seen.

Council findings varied with the facts and the urgency of the case, and although many complaints were dropped after being reviewed, other protests were supported against print and electronic news handlers.

The Press and Watergate

The newspapers produced a mixed record with respect to the criminal acts and other scandals of the Nixon administration. A large number of news editors dismissed the Watergate break-in and burglary of the Democratic national headquarters in Washington, D.C., on June 17, 1972, as a "caper" worth little attention and so relegated it to a small, inconspicuous space. However, the *Washington Post* recognized that five men in business suits, wearing surgical gloves and equipped with a walkie-talkie, were not ordinary burglars. The *Post* not only placed the puzzling unlawful entry on page 1, but put a staff to work seeking the motive. Through one frustration after another, the *Post* editors, including Benjamin C. Bradlee and Barry Sussman, and two reporters, Bob Woodward and Carl Bernstein, dug for the facts. In the meantime the White House, as the public came to know later, engaged in a gigantic cover-up, led by Nixon himself. The presidential press secretary sought to mislead the news media by insisting that there was nothing to hide and by ridiculing the persistence of the *Post* staff.

As the screen of deception began to crack, other newspapers followed the *Post.* Early recruits to the investigative and reporting functions included the *New York Times, Los Angeles Times, Wall Street Journal,* and *Christian Science Monitor.* For example, disclosure that Spiro T. Agnew was under the federal inquiry that led to his no-contest plea and resignation from the vice-presidency first appeared in the *Wall Street Journal.* In time the press as a whole found it necessary to print Watergate and related news generously. When the electronic networks reported the shocking developments each day, newspapers had little choice but to do as much. Some of Nixon's defenders accused the media of seeking vindictively to destroy the president and his administration. That thesis did not stand up in view of the fact that an overwhelming 94 percent of U.S. newspapers had supported Nixon in his bid for reelection in 1972. Over most of two years the *New York Times* devoted more space to the Senate hearings into Watergate scandals, Nixon's income taxes and associated matters, and the subsequent impeachment proceedings and pardon than to any other domestic concern. Eventually some of Nixon's strongest backers, such as the *Chicago Tribune* and the *Saint Louis Globe-Democrat,* altered their editorial position markedly and called him to strict account on his misconduct.

Newspapers and the Courts

The First Amendment to the Constitution prohibits Congress from passing any law "abridging the freedom of speech, or of the press," and the Supreme Court in *Gitlow* v. *New York* (1925) declared that "freedom of speech and of the press [are] protected by the due process clause of the Fourteenth Amendment from impairment by the states." Moreover, most states wrote strong free-press provisions into their constitutions. Even so, many issues arose, particularly in the half century after World War I, that brought press freedom into legal controversy.

Other than the cases related to World War I, the first important free-press test was decided by the Supreme Court in 1931 in *Near* v. *Minnesota.* At issue was a state law imposing prior censorship against comment on alleged wrongdoing by public officials. The law was voided unanimously. In 1936 the Supreme Court, in *Grosjean* v. *American Press Company,* invalidated Huey Long's newspaper gag act. In 1941, in *Times-Mirror Company* v. *Superior Court,* a five-to-four decision ruled in favor of wide latitude in critical comment on a pending case. The unanimous decision in *Craig* v. *Harney* in 1947 upheld the *Corpus Christi* (Tex.) *Call-Times'* defense against a contempt proceeding arising from comment on a trial involving private rather than public persons.

The 1960's and 1970's brought a series of major free-press cases. In *New York Times Company* v. *Sullivan,* involving the wording of a civil rights advertisement, the Supreme Court unanimously held in 1964 that a public official could not recover libel damages without proving malice. Also unanimously, the Supreme Court in *Brandenburg* v. *Ohio* voided a state criminal syndicalism law in 1969 as violating the rights of free speech and free press. The most important decision of the decade and one of the most important in American history came in the Pentagon Papers case in 1971. Involving the *New York Times* and the *Washington Post,* but also inferentially the press as a whole, the issue was whether the Nixon administration could enjoin publication of official papers relating to the Indochinese war. The holding of six justices was that the government did not meet its burden of showing justification for prior restraint. In a five-to-four decision in 1972 the Supreme Court ruled against Earl Caldwell of the *New York Times,* television newscaster Paul Pappas of New Bedford, Mass., and Paul Branzburg of the *Louisville Courier-Journal,* who argued against disclosing news sources before a grand jury. A crucial free-press victory came in 1974 in *Miami Herald Publishing Company* v. *Tornillo*, when the Supreme Court unanimously voided Florida's so-called right-of-reply statute requiring equal space in answering criticism.

Rather than disclose their news sources some reporters served contempt-of-court jail sentences. For example, William Farr of the *Los Angeles Times* served forty-six days in 1973 before being freed on appeal by Supreme Court Justice William O. Douglas. The press gained when Congress passed the 1975 Freedom of Information Act, which opened news sources in the federal government usually closed before.

The "New Journalism"

In the late 1960's and into the 1970's unorthodox developments in the press came to be called the "new journalism." The term was used to embrace a wide range of writing—a partially imaginative "nonfiction" as news writing on current events as well as on the "pop culture"; school and campus and other so-called "underground" papers; the community-oriented journalism reviews, both professional and academic; the "alternative" weeklies that stressed local investigations and sharp commentaries; and publications that dealt with pointed problems, such as the environment, the feminist movement, and pressing social issues. The writers included Gay Talese, Tom Wolfe, Lillian Ross, Norman Mailer, Truman Capote, and Jimmy Breslin. Among the new-style papers were the *Maine Times*, Manhattan's *Village Voice*, the *Texas Observer*, *Cervi's Rocky Mountain Journal*, and the *San Francisco Bay Guardian*. A category of writers known as "advocates" included James F. Ridgeway, Nicholas von Hoffman, Gloria Steinem, Pete Hamill, and Jack Newfield. In the electronic media account was taken of "alternative broadcasting"—public access television and television sponsored by viewers. Although the field was subject to almost continuous change, the term "new journalism" persisted for want of a more exact description. Some of its critics held that it was neither new nor journalism.

Newspaper Rise and Decline

In the half century from 1800 to 1850, the number of dailies increased tenfold, from 24 to 254. Total daily circulation did not quite quadruple; it was 200,000 in 1800 and 758,000 in 1850. Through the 19th century each decade saw increases in the number of dailies, 387 in 1860 with a circulation of 1,478,000 to 574 in 1870 with a circulation of 2,601,000. Technological improvements made larger press runs possible, and as the number of dailies tripled—971 in 1880; 1,610 in 1889; 2,226 in 1899; and 2,600 in 1909—circulation rose at a faster rate. The circulation figures for those same years were 3,566,000; 8,387,000; 15,102,000; and 24,212,000. The 1909 total of 2,600 was essentially the high mark in the number of daily newspapers. By 1920 the total had declined to 2,324. Circulation continued to rise, reaching 31 million by 1920.

In the 1920–30 period the number of dailies decreased by about 100. In 1930 there were 2,219 dailies, but the total circulation reached 45,106,000. Under the pressure to combine, the number of dailies dropped in 1941 to 1,857, a decline that continued in the 1940's until the total fell to 1,744. After about 1945 there was a leveling off through the 1950's and 1960's. In the early 1970's the number of dailies held rather steady while the circulation total rose slightly. In 1970 there were 1,748 dailies, with a circulation of 62,107,000; by 1973 there were 1,774 dailies with a circulation of 63,147,000. A major influence was the rise of the electronic media as a means of communication. Where a century earlier, major cities might have had as many as 10 dailies, in 1974 only two cities—New York and Chicago—had 4 and only three—Philadelphia, Boston, and San Antonio—had 3 dailies.

News Wire Services

The major services for the transmission of news and pictures by wire or radio, the Associated Press and United Press International, were started in 1848 and 1907, respectively. The United Press Association merged with a Hearst wire service, the International News Service, in 1958 to form United Press International.

Education in Journalism

The American Press Institute at the Columbia University Graduate School of Journalism, the Nieman Foundation at Harvard, and other programs at academic institutions provided opportunities for practicing newspaper workers to improve their professional knowledge and abilities. The University of Missouri School of Journalism, dating back to 1908, maintained a national Freedom of Information Center. Programs of prizes and awards, such as those established by Joseph Pulitzer in 1917, emphasized meritorious service in reporting, correspondence, editorial writing, cartooning, criticism, and other areas. Many newspapers had overlooked their own shortcomings, and for years the press's own critics, Silas Bent, Will Irwin, A. J. Liebling, Oswald Garrison Villard, and George Seldes, wrote for a small but growing audience. By the mid-1970's the press was listening as never before and striving to work on a higher plane.

BIBLIOGRAPHY

W. K. Agee, ed., *The Press and the Public Interest.*
James Aronson, *Deadline for the Media.*
B. H. Bagdikian, *The Information Machines.*
Alfred Balk, *A Free and Responsive Press.*
J. A. Barron, *Freedom of the Press for Whom?*
Silas Bent, *Ballyhoo: The Voice of the Press.*
S. M. Bessie, *Jazz Journalism.*
W. G. Bleyer, *Main Currents in the History of American Journalism.*
Herbert Brucker, *Communication Is Power.*
F. L. Bullard, *Famous War Correspondents.*
Robert Cirino, *Don't Blame the People.*
H. M. Clor, ed., *The Mass Media and Modern Democracy.*
E. E. Dennis and W. L. Rivers, *Other Voices: The New Journalism.*
Edwin Emery and H. L. Smith, *The Press and America.*
P. L. Fisher and R. L. Lowenstein, *Race and the News Media.*
J. C. Goulden, *Truth Is the First Casualty.*
Laurence Greene, *America Goes to Press.*
Gerald Gross, ed., *The Responsibility of the Press.*
W. A. Hachten, *The Supreme Court on Freedom of the Press.*
Stephen Hess and Milton Kaplan, *The Ungentlemanly Art.*
John Hohenberg, *Free Press, Free People.*
R. M. Hutchins, *A Free and Responsible Press.*
A. M. Lee, *The Daily Newspaper in America.*
R. W. Lee, ed., *Politics and the Press.*
A. J. Liebling, *The Wayward Pressman.*
C. E. Lindstrom, *The Fading American Newspaper.*
L. M. Lyons, ed., *Reporting the News.*
R. E. McCoy, *Freedom of the Press.*
A. K. MacDougall, ed., *The Press: A Critical Look From the Inside.*
Lester Markel, *What You Don't Know Can Hurt You.*
J. C. Merrill, *The Elite Press.*
Dale Minor, *The Information War.*
F. L. Mott, *American Journalism.*
William Murrell, *A History of American Graphic Art.*
R. E. Park, *The Immigrant Press and Its Control.*
W. L. Rivers and M. J. Nyhan, *Aspen Notebook on Government and the Media.*
Victor Rosewater, *History of Co-operative News-Gathering.*
B. W. Rucker, *The First Freedom.*
R. A. Rutland, *Newsmongers: Journalism in the Life of the Nation.*
P. M. Sandman, D. M. Rubin, and D. B. Sachsman, *Media.*
Martin Sheridan, *Comics and Their Creators.*
Upton Sinclair, *The Brass Check.*
I. F. Stone, *In a Time of Torment.*
John Tebbell, *The Media in America.*
O. G. Villard, *The Disappearing Daily.*
E. S. Watson, *A History of Newspaper Syndicates in the United States.*

— IRVING DILLIARD

NEWSPAPERS SINCE THE 1950S

By the early 1990s there were 9,000 newspapers published in the United States, about 1,600 of them dailies. Both their number and combined circulation of 60 million have changed little since the 1950s. Newspapers still receive the lion's share of dollars invested in advertising. In the mid-1990s most newspapers earned handsome profits, but the industry was gloomy because circulation had grown more slowly than the population, and papers were not attracting young readers. With increased competition for advertising money from television and magazines (usually three-quarters of a paper's income), some publishers tried to reach nonsubscribers with "shoppers," inserts filled with retail ads, while others changed content to match reader survey responses.

Other changes since the 1970s included the adoption in 1973 by journalists of a new voluntary code of ethics, and in several cities they published journals, including the *Columbia Journalism Review* and *American Journalism Review,* in which they criticized their own publications. The National News Council, which investigated complaints of unethical behavior against the largest newspapers and the wire services, was abandoned after eleven years in 1984, but a few publishers supported local versions. In 1995 newspapers employed fewer than 500,000 staff and other workers nationwide.

By the early 1990's, only a handful of cities still supported competing dailies, leading many papers to avoid endorsing political candidates.

The newspaper as a local institution changed in 1982 when Gannett Company, the largest newspaper chain, launched *USA Today,* which quickly became the number two newspaper in the country. Like the *Wall Street Journal,* which has the highest circulation, *USA Today* utilizes satellites to print in several locales. These two national dailies are followed by the *Los Angeles Times* and the *New York Times,* both with circulations of more than a million, The *Washington Post,* the *New York Daily News,* and *New York Newsday* reported circulations in excess of 750,000. More than 100 others exceed 100,000. Smaller dailies received the Pulitzer Prize for Meritorious Public Service during the 1970s and 1980s, including the *Anchorage Daily News* (1976, 1989), the *Lufkin (Texas) News* (1977), the *Jackson (Miss.) Clarion-Ledger* (1983), and the weekly *Point Reyes (Calif.) Light* (1979).

The decades-long rush toward chain ownership abated in the early 1990s, in part because there were few privately owned dailies left to acquire. Only a handful of cities still supported competing dailies, leading many papers to avoid endorsing political candidates. Instead, many added op-ed pages, in which they publish columnists with diverse views. By the late 1980s computer terminals had replaced typewriters in newsrooms and offset printing was almost universal, which led to the increased use of color in photographs, illustrations, and maps. Technological improvements weakened the printing craft unions, causing the number of labor strikes to decline. The foreign-language press changed to serve the immigrants from Asia and Central America, and the *Miami Herald*, among others, prints editions in Spanish. The African-American press became more economically viable, thanks to increased advertising, and there was a trend toward consolidation. The *Afro-American* published editions in Washington, Baltimore, and other cities, while the *Chicago Daily Defender* acquired the *Michigan Chronicle* in Detroit.

BIBLIOGRAPHY

Newspaper Association of America, *Facts About Newspapers* (Reston, Va., 1994).

Richard A. Schwarzlose, *Newspapers: A Reference Guide* (New York, 1987).

— JOHN D. STEVENS

NEZ PERCE WAR

Nez Perce War (1877). The various bands of the Nez Perce Indians, occupying a large area in the region where Washington, Oregon, and Idaho meet, had always been on friendly terms with the whites, and the Stevens Treaty of 1855 had guaranteed them a large reservation in their homeland. But when gold was discovered in 1860 swarms of miners and settlers intruded upon their lands. In 1863 some of the chiefs signed a new treaty, agreeing to move to the much smaller Lapwai Reservation in Idaho; but Chief Joseph and his southern Nez Perce refused to leave their Wallowa Valley home in northeastern Oregon, Joseph being under the influence of Smohalla, a nativistic prophet of a small Sahaptin tribe living along the Columbia River who preached that the Indians should reject the things of the white man and return to their native ways.

Joseph did not want war, and at the council held at Lapwai in May 1877 he agreed to move his people to the reservation. Hostilities were precipitated when a few young warriors killed some settlers in revenge for outrages. Troops under Gen. O O. Howard moved against the Indians, who, fighting defensively, defeated the soldiers in several battles, notably at White Bird Canyon in Idaho on June 17. Joseph executed a skillful retreat across the Bitterroot Mountains in an attempt to reach Canadian territory, but on Oct. 15, 1877, within thirty miles of the border, he was surrounded by the troops of Gen. Nelson A. Miles and forced to surrender. With only 300 warriors, Joseph had opposed troops numbering 5,000, traveling more than 1,000 miles in four months with a band that included women and children.

Chief Joseph (ca. 1840-1904) led the Nez Perce in resisting an illegal treaty ceding their land to the U.S. government. When peaceful measures failed, he tried to get his people to the safety of Canada. Though the Nez Perce defeated the U.S. army in several battles, they were stopped short of the Canadian border. Joseph was captured and lived out the rest of his life on a reservation in Washington state, declaring "I will fight no more forever." (Library of Congress/Corbis)

BIBLIOGRAPHY

Merrill D. Beal, *"I Will Fight No More": Chief Joseph and the Nez Perce War.*

Francis Haines, *The Nez Percés.*

Alvin M. Josephy, *The Nez Percé Indians and the Opening of the Northwest.*

— KENNETH M. STEWART

NIAGARA MOVEMENT

Niagara movement, a black movement composed mainly of intellectuals and professionals, organized in 1905 under the leadership of W. E. B. Du Bois and William Monroe Trotter for the purpose of initiating aggressive action to secure full citizens rights for black Americans. Its name came from the location of the organizational meeting in Niagara Falls, Ontario, Canada, to which Du Bois and his colleagues had gone after having been refused accommodations on the U.S. side of the border. The movement reflected the opposition among blacks both to the patterns of racial discrimination that had become standard practice in all parts of the country and to the accommodation and gradualism advocated by Booker T. Washington. It placed responsibility for the status of U.S. race relations on the attitudes and actions of whites and declared that blacks would be satisfied with nothing less than full civil rights. It called for the abolition of all legal distinctions based on race and color.

In 1906 the movement held its first national meeting at Harpers Ferry, W.Va., where it issued to the nation a strongly worded proclamation: "We claim for ourselves every right that belongs to freeborn Americans—political, civil and social. . . . We want full manhood suffrage, and we want it now, henceforth and forever." Among those attending the meeting were relatives of blacks who died in support of the abolitionist John Brown and a son of Frederick Douglass.

The selection of Harpers Ferry as the meeting place and the strength of its statements caused the Niagara movement to be viewed as radical and caused some black intellectuals and professionals to refuse to associate themselves with it. Strongly opposed to the movement was Booker T. Washington of Tuskegee Institute in Alabama, who because of his influence on the distribution of philanthropic gifts to education and on the appointment of blacks to government jobs was the strongest force in the black community of the nation. Washington's opposition, along with a split that developed between Du Bois and Trotter, weakened the movement to the point of ineffectiveness within a few years. In 1909, Du Bois and other blacks from the Niagara movement joined with a group of white liberals in the formation of the National Association for the Advancement of Colored People (NAACP).

The Niagara movement accomplished little during its brief history. Its importance lay in its outspoken opposition to Jim Crow laws, reflecting the dissatisfaction of Afro-Americans with their condition in the United States, and in its articulation of a position contrary to that of Washington. Coming as it did in the Progressive period, it revealed the lack of support for reform in race relations among white Progressive leaders. It is important also as a forerunner of the NAACP.

BIBLIOGRAPHY

Francis L. Broderick, *W. E. B. Du Bois: Negro Leader in a Time of Crisis.*

Stephen R. Fox, *The Guardian of Boston: William Monroe Trotter.*

Elliott M. Rudwick, "The Niagara Movement," *Journal of Negro History,* vol. 42 (1957).

— HENRY N. DREWRY

NINETEENTH AMENDMENT

The movement for the enactment of the Nineteenth Amendment of the U.S. Constitution, which gave women the vote, began at the Seneca Falls Convention of 1848, when, on the insistence of Elizabeth Cady Stanton, a resolution was adopted declaring "that it is the duty of the women of this country to secure to themselves their sacred right to the elective franchise." Following the Civil War continuous work began for adoption of an amendment to the Constitution stating that "The right of citizens of the United States to vote shall not be denied or abridged by the United States or by any state on account of sex."

The Nineteenth Amendment, which gave women the vote, grew out of pressures for equal rights set in motion at the 1848 Seneca Falls Convention organized by Elizabeth Cady Stanton.

On Jan. 9, 1918, President Woodrow Wilson came out in favor of the amendment, and the next day the House of Representatives passed it; but the Senate failed to act before the congressional session ended. In May 1919, soon after the Sixty-sixth Congress met, the House again acted favorably, and in June 1919 the Senate gave approval. Wisconsin, the first state to ratify, acted June 10, 1919. On Aug. 26, 1920, Tennessee cast the decisive favorable vote, the thirty-sixth, making the measure part of the law of the land.

BIBLIOGRAPHY

E. C. Stanton, S. B. Anthony, M. J. Gage, I. H. Harper, eds., *The History of Woman Suffrage.*

— MARY WILHELMINE WILLIAMS

NIXON, RESIGNATION OF

On Aug. 9, 1974, in a letter delivered to Secretary of State Henry Kissinger at 11:35 A.M., President Richard M. Nixon wrote, "I hereby resign the office of President of the United States." He thus became the first president ever to do so. On the preceding evening, Nixon announced his decision in an address to the nation, and spoke regretfully of any "injuries" committed "in the course of events that led" to it. Nixon noted the painfulness of his decision: "I have never been a quitter. To leave office before my term is completed is opposed to every instinct in my body. But as president I must put the interests of America first."

On the morning of Aug. 9, Nixon bade an emotional, sometimes tearful, farewell to his cabinet and White House staff. He then flew home to California, where he had begun his political career. With Mrs. Nixon, their daughter Tricia, and her husband, Edward F. Cox, the outgoing president landed at El Toro Marine Base and was taken by helicopter to La Casa Pacifica, his seaside villa near San Clemente.

At the moment that Nixon's letter of resignation was handed to the secretary of state, Vice-President Gerald R. Ford assumed the powers of the president, and slightly more than half an hour later he took the oath of office. In his address, President Ford expressed prayerfully the hope, "May our former president, who brought peace to millions, find it for himself."

Nixon's resignation was rooted in the Watergate and other scandals that plagued his second term and eroded the political strength derived from his overwhelming reelection in 1972. Two late-hour events forced Nixon to resign. In late July 1974 the House Judiciary Committee adopted three articles of impeachment, delineating many specific charges against the president. Less than a week earlier, on July 24, the Supreme Court, in an 8–0 decision, had ruled, in *United States* v. *Nixon*, that he must provide quantities of tapes of White House conversations required in the criminal trials of his former subordinates. The tapes disclosed that Nixon had participated as early as June 23, 1972, in the cover-up of the Watergate burglary, thus contradicting his previous denials. His remaining congressional and public support swiftly collapsed and made his impeachment a certainty. Its course was halted by his resignation.

Nixon took the step after Republican Sen. Barry Goldwater of Arizona disclosed that no more than fifteen votes existed in the Senate against impeachment, far short of the thirty-four necessary if Nixon hoped to escape conviction. White House Chief of Staff Alexander M. Haig, Jr., and Kissinger urged Nixon to step down in the national interest.

By resigning, Nixon avoided the disgrace implicit in a successful impeachment, and he preserved the pension rights and other perquisites of a former president that would have been lost. In impeachment, the Senate would have rendered an authoritative judgment concerning Nixon's conduct. By resigning, he would be able to characterize his presidency himself in terms that were minimally culpable. He acknowledged only that "if some of my judgments were wrong—and some were wrong—they were made in what I believed at the time to be in the best interests of the nation."

On Sept. 8, 1974, President Ford pardoned Nixon for all federal crimes that he "committed or may have committed or taken part in" while in office. The pardoning of the former president prior to his possible indictment, trial, and conviction, although supported by a U.S. Supreme Court ruling in *Ex parte Garland*, 4 Wallace 333 (1867), provoked criticism that the pardon was a cover-up of Nixon's cover-up of Watergate.

— LOUIS W. KOENIG

NORTH AMERICAN FREE TRADE AGREEMENT

North American Free Trade Agreement (NAFTA). The General Agreement on Tariffs and Trade (GATT), which went into effect in 1948 in the wake of World War II, sought to expand free trade by reducing tariffs between the twenty-three signatory nations. With the gradual privatization of state-run industries and economies, its membership expanded to ninety-six nations in 1988, and tariff barriers were reduced. A strong supporter of GATT throughout its history, the United States in 1986 began to urge that GATT move beyond the reduction of trade barriers and that its agenda include foreign investment, services, agriculture, and intellectual property rights. Many viewed this as an attempt to loosen environmental and social regulations that might hamper access to resources throughout the world. While perhaps seeking to increase investment opportunities for corporate interests, the United States by the mid-1980s was clearly on the defensive economically. Once the leading creditor nation in the world, it had become the largest debtor nation and suffered from what some feared was a perpetual trade deficit.

Increasing competition from Pacific and European countries caused the United States to begin trying to assemble a dollar-dominated block in the American hemisphere. This desire led first to the Free Trade Agreement (FTA) with Canada, which went into effect on Jan. 1, 1989, and then to an expanded trilateral agreement with Canada and Mexico, the North American Free Trade Agreement, which went into effect on January 1, 1994. A multivolume, fifteen-pound document, NAFTA at its simplest level set up a schedule for the elimination of tariffs over a fifteen-year period. Given the earlier agreement between the United States and Canada, NAFTA dealt primarily with restructuring trade between the United States and Mexico and between Mexico and Canada. All tariffs between the United States and Canada would end by the year 1998;

those between the United States and Mexico would be eliminated by 2008. The agreements, however, much like the expanded agenda for GATT, covered more than the elimination of trade barriers and led to divisive debate in all three countries. While few objected to freer trade, the opponents of the FTA with Canada and, later, NAFTA were many and vociferous. Concerns among Canadians in 1988 and Mexicans in 1992 reflected a lingering view of the United States as a powerful nation that might yet seek to swallow up or strangle its neighbors. While some critics employed a powerful emotional rhetoric reminiscent of the days when the United States was roundly condemned as the Colossus of the North, others focused on the perceived need to protect Canadian and Mexican sovereignty, which they saw as threatened by expanded U.S. investment in such crucial national resources as oil and in institutions such as banking. Given the unequal status between themselves and their powerful neighbor, these opponents argued, both Canada and Mexico risked becoming in effect economic colonies of the United States.

In 1988 Canadians voiced many of the same concerns expressed by labor leaders and environmentalists in the United States in the early 1990s. Because Canada was already part of GATT, Canadians questioned the necessity of the FTA and the benefit to Canada of tying itself more closely to the largest debtor nation in the world. They argued that the movement of jobs from Canada to the United States, already a problem because of lower U.S. labor costs, would accelerate and that Canada's higher standards of environmental regulation and social programs would be threatened by U.S. investment and business practices. The debates over NAFTA that raged in all three North American countries in the early 1990s thus reflected not only old suspicions and prejudices but the confusion and uncertainty engendered by the end of the cold war, the increasingly global problems of overpopulation and pollution, and the growing interdependency of economies, as well as suspicion that the only ones who would benefit from the new agreements would be the transnational corporations, which many observers considered already too powerful and unregulated. By far the most emotional issue in all three countries was the effect of NAFTA on employment. While proponents of NAFTA stressed that implementation would ultimately create jobs, the fear of job loss inspired many opponents. The negotiations commenced and continued during a period of global recession and high unemployment. While the movement of jobs from Canada to the United States and from the United States to Mexico had preceded the FTA and NAFTA negotiations, labor groups in both the United States and Canada were unshakable in their opposition.

As the leaders of both Mexico and the United States sought to assuage the fears of those at home who opposed NAFTA, the fate of the pact had implications beyond the borders of North America in the early 1990s. When President George Bush and Mexican President Carlos Salinas de Gortari announced in June 1990 the possibility of a free trade agreement between Mexico and the United States, Bush also announced the Enterprise for the Americas Initiative, which envisioned a free trade block stretching from Alaska to Tierra del Fuego. This announcement preceded a dizzying number of new trading alignments within Latin America, including the agreement among Argentina, Brazil, Paraguay, and Uruguay in March 1991 to establish MERCOSUR, which pledged to integrate their economies by 1995, and numerous framework trade agreements between the United States and its southern neighbors. Most of these proposals received little attention, and public debate remained focused on the free trade agreement with Mexico.

While NAFTA proponents stressed that the agreement would ultimately create jobs, fears of job loss prompted widespread opposition.

Throughout the course of the NAFTA negotiations, which began in February 1991, more than economics was at stake. The creation of a multinational trading bloc represented a political as well as an economic objective. Correctly or not, Latin American leaders by the early 1990s had come to see the opportunity to move closer to the United States economically as a way to move their countries politically along a modern path of reform. At stake, then, was more than an economic reordering of the relationship among the three North American countries; achievement of a foreign policy objective—strengthening political ties throughout the hemisphere—was also on the line. NAFTA was approved by the U.S. Congress in November 1993. A complicated and cumbersome document largely unread by proponents and opponents alike, it included concessions made on all sides, because leaders in the United States, Mexico, and Canada sought to effect its passage, promote their own economies, and protect the frailest components of those economies.

[See also Canada, Relations with; General Agreement on Tariffs and Trade; Mexico, Relations with.]

BIBLIOGRAPHY

Marjorie Montgomery Bowker, *On Guard for Thee: An Independent Review of the Free Trade Agreement* (Quebec, 1988).

Victor Bulmer-Thomas, Nikki Craske, and Monica Serrano, eds., *Mexico and the North American Free Trade Agreement: Who Will Benefit?* (New York, 1994).

John Cavanagh et al., eds., *Trading Freedom: How Free Trade Affects Our Lives, Work, and Environment* (San Francisco, 1992).

— MARY COMMAGER

NORTH ATLANTIC TREATY ORGANIZATION

North Atlantic Treaty Organization (NATO). The signing of the North Atlantic Treaty on Apr. 4, 1949, marked the end of a tradition of nonentanglement with European powers that had begun in 1800 with the termination of the Franco-American alliance of 1778. The treaty linked the United States with eleven other nations—Canada, Iceland, the United Kingdom, France, Belgium, the Netherlands, Luxembourg, Norway, Denmark, Portugal, and Italy. The proximate cause of this transformation in U.S. foreign relations was the Soviet communist menace to Western Europe. Initiative for the alliance came from Europe. In 1947 the administration of President Harry S. Truman had announced the Truman Doctrine, which established the principle of providing assistance to countries threatened by communist takeover, and the Marshall Plan, a program for the economic reconstruction of Europe that also included containment of communism as one of its goals. Worried that these measures did not provide sufficient security against communist subversion or Soviet pressures, however, the European nations sought a binding pledge from the United States. They received it in the form of Article 5 of the treaty, which stated that an attack on one member would be considered an attack on all. The allies in turn pledged to build their defenses, integrate their military forces, and prove through self-help and mutual assistance to be worthy of the U.S. commitment.

The alliance itself had little military significance in 1949. Its members assumed that the fact of U.S. adherence to the treaty would be sufficient to deter external attack and that a modest U.S. military assistance program would be sufficient to inhibit internal subversion. In 1950 the Korean War shattered these assumptions. If the Soviets were testing American resolve in a divided Korea, they might conceivably make their next move in a divided Germany. Fear of attack impelled the allies to expand the alliance into a military organization, under a Supreme Allied Commander in Europe (SACEUR) and in the Atlantic (SACLANT). A political headquarters was established in Paris in 1952. A vast military assistance program begun in the summer of 1950 was to raise the size of the ground forces to fifty divisions to cope with a potential Soviet invasion of the West. Greece and Turkey were brought into the alliance in 1952 to shore up the southeastern flank of NATO. West Germany entered the alliance in 1955 only after resistance from its neighbors, France in particular, had been overcome. From 1950 onward the purpose of the alliance was military rather than political. Throughout the 1950s and 1960s the SACEURs, beginning with General Dwight D. Eisenhower, were dominant figures, overshadowing the civilian secretaries-general. Although the drive to build up a large standing army waned in the 1950s, to be replaced by emphasis on nuclear weapons—tactical, intermediate, and by the end of the decade, intercontinental—the concern of the NATO allies remained centered on military security and U.S. authority remained self-evident.

By the late 1950s, however, there were clear signs of discontent among the allies, which gathered strength in the 1960s. Part of the problem was the increasing resentment of the U.S. nuclear monopoly as expanding economies in the European Economic Community generated a self-confidence that had been lacking earlier. At the same time Soviet technological achievements, epitomized by the Sputnik earth satellite in 1957, both stimulated interest of the allies in building their own nuclear weapons and cast doubt on the support of the United States if its own cities were vulnerable to Soviet intercontinental ballistic missiles (ICBMs). Efforts on both sides of the Atlantic to shore up the alliance faltered in the face of a rising Soviet threat. An ambitious attempt to create a multilateral force in Europe, armed with nuclear weapons, collapsed in 1964 because of U.S. unwillingness to turn over control of the weapons to the allies. President Charles de Gaulle's France withdrew its military participation in 1966 but remained a member of the NATO alliance, and NATO's headquarters moved in the following year from Paris to Brussels.

The events of the late 1980's—including Germany's reunification and the Warsaw Pact's dissolution—furthered NATO's achievement of its primary goal: removal of the communist menace.

In 1967 the Harmel Initiative, named for Belgium's foreign minister, reinvigorated the alliance by having

NATO use détente as well as defense as a major objective. On the assumption that coexistence with the Soviet bloc was a reality, the NATO allies in the 1970s negotiated with the Soviet-controlled Warsaw Pact nations on such issues as reducing nuclear and conventional weaponry and accepting the postwar boundaries of East Germany and Poland. The periodic crises in the 1950s and 1960s over the status of West Berlin, which had led to the Berlin Wall and confrontation between Soviet and American tanks in 1961, seemed to have ended. There was still an uneasiness among the allies when détente did not prevent the Soviet Union from building up offensive nuclear weapons at a time when the United States was reducing its own defense effort. Chairman Leonid Brezhnev's Soviet Union was less volatile than that of Premier Nikita Khrushchev but was no less threatening. Europeans were particularly worried about intermediate-range ballistic missiles targeted on their cities. Soviet behavior induced the allies to follow a dual-track system of both increasing defenses and reviving détente. Although ICBMs based in the United States and Polaris missiles on U.S. submarines effectively neutralized Soviet missiles, European insecurity required deployment of U.S. cruise and Pershing II missiles in five European countries to ease their fears. The United States asked for major increases in NATO defense expenditures, and, in the administrations of Presidents Jimmy Carter and Ronald Reagan, committed itself to massive increases. The Soviet Union at first refused to accept mutual reductions, on the mistaken assumption that Western antinuclear public opinion would prevent the deployment of U.S. missiles. When President Mikhail Gorbachev came to power in the mid-1980s, however, he sought to deescalate the conflict; the Soviet economy could not withstand new burdens that would result from further military competition with the United States. Negotiations that had been interrupted in 1983 while the Soviets attempted to intimidate the West resumed in 1985.

The rush of events at the end of the 1980s—reunification of Germany and dissolution of the Warsaw Pact and of the Soviet Union itself—ended in NATO's achievement of its initial goal, removal of the communist menace. In the mid-1990s NATO's sixteen nations, including Spain since 1982, were seeking new functions for the organization. Until such could be found, the disarray in the former Soviet empire postponed any measures to terminate the Atlantic alliance.

[See also Arms Race and Disarmament; Cold War.]

BIBLIOGRAPHY

David P. Calleo, *Beyond American Hegemony: The Future of the Western Alliance* (New York, 1987).

Lawrence S. Kaplan, *NATO and the United States* (New York, 1994).

Stanley R. Sloan, *NATO's Future* (Washington, D.C., 1985).

— LAWRENCE S. KAPLAN

NORTHWEST PASSAGE

From 1497 to 1800, when it was believed that the riches of the Orient could be reached via a ship route around the northern extremities of North America, a northwest passage was the goal of many explorers. Further stimulus was provided by the papal bull of 1493 that barred all southern trade routes to countries other than Spain and Portugal. The most important explorers of this period were John Cabot (1497–98), Jacques Cartier (1534–35), Martin Frobisher (1576), John Davys (1585–87), and Henry Hudson (1610–11). They covered most of the shoreline and inlets of the northeastern section of the North American continent. By directing attention to certain areas for further search while negating others, they contributed to future exploration for a passage. William Baffin (1610), however, gave the quest a decided setback when, as a result of his one voyage to the Arctic, he declared that Baffin Bay was entirely landlocked.

Later the search for a water route took a more practical bent, a filling-in of geographical and scientific data. After the Napoleonic Wars, British naval officers under the supervision of John Barrow, second secretary of the admiralty, renewed exploration of the North American Arctic. The combined exploits of expeditions led by W. E. Parry (1819–20, 1821–23), John Franklin and John Richardson (1819–22, 1825–27), John Ross (1829–33), and R. J. L. M. McClure (1850–54) resulted in eventual success. Roald Amundsen (1903–06), a Norwegian, was the first to sail all the way from the Atlantic to the Pacific. Henry A. Larsen (1940–42), a sergeant in the Royal Canadian police, crossed eastward in the schooner *Saint Roch* along the same shallow route. In 1944, Larsen made the return journey in the same ship, following a deep-water route this time. In 1954 Capt. O. C. S. Robertson of the Royal Canadian Navy traversed the deep-water route westward with the icebreaker *Labrador*. In 1956 three U.S. Coast Guard vessels—*Storis, Spar*, and *Bramble*—led by the Canadian icebreaker *Labrador*, made the passage westward through the treacherous Bellot Strait, between Boothia Peninsula and Somerset Island.

The Northwest Passage consists of five possible routes through the Canadian Arctic archipelago, but only two are practical and only one is deep enough for large ships. The deep-water route extends westward from Baffin Bay through Lancaster Sound, Barrow Strait, Viscount Melville Sound, Prince of Wales Strait, and Amundsen

Gulf to emerge into the Beaufort Sea. In an attempt to determine the type of tanker needed to reach Alaska's oil-rich north shore by a northern route, a $50 million project was begun in 1969 by three major oil companies. The *Manhattan*, the largest and most powerful ship built in the United States, was converted to a research vessel and the world's largest icebreaker. Accompanied by other icebreakers, the *Manhattan* sailed on Aug. 24, 1969, entering the Northwest Passage on Sept. 5. On Sept. 14 it reached Point Barrow, after breaking through 650 miles of ice. Although the voyage was made during the most favorable season for ice navigation, hull damage was sustained. Atomic submarines also have navigated an under-the-ice route across the North Pole via the Bering Strait to the Atlantic Ocean east of Greenland. Continued advances in technology may well render surface ship transport through the Northwest Passage economically feasible in the future.

BIBLIOGRAPHY

Ernest S. Dodge, *Northwest by Sea.*
Bern Keating, *The Northwest Passage.*
L. P. Kirwan, *A History of Polar Exploration.*
Jeannette Mirsky, *To the North.*
U.S. Department of the Navy, *Toward the Poles.*

— EDWIN A. MACDONALD

NORTHWEST TERRITORY

Northwest Territory, officially the "Territory Northwest of the River Ohio," included the Old Northwest when it was established by Congress July 13, 1787. The Ordinance of 1785 had already provided for the survey of the public land in townships, each six miles square and divided into thirty-six sections of 640 acres. Payment for the land was permitted in specie, or in Continental certificates, and, for one-seventh, the land warrants issued to revolutionary soldiers were accepted. The ordinance set aside section sixteen in each township for the support of education.

The Ordinance of 1787 outlined the governmental framework. At first there would be an arbitrary administration, with a governor, three judges, and a secretary elected by and responsible to Congress. When the population included 5,000 free white males of voting age, the territory would have local autonomy, with a legislative assembly, although Congress would still choose the governor. Finally, when any one of the stipulated divisions contained 60,000 free inhabitants, it would be admitted into the Union as a state. An important clause in the ordinance forbade slavery in the Old Northwest. The two ordinances, modified to meet changing conditions, remained the basic principles for the organization of the Old Northwest and set precedents for later territorial development.

In 1787 the Northwest Territory had a widely scattered population of some 45,000 Indians and 2,000 French. The first legal American settlement was made at Marietta (present-day Ohio), Apr. 7, 1788. Gov. Arthur Saint Clair inaugurated the territorial government, July 15, 1788, forming Washington County between the eastern boundary and the Scioto. In January 1790 he established Hamilton County between the Scioto and Miami rivers and in March he set up Saint Clair County along the Mississippi north of the Ohio. Winthrop Sargent, secretary of the territory, then organized Knox County between the Miami and Saint Clair County, and in 1796 he formed Wayne County with Detroit as the county seat. From these basic counties others were set off as population increased.

Because of a fear of attacks by Indians the earliest settlements were confined to the Ohio Valley, but after Gen. Anthony Wayne's decisive victory at Fallen Timbers, Aug. 20, 1794, and the subsequent Treaty of Greenville the greater part of Ohio was opened up. Population increased so rapidly that the autonomous stage of government was inaugurated Sept. 4, 1799, with the first meeting of the territorial assembly. Owing to the distance between many of the settlements a division of the territory became necessary, and in 1800 the area west of a line north from the mouth of the Kentucky River was set off as Indiana Territory. The diminished Northwest Territory was further decreased in 1803, when Michigan was annexed to Indiana.

A movement for statehood began, which was aided by the Jeffersonian Republican national victory in 1800. Although the territory had approximately only 42,000 inhabitants on Apr. 30, 1802, Jefferson approved the necessary enabling act. With the first meeting of the state legislature, Mar. 1, 1803, the Northwest Territory gave place to the state of Ohio.

BIBLIOGRAPHY

B. W. Bond, Jr., *Civilization of the Old Northwest.*
R. C. Downes, *Frontier Ohio, 1788–1803.*

— BEVERLEY W. BOND, JR.

NUCLEAR POWER

Nuclear power, in physics, refers to energy produced by fission, when atoms are split, or by fusion, when two nuclei of a light atom are fused to form a single nucleus. The energy produced can be used for weapons or for peaceful purposes. The phrase is also used to designate those nations that have nuclear weapons. The nations that have declared they have nuclear weapons are China,

France, the former Soviet Union, Great Britain, and the United States. The breakup of the Soviet Union in the early 1990s resulted in the addition of Byelarus, Kazakhstan, and Ukraine as nuclear-weapon states because the nuclear missiles and storage sites placed on their territory by the Soviet Union became the property of these newly independent states. All three have declared their intention to transfer their weapons to Russia. In addition, a number of nations, such as India, Pakistan, and North Korea, are believed to have the capacity to develop nuclear weapons within a few months. Others, such as Israel, are suspected of having developed one or more such weapons secretly.

Nuclear power also refers to plants and industry that generate electric power from nuclear sources. Nuclear power plants differ from hydroelectric plants, which generate electricity from the force of flowing water, and coal-, oil-, or gas-fired electric plants, which generate electricity from the heat drawn from burning fossil fuels. Nuclear power plants generate steam to drive electric turbines by circulating liquid through a nuclear reactor. The reactor produces heat through the controlled fission of atomic fuel. Normally the fuel for power reactors is slightly enriched uranium. In 1951 the U.S. Atomic Energy Commission built the first nuclear reactor to generate electric power. The increasing availability of uranium ore at that time and the resulting reduction in price of this essential fuel increased interest in commercial exploitation of the new technology. Nuclear reactors have several advantages over power generation using other fuels. Unlike fossil fuels, nuclear fuel does not foul the air and is not dependent on oil imports from unstable parts of the world. The rising costs of the world's diminishing coal, oil, and natural gas resources and the limitation on the number of hydroelectric power plants that can be built could be overcome by nuclear plants. The attraction of electricity generated by nuclear power was not limited to the United States. Industrial and some developing nations embarked on ambitious programs of their own. By 1966 nuclear power generators were being built or operating in five countries. By the beginning of the 1980s there were 100 nuclear power plants in the United States.

One of the by-products of nuclear power generation is plutonium, a material that can be chemically processed for use in nuclear weapons. The danger of such use by nonnuclear nations led to international safeguards under the 1968 Nuclear Nonproliferation Treaty. In Article III signatory nations agreed to inspections by the International Atomic Energy Agency (IAEA), "with a view to preventing diversion of nuclear energy from peaceful uses to nuclear weapons or other nuclear explosive devices." Most of the world's nuclear and nonnuclear nations signed this treaty. Iraq in 1992 and North Korea in 1994 were subjected to IAEA inspections that proved treaty violations in the former and raised serious suspicions about the latter. Both nations were signatories of the treaty, although North Korea announced its withdrawal some months prior to inspection. Iraq's nuclear-weapon production facilities were discovered as a result of a series of highly intrusive IAEA inspections and were subsequently destroyed by the United Nations.

When Congress passed the Atomic Energy Act of 1954, it approved President Dwight D. Eisenhower's Atoms for Peace program, which included commercial development of nuclear reactors for the purpose of generating electric power. During the 1960s electricity generated by nuclear power contributed 1 to 2 percent of the nation's energy total. Since then that percentage has grown steadily, surpassing the proportion from hydroelectric sources in 1984. By 1990 nuclear power amounted to one-fifth of the nation's total generation of electricity. By 1992 nuclear generation reached 619 billion net kilowatt hours, more than double the amount generated in 1979, when the Three Mile Island accident produced an adverse effect on U.S. development of nuclear power plants.

President Eisenhower's Atoms for Peace program included commercial development of nuclear reactors for generating electric power.

In reaction to the 1973 oil embargo, U.S. consumers temporarily used less energy, which diminished the rate of growth in electricity generation. As a result of this and other factors, such as higher construction costs, delays brought on by antinuclear protests, increased operating costs resulting from new federal regulations, and uncertainties about disposal of high-level radioactive waste, no requests for construction of new nuclear power plants had been received by the Nuclear Regulatory Commission since 1978. The level of generation was still rising, however, because plants started in the 1970s had gone on-line, and modernization after 1979 made power plants more efficient. The rising production trend was expected to continue until the beginning of the twenty-first century, then level off and begin to fall, unless more nuclear plants were built.

[See also Arms Race and Disarmament; Nuclear Regulatory Commission; Strategic Arms Limitations Talks; Three Mile Island.]

BIBLIOGRAPHY

Department of Energy, Energy Information Administration, *Annual Energy Outlook 1994* (Washington, D.C., 1994), and *1992 Energy Facts* (Washington, D.C., 1993).

Daniel Deudney and Christopher Flavin, *Renewable Energy: The Power to Choose* (New York, 1983).

Peter Mannfield, *World Nuclear Power* (New York, 1991).

— ROBERT M. GUTH

NUCLEAR REGULATORY COMMISSION

The attraction of nuclear power has been dimmed since its beginnings by the danger of accidents. Governments faced a dilemma between promoting what was for many years seen as the promise of clean and cheap power and the need to regulate commercial development to protect public safety and the environment. The Nuclear Regulatory Commission (NRC) was created as the U.S. government's regulator. Established under the Energy Reorganization Act of 1974, it inherited licensing and regulatory authority from its predecessor, the Atomic Energy Commission. The NRC licenses and regulates the construction and operation of civilian nuclear reactors and the possession, use, processing, handling, and disposal of nuclear materials. It issues rules and standards to protect public health and safety and the environment from the dangers of commercial nuclear programs and inspects them for adherence to NRC rules. The five commissioners are appointed by the president (who also selects the chair) for five-year terms. A maximum of three commissioners may be of the same political party. The NRC's major program responsibilities are administered by the Offices of Nuclear Reactor Regulation and Nuclear Material Safety and Safeguards. Field operations are conducted from regional offices in Atlanta, Philadelphia, Chicago, Dallas, and San Francisco. NRC headquarters is in Bethesda, Md. The Office of Nuclear Reactor Regulation licenses construction and operation of nuclear reactors and seeks to ensure their safe and environmentally sound operation. Since the late 1970s, however, applications for new construction of nuclear power plants have dwindled to the point where safety of operations and environmental inspections and reviews have become the office's principal business. The Office of Nuclear Material Safety and Safeguards oversees uranium mines, mills, and recovery facilities for the proper processing, handling, transportation, storage, and prevention of theft and sabotage of nuclear materials. The Office of Nuclear Regulatory Research develops safety and environmental standards for the operation of nuclear facilities and management of nuclear waste. It sponsors research on which to base standards and to support the NRC's responsibilities for evaluating accidents and predicting risk.

Established to relieve tension between the development and regulation of nuclear power, the NRC found itself divided between responsibilities for safety and environmental protection and the profitability of the nuclear power industry. Public confidence in nuclear power was undermined by the Mar. 28, 1979, accident at the Three Mile Island nuclear plant near Harrisburg, Pa., in which a cooling-system failure of one reactor led to a partial exposure of its uranium core, threatening an explosion and wide release of radioactivity until the crisis was contained twelve days later. The NRC received scathing criticism for lax enforcement and poor preparation for emergencies from the commission investigating the accident. Inevitably more stringent regulation followed, leading to increased costs for new plants. Industry budgets had to deal with lengthening start-up times that were already seen as excessive and account for expensive cleanup in the event of another accident. As of 1995 no applications to build new commercial nuclear power plants had been received since the 1979 accident and projects for the construction of new plants were abandoned in the 1980s. The cost of electricity produced by earlier plants and those completed since the accident rose steadily into the 1990s and were projected to continue rising. Environmental concerns linked to fossil fuels may well drive costs of nonnuclear power generation up to the point where nuclear generation again may look commercially attractive.

[See also Atomic Energy Commission; Nuclear Power; Three Mile Island.]

BIBLIOGRAPHY

Philip L. Catelon and Robert C. Williams, *Crisis Contained: The Department of Energy at Three Mile Island* (Carbondale, Ill., 1982).

Fred Clement, *The Nuclear Regulatory Commission* (New York, 1989).

Union of Concerned Scientists, *Safety Second* (Bloomington, Ind., 1987).

— ROBERT M. GUTH

NUCLEAR TEST BAN TREATY

Nuclear Test Ban Treaty was largely a result of worldwide public pressure to eliminate the health hazard of radioactive fallout from exploding atom bombs. By 1954 governments felt that pressure to be sufficiently strong to deal with the problem seriously. Previously, banning nuclear tests had been a minor aspect of general and futile disarmament talks. On May 10, 1955, the Soviet Union seized the initiative by making the test ban a major point in its general disarmament proposal. Although in the course of time it changed the details of the proposal, it consistently favored a simple prohibition of testing nuclear devices. The American government rejected this idea for several years, arguing that without an international inspection system a test ban or disarmament in general would be dangerous to national security and that, besides, a "clean" bomb would soon be developed, making a test ban superfluous. The resulting debate between the Soviet Union, the United States, and Great Britain merely served to arouse public opinion further. The controversial issue figured prominently in the American presidential elections of 1956 and 1960. On Jan. 12, 1957, the American government felt obliged to announce the conditions under which it would consider a test ban and thereby allowed the problem to be dealt with separately from general disarmament negotiations. But it took another six and a half years before an independent agreement could be reached, and, ironically, by that time the motivation for conciliatory attitudes had changed in the United States and the Soviet Union, although not in Britain.

In the Soviet Union, the growing rift with China in the early 1960's made a test ban agreement desirable.

The negotiations during this period paralleled the vicissitudes of the cold war. For instance, in 1958 the three governments each renounced independently any further tests but soon after resumed them, mainly for political reasons. After the U-2 spy plane incident and the cancellation of the Paris summit conference in 1960, negotiations slowed down considerably and at times were even integrated again with the hopeless general disarmament talks. In spite of public demands in many countries for a test ban, it was clear that the negotiations were decisively affected by considerations of foreign policy, national security, and cold war propaganda. A gradual rapprochement between the United States and the Soviet Union on the test ban question was caused by changing incentives on both sides to reach agreement. In the United States, preoccupation with a nuclear balance of power and a general inspection system for disarmament was partly replaced by a desire to prevent the enlargement of the "nuclear club." In the Soviet Union the growing split with China made a test ban agreement desirable. Very likely also, the development of reconnaissance satellites made on-site inspection increasingly unimportant to the United States and the Soviet Union.

On Aug. 27, 1962, the United States, in a major concession, and the United Kingdom presented a draft treaty resembling a Soviet proposal of Nov. 28, 1961, both calling for the end of tests in the atmosphere, in space, and under water. The problem of underground tests was left unmentioned because the parties were too far apart in their views. The Cuban missile crisis and its settlement provided the final impetus to conclusive action. On Aug. 5, 1963, the United States, Great Britain, and the Soviet Union signed an agreement in Moscow, open for signature to all other nations. All test explosions of nuclear weapons or other devices in the atmosphere, in space, and under water were prohibited. The signatories also promised not to participate in any way in such tests by others. More than 100 acceded to the treaty. Among them was India but not France and China. The treaty was hailed as a precedent for other disarmament measures, as a means for stopping the spread of nuclear weapons to other nations, and as a major contribution to the reduction of international tensions. Subsequent events showed that these hopes were not fully realized.

BIBLIOGRAPHY

Arthur H. Dean, *Test Ban and Disarmament: The Path of Negotiation.*

Harold K. Jacobson and Eric Stein, *Diplomats, Scientists, and Politicians: The United States and the Nuclear Test Ban Negotiations.*

Mary Milling Lepper, *Foreign Policy Formulation: A Case Study of the Nuclear Test Ban Treaty of 1963.*

David E. Mark, *Die Einstellung der Kernwaffenversuche.*

— WERNER LEVI

NULLIFICATION

Nullification, the act by which a state suspends, within its territorial jurisdiction, a federal law. The doctrine of nullification evolved from the theory that the Union was the result of a compact between sovereign states, that the Constitution was a body of instructions drawn up by the states for the guidance of the general government, that the states were the rightful judges of infractions of the Constitution, and that the states were not bound by the acts of their agent when it exceeded its delegated powers. The right of nullification was first asserted by Virginia and Kentucky in their resolutions of 1798. The Kentucky resolutions of 1799 boldly asserted that nullification was the "rightful remedy" for infractions of the Constitution. Only fifteen years later the fundamental principles of nullification were again invoked by the action of the Hartford Convention of 1814. Georgia not only nullified the decisions of the

A Matthew Brady photograph of the American statesman John C. Calhoun, who served as Vice President under both John Quincy Adams and Andrew Jackson. (Library of Congress/Corbis)

Supreme Court in its controversy with the Cherokee in the early 1830's but also prevented their enforcement. Several northern states nullified the Fugitive Slave Law of 1850 by the passage of personal liberty laws.

The most notable example of nullification occurred in South Carolina after opposition to the protective tariff began to develop in the South in the 1820's. This hostility mounted to such proportions that the legislature of South Carolina in 1828 printed and circulated Sen. John C. Calhoun's *Exposition*, which reaffirmed the doctrines of 1798 and formulated a program of action—the interposition of the state's veto through the people in sovereign convention assembled. The South Carolinians then waited, expecting the administration of President Andrew Jackson to reduce the tariff. When Congress enacted a tariff act in 1832 that proclaimed protection a permanent policy, the nullifiers carried the issue to the people. They won control of the legislature and called a state convention (Nov. 19, 1832). This body adopted the Ordinance of Nullification declaring the tariff acts of 1828 and 1832 oppressive, unconstitutional, null and void, and not binding on the people of South Carolina. Appeals to the federal courts were forbidden, and state officials were required to take an oath to support the ordinance. The legislature later passed acts necessary to put the ordinance into effect. South Carolina expected other southern states to follow its lead, but none supported nullification, although several protested against protective tariffs.

Jackson issued a proclamation on Dec. 10, 1832, in which he denounced nullification as rebellion and treason and warned the people of South Carolina that he would use every power at his command to enforce the laws. In a message to Congress he urged modification of the tariff and, later, asked the passage of a "force act" to enable him to use the army and navy in enforcing the law. Before the date set for the ordinance to take effect, Feb. 1, 1833, measures for reducing the tariff were introduced in Congress. Consequently, a South Carolina committee, empowered by the convention to act, suspended the ordinance until Congress should take final action. Both the Force Act and the Compromise Tariff were passed by Congress, and both were approved by the president early in March. The convention reassembled on Mar. 11, 1833, and rescinded the Ordinance of Nullification, but nullified the Force Act. The nullifiers, who had claimed their action peaceable, argued that the reduction of the tariff duties amply justified their position and action.

The doctrine of nullification was again raised in 1954, when the Supreme Court declared racial segregation unconstitutional in *Brown* v. *Board of Education of Topeka.* No state, however, chose to call a special state convention to nullify the decision, but chose instead to evade compliance, especially through state legislation and litigation.

BIBLIOGRAPHY

H. V. Ames, *State Documents on Federal Relations.*

Frederic Bancroft, *Calhoun and the South Carolina Nullification Movement.*

C. S. Boucher, *The Nullification Controversy in South Carolina.*

John R. Schmidhauser, *The Supreme Court as Final Arbiter in Federal-State Relations, 1789–1957.*

— FLETCHER M. GREEN

NURSING

The origins of American nursing can be traced, in part, to the humanitarian ideals, sanitary reforms, and scientific progress characteristic of medicine in the late

19th century. Although no longer monopolized by the moralism of the religious orders, nursing attracted many women because of its ideals of service. The hygienic values of the sanitary reformers were incorporated into the designs of hospitals, by then viewed as institutions exclusively devoted to the care of the sick. In these hospitals, physicians could attend to a larger number of patients and they could offer an ever-increasing array of technically effective services. With the advent of new diagnostic and therapeutic instruments (for example, thermometers, sphygmomanometers, hypodermic needles) and the rise of the new surgery made possible by anesthetics and antiseptic techniques, patients needed responsible attendants, and physicians needed knowledgeable assistants. By 1873 four hospitals were operating schools of nursing: the New England Hospital for Women and Children in Boston; Massachusetts General Hospital in Boston; New Haven Hospital in New Haven, Conn.; and Bellevue Hospital in New York City. These early schools, though, provided mostly apprenticeship training, at best.

Hospital administrators soon realized that improved nursing care diminished mortality and morbidity on the wards and that young, idealistic women could be encouraged to care for the sick in return for training and "board and keep." In 1873 there were 178 hospitals in the United States; by 1909 the number had increased to more than 4,000. By 1893 there were 225 hospital nursing schools, and by 1900, at least 432. The students learned from older nurses, matrons, or superintendents, and physicians who volunteered to give lectures or demonstrations. In 1907 Columbia University appointed Mary Adelaide Nutting as the first full-time American professor of nursing.

Nutting had been one of the first graduate nurses to urge the establishment of a professional journal for nursing. After several years of struggle, the *American Journal of Nursing* appeared in 1900. Prior to that, Nutting's predecessors at the Johns Hopkins Hospital School of Nursing, Isabel Hampton and Lavinia Dock, had been instrumental in the establishment of two professional nurse associations: the American Society of Superintendents of Training Schools for Nurses of the United States and Canada (1894) and the Nurses Associated Alumnae of the United States and Canada (1896). By 1912 the former group, now known as the National League of Nursing Education, and the latter group, now known as the American Nurses' Association, adopted the *American Journal of Nursing* as their official publication. In recognition of the growing number of public health nurses who worked in homes, clinics, schools, and industries, the National Organization for Public Health Nursing was organized in 1912.

By 1914 forty-one states had adopted nurse practice acts, thereby establishing state boards of nurse examiners. The graduates of schools approved by these boards were authorized to use the title "Registered Nurse" (RN). Many of these state boards established criteria for evaluating schools, but standards were not very high.

With cues from the successful reforms in medical education, nurse educators undertook a thorough evaluation of nursing schools between 1913 and 1937. The National League of Nursing Education prepared a standardized curriculum that was gradually adopted. Between 1929 and 1937, nursing schools reduced their enrollment, made admission qualifications more rigid, eliminated monthly stipends for hospital services, and discharged students with poor grades. A truly national program of accreditation became effective with the formation of the National Nursing Accrediting Service in January 1949.

As the demand for nurses became particularly acute during and after World War II, the problems of balancing quality and quantity loomed large. Fraught with considerable intramural squabbling, several kinds of educational programs evolved. The majority remained in hospitals; they included short-term training programs for practical or vocational nurses and diploma programs that afforded eligibility for licensure after two or three years of study. In 1957, 81.9 percent of American nursing schools were under hospital or noncollegiate control. Of nurses graduating in 1963, 82.5 percent received diplomas from 874 hospital schools. Some nurse educators believed that nursing education must be interdigitated with baccalaureate education. The University of Minnesota offered the first baccalaureate degree program in 1909. By 1929 there were 32 such programs; by 1962, 174. In that year, 13.8 percent of 31,000 nurse graduates had received baccalaureate degrees. The third major approach involved numerous junior colleges that appeared after World War II. In 1962, 3.7 percent of nursing graduates were trained in 69 associate degree programs mostly affiliated with these junior colleges. By 1973 there were 574 such programs, along with 305 baccalaureate degree programs and 494 diploma programs. The trend has been toward an increase in baccalaureate and associate degree programs and a decrease in diploma programs.

After 1925 nurses experienced severe social and scientific stresses in their quest for professional status. Primarily women until the 1960's, nurses have participated in the many vicissitudes of the woman's rights movement. The demands of marriage and family together with the competitive attractions of other occupations and professions have influenced the evolution of nursing in a profound way. Professionally, nurses have acquired an extraordinary new array of scientific and technical responsibilities. Rapidly accepting many new tasks in operating rooms, on the wards, and in outpatient clinics, nurses have even begun to specialize in the same fashion as physicians. Furthermore, the advent of the pediatric nurse practitioner program in the 1960's has given rise to a new group of nurse professionals whose functions are very similar to those of some orthodox medical practitioners.

BIBLIOGRAPHY

Richard A. Shryock, *The History of Nursing.*

— CHESTER R. BURNS

NURSING SINCE THE 1960S

Since the 1960s nurses have expanded their knowledge, practice, and independence. With congressional legislation authorizing Medicare and Medicaid, enormous numbers of people sought primary-care services. Aware that there were not enough physicians, Congress authorized federal funding to hospitals, clinics, and schools of nursing that offered training in ambulatory, primary care to nurses. In the ensuing years, certified nurse practitioners (CRNPs) developed specialties in pediatrics, geriatrics, and women's health, joining nurse-midwives, visiting nurses, and nurse-anesthetists who had practiced more independently than other nurses from the early years of the twentieth century. Nurses' roles in the acute care of hospitalized patients also enlarged. Advances in medical science and technology from World War II greatly increased the invasiveness of procedures and risk to patients of hospital care. Nurses and physicians worried about patients residing unobserved in semiprivate rooms, as patients utilized the coverage offered by health-insurance plans to avoid hospitalization in wards. Nurses responded by grouping their sickest patients in areas that could be more intensely monitored. The first such arrangements took the form of recovery rooms following surgery. Coronary-care units followed, and by the 1990s critical-care units existed for patients with almost every kind of organ dysfunction. Intensive nursing care gave these units their character, and critical care evolved as a specialty of expert nurses. The American Association of Critical Care Nurses, founded in 1969, began the journal *Heart and Lung* and rapidly became nursing's largest specialty organization.

The two major nursing fields started to merge in the 1990s. Hospitals began to hire nurse practitioners in specialties as substitutes for medical house staff residents. Clinical nurse specialists began to develop physical examination and diagnostic skills. Hospitals thus hired nurses to deliver medical services and often chose minimally trained substitutes to give nursing care. In the 1960s the American Nurses' Association and the National League for Nursing recommended the baccalaureate degree for beginning professional nurses. Community college and hospital program graduates were to be designated "technical nurses." Licensed practical nurses would continue to graduate from hospital and high school programs. State legislatures balked at passing such proposals, and by 1994 only North Dakota had passed the legislation. Although enrollments in programs that prepared registered nurses reached an all-time high of 257,983 in 1992 (from 230,803 in 1973), only 102,128 were baccalaureate enrollees, 132,603 were associate degree candidates, and 23,252 were hospital diploma program participants. Men comprised 12 percent of these enrollees, up from 7 percent a decade earlier. Meanwhile, graduate nursing programs were increasing. In 1973 eight doctoral programs in nursing enrolled 375 students. By 1992 fifty-four doctoral programs had 2,727 students enrolled. By the mid-1990s employers generally required nursing researchers, educators, and administrators to hold doctorates.

[See also Health Care; Nursing.]

BIBLIOGRAPHY

Barbara Melosh, *"The Physician's Hand": Work Culture and Conflict in American Nursing* (Philadelphia, 1982).

Susan M. Reverby, *Ordered to Care: The Dilemma of American Nursing* (New York, 1987).

— ELLEN D. BAER

OIL CRISES

In 1973–1974 and 1979 the United States experienced shortages of gasoline and other petroleum products because of reduced domestic oil production, greater dependence on imported oil, and political developments in the oil-rich Middle East. Historically, the United States had supplied most of its own oil, but in 1970 U.S. oil production reached full capacity. Imported oil, especially from the Middle East, rose from 19 percent of national consumption in 1967 to 36 percent in 1973. The Arab-Israeli War of 1973 contributed to the first oil crisis. At that time, Saudi Arabia controlled 21 percent of the world's oil exports. After Egypt and Syria attacked Israel in October and the United States came to Israel's aid, oil ministers from the five Persian Gulf states and Iran cut their monthly production by 5 percent to discourage international support for Israel. They banned oil exports to Israel's allies, including the United States, the Netherlands, Portugal, South Africa, and Rhodesia (Zimbabwe). World oil prices jumped from $5.40 per barrel to more than $17. Retail gasoline prices in the United States increased 40 percent, and consumers often faced long lines at service stations. To conserve gasoline and oil, President Richard M. Nixon reduced the speed limit on national highways to 55 miles per hour and encouraged people to carpool and to lower their house thermostats. It was Israeli victories and U.S. arrangement of Arab-Israeli negotiations and not domestic programs, however, that helped end the embargo in March 1974.

The Organization of Petroleum Exporting Countries (OPEC) continued to keep world oil prices high, which slowed the world economy. In 1973–1975 the U.S. gross national product declined by 6 percent and unemployment doubled to 9 percent. The economies of Europe and Japan also suffered, but the developing countries that lacked money to pay for expensive oil suffered most. In 1975 Congress established fuel-efficiency standards for U.S. automobiles to reduce energy costs and dependency on foreign oil. President Jimmy Carter urged additional steps. By the late 1970s the United States was exploring both old (coal) and new (solar, thermal, and wind) sources of energy.

A second oil crisis followed the collapse of the government of the shah of Iran and suspension of Iran's oil exports in December 1978. Iran was the world's second-largest exporter of oil. If buyers, including oil companies, manufacturers, and national governments had not panicked, however, this second oil shortage would not have been so severe. Gasoline prices rose, and people again waited in lines at service stations. These factors, combined with the hostage crisis in Iran, contributed to President Carter's defeat in the 1980 election. The worst of the second crisis was over by 1980. In late 1985 a drop in world oil prices (from $32 to $10 per barrel) gave American consumers a sense that the crisis had ended, but concerns about the increasing U.S. dependence on foreign oil remained in the 1990s.

[See also Hostage Crises; Middle East, Relations with.]

BIBLIOGRAPHY

Daniel Yergin, *The Prize: The Epic Quest for Oil, Money, and Power* (New York, 1991).

— KENNETH B. MOSS

OKLAHOMA CITY BOMBING

Oklahoma City Bombing (April 19, 1995), in which a bomb composed of a fertilizer called ammonium nitrate mixed with fuel oil destroyed the Alfred P. Murrah federal building in Oklahoma City, Okla., killing 168 people, including fifteen children in a day-care center. The building housed branches of federal departments including the Bureau of Alcohol, Tobacco, and Firearms, thought initially to be the target of the bomb. The worst act of terrorism in U.S. history, the blast sent Americans into mourning and deep apprehension over civil disorder. President Bill Clinton led a national day of sorrow on Sunday, April 23. For seventeen days after the explosion rescue teams from around the nation combed the rubble seeking survivors and excavating bodies, often under hazardous conditions. Shortly after the blast Federal Bureau of Investigation agents arrested Timothy McVeigh, a former U.S. Army sergeant with extreme right-wing views, as the principal suspect in the bombing. McVeigh, authorities believed, rented a truck in Kansas, filled it with the combustible mixture, and drove it to Oklahoma City. He allegedly parked the truck in front of the Murrah building, lit the fuse, and walked away; witnesses identified him at the scene. Federal authorities believed he acted to avenge destruction of the Branch Davidian cult in Waco, Tex., which took place on the same date two years earlier, and because he feared federal revocation of the constitutional right to carry guns. On Aug. 16 McVeigh and a friend from his time in the army, Terry Nichols, were arraigned in federal court under extraordinary security; both pleaded not guilty to charges that they had carried out the terrorist attack in Oklahoma City. Another army friend, Michael Fortier, under threat of indictment, testified to government officials against McVeigh and Nichols. Fortier reportedly was promised lesser charges in exchange for testimony. After eliminating leads concerning other unknown participants (John Does) in the bombing, federal investigators declared that McVeigh and Nichols acted alone and not in conspiracy with any organization. Attorney General Janet Reno announced that the government would seek the death penalty if the pair were convicted. McVeigh's extreme views directed media attention to conservative radio talk-show hosts and "citizen militias" vowing to execute federal agents infringing Second Amendment rights, although all disavowed any connection with the bombing. Incredibly, one talk-show host blamed the government for the explosion while another, G. Gordon Liddy, advised on the best methods to assassinate federal agents. The FBI sought links between McVeigh and far-right militia groups. President Clinton called for stronger antiterrorist laws, although support for additional statutes was lukewarm among Republicans and civil rights proponents.

[See also Terrorism; Waco Siege.]

— GRAHAM RUSSELL HODGES

OKLAHOMA SQUATTERS

Oklahoma Squatters were settlers upon lands not yet opened to white settlement or to which the title was in dispute. As early as 1819 white settlers attempted to occupy lands in the southeastern part of Oklahoma that were claimed by the Osage, but they were removed by the military. The region between the two branches of Red River, known as Greer County, was claimed by both Texas and the United States; it was also entered by settlers soon after 1880, although a presidential proclamation warned them not to occupy it until the question of title had been settled.

During the period from 1879 to 1885 a large number of so-called boomers, under the leadership of C. C. Carpenter, David L. Payne, and W. L. Couch, sought to settle as squatters upon the unassigned lands of central Oklahoma, but were removed by U.S. soldiers. Just prior to each of the various openings of lands to settlement a number of people entered upon the land before the date set for the opening. These were known as Sooners. Many other white persons entered the Indian Territory without the permission of the governments of the Five Civilized Tribes and stubbornly resisted removal. These were in reality squatters, although they were commonly called intruders.

Members of Troop C of the Fifth Cavalry, which arrested boomers and squatters prior to the opening of Oklahoma, in 1888. (The National Archives/Corbis)

BIBLIOGRAPHY

J. S. Buchanan and E. E. Dale, *A History of Oklahoma.*
E. E. Dale and J. L. Rader, *Readings in Oklahoma History.*

— EDWARD EVERETT DALE

"OLD HICKORY"

Because of his endurance and strength, Andrew Jackson was given this nickname in 1813 by his soldiers during a 500-mile march home from Natchez, Miss., to Nashville, Tenn. He was affectionately known by this name among his friends and followers for the rest of his life.

BIBLIOGRAPHY

J. Parton, *Life of Andrew Jackson,* vol. I.

— P. ORMAN RAY

OLD NORTHWEST

Old Northwest included some 248,000 square miles, approximately between the Ohio and Mississippi rivers and the Great Lakes. The Definitive Treaty of Peace of 1783 awarded this territory to the United States and, after the different states had ceded their claims, it became a public domain organized as the Northwest Territory.

BIBLIOGRAPHY

F. A. Ogg, *The Old Northwest.*

— BEVERLEY W. BOND, JR.

OLIVE BRANCH PETITION

After the first armed clashes at Lexington and Bunker Hill in Massachusetts in 1775, the newly organized Continental Congress decided to send a petition to George III, setting forth the grievances of the colonies. Knowing the king's violent opposition to the idea of dealing with the colonies as a united group, each of the congressional delegates signed the paper as an individual. Further, to show their amicable intent, they made Richard Penn, descendant of William Penn and a staunch Loyalist, their messenger. When Penn reached London on Aug. 14, 1775, the king refused to see him or to receive his petition through any channel.

BIBLIOGRAPHY

Edmund C. Burnett, *The Continental Congress.*
Merrill Jensen, *The Founding of a Nation.*

— ALVIN F. HARLOW

An 1870 wood engraving entitled "Free Love and Its Votaries, or American Socialism Unmasked" shows women working in a silk factory at the Oneida Colony. (Library of Congress/Corbis)

ONEIDA COLONY

Oneida Colony, established in 1848 between Syracuse and Utica, in New York State, was America's most radical experiment in social and religious thinking. From literal concepts of perfectionism and Bible communism the colony advanced into new forms of social relationships: economic communism, the rejection of monogamy for complex marriage, the practice of an elementary form of birth control (*coitus reservatus*), and the eugenic breeding of stirpicultural children. John Humphrey Noyes, leader of the group, was a capable and shrewd Yankee whose sincere primitive Christianity expressed itself in radically modern terms. His fellow workers had experienced complete religious conversion and boldly followed him into a communal life that rejected the evils of competitive economics while it kept realistically to the methods of modern industry, believing that socialism is ahead of and not behind society.

From the inception of the colony the property grew to about 600 acres of well-cultivated land, with shoe, tailoring, and machine shops, the latter producing commercially successful traps and flatware among other items; canning and silk factories; and great central buildings and houses for employees. The group also formed a branch colony in Wallingford, Conn. Assets had reached more than $550,000 when communism was dropped. Health was above the average, women held a high place, children were excellently trained, work was fair and changeable, and entertainment was constant.

In 1879, forced by social pressure from without and the dissatisfaction of the young within, monogamy was adopted, and within a year communism was replaced by joint-stock ownership. In its new form, Oneida continued its commercial success, but as a conventional company. During the 20th century, the Oneida Company was noted for its production of fine silver and stainless steel flatware.

BIBLIOGRAPHY

W. A. Hinds, *American Communities.*
J. H. Noyes, *History of American Socialism.*
R. A. Parker, *A Yankee Saint.*

— ALLAN MACDONALD

OPEN DOOR POLICY

Three interrelated doctrines—equality of commercial opportunity, territorial integrity, and administrative integrity—constituted the American idea of the Open Door in China. Formally enunciated by Secretary of State John Hay in 1899 and 1900, the Open Door policy emerged from two major cycles of American expansionist history; the first, a maritime cycle, gained impetus from the new commerial thrust of the mid-19th century and blended into the new cycle of industrial and financial capitalism that emerged toward the end of the century and continued into the 1930's. Thereafter, its vitality ebbed away as political and economic forces posed a new power structure and national reorganization in the Far East.

The first cycle of Open Door activity developed through the mid-19th-century interaction of the expansion of American continental and maritime frontiers. The construction of the transcontinental railroads gave rise to the idea of an American transportation bridge to China. The powers behind the lush China trade, headquartered in the mid-Atlantic and New England coastal cities, established commercial positions on the north Pacific coast and in Hawaii in order to transfer furs and sandalwood as items in the trade with the Chinese. The resulting expansion of maritime commerce was coordinated with the American investment in whaling; the great interest in the exploration of the Pacific Ocean and the historic concern for the development of a short route from the Atlantic to the Pacific across Central America; a growing American diplomatic, naval, and missionary interest in eastern Asia; the opening of China to American trade on the heels of the British victory in the Anglo-Chinese War of 1839–42 via the Cushing Treaty of 1844; and the push into the Pacific led by Secretary of State William H. Seward that culminated in the purchase of Alaska in 1867 and the Burlingame Treaty of 1868.

Throughout this period the United States adapted British commercial policy to its own ends by supporting the notion of free and open competition for trade in international markets, while denouncing British colonial acquisitions and preferential trade positions. The European subjection of China by force and the imposition of the resulting treaty system gave American maritime interests an opportunity to flourish without a parallel colonial responsibility or imperial illusion. The expansionist thrust of this cycle of mercantile exchange and trade reached its peak with the onset of the Spanish-American War in 1898 and the great debate over the annexation of Hawaii and the Philippines during President William McKinley's administration.

The second cycle of expansionist development sprang from the advent of industrial capitalism and the requirements of commercial American agriculture for export markets, bringing together a peculiarly complex mixture of farm and factory interests that had traditionally clashed over domestic economic policy and legislation. A mutually advantageous world view of political economy was welded as both interests prepared to move into and expand the China market. As the increasing commercialization of American agriculture led to a need for greater outlets for American grain and cotton manufactured goods, China was becoming also a potential consumer of the products of American heavy industry, including railroad equipment, and of oil products. At the same time, outlets were needed for the investment of growing American fortunes, and it was speculated that the modernization of China through the expansion of communication and transportation would, in turn, increase the demand for the products of American economic growth.

Critics of Secretary of State John Hay's policy assert that the Open Door formula "was already an old and hackneyed one at the turn of the century," that its "principles were not clear and precise," and that it could not "usefully be made the basis of a foreign policy." It may well be that American announcements on behalf of China's territorial integrity did create an erroneous "impression of a community of outlook among nations which did not really exist." But it was a foreign policy expressive of national ambition and protective of American interests, actual and potential. It was stimulated by international rivalry at the end of the 19th century for control of ports, territories, spheres of influence, and economic advantage at the expense of a weak China. It was manipulated through the influence of British nationals in the Imperial Maritime Customs Service (established by the foreign treaty system) who were intent on protecting their vested administrative interests even at the expense of their own country's position in China. And it was a time-honored administrative tactic that attempted to strengthen the American position in China by cloaking its claims in the dress of international morality on behalf of China's territorial and political independence while simultaneously protecting the interests of the powers in maintaining the trade and political positions already acquired there. Dealing as Hay did from an American bias in developing a position of power without admitting the power of an already existing ambition in China, the tactic of the Open Door served full well to initiate a chain of Open Door claims that steadily expanded up to World War I and beyond.

The Open Door Policy was stimulated by international rivalry at the end of the nineteenth century for control of ports, territories, and spheres of influence.

Hay's Open Door notes to Germany, Russia, and England in 1899, and later to the other powers, are conventionally interpreted as an attempt to bluff them into accepting the American position in China, whereas actually they announced the decision of the United States to press its interests on its own behalf.

From that time forward the United States mingled in the international rivalries in Manchuria as well as in China proper. At first anti-Russian in Manchuria and intent on extending American railroad, mining, and commercial privileges there, the United States then became anti-Japanese after the Russo-Japanese War of 1905, although it was not able to make a definitive commitment of national resources and energy. Influenced by the caution of President Theodore Roosevelt, in the Taft-Katsura Agreement of 1905 and the Root-Takahira Agreement of 1908, the United States recognized Japan's growing power in eastern Asia in return for stated Open Door principles and respect for American territorial legitimacy in the Far East. Later, during the administration of President William Howard Taft, the United States attempted to move into Manchuria and China proper via Open Door proposals on behalf of American railroad and banking investment interests in 1909 and 1913, and in so doing made overtures of cooperation with the European powers as well as with Russia and Japan. During President Woodrow Wilson's administrations the United States veered from side to side: it attempted to protect its stake in China by opposing Japan's 21 Demands on China in 1915, and then it attempted to appease Japan's ambitions in Manchuria by recognizing the Japanese stake there in the Lansing-Ishii Agreement of 1917.

Five years later, at the Washington Armament Conference negotiations, the Open Door outlook was embedded in the details of the Nine-Power Treaty, which called for the territorial and administrative integrity of China and equality of trade opportunity without special privileges for any nation; there also began plans for the abolition of extrality, the system of legal rights and privileges that foreigners enjoyed in China, which placed them beyond the reach of the government.

During the period 1929–33, Manchuria came to the forefront of American Open Door concerns, with the invocation of the Kellogg-Briand Pact of 1927 against Japan's use of force in Manchuria. By 1931, Secretary of State Henry L. Stimson had established the continuity of American policy by linking the principles of the Kellogg-Briand Pact with those expressed in the Nine-Power Treaty of 1922. A year later, in 1932, Stimson made history by articulating his non-recognition doctrine, regarding Japan's conquest of Manchuria and the establishment of the puppet state of Manchukuo.

From that point onward, throughout the 1930's and on to World War II, the United States, led by Secretary of State Cordell Hull, maintained growing opposition to Japan's aggrandizement in the sphere of China and the enlargement of Japan's ambitions throughout Southeast Asia.

BIBLIOGRAPHY

John K. Fairbank, *The United States and China.*
George Kennan, *American Diplomacy 1900–1950.*
William A. Williams, *The Shaping of American Diplomacy.*

— CHARLES VEVIER

OPINION POLLS

Opinion polls in the United States primarily involve measuring public views through surveys. Polling gained legitimacy after the 1936 presidential election, when three pollsters, including George H. Gallup, correctly predicted Franklin D. Roosevelt's victory. The *Literary Digest* incorrectly picked Roosevelt's opponent, basing its forecast on responses mailed in by 2 million Americans. The pollsters instead used scientific sampling, which established that predictions made from polling a small random sample, usually 1,200 people, can be equally or more valid than asking a million respondents. When pollsters incorrectly predicted the 1948 presidential election results, picking George Dewey over Harry S. Truman, it was not because samples were too small but because they were improperly drawn and thus not representative. The 1948 embarrassment led to procedures that resulted in increasing acceptance. Polling organizations now emphasize reliability, whether similar results would occur if the same survey was conducted repeatedly, and validity, whether the survey measured what it was designed to measure.

From its onset, polling raised concerns about the effect on voting and other public behavior. Some early critics argued that polls did not merely measure opinion but affected it. Later research found that while voters may be influenced by poll results early in a campaign, the effects decrease as election day nears. Many observers voiced concerns following the 1980 presidential election about exit polling, interviews conducted as people left voting sites, fearing that early reports of the results could affect voter turnout in later time zones. Although exit polls are still conducted, many feel that their impact has been exaggerated. Of greater concern during and since the presidency of Ronald Reagan (1981–1989) has been the inclusion of communication, polling, and media specialists in the White House who have become barriers between the president and the public. The combined expertise of these specialists, who favor nostalgic posturing, sound bites, and negative advertising, may be responsible for even lower voter turnout. After reaching new heights in the 1988 and 1992 presidential campaigns, negative ads and polls influenced by them became even more prevalent in the 1994 midterm elections when 70 percent of campaign budgets for national office went to media and polling consultants. "There's not a competitive race in the country that doesn't use a poll," Democratic pollster Mark Mellman said in 1994, adding, "You've got to point out the faults of your opponent or you'll get creamed." The marketing of modern politicians as though they were commercial products, using computerized mass mailings and phone banks, minimizes discussion of serious issues, dehumanizes politics, and devalues leadership. As of the mid-1990s neither the American people nor their elected representatives seemed prepared to question the impact of polling and negative advertising on the U.S. political system.

[See also Campaigns, Presidential; Public Opinion.]

— KATHLEEN B. CULVER

ORDINANCES OF 1784, 1785, AND 1787

Ordinances of 1784, 1785, and 1787 were enacted in connection with the development of a policy for the settlement of the country northwest of the Ohio River. The establishment of the government of the Confederation was delayed several years over the issue of the disposition of the western lands. Seven states had western land claims, six had none; and the latter refused to join the Confederation until the former should cede their lands to the new government, to be utilized for the common benefit of all the states.

In 1780 New York led the way by giving up all claim to the western lands, whereupon Congress passed a resolution pledging that the lands the states might cede to the general government would be erected into new states that should be admitted to the Union on a basis of equality with the existing states. This vital decision made possible the future extension of the nation across the continent, for it is unthinkable that without it the people west of the Alleghenies would ever have submitted to a state of permanent dependence upon the original states.

Connecticut and Virginia followed New York, and the Confederation was established, Mar. 1, 1781. With the close of the Revolution the problems of reorganization became more insistent, and among them the disposition of the western country loomed foremost. Among various projects propounded, one by Thomas Jefferson, which Congress enacted (Apr. 23), became known as the Ordinance of 1784. It provided for an artificial division of the entire West into sixteen districts, each district eligible for statehood upon attaining a population of 20,000. Although subsequently repealed, the Ordinance of 1784 contributed to America's developing colonial policy its second basic idea: the establishment of temporary governments, under the fostering oversight of Congress, until a population sufficient for statehood should be attained.

Next year (May 20, 1785) the ordinance "for ascertaining the mode of disposing of lands in the Western territory" was enacted. Since the dawn of civilization individual landholdings had been bounded and identified by such marks as trees, stakes, and stones, and in the absence of any scientific system of surveying and recording titles of ownership to them, confusion, with resultant disputes and individual hardships, existed. In its stead, the Ordinance of 1785 provided a scientific system of surveying and subdividing land with clear-cut establishment of both boundaries and titles. The unit of survey is the township, six miles square, with boundaries based on meridians of longitude and parallels of latitude. The townships are laid out both east and west and north and south of base lines crossing at right angles; within, the township is subdivided into thirty-six square-mile sections, and these, in turn, into minor rectangles of any desired size.

In March 1786 a group of New Englanders organized at Boston the Ohio Company of Associates. The leaders were able men of affairs who had very definite ideas concerning the colony they proposed to found. They opened negotiations with Congress, which made the desired grant of land, and on July 13, 1787, enacted the notable ordinance (which the petitioners had drafted) for the government of the territory northwest of the Ohio. It provided for a temporary government by agents appointed by Congress; but when the colony numbered 5,000 adult free males, a representative legislature was to be established, and upon the attainment of 60,000 population the territory would be admitted to statehood.

The ordinance also provided for the future division of the territory into not less than three nor more than five states; and it contained a series of compacts, forever unalterable save by common consent, safeguarding the rights of the future inhabitants of the territory. These established religious freedom, prohibited slavery, and guaranteed the fundamental rights of English liberty and just treatment of the Indians; a notable summary of the fundamental spirit of New England was supplied in the declaration that "Religion, morality, and knowledge being necessary to good government and the happiness of mankind, schools and the means of education shall forever be encouraged."

The Ordinance of 1784 contributed a fundamental idea to America's colonial system. Those of 1785 and 1787 still remain as landmarks in the orderly development of the American scheme of life.

[See also Northwest Territory.]

BIBLIOGRAPHY

B. A. Hinsdale, *The Old Northwest.*
W. E. Peters, *Ohio Lands and Their Subdivisions.*
M. M. Quaife, *Wisconsin, Its History and Its People.*

— M. M. QUAIFE

OREGON MISSIONS

Attention was called to the need for Christian work among the Indians of the Pacific Northwest by an appeal made to Gen. William Clark of Saint Louis in 1831 by four Flathead Indians, who had journeyed from the Oregon Country asking that they be given religious instructors. A description of this visit was first published in the *Christian Advocate and Journal* of New York in 1833 and was widely copied in other religious journals. The Methodists immediately recommended the establishment of an Oregon mission, and Jason Lee, a young New Englander, was appointed to head it. By September 1834, he and his party had reached Fort Vancouver, on the Columbia River. A mission among the Flathead being found to be impracticable, Lee established a mission in the Willamette Valley. A year later the American Board of Commissioners for Foreign Missions resolved to found a mission in the Pacific Northwest and commissioned Marcus Whitman and Henry H. Spalding to carry out the enterprise. Work was begun near what is now Walla Walla, Wash., and soon a prosperous mission was in operation. Both Lee and Whitman became interested in bringing colonists to Oregon, a policy that their mission boards did not approve. Largely because of this fact Lee was removed. Whitman and his wife with twelve other persons were murdered by the Indians in 1847.

Roman Catholic missionaries were also active in the same region, where their work was favored by the Hudson's Bay Company as being less likely to interfere with the fur trade. Under the intrepid Jesuit, Father Pierre Jean De Smet (1840–46), Catholic missions were established in the region and within a few years 6,000 converts were claimed.

BIBLIOGRAPHY

C. J. Brosnan, *Jason Lee, Prophet of the New Oregon.*
Clifford M. Drury, *Marcus Whitman, Pioneer and Martyr.*
E. Lavelle, *The Life of Father DeSmet, S.J., 1801–1873.*

— WILLIAM W. SWEET

OREGON TRAIL

Oregon Trail was first dimly traced across the country from the Missouri River to the Columbia River by explorers and fur traders. After 1842 it was worn into a deeply rutted highway by the pioneers in their covered wagons. In 1805 the course of Meriwether Lewis and William Clark in the region of the Snake and Columbia rivers covered a portion of what was later to be the famous pioneer highway. A few years later (1808) a party of the Missouri Fur Company traveled through the South Pass in Wyoming, and thus discovered an important part of the trail. A party of fur traders from Astoria, under Robert Stuart, returned to the East in 1812 largely following the route that later became the Oregon Trail. Two independent American fur traders, Capt. Benjamin L. E. de Bonneville and Capt. Nathaniel J. Wyeth, between the years 1832 and 1836, led their companies over this route. Knowledge of the trail as a passable route was current among the traders on the frontier and became common property. For the companies of settlers this knowledge was available in two forms: traders who had been over the route and were willing to hire out as guides; and printed guidebooks compiled by enterprising travelers. These guidebooks appeared surprisingly early and the copies that reached the end of the trail were thumbed and worn.

The distances on the trail were calculated with a high degree of accuracy. One of the old guidebooks (J. M. Shively, *Route and Distances to Oregon and California* [1846]) gives a tabulation of the distances of the established trail. The points used to mark the way were selected for a variety of reasons—conspicuous landmarks, difficult streams to ford, and infrequent posts at which a few supplies might be obtained. This guidebook marks the way from the Missouri River to the mouth of the Columbia River as follows:

	Miles
From Independence to the Crossings of Kansas	102
Crossings of Blue	83
Platte River	119
Crossings of South Platte	163
To North Fork	20
To Fort Larima [Laramie]	153
From Larima to Crossing of North Fork of the Platte	140
To Independence Rock on Sweet Water	50
Fort Bridger	229
Bear River	68
Soda Springs	94
To Fort Hall	57
Salmon Falls	160
Crossings of Snake River	22
To Crossings of Boise River	69
Fort Boise	45
Dr. Whitman's Mission	190
Fort Walawala [Walla Walla]	25
Dallis Mission [The Dalles]	120
Cascade Falls, on the Columbia	50
Fort Vancouver	41
Astoria	90

The author could well have left off the last ninety miles and given the distance into the Willamette Valley, which was the destination of most of the travelers.

The interest in Oregon became so widespread along the frontier about 1842 that emigrating societies were formed to encourage people to move to Oregon. By lectures, letters, and personal visits, members of these societies secured recruits for the long journey. Independence, Mo., was the most frequent place of departure, and shortly after leaving there the companies commonly organized a government by electing officers and adopting rules of conduct. The emigrants gathered in time to leave in the early spring, so as to take advantage of the fresh pasturage for their animals and to allow all possible time for the long journey.

So deeply worn was the Oregon Trail that generations after the last covered wagon rolled by, hundreds of miles of the trail could still be traced.

From Independence the companies followed the old Santa Fe Trail, a two days' journey of some forty miles to where a crude signpost pointed to the "Road to Oregon." At Fort Laramie, where the trail left the rolling plains for the mountainous country, there was an opportunity to overhaul and repair wagons. The next point where repairs could be made with outside help was Fort Bridger, some 394 miles beyond Laramie and about 1,070 miles from Independence. The trail used South Pass through the Rockies. It is a low pass less than 7,500 feet above sea level and was easily passable for the heavy covered wagons. The difficulties of travel greatly increased on the Pacific side. Much barren country had to be crossed under conditions that wore out and killed the already exhausted horses and oxen. At Fort Hall, in the Snake River country, the first emigrants gave up their wagons and repacked on horses; but after a short while determined individuals refused to do this and worked a way through for their wagons. The Grande Ronde Valley, in northeast Oregon, offered grass to recruit the worn beasts of burden before the travelers attempted the almost impassable way through the Blue Mountains. Emerging from these mountains the emigrants followed the Umatilla River to the Columbia River, which they followed to Fort Vancouver, the last portion often being made on rafts. The journey of some 2,000 miles over the Oregon Trail was the greatest trek of recorded history.

The wagon traffic on the Oregon Trail during the 1840's and 1850's became so heavy that the road was a clearly defined and deeply rutted way across the country. When the ruts became too deep for travel, parallel roads were broken. So deeply worn was the Oregon Trail that generations after the last covered wagon had passed over it hundreds of miles of the trail could still be traced. To the awed Indians it seemed the symbol of a nation of countless numbers.

The 2,000 miles of the Oregon Trail tested human strength and endurance as it has rarely been tested. The trail was littered with castoff possessions, often of considerable monetary as well as great sentimental value. Worn draft animals that could no longer drag the heavy wagons and even the most prized possessions had to be left standing beside the trail. Carcasses of the innumerable dead cattle and horses were left along the trail while the bodies of the human dead were buried in shallow graves. The diaries of the overland journey note with fearful monotony the number of new graves passed each day. Cholera was then the terrible scourge of these pioneers.

From 1842 through the 1850's the companies came over the trail in large numbers, to dwindle away in the 1860's. The bitter experiences of the first companies, who knew so little about equipment, were passed on to the later companies, and as the years went by the travelers were able to use better-adapted equipment. Specially constructed wagons became available; oxen largely replaced horses; and supplies were selected more wisely. The route became easier to follow and even included crude ferries at some of the most difficult river crossings. Nevertheless, up to the day that the last covered wagon was dragged over the rutted highway, the Oregon Trail was the way of hardship and danger that tested the pioneer stock of the West.

BIBLIOGRAPHY

David Lavendar, *Westward Vision: The Story of the Oregon Trail.*

— ROBERT MOULTON GATKE

OREGON TREATY OF 1846

Oregon Treaty of 1846 fixed the boundary between the United States and British America at the forty-ninth parallel west of the Rocky Mountains except at the western terminus of that line, where it was to swerve southward around Vancouver Island and out through Juan de Fuca Strait, north of what is today Clallam County, Wash. By the Convention of 1818, renewed in 1827, the United States and Great Britain had agreed that the country claimed by either west of the Rockies be free and open to the citizens of the two powers. Acting under a joint resolution of Congress (Apr. 27, 1846), President James K. Polk transmitted the year's notice for the termination of that treaty, expressing the hope that this would hasten a friendly settlement. George Hamilton Gordon, Lord Aberdeen, the British foreign minister, then drafted a treaty (May 18, 1846), which was accepted by President Polk and the Senate (June 15, 1846). The election of Polk as president in 1844 on a platform that demanded the whole Oregon Country, its rapid settlement by Americans, the purpose of the Hudson's Bay Company to move its main establishment from Fort Vancouver on the Columbia River to Victoria on Vancouver Island, and the adoption by Great Britain and the United States of mutual beneficial tariff policies in 1846—repeal of the British Corn Laws (June 26) and passing of the Walker tariff (July 30)—were factors in influencing a settlement of this boundary dispute at this time.

BIBLIOGRAPHY

S. F. Bemis, *A Diplomatic History of the United States.*
R. C. Clark, *A History of the Willamette Valley, Oregon.*

— R. C. CLARK

ORGANIZATION OF AMERICAN STATES

Organization of American States (OAS) had its genesis in the Ninth International Conference of American States, assembled in Bogotá, Colombia, in March 1948. At that meeting a charter was adopted formalizing the inter-American system, its key structural features being (1) a council of the OAS to manage the organization's business, (2) subsidiary councils (cultural, economic and social, and juridical), and (3) the Pan-American Union, to function as the general secretariat. General inter-American conferences were to be held every five years, and provision was made for the convocation of consultative meetings of foreign ministers to deal with threats to the Western Hemisphere.

Regular inter-American conferences under the OAS aegis began in 1954 in Caracas, Venezuela, and special conferences have been held at Punta del Este, Uruguay (1961); Washington, D.C. (1964); Rio de Janeiro (1965); and Buenos Aires (1967). Matters dealt with have included internal organizational rearrangements, hemispheric security, and the formation of the Alliance for Progress. Consultative meetings occurred in Washington (1951, 1964, 1965, 1967), Santiago, Chile (1959), San José, Costa Rica (1960), Punta del Este (1962), and Buenos Aires (1967). The principal issues were the stance of the Americas in the Korean conflict, the aggression of the Dominican Republic against Venezuela, the threat of communism and the Cuban revolution, and U.S. intervention in the Dominican Republic.

Given the distribution of economic and military power in the Western Hemisphere, U.S. participation in the OAS has been crucial in most respects. It was on U.S. initiative that the organization came into being, and its operational costs are defrayed mostly by the United States. Thus, it is not surprising that the choice of issues considered and the nature of the resolutions passed by that body have tended to reflect U.S. interests and positions, although not as categorically as political realities might lead one to expect.

BIBLIOGRAPHY

Mary Margaret Ball, *The OAS in Transition.*

— FRANCISCO S. PÉREZ-ABREU

P

PACIFISM

Four unique types of pacifism have entered American life and politics: (1) conscientious objection to war, resulting in personal refusal to participate in war or military service; (2) opposition to, and renunciation of, all forms of violence; (3) a strategy of nonviolent action to overcome specific injustices or to bring about radical change in the social order; and (4) a "positive testimony" to a way of life based on conviction of the power of love to govern human relationships.

Conscientious objection to war was a central doctrine of the "historic peace churches" (Brethren, Mennonites, and Quakers), which held war to be in fundamental contradiction to their religious faiths. In prerevolutionary Pennsylvania, Quakers tried with some success to apply their pacifist convictions in the colony that William Penn had established as a "holy experiment," a colony where they could live at peace with each other and with all persons, including their Indian neighbors. The Revolution, however, split the Quakers on the issue of political pacifism and led to their permanent withdrawal as an organized religious body from political responsibility. This returned pacifism to the individual for decision—on refusing to fight, pay taxes for military purposes, or in other ways support the war "system."

The number of objectors and the form of their objection varied with the moral appeal of each war, reaching a climax of opposition to U.S. military action in Vietnam and Cambodia in the late 1960's. Probably one out of five of those of draft age during this period were exempted from military service because of conscientious objection (although many of these were ostensibly deferred for other reasons, because local draft boards did not wish to acknowledge such claims formally). An unprecedented, though unspecified, number of draftees were discharged from military service or were absent without leave (AWOL) because of objections after induction. In addition, a substantial number were imprisoned because they refused to fight or to be inducted.

During this time, pacifist ranks reached out to most denominations, and many of the country's religious leaders were included. Also, persons whose objection to war stemmed from humanitarian or philosophical convictions, rather than religious training and belief—the criterion for conscientious objection specified in the Selective Training and Service Act of 1940—were legitimized by a succession of Supreme Court decisions.

Meanwhile, pacifists in the 20th century had again gone political in attempts to prevent war and keep the United States out of war. They were a principal force in the American peace movement and were often at odds with those who urged a collective-security system with international military sanctions as the most effective approach to maintaining peace.

The second form of pacifism abjures violence in any form and sees violence operating not only in outright war but also through social institutions that permit human exploitation and discrimination and that rely on repression and force to maintain "law and order." Consequently, the major goal of such pacifists has been social reform. The core of the American antislavery movement was largely pacifist. For example, in the 1750's John Woolman preached to his fellow Quakers that slavery was incompatible with their professed respect for "that of God in every man." Social pacifism also infused the struggle for prison reform, the fight against capital punishment, the championing of women's rights, efforts to improve care of the mentally ill and retarded, and the securing of civil rights for all minorities.

Social-reform pacifists were in direct conflict with those who insisted that effective action demanded violence. They found themselves denounced as soft-headed dupes, if not outright lackeys, of the entrenched oppressors. To this, pacifism responded with its third pattern—a strategy of nonviolent direct action. Modeled on Mahatma Gandhi's philosophy of civil disobedience (*satyagraha*), sit-ins (put to an early test by some unions in the industrial conflicts of the 1930's), marches (which achieved dramatic impact with the "stride toward freedom" from Selma to Montgomery, Ala., of Martin Luther King, Jr., who called for an end to racial discrimination), vigils (usually conducted by smaller groups with a strong religious motif), and boycotts (as notably organized by César E. Chavez, 1965–70, on behalf of grape pickers striking against California growers) became expressions of nonviolent protest. These actions were characterized by extraordinary self-discipline, even when met by violent counteraction.

Pacifist influence was fractured by a succession of violent events. The assassination of King silenced the most effective spokesman for nonviolence at a time when militants among blacks and others in the civil rights movement were clamoring for confrontation by force. Later, a sense of helplessness swept over the peace movement when President Richard M. Nixon moved to extend the war into Cambodia and substituted massive, electronically controlled bombing and mining for the presence of most American draftees in Vietnam. But backlash against the civil rights and peace movements demonstrated that a wide base of nonpacifist values existed throughout America, especially in middle-income ethnic groups. The collapse of the George S. McGovern campaign for the presidency in 1972 seemed to bury the hopes for effective political expression of pacifist concerns, leaving a vacuum of disillusionment that militants eagerly sought to fill.

A backlash against the civil rights and antiwar movements showed a wide base of nonpacifist values existing throughout American society.

Two influences combined to generate a fourth type of pacifism. Many conscientious objectors became increasingly troubled by the essentially negative posture of their position. Mere objection, whether to war or to injustice generally, failed to satisfy their concern with creating the conditions for a human community. Second, there was a growing feeling that societies, and American society in particular, were past reforming and that peace would have to be sought within a small group of kindred souls. Both influences moved toward a definition of pacifism as a total philosophy of life and toward experimentation with human relationships in which love would replace violence. These two expressions of pacifism, however, differed in focus. The first emphasized an outward "testimony" by which the principles of cooperative community could be demonstrated to others as a viable way of life. This was the original intent of the Civilian Public Service program, which had been organized voluntarily by the historic peace churches to offer an alternative to military service during World War II. Conscientious objector units worked, with commendable accomplishments, on conservation and park projects, in fire fighting and disaster relief, in mental health hospitals and schools for retarded children, and as "guinea pigs" for medical research. The effectiveness of the testimony-by-work approach was seriously undermined, however, by Selective Service control and the inescapable consciousness that the testifiers were in fact conscripts, not volunteers.

The second approach rejected society in favor of a commune of persons willing to live simply on a share-alike basis and as independently as possible from the requirements of the so-called system (including fixed employment). The new communes followed the long tradition in America of experimental communities devoted to the ideal of self-sufficient and harmonious living.

In the mid-1970's pacifism in America seemed to have returned to its pristine base of individual conviction. But the activism of the 1960's had left both a commitment to conscientious objection to war and a sensitivity to social injustice that encompassed a much broader reach of American life than ever before.

BIBLIOGRAPHY

American Friends Service Committee, *Speak Truth to Power.*

Peter Brock, *Pacifism in the United States: From the Colonial Era to the First World War.*

Charles Chatfield, *For Peace and Justice: Pacifism in America, 1914–1941.*

Merle E. Curti, *Peace or War: The American Struggle, 1636–1936.*

Martin Luther King, Jr., *The Trumpet of Conscience.*

Peter Matthiessen, *Sal si puedes: César Chavez and the New American Revolution.*

Mulford Q. Sibley, *The Quiet Battle.*

Mulford Q. Sibley and Philip E. Jacob, *Conscription of Conscience: The American State and the Conscientious Objector, 1940–1947.*

— PHILIP E. JACOB

PANAMA CANAL TREATY

Panama Canal Treaty (1977). The genesis of the 1970s agreements between Panama and the United States lay in increasing Panamanian discontent over existing treaty relationships with the U.S. government. The 1903 Hay-Bunau-Varilla Treaty had granted "in perpetuity" to the United States a canal zone within which the United States could exercise "all the rights, power, and authority" of a sovereign state. Severe rioting in January 1964 led to twenty-one Panamanian deaths and considerable destruction of U.S.-owned property. In December of that year President Lyndon B. Johnson promised negotiations to abrogate the 1903 treaty. The following year Johnson and Panamanian President Marco Aurelio Robles announced agreement on a set of principles to guide subsequent negotiations. Draft treaties were completed and initialed by late June 1967, but leakage of the terms to the press stirred opposition in both countries and led to the shelving of the covenants.

An October 1968 coup in Panama brought to power Guardia Nacional Colonel Omar Torrijos Herrera. A chance conversation two years later between President Richard M. Nixon and Panamanian President Demetrio Lakas led to resumption of negotiations between the two countries. In May 1973 Panamanian Foreign Minister Juan Antonio Tack formulated a set of principles (similar to the Johnson-Robles principles of 1967) to undergird any U.S.-Panama agreement. Secretary of State Henry Kissinger signed a modified version of the Tack principles in 1974. The administration of President Gerald R. Ford could not obtain Pentagon support for the proposed treaties until the autumn of 1975. President-elect Jimmy Carter in January 1977 requested a review of negotiations and subsequently authorized a resumption on the basis of the Tack-Kissinger principles. Treaties following the terms of the 1967 principles were signed by Carter and Torrijos on Sept. 7, 1977.

The Panama Canal Treaty stated that the United States would maintain control of the waterway until Dec. 31, 1999, and Panama would assume a greater role in the canal's operation, maintenance, and defense. An increasing percentage of canal revenues would accrue to Panama during the transition period. A second agreement, the Neutrality Treaty, required Panama to keep the canal neutral and open to all nations, with the United States and Panama pledged to guarantee neutrality. A Carter-Torrijos "statement of understanding" was issued as a clarification of two articles of the Neutrality Treaty. Each country could act to defend the canal "against any aggression or threat," although this did not mean that the United States could intervene in Panama's internal affairs. Both treaties were approved by plebiscite in Panama on Oct. 23, 1977, but final congressional approval took two years. Republican Senator Dennis DeConcini of Arizona proposed an amendment to the Neutrality Treaty stating that in the event of the closure of the canal the United States and Panama independently had the right to take any necessary steps to reopen it, including use of force. With this amendment the U.S. Senate approved the Neutrality Treaty on Mar. 16, 1978, by a vote of 68 to 32. The Canal Treaty was ratified by the same margin on April 18. It contained an amendment introduced by the Senate leadership stating that nothing in either treaty would have as its purpose or would be interpreted as a right of intervention in the internal affairs of Panama. President George Bush may have violated this amendment when he ordered the invasion of Panama in 1989 to capture General Manuel Antonio Noriega. Enabling legislation for the two treaties passed the House and Senate late in September 1979; both treaties went into effect on Oct. 1, 1979.

[See also Panama Invasion.]

BIBLIOGRAPHY

William J. Jorden, *Panama Odyssey* (Austin, Tex., 1984).

— RICHARD W. TURK

PANAMA, DECLARATION OF

Declaration of Panama was adopted at Panama City on Oct. 3, 1939, by the Consultative Meeting of Foreign Ministers of the American Republics. To deal with conditions created by the outbreak of war in Europe in early September 1939, sixteen resolutions or sets of resolutions and declarations were adopted. These dealt with such matters as economic cooperation, continental solidarity, neutrality, humanization of war, and contraband of war. But the most widely publicized was No. XIV, entitled "Declaration of Panama," which consisted of a preamble and four declarations. The first declaration stated that American waters should be "free from the commission of any hostile act by any non-American belligerent nation, whether such hostile act be attempted or made from land, sea or air." These waters were defined to include a strip averaging about 300 miles in width extending southward from the eastern end of the United States-Canada boundary, around South America, and northward to the western end of the boundary between the United States and Canada.

In the second declaration it was stated that the republics would attempt, "through joint representations," to secure compliance with the declaration by the belligerents. Provision was made in the third declaration for further consultation, if necessary, to "determine upon the measures" to be undertaken "to secure the observance" of the declaration. The fourth declaration provided for individual or collective patrols by the republics of "the waters adjacent to their coasts . . . whenever they may determine that the need therefor exists."

— ERIK MCKINLEY ERIKSSON

PANAMA INVASION

Panama Invasion (1989). The invasion of Panama by U.S. forces in December 1989 was designed in part to end the rule of General Manuel Antonio Noriega. A graduate of the Peruvian Military Academy in 1962, he had supported Colonel Omar Torrijos Herrera, the ruler of Panama, during an attempted coup against the latter in 1969. Noriega soon became head of the Panamanian military intelligence service and served Torrijos for a decade as chief of security. Two years after Torrijos's death in an airplane crash in 1981, Noriega became commander of the Guardia Nacional, renamed the Panama Defense Forces (PDF). Torrijos and subsequently Noriega aided the U.S.-sponsored Contras with arms and supplies in their struggle against the Sandinista regime in Nicaragua. Noriega's involvement with the Medellín drug cartel in the 1980s and the emergence of Panama as a money-laundering site proved far more lucrative than receiving U.S. support because of assistance to the contras.

In 1987 a feud between Noriega and his chief of staff, Roberto Diaz Herrera, led to Diaz's publicly charging Noriega with crimes and encouraged Panamanian opponents to demand Noriega's resignation. Noriega responded with arrests and brutality. Secret negotiations between Panamanian and U.S. representatives designed to facilitate Noriega's departure broke down. The U.S. Justice Department filed indictments against Noriega in federal court; soon afterward the U.S. government imposed a series of economic sanctions. The United States sent additional military forces to the Canal Zone in Panama, recalled its ambassador, and encouraged PDF officers to overthrow Noriega. An attempted coup in 1989 failed and led to executions. The media criticized President George Bush and Secretary of Defense Richard Cheney for failing to provide more support to the coup leaders. The U.S. military drew up plans for an invasion, which began when a U.S. serviceman died from gunfire outside PDF headquarters on Dec. 16, 1989.

Operation Just Cause began December 20 and lasted through December 24. The PDF numbered 5,000, augmented by 8,000 paramilitary troops organized in "dignity battalions." The 13,000 U.S. troops stationed in Panama were reinforced by an additional 9,000. Fighting centered around Noriega's headquarters in Panama City. Noriega took refuge with the papal nuncio (the Vatican's representative in Panama), but surrendered on Jan. 3, 1990. Twenty-three U.S. soldiers were killed during the invasion. Panamanian deaths—military and civilian—exceeded 500. U.S. public opinion supported the operation but many foreign governments did not. A new civilian regime took control in Panama and the country experienced severe economic problems and a troubled security situation for months afterward. Noriega became a federal prisoner in Miami on Jan. 4, 1990; he was tried and convicted in April 1992 of cocaine smuggling and imprisoned. Political and economic stability remained an elusive commodity in Panama; nationalist resentment against the United States surged, and by 1995 Noriega's adherents may have regained a degree of authority in Panama.

[See also Panama Canal.]

BIBLIOGRAPHY

Edward M. Flanagan, Jr., *Battle for Panama: Inside Operation Just Cause* (Washington, D.C., 1993).

— RICHARD W. TURK

PANIC OF 1837

During the period 1830–36 enormous state debts had piled up from the construction of canals and railroads and in the chartering of new banks among the settled states. At the same time many state banks, which after 1833 held deposits of government funds, expanded their credit; land speculation was common in all sections of the country; and imports exceeded exports. In 1836 three events occurred that precipitated a crisis. To check the land speculation President Andrew Jackson, on July 11, 1836, issued a specie circular, which required all payments for public lands to be made in specie, thus cramping the operations of the banks financing the western land speculation. On June 23, 1836, Congress passed an act to distribute the surplus revenue in the U.S. Treasury among the states, thereby causing the depository banks to contract their credit. To make matters worse, a financial crisis in England caused many British creditors to call in their loans, while the failure of American crops lessened the purchasing power of farmers. On May 10, 1837, the New York banks suspended specie payment, a move followed by most of the banks in the country. After resumption in 1838, Philadelphia banks suspended specie payments, Oct. 9, 1839, and there were additional widespread suspensions in 1842. The depression lasted until 1843 and was most severely felt in the West and the South. There was a general suspension of public works, a demand for more stringent banking laws, widespread unemployment, and state defalcations and repudiations. The Independent Treasury System was established in 1840 partly as a result of the panic, and the universal distress contributed to the defeat of Martin Van Buren for president and the return of the Whigs to power in that same year.

BIBLIOGRAPHY

R. C. McGrane, *The Panic of 1837.*
W. B. Smith, *Economic Aspects of the Second Bank of the United States.*

— REGINALD C. MCGRANE

PANIC OF 1893

Panic of 1893, a spectacular financial crisis the background of which is found in the usual factors of the business cycle, together with an inflexible banking system. Capital investments in the 1880's had exceeded the possibilities of immediately profitable use, and the trend of prices continued generally downward.

The uneasy state of British security markets in 1890, culminating in the liquidation of the British banking house of Baring Brothers and Company, stopped the flow of foreign capital into American enterprise, and the resale of European-held securities caused a stock market collapse in New York and substantial exports of gold. The panic that seemed inevitable that autumn turned instead to uneasy stagnation as the huge exports of agricultural staples the next two years reestablished gold imports and postponed the crisis. A high degree of uncertainty returned in the winter of 1892–93, aided by the well-publicized danger that the country would be forced off the gold standard by the decline in the U.S. Treasury's gold reserve, which bore the brunt of the renewed exports of gold and also suffered from decreased federal revenues and heavy expenditures, including the purchases of silver under the Sherman Silver Purchase Act of 1890.

The Philadelphia and Reading Railroad failed in February, and the gold reserve fell below the accepted minimum of $100 million in April 1893. The National Cordage Company failed in May and touched off a stock market panic. Banks in the South and West were especially hard pressed, and nearly 600 in the entire country suspended, at least temporarily. By the end of 1893 about 4,000 banks had collapsed, and there were more than 14,000 commercial failures. This condition continued throughout the summer, and all currency was at a premium in New York in August.

Many of President Grover Cleveland's advisers had been urging him to force repeal of the Silver Purchase Act, since his election the previous November. The panic atmosphere furnished the opportunity, and repeal was advanced as the one absolute cure for the depression. By Oct. 30 it had passed both houses of Congress. In the meantime, imports of gold had stabilized the monetary situation in New York somewhat, but the depression continued. The winter of 1893–94 and the summer following witnessed widespread unemployment, strikes met by violence, and a march on Washington, D.C., by a group of jobless men seeking relief, known as "Coxey's Army"—all part of the human reaction to the tragedy. The depression did not lift substantially until the poor European crops of 1897 stimulated American exports and the importation of gold. The rising prices that followed helped to restore prosperous conditions.

BIBLIOGRAPHY

J. A. Barnes, *John G. Carlisle: Financial Statesman.*

O. M. W. Sprague, *History of Crises Under the National Banking System.*

Otto C. Lightner, *History of Business Depressions.*

— ELMER ELLIS

PANIC OF 1929

Panic of 1929 had so many causes that, historically, the remarkable fact is that its magnitude surprised many economists who were keeping a close watch on the situation. Wesley C. Mitchell, however, one of the greatest American economists, was never carried away by the climate of speculative prosperity. Writing in the spring of 1929 he said that "recent developments may appear less satisfactory in retrospect than they appear in prospect. . . . Past experience . . . suggests that the pace will slacken presently, and that years may pass before we see such another well-maintained advance." Basic among the factors leading to the instability feared by Mitchell were a volume of annual private and corporate savings in excess of the demand for real capital formation, a large export trade in manufactured goods supported by foreign lending, a low-discount Federal Reserve policy designed to support the British pound, an increasing use of stock-exchange securities rather than commercial paper for bank loans, the failure of wages or mass consumption to continue to rise much after 1926, a rapid increase in urban and suburban mortgage debt on speculative properties, sharply rising local government indebtedness, and increasing depression in a large part of the agricultural sector.

Some of these factors have been common to all American boom periods. The three that particularly characterized and ultimately undermined the pre-1929 boom were an insufficient increase in consumer demand to encourage the use of savings in productive domestic investment, the financial relations with foreign nations, and the change in the character of bank assets.

The period of prosperity from 1924 to late 1926 had been largely aided by installment buying of consumer durable goods, particularly automobiles; real estate investment; and construction. When this boom ended with a temporarily saturated automobile market in 1927, a depression of some duration was to be expected, but the speculative construction boom, supported greatly by state and local expenditures, showed surprising vitality until mid-1929; the Federal Reserve Board pursued a relatively easy money policy; and exports continued to be buoyed up by large foreign lending. To this extent the boom of 1927–29 may be regarded as partly dependent on government policies ranging all the way from borrowing too freely for street paving in new developments to failure to aid declining agriculture. But to put the blame on government at all levels would be to neglect the optimism of American big businessmen and financiers and their failure to face the long-run instabilities in the situation until a runaway stock-market boom had made orderly retreat impossible.

It is estimated—reliable data are still restricted by government regulations—that the income of the top 10 percent of receivers, who in those days did nearly all the net saving, was advancing rapidly. When the opportunities for real, labor-employing investment sagged after 1926, the money of the top-income group went into luxury purchases and the stock, bond, or mortgage markets. This development in turn gave the incentive of "easy money" to all kinds of speculative operators. In utilities and railroads, particularly, the pyramided, or many-staged, holding company structure was used by such insiders as Samuel Insull, Sidney Z. Mitchell, and Mantis J. and Oris P. Van Sweringen to put together and control vast business empires in which the costs of management and the burden of indebtedness rose rapidly. Investment trust companies, formed to give small investors the security of diversification, also became agencies for gaining control of companies—in other words, power structures for the insiders. Banks, in order to keep their depositors' money employed, often made large loans on the security of huge blocks of the common stock of a single company.

In June of 1929, sensitive economic indices began turning downward and some bankers were becoming alarmed by the continued rise of the stock market; in August the Federal Reserve Board tightened credit by raising the discount rate. The immediate effect of this action was adverse, as some of the Federal Reserve Bank officers had feared. Higher interest rates attracted not only more domestic capital into call loans on the stock market but also much foreign capital as well, applying a final lash of the whip to the runaway boom in security prices.

The stock market reached its peak right after Labor Day, 1929. It declined only slightly during September and early October, but on Friday, Oct. 18, it began to decline rapidly; from then until mid-November there was a series of panic days, the first of which was Oct. 24 and the worst, Oct. 29, the most devastating day in the history of the stock exchange. Yet during the whole month-long decline, the Standard and Poor stock-market index fell less than 40 percent and public statements held that no harm had been done to normal business.

Some of the unseen factors that were to turn the stock-market decline into an unforeseen and unprecedented depression were big bank loans that could not be liquidated, forcing the banks, by law, to post capital sufficient to cover the deficiency between a loan and the market value of its collateral; the pressure of the failure of weak banks on stronger ones; the collapse of Central European finance in 1931; the decline in the total of all forms of government spending for public works from 1930 to 1936; a monetary policy by the Federal Reserve banks that vacillated between meeting domestic needs and meeting foreign needs; and the failure of any large capital-consuming technological development to restimulate private investment. One might also add the general failure of economists, politicians, and businessmen to understand the relations of income distribution, demand, and investment, which were to be clarified in the mid-1930's by John Maynard Keynes.

Walter Thornton bids farewell to his snappy roadster, after the stock market crash of 1929. (UPI/Corbis-Bettmann)

BIBLIOGRAPHY

John Kenneth Galbraith, *The Great Crash, 1929.*

Wesley C. Mitchell, *Recent Economic Changes,* vol. II.

— THOMAS C. COCHRAN

PARIS, TREATY OF (1763)

Treaty of Paris, between Great Britain, France, and Spain, brought to an end the French and Indian War. In 1755 Great Britain had been willing to limit its jurisdiction in the interior of North America by a line running due south from Cuyahoga Bay on Lake Erie to the fortieth parallel and southwest to the thirty-seventh parallel, with the proviso that the territory beyond that line to the Maumee and Wabash rivers be a neutral zone. The British claimed, however, an area that would have included all the land between the Penobscot and Saint Lawrence rivers and the Gulf of Saint Lawrence and the Bay of Fundy, as well as the peninsula of Nova Scotia. The result of the British victory was an extension of British demands on France to include the cession of all of Canada to Great Britain and the advancement of the boundary of the continental colonies westward to the Mississippi River. Both these demands, together with the right to navigate the Mississippi, were granted to Great Britain in the treaty. Cuba, conquered by the British, was returned to Spain, which to offset this gain ceded East Florida and West Florida to Britain. As compensation for its losses, Spain received from France by the Treaty of Fontainebleau (1762) all the territory west of the Mississippi River and the island and city of New Orleans. France retained only the islands of Saint Pierre and Miquelon off the south coast of Newfoundland, together with the privilege of fishing and drying fish along the northern and western coasts of Newfoundland as provided in the Treaty of Utrecht (1713). In the West Indies, Great Britain retained the islands of Saint Vincent, Tobago, and Dominica; Saint Lucia, Martinique, and Guadeloupe were returned to France. The Treaty of Paris left only two great colonial empires in the Western Hemisphere, the British and the Spanish.

BIBLIOGRAPHY

Kate Hotblack, "The Peace of Paris, 1763," *Transactions of the Royal Historical Society*, vol. 2, 3rd series.

Theodore C. Pease, *Anglo-French Boundary Disputes in the West, 1749–1763.*

Max Savelle, *The Diplomatic History of the Canadian Boundary, 1749–1763.*

— MAX SAVELLE

PARIS, PEACE OF (1783)

During the American Revolution, Great Britain became successively engaged in war with the American colonies, France, Spain, and the Netherlands. When the conflict came to an end treaties of peace between those four powers respectively and Great Britain were made. Preliminary articles were signed at Paris between the United States and Great Britain on Nov. 30, 1782, and between the Netherlands and Great Britain on Sept. 2, 1783. On Sept. 3, 1783, three definitive treaties of peace between Great Britain and the United States, France, and Spain were signed.

The Definitive Treaty of Peace, between the United States and Great Britain, was signed at Paris because the British plenipotentiary, David Hartley, declined to go to Versailles for that purpose, although that course was desired by the American commissioners—John Adams, Benjamin Franklin, and John Jay. The signing of the treaty with the United States took place in the morning, and after word thereof was received at Versailles the treaties with France and Spain were there signed between noon and one o'clock. Thus, it is erroneous to speak of the Definitive Treaty of Peace between the United States and Great Britain as the Treaty of Versailles.

BIBLIOGRAPHY

Richard B. Morris, *The Peacemakers: Great Powers and American Independence.*

Richard W. Van Alstyne, *Empire and Independence: The International History of the American Revolution.*

— HUNTER MILLER

PARIS, TREATY OF (1898)

Treaty of Paris, terminated the Spanish-American War. Under its terms Spain relinquished all authority over Cuba and ceded to the United States Puerto Rico, the Philippine Islands, and Guam, in exchange for $20 million as the estimated value of public works and nonmilitary improvements in the Philippines. Hostilities had been suspended Aug. 12, and on Oct. 1 the five U.S. commissioners, headed by former Secretary of State William R. Day, opened negotiations with the Spanish commissioners in Paris. The most difficult questions encountered were the disposition of the Philippines, which Spain was reluctant to relinquish, and

Under the Treaty of Paris that ended the Spanish-American War in 1898, Spain ceded to the U.S. all authority over Cuba, Puerto Rico, the Philippines, and Guam.

of the $400 million Spanish debt charged against Cuba, which the Spanish wished assumed by either Cuba or the United States. Eventually Spain yielded on both points. An attempt by the U.S. commissioners to secure the island of Kusaie in the Carolines was blocked by Germany, which had opened negotiations for the purchase of these islands. The treaty was signed Dec. 10. The Senate, after bitter debate over the adoption of an imperialistic policy, exemplified in the annexation of the Philippines, consented to ratification by a close vote on Feb. 6, 1899. The treaty was proclaimed Apr. 11, 1899.

BIBLIOGRAPHY

E. J. Benton, *International Law and Diplomacy of the Spanish-American War.*

Julius W. Pratt, *Expansionists of 1898.*

— JULIUS W. PRATT

PARKS, NATIONAL, AND NATIONAL MONUMENTS

Of the 31 million acres in the National Park System in 1975, 15.6 million were in the thirty-eight national parks and 9.8 million in the eighty-one national monuments. Often called the crown jewels of the park system, national parks can be established only by act of Congress. Congress may also authorize national monuments, but most of them have been established by presidential proclamation under the Antiquities Act of 1906, which was passed to protect endangered archaeological and scientific sites on federal lands. Whereas the term "monument" is used in Europe principally to describe works of nature and in America most commonly to refer to statues or stone shafts, both meanings are included in the National Park System's usage—which comprehends, for example, both Death Valley and the Statue of Liberty.

Every president from Theodore Roosevelt to Lyndon B. Johnson proclaimed at least one national monument to protect scientific or historical sites, placing them under the supervision of the Department of the Interior, Department of Agriculture, or War Department, and in a number of instances the designation served to protect significant areas until park status could be conferred on them. National parks that were formerly national monuments are Lassen Volcanic, Grand Canyon, Acadia, Zion, Carlsbad Caverns, Bryce Canyon, Grand Teton, Olympic, Petrified Forest, Arches, and Capitol Reef.

The sixty-two areas transferred to the National Park Service by executive order in 1933 included the Statue of Liberty, nine other national monuments of the War Department, and Fort McHenry National Park, which was redesignated a national monument in 1939. The order also transferred fourteen national monuments from the Department of Agriculture's Forest Service to the Park Service, including Mount Olympus, Wash., most of which became Olympic National Park in 1938. Bandelier National Monument in New Mexico, containing ruins of cliff dwellings, was transferred from the Department of Agriculture to the National Park Service in 1932; Custer Battlefield, Mont., from the War Department in 1940; and Fort Sumter, S.C., from the Department of the Army in 1948.

A national park must possess nationally significant lands or waters of such superior quality, beauty, or scientific importance that it is imperative to protect them. While both national parks and national monuments must possess features that merit commitment to national care, a national park should contain two or more such features whereas a national monument need not. National parks are relatively spacious (see Table 1); national monuments may be any size. The two largest National Park Service areas in 1975 were national monuments in Alaska, Glacier Bay and Katmai, both of which may become national parks. All national parks are categorized as natural, rather than historical, areas except Mesa Verde, Colo.

The thirty-five national monuments categorized as natural areas are Glacier Bay and Katmai, Alaska; Chiricahua, Organ Pipe Cactus, Saguaro, and Sunset Crater, Ariz.; Channel Islands, Devils Postpile, Joshua Tree, Lava Beds, Muir Woods, and Pinnacles, Calif.; Death Valley, Calif.-Nev.; Black Canyon of the Gunnison, Colorado, Florissant Fossil Beds, and Great Sand Dunes, Colo.; Dinosaur, Colo.-Utah; Biscayne, Fla.; Craters of the Moon, Idaho; Agate Fossil Beds, Nebr.; Lehman Caves, Nev.; Capulin Mountain, Fossil Butte, and White Sands, N.Mex.; John Day Fossil Beds and Oregon Caves, Oreg.; Badlands and Jewel Cave, S.Dak.; Cedar Breaks, Natural Bridges, Rainbow Bridge, and Timpanogos Cave, Utah; Devils Tower, Wyo.; and Buck Island Reef, V.I.

The forty-six national monuments categorized as historical areas are Russell Cave, Ala.; Canyon de Chelly, Casa Grande Ruins, Hohokam-Pima, Montezuma Castle, Navajo, Pipe Spring, Tonto, Tumacacori, Tuzigoot, Walnut Canyon, and Wupatki, Ariz.; Cabrillo, Calif.; Yucca House, Colo.; Hovenweep, Colo.-Utah; Castillo de San Marcos, Fort Jefferson, and Fort Matanzas, Fla.; Fort Frederica, Fort Pulaski, and Ocmulgee, Ga.; Effigy Mounds, Iowa; Saint Croix Island, Maine; Fort McHenry, Md.; Grand Portage and Pipestone, Minn.; George Washington Carver, Mo.; Custer Battlefield, Mont.; Homestead and Scotts Bluff, Nebr.; Aztec Ruins, Bandelier, Chaco Canyon, El Morro, Fort Union, Gila Cliff Dwellings, Gran Quivira, and Pecos, N.Mex.; Castle Clinton and Fort Stanwix, N.Y.; Statue of Liberty, N.Y.-N.J.; Mound City Group, Ohio; Fort Sumter, S.C.; Alibates Flint Quarries and Texas Panhandle Pueblo Culture, Tex.; Booker T. Washington and George Washington Birthplace, Va.

Table 1

NATIONAL PARKS

NAME	LOCATION	ORIGIN	ACREAGE	1974 VISITORS
Yellowstone	Wyo.-Idaho-Mont.	1872	2,219,823	1,937,800
Sequoia	Calif.	1890	386,823	686,900
Yosemite	Calif.	1890	760,917	2,343,100
Mount Rainier	Wash.	1899	235,404	1,495,500
Crater Lake	Oreg.	1902	160,290	525,000
Wind Cave	S.Dak.	1903	28,060	855,700
Platt	Okla.	1906	912	3,903,500
Mesa Verde	Colo.	1906	52,036	446,700
Glacier	Mont.	1910	1,013,598	1,406,600
Rocky Mountain	Colo.	1915	263,793	2,501,100
Hawaii Volcanoes	Hawaii	1916	229,177	1,613,100
Lassen Volcanic	Calif.	1916	106,372	408,700
Mount McKinley	Alaska	1917	1,939,492	425,500
Grand Canyon	Ariz.	1919	1,218,375	2,028,200
Acadia	Maine	1919	37,601	2,734,900
Zion	Utah	1919	146,571	941,300
Hot Springs	Ark.	1921	5,801	2,314,500
Carlsbad Caverns	N. Mex.	1923	46,755	672,400
Bryce Canyon	Utah	1924	37,277	410,300
Great Smoky Mountains	N.C.-Tenn.	1926	517,014	10,447,200
Shenandoah	Va.	1926	190,445	2,215,300
Mammoth Cave	Ky.	1926	52,129	1,740,000
Grand Teton	Wyo.	1929	310,418	2,936,800
Isle Royale	Mich.	1931	539,280	13,900
Everglades	Fla.	1934	1,400,533	1,000,000
Big Bend	Tex.	1935	708,118	191,300
Olympic	Wash.	1938	897,886	2,479,300
Kings Canyon	Calif.	1940	460,136	1,224,400
Virgin Islands	V.I.	1956	14,470	298,200
Haleakala	Hawaii	1960	27,824	441,300
Petrified Forest	Ariz.	1962	94,189	789,200
Canyonlands	Utah	1964	337,570	59,000
Guadalupe Mountains	Tex.	1966	79,972	39,400
Redwood	Calif.	1968	62,286	328,300
North Cascades	Wash.	1968	504,785	885,300*
Voyageurs	Minn.	1971	219,128	no count
Arches	Utah	1971	73,398	171,300
Capitol Reef	Utah	1971	241,865	234,000

* Includes visits to two adjacent national recreation areas.

Legislation presented in Congress on Dec. 17, 1973, would preserve for all present and future generations scenic, wildlife, and archaeological wonders of Alaska. The polar bear would come under National Park Service protection for the first time. Wolf packs, mountain goats, brown grizzly bears, caribou, Dall sheep, endangered species of whale, rare birds, and birds migrating to six continents would be protected, as would Eskimo and Indian cultures, archaeological sites, mountain ranges, unspoiled river valleys, glaciers larger than Rhode Island, and tundra and mountain wilderness. Four new national parks, four new national monuments, and two other parklands would achieve this purpose. The proposed national parks would take in 21.48 million acres, added to which would be a 3.18-million-acre expansion of Mount McKinley National Park, to include the south half of North America's highest peak.

BIBLIOGRAPHY

John Ise, *Our National Park Policy.*

National Park Service, *Index of the National Park System*, and *Public Use of the National Parks.*

Thomas A. Sullivan, *Proclamations and Orders Relating to the National Park Service up to Jan. 1, 1945.*

Hillary A. Tolson, *Laws Relating to the National Park Service*, supp. II.

— JOHN VOSBURGH

PARKS, NATIONAL

Of the 83.3 million acres in the National Park System in 1994, 50.4 million were in the fifty-four national parks and 2.06 million in the seventy-three national monuments. The remaining acres can be accounted for in other areas in the system—such as national seashores, national scenic trails, and national historic sites—that are not designated as national parks or national monuments. During the administrations of Richard M. Nixon, Gerald R. Ford, Ronald Reagan, and George Bush, national monuments were created by congressional action. President Jimmy Carter, acting under the powers assigned presidents by the Antiquities Act of 1906, created national monuments in Alaska by proclamation.

Between 1974 and 1994 fifteen areas that were formerly national monuments became national parks: Badlands, Biscayne, Channel Islands, Death Valley, Dry Tortugas, Gates of the Arctic, Glacier Bay, Great Basin, Katmai, Kenai Fjords, Kobuk Valley, Joshua Tree, Lake Clark, Saguaro, and Wrangell–St. Elias. The Theodore Roosevelt National Memorial park, created in 1947, was redesignated a national park in 1978, and in 1988 the National Park of American Samoa was established. The two largest National Park Service areas in 1995 were Wrangell–St. Elias and Gates of the Arctic, both in Alaska. In 1977 the National Park Service classification system that divided units into natural, historical, and recreational areas was abolished because these categories became difficult to apply, as some areas contained multiple attributes. National parks and national monuments are often, however, classified informally according to their primary attributes.

The twenty-nine national monuments categorized as primarily natural areas are Aniakchak, Alaska; Chiricahua, Organ Pipe Cactus, Sunset Crater Volcano, Arizona; Devils Postpile, Lava Beds, Muir Woods, Pinnacles, California; Black Canyon of the Colorado, Gunnison, Dinosaur, Florissant Fossil Beds, Great Sand Dunes, Colorado; Craters of the Moon, Hagerman Fossil Beds, Idaho; Agate Fossil Beds, Nebraska; Capulin Volcano, El Malpais, White Sands, New Mexico; John Day Fossil Beds, Oregon Caves, Oregon; Congaree Swamp, South Carolina; Jewel Cave, South Dakota; Cedar Breaks, Natural Bridges, Rainbow Bridge, Timpanogos Cave, Utah; Buck Island Reef, Virgin Islands; Devils Tower, Fossil Butte, Wyoming.

The forty-three national monuments categorized as primarily historical areas are Russell Cave, Alabama; Cape Krusenstern, Alaska; Canyon de Chelly, Casa Grande Ruins, Hohokam Pima, Montezuma Castle, Navajo, Pipe Spring, Tonto, Tuzigoot, Walnut Canyon, Wupatki, Arizona; Cabrillo, California; Hovenweep, Yucca House, Colorado; Castillo de San Marcos, Fort Matanzas, Florida; Fort Frederica, Fort Pulaski, Ocmulgee, Georgia; Effigy Mounds, Iowa; Poverty Point, Louisiana; Fort McHenry, Maryland; Grand Portage, Pipestone, Minnesota; George Washington Carver, Missouri; Little Bighorn Battlefield, Montana; Homestead, Scotts Bluff, Nebraska; Aztec Ruins, Bandelier, El Morro, Fort Union, Gila Cliff Dwellings, Petroglyph, Salinas Pueblo Missions, New Mexico; Castle Clinton, Fort Stanwix, Statue of Liberty, New York; Fort Sumter, South Carolina; Alibates Flint Quarries, Texas; Booker T. Washington, George Washington Birthplace, Virginia.

The most significant service acquisitions between 1974 and 1994 were in Alaska. Under the Alaska Native Claims Settlement Act of 1971 the secretary of the interior was given the discretion to withdraw up to 80 million acres of Alaskan lands that would qualify as units operated by one of the following agencies: National Park Service, Forest Service, or Fish and Wildlife Service. In 1973 Secretary Rogers C. B. Morton recommended that 32.3 million acres be withdrawn for parks. Congress had five years to act on the secretary's recommendation, which would double the size of the lands administered by the Park Service. There was strong opposition from commercial interests and from hunters who urged Congress to create preserves that permitted sport hunting and trapping, rather than parks that prohibited those activities. Representative Morris K. Udall of Arizona drafted a bill that created national preserves but it was defeated in May 1978.

It appeared that the five-year limit for Congress to act would expire and the withdrawn areas would revert to public lands. On Dec. 1, 1978, President Jimmy Carter proclaimed fifteen new national monuments and made additions to two others. He proclaimed the withdrawn lands as monuments to allow Congress time to draft legislation concerning their status. In 1980 Congress agreed to an Alaskan lands bill, and on December 2 President Carter signed the Alaska National Interest Lands Conservation Act into law, redesignating seven monuments as national parks and increasing the acreage of the National Park Service by more than 47 million, much more than the 32.3 million Secretary Morton had recommended for withdrawal. Five of the seven parks were accompanied by national preserves, allowing sport hunting and trapping.

BIBLIOGRAPHY

Barry Mackintosh, *The National Parks: Shaping the System* (Washington, D.C., 1991).

National Park Service, *The National Parks: Index 1993* (Washington, D.C., 1993).

— JON E. TAYLOR

PATENTS AND U.S. PATENT OFFICE

The American legal and administrative system for issuing letters patent to inventors has attempted since the colonial period to encourage invention and the growth of industry by granting monopolies. Detailed requirements for this valuable privilege have been imposed to prevent the continuance of the monopoly beyond a limited period. The rare colonial approval of monopolies for the purchase, production, and sale of commodities derived from the British crown's authority to grant such monopolies in the national interest. This authority was restricted in scope by *Darcy* v. *Allien* (1602), which invalidated the patent of Queen Elizabeth I for the manufacture of playing cards because she failed to show that the process was an invention; the monopoly was therefore not considered to be in the national interest. Monopolistic practices, such as engrossing, regrating, and forestalling, had already been declared illegal under the common law. These decisions served as the basis for the 1623 Statute of Monopolies, which authorized monopolics only to "the true and first inventor" of a new manufacturing process. The monopolies were limited to fourteen years, presumably an adequate period to train apprentices in the new technology and to receive the deserved monetary benefits. Continuation of the monopoly was to be prevented when the apprentices became independent.

With this background the general court of Massachusetts Bay Colony granted monopolies for stated periods, with the objective of encouraging domestic industry. Benefits to inventors or innovators were either in the form of monopolies or monetary grants by the colony for each sale of the patented item. Since the Articles of Confederation made no mention of patents, individual states continued the precedent established in colonial Massachusetts. Maryland, for example, granted patents to James Rumsey for his steamboat and to Oliver Evans for his milling machinery. Evans' invention was also patented in most other states.

In 1790 Congress passed the first patent law under the constitutional power, provided in Article I, Section 8, "to promote the Progress of Science and useful Arts, by securing for limited Times" exclusive rights of inventors to their discoveries. The act provided that petitions for patents would be forwarded to the secretaries of state and war and to the attorney general, that any two members of this patent board could approve a fourteen-year patent, and that the attorney general was to submit the approved patent for the president's signature. When Thomas Jefferson was secretary of state, he played the leading role in this procedure, and his department was the registry for the system. Jefferson, a notable inventor, had a deep interest in science and technology. Because of his abhorrence of monopoly, he applied strictly the rule of novelty and usefulness to each application. Only three patents were approved in 1790.

Objections to delays in processing petitions and the narrow interpretation of the 1790 act resulted in passage in 1793 of a new law, providing for termination of the board and an administrative structure for examining the merits of the petitions. The secretary of state was to register the patents and appoint a board of arbiters when two or more petitioners claimed the same invention (known as an interference proceeding). The law left to the courts any disputes about the validity of the petitioners' claims. But it seemed to many that the courts were excessively concerned with patent litigation and that the judges were in general unqualified to adjudicate disputes about claims of priority and technical questions. The volume of petitions under the 1793 act caused Secretary of State James Madison to establish in 1802 the Patent Office, under Commissioner William Thornton, to administer the department's responsibilities for the patent system. It was Thornton who, in September 1814, saved the patent files from destruction by British troops.

Chiefly through the efforts of Sen. John Ruggles, a persistent critic, the patent law was again completely rewritten on July 4, 1836. The new law gave the Patent Office responsibility for examining petitions and for ruling on the validity of the claims for an invention, its usefulness, and its workability. The law provided that the fourteen-year monopoly could be extended for an additional seven years if a special board (later, the commissioner of patents) found that the patentee encountered unusual problems in producing and marketing his device. In 1861 Congress withdrew this authority to extend patents and reserved such grants to itself; to give the patentee additional time for producing and marketing new products, Congress increased the monopoly period to seventeen years.

The 1836 patent law gave the Patent Office responsibility for ruling on the validity of the claims for an invention, its usefulness, and its workability.

In 1839, Congress initiated a historically important program for the Patent Office by authorizing it to disseminate seeds and to collect and publish data of interest to farmers. The agricultural division of the office was thus the predecessor of the Department of Agriculture, established in 1862. Since 1930 the Patent Office has issued patents for a "distinct and new variety" of asexually produced plants, thus renewing an early interest in promoting agriculture.

Congress codified and modified the various patent laws in 1870. It added the power to issue trademark patents to the authority under an 1842 act for granting design patents. The 1870 act delegated copyright responsibilities, some of which had been in the Patent Office, to the Library of Congress. It also sanctioned the procedures for adjudicating interferences by establishing the Office of the Examiner of Interferences. During the next decades the Patent Office, which had been transferred to the Department of the Interior when that was created in 1849 and to the Department of Commerce in 1925, developed its basic organization and essential procedures. Executive and managerial authority were vested in the commissioner of patents, one or more assistant commissioners, and the Office of Administration. The solicitor assumed jurisdiction over all legal matters and, particularly, the extensive litigation to which the commissioner was a party. A registry office, under several name changes, registered patent applications and assignments of approved patents, published and distributed patent specifications, and organized a scientific and technical library. The chief operating function of examining the claims assigned by the registry unit was delegated to several patent examining divisions. Separate units processed trademark applications. Boards with important staff functions—such as the Trademark Trial and Appeal Board, the Board of Patent Interferences, and the Board of Appeals—began adjudicating appeals to reverse examiners' findings with regard to invention and design patents, trademark disputes, and interferences. An office was also established to study and advise the commission on policies and actions under international patent and trademark agreements. Beginning in the 1960's the Patent Office included advisers on the use of automatic data-processing systems for recording, classifying, and examining patents.

Although the patent system has long played a significant role in the history of American science and technology, it has had considerable adverse criticism. Critics—for example, in the 1938 hearings of the Temporary National Economic Committee—have claimed that the system has fostered monopoly by creating producers who, by superior technology protected by a series of patents and delays in patent proceedings, corner a large part of the market. Critics have also accused the system of suppressing inventions to delay change. Advocates, probably a large majority, have called attention to the incentive of reward, to antitrust proceedings when companies become too dominant in an industry, to the right of a patentee not to sell his product, and to the importance of Patent Office publications in disseminating specifications and drawings of inventions. Since the founding of Thomas Edison's laboratory in 1876, most of the significant inventions have been developed by institutional research sponsored by the federal government, universities, and private companies.

BIBLIOGRAPHY

Levine H. Campbell, *The Patent System of the United States, so far as It Relates to the Granting of Patents: A History.*

Harry Kursh, *Inside the U.S. Patent Office.*

U.S. Patent Office, *Rules of Practice in Patent Cases.*

— MEYER H. FISHBEIN

PATROONS

On June 7, 1629, the directorate of the West India Company granted, and the States General of the Netherlands approved, a charter of freedoms and exemptions, which provided for the grant of great estates, called patroonships, to those members of the company who were able to found settlements of fifty persons within four years after giving notice of their intentions. The patroon, after extinguishing the Indian title by purchase, was to hold the land as a "perpetual fief of inheritance" with the fruits, plants, minerals, rivers, and springs thereof. He was to swear fealty to the company and have the right of the high, middle, and low jurisdiction. Before the end of January 1630, patroonships had been registered by Michiel Pauw, for Pavonia, on the west side of the Hudson River, across from Manhattan Island; by Samuel Godyn, for the west side of the Delaware River; by Albert Coenraets Burgh, on the east side of the Delaware River; by Samuel Blommaert, for the Connecticut River; and by Kiliaen van Rensselaer, for Rensselaerswyck, around Fort Orange on the Hudson. With the single exception of Rensselaerswyck, these grants were unsuccessful. The difficulties of transportation across the Atlantic Ocean, lack of cooperation from the company, quarrels with the authorities at New Amsterdam, Indian troubles, and the difficulties of management from 3,000 miles away were all factors in their failure. In 1640 the revised charter reduced the size of future patroonships, but the same factors contributed to prevent the success of these smaller grants. At the close of Dutch rule all but two of the patroonships had been repurchased by the company.

BIBLIOGRAPHY

A. C. Flick, ed., *History of the State of New York,* vol. I.

— A. C. FLICK

PAWNEE

When first contacted by Europeans, perhaps as early as 1541 by the expedition of Francisco Vásquez de Coronado, the Pawnee, an American Indian tribe in the Great Plains, lived in the present state of Nebraska on the middle course of the Platte River and the Republican fork of the Kansas River. Three main branches or bands of the Pawnee spoke a single Caddoan language, while a fourth group, virtually a separate tribe, the Skidi, spoke a variant dialect. The Caddoan languages were spoken in the regions to the south, by the Caddo and Wichita, for example. If Caddoan, as some suggest, relates to a broader Hokan, sometimes designated as a Hokan-Siouan phylum, the origins of the Pawnee as well as those of the Arikara, a prominent related offshoot, may be traced to the southeast. Such a notion is borne out by the retention by the Pawnee of river-bottom agriculture, a trait carried by the Arikara from the Pawnee to the Siouan Mandan and Hidatsa. A large Plains tribe, with perhaps 10,000 members in 1780, the Pawnee stressed both the permanent farming village and forays far afield for horses and military honors. Although the Pawnee shared basic elements of Plains Indian culture with neighboring tribes, they were known for the ceremony of the morning star, a ritual involving human sacrifice for communal good. Somewhat off the paths of east-west settlement, the Pawnee enjoyed fairly benign relations with Europeans and were often employed as U.S. Army scouts.

BIBLIOGRAPHY

George E. Hyde, *Pawnee Indians.*

— ROBERT F. SPENCER

PEACE CORPS

As an idea, the Peace Corps originated with Democratic Representative Henry S. Reuss of Wisconsin and Senator Hubert H. Humphrey of Minnesota in the late 1950s. Both advocated sending U.S. volunteers into developing nations to help alleviate poverty, illiteracy, and disease. Democratic presidential candidate John F. Kennedy adopted the idea in 1960. The Peace Corps appealed to Kennedy's notion of service to country and humanity; it also had the potential for encouraging goodwill for the United States among developing nations. The Soviets and Chinese, in Kennedy's opinion, were far ahead of the United States in cultivating friendships among nations emerging from colonialism after World War II. He wanted the Peace Corps to counter communist aims in developing nations by demonstrating U.S. democratic values. President Kennedy moved quickly, appointing his brother-in-law, Sargent Shriver, to create the Peace Corps. Shriver built the agency in a matter of weeks. The president signed an executive order on Mar. 1, 1961, temporarily establishing the Peace Corps, and in September, Congress voted to create a permanent corps. Appointed its first director, Shriver worked to develop a system for recruiting, training, transporting, supplying, and caring for overseas volunteers. His drive helped the Peace Corps gain independent status from other U.S. foreign policy agencies. Although directors of the Peace Corps are political appointees and have changed the focus of the organization somewhat as presidential administrations changed, the Peace Corps has remained relatively free from use as a direct foreign policy instrument.

Sargent Shriver, the Peace Corps' first director, helped ensure that the Corps would remain relatively free from use as a tool of foreign policy.

After the end of the cold war the Peace Corps' goals remained unaltered. It seeks to promote world peace and friendship through interaction of the volunteers with their hosts. Volunteers spend two years in a host country that requests Peace Corps help, aiding in whatever ways the host desires. Tasks range from teaching and community organizing to assistance in agriculture.

The corps concentrates on small, personal projects and has three broad aims—providing trained workers for developing nations, promoting understanding of the United States and its values, and increasing volunteers' understanding of the perspectives and values of people in developing nations. Despite attacks, low funding, and internal problems the Peace Corps survives as a popular agency. Since 1961 it has sent more than 140,000 volunteers to ninety-nine nations. The agency cannot keep pace with demands for volunteers. Charges of cultural imperialism have been leveled, but the agency responds that it does not seek to replace traditional societies' values with those of the United States but rather to act as a bridge between cultures. The Peace Corps continues to receive bipartisan congressional support.

BIBLIOGRAPHY

Gerard T. Rice, *The Bold Experiment: JFK's Peace Corps* (Notre Dame, Ind., 1985).

— JOEL D. SHROCK

PEACE MOVEMENTS

Two kinds of peace movement have been prevalent in America. One kind has opposed particular wars in which the United States has been involved; the other, most active in peacetime, has concentrated on advocating long-term mechanisms for the peaceful settlement of international disputes. Pacifists have taken part in both kinds of peace movement, but they have rarely constituted the most important segment.

Between the American Revolution and World War I, the major American wars were opposed by disparate groups that were unsympathetic to the purposes of a specific war. Opposition to the War of 1812 was centered among conservative Federalists in New England, who flirted with the idea of seceding from the Union in the Hartford Convention of 1814. They opposed the disruption of trade with Britain that the war entailed, and they feared that the territorial expansion desired by the promoters of the war would diminish the power of the eastern states in national politics. The Mexican War (1846–48), on the other hand, was opposed most strongly by northern critics of slavery, who attacked the war as a slaveholders' plot to add new land for the expansion of slavery. These same people, except for a small group of pacifists, strongly supported the northern cause in the Civil War. Opposition to the Civil War was generally of a conservative, often racist, nature, based on opposition to the use of the federal government's power to take action against slavery. The Spanish-American War of 1898 was almost universally popular in the United States at first; the opposition that emerged was directed at the decision of President William McKinley's administration to keep the Philippines and suppress the Filipinos by force, an opposition centered among reformers who saw imperialism as contrary to American ideals.

During the long intervals between these wars, the second type of peace movement grew at a more or less steady pace. The first local peace society was formed by David Low Dodge in New York in 1815, and the nationwide American Peace Society followed in 1828. Led chiefly by William Ladd, this group flourished during the social reform agitation of the 1830's, distributing tracts attacking the folly of war and advocating proposals such as a congress of nations and arbitration treaties. In 1846 Elihu Burritt and others who objected to the moderate policies of Ladd's successors formed the League of Universal Brotherhood, which within a few years claimed 20,000 American and 20,000 British members. Its members took an oath never to support any war for any purpose. It undertook peace propaganda and was in large measure responsible for a series of "universal peace congresses" held in various European cities between 1848 and 1853.

Except for a small number of people who clung to an absolute pacifism—notably Burritt and William Lloyd Garrison—the great majority of those active in the peace groups supported the Civil War. The American Peace Society spoke for them when it claimed that the war was an unlawful rebellion against authority, not a genuine war, and George Beckwith, the society's leader, repeatedly spoke against any concessions to the Confederacy. The society continued in existence during the war, however, and resumed its propaganda activities after the armistice. It was joined by the Universal Peace Union, founded by pacifists in 1866 and headed by Alfred Love, a Philadelphia merchant. Both organizations placed considerable stress on arbitration of disputes between nations, and their pressure helped encourage a growing willingness on the government's part to negotiate treaties promising to submit future disputes to arbitration. The Universal Peace Union, unlike most peace groups before or since, also concerned itself with labor disputes in the United States; it took a middle-ground position favoring arbitration as an alternative to strikes and lockouts. As before the Civil War the peace movement consisted mainly of upper-middle-class people, such as lawyers, preachers, and merchants, although there were few wealthy businessmen in its ranks.

The Spanish-American War and, more important, the American conquest of the Philippine Islands that followed Spain's surrender marked the first large-scale use of American troops outside the North American continent. The American Anti-Imperialist League, formed in 1899 and centered in Boston, organized a persistent opposition to the American invasion. The Democratic party's 1900 presidential candidate, William Jennings Bryan, made opposition to the Philippine annexation his main campaign issue and received much support for it even though he lost the election. Bryan's defeat, together with the waning of Filipino military resistance, did much to deflate the antiimperialist movement. During its heyday it had managed to offer principled opposition to an American war and also to point out (as the traditional peace movement had not done) the connection between economic expansionism and war.

During the next decade and a half, before the outbreak of World War I in 1914, the traditional peace movement flourished. It acquired some wealthy backers, such as Andrew Carnegie, who sponsored the Carnegie Endowment for International Peace. Most of the new converts to the peace movement were far from being pacifists; their primary concern was with the fashioning of mechanisms to ensure international order without war. Their growth reflected the new status of the United States as the world's leading manufacturing power with a strong stake in international diplomacy. At the same time, there was increasing concern within churches, especially of the Protestant denominations, about peace: for example, it has been estimated that more than 50,000 sermons were preached in behalf of peace on the Sunday before Christmas in 1909.

After the outbreak of war in Europe in 1914, most of the peace movement came to reconcile itself to the idea of American intervention, which came in April 1917. New organizations, such as the American Union Against Militarism, the Emergency Peace Federation, and the Women's Peace Party, took on the burden of trying to stave off American entry into the war. The main left-wing groups of that period, the Socialist party and the Industrial Workers of the World, also vigorously denounced the war as a dispute between rival imperialists. Once war was declared, the nominal peace groups generally gave full support, as when the American Peace Society newspaper seriously declared, "We must aid in the starving and emaciation of a German baby in order that he, or at least his more sturdy little playmate, may grow up to inherit a different sort of government from that for which his father died."

Some opposition groups did remain active during the war. The American Union Against Militarism spawned a civil liberties bureau, later to become the American Civil Liberties Union, which worked on behalf of conscientious objectors to conscription during the war. Liberal and Socialist critics of the war formed the People's Council of America for Democracy and Terms of Peace to advocate an early peace. But governmental repression on all levels was fierce. The People's Council searched in vain for a city to meet in; dozens of Socialist publications were denied access to the mails; hundreds of national and local leaders of the Industrial Workers of the World were jailed; and 2,000 people were arrested altogether on charges of disloyal speech. The fact that considerable grass-roots opposition to the war still existed was shown by the increased vote given to Socialist party candidates in many local elections; but the opposition was given no room to mobilize on a national level.

In the two decades after the 1918 armistice a strong disenchantment with the aims and results of World War I spread among the American public. It was reflected not only in revisionist writings about the war but also in the renewed growth of peace organizations. Both the more conservative groups aligned with the Carnegie Endowment and such pacifist groups as the Fellowship of Reconciliation flourished during that period. Peace activity was especially marked on college campuses, as an estimated half million students took part in rallies against war at the peak of the student activity in 1936. Disillusionment with war was so widespread that Congress passed a series of neutrality acts in the 1930's aimed at preventing the United States from being drawn into a future war. As war drew nearer in Europe and Asia at the end of the decade, the antiwar consensus eroded and the neutrality legislation was circumvented or repealed. German attacks against France and Britain in 1940 and Russia in 1941 reconciled most people, including a great majority of liberals and radicals, to American support for the Allies. Once the United States entered the war officially in December 1941, American participation received a more nearly unanimous domestic support than in any previous war in the nation's history. Public opposition to the war was almost nonexistent. Of the prewar peace groups, the most active during the war were those that worked to influence the government in the direction of creating a permanent world organization on the basis of the wartime alliance. Pacifists still refused to accept the war—while preferring the Allied cause to that of Germany and Japan—but a great many of those who had espoused an absolute pacifism in the 1930's abandoned their previous position.

With the breakup of the wartime alliance and the beginning of the cold war against the Soviet Union in the late 1940's, the wartime consensus on foreign policy at first fell apart and was then reimposed by repression. In the immediate aftermath of World War II, war weariness and demonstrations by soldiers who wanted to come home forced a much more rapid demobilization of the armed forces than had been planned. But cold war tensions soon made possible a peacetime draft and increasingly tight alliances with conservative regimes around the world. Critics of the government's stance came to be branded either as subversives or as dupes of world communism. The outbreak of war in Korea (1950) exacerbated this tendency, and pacifist, as well as radical, groups were reduced to the lowest point of their peacetime influence in at least half a century. The Korean War was by no means popular in the United States, but this fact sprang simply from war weariness, and there was no peace movement of any size that could claim credit for the war's unpopularity.

The Korean armistice in 1953 and a general relaxation of cold war tensions in the mid-1950's, together with a decline in the worst aspects of repression, enabled a peace movement to emerge again in 1957. The issue of nuclear testing was seized upon, both as a symbol of the menace of nuclear war and as an immediate hazard. Thousands of scientists signed a petition against atmospheric nuclear testing, and the National Committee for a Sane Nuclear Policy (SANE) was formed in 1958 by liberals and pacifists. Women Strike for Peace, the Student Peace Union, and the Committee for Nonviolent Action were formed within the space of a few years. Agitation by this new peace movement contributed to the defeat of the proposals under President John F. Kennedy's administration for a far-reaching civil defense program (which the peace groups argued would make war seem more acceptable) and, on the other hand, helped lead to the negotiation of a limited ban on nuclear testing by the United States and the Soviet Union in 1963. The peace movement was not able to slow the steady increase in military appropriations, which accelerated under Kennedy.

The American intervention in Vietnam, which reached major proportions in 1965, elicited a strong and ultimately effective peace movement. The first national demonstrations against the war, called by the Students for a Democratic Society, drew upward of 20,000 young people to Washington, D.C., in April 1965. Within two years, perhaps as many as half a million persons took part in the spring 1967 antiwar marches in New York City and San Francisco. On college campuses a draft-resistance movement gained momentum, and on scores of campuses there were obstructive sit-ins against recruiters for the armed forces and for the Dow Chemical Company, which manufactured napalm used in Vietnam. As more and more liberals joined radicals in turning against the war, President Lyndon B. Johnson's popularity within his own Democratic party began to suffer badly. Amid poll reports that showed him a certain loser to antiwar Sen. Eugene McCarthy in the Wisconsin presidential primary, Johnson withdrew as a presidential candidate in March 1968.

During the administration of President Richard M. Nixon the ranks of protesters swelled. Probably several million persons took part in activities during the antiwar moratorium in October 1969, and on Nov. 15 the largest antiwar demonstration in the nation's history took place in Washington, D.C. In May 1970 hundreds of college campuses were shut down during a nationwide student strike to protest an American invasion of Cambodia. Because of general disillusionment and the growing protest movement, the Democratic majority in Congress began to pressure the Nixon administration for an end to the war. The administration signed a peace treaty on Vietnam in January 1973 and in the summer of that year was forced by Congress to end American bombing of Cambodia, the last element of direct participation by American forces in the Indochina war.

BIBLIOGRAPHY

Charles Chatfield, *For Peace and Justice.*
Merle Curti, *The American Peace Crusade.*
H. C. Peterson and Gilbert Fite, *Opponents of War, 1917–1918.*
Thomas Powers, *The War at Home.*
Daniel B. Schirmer, *Republic or Empire.*
Lawrence S. Wittner, *Rebels Against War.*

— JAMES P. O´BRIEN

PEACE MOVEMENTS SINCE THE 1970S

U.S. citizens take part in peace movements for a variety of reasons. Some limit their commitment to specific antiwar activities, particularly during military conflicts. Others champion internationalism, supporting worldwide peace organizations. Many are pacifists, religious or secular. Some believe that large standing armies pose a threat to liberty and democracy. Many link peace to such other interests as feminism, socialism, civil rights, or environmentalism. With the end of the Vietnam War in 1975 the broad coalition of peace activists who had come together to protest the longest conflict in U.S. history broke down once again into smaller groups addressing a range of concerns.

Protests against the nuclear arms race, which had been a focus of peace groups since the 1950s, intensified in the 1980s in response to the Ronald Reagan administration's buildup of the U.S. nuclear arsenal. In the early 1980s the nonviolent Livermore Action Group sought to close the Lawrence Livermore National Laboratory in California, which produced nuclear weapons. Such actions reinforced the wider nuclear freeze campaign, a movement that in November 1982 led to the largest voter referendum on any issue in U.S. history.

More than 11.5 million Americans, 60 percent of those voting on the freeze issue, supported the measure. The freeze issue appeared on the ballot in states and localities across the country. Twelve state legislatures, 321 city councils, 10 national labor unions and international bodies endorsed the effort by the United States and Soviet Union to ban mutually the testing, production, and deployment of nuclear weapons. One result of the movement was the Intermediate-Range Nuclear Forces (INF) Treaty of 1988 with the Soviet Union.

Activists also linked the huge U.S. military budget with neglect of such human needs as education, health care, and housing for the poor, which led to ambitious campaigns against such costly projects as the B-1 bomber, the MX missile system, and the Strategic Defense Initiative ("Star Wars"). Peace groups were critical of U.S. military interventions in Grenada (1983) and Panama (1989), and to a lesser extent, in Somalia (1992), challenging the morality as well as the effectiveness of using military means to achieve political, economic, or even humanitarian ends. Although the brief Gulf War of 1991 elicited overwhelming public support in favor of halting Iraq's aggression against Kuwait, many peace activists criticized the George Bush administration for engaging in a war they believed was more about U.S. dependency on Middle East oil than about freedom for the citizens of Kuwait. Elsewhere, protests were aimed at the Reagan administration for its support of the Contras seeking to overthrow the Sandinista government in Nicaragua, where in 1990 U.S. peace organizations monitored free elections.

A unique aspect of the peace movement since the 1970s has been the surge of feminist involvement. Awareness generated by the 1975–1985 United Nations Decade for Women resulted in international networks concerned with global issues of war, economic crises, and the rights of women. In 1980 and 1981 women encircled the Pentagon to oppose war. New York State in 1983 witnessed the massive Women's Encampment for the Future of Peace and Justice sited next to the Seneca Army Depot, a nuclear weapons storage facility. The 1987 Mother's Day action at the Department of Energy's nuclear test site near Las Vegas enlisted thousands of women from throughout the country. As in the past, peace movements appealed most to middle-income women, clergymen, educators, college students and people in their twenties, and some business leaders. Geographically, their centers of strength were in college towns, the large metropolitan areas of the Northeast and Midwest, and along the West Coast.

[See also Arms Race and Disarmament; Grenada Invasion; Gulf War of 1991; Human Rights; Panama Invasion; Strategic Defense Initiative; Women's Movement.]

On August 28, 1968, anitwar demonstrators in Chicago attempting to march from Grant Park to Convention Hall are greeted by National Guardsmen wearing gas masks and holding their rifles at the ready. Police resorted to using tear gas as thousands of protestors broke through National Guard and police lines. (UPI/Corbis-Bettmann)

BIBLIOGRAPHY

Charles Chatfield, *The American Peace Movement: Ideals and Activism* (New York, 1992).

Barbara Epstein, *Political Protest and Cultural Revolution* (Berkeley, Calif., 1991).

Charles F. Howlett, *The American Peace Movement: References and Resources* (Boston, 1991).

Lawrence S. Wittner, *Rebels Against War: The American Peace Movement, 1933–1983* (Philadelphia, 1984).

— CHARLES F. HOWLETT

PEARL HARBOR

Pearl Harbor naval base on the south coast of Oahu, Hawaiian Islands, six miles west of Honolulu, is large enough to accommodate the entire U.S. fleet. First in 1845 and again in 1875 attention was called to Pearl Harbor as a defense post for Hawaii and for the west coast of the United States. In 1887 the Hawaiian government granted the United States exclusive use of Pearl Harbor as a fueling and naval repair station. In 1908 the Navy Department dredged and widened the entrance channel. In 1919 a huge drydock was completed, and in 1926 the channel was again deepened and widened. It was designated as a naval, military, and airplane base, and all needed facilities were established, including ammunition dumps, machine shops, radio towers, a hospital, an airplane base on Ford Island in the harbor, barracks for military and naval personnel, and extensive fuel oil storage facilities. Pearl Harbor served as a port of observation in the mid-Pacific, as a defense lookout for the west coast of the United States and Alaska, and as a base for the Pacific fleet.

On July 16, 1940, a militant government came into power in Japan, favoring Germany in its war against the Soviet Union and Western Europe. Relations with the United States became strained. President Franklin D. Roosevelt proposed a meeting with the Japanese prime minister, Prince Fumimaro Konoye, to adjust differences between the two countries, but the offer only strengthened the hands of the Japanese militarists. Further negotiations between the two governments followed, but to no avail. The war in Europe seemed to be favoring Germany, with which the Japanese wanted to form an alliance, as the United States government was trying to halt Japanese aggression in Manchuria and to prevent the making of an alliance with Germany.

On Oct. 18, 1941, a new Japanese government, more militant than its predecessor, came into power, headed by Hideki Tojo, and all efforts at conciliation failed. On Nov. 14, 1941, U.S. army and navy commanders in the Pacific area, including Pearl Harbor, were warned to be on the alert for a surprise Japanese attack; on Nov. 27 a dispatch declaring itself to be a "war warning" was sent to Pearl Harbor—but American authorities thought that the Philippines or Malaysia would be the target.

In the meantime a Japanese carrier task force had left the Kurile Islands in northern Japanese waters on Nov. 25, moving eastward for a surprise attack on the American naval base at Pearl Harbor, despite the opposition of the Japanese Emperor Hirohito and his supporters. Despite the several warnings—all of them vague and uncertain, however, about the objective of the rumored Japanese attack—the commanders at Pearl Harbor, both naval and military, were unimpressed and continued to concentrate on their training programs rather than on making preparations for any sort of a surprise naval attack. No effective security patrol had been established.

On Saturday, Dec. 6, 1941, many army and navy personnel were on the usual weekend shore leave, some to return to their posts late that night and some early the next day. At about 3:30 A.M., local mean time, on Dec. 7, a patrolling minesweeper reported the presence of an unidentified midget submarine outside the harbor to the destroyer *Ward*, also on night patrol. No report was made to the commandant until the *Ward* radioed at 6:54 A.M. that it had sunk a submarine, but the information was delayed in reaching the high command; also the harbor gate had not been closed. Virtually the entire U.S. fleet of ninety-four vessels, including eight battleships, was concentrated at Pearl Harbor; the disposition of troops, airplanes, and antiaircraft guns made effective defense nearly impossible.

At 7:55 A.M. on Dec. 7, 1941—a "day that will live in infamy"—the first waves of Japanese bombers attacked airfields and the fleet, particularly the battleships, anchored in the harbor. A second wave came over at 8:50 A.M. Not a single American plane in the area could be got into the air except a fighter squadron at Haleiwa, some miles away, which the Japanese had overlooked. Several of the smaller vessels were able to get into action briefly against Japanese submarines. When the last attacking Japanese planes returned to their carriers at about 9:45 A.M. Pearl Harbor was a smoking shambles. The attackers were unopposed. Every American airplane was either destroyed or disabled; the battleships were sunk or disabled; and other naval craft in the harbor had suffered a like fate. Of the personnel in the area, 2,403 were lost; the wounded totaled 1, 176. Fortunately, the three carriers of the Pacific fleet were not in the harbor.

Word of the disaster reached Washington, D.C., at about 2:00 P.M., eastern standard time. The next day, Dec. 8, Roosevelt appeared before Congress and asked for recognition of a state of war. It was granted promptly, with one dissenting vote.

When the last attacking Japanese planes returned to their carriers at about 9:45 A.M., Pearl Harbor was a smoking shambles.

When news of the attack on Pearl Harbor reached the people of the United States, the nation was shocked that such a thing could happen at a time when it was generally known that relations with a boasting, belligerent Japan were strained almost to the breaking point. It was necessary for the president to do something without delay to satisfy public clamor, and so, on Dec. 18, 1941, he appointed a commission under the chairmanship of Owen J. Roberts of the U.S. Supreme Court to inquire into the matter and make an immediate report fixing the responsibility. The report, rendered in January 1942, placed the responsibility and the blame squarely on Rear Adm. H. E. Kimmel and Gen. Walter C. Short, the navy and army commanders at Pearl Harbor. There were many responsible people in and out of Washington who felt that the commission had not reached the heart of the matter, but merely produced scapegoats to satisfy the public—that Kimmel and Short had been sacrificed to political expediency. Both of them were relieved of their commands and retired. Adm. Harold R. Stark, chief of naval operations, was reduced in authority and transferred to an innocuous assignment in Great Britain; Gen. George C. Marshall, army chief of staff, went unscathed. It was generally considered that while none could be accused of culpable negligence, a lamentable lack of judgment could be charged to Kimmel, Short, and Stark.

As time passed, however, it came to be generally agreed that responsibility for their faulty evaluation must be shared by those in Washington who had been slow in relaying information about the fast-moving developments to the commanders in Hawaii. Moreover, everyone concerned had underestimated Japanese capabilities.

BIBLIOGRAPHY

E. J. King and W. M. Whitehill, *Fleet Admiral King: A Naval Record.*
Samuel Eliot Morison, *The Rising Sun in the Pacific, 1931–1942.*

— THOMAS ROBSON HAY

PENDLETON ACT

Pendleton Act (Jan. 16, 1883), the federal government's central civil service law, was written by Dorman B. Eaton, sponsored by Sen. George H. Pendleton of Ohio, and forced through Congress by public opinion. It exempted public officials from political assessments. The Civil Service Commission was reestablished to prepare rules for a limited classified civil service, which the president could expand at discretion. Competitive examinations were to determine the qualifications of applicants, while appointments were to be apportioned among the states according to population.

BIBLIOGRAPHY

C. R. Fish, *The Civil Service and the Patronage.*

— CHESTER MCA. DESTLER

PENNSYLVANIA GERMANS

Pennsylvania Germans, commonly but erroneously called "Pennsylvania Dutch," are a distinctive people with a history all their own and should not be confused with the general mass of German-Americans. Among the first settlers entering Pennsylvania under Penn's charter, they increased somewhat slowly at first, but after 1727, when the heavy Palatine immigration set in, their increase was rapid. At the time of the Revolution the Pennsylvania Germans composed about a third of the population of the province.

Settling in the southeastern part of the colony, between the English on the east and the Scotch-Irish on the west, they occupied a well-defined geographic area, frequently referred to as Pennsylvania-German Land, where they still predominate overwhelmingly. This region embraces the counties of Northampton, Lehigh, Berks, Lancaster, Lebanon, and York, and adjacent districts, although many Pennsylvania Germans are found elsewhere in the state. In the area occupied by them in predominant numbers they developed a distinctive civilization that, by reason of the Pennsylvania-Dutch dialect and a strong ethnic consciousness, together with a certain conservatism, tends to perpetuate itself. Although considerably modified by the assimilating influences about them, the distinctive characteristics of the Pennsylvania Germans have persisted to a remarkable degree, especially in the rural districts.

BIBLIOGRAPHY

Richard O'Connor, *The German-Americans.*
Ralph Wood, ed., *The Pennsylvania Germans.*

— WAYLAND F. DUNAWAY

PENTAGON PAPERS

The so-called Pentagon Papers comprise a forty-seven-volume study of the American involvement in the Vietnam War. Commissioned by Secretary of Defense Robert S. McNamara under the administration of President Lyndon B. Johnson, during an interval of impasse and frustration in the war, the study includes internal working papers from the four presidential administrations of the years 1945–68, with analytical commentary, or about 4,000 pages of documents and 3,000 pages of analysis, prepared by thirty-six military and civilian analysts. Initially, twenty sets of the papers were printed early in President Richard M. Nixon's administration, which largely ignored them until they were published in the *New York Times.*

While working for the Rand Corporation in 1969 in Santa Monica, Calif., which contributed to the Pentagon Papers study, Daniel Ellsberg decided that the American people should know about the actions of their government as depicted in the papers; aided by Anthony J. Russo, he copied the study and released it to newspapers. In 1971 the *New York Times* and other newspapers published the papers. After several installments appeared, the Justice Department obtained an injunction barring further publication. However, in *The New York Times* v. *United States* (1971), the Supreme Court ruled that the government failed to satisfy the exacting burden of proof necessary to justify prior restraint and had therefore infringed on the First Amendment's guarantees of freedom of the press.

Subsequently, Ellsberg and Russo were indicted for espionage, theft, and conspiracy; but in 1973, U.S. District Judge William M. Byrne, Jr., terminated the case on grounds of gross government misconduct. Byrne cited many violations of procedure and an alleged break-in by government officials at the office of Ellsberg's psychiatrist in a quest for evidence to discredit the defendant. During the case White House officials improperly approached Byrne concerning his possible appointment to the vacant Federal Bureau of Investigation directorship, which raised questions of propriety.

The Pentagon Papers are a mine of historical raw material, an inside view of government decisionmaking, available for scholarly scrutiny extraordinarily soon after the events they generated. The papers drew upon sealed files of the Defense Department, important presidential orders, and diplomatic papers. But the papers are also incomplete, for they do not include secret and important White House documents revelatory of presidential attitudes and purposes; nor do the papers include important and voluminous documents concerning the war's diplomacy.

The papers can be interpreted in conflicting ways, largely depending on the evaluator's own assessment of U.S. involvement in the Vietnam War: If it is deemed a horrendous mistake, the papers are a chronicle of failure, instigated by outmoded cold war doctrines and President John F. Kennedy's 1960 inaugural commitment to pay any price and bear any burden to bar the loss of further territory to Communist control. But the Pentagon Papers can also be interpreted as proving the viability of such concepts and as detailing the remarkable collaboration of four administrations, of both major parties, in perpetuating a commitment to an ally and in long pursuing a costly, eventually unattainable, goal—the prevention of victory in Vietnam to Communist forces.

The papers support several particular findings. For example, the war was closely controlled by civilian leaders; military leaders, reluctant to undertake the venture

Daniel Ellsberg, who "leaked" the Pentagon Papers, attends a Washington, D. C. conference sponsored by the Center for National Security Studies. Critics seeking accountability and control over the Central Intelligence Agency were called to testify, and the Senate Foreign Relations Committee authorized an investigation of evidence that official testimony had been misleading about the CIA's involvement in Chile. (UPI/Corbis-Bettmann)

and doubting its strategic significance, were constantly concerned that they would not be allowed to enlarge the war sufficiently to establish a clear advantage over Communist forces. And the papers reveal that the United States entered the war and increased its commitment always by thoroughly deliberated steps, not by casual decision or through faulty intelligence.

Although civilian leaders controlled the war, military considerations surpassed political factors at most stages. Each presidential administration was captive to a resolve not to abandon the war—not to repeat the 1938 appeasement of Munich (which American leaders well remembered), not to sacrifice Vietnam as Czechoslovakia had been sacrificed before World War II. The Pentagon

Papers reflect a belief in the domino theory, the supposition that the fall of one Asian nation into Communist hands would lead progressively to the fall of others. Even the Soviet-Communist China split did not raise doubts among American decisionmakers about the necessity of continuing the war. Each president, caught in a dilemma caused by anxiety to avoid defeat by a minor enemy and by fear of bringing Communist China or the Soviet Union into the war, was reluctant to escalate the war, a mood that was camouflaged by expansive public rhetoric urging the nation to "stay the course" and "pay the price."

The Pentagon Papers are replete with the cold, assured prose of efficiency experts, social-science gamesmanship, and probability theory: The war's choices are "options," countries and peoples are "audiences," and threats and escalations become "scenarios." They show that, generally, the executive decisionmakers constituted a tightly knit inner government that easily perpetuated itself from one presidency to the next.

BIBLIOGRAPHY

Mike Gravel, ed., *The Pentagon Papers.*
Lyndon Baines Johnson, *The Vantage Point.*

— LOUIS W. KOENIG

PEQUOT WAR

Pequot War (1636–37). Prior to any white settlement in Connecticut trouble had developed between Dutch traders and the Pequot, who were located in the southeastern part of the region and who claimed control over the tribes farther west. Capt. John Stone, an English trader, and several companions were killed by the Pequot on board their ship in the Connecticut River in 1633, as was Capt. John Oldham in 1636 at Block Island, at the entrance to Long Island Sound, which led to a fruitless attack by a Massachusetts Bay expedition.

Both sides began preparations for further hostilities. Capt. John Underhill with a score of men arrived early in 1637 to strengthen Saybrook Fort, located at the mouth of the Connecticut River, while in April some Pequot made an attack on Wethersfield further north, near Hartford, killing nine persons. It was this latter event that led the general court of the recently settled river towns—Windsor, Hartford, and Wethersfield—on May 1, 1637, to declare war on the Pequot. Ninety men were levied, supplied, and placed under command of Capt. John Mason. Accompanied by eighty Mohegan under Uncas, they soon made their way down the river to Saybrook. Joined by Capt. Underhill and twenty Massachusetts men, Mason took his party in boats to the country of the Narraganset, where he conferred with their chief, Miantonomo, and received further aid. A two-day march overland brought the party to the Pequot fort near present-day Mystic. The fort was surprised and burned (May 26). Only seven Indians escaped the slaughter. Mason and his men attacked a second Pequot stronghold two miles away the same night. About 300 braves from other Pequot towns decided that their only safety was in flight and started with their women and children for the Hudson River. Meanwhile, the Mason party, reinforced by forty Massachusetts men, returned to Saybrook, while Capt. Israel Stoughton and 120 additional Massachusetts men arrived at New London harbor. After a conference, it was decided to pursue the fleeing Pequot, who were soon caught in Sasqua swamp, near present-day Southport, Conn. Through the intervention of Thomas Stanton the women and children were led out of the swamp before the attack was made. The fight on July 13 resulted in the escape of about 60 Pequot and the capture of 180, who were allotted to the Mohegan, Narraganset, and Niantic and absorbed into their tribes. Many of those who escaped were hunted down, while chief Sassacus was slain by the Mohawk and his scalp sent to Hartford. The Pequot, as a separate tribe, ceased to exist.

BIBLIOGRAPHY

Alden T. Vaughan, *New England Frontier: Puritans and Indians, 1620–1675.*

— GEORGE MATTHEW DUTCHER

PERRY'S EXPEDITION TO JAPAN

In response to a growing desire in the United States for commercial relations with Japan, closed to foreigners for almost two and a half centuries except for a carefully restricted trade with the Dutch, President Millard Fillmore dispatched an expedition to Japan in 1852 under the command of Commodore Matthew Calbraith Perry. Its objectives were to arrange for the protection of American seamen and property involved in shipwrecks off the Japanese coast; to obtain permission for American vessels in the Asiatic trade to secure provisions, water, and fuel; and to induce the Japanese government to open up one or more of its ports for trade. A further goal suggested by Perry was the acquisition of one of the outlying Japanese islands for use as an American naval base or coaling station, but this proposed move was rejected by the president.

Perry's mission, although pacific in character, was intended to impress upon the Japanese, through a show of force, the determination of the United States to enter into treaty relations. Thus, a considerable squadron, first of four war vessels and later of seven, was provided Perry. A first visit was made to the Bay of Yedo (Tokyo) in July 1853, and Perry formally delivered a letter from President Fillmore to the emperor of Japan. Perry informed the Japanese authorities that he would return early the next year for a definite answer to the proposals embodied in the letter, and he then withdrew his ships to the China coast.

A second visit took place in February 1854, and conversations were commenced, near the site of present-day Yokohama, looking toward conclusion of a treaty of peace and amity. Perry's firm insistence on American rights, backed up by the strength of his naval force, and conditions within the empire combined to convince the Japanese authorities to abandon their traditional policy of seclusion. On Mar. 31, 1854, the Treaty of Kanagawa, opening Japan to trade and also providing for the care of shipwrecked Americans and for facilities to supply American ships, was duly signed.

BIBLIOGRAPHY

Foster Rhea Dulles, *Yankees and Samurai.*

Samuel Eliot Morison, *Old Bruin: Commodore Matthew C. Perry, 1794–1858.*

Matthew C. Perry, *The Japan Expedition, 1852–1854: The Personal Journal of Commodore Matthew C. Perry.*

— FOSTER RHEA DULLES

PETITION, RIGHT OF

Right of Petition guarantees a citizen the opportunity to communicate with his government. In the United States it arises from the First Amendment to the Constitution, which provides that "Congress shall make no law respecting . . . the right of the people peaceably to assemble, and to petition the Government for a redress of grievances." Most state constitutions make a similar provision, and the Supreme Court extended the First Amendment right of petition, through the Fourteenth Amendment, to prohibit infringement by a state, in *De Jonge* v. *Oregon,* 299 U.S. 353 (1937). Originally, peaceful assembly was part of the right to petition. Its independent standing shows both the early importance of petition and the growth of protected expression. Lobbying and bills for private relief are covered. The right has been extended beyond grievances to encompass anything within the jurisdiction of government, including issues of highest national policy. There is no right to action on a petition, only to consideration.

In 1215, Articles 40 and 61 of the Magna Charta established a limited right of petition to four of twenty-five English barons acting as guardians of the charter. Until 1414, when it declared itself "as well assenters as petitioners," even Parliament stood only as a petitioner. The Declaration of Right of 1689 protected the British subject from government retaliation for exercising the right of petition by providing that "Prosecutions for such Petitioning are Illegall." The use of petitions increased greatly in the 18th and 19th centuries but is now of little significance in Parliament and is limited by technical requirements.

Although the American Declaration of Independence proclaimed, "We have Petitioned for Redress in the most humble terms: Our repeated Petitions have been answered only by repeated injury," American history is marked by government opposition to the right of petition. Following passage of the gag resolutions of May 1836, which tabled petitions to abolish slavery, former president John Quincy Adams, then a representative from Massachusetts, said, "I hold this . . . to be a direct violation of the Constitution." But in January 1840 the House of Representatives enacted a standing rule providing "no petition . . . praying the abolition of slavery . . . shall be received by this House, or entertained in any way whatever." The rule was repealed in December 1844. Jacob Coxey's army of the unemployed invoked the right of petition in 1894, only to be arrested for walking on the grass of the Capitol. In 1918 petitioners seeking repeal of espionage, sedition, and military recruitment laws were jailed. Veterans petitioning Congress for bonuses were routed by soldiers and their camps burned in 1932.

What has become the American right of petition was slowly wrested from a monarch who originally did not have to hear any grievance.

The 1960's and 1970's witnessed a great increase in mass petitioning. In 1965, Martin Luther King, Jr., led petitioners from Selma to the state capitol in Montgomery, Ala., seeking the right of blacks to vote, but the governor failed to appear to receive their petition. The Poor People's Campaign in 1968 presented to all three branches of the federal government the most comprehensive petitions in American history, with the warning "Heed the poor, America." The Vietnam Veterans Against the War petitioned the Congress to end the war in Indochina, by activity ranging from formal testimony to hurling their medals for service, heroism, and combat wounds on the Capitol steps in 1971.

What has become the American right of petition was slowly wrested from a monarch who originally did not have to hear any grievance and could do no wrong for which redress could be obtained in law. The U.S. Supreme Court, in its first test of the right, said, "The very idea of a government, republican in form, implies a right on the part of its citizens . . . to petition for a redress of grievances" (*United States* v. *Cruikshank*, 92 U.S. 542 [1876]). No right more sensitively measures the vitality of a republic and its responsiveness to the people.

— RAMSEY CLARK

PHILADELPHIA RIOTS

On May 6–8 and July 5–8, 1844, riots in Philadelphia climaxed the first phase of American nativistic agitation. Both periods of rioting followed minor clashes between Irish Catholics and native political organizations. Disorder quickly spread, as Protestants, their antipathies heightened by antipapal propagandists and by a recent Catholic attempt to end Bible-reading in the public schools, began systematic attacks on foreigners. During the actual rioting, Philadelphia resembled a war-torn city: military companies fought in the streets, cannon were mounted in the public squares, Catholic churches were burned, and hundreds of immigrants' homes were sacked by pillaging mobs. A score of persons were killed and nearly 100 wounded before militia ended the mob rule. Public reaction against this violence contributed to the downfall of the American Republican party and sent the whole nativistic movement into temporary eclipse.

BIBLIOGRAPHY

Ray A. Billington, *The Protestant Crusade.*

— RAY ALLEN BILLINGTON

PHONOGRAPH

The concept of a device to record and reproduce sound goes back as far as Cyrano de Bergerac's *Comic History of the States and Empires of the Moon*, written in 1656. The prehistory of an actual instrument to record sound is at least as early as the Phonautograph of Léon Scott in Paris in 1857. This was used for recording and analyzing the pattern of sound waves as registered on the smoked surface of a metal cylinder. Because of the fragility of the film of lampblack it was not possible to play back the sound, nor is there any indication that such a course was even conceived. The machine did contain the essential elements later used in the phonograph, but it recorded laterally rather than vertically to the record surface, as Thomas A. Edison's machine did. Scott recorded on both cylinders and disks, and it may be that one of his instruments sparked the concept of Charles Cros, who in April 1877, twenty years later, lodged a sealed description of a proposed phonograph, including the name, with the French Academy of Sciences. This was published in October 1877. Meanwhile, on July 30, 1877, Edison filed a provisional specification with the British patent office and on Dec. 24, 1877, applied for a U.S. patent. His tinfoil phonograph was announced to the public in *Scientific American* on Nov. 17, 1877. As demonstrated at that time it was an impractical machine, little more than an interesting toy using fragile tinfoil records of little durability. He put it aside to devote his energies to developing the incandescent lamp, which promised greater returns.

In 1880, when Alexander Graham Bell received the $20,000 Volta Prize from the French Academy of Sciences for his work with the telephone, he founded the Volta Laboratory in Washington, D.C. Acoustical research, including work on both the telephone and the phonograph, was conducted at this laboratory. The most far-reaching result was a patent issued in 1886 to Chichester A. Bell and Charles Sumner Tainter, which included cutting the sound track into wax as opposed to indenting tinfoil, as described in Edison's patent. Although the issue was warmly contested, a distinction between the two methods was upheld by the courts, and Edison was obliged to operate under a license from the Bell and Tainter patent, although he had used the method before its issuance.

Early phonograph records gave little volume and were not durable. They had to be duplicated either mechanically by pantograph or acoustically. Neither method was satisfactory. These limitations were overcome by Emile Berliner in a series of patents between 1887 and 1895. The patents covered a wax-coated zinc disk on which the sound waves were cut laterally through the wax to the zinc. The exposed metal was then etched according to the pattern recorded in the wax. This process made a very durable loud-volume record described as sounding "like a partially educated parrot with a sore throat and a cold in the head." After several playings the harshest of the tones were softened, and the background or surface noise abated somewhat. A matrix or impression made from this original was successfully used to mold duplicates in hard rubber. The material was changed late in 1897 to a shellac composition, but it still depended on an etched zinc original.

In 1901 a patent was issued to Joseph W. Jones for cutting the original records in wax that was subsequently electroplated to allow duplication. The patent came as a surprise to Eldridge R. Johnson, who, in addition to manufacturing Berliner graphophones, had been making records by the same process, independently devised. After intense legal maneuvering Johnson was able to continue using the technique and in 1901 formed, with these records, the famous Victor Talking Machine Company. Edison met the challenge of greater volume and fidelity by perfecting his "gold molding" process, which had been initiated in 1892. Unfortunately, some of his earlier patents had revealed enough about the process to enable competitors to introduce successful records molded in Celluloid, a superior substance Edison was not able to use for many years because of patents held by others.

Although Edison's business expanded at a rapid rate for years, it never was able to overcome the lead taken by disk records and machines, particularly in the urban market. All aspects of the record business felt increasing competition from radio, starting in the 1920's. At the same time electricity began to be applied with very good effect to problems of the phonograph business that had never been satisfactorily resolved by purely acoustical and mechanical means. Electrical recording had been conceived and experimented with as early as 1882 by Berliner, but the telephone transmitter was too limited in tonal range for the successful conversion of music to electrical impulses.

Electrical recording was conceived and experimented with as early as 1882 by Emile Berliner.

A wire recorder foreshadowing tape recordings was invented in 1898 by the Danish electrical engineer Valdemar Poulsen, but it was largely unsuccessful for want of a suitable means of adequate amplification. The advent of the vacuum tube made suitable amplification easy, and mechanical recording became obsolete. The actual work was accomplished by Joseph P. Maxfield, H. C. Harrison, and associates at the Western Electric Company, the manufacturing branch of Bell Telephone, during 1924, making possible the manufacture of records that could reproduce a much greater range of cycles per second at a much higher volume. Coupled with the exponential horn advocated by Clinton R. Hanna and Joseph Slepian, these new records led to the creation of the Orthophonic Victrola, the last significant nonelectric phonograph to be produced. It was available with a record changer, not in itself a new development, but significant as the immediate forerunner of the coin-operated jukeboxes of the 1930's, produced by such makers as the Capehart, Seeburg, and Wurlitzer companies.

By that time all reproduction from records was electronic, following the trend set by recording techniques of a few years earlier. The new players were called radio-phonographs, and their history is closely allied to radio and high-fidelity technology. Record development made substantial advance in this era. During World War II, because of a shortage of shellac, a plastic, Vinylite, was substituted. This flexible material made the records unbreakable and greatly reduced surface noise. It was softer than the old shellac composition, and so it became desirable to reduce needle pressure. The weight of the needle was reduced, and a permanent sapphire needle was introduced, whose shape remained constant over a long time and closely conformed to the profile of the record groove, giving better support. This development made possible more closely spaced grooves and a longer playing time for each record. In 1948 the Columbia Record Company introduced microgroove records that made 33 1/3 revolutions per minute, the first to be made specifically for use only with a permanent stylus, the long-extinct Edison records excepted.

Electronics, low needle pressure and minimal record wear, very low surface noise, and long playing led to the development of stereophonic recording and playback, not a new concept but never before successfully implemented. A Parisian, Clément Ader, received a German patent for the telephone transmission of such sound in 1881, and various experiments were made in stereophonic radio broadcasting in the 1920's and 1930's. A. D. Blumlein of the Columbia Company in England patented, in 1930, a system of cutting the two separate recordings needed for stereo in one groove; one is recorded laterally and the other by the hill-and-dale technique. By early 1958 nine record companies were producing long-playing stereophonic records, and the necessary cartridges and switching gear were available at modest prices. This was the year stereo made its great leap into the consumer field. The greatest subsequent advance by the mid-1970's was the development of quadraphonic sound. This is achieved by either of two competing approaches. First to be marketed, in 1970, was the "Matrix" system invented by Peter Scheiber in 1969. The other is the "discrete" system originally developed by Victor of Japan between 1968 and 1971 and first introduced into the United States in 1972. Records in either system may be satisfactorily reproduced with all monaural and stereophonic equipment. Because of complex electronic requirements, reproduction in quadraphonic sound depends on compatible specialized equipment.

BIBLIOGRAPHY

William F. Boyce, *Hi-Fi Stereo Handbook.*

Roland Gelatt, *The Fabulous Phonograph, From Tin Foil to High Fidelity.*

Théodose Achille Louis Du Moncel, *The Telephone, the Microphone and the Phonograph.*

Harry F. Olson, *Modern Sound Reproduction.*

Oliver Read and Walter Welch, *From Tin Foil to Stereo, Evolution of the Phonograph.*

— EDWIN A. BATTISON

PHOTOGRAPHIC INDUSTRY

In 1839 the Frenchman Louis J. M. Daguerre introduced in Paris the first commercial photographic process, the daguerreotype. This novel process produced unique positive images on silvered plates that were exposed in cameras. Because of the perishability of the photosensitive materials and the complexity of the process, the practice of daguerreotypy, which soon became popular in the United States, was restricted to technically oriented persons who produced their own photosensitive materials at the site of the picture-taking. The daguerreotypists obtained the requisite optical apparatus from small optical instrumentmakers and chemical supplies from domestic and foreign chemical manufacturers. Within a decade the number of professional daguerreotypists increased substantially, and specialized photographic supply houses arose in the larger cities.

During the mid-1850's a variety of wet collodion processes replaced the daguerreotype. Fluid collodion served as carrier for the photosensitive halogen salts. At the site of exposure the photographer flowed the salted collodion onto glass for direct positive images in the ambryotype process, onto japanned iron plates for direct positive images in the tintype process, and onto glass for a negative from which a positive image was printed onto photosensitive paper in the popular negative-positive process. Owing to the perishability of the photosensitive negative and positive materials, their production remained with the professional photographers. The change in technology did influence many of the small producers of supplies for the photographer: for example, the Scovill Manufacturing Company of Waterbury, Conn., which had become the principal American producer of unsensitized daguerreotype plates, shifted its product line. While small producers of such new photographic supplies as tintype plates and unsensitized print paper did emerge in the 1860's and 1870's, the most powerful firms in the industry were the Anthony and the Scovill companies, which dominated the jobbing function in photographic supplies and also engaged in the production of photographic papers, chemicals, cameras, and albums.

In the early 1880's dry gelatin supplanted wet collodion as the carrier of photosensitive salts on negative glass plates. Because the gelatin carrier preserved the photosensitivity of the halogen salts for many months, the technological change permitted centralized factory production of photosensitive materials for the first time. The traditional marketing and production companies in the industry did not take the lead in producing plates and papers; new firms assumed production leadership—Cramer, Seed, and Hammer in Saint Louis; American Aristotype in Jamestown, N.Y.; Eastman in Rochester, N.Y.; Stanley in Boston; and Nepera Chemical in Yonkers, N.Y. Many of them developed marketing departments independent of the jobbing firms of Scovill and Anthony. Although gelatin plates simplified the practice of photography and increased the number of amateur photographers, the technical complexities still deterred most people from practicing photography.

In 1884 George Eastman, despairing of the intense price competition in the dry-plate market, sought with William H. Walker, a Rochester cameramaker, to develop an alternative to dry plates. Improving substantially on a commercially unsuccessful system sold by Leon Warnerke in the 1870's in Britain, they introduced in 1885 a roll-film system. It consisted of a roll holder that slid into the back of the camera instead of the glass plates, and it employed roll film as the negative replacement for the glass plate. Although the well-designed and mass-produced Walker-Eastman roll holder met with enthusiasm initially, the lack of transparency of the paper film first employed by Eastman and the technical complexity of the later stripping film discouraged professional and amateur photographers from adopting the system. Recognizing the failure of this carefully patented system, Eastman reconceived his market and the roll-film system. In 1888 he addressed the enormously large and previously untapped mass amateur market by isolating the technical complexities from picture taking and by providing factory service to perform the technical functions. He added to the company's established production of photosensitive materials by designing a simple-to-operate, highly portable roll-film camera, the Kodak, and by providing factory service that included the unloading and reloading of the camera with film and the developing and printing of the pictures. With a highly successful advertising campaign featuring the slogan "You press the button—we do the rest," Eastman inaugurated photography for novices and revolutionized the industry. During the next decade numerous improvements were introduced, including a Celluloid base for film and daylight-loading film cartridges. The Eastman Kodak Company's tight patent control on the film system and its policy of continuous innovation helped it establish and maintain an almost exclusive position in the market.

As Eastman Kodak grew in size, it sought to broaden and strengthen its nonamateur product line by acquiring, during the decade from 1898 to 1908, a number of photographic-paper, plate-camera, and dry-plate companies in the United States and in western Europe. Despite the existence of a number of large competitors—including Ansco (a merger of the two old firms of Anthony and Scovill), Defender, Cramer, and Hammer in the United States; Ilford in Britain; and AGFA in Germany—Eastman Kodak held a substantial market share in photographic materials and apparatus both at home and abroad by 1910. George Eastman helped the company maintain this position through his continued emphasis on product quality, innovations, and patents. In recognition of the increasing importance of chemistry and physics to the industry, Eastman established in 1912 the Eastman Kodak Research Laboratory and appointed as its director the British photochemist C. E. Kenneth Mees. Within a decade of its founding the laboratory began to have a direct influence on the output of the Eastman Kodak production lines.

The introduction of the roll-film system stimulated the development of cinematographic apparatus. Early in the 20th century, concurrent with the rapid growth of amateur photography, an American cinematographic industry began to emerge, with innovators in cine projection equipment assuming the initial leadership. At the end of the first decade of the century a number of firms producing apparatus and commercial films combined their patents and other assets to form the Motion Picture Patents Company. It sought, through the control of basic apparatus patents and of the distribution of unexposed film, to limit competition in the motion picture industry, but adverse court decisions in an antitrust suit and a series of product and marketing innovations brought about the demise of the organization within a decade. Large new corporations that integrated production, distribution, and exhibition functions—and employed such innovations as multireel films and motion picture stars—emerged by 1920 as the new leaders of the cine industry. These included Paramount, Fox, and Loew. The introduction of sound films in the late 1920's altered this structure somewhat as the innovators, Warner and RKO, joined the small group of leaders.

Meanwhile, the rapidly growing demand for raw cine film greatly stimulated film production at Eastman Kodak. After 1909 the production of cine film substantially exceeded the production for still photography. Although the company carefully avoided entry into the professional cine field, the territory of its largest customers, it did introduce home movie equipment with nonflammable film in the early 1920's. From the late 1920's onward the company developed and introduced a series of color processes for motion pictures. During the middle 1940's the motion picture industry enjoyed its greatest success, but soon the introduction of television inaugurated a quarter-century of decline. In response the industry introduced spectaculars; three-dimensional and widescreen productions; new exhibition methods, such as drive-in and shopping-center theaters to replace the giant downtown movie palaces of an earlier era; and, later, low-budget, sensational movies featuring sexuality and violence.

In still photography between World War I and World War II the German industry began to compete with the American. Whereas only minor improvements had been made in cameras for amateurs and in the reflex camera introduced to professional photographers at the turn of the century, German camera-makers, influenced by cinematography, introduced in the early 1920's small 35-mm cameras that appealed to journalists and serious amateur photographers. Also, in the late 1920's Ansco, which had faltered since its founding because of limited capital and technical resources, sold its assets to the I. G. Farben-Industrie and became the American outlet for the research-oriented German photographic industry. With the advent of World War II the U.S. government assumed ownership and operation of the firm, and the government relinquished ownership only in 1965, when the firm became a public corporation, General Aniline and Film (GAF).

In the post–World War II period four developments were of particular importance to the American industry. First, Eastman Kodak, as a result of its research and development, successfully introduced and promoted color-print photography. Second, Japan, manufacturer of high-quality miniature cameras for the serious amateur photographer, developed a dominant influence in that specialized sector of the American and international market. Third, in 1948 the Polaroid Corporation introduced to the market a new system of photography that produced finished prints direct from the camera. Edwin H. Land, designer of the Polaroid camera and principal researcher and shareholder in the firm, developed a well-protected system of patents that created an unassailable market position for his company. Fourth, Eastman Kodak, in response to the Polaroid challenge, introduced a series of Instamatic camera systems that further simplified negative-positive picture-taking. Three of these four developments reflect the importance of the research-and-development strategies and of the mass amateur-market emphasis of the American industry in its maintenance of international dominance in the 1970's despite the competitive efforts of German and Japanese firms.

BIBLIOGRAPHY

Reese V. Jenkins, *Images and Enterprise: Technology and the American Photographic Industry, 1839–1925.*

Robert Taft, *Photography and the American Scene.*

— REESE V. JENKINS

PHOTOGRAPHY

During the final decades of the twentieth century photography became easy for unskilled practitioners. The cumbersome method introduced by Louis J. M. Daguerre in 1839 had given way to affordable 35-mm compact automatics. Photographic images in silver, color dyes, and printers' ink had spread around the world. Innovations in moving film made faraway events accessible through simultaneous broadcast. Professional photographers were typically in the forefront of technology and trends. To compensate for the disappearance of skilled portraiture and documentation in the wake of the 35-mm revolution, photographers turned to publishing and advertising. Their camera of choice was a 2¼-inch format equipped with motor drives and used with multiple lenses and sophisticated artificial lighting. Fine-art photographers devoted considerable energy to experimenting with equipment, format, film, and paper, and their subjects tended toward the eclectic. Since the late 1940s they have attempted to capture "private realities," a quest that drew inspiration from such sources as Eastern religious philosophies, psychoanalytic theory, and abstract expressionist painting. The popularity of this form in the United States stemmed from the postwar economic boom, the ability of former military personnel to attend art schools and colleges at federal expense, and the founding of the Institute of Design, the Western Hemisphere version of the Bauhaus, which advocated a "new vision" of interpreting common places in personal ways. New vision photographers experimented with equipment and format, frequently contriving a final image from collages, montages, and multiple exposures.

The straight tradition popularized by Edward Weston remained the dominant but far from the only style in professional photography in the late twentieth century. A gifted photographer, educator, and author, Minor White encouraged his followers to reveal "things for what they are" as well as "for what else they are." His advocacy of the "equivalent image" produced a cultlike following in the 1960s that continued into the 1990s. White's influence led photographers with a mystic bent to seek spiritual oneness with nature. With large-format cameras they photographed such natural phenomena as gnarled trees, tumultuous ocean waves, and dew-tinged leaves and petals. Photographers like Walter Chappell and Paul Caponigro struggled to evoke the mystic divinity of nature itself. Aerialists like Bradford Washington went aloft to invest nature with stunning abstractions of shifting land masses and geometrical farmlands.

Photographers took to the streets in the 1950s and 1960s using handheld units to frame reality with sardonic or ironic twists. Like the painter Andy Warhol, these photographers opted for the vernacular and emblems of popular culture. Modern masters like William Klein, Garry Winogrand, and William Wegman chose human (and in Wegman's case, canine) interaction among artifacts, whereas Elliott Erwitt, who beginning in the late 1940s has taken pictures of everyday scenes from around the world, preferred symbols largely free of human encroachment, although one well-known sequence shows the world of humans from a dog's point of view. Bruce Davidson and Diane Arbus sought odd faces in out-of-the-way places and captured them with a dignity previously reserved for the wealthy and classically beautiful.

United Press International and the Associated Press, the largest news wire services in the U.S., began transmitting pictures electronically in 1987.

Underlying the achievements of all photographers since the 1970s were technological improvements in cameras. The single-lens reflex camera became smaller and more reliable, with large-format cameras revamped to fit the computer age. In 1972 the Polaroid camera was improved with the SX-70 system, which was in turn supplanted by the 600 system, featuring automatic focus, electronic flash, and battery together with high-speed color film. In the last quarter of the twentieth century both black-and-white and color-positive-and-negative film vastly improved in speed and resolution. Infrared film sensitive to light invisible to the human eye had wide use in science. In the 1990s both Agfa and Ilford marketed wide-latitude film that joined dye couplers with silver halides to form images.

Electronic cameras, introduced in the early to mid-1990s, became increasingly sophisticated and easy to use, producing high-resolution photos and spelling the end of film photographic processes in certain quarters, notably news coverage. In 1987 United Press International and Associated Press, the largest news wire services in the United States, began transmitting pictures electronically. Still-picture versions of camcorders or videocameras (which themselves gained wide use as observation and surveillance tools in prisons, hospitals, courts, schools, and banks and were employed to help diagnose injuries and perform such surgery as laparoscopy) came into being, and digital cameras enabled photographers to store pictures on computer chips, which can be downloaded and tinkered with on a personal computer, obviating the need for the darkroom. Despite industry predictions that digital cameras were poised to do to the traditional silver halide photography market what camcorders did to Super-8 home movies, their high cost made acquisition prohibitive to the average consumer, although a camcorder could be converted into a digital camera for under $200. Digital imaging and computer manipulation of photos led to the use of faked and "enhanced" pictures in magazines, on television, and in newspapers. A 1994 *Time* magazine cover featured a digitally altered image of O. J. Simpson's mug shot, taken when he was arrested for the murder of his former wife and one of her friends. Among applications by the scientific community was the use in 1994 of digital image processing of conventional photographs to reveal detailed views of the sun's corona during an eclipse.

BIBLIOGRAPHY

Ian Jeffrey, *Photography: A Concise History* (New York, 1981).

Beaumont Newhall, *The History of Photography: From 1839 to the Present*, 5th ed. (Boston, 1982).

Johann Willsberger, *The History of Photography* (Garden City, N.Y., 1977).

— EVELYN S. COOPER

PIEDMONT REGION

Piedmont region, geographically, the area of the eastern United States lying at the foot of the easternmost ranges of the Appalachian mountain system; historically, all the territory between these ranges and the fall line on the rivers. Below the falls many of the rivers are tidal estuaries, and the region is known as Tidewater. Upcountry and backcountry are other terms sometimes used to designate the Piedmont region. The division of the Atlantic coastal plain into two regions has been profoundly important in American history. The Tidewater region, settled first, became the locale of conservative planters, merchants, and politicians. The Piedmont region was settled later, primarily by less wealthy and less cultured individuals. There they became small farmers rather than great planters or merchants. Socially and economically democratic, Piedmonters were generally at odds with the Tidewater population. Early sectionalism in America was based mainly on this differentiation. The gradual elimination of political discrimination and improved transportation have decreased but not eradicated the sectional significance of the Piedmont region.

BIBLIOGRAPHY

Charles Henry Ambler, *Sectionalism in Virginia.*

— ALFRED P. JAMES

PIKES PEAK

Pikes Peak, a famous mountain, altitude 14,110 feet, located in the Front Range of the Rocky Mountains in El Paso County, Colorado, was discovered in November 1806 by Lt. Zebulon M. Pike. Pike failed to ascend the peak because of heavy snow. It was first ascended by Edwin James, J. Verplank, and Z. Wilson of Maj. Stephen H. Long's expedition on July 14, 1820; Long named the peak after James, but popular usage by trappers and others of the name "Pikes Peak' " led to an official name change. Pikes Peak is the center for the region of Garden of the Gods, Manitou Hot Springs, the Ute Pass Highway, and the Cripple Creek gold mines. It is of historical significance as a landmark of early traders and trappers and as the name of the region now known as Colorado. The discovery of gold in 1858 brought large numbers to the region. Although many returned home in disappointment, further discoveries in 1859 attracted thousands more who crossed the Plains with the slogan "Pikes Peak or Bust" and who gradually opened up the various mining camps near Pikes Peak or settled in the valleys of the state.

BIBLIOGRAPHY

Enos A. Mills, *Rocky Mountain Wonderland.*

John O'Byrne, *Pikes Peak or Bust.*

— MALCOLM G. WYER

PIKE'S SOUTHWESTERN EXPEDITION

Pike's Southwestern Expedition (1806–07), conducted by Lt. Zebulon M. Pike and a small band of U.S. soldiers, was organized to explore the Arkansas and Red rivers, to gather information about the abutting Spanish territory, and to conciliate the Indian tribes in the newly acquired territory of the United States extending southwestward toward Santa Fe and the Spanish border. Leaving Fort Bellefontaine (near Saint Louis) on July 15, 1806, the party traveled to the Pawnee towns in Kansas and then by way of the Arkansas River into Colorado. From here it crossed, in midwinter, the Sangre de Cristo Range to the Conejos, a tributary of the Rio Grande in New Mexico, and built a fort nearby. Learning of Pike's expedition in their territory, Spanish officials sent a detachment of soldiers to bring the men to Santa Fe. From there the Spanish authorities conducted Pike to Chihuahua and then by a circuitous route to the American border at Natchitoches, La., on July 1, 1807.

Pike's narrative, *An Account of Expeditions to the Sources of the Mississippi and Through the Western Parts of Louisiana*, published in 1810, afforded his countrymen their first description of the great Southwest, including military information valuable to the federal government. His men, few in number and poorly equipped, had braved possible Indian attack, the perils of starvation, the exposure of the Colorado Rockies in midwinter, and the prospect of perpetual confinement in a Spanish prison. Pike's journal was a valuable addition to the literature of New World exploration.

[See also Louisiana Purchase.]

BIBLIOGRAPHY

Elliott Coues, ed., *The Expeditions of Zebulon M. Pike.*
S. H. Hart and A. B. Hulbert, eds., *Zebulon Pike's Arkansaw Journal.*
M. M. Quaife, ed., *The Southwestern Expedition of Zebulon M. Pike.*

— M. M. QUAIFE

PIKE'S UPPER MISSISSIPPI EXPEDITION

Pike's Upper Mississippi Expedition (1805–06). The acquisition of Louisiana in 1803 initiated a notable period of western exploration in which Lt. Zebulon M. Pike played a leading role. On Aug. 9, 1805, he left Saint Louis with twenty soldiers on a 70-foot keelboat to explore the Mississippi River to its source, conciliate the Indians in the area, assert the authority of the United States over British traders, and procure sites for military posts. Near Little Falls, Minn., Pike built a log fort and traveled for weeks in midwinter by sled and toboggan, ascending to what he thought were the upper reaches of the Mississippi and falsely named Leech Lake as the source of the river. He also met with British traders, urging them to obey the laws of the United States, held councils with the Indians, and made geographical observations. He returned to Saint Louis on Apr. 30, 1806, with a record of achievement that won him the appointment to lead an expedition to the far Southwest. Although he had accomplished all that had been expected of him, the federal government neglected to follow up his achievement, whose chief practical result was its addition to existing geographical knowledge.

BIBLIOGRAPHY

Elliott Coues, ed., *The Expeditions of Zebulon M. Pike.*
W. W. Folwell, *History of Minnesota*, vol. I.

— M. M. QUAIFE

PILGRIMS

Pilgrims consisted of thirty-five members of an English Separatist church living in Leiden, the Netherlands, who, with sixty-six English sectarians and servants, sailed from Plymouth, England, on Sept. 16, 1620, on the *Mayflower* and founded Plymouth Colony in New England in December. Although outnumbered by the English contingent, the Leiden group were the prime movers and the backbone of the migration, and the Pilgrims are generally associated with the Leiden congregation of which they were a part. The congregation, one of many Puritan sects that opposed the Elizabethan Established Church settlement, originated at Scrooby, Nottinghamshire, England, an obscure village on a manor of the archbishop of York. Led by William Brewster, the archbishop's bailiff who had become a Puritan while at Cambridge, the sect formed as a Separating Congregationalist church between 1590 and 1607. By 1607 the congregation embraced 100 or more rural folk, including Elder Brewster; William Bradford, son of a prosperous Austerfield farmer; and John Robinson, nonconformist Cambridge graduate who became their minister in 1607.

A minority of Scrooby village, the congregation was perse-

The landing of the pilgrims at Plymouth Rock, in Massachusetts Bay, in December 1620. Plymouth Plantation was established by charter in the following year. (Corbis-Bettmann)

cuted by conforming neighbors and "investigated" by the Ecclesiastical Commission of York in November 1607. Thus, believing firmly in ecclesiastical independence and to avoid contamination in England, they determined to ensure religious and ecclesiastical purity by emigrating to Holland, where other English sectaries found liberty to worship and lucrative employment. After embarrassing difficulties with English officials, about 100 escaped to Amsterdam by August 1608, but Amsterdam heterodoxy troubled them. In May 1609, with Dutch permission, they settled at Leiden, where the local cloth industry largely employed their labors and the university stimulated their leaders. At Leiden the congregation approximately tripled in numbers (1609–18), and its polity and creed crystallized under the able leadership of Robinson and Brewster.

But as years passed they grew troubled and discontented. Their work was hard, their incomes small, and their economic outlook unfavorable. Their children were losing touch with their English background, and they lacked that ecclesiastical and civil autonomy deemed necessary for their purity and proper growth. Thus, they decided in the winter of 1616–17 to move to America, to the northern part of the Virginia Company's grant, under English protection, where they hoped to establish a profitable fishing and trading post. Deacon John Carver and Robert Cushman negotiated with the Virginia Company in the summer of 1617, hoping for official guarantees against English ecclesiastical interference. The Virginia Company encouraged them and gave them a charter (June 9, 1619). But they needed capital. When in February 1620 Thomas Weston, London Puritan merchant, proposed that they employ a charter that his associates held from the Virginia Company (dated Feb. 20, 1620, in the name of John Peirce and associates) and form a joint-stock company for seven years to repay financing of the trip, the Leiden people accepted. Specific terms were drawn up.

A bare majority, however, voted to remain in Leiden. The minority, taking Brewster as their "teacher," prepared to depart. A sixty-ton vessel, the *Speedwell*, was outfitted, and all was in readiness to sail when difficulties with the London financiers paralyzed the enterprise until June 10, when Cushman persuaded Weston to continue cooperation. The London associates hired the *Mayflower*, which by mid-July was provisioned and ready to sail. Aboard were some eighty men, women, and children, most of them engaged by Weston as laborers or servants, and probably not of the Separatist persuasion. On July 22 the Leiden people left Delftshaven in the *Speedwell* and joined the *Mayflower* at Southampton. There they quarreled over business terms with Weston, who finally left them "to stand on their own legs" and, with no settlement, they sailed on Aug. 15. But the *Speedwell* proved unseaworthy and, after repairs at Dartmouth and Plymouth, the decision was made to sail on the *Mayflower* alone. On Sept. 16, with some eighty-seven passengers, fourteen servants and workmen, and a crew of forty-eight, the *Mayflower* sailed from Plymouth. Only two of those aboard—Brewster and Bradford—came from the original Scrooby congregation.

After an uneventful voyage Cape Cod was sighted on November 19, north of the limit of their patent. There, deliberately abandoning their patent—which had given them legal departure from England—they determined to settle without legal rights on Massachusetts Bay. To quiet murmurs of the London men and maintain order, forty-one adult males drew up and signed the famous Mayflower Compact on Nov. 21, 1620, in which they pledged to form a body politic and submit to majority rule. The same day they landed in what is now Provincetown harbor. After considerable searching they discovered a harbor (Plymouth Harbor) on Dec. 21, landed the *Mayflower* there (Dec. 26), and spent the remainder of the winter building the town, combating illness (which reduced their number by forty-four by April). In March 1621, they chose a governor and other officers, but not until November 1621, when Weston arrived in the *Fortune*, did they come temporarily to terms with the London financiers and receive from the Council for New England a charter (dated June 11, 1621) that gave legal birth to Plymouth Plantation.

BIBLIOGRAPHY

William Bradford, *History of Plymouth Plantation.*

John Demos, *A Little Commonwealth: Family Life in Plymouth Colony.*

George D. Langdon, *Pilgrim Colony: A History of New Plymouth, 1620–1691.*

— RAYMOND P. STEARNS

PIONEERS

The terms "frontiersmen," "early settlers," and "pioneers" are applied indiscriminately in American history to those who, in any given area, began the transformation of the wilderness and the prairie into a land of homes, farms, and towns. In common usage, explorers, fur traders, soldiers, and goldseekers are not classed as pioneers unless they later settled down more or less permanently. They were the vanguard, the scouts of the westward movement. The pioneers constituted the shock troops of the main army.

Numerous differences with respect to region, period, and origin make it impossible to present a uniform description of the American pioneers. The English colonists were the first pioneers, but there were striking differences in character, purpose, and modes of life among the first inhabitants of such colonies as Massachusetts Bay, Pennsylvania, Virginia, and Georgia. The Germans and Scotch-Irish who pioneered the way into the interior of Pennsylvania and into the backcountry of Virginia and the Carolinas differed from their fellow settlers of English origin. By the time settlers began to pour over the mountains into the Mississippi Valley some of these differences were modified by the leveling effect of frontier experiences, but there were still noticeable variations in the types of pioneers and pioneer life. The first settlers in the various and distinct geographical regions of the Far West differed in some respects from each other and from the pioneers of the Middle West.

Some general similarities in character, motives, qualities, and life on the frontier may, however, be pointed out. It is safe to say that the pioneers as a class were people who had been in some degree and for some reason dissatisfied, maladjusted, or unsuccessful in the communities, whether in the United States or in Europe, from which they migrated. At the same time they were hardy, venturesome, optimistic, and willing to undertake the dangers and labors of taming the wilderness. The completely satisfied and the timid were not attracted to the outer fringe of civilization.

In general, pioneers as a class were people who had been somehow dissatisfied, maladjusted, or unsuccessful in the communities from which they migrated.

In one form or another, the desire to improve their economic status was undoubtedly the most universal and constant motive that impelled the pioneers westward. Cheap and fertile land was the most potent lure, and thus the term "pioneers" is confined largely to those who went west to take up land and make farms for themselves, although many were attracted by the opportunities for trade, mechanical occupations, and professional practice in newly established towns. Not all the pioneers were any more successful in their new homes than they had been in the places from which they came. A lengthy record of frontier failures, shiftlessness, and degeneration could be compiled from the writings of travelers and observers. Furthermore, numerous pioneers, finding their expectations too rosy-hued, sold out after a few years and went back to their native lands or towns.

Everywhere the lives of the pioneers were conditioned by the wilderness environment. Their homes were built of whatever materials the region afforded. The log cabin, with its earthen or puncheon floor, leaky roof, fireplace, and crude furniture, was the typical pioneer dwelling wherever trees were available. On the prairies, and especially in Kansas, Nebraska, and the Dakotas, the sod house took the place of the log cabin, whereas in some sections of the Southwest the adobe hut was the prevailing type of shelter. There is ample evidence that these crude and cheerless homes were often a severe trial to the wives and mothers. Their long days were filled with arduous and multitudinous tasks to be performed without what would now be regarded as the barest necessities. Both men and women suffered the psychological hardships of pioneer life—loneliness, fear of Indians, homesickness for relatives and old friends, and worry in times of sickness.

Unremitting toil was likewise the lot of the pioneer men whose visions were fixed on productive farms yielding a competence for themselves and their families. The task of clearing land covered with trees was one requiring strength and perseverance, and many years would pass before a quarter-section farm could be completely freed of trees and stumps. A small clearing was first made for vegetables, and thereafter for several years the pioneer farmer devoted himself alternately to planting and caring for crops among trees deadened by girdling and to cutting down trees, rolling them into piles, burning or splitting them into fence rails, and afterward digging, chopping, and burning out the tenacious stumps. On the prairies the work of preparing land for cultivation was less difficult, but the breaking of the tough sod was by no means an easy task.

Food was usually plentiful. Pork was the meat most widely eaten in pioneer days, supplemented by wild game as frequently as possible. Wild fruits were available in some sections. Vegetables were raised in considerable variety, and corn in the form of cornmeal or hominy was a customary feature of the diet. Clothing as a rule was homemade of linsey-woolsey, a combination of linen and wool; and not infrequently the father made the shoes for the family.

With allowance for some exceptions, the pioneers as a whole were not a healthy people. The first settlements were often in the forests or on lowlands along streams. Poorly constructed dwellings and the exposure of pioneer life resulted in weakened constitutions. Because of these and other factors, epidemics frequently took a terrible toll in frontier communities. The rate of infant mortality was extremely high, and early graves claimed a shockingly great proportion of the mothers.

Pioneer life, however, was not all hardship, labor, and suffering. The pioneers were known generally to be a gregarious people, who seized every possible occasion to get together with their neighbors—at cabin raisings, logrollings, corn huskings, quilting parties, weddings, and camp meetings. They were generous and hospitable to strangers and travelers. All told, they were people well fitted to lay the foundations of civilization in the wilderness.

BIBLIOGRAPHY

Ray Allen Billington, *Westward Expansion: A History of the American Frontier.*

Bernard De Voto, *Year of Decision, 1846.*

David Lavendar, *Westward Vision: The Story of the Oregon Trail.*

C. F. McGlashan, *History of the Donner Party, A Tragedy of the Sierras.*

George R. Steward, *The California Trail: An Epic With Navy Heroes.*

— DAN E. CLARK

PIRACY

From the early 17th century to the early 19th century the Atlantic and Gulf coasts were the sites of operations for numerous pirates who preyed on American shipping and caused great losses in ships and lives.

From New England's earliest settlement, its shipping suffered from pirates on its coast. In 1653 Massachusetts made piracy punishable by death; and its governors sometimes sent out armed ships to attack offshore pirates. On the other hand, colonial governors after 1650 granted "privateering" commissions to sea desperadoes and winked at their piracies—a popular procedure then. The Navigation Acts, passed by Great Britain from 1650 to 1696 halted all foreign ships from trading in the American colonies and led to colonial smuggling and eventually to piracy. Colonial merchants and settlers bought pirates' stolen goods and thus obtained necessary commodities at a cheap price. New York, Newport, R.I., and Philadelphia were rivals in this scandalous trade, with Boston, Virginia, and the Carolinas also buying stolen goods.

Richard Coote, Earl of Bellomont, was appointed governor of New York and New England in 1697 with orders to "suppress the prevailing piracy that was causing so much distress along the coast" and in that same year reported general colonial connivance with pirates, especially in New York, Rhode Island, and Philadelphia. One New York merchant secured $500,000 in seven years through the promotion of piracy.

The highest number of piracies was committed during the period 1705–25, and 1721–24 saw a reign of terror on the New England coast. English men-of-war ended this peril, but after the American Revolution piratical attacks on U.S. ships by French "privateers" brought on an undeclared war between France and the United States and led to the creation of the U.S. Navy. Piratical operations of English men-of-war on U.S. coasts and the high seas—including the impressment of American seamen—led to the War of 1812. The period 1805–25 witnessed a resurgence of piracy, which led to the maintenance and increase of the U.S. Navy, then busy at suppressing piracy and convoying ships. Over 3,000 instances of piracy were recorded between 1814 and 1824—half of them on U.S. shipping.

Beginning in 1805 the navy was engaged in warring on pirates on the Louisiana and Gulf coasts, which had long been haunted by pirates. The Barataria pirates were driven out in 1814, as well as the Aury-Laffite pirates from Galveston, Texas, in 1817. In 1816–24 the United States faced a perplexing problem in handling the piratical "privateers" of the new Latin-American republics. Congress finally was so angered by these freebooters' depredations that in 1819 an act was passed prescribing the death penalty for piracy.

The Spaniards of Cuba and Puerto Rico sent out many pirates who captured American ships, murdered their crews, and nearly brought on a war between the United States and these two colonies of Spain. Congress denounced "this truly alarming piracy" in 1822, and in 1823–24 dispatched a strong naval squadron to suppress these pirates. By 1827 piracy had ended on all U.S. coasts.

BIBLIOGRAPHY

George Francis Dow and John H. Edmonds, *The Pirates of the New England Coast.*

Gardner W. Allen, *Our Navy and the West Indian Pirates.*

George Wycherley, *Buccaneers of the Pacific.*

— GEORGE WYCHERLEY

PLANK ROADS

Plank roads, introduced into the United States from Canada about 1837, were first constructed in the state of New York and were widely adopted in South Carolina, Illinois, Ohio, and Michigan. Thousands of miles were built at a mileage cost of from $1,000 to $2,400. Roadways were first well drained, with ditches on either side. Then planks, 3 or 4 inches thick and 8 feet long, were laid at right angles to stringers, which were placed lengthwise on the road. Planks were prepared by portable sawmills that were set up in neighboring forests. For a time plank roads successfully competed with railroads, but were eventually replaced by paved roads.

BIBLIOGRAPHY

B. H. Meyer, *History of Transportation in the United States Before 1860.*

— CHARLES B. SWANEY

PLANTATION SYSTEM OF THE SOUTH

Plantation system of the South was developed to meet the world demand for certain staple crops. While in 17th-century England the word "plantation" meant a colony, the relationship between the London Company and its plantation—Virginia (1607–24)—meant far more than that. The company transported the settlers, who were to be laborers, provided the taskmasters, fed and clothed the workers, and received the proceeds of their labor. Ten years' experience revealed numerous defects in operating a whole colony as one estate. Consequently, the company's possession was divided into smaller industrial units and private ownership granted; and when Virginia passed to the English crown (1624), it became a commonwealth of independent farms and private plantations. While tobacco was already known and used in England, the discovery in 1616 of a new method of curing it increased the demand and spurred large-scale production. The demand for labor thus created was filled by African slaves brought to the New World by Dutch traders, resulting in the adaptation of slaves to the system. This was the distinguishing feature of the plantation industry, because the racial factor and slave status of the laborers produced a fairly rigid regimentation. By the end of the 17th century the Virginia system was a model for the other southern colonies.

As finally evolved, the system employed large laboring forces (1,000 acres and 100 slaves was considered a highly productive unit), a division of labor, and a routine under the direction of a central authority to produce tobacco, rice, sugar, and cotton in large quantities for domestic and foreign markets. While tobacco and rice were important in the evolution of the system, cotton was the greatest force in making it dominant in southern economic life. The introduction of sea island cotton into Georgia (1786) and the invention of the cotton gin by Eli Whitney (1793) made possible the profitable growing of short staple cotton, and enabled the South to supply the English textile industry with the commercial quantities of raw cotton so urgently demanded. In 1800 the South exported 35,000 bales, in 1820 more than 320,000, and in 1860, 5 million bales. The plantation industry was in reality the "big business" of the antebellum South.

While seemingly affluent, the plantation system was financially dependent on the eastern cities, especially New York, where cotton was marketed.

The plantations were self-sustained communities, with slave quarters, storehouses, smokehouses, barns, tools, livestock, gardens, orchards, and fields. The slaves were usually worked in gangs, although the task system was not uncommon; skilled slaves were employed in their special capacity; and care was taken to keep as large a number of slaves as possible busy throughout the year. The larger the plantation the more highly organized it was apt to be. In the absence of the owner, the establishment was directed by his agent, usually the overseer.

Climate and soil largely determined the location of the plantation system. The upper South (Maryland, Virginia, Kentucky, North Carolina) produced tobacco; the South Carolina and Georgia tidewater produced sea island cotton and rice; the rich bottoms of Louisiana, sugar cane; and throughout the Piedmont region short staple cotton held sway. Because slave labor was used, the "black belts" were identical with the plantation zones. After its development in Virginia, the plantation regime spread southwest with the national territorial expansion, until in 1860 most of the climatic zone available for staple production was affected.

The entire social and economic life of the South was geared to the plantation industry, although in 1850 two-thirds of all the white people of that section had no connection with slavery, and 1,000 families received over $50 million per year in contrast with about $60 million for the remaining 666,000 families. This concentration of wealth produced an economic power that dominated every field, similar to that of the northern industrial magnates of 1880.

While seemingly affluent, the plantation system was financially and commercially dependent on the eastern cities, especially New York. Such dependency reduced southern cities to mere markets and sent fluid capital as payment for insurance, freights, tariffs, and warehouse fees to New York and Philadelphia. Cotton was usually marketed through New York, and plantation supplies were purchased there or from northern agencies in the South. Soil exhaustion and erosion increased with the expansion of agriculture, the causes being the nature of the southern terrain, improper methods of cultivation, the lack of commercial fertilizer (before 1850), together with the continuous cultivation of the staples on the same land. A more efficient organization and operation of the system was imperative by 1860.

The plantation system with slave labor was destroyed by the Civil War and the decade of Reconstruction that followed. Some plantations operated thereafter on a crop-sharing basis under a centralized authority, as for example "Dunleith," in the Yazoo-Mississippi delta. Others operated on a wage-labor basis, but the vast majority broke up into small farms, operated by the individual owner, tenant, or sharecropper.

BIBLIOGRAPHY

John W. Blassingame, *The Slave Community.*

Eugene D. Genovese, *The World the Slaveholders Made: Two Essays in Interpretation.*

Robert M. Myers, ed., *The Children of Pride.*

— RALPH B. FLANDERS

PLASTICS

Natural plastics include horn, hoof, shell, shellac, and certain tars; animal horn, hoof, and tortoiseshell are albumenoids called keratin. Horn is plasticized by boiling water and then may be split, flattened, and delaminated along the annual growth rings. These thin laminates are molded, self-bonded, colored, carved, and machined. Animal-hoof glues are basic adhesives.

From horn, the horners, or hornsmiths, who came to America from England early in the 18th century fabricated combs, buttons, spoons, and other products; their lanthorn windows were converted to glass after 1740.

Combmaking from horn and shell was a business concentrated in Leominster, Mass., and Leominster plastics pioneers adapted to Celluloid, Bakelite, and acetate as the industry matured. Molding, extrusion, and calendering of plastics were pioneered by the rubber industry. The basic Edwin Chaffee rubber calender of 1833 is still used for coating fabrics and paper with vinyl, polyethylene, and other plastics. Molders of plastics followed the mold and pressing procedures of the rubber workers as they started to mold gutta-percha and shellac.

Gutta-percha, a rubberlike product of several trees of Malaysia, was introduced in Europe in 1832, and gutta-percha became the generic name for molded plastics, even though they were molded of shellac, rubber, or the pitch-bonded fillers. Shellac preparations, especially shellac-bonded wood flour, became important for molding and laminating and continued in that use until replaced by synthetics after World War II; shellac was the principal material used in phonograph records before the appearance of vinyl.

Nitrocellulose, a product of the action of nitric acid on cotton, was discovered in Germany in 1845. Its flammability ultimately brought it into use as a military propellant, under the name "guncotton." Solutions of nitrocellulose left, on evaporation, a plastic film that was called collodion, used in photography as early as 1851. At the same time, the compounding of nitrocellulose with other materials, especially camphor, was found to yield a bulkier plastic material. Introduced in England, molded nitrocellulose products were popular but less than satisfactory until technically improved by John W. Hyatt of Albany, N.Y., who introduced injection molding, solvent extrusion (forcing molten plastics through an opening), blow molding (similar to glass blowing), and other fabrication techniques. Hyatt's Celluloid, as he called it, introduced in 1869, made possible George Eastman's roll-film camera; Thomas A. Edison's motion picture; new forms of dentures, spectacle frames, collars, and side curtains; and a host of novelties. It also gave rise to a worldwide business and spawned many companies in the United States. The Celluloid Manufacturing Company (later Celanese), established in 1871, gave birth to the Hercules Plastics Corporation and the Atlas Powder, Nixon Nitration, and Foster Grant companies.

The combustibility of Celluloid placed a severe limit on its use, and a continuous attempt to produce similar, but nonflammable, plastics by reacting cotton with acids other than nitric acid yielded a cellulose acetate resin about 1890. One of its first uses was in the coating of airplane wings, but in 1908 it was replacing Celluloid in photographic film.

Bakelite, made from phenol and formaldehyde, is often considered the first truly synthetic plastics material, as its ingredients are not found in nature in a pure form. It takes its name from Leo H. Baekeland, a Belgian immigrant to the United States, who devoted the years 1902–10 to an attempt to reduce to a usable form the sticky product of certain organic reactions. The resin he succeeded in hardening by heat appeared just in time to serve as an insulating material in the embryonic electrical and automotive industries. Bakelite triggered the explosive growth of industrial plastics materials and remains one of the most important of them.

Other new plastics materials appeared with increasing frequency, including new urea resins resembling Bakelite. The process of thermosetting appeared in 1928, acrylics and polyethylene in 1931, vinyl resins in 1933, melamine in 1937, styrene about 1937, Teflon and epoxy in 1938, nylon in 1939, silicones in 1943, polypropylene in 1954, plastic foams (for example, urethane) about 1955, polycarbonate in 1959, and polysulfone in 1965.

Many of these materials had been discovered in the mid-19th century, when chemists—almost exclusively Europeans—were studying the properties of newly isolated organic compounds. Many of them exhibited polymerization, the property of agglomerating into large molecules having plastic properties for which nobody at the time felt any need. The early manufacturers naturally suggested uses, but their principal problem was in giving the plastics materials a usable form, and this was largely a mechanical problem. Hyatt had pioneered in the use of heat and pressure, extrusion, and blow molding. But these innovations were merely the beginning of plastics-forming technology, and subsequent improvements owed almost as much to European as to American enterprise. In the United States the Tennessee Eastman Company in particular developed cellulose acetate; E. I. Du Pont de Nemours, Celanese; and the research firm of Arthur D. Little concerned itself with the improvement of industrial thermoplastic resins. James T. Bailey, a glass technologist, in 1938 developed an automatic machine combining hot extrusion with blow molding for the manufacture of bottles. In 1947 he developed the "layflat tubing process" for film manufacture. In 1937 Ellis Foster introduced low-pressure molded plastics with glass filament reinforcement. W. H. Willert's reciprocating screw plasticizer-plunger of 1952 facilitated both injection and blow molding.

By the mid-1970's plastics were proven to be one of the answers to many of the pollution and waste disposal problems. Biodegradable materials had become available, and all plastics could be burned to convert their total energy values into heat. Flame retardant additives eliminated the combustion hazards that were present in the early plastics.

BIBLIOGRAPHY

J. Harry DuBois, *Plastics History, USA.*

Williams Haynes, *Cellulose, The Chemical That Grows.*

Carl B. Kaufman, *Grand Duke, Wizard and Bohemian—A Biographical Profile of Leo Hendrik Baekeland.*

M. Kaufman, *The First Century of Plastics.*

John K. Mumford, *The Story of Bakelite.*

— J. HARRY DUBOIS

PLATT AMENDMENT

Platt Amendment was the basis for Cuban-American relations from 1901 to 1934. Following the Spanish-American War the problem of the future relations between the United States and Cuba became a matter of earnest consideration in both countries. For the purpose of finding a solution, Gen. Leonard Wood, head of the U.S. military government in Cuba, convened the Cuban constituent assembly on Nov. 5, 1900, and instructed it to render an opinion on what the future relations "ought to be." Two unsatisfactory proposals were later submitted, whereupon the United States drew up its own plan. Although much of it was drafted by Secretary of War Elihu Root, it became known as the Platt Amendment after Sen. Orville H. Platt of Connecticut, chairman of the Senate committee on Cuban relations. To insure its passage it was attached as a rider to the army appropriations bill for the fiscal year ending June 13, 1902. It contained eight articles, the substance of which were: (I) Cuba was to make no treaty that would impair its independence, nor was it to alienate Cuban territory to a foreign power; (II) Cuba was not to assume or contract any public debt beyond its ability to meet out of "ordinary revenues"; (III) Cuba was to permit the United States "to intervene for the preservation of Cuban independence, the maintenance of a government adequate for the protection of life, property and individual liberty, and for discharging the obligations with respect to Cuba imposed by the Treaty of Paris on the United States now to be assumed and undertaken by the government of Cuba"; (IV) all acts of the United States during the occupation were to be validated; (V) Cuba was to continue the sanitation program started by the United States and, if necessary, extend it; (VI) title to the Isle of Pines was to be decided later; (VII) coaling and naval stations chosen by the United States were to be sold or leased; (VIII) the articles were to be embodied in a permanent treaty with the United States.

When the articles were submitted to the Cuban convention with the demand that they be incorporated into the Cuban constitution, a storm of indignation arose. The convention at first refused to agree and sent a delegation to Washington to protest. Particularly objectionable was Article III, which was viewed as depriving Cuba of its sovereign rights. In spite of assurances given by Root that the United States interpreted its right to intervene as applying only when Cuban independence was threatened by internal anarchy or foreign attack, the convention continued to balk. Not until the United States threatened to remain in the island did the convention, on June 13, 1901, agree to accept it. On May 22, 1903, the articles were written into a formal treaty. The arrangement, never popular in Cuba, aroused increasing bitterness as time went on, especially when later administrations at Washington showed a tendency to ignore the Root interpretation. While armed intervention was seldom resorted to, except in 1906–09 and again in 1917, there were numerous occasions when the United States exerted pressure of some sort. This so-called "intermeddling and interference" strengthened the demand for the repeal of the Platt Amendment, to which the United States acceded on May 29, 1934.

BIBLIOGRAPHY

David F. Healy, *The United States in Cuba, 1898–1902: Generals, Politicians, and the Search for Policy.*

— L. J. MEYER

PLEDGE OF ALLEGIANCE

As part of the celebration to mark the 400th anniversary of the discovery of America, President Benjamin Harrison in 1892 called for patriotic exercises in school. The pledge of allegiance, taken from a children's magazine, the *Youth's Companion,* was first recited by public-school children as they saluted the flag during the National School Celebration held that year. In 1942 Congress made the pledge part of its code for the use of the flag.

The Pledge of Allegiance, taken from a children's magazine, the Youth's Companion, *was first recited by public school children in 1892.*

Authorship of the pledge was claimed by Francis Bellamy, an associate editor of the *Youth's Companion,* in 1923. The original wording was expanded by the National Flag Conference of the American Legion in 1923 and 1924, and the words "under God" were added by Congress in 1954. The text of the pledge is as follows: "I pledge allegiance to the flag of the United States of America and to the Republic for which it stands, one Nation under God, indivisible, with liberty and justice for all."

— NORMA FRANKEL

PLESSY V. FERGUSON

Plessy v. *Ferguson,* 163 U.S. 537 (1896), upheld the validity of an 1890 Louisiana statute that required railroads operating in that state to provide "equal but separate accommodations for the white and colored races." For nearly sixty years after the *Plessy* decision the separate-but-equal doctrine enabled states to legislate segregation of races in almost all areas of public activity. In *Gong* v. *Rice,* 275 U.S. 78 (1927), the Court decided that a child of Chinese ancestry who is a citizen is not denied equal protection by being assigned to a public school provided for black children, when equal facilities are offered to both races.

Beginning in 1938, cases in the field of higher education foreshadowed the demise of the separate-but-equal doctrine, but it was not until the landmark ruling in *Brown* v. *Board of Education of Topeka* (1954) that the Supreme Court categorically held that "separate educational facilities are inherently unequal" and consequently a violation of the equal protection clause of the Fourteenth Amendment. After *Brown,* the Court quickly extended its desegregation principle to all varieties of public facilities, such as parks and golf courses. Although not explicitly overruled by the Court, the separate-but-equal formula, first enunciated in *Plessy,* has been tacitly buried as a legal doctrine.

BIBLIOGRAPHY

Alexander M. Bickel, "The Original Understanding and the Segregation Decision," *Harvard Law Review,* vol. 69 (1955).
Harold W. Chase and Craig R. Ducat, eds., *Corwin's Constitution and What It Means Today.*
J. Skelly Wright, "Professor Bickel, the Scholarly Tradition, and the Supreme Court," *Harvard Law Review,* vol. 84 (1971).

— HAROLD W. CHASE AND ERIC L. CHASE

POCKET VETO

Pocket veto, an indirect veto by which a U.S. president negates legislation without affording Congress an opportunity for repassage by an overriding vote. The Constitution (Article I, Section 7) provides that measures presented by Congress to the president within ten days of adjournment (not counting Sundays) and not returned by him before adjournment fail to become law. They are said to have been pocket vetoed. First employed by President James Madison, the pocket veto has been used by every president since Benjamin Harrison. Between 1789 and September 1972, 955 of the 2,260 vetoes recorded—or 42 percent—were pocket vetoes. During that period nine presidents, the last of whom was Dwight D. Eisenhower, pocketed more measures than they returned to Congress disapproved. Controversy over the practice has focused on the definition of "adjournment": presidential usage has included brief recesses, whereas congressional critics have argued that the term intends only lengthy or *sine die* adjournments.

BIBLIOGRAPHY

Joseph E. Kallenbach, *The American Chief Executive: The Presidency and the Governorship.*

— NORMAN C. THOMAS

POLAR EXPLORATION

Exploration of the polar regions from North America began with the expedition of the 60-ton vessel *Argo* from Philadelphia in 1753 to explore, survey, and map the coast of Labrador to the entrance into Hudson Bay. John Churchman's petition to Congress in 1789 to subsidize his proposed expedition to Baffin Land (now Baffin Island) for scientific observations was rejected. Sealers and whalers—especially from New England—approached the arctic waters in Smith Sound and, in Antarctica, reached the Antarctic Peninsula. James Eights, a geologist on the Palmer-Pendleton sealing and exploring expedition to antarctic waters in 1829–31, postulated an antarctic continent. The U.S. exploring expedition of 1838–42 under Charles Wilkes explored, surveyed, and mapped the edge of the antarctic continent in the area near the Antarctic Peninsula and for 1,500 miles along the coast of East Antarctica, now called Wilkes Land.

Systematic exploration of the polar regions by the United States began in the 1840's. Inspired in part by a humanitarian interest in searching for Sir John Franklin's expedition, lost in the Canadian Archipelago, it was also in response to the clamor of sealers and whalers for arctic maps and geographical information and in response to the burning scientific interest of Matthew Fontaine Maury in the Arctic, especially its so-called open polar sea. As head of the U.S. Navy's Depot of Charts and Instruments, Maury was directly responsible for sending the first (Edwin Jesse De Haven, 1850–51) and second (Elisha Kent Kane, 1853–55) Grinnell expeditions into the North American Arctic, in which Kane reached 80°40′, and for encouraging the Isaac I. Hayes expedition (1860–61), in which Hayes reached 81°35′. These expeditions opened the route to the North Pole through Smith Sound. The navy also dispatched an exploring expedition, under John Rodgers and Cadwalader Ringgold (1853–56), to the North Pacific Ocean and into the Arctic Ocean to Wrangel Island to explore, survey, and map. In the late 1850's Maury sought in vain to get the active cooperation of the major nations in an assault on the South Pole combined with an exploration of Antarctica.

The Civil War delayed further official efforts in polar exploration until the ill-fated U.S.S. *Polaris* expedition under Charles Hall (1871–73) to the northeast coast of Greenland, during which Hall died and crew members suffered a very severe winter. In a disastrous expedition, the U.S.S. *Jeannette* under George De Long (1879–81) penetrated the Arctic Ocean through the Bering Strait, was beset in the ice, and for more than two years drifted west across the top of Siberia to a point near the mouth of the Lena Delta, where it was crushed. The purchase of Alaska in 1867 initiated a broad program of exploration, surveying, and mapping by various government agencies—notably the Geological Survey, Coast and Geodetic Survey, navy, army, and revenue service—that has continued to the present. During the International Polar Year (1882–83) the Army Signal Office established stations at Point Barrow, Alaska, under P. Henry Ray and in Lady Franklin Bay (Fort Conger), Ellesmere Island, under A. W. Greely, from which extensive explorations and surveys were made of Ellesmere Island and the north coast of Greenland.

From 1885 to 1920 the dominant effort in polar exploration was to attain the North Pole. Although these explorations were private, they did have varying amounts of federal aid and active support. Most important were the seven successive explorations of Ellesmere Island, northern Greenland, and the adjoining Arctic Ocean by Robert E. Peary (1886–1909) that resulted in his reaching the North Pole on Apr. 6, 1909. Others include Frederick A. Cook's explorations of Ellesmere and Axel Heiberg islands (1907–09); and the Baldwin-Ziegler (1901–02) and the Fiala-Ziegler (1903–05) expeditions to Franz Josef Land in ill-fated attempts to reach the pole. The Jesup North Pacific expedition (1897–1902) and the Harriman Alaska expedition (1899) were privately subsidized scientific explorations, as were the National Geographic Society glaciological surveys of Alaska (1912–19). The Crocker land expedition, led by Donald B. MacMillan (1913–17), explored extensively in northwestern Greenland and Ellesmere Island. U.S. polar exploration had become almost exclusively arctic-oriented, although shortly after his return from the north in 1909 Peary strongly advocated sending expeditions to Antarctica, and at about the same time, Robert C. Murphy began his long life of scientific research in Antarctica with his ornithological and other observations in South Georgia (1912–13).

The introduction of the airplane into polar exploration changed the character and extent of U.S. activity by private as well as by government agencies between 1919 and 1941. Four U.S. Army Air Service aircraft flew from New York City to Nome, Alaska (1920). This was followed by a succession of momentous flights that went far in opening to view extensive areas of both the Arctic and the Antarctic. The arctic flights included the Roald Amundsen–Lincoln Ellsworth flight in 1925 from Spitsbergen north across the Polar Sea to eighty-eight degrees north latitude; the Donald B. MacMillan–U.S. Navy (Richard E. Byrd) expedition (1925) to northwest Greenland, with flights by Byrd especially into Ellesmere Island; Byrd's flight from Spitsbergen to the North Pole and return in 1926; the George Hubert Wilkins–Carl Ben Eielson flight from Point Barrow, Alaska, across the Arctic Ocean to Spitsbergen in 1928; Wilkins' extensive flights and surveys of the Arctic Ocean north of Canada toward the pole in 1937–38; and Charles A. Lindbergh's survey flight of Greenland in 1931 for an arctic air route.

Significant terrestrial scientific explorations during the interwar years include those of Louise A. Boyd in the Norwegian and Greenland seas and along the east coast of Greenland (1928–41); the first exploration by a submarine, the *Nautilus*, below the ice of the Arctic Ocean northwest of Spitsbergen, by Wilkins (1931); a succession of scientific expeditions to western Greenland made by the University of Michigan under William H. Hobbs (1926–31); and the glaciological and topographic surveys in Alaska of the American Geographical Society (1926–41), led by William Fields and Walter A. Wood, and of the National Geographic Society (1919–41).

Following quickly upon initial successes flying in the Arctic, the United States directed its interests to Antarctica. Prior to World War II notable flights to Antarctica included flights by Wilkins in 1928–30 along most of the Antarctic Peninsula; four flights by Ellsworth (1933–39), including his long flight of 1935 from the northern tip of the Antarctic Peninsula to the Ross Ice Shelf beyond Marie Byrd Land; and Byrd's flight from Little America to the South Pole in November 1929. Byrd planned and commanded the first (1928–30) and second (1933–35) Byrd Antarctic expeditions, based at Little America I and II, and the U.S. Antarctic Service (1939–41) expedition, based at Little America III in West Antarctica and Stonington Island in the Antarctic Peninsula. From these bases Byrd and his staff carried out far-reaching air-and land-survey explorations into largely unknown regions, greatly modifying the map of West Antarctica and setting the pace for large-scale post–World War II activities.

During World War II the United States used its records of previous expeditions in the Arctic in a vast program of establishing transarctic air routes; locating air bases and meteorological and other scientific stations; and developing logistic support forces, especially in Alaska, northern Canada, Greenland, and Iceland. The U.S. Weather Bureau, Coast Guard, navy, army, and army air corps played leading roles in this further exploration.

Commander Richard Byrd awarded a medal by President Franklin D. Roosevelt in 1933 for his Antarctic exploration. (Corbis-Bettmann)

Following World War II, through about 1956, the United States carried out an accelerated program of polar exploration and scientific investigation, primarily to test and improve on the experiences of the war years. In Antarctica the government launched an all-out program of exploration by the U.S. Navy Antarctic Developments Project (Operation Highjump, 1946–47), which involved ships, airplanes, over-snow vehicles, and personnel—the largest expedition ever sent to Antarctica. This program included the first use of helicopters and icebreakers in the area. Much of the continent was surveyed and mapped. The last private expedition to Antarctica was conducted by Finn Ronne as the Ronne Antarctic research expedition (1947–48). It explored, surveyed, and mapped in the Antarctic Peninsula, south into the Weddell Sea, and west around Alexander I Island. These expeditions were followed by the U.S. Navy Second Antarctic Developments Project (Operation Windmill, 1947–48), which explored, surveyed, and mapped the Ross Sea, the coast of West Antarctica, and Wilkes Land. During the austral summer of 1954–55, the icebreaker U.S.S. *Atka* circumnavigated the continent surveying the icefront and inspecting sites for bases for scientific stations to be used during the forthcoming International Geophysical Year (1957–58).

During World War II the U.S. used its records of previous arctic expeditions in a vast program of establishing transarctic air routes and locating air bases.

In the Arctic the decade after 1945 saw routine scientific (meteorological and geophysical) flights between Fairbanks and the North Pole, extensive surveys of the Arctic Ocean leading to the location and mapping of ice islands and their occupation by scientific stations; a continuous succession of army, navy, and air force logistic and scientific operations, often with Danish or Canadian collaboration; the establishment of the U.S. Navy Arctic Research Laboratory at Point Barrow, Alaska; successive penetrations of the Canadian Archipelago by navy task forces in experiments in logistics and tests; exploration for the building of the Distant Early Warning line; and surveys by navy task forces of the coast of northwest Greenland and of Ellesmere Island for bases, which culminated in the building of the giant Thule air base in Greenland.

The scientific aspect of U.S. polar exploration has been greatly accelerated since the beginning of the International Geophysical Year (1957–58), especially in Antarctica, where a remarkably high degree of international cooperation and participation has resulted from the Antarctic Treaty (June 21, 1961), signed by twelve governments. The logistics for a large program of permanent and temporary bases in Antarctica, as carried out by the U.S. Naval Support Force, and a scientific program directed by the Office of Polar Programs in the National Science Foundation have both been discussed in *Antarctic Journal of the United States* and its predecessor publications since 1959.

In the Arctic the program of exploration since World War II has been wide-ranging, including oceanographic and hydrographic surveys by U.S. Navy and Coast Guard ships of Chukchi, Beaufort, Greenland, and Norwegian seas and the continental shelf of the lands fronting onto the Arctic Ocean; the full transect of the Arctic Basin by nuclear inertial guidance submarines; an extensive program of long-range observational geophysical and aerial mapping; and the permanent establishment of a variety of scientific and logistic bases at strategic sites throughout the North American sector, some of which are on drifting ice islands. These activities have been discussed in *Arctic: Journal of the Arctic Institute of North America, Montreal* (since 1946) and in the *Polar Record*, published by Scott Polar Research Institute, Cambridge, England (since 1931).

BIBLIOGRAPHY

Kenneth J. Bertrand, *Americans in Antarctica, 1775–1948.*

Herman R. Friis and Shelby G. Bale, Jr., *United States Polar Exploration.*

L. P. Kirwan, *A History of Polar Exploration.*

Paul A. Siple, *90° South: The Story of the American South Pole Conquest.*

— HERMAN R. FRIIS

POLICE

The ultimate basis of legal order is the likelihood that laws will be enforced, by physical coercion if need be. Police are the normal repository of these enforcement powers, holding a monopoly on the legitimate means of force in a society. They are responsible for maintaining the public order; promoting the public health, safety, and morals; and preventing and detecting violations of laws within a political jurisdiction.

Although continental European countries have traditionally maintained some form of national, professional police forces since the 17th century, the decentralized, local nature of American police agencies reflects their Anglo-Saxon origins. Before the 19th century England and its colonies relied on constables or sheriffs to maintain order, and their offices were outgrowths of still earlier localized systems of maintaining order, such as mutual pledges, tithing, and the watch and ward, or nightwatch.

The problems of lawlessness and disorder associated with industrialization and urbanization highlighted the inadequacies of these prior systems. The London Metropolitan Police force, established in 1829, is generally regarded as the first modern city police department. Although Boston employed night-watchmen as early as 1636 and added a daywatch in 1838, the first consolidated city police force in America was created in New York in 1844. Early departments were characterized by political influence, corruption, and inefficiency. In the absence of urban problems, rural areas continued to be served by sheriffs.

Texas established a state police force, the Texas Rangers, in 1835, but most state police forces were not created until the 20th century, partly in response to problems posed by the automobile. While there is no federal police force as such, many police activities are performed by the Federal Bureau of Investigation, established in 1908, and a variety of specialized agencies, most of which are within the Department of Justice, the Treasury Department, and the Department of Defense.

BIBLIOGRAPHY

David J. Bordua and Albert J. Reiss, in Paul F. Lazarsfeld, ed., *The Uses of Sociology.*

— BARRY C. FELD

POLICE SINCE THE EARLY 1970S

In the early 1990s, the United States had more independent police agencies than any other country. Estimates have been as high as 40,000, but contemporary estimates range from 20,000 to 25,000. These figures contrast with such countries as Ireland and Israel, which have single national police forces, and with those countries whose multiple forces are centrally coordinated, such as France and Great Britain. It is at least partly by design that the United States has neither a single national police force or a centrally coordinated system of multiple agencies. Local control of police appeared to be a guarantee against the acquisition of too much political power by police. The Federal Bureau of Investigation has some characteristics of a national police force, but its jurisdiction is limited by other federal police agencies, as well as by state and local police forces. Many critics use what they regard as the serious abuses of power by J. Edgar Hoover, who headed the FBI for forty-eight years (1924–1972), to argue against greater centralization.

In 1995 there were more than sixty federal agencies with law enforcement powers. The FBI, U.S. Marshals Service, Immigration and Naturalization Service, and Drug Enforcement Administration are in the Department of Justice. Within the Department of the Treasury are the Secret Service, Customs Service, and Bureau of Alcohol, Tobacco and Firearms. The police power of this last agency was brought to the attention of the American public by its 1993 raid on the Branch Davidian complex in Waco, Texas. Federal police agencies have specialized law enforcement functions, but their geographical jurisdiction extends throughout the United States. Although the jurisdictions of state and local agencies are limited to territory governed by state or local political authorities, they have general law enforcement powers within their territories. There are some legal extensions to the geographically limited authority of local police. Buffer zones can extend beyond city or county lines within which police have full authority, and officers often have the authority to engage in "hot pursuit" of a suspect across boundaries that would normally define their jurisdiction. The Texas Rangers, founded in 1835, before Texas became a state, became the first state police force. Pennsylvania established a state police force in 1905, and the other states, except for Hawaii, have followed suit. The law enforcement powers of state police vary from one state to another. State National Guard units, normally federally controlled army or air force units, can also be used by the governors of states as domestic police agencies in times of emergency. Sheriffs are county officials, generally elected to office. Although the list of tasks typically performed by sheriff departments is long, responsibilities vary from one department to another. In addition to law enforcement, sheriffs usually have charge of county jails and can be officers of the county court, enforcing courtroom security and serving legal notices, such as warrants, subpoenas, and foreclosures. Sheriff departments sometimes receive criticism because of their connection to politics and frequent failure to uphold professional standards for recruitment and training.

In 1995 there were more than sixty federal agencies with law enforcement powers, including the FBI and the Bureau of Alcohol, Tobacco, and Firearms.

Police departments have become more professional by raising recruitment standards, increasing recruit training, and using advanced technology and the results of specialized research. Scientific police work began in Europe, with development of fingerprinting and other modern methods of crime detection, and U.S. police departments began to adapt the European model to the United States in the early twentieth century. There has been an increase in use of technology, from the introduction of radio-dispatched patrol cars in the 1930s to the use of computerized databases in the 1990s. Many police agencies now require recruits to have college degrees, and a growing number of programs in criminal justice have attracted students hoping to pursue careers in police work. The professionalization of the police was in response not only to the technical demands of law enforcement but also to repeated discoveries of corruption in police departments. In New York City the 1972 report of the Knapp Commission, appointed to investigate the corruption allegations of Detective Frank Serpico, stated that 15,000 New York City police officers, half the members of the department, were taking illegal payoffs. In 1986 police officers in Boston were found to have been stealing and fixing police promotion exams, and officers in New York and Philadelphia were accused of participation in gambling and drug operations. The beating of Rodney King in 1991 by Los Angeles police officers led to widespread investigations throughout the country of police racism and excessive use of violence.

Since the early 1970s police departments have recruited more women and minorities through the efforts of progressive police leaders and because of the legal requirements for equal employment and affirmative action. Recruitment of minorities was part of attempts to improve relationships between police and communities. Such incidents as the videotaped beating of King dramatized the need for police who are both highly professional and committed to the welfare of people within their jurisdictions. After the riots following acquittal of the officers who beat King, former Philadelphia Police Commissioner Willie Williams was appointed the first African-American police chief in the history of Los Angeles.

[See also Crime; Federal Bureau of Investigation; Justice, Department of; Los Angeles Riots; Waco Siege.]

BIBLIOGRAPHY

David H. Bayley, *Patterns of Policing: A Comparative International Perspective* (New Brunswick, N.J., 1995).

Randy LaGrange, *Policing American Society* (Chicago, 1993).

— RICHARD W. MOODEY

POLISH AMERICANS

The arrival of Poles at the Jamestown colony in Virginia on Oct. 1, 1608, initiated the Polish presence in America. The London Company recruited Poles, most probably to manufacture pitch, tar, and soap. When the hard-working Poles were denied the vote in the Virginia House of Burgesses in 1619, they objected and won the franchise. Few Poles, however, reached the colonies before the American Revolution. Kazimierz Pulaski and Tadeusz Kościuszko were the earliest Polish political émigrés. Pulaski served as a volunteer in the Continental army from 1777 to 1778 and then was made a general and ordered to organize a cavalry corps; he was mortally wounded at the Battle of Savannah in October 1779. Kościuszko was appointed colonel of engineers in the Continental army in 1776, and his fortifications at Freeman's Farm (Bemis Heights), N.Y., ensured the American victory at Saratoga in 1777. A scattering of exiles and émigrés followed in the first half of the nineteenth century.

The character of Polish migration changed in 1854, when 150 Silesian peasants settled Panna Maria, Texas, near San Antonio. Driven by what was unavailable at home, especially after the Polish Insurrection of 1863, Poles came to the United States, according to Henryk Sienkiewicz, a Nobelist in literature (1905), "in search of bread and freedom." They planted urban villages in the midwestern industrial states of Illinois, Michigan, Wisconsin, Ohio, Minnesota, and Indiana and in the Atlantic coast states of New York, Pennsylvania, New Jersey, Massachusetts, Connecticut, Maryland, Delaware, Rhode Island. Polish settlements were particularly dense in metropolitan New York, Chicago, Detroit, Philadelphia, Milwaukee, Buffalo, Pittsburgh, Cleveland, Minneapolis–St. Paul, Boston, and Baltimore. They labored in steel and linen mills, factories, and mines, while only 10 percent made their way into agriculture. Polish immigrants organized a complex community infrastructure between 1854 and World War II. More than 950 Roman Catholic and Polish National Catholic parishes, 585 parochial schools, national insurance fraternal organizations (Polish National Alliance, Polish Roman Catholic Union, Polish Women's Alliance, and Polish Falcons), a Polish language press, and athletic, cultural, social, and political clubs and organizations. The 1930 U.S. Census counted 3,342,198 Polish immigrants and their descendants.

During World War I (1914–1918), Polish Americans lobbied the administration of President Woodrow Wilson on behalf of Poland's independence. In the interwar period, the Polish-American community pursued domestic priorities. Citizens clubs helped members acquire citizenship and political recognition. During and after the Great Depression, Polish Americans voted for Franklin D. Roosevelt and his New Deal and joined labor unions. By 1945 they constituted nearly 10 percent of the Congress of Industrial Organizations. The outbreak of World War II in September 1939 altered the Polish-American community's development. Following the Soviet occupation of Poland in 1944, 190,771 political émigrés, soldier-exiles, and displaced persons entered the United States between 1949 and 1956. The Polish American Congress, founded in 1944, articulated postwar Polish-American concerns, including the socioeconomic advancement of Americans of Polish origin. Polish settlements in the United States declined after World War II, as educational levels rose and Polish Americans joined the exodus from inner cities. A limited ethnic revival occurred in the 1970s, a response to the blight of ethnic humor in the media. The election of Pope John Paul II in 1978 stimulated Polish-American pride, as did the creation of the Solidarity movement in Poland in 1980.

Most descendants of pre-World War I Polish immigrants became Americanized, but the appearance of a more liberal communist government in Warsaw in 1956 reopened direct migration from Poland, reinforcing declining Polish communities in the United States. The Immigration and Naturalization Act of 1965 also shaped Polish migration to the United States. Between 1965 and 1990 there were 178,384 immigrants, along with 957,360 nonimmigrants, temporary visitors who claimed to be tourists but actually sought work. In addition, 35,131 Solidarity-era political refugees arrived in the 1980s. The arrival of more than one million immigrants, nonimmigrants, and refugees helped Polish-American communities survive. The 1990 U.S. Census recorded 9.4 million Americans of Polish descent.

A century ago peasants and unskilled laborers were the majority in the immigrant community. Since World War II, however, Polish Americans' income, education levels, and occupational mobility increased, as did their percentages in the professions, management, research and education, and in technical jobs. Americans of Polish origin who have achieved professional acclaim include Senator Edmund S. Muskie and Representative Dan Rostenkowski; Stanislaw Ulam (physics); Zbigniew Brzezinski (political science); Arthur Rubenstein, Liberace, and Bobby Vinton (music); Pola Negri, Gloria Swanson, and Charles Bronson (motion pictures); Nobel laureate Czeslaw Milosz and novelist Jerzy Kosinski; General John Shalikashvili; and baseball's Stan Musial and Carl Yastrzemski, while Polish Americans have played on every National Football League team.

Polish Americans in the 1990s were still concentrated in the states where their ancestors settled, but they joined the migration to the Sunbelt states. They are part of the American tapestry, but retain ties to their ancestral homeland. Polish Americans hailed the fall of communism in 1989 but remained anxious about Poland's security and lobbied for Poland's admission to the North Atlantic Treaty Organization and European economic and political associations.

BIBLIOGRAPHY

Andrzej Brozek, *Polish Americans, 1854–1939* (Warsaw, 1985).

John J. Bukowcyzk, *And My Children Did Not Know Me: A History of Polish-Americans* (Bloomington, Ind., 1987).

Waclaw Kruszka, *A History of Poles in America to 1908* (Washington, D.C., 1905–1908), trans. and repr., James S. Pula, ed. (1993–1995).

W. S. Kuniczak, *My Name Is Million: An Illustrated History of the Poles in America* (New York, 1978).

Helena Znaniecka Lopata, *Polish Americans*, rev. ed. (New Brunswick, N.J., 1994).

James S. Pula, *Polish Americans: An Ethnic Community* (New York, 1995).

— STANISLAUS A. BLEJWAS

POLITICAL ACTION COMMITTEES

Political Action Committees (PACs), groups that collect monies from their members or politically like-minded citizens, represent a single interest group, such as a labor union, corporation, or industry, or such socioeconomic issues as abortion or the environment. PACs use their monies to influence the legislative and executive branches of government. Even foreign powers have PACs working in the halls of state legislatures and Congress. Participation in PACs is not always voluntary. Groups put pressure on the men and women who work for them by inviting them to participate either monetarily or as volunteers. The hidden message often is that those who give money to PACs will be looked upon favorably by the organization in the form of promotions and pay raises. PACs attempt to gain support for their interests by contributing to political campaigns, hoping that their favors will be returned once candidates reach office. Even when candidates eschew PAC money, the very existence and need for that money assures that, for the most part, only independently wealthy candidates can compete with those who take PAC money. The most insidious thing about PACs is that they continue to be part and parcel of a political process that assures that those with the most money will have the most access and influence in the system.

PACs appear to be an ineradicable part of a political process that assures that those with the most money have the most influence.

The origin of PACs can be traced to the American labor movement and the Congress of Industrial Organizations (CIO). The first political action committee was formed during World War II, after Congress prohibited the assets of organized labor from being used for political purposes. The CIO created a separate political fund in 1943 to receive and spend voluntary contributions and called it the Political Action Committee. After the CIO merged with the American Federation of Labor, a political action committee called the Committee on Political Education (COPE) was formed in 1955. Other PACs, such as the American Medical Political Action Committee (AMPAC) and the Business-

Industry Political Action Committee (BIPAC), were formed in the 1950s and 1960s, but it was not until the reform legislation of the 1970s that the number of PACs began to increase significantly.

While labor unions formed PACs during the 1940s, corporations were not allowed to support candidates until the Federal Campaign Act (FECA) of 1971, which allowed corporations to use their money to set up PACs. In 1974 and 1976 FECA was amended, giving trade associations and corporations a new role in politics. As a result, FECA changed its guidelines for raising political money, sparking a tremendous growth in the number of PACs and the amount of money spent to influence the political system. Even though revisions in FECA set limits on the amount of money PACs could contribute to individual candidates and political campaigns ($5,000) and set a $1,000 limit on individual contributions per candidate per election, PACs were able to get around these limitations and still influence the political system. In fact, PACs often receive guidance from the lobbyists who work directly in the halls of state legislatures and Congress. While it is conflictive and often forbidden to have labor unions, for example, use their members' dues for political influence, there is no question that such arrangements are made.

Observers have argued for reform of the election process, insisting that PAC money should be eliminated or at least severely limited. Even where there are legal limits, individuals and groups have gotten around them by giving so-called "soft money" to political parties instead of directly to candidates. Officially, soft money is supposed to be used for party housekeeping, but in fact parties manage to pass on their cash to candidates. Gifts of soft money tend to obligate party managers to PACs and their political goals. In fact, the very existence of PACs since the 1970s has run up the tab on elections to the point that a single congressional contest may involve the expenditure of $1 million or more. For example, in 1974 approximately 600 PACs gave $12.5 million to congressional candidates. In 1988 the number of PACs had increased seven times (approximately 4,200 with $132 million in contributions to primarily incumbents). This increase raised public criticism of PACs and led to congressional proposals to eliminate them in 1991–1992, but no significant action was taken. According to the Center for Responsive Politics, there were 3,954 registered PACs in existence at the end of 1994, but only 3,001 were active.

BIBLIOGRAPHY

W. Lance Bennett, *The Governing Crisis: Media, Money, and Marketing in American Elections* (New York, 1992).

William J. Keefe and Morris S. Ogul, *The American Legislative Process: Congress and the States*, 5th ed. (Englewood Cliffs, N.J., 1981).

Frank J. Sorauf, *Money in American Elections* (Boston, 1988).

F. Wertheimer and Susan Weiss Manes, "Campaign Finance Reform," *Columbia Law Review* 94 (May 1994).

— ALAN CHARTOCK

"Join or Die": the first American political cartoon, originally published by Benjamin Franklin in his Pennsylvania Gazette, *1754. (The Granger Collection)*

POLITICAL CARTOONS

The history of American political cartoons can be divided into three eras, defined by the medium in which the cartoons were presented to the public—as prints, in magazines, and in newspapers. In the first era, which spanned from the 1750s to the 1870s, most cartoons were sold as steel engravings or, after

1820, lithographs. During the second era, from the 1840s to the beginning of the twentieth century, most cartoons appeared in magazines, either as woodcuts or lithographs. This was the first golden age of the political cartoon, when Thomas Nast of *Harper's Weekly* and Joseph Keppler of Puck made the political cartoon a tool for reform. The third era dawned in 1884, when publisher Joseph Pulitzer began printing political cartoons on the front page of the *New York World.* Since then the political cartoon has become a staple of the editorial pages of daily newspapers. Important newspaper cartoonists of the late nineteenth century and the first half of the twentieth century include Homer Davenport (*New York Journal*), John T. McCutcheon (*Chicago Tribune*), Jay Norwood ("Ding") Darling (*Des Moines Register*), and Daniel Robert Fitzpatrick (*St. Louis Post-Dispatch*), the last three of whom received Pulitzer Prizes. The cartoons of Herbert L. Block ("Herblock"), who received the first of three Pulitzers in 1942, have appeared in the *Washington Post* since 1946.

Many critics regard the period from the mid-1960s to the mid-1990s as the second golden age of cartooning. The period began when Patrick Oliphant emigrated from Australia to the United States in 1964 to work for the *Denver Post.* Unlike his predecessors, who tended to support one political party or the other, Oliphant made fun of all politicians. His satiric cartoons, full of demeaning caricatures of well-known politicians, prompted a generation of Americans once again to regard the political cartoon as a tool of reform. Those who have followed in Oliphant's footsteps include Jeff MacNelly (*Richmond News Leader* and later *Chicago Tribune*), Mike Peters (*Dayton Daily News*), Tony Auth (*Philadelphia Inquirer*), Doug Marlette (*Charlotte Observer, Atlanta Constitution,* and later *New York Newsday*), and Jim Borgman (*Cincinnati Enquirer*), all of whom have won the Pulitzer Prize for Editorial Cartooning. None of these cartoonists' work, however popular, had the impact of Garry Trudeau's comic strip "Doonesbury," which began in 1970 and was the first comic strip to be awarded the Pulitzer for editorial cartooning (1975). Because of its treatment of such controversial content as abortion, "Doonesbury" has been "censored" with some frequency (that is, certain strips have not been included by some newspapers that routinely run the strip). By the mid-1990s "Doonesbury" was appearing daily in more than 1,000 newspapers.

BIBLIOGRAPHY

The Best Editorial Cartoons of the Year (Gretna, La., annually since 1972).

Stephen Hess and Milton Kaplan, *The Ungentlemanly Art: A History of American Political Cartoons* (New York, 1975).

Richard Samuel West, *Satire on Stone: The Political Cartoons of Joseph Keppler* (Urbana, Ill., 1988).

— RICHARD SAMUEL WEST

POLK DOCTRINE

President James K. Polk's first annual message, Dec. 2, 1845, reaffirmed the Monroe Doctrine and at the same time extended the scope and narrowed the boundaries of the Monroe-Adams dictum by announcing American determination "that no future European colony or dominion shall, with our consent, be planted or established on any part of the North American continent," and American intention to resist "any European interference . . . " there. He thus added to the original idea of noncolonization of unoccupied territory that of "dominion," which has been defined as including acquisition "by voluntary transfer or by conquest of territory already occupied"; and emphasized opposition to "any interference." He also restricted the geographical radius of his prohibition to North America. This doctrine, applied in 1848 to discourage Yucatán from voluntarily ceding itself to some European power, was looked upon by Latin-American nations as a limitation upon their sovereignty.

BIBLIOGRAPHY

S. F. Bemis, ed., *The American Secretaries of State and Their Diplomacy,* vol. V.

— L. ETHAN ELLIS

POLL TAX

A tax levied on each person within a particular class (for example, adult male) rather than on his property or income is called a poll, head, or capitation tax. Poll taxes were employed in all the American colonies at one period or another. It was Virginia's only direct tax for years, and before the Revolution Maryland had practically no other direct tax. Poll taxes continued to be levied by most states through the 19th century and well into the 20th. In 1923 thirty-eight states permitted or required the collection of poll taxes. The amount of the tax varied from one to five dollars, and the proceeds were often allocated to specific public facilities, such as state schools or roads.

For many years states (five states as late as 1962) used the poll tax as a means of discouraging blacks from registering to vote by making the payment of the tax a prerequisite to the exercise of the right to vote. And the Supreme Court periodically upheld the states' right to do so, as in *Breedlove* v. *Suttles,* 302 U.S. 277 (1937).

In 1964 the Twenty-fourth Amendment to the Constitution was ratified, nullifying all state laws requiring payment of a poll tax as a condition "to vote in any [federal] primary or other [federal] election." Because the amendment made no mention of purely state elections, a few states continued the levy as a prerequisite for voting in state elections until 1966, when the Supreme Court, in *Harper* v. *Virginia Board of Elections*, 383 U.S. 663, ruled that a state violates the Fourteenth Amendment "whenever it makes the affluence of the voter or payment of any fee an electoral standard."

BIBLIOGRAPHY

Thomas I. Emerson and David Haber, *Political and Civil Rights in the United States.*

— HAROLD W. CHASE AND ERIC L. CHASE

POLYGAMY

Polygamous living has been a custom practiced by certain sects and minorities, the most important of these in the United States being the Mormons and the Oneida Perfectionists. In the antebellum South, slaves were encouraged or permitted to mate according to the wishes of their owners, sometimes polygamously.

What is essentially polygamous living is practiced by many persons secretly, or with the knowledge of limited circles of acquaintances who approve or tolerate the situation. It is distinguished from prostitution in that it involves continuity of relationship, with affection and responsibility toward the extra mate. Such relationships, indicated by the terms "concubine," "mistress," and "lover," among others, have been described as occurring in many places in the American colonies and throughout American history. Toleration has varied from time to time and from place to place. Adultery is a crime in many states but is seldom prosecuted criminally. More often it forms the ground for a civil suit for divorce by the innocent party. Occasionally a person, concealing the facts or ignorant of the law, goes through the form of a marriage ceremony with his second or illicit partner; this constitutes bigamy, which is a crime, and furthermore the marriage thus attempted is legally null and void. Many divorces, if contested in the courts of the home state, would be found invalid, and hence the remarriage of the parties would be bigamous. In such case a civil suit for property is much more likely, in practice, than a criminal prosecution for bigamy. Some writers have said that the high U.S. divorce rate results in a form of "serial polygamy," as distinguished from "simultaneous polygamy."

BIBLIOGRAPHY

A. W. Calhoun, *A Social History of the American Family.*
E. R. Groves, *The American Family.*

— JOSEPH K. FOLSOM

PONCE DE LEÓN'S DISCOVERY

Ponce De León's discovery of Florida in 1513 added the mainland of North America to the Spanish dominions. In 1512 Juan Ponce de León secured a royal grant, with the title of *adelantado*, to conquer the island of Bimini to the north of Cuba where the fountain of youth presumably was located. Sailing from Puerto Rico on Mar. 3, 1513, he sighted the mainland on Mar. 27, and on Apr. 2 landed just north of the present site of Saint Augustine. The region was named Florida in honor of the Easter season. Reembarking, Ponce de León explored the eastern shore of Florida, doubled the cape, and passed along the Florida Keys, which he called the Martyrs. He continued along the western coast, probably reaching Pensacola Bay, and returned to Puerto Rico on Sept. 21. Besides taking possession of Florida, he discovered the Bahama Channel. Returning to Spain in 1514, he received a grant to colonize the islands of Florida and Bimini, but it was not until 1521 that he undertook the second expedition from Puerto Rico to Florida. Reaching the peninsula probably at Charlotte Harbor on the western coast, he and his party were attacked by hostile Indians, and in a battle the *adelantado* was severely wounded. The effort at colonization was abandoned, and the expedition returned to Havana, Cuba, where Ponce de León died.

BIBLIOGRAPHY

Frederick A. Ober, *Juan Ponce de León.*

— ROSCOE R. HILL

PONTIAC'S WAR

Pontiac's War (1763–64), an uprising of Indians in 1763 after the end of the French and Indian War, in opposition to British expansion in the Great Lakes area. The leader and instigator of the struggle was an Ottawa chief named Pontiac, who devised a plan for a general uprising of the Indians and for a systematic destruction of the British forts and settlements. Pontiac seems to have been under the influence of the Delaware Prophet, who had earlier preached a return to the old Indian ways. Pontiac had long been hostile to the English and had fought against them at Gen. Edward Braddock's defeat in 1755.

Most of the Indians of the Great Lakes area had been on better terms with the French than with the English, and they were outraged when the British commander, Gen. Jeffrey Amherst, issued new and strict regulations that banned the credit and gifts that the Indians had been accustomed to receiving from the French.

Pontiac, following the teachings of the Delaware Prophet, attempted to forge unity among the Indians of the area and to induce them to join the Ottawa in a war against the English; he was convinced that the friendly French were preparing to reconquer their lost territories. Meanwhile, English settlers were moving into the area. Pontiac succeeded in convincing the Delaware, Shawnee, Chippewa, Miami, Potawatomi, Seneca, Kickapoo, and others that they should join him in his war on the British. In the spring of 1763 Pontiac convened a council of the Indian allies at the mouth of the Ecorse River, a few miles from Detroit, where he incited the hundreds of attending warriors to drive out the British.

The aroused warriors, at the end of May 1763, attacked every British fort in the area, taking eight out of ten of them and killing the garrisons. The main fortifications, Fort Pitt and Detroit, were, however, successfully defended, although under siege by the Indians. Because of the central location and military importance of Detroit, Pontiac himself directed the attack on it. He had planned a surprise attack; but the post commander, Maj. Henry Gladwin, was warned in advance, and the gates were closed. Pontiac laid siege to the fort, a tactic that was without precedent in Indian military history. During the summer the fort was relieved by reinforcements and military supplies from Niagara, but Pontiac continued to besiege it until November. Realizing that he could expect no assistance from the French and suffering defection of his Indian allies, Pontiac retreated to the Maumee River. Col. John Bradstreet entered Detroit with troops on Aug. 26, 1764, and prevented a renewal of the siege; but a formal peace was not concluded until July 24, 1766. Pontiac was unsuccessful in arousing the tribes along the Mississippi River to another effort, and in 1769 he was killed by an Illinois Indian.

BIBLIOGRAPHY

Francis Parkman, *History of the Conspiracy of Pontiac.*
Howard H. Peckham, *Pontiac and the Indian Uprising.*

— KENNETH M. STEWART

PONY EXPRESS

During the late 1850's the question of the best route for the overland mail to California was a topic of great interest in the Far West. In September 1857 a contract was granted to John Butterfield and his Overland Mail Company, which began operation one year later over a circuitous southern route. The shortest time made on this route was twenty-two days. Many Californians, including Sen. William M. Gwin, believed that a central route was entirely feasible and would expedite the carrying of mail to the coast. It was Gwin who, early in 1860, induced William H. Russell, of the freighting firm of Russell, Majors and Waddell, to demonstrate the practicability of a central route in a dramatic manner by establishing a pony express. Of course, the hope of securing a lucrative mail contract was the motivating factor with the company.

Changing mounts at a Pony Express station. The mail system was inaugurated on April 3, 1860, and ended only a year later, when telegraph service was established. Engraving by Frederick Remington. (Corbis-Bettmann)

The project was pushed vigorously. Starting at Saint Joseph, Mo., the route in general followed the well-known Oregon-California trail by way of Fort Kearny and Scottsbluff (Nebraska), Fort Laramie, South Pass, and Fort Bridger (Wyoming), and Salt Lake City. From there the trail went around the southern end of the Great Salt Lake, by way of Fort Churchill, Carson City (both in Nevada), and Placerville (California) to Sacramento. Stations were built at intervals of about fifteen miles, wherever stage stations did not already exist. Fleet, wiry, Indian ponies were purchased; and young, courageous, lightweight riders were hired. On Apr. 3, 1860, the service was inaugurated. It was like a giant relay, in which about seventy-five ponies participated in each direction. At each station the riders were given two minutes in which to transfer the saddlebags to fresh ponies and be on their way again. After riding a certain distance, one rider would hand the mail over to another, and so on, until the destination was reached. Day and night, summer and winter, over dusty plains and dangerous mountain trails, and frequently in the midst of hostile Indians, the ponies and their riders galloped at their best speed over the sections of the route allotted to them.

During the eighteen months of the operation of the pony express only one trip was missed. The service was weekly at first and later semiweekly. The best time ever made was in November 1860, when news of President Abraham Lincoln's election was carried in six days from Fort Kearny to Fort Churchill, then the termini of the telegraph lines that were being built from the Missouri River and California. When the two telegraph lines were joined on Oct. 24, 1861, all need for the pony express was eliminated.

The pony express was disastrous to the fortunes of Russell, Majors and Waddell. The cost of operation was greatly in excess of the revenue. In fact the company was virtually ruined by the experiment and was disappointed in its hope of gaining a valuable mail contract, which went to another firm. Furthermore, the enterprise was not even necessary as a demonstration of the feasibility of a central route. The outbreak of the Civil War made the selection of such a route inevitable.

BIBLIOGRAPHY

William Banning and George H. Banning, *Six Horses.*
Glenn D. Bradley, *The Story of the Pony Express.*
Le Roy Hafen, *The Overland Mail, 1849–1869.*

— DAN E. CLARK

POOR RICHARD'S ALMANAC

Poor Richard's Almanac (1732–96), published in Philadelphia by Benjamin Franklin, contained, in addition to the usual almanac information on the weather, tides, eclipses, and medicinal remedies, maxims, saws, and pithy sayings written by Franklin. Each edition of *Poor Richard's Almanac* saw an increase in sales until 10,000 copies were printed annually, approximately one for every hundred people in the colonies. It eventually became the second most popular book in the American colonies, the Bible being first. It is probable that Franklin ceased to write for the almanac after 1748, when he began to devote most of his time and energy to public affairs, although he continued as its editor and publisher. In 1757, after editing the 1758 edition, he disposed of the almanac, which continued to appear until 1796. In 1758 Franklin collected the best of his writings from *Poor Richard's Almanac* in *Father Abraham's Speech,* more commonly known as *The Way to Wealth.*

BIBLIOGRAPHY

Benjamin Franklin, *Papers.*
Carl Van Doren, *Benjamin Franklin.*

— E. H. O'NEILL

POPULAR SOVEREIGNTY

Popular sovereignty, in a general sense, means the right of the people to rule. "Squatter sovereignty" literally means the right of people living anywhere without a government to form a body politic and practice self-government. When the theory that the people of a federal territory had the right to determine the slavery question for themselves was first enunciated, it was dubbed "squatter sovereignty" by its opponents. The term has persisted and is often used as the equivalent of popular sovereignty.

When Lewis Cass, senator from Michigan and later secretary of state, in a letter to A. O. P. Nicholson dated Dec. 24, 1847, declared that he was "in favor of leaving the people of any territory which may hereafter be acquired, the right to regulate [slavery] themselves, under the great general principles of the Constitution," he made the first clear statement of the principle of popular sovereignty. Acts organizing the territories of Utah and New Mexico were passed in 1850. In neither territory was slavery prohibited or protected. It was simply provided that each of the territories should be admitted with or without slavery as its constitution might specify.

Sen. Stephen A. Douglas of Illinois made the Kansas-Nebraska Act a popular sovereignty measure that repealed the antislavery provision of the Missouri Compromise of 1820. That popular sovereignty would produce a bitter struggle for Kansas was as difficult to foresee as was the Civil War. The conflict that followed the passage of the Kansas-Nebraska Act was really decided by the forces controlling the westward movement of the 1850's. So superior were the drawing qualities of northern and southern frontier areas in competition with Kansas that only a small proportion of the migrating colonists reached that territory before 1860. The conditions prevailing between 1854 and 1860 were such that those interested in making Kansas a slaveholding state had no chance of success. Even the modest contingent from the North, largely from Ohio, Indiana, and Illinois, greatly outnumbered the contribution from the entire South to Kansas. The southerners who settled in the territory were mainly nonslaveholders from the upper South, and many of them voted with the free-state element, when, on Aug. 2, 1858, it was finally determined by a large majority that Kansas would not become a slaveholding state. Douglas' debates with Abraham Lincoln (Aug. 21–Oct. 15, 1858) came after the people of Kansas had made this decision, and there was no remaining federal territory where the conditions were so favorable to slavery.

Douglas opposed the admission of Kansas under the Lecompton Constitution on the ground that popular sovereignty had not been fairly applied when that constitution was first submitted to the people. Through the aid of Republicans, he won the Lecompton fight, which preceded the debates with Lincoln. The Dred Scott decision had come a year before the Lecompton contest. The opinion of Chief Justice Roger B. Taney troubled the leaders of the new Republican party, because it ran directly counter to the Wilmot Proviso principle. Lincoln believed that Taney had also played havoc with popular sovereignty, although Douglas declared that he had accepted the Court's decision. Before the beginning of the debates, the logic of the situation caused Douglas to discuss the effects of the decision on his principle of nonintervention. His Freeport Doctrine, in response to Lincoln's famous second question as to how the doctrine of popular sovereignty could be reconciled with the Dred Scott decision, was not new to either of the senatorial candidates. The assertion of Douglas that slavery could not exist in any territory where the territorial legislature refused to provide the necessary police regulations squared with the facts, and the people of a territory really could decide for themselves regardless of how the Supreme Court might in the future decide the abstract question of the right of a territorial legislature to prohibit slavery. When Sen. Albert G. Brown of Mississippi complained on the floor of the Senate on Feb. 23, 1859, that "Non-action goes a great way to exclude slave property from a territory, further perhaps than to exclude any other property," he was virtually repeating what Douglas had asserted at Freeport. On the basis of his belief that territorial legislatures would exclude slavery by nonaction, Brown voiced the demand that Congress provide the necessary legislation. It was then that Douglas added the second and final corollary to the doctrine of popular sovereignty, when he proclaimed that he would "never vote for a slave code in the territories by Congress."

[See also Compromise of 1850; Lecompton Constitution.]

BIBLIOGRAPHY

Eugene H. Berwanger, *The Frontier Against Slavery: Western Anti-Negro Prejudice and the Slavery Extension Controversy.*

Eric Foner, *Free Soil, Free Labor, Free Men.*

James A. Rawley, *Race and Politics: Bleeding Kansas and the Coming of the Civil War.*

— WILLIAM O. LYNCH

POPULISM

Populism emerged in the politically turbulent decade of the 1890's. It grew out of an agrarian movement of protest against some of the consequences of industrialization, reached its greatest intensity in the depression crisis following the panic of 1893, and lost its driving force just when success seemed imminent, during the presidential election of 1896.

For several reasons American agriculture had always moved in the direction of extensive, rather than intensive, farming. An abundance of land, a chronic shortage of labor, and improvements in agricultural technology had all led to an emphasis on productivity per man-hour rather than productivity per acre. Post-Civil War expansion of the railroad network and development of agricultural machinery had opened up vast areas of new land in the trans-Mississippi West. Between 1870 and 1900 the amount of farmland under cultivation doubled. Increased agricultural production in the United States—combined with increased production of agricultural regions in Canada, Australia, the Ukraine, and South America—contributed to a secular, or long-term, decline in agricultural prices throughout the world. In the United States the wholesale index of farm products went from 112 in 1870 to 71 in 1890. The total value of those products was on the rise, however, and not all farmers experienced a reduction of income as a result of price declines. Those who commanded sufficient capital to conduct their operations without incurring overburdening debts were usually able to succeed. Indeed, per capita farm income actually increased in the three decades after 1870.

Many farmers nevertheless experienced difficulties, and the incidence of rural distress in the late 1880's and the 1890's was particularly great in two of the nation's major agricultural areas: the old cotton-growing region of the South and the recently settled Plains region of the West. In the South heavy reliance on a single crop made farmers peculiarly subject to the deleterious effects of falling world prices. In the West the subhumid climate of the Plains made farming more costly and more risky than in eastern areas, where drought was less common. But in the early 1880's precipitation had been unusually great, and the promise of future prosperity had stimulated a land boom that, in turn, encouraged farmers to borrow more heavily than was justifiable. When the boom collapsed in the winter of 1887–88, the per capita private debt in Kansas was four times that in the nation as a whole. The maintenance of a crop-lien system in the South after the Civil War and the high rate of mortgage foreclosures in the Plains area during the late 1880's and the 1890's are indications of a relatively large number of marginal farms in both areas. And it was in the South and the trans-Mississippi West that agrarian causes won the most enthusiastic support; there the late 19th-century movement to organize farmers made the most significant gains.

Populism, which grew out of an agrarian protest movement, lost its force just when success seemed imminent, during the presidential election of 1896.

The wave of agrarian protest that culminated in the Populist movement began with formation of local farmers' alliances in Texas and Arkansas during the 1870's. In the following decade those early organizations merged to form the National Farmers' Alliance and Industrial Union, popularly known as the Southern Alliance to distinguish it from the smaller Northwestern Alliance, founded in Chicago in 1880. Emphasizing economic activities, both organizations recruited members during the 1880's and by the end of the decade could claim a combined membership of more than a million. The two alliances failed to unite as a political party, but they did hold concurrent conventions at Saint Louis in December 1889. There they agreed on the desirability of several measures, including an inflationary currency, government ownership of railroads, and legislation against alien landholding.

Sustained by the thought of a common purpose, leaders of dissident agrarians mustered their forces for the congressional and state elections of 1890. With the help of interested groups they formed independent parties in Kansas, Nebraska, the Dakotas, Minnesota, Colorado, Michigan, and Indiana. In the South members of the alliance concentrated on gaining influence within the Democratic party. The results were encouraging enough to arouse extensive support for a new national party, for aside from winning control of several state offices, the agrarians sent nine representatives and two senators to Congress. After a series of preliminary meetings the People's party came into being at a convention in Omaha, Nebr., in July 1892. Delegates nominated Iowa's James B. Weaver and enthusiastically adopted a platform calling for remedial legislation in the three areas of land, transportation, and finance. Specific planks included demands for free coinage of silver, an increase in the circulating medium, a graduated income tax, postal savings banks, government ownership of railroad and telegraph lines, and reclamation of alien landholdings. While Populists did not accomplish all they had hoped to achieve in the election, Weaver did carry four states and win twenty-two electoral votes.

The returns of 1892 proved gratifying enough to preserve optimism within the People's party, and after the onset of a severe depression in 1893, party organizers sought to take advantage of widespread economic discontent. In some areas they broadened their program to win the support of organized labor, Socialists, and advocates of the single tax; Populists of Wisconsin and Illinois, for example, even went so far as to endorse collective ownership of the means of production and distribution. But of all proposals with which the Populist party was identified, the free silver plank of the 1892 platform seemed to have the greatest appeal to voters. During the hard times of the 1890's, monetary reform could be presented not only as a stimulant to agricultural prices but also as a cure for the depression. Yet the attractions of silver divided Populist leadership. A middle-of-the-road faction, seeing bimetallism as an incidental issue, argued for a broader program, or at the least for adherence to the entire Omaha platform; fusionists, on the other hand, attracted by the possibility of victory, were persuaded that the People's party should join forces with others in the free silver camp. Confident that they could dominate affiliations with other groups, the fusionists looked forward to the election of 1896 as an opportunity to win the day for their entire platform by capturing the nation's free-silver sentiment.

The fusionist strategy prevailed, but Populists of each persuasion were disappointed in the way events unfolded. Assuming that both Republicans and Democrats would stand behind the gold standard and identify themselves with commercial and industrial interests, People's party leaders scheduled their national convention to follow the major party conventions. In so doing they hoped to pick up the support of disaffected silverites in both major parties. Contrary to expectations, however, bimetallists dominated the Chicago convention of the Democratic party; nominated the silverite William Jennings Bryan; and adopted a free-silver plank. When Populists convened in the wake of Bryan's dramatic triumph at Chicago, they found themselves facing distasteful alternatives: they could nominate their own candidate and defeat monetary reform, or they could endorse Bryan and destroy the People's party by merging with the Democrats. After a long and painful struggle, delegates accepted the second alternative.

As an organized political force, the Populist movement thus met defeat even before the candidates of 1896 entered the climactic stage of the campaign; and William McKinley's convincing triumph over Bryan removed whatever consolation the Populists might have salvaged from the election. With the return of prosperity after 1897, the United States moved into a new era in which agricultural interests developed new techniques, new organizations, and new strategies. Farm organizations gained considerable political influence as pressure groups in the 20th century, but the hope of building a national party on agrarian principles had disappeared.

BIBLIOGRAPHY

Robert F. Durden, *The Climax of Populism.*
John D. Hicks, *The Populist Revolt.*
Stanley L. Jones, *The Presidential Election of 1896.*
Norman Pollack, *The Populist Response to Industrial America.*
C. Vann Woodward, *Origins of the New South.*

— PAUL W. GLAD

POSTAL SERVICE, UNITED STATES

Since its establishment in 1970, the United States Postal Service (USPS), an independent agency of the executive branch of the government, has become a self-supporting corporation. Although the Postal Service is legislatively enjoined to achieve and maintain financial independence, unlike private corporations, it must provide cost-effective service and carry out federal policies. When the USPS sought to reduce costs during the 1970s and 1980s by consolidating services and closing local branches, public disapproval caused Congress to override such plans. As a self-sustaining corporation operating within the competitive private sector, the USPS strives for efficiency and innovation. It has computerized its operations; added Express Mail, an overnight service and the first new official class of mail since 1918; introduced Mailgrams, electronic messages delivered but not originating in writing; and in 1983 expanded the ZIP (Zone Improvement Program) code sorting system, first introduced in 1963 from five to nine digits. Despite competition from private-sector carriers, the USPS in the 1990s was the largest carrier of the world's mail (161 billion pieces annually), at rates lower than those of nearly all other letter carriers worldwide. The USPS achieves this standard even as its status as a federal agency imposes additional demands. The USPS must publicize and enforce legislation concerning interstate commerce, narcotics trafficking, business fraud, selective service registration, and the distribution of materials deemed pornographic. In 1992 there were 39,595 post offices, stations, and branches in the United States and possessions; in 1993 the USPS employed almost 780,000 employees, second only to the Department of Defense.

BIBLIOGRAPHY

United States Postal Service, *History of the U.S. Postal Service 1775–1981* (Washington, D.C., 1982).

— KERRY A. BATCHELDER

POTOMAC RIVER

Potomac River drains the western slopes of the central Allegheny Mountains of West Virginia into the Chesapeake Bay. Two main streams, the North Branch and the South Branch, and several minor streams unite to form the upper Potomac. A freshwater river for 287 miles, the Potomac below Washington, D.C., is a tidal estuary 125 miles in length and from 2 to 8 miles wide.

Spaniards probably reached the Potomac estuary before 1570. Capt. John Smith visited, described, and mapped it in 1608. Capt. Samuel Argall, deputy governor of Virginia, and others sailed its waters in the next decade. In the late 1620's Virginia traders frequented its waters and shores. Probably agents of George Calvert before 1632 explored the upper Potomac. After the founding of Maryland in 1634, the Potomac was the early passageway of the colony. In following decades its southern shores were gradually settled by Virginians. But owing to the falls above Washington, D.C., and at Harpers Ferry the upper Potomac was long unimportant. In the second quarter of the 18th century, Germans and Scotch-Irish crossed it into the Shenandoah Valley, and about 1740 Thomas Cresap, militant Marylander, settled at Oldtown (also called Shawanese Oldtown) above the junction of the South Branch and the Potomac, in western Maryland. Slowly the Potomac Valley became a pathway to the Ohio Valley, utilized by the Ohio Company of Virginia, by George Washington, and by Gen. Edward Braddock. Over this route traveled the first settlers to the Monongahela country. Its utilization was the basis of later enterprises, such as the Potomac Company of 1785, the Cumberland Road of

1807, the Baltimore and Ohio Railroad of 1827, and the Chesapeake and Ohio Canal Company of 1828.

BIBLIOGRAPHY

Corra Bacon Foster, *Early Chapters in the Development of the Potomac Route to the West.*
Paul Wilstach, *Potomac Landings.*

— ALFRED P. JAMES

POTSDAM CONFERENCE

Potsdam Conference (July 17–Aug. 2, 1945), the last meeting during World War II of the three allied chiefs of state—President Harry S. Truman, Prime Minister Winston Churchill, and Marshal Joseph Stalin. Germany, but not Japan, had already surrendered. Truman, Churchill (who was replaced during the conference by the new prime minister, Clement Attlee, after the British elections), and Stalin fixed terms of German occupation and reparations and replaced the European Advisory Commission (set up at the Moscow Conference of Foreign Ministers in October 1943) with the Council of Foreign Ministers of the United States, Great Britain, France, and Russia, charged with preparing peace terms for Italy, Romania, Bulgaria, Austria, Hungary, and Finland. Since Russia had not yet declared war on Japan, the Potsdam Declaration (July 26, 1945) was signed by the United States and Great Britain only, although with China's concurrence. The declaration called for Japan to surrender but gave assurances that it would be treated humanely. Although the discussions were fairly cordial, the American delegation, disturbed by indications of Russian noncooperation, left Potsdam in a far less optimistic mood than President Franklin D. Roosevelt's delegation had left Yalta.

— CHARLES S. CAMPBELL

POVERTY

Poverty, especially in its most tangible forms of hunger and homelessness, continued to plague the United States as the twentieth century drew to a close. Poverty challenges the belief that hard work will be rewarded, and that all U.S. citizens have equality of opportunity. Poverty is defined as either a relative measure of money or material goods of one person in relation to others or as an absolute measure of how a person can meet the minimum requirements for survival. The most commonly used, although widely disputed, measure of poverty in the United States is an absolute measure, known as the poverty line. This is an amount of money calculated by multiplying the Department of Agriculture's Economy Food Plan by three (assuming therefore that food constitutes one-third of a family's expenditures). Developed for purposes of research, the measure was never meant to mark eligibility for social programs. The poverty threshold in 1994 was $15,141 a year for a family of four. In that same year, and by that measure, 14.5 percent of Americans lived in poverty. The poverty rate was not evenly distributed throughout the U.S. population. In 1994 it was 11.7 percent among whites, 30.6 percent among African Americans, and 30.7 percent among Hispanics. Also of concern was that 21.8 percent of all children in 1994 were poor.

The persistence of poverty in the U.S. challenges the belief that hard work will be rewarded, and that all citizens have equality of opportunity.

The first large-scale effort to confront poverty on a national basis in the United States was during the Great Depression of the 1930s, when as much as 25 percent of the workforce was unemployed. No longer were religious and voluntary associations, which had given charity to the "deserving" poor, able to provide for those out of work. The Great Depression also underlined the structural problems (epitomized by the stock market crash of 1929) creating poverty, as opposed to the wage earner's lack of morality or personal failings. The Social Security Act of 1935 introduced the nation to social insurance, unemployment insurance, and public assistance. During the early 1960s President John F. Kennedy helped focus the nation's attention on the 22.2 percent of the population (in 1960) living in poverty. During President Lyndon B. Johnson's administration (1963–1969), legislation collectively known as the War on Poverty increased federal spending for the poor and helped bring the poverty rate down to 12.1 percent by 1969. One of the philosophical innovations of this era was the concept of "maximum community participation" of the poor. The poor became community action workers and sat on boards of antipoverty agencies.

Throughout the 1970s and 1980s there was widespread disillusionment with antipoverty efforts and a disdain for welfare programs that many observers saw as sapping people's work ethic. Under the administration of Richard M. Nixon (1969–1974), spending for the poor increased, contrary to the public impression of that Republican president's policies. Ronald Reagan's administration (1981–1989), however, promoted a "new federalism" to reduce the federal role in providing for the poor. Programs for the poor remained, but with restricted eligibility. During the administration of Bill Clinton, the Republican Congress, in alliance with Republican governors, continued the effort to transfer the responsibility for the poor from the federal government to the states, over the objections of the Democratic minority and President Clinton.

In the 1990s Americans were still debating ways to battle poverty. Especially disturbing was the homelessness and lack of opportunity facing the inner-city poor. Measures such as eliminating the welfare program available in some states for single, chronically unemployed persons, limiting the duration of receipt of welfare, or tying eligibility to work training or educational programs were hotly disputed. The most radical of the new proposals was the elimination of the federal commitment to provide subsistence payments to poor children through the Aid to Families with Dependent Children program. Instead, states would be given smaller sums of money and be allowed to decide who would get benefits and how much they would get, and benefits would not go to children born to teenage mothers or to children born to women already receiving assistance. Self-help and empowerment again become key phrases in discussions of antipoverty efforts and were implemented by agencies such as Habitat for Humanity, which involved the poor in rehabilitating housing.

[See also Reaganomics; Welfare.]

BIBLIOGRAPHY

Irene Glasser, *Homelessness in Global Perspective* (New York, 1994).

Michael B. Katz, *The Undeserving Poor: From the War on Poverty to the War on Welfare* (New York, 1989).

Sar A. Levitan, *Programs in Aid of the Poor*, 6th ed. (Baltimore, 1990).

William Julius Wilson, *The Truly Disadvantaged: The Inner City, the Underclass, and Public Policy* (Chicago, 1987).

— IRENE GLASSER

POWELL'S EXPLORATIONS

John Wesley Powell, professor of geology at the Illinois State Normal University, led two major expeditions down the Colorado River in the 19th century. Powell gained national prominence as a scientist because of these explorations and his findings. The first expedition, the more important one historically, was made in 1869. Powell organized a company of eleven men and in May, aboard four boats, entered the Colorado where the Union Pacific Railroad crosses the Green River, in western Wyoming. The expedition explored the length of the Green and Colorado rivers to the mouth of the Virgin River, in southeastern Nevada, passing through precipitous canyons and traversing treacherous rapids and waterfalls. The party did not emerge until Aug. 29, after a journey of 900 miles. So dangerous were the rapids that three of the men deserted before the end of the journey. Powell reported the expedition to Congress, which in 1870 appropriated funds for the exploration of adjacent rivers and territories. Powell undertook a second expedition (1871–72), which was the more scientifically productive of the two, and which included such eminent geologists as Grove Karl Gilbert and Clarence Dutton and the archaeologist William H. Holmes. The collaboration of these men did much to formulate the basic principles of structural geology. As a result of the second expedition's success, Powell was named director of the Survey of the Rocky Mountain Region in 1877. Two years later all local surveys were merged in the U.S. Geological Survey, and Powell was made chief of this bureau in 1881; he served as chief until 1894. Among Powell's important publications resulting from his Colorado River explorations are *The Exploration of the Colorado River of the West* (1875) and *The Geology of the Eastern Portion of the Uinta Mountains* (1876).

BIBLIOGRAPHY

F. S. Dellenbaugh, *Canyon Voyage*.

R. B. Stanton, *Colorado River Controversies*.

Wallace Stegner, *Beyond the Hundredth Meridian: John Wesley Powell and the Second Opening of the West*.

POWHATAN CONFEDERACY

Powhatan Confederacy, a 17th-century chiefdom established by conquest among the Algonkin-speaking Indians of the Virginia coastal plain. Chief Powhatan (properly the name of his principal village) inherited dominion over some seven local groups ("tribes"). Thereafter he extended his sway north and south on the tidewater plain and across Chesapeake Bay to its eastern shore, until it embraced some thirty tributary groups, having an estimated population of 9,000. The center of Powhatan's domain lay on the James, Pamunkey, and Mattaponi rivers; yet within it the Chickahominy preserved their independence. Farmers who supplemented their agricultural produce through fishing, hunting, and gathering, these Virginia Algonkins dwelt in villages that were often fortified; the largest had over 200 inhabitants.

For the most part status among the leading families rested on a combination of wealth and ability. Powhatan exacted annual tribute from subordinate chiefs, and his own fields were worked by his immediate subjects. Opechancanough, one of two brothers who were to succeed him, had his seat at Pamunkey, a principal tributary. Beneath the chiefs in their various villages were officials serving both as advisers and as war leaders. Buttressing the ruling class was a priesthood serving in major villages at temples, each of which housed the image of a tribal deity together with the bones of past chiefs.

Powhatan and his chiefdom played a vital role in the early history of the Virginia colony. The early settlers were dependent for sustenance on the purchase or seizure of Indian foodstuffs, and during the "starving time" in 1609 some were lodged with the Indians. Powhatan was treated by the English as minor, barbaric royalty, and the marriage of his daughter Pocahontas to John Rolfe was instrumental in concluding peace between him and the English, freeing the latter to subdue the intervening Chickahominy. With the death of Powhatan in 1618, power passed by turns to Opechancanough, who remained obdurate and who in 1622 led his people into sudden and concerted war against the colonists. The colonists rallied from the blow and launched merciless reprisals until 1631. In 1644 the aged chieftain essayed a last, desperate campaign that ended in his defeat and death. Thereafter, the Virginia colony, in an early form of indirect rule, incorporated the chiefdom in subordinate status. In the last official act of the Tributary chiefs, as they were by then known, a delegation participated in the Treaty of Albany (1722) with the Iroquois.

BIBLIOGRAPHY

James Mooney, "Powhatan," in F. W. Hodge, ed., *Handbook of American Indians North of Mexico.*

Theodore Stern, "Chickahominy: The Changing Culture of a Virginia Indian Community," *American Philosophical Society Proceedings*, vol. 96 (1952).

— THEODORE STERN

PRESBYTERIANISM

The name of the Presbyterian church is derived from its form of church government by a hierarchy of church courts composed of both teaching (clerical) and ruling (lay) elders, or presbyters. Doctrinally, Presbyterian churches are part of the Reformed tradition, founded by John Calvin of Geneva in the 16th century. Their most widely accepted standard is the Westminster Confession of Faith, which was drafted in 1646, during the English Civil War. The theology of the confession was influenced chiefly by the Puritan tradition. It stresses the role of the divine decrees, the use of the covenant system, the identification of the Lord's Day with the Christian sabbath, and the subjective operation of grace.

Although the Scotch-Irish have exerted considerable influence on the development of American Presbyterianism, the church has never been merely a reproduction of the Church of Scotland. Francis Mekamie, often called the founder of American Presbyterianism, organized the Presbytery of Philadelphia in 1706. By 1716 the church was large enough to form itself into a synod representing four presbyteries and thirty ministers. A large number of these clergymen were from New England, and conflict between the Scotch-Irish, led by John Thomson, and those clergymen was characteristic of early Presbyterian history. The original dispute concerned the terms of subscription to the Westminster standard, and implicitly the issue of the independence of the American church. It was settled by a compromise in 1729 that adopted a looser form of subscription than was current in Europe.

Presbyterian churches are part of the Reformed tradition founded by John Calvin of Geneva in the sixteenth century.

The Presbyterian church was both active in the Great Awakening and deeply divided over its significance. The center of Presbyterian Evangelical Calvinism was the Log College, established by William Tennent to train clergymen. Its graduates, partly under the influence of the Dutch Reformed pastor Theodore Frelinghuysen, were active revivalists and tended to form their own ecclesiastical party. Gilbert Tennent, the son of William, was the leader of the small revival that swept the middle colonies in the 1730's and was later a leading supporter of the evangelistic tours of George Whitefield. As the revival grew, so did tension between the two parties in the church. In 1741 Gilbert Tennent preached the so-called Nottingham sermon, "The Danger of an Unconverted Ministry," which heralded the coming division of the church into the Synod at New York, or New Side, formed by the Tennents and John Dickenson, and the Synod of Philadelphia, or Old Side, headed by Thomson. A reconciliation occurred only after the New Side made diplomatic advances to the Old Side pastors. But the controversy lay just beneath the surface, and the theological issues raised by evangelicalism were to contribute to the later Old School–New School schism.

In 1801 the Presbyterians joined the Congregationalists in the Plan of Union, which was intended to promote a joint endeavor in the winning of the West. The success of the plan, however, caused controversy, and as Congregationalism drifted toward a more liberal theology, it was abrogated. Most of the churches founded under the plan adhered to the New School theology.

Although the spread of Presbyterianism was initially hampered by its insistence on a learned ministry, its high standards enabled it to become the educator of the West. Presbyterians were the great college founders of the region, and, in the period before the Civil War, exercised the greatest cultural influence on that emerging society.

The question of slavery lay beneath many of the struggles in the Presbyterian church prior to the Civil War, and despite attempts by church leaders to resolve the issue, it refused to disappear. Although the abrogation of the Plan of Union in 1837 and the division of the church into New School and Old School groups were ostensibly over theological issues, it appears that the question of race was a hidden item on the agenda of the southern delegations. The New School Presbyterians were unable to maintain unity after 1857, when the small number of southern evangelicals withdrew from the parent body. The Old School remained united until hostilities actually began. After the Civil War, Old School and New School factions in both the North and South reunited, leaving the main division in Presbyterianism on regional lines, and as late as 1958 the Presbyterian Church in the United States (southern) refused merger with the northern body.

Since the Civil War the Presbyterian churches have been troubled by theological controversies that have threatened to destroy their precarious unity. The most serious of these was the fundamentalist-modernist controversy in the early part of the 20th century. The Old School theologians of Princeton Seminary formulated the defense of the traditional understanding of scripture against the higher criticism. In 1892 the general assembly of the northern church accepted the Princeton interpretation of the issue and suspended several seminary professors, most notably Charles A. Briggs of Union Seminary, from the ministry. In 1910 the general assembly passed a resolution declaring five fundamentals (inerrancy of the Bible, the virgin birth, substitutionary atonement, bodily resurrection, and the miracles of Christ) necessary articles of belief. Because of this decision, further discussion moved underground until the 1920's, when it reemerged over the teachings of Harry Emerson Fosdick, a Baptist serving the First Presbyterian Church of New York City. Given the choice of conforming or resigning, Fosdick resigned.

Since the early 1960's there have been signs that the Presbyterian church, at least in the North, has moved toward greater theological comprehensiveness. Following the merger of the Presbyterian Church in the United States of America and the United Presbyterian Church of North America in 1958, the new church began examining its confessional standards. The result of its deliberations was the adoption of the Book of Confessions, which added to the traditional Westminster standard such traditional symbols as the Apostles Scots Confession of 1560 and such modern statements of faith as the Barmen Declaration (1934) and the Confession of 1967. Although some lay groups protested the new position, it seemed to be firmly established in the mid-1970's.

The principal Presbyterian denominations and their 1974 membership figures are Associate Reformed Presbyterian Church, 28,711; Cumberland Presbyterian Church, 87,838; Orthodox Presbyterian Church, 14,871; Presbyterian Church in the United States (southern), 951,788; Reformed Presbyterian Church of North America, 5,560; Second Cumberland Presbyterian Church, 30,000; and United Presbyterian Church in the United States of America (northern), 2,908,958.

BIBLIOGRAPHY

Charles A. Anderson, *The Presbyterian Enterprise.*

Gaius Jackson Slosser, *They Seek a Country: The American Presbyterians.*

Ernest Trice Thomson, *Presbyterians in the South.*

Leonard J. Trinterud, *The Forming of an American Tradition: A Reexamination of Colonial Presbyterianism.*

— GLENN T. MILLER

PRESERVATION MOVEMENT

The historic-preservation movement in the United States—the varied aspirations and actions of Americans to save their tangible historical and cultural heritage—began in 1850 when New York State became the first agency, public or private, to preserve officially a historic house as a museum: the Hasbrouck House, George Washington's headquarters at Newburgh, N.Y. Although there was great national enthusiasm to memorialize the first president, Congress rejected three proposals that the U.S. government acquire Mount Vernon, Washington's estate in Virginia. In 1858 a private group, the Mount Vernon Ladies' Association of the Union, rescued the estate.

The first federally purchased historic house was the Custis-Lee Mansion in Arlington, Va.; it was bought in 1883. The first federal park tract protected for historic value was Casa Grande, an excavated Indian pueblo in Arizona that was acquired by authorization of Congress in 1889.

The U.S. preservation movement can be followed through national legislation. The passage of the Antiquities Act in 1906 (Public Law 209) authorized the president to declare as national monuments historic landmarks, historic and prehistoric structures, and other objects of historic or scientific value located on lands owned or controlled by the government. The Historic Sites Act of 1935 (Public Law 74–292) declared it a national policy to preserve for public use historic sites, buildings, and objects of national significance for the people of the United States. The National Trust for Historic Preservation of 1949 authorized the establishment of a nonprofit, educational corporation to further the purpose of the Historic Sites Act; to facilitate public participation in preservation through service, education, and counsel; and to accept and administer properties significant in American history and culture for the public.

The National Historic Preservation Act of 1966 (Public Law 89–665) reaffirmed the national policy for preservation, acknowledged that governmental and nongovernmental preservation programs up to that time were inadequate to preserve the national heritage, and stated that although the major preservation burdens were borne and major efforts initiated by the private sector, the federal government should accelerate its activities and give maximum encouragement to the National Trust for Historic Preservation and to local and state governmental efforts. The preservation program of the National Park Service, a bureau of the Department of the Interior, was strengthened. Also, the National Register for Historic Places—which lists districts, sites, buildings, structures, and objects of local, regional, state, and national significance—was expanded. Heads of federal agencies were required to consider the effect on National Register properties of proposed federal projects. Conflicts between projects and properties were to be reported for comment to the Advisory Council on Historic Preservation, a unit established by the act. The act also authorized grants to the states for 50 percent of the cost of preparing statewide historic-preservation plans and historic-site surveys and gave assistance to preservation projects. Matching grants were authorized to the National Trust for its educational, technical, and properties programs.

Other national legislation that assists in the preservation of the American historical and cultural heritage includes the amended Surplus Property Act, 1944; the National Foundation on the Arts and the Humanities Act, 1965; the National Museum Act, 1966; the Demonstration Cities and Metropolitan Development Act, 1966; the Transportation Act, 1966; and the National Environmental Policy Act, 1969.

The 1966 National Historic Preservation Act and subsequent national preservation legislation were instigated by the rapid development of available land following World War II. Urbanization and increasing population brought highway construction, commercial and residential development, industry, and other developments that posed preservation problems.

Since 1850 historic preservation has developed from a pastime to a national movement. Preservationists work for private historical societies and action groups and for local, state, and federal public agencies. They are involved in the protection of one or many structures or a district with a total character greater than the sum of its individual elements. The National Trust sets national standards and provides direction for its members and the general public. In 1975 it had more than 75,000 individual members and affiliated organizations and a $5.8 million annual budget; it owned thirteen historic properties, which from June 1974 to June 1975 were visited by more than 230,000 people.

Government and such private groups as the National Trust are attempting to make preservation relevant to people of all income levels and to all racial and ethnic groups. Every American has a history and should have a tangible cultural heritage. Preservationists are concerned not only with the restoration and viewing of prime landmarks; they also advocate the rehabilitation of properties of lesser importance for rescue. The variety of properties in the urban and rural environment is vital to the quality of American life.

In the past, persons concerned about cultural values were not activists but appreciators; they were busy recording history and quietly enjoying it. Today preservationists are vigilantes participating in progress and are helping to make history by causing cultural values to be considered in all planning and development.

BIBLIOGRAPHY

David E. Finley, *History of the National Trust for Historic Preservation, 1947–1963.*

Robert R. Garvey and Terry B. Morton, "The United States Government in Historic Preservation," *Momentum*, vol. 2 (1968).

Charles B. Hosmer, Jr., *Presence of the Past—A History of the Preservation Movement in the United States Before Williamsburg.*

U.S. Conference of Mayors and the Ford Foundation, Special Committee on Historic Preservation, *With Heritage So Rich.*

— TERRY B. MORTON

PRESIDENT

The office of the president, created by the U.S. Constitution, is a depository of vast powers. First, there are the powers conferred by the Constitution. For example, the Constitution vests the executive power in the president and charges him to take care that the laws are faithfully executed. He is also commander in chief of the armed forces. Some of his constitutional powers, such as the veto, pertain to the legislative process.

Much of a president's authority is delegated to him by statute, to enable him to implement national policies. Covering a wide array of topics, from organization of the executive branch to tariffs and from labor-management relations to policy on national resources, such authority reflects the variety of functions and services of the late 20th-century American government. These powers, like the president's constitutional powers, are frequently granted in broad language and confer upon him considerable discretionary authority. The very complexity of modern government also means that many of these powers are not so much exercised by the president directly as by subordinates, in his name.

The presidency has been shaped in part by recurring periods of emergency and peril, during which the executive power tends to thrive and expand.

The third kind of power exercised by the president of the United States is extraconstitutional—what John Locke defined as the power to act "according to discretion for the public good without the prescription of law." A good example may be seen in some of the actions of President Abraham Lincoln during the Civil War: unauthorized expenditures of funds and independent raising of an army. In almost every instance of national emergency—a devastating depression, a major war—presidents have exceeded their constitutional and legal powers, and such actions have generally been legitimized through public approval. Such a tradition is at the core of the modern presidency: that the president as the sole representative of all the people possesses great power to preserve and protect the nation.

The presidency is an evolving, rather than a static, institution. While it is encrusted with custom and tradition, as an office it differs significantly from what was envisioned for it by its founders. It is a mixture of traditional and newly acquired functions. Like other institutions, the U.S. presidency has been conditioned by the forces and pressures that affect society generally and has thus been significantly altered over the years. Among the factors that have influenced its development are the following: (1) democratization of the means of nominating and electing the chief executive, lending substance to the claim that he is the only official elected by all the people; (2) ambiguity in the constitutional phrases defining presidential power and duties; (3) expansion in the role of the government, and the consequent creation of a vast bureaucracy under the president; (4) recurring periods of emergency and peril, during which the executive power seems to thrive and expand; and (5) the rise of the United States as a major world power and the preoccupation with foreign policy in the political arena, an area in which the president has long-standing advantages over the other branches of the government.

The office of president is also subject to the influence of personality. Each occupant of the office brings a personal dimension to it: his own political skills and abilities, his own vision and goals. Throughout history a number of broad presidential types have emerged. One is a literalist president, who functions in close obedience to the letter of the Constitution and the traditional separation of powers. Presidential powers are seen by such an incumbent mainly in a negative sense, restricting and confining; to him, Congress is in many ways the preeminent branch, needing little guidance or direction from the president. Such a chief executive plays the political role sparingly, preferring to remain above the battle. In the 19th century there were many such presidents—James Buchanan, Franklin Pierce, Ulysses S. Grant, James A. Garfield. Examples of 20th-century presidents of this type would include William H. Taft, Warren G. Harding, and Calvin Coolidge. At the other end of the continuum is a strong president. Such a president views his powers with a maximum liberality and, in the process of using them, frequently incites constitutional controversies; he establishes new precedents and breaks old ones. The emphasis of his activity is political, not legalistic. The president sees himself not merely as an administrative officer, but, in John F. Kennedy's phrase, as "the vital center of action in our whole scheme of government." This interpretation of function is represented by Andrew Jackson, Lincoln, Woodrow Wilson, Theodore Roosevelt, Franklin D. Roosevelt, and Kennedy. The third type of president takes a position about midway between the first two. He sometimes emphasizes the purely administrative aspects of the presidency and at other times the broader dimensions of the office. At one time he defers to Congress; subsequently he pushes and prods the legislators. The distinctive trait of such a president is that he views the essential presidential function defensively, using executive energy and weapons (such as the veto) to maintain an existing equilibrium. Examples include John Adams, John Quincy Adams, Martin Van Buren, and Grover Cleveland. Dwight D. Eisenhower might also belong in this category. Most modern commentators suggest that regardless of a particular incumbent's theory or view of the presidency, national demands and expectations push a president more and more to adopt the strong role.

The presidency has been a fairly flexible and adaptable institution. Originally selected by a few, the president is now popularly elected. Many 19th-century presidents regarded themselves primarily as administrators, but 20th-century presidents have performed a greater variety of roles, ranging from chief legislator to guardian of domestic peace and manager of prosperity. To help a president perform his expanded duties, an array of advisers, offices, and councils has been created, so that in some respects the presidency has been institutionalized. And it is likely that this development and adaptation will continue. The presidency will probably remain the focus of great demands and expectations. Its tasks and duties are so varied and complex and of such significance to the nation and the world that it has become one of the most powerful positions in the world. At the same time the circumstances of the age have subjected the president's leadership, domestic and foreign, to many limitations. His powers seem vast, but he is constrained in ways unknown to his predecessors, and when his powers are measured against the problems he confronts, they do not seem so great. And as a repository of high public hopes and expectations, presidential action or inaction must inevitably disillusion some people.

BIBLIOGRAPHY

Dorothy Buckton James, *The Contemporary Presidency.*
Louis Koenig, *The Chief Executive.*
Dale Vinyard, *The Presidency.*
Aaron Wildavsky, *The Presidency.*

— DALE VINYARD

PRESIDENCY

The American presidency has undergone a major transition since the 1970s. The president has vastly greater power than any official to lead the citizenry by setting the national agenda and determining foreign policy. Far more than his predecessors, however, the contemporary president must negotiate with Congress, the judiciary, cabinet departments, and executive and independent agencies, all of which have become more assertive. The president also faces ever-greater pressure from an electorate increasingly less loyal to political parties, from special interest groups that are well-financed and from media that are investigative. The president's international influence has been eroded by the rise of other industrial nations and Third World countries. Further, although the United States has unrivaled military strength and the world's largest economy, in the post-cold war era the president's command of nuclear weapons and foreign aid is not as effective as before to resolve conflicts and align nations, and the public is reluctant to approve U.S. participation in international peacekeeping or nation-building operations.

President Franklin D. Roosevelt (1933–1945) established the modern presidency. He acted as chief legislative whip and established the executive office of the president by moving the Bureau of the Budget into the White House offices in 1939, thereby expanding federal authority. His administrators managed New Deal programs and a wartime economy, and he exercised extraordinary diplomatic-military authority through executive agreements and summit conferences. Presidents expanded their power in the next decades by using the Bureau of the Budget and Council of Economic Advisers to assess the costs of legislative programs and national economic policy, marshaling federal authority to enforce Supreme Court desegregation rulings and civil rights laws and commanding television time for addresses and press conferences to advocate policies. Notably, President Lyndon B. Johnson (1963–1969) focused his political-legislative skills on his Great Society's commitment to voting and social welfare rights.

Presidential power over foreign affairs grew even more markedly. Harry S. Truman (1945–1953) became the first president to send troops to fight a major war—in Korea—and to station them abroad—in Western Europe—without formal approval from Congress. President Dwight D. Eisenhower (1953–1961) unilaterally approved military and covert actions against foreign governments. President John F. Kennedy (1961–1963) denied Congress a role in crises over Cuba and Vietnam. President Johnson used an incident in the Gulf of Tonkin in 1964 to persuade Congress to authorize almost unlimited retaliation, which led to a decade of war in Vietnam. Mounting protest against the Vietnam War, which television brought graphically into American homes, forced Johnson to forgo a reelection bid in 1968.

Richard M. Nixon, a Republican with a "southern strategy," was elected president in 1968 by promising not only to end the Vietnam War but to maintain a "law and order" administration, to reduce executive branch intervention in economic and social welfare matters, and to appoint conservative Supreme Court judges who would not "legislate" from the bench. Despite these pledges, the Nixon presidency (1969–1974) proved to be as "imperial" as any other. It enlarged and delegated authority to White House staff, expanded the Bureau of the Budget in 1970 into an even more powerful Office of Management and Budget (OMB), and impounded congressionally allocated funds, a virtual line-item veto. In 1971 Nixon instituted wage and price controls, suspended international convertibility of the dollar, and imposed a surcharge on imports. At the same time he outspent Johnson's Great Society, becoming the only cold war president to spend more on human resources programs than defense. Under Nixon the White House dominated foreign policy. It expanded the Vietnam War by secretly bombing Cambodia, intensified the warfare in Laos, and vastly increased bombing of North Vietnam. He restructured the National Security Council (NSC) to rival the Department of State and authorized his NSC adviser to use secret diplomacy to destabilize other governments, opened relations with the People's Republic of China, and negotiated to conclude the Vietnam War. Nixon also established a tenuous détente with the Soviet Union.

Congress gradually reasserted its authority at home and abroad during the Nixon era. It refused to confirm two Supreme Court nominees (although Nixon did appoint four justices who greatly influenced Court opinions) and passed the Budget and Impoundment Control Act of 1974, creating the Congressional Budget Office to counter OMB functions. In 1969 the Senate resolved that a national commitment to use U.S. forces or finances to aid another country required formal approval from Congress. In 1970 Congress repealed the Gulf of Tonkin Resolution and prohibited use of past or present appropriations to finance U.S. combat in Laos, Cambodia, and North and South Vietnam after August 1973. The Case-Zablocki Act of 1972 mandated that the president report all executive agreements to Congress within sixty days. The War Powers Act of 1973, passed over Nixon's veto, limited the president's use of troops abroad without formal congressional approval to sixty to ninety days, although the law conceded the president's authority to commit troops initially. In 1983 the Supreme Court, in an unrelated case, ruled that legislative vetoes (that is, Congress's right to overturn executive branch action either by withholding approval or voting to disapprove) such as provided in the War Powers Act were unconstitutional. In addition, since 1973 every president has sent troops abroad with scant reference to the War Powers Act.

The Watergate scandal during Nixon's second term brought the presidency into disrepute. White House aides and other officials were convicted for sanctioning or covering up a break-in at Democratic National Committee headquarters during the 1972 presidential campaign, a grand jury named the president an unindicted co-conspirator, and the House Judiciary Committee voted impeachment articles. In August 1974 Nixon became the first president to resign the office. Watergate was the worst White House scandal in U.S. history because it violated civil liberties and the political process and produced enduring public cynicism about the presidency and politics, but it also created a framework for scrutinizing alleged presidential transgressions. This included investigation by congressional committees and special prosecutors and a unanimous Supreme Court ruling that the president's executive privilege does not reach to withholding evidence in a criminal proceeding.

The presidency in the decade following Watergate and the end of the Vietnam War appeared at least temporarily weakened. President Gerald R. Ford (1974–1977) lacked a national constituency when he assumed the office following Nixon's resignation, and he undercut his support by pardoning Nixon. Ford's successor, President Jimmy Carter (1977–1981), lacked congressional allies, and his call for zero-based budgeting won no favor with federal officials, but he was able to broker Middle East peace accords and gain passage of the Panama Canal Treaty in 1978. His presidency foundered on matters beyond White House control: an energy crisis; inflation; the Soviet invasion of Afghanistan; and a revolution and hostage-taking in Iran.

Congressional and blue-ribbon panel investigations of the Iran-contra affair proved only that the president had given his aides license, not instruction, to violate the law.

Ronald Reagan won the presidency in 1980 by promising to minimize the size and scope of the federal government and to restore marketplace freedom and offering a foreign-military policy to regain U.S. global primacy. He identified closely with his party and capitalized on resurgent Republicanism in the older South as well as in newer Sunbelt regions and on rising religious fundamentalism. His victory catalyzed growing opposition to higher taxes and social welfare payments, administrative agency rulemaking, judicial decisions giving legal status to socially based rights, and animus toward the Soviet Union and terrorism. Reagan used both old and new political devices to strengthen his presidential power. He galvanized popular support with media messages, and used OMB's fiscal analyses and oversight of agency budgets and legislative proposals to slash social welfare, reduce taxes, and increase military spending. His economic policies, dubbed "Reaganomics," led to record budget deficits that necessitated cuts in social programs, prevented new entitlements, and created policy formation by budget priority. Reagan speeded deregulation. During his eight-year presidency, he appointed more than half of all federal judges—although Congress in 1987 rejected his controversial Supreme Court nominee, Robert Bork, who favored recent Supreme Court decisions that narrowed individual rights.

In foreign affairs Reagan undertook a vast nuclear weapons buildup, deployed forces to Lebanon, invaded Grenada, bombed Libya, and approved extensive covert activity in Central America. After difficult summit meetings with Soviet leaders, he reversed course in 1987–1988 to effect the most significant nuclear arms reduction since the start of the cold war. His presidency was jolted by the revelation that NSC officials had broken the law and lied under oath to Congress while exchanging arms for hostages with Iran and supporting covert actions in Central America. Congressional and blue-ribbon panel investigations of the Iran-Contra scandal proved only that the president gave his aides license, not instruction, to violate the law.

The popular Reagan propelled Vice President George Bush into the White House in 1988. Bush's forceful foreign policies against dictators in Panama and Iraq raised his standing to extraordinary heights in 1991, but he lost reelection a year later to a relatively unknown Democrat, Governor Bill Clinton of Arkansas, whose campaign emphasized domestic issues and benefited from sharp criticism of Bush's economic policies by an independent presidential candidate, billionaire businessman Ross Perot. Despite initial difficulties, Clinton won passage of the North American Free Trade Agreement in 1993 and a sharply modified economic program that raised taxes on high incomes, reduced burdens on lower income groups, and slowed the growth of annual budget deficits, but also included only modest appropriations for education and job programs. Clinton also appointed two moderate Supreme Court justices, Ruth Bader Ginsburg and Stephen G. Breyer. Most significantly, however, after appointing his wife, Hillary Rodham Clinton, to head a task force on national health care reform, the president failed to gain necessary support for its complex proposal intended to guarantee health coverage for all Americans and to contain health care costs, which had risen to 14 percent of the gross national product.

The Clinton presidency achieved moderate success in foreign policy despite a setback in 1993 when eighteen U.S. soldiers, part of a United Nations mission in Somalia, were killed by rebel forces, leading to the withdrawal of U.S. troops. Nonetheless, the Clinton administration helped to broker historic accords, signed at the White House, that initiated mutual recognition between Israel, the Palestinian Liberation Organization, and Arab autonomy on the West Bank and Gaza Strip. In 1994 Clinton effected a successful military—and peaceful—intervention to restore a democratically elected government in Haiti. The Clinton administration also fostered negotiations in 1995 intended to end four years of raging civil-religious war among Croatians, Bosnian Muslims, and Bosnian Serbs in the former Yugoslavia.

The Clinton presidency suffered a sharp political decline when the Republicans, who promoted term limits for federal officials and vastly reduced federal commitment—and greater state control—over social welfare programs, swept the congressional elections in 1994 and gained control of both houses of Congress for the first time in forty years. The Republican victories shifted the initiative for legislation from the White House to Congress, which rejected term limits but by the end of 1995 had prepared an economic program that proposed a balanced budget within seven years, lower taxes for high-income earners, and greatly reduced federal expenditures but more latitude for state controls for entitlement programs, including welfare (Aid for Families with Dependent Children) and Medicare and Medicaid. As 1996 opened it was unknown whether the president would try to compromise with Congress or veto the legislation and seek a new political mandate in the presidential election in the fall.

Post-Watergate presidents seem subject to unrelenting investigation of their personal as well as political behavior by Congress, special prosecutors, newspapers, and TV and radio talk shows. By 1995 the branches of government were more separate than ever before. Congress was voting programs and agency administrators and federal judges were making decisions that showed little deference for White House policy. A better-informed public was ready to change parties because of issues. The president still had unrivaled power to command public and congressional attention with policy statements, whether from the Oval Office or on talk shows. He had assistants to draft legislation and form political strategy. The OMB could bargain with congressional budget committees. The president retained almost unlimited power in foreign policy crises and great latitude in general to advance the national interest, even by reversing course with former adversaries, as Nixon did with China and Reagan did with the Soviet Union. Although constraints on presidential authority induced more accountability, they did not weaken the presidency, but even with great power, future presidents may find it more difficult to effect solutions to such problems as crime, poverty, drug addiction, and racial antipathy, as well as civil-religious wars, human rights violations, and nuclear proliferation.

[See also Budget, Federal; Campaigns, Presidential; Democratic Party; Iran-Contra Affair; Reaganomics; Republican Party; Third Parties and Independents; War Powers Act; Watergate, Aftermath of.]

BIBLIOGRAPHY

Ryan J. Barrileaux, *The Post-Modern Presidency: The Office After Ronald Reagan* (New York, 1988).

Fred I. Greenstein, ed., *Leadership in the Modern Presidency* (Cambridge, Mass., 1988).

Richard E. Neustadt, *Presidential Power and the Modern Presidents: The Politics of Leadership from Roosevelt to Reagan*, rev. ed. (New York, 1990).

Malcolm Shaw, ed., *The Modern Presidency: From Roosevelt to Reagan* (New York, 1987).

— ARNOLD A. OFFNER

PRESIDENTIAL SUCCESSION

Article II, Section 1, of the U.S. Constitution provides for the succession of the vice-president to the presidency of the United States in case of the death or resignation of the president or his removal from office. Eight presidents had died in office by 1975: William Henry Harrison, Zachary Taylor, Abraham Lincoln, James A. Garfield, William McKinley, Warren G. Harding, Franklin D. Roosevelt, and John F. Kennedy. One president, Richard M. Nixon, had resigned.

Before ratification of the Twenty-fifth Amendment in 1967, there was no clearly defined constitutional line of succession if the vice-president should succeed to the presidency and then die, but Congress, in 1947, had provided by law for such an eventuality by establishing a line of succession. The speaker of the House of Representatives was placed next in line after the vice-president; next came the president pro tempore of the Senate; and then the members of the cabinet, beginning with the secretary of state. An earlier act (1886) had placed the members of the cabinet in line after the vice-president.

The Twenty-fifth Amendment provides a means of filling the vice-presidential post in case of a vacancy, which had occurred sixteen times by 1975: seven vice-presidents had died in office, one had resigned, and eight had succeeded to the presidency. The amendment empowers the president to nominate a vice-president, subject to confirmation by Congress (majority vote in both chambers). If so confirmed, the new vice-president would then be eligible for succession to the presidency. This amendment was first used in 1973 upon the resignation of Spiro Agnew, when President Nixon nominated Rep. Gerald R. Ford for the position. Subsequently, when Nixon resigned and Ford became president, Ford nominated Gov. Nelson Rockefeller for the post.

The Twentieth Amendment, ratified in 1933, deals with another possible problem: if the president-elect dies or fails to qualify for office by the date of the inauguration, the vice-president-elect shall act as president. Furthermore, if neither the president-elect nor the vice-president-elect qualifies, Congress is empowered to declare who shall act as president.

BIBLIOGRAPHY

Harold W. Chase and Craig R. Ducat, eds., *Corwin's The Constitution and What It Means Today.*

— DALE VINYARD

PRICE-FIXING

Price-fixing, a government action dating back to the time of Hammurabi, varies from restraints in inflation and discrimination to supports in time of deflation. Enforcement of restraints is difficult. Fixing prices by private agreement, ancient and common in business practice, is typically secret, unenforceable, and against public policy.

Northern colonial communities routinely regulated prices of necessaries. New York ordinances provoked strikes by coopers (1680) and bakers (1741). Massachusetts fixed beaver and corn as currency (1630) and set silver's value in previous contracts from 1727. Direct wage regulation was also common.

Unprofitable tobacco plagued colonial Virginia except in intervals such as 1682–1702. Its minimum prices of 1632–40, forbidden by royal ordinance in 1641, were followed by repeated stinting acts. Virginia also passed numerous rating acts equating tobacco currency to sterling.

Aside from Congress fixing the price of gold and silver, the federal government took little action between 1775 and 1917. The Continental Congress sidestepped the inflation problem. New England drafted schedules at price conventions in 1776–78, but Connecticut alone put them into effect. Enforcement proved impossible. Civil War prices remained largely free—northern foods were surprisingly cheap until 1864. Evidently the Confederacy's controls started too late to permit enforcement. By October 1864 compliance was so poor that legal ceilings, although extremely high, averaged only 37 percent of published market prices.

> *Fixing prices by private agreement—a common business practice since ancient times—is typically secret, unenforceable, and against public policy.*

In World War I the War Industries Board imposed selective controls effectively and accumulated administrative experience. In 1942–45 the Office of Price Administration approached complete regulation of all prices and rents. Many orders began with a "freeze" (seller's prior maximum price) to be replaced later by "flat" pricing (uniform ceilings for comparable sellers). Upward adjustments were limited to hardship cases. Once begun, controls extended because goods flowed toward free markets. Black markets began flourishing near the end of the war, and practically all prices zoomed upward after the lid was lifted in 1946. Several states then assumed rent controls.

The Office of Price Stabilization imposed milder regulations during the Korean War. The persistence of creeping inflation during the late 1960's prompted the administration of Lyndon B. Johnson to establish guidelines on wage increases and pressure large concerns against raising prices. President Richard M. Nixon established the Cost of Living Council, the Price Commission, and the Pay Board, attacking the problem at strategic points, but avoiding enforcement of the World War II variety. Prices were still inching upward in 1975 despite much unemployment here and there.

After 1865, declining prices, cutthroat competition, and the emergence of giant concerns led eventually to the Granger laws and the Interstate Commerce and Sherman Antitrust acts. The utility policy set maximum rates to protect users, whereas the railroad policy also enforced minimum rates to protect small shippers. Later legislation follows these general objectives.

The Great Depression saw federal and state efforts to restore prices to former levels ("reflation"). Gold was boosted from $20.67 to $35 per troy ounce. The National Industrial Recovery Act let industries enact codes including minimum prices and wages (declared unconstitutional in 1935). The Agricultural Adjustment Act (also declared unconstitutional, in 1936) and later legislation provided higher prices and production controls. Still in effect in 1975, the parity-price program aimed to assure growers of leading crops prices in line with the prices they were paying. Minimum retail milk prices came in federal marketing areas and many states, and were also still in effect in 1975. Chain-store price cutting was attacked in the 1930's by fair-trade laws in forty-five states, allowing manufacturers to set minimum retail prices. The general inflation after 1945 saw several such laws repealed or invalidated in court, reflecting a notable shift of public policy away from favoring price supports.

Common and statute law treats price agreements as conspiracies in restraint of trade, but enforcement since 1711 has commonly taken the price situation into account. Beginning in 1817 saltmakers in western Virginia entered a long series of price and production agreements without court interference. Salt prices were low and other prices were declining. In *United States* v. *Trenton Potteries Company* (1927), however, the Supreme Court decided in favor of the government, rejecting contentions that the agreed-upon prices were not unreasonable. The most notable Supreme Court action came in 1961 (*United States* v. *General Electric et al.*), resulting in heavy fines, imprisonment of seven executives, and huge refunds. Nevertheless, agreements promise so much security to sellers that they may be expected to persist at various levels of trade.

The quotation of steel and cement prices from basing points was held illegal, as an aid to collusion by the Court in 1948 (*Federal Trade Commission* v. *Cement Institute et al.*), after buyers reported identical bids from various sellers. Retail prices of gasoline and new automobiles were still quoted in this way in the mid-1970's.

BIBLIOGRAPHY

Thomas S. Berry, *Western Prices Before 1861.*

Lewis C. Gray and Esther K. Thompson, *History of Agriculture in the Southern United States to 1860.*

Harvey C. Mansfield, *Short History of the OPA.*

Dudley F. Pegrum, *Public Regulation of Business.*

W. B. Weeden, *Economic and Social History of New England.*

Chester W. Wright, *Economic History of the United States.*

— THOMAS SENIOR BERRY

PRIMARY, DIRECT

The most widely used system in the 20th century for nominating candidates of a political party for elective office is the direct primary. Potential candidates of a given party for an office must obtain a designated minimum number of signatures of party members to allow their names to be printed on the ballots. Those candidates are then voted on by all the members of the given party in the election district on a prescribed date, ranging from early April to late September, according to state election laws and procedures. The winners of the direct primary for each office for each political party are allowed to represent their respective parties in the general election that takes place several months after the direct primary.

Before the early 1900's nominations for public office were made by the congressional and legislative caucuses' declaring nominees (from the birth of the United States through 1830) or by delegate conventions (from the 1830's until the early 1900's). Robert M. La Follette's Progressive movement in Wisconsin gave impetus to the principle of nominating candidates by direct voting of party members.

Democrats in Crawford County, Pa., first used the system on Sept. 9, 1842; the Republicans started to use the "Crawford County system" in 1860. Slowly but steadily, this system for nominating candidates became the standard method. It was accepted voluntarily at first and later enacted into state election laws.

Two types of direct primaries exist: closed and open. A closed primary, used by almost all states, is a direct primary in which evidence of party membership is required, either by enrollment before the election or by a statement of allegiance at the polls when the voter asks for the ballot of a given party. An open primary is a direct primary in which no party membership test is given, no record of the voter's choice of party ballot made, and no challenge made as to party affiliation.

BIBLIOGRAPHY

Charles E. Merriam and Louise Overacker, *Primary Elections.*
National Municipal League, *A Model Direct Primary Election System.*

— RONALD F. STINNETT

PRINTING PRESS, EARLY AMERICAN

For over 100 years printing in America was done on presses imported from Europe. In 1750 Christopher Sower of Germantown, Pa., contrived a press for himself, but American manufacture did not begin until 1769 when Isaac Doolittle, a clockmaker of New Haven, Conn., built a press for William Goddard of Philadelphia. Around 1800, Adam Ramage, a Scotsman, began to manufacture in Philadelphia the presses that bore his name. All of these presses were of primitive design, operated by a hand lever that applied pressure to the platen by a central screw, held in a framework of wood. Ramage subsequently improved the press, enlarged the screw, and used more metal parts. He adapted or copied European innovations and carried on a sizable manufacturing business. In 1816 George Clymer made his Columbian press, which substituted direct leverage for the screw; and Otis Tuft used a toggle joint in place of the screw. Other pressmakers were John I. Wells of Hartford and Samuel Rust and Peter Smith of New York. The latter brought out the Washington handpress but sold the patent in 1825 to R. Hoe and Company. The power press was then coming into use, but these handpresses were used in smaller offices for many years.

The first regular manufacture of type in America was begun in 1769 by Abel Buell of Killingworth, Conn.; Buell's foundry was aided by the Connecticut assembly. German type was cast in 1770 by Christopher Sower, Jr., in Germantown. The Philadelphia firm of Binny and Ronaldson, established in 1796, was the first extensive typefoundry in America.

The first American printing press, brought to America by Stephen Day and established at Harvard in 1640. Undated photograph. (Corbis-Bettmann)

BIBLIOGRAPHY

Thomas MacKellar, *The American Printer.*
L. C. Wroth, *The Colonial Printer.*

— MILTON W. HAMILTON

PRISONERS OF WAR AND MISSING IN ACTION

Prisoners of War and Missing in Action (POWs and MIAs), an important legacy of the Vietnam War, with ramifications for both American domestic politics and U.S. relations with Vietnam. By the terms of the Paris Peace Accords of 1973, which ended U.S. involvement in Vietnam, the Democratic Republic of Vietnam (North Vietnam) agreed to release all American POWs that it was holding. North Vietnam, although having acceded to the Geneva Convention of 1949, which classified prisoners of war as "victims of events" who were entitled to "decent and humane treatment," had insisted that the crews of U.S. bombers were guilty of "crimes against humanity," and returning POWs told stories of mistreatment by their captors. The emotions stirred by evidence of mistreatment were magnified by reports that not all POWs had been returned and that Americans were still being held captive. These impressions of an inhumane Vietnamese government (officially called the Socialist Republic of Vietnam following the North's victory of 1975, which reunified the country) were reinforced by the plight of "boat people" fleeing Vietnam and Vietnam's invasion of Cambodia in 1978. These events helped to solidify public and congressional support for nonrecognition of Vietnam and a trade embargo.

The United States made "full accountability" of MIAs a condition of diplomatic recognition of Vietnam. At the end of the war, 1,750 Americans were listed as missing in Vietnam (another 600 MIAs were listed in neighboring Laos and Cambodia). The United States also insisted that Vietnam assist in the recovery of remains of MIAs who were killed in Vietnam and in the return of any individuals who might have survived the war. Of particular concern were the "discrepancy cases," where individuals were believed to have survived an incident (for example, bailing out of an aircraft and having been reportedly seen later) but were not among the returning POWs.

The POW and MIA controversy triggered a rigorous debate and became a popular culture phenomenon in the late 1970s and 1980s, despite Pentagon and congressional investigations that indicated there were no more than 200 unresolved MIA cases out of the 2,266 the Department of Defense still listed as missing and about a dozen POWs unaccounted for. (Approximately 300,000 North and South Vietnamese are still considered MIAs.) President Ronald Reagan, speaking before the National League of POW/MIA Families in 1987, stated that "until all our questions are fully answered, we will assume that some of our countrymen are alive." The Vietnam Veterans of America, which sent several investigating groups to Vietnam in the 1980s, helped renew contacts between the U.S. and Vietnamese governments. Accordingly, agreements were reached between Vietnamese authorities and representatives of the Reagan administration that resulted in cooperation in recovering the remains of American casualties. Several hundred sets of remains were returned to the United States beginning in the late 1980s. In addition, progress was made in clarifying "discrepancy cases." The question resurfaced in the 1990s about whether President Richard Nixon and Secretary of State Henry Kissinger had done all they could during peace negotiations to free servicemen "knowingly" left behind or whether they both were so desperate to get out of Vietnam that they sacrificed POWs. Both Nixon and Kissinger maintained that it was the "doves" in Congress at the time who prevented any effective military action to find out the truth about POWs when it was still possible to do so in the summer and spring of 1973. On Feb. 3, 1994, with the approval of the Senate and business community, President Bill Clinton removed the nineteen-year trade embargo against Vietnam, and the Vietnamese government cooperated with veterans groups in locating the remains of U.S. soldiers and returning remains to the United States for burial, including those of nine soldiers in October 1995.

BIBLIOGRAPHY

Frederick Z. Brown, *Second Chance: The United States and Indochina in the 1990s* (New York, 1989).

— GARY R. HESS

PRIVATEERS AND PRIVATEERING

The operations of Sir John Hawkins, Sir Francis Drake, and other 16th-century Elizabethan freebooters are often considered the historical starting point of privateering in America. But the participation of privately armed American colonists in the wars of England did not begin until more than a century later, during King William's War (1689–97). During Queen Anne's War (1702–13), a considerable number of privateers were commissioned by the colonial governors. Relatively few took to the sea during the short war with Spain in 1718, but under royal warrants the American governors, in 1739, again issued letters of marque and reprisal against Spain. In King George's War (1744–48) privateering began to assume the proportions of a major maritime business, and it is said that during the French and Indian War (1754–63) 11,000 Americans were engaged in such operations.

Upon the commencement of hostilities with the mother country in 1775, most of the colonies, notably Massachusetts and Rhode Island, issued letters of marque and reprisal, and three months before the Declaration of Independence, the Continental Congress sanctioned privateering "against the enemies of the United Colonies." The 1,151 American privateers operating during the Revolution captured about 600 British vessels, of which 16 were men-of-war. During the last three years of the war, the privateers carried the brunt of the fighting at sea. By 1781 there were in commission only three public cruisers, but 449 privately armed cruisers carrying 6,735 guns were in service. Although the operations of the privateers had been not only financially profitable but also an invaluable aid to the navy, the U.S. government soon joined the movement in Europe to abolish privateering. It reversed its position in 1798 in the face of the arrogant depredations of armed vessels sailing under the authority of republican France. Congress first dealt with this threat in an act of June 25, 1798, allowing American merchantmen to arm themselves for defensive purposes. An act of July 9, 1798, authorized them to apply for special commissions to make offensive war on all armed French vessels. By the close of the year at least 428 merchantmen had been armed (probably three-fourths of these had received official commissions), and before the close of hostilities in 1801, upward of 1,000 vessels had been armed. Since the armed merchantmen were not allowed to prey on unarmed commerce, fighting was generally secondary to trading; nevertheless, there were some notable encounters and valuable captures. In the War of 1812, 515 letters of marque and reprisal were issued, under which 1,345 British vessels are known to have been taken. All the seaboard states from Maine to Louisiana sent privateers to sea against Great Britain in either the Revolution, the War of 1812, or both, but the numbers contributed by each state varied greatly. Massachusetts led with a total of at least 457 ships, and Maryland followed with 281; in contrast, New Jersey and North Carolina probably contributed not more than four ships each.

With the return of world peace in 1815, many American and European privateers were unwilling to return to peaceful pursuits; some found service in Latin-American revolutions, and others became pirates. For the next twenty-five years the U.S. Navy was much engaged in the suppression of piracy. The Republic of Texas resorted to privateering in the early stage (1835–37) of its protracted war with Mexico. The United States, with its naval superiority, did not find it expedient to issue letters of marque and reprisal during the Mexican War (1846–48). The United States declined to accede to the Declaration of Paris (1856), outlawing privateering among the principal world powers, but when the Confederate States of America issued letters of marque, President Abraham Lincoln endeavored to treat the Confederate privateers as pirates, until he was checked by retaliatory measures. The privateers sailing from Louisiana, North Carolina, and South Carolina in 1861 enjoyed as profitable cruises as had their predecessors of 1812; but Confederate privateering declined after the first year, and a volunteer naval system was instituted. The United States' attempt at privateering in 1863 proved abortive, as did Chile's attempt against Spain in 1865, and privateering ended throughout the world with the downfall of the Confederacy.

BIBLIOGRAPHY

C. W. Kendall, *Private Men-of-War.*
W. S. Maclay, *A History of American Privateers.*
W. M. Robinson, Jr., *The Sea Dogs of Texas.*
W. M. Robinson, Jr., *The Confederate Privateers.*

— WILLIAM M. ROBINSON, JR.

PROCLAMATION OF 1763

Proclamation of 1763, a document issued by the British government regulating the settlement of land in North America. It was prepared in part by William Petty Fitzmaurice, Lord Shelburne, president of the Board of Trade, but was completed after his resignation by his successor, Wills Hill, Lord Hillsborough, and was proclaimed by the crown on Oct. 2. By it, parts of the territory in America acquired through the Treaty of Paris earlier in the year were organized as the provinces of Quebec, East Florida, West Florida, and Grenada; the laws of England were extended to these provinces; and provision was made for the establishment of general assemblies in them. Settlement within the new provinces was encouraged by grants of land to British veterans of the French and Indian War.

The part of the proclamation most significant for American history was that aimed at conciliating the Indians. The governors of the provinces and colonies were forbidden to grant lands "for the present, and until our further Pleasure be known . . . beyond the Heads or Sources of any of the Rivers which fall into the Atlantic Ocean from the West and North West." An Indian reservation was thus established south of the lands of the Hudson's Bay Company, west of the province of Quebec and of the Appalachian Mountains, and north of the boundary line of the Floridas, the thirty-first parallel. Settlement upon the Indian lands was prohibited, and settlers already on such lands were commanded "forthwith to remove themselves." Furthermore, private purchases of land from the Indians were forbidden; those that had been made in the Indian reservation were voided; and future purchases were to be made officially, by the governor of the colony involved, for the crown alone. Indian traders were to be licensed and to give security to observe such regulations as might be promulgated.

Although the proclamation was issued hurriedly at the time of Pontiac's War, the sections relating to the Indian lands and Indian trade had been maturely considered. For more than a decade successive ministries had been dissatisfied with the management of Indian relations by the different colonies. The rivalry among the colonies for Indian trade, and in some cases for western lands, had led to abuses by the governors of their power over trade and land grants. Attempting to advance their own interests or those of their respective colonies, the governors ignored the interests of the Indians and aroused a justified resentment. The success of the French in conciliating the Indians was an argument in favor of a unified system of imperial control of Indian affairs and the restriction of settlement.

The appointment in 1756 of two superintendents of Indian affairs, for the northern and southern districts, had been the first step toward the British government's control of Indian relations. Thereafter, the letters of Sir William Johnson, superintendent of the northern Indians, informed the Board of Trade of Indian grievances and urged the fixing of a line west of which settlement should be prohibited. The danger from the Indians during the French and Indian War automatically fixed such a line at the Appalachian Mountains, and after the war proclamations by the military authorities continued this line. Settlers, however, disregarding the proclamations, swarmed over the mountains, and their encroachments were one of the causes of Pontiac's War. The proclamation of 1763 was an attempt to check the advance of pioneering until some agreement securing the Indians' consent to such settlement could be made. The proclamation fixed the settlement line temporarily at the watershed—a conspicuous landmark—but did not and was not intended to change the boundaries of the old colonies; nevertheless, it was resented in the colonies as an interference in their affairs. After Pontiac's War, negotiations with the Indians resulted in the treaties of Hard Labor, Fort Stanwix, and Lochaber, by which a new line, more acceptable to the colonists, was drawn. In 1774 the Quebec Act added the remainder of the Indian reservation north of the Ohio River to the province of Quebec, but this act aroused resentment in some of the thirteen colonies already close to rebellion, since it was seen as an attempt to deprive them of their claims to western lands.

BIBLIOGRAPHY

C. W. Alvord, *Mississippi Valley in British Politics.*

— SOLON J. BUCK

PROGRESSIVE MOVEMENT

Progressive Movement was a diffuse reform effort of the first two decades of the 20th century. It had supporters in both major political parties and pursued a number of goals, ranging from prohibition and woman suffrage to antitrust legislation, industrial regulation, tax reform, and workmen's compensation. Some historians, noting the variety of politicians and issues embraced by the term, have questioned the propriety of speaking of anything so coherent as a "movement." The term nevertheless usefully describes the attempt to depart from 19th-century laissez-faire policies and to make government both more democratic and more effective in redressing the imbalances of power that large-scale industrialism had produced. In 1912 some of the people committed to those goals formed an important third party, the Progressive, or Bull Moose, party.

The new party's origins can be traced to Theodore Roosevelt's presidency, 1901–09. Roosevelt's proposals for the regulation of transportation and industry, tax reform, labor laws, and social welfare legislation helped to shape a loose coalition of Republican senators and representatives, mostly from the Midwest, who were eager to make their party an instrument of reform. To continue the advances his administration had made, Roosevelt handpicked his successor for the Republican presidential nomination in 1908, William Howard Taft, who was thought to be friendly to the midwestern progressives while still acceptable to the conservative wing of the party.

The Progressive Movement, with supporters in both major political parties, pursued goals ranging from prohibition and woman suffrage to industrial regulation and tax reform.

Once in the White House, Taft proved so much more responsive to the Republican Old Guard than to the progressives that he produced a fateful rebellion within his party. The battle lines began to form during the special session of Congress that Taft called in 1909 to draft new tariff legislation. At the outset the progressives tried to enlist Taft's help in their fight to restrict the powers of the autocratic, reactionary speaker of the House, Joseph G. ("Uncle Joe") Cannon of Illinois. Taft, although sympathetic to the progressives' campaign against the speaker, refused to give them sufficient aid, and Cannon survived the fray with his powers only slightly reduced. Taft also disappointed the midwesterners on the tariff issue, where they expected his support for lower schedules. Again he had proved an undependable ally, and the new Payne-Aldrich tariff actually raised import rates. At the same time Taft wavered in his commitment to income tax legislation, another cherished progressive goal.

In the regular session of Congress Taft intensified progressive disaffection by proposing in his railroad bill a court of commerce to adjudicate disputed rulings of the Interstate Commerce Commission. Almost all the courts had proved unfriendly to regulatory measures, and progressives wanted to curb judicial power, not extend it. Taft further alienated progressives when he supported his secretary of the interior, Richard A. Ballinger, against Gifford Pinchot, the chief forester in the Department of Agriculture, who charged that Ballinger had betrayed Roosevelt's conservation policies.

The progressive ranks included senators Robert M. La Follette of Wisconsin, Jonathan P. Dolliver and Albert B. Cummins of Iowa, Albert J. Beveridge of Indiana, Moses E. Clapp of Minnesota, Joseph L. Bristow of Kansas, William E. Borah of Idaho, Jonathan Bourne of Oregon, and Rep. George W. Norris of Nebraska. By 1910 Taft had resolved to purge the insurgents, as they were known, in the election of that year. But the results boded ill for Taft. The Republican Old Guard suffered widespread casualties at the polls; the Democrats gained control of the House for the first time in eighteen years. The "Grand Old Party" was left more bitterly divided than ever.

In the wake of the election the insurgents formed the National Progressive Republican League in a meeting at La Follette's home on Jan. 21, 1911. Ostensibly created to advocate progressive principles, the league was widely regarded as a device for La Follette to wrest the Republican presidential nomination from Taft in 1912. That suspicion was confirmed when La Follette, on June 17, 1911, announced his candidacy for the nomination.

Theodore Roosevelt, in the meantime, had watched the developing schism in his party with increasing discomfort. Although he campaigned for both regulars and insurgents in the election of 1910, he showed his progressive sympathies in a famous speech expounding his "New Nationalist" philosophy at Osawatomie, Kans., on Aug. 31, 1910. Still, while rankled by Taft's policies, Roosevelt remained aloof from the National Progressive Republican League. Many of its members preferred him to La Follette as a presidential nominee, but Roosevelt remained convinced until well into 1911 that 1912 would be a Democratic year; better to stick with Taft and let the Old Guard bear responsibility for defeat, he reasoned, thus clearing the way for reorganization of the party along progressive lines before the 1916 election.

On Oct. 27, 1911, the Taft administration announced its intention to bring an antitrust suit against the United States Steel Company. The suit attacked U.S. Steel's 1907 acquisition of the Tennessee Coal and Iron Company, a merger that Roosevelt, then president, had personally approved in a meeting with J. P. Morgan. Incensed at Taft's repudiation of that decision, and at the implication that he had been a party to wrongdoing, Roosevelt announced late in February 1912 that his "hat was in the ring." Most of La Follette's backers, many of whom had been covertly promoting Roosevelt's candidacy, almost immediately declared their support for the former president. There followed a bitter series of battles for delegates to the Republican National Convention, scheduled to meet June 18, 1912, in Chicago. Taft, by organizing the largely black Republican delegations from the southern states and by controlling the national committee, clearly had the upper hand. Of the 254 contested seats at Chicago, 235 went to pro-Taft delegates, and only 19 to Roosevelt men. On a vote of 561 to 107 the convention nominated Taft, while 344 Roosevelt delegates simply refused to vote. Roosevelt, backed by many of the rank and file but by few party professionals, determined to abandon his lifelong Republicanism and form a new party. Assured of financial support by publisher Frank A. Munsey and by George W. Perkins, an associate of J. P. Morgan and a director of U.S. Steel and International Harvester, Roosevelt called for the first Progressive National Convention to meet in Chicago on Aug. 5, 1912.

That convention, made up of reformers of every stripe but dominated by urban, middle-class persons with little previous experience in national politics, adopted a remarkably advanced platform. Condemning what it called "the unholy alliance between corrupt business and corrupt politics," the platform called for the adoption of primary elections; the short ballot; initiative, referendum, and recall measures; the direct election of U.S. senators; and woman suffrage. It advocated federal legislation establishing minimum standards of industrial safety and health; minimum wages for women; the eight-hour day in many industries; medical, old-age, and unemployment insurance; stronger regulation of interstate business (Perkins, to the distress of many delegates, succeeded in eliminating an antitrust plank from the platform); a tariff commission; public ownership of natural resources; graduated income and inheritance taxes; improved educational services for immigrants; and government supervision of securities markets. It endorsed collective bargaining, the establishment of industrial research laboratories, government-business cooperation to extend foreign commerce, the creation of a department of labor, and the prohibition of child labor. It strongly opposed the power of the courts to nullify social and economic legislation.

Roosevelt and Gov. Hiram W. Johnson of California, vice-presidential nominee, running best in the big cities, finished second in the national balloting, with 4.1 million popular and 88 electoral votes. But at the state and local levels, the party did less well. It was able to field full slates in only fifteen states. Including incumbent Republicans who had joined the Progressives, the party in 1913 could count only one governor, two senators, sixteen representatives, and 250 local elected officials. Many Progressives blamed their relatively poor showing at the polls on the influence of Perkins, who, they claimed, had too close an association with Wall Street. Roosevelt, however, stood by Perkins and in 1913 thwarted an attempt to oust him from the chairmanship of the national executive committee.

When the elections of 1914 produced more disasters for the party (every important Progressive save Hiram Johnson was defeated) and when, after the outbreak of World War I, the questions of neutrality and preparedness threatened further to divide it, many Progressives began to consider fusion with the Republicans. The two parties held their presidential nominating conventions simultaneously in June 1916, in Chicago. There, after Roosevelt had declined the Progressive nomination, the national committee, on a divided vote, agreed to endorse the Republican candidate, Charles Evans Hughes. Most Progressives thereupon rejoined the party they had left in 1912, a few became Democrats, and a diehard contingent persevered until April 1917, when in a final convention in Saint Louis it merged with the Prohibition party.

The Progressive bolt, by splitting Republican strength, had made possible Woodrow Wilson's victory in 1912. It had also removed liberal influence from the Republican party just when liberals were on the verge of controlling it. When they returned four years later, they were largely without power; their departure had helped to ensure conservative dominance of the Republican party for some years to come. Their action had, however, demonstrated the strength of liberal sentiment in the country and helped move the Democrats in a progressive direction. Wilson, especially in 1915–16, pursued several policies calculated to woo the Progressive voters of 1912 into the Democratic ranks. And the Progressive platform of 1912 constituted a charter for liberal reform for the next fifty years.

BIBLIOGRAPHY

Alfred D. Chandler, Jr., "The Origins of Progressive Leadership," in Elting E. Morison, ed., *The Letters of Theodore Roosevelt*, vol. VIII.

Benjamin Parke DeWitt, *The Progressive Movement.*

George E. Mowry, *Theodore Roosevelt and the Progressive Movement.*

Robert H. Wiebe, *The Search for Order, 1877–1920.*

— DAVID M. KENNEDY

PROGRESSIVE PARTY

Progressive Party (1947–52). Established in 1947 and expiring shortly after the 1952 national elections, the Progressive party claimed that it was the true heir to the philosophy of Franklin D. Roosevelt and condemned the administration of Harry S. Truman for its alleged failures at home and abroad. The party opposed the administration's loyalty-security program, called for bolder civil rights and welfare measures, charged that the large military budgets fostered bellicosity, blamed the administration in large measure for the cold war, and offered a policy of accommodation with the Soviet Union. In 1948 the party selected as its candidates Henry A. Wallace, formerly vice-president under Roosevelt, and Glen H. Taylor, senator from Idaho. Polls initially predicted that the party would receive about 7 percent of the popular vote, cut into Democratic strength, and cost Truman the election. But the Czechoslovakian coup and the Berlin blockade, both interpreted widely as proof of Communist aggression, and the charges of growing Communist influence in the party cut deeply into its potential support. The party won 1,157,172 votes, or 2.4 percent of the popular vote, with more than 60 percent of that from New York and California and most of it from New York City and Los Angeles. The crushing defeat, growing anticommunism in America, and renewed charges of Communist domination soon weakened the party. In 1950 it was injured when its executive board opposed American intervention in the Korean War, and Wallace, along with many others, resigned. In 1952 the party ran Vincent W. Hallinan, an attorney, and Charlotta Bass, a black newspaper publisher, and received 140,023 votes, 56,647 of those from New York City.

— BARTON J. BERNSTEIN

PROHIBITION

The ratification of the Eighteenth Amendment to the U.S. Constitution, completed Jan. 29, 1919, and the subsequent enactment by Congress of the Volstead Act marked the culmination of a long campaign in the United States against the manufacture and sale of alcoholic beverages. Although the origin of the movement is to be found in colonial protests against the excessive use of intoxicants, the temperance crusaders did not turn from moral suasion to legal coercion until the middle of the 19th century. Thereafter, three periods of legislative activity are apparent. First, between 1846 and

1855, following the lead of Maine, thirteen states passed prohibition laws. Within a decade, however, nine of these measures had been either repealed or declared unconstitutional. After Kansas, in 1880, had written prohibition into its constitution, there was a revival of the temperance movement, stimulated by the persistent efforts of the Prohibition party (1869), the Woman's Christian Temperance Union (1874), and, most powerful of all, the Anti-Saloon League (1893). Again results were impermanent, for by 1905 only Kansas, Maine, Nebraska, and North Dakota were prohibition states.

The failure of the brewers and distillers to set their houses in order and the judicious political tactics of the Anti-Saloon League prepared the way for the final drive to outlaw the saloon. A wide range of motivations influenced the voters as they went to the polls under local option laws in the various states. The ardent reformers relentlessly pressed their arguments that the liquor interests represented a demoralizing force in American politics, that the mechanization of industry placed a premium upon the sober employee, and that the taxpayer really paid the bills for a business that was filling the poorhouses and prisons with its victims. On the eve of the United States' entrance into World War I, there were prohibition laws in twenty-six states, of which thirteen could be described as "bone-dry." Wayne B. Wheeler, Ernest H. Cherrington, and other leaders of the Anti-Saloon League, who had already mobilized the forces of evangelical Protestantism, were quick to associate prohibition with winning the war. Congressional action reinforced their arguments.

By December 1917, both the Senate and the House of Representatives had approved a resolution, originally proposed by Sen. Morris Sheppard of Texas, to add an amendment to the Constitution prohibiting the "manufacture, sale or transportation" of intoxicating liquors for beverage purposes. Within thirteen months ratification by the legislatures of three-quarters of the states had been secured, and a year later the Eighteenth Amendment went into effect. Meanwhile, Congress had placed restrictions upon the manufacture of intoxicants, to conserve grain during the war, and had provided that from July 1, 1919, until the termination of the war (which actually ended in 1918) no distilled spirits, beer, or wine should be sold for beverage purposes.

The opponents of Prohibition soon directed their attack against the efforts of governmental agents to enforce the law. They approved the banishment of the saloon, but they insisted that it had been replaced by illegal "speakeasies" and nightclubs; that the illicit traffic in intoxicants was breeding "rum runners," racketeers, and gangsters; that corruption was rampant in federal and state enforcement units; and that disrespect for all law was becoming a characteristic of those who flouted the liquor laws with impunity. The supporters of the Eighteenth Amendment, on the other hand, admitted that enforcement was far from perfect but proclaimed Prohibition's benefits—reduced poverty, increased bank deposits, and expanding industry. For them it

Federal agents pour bootleg whiskey into sewer during Prohibition, enacted by the 18th Amendment to the Constitution in 1919. Popular disgust over the failure of enforcement led to its repeal in 1933. (Corbis-Bettmann)

was a basic factor in the nation's prosperity from 1923 to 1929.

But popular disgust over the failure of enforcement grew so steadily, especially after the onset of the Great Depression, that the Democratic National Convention in 1932 demanded repeal of the Eighteenth Amendment. The Democratic landslide in the November elections persuaded Congress that the time for action had come. In the short session (Feb. 20, 1933) a resolution was approved providing for an amendment to accomplish repeal. Submitted to conventions in the several states, the Twenty-first Amendment was ratified in less than a year. Before ratification, Congress, on Mar. 22, 1933, had legalized the sale of beverages containing no more than 3.2 percent alcohol, wherever state law did not contravene.

Repeal of the Eighteenth Amendment ended the first experiment on the part of the American people in writing sumptuary legislation into the fundamental law of the land. The liquor problem was turned back to the states.

BIBLIOGRAPHY

J. C. Furnas, *The Life and Times of the Late Demon Rum.*
Charles Merz, *Dry Decade.*
Andrew Sinclair, *Prohibition: The Era of Excess.*
James H. Timberlake, *Prohibition and the Progressive Movement.*

— JOHN KROUT

PROHIBITION PARTY

Prohibition Party, oldest of the third parties in the United States, was organized in 1869 after nearly three-quarters of a century of temperance agitation had failed to influence the platforms of the major parties. The campaign of 1872 marked its initial appearance in national politics. Nine states were represented at its first national convention in Columbus, Ohio, Feb. 22, 1872. James Black of Pennsylvania was nominated for president. Prior to 1872 Prohibition candidates for state offices had been nominated in some states. In its early years the party was strongest in Ohio and New York, holding the balance of power in the latter in the presidential election of 1884. Candidates have appeared in every presidential campaign since 1872 but have never won any electoral votes. The peak of the party's popular support was reached in 1892 when its candidate for president, John Bidwell, received 271,000 votes. In 1896 the money question temporarily split the party.

Through its educational activities and its strong appeal to the moral sentiment of the people, the party exerted an influence for a more effective governmental policy toward the liquor problem. While its primary object has been the prohibition of the manufacture and sale of intoxicating liquors, it has advocated other political, economic, and social reforms, many of which have subsequently been endorsed by the major parties.

BIBLIOGRAPHY

W. B. Hesseltine, *The Rise and Fall of Third Parties.*
Howard P. Nash, *Third Parties in American Politics.*

— GLENN H. BENTON

PROPERTY QUALIFICATIONS

The Twenty-fourth Amendment to the Constitution (Jan. 23, 1964) effectively outlawed property qualifications for voting in federal elections by abolishing all poll or other taxes as requirements for voting. This prohibition was extended to state elections by a 1966 Supreme Court decision (*Harper* v. *Virginia Board of Elections*), which held that state poll taxes were in violation of the Fourteenth Amendment's requirement of equal protection of the laws. A 1973 Supreme Court decision, however, permitted states to limit voting to property owners in "special" districts. In a six-to-three decision, the majority held that a state "could rationally conclude that landowners are primarily burdened and benefited by the establishment and operation of watershed districts, and may condition the vote accordingly."

The rationale behind property qualifications in the American states was that only property owners possessed "stock" in the state, which was regarded as a corporation. Almost all states had property requirements for voting at the time of the American Revolution. The Massachusetts requirement was typical, requiring that a voter had to own either real estate yielding an annual income of 40 shillings or other property worth £40.

In the early 19th century the newly admitted western states had few property requirements for voting, and the eastern states tended to reduce the requirements. For example, when Ohio became a state in 1803 the only property requirement for voting was that voters pay a county tax, or "work out" a tax on the public highway. By 1820 even Massachusetts gave the vote to those who paid a county or state tax. By the time of the Civil War virtually all property requirements for voting had been eliminated. After the Civil War many southern states enacted poll taxes in order to disfranchise blacks.

— JOHN H. FENTON

PROSPECTORS

Prospectors are persons who explore for minerals. For many 19th-century American prospectors the hope of

A prospector pans for gold in a river in this undated photograph. For many 19th-century prospectors, striking it rich was a lifelong preoccupation. (Corbis-Bettmann)

one day striking it rich was a lifelong preoccupation. William Green Russell is typical. Twice (1849 and 1853) he went from the Georgia gold mines to California's rich deposits. In 1858 he led a party to the foothills north of Pikes Peak and found the placer deposit that, greatly exaggerated, precipitated the Pikes Peak gold rush. In 1859 he led another party from Georgia to rich deposits in Russell Gulch above Central City, Colo. After the Civil War he returned again to Colorado, and the last two summers before he died he spent placer mining in the San Luis Valley.

Most prospectors were not placer miners by trade as was Russell. George Jackson was a hunter and trapper who was first touched by the gold fever during the California rush. When he made his discovery at Idaho Springs, Colo., he was equipped with a hunting knife and tin cup instead of a pick and pan. Bob Womack, who precipitated the Cripple Creek gold rush in 1893, was a cowboy and ranch hand who had the gold fever. Even when riding the range he could not resist picking up unusual pieces of rock. George Washington Carmack, who discovered Bonanza Creek in the Klondike on Aug. 10, 1896, combined prospecting and trading with the Yukon Indians.

The 19th-century prospectors' explorations accelerated the settlement of the West. The influx of miners and then settlers after gold discoveries forced the Cherokee from Georgia, the Sioux from the Black Hills of South Dakota, and the Arapaho, Cheyenne, and Ute from Colorado.

By the mid-20th century prospecting in the United States was being done, for the most part, by representatives of giant corporations, who relied heavily on geological research and sophisticated detection equipment. Increasingly, the minerals being sought were those related to energy production, notably petroleum and uranium.

BIBLIOGRAPHY

G. C. Quiett, *Pay Dirt.*

— PERCY S. FRITZ

PROTESTANTISM

All Christians believe that there is one God, that God is revealed in Jesus of Nazareth, the Christ, and that the purpose of the church is to worship God and live in the way of Christ. Historically, three different Christian faith communities—Roman Catholic, Eastern Orthodox, and Protestant—developed, each with a distinctive way of understanding and living out those beliefs. The word "protestant" was applied to Martin Luther and others who in the Reformation of sixteenth century Europe protested certain beliefs and practices of the Roman Catholic church. Protestants came to North America from Europe to gain religious and economic freedom. They helped shape the New World forms of capitalism and democracy as well as religion. Protestants were in turn changed and shaped by pioneer life, democracy, the federal form of government, capitalism, and slavery. The historic Protestant theological foundation rests on three "alones" and one "all." A person is saved (reconciled with God, others, and self) through God's grace (unearned love) rather than through human works, rituals, sacrifices, or beliefs (grace alone). Such grace is available to anyone through trust in God (faith alone). God is revealed in the Bible (Scripture alone). Every believer has equal access to God, especially by reading the Bible, without going through the priests and rituals of the church (the priesthood of all believers). Thus, Protestantism is a faith of freedom and a faith in freedom. There exists in its very nature, however, a paradox that hovers over the line between inclusion and exclusion. The doctrines of grace alone, faith alone, and the priesthood of all believers are inclusive. The doctrine of Scripture alone, however, is exclusive. If God is revealed in the Bible, then everyone has access to the one revealed truth. Those who do not choose to accept it are excluded by their own choice.

Protestants have never resolved the tension between the inclusive and exclusive dimensions of their faith. Sidney Mead described the United States as "a nation with the soul of a church." This soul was expressed politically in democracy and personal responsibility. It took form culturally in the ethic of hard work and personal morality. The United States was formed largely by this basic Protestant principle of individual freedom and responsibility, producing a new "social contract." Nonetheless, exclusion was built into this religious social contract because it existed primarily for white males and not even for all of them. Indentured servitude was a part of early U.S. life. Immigrant groups such as the Irish had to struggle against severe prejudice before being accepted into the contract. Native, African, Asian, and Hispanic Americans were both overtly and covertly omitted from the American dream. Although women of all races often worked as equal partners with men under harsh conditions, they had very few legal rights and their social position was severely circumscribed. The U.S. story, however, despite the marginalization of many people, was one of expansion and growth. Protestant churches, especially those that adapted to frontier conditions, participated in that growth. By 1960 approximately 60 percent of all U.S. citizens identified themselves as Protestant.

In 1993, according to the *Yearbook of American and Canadian Churches*, the largest Protestant religious groups in the United States were Baptist (33.5 million), Methodist (14.6 million), Pentecostal (10.1 million), Lutheran (8.3 million), Latter-day Saints (4.5 million), and Presbyterian (4.2 million). These and other groups were further divided into approximately 150 groups of associated churches, ranging in size from the 15 million members of the Southern Baptist Convention to the 420 members of the United Christian Church.

Since the 1960s, however, Protestantism has divided not along traditional denominational lines of theology but along the battle lines of social issues. Fewer Protestants think of themselves as Baptist or Methodist or Presbyterian. They identify themselves, consciously or unconsciously, as conservative or liberal, moderate or fundamentalist, charismatic or feminist, Native American or African American. Divisions have focused on issues of abortion, the cold war, consumerism, politics, race, television, family values, gambling, gender, and homosexuality. Religious differences have centered on such issues as inclusive (that is, not exclusively male) language, especially about God; prayer in public schools; biblical inerrancy; ecumenism; denominational control; church growth or lack of it; the role of women, especially in the ministry; and theology, especially specifically focused theologies such as liberation, feminist, and black.

These are all issues of inclusion and exclusion. Can women, homosexuals, fetuses/unborn children, ethnic minority persons, or communists be included in the church and the social contract? Should those be excluded who do not believe the Bible is without error, or those who participate in politics, get divorces, have children out of wedlock, or believe in evolution? Who is excluded by the nature of those prayers, or by prayer itself? Denominations, as associations of churches with common beliefs and practices, once provided fairly clear lines of inclusion and exclusion. In the 1990s, however, they were more administrative than theological.

Protestantism also has been shaped by religious consumerism. People choose a congregation because it meets their current needs and beliefs, not because of its denomination. They "church shop" and pick the congregation with the best youth program, the newest music, or the most congenial preaching. Even after making their choice they may not know what, if any, denomination they have selected. They tend to choose large congregations rather than small ones, causing decline in older denominations that have many small churches.

Debates of inclusion-or-exclusion have questioned whether women, the unborn, ethnic minority persons, homosexuals, or communists should be included in the church and the social contract.

Since the 1970s population has shifted from the Northeast and Midwest to the Sunbelt. The shift from rural areas to large metropolitan areas has continued. Such older mainline denominations as Methodists and Presbyterians were heavily invested in church buildings and institutions in the industrial Rustbelt and in declining agricultural areas. As in earlier periods of U.S. history, newer, more conservative groups, such as pentecostals, were able to respond more readily. They established congregations where the people went. They grew as the more established denominations declined. Many of the most noticed churches do not even belong to denominations but are "megachurches" founded by entrepreneurial ministers who use television and modern fund-raising to build independent ministries. A large pool of new members for Protestant churches is composed of former Roman Catholics who no longer feel comfortable with the Catholic hierarchical structure, theology, or certain Catholic social stances, especially abortion, celibate clergy, and the place of women in church leadership.

In the 1960s and 1970s, several formal denominational mergers took place. Many Protestants talked about an "ecumenical imperative" to overcome denominational differences and witness to the unity of Christ through the unity of the church. Interdenominational ecumenism has now become almost irrelevant, however, because denominations no longer provide religious and social identity. This new ecumenism operative in Protestantism is based on individual Christians or, in some cases, congregations, joining together around issues. This creates tensions within denominations as their members are no longer united by theology but divided by issues of biblical inerrancy, speaking in tongues, abortion, homosexuality, women in ministry, and so forth. Almost every denomination has two or more groups in constant conflict with one another over who controls the denominational administration, theological schools, and missions.

Protestants are still individualistic, but it is an individualism based more on experience, practice, and social stance than upon theology. Protestants are as informed in spiritual practice by popular psychology and television talk shows as they are by traditional Christianity or denominational programs and literature. Although Protestants cannot agree on who should be excluded, there is considerable agreement on who should be included. Few denominations and congregations have succeeded in becoming interracial, but many have admitted women to full positions of leadership, both lay and clergy. They are increasingly sensitive to other marginalized persons, such as the physically challenged. They have transformed orphanages into homes for abused children and created retirement facilities for the burgeoning elderly population. Conservatives, liberals, moderates, charismatics, and feminists join together across lines of exclusion to feed the hungry, strengthen families, encourage the addicted, and comfort those afflicted by natural disasters.

[See also African-American Religions and Sects; African Methodist Episcopal Church; Fundamentalism; Jehovah's Witnesses; Latter-day Saints, Church of Jesus Christ of; Mennonites; Methodists; Presbyterianism; Puritans and Puritanism; Quakers; Reformed Churches.]

BIBLIOGRAPHY

Harold Bloom, *The American Religion: The Emergence of the Post-Christian Nation* (New York, 1992).

Roger Finke and Rodney Stark, *The Churching of America 1776–1990* (New Brunswick, N.J., 1992).

George W. Forell, *The Protestant Faith* (Englewood Cliffs, N.J., 1960).

C. Eric Lincoln and Lawrence H. Mamiya, *The Black Church in the African American Experience* (Durham, N.C., 1990).

Sidney E. Mead, *The Nation with the Soul of a Church* (New York, 1975).

— JOHN ROBERT MCFARLAND

PUBLIC DOMAIN

The public domain is distinguished from national domain and acquired land. National domain arises from political jurisdiction; acquired land is either bought or received as gifts for national parks, monuments, forests, wildlife refuges, post-office sites, and other such purposes. The first portion of the public domain or public land was created by cessions of their western land claims by seven of the original thirteen states: Massachusetts, Connecticut, New York, Virginia, North Carolina, South Carolina, and Georgia. These seven states retained the ungranted land within their present boundaries as did the other original states and Maine, Vermont, West Virginia, Kentucky, Tennessee, and Texas. Between 1802 and 1867 huge additions to the national domain and the public domain were made through the Louisiana Purchase in 1803, the Florida Purchase in 1819, the annexation of Texas in 1845 and the Texas cession of 1850, the division of the Oregon country in 1846, the huge purchase from Mexico in 1848, the Gadsden Purchase of 1853, the purchase of Alaska in 1867, and the annexation of Hawaii in 1898.

From the outset there were two views concerning the policy that should govern the disposal of the public lands. The first, sponsored by Alexander Hamilton, was that the government's need of money to retire its revolutionary war debt and to meet its expenses required it to pledge the public domain for the payment of that debt and to extract from it the greatest possible income. The other view, held by Thomas Jefferson, was that farmer-owners with a stake in the land made the most responsible citizens and that the public lands should be easily accessible to them at little cost. Hamilton's view prevailed for a time and, indeed, was reluctantly accepted by Jefferson, who yielded to necessity. The basic established price varied from $1.00 to $2.00 per acre until 1820, when credit was abolished and the minimum price became $1.25 per acre. This may not have been a high price to the investors Hamilton hoped would purchase large tracts of land, but to frontiersmen lacking capital or credit it was more than they could raise. Their solution was to squat on public land, improve it, and try to raise a crop or two to make their payments before their trespass was discovered. Squatters wanted protection against speculators who might try to buy their somewhat improved tracts. Squatters protected themselves through claim associations, which provided mutual assistance to all members. But the squatters also wanted the legal recognition of their right of preemption—that is, a prior right to purchase their claim before auction at the minimum price, without having to bid against speculators. They won a number of special preemption acts and in 1841 sustained a major victory with the adoption of the Distribution-Preemption Act, which permitted persons to settle anywhere on surveyed land in advance of its official opening; to improve the land; and, when the auction was announced, to purchase up to 160 acres at the minimum price of $1.25 an acre. Squatterism—first banned, although not successfully; then tolerated; and finally sanctioned—had thus prevailed, and a major breach in the revenue policy was made.

In 1854 the Graduation Act provided a further breach by reducing the price of land that had been on the market for ten or more years in proportion to the length of time it had been subject to sale, the lowest price being 12.5 cents. In 1862 the West gained its major triumph in the Homestead Act, which made public lands free to settlers who would live on and improve tracts of up to 160 acres for five years. Unfortunately, a substantial portion of the best arable lands had already been alienated through sale to speculators, grants to states, and direct grants to corporations to aid in the construction of canals and railroads. Grants to states and railroads alone amounted to well over 300 million acres. All this land was to be sold for the market price and was beyond the reach of many pioneer settlers.

Individual speculators and land companies invested heavily in land during boom periods, 1816–19, 1833–37, and 1853–57. Holdings of from 10,000 to 50,000 acres were not uncommon; a score or more ranged up to 100,000 acres; and partnerships held as much as 500,000 acres. By anticipating settlers, investors, as well as land grant railroads and states, raised the cost of farmmaking; dispersed population widely on the frontier; delayed the introduction of roads, churches, and transportation facilities; contributed to the early appearance of tenancy; aggravated relations with the Indians; and in some regions were responsible for the development of rural slums. On the other hand, they provided credit to hard-pressed pioneers; aided in bringing settlers to the West through their advertising and promotional works; and introduced improved farming techniques that by example contributed to better agricultural practices. At the time public attention centered on the damaging effects of intrusions by speculators and led to demands for the limitation in the sale of public land and the halt to further grants to railroads. After the adoption of the Homestead Act, little newly surveyed land was opened to unlimited purchase, although unsold land that had been offered previously continued to be subject to unrestricted entry.

Farmers in the High Plains west of the ninety-ninth meridian, where the annual rainfall was less than 20 inches and where a portion of the land had to be left fallow each year, needed more than 160 or even 320 acres for the extensive cultivation that was necessary. Congress met this difficulty by increasing the quantity that farmmakers could acquire by enacting the Timber Culture Act of 1873, the Desert Land Act of 1877, and the Timber and Stone Act of 1878. Combined with the Preemption and Homestead acts, these measures permitted individuals to acquire up to 1,120 acres in the semiarid High Plains and in the inter-mountain and desert regions. Like all poorly drafted land legislation, the acts became subject to gross abuse by grasping persons anxious to engross as much land as possible through the use of dummy entrymen and roving, uprooted people willing to serve their ends.

Growing criticism of the abuse of the settlement laws and the laxity of the land administration led in 1889–91 to the adoption of a series of measures to restrict total acquisition of public lands under all laws to 320 acres, to halt all purchases of potential agricultural lands other than those specifically intended for farmmaking, and to eliminate or insert additional safeguards in acts most subject to abuse.

The National Park Service was established in 1916 to administer and protect areas of exceptional natural beauty.

Notwithstanding the extensive abuse of the land system and its incongruous features that somewhat minimized the effectiveness of the measures designed to aid homesteaders in becoming farm owners, the public land states enjoyed a remarkable growth rate. In the 1850's, the first decade for which there are statistics, 401,000 new farms were created in the public land states. Thereafter the number grew even more rapidly. By 1890 additional farms numbering 2 million had been established in the public land states. Never before had so many farmers subjected such a large area to cultivation as occurred in those years.

The censuses of 1880 and 1890, giving alarming figures of mortgage debt outstanding on farms and the high proportion of farms that were tenant-operated, combined with the growing feeling that soils, minerals, and forests were being wastefully used, turned people's

SUMMARY OF ACCESSIONS OF THE UNITED STATES

	National Domain (acres)	Public Domain (acres)
Area conceded by Great Britain in 1783 and by the Convention of 1818 (Lake of the Woods boundary)	525,452,800	
Cessions of seven states to the United States		233,415,680
Louisiana Purchase (1803)	523,446,400	523,446,400*
Florida Purchase (1819)	43,342,720	43,342,720*
Red River Basin (Webster-Ashburton Treaty, 1842)	29,066,880	29,066,880
Annexation of Texas (1845)	247,050,480	
Oregon Compromise (1846)	180,644,480	180,644,480
Treaty With Mexico (1848)	334,479,360	334,479,360*
Purchase From Texas (1850)		78,842,880
Gadsden Purchase (1853)	18,961,920	18,961,920*
Alaska Purchase (1867)	365,481,600	365,481,600
Hawaiian Annexation (1898)	3,110,820	

* Between 40 million and 50 million acres included in the public domain were in private claims of land granted by Great Britain, France, Spain, and Mexico, which when proved valid were patented and were not subject to disposal by the United States.

thoughts to further reform in land management and to conservation. Instead of a policy of transferring all public lands to individuals, railroads, and states as rapidly as possible, it was determined to retain a portion of the land in public ownership. To this end, an amendment to the General Revision Act of 1891 authorized the president to withdraw from public entry forest lands on which organized management policies could be introduced. Under President Theodore Roosevelt's leadership gross withdrawals were pushed to nearly 160 million acres.

Next in the planned use of the natural resources by government was the Reclamation Act (Newlands Act) of 1902, which provided that the income from the sale of public lands be used for construction of high dams on western rivers to store water for the irrigation of dry lands and thus to provide for a new farmers' frontier. With supplementary appropriations for construction of dams, the government gave an enormous boon to the development of the eleven far western states; but the provisions of the act that were designed to make small farmers the major beneficiaries (the antispeculator and excess-lands provisions) have been frustrated, and instead large individual and corporate owners have derived the greatest returns.

In 1916 the National Park Service was created to administer areas of superlative natural beauty that were being set aside from the public lands as permanent reserves—Yosemite, Yellowstone, Hot Springs, Glacier, Sequoia, Mount Rainier, Grand Canyon, and Crater Lake. These and other places of outstanding aesthetic, geologic, and historical interest were thus prevented from despoilment by curiosity seekers and commercial interests.

Rapid and unscientific exploitation of mineral lands by destructive and wasteful practices induced Roosevelt to order the withdrawal of 66 million acres suspected of being underlain with valuable coal deposits and a smaller acreage of suspected oil-bearing land. Lands having coal, potash, phosphate, and nitrate deposits were also withdrawn from entry, although the surface rights might be left alienable. In 1920 the Mineral Leasing Act provided some control over the exploitation of these withdrawn lands for the first time and, as a sweetener to the West, allocated 37.5 percent of the proceeds from leasing to the states in which the lands were located and 57.5 percent to reclamation projects, thereby assuring a principal and growing source of funds for such projects. The remaining 5 percent went to the states in which lands were allocated for schools.

Roosevelt was also persuaded by his conservation-minded advisers, notably Gifford Pinchot, to withdraw 3.45 million acres of public lands as possible sources for power sites. Under the Water Power Act of 1920 a system of licensing the power sites was authorized, but it was not until the 1930's and 1940's that the great hydroelectric power development of the federal government was undertaken.

The last important withdrawal of public lands from entry was made in 1934. The harmful effects of overgrazing on the ranges of the West had become so evident that even the livestock industry was persuaded to accept federal control. It was provided that in the future the remaining grazing lands in public ownership were to be leased under close supervision. To administer these lands a Division of Grazing was set up in the U.S. Department of the Interior. Congress preferred to create a new administrative agency rather than to permit the Forest Service, which had gained much valuable experience in administering the range lands within the national forests, because this latter agency had shown independence as well as excellent judgment in protecting its lands. The Division of Grazing started off well, but it also ran into bitter opposition for its failure to play politics, was virtually starved by Congress by inadequate appropriations, and was later consolidated with the General Land Office in the Bureau of Land Management.

A century and a half of unparalleled prodigality in managing the public domain had made possible the alienation of most of the best agricultural, forest, and mineral lands of the United States, but there still remained a noble fragment in federal ownership under organized management. By the 1970's there were 186 million acres in the national forests, 26 million acres of which were acquired land bought for watershed protection and other conservation objectives. They included stands of Douglas fir, sugar pine, ponderosa pine, and Sitka spruce in California, Oregon, Washington, and the Rocky Mountain states, where steeply sloped land must be carefully protected from fire and overgrazing to prevent silting of reservoirs and irrigation districts. In the mid-1970's the Bureau of Land Management (BLM) administered 140 million acres in grazing districts and remaining desert lands and some 300 million acres of unsurveyed land in Alaska, subject to selection by the state of 103.35 million acres and by the native tribes of 40 million acres, as provided in legislation of 1972. Included in the BLM lands are some of the richest stands of Douglas fir, the result of the forfeiture of the Oregon and California railroad land grant.

Best known of the public lands are the 19 million acres in the national parks, part of which came from the public domain and part through gift (Mount Desert Island) or exchange of public land outside the parks for privately owned inholdings. Of the original 1.23 million acres in the fifty states, the public domain comprised some 350 million acres in 1975. Public policy in the mid-1970's was directed to acquiring additional tracts of seashore, mountain, and lakeside to meet the recreational needs of an expanding population with more time for outdoor enjoyment.

BIBLIOGRAPHY

Paul W. Gates, *History of Public Land Law Development; One Third of the Nation's Land: A Report to the President and to the Congress by the Public Land Law Review Commission.*

— PAUL W. GATES

PUBLIC LAND COMMISSIONS

Public Land Commissions were established by the U.S. government on four occasions to review federal land policies and to make recommendations for their improvement or redirection. The first of these was authorized by Congress in 1879, when widespread abuse of the settlement laws existed; corruption was prevalent in the local land offices and in the awarding of lucrative surveying contracts; the General Land Office was understaffed and far behind in its work; and a mass of conflicting land laws and administrative orders required revision. Five distinguished men long associated with public land administration were appointed to the commission, the best known of whom was John W. Powell, explorer of the Grand Canyon and author of the *Report on the Lands of the Arid Region.* The testimony they took during a three-month tour of the West revealed scandalous management of the surveys, illegal sale of relinquishments, and exploitative activities by land attorneys and agents, and it indicated that serious damage was being done to rich valley lands in California by hydraulic mining. Recommendations for change included abolition of the unnecessary receivers' office in each land district, better salaries for the staff of the General Land Office, classification of the public lands, sale of the grazing lands, and exchange of lands between the railroads and the government to block areas for more effective management. Congress was not moved to action, although some of the reforms were adopted in 1889–91, by which time the best of the arable land had gone into private ownership. Thomas Donaldson, a member of the commission, left its most lasting contribution, *The Public Domain,* a 1,300-page history and analysis of land policies that has since become a basic source of information about land policies. It bore down heavily on the misuse of the settlement laws.

Western livestock, lumber, and mining interests did not like the dynamic leadership of Roosevelt's appointee, Gifford Pinchot, one of the founders of the modern conservation movement.

In 1903 President Theodore Roosevelt appointed the second commission with Gifford Pinchot, then head of the Bureau of Forestry in the Department of Agriculture, as its most important member. After hearings in Washington, D.C., and in the West, the commission recommended the repeal of the Timber and Stone Act of 1878, as had the first commission. It also urged the appraisal of timber and other lands before they were sold; the establishment of grazing districts to be administered by the Department of Agriculture, with fees to be charged for use of the public ranges for grazing; the repeal of the lieu land feature of the Forest Management Act of 1897; and additional safeguards in the Homestead Act of 1862 and Desert Land Act of 1877. Congress was not receptive, although the lieu land provision was repealed and the forest reserves were transferred from the Department of the Interior to the Agriculture Department's Bureau of Forestry under Pinchot.

Western livestock, lumber, and mining interests did not like the dynamic leadership of Pinchot, one of the founders of the modern conservation movement, and they brought about his dismissal by President William Howard Taft in 1910. These interests were pressing for the cession of the public lands to the states in which they were located, thereby reviving an issue that had agitated the public land states for a century. They also opposed executive withdrawals of public lands that kept them from entry by private individuals and companies. They wanted no more government controls on public lands. Until 1929 their influence was responsible for relaxation of controls in the Department of the Interior, while the public lands were being overgrazed and their carrying capacity was seriously declining. Conservationist forces were not moribund but rather were regrouping their forces to protect the national forests from passing into private hands and to provide management of the public domain rangelands previously uncontrolled. President Herbert Hoover may have sensed this ground swell and shrewdly decided to anticipate it with a proposal to convey the remaining public lands not subject to controlled use by a government agency to the western states, which, he said, had "passed from swadling cloths and are today more competent to manage" them than the federal government. In response to his request, Congress authorized the appointment of the third commission, known as the Committee on the Conservation and Administration of the Public Domain. A carefully picked committee, dominated by westerners, recommended that the public lands, minus mineral rights, be turned over to the states in the hope that they would establish grazing control but that if they did not, the United States should undertake to do so in the recalcitrant states. The committee also recommended a procedure to eliminate those portions of the national forests it was not deemed desirable to retain. Conservationists throughout the country, not agreeing with the president that the record of the states was better than that of the National Forest Service in administering both forest and rangelands under its jurisdiction, sprang to arms in opposition to the recommendations. Most western states were also distressed at the recommendations, for they felt that without the mineral rights there was little to be gained from the cession of the lands. No action was taken.

The fourth and best-financed of the public land commissions came into existence in 1964, when many issues affecting the public lands were in need of serious attention and measures relating to them were already under consideration in Congress. Rather than deal with these questions in a piecemeal fashion, Congress decided to create the Public Land Law Review Commission, which, through use of the best expert aid in the universities and government agencies, would attempt an overall examination of the many overlapping and conflicting programs and make recommendations to the Congress for new legislation. Again, failing to recognize that the public lands belong to the nation and that people of all states are deeply concerned about their management, whether they are national forests, parks, grazing districts, or wildlife refuges, the commission was strongly slanted toward the western viewpoint. Its final report, *One Third of the Nation's Land*, contained homilies about planning for future needs and multiple use but placed emphasis on giving commercial interests more leeway in utilizing and acquiring ownership of the public lands, although requiring that they pay more for those privileges. The report showed westerners' dislike of the use of executive authority to effect land withdrawals, opposition to higher fees for grazing privileges, and preferences for state, as against federal, administrative authority. It also reflected the general public's concern for retaining public lands in government ownership and for multiple use of the lands, but it favored "dominant use," which was generally interpreted to mean timber cutting and mining above other uses. Conservationists long accustomed to regarding the National Forest Service as the best administrative agency dealing with land matters were troubled by the proposal to consolidate it with the Bureau of Land Management. Environmentalists feared that the commission's failure to recommend the repeal of the Mining Act of 1872, which had been responsible for some of the most serious errors of the past in land administration, showed a marked insensitivity to public attitudes.

BIBLIOGRAPHY

Paul W. Gates with a chapter by Robert W. Swenson, *History of Public Land Law Development.*

— PAUL W. GATES

PUBLIC OPINION

Public opinion, a term that has been in common usage in the United States since the latter part of the 18th century. No definition has won general acceptance, although many have been suggested. Analysis of many of these led Harwood L. Childs, Princeton University professor of politics, to conclude in 1962 that public opinion is "used to refer to any collection of individual opinions." Opinion pollsters and scholars of the 20th century customarily define the specific collections of persons to whom they refer as various "publics" rather than "the public." In general usage the term often implies the opinion of the public at large, a considerable majority of all the people, or of the voting public.

The vagaries of definition have hardly detracted from interest in public opinion. Over the years a great deal of attention has been given to the subject by politicians, journalists, historians, and social scientists, for however defined, public opinion is widely recognized as being vitally related to many democratic processes—not only governmental, but social and economic as well. Such has not always been the case. In its earliest usage the "public" in "public opinion" was equated with "the people" or, more specifically, the landholders or propertyowners in whom the franchise was vested.

The general thesis that the political history of the United States has been largely a long struggle between vested rights and the public interest, with the former being gradually eroded as popular suffrage and individual rights have expanded, provides a loose frame of reference for changes in the broad usage of the term "public opinion."

Public opinion is commonly associated with concepts integral to democracy and consequently receives very close attention. Majority rule, consent of the governed, and representative government can hardly be discussed without reference to public opinion; nor can referenda, for example, or propaganda.

Consideration of public opinion is morally and ethically essential in the context of government in the United States and in most other countries of the free world; it is a practical necessity for any form of government. Consequently, systematic efforts to measure and evaluate the opinions of masses of people and special groups of people are more or less universal. By no means limited to governmental agencies, such efforts are undertaken by private and institutional agencies interested in public opinion from various perspectives.

Public opinion research burgeoned after 1935. Both American and world associations for public opinion research came into being. The Gallup Poll, originated by George H. Gallup in the 1930's, became the prototype of public opinion polling around the world, as many other widely known polling organizations were developed, mostly in the decade 1935–45: the Harris Poll, the Opinion Research Corporation, and the National Opinion Research Center; many regional, state, and even local companies; and nonprofit research groups, such as the Bureau of Applied Social Research at Columbia University, the Survey Research Center at the University of California, Berkeley, and the Survey Research Center at the University of Michigan. Many of these and other organizations belong to the National Council on Public Polls (founded 1969), which distributes information to journalists, broadcasters, and public officials concerning appropriate standards for conducting public opinion polls and reporting on their results.

Consideration of public opinion, besides being morally and ethically essential in a free country, is a practical necessity for any form of government.

A number of these polling organizations specialize in predicting voting behavior in national, state, and local elections based on surveys of samples of the voting population. Their published and private reports on the popularity of political figures and on trends in public opinion and attitude on a variety of topics are also well known. Other organizations study more esoteric and philosophical problems of public opinion, the opinions of special publics, methodology of survey research, propaganda and mass communications, and opinion formation and leadership. Commercially oriented organizations tend toward market research activities, such as studying the psychological motivations behind buying behavior and corporate-image analyses. Some limit their practice to, or specialize in, advising political officeholders and candidates about their images or popularity and the implications of alternative actions or positions they might take—all based, at least in part, on public opinion research.

Substantial efforts are made to relate opinions or attitudes to actions and to determine the reasons for the development of opinions and attitudes and the relationship of education, mass communications, propaganda, cultural, and societal factors to both public opinion and behavior. Elections, the adoption of legislation, and the formation and implementation of public policies frequently provoke complex analyses of their relationship to public opinion. In 1961 V. O. Key, Jr., epitomized the views of many social scientists when he said that "the sharp definition of the role of public opinion as it affects different kinds of policies under different types of situations presents an analytical problem of extraordinary difficulty."

Since the early years of the Republic there has been a tendency for some observers to attempt to correlate an increasingly well-informed populace and electorate with the expansion of democratic processes in the sense of making governmental policies and practices more responsive to public opinion. Faith in this potential has persisted despite parallel increase in the awareness of the extent to which the United States functions as a pluralistic society with a constant need to balance complex interests. Political theorists and realists alike have tended to believe that such factors as the spread of public education and the development of mass media of communication inevitably engender increased governmental responsiveness to public opinion, in terms of both broad policies and specific issues concerning which the voting public can conceivably become well informed.

During the first half of the 20th century, techniques for manipulating and controlling public opinion and actions based on these advances began to be recognized as an increasing threat to such hopes. This was especially true as these techniques were successfully exercised in the form of propagandist activities by national governments and powerful social and economic institutions, sometimes working in concert. Phrases such as "the engineering of consent" to describe opinion formation processes began to suggest the effectiveness of forces antithetical to the leadership of informed public opinion.

To some observers the development of enlightened public opinion has seemed unlikely. They have viewed the role of public opinion in a democracy as an inherent defect in the form of government and likely to bring about its downfall as the technological revolution and international tensions combine to require governmental action of a degree of sophistication that the great mass of the people cannot and will not support. Others believe that the masses of people and their institutions are being corrupted by the propagandist activities of elected officials and leaders who constitute a sort of democratic ruling class. For example, in the 1960's the French historian Jacques Ellul concluded that tools of propaganda and not public opinion guide men's destinies and that the very prospects for democratic freedom are bleak unless the peoples of all the world soon awaken to this danger and take appropriate action to protect themselves. Simultaneously, in the United States, Key declared that "the critical element for the health of a democratic order consists in the beliefs, standards and competence of those who constitute the influentials, the opinion leaders . . . if a democracy tends toward indecision, decay and disaster, the responsibility rests here, not in the mass of the people."

BIBLIOGRAPHY

Harwood L. Childs, *Public Opinion: Nature, Formation and Role.*
Jacques Ellul, *Propaganda: The Formation of Men's Attitudes.*
V. O. Key, Jr., *Public Opinion and American Democracy.*
Walter Lippmann, *Public Opinion.*

— PAUL M. DOUGLAS

PUEBLO REVOLT

Pueblo Revolt (1680–96), in New Mexico, was engineered by Popé, a Tewa Indian of San Juan Pueblo, one of forty-seven Pueblo religious leaders who in 1675 had been flogged by the Spaniards for practicing Pueblo religious rites. The Spanish, who then numbered only about 2,500 in all of New Mexico, had been making strenuous efforts to extirpate pagan beliefs and ceremonies, and potential rebellion had been brewing among the Indians. The Spanish colony itself had approached the brink of demoralization and disorganization because of persistent conflict between the ecclesiastical and civil authorities. Popé preached a return to the old Indian ways, plus the elimination of the missions and the driving out of the Spaniards. He held secret meetings in an effort to unify the Pueblo, who had been too disunited for effective action. A day for simultaneous uprising was agreed upon, but word leaked out in advance. Nevertheless, all the Pueblo north of Isleta, N.Mex., participated. In a concerted uprising the Indians destroyed all the missions and killed about 400 Spaniards. The rest of the Spaniards fled south to El Paso. Attempts at reconquest by the Spaniards were unsuccessful prior to 1692, by which time the brief unity of the Pueblo had been shattered by internal dissension. In 1692 the Spanish expedition under Diego de Vargas was resisted by some Pueblo but not by others. Santa Fe was taken, and by 1696 Spanish control over the Pueblo of the Rio Grande area had been firmly reestablished.

BIBLIOGRAPHY

J. M. Espinosa, *First Expedition of Vargas Into New Mexico, 1692.*
Franklin Folsom, *Red Power on the Rio Grande.*
C. W. Hackett and C. C. Shelby, *Revolt of the Pueblo Indians of New Mexico and Otermin's Attempted Reconquest, 1680-1682.*
Robert Silverberg, *The Pueblo Revolt.*

— KENNETH M. STEWART

PUERTO RICAN AMERICANS

Although Puerto Ricans began migrating to the United States soon after the turn of the twentieth century (2,000 from 1900 to 1909), it was not until the 1940s that they did so in large numbers (151,000 from 1940 to 1949). Puerto Ricans settled in major cities, including New York, Chicago, Boston, and Philadelphia, as well as such smaller cities as Albany and Buffalo, N.Y.; Cleveland; Hartford, Conn.; and Worcester, Mass. There was a decrease in the number of migrants in the 1960s (145,000), but that trend reversed in the 1970s, although some 160,000 mainland residents returned to Puerto Rico during that decade. In 1994 Puerto Ricans and those of Puerto-Rican descent in the United States numbered close to 3 million.

Studies of the Puerto Rican population in the United States have commonly treated it either as a divided nation or as an ethnic minority. The first conceptualization considers the migratory experience within the context of international capitalism. Expanding urban industry absorbed surplus labor from the "colony" during and after World War II. Shrinking economic opportunities on the mainland beginning in the 1960s halted the flow and eventually resulted in return migration, a phenomenon peculiar to Puerto Ricans because of their status as U.S. citizens since 1917. In the 1970s and 1980s, however, a "brain drain" occurred in Puerto Rico because of limited employment opportunities in certain fields for overqualified individuals, causing many in search of more competitive salaries and higher standards of living to move to U.S. cities. The second scholarly construction treats migrants as an ethnic minority being integrated into mainstream American culture. It emphasizes the conditions Puerto Ricans encountered when they arrived and explains their adaptation in terms of the available resources and social-service programs. This interpretation attributes return migration either to the failure of Puerto Ricans to adapt to the host country and their desire to seek refuge among family and friends on the island or to the inability of U.S. agencies to provide the necessary wherewithal for integration.

Government officials on both the mainland and the island have considered migrants and return migrants as a problem. In U.S. cities the first wave of Puerto Ricans became the target of much discrimination because of skin color, level of education, and cultural differences. The second and third generation reacted by developing "cultural" traits that would ensure survival. Gang violence, later connected to drug use, was one of the coping strategies stereotyped by sensational and insensitive media. Equally recognizable has been ghettoization, social marginalization, unstable household income, and high levels of unemployment and high school dropout rates. On the island a large number of Puerto Ricans rejected the first wave of return migrants. Most natives' understanding of and sympathy for the mainland experience was limited. To them, *nuyoricans* seemed aggressive, lacking in culture, and, probably most important, unable or unwilling to speak Spanish. The sources of conflict did not disappear and the situation became more manageable in the late 1980s only because it was more familiar.

On their part, migrants and their descendants have created a distinctive culture by appropriating elements from the societies of origin and destination. In every large U.S. city Latin markets provide ingredients for a diet in which indigenous and African food conforms to more American tastes. Church and community organizations promote traditional religious and social rituals, such as christenings or young women's fifteenth-birthday celebrations, and coordinate the commemoration of important U.S. events, such as the birthday of Martin Luther King, Jr., or Independence Day. Salsa, the Afro-Latin rhythm born in Spanish Harlem, became a popular staple of the U.S. commercial music world. Moving comfortably among constituencies and the larger American public, Puerto-Rican educators, politicians, and civil servants reinforced and even institutionalized these rich cross-cultural contributions.

[See also Hispanic Americans.]

BIBLIOGRAPHY

José Hernández Alvarez, *Return Migration to Puerto Rico* (Berkeley, Calif., 1967).

Center for Puerto Rican Studies, *Labor Migration Under Capitalism: The Puerto Rican Experience* (New York, 1979).

Luis Nieves Falcón, *El Emigrante Puertorriqueño* (Rio Piedras, P.R., 1975).

— TERESITA MARTÍNEZ-VERGNE

PULLMAN STRIKE

As a result of the panic of 1893, various railroad companies suffered heavy losses, which led them to curtail their operations and to reduce the wages of their employees. The Pullman Palace Car Company, which manufactured railroad sleeping cars, lowered the wages of its employees an average of 25 percent. This company, organized in 1867, carried on its chief operations at Pullman, a town which it owned just south of Chicago. When wages were reduced, no reduction was made in the rentals and fees charged employees in the company town. About 4,000 disgruntled employees joined Eugene V. Debs's American Railway Union in the spring of 1894. On May 11, 1894, about 2,500 Pullman employees quit work and forced the closing of the shops. Thereafter attempts were made to arbitrate the differences between the company and its employees, but the former took the view that there was nothing to arbitrate. Nor would the company consent to bargain with the union, although Pullman officials expressed readiness to deal with employees individually.

The Pullman Palace Car Company in 1894 lowered its employees' wages by 25 percent, but made no reduction in the rentals and fees charged in the company town near Chicago.

The local strike soon developed into a general railroad strike, when members of the American Railway Union refused to handle Pullman cars. First, twenty-four Chicago-based railroads, whose affairs were handled by the General Managers' Association, were tied up. This led to a general railroad tie-up throughout the western United States by June 28. In another two days the strike had spread to practically all parts of the country. One result was serious delay in the transportation of mail. At this juncture federal judges William A. Woods and Peter S. Grosscup issued a "blanket injunction," prohibiting all interference with trains. The injunction was defied, and violence was resorted to by the strikers. Thereupon, President Grover Cleveland ordered federal troops into Chicago on July 4. Following their arrival, there was much mob violence and destruction of railroad property. Rioting occurred in cities as far west as Oakland, Calif., and on July 5, federal troops were put on strike duty in California. By July 13 some trains were running under military guard, and a few days later the strike was broken. By July 20 all federal troops were out of Chicago. During the strike Debs was arrested and his subsequent conviction for violation of a federal injunction led to a lengthy campaign to curb the use of blanket injunctions in labor disputes. This campaign ultimately resulted in the passage of the Norris–La Guardia Anti-Injunction Act of 1932.

BIBLIOGRAPHY

W. H. Carwardine, *The Pullman Strike.*
Almont Lindsey, *The Pullman Strike.*

— ERIK MCKINLEY ERIKSSON

PUNISHMENT, CRUEL AND UNUSUAL

The Eighth Amendment to the Constitution of the United States declares: "Excessive bail shall not be required, nor excessive fines imposed, nor cruel and unusual punishments inflicted." The amendment is almost identical to the tenth guarantee in the English Bill of Rights of 1689; however, the words "ought not to be required" appear in the English document, instead of the more positive words "shall not be required." Considered a fundamental guarantee of liberty, prohibition of "cruel and unusual punishments" was included in a number of the original state constitutions of the revolutionary period, notably those of Virginia, Maryland, North Carolina, and Massachusetts. Naturally, when a national Bill of Rights was adopted in 1791, the guarantee was included to prevent excesses by the government such as had been common in 17th-century England.

In the 1960's the issue of whether capital punishment was "cruel and unusual" became prominent. Civil libertarians contended that, in view of changing societal attitudes, killing criminals was per se objectionable and that the death sentence was being so rarely meted out in applicable cases that its imposition had become arbitrary and discriminatory. In 1972 the U.S. Supreme Court, in *Furman* v. *Georgia*, did strike down all capital punishment statutes, but only on the grounds that the death sentence was being administered arbitrarily. In the wake of the decision several states enacted laws that, in essence, mandated capital punishment for certain crimes, removing any discretion judges or juries had in handing down the sentence.

BIBLIOGRAPHY

E. M. Eriksson and D. N. Rowe, *American Constitutional History.*
C. Ellis Stevens, *Sources of the Constitution of the United States.*

— ERIC MCKINLEY ERIKSSON

PURITANS AND PURITANISM

The terms "Puritans" and "Puritanism" originated in England in the 1560's, when they were used to describe the people who wished to reform the Church of England beyond the limits established by Queen Elizabeth I and who strove to "purify" it of what they considered the remnants of Roman Catholicism. Puritanism was first formulated as an ecclesiastical protest and was at the beginning devoted to attacking clerical vestments, the use of medieval ceremonial, and the structure of the official hierarchy; Puritans wished to substitute a church government modeled upon the example of the apostles in the New Testament. However, this preoccupation with polity and ritual must be interpreted as an expression rather than the substance of Puritanism. Puritans were men of intense piety, who took literally and seriously the doctrines of original sin and salvation by faith; they believed that true Christians should obey the will of God as expressed in divine revelation, and they condemned the Church of England because they found its order impious and anti-Christian. After 1603 their opposition to the church became allied with the parliamentary opposition to the royal prerogative; in the 1640's Puritans and Parliamentarians united in open warfare against Charles I.

Puritanism was thus a movement of religious protest, inspired by a driving zeal and an exalted religious devotion, which its enemies called fanaticism, but which to Puritans was an issue of life or death. At the same time, Puritanism was connected with the social revolution of the 17th century and the struggle of a rising capitalist middle class against the absolutist state. It was a religious and social radicalism that in England proved incapable of maintaining unity within its own ranks and, during the 1650's, split into myriad sects and opinions. The process of division began in the 16th century when "Separatists" broke off from the main body of Puritans. A small congregation of these extremists fled to America and established the Plymouth colony in 1620, although the major contribution of Puritanism to American life was made through the settlement established by the Massachusetts Bay Company at Boston in 1630. This band of Puritans was inspired to migrate by a conviction that the cause had become hopeless in England after the dissolution of the Parliament of 1629. Within the next decade some 20,000 persons came to Massachusetts and Connecticut and there built a society and a church in strict accordance with Puritan ideals. Ruled by vigorous leaders, these colonies were able to check centrifugal tendencies, to perpetuate and to institutionalize Puritanism in America long after the English movement had sunk into confusion and a multiplicity of sects. Yet in so far as Puritanism was but the English variant of Calvinism and was theologically at one with all Reformed churches, New England Puritanism must be viewed as merely one of the forms in which the Calvinist version of Protestantism was carried to America; its influence, therefore, must be considered along with that of Scotch-Irish, Dutch, or French Protestantism.

In the United States the word Puritanism has become practically synonymous with New England, simply because New England (except for Rhode Island) achieved a social organization and an intellectual articulation that trenchantly crystallized the Puritan spirit. Puritanism can be said to have affected American life wherever Calvinism has affected it, but most markedly at those points where persons of New England origin have been influential.

BIBLIOGRAPHY

William Haller, *The Rise of Puritanism.*

M. M. Knappen, *Tudor Puritanism.*

Perry Miller and T. H. Johnson, *The Puritans.*

R. H. Tawney, *Religion and the Rise of Capitalism.*

— PERRY MILLER

Q

QUAKERS

Quakers, members of the Society of Friends, first came to America shortly after Quakerism emerged from the ferment of the Puritan Revolution in England. The society was founded by George Fox, who began preaching in 1647, as a democratic, apostolic Christian sect, and since it had no place for priest or minister, bishop or presbyter, it seemed to threaten church and government alike. Fox's doctrine that God's Inner Light illuminates the heart of every man and woman converted many who, despite fierce persecution, roamed the dales and towns of England as ministers of the new gospel. Ann Austin and Mary Fisher carried the message to Barbados in 1655 and thence to Boston in 1656. There the Puritan authorities imprisoned them, burned their Quaker books, and finally shipped them back to Barbados. Zealous Quaker missionaries, continuing to invade the Massachusetts Bay Colony, suffered fines, flogging, and banishment. Three men and one woman who defied the ban were hanged on Boston Common between 1659 and 1661. In Rhode Island, on the other hand, leading families embraced the new faith and established the "yearly meeting" for worship and church business at Newport in 1661. Quakers appeared in Maryland in 1656 and in Virginia in 1657. When Fox himself visited the colonies in 1672 he found Friends scattered all along the mainland coast from North Carolina to New England.

Continuing persecution at home prompted an increasing emigration of British Quakers to the New World. Settlements in West Jersey preceded the "Holy Experiment" that William Penn, convert to Quakerism, undertook in 1681 in Pennsylvania. Thousands of British Quakers and a few Rhineland pietists found refuge in Penn's colony. Uniting with their brethren in New Jersey and Delaware, the Pennsylvania Friends organized a yearly meeting in 1681, which became the most influential in America. Other yearly meetings, independent of the Philadelphia meeting but in close touch with it, took form in Maryland (1672), New York (1695), and North Carolina (1698). Each followed the pattern of church organization that had developed in England; subordinate quarterly meetings were established, with monthly meetings the basic congregational units of the society. Friends met for worship to wait upon the Lord, maintaining a silence broken only by occasional sermons and prayers by men and women who felt the Spirit move them. They renounced ritual and the outward sacraments and eschewed music and art. The very simplicity of their worship and the austerity of their meetinghouses made for a certain dignity and beauty, and the uprightness of their lives lent grace to the plainness of Quaker speech and apparel.

As persecution almost ceased after the British Toleration Act of 1689, except for occasional fines for refusal to do military service or pay tithes to an established church, quietism rather than active proselytism became the rule. Friends perfected their organization as a "peculiar people" and punished by disownment breaches of the discipline, such as marrying out of the society. Although in colonies such as Pennsylvania they had played a prominent role in government, they withdrew from politics after the mid-18th century, primarily because of the conflict between their pacifism and the military necessities of the French and Indian War and the American Revolution. After the Revolution the westward movement drew many of them, particularly from Virginia and North Carolina, over the mountains to the slave-free soil of the Northwest Territory. Gradually they spread to the Pacific Coast, establishing yearly meetings in Ohio (1813), Indiana (1821), Iowa (1863), Kansas (1872), Illinois (1875), Oregon (1893), California (1895), and Nebraska (1908). Another stream of emigration led through western New York and into Ontario, Canada.

The evangelical movement that splintered 19th-century American Protestantism also brought schism to the Society of Friends. The Great Separation of 1827–28, beginning in Philadelphia, produced Orthodox and Hicksite groups, the former evangelical and the latter more Unitarian in tendency. The Hicksites avoided further separations and united in the biennial General Conference in 1902. But among the Orthodox, evangelicalism produced schism after schism, beginning with a small Wilburite, or Conservative, separation in New England in 1845. The Philadelphia yearly meeting forestalled further division by ceasing to correspond with other Orthodox bodies in 1857 and by refusing to join the Orthodox Five Years Meeting, which began to take form in 1887. The isolation and evangelicalism of the western frontier so affected Friends in the West that their "churches," paid pastors, and missionary activities made them hardly distinguishable from their non-Quaker evangelical neighbors.

Theological differences diminished in the 20th century among Friends in the eastern United States and Canada, who largely followed the older Quaker practice of unprogrammed, nonpastoral worship. A series of reunions of the Orthodox and Hicksite yearly meetings took place, beginning in Philadelphia, New York, and Canada in 1955. On the other hand, the fundamentalist-modernist controversy gave fresh life to evangelical fervor in some western Orthodox meetings. Oregon withdrew from the Five Years Meeting in 1926—after 1965 called Friends United Meeting—as did Kansas in 1937; and in 1966 they both joined Ohio and Rocky Mountain yearly meetings in forming the Evangelical Friends Alliance.

The Quaker doctrine of the Inner Light encouraged humanitarian social activities even as it had fostered religious mysticism and quietism. Whereas Quakers had attacked the slave trade and slavery in the 18th and 19th centuries and made notable contributions in the fields of Indian relations, prison reform, education, woman's rights, temperance, and the care of the insane, their modern descendants sought to apply Quaker principles to the problems of war and social maladjustment. The American Friends Service Committee, organized in 1917 to enable Friends to substitute noncombatant relief work for military service, united all Quaker groups in promoting their peace testimony. The committee's pioneering in crisis situations in the United States and abroad brought them and their English counterpart, the Friends Service Council, the Nobel Peace Prize in 1947.

The Quaker doctrine of the Inner Light encouraged humanitarian social activities even as it had fostered religious mysticism and quietism.

Friends opposed the Vietnam War from the beginning and highlighted their peaceful campaign against the war by attempting to bring relief to suffering civilians on both sides. As in World War II some went to prison rather than have anything to do with the Selective Service System, while others accepted alternative service under civilian auspices. Most avoided the more militant peace demonstrations of the 1960's, but some of the younger members came to believe that only through a radical approach to militarism, racism, poverty, and other sources of social unrest could they measure up to the standards of early Quakerism.

No longer a peculiar people in matters of dress and language, no longer rigid in enforcing a strict discipline against mingling with the world's people, no longer disowning people for marrying out of meeting or even for accepting military service if conscience so dictated, 20th-century Quakers showed great diversity among themselves and many similarities to other Christians around them. Nevertheless, their peace testimony in particular and their emphasis on the Inner Light set them apart as a unique group, and for all their diversity they joined together in 1937 in a Friends World Committee for Consultation, which drew Quakers together from throughout the world. In 1973 the Society of Friends included approximately 118,000 members in the United States and Canada. While rural membership seemed to be declining somewhat, new growth in metropolitan areas and university centers indicated an increasing interest in Quaker principles and their application to religious worship and the problems of modern life.

BIBLIOGRAPHY

Errol T. Elliott, *Quakers on the American Frontier.*
Daisy Newman, *A Procession of Friends: Quakers in America.*
Elbert Russell, *The History of Quakerism.*

— THOMAS E. DRAKE

QUARTERING ACT

The first quartering act in the colonies was passed in March 1765 for a two-year term; it required the colonies to provide barracks for British troops. A second act, 1766, provided for quartering troops in inns and uninhabited buildings. The Quartering Act of June 2, 1774, known as one of the Coercion Acts, was passed by Parliament to permit effective action by the British troops sent to Boston after the Tea Party in 1773. In 1768 the Boston Whigs, taking advantage of the absence of barracks in Boston, had attempted to quarter the British troops in Castle William (a fort on an island in Boston harbor) rather than in the town itself where they were urgently needed. To forestall a like effort, the Quartering Act of 1774 provided that when there were no barracks where troops were required, the authorities must provide quarters for them on the spot; if they failed to do so, the governor might compel the use of occupied buildings. The Boston patriots, however, refused to allow workmen to repair the distilleries and empty buildings that Gen. Thomas Gage had procured for quarters and thus forced the British troops to remain camped on the Boston Common until November 1774.

BIBLIOGRAPHY

Edward Channing, *History of the United States*, vol. III.

— JOHN C. MILLER

QUEEN ANNE'S WAR

Queen Anne's War (1702–13) was the American counterpart of the War of the Spanish Succession, which was fought in Europe from 1701 to 1714. Fundamental issues, including the rivalry of France and England in America, had been left unsolved by the Treaty of Ryswick (1697). They were revived upon the acceptance of the Spanish throne by a grandson of Louis XIV of France in November 1700. The threat of Bourbon domination in Europe and in French and Spanish America caused William III of England and the Dutch Netherlands to ally (Sept. 7, 1701) with Holy Roman Emperor Leopold I, a member of whose Hapsburg family claimed the Spanish throne. On May 4, 1702, two months after Anne had succeeded William as sovereign of England, the three allied powers jointly declared formal war on France.

In America the war was fought in the West Indies and on the Carolina and New England frontiers. In the summer of 1702 the English captured the West Indies island of Saint Christopher, but Adm. John Benbow's action against a French squadron along the Spanish Main was indecisive. After the English failure to take Guadeloupe in 1703, military activity in the West Indies was restricted to privateering, from which English colonial trade suffered. In December 1702 South Carolinians destroyed the town, not the fort, of Spanish Saint Augustine; and in 1706 a Franco-Spanish fleet was repulsed from the harbor of Charleston.

In the North, New England bore the brunt of the war against the French in Canada. Until 1709 neither New York nor England rendered material assistance. English settlements, including those at Wells and Saco (Maine) and Deerfield, Reading, Sudbury, and Haverhill (Massachusetts), became the victims of barbarous French and Indian raids. After retaliatory attacks on Port Royal, led in 1704 by Col. Benjamin Church and in 1707 by John March, had failed, the English colonists secured, in 1709, Great Britain's promise of aid for expeditions against Quebec and Montreal. These projected campaigns under Samuel Vetch and Francis Nicholson were abandoned in October 1709, after the promised British force had been diverted to Portugal. In the following year a British contingent arrived, secured by Nicholson and Peter Schuyler in London. With that support, colonial troops, led by Nicholson and Sir Charles Hobby took Port Royal in October 1710. The capture of Port Royal, renamed Annapolis Royal, signified the fall of Acadia to Great Britain.

The new Tory government in England, dominated by Robert Harley and Henry St. John and interested in obtaining the asiento (a license from Spain to sell slaves in its colonies) for the projected South Sea Company, disavowed the contention of John Churchill, Duke of Marlborough, that the European fronts were alone decisive, and dispatched an expedition to support colonial troops in attacks on Quebec and Montreal. However, on Aug. 23, 1711, ten of the expedition's ships were wrecked with the loss of nearly 750 men on the rocks above Anticosti Island in the Saint Lawrence, and the rest of the expedition returned to England.

Meanwhile, in 1711, peace negotiations had begun in Europe. In October 1712, American colonial governors received a royal proclamation of an armistice, and on Apr. 11, 1713, Queen Anne's War was concluded by the Treaty of Utrecht.

BIBLIOGRAPHY

E. B. Greene, *Provincial America.*
F. Parkman, *A Half-Century of Conflict.*
G. M. Trevelyan, *England Under Queen Anne.*

— E. B. GRAVES

R

RADICAL REPUBLICANS

Radical Republicans, the determined antislavery wing of the Republican party during the first twenty years of its existence, beginning in the mid-1850's. Opposed to further compromises with slaveholders before the Civil War, they became the most persistent advocates of the emancipation of slaves during the conflict and of the elevation and enfranchisement of blacks afterward.

Veterans of the free-soil and antislavery movements, the radical Republicans played an important role in the founding of the Republican party as an organization committed to the restriction of slavery. Successful in keeping the party true to the free-soil principle, radical Republicans blocked concessions to retain the southern states' loyalty during the secession crisis and cooperated with President-elect Abraham Lincoln in defeating the Crittenden Compromise. They also demanded the retention of Fort Sumter and strongly supported the president in his refusal to evacuate it.

When the Civil War broke out, the radicals insisted on its vigorous prosecution. For this purpose they helped organize and dominated the Joint Committee on the Conduct of the War and agitated for the dismissal of conservative generals, notably George B. McClellan. They favored the confiscation of enemy property, the establishment of the state of West Virginia, and the raising of black troops. Above all, they never ceased to work for the liberation of the slaves.

The radicals' emphasis on speedy emancipation often brought them into conflict with Lincoln. They deplored his reversal of John C. Frémont's order to end slavery in Missouri, criticized his failure to oust conservative cabinet members, and demanded that he take immediate steps to abolish servitude. Their clashes with the president were formerly considered proof of their irreconcilable differences with him, but mid-20th-century historians stress the essential similarities between Lincoln and his radical critics. In many respects he tended to sympathize with their aims, if not with their methods, and he was thus able to make use of their energy and zeal to achieve the essential racial progress that he gradually came to favor.

In the controversy about Reconstruction the radicals were the main proponents of the protection of black rights in the South. Instrumental in the passage of the Wade-Davis Bill (1864), which would have freed all remaining slaves and set forth a stringent plan of reconstruction, they mercilessly denounced Lincoln when he vetoed it. Nevertheless, the president later not only cooperated with them in effecting the passage of the Thirteenth Amendment but also in his last speech endorsed at least in part their demand for black suffrage in Louisiana.

The radical Republicans at first welcomed President Andrew Johnson's accession. As a southern Unionist who had been a member of the Committee on the Conduct of the War, he was considered sufficiently stern to impose rigorous conditions on the defeated insurgents. But when he insisted on his mild plan of Reconstruction, the radicals took the lead in the congressional struggle against him. Their tireless agitation induced the moderates to cooperate in passing various measures for the protection of the blacks: the Fourteenth Amendment, the Freedmen's Bureau, and the civil rights acts may be cited as examples. The group was also responsible for the inauguration of radical Reconstruction. Because of the president's interference with Republican policies in the South, the radicals provided the impetus for his impeachment, although they suffered a severe blow in their failure to secure his conviction.

During the administration of President Ulysses S. Grant, their influence gradually waned, although they were able to maintain enough enthusiasm to enable the party to pass the Fifteenth Amendment, implement Reconstruction, and enact enforcement bills as well as one last civil rights measure. But the weakening of the reform spirit, the death and retirement of leading radicals, and the emergence of new issues contributed to their decline. Then came the panic of 1873, and when the Democrats recaptured the House of Representatives in 1874, the end of radicalism was in sight.

Because they never possessed a cohesive organization, the exact identification of individual radicals is difficult. Some Republicans were always radicals; others cooperated only at certain times. Among the most consistent radicals were Charles Sumner, Thaddeus Stevens, Benjamin F. Wade, Zachariah Chandler, and George W. Julian. Benjamin F. Butler, John A. Logan, and Henry Winter Davis were identified with the group after 1862; Lyman Trumbull collaborated only before that time. The test of radicalism was always the degree of commitment to reform in race relations; on all other issues, individual radicals differed. Protection and free trade, inflation and hard money, woman's rights and labor reform—all had their advocates and opponents. The only issues that held them together were those of opposition to slavery and insistence on fair treatment of the freedmen.

Just as different radicals had conflicting views on many economic and social questions, so were they also motivated by widely disparate incentives. While some were undoubtedly conscious of the party advantages of black suffrage in the South, many were sincerely devoted to the ideal of racial justice. Often accused of vindictiveness, they were not primarily interested in revenge and failed to punish severely any of the prominent Confederates. Because practical and ideological considerations did not necessarily conflict, such leaders as Stevens could publicly admit the influence of both. The radical Republicans' importance lies in their successful pressure for reform as evidenced in emancipation and the passage of the Thirteenth, Fourteenth, and Fifteenth amendments.

BIBLIOGRAPHY

Harold M. Hyman, ed., *The Radical Republicans and Reconstruction, 1861–1870.*

Grady McWhiney, ed., *Grant, Lee, Lincoln and the Radicals.*

David Montgomery, *Beyond Equality: Labor and the Radical Republicans, 1862–1872.*

Hans L. Trefousse, *The Radical Republicans: Lincoln's Vanguard for Racial Justice.*

T. Harry Williams, *Lincoln and the Radicals.*

— HANS L. TREFOUSSE

RADICALS AND RADICALISM

The derivation of the word "radical" from the Latin *radix* ("root") gives only a vague clue to its meaning in modern thought and history. It is, of course, a significant term in mathematics. But the word has also been used in a number of other fields and in a variety of contexts. Thus, one can speak of radical views in philosophy, science, art, or architecture (Frank Lloyd Wright, for example, was once thought of as a radical in architecture). The term is often used to designate a person who wishes to alter drastically any existing practice, institution, or pattern of conduct. It may be used to designate any outlook or person appearing to be unorthodox or atypical and in this sense connotes opposition to whatever is regarded as accepted or established. Thus, it is sometimes used derogatorily to discredit the views of opponents.

"Radical" and "radicalism" are words used frequently in politics and fields related to politics. The radical is sometimes seen as the individual or position reflecting the most "leftward" view. It is therefore common to designate points on the political spectrum as radical, liberal, conservative, and reactionary. In the 20th century the term is sometimes employed to designate any view considered extreme, whether of the "left" or of the "right": hence, during the presidential campaign of 1964 candidate Barry Goldwater was not infrequently called a "radical of the Right." But some view radicalism as any outlook, proposal, or program seeking basic change in the direction of greater economic, social, or political equality.

The term radical *is often used to designate someone who wishes to alter drastically any existing practice, institution, or pattern of conduct.*

Whatever the precise meaning attached to such words as "radical" and "radicalism" it seems they are designations that can be understood best in relation to the contexts within which they are used. They are relative terms: a position is radical in comparison with other positions that may be taken, and what is regarded as radical in one generation may be orthodox or nonradical in another. For example, Victoria Claflin was a radical in the feminist movement of the late 19th century in her advocacy not only of woman's suffrage but also of free love, but she might be regarded as less radical in the context of the feminist movement of the 1970's.

The 18th- and early 19th-century advocates of reform in the British Parliament were seen as radical, as were the utilitarians and Chartists. In pre-Civil War America many of the utopian community experiments could be described in similar terms (the Oneida Community of John Humphrey Noyes, for instance, which stressed communism in material and sexual spheres and advocated fundamental changes in the status of women). The Workies, a political party organized in 1829, was radical, as were William Lloyd Garrison and other abolitionists. The abolitionist movement as a whole was sometimes described as having conservative, moderate, and radical wings; and somewhat similarly the 19th-century peace movement was said to consist of conservatives (who thought that while war in general must be opposed, defensive wars were permissible) and radicals (who viewed all war, including so-called defensive war, as morally wrong and impermissible).

Immediately after the Civil War the label Radical Republican came to be attached to Republican party leaders who, in the manner of Thaddeus Stevens and Charles Sumner, pressed more aggressively than most

Republicans for guarantees of social and political equality for newly emancipated slaves and advocated somewhat harsh measures against the former Confederacy.

Radicalism in politics from 1865 to World War I was centrally associated with proposals to alter fundamentally the "capitalist" economic and social system. In varying ways radicals demanded far-reaching changes in property relations, in distribution of wealth and income, or in the status of labor. The Knights of Labor were originally thought of as radical, as were the members of the Greenback Labor party, the Free Silver men, the Single Taxers of Henry George, and many leaders of the so-called Populist revolt. There were several types of so-called agrarian radicals, who advocated drastic change in the agricultural economy and society. Then there were the Socialist groups, such as the Socialist Labor Party, established in 1877, and the American Socialist Party, founded in 1901. The anarchists should also be mentioned, and their leaders, Emma Goldman and Alexander Berkman, for example. American syndicalism was represented by the Industrial Workers of the World, founded in 1905, which from its birth until the end of World War I symbolized for many all that was supposedly iniquitous in radicalism as a whole.

With the decline of socialism and anarchism after World War I, the center of much radicalism in the public mind came to be concentrated in the so-called Communist movement and its "front" groups. "Bolshevist," "Communist," "Red," "subversive," and "radical" were often used interchangeably, both by citizens and by congressional and state legislative investigating committees. During the 1950's "Communist radicals" became the targets of Sen. Joseph McCarthy's campaigns, and "McCarthyism" became a kind of shorthand for "antiradicalism." In the heyday of McCarthyism fundamental criticism in any area of American life was at an ebb and new radical movements were correspondingly rare.

During the 1960's many leaders and movements appeared that were called radical either by themselves or by their critics. Students for a Democratic Society (SDS) was one such group, with its criticism both of the Old Left (the Marxists) and of orthodox American politics. The student protest movement, centering in such institutions as the University of California, Berkeley, was variously described as being radical in general or as having a radical wing. Many thought of the Civil Rights Movement as an exemplification of radicalism, and many held that Martin Luther King, Jr., advocated radical solutions. Before his assassination in 1968 King was regarded by many as nonradical, the mantle of radicalism having passed to such leaders as Stokely Carmichael and H. Rap Brown. The peace movement of the 1960's, which concentrated on ending the Vietnam War, produced a number of self-styled radicals and leaders who were seen by others as radical. The veteran peace leader A. J. Muste described himself as a radical pacifist, and several of his associates, including David Dellinger, saw themselves in a similar light. Nonregistrants under the Selective Service law were viewed by many as radicals.

It is highly characteristic of the American experience that many proposals that at one time were described as radical, and even as unthinkable, should later be adopted as public policy. The list is a long one, including federal income taxes (originally described by many opponents as a kind of communism), collective bargaining, and Social Security. Some of the immediate demands included in the Socialist party platform of 1912—radical in their day—came to be embodied in New Deal legislation enacted after 1933.

The functions of American radicalism, viewed as sharp social criticism and pleas for fundamental changes in society, have been described as manyfold: to challenge an ever-present and strong tendency to social complacency; to emphasize the proneness of a society to fall away from its professed ideals; to point out the frequently gross inadequacy of moderate remedies; and to provide the drastically unorthodox paradigms seemingly so essential for stimulation of creative public discussion.

BIBLIOGRAPHY

Benjamin R. Epstein, *The Radical Right.*

Christopher Lasch, *The New Radicalism in America.*

Sidney Lens, *Radicalism in America.*

Staughton Lynd, *Intellectual Origins of American Radicalism.*

— MULFORD Q. SIBLEY

RADIO

When radio first appeared in the United States in the early 1920s, it created an entirely new medium of entertainment—a "theater of the mind." By the 1930s listening to the radio became the most common home activity of families. All network programming was planned around the family. Women were offered daily dramatic serials during mornings and afternoons, nearly all sponsored by manufacturers of soap or detergent products ("soap operas"). Children were served adventure shows in the late afternoons. News and commentary programs followed. From 7:00 P.M. on, dramas and variety shows were broadcast for the entire family. Programming by and large was controlled by four national networks: the Radio Corporation of America's (RCA) National Broadcasting Company, with two networks (NBC-Red and NBC-Blue); the Columbia Broadcast-

On Halloween night in 1938, Orson Welles broadcast a dramatization of the science fiction book War of the Worlds *that caused near hysteria among the listening audience. A newspaper headline the next day read "Panic Grips Nation as Radio Announces 'Mars Attacks World.'" (The Granger Collection, New York)*

ing System (CBS); and the Mutual Broadcasting System (MBS). Because RCA owned two networks, the Federal Communications Commission ordered it to divest one, which it did in 1943, with NBC-Blue becoming the American Broadcasting Company.

Radio produced its own celebrities, few of whom could duplicate their successes in motion pictures. Jack Benny, Fred Allen, George Burns and Gracie Allen, Major Bowes, and Fanny Brice became extensions of virtually every U.S. family during radio's "golden age." For a time the most popular program featured a ventriloquist, Edgar Bergen, whose inability to keep his lips from moving doomed his attempts in later years to translate his show to television. It was the overwhelming popularity of Bergen and his dummy, Charlie McCarthy, a show that attracted one-third of all radio listeners, that may have prevented a national panic on Halloween of 1938. That night actor Orson Welles, whose "Mercury Theater on the Air" attracted a mere 3.6 percent of the national radio audience, broadcast a dramatization of the science-fiction book *War of the Worlds* by British author H. G. Wells that caused a near panic among the audience. A newspaper headline next day related that "Radio War Terrorizes U.S."; another read, "Panic Grips Nation as Radio Announces 'Mars Attacks World.'" The program demonstrated the power of radio's possible manipulation of the public's imagination.

Radio has had a marked effect on politics and reporting. President Franklin D. Roosevelt, whose voice rivaled those of the actors of the day, mobilized support for his New Deal in the 1930s by taking his message directly to the electorate via radio in "fireside chats." In the 1940s he used them to arouse the nation's patriotic ardor. When war came, first to Europe, then to the United States, radio was brought into the living rooms of Americans with on-the-scene reports from such correspondents as Edward R. Murrow, Walter Cronkite, William L. Shirer, Howard K. Smith, and Eric Sevareid.

With the advent of television—and concurrent development of the transistor—following World War II, radio was transformed into a portable jukebox, with networks becoming little more than headline news services. Independent stations appealing to niche audiences developed—stations with music appealing to older listeners, stations aimed at teenagers, and stations directed at ethnic minorities. With the emergence of new stations on the FM band by the 1970s, the niches were themselves partitioned. Stations were classified as "contemporary," "adult," "album-oriented," "urban," or described by a dozen other tags. FM broadcasting, with its superior fidelity, overtook established AM stations, in numbers and popularity. Between 1975 and 1995 FM stations in the United States nearly doubled to 5,000, and AM stations declined from 4,700 to 4,200.

With broadcasting companies downgrading their radio networks to insignificance, independent syndicators in the 1970s began providing special programming. A program hosted by Los Angeles disc jockey Casey Kasem, featuring a "countdown" of the top forty songs of the week, became the first program to attract a sizable national audience since radio's heyday in the 1930s and 1940s. In the mid-1970s a program syndicator, Westwood One, achieved a dominant position, eventually purchasing Mutual and NBC radio and signing Kasem to a long-term, multimillion-dollar contract. Its success was attributed to cost efficiencies achieved by distributing programs via satellite rather than by land lines. In 1980 Sony introduced the Walkman, a transistorized radio-cassette player that provided concert-hall sound in a package weighing only a few ounces. Demand became so great that a year after its introduction, there was still a month-long wait at many retailers. Ironically, competition with Walkman-type devices in the 1980s came from hefty portable players, or "boom boxes," that could blast the sound of popular radio stations through entire neighborhoods.

Because of the inferior tone quality of AM, many radio stations on that band turned to all-news and all-talk formats, where high fidelity was of little importance. News stations rehashed summaries of the day's events every twenty minutes—presumed to be the average length of an automobile commute. Indeed, all radio programmers recognized that most of their audiences listened in cars, so frequent traffic reports also became obligatory.

Initially, talk shows appealed to middle-aged audiences that appeared to delight in airing their personal problems through call-ins to station hosts, but in the early 1990s two utterly dissimilar national talk-show personalities, Howard Stern and Rush Limbaugh, rose to national prominence, overhauling the medium in the process. Stern's scatological satires made him the most listened-to personality on the air—even as federal regulators fined stations he appeared on for broadcasting obscene material. Limbaugh's humorous conservative broadcasts similarly caught on and produced a host of imitators. He and his cohorts were widely credited with helping the Republican party win a majority in both houses of Congress in 1994.

[See also Television.]

BIBLIOGRAPHY

Erik Barnouw, *A History of Broadcasting in the United States*, 3 vols. (New York, 1966–1970).

— LEW IRWIN

RAILROADS

The earliest railroads in the United States were short wooden tramways connecting mines or quarries with nearby streams, upon which horses could draw heavier loads than on the common roads. The idea of the railroad as it came to be, tracks on which trains of cars are pulled by mechanical power in common-carrier service, was first expounded by Col. John Stevens of Hoboken, N.J., who in 1812 published his *Documents Tending to Prove the Superior Advantages of Rail-Ways and Steam Carriages Over Canal Navigation.* On Feb. 6, 1815, he secured a charter from the New Jersey legislature authorizing the building of a railroad across the state, but he was unable to enlist the capital necessary for construction.

The first charter under which a railroad was built in the United States was that of the Granite Railway of Massachusetts, a three-mile line built in 1826, which used horses to haul stone for the building of the Bunker Hill monument from quarries at Quincy.

The first railroad incorporated as a common carrier of passengers and freight, the Baltimore and Ohio, was chartered by the state of Maryland on Feb. 28, 1827. Construction was started with due ceremony on July 4, 1828, and the first passengers were carried in January 1830 in single cars drawn by horses.

Experiments with steam locomotion were already under way. Stevens had built a tiny locomotive that ran on a circular track on his estate in 1825. More significant was the *Stourbridge Lion*, imported from England by the Delaware and Hudson Canal and Railroad for use on the line of rails connecting its mines with its canal. On its one trial trip on Aug. 8, 1829, the *Lion* proved to be too heavy for the track and was not used again as a locomotive. In August 1830 the Baltimore and Ohio experimented with the *Tom Thumb*, an engine whose diminutive size was indicated by its name. It was built and operated by Peter Cooper.

The essential elements of a railroad in the modern sense—track, trains of cars, mechanical locomotive power, and public service as a common carrier—were first combined on the South Carolina Canal and Rail Road Company (later included in the Southern Railway system) when, on Dec. 25, 1830, it inaugurated scheduled service on the first six miles of its line out of Charleston with the steam locomotive *Best Friend*, the first to pull a train of cars on the American continent. Three years later the line was opened to Hamburg, a terminus across the river from Augusta, Ga., 136 miles away, making it at the time the longest railway in the world.

Railroads opened for operation by steam power in the early 1830's included the Mohawk and Hudson, earliest link in the future New York Central system, over which the locomotive *DeWitt Clinton* pulled a train of cars between Albany and Schenectady on Aug. 9, 1831; the Camden and Amboy, later part of the Pennsylvania system, on which the British-built *John Bull* was placed in service at Bordentown, N.J., also in 1831; the Philadelphia, Germantown and Norristown, later part of the Reading, on which *Old Ironsides*, built by Matthias Baldwin, first ran in 1832; and the railroad connecting New Orleans with Lake Pontchartrain, afterward part of the Louisville and Nashville, on which the first locomotive in the Mississippi Valley made its initial scheduled run on Sept. 17, 1832.

By 1835 railroads ran from Boston to Lowell, the beginnings of the future Boston and Maine; to Worcester, first link in the Boston and Albany; and to Providence, the genesis of the New York, New Haven and Hartford. The Petersburg Railroad, later part of the Atlantic Coast Line, ran from the Virginia city whose name it bore south into North Carolina. The Baltimore and Ohio had built a branch to Washington, D.C., and had pushed its main line westward to the Blue Ridge. Countering this effort by Baltimore to reach out for the trade of the West, several New York businessmen had started the New York and Erie, headed westward for Lake Erie through the southern tier of counties of the state. The state of Pennsylvania, not to be outdone, had opened a hybrid route between Philadelphia and Pittsburgh, using two stretches of canals, a railroad operated with both locomotives and horses, and a series of inclined planes by which cars were raised and lowered over the Alleghenies.

Pennsylvania was not the only state to undertake the building of a railroad. North Carolina, acting through corporations in which the state was a majority stockholder, built and owned lines that came to constitute a substantial segment of the Southern Railway, which operates them under lease. Georgia, acting directly, built, and later leased to the Louisville and Nashville, an important link between Georgia and Tennessee. Virginia became a large stockholder in the Richmond, Fredericksburg and Potomac. Less fortunate were the railroad ventures of the states of Michigan and Illinois, which embarked prematurely on ambitious state transportation schemes that failed and were sold to private companies. One of the most successful ventures in public ownership was the Cincinnati Southern, a line built and owned by the city and operated under lease by the Southern Railway system.

1840–60

By 1840, the end of the first decade of the railroad era, 2,800 miles of railroad were in operation in the United States, with mileage in every seacoast state and in Kentucky, Ohio, Indiana, Michigan, and Illinois. In the second decade of railroad development, mileage more than trebled, reaching a total of 9,000 miles. Lines had been opened in Vermont and Wisconsin, and missing links had been supplied, so that by 1850 it was possible to travel by rail between Boston and Buffalo, with numerous changes of cars, and between Boston and Wilmington, N.C., with occasional gaps covered by steamboat.

By 1850, also, there had been developed a standard American-type locomotive, with a four-wheel swivel leading truck and four driving wheels, coupled. The design was simple, powerful, and easy on the track. It became the ancestor of a variety of heavier and more powerful types for freight and passenger service, but itself remained the backbone of the locomotive fleet until almost the end of the century.

In the decade of the 1850's railway mileage again more than trebled, as the ambitious efforts of the Atlantic seaports to reach the West were fulfilled. New York was connected with the Great Lakes, both by the Erie Railroad and by way of Albany and the New York Central, formed in 1853 by the consolidation of a dozen small railroads between the Hudson River and Buffalo. Philadelphia established an all-rail connection with Pittsburgh, and Baltimore reached the Ohio at Wheeling early in the 1850's.

By 1840, the end of the first decade of the railroad era, 2,800 miles of track were in operation in the U.S.

Before these lines reached their trans-Allegheny goals, other lines were being built across the more open and level country of the Middle West. Chicago was entered from the East in 1852 almost simultaneously by two lines, the Michigan Central and the Michigan Southern, both of which were later included in the New York Central system. Already, lines were building west from Chicago—the Galena and Chicago Union (later the Chicago and North Western), which brought the first locomotive to the future rail center on a Great Lakes sailing vessel, and the Chicago and Rock Island, which reached the Mississippi River in February 1854. Only a year later a route between Chicago and East Saint Louis afforded another rail connection between the East and the Mississippi, while in 1857 two such connections were added—the direct route from Baltimore via Cincinnati and, to the south, a route between Charleston and Savannah, on the Atlantic, and Memphis, on the Mississippi.

But before the rails reached the great river from the East, railroads had started from the west bank. The first locomotive to turn a wheel beyond the Mississippi ran on Dec. 9, 1852, on the Pacific Railroad of Missouri (later the Missouri Pacific) from Saint Louis five miles westward. In 1856 the Iron Horse crossed the Mississippi on the first railroad bridge, that of the Rock Island line, later called the Chicago, Rock Island and Pacific. Before the end of the decade, the railroad had reached the Missouri on the tracks of the Hannibal and Saint Joseph (later part of the Burlington lines).

For the most part these routes had been built as separate local lines, in many instances lacking the physical connections without which through movement of freight and passengers was impossible. One road built as a unit was the Illinois Central, a north-south line connecting East Dubuque and Cairo, with a "branch" from Centralia to Chicago. Chartered in 1851, the line of more than 700 miles was completed in 1857.

One factor in the successful building of the Illinois Central was the grant by the federal government to the state of Illinois, and through that state to the railroad corporation, of vacant lands from the public domain in Illinois as an aid to financing the construction of the line. This grant, and a like grant of lands in Alabama and Mississippi to the Mobile and Ohio Railroad, which was to be built northward, was the beginning of a policy of making such grants-in-aid for railroad building, following an earlier precedent of such grants-in-aid for canals and wagon roads. Lands were granted to railroads in alternate sections of one mile square, for distances of from six to twenty miles on either side of the line. The government retained title to alternate sections, making a checkerboard pattern of private and government ownership. The purposes of the grants were to use vacant and unsalable lands lacking transportation and to encourage the building of railroads into undeveloped regions, thereby attracting settlers, adding value to the lands retained by the government, increasing production and taxable wealth, and unifying the nation.

During the twenty-one years the policy was in effect, from 1850 to 1871, federal land grants were made to aid in the building of less than 10 percent of the railroad mileage of the United States, by which some 131 million of the approximately 1.4 billion acres of public lands owned in 1850 were transferred to private ownership. The value of the lands granted as of the time of the grants was approximately $125 million. In return for the grants the railroads carried government freight, mail, and troops at reduced rates until 1946, when the arrangement was ended by act of Congress. By that time land grant rate deductions for the government amounted to a total of more than $1 billion.

In the 1850's, railroad building was started in newly annexed Texas, where the Buffalo Bayou, Brazos and Colorado was opened from present-day Houston westward toward Richmond, Tex., in 1853, and in the new state of California, where the Sacramento Valley was opened in 1856 from navigable waters at Sacramento to Folsom (both later part of the Southern Pacific system).

1861–65

With the coming of the Civil War, the building of new railroads was slowed down somewhat, but the existing railroads were called upon to play essential roles in the struggle. Even before war started, the east-west railroads, tying the Northwest to the Northeast rather than to the lower Mississippi Valley, had been largely decisive in determining the attitude of the interior states of the North. More than two-thirds of the 1861 mileage and an even greater proportion of railroad transportation capacity lay in the states that adhered to the Union. Invasion of the South soon reduced even the small percentage of the railroad mileage in Confederate hands. It is not too much to say that relative railroad strength was a decisive factor in the "first railroad war."

On the railroads of both sides there were remarkable transportation achievements. The outcome of the first Battle of Bull Run was determined by troops shifted by rail from the Shenandoah Valley to the vicinity of Manassas, Va. A major rail movement was the transfer of the Confederate Army of Tennessee from Tupelo, Miss., to Chattanooga, via Mobile, Ala., and Atlanta, preparatory to the launching of Gen. Braxton Bragg's Kentucky campaign. A more remarkable accomplishment was the movement of Gen. James Longstreet's army corps from Virginia through the Carolinas and Georgia, just in time to win the Confederate victory of Chickamauga, Ga. Most remarkable of all was the movement of Gen. Joseph Hooker's two corps of 22,000 men over a distance of 1,200 miles from Virginia to the vicinity of Chattanooga, via Columbus, Indianapolis, Louisville, and Nashville.

More important even than these spectacular shifts of large army units from one strategic field to another was the part played by the railroads in the day-to-day movement of men, food, ammunition, matériel, and supplies from distant sources to the combat forces. Movements of this sort reached a climax in Gen. William Tecumseh Sherman's campaign for the capture of Atlanta in the summer of 1864, when his army of 100,000 men and 35,000 animals was kept supplied and in fighting trim by a single-track railroad extending nearly 500 miles from its base on the Ohio River at Louisville.

1865–1916

There had been agitation for a transcontinental railroad since 1848 at least, and during the 1850's the topographical engineers of the army had explored five routes. Ultimately railroads were built on all those routes, but sectional jealousies and the immensity of the task prevented such an undertaking until the Civil War removed the southern routes from consideration and, at the same time, made imperative the need for better communication with the Pacific coast. Congress accordingly passed, and President Abraham Lincoln signed on July 1, 1862, a bill authorizing a railroad between the Missouri River and California, to be built on the central, or "overland," route.

The president designated Council Bluffs, Iowa, as the starting point. Construction was undertaken by the Union Pacific, building westward from Omaha, and by the Central Pacific (later part of the Southern Pacific), building eastward from Sacramento, Calif. On May 10, 1869, the construction crews met and joined tracks at Promontory, Utah, in the mountains north of the Great Salt Lake. The junction was celebrated by the ceremony of driving a golden spike, as the telegraph instruments clicked out to the waiting and rejoicing United States the message "The last rail is laid . . . the last spike driven. . . . The Pacific Railroad is completed."

The first transcontinental route was built as a "great military highway" in the words of Sherman, and was not expected to be self-supporting. Construction was aided by land grants and by government loans, frequently and erroneously described as gifts, despite the fact that the loans were repaid in full with interest. Later transcontinental routes were not aided by loans but in most instances received grants of land, in return for which they carried government traffic at reduced rates.

The second transcontinental connection was supplied in 1881 when the Atchison, Topeka and Santa Fe, building westward, met the Southern Pacific, building eastward, at Deming, N.Mex. The Southern Pacific continuing to build eastward, met the Texas and Pacific at Sierra Blanca, Tex., in 1882 and, by further construction and acquisition of lines, established a through route to New Orleans in 1883. In the same year California was reached by a line built by the Santa Fe westward from Albuquerque, N.Mex., forming still another transcontinental route.

The construction crews joined tracks at Promontory, Utah, on May 10, 1869; when the golden spike was in place, the transcontinental railroad was complete.

The first route to reach the Pacific Northwest was opened in 1883 by the Northern Pacific, built through the northernmost tier of states. A second route to the Northwest was opened a year later when the Oregon Short Line, built from a junction with the Union Pacific, joined tracks with the Oregon Railway and Navigation Company (both later part of the Union Pacific system).

In 1893 a third route to the Pacific Northwest, and the first to be built without the aid of land grants, was completed by the Great Northern. The extension to the coast of the Chicago, Milwaukee and Saint Paul, which added "Pacific" to its name, was completed in 1909, also without the aid of land grants.

The Union Pacific route to southern California was completed in 1905 by the San Pedro, Los Angeles and Salt Lake, while another route to northern California was opened in 1910 when the Westem Pacific effected a junction at Salt Lake City with the Denver and Rio Grande Western.

Meanwhile, railroad construction continued in the older portions of the United States, closing the gaps in the rail net. Between 1860 and 1870, despite the interruption of the Civil War, total mileage increased from 31,000 to 53,000 miles. This rate of growth was exceeded in the 1870's when 40,000 miles of new line were built.

The decade of the 1880's recorded the greatest growth in railway mileage, with an average of more than 7,000 miles of new line built each year. By the end of the decade the conversion from iron rail to the stronger, more durable, and safer steel rail was largely completed. The same decade also saw the standardization of track gauge, of car couplers, of train brakes, and of time, all essential steps toward a continent-wide commerce by rail.

The earlier railroads were built to serve the interests of particular points and, for the most part, without thought of future interconnection with other lines. Under such circumstances the question of gauge, or the width of track between rails, was of small importance. Altogether twenty-four different gauges have been used in the United States, ranging from 2 feet to 6 feet. By the 1880's gradual adjustment had brought about general agreement on two gauges. One of 5 feet predominated in the South. The other, predominant in the rest of the country, was 4 feet, 8.5 inches, a width originally used in England by George Stephenson, which had spread to the United States through the importation by early railroads of English-built locomotives. In 1886 the railroads of the South changed their gauge to conform, and the odd figure of 4–8.5 became "standard gauge" for all but a limited mileage of narrow-gauge railroads.

Along with standardization of track gauge, cars and locomotives had to be standardized to make it possible for the cars of any railroad to run on the tracks and in the trains of every other railroad. Car couplers, for example, had to work not only with other couplers of like design but also, as cars went from road to road, with those on other lines. As new models of couplers were introduced, they had to work with those already in use. As early as 1869, the Master Car Builders' Association, one of the ancestors of the Association of American

Railroads, had begun tests of various types of couplers designed to replace the simple but unsafe and unsatisfactory link-and-pin device. Altogether more than 3,000 patents were issued for various forms of safety couplers. Forty-two were considered practical enough to warrant consideration in a series of tests at Buffalo beginning in 1885, which resulted in the adoption, in 1887, of the design of Eli H. Janney as standard. Vastly modified and improved, the basic principle remained standard in the 1970's.

As in the case of couplers, interchange of freight cars between railroads required standardization of brakes. Early trains were stopped by hand brakes, set on each car by brakemen. Efforts to control the setting of brakes from the locomotive were unsuccessful until, in 1869, George Westinghouse devised his first air brake for passenger trains. Three years later he developed an improved system in which the brakes would be applied automatically if the train was accidentally separated. These brakes were installed on most passenger cars within the next decade, but the problem of a satisfactory brake for freight trains remained. In 1886 and 1887 exhaustive tests were conducted on the Chicago, Burlington and Quincy at Burlington, Iowa, which resulted in the adoption of a quick-acting brake for freight trains. With further improvements, especially those adopted in 1933 after exhaustive laboratory and road tests, the air brake remained fundamental in train operation.

Another feature of railroad operation standardized in the 1880's was time. Previously, each locality had used its own sun time, while each railroad had its own standard, usually the local time of its headquarters or of some important city on the line. There were altogether nearly a hundred different railroad times, bringing about unimaginable confusion. On Nov. 18, 1883, under an arrangement put into effect by the General Time Convention (another predecessor organization of the Association of American Railroads), all railroad clocks and watches were set on a new standard time with four zones one hour apart. Within a short time most localities abandoned their particular times and conformed to the system of Eastern, Central, Mountain, and Pacific time zones set up by the railroads. The system of standard time continued under railroad auspices until 1918, when by act of Congress it was placed under control of the Interstate Commerce Commission (ICC).

The ICC itself dates from the 1880's. Early attempts to regulate railroad rates and practices by action of the states had been only partially successful, although in 1876 the so-called. Granger laws had been upheld by the U.S. Supreme Court for intrastate application. In 1886, however, the Court held, in *Wabash, Saint Louis and Pacific Railroad Company* v. *Illinois*, that Congress had exclusive jurisdiction over interstate commerce and that a state could not regulate even the intrastate portion of an interstate movement. Efforts had been made for a dozen years before to have Congress enact regulatory legislation. The decision in the *Wabash* case brought these efforts to a head and resulted in passage on Feb. 4, 1887, of the Interstate Commerce Act, which created the ICC. Subsequent enactments, notably those of 1903, 1906, 1910, 1920, 1933, 1940, and 1958, broadened the commission's jurisdiction and responsibilities, increased its powers, and strengthened its organization.

In 1888 the first federal legislation dealing with relations between railroads and their employees was passed. This enactment applied only to employees in train and engine service, who were the first railway employees to form successful unions—the Brotherhood of Locomotive Engineers in 1863, the Order of Railway Conductors in 1868, the Brotherhood of Locomotive Firemen and Enginemen in 1873, and the Brotherhood of Railroad Trainmen in 1883. These, with the Switchmen's Union of North America, organized in 1894, constitute the "operating" group of unions. "Nonoperating" crafts formed organizations at various dates—the telegraphers (1886), the six shop-craft unions (1888–93), the maintenance-of-way employees (1891), the clerks and station employees (1898), the signalmen (1901). Nevertheless, the Erdman Act (1898) and the Newlands Act (1913), providing various measures of mediation, conciliation, arbitration, and fact-finding in connection with railway labor disputes, dealt with train service cases only.

Between 1890 and 1900 another 40,000 miles were added to the railroad net, which by the turn of the century had assumed its main outline. After 1900, still another 60,000 miles of line were built, to bring the total of first main track to its peak of 254,000 miles in 1916. Mileage of all tracks, including additional main tracks, passing tracks, sidings, and yards reached its maximum of 430,000 miles in 1930. By 1960, mileage of line declined to approximately 220,000, and miles of tracks of all sorts had declined to 390,000. This reduction in mileage was the result of many factors, including the exhaustion of the mines, forests, and other natural resources that were the reason for being of many branch lines; intensified water and highway competition; and the coordinations and consolidations that made many lines unnecessary. In 1916 more than 1,400 companies operated 254,000 miles of line; in 1960, fewer than 600 companies operated 220,000 miles of line—but the reduced mileage had more than double the effective carrying capacity of the more extensive network.

1917–41

Railroad mileage was at its peak when, in April 1917, the United States entered World War I. Immediately the railroads established the Railroads' War Board to coordinate their work in meeting increased transportation demands. Increased service was achieved, but by December it was apparent that a voluntary organization of this kind could not cope with all the many difficulties: congestion arose from abuse by government organizations of the privilege of demanding priority and preference for cars, loading them even when they could not be unloaded promptly at destination, and further complications arose from the failure to suspend for the emergency the application of the antitrust laws and the antipooling provisions of the Interstate Commerce Act. On Dec. 26, 1917, President Woodrow Wilson issued his proclamation taking over the railroads for operation by the government, to start Jan. 1, 1918.

Operation of the railroads by the U.S. Railroad Administration lasted for twenty-six months, until Mar. 1, 1920. From the standpoint of meeting the transportation demands of the war, the operation was creditable. From a financial point of view, it resulted in losses, largely because of increased wages and prices not compensated for by increases in rates and fares, which amounted to an average of nearly $2 million a day for the period of government operation.

Congress voted to return the railroads to private operation and set up the terms of such operation in the Transportation Act of 1920. Among the changes in government policy was recognition of a measure of responsibility for financial results, found in the direction to the ICC to fix rates at such a level as would enable the railroads, as a whole or in groups, to earn a fair return on the value of the properties devoted to public service. This provision was frequently described as a government guarantee of railroad profits, although there was no guarantee of earnings. Commercial conditions and competitive forces kept railway earnings well below the contemplated level, and the government was not called on to make up the deficiency.

Another shift in government policy related to consolidation of railroads, previously frowned upon but encouraged by the Transportation Act of 1920. The change in policy stemmed from the fact that consolidation in one form or another had been from early times the way of growth of the major systems, some of which included properties originally built by a hundred or more companies. Accordingly the 1920 law directed the ICC to work out a scheme of consolidation for the railroads, a requirement of which the commission was relieved at its own request in 1933.

The 1920 act also set up the U.S. Railroad Labor Board, with jurisdiction extending to all crafts of employees and with power to determine wage rates and working conditions, although without power to enforce its decisions otherwise than by the force of public opinion. The first nationwide strike on the railroads took place in 1922, when the shopmen struck against a Labor Board decision reducing wages. The strike failed, but its aftereffects were such that in the Railway Labor Act of 1926, agreed to by the unions and the railroads, the Labor Board was abolished and the principles of the earlier labor legislation, with their reliance on mediation and conciliation, were restored, with improved machinery for making them more effective. The 1926 law was amended in important particulars in 1934, at the instance of the Railway Labor Executives Association, an organization of the "standard" railway unions formed in 1929.

The first nationwide railroad strike took place in 1922, when shopmen struck against a Labor Board decision reducing wages.

In 1934, also, the Railroad Retirement Act was passed as the first of the Social Security measures of the New Deal period. This legislation was declared unconstitutional, but in 1937 a retirement and unemployment insurance system was set up under legislation agreed upon by the Railway Labor Executives Association and the Association of American Railroads, an organization of the industry formed in 1934.

While railway mileage was shrinking in the two decades between World War I and World War II, the same years saw the introduction of numerous innovations in railroad plant, equipment, and methods, which greatly increased capacity and efficiency. The wooden car virtually disappeared. The steam locomotive became more powerful and more efficient. The diesel locomotive was introduced in passenger service in 1934 and in freight service in 1941. Passenger car air conditioning was introduced in 1929, and the first all air-conditioned train was operated in 1931. Streamlining was added to passenger train service, beginning in 1934. Passenger train speeds were increased, and overnight merchandise freight service for distances of more than 400 miles was inaugurated. Centralized traffic control and train operation by signal indication multiplied the capacity of single-track lines and even made it possible to take up trackage that was no longer required. Car retarders increased the speed and capacity, as well as the economy, of handling trains in terminal yards. Methods of operation, including car supply and distribution, particularly through the operations of the Car Service Division of the Association of American Railroads, were so improved that periodic general car shortages were no longer experienced.

1942–60

The combined effect of these and other improvements in plant, methods, and organization was such that the railroads, continuing under private operation, were able to meet all transportation demands during World War II. With one-fourth fewer cars, one-third fewer locomotives, and nearly one-third fewer men than they had in World War I, the railroads handled double the traffic of the first war and did so without congestion or delay.

In spite of wartime increases in wages and the prices of materials and supplies, railway rates and fares were no higher at the end of the war than they were when war began. As a result of postwar increases in wages average hourly earnings of employees went up from approximately $1 an hour to more than $2.50 an hour, and the level of prices paid for materials and supplies more than doubled in fifteen postwar years. In the same period the average revenue received for hauling a ton of freight one mile went up from about 1 cent to 1.5 cents, and the average charge for carrying a passenger one mile went up from about 2 cents to a little less than 3 cents. At the same time competitive forces reduced the railroads' share of the total transportation movement.

In May 1946, President Harry S. Truman, acting under his war powers, seized the railroads as a means of dealing with a nationwide strike by the engineers and trainmen, which had paralyzed the railroads for two days. Similar strike threats by other groups of unions brought similar seizures by the government in 1948 and again in 1950, the latter lasting nearly two years. In 1951 Congress amended the 1934 Railway Labor Act by removing the prohibition against compulsory union membership as a condition of holding a job on the railroads, thereby permitting the establishment of the union shop by negotiation, and such agreements were negotiated on most railroads.

Throughout the postwar years the railroads carried forward a program of capital improvements, with expenditures for such purposes averaging more than $1 billion yearly. The most striking and significant change was the displacement of the steam locomotive by the diesel-electric. Other major developments included the wider use of continuous welded rail in lengths of a quarter-mile, a half-mile, and even longer; the wide use of off-track equipment in maintenance-of-way work; the development of new designs of freight cars to make them ride more smoothly; the introduction of container or trailer-on-flat-car service, commonly called piggybacking; and the development of the automatic terminal with electronic controls, known as the push-button yard.

In passing the Transportation Act of 1958 Congress somewhat relaxed regulatory requirements on the railroads, providing, in effect, that competitive cost factors be given greater consideration in determining the lawfulness of rates, so long as the rates proposed were compensatory to the carrier and not discriminatory, as they were among shippers.

In 1959 Congress amended the Railroad Retirement Act and the Unemployment Insurance Act, increasing the benefits and the taxes levied to pay them: the measures provided for the financing of retirement by taxes on both companies and employees, half and half, and of unemployment insurance by taxes on the companies alone, without contribution from the employees.

As 1959 ended, railroads and employees were engaged in negotiations over wages and working conditions. The companies were seeking changes in rules that, it was charged, compelled payment for work not done and not needed. The operating unions denied the charge, maintaining that the rules under criticism were necessary for safety and the protection of the right of employees. Besides the dispute over featherbedding, with the operating unions only, negotiations over wages were in progress with all the employee organizations.

1961–74

In the seventh decade of the 20th century American railroads achieved some technical gains, but in other areas they suffered both real and relative losses. Total mileage operated declined from 216,000 miles in 1961 to 202,000 miles in 1973. In those twelve years total operating revenues for the industry climbed from $9.2 billion in 1961 to an all-time high of about $14.8 billion in 1973, but much of the increase was caused by inflation. Freight revenue increased in importance, climbing from 84 percent to 93 percent of the total operating revenue. While freight carloading declined, because of the use of larger and larger cars, there was a significant increase in total ton-mileage, and the 852 billion ton-miles reached in 1973 was a record high. However, the railroads' share of total intercity commercial freight was still declining, dropping from 43 percent in 1961 to about 38 percent in 1973. The discontinuance of hundreds of passenger trains and the growing popularity of jet air travel caused an even greater decline in rail passenger service. The 10.3 billion passenger-miles in 1974 was only about 50 percent of the 1961 figure, and the railroads' share of all passenger traffic declined from 26 percent in 1961 to less than 6 percent in 1973. By the early 1970's a major portion of the remaining rail passenger mileage was urban commuter traffic.

During the 1960's and early 1970's rises in freight rates and passenger fares roughly matched the growing inflation. Between 1961 and 1974 average freight rates increased from 1.37 cents to 1.85 cents per ton-mile, while average passenger fares climbed from 3.08 cents to 5.22 cents a mile. The total investment in the railroad industry grew but modestly in these years, increasing from $35.1 billion in 1961 to $37.4 billion in 1972. Nor was there much favorable news on the profit front, since the rate of return for the entire industry ranged from a low of 1.73 percent to a high of 3.90 percent, averaging only 2.46 percent for the period, significantly lower than the average rate of 3.45 percent for the 1950's and 4.25 percent for the 1940's.

The rather bleak financial picture was in part relieved by the achievement of modest technological advances. Innovation was especially notable in freight service. There was a slight drop in the number of freight cars in service, but the average capacity per car increased by nearly 25 percent. This factor plus greater daily car mileage resulted in a significant gain in the net ton-miles per freight-train hour.

In 1971 most railroad passenger service was taken over by the federally sponsored National Railroad Passenger Corporation, better known as Amtrak.

A major reduction in "hot boxes" (overheated journal bearings) was achieved during the 1960's. Improved lubrication plus infrared detection devices placed trackside reduced the number of set-out freight cars (those left on a siding because of a hot box) by more than 90 percent. Started in the late 1960's a program of automatic car identification (ACI) began providing the industry with a nationwide computer car-locating system. By the late 1960's many railroads were using sophisticated computers to help handle the mountains of paperwork that go with nearly every railroad operation. Almost 10,000 miles of Centralized Traffic Control (CTC) was installed during the decade, and CTC signaling was in use on about 40,000 miles of road by 1972.

New types of freight service were also appearing or being expanded. Piggyback freight service, introduced in the 1950's, continued to grow: such carloadings more than doubled between 1961 and 1968 and in the latter year amounted to almost 5 percent of the total carloadings for the year. A great increase was achieved in the railroad movement of new motor vehicles: in the late 1950's such traffic was about 90 percent by highway rack truck; in the early 1960's specially built railroad trilevel rack cars carried more and more of this traffic, and between 1969 and 1972 railroads delivered more than 50 percent of all automobiles produced. The railroads also rebuilt a declining coal traffic by introducing "unit trains"—whole trains of permanently coupled cars that carry bulk tonnage to a single destination on a regular schedule—thus reducing rates. The unit coal trains were so popular that the idea was soon extended to the shipment of grain, ore, pulpwood, and even trash and garbage.

Passenger service dropped off sharply in the 1960's. In 1961 passenger service was offered on more than 40 percent of the nation's rail network, whereas by 1971 passenger trains were running on less than 20 percent of the national mileage. Early in 1969 a government-sponsored project for high-speed passenger service in the Northeast Corridor was started when Metroliner service was provided between New York City and Washington, D.C. In May 1971 most railroad passenger service was taken over by the federally sponsored National Railroad Passenger Corporation, soon to be known as Amtrak. Amtrak provided passenger service consisting of about 1,300 trains a week, running over 20,000 miles of track on twenty-two different railroads, and serving 340 American cities. The financial support provided by the government assured at least some continuing rail passenger service for the immediate future.

In these years the railroad labor picture was marked by a continued drop in the work force accompanied by a marked increase in wages and salaries. Increased productivity plus the loss of some traditional rail traffic in the 1960's caused the total number of rail workers to drop from 717,000 in 1961 to 525,000 in 1974, a decline of more than 25 percent.

Wage rates and pay scales for railroad workers climbed rapidly. Between 1961 and 1974 average annual earnings per employee climbed from $6,444 to $14,235. The average straight time hourly rate rose from $2.72 to $5.84, more than doubling over the thirteen-year period. In general terms, railroad wages were climbing twice as fast as the cost of living. As it had for some time, the total cost of railroad labor, including fringe benefits and payroll taxes, continued to total just over 50 percent of all railway operating revenues.

The featherbedding issue, which railroad management had first raised in 1959, continued to color all railroad labor relations. One of the most difficult aspects of this problem, the issue of the employment of firemen in freight diesels, was finally resolved during 1972. Also by 1972 "full crew" laws had been eliminated in nearly all the states of the union. As in the case of the settlement concerning diesel firemen, fairly generous employment-security provisions were provided for those workers employed at the time of the repeal of the "full crew" laws.

A major development was the trend toward merger or consolidation: in the late 1950's there were 116 Class I railroads operating in the nation, and by 1973 this number had been reduced to just over 60. Between 1959 and 1964 the Norfolk and Western expanded by taking over the Virginian, the Wabash, and the Nickel Plate. During the same years the Chesapeake and Ohio gained control of the larger Baltimore and Ohio. Farther south the Atlantic Coast Line and the Seaboard Air Line merged in 1967 to become the Seaboard Coast Line. Between 1962 and 1968 long involved proceedings between the New York Central and the Pennsylvania resulted in a new consolidated 21,000-mile system, the Penn Central, which included the New York, New Haven and Hartford. And in 1970 approval was given for the mammoth 23,500-mile Burlington Northern system, a merger of the Great Northern, the Northern Pacific, and the Chicago, Burlington and Quincy.

Extensive operational savings were projected and claimed for nearly every proposed railroad merger, and often such economies were realized, when the consolidation was orderly and well planned. The merger problems facing the Penn Central in the first two years of its corporate existence were so difficult that the railroad was forced into bankruptcy in the summer of 1970. Part of the Penn Central's problem was that it was operating hundreds of miles of route-mileage that generated very little profitable traffic. This same condition was largely responsible for the bankruptcy of several other eastern railroads in the early 1970's.

Throughout these years the role of government in railroad affairs continued to be a dominant one. While federal controls had been somewhat lessened by the Transportation Act of 1958, most railroad managers still believed their industry to be overregulated. Nor did they feel that any significant improvement came with the establishment, in 1966, of the new Department of Transportation. When the newly merged Penn Central went into bankruptcy in 1970, Congress did pass legislation that provided some indirect financial support. But in the early 1970's the continuing low rate of return on the investment, the increased concern over railroad safety, and the threat of additional bankruptcy for eastern lines all tended to deepen the sense of crisis within the industry. In some quarters a renewed consideration of possible nationalization of the nation's railways was favored, while in others it was believed that the federal government might, through new legislation, achieve some solution to the problems facing American railroads.

RAILROADS, SKETCHES OF PRINCIPAL LINES

Atchison, Topeka and Santa Fe

Chartered in 1859 to connect Atchison and Topeka, Kans., the Atchison, Topeka and Santa Fe expanded rapidly. Through a combination of construction, purchases, and leases the road by 1889 had become a 7,000-mile system stretching from Chicago westward to the Pacific coast and southward to the Gulf of Mexico. It was a pioneer in the use of diesel locomotives, especially in freight service. The system of just under 13,000 miles made the Santa Fe first in mileage in the middle decades of the 20th century.

Boston and Maine

The first of the 111 companies absorbed into the Boston and Maine was the Boston and Lowell, chartered in 1830. The name "Boston and Maine" dates from 1835. In the early 1970's the railroad operated 1,500 miles of line in Massachusetts, New Hampshire, Maine, Vermont, and New York.

Burlington Northern

In 1970 the ICC approved the merger of the Chicago, Burlington and Quincy, the Great Northern, and the Northern Pacific into the Burlington Northern. The combined trackage of 23,500 miles made it the longest railroad system in the nation.

CHICAGO, BURLINGTON AND QUINCY. The original unit of the Burlington system was the Aurora Branch Railroad, a 12-mile line chartered in Illinois in 1849. It expanded through the amalgamation of some 200 railroads into a system that in the early 1970's extended from Chicago and Saint Louis to Minneapolis-Saint Paul and thence to Montana, Wyoming, Colorado, and the Gulf coast of Texas. The Burlingtonpioneered in the development of streamline passenger equipment with the introduction of the first Zephyr in 1934.

GREAT NORTHERN. The original line included in the Great Northern was the Saint Paul and Pacific, which started in 1862 to build northward and westward from Saint Paul. After James J. Hill secured control, the emphasis was on building to the west, although the line was built north to Winnipeg, Manitoba, Canada. The transcontinental line was opened in 1893. In the early 1970's the company operated 8,200 miles of road, extending from Minneapolis-Saint Paul and the head of the Great Lakes to Vancouver, British Columbia; Seattle; and Portland, Oreg.

NORTHERN PACIFIC. The first of the northern transcontinental lines, the Northern Pacific, was chartered by an act of Congress, signed by President Abraham Lincoln on July 2, 1864. Construction of the line to connect the head of the Great Lakes with Portland, Oreg., was started in 1870 and completed in 1883. In the early 1970's the company operated 6,700 miles of line, extending from Minneapolis-Saint Paul and Duluth-Superior, on Lake Superior, to Seattle and Tacoma, Wash., and Portland.

Central of Georgia

Chartered in 1833 as the Central Railroad and Banking Company of Georgia to build a railroad from Savannah to Macon, the Central of Georgia operated 2,000 miles of line in Georgia, Alabama, and Tennessee in the early 1970's. It should not be confused with the Georgia Railroad between Augusta and Atlanta, built and owned by the Georgia Railroad and Banking Company, also incorporated in 1833, and operated under lease after 1882. Nor should it be confused with the Western and Atlantic Railroad, under which name the state of Georgia built a line between Atlanta and Chattanooga, still owned by the state and operated under lease by the Louisville and Nashville.

Chesapeake and Ohio

The 22-mile Louisa Railroad, chartered in Virginia in 1837, had grown into the 5,100-mile Chesapeake and Ohio system by the early 1970's, extending from Hampton Roads, Va., and Washington, D.C., to Louisville, Ky., Chicago, the Straits of Mackinac, and the western shore of Lake Michigan (by car ferry). In 1947 the railroad absorbed into its system the Père Marquette. Between 1960 and 1963 it took over the larger Baltimore and Ohio, when that line was in financial trouble.

BALTIMORE AND OHIO. Chartered in 1827 (the oldest charter under which a railroad operated in the early 1970's), the Baltimore and Ohio was built to Wheeling on the Ohio River by late 1852. Later through construction and the acquisition of other lines it expanded northward to Philadelphia and New York City and westward to Saint Louis and Chicago, extending its mileage to 5,500.

Chicago and North Western

Chartered in 1848, the Galena and Chicago Union was the first railroad to serve Chicago. It became the Chicago and North Western in 1859. Eight years later it was the first line to reach the Missouri River at Omaha, where it connected with the Union Pacific. In 1910 the Chicago and North Western was the first railroad to sponser the "Safety First" movement. Serving the region between the Great Lakes and the Rockies, it acquired the Chicago Great Western in 1968, thus extending its system to 10,700 miles.

Chicago, Milwaukee, Saint Paul and Pacific

The earliest "ancestor" of the Chicago, Milwaukee, Saint Paul and Pacific was chartered in 1847 to build a line across Wisconsin to the Mississippi River. By 1900 the Chicago, Milwaukee and Saint Paul operated between the Great Lakes and the Missouri River. Between 1905 and 1909 the line was extended to the Pacific coast, and during the next decade some of the mountain route was electrified. In 1921 the line was extended into Indiana. With more than 150 companies consolidated in the system, the Milwaukee operated about 10,200 miles in 1973. Early in that year the line decided to shift to diesel power on its two mountain electrified divisions.

The earliest "ancestor" of the Chicago, Milwaukee, Saint Paul and Pacific Railroad was chartered in 1847 to build a line across Wisconsin to the Mississippi River.

Chicago, Rock Island and Pacific

Incorporated in 1847 to build from Rock Island to LaSalle, Ill., but built from Chicago under an amended charter, the Chicago, Rock Island and Pacific was the first railroad to bridge the Mississippi, in 1856. It operated 7,500 miles of line in the early 1970's, extending from Chicago, Saint Louis, and Memphis on the east, to Minneapolis-Saint Paul on the north, Colorado and New Mexico on the west, and the Texas and the Louisiana Gulf coast on the south.

Delaware and Hudson

The original company, the Delaware and Hudson Canal Company, chartered in 1823, built a canal and a railroad to bring out coal from Carbondale, Pa., to Rondout, N.Y., on the Hudson River. On this line, in 1829, the first steam locomotive to turn a wheel on an American railroad made its first, and only, run. The original canal was abandoned in 1898. The system, extending through upstate New York to Montreal, Quebec, Canada, was built up by acquisition and construction to over 700 miles.

Denver and Rio Grande Western

Chartered in 1870 by Denver interests, the Denver and Rio Grande Western built a narrow-gauge line that reached a large part of southern and western Colorado and extended to Salt Lake City. By 1890 main lines had been converted to standard gauge. Consolidation with the Denver and Salt Lake, with its Moffatt Tunnel through the crest of the Rocky Mountains, and construction of a new cutoff connection with the original main line shortened the distance between terminals by 175 miles. In the early 1970's the road operated 1,900 miles, of which some was narrow gauge.

Erie Lackawanna

A 2,900-mile road, the Erie Lackawanna was formed in 1960 out of two lines, the Delaware, Lackawanna and Western and the Erie.

DELAWARE, LACKAWANNA AND WESTERN. Chartered in 1851 to build an outlet for the coal of the Lackawanna Valley in Pennsylvania, the Liggitt's Gap Railroad was extended west to Buffalo, north to Lake Ontario, and east to New York via Hoboken, N.J., becoming the Delaware, Lackawanna and Western.

ERIE. Chartered as the New York and Erie, in 1832, to build from Piermont, N.Y., on the Hudson, to Dunkirk, on Lake Erie, the Erie completed a 6-foot-gauge track in 1851. The financial and corporate history of the road was checkered in the extreme, but after a reorganization in 1941, it began a career of solid success. Before merging with the Lackawanna in 1960, the Erie operated 2,300 miles, extending from New York City to Buffalo, Cleveland, and Chicago.

Florida East Coast

The railroad that extends from Jacksonville to Miami, the Florida East Coast, is the result of the vision and determination of one man, Henry M. Flagler. Retiring from the Standard Oil Company at the age of fifty-three, he went to Saint Augustine, then reached only by a narrow-gauge railroad from the Saint Johns River. Acquiring the railroad in 1885, he steadily pushed it southward, reaching Miami in 1896. The overseas extension, built across the Florida keys and stretches of open sea, reached Key West in 1912, the year before Flagler's death. In 1935 the extension suffered severe hurricane damage and was abandoned as a railroad, to become the overseas highway to Key West.

Grand Trunk Western

A subsidiary of the Canadian National Railways, the Grand Trunk Western was built from Port Huron and Detroit across Michigan, Indiana, and Illinois, reaching Chicago in 1881, and then extended to Milwaukee, via cross-lake car ferry. The tunnel under the Saint Clair River, connecting the western extension with the parent Grand Trunk, was completed in 1891. In the early 1970's the Grand Trunk Western operated nearly 1,000 miles. Other Canadian National subsidiaries in the United States include the grand Trunk to Portland, Maine, opened in 1853, and the Central Vermont, acquired in 1899.

Illinois Central Gulf

A 9,500-mile-line, the Illinois Central Gulf was the result of the 1972 merger of the Gulf, Mobile and Ohio and the Illinois Central.

GULF, MOBILE AND OHIO. The Gulf, Mobile and Ohio dates from 1940, when the corporation was formed by the consolidation of the Gulf, Mobile and Northern (itself a 1917 consolidation of earlier small railroads) with the Mobile and Ohio, which in the decade before the Civil War built a through line from Mobile, Ala., to Columbus, Ky., and afterward extended it to Saint Louis. In 1947 the firm absorbed the Alton, originally the Chicago and Alton, which dated from 1847. At the time of its merger with the Illinois Central the Gulf, Mobile and Ohio had a 2,700-mile system extending from Chicago and Kansas City, Mo., to Mobile and New Orleans.

ILLINOIS CENTRAL. Incorporated in 1851, the Illinois Central was still operating in the early 1970's under its original charter, which called for a 705-mile railroad within the state of Illinois. Along with the Mobile and Ohio, the Illinois Central received the first railroad land grant provided by the federal government. After the Civil War a southern line to the Gulf was acquired. At the time of the 1972 merger the Illinois Central operated a 6,700-mile system in fourteen states, extending from Chicago west to the Missouri River and south to New Orleans and Birmingham, Ala.

Lehigh Valley

Originally chartered as the Delaware, Lehigh, Schuylkill and Susquehanna for the purpose of hauling coal from the vicinity of Mauch Chunk, Pa., the Lehigh Valley adopted its present name in 1853. The line expanded to 925 miles, reaching the Niagara frontier on the west and New York on the east. In the process it acquired numerous other lines, some dating back to 1836.

Louisville and Nashville

Chartered in 1850, the Louisville and Nashville completed its line between the cities whose names it bears in 1859. Continuing to operate under its original charter, the railroad constructed and acquired some seventy-five other lines and by the early 1970's had created a 6,300-mile system extending from Chicago, Cincinatti, and Saint Louis to Memphis, Atlanta, and New Orleans. The oldest existing part of the railroad was the line between Lexington and Frankfort, Ky., chartered in 1830, opened for traffic in 1834, and acquired by the Louisville and Nashville in 1881.

Missouri, Kansas and Texas

The Union Pacific, Southern Branch, a road chartered in 1865, was the first of several short roads to make up the Missouri, Kansas and Texas, organized in 1870. A line from Junction City, Kans., was built southward to the southern border of Kansas by 1870, and to the Texas line by 1872. Subsequent expansion by the end of the century created a system of 2,600 miles extending from Saint Louis and Kansas City, Mo., to San Antonio and Houston.

Missouri Pacific

The Pacific Railroad of Missouri, the earliest part of the Missouri Pacific, was chartered on July 4, 1851, to build a line of 5.5-foot gauge from Saint Louis to the West Coast. The first locomotive west of the Mississippi ran on the first 5 miles of this railroad in December 1852. By construction and consolidation, the road extended from Saint Louis, Memphis, and New Orleans to Omaha; Pueblo, Colo.; Laredo, Tex.; and the Gulf coast, operating nearly 9,000 miles.

Norfolk and Western

The City Point Railway, a 9-mile line between Petersburg, Va., and the James River, chartered in 1836, is the oldest part of the Norfolk and Western. It grew into the Southside Railroad, which, with connections, stretched across southern Virginia from tidewater to Tennessee and with extensions westward into the coal fields, and became the basis of the Norfolk and Western. The railroad grew to 2,700 miles with the addition of the Virginian in 1959. In 1964 two other roads, the Nickel Plate and the Wabash, were added, creating a system of 7,600 miles.

NEW YORK, CHICAGO AND SAINT LOUIS. The Nickel Plate Road, as the New York, Chicago and Saint Louis is usually called, was opened for operation between Buffalo and Chicago in 1882; the last spike, driven at Bellevue, Ohio, was nickel plated. Control soon passed to the New York Central, which acquired the road rather than have it fall into unfriendly hands. In 1916 control was sold to Mantis James Van Sweringen and Oris Paxton Van Sweringen, two brothers interested in Cleveland real estate. They later added the Lake Erie and Western and the Toledo, Peoria and Western to the Nickel Plate; subsequently the Wheeling and Lake Erie was added. In the early 1970's the system operated 2,200 miles, extending from Buffalo and Wheeling to Chicago and Peoria, Ill., and Saint Louis.

WABASH. The Northern Cross, 12 miles long, built in 1838, was the first railroad in Illinois and the earliest part of the Wabash. It became a system of nearly 3,000 miles, one of the few operating in both the East and the West, stretching from Buffalo and Toledo to Saint Louis, Kansas City, Mo., Omaha and Des Moines. A separately operated subsidiary, the Ann Arbor Railroad, with car ferries across Lake Michigan, extended the system.

Penn Central

After long years of negotiation the Pennsylvania New York Central Transportation Company was created in 1968 out of the New York Central, the Pennsylvania and the New York, New Haven and Hartford. The problems facing the 21,000-mile Penn Central in the first two years of its corporate existence were so great that the line was forced into bankruptcy in the summer of 1970. Congress passed legislation that provided some indirect financial aid, but after nearly three years of receivership the Penn Central was still operating hundreds of miles of excess track that produced very little profitable traffic.

NEW YORK CENTRAL. The Mohawk and Hudson, the oldest of the many companies that made up the New York Central, was incorporated in 1826 and ran its first train in 1831. The Hudson River Railroad was added to the New York Central (organized in 1853) in 1869, to be followed in the course of time by the Lake Shore and Michigan Southern, the Michigan Central, the Big Four, the Boston and Albany, the West Shore, the Toledo and Ohio Central, and other railroads, including the separately operated Pittsburgh and Lake Erie. The system grew to more than 10,000 miles, extending from Montreal, Boston, and New York to the Straits of Mackinac, Chicago, and Saint Louis.

The Mohawk and Hudson, the oldest of the many companies that made up the New York Central, was incorporated in 1826 and ran its first train in 1831.

NEW YORK, NEW HAVEN AND HARTFORD. Earliest of the approximately 125 companies that made up the New York, New Haven and Hartford was the Boston and Providence, chartered in 1831 and in operation by 1834. The Hartford and New Haven, incorporated in 1833, connected New Haven with Springfield, Mass., by 1844, the year in which a railroad was chartered to connect New Haven with New York. This line, providing the first all-rail service between Boston and New York via Springfield, was opened in 1848. The Shore Line, operating between New Haven and Providence, was leased in 1870. The New York, New Haven and Hartford thus came to operate 1,800 miles, serving southern New England and New York. Between 1907 and 1914 the railroad installed the first railroad electrification using high-voltage alternating-current transmission between New York and New Haven.

PENNSYLVANIA. Long known as the "standard" railroad, because of the high quality of its property and operation, the Pennsylvania for decades took pride in its unbroken record of dividend payments. It was chartered in 1846 to build a line between Harrisburg and Pittsburgh, paralleling the state's canal and inclined-plane system. By purchase, lease, and construction the line was expanded to a system of 10,000 miles, extending eastward to Philadelphia, New York, Washington, D.C., and Norfolk, Va., and westward to Chicago and Saint Louis. The oldest segment of the system was the pioneer Camden and Amboy, chartered by New Jersey in 1830 and completed in 1834. The first "T" rail was rolled in a design whittled out by Robert Stevens, son of Col. John Stevens, while on a voyage to England to purchase rail for Camden and Amboy. The design became the basis of rail used throughout the world.

Pullman Company

George M. Pullman built his first sleeping cars (rebuilt coaches of the Chicago and Alton) in 1858. His first completely Pullman-built car was finished in 1864. By the end of the century the name "Pullman" was substantially synonymous with the sleeping-car business, although the company also manufactured passenger and freight cars. As a result of an antitrust suit, the enterprise was required to divest itself of either the car-manufacturing or the car-operating business. In 1947 the latter was taken over by fifty-seven railroads.

Reading

The Reading Company, which operated 1,200 miles of line in Pennsylvania, New York, and Delaware in the early 1970's, was a successor company to the Philadelphia and Reading Railroad, incorporated in 1833, although parts of the line had been built by still earlier companies. It was on one of these predecessor lines, the Philadelphia, Germantown and Norristown, the *Old Ironsides*, the first locomotive built by Matthias Baldwin, ran in 1832. In the 1970's the Readin owned a majority of the stock of the Jersey Central Lines.

Saint Louis-San Francisco

The Saint Louis-San Francisco, started in 1866, was planned to run from Springfield, Ill., to the Pacific coast; but its point of origin was changed to Saint Louis, and it never reached the California city whose name it bears. It developed as a system of some 4,800 miles, stretching from Saint Louis and Kansas City, Mo., to Oklahoma and northern Texas, on the southwest, and to Alabama and Florida, on the southeast. The "Frisco" is one of the few systems to operate in both the West and the Southeast.

Saint Louis-Southwestern

The "Cotton Belt," as the Saint Louis-Southwestern is commonly called, started as a Tyler Tap Railroad, chartered in 1871, to build a connection from Tyler, Tex., to a main-line railroad. The enterprise expanded to a system of 1,500 miles, connecting Saint Louis and Memphis with Fort Worth, Dallas, and Waco, Tex. The present name of the company dates from 1891.

Seaboard Coast Line

In 1967 two major southern railroads, the Atlantic Coast Line and the Seaboard Air Line, merged to form the Seaboard Coast Line.

ATLANTIC COAST LINE. The Richmond and Petersburg was chartered in 1836 to connect those two Virginia cities. The Atlantic Coast Line was created out of the Richmond and Petersburg and dozens of other southern railways. Service south of Virginia was possible with the acquisition of lines serving the Carolinas, Georgia, Alabama, and Florida. It became the Atlantic

Coast Line in 1900, when the parent company absorbed its southern connections. In the early 1970's the railroad operated 5,600 miles of line and had substantial interests in the Louisville and Nashville, the Clinchfield, and other roads.

SEABOARD AIR LINE. The name "Seaboard Air Line" was first applied in 1889 to a loose operating association of a half a dozen separate connecting railroads in Virginia and the Carolinas. The oldest line was the Portsmouth and Roanoke, chartered in 1832, which was built from Portsmouth, Va., to Weldon, N.C. In 1900 the several railroads were consolidated and, by acquisition and construction, they grew into a system of 4,000 miles extending from Norfolk and Richmond through the Carolinas and Georgia to Birmingham and Montgomery, Ala., and to both coasts of Florida.

Soo Line (Minneapolis, Saint Paul and Sault Sainte Marie)

Chartered in 1873 by businessmen of Minneapolis to build a line eastward to the Canadian border at Sault Sainte Marie, the Soo Line reacherd the sault in 1887. By the same time it had extended westward into the Dakotas, finally building to a western connection with the Canadian Pacific at Portal, N.Dak. After 1909 the Soo Line operated the Wisconsin Central, effecting an entrance into Chicago. The 4,600-mile system became a separately operated subsidary of the Canadian Pacific in the 1940's.

Southern Pacific

The beginnings of the Southern Pacific were in Louisiana, Texas, and California. In Louisiana the New Orleans, Opelousas and Great Western Railroad was chartered in 1850 to build from New Orleans westward. In the same year, in Texas, the Buffalo Bayou, Brazos and Colorado was chartered; it was in operation by 1852. The Sacramento Valley Railroad also was started in 1852 in California. The Central Pacific, incorporated in California in 1861, undertook the task of building a railroad eastward over the Sierra Nevada and, in 1862, was selected to build the western leg of the first transcontinental route. The Southern Pacific, incorporated in California in 1865, built south and east, to become part of the second transcontinental route. The interests of the Central Pacific and the Southern Pacific were closely linked as early as 1870. In 1934 the twelve companies making up the Southern Pacific interests in Texas and Louisiana were consolidated into the Texas and New Orleans Railroad. In the early 1970's the Southern Pacific system operated more than 13,000 miles of line.

Southern Railway

The Southern Railway was formed in 1894, when the purchasers of the Richmond and Danville were authorized to acquire the East Tennessee, Virginia and Georgia, and other lines, among them the pioneer South Carolina Railroad. The system came to include the separately operated Cincinnati, New Orleans and Texas Pacific; Alabama Great Southern; New Orleans and Northeastern; Georgia, Southern and Florida; and Carolina and Northwestern railroads. A total mileage of 8,000 in the early 1970's extended from Washington, D.C., Cincinnati, and Saint Louis to New Orleans, Mobile, and Florida.

Texas and Pacific

Chartered by act of Congress in 1871, the Texas and Pacific took over the barely started projects of the Southern Pacific (a company in no way related to the later company of that name), formed in 1856; the Memphis, El Paso and Pacific, also formed in 1856; and the Southern Transcontinental, organized in 1870. From northeast Texas, at Marshall and Texarkana, lines were built westward toward El Paso and eastward to New Orleans. In 1882, at Sierra Blanca, Tex., 90 miles east of El Paso, the Texas and Pacific met the crews of the Galveston, Harrisburg and San Antonio, building the Southern Pacific line eastward. Joint trackage was arranged, effecting an entrance into El Paso for the Texas and Pacific. The new line to New Orleans was completed in 1882, with full service starting early in 1883. In the early 1970's the company operated 2,100 miles of line.

Union Pacific

The Union Pacific was incorporated by act of Congress in 1862, to build westward from the Missouri River to meet the Central Pacific of California, building eastward. To the approximately 1,000 miles of the original main line, the company added the Kansas Pacific; Denver Pacific; Oregon Short Line; Oregon-Washington Railway and Navigation Company; San Pedro, Los Angeles and Salt Lake; and other railroads. The property was extensively improved after it came under the con-

> *The Union Pacific was incorporated by act of Congress in 1862 to build westward from the Missouri River to meet the Central Pacific of California, building eastward.*

trol of Edward H. Harriman in 1897. In the early 1970's it operated nearly 9,500 miles of line, extending from Council Bluffs, Iowa, Omaha, Nebr., Saint Joseph, Mo., to Portland, Oreg., Seattle and Spokane, Wash., and Los Angeles.

Western Pacific

The latest of the transcontinental connections in the United States to be formed was the Western Pacific, organized in 1903 and opened for service between Salt Lake City and Oakland-San Francisco, Calif., in 1909. A branch line connecting with the Great Northern, opened in 1931, added a north-south route to the original east-west line of the railroad. Total mileage, including the subsidiary Sacramento Northern, was approximately 1,500 in the early 1970's.

BIBLIOGRAPHY

Association of American Railroads, *Yearbook of Railroad Facts.*
Stewart H. Holbrook, *The Story of American Railroads.*
Robert G. Lewis, *Handbook of American Railroads.*
John F. Stover, *The Life and Decline of the American Railroad.*

— ROBERT S. HENRY AND JOHN F. STOVER

RAILROAD STRIKE OF 1877

The depression of the 1870's reached its lowest point in 1877, a year that was marked by repeated wage reductions, particularly in the railroad industry. Militant feeling among trainmen expressed itself in spontaneous outbreaks. On July 17, 1877, after a new 10 percent wage reduction went into effect, trainmen halted freight cars of the Baltimore and Ohio Railroad at Martinsburg, W.Va. When the local militia proved sympathetic, President Rutherford B. Hayes, upon request of the governor, sent Gen. Winfield S. Hancock and 200 federal soldiers to the scene, and the strike ended there, but not before it had begun spreading over the nation. At Baltimore, a mob surrounded the state armory, fought with the soldiers, and attempted unsuccessfully to burn the building. At Pittsburgh, where popular feeling was strongly against the railroads, militia, ordered from Philadelphia, was besieged in a roundhouse and narrowly escaped the flames of a fire begun at the shops. Sympathetic strikes in other cities brought further news of rioting. A wave of reaction followed as courts and legislators revived the obsolete doctrines of conspiracy. The precedent of federal troops in industrial disputes became an active one, and the states strengthened their policing activities. Radical labor parties found expression in a new rift between classes.

BIBLIOGRAPHY

Samuel Yellen, *American Labor Struggles.*

— HARVEY WISH

RAILROAD STRIKES OF 1886

During 1884–85, the Knights of Labor succeeded in winning four of the five major railroad strikes. Although Jay Gould, whose railway system had fought the Knights, expressly agreed to show no antiunion discrimination, he secretly prepared to break the power of the order. The Knights, encouraged by their victories, pressed for full observance of the agreement, and when the Texas and Pacific Railroad office at Marshall, Tex., discharged its union foreman, a general strike was ordered for Mar. 1, 1886, on the issue of union recognition and a daily wage of $1.50 for the unskilled. Under the leadership of Martin Irons, 900 men struck, tying up 5,000 miles of railway in the central states, and the struggle soon took on the aspect of a crusade against capital. Gould would neither arbitrate unless the workers first returned to work nor would he reinstate discharged strikers. After two months, marked by occasional violence and the employment of federal troops, the strike collapsed on May 3. This defeat discredited industrial unionism and its proponent, the Knights of Labor, assuring the subsequent victory of the craft unions as exemplified by the American Federation of Labor.

BIBLIOGRAPHY

J. R. Commons and others, *History of Labor in the United States,* vol. II.

— HARVEY WISH

RALEIGH'S LOST COLONY

The group usually designated as the Lost Colony cleared from Plymouth, England, in three small ships on May 8, 1587, and reached Roanoke Island in the Albemarle region of the present state of North Carolina on July 22. The region then was known as Virginia. The colony was composed of 91 men, 17 women, and 9 boys, a total of 117 persons. Sir Walter Raleigh named John White, who led the expedition, governor of the colony, which was incorporated as "the Governour and Assistants of the Citie of Ralegh in Virginia." White, an artist, had been a member of the Ralph Lane colony of 1585–86, as had several other members of his colony.

The colonists had not intended to stop permanently on Roanoke Island; they had been instructed by Raleigh to pick up fifteen men left there by Sir Richard Grenville and to proceed on to the Chesapeake region, where a more suitable English base for action against the Spanish might be established. They were frustrated in this plan by the pilot of the expedition, who set them ashore, where they occupied the houses and fort abandoned the previous year by Lane's unsuccessful colony.

From the first the Roanoke colonists, inheriting the enmity Lane had provoked, encountered the hostility of Indians on the mainland opposite the island, although they enjoyed the friendship of Manteo and his kinsmen from the island of Croatoan (probably present-day Hatteras) to the south. On Aug. 18 Ellinor (or Elyoner) White Dare, daughter of Gov. John White and wife of Ananias Dare, gave birth to a daughter, Virginia, the first English child born in America. Soon thereafter controversy arose about who should return to England for supplies. It was decided that White should go, and on Aug. 27 he reluctantly sailed. When White reached England the danger of the threatened Spanish armada overshadowed all else. White was not able to come back to Roanoke Island until August 1590. He discovered no trace of the colony except the letters "C R O" carved on a tree and the word "CROATOAN" cut on the doorpost of the palisade. The colonists had agreed to leave a sign if they moved from Fort Raleigh.

The fate of Raleigh's colony remains a mystery. It has usually been assumed that the colonists went to the friendly Croatoans, but it has also been suggested that they were victims of the Spanish. Settlers at Jamestown after 1607 were told by Indians that some of the colonists from Roanoke Island, apparently trying to make their way to Chesapeake Bay, were caught between two warring bodies of Indians not far from their destination and slaughtered. Chief Powhatan had been present and had some utensils that he said had been in the possession of the colonists. Rumors circulated in Virginia that a few had escaped and were held by Indians to engage in metalwork, but attempts to find them failed.

Though it was assumed that the colonists went to the friendly Croatoans, or were victims of the Spanish, the fate of Raleigh's colony remains a mystery.

In England in 1594, seven years after the sailing of the colonists, relatives of a youth, John Dare, natural son of Ananias Dare of the Parish of Saint Bride's, Fleet Street, London, petitioned the court that he be awarded his father's property. Under the common law of England an unaccounted-for absence of seven years was necessary for a ruling of presumed death. In 1597 the petition was granted and the Lost Colony legally recognized as lost.

BIBLIOGRAPHY

William S. Powell, "Roanoke Colonists and Explorers: An Attempt at Identification," *North Carolina Historical Review*, vol. 34.

David B. Quinn, *The Roanoke Voyages.*

— WILLIAM S. POWELL

RALEIGH'S PATENT AND FIRST COLONY

On Mar. 25, 1584, Queen Elizabeth renewed Sir Humphrey Gilbert's patent of 1578 in the name of Gilbert's half-brother, Walter Raleigh, giving him and his heirs and assigns the right to explore, colonize, and govern "such remote, heathen, and barbarous lands not actually possessed of any Christian prince, nor inhabited by Christian people." The settlers planted within this grant were to have "all the privileges of free Denizens, and persons native of England," and all laws passed must be in harmony with the laws of England.

On Apr. 27, 1584, Raleigh sent out an expedition led by Philip Amadas and Arthur Barlowe, who were instructed to explore the country and decide on the site for a future colony. Coming via the West Indies, they reached the North Carolina coast early in July. They entered Albemarle Sound, took possession of the country in the name of the queen, and a few days later landed at Roanoke Island where they feasted as guests of the Indians at a small village. After two months spent in exploring and trading with the Indians, they returned to England with reports of the beautiful country, the friendly Indians, the abundance of game and fish, and the soil that was "the most plentiful, sweete, fruitfull and wholsome of all the worlde." Queen Elizabeth was pleased; she named the new land "Virginia" and knighted Raleigh.

In April 1585 Raleigh sent out a colony, consisting of 108 men, with Ralph Lane as governor and Sir Richard Grenville in command of the fleet. This colony landed at Roanoke Island on July 27. About a month later, Grenville returned to England, leaving behind the first English colony in America. Lane built a fort and "sundry necessary and decent dwelling houses," and from this "new Fort in Virginia," Sept. 3, 1585, he wrote Richard Hakluyt in London the "first letter in the English language written from the New World." The Lane colony spent most of its time in a vain quest for gold. Soon supplies began to run low and had to be obtained from the Indians, who were becoming more and more unfriendly. War finally broke out in the spring of 1586. Lane won an easy victory, but unrest and distress continued to increase. When Sir Francis Drake's fleet appeared along the coast and offered to take the colony back to England, Lane consented and they departed after having been on Roanoke Island for about ten months.

About two weeks later, Grenville arrived with supplies, finding the colonists gone. He soon returned to England, but being "unwilling to loose possession of the countrey which Englishmen had so long held," he left fifteen men on Roanoke Island, "furnished plentifully with all manner of provisions for two years." When the next Raleigh colony, headed by John White, arrived at Roanoke in July 1587, they found only the bones of one of the men Grenville had left and the fort and houses in ruins.

[See also Raleigh's Lost Colony.]

BIBLIOGRAPHY

C. W. Sams, *The First Conquest of Virginia.*

— HUGH T. LEFLER

REAGANOMICS

Reaganomics is the broad term used to describe President Ronald Reagan's economic policy during the 1980s. It was outlined in a document presented to Congress shortly after the 1980 election, entitled *America's New Beginning: A Program for Economic Recovery.* The program called for budget reforms to cut the rate of growth in federal spending; a series of steps to cut personal income taxes and business taxes; a far-reaching program of regulatory relief; and a commitment to a monetary policy for restoring a stable currency and healthy financial markets. Based largely on the principles of supply-side economics, the program was designed to lift the nation's economy out of its deepest recession since the Great Depression by reducing the federal government's economic role. By shifting federal revenues to a less restricted private sector through tax reduction, President Reagan expected to reinvigorate the economy. At the same time he hoped to reduce, or even eliminate, the federal deficit, a task made more difficult by another political goal—increasing defense spending.

With assistance from the Republican minority and a cadre of conservative Democrats, many of Reagan's congressional initiatives were passed. Although the nation remained mired in recession for the first two years of his administration, a robust recovery soon turned into the longest peacetime economic expansion in U.S. history, ending only in 1990. More than 18 million jobs were created during the economic expansion from 1983 to 1990, unemployment fell, and inflation dropped from 12.5 percent in 1980 to 4.4 percent in 1988, but the growth came at a price. Unable to cut federal spending, Reagan oversaw a tripling of the federal debt to $2.7 trillion and a quadrupling of the annual trade deficit to $137 billion. The legacy of Reaganomics is a matter of intense debate. In 1980 George Bush, an unsuccessful presidential candidate in the Republican primaries, dubbed Reagan's policies "voodoo economics." Bush and others were skeptical about whether Reagan could cut taxes, increase defense spending, and balance the budget. Critics charge that government spending cuts came at the expense of the poor and that tax cuts almost exclusively benefited the wealthy, increasing the gap between rich and poor. Reagan's economic policies, they add, unleashed a "decade of greed" and rampant speculation that led to the 1987 stock market crash and the 1990 recession. Further, they say, the federal deficit will serve as a drag on the nation's economy for generations. Reagan's supporters say that virtually all sectors of the economy benefited from his economic policies, that he reduced the rate of federal spending growth, and that the federal debt as a percentage of the nation's gross national product decreased. They add that the Democratic majority in Congress thwarted Reagan's efforts to make deeper cuts in federal spending and eventually undermined his tax policies with tax reforms in 1986 and 1990.

In 1980 George Bush, as a candidate in the Republican primaries, dismissed Reagan's fiscal plans as "voodoo economics."

[See also Wall Street.]

BIBLIOGRAPHY

Lou Cannon, *President Reagan: The Role of a Lifetime* (1991).
"The Real Reagan Record," *National Review* (Aug. 31, 1992).

— ERIK BRUUN

RECIPROCAL TRADE AGREEMENTS

In the election of 1932 the Democrats came to power on a program involving "a competitive tariff" for revenue and "reciprocal trade agreements with other nations." Cordell Hull, President Franklin D. Roosevelt's secretary of state, was the driving force behind congressional action in getting the Trade Agreements Act made law on June 12, 1934. The new act, in form an amendment to the 1930 Tariff Act, delegated to the president the power to make foreign-trade agreements with other nations on the basis of a mutual reduction of duties, without any specific congressional approval of such reductions. The act limited reduction to 50 percent of the rates of duty existing then and stipulated that commodities could not be transferred between the dutiable and free lists. The power to negotiate was to run for three years, but this power was renewed for either two or three years periodically until replaced by the Trade Expansion Act of 1962.

Although Congress gave the State Department the primary responsibility for negotiating with other nations, it instructed the Tariff Commission and other government agencies to participate in developing a list of concessions that could be made to foreign countries or demanded from them in return. Each trade agreement was to incorporate the principle of "unconditional most-favored-nation treatment." This requirement was necessary to avoid a great multiplicity of rates.

After 1945 Congress increased the power of the president by authorizing him to reduce tariffs by 50 percent of the rate in effect on Jan. 1, 1945, instead of 1934, as the original act provided. Thus, duties that had been reduced by 50 percent prior to 1945 could be reduced by another 50 percent, or 75 percent below the rates that were in effect in 1934. But in 1955 further duty reductions were limited to 15 percent, at the rate of 5 percent a year over a three-year period, and in 1958 to 20 percent, effective over a four-year period, with a maximum of 10 percent in any one year.

In negotiating agreements under the Trade Agreements Act, the United States usually proceeded by making direct concessions only to so-called chief suppliers—namely, countries that were, or probably would become, the main source, or a major source, of supply of the commodity under discussion. This approach seemed favorable to the United States, since no concessions were extended to minor supplying countries that would benefit the chief supplying countries (through unconditional most-favored-nation treatment) without the latter countries' first having granted a concession. The United States used its bargaining power by granting concessions in return for openings to foreign markets for American exports.

Between 1934 and 1947 the United States made separate trade agreements with twenty-nine foreign countries. The Tariff Commission found that when it used dutiable imports in 1939 as its basis for comparison, U.S. tariffs were reduced from an average of 48 percent to an average of 25 percent during the thirteen-year period, the imports on which the duties were reduced having been valued at over $700 million in 1939.

During World War II the State Department and other government agencies worked on plans for the reconstruction of world trade and payments. They discovered important defects in the trade agreements program, and they concluded that they could make better headway through simultaneous multilateral negotiations. American authorities in 1945 made some far-reaching proposals for the expansion of world trade and employment. Twenty-three separate countries then conducted tariff negotiations bilaterally on a product-by-product basis, with each country negotiating its concessions on each import commodity with the principal supplier of that commodity. The various bilateral understandings were combined to form the General Agreement on Tariffs and Trade (GATT), referred to as the Geneva Agreement, which was signed in Geneva on Oct. 30, 1947. This agreement did not have to be submitted to the U.S. Senate for approval because the president was already specifically empowered to reduce tariffs under the authority conferred by the Trade Agreements Extension Act of 1945.

From the original membership of twenty-three countries, GATT had expanded by the mid-1970's to include more than seventy countries, a membership responsible for about four-fifths of all the world trade. During the numerous tariff negotiations carried on under the auspices of GATT, concessions covering over 60,000 items had been agreed on. These constituted more than two-thirds of the total import trade of the participating countries and more than one-half the total number of commodities involved in world trade.

With the expiration on July 30, 1962, of the eleventh renewal of the Reciprocal Trade Agreements Act, the United States was faced with a major decision on its future foreign trade policy: to choose between continuing the program as it had evolved over the previous twenty-eight years or to replace it with a new and expanded program. The second alternative was chosen by President John F. Kennedy when, on Jan. 25, 1962, he asked Congress for unprecedented authority to negotiate with the European Common Market for reciprocal trade agreements. The European Common Market had been established in 1957 to eliminate all trade barriers in six key countries of Western Europe: France, West Germany, Italy, Belgium, the Netherlands, and Luxembourg. Their economic strength, the increasing pressure on American balance of payments, and the threat of a Communist aid and trade offensive led Congress to pass the Trade Expansion Act of 1962. This act granted the president far greater authority to lower or eliminate American import duties than had ever been granted before, and it replaced the negative policy of preventing dislocation by the positive one of promoting and facilitating adjustment to the domestic dislocation caused by foreign competition. The president was authorized, through trade agreements with foreign countries, to reduce any duty by 50 percent of the rate in effect on July 1, 1962. Whereas the United States had negotiated in the past on an item-by-item, rate-by-rate basis, in the future the president could decide to cut tariffs on an industry, or across-the-board, basis for all products, in exchange for similar reductions by the other countries. In order to deal with the tariff problems created by the European Common Market, the president was empowered to reduce tariffs on industrial products by more than 50 percent, or to eliminate them completely when the United States and the Common Market together accounted for 80 percent or more of the world export value. The president could also reduce the duty by more than 50 percent or eliminate it on an agricultural commodity, if he decided such action would help to maintain or expand American agricultural exports.

After Kennedy's death, President Lyndon B. Johnson pushed through a new round of tariff bargaining that culminated in a multilateral trade negotiation known as the Kennedy Round. The agreement reached on June 30, 1967, reduced tariff duties an average of about 35 percent on some 60,000 items representing an estimated $40 billion in world trade, based on 1964 figures, the base year for the negotiations. As a result of the tariff-reduction installments of the Kennedy Round, by 1973 the average height of tariffs in the major industrial countries, it is estimated, had come down to about 8 or 9 percent.

Although both Johnson and President Richard M. Nixon exerted pressure on Congress to carry some of the trade expansion movements of the Kennedy Round further, Congress resisted all proposals. The crisis in foreign trade that developed in 1971–72 was the result of stagnation as well as of an unprecedented deficit in the U.S. balance of payments. Some pressure groups from both industry and labor tried to revive the protectionism that had flourished before 1934, but they had had small success except on petroleum imports by the mid-1970's.

BIBLIOGRAPHY

Grace Beckett, *The Reciprocal Trade Agreements Program.*

Sidney Ratner, *The Tariff in American History.*

— SIDNEY RATNER

RECONSTRUCTION

The question of the restoration of the seceded states to the Union became an issue long before the surrender at Appomattox, Va., on Apr. 6, 1865. According to the Crittenden-Johnson Resolutions of July 1861, the object of the war was to restore the Union with "all the dignity, equality, and rights of the several States unimpaired." But as the conflict progressed, it became evident that this objective was impossible to achieve. Congress refused to reaffirm its policy; President Abraham Lincoln appointed military governors for partially reconquered states; and radicals and moderates debated the exact status of the insurgent communities.

The president viewed the process of wartime reconstruction as a weapon to detach southerners from their allegiance to the Confederacy and thus shorten the war. Consequently, on Dec. 8, 1863, he issued a proclamation of amnesty that promised full pardon to all but a select group of disloyal citizens. Wherever 10 percent of the voters had taken the oath of allegiance, they were authorized to inaugurate new governments. All Lincoln required was their submission to the Union and their acceptance of the Emancipation Proclamation.

The president's plan encountered resistance in Congress. Perturbed by his failure to leave Reconstruction to the lawmakers and anxious to protect Republican interests in the South, Congress, on July 2, 1864, passed the Wade-Davis bill, a more stringent measure than the "10 percent plan." Requiring an oath of allegiance from 50, rather than 10, percent of the electorate before new governments could be set up, the bill prescribed further conditions for prospective voters. Only those able to take an "ironclad oath" of past loyalty were to be enfranchised, and slavery was to be abolished. When Lincoln pocket-vetoed the measure, its authors bitterly attacked him in the Wade-Davis Manifesto. After the president's reelection, efforts to revive the Wade-Davis bill in modified form failed. Congress refused to recognize the "free-state" governments established in accordance with Lincoln's plan in Louisiana and Arkansas, and so Lincoln's assassination on Apr. 14, 1865, left the future of Reconstruction in doubt.

What Lincoln would have done if he had lived is difficult to establish. It is known that as soon as Gen. Ulysses S. Grant had forced Gen. Robert E. Lee to surrender, the president withdrew his invitation to members of the Confederate legislature of Virginia to reassemble: his wartime plans are evidently not necessarily a guide to his peacetime intentions. It is also clear that he was not averse to the enfranchisement of qualified blacks. He wrote to this effect to the governor of Louisiana and touched on the subject in his last public address, on Apr. 11, 1865. But his larger policy had not yet fully matured.

With the end of war the problem of Reconstruction became more acute. If the seceded states were to be restored without any conditions, local whites would soon reestablish Democratic rule. They would seek to reverse the verdict of the sword and, by combining with their northern associates, challenge Republican supremacy. Moreover, before long, because of the end of slavery and the lapse of the Three-fifths Compromise, the South would obtain a larger influence in the councils of the nation than before the war.

The easiest way of solving this problem would have been to extend the suffrage to the freedmen. But in spite of an increasing radical commitment to votes for blacks, the majority of the party hesitated. Popular prejudice, not all of it in the South, was too strong, and many doubted the feasibility of enfranchising newly liberated slaves. Nevertheless, the integration of the blacks into American life became one of the principal issues of Reconstruction.

Lincoln's successor, Andrew Johnson, was wholly out of sympathy with black suffrage. A southerner and former slaveholder, Johnson held deep prejudices against blacks, who, he believed, should occupy an inferior place in society. He was willing to concede the vote to the very few educated or propertied blacks, if only to stop radical agitation, but he did not even insist on this minimum. Based on his Jacksonian convictions of an indestructible Union of indestructible states, his Reconstruction policies in time of peace resembled those of his predecessor in time of war. But they were no longer appropriate.

Johnson's plan, published on May 29, 1865, called for the speedy restoration of southern governments based on the (white) electorate of 1860. High Confederate officials and all those owning property valued at more than $20,000 were excluded from his offer of amnesty, but they were eligible for individual pardons. Appointing provisional governors who were to call constitutional conventions, Johnson expected the restored states to ratify the Thirteenth Amendment abolishing slavery, nullify the secession ordinances, and repudiate the Confederate debt.

How Lincoln would have handled the postwar Reconstruction is difficult to establish, but it is certain that his successor, Andrew Johnson, was averse to black suffrage.

In operation the president's plan revealed that little had changed in the South. Not one of the states enfranchised even literate blacks. Some balked at nullifying the secession ordinances; others hesitated or failed to repudiate the Confederate debt; and Mississippi refused to ratify the Thirteenth Amendment. Former insurgent leaders, including Alexander H. Stephens, the vice-president of the Confederacy, were elected to Congress. Several states even passed black codes that in effect remanded the blacks to a condition not far removed from slavery.

The reaction of northerners to these developments was not favorable. When Congress met in December, it refused to admit any of the representatives from the seceded states. All matters pertaining to the restoration of the South were to be referred to the newly created Joint Committee of Fifteen on Reconstruction.

Johnson had to make a choice. Either he could cooperate with the moderate center of the party or, by opposing it, break with the overwhelming majority of Republicans and rely on the small minority of conservatives and the Democrats. When Lyman Trumbull, the moderate chairman of the Senate Judiciary Committee, framed the Freedmen's Bureau and civil rights bills largely for the protection of the blacks, the president, unwilling to compromise on the subject of race and federal relations, refused to sign them. As a result, the moderates cooperated increasingly with the radicals, and the civil rights bill veto was overridden on Apr. 9, 1866.

Congress then developed a Reconstruction plan of its own: the Fourteenth Amendment. Moderate in tone, it neither conferred suffrage on the blacks nor exacted heavy penalties from the whites. Clearly defining American citizenship, it made blacks part of the body politic, sought to protect them from state interference, and provided for reduced representation for states disfranchising prospective voters. If Johnson had been willing to accept it, the struggle over Reconstruction might have been at an end. But the president was wholly opposed to the measure. Believing the amendment subversive of the Constitution and of white supremacy, he used his influence to procure its defeat in the southern states, an effort that succeeded everywhere except in Tennessee, which was admitted on July 24, 1866. At the same time, he sought to build up a new party. The rival plans of Reconstruction thus became an issue in the midterm elections of 1866, during which four national conventions met, and Johnson on his "swing around the circle" actively campaigned for his program. His claims of having established peace in the South were weakened by serious riots in Memphis and New Orleans.

The elections resulted in a triumph for the Republican majority. Since the president was still unwilling to cooperate, Congress proceeded to shackle him by restricting his powers of removal (Tenure of Office Act) and of military control ("Command of the Army" Act). In addition, it passed a series of measures known as the Reconstruction Acts, which inaugurated the congressional or "radical" phase of Reconstruction.

The first two Reconstruction Acts divided the South (except for Tennessee) into five military districts, enfranchised blacks, and required southern states to draw up constitutions safeguarding black suffrage. The new legislatures were expected to ratify the Fourteenth Amendment, and certain Confederate officeholders were for a time barred from voting and from officeholding.

The president refused to concede defeat. After his vetoes of the Reconstruction Acts were not sustained, he sought to lessen their effect as much as possible. His lenient interpretation of the law led to the more stringent third Reconstruction Act (July 19, 1867), which only spurred him to further resistance. On Aug. 12 he suspended Edwin M. Stanton, his radical secretary of war. After appointing Grant secretary ad interim, he also removed several radical major generals in the South. Democratic successes in the fall elections greatly encouraged him.

Johnson's intransigence resulted in a complete break with Congress. Because the radicals lacked a majority, their first attempt to impeach him failed, on Dec. 7, 1867. But when the Senate reinstated Stanton and the president dismissed him a second time, the House acted. Passing a resolution of impeachment on Feb. 24, 1868, it put Johnson on trial before the Senate. Because of moderate defections and the weakness of the case, he was acquitted by one vote, on May 16 and 26. His narrow escape once more encouraged southern conservatives, so that it was difficult for Grant, elected president in November 1868, to carry congressional Reconstruction to a successful conclusion.

During 1867 and 1868 radical Reconstruction had been gradually initiated. Despite conservative opposition—Congress had to pass a fourth Reconstruction Act easing requirements before the constitution of Alabama was accepted; the electorate ratified the new charters in all but three states—Mississippi, Texas, and Virginia. Accordingly, in the summer of 1868 the compliant states were readmitted and the Fourteenth Amendment declared in force. Because Georgia later excluded blacks from its legislature and because Mississippi, Texas, and Virginia, for various local reasons, did not ratify their constitutions on time, those four states were subjected to additional requirements. These included the ratification of the Fifteenth Amendment, prohibiting the denial of suffrage on account of race. After complying with the new demands, these states too were restored to their places in the Union in 1870, and the amendment was added to the Constitution.

Historians have long argued about the nature of the radical governments. According to William A. Dunning and his school, they were characterized by vindictiveness, corruption, inefficiency, and ruthless exploitation of southern whites. Northern carpetbaggers, local scalawags, and their alleged black tools supposedly trampled white civilization underfoot. Some scholars have questioned these assumptions. Pointing out that the radical governments succeeded in establishing systems of public education, eleemosynary institutions, and lasting constitutions, modern experts have discarded the concept of "black Reconstruction." Black legislators were in a majority only in South Carolina, and even there their white allies wielded considerable influence. Conceding the presence of corruption in the South, these historians have emphasized its nationwide scope. They have tended to show that the new governments deserved credit for making the first efforts to establish racial democracy in the South and that many radical officeholders, black and white alike, did not compare unfavorably with their conservative colleagues.

For a time blacks continued to vote, though in decreasing numbers, and by the turn of the century they had been almost eliminated from southern politics.

But the experiment could not last. The rapid disappearance, by death or retirement, of radical Republicans, the granting of amnesty to former Confederates, the conservatives' resort to terror, and a gradual loss of interest by the North would have made Reconstruction difficult in any case. These problems were complicated by the blacks' lack of economic power—Johnson had gone so far as to return to whites lands already occupied by freedmen. Factionalism within the dominant party increased with the rise of the Liberal Republicans in 1872, and the panic of 1873 eroded Republican majorities in the House. The Supreme Court, which had refused to interfere with Reconstruction in *Mississippi* v. *Johnson* (1867) and *Georgia* v. *Stanton* (1867), began to interpret the Fourteenth Amendment very narrowly, as in the Slaughterhouse Cases (1873). Such a tendency foreshadowed the Court's further weakening of not only the Fourteenth Amendment but also the Fifteenth Amendment, in *United States* v. *Cruikshank* (1876) and

United States v. *Reese* (1876) and its invalidation in 1883 of the Civil Rights Act of 1875 in the Civil Rights Cases.

The end of Reconstruction came at different times in the several states. Despite the passage of three Federal Force Acts during 1870 and 1871, the gradual collapse of the radical regimes could not be arrested. In some cases terror instigated by the Ku Klux Klan and its successors overthrew Republican administrations; in others, conservatives regained control by more conventional means. By 1876 Republican administrations survived only in Florida, Louisiana, and South Carolina, all of which returned disputed election results in the fall. After a series of economic and political bargains enabled Rutherford B. Hayes, the Republican candidate, to be inaugurated president, he promptly withdrew federal troops, and Reconstruction in those states also came to an end. For a time blacks continued to vote, although in decreasing numbers, but by the turn of the century they had been almost eliminated from southern politics.

Reconstruction thus seemed to end in failure, and the myth of radical misrule embittered relations between the sections. But in spite of their apparent lack of accomplishment, the radicals had succeeded in embedding the postwar amendments in the Constitution, amendments that were the foundation for the struggle for racial equality in the 20th century.

BIBLIOGRAPHY

Herman Belz, *Reconstructing the Union: Theory and Policy During the Civil War.*

Michael Les Benedict, *A Compromise of Principle.*

William R. Brock, *An American Crisis: Congress and Reconstruction, 1865–1867.*

La-Wanda Cox and John H. Cox, *Politics, Principle, and Prejudice, 1865–1866.*

John Hope Franklin, *Reconstruction After the Civil War.*

Eric L. McKitrick, *Andrew Johnson and Reconstruction.*

Rembert W. Patrick, *The Reconstruction of the Nation.*

J. G. Randall and David Donald, *The Civil War and Reconstruction.*

Kenneth P. Stampp, *The Era of Reconstruction.*

— HANS L. TREFOUSSE

RECONSTRUCTION ACTS

Reconstruction Acts, a series of laws designed to carry out the congressional program of Reconstruction. The first Reconstruction Act (Mar. 2, 1867) divided all southern states except Tennessee into five military districts to be commanded by general officers. Conventions chosen by universal male suffrage were to frame constitutions, which would then have to be accepted by the electorate. After completing these steps and ratifying the Fourteenth Amendment, the southern states would be deemed ready for readmission as full-fledged members of the Union. Insurgents disfranchised for their participation in rebellion were denied the right to vote.

When southerners refused to take steps to call conventions, a supplementary Reconstruction Act (Mar. 23, 1867) provided that the commanding generals initiate the voting process. Registrars were required to take an "ironclad oath," and the electorate was to vote on the question of holding a convention. Because Attorney General Henry Stanbery interpreted the law in such a way as to favor the conservatives, a second supplementary Reconstruction Act (July 19, 1867) declared that the state governments were strictly subordinate to the military commanders, broadly defined the disfranchising clauses, and spelled out the generals' right to remove state officers. After the conservatives in Alabama had defeated the radical state constitution by registering but not voting, a third supplementary Reconstruction Act (Mar. 11, 1868) enabled a majority of the actual voters, rather than of the registrants, to ratify. The first three of these measures were passed over President Andrew Johnson's veto; the last became law without his signature.

The Reconstruction Acts were the result of Johnson's refusal to modify his policies in conformity with the wishes of the majority of the Republican party. His own plan of Reconstruction was so mild as to fail to protect either the freedmen in the South or the interests of the Republican party in the country. Consequently, when the voters rejected his policies in the fall of 1866 and all southern states except Tennessee refused to ratify the Fourteenth Amendment, the radicals demanded more stringent legislation. Thaddeus Stevens, who had originally advocated a more comprehensive measure, then reported a bill remanding the South to military rule, but the pressure of moderates forced him to agree reluctantly to Sen. John Sherman's amendments providing for a possible method of restoration.

Although the purposes of the acts were ostensibly achieved with the inauguration of radical governments in the South, in the long run they must be deemed a failure. In state after state conservative rule was eventually restored and blacks once more subordinated to whites. The revolutionary effect often ascribed to the acts because of their emphasis on black suffrage has been exaggerated. While modern historians have criticized them for ambiguities and imperfections, they are no longer considered unprovoked examples of vindictive radicalism. Their principal importance lies in their hastening the ratification of the Fourteenth Amendment.

BIBLIOGRAPHY

John Hope Franklin, *Reconstruction After the Civil War.*
Eric L. McKitrick, *Andrew Johnson and Reconstruction.*
J. G. Randall and David Donald, *The Civil War and Reconstruction.*
Kenneth M. Stampp, *The Era of Reconstruction, 1865–1877.*

— HANS L. TREFOUSSE

RED RIVER INDIAN WAR

Red River Indian War (1874–75). As a result of the Treaty of Medicine Lodge (Barber County, Kans.), in October 1867, the Comanche, Kiowa, and Kataka were put on a reservation about the Wichita Mountains and the Arapaho and Cheyenne on another farther north (both within western Oklahoma). The Indians, not content to accept a sedentary life, again and again slipped away to raid the borders of Kansas, Colorado, New Mexico, and Texas. During the summer of 1874, Gen. Philip H. Sheridan was ordered to conduct a punitive campaign against the refractory Indians. Soon thereafter both cavalry and infantry under the command of colonels Nelson A. Miles, George Buell, John W. Davidson, and Ranald S. Mackenzie and Maj. William Price advanced from their posts in Texas, New Mexico, and Indian Territory against the hostile Indians who were encamped along the Red River, its tributaries, and the canyons of the Staked Plain (Liano Estacado) in west Texas and southeastern New Mexico. More than fourteen pitched battles were fought before the Indians submitted and returned to their reservations. Seventy-five of their leaders were sent to Florida for confinement.

BIBLIOGRAPHY

W. S. Nye, *Carbine and Lance.*
C. C. Rister, *The Southwestern Frontier, 1865–1881.*

— C. C. RISTER

REFERENDUM

There are many ways of classifying or categorizing a referendum, but one prime characteristic is common to all its various manifestations: a referendum generally involves the submission of a public-policy measure or question directly to the people at a formal election for their approval or disapproval. Such referenda may be compulsory or advisory, constitutional or legislative, local or statewide in nature. Questions posed to the public on a referendum ballot may deal with proposed changes in state constitutional provisions, in city charters, in state laws, or in levels of school taxes or bonding.

In terms of mere volume, the public referendum no doubt finds its heaviest use among the thousands of local governmental units where state constitutions or state laws stipulate voter approval before public resources may be either sought or spent or before certain governmental functions may be either added or abolished.

The Massachusetts constitution of 1780 is usually credited with introducing the use in the United States of statewide constitutional referenda on the adoption or rejection of new constitutions or on the adoption or rejection of amendments to existing constitutions. Use of the statewide legislative referendum came somewhat later. After an early beginning in Texas (1840's) major impetus for legislatures to submit measures to the voters for their approval before they could become law did not develop until the end of the 19th century and the first two decades of the 20th century.

Questions posed to the public on a referendum ballot may deal with proposed changes in city charters, in state laws, or in levels of school taxes or bonding.

The Progressive movement viewed the legislative referendum—along with the initiative, the recall, and the primary—as part and parcel of urgently needed governmental reforms through wider and more direct forms of citizen participation.

By 1975 provision for the use of the legislative referendum could be found in the constitutions of at least twelve states—Colorado, Georgia, Maine, Michigan, Missouri, Montana, New Jersey, North Carolina, Oklahoma, Oregon, Vermont, and Washington. An even larger number of states permitted a citizen-initiated legislative referendum on the filing of a petition (containing a specified number of signatures) with the secretary of state. This group of twenty-three states includes Alaska, Arizona, Arkansas, California, Colorado, Idaho, Kentucky, Maine, Maryland, Massachusetts, Michigan, Missouri, Montana, Nebraska, Nevada, New Mexico, North Dakota, Ohio, Oklahoma, Oregon, South Dakota, Utah, and Washington.

Although infrequently called into operation when compared with the hundreds of constitutional amendments and thousands of local issues, the approximately half-a-dozen legislative referenda voted on annually have been employed to ascertain the public will on a wide variety of legislative subject matters. Two major categories appear frequently: referenda dealing with changes in governmental machinery or organization and those addressing themselves to fiscal or financial matters. Since many of these issues included proposals for higher taxes or for the establishment of additional governmental agencies or departments, the electoral responses to such referenda not surprisingly have more often been negative than positive.

Voters who view the extension of public services as socially desirable and therefore consider it proper for state or local governments to enhance their functions and operations have become more and more disenchanted with the usefulness of the referendum as an instrument for change. Such disillusionment with "plebiscitary democracy" has been reinforced when the usual low voter-turnout at referendum elections (averaging about 30 percent or less in most communities) quite often accrued to the distinct advantage of individuals and groups with ample resources to strengthen and favor the cause of the status quo. The referendum has also come under increasing criticism for inviting campaign strategies that tend to exacerbate racial antagonisms in legislative issues affecting changes in the development of housing, urban renewal, and neighborhood school patterns.

In theory at least, the referendum, whether initiated by the action of citizens or of the legislature, remains a viable "populist" device in the arsenal of direct democracy whenever the instrumentalities of representative democracy fail to function in the interest of the general public.

BIBLIOGRAPHY

Penelope J. Gazey, "Direct Democracy: A Study of the American Referendum," *Parliamentary Affairs* (Spring 1971).

Howard D. Hamilton, "Direct Legislation: Some Implications of Open-Housing Referenda," *American Political Science Review* (March 1970).

— G. THEODORE MITAU

REFORMED CHURCHES

Reformed churches are the American representatives of Dutch Calvinism. Their first American congregation, the Collegiate church in New York City, was established in 1628 and was still functioning in 1975. The church was divided by the Great Awakening over the issue of evangelism and its relationship to the church in the Netherlands. The church was reunited in 1771 under the ultimate authority of the home church, but it declared itself independent in 1819. The largest schism in the history of the movement occurred in 1822 when the Christian Reformed Church left the parent body. Although the early strength of the church was concentrated in the New York-New Jersey area, migrations to Michigan and Iowa in the 1850's gave the church a firm midwestern basis. The principal Reformed denominations in 1974 were the Christian Reformed Church, 287,114 members; Reformed Church in America, 366,381; Protestant Reformed Church in America, 3,000; and Reformed Church in the United States, 4,008.

BIBLIOGRAPHY

Herman Hoeksema, *The Protestant Reformed Churches in America: Their Origin, Early History and Doctrine.*

Diedrich Kromminga, *The Christian Reformed Church: A Study in Orthodoxy.*

Frederick James Zwierlein, *Religion in New Netherland 1623–1664.*

— GLENN T. MILLER

REGISTRATION OF VOTERS

Because of widespread election fraud in the 19th century by the use of such devices as "repeaters" and "tombstone" voters, almost every state requires that a person register in order to vote. The first voter registration law was enacted in Massachusetts in 1800, and similar laws were soon enacted in other New England states. Most large cities initiated registration laws between 1850 and 1900, but many laws were inadequate and election fraud was common. Since 1900 reform legislation has made registration laws more effective.

To register, the voter appears before county or city election officials during a set period and establishes his or her right to vote. In most states the individual must be at least eighteen years old; be an American citizen; and have lived in the state thirty days. Once the person is registered, his or her name appears on registration lists and is checked off when he or she votes. The registration lists are public documents and are available for inspection to check the qualifications of voters or for use in campaigning. Registration may be either permanent or periodic. Under permanent registration the voter's name stays on the list as long as the voter resides at the same address. In a few states a person is dropped from the list if he or she fails to vote in two successive elections. Periodic registration requires voters to reregister at certain times. This practice keeps the registration lists current but is often inconvenient for voters.

Unnecessarily restrictive registration laws have kept many persons from voting. In 1970 Congress passed a voting rights act that replaced the confusing pattern of state residency requirements with a uniform national law for presidential elections. The law also permits absentee registration and voting. The Supreme Court ruled in 1972 (*Dunn* v. *Blumstein*) that states may not require residency of more than thirty days in federal elections. By contrast, in 1973 the Court ruled that states may have a residency requirement of fifty days for state and local elections.

The nature of voter registration and the high mobility of the American people are major factors leading to low voter-turnout. Nationwide approximately 75 percent of those eligible to vote are registered. In 1972 nearly 62 million Americans of voting age did not vote in the presidential election, and in the 1974 congressional elections there was only a 38 percent nationwide turnout. In many Western European countries the government takes the initiative in registering voters, and in some countries there are compulsory registration laws. The result is high rates of voter turnout. The U.S. Senate in 1973 passed a bill to allow all potential voters in federal elections to register by postcard, but the bill was not approved by the House of Representatives.

BIBLIOGRAPHY

Joseph P. Harris, *Model Voter Registration System*, and *Registration of Voters in the United States*.

— DAVID C. SAFFELL

REGULATORS

Regulators, irregular armed combinations, organized in numerous southern communities after the Civil War to obstruct the welfare activities of the Freedmen's Bureau. These local self-appointed committees of vigilantes, known also as "Black-Horse Cavalry" and "Jayhawkers" in Georgia and Louisiana, generally rode at night, in disguise, employing arson, murder, and mutilation to terrorize the freedmen and prevent the exercise of their rights to make labor contracts and to migrate. The Regulators resembled the Ku Klux Klan (organized 1866) in the methods employed, but they lacked the hierarchical organization and the political aims of the Klan.

— MARTIN P. CLAUSSEN

RELIGIOUS LIBERTY

Religious liberty is perhaps the greatest contribution America has made both in the realm of politics and of religion. At the time of the establishment of the American colonies there was no country in Europe without a state church, and everywhere, with the possible exception of Holland, unity of religion was considered essential to the unity of the state. There is a mistaken notion, widely held, that the Reformation more or less automatically brought about religious liberty, but nothing is farther from the truth. The Reformation resulted in the establishment of numerous national churches, as in England, Scotland, Holland, and the Scandinavian countries, which were as intolerant of Roman Catholicism and the small dissenting sects as Roman Catholicism was intolerant of them.

Besides the national churches that arose out of the religious and political upheaval of the Reformation, there also developed numerous small sects, generally poor and despised, most of them taking as their pattern the primitive church of the first three centuries. These small minority bodies generally stood for the separation of church and state and for complete religious liberty. It is an important fact to bear in mind that religious liberty and the separation of church and state have been principally advocated by the small minority sects and never by the great state churches. The English Baptists, a small despised sect, took over the principles of the Anabaptists of the continent and held to religious liberty as their first and greatest principle. The Quakers also became the advocates of freedom of conscience. Another source of the principle of religious liberty is found in the work of such 16th- and 17th-century political philosophers as Sir Thomas More, who pictured in his ideal state one where there was complete religious liberty, and John Locke, who wrote an important series of essays on religious toleration.

The American colonies became the first place in the world where complete religious liberty was actually tried in a political state. Roger Williams, the founder of Rhode Island, had become thoroughly imbued with this idea, and when he established Rhode Island the principle was there put into operation. Another factor that made the American colonies a fruitful place for the growth of this principle was the fact that a majority of the colonies were begun as proprietary grants, where the governments as well as the land were controlled by the same person or groups of persons. This meant that, in order to attract settlers to buy and settle the land, persecuted religious groups from almost every country in western Europe were invited to come to these colonies. Thus, William Penn; Cecilius Calvert, Lord Baltimore; and the proprietors of the Carolinas and Georgia welcomed the persecuted sectaries. Still another factor creating an environment in America favorable to religious liberty was the fact that, by the end of the colonial period, a great majority of the population throughout the colonies was unchurched, and unchurched people generally are opposed to granting special privileges to any one religious body. It is an interesting and significant fact that the political leaders who led in the movement to separate church and state with the establishment of independence, such as James Madison and Thomas Jefferson, were nonchurch members. Of all the colonial religious bodies the Baptists were the most tenacious in their advocacy of religious liberty and as a whole made the largest contribution toward its achievement.

The American colonies became the first place in the world where complete religious liberty was actually tried in a political state.

In the colonies south of Pennsylvania the Anglican church was established by law, but only in Maryland and Virginia was it a factor of significance. In Massachusetts, Connecticut, and New Hampshire the Congregational church was the privileged body, but by the end of the colonial period the factors noted above had considerably relaxed control. The great colonial awakenings had strengthened the dissenting bodies especially in the middle and southern colonies and the coming of the Revolution gave them an opportunity to bargain for greater privileges.

Although there were no direct religious issues involved in the revolutionary war, the disturbed political and social situation that it created, together with the necessity for the formation of new governments, gave opportunity for the new principle, religious liberty, to be incorporated in the new constitutions as they were adopted. Thus, the new state and federal constitutions simply took over, in this respect, what already was to a large degree in practical operation.

BIBLIOGRAPHY

Sanford H. Cobb, *Rise of Religious Liberty in America.*
M. L. Greene, *The Development of Religious Liberty in Connecticut.*
E. F. Humphrey, *Nationalism and Religion in America.*
H. R. McIlwaine, *Struggle of the Protestant Dissenters for Religous Toleration in Virginia.*

— WILLIAM W. SWEET

REMOVAL ACT OF 1830

In his first annual message to Congress on Dec. 8, 1829, President Andrew Jackson recommended legislation looking to the removal of the Indians from east of the Mississippi River. A bill was introduced in the House of Representatives, Feb. 24, to carry this recommendation into effect. Although bitterly opposed in and out of Congress, it was enacted by a close vote, May 28, 1830. It authorized the president to cause territory west of the Mississippi to be divided into districts suitable for exchange with Indians living within any state or territory of the United States for lands there claimed and occupied by them and authorized the president to make such exchange.

BIBLIOGRAPHY

Grant Foreman, *Indian Removal.*

— GRANT FOREMAN

REPARATION COMMISSION

Reparation Commission (1920–30) was directed by articles 231–235 of part VIII of the Treaty of Versailles to estimate damage done by Germany to Allied civilians and their property during World War I and to formulate methods of collecting assessments, since the Paris conferees had become deadlocked on the issue. In June 1920 the Supreme Council decided that Germany should pay at least 3 billion gold marks for thirty-five years, the total not to exceed 269 billion marks. Within this frame, and after sanctions had been applied because of German defaults, the commission, on advice of a committee of experts, reported to the Supreme Council in April 1921 that damages amounted to 132 billion marks and recommended annual payments of 2 billion marks and 26 percent of German exports, with a cash payment of 1 billion marks by Sept. 1. Economic and monetary chaos in Germany coupled with resentment at the reparations scheme brought a Franco-Belgian force into the Ruhr. By the time of complete collapse of the German mark in 1923, accompanied by dislocation of world trade, there had been paid in cash, commodities, and services an amount that was estimated by the commission at approximately 10.5 billion gold marks, by the Germans at something over 42 billion marks, and by various economists at sums somewhere between these extremes. Of this indeterminate amount the United States received nothing of the reparations per se, although considerable sums had been paid to reimburse expenses of the Army of Occupation, damage in the United States, and the like.

In 1922 Secretary of State Charles E. Hughes had suggested, although the United States not being a party to the Treaty of Versailles technically had nothing to do with the matter, that the whole issue be taken out of politics and adjusted on economic principles, and intimated that the services of American experts might be available. Accordingly, a committee set up to study German finances, with Charles G. Dawes as chairman, worked out a plan to go into effect on Sept. 1, 1924, with a sliding scale of annuities in cash and kind, together with suggestions how revenues should be raised and payments distributed. In the opinion of competent economists the plan worked fairly well, at least in the short run, providing for the payment of nearly 10 billion marks to the creditors and at the same time allowing stabilization of German currency and an upward trend in German economic life, even though no definite aggregate total had been fixed. Desire on the part of the creditor powers to arrange a definitive settlement and to have turned into marketable bonds Germany's future obligations brought a second committee of experts, even though Germans were afraid of the effect such an arrangement would have on them. The conference, meeting under the chairmanship of Owen D. Young in the spring of 1929, produced a new plan that, somewhat modified by the Reparation Commission especially on the insistence of Great Britain, arranged for annuities running until 1988 and aggregating with interest 121 billion marks. On May 17, 1930, the Young Plan went into operation and on that day the Reparation Commission ceased operations. In barely two years, however, payments stopped with the moratorium proposed by President Herbert Hoover, effective June 30, 1931, after a sum of 2.871 billion marks had been turned over to the creditor nations. Thenceforward, to all intents and purposes reparations were suspended regardless of the Lausanne Agreement (July 9, 1932), which attempted to replace the Young Plan with a set of new and reduced obligations.

In American popular estimation reparations were tied to debts owed the United States by various governments that had been ranged against Germany in World War I or had been advanced loans subsequently. The U.S. government, however, never acknowledged any such relationship even though such payments as had been made on these debts actually had been derived from Germany.

BIBLIOGRAPHY

David Felix, *Walter Rathenau and the Weimar Republic: The Politics of Reparations.*

— L. B. SHIPPEE

REPRESENTATION

Alexander Hamilton, in *The Federalist,* called representation a principle, imperfectly known to the ancients, which has made most of its progress toward perfection in modern times, and a powerful means by which the excellencies of republican government may be retained and its imperfections lessened or avoided. The idea of representation is absent from Aristotle's *Politics,* partly because a state so large that it required representation would have seemed too large for political excellence to classical political theorists.

The democracy of the modern world has generally been representative democracy. Pure democracy, in which the politically qualified members of the community meet together to discuss and decide public questions, is suitable only for small communities with simple collective needs. All the members of modern democratic communities cannot personally assemble to make laws in one gigantic town meeting. Rather the community is represented by individuals who can legislate for the people more effectively than the people can legislate directly themselves.

Hobbes defined a representative as one who has been given authority to act in the name of another, so that whatever the representative does is considered the act of the represented.

A representative is someone who will be held responsible by those for whom he acts, who must account for his actions. If the representative's actions bear no relation to his constituents' needs or interests, he is not representing his constituents. Should a representative act on his own judgment of what is in the national interest, or should he be a faithful servant of his constituency's expressed will? There are those who argue that the representative must act independently, on his own judgment, and that his job is to adapt the constituent's separate interests into the national interest. Others stress the popular mandate given a representative by those for whom he acts and say he has an obligation to do what they expect of him, to act as if they were acting themselves.

A representative, said Thomas Hobbes, is a man who acts in the name of another, who has been given authority to act by that other, so that whatever the representative does is considered the act of the represented. Representation is authority, the right to make commitments for another. Within limits, the representative is free to do as he pleases, at least insofar as his constituents are concerned. According to Hobbes, every government is a representative government in that it represents its subjects. Edmund Burke thought of a representative essentially as representing, not individuals, but the large, stable interests that constitute the national interest. The duty of each representative is to determine the good of the whole, and the selfish wishes of parts of the nation or the wills of individual voters are irrelevant. The representative must discover the national interest. Since the relation of each representative is to the nation as a whole, he stands in no special relation to his constituency. He represents the nation, not merely those who elected him. Therefore the representative is like a trustee: his obligation is to look after his constituents, not to consult or obey them. John Stuart Mill said that what distinguishes a representative assembly from any other collection of people is its accurate correspondence to the larger population for which it stands. To be representative, a legislature must be a mirror that accurately reflects the various parts of the populace. According to Mill, every man needs to have his vote count equally because no one can know or defend his particular interest as well as he. Mill was much more inclined to think of the representative as an agent than as a trustee.

BIBLIOGRAPHY

J. Roland Pennock and John W. Chapman, eds., *Representation (Nomos X).*

Hannah F. Pitkin, *The Concept of Representation.*

— MORTON J. FRISCH

REPRESENTATIVE GOVERNMENT

Representative government, government that represents all the people, giving effect to their opinions and interests, not imposing on them the opinions and interests of their rulers. Representative government, which emerged in the 17th century, had come to be virtually universal by the mid-20th century in the sense that most governments claimed to be representative, for much of world opinion condemns governments that rule contrary to popular opinions and interests. Representative government in its present form, moreover, is democratic government. The ancient democracies lacked the representative principle, having neither the geographic extent nor the large populations that later called the principle into play.

According to the modern theory of representative government, democratic government deals with its problems most competently and protects the liberties of the people most effectively when assemblies are composed of representatives of the citizenry rather than of the citizens themselves en masse. The presumption is that representatives will be capable men who will deliberate wisely in the interests of the people and not misrepresent their interests. Representative government can be made less democratic either through suffrage limitations (limiting voters) or representative qualifications (limiting those who may be elected).

Since the practice of politics and government requires the exercise of discretion in variable circumstances, direct democracy is practicable only in a small country in which the populace can meet as a body often enough to consider new circumstances. The theorists of modern representative government—notably Edmund Burke; Alexander Hamilton, James Madison, and John Jay, the authors of *The Federalist* (1788); and John Stuart Mill—preferred a large country as more favorable to liberty and more powerful and insisted upon representative government allowing discretion to representatives to deal with changing circumstances. The authors of *The Federalist* hoped and intended that the representatives of the American people would "refine and enlarge" the views of their constituents and that they would be governed not by temporary and partial considerations, but by the true interests of the country.

Mill, in *Representative Government* (1861), argued that representatives should have the responsibility of thinking about and discussing public issues in the interest of the whole, that they should not merely reflect the views of their constituencies. But he also argued that they should not actually govern. The functions of government, he believed, require highly skilled, experienced, well-trained individuals. He advocated. that experts should govern, while being controlled by representatives of the people; the representatives would not constitute the government, but act for the people to control the government. And he warned that effective representative government would require that a balance be maintained between the representative assembly and the government.

Jean-Jacques Rousseau, on the other hand, contended that representative government is undesirable, because responsibility is removed from the hands of the citizens, that there is no way to institutionalize or guarantee that the representative's vote will always coincide with the will of those he represents. But confronted with nations too large to allow all citizens to meet in a common body, representation becomes an unfortunate necessity. Rousseau proposed that the representatives should be elected by local assemblies of all the citizens and be given complete instructions. Opposing the use of independent judgment by the representatives, he further proposed that every new question should be referred back to the electors, to ensure an expression of the general will.

The problem of modern representative government—of which Rousseau was well aware—is how to govern the people without instructing or educating them. The people must be governed; but if they are instructed or educated, they are no longer simply represented. They are ruled. A representative is supposed to act on behalf of others, in their place, in their name, for their sake, in accordance with their opinions and interests, in order to please or satisfy them, as they would have acted themselves. But it is difficult, if not impossible, to have a democratic government that governs the populace without imposing any views or opinions on it.

BIBLIOGRAPHY

Benjamin Fletcher Wright, "Direct and Representative Democracy," in Wright, ed., *The Federalist.*

— MORTON J. FRISCH

REPUBLICAN PARTY

Failure of the established American political parties to contain sectional conflict over the status of slavery in the new territories stimulated organizations of protest throughout the free states in the two decades before the Civil War. The sentiment of northern farmers and workingmen was crystallized by the Kansas-Nebraska Act of 1854, which repealed the Missouri Compromise.

The Republican name was first adopted at a protest meeting in Ripon, Wis., on Feb. 28, 1854, and the first convention of a Republican state party was held "under the oaks" at Jackson, Mich., on July 6, 1854. Local and congressional election victories followed in several states. The new party included politicians and voters who had previously given their allegiance to the northern (or "Conscience") Whigs, the Free Soil party, the free Democrats, and the nativist American (or "Know-Nothing") party. The name "Republican" was taken from that of the Jeffersonian Republicans, the party of Thomas Jefferson, who was recognized as the spiritual leader of the 1854 protests. Jefferson was seen as an opponent of slavery (or at least of its expansion), champion of the concept of a nation of small landholders, and leader of radical opposition to the established aristocracy.

The sentiments of the new party were firmly agrarian and radical. Opposition to the slavocracy was coupled with support for new railroads, free homesteads, and the opening of the West by free labor. Support for the protective tariff was added in an appeal to the manufacturing (as opposed to the plantation) interest.

The 1856 Republican National Convention nominated John C. Frémont of California as its candidate for the presidency. Frémont was defeated, but he carried eleven states, establishing the organizational base of the new party. Winning every free state in 1860, Abraham Lincoln moved to consolidate his political support, but he could not deter the southern secessionists. Lincoln selected the preservation of the Union as the issue of broadest appeal, emancipating the slaves only when the political time was ripe. The party was known as the Union party for Lincoln's reelection campaign of 1864, for which Andrew Johnson of Tennessee was nominated as vice-president to attract future southern support.

After Lincoln's assassination, Radical Republicans in Congress asserted party leadership. They did not regard Johnson as a Republican, and the Tennessean's efforts to enact Lincoln's policies of reconciliation with the South led only to his impeachment. Reconstruction policies drove the southern Whigs into the Democratic party and created the Solid South. Republicans demonstrated their party's sectional nature by nominating former Union soldiers, as long as any were available—Ulysses S. Grant, Rutherford B. Hayes, James A. Garfield, Benjamin Harrison, and William McKinley—and Republicans occupied the White House for all but eight of the thirty-two years following Lincoln's first election. But the national strength of the two parties was remarkably equal; in the popular vote the majority alternated between them. Resolving the contested election of 1876 between Hayes and Samuel J. Tilden, Republicans abandoned the freedman to the mercies of the southern whites in return for a renewed lease on the White House.

McKinley's election in 1896 constituted the defeat of radical, lower-class reform as personified by populism and William Jennings Bryan. It established the Republicans as the normal majority party, representing industrial progress, northern farmers, middle-class respectability, eastern urban labor, and even college presidents. McKinley was assassinated during his second term, and Theodore Roosevelt became president. After reelection in his own right in 1904, Roosevelt assumed leadership of the Progressive movement, making the Republicans also the party of conservation and reform. Only a feud between Roosevelt and his successor, William Howard Taft, brought about the Democratic victory that installed Woodrow Wilson in the White House in 1913—the only break in thirty-six years of Republican domination.

With the exception of Roosevelt, Republican presidents followed the pattern imposed on Andrew Johnson into the 20th century. Warren G. Harding and Calvin Coolidge personified this Whig tradition, which subordinated executive leadership to the legislature. Although a Progressive by background, Herbert Hoover shared this limited concept of presidential power, and it proved inadequate to the demands of the Great Depression. Hoover's defeat for a second term by Franklin D. Roosevelt was followed by the stunning defeat of Alfred M. Landon, the Kansas Progressive, in 1936. The Republicans were cast in a long-term minority role.

As the New Deal forged a majority by adding organized labor, urban minorities, and intellectuals to the base of the South, the Republicans came to be regarded as the party of eastern big business and midwestern farmers. Conservative (and some isolationist) Republicans predominated in Congress, while presidential nominations were controlled by the eastern, liberal, internationalist wing of the party. The era's defeated Republican candidates were Wendell L. Willkie in 1940 and Thomas E. Dewey in 1944 and 1948. Dwight D. Eisenhower's phenomenal personal popularity made inroads even into southern Democratic allegiances and won him the presidency in 1952 and 1956, but little of his popularity was transferred to the Republican party. "Ike" had a Republican Congress for only two of his eight years in office, and his vice-president, Richard M. Nixon, lost narrowly to John F. Kennedy in 1960. Four years later, Republican delegates from the South and West repudiated the eastern leadership by nominating Barry Goldwater, an avowed conservative. Goldwater carried only his native Arizona and five states of the Deep South against Lyndon B. Johnson.

In 1968 Nixon claimed the moderate position between liberal and conservative Republicans and won the nomination easily. In a three-way contest, George C. Wallace won 13 percent of the vote, and Nixon edged out Hubert H. Humphrey for a plurality, while the Democrats recaptured Congress. Winding down American involvement in the Vietnam War, Nixon visited the Soviet Union and China, striving for a "generation of peace." In 1972 he defeated Sen. George McGovern in a historic personal landslide, failing to carry only Massachusetts and the District of Columbia. But Nixon offered little support to other Republican candidates, and the Democrats retained control of Congress.

The Watergate burglary was raised as an issue in the 1972 campaign but received little public attention. Beginning in 1973, press exposures, congressional investigations, and court proceedings revealed the complicity of Nixon administration officials in that crime and others. Tainted by an unrelated Maryland scandal, Vice-President Spiro T. Agnew resigned in October 1973 rather than face indictment. Invoking the Constitution's Twenty-fifth Amendment for the first time, Nixon appointed House Minority Leader Gerald R. Ford to replace Agnew. When Nixon was forced by a Supreme Court decision to release tape recordings that proved he had known of his leading aides' involvement in Watergate, he resigned his office (August 1974) rather than face impeachment proceedings, which had been voted by the House Judiciary Committee.

Gerald Ford's accession to the presidency was greeted with relief because of his apparent honesty and plainspokenness. But this image was immediately tarnished when he pardoned Richard Nixon, and conservative Republicans were affronted when Ford appointed Nelson Rockefeller as vice-president. Ford retained the foreign policy leadership of Henry Kissinger, who had served Nixon, and frequently used the veto power in domestic matters. During 1975, the Democratic majority in Congress did not present a coherent opposition. Ford's chief political problem as 1976 began was a conservative challenge for the Republican presidential nomination from former Gov. Ronald Reagan of California.

BIBLIOGRAPHY

George H. Mayer, *The Republican Party, 1854–1966.*
Malcolm Moos, *The Republicans.*

— KARL A. LAMB

REPUBLICAN PARTY FROM 1968 UNTIL PRESENT DAY

With the exception of Jimmy Carter's one term as president (1977–1981), Republicans dominated the presidency from 1968 until 1992. This record stood in striking contrast to the previous thirty-six years, when only one president, Dwight D. Eisenhower, carried the Republican banner. On all other levels of competition since the 1970s—party registration, seats in Congress, governorships, and state legislatures—Republicans as a rule ran behind the Democrats, although the discrepancy varied with each category and from year to year. In the 1980s the party undertook a shift to the ideological right, leading to virtual disappearance of a familiar force in American politics—the liberal Republican. Republican gains at the start of the 1970s stemmed as much from problems of the Democrats as from broad approval of Republican policies. The Republicans did profit from an end to the once "solid" Democratic South, at least in presidential politics. While southern Democrats continued to dominate on a reduced scale in state and local contests, a solid Republican South emerged in presidential races. Republican planners in the early 1970s hoped for a "southern strategy." More important to Republican fortunes was the Democratic association with the Vietnam War and its consequences in the late 1960s and early 1970s—demonstrations and riots, youth rebellion, emergence of a radical left—all of which divided the Democrats and seemed to challenge revered American principles.

In turning in 1968 to a centrist presidential candidate, Richard M. Nixon, Republicans sought to end their internal divisions of the 1960s. Brought into office in a close contest, the ticket of Nixon and Governor Spiro T. Agnew of Maryland overpowered the Democrats four years later with 61 percent of the popular vote. Democratic candidates Senator George McGovern and Sargent Shriver won only Massachusetts and the District of Columbia. Although Nixon had initially been elected on a law-and-order southern strategy campaign, desegregation continued in the southern states, albeit at times with little assistance from the president. His record on social and economic programs was mixed, but it contained more than expected by either conservatives or liberals. While he abolished the Office of Economic Opportunity, he proposed a family assistance plan, which failed to pass Congress, and supported proposals for environment control and consumer protection. Nixon was the only post-World War II president whose budgets, from 1970 through 1975, contained more spending on human resource programs than for defense.

Nixon's most visible achievements were in foreign affairs, where moves to reverse twenty years of hostility with the People's Republic of China and to pursue détente with the Soviet Union surprised liberals and caught rightist critics off guard. While the war in Vietnam continued through his first term, Nixon's plan of Vietnamization steadily reduced the U.S. commitment. By 1972 he could claim that peace was within sight. Although no viable peace was achieved, the margin of victory occurred because of the division of the opposition and a perception of the Democrats as the party of disorder and of McGovern as the candidate of the radical left. Nixon's victories brought factions within the Republican party together after Barry Goldwater's defeat by Lyndon Johnson in 1964. Republicans elected 192 members of the House of Representatives in 1968 and again in 1972, the largest number since 1956 and the largest until the 1990s. Between 1970 and 1992 in the House, only in 1972 did the margin by which Democrats outnumbered Republicans drop beneath fifty, and the number frequently stood at 100 or more. During the Nixon years the party had a deficit of at least ten seats in the Senate.

Nixon's visit to China and his pursuit of détente with the Soviet Union surprised liberals and caught rightist critics off guard.

Rather than build on their gains, Republicans squandered them in the scandals of the early 1970s. First came the problems of Vice President Agnew, who, faced with charges of receiving bribes, pleaded no contest and resigned in October 1973. Nixon was by this time deeply involved in the Watergate affair, illegal activities against the Democrats and efforts to hide the truth. The Watergate tapes—secret recordings in the Oval Office—revealed that Nixon had obstructed justice by participating in efforts to conceal the origins of the scandal and repeatedly lied about the Watergate cover-up from June 1972 to August 1974. Rather than face impeachment and likely removal from office, he resigned on Aug. 9, 1974. The Watergate scandal went beyond the president. Republicans faced charges ranging from arrogant and mean-spirited behavior to shadowy fund-raising and various forms of illegal activity. Several government officials went to prison. The political fallout was immediate. The Republicans lost five Senate seats in 1974, leaving Democrats in control, 60–37. The Democratic margin in the House grew from 49 to 147. Republicans controlled legislatures in only five states, and whereas in 1970 they outnumbered Democrats in governorships by thirty-two to eighteen, in 1975 there were thirty-six Democratic governors to thirteen Republicans. Lopsided Democratic majorities in Congress held up in the election of 1976. Republicans could take encouragement from the fact that in the 1976 presidential election Gerald R. Ford, who replaced Agnew in 1973 and thus was on hand to serve out the final two and a half years of Nixon's presidency, came close to being elected over Carter.

After 1976 the Republicans did not stay down long. Changes in party procedure, economic thought, and the political climate helped produce a comeback in the 1980s. The Republican National Committee shifted fund-raising from large contributors to direct mailings and use of computer technology, acquiring substantially larger sums of money and a broader base. Several forces combined to produce an enlarged ultraconservatism, the New Right. First came the appeal in the nation, if not the world, of supply-side economics, the thesis that prosperity depended upon sharp reduction of taxes, especially in the highest brackets. Many people concluded that a divided and guilt-ridden America had become impotent in the aftermath of the Vietnam War, a charge seemingly made unchallengeable in the humiliating hostage crisis with Iran that began in 1979. Because Carter was president at the culmination of this post-Vietnam syndrome, blame was laid at his feet. Republicans continued to mobilize white voters in the South and Southwest, conspicuously through politicization of the religious right—white evangelicals disturbed with reform movements that favored affirmative action in the workplace and educational institutions, abortion, feminism, and homosexual rights. While strongest in the South, the religious right showed strength in other states.

The 1980s marked the high point of Republican domination during the post-World War II era. Ronald Reagan defeated Carter in 1980 by nearly 10 percent of the popular vote and Republicans won control of the Senate for the first time since 1954. Despite gaining thirty-three seats in the House, they could come no closer to the Democrats than fifty-one. A man of strong feelings rather than intellect, Reagan was a superb communicator who emerged as spokesman of neoconservative ideas—hostility to social programs, freedom of economic enterprise (expressed mostly in lower taxes), traditional values, and patriotism expressed in U.S. military power. Inspired by a tax cut (with no corresponding reduction in government spending) and by the admonition that it was proper, even American, to seek personal gain, the economy began a long surge. Interest rates and inflation went down. Massive increases in military spending and the president's skirmishes with foreign adversaries such as the dictator of Libya were indications that America "was back." Seemingly every Republican (and some Democrats) signed on to the program of nationalism and conservatism; scarcely anywhere could one find anyone who wore the label of liberal Republican. The high point came in the election of 1984 when the ticket of Reagan and George Bush defeated Walter Mondale and Geraldine Ferraro with 59 percent of the popular vote; the Democrats won only Minnesota (Mondale's home state) and the District of Columbia.

The scope of the Republican victory in 1984 was illusory. Republicans retained control of the Senate but made a disappointing gain of only fourteen seats in the House, leaving Democrats with a margin of eighty-one seats. The erosion of Republican power began. Democrats recaptured the Senate in 1986 and established a ten-seat margin that would carry into the 1990s. The majority in the House grew and by 1991 had reached 100. Republicans did narrow Democratic domination of governors' races. By Reagan's second term, however, it was possible to charge that the benefits of Reaganomics, as the economic program was called, had gone largely to the wealthy. The boom of the 1980s rested on borrowed money, leading to soaring budget deficits and a trade deficit that for a single year passed $150 billion. Reagan's popularity continued to befuddle opponents, but his presidential style came under criticism, notably in the Iran-Contra affair, a drawn-out scandal that raised constitutional questions about the conduct of foreign policy within the White House.

The 1980's marked the high point of Republican domination during the post–World War II era.

If the Reagan revolution was not fully a Republican revolution it continued to promote party fortunes in retaining the presidency in 1988. Victory of the Republican ticket of Vice President Bush and Senator Dan Quayle (by 54 to 46 percent) rested on the same coalition that had elected Reagan: the South, Great Plains, Rocky Mountain area, California and key industrial states, white Protestants (notably evangelicals), and partial support of white Catholics. Out of conviction or expediency, the Bush administration pledged more conservatism, more Reaganism. Encouraged by unexpected developments in foreign affairs, the new president received a high approval rating, and at one juncture it passed even that of Reagan. In speed and apparent fullness of victory, the Gulf War of 1991 dazzled the American people. Republicans claimed that the collapse of communism and of the Soviet Union, which occurred during 1989–1991 also were victories of Presidents Reagan and Bush. Bush's fall from grace, if more gradual than the rise, was equally profound. Problems that appeared earlier in the 1980s caught hold—budget and trade deficits, plant closings, and increasing unemployment. Conservatives who had claimed that growth in the 1980s had come from diminished government activity could not now urge more government involvement. In Governor Bill Clinton and Senator Al Gore the Democrats in 1992 offered young opponents who promised something new for the nation. Entry into politics of Ross Perot, an eccentric and appealing billionaire, complicated the political picture. Perot's message that something was seriously wrong in Bush's America did not bode well for the incumbent Republican. On the surface the defeat of Bush and Quayle was devastating—less than 38 percent of the popular vote and more reduction of Republican strength in Congress. The magnitude of the loss was offset by the size of the Democrat victory—Clinton and Gore received only 43 percent of the popular vote.

Ending twelve years of Republican control of the presidency did not end the contest for party leadership and direction. The party reevaluated the wisdom of being identified as a rightist organization with narrowly defined social and economic positions. An immediate problem of the mid-1990s was how the party would treat the religious right, a group that pledged votes, vigor, and money but that angered some Republicans and showed signs of producing diminishing returns. If the Republicans had received their best marks in managing world affairs, they had to answer charges that they were a party of whites, a nativist group in a nation increasingly immigrant, a party whose policies favored an economic elite. Debates in Congress over post-cold war foreign policy, health care, and crime reinforced this view. By the 1994 midterm elections, the most conservative Republicans at the state and national level had won the battle to redefine the party. Rallying around their "Contract with America," they marched to an astonishing partisan victory at the polls. Playing to the anxieties of Americans about big government and higher taxes, and perceptions of President Clinton's ambivalence and weakness as a leader, the Republican party gained its first Senate majority in eight years, its first majority of governors since 1970, and its first House majority in thirty years and only the second since 1930. Not a single Republican incumbent senator, governor, or House member was defeated. The formerly Democratic "Solid South" left Republicans with 16 of 28 southern and border senators, 7 of the 14 southern governorships, and 73 of 139 southern representatives. When the dust cleared, control of Congress and of the Republican party was in the hands of Majority Leader Robert J. Dole in the Senate and Speaker Newt Gingrich in the House. Many pundits predicted that the long-awaited national party alignment had taken place—from Democratic dominance to Republican—not unlike the shift that had taken place in 1930 and 1932. It remained to be seen how valid that assessment would be—if the remarkable Republican gains of 1994 would be far-reaching.

[See also Democratic Party; Iran-Contra Affair; Reaganomics; Watergate, Aftermath of.]

BIBLIOGRAPHY

Sidney M. Milkis, *The President and the Parties* (New York, 1992).

A. James Reichley, *The Life of the Parties: A History of American Political Parties* (New York, 1992).

— ROSS GREGORY

RESERVATION SYSTEM, TERMINATION OF

After World War II there were strong pressures in Congress to terminate the Indian reservation system and accelerate the liquidation of the government's responsibilities to the Indians. In 1953 the House of Representatives passed Concurrent Resolution 108, providing for a speedy end to federal supervision of the Indians of five designated states and of seven other tribes. Termination laws were enacted for the Menomini of Wisconsin, the Klamath of Oregon, and a few other small groups, despite intense opposition by Indians throughout the country. The effects of the laws on the Menomini and Klamath were disastrous, and many members of the tribes were soon on the public assistance rolls. President John F. Kennedy in 1961 halted further termination, and the administrations of President Lyndon B. Johnson and President Richard M. Nixon also recognized that the policy had been in error and that it should be replaced by a policy of encouraging Indian

Small children stand by the government school building on the Lac du Flaubeau Indian Reservation in Vilas County, Wisconsin in 1906. USDA-Forest Service/Corbis.

self-determination, with continuing government assistance and services.

BIBLIOGRAPHY

Vine Deloria, Jr., *Custer Died for Your Sins.*

D'Arcy McNickle, *Native American Tribalism: Indian Survivals and Renewals.*

— KENNETH M. STEWART

RESERVED POWERS OF STATES

The Constitution of the United States created a government of enumerated powers. The framers intended that all powers not conferred on the national government by the Constitution nor denied by that document to the states should be retained by the states. In the ratifying conventions questions were raised as to why such an important matter had been left to inference. The First Congress reflected this feeling of uneasiness in proposing a series of amendments. Ten of these were ratified by the states. The Tenth Amendment states, "The powers not delegated to the United States by the Constitution, nor prohibited by it to the States, are reserved to the States respectively, or to the people." This amendment securely established the United States as a federal state composed of a central government and a number of constituent state governments, each possessing powers independent of the other.

In Article I, Section 8, of the Constitution, in seventeen clauses, the powers of Congress are set forth. Except in a few instances no state may exercise any of these. To the powers expressly conferred on the national government by the Constitution, the U.S. Supreme Court has, by a consistent policy of broad construction, added many implied powers. It has also pointed out that the national government possesses certain inherent powers by virtue of its sovereign character. No state may invade these fields. These are the powers delegated to the United States that are referred to in the Tenth Amendment.

The powers prohibited to the states by the Constitution are found principally in Article I, Section 10, and in the Fourteenth, Fifteenth, Nineteenth, Twenty-fourth, and Twenty-sixth amendments. By Article I, Section 10, the states are forbidden absolutely to enter into treaties, alliances, or confederations; to grant letters of marque; to coin money; to emit bills of credit; to make anything but gold or silver coin tender in payment of debts; to pass bills of attainder, ex post facto laws, or laws impairing the obligation of contracts; and to grant titles of nobility. They are also prohibited, except with the consent of Congress, from laying duties on imports or exports (with certain exceptions), from laying duties of tonnage, keeping troops or ships of war in time of peace, entering into agreements or compacts, and engaging in war. The Fourteenth Amendment forbids the making or enforcing of any state law that shall abridge the privileges and immunities of citizens of the United States; the deprivation of any person of life, liberty, or property without due process of law; or the denial of equal protection of the laws. The Fifteenth Amendment restrains the power of the states to define the qualifications of electors by forbidding discrimination on the grounds of race, color, or previous condition of servitude; the Nineteenth, on the basis of sex; the Twenty-fourth, by reason of failure to pay any poll tax or other tax; and the Twenty-sixth, on the grounds of age. All of these things states may not do except upon the conditions specified in the Constitution. But all remaining powers of government are theirs.

The Supreme Court of the United States is the final arbiter in case of conflict between a state and the national government over the right to exercise a governmental power. On occasion, as in the Child Labor Cases, the Court has declared acts of Congress invalid because they invaded the reserved powers of the states. On many other occasions state statutes have been declared void as invasions of the power of the national government.

BIBLIOGRAPHY

J. M. Mathews, *The American Constitutional System.*

Samuel P. Orth and Robert E. Cushman, *American National Government.*

— HARVEY WALKER

RESERVED POWERS OF THE PEOPLE

The Tenth Amendment reserves all powers not granted to the United States by the Constitution, nor prohibited by it to the states, to the states respectively or the people. It seems clear that the people referred to were the people of the several states, not the people of the United States. Thus viewed, the phrase "to the people" is a pronouncement of a political theory of popular sovereignty—a recognition of the right of the people to create and alter their state governments at will.

If the people of a state merely established a government, placing no limitations upon its powers, the legislative branch would possess all of the authority implied by the Tenth Amendment. But state constitutions commonly go much further than this. Bills of rights to protect the citizen of the state from his state government are found in every state constitution. In many states the people have reserved to themselves the power to propose new laws through the initiative or to require the submission to popular vote of laws passed by the legislature through the referendum. As state constitutions grow longer, more and more subjects are removed from legislative competence and are made subject to alteration only by popular vote. Such reservations of power as these give content to the final phrase of the Tenth Amendment.

In another sense it may be said that the effect of the amendment was to guarantee to the citizens of the states the continuation of the legal rights and duties that had been built up by the courts in the common law. Or from still another point of view it is an embodiment in legal phraseology of the right of revolution asserted in the Declaration of Independence. Thus it may be interpreted as an effort on the part of the First Congress to suggest that each citizen might possess a sphere of privacy that should be inviolate from interference by his government.

— HARVEY WALKER

RESETTLEMENT ADMINISTRATION

Before 1933 agricultural economists had deplored the wasteful and destructive use to which much land was being put in the United States and had urged the adoption of certain controls in land use and the retirement from cultivation of badly eroded and submarginal lands. The conservation-minded New Deal undertook to retire submarginal land as part of its agricultural adjustment program. The Resettlement Administration was created in May 1935 to administer the land retirement program and to resettle the displaced farmers on other areas. It was also given responsibility for the efforts being made to enable tenants to become homeowners. In 1937 the Resettlement Administration was transferred to the Department of Agriculture, where it became the Farm Security Administration.

— PAUL W. GATES

RESOLUTION, LEGISLATIVE

Three classes of resolutions are used by Congress. The simplest resolution is one by which one house deals with its own affairs, and such a resolution is not called to the attention of the chief executive or the other house. It may be used, for example, to create an investigating committee, to authorize the printing of special reports, to allow committees to increase their staffs, or to amend its own rules of procedure. Since 1932 some legislation empowering the president to reorganize executive bureaus and to set salaries for federal executives, judges, and members of Congress has provided that the presidential proposals would go into effect unless either house, by a simple resolution, disapproved within a limited time.

Joint resolutions must be approved by both houses and the chief executive, who may also veto them.

Concurrent resolutions involve action by both houses. They are without force and effect beyond the confines of the Capitol; they do not go to the president for approval or disapproval. They may be used to express an opinion or purpose of Congress, as in the case of the 1962 Berlin Resolution declaring it to be the sense of Congress that all necessary means were to be used to prevent Soviet violation of Allied rights in Berlin. More often, they are used to make corrections in bills passed by both houses, to amend conference reports, to fix a time for a joint session to hear an address by the president, or to fix a time for adjournment, for example.

Joint resolutions must be approved by both houses and the chief executive, who may also veto them, with the exception of joint resolutions proposing amendments to the Constitution, which are not submitted to the president. Joint resolutions have the force and effect of law, but they are ordinarily used for minor legislative purposes, such as invitations to foreign governments, extensions of existing laws, or corrections of errors in bills that have already been signed into law by the president. Joint resolutions have been employed for important foreign policy actions—for example, the annexation of Texas (1845) and the delegation to the president of broad powers in the conduct of the Vietnam War, by the Gulf of Tonkin Resolution (1964).

BIBLIOGRAPHY

Clarence Cannon, *Cannon's Procedure in the House of Representatives.*
Congressional Quarterly, *Guide to the Congress of the United States.*
George B. Galloway, *The Legislative Process in Congress.*

— D. B. HARDEMAN

REVENUE, PUBLIC

Public revenue has been derived from a changing array of tax sources in the United States. Before 1913 customs duties on imports and proceeds from the sale of public lands constituted the major part of the revenue of the federal government. Thereafter taxes on the income of individuals and corporations became the dominant source of government income.

Excise taxes on the sale of selected commodities—notably alcohol, tobacco, and automobiles—provide an important, but lesser, source of revenue. After the 1930's a rapid expansion occurred in social security taxes and other employment-related "contributions" that are, in turn, dedicated to financing specific social insurance benefits.

In the fiscal year 1972 the federal government received about $86 billion, or 43 percent of its total revenue of $198 billion, from the progressive personal income tax. Another $30 billion, or 15 percent, came from the corporate income tax. Social insurance taxes and contributions accounted for $54 billion, or 28 percent. Excise, estate, and gift taxes; customs duties; and miscellaneous receipts produced a total of $28 billion, or 14 percent.

State governments, in contrast, have generally depended most heavily on sales taxes, although most have adopted personal and/or corporate income taxes as sources of supplementary revenue. Through grants-in-aid, the federal government has financed major shares of state expenditures for highways and public assistance.

Cities, counties, and other local governments raise the bulk of their income from the traditional taxes on property values. The larger cities, particularly, have levied payroll taxes in an effort to obtain revenue from commuters, who work in the central city but live in adjacent suburbs. State and federal governments have financed rising proportions of education and other local activities, in response to the slow growth in the yield of fixed-rate property taxation.

Overall, revenues raised by state and local governments rose from $18.8 billion in 1951 to $114.8 billion in 1971. These funds were supplemented by $2.3 billion of federal grants in 1951 and $26.9 billion in 1971.

— MURRAY L. WEIDENBAUM

REVOLUTION, AMERICAN

A special place in the national consciousness is reserved for the American Revolution. Its "sanctifying power" arises from the virtual unanimity with which all shades of American political opinion, from Left to Right, regard it as the seedbed of the subsequent development of the nation. Unlike other wars in American history, the Revolution was not followed by a lengthy period of recrimination and self-doubt by participants, nor did it become the object of revisionism by historians seeking to explain away the country's participation or criticizing the leadership that precipitated it. The Loyalist critics of the event had virtually no audience either in America or in Great Britain for a century thereafter. The lost cause of the Loyalists aroused none of the sentimental affection that southerners managed to excite for their cause after the Civil War. Despite such unanimity there is considerable disagreement among historians about the causes, nature, and consequences of the Revolution. Some aspects of the event remain undisputed: it changed the colonies into independent states, replaced monarchy with republicanism, and welded thirteen separate polities into a union based on the unique principle of divided sovereignty—that is, federalism. While an American nationalism did not precede the rupture with England, the end of the war saw the emergence of characteristics uniquely American: a sense of optimism arising from the relative ease with which the war was won; a belief in the superiority of "militia" soldiers and amateur diplomats over professionals; a rejection of Europe as the home of monarchies, war, and political corruption; and a commitment, however inchoate in the revolutionary era, to the principle that good government is republican government, without the privileges and inequalities of the European order.

The view that the new American nation personified a novel social and political ethic and was not merely a transplanted fragment of the Old World was expressed by contemporaries on both sides of the Atlantic. Thomas Paine, the propagandist of independence, was convinced that by 1783 Americans had become so transformed by the Revolution that their very "style and manner of thinking" were different; and a French observer, Brissot de Warville, was astounded to find how deeply the new Americans believed that "all men are born free and equal." In the 20th century, historians have come to perceive in the American Revolution the first of a whole wave of such phenomena in the Western world, an age of democratic revolutions, expressive of the near-universal aspiration for popular government and of the principle that public power must arise from those over whom it is exercised. In short, then, the American Revolution was more than a colonial revolt against a mother country: it was the beginning of the assault on the ideas and institutions of the "old regime," both in the New World and in the Old World; and its course has not yet been run. Critics on the American Left in the 20th century cavil largely over the incompleteness of the Revolution, the missed opportunities during that upheaval for improving the lot of women, blacks, servants, and children and for restructuring the social, as well as the political, order. Whatever the angle of vision, however, the American Revolution is understood as a momentous event for the history of the world as well as for the future United States.

Background

Years afterward John Adams declared that the Revolution was not synonymous with the War for Independence—that the latter began at Lexington and Concord, but the former occurred long before "in the minds and hearts of the people." The real revolution was the radical change in the colonists' principles and opinions, and this could be traced back to "the history of the country from the first plantation in America." The statement is both true and untrue. The preconditions for the separation from the mother country were surely rooted in the colonial past, but their existence in no way foretold the inevitability of the rupture of the British Empire. Two months after the Battle of Concord, Thomas Jefferson affirmed his cordial affection for continued union with Britain, a view restated officially by the Continental Congress in its Declaration of Causes of Taking up Arms (July 6, 1775): "We mean not to dissolve that union which has so long and so happily subsisted between us. . . . We have not raised armies with ambitious designs of separating from Great Britain." And yet the Revolution arose from a set of conditions that made many, perhaps most, Americans receptive to the idea of independence by 1776. These conditions, of long-standing development, included (1) a system of imperial regulation that subordinated the colonial polity to the administrative direction of officials in London; (2) a web of economic controls, generally

Years afterward, John Adams said that the War for Independence began at Lexington and Concord, but the Revolution occurred long before, "in the minds and hearts of the people."

designated as the mercantile system, that restricted colonial trade, manufacturing, and fiscal policy by parliamentary legislation; (3) the laxity of enforcement of both the political and the economic controls, permitting the colonies to develop, in effect, a wide degree of autonomy in the years before 1763; (4) the conceptualization in the American mind during the years of "salutary neglect" of the rights to self-government as arising not from royal favor but from the intrinsic character of the British constitution and from those natural laws that the European Enlightenment professed to be the normative feature of the political world in the same sense that Newtonian mechanics determined the shape of the physical universe; (5) the series of British measures, beginning in the mid-18th century, designed to tighten the bonds between colonies and mother country and to reassert the primacy of imperial over colonial interests; and (6) the colonial response to these "triggers of rebellion," which assumed the character not merely of specific reactions to British measures but of an American world view that saw in the combination of imperial regulations a generalized threat to the liberties of the colonists and a conspiracy to reduce them to political vassalage.

English Mercantilism

Historians writing in the century following independence were wont to attribute primary responsibility for the Revolution to the British mercantile system. Thus, the 19th-century historian George Bancroft solemnly asserted that although there were many sources of the torrent that became the Revolution, "the headspring which colored all the stream was the Navigation Act." Bancroft was referring to the cluster of regulatory acts passed by Parliament between 1660 and 1696 and generally designated as the Acts of Trade and Navigation. Originally intended to bar the Dutch from the imperial carrying trade, the laws came to constitute a comprehensive pattern of regulation of Anglo-American commerce. They confined trade between America and England to ships that were manufactured and manned by Englishmen (or Americans); enumerated a variety of American natural products that must be shipped to or through English ports; required goods of European or Asian origin to be imported into the colonies via England; and levied high duties on non-English sugar and molasses imported into the colonies (the latter by an act of 1733). To prevent colonial exporters from evading English duties by first shipping their products to other colonial ports, these taxes were collected at the port of shipment. Complementing the commercial regulations were laws limiting colonial manufacturing and export of woolens (1699), hats (1732), sailcloth (1736), and finished iron (1750); and a series of acts prohibiting the minting of colonial coins, the establishment of banks, and the issue of paper money except under the most extraordinary (usually wartime) circumstances.

Superficially these laws appeared to place the colonies in an economic straitjacket, compelling them to concentrate their labors on the production of raw materials needed in England and making them dependent on the mother country for their finished products. As in most colonial economies the consequence was to create heavy and increasing trade deficits in the colonies and an imbalance of payments in Britain's favor. In the absence of accurate and complete statistics, the extent of this imbalance can only be estimated. It was greatest in New England and the Middle Colonies, which raised few products for export to Great Britain, and smallest in the southern colonies, which could use their exports of tobacco, rice, indigo, and naval stores to pay for their British imports. Overall the colonial trade deficit with England ranged from £67,000 annually during the decade 1721–30 to almost £900,000 annually during the years 1751–60. There is little evidence, however, that these deficits were major causes of colonial complaint. Further, they were offset by colonial profits earned in trade with southern Europe and the West Indies, funds brought to America by immigrants, and expenditures by the British government for the defense and administration of the colonies. The view of some modern economic historians is that no actual deficits were incurred by the colonies throughout the 18th century and that the benefits of membership in the British Empire (protection of the British navy, favorable insurance and shipping rates, bounties, and preferential tariffs) offset the costs to such a degree that the net burden imposed on the colonists by the Navigation Acts was no more than

25 cents per capita annually, or between 1 and 2 percent of national income.

The restrictive character of the regulations on manufacturing and currency may have been exaggerated as well. It is unlikely that a large-scale woolen industry would have developed in America in any case, given the superiority of British woolens; the hat industry expanded despite British restrictions; and some colonial industries actually profited from British regulatory legislation. There were more forges and furnaces in America than in England and Wales, and by 1775 one-seventh of the world's iron was being produced in British North America. American shipyards contributed one-third of all the vessels in the empire trade, and three-quarters of the ships in the colonial carrying trade were American. British legislation did not prevent the development of active distilling, glass, stoneware, milling, and meat-packing industries in the colonies or of the profitable fur business. Despite British currency restrictions, the colonies appear to have acquired enough specie from their international trade and enough paper money from periodic local emissions to meet their needs; in the Middle Colonies, particularly, the paper money was neither largely inflated nor badly managed. The observations of European travelers about the well-being of Americans, the rise of colonial fortunes, the high rate of wages, and the relatively high economic growth rate all attest to the general prosperity of colonial America as adequately as a statistical estimate that, in 1967 dollars, the per capita physical wealth of the free population in 1774 (excluding cash, servants, and slaves) was $1,086, making colonial Americans better off than most Europeans at the time and as well off as 19th-century Americans. Clearly, the American Revolution was not the product of economic privation.

On the other hand, neither the benefits nor the burdens of English mercantilism were evenly distributed within the colonies, nor can statistical evidence document the frustrations, irritations, and personal hardships created by British economic restrictions. It is impossible to calculate how much more colonial energy and capital would have been invested in manufacturing had obstructive legislation not acted as a deterrent. Surely the price of imports was raised by the inability of Americans to purchase under competitive conditions from other than English sources, and the price of exports was correspondingly depressed by being confined to English outlets. The merchants of New England and the Middle Colonies were often able to meet their trade balances with Great Britain only by illicit trade with the West Indies, and smuggling everywhere eased somewhat the burdens of lawful observance of the Navigation Acts. Southern planters traded so exclusively with the mother country and were so dependent on its credits that they found themselves saddled, by 1776, with a huge debt, prompting Jefferson to quip wryly that Virginians were "a species of property annexed to certain mercantile houses in London." The condition reflected the extravagance of the Virginia aristocrats and the limitations of a one-crop economy as much as involuntary participation in the British mercantile system. Perhaps the most important explanation for the ability of Americans to prosper within British mercantilism was the failure of the mother country before 1763 to make the system fully operative and of the colonies to observe all its strictures.

Old Colonial System

Britain's colonies in North America were not settled according to any comprehensive plan, and during most of the 17th century they received little direction from the imperial government. Although the crown after 1625 asserted its jurisdiction over all the colonies, it developed no overall administration for them. In 1675 a committee of the Privy Council, designated the Lords of Trade, was given general responsibility for the political and economic direction of the colonies, but during its ten-year life it failed to construct a system for ensuring colonial subordination to royal authority. In 1696 a new body, the Board of Trade, was established to handle colonial affairs. Although having an advisory function only, its eight permanent members became the crown's and Parliament's experts on colonial matters, reviewing all colonial legislation, writing instructions for colonial governors, hearing complaints from colonial assemblies and royal officials, and recommending appropriate action to the king and Parliament. Not until 1768 was a secretary of state for American affairs created as a separate cabinet post. Above the Board of Trade sat the Privy Council, which disallowed colonial laws, heard appeals from colonial courts, and appointed colonial governors and approved their instructions.

A host of other officials assisted in administering the empire: the bishop of London, with ecclesiastical jurisdiction over the colonies; the treasury and the customs board, with responsibility for the collection of duties and revenues; and the Admiralty and the War Office, supervising the army and navy in America. But the linchpin of empire was the royal governor, who sat in all the colonies except Connecticut and Rhode Island, where by charter right the governor was elected. With wide powers to appoint local officials, to grant land, to hand down pardons, to hear lawsuits on appeal, to command the militia, to veto legislation, and to convene and dismiss the provincial assembly, the governor possessed in theory all the majesty of the crown itself within the colony over which he held sway as "captain general and governor in chief."

But practice did not comport with theory, and in the divergence between the two lay both the strength and the weakness of the imperial system. In America the governor's extensive prerogatives were effectively weakened by the rising power of the assemblies, controlled by local elites, who by 1776 dominated the political, social, and economic life of their colonies. Using as levers their power to levy taxes and to disburse funds, the assemblies wrested a variety of other powers from the chief executive simply by threatening to withhold the grant of his annual salary unless he complied with their legislative wishes. Without permanent salaries guaranteed from England, governors became complaisant, even if this meant a rebuke from the authorities in London. By 1776 the assemblies not only possessed fiscal power but, through it, controlled the appointment of local officials whose salaries they determined. In addition, they largely set the qualifications for membership in the house, established franchise requirements, and denied the governor's council the right to amend money bills—and they claimed such rights by virtue of the status of each as a miniature House of Commons.

Governors were generally unequal to the contest with the assemblies. Largely English-born, serving short terms in their colonial posts, they never acquired enough familiarity with local politics to learn to manage the assembly or to build political machines of their own. The patronage powers through which they might have created countervailing forces were undermined by the absence of an independent gubernatorial purse and by the failure of the home authorities to honor gubernatorial nominations. As early as 1670 one chief executive complained that the assembly's fiscal powers had "left his Majesty but a small share of the Sovereignty." A strong governor was likely to arouse complaints to London from the colonists about his "uneasy administration." A compliant governor would be admonished by the Board of Trade for his weakness. The problem, as described by Gov. Jonathan Belcher of Massachusetts, was to "steer between Scylla and Charybdis; to please the king's ministers at home, and a touchy people here." Only the most extraordinary of chief executives was capable of resolving the dilemma, and the men sent to administer the American colonies were far from extraordinary. They may not have been the "decayed courtiers and abandoned, worn-out dependents" that one colonist complained of, but even friends of the crown, such as New York merchant John Watts, were convinced that "better men must be sent from home to fill offices or all will end in anarchy."

The shortcomings of imperial administration in the colonies were paralleled by weaknesses in the machinery of government in London. The Board of Trade possessed only recommendatory powers; it shared responsibility for the colonies with too many other official agencies. The most important single office in colonial administration before 1768 was that of secretary of state for the Southern Department—and the post was held by no fewer than twenty-three men between 1696 and 1768. The damage created by such instability was acute. Colonial problems received only short-term attention in London, while the colonial governors, who might have provided the needed strength and stability for imperial administration, had their authority undermined by inadequate support in England and by the challenge of powerful assemblies in America. In cases of conflict between provincial assemblies and royal governors, the inclination of British officials was to concede to the American legislatures, especially during wartime, when the colonies were relied on as reservoirs of men and money. The objective, in the words of the Board of Trade, was to make government in the colonies "as easy and mild as possible."

Even friends of the crown, such as New York merchant John Watts, were convinced that "better men must be sent from home to fill [governors'] offices or all will end in anarchy."

The relationship between colonies and mother country by 1763 has been described as an "uneasy connection." The colonies had achieved a wide measure of political competence. They had their own political institutions, controlled by the local elites who governed with the support and even the participation of a relatively broadly based constituency. The economic prosperity of the colonies added to their sense of self-importance. That this *de facto* autonomy existed within a theoretical framework that held the colonies to be inferior polities within the empire troubled Americans not at all so long as no real effort was made by Britain to have practice conform to theory. When after 1763 Great Britain undertook to do just that, the crisis was precipitated.

Crisis of Empire

The old British Empire was set on the road to disruption when authorities in London decided to end the policy of accommodation, or salutary neglect, that had characterized colonial administration throughout much of the 18th century and to bring the American provinces under stricter control. The need for a less "slovenly and chaotic" system of governance was evident in the late 1740's, as governors deluged the Board of Trade with complaints about the intractability of their assemblies and the perpetual encroachments of local legislatures on the royal prerogative. One consequence was the establishment of a regular packet service in 1755 between England and America to speed up the process of decisionmaking. Another was instructions to all governors to enforce the Navigation Acts rigorously, to secure permanent salaries for royal officials, and to disapprove any fiscal legislation that permitted the assemblies to spend money without the order of the governor. The outbreak of the French and Indian War (or the Great War for Empire) in 1754 temporarily halted the campaign to reduce the autonomy of the colonies, but the war itself emphasized the need for the effort.

The cost of the conflict with France doubled the British national debt and added £8 million to the British annual budget. For this expenditure on their behalf, the American colonies appeared to show little gratitude. Colonial manpower contributed minimally to the military effort; colonial assemblies had only grudgingly met their financial obligations to support the troops engaged in their own defense; and, worse, colonial merchants engaged in illicit private trade with the enemy in the midst of the armed contest. The acquisition from France and Spain of the tramontane West, Canada, and Florida enlarged the task of imperial government considerably. The new territories had to be administered; the Indian tribes that had aided Britain during the war had to be assured against spoliation of their hunting grounds by covetous settlers; a permanent army of regulars had to be stationed in the American colonies for their defense and for keeping the peace with the Indians. As a matter of equity no less than of financial necessity, the colonies were to be required to share the new burdens of empire. More, the weak links in the commercial connection between Britain and the colonies had to be strengthened. A system of customs collection that required an outlay of from £7,000 to £8,000 a year to produce a return of under £2,000 appeared ridiculous to British officials. In a comprehensive report to the Privy Council in October 1763, the Board of Trade warned that the proper regulation of colonial commerce was "of immediate Necessity, lest the continuance and extent of the dangerous Evils . . . render all Attempts to remedy them hereafter more difficult, if not impracticable."

Under the leadership of George Grenville and Charles Townshend the British ministry took steps between 1763 and 1767 to ward off the threatened evils. A royal proclamation in 1763 placed a temporary limit on further western settlement and established stricter regulations for carrying on the fur trade in Indian territory. Customs collectors formerly living at ease in Britain while deputies in America did their work were ordered to their colonial posts. An American board of customs commissioners was established at Boston, and a new system of vice-admiralty courts was created to try offenses under the Acts of Trade—in juryless courts. The Quartering Act (1765) required the colonies to defray the cost of housing a 10,000-man standing American army. The Currency Act (1764) strictly enjoined the colonial assemblies from emitting any further paper money as legal tender. And to defray at least half the cost of the new American military establishment and to provide funds for a permanent civil list in the colonies, a whole range of new taxes and duties was mandated: a tax on newspapers and legal and commercial documents (Stamp Act, 1765); lower but strictly enforced duties on the importation of foreign molasses (Revenue Act, 1764); and new duties on imported lead, glass, paint, paper, and tea (Townshend Acts, 1767).

However defensible and propitious from the British point of view, the efforts at tightening the reins of imperial administration could scarcely have come at a less opportune time in America. Flushed with the victory over the French, the colonists saw themselves as the saviors of the British Empire in America. The removal of the enemy in Canada decreased their military dependence on England, and their heightened sense of independence and self-confidence led them to expect a more important, not less important, role in the empire. Colonial assemblies, already in the ascendancy before the war began, increased their powers during the conflict as they successfully appealed over the heads of the governors to William Pitt as war minister; and the governors had many of their own powers usurped by the British army and navy commanders in America. Finally, the economic climate was insalubrious for new British taxes, for the artificial prosperity of wartime was followed by a recession, reflected in a shortage of specie, declining land values, and the end of the French West Indian trade.

The introduction into this volatile situation of a range of unaccustomed impositions appearing to alter the traditional relationship between the colonies and England produced almost predictable results. The new imperial program was denounced not only as unjust and burdensome but also as unconstitutional; and the heart of the American objection in the long run was that whatever the logic or necessity of the program, it lacked the essential element of colonial consent. For Americans, whose conception of empire had become that of a greater England in which the colonies functioned as partners rather than as subordinates, the Grenville-Townshend measures bore the marks of insult and illegitimacy.

The colonists may well have been able to afford the new taxes. The rum industry probably would not have been ruined by the higher duties on French sugar and the more strictly enforced duties on French molasses. The Stamp Act would not have drained the colonies of specie: the monies collected would have been spent in America to support the British military establishment there. The new customs duties would have been passed on by importers to American consumers, whose tax burden was some fifty times less than that of English taxpayers. But whatever the economic basis of their dissent, the Americans framed their protests during the next decade in the context of their "ancient, legal, and constitutional rights" not to be taxed without their own consent. "The question is not of the expediency of the Stamp Act," the British commander in Boston, Gen. Thomas Gage, informed the secretary of state, "or of the inability of the colonists to pay the tax; but that it is unconstitutional, and contrary to their rights." When the British denied the charge on the grounds that the colonists were "virtually" represented in Parliament, as were all other Englishmen, whether they participated directly in the election of representatives or not, Americans responded that the interests of the colonists could never be adequately represented in a body 3,000 miles away. When one American publicist, Daniel Dulany, objected to the stamp tax as a novel "internal tax" intended for revenue purposes exclusively, Parliament countered with "external" duties designed to regulate trade. The New York Assembly thereupon responded for the colonies that "all impositions, whether they be internal taxes, or duties paid for what we consume, equally diminish the estates upon which they are charged"; and John Dickinson, in his enormously influential *Letters From a Farmer in Pennsylvania to the Inhabitants of the British Colonies* (1767–68), enlarged the grounds of colonial opposition by insisting that any "Act of Parliament commanding us to do a certain thing . . . is a tax upon us for the expence that accrues in complying with it."

As they argued their case, the colonists came to formulate a well-rounded constitutional theory representing an American consensus: The British constitution fixed the powers of Parliament and protected the liberties of the citizen; such a constitution could not be changed by the stroke of a pen; the powers of Parliament were limited; and those powers were specifically limited with regard to the American colonies by their immutable right to legislate for themselves in matters of internal concern. No objection was raised to Parliament's exercise of broad general authority in imperial affairs, but the demand was made that the line between imperial and American concerns be clearly defined and scrupulously observed. Just as a delicate and proper balance existed between the elements of the British government—king, lords, and commons—so the division needed to be observed in the colonies between the prerogative power of the crown and the lawful rights of the provincial assemblies. When Britain taxed the colonies, authorized searches of private homes without specific warrant through writs of assistance, tried Americans in juryless courts, and placed American judges at the mercy of the executive by appointments "at the pleasure of the Crown" rather than "during good behavior," it denied Americans rights that Englishmen at home possessed. If Americans were indeed entitled to the "rights of Englishmen," then such rights implied equality of treatment for Britons wherever they resided. By stressing the constitutionality of their own position, American leaders sought to legitimize their cause and to place Britain on the defensive. As Richard Dana put the matter on the occasion of the Revolution's first centennial, "We were not the revolutionists. The King and Parliament were . . . the radical innovators. We were the conservators of existing institutions."

The heavy emphasis that Americans placed on constitutional forms of protest bespoke the essential conservatism of the colonial leadership—lawyers, merchants, and planters. But the protesters were not unwilling to employ more forcible means of expression to achieve their ends. These other "necessary ingredients" in the American opposition were economic coercion by the boycott of British imports, a technique used against both the Stamp Act and the Townshend Acts; mob violence, such as the intimidation of stamp distributors, the public humiliation of customs informers, street rioting, and effigy burning; and outright defiance of the law, including the refusal to do business with stamped documents, the publication of newspapers on unstamped paper, and the refusal of the New York Assembly to vote the funds required for troop support under the Quartering Act. That the violence was more tempered in America than in Europe's popular disturbances is explained not only by the reluctance of the American leadership to resort to force except under the most disciplined controls but also by the absence of the kind of official constabulary that might have interposed counterforce and thus produced heightened violence. To conservatives there was obvious danger in enlisting the mob, both because of the ease with which violence could be shifted from imperial to local objects of hostility and because of the opening that would be provided for the politically inarticulate to become part of the body politic.

The Americans' emphasis on constitutional forms of protest showed the essential conservatism of the colonial leadership—lawyers, merchants, and planters.

The furious American protests engendered by the Grenville-Townshend program took British officialdom by surprise. All the new imperial measures had been approved by large parliamentary majorities, and little attention had been given to the consequences. Horace Walpole's classic statement about the passage of the Stamp Act stands as testimony to the state of British insouciance: "Nothing of note in Parliament but one slight day on American taxes." In the face of the colonial onslaught, Parliament retreated: it repealed the Stamp Act in 1766 and the Townshend Acts in 1770; and it modified the Proclamation of 1763 so as to permit gradual movement of settlers and fur traders to the West. The retreat was prompted by the damage done to British economic interests by the colonial boycotts. British exports dropped 20 to 40 percent during the protest movements of 1765–66 and 1767–70; the Townshend duties were estimated to have produced £3,500 in revenue at a cost to British business of £7.25 million. On the issue of its right to tax the colonies, Parliament did not retreat at all. In the Declaratory Act (1766), which accompanied the repeal of the stamp duties, it asserted unequivocally its power "to make laws and statutes . . . to bind the colonies and people of America . . . in all cases whatsoever"; and when it repealed the Townshend duties, it retained a tax on tea to reaffirm that power.

Between 1770 and 1773, incidents in the colonies maintained and even escalated the mutual suspicions already generated between representatives of British authority and spokesmen of the colonial position: a clash between some of New York City's citizens and British soldiers over the destruction of a liberty pole on Jan. 19, 1770 (the Battle of Golden Hill); the encounter between Bostonians and English soldiers on Mar. 5, 1770, resulting in the death of five Americans (the Boston Massacre); the destruction of a British customs schooner, the *Gaspée*, by the irate citizens of Rhode Island on June 9, 1772; and a protracted controversy that continued throughout these years between the South Carolina Assembly and the governor over the legislature's right to disburse funds without the approval of the chief executive or his council (the Wilkes Fund controversy). In Massachusetts such radicals as Samuel Adams used each anniversary of the Boston Massacre to remind Bostonians of the need for eternal vigilance to prevent the utter extinction of American liberties by British armies. In all the northern colonies the period witnessed a wave of fear on the part of dissenting religious sects over the proposal initiated by some Anglican clergymen, notably Samuel Seabury and Thomas Bradbury Chandler, to strengthen the Church of England in the colonies by appointing a resident bishop. Overly suspicious colonists saw in the proposal a move to enlarge the encroachments of British temporal power by adding to it ecclesiastical suzerainty.

Underneath all the specific irritants in the Anglo-American relationship was the overriding constitutional-legal question of how the claims of two contending centers of political power could be reconciled. Disclaiming independence, the colonists came to conceive of the empire as a divided sovereignty, part being exercised by the English Parliament and part inhering in the respective colonial assemblies. To English Whigs, whose Glorious Revolution had in 1688 wrested independent powers from the crown and vested them in the "King *in* Parliament," it seemed that any diminution of parliamentary sovereignty would only enhance that of the crown. The idea of a commonwealth of autonomous sovereignties seemed chimerical: either Parliament had all power to govern the colonies or none at all. Americans gradually came to prefer the second alternative. Their reluctant acceptance of the idea of separation from the British Empire was given emotional support by the conviction that Britain had lost its ancient virtue, corrupted its constitution, and abandoned the liberties of its citizens. America must not go the way of Britain. The example of classical antiquity was cited as proof of the ease with which republics could become captured by despots when a free people failed to resist encroachments on their liberties by power-hungry officials. The writings of English radical thinkers of the early 18th century, particularly Thomas Gordon and John Trenchard, provided evidence of the dangers to liberty even in Whig England, in the form of standing armies, patronage-ridden parliaments, corrupt ministers, controlled elections, and grasping priests and bishops. The republication of these writings—*Cato's Letters* and the *Independent Whig*—in American newspapers and pamphlets revealed the readiness of the colonists to accept the reality of such danger and, at the same time, heightened their fears of its imminence. The spirit of Puritanism was summoned up to warn Americans of the threat to their souls if they failed to purge themselves of the evil of political, as well as moral, corruption. And John Locke's familiar compact theory of government provided theoretical justification for the last resort of a free people whose liberties were infringed by an arbitrary government: dissolution of the original compact.

For such modern historians as Bernard Bailyn, the emergence of this American ideology—integrating constitutional theory, legal abstractions, political grievances, and economic and social discontent into a comprehensive set of values, beliefs, and attitudes—explains the outbreak of the Revolution and makes understandable its character and consequences. America's response to British measures, in this view, was less the result of economic despair, social unrest, or religious oppression than of fear that traditional colonial liberties were being deliberately destroyed by acts of British power. The mood evoked by these fears was not merely a defensive adherence to a cherished past when American liberties were secure, but a buoyantly optimistic vision of the future; for the obligation now imposed on Americans was not merely to preserve their own virtue and freedom but also to "rouse the dormant spirit of liberty in England"—that it was a "great and glorious cause." Colonial leaders felt that the eyes of all Europe were upon them: "If we fail, Liberty no longer continues an inhabitant of this Globe," James Allen, a Philadelphian, confided to his diary on July 26, 1775. And Paine gave the idea consummate expression in *Common Sense*: "Every spot of the old world is over-run with oppression. Freedom hath been hunted round the Globe. . . . O! receive the fugitive and prepare an asylum for mankind."

By 1776, Americans possessed the machinery for revolution as well as the ideology. At the local level, militants had organized groups called Sons of Liberty to carry on the agitation against the Stamp Act. While the Sons engaged in intercolonial correspondence with each other, no real union was effected. A more serious instrumentality of intercolonial action was the system of committees of correspondence initiated by the Virginia legislature in 1773. Other colonial assemblies took up the idea, and a network of official legislative committees was soon in existence to concert uniform efforts against British measures. In 1773 Great Britain unwittingly put the system to the test by the enactment of the Tea Act, a blunder of the most momentous consequence. The act aimed to save the East India Company from bankruptcy by permitting it to sell its large tea surpluses directly in America, without payment of the usual British reexport duties. The measure threatened to undercut the business not only of colonial smugglers but also of lawful merchants who usually acted as consignees of the company's tea. Tea "parties" in a number of colonies destroyed the company's product before it could be distributed. The most famous act of destruction was the dumping of 90,000 pounds of tea in Boston harbor on Dec. 16, 1773. When Parliament in 1774 punished Massachusetts by a series of acts—the so-called Intolerable Acts—that included the suspension of the province's charter of government and the closing of the port of Boston, the intercolonial apparatus of committees of correspondence went into action. Relief supplies were sent from everywhere to the beleaguered city, and a congress of the colonies convened in Philadelphia on Sept. 5, 1774.

By passing the Tea Act of 1773, Britain unwittingly committed a blunder of the most momentous consequence.

"No one circumstance could have taken place more effectively to unite the colonies than this manoeuvre of the tea," John Hancock noted. The issue debated in Philadelphia at the Continental Congress was not the East India Company's monopoly, or even the tea tax, but the larger issue of the rights of the colonies and their constitutional relationship with Great Britain. The Declaration of Colonial Rights and Grievances reaffirmed the colonists' right to "a free and exclusive power of legislation in their several provincial legislatures"; a conservative proposal of reconciliation by Joseph Galloway of Pennsylvania, hinging on an American parliament as an "inferior and distinct branch of the British legislature," was rejected; and a comprehensive nonimportation, nonexportation, and nonconsumption agreement was adopted. By the meeting of the Second Continental Congress on May 10, 1775, hostilities had already commenced. Blood had been shed at Lexington and Concord on Apr. 19, and in all the colonies militia units were being organized and armed. With the appointment on June 15 of George Washington to command an American army, the colonies were ready for civil war. The Revolution had begun, but its objectives were not yet clearly defined.

Conciliation or Independence

Americans of all shades of political opinion in 1775 were prepared to fight for their rights, but not all favored a separation from Britain. Only a minority of the Second Continental Congress agreed with John Adams that "the cancer is too deeply rooted and too far spread to be cured by anything short of cutting it out entire." Congress was controlled by moderates, sentimentally attached to the empire, admiring of its institutions, and deeply respectful of the virtues of the British constitution. They feared the consequences of a total rupture: the danger to their persons and property as rebels should their challenge to authority fail, and the equal danger that success would bring social upheaval and mob rule. Could an independent America, shorn of British protection, prevent a foreign invasion? The mood of the moderates was perhaps best expressed by Thomas Jefferson's cautionary note in the later Declaration of Independence: "All experience hath shewn, that mankind are more disposed to suffer, while evils are sufferable, than to right themselves by abolishing the forms to which they are accustomed."

Many conservatives clung to the hope that friends of America in Great Britain would bring about a change in the ministry and thereby end colonial grievances. These hopes were shattered by the failure of every plan of accommodation that emanated from Britain before 1776. A proposal by William Pitt the Younger that Parliament renounce taxation of the colonies in return for American acceptance of parliamentary sovereignty was overwhelmingly beaten in the House of Lords. A conciliatory resolution sponsored by the prime minister, Frederick North, known by courtesy as Lord North, to forbear taxing any colony that made adequate voluntary contributions for the support of the empire was rejected by the Continental Congress as unduly vague. A scheme offered by a Scottish nobleman, Thomas Lundin, the titular Lord Drummond, going further than North's plan in promising a "formal Relinquishment" of all future parliamentary claims to colonial taxes and a permanent imperial constitution, failed when Drummond could not produce an official stamp of approval.

Colonial militants were content to allow the force of events to dash the hopes of the conciliationists, and Britain contributed effectively to this end. The king rejected the so-called Olive Branch Petition of the Continental Congress in August 1775 and declared the colonies to be in open rebellion. A few months later a royal proclamation interdicted all trade with the colonies. Sentiment for independence was increasingly aired in the press and was given its clearest expression in Paine's pamphlet *Common Sense*, which appeared in January 1776. Its sale was extraordinary and its impact enormous. In their extralegal associations, Americans had already come to accept the republican idea that all power stemmed from the people. Paine articulated the idea in more uncompromising language: Monarchy was an "exceedingly ridiculous" invention of the devil; the king of Great Britain was a "royal brute"; America gained nothing by its connection with Britain; the tie was a liability, involving America in Europe's wars; and it was time to part. Less logical than emotional, Paine's pamphlet summed up in fervid language all the deep-seated fears and hopes that had been latent in the American mind for a half-century: colonial resentment of inferior status; the New World's rejection of the Old World; the child's demand for recognition as an adult; and America's optimism that it represented the opportunity of creating a political Zion for all mankind in the New World, just as the Puritans had sought to build in Massachusetts a model for wayward England. Paine reassured Americans that they need not fear the separation from Englishmen abroad: they were indeed a different people, not Britons transplanted but new men in a new world. A few years later the Frenchman M. G. J. de Crèvecoeur, who became a naturalized American, summed up the sentiment in *Letters From an American Farmer* (1782): "He is an American, who leaving behind him all his ancient prejudices and manners, receives new ones from the new mode of life he has embraced, the new government he obeys, and the new rank he holds. . . . Here individuals of all nations are melted into a new race of men."

Declaration of Independence

On June 7, 1776, Richard Henry Lee of Virginia introduced into Congress a resolution declaring the colonies "free and independent states." On July 2, it was adopted. The negative phase of the Revolution was thus ended. Americans gave up the hope of restoring the past and of reconstituting their former relationship with Britain. In the Declaration of Independence, adopted on July 4, they voiced their aspirations for the future as well as their rejection of the past. The Declaration's lengthy indictment of George III and its detailed enumeration of colonial grievances were history; the almost incidental preamble, expounding the principles of equality and popular government, was prophecy. It is unlikely that the conservative signers of the document fully recognized its revolutionary implications. Fifty years later Americans came to appreciate how quintessentially it expressed the primal truths of democratic government; a hundred years later President Abraham Lincoln recognized how perfectly the principles of the declaration served as a "standard maxim" for all free societies, "familiar to all, and revered by all; constantly looked to . . . and augmenting the happiness and value of life to all people of all colors everywhere." The invocation of the declaration by South Americans and Hungarians in the 19th century and by black militants in the United States and emerging nations of Asia and

Africa in the 20th century attests the validity of Carl Becker's observation that the philosophy of human rights imbedded in Jefferson's preamble is applicable "if at all, not for Americans only, but for all men." Thus, what was intended as a timely public vindication of the revolt of a single people became a timeless universal political testament.

Loyalists

A substantial minority of Americans declined to opt for independence, and for their refusal they suffered historical neglect for almost two centuries. To the patriots, the Loyalists were traitors to the American cause. Those Loyalists who adhered to their position even after the war ended fled to other parts of the empire, where their voices were not heard by the citizens of the new United States. Other Loyalists remained quietly in their former homes, not daring to call attention to their earlier stand. For republican America the Loyalists were the un-Americans, and they passed from the collective memory.

Estimates of their number vary. Loyalists themselves assured the British government at the outset of the conflict that the majority of colonists were loyal to the mother country. John Adams, some forty years after the event, noted that one-third of the colonial population opposed the Revolution. Both figures are undoubtedly high. More recent estimates suggest that between 15 and 30 percent of the population was loyal to Britain. From 15,000 to 30,000 served in British regular or militia units during the war, and about 60,000 to 100,000 went into exile after the Revolution ended. Some 5,000 eventually made claims to the British government for losses incurred by their loyalty to the crown. Geographically the centers of Loyalist strength were those areas occupied by British troops, either because it was unhealthy to be a rebel in those places or because Loyalists gravitated to garrison towns for protection. New York, Georgia, South Carolina, and North Carolina produced the largest number of Loyalists; Virginia, Maryland, and Delaware, probably the fewest.

Early patriot historians tended to denigrate the Loyalists by characterizing them as the old, the cowardly, the rich and wellborn, and the political reactionaries, but later research has discounted all such categorization. Loyalists came from every segment of the population and from all social and occupational groups and represented every shade of political opinion. Most were probably small farmers, as were most Americans at the time. Obviously, most high officeholders under the crown remained loyal, as did most Anglican ministers in the northern colonies; for the latter, the king was head of the Church of England and was thereby owed spiritual as well as temporal obedience. Yet in the South, most Anglican ministers joined the patriot ranks. Wealthy merchants and landowners, fearful of social instability and the political democracy of republican government, elected to remain with monarchical Britain; but Charles Carroll of Maryland, reputedly the wealthiest man in the colonies, became a rebel. So did many other prominent merchants and landholders. One historian has suggested that loyalism enlisted the support of cultural minorities, such as the Quakers and Highland Scots, because they felt threatened by the drive to cultural uniformity that might be expected of an independent United States; they felt more secure under British rule. Another historian views loyalism as essentially a matter of temperament and disposition, engaging men of timid character who feared the dangers ahead more than the disabilities of the present. Still another has mustered evidence that loyalism was the choice of older elites and established families, patriots comprising the rising and ambitious political and social leadership.

It is unlikely that the friends of Britain deserved the appellation "Tory," with which they were often branded. Their political beliefs, like those of the patriots, were largely Whig. They objected to parliamentary taxation, defended the right of the colonists to govern themselves, and were as suspicious of corruption in the British ministry as were their rebellious neighbors. They were not absolute monarchists but rather "good Whigs" and devotees of the principles of John Locke. What differentiated them from the patriots was that they did not think British provocations extreme enough or the alleged conspiracy against American liberties imminent enough to warrant political parricide. Their inability to feel the moral indignation of other Americans explains their failure to publicize their case more vigorously in print. Many were sure the crisis of 1774–76 would pass, as had the earlier crises. They saw no need for an intercolonial organization to combat the Sons of Liberty, no need to present a lengthy exposition of the merits of loyalty. The prospective rebels, in their view, were the ones who had to make a case. When the Loyalists realized how well the rebels were succeeding, it was too late for the king's friends to make their own bid for public support.

The ultimate tragedy of the Loyalists is illustrated by the fate of the 7,000 who exiled themselves to Great Britain. They returned "home" because they felt more British than American, but they soon discovered that they were not welcomed by Englishmen and that they were not at home in Britain. Those Loyalists who remained in America during the Revolution suffered harassment, physical assault, incarceration, banishment, and confiscation of property. In some regions, such as New York, the civil war fought between Loyalists and patriots assumed bloody proportions. Yet when the war ended, many Loyalists were permitted to resume their old places in their native states and to become quietly reintegrated into the life of the American republic.

Diplomacy

Although the Declaration of Independence represented America's rejection of the Old World, the Revolution was from its inception pursued in an international context. The revolutionary crisis was itself an outcome of the great war between France and Britain for supremacy of North America. In weighing the decision for independence, European considerations were never far from the minds of the American leadership. Some opposed independence precisely because an America standing alone would be prey to foreign foes; others opposed independence until there was assurance of foreign support for the new republic. Still others urged independence out of fear that Great Britain would partition North America with France and Spain in return for their aid in suppressing the rebellious colonies. One purpose of the Declaration of Independence was to enlist the sympathetic ear of a candid world" and to state the causes of separation in such a way as to ensure the "decent respect" of the "opinions of mankind." Few Americans believed that they could fight a successful war without aid from abroad. Thus, the United States entered nationhood with the same diplomatic ambivalence it was to exhibit thereafter: a desire to be free of the intrigues and politics of Europe, mixed with the conviction that the fate of the New World was indissolubly linked with that of Europe. Testifying to this ambivalence was America's dualistic stand: isolationism in separating from Great Britain, accompanied by involvement in European politics through a binding alliance with Britain's traditional foe, France, as an essential ingredient in the success of that separation.

The revolutionary crisis was itself an outcome of the great war between France and Britain for supremacy in North America.

The alliance with France of 1778 reflected the colonies' desperate need for men, money, arms, and recognition, not any emergent affection for the Bourbon monarchy. France, in turn, found the alliance a useful tool in its long-range diplomatic struggle to reduce the power of Great Britain; it did not have any enthusiasm for colonial uprisings or republican government. France began sending supplies to the colonies secretly even before independence was declared and unofficially from 1776 to 1778. It required the American victory at Saratoga in October 1777 to convince the French that an open and official alliance could be risked. A commercial treaty assured each signatory of "most favored treatment" in its trade with the other; a political compact united the two countries in the war against Britain, each agreeing not to make peace without the consent of the other.

The French liaison was enormously useful to the colonists. French gunpowder made possible the victory at Saratoga, and the presence of the French fleet off the Virginia coast assured the defeat of Gen. Charles Cornwallis at Yorktown in 1781. French monetary aid amounting to $7 million constituted a substantial contribution to the precarious war chest of the American states; French seaports provided refuge for American privateers; and French recognition lifted American morale. On the negative side, the entry of Spain into the war in 1779 as an ally of France confused the objectives of the conflict, for Spain was interested in recapturing Gibraltar from Britain and was assured of French assistance, thus linking the American cause to Spain's European interests. The French alliance proved even more embarrassing to the new United States when it sought in the years after the Revolution to pursue an independent diplomatic course. It was not until 1800 that the vexatious treaties were canceled, during the administration of President John Adams.

That the alliance with France was a mixed blessing was made evident during the peace negotiations with Great Britain. Technically, the American peace commissioners—Benjamin Franklin, John Adams, and John Jay—were barred from undertaking negotiations without the consent of the French ally; but there is ample evidence that French officials were prepared to terminate the war early without American consent and on terms that would have left the British in possession of considerable American territory. The boldness of America's "militia" diplomats in negotiating a treaty and then presenting it as a *fait accompli* to their French ally was rewarded by extraordinarily favorable terms. By the Treaty of Paris of 1783, to which France ultimately acceded, the United States secured recognition, all of the trans-Appalachian West to the Mississippi River, and the liberty of fishing off the Newfoundland banks. In return the United States promised to place no lawful impediments in the way of the collection of private British prewar debts in the United States and to recommend to the states the restoration of confiscated Loyalist property. The concessions were a small price to pay for two crucial gains: independence and a continental domain for thirteen seaboard states.

Home Front

The two major problems confronting the united colonies in the Revolution were manpower and money; and both stemmed from the absence of any effective centralized political authority through which concerted action by all thirteen commonwealths could be achieved. The problem of effective authority was solved only in 1781 by the ratification of the Articles of Confederation, creating "a firm league of friendship." But by then, the war was virtually over. The political instrumentality by which the states acted at the national level throughout the war was the Continental Congress. It functioned without specific constitutional authority and operated on the principle of government by supplication. Its decisions were not laws but requests to the sovereign states. In securing supplies and military services, the Congress in effect borrowed on the security of the good faith of the United States and its future ability to honor its wartime commitments to suppliers and soldiers.

Both the Congress and the states relied heavily on paper money or bills of credit to finance the war, the former issuing over $200 million worth and the states about as much. By 1780 the acceptability of national currency had dropped to 2.5 percent of its face value, giving rise to the phrase "not worth a continental." Price inflation was correspondingly fierce; Philadelphia prices, for example, increased 100 percent in three weeks during May 1779. The effect was to impose an enforced tax on most of the public, which by modern standards is a harsh, but not uncustomary, way of financing a war. State price-fixing failed to curb the inflationary spiral, and workers struck for higher pay in several states, including New York, Pennsylvania, and North Carolina; merchants made huge profits from the artificial war-boom economy, and so did farmers, who made up 90 percent of the population, as the demands of both armies for foodstuffs provided them with a ready market for their produce. Congress issued bonds, or loan-office certificates, bearing 4 and 6 percent interest; borrowed abroad, largely from France but also from Holland and Spain; made requisitions for money and commodities directly on the individual states; and secured some funds through the sale of confiscated ships and other enemy property. By early 1781 the whole system was so chaotic that Robert Morris was appointed superintendent of finance to reorganize it. Morris succeeded in rationalizing the various forms of paper credit and in issuing new bank notes through the medium of the quasi-public Bank of North America. Redemption of its notes was expected to come from a variety of excise taxes and customs duties, but Congress never approved the tax program upon which the Morris fiscal plan was structured.

Manpower was in as short supply as money, again resulting from the absence of a centralized political authority possessing coercive powers. The American forces consisted of two basic types, the Continental Line, or regulars, and the state militia. Altogether, almost 400,000 men served in one or the other, but the figure is deceptive. Few of the 230,000 men who were in the Continental army were long-term enlistees. Some served for terms as brief as three months, and Washington never had more than 20,000 men in his command at any one time. The militia, totaling some 165,000 men, were not much more useful in major campaigns than the short-term regulars. At the critical Battle of Yorktown, almost half of Washington's command consisted of French troops. Regulars served by enlistment, having been attracted by numerous bounties in cash and land. Frequently state recruiters competed with Continental recruiters for men. Militiamen were conscripted, with the option of providing substitutes or paying fines for not serving. Deserters were not uncommon, being estimated at half of the militia and one-third of the Continentals during the course of the war. The most spectacular of the many mutinies in the ranks was that of the Pennsylvania Line in January 1781. Whatever the causes of their disaffection, virtually none of the deserters or the mutineers went over to the British; neither did many of the American prisoners who were incarcerated in miserable British prison ships in New York harbor.

An estimated 5,000 blacks served in the American forces; the largest source was the New England states. At first, only free blacks were accepted in the army, but as manpower became short, slaves were drafted for military service in all states except South Carolina and Georgia. Blacks also served as spies, messengers, guides, naval pilots, and construction workers. They were not organized in segregated units but fought side by side with white soldiers. The recruitment, voluntarily and involuntarily, of white servants, vagrants, and convicts, along with free and bonded blacks, lent substance to the British denigration of the American forces as a "rabble in arms." But it was something else, something the British could not appreciate: a citizen army, with high morale and extraordinary powers of survival, which provided almost a half-million Americans with a political education in the merits of republican government. The highest tribute paid to this "rag, tag, and bobtail" army was the contrast made by the Marquis de Lafayette, Marie Joseph du Motier, between American and European soldiery: "No European army would suffer the tenth part of what the Americans suffer. It takes citizens to support hunger, nakedness, toil, and the total want of pay." Paine offered still another explanation of the victory of America's citizen soldiers: "It is not a field . . . but a cause that we are defending."

Results of the Revolution

The American Revolution began as a quest for political independence on the part of thirteen British colonies in North America. The patriot leaders of 1776 did not intend to make a social revolution as well, nor did they mean their war for independence to be a clarion call to colonial peoples everywhere to take up arms against their own imperial masters. The mystery and enduring fascination of the Revolution is that it overflowed its narrow banks and produced consequences greater than intended. The war disrupted existing social institutions, enlarged the body politic, and established new standards by which to measure social progress. The suspicion of power and privilege and the assumption that men had "a common and an equal right to liberty, to property, and to safety; to justice, government, laws, religion, and freedom" became the yardsticks by which institutions in the new republic were tested, immediately and in the distant future. The specific evidences of change were not always spectacular. Bills of personal rights were included in the constitutions of the new states; governors were made elective and often shorn of traditional executive powers; the state legislatures were less dominated by wealthy elites than before. Blacks were freed in some northern states; provision for their future emancipation was made in others; and antislavery sentiments spread even in southern states. Official churches disappeared in all but three of the states, and religious freedom was guaranteed in all of them. Confiscated Loyalist estates were broken up, and some of the property found its way into the hands of small farmers.

The American Revolution began as a quest for political independence; the patriot leaders of 1776 did not intend to make a social revolution as well.

But the optimism engendered by the Revolution constitutes the real measure of its transforming character. Slavery did continue; the new men in politics were neither libertarian nor proletarian; the new state governments were still controlled by elites; discrimination against religious minorities did not cease; and women remained second-class citizens in a male society. But there was universal expectation that the road to improvement had been opened. To liberal thinkers in Europe as well as in America, the success of the American Revolution gave hope of a roseate future. An Englishman, Richard Price, viewed events in the New World as opening up "a new prospect in human affairs" and "a new era in the history of mankind." The old regime had been assaulted and its defenses breached. The French philosopher Anne Robert Jacques Turgot, Baron de l'Aulne, agreed with Price: America was "the hope of the human race," and he speculated that it might become the model. Fifty years after writing the Declaration of Independence, Jefferson was confident that its liberal principles would be the signal for arousing men everywhere to burst the chains of bondage that kept them in vassalage to the old order. For these men the American Revolution was the fruition of the European Enlightenment. The Old World through its philosophers had imagined the Enlightenment; the New World in the American Revolution had institutionalized it. It was for later generations of Americans to perfect the design of those institutions and to spell out more fully the implications of the democratic ideology to which the Revolution had given birth.

BIBLIOGRAPHY

John Alden, *The American Revolution*, and *A History of the American Revolution*.

Charles M. Andrews, *The Colonial Background of the American Revolution*.

Bernard Bailyn, *The Ideological Origins of the American Revolution*.

Carl Becker, *The Declaration of Independence*.

Samuel F. Bemis, *Diplomacy of the American Revolution*.

William A. Benton, *Whig-Loyalism*.

Carl Bridenbaugh, *The Spirit of '76: The Growth of American Patriotism Before Independence*.

Wallace Brown, *The Good Americans*.

Weldon A. Brown, *Empire or Independence*.

Edmund C. Burnett, *The Continental Congress*.

Robert M. Calhoon, *The Loyalists in Revolutionary America*.

Ian R. Christie, *Crisis of Empire: Great Britain and the American Colonies, 1754–1783*.

Elisha P. Douglass, *Rebels and Democrats*.

Joseph A. Ernst, *Money and Politics in America, 1755–1775*.

E. James Ferguson, *The American Revolution*.

Lawrence H. Gipson, *The Coming of the Revolution*.

Everts B. Greene, *The Revolutionary Generation*.

David Hawke, *A Transaction of Free Men*.

John Head, *A Time to Rend*.

Don Higginbotham, *The War of American Independence*.

J. Franklin Jameson, *The American Revolution Considered as a Social Movement*.

Merill Jensen, *The American Revolution Within America*, and *The Founding of a Nation: A History of the American Revolution*.

Lawrence S. Kaplan, *Colonies Into Nation*.

Bernard Knollenberg, *Growth of the American Revolution*, and *Origin of the American Revolution*.

Stephen G. Kurtz and James H. Hutson, eds., *Essays on the American Revolution.*
Benjamin Labaree, *The Boston Tea Party.*
Piers Mackesy, *The War for America.*
Pauline Maier, *From Resistance to Revolution.*
John C. Miller, *Origins of the American Revolution,* and *Triumph of Freedom.*
Broadus Mitchell, *The Price of Independence: A Realistic View of the American Revolution.*
Edmund S. Morgan, *The Birth of the Republic.*
Edmund S. Morgan and Helen M. Morgan, *The Stamp Act Crisis.*
Richard B. Morris, *The American Revolution Reconsidered,* and *The Peacemakers.*
William H. Nelson, *The American Tory.*
Allan Nevins, *The American States During and After the American Revolution.*
Mary Beth Norton, *The British-Americas.*
Howard H. Peckham, *The War for Independence.*
Benjamin Quarles, *The Negro in the American Revolution.*
Arthur M. Schlesinger, *The Colonial Merchants and the American Revolution,* and *Prelude to Independence: The Newspaper War on Britain.*
Marshall Smelser, *The Winning of Independence.*
Paul H. Smith, *Loyalists and Redcoats.*
William C. Stinchcombe, *The American Revolution and the French Alliance.*
Carl Van Doren, *Secret History of the American Revolution.*
Claude H. Van Tyne, *The Loyalists in the American Revolution.*
Willard M. Wallace, *Appeal to Arms: A Military History of the American Revolution.*
Esmond Wright, *Fabric of Freedom.*
Arthur Zilversmit, *The First Emancipation.*
Hiller Zobel, *The Boston Massacre.*

— MILTON M. KLEIN

REVOLUTIONARY WAR, AMERICAN ARMY IN THE

The American army of the Revolution came into existence almost by accident, and it developed gradually. It stemmed from the various local minutemen, alarm companies, and volunteers who had sprung to arms to meet the British expedition against Lexington and Concord and pursued the redcoats back to Boston on Apr. 19, 1775. Many of these men remained to besiege the city, and they were joined by volunteers from other New England colonies in the weeks that followed. At first there was no overall command, no definite enlistments, and only such discipline as the natural decency of the men provided. Some colonies, especially Massachusetts and Connecticut, attempted to meet the crisis by appointing officers and enlisting volunteers for the rest of the year. They even organized expeditions such as the one against Fort Ticonderoga in May 1775, but still confusion reigned. Finally the Massachusetts Provincial Congress sent an urgent appeal to the Continental Congress in Philadelphia asking it to adopt the new army and provide direction. The Congress responded. On June 14 it authorized the raising of ten companies of riflemen in Virginia, Maryland, and Pennsylvania as the nucleus of a new national army, and on June 15 it appointed George Washington of Virginia commander in chief. By July 3 Washington had arrived in Cambridge, Mass., to take command, and a few weeks later the rifle regiments joined him.

The new commander immediately set out to bring order from chaos. Appealing to patriotism to maintain discipline and hold men in camp, he developed in conjunction with a congressional committee a plan of organization that was ready by September. This plan called for a Continental army of twenty-six regiments or battalions of infantry with a strength of 728 men each, one regiment of riflemen, and one of artillery, for a total of 20,372 men. Each of the infantry regiments was to consist of eight companies of 86 men, 4 officers, and 8 regimental staff officers. All were to be enlisted until the end of 1776 and responsible only to the Continental Congress. The effective date for the new organization was to be Jan. 1, 1776, but when that day arrived, arrangements were far from complete. Many men considered the enlistment period too long. Others hesitated to serve under new officers whom they had not selected themselves. Officers who had achieved high rank in the existing thirty-eight volunteer regiments were reluctant to accept lower ranks in the Continental army. By March, when the spring campaign began, only 9,170 men had joined the ranks. This was less than half the desired number, and Washington had to rely on help from local militia units in order to obtain an adequate operating force.

General Washington never had as many as 15,000 able-bodied troops under his command at any one time; the usual number was about 10,000.

Congress authorized additional regiments. The rifle and artillery regiments became a corps and a brigade, respectively. Cavalry, light infantry, and artificer regiments were added, as well as special mixed units called legions. Still the Continental army, or Continental line as it was sometimes called, remained throughout inadequate to conduct a campaign entirely by itself. Before the end of the war, Congress had authorized eighty-eight battalions totaling 80,000 men, but the quota was never met. Some of the regiments were never raised; others were always under strength. The actual number of men under arms varied, but the best estimates indicate that Washington never had as many as 15,000 able-bodied Continentals under his command at any one time; the usual number was about 10,000. To muster an adequate force, he had to rely on state regiments and on local militia organizations called out for short-term emergencies in their local areas. Almost all major actions and campaigns were fought with a mixture of these three types of troops, even after 1776 when Congress began to recruit soldiers for longer periods—usually three years or the duration of the war.

In its recruiting, Congress relied almost entirely on volunteers. Some states used a quota system requiring either men or money. There were offers of bounties in money or land to induce enlistment or to make it financially possible for a man to sign up. After much discussion it was agreed that all free men regardless of color were welcome, and many regiments numbered blacks among their veterans. By the end of the war, in fact, the Rhode Island regiment was almost entirely black because of that state's policy of purchasing the freedom of any slave willing to enlist.

The basic weapon of the Continental infantryman was the smoothbore flintlock musket. It was an inaccurate weapon at best. A good marksman could only expect to hit a target the size of a man at 100 yards, but this lack of precision was not important in 18th-century warfare. In the tactics followed by all armies, the important thing was to lay down a field of fire and saturate it with bullets through volley firing; thus, speed of loading was critical, and a well-trained soldier could be expected to load and fire four times a minute, using a paper cartridge. The rifle, a much more accurate firearm, took considerably longer to load, and so it was used primarily for sniping, long-range shooting, and other special tasks. The rifleman, whose weapon did not have a bayonet, was useless in the hand-to-hand combat that decided many actions; at close quarters only the infantryman with his musket and bayonet could perform satisfactorily. Cavalrymen carried either pistols, musketoons, or carbines but generally scorned them; they considered the saber the only really useful weapon for a horseman.

In order to perform properly with any of these arms, it was necessary to establish a uniform drill. The older veterans at Boston had for the most part followed the manual first published by British Gen. Humphrey Bland in 1727, entitled *A Treatise of Military Discipline.* About 1768 there was a general shift, at least in New England, to a simplified drill prepared for the militia of Norfolk in 1759. Timothy Pickering of Salem, Mass., further simplified the "Norfolk Discipline," as it was called, in *An Easy Plan of Discipline for a Militia,* published in 1775. Some colonies adopted the regular British army manual of 1764. Thus, there were at least three different systems of discipline in use during the early years of the war. They were generally similar, but there were minor differences that could cause confusion in a crisis.

The man who providentially arrived to correct this potential hazard was Baron Friedrich Wilhelm von Steuben. A born teacher and drillmaster, von Steuben hammered the Continental soldiers into well-trained and disciplined units during the bleak winter of 1778 at Valley Forge. As part of his program he prepared a new drill manual with ideas borrowed freely from British, German, and French sources. He simplified and sharpened commands; reduced the number of motions required for firings and maneuvers; and, most important of all, changed the line of battle from three ranks to two, achieving more maneuverability. The first edition of his manual, *Regulations for the Order and Discipline of the Troops of the United States,* was published in 1779, and it remained the basic manual for American soldiers for more than twenty-five years.

Under von Steuben's guidance the Continental became a first-class soldier in the approved European tradition. Contrary to popular belief, he did not hide behind trees and fences to snipe at enemy troops. Such tactics were sometimes used by militiamen, as at King's Mountain, but the American regular met the British army on its own terms, in open fields, drawn up in line of battle. He learned to make and receive fierce bayonet charges, and in such notable attacks as at Stony Point and the assault on the British redoubt at Yorktown, he charged with unloaded musket, relying solely on cold steel.

A major general in the Continental army, von Steuben was only one of a number of foreign officers who offered their services to the Americans. American representatives in Europe, such as Silas Deane and Benjamin Franklin, were besieged with offers. Some of these volunteers made outstanding contributions, notably Marie Joseph du Motier, Marquis de Lafayette; Johann Kalb; Casimir Pulaski; and Thaddeus Kosciusko. Others, such as Philippe Tronson du Coudray, were either arrogant or incompetent or both and nearly produced a revolt by American officers who found themselves being superseded. The situation became so bad, in fact, that Washington and Congress soon reversed the policy of welcoming foreign officers and began actively to discourage them.

With rare exceptions, notably the Battle of King's Mountain, the militia and state line units that supplemented the Continental army were ineffective by themselves. When used for delaying tactics and backed by Continentals, as at Guilford Courthouse and Cowpens, they performed useful service. Among the state line regiments, the outstanding unit was the Illinois Regiment of the Virginia State Army. Under its commander, George Rogers Clark, it captured Cahokia, Kaskaskia, and Vincennes and thus established American claims to the Middle West.

BIBLIOGRAPHY

Fred Anderson Berg, *Encyclopedia of Continental Army Units.*

Francis B. Heitman, *Historical Register of Officers of the Continental Army.*

Harold L. Peterson, *The Book of the Continental Soldier.*

Hugh F. Rankin, *The North Carolina Continentals.*

— HAROLD L. PETERSON

REVOLUTIONARY WAR, BRITISH ARMY IN THE

Although in April 1775 the authorized strength of the British army was 48,647, the army numbered only about 32,000 men, of whom 6,991 were in America. By March 1782, through desperate recruiting and impressment and the hiring of German regiments, the total had risen to 113,000 effectives, exclusive of regulars in Ireland, armies of the East India Company, and paid militia. That total included 8,756 in the West Indies and 46,000 in North America, and of the latter, two-thirds were Germans or American provincials.

The Western Hemisphere contained four independent commands: (1) the Lesser Antilles, (2) Jamaica, (3) the new province of Quebec, and (4) the sprawling mass composed of Nova Scotia, the thirteen colonies on the Atlantic seaboard, and the Floridas, Bahamas, and Bermudas. The rich islands of the two West Indian commands were imperiled when France, Spain, and the Netherlands joined in America's struggle, and Great Britain was therefore induced to divert into that theater armament critically needed along the North American coasts. More than any other factor, it was the predicament of the West Indies that hastened British defeat. But patriot leaders, naturally, were preoccupied with the Quebec command and the other North American command, whose headquarters lay in New York between 1776 and 1783. As War Office and Admiralty functions were purely administrative, operation control over these four commands (but only these) lay with the secretary of state for the American department, who, between 1775 and 1782, was Lord George Sackville-Germain. Because the prime minister, Lord Frederick North, chose to wage parliamentary politics rather than war, the final arbiter of domestic and global priorities could only be the king. Satisfactory distribution of operational responsibilities never emerged, because of lack of comity among the cabinet and the services, and because global communications lay at the mercy of wind and weather; the army was considered of only secondary importance in comparison with the navy, and empire had spread too far for communication to be maintained by preindustrial technology.

Socially the army was, along with an established church, a form of outdoor relief for disinherited brothers of rural landlords, a price the nation paid to maintain primogeniture. In all about 2,000 British officers served in America during the war. Commonly they were promoted gratis to fill vacancies caused by death, or else, with permission, they bought commissions from previous holders and could sell out at any time; in 1783 most of those still serving reverted to the reserve on half pay for life. A few were members of Parliament, a dozen were baronets, and at least seventy-eight were peers or sons of peers; these and scores of others possessed such political connections as to make a travesty of discipline.

As marksmen, the British were no match for the Continentals; it was estimated in 1776 that the British fired 1,400 shots for each American killed.

By contrast, private soldiers represented strictly nonpolitical Britain. Those serving in 1775 had largely enlisted for life or according to regimental contract; others, later, for three years or until the "rebellion" ended, at the crown's option. Voluntary enlistment, highly unpopular, was stimulated by bounties; by acceptance of Roman Catholics, previously excluded; and by the creation of dozens of new regiments, whose cadres recruited partly at private expense in order to obtain commissions. Also convicts were pardoned on condition of enlistment: in Britain, it has been said, "every gaol became a recruiting depot." After the Revolution merged with foreign war, press acts of May 1778 and February 1779 provided for conscripting the unemployed poor—but not voters—for service of five years or the duration of war. Although a latent purpose was certainly control of the poor, the fear of riots permitted only casual conscription. Given a base pay of eight pence per day minus deductions for food, clothing, repair of arms, and Chelsea Hospital (a pension fund), the rank and file seldom saw money except as proceeds of crime. Until July 1778 all supplies and provisions for the American theater, except fresh meat, came from Europe; after France intervened, shipments were often delayed and damaged or spoiled. For bachelors the horrors of service were avoided by simple desertion—in Ireland one-sixth of the soldiers deserted each year—and for married men they were tempered by the presence of wives and children, for whom they drew rations; bad as it was, the regiment was literally the soldier's home. Yet discipline was ferocious; severe floggings were administered as well to women (100 lashes) as to men (1,000 lashes). Nevertheless, death sentences were seldom carried out. Difficulties of recruitment and transport made conservation of men the paramount concern; major engagements had to be avoided, and no commander dared exploit an advantage if he would thereby diminish compactness and facilitate desertion. In brief, although the background explanations differ, the redcoats and the ragged Continentals were remarkably similar in character and circumstances. Patriotic assumptions that the Continental rank and file were superior in spirit, because they were free citizens of a threatened land, have not yet been validated by intensive research in the rosters of both armies, to compare them in social composition and in the statistical indices of morale.

Disease took a heavy toll of all ranks in southern campaigns and West Indian service. Battle casualties were also higher than had been usual, because of American emphasis on marksmanship. Reared in an open country less rich in game, the British relied less on the musket than on the bayonet. Rather than aim the piece, they pointed it, fired hit-or-miss, and then endeavored to rout the enemy with a bayonet charge. It was estimated in 1776 that 1,400 shots were fired by the British for each American killed. Accustomed to meager risk and to substantial cavalry support, red-coats at first maintained their usual solidity, but American conditions gradually forced on them new conceptions of looseness, flexibility, and firepower. Even before 1775 an "Americanization" of the army had begun, and the Revolution broadened and sealed the shift.

BIBLIOGRAPHY

John Adlum, *Memoirs of the Life of John Adlum in the Revolutionary War.*

Henry Belcher, *The First American Civil War*, vol. I.

Edward E. Curtis, *The Organization of the British Army in the American Revolution.*

J. W. Fortescue, *The History of the British Army*, vol. III.

Piers Mackesy, *The War for America, 1775–1783.*

John Shy, *Toward Lexington: The Role of the British Army in the Coming of the American Revolution.*

Christopher Ward, *The War of the Revolution*, vol. I.

— HENRY J. YOUNG

REVOLUTIONARY WAR, FOREIGN VOLUNTEERS IN

The ideal of human liberty actuating the colonies in 1776 found response in the hearts of many Europeans, especially in France. A small proportion of those who wrote Benjamin Franklin offering their services actually reached America. The first secret aid ships of Pierre Augustin Caron de Beaumarchais, the *Mercure* and the *Amphitrite*, landed about thirty volunteers in March and April 1777 at Portsmouth, Va. A few stragglers and four royal engineers, the latter sent for by Congress, reached Philadelphia in June from the West Indies, while Marie Joseph du Motier, Marquis de Lafayette, and his eleven officers, making their way over intolerable roads from Charleston, arrived in July. More than half of these men were rejected by Congress and had their expenses paid back to France.

Among the most notable of those commissioned were: Charles Armand, Marquis de la Rouërie; Pierre Charles l'Enfant, later designer of the insignia of the national capital; Philippe Tronson du Coudray, drowned in September in the Schuylkill River; Thaddeus Kosciusko, a Lithuanian, who arrived in 1776 and built the fortifications at West Point; Louis Lebegue DuPortail, who fortified Valley Forge; and Casimir Pulaski, a Polish count, who was killed at Savannah, Ga., in 1779. Only two of Lafayette's officers were retained by Congress: Johann Kalb (Baron de Kalb), killed at Camden, S.C., in 1780, and the latter's aide Paul Dubuisson, wounded and made prisoner there.

The last secret aid volunteers to arrive came on the *Flamand* in December 1777, sent by Beaumarchais: among them were Baron Friedrich von Steuben and his interpreter, Pierre Étienne Du Ponceau, the latter of whom remained in America and became a noted lawyer in Philadelphia.

BIBLIOGRAPHY

Thomas Balch, *The French in America.*

E. S. Kite, *Duportail and the French Engineers.*

— ELIZABETH S. KITE

RIOTS

The English Riot Act of 1715 made it a felony for twelve or more persons to gather together and disturb the peace. As part of the common law practiced in the American colonies and the United States, a riot could consist of as few as three persons, assembled for a common purpose, who behaved so as to cause observers to fear disturbance of the peace. Most events characterized as riots, however, involve more people, and sociologists and social psychologists now treat riots as instances of "collective behavior" or "crowd psychology." The common law definition of a riot allows public officials to break up even a peaceful assembly, if participants behave in such a way as to cause observers to fear disruption of civic peace. Whether actions of publicly assembled people cause a riot depends very much on point of view. The Boston Massacre of 1770 occurred when British troops fired into what they regarded as a rioting crowd, and the Boston Tea Party of 1773 was, to British authorities, another riot. From a later American perspective these were not unfortunate breaches of civic peace but events leading to the revolutionary war. When people protest against injustice they often view their action as a legitimate uprising, while those against whom the protest is directed are likely to define it as a riot.

The Constitution was a compromise between those who favored democratic self-government and those who feared that democracy would degenerate into mob rule. The First Amendment guarantees the "right of the people peaceably to assemble, and to petition the Government for a redress of grievances." Freedom of assembly establishes legitimacy of peaceful demonstrations, but it is widely held that crowds are more irresponsible than the individuals they comprise. From the perspective of those in authority, crowds must be kept under control. A riot is not just a failure to keep the people under control, but it is also an occasion for using force to gain control. The right of people to assemble is balanced by the right of authorities, established in common law, to declare an assembly a threat to civic peace.

One of the worst waves of riots was occasioned by the military draft during the Civil War. The Conscription Act of 1863 not only required men to fight for a cause in which many did not believe, but allowed any man drafted to avoid service by finding a substitute or paying $300. There were riots across the country, but the worst were in New York City in July 1863, where there were many poor Democrats who both sympathized with the South and resented the ability of the rich to buy out of military service. It took four days and a combination of police, militia, army, navy, and West Point cadets to quell the rioting.

The history of labor unions has been punctuated by civil disturbances. The weapon of unions has been the strike, and strikes have often resulted in violence. Workers struck against the Carnegie Steel Company in Homestead, Pa., in 1892, and the company hired Pinkerton detectives to protect the strikebreakers brought in by the company. The battle between strikers and detectives led the governor to call in the state militia, which broke the strike. Strikers often engage in picketing to publicize their grievances, discourage the public from patronizing the business being struck, and prevent strikebreakers from taking their jobs. Both strikes and picketing have resulted in court decisions and legislation to protect workers, owners, and the peace. The courts have usually frowned on protecting civil disorder or violence, most recently in the case of protesters outside of abortion clinics.

Veterans, impoverished by the Great Depression, marched on Washington, D.C., in 1932 and camped out in fields and government buildings. They were supporting passage of a bill to grant them immediate payment of their World War I bonus. After the bill was defeated in Congress approximately 2,000 of the 15,000 veterans refused to leave the capital, and some government officials feared that the veterans would disturb the peace. When attempts by local police to remove the veterans resulted in four deaths, Army Chief of Staff General Douglas McArthur, on orders from President Herbert Hoover, sent in U.S. troops, which set fire to the camps and drove the "bonus marchers" from the city.

The worst draft riots in 1863 were in New York City, where many poor Democrats sympathized with the South and resented well-to-do northerners' ability to buy their way out of service.

The unpopular and undeclared Vietnam War, and the use of the draft to provide soldiers for it, was the occasion for many antiwar demonstrations. In the summer of 1968 civil rights and antiwar protesters joined in a march outside the Democratic National Convention in Chicago. One of the reasons for emphasis on nonviolence in the civil rights and antiwar movements in the 1960s was to make it more difficult for officials to declare a march or demonstration a riot. In Chicago, however, city and party officials viewed the march as a potential riot, and Mayor Richard J. Daley sent in busloads of police. Protesters and sympathizers described what happened as a police riot, claiming the protest peaceful and nonviolent until police attacked. Defenders of the police argued that television cameras recorded only violence of the police, not provocations of demonstrators.

A 1968 report of the National Advisory Commission on Civil Disorders identified white racism and resulting feelings of hopelessness and powerlessness on the part of African Americans as the cause of race riots during the 1960s. The same reasoning could be applied to actions taken by members of the American Indian Movement, who occupied Alcatraz in San Francisco Bay in 1969, and Wounded Knee on the Pine Ridge Reservation in South Dakota in 1973. Different factors, however, were identified as the causes behind the disturbances in Los Angeles during the summer of 1992, when Hispanics and Koreans as well as African Americans took to the streets. The actions followed the acquittal of white police officers who had beaten Rodney King, a black man. The beating was videotaped and shown so often on national television that many Americans, white as well as black, saw the acquittal as a miscarriage of justice. It was argued that the beating was only an occasion for the rioting, the latter being an expression of frustration on the part of poor racial groups in Los Angeles. According to this argument, the Los Angeles uprising of 1992 had more to do with class than with race. The difficulty Americans had in categorizing what happened in Los Angeles in 1992 demonstrates the continuing debate in the United States over what distinguishes a riot from legitimate protest over injustice.

[See also Alcatraz; American Indian Movement; Draft Riots; Los Angeles Riots.]

BIBLIOGRAPHY

Robert Gooding-Williams, ed., *Reading Rodney King, Reading Urban Uprising* (New York, 1993).

Barbara Salert, *The Dynamics of Riots* (Ann Arbor, Mich., 1980).

— RICHARD W. MOODEY

ROANOKE ISLAND, CAPTURE OF

On Feb. 8, 1862, Union Gen. A. E. Burnside, with an overwhelming force of vessels and men, overran the weakly fortified Confederate positions on Roanoke Island, N.C. The capture of this strategic island enabled Union troops to occupy Elizabeth City and to overrun many North Carolina counties bordering on Albemarle Sound.

BIBLIOGRAPHY

S. A. Ashe, *History of North Carolina,* vol. II.

— RICHARD E. YATES

A 1907 caricature of the industrialist Edward H. Harriman, with the railroads of America all heading toward his mouth. The original caption reads "Design for a Union Station." (Library of Congress/Corbis)

ROBBER BARONS

Robber Barons, a term that is widely used in describing big businessmen of the late 19th century. It implies that entrepreneurial policies and practices during the Gilded Age, as Mark Twain first called it, were characterized by a ruthless and unscrupulous drive for monopoly and economic power. The origins of the term are not precise. Edwin L. Godkin, editor of the *Nation,* used it in 1869; at about the same time Sen. Carl Schurz of Missouri used the phrase in a speech. Contemporaries Charles Francis Adams, Jr., and Henry Demarest Lloyd contributed strongly to the image by denouncing the activities of the new moguls.

During the Progressive period of the early 20th century various muckraking writers, such as Ida M. Tarbell and Gustavus Myers, did much to crystallize the stereotype of the businessman as a destructive agent in society. The 1920's witnessed a dramatic swing of the pendulum to the other side as the nation enjoyed apparent prosperity and the businessman reached the zenith of his popularity. Even Tarbell, who in the Progressive years had scathingly attacked the Standard Oil Company, produced a laudatory biography of Judge Elbert H. Gary of the United States Steel Corporation.

Then came October of 1929. The businessman came crashing from his pedestal of popular acclaim as the nation sank deeper and deeper into the despair accompanying the economic frustrations of the 1930's. The term, "robber barons" became a permanent part of the historian's vocabulary with the publication in 1934 of Matthew Josephson's *The Robber Barons: The Great American Capitalists, 1861–1901.* Numerous volumes during the 1930's echoed the view of big business as decadent.

As World War II approached and the economy rebounded, the businessman received his reprieve and historians began viewing the "robber baron" from a more positive vantage point. A school of historians known as revisionists was led by Allan Nevins, in a biography of John D. Rockefeller (1940); Louis M. Hacker, in the *Triumph of American Capitalism* (1940); and Thomas C. Cochran and William Miller, in the *Age of Enterprise* (1942). After World War II this ever-increasing number of historians and economists attempted to evaluate the late-19th-century businessman in a less emotional, more objective way. Rather than concentrate on the destructive characteristics of the moguls, the revisionists examined their creative contributions and attempted to ascertain the reasons for the growth of big business in the evolution of American society more clearly.

— THOMAS BREWER

ROCKEFELLER FOUNDATION

Rockefeller Foundation was established by John D. Rockefeller and chartered on May 14, 1913, under the laws of the state of New York, "to promote the well-being of mankind throughout the world." Within a few years after its organization, Rockefeller had given the foundation approximately $182 million. By the end of 1974 the foundation had paid out close to $1.18 billion from income and principal.

During its first fifteen years the foundation devoted itself almost entirely to public health and the medical sciences. The foundation's field staff extended campaigns against hookworm from the American South into many lands and undertook control measures against other communicable diseases, particularly malaria and yellow fever. The need for trained people led to the support of medical education and to the development of strategically placed schools of public health. The development of the vaccine against yellow fever in 1937, a joint effort of foundation field staff and laboratory investigators, culminated two decades of worldwide health activities. By 1929 the work of the foundation had been rounded out to include support of the natural sciences, the social sciences, and the arts and humanities. From support of investigations of basic physiological processes that were then little understood came, many years later, great advances in such fields as biochemistry, molecular biology, and human genetics; much demonstrably valuable work was supported at the same time in international relations, economics, and cross-cultural research and teaching.

About 1952 the foundation began to reduce the support of science and scholarship in the West, by then well funded from other sources, to help apply existing knowledge to the solution of the overwhelming problems of the developing world. The foundation's pioneering operating programs in agriculture, initiated in Mexico in 1943, led to greater per-unit production of food crops in many countries. These programs, as well as population stabilization efforts and the strengthening of selected universities to serve the needs of their regions, were being continued in the 1970's with a greater emphasis on their economic and social consequences. In the United States, grantmaking efforts to bring about equality of opportunity, a renewed emphasis on America's cultural identities, and a concern for the technological impact on the environment became the foundation's main thrusts. A modest program in international relations sought to resolve conflict inherent in transnational issues.

Although the foundation is both an operating and a grantmaking organization, much of its program lies in the support of other agencies and in the training, through fellowships, of competent people in its fields of interest. Between 1915 and 1975 more than 10,000 men and women—primarily from the developing countries—received study awards. Awards are now also available for competition among American scientists and scholars in the fields of agriculture, the humanities, and population, as well as the environment, minority-group education, conflict resolution, and the arts.

BIBLIOGRAPHY

Rockefeller Foundation, *Annual Report.*

— JOHN H. KNOWLES

ROCKY MOUNTAINS

Rocky Mountains, a vast mountain system that extends from northern Mexico to northwest Alaska, a distance of more than 3,000 miles, and forms the continental divide. Spanish pioneers in Mexico were the first white men to see the Rocky Mountains. Francisco Vásquez de Coronado, in 1540, was the first to see the U.S. Rockies. The presence of precious metals in the region of the mountains induced the earliest exploration and first settlements, by Spaniards in the southern portion of the Rockies.

From the east, via the Great Lakes, came the French. As early as 1743, members of the La Vérendrye family saw the "shining mountains" in the Wyoming region. Frenchmen and then Englishmen, hunting furs, followed Canadian streams to the western mountains. Then came the pelt-hungry Americans up the Missouri River and its tributaries. The trappers and traders, first gathering beaver skins and later buffalo hides, became the mountain men, who were the real trailblazers of the central Rockies. Their pack trains and wagons broke the practicable trails into and over the mountains.

The Louisiana Purchase (1803) was without definite boundaries, but the original French claim to the drainage area of the Mississippi River indicated the crest of the Rockies as the western boundary. Meriwether Lewis and William Clark, in the Northwest (1804–06), and Zebulon M. Pike, in the Southwest (1806–07), led the first official expeditions for the United States into the Rocky Mountains. Their reports were more favorable than that of Maj. Stephen H. Long, who, in 1820, came to the base of the mountains and labeled the adjoining high plains the "Great American Desert." To the westward-moving flood of homeseekers, these plains, the Rocky Mountains, and intervening plateaus were uninviting for settlement, and the homesteaders traveled another 1,000 miles to the Pacific coast, over trails determined by mountain topography. In southern Wyoming, where the Rockies flatten to a high plain, South Pass became the gateway to Oregon. Participants in the Mormon trek of 1847 and the California gold rush of 1849 used this same crossing of the continental divide. Gold discoveries during the 1850's and 1860's led to permanent settlement in the Rockies and eventually to the formation of the mountain states.

The agriculture that followed mining in the West was determined by the mountains. The high regions catch the snows that make the rivers, and these feed the irrigation canals that make farming possible in the semiarid country east of the Rockies. These same geographical factors later inspired reservoir construction and reclamation and tramontane water diversion projects. The vital importance of mountain watershed protection led to national forest conservation, as lumbering became an important industry in the more heavily wooded areas of the Rockies.

The locations of cities and towns were fixed by the mountain geography, as were the routes of the transcontinental railroads. The automobile highways were also similarly directed.

Discoveries of gold during the 1850's and 1860's led to permanent settlement in the Rockies and eventually to the formation of the mountain states.

The federal government has established four national parks in the Rocky Mountain region: Yellowstone National Park in Wyoming, Montana, and Idaho (Mar. 1, 1872), which is the world's greatest geyser area; Glacier National Park in Montana (May 11, 1910); Rocky Mountain National Park in Colorado (Jan. 26, 1915), which includes 410 square miles of the Rockies' Front Range; and Grand Teton National Park in Wyoming (Feb. 26, 1929), which includes the winter feeding ground of the largest American elk herd.

BIBLIOGRAPHY

W. A. Atwood, *The Rocky Mountains.*

R. G. Thwaites, *A Brief History of Rocky Mountain Exploration.*

— LEROY R. HAFEN

ROE V. WADE

Roe v. *Wade*, 410 U.S. 113 (1973), which established a woman's constitutional right to choose to have an abortion, set one of the most controversial precedents in the history of the Supreme Court. By a vote of seven to two, the Court invalidated Texas and Georgia laws prohibiting abortion except when necessary to save the mother's life. "Jane Roe" was the pseudonym of Norma McCorvey, a pregnant woman who challenged the Texas statute. The law prevented her from terminating the pregnancy (she gave her daughter up for adoption), but her case won that right for other women. Justice Harry Blackmun's majority opinion relied on the right of privacy recognized eight years earlier in *Griswold* v. *Connecticut.* "This right," he declared, "is broad enough to encompass a woman's decision whether or not to terminate her pregnancy." The Court acknowledged that the right to choose an abortion based on a private decision between a woman and her doctor was not absolute. Like all rights it could be infringed if government had a compelling interest in doing so.

Texas had advanced two justifications for abortion laws: protecting the mother's health and preserving prenatal life. The Court ruled that each interest became compelling at a different stage of pregnancy. No restrictions were justified in the first trimester (three months). Concern for maternal health justified appropriate regulations, but not prohibition, in the second trimester, when abortion became more risky than going to term. The question of prenatal life was more complex. If, as many people believe, human life begins at conception, the state has not only the power but the duty to protect the constitutional rights of the fetus. *Roe* concluded that "the word 'person' as used in the Fourteenth Amendment does not include the unborn." The state's interest in "potential life" became compelling, however, when the fetus could survive outside the mother's body. Since viability occurred at approximately the end of the sixth month, a state could prohibit third-trimester abortions—except when necessary to save the mother's life.

Although *Roe* was not based on the equal protection clause, it was a victory for women's rights. The need for reproductive choice, regardless of the exact judicial rationale, is indicated by the fact that 1.5 million elective abortions are performed in the United States every year. The Court's opinion, however, received widespread criticism even from those who were positive or neutral about the result. The justices evinced little awareness of the considerable differences between birth control, the issue in *Griswold*, and abortion. If Justice Harry Blackmun emphasized the possible devastating effect of unwanted pregnancy, he did not explain why bearing an unwanted child was worse than many other things government forces upon individuals. *Roe* also did not explain why, if no legal, medical, or philosophical consensus exists on when life begins, a state cannot decide that it begins at conception. The public reaction to *Roe* v. *Wade* made reproductive choice one of the country's most debated issues and even inspired presidential selection of justices expected to overturn *Roe*. Decisions upholding indirect restrictions have weakened the impact of *Roe*. In practice only adult women who have access to abortion and can afford it have the right to choice.

[See also Abortion; Women's Movement.]

BIBLIOGRAPHY

Judith A. Baer, *Women in American Law* (New York, 1991).
Joan Hoff, *Law, Gender and Injustice* (New York, 1991).

— JUDITH A. BAER

ROSENBURG CASE

On Apr. 5, 1951, Julius Rosenberg and his wife Ethel, natives of New York City, were sentenced to death after being found guilty of furnishing vital information on the atomic bomb to Soviet agents in 1944 and 1945. Julius Rosenberg had been an electrical engineer. Evidence against the pair was supplied by Ethel Rosenberg's brother, David Greenglass, who was himself sentenced to fifteen years' imprisonment. Also involved was Morton Sobel, sentenced to thirty years. Despite worldwide appeals to President Dwight D. Eisenhower to commute their sentences, the Rosenbergs were executed at Sing Sing Prison on June 19, 1953.

Controversy continued over the tactics used by government agencies during the trial; in particular, charges were made that the Federal Bureau of Investigation tampered with the evidence. In 1975 Michael and Robert Meeropol, the sons of the Rosenbergs (who had taken the surname of their adoptive parents), won a court battle forcing the government to release hitherto secret documents relating to the case.

BIBLIOGRAPHY

Louis Nizer, *The Implosion Conspiracy.*
Walter Schneir and Miriam Schneir, *Invitation to an Inquest.*

ROUGH RIDERS

Rough Riders, officially the First U.S. Cavalry Volunteers, was the most widely publicized single regiment in American military history. It was recruited for the

Theodore Roosevelt in the uniform of a rough rider, 1898. (Corbis-Bettmann)

Spanish-American War, its members coming from the cattle ranges and mining camps and from the law enforcement agencies of the Southwest. Such personnel offered brilliant copy for the flamboyant and unrestrained war correspondents of the era, and the unit's commanding officers further enhanced its image. Leonard Wood, of the Army Medical Corps, left his post as White House physician to accept the colonelcy; Theodore Roosevelt became lieutenant colonel. Neither was trained for line command, but both had exceptionally colorful personalities.

The Rough Riders had a brief training period at San Antonio in the spring of 1898 and then entrained for Tampa, Fla. There the unit's horses were abandoned, and in the chaos of embarkation, only slightly more than half the regiment left Florida. The fragment that did reach Cuba lived up to its advance publicity. From Las Guásimas, after which Wood was promoted to a brigade commander, to San Juan Hill, the Rough Riders' attacks were often unconventional but usually successful.

BIBLIOGRAPHY

Theodore Roosevelt, *The Rough Riders.*

— JIM DAN HILL

S

SACCO-VANZETTI CASE

Nicola Sacco, a skilled shoeworker born in 1881, and Bartolomeo Vanzetti, a fish peddler born in 1888, were arrested on May 5, 1920, for a payroll holdup and murder in South Braintree, Mass.; a jury, sitting under Judge Webster Thayer, found the men guilty on July 14, 1921. Complex motions relating to old and new evidence, and to the conduct of the trial, were argued before Thayer, the Massachusetts supreme court, and a special advisory commission serving the governor; the accused did not prevail and were executed on Aug. 23, 1927.

Among the legal issues were these: prejudicial behavior by the prosecutor, complemented by an often inept defense; profane and violent prejudice by the judge against the defendants, expressed outside the courtroom and possibly implicit in his behavior on the bench; possible perjury by a state police captain; refusal to deal with a set of circumstances pointing more exactly to a group of professional criminals; inexpert presentation of ballistics evidence; and failure of the evidence as a whole to remove "reasonable doubt." Throughout the trial the men were disadvantaged by their declared philosophical anarchism, their status as unassimilated alien workers, and the general "Red baiting" atmosphere of the times. Scholarly legal opinion overwhelmingly holds that apart from the question of guilt or innocence, the case is an extremely serious instance of failure in the administration of justice.

Within the United States, Sacco and Vanzetti received from the start the help of compatriots, fellow anarchists, and scattered labor groups. By 1927 they had the support in money, action, and words of major liberal figures, concerned men of law, numerous writers, and, increasingly, organized labor and the Communist party leadership. Nevertheless, it is clear that the majority of persons in the United States who held an opinion, and they were in the millions, believed the verdict sound and approved of the death penalty. By 1927 the case had become a worldwide issue, with many demonstrations against U.S. embassies.

By 1970 the case had inspired 7 novels, 7 plays, 3 television presentations, and 150 poems. Important are Upton Sinclair's novel *Boston* (1928) and Maxwell Anderson's play *Winterset* (1935). Ben Shahn, the artist, produced a notable series of gouaches on Sacco and Vanzetti. The letters written by the men themselves, during their seven years in prison, are regarded by many as the most profoundly human and genuinely literary commentary on the case.

BIBLIOGRAPHY

The Sacco-Vanzetti Case: Transcript of the Record.
Herbert B. Ehrmann, *The Case That Will Not Die.*
Osmond K. Fraenkel, *The Sacco-Vanzetti Case.*
G. Louis Joughin and Edmund M. Morgan, *The Legacy of Sacco and Vanzetti.*
Robert H. Montgomery, *Sacco-Vanzetti: The Murder and the Myth.*
Nicola Sacco and Bartolomeo Vanzetti, *Letters.*

— LOUIS JOUGHIN

SAND CREEK MASSACRE

On Nov. 29, 1864, Colorado militiamen descended upon an encampment of Southern Cheyenne at Sand Creek, thirty miles northeast of Fort Lyon in southeastern Colorado Territory, killing about a third of a band of 500, most of whom were women and children. The chief of the Cheyenne, Black Kettle, had tried to keep peace with the whites, but there had been a number of incidents and clashes between white gold miners and the Indians of the area. Indian activity had endangered lines of communication between Denver and the Missouri River. Chief Black Kettle, following instructions after a conference with the governor and having been guaranteed safe conduct, had brought his band to Sand Creek and had placed them under the protection of the fort. Despite the peaceful intentions of the Cheyenne, they were the object of a vicious attack by the Colorado volunteers under Col. J. M. Chivington and were slaughtered, mutilated, and tortured, although the militiamen were so undisciplined that many of the Indians managed to escape. The wanton massacre was a cause of further Indian warfare in the Plains, as the Cheyenne warriors, most of whom had been away hunting at the time of the massacre, joined with the Sioux and Arapaho in new attacks on the settlers.

BIBLIOGRAPHY

Stan Hoig, *The Sand Creek Massacre.*

— KENNETH M. STEWART

SAUK PRAIRIE

Sauk Prairie, a large and fertile prairie that stretches along the Wisconsin River, rimmed by the bluffs of the Baraboo Range, in Sauk County, Wis. On this prairie the Sauk settled about the middle of the 18th century, after having been driven from the shores of Green Bay by the French. The first British officer in Wisconsin, who occupied Fort Edward Augustus at Green Bay, 1761–63, made a treaty of alliance with the Sauk chiefs, who professed their friendship for the British newcomers. When the explorer Jonathan Carver in 1766 passed along the Fox-Wisconsin waterway, he found a large and prosperous village of the Sauk on the prairie, and noted that the loss of the friendship of this large tribe would be disastrous for the British cause in the West. This was tested after the outbreak of the American Revolution, when in 1777 Capt. Charles Michel de Langlade, of the British Indian department, sent his nephew, Charles Gautier de Verville, to arouse the Wisconsin Indians for auxiliaries in Canada to assist in repelling the American invasion. Gautier arrived at the Sauk village in Sauk Prairie in May 1778, only to find that he had been preceded by a "rebel belt," that is, by a messenger from the tribes of the eastern United States, to engage the western Indians to come to the support of Gen. George Washington's army. At the same time a Spanish messenger from Saint Louis arrived bidding for the Sauk trade and alliance.

Thus in the heart of Wisconsin was heard the repercussion of the contest being waged between the British and the colonies, with the outlying support of the Spanish officials. Gautier succeeded in securing a number of Sauk for Langlade's party; but the tribe began moving to the Mississippi near the mouth of Rock River, in what is now northwest Illinois, in order to approach the Spanish and the Americans of the Illinois settlements, which were captured by George Rogers Clark in July 1778. Thereafter, the Sauk forsook for a time their British alliance for that of Clark and the Americans.

BIBLIOGRAPHY

L. P. Kellogg, *British Régime in Wisconsin and the Northwest.*

— LOUISE PHELPS KELLOGG

SAVINGS AND LOAN CRISIS

One of the most dramatic financial stories of the 1980s was the collapse of hundreds of savings and loan institutions (S&Ls, also known as "thrifts") that had became insolvent in the wake of federal deregulation of the industry. As mandated by law, the government stepped in to protect the federally insured depositors of the failed thrifts, at a cost of billions of dollars. Traditionally, S&Ls had provided savings accounts and long-term residential mortgages and had been restricted by government regulation from offering most other types of financial services. With the failure of many S&Ls in the Great Depression, the Federal Savings and Loan Insurance Corporation (FSLIC) was created in 1934 to protect depositors' money. This system worked well in an environment of stable or falling interest rates, but the industry faced severe pressure from rising interest rates in the late 1960s and throughout the 1970s. S&Ls were forced to pay higher short-term rates to attract and keep deposits but could not increase revenue from the long-term, fixed-interest-rate home mortgages they had issued. In 1966 Congress placed a limit on the interest S&Ls could pay on deposits, setting it slightly higher than the rate allowed to banks. This limitation hurt S&Ls in the 1970s as investors began to shift money to higher-paying Treasury bills and newly created money market mutual funds. At the same time, most S&Ls continued to be prohibited from issuing adjustable-rate home mortgages.

Congress attempted to address these problems through a process of deregulation that started in 1980, when the Depository Institutions Deregulation and Monetary Control Act began to phase out interest-rate ceilings on deposits, allowed S&Ls to compete with banks in offering interest-paying checking accounts, and raised federal insurance on deposits to $100,000 per account. Problems continued and in 1981 for the first time the S&L industry as a whole was unprofitable. The Garn–St. Germain Depository Institutions Act of 1982 extended deregulation by authorizing S&Ls to issue adjustable-rate mortgages, permitting up to 40 percent of assets to be invested in nonresidential real estate loans and up to 10 in commercial loans and generally easing net worth and ownership requirements to give S&Ls more flexibility. Concurrently, several states liberalized their own regulation of state-chartered S&Ls, even as these non-federally chartered institutions still qualified for FSLIC deposit insurance.

The S&L industry grew dramatically. Assets soared from $686 billion in 1982 to $1.1 trillion in 1985. In the same period assets held in the traditional home mortgage market fell from 64.7 percent to 38.1 percent. Much of the increased asset base came from large (usually $100,000) deposits gathered nationally by "money brokers," such as Wall Street securities firms. Certain S&Ls, especially in Texas, Florida, Colorado, Arizona, and California, used their new powers to invest heavily in commercial real estate and even riskier investments, such as the high-paying, low-credit-rated "junk bonds" issued by Wall Street firms in the 1980s. The lavish personal expenditures and flamboyance of some S&L executives, many of whom were new to a traditionally low-key industry, garnered public attention. The fundamental problem that brought down many of these high-flying S&Ls was their inordinate exposure to high-risk and unsound investments that in the Southwest turned sour after oil prices plummeted in the mid-1980s. The high rates of interest paid to depositors and the fact that deposits were federally insured were a formula for disaster. Ultimately, government would be liable for the greed and excess of a certain part of the S&L industry.

Many high-flying S&Ls were brought down by their inordinate exposure to high-risk and unsound investments that turned sour after oil prices plummeted in the mid-1980's.

As early as 1985 officials of the Federal Home Loan Bank Board (FHLBB), which regulated S&Ls, were aware of these problems and began to try to deal with them. They were hindered for several years by the failure of Congress to support them and by intervention of lawmakers on behalf of specific S&Ls. Still, quicker action by the FHLBB would not have eliminated the bad loans and investments already on the books of S&Ls. To close insolvent institutions required increased capitalization of the FSLIC insurance fund. Congress in 1987 approved a limited increase, inadequate to make much of a dent in the problem. Less money for the FSLIC meant fewer bad S&Ls could be closed, and House Majority Leader Jim Wright of Texas intervened on behalf of a group of Texas S&L owners. The FSLIC requested $15 billion in additional funds but received less than half that amount. The most celebrated case of successful lobbying to thwart federal regulators was that of the "Keating Five." Charles H. Keating, Jr., enlisted the aid of five senators—Alan Cranston of California, Dennis DeConcini and John McCain of Arizona, Donald W. Riegle, Jr., of Michigan, and John Glenn of Ohio—on behalf of his troubled Lincoln Savings and Loan. Keating contributed a total of $1.4 million to the campaign funds of these senators and was able to keep going until 1989, when Lincoln closed at an estimated cost to taxpayers of $2.5 billion. He later served a prison term for securities violations, and the five senators, particularly Cranston, were reprimanded by their colleagues.

Faced with limited congressional cooperation, the FHLBB in 1988 began to close insolvent S&Ls by arranging for their acquisition by outside investors; 205 S&Ls were disposed of in this fashion. The full dimensions of the problem, however, required the attention of President George Bush and Congress, which led in 1989 to the Financial Institutions Reform, Recovery, and Enforcement Act (FIRREA). This sweeping legislation authorized initial borrowing of an additional $50 billion to support the cleanup and established a new agency, the Resolution Trust Corporation (RTC), to carry out this task. The FHLBB was abolished and regulation of the remaining healthy S&Ls was lodged in the Office of Thrift Supervision in the Department of the Treasury. The FSLIC was merged into the Federal Deposit Insurance Corporation, which insured commercial bank deposits. Higher insurance premiums, much tighter net worth requirements, and restrictions on lending and investment practices were placed on S&Ls. This caused additional institutions that had not been greatly involved in the excesses of the 1980s to be closed or merged with banks. By 1995 the RTC had sold or merged 747 insolvent thrifts, leaving a smaller but presumably healthier industry. The cost to taxpayers under FIRREA was $180 billion, significantly higher than the initial expectations when the RTC was created but ultimately less than other estimates, which ranged as high as $500 billion. In any case, the savings and loan crisis was a sobering experience that raised many questions about business, government, and politics in the United States in the late twentieth century.

[See also Banking and Finance; Corruption, Political; Reaganomics.]

BIBLIOGRAPHY

Edward J. Kane, *The Gathering Crisis in Federal Deposit Insurance* (Cambridge, Mass., 1985).

Lawrence J. White, *The S&L Debacle* (New York, 1991).

— JOHN B. WEAVER

SCAB

Scab, a term of opprobrium applied to one who takes the job of a union worker during a strike. The word was used in 1806 at a trial in Philadelphia of eight workingmen for intimidation of nonunion men. A journeyman shoemaker testified that when he came to America from England in 1794, he was notified that he must either join the shoemakers' union or be considered a "scab" and be forbidden to work with union men. The word "scab" did not come into public notice until about 1885–86, when unions were coalescing into great national organizations. Its meaning had to be explained to a congressional committee in the latter year.

BIBLIOGRAPHY

Mary Ritter Beard, *The American Labor Movement.*

— ALVIN F. HARLOW

SCALAWAG

Scalawag, the term of opprobrium applied by conservative southerners to those native whites who joined with the freedmen and the carpetbaggers in support of Republican policies during Radical Reconstruction. The word, originally used to describe runty or diseased cattle, came to be a synonym in the antebellum period for a "mean fellow, a scape grace," and acquired its political connotations after the war.

Scalawags came from all elements of southern society. In the states of the upper South, where they were most numerous, white Republicans were generally hill-country farmers characterized by their Unionist sympathies. In contrast, those in the Deep South came from elements of the planter-business aristocracy with Whig antecedents. The role of the scalawags in Reconstruction has generally been underrated. Comprising approximately 20 percent of the white electorate, they often provided the crucial margin of victory for the Republicans. In the constitutional conventions of 1867–68 and the subsequent state governments they exerted leadership disproportionate to their popular strength.

BIBLIOGRAPHY

Warren A. Ellem, "Who Were the Mississippi Scalawags?" *Journal of Southern History,* vol. 38 (May 1972).

John Hope Franklin, *Reconstruction After the Civil War.*

Allen W. Trelease, "Who Were the Scalawags?" *Journal of Southern History,* vol. 29 (November 1963).

— WILLIAM G. SHADE

SCOPES TRIAL

The fundamentalist movement, which arose in the United States about 1910, led to the passage of laws in Tennessee, Mississippi, and Arkansas forbidding the teaching of the theory of evolution in the public schools and colleges of the state. In 1925, in Tennessee, a twenty-five-year-old high school teacher, John Thomas Scopes, was tried for violating the state's "monkey law" (the Butler Act of Mar. 21, 1925). The case began with an argument between Scopes and three friends, on May 5, 1925, in a drugstore in Dayton. They decided to engineer a test case to settle the law's constitutionality and incidentally to "put Dayton on the map."

The Monkey Trial, as it was popularly known, began on July 10 and aroused enormous interest. William Jennings Bryan, political leader and ardent fundamentalist, served as a volunteer lawyer for the prosecution, while Scopes had as defenders

Defense attorney Clarence Darrow (left) and prosecutor William Jennings Bryan presided over the Scopes "Monkey Trial" in 1925, in which a Tennessee high school teacher was charged with violating state law by teaching the theory of evolution. The sensational trial resulted in a guilty verdict, which was later overturned on appeal. (Corbis-Bettmann)

several eminent attorneys, including Clarence S. Darrow. Judge John T. Raulston tried to run a fair and orderly trial, but this proved hard in the circus atmosphere that sprang up in the normally quiet, conservative town. Dayton swarmed with evangelists, eccentrics, and traveling showmen, some of whom exhibited tame chimpanzees.

The defense planned to attack the law on three main constitutional grounds: first, that it violated the First and Fourteenth amendments to the Constitution by writing into the law a religious doctrine, namely fundamentalist creationism; second, that it was unreasonable in that it forbade the teaching of a well-established fact of nature; and third, that it was vague, because it did not say whether it meant "teach" in the sense of "set forth" or "explain" or in the sense of "advocate" or "recommend." To prove the second point, the defense brought to Dayton a dozen scientists to testify to the overwhelming evidence for evolution. The prosecution, however, succeeded in having such testimony excluded as irrelevant, so the scientists remained merely spectators.

Toward the end of the trial, Darrow called Bryan as an expert witness on the Bible. Fearing for the floor of the old courthouse because of the number of spectators, Judge Raulston had moved the trial out on the lawn. In an hour and a half of grilling, Darrow showed that Bryan, although a man of many attractive qualities, knew nothing about many subjects on which he had pontificated and could not understand scientific reasoning. On the next day, Raulston expunged the Darrow-Bryan debate from the record and called in the jury. Darrow hinted that he wanted a guilty verdict to make possible an appeal. The jury obliged, and Scopes was fined $100.

When the case was appealed, the Tennessee Supreme Court set aside the verdict because the judge had committed a legal blunder in levying the fine. At the courts' suggestion, the prosecution nol-prossed the bizarre case. Scopes, who admitted that he had never taught evolution at all (he had been too busy coaching the football team), became a geologist. Bryan died in his sleep five days after the trial. The Butler Act was repealed in 1967, and shortly thereafter the two remaining laws prohibiting the teaching of evolution were found unconstitutional.

BIBLIOGRAPHY

L. Sprague de Camp, *The Great Monkey Trial.*
Ray Ginger, *Six Days or Forever?*

— L. SPRAGUE DE CAMP

SCOTCH-IRISH

Scotch-Irish, a people, in the American colonies and the United States, emanating from the Scottish Protestants who were transplanted to Ulster, Ireland, chiefly during the 17th century, and from their descendants. The migrations from Scotland to Ulster, begun during the years from 1607 to 1609 under the sponsorship of James I, continued intermittently throughout the century. By the close of the 17th century, adverse economic conditions and political and religious disabilities arose, creating in them a desire to leave Ireland. Their farms were owned by absent English landlords who demanded high rentals; parliamentary regulation, 1665–80, seriously impaired their cattle-raising industry; the Woolens Act of 1699, which forbade the exportation of wool from Ireland, rendered sheep raising unprofitable; an act of Parliament in 1704, excluding Presbyterians from holding civil and military offices, denied them a voice in government; and the government taxed them to support the Anglican church, in which they did not worship. Consequently, thousands of these people from Ulster, with their Scotch heritage, their experience in colonization, and their Presbyterian faith, emigrated to America.

The Scotch-Irish began to arrive in the American colonies as early as the middle of the 17th century, if not before, and continued to settle in small numbers until about 1715. This influx was greatly accelerated after 1717, because of efforts of English landlords to increase rentals on Ulster farms held under long-term. leases that were expiring in that year. Thereafter, a steady stream of Scotch-Irish poured into American ports, as many as 10,000 reputedly arriving in Pennsylvania within a single year. The total number of these immigrants to America has never been definitely ascertained, but various studies indicate that in 1790 probably 6 percent of the total U.S. population, or approximately 225,000 people, were Scotch-Irish or of Scotch-Irish extraction.

On their arrival in America, they scattered themselves widely and established clusters of settlement in every colony. Their tendency was to penetrate to the frontiers, however, following the main channels of migration to the fertile lands along the streams and in the valleys of the mountains of the backcountry. While Scotch-Irish immigrants arrived in nearly every port along the Atlantic seaboard, Baltimore and Philadelphia were the chief ports of entry. From Baltimore many of these settlers followed the Potomac River westward to the Shenandoah Valley and turned southward into the back counties of Maryland, Virginia, and the Carolinas or went westward to the Monongahela country in southwestern Pennsylvania; others went northward along the Susquehanna River and into the valleys between the mountain ranges in Pennsylvania. From Philadelphia, many followed the Delaware River to the north or went westward to the frontier. Thus, while Scotch-Irish settlers were found in every colony, the frontier regions of Pennsylvania and the southern colonies received the greater contingents. Approximately 65,000 Scotch-Irish settled in the piedmont of North Carolina between 1739 and the Revolution. As the frontiers moved westward across the continent, the Scotch-Irish and their descendants, usually among the vanguard of settlers, migrated to the newer regions. While they may now be found in every state in the Union, they settled in greater numbers in Tennessee, Kentucky, Missouri, Ohio, Indiana, and Illinois.

Scotch-Irish contributions to the development of the United States have been great. Rugged and daring, they made fine settlers on the more extended frontiers; their educated ministers gave an effective intellectual leadership and stimulated the founding of many institutions of higher learning; and their qualities for leadership and their inclination for politics produced from among them fine political leaders in every generation.

BIBLIOGRAPHY

R. J. Dickson, *Ulster Emigration to Colonial America, 1718–1775.*
Ian C. Graham, *Colonists From Scotland.*
E. R. Green, ed., *Essays in Scotch-Irish History.*
James G. Leyburn, *The Scotch-Irish.*

— R. J. FERGUSON

SCOTTSBORO CASE

In April 1931 in Scottsboro, Ala., eight of nine black teenagers were convicted and sentenced to death for allegedly raping two white women. (The ninth was sentenced to life imprisonment.) From 1931 to 1937, during a series of appeals and new trials, the case grew to an international cause célèbre as the International Labor Defense (ILD) and the Communist Party of the U.S.A. spearheaded efforts to free the "Scottsboro boys." In 1932 the U.S. Supreme Court concluded that the defendants had been denied adequate counsel (*Powell* v. *Alabama*), and the following year Alabama Judge James Edwin Horton ordered a new trial because of insufficient evidence. In 1935 the Supreme Court again ruled in favor of the defendants by overturning convictions on the ground that Alabama had systematically excluded blacks from jury service (*Norris* v. *Alabama*).

But public opinion in Alabama had solidified against the Scottsboro youths and their backers, and each successful appeal was followed by retrial and reconviction.

Defense attorney Samuel Liebowitz talks over the case with his client Heywood Patterson, thrice convicted and thrice doomed defendant in the Scottsboro cases, while behind him stands Clarence Norris. (UPI/Corbis-Bettmann)

Finally, in 1937, defense attorney Samuel Leibowitz and the nonpartisan Scottsboro Defense Committee arranged a compromise whereby four of the nine defendants were released and the remaining five were given sentences ranging from twenty years to life. Four of the five defendants were released on parole from 1943 to 1950. The fifth escaped prison in 1948 and successfully fled to Michigan. In 1966 Judge Horton revealed theretofore confidential information that conclusively proved the innocence of the nine defendants.

BIBLIOGRAPHY

Dan T. Carter, *Scottsboro: A Tragedy of the American South.*

— DAN T. CARTER

SEARCH AND SEIZURE, UNREASONABLE

The American colonists' hostility to general warrants, which authorized the apprehension of unnamed persons and indiscriminate search of their papers, and writs of assistance, which empowered customs officials to search, at their will, wherever they suspected uncustomed goods to be, is reflected in the Fourth Amendment to the U.S. Constitution, which prohibits "unreasonable searches and seizures" and requires that warrants be issued upon "probable cause, supported by oath or affirmation, and particularly describing the place to be searched, and the person or things to be seized."

Unless exceptional circumstances exist, such as the need to act swiftly to prevent the destruction of evidence, an officer may not search simply because he has "probable cause," or reasonable grounds, to do so; he must obtain a search warrant, a written authorization by a judicial officer. An arrest may be made without a warrant, even though it is practicable to obtain one. "Incident to the arrest," the person may then be searched without a warrant, as may the area "within his immediate control," in order to protect the arresting officer against attack by hidden weapons or to prevent the destruction of evidence. In the 1968 so-called stop-and-frisk cases, the U.S. Supreme Court held that an officer who lacks adequate grounds to make an arrest or search may nevertheless briefly detain a person in a public place and frisk him—that is, conduct a carefully limited search of the outer clothing of such a person to discover weapons.

The U.S. Supreme Court, in *Mapp* v. *Ohio* (1961), held that the Fourth Amendment is enforceable against the states through the due process clause of the Fourteenth Amendment and requires the exclusion of illegally seized evidence in state, as well as federal, prosecutions. This decision overturned *Wolf* v. *Colorado* (1949). By 1975 the continued vitality of this doctrine, known as the "exclusionary rule," appeared to be in serious jeopardy. It had been criticized by numerous legal commentators and law enforcement officials and, in 1971, by Chief Justice Warren E. Burger as not worth the high price it extracts from society—the release of many guilty criminals.

BIBLIOGRAPHY

Jacob Landynski, *Search and Seizure and the Supreme Court.*

Wayne LaFave, " 'Street Encounters' and the Constitution," *Michigan Law Review*, vol. 67 (1968).

Dallin Oaks, "Studying the Exclusionary Rule in Search and Seizure," *University of Chicago Law Review*, vol. 37 (1970).

— YALE KAMISAR

SECESSION, ORDINANCE OF

Ordinance of secession was the enactment in legal form by which eleven southern states withdrew from the Union in 1860–61. According to the compact theory of union, sovereign states had entered the partnership by ratifying the Constitution of the United States. Secession, therefore, was achieved by a repeal of the act of ratification. This was accomplished in each state by a convention, elected for the purpose, as the instrumentality of government most nearly expressive of the sovereign will of the people.

BIBLIOGRAPHY

D. L. Dumond, *The Secessionist Movement, 1860—1861.*

— C. MILDRED THOMPSON

SECESSION, RIGHT OF

The southern states of the American Union were advancing no new theory when they appealed to and exercised the right of secession in 1860–61. Publicists and statesmen had championed the right from the beginning of American independence. The right of a people to establish, alter, or abolish their government and to institute a new one if their safety and happiness demanded it was a fundamental principle of the American Revolution. This idea was the basis of the threat of both Vermont and Kentucky during the 1780's to separate from the Confederation and set up independent governments, or to ally with some foreign power.

More specifically the right of secession was based on the doctrine of state sovereignty and the compact theory of the Union. James Madison stated this theory very clearly when he wrote: "Our governmental system is established by compact, not between the Government of the United States and the State Governments but between the states as sovereign communities, stipulating each with the other. . . . "

South Carolina nullified the tariff acts of 1828 and 1832 and signified its intention of seceding if the federal government attempted coercion.

The first serious threat of secession came in 1798 when the Democratic-Republicans, smarting under Federalist legislation, talked of separation. John L. Taylor, a prominent North Carolina judge, openly advocated secession, but the more moderate views of Thomas Jefferson prevailed, and Virginia and Kentucky adopted their resolutions condemning the legislation as unconstitutional, null and void, and proclaiming the right of the states to interpose or nullify such acts. Jefferson's purpose was to appeal to the people in the election of 1800, rather than to apply either nullification or secession.

After Jefferson's presidential victory in 1801 the New England Federalists sought a remedy against Democratic domination. Sen. Timothy Pickering of Massachusetts said that "the principles of our Revolution point to the remedy—a separation." The purchase of Louisiana further antagonized the Federalists, and the Essex Junto planned a new confederacy composed of New England and New York, "exempt from the corrupt . . . influence and oppression of the aristocratic democrats of the South." Alexander Hamilton blocked their efforts, but Rep. Josiah Quincy of Massachusetts still maintained in 1811 that the admission of Louisiana would dissolve the Union. The disgruntled Federalists of New England resorted to treasonable action in opposing "Mr. Madison's war," and in 1814 met in the Hartford Convention behind closed doors and in utmost secrecy. There is little doubt that their object was the dissolution of the Union and the formation of a New England confederacy if their program of constitutional reform failed. Fortunately the news of the peace treaty prevented action.

The next rumblings of discontent were heard in the southern states. Threats of separation were made over both the Missouri question and the Indian controversy, and the tariff issue brought these threats to the very threshold of action. South Carolina nullified the tariff acts of 1828 and 1832 and signified its intention of seceding if the federal government attempted coercion.

Slavery in the territories caused both North and South to threaten to secede. John Quincy Adams thought the free states would secede if Texas were annexed, and the southern leaders threatened separation if slavery were excluded from the Mexican cession. This controversy culminated in the assembling of the Nashville Convention of 1850 and of state conventions in several southern states. These conventions reluctantly accepted the Compromise of 1850 and secession was halted. The abolitionists called a convention of all the free states to meet at Cleveland in 1857 to consider separation, but the depression prevented the meeting.

The threat of secession was the last resort of the minority to protect its interests under the Constitution, and was constantly present from the Revolution to the Civil War.

[See also Declaration of Independence; Missouri Compromise; Nullification.]

BIBLIOGRAPHY

Alpheus Thomas Mason, ed., *The States Rights Debate: Anti-Federalism and the Constitution.*

Paul C. Nagel, *One Nation Indivisible: The Union in American Thought, 1776–1861.*

— FLETCHER M. GREEN

SECESSION OF SOUTHERN STATES

On Abraham Lincoln's election to the presidency, the governor of South Carolina, William H. Gist, recommended and the legislature called a state convention (that being the method by which the Constitution of 1787 was ratified), which met amidst great excitement on Dec. 20, 1860. By a unanimous vote the convention passed an ordinance dissolving "the union now subsisting between South Carolina and other States." The convention issued a Declaration of Immediate Causes, expressing the states' rights view of the Union, and appointed commissioners to other southern states and to Washington, D.C. This action seemed precipitate by many who favored further efforts to secure constitutional rights (through an all-southern convention, appeals to the North, or compromise through Congress). But South Carolina had assurances that other states would follow, and many thought that better terms might be made out of the Union than in it. Overriding minorities, six other states by conventions passed ordinances of secession early in 1861: Mississippi, Jan. 9 (84 to 15); Florida, Jan. 10 (62 to 7); Alabama, Jan. 11 (61 to 39); Georgia, Jan. 19 (164 to 133); Louisiana, Jan. 26 (113 to 17); and Texas (over the opposition of Gov. Sam Houston), Feb. 1 (166 to 8), thus completing the secession of the lower South. Nearly all who voted against secession did so because they doubted its expediency, not the right.

President James Buchanan, believing secession unconstitutional but considering himself without authority to coerce, and anxious not to give the upper South cause for secession, was determined not to risk war by an overt act in protecting federal property (such as forts, arsenals, and post offices) and sustaining the operation of federal laws. The South Carolina commissioners, sent to negotiate with Buchanan for the peaceful division of property and debts, demanded that Maj. Robert Anderson, then occupying Fort Sumter in Charleston harbor, evacuate that post, inasmuch as continued federal occupancy was inconsistent with the sovereignty of South Carolina. This he refused to do. Meanwhile Congress, despite an address from some southern members saying that "All hope of relief in the Union, through the agency of committees, Congressional legislation, or constitutional amendments, is extinguished," was sifting compromise proposals. Of these the Crittenden Compromise, involving the extension of the Missouri Compromise line, was the more hopeful, but it failed to get the support of the Republican leaders, as did Kentucky Sen. John J. Crittenden's suggestion for a national referendum. More certain was the failure (because opposed by the extremists on either side) of the Washington Peace Conference (Border Slave State Convention) that, two months later, presented proposals similar to Crittenden's.

With compromise failing and with Buchanan taking a firmer attitude as he became less hopeful of peace and union (he sent the *Star of the West* to reinforce Sumter), representatives from the seceded states met at Montgomery on Feb. 4, 1861, to organize a new nation. Lincoln's inaugural promise "to hold, occupy, and possess the property and places belonging to the government," coupled with his assertion that "Physically speaking, we cannot separate," seemed none the less threatening by his assurance, "The government will not assail you." Peaceful secession seemed remote after Lincoln's fateful decision to relieve Fort Sumter, the firing on the fort on Apr. 12, and Lincoln's call for volunteers three days later. This practical state of war compelled the states of the upper South to make a reluctant choice between the Confederacy and the Union.

Earlier in April the Virginia convention voted against secession (88 to 45), preferring a conference of the border states and further discussions with Lincoln. But two days after the call for volunteers the convention, Apr. 17, adopted the ordinance of secession (88 to 55), which was ratified by popular vote on May 23, although the convention had entered into a military league with the Confederacy on Apr. 24. In Arkansas opinion was very evenly divided (a popular referendum had been set for Aug. 5), but the governor rejected Lincoln's call for militia, and on May 6 the convention passed the secession ordinance (65 to 5). Tennessee, like Virginia, had large nonslaveholding sections where many people for geographic, economic, or social reasons did not feel that their interests would be served by the Confederacy. The legislature on Jan. 19 provided for a popular vote for delegates to a convention and for the convention itself, which was rejected (Feb. 9) by a vote of 68,282 to 59,449. After the firing on Fort Sumter and the threat of coercion, the legislature ratified a league with the Confederacy (May 7) and authorized the governor to raise a force of 55,000 men. On June 8 the people voted for secession (104,913 to 47,238). The opposition to secession in western Virginia led to the formation of a separate state; a like movement in eastern Tennessee proved abortive. The unanimous vote for secession by the convention of North Carolina, the last state to secede (May 20), was clearly the result of Lincoln's proclamation. The border slave states of Kentucky, Maryland, Delaware, and Missouri did not secede, and Kentucky's attempted neutrality failed.

BIBLIOGRAPHY

William Barney, *The Road to Secession.*
Steven A. Channing, *Crisis of Fear: Secession in South Carolina.*
Avery O. Craven, *The Coming of the Civil War.*
D. L. Dumond, *The Secessionist Movement, 1860–61.*
Kenneth Stampp, *And the War Came.*

— R. H. WOODY

SECRET SERVICE, UNITED STATES

United States Secret Service was created on July 5, 1865, as a bureau of the Department of the Treasury, to suppress rampant counterfeiting. It was estimated during the Civil War that one-third of the currency in circulation was counterfeit. Because there were approximately 1,600 state banks designing and printing their own notes and each note bore a different design, it was difficult to distinguish one of the 4,000 varieties of counterfeit notes from the 7,000 varieties of genuine notes. It was hoped that the adoption of a national currency in 1863 would resolve the problem. But it, too, was soon counterfeited extensively, so that it became necessary for the government to take enforcement measures.

In addition to the suppression of counterfeiting, the Secret Service was often requested to conduct investigations later assigned to other government agencies. These investigations included such matters as mail frauds, bank and train robberies, bounty claims, illicit traffic in whiskey, Ku Klux Klan activities, and counterespionage (during the Spanish-American War and World War I). The Secret Service continues to suppress forgery and fraudulent negotiation or redemption of government checks, bonds, and other obligations or securities of the United States.

Since its inception, the Secret Service has greatly expanded. After the assassination of President William McKinley in Buffalo, N.Y., in 1901, it was assigned to protect President Theodore Roosevelt, although legislation authorizing presidential protection by the Secret Service was not enacted until 1906. In 1913 such protection was also authorized for the president-elect, and in 1917 for members of the president's immediate family. An act of Congress in 1951 authorized the Secret Service to protect the vice-president. Protection was also later extended to the vice-president-elect, a former president and his wife during his lifetime, the widow of a former president until her death or remarriage, and minor children of a former president until they reach sixteen years of age. Protection for major presidential and vice-presidential candidates was authorized in 1968; recipients of such protection are designated by the secretary of the Treasury after consultation with an advisory committee.

On Mar. 19, 1970, President Richard M. Nixon signed legislation establishing the Executive Protective Service, a uniformed division of the Secret Service. This increased the size and responsibilities of the former

White House Police Force. The Executive Protective Service protects the White House and foreign missions in the metropolitan area of the District of Columbia. In January 1971 Congress enacted legislation authorizing the Secret Service to protect a visiting head of a foreign state or foreign government and, at the direction of the president, other distinguished foreign visitors to the United States and official representatives of the United States performing special missions abroad.

BIBLIOGRAPHY

Harry E. Neal, *The Story of the Secret Service.*

— JAMES J. ROWLEY

SECRET SOCIETIES

Secret societies existed in rudimentary form among primitive peoples and have appeared in all lands and ages, but they have been especially numerous and active in the United States. Organized, in most instances, for the social and moral welfare of their members and to promote good fellowship and patriotism, secret societies have apparently met a deep-seated psychological need in the American people. In addition they have done a great amount of charitable and educational work that has been of advantage to the general community. Freemasonry, the ritual and philosophy of which have influenced many similar organizations, was introduced from Great Britain about 1730; the Independent Order of Odd-fellows was brought over from the same country in 1819. A roster of indigenous societies would reach encyclopedic proportions. A few well-known ones are the Knights of Pythias, founded in 1864; the Benevolent and Protective Order of Elks, 1868; the Knights of Columbus, 1882; and the Loyal Order of Moose, 1888.

A strong popular prejudice against secret societies in the 1820's was directed not only at the Masons but at college fraternities.

For a decade following 1826 there was a strong popular prejudice against secret orders. While directed primarily against the Masons, this prejudice was even directed against college fraternities, which during this period were under popular disfavor and which were the subjects of an extensive literature of exposure and denunciation in the press. The movement soon subsided; Masonry quickly revived; new societies were formed; and ritual and secrecy were effectively used to promote a wide variety of causes—temperance, liquor control, agricultural improvement, life insurance, and the betterment of the underprivileged. Local societies occasionally showed vigilante proclivities, pursuing alleged evildoers with tar and feathers, birch rods, or even more lethal weapons.

The subversive and revolutionary secret society, so common in European countries, has had an unfruitful field in America, although the prerevolutionary activity of the Sons of Liberty, the disloyal operations of the Knights of the Golden Circle during the Civil War, and the Molly Maguires in the post-Civil War period are somewhat analogous. Antiforeign and anti-Catholic prejudice produced the secret Know-Nothing party in the 1850's, and history repeated itself seventy years later in the similar activities of the revived Ku Klux Klan. For the most part American secret societies have avoided direct participation in politics, but the mere existence of large and cohesive bodies of brethren has made them a factor to be considered by politicians.

BIBLIOGRAPHY

Arkon Daraul, *A History of Secret Societies.*

— W. A. ROBINSON

SECTIONALISM

The United States is by no means a homogeneous entity in regard to such characteristics as physiography, geography, topography, ecology, and climate. Understanding the nation comes more easily when one thinks of it in terms of regions: the Appalachian Mountains, the Mississippi watershed, the Great Plains, the Rocky Mountains, the Far West. The United States is filled with economic diversity as well. The economy of the tidewater South is not the same as that of the Ozark Mountains; the economy of the upper Great Plains is strikingly different from that of the American Southwest; New England's economic status and problems sharply contrast with those in areas around the Great Lakes. Political interests of Americans living in these and other regions of the United States have been affected by the physical and economic characteristics of the separate regions. Despite the fact that the nation has gained a degree of political cohesion because of the presence of national political parties, regional influence on leaders and members of those parties has had great impact; political sectionalism has been the result. Of the many factors contributing to sectionalism, the economic interests of the people in a given region or regions are the most important.

The spirit of sectionalism and its manifestations have been present throughout American history, and every major region of the nation has strongly espoused its sectional interests at one time or another. Charles Pinckney's statement "When I say Southern, I mean Maryland, and the states to the southward of her" was made when the Constitutional Convention was bogged down over the question of the economic interests of the South. Although less cohesive than the South, the middle states at that time expressed united concern for the protection of their grain exports. New England sectionalism appeared during the War of 1812, when citizens of that region generally criticized "Mr. Madison's war." Pioneers who drove the frontier westward quickly developed loyalties to their new regions, soon advancing the economic and political interests of their section.

During the first half of the 19th century the United States consisted of three large and rather ill-defined regions: the North (the area north of the Ohio River and the Mason-Dixon Line); the South (the region below that boundary); and the West (the large area west of the Appalachian Mountains). To a large extent the history of the United States from 1800 to 1865 is the history of the relationship of those three regions. The positions and interactions of the people and leaders of these regions on a number of economic issues revealed militant sectionalism.

The question of how the United States should dispose of its vast public lands divided the nation. Northerners and southerners generally believed that the western lands should be sold to the highest bidder, gaining revenue for the U.S. Treasury. Westerners were not yet advocating that the land be given away (as they did after the Civil War), but they did favor a policy of charging settlers only a minimum amount of money for the land. Trade between North and West was advanced when somewhat better transportation facilities were developed, and both sections' economies improved as the West supplied the North with food and the North shipped the West needed manufactured goods. When states and private enterprise did not provide enough means of transportation between the two regions, northerners and westerners demanded that the national government construct additional internal improvements at national expense. The South did not stand to gain by the building of national canals and roads, and it objected to national money being spent on such projects. As the North developed more industry it demanded that Congress pass a protective tariff; the South remained primarily an agricultural region, trading cotton and tobacco in European and world markets, and it preferred that the nation adopt low tariff rates. The West was divided on the tariff: the Northwest favored a high tariff, while the Southwest desired low rates.

Thus, no two sections had identical interests, and the West was divided within itself on the tariff question. Under the circumstances, the sections engaged in much political maneuvering to obtain the economic advantages each desired for itself. The tariff dispute brought a crisis in 1832, when South Carolina took the extreme action of nullifying a tariff law passed by Congress. A compromise resolved the disagreement, but the events were a portent of future sectional conflict.

The question of the expansion of slavery into the western territories overshadowed all other sectional concerns in the twenty years prior to the Civil War. Northerners hoped to prohibit the spread of slavery, while southerners believed they had the right to take their slaves wherever they migrated. The economic and political implications of the slavery dispute were great, and soon these subjects became intertwined with sectional prestige and honor. The annexation of Texas, the Wilmot Proviso, the Mexican War, and the admission of California as a state all became primarily sectional issues, on which leaders of both North and South staked their political future. The two sections were driven farther apart in the decade of the 1850's, until war became the only means by which to settle their differences. The Civil War was the ultimate consequence of extreme sectionalism. Although the Civil War abolished slavery and held together a badly divided nation, sectionalism did not die at Appomattox. During the Reconstruction era political and economic interests dominated the actions of many of the nation's leaders, both northern and southern. These activities intensified sectional feelings, creating bitterness that lasted well into the 20th century.

After Reconstruction various regions manifested sectionalism from time to time, but the region most closely associated with that concept remained the South. The development of what became known as the Solid South, the relegation of the freed black to a position of inferiority, and the status of the South as an economic appendage of the North were all manifestations of a nation not yet free of severe sectional differences. By mid-20th century the Solid South was breaking up; southern states began to cast electoral votes for Republican presidential candidates, and state Republican parties became more competitive with the dominant Democrats. At the same time blacks demanded and received some of the rights of American citizens, and white southerners learned to live with the new status of black southerners. The southern economy continued to be greatly influenced by northern corporations, but southern companies were established and in some instances competed with the outsiders. In any case, the southern economy prospered because of the presence and growth of industry, the South's standard of living rose, and southerners had increased purchasing power. All these factors combined to diminish the concept of sectionalism in the South, although it continued to be a political and economic factor between rural and urban areas around the nation.

BIBLIOGRAPHY

Monroe Billington, *The American South: A Brief History.*

Avery O. Craven, *The Growth of Southern Nationalism, 1848–1861.*

David Brion Davis, *The Slave Power Conspiracy and the Paranoid Style.*

William B. Hesseltine, "Regions, Classes and Sections in American History," *Journal of Land and Public Utility Economics,* vol. 20 (1944), and "Sectionalism and Regionalism in American History," *Journal of Southern History,* vol. 26 (1960).

Kenneth M. Stampp, *The Era of Reconstruction, 1865–1877.*

Charles S. Sydnor, *The Development of Southern Sectionalism, 1819–1848.*

George Brown Tindall, *The Emergence of the New South, 1913–1945.*

Frederick Jackson Turner, *Rise of the New West, 1819–1829, The United States, 1830–1850: The Nation and Its Sections, and The Significance of Sections in American History.*

C. Vann Woodward, *Origins of the New South, 1877–1913.*

— MONROE BILLINGTON

SEDITION ACTS

Two national sedition acts had been passed in the United States by the mid-1970's. The first, passed by the Federalist-dominated Congress of 1798, was intended to halt Democratic-Republican attacks on the government and to ferret out pro-French sympathizers in case of war with France. Two complementary alien acts allowed the government to deport French and pro-French foreigners who were generally supporters of the Democratic-Republican party. The second sedition act, passed during World War I, was aimed at subversives, such as pacifists or "Bolsheviks" who interfered with the war effort.

The Sedition Act of 1798 reestablished the English common law on seditious libel, but with some important changes. The new law accepted the idea of jury determination of sedition and also allowed truth to be considered in defense. Whether or not the act violated the First Amendment's intention of abolishing seditious libel was not established at the time, but certainly the partisan use of the act added weight to the Democratic-Republican conviction that it did so. The act expired in 1801, and during President Thomas Jefferson's tenure in office all persons convicted under the act were pardoned; Congress eventually voted to repay all fines levied against the convicted. Although the act expired before its constitutionality could be tested, it was generally assumed to be unconstitutional, and in 1964 the Supreme Court flatly declared it inconsistent with the First Amendment in *New York Times Company* v. *Sullivan.*

The Sedition Act of 1918 made it a felony to interfere in the war effort; to insult the government, the Constitution, or the armed forces; and "by word or act [to] support or favor the cause of the German Empire or its allies in the present war, or by word or act [to] oppose the cause of the United States." The most vital difference between this act and that of 1798 was the emphasis in 1918 on criticism of the government and its symbols as opposed to the listing of individual officers in the 1798 act. The most significant statement of judicial opposition to the Sedition Act of 1918 is contained in the dissenting opinions of justices Oliver Wendell Holmes and Louis D. Brandeis in *Abrams* v. *United States* (1919). The national hysteria produced by the war, climaxing in the Red scare and the Palmer raids (mass arrests of political and labor agitators, under the auspices of Attorney General A. Mitchell Palmer), ran its course by the early 1920's, and the Sedition Act was repealed in 1921. Similar acts passed by the states resulted in litigation reaching the Supreme Court. The most notable decision in this area was *Gitlow* v. *New York* (1925), in which the Court began extending the strictures of the First Amendment to the states.

Although the Alien Registration Act of 1940, better known as the Smith Act, is not called a sedition act, it had that as a major purpose. Rather than forbidding criticism of government officers, the Smith Act prohibits advocacy of forceful overthrow of the government and makes it a crime to belong to an organization subsequently found to be guilty of advocating forceful removal of the government. Interpretations of such laws as these are generally determined by whether one sees them as necessary to national security or as threats to freedom of speech and press.

BIBLIOGRAPHY

Zechariah Chaffee, Jr., *Freedom of Speech.*

Leonard W. Levy, *Legacy of Suppression.*

— JOSEPH A. DOWLING

SEGREGATION

Segregation, in American history, refers to attempts by the white, Anglo-Saxon majority to separate and keep apart from themselves certain minority groups such as Afro-Americans, Indians, immigrants, and Mexican-Americans. During the colonial period and early years of the United States, white Americans generally kept themselves apart from the Indians whose lands they preempted. This action became official government policy shortly after the Civil War, when Indians were separated from whites by a reservation system. European and Oriental immigrants were crowded into the ghettos of the larger urban centers of the nation, and the Mexican-Americans of the Southwest were similarly segregated from whites. Segregation has existed throughout the nation's history and in all regions, but it has been most closely associated with the South and the efforts of southern whites to relegate blacks to a position of inferiority. Segregation of the white and black races was a recognized element in the pre-Civil War slave system; and after slavery was abolished, white southerners were determined to continue racial separation. Examples of black integration into white society existed in the Reconstruction South, but many more instances of segregation occurred, and after a brief period of uncertainty regarding the relative relationship of the two races, segregated conditions crystallized, placing the black citizen at a disadvantage in social, political, educational, and economic spheres.

Several southern states early passed laws forbidding blacks to ride in first-class passenger railway cars, and numerous local ordinances requiring racial segregation in most public facilities followed. The enactment of these laws stimulated the U.S. Congress to pass the Civil Rights Act of 1875, to assure equal accommodations in public conveyances, inns, theaters, and other places of public entertainment. In 1883 the Supreme Court ruled this act unconstitutional, declaring that states could not abridge the privileges of American citizens but pointedly excluding individuals and private corporations from this restriction. When blacks complained that railroads discriminated against them, the Interstate Commerce Commission ruled that the railroads must provide equal facilities for members of both races. Even though facilities for blacks were never equal, the Supreme Court upheld the validity of a separate-but-equal transportation law in the *Plessy* v. *Ferguson* (1896) decision. The separate-but-equal concept spread to other areas, particularly education, in the years that followed, and it went without successful challenge for nearly sixty years. In the meantime, southerners had circumscribed many areas of contact between the races. City governments and state legislatures adopted ordinances prohibiting certain activities by blacks. Unwritten laws, regulations, customs, traditions, and practices restricting the freedom of blacks in all parts of the country also developed. From 1900 to the beginning of World War II, the injustices and inequities of racial discrimination were present in the South in almost every area of human activity. Transportation and residential restrictions were commonplace. Public parks, golf courses, swimming pools, and beaches were segregated. Marriage between the races was made illegal in most southern states. Most southern hotels, restaurants, and theaters refused the patronage of blacks, while movie houses reserved separate sections or balconies for them. Sports and recreational activities were segregated, and hospitals, prisons, asylums, funeral homes, morgues, and cemeteries provided separate facilities.

A segregated drinking fountain in the American South. The "separate-but-equal" concept allowed segregation of public facilities, and wasn't successfully challenged until 1954. (Corbis-Bettmann)

Segregation was not limited to the South. A few thousand free blacks lived in the North and West during the time of slavery, and discriminatory practices toward them were not uncommon. As the black population in the North and West grew after the abolition of slavery, restrictions increased. This was especially true during and after World War I, when great numbers of southern blacks moved northward and westward in search of economic opportunity. Some northern and western states passed statutes prohibiting intermarriage. Separate schools were often permitted and sometimes required. *De facto* segregation occurred in residential housing and restrictive covenants were commonplace in many neighborhoods; as a result, blacks crowded into the ghettos of the northern and western cities. Prejudicial attitudes of northerners and westerners forced blacks into subservient positions in many areas of life, especially public accommodations, even though by law blacks were equal.

Another great surge of black migration out of the South occurred during World War II, and while the migrants sometimes improved their economic status, they experienced *de facto* segregation in the North and West. Blacks were unhappy with these restrictions to their freedom, especially since they were helping the nation fight a war to free the world's enslaved peoples. They demanded that both *de jure* and *de facto* segregation throughout the United States be abolished. The federal government responded to one of these demands when President Harry Truman ordered the desegregation of the armed forces, after which racial discrimination was officially abolished in all three branches of the military. Since segregated facilities in education were transparently unequal, blacks also attacked this line of inequality. Even before World War II, blacks had initiated steps to break down the states' biracial school systems. In 1938 the Supreme Court had ruled in the *Gaines* case that Missouri must provide legal training in the state for blacks equal to that for whites. Shortly after the war, similar lawsuits in Oklahoma and Texas were successful, and black graduate and professional students were permitted to attend those states' public-supported universities. Lawsuits against public school systems followed. In 1954, in *Brown* v. *Board of Education of Topeka*, the Supreme Court rejected the separate-but-equal fiction, declaring that separate school facilities were inherently unequal and in violation of the equal protection clause of the Fourteenth Amendment. Desegregation of schools proceeded at a relatively slow pace, and in 1969 the Supreme Court ruled that school segregation must end "at once." Controversies over implementation existed in the 1970's, although much progress had been made in the twenty years after the *Brown* decision.

Blacks also pressed for other concessions rightfully theirs: equal employment opportunities, nondiscriminatory accommodations in private and public facilities, fair housing conditions, and the franchise. Beginning in 1957 the U.S. Congress passed a series of civil rights acts, the first since Reconstruction. Included among them were bills establishing the Fair Employment Practices Commission and the Civil Rights Commission, both of which directed their efforts to redressing the grievances of minority groups. The post-World War II "civil rights revolution" revealed the progress and problems in the nation's attempt to abolish racial segregation.

BIBLIOGRAPHY

Charles S. Johnson, *Patterns of Negro Segregation.*
Milton R. Konvitz and T. Leskes, *A Century of Civil Rights.*
Charles S. Mangum, Jr., *The Legal Status of the Negro.*
Charles E. Silberman, *Crisis in Black and White.*
C. Vann Woodward, *The Strange Career of Jim Crow.*

— MONROE BILLINGTON

SEMINOLE

Seminole, one of the Five Civilized Tribes, lived chiefly in Florida and Oklahoma in the 20th century. They were originally of Muskhogean stock and spoke Muskogee or Hitchiti. In the early 18th century they were associated with the Lower Creek on the Chattahoochee River in Georgia, but they began to move into Florida after 1700. By 1775 they had become known as the Seminole, which means "separatist" or "wild people." Their numbers were later augmented by Upper Creek, members of conquered tribes, and a considerable number of fugitive black slaves from Georgia. Although the Seminole were town dwellers, they derived their living from farming, supplemented by hunting and trading; they developed a complex social organization in which military prowess played a major role.

During the Spanish domination of Florida the relative weakness of Spanish control allowed the Seminole to develop without interference. From 1763 to 1783, while Florida was in British hands, the tribe was for the most part on good terms with the authorities, and during the American Revolution it was pro-British. The end of the Revolution brought the Seminole into conflict with their Georgia neighbors over the Indian policy of giving refuge to runaway slaves. During the War of 1812 a number of Seminole raids on the Georgia border and retaliatory expeditions from the United States took place, culminating in the first Seminole War (1816–18) and Andrew Jackson's punitive expedition in 1818. The acquisition of Florida by the United States through the Adams-Onís Treaty of 1819 brought the Seminole under American control.

Eventually subdued by U.S. forces, the tribe signed the Treaty of Camp Moultrie (1823), agreeing to its removal from tribal lands in Florida to a reserve in the West. The treaty was repudiated by a large portion of the tribe, led by Micanopy and Jumper, and border raids continued. The influx of white settlers into Florida brought renewed pressure for removal; and the treaties of Payne's Landing (1832) and Fort Gibson (1833) were negotiated with a few Seminole chiefs stipulating that the tribe should move to Creek lands in the West. Again a major part of the tribe resisted, and a series of attacks led by Osceola escalated into the second Seminole War (1835–42). At the end of that war most of the hostile Seminole were removed to the Creek lands west of the Mississippi. Until 1860 the Seminole's relations with the United States continued to be troubled by dissatisfaction with their new lands and conflict with slaveholders over runaway slaves. During the Civil War the Seminole were divided in sentiment, but most tended to support the Union, participating in the Union victory at Honey Springs in July 1863.

The end of the Revolution brought the Seminole into conflict with their Georgia neighbors over the Indian custom of giving refuge to runaway slaves.

The Seminole Treaty of 1866 provided for a new reservation of 200,000 acres (creating what is now Seminole County, Okla.) and a grant of $235,362 and marked the beginning of a period of relative peace and stability for the tribe. In 1901 the Seminole became U.S. citizens, and by 1902 land allotments in severalty had been made to all Seminole citizens. Tribal government was extinguished in 1906. Oil production began on a large scale in Seminole country in 1923 and 1924, providing an impetus to economic development. In 1967 a federal claims court upheld a 1964 verdict of the Indian Claims Commission that the Seminole had been illegally deprived of some 32 million acres in Florida, paving the way for compensation. By 1970 there were some 5,055 Seminole living in Oklahoma and Florida.

BIBLIOGRAPHY

Grant Foreman, *The Five Civilized Tribes.*
Harry Henslick, "The Seminole Treaty of 1866," *The Chronicles of Oklahoma,* vol. 48.
Edwin C. McReynolds, *The Seminoles.*
John K. Mahon, *History of the Second Seminole War, 1835–1842.*

— DOROTHY TWOHIG

SEMINOLE WARS

In 1816 the United States built Fort Scott near the confluence of the Flint and Chattahoochee rivers on the border between Georgia and Florida, which was then under Spanish control. Across the Flint was a Mikasuki settlement called Fowlton. Neamathla, the chief there, used the village as a base from which to stage raids into the southeastern United States and as a collecting point for loot and runaway slaves. He was, through long conditioning, violently anti-United States. There was no united confederation of Indians in Florida, only the Mikasuki, the Seminole, and some splinter groups who cooperated unsystematically.

Neamathla's hostility caused Brig Gen. Edmund P. Gaines, commanding at Fort Scott, to send 250 men under Col. David Twiggs to Fowlton. The result was a small battle on Nov. 21, 1817, the opening action of the first Seminole War (1817–18). After that battle the Mikasuki retreated eastward toward the Suwannee River, where they could achieve loose cooperation with the Alachua band across the river.

In January 1818 President James Monroe's administration sent Maj. Gen. Andrew Jackson to Florida "to conduct the war in the manner he may judge best." Jackson reached Fort Scott on Mar. 9, 1818. His force quickly built up to 1,500 white men and 2,000 Creek Indians. With it he followed the Indians eastward, destroying their villages. By early April he had broken all Indian resistance west of the Suwannee River. He next turned his force against the scattered points held by the Spanish in that area, all of which he conquered.

Monroe quickly returned Jackson's conquests to Spain, but the first Seminole War had convinced the Spanish government that it would be in its interest to deed Florida to the United States before it was lost through conquest. The transfer was completed in 1821, and without their being consulted the Florida Indians, including the Seminole, went with the peninsula. Then, in 1830, Congress passed the Indian Removal Act, to transplant all the eastern Indians somewhere west of the Mississippi River. When applied to the Florida Indians, the Removal Act brought on the second Seminole War (1835–42).

On Dec. 28, 1835, Osceola, the guiding spirit of resistance to removal, directed the murder of Indian agent Wiley Thompson at Fort King and, simultaneously, the massacre of two companies commanded by Maj. Francis L. Dade. The Indians then rapidly devastated northeastern Florida and won two sharp victories over the white men.

Jackson, by then president, sent Maj. Gen. Winfield Scott, a hero of the War of 1812, to replace Brig. Gen.

Duncan L. Clinch. Scott tried to use classical military methods, but the Indians countered with guerrilla tactics that rendered his campaign all but futile. Jackson, relieving Scott in May 1836, temporarily invested the governor of Florida Territory, Richard K. Call, with the command and in December assigned Maj. Gen. Thomas S. Jesup to Florida.

Jesup was the pivotal figure in the war. He had scant respect for Indians, and after they breached the faith a few times, he abandoned the conventions of so-called civilized war. He estranged the blacks from their Indian allies, experimented with bloodhounds, forced captives on pain of death to betray their friends, and violated flags of truce and promises of safe conduct. Under a flag of truce he seized the charismatic Osceola in October 1837. The largest pitched battle was fought near Lake Okeechobee on Christmas Day 1837, with Gen. Zachary Taylor in immediate command. By the time Jesup was relieved in May 1838 about 100 Indians had been killed and 2,900 captured.

During the next four years the leadership on both sides changed frequently. There was no central Indian command, but Wild Cat, Sam Jones, Tiger Tail, and Halleck Tustenuggee emerged as forceful leaders. U.S. operations were more centrally directed under the successive commands of Taylor, Walker K. Armistead, and William J. Worth. All three had to learn to use only Indian tactics. By 1842, when there were no more than 300 Seminole left in Florida, Worth recommended that the government end its attempts to force them to leave. After some delay, the War Department directed him to implement his recommendation. Accordingly, the few remaining Indians formally agreed in mid-August 1842 to confine themselves to the area south of Pease Creek and west of Lake Okeechobee. Their agreement with Worth, in no way a treaty, brought an end to seven years of war.

Florida became a state in 1845, and since conditions on the border continued to be sensitive, it sought to expel the Seminole completely. To placate the state, the federal government began to build roads into the Indian preserve and to curtail white trade with the Indians. Military patrols and survey parties found their way south of Pease Creek. One such patrol, under Lt. George L. Hartsuff, vandalized some property deep in Indian country. That property happened to belong to the foremost Seminole leader, Billy Bowlegs. This heedless act set off the explosion that ever-increasing encroachments had prepared. Bowlegs, leading thirty-five warriors, attacked Hartsuff's detachment at dawn on Dec. 20, 1855, inflicting six casualties. Nearby white people scurried for the forts, and the third Seminole War (1855–58) was under way.

At the start of the third war there were perhaps 360 Seminole in Florida, 120 of them warriors. The United States enlarged its regular force to 800 and summoned into service 1,300 Florida volunteers. This force in time was placed under the command of Brig. Gen. William S. Harney, a hardened Indian fighter with experience in Florida tactics. Since the Indians did their best to avoid pitched battles, Harney sent his detachments into the remotest haunts to ferret them out. That method finally brought the chiefs to a conference at Fort Myers on Mar. 15, 1858. There 165 persons, including Billy Bowlegs, surrendered and were shipped west. Bowlegs returned to Florida in December 1858 and helped to persuade another 75 to migrate. This left roughly 125 Florida Seminole, who were never thereafter forced or persuaded to leave their homeland.

BIBLIOGRAPHY

Charles H. Coe, *Red Patriots: The Story of the Seminoles.*
James W. Covington, *The Story of Southwestern Florida,* vol. I.
John K. Mahon, *History of the Second Seminole War.*
Edwin C. McReynolds, *The Seminoles.*
James Parton, *Life of Andrew Jackson,* vol. II.

— JOHN K. MAHON

SEVENTEENTH AMENDMENT

Demand for the popular election of U.S. senators appeared in the 1830's, but the prestige and general effectiveness of the upper chamber were then such that little headway was made until after the Civil War. Popular belief that the Senate had deteriorated, recurrent cases of buying election from venal legislatures, corporate influence in selecting candidates, and other unsatisfactory features of the existing system gave a tremendous impetus to the movement. A proposed amendment to the Constitution, making direct election possible, passed the House several times, but it was not until 1912 that the Senate finally accepted the inevitable. Ratification followed, and the amendment became effective May 31, 1913.

BIBLIOGRAPHY

George H. Haynes, *The Senate of the United States: Its History and Practice.*

— W. A. ROBINSON

SHAKERS

Shakers, members of the United Society of Believers in Christ's Second Coming. The movement was founded by Ann Lee Standerin, or Stanley, on the basis of revelations to her that the Second Coming would be in the form of a woman and that she was that woman. When she and her followers moved from England to the New World in 1774 and established themselves at what was to become Watervliet, N.Y., in 1776, they adopted a communal rule of life for their society. The movement was deeply influenced by the popular millennianism of the time. Believing themselves to be the vanguard of the new age, the Shakers sought to be an intercessory remnant that would call all men to blessedness. Their well-known practice of celibacy was related to their millennial beliefs: there was no need to procreate, since the end was near. They acquired children for their communities through adoption. Although the Shakers shared many beliefs with the Quakers and other Evangelical groups, they were distinctive in their adherence to spiritualism and the important place they gave to seances in their worship. The morality of the sect was simple: they believed that the practice of the twelve virtues and four moral principles was enough to raise man from the animal to the spiritual state. The name Shaker came from a ritual form of dancing that often became quite frenzied. The Shakers reached their largest membership (6,000) before the Civil War and have declined continually since that time. By 1974 no brothers and only twelve Shaker sisters were left. Most people know of the sect through its furniture, which was classical in its functional simplicity and noted for its fine workmanship.

BIBLIOGRAPHY

Edwards D. Andrews, *The People Called Shakers.*

— GLENN T. MILLER

A sharecropper and his daughter stand in the doorway of their shack home in New Madrid County, Missouri, May 1938. (Library of Congress/Corbis)

SHARECROPPER

Sharecropper is a farm tenant who pays rent with a portion (usually half) of the crop he raises and who brings little to the agricultural operation besides his labor and that of his family. Although sharecropping had largely disappeared by the 1970's, it was once prevalent in the South. A product of Reconstruction, it was partially a response to the scarcity of liquid capital in the South following the Civil War. But its primary purpose was to establish a stable, low-cost work force that would replace slave labor, and it thus represented the bottom rung in the southern tenancy ladder.

Working usually under close supervision, the sharecropper often lacked title to his harvest, a factor that distinguished him from a share tenant. The landlord usually furnished working stock, tools, half the necessary fertilizer, housing, fuel, and seed, varying the amounts according to the land area that the cropper and his family could cultivate.

Most sharecroppers depended on credit, which they got from independent merchants or, more frequently, from landlord-operated commissaries. Interest rates ranged from 10 to 60 percent. The security on these loans was a lien against the tenant's forthcoming crop. At harvest, the landlord established the crop's worth, subtracted what was owed him, and remitted the remainder to the tenant. The cropper's cash return was almost always low and was often swallowed up by his debt.

Concerned by the extent of sharecropping and other forms of tenancy, Congress in 1937 passed the Bankhead-Jones Farm Tenant Act, sponsored by Alabama Sen. John H. Bankhead and Texas Rep. Marvin Jones, to help renters of all types acquire their farms by empowering the Farm Security Administration to lend money to tenants who desired to purchase land. Government-aided purchase programs, the mechanization of southern agriculture, and the lure of urban employment caused the number of sharecroppers to drop from 776,278 in 1930 to 121,037 in 1959, the last year that the federal agricultural census identified croppers as a separate group.

BIBLIOGRAPHY

Calvin L. Beale, "The Negro in American Agriculture," in John P. Davis, ed., *The American Negro Reference Book.*

David Eugene Conrad, *The Forgotten Farmers*; Oscar Zeichner, "The Transition From Slave to Free Agricultural Labor in the Southern States," *Agricultural History*, vol. 13 (1939).

— DAVID E. BREWSTER

SHAWNEE

Shawnee, a southern tribe of the Algonquin, are first recognized as inhabiting the Cumberland basin in what is now Tennessee with an outlying colony on the Savannah River in South Carolina. The latter group was the first to abandon its southern hunting grounds, in a migration lasting from about 1677 to 1707 and caused by friction with the nearby Catawba who were favored by the whites. Their new homes were in the valleys of the Susquehanna and Delaware rivers, but congestion soon caused them to remove to the waters of the upper Ohio Valley in a migration lasting from about 1720 to the years of the French and Indian War (1754–63). The Shawnee on the Cumberland began retreating north as the result of friction with the Cherokee and Chickasaw about 1710 and began to merge with their brethren from the east in a group of villages on the Ohio River from what is now Tarenturn, Pa., to the mouth of the Scioto in Ohio—hunting in the forests on both sides of the river.

The Shawnee were the spearhead of resistance to advancing settlement in that period of frontier warfare lasting from 1755 to 1795, supporting and being supported first by the French and then by the English. By 1795 their homes were in the valley of the upper Miami, and the Treaty of Greenville of that year forced them to retreat to Indiana. A movement for confederated Indian regeneration and resistance to further white expansion developed under the leadership of the Shawnee brothers, Tecumseh and Tenskwatawa (the Shawnee Prophet), but met disaster in the Battle of Tippecanoe in 1811. The loss to the Indians of British support, as the result of the War of 1812, hastened the rapid dispersion of the Shawnee. The main body is now incorporated with the Cherokee in Oklahoma.

BIBLIOGRAPHY

C. C. Trowbridge, *Shawnese Traditions.*

Glenn Tucker, *Tecumseh: Vision of Glory.*

— R. C. DOWNES

SHAWNEE AND DELAWARE MIGRATION

Shawnee and Delaware Migration to the Ohio Valley from the Susquehanna and Delaware river valleys, which took place from about 1720 to 1753, was important in the period leading up to the French and Indian War. It not only brought Indian life and power to a French area that had been uninhabited, but it also diminished English influence through the loss of those tribes. Moreover, in the Ohio region the eastern Shawnee merged with their western brethren who had migrated from the Cumberland Valley.

The migration was caused by the encroachment of whites; by such aggravations as the Walking Purchase of 1737, in which the Delaware were forced to relinquish about 1,200 square miles in eastern Pennsylvania; by the decline of hunting and knowledge of better hunting grounds in the West; by the probability that the Iroquois would not be able to keep them out of the new grounds; and by encouragement from both French and English traders. In the competition for the furs of the new region the English got the lion's share. But the fact that the English trade was accompanied by uncontrolled rum selling and unpunished fraud caused many Shawnee and Delaware to prefer the French, with whom their leaders were in touch from the beginning of the migration. They were well-disposed toward French expansion, which culminated in the French occupation of the Forks of the Ohio (1754) and the erection of Fort Duquesne that same year. The English, first through the Pennsylvania colonial government and later through the Iroquois overlords of the Shawnee and Delaware, sought in vain to bring the migrants back to English protection. Although the Iroquois scolded their dependents, they went no farther, and the failure of the Pennsylvania government to establish an Indian department impressed the Indians with the inability of the English to make their traders behave.

During the French and Indian War when the western Shawnee and Delaware, supporting the French, sought to wipe out the interior Pennsylvania settlements, the status of those remaining in the East was imperiled. The reassertion of English supremacy caused most of these to join the western tribesmen. After 1763 all were again under English influence.

BIBLIOGRAPHY

R. C. Downes, *Indian Relations in the Ohio Valley.*

— RANDOLPH C. DOWNES

SHAYS'S REBELLION

Shays's Rebellion (August 1786-February 1787), in western and central Massachusetts, was the outstanding manifestation of the discontent widespread throughout New England during the economic depression following the Revolution. Many small property holders in Massachusetts were losing their possessions through seizures for overdue debts and delinquent taxes; many faced imprisonment for debt. Town meetings and county conventions petitioned for lightening of taxes (disproportionately burdensome to the poorer classes and western sections); sought suspension, abolition, or reform of certain courts and revision of the state constitution; and especially urged the issue of paper money, but were stubbornly opposed on most points by the legislature. Lacking, in many cases, property qualifications for voting and thus unable to look for relief through the ballot, the malcontents, beginning at Northampton, Aug. 29, resorted to massed efforts to intimidate and close the courts to prevent action against debtors. Fearful they might be indicted for treason or sedition by the state supreme court at Springfield, in late September they appeared there in armed force. Daniel Shays, revolutionary veteran and local officeholder of Pelham, emerged as leader, demanding that the court refrain from indictments and otherwise restrict its business. A clash with neighborhood militia under Maj. Gen. William Shepard was avoided when both bands agreed to disperse. The court adjourned.

Indirectly, Shays's rebellion strengthened the movement culminating in the adoption of the U.S. Constitution.

In January the insurgents returned to Springfield for supplies from the Confederation arsenal there, a move foreseen by state and federal authorities. Federal preparations for arsenal defense were masked by announcement that requisitioning of forces was necessitated by menacing Indians on the frontier. Adequate government funds were not forthcoming for either federal or state troops, but Gen. Benjamin Lincoln secured for the latter some $20,000 from private individuals. Shepard's forces repulsed the Shaysites' attack on the arsenal (Jan. 25); Lincoln's men dispersed a nearby insurgent force under Luke Day. Marching to Petersham through a blinding snowstorm, Lincoln surprised and captured most of the remaining insurgents early in February, and the rebellion soon collapsed. Shays escaped to Vermont; eventually, with about a dozen others condemned to death, he was pardoned. James Bowdoin, governor during the insurrection, was defeated at the next election; reforms in line with the Shaysites' demands were soon made, and amnesty granted with few exceptions. Alarmed by "this unprovoked insurrection" of "wicked and ambitious men," some conservatives despaired of republican institutions. Far greater numbers viewed the rebellion as proof of need for a stronger general government, capable of suppressing such uprisings, or, better still, preventing them by improving economic conditions throughout the United States. Thus, indirectly, the rebellion strengthened the movement culminating in the adoption of the U.S. Constitution.

BIBLIOGRAPHY

Merrill Jensen, *The New Nation: A History of the United States During the Confederation, 1781–1789.*

G. R. Minot, *The History of the Insurrections in Massachusetts.*

J. P. Warren, "The Confederation and the Shays Rebellion," *American Historical Review* (October 1905).

— LOUISE B. DUNBAR

SHENANDOAH VALLEY

Shenandoah Valley, that part of the great valley between the Allegheny and the Blue Ridge mountains extending from the Potomac River at Harpers Ferry south to the watershed of the James River a few miles southwest of Lexington, Va. There are three parts of the Shenandoah Valley: the lower, extending from the Potomac forty miles south, settled chiefly by English immigrants from tidewater Virginia; the middle, from near Strasburg to the vicinity of Harrisonburg, settled almost wholly by Germans; and the upper, from Harrisonburg to the waters of the James, originally more wooded than the middle and lower valley. This last was the part chosen by the Scotch-Irish immigrants, most of whom came down from Pennsylvania.

There were travelers into the valley at least fifty years before Gov. Alexander Spotswood's expedition of the Knights of the Golden Horseshoe in 1716, and the larger movement of Germans led by Jost Hite in 1732, and of Scotch-Irish led by John Lewis in the same year. Settlers were known near Shepherdstown, in what is now northeastern West Virginia, in 1717; Adam Miller had settled in the present Page County by 1726; and there were settlers near Luray in 1727.

The lower valley became the seat of slavery and tobacco, the settlers adhering to the church of England; while the middle valley, marked by large barns and rolling meadows, was settled by quiet, home-loving "Valley Dutch" people who were Lutheran. The upper valley, whose inhabitants were Presbyterian in religion and Scotch-Irish in politics, was known for its fierce democracy, its exploring hunger for land, and its Indian wars. The lower valley was linked closely with tidewater Virginia geographically and socially; George Washington served in the House of Burgesses as delegate from Frederick County before he represented Fairfax. The middle valley, including Augusta County, extended to "the Great South Sea, including California," and held its county court at times near Fort Duquesne, the present city of Pittsburgh.

BIBLIOGRAPHY

Samuel Kercheval, *History of the Valley of Virginia.*

— JAMES ELLIOTT WALMSLEY

SHERMAN ANTITRUST ACT

Sherman Antitrust Act, enacted July 2, 1890, was the first federal law directed against industrial combination and monopoly. Once considered a great landmark in the relations between government and business, it was more certainly an example of the ambivalence that has characterized the American people and government as they have sought to enjoy the benefits of big business while distrusting its methods and economic power.

In the twenty-five years following the panic of 1873, the United States experienced the first wave of industrial combination. Consolidation took many forms, but the most publicized was the "trust" device. With the 1880's an antimonopoly movement pledged to the destruction of the trusts had taken political form in several states, and by 1890 fifteen states had enacted antitrust statutes. These efforts proving ineffective, there was a growing demand for federal action, led by small entrepreneurs complaining of the unfair trade practices of monopolistic firms. In response to this demand, Congress, by a large bipartisan majority, passed the Sherman Antitrust Act. Fortuitously associated with the name of Sen. John Sherman of Ohio, its prime authors were the leading Republican members of the Senate Judiciary Committee—George F. Edmunds of Vermont and George F. Hoar of Massachusetts.

The key provision of the act was incorporated in the first of its eight sections: "Every contract, combination in the form of trust or otherwise, or conspiracy, in restraint of trade or commerce among the several states, or with foreign nations, is hereby declared to be illegal." In the Judiciary Committee it had been decided not to attempt to define a "combination" or "trust," not to include intrastate commerce, and not to widen the prohibition to include combinations in restraint of production as well as trade. Although some writers have seen this delimitation as proof of a determination by its authors to conciliate big business and deceive the public, the act in fact represented caution, not conspiracy. Anxious to encourage economic growth while curbing monopoly, the authors of the Sherman Act sought to fashion a law that would find clear justification in the commerce clause of the Constitution and make clear the authority of the federal judiciary to enforce the common-law prohibition against illegal combinations "in restraint of trade."

The subsequent history of the act is a story of periodic bursts of attention and long-term declining importance. During the 1890's the Justice Department sought few indictments under the act, and when it was stirred to action, as in the attempt to break up the sugar trust, the Supreme Court interpreted the act so strictly as to render its prohibitions meaningless. The only successful prosecutions under the Sherman Act in the 1890's were those waged against labor unions, such as *United States* v. *Debs* (1894). The presidency of Theodore Roosevelt witnessed an effort to revive the act as an instrument of federal regulation of big business, but the effort was largely unsuccessful. The few trusts that were ordered dissolved soon reappeared in another guise, and Roosevelt was himself prepared to distinguish between "good" and "bad" trusts. That distinction later received judicial sanction in a Supreme Court opinion of 1911 (*United States* v. *American Tobacco Company*) that only combinations in "unreasonable" restraint of trade were subject to the penalties of the Sherman Act. With the administration of Woodrow Wilson, the Clayton and Federal Trade Commission acts were passed (1914); when later presidents engaged in bouts of trust-busting, they used primarily these instruments and the cease-and-desist orders of the regulatory commissions. Since the administration of Franklin D. Roosevelt and the New Deal, the Sherman Antitrust Act has played only a comparatively minor role in the relations of big business and the federal government.

Although insufficient to the task assigned, the act was noteworthy as a pioneer measure in the field of federal regulatory legislation. It remains of continuing historical significance as an illustration of the ambivalent attitude of the American public and Congress toward the problem of industrial combination.

BIBLIOGRAPHY

Hans B. Thorelli, *The Federal Antitrust Policy: Origination of an American Tradition.*

— RICHARD E. WELCH, JR.

SHERMAN SILVER PURCHASE ACT

In 1890 a certain group of congressmen was anxious to enact the McKinley tariff bill, and the advocates of silver currency were urging the enactment of a bill providing for the free coinage of silver. While the silver advocates had a majority in the Senate, powerful enough to force the House into line, they were advisedly fearful that President Benjamin Harrison would veto a free coinage bill, even if it were attached as a rider to a tariff bill that he otherwise favored. As a practical solution to this dilemma the "silver" senators determined to adopt not a free coinage measure but the nearest possible approach to it. A compromise bill, the Sherman Silver Purchase Act, named for Sen. John Sherman of Ohio, became law on July 14, 1890. The act provided for the issuance of legal tender notes sufficient in amount to pay for 4.5 million ounces of silver bullion each month at the prevailing market price. Then enough silver dollars were to be coined from the bullion purchased to redeem all the outstanding Treasury notes issued in this manner. The notes were made full legal tender except where otherwise expressly stipulated in the contract, and were made redeemable on demand either in gold or silver coin at the discretion of the secretary of the Treasury, although the act went on to declare it to be "the established policy of the United States to maintain the two metals on a parity with each other upon the present legal ratio or such ratio as may be established by law."

With the passage of the Sherman Act there were three kinds of currency, substantial in amount, which the federal government had to keep at par with gold: greenbacks, silver certificates, and Treasury notes. The direct effect of the Sherman Act was twofold: first, it increased the circulation of redeemable paper currency in the form of Treasury notes by $156 million, and second, it accentuated the drain on the government's gold reserves by requiring the Treasury notes to be redeemed in gold as long as the Treasury had gold in its possession. The financial crackup in Argentina and the resultant liquidation in Great Britain, involving the failure of the banking house of Baring Brothers and Company, eventually forced an exportation of gold from the United States to Great Britain, and this exodus, coupled with an extraordinary stringency in the money market induced by unusually heavy demand for funds evoked by the industrial activity in the West and South, created a situation bordering on panic in the latter part of 1890.

Some respite from this taut financial situation was gained by the extraordinary grain crop of 1891 in the United States and the European crop shortage, as a consequence of which the exports of gold were transformed into imports, which in turn made bank reserves ample and the money market easy. But this respite was short-lived. The arbitrary issues of Treasury notes again began to undermine public confidence. The Treasury's already precarious position ensuing from a policy of increased governmental expenditures, the marked growth of U.S. indebtedness to foreign nations, and the reduction in custom receipts brought about by the McKinley Tariff was aggravated by the additional drain on the Treasury's resources that the redemption of the Treasury notes entailed. The cumulative effect of the foregoing factors culminated in the panic of 1893, which was characterized by a fear of the abandonment of the gold standard because of the depletion of the government's gold reserve. The panic was checked in the autumn of 1893 by the repeal of the Sherman Act.

BIBLIOGRAPHY

W. Jett Lauck, *The Causes of the Panic of 1893.*

— FRANK PARKER

SHIPBUILDING

Shipbuilding was one of the leading industries before the American Revolution, especially in New England. There were two important reasons for the prosperity of the industry. First, the English Navigation Acts, which prohibited the carrying of goods between England and the colonies in foreign ships, classified colonial-built ships as English built. The other reason was economic. With an abundant supply of oak and pine growing almost to the water's edge, a vessel could be built in America for about 30 percent less than in England, where timber, increasingly scarce, had to be carried great distances to the shipyards. British shipowners snapped up these American bargains, and on the eve of the Revolution a third of the vessels in British registry were American built. That lucrative situation ended with independence in 1783 and would not be revived until 1849, when Britain abolished the Navigation Acts.

The next American shipbuilding boom came between the mid-1840's and the mid-1850's, when a series of outside stimuli, ranging from Irish rainfall to California gold, produced the so-called Golden Age of American shipbuilding. During that decade American shipping almost overtook the British in quantity and far surpassed it in quality. For those ready to pay the price, excellent crack packets and clippers could be built on New York's East River or around Boston harbor. Good substantial cargo carriers could be built more cheaply along the Maine coast, particularly at Bath, Casco Bay, and the central coast. The American Civil War brought this era to a close.

An entirely new picture emerged after the Civil War. With Britain turning out compound-engine freighters in large quantities, American square-riggers were gradually squeezed out of most of the deep-sea trades, except for Maine's excellent Down Easters. Because cheaper coal and iron were available to foreign shipbuilders, the old 30 percent cost differential in favor of American vessels now turned into a 30 percent differential advantage for the foreign iron (and later steel) steamships. The American merchant marine also declined as the U.S. government failed to follow other maritime nations in adequately subsidizing its shipping. In addition, the government failed to build up its navy for a period of twenty years after the Civil War. The shipbuilding industry could not overcome these handicaps, even though there was an increasing demand for ships to carry the growing commerce along the coast and on the Great Lakes.

Thanks to an abundance of oak and pine growing almost to the sea's edge, a vessel could be built in America for about 30 percent less than in England.

World War I marked the beginning of an extraordinary period of American shipbuilding activity. Total tonnage was only 225,122 tons in 1915, but was over 12 million tons between 1917 and 1922. This notable increase in tonnage enlarged the merchant marine of the United States so greatly that there was little demand for new tonnage after the boom ended. Naval construction was reduced by the international disarmaments agreements in the 1920's, and in 1929 amounted to only 128,976 tons, the lowest amount since 1830.

World War II saw tremendous construction programs, in which the navy spent $19 billion, building everything from landing craft up to superdreadnoughts and carriers. The Maritime Commission spent $13 billion constructing 5,777 ships, including 2,708 of the standardized 10-knot Liberty ships; 414 of the faster 16.5-knot Victory ships, also of around 10,000 deadweight tons; 541 of the C-2s, C-3s, and other so-called tailor-made ships of the long-range program; and 702 tankers.

The end of the war brought another postwar shipbuilding slump. In 1956 only two freighters and six tankers were under construction. The postwar construction, however, did produce some distinctive new types of ships. The liner *United States*, built in 1952, established a record as the fastest afloat. The use of nuclear power was initiated by the submarine *Nautilus*, which was followed by several other nuclear-powered submarines. Nuclear reactors also powered the giant carrier *Enterprise* and the passenger liner *Savannah*.

The Merchant Marine Act of 1970 came as a blessing to the dwindling shipbuilding industry. It authorized construction subsidies to a wide range of vessels, especially the bulk and bulk-oil carriers. Although the act's programs were later cut back in budget reducing moves, numerous large contracts were let. In 1973 U.S. shipbuilders had approximately 3.2 million gross registered tons under construction or contract.

BIBLIOGRAPHY

E. G. Fassett, *The Shipbuilding Business in the United States of America.*

L. C. Kendall, *The Business of Shipping.*

— ROBERT G. ALBION

SHIPPING ACT OF 1916

Shipping Act of 1916 created the U.S. Shipping Board empowered to construct or buy vessels for use in commerce or as naval and military auxiliaries and to operate them or lease or sell them to American citizens. In time of emergency the transfer or sale of American-flag ships to foreign registry or ownership was restricted and the president was given power to conscript vessels. Various practices, including deferred rebates, were declared unfair and prohibited to ocean common carriers.

— FRANK A. SOUTHARD, JR.

SILVER DEMOCRATS

Silver Democrats, a term used at various times after 1878 to refer to those members of the Democratic party who were active advocates of free coinage of silver at the 16 to 1 ratio. More general use of the term "Silver Democrats" followed the inauguration of President Grover Cleveland in 1893 and his calling of a special session of Congress to repeal the Sherman Silver Purchase Act of 1890, which required the U.S. Treasury to buy virtually all silver mined in the United States. This repeal split the party wide open, with Silver Democrats in opposition to the administration, which in turn used every means at its command to force Democrats in Congress to support the administration's plan. From 1893 until the national convention of July 1896, the Silver Democrats were a large faction of the party at odds with the official leadership. That convention was a test of strength between the administration and the Silver Democrats, and had the latter lost, undoubtedly many of them would have joined the other free-coinage factions in support of a fusion candidate. But their complete victory at the convention made the Silver Democrats the regulars beyond question, and the term tended to fall into disuse. This result was encouraged also by the decline of free coinage as a political issue. Nevertheless, the platform of 1900 was a Silver Democratic document, and only in 1904 was free coinage repudiated by the party's candidate, Alton B. Parker.

BIBLIOGRAPHY

J. F. Rhodes, *History of the United States.*

— ELMER ELLIS

SILVER PROSPECTING AND MINING

Silver sometimes occurs in ore as native silver in lodes or veins that run to great depths underground. The outcroppings of such ores identify the lode to the prospector. This silver can be recovered by crushing the ore in a stamp mill, passing it over copper plates coated with mercury, and separating the amalgam by driving off the mercury with heat. Most silver ores are more complex. Silver is usually chemically combined with gold, lead, copper, or other metals, and the identification of these ores is much more difficult than those containing native silver. The complex ores also require more intricate metallurgical processes for separation.

Silver mining in the United States began at an early period. The Spanish had worked small mines during their occupation of New Mexico, California, and Texas. Small amounts of silver also were recovered by mining in New Hampshire after 1828 and in Virginia and Tennessee after 1832. Large-scale silver mining had its beginning in Nevada after 1859, when Peter O'Riley and Patrick McLaughlin, prospecting the area eastward from the California gold fields, staked the Ophir, or Comstock, lode. They were looking for gold, but their happy discovery developed into a bonanza mine that yielded more silver than gold. The Comstock ores were so rich that within two decades more than $300 million worth of silver and gold had been extracted.

The Comstock experience of goldseekers finding silver became a pattern repeated in various parts of the American West in the years that followed. At Georgetown, Colo., an original gold placer camp developed as the center of a silver-producing district after the opening of the Belmont lode in 1864. Also in Colorado, the gold camp of Oro City was almost a ghost town when ores of carbonate of lead with a rich silver content were discovered in 1877 and the greatest of Colorado silver cities, Leadville, was born. Again, gold prospectors accidentally discovered the Bunker Hill and Sullivan mines in the Coeur d'Alene district of Idaho.

Concentrating mills and smelters, necessary for treating complex silver ores, were not available in the United States until 1866–68. Thomas H. Selby at San Francisco; W. S. Keyes at Eureka, Nev.; A. W. Nason at Oreana, Nev.; and Nathaniel P. Hill at Blackhawk, Colo., were pioneers of the smelting industry in the United States. Recovered metals such as lead and copper became increasingly significant byproducts of the silver smelters.

The prosperity of the silver mining industry in the United States during the 19th century was intimately related to the currency policy of the federal government, particularly after the demonetization of silver in 1873. Many of the largest producing silver mines in the country, including those at Leadville, Aspen, and Silver Cliff in Colorado, those of the Silver Reef district in Utah, the Idaho mines, and the mines in the Butte district in Montana, were opened after 1873. During the quarter of a century that followed, while the nation debated the questions of silver purchases and coinage, the huge quantities of silver produced by these mines depressed the price, already reduced by demonetization. With the repeal of the Sherman Silver Purchase Act in 1893, the domestic silver market fell to levels so low that many mines suspended operations.

The industry recovered sufficiently to make the years 1911–18 the peak years in volume of production; an annual average of 69,735,000 fine ounces of silver were produced during those years. Then continuing low prices for silver and high production costs limited activity in mining. After 1920 the Coeur d'Alene district of Idaho was the leading silver-producing region in the country. In 1970 Idaho produced 42 percent of the 45,006,000 fine ounces of silver mined in the United States; most of the other silver came from mines in Arizona, Utah, and Montana.

BIBLIOGRAPHY

W. R. Crane, *Gold and Silver.*
Rodman Wilson Paul, *Mining Frontiers of the Far West, 1848–1880.*
Thomas Arthur Rickard, *History of American Mining.*
U.S. Bureau of Mines, *Minerals Yearbook* (1971).

— CARL UBBELOHDE

SIOUX WARS

The first clash between the Sioux and American troops occurred in 1854, near Fort Laramie, Wyo., when Lieutenant J. L. Grattan and eighteen men were killed. In retaliation, Gen. W. S. Harney in 1855 attacked a camp of Brulé Sioux near Ash Hollow, Neb., and killed about a hundred. Following the battle, the Brulé chief, Spotted Tail, was imprisoned, and the Sioux country was peaceful for a while. With the beginning of the Civil War, regular army troops were withdrawn from the Plains area, to be replaced by state and territorial militiamen in attempting to keep the Indians peaceful.

In Minnesota the Eastern (or Santee) Sioux had ceded much of their land, reserving for themselves territory along the Minnesota River under the provisions of the 1851 Treaty of Traverse des Sioux. White settlers soon began to press in upon the Sioux holdings, and white traders cheated the Sioux, until in August of 1862 there was a Sioux uprising in Minnesota under the leadership of Little Crow. The revolt was crushed in September, after which some of the dispersed Sioux sought refuge in Canada, while others joined the Teton Sioux in the plains of South Dakota.

The Teton were not generally hostile to the whites until 1865, when they joined with the Arapaho and Cheyenne in attacking emigrants on the Bozeman Trail to the Montana goldfields. In 1865 the Teton under Chief Red Cloud defeated an army unit at the Upper Platte Bridge, destroying this important link on the trail to the West.

A peace treaty had guaranteed the Sioux could keep the Black Hills in perpetuity, but a discovery of gold in 1874 brought in a rush of gold prospectors.

With the end of the Civil War, regular federal troops were rushed to the Plains in an attempt to pacify the Indians, but the Sioux were aroused by the government's intention to erect forts along the Bozeman Trail. Red Cloud's War (1866–67) followed, during which the Sioux attacked wagon trains, halted traffic on the trail, and laid siege to the forts. On Dec. 21, 1866, Capt. William J. Fetterman and eighty troopers were annihilated by Red Cloud's warriors. In 1868 the government agreed to abandon the trail and forts and Red Cloud signed a treaty of peace at Fort Laramie.

The treaty had guaranteed the possession in perpetuity of the Black Hills by the Sioux, but in 1874 there was a rush of gold prospectors into the area. The consequence was the Black Hills War in 1876, in which Gen. George Armstrong Custer and his troops were killed at the Battle of the Little Bighorn on June 25. The Sioux separated after the battle, and Gen. George Crook defeated American Horse's band at Slim Buttes on Sept. 9. Sitting Bull was pursued to Canada by Gen. Nelson A. Miles. Crazy Horse and his Oglala fought on until they were induced by hunger to surrender on Jan. 7, 1877.

Relative peace then prevailed until the final Sioux uprising, sometimes called the Messiah War, which attended the religious excitement of the Ghost Dance in 1890. On Dec. 15 Chief Sitting Bull was killed by Indian police who had been sent to arrest him, and the pacification of the Sioux was completed on Dec. 29 with the massacre of some 300 Sioux at the so-called Battle of Wounded Knee.

BIBLIOGRAPHY

Kenneth Carley, ed., *The Sioux Uprising of 1862.*
George E. Hyde, *A Sioux Chronicle.*
Roy W. Meyer, *History of the Santee Sioux.*
James C. Olson, *Red Cloud and the Sioux Problem.*
Robert M. Utley, *The Last Days of the Sioux Nation.*
Stanley Vestal, *Sitting Bull, Champion of the Sioux.*

— KENNETH M. STEWART

SIXTEENTH AMENDMENT

Sixteenth Amendment, the amendment to the U.S. Constitution authorizing Congress to impose a federal income tax. When the Supreme Court invalidated, in 1895, the income tax of 1894 in *Pollock* v. *Farmers Loan and Trust Company*, the decision aroused widespread disapproval on the grounds that as long as tariff duties and excises constituted the main source of federal revenue, those best able to pay were escaping a fair share of the tax burden. It was also argued that federal outlays were bound to increase in the future, that emergencies like war could require vast federal expenditures, and that additional taxing power was therefore needed. In view of the limitation imposed by the Supreme Court, a constitutional amendment empowering Congress to lay income taxes without apportionment among the states was the only way out of an impasse. In 1908 the Democratic platform endorsed such an amendment, and it was widely supported by the progressive wing of the Republican party. President William Howard Taft eventually recommended submission of an amendment to the states, and the necessary resolution passed both houses of Congress by overwhelming majorities in July 1909. The necessary ratifications were forthcoming, and the amendment was declared effective Feb. 25, 1913.

BIBLIOGRAPHY

E. R. A. Seligman, *The Income Tax.*
A. C. McLaughlin, *Constitutional History of the United States.*

— W. A. ROBINSON

SKYSCRAPERS

The skyscraper may be defined as a multistory elevator office building, usually of skeleton frame construction. The first skyscrapers were built in the United States in the last quarter of the 19th century, but since that time the form has been borrowed by many countries throughout the world.

The skyscraper's beginnings can be traced back to such structures as the Equitable Life Building (Gilman,

Kendall, and Post, 1868–70), the Western Union Building (George B. Post, 1873–75), and the Tribune Building (Richard M. Hunt, 1874–75), all in New York City. They were among the first buildings to use elevators to make accessible office space on higher floors.

Skeleton frame construction, which made buildings of more than ten stories economically feasible, was perfected in Chicago by William LeBaron Jenney in the Home Life Insurance Building (1883–85) and by Holabird and Roche in the Tacoma Building (1887–89). In the Wainwright Building (Saint Louis, 1890–91) Adler and Sullivan clad the metal frame with a functional design that expressed not only its structural system but also its use as a tall office building; they thus produced one of the finest examples of early skyscraper architecture.

In the East architects were moving in a different direction. The Ames Building by Shepley, Rutan, and Coolidge (Boston, 1889) represented the Romanesque mode as revived by H. H. Richardson. The New York Life Insurance Building by McKim, Mead and White (Kansas City, 1890) employed Italian Renaissance motifs. Bruce Price, in the American Surety Building (New York, 1894–95), conceived of the skyscraper as a classic column divided into base, shaft, and capital. The tower concept had many followers, as exemplified by the Singer Tower (Ernest Flagg, 1906–08), the Woolworth Building Tower (Cass Gilbert, 1913), the Chrysler Tower (William Van Alen, 1929), and the Empire State Building (Shreve, Lamb and Harmon, 1930).

The Empire State Building was, for decades, the world's tallest building until the opening in 1970 of the twin-towered World Trade Center in New York City. That, in turn, was soon superseded as the tallest building by the Sears Tower in Chicago.

New York City's Rockefeller Center (Reinhard and Hofmeister; Hood, Godley and Fouilhoux; Corbett, Harrison and MacMurray, 1928–40) marked the beginning of a trend toward open large-scale planning. The tendency toward modest development and landscaped environment was continued in such works as Lever House by Skidmore, Owings and Merrill (New York, 1952) and the Seagram Building by Ludwig Mies Van Der Rohe and Philip Johnson (New York, 1958). By the early 1970's, as urban congestion increasingly came to be perceived as a major problem, a number of cities were offering tax and other incentives to developers to plan for open space around tall office buildings.

BIBLIOGRAPHY

Carl W. Condit, *American Building Art: The 19th Century*, and *The Rise of the Skyscraper*.

Henry Russell Hitchcock, *Architecture 19th and 20th Centuries*.

— WINSTON WEISMAN

SLAVE INSURRECTIONS

Rebellion and conspiracy to rebel were the forms of protest that the victims of American slavery most often took against those who enslaved them. They involved careful planning, collective action, and the willingness to stake one's life on a cause that had little chance of success. As an attack on the ultimate in undemocratic practices, these unsuccessful attempts and the labors of their leaders can be viewed as being in the tradition of the ideals of the Declaration of Independence and as promoting the concept of individual freedom and human dignity. The oppression against which they fought and the odds against their success were far greater than those encountered by the patriots who made the American Revolution.

Until well into the 20th century, historians tended to play down unrest among slaves and to picture insurrections as seldom occurring in the United States. This mythology both reflected and was needed to support slavery and the Jim Crow practices that followed emancipation. Post-World War II historians find that the evidence warrants a different interpretation. More than 250 cases have been identified that can be classified as insurrections, and periodic expressions of fear among whites of slave revolts can be documented. Further evidence exists in the slave codes and the records of punishment. It is difficult to be definitive on this matter, because of the obvious policy of silence regarding such events, the bias of the records maintained by those supporting slavery, the difficulty of distinguishing between personal crimes and organized revolts, and the quick spread of rumors. However, there is now general agreement that dissatisfaction with their condition was characteristic among slaves and that insurrection was more frequent than earlier historians had acknowledged. A unique record of slave convictions in the state of Virginia for the period 1780–1864 gives support to the revisionist. Of a total of 1,418 convictions, 91 were for insurrection and 346 for murder. When this is added to the several recorded examples of plots and revolts in the state in the 17th and early 18th centuries, the record for that state alone is impressive.

The first slave revolt in territory that became the United States took place in 1526 in a Spanish settlement near the mouth of the Pee Dee River in what is now South Carolina. Several slaves rebelled and fled to live with Indians of the area. The following year the colonists left the area without having recaptured the slaves. Insurrection in the British colonies began with the development of slavery and continued into the American Revolution. The most serious of the period occurred in New York and in South Carolina. In 1712 a slave conspiracy in New York City led to the death of nine whites and the wounding of five or six others. Six of the rebels killed themselves to avoid capture. Of those taken into custody twenty-one were executed in a variety of ways. Some were hanged, others burned, one broken on the wheel, and one hanged in chains as an example to other would-be insurrectionists. In 1739 an uprising known as Cato's Revolt took place at Stono, S.C., near Charleston. Blacks seized guns and ammunition and fought the militia before being defeated. Approximately twenty-five whites and fifty blacks were killed. In 1741 a conspiracy among slaves and white servants in New York City led to the execution of thirty-one blacks and four whites.

The successful slave revolt in Haiti during the French Revolution led to a series of plots in the South. Others followed up to the Civil War. Of these Gabriel's Revolt, the plot of Denmark Vesey, and Nat Turner's Revolt were the most significant.

In 1800 Gabriel Prosser and Jack Bowler planned a revolt to involve thousands of slaves in the Richmond area. Authorities became aware that something was under way, and James Monroe, then governor of Virginia, ordered that precautions be taken. In spite of this the leaders planned to proceed on Saturday, Aug. 20. On that day there occurred what a contemporary described as "the most terrible thunder accompanied with an enormous rain, that I ever witnessed in the state." Nevertheless, over a thousand armed slaves gathered only to find that a bridge over which they had to pass had been washed away. On the same day an informer gave specifics of the plot to authorities. Many arrests were made, including Prosser and Bowler. Thirty-six slaves, including the leaders, were executed.

In 1822 Denmark Vesey, a black who had purchased his freedom in 1800, planned an uprising in the area of Charleston. With able assistance from such leaders as Peter Poyas and Mingo Harth many slaves over a large area were involved. The plan was to attack Charleston on the second Sunday in July, Sunday being a day on which it was customary for many blacks to be in the city and July being a time when many whites were vacationing outside the city. Weapons were made and information secured as to the location where arms and ammunition were stored. However, betrayal led Vesey to move the date ahead one month; but before action could be taken, further information led to the arrest of the leaders. Vesey and thirty-four others were found guilty and hanged.

In 1831 Nat Turner led a revolt in Southampton County, Va. Slaves killed over seventy whites and caused panic over a wide area. Soldiers defeated the rebels, and Turner and others were executed.

Some generalizations can be made about these insurrections. They involved mainly slaves, with only occasional participation by free blacks and rare involvement of whites. They were stimulated by factors and events external to the local situation—such as the revolution in Haiti—and each uprising brought a new crop of repressive laws. The measure of the importance of these revolts is not determined by their failure to free slaves but by the information they provide about slaves and their reactions to the institution of slavery.

BIBLIOGRAPHY

Herbert Aptheker, *American Negro Slave Revolts.*

Nicholas Halasz, *The Rattling Chains.*

Marion D. Kilson, "Toward Freedom: An Analysis of Slave Revolts in the United States," *Phylon,* vol. 25 (1964).

— HENRY N. DREWRY

SLAVERY

Africans, or Negroes, as they were also called by European slave traders, were first brought to the British continental colonies in August 1619 when a Dutch frigate sold twenty black captives to settlers in Jamestown, Va. It is not certain whether these black bondsmen were indentured servants or slaves, but it seems clear that from the time of their arrival in British America, blacks were treated as inferiors to all whites, indentured or free.

By the year 1640 some blacks in Virginia were actually being held in perpetual bondage as *de facto* slaves and some of their children had inherited the same obligation, while others remained contracted servants or had been set free by their masters. After that date the bonds of black servitude tightened in the colony. The rising costs of free and indentured labor added to the availability of cheap African labor that could be compelled to serve for life, and Anglo-Saxon color prejudices led to the transformation between 1640 and 1660 of informal black slavery into black chattel bondage sanctioned by law. By the 1660's Virginia had enacted a series of laws giving statutory recognition to the institution of slavery and consigning blacks to a special and inferior status in society.

As slavery evolved in Virginia, it appeared in the other British colonies. By the end of the 17th century it had gained legal recognition throughout British America and had become the presumed status of all blacks. Along the southern seaboard, where environmental conditions were suitable for the production of staple crops, such as tobacco, rice, and cotton, slavery took firm root. The institution never took strong hold in the middle Atlantic and New England settlements. Less temperate climates, rockier terrain, and a predominantly commercial economy supplemented by subsistence agriculture prevented settlers from duplicating on northern soil the lucrative plantation economy developing in the South. Nevertheless, huge profits were reaped by those northerners, particularly merchants in Massachusetts and Rhode Island, who were involved in the Atlantic slave trade.

In all of the colonies, despite various social and ecological differences, enslaved blacks suffered a gradual erosion of their status; by about 1700 they had reached their complete debasement, being regarded as human property. Each region, out of fear, antimiscegenationist sentiments, and racial prejudice, passed in the course of the 18th century elaborate sets of slave codes to regulate slave activity and to protect white society against black uprisings. Slaves were denied the right to marry, own property, bear arms, or defend themselves against assault. So that baptized slaves and children fathered by white men could not escape enslavement, colonial legislatures ruled that conversion to Christianity had no effect upon a person's condition, bond or free, and that status was determined by the race of the mother.

As imperfections in the system were corrected and as slave importations from Africa and the Caribbean increased in the 18th century, the slave population in the English colonies grew to large proportions, expanding from 20,000 in 1700 to 500,000 by the time of the American Revolution. The majority of the slaves were concentrated in those colonies along the southern seaboard in which tobacco, rice, indigo, and cotton were the important crops. South Carolina had a slave population in 1765 of 90,000 out of a total population of 130,000, and Virginia had a population of 120,000 slaves out of a total of 290,000 in 1756. The numbers of slaves never attained such levels in the North, where only in New York and Rhode Island, because of their extensive agricultural enterprises, were sizable groups of blacks concentrated.

Because of its tenuous base north of the Potomac River, the institution of slavery was unable to survive the attack directed against it there during the revolutionary war era. Strong abolitionist impulses inspired by the Quakers, the libertarian ideals of the war for independence, black freedom petitions, and the marginal importance of slavery to the North's economy produced between 1780 and 1804 a number of state court decisions and laws gradually abolishing slavery in New England and the middle Atlantic states. The institution remained basically untouched in the South, which was heavily dependent upon slave labor. Despite the antislavery pronouncements of some liberal southern statesmen, such as Thomas Jefferson, emancipation of the slaves was widely regarded as an impractical and irresponsible act that was detrimental to the economy and harmful to the blacks who allegedly benefited from their masters' paternalistic care.

To avoid disruptive conflict with the South and thereby hold together the newly formed republic, the framers of the U.S. Constitution agreed at the Constitutional Convention, held in Philadelphia in September 1787, to several compromises favorable to southern interests. The Constitution included a provision by which, for purposes of congressional apportionment, a slave was to be counted as three-fifths of a person; an extension of the slave trade until 1808; and a fugitive slave clause, which ensured the return of runaway slaves to their masters. Although the Constitution proved to be a conservative compact between northern commercialists and the southern aristocracy, the passage by Congress in 1787 of the Northwest Ordinance, which prevented the expansion of slavery into the midwestern territories, and the closing in 1808 of the African slave trade greatly restricted the future development of American slavery and deeply affected its character.

Congressional barriers against western expansion and exclusion from the international slave trade did not result, as some emancipationists had hoped, in the natural death of southern slavery. The institution had become by the late 1780's a viable economic system so intricately woven into the social fabric of southern life that black emancipation was never seriously considered. Growing demands in the world and domestic markets for cotton and the invention of the cotton gin in 1793 by Eli Whitney, which revolutionized the production of southern cotton, made slavery at the turn of the century an even more profitable enterprise, believed to be absolutely essential to the southern economy and society.

Because of its heightened commercial value and improved means of production, cotton soon became the staple crop throughout much of the South, spreading from the southeastern states, which until about 1800 had grown most of the nation's cotton, into the virgin lands acquired through the Louisiana Purchase of 1803. By the 1830's the fertile Gulf Coast states of Mississippi, Alabama, and Louisiana dominated an American cotton industry that was producing three-fourths of the world's supply.

With the rise of the southern cotton kingdom came increased demands by the planters for slave labor. For a brief period continued imports from Africa had been relied upon, but after the 1808 prohibition, planters were forced to turn to the domestic slave trade then being developed by states in the upper South, such as Virginia and Maryland, which had an excess supply of slaves. During the four decades preceding the Civil War, the domestic slave trade accounted for the transfer of about 200,000 slaves from the soil-exhausted Chesapeake Bay region to the alluvial Black Belt area, where cotton had become "king." Despite its volume, the domestic slave trade failed to supply planters in the lower South with the number of slaves needed on their extensive cotton fields. Since Congress could not be persuaded to reopen the trade with Africa, the planters had no choice but to increase their slave force by natural reproduction.

Out of economic necessity, American slaveowners generally created on their plantations material conditions conducive to the natural production of a large indigenous slave population. Of all the slave systems in the New World, it was only in North America that the slave population grew naturally to large proportions. Existing on the fringes of the Atlantic basin slave trade, the United States probably imported not more than about 430,000 slaves from Africa, less than 5 percent of the estimated total involuntary immigration of blacks to the Western Hemisphere. The growth of the slave population from 750,000 in 1790 to over 4 million in 1860, an increase of about 30 percent each decade, was attributable almost entirely to natural reproduction.

American slaveholders put their vast black work force to effective use, utilizing it in various capacities, not all of which was agriculturally based. Almost half a million slaves were employed in nonagricultural pursuits in the cities, towns, and labor camps of the antebellum South. Because of the special skills many slaves had acquired and the low costs of unfree labor, there was, throughout much of the antebellum era, a great demand among southern urbanites and industrialists for slave artisans and factory workers.

By the 1830's, virtually all opposition among southern whites to the institution of slavery had disappeared.

The farm or plantation remained nonetheless the slave's typical environment. In 1860 more than half of North America's 4 million slaves lived in the countryside on plantations worked by 20 or more slaves, but the bulk of the slave population was owned by a distinctly small segment of southern society. On the eve of the Civil War there were only 385,000 slave-holders in a free white population of 1.5 million families. Therefore only one-quarter of southern whites had a vested economic interest in slavery. But aspirations of one day belonging to the planter class, deeply ingrained racial prejudices, and psychological gratification derived from their superiority over the degraded blacks caused nonslaveholders to support an economic system that conflicted with their own class interests.

By the 1830's, virtually all opposition among southern whites to the institution of slavery had disappeared. Public reactions to mounting abolitionism in the North and increasing fears of slave insurrections in their own states silenced or drove into exile any remaining southern advocates of emancipation. To stifle all dissent, the South constructed an elaborate ideological and militant defense of slavery. Headed by George Fitzhugh, the proslavery ideologue of Virginia, southern apologists, including politicians, clergymen, social scientists, and natural scientists, popularized arguments that slavery was a positive good, divinely ordained, and that blacks were inherently inferior to whites.

Convinced of black inferiority and of the sanctity of slavery, southerners of all classes were prepared to protect the system by force if necessary. Service on the slave patrols and militia units instituted throughout the South to crush any internal or external threats was considered a civic duty and contributed to the emergence of a martial spirit in the region that verged on fanaticism and gave more authoritarian and coercive features to the slave system itself. Yet, absolute control of slave activity was never achieved. Unlike the modern concentration camp, which possessed the sophisticated means to induce widespread infantilism among its inmate population, the plantation, even under the harshest of conditions, was not so totalitarian a system that it was able to reduce its black work force to obsequious childlike dependents.

From dawn to dusk and sometimes long after dark during the harvest season, the slaves toiled under the supervision of either their masters, hired overseers, or trusted slaves called drivers; both brutal force and a complex system of rewards were used to get them to work efficiently. The daily routine of extended hours at forced labor was rarely interrupted except for a brief meal in the afternoon, and work in the fields only came to a full halt on Sundays and special holidays, such as Christmas. Consequently, it was usually only at night that the slaves enjoyed any respite from their labor. But as much as their lives were regimented by the plantation, the slaves often developed personalities strong enough to withstand the full psychological brunt of slavery's negative impact.

A communal spirit developed in the slave quarters, where the slaves were free of the constant scrutiny of their masters. The semiautonomous black culture created there out of both fragmentary African traditions and the American experience was among the chief factors protecting black personalities against adverse psychological change. The slave community, with its own hierarchy of male and female leaders, strong family ties, folklore, and spiritual beliefs, provided the slaves with the psychic ability to endure their oppression and the mental capacity to envision a better future, if not for themselves, for their children. Those slaves who were fully socialized to the slave system probably longed for a heavenly reward in the afterlife and passively accepted their subjugation, but many others who were less submissive sought to make the most out of their immediate conditions through subtle and overt forms of resistance.

A particular set of impersonal factors, including geography, demography, and political stability, generally prevented the development in the United States of physical and social conditions conducive to slave uprisings. Unlike the situation in the Caribbean and Latin America, where the large ratio of slaves to their masters, political unrest, and the rugged terrain of the interior facilitated slave insurrections, conditions in North America militated against them. So formidable were the obstacles to rebellion in the United States that, for the most part, slaves could not think realistically of collective violence.

"Day-to-day resistance," expressed in malingering, work slowdowns, sabotage, arson, self-mutilation, and the feigning of illness or incompetence, was a more common form of the Afro-American slaves' opposition to the slave system. Black culture was also used as a subtle instrument of protest by the slaves. Masked in inoffensive language, slave sermons, spirituals, and folklore often contained subversive themes and messages that contributed to the cultivation in the slave quarters of a tradition of resistance to white oppression.

More overt examples of slave unrest are represented in the numerous attempts by slaves to run away to the free states in the North or to Canada. As perilous as such undertakings were, thousands of slaves tried to secure their freedom by fleeing from the South. Numerous slaves succeeded in their flight for freedom, mainly with the assistance of free blacks working as "agents" for the "Underground Railroad," such as Harriet Tubman. The most dramatic, but also rarest, form of slave protest was open rebellion. Historians have been able to identify some 250 instances of slave conspiracies and revolts in North America, the most noted of which were the Gabriel Prosser plot of 1800 in Henrico County, Va.; the Denmark Vesey conspiracy of 1822 in Charleston, S.C.; and the Nat Turner rebellion of 1831 in Southampton County, Va.

Except for the very rare occasion when rebel slaves managed to escape into the wilderness and form maroon societies, the rebellions were ruthlessly crushed and their leaders brutally executed. Repressive laws usually followed to terrorize the slave and free black population of the South into total submission. To protect the slave system against northern-based attacks, southern politicians, led by John C. Calhoun of South Carolina, upheld the principle of states' rights in Congress and sought to maintain a balance in the Senate between free and slave states. These efforts were intensified during and after the Missouri Compromise of 1820, which resulted in the admission of Missouri to the Union as a slave state. Through the diplomacy of Speaker of the House Henry Clay, the compromise preserved the delicate balance of power then existing between the free and slave states but served notice to the South of the growing opposition in other sections of the country to the issue of slavery and its expansion.

The 1884 painting, "The Last Moments of John Brown," by Thomas Hovender, depicts the militant abolitionist being led to the gallows. (Corbis-Bettmann)

With the extension of America's borders to the Pacific in the 1840's, northern industrialists and farmers, for economic, political, and constitutional reasons, took a stand against the expansion of slavery into the newly acquired territories west of the Louisiana Purchase. Growing sectional strife over the issue reached a climax in the 1850's. The admission of Texas to the Union in

1845 as a slave state and the problem of slavery in the territories won from Mexico in 1848 led to a long and disruptive constitutional debate. Senators Stephen A. Douglas of Illinois and Henry Clay of Kentucky produced an omnibus bill, known as the Compromise of 1850, which temporarily settled the dispute and succeeded in preventing the threatened secession of the South from the Union. In the end, the compromise only provided an uneasy truce between the two sections. The illusory peace it created rapidly disintegrated under a wave of new disputes stemming from the slavery issue.

Tempers inflamed by the passage of the stringent Fugitive Slave Act (a proslavery provision of the Compromise of 1850), Harriet Beecher Stowe's novel *Uncle Tom's Cabin* (1852), the Kansas-Nebraska Act and conflict of 1854, and the Dred Scott Supreme Court decision of 1857 brought the nation to the brink of war. When white abolitionist John Brown and his interracial band attacked the federal arsenal at Harpers Ferry, Va. (now West Virginia), in 1859 to incite a general slave insurrection and Republican Abraham Lincoln of Illinois was elected president in 1860, most whites in the South were convinced that the only way to preserve southern civilization was to secede from the Union. In late 1860 and early 1861, seven Deep South states proceeded to secede from the Union, and on Apr. 12, 1861, South Carolina troops fired upon Fort Sumter, beginning the Civil War.

When Lincoln dispatched federal troops to repress the rebels, he had no intention of freeing the slaves. His sole aim was restoration of the Union. Still, slavery was the fundamental cause of the conflict, and the issue of emancipation could not be indefinitely avoided by the president. Union generals in the field quickly recognized that freeing of the slaves would cripple the southern war effort and attract thousands of freed blacks to the side of the North. Fearful, however, of driving the loyal slave states of Maryland, Delaware, Missouri, and Kentucky into the Confederate camp, Lincoln resisted freeing the slaves and even prevented for a time the enlistment of free blacks into the Union army.

Initially, most northerners supported Lincoln's limited war aims and his opposition to black troops, but military expediency and growing moral concern soon transformed the conflict into a crusade to free the slaves as well as to save the Union. Abolitionists and Radical Republicans gradually convinced Congress and much of the general public of the need to abolish slavery, which was seen as the cornerstone of the Confederacy. Under mounting pressures from these groups and because of military necessity, Lincoln reluctantly altered his position on black soldiers and emancipation. In the spring and summer of 1862, Lincoln signed legislation abolishing slavery in the District of Columbia, banning slavery in the territories, and freeing slaves who escaped to northern lines. These actions were followed in the fall by decisions to authorize the enlistment of black volunteers into the army and to issue a preliminary emancipation proclamation.

Had the Confederacy surrendered in 1863, Lincoln might not have issued the Emancipation Proclamation, and southerners would have retained possession of their slaves.

By the terms of the preliminary announcement, issued by Lincoln in September 1862, all slaves in those states still in rebellion on Jan. 1, 1863, would be freed. Slaves in the loyal border states and in areas occupied by Union forces were excluded from the ruling, revealing the president's continued ambivalence toward general emancipation. Had the Confederates surrendered within a period of 100 days, the South might have been able, under the provisions of Lincoln's proclamation, to retain its slaves. But no concession short of independence was acceptable to southerners. The Confederacy refused to surrender, forcing the president to issue the Emancipation Proclamation on its scheduled date. Presented to the nation as a necessary war measure, the edict legally freed over 3 million slaves held in rebel territory and enabled freedmen to serve in the Union army. Issuance of the proclamation was acclaimed at home and abroad as a great humanitarian act, but the document was flawed. It left in bondage some 800,000 slaves in the border states and in areas controlled by the federal government. They were not freed until the adoption in December 1865 of the Thirteenth Amendment, which formally brought to an end nearly 250 years of black slavery in America.

BIBLIOGRAPHY

Herbert Aptheker, *American Negro Slave Revolts.*
John W. Blassingame, *The Slave Community.*
Philip Curtin, *The Atlantic Slave Trade.*
Melvin Drimmer, ed., *Black History.*
Robert William Fogel and Stanley L. Engerman, *Time on the Cross.*
Winthrop Jordan, *White Over Black.*
John Hope Franklin, *From Slavery to Freedom.*
Eugene Genovese, *Roll, Jordan, Roll.*
August Meier and Elliot Rudwick, *From Plantation to Ghetto.*
Benjamin Quarles, *The Negro in the Making of America.*

Kenneth Stampp, *The Peculiar Institution.*
Allen Weinstein and Frank Otto Gatell, *American Negro Slavery.*

— WILLIAM R. SCOTT

SLAVE STATES

Slave States were those states where, prior to the Civil War, slaveholding was sanctioned by law. This was the case in all the states in 1776. Under the influence of the American Revolution, slavery disappeared from those areas north of Delaware and Maryland. Pennsylvania moved against it in 1780, Massachusetts abolished it by court action in 1783, and Connecticut and Rhode Island passed laws prohibiting slavery in 1784. New York in 1785 and New Jersey in 1786 passed manumission acts that were followed by more effective legislation in 1799 and 1804. The Northwest Ordinance (1787) prohibited the establishment of slavery in any state formed in that territory. But the trend did not continue. The Compromise of 1820 had been worked out to define the territory from which slave states might develop, and by 1845 nine new slave states had entered the Union. Efforts to add additional slave states and to prevent the spread of slavery led to fighting in Kansas and became a major national issue in the 1850's. On the eve of the Civil War the slave states were Alabama, Arkansas, Delaware, Florida, Georgia, Kentucky, Louisiana, Maryland, Mississippi, Missouri, North Carolina, South Carolina, Tennessee, Texas, and Virginia.

— HENRY N. DREWRY

SLAVE TRADE

African slaves were first brought to the New World shortly after its discovery by Christopher Columbus (there are records of them in Haiti in 1501), but the slave trade proper did not begin until 1517. It was largely the inspiration of Bartolomé de Las Casas, later the bishop of Chiapas, Mexico, who had seen that the Indian slaves "died like fish in a bucket," as one indignant Spaniard remarked, while "these Negroes prospered so much . . . [they] would never die, for as yet none have been known to perish from infirmity." In an effort to save the Indians, Las Casas suggested the wholesale importation of black slaves, a suggestion he was later bitterly to regret. In response to his plea, Charles V of Spain issued the Asiento, a contract giving the holder a monopoly on importing slaves to the Spanish dominions; Charles gave it to a favorite courtier. For the next two centuries the Asiento was to be a much coveted prize in European wars and treaties.

Portugal claimed the west coast of Africa as a result of expeditions sent out by Prince Henry the Navigator and at first controlled the export of slaves. Many of the words associated with the trade came from the Portuguese, such as "palaver" (a conference), "barracoon" (a slave pen), "bozal" (a newly captured black), "panyaring" (kidnapping), and "pickaninny" (a child). Portugal's hegemony was soon challenged by French, Dutch, Swedish, Danish, Prussian, and English slavers, but Portugal managed to retain control of the area south of the Bight of Benin and did until 1974. The various slaving companies erected a series of great forts, built on the design of medieval castles, along the coast of Africa. The castles, some of which are still standing, served the double purpose of acting as barracoons for the slaves and as protection against native attacks.

The slaving territory extended roughly from the Senegal River to Angola. The Bight of Benin provided so many slaves that it became known as the Slave Coast, mainly because it included the mouths of the Niger River, to which slaves were shipped down from the interior by canoe in large numbers. Some of the African tribes particularly associated with the trade were the Mandingo, Ashanti, Yoruba, Ewe, and Ibo.

Slavery was a recognized institution in Africa but consisted mainly of domestic slaves, for the continent was not industrialized and so had no market for large crops raised by slave labor. Some of the Mandingo nobles owned a thousand slaves. The local kings sold their surplus slaves, as well as criminals, debtors, and prisoners of war, to the European traders. In times of famine, parents often sold their children. These sources did not meet the constantly growing demand, and soon slave-catching raids were organized by the coastal tribes, using firearms supplied by the slavers. Even tribes reluctant to cooperate with the Europeans were forced to do so, because without firearms they would have been enslaved by their neighbors.

England, as the outstanding sea power, gradually came to control the trade. The first English slaver was John Hawkins, one of the most famous Elizabethan sea dogs. Hawkins engaged in a series of raids, beginning in 1560, on native communities along the coast, selling his captives in Spanish possessions in defiance of the Asiento. Queen Elizabeth called the business "detestable," but once aware of Hawkins' profits she became a shareholder in his subsequent voyages. Francis Drake as a young man also took part in the trade.

At first the English colonies in North America depended on European indentured servants for labor. When the supply of such individuals began to run short, the colonists turned to slaves. The first black slaves were landed in Jamestown, Va., in 1619. They were regarded as indentured servants, but by the middle of the 17th century slaves had come to be considered human chattels. All the colonies had slaves, but as the plantation system developed in the South, the slaves became concentrated there. Slavery was abolished in the northern colonies, principally as an inducement to white laborers to emigrate, but the New England colonies continued to take an active part in the slave trade itself, providing ships and crews and selling the slaves south of the Mason-Dixon Line. The trade expanded rapidly after 1650. It is thought that only 900,000 slaves were exported to the colonies during the whole of the 17th century, but by 1750, 100,000 slaves a year were arriving. There was an increasing demand for sugar, tobacco, rice, and later cotton, crops that could be supplied most profitably by slave labor.

In 1662 the Royal Adventure Trading Company (reincorporated as the Royal African Company in 1663) was founded in England and bought up all the castles along the coast, thinking this would give it a monopoly of the trade. By this time the tribal kings were as deeply involved in the trade as the Europeans, so the castles with their elaborate system of defense had become an anachronism. The company went bankrupt in 1750.

By the 18th century, the actual slave catching was done mainly by such warlike inland tribes as the Ashanti and the Dahomey, with the coastal tribes acting as middlemen. The slaves usually came from 200 to 300 miles inland, often much further. Mungo Park traveled 500 miles with a slave coffle (slave gang). To prevent escape, two slaves were often yoked together by means of a stick with a fork at each end into which the slaves' necks were fastened. The coffle was then marched to the coast, where the slaves were kept in a barracoon usually presided over by a European called a factor. When enough slaves had been collected, they were ferried out by canoe to the ships waiting off shore. The task of ferrying was generally conducted by the Krumen, a tribe of fishermen that came to specialize in this work.

In 1713 the Treaty of Utrecht gave England the Asiento and a virtual monopoly of the trade north of the equator. There followed a great boom in the slave trade. Liverpool was largely built on money made from the trade. So many slaves were exported that the Africans were convinced that white men were cannibals who existed solely on human flesh, as they could think of no other explanation for the enormous demand.

The American colonies developed triangular trade in the mid-18th century. A captain would load up with trade goods and rum and sail to Africa, where the goods would be exchanged for slaves. He would then land his slaves in the West Indies and take on a cargo of molasses, which he would transport to New England to be made into rum. In this way a captain was never forced to sail with an empty hold and could make a profit on each leg of the voyage. The base of the triangle, the run across the middle of the Atlantic, became known as the Middle Passage. At first slavers attempted to make some provisions for the welfare of their human cargo, such as "loose packing" (not overcrowding the slaves), arguing that the fewer the slaves who died, the greater the profits. Later most slavers became convinced that it was more profitable to pack slaves into every available square foot of space and make a run for it, a practice called "tight packing." With good winds the voyage could be made with little loss of life in two months, but with contrary winds most of the human cargo would be lost.

By the 18th century, the actual catching of slaves was done mainly by such warlike inland tribes as the Ashanti and the Dahomey, with the coastal tribes acting as middlemen.

Since the slaves were packed "spoon fashion" with "no more space than a man would have in his coffin," it was necessary to bring small groups, heavily shackled, on deck for short periods and force them to "dance" to restore their blood circulation. Nets had to be rigged along the ship's sides to prevent the slaves from leaping overboard and drowning themselves. Many refused to eat and had to be force-fed by a device called the "speculum ores," which resembled a funnel and was forced down the slave's throat. Then "slabber sauce," made of palm oil, horse beans, and flour, was poured down the funnel. Many died of the flux (dysentery), smallpox, and what the slavers called "fixed melancholy," or simply despair. A few captains were more merciful, such as Hugh Crow, who was awarded a bounty by the Anti-Slave Society for making a series of runs without losing a single slave; John Newton, who later became a clergyman; and Billy Boates, who was actually able to arm his slaves to beat off the attacks of privateers.

By the end of the 18th century there began to be strong moral opposition to the slave trade, although many considered it an economic necessity and the only method of providing manpower. In America, the fight against the trade was led by such men as John Woolman and Anthony Benezet. In England, the antislavery forces were led by Thomas Clarkson and William Wilberforce. Great Britain abolished the trade in 1807, and the United States did the same in 1808. The other European and South American countries gradually followed suit, either from pressure exerted on them by Great Britain or from honest conviction.

The trade continued to increase despite the prohibition. The invention of the cotton gin in 1793 and the development of the power loom, which created an unlimited demand for cotton, resulted in fresh demands for slaves. The value of a prime field hand rose from $500 to $1,500. Theodore Canot, a famous slave smuggler, left records of his voyages showing that on a single successful trip he made a net profit of $41,439. Two or three such voyages could make a man wealthy for life. The slavers started using fast ships—the forerunners of the clipper ship—which were rarely caught by the old-fashioned frigates sent by the British to patrol the African coast. As slavery was still legal in Africa, the native rulers continued to erect barracoons along the coast and await cruising slavers, which would signal, usually by flags, that they were in the market for a certain number of slaves. The slaves would be ferried out and loaded in only two or three hours; the slaver would then hoist all sails and run for the West Indies. Unless a frigate was able to catch a slaver with sails furled in the act of loading, capture was highly unlikely, although after the British had managed to capture a few slavers and used them as patrol vessels, the odds were more even.

A tangle of legal restrictions was imposed on the slaving squadron. Many nations, including the United States, refused to allow any ship flying their respective flags to be searched by the British even though it could be proved that the ship was using the flag illegally. As a result, slavers carried with them a number of different flags and appropriate papers to frustrate the frigates. To be condemned as a slaver, a ship had to be carrying slaves when boarded. This resulted in slavers tying their captives to the anchor chain and then, if in danger of capture, dropping the anchor over the side, dragging the slaves with it. Even if this was done in full view of the pursuing frigate, the ship could not be seized if no slaves remained onboard.

Slavers were declared pirates by both the United States and Great Britain under the treaty of 1820 and could be hanged, although this sentence was in fact not carried out until a later period. In 1839 the Equipment Clause was passed, authorizing a frigate's captain to seize a ship if it was obviously fitted out as a slaver with slave decks, large amounts of extra water casks, shackles, and grilled hatches. The Webster-Ashburton Treaty of 1842, between Great Britain and the United States, provided for American warships to cruise along the coast with the British vessels so that if a suspected slaver was flying American colors, the American warship could pursue it. This joint cruising was largely a failure. Few American frigates were ever sent, and most of those did not take their duty seriously. Some of them were under the command of southern officers who sympathized with the slavers, but a few American captains, such as Commodore Andrew Foote, did make an honest effort to suppress the trade and succeeded in making some captures.

In 1840 Capt. Joseph Dennan of the British navy, tired of seeing the barracoons packed with slaves along the coast, finally burned them after freeing the captives. The African monarchs angrily protested, but Parliament supported Dennan, although a few years before he would have been court-martialed for such an act. As a result, the barracoons had to be relocated far inland, which made loading the slaves onto ships much more difficult. Brazil was notorious for openly practicing the trade even though it had declared against it, and so in 1849 British Adm. Barrington Reynolds sailed into the port of Rio de Janeiro and burned all the slavers that he could find lying at anchor. To the populace's furious protests, Don Paulino, the Brazilian foreign minister, could only reply, "When a powerful nation like Great Britain is evidently in earnest, what can Brazil do?" To avoid the slaving squadron, some slavers dared to make the long and dangerous cruise around the Cape of Good Hope and load with slaves in East African ports, especially Zanzibar. A few thousand slaves were shipped in this way until the British sent paddlewheel frigates to stop the practice.

Meanwhile, slaves continued to be run into southern ports. In 1860 Capt. Nathaniel Gordon of the *Erie* was captured with a cargo of slaves. At President Abraham Lincoln's command, Gordon was hanged in New York, although troops had to be called out to prevent mobs from rescuing him.

With the abolition of slavery in the United States and the end of the Civil War, the trade largely came to an end. A few cargoes were probably run to Brazil in the 1870's and possibly even in the early 1880's, but to all intents and purposes, the trade was finished. In 1867 the slaving squadron was withdrawn.

Some 15 million blacks were exported from Africa during the 300 years of the slave trade. The number who died in native wars growing out of the slave trade was at least three times that figure. For Europeans and Americans, the trade provided much of the capital that financed the Industrial Revolution and supplied the labor that developed the American South and Southwest. For Africans, it was a disaster. It bled dry great sections of the continent, leaving communities so weak that they could not harvest crops; encouraged local wars; and discouraged development of the continent's resources, because the trade was so enormously profitable nothing else could compete with it.

BIBLIOGRAPHY

Theodore Canot, *Adventures of a Slave Trader.*
Captain Colomb, *Slave-Catching in the Indian Ocean.*
Basil Davidson, *Black Mother.*
Elizabeth Donnan, ed., *Documents Illustrative of the History of the Slave Trade to America.*
W. E. B. Du Bois, *The Suppression of the Slave Trade.*
Christopher Lloyd, *The Navy and the Slave Trade.*
Daniel Mannix and Malcolm Cowley, *Black Cargoes.*

— DANIEL MANNIX

SLUMS

Slums are seriously blighted residential districts that contribute to the social disorganization of their inhabitants. Slums have appeared in most cities, particularly in those of rapid growth and increasing heterogeneity. Except for scattered tenements that became overcrowded, the slow-growing cities in the American colonies escaped the blighting effects of slums until their increased size in some cases made the primitive sanitary facilities unwholesome. Poverty and other hardships abounded, but it was not until 1832, when the ravages of cholera exacted a heavy toll among the inhabitants of congested urban districts, that a few observant citizens in New York, Philadelphia, and Boston became aware of the existence there of wretched slums. In smaller towns these afflictions could still be attributed to an angry deity, but in New York a health survey by Dr. John H. Griscom prompted the formation in 1842 of the Association for Improving the Conditions of the Poor. Yet many members regarded it as only one of over a hundred charities, and the early attempts of its leaders to expose the evils of congestion had little effect, despite such reports as one in 1853 that pointed out the crowding of 18,456 persons into 3,742 cellars. The draft riots of 1863 revealed for the first time the extent of alienation that had developed in the slums. As a result the Citizens' Association made its appearance and appointed a council of hygiene and public health, which conducted an investigation that prompted the adoption of the first tenement house law in 1867.

Although the existence of slums was recognized, the causes and character of their growth were so poorly understood that successive housing reforms were vitiated. The rapid influx of poor Irish and German immigrants in the 1840's and 1850's inundated the older districts of Albany, New Orleans, and some other, smaller cities, as well as New York, Philadelphia, Baltimore, and Boston. Many substantial old houses and some warehouses, too, were hastily converted into multiple residences with minimal sanitary facilities, and flimsy annexes were added, often covering the last square inch of available land. When the early housing codes in New York City endeavored to preserve some open space and, later, to ban dark rooms, the builders added additional floors and provided airshafts that carried foul odors and sounds into every apartment. The increased density thus provided made it profitable to replace the less-substantial houses of an earlier day with solid rows of five- and six-story tenements that extended over wide districts and attracted only the poorest residents. A mounting influx of newcomers in the last decades of the century dumped thousands of Germans, Jews, Poles, Russians, and Italians into the vast expanse of tenements, where they competed for control of ethnic colonies and strove to ameliorate the slum environment by the introduction of their native customs.

Ethnic colonies appeared in most northern cities and in New Orleans in the South by midcentury, when over half the urban population was of foreign birth or parentage. Some, particularly in the German and Jewish colonies, which included many migrants who had urban experience abroad, successfully developed ethnic neighborhoods or ghettos that maintained wholesome communities and made vital cultural contributions to the growing cities. But as the streams of immigrants shifted and successive waves of eastern Europeans and Italians crowded their Irish and German predecessors out of the old districts, the ravages of time combined with the blight of poverty and the tensions of a new invasion to transform struggling ghettos into wretched slums.

The public awareness of the slums, induced by revealing accounts, such as those of Jacob Riis in New York and Jane Addams in Chicago, helped to support the social settlements in their endeavor to assist the residents of blighted districts develop wholesome communities. Together the settlement workers and neighborhood leaders pressed for increased civic provisions for health and safety and for the public enforcement of building codes, as well as for playgrounds and schools and finally for public housing. But their accomplishments were often dissipated and forgotten as the more promising and successful residents moved away or an influx of dissident newcomers brought a renewed struggle for local identity and survival. Each fresh invasion not only added new complications, contributing to social disorganization, but also deteriorated the housing stock. A federal survey in 1893 found the worst slum districts largely concentrated in New York and Chicago, but later studies found them widely present in most older cities of the Northeast.

The sudden drop in the tide of immigrants during World War I brought a sharp decline in the density of many old ethnic districts. In several heavy-industry cities in the North, where the wartime demand for labor had prompted efforts to import blacks from the South, a new invasion of the oldest slum districts commenced, producing violent race riots in a few cities. The migration from the South dropped off after the armistice, when the influx from southern and eastern Europe resumed until checked by the exclusion acts of the 1920's. The problems of the slums appeared to subside during the prosperous 1920's, in part because of the drastic reduction in the number of new immigrants, a situation that continued in the early years of the depression that followed. As unemployment and poverty spread, the influx of newcomers, and consequently the densities of the slum populations, declined. Moreover, the new federal relief measures brought the first public housing projects, among other welfare benefits, to some of the worst slum districts.

The sudden drop in the tide of immigrants during World War I brought a sharp decline in the density of many old ethnic districts.

But the respite was short-lived in most cities. World War II stimulated a movement of blacks from the South that continued in the postwar years. The settlement of these blacks in old immigrant districts spurred the migration of former residents to the outskirts and suburbs, creating inner-city black ghettos that added the new dimensions of color and prejudice to the problems of the slums. As the migration continued, the expansion of these areas threatened both the downtown business districts and the nearby residential neighborhoods to which some of the older immigrant groups had removed. As the tension increased, focusing attention on the slums, the pressure for federal action mounted, spurring an expansion of the public housing program as a means of eradicating the slums. Unfortunately the demolition of old tenements had the effect of scattering their inhabitants, and in the face of a continued influx of blacks and a new influx of Puerto Ricans the search for new housing was intensified. Efforts to locate the new projects in outlying wards met stiff neighborhood resistance; the result was a concentration of the low-cost units in high-rise blocks that in some cities exceeded the worst densities of the old slums. And when key locations near the business district were cleared for commercial or high-rental developments, the charge of black removal added to the mounting tensions, which finally erupted in a contagion of inner-city riots of unprecedented violence in the 1960's. The rioting eventually subsided, and the introduction of new model-city participatory programs for the redevelopment of blighted districts offered federal assistance for their rejuvenation. The federal effort fostered the newly developing sense of black pride, which brought a surge for black power that helped to determine the character of some new housing projects in inner-city areas. Their combined efforts proved insufficient, however, to counteract the blighting effects of poverty, unemployment, and race prejudice. Frustrated by the limited accomplishments, the federal government terminated the model-city projects and merged its subsidies in a block-grant system that turned responsibility for the fate of the slums back to the cities.

BIBLIOGRAPHY

Charles Abrams, *The City Is the Frontier.*
Roy Lubove, *The Progressives and the Slums.*
Jacob Riis, *How the Other Half Lives.*

— BLAKE MCKELVEY

SMALLPOX

Smallpox in its classic form is an acute, highly contagious disease with an average fatality rate for untreated cases of about one in six to one in four. Survivors are often permanently disfigured or disabled. First clearly described by medieval Arab writers, smallpox was by the 17th century a common disease of children in Europe. Brought to the Americas by explorers and settlers, it destroyed many Indian tribes. It became epidemic several times in the British colonies in the 1600's and occasioned the first colonial medical publication, Thomas Thacher's *A Brief Rule to Guide the Common-People of New-England How to Order Themselves and Theirs in the Small Pocks, or Measels* (Boston, 1678). To prevent the introduction and spread of the disease, the New England colonies created an elaborate system of quarantine and isolation during the 18th century.

About 1700, reports began reaching England about the practice, called inoculation, of inserting matter from a pustule of a smallpox patient into superficial incisions in the arms of persons who had not had the disease. The person so inoculated generally had a comparatively mild case of smallpox. Like natural smallpox, inoculated smallpox conferred lifelong immunity. After reading an account in the Royal Society's *Philosophical Transactions,* Cotton Mather persuaded Dr. Zabdiel Boylston to try it in 1721, when smallpox next became epidemic in Boston. A violent controversy ensued as Mather and Boylston were accused of spreading the disease. Statistics showed, however, that the case fatality rate for inoculated smallpox was much lower than for natural. In

Boston in 1721 there were 5,759 cases of natural smallpox, with 842 deaths (nearly 8 percent of the total population), and 287 inoculated cases, with only 6 deaths. Subsequent experiences were generally more favorable, so that inoculation became widely accepted, especially among those who expected to be exposed to the disease. Inoculation entailed some risk, and, if unregulated, could expose the community to the hazard of contagion. Several colonies passed laws prohibiting inoculation except during epidemics or in isolated hospitals. Many communities were thus able to avoid smallpox altogether for years. In the Middle Colonies, by contrast, inoculation was freely allowed, and in Philadelphia smallpox spread widely at frequent intervals, just as in British towns of comparable size. After the first year of the Revolution, American recruits were regularly inoculated, which made smallpox a minor threat to the effectiveness of the army. Although inoculation could not eliminate smallpox—it was, after all, a form of the disease itself—it could, when properly regulated and publicly supported, contribute significantly to reducing the death rate.

Of the 26 countries reporting smallpox morbidity to the League of Nations from 1921 to 1930, the U.S. had the highest attack rate of any nation except India.

In 1798 the English physician Edward Jenner introduced vaccination—that is, the inoculation of cowpox, a naturally occurring disease among dairy cattle and dairy workers—using techniques virtually identical to those used for the inoculation of smallpox (now known also as variolation). Vaccination, according to Jenner, was never fatal, did not spread naturally, and offered permanent protection against smallpox. Since then vaccinia has replaced cowpox virus as the usual inoculum and Jenner's conclusions have been found to be not strictly true; in particular, periodic revaccination is necessary for full protection. Compared to variolation, however, Jennerian vaccination was an immeasurable advance—probably the greatest single advance in preventive medicine ever achieved. Despite inevitable opposition, misuse, and errors, it was rapidly accepted around the world.

Soon after Jenner's announcement it was reported in the United States in medical publications and in newspapers. Several physicians sought to import vaccine; with one minor exception, the first to do so successfully was Benjamin Waterhouse, who vaccinated his son Daniel on July 8, 1800. At first Waterhouse sought outrageous profits from his temporary monopoly, but soon other physicians received vaccine from England independently; thereafter Waterhouse actively promoted its use. Vaccine institutes were promptly organized to treat the poor free, the first under James Smith in Baltimore in 1802. Smith later received an appointment as U.S. agent of vaccination under an 1813 act of Congress.

Vaccination was not universal in the 19th century. During the Civil War the Union army experienced some 19,000 cases and 7,000 deaths from smallpox. Preservation of live vaccine virus was difficult, and the vaccine sometimes became contaminated with other pathogenic microorganisms. The introduction of animal vaccine produced in calves in 1870 and of glycerinated lymph somewhat later helped to obviate these difficulties. As health departments began urging compulsory vaccination, especially after the pandemic of 1870–75, antivaccination societies were founded. Alleging the dangers of the introduction of other diseases, the infringement of personal liberty, and the ineffectiveness of vaccination, the antivaccinationists were supported by patent medicine interests, homeopaths, and others who opposed government regulation of drugs or of medical practice. As a result, the United States, of the twenty-six countries reporting smallpox morbidity to the League of Nations in 1921–30, had the highest attack rate of any nation except India. The great majority of cases in the United States were a relatively mild form known as alastrim, with a case fatality rate of less than 1 percent. Nevertheless, during an outbreak of classic smallpox in 1924–25 imported from Canada, some 1,270 deaths occurred. The use of vaccination increased substantially during the 1930's and World War II, and the incidence of smallpox since then has been extremely small. In the 1960's, as deaths from the occasional rare complications of vaccination in many countries outnumbered those from smallpox itself, the question was seriously raised whether vaccination should be continued as a standard routine. In 1967 occurrences of smallpox were reported to the World Health Organization (WHO) from forty-three countries; in thirty it was considered endemic. In that year the WHO began a program of intense surveillance and vaccination aimed at eradicating the disease. During 1974 smallpox was reported in only nine countries; in only three—India, Bangladesh, and Ethiopia—was the disease considered endemic, and the prospect of complete eradication within another two or three years appeared bright.

BIBLIOGRAPHY

John B. Blake, *Benjamin Waterhouse and the Introduction of Vaccination: A Reappraisal,* and *Public Health in the Town of Boston 1630–1822,* Harvard Historical Studies, vol. LXXII.

A. W. Hedrich, "Changes in the Incidence and Fatality of Smallpox in Recent Decades," *Public Health Reports,* vol. 51 (1936).

A. J. Rhodes and C. E. Van Rooyen, *Textbook of Virology.*

World Health Organization, "Smallpox in 1974," *WHO Chronicle,* vol. 29 (April 1975).

— JOHN B. BLAKE

SMITH ACT

Smith Act (June 28, 1940) provides for the registration and fingerprinting of aliens living in the United States and declares it unlawful to advocate or teach the forceful overthrow of any government in the United States or to belong to any group advocating or teaching such action. Passage of the act reflected American anxiety over Germany's rapid conquest of Western Europe at the beginning of World War II and over Communist-inspired strikes intended to injure American defense production. The act has been strongly criticized on the ground that it interferes with freedom of speech, guaranteed by the First Amendment. In a famous case, *Dennis* v. *United States,* concerning the conviction of eleven Communists under the act, the Supreme Court in 1951 upheld its constitutionality. In 1957, however, in *Yates* v. *United States,* the Court held that the teaching or advocacy of the overthrow of the U.S. government that was not accompanied by any subversive action was constitutionally protected free speech not punishable under the Smith Act.

BIBLIOGRAPHY

Edward S. Corwin, "Bowing Out 'Clear and Present Danger,'" *Notre Dame Lawyer,* vol. 27.

Wallace Mendelson, "Clear and Present Danger: From Schenck to Dennis," *Columbia Law Review,* vol. 52.

— CHARLES S. CAMPBELL

SMITH EXPLORATIONS

Jedediah Strong Smith, fur trader and explorer, joined William Henry Ashley's expedition in 1822 to establish the Rocky Mountain Fur Company. The expedition began at Saint Louis and ascended the Missouri River. In the spring of 1824 Smith headed the first party of Americans to travel through South Pass (Wyoming), which later became the gateway for westward migration. In the summer of 1826 Smith led a party from the Great Salt Lake in Utah to southern California—the first group of Americans to reach the Spanish settlements by an overland route. In June 1827 he and two companions returned to the Great Salt Lake by the central route—the first white men to cross the Sierra Nevada and the Great Salt Desert from west to east. Shortly afterward he set out again for California, with eighteen men, ten of whom were massacred by Mohave on the Colorado River. In 1827–28 he traveled up the Pacific coast, opening up a new route to Fort Vancouver on the Columbia River. Smith lost all but three of his men by massacre on the Umpqua River in Oregon. In 1829 he explored the Snake River country, and the following year he returned overland to Saint Louis. In the spring of 1831 he set out with a wagon train for Santa Fe, N.Mex., and while seeking water for his party was killed by the Comanche on the Cimarron River in southwestern Kansas on May 27.

BIBLIOGRAPHY

H. C. Dale, *The Ashley-Smith Explorations and the Discovery of the Central Route to the Pacific.*

Maurice S. Sullivan, *The Travels of Jedediah Smith.*

— JOHN G. NEIHARDT

SOCIAL GOSPEL

Social Gospel, a late 19th- and early 20th-century American Protestant reform movement attempting to apply the principles of Christianity to the social and economic problems that resulted from increased industrialization, urbanization, and immigration following the Civil War. The movement had its origins in Unitarianism's emphasis on the social side of Christianity during the early 1800's, but it did not become a major force until the 1880's. At that time, the rise of labor organizations and the resulting labor disturbances brought the accusation from labor that the church was more sympathetic to capital than to labor. This stirred liberal church leaders to a study of the implications of the teachings of Jesus on social and economic questions. Among the early leaders in the movement were Washington Gladden, Richard Theodore Ely, Charles Monroe Sheldon, Walter Rauschenbusch, and Shailer Mathews. Their teachings and writings, which advocated the abolition of child labor, a shorter work week, improved factory conditions, and a living wage for all workers, as well as prison reform and changes in the free-enterprise system, exercised widespread influence. They aroused a lively social consciousness within the major denominations that led to the establishment of various kinds of social-service agencies and the adoption of liberal social programs.

BIBLIOGRAPHY

Washington Gladden, *Tools and Man: Property and Industry Under the Christian Law,* and *Applied Christianity.*

Shailer Mathews, *The Church and the Changing Order.*
Walter Rauschenbusch, *Christianity and the Social Crisis.*

— WILLIAM W. SWEET

SOCIALIST MOVEMENT

Socialism is an outlook or a social philosophy that advocates that the major instruments of production, distribution, and exchange should be owned and administered by society for the welfare of all rather than for the benefit of a few. Basically, socialism would abolish private property in major producers' goods or capital while usually retaining it in consumers' goods. The gap between lowest and highest personal incomes would be drastically reduced, and there would be an expansion of "free" goods and services (Socialists often advocate not only free parks and schools but also free public transport, health services, and legal services). There have been many schools of Socialist thought, the varying perspectives often turning on differences in strategy and on interpretation of ultimate goals.

In American history the Socialist movement began during the early part of the 19th century, when communitarian experiments, gaining their inspiration from such Europeans as Charles Fourier, Étienne Cabet, and Robert Owen, were established. Brook Farm, founded in 1841 and associated with several of the Transcendentalists, was Socialist in spirit. The Oneida Community in New York State, founded by John Humphrey Noyes in 1848, might also be described as reflecting one variety of socialism, although it went further in the direction of communism than socialism in general.

After the publication of Karl Marx's and Friedrich Engels' *Communist Manifesto* (1848), a new type of socialism appeared, generally called Marxism. Analyzing the dynamics of industrial society, Marx and Engels foresaw the day when industrial capitalism would disintegrate and socialism would arise in its place. Generally speaking, Marx and Engels believed that socialism was likely to develop first in the most highly industrialized societies, where accelerating class consciousness would play an important role.

After the Civil War the influence of Marxian socialism began to be felt in the United States. Along with native American Socialist currents, it challenged the framework of American capitalism. The hard times of the 1870's and 1880's stimulated the development of the movement. In 1877 the Socialist Labor party was established. Edward Bellamy's followers in the Nationalist movement a decade later were fundamentally Socialist, and many Populists (organized in 1892) had somewhat the same point of view. In 1897 the Social Democracy of America was launched by Eugene V. Debs. Out of it emerged the Social Democratic party in 1898—which, with other groups, established the Socialist party of America in 1901.

From 1901 to World War I the Socialist party waxed in strength. By 1912 it had enrolled 118,000 members. Its leader, Debs, was favorably received both in industrial areas and among many farmers (as in Oklahoma). In 1920, while in prison for opposing World War I, Debs received 919,799 votes for the presidency. The party began to disintegrate after the Bolshevik revolution in Russia in 1917. Dissidents formed the Communist party and the Communist Labor party; in 1920 another splinter group established the Proletarian party. Debs's successor as leader of the Socialist party, Norman Thomas, ran for the presidency six times (1928, 1932, 1936, 1940, 1944, and 1948), but only once, in 1932, did he win a substantial vote (881,951).

One of the most common explanations for the decline of American socialism is the U.S.'s relatively high standard of living.

By the 1950's the formal Socialist movement in the United States had been reduced greatly. The Socialist party ceased to run candidates for the presidency after 1956. Although other groups called Socialist continued to exist and to nominate candidates, their electoral strength was small: in the 1968 presidential election the Socialist Labor party won 52,588 votes and the Socialist Workers party (Trotskyite), only 41,300.

Scholars have long been concerned to explain the decline of American socialism, but they have differed among themselves in their emphases. Causes often listed to account for the disintegration of the movement have been the relatively high standard of living enjoyed by American workers, making socialism less attractive to those who were supposed to be its vanguard according to Marx; a labor movement that has been relatively unsophisticated politically; the development of the New Deal, which some Socialists thought of as moving toward their goals; and the many internal feuds that weakened the movement, particularly after 1917.

BIBLIOGRAPHY

Donald D. Egbert, Stow Persons, and T. D. Seymour Bassett, eds., *Socialism and American Life.*
H. W. Laidler, *A History of Socialist Thought.*
James Weinstein, *The Decline of Socialism in America, 1912–1925.*

— MULFORD Q. SIBLEY

SOCIALIST PARTY OF AMERICA

Socialist Party of America was formed in July 1901 by a union of Eugene V. Debs and Victor L. Berger's Social Democratic party and Morris Hillquit's wing of the Socialist Labor party. The Socialist party gave to American radicalism, normally fragmented and divided, a unique era of organizational unity. Only the tiny Socialist Labor party and, later, the Industrial Workers of the World remained outside. The Socialist party incorporated surviving elements of western populism; until 1918 the highest percentage of its popular vote came in states west of Mississippi (Oklahoma boasted the largest state organization). The party was also well entrenched in the labor movement: the Socialist candidate captured almost one-third of the vote for the presidency of the American Federation of Labor in 1912. In that year, too, the Socialists reached the high point of their electoral success: Eugene V. Debs, running for the U.S. presidency, gained 6 percent of the vote; and some 1,200 Socialists were elected to public office, including seventy-nine mayors.

The party's growth stopped after 1912, but the following years can be characterized as a time of consolidation rather than as a time of decline. For once departing from its policy of inclusiveness, the party in 1913 cast out the syndicalist wing led by William D. Haywood. By eliminating the one group not committed to political action, the Socialist party became more cohesive without altering the balance between the right and left wings. World War I severely tested, but did not undermine, the Socialist movement. Unlike its western European counterparts the American party adhered to the stand of the Second International against war. The enunciation of that position at the Saint Louis convention of April 1917 did drive out prominent prowar members, but it did not split the party. Wartime persecution hurt the movement: Debs and many others went to prison; vigilante action and the barring of Socialist literature from the mails weakened outlying bodies, especially in the western states. These setbacks were more than counterbalanced by the rapid growth of the party's foreign-language federations and by the tapping of antiwar sentiment, as was evident in the party's strong showing in wartime elections.

Eugene V. Debs (1855-1926), American Socialist and organizer of the Social Democratic Party in the United States. Undated photograph. (Corbis-Bettmann)

The Bolshevik revolution in Russia (1917) was the turning point. The problem was not the event itself—this was universally hailed by American Socialists—but whether it provided a model for the United States. The left wing, and especially the foreign-language federations, believed that it did, and they were sustained by instructions coming from the Third Communist International in 1919. The party leaders thought otherwise: they did not think that the United States was ripe for revolution, nor were they willing to reconstitute the party along Leninist lines. With the left wing about to take over, the established leadership in May 1919 suddenly expelled seven foreign-language federations and the entire Michigan party and invalidated the recent elections to the national executive committee.

A decisive break with the past had occurred. Not only was American radicalism permanently split between Communists and Socialists, but the latter had lost their authenticity as a movement of radical action. By 1928 Socialist membership was not a tenth of the 1919 level, and although it experienced some revival during the 1930's, the party never regained either its popular base or the electoral appeal of earlier years. Having lost its left wing, moreover, the Socialist party evolved into an essentially reformist movement whose appeal was largely to the urban middle class. The new national leadership after the death of Debs in 1926 symbolized the change: Norman Thomas was a Princeton graduate, a former Presbyterian minister who had come to socialism via pacifism and the appeal of conscience. After 1956 the Socialist party ceased to nominate presidential candidates and increasingly viewed itself as an educational rather than a political force. In 1972 the Social Democratic Federation, a moderate wing that had split away in 1936, was reunited with the Socialist party; at the end of 1972 the name was changed to Social Democrats USA. In the 1972 presidential election, the united party supported George McGovern and took as its principal job the rallying of the liberal and labor vote for the Democrats. With a claimed membership of roughly 20,000, the Social Democrats in 1974 pledged to work with the Democratic party and the trade union movement toward Socialist goals and "to transform the Democratic Party into the Social Democratic Party."

BIBLIOGRAPHY

David A. Shannon, *The Socialist Party of America.*
James Weinstein, *The Decline of Socialism in America.*

— DAVID BRODY

SOCIAL SECURITY

Social Security is the largest, costliest, and most successful domestic program in the history of the United States. Through its 1,300 local branches, ten regional headquarters, and central offices in Baltimore and Washington, the Social Security Administration issues 500 million checks a year. Officials deal with old-age and survivors benefits, assess the needs of disabled workers, and provide eligible senior citizens with hospital insurance and supplemental medical insurance under Medicare. The administration's error rate is under 3 percent—a remarkable achievement for any bureaucracy. Beginning in the 1980s fear arose because of the program's imminent bankruptcy, but a majority of Americans continued to express considerable confidence in the system. Social security, Democratic Senator Bill Bradley declared in 1983, is "the best expression of community that we have in this country today."

Social security was designed to enable ordinary people to cope with the "risks" associated with loss of wages. Although Americans now tend to view it as a program for the elderly, its New Deal architects perceived old-age dependency in the context of family networks that changed with the generations. As Franklin Delano Roosevelt told Congress in 1934, "If, as our Constitution tells us, our federal government was established among other things, 'to promote the general welfare,' it is our plain duty to provide for the security upon which welfare depends. . . . Hence I am looking for a sound means which I can recommend to provide at once security against several of the great disturbing factors of life, especially those which relate to unemployment and old age. . . . These three objectives—the security of home, the security of livelihood, and the security of social insurance—are, it seems to me, a minimum of the promise that we can offer to the American people."

Social Security is the largest, costliest, and most successful domestic program in U.S. history.

The Social Security Act of Aug. 14, 1935, largely met Roosevelt's expectations by mounting a two-pronged attack on old-age dependency. A federal-state partnership was established under Title I, which gave men and women over sixty-five years of age assistance if deemed eligible. (Because no national guidelines were established, southern states managed to circumvent the spirit of the provision and maintain racial discrimination. Still, procedures were established to enable applicants to appeal; this made old-age assistance a right, not a gratuity.) To reduce old-age poverty, employers and employees were expected to contribute 0.5 percent each (for a total of 1 percent) of the first $3,000 of an employee's salary for a retirement pension. The 1935 act dealt with the needs of younger citizens as well. Titles III and IX established a mechanism for unemployment compensation. Title IV launched what would eventually become Aid for Families with Dependent Children; Title X assisted the blind. Under Title V states received money for crippled children, rural public health services, and vocational rehabilitation; the U.S. Public Health Service received training funds under Title VI. The Social Security Board was authorized (Title VII) to evaluate programs. Although Title XI gave Congress "the right to alter, amend, or repeal any provision of this Act," President Roosevelt knew his program was safe: "We put those payroll contributions there so as to give the contributors a legal, moral, and political right to collect their pensions and unemployment benefits. With those taxes in there, no damn politician can ever scrap my social security program."

In 1939 Title II benefits were extended to widows and other family members of contributing workers. Whereas private insurance would have required an increase in taxes on grounds of equity, no new Federal Insurance Contribution Act (FICA) taxes were levied, showing a social-welfare orientation. Disability provisions were added in the 1950s, medicare in 1965. The 1972 amendments combined assistance provisions into a supplemental security income program, which established the nation's first poverty floor. That same year automatic cost-of-living adjustments were added. As its creators envisioned in the depths of the Great Depression, by the mid-1970s nearly every worker paid taxes on his or her wages. In principle, nearly all U.S. citizens were eligible for entitlements at some point in their lives. President Gerald Ford (1974–1977) first confronted the fiscal problems associated with expanding social security. To strengthen the system, President Jimmy Carter (1977–1981) adjusted benefit schedules and imposed steep tax increases. Although the 1983 amendments shored up financing of the retirement program, public confidence in the system's future remained shaky. The disability insurance program remains volatile; neither experts nor policymakers seem able to define "disability" in a consistent manner.

[See also Medicare and Medicaid; New Deal; Social Security; Taxation.]

BIBLIOGRAPHY

W. Andrew Achenbaum, *Social Security: Visions and Revision* (New York, 1986).

Martha Derthick, *Agency Under Stress: The Social Security Administration in American Government* (Washington, D.C., 1990).

Eric R. Kingson and Edward D. Berkowitz, *Social Security and Medicare: A Policy Primer* (Westport, Conn., 1993).

— W. ANDREW ACHENBAUM

SOCIAL WORK

The profession of social work in the United States developed early in the 20th century among persons employed in local and state charitable organizations. Although governmental auspices predominated in institutions, hospitals, and prisons, innovative ideas tended to come from such settlement houses as Henry Street in New York and Hull House in Chicago, as well as from such charity organization societies houses in Boston, New York, and Baltimore. By World War I paid workers were displacing wealthy volunteers in many agencies. Professional associations emphasized communication between members, ethics, quality in education and performance, research and writing, and improved working conditions. Six such organizations merged in 1955 to form the National Association of Social Workers (NASW).

Social work education started in New York City in 1898 with an agency-sponsored summer school. Collegiate auspices (Simmons College and Harvard) were achieved in Boston in 1904, and by 1930 two-year graduate programs were becoming standard. In 1975 eighty-one universities in the United States offered masters degrees and thirty-one offered doctoral degrees in social work. Nevertheless, staff needs were so great in a rapidly expanding field that membership in NASW, previously limited to those with masters degrees, was opened to graduates of 135 accredited undergraduate programs.

Emphasis in the profession has always been divided between effecting "retail" individual social adjustments and "wholesale" solutions through institutional change. The latter approach reached a high point in 1912 when Theodore Roosevelt, then candidate for the U.S. presidency, incorporated large sections of a social work report on standards of living and labor in the Progressive (Bull Moose) platform. Following World War I, with reform in eclipse, enthusiasm for Freudian psychology shifted the emphasis of social work toward adjustment of individuals. This trend was confirmed in the schools during the New Deal, when many reform-minded teachers were drawn into administration of the Social Security Act and other new programs. In the post-World War II era the National Mental Health Act financed a further sharp, unbalanced increase in the psychiatric aspect of social work with the institution of the War on Poverty and other programs of the 1960's.

Notable early leaders of social work include Mary Richmond (1861–1928), Jane Addams (1860–1935), Richard Cabot (1868–1939), and Harry Hopkins (1890–1946). The influential magazine The Survey, until its demise in 1952, was a principal interpreter of social work concerns.

BIBLIOGRAPHY

Arthur E. Fink, C. Wilson Anderson, and Merrill B. Conover, *The Field of Social Work.*

Robert Morris, *The Encyclopedia of Social Work.*

Ralph E. Pumphrey and Muriel W. Pumphrey, *The Heritage of American Social Work.*

— RALPH E. PUMPHREY

SOCIETY FOR THE PREVENTION OF CRUELTY TO CHILDREN

In April 1874 the American Society for the Prevention of Cruelty to Animals rescued and obtained the protection of the state for Mary Ellen Wilson, a mistreated child. In April of 1875, as a direct result of this case, the first child protective agency, the New York Society for the Prevention of Cruelty to Children, was incorporated.

Child protection services are accepted as a responsibility of every community and, under public or private auspices, are to be found in every state.

During the ensuing quarter century more than 150 similar societies were formed across the country. The primary objective of such agencies is the protection of abused and neglected children. Upon receipt of a complaint alleging child neglect or abuse, the child protective agency investigates and offers indicated services to correct unwholesome home conditions and, in appropriate situations, secures protection of the child by legal proceedings. Child protective services are accepted as a responsibility of every community and, under public or private auspices, are to be found in every state.

— THOMAS BECKER

SOLDIERS AND SAILORS CONVENTIONS

Soldiers and Sailors Conventions (1866), political gatherings held during the political campaign waged by President Andrew Johnson and his conservative supporters against the Radical Republicans as they sought to influence the outcome of fall elections. Attempting to show themselves as national in scope and thus the true party of the Union, Johnson and his supporters met at the National Union Convention in Philadelphia, on Aug. 14. Former Union and Confederate officers, many prominent Copperheads, and a large number of moderate southern Democrats who favored Johnson's Reconstruction policies participated in the gathering, which became known as the Arm-in-Arm Convention.

At a second meeting on Sept. 17, conservative federal veterans, led by generals Thomas Ewing, Jr., Gordon Granger, George Armstrong Custer, John Alexander McClernand of Illinois, and J. B. Steedman of Ohio, urged support of the president's policies of conciliation and immediate restoration of the seceded states to the Union. Gen. John Ellis Wood, who presided, denounced the abolitionists as "revengeful partisans with a raging thirst for blood and plunder." Many leaders joined in a round robin attacking Edwin M. Stanton, secretary of war.

The Radicals countered by calling northern and southern supporters of congressional Reconstruction policies to a gathering at Philadelphia on Sept. 3. A second group, mostly former military men, met at Pittsburgh in the Soldiers and Sailors Convention (Sept. 25). Gen. Jacob Dolson Cox, of Ohio, was permanent president. The convention's resolutions, drafted by Benjamin Franklin Butler, "the hero of Fort Fisher," endorsed the Fourteenth Amendment as "wise, prudent and just" and denounced the Johnson policies.

BIBLIOGRAPHY

G. F. Milton, *The Age of Hate.*

— GEORGE FORT MILTON

SONS OF LIBERTY (AMERICAN REVOLUTION)

Sons of Liberty (American Revolution), radical organizations formed in the American colonies after Parliament's passage of the Stamp Act in 1765. Societies sprang up simultaneously in scattered communities, an indication that although leadership was an important factor in agitating American independence, there existed among the people a considerable degree of discontent over parliamentary interference in colonial affairs. New York and Boston had two of the largest and most active Sons of Liberty chapters.

The organizations constituted the extralegal enforcement arm of the movement for colonial self-government. Members circulated patriotic petitions, tarred and feathered violators of patriotic decrees, and intimidated British officials and their families. They stimulated a consciousness of colonial grievances by propaganda. They conducted funerals of patriots killed in street brawls; promoted picnics, dinners, and rallies; drank toasts to the honor of historic leaders of liberty; denounced British tyranny; and hanged unpopular officials in effigy. Upon discovering that British authorities were unable to suppress them, the Sons of Liberty issued semiofficial decrees of authority and impudently summoned royal officials to "liberty trees" to explain their conduct to the people.

BIBLIOGRAPHY

Roger Champagne, "The Military Association of the Sons of Liberty," *New York Historical Society Quarterly,* vol. 41.

E. S. Morgan and H. M. Morgan, *The Stamp Act Crisis.*

— LLOYD C. M. HARE

SONS OF LIBERTY (CIVIL WAR)

Sons of Liberty (Civil War), a secret organization of Copperheads, strongest in the Northwest, was formed in 1864 by the reorganization of the Order of American Knights, with C. L. Vallandigham of Ohio, then in exile in Canada, as supreme commander. The 300,000 members were sworn to oppose unconstitutional acts of the federal government and to support states' rights principles. They opposed the draft and discouraged enlistments. Confederate agents in Canada attempted unsuccessfully to promote a so-called Northwest Conspiracy, which involved using the Sons of Liberty to form a Northwestern Confederacy. Six members of the organization were arrested and tried for treason at Indianapolis in September and October 1864. Three were condemned to death but never executed.

BIBLIOGRAPHY

E. J. Benton, *The Movement for Peace Without a Victory During the Civil War.*

— CHARLES H. COLEMAN

SOONERS

Sooners were those persons who illegally entered certain lands in the Indian Territory prior to the date set by the U.S. government for the opening of the lands to settlement. The term was first used in connection with the settlement of the so-called Oklahoma Lands in 1889. A proclamation issued by President Benjamin Harrison authorized settlement of these lands as of noon, Apr. 22, and forbade any person to enter them earlier. Those who did so came to be called Sooners. The term was also used at later openings of Indian Territory lands to settlement.

BIBLIOGRAPHY

J. S. Buchanan and E. E. Dale, *A History of Oklahoma.*
J. B. Thoburn, *History of Oklahoma,* vol. II.

— EDWARD EVERETT DALE

SOUTH, ANTEBELLUM

If, as has been said, the South is today a history in search of a country, such an assertion would not have been true during most of the antebellum period. The considerable interest in the history of the South developed in the post-Civil War period, when there was a golden age to remember and its passing to lament. The revolutionary war stimulated some historical writing, but otherwise there was relatively little attention given to the history of a society not yet fully sectionally conscious. During the years of early settlement the indefinite boundaries of its several colonies, established by the whims of English monarchs, were of no great moment; reference to the Chesapeake country, the Carolina-Georgia lowlands, and the backcountry inland from these two areas defined the life experiences of the settlers much more realistically. As economic and political focuses developed in the 18th century—such centers as Saint Marys and Annapolis, Md.; Jamestown and Williamsburg, Va.; New Bern, Edenton, and Charleston in the Carolinas; and, later, Nashville, Natchez, and New Orleans—colony and state entities became administratively and jurisdictionally functional and served to give separate identities to populations within them.

The Old South never achieved a single outstanding urban focus; New York handled at least as much of the South's trade as did Charleston, New Orleans, or Baltimore, which in 1860 was its largest city. On the eve of the Civil War the South was still overwhelmingly rural, and its towns and small cities were gracious plantation capitals dominated more by planters than by merchants. It had by that time developed a planter gentry that exercised an economic and political influence in each southern state, as well as in the nation, out of all proportion to its numbers. By 1850 planters were being separately enumerated in the U.S. census. Behind the great planters, possessing thousands of acres and hundreds of slaves, ranged a larger number of small planters and an even larger number of white yeoman farmers. Behind these came poor whites, free blacks, black slaves, and scattered Indian groups. By 1860 the Old South had achieved a heterogeneity that linked into an organic whole the parts of its massive and varied geographical areas from Maryland to eastern Texas and moved it toward a political and cultural unity.

In this area there developed and spread a distinctive institution—the plantation—not present in the European or African traditions of the settlers or in any other part of continental North America. It shared certain characteristics with the English manor, Old Testament Hebrew patriarchal society, the classical Greek state, and the Roman latifundium, but it had a distinct mode of its own. It produced agricultural staples for sale, not for local consumption. It was the driving force behind the settlement of the land and of the westward expansion of southern civilization. Plantations largely determined the settlement, distribution, and tasks of labor not only on the estates themselves but also in the farm areas symbiotic to them. They accommodated the relationships between people of diverse race, nationality, and culture and, in doing so, provided order, stability, and continuity; and they set the stage for the identification of the white people of the area as southerners and for the class and racial stratification of the whole population.

The plantation was a distinctive institution not found in the European or African traditions of the settlers, or in any other part of continental North America.

Southern civilization had its inception in the 1607 settlement of Englishmen at Jamestown, Va., and modified English traditions and institutions continued to dominate southern society into the late 20th century. of the South's white population in 1860—about 60 percent of the total—no less than two-thirds was of English stock; persons of Scottish and Scotch-Irish descent made up about one fifth; and the balance of the white population was made up of smaller percentages of French, Spanish, German, and Celtic-Irish descendants. The southern black population—about 40 percent—accounted for about nine-tenths of the black population of the United States.

The London (later, Virginia) Company initiated what was originally intended to be a trading factory at Jamestown, after the precedent of Italian and English trading factories in the Baltic and the Levant, but trade with the native Indians proved unprofitable. The economic motive explicit in the enterprise was realized after 1619 in the production of tobacco, an addictive drug with a market elastic enough to pay the cost of production in Virginia and of transportation to England and yet yield a profit. Entrepreneurial tobacco plantation agriculture began an independent development in Virginia and Maryland in the early 17th century; the rice and indigo plantations of South Carolina and the sugar plantations of Louisiana were African and/or West Indian transplants in the early 18th century.

Like the tobacco plantation, the rice, indigo, and sugar plantations were territorially delimited; they did not undergo any significant westward expansion, as did cotton plantations. Following the invention of the cotton gin in 1793 and the surging demand for raw cotton in England incident to the Industrial Revolution, it was the cotton planters who mobilized the tremendous energy necessary to cross southern state boundaries, and by 1860 they had carried the institution of the plantation all the way to eastern Texas. South Carolina, the leading cotton-producing state, was the focus of secessionist activities.

An analysis of the bases of the civilization of the Old South falls conveniently into three contexts: the regional, the sectional, and the cultural. The regional South is delineated in demographic, ecological, and economic terms; the sectional South, in political and ideologic terms; and the cultural South, in terms of its way of life. The plantation was the active institutional determinant in all three respects.

The South as region or as subregion was originally differentiated from the rest of North America as a specialized territorial division of labor along with eastern Mexico, central America, northern and northeastern South America, and the islands of the West Indies for the production of tropical and subtropical agricultural staples for the markets of Europe. Because of the relative cheapness of water transportation, plantation America hugged the islands and coastlands of the Atlantic, the Caribbean, the Gulf of Mexico, and the rivers that emptied into those waters. The area now called the South, with outlets along the Atlantic coast and the Gulf of Mexico, was the northern part, or subregion, of the larger plantation region. It was, and is, the only region of the United States that fronts the sea on two sides, and it has a total shoreline of nearly 3,000 miles, greater than the rest of the United States, North and West, combined.

Those parts of the New World where colonial wares profitably could be produced were areas of what H. J. Niebor, in his *Slavery as an Industrial System* (1910), calls "open resources," areas where there was more land than there was labor to till it and where men of capital and enterprise competed with each other for such workers as could be made available. It was in response to this situation that white indentured servitude, Indian slavery, and, far more important, black slavery were introduced. In consequence, the society became biracial, with blacks and whites in the plantation areas intermixed on the same land. There was a concentration of white yeoman farmers and squatters in the more inaccessible and less fertile areas.

In the course of bringing land into new, and presumably higher, economic uses, the plantation became a political institution, a little state or subdivision of the state, within which a monopoly of authority was exercised by the planter. On the unruly southern frontier the planter, himself often lawless, established law on his own plantation, privileged to reward and punish even by the occasional exercise of the power of life and death, especially in the early years. By virtue of his authority he pursued a sort of military agriculture, employing a hierarchically ordered, regimented labor, imported and distributed as a utility. The people thus imported—black Africans—interbred with some of the whites in authority over them, especially where there was an imbalance of the sexes. The concept of race, already present in the Atlantic slave trade, became much more than a physical anthropological expression, for it was elaborated into a set of symbols and dogmas to set the races apart and keep both the mixed and the unmixed portions of the nonwhite population within the ranks of the laboring caste. It thus became a political idea, and although most of the mixed population—almost half a million people—had by 1860 become free blacks, they were not yet free men. Between 1830 and 1860 the subject of the free black surpassed the subject of slavery as the most discussed problem of the Old South, but it was caste, as well as slavery, together with the idea of race implicit in them, that set the South off against the North in a sectional bipolarity.

"I shall recognize as tests of sectionalism all those methods by which a given area resists national uniformity," wrote Frederick Jackson Turner in *The Significance of Sections in American History*. In these terms the South became "the South" as a section rather than a region or subregion. The northern part of plantation America became part of a political entity, the United States, to which other parts of the Gulf-Caribbean-Atlantic region did not belong; and from the years of the American Revolution on, there was a mounting conflict of interest between the South and the other sections of the Union. During the Constitutional Convention, in the words of Charles C. Pinckney of South Carolina, "a real distinction between northern and southern interests arising from the character of their means of livelihood" became apparent. It was to become more apparent when events such as the War of 1812, the nullification controversy, the Nat Turner slave rebellion in 1831, the war with Mexico (1846–48), the failure of compromise efforts, and John Brown's raid at Harpers Ferry (1859) fanned the flames of sectional opposition. It was as if an institutional fault line extending westward from the Mason-Dixon line broke the continuity of northern and southern social systems. The plantation had intruded an alien social stratum into the southern system, which threw all other institutions out of line with their northern counterparts. Revolutionary abolitionists in the North began an attack on the evils of slavery and the dark purposes of "the slave power" that broadened into a condemnation of the South generally. Southerners responded with equal intemperance. In the processes of attack and counterattack the interests and customs of each society, and especially of the South, came to be regarded by the members of each as essential to survival and thus to be defended at all costs.

Such considerations introduce the South as a culture area, as ethnologists tend to think of culture, characterized by those intangible aspects of a civilization that are felt rather than satisfactorily apprehended intellectually and expressed verbally. Southern culture is manifest in a climate of conventional understandings that are difficult to fix in terms easily understood by nonsoutherners. A map of plantation societies around the world, past and present, shows the South to have been the largest such society the world has ever known. Millions of people grew up and lived in this system of society and knew no other, or very little of any other, having little opportunity for comparison and contrast with other cultures. The southern region in the larger world community and the individual plantation in the forest were highly isolated, and the resultant culture was a product of isolation. The culture of the Old South was a way of life, a distinctive style of living, taken for granted and requiring no analysis or explanation. A young woman visiting in New York was "surprised to hear of 'plantation customs' said to exist" in the South. Thus, it is not surprising that the storytellers of the Old South could, like Jane Austen, apply themselves to the telling of the tale itself "by agreeing with society and being at peace with it." The resulting literature emphasized manners and chivalry and was generally romantic.

In terms of Matthew Arnold's idea of culture as the cultivation of "what is best and noblest in us," those attributes of a civilization that can be pointed to, praised, and refined, the Old South exhibited itself in the literary societies of its colleges and universities, the achievements of its scientists, its oratory, its literary periodicals, its architecture, its literature, its statesmen, and its theologians. There were eminent southern men of achievement in all such areas. Southern ethnocentrism has perhaps overpraised both them and the society that produced them, but such overpraise is a sin of ethnocentrism generally. The ingredients of a high civilization were present in the lives of the plain folk of the South—such as gardens, balladry, folk sermons, and culinary art—yet few creative masterpieces of an enduring nature were inspired by them.

The plantation system gave southerners the sense of belonging to an ordered civilization and, in the 1850's, occasioned the first use of the word sociology *in America.*

The regional, sectional, and cultural aspects of the Old South came together to form a social system at the center of which was the institution of the plantation supported by a series of satellite institutions. The "plantation system" and "the South" became almost synonymous, and although not every southerner lived within the physical bounds of a plantation, perhaps all properly called southerners lived within the plantation system. The plantation took on a familial form, modifying the family within itself as well as the families of all classes symbiotic to it, whether deriving from Europe or from Africa. There was little place for free public schools until near the end of the pre-Civil War period, but academies were fairly numerous, and state and denominational colleges drew students from among the sons of the smaller planters as well as the affluent ones. These educational institutions, as well as military schools, functioned within the plantation system to indoctrinate and to support it. Protestant, Roman Catholic, Jewish, and even such black religious organizations as there were came to be part of the system and to serve it by seeking to transfer attention from the ills of this world to salvation in the next. The county developed as a primary social, as well as governmental, unit, with the plantation often functioning as an informal, but effective, subdivision. The states, too, came under control of planter oligarchies. All lived under the laws sponsored by plantation interests, even where the institution was not physically present and where the system tapered off, somewhat diluted, toward piedmont and mountain areas. It was a system that gave southerners the sense of belonging to an ordered civilization and led to the first use of the word "sociology" in America, notably by Henry Hughes and George Fitzhugh in the 1850's. Sociology, according to Fitzhugh, was the descriptive social science of the South, just as its enemy, political science, was that of the North.

BIBLIOGRAPHY

U. B. Phillips, *Life and Labor in the Old South.*

David Potter, *The South and the Sectional Conflict.*

Wendell Holmes Stephenson, *A Basic History of the Old South.*

Edgar T. Thompson, *Plantation Societies, Race Relations, and the South.*

— EDGAR T. THOMPSON

SOUTHERN CHRISTIAN LEADERSHIP CONFERENCE

An outgrowth of the Montgomery [Ala.] Improvement Association (which was founded in 1955 and led by Martin Luther King, Jr.), the Southern Christian Leadership Conference (SCLC), based in Atlanta, was formed in 1957 as a "non-sectarian coordinating agency" for "nonviolent direct mass action." The first major civil rights organization to originate in the South, the SCLC was a Southwide umbrella of loosely affiliated organizations, mostly of black Baptist churches, that sought "full civil rights and total integration of the Negro into American life." Amorphous in organization, SCLC's principal force was symbolic, especially through its president, King. By filling the ideological and generational vacuum between the more conservative National Association for the Advancement of Colored People (1909) and National Urban League (1910), on the one hand, and the more radical Congress of Racial Equality (1942) and Student Nonviolent Coordinating Committee (1960), on the other, SCLC added prestige, respectability, and money to the civil rights movement, especially between the time of King's winning of the Nobel Peace Prize in 1964 and his assassination in 1968.

BIBLIOGRAPHY

Kenneth B. Clark, "The Civil Rights Movement: Momentum and Organization," in Talcott Parsons and Kenneth B. Clark, eds., *The Negro American.*

August Meier, "On the Role of Martin Luther King," *New Politics,* vol. 4 (1965).

— HUGH DAVIS GRAHAM

SOUTH PASS

South Pass, the most celebrated of the passes in the Rocky Mountains, because through it ran the great emigrant trail to Oregon and California. It is located in Wyoming at the southern end of the Wind River Mountains. The approach to the pass is so gradual that, in the words of explorer John C. Frémont, "the traveller, without being reminded of any change by toilsome ascents, suddenly finds himself on the waters which flow to the Pacific Ocean." There are claims that John Colter discovered the South Pass in 1807 or 1808 and that Robert Stuart and the returning Astorians crossed it in 1812, but both claims are disputed. It is certain that the effective discovery was made in 1824 by Thomas Fitzpatrick, a fur trader. Capt. Benjamin L. E. Bonneville first took wagons over the pass in 1832, and a few years later it became the mountain gateway on the Oregon Trail.

BIBLIOGRAPHY

Hiram M. Chittenden, *The American Fur Trade of the Far West.*

E. W. Gilbert, *The Exploration of Western America, 1800–1850.*

— DAN E. CLARK

SPACE PROGRAM THROUGH PROJECT APOLLO

See NATIONAL AERONAUTICS AND SPACE ADMINISTRATION

SPACE PROGRAM

The U.S. civil space program went into something of a holding pattern after completion of Project Apollo in December 1972. For the next decade the major program of the National Aeronautics and Space Administration (NASA) was the development of the Space Transportation System, a reusable space shuttle that was supposed to be able to travel back and forth between the Earth and space more routinely and economically than the spectacular but expensive series of missions that had followed the Apollo 11 moon landing on July 20, 1969. Between the autumn of 1969 and early 1972, NASA leaders worked to convince President Richard M. Nixon that the shuttle was an appropriate follow-on project to Apollo. They were successful on Jan. 5, 1972, when the president issued a statement announcing the decision to "proceed at once with the development of an entirely new type of space transportation system designed to help transform the space frontier of the 1970s into familiar territory, easily accessible for human endeavor in the 1980s and 1990s." The shuttle became the largest, most expensive, and most highly visible project undertaken by NASA after its first decade, and it has continued to be a central component of the space program.

The space shuttle that emerged in the early 1970s consisted of three primary elements: a delta-winged orbiter spacecraft with a large crew compartment, a fifteen-by-sixty-foot cargo bay, and three main engines; two solid rocket boosters (SRBs); and an external fuel tank housing the liquid hydrogen and oxidizer burned in the main engines. The orbiter and SRBs were reusable. The shuttle was designed to transport up to 45,000 pounds of cargo into near-Earth orbit for a planned space station, to be located 115 to 250 miles above the earth, and to accommodate a flight crew of ten (although seven would be more common) for a basic space mission of seven days. For its return to earth, the orbiter was designed to have a cross-range maneuvering capability of 1,265 miles to meet requirements for liftoff and landing at the same location after only one orbit. This capability satisfied Department of Defense requirements for a shuttle that could place in orbit and retrieve reconnaissance satellites.

NASA began developing the shuttle soon after the president's announcement with the goal of flying in space by 1978, but because of budgetary pressure and technological problems the first orbital flight was delayed until 1981. There was tremendous excitement when *Columbia*, the first operational orbiter, took off from Cape Canaveral, Fla., on Apr. 12, 1981, six years after the last U.S. astronaut had returned from space following the Apollo-Soyuz Test Project in 1975. After the two-day test flight, the nation watched with excitement as the shuttle landed like a conventional airplane at Edwards Air Force Base in California. The first flight was a success, and both NASA and the media proclaimed the beginning of a new age in space flight, an era of inexpensive and routine access to space for many people and payloads. Speculation abounded that within a few years shuttle flights would take off and land as predictably as airplanes and that commercial tickets would be sold for regularly scheduled "spaceline" flights.

In the mid-1970's, speculation abounded that shuttle flights would soon "take off" and that commercial tickets would be sold for regularly scheduled "spaceline" flights.

As it turned out, the shuttle program provided neither inexpensive nor routine access to space. By January 1986 there had been only twenty-four shuttle flights; in the 1970s NASA had projected more flights than that for every year. Although the system was reusable, its complexity, coupled with the ever-present rigors of flying in an aerospace environment, meant that turnaround time between flights was several months instead of several days. Missions were delayed for all manner of problems, and it took thousands of work hours and expensive parts to keep the system performing. Observers began to criticize NASA for failing to meet expectations. Analysts agreed that the shuttle had proven neither cheap nor reliable, both primary selling points, and that NASA should not have used those arguments in building a political consensus for the program. By 1985 there was general agreement that the effort had been both a triumph and a tragedy. An engagingly ambitious program had developed an exceptionally sophisticated vehicle, one that no other nation on earth could have built at the time. At the same time, the shuttle's much-touted capabilities had not been realized. Criticism reached its height following the tragic loss of *Challenger* and its crew of seven in an explosion during a launch on Jan. 28, 1986. Pressure to get the shuttle schedule more in line with earlier projections had prompted NASA workers to accept operational procedures that fostered shortcuts and increased the opportunity for disaster, although that was not the entire reason for the explosion. Several investigations followed the accident, the most important being the blue-ribbon commission mandated by President Ronald Reagan and chaired by William P. Rogers. It found that the *Challenger* accident resulted from a poor engineering decision, an O-ring used to seal joints in the SRBs that was susceptible to failure at low temperatures.

Following the *Challenger* accident, the shuttle program went into a two-year hiatus while NASA redesigned the SRBs and revamped its management. James C. Fletcher, NASA administrator between 1971 and 1977, was brought back and given the task of overhauling the agency. NASA invested heavily in safety and reliability programs and restructured its management. Most important, engineers added a way for the astronauts to be ejected from a malfunctioning shuttle during launch. Another decision resulting from the accident was to increase the use of expendable launch vehicles. The space shuttle finally returned to flight on Sept. 29, 1988, with the launch of *Discovery*. Through April 1993 NASA launched an additional thirty shuttle missions without an accident. Each undertook scientific and technological experiments ranging from deployment of space probes, such as the *Magellan* Venus radar mapper in 1989 and the Hubble Space Telescope in 1990 to the continued *Spacelab* flights in 1991 for the European Space Agency (which NASA had undertaken in 1983) and a dramatic three-person extravehicular activity (EVA) in 1992 to retrieve a satellite and bring it back to earth for repair. Through all these activities, a good deal of realism about what the shuttle could and could not do began to emerge.

In addition to the shuttle, the space program initiated a series of spectacular science missions in the 1970s. Project Viking was the culmination of an effort begun in 1964 to explore Mars. Two identical spacecraft were built, each consisting of a lander and an orbiter. Launched on Aug. 20, 1975, *Viking 1* landed on July 20, 1976, on the Chryse Planitia (Golden Plains). *Viking 2* was launched on Sept. 9, 1975, and landed Sept. 3, 1976. One of the scientific activities of the project was an attempt to determine whether there was life on Mars, but the Viking landers provided no clear evidence for living microorganisms in soil near landing sites. One of the most important space probes undertaken by the United States was initiated because the Earth and all the giant planets of the solar system were due to gather on one side of the sun in the late 1970s. This geometric lineup made possible close observation of all planets in the outer solar system (with exception of Pluto) in a single flight, which was called the Grand Tour. The flyby of each planet would bend a spacecraft's flight path and increase velocity enough to deliver it to the next destination, which would occur through a complicated process known as gravity assist (something like a slingshot effect), thereby reducing the flight time to Neptune from thirty years to twelve. Project Voyager was a satellite reconnaissance in which two Voyager spacecraft were launched from Kennedy Space Center in 1977 to photograph Jupiter and Saturn. As the mission progressed, with achievement of all objectives at Jupiter and Saturn in December 1980, flybys of the two outermost giant planets, Uranus and Neptune, proved possible—and irresistible. *Voyager 1* and *Voyager 2* explored all the giant outer planets, including their rings and magnetic fields and forty-eight of their moons.

The $2 billion Hubble Space Telescope project received much media attention in the early 1990s. A key component of the telescope was a precision-ground 94-inch primary mirror shaped to within microinches of perfection from ultralow-expansion titanium silicate glass with an aluminum-magnesium fluoride coating. The telescope was launched from the space shuttle in April 1990, and the first photos provided much better images than pictures of the same target taken by ground-based telescopes. Controllers then began moving the telescope's mirrors for better focus, and although focus sharpened, the best image still had a pinpoint of light encircled by a hazy ring or "halo." Technicians concluded that the telescope had a spherical aberration, a mirror defect one twenty-fifth the width of a human hair that prevented Hubble from focusing all light to a single point. Many observers believed the spherical aberration would cripple the forty-three-foot-long telescope, and NASA received much criticism, but scientists found a way to work around the abnormality with computer enhancement. Because of difficulties with the mirror, NASA launched *Endeavour* in December 1993 on a mission to insert corrective lenses on the telescope and to service other instruments. During a weeklong mission *Endeavour's* astronauts conducted a record five space walks and completed all programmed repairs. The images returned afterward were more than an order of magnitude better than those obtained before.

During the 1980s plans were put forth for a new generation of planetary exploration. The Reagan administration called for a permanently occupied space station in 1984. Congress made a down payment of $150 million for space station *Freedom* in the fiscal year 1985 NASA budget. From the outset both administration officials and NASA intended *Freedom* to be an international program. Partners abroad, many with their own rapidly developing space capabilities, could enhance the effort. NASA leaders pressed forward with international agreements among thirteen nations to take part, but almost from the outset *Freedom* was controversial. Debate centered on costs versus benefits. The projected cost of $8 billion had tripled within five years. NASA pared away at the budget, and in the end the project was satisfactory to almost no one. In the late 1980s and early 1990s a parade of space station managers and NASA administrators, each attempting to rescue the program, wrestled with *Freedom* and lost. In 1993 the international situation allowed NASA to include Russia in the building of an international space station, a smaller and cheaper successor to *Freedom.* On Nov. 7, 1993, a joint announcement was made by the United States and Russia that they would work with other international partners to build a station for benefit of all. Even so, the space station remained a difficult issue as policymakers confronted competing national programs. Even more troubling for the space program was the ambitious Space Exploration Initiative (SEI), which would return people to the moon by the year 2000, establish a lunar base, and, using the space station and the moon as bases, reach Mars by 2010. The price tag was estimated at $700 billion over two decades. Congress refused to fund SEI despite lobbying by Vice President Dan Quayle as head of the National Aeronautics and Space Council, an advisory group to President George Bush. Although the president castigated Congress for not "investing in America's future," members believed such a huge sum could be better spent elsewhere. "We're essentially not doing Moon-Mars," Senator Barbara Mikulski of Maryland declared bluntly.

Although President Bush scolded Congress for not "investing in America's future," members believed the huge sums in question could be better spent here on earth.

By 1993 the highly successful *Magellan* mission to Venus had provided data about that planet. The *Galileo* mission to Jupiter had become a source of concern because not all systems were working, but it also returned useful data. The ill-fated *Mars Observer* reached its destination in 1993 but was lost as a result of an onboard explosion. Thus, as the U.S. space program approached the last years of the twentieth century its reputation had been tarnished by debates about the space station and SEI, the initial failure of the Hubble Space Telescope, and the deficiency of *Galileo,* to say nothing of the *Challenger* accident. The fate of the space station program was undecided in 1994, on the twenty-fifth anniversary of the first moon landing, but both it and the stillborn Space Exploration Initiative pointed up the difficulty of building a constituency for large science and technology programs.

[See also Challenger *Disaster; National Aeronautics and Space Administration.]*

BIBLIOGRAPHY

Roger E. Bilstein, *Orders of Magnitude: A History of the NACA and NASA, 1915–1990* (Washington, D.C., 1989).

Wernher von Braun, Frederick I. Ordway III, and Dave Dooling, *History of Rocketry and Space Travel,* 3rd ed. (New York, 1986).

Roger D. Launius, *NASA: A History of the U.S. Civil Space Program* (Melbourne, Fla., 1994).

Howard E. McCurdy, *Inside NASA: High Technology and Organizational Change in the U.S. Space Program* (Baltimore, 1993).

Walter A. McDougall, *The Heavens and the Earth: A Political History of the Space Age* (New York, 1985).

— ROGER D. LAUNIUS

SPANISH-AMERICAN WAR

The sinking of the battleship *Maine* in Havana harbor on Feb. 15, 1898, provided a dramatic *casus belli* for the Spanish-American War, but underlying causes included U.S. economic interests ($50 million invested in Cuba; $100 million in annual trade, mostly sugar) as well as genuine humanitarian concern over long-continued Spanish misrule. Rebellion in Cuba had erupted violently in 1895, and although by 1897 a more liberal Spanish government had adopted a conciliatory attitude, U.S. public opinion, inflamed by strident "yellow journalism," would not be placated by anything short of full independence for Cuba.

The *Maine* had been sent to Havana ostensibly on a courtesy visit but actually as protection for American citizens. A U.S. Navy court of inquiry concluded on Mar. 21 that the ship had been sunk by an external explosion. Madrid agreed to arbitrate the matter but would not promise independence for Cuba. On Apr. 11, President William McKinley asked Congress for authority to intervene. Congress, on Apr. 19, passed a joint resolution declaring Cuba independent, demanding the withdrawal of Spanish forces, directing the use of armed force to put the resolution into effect, and pledging that the United States would not annex Cuba. On Apr. 25 Congress declared that a state of war had existed since Apr. 21.

The North Atlantic Squadron, concentrated at Key West, Fla., was ordered on Apr. 22 to blockade Cuba. The squadron, commanded by Rear Adm. William T. Sampson, consisted of five modern battleships and two armored cruisers, after the *Oregon* completed its celebrated sixty-six-day run around Cape Horn and joined the squadron. The Spanish home fleet under Adm. Pascual Cervera had sortied from Cadiz on Apr. 8, and although he had only four cruisers and two destroyers, the approach of this "armada" provoked near panic along the U.S. East Coast, causing Sampson to detach a flying squadron under Commodore Winfield Scott Schley to intercept Cervera.

Spanish troop strength in Cuba totaled 150,000 regulars and 40,000 irregulars and volunteers. The Cuban insurgents numbered perhaps 50,000. Initial U.S. strategy was to blockade Cuba while the insurgents continued the fight against the Spanish, with the expectation of an eventual occupation of Cuba by an American army. At the war's beginning, the strength of the U.S. Regular Army under Maj. Gen. Nelson A. Miles was only 26,000. The legality of using the National Guard, numbering something more than 100,000, for expeditionary service was questionable. Therefore, resort was made to the volunteer system used in the Mexican War and Civil War. The mobilization act of Apr. 22 provided for a wartime army of 125,000 volunteers (later raised to 200,000) and an increase in the regular army to 65,000. Thousands of volunteers and recruits converged on ill-prepared southern camps; there was a shortage of weapons, equipment, and supplies; and sanitary conditions and food were scandalous.

In the Western Pacific, Commodore George Dewey had been alerted by Acting Secretary of the Navy Theodore Roosevelt to prepare his Asiatic Squadron for operations in the Philippines. On Apr. 27 Dewey sailed from Hong Kong with four light cruisers, two gunboats, and a revenue cutter—and, as a passenger, Emilio Aguinaldo, an exiled Filipino insurrectionist. Dewey entered Manila Bay in the early morning hours on May 1. Rear Adm. Patricio Montojo had one modern light cruiser and six small antiquated ships, a force so weak that he elected to fight at anchor under protection of Manila's shore batteries. Dewey closed to 5,000 yards and shot Montojo's squadron out of the water, but he had insufficient strength to land and capture Manila itself. Until U.S. Army forces could arrive, the Spanish garrison had to be kept occupied by Aguinaldo's guerrilla operations.

In the Atlantic, Cervera managed to elude both Sampson and Schley and to slip into Santiago on Cuba's southeast coast. Schley took station off Santiago on May 28 and was joined four days later by Sampson. To support these operations a marine battalion on June 10 seized nearby Guantánamo to serve as an advance base. Sampson, reluctant to enter the harbor because of mines and land batteries, asked for U.S. Army help. Maj. Gen. William R. Shafter, at Tampa, Fla., received orders on May 31 to embark his V Corps. Despite poor facilities, he had 17,000 men, mostly regulars, ready to sail by June 14 and by June 20 was standing outside Santiago. Sampson wanted Shafter to reduce the harbor defenses; Shafter was insistent that the city be taken first and decided on a landing at Daiquiri, east of Santiago. On June 22, after a heavy shelling of the beach area, the V Corps began going ashore. It was a confused and vulnerable landing, but the Spanish did nothing to interfere. Once ashore, Shafter was joined by insurgent leader Calixto Garcia and about 5,000 revolutionaries.

Wisconsin troops passing the Customs House at Ponce, Puerto Rico, on their way to the front, during the Spanish-American War, in 1898. (The Granger Collection, New York)

Between Daiquiri and Santiago were the San Juan heights. Shafter's plan was to send Brig. Gen. Henry W. Lawton's division north to seize the village of El Caney and then to attack frontally with Brig.

Gen. Jacob F. Kent's division on the left and Maj. Gen. Joseph Wheeler's dismounted cavalry on the right. The attack began at dawn on July 1. Shafter, sixty-three years of age and weighing more than 300 pounds, was soon prostrated by the heat. Lawton was delayed at El Caney by stubborn enemy resistance and failed to come up on Wheeler's flank. Wheeler, one-time Confederate cavalryman, sent his dismounted troopers, including the black Ninth and Tenth cavalries and the volunteer Rough Riders, under command of Lt. Col. Theodore Roosevelt (he had left the navy to seek a more active role in the war), against Kettle Hill. Kent's infantry regiments charged up San Juan Hill covered by Gatling-gun fire. The Spanish withdrew to an inner defense line, and as the day ended, the Americans had their ridge line but at a cost of 1,700 casualties.

Shafter, not anxious to go against the Spanish second line, asked Sampson to come into Santiago Bay and attack the city, but for Sampson there was still the matter of the harbor defenses. He took his flagship eastward on July 3 to meet with Shafter, and while they argued, Cervera inadvertently resolved the impasse by coming out of the port on orders of the Spanish captain general. His greatly inferior squadron was annihilated by Schley, and on July 16 the Spaniards signed terms of unconditional surrender for the 23,500 troops in and around the city.

On July 21 Miles sailed from Guantánamo in personal charge of an expedition to Puerto Rico. He landed near Ponce on July 25 and against virtually no opposition began a march to San Juan, which was interrupted on Aug. 12 by the signing of a peace protocol.

At the end of July, the VIII Corps, some 15,000 men, mostly volunteers, under Maj. Gen. Wesley Merritt, had reached the Philippines. En route, the escort cruiser *Charleston* had stopped at Guam and accepted the surrender of the island from the Spanish governor, who had not heard of the war. Because of an unrepaired cable Dewey and Merritt themselves did not hear immediately of the peace protocol, and on Aug. 13 an assault against Manila was made. The Spanish surrendered after token resistance.

In Cuba tropical diseases reached epidemic proportions, and a number of senior officers proposed immediate evacuation. This was embarrassing for the army, but it also hastened the removal of thousands of fever patients to a camp at Montauk Point, Long Island, and gave impetus to the successful campaign against yellow fever by the U.S. Medical Corps.

The peace treaty signed in Paris on Dec. 10, 1898, established Cuba as an independent state, ceded Puerto Rico and Guam to the United States, and provided for the payment of $20 million to Spain for the Philippines. Almost overnight the United States had acquired an overseas empire and, in the eyes of Europe, had become a world power. The immediate cost of the war was $250 million and about 3,000 American lives, of whom only about 300 were battle deaths. A disgruntled Aguinaldo, expecting independence for the Philippines, declared a provisional republic, which led to the Philippine insurrection that lasted until 1902.

BIBLIOGRAPHY

R. A. Alger, *The Spanish-American War.*

F. E. Chadwick, *The Relations of the United States and Spain: The Spanish-American War.*

G. A. Cosmas, *An Army for Empire.*

F. Freidel, *The Splendid Little War.*

H. W. Wilson, *The Downfall of Spain.*

— EDWIN H. SIMMONS

SPEAKER OF THE HOUSE OF REPRESENTATIVES

Although the concept of the speaker of the House was borrowed from the British House of Commons and some colonial assemblies, the speaker-ship of the U.S. House of Representatives has developed into a uniquely original institution. The speaker is the first officer named in the U.S. Constitution: "The House of Representatives shall clause their Speaker and other Officers . . . " (Article I, Section 2). There is no requirement that the speaker be a House member, or even an American citizen, but in 1789 the House chose a member, Frederick A. C. Muhlenberg, as its first speaker, and the tradition of choosing from its membership has continued. Through the personal impact of its many competent occupants, the speakership has come to be regarded as second only in power and importance to the presidency. Standing behind the vice-president in succession to the presidency, several speakers have been only one step away from the highest office in the land—for example, Sam Rayburn, when the administration of Harry S. Truman was without a vice-president (1945–49); and Carl Albert, after the resignation of Vice-President Spiro T. Agnew (1973), and again after the resignation of President Richard M. Nixon (1974). In diplomatic protocol the speaker ranks third—behind the president and vice-president, but ahead of the chief justice of the Supreme Court—for purposes of seating at official and social functions. The speaker is given a salary in addition to that received as a member of the House and a substantial expense account.

The speaker of the House plays a variety of roles. His first duty is to preside over the House of Representatives. Every two years, at the beginning of each new

Congress, the House must elect its speaker before it can conduct its business; although the speaker is elected by the votes of a majority of all House members, in practice the House merely ratifies the choice of the majority party membership. He interprets the rules of the House, and his rulings can be overturned by a majority of the House, although from 1931 to 1975 not a single ruling was reversed. He preserves order, enforces the rules, refers bills and resolutions to the appropriate committees, and prevents dilatory tactics from paralyzing House action. He chooses the member who will preside as chairman of the Committee of the Whole, where the House conducts much of its important business. The speaker has a unique relationship with the president. In private conversations and in more formal meetings, he presents the views of the House members to the president and in turn reports the views of the president to House members informally.

The Speaker of the House enforces the rules, refers bills to the appropriate committees, and prevents delaying tactics from paralyzing House action.

Until the early 20th century, the speakership was a highly partisan office, used by the majority to work its will. The tradition then developed of a scrupulously fair presiding officer who considers it one of his highest duties carefully to protect the rights of every minority member under the rules of the House. But in his role as leader of his political party in the House, there is no pretense of nonpartisanship. The speaker has great influence in placing his party's members on committees. (Until the House internal revolution in 1910, the speaker for years had named all committee chairmen and appointed all committee members for both majority and minority parties.) He negotiates many internal matters with the minority leader, such as the membership ratio between parties on committees, and he names members of conference committees to negotiate differences with the Senate. Another important power is his right to name several hundred members of special boards and commissions. The speaker is also influential in determining which bills the House will consider.

The speaker's power over the political fortunes of his party's House members is substantial, particularly for new members. His favor can greatly advance a newcomer's career in the House; his disfavor usually has a retarding, even a blighting, effect. The speaker can aid a candidate through letters of endorsement, speeches in the candidate's home district, disbursement of campaign funds, and intervention with local party leaders. The speaker usually wields significant power in the selection of his party's presidential and, at times, vice-presidential candidates. On numerous occasions he has served as presiding officer and keynote speaker of his party's national conventions. Nevertheless, the office of speaker of the House has not been a stepping-stone to the presidency; as of 1976 James K. Polk was the only former speaker ever elected president.

Time-consuming, but a source of power in the House, are the speaker's many housekeeping responsibilities. Under law and House rules, he has control over the south, or House, end of the Capitol building and grounds, and the House office buildings. The assignment of offices, and of storage and parking space, provides him with additional valuable patronage.

BIBLIOGRAPHY

Congressional Quarterly, *Guide to the Congress of the United States.*
Mary P. Follett, *The Speaker of the House of Representatives.*

— D. B. HARDEMAN

SPECIE PAYMENTS, SUSPENSION AND RESUMPTION OF

Under a system of specie payments it is required by law or custom that fiduciary money, usually in the form of bank notes or government paper money issues, be redeemed at par and upon request of the issuing bank or the Treasury in metallic coin. Since the Founding Fathers remembered with distaste the paper-money inflation of the Revolution and the excesses of some of the states during the Confederation, the decision for a specie standard of value was implicit in the constitutional grant of power to Congress "to coin Money" and "regulate the Value thereof" and in the prohibition that the states refrain from emitting bills of credit or making anything but gold or silver a legal tender.

The maintenance of specie payments in the United States was difficult from the outset. Alexander Hamilton had recommended in 1791, and Congress adopted in 1792, a bimetallic standard of value, under which the dollar was defined in terms of both silver and gold. By adopting the then prevailing market ratio of 15 to 1 as the mint ratio, Hamilton hoped to keep both metals in monetary circulation. Unfortunately, soon after coinage began, the international market price of silver began to fall and gold was hoarded or exported to Europe. It even proved difficult to keep the newly coined silver dollars in circulation, because they were accepted at a higher value in the Spanish possessions. Therefore, the nation for many years was only nominally on a specie standard, particularly in the less-developed regions where a barter system prevailed. In 1834 an attempt was made to bring gold back into monetary circulation by reducing the gold content of the dollar from 24.7 to 23.2 grains while maintaining the silver dollar at 371.25 grains. This meant a new mint ratio of silver to gold of 16 to 1. This ratio undervalued silver, since the international market ratio of the time was about 15.75 to 1. Consequently, silver tended to disappear from circulation, while an increasing number of gold coins were minted and used. Essentially, after 1834 and until 1934, the dominant standard of value in the United States was gold coin.

A basic difficulty in maintaining specie payments during the 19th century was America's usually unfavorable balance of trade. The tendency for specie to be exported in payment for goods was exacerbated in times of war and economic crisis. Also, until 1864, when the National Banking System was established, it was difficult to control the paper bank-note issues of the state-chartered banks. The Supreme Court had decided that the constitutional prohibition against the state issue of bills of credit did not apply to state-chartered banks, which proceeded to issue bank notes far in excess of their ability to maintain specie payments. In wartime, moreover, the federal government was under great pressure to meet its needs for revenue through the issue of irredeemable paper money.

In 1814–15, specie payments were suspended by most of the banks and by the U.S. Treasury in some sections of the country. The unregulated credit expansion of the banks, combined with the wartime issue of Treasury notes, was responsible. Coin payments were resumed in February 1817. Another great credit expansion fostered by the policies of the second Bank of the United States culminated in the panic of 1819 and a severe depression during which most banks in the South and West refused to pay specie.

The years 1830–37 were marked by solid economic development as well as by feverish speculation in land. This eventually led to the panic of 1837 and a nationwide suspension of specie payments. Factors involved in the suspension included a doubling of bank circulation between 1830 and 1837; Andrew Jackson's Specie Circular of July 11, 1836, which halted the land boom; and the distribution of a government surplus, which removed much hard money from the less-developed regions of the country. Perhaps of more importance was the cessation of European investment, followed by large exports of specie. Partial resumption was achieved prematurely in 1838. Continuing outflows of metallic coin brought another suspension in 1839. Finally specie payments resumed in 1842.

The cycle repeated itself in the 1850's. Railroad and industrial expansion was fueled by heavy domestic and foreign investment. State bank-note issues increased and speculation was prevalent. In 1857 capital imports from Europe slackened and the flow of California gold decreased. Money became tight. On Aug. 24 the failure of the Ohio Life Insurance and Trust Company precipitated a panic in New York City that spread to the rest of the country. Specie payments were suspended. They were resumed six months later.

The most serious deviation from the specie standard occurred in the years 1862–79. The departure from gold payments by the banks and the government on Dec. 30, 1861, was forced by the domestic hoarding and export of specie, which had gathered momentum as the domestic military situation deteriorated and as a war with England seemed imminent. Another cause was the failure of Secretary of the Treasury Salmon P. Chase to recommend drastic increases in taxes and his use of demand Treasury notes, a form of paper money.

In February 1862 the government began issuing U.S. notes, better known as "greenbacks." These notes were legal tender and by 1865 had been issued to the amount of $431 million. While the issuance of the greenbacks had not caused the suspension of specie payments, the failure of Secretary of the Treasury Hugh McCulloch's contraction program after the Civil War made resumption very difficult. Contraction of the greenbacks was strongly resisted by powerful economic groups because of its deflationary impact. The obvious solution would have been a devaluation of the gold content of the dollar.

The tactic of letting the country's economy grow up to the currency supply was adopted instead. On Jan. 14, 1875, Congress passed the Resumption Act, which provided that coin payments be resumed on Jan. 1, 1879.

Despite the Free Silver agitation of the late 19th century, the United States adhered to the gold standard. Attempts by western and southern agrarians to restore silver to its ancient monetary function were rebuffed by the ruling conservative administrations. Such measures as the Bland-Allison Act of 1878 and the Sherman Silver Purchase Act of 1890 simply provided a subsidy to the silver mine owners of the West. The defeat of William Jennings Bryan in 1896 effectively squelched the silver movement, and the Gold Standard Act of 1900 legally placed the nation's money on the monometallic basis, which had been *de facto* since 1879.

Difficulties in maintaining gold payments were encountered in 1893 and 1907. The basic problem was the maintenance of an adequate reserve for redemption of fiduciary money in the face of domestic hoarding and a persistent export of gold. The panic of 1907 was caused by unsound bank investments.

A deviation from the gold standard occurred shortly after the United States entered World War I. Large gold exports seemed to threaten the base of the monetary and credit structure. On Sept. 7 and Oct. 12, 1917, President Woodrow Wilson placed an embargo on exports of coin and bullion. These restrictions were removed in June 1919.

The economic cataclysm of the 1930's marked the end of a legitimately defined specie standard of value in the United States. The 1929 stock market crash was followed by more than 5,000 bank failures in three years. The international nature of the crisis was signaled by England's abandonment of the gold standard in September 1931. Gold began to be hoarded, and the specie basis of the system was further threatened by gold exports. In the two weeks preceding the inauguration of President Franklin D. Roosevelt on Mar. 4, 1933, the Federal Reserve banks lost more than $400 million in gold, bringing the reserve down almost to the legal minimum. Several states had already declared banking "holidays" when Roosevelt, on Mar. 6, issued an executive order closing all banks for four days and prohibiting them from exporting, paying out, or allowing the withdrawal of specie. By the end of March most banks had been allowed to reopen, but specie payments were not resumed. By further executive orders issued in April 1933 the break with the gold standard was made more complete. No person or institution was permitted to hold gold or gold certificates. An embargo was placed on all international transactions in gold except under license issued by the secretary of the Treasury. By a joint resolution on June 5, Congress declared void the "gold clause" in government bonds and private obligations. For the first time the United States had deliberately abandoned the gold standard *de jure.*

Within three years of the 1929 stock market crash, more than 5,000 banks had failed.

After fluctuating in value in international money markets for nearly two years, the dollar was finally stabilized under the terms of the Gold Reserve Act and a presidential order in January 1934. The new dollar was defined as 13.71 grains of fine gold, which marked a devaluation to 59.06 percent of its former value. On this basis Secretary Henry Morgenthau announced the Treasury's willingness to buy and sell gold at the new rate of $35 per ounce. It now became possible to obtain gold bullion for making international payments, but domestically the country continued on an irredeemable paper standard, which made gold holdings by citizens illegal.

This "bastardized" gold standard endured for thirty-seven years. Operating under a favorable balance of payments, the United States amassed a gold reserve amounting to more than $24 billion in 1949. After that time, deficits in the international balance reduced the gold stock until it amounted to only about $10 billion by 1971. The continuing deterioration of the balance of payments and the threat to the gold stock impelled President Richard Nixon on Aug. 15, 1971, to order that the Treasury cease all purchases and sales of gold. As of 1975 the dollar was not maintained either at home or abroad at any fixed value in terms of gold; it is uncertain whether gold will regain a place in the monetary system of the nation.

BIBLIOGRAPHY

Bray Hammond, *Banks and Politics in America From the Revolution to the Civil War.*

Broadus Mitchell, *Depression Decade.*

Robert P. Sharkey, *Money, Class, and Party.*

Paul Studenski and Herman E. Krooss, *Financial History of the United States.*

Peter Temin, *The Jacksonian Economy.*

Irwin Unger, *The Greenback Era.*

— ROBERT P. SHARKEY

SPIES

Only once has America ever entered a war with an adequate espionage service in actual operation; that war was the Revolution. Many months before the Battle of Lexington (April 1775), Paul Revere and a group of patriots, mostly his fellow "mechanics," had begun to keep British Gen. Thomas Gage's troops under secret observation and had set up a secret courier service in Boston and the surrounding countryside. It was this group that kept the patriot leaders continually informed and gave early warning of the proposed march to Lexington and Concord. Unfortunately, it failed to detect the leading British secret agent, who was performing similar services for Gage—Benjamin Church, a member of the Massachusetts Provincial Congress and, in 1755, Gen. George Washington's medical director.

Unfortunately, the espionage service of Revere's group covered only parts of New England and was allowed to lapse when New York became the theater of operations in 1776. Although Washington could easily have established a secret service before occupying New York, and especially while actually in occupation there, he failed to do so. When he had been driven to Harlem by the British, and the need for spies had become pressing, Washington sent out Nathan Hale—a brave and devoted man, but completely untrained and without code, cipher, a system of "safe houses," or communication lines. One carrier pigeon could have brought Washington the information he needed (which Hale had collected but could not send). It would probably also have saved Hale's life, for he would not then have been forced to carry the incriminating papers found on his person when he was captured and executed by the British in September 1776. After this needless tragedy, Washington did at last set up an intelligence network in Manhattan, New Jersey, and Long Island, which did admirable service throughout the rest of the war, losing surprisingly few of its very active spies. The Culpers kept up a continuous flow of information from Manhattan and Long Island, using a secret ink invented by Sir James Jay, a physician and the brother of John Jay.

When it became obvious that British Gen. William Howe might move to Philadelphia, Washington did not repeat his New York blunder but saw to it that a well-organized American spy net was waiting for the British when they marched in. After preliminary work by Gen. Thomas Mifflin, Maj. John Clark maintained a flow of copious and accurate information from the city for Washington's benefit. For Howe's benefit, Clark was also able to supply some ingeniously falsified "official" documents from American headquarters written by Washington himself. On one occasion an amused American agent heard a British staff officer commenting on the assured accuracy of certain documents, which, he boasted, had come directly from Washington's headquarters—as indeed they had. Washington's headquarters were themselves penetrated by Ann Bates, a young Tory matron working for Sir Henry Clinton.

As the Civil War approached, the federal government repeated its previous blunder by neglecting to prepare an espionage system in advance. In the meantime, Capt. Thomas Jordan, a Virginian on duty in the War Department, set up a ring of Confederate spies in Washington, D.C., with code, cipher, and courier service, which he handed over to Rose O'Neal Greenhow. Her lax security soon destroyed the ring, but not before it had supplied Confederate Gen. Pierre Beauregard with Union Gen. Irvin McDowell's exact marching orders for Bull Run.

The first Union efforts at espionage in 1861, under Allan Pinkerton, Lafayette Baker, and William Alvin Lloyd, a private spy employed by President Abraham Lincoln, were mainly failures, but as the war continued Union intelligence became very skillful. Elizabeth Van Lew, a Union loyalist living in Richmond, began spying for the Union as soon as the war started and built up a large network in Richmond, which was later taken into the much larger system directed by Gen. George Henry Sharpe for Gen. Ulysses S. Grant's forces. During the siege of Richmond, Van Lew was able to send a Richmond newspaper regularly and a bouquet of flowers frequently through Confederate lines for Grant's breakfast table.

"Sheridan's Scouts," commanded by Union Maj. H. H. Young, kept its men continually in the Confederate ranks and even in Gen. Jubal A. Early's headquarters. Gen. Philip H. Sheridan himself said he owed the victory at Winchester, Va., to information from a Quaker schoolmistress inside the town. James A. Campbell, one of Sheridan's scouts, found the courier who located her. Union Gen. G. M. Dodge operated a network of nearly 100 secret agents throughout the Confederacy during most of the war.

The Spanish-American War was too short to permit the development of an adequate intelligence system. Lt. Andrew Summers Rowan's secret visit to the Cuban revolutionary Gen. Calixto García Íñiguez in 1898 was a brilliant feat, but the fact that the War Department did not know where to find an important ally is dismal evidence of the sad state of its secret service.

A modern military intelligence division had been organized some years before World War I, and the navy by this time had created the Office of Naval Intelligence. These were largely devoted to analyses of "overt" information, coming through attachés and published sources. Before the war was over, however, there was a large and effective spy system in Europe, and the army was making remarkable advances in breaking codes and ciphers.

As World War II approached, the armed forces began to enlarge their intelligence services, mainly by calling in specially qualified reserve officers. A new espionage service was organized, but it was obvious that operations would have to be larger than the United States had ever organized before. Instead of allowing the army and navy to enlarge upon the work they were already doing, President Franklin D. Roosevelt set up the Office of Strategic Services (OSS). Like all improvised services, the OSS made some serious blunders, but it did a great deal of useful espionage and sabotage. Its success in persuading the German commanders in Italy to lay down their arms in defiance of the Nazi government was alone sufficient to justify its existence. Its successor, the Central Intelligence Agency (CIA), has since continued its work on a permanent basis. The control of German sabotage attempts was much improved over that of World War I, and numerous German spies and saboteurs were promptly captured and executed by the military authorities—for example, the spies landed secretly by submarine in Florida and on Long Island (N.Y.). On the Western Front, the detachment of German troops disguised in American uniforms infiltrated into the American lines were also detected, captured, and used either to assist the Americans or executed.

BIBLIOGRAPHY

John Bakeless, *Spies for the Confederacy, and Turncoats, Traitors, and Heroes.*

Lafayette C. Baker, *History of the U.S. Secret Service.*

W. G. Beymer, *On Hazardous Service.*

James D. Bulloch, *Secret Service of the Confederate States in Europe.*

Allen Dulles, *Secret Surrender.*

Lewis Einstein, *Divided Loyalties.*

T. M. Johnson, *Our Secret War.*

— JOHN BAKELESS

SPOILS SYSTEM

"To the victor belong the spoils of the enemy" is the motto of the spoilsmen, proclaimed in 1832 by Sen. William L. Marcy of New York. In essence, the spoils system is an arrangement in which loyalty and service to a political party is the primary criterion for appointment to public office. Under the system, following an election, incumbent officeholders are summarily removed and replaced by those faithful to the victorious party. These dismissals are defended by the premise that rotation in office is an integral part of the democratic process. The theory is that one person is as capable as another in performing the duties of public office. One of the most criticized excesses of the spoils system is the assessment of a portion of the salary of politically appointed officeholders by the party to help it cover its expenses, particularly those of the political campaign. The spoils system provides the opportunity for party leaders to create a functional political machine to do their bidding. It makes a career in public service difficult and thus discourages many of the better-qualified citizens from seeking public office.

The spoils system was hardly a new phenomenon when the U.S. Constitution went into effect in 1789. The marketing of public offices predates the Roman Empire and has throughout history affected the development of political institutions in all parts of the world. But it is under a two-party system, such as has prevailed in the United States, that the spoils system is most prosperous.

Despite President George Washington's statement that government jobs should be filled by "those who seem to have the greatest fitness for public office," during his second administration, after the rise of the party system, he appointed people on the basis of loyalty to the Federalist party. His successor, John Adams, on leaving office in 1801, made his famous "midnight appointments," including John Marshall's appointment as chief justice of the Supreme Court. When Thomas Jefferson became president, he found himself engulfed by Federalists, who dominated the government. Consequently, he replaced many Federalists with fellow Democratic-Republicans while professing to make fitness for office the only qualification for appointment.

The spoils system makes a career in public service difficult and thus discourages many of the better-qualified citizens from seeking public office.

Andrew Jackson, who assumed office in 1829, developed and justified the spoils system. Jackson's contribution to the spoils system was that he was the first to articulate, legitimize, and establish it in the American political context. Ironically, Jackson himself was elected largely by accusing his predecessor, John Quincy Adams, of patronage practices during his administration.

Historians have tended to overemphasize the role of Jackson in introducing the spoils system into national politics. Despite all the publicity he gave to the spoils system, Jackson actually removed very few officeholders. It is estimated that during his tenure of office (1829–36) only one-tenth to one-third of all federal officeholders were replaced. Jackson believed in the theory of rotation in office, and he reasoned that political patronage could give the common man the opportunity to participate in government. He was dismayed that one social class, the "aristocracy," had monopolized public office since the birth of the Republic. The worst that can be said of Jackson is that his administration helped to perpetuate an extant political practice. He is hardly more to blame than Jefferson for its introduction. Each removed about the same proportion of officeholders, and each made appointments on a partisan basis.

The spoils system grew by leaps and bounds after the close of the Jacksonian era. Thereafter, each successive administration engaged in wholesale removals of political opponents in favor of the loyal supporters of the victorious candidate. When Abraham Lincoln became president in 1860, he removed over 75 percent of the incumbent officeholders he inherited from his predecessors, the most sweeping use of the spoils system to date.

The unrestrained use of the spoils system continued until after the Civil War, characterized by the scandals and corruption of the Grant era. It was not until the assassination of President James A. Garfield in 1881 by a demented officeseeker who personally blamed the president for his rejection that efforts to reform the system met with any success. In 1883 Congress enacted the Pendleton Act, which created the Civil Service Commission and a merit system for appointments to lower federal offices. Since then, successive presidents have, with few exceptions, extended the Civil Service classification list, so that by the mid-1970's more than 90 percent of all nonelective federal positions were included. Eligibility for these offices is determined by competitive examinations. Nevertheless, there are still thousands of officeholders who are not on the classification list whose jobs are considered political spoils for the victorious party.

BIBLIOGRAPHY

Lee Benson, *The Concept of Jacksonian Democracy.*

John M. Dobson, *Politics in the Gilded Age: A New Perspective on Reform.*

Ari A. Hoogenboom, *Outlawing the Spoils: A History of the Civil Service Reform Movement, 1865–1883.*

Martin Tolchin and Susan Tolchin, *To the Victor . . . : Political Patronage From the Clubhouse to the White House.*

— DONALD HERZBERG

"SQUARE DEAL"

"Square Deal," a picturesque phrase used with political significance by Theodore Roosevelt while he was president to symbolize his personal attitude toward current topics of the period. He first used the phrase in Kansas while on a tour of the western states as he explained the principles later to be embodied in the platform of the Progressive party. The "square deal" included Roosevelt's ideals of citizenship, the dignity of labor, nobility of parenthood, great wealth, success, and the essence of Christian character. Later it was applied to industry. The phrase was extremely popular in 1906.

BIBLIOGRAPHY

Theodore Roosevelt, *A Square Deal.*

— FRANK MARTIN LEMON

STAMP ACT

By 1763 British and colonial arms had driven French power from Canada. The extension of the British colonial empire raised new and serious problems. The conquest of Canada brought under British rule disaffected French and hostile Indians. In 1763 Indians led by Pontiac, fearing British rule and colonial encroachment on their land, fell on the frontier settlements in a devastating attack. It was clear that garrisons were needed on the long border to guard the colonists against Indian attack and the Indians against predatory whites. It was equally clear that the control of frontier affairs could no longer be left to the separate colonies with their conflicting interests. Frontier problems became more than ever a matter of common concern to be met and solved by the British government as the central authority.

The garrisoning of the border meant a heavy expense, and at once the financial question became a decisive factor. The estimates fixed £320,000 as the cost of supporting an American army of 10,000 men for defense in the mainland colonies and the West Indies. Where should this financial burden fall? The French war had doubled the British national debt, bringing it to the sum of £130,000,000 with a yearly interest charge of £4,500,000. In addition to the support of a colonial military force, increased estimates were necessary to maintain British naval supremacy. So heavy was the strain on the British taxpayer that the ministry decided to call on the colonies to share the expense of the American army. This decision once made, another decisive question arose. Should the colonial share be levied by the several colonial representative bodies or by the British Parliament? In the past, Parliament had not taxed the colonies for revenue purposes. In time of imperial wars, royal requisitions were sent to the colonies to raise and pay troops to cooperate with the British forces. But the realities of the French and Indian War plainly showed that the requisition system was inefficient and unfair. A general lack of vigorous cooperation impaired military operation. The military burden was not equitably distributed, a few colonies responded loyally, some half-heartedly, others far short of their abilities. This conduct led during the war to proposals to tax the colonies by act of Parliament. The Indian uprising under Pontiac further revealed that the colonies could not be depended on for adequate frontier defense, nor would they share the burden equitably.

The Stamp Act of 1765 required the use of stamps on all legal and commercial papers, pamphlets, newspapers, playing cards—and, to Parliament's surprise, it outraged the colonists.

These facts decided the British ministry to resort to the levy of a parliamentary tax on the colonies. The first step was the passage of the Sugar Act of 1764. The old severe duties on colonial trade with the foreign West Indies were reduced in the hope that it would yield some revenue, probably £45,000. This was held to be less than the colonial share, and Sir George Grenville, chancellor of the Exchequer, proposed a stamp tax on the colonies. He deferred the plan a year to give the colonies an opportunity to suggest means more to their liking. They protested strongly against a stamp act and suggested nothing more than taxation by the colonial assemblies as of old. Grenville conferred with the colonial agents in London, among them Benjamin Franklin of Pennsylvania and Jared Ingersoll of Connecticut. The agents pleaded for the old method of raising revenue in the colonies. To this Grenville countered by asking if the colonies could agree on the quotas each should raise and whether it was certain every colony would raise its quotas. In the light of past experience, the agents had no answer to these questions. And so Parliament proceeded to pass the Stamp Act of 1765 with a heavy majority. The use of stamps was required on all legal and commercial papers, pamphlets, newspapers, almanacs, cards, and dice. The law provided for a Stamp Office in London, an inspector for each of the colonial districts, and a stamp distributor for each colony. The estimated yield from stamps ranged from £60,000 to £100,000, collected in both mainland colonies and the West Indies. The combined revenues of the Sugar and Stamp acts, £105,000 to £145,000, would meet less than half the cost of the American garrison forces.

Few in England realized the significance of the stamp tax. Parliament, in harmony with the rule not to receive petitions against revenue bills, did not heed the colonial protests. The ministers and Parliament felt that the law was a fair solution of a pressing problem. Even the colonial agents failed to understand the colonial temper. Franklin nominated a stamp distributor for Pennsylvania and Ingersoll accepted the post for Connecticut. News of the Stamp Act blew up a colonial storm. Parliamentary taxation for revenue was an innovation that threatened the very foundation of colonial self-government and outraged the precious right of Englishmen to be taxed only by their consent. Colonial opposition nullified the Stamp Act in 1766.

BIBLIOGRAPHY

John R. Alden, *General Gage in America.*

Lawrence H. Gipson, *The Coming of the Revolution, 1763–1775.*

Edmund S. Morgan and Helen M. Morgan, *The Stamp Act Crisis.*

John Shy, *Toward Lexington: The Role of the British Army in the Coming of the American Revolution.*

— WINFRED T. ROOT

STAMP ACT CONGRESS

Stamp Act Congress (1765). The Stamp Act and other recent British statutes menaced self-rule in all the colonies and thus furnished a principle of union. The House of Representatives of Massachusetts, appreciating the value of united effort, issued in June a call to all the colonies to send delegates to New York City. Nine colonies responded, and a total of twenty-seven delegates met in the City Hall from Oct. 7 to Oct. 25. They framed resolutions of colonial rights and grievances and petitioned king and Parliament to repeal the objectionable legislation. They held that taxing the colonies without their consent violated one of the most precious rights of Englishmen. Since distance precluded colonial representation in the British Parliament, they could be taxed only by their local assemblies in which they were represented. The congress is significant in that parliamentary threats to colonial self-control fostered the movement that slowly brought to maturity the spirit and agencies of national unity.

BIBLIOGRAPHY

C. H. Van Tyne, *Causes of the War of Independence.*

— WINFRED T. ROOT

STANDARD OIL COMPANY

Standard Oil Company, an Ohio corporation, was incorporated on Jan. 10, 1870, with a capital of $1 million, the original stockholders being John D. Rockefeller (2,667 shares); William Rockefeller (1,333 shares); Henry M. Flagler (1,333 shares); Samuel Andrews (1,333 shares); Stephen V. Harkness (1,334 shares); O. B. Jennings (1,000 shares); and the firm of Rockefeller, Andrews and Flagler (1,000 shares). It took the place of the previous firm of Rockefeller, Andrews and Flagler (formed 1867), whose refineries were the largest in Cleveland and probably the largest in the world at that time. Important extensions were immediately made. Thanks partly to these refineries, partly to superior efficiency, and partly to the threat of the South Improvement Company, Standard Oil early in 1872 swallowed practically all rival refineries in the Cleveland area. The roster of stockholders on Jan. 1, 1872, was slightly increased, and the capital raised to $2.5 million. Coincidentally with the conquest of Cleveland, Standard Oil began reaching out to other cities. In 1872 it bought the oil transporting and refining firm of J. A. Bostwick and Company in New York; the Long Island Oil Company; and a controlling share of the Devoe Manufacturing Company on Long Island. In 1873 it bought pipelines, the largest refinery in the oil regions, and a half interest in a Louisville refinery. The acquisition of the principal refineries of Pittsburgh and Philadelphia was carried out in 1874–76, while in 1877 Standard Oil defeated the Pennsylvania Railroad and the Empire Transportation Company in a major struggle, taking possession of the pipelines and refineries of the latter. Another war with the Tidewater Pipeline resulted in a working agreement that drastically limited the latter's operations. By 1879 Standard Oil, with its subsidiary and associated companies, controlled from 90 percent to 95 percent of the refining capacity of the United States, immense pipeline and storage-tank systems, and powerful marketing organizations at home and abroad. Under John D. Rockefeller's leadership it was the first company in the world to organize the whole of a huge, complex, and extremely rich industry. In 1875 the stock of Standard Oil was increased to a total of $3.5 million, the million dollars of new stock being taken by Charles Pratt and Company; Warden, Frew and Company; and Harkness. In 1879 there were thirty-seven stockholders, of whom Rockefeller, with 8,894 shares, held nearly three times as much as any other man.

While Standard Oil of Ohio remained legally a small company with no manufacturing operations outside its state, practically it was the nucleus of an almost nationwide industrial organization, the richest and most powerful in the country. Its articles of incorporation had not authorized it to hold stock in other companies nor to be a partner in any firm. It had met this difficulty by acquiring stocks not in the name of Standard Oil of Ohio, but in that of some one prominent stockholder as trustee. Flagler, William Rockefeller, Bostwick, and various others served from 1873 to 1879 as trustees. Then in 1879 the situation was given more systematic treatment. All the stocks acquired by Standard Oil and held by various trustees, and all the properties outside Ohio in which Standard Oil had an interest, were transferred to three minor employees (George H. Vilas, Myron R. Keith, George F. Chester) as trustees. They held the stocks and properties for the exclusive use and benefit of Standard Oil's stockholders and distributed dividends in specified proportions. But while this arrangement was satisfactory from a legal point of view, it did not provide sufficient administrative centralization. On Jan. 2, 1882, therefore, a new arrangement, the Standard Oil Trust Agreement, set up the first trust in the sense of a monopoly in American history. All stock and properties, including that of the Standard Oil proper as well as of interests outside Ohio, were transferred to a board of nine trustees, consisting of the principal owners and managers, with John D. Rockefeller as head. For each share of stock of Standard Oil of Ohio, twenty trust certificates of a par value of $100 each were to be issued. The total of the trust certificates was therefore $70 million, considerably less than the actual value of the properties. Standard Oil's huge network of refineries, pipes, tanks, and marketing systems was thus given a secret, but for the time being satisfactory, legal organization, while administration was centralized in nine able men with John D. Rockefeller at their head.

This situation lasted until 1892, Standard Oil constantly growing in wealth and power. Then, as the result of a decree by the Ohio courts, the Standard Oil Trust dissolved, and the separate establishments and plants were reorganized into twenty constituent companies. But by informal arrangement, unity of action was maintained among these twenty corporations until they were gathered into a holding company (Standard Oil of New Jersey) in 1899. Then in 1911 a decree of the U.S. Supreme Court forced a more complete dissolution. Rockefeller remained nominal head of Standard Oil until 1911, but after 1895 he had surrendered more and more of the actual authority to his associates, with John D. Archbold as their chief.

BIBLIOGRAPHY

Ralph W. Hidy and Muriel E. Hidy, *Pioneering in Big Business, 1882–1911.*

Allan Nevins, *Study in Power: John D. Rockefeller.*

Harold F. Williamson, *The American Petroleum Industry.*

— ALLAN NEVINS

"STAR-SPANGLED BANNER"

"Star-Spangled Banner" was inspired by the British attack on Fort McHenry in the War of 1812. On the night of the attack, Francis Scott Key, a young Baltimore lawyer, together with a group of friends had gone to the British admiral to seek the release of a prominent physician who had been captured. Because of plans for the attack, Key and his companions were detained on ship in the harbor and spent the night of Sept. 13–14, 1814, watching the British bombard the fort. Key felt sure that the attack had been successful, but when dawn disclosed the American flag still flying, Key's emotions were so stirred that he wrote the words of the "Star-Spangled Banner" on the back of an envelope. He adapted them to a then popular drinking song, "To Anacreon in Heaven," probably written by British composer John Stafford Smith. The original version was printed as a handbill the next day; a week later it appeared in a Baltimore newspaper. Later Key made a complete draft. The song soon became in fact the national anthem, but it was not until 1931 that Congress officially recognized it as such. Despite its prominence

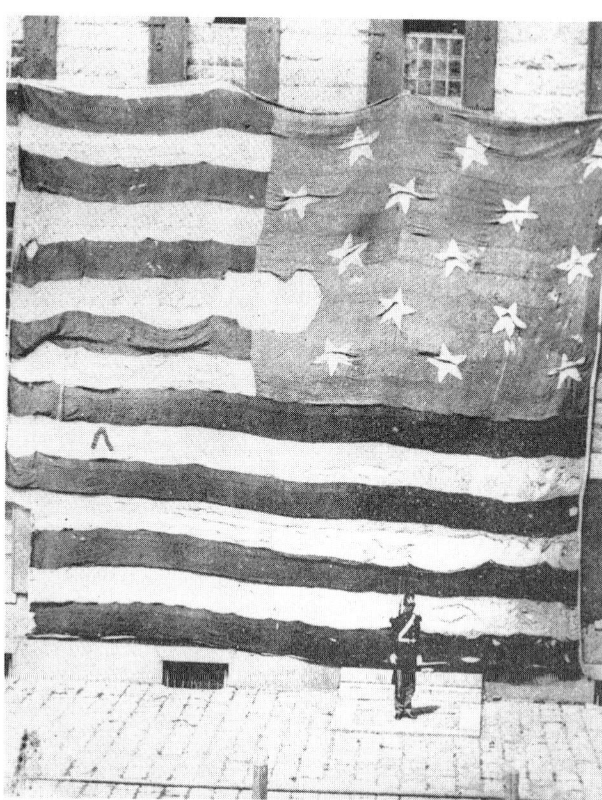

The flag from Fort McHenry, Baltimore, Maryland, that inspired Francis Scott Key to write the national anthem. The flag is now on display at the Smithsonian Institution in Washington, D.C. (Corbis-Bettmann)

there are few people who know more than the first stanza of the "Star-Spangled Banner," and many have found the melody difficult to sing. Numerous attempts have been made to simplify the music, but none has been generally accepted. The actual "star-spangled banner" that flew over Fort McHenry is on display in the Smithsonian Institution.

BIBLIOGRAPHY

John Tasker Howard, *Our American Music.*

— E. H. O'NEILL

STARVING TIME

Starving Time, the term used to refer to the food shortage at Jamestown in the winter of 1609–10. There was a similar shortage of food at Plymouth in the spring of 1622. The Jamestown starving time was relieved by the arrival of a ship from England, that at Plymouth by the arrival of a fishing vessel via Virginia.

BIBLIOGRAPHY

L. G. Tyler, *England in America.*
William Bradford, *History of Plymouth Plantation.*

— MATTHEW PAGE ANDREWS

STATE CONSTITUTIONS

In the American federal union each of the United States has operated at all times under a written constitution of its own. For eleven of the original states this was a matter of necessity, not of choice. The royal provinces and proprietary colonies had been governed under charters that were not at all suited to independence. Only the two largely self-governing colonies were willing to retain their charters long after the Revolution—Connecticut until 1818 and Rhode Island until 1842. By 1780 each of the other states had adopted a new constitution, and four acted even before independence was formally declared. Several of the earliest constitutions were hastily drawn and soon replaced, but others served for years with only minor changes. Indeed, the Massachusetts constitution of 1780, although extensively revised, still remains in force, the oldest in America. It was also the first to be framed by a convention elected especially for that purpose and referred to the voters for their approval. In all other states the first revolutionary constitutions were the work of provincial congresses or assemblies. Among their members were many men who were soon to distinguish themselves in national affairs: John Rutledge in South Carolina, James Iredell in North Carolina, George Mason, Patrick Henry, and James Madison in Virginia, Benjamin Franklin in Pennsylvania, John Jay and Gouverneur Morris in New York, and John Adams in Massachusetts.

The revolutionary constitutions varied greatly in form and substance. Pennsylvania's was the most radical. It created a plural executive, a unicameral legislature, and a council of censors to investigate the government every seven years. Maryland's was probably the most conservative, if only for the high property qualifications it set for officeholders—£500 for representatives, £1,000 for senators, and £5,000 for governor. In all but a few states the legislative power was supreme. Only in New York and Massachusetts, among the states with new constitutions, was the governor elected by the people and given broad powers. Even in Connecticut and Rhode Island, where the governor had long been popularly elected under the colonial charters, the executive branch was dominated by the legislature. The judiciary was no less subordinate. In all but four states judges were elected by the legislature and served more or less at its pleasure. In New York, on the other hand, judges were not only appointed, four of them served on a council of revision with the governor to review all bills about to be enacted into law.

By 1787, when the new federal constitution was being drawn, its framers were able to draw on the states' own rich and varied constitutional experience. In some matters they rejected state constitutional precedents altogether. They were determined, above all, to strike a more even balance between the legislative, executive, and judicial departments than the states had been able to achieve. In separating the three departments and making them structurally independent of each other, the framers were no doubt influenced by the writings of Polybius, John Locke, and Charles de Secondat, Baron de Montesquieu, but the doctrinal precedents closest at hand were the constitutional prescriptions, although not the practice, in Virginia, Maryland, Georgia, Massachusetts, and, after 1784, New Hampshire. In most states both the executive and judicial departments were too weak to furnish a suitable model, but the framers did draw on the experience in three states. The president was to be elected only indirectly by the voters in much the same way state senators were elected in Maryland, although in his case the electors were for a time twice removed from popular vote. He was also given the same broad powers enjoyed by the governor of New York to "take care" that the laws are faithfully carried out, to pardon and reprieve offenses against the law, to inform the legislature at every session about the state of public affairs and recommend bills for it to enact, and to call it into special session. The president was also given the same veto over legislation granted the governor under the Massachusetts constitution. Similarly, federal judges were made appointive in the same way as state judges in Maryland, Massachusetts, and New Hampshire, by the chief executive with the consent of an advisory body to serve during good behavior. Finally, the Bill of Rights, which was added to the federal constitution in 1791, merely followed the example first set by Virginia in 1776.

The fifty state constitutions that are in effect vary greatly in age, length, and form. Only nineteen states, as of 1973, still operated under the constitution with which they entered the Union, and even these were extensively revised. Nine states, all but one in the South, have had at least five constitutions, and one, Louisiana, no less than ten. Three states have constitutions that date back to the 18th century—Massachusetts (1780), New Hampshire (1784), and Vermont (1793). Nine other state constitutions were adopted before 1860. Seventeen others, on the other hand, were adopted in the 20th century, and of these, twelve since World War II. Nearly half, twenty-one, were adopted between 1860 and 1899, when new constitutions had to be framed both for the new western territories and the states of the defeated Confederacy. The state constitutions presently in force vary even more in length. Those which are briefest tend to be either the earliest or the latest. The southern constitutions, on the other hand, are by far the longest, because they are loaded down with detailed provisions more appropriate to a statutory code. Their average length is twice that of the western states and more than three times that of the New England and midwestern states. Louisiana's, indeed, is in a class by itself: its more than a quarter of a million words make it ten times longer than the average of the other forty-nine states and thirty-five times longer than the federal constitution.

Only in their basic organization do all fifty constitutions follow a common pattern. In every state except Vermont a preamble declares the constitution to have been ordained by the people or, in Tennessee, by their delegates and representatives. Unlike the federal constitution, all but a few abound with references to the Deity, and a few still allude to an original social compact and to natural rights. In every state the legislative, executive, and judicial powers are vested in separate and distinct departments. In most states the legislative power is defined quite expansively. Only eleven states, in fact, vest their state legislature expressly with the police power. Hawaii and Oklahoma extend the legislative power to "all rightful subjects of legislation," and New Mexico and Oregon to "all powers necessary to the legislature of a free state." Three others provide that the legislature's authority is not restricted either because certain powers have been enumerated, as in Alaska and Oklahoma, or because others previously conferred have been omitted, as in Virginia. Yet in every state the legislature is effectively barred from exercising such sweeping power either by detailed restriction on its use or by an equally expansive guarantee of personal rights. In no less than thirty-five states political power is declared to be inherent in, or derived from, the people, and in thirty states unenumerated rights are reserved to the people. The same doctrine of popular sovereignty is implied in every other state constitution. In construing their state's constitution, moreover, state courts have usually taken a restrictive view of state legislative power and a broad view of personal, especially property, rights, which the legislature is bound to accept. It is ironic, although perhaps no longer relevant, that the power on which the practice rests—judicial review—is not explicitly provided in any state constitution.

In most states the constitution has become so detailed and rigid as to require frequent change. In every state, amendments or revisions may be proposed either by the legislature itself or by an elective convention called especially for that purpose. Increasingly, legislatures and conventions have come to rely on appointive commissions to study the constitution and to recommend proposals for its revision. Fourteen states, all but five west of the Mississippi, also permit the voters to initiate constitutional amendments. Specific amendments are usually proposed by the legislature or the voters; more thoroughgoing revision, by constitutional conventions or commissions. In Delaware, proposals to amend or revise the constitution become effective as soon as the legislature or convention has taken final action. In every other state, proposed changes must be referred to the voters for their approval. In the two centuries since 1776, at least 226 constitutional conventions have been held, 136 constitutions framed and adopted, and well over 5,000 amendments approved, most of them by popular vote. Indeed, Americans can be said to have had more experience in making constitutions than any other people in history.

BIBLIOGRAPHY

Cynthia E. Brown, *State Constitutions Conventions From Independence to the Completion of the Present Union, 1776–1959: A Bibliography.*

Robert B. Dishman, *State Constitutions: The Shape of the Document*; Legislative Drafting Research Fund, *Constitutions of the United States—National and State*, and *Index Digest of State Constitutions.*

Allan Nevins, *The American States During and After the Revolution, 1775–1789.*

Albert L. Strum, *Thirty Years of State Constitution-Making, 1938–68.*

— ROBERT B. DISHMAN

STATE, DEPARTMENT OF

The Constitution empowers the president to appoint diplomats and consuls to represent the United States abroad. Since 1789 their work has been directed by the Department of State. For much of the nineteenth century, appointments to the diplomatic and consular services were used to reward political contributors and the party faithful. The 1890s witnessed the first lasting steps to end this arrangement and to base appointments on demonstrated merit. By the time the United States entered World War I not only had the consular service and that portion of the diplomatic corps below the rank of ambassador or minister been taken out of politics, but the foundations and structural outline for a career foreign service had been put into place.

Appointments now were made to the services only after examination and incumbents were not turned out of office when the other political party captured the White House. The State Department's operations and its links with the field foreign service were systematized, primarily through development of the geographic bureaus, which have been the basis for much of the department's organization ever since. In 1924 the Rogers Act, drafted in the State Department, merged the diplomatic and consular services into the Foreign Service of the United States. Many of the reforms of prior years, such as appointment only after competitive examination, were given statutory authority.

In the 1990s, there were approximately 4,700 Foreign Service officers (FSOs) working at some 250 diplomatic and consular offices abroad as well as at the State Department in Washington, D.C., in four major areas: political reporting and analysis; economic reporting and analysis; consular affairs (primarily handling visa applications and assistance to U.S. citizens); and administration. Even before the Rogers Act, the proportion of chiefs of mission coming from the career service had reached 50 percent. In the decades that followed, and particularly with the great increase in the number of nations after World War II, roughly a 70:30 ratio came to prevail. From the 1960s to the mid-1990s about 70 percent of such appointments went to career FSOs and 30 percent to political appointees. That ratio was slightly more favorable for FSOs under President Jimmy Carter (75:25) and slightly less favorable under Ronald Reagan (67:33). Some commentators have observed that the United States is the only major country that chooses large numbers of its envoys from outside its career service and that both Republican and Democratic presidents have dealt in "bought commissions" for ambassadorial appointments. Others note that in some instances a president may need to appoint to a foreign capital a person in whom he has confidence or with whose views he is in agreement. This sentiment is by no means new, as illustrated by Woodrow Wilson's letter, four months into his presidency, to a State Department official: "Every day, I feel more and more keenly the necessity of being represented at foreign courts by men who easily catch and instinctively themselves occupy our point of view with regard to public matters."

The four major areas of the State Department are political reporting and analysis; economic reporting and analysis; consular affairs (including visas); and administration.

Since the Rogers Act, changes in the organization of the Foreign Service have demonstrated an almost continuous effort to adapt the foreign affairs machinery to changing circumstances. The Foreign Service Act of 1980, for example, created a Senior Foreign Service for older officers, fostering the advancement of younger FSOs. A principal problem for the State Department has been that it has not been alone in representing the nation abroad, much less in helping the president formulate and conduct foreign policy. The State and Commerce departments have clashed over certain issues involving foreign trade promotion since the Commerce Department was created in 1903, and since World War II foreign affairs agencies have proliferated. One observer counted sixty-one in 1971 and a study in 1993 found eighty-seven. At the typical U.S. embassy abroad fewer than 20 percent of the personnel are State Department people. At home, the department has had to contend in policy planning matters not only with a much enlarged Defense Department but with agencies traditionally domestic in their orientation, such as the Departments of the Treasury and Agriculture, as foreign and domestic questions have become more intertwined.

The State Department's chief competitor in Washington, D.C., has been the National Security Council (NSC), created in 1947 by the National Security Act. Particularly since the John F. Kennedy administration (1961–1963), the NSC has built a large staff to contend with State for the ear of the president and his staff. Several presidents have relied more on the national security adviser than the secretary of state, and they have appointed strong and articulate academics to the former post, such as Kennedy's McGeorge Bundy, Richard Nixon's Henry Kissinger, and Jimmy Carter's Zbigniew Brzezinski. An example of a president bypassing the secretary of state occurred in the summer of 1980, when Secretary of State Edmund Muskie and other State Department officials learned only from newspaper accounts that President Carter had two weeks earlier issued a directive revising the U.S. nuclear war strategy; by contrast, the Defense Department and the NSC had taken part in the decision.

During the Ronald Reagan (1981–1989) and George Bush (1989–1993) administrations, the secretary of state's role vis-à-vis the national security adviser was strengthened, primarily because of the forcefulness of Secretaries of State Alexander Haig, George P. Shultz, and James Baker. Yet even Secretary Shultz felt obliged in 1986 to cable all U.S. ambassadors with a warning not to bypass him by communicating directly with the national security adviser. It is clear that the traditional concept of a State Department serving the president as the only agency for foreign policy development, as well as having nearly total responsibility for official contacts and relations with other nations, has not been a viable one since at least the late 1940s. Critics frequently have called upon the State Department to coordinate the activities of the various foreign affairs agencies, a task more easily said than done.

Another problem for the State Department has been its lack of a domestic constituency. During the first years of the twentieth century, department officials were able to mobilize support from the business community for their work on behalf of promoting foreign trade and reforming the consular and diplomatic services. Most of this support was soon diverted to the Commerce Department's commercial attachés. Other agencies, such as the Departments of Defense and Agriculture, have developed powerful domestic pressure groups lacking in the Department of State.

Social changes in the United States and the world also have left their marks on the State Department and Foreign Service. Among these are changes in the roles of women. Increasingly, wives of FSOs have demonstrated a strong desire for careers of their own, yet traditionally they have acted as unpaid hostesses and until 1972 were even included as an element in their husbands' annual performance evaluations. In 1978 the department established the Family Liaison Office, which received legislative sanction in the Foreign Service Act of 1980, to help with careers for spouses. The 1980 act also provided for retirement and survivor benefits for divorced spouses. Women Foreign Service officers likewise gained ground. As late as 1971 a woman FSO was expected to resign if she married and women were routinely assigned to consular rather than to diplomatic work. Also in 1971 the first sex discrimination suit was filed against the department. *Palmer* v. *Shultz* (1985) held that the department did not discriminate but was reversed the next year, resulting in cancellation of the 1989 foreign service examination while the department worked to take corrective action as prescribed by the court.

Concern that the Foreign Service contained too small a proportion of minorities and women led to concerted efforts to recruit and retain persons from both groups. Hence, the department has pursued affirmative action, as it did in the early twentieth century for white male Democrats from the South in order to create the fact and the image of greater political diversity in the foreign service. By the late 1980s and early 1990s the department's efforts were achieving results. From 1987 to 1993 women and minorities eligible for promotion were advanced at rates slightly higher than other eligible FSOs. The push for affirmative action did not slacken with the advent of the Bill Clinton administration and its advocacy of a government that "looks like America." Meanwhile, with much less attention, the composition of the service also has been changing in terms of the college background of officers, with a pronounced decline in the proportion possessing Ivy League degrees and a significant rise in the fraction of alumni from state universities.

Another development greatly affecting the Foreign Service has been the growing incidence of terrorism directed at U.S. embassies abroad, of which the Iranian hostage situation of 1979–1981 was only the most prominent and dramatic. By 1981 the State Department was offering a two-day seminar on how to avoid and survive terrorist attacks, and by early 1983 some 15 percent of the department's expenditures were used to protect U.S. personnel and facilities. In 1986 the Bureau of Diplomatic Security was established at State, and in that same year Congress voted to provide U.S. government employees taken hostage by terrorists cash payments of not less than half the worldwide average per diem. The reference by Secretary of State John Foster Dulles (1953–1959) to Foreign Service officers as "soldiers in the front line trenches of our foreign policy" was taking on additional meaning in the last quarter of the twentieth century.

[See also Commerce, Department of; Defense, Department of; Terrorism.]

BIBLIOGRAPHY

Barry M. Rubin, *Secrets of State: The State Department and the Struggle Over U.S. Foreign Policy* (New York, 1985).

Andrew L. Steigman, *The Foreign Service of the United States: First Line of Defense* (Boulder, Colo., 1985).

Richard Hume Werking, "Department of State," in Donald R. Whitnah, ed., *Government Agencies* (Westport, Conn., 1983).

— RICHARD HUME WERKING

STATES' RIGHTS

Advocates of the principle of states' rights believe that considerable governmental authority should be located in the separate and collective states of the United States. The concept of states' rights arose as an extension of colonial rights, which Americans had claimed when they were still under the British crown. This idea underlay the American Revolution, and it was present during the Confederation period. When the Constitutional Convention met in 1787, states' rights proponents pressed to include their ideas in the Constitution, but there was also the desire for a strong national government, with minimal power residing with the states. Adopted at that convention was a federal system, a reasonably satisfactory compromise reconciling state and national power. In 1791 the Tenth Amendment was added to the Constitution, which spelled out the states' rights doctrine: "The powers not delegated to the United States by the Constitution, nor prohibited by it to the States, are reserved to the States respectively, or to the people." A large part of American history from that time until 1865 was the story of the push and pull of the national and state governments in their attempts to define their relationships to each other and to protect their respective powers. In 1798 the promulgation of the Kentucky and Virginia Resolutions, which protested acts passed by the national Congress, were manifestations of states' rights. The Hartford Convention of 1814, called by New Englanders who disagreed with President James Madison's wartime policies, was another example of states' rightism.

The idea of states' rights arose as an extension of colonial rights, underlay the American Revolution, and was present during the Confederation period.

Although various individual states and groups of states from time to time appealed to the principle of states' rights for their political and economic protection, the South is the section of the country most often associated with the doctrine. In the first half of the 19th century, when disputes arose over the tariff, the national bank, public land policies, internal improvement, and the like, southern leaders used arguments based on states' rights in their attempts to protect their economic interests. They usually lost these battles to maintain their economic power, and their appeals to a constitutional principle went unheeded. Overriding all the other disputes was the question of the extension of slavery into the American territories. Southern states fell back on the states' rights principle once again when northerners argued that slavery should not expand. Various events of the 1850's, including the Compromise of 1850, the Kansas-Nebraska controversy, the formation of the Republican party, civil strife in Kansas, the Dred Scott decision, and John Brown's raid, and the election of Abraham Lincoln as president in 1860 were closely related to the slavery and states' rights controversies and led directly to the Civil War. That war established the supremacy of the national government and relegated the states to lesser political and economic positions. Disputes arose from time to time about the relationship of the national and state governments, and invariably the national government emerged the victor. In the first half of the 20th century, southern politicians continued to speak about states' rights, but this was often nothing more than oratory designed to please southern voters.

After midcentury, when the power, size, and authority of the national government became greater and more complex, many Americans began to have misgivings about the shortcomings of a massive government essentially run by bureaucrats. Those politicians who talked about states' rights often found they had more receptive audiences than previously. Controversies over the administration of welfare programs and other social services gave states' rights advocates issues that they could exploit. More important, the cry for states' rights was often a thinly disguised but firm stand against racial integration in regard to education, public accommodations, politics and voting, housing, and jobs, areas that states' righters insisted were within the sphere of the states. But the revival of states' rights arguments in the third quarter of the 20th century had little basic impact on the general locus of political power. The national government continued to be more powerful, the states remaining in secondary roles. The attempts of the Founding Fathers to divide sovereignty between national and state governments laid the basis for many controversies throughout the nation's history, but on the whole the structure of government that they established functioned well. Save for the Civil War, disputes had been compromised peacefully. Even as the national government gained more power within the limits of the Constitution after the mid-20th century, there appeared to be no prospect of a serious revolt over the diminishing rights of the states.

BIBLIOGRAPHY

Avery O. Craven, *Civil War in the Making, 1815–1860.*

William W. Freehling, *Prelude to Civil War: The Nullification Controversy in South Carolina, 1816–1836.*

Arthur Meier Schlesinger, "The State Rights Fetish," *New Viewpoints in American History.*

Charles S. Sydnor, *The Development of Southern Sectionalism, 1819–1848.*

— MONROE BILLINGTON

STATUE OF LIBERTY

Statue of Liberty, properly *Liberty Enlightening the World*, is located on Liberty (formerly Bedloe's) Island in New York Harbor. It was conceived by the French sculptor Frédéric August Bartholdi and cost approximately 1 million francs, a sum raised by conscription. A gift to the United States from the people of France, the colossal copper figure was shipped in sections in 1885 and unveiled on Oct. 28, 1886. President Grover Cleveland accepted it in a belated commemoration of a century of American independence. From the pedestal to the top of the upraised torch, the height is 152 feet; the overall height is 302 feet. The Statue of Liberty has served as the symbol of welcome to millions of immigrants.

— IRVING DILLIARD

STEAMBOATS

The idea of steam-powered boats intrigued men before the days of James Rumsey, John Fitch, and Robert Fulton. Practical steamboat experiments began with the double-acting engine in 1782; both Rumsey and Fitch operated their boats two years before George Washington's inauguration (1789). Successful commercial navigation is usually dated from the voyage of Fulton's *Clermont* in 1807. Thereafter, steamships were launched for deep-sea passage and for the swift streams of the tidewater and Mississippi Valley, whose tortuous curves and shallow sandbar-studded waters required high-powered, light draft boats. The first steamboat on western waters, the *New Orleans*, was built from Fulton-Livingston patents in 1811. It was a 300-ton, two-masted side-wheeler with boiler, engine, and vertical stationary cylinder placed in its open hold. The bow was reserved for freight—the cabins were aft of the machinery. In 1813 Daniel French launched the 25-ton *Comet*, a stern-wheeler featuring vibrating cylinders. The *New Orleans* and *Comet* served as models until 1816, when Henry M. Shreve built his second steamboat, the 403-ton *Washington*, although his earlier craft, the *Enterprise*, had been the first steamboat to ascend the Mississippi and Ohio rivers from New Orleans to Louisville, Ky. Shreve contributed three ideas to the *Washington*: he placed the machinery and cabin on the main deck; used horizontal cylinders with vibrations to the pitmans; and employed a double high-pressure engine. He also introduced the second deck, which became standard on all western steamboats thereafter. Subsequent marine architecture simply improved on these features.

A generation passed before the floating palaces of the Mark Twain era evolved. Steamboats increased in tonnage; they boasted ornate cabins and private staterooms, bars and barber shops, bands and orchestras, and steam whistles and calliopes. Steam was used to work the capstan, handle the spars, or swing the stage. An auxiliary engine, or doctor, pumped water into the boiler. Coal gradually replaced wood, and the electric searchlight was substituted for the wood torch. Spacious decks with promenades were built high above the main deck—the texas (for the crew) and the pilot house being placed high above all. In 1843 the second *J. M. White* was launched at Pittsburgh. It was 250 feet long, with a 31-foot beam and an 8.5-foot hold, and had seven boilers, 30-inch cylinders, and a 10-foot stroke. In 1878 the third *J. M. White* was built at Louisville at a cost of more than $200,000. It was 325 feet long, with a 50-foot beam and an 11. 5-foot hold. It had ten boilers 34 feet long, and its cylinders were 43 inches in diameter with an 11-foot stroke. The main cabin was 260 feet long. It could carry 8,500 bales of cotton. The record load of 9,226 bales of cotton was carried by the *Henry Frank* in 1881. It would have taken a season of hard work for the *New Orleans* to carry this amount.

BIBLIOGRAPHY

E. W. Gould, *Fifty Years on the Mississippi.*

W. J. Petersen, *Steamboating on the Upper Mississippi.*

— WILLIAM J. PETERSEN

STEAM POWER AND ENGINES

The first useful steam engine was developed in England by Thomas Newcomen and was put into operation by 1712. By 1730 the engine was not uncommon in western Europe, and in 1755 the first steam engine began operation in the American colonies, at a copper mine in Belleville, N.J. This engine, built by the British firm of Joseph Hornblower, was followed by another in Philadelphia, built in 1773 by Christopher Colles. Three years later a third engine was at work, raising water for New York City waterworks. The Newcomen engines were large, expensive, and cumbersome. Except for draining valuable mines or providing water for large cities, they were not economically attractive in America, where waterpower suitable for manufactures was reasonably plentiful along the eastern seaboard.

Providing power for transportation was a greater problem. The Newcomen engine was too bulky for such purposes, but after the improvements made by James Watt beginning in 1764, it occurred to many that the steam engine might be applied to propelling boats. Beginning in 1785 more than a dozen American inventors tried to build steamboats, including Jehosaphat Starr, Apollos Kinsley, Isaac Briggs, William Longstreet, Elijah Ormsbee, John Stevens, Daniel French, Samuel Morey, James Rumsey, and Nathan Read. They were all handicapped by having to build their own engines (the export of which was forbidden by England) with inadequate machine-shop facilities and limited knowledge of steam technology. The most successful inventor was John Fitch, who established regular steamboat service between Philadelphia and New Jersey in 1790.

The complexity of applying steam power to navigation led some of these inventors to turn to the simpler problems of supplying stationary power. The Soho works in New Jersey, which had helped Stevens on his steamboat, began in 1799 to build two large engines for a new waterworks in Philadelphia. The head of the shops, Nicholas J. Roosevelt, was later a partner of Robert Fulton in operating the first commercially successful steamboat (1807). Robert Livingston, a partner of Fulton and brother-in-law of Stevens, was also associated with Benjamin Henry Latrobe, a British physician-architect with a knowledge of steam engines, and a number of workmen who had built and operated engines in England. Some of the most prominent emigrant British engineers were James Smallman, John Nancarrow, and Charles Stoudinger; their knowledge, along with that of other British engineers, was the single most important source of new technological information for American inventors and engine builders.

In 1802 Oliver Evans of Philadelphia became the first American to make steam engines for the general market. He was followed by Smallman in 1804, and with the addition of Daniel Large and others, that city soon became the center of engine building. New York City, where Robert McQueen and James Allaire had been patronized by Fulton, became another center of engine manufacture. During the War of 1812 the building and use of engines spread to the western states. The first engine built in Pittsburgh (for a steamboat) was completed in 1811. The following year Evans opened a Pittsburgh branch of his Philadelphia Mars Iron Works. With the addition of such pioneer builders as Thomas Copeland, James Arthurs, Mahlon Rogers, and Mark Stackhouse, Pittsburgh too became a center of steam engineering. The first engine shop in Kentucky was opened in Louisville in 1816 by Thomas Bakewell and David Prentice. Work in Cincinnati, Ohio, began soon afterward, and by 1826 that city had five steam-engine factories. This western activity was brought about in part by the widespread use of steamboats on the western waters, the demand for engines on southern sugar plantations, the easy accessibility of iron and coal around Pittsburgh, and, initially, the dislocations of eastern trade caused by the War of 1812.

By 1838 steam power was widely accepted all over the United States. In that year 3,010 steam engines were counted in a federal census. Of these, 350 were used on locomotives, 800 on steamboats, and 1,860 were stationary. This last category included those that ran mills of all descriptions, were at work on farms and plantations, and raised water for cities. Pennsylvania accounted for the largest number (383) of stationary engines, Louisiana was second with 274, and Massachusetts had 165. Except for Louisiana, where the engines were typically used on large sugar plantations to grind cane, most of these were located in cities. Of the 383 engines in Pennsylvania, 133 were at work in Pittsburgh and 174 in Philadelphia; of the 165 engines in Massachusetts, 114 were in or around Boston. The steam engine had a profound effect on the nature of cities. Formerly centers only of trade, culture, and government, they now became centers of manufacturing and, consequently, the home of a large class of factory operatives. As long as factories and mills had depended on waterpower, such a development in cities had been impossible.

By the middle of the 19th century, virtually every American city contained shops producing steam engines and had a large number of the machines at work. Imported engines were not important in the trade, although American engines were regularly exported. Northern-made engines in the South were used not only on plantations but also in other extractive processes carried out in rice mills, cottonseed oil mills, cotton gins and presses, and the saline wells of western Virginia. Most important, these engines found increasing use in cotton textile mills scattered throughout the region. Southern cities, notably Charleston, S.C., and Richmond, Va., became manufacturing centers in their own right, basing their activity to a considerable extent on steam.

As the first machine necessarily made of iron, the steam engine had a critical influence on the development of the iron industry. Previously, most iron had been used in a wrought form. Most engine parts were cast, however, and the improvements in casting technique forced by engine development were available for use in making other machines as well. In addition, rolling mills began to multiply only when boiler plate came into demand from engine builders. These boiler-plate makers in turn became the first to construct iron boats.

As the first machine necessarily made of iron, the steam engine had a critical influence on the development of the iron industry.

The harnessing of steam engines to railroad locomotion, of course, increased the demand for rails as well as engines. In a circle of improvement, steam engines were used to drive rolling mills, provide blast for furnaces, and run drilling machines, lathes, and other iron-working machines, all of which made it easier to produce and work iron and led to improved steam engines. The demand for coal, both for iron furnaces and steam boilers, was also greatly stimulated.

There were essentially three types of steam engines used in the country before the introduction of the turbine late in the 19th century. The first engines were of the Newcomen type. After the introduction of Watt's improvements in this engine, no more of the old style were built. Watt's atmospheric engine was widely popular for both stationary use and for the eastern steamboats, such as Fulton's *Clermont.* It was largely superseded by the high-pressure engine of Evans. The piston of the Newcomen-type engine was actuated by introducing steam under it, condensing the steam with cold water, then allowing the weight of the atmosphere (about 15 pounds per square inch) to push the piston down. Watt's key improvement was to provide a separate condenser, which would conserve heat and make the piston "double-acting" by introducing steam alternately on both sides of the piston. Evans' further improvement consisted in using the force of the steam itself (at 100–200 pounds per square inch) to drive the piston directly, allowing it to escape into the atmosphere uncondensed. The power of the Watt engine could usually be increased only by enlarging the cylinder. With Evans' Columbian engine, only the steam pressure need be increased. Because it provided more power in a smaller space, his engine quickly became standard on western steamboats and eventually on locomotives.

Subsequent efforts at improvement went in two directions: first, toward further refinements of the reciprocating engine, especially by such improved valve actions as that of George Corliss of Rhode Island, and second, toward a rotary engine. Hundreds of patents were taken out for such devices before the successes of such late 19th-century inventors as Charles Gordon Curtis in developing the steam turbine. In the 20th century steam power has remained of primary importance only in the generation of electricity in power plants, although its potential use in automobiles periodically receives attention.

BIBLIOGRAPHY

G. Bathe, *Oliver Evans.*

H. W. Dickinson, *Robert Fulton, Engineer and Artist.*

T. Hamlin, *Benjamin Henry Latrobe.*

C. Pursell, *Early Stationary Steam Engines in America.*

— CARROLL PURSELL

STEEL STRIKES

Strikes in the basic steel industry fall into three periods: historic unsuccessful recognition struggles culminating in the 1937 "Little Steel" strike; a period of frequent strikes that followed National War Labor Board control and ended with the long 1959 strike; and the period between 1960 and 1975, which was free from strikes.

Before the 1935 National Labor Relations Act, with its provision for certification elections, the union-recognition issue was resolved not by ballot but by brute force. The Homestead strike of 1892 was followed by other landmark violent strikes, in 1901, 1909, and 1919. In 1919 the U.S. Steel Corporation defeated a massive organizing attempt by twenty-four unions led by the American Federation of Labor (AFL). After driving out the Amalgamated Iron and Steel Workers in 1909, U.S. Steel maintained an open-shop policy until the recognition of the Steel Workers' Organizing Committee of the Congress of Industrial Organizations (CIO) in the John L. Lewis—Myron C. Taylor discussions of 1937. The rest of the steel companies, known collectively as "Little Steel," delayed recognition of the union in 1937 by defeating the steelworkers in the last of the violent and bitter struggles. Union demonstrators at the Republic Steel Corporation plant in Chicago were fired on by the police, and ten were killed; two others were killed by special deputies at Republic's plant in Massillon, Ohio.

Free collective bargaining between the Steelworkers Union and the industry essentially began in 1946. Between 1946 and 1959 the union had the contractual right to strike ten times and struck five. Most of these strikes lasted about one month (1946, 1949, 1956). The 1952 strike was of two months' duration and the 1959 strike went on for more than three months. These were all peaceful and orderly strikes in which the companies made no attempt to operate the mills.

The struggle for recognition was over. Collective bargaining in steel was industrywide, with negotiation ultimately between the union and a coordinating committee of large companies. When the union struck it shut down the industry. This typically brought some form of government intervention in what were regarded as national emergency situations. The 1952 strike created a constitutional crisis in which the Supreme Court ruled that President Harry S. Truman's seizure of the mills was unconstitutional. The 116-day 1959 strike was ended by the Supreme Court, which upheld a national emergency injunction.

The 1959 struggle marked a turning point. Crisis bargaining gave way to joint study under the auspices of the Human Relations Committee. In this new relationship subcommittees worked constructively on many issues. Political upheaval in the union in 1965 ended formal joint study. Complex and difficult negotiations on three levels—the plant, the corporation, and the industry—took place in 1965, 1968, and 1971. In an unprecedented breakthrough, the parties agreed in 1973 to a no-strike pledge for their 1974 negotiations with submission of unresolved issues to arbitration.

BIBLIOGRAPHY

J. H. Fitch, *The Steel Workers.*

Walter Galenson, *The CIO Challenge to the AFL: A History of the American Labor Movement, 1935–1941.*

John A. Garraty, "U.S. Steel Versus Labor: The Early Years," *Labor History,* vol. 1 (1960).

E. Robert Livernash et al., *Collective Bargaining in the Basic Steel Industry.*

— E. ROBERT LIVERNASH

STRATEGIC ARMS LIMITATION TALKS (SALT)

From November 1969 until June 1979, the United States and the Soviet Union negotiated limitations on their strategic nuclear arms. Two sets of agreements were reached—the SALT I accords signed at the first summit meeting of President Richard M. Nixon with Soviet leader Leonid I. Brezhnev in Moscow in May 1972, and the SALT II Treaty signed at the only summit meeting between President Jimmy Carter and Brezhnev, in Vienna in June 1979. These were the first substantial arms control agreements between the two countries. Originally proposed by the United States in December 1966, the Soviet Union equivocated until May 1968, when the Soviets had numerical strategic parity in sight. A planned opening of SALT at a summit meeting in September 1968 was derailed by the Soviet-led Warsaw Pact occupation of Czechoslovakia in August. With the defeat of the Democrats in the 1968 presidential election, SALT had to await a new administration and its review of defense and foreign policies. The delay of the opening of SALT from fall 1968 to late fall 1969 had one significant adverse effect; during that year the United States successfully tested and developed deployable MIRV (multiple, independently targeted reentry vehicle) warheads for its strategic missiles—five years ahead of the Soviet Union. As a result, the negotiations placed no restrictions on MIRV technology, seriously undercutting the value of the SALT I and SALT II agreements limiting strategic offensive arms.

Two SALT I accords were reached in January 1972—the Antiballistic Missile (ABM) Treaty, which severely limited ABM defenses, and the Interim Agreement on the Limitation of Strategic Offensive Arms, which froze the total number of strategic missile launchers pending further negotiation of a more comprehensive treaty limiting strategic missiles and bombers. (A separate agreement on measures to avert accidental use of nuclear weapons had been concluded in September 1971.) The

ABM Treaty, of indefinite duration, restricted each party to two ABM sites, with 100 ABM launchers at each. (In the only later amendment to the treaty, a 1974 protocol, the two parties agreed to forgo one of those sites, so that each was thereafter limited to a single deployment location.) Further constraints included a ban on the testing and deployment of land-mobile, sea-based, air-based, and space-based systems. Only fixed, land-based ABM systems could be deployed at the one allowed site. The Soviet Union kept its existing ABM deployment around Moscow. The United States completed its deployment at a site for defense of intercontinental ballistic missile (ICBM) launchers near Grand Forks, S.Dak., but in 1975 mothballed the complex as too expensive. The ABM Treaty was a solid achievement in arms limitation, although agreement was facilitated by doubts on both sides as to the cost-effectiveness of available ABM systems. While the treaty headed off a costly and useless ABM deployment race, it did not have the desired effect of also damping down deployment of strategic offensive missiles, especially because MIRVs were not constrained.

The Interim Agreement froze the level of land- and sea-based strategic missiles (permitting completion of launchers already under construction). The Soviet Union had a quantitative advantage with 2,348 missile launchers to 1,710 for the United States. This was, however, offset in two important ways. First, neither strategic bombers nor forward-based nuclear delivery systems were included, and the United States had a significant advantage in both categories. Second, although the Soviet Union had more missile launchers and deployed missiles, the United States had a larger number of strategic missile warheads and by 1972 had already begun deploying MIRV warheads. Overall, the Interim Agreement placed only modest limits on strategic missiles. In contrast to the ABM Treaty, it was not significant as an arms control measure.

SALT II was the name given to the follow-on negotiation of a treaty to replace the SALT I Interim Agreement. These talks lasted from November 1972 to June 1979. The SALT II Treaty provided equal levels of strategic arms (2,400, to be reduced over time to 2,200, strategic delivery vehicles) and included strategic bombers as well as strategic missiles. Intended to be in effect for ten years, during which a third SALT negotiation for further reductions was envisaged, the SALT II Treaty fell afoul of the collapse of the Soviet-American détente of the 1970s after the Soviet occupation of Afghanistan in 1979 and was never ratified. Its major constraints, however, were formally observed by both sides until 1986, and for all practical purposes even after the dissolution of the Soviet Union.

In 1982, under the administration of President Ronald Reagan, a new series of negotiations, the Strategic Arms Reduction Talks (START), succeeded SALT. In July 1991 the START I Treaty was signed in Moscow by President George Bush and Soviet President Mikhail Gorbachev. In January 1993 the START II Treaty was also signed in Moscow, by Bush and Russian President Boris Yeltsin. The treaties involved increasingly substantial reductions, but even so, START I brought the level of strategic warheads down only to about the SALT II level, and START II down to the SALT I level.

The SALT process was a success in demonstrating that adversaries could reach arms limitation agreements, but owing to the very cautious and conservative approaches of both sides, the limitations on strategic offensive arms were unable to keep up with the military technological advances given precedence by the two countries. The ABM Treaty, buffeted mainly by revived U.S. interest in President Reagan's Strategic Defense Initiative (SDI) of 1983, survived the decade before the SDI was abandoned. It remained an effective arms control agreement. Pursuant to the SALT I agreements a Standing Consultative Commission (SCC) was established to resolve questions regarding the meaning of and compliance with the SALT agreements. It was also stipulated that there would be no interference with the use of national technical means of verification, such as observation satellites. SALT thus helped at least to stabilize, if not greatly reduce, the military balance. The SALT process and the agreements reached, while causing some friction and disagreements, contributed to the overall political détente of the 1970s. While not sufficient to sustain that détente, the SALT process helped ensure that even under renewed tension the risk of nuclear war remained low.

[See also Arms Race and Disarmament; Cold War; Strategic Defense Initiative.]

BIBLIOGRAPHY

John Newhouse, *Cold Dawn: The Story of SALT* (New York, 1973).
Gerard C. Smith, *Doubletalk: The Story of SALT I* (New York, 1980).
Strobe Talbott, *Endgame: The Inside Story of SALT II* (New York, 1979).
Thomas W. Wolfe, *The SALT Experience* (Cambridge, Mass., 1979).

— RAYMOND L. GARTHOFF

STRATEGIC DEFENSE INITIATIVE (SDI)

Strategic Defense Initiative, known to its critics as "Star Wars," was introduced in 1983 by President Ronald Reagan as a new and highly effective program to protect the United States from nuclear attack. SDI would have employed infrared detectors and exotic weapons, such as high-powered lasers to identify, track, and destroy incoming ballistic missiles. Traveling at the speed of light, a satellite-based laser beam could engage an enemy missile soon after launch. According to President Reagan, SDI would safeguard the nation, making nuclear weapons "impotent and obsolete." Despite its attraction, the proposal evoked immediate opposition. Critics questioned the legality of SDI because space-based antimissile weapons were prohibited by the 1972 ABM (antiballistic missile) Treaty. Moreover, they claimed that the system would require many major technological breakthroughs and would be prohibitively expensive (estimates ran as high as $1 trillion). They also claimed that SDI would be vulnerable to many countermeasures, and the immensely complex computer code required for battle management could never be tested and was unlikely to work. The administration argued that all the technical problems could be overcome with an aggressive research program, which was legal under its interpretation of the ABM Treaty. During the Reagan administration and that of George Bush (from 1981 to 1993), Congress funded the program at levels substantially below administration requests. As technical difficulties arose, the program was modified to emphasize more conventional weapons such as small heat-seeking rockets ("brilliant pebbles"). President Bill Clinton's first secretary of defense, Les Aspin, promoted theater missile defenses by substituting ground-based missile defense systems for space-based ones. In effect this proposal put an end to SDI, a course made easier by the collapse of the Soviet Union and the end of the cold war.

According to President Reagan, the Strategic Defense Initiative—also known as "Star Wars"—would make nuclear weapons "impotent and obsolete."

[See also Arms Race and Disarmament.]

BIBLIOGRAPHY

Steven Anzovin, ed., *The Star Wars Debate* (New York, 1986).

Robert M. Lawrence, SDI: *A Bibliographic and Research Guide* (Boulder, Colo., 1987).

— LEO SARTORI

STUDENT NONVIOLENT COORDINATING COMMITTEE

Student Nonviolent Coordinating Committee (SNCC) was founded in April 1960, to coordinate the southern black college-student nonviolent direct-action protests against lunch-counter segregation that had arisen earlier in the year. As this phase of the southern black protest movement subsided toward the end of the year, with the dropping of the color bar at many chain and department store dining facilities in Texas and the upper South, SNCC changed from a committee coordinating campus-based groups to a staff organization that initiated its own projects in local communities. SNCC played a central role in the desegregation and voter registration campaigns that followed in the Deep South. Operating in the most oppressive areas, its dedicated workers became celebrated for their courage in the face of white intimidation. Despite noteworthy accomplishments, the millenarian SNCC people became disillusioned with their failure radically to reshape southern society in a few short years. In the radical vanguard of the black protest movement, by 1966 they adopted an ideology of black separatism and revolutionary violence—a transformation accompanied by the rapid decline and ultimate disappearance of the organization. Yet SNCC had made a key contribution to the important social changes that had occurred in the South.

The Student Nonviolent Coordinating Committee, founded in 1960 for peaceful direct action, had by 1966 shifted to an ideology of black separatism and revolutionary violence.

— AUGUST MEIER

SUBWAYS

Street congestion in the larger American cities was becoming intolerable in the late 19th century. Elevated railroads were built in three of the largest cities, New York, Chicago, and Boston, but were unsatisfactory because of noise, unsightliness, and depreciation of adjacent property values. Subways had been discussed in New York City in 1860, but the idea was dropped because of enormous cost. Between 1895 and 1900 Boston removed 1.7 miles of trolley-car tracks from crowded streets and placed them underground. Later these tunnels were extended and integrated with the city's system.

By 1900, when New York City's first contract for a subway was let, a billion passengers a year were riding crowded, slow streetcars. As the city grew and spread out, faster movement was necessary. The first subway line was opened by the Interborough Rapid Transit Company on Broadway in 1904. An extension to Brooklyn followed, and a tunnel under the East River was completed in 1908. By 1930 the Interborough operated 224 miles of subway and 139 miles of elevated line. The Brooklyn Rapid Transit Corporation developed a network of lines in Brooklyn and entered Manhattan by three tunnels under the East River, the last completed in 1924. The Hudson and Manhattan Tubes, completed in 1911, connected Manhattan with Jersey City, Hoboken, and Newark, N.J.

Philadelphia opened its first subway in 1907. After 1920 Newark, Saint Louis, and Los Angeles placed short sections of their surface-car lines underground. Between 1900 and 1910 a system of freight subways was built under downtown Chicago, but in the 1930's it was superseded by the motor truck. New York's private companies were supplemented by a city-owned system that completed its Eighth Avenue line in 1932. Most of the elevated lines in Manhattan were gradually abandoned, and the private companies and city system were merged under a transit authority in 1940. A Second Avenue subway and an additional East River tunnel, planned for many years, had construction halted in 1975 because the city was short of funds.

Between 1938 and 1943 a short subway was built in Chicago to supplement the elevated lines. Two new subways planned to replace the Loop and other elevated roads were held in abeyance in the mid-1970's because of the heavy deficits of the Chicago Transit Authority. The Bay Area Rapid Transit (BART) system in the San Francisco area, opened in 1973–74, comprises 75 miles of line, of which 16 are in tunnels under the city connected to the aboveground East Bay trackage by a four-mile tunnel under San Francisco Bay. In 1976 the first stage of a comprehensive metropolitan transit system, 4.5 miles of subway, was scheduled to open in Washington, D.C. The systems of the 1970's featured quiet, air-conditioned, and automated cars. More modern equipment was rapidly replacing older cars on New York's system, which in the 1970's was the most extensive and heavily patronized in the world.

BIBLIOGRAPHY

Interborough Rapid Transit Company, *The New York Subway: Its Construction and Equipment.*

James R. Walker, *Fifty Years of Rapid Transit, 1864–1917.*

Edward E. White and Muriel F. White, *Famous Subways and Tunnels of the World.*

— ERNEST W. WILLIAMS

The first subway trip for paying passengers on Chicago's new subway, October 18, 1943. Chicago's system was preceded by subway networks in several cities, including an extensive, city-owned system in New York City. (UPI/Corbis-Bettmann)

SUFFRAGE, EXCLUSION FROM THE

It is generally estimated that because of state property and taxpaying qualifications, fewer than one-fourth of all white adult males were eligible to vote in 1787–89, the time the U.S. Constitution was being ratified. The history of the suffrage in the United States since then has been one of steady expansion, partly through constitutional amendments and partly through legislation. The states had largely abandoned the property qualifications for voting by 1850. The Fifteenth Amendment, ratified in 1870, forbade denial of the right to vote "on account of race, color, or previous condition of servitude." The Nineteenth Amendment, which was adopted in 1920, prohibited denial of the right to vote on account of sex. The poll tax was outlawed for federal elections by the Twenty-fourth Amendment (1964) and for state elections by a Supreme Court decision (*Harper* v. *Virginia Board of Elections*, 383 U.S. 663, 1966). The Twenty-sixth Amendment, ratified in 1971, lowered the age limit for all federal and state voting to eighteen. Various obstacles to Afro-American suffrage were progressively eliminated by Supreme Court decisions—for example, the white primary in 1944 (*Smith* v. *Allwright*, 321 U.S. 649) and the "reasonable interpretation" of the Constitution test in 1965 (*Louisiana* v. *United States*, 380 U.S. 145)—and by federal legislation, notably the Voting Rights Act of 1965, which outlawed literacy, educational, "good character," and voucher devices aimed at keeping black suffrage to a minimum. Lengthy local residential qualifications for voting eligibility were declared unconstitutional by the Supreme Court in 1972 (*Dunn* v. *Blumstein*, 31 Lawyers Edition, U.S. Supreme Court Reports, Second Series 274). Unequal voting power resulting from malapportionment was held unconstitutional in a notable series of Court decisions beginning with *Baker* v. *Carr*, 369 U.S. 186 (1962). Thus, by 1972 all persons over eighteen, of whatever sex, color, or race, were legally entitled to vote. The remaining obstacles to voting were largely administrative in character and related to such matters as registration procedures and the times, places, and manner of holding elections.

BIBLIOGRAPHY

Richard Claude, *The Supreme Court and the Electoral Process.*

— DAVID FELLMAN

SUGAR ACTS

Throughout the American colonial period the British Empire was dependent on its West India islands for sugar. The rich sugar planters, residing in England, became politically powerful, and in 1733 secured the enactment of the Molasses Act. Under this law foreign molasses, imported into any British colony, was subject to an import duty of six pence per gallon. The object was not taxation, but to give the British sugar planters a monopoly of the American molasses market. The law was opposed by the New England merchants, especially in Massachusetts and Rhode Island, on the ground that the resultant increased price of rum would injure both the fishing industry and the trade to Africa. The protests were ineffective, and the dire results failed to develop. Opposition to the law died down, especially as there was little systematic effort to enforce it. The sugar planters discovered that the Molasses Act was of little value to them, and what they most needed was a larger market in Europe, which they got through a rebate of the import duties on sugar exported to the Continent. In time the British rum distilleries absorbed the British molasses, while there was no market for that from the growing French sugar industry. This situation made French molasses cheap, and there developed a well-organized colonial evasion of the import duty.

In 1764 George Grenville, chancellor of the Exchequer, had enacted a new sugar act, by which he undertook to end the smuggling trade in foreign molasses and at the same time secure a revenue. The duty on foreign molasses was lowered from six to three pence a gallon, the duties on foreign refined sugar were raised, and an increased export bounty on British refined sugar bound for the colonies was granted. The net result was to give the British sugar planters an effective monopoly of the American sugar market; smuggling of foreign sugar became unprofitable; and the old illicit trade in foreign molasses was disturbed. Americans had been importing large quantities of foreign molasses on which they paid, by collusion, total sums that averaged somewhere between half a penny and a penny a gallon. Most of this money went into the pockets of the customs officials instead of the treasury. Under the act of 1764, the three pence was more than the traffic would bear, if the law was enforced. There were violent protests at first; two years later the duty was lowered to one penny a gallon, applied alike to foreign and British imports, and the protests on the molasses duty came to an end. At this lower rate it was an important revenue producer and yielded annually from 1767 to 1775 an average of £12,194 per year.

Under the Sugar Act (and contrary to custom), any ship caught with any article on board before bond covering that article had been given was subject to seizure and confiscation.

Other phases of the Sugar Act of 1764 were far more irritating than was the lowered duty on molasses. One was a new duty on wine imported from Madeira, which prior to this time had come in duty free and was the main source of profit for the fish and food ships returning from the Mediterranean. This part of the Sugar Act led to few direct protests, but did produce some spectacular attempts at evasion, such as the wine-running episode in Boston involving a ship belonging to Capt. Daniel Malcolm, in February 1768. The provisions that produced the most irritation were new bonding regulations compelling ship masters to give bond, even when loaded with nonenumerated goods. The worst feature was a provision that bond had to be given before any article enumerated or nonenumerated was put on board. Under American conditions it was impossible for a shipmaster to give a new bond at a customhouse before he took on board every new consignment of freight. The universal practice was to load first, then clear and give bond. Under the Sugar Act any ship caught with any article on board before bond covering that article had been given was subject to seizure and confiscation. The customs commissioners made this provision a source of private profit to themselves. The most notorious seizures for technical violations of the bonding provision included John Hancock's sloop *Liberty* (June 10, 1768) and the *Ann* belonging to Henry Laurens of South Carolina.

BIBLIOGRAPHY

F. W. Pittman, *Development of the British West Indies, 1700–1763.*

— O. M. DICKERSON

SUGAR INDUSTRY

In colonial America sugar was made from maple sap for household use and for local trading. With the acquisition of Louisiana in 1803, the United States acquired a small, but rapidly growing, sugar industry. Major improvements were made in the manufacture of sugar, including the introduction in the 1820's of steam power for crushing cane and the invention in the 1840's by Norbert Rillieux, a Louisiana Creole, of a multiple-effect system for evaporating cane juice, which replaced the open kettle boilers and revolutionized sugar manufacture.

Prior to 1861, most Louisiana cane sugar was shipped to cities throughout the Mississippi Valley and the East Coast, and much of it was consumed in the form of raw sugar. Refiners in eastern cities imported raw sugar from the West Indies and, by a refining process of melting the sugar, clarifying the juice in boneblack filters, and centrifugal drying, produced a dry, white sugar.

In the 20th century further improvements occurred in sugar culture and manufacture. Just as horses and mules replaced oxen in cultivation prior to 1840, tractors replaced mule power in the 1920's and 1930's. Since World War II, mechanical harvesters have replaced much of the handcutting of cane. In the late 19th and early 20th centuries, the cultivation of sugar beets spread throughout the central and western states from the Great Lakes to California, and in both cane and beet processing, large expensive central mills dominated the manufacture of sugar.

By the 1960's the refining branch of the sugar industry was dominated by large corporations and was concentrated in coastal cities, especially New York, New Orleans, Savannah, Baltimore, Philadelphia, Boston, and San Francisco. Refiners process raw sugar from Louisiana, Florida, Hawaii, Puerto Rico, and foreign countries.

In 1970 more than 6 million tons of raw sugar (cane and beet) were produced in the United States and its possessions, and an additional 5 million tons were imported from foreign countries. Refined sugar was marketed in more than 100 varieties of grades and packaging to meet highly specialized demands. Per capita sugar consumption in the United States increased rapidly during the 20th century and by the 1970's had been stabilized at about 100 pounds per year.

BIBLIOGRAPHY

Victor S. Clark, *History of Manufactures in the United States.*
J. Carlyle Sitterson, *Sugar Country: The Cane Sugar Industry in the South, 1753–1950.*
U.S. Beet Sugar Association, *The Beet Sugar Story.*
U.S. Department of Agriculture, *Agricultural Statistics* (1971).

— J. CARLYLE SITTERSON

SUMMIT CONFERENCES, PRESIDENTIAL

Summit Conferences, Presidential, denote personal diplomacy at the highest levels of government. They are based on the assumption that U.S. presidents, possessing the ultimate power over questions of peace and war, can in direct conversations with other heads of state resolve disagreements too long protracted, perhaps dangerously, by lesser officials. For that reason well-publicized exchanges between national leaders, even when they achieve nothing, offer reassurance to a troubled world that current conflicts, however bitter, exist far below the threshold of war. Presidential summitry implies that the country's interests, power, and prestige are directly engaged in the issues of the day. There were occasions before the dramatic events of the late 1930s when presidents participated in international gatherings or conferred privately with leaders of other countries, but those occasions scarcely passed as summit conferences, which supposedly address troublesome international issues head-on. Formal or ceremonial state visits had slight diplomatic significance, or perhaps none at all.

It is not strange, therefore, that the experience of the United States in summitry began with Franklin D. Roosevelt's efforts to influence the course and consequences of World War II. At the Atlantic Conference aboard the *Augusta* off Newfoundland in August 1941, Roosevelt and British Prime Minister Winston Churchill framed the Atlantic Charter to define their wartime goals. At Casablanca in January 1943 Roosevelt and Churchill agreed on basic war plans, and Roosevelt proclaimed the Allied goal of unconditional surrender. In late November 1943 Roosevelt conferred with China's Chiang Kai-shek in Cairo and then continued on to Tehran for his first tripartite summit with Churchill and the Soviet leader Joseph Stalin. Early in December he returned to Cairo for a minor summit with Churchill and President Ismet Inönü of Turkey. At Yalta in February 1945 Roosevelt held his second and final summit with Churchill and Stalin. President Harry S. Truman terminated the wartime tripartite summits at Potsdam in July and August of 1945. With the emergence of the cold war, summit conferences with the Soviet Union were rendered elusive by Washington's demands that the Kremlin first abandon its objective of advancing world revolution, discard its aggressiveness, and appear ready to fulfill any international agreements by demonstrating its good faith.

Churchill used the term "summit" in calling for a conference at the highest level in the spring of 1953. Denying that the USSR was prepared to fulfill one or more of the country's established requirements, President Dwight D. Eisenhower refused for two years to attend a summit with the Soviet leaders. Retreating under domestic and world pressure, Eisenhower attended the Geneva Big Four Conference of July 1955. Despite its outward display of cordiality, the Geneva summit achieved very little. In November 1957 Kremlin leaders launched a crusade for another summit. The Eisenhower administration demanded that any future summits have adequate preparation, an agreed-upon agenda, and reasonable assurance of success. It was also decided to seek the approval of regional allies, usually registered in a presummit foreign ministers conference. Soviet leaders argued that presummit conferences eliminated the possibility of diplomacy among equals. Again with considerable reluctance, Eisenhower attended the Paris summit of 1960 only to face an angry Nikita Khrushchev, who quickly terminated the conference because of the president's refusal to apologize for sending spy planes across Soviet territory.

For President Richard M. Nixon summitry became symbolic of his effort to advance the spirit of détente between the United States and the communist powers. His summitry began with his trip to China in February 1972—a spectacular media event. His Moscow summit with Soviet leader Leonid Brezhnev in late May 1972 marked the high point of official Soviet-American cordiality during the cold war. In addition to the SALT I Treaty on nuclear weapons, the two leaders signed a variety of lesser agreements to extend the interests binding the two countries together. The two succeeding Nixon-Brezhnev summits, in Washington and Moscow, were anticlimactic. Both countries had reached the outer limits of successful coexistence. Nixon's East-West summits never overcame the doubts and antagonisms that characterized the cold war. President Ronald Reagan's four summits with Mikhail Gorbachev, beginning with the Geneva summit of November 1985 and ending with the Moscow summit of May 1988, marked the beginning of the end of the cold war itself. President George Bush's summit with Gorbachev at Malta in December 1989 continued that trend into the post-cold war era.

President Reagan's four summits with Soviet leader Mikhail Gorbachev between 1985 and 1988 marked the beginning of the end of the cold war.

Noted critics of summitry, such as British diplomat Harold Nicolson and former U.S. ambassador George F. Kennan, warned that diplomacy among heads of states would lack the time and knowledge that professionals could bring to the task. In practice the summits scarcely engaged those present in diplomacy. Such gatherings permitted an exchange of views, extensive socializing, and photo opportunities in abundance, interspersed occasionally with the signing of agreements prepared laboriously by professional diplomats over long periods of time. Thus, summitry was designed less to settle disputes then to publicize agreements already reached. In personalizing such agreements, summits enabled those attending to exaggerate their achievements and thereby enhance their stature as world leaders. Presidents, responding to global expectations, possessed the authority to make concessions not permitted to those obligated to defend established policies. In practice, however, successive presidents refrained from exercising their special prerogatives as heads of the nation's foreign policy establishment. Still, their presence at the summits was a reminder that presidents, not others, carried the responsibility for the country's external policies.

Summits invariably reflected the political, military, and diplomatic realities of the time with little capacity to change them. If presidents on occasion chose to be their own secretaries of state, they seldom revealed that proclivity at the summits.

[See also Arms Race and Disarmament; Atlantic Charter; China, Relations with; Cold War; Potsdam Conference; Strategic Arms Limitation Talks; Summit Conferences; Yalta Conference.]

BIBLIOGRAPHY

Elmer Plischke, *Summit Diplomacy: Personal Diplomacy of the President of the United States* (Westport, Conn., 1974), and *Diplomat in Chief: The President at the Summit* (New York, 1986).

— NORMAN A. GRAEBNER

SUMTER, FORT

Fort Sumter, situated on a sandbar at the mouth of the harbor of Charleston, S.C., and commanding the sea approach to the city, draws its significance from the important part it played in the Civil War. On the night of Dec. 26, 1860, following the passage of the Ordinance of Secession (Dec. 20) by South Carolina, Maj. Robert Anderson, in command of the Union forces at Charleston, removed his garrison from Fort Moultrie, on Sullivan's Island, to Fort Sumter where he believed he would be in a better position for defense in the event of hostilities. President James Buchanan, whose term of office would expire on Mar. 4, 1861, avoided the momentous decision of whether to recall Anderson or send an expedition to reinforce him at the risk of provoking war. Upon assuming the office of president, Abraham Lincoln, Buchanan's successor, met the issue by dispatching a fleet to relieve the fort. With this fleet momentarily expected at Charleston, Gen. Pierre G. T. Beauregard, in command of the Confederate forces, offered Anderson a final opportunity to evacuate. This was not accepted, and at 4:30 on the morning of Friday, Apr. 12, the Confederate batteries opened fire on Fort Sumter. On Apr. 13, after a bombardment of thirty-four hours, Anderson surrendered; the Civil War had begun.

On Apr. 7, 1863, Fort Sumter, then garrisoned by Confederates and commanded by Col. Alfred Rhett, was attacked by a Union fleet of nine ironclads under the command of Adm. Samuel F. Du Pont. This engagement, which lasted only two hours and twenty-five minutes, was far-reaching in its effects. While it inflicted on the United States one of the greatest defeats in its naval history, it was conducted on a sufficiently large scale to bring out the strength as well as the weakness of the new type of fighting ship, and inaugurated the era of the modern steel navy.

In August 1863 the great siege of Fort Sumter, by combined Union naval and land forces, began and lasted for 567 days. During this period the fortification was subjected to three major bombardments (the first from Aug. 17 to Aug. 23), totaling 117 days of continuous fire, day and night. For 280 days it was under fire "steady and desultory." Projectiles to the number of 46,053, weighing 3,500 tons, were hurled against it. Casualties (with a normal complement of officers and men of 300) were 53 killed and 267 wounded. After the first bombardment of sixteen days the fort had been pronounced "silenced and demolished." But it was rebuilt under fire by its defenders. This occurred again after both the second and third bombardments. During this protracted and successful defense, commanding Confederate officers were successively: Col. Alfred Rhett; Maj. Stephen Elliott, Jr.; Capt. John C. Mitchell; and Capt. Thomas A. Huguenin. Maj. John Johnson was engineer officer in charge during the entire siege, and much of the credit for the defense was attributed to his skill and resourcefulness.

Fort Sumter was never surrendered by the Confederates. On Feb. 17, 1865, when the approach of Gen. William Tecumseh Sherman's army of 70,000 made the evacuation of the whole Charleston sector inevitable, the fort was closed and abandoned.

Fort Sumter National Monument was established by the U.S. government in 1948.

BIBLIOGRAPHY

Richard Current, *Lincoln and the First Shot.*

DuBose Heyward and Herbert Ravenel Sass, *Fort Sumter, 1861–1865.*

— DUBOSE HEYWARD

SUPREME COURT

Supreme Court, created by the Judiciary Act of 1789, originally consisted of a chief justice and five associate justices. Congress has varied the size of the Court from time to time, but since 1869 the Court has included a chief justice and eight associate justices. In 1936–37 President Franklin D. Roosevelt proposed that Congress add six more places on the Court, in an effort to secure more favorable decisions, but this attempt to "pack" the Court failed.

All justices are appointed by the president, subject to confirmation by the Senate. It is unusual for the Senate to refuse to confirm a presidential nomination; there were only three such cases in the first seventy-five years of the 20th century. President Herbert C. Hoover's nomination of Circuit Judge John J. Parker and President Richard M. Nixon's nomination of Clement F.

Haynsworth, Jr., and George H. Carswell, also circuit judges, failed to win Senate approval. Political considerations are usually important factors in the nomination and confirmation process. A president will generally select members of his own political party, although there have been a few exceptions, and he tends to prefer men who share his basic political philosophy. The appointee's philosophy is invariably a subject of extensive inquiry and debate both in the Senate Judiciary Committee and on the floor of the Senate.

The justices of the Supreme Court hold office for life—the Constitution says "during good Behaviour"—and can be removed from office only by the impeachment process, which requires a two-thirds vote of the Senate. No Supreme Court justice has ever been impeached, although a serious attempt was made to remove Justice Samuel Chase in 1805. Most justices are well beyond middle age when first appointed to the Court, but they have enjoyed unusual longevity; in all, by 1975 there had been only a hundred men on the Court, and Warren E. Burger, who was appointed to the center chair in 1969, was only the fifteenth chief justice in the Court's history.

Six justices are necessary to constitute a quorum. The regular term of the Supreme Court begins on the first Monday in October each year and generally ends some time the following June. In unusual circumstances involving matters of urgent public concern the Court may decide to hold a special term during the summer recess.

The Court disposes of a large number of cases each year. For example, in the 1971 term 4,500 cases were filed, 3,645 cases were disposed of, oral argument was heard in 177 cases, and 129 opinions were written. A handful of cases involved suits between states, but most cases came up from the lower federal courts and the state courts. The normal procedure of the Court is to hear oral arguments from Monday through Thursday for two weeks and then to recess for two weeks. Since 1955 it holds its conferences, at which decisions are reached, on Fridays instead of Saturdays.

When cases are filed with the Court they are placed on one of three dockets: the original docket (which consists of suits between states), the appellate docket (which consists of the review of lower-court decisions), and the miscellaneous docket (which includes appeals *in forma pauperis* and applications for such extraordinary writs as habeas corpus, mandamus, and prohibition).

The Supreme Court's main business is to review appeals from the lower federal courts and from the state courts in cases raising federal issues—that is, questions of law arising under the federal Constitution, an act of Congress, or a treaty of the United States. The appellate jurisdiction of the Supreme Court is subject to regulation by Congress. According to prevailing statutes, cases reach the Court by writ of certiorari, by appeal, or by certification.

The granting of a writ of certiorari is wholly within the discretion of the Court. Under its own rules of practice the writ is granted on the vote of at least four justices, which is an exception to the general rule that all business is controlled by majority vote. The whole tendency of legislation, since the adoption of the Judiciary Act of 1925, has been to expand the classes of cases in which the Court may exercise discretion, and to narrow the range of cases the Court is obliged to take. Speaking generally, the Court grants certiorari only if the case involves a matter of considerable public importance. About 90 percent of petitions for certiorari are denied.

Cases that reach the Supreme Court by appeal are technically within the compulsory jurisdiction of the Court. At the turn of the century, however, it invented the device of dismissing an appeal if it does not involve a substantial federal question. A large majority of appeals from the highest state courts are dismissed each year for lack of a substantial federal question. It follows that, for the most part, the Court hears only those cases it believes to be in the public interest to review, since it exercises almost total control over its dockets.

Finally, several courts, mainly the federal courts of appeal and the court of claims, may choose to send a case to the Supreme Court by certifying the issues to be settled. In these instances, which are very few in number, the decision for Supreme Court review is made by the lower court. No state court may certify appeals in this fashion.

The Constitution gives the Supreme Court original jurisdiction over cases between states. The states often sue each other over a variety of issues, such as boundaries, water rights, debts, and pollution, and these cases are heard directly by the Supreme Court. Since the Court is not equipped to sit as a trial court, when it deals with an interstate dispute it appoints a distinguished lawyer or former judge to sit as a special master. The master conducts the evidentiary hearing, after which he makes recommendations on which the Court ultimately acts. In settling serious disputes between two or more states in a rational and judicial manner the Court performs an important and essential function that helps reduce inevitable tensions between the states.

The Court is both a judicial and a political institution. As a judicial body it deals with cases between adversary parties according to the traditional usages and rhetoric of law courts. It is political in the sense that its decisions extend far beyond the actual parties of record and thus declare fundamental policy for the whole country. Above all, having the power of judicial review, the Court may declare federal and state statutes to be unenforceable if found to be in conflict with the Constitution. Since the great power-limiting clauses of the Constitution, such as the due process and equal protection guaranties, are phrased in very broad and generous language, the Court has much room in which to maneuver. In seeking to cope with such seminal concepts as the separation of powers and the rights of the individual the Court may well be described, in the language of the British jurist James Bryce, as both "the living voice of the Constitution" and "the conscience of the people."

As the ultimate interpreter of the Constitution, the Supreme Court has had the delicate function of drawing the line between the power of the national government and that of the state governments and thus has served as the umpire of the federal system. It has also had the responsibility of drawing the lines between individual liberties and permissible social controls. In a highly pluralistic nation it has been charged with the responsibility of finding tolerable balances between its many segments. Thus, the Supreme Court has always occupied a pivotal and highly visible position in the American political and governmental world. It has rarely been far removed from the eye of the recurrent political storms that have appeared in the course of American history. Thomas Jefferson, for example, waged political warfare against a Court drawn from his opposition, the Federalist party, and headed by a masterful adversary, Chief Justice John Marshall. During the fateful years leading to the Civil War the Court was deeply embroiled in controversies created by the existence of slavery and reached a new low in popular acceptance with its 1857 decision in the Dred Scott case. During the Reconstruction period the Court had to come to grips with the constitutional significance of a Union victory and gave great offense to the radicals, who were determined to pursue a far more drastic program than the justices were willing to accept. Later in the century a conservative Court, dominated by aging justices, frustrated the efforts of reformers to tax incomes and regulate monopolies. Between 1933 and 1937 a determined majority of five justices defeated many important New Deal statutes through a strict construction of the Constitution. On the other hand, under the leadership of Chief Justice Earl Warren in the 1950's and 1960's, the Court read the Constitution generously to extend the rights of the individual, such as the rights of free speech and of religious conscience and the rights of persons accused of crime. Whether the balance had been shifted too far in favor of persons accused of crime became a leading public issue in the United States. With the appointment of a new chief justice and three associate justices during his first three years in office, Nixon laid the foundation for a new shift of emphasis in a more conservative direction. Particularly in the field of the rights of persons accused of crime, the Court over which Chief Justice Burger presided after 1969 tended to limit some of the decisions of the Warren Court.

BIBLIOGRAPHY

Paul A. Freund, *The Supreme Court of the United States.*

— DAVID FELLMAN

SUPREME COURT AFTER THE WARREN COURT

In 1969 Chief Justice Earl Warren retired from the Supreme Court, bringing to an end the "Warren revolution," a period of unprecedented judicial activism in protection of personal rights ranging from the landmark *Brown* v. *Board of Education of Topeka*, 347 U.S. 483 (1954), which fueled the civil rights movement of the 1950s and 1960s, to *Miranda* v. *Arizona*, 384 U.S. 436 (1966), which protected citizens from arbitrary police interrogation. While many observers expected the Court of Warren Earl Burger (1969–1986), with four justices including the chief justice appointed by President Richard M. Nixon, to undo the Warren revolution, matters did not turn out that way. No important Warren Court decision was overruled; some were narrowed but others were not only applied but expanded.

During the Warren Court years, a new activism in protection of personal rights became the judicial hallmark. Strict scrutiny became the primary legal tool to broaden individual rights by reinterpreting the First Amendment, the procedural guarantees of the Bill of Rights (incorporated into the Fourteenth Amendment), the equal protection clause of the Fourteenth Amendment. For the most part the Burger Court continued this liberal jurisprudential trend, but it did more than merely confirm Warren Court jurisprudence. It reintroduced substantive due process to protect personal rights—a doctrine not employed widely since the first quarter of the twentieth century, under which due process was employed to review the reasonableness of laws. The outstanding example was the decision in *Roe* v. *Wade*, 410 U.S. 113 (1973), which ruled that there was a constitutional right to an abortion during the first three months of pregnancy. The right was based on the constitutional right of privacy that had been recognized by the Warren Court. *Roe* was as activist as any Warren Court decision—based on "policy" judgments that led to recognition of a new right not enumerated in the Bill of Rights.

The Burger Court also substantially expanded other women's rights. While it never declared sex a suspect classification under the Fourteenth Amendment, it did establish a "middle" or "heightened" level scrutiny test for sex discrimination cases as the result of three decisions between 1971 and 1976. In the first of these rulings, *Reed* v. *Reed*, 404 U.S. 71 (1971), the Supreme Court invalidated for the first time in its history a statute on the grounds of sex discrimination. In the second, *Frontiero* v. *Richardson*, 411 U.S. 677 (1973), the Court came within one vote of declaring sex a suspect classification. In the third, *Craig* v. *Boren*, 429 U.S. 190 (1976), the Court ruled that "classification by gender must serve important governmental objectives and must be substantially related" to the achievements of these objectives. This new standard has been applied to cases involving women since 1976.

The Burger Court also aided the cause of desegregation of public schools with its decision in *Swann* v. *Charlotte-Mecklenburg Board of Education*, 402 U.S. 1 (1971), which vested broad remedial power in the courts to ensure desegregation, including extensive busing. The *Brown* principle was also expanded to uphold affirmative action programs. As Justice Sandra Day O'Connor, the first woman justice to sit on the Court, later concluded, "We have reached a common destination in sustaining affirmative action against constitutional attack." The same was true in other areas, including the First Amendment, reapportionment, and equal protection. In all these areas the Warren principles remained. The Burger Court dealt with other crucial constitutional issues. *United States* v. *Nixon*, 418 U.S. 683 (1974), brought the Court into the Watergate scandal by ruling that the president could not retain subpoenaed tapes by claiming executive privilege. Its decision led directly to the first resignation of a U.S. president.

Under Chief Justice William H. Rehnquist (1986–), the Court reflected the rightward tilt in U.S. politics affirmed in the 1994 midterm congressional elections, in which Republicans gained control of Congress for the first time since the 1950s. Under the leadership of this conservative activist the Court began to shape a new constitutional case law undoing some of the work of its predecessors. A definite change in direction was manifested in the Rehnquist Court's decisions on civil rights and criminal law. In *Richmond* v. *J. A. Croson Company*, 488 U.S. 469 (1989), the Court struck down a Richmond, Virginia, affirmative action plan, known as set-asides, under which prime contractors awarded city contracts were required to subcontract at least 30 percent of each contract to minority business enterprises. Set-asides represented a form of affirmative action introduced by the Nixon administration, but the Rehnquist Court ruled that the Fourteenth Amendment required strict scrutiny of all race-based action by state and local governments. Without proof of intentional discrimination by the city, the Richmond plan could not be upheld. The argument that the city was attempting to remedy discrimination, as shown in the disparity between contracts awarded in the past to minority businesses and the city's minority population, was rejected. The Burger Court, in *Fullilove* v. *Klutznick*, 448 U.S. 448 (1980), had sustained federal works programs that set aside 10 percent of the value of contracts for businesses owned by blacks and other minorities. In *Adarand Constructors* v. *Peña* 115 S.Ct. 2097 (1995), however, five justices of the Rehnquist Court cast grave doubt on the continued validity of *Fullilove*. Although neither the federal construction program involved in the case or federal affirmative action in general was declared unconstitutional, strict scrutiny was for the first time applied to federal as well as state affirmative action programs, casting doubt on the validity of many such programs.

Under Chief Justice Rehnquist, the Court reflected the rightward tilt in U.S. politics affirmed in the 1994 midterm congressional elections.

Other Rehnquist Court decisions shifted the burden of proof in civil rights cases, holding that plaintiffs, not employers, had the burden of proving that a job requirement shown statistically to screen out minorities was not a "business necessity." Employers were permitted to show by only a preponderance of the evidence rather than by clear and convincing evidence (a higher burden of proof) that refusals to hire were based on legitimate and not discriminatory reasons. The Rehnquist Court also refused to invalidate a death sentence imposed upon a black defendant despite a detailed statistical study that showed black defendants who killed white victims were far more likely to receive the death penalty than white defendants. The Court stressed that there was no proof that the decision-makers in this particular case acted with discriminatory purpose.

From 1973 to 1989 the Supreme Court struck down most attempts by states to place restrictions on women's constitutional right to abortions. In *Webster* v. *Health Reproductive Services*, 492 U.S. 490 (1989), the Rehnquist Court upheld restrictions on abortions but refused to overrule the fundamental right to abortion declared in *Roe.* In *Planned Parenthood of Southeastern Pennsylvania* v. *Casey,* 112 S. Ct. 2791 (1992), the Rehnquist Court again declined to overrule *Roe,* although it did uphold a variety of other restrictions on abortion.

Rehnquist Court decisions also marked the beginning of a trend in favor of property fights. For the first time in years, the Court began to stress the constitutional prohibition against taking property without compensation. Noteworthy in such cases was the Court's use of heightened scrutiny to review the merits of land-use regulations in deciding whether a challenged regulation required judicial invalidation in the absence of compensation. Indeed, the Court implied that claims of unconstitutional takings (whether by acquisition or regulation) fall into a particularly sensitive constitutional category comparable to that of freedom of speech. As the chief justice stated in a 1994 case, "We see no reason why the Takings Clause . . . should be relegated to the status of poor relation." The Court's decisions on takings without compensation signaled a tilt in favor of property rights and away from the strong preference given to personal rights by the Warren and Burger courts. Nonetheless, significant Warren Court criminal-procedure decisions remained a part of Rehnquist Court jurisprudence. The key Warren criminal trilogy—*Gideon* v. *Wainwright,* 372 U.S. 335 (1963); *Mapp* v. *Ohio,* 367 U.S. 436; and *Miranda* v. *Arizona,* 384 U.S. 436 (1966)—continued to be followed, although some of their doctrines were narrowed. When the Rehnquist Court struck down New York City's legislative apportionment in *Board of Estimate* v. *Morris,* 489 U.S. 688 (1989), it relied on the Warren Court's one-person, one-vote principle.

By the end of the Court's session in 1995 a conservative majority began to assert itself in a series of five-to-four decisions. Thus, it ruled that race cannot be the primary factor in redrawing congressional districts, held against Kansas City's ambitious court-ordered program for desegregating schools, permitted Boston's St. Patrick's Day parade organizers to exclude homosexuals from participating, upheld drug-testing of student athletes, limited lawsuits by prisoners protesting prison conditions, decided that the University of Virginia violated the free speech rights of students when it denied funding for a Christian student newspaper, and similarly found that Ohio could not prevent the Ku Klux Klan from erecting a cross in a public park.

[See also Brown *v.* Board of Education of Topeka*;* Miranda *v.* Arizona*;* Roe *v.* Wade*; Watergate, Aftermath of.]*

BIBLIOGRAPHY

David P. Currie, *The Constitution in the Supreme Court: The Second Century, 1888–1986* (Chicago, 1990).

Robert McCloskey, *The American Constitution,* 2nd ed. (New York, 1994).

David M. O'Brien, *Storm Center: The Supreme Court in American Politics,* 2nd ed. (New York, 1990).

William H. Rehnquist, *The Supreme Court: How It Was, How It Is* (New York, 1987).

David G. Savage, *Turning Right: The Making of the Rehnquist Court* (New York, 1992).

Bernard Schwartz, *The Ascent of Pragmatism: The Burger Court in Action* (Reading, Pa., 1990), *A History of the Supreme Court* (New York, 1993), and *Decision: How the Supreme Court Decides Cases* (New York, 1996).

James F. Simon, *The Center Holds: The Power Struggle Inside the Rehnquist Court* (New York, 1995).

William M. Wiecek, *Liberty Under Law: The Supreme Court in American Life* (Baltimore, 1988).

— BERNARD SCHWARTZ

SWEATSHOP

Sweatshop, an undesirable work environment characterized by job insecurity, low wages, long hours, and poor, often unhealthful, working conditions. Such work may be located in quarters provided by the employer, in which case a "shop" literally exists. But "sweated" workers frequently labor in their living quarters, so that the designation "shop" is figurative.

Work situations of this sort most commonly arise in industries of intense competition, where low capital requirements afford firms great ease of entry into and exit from the industry and where production processes require large amounts of relatively unskilled labor. Secondary earners (women and children) drawn from low-income households and primary earners (male and female) without alternative employment opportunities are the most frequent victims of sweating. Historically, the garment trades and cigar manufacturing in the years 1880–1910 provide outstanding examples of sweated trades in the United States. Competitive pressures forced wages down to levels that bore little relation to living costs. Recently arrived immigrant workers in these industries, and even the employers and subcontractors who sweated them, were relentlessly pitted against one another in their efforts to earn an income. Perhaps the best example in the 1960's and 1970's of a sweated trade would be that involving migrant farm workers.

The first extensive public exposure of sweating was made in England in 1889–90 by the Select Committee of the House of Lords on the Sweating System, although the practice undoubtedly predated these investigations by a wide margin. In the United States, the first public effort to deal with the problem took the form of a law prohibiting the production of tobacco products in living quarters (New York, 1884). This legislation and similar state laws requiring the registration and/or inspection of homework were, where sanctioned by the courts, generally ineffective. Union organization and collectively bargained standards, such as arose in the garment trades in 1910–20, were the most effective deterrents to sweating. The passage of federal minimum-wage and maximum-hour legislation in 1938 also contributed in important measure to this end everywhere except in agriculture.

BIBLIOGRAPHY

J. Seidman, *The Needle Trades.*

— H. M. GITELMAN

T

TAFT-HARTLEY ACT

Taft-Hartley Act, officially known as the Labor-Management Relations Act, was enacted on Aug. 22, 1947. Sponsored by Sen. Robert A. Taft and Rep. Fred Hartley, it amended the National Labor Relations Act of 1935 (Wagner Act) in reaction to the unregulated growth of organized labor and certain alleged abuses of power by some labor leaders. A disorderly state of industrial relations was portrayed by the Republican congressional candidates in 1946, and, for the first time since 1930, Republican majorities were established in both houses of Congress, which allowed for passage of the Taft-Hartley Act by overriding the veto of Democratic President Harry S. Truman.

The depression of the early 1930's dramatized the organized power of industry in contrast to the unorganized weakness of the work force. To counter this condition, Congress enacted the National Industrial Recovery Act (NIRA) in 1933, which, coupled with the National Labor Board established by executive order that year, began a period of federal control of prices, wages, and hours. A subsequent amendment to NIRA gave employees the right to organize and bargain collectively free from the interference, restraint, or coercion of their employers. Under the act, union membership, particularly in the coal industry, expanded rapidly. The National Labor Relations Board, however, was short-lived, for in May 1935 the Supreme Court ruled NIRA unconstitutional. One month after that decision, Congress enacted the National Labor Relations Act, also called the Wagner Act, which gave employees the right to organize and bargain collectively free from employer interference and provided the machinery for enforcing that right. The act established a threefold process to achieve its aims. First, a three-man National Labor Relations Board was set up, with provision for a staff and field organization to administer the law; second, provision was made for board-conducted elections through which employees would select representatives for bargaining purposes; and third, the act defined five sets of employer practices designated "unfair labor practices," which the board was given the power to determine and prohibit.

Critics of the Wagner Act sued immediately to have it declared unconstitutional. In 1937 the Supreme Court declared the act constitutional. With that issue settled, the critics changed their strategy, and began a congressional effort to have the act amended. With the problems of World War II concerning the nation, the drive for amendment was unsuccessful, and between the years 1935 and 1947, union membership expanded from three million to fifteen million. In some industries, such as coal mining, construction, railroading, and trucking, four-fifths of the employees were working under collective bargaining agreements, and union leaders wielded great power. In 1946 a wave of strikes developed, which closed steel mills, ports, automobile factories, and other industries. With the birth of the cold war era, fears of Communist-dominated unions contributed to the climate that prompted passage of the Taft-Hartley Act.

Whereas the preamble of the Wagner Act limited the blame for labor disputes obstructing commerce to employers, the Taft-Hartley Act extended the blame to the conduct of unions. The definition of unfair labor practices by employers was tightened, thereby allowing employers to speak more openly in labor controversies. The freedom of unions in the exercise of economic pressure was limited by the designation of six unfair union labor practices. Other major changes consisted of allowing the employees the right to reject organization; the closed shop agreement was outlawed; state right-to-work laws were given precedence over the Taft-Hartley provision for union shops by majority vote of the workers; unions were prohibited for the first time from engaging in secondary strikes; unions could be sued as entities; political contributions and expenditures of unions were restricted; internal union affairs were regulated and reports were required to be filed; no benefits were accorded any labor organization, under the act, unless the union officers filed affidavits showing that they were free from Communist Party affiliation or belief; and the power of "discretionary injunction" was restored to the courts. The act remained unchanged until further union restrictions were enacted in amendments to it, through passage of the Landrum-Griffin Act in 1959.

BIBLIOGRAPHY

A. Cox and D. Bok, *Labor Law, Cases and Materials.*

— DAVID MANDEL AND ALFRED J. PETIT-CLAIR, JR.

TAMMANY HALL

Patterned after the prerevolutionary Sons of Saint Tammany, named for Tamanend, a legendary Delaware chief, the Society of Saint Tammany or Columbian Order was founded in May 1789 by William Mooney as a patriotic, fraternal society with an elaborate Indian ritual. Its members, called "braves," were a familiar sight in the early days of the Republic as, dressed in fanciful Indian costumes and led by their thirteen sachems, they marched in Independence Day and Evacuation Day parades, retiring to their wigwam in the long room of Martling's Tavern to drink toasts to the men and causes they supported. One early sachem stated that the society "united in one patriotic band, the opulent and the industrious, the learned and the unlearned, the dignified servants of the people and the respectable plebeian, however distinguished by name, or sentiment, or by occupation."

Enthusiastically pro-French and anti-British, the Tammany Society became identified with Thomas Jefferson's Democratic-Republican party. Under the leadership of Matthew Davis, Tammany joined ranks with the Aaron Burr faction in New York City, which opposed the faction headed by De Witt Clinton. The Federalist members resigned from the society and Tammany lost all pretense of nonpartisanship. The society prospered, however, and in 1812, boasting some 1,500 members, moved into the first Tammany Hall at the corner of Frankfurt and Nassau streets. In the "labyrinth of wheels within wheels" that characterized New York politics in the early 19th century, Tammany was the essential cog in the city's Democratic wheel, and carried New York for Andrew Jackson and Martin Van Buren in the elections of 1828 and 1832.

The adoption by the state legislature in 1826 of universal white male suffrage and the arrival each year of thousands of immigrants changed the character of New York City and of its politics. Despite some early xenophobia, the Tammany leaders rejected the nativism of the Know-Nothing party, and realizing the usefulness of the newcomers, led them to the polls as soon as they were eligible to vote; in turn, the new voters looked to the local Democratic district leader as a source of jobs and assistance in dealing with the intricacies of the burgeoning city bureaucracy. As the city grew, so did the opportunities for aggrandizement in the form of franchises, contracts, and patronage for Tammany supporters. The venality of the board of aldermen—most of them Tammany men—in the 1850's earned them the title of the Forty Thieves, and it was a rare alderman who did not retire from public service a substantially richer man. Upon the election of Fernando Wood as mayor in 1854, city hall became and remained a Tammany fiefdom—except for the one-term reform administrations of William L. Strong (1894), Seth Low (1901), and John Purroy Mitchell (1913)'until the advent of Fiorello La Guardia in 1933.

With the elevation of William Marcy Tweed, an alumnus of the Forty Thieves, to grand sachem of the Tammany Society in 1863, the fraternal organization was subsumed by the political, and to all but purists the two remained inextricably fused. Under Tweed, Tammany became the prototype of the corrupt city machine, and for a time its power extended to the state capital after Tweed succeeded in electing his own candidate, John Hoffman, governor. The corruption of the Tweed Ring was all pervasive. Tweed and his associates pocketed some $9 million, padding the bills for the construction of the infamous Tweed Courthouse in City Hall Park. The estimated amounts they took in graft, outright theft, real estate mortgages, tax reductions for the rich, and sale of jobs range from $20 million to $200 million. Tweed ended his spectacular career in jail, following an exposé of the ring by the *New York Times* and *Harper's Weekly*, whose famous cartoonist, Thomas Nast, lashed out at the boss week after week, depicting him in prison stripes and Tammany as a rapacious tiger devouring the city. "Honest" John Kelly turned Tammany into an efficient, autocratic organization that for several generations dominated New York City politics from clubhouse to city hall. He spurned the outright thievery of the Tweed Ring, preferring what George Washington Plunkitt called "honest graft."

The venality of the board of aldermen—most of them Tammany men—in the 1850's earned them the title of the Forty Thieves.

Kelly's successor as Tammany leader was Richard Croker, who was somewhat more in the Tweed mold; he took advantage of the smooth-running Kelly machine to indulge his taste for thoroughbred horses, fine wines, and high living. Through a combination of "honest graft," police corruption, and the protection of vice, Croker became a millionaire. In 1898 the consolidation of New York City with the City of Brooklyn and the towns and villages of Queens and Richmond to form Greater New York gave Tammany new opportunities. Croker was forced to resign in 1901 following the revelations of the Lexow investigation of the New York City police department that exposed a network of corruption involving police, judges, saloonkeepers, and the city's underworld. A $300 bribe got a young man a job as a police officer; $2,500 advanced him to sergeant; and $10,000 merited a captaincy, a job with a yearly salary of less than $3,000. Croker initiated the alliance between Tammany and big business, but Charles Francis Murphy, his successor, perfected it. Contractors with Tammany connections built the skyscrapers, the railroad stations, and the docks. A taciturn former saloonkeeper who had been docks commissioner during the administration of Mayor Robert A. Van Wyck, Murphy realized that the old ways were no longer appropriate. He set about developing the so-called New Tammany, which, when it found it was to its advantage, supported social legislation; sponsored a group of bright young men like Alfred E. Smith and Robert Wagner, Sr., for political office; and maintained control of the city by its old methods. Murphy died in 1924 without realizing his dream of seeing one of his young men, Al Smith, nominated for the presidency. Murphy was the last of the powerful Tammany bosses. His successors were men of little vision, whose laxity led to the Seabury investigation of the magistrates courts and of the city government.

In 1932 Mayor James J. Walker was brought up on corruption charges before Gov. Franklin D. Roosevelt but resigned before he was removed from office. In retaliation the Tammany leaders refused to support Roosevelt's bid for the Democratic nomination for president, and tried to prevent Herbert H. Lehman, Roosevelt's choice as his successor, from obtaining the gubernatorial nomination. As a result, the Roosevelt faction funneled federal patronage to New York City through the reform mayor, La Guardia (a nominal Republican). The social legislation of the New Deal helped to lessen the hold of the old-time district leaders on the poor, who now could obtain government assistance as a right instead of a favor. Absorption of most municipal jobs into civil service and adoption of more stringent immigration laws undercut the power base of the city machines. Carmine G. De Sapio briefly revived Tammany Hall in the 1950's, but the day of the old-time boss was over. New York Democratic politics was rife with reformers who were challenging the organization; De Sapio lost control of his Greenwich Village district to reformers in 1961. Shortly thereafter the New York County Democratic Committee dropped the name Tammany; and the Tammany Society, which had been forced for financial reasons to sell the last Tammany Hall on Union Square, faded from the New York scene.

BIBLIOGRAPHY

Alexander B. Callow, Jr., *The Tweed Ring.*

Seymour J. Mandelbaum, *Boss Tweed's New York.*

Warren Moscow, *The Last of the Big Time Bosses: The Life and Times of Carmine De Sapio and the Decline and Fall of Tammany Hall.*

Jerome Mushkat, *Tammany: The Evolution of a Political Machine, 1789–1865.*

M. R. Werner, *Tammany Hall.*

— CATHERINE O'DEA

TARIFF

Tariff, a duty levied on goods coming into the ports of a nation from foreign sources (called a specific duty if levied at so much per article or unit of weight or measure; called ad valorem if levied at so much per dollar value). Tariffs may be essentially either for the purpose of raising revenue or for protecting the domestic economy; that is, a low tax may be levied that discourages importations only a little but brings in money to the treasury for helping maintain the government, or on the other hand, a high tax may block the flow of incoming goods in whole or in part and thus theoretically encourage domestic production. A policy of absolutely unhampered economic intercourse is described as free trade. This practice of levying no duties either on imports or on exports is based on the premise that each politicogeographic unit should produce what it can produce best and most cheaply. Thus without the maintenance of high-cost production and its consequent high prices, consumers, whether they be buyers of finished goods or purchasers of raw materials for processing, theoretically enjoy both quality and cheapness. As a practice and as a philosophy of the national government of the United States, levying import duties was born with the Constitution, while the stipulation was clearly made that exports should not be subject to duties.

The Democratic party, under whatever name it has been designated since the beginning of the nation, has traditionally, though not exclusively, sponsored low tariff rates. As a consequence it was long referred to as a free trade party, a term habitually applied both in Europe and in the United States to all parties and individuals advocating low duties. Sensing the inaccuracy of the term "free trade," the Democrats came eventually in the late 19th century to designate their policy as favoring "tariff for revenue only." Even that was a selective term, for it meant, whether specifically put into words or not, revenue exacted from those most able to pay or from those who bought extravagantly. Salt, sugar, coal, flour, and other essentials of human beings regardless of their incomes were exempted whenever possible. Leather for harness, coarse cloth, cheap dishes, lumber, and similar products used by the poor in their quest of livelihood were taxed lightly on the theory that even if there was no competition, domestic manufacturers might use the rates as an excuse for maintaining high prices. Luxuries, however, might bear heavier levies than protectionists would demand. Whether the rates have been high or low, revenue has been an important aspect of the U.S. tariff. With the exception of two years, 1814–15, during war with England, and a short period in the middle 1830's, when the land boom was at its height, money for the maintenance of the government until 1860 was derived overwhelmingly from the customs dues. From 1868 until the end of the first decade of the 20th century the tariff, thoroughly protectionist, was, except for a half dozen years in the 1890's, still the greatest single contributor of revenue. The two basic premises of the argument of the advocates of low tariff rates were that unrestricted trade in the short run prevented exactions of the many by the few and in the long run promoted a rising standard of living among all the people. In the years after the Civil War many noted intellectuals joined the farmers, workmen, and others in a vigorous attack on the high rates. Before the administration of Woodrow Wilson (1913–20), however, only a few abortive reductions were achieved.

High tariffs were achieved largely through promises of prosperity by political leaders and backed by aggressive and generous manufacturers.

The theory of a protective tariff has origins deep in American history. Colonial experience shaped some of the protectionist thought; and in the early years of the government, especially after the War of 1812, it became obvious that the development of basic domestic industries was necessary if the people wanted to escape the economic-financial subservience of colonial days. Although the first tariff laws were in part dictated by a deep concern with encouraging domestic industries, protection as such did not begin until after 1816, suffered a decline in the 1840's and 1850's, and rose to dominance with the burgeoning industry of the second half of the 19th century. The two primary arguments of the protectionists were; first, that high duties defended infant industries against competition and permitted them to grow into producers for the nation and, second, that high duties benefited the workman by giving him more days of work at higher rates of pay. Prosperity and protection as allies were set forth in bold strokes by Alexander Hamilton in the first years of the nation's history and brilliantly portrayed by Henry Clay in the first half of the 19th century; but it was in the twenty years preceding 1900 that the full dinner pail, the smoking factory chimney, and the happy laborer were forged into a seemingly indestructible industrial montage. There were other arguments. Political, economic, and often patriotic groups declared vehemently for protection of home industries against specific low-cost foreign competition (as, at times, in the case of sugar) even though the cost to consumers was frequently much higher than the gain to the producers. Others demanded tariffs to equalize in general the disadvantages of the United States in competition with the low-cost, low-wage products of the world. And always there was the argument, emphasized again after World War II, that preservation and promotion of strategic industries and arts are essential to national survival.

Whatever the theories advanced, high tariffs were achieved largely through promises of prosperity by eminent political leaders, backed by aggressive and generous manufacturers. Effective, too, was the fact that legislators, whatever their importance, were forced to support bills providing protection of products of other regions in order to obtain privileges demanded by the economic interests of their own constituents. The bitterest criticisms of protection were that industrialists, selling in a closed market, exacted unwarranted profits from consumers; that high tariffs mothered trusts and monopolies; that "infant industries" never grew to maturity; and that the duties were a tax as clearly (as Grover Cleveland put it) as though the tax gatherer called at stated intervals and collected the tolls.

Tariff Commissions

THE REVENUE COMMISSIONS. Section 19 of the Internal Revenue Act of Mar. 3, 1865, authorized the secretary of the Treasury to appoint a commission of three persons to "inquire and report" on how much money should be raised by taxation to meet the needs of the government, the sources from which it should be drawn, and the "best and most efficient mode of raising the same." The commission was neither impartial nor nonpolitical. David A. Wells, scientist, teacher, and author, and recent but ardent convert to protection, was chairman. Stephen Colwell, former lawyer, ironmaker, and active member of the American Iron and Steel Association, was also an easterner and a protectionist. Western agrarian, Democratic, and other minority interests were represented by Samuel S. Hays, comptroller of the city of Chicago. Wells and Colwell were anxiously watched and carefully instructed by Henry C. Carey, Philadelphia's high priest of high tariff.

Colwell became within a short time merely an adviser to the industrialists about how to organize and present their demands. Wells, on the other hand, began to question a policy of protection, especially after the new tariff bill, based in part on his recommendations, was put before the House on June 25, 1866. In July leaders of the hopelessly entangled Congress substituted for the commission the new office of Special Commissioner of the Revenue. Wells, appointed to the position, began the basic preparation for another bill, which he soon found was doomed to failure. Even the commissioner himself was drawn into the welter of confusion that was created by the interplay of selfish interests and was finally beaten into the ranks of the tariff reformers. The office came to an end on June 30, 1870.

TARIFF COMMISSION OF 1882. In December 1881 President Chester A. Arthur, confronted with domestic and foreign economic disturbances and plagued with a Treasury surplus of $100 million, recommended a tariff commission. The Democrats bitterly opposed the measure, not only on the premise that the commission would be protective but also on the assumption that the congressmen were more familiar with the needs of the people than the members of a commission could be. Not a single member of the commission as appointed was an advocate of tariff reform. John L. Hayes, secretary of the Wool Manufacturers' Association, was named chairman. Despite bias the report of the commission as submitted to Congress cited facts to show that some of the high rates were injurious to the interests supposed to be benefited. Reductions in the general tariff were recommended, though sometimes, as the chairman of the commission wrote, as "a concession to public sentiment, a bending of the top and branches to the wind of public opinion to save the trunk of the protective system." No basic changes were made, and the Democrats, when they returned to power in the House in December 1883 let the commission die.

TARIFF BOARD. Sensing the difficulties that might arise in applying reciprocity provisions (limited reciprocity plans had been included in both the McKinley and the Dingley tariffs), the Republicans in the Payne-Aldrich tariff of 1909 authorized the president to employ such persons as might be required in the discharge of his duties. President William Howard Taft, using the loosely worded authority that was his, created in September the Tariff Board, with Henry C. Emery, professor of political economy at Yale, as chairman. The board, in cooperation with the State Department, made studies of discriminatory practices on the part of foreign states and, in addition, investigated American industries in relation to cost of production, duties demanded, and duties already exacted for their benefit. But the board's life was short. The protectionists, already under heavy challenge, feared it was a new threat to their supremacy. The Democrats, suspecting anything Republican as protectionist, refused in 1912 to make appropriations for its continuance.

TARIFF COMMISSION OF 1916. President Wilson in 1916 appointed what is often referred to as the first nonpartisan tariff commission. There was, he said, a world economic revolution and the changes accompanying it were so rapid that congressmen, already overwhelmed by the magnitude of their duties, had neither time nor means for the inquiry necessary to keep them informed. Headed by Frank W. Taussig until 1919, the commission survived despite accusations of partisanship and occasionally of incompetence.

The work of the commission was first used in the preparation of the incongruous Fordney-McCumber tariff of 1922. That legislation not only continued the commission but also increased its powers. The president was authorized—on recommendation of the Tariff Commission—to raise or lower duties by not more than 50 percent of the ad valorem rate on articles that threatened to capture American markets because of a higher cost of production. Although it was obvious that Europe could pay its huge debt to the United States only through the shipments of goods, the Tariff Commission under the Smoot-Hawley tariff continued its cost investigations.

Tariff Powers of the President

Always a potentially significant force in the direction of the tariff despite the jealously guarded rights of the legislators, the president in the 20th century has become a powerful factor both in shaping and in applying the tariff. The authority necessary to carry out the reciprocity provisions of the tariffs of 1890 and 1897 was carefully circumscribed, but in 1909 the president was given rather broad powers in the Payne-Aldrich bill. These powers were further enlarged in 1922, when, in the Fordney-McCumber Tariff Act he was delegated the right, after hearings and a favorable report by the Tariff Commission, to raise or lower established duties by 50 percent without further reference to Congress. Challenged by a New York importer, this action was upheld in *J. W. Hampton, Jr., and Company* v. *United States,* 276 U.S. 394 (1928). The cost equalization formula that, until the early 1930's, underlay the flexible provisions tended to increase the tariff.

The forces that have made tariff a subject of concern to the American people have varied from time to time both in nature and intensity; the purposes for levying duties have been always complex and sometimes uncertain. Generally, the history of the tariff in the nation can be divided into three great periods: from 1789 to 1860, from 1860 through the second quarter of the

20th century, and from the depression years of the 1930's into the post-World War II period.

Tariff of 1789

Controversy over tariff for revenue only and tariff for protection began with the First Congress. A bill of 1789, presented by James Madison as a simple means of raising money, emerged as a partially protective measure. Several states, particularly Massachusetts and Pennsylvania, were able to impose ad valorem duties ranging from 5 percent to 15 percent in defense of leading articles of manufacture in the new nation. Some agricultural products were included also, and specific duties with the obvious intent of promoting home output were levied on certain articles of common use, such as nails and glass.

As early as 1790 Secretary of the Treasury Hamilton had begun to collect information on the condition of and the attitude toward industry in the various states. On Dec. 5, 1791, he submitted his brilliant Report on Manufactures, but his pleas for further protection were ignored. Congress did make many changes by increasing duties on special items and by enlarging the free list of raw materials, but the general level remained much the same.

Tariff of 1816

In less than a fortnight after war was declared by the United States against Britain in 1812, Congress doubled all import duties and levied additional restrictions on all goods brought in in foreign bottoms. An embargo a year later almost destroyed the already crippled commerce. Rehabilitation began immediately after the war. All restrictions (both on tonnage and on goods) based on nationality of vessels were soon repealed—providing, of course, that all foreign discriminations were abolished also. American commerce, less restrained than it had ever been, began to flourish. But the per capita debt of the nation had more than doubled; prices were declining; and England, eager to regain its sales abroad, began dumping its surplus goods onto the markets of the United States for whatever they would bring.

The tariff problem was confused. John C. Calhoun, though warned of the penalties that must fall on agriculture, sponsored high duties in the hope of stimulating cotton manufacturing and cotton sales. Other nationalists, especially in the South and West, hostile toward England and resentful of the nation's dependence on Europe for munitions and military supplies of various kinds, joined the clamor for high rates. But it was the owners of the iron mills and textile plants that had grown up with such astounding rapidity during the war who cried out the loudest. "Infant industries" that had saved the nation deserved, they said, rates high enough to make their continued operation possible, even though they were obviously inefficient. To further complicate the traditional alignment on the tariff question, Daniel Webster spoke out against protection for New England, where the commercial and shipping aristocracy, though weakening, still dominated.

The South was becoming a bitter enemy of a tariff system that seemed to benefit only manufacturers.

The bill that was finally passed in April 1816 marks the beginning of tariff for protection. Cotton and woolen goods and pig iron and hammered and rolled bars were especially favored. Estimates of the general average rate of protection have varied from 30 percent to 45 percent. The argument for higher rates continued. Clay wished to protect the "home market" for the benefit of agrarians and industrialists alike—and the profits derived were to be used for internal improvements. His "American system" envisioned increasing wages for the industrial workers and rising prices for the farmers. The situation, however, was changing. The South was becoming a bitter enemy of a tariff system that seemed to benefit only manufacturers. Deluded by false hopes of quick prosperity that would spread transportation across the Appalachians and bring pounding factories to their section, growers of foodstuffs and also of hemp, flax, and wool in western Pennsylvania, Ohio, Indiana, Illinois, Kentucky, and Missouri joined the middle Atlantic states in an incongruous protectionist alliance and in 1824 passed a new tariff that not only raised the rates of 1816 substantially but also placed duties on such untaxed products as lead, glass, hemp, silk, linens, and cutlery.

"Tariff of Abominations"

The woolen manufacturers especially were dissatisfied with the protection afforded by the tariff of 1824, and the mild recession of 1825 spread discontent. In 1827 the deciding vote of Vice-President Calhoun alone defeated a bill that would have raised the ad valorem duty on the most used woolen cloth to about 70 percent. In that same year delegates from more than half the states, in a meeting at Harrisburg, Pa., spoke out dramatically for general tariff increases. Angry protests arose against what were regarded as unneeded and unwarranted levies, particularly in the South. The tariff issue, in fact, had become not only sectional but partisan as well. Andrew Jackson, smarting from the injustices of the assumed "corrupt bargain" of 1824, was determined to win enough followers to send him to the White House.

His supporters are charged with constructing a tariff in such a way that its anticipated defeat would isolate New England but bring enough support in New York, Pennsylvania, and the West—when joined with the vote of the South—to elect the general. Jackson was not personally involved in the plan, and neither were at least some of the men who pushed the measure through Congress in 1828; but there was some substance to the remark of John Randolph that the bill was concerned only with the manufacture of a president.

Cottons, woolens, iron, hemp, flax, wool, molasses, sailcloth, and whatever else could be protected was protected in the new bill. The tax on raw wool, molasses, and sailcloth, along with many others, irked the New Englanders, but enough of them voted for the measure to pass it. Nobody was pleased; the phrase "tariff of abominations" was bandied about everywhere and in the South became a rallying point for nullificationists.

Compromise Tariff of 1833

The protests of 1828, coupled with the budding Treasury surplus, soon forced the protectionists to desert in part the infant industry doctrine in favor of the pauper-labor argument. Clay, hoping to quell rising criticism, pushed through Congress in 1832 a bill that removed most of the objectionable features of the "abominations" tariff and lowered general duties slightly below those of 1824. But in November 1832 South Carolina declared the act (as well as its predecessor) null and void. Jackson—with much meaningless bluster—took a firm stand. He swore he would collect the revenue; and he asked Congress for a force act authorizing the use of military power in dealing with the situation.

Clay and Calhoun worked out a compromise plan to give seeming victory to all involved. By skillful congressional manipulation they both revised the tariff and passed the force bill on the same day—Mar. 1, 1833. To please the South they enlarged the free list and stipulated that all rates above 20 percent should be lowered to that level by June 30, 1842. To placate the protectionists they provided for gradual reduction of one-tenth every two years until 1840 (the remaining six-tenths was to be removed in the last six months). The compromise tariff was replaced shortly after it expired by a hurriedly prepared measure that reversed temporarily the downward trend of duties. But because financial and business conditions had improved, the trend turned downward again in the Walker Act of 1846, and further reductions were made in 1857.

Morrill Tariffs

The first of the Morrill tariffs, enacted Mar. 2, 1861, was precipitated by the panic of 1857, which drastically affected federal revenue. Succeeding acts in 1862, and 1865 raised the rates to undreamed-of heights. Revenue was not completely forgotten, but the need to assuage American manufacturers upon whose products heavy internal revenue taxes had been levied was far more important. The end of the Civil War and a growing Treasury surplus soon brought repeal of most of the internal revenue levies except for those on such items as liquors and tobacco. The Morrill tariffs, however, remained basically undisturbed until 1890, when they were raised. Although some modest efforts at tariff reductions began soon after the war, the moderate proposals of 1866, 1867, 1872, 1875, 1883, and other years brought no real changes.

The Democrats won the speakership of the House of Representatives in 1875 (and held it with the exception of one term, 1881–83, until 1889), but it was not until December 1883 that the southern and border states tariff-revisionist wing of the party—with the help of midwestern farmers—stripped Samuel J. Randall of Pennsylvania, Democrat and staunch friend of industry, of his power and elected John G. Carlisle of Kentucky to the speakership. Early in 1884 William R. Morrison introduced a bill to reduce the tariffs by a horizontal 20 percent, with no rates lower than those of the Morrill Act of 1861. But Randall and his forty protectionist followers representing Ohio wool growers, Louisiana sugar producers, and a handful of other small interests in the House defeated the measure. The election of President Cleveland in 1884 brought no immediate help. A depression had strengthened the protectionists, the silver issue had disturbed the political situation, and, despite remarks that "The Old Hose Won't Work" any more (bloody shirt issue in putting out the tariff reform fire), the Democratic party—to the profit of the industrialists—still lay faintly in the shadow of the political charges of treason. Moreover, Carlisle was too theoretically democratic to be ruthless; Cleveland was too adamant to be politic; and the Democrats were too divided to use their power effectively.

President Cleveland, after the Morrison bills had failed again in 1885 and 1886, decided to make the tariff alone the subject of his message to Congress in December 1887. In July the next year a very real reform tariff prepared by Rep. Roger Q. Mills was passed in the House with only four Democratic votes in opposition. Randall had lost his power, and the decision on protection was left to the Republican Senate.

McKinley Tariff of 1890

The Republicans chose to regard the election of Benjamin Harrison to the presidency in 1888 as a mandate for higher tariffs. Rep. William McKinley's bill, pushed by sheer ruthlessness through the House by Speaker Thomas B. Reed, was reshaped in the Senate. That body, in fact, was for the next nineteen years the major force in tariff legislation. Taxes on tobacco and alcohol were reduced, but the tariff duties were raised appreciably, with protection as the primary purpose. Bounties were given sugar growers, and for the first time a reciprocity provision was included.

Wilson-Gorman Tariff of 1894

Since they had won the House in the fall elections of 1890 and the presidency and the Senate two years later, success seemed within reach of the tariff-reform Democrats, but the golden hopes of reductions soon faded. The Harrison administration had stripped the Treasury of its surplus, a paralyzing panic fell on the country in April, and Cleveland split his party into bitter factions by his determined repeal of the Sherman Silver Purchase Act in a special session of Congress in the late summer of 1893. The bill that William L. Wilson introduced in the House early in 1894 fell in the Senate into the hands of Arthur P. Gorman of Maryland, a protectionist Democrat, and was completely re-shaped; 634 amendments were added by various interests. The House majority made a dramatic stand, but the Senate had its way, and Cleveland, having declared that "party perfidy and party dishonor" had been involved in its making, let the Wilson-Gorman bill become a law without his signature.

Dingley and Payne-Aldrich Tariffs

After victory in the campaign of 1896, the Republicans turned not to gold but to the tariff, and, despite swelling opposition to protection even within their own party, maintained for more than a decade the highest duties in American history up to that time. It took just thirteen days to push through the House the bill that Nelson W. Dingley introduced in March 1897. After 872 amendments and two months of argument in the Senate, the bill emerged from Congress with the highest duties ever passed. But with growing opposition from the intellectuals and increasing protests from the people and their liberal representatives, tariff was becoming politically dangerous. President Theodore Roosevelt chose to avoid the issue altogether. By 1908, however, pressure for reduction had become so great that even the Republican party seemed in its platform to promise downward revision.

The moderate House bill that Sereno E. Payne submitted early in 1909 was quickly passed. Nelson W. Aldrich reshaped it in the Senate; a total of 847 amendments were made, almost wholly in the interest of higher duties. Despite some concessions to President Taft and brilliant opposition by the Republican insurgents, the tariff remained protectionist, and Taft ineptly praised the measure as the best ever passed.

Underwood Tariff of 1913

In tariff philosophy President Wilson represented not only the majority of his party but also the thought of the intellectuals, who had long been questioning the prevailing protectionist practice of the nation. Comprehending in part at least the currents of change that were sweeping the nation into the world, he turned his knowledge of theoretical and practical politics to the task of reshaping domestic policy in many fields. Soon after Rep. Oscar W. Underwood of Alabama revealed his tariff proposals to the special Congress in 1913, the long-familiar lobbyists, a significant force in tariff legislation, flocked into Washington. The president struck out in a biting condemnation and the "third house" departed. Approved by the Senate with few changes, the measure became effective in October, providing the first real and consistent reductions since the tariffs of 1846 and 1857. The free list was greatly enlarged, 958 rates were reduced, 307 were left unchanged, and fewer than a hundred were increased. Rates averaged roughly 26 percent; some had not been lower since the first tariff.

In tariff philosophy President Wilson represented not only the majority of his party but also the thought of the intellectuals, who questioned prevailing protectionist practices.

Unfortunately the low duties never had a chance to prove themselves because of the start of World War I. The conflict with Germany and its satellites, when the United States joined the Allies, brought not only increasing prices but also new producing plants, hurriedly and expensively built. The inevitable cry against foreign competition was certain to come up when war's end brought reconversion to peacetime needs with its accompanying costly production and its shrinking days of work, declining wages, and lessening demand for agricultural and other extractive products. New industries were also to fight for benefits.

Fordney-McCumber and Smoot-Hawley Tariffs

Pulling the nation out of its economic difficulties by increasing protection in the dozen critical years after World War I was attempted by an emergency tariff of 1921, which was designed to soothe the discontented farmers and check some beginning imports from Europe. But it was the bill introduced in the House by Joseph W. Fordney the next year and taken up in the Senate by Porter J. McCumber that sought to withdraw the nation from the economic world as others were attempting to isolate it from the political world. Equalization in an exaggerated form in part determined the details, and nationalistic ambitions gave it spirit. The farmers were again promised impossible prosperity by the levying of duties on products already in overabundance at home. The rates in general were the highest in American history, and a flexible provision by which the president could revise rates up or down by 50 percent ensured maintenance of the equal-cost-of-production principle. Conditions did not improve materially, and the only answer politics had to offer was more protection. The rates of the Smoot-Hawley Act of June 1930 set a new record in restrictive legislation and brought much-deserved criticism. More than a thousand members of the American Economic Association petitioned President Herbert Hoover to veto the bill. Other economic and financial organizations, as well as individuals, joined the rising protest that spread over the world. European nations not only spoke out boldly but also passed retaliatory laws. The depression grew worse, war-debt payments from Europe ceased, and, as a result of a combination of circumstances, world economy ground to a standstill.

Tariffs by Reciprocity Agreements

Sen. Cordell Hull of Tennessee was among the few men in Congress during the depression who insisted that national prosperity depended on freeing the commerce of the world rather than on restricting it. He became secretary of state in the administration of President Franklin D. Roosevelt and in 1934, by authority of the Reciprocal Trade Agreements Act of that year, inaugurated a series of executive agreements with foreign nations by which he in part freed trade not only for the United States but, also, by applying the most-favored-nation clause principle, for other nations as well. But there was little time for rehabilitation. World War II, with its appalling destruction, soon swept over Europe and Asia. Old nations and new were plagued by poverty. They needed everything but had no money with which to buy, and the United States, surfeited with goods, real and potential, had no place to sell. A profound change was beginning in world economy. International interdependence, particularly in trade, was becoming clear even to the most nationalistic. In the United States it was obvious also that Europe, the major prewar market of the United States, must be restored. Thus the Marshall Plan, the Point Four program, and various other governmental and private restorative measures were instituted. Money was poured into Europe to rebuild the devastated industrial plants and restore the ravished farms. Military forces were established to protect the struggling nations, and the money necessary to support them joined other money in putting Europeans back to work.

Everywhere trade practices underwent radical changes as the economic structure was rebuilt. In the United States tariff had already ceased to be a strictly domestic and almost wholly political issue. Foreign considerations had become a major factor in the formulation of tariff policy: tariff making was losing its purely national aspects (dominated by Congress) and was becoming an international problem centered primarily around the president and his executive and diplomatic agents (the State Department was soon to be denied any substantial part in tariff making decisions). Bolstered by liberal philosophers and by economists in the tradition of Adam Smith, the conviction that trade could flourish only when it was free was slowly finding acceptance among governments.

The tragic postwar economic situation that so drastically changed world thinking concerning trade brought many reform efforts. It was obvious that a free world economy required an international mechanism for payments. Even before the war had ended a conference at Bretton Woods in New Hampshire in the summer of 1944 set up the basic machinery for a world monetary system. The two significant units were the International Monetary Fund (IMF) and the International Bank for Reconstruction—known simply as the World Bank. Labeled a failure by many individuals and groups, the two have served their purposes as a beginning experiment. But burdened with an impossible gold redemption task that the United States had unsuccessfully attempted in the 1890's, pulled in diverse and often contradictory directions by academic specialists, faced by an overvalued dollar that was impossible to change except multilaterally, and hampered by nationalistic jealousies and political resentments, these two organs became the chief centers around which gathered the disenchanted in the late 1960's to discredit the philosophy of free trade in the world.

Economic restoration after World War II rested heavily on American money and on international reform in tariff duties. The General Agreement on Tariffs and Trade (GATT), formulated by many nations in Geneva in 1947 and devoted in large part to the reduction of tariffs and the abolition of trade discriminations, was firmly established by January 1948. The United States, largely ignoring the International Trade Organization (ITO), actively participated in the work of GATT from the beginning. Although tariff reform in the nation was still governed by the Trade Agreements Act of 1934 and its many extensions (eleven by 1958), significant reductions in U.S. duties were made in the immediate postwar years, incorporating the established principle that the president had the power to raise or lower rates, within limits, without reference to Congress. Conscious of the fact that rate reductions bring inevitable economic impositions, real or assumed, the tariff reformers provided protective safeguards against injuries to industries through "peril point" judgments and "escape clause" decisions. A peril point judgment was the rate of duty determined through study by the Tariff Commission, before negotiations were entered into, which the commission judged to be the minimum that would not injure the particular industry involved. If the president disregarded the judgment, he was required to explain his reasons to Congress. Escape clause decisions provided for relief from injuries after rate reductions had been agreed on. The president, the Congress, the Tariff Commission itself, or any interested party could invoke the escape clause on the assumption that the existing duties were imposing economic hardships on an industry or industries. The commission was required to study each complaint and recommend a course of action. The president might or might not follow the commission's recommendations, although by later amendment any rejection could be reversed by a two-thirds vote of the Congress. Despite the reluctance of the lawmakers to share their power, much had been accomplished in economic legislation by the end of the 1940's, and the tariff rates had been reduced for the most part to the levels of the Wilson administration.

In 1957 France, Belgium, West Germany (German Federal Republic), Luxembourg, Italy, and the Netherlands joined together in the European Economic Community (EEC, most often referred to as the Common Market). Great Britain, Sweden, Norway, Denmark, Austria, Switzerland, and Portugal (Finland became an associate member in 1961) formed the European Free Trade Association (EFTA) three years later. Although these memberships later shifted and similar-minded organizations were formed in South America and elsewhere, it was clear by the beginning of the 1960's that a world revolution in economic action and thought had attained a commanding stature if not maturity. The European organizations and the United States were in themselves a loose common unit that soon came to be referred to as the Atlantic Community.

1960–72

Although a rising undercurrent of bitterness was everywhere apparent in the economic relations of the somewhat united free world, the 1960's opened on an expanding economy. The Democrats, traditional liberals in trade regulations, had won the presidency under John F. Kennedy in the November elections in 1960; and already ministers were preparing for a session in Geneva to set up ground rules for the coming meeting of GATT, called "rounds" in the parlance of the new trade world. But the last extension of the Reciprocal Trade Agreements Act of 1934 was to expire in June 1962, and a new law was needed if the dream of the reformers was to be achieved.

On Jan. 25, 1962, Kennedy set forth the existing complexities in a message to Congress. There were three basic areas on which he dwelt: the economic realities and possibilities of the new Atlantic Community, which might even reach out to the developing countries; the gains to be had by unchaining international commerce from the protective tariffs, quotas, and other restrictions by which it was bound; and the political imperatives involved in creating and preserving a powerful and prosperous free world. Common economic growth was the key factor involved, he said, but economic growth depended on a relatively free exchange of goods, and a free exchange of goods depended in turn on agreements reached through orderly and accepted cooperative action on the part of the participating nations.

In the legislation he proposed, Kennedy sought power not only to make tariff revisions at home but also to bargain with authority abroad, either within GATT or individually. He advocated an "open partnership" in which all free nations, and the developing countries as well, could share by opening their markets freely. Kennedy argued that the United States had nothing to lose in pressing for open markets at home and abroad; it could lose, he emphasized, only if the Common Market, for example, should throw up a tariff wall that halted the flow of American goods. The two great Atlantic economic units would, he said, "either grow together or . . . apart." Foreign imports, he argued, could do little damage to the United States because of its tremendous industrial potential; cheap labor, he added, would always be smothered by the greater American productivity per man hour.

President Kennedy advocated an "open partnership" in which all free nations could share by opening their markets freely.

A bill, made up of permissions and prohibitions, was enacted as the Trade Expansion Act in late summer

1962. The president was authorized to take various actions designed to stimulate economic growth at home, promote trade and peaceful relations abroad, and prevent Communist penetration of the free world or the markets of its potential friends, mostly the developing nations. He was also given permission to make across-the-board tariff cuts of 50 percent or more on a most-favored-nation basis, to include agricultural items in the negotiations, and to reduce tariff levies up to 100 percent on a few items. Tariffs of 5 percent or less, mostly in deference to Canadian trade, could be entirely eliminated, as could the duties on certain tropical products. The chief executive was required, however, to insert certain terminal dates on all items negotiated, consult the Tariff Commission and the departments concerned, and withhold most-favored-nation status from any country dominated by communism (later relaxed in the case of Poland and Yugoslavia). He was directed also to reserve any article from negotiation that was protected by action under the escape clause and any products included in the act's national security amendment, as, for instance, petroleum.

Early in 1963 the free world began preparations for an international conference under the auspices of GATT in the hope of lowering tariff and other barriers throughout the Atlantic Community, but there were difficulties. President Charles de Gaulle of France had in January vetoed England's entrance into the Common Market. Moreover, several European leaders were not enthusiastic about Kennedy's Trade Expansion Act; and some Americans thought it a good time to have a general showdown. The free-world monetary system was under attack; America's balance-of-payments deficit was causing alarm; and American capital was pouring out to Europe to build industrial plants, which provoked both European resentments and American criticisms.

The general meeting of GATT, called the Kennedy Round, convened at Geneva on May 16, 1964. Present were more than 600 delegates from eighty-two countries. Christian A. Herter, armed with fifty-five volumes of hearings—including the Tariff Commission's advice—led the American delegation. Common understanding was lacking: it was, for instance, utterly impossible to give a uniform classification to the multitude of products from the various nations assembled. The largely English-speaking group at the conference—dominated by the United States—found itself for the first time in tariff history faced by an equally powerful European bargaining group, the representatives of the Common Market. Directed chiefly by De Gaulle, these leaders, it seemed, were as much interested in demonstrating their might as they were in developing a workable economic system. De Gaulle and his followers were convinced that such existing institutions as the IMF and GATT were creatures of England and the United States and were more concerned with new creations, especially in the monetary field, than with mere modifications. The third group at the conference represented the developing countries, nations scattered over Asia, Africa, and Latin America. Some of them, no older than the war that had directed the forces drawing the delegates to Geneva, were painfully poor. Their leaders were convinced that all existing economic organizations had been created to aid the developed countries and hinder the developing countries—and they forewarned the powerful in the group of their future potential. In the meantime, they lodged their hopes in the United Nations.

Because the old method of settling rates item by item had become virtually impossible, the United States at the opening of the meeting immediately proposed a 50 percent linear reduction across-the-board on a most-favored-nation basis. Opposition arose immediately. The argument was that European tariffs were much lower in general than those of the United States and that, even with a 50 percent reduction, American rates would still remain much higher. The Common Market delegates, led by France, submitted an *écrêtement*, or harmonization plan, to lower tariffs halfway from their existing levels to a fixed target level—10 percent for manufactures, 5 percent for semimanufactures, and zero for raw materials. The linear proposal eventually won out, but there was much controversy over equalizing the cuts in cases of wide differences in rates. In order to avoid petty negotiations, it was stipulated that the higher rate must be double the lower rate and that the higher rate must exceed the lower by 10 percentage points; in such cases reductions were limited to 25 percent.

Changing production patterns and shifting consumption habits had created problems in the agricultural areas and the American delegation offered few concessions. The developing countries, which concentrated on the production of tropical fruits, further complicated the agricultural problem; special industries, such as textiles in Taiwan, Hong Kong, South Korea, and other countries, evoked protests against cheap labor. Non-tariff restrictions, especially if they nullified a tariff agreement, stirred bitter dissensions—they could, in fact, destroy the hopes of the meeting. There were also protests against the American Selling Plan (ASP), which used domestic prices for determining tariff rates in the benzenoid chemical and two other minor fields. Agreements were arrived at with difficulty. One delaying factor was that many countries were reluctant to accept proposals in one area while other areas were still being negotiated. There was no generally accepted body of statistics on which to base judgments, and there was no absolute means of identification of goods, for similar names did not always mean similar goods.

For nearly four years the GATT delegates argued over reducing international tariff barriers equitably. The United States feared that high support prices, variable import levels, and export subsidies might eliminate old markets in Europe for its agricultural products. (There were reasons to believe that a general loss in sales might result even if there were no nontariff barriers, for the six nations were now surrounded by a common tariff wall.) On the other hand, France in particular and the Common Market in general cherished the dream of shifting domination of the new free-world economics to Europe.

The achievements of the international meeting were substantial. The United States won its initial argument over the method to be used in reducing rates. The escape clause was appreciably modified as the government for individual plants—not a complete industry—assumed responsibility for training and otherwise aiding workers who had lost their jobs and also for reestablishing the displaced industrialist. Tariff reductions, although disappointing in many ways, were, in view of the enormity of the opposing factors, indeed remarkable. The average rate arrived at was slightly more than 35 percent; 66 percent of the imports of the industrialized countries—except meat, cereal, and dairy products—were either freed of duty or subject to 50 percent or more reduction. On the other hand little was done concerning tariffs on such items as iron and steel, textiles, clothing, and fuel. Although the United States made some concessions, the developing countries benefited only slightly. Most nations were disappointed, but the agreement was signed on Jan. 30, 1967.

While the delegates from the United States were urging free international trade at Geneva, many factory owners and factory workers at home were pressing hard for a return to a protective tariff. Americans generally were angered by European grumbling about NATO, the IMF, and the ASP; and their anger was heightened when European leaders—such as Chancellor Willy Brandt of West Germany—spoke from their prospering nations to say that although American sacrifices were appreciated, they were, after all, for the good of the United States. The European countries were working together; Canada refused to join any group; the countries of the New World (Mexico, Central America, and South America) were in the developing stage; and it appeared the United States might be standing alone. In addition the balance of trade had swung heavily against the United States in the late 1950's for several reasons: tourist expenditures abroad increased; Japan began to challenge the great export nations of the world; steel from formerly noncompetitive mills began to compete with U.S. markets; automobiles and textiles in particular, as well as other products, began to set records in American sales; and the balance of payments deficit, spurred by the high prices that inflation and the overvalued dollar had created, brought disruptions in the free-world monetary system that rested heavily on the American dollar and the American gold reserve.

While the U.S. delegates in Geneva urged free international trade, many factory owners and workers at home were pressing hard for a return to a protective tariff.

Academic arguments that the world could not live unless its goods were freely exchanged did little to check the rising resentments that by late 1968 had prompted the introduction of 717 bills in Congress to impose quotas on imports and the exertion of many legislative efforts in the states to require American-made products in public construction projects. The difficulty was that the advocates of free trade were talking about long-time gains, whereas farmers, industrialists, and laborers were thinking of short-time losses. In the quarrel between the United States and the Common Market, equality in trade was in some degree maintained by a give-and-take bargaining that has been called tit-for-tat exchanges, and in the monetary area by *ad hoc* agreements.

By 1970 the protectionist movement had achieved its greatest intensity since the days of the Great Depression. Industrialists were thoroughly convinced that the escape clause as modified in the 1962 Trade Expansion Act was no friend of the manufacturers and that the Tariff Commission and other agencies concerned were interested only in economic philosophy. There was not a single favorable finding under the law from 1962 to 1969; and the outward flow of American capital furthered the protectionist movement.

After coming into office in January 1969, President Richard M. Nixon reduced American commitments in Vietnam, but he had only limited success in stopping inflation and reducing unemployment. Congress, urged by many groups at home and irked by French and Japanese protective actions abroad, was by late 1970 pushing hard toward restrictive legislation. On June 29, 1971, the cry went up, "Stop the flow of imports!"

"Save American Jobs!" as a thousand members of the International Union of Electrical, Radio, and Machine Workers marched down Constitution Avenue in Washington, D.C., and on to Capitol Hill to take their message to the lawmakers. The message was a familiar one, and it fell on sympathetic ears in Congress. The Burke-Hartke Act, which provided that the nation should, in effect, return to the tariff rates of the Smoot-Hawley law of 1930, was passed.

On Aug. 15, 1971, Nixon, in an effort to reduce unemployment, slow inflation, better the monetary situation, and improve the balance-of-payments deficit, froze wages, prices, and rents for a period of ninety days and recommended to Congress a limited but aggressive action that included a buy-American policy for capital goods. In international trade he suspended dollar redemptions in gold and imposed a 10 percent surtax on dutiable imports. The surtax, soon removed, had no appreciable effect on the amount of goods coming into American ports, but the "Nixon Shock," despite some fears to the contrary, did tend to stabilize the critical monetary situation. At the same time foreign reaction to the Burke-Hartke Act was quick and uncompromising. Some European countries placed immediate restrictions on American goods; and in November at a meeting of 102 nations on Ibiza, a small Spanish island off the east coast of Spain, a common and biting retaliation was agreed on. An escalation clause provided for progressively harsher penalties as the time of enforcement of the offending law lengthened. Pressure for repeal of the Burke-Hartke Act soon appeared in the United States, and was backed by many groups, including labor. On Dec. 24, 1971, Congress repealed the act. At the beginning of 1972 world leaders—and particularly Secretary of State William P. Rogers—were speaking out for freer international trade, although self-interest and resentments were all too obvious.

On July 16, 1972, sixteen nations met in Brussels to draw up plans for the formation of the largest economic unit in the free world. The six nations of the Common Market were to be joined on Jan. 1, 1973, by Great Britain, Denmark, Norway, and Ireland; the admission of Sweden, Switzerland, Austria, Finland, Iceland, and Portugal to limited membership was to make up the sixteen-nation unit. (Nine of the sixteen had been members of EFTA.) The many problems to be resolved included common tariffs, internal harmonizations, and the old problem of ultimate destination. Moreover, it was necessary to set forth clearly rules of origin. When it appeared that the new trade group might foster further restrictions, the United States objected vigorously, and controversies stirred further resentments among the Europeans, already quarreling among themselves. Unity, it seemed to some, was falling apart. Norway, with only 0.5 percent unemployment and one of the highest standards of living in the world, feared that its economic welfare was being threatened and voted 53.6 percent against joining the new Common Market. Inflation, sweeping over Europe and Japan, further threatened unity. Gold, with a two-tier price, was being bid higher in Europe by speculators as it grew scarcer in the United States. George P. Schultz, secretary of the Treasury, proposed on Sept. 26, 1972, at a meeting of the IMF several pointed reforms to be made in the monetary system; though approved, they brought no immediate action.

Even some of the leaders of the movement to liberate world commerce had faltered. In midsummer Karl Schiller, West Germany's economic and finance minister and perhaps Europe's staunchest defender of free trade, resigned. In the United States, Rep. Wilbur D. Mills, chairman of the powerful House Ways and Means Committee, wavering in his long-time devotion to free trade, declared that he would support higher tariffs and import quotas unless "some other countries mended their ways."

Troubles fell thick and fast on the nation during 1973–75, and international trade continued to stir up controversy. The dollar, devalued for the second time in February 1973, was further deteriorated by the subsequent currency float; and at the end of the year a gasoline shortage developed, following the oil embargo by the Arab nations in October. The economic situation worsened in 1974, and by midyear the nation was in a deep recession. Unemployment continued to increase, surpluses continued to pile up, and prices continued to climb upward. Trade regulations lost some of their immediacy, but in 1976 the principle of a relatively free international commerce remained a fundamental necessity in the minds of the leaders of the concerned nations.

BIBLIOGRAPHY

Robert E. Baldwin, *Nontariff Distortions of International Trade.*

Robert E. Baldwin and others, *Trade Growth and the Balance of Payments.*

James A. Barnes, *John G. Carlisle: Financial Statesman.*

William Beveridge, *Tariffs: The Case Examined.*

Kenneth W. Dam, *The GATT: Law and International Economic Organization.*

Herbert R. Ferleger, *David A. Wells and the American Revenue System.*

J. Frank Gaston, *Border Taxes and International Economic Competition.*

Harry Gordon Johnson, *Aspects of the Theory of Tariffs.*

Kenneth C. Mackenzie, *Tariff Making and Trade Policy in the United States and Canada.*

Allan Nevins, *Grover Cleveland: A Study in Courage.*

Howard Samuel Piquet, *The United States Trade Expansion Act of 1962.*
Ernest H. Preeg, *Traders and Diplomats: An Analysis of the Kennedy Round.*
William A. Robinson, *Thomas B. Reed: Parliamentarian.*
Frank W. Taussig, *The Tariff History of the United States.*

— JAMES A. BARNES

TAXATION

Taxation is the imposition, by a national government or by a government of one or more of its subdivisions, of compulsory contributions on the subjects of a government for meeting all or part of the expenditures of that government. The taxes imposed during the course of American history have changed as the original group of agricultural-mercantile colonies has evolved into an industrial, urban world power. The American tax system has reflected modifications in the ownership and control of property and business enterprise and has responded to the rise of a government bureaucracy, capable of improving economic records, tax-appraisal valuations, and collection techniques. The clash of different economic groups over what the goals of government expenditures should be and the proper means of raising revenue accounts for much of the specific tax legislation proposed and enacted over the years. Some influence on tax policy has come from statesmen, reformers, and fiscal experts who placed the national welfare, as they saw it, above narrow partisan politics. The advancement of social welfare through wise governmental fiscal policy in peace and war justifies the dictum of Justice Oliver Wendell Holmes: "Taxes are the price we pay for civilization."

Colonial Period

Throughout the 17th century and the first few decades of the 18th century, the government expenditures of the colonies were relatively simple and limited; both colonial taxations and the customs duties imposed by the British trade and navigation laws in that period were light. The taxing systems of the colonies varied according to the economic and political conditions in the three main sections of the country. The New England colonies favored a poll (capitation or head) tax; a tax on the gross produce of the land, which was finally developed into a general property tax; and a faculty tax (an arbitrary tax on the assumed income or earnings of laborers, artisans, and tradesmen). The southern colonies, dominated by large landowners, preferred import and export duties, supplemented at times by the poll tax. The middle Atlantic colonies evolved a mixed system of import duties, excises on beverages, and property taxes. All the colonies resorted at one time or another to import and export duties for revenue purposes. The colonies, notably in New England, used an indirect form of taxation or forced loan from their people whenever they issued paper money that depreciated greatly in value. Although Parliament prohibited the further issuance of legal tender bills of credit in 1751 in New England and in 1764 in all the other colonies, as late as 1774 some $12 million in such paper money was estimated to be in current use. In all the proprietary colonies, except New Netherland, quitrents (very light annual feudal payments on all grants of land) were imposed, but widespread resistance by the colonists brought very little revenue except in Maryland, Virginia, and Pennsylvania.

The local colonial governments maintained themselves by fees, fines, and compulsory contributions of services; by voluntary monetary contributions early in colonial history; and by taxes on real and personal property throughout the rest of the colonial period. The poll tax was a tax levied on all persons, generally adult males, in a community, free or slave, without any regard for the size of the income or property of the person upon whom the tax was based. Although the poll tax was usually low, it bore most heavily on low-income groups, except in the case of slaveowners, especially in wartime. The poll tax was utilized in all the colonies, particularly in the South during the 17th century. The local governments of Virginia, North Carolina, and Maryland relied greatly on poll taxes to meet their needs. Payment was frequently made in produce, for example, tobacco.

Until the end of the French and Indian War in 1763, England never attempted to collect much revenue from the colonies.

The property tax developed in the 17th century in New England and then spread to the middle colonies. It never took root in the southern colonies, although it was used for a few years during the fiscal crises of war. Property in New England was originally supplementary to the poll and faculty taxes as a tax base. Property taxes were frequently imposed only on selected types of real and personal property, especially land, houses, livestock, ships, and mills. Often these types of property were taxed according to rather arbitrary schedules of statutory values, with different rates applicable to different types of property. Both the colonial and local governments in New England and the middle colonies used these property taxes as important sources of revenue, but the southern ruling groups resisted the use of such taxes until the American Revolution.

Until the end of the French and Indian War in 1763, England never attempted to collect much revenue from the colonies. The small amount collected was used chiefly to regulate trade according to the Navigation Acts, beginning in 1660. In 1765 Parliament passed the historic Stamp Act, which, contrary to precedent, was an internal tax imposed from without. The resentment against this tax, and against the 1764 sugar tax, was intensified by the economic depression following the 1763 peace treaty with France and led the colonists to oppose all forms of taxation by England on the new principle of "no taxation without representation." Although the Stamp Act was repealed the next year, Parliament in 1767 revived its tax policy and imposed import duties on certain commodities through the Townshend Acts. A strong colonial nonimportation movement caused Parliament in 1770 to repeal all these duties, except that on tea. The reconciliation with the colonists lasted two years; it ended with the Boston Tea Party in 1773, Parliament's Coercive Acts in 1774, and the battles of Lexington and Concord in 1775.

Revolution and Confederation Period

The organization and support of the revolutionary militia were sustained at first by the various colonies, which obtained the requisite funds out of the established revenue sources and the issuance of paper money. In 1775 the Continental Congress authorized an army and navy, a committee for foreign affairs, the supervision of the frontier Indians, and the administration of the post office. Revenue was needed for these activities. Although heavy war taxes might have been desirable, the colonies had not granted to the Continental Congress the power to levy taxes. The Congress assumed the power to contract debts, but it could only apportion the sums that it needed among the colonies and ask them to remit. These requisitions on the colonies could not be imposed by force by any central authority and were little honored. The total receipts from the colonies, measured in gold, has been estimated at $5.8 million. In 1780 Congress demanded tax payments through specific supplies of food and fodder, but this new system resulted in great waste and inefficiency and proved to be of small value. Consequently, Congress depended for its revenue mainly on the issuance of paper money and on domestic and foreign loans. The colonial or state governments, unlike the Continental Congress, had the power to levy taxes. The New England states, New Jersey, and Maryland used this power during the Revolution to cover their expenses, to retire their own early currency issues, and to raise part of their contributions to the Continental government. New York, Pennsylvania, and the southern states made no attempt to levy direct taxes, but they raised some revenue from indirect taxes and relied generally on their own paper money and loans to meet their needs.

In 1781 the Articles of Confederation went into effect after the Continental Congress had been operating for some years as a revolutionary and extralegal, but *de facto*, coordinating and directing government, national though not centralized. The articles did not confer upon the Congress the right to levy taxes, but they empowered Congress to contract debts and to apportion the sums needed to cover its expenses among the states in proportion to the value of the land, buildings, and improvements thereon within each state. The taxes for paying that proportion were to be "laid and levied by the authority and direction of the legislatures of the several States, within the time agreed upon by the United States, in Congress assembled." Some states attempted to meet the requisitions of Congress, but the majority proved indifferent. In order to obtain funds for current expenditures or payment of interest on the national debt, Congress proposed, first in 1781 and then in 1783, that it be granted power to levy specific customs duties on certain classes of imports. These proposals were blocked, by Rhode Island in the first instance and by New York in the second. Efforts in 1781–82 to secure approval for a Confederation land tax, a poll tax, and a liquor excise were equally fruitless.

1789–1865

The Confederation government never managed to obtain enough revenue from its requisitions to cover its expenditures between 1781 and September 1789 and had to depend on foreign and domestic loans to meet most of its current expenses. Although the achievements of the Confederation are greater than many of its past critics have allowed, there is no doubt that the framers of the new constitution of 1787 strengthened the national government by empowering Congress "To lay and collect Taxes, Duties, Imposts and Excises, to pay the Debts and provide for the common Defence and general Welfare of the United States" (Article i, Section 8). But certain limitations were imposed: all duties, imposts, and excises were to be (geographically) uniform throughout the United States; direct taxes were to be laid in proportion to the population: no duties were to be imposed by Congress on articles exported from any state. On the other hand, no export or import duties were to be imposed by any state without the consent of Congress. Direct taxes were generally understood at that time to be taxes on land and poll taxes—and this interpretation was sanctioned by U.S. Supreme Court decisions from 1796 until 1881. The general welfare clause was capable of a narrow and a broad construction in relation to the spending and taxing powers of Congress, but after a century and a half of debate Alexander Hamilton's interpretation came to prevail against James Madison's more restricted one, and Congress has been deemed the authority fit to decide the proper objects of government spending and the appropriate tax measures needed therefor. Congress was not originally circumscribed in its taxing power by constitutional tax exemptions for the instrumentalities of state government, the salaries of state and federal judges, and the holders of state and municipal offices; these limitations on Congress arose from judicial legislation by the Supreme Court after the Civil War.

The first use by Congress of its tax powers was in the passage of the tariff act of July 4, 1789; from that date until the Civil War the federal government derived its main revenue from its receipts from customs duties on goods imported into the United States, for the American people were by their past political experience hostile to internal taxation. But when the early customs duties failed to produce adequate revenue, Congress established an internal revenue system that has grown from a few excise taxes on distilled spirits, carriages, and other commodities or transactions to personal and corporate income taxes, estate and gift taxes, railroad compensation taxes, social security taxes, and excess profits taxes. In addition to receipts from these taxes, the national government has received income from such other sources as the sale of public lands, surplus postal receipts, the proceeds of government-owned securities, Panama Canal tolls, proceeds from the sale of surplus property, and seigniorage. From 1791 to 1802 Congress experimented with excise taxes on all distilled spirits (1791); on carriages, the sale of certain liquors, snuff manufacture, sugar refining, and auction sales (1794); and with stamp duties on legal transactions, including a duty on receipts for legacies and probates of wills—the first step in the development of the federal inheritance tax (1797). The first direct tax was imposed in 1798 on all dwelling houses, lands, and slaves between twelve and fifty. Congress set the specific sum to be collected and then apportioned it among the states according to the size of each state's population.

The unpopularity of the 1791 tax led to the Whiskey Rebellion in 1794 and was a major factor in the 1802 abolition of the Federalist system of excise duties and direct taxes, with the exception of the salt tax (eliminated in 1807). For revenue President Thomas Jefferson relied on customs receipts, land sales, and the postal services. The War of 1812 forced Congress to adopt new internal taxes: direct taxes on houses, lands, and slaves were enacted in 1813, 1815, and 1816 for some $12 million and apportioned among the states on the basis of the 1810 census. Congress also enacted duties on liquor licenses, auction sales, carriages, refined sugar, distilled spirits, and certain other articles. But these duties and the direct taxes were repealed late in 1817 in response to popular pressure. If the war had not ended in 1815, Congress might have adopted the inheritance tax and income tax recommended early that year by Alexander J. Dallas, President Madison's secretary of the Treasury. From 1817 until the outbreak of the Civil War, the national government made no use of excise, stamp, income, inheritance, or direct property taxes. Government expenses were met principally from customs duties, supplemented by the income from the sale of public lands. When the revenues were inadequate for brief periods, the Treasury secured temporary loans and thus avoided new internal taxes, even during the war with Mexico. Between 1817 and 1857 it was necessary fourteen times to issue Treasury notes or to raise loans, but the revenues in the following years restored the balance in favor of the government.

From 1817 until the outbreak of the Civil War in 1861, the federal government made no use of excise, stamp, income, inheritance, or direct property taxes.

The panic of 1857, the consequent drop in national income, and the failure to tap new tax resources resulted in a series of Treasury deficits that were increased by the secession of southern states and the outbreak of the Civil War. Salmon P. Chase, secretary of the Treasury, feared to impose heavy taxation and wished to rely mainly on the sale of government bonds, tariff increases, and the proceeds from the sale of public lands. But the public and Congress proved to be wiser than he and backed the introduction of a massive internal tax program. Congress passed a series of internal revenue bills between 1861 and 1865 that revived the direct tax, introduced the first national income tax and genuine national inheritance tax, and restored such old excise taxes as those on spirituous and malt liquors, tobacco, and carriages. It also developed an immense number of new excise taxes, on manufactured goods (especially luxuries); the gross receipts of transportation and insurance companies; the circulation, deposits, and capital of banks; stamps on legal documents and instruments of evidence; and licenses for carrying on certain trades, professions, and businesses. The Civil War income tax laws granted exemptions first to those with income under $800, then under $600. The principle of progressive income taxation was embodied in both the 1862 and 1864 internal revenue acts, as was the important administrative device of tapping revenue at the source. No exemption was given to income derived from state instrumentalities until the U.S. Supreme Court ruled in *Collector* v. *Day* (1871) that Congress could not tax the instrumentalities of state government, including the salary of a state judge. (This doctrine was later extended in 1895 in *Pollock* v. *Farmers' Loan and Trust Company* to exempt the holders of state and municipal bonds from paying national income taxes on income from such securities.) Although the Confederate States of America failed to establish an independent southern nation, their tax system deserves some brief mention. Jefferson Davis' successive secretaries of the treasury, Christopher G. Memminger and George A. Trenholm, had an impossible task. But they persuaded their congress to pass a direct tax; an income tax; a property tax on naval stores, agricultural products, and all kinds of money and currency on hand and on deposit; a tax on profits from any business; and a license tax. These taxes, enacted between 1861 and 1865, were insufficient, and the Confederacy resorted to issuing bonds and paper money, only to end in fiscal chaos.

1866–1913

Once the Civil War was over, national governmental expenditures declined, and taxes were reduced. Internal revenue taxes were gradually repealed between 1866 and 1883, after which the only commodities taxed were liquor and tobacco. The political pressure of diverse manufacturing and banking groups led first to the reduction of the income tax in 1867 and 1870 and then to its expiration in 1872, despite the opposition of the merchant and farm groups, which feared that abolition of the income tax would strengthen governmental reliance on the protective tariff for revenue. The taxes on legacies and successions were repealed in 1870 for the same reasons as was the income tax. Yet agrarian and labor discontent from 1873 on resulted in repeated proposals for the restoration of the income tax by southern and western congressmen; the Greenback, Antimonopoly, and Populist parties; and the Knights of Labor. In 1894 Congress passed a 2 percent tax on all personal and corporate income over $4,000; gifts and inheritances were included in income. The Supreme Court had held in 1796 that the only direct taxes in a clear constitutional sense were poll taxes and taxes on land (*Hylton* v. *United States*). The Civil War income tax laws had been upheld by the Supreme Court in 1881 (*Springer* v. *United States*) on the ground that an income tax was not a direct tax. But powerful financial interests feared the impact of the 1894 income tax law on the accumulation of great fortunes and brought three suits before the Supreme Court that resulted in the Court's handing down two decisions in 1895 that reversed a century of legal precedent (*Pollock* v. *Farmers' Loan and Trust Company*). The first decision (Apr. 8, 1895) declared that the tax on rents or income from property was a direct tax, had to be apportioned among the states according to population, and was unconstitutional unless so apportioned. The tax on income from municipal bonds was nullified as an infringement by the national government on the borrowing power of the state and its instrumentalities. On May 20, 1895, the full Court, by a five-to-four decision, ruled that a tax on income from personal property was a direct tax. Although the whole Court agreed that a tax on the income from professions, trades, or employments was valid, the majority of five held the entire income tax invalid. This judicial veto of Congress led to intense political pressure by small business, farm, and labor groups through the Populist, Democratic, Socialist Labor, and Socialist parties for the adoption of the Sixteenth Amendment to the Constitution. With its ratification in 1913, the taxation of personal income by the national government became a valid, permanent, and major source of revenue.

The Spanish-American War in 1898 forced the sound-money, conservative war finance group in Congress to nearly double the tobacco and beer taxes, to adopt special stamp and occupation taxes, and to impose a tax on legacies and distributive shares of personal property, graduated both according to the degree of relationship and the amount of the estate, with general exemption for estates under $10,000 and for all property passing to the surviving husband or wife. The rate rose to 15 percent on bequests from estates of over $1 million to more distant relatives, strangers in blood, and "bodies politic or corporate." The emphasis of the tax was on the transmission of the property, which made the tax in a technical sense a modified estate duty rather than an inheritance tax.

The passage of this radical statute was partly the result of the resurgence of the inheritance tax movement in the late 1880's and 1890's. Although there had been several state inheritance taxes of one kind or another before 1885, a collateral inheritance tax law passed by New York in 1885 became a model for many states adopting such taxes in the next few years. In 1892 New York, by imposing an inheritance tax on direct heirs, gave an impetus to other states. Having upheld the constitutionality of the federal Civil War inheritance tax in 1874 in *Scholey* v. *Rew*, the Supreme Court upheld the constitutionality of state inheritance taxes in 1896 and

1898 in *United States* v. *Perkins* and *Magoun* v. *Illinois Trust and Savings Bank.* To get around the restrictions of the 1895 *Pollock* decision, the Court held in *Knowlton* v. *Moore* (1900) that the 1898 federal inheritance tax was valid as an indirect excise tax not subject to the Constitution's apportionment requirement and not violating its uniformity requirement. Shortly thereafter Congress first lowered many of the war revenue taxes and then repealed them all.

The continuing resentments of small businessmen, farmers, and workers against big business erupted into the Progressive movement, which had as a major objective the passage of a federal income tax law notwithstanding the 1895 decisions. To prevent the passage of such a law, conservative Republicans put through Congress in 1909 the first federal corporation tax since the Civil War, a mild 1 percent tax on the net income above $5,000 of every corporation organized for profit. This tax was an extension of the general taxation of corporations by states, which Pennsylvania had initiated in 1840 with a tax on dividends and had developed by 1868 into a tax on corporate net income. Opponents of this new form of federal taxation appealed to the Supreme Court to follow the *Pollock* precedent, but the Court decided that the 1909 tax was not a direct tax but an excise that could be based on the entire corporate income, including income from nontaxable property, such as municipal bonds and other property not directly or actively used in the corporate business. In 1913 the Sixteenth Amendment was adopted, with its explicit grant of power to Congress to levy income taxes without apportionment among the states. This sanctioned the 1913 federal income tax law with a progressive rate scale that had as its maximum a 7 percent tax on personal net income over $500,000, as well as a 1 percent tax on corporate net income. The Supreme Court affirmed the constitutionality of the 1913 income tax in *Brushaber* v. *Union Pacific Railroad Company* (1916).

1914–40

The outbreak of World War I led to increased American defense and (after 1917) war expenditures and a series of new tax laws designed to meet about one-third of the total war costs, with the remainder to be met by large-scale public borrowings. Congress passed four major revenue acts between October 1914 and February 1919 that increased the rates of the recently adopted corporation and personal income taxes to unprecedented heights and added a special tax on munitions manufacturers, an estate tax, an excess profits tax, a war profits tax, transportation taxes, and a wide variety of new excise taxes on goods and services, mainly luxuries and amusements. The duties on fermented liquors, wines, and tobacco were raised. The principle of progression was applied to the corporation, estate, personal income, excess profits, and war profits taxes so as to increase the burden on high incomes and large fortunes. The income tax exemption was lowered to $1,000 for single persons and $2,000 for married persons. The tax on personal incomes rose to 77 percent on income over $1 million. The excess profits tax was based on the profits in excess of the normal prewar profits during 1911–13, measured as a percentage of the invested capital for the taxable year, and was designed to minimize high war profits that represented windfalls to those engaged in wartime business enterprise. A tax was imposed on undistributed corporation profits that were retained as surplus above the requirements of the business for purposes of avoiding income taxes, but this provision proved ineffectual and was repealed in 1918. All these taxes, especially the income and excess profits taxes, produced a higher percentage of the federal government's war revenue than did the taxes in the Civil War or any other previous American war. The Treasury resorted to four great bond issues during 1917–18; the four Liberty Loans produced a total of $17 billion. This bond total was increased to $21.5 billion by the 1919 Victory Loan. Most of these loans carried tax exemption privileges that made them attractive to investors and offered opportunities for tax avoidance. Two factors that reduced the war revenue from taxes were the sharp drop in imports and customs duties that followed the outbreak of war in Europe and the loss in revenue caused by state and federal prohibition laws passed between 1914 and 1918.

During the New Deal, tax laws were passed to prevent an unjust concentration of wealth and economic power and to induce business to adopt certain recovery policies.

After World War I Congress gradually repealed the special war taxes, notably the excess profits tax, and made sharp reductions in corporate and personal income, as well as estate, tax rates. A federal gift tax was introduced in 1924 to counteract widespread avoidance of federal estate taxes; it was repealed in 1926, only to be restored in 1932 as a permanent part of the federal tax structure. In 1924 Congress tried to promote uniformity in state inheritance taxation by providing credit up to 25 percent of the federal estate tax for the amount of any estate, inheritance, legacy, or succession taxes paid to any state or territory on any property included in the gross estate. This credit was increased to 80 percent in 1926 and has remained at that level. But this tax credit did not produce much uniformity in state taxes or in state tax rates. Most states absorbed the federal credit by supplementing their inheritance taxes with estate taxes.

The 1929 depression forced Congress and President Herbert Hoover into late antidepression fiscal spending and into raising the corporate and personal income tax rates; doubling the estate tax rates; reenacting the gift tax; and imposing numerous manufacturers excise taxes and sales taxes on gasoline, luxury, and sporting articles, and special taxes on bank checks, bond transfers, and telephone, telegraph, and radio messages in a futile effort to balance the federal budget. With the inauguration of President Franklin D. Roosevelt in 1933 and the institution of his New Deal policies for relief, recovery, and reform, massive government spending to finance unemployment relief and public works destroyed the balanced federal budget. Tax laws were passed to prevent an unjust concentration of wealth and economic power and to induce business to adopt certain recovery policies. In 1933 Congress enacted a corporation excess profits tax, a capital stock tax, and an increase in the gasoline tax. Under the Agricultural Adjustment Act of 1933, farmers were paid for curtailing their acreage of certain commodities through taxes imposed on the first processor of the commodities in question. This tax was abandoned after the Supreme Court ruled the act unconstitutional in *United States* v. *Butler* (1936). In 1934–35 the surtax rates on personal income and the rates of the estate and gift taxes were increased, and a tax was imposed on the undistributed net income of personal holding companies. In 1935 the corporate income tax and the excess profits tax were made higher, on a progressive scale. In the same year the Social Security Act established old-age insurance for qualified workers through payroll taxes on both employers and employees and unemployment insurance through a payroll tax on employers, providing for a 90 percent credit for an unemployment tax paid to any state. In 1936 a graduated undistributed corporate income or profits tax was levied in order to induce corporations to distribute their earnings to their stockholders. This highly controversial measure was modified in 1938 and repealed in 1939. Partly as compensation for this repeal, the corporate income tax was increased in 1938 and 1939. The Public Salary Act of 1939 extended the federal income tax to the salaries of federal judges and state employees and officials; in return, the federal government permitted nondiscriminatory state taxation of the salaries of federal employees and officers. The Court supported this reciprocity action in *Graves* v. *O'Keefe* (1939).

1940–73

The invasion of Poland by Nazi Germany in September 1939 put the economy of the United States on a semiwar basis in terms of military expenditure and revenue measures, and the declaration of war against Japan in December 1941 brought with it a full-fledged war economy. The federal expenditures for the period July 1, 1940, to Aug. 31, 1945, totaled $337 billion, of which $304 billion was devoted to national defense. In the longer period from July 1, 1940, to June 30, 1946, federal spending reached $379 billion for military and nonmilitary expenditures. This sum was ten times the amount spent during World War I and one hundred times that spent during the Civil War. The national debt rose from $42.9 billion at the end of 1940 to $270 billion at the end of the fiscal year 1946. Of the $380 billion received as revenue during the period from June 1940 to December 1945, about 40 percent came from taxes, a higher percentage than that of World War I or of the Civil War. This record was achieved by the passage of six important revenue bills between June 1940 and May 1944. These acts raised progressively the rates on personal income to a maximum of 94 percent on income over $200,000, while lowering the exemption to $500 per person, whether married, single, or dependent. Thus the number of persons paying income taxes rose from 4 million in 1939 to 42.7 million in 1945. The lowering of the exemption restrained inflation and was accompanied by the enactment of heavy excises on commodities needed for military purposes in order to limit their consumption by civilians. To prevent war profiteering, drastic increases in corporate and excess profits taxes were enacted, as were price controls and other measures. The excess profits tax, reintroduced in 1940, rose to a gross rate of 95 percent and a net rate of 85.5 percent, inasmuch as a postwar credit of 10 percent of the amount due was given. Excess profits, as finally determined, were those in excess of 95 percent of the average earnings of the base period, 1936–39, or the amount of a specified percentage of the invested capital. The combined normal and surtax corporation tax rate was raised from 19 percent in 1940 to 40 percent by 1942. But these high personal and corporate tax rates were tempered by various provisions. Individuals were granted personal deductions for unusually large medical expenses and a generous optional standard deduction. Moreover, the rule was established that no person was required to pay more than 90 percent of his income in taxes. Similarly, the aggregate of the corporation and excess profits tax could not exceed 80 percent of the income. Business losses, suffered either by individuals or corporations, could be carried back or forward for two years to reduce taxable income. An important innovation was the transfer of the payment of personal income taxes from a deferred to a current basis. Congress forgave about three-fourths of the taxes due in 1942 to ease the shift. Substantial revenue was obtained from the excise taxes on distilled spirits, wines, fermented malt liquors, tobacco, transportation of persons and property, telephone and telegraph messages, theater admissions, and manufactures. The rates of the estate and gift taxes were greatly increased in 1941, mainly by making the maximum rate of each apply to that portion of net estates and net gifts exceeding $10 million, instead of $50 million.

Despite such tax increases, about 60 percent of war expenditures had to be paid through borrowing. The Treasury offered three different types of savings bonds, as well as the usual long-term bonds and short-term obligations to corporations and high-income investors: certificates of indebtedness; Treasury bills running for seventy-one to ninety-one days; and tax savings notes, acceptable at par and accrued interest. Between December 1942 and December 1945, Americans bought $156 billion in war bonds. Although individuals bought about 25 percent of the total defense-war offerings of the U.S. government, the commercial banks and the federal reserve banks took 38 percent. As a result the money supply between 1941 and 1945 doubled, although it did not affect price levels proportionately until the removal of price controls after the war.

Shortly before Japan surrendered in September 1945, Congress began easing the tax capital-reconversion burdens of American businesses through the 1945 Tax Adjustment Act. In November Congress passed the Reconversion Tax Act, which repealed the capital stock tax and the excess profits tax, the latter effective at the end of 1945. Corporate and personal income tax rates were moderately reduced, and tax exemptions were given to members of the armed forces below the rank of a commissioned officer on service pay received during the war. With presidential support Congress postponed reduction of many of the wartime excise taxes that were due to expire—and most of these "temporary" taxes continued. In 1948 Congress overrode President Harry S. Truman's veto and made large reductions in the personal income, estate, and gift taxes. Husbands and wives were allowed to divide their incomes on joint income tax forms and thereby reduce their taxes. The new estate and gift tax law permitted a husband or wife in a common-law state to transfer 50 percent of his or her property to a spouse without taxation, provided that the receiver of the property obtained complete control of it and included it in his or her estate at death for taxation purposes. This marital deduction provision eliminated the long-standing advantage that residents of community-property states had had over residents of common-law states.

The trend to lower taxes was halted by the outbreak of the Korean War in June 1950. In three revenue bills enacted during 1950–51 Congress raised personal and corporation income taxes to World War II levels, in some instances even higher; reimposed an excess profits tax; and increased excise taxes above World War II rates. In 1954, one year after the Korean War ended, Congress repealed the excess profits tax and enacted a comprehensive downward revision of the income tax, both to stimulate business enterprise and to remove inequalities in the treatment of taxpayers. Between 1950 and 1958 the Social Security taxes and the accompanying benefits were raised on five different occasions. A few changes in the excise taxes were also made, the biggest of which were the increases affecting motorists to aid in financing the highways.

In 1948 Congress overrode President Truman's veto and made large reductions in the personal income, estate, and gift taxes.

Although recessions occurred in 1957–58 and 1960–61, the administration of President Dwight D. Eisenhower did not enact any tax reduction program to stimulate recovery. But President John F. Kennedy counteracted the recession of 1961 with a $6.2 billion increase in government spending and an investment tax credit for businessmen. After Kennedy's assassination in 1963, President Lyndon B. Johnson pushed through Congress in 1964 a bill providing $11.5 billion in income tax reductions for the calendar years 1964 and 1965. The rate scale for individual income taxes was reduced from a range of 20–91 percent to 14–70 percent; for corporations the combined normal and surtax rate was reduced from 52 to 48 percent. The 7 percent investment credit in the Revenue Act of 1962 was simplified and broadened. These changes dropped the unemployment rate in 1965 to 4.5 percent and in 1966 to 3.8 percent. In June 1965 Congress scaled down the excise taxes that still remained from the Korean War to all but a few major taxes levied for sumptuary and regulatory reasons and as user charges. The reduction of almost $5 billion was made in several yearly steps from 1965 to 1969.

In March 1966 Congress enacted a Tax Adjustment Act that provided for withholding (effective May 1, 1966) personal income taxes at graduated rates ranging up to 30 percent instead of at a flat rate of 14 percent. It also liberalized and restricted the rules for tax-option corporations; increased greatly the tax benefits for retirement plans of the self-employed; and restructured, in the Foreign Investors Tax Act of 1966, the rules for taxation of the U.S. income of nonresident aliens and foreign corporations. Congress suspended until 1968 the investment credit and accelerated depreciation benefits for many assets.

In January and August of 1967 President Johnson asked Congress to enact a surtax on individual and corporate income taxes. Congress took no action on his request until June 1968, when it enacted a 10 percent surtax, made retroactive to April 1968 and scheduled to expire on June 30, 1969. Scheduled reductions in the telephone and automotive excise taxes were again postponed. The surtax specifically exempted low-income taxpayers from the additional personal income tax liabilities. In addition to the tax measures, the Revenue and Expenditure Control Act of 1968 required a $6 billion reduction in federal spending during fiscal year 1968 and a reduction of $10 billion in proposed new obligational authority in the budget for fiscal year 1969. Another important tax law, enacted in January 1968, provided for an increase in Social Security payments of 13 percent for all beneficiaries. The amount of earnings subject to this tax and creditable toward benefits was increased from $6,600 to $7,800, effective Jan. 1, 1968.

When President Richard M. Nixon assumed office in January 1969 he promptly sought retention of the 10 percent surtax until June 1970. Congress first extended the surtax at 10 percent through Dec. 31, 1969, and then extended it at 5 percent for the first six months of 1970. This last provision was incorporated into the Tax Reform Act of 1969 in order to force the Nixon administration's commitment to that law. The Tax Reform Act of 1969 was the most widespread tax reform measure in the history of American tax legislation. The reform highlights included (1) stricter rules on the creation and operation of private charitable foundations in order to prevent their being used for the personal tax benefit of their founders; (2) the reduction of the percentage depletion for oil and gas production from 27.5 to 22 percent; (3) the imposition of ordinary income tax rates on charitable contributions of appreciated property, such as inventories or securities, on which there would be short-term capital gains; (4) the elimination of a long-standing 25 percent ceiling on long-term capital gains for those with such gains in excess of $50,000 a year; and (5) the imposition of a minimum tax of 10 percent on "tax preference" (tax-free) income in excess of $30,000 a year. Substantial tax-relief measures were also incorporated in the Tax Reform Act of 1969. These measures included (1) a four-step increase in the deduction for personal dependency from $600 in 1969 to $750 in 1973; (2) the removal of 5.5 million low-income taxpayers from the tax rolls by a new minimum standard deduction set at $1,100 for 1970, $1,050 for 1971, and $ 1,000 for 1972; and (3) a gradual increase in the standard deduction for taxpayers (not itemizing their tax returns) from 10 percent of income, with a $1,000 ceiling, to 15 percent, with a $2,000 ceiling, in 1973.

Starting in August 1971, Nixon's fiscal policy became expansionary as his concern over recession exceeded his fear of inflation. As a result significant federal tax changes, embodied in the Revenue Act of 1971, went into effect at the beginning of 1972. These changes included a 7 percent investment tax credit, a repeal of the 7 percent automobile excise tax, and an increase in the personal income tax exemption for 1972. The investment tax credit was intended to increase corporate profit as a means of stimulating investment. The repeal of the automobile excise tax contributed greatly to the substantial increase in car sales during 1972. The personal income tax exemption of $750 for 1972, along with the low-income allowance (minimum standard deduction) of $1,300, eliminated the personal income tax for people having incomes below the poverty level. In another 1971 statute Social Security benefits were raised by 10 percent, and the taxable earnings base for such taxes was increased from $7,800 to $9,000, effective January 1972.

In 1972 Nixon's fiscal strategy shifted from stimulating the economy to holding the budget down and avoiding an excessive deficit. In the tax field an act of Congress, approved July 1, 1972, increased Social Security benefits by 20 percent, effective September 1972, and enlarged the taxable earnings base, first to $10,000, effective January 1973, and then to $12,000, effective January 1974. The relevant employee-employer tax rates were each increased from 4.6 percent in 1971 to 5.5 percent by 1973. The law also authorized an automatic increase in benefits and the taxable earnings base whenever the cost of living rose more than 3 percent in any year and no legislative benefit increase had been enacted or become effective in the previous year. This was a revolutionary legislative advance to protect the low- and middle-income classes from the ravages of inflation. An additional 5.6 percent increase in Social Security benefits, effective July 1, 1974, was enacted in July 1973.

The most important fiscal development in 1972, however, was the initiation of revenue sharing between the national and state governments, enacted into law in October 1972. This legislation followed some eight years of debate over the structure of intergovernmental fiscal relations: whereas federal grants-in-aid had been restricted to specific programs authorized by Congress and had been made in most instances to the states, to be redirected in part to local governments, revenue sharing was to provide generally unrestricted grants directly to state and local governments. The State and Local Assistance Act of 1972 specified the distribution of $5.3 billion for the calendar year 1972. The amount for distribution was to increase annually until it reached $7.2 billion in 1976. A third of the funds were to go to the states and two-thirds to the local governments.

State and Municipal Taxation

State taxation in the United States from 1774 to 1789 followed the sectional pattern of taxation established before the American Revolution. In 1789 the states gave up the use of export, impost, and tonnage duties. During the 19th century state taxation was restricted mainly to general property tax, although some states introduced special bank taxes, insurance company taxes, general corporation taxes, and inheritance taxes. But none of these levies produced more than a slight fraction of a state's total revenue. Toward the end of the 19th century the states began to depend in large measure on taxes other than the general property tax, which as late as 1902 furnished 52 percent of the revenue of the states. Corporation and personal income taxes became increasingly important after 1911; and after 1920 gasoline taxes became another leading source of state revenue. By 1940 property taxes supplied only one-sixteenth of state tax revenue. By 1970 the ratio was one-fiftieth. Since the 1930's the chief state taxes, in addition to the corporation and individual income taxes, have been the general sales tax, the gasoline tax, and the payroll tax for unemployment insurance. Specific state taxes on the retail sale of tobacco products and alcoholic beverages also produced revenue, although they and the state inheritance and estate taxes brought in considerably less revenue than the four principal state taxes. Generally, a sales tax is paid by the consumer on retail purchases of all commodities except those specifically excluded and, in some states, of certain services, usually public utilities and amusements. Several states include in their sales tax structure fractional-rate business occupation levies on sales by manufacturers or wholesalers, or both. A few states also use the retail sales tax supplemented by business taxes on the gross receipts of businesses at all stages of production and distribution, including the retail. One state, Indiana, introduced a retail sales tax in 1963 and adopted a small tax credit against the income tax as a relief measure for low-income persons. The state payroll taxes for unemployment insurance are the result of a 90 percent credit to each state for the tax that employers would otherwise have been required to pay in full to the federal government under the Social Security Act of 1935.

By 1900 the general property tax used by counties, municipalities, and other local governing authorities as their principal source of revenue had become a selective tax on real estate and business personalty (that is, equipment and inventory) and has remained so ever since. As the cost of local government increased with the accelerated growth of cities, the consequent shift from low to high rates in the general property tax led to severe criticism of the prevailing undervaluation of real property and inadequate assessment of personal property, especially stocks, bonds, notes, and mortgages. Improvements in tax administration and the establishment of local boards of review and equalization and of state tax commissions were accompanied by a marked development in the practice of dividing certain state-collected taxes between state and local governments and, in the 20th century, by state governments relying less on property taxes. Several states ceased to tax property and left that source of revenue to cities, counties, and other local units of government. Most cities and some counties have also derived some revenue from local licenses, permits, and various fees. Increasingly after World War II, local governments began imposing payroll, income, sales, gasoline, automobile, and other taxes as supplements to their property taxes. Nevertheless, the property tax in 1970 accounted for 85 percent of all local revenue. Its importance was greatest for school districts (98 percent), townships (93 percent), and counties (88 percent). Its contribution was somewhat lower (67 percent) for municipalities, which had developed additional revenue sources. As inflation in the 1970's became more burdensome to state and local taxpayers, Congress, in October 1972, inaugurated its revenue-sharing program in an effort to ease state and local tax problems. Recent court decisions that aim at equalizing the quality of education and the tax funds for all school districts within a state will probably increase the importance of state income taxes and lower that of local property taxes.

Trends in Tax Policy

Certain major trends in the American tax system deserve careful consideration. Total American tax collections—local, state, and federal—increased from 6.2 percent of the gross national product (GNP) in 1902 to 30 percent in 1970, largely because international tensions and wars made it necessary for the U.S. government to maintain and increase outlays for military purposes and for foreign aid. These, combined with heavy postwar federal debt interest, the cost of aid to veterans, and domestic welfare expenditures and farm aid, prevented any significant reduction in federal taxes. At the same time, state and local governments, subject to increased demands for schooling, housing, and other services, have had to raise the revenue they receive through taxes. These unprecedented revenue demands came while the GNP, between 1940 and 1973, expanded fourfold (measured in constant 1958 dollars). Tax yields rose at the same time that most taxpayers were able to increase their consumer purchases.

Total American tax collections—local, state, and federal—increased from 6.2% of the GNP in 1902 to 30% in 1970, largely to pay for military and foreign aid outlays.

Before 1940 federal tax collections constituted about 33 percent of the total for all governmental units—local, state, and federal. The federal share of taxes rose in World War II to 80 percent. By 1970 it seemed to stabilize at 66 percent, albeit still exceeding state and local shares. In 1970 personal and corporate income taxes produced 48 percent of all U.S. tax revenue. Next in importance are sales, commodity, and service excise taxes, especially those on tobacco and liquor, which constituted 18 percent of the 1970 total. The share of payroll taxes was also 18 percent; that of the property tax, although crucial in local finance, was only 12 percent of the combined. federal, state, and local tax revenue in 1970.

Income Taxes

The American income tax system dates back to the faculty taxes (arbitrary taxes on the assumed earnings of workers, artisans, and tradesmen) adopted by various New England and middle Atlantic colonies in the 17th and 18th centuries. In the 19th century most states abandoned the faculty tax. The success of the 1911 Wisconsin income tax law encouraged many other states to adopt similar laws between World War I and World War II. By 1971 general individual income taxes had been adopted in thirty-seven states, the corporation income tax in forty-three states, and local income taxes in ten states.

Between 1861 and 1865 Congress passed four income tax laws. In 1872 the tax was permitted to lapse because its yield threatened the high protective tariff system. In 1894 Congress imposed an income tax that the U.S. Supreme Court, in 1895, declared unconstitutional. This action led, in 1913, to the ratification of the Sixteenth Amendment, which empowered Congress to impose personal income taxes without their apportionment among the states in accordance with the census. The 1913 federal income tax applied to wages, salaries, interest, dividends, rents, entrepreneurial incomes, and capital gains. The rate was 1 percent on net income over $4,000 and 7 percent on net income over $500,000. Subsequent rates and exemptions changed often. Maximum marginal rates reached 77 percent in 1918, 94 percent in 1944–45, and 92 percent in 1952–53. They sank to 24 percent in 1929, then rose to 79 percent from 1936 to 1939. From 1954 to 1962 the maximum rate was 91 percent; in 1971, 70 percent. A special Vietnam War surcharge went into effect at 7.5 percent of tax in 1968, 10 percent in 1969, and 2.5 percent in 1970. Exemptions decreased markedly during World War I and World War II. This downward trend made the income tax a tax on the masses instead of a tax on the high-income groups.

The corporation income tax rate started at 1 percent in 1909. It then rose to 12 percent during World War I; 13.5 percent during 1926–27; 40 percent during World War II; and 52 percent during the Korean War. The Revenue Act of 1964 cut the rate to 50 percent for 1964 and to 48 percent for subsequent years. The Vietnam War surcharge was extended to corporations at 10 percent of tax in 1968–69 and 2.5 percent in 1970. From 1909 to 1935 the corporation income tax was levied at a flat rate on taxable income. But since 1936 a relatively simple graduation system has prevailed. In 1936–37 Congress experimented with a surtax on undistributed corporate profits.

After 1913 a number of significant changes in the federal income tax structure occurred: for example, the introduction in 1917 of a credit for dependents and a deduction for charitable contributions, the allowance in 1918 of depletion deductions for mines and oil and gas wells, the adoption in 1921 of preferential rates for long-term capital gains, the taxing in 1939 of previously exempted salaries of local and state officials, the discontinuance in 1941 of tax-exempt federal bonds, the enactment in 1948 of "income splitting" for married couples, the allowance in 1954 of accelerated depreciation deductions for business equipment and buildings, the replacement in 1969 of the minimum standard deduction by a low-income allowance, and the adoption that same year of a minimum tax on selected preference income and a top marginal rate of 50 percent on earned income. Many of these changes benefited high-income groups and so eroded the personal income-tax base that it came to only 43 percent of personal income.

Internal Revenue

The first period during which internal taxes were used to support the U.S. government was from 1791 to 1802. Hamilton, the first secretary of the Treasury, advocated a system of excise taxes and proper collection machinery. Between 1791 and 1798 Congress imposed taxes on distilled spirits, carriages, refined sugar, snuff, property sold at auction, and legal transactions. A direct tax on dwelling houses, lands, and slaves between twelve and fifty was also imposed. Although the revenue was meager, strong opposition to the excise taxes, especially from the Antifederalist party, led to the Whiskey Rebellion in 1794 and the abolition of the Federalist excise system in 1802. The federal government relied on revenue from the tariff until the war with England in 1812 forced Congress to impose various internal excise taxes as well as a direct tax on dwelling houses, lands, and slaves. But when the war ended and the Tariff Act of 1816 brought in high revenues, Congress abolished the direct taxes and excise taxes it had imposed during the war. From then until the outbreak of the Civil War the federal government made no use of any internal taxes.

During the Civil War, Congress enacted four income tax laws and imposed an inheritance tax and a wide variety of excise taxes on a long list of commodities, including alcoholic beverages and tobacco. The income tax was especially productive—it brought in about 15 percent of total federal taxes in 1866 but was allowed to expire in 1872. During the postwar period, most of the excises and the inheritance tax were repealed. Taxes on alcoholic beverages and tobacco were continued, however, and steadily increased in importance.

In 1894 an income tax law was enacted, although it was declared unconstitutional in 1895. During the Spanish-American War of 1898 new miscellaneous excise taxes and an inheritance tax were levied, but the excises had been largely repealed by 1902, and the inheritance tax was repealed a few years later. In 1909 a corporation excise tax was imposed on the net income of corporations, largely to block action on the Sixteenth Amendment. But this amendment was ratified and led to the income tax law of 1913.

With the advent of World War I, the income tax became the most significant source of federal revenue. By 1917 income tax collections surpassed customs revenues, and by 1920 they accounted for about two-thirds of total federal tax revenues. Additional wartime revenues were derived from newly imposed estate, capital stock, and excess profits taxes, and also from a large number of excise taxes on specific commodities and services.

During the prosperous 1920's, four tax reduction acts were passed. Although personal and corporate income tax burdens were lessened, the annual income tax receipts made up the major part of total federal tax revenue during that decade—most of the excise taxes had been either repealed or greatly reduced, with the important exception of the tax on tobacco. The alcoholic beverage tax, although a high revenue producer until 1919, produced little revenue during Prohibition.

During the Great Depression and the New Deal an attempt was made to maintain federal revenues by raising various existing taxes and imposing some new ones. But tax revenues decreased until 1935, when a gradual upswing began. Part of the increase was accounted for by revenue from the tax on alcoholic beverages after the repeal of Prohibition in 1933. Other increases came from the estate tax (imposed in 1916) and the gift tax (reimposed in 1932); they accounted for nearly 10 percent of federal tax revenues for several years. In the mid-1930's important employment taxes were introduced to finance the old-age Social Security, unemployment insurance, and railroad retirement programs. In the same decade several short-lived taxes were imposed under the Undistributed Profits and Agricultural Adjustment acts of 1933.

During World War II the overriding importance of the individual and corporate income taxes in the federal tax structure was established. Sharp increases in tax rates, reductions in personal exemptions, and the reintroduction of the excess profits tax coincided with a massive expansion of income and profits, to raise income and profits tax revenues from a 1940 level of $2 billion to over $35 billion in 1945. Whereas individual income tax had previously applied to only a small percentage of the population, it was now broadened to cover most of the working population. The withholding system was introduced to facilitate payment and collection. During 1944–45 individual income tax rates ranged from 23 to 94 percent—a historic high. Excise taxes were increased on tobacco, liquor, travel, and telephone service.

In 1945 and 1948 Congress enacted major income tax reductions and repealed the excess profits tax, the capital-stock tax, and the declared-value excess profits tax. By 1950 income and profits tax revenues had declined by one-fifth from the 1945 level. The Korean War led to the enactment of three major revenue acts between September 1950 and October 1951. As a result individual and corporate income tax rates were increased and the excess profits tax was reimposed. In 1954 individual income tax rates were reduced to pre-1951 levels, and the excess profits tax was allowed to expire at the same time that an excise tax reduction law was passed.

During 1944–45, individual income tax rates ranged from 23 to 94%—a historic high.

A new fiscal policy designed to stimulate economic growth and high-level employment was responsible for the major income tax deductions that were provided in the Revenue Act of 1964. In 1969 the adoption of a low-income allowance eliminated from the income tax rolls nearly all individuals and families who are officially classified as poor. Congress established a special Vietnam War surcharge to the individual income tax for the period 1968–70, although its rates varied yearly. In 1970 internal taxes accounted for 90 percent of U.S. government receipts.

Taxation in Territories and Possessions

Article IV, Section 3, of the U.S. Constitution empowers Congress to admit new states "into this Union" and "to dispose of and make all needful Rules and Regulations respecting the Territory or other Property" of the United States. Until Puerto Rico, the Philippines, and Hawaii were annexed in 1898, there was no question that the Constitution "followed the flag." But in the so-called Insular Cases of 1901 the Supreme Court drew a distinction between "incorporated" and "unincorporated" territories. In the case of incorporated territories, the entire Constitution and the laws and treaties of the United States apply, including those constitutional provisions and statutes relating to federal taxation. In the case of unincorporated territories, Congress, subject to Supreme Court rulings, has almost unlimited power of legislation for such territories. In either case, the citizens of the territories have been subject to federal taxation without representation in Congress.

With the admission of Hawaii and Alaska to the Union as states in 1959, there were no longer any incorporated territories, that is, territories that Congress had determined should be groomed for statehood. The largest remaining territory, Puerto Rico, had the unique status of commonwealth.

In tariff matters the U.S. Supreme Court decided in 1901 in one of the Insular Cases, *Downes* v. *Bidwell*, that Congress had the right to impose a duty on imports from Puerto Rico, despite the constitutional provision that all duties, imposts, and excises must be uniform throughout the United States. In practice, however, tariff duties have not been levied on Puerto Rican goods. Thereafter this uniformity of taxation clause did not apply to unincorporated territories.

On the subject of local taxation the national government has permitted a considerable measure of local autonomy, even in the unincorporated territories. Persons and property in the District of Columbia, however, are subject to both taxation and budgetary appropriation by Congress, even though the district is governed by a city council appointed by the president. Congress has limited the imposition of federal income and estate taxes on U.S. citizens who are bona fide residents of the unincorporated territories. The detailed rules are to be found in the U.S. Internal Revenue Code.

BIBLIOGRAPHY

Harold W. Chase and Craig R. Ducat, *Corwin's Constitution and What It Means Today.*

John Chommie, *The Internal Revenue Service.*

Lillian Doris, ed., *The American Way in Taxation: Internal Revenue, 1862–1963.*

John F. Due, *Sales Taxation.*

L. L. Ecker-Racz, *The Politics and Economics of State-Local Finance.*

Richard B. Goode, *The Corporation Income Tax,* and *The Individual Income Tax.*

Richard A. Musgrave and Peggy B. Musgrave, *Public Finance in Theory and Practice.*

Dick Netzer, *Economics of the Property Tax.*

Joseph A. Pechman, *Federal Tax Policy.*

Sidney Ratner, *Taxation and Democracy in America.*

Stanley S. Surrey, *Pathways to Tax Reform.*

— SIDNEY RATNER

TEAPOT DOME OIL SCANDAL

In 1921, by an executive order, President Warren G. Harding transferred control of the naval oil reserves at Elk Hills, Calif., and Teapot Dome, Wyo., from the Department of the Navy to the Department of the Interior; the transfer was made with the approval of Secretary of the Navy Edwin Denby. The following year Secretary of the Interior Albert B. Fall leased, without competitive bidding, the Teapot Dome fields (Apr. 7) to Harry F. Sinclair, president of the Mammoth Oil Company, and the Elk Hills fields (Apr. 25, Dec. 11) to Edward L. Doheny, a personal friend.

In 1923 Sen. Thomas J. Walsh of Montana led a Senate investigation of the leases and found that in 1921 Doheny had lent Fall $100,000 (without interest) and that shortly after Fall's retirement as secretary of the interior (March 1923) Sinclair had loaned Fall $25,000. Fall was convicted of accepting bribes, sentenced to one year in prison, and fined $100,000. Sinclair and Doheny were acquitted of bribery charges, but Sinclair was later sentenced to nine months in prison for contempt of court. Two Supreme Court decisions in 1927 declared the Elk Hills lease (Feb. 28) and the Teapot Dome lease (Oct. 10) invalid, and the fields were returned to the U.S. government.

BIBLIOGRAPHY

Burl Noggle, *Teapot Dome: Oil and Politics in the 1920's.*
Morris R. Werner and John Starr, *Teapot Dome.*

TELECOMMUNICATIONS

Beginning in the 1870s the Bell Telephone Company dominated the nation's phone network, known as the Bell System, including long-distance service under its subsidiary, American Telephone & Telegraph (AT&T). In the late 1960s, however, AT&T faced pressure from the U.S. government to break its protected monopoly. In 1969 government regulators allowed MCI Communications to sell long-distance service and connect with the AT&T network. In 1984 a federal court decision allowed AT&T to retain its long-distance service and manufacturing and research operations but forced the company to divest itself of the seven regional Bell operating companies, the so-called Baby Bells, and agree to purchase equipment from other companies besides its subsidiaries. The implications of the divestiture of AT&T in 1984 were far-reaching. At first there was confusion as customers began paying phone bills to both a local phone company and a long-distance company. Soon consumers adjusted to a variety of long-distance companies, such as AT&T, MCI, and Sprint, and many companies began to sell phone equipment to consumers.

By the mid-1990s new technologies had rapidly changed the telecommunications market. The expanded use by the 1980s of fiber-optic cable in network systems enabled companies to transmit telephone calls by digital technology, which conveys information about the transmitted signal through a numerical code rather than representing it, as is done with analog technology. This change resulted in improved clarity on phone lines, but in the mid-1990s as many as half the phones in the United States still relied on analog technology to send a signal between the network system and the home or office. For computers and fax systems to use analog technology, it was necessary to provide them with a modem, which converts the digital message into audio signals. Increasingly, some argued that telephones did not need to rely on traditional network systems and that a radio signal or even a satellite transmission could be used, which was the basis of the expanding mobile and cellular phone business. Between 1990 and 1992 the number of cellular phones in the United States increased from 4 million to 9 million. In fact, because of the accelerating integration of technologies related to computers, telephones, and cable television, and other entertainment media seemed uncertain by the mid-1990s. Companies that provided the network system for telephones wanted changes in U.S. laws that would enable them to carry entertainment shows into homes in order to challenge cable television. During the early and

Secretary of the Navy Edwin Denby announces to reporters in 1923 that he will not resign from his post, despite his implication in the Teapot Dome scandal. Denby had approved the transfer of valuable government oil fields that were later illegally leased. (Library of Congress/Corbis)

mid-1990s a number of agreements and mergers between telecommunications and entertainment companies occurred that reflected new technological capabilities. Likewise, the regional Bell companies wanted Congress to revise existing laws so that they could compete directly against AT&T and other companies in the manufacture of telecommunications equipment.

[See also Computers; Telephone.]

BIBLIOGRAPHY

Irwin Lebow, *Information Highways and Byways: From the Telegraph to the 21st Century* (New York, 1995).

Steven Lubar, *InfoCulture: The Smithsonian Book of Information Age Inventions* (Boston, 1993).

E— KENNETH B. MOSS

TELEGRAPH

The creation of a worldwide electromagnetic telegraph system during the 19th century was the first in a series of technological revolutions in communication and had unforeseen but profound social, political, military, and economic consequences. Within a single generation the telegraph virtually eliminated the barriers of time and space, and communication between Europe and America was reduced to seconds from days or weeks. The impact of the telegraph was especially evident in the United States, where it became one of the first great industrial monopolies. It was used by both the North and South during the Civil War.

The telegraph also helped to encourage settlement of the West, the growth of cultural nationalism, and the creation of other large industries, including the railroad. In its evolution the telegraph industry followed the pattern of American political history—the early autonomous companies were succeeded first by an ineffective confederation and then by the centralized control of the Western Union Company.

The requisite technical elements of the telegraph became available by the mid-1830's with the discoveries of Alessandro Volta, Hans Christian Oersted, Joseph Henry, and other electrical scientists. The potential social utility of the telegraph was soon perceived by a number of men, including Samuel Morse, a professor of art at New York University (NYU). Although Morse lacked both the technical skills and capital needed to convert the concept into a practical commercial system, he proved to be a charismatic leader and persuasive lobbyist. Important contributions to the development of a successful system were made by Morse's associates Leonard D. Gale and Alfred Vail. Gale, a professor of chemistry at NYU, was familiar with Henry's research. Vail was not only an inventive engineer but also was able to utilize the facilities of his family's iron works. A major innovation (generally attributed to Vail) was the introduction of the famous "Morse Code," a bisignal code that has since evolved into the pulse code system used in digital computers and space telemetry systems. Although Morse and his associates conducted a public demonstration of their new communications system in 1838, their first intercity line was not completed until 1844. This was a forty-mile line between Washington, D.C., and Baltimore and was built with the aid of a $30,000 congressional appropriation awarded in 1843. One of the first uses of the new line was to transmit news from the national political conventions of 1844 from Baltimore to Washington.

When Congress, already divided by sectional ideological differences over internal improvements policy, declined to develop the telegraph as a national public utility, Morse and his associates organized the Magnetic Telegraph Company in 1845 to promote and expand the system. The next decade was marked by a somewhat chaotic expansion and the creation of many small competing telegraph companies. By 1852 the United States had about 15,000 miles of telegraph lines—more than half the world's total. The Western Union Company, which eventually established an effective national monopoly of the industry, was organized in 1856. The first transcontinental line was completed in 1861.

The successful laying of a transatlantic telegraph cable was one of the epic engineering achievements of the 19th century. Cyrus West Field, a young American entrepreneur, provided the leadership for this project, although the cable and most of the capital came from England. The first cable became operational in 1858, setting off jubilant celebrations that were terminated by the early failure of the cable. Final success was achieved in 1866, and electrical communication with Europe has since been continuously maintained.

World attention was first directed to the military implications of the telegraph by its use in the American Civil War to control not only the movement of troops and supplies but also field tactics. Mobile telegraph units were used to coordinate the latter. The postwar period was marked by continuing expansion and increased standardization of apparatus and operating procedures as the Western Union Company achieved dominance in the industry. Innovations were mainly directed toward increasing the information-handling capacity of telegraph lines by multiplexing techniques invented by Thomas Edison, Alexander Graham Bell, and others. A new era in telegraphy began during the last decade of the century with the advent of Guglielmo Marconi's wireless telegraphy system. The two systems developed comparatively independently until after

1912, when the introduction of electronic amplifier devices led to "wired wireless" systems. These systems were capable of transmitting telegraphic code, voice, and photographs either by wires or through air. This productive synthesis led directly to the development of television during the 1930's. The realization that a wide variety of information, including logic, could be expressed and transmitted by telegraphic pulses has become the basis for both a comprehensive theory of communication and large new industries devoted to data processing and to various modes of remote electrical communication.

BIBLIOGRAPHY

E. A. Marland, *Early Electrical Communication.*

Robert Luther Thompson, *Wiring a Continent: The History of the Telegraph Industry in the United States, 1832–1866.*

— JAMES E. BRITTAIN

TELEPHONE

In less than a century the telephone evolved from a scientific curiosity into a vital communication system affecting international relations, business management, and the everyday activities of individuals. Its diverse uses include rural party lines, multistory interoffice communication lines, and the famous "hot line" between Washington, D.C. and Moscow. The technical feasibility of an electromagnetic telephone based on the conversion of fluctuating sound waves in air into fluctuating electrical currents in long wires appears to have been recognized by several inventors by the early 1870's. Their interest was generally an outgrowth of efforts to increase the information-handling capacity of existing telegraph circuits by using some form of harmonic telegraphy. The most famous of these inventors was the Scottish immigrant Alexander Graham Bell, whose strategic telephone patent led to the organization of the largest industrial corporation in the world. Bell and his assistant, Thomas A. Watson, achieved the first successful transmission of articulate speech in March 1876, and Bell gave the first public demonstration at the Philadelphia Centennial Exposition later the same year. The Bell Telephone Company, which eventually became the American Telephone and Telegraph Company, was organized in 1877 to develop a commercial system.

The telephone industry has undergone three major phases of technical development since 1876. The first was a preelectronic phase that lasted until the eve of World War I. Numerous inventors, engineers, and scientists made significant theoretical and practical contributions during this period. Among the more important innovations were the carbon transmitter, central switchboards, multicircuit cables, hard-drawn copper wire, loading coils, and the four-parameter transmission theory. The first circuits were carried by poles, but the resultant congestion in urban areas soon led to legislative pressures to convert these to underground lines. This difficult problem was eventually solved by engineers of the Bell System with paper-insulated cable pairs and loading coils. The design of long-distance circuits between cities proved equally difficult. An experimental line between Boston and New York City was first completed in 1884 using hard-drawn copper wire. The introduction of loading coils during the first decade of the 20th century made feasible a 2,000-mile circuit without amplifiers. Following a brief litigious encounter with the Western Union Company that was resolved in 1879, the Bell Company maintained an effective monopoly of the industry in the United States until the expiration of Bell's patents in the 1890's. Despite a few years of intense competition from independent companies, the dominance of the Bell System was not successfully challenged, and most of the smaller companies were finally absorbed or went out of business. After the "postalization" of the telephone industry in England in 1912, the United States was the last major country with a privately owned telephone system. Although there was a strong movement, especially during the administration of Woodrow Wilson, to follow the British example, this was not done (except for a one-year period beginning in August 1918).

Alexander Graham Bell's telephone patent led to the organization of the largest industrial corporation in the world.

The second major phase of development, which followed the introduction of electronic vacuum-tube amplifiers in 1912, lasted until World War II. The new device enabled the first transcontinental conversation by wire in 1915. The first transatlantic radio telephone conversation using vacuum-tube techniques was achieved by Bell System engineers the same year. The advent of radio-electronic methods enabled the completion of a worldwide telephone system during the 1920's. The capacity of wire circuits was also greatly increased during the interwar years with the use of wave filters, negative feedback amplifiers, and wide-band coaxial transmission lines. Ultimately a combination of these features led to the successful completion of the first transatlantic telephone cable with built-in amplifiers in 1956. Another significant development during the 1920's was the introduction of automatic dialing in larger cities using complex banks of electromechanical switches.

The third major phase in the evolution of the telephone was stimulated by the introduction in 1948 of solid-state amplifiers and switching circuits and the application of microwave techniques similar to those used in radar systems during World War II. The new semiconductor devices enabled the replacement of vacuum tubes and electromechanical switches by more reliable, faster, and more economical solid-state circuits. These and other techniques, including pulse-code modulation and theoretical advances in information theory, have opened a range of new possibilities in telephony that are still being introduced. Microwave links capable of carrying television as well as numerous telephone channels were introduced by the Bell System in 1946. Similar techniques were used in the design of the first international communications earth satellite, Telstar, which was launched in July 1962.

BIBLIOGRAPHY

American Telephone and Telegraph Company, *Events in Telephone History.*

Robert V. Bruce, *Bell: Alexander Graham Bell and the Conquest of Solitude.*

Percy Dunsheath, *A History of Electrical Engineering.*

David A. Hounshell, "Elisha Gray and the Telephone: On the Disadvantages of Being an Expert," *Technology and Culture*, vol. 16 (1975).

— JAMES E. BRITTAIN

TELEVISION

Television originated in 19th-century concepts of converting photographic images into an electrical impulse equivalent. In 1873 the telegraph engineer Willoughby Smith noted that the electrical resistance of selenium changed when exposed to light. Various possibilities were soon explored, particularly in France and England, concerning a practical optical-electrical conversion system. But the basic problem of converting the image was unresolved until 1884, when Paul G. Nipkow of Germany designed a scanning disc with the potential for sequentially transmitting individual segments of the picture. Although Nipkow's apparatus was too crude to permit useful results, the advent of vacuum-tube amplifiers and practical phototubes by 1920 made a commercial system feasible.

In the period 1925–30 both John Logie Baird of England and Charles Francis Jenkins of the United States developed scanning disc systems to the point of quasi-commercial application. The Jenkins Laboratories of Washington, D.C., began operation of station W3XK in 1928. By 1931 some two dozen stations employing low-definition scanning (30–60 lines) were in service. The Jenkins Television Corporation marketed receivers in finished cabinets and claimed that it met most of its operating expenses from sets sold to the public.

Notable experimental work and programming with the Nipkow disc system were done by several other groups, including the General Electric Company and the University of Iowa. One advantage of the early TV broadcasts was the use of low frequencies (2,000 kilohertz range) and hence great distance capability. But the picture definition was clearly unsuitable for a viable service.

Suggestions for electronic television arose soon after the development of the cathode ray tube by Karl Ferdinand Braun and J. J. Thomson about 1900. But several key problems in the area of electron optics remained unresolved. Work on the optical-electrical conversion (camera) tube was done principally by Philo Taylor Farnsworth, an independent inventor, and Vladimir K. Zworykin, working first at Westinghouse and later with Radio Corporation of America (RCA). In 1923 Zworykin applied for a patent that described an all-electronic scanning system. The application became involved in a seven-way interference proceeding (including interference with Farnsworth), and the patent issue was delayed until 1938. Nevertheless, Zworykin's camera device, the iconoscope, had certain intrinsic advantages in terms of image intensification and predominated in the experimental research of the late 1930's. Farnsworth's image dissector tube, electron-multiplier, and other contributions in electronic circuit design were still crucial to the technology, and, in practice, cross-licensing of the inventions of both parties was necessary for the early commercial growth of television.

The low-definition, mechanical-scanning service did not disappear overnight. Some systems persisted into the late 1930's. Electronic methods sometimes incorporated mechanical scanners at the transmission end; but by 1938 the all-electronic era had begun and engineering standards were remarkably close to those in use in the 1970's. Receivers were first marketed in the New York City area by both DuMont and RCA. By the summer of 1939 the National Broadcasting Company provided extensive programming over station W2XBS New York, with service specially geared for the New York World's Fair. Much of this development was attributed to the RCA research program implemented by David Sarnoff.

In December 1939 the Federal Communications Commission (FCC) tentatively adopted rules to permit a sponsored program service in which fees collected supported further experimental work. A number of conflicts arose, however, and the industry was compelled to examine all aspects of the new technology through a group called the National Television Systems Committee (NTSC). Full commercial program service was authorized by the FCC on July 1, 1941. The engineering standard of 525 picture lines, 30 frames per second, was officially adopted.

Color television originated with the work of Herbert Eugene Ives of Bell Telephone Laboratories in the late 1920's. Baird in England had some success by 1938 with rotating color discs and a cathode ray tube. But Peter Carl Goldmark of CBS Laboratories achieved the most notable success in the United States with a high definition color system by 1940. Program transmissions were extended in 1945 employing developmental UHF (ultrahigh frequency) stations in New York City. By 1950 the CBS system (termed "field-sequential") was of sufficient quality to offer serious consideration for commercial adoption. The main drawback was the use of a rotating color wheel and noncompatibility with the monochrome service. Official authorization was delayed by litigation until Apr. 1, 1951; but the successful development of an all-electronic system by RCA led to some reconsideration and a revised set of standards formulated by the NTSC. The NTSC system was authorized for broadcasting in 1953. But more than a decade elapsed before improvements in electron-optics and circuit design made color receivers attractive enough for large-scale purchase by the general public. By the mid-1970's advances in solid-state engineering further reduced the size, and weight of consumer-TV products and created great economies in energy consumption.

BIBLIOGRAPHY

Albert Abramson, *Electronic Motion Pictures.*

— ELLIOT N. SIVOWITCH

TELEVISION AT THE END OF THE TWENTIETH CENTURY

At the end of the twentieth century television was the primary leisure activity of most Americans and their most likely source for news. The medium had changed markedly since the mid-1970s, when three national networks, ABC, CBS, and NBC, dominated television; 87 percent of all TV stations were affiliated with a network. In the evening, when most Americans watched television, 90 percent of all sets were tuned to a network program. The networks fought for first place in audience ratings. Because advertisers sponsoring programs paid more for large audiences, high ratings meant millions of dollars. The networks spared no expense to lure viewers.

Network rivalries were fierce in the mid-1970s. ABC, long the weakest of the three networks in terms of popular programming and affiliates, gradually achieved parity with CBS and NBC, winning younger viewers with situation comedies like *Happy Days* and *Three's Company.* The latter's sexually teasing qualities, apparent in another ABC hit, *Charlie's Angels,* about three female private detectives, encouraged imitation by CBS and NBC. ABC also poured resources into its long-dormant news division, which by the 1980s enjoyed an equal rating with its competitors. ABC also benefited from television sets equipped to receive ultra high frequency (UHF) channels 14 through 83, relying on UHF stations for affiliates. In 1967 just under half of all viewers had sets equipped to receive UHF; eight years later the number was 90 percent. UHF ultimately undermined all three networks; UHF stations began operations without network affiliation. "Independent stations" increased from 13 percent in 1975 to 39 percent in 1987. They began counterprogramming, especially in the early evening, with game shows and other entertainment to compete with the network news shows. Availability of stations unaffiliated with ABC, CBS, or NBC encouraged formation of a fourth network, Fox, in 1986.

The three original networks underwent changes in ownership in 1986. General Electric purchased NBC, Capital Cities purchased ABC, and the investor Lawrence Tisch bought CBS. To their dismay the new proprietors found themselves in a cost squeeze. In the 1970s inflation had allowed networks to pass along to advertisers higher production expenses. Sponsors, affected by the inflation psychology, did not protest. A decade later, with inflation falling, demand for national time softened; the networks no longer enjoyed a seller's market. Although programming costs continued to rise, advertisers refused to make up the increases. Even network news divisions, sources of industry pride, had to lower expenses. Staffs were cut and domestic and overseas bureaus pared or shut. Each network looked for cheaper programming, including more news shows. Despite lavish salaries awarded a few newscasters, news programs such as CBS's *48 Hours* cost less than entertainment series. The networks produced the news shows and did not have to share their profits with independent producers in Hollywood. Despite reductions in operating expenses the three networks' woes worsened; profits fell 50 percent between 1984 and 1988. By the mid-1990s Fox emerged as a serious rival of the big three. Like ABC in the 1970s, Fox succeeded with comedies like *The Simpsons* and *Married . . . With Children,* as well as a sexy dramatic series, *Beverly Hills 90210*, which appealed to the younger viewers coveted by advertisers. In 1994 Fox outbid CBS for the rights to telecast National Football League games, which the latter network had aired since the 1950s. A year later Fox led CBS in many large TV markets.

Cable television proved the greatest blow to the networks' oligopoly. Cable required a monthly fee to enhance reception but offered many more choices in programming. In a typical viewing area in the 1980s a noncable household had seven channels; a cable household thirty-three. In the 1990s experts predicted as many as 500 cable channels might eventually be available. Cable systems had entered some areas to improve reception, not choice, as early as 1949, but the Federal Communications Commission (FCC) and local governments, which regulated underground wiring connecting households to cable, discouraged the new system until the mid-1970s. Over the next years government oversight relaxed. Households with cable increased from 15 percent in 1975 to 60 percent in 1994. It was not until the late 1980s that the networks recognized cable's threat. Earlier they had started cable channels but their involvement was halfhearted; their emphasis remained over-the-air broadcasting.

Meanwhile, the Public Broadcasting System (PBS), established in 1967 and partly supported by federal and state sources, lost viewers and programming to cable outlets emphasizing culture. The Cable News Network (CNN) established a small but devoted following and was boosted by the Gulf War of 1991 and the sensational murder trial of O. J. Simpson four years later. In 1992 CNN programs combined with radio talk shows to assist the independent presidential candidacy of the Texas billionaire Ross Perot, initially ignored by the networks. Democratic nominee Bill Clinton similarly used "alternative media," including the all-music MTV channel.

One network response to cable television was to make programs more "realistic," with explicit offerings of sex and violence.

Communication satellites benefited cable TV. In the mid-1970s several companies, including independent stations in Atlanta, New York, and Chicago, began relaying signals off satellites and making them available to cable companies across the country. Pay-cable outlets led by Home Box Office offered recently released and uncut feature films together with original programming. In late 1993 more than one-fourth of all households with television sets received one or more pay cable outlets. The videocassette recorder (VCR) delivered another blow to the networks. Sales of VCRs began in the early 1980s and by the mid-1990s four out of every five households with televisions had VCRs. Although some owners used VCRs to tape network shows to watch later, many more rented feature films, especially on weekends, which greatly reduced TV viewing. The effects of cable and VCRs were clear by the early 1990s. The network share of evening prime time fell to 60 percent. In 1980 three-fourths of viewers tuned to network evening newscasts; by 1992 that share had fallen almost to half.

One response to cable, seen at NBC in the early 1980s, was to make programs more "realistic," more like uncut movies on pay channels, with explicit treatment of sex and violence. Relaxed standards in feature films and popular music inspired this new realism. Being frank about sex and violence on television, however, infuriated parents, members of Congress, and conservative pressure groups, who accused the networks of contributing to a decline of national morality. In 1992 Vice President Dan Quayle condemned the TV series *Murphy Brown* for having the title character give birth out of wedlock. Relatedly, the news divisions were anxious to boost their programs' appeal and compete with many more channels. Network newscasts began to mimic local stations, which had never taken their responsibilities as seriously as had the networks. Especially at CBS, less attention was devoted to international and national news and more to human interest stories and segments on helping viewers cope with medical and financial matters. News programs competing against entertainment shows in the evening began to imitate the "tabloid" or sensational programs aired by Fox and independent producers.

[See also Advertising; Music Television; Radio.]

BIBLIOGRAPHY

Ken Auletta, *Three Blind Mice* (New York, 1992).
James L. Baughman, *The Republic of Mass Culture* (Baltimore, 1992).

— JAMES L. BAUGHMAN

TELLER AMENDMENT

Teller Amendment, a disclaimer on the part of the United States in 1898 of any intention "to exercise sovereignty, jurisdiction or control" over the island of Cuba when it should have been freed from Spanish rule. It was proposed in the Senate by Henry M. Teller of Colorado and adopted, Apr. 19, as an amendment to the joint resolution declaring Cuba independent and authorizing intervention. Spain declared war on the United States five days later.

BIBLIOGRAPHY

J. F. Rhodes, *The McKinley and Roosevelt Administrations.*

— JULIUS W. PRATT

TEMPERANCE MOVEMENT

Although the temperance movement originated in the sporadic attempts to curb the use of intoxicants during the 17th century, the first temperance society in America was formed in 1808 at Moreau, Saratoga County, N.Y., by Billy J. Clark, a physician. Clark had been much impressed by Benjamin Rush's *An Inquiry Into the Effects of Spirituous Liquors on the Human Mind and Body* (first published in 1784), for it confirmed his own ideas based on long observation of intemperance among his patients. The forty-four members of the unique society signed a pledge to "use no rum, gin, whisky, wine or any distilled spirits . . . except by advice of a physician, or in case of actual disease." It was no ironclad pledge, but it became the model for other groups opposed to intemperance.

More important than the work of Clark was the influence of Lyman Beecher, pastor at East Hampton, N.Y. He was inspired by Rush's essay to preach a series of sermons in 1810 against the current drinking customs. Entering on a pastorate at Litchfield, Conn., the following year, Beecher persuaded the political and ecclesiastical leaders of the "standing order," fearful of the tendency of the "ungodly" to join the Jeffersonian Republicans, that it was essential to organize in order to save the state from "rum-selling, tippling folk, infidels and tuff-scruff." From this agitation came the Connecticut Society for the Reformation of Morals (May 19, 1813), which was dedicated to the suppression of drunkenness, gambling, and general lawlessness. Meanwhile, the Massachusetts clergy, supported by Federalist politicians, had organized their campaign against intemperance (February 1813) under the leadership of Jedidiah Morse and Jeremiah Evarts. Auxiliary societies were soon formed in New England and New York, but for a decade no phenomenal victories were won.

Not until 1825 were the forces of evangelical Protestantism really mobilized for the temperance crusade. In that year Lyman Beecher again stirred his parishioners with powerful sermons, which were printed and widely distributed. The response to his appeal quickly took form; on Feb. 13, 1826, sixteen clergy and laymen in Boston signed the constitution of the American Society for the Promotion of Temperance. Their action revealed a new spirit. The temperance reformers were now under divine compulsion to send out missionaries to preach the gospel of total abstinence from the use of strong spirits. Using an effective system of state, county, and local auxiliaries, the Boston society soon claimed to be national. Voluntary contributions enabled it to support agents who visited every part of the country striving to affiliate all temperance groups with the national society. By 1834 there were auxiliaries in every state and approximately 5,000 locals and 1 million pledge signers were affiliated with them. Two years later there were eleven weekly and monthly journals devoted solely to temperance, while many religious periodicals carried news of the reform movement. Despite limited financial resources, the reformers printed and distributed millions of tracts. In song and story, in pageant and play, in essay and sermon, the temperance plea was presented to the nation.

In 1836, at the annual convention of the American Temperance Union (ATU), sponsored by the American Temperance Society, dissension appeared within the ranks. The delegates wrangled over three proposals: (1) to denounce the antislavery reformers and placate the southern temperance societies; (2) to sponsor legislation against the liquor traffic; and (3) to adopt a pledge of "total abstinence from all that can intoxicate." The convention avoided a decision on the first two proposals, but by a narrow majority adopted the total abstinence pledge. As a result there was a noticeable decline in the membership of the societies affiliated with the ATU, for many insisted that abstinence and temperance were not synonymous and vigorously opposed placing wines and malt beverages under the ban.

The ground thus lost was more than regained during the decade of the 1840's, as the Washington Temperance Society revival brought a remarkable increase in pledge signers. Labeling themselves reformed drunkards, the Washingtonians in the spring of 1841 began to stage sensational "experience meetings," which aroused the interest of thousands who had not been reached by the literary propaganda of the older societies. The emotionalism of such meetings was contagious, and the most successful temperance lecturer of the day, John B. Gough, soon utilized it in winning converts. While Washingtonianism was at its height, Father Theobald Mathew, whose campaign against intemperance among his fellow Irish countrymen had won worldwide acclaim, undertook a speaking tour through the United States. Between July 1849 and November 1851, according to the *New York Herald*, he traveled 37,000 miles and administered the pledge to almost 500,000 Catholics.

Beneath the surface the temperance movement had been slowly converted into a campaign for prohibition. A few leaders had long been eager to direct the force of law against the liquor traffic; they had denounced the licensing of retail dealers in intoxicants; they had supported such legislation as the "fifteen gallon law" of Massachusetts (1838), which forbade the sale of less than fifteen gallons of spirituous liquors "and that delivered and carried away all at one time." The demand for statewide prohibition was most ably expressed in Maine, where Neal Dow, a successful merchant of Portland, had committed the temperance groups to the policy of legal coercion. In 1846 the legislature passed an act that prohibited the retail sale of intoxicants. Not satisfied, Dow's followers secured a truly prohibitory statute in Maine in 1851. New York State put a law into effect prohibiting the sale of intoxicants in 1845, but the law was repealed in 1847.

The Anti-Saloon League and other temperance forces succeeded in securing passage in 1919 of an amendment outlawing the manufacture and sale of alcoholic beverages.

In September 1869 delegates from twenty states met in Chicago to form the Prohibition party. Its purpose was to seek legislative prohibition of the manufacture, transport, and sale of alcoholic beverages. The party failed to gain the support of either the Democrats or the Republicans, and in 1872 began to nominate its own presidential candidates. At first the Prohibition party candidates received only a few votes, but by 1892 their candidate, John Bidwell, received 265,000 votes. Three years later the nonpartisan Anti-Saloon League was formed by members of temperance groups and evangelical Protestant church groups. It too sought government control of liquor.

The temperance movement was aided during World War I by the enforcement of conservation policies that limited the output of liquor. By 1919 temperance forces, most notably the Anti-Saloon League, had succeeded in securing passage of the Eighteenth Amendment to the U.S. Constitution, which prohibited the manufacture, sale, import, and export of alcoholic beverages. But bootlegging and smuggling of intoxicating beverages increased so rapidly that the enforcement of national prohibition was extremely difficult. The Twenty-first Amendment (1933) repealed Prohibition. Thereafter the temperance movement waned, local option was put into effect in a number of states, and by 1966 no statewide prohibition law existed in the United States.

BIBLIOGRAPHY

Herbert Asbury, *The Great Illusion.*
J. R. Gusfield, *Symbolic Crusade.*
J. A. Krout, *The Origins of Prohibition.*

— JOHN A. KROUT

TENEMENTS

Tenements are legally defined as multiple dwellings, buildings in which more than three families live independently under one roof. Unlike apartment houses, they became notorious, for their degraded condition, the result in many cases of absentee landlordism. In the 19th and 20th centuries poor housing was rampant in New York City and in the major cities of the eastern seaboard, the South, and the Midwest. Few people spoke out against these slums.

The first Real Property Inventory (RPI), which was conducted in the 1930's during the Great Depression, revealed that the tenement house was not restricted to New York City. The RPI report indicated that President Franklin D. Roosevelt's "One third of the nation . . . " was indeed ill housed. New York's Lower East Side found its parallel in Chicago's West Side and in every city in the nation; and conditions were even worse in the inflammable wooden three-decker tenements of Boston's Dorchester and in small mill towns throughout the country where factory housing was invariably condensed in an attempt to keep it readily accessible to the industrial plants it served.

The battle for housing reform in New York City, for example, was a painfully slow series of investigations, reports, laws, and amendments (and in the last quarter of the 20th century poor conditions still prevailed in great sections of the city). In 1867 about two-thirds of the city's population lived in tenement houses. As apartment houses were not built before 1869, this left the remaining one-third living in quarters above stores, and in hotels and boardinghouses—only a relatively small number lived in privately owned townhouses.

As early as 1842 John H. Griscom, a New York City inspector, drew attention to the fact that cellars were being used as dwellings. In 1846 the Association for Improving the Condition of the Poor reported on the living conditions of tenement dwellers. In 1857 the State Legislative Committee on the Condition of Tenement Houses pointed out the close relationship of poverty to a decline in morality.

Progress was made at last in 1860, when a law requiring fire escapes was passed; in 1862 the Department for the Survey and Inspection of Buildings was established. In 1866 the Metropolitan Board of Health was created and on May 14, 1867, the first Tenement House Law, establishing minimum standards for room size, ventilation, and sanitation, was passed. It proved beneficial but was weakened by the discretionary powers vested in the Board of Health. In 1879 a meeting at Cooper Union led to the formation of a mayor's committee that advocated the construction of model tenements. The Improved Dwellings Association implemented this with a program of construction. The second Tenement House Law, an amendment of the one of 1867, was passed in 1879, requiring that tenements henceforth constructed occupy not more than 60 percent of the lot. A competition held in the same year resulted in the notorious "dumbbell" tenement, so called because the plans called for a dumbbell-shaped building. In 1887 a further amendment to the law provided for the permanent Tenement House Commission and was applied for the first time to old buildings that were being enlarged or altered.

Jacob A. Riis's revealing book, *How the Other Half Lives* (1890), helped create a state commission, headed by Richard Watson Gilder. Founded in 1894, the commission investigated conditions and wrote a voluminous report. In 1896 the City and Suburban Homes Company was formed, which built tenement houses throughout the city, using Ernest Flagg's competition-winning designs. In 1899 Flagg also designed the first fireproof tenement.

In 1900 the Charity Organization Society held a competition that resulted in the "new law" tenement, which supplanted the "dumbbell" plan. That year Gov. Theodore Roosevelt appointed the Tenement House Commission with Robert W. DeForest as chairman, for which Lawrence Veiller and I. N. Phelps Stokes drafted the Tenement House Act of 1901. This law forbade the construction of "old law" tenements, and the next year the separate Tenement House Department was created for New York City.

Tenement houses in New York City go back to the mid-1820's, when one was reputedly built at 65 Mott Street. In 1833 Henry Burgh, the humanitarian, built a row of tenements at the northeast comer of Water and Scammel streets. In 1850 a model tenement, Gotham Court, was built on a long narrow lot at 26 Cherry Street. It was destined to become the most squalid of them all. Setting a worthy precedent, Alfred T. White built three radically new model tenements in Brooklyn, Home Buildings (1877), Tower Buildings (1879), and Riverside (1890). Investing at low interest rates, the City and Suburban Homes Company, the Stokes family, and several philanthropists constructed model tenements that were designed by some of the most progressive architects of the day. From these model tenements, built from the 1890's through the 1920's, with their ample provisions for light and air, it was an easy step to the first housing project, Knickerbocker Village, constructed in 1934.

BIBLIOGRAPHY

Robert W. DeForest and Lawrence Veiller, *The Tenement House Problem.*

James Ford, *Slums and Housing.*

Roy Lubove, *The Progressives and the Slums,* and *I. N. Phelps Stokes: Tenement Architect.*

I. N. Phelps Stokes, *The Iconography of Manhattan Island, 1498–1909.*

Jacob A. Riis, *How the Other Half Lives.*

— ALAN BURNHAM

TEN-FORTIES

Ten-forties, gold bonds issued during the Civil War that were redeemable after ten years and payable after forty years. Authorized by Congress (Mar. 3, 1864) to allow greater freedom in financing the Civil War, their low 5 percent interest made them unpopular. Bond sales declined rapidly and forced the Treasury to resort to short-term loans.

BIBLIOGRAPHY

D. R. Dewey, *Financial History of the United States.*

— CHESTER MCA. DESTLER

TENNESSEE VALLEY AUTHORITY

A government-owned dam and nitrate-producing facility at Muscle Shoals, on the Tennessee River in northwestern Alabama, completed too late to produce the intended munitions for World War I, became the seedling of an audacious experiment in river valley development—the Tennessee Valley Authority (TVA). Nebraska Sen. George W. Norris in the 1920's hoped to build more dams comparable to Wilson Dam at Muscle Shoals and bring public control to the Tennessee River. Almost singlehandedly he held the dam in government ownership until the vision of President Franklin D. Roosevelt expanded it in 1933 into a broader conception of multipurpose development and regional planning. In 1933, prodded by Roosevelt, Congress enacted the Tennessee Valley Act.

The New Deal could not have designated a river valley more appropriate for control and development. The Tennessee drains a seven-state area of 40,000 square miles, where 52 inches of annual rainfall often brought damaging floods. The region was poor, its 3 million people earning only 45 percent of the average national per capita income. Roosevelt and the first directors of the TVA—Chairman Arthur E. Morgan, David Lilienthal, and Harcourt A. Morgan—envisioned a publicly owned corporation, nationally financed but based in the region, which would harness the unruly Tennessee River, holding back its floods and drawing electric power from its torrent. But the TVA was to be more than a flood control and power agency. It was seen as a regional planning authority, with a wide mandate for such undertakings as economic development, recreation, reforestation, and the production of fertilizer.

The agency's early years were filled with controversy. Private utilities fought TVA power policies in the courts, and an internal feud between Chairman Arthur Morgan and directors Lilienthal and Harcourt Morgan unsettled the agency's direction until 1938. But by 1941 the authority was able to show stunning progress. It operated eleven dams with six more under construction and was selling low-cost electric power to 500,000 consumers in six states. TVA technicians developed a concentrated phosphate fertilizer well adapted to the soils of the area, and 25,000 demonstration farms instructed local citizens in the benefits of more scientific farming. During World War II, 70 percent of TVA power went to defense industries, chief among them the Oak Ridge atomic project.

During World War II, 70% of TVA power went to defense industries, chief among them the Oak Ridge atomic project.

The agency survived criticism from conservatives in the 1940's and 1950's, and by the early 1970's claimed an impressive record. In 1972 it was estimated that $395 million in flood damages had been averted by the authority's dams since 1936; freight traffic on the Tennessee, which had been 1 million tons in 1933, had increased to 27 million tons annually; and power revenues came to $642 million, of which TVA returned $75 million to the U.S. Treasury. Two million residential consumers, along with industry, used TVA power in 1972, paying half the national average per kilowatt hour. TVA technicians demonstrated new fertilizers and advised farmers on crop diversification. The agency encouraged recreational development and ceded much parkland to local governments. Roosevelt called the South the nation's number one economic problem in the 1930's, and TVA appears to have been one of the major reasons for the economic growth of the area during the decades after World War II.

Attacked in the beginning for being too radical, TVA later found itself criticized for being too conciliatory to established interests and traditional ideas. Director Lilienthal claimed that TVA practiced "grassroots democracy" by reaching out in a massive educational effort to involve the dispersed rural population of the valley. But critics saw mostly manipulation in this approach and scored the agency's decision to work through the existing institutions for agricultural field work—the land grant colleges, the Department of Agriculture's Extension Service, and county agents—even though they were dominated by the more affluent white farmers. Undeniably, TVA had made an early decision not to challenge the region's agricultural power structure or its racial customs, a decision that brought crucial local support for TVA power programs but also charges of the abandonment of early ideals. Not intended in the beginning to be primarily a producer of electric power, TVA gradually allowed electricity to overshadow its other interests, and thus found itself in the 1960's the nation's largest single user of strip-mined coal (80 percent of TVA power is now generated in coal-burning plants). Soon the agency was the recipient of attacks from angry environmentalists who had repudiated TVA's developmental ethic. These troubles seemed to be the price that the agency had to pay for its successful (but singleminded) economic development of the Tennessee Valley region.

BIBLIOGRAPHY

David E. Lilienthal, *TVA: Democracy on the March.*
Marguerite Owen, *The Tennessee Valley Authority.*
Philip Selznick, *TVA and the Grass Roots.*

— OTIS L. GRAHAM, JR.

TENURE OF OFFICE ACT

Tenure of Office Act, passed by Congress Mar. 2, 1867, over President Andrew Johnson's veto, was designed to restrict greatly Johnson's appointing and removing power. The Senate's consent was required for removals in all cases in which its consent was necessary for appointment. At first the design seems not to have been that of protecting any particular cabinet member—these officers were expressly excepted—but rather Republican appointees in general. But after considerable debate a proviso was inserted that cabinet members should hold office during, and for one month after, the term of the president who made the appointment, subject to removal only with the Senate's consent. Violation of the act was made a high misdemeanor. When Johnson attempted to remove Secretary of War Edwin M. Stanton the Radical Republican Congress proceeded with its long-laid plans for the impeachment and trial of the president. As Stanton was not a Johnson appointee, the act could not be applied to him. Passed during, and as part of, the struggle between Johnson and Congress over Reconstruction, sections of the act were repealed early in Ulysses S. Grant's first administration; the rest of the act was repealed Mar. 5, 1887.

BIBLIOGRAPHY

D. M. Dewitt, *The Impeachment and Trial of Andrew Johnson.*

R. W. Winston, *Andrew Johnson.*

— WILLARD H. SMITH

TERRITORIES OF THE UNITED STATES

Territories of the United States are those dependencies and possessions over which the United States exercises jurisdiction. Until the turn of the 19th century, American experience was almost exclusively directed to the creation of territorial governments within the continental United States. The force of the Northwest Ordinance of 1787 set the precedent that territorial status was a step on the path to statehood, during which time residents of the territories maintained their citizenship and their protections under the Constitution. Alaska and Hawaii, admitted in 1959, were the last of the territories to become states and the only exceptions to the pattern of contiguity with existing states and territories. Although new states were admitted, in the 20th century the United States entered an era when the appropriate destiny of its territorial acquisitions was not necessarily statehood.

For the Spanish possessions ceded to the United States in 1898, the peace treaty did not include the promise of citizenship found in earlier treaties of annexation. Subject only to the limitations of the Constitution, Congress was free to determine the political status and civil rights of the inhabitants. In the Insular Cases, decided in 1901, the Supreme Court held that Congress could distinguish between incorporated and unincorporated territories and that the full guarantees and restraints of the Constitution need not be applied to the latter. Congress uniformly chose to treat its new acquisitions as unincorporated territories and so enjoyed a flexibility not present in the earlier pattern of territorial government.

In common with other dependencies Puerto Rico was initially subject to military control, although this period was brief. Its inhabitants became U.S. citizens in 1917. Civil government with a gradual broadening of self-rule culminated in an act of Congress in 1950 that authorized Puerto Rico to formulate and adopt its own constitution, which came into effect in 1952. The result was the organization of Puerto Rico as a commonwealth defined as "a politically organized entity . . . in which power resides ultimately in the people, hence a free state, but one which is at the same time linked to a broader political system in a federal or other type of association, and therefore does not have independent or separate existence." While commonwealth status is not the equivalent of statehood and did not terminate U.S. authority, the agreement that neither Congress nor the president should annul Puerto Rican legislation guaranteed the commonwealth the maximum degree of autonomy accorded to any of the territories.

The Virgin Islands were purchased from Denmark in 1917 and citizenship was conferred in 1927. Its political status has been determined by acts of Congress enacted in 1936 and 1954. While the powers of its unicameral legislature were expanded and the inhabitants elected their own governor, territorial government remained closely defined and limited.

Guam did not attract significant attention until World War II, after which it became the site of major military installations. Guamanians became citizens in 1950, framed and adopted a constitution in 1969, and since 1970 have elected their governor as well as members of the legislature. Congressional revisions of the Organic Act permitted Guam its constitution.

American Samoa became a distinct entity in 1899 and remained under the administration of the U.S. Navy until 1951. In 1960 a constitution was formulated with Samoan participation and was then accepted and promulgated by the secretary of the interior. In 1975 Samoa still continued as the responsibility of the Department of the Interior. Its people were nationals rather than citizens of the United States.

The Treaty of 1903, by which the United States acquired the Panama Canal Zone, gave the United States in perpetuity the freedom to exercise all rights and powers as though it were sovereign. A governor was appointed by the president with full authority to administer the zone. In 1967 an attempt to revise the political status of the Canal Zone failed; American proposals were unacceptable to the Republic of Panama.

With the exception of Guam, islands of the Caroline, Marshall, and Mariana groups have been held by the United States as trust territories under the United Nations since 1947. The trust agreement charges the United States with the development of the islands toward "self-government or independence." Administrative responsibility rests with the Department of the Interior. In 1965 the Congress of Micronesia held its first session; as of 1975 it continued as an important means of expressing Micronesian needs and aspirations.

BIBLIOGRAPHY

Department of State, *Bulletins*, vol. 61 (Sept. 8, 1969), vol. 63 (Sept. 21, 1970), vol. 66 (June 12, 1972).

Whitney T. Perkins, *Denial of Empire: The United States and Its Dependencies.*

— ROBERT L. BERG

TERRORISM

Terrorism uses low levels of violence or intimidation for political ends. U.S. terrorist groups have been racist (Ku Klux Klan, Black Panthers), nationalist (Puerto Rican Liberation Army), opposed to a strong central government (Posse Comitatus), antiwar (Weathermen, Symbionese Liberation Army), and xenophobic and anti-Semitic (neo-Nazi skinheads). From 1985 to 1993 there were five to ten terrorist incidents in the United States annually, mostly bombings and arson, with about the same number of suspected and prevented incidents. The first incident of international terrorism against the United States occurred just before the Algeciras Conference in 1904, when the Moroccan chief Ahmed ibn-Muhammed Raisuli kidnapped Ion Perdicaris, a naturalized American citizen, from his villa near Tangier. Secretary of State John Hay telegraphed the U.S. consul-general in Tangier demanding "Perdicaris alive or Raisuli dead." The public acclaimed the tough handling of the incident, but an unpublished part of the telegram had warned the consul to avoid force without specific instructions.

This photo of Particia Hearst was released by the Symbionese Liberation Army on Apr. 3, 1974, together with a tape recording of Hearst claiming that she had joined the terrorist SLA after having been kidnapped 58 days before. (UPI/Corbis-Bettmann)

The Department of State has kept statistics on international terrorism since 1968. The data show that U.S. citizens and property have been the most frequent targets of terrorism—about 20 percent of all international incidents in 1985 and more than 40 percent in 1990. In 1975 American citizens suffered 36 percent of the casualties from international terrorism; in 1985, 21 percent; and in 1990, only 5 percent. U.S. casualties peaked at 386 (271 fatalities, 115 wounded) in 1983, when on October 23, 241 marines died when a member of the Islamic Jihad drove a truck loaded with dynamite into the barracks at the Beirut International Airport. The level of terrorism has been directly related to U.S. foreign policy. There were, for example, some 160 terrorist attacks worldwide within six weeks of the start of the Gulf War in January 1991. The most significant international terrorist act against the United States was the seizure of the U.S. embassy in Tehran, Iran, on Nov. 4, 1979. Fifty-two Americans were held for 444 days with the collusion of the Iranian government. They were released on Jan. 20, 1981, in return for the $6 billion in Iranian assets frozen in U.S. banks. The event helped defeat Jimmy Carter in the 1980 presidential election. The worst incident of international terrorism within the United States was the Feb. 26, 1993, bombing in New York City of the World Trade Center, the tallest building in the nation's most populous city. Six people were killed and more than 1,000 injured by explosives equal to 1,500 pounds of TNT.

The U.S. government has demanded the extradition of terrorists, trained foreign antiterrorist forces, launched air strikes, and enforced trade sanctions against states that support terrorism. It also has traded weapons to Iran for hostages kidnapped in Lebanon and reportedly paid $3 million to Sheik Mohammed Hussein Fadlallah, who organized the 1983 bombing of the marine barracks, not to attack U.S. interests in Beirut again. International terrorism accounted for fewer than 2,000 deaths during 1970–1979 and just over 4,000 fatalities during 1980–1989. Terrorism has been more frightening and dangerous than these statistics indicate, however, because terrorists have targeted civilians and attempted to destabilize governments.

[See also Beirut Bombing; Fundamentalism; Hostage Crisis; Oklahoma City Bombing; White Supremacists.]

BIBLIOGRAPHY

Walter Laqueur, *The Age of Terrorism* (Boston, 1987).
John L. Scherer, ed., *Terrorism* (Minneapolis, 1986–, quarterly).
U.S. Department of State, *Patterns of Global Terrorism* (Washington, D.C., annually).
Alexander Yonah, ed., *Terrorism: An International Journal* (New York, 1977–1991, quarterly).

— JOHN L. SCHERER

TEXAS V. *WHITE*

Texas v. *White*, 7 Wallace 700 (1869), an attempt by the Reconstruction governor of Texas to prevent payment on federal bonds disposed of by the secessionist state government in payment of supplies for the Confederacy. The Supreme Court acknowledged the governor's competence to sue on the ground that Texas was now, and had never ceased to be, a member of "an indestructible Union"; hence the ordinance of secession was void. The president's Reconstruction acts were termed "provisional" with permanent authority on this subject vested in Congress. As to the immediate issue, the Court denied the power of the secessionist government to dispose of state property for purposes of rebellion. The decision was overruled in 1885 in *Morgan* v. *United States* (113 U.S. 476, 496).

BIBLIOGRAPHY

Charles Warren, *The Supreme Court in U.S. History.*

— HARVEY WISH

TEXTILES

Technology

All the technological elements of the European handicraft textile trades, except possibly the Dutch ribbon loom, came to America with the colonists. The preparation of wool and cotton yarn required hand cards and spinning wheels (the spindle wheel and the bobbin-and-flyer wheel). The preparation of linen yarn required scutching boards and knives, brakes, hackles, and the bobbin-and-flyer wheel. Reels, swifts, pirn winders, warping bars, and handlooms figured in weaving, and the finishing of woolen cloth entailed fulling stocks, teasle handles, and shears. All operations, apart from fulling, could be adequately performed in the home. Despite England's mercantilist policies, aimed at relegating colonial manufacturing to the household subsistence level, the regional standardization in New England of at least one technique (yarn numbering) suggests a measure of professionalism, if not capitalism, in the trade.

Fortuitously, the American Revolution coincided with Britain's industrialization. Between the revolutionary war and the War of 1812 the immigration of British artisans and the promotion of the American interest in manufacturing brought the new British industrial techniques of manufacturing textiles to the United States. In defiance of British prohibitory laws, the essential components of the new cotton processing system (the picker, card, drawing frame, roving can frame, double speeder, jenny, mule, waterframe, throstle, twisting frame, warping mill, power loom, and roller printing machine) crossed the Atlantic as whole machines, parts, plans, or mental images. Likewise, the elements of the new woolen manufacturing system (the picker, card, billy, jenny, jack, warping mill, fly-shuttle hand loom, gig mill, and screw press) were smuggled out of Britain. This period of technological acquisition and industrial experimentation also witnessed the invention of three important labor-saving devices by Americans: the cotton gin, by Eli Whitney (1794); the rotary cloth shear, by Samuel G. Dorr (1792); and card clothing machines, by Amos Whittemore (1797) and Pliny Earle (1803).

By the 1830's the factory system, utilizing the new powered machinery, emerged as the dominant organizational form in the cotton and woolen industries. During the initial period of industrialization, 1814–40, product market competition and America's endowment of the factors of production impelled manufacturers to make capital-intensive modifications of the British technology. Conforming to a number of labor-saving manufacturing principles (large-scale production; production of standardized, lower-quality yarns and cloths; vertically integrated manufacturing; flow production; extended use of inanimate power; high operating speeds; consolidation of mechanical processes; maximum mechanical control and work; and automatic fault detection), a variety of significant innovations appeared. Inventions important for cotton manufacturing were the railway drawing head, by William B. Leonard (1833); roving speeders, by George Danforth (1824) and Gilbert Brewster (1829); the roving frame differential gear, by Asa Arnold (1823); cap spinning, by Charles Danforth (1828); ring spinning, which raised spindle speeds from 3,000 to 6,000 revolutions per minute, by John Thorp (1828); self-acting loom temples, by Ira Draper (1816); the dobby head for fancy power-loom weaving, by William Crompton (1837); and stop motions for the warping frame, by Paul Moody (1816), and for the drawing frame, by Samuel Batchelder (1832). The use of self-acting cotton mules, some from England, spread in the 1830's and 1840's. In woolen manufacturing, John Goulding's condenser (1826), the woolen power loom (1820's), and Crompton's dobby head effected the greatest savings.

Orders for equipment softened the machine-building industry and brought a period of relative technological stagnation between the 1840's and about 1870, when immigration, the Civil War, and the westward movement stimulated the demand for textiles. Apart from George Wellman's self-stripping card (1853) and the popularization of ring frames, improvements in cotton machinery came from England: fly frames for better quality yarns after 1840 and a highly productive slasher after 1867. In the woolen industry the Apperly intermediate card feed, also from England, and self-acting winding devices for spinning jacks were introduced in the 1860's. In weaving, Crompton increased fancy broadloom speeds to eighty-five picks per minute (1857) and Lucius J. Knowles invented a more rugged head motion and, similarly capital-saving, the openshed principle (both 1863). Use of the rotary fulling mill, claimed by American and British patentees, spread in the 1840's. Probably the most significant innovations of this period were Erastus B. Bigelow's jacquard power loom for weaving Brussels carpets (1846–48) and Elias Howe's sewing machine (1846).

After 1870 inventive effort was directed toward labor-saving, rather than capital-and-labor-saving, improvements. High speeds, simple designs, hard-wearing construction, large capacity, automatic feeding and control, and further mechanization of manual tasks were introduced to compensate for the limitations of the unskilled immigrant labor force. The most spectacular results occurred in the cotton industry. In cards, higher capacities were complemented by the perfected self-clearing action of the revolving flat card, imported from England in 1885. With the rise of the competitive southern cotton industry in the 1880's, the northern mills turned to the manufacture of finer goods. To make these, Heilmann-type combers, invented in 1845, were brought from Europe. American combers, first built in the 1890's, culminated in the Whitin model of 1904–05, which out-paced European models in simplicity, speed, and capacity.

But spinning and weaving underwent the most far-reaching changes. Buying up spindle patents and manufacturing the best of them, George Draper and Sons of Hopedale, Mass., created a revolution in ring spinning. For example, Francis J. Rabbeth's spindle (1878), with its lightweight and self-centering features, raised spindle speeds up to 10,000 revolutions per minute. Between 1871 and 1890, George O. Draper (not to be confused with George Draper) calculated, the new spindles saved the industry $100 million. Certainly they spelled extinction for the cotton mule.

The automatic loom, developed by a group of Draper engineers (1888–94), incorporated James H. Northrop's bobbin changer, a self-threading shuttle, a weft feeler, and Charles F. Roper's warp stop motion (the first really successful one). Whereas the common power loom had to be halted every five minutes for the shuttle to be replenished manually, the automatic loom could weave indefinitely. Consequently, one weaver could run about twenty-four automatic looms, compared to about eight common ones. Supporting these major advances were many accessory ones, such as the Barber knotter (1900), which saved 10 percent in spooling time, and numerous incremental improvements recorded in thousands of patent specifications.

Capital-intensive trends continued in other branches of the textile industry. William C. Bramwell's automatic card feed (1876) and the belated adoption (1870's) of the English automatic mule stood out in woolen manufacturing. Higher throwing speeds and the automatic loom (about 1916) gained the largest labor savings for the silk industry. And in knitting, the perfection of the automatic, seamless, circular knitting machine by J. L. Branson and E. R. Branson (1899) and others gave an enormous fillip to the hosiery trade.

The discovery of polymer fibers, beginning with nylon, made it possible to program a fiber with particular chemical properties for specific uses.

The rise of modern science transformed the nature of textile innovation. Traditionally, progress had come from empirical effort in mechanical engineering, applied mostly to the physical manipulation of natural fibers. But advances began to spring from fundamental research in the laboratory. The succession of synthetic dyes discovered after 1856 reduced labor costs, widened color ranges, improved color consistency, and encouraged better fabric designs. Synthetic fibers presented more profound changes. Viscose rayon and acetate, pioneered in Europe and commercially manufactured in America after 1910 and 1918, respectively, had begun to challenge the supremacy of the natural fibers in many of the weaving and knitting branches by the 1930's. The discovery of polymer fibers, beginning with nylon, developed 1928–38 by Wallace H. Carothers of E. I. Du Pont de Nemours and Company, eventually made it possible to program a fiber with particular chemical and physical properties for specific uses.

In traditional yarn and cloth manufacturing, labor-saving innovations continued. Fernando Casablancas' long draft roving and spinning heads (1913) were adopted in the U.S. cotton industry in the 1930's to give economies in roving and better yarns from mixed fiber lengths (the result of more scientific cotton cultivation). And the continuous spinning principle was at last applied to wool in Durrell O. Pease's woolen ring spinning frame (1888–95), developed by the Whitin Machine Works (1928–31). It completely ousted the woolen mule in the 1940's and 1950's.

Technical developments in the 1950's and 1960's included such revolutionary devices as nonweaving techniques for making carpets and disposable clothing and breakspinning in which twist is inserted without package rotation. In traditional processing, labor and capital savings were pursued through electronic and mechanical automation (as in carding or jacquard knitting), greater capacities (as in roving and spinning packages), and higher speeds (as in water-jet looms that weave at 500 picks per minute or in automatic knitting machines that knit 4 million stitches per minute).

— DAVID J. JEREMY

Industry

Cotton textile manufacture was the first American industry to make the transition from a handicraft to the factory system and to develop the automated technology necessary for large-volume production. The early history of the industry was characterized by a high return on investment, which eventually attracted new entrants and resulted in the industry's rapid maturation into a highly competitive, cyclical business. Expansion of capacity was rapid and steady, until by 1900 the textile industry was probably the nation's largest single employer of industrial labor and producer of machine-made goods—but the expansion was accompanied by a deterioration of working conditions that nurtured social antagonisms.

The first phase of the textile industry's development took place in the 1790's, when Samuel Slater introduced the automated carding and spinning machinery that Richard Arkwright and Jedediah Strutt had recently developed in England. Backed by Rhode Island mercantile capital, Slater organized in southern New England a number of small, power-driven spinning factories. The second phase of the industry's development began during the War of 1812, when a group of Boston merchants led by Francis Cabot Lowell and Nathan Appleton entered the industry with their large financial resources. To Slater's preparatory machinery they added a power loom and a number of related features that contributed the final components necessary for the application of power and automation to textile manufacturing processes. Between 1820 and 1830 they organized a number of large and very profitable factories at Waltham and Lowell, Mass.

These developments came at a time when Boston mercantile capital was seeking domestic outlets for investment, and the textile industry, one of the few industries suitable for large-scale investment, was ideal. As other Boston merchants sought to invest in the industry, the Lowell group saw an opportunity to profit from the organization of new enterprises. At Lowell they established a promotional corporation that sold land, waterpower, and machinery at a large profit to new manufacturing corporations, which they themselves organized. More profits followed from the sale of stock in those enterprises to other merchants. So successful were the Lowell promotional operations that other entrepreneurs sought to repeat them elsewhere, thus precipitating an industrial boom that was without precedent in American history. The Lowell industrial pattern was repeated in numerous New England towns between 1830 and 1850—Lawrence, Chicopee, and Holyoke, Mass.; Manchester, Somersworth and Dover, N.H.; and Saco and Lewiston, Maine.

The promotional pattern developed at Lowell had serious implications for the industry's future. Each of the industrial centers had large investments in real estate, waterpower, and machine-shop facilities, which could be productively employed only through the expansion of the industry. There were many instances in which the owners of the industrial developments themselves started new mills principally to provide markets for their waterpower, mill sites, and machinery. The industry thus continued to expand at a furious rate in good times and bad, and capacity increased without regard to market demand.

Entry into the textile industry was facilitated because of the existence of the numerous machine shops in New England that made the latest machinery available to new entrants on attractive terms. When the South began to industrialize after the Civil War, it was able to import from New England the technology and equipment necessary to build a large textile industry rapidly. This fact, and the availability of cheap labor, explains the rapid rise of the industry in that area. Throughout the expansionist period capacity and machine productivity increased steadily, the prices of all products fell, and profit margins shrank. By 1850 conditions in the industry had deteriorated to the point where profitability was marginal and the pattern of earnings highly cyclical.

The textile industry's exponential growth pattern had a number of effects on American society. It provided

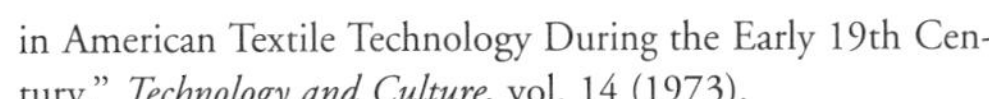

low-cost cotton goods to an expanding national population, and some of its sophisticated technology permeated other industries. The profits, marginal as they were at times, provided the venture capital that eventually developed the railroad, mining, communications, and other industries. The southern plantation system was provided for many years with an expanding market for its cotton, and thus slavery was given an economic *raison d'être*, which it might not otherwise have had. Management in the factories, faced with the relentless task of exacting a return on capital in the face of shrinking profits, constantly sought ways to reduce labor costs. Working conditions invariably deteriorated in the factories, precipitating lockouts, strikes, riots, and eventually the development of antagonisms between capital and laboring classes. In Massachusetts and the other industrial areas, these antagonisms brought about social, constiutional, and ethnic conflicts that became part of the American political heritage.

BIBLIOGRAPHY

Arthur H. Cole, *The American Wool Manufacture.*

George S. Gibb, *The Saco-Lowell Shops, Textile Machine Building in New England, 1813–1849.*

David J. Jeremy, "British Textile Technology Transmission to the United States: The Philadelphia Region Experience, 1770–1820," *Business History Review*, vol. 47 (1973), and "Innovation in American Textile Technology During the Early 19th Century," *Technology and Culture*, vol. 14 (1973).

James Montgomery, *A Practical Detail of the Cotton Manufacture of the United States of America.*

Robert V. Spalding, *The Boston Mercantile Community and the Promotion of the Textile Industry, 1813–1860* (unpublished doctoral dissertation, Yale University, 1963).

Caroline F. Ware, *The Early New England Cotton Manufacture: A Study in Industrial Beginnings.*

— ROBERT V. SPALDING

THANKSGIVING DAY

After the first harvest of the Plymouth, Mass., colonists in 1621, Gov. William Bradford appointed a day of thanksgiving and prayer. Another in 1623 celebrated a fall of rain after a drought. After 1630 an annual thanksgiving came to be observed after harvest, and other New England colonies took up the practice in desultory fashion. During the revolutionary war the Continental Congress recommended days of thanksgiving, and in 1784 it decreed a special one for the return of peace. President George Washington proclaimed one on Nov. 26, 1789, at the setting up of the new government, and another in 1795 for general benefits. President James Madison in 1815 again asked the nation to give thanks for peace. By 1830 New York had adopted the day as an annual custom, and other northern states followed its lead. In the South the custom did not appear until 1855, when it was adopted by Virginia, and thereafter by the other southern states. President Abraham Lincoln in 1863 began the practice of a national proclamation, fixing the fourth Thursday (later in the 19th century it came to be regularly the last Thursday) in November, although he had no power to order a holiday in the various states. In 1939 President Franklin D. Roosevelt upset the precedent of several decades' standing by proclaiming Nov. 23 as Thanksgiving Day (the third Thursday). Many governors refused to accept

The 18-member Raymond Baker family of Joliet, Illinois, enjoys Thanksgiving dinner in 1948. In 1941, Congress enacted a resolution fixing the fourth Thursday of November as Thanksgiving Day, a national holiday. (UPI/Corbis-Bettmann)

this date, and in their states Nov. 30 was the accepted festival, although a few actually authorized the celebration of both dates. Roosevelt also proclaimed the third Thursday in November of 1940 and 1941 as days of thanksgiving, but the disagreement as to the day on which the holiday should be celebrated continued. Therefore, Congress enacted a resolution in 1941 setting the fourth Thursday of November as Thanksgiving.

BIBLIOGRAPHY

Robert J. Myers and others, *Celebrations: The Complete Book of American Holidays.*

— ALVIN F. HARLOW

THEATER

Although professional theater did not develop in America until the middle of the 18th century, amateur performances were recorded as early as 1598, when a Spanish *comedia* was acted on the banks of the Rio Grande near the site of present-day El Paso, Tex. The first known performance in the English colonies, an amateur production of a playlet called *Ye Bare and Ye Cubb*, was presented in Virginia in 1665. The performers were arrested for presenting the play but were found "not guilty of fault." Productions by student actors took place at Harvard (1690) and at William and Mary (1702), and between 1700 and 1750 a number of performances by strolling amateurs with professional aspirations were seen at Williamsburg, Va., New York City, Philadelphia, and other major towns. But not until 1752 did the first important professional actors, a company led by Lewis Hallam, appear in the colonies.

The Hallam troupe, a family operation that had played at English fairs and at their own small playhouse in London, was typical of the modest touring company that flourished in the English provinces during the 18th century. They brought with them characteristic provincial ideas about theatrical organization and management that were to dominate theater practice in America until the Revolution and to set the pattern for later companies. The Hallams arrived in September 1752 in Williamsburg and in the next three years performed there and at simple, improvised playhouses in New York, Philadelphia, and Charleston, S.C. In 1755 the troupe sailed for Jamaica, where a theater operation under David Douglass was already established. The next year Hallam died, and in 1758 his widow married Douglass, who took over the company, which continued to perform in Jamaica and on the mainland. Douglass was successful in establishing the first fairly substantial permanent theater buildings in the colonies, among them the Southwark Theatre in Philadelphia, opened in 1766, and the John Street Theatre in New York, opened in 1767. In 1775, after the Continental Congress banned all "exhibitions of shews, plays, and other expensive diversions and entertainments," Douglass left permanently for Jamaica. The prohibition against theater was more honored in the breach, and the Revolution marked a return to amateur performance by both British and American troops. Also, a small group of amateur plays were written on patriotic themes—the first major burst of playwriting in the colonies.

After the war, members of Douglass' troupe soon returned to America, competing with other new companies and helping the rapid expansion of theater along the eastern seaboard. By the 1790's there were four principal professional circuits in the East, centered at Charleston, Philadelphia, New York, and Boston. The theatrical fare offered on these circuits consisted mostly of English plays, although an increasing number of turn-of-the-century American writers were writing plays. They included Royall Tyler, author of *The Contrast* (1787), the best-known early American play; the painter and theater manager William Dunlap; and John Howard Payne, the first American to achieve international recognition as a playwright. By 1800 most important eastern cities possessed relatively handsome and well-equipped theater buildings, generally similar to the better English provincial theaters in their appointments and decoration.

West of the Alleghenies, professional performance conditions remained as primitive as they had been in the East during the Hallam era. Troupes toured by flatboat or wagon, setting up whenever and wherever there was a chance of attracting a profitable crowd. Samuel Drake, for example, who toured as far as Kentucky in 1815, carried only the few simple sets and equipment necessary to turn any convenient room into a crude theater. By the late 1830's some of the problems of adequate staging were solved through the use of showboats to bring theater to major river towns. Among the pioneer professional companies in the West were those of James H. Caldwell, who performed in the Mississippi Valley towns in the 1820's and 1830's, and the troupe formed by Noah Miller Ludlow and Solomon Franklin Smith, which by the 1840's had become the leading theatrical organization in the West.

In the East theater continued to expand during the first half of the 19th century, although the perilous financial climate of the period led to managerial difficulties and a number of bankruptcies. Hard-pressed managers hit on many schemes to attract patrons, among them the importation of foreign stars to perform with local stock companies. During the 1820's and 1830's such famous foreign performers as Edmund Kean, William Charles Macready, Charles Kemble and his daughter, Fanny Kemble, and Lucia Elizabeth Mathews, known as Mme. Vestris, toured the United States, along with an increasing number of lesser European actors. At first, star tours tended to be restricted to the major theatrical centers of the East, but as transportation improved and the touring concept proved itself, stars ranged farther and farther West. In many ways touring stars represented a mixed blessing for local stock companies, for they often demanded and got immense salaries for slipshod and poorly rehearsed work, and frequently caused dissension among local acting companies whose members felt they were doing nothing except supporting the star.

For the most part, early 19th-century stock actors, like the touring stars, were English and trained initially in the English theater. Gradually, a small group of talented and imaginative native actors developed, among them Edwin Forrest, the first American actor to gain international fame. Forrest popularized a so-called "American" school of acting, a highly athletic performance style that contrasted sharply with the relatively restrained acting of such touring English stars as Kemble and Macready and that became extremely popular with the American theatergoer.

Much of Forrest's success came in new American plays, a number of them built around native themes or characters. One of Forrest's major roles was the part of the heroic Indian chief in *Metamora, or the Last of the Wampanoags* (1829), by John Augustus Stone. The "noble savage" character had already appeared earlier in several plays by George Washington Parke Custis, and from the 1830's to the Civil War era the romantic Indian play provided a staple of American entertainment. After the war increasing controversy between whites and Indians led to a far less heroic portrait of the Indian on the stage.

Also popular toward the middle of the century were plays featuring the so-called "Yankee." A simple and often naive figure, but invariably earnest, stout-hearted, and patriotic, the Yankee was first seen in the character of Jonathan in Tyler's *The Contrast.* Over the years a line of "Yankee specialists" developed, and between about 1830 and 1850 dozens of tailor-made Yankee plays appeared. If the Yankee stood for rural values and standards, urban life was represented by the figure of the volunteer fireman. The fireboy appeared initially as the diamond-in-the-rough Mose the Bowery Bhoy in Benjamin A. Baker's *A Glance at New York in 1848* (1848), the first of many city lowlife comedies that were in vogue until the 1860's.

Large cities offered a wide choice of entertainments at mid-century, including such curiosities as panoramas and dioramas, which featured highly realistic scenes of famous places or well-known historical events, and the "dime" museum, an institution popularized by the showman Phineas T. Barnum, Barnum's American Museum in New York City, first opened in 1842, combined an exhibition of freaks and curiosities with a highly respectable variety entertainment or play presented in a so-called "lecture room." One of the attractions in Barnum's lecture room was a dramatized version of Harriet Beecher Stowe's sensationally popular novel *Uncle Tom's Cabin.* Within a few years after the novel's appearance in 1852, dramatic versions were appearing at theaters all over the country, with touring companies of "Tommers" performing in tents in the most remote areas. The traveling Tom Show continued to attract audiences in small towns and rural areas throughout the century, and in some cases represented the only theater to be seen in isolated areas except for the occasional medicine show, free entertainment by traveling quacks who hawked medicine between the acts.

Immensely popular at mid-century was the minstrel show, a uniquely American form of variety performance that featured white entertainers in blackface presenting songs, jokes, dances, and comedy sketches. The professional minstrel troupes flourished from about 1850 to 1870. The form gradually declined, and by World War I only a handful of professional companies continued to perform, although amateur minstrelsy could still be seen for some years to come. Also in demand at mid-century were burlesques, in which well-known plays, novels, events, and personalities were parodied in light musical productions. Among the best-known burlesques were those created by John Brougham and George W. L. Fox. Fox also helped to popularize a version of traditional English pantomime in the United States through his production of *Humpty Dumpty* (1868), successive editions of which appeared throughout his life.

By the middle of the 19th century, professional theater troupes had reached the Far West, spurred by the appearance of gold in California in 1848, the discovery of the Comstock lode in 1859, and other major mining strikes. Troupes in the West were also fostered by the Mormons, who were vitally interested in theater and, after 1865, sponsored a resident professional company in Salt Lake City, Utah. In 1869 the first transcontinental railroad opened the entire West to touring companies.

The number of resident stock companies in America gradually increased; there were about fifty on the eve of the Civil War. Among the best was the company formed in 1853 at the Arch Street Theatre in Philadelphia by John Drew and Louisa Lane Drew, the founders of the famous Drew-Barrymore theatrical dynasty. Although the stock company remained the major producing organization in most urban areas, its form was altered by new developments. Companies relied less, for example, on producing many plays in rotation, choosing instead to limit the number of plays and give each a relatively long run. By the last quarter of the century local repertory had been almost totally destroyed by the long-run concept and the touring company. As railroad connections continued to improve throughout the United States, so-called "combination" companies—essentially packages made up of a long-running play or plays, a star, and a company of supporting players—began to appear more and more frequently. Gradually local stock companies were forced into the unenviable position of performing in their own theaters only when those theaters were not occupied by more popular and prestigious combination productions. By 1900 there was scarcely a resident stock company left in business.

As the touring show replaced the stock company, critical booking problems developed for theater owners and managers, who were forced to book each show of the season separately, and often from a different producer. This situation led to the increased use of booking agents and, in 1896, to the so-called "Theatrical Syndicate"—a group of entrepreneurs headed by Charles Frohman—which offered managers a full season of first-class road shows on the understanding that the managers book only through the syndicate. It gradually gained control of important theaters throughout the country. Uncooperative managers and producers were often forced out of business, and stars who refused to appear in syndicate shows often found it impossible to obtain any theater in which to perform. The syndicate was opposed by a number of powerful figures in the American theater, among them the actress Minnie Maddern Fiske and her husband, the dramatist and editor Harrison Grey Fiske, as well as by David Belasco, James A. Herne, and James O'Neill, a prominent actor and the father of the playwright Eugene O'Neill. The Shubert brothers, Sam S., Lee, and Jacob J., also opposed the syndicate. Setting up a rival operation, the Shuberts gradually wrested more and more control from the syndicate until, by 1916, it was no longer an effective force in the theater.

The 19th-century theater witnessed a growth of interest in both realism and spectacle. By the last third of the century, elaborate machinery was being developed at major theaters to handle an increasingly complex and detailed stagecraft and one that relied more heavily on the three-dimensional box setting. Booth's Theatre, for example, erected in 1869 in New York City by the actor Edwin Booth, substituted a flat floor, stage elevators, and an elaborate overhead rigging system for the traditional raked stage and wing and groove scenery borrowed from the English stage and found in most American theaters built from the 18th century on. Steele MacKaye, an actor, playwright, producer, and theater manager, created a stage that was even more complex technically at his Madison Square Theatre (1879); it had a huge double elevator stage, permitting complete scene changes in about 40 seconds.

The interest in realistic scenery and staging found its most famous exponent in Belasco, a former employee of MacKaye, who presented onstage such naturalistic coups as a completely equipped Childs' Restaurant and a genuine boardinghouse bedroom, which he purchased and reerected as a stage setting. Realism and spectacle presented difficult staging problems for touring companies, which were often forced to work in theaters outfitted only with traditional stage machinery, much of it of doubtful quality. The motion picture, introduced to Americans toward the end of the century, provided a medium that could satisfy an audience's desire for local color and spectacle in meticulous detail. The first motion-picture theater was opened in 1905 in McKeesport, Pa.; within four years there were 8,000 more scattered about the United States. Ultimately they offered formidable competition to legitimate and variety theaters, and the appearance of talking pictures in 1927 was a serious blow to live theater.

By the last quarter of the century a number of professional playwrights had emerged, including MacKaye, Bronson Howard, Bartley Campbell, and Augustus Thomas. Among the most notable were William Clyde Fitch; the playwright-actor William Gillette, best known for his Civil War melodrama *Secret Service* (1895) and his adaptation from the stories of Sir Arthur Conan Doyle, *Sherlock Holmes* (1899); and Herne, author of the important realistic drama *Margaret Fleming* (1890). The farces of Charles H. Hoyt and Edward Harrigan were an important contribution to the stage of the day, as the plays of George M. Cohan were in the first years of the new century. The burlesque tradition established by Brougham, Fox, and others, which featured scantily clad dancers, moved farther in the direction of the musical variety show, which it was to become in the 20th century. Vaudeville, which had developed out of the earlier male-only variety shows, had become a vital force in American entertainment and was to remain so until its decline in the 1930's. The Yiddish Theater in New York, at a low ebb around the turn of the century, was shortly to begin a period of great creativity and prosperity under the leadership of such figures as Maurice Schwartz and Rudolph Schildkraut.

For the most part, American theater in the first years of the 20th century was parochial and avowedly commercial, with few really first-rate playwrights and little interest among theater people in innovative production techniques or in the experiments taking place in European theaters. Gradually, the work of European playwrights, directors, and stage designers began to make its influence felt in the United States. The plays of Henrik Ibsen and George Bernard Shaw were produced in America, and by World War I American audiences had seen Dublin's Abbey Theatre (1911), Sergei Diaghilev's Ballets Russes (1916), and Jacques Copeau's company (1917), as well as Max Reinhardt's starkly designed production of *Sumurun* (1912). Other European experiments in stage and costume design—generally referred to collectively as the "new stagecraft"—were brought to the United States in the work of Joseph Urban, the Viennese designer who joined the staff of the Boston Opera Company during the 1911–12 season, and in the efforts of two young European-trained American designers, Robert Edmond Jones and Lee Simonson.

Among the most important influences from Europe was the so-called "independent theater" movement, a name given to the experimental theater groups that arose in the last quarter of the 19th century in France, Germany, England, and Russia. The result in the United States was a number of "little theaters" that drew their inspiration from the independent theater tradition. Among the best known were the Neighborhood Playhouse and the Washington Square Players, both established in New York in 1915, and the Provincetown Players, founded at Provincetown, Mass., the same year and relocated in New York in 1916. By the early 1920's one branch of the Provincetown Players under Eugene O'Neill, Kenneth Macgowan, and Jones was presenting daring experiments in playwriting and production. The Washington Square Players became the Theatre Guild in 1918 and, under the leadership of director Philip Moeller and Simonson, presented a number of excellent plays.

Ironically, the misery and dissent of the Great Depression produced some of America's most interesting theater work, much of it antiestablishment or experimental in approach. An active workers' theater movement, which led to the production of many Socialist protest plays, had begun to develop as early as the mid-1920's. In 1933 the Theatre Union was formed in New York to coordinate the activities of the rapidly developing workers' theater groups around the country. By 1937 the Theatre Union had failed, and by the beginning of World War II workers' theater in America had largely disappeared. Meanwhile the Federal Theatre Project was established in 1935 in an attempt to help alleviate unemployment in the theater. The Federal Theatre presented more than a thousand productions around the country, the most famous of which were the "Living Newspapers," documentary performances that focused on such topics as slum housing and rural electrification. The political flavor of much of the Federal Theatre's work led to congressional hearings, and in 1939 its funds were discontinued. Out of the Federal Theatre came the experimental Mercury Theatre, founded in 1937 by Orson Welles and John Houseman, and perhaps best known for its anti-Fascist *Julius Caesar*, produced the same year.

In 1923–24 Konstantin Stanislavski's Moscow Art Theatre toured the United States. Two of the actors, Richard Boleslavski and Maria Ouspenskaya, remained in America after the company returned to Russia, and from 1923 to 1930 they ran the American Laboratory Theatre, which first popularized the Stanislavski System of actor training in America. In 1930 former students at the American Laboratory Theatre were influential in founding the Group Theatre, modeled on Stanislavski's organization and perhaps the most important American theater company of the 1930's. Among those associated with the Group Theatre were Harold Clurman, Cheryl Crawford, Elia Kazan, Lee Strasberg, and Stella Adler, a member of the distinguished Yiddish Theater family. The Actors Studio, founded by Strasberg, Crawford, and Kazan in 1947, became the home of the Stanislavski System in America. The Playwrights' Company, founded in 1938 in an attempt to get productions by major dramatists on stage in spite of the depression, continued to be a force in the American theater until 1960.

Between World War I and World War II the United States began to produce playwrights of international reputation, among them Maxwell Anderson, Sidney Howard, Robert E. Sherwood, Philip Barry, Elmer Rice, S. N. Behrman, Thornton Wilder, Clifford Odets, and Lillian Hellman. Perhaps America's most important playwright was O'Neill, author of such works as *Anna Christie* (1921), *The Hairy Ape* (1922), *Desire Under the Elms* (1924), *Ah, Wilderness!* (1933), and *Long Day's Journey Into Night*, written in 1940–41 and posthumously produced in 1956.

The years after World War II witnessed the development of a number of other new playwrights, notably Tennessee Williams, author of *The Glass Menagerie* (1945), *A Streetcar Named Desire* (1947), and *Cat On a Hot Tin Roof* (1955), and Arthur Miller, whose most significant works include *Death of a Salesman* (1949), *The Crucible* (1953), and *A View From the Bridge*

(1955). In the 1960's, Broadway produced a capable and talented commercial playwright, Neil Simon, and the sensitive and potentially significant writer Edward Albee, author of *Who's Afraid of Virginia Woolf?* (1962) and *Tiny Alice* (1964).

In the same period the American musical comedy was developed to a high level in such work as *Oklahoma!* (1943), by Oscar Hammerstein II and Richard Rodgers and based on the popular Lynn Riggs play *Green Grow the Lilacs* (1931), and the musicals of Alan Jay Lerner and Frederick Loewe—*Brigadoon* (1947) and *My Fair Lady* (1956). Other important musical comedies included *Gentlemen Prefer Blondes* (1949) and *Funny Girl* (1964) by Jules Styne and *West Side Story* (1957) by Leonard Bernstein and Arthur Laurents.

In spite of such capable work, Broadway theater offerings continued to decline in both number and quality, the victims of rising ticket prices and growing competition from television. The postwar era was marked, however, by a flurry of regional theater activity, including the founding of Theatre 47 (1947) in Dallas by Margo Jones, the Arena Stage (1949) in Washington, D.C., the Actors' Workshop (1952) in San Francisco, and the Minnesota Theatre Company (1963) in Minneapolis, with Sir Tyrone Guthrie as director. Interest in regional theater continued throughout the 1960's, although the early 1970's witnessed a great deal of financial anxiety on the part of theaters outside New York, as well as those on Broadway. But many of the summer stock companies founded during the postwar period have succeeded, and light summer theater entertainment is available throughout the country.

The problems that beset the New York theater in the 1950's led to the growth of the off-Broadway movement, which featured low-budget, often experimental productions of plays that could not get a hearing on Broadway. Among them were the works of the French "Absurdist" playwrights—Jean Genêt, Eugene Ionesco, and Samuel Beckett. Important off-Broadway organizations included the Circle in the Square, founded in 1951 by José Quintero and Theodore Mann, and the Phoenix Theatre, founded in 1953 by Norris Houghton and T. Edward Hambleton.

The Living Theatre (1948), directed by Julian Beck and Judith Malina, began as an off-Broadway troupe, then became part of the later off-off-Broadway movement. Centering around experimental performance, off-off Broadway attained international importance through such play-producing organizations as Ellen Stewart's Cafe La Mama (1962), later the La Mama Experimental Theatre Club, Al Carmines' Judson Poets' Theater (1961) at the Judson Memorial Church on Washington Square in Greenwich Village, and Theatre Genesis at Saint Mark's Church-in-the-Bowery in the East Village. The same period produced a number of experimental theater companies, which depended less on the work of playwrights than on productions created out of group exercises and improvisation. Along with the Living Theatre, other important companies working in this way included Joseph Chaikin's Open Theater and Richard Schechner's Performance Group. In the 1960's and 1970's much interest was generated by the Ontological-Hysteric Theater (1968), an experimental group directed by Richard Foreman. Since 1955 the activities of experimental theater in America have been covered by the *Drama Review* (formerly the *Tulane Drama Review*), a New York magazine devoted to avant-garde performance.

BIBLIOGRAPHY

O. S. Coad and Edwin Mims, Jr., *The American Stage.*

Alan S. Downer, *Fifty Years of American Drama, 1900–1950.*

John Gassner, *Theatre at the Crossroads Plays and Playwrights of the Mid Century American Stage.*

Barnard Hewitt, *Theatre USA, 1668 to 1957.*

Richard Moody, *America Takes the Stage: Romanticism in American Drama and Theatre, 1750–1900.*

Montrose J. Moses and John Mason Brown, *The American Theatre As Seen by Its Critics, 1752–1934.*

Arthur Hobson Quinn, *A History of the American Drama from the Beginning to the Civil War,* and *A History of the American Drama from the Civil War to the Present Day.*

Carl J. Stratman, *Bibliography of the American Theatre, Excluding New York City.*

Gerald Weales, *American Drama Since World War II.*

Garff B. Wilson, *A History of American Acting.*

— BROOKS MCNAMARA

THEATER SINCE THE 1960S

Profound changes began to occur in theater during the 1960s, establishing patterns that prevailed into the 1990s. The major development was decentralization of the professional theater, which provided careers for artists outside New York City and made professional theater accessible to audiences throughout the United States. Theaters were most often established as not-for-profit operations, heavily dependent on local and federal support. The regional shift occurred because rising production costs in New York discouraged risk taking and admission prices gradually increased (in 1994 Broadway theater tickets reached a high of $75). By the early 1990s, 300 not-for-profit professional theaters were playing to more than 16 million people annually. Despite the demise of forty theaters between 1980 and 1993, largely the result of economic pressure, in the early 1990s not-for-profit theaters were a $366 million industry.

One interesting result of the spread of American theater was transference of successful productions by regional theaters to New York (and national or international recognition), beginning with the Washington, D.C., Arena Stage production of Howard Sackler's *The Great White Hope* in 1976. Since then major American plays have frequently originated outside New York: David Mamet's *Glengarry Glen Ross* (Chicago's Goodman Theatre, 1984), Marsha Norman's *'night, Mother* (American Repertory Theatre in Cambridge, Mass., 1983), Herb Gardner's *I'm Not Rappaport* and *Conversations with My Father* (both presented first at the Seattle Repertory Theatre), and all of the plays by African-American playwright August Wilson, beginning with *Ma Rainey's Black Bottom* (Yale Repertory Theatre, 1984). Sixteen of the seventeen Pulitzer Prizes in drama (1976–1993) went to plays developed by not-for-profit companies. The winner of the 1992 prize, Robert Schenkkan's *The Kentucky Cycle* was seen first in Seattle in 1991. The 1993 winner, Tony Kushner's *Angels in America*, received the prize several weeks before its Broadway opening, after development in London, San Francisco, and Los Angeles.

A residual effect of the socially committed, aesthetically radical theater artists of the late 1950s and early 1960s, and in opposition to theater epitomized by Broadway, was an avant-garde theater centered in the Off-Broadway and Off-Off-Broadway districts and in major cities throughout the country. This avant-garde theater paralleled the winding down of the Vietnam War. Stimulated by the English-born director Peter Brook and the Polish national Jerzy Grotowski, it sought to strip away old conventions and reach what Brook and Grotowski called a "holy" core or essence. Experiment led to changes in style and structure and encouraged new topics and such cross-disciplinary hybrids as dance-theater, performance art, docudrama, environmental theater, guerrilla theater, and New Vaudeville. Eschewing conventional plots and characters, director-playwrights Richard Foreman, Lee Breuer, and Robert Wilson emerged in the 1970s, and such ensembles as Mabou Mines and the Wooster Group turned from polemic to self-reflective visionary and aural images. In the 1980s a more conservative atmosphere encouraged radical artists—for example, Eric Bogosian, Laurie Anderson, Karen Finley, Spalding Gray, and Anna Deavere Smith—to explore social and political issues in more personal ways. The controversial authorial voice of stage directors, which began in the 1970s, intensified in the work of JoAnne Akalaitis, Meredith Monk, Elizabeth LeCompte, Anne Bogart, and Peter Sellars.

All the while there was an expansion of demographics on stage and in the audience. The voices of African Americans, Latinos, Asians, gays, and women, in the past on the fringe, reached the centers of theater. Previously marginalized artists moved into positions of considerable visibility. Pulitzer Prizes were won by Beth Henley (*Crimes of the Heart*, 1981), Marsha Norman (*'night, Mother*, 1983), and Wendy Wasserstein (*The Heidi Chronicles*, 1989), raising by half the number of Pulitzers in drama awarded to women since their inception in 1918. The African-American director George C. Wolfe became producer of the New York Shakespeare Festival, a major not-for-profit theater established by Joseph Papp (1921–1991). In 1993 the National Endowment for the Arts appointed as its head actress Jane Alexander, the first artist to hold this post.

Commercial theater since the early 1970s, despite unwillingness to experiment and despite soaring production costs, has enjoyed considerable prosperity, with long runs of spectacular musicals, many imported from abroad, such as *Cats, Les Misérables, Phantom of the Opera, Miss Saigon, Sunset Boulevard*, and others with small-cast plays. Major figures included playwright Neil Simon, whose *Lost in Yonkers* (1991) won the Pulitzer Prize, and composer-lyricist Stephen Sondheim, who continued to be the most original American creator of musical theater. Playwrights who first gained attention in the 1970s, such as John Guare, Terrence McNally, and August Wilson, became major voices in the theater by the late 1980s. By the mid-1990s, however, despite productions dealing with controversial subjects (*Kiss of the Spider Woman, Angels in America*), Broadway continued to be dominated by musical revivals (*Guys and Dolls, Crazy for You, She Loves Me, Joseph and the Amazing Technicolor Dreamcoat, My Fair Lady, Damn Yankees, Show Boat*).

BIBLIOGRAPHY

C. W. E. Bigsby, *Modern American Drama, 1945–1990* (New York, 1992).

Mary C. Henderson, *Theater in America: 200 Years of Plays, Players, and Productions* (New York, 1986).

Don B. Wilmeth and Tice L. Miller, *Cambridge Guide to American Theatre* (New York, 1993).

— DON B. WILMETH

THIRD PARTIES

Although the fortunes of the various third (or "minor") political parties have waxed and waned, there have been few periods since the middle of the 19th century in which the American party system has been without them. Diverse both in origin and in goals, third parties have had in common only the fact that they have been largely noncompetitive within the American two-party system.

Some of the American third parties have been marked by overriding commitments to issues—whether to a single issue, a cluster of issues, or a full-blown ideology—such as the antislavery Liberty and Free Soil parties of the 1840's and 1850's, the agrarian protest parties of the post–Civil War period (Greenback and Populist parties), and the Socialist parties of the 20th century (Socialists, Socialist Workers, and Socialist Laborites). While these parties have rejected to varying degrees the usual political pragmatism and thus the electoral competitiveness of the major parties, some of them have been electoral parties in the more conventional sense. The National Progressive ("Bull Moose") party of 1912 and the Dixiecrat party of 1948, for example, did plan on some form of electoral success resulting from the operation of the electoral college, the former by winning statewide pluralities in a three-way race and the latter by preventing the major parties from winning the necessary majority in the electoral college.

In organizational form, too, American third parties have been diverse. A good many of them have been small organizations with national memberships but with little or no state or local apparatus. Others have developed the layers of party committees found in the major parties, especially in states or localities in which they have been strong. Still others, such as George Wallace's American Independent party in the 1960's and 1970's, have largely been national movements centering around a single person and maintaining only those local organizations necessary to achieve access to the ballot in the states. Finally, some especially evanescent third parties have had virtually no organization, national or local; this has been the case especially in those parties formed for tactical advantage in specific elections—for example, the Dixiecrats of 1948.

The electoral effect and importance of the third parties have not been great. Since the formation of a stable two-party system around the time of the Civil War, no third party has won a presidential election. Only the National Progressive Party of 1912, with Theodore Roosevelt as its candidate, came in second. Only four other third parties have even carried a state in a presidential election: the Populists in 1892, the Progressives in 1924, the Dixiecrats in 1948, and the American Independents in 1968. (Technically, the candidates of the Dixiecrats in 1948 carried several states as the official candidates of the Democratic parties of those states.) In many other presidential elections the total vote for all third-party candidates amounted to less than 1 percent of the total vote, and in 1964 it dipped to less than 0.2 percent. Indeed, many of the third parties by the middle of the 20th century found it increasingly difficult both to get on the ballots of the states and to muster the resources for a campaign.

Some third parties have enjoyed at least short periods of electoral success in some states and localities. Some have controlled local office for varying periods of time; the Socialist party, for example, held many mayorships before World War I, including those in Cincinnati and Milwaukee. In 1968 and afterward, the predominantly black National Democratic party of Alabama elected a number of local officials in that state. Some third parties have even managed to win governorships and to control state legislatures. The Nonpartisan League (which despite its name was indeed a party) controlled the North Dakota governorship and legislature from World War I into the 1920's, and its offshoot, the Farmer-Labor party of Minnesota, controlled that state's governorship and showed substantial strength in the legislature throughout the 1930's. Other local parties functioned by capturing one of the two major parties in the primary and running its candidates under that party's label; the Wisconsin Progressives so operated within the Republican party until the 1930's.

The success of the third parties in nonelectoral politics is less easy to assess. They have been thought of generally as instruments of protest, as having nurtured unpopular ideas and policies into popularity. It is true, for instance, that a number of the social and economic reforms that were enacted nationally in Franklin D. Roosevelt's New Deal had long been featured in the platforms of such third parties as the Socialist party. Nevertheless, it is difficult to say whether these reforms would have languished without early third-party sponsorship. Perhaps it would be more accurate to say simply that many social reform movements have managed to gain support in the United States through a number of avenues, including the third parties.

BIBLIOGRAPHY

William B. Hesseltine, *The Rise and Fall of Third Parties.*
Richard Hofstadter, *The Age of Reform.*
George Thayer, *The Farther Shores of Politics.*

— FRANK J. SORAUF

THIRD PARTIES AND INDEPENDENTS

The decline since 1960 in identification among the electorate with either the Republican or Democratic parties contributed to a proliferation of minor parties and two of the most successful independent presidential tickets in U.S. history. Third parties in the United States have always been quite diverse in goals and organization. With the exception of Alabama Governor George Wallace's American Independent party in the presidential election of 1968, the only aspect such parties have had in common is their failure to influence the electoral process. Wallace's party exemplified the third party as protest vote, and his strength at the polls (13.5 percent of the total) inspired the administration of Richard M. Nixon to adopt rhetoric and policies specifically designed to capture Wallace's traditionally Democratic followers for the Republican party. Wallace competed in the Democratic primaries in 1972 but was shot in an assassination attempt, and the party he founded faded into obscurity.

Most third parties are ideologically based, and purity of doctrine is more important than pragmatic efforts to build a campaign organization and establish a coalition of voters. The Marxist parties—Socialist Workers, Communist, Socialist Labor, Workers World, Socialist—are cases in point. All remained active through the 1980s, but none received more than one-tenth of 1 percent of the votes cast, in part because state laws make it difficult for third-party candidates to qualify to be on ballots. The Libertarian party has achieved greater success on the far right of the political spectrum. Emphasizing individual freedom, an unregulated market economy, and voluntarism (even to the extent of opposing the power of taxation), the Libertarians have contested most national and many state offices. Their presidential candidate in 1980, Ed Clark, received just over 1 percent of the vote, and the 1992 candidate, Andre Marrou, .28 percent. A few minor parties focus essentially on a single issue, much like interest groups. The Prohibition party continued to field presidential candidates, although it drew only a few thousand votes per election and only 985 votes in 1992. The Citizens party, founded by Barry Commoner in 1969 and similar to the Green parties in Europe, qualified for federal matching funds in 1984 but attracted only 72,000 presidential votes. The Right-to-Life party, which opposes abortion, has received even fewer votes.

Far more impressive than third parties has been a series of independent candidates. Former Democratic Senator Eugene McCarthy drew almost 1 percent of the vote nationally in the 1976 presidential election. Republican John Anderson qualified for federal matching funds in 1980, initially while contesting his own party's primaries and then as an independent in the general election. He spent almost $15 million on the campaign and captured 6.6 percent of the popular vote. In 1990 maverick Republican Lowell Weicker won the governorship of Connecticut as an independent, while Bernard Sanders of Vermont ran as an independent for the U.S. House of Representatives and became the first Socialist elected to Congress since World War I. In the 1992 presidential campaign Texas billionaire Ross Perot ran as an independent and captured almost 19 percent of the popular vote (the best third-party showing since Theodore Roosevelt ran as a Progressive in 1912), even though he dropped out of the race for ten weeks in midsummer. Perot created a tightly controlled campaign organization, designed primarily to obtain signatures to qualify him for the ballot in every state. He spent tens of millions of his own dollars on lengthy network television "infomercials," $3 million on election eve alone. He was also the first third-party candidate to be included in televised presidential debates. Perot's success illustrated both widespread disaffection with the major parties and the crucial importance of money in politics.

BIBLIOGRAPHY

Earl R. Kruschke, *Encyclopedia of Third Parties in the United States* (Santa Barbara, Calif., 1991).

Frank Smallwood, *The Other Candidates: Third Parties in Presidential Elections* (Hanover, N.H., 1983).

— KEITH IAN POLAKOFF

THIRTEENTH AMENDMENT

Thirteenth Amendment, which abolished slavery, was one of the so-called Civil War amendments. As a compromise measure before the war began, Congress had adopted a resolution in February 1861 for an amendment that would deny it the power to abolish slavery in any state. But as the war progressed both the president and Congress became convinced that the federal government must assume power over slavery. By the Confiscation Acts of 1861–62, slaves of disloyal owners were subject to forfeiture to the national government and could thereby be freed. The Emancipation Proclamation, Jan. 1, 1863, as a war measure, declared free the slaves in the parts of the Confederacy still unconquered. At the end of the war existing laws and proclamations left the slaves of loyal owners untouched and did not apply to the whole of the slave-owning region; they provided for freeing the slaves, but did not abolish slavery as an institution. While slavery was virtually dead, its legal status was neither complete nor necessarily permanent. It was generally recognized that an amendment to the U.S. Constitution was required to clarify the legal issues. Resolutions had been introduced in both houses of Congress as early as December 1863, in the House by Rep. James M. Ashley of Ohio, and in the Senate by John Brooks Henderson of Missouri and by Charles Sumner of Massachusetts. In its final form the resolution was reported to the Senate by Lyman

Trumbull of Illinois, chairman of the Judiciary Committee. The phraseology used was almost identical with the slavery prohibition of the Northwest Ordinance of 1787. The second section of the amendment expressly gave Congress the power of enforcement by appropriate legislation.

At the end of the Civil War, existing laws and proclamations provided for freeing the slaves, but did not abolish slavery as an institution.

The resolution passed the Senate, Apr. 8, 1864, by a vote of 38 to 6. In the House it failed at first (June 15, 1864) to secure the necessary two-thirds vote, but passed later, 119 to 56, with 8 representatives not voting (Jan. 31, 1865).

Ratification of the amendment by the former seceded states was required as part of President Andrew Johnson's Reconstruction program, and eight of these states were counted officially in the three-fourths of the states necessary to ratification. These states were not considered states in the Union by Congress in the Reconstruction Acts of 1867, but their ratification of the amendment was not invalidated. The amendment was proclaimed ratified, and "valid as part of the Constitution of the United States," on Dec. 18, 1865.

BIBLIOGRAPHY

J. G. Randall, *The Civil War and Reconstruction.*

James Ford Rhodes, *History of the United States, 1850–1877,* vol. IV.

— C. MILDRED THOMPSON

THREE MILE ISLAND

Three Mile Island, site of the worst nuclear power program mishap in the history of the United States, is located in the Susquehanna River near Harrisburg, Pennsylvania. The event, which could easily have become a major disaster, shook public confidence in nuclear technology. The seven-day emergency began on Mar. 28, 1979, at Unit 2, one of two nuclear power plants built on the island in the early 1970s. The plant's operators initially mishandled the accident, and the resulting emergency was poorly managed by technical experts as well as state and federal officials responsible for public safety. The seriousness of the accident became clear, however, when both Governor Richard L. Thornburg of Pennsylvania and President Jimmy Carter visited the stricken plant while its operators were still struggling to resolve the menacing situation. A combination of faulty design and human error caused the problem. An overheated reactor core whose protective coolant was largely gone resulted in reactor temperatures as high as 4,300 degrees and the accidental release of radiation into the atmosphere. The event could have led to core temperatures so high (5,200 degrees) that the core would have melted through its base, resulting in unprecedented damage to the containment structure. Although a nuclear meltdown had never occurred, there was little doubt that such an event could have caused a release of deadly radiation into the atmosphere many times greater than the fallout created by the atomic bomb exploded at Hiroshima in the final days of World War II. The population around Three Mile Island and possibly—depending on prevailing winds—hundreds of miles away would have been in deadly peril. Government analysts calculate that, at the height of the crisis, the Three Mile Island reactor was within approximately one hour of a meltdown. The lessons learned at Three Mile Island led to stricter supervision and design modifications that, together with the prospects of high cleanup costs, such as those incurred at the stricken Pennsylvania plant, made earlier profit expectations unrealistic. Thus, the accident had a strong negative effect on the nuclear power industry's plans for building new plants.

[See also Nuclear Power; Nuclear Regulatory Commission.]

BIBLIOGRAPHY

Philip L. Cantelon and Robert C. Williams, *Crisis Contained: The Department of Energy at Three Mile Island* (Carbondale and Edwardsville, Ill., 1982).

Fred Clement, *The Nuclear Regulatory Commission* (New York, 1989).

Daniel F. Ford, *Three Mile Island: Thirty Minutes to Meltdown* (New York, 1982).

Mike Gray and Ira Rosen, *The Warning: Accident at Three Mile Island* (New York, 1983).

President's Commission on the Accident at Three Mile Island, *The Need for Change: The Legacy of Three Mile Island* (Washington, D.C., 1979).

— ROBERT M. GUTH

TIDEWATER

Tidewater is a term commonly used in American history to designate that part of the Atlantic coastal plain lying east of the points in rivers reached by oceanic tides. This region, the first to be occupied by settlers from the Old World, slowly became the habitat of comparative wealth. Merchants and shippers in the towns and planters growing tobacco, rice, indigo, and cotton dominated the tidewater population. Since the tidewater coastal area is so narrow in New England the terminology is more applicable elsewhere, particularly in the middle Atlantic and south Atlantic regions of the English colonies and the later states of the federal Union. First to settle and the earliest to be established economically, socially, and politically, the inhabitants of the tidewater regions secured control of the government. Almost inevitably they used the machinery of government for their own benefit and in accordance with their own traditions and ideals, and they resisted any effort to weaken their control. But the later population, composed largely of small farmers, which moved beyond into the piedmont region, found this tidewater domination of government both unfair and injurious. A serious and long-standing sectional conflict resulted. Sometimes, as in the case of Bacon's Rebellion of 1676 in Virginia, the Paxton riots of 1764 in Pennsylvania, and the Regulator movement of 1768–71 in North Carolina, the conflict resulted in open warfare. At times manipulation and compromise kept violence down. But on all occasions the serious conflict in ideals and interest had to be taken into consideration. The political history of the colonies, and later the states, can only be interpreted adequately in the light of this conflict.

Control of the government by the tidewater element of the population was maintained largely by a device of disproportional representation that was widely in operation from Pennsylvania to Georgia. Another device was restricted suffrage, wherein a heavy property qualification was used to the advantage of the wealthy of the tidewater and to the disadvantage of the poorer inhabitants of the interior. Using these devices to control the legislatures, the tidewater element pursued policies in regard to the Indians, debts, and taxes that were of most benefit to the tidewater population and therefore often injurious to the up-country population.

BIBLIOGRAPHY

F. J. Turner, *Sectionalism in American History.*

— ALFRED P. JAMES

TITANIC, SINKING OF THE

The largest ship in existence at the time, the White Star liner *Titanic*, bound for New York on its maiden voyage with 2,223 persons aboard, struck a partly submerged iceberg in the North Atlantic at 11:40 P.M. on Apr. 14, 1912. It sank 2 hours and 40 minutes later, with the loss of 832 passengers and 685 of the crew. Ocean wireless telegraphy was in its infancy then; many ships carried no radio; others had only a day operator. The liner *Californian* was only a few miles distant at the time, but its operator was asleep and its instruments silent. The eastbound liner *Carpathia*, fifty-six miles distant, caught the *Titanic*'s distress signal, sped to the scene, picked up over 700 survivors, and returned to New York. There was bitter criticism of the *Titanic*'s construction, of its shortage of lifeboats, of its high speed after receiving iceberg warnings, and of the *Californian*, whose crew admitted seeing rockets from the *Titanic*, but "didn't know what they meant." Among those who lost their lives were John Jacob Astor IV, Benjamin Guggenheim, and Charles Thayer.

BIBLIOGRAPHY

Lawrence Beesley, *The Loss of the Titanic.*
Walter Lord, *A Night to Remember.*

— ALVIN F. HARLOW

TOBACCO INDUSTRY

John Rolfe's experiments in 1612 to develop a tobacco to replace the indigenous variety, one suitable for commerce, soon produced a major exportable staple for colonial Virginia, Maryland, and North Carolina and ultimately a commercial commodity for some twenty states. The exportation of over 100 million pounds annually to England by the eve of the Revolution is ample evidence of its economic significance in the colonial period. The tobacco industry had regained its prewar productivity by 1790, when about 78 percent of the crop was exported. Although the United States exported 500 million pounds in 1970, this constituted only 25 percent of the total production. The remainder was consumed domestically.

One of the most conspicuous developments in the tobacco industry in the century and a half following the Revolution was its geographical expansion as a commercial staple. The decline and later end of tobacco production in postrevolutionary tidewater Virginia was accompanied by a comparable expansion into the piedmont district of Virginia and North Carolina and into South Carolina and Georgia by the early 1790's. What promised to be an important staple in South Carolina and Georgia was soon displaced by cotton for almost a century. By 1800 tobacco was emerging as a staple in Kentucky and Tennessee. During the next half century Florida, Louisiana, Missouri, Ohio, Arkansas, Indiana, Pennsylvania, New York, Connecticut, and Massachusetts began to produce tobacco commercially. Southern Wisconsin joined the ranks on the eve of the Civil War. In the late 19th and early 20th centuries, northern Wisconsin, Minnesota, South Carolina, Georgia, and Alabama became tobacco-producing states.

In addition to geographical expansion, another significant development in the 19th century was the gradual differentiation of tobacco into several distinctive types. This development resulted principally from the spread of the culture to new and different soil compositions, hybridization, and the development of three distinct curing methods (flue, dark-fired, and air). Different types of soil produce different types of tobacco. The new soil types thus explain why tobacco became a staple commodity only in certain states and in limited areas within these states. Changes in the popular method of consuming tobacco and the increase in per capita consumption also had a profound effect on the development of the various tobaccos. At the end of the colonial period all American tobacco tended to be classified as one type (Oronoco) and was consumed at home and abroad in two principal ways: it was smoked in clay pipes or ground up and used as snuff. During the first half of the 19th century chewing became the chief method of consuming tobacco and remained so until near the end of the century. Chewing is especially important in accounting for the rapid expansion of tobacco west of the Alleghenies. The darker tobaccos from the virgin soil of this area were popular for making the chewing plug and twist. The brighter tobacco produced in Virginia, North Carolina, Maryland, and Ohio was stimulated by the demand for a yellow leaf in which to wrap the dark licorice-laden chewing plug. The chewing public demanded that the "quid" be pleasing to the eye as well as to the taste.

In the antebellum period cigar consumption grew large enough to cause farmers in New England, New York, and Pennsylvania to try their hand at growing Cuban tobacco. The infant industry was soon stimulated by the growing popularity of cigars following the Mexican War. Chewing-tobacco consumption peaked and began its decline by the 1890's; cigar consumption continued to rise until 1907, and the production of cigar tobacco spread to Wisconsin, Florida, and Georgia.

Long before chewing and cigar consumption reached their peak of consumption, Americans returned to pipe smoking in large numbers and added the cigarette habit, which was introduced to Europeans during the Napoleonic campaigns and spread throughout Europe during the Crimean War. The smoking fad, aided by the perfection of American cigarette-manufacturing machines in the 1870's, rejuvenated the bright-tobacco industry in the southern states, including its spread into South Carolina, Georgia, and Florida, as well as the Burley-tobacco industry of Kentucky and Tennessee. By 1921 the cigarette had become the chief means of consuming tobacco in the United States and made the bright tobacco of the southern states the world's leading tobacco crop. In the 1970's cigarettes accounted for about 80 percent of the tobacco consumed in the United States, cigars about 10 percent, and snuff less than .015 percent. Bright tobacco constitutes over one-half of the total production and about 80 percent of the total leaf exported by the United States.

In 1970 American tobacco farmers received $1.5 billion for their crop. Tobacco provided a livelihood for thousands of farmers, factory workers, wholesale and retail tobacco sellers, and many more. The tremendous mechanization in the tobacco belts after World War II was an important stimulus to farm-machinery manufacturers, and the filter cigarette, which became popular in the 1950's, aided the expanding synthetic fibers industry. Given the federal, state, and local taxes levied on the enormous quantities of tobacco consumed annually in the United States, few U.S. commodities have contributed more to the American economy, despite its condemnation as a health hazard.

BIBLIOGRAPHY

L. C. Gray, *History of Agriculture in the Southern United States to 1860.*

G. M. Herndon, *William Tatham and the Culture of Tobacco.*

Meyer Jacobstein, *The Tobacco Industry in the United States.*

J. C. Robert, *The Story of Tobacco in America.*

N. M. Tilley, *The Bright-Tobacco Industry.*

— G. MELVIN HERNDON

TOBACCO INDUSTRY SINCE THE 1970S

Despite decades of turmoil caused by medical evidence that tobacco use creates a health hazard, in the mid-1990s the tobacco industry still maintained its important position in the U.S. economy. The industry enjoyed political and social approval during the first half of the twentieth century, although its pricing policies and advertising practices sometimes drew public ire. After the Supreme Court broke up the American Tobacco Trust in 1911, six corporations—American Tobacco, R. J. Reynolds, Philip Morris, Brown and Williamson, Liggett and Myers, and P. Lorillard—dominated cigarette manufacturing. Cigar, pipe, and chewing tobacco manufacturers likewise tended toward concentration, led by U.S. Tobacco. In 1946 the Supreme Court upheld lower court findings that cigarette manufacturers had tacitly fixed prices, albeit through collusion rather than formal agreement. Beginning in the 1950s the Federal Trade Commission (FTC) regularly issued cease-and-desist orders against tobacco manufacturers for misleading advertising, which made health claims in such slogans as "A Treat Instead of a Treatment" and "Not a Cough in a Carload." Despite such interventions cigarette smoking was encouraged by the government and even the Red Cross during both world wars and was adopted by many Americans as chic, convenient, and socially acceptable. Movies, advertising, and Prohibition promoted increased use of tobacco products. In 1920 the industry sold 298,590 metric tons of tobacco (or 11.3 grams per adult per day); by 1950 that number had risen to 511,880 (12.7 grams per adult per day). Increased use of cigarettes accounted for most of the growth. More than half of men and about a third of women smoked regularly in 1950.

Beginning in the 1950's the Federal Trade Commission regularly issued cease-and-desist orders against tobacco manufacturers for misleading advertising.

Medical studies regarding the safety of cigarette smoking threatened tobacco's economic and political status. During the early 1950s British and U.S. physicians, together with organizations like the American Cancer Society, began to publicize epidemiological studies showing a long-suspected association between cigarette smoking and cancer as well as heart disease and other ailments. Newspapers and magazines such as the *Reader's Digest* published articles condemning smoking, producing the first national health scare. As a result, in 1953 and 1954 both tobacco stock prices and cigarette consumption declined. Manufacturers responded in several ways: exporting to other markets, producing filter-tip cigarettes, and launching new advertising and public relations campaigns. Exports climbed after 1955, from 15 million cigarettes to 25 million ten years later; they increased more rapidly after 1970. The popularity of filter tips grew because smokers thought they were safer than regular cigarettes. Before 1953 just one brand of filtered cigarettes was sold in the United States, but each of the major companies put at least one brand on the market in 1953 or 1954; market share grew from 1 percent in 1950 to 19 percent in 1955. The industry spent $38 million on television, magazine, and newspaper advertising in 1954. It promoted filtered cigarettes, although not all filters were effective and some, such as one made of asbestos, were harmful.

Forbidden by a 1911 antitrust order to form a trade association, cigarette manufacturers engaged a New York public relations agency, Hill and Knowlton, which advised company presidents to recruit public relations firms, growers, and warehouses to create the Tobacco Industry Research Committee (TIRC). TIRC's mission was to provide research money for study of issues related to smoking and cancer and to conduct a public relations program. TIRC representatives insisted that because a clinical link between smoking and lung cancer had not been proven (which was true) more research should be conducted. In 1958 the Hill and Knowlton agency created the Council for Tobacco Research, responsible for scientific research only, and the Tobacco Institute, the industry's lobbying and public relations arm.

The 1964 U.S. surgeon general's *Report on Smoking and Health* created a second national health scare. Based on more than 4,000 published studies on tobacco use, the report indicated that without question smoking was hazardous and that the problem warranted remedial action. Two-thirds of the adults in a government survey that year said they believed smoking caused lung cancer, up from two-fifths the previous year. This widespread and growing belief brought a threat of federal regulation but neither the FTC or the Food and Drug Administration took decisive action, and the U.S. Department of Agriculture continued to provide subsidies to tobacco farmers. Congress divided on the issue of tobacco and health, usually to the industry's benefit. The first hearings on smoking and health took place in 1957, when a House committee found that the FTC had not adequately reacted to deceptive advertising about filters. After the surgeon general's report Congress in 1965 passed the Cigarette Labeling and Advertising Act, which required that all cigarette packages and advertisements contain the warning label "Caution: Cigarette Smoking May Be Hazardous to Your Health." Critics found the warning weak because it said "may be" rather than "is" and because it did not include warnings about lung cancer or other diseases. The industry opposed any label but accepted the 1965 version; ironically, the label later provided legal protection for the industry, which could prove that after 1965 smokers had been aware of potential risks associated with tobacco use but chose to smoke anyway.

Congressional investigation of cigarette advertising and an aggressive campaign that used the Federal Communications Commission's Fairness Doctrine to gain free air time for antismoking messages led manufacturers in 1970 to remove all cigarette ads from television and radio, while Congress continued to fund research on how to grow more and better tobacco. Revenue from tobacco taxes made it difficult for Congress to be decisive about regulating cigarette smoking. In 1964 annual federal taxes on cigarettes totaled $2 billion; state taxes brought in well over $1 billion.

Despite growing criticism of the industry, tobacco manufacturers never acknowledged that their products were harmful or addictive, although they offered filter tips and took steps to lower the amounts of tar and nicotine in cigarettes. Tobacco remained a legal product and tobacco interests gained exemptions from such measures as the Consumer Product Safety Act, the Fair Packaging and Labeling Act, the Hazardous Substances Act, and the Toxic Substances Control Act. During the 1980s tobacco corporations diversified by purchasing less controversial companies, such as Nabisco and General Foods, which helped protect stock prices. Exports, especially to Asia, continued to rise. Fifty years after the first major health scare the tobacco industry was valued at $50 billion and had 50 million consumers worldwide.

A wave of civil lawsuits against the tobacco industry also reflected smokers' concerns; between the mid-1970s and 1995 more than 400 unsuccessful lawsuits were filed. The companies responded with a no-compromise legal strategy. They defended every claim regardless of cost through trials and appeals. Tobacco attorneys outspent and outlasted plaintiffs who ran out of money or died while litigation lingered. In 1994, however, the first class-action suits were brought against tobacco companies, including a suit by sixty law firms in five states. The suit represented up to 40 million smokers and 50 million former smokers claiming to be addicted or damaged or both by tobacco products. The solidarity of the tobacco companies against lawsuits and regulation was shattered in March 1996, when the Liggett Group (the fifth-largest company but with only a 2 percent market share) agreed to settle its part of the suit. Liggett agreed to payments for an antismoking campaign, not to oppose new government regulations, and to make the first damage payments ever by a tobacco company. Shortly thereafter, two former Philip Morris employees confirmed charges against the tobacco companies of manipulation of nicotine levels to keep smokers hooked. Other class-action suits were pending as well, including one against Philip Morris involving 60,000 flight attendants who said they were forced to inhale secondary smoke in airline cabins before smoking on airplanes was banned. In February 1994 the state of Florida decided to sue the tobacco companies for the Medicare costs it incurred in treating smokers; West Virginia, Minnesota, and Mississippi filed similar suits.

[See also Advertising; Environmental Protection Agency; Food and Drug Administration.]

BIBLIOGRAPHY

John C. Burnham, *Bad Habits* (New York, 1993).
A. Lee Fritschler, *Smoking and Politics*, 4th ed. (Englewood Cliffs, N.J., 1989).
Robert L. Rabin and Stephen D. Sugarman, eds., *Smoking Policy: Law, Politics, and Culture* (New York, 1993).
Robert Sobel, *They Satisfy: The Cigarette in American Life* (Garden City, N.Y., 1978).
Susan Wagner, *Cigarette Country* (New York, 1971).
Thomas Whiteside, *Selling Death* (New York, 1971).

— KAREN S. MILLER

TOLERATION ACTS

In Rhode Island the code of 1644 granted full freedom of worship, a principle confirmed by the royal charter of 1663. In Pennsylvania the great charter of 1682, written by William Penn, provided for religious liberty to all who acknowledged God. In 1706, under the pressure of royal authority, religious and political liberty was denied to Jews, Catholics, and Socinians. In Maryland the Toleration Act of 1649 guided the policy of the proprietors except for the period 1654–58. The royal charter of 1732 creating Georgia confirmed religious liberty for all except Catholics.

John Lord Berkeley and Sir George Carteret, grantees of New Jersey, in their concessions of 1665, and the Carolina proprietors, in their proposals of 1663, offered liberty of worship to attract settlers. When the Jerseys came into the control of Quakers and others religious liberty continued—in West Jersey by the law of 1681, East Jersey, 1683.

The Congregational church was legally established in Massachusetts and Connecticut. Taxpayers were required by law to contribute to the support of the Puritan church and ministry. The strong protest of dissenters in Massachusetts found a response in the law of 1731 exempting Quakers from this burden; a few years later Baptists and Episcopalians were relieved. In Connecticut the Toleration Act of 1708 provided freedom of worship but gave no release from paying rates to the established church. However, in 1727–29 Quakers, Baptists, and Episcopalians were exempted.

In the late 1600's and early 1700's, taxpayers in Massachusetts and Connecticut were required by law to contribute to the support of the Puritan church and ministry.

The Episcopal church was legally established early in Virginia; in Maryland and the Carolinas in the first part of the 18th century; and in 1758 in Georgia. The church was not strong except in Virginia and South Carolina. In all the colonies the dissenters were a growing majority. The church did not invade the religious liberty of others in South Carolina, and in Virginia and Maryland dissenters were granted the benefits of the English Toleration Act of 1689.

The American Revolution reinforced the doctrines of individual liberty, particularly religious freedom. Most state constitutions framed in this era sanctioned freedom of conscience in religion in full or qualified manner. The connection of church and state continued in Connecticut until 1818, in Massachusetts until 1833, but in other states it was abolished early. The Northwest Ordinance of 1787 extended the principle of liberty of worship to the Northwest Territory. On a national scale the Constitution (Amendment I) forbade Congress to abridge the free exercise of religion.

BIBLIOGRAPHY

Sanford H. Cobb, *The Rise of Religious Liberty in America.*

— WINFRED T. ROOT

TOM THUMB

Tom Thumb, a locomotive built by Peter Cooper for use on the new Baltimore and Ohio Railroad, which at the beginning used horses as motive power. In its test in 1830 the engine, on a double track line out of Baltimore, raced against a car drawn by a horse. It would have beaten it had not a pulley belt slipped off.

BIBLIOGRAPHY

Edward Hungerford, *The Story of the Baltimore #38; Ohio Railroad.*

— ALVIN F. HARLOW

TONKIN GULF RESOLUTION

Two attacks by North Vietnamese torpedo boats on U.S. destroyers (Aug. 2 and 4, 1964) in the Gulf of Tonkin set in motion the events that led to a congressional resolution on Aug. 7, 1964. On the grounds that these attacks represented a "systematic campaign of aggression by North Vietnam against South Vietnam," Congress jointly resolved, with only two senatorial dissents, to support President Lyndon B. Johnson's determination "to take all necessary measures to repel any armed attack against the forces of the United States." The Tonkin Gulf Resolution precipitated a vast increase in America's military involvement in South Vietnam. Subsequent questions about American destroyers being in North Vietnam waters at the time of attack raised charges that the Johnson administration had courted a crisis. National disillusionment over the Vietnam War led to the resolution's repeal on Jan. 13, 1971.

— LAWRENCE S. KAPLAN

TORPEDO WARFARE

The direct ancestor of the modern torpedo was the self-propelled, or "automobile," torpedo developed in the 1860's by Robert Whitehead, an Englishman in the employ of the Austrian navy. The Whitehead torpedo was a cigar-shaped weapon that carried an explosive charge in its nose. It was powered by a small reciprocating engine and could be set to run at a predetermined depth. By the 1870's the automobile torpedo had been adopted by all the major navies. The first sinking of a warship by the new weapon occurred in 1891 during the Chilean civil war when the ironclad *Blanco Encalada* was sunk by a Whitehead torpedo.

During the next twenty years the torpedo increased rapidly in speed, range, and explosive power. By the eve of World War I the effective range of the torpedo was just under 7,000 yards, and its top speed was over 40 knots. The 21-inch torpedo, the largest then in general use, had a bursting charge of 700 pounds of explosive.

Until about 1900 the principal carrier of the torpedo was the torpedo boat, a small, very fast vessel especially designed for torpedo attacks. The first U.S. torpedo boat, the *Cushing*, was approved for construction in 1886 and completed in 1890; it had a maximum speed of 23 knots and an armament of three 6-pounders and three 18-inch torpedo tubes on a displacement of 116 tons. As a protection against such vessels large warships acquired batteries of smaller caliber quick-firing guns that could be used to ward off a torpedo-boat attack. Beginning in the 1890's the major powers began to develop a new type of warship, the torpedo boat destroyer, or simply "destroyer," a large, faster torpedo vessel with a gun armament heavy enough to outfight a torpedo boat. By the outbreak of World War I the destroyer, now grown to a vessel of about 1,000 tons, had largely usurped the function of the torpedo boat and was valuable for patrol and the escort of convoys.

The warship that was destined to make the most effective use of the torpedo was the submarine. During World War I German submarines sank more than 11 million tons of British merchant shipping, forced the British battle fleet to take extraordinary precautions in its operations, and came close to winning the war for the Central Powers.

Between the wars the torpedo-carrying airplane, or torpedo plane, added a new dimension to torpedo warfare. In World War II this new weapon played a prominent part in naval operations. A small force of British "swordfish" torpedo planes put half the Italian battle fleet out of action at Taranto harbor in 1940, and the following year the Japanese achieved even more spectacular successes when their torpedo planes, carrying a new type 24-inch torpedo, helped to cripple the American fleet at Pearl Harbor and sank the new British battleship *Prince of Wales* and the battlecruiser *Repulse* off the coast of Malaya.

In World War II the submarine proved even more formidable as a torpedo carrier than in World War I. Tonnage losses to German U-boats rose into the millions before the Allies were finally able to win the long Battle of the Atlantic. In the Pacific, American submarines devastated the Japanese merchant marine and accounted for 28 percent of all Japanese naval shipping sunk in the course of the war.

BIBLIOGRAPHY

Bernard Brodie, *Seapower in the Machine Age.*

— RONALD SPECTOR

TOWNSHEND ACTS

Townshend Acts, four acts imposed on the American colonists by Parliament in June-July 1767. They take their name from Charles Townshend, chancellor of the Exchequer and head of the British government at the time they were enacted.

The first act, passed on June 15, suspended the New York assembly from further legislative activities until it complied with the provisions of the Quartering Act of 1765, which required colonies to supply British troops with barracks or other shelter; straw for bedding; cooking utensils; firewood for cooking and heating purposes; and a ration of rum, cider, or vinegar to combat scurvy. Four years earlier Pontiac's War had demonstrated the danger of leaving the army units scattered in small garrisons throughout the West, where they could be attacked and destroyed in detail. Gen. Thomas Gage, commander in chief in America, decided to skeletonize the western garrisons and concentrate all available troops in central reserves to be dispatched to any place they were needed. New York was selected as the best place for the reserves, and troops were ordered there, which imposed an unforeseen financial burden on that province. Apparently the amount of expenditures would vary, not with the plans of the assembly, but with the whims of the commanding general. The New York assembly made its usual appropriation for a limited number of troops, but refused to appropriate for additional quarters in New York, especially as there was still ample room in the barracks at Albany. The Suspending Act forbade the assembly to carry on any other business until it had met fully the demands of Gage. As assemblies were summoned, prorogued, and dissolved by order of the governor, representing the crown, this assumption of authority on the part of Parliament created serious concern in America. It was a weapon that might be used to invade other American rights and enforce other laws that the colonists considered unjust and unconstitutional.

The second act was the Revenue Act, passed on June 29. It levied import duties payable at American ports on white and red lead, painters' colors, various kinds of paper, glass of all kinds, and three pence a pound on tea. All of these articles were legally importable only from Great Britain. It was the second time in the history of the empire that commercial regulations affecting the colonies had been adopted for revenue purposes. All other laws, except the Sugar Act of 1764, had been for the purpose of protecting some industry within the empire. For this reason men like Sir William Pitt, Edmund Burke, and Barlow Trecothic assailed this law as anticommercial. Instead of encouraging British industry, it discouraged English manufacture, and by taxation encouraged a competing industry in the colonies or discouraged the use of the articles singled out for taxation.

The revenue arising from these new colonial taxes was to go first to the cost of collection, then to support an independent civil establishment in America—that is, judges, governors, and other crown employees were paid from this fund instead of being dependent, as they always had been for their salaries, on annual appropriations of the local assemblies. This use of the money struck at the very foundation of American political liberty. During the past half-century the colonies had achieved almost complete local self-government through financial control of the royal officers. To put judges and governors beyond all local control and at the same time make them dependent upon the ministry for the tenure of their offices and their pay was to set up what many Americans considered despotic control. Resistance to a program of political enslavement took the form of agitation; nonimportation agreements; open evasion of the duties in some cases; promotion of American spinning, weaving, glass, and paper industries; and open hostility to the enforcing officers.

During the past half-century the colonies had achieved almost complete local self-government. Then came the Townshend Acts.

The new taxes were to be collected by a Board of Customs Commissioners, established by the third Townshend Act, also passed on June 29. The board was stationed at Boston and was given complete control over all customs in America. It was empowered to revise and reorganize the entire American customs; discontinue old or establish new ports of entry; appoint customs officers, searchers, spies; hire coast-guard vessels, provide them with search warrants, and in general do whatever seemed necessary to them to enforce the revenue laws.

Costs of this new and very costly establishment were to be paid out of the revenue and out of seizures. As the revenue law itself was unpopular and considered by the colonists unconstitutional, the enforcement officers met with resistance in some cases, as in the seizure of the *Liberty* and the burning of the *Gaspée.* The real or fancied opposition led the customs commissioners to ask for troops, and large forces were hurried to Boston in September 1768, where they were quartered in the city contrary to the Quartering Act. For more than nine months Boston was practically under military rule. There was friction between the people and the soldiers. The people of Massachusetts appealed to other colonies through protests and through *The Journal of the Times,* an ostensible day-to-day account of actual conditions in Boston. This was widely published in American and British papers. Most of the troops were withdrawn in 1769, but two regiments were left. One of these, the Twenty-ninth, was involved in the Boston Massacre, Mar. 5, 1770, after which all troops were withdrawn. With the repeal of all duties, except that on tea, in 1770, the controversy gradually quieted down, until aroused anew by the tea controversy and the Boston Tea Party in 1773.

The fourth act, passed on July 2, repealed the inland duties on tea in England and permitted it to be exported to the colonies free of all British taxes.

It has been said that Townshend sought to raise revenue in America by enforcing the Navigation Acts. Such statements are without foundation. The only navigation act that could yield a revenue was 25 Charles II, which levied export duties on enumerated products shipped from one British colony to another. This was purely regulative and was designed to prevent enumerated products being shipped to Europe in competition with the direct trade from England. The collections under this law after 1767 were not increased; for the fifteen years 1749–63 the collections had averaged £1,395 annually; and for the six years ending with 1774 under the Townshend Acts, they averaged only £778 per year—an actual decrease of more than £600 per annum under the Townshend Acts. The increased revenues came from the Sugar Act and from the Townshend Revenue Act.

BIBLIOGRAPHY

Edward Channing, *History of the United States.*

— O. M DICKERSON

TRADING POSTS, FRONTIER

From the establishment of Jamestown (1607) until the end of Indian treatymaking (1871), traders and trading posts were important factors in border relations. By 1774 Albany and Oswego, N.Y., were major trade centers for the Iroquois and other northwestern tribes. At both places Indians would exchange their furs for guns, ammunition, hatchets, knives, kettles, and blankets. And during the period of colonial rivalries, Spain and France also had their strategic trading posts. Mobile (1710), Natchitoches (established by Louis Juchereau de Saint Denis, 1713), Natchez (established by Jean Baptiste Le Moyne, Sieur de Bienville, 1716), and Saint Louis, Mo. (established by Pierre Laclède and his stepson, René Auguste Chouteau, 1764), were only a few maintained in the Mississippi Valley and from New Orleans to Pensacola.

After American independence, President George Washington proposed, and Congress inaugurated (1796), the setting up of government factories and trading posts, and every border fort became a trade center. But bitter opposition by individual traders led to the abandonment of the policy in 1822. Moreover, American influence with frontier tribes up to 1814 was hampered by British trader influence. Not until 1795 would England agree to surrender occupied posts within the northern boundary of the United States. And English traders at Detroit continued to sell war supplies to tribes of the Ohio and Mississippi valleys until after 1814.

Shortly after American occupation of the Louisiana Territory (1804), trading posts were established throughout the trans-Mississippi West. Saint Louis was the center for supplying traders and posts within the Pacific Northwest and Midwest, and New Orleans the Southwest. Missouri traders had built Fort Lisa by 1813 and Fort Benton (at the mouth of the Big Horn, not to be confused with Fort Benton on the Upper Missouri) by 1821, and John Jacob Astor had set up a post at Astoria on the Columbia River in 1811. Astor's organization encountered severe competition from the Hudson's Bay Company, which had several posts in the same region. Sutter's Fort on the American River (1841) in California was the best-known trading station in California; farther east, Fort Bridger and Fort Laramie became well known by the early 1840's.

In the greater Southwest posts were equally important as factors in advancing the frontier. At the three forks of the Arkansas, in present Oklahoma, Auguste Pierre Chouteau and other traders had established their posts by 1815; later Chouteau built another near present Purcell (1835). The best-known trading post in the Southwest during the 1830's was Bent's Fort on the Arkansas, begun by Charles and William Bent, Ceran

St. Vrain, and Benito Vasquez (1828–29). In Texas, posts were established during the days of the republic near modern Waco (Torrey's) and higher up on the Brazos River (the Barnards). From these and other posts vast quantities of trade goods were exchanged for furs and buffalo hides taken by the Indians.

BIBLIOGRAPHY

Hiram Chittenden, *The American Fur Trade of the Far West.*
Clarence A. Vandiveer, *The Fur-Trade and Early Western Exploration.*

— C. C. RISTER

TRAIL OF TEARS

Trail of Tears was the name given by the Cherokee to the forced journey in 1838 from their lands in Georgia through Kentucky, Illinois, and Missouri to Oklahoma. This removal was based on the signing by a minority of the Cherokee leaders of the Treaty of New Echota in 1835, under the terms of which the Cherokee were to surrender their lands and move west of the Mississippi. The document was overwhelmingly repudiated by most of the tribe, and they refused to move; but the state of Georgia obtained a court order for Cherokee removal, to be accomplished by military force. Troops under Gen. Winfield Scott rounded up the Indians and drove them into concentration camps, where they were held until they were sent on the long journey in detachments of about 1,000 each. In all, some 15,000 Cherokee were forced to move when local whites ran off their livestock and plundered and burned their homes. The journey was made mostly on foot, beginning in October and November, and as winter came on, many of the Cherokee fell ill and died en route. The journey was mismanaged, and there was a shortage of supplies; the escorting troops rushed the Indians onward, refusing to allow them to minister to their sick or bury their dead. On this Trail of Tears, one of the most pathetic episodes in American history, some 4,000 Cherokee perished.

BIBLIOGRAPHY

Grant Foreman, *Indian Removal.*
Dale Van Every, *The Disinherited.*
Grace S. Woodward, *The Cherokees.*

— KENNETH M. STEWART

TRAIN ROBBERIES

Train robberies were more frequent in America than anywhere else in the world in the latter half of the 19th century. In part caused by the vast stretches of sparsely inhabited country that permitted the robbers to escape undetected, the robberies were also made easier by carelessness and lack of adequate protection. The first train robbery on record was that of an Adams Express car on the New York, New Haven and Hartford Railroad, which was rifled of $700,000 between New York and New Haven in 1866. That same year the first train holdup by the four Reno brothers occurred in southern Indiana. The gang took the express messenger's keys from him at gunpoint and robbed the safe of $13,000. Some members of the gang were arrested but never tried. A year later another gang repeated the exploit in the same neighborhood. After one of the Reno brothers was arrested in 1867, the remainder of the gang staged a number of bold bank and train robberies in southern Indiana and Illinois in 1868. They were traced by the Pinkerton Detective Agency, just then coming into prominence. After they were jailed, the brothers, except John, were executed by vigilantes before their cases came to trial. The Farringtons operated in 1870 in Kentucky and Tennessee; and Jack Davis of Nevada started operations at Truckee by robbing an express car of $41,000. He had learned his trade robbing stagecoaches in California a few years earlier.

The year 1870 marked the height of train robberies, East and West. An express car was robbed at Albany in that year and the messenger shot. In those days care was not taken to lock the express and baggage end doors and the cars were frequently used for loafing and smoking. The picturesque and daring Jesse James gang began to operate in 1873 near Council Bluffs, Iowa. No other robbers are so well known, and legends and songs cluster about their deeds. For nine years they terrorized the Middle West, and only after Jesse was shot by a confederate and his brother Frank retired to run a Wild West show did trainmen breathe more freely. Sam Bass in Texas, the Dalton boys in Oklahoma, and Sontag and Evans in California are other robbers with well-known records. After 1900 the number of holdups declined conspicuously.

BIBLIOGRAPHY

A. F. Harlow, *Old Waybills.*

— CARL L. CANNON

TRANSCENDENTALISM

Transcendentalism, a philosophical term developed by the German philosopher Immanuel Kant that embodies those aspects of man's nature transcending, or independent of, experience. It became the inspiration of a liberal social and cultural renaissance in New England during 1830–45 and received its chief American expression in Ralph Waldo Emerson's individualistic doctrine of self-reliance. In 1836 Emerson and a radical wing of Uni-

American poet, essayist, and lecturer Ralph Waldo Emerson was a central figure of the philosophical, social, and literary movement that came to be known as New England Transcendentalism. (Library of Congress/Corbis)

tarians formed the Transcendental Club as a discussion group; Margaret Fuller's *Dial* later (1840–44) became its leading organ. Experiments in "plain living and high thinking" like Brook Farm and Fruitlands attracted the exponents of a new self-culture; and social utopians, from vegetarian enthusiasts to abolitionists, found a congenial atmosphere within the movement.

BIBLIOGRAPHY

H. C. Goddard, *Studies in New England Transcendentalism.*

— HARVEY WISH

TRANSPORTATION, DEPARTMENT OF

In a message to Congress in March 1966, President Lyndon B. Johnson outlined a proposal for a unified transportation authority, and in October Congress established the Department of Transportation (DOT). In April 1967 President Johnson activated the new department, which was headed by a cabinet-level secretary of transportation. The new department, which brought together about 90,000 employees from more than thirty formerly separate agencies, was given responsibility for federal investments in transportation and for creating an economical, efficient, and safe national transportation system, taking into account environmental standards and national defense. It did not take over the regulatory activities of the Civil Aeronautics Board (dissolved in 1984), the Interstate Commerce Commission, or Federal Maritime Commission. In 1981, however, the Maritime Commission, renamed the Maritime Administration, was transferred by Congress to DOT. Officials responsible for the nation's overall system of transportation report to the secretary of transportation, as do the administrators of nine special operating divisions, most of which are devoted to specific modes of transportation. Responsible for the general transportation system are a deputy secretary, a general counsel, and assistant secretaries for budget and programs, policy and international affairs, governmental affairs, public affairs, and administration. The nine operating divisions are the United States Coast Guard, Federal Aviation Administration, Federal Highway Administration, Federal Railroad Administration, National Highway Traffic Safety Administration, Urban Mass Transportation Administration, Saint Lawrence Seaway Development Corporation, Research and Special Programs Administration, and Maritime Administration. Although the administrators of these divisions report to the secretary of transportation, they are appointed by the president and must be confirmed by the Senate.

Railway transportation was in crisis in the late 1960s, and DOT participated in the creation of the National Railroad Passenger Corporation (Amtrak), established in 1971, and Consolidated Railroads (Conrail), established in 1976 primarily as a freight carrier. Both were chartered by the federal government as quasi-public, profit-making corporations. They have not been profitable, however, and have required federal subsidies. In 1987 the federal government sold its shares of Conrail stock as part of President Ronald Reagan's privatization program. Amtrak, however, through a combination of rate hikes, cost cutting, and effective marketing, managed to reduce its reliance on federal subsidies. The secretary of transportation is one of the nine members of the Amtrak board.

A related but autonomous agency is the National Transportation Safety Board (NTSB), established by the same act that created DOT. NTSB is a five-member board, appointed by the president, that reports directly to Congress. It is responsible for investigating accidents involving all forms of transportation, taking over investigations formerly carried out by the Civil Aeronautics

Board and the Interstate Commerce Commission. In practice, much of the initial accident investigation is carried out by the operating division within DOT that has jurisdiction over the mode of transportation involved in the accident.

BIBLIOGRAPHY

Robert C. Lieb, *Transportation: The Domestic System*, 2nd ed. (Reston, Va., 1981).

Roy J. Sampson, Martin T. Farris, and David L. Shrock, *Domestic Transportation: Practice, Theory, and Policy*, 5th ed. (Boston, 1985).

— RICHARD W. MOODEY

TRAPPING

Trapping continues to be a part-time occupation for many rural Americans. Until the middle of the 19th century trapping was a prime factor in the process of westward movement, for professional trappers and traders not only developed a source of wealth for a growing nation but, more importantly, they explored the rivers, blazed trails through unmapped forests, brought hostile Indians under control, made known the agricultural values of the wilderness, and extended American holdings to the Pacific Ocean. The American trapper, as a type, may well be identified as that picturesque mountain man of the Rocky Mountain region who during the first half of the 19th century worked out of the fur trade center, Saint Louis, in a struggle against nature and British antagonists in winning the West for the United States. This American trapper did not arrive ready-made to succeed Meriwether Lewis and William Clark in further penetration of the western country. He evolved through many stages from the Pilgrim trapper of 1620, from the Dutch trader of the Connecticut and Hudson rivers, from the Frenchman of Green Bay, from the British North West Company agent, from the Hudson's Bay Company voyageur, and from the backwoodsman of Kentucky and Tennessee. From some of these he inherited a psychological character that made him indomitable; from all he borrowed his technique and his material equipment.

The upper Missouri trapper of 1830 was a composite picture of the many types that had dared the wilderness through 200 years of westward progress. With him he took a method that had its beginnings in the Indian trade on the Saint Lawrence and Potomac rivers and a paraphernalia that sprang from roots deep in the countries of Europe. Many of his items of equipment and objects of trade had not changed in two centuries of use in America. In following his profession, the trapper of the upper Missouri traveled with a company of companions who were employed by one of the established trading firms of Saint Louis or who worked out of that city as free and independent trappers. Zenas Leonard, writing of his arrival with the Gant and Blackwell party in beaver country at the junction of the Laramie and Platte rivers on Aug. 27, 1831, gives the following description of procedure:

> Captain Gant gave orders to make preparations for trapping. The company was divided into parties of from 15 to 20 men, with their respective captains placed over them, and directed by Captain Gant in what direction to go. Captain Washburn ascended the Tiber Fork; Captain Stephens, the Laramie; Captain Gant, the Sweetwater—all of which empty into the River Platte near the same place. Each of these companies were directed to ascend these rivers until they found beaver sufficiently plenty for trapping, or until the snow and cold weather compelled them to stop, at which event they were to return to the mouth of the Laramie River to pass the winter together.

Osborne Russell, who trapped in the Yellowstone Park country in the 1830's and 1840's, wrote:

> The trapper extracts this substance [castoreum, the trapper's bait] from the scent glands of the beaver and carries it in a wooden box. He sets his steel trap in the water near the bank about six inches below the surface, throws a handful of mud upon the bank about one foot from the trap, and puts a small portion of the castoreum thereon. After night, the beaver comes out of his lodge, smells the fatal bait 200 or 300 yards distant, and steers his course directly for it. He hastens to ascend the bank, but the trap grasps his foot and soon drowns him in the struggle to escape.

Beaver no longer constitutes the chief item in the American fur trade, and Saint Louis has competition from the raw fur dealers in Chicago, New York, Saint Paul, and other large centers of fur trade. Trapping in the United States in the 1970's brought largest returns in muskrat, fox, nutria, lynx, opossum, and raccoon, and the volume of business was far greater than it had ever been during the days of the mountain man. The significance of the trapper and trapping in the history of the United States is not to be judged by volume of furs traded, however. Their influence on the course of empire is not reflected in the bare statistics of commercial returns.

BIBLIOGRAPHY

Robert Glass Cleland, *This Reckless Breed of Men: The Trappers and Fur Traders of the Southwest.*

L. R. Hafen, *The Mountain Men and the Fur Trade of the Far West.*

Carl P. Russell, *Firearms, Traps and Tools of the Mountain Men.*

— CARL P. RUSSELL

TREASON

The U.S. Constitution (Article III, Section 3) restrictively defines treason against the United States and denies Congress authority to enlarge the constitutional definition. State constitutions contain similar limiting definitions of treason against a state. By these definitions treason "shall consist only in adhering to . . . Enemies" of the nation or state, "giving them Aid and Comfort," or "in levying War against" the nation or state. Enemies are only those opponents against whom the nation has formally declared war. Aid and comfort can be any form of benefit, in fact, tendered to the enemy. The concept marches with the times; thus, in World War II aid and comfort included propaganda radio broadcasts intended to lower the morale of U.S. troops.

Old English authority defines "levying of war" as any group action aimed at preventing by violence the enforcement of any statute or order of the sovereign. American authority takes a more restrictive view; spontaneous group violence against lawful authority or organized violence against the enforcement of a particular law may be prosecuted as the less serious crimes of riot or unlawful assembly, but war is levied only by organized group effort to overthrow the government.

During World War II, the working definition of treason would include propaganda radio broadcasts intended to lower the morale of U.S. troops.

Under either heading of treason the federal and state constitutions require that government prove that a defendant has committed an overt act in pursuing his treasonable intention—that is, it does not suffice merely to prove a treasonable intention—and that the act be proved by "the testimony of two witnesses to the same overt act, or on confession in open court." The act need not itself evidence treasonable intent. But if the act does not plainly give aid to enemies or levy war, the U.S. Supreme Court has intimated that evidence of the act's context, to show its character as aid or levying, may also have to be supplied by two witnesses. Treason may be committed by citizens within or outside the country, and probably by noncitizens who by residence accept the benefits of the legal order. The Constitution empowers Congress to define penalties for treason but stipulates that "no Attainder of Treason shall work Corruption of Blood, or Forefeiture except during the Life of the Person attainted."

BIBLIOGRAPHY

James Willard Hurst, *The Law of Treason in the United States.*

— JAMES WILLARD HURST

TREASURY, UNITED STATES

The U.S. Treasury was created by act of Congress on Sept. 2, 1789. Alexander Hamilton, the first secretary of the Treasury, besides collecting and disbursing the public revenue, made the Treasury a prime agency for promoting the economic development of the country. Since the depression of the 1930's, the regulatory functions of the Treasury have been articulated and elaborated. The secretary, in formulating Treasury policy, meets regularly with the director of the Bureau of the Budget and the chairman of the Council of Economic Advisers; frequently the chairman of the Federal Reserve Board is included. With maximum statistical information they seek to analyze the economic outlook and to coordinate official actions.

The four basic responsibilities of the Treasury are (1) to frame and recommend financial, tax, and fiscal measures; (2) to serve as financial agent for the U.S. government; (3) to enforce certain laws; and (4) to manufacture coins and currency. The Treasury formerly included agencies that have since become autonomous with the expansion of the national government, notably the postal service, the Coast Guard, the Bureau of Narcotics, and the parent agencies of the departments of the Interior, Commerce, and Labor. Other wide and varied powers and duties have gradually devolved on the Treasury, with a corresponding proliferation of policymaking and administrative officers and staffs.

Besides his domestic concerns, including management of the public debt, the secretary of the Treasury represents the United States in foreign financial organizations, including the International Monetary Fund, the International Bank for Reconstruction and Development, the Inter-American Development Bank, and the Asian Development Bank.

More than 80 percent of the Treasury's annual appropriation (more than $35 billion in 1975; 1976 estimate, $43 billion) and 90 percent of the personnel are assigned to revenue collection. Principal internal sources are individual and corporation income taxes;

excise, estate, and gift taxes; and employment taxes under the Social Security system. The work is done in seven regions, with a computer center at Martinsburg, W. Va. The treasurer of the United States receives, holds, and pays out public moneys; 640 million checks were issued in 1971, and the number increases by about 3 percent a year. Operating cash is deposited in thirty-six Federal Reserve banks and branches.

The Customs Bureau, besides operating collections at 291 ports of entry, enforces numerous programs protecting health and agriculture. The Office of the Comptroller of the Currency (with a staff of 1,650 examiners) oversees 4,600 national banks. The Bureau of Engraving and Printing produces paper money and postage and food stamps; the Mint produces coins. The Secret Service enforces laws against counterfeiting and guards the president and other high officials and their families, presidential candidates, and visiting foreign dignitaries. The Bureau of Alcohol, Tobacco, and Firearms is charged with preventing illicit trade in these commodities; the Office of Management assists the president in framing the government's fiscal program. The Treasury also has savings bonds continuously on sale at 30,000 issuing agencies.

The internal structure of the Treasury, to insure faithful performance by different divisions, is essentially what Hamilton devised at its inception.

BIBLIOGRAPHY

U.S. Government Organization Manual (1975–76).

U.S. Budget in Brief, Fiscal Year 1976.

Harley H. Hinhichs, "The Treasury Department," *National Journal* (Nov. 1, 1969).

— BROADUS MITCHELL

TREASURY, DEPARTMENT OF THE

Department of the Treasury established in 1789, consisted in 1995 of sixteen departmental offices and eleven operating bureaus: the Customs Service (established in 1789); U.S. Mint (1792); Internal Revenue Service (1862); Bureau of Engraving and Printing (1862); Office of the Comptroller of the Currency (1863); Secret Service (1865); Bureau of the Public Debt (1919); Financial Management Service (1920); Federal Law Enforcement Training Center (1970); Bureau of Alcohol, Tobacco, and Firearms (1972); and the Office of Thrift Supervision (1989). The Treasury Building in Washington, D.C., was declared a national historic landmark on Oct. 18, 1972. Secretary of the Treasury Salmon P. Chase's Civil War office, the office used by President Andrew Johnson for six weeks in 1865, and the Cash Room were restored with private funds.

The secretary of the Treasury is the chief adviser to the president on fiscal and financial affairs and plays a key role in the formulation and execution of domestic and international economic policy. Since 1970 the Treasury Department has played a central role in important international events. The Treasury, with support from other U.S. agencies, developed comprehensive proposals for reform of the international monetary system after the collapse in the early 1970s of the Bretton Woods system (the world payments system of fixed exchange rates for major currencies centered on the dollar and its convertibility into gold). It took the lead in the Smithsonian Agreement of 1971 (a last attempt to realign fixed rates and bolster the Bretton Woods system); revision of the articles of the International Monetary Fund in the mid-1970s, the basis for a new system of management of floating exchange rates; and the Plaza Accord of 1985 (the first substantive effort by the United States, United Kingdom, France, Germany, and Japan to coordinate their economic policies, including exchange rate policies). Through the Office of the Assistant Secretary for International Affairs, the Treasury Department was also the architect of the U.S. government's yen-dollar talks and two other bilateral financial consultations with Japan in the 1980s aimed at liberalizing Japan's capital markets.

Treasury played a key role in the major tax reforms of the 1970s and the 1980s. Significant peacetime U.S. tax reforms took place during the administration of President Ronald Reagan (1981–1989), when the economic and legal staffs of the Office of the Assistant Secretary for Tax Policy helped draft the Economic Recovery Tax Act of 1981 and the Tax Reform Act of 1986. The staffs also played a key role in the formulation of the deficit reduction bills passed in 1990 and 1993. The Treasury Department also administered the revenue sharing program, an initiative of President Richard M. Nixon's administration that distributed $82.6 billion among 39,000 states, cities, and other general-purpose local governments between the program's enactment in 1972 and its repeal in 1986.

The Office of the Assistant Secretary for Economic Policy participated actively in the formulation of the four phases of wage and price controls (Aug. 15, 1971–Apr. 30, 1974); studied the impact of changes in the financing and benefit structure of the Social Security Trust Fund and provided input for the major reforms enacted in 1983; analyzed the hospital cost containment proposal of President Jimmy Carter's administration in 1980 and President Bill Clinton's health care reform proposal of 1993–1994; and analyzed the deficit reduction packages of the George Bush and Clinton administrations.

The U.S. government securities market is the largest and most liquid securities market in the world. Sales of Treasury securities to the public raise funds to cover the shortfall between the government's receipts and expenditures and to refinance debt. The public debt amounted to $371 billion on June 30, 1970. On Sept. 30, 1994, it was $4.7 trillion. More than half that amount, $2.7 trillion, was in marketable securities held by private investors. Nonmarketable Treasury securities, including U.S. savings bonds, and marketable debt held by government accounts and the Federal Reserve System, make up the rest of the public debt.

The Office of the Under Secretary for Domestic Finance, which develops the legislative and regulatory financial institutions policy for each presidential administration, developed the Financial Institutions Reform, Recovery, and Enforcement Act of 1989, which addressed the savings and loan crisis. The Fiscal Assistant Secretary's Office manages the government's cash balances. The Office of the Under Secretary for Enforcement oversees the government's second largest law enforcement complement. The Internal Revenue Service (IRS), the largest bureau of the Treasury Department, collects more than $1 trillion each year in tax revenue. Although income taxes account for the bulk of this amount, the IRS also collects corporate, excise, and estate and gift taxes. Electronic filing of tax returns was initiated in 1986, and passage of the Taxpayer's Bill of Rights in 1988 strengthened protections for individual taxpayers. The Bureau of Engraving and Printing produced U.S. paper money only in its Washington, D.C., plant until 1991, when it opened a second currency facility in Fort Worth, Texas. The savings and loan crisis of the 1980s led to the creation of the Office of Thrift Supervision in 1989, replacing the Federal Home Loan Bank Board.

[See also Banking and Finance; Budget, Federal; Savings and Loan Crisis.]

BIBLIOGRAPHY

Mark Walston, *The Department of the Treasury* (New York, 1989).

— ABBY L. GILBERT

TREATIES WITH FOREIGN NATIONS

In international usage the term "treaty" has the generic sense of "international agreement." Rights and obligations, or status, arise under international law irrespective of the form or designation of an agreement. But in constitutional usage, treaties are sometimes distinguished from less formal agreements by special requirements for negotiation or ratification, limitations of subject matter, or distinctive effects in domestic law. The Constitution of the United States distinguishes treaties from other agreements and compacts in several ways.

The first way is that only the federal government can conclude a "Treaty, Alliance, or Confederation"; states can make an "Agreement or Compact" with other states or with foreign powers but only with consent of the Congress (Article I, Section 10). Although there is no explicit authorization for the national government to conclude an agreement or compact (that is, what is usually called an executive agreement), the power probably results from other delegated powers and is frequently exercised.

The second way is that treaties are negotiated and ratified by the president, but he must obtain the advice and consent of the Senate, two-thirds of the senators present concurring (Article II, Section 2, Clause 2). This was understood by President George Washington to include advice concerning both negotiations and ratification. He attempted oral consultation of the Senate at an executive council concerning a proposed treaty with the southern Indians, but after a frustrating experience he declared "he would be damned if he ever went there again." His successors followed his example, so that advice and consent came to be confined to ratification. Is the Senate the most appropriate body for legislative assent? It has often been charged with delay and obstruction, especially after its defeat of the League of Nations Covenant and, even after substantial acceptance by other signatories of reservations it proposed, of the Statute of the Permanent Court of International Justice. These are not representative instances; careful studies of the overall record show little evidence of undue delay or obstruction. It can be argued that approval by both houses of Congress would be more representative of the people, but this would lengthen legislative consideration without assuring improvement.

The third way that the Constitution distinguishes treaties from "agreements and compacts" is that treaties made under authority of the United States are stated to be part of the supreme law of the land (with the Constitution and statutes "made in pursuance thereof"), which judges in every state are bound to enforce (Article VI, Section 2). Sen. John W. Bricker argued that "under authority of the United States" did not so clearly as "in pursuance thereof" compel conformity with the Constitution and proposed amendments to close this "gap." But the Supreme Court has often indicated that it would hold unconstitutional treaties to be void; it has not in fact had occasion to do so (*Missouri* v. *Holland*, 252 U.S. 416 [1920]; *Reid* v. *Covert*, 354 U.S. 1 [1957]). Treaties are internationally obligatory on exchange or deposit of ratifications. In domestic law this is true only when the treaty is "self-executing" (that is, intended to be, and so detailed it can be, directly applied by administrative officers); otherwise it is held to be directed to Congress for legislative implementation (*Foster* v. *Neilsen*, 2 Peters 253 [1829]). Presumably, executive agreements, which are not mentioned in the supremacy clause, are subordinate to federal statutes and void if in conflict with them (*United States* v. *Guy W. Capps, Inc.*, 204 Federal Reporter, Second Series 655 [4th Circuit, 1953]; affirmed on other grounds, 348 U.S. 296 [1955]). Although not listed as part of the supreme law of the land, they may, as statements of foreign policy, supersede conflicting state policies (*United States* v. *Belmont*, 301 U.S. 324 [1937]; *United States* v. *Pink*, 315 U.S. 203 [1942]).

Fifteen treaties were concluded prior to the Constitution of 1789, using procedures made difficult by political decentralization. They were negotiated by commissioners appointed and instructed by the Continental Congress and ratified by the Congress. Technically the assent of all thirteen colonies was required until ratification of the Articles of Confederation in 1781, and thereafter of nine. The Treaty of Alliance with France (1778) and two related treaties were ratified by a vote recorded as unanimous, yet it is clear two states were not represented and doubtful whether representatives of two others were present. Even after creation of the Department of Foreign Affairs (1781), treaties were negotiated under special instructions of the Congress. When John Jay was appointed in 1786 to negotiate a convention with Spain, Congress refused his request for a committee to instruct him and directed him not to accept Spanish proposals until approved by Congress. He initialed an understanding that provided commercial reciprocity and territorial guaranties conditioned upon temporary relinquishment by the United States of navigation on the lower Mississippi. A bitter debate followed in Congress, seven eastern and northern states favoring this bargain and six southern and southwestern states opposing it. As nine votes evidently could not be mustered for ratification, negotiations were dropped. References to this incident in the Constitutional Convention and ratification conventions in Virginia and North Carolina show that it influenced the mode of ratification incorporated into the Constitution. Despite difficulties the pre-Constitution Congress concluded the Treaty of Paris (1783) ending the revolutionary war; arrangements for refinancing debts to France (1782, 1783); commercial treaties with the Netherlands (1782), Sweden (1783), and Prussia (1785); the Treaty of Peace and Friendship with Morocco (1786); and a consular convention with France (1788).

At first treatymaking under the Constitution was concerned mainly with avoiding entanglement in the Napoleonic Wars and consolidating the territorial position of the new republic. Jay's Treaty (1794) with Great Britain provided a *modus vivendi* designed to preserve the bulk of American neutral rights by some concessions and to resolve continuing problems of the 1783 peace settlement. It led to successful arbitrations that stimulated further use of arbitration. Early treaties with the Barbary states secured unmolested transit for merchant ships by paying subsidies (Algiers, 1795; Tripoli, 1796; Tunis, 1797); then President Thomas Jefferson's navy vigorously attacked the pirates and secured remission of these payments (Tripoli, 1805; Algiers, 1815, 1822; Tunis, 1824). By the Treaty of San Lorenzo (1795), usually called Pinckney's Treaty, Spain granted the United States the right to deposit river cargoes in New Orleans for transshipment, and in 1800 a basic commercial convention was concluded with France. The Spanish violated their agreement, but Mississippi River valley rivalries ended with the treaty with France (1803), which ceded Louisiana to the United States and partly adjusted claims from French spoliations. By the Adams-Onís Treaty with Spain (1819) the United States obtained East Florida, the relinquishment of Spanish claims to West Florida, and Oregon Territory north of the forty-second parallel. Following the War of 1812 a series of treaties adjusted relationships with Great Britain: exchange of prisoners (1813); the Treaty of Ghent (1814), concluding peace; a commercial treaty (1816); demilitarization of the Great Lakes (1817); and the Convention of 1818 on coastal fisheries and the northern boundary.

Fifteen treaties were concluded before the Constitution of 1789, using procedures made difficult by political decentralization.

Thereafter attention turned to the westward movement that rounded out the continental domain and to external trade, both of which were dominant themes in treatymaking during the remainder of the century. Territorial additions and changes were marked by the Webster-Ashburton Treaty (1842), which adjusted the northeastern boundary; the treaty of 1846, carrying the northern boundary through Oregon Territory at the forty-ninth parallel; the Treaty of Guadalupe Hidalgo (1848), concluding the Mexican War and fixing the boundary with Mexico except as modified by the Gadsden Purchase Treaty (1854); and the treaty whereby Russia ceded Alaska (1867). Because of difficulties in securing Senate approval of treaties, Texas (1845) and the Hawaiian Islands (1898) were annexed by congressional joint resolutions, providing fuel for argument that a majority vote in both houses of the Congress would provide a more flexible mode of consent to ratification. In 1846 the United States obtained from New Granada (now Colombia) rights to construct transit across the Isthmus of Panama, but conflicting interests of Britain in Central America delayed plans for a canal and led to a compromise in the Clayton-Bulwer Treaty (1850). In spite of British withdrawal from the Mosquito Coast, American opinion continued to be hostile to this treaty because of provision for joint control of the projected canal, which many considered inconsistent with the Monroe Doctrine. Finally the United States initiated fresh negotiations, which produced the Hay-Pauncefote Treaty (1901), opening the way for construction by the United States of a canal to be maintained as an international waterway. Failure to secure ratification by Colombia of the Hay-Herrán Treaty (1903) for construction of the canal led to the Panamanian revolution, rapid recognition of Panama by the United States, and conclusion with Panama of a treaty (1903) that granted the United States the Canal Zone in perpetual leasehold. The Treaty of Paris (1898) ended the Spanish-American War, with cession of the Philippine Islands, Puerto Rico, and Guam. Cuban independence was guaranteed by the Platt Amendment, incorporated into the Treaty on Relations With Cuba of 1903, the United States obtaining a lease of Guantánamo Bay for a naval base. At Cuba's request the Platt Amendment was abrogated in 1934, but the leasehold was reaffirmed. The Virgin Islands were purchased by agreement with Denmark in 1916.

Commercial relations with an ever-expanding group of states led to numerous regulatory conventions. Early treaties of commerce and navigation arranged tariff concessions reciprocally; rights of merchant ships in foreign waters; and definition of consular functions in relation to nationals, national vessels, and exports. Most-favored-nation clauses were of the conditional type, extending benefits given the most-favored-nation only if reciprocal concessions were made. Even when not explicit, courts inferred such a condition from reciprocity clauses in which third states received special benefits in return for compensatory concessions, apparently upon analogy to the common-law requirement of consideration in contracts. The inappropriateness of applying this private-law doctrine to treaties, particularly those with countries not part of the English common-law system, was later conceded. After 1923 use of the conditional clause was abandoned. Later commercial conventions show stronger establishment clauses granting reciprocally to nationals of the other party rights to conduct commercial and industrial enterprises, to acquire property for residential and business purposes, and to employ agents and workers. Growth in the 20th century of corporate enterprise in foreign countries led to provisions for protection and regulation of it. Since World War II there has been emphasis on aid for reconstruction, military assistance, and financial and technical assistance for development. This has led to numerous treaties, followed by executive agreements elaborating detailed applications of programs authorized in treaties or basic statutes. Similarly, many conventions have elaborated principles of reciprocal trade agreements acts, later of the General Agreement on Tariffs and Trade (1948), and of the Chicago Air Convention (1944) regulating international air transport.

Commercial relations have increased violations of the rights of nationals, producing international claims sponsored by governments. Consequently many conventions have been concluded creating commissions to hear one or a series of claims, with supplementary *compromis* to arrange details of jurisdiction and procedure. Following a continuing policy the United States has also concluded both *ad hoc* and permanent arbitral agreements for adjustment of public injuries. The Treaty of Washington (1871) for adjustment of the Alabama Claims, the treaty of 1892 for arbitration of disputes over pelagic sealing in the Bering Sea, and creation of the Permanent Court of Arbitration (Hague Peace Conferences, 1899, 1907) are 19th-century examples. More recently the Root treaties of 1908–09 limited arbitration to disputes of a "legal nature" and those not affecting "the vital interests, the independence, or the honor" of the signatories, or "interests of third parties," exceptions unfortunately embracing matters most needing arbitration. They were omitted from the Taft-Knox Treaties of 1911. The Bryan Treaties of 1913–14 contained a "cooling-time" provision suspending hostilities pending investigation and report. The United States also made arbitral commitments under the United Nations Charter (1945) and the General Treaty of Inter-American Arbitration (1929).

There are early cases of extradition by the United States of fugitives from justice without treaty; this is no longer permitted. Beginning with Jay's Treaty and the Webster-Ashburton Treaty of 1842 with Britain, the United States has concluded extradition treaties with most countries. The older ones listed specific offenses for which extradition would be granted. Since the 1930's some treaties, particularly multilateral conventions, omit lists, authorizing extradition for any offenses punishable under the laws of both states ("double criminality"). The United States is a party to the multilateral

Montevideo Convention on Extradition (1933), which has helped to unify practice among Western Hemisphere states.

There are early cases of extradition by the U.S. of fugitives from justice without treaty; this is no longer permitted.

Beginning with the Red Cross Convention of 1854, the United States has concluded multilateral treaties, but these totaled only seventy before 1914, nearly half the products of the Hague Conferences, which codified international law regulating warfare and created the Permanent Court of Arbitration; the Central American Peace Conference of 1907, which set up the short-lived Central American Court of Justice; and several Pan-American conferences. Others regulated or created agencies to regulate weights and measures, submarine cables, exchange of documents, protection of industrial and literary property, sanitation and public health, wireless telegraphy, salvage, the African slave trade, white slavery, and safety at sea. There was one important political convention, the General Act of the Algeciras Conference (1906). The Declaration of London (1909), codifying the law of maritime neutrality, was not ratified. Since World War I, efforts have continued to organize the international community by multilateral conventions, which have become numerous. Two international organizations with comprehensive functions were created: the United States rejected the League of Nations Covenant and the Statute of the Permanent Court of International Justice, then initiated the Kellogg-Briand Pact (1928) for renunciation of aggressive war, and ratified the Charter of the United Nations and the Statute of the International Court of Justice (1945). It has participated in formation of the Organization of American States (1948), with consultative and security functions, and in many Pan-American agreements for economic and cultural cooperation. Beginning in 1947 it constructed a network of defensive alliances, including the North Atlantic Treaty Organization (1947) and the Southeast Asia Treaty Organization (1954). It also joined many international administrative unions with specialized economic and social functions, the more important of which are affiliated with the United Nations as specialized agencies. Multilateral lawmaking conventions have been used increasingly for codification and development of international law. Although the United States has been active in formulating such conventions and has ratified four dealing with the law of the sea (1958) and two regulating diplomatic and consular activity (1960, 1962), it has not ratified the Convention on the Law of Treaties (1968) nor the Genocide Convention (1949), a number of conventions for international protection of human rights, and most of the numerous International Labor Organization conventions. Its reluctance stems from pressures by those who fear conflicts with domestic jurisdiction or invasion of areas of state legislative competency—not legal but certainly political difficulties.

Until 1950 U.S. treaties were annually published in *Statutes at Large*; since then they have been published in the series *United States Treaties and Other International Agreements.*

BIBLIOGRAPHY

Charles I. Bevans, ed., *Treaties and Other International Agreements of the United States of America, 1776–1949.*

Charles Butler, *The Treaty-Making Power of the United States.*

Elbert M. Byrd, *Treaties and Executive Agreements in the United States.*

Samuel B. Crandall, *Treaties, Their Making and Enforcement.*

Royden J. Dangerfield, *In Defense of the Senate: A Study in Treaty Making.*

Robert T. Devlin, *The Treaty Power Under the Constitution of the United States.*

Harry G. Hawkins, *Commercial Treaties and Agreements: Principles and Practice.*

Ralston Hayden, *The Senate and Treaties, 1789–1817.*

Louis Henkin, *Foreign Affairs and the Constitution.*

Charles Cheney Hyde, *International Law Chiefly as Interpreted and Applied by the United States.*

C. H. McLaughlin, "The Scope of the Treaty Power in the United States," *Minnesota Law Review*, vols. 42 (1958) and 43 (1959).

Richard C. Snyder, *The Most-Favored-Nation Clause.*

— C. H. WCLAUGHLIN

TRESPASS ACT

Trespass Act (1783), an act contrary to the provisions of the Definitive Treaty of Peace, was passed in New York at the insistence of Gov. George Clinton. Primarily designed to benefit the owners of real estate in or about New York City whose property had been occupied by the British during the Revolution, it permitted the owners of such real estate to sue to recover rents and damages. A large number of actions were started under the law. Chief Justice Richard Morris of the New York Supreme Court was awarded a judgment of £5,000 against former Gov. William Tryon for damages to a farm worth only a third that sum. When Mayor James Duane, in the mayor's court of New York City, virtually pronounced the act unconstitutional in the case of *Rutgers* v. *Waddington*, the legislature censured him, and some members sought to remove him from office. Alexander Hamilton, under the name of "Phocion," wrote a pamphlet in 1784 denouncing the harsh treatment of the Loyalists and appealing to Congress and the states to observe the treaty of peace with respect to them. He was answered by Isaac Ledyard, as "Mentor"; and the controversy continued until 1788, when under the influence of Hamilton, John Jay, Philip J. Schuyler, Duane, and Robert R. Livingston, the legislature repealed all laws contrary to the treaty of peace.

BIBLIOGRAPHY

A. C. Flick, *Loyalism in New York During the American Revolution.*

— A. C. FLICK

TRIANGULAR TRADE

Unlike the tobacco and sugar colonies, the mainland English colonies north of Maryland did not, from their beginnings, have great staple products readily exportable directly to England in exchange for European goods. Yet, in order to maintain their accustomed European standards of living and to support an expanding economy, their relatively heavy populations demanded large imports of European manufactured wares—hardware, kitchen utensils, furniture, guns, building materials, farm tools, and textiles. Thus, from earliest times their imports from England exceeded their direct exports to England. Moreover, after 1660, many of their exportable surpluses—fish, cereals, and meats—were forbidden in England. As they were unable or forbidden by law to manufacture their needs in the colonies, they were forced to balance their trade by engaging in complex trading enterprises, to dispose of diversified surpluses in non-English markets in order to provide purchasing power in England. One means to redress the unfavorable English trade balance was the triangular trade, sometimes called the "three-cornered," or "roundabout," trade.

The triangular trade did not conform to a constant mercantile pattern. In its simplest form, near the mid-18th century, its three corners were, in sequence, a port in the northern colonies (most commonly Boston or Newport, R.I.), the Gold Coast of Africa, and a port in the West Indies (often Kingston, Jamaica). For example, the brigantine *Sanderson* of Newport sailed in March 1752 with a crew of nine and a cargo of 8,220 gallons of rum, some short iron bars ("African iron," used as currency among African natives), flour, pots, tar, sugar, shackles, shirts, provisions, and water. When the ship reached Africa, the cargo was exchanged for fifty-six slaves, 40 ounces of gold dust, and about 900 pounds of pepper. Proceeding to Barbados (June 17, 1753), the captain sold the slaves at £33 to £56 per head and disposed of the gold dust and pepper—with net proceeds of £1,324. Of this, £11,17s. was spent for fifty-five hogsheads of molasses and three hogsheads, twenty-seven barrels of sugar; the remainder due the captain was paid in bills of exchange drawn upon Liverpool. The *Sanderson* then returned to Newport.

Cargoes, routes, and ports varied. Although the main cargo on the first leg was generally rum and "African iron," it sometimes consisted of cloth or trinkets. The chief cargo on the second leg of the voyage—the infamous middle passage—was slaves, but occasionally it consisted of gold dust, condiments, ivory, or wines purchased en route at the Wine Islands, Spain, or France. On the homeward voyage, besides molasses and sugar, salt, wines, condiments, cotton, dyewoods, rice, tobacco, silver, bills of exchange, and slaves occasionally made up the cargo—any wares, in fact, that could be used at home or sold in England. In another variant of the trade, a New England, New York, or Philadelphia vessel carried fish, tobacco, or lumber to Lisbon, Cádiz, Gibraltar, or other Mediterranean ports, exchanged the cargo for European goods, traded in the West Indies for molasses, sugar, silver, or bills of exchange, and returned home.

Roots of the triangular trade extended into early Massachusetts commerce, although the trade itself did not flourish until after 1700. In the 1640's New England sales of fish and lumber in Spain and concurrent commerce with the West Indies must have suggested the roundabout trade; and in the 1650's New England vessels engaged directly in the African slave trade. But the monopoly of the Royal African Company (1672–97) closed to colonial vessels legal slave trade to the West Indies. Meanwhile, New England trade with the sugar colonies reached enormous proportions, and the uses of rum in the Indian trade and in the fisheries came to be widely recognized. Twenty-five years after Parliament threw open the slave trade (1697), rum—increasingly of New England origin—displaced French brandy in the African slave trade. Rum distilleries arose everywhere in New England after about 1700; Newport alone had twenty-two in 1730, Massachusetts had sixty-three in 1750. To a lesser extent they also developed in New York and Philadelphia. By 1770, three-fourths of the imports from the West Indies to northern colonies consisted of rum, molasses, and sugar. After 1715 much of these derived illegally from the French sugar islands, giving rise to English demands for the widely ignored Molasses Act of 1733 and the revolution-provoking Sugar Act of 1764. The importation of rum's baser cane equivalents and the growth of distilleries in the colonies were in direct proportion to the growth of the triangular trade.

Centered in New England, principally at Newport and Boston, the triangular trade extended to New York and Philadelphia and engaged hundreds of vessels before the Revolution, mostly small ships of 100 tons or less. Prominent merchants, notably Peter Faneuil of Boston, took the lead in the business and sold countless slaves in the West Indies, from which most went to Spanish colonies, and some to New England, New York, Philadelphia, and the southern mainland. Profits arising from the trade not only materially assisted in balancing the colonies' trade with England (adverse to an extent of £1,232,000 in 1770), but also accumulated great private capital surpluses in the colonies, capital of great value in developing subsequent American business enterprise.

BIBLIOGRAPHY

Robert G. Albion and others, *New England and the Sea.*

Bernard Bailyn, *The New England Merchants in the Seventeenth Century.*

Thomas C. Barrow, *Trade and Empire: The British Customs Service in Colonial America.*

Richard Dunn, *Sugar and Slaves: The Rise of the Planter Class in the English West Indies, 1640–1713.*

— RAYMOND P. STEARNS

TRUMAN DOCTRINE

On Mar. 12, 1947, President Harry S. Truman asked Congress for $400 million for the defense of Greece and Turkey from the pressure of Soviet communism. On May 15, Congress, although the country was officially at peace, voted the money, thus sanctioning a radical departure from the traditional policy of "nonentanglement" in European affairs. Truman indicated that this departure was to be more than temporary when he declared it to be a general principle of American policy "to help free peoples to maintain . . . their national integrity against aggressive movements that seek to impose upon them totalitarian [Communist] regimes."

— CHRISTOPHER LASCH

"TRUST-BUSTING"

"Trust-Busting," a term that originated during the administration of Theodore Roosevelt, which marked the turn from an apathetic policy in enforcement of the Sherman Antitrust Act of 1890 to one of energetic prosecution of lawbreakers in big business. In the phrases of the period, trust-busting might be defined as "wielding the Big Stick" against "malefactors of great wealth."

BIBLIOGRAPHY

Walter Lippman, *Drift and Mastery.*

— MYRON W. WATKINS

TRUSTS

Authorities on trusts agree that the term has been so broadly used that a precise definition is impossible. The economist Eliot Jones limits it to an industrial monopoly, and that is the general practice, although banking combines have been known as money trusts, public utilities have been called power trusts, and railroad companies and labor organizations have been prosecuted under the federal antitrust laws. On the other hand, local monopolies are not trusts. It is the attempt, or even the ability, to set prices in a national market, or even a large portion of it, that makes a concern a trust.

National monopolies first became apparent in American industry after the Civil War. Cheaper transportation made possible by ever more efficient railroads widened markets. More complex and costly machinery, often financed with borrowed funds (greater fixed costs), made maximum output increasingly desirable so as to reduce the cost per item manufactured. And when the economy was depressed, fewer businesses could afford to shut down temporarily—which tended to lead to overproduction. That, in turn, made competition more cutthroat than it had been under earlier conditions of high variable costs. Survival seemed to depend on solving the overproduction predicament, and businessmen favored one of two solutions. The first was increasing the demand—finding additional customers—and so advertising, salesmanship, and other marketing techniques developed rapidly. The other was decreasing the supply and raising the price, which required the formation of a monopoly. It first took the form of pooling agreements that limited production, fixed prices, centralized selling, and set quotas, but since these were unenforceable under the common law, they were often broken. The first trust was the Standard Oil Company, the organizational nature of which was secret in 1879 when it was founded, but amended and publicized in 1882, when it was renamed the Standard Oil Trust. The stockholders in numerous refining, pipeline, and other companies assigned their stock to a board of nine trustees at a stipulated price and received trust certificates. The trustees had legal and voting rights in the stocks; and the stockholders received the profits. This ingenious system was soon copied by other industries: the American Cotton Oil Trust was set up in 1884, the National Linseed Oil Trust in 1885, and the Distillers and Cattle Feeders Trust, known as the whiskey trust, in 1887.

Public agitation over the size and power of these giant organizations led to the testing of their legality in state courts, which decided that entering into such agreements was beyond a corporation's powers. Congress passed the Sherman Antitrust Act on July 2, 1890, section 1 of which states that "every contract, combination . . . or conspiracy in restraint of trade or commerce among the several states . . . is . . . illegal." Between 1891 and 1897 only fifty combinations capitalized at $1 million or more were formed, most of them of the property-holding type. The depressions covering most of these six years were, of course, also a discouraging factor.

Antitrust legislation was not effective for long. The Supreme Court seemed to draw the teeth of the Sherman Act in 1895 in *United States* v. *E. C. Knight Company* by ruling that the control of 98 percent of the sugar refining in the country was not illegal because it took the form of manufacturing in one state and not commerce between states. Said the Court, "Commerce succeeds to manufacture, and is not a part of it." In addition, a satisfactory substitute for the trustee device was found when New Jersey in 1889 and 1893, then Delaware, Maine, and other states, authorized corporations receiving charters from them to hold stock in other corporations, a right not previously enjoyed. The security holding company, which this made possible, differed from the trustee system in that ownership was substituted for trusteeship.

Between 1898 and 1903 trusts were formed in rapid succession. The census of 1900 showed 185 industrial combinations, seventy-three of them capitalized at $10 million or more, turning out 14 percent of the industrial products of the nation; 1901 witnessed the founding of the billion-dollar U.S. Steel Corporation; and by 1904 there were 318 trusts that controlled 20 percent of the manufacturing capital of the country. The so-called rich man's panic of 1903 brought the movement to a close.

The Supreme Court ruled that one firm's control of 98 percent of U.S. sugar refining was not illegal because it took the form of manufacturing in one state and not commerce between states.

Meanwhile the government had won a few minor cases with the Sherman Act; Theodore Roosevelt had become president; and reform fever had begun to sweep the nation. The trust-busting movement began with the Supreme Court decision of Mar. 14, 1904, against the Northern Securities Company, a security holding company formed to unite two great competing railroad systems in the Northwest. Suits were brought against forty-four trusts and combinations during Roosevelt's administration and against ninety more under President William Howard Taft.

The trusts became better behaved. The ruthless extermination of rivals that had characterized the oil and cash-register trusts gave way to a more tolerant system of letting the independents live if they would adhere to the trust's price policy and so keep business stable and profits at a maximum. These milder tactics bore fruit in 1911 when the Supreme Court announced in *Standard Oil Company of New Jersey et al.* v. *United States* and *United States* v. *American Tobacco Company* that these trusts were being dissolved because they were acting in "unreasonable" restraint of trade. The implication of this renowned "rule of reason" was that "good" trusts would not be broken up in the future. The following year the Court went a step further in the Terminal Railroad Association case and contended that even a trust that had acted in restraint of trade should be tolerated, if it could be used for legitimate purposes.

In the 1912 presidential election campaign Woodrow Wilson advocated a "New Freedom," of which the keynote was the restoration of free competition in trade and industry; and in 1914 his administration secured the passage of the Clayton Antitrust and Federal Trade Commission acts. The Clayton Act condemned such business practices as local price discrimination, tying contracts, interlocking directorates, and even the acquisition by one corporation of the stock of another in the same business, if the consequences were monopolistic. The Federal Trade Commission Act forbade "unfair methods of competition in commerce," a broad term that was left to the commission to enforce and the courts to continue to interpret. But the "New Freedom," handicapped by greater judicial tolerance of trusts and by the outbreak of World War I, died young.

There are several explanations for the public's subsequently less hostile attitude toward trusts. World War I had taught businessmen in all lines the advantages of concerted action; it had showed the public that a rising price level was probably caused more by monetary factors than by monopoly exploitation; and it had bred a cynical attitude toward reform. The Webb-Pomerene Act of 1918 and the Merchant Marine Act of 1920 permitted American concerns to combine to some extent in their foreign business. When the Supreme Court did not dissolve the U.S. Steel Corporation in 1920, despite its control of over half the nation's steel output and such evidence as a price of $28 a ton for steel rails maintained for ten years, a new trust movement got under way. The merger became the chief method of combination because the Clayton Act virtually forbade large-scale commercial combination by stock purchase. However, public utility empires still used the holding company device. It has been estimated that there were over 500 combinations during the administration of President Calvin Coolidge. During the prosperous years of the 1920's businesses in the same line were permitted increasingly to compare recent statistical information; basing point systems grew in popularity; and in *Appalachian Coals, Inc.* v. *United States* in 1933 a joint sales agency, including producers of 75 percent of the output, was judged not contrary to the antitrust laws.

The great amount of price-cutting that took place during the Great Depression led to criticism of the predatory character of competition and to considerable talk of the need for a more planned economy. During the administration of President Franklin D. Roosevelt, under the National Industrial Recovery Act of 1933, trade associations and other industrial groups were permitted to control prices and to determine production and were encouraged to draw up codes of fair competition; they were promised that any action taken in compliance with an approved code would not subject them to prosecution under the antitrust laws. The Federal Trade Commission was to enforce these codes. Within the first month over 400 of the eventual total of 677 codes were filed, and many were too hastily approved. Code groups were permitted many liberties forbidden under the antitrust laws, especially the soft coal, petroleum, lumber, and cleaning and dyeing businesses. The suspension of over forty years of antitrust legal precedents left the courts bewildered. The Supreme Court's decision in *Schechter* v. *United States* in May 1935 brought this experiment in industrial self-government to an end.

Two subsequent laws slightly altered antitrust legislation. The Robinson-Patman Act (1936) sought to define the types of wholesale price discrimination that should be prohibited, and the Miller-Tydings Act (1937) gave force in interstate commerce to the resale price maintenance laws existing in most states and represented a lessening of competition.

On June 16, 1938, Congress authorized the appointment of the Temporary National Economic Committee, with Sen. Joseph C. O'Mahoney as chairman, to investigate the growing concentration of economic power and recommend appropriate legislation. That committee's lengthy hearings, starting Dec. 1, 1938, and its final report again indicated the need to curb the trusts. Thurman Arnold of the Antitrust Division of the Justice Department began litigation against many big companies. Then World War II broke out and, as in World War I, the government suspended prosecution of the trusts and encouraged cooperation among industries in the interest of efficiency. The Office of Price Administration even found this concentration of economic power useful in effecting price controls.

Between 1937 and 1948 the government instituted more antitrust suits than in any previous decade; the government generally won but imposed mild penalties. The most famous case, started in 1937, involved the Aluminum Company of America (Alcoa). In 1945 the Circuit Court of Appeals, in a decision written by Judge Learned Hand, reversed an essential principle of the 1920 U.S. Steel case by ruling that great size, and certainly 90 percent control of the aluminum industry, was a violation of the law—good behavior notwithstanding. Subsequent decisions slightly modified this stand. To provide Alcoa with the desired competition, the government sold its wartime aluminum plants to two newly established competitors. About 1946 the Antitrust Division began investigations of 122 companies. Major targets were the Du Pont Company with its large General Motors holdings (a case won by Antitrust in 1957), the Atlantic and Pacific Tea Company, and the Pullman Company. One of Antitrust's greatest victories was the Supreme Court's order in 1948 to the Cement Institute to abandon its basing-point system, for the decision obliged some twenty-five other industries, among them steel, to give up their basing-point systems as well.

By 1950 a few corporations had incomes greater than that of any state or city government in the country, and the size of these empires and the power of their rulers caused anxiety. In 1950 Congress passed the Celler-Kefauver Act, which forbade a company to acquire all or part of the assets of another if the consequence would be to reduce competition. Nevertheless, between 1950 and 1969 some 17,000 mergers took place. Some ran into trouble. When the Brown Shoe Company, controlling 4 percent of the market, acquired the Kinney Shoe Company, controlling 1.5 percent, the Supreme Court in 1962 ordered divestiture on the ground that in some lines of shoes, or in some cities, a dangerous horizontal concentration would result. That decision greatly strengthened the hand of Antitrust.

Although aware that a merger would not be tolerated, some companies colluded to fix prices anyway. In 1961 the General Electric Company, the Westinghouse Electric Corporation, and twenty-seven other electrical equipment manufacturers were convicted of using an elaborate secret code to fix the prices of their products. It was a shocking revelation—and the court gave seven company officials jail sentences and imposed $1.8 million in fines.

During the 1960's many of the mergers were conglomerates that Antitrust at first believed could not be shown to lessen competition. But after about 1969 the Federal Trade Commission increased its attack on mergers, even of the general sort, as in obliging Procter and Gamble to divest itself of the Clorox Company.

Meanwhile in the fair trade segment of antitrust activity many state legislatures and courts outlawed the practice of legalizing resale price maintenance policies in interstate commerce, despite the McGuire-Keogh Act of 1952—and the number of discount houses mushroomed.

The trust situation changed in several ways between the 1920's and the 1970's. In 1971 there were 129 industrial corporations whose annual sales exceeded $1 billion—and the General Motors Corporation, the Ford Motor Company, and the Chrysler Corporation controlled 97 percent of American passenger car production. Many critics argued that the nation's most powerful monopolies were no longer confined to its industries; they also included some of its labor unions. By the Clayton Act of 1914 and the Norris-La Guardia Act of 1932, unions were virtually exempt from antitrust prosecution. Reluctance of elected officials to act against them also protected them. Yet such a situation sometimes had unforeseen benefits, such as providing a countervailing power to the industrial monopoly. Ralph Nader and his so-called organized consumerism emerged in the 1960's as another countervailing power. Finally, from the 1930's on, the federal government itself, in order to solve the problem of overproduction or overcapacity, organized or encouraged its own monopoly, somewhat as John D. Rockefeller had once done. The Agricultural Adjustment Administration of 1933 was essentially a government-sponsored farmers trust to limit production and raise the level of farm prices. Admittedly the government, not private citizens, directed the program, but this monopoly, like others, exploited consumers.

The United States and Great Britain have used seven methods to deal with trusts. They are regulating the industry, as Congress did to the railroads by the Interstate Commerce Act of 1887; setting up a government yardstick, as the Tennessee Valley Authority was intended to do; not interfering—in the hope that competition will somehow reappear; imposing heavy taxes on monopoly profits; keeping tariffs low to make foreign competition effective, as Great Britain did until 1931; nationalizing offending industries, as Great Britain has also done; and ordering the trusts to break up, as the Supreme Court did to Standard Oil of New Jersey in 1911. American antitrust legislation has used dissolution as its chief remedy and form of punishment, but that approach has not always been especially successful: the thirty-four parts of Standard Oil of New Jersey remained for a time after 1911 a trust operating under an interlocking directorate.

BIBLIOGRAPHY

T. W. Arnold, *The Folklore of Capitalism.*

Corwin Edwards, *Maintaining Competition.*

F. A. Fetter, *The Masquerade of Monopoly.*

G. C. Fite and J. E. Reese, *An Economic History of the United States.*

Ralph Hidy and Muriel Hidy, *Pioneering in Big Business.*

Eliot Jones, *The Trust Problem.*

D. L. Kemmerer and C. C. Jones, *American Economic History.*

Ross Robertson, *History of the American Economy.*

G. Stocking and M. W. Watkins, *Monopoly and Free Enterprise.*

Ida Tarbell, *The Standard Oil Company.*

Simon Whitney, *Anti-Trust Policies.*

— DONALD L. KEMMERER

TUBERCULOSIS

Under such names as phthisis and consumption, tuberculosis was one of the great killer diseases throughout much of American history. It was a familiar complaint and for this reason went virtually unnoticed among the great pestilential outbreaks of smallpox, yellow fever, and other more dramatic diseases. Although an age-old disorder, its incidence began rising in the 18th century and reached a peak in America and western Europe around the mid-19th century. The extent of tuberculosis in the colonial period is difficult to estimate, since the disease was not fully understood and the most common terms for it, consumption and phthisis, were too inclusive. Cotton Mather, for example, suggested that many venereal complaints were hidden under the term consumption.

By the early 19th century tuberculosis was recognized as a leading cause of death, but neither its cause nor cure was known; the public accepted it as an inevitable part of life, and the medical profession was at a complete loss. English and American physicians, unlike those of Italy, did not believe the disease to be communicable. The two most common forms of therapy involved either shutting the patient in a closed room away from all drafts (and fresh air) or else urging him to seek a warmer climate. Florida was the first choice, but later the Southwest was settled, and it quickly became the mecca for "lungers," as tubercular patients were often known. For a brief period in the mid-19th century many northern patients flocked to the Louisiana sugarcane mills during the harvest season, where the high

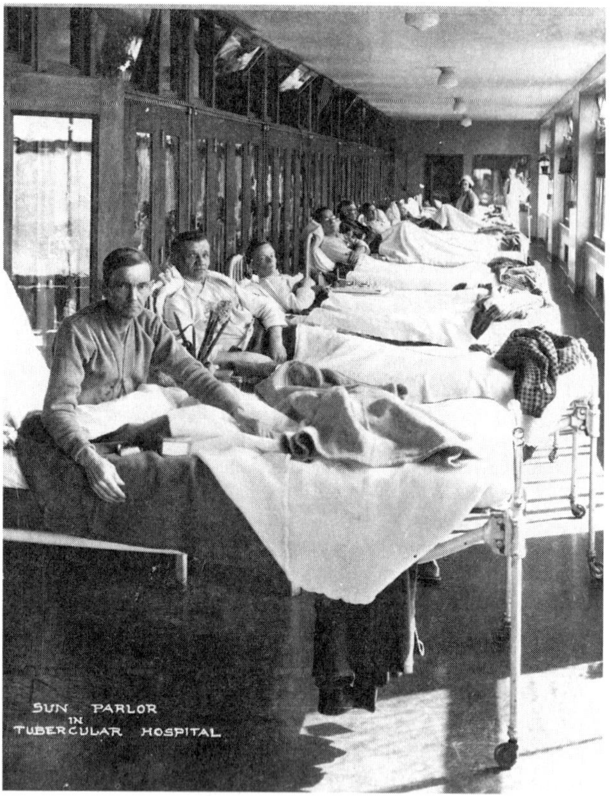

Soldiers in the tuberculosis hospital, Soldiers National Home, Dayton, Ohio. A large-scale public health program in the early 20th century brought a sharp reduction in the tuberculosis death rate. (Library of Congress/Corbis)

humidity and fumes from the cane syrup were reputed to cure many cases.

Even the best of physicians could do little to alleviate or cure the disease. As late as 1881 Austin Flint, in his standard textbook *The Principles and Practice of Medicine,* stated that tuberculosis was "non-communicable" and attributed it to such causes as hereditary disposition, unfavorable climate, sedentary indoor life, defective ventilation, and "depressing emotions." But the following year Robert Koch announced the discovery of tubercle bacilli (*Mycobacterium tuberculosis*) and showed it to be the cause of the disease. This major discovery created considerable stir, but it took another twenty years before the American medical profession became convinced that the disease was communicable.

Meanwhile two significant developments were taking place. First, for reasons still not clear, the incidence of tuberculosis was beginning to decline. The death rate from tuberculosis in leading American cities was in excess of 400 per 100,000 population during the early years of the 19th century. The Boston bills of mortality for 1812–21, for example, show a tuberculosis death rate of approximately 472 per 100,000 population. By 1900 the estimated rate for the major American cities was down to about 200. The second development was the appearance of tuberculosis sanatoriums, a movement that was in full swing in western Europe by the mid-19th century. The American pioneer in this field was Edward L. Trudeau, who probably contracted tuberculosis while caring for his brother. Despite the fact that he himself was a physician, his symptoms were not recognized until the disease was well advanced. When a stay in the South failed to bring improvement and his condition was considered hopeless, he resolved to spend his last days in the Adirondacks, at that time a wilderness area that had always appealed to him. His health steadily improved in the outdoor life, and in 1884 he opened a small sanatorium at Saranac Lake, N.Y., modeled on one of the European establishments. Encouraged by its success, in 1894 he established a laboratory devoted to the study of tuberculosis. Trudeau's reputation grew rapidly, and the relatively high recovery rate of his patients gave new hope to thousands of consumptives. Within a few years sanatoriums appeared throughout the United States, and the emphasis in tubercular therapy came to be placed upon rest, fresh air, and a sound diet.

This rest therapy in the early years of the sanatoriums obtained considerable success, but the 20th century brought further improvements in diagnosis and treatment. The impact of the bacteriological revolution and the advent of roentgenology opened a new era in diagnosis, and the introduction of surgical collapse and surgical section revolutionized treatment in advanced cases.

These developments paved the way for large-scale public health programs. The New York City Health Department took the initiative in 1889 by commissioning three of its consultants, one of whom was Hermann M. Biggs, to investigate tuberculosis. The resulting report, which clearly stated that the disease was communicable and preventable, is a medical classic. The Health Department found the medical profession generally hostile to these findings but nonetheless published a circular in several languages entitled "Rules to be Observed for the Prevention and Spread of Consumption." A subsequent report by Biggs in 1893 led the department to take more positive action. A greater effort was made to educate the public about the disease, and physicians were urged to report their cases. As it became clear that tuberculosis was a communicable disorder and that physicians were not cooperating, the department passed an ordinance in January 1897 making case reporting compulsory. Despite a chorus of outraged cries from medical societies and journals, the Health

Department pushed ahead with its tuberculosis program. In the succeeding years public health nurses were assigned to visit homes of patients, and diagnostic clinics, a municipal sanatorium, and the first tuberculosis preventorium for children were added to the department's facilities. Even more important in the battle against tuberculosis was the department's educational program designed to make the public aware of the disease and to teach both patients and their families to take necessary precautions. Other city and state health departments soon established similar programs. In the process of educating the public, they received considerable help from the many voluntary tuberculosis associations.

This large-scale attack mounted in the 20th century brought a sharp reduction in the national tuberculosis death rate for the first quarter of the century and a more gradual fall in the rate in the ensuing years. In 1943 the introduction of streptomycin brought a new weapon to bear, but neither it nor isoniazid (1953) proved decisive. Preeminently a social disease, tuberculosis still exists among older inhabitants of urban skid rows and in certain poverty areas, but it is no longer a serious problem in the United States.

BIBLIOGRAPHY

René Dubos and Jean Dubos, *The White Plague, Tuberculosis, Man and Society.*

John Duffy, *A History of Public Health in New York City, 1866–1966.*

Selman A. Waksman, *The Conquest of Tuberculosis.*

— JOHN DUFFY

TUSCARORA WAR

Tuscarora War (1711–13), was fought in eastern North Carolina. The lower Tuscarora, led by Chief Hencock, were moved to attack their white neighbors chiefly because of the vicious practices of white traders—who kidnapped their young to sell into slavery—and because of their alarm at settlers' encroachments on their hunting grounds. A sudden massacre (September 1711) almost overwhelmed the white colony. New York officials persuaded the warlike Seneca, related to the Tuscarora, not to enter the fray. Virginia aided by overawing the upper Tuscarora into neutrality and, later, nominal alliance. South Carolina's assistance was more apparent. Col. John Barnwell led a relief expedition of about 50 whites and more than 350 Indian allies. Although his campaign (January–April 1712) weakened the enemy, it ended in a poorly observed truce. A second South Carolina expedition was commanded by Col. James Moore; it consisted of 33 whites and almost 1,000 Indian warriors. The main body of the enemy took refuge in Fort Nohoroco, near present-day Snow Hill, N.C. A three-day engagement resulted in its capitulation (March 1713) and in Tuscarora acceptance of a drastic treaty of peace. Most of the Tuscarora trekked northward and joined their kindred; thereafter the Five Nations were known as the Six Nations. Native opposition having been shattered, North Carolina's westward expansion began in earnest.

BIBLIOGRAPHY

W. Clark, "Indian Massacre and Tuscarora War 1711–13," *The North Carolina Booklet*, vol. II (1902–03).

— W. NEIL FRANKLIN

TUSKEGEE INSTITUTE

In 1881 Lewis Adams, a mechanic and former slave, and George W. Campbell, a banker and former slaveowner, both of Tuskegee, Ala., saw the need for the education of black youth in Macon County and secured a charter, which appropriated $2,000 annually for teachers' salaries, from the state legislature. Booker T. Washington was chosen to head the school, and the coeducational Tuskegee Normal and Industrial Institute (the name was shortened in 1937) was established by an act of the Alabama general assembly on Feb. 12, 1881. Washington became the first principal and opened the school on July 4. Spectacular growth and development took place under Washington and continued under his successors: Robert Russa Moton, Frederick D. Patterson, and Luther H. Foster.

Tuskegee Institute is a small university offering undergraduate degrees in six major areas—arts and sciences, applied sciences, education, engineering, nursing, and veterinary medicine—and work at the master's level in each area except nursing. The program is fully accredited, by the Southern Association of Colleges and Schools, and many of the professional areas are approved by national agencies.

Enrollment, predominantly undergraduate, was 3,000 in 1973, with students representing twenty-nine states, the District of Columbia, and seven foreign countries. Twenty-five degree-granting courses make up the curricula of six areas. Physical facilities include 4,925 acres of land and 159 buildings.

— DANIEL T. WILLIAMS

TWEED RING

Tweed ring, led by William Marcy Tweed, New York State senator and political boss, robbed the New York City treasury of a minimum of $30 million in the thirty months ended July 31, 1871. Another audit estimated that the Tweed Ring proper, which began in 1869, and its immediate forerunner, looted the city of between $45 million and $50 million in the three years and six months beginning Jan. 1, 1868. An aldermanic investigation (1877) raised this figure to $60 million. Matthew J. O'Rourke, a journalist who, while county bookkeeper, exposed the frauds, reckoned $200 million as the total stealings of the ring and the lesser Tweed rings from Jan. 1, 1865, to July 31, 1871. This included fraudulent bond issues, the sale of franchises, tax reductions, and other official favors, of an approximate worth of $125 million.

The Tweed Ring's takings from the New York City treasury over a three-year period were estimated at between $30 million and $50 million.

When the ring came into being on Jan. 1, 1869, it seemingly had nothing to fear. Tweed's man, John T. Hoffman, had that day been inaugurated governor of the state; and in New York City Tweed was sovereign. He controlled the police, the district attorney, the courts, and most of the newspapers. A Democrat, he silenced the Republican party by putting scores of its leaders on the payroll—his own or the taxpayers'. He took over the city's lone reform organization in like manner. The ring members were Mayor A. Oakey Hall, known as the "elegant Oakey"; City Comptroller Richard B. Connolly, alias "Slippery Dick"; City Chamberlain Peter Barr Sweeny, otherwise "Bismarck" or "Brains"; and Tweed, president of the Board of Supervisors and leader of Tammany Hall.

The ring's methods called for unscrupulous contractors, merchants, and others who dealt with the municipality. The original plan called for mulcting the city out of one dollar for every two paid out. Drunk with avarice, the ring's share was gradually increased until checks were drawn to imaginary individuals, firms, hospitals, and other charitable institutions. The ring's recklessness and the magnitude of its thefts shoved the city to the verge of bankruptcy. This, coupled with a struggle between Tweed and the reformer Samuel J. Tilden for Democratic party control, led to the ring's undoing.

Promises to publish a complete list of the ring's beneficiaries and to sue them all were broken because too many influential people were involved. Three of the ring judges, George G. Barnard, John H. McCunn, and Albert Cardozo, were impeached. The first two were removed; Cardozo resigned. Tweed, reputedly worth $12 million at the peak of his power, was made the scapegoat. He made a partial confession. His offer to tell all if permitted to die outside prison walls was spurned. He died in Ludlow Street jail on Apr. 12, 1878.

BIBLIOGRAPHY

Denis Tilden Lynch, *Boss Tweed*, and *The Wild Seventies*.
S. J. Mandelbaum, *Boss Tweed's New York*.

— DENIS TILDEN LYNCH

TWELFTH AMENDMENT

The U.S. Constitution originally provided that "the Person having the greatest Number of Votes shall be the President, if such Number be a Majority of the whole Number of Electors appointed; and if there be more than one who have such Majority, and have an equal Number of Votes, then the House of Representatives shall immediately chuse by Ballot one of them for President." It soon became evident that this arrangement was not satisfactory. The almost inevitable result was a lack of harmony between the president and vice-president, since two candidates from the same party would not normally be at the top of the list. In case of the death of the president, a change of party control in the middle of the four-year term would result, without any mandate from the people.

In 1800 an acute situation developed. Thomas Jefferson and Aaron Burr not only received the largest number of votes, but the same number; it was, therefore, necessary for the House of Representatives to break the tie. While provision had been made for this contingency, its actual occurrence almost precipitated a crisis. The Federalists were restrained only with difficulty from frustrating the expressed will of the electorate, and throwing the election to Burr. Steps were promptly taken to prevent the recurrence of such a situation.

The Twelfth Amendment, having passed the Senate on Dec. 2, 1803, was proposed to the states by Congress on Dec. 9, following its passage by the House. There were at the time seventeen states in the Union; the approval of thirteen was necessary for ratification. The legislature of New Hampshire, by its approval of the amendment on June 15, 1804, made that state the thirteenth to ratify. But the governor vetoed the action, and if his veto was valid—which it probably was not—then the ratification by Tennessee on July 27, 1804, was decisive. Formal notice of ratification was made by Secretary of State James Madison on Sept. 25, 1804, in time for its provisions to be effective in the presidential election of 1804.

[See also Jefferson–Burr Election Dispute.]

BIBLIOGRAPHY

Edward Stanwood, *History of the Presidency.*

W. W. Willoughby, *Constitutional Law of the United States.*

— W. BROOKE GRAVES

TWENTY-FIRST AMENDMENT

Twenty-first Amendment, providing for repeal of the Eighteenth Amendment, was proposed by Congress in February 1933, ratified by the thirty-sixth state within ten months, and proclaimed to be in effect Dec. 5, 1933. At the time only eleven states had provisions in their constitutions concerning prohibition but among these were some curious ones. Kentucky, for example, permitted liquor to be used medicinally, the patient prescribing the dosage for himself. The Twenty-first Amendment apparently permits states to levy an import tax on alcoholic beverages, operative against goods produced in other states, thereby modifying the provision of Article I of the Constitution prohibiting state imposts or the barring of importation altogether.

— ROBERT G. RAYMER

TWENTY-SECOND AMENDMENT

Sent to the states by the Eightieth Congress, Mar. 21, 1947, the Twenty-second Amendment to the U.S. Constitution became effective on Feb. 26, 1951. It provides that "No person shall be elected to the office of the President more than twice." The amendment was the result of agitation following President Franklin D. Roosevelt's breaking of the two-term tradition by running for and being elected to a third and a fourth term. A qualifying clause prevented President Harry S. Truman, who as vice-president became president upon the death of Roosevelt, Apr. 12, 1945, from running for reelection more than once. During President Dwight D. Eisenhower's term of office there was some effort to repeal the amendment in order to enable him to seek a third term. After Eisenhower left office in 1960, such efforts abated.

There were initially some fears that the amendment would render a president less effective in the last two years of his second term, but such did not prove to be the case in Eisenhower's last years. Malcolm Moos, aide to Eisenhower, observed, " . . . it may be that the President is using the Twenty-second Amendment as a political weapon aimed at Congress. In other words, the President can gain support for his policies because he can convince the people he has nothing to gain personally. The amendment eliminates self-interest.

— THOMAS ROBSON HAY AND HAROLD W. CHASE

TWENTY-THIRD AMENDMENT

Proposed by Congress on June 17, 1960, the Twenty-third Amendment to the U.S. Constitution was ratified on Mar. 29, 1961. The amendment grants the right to vote in federal elections for three electors for president and vice-president to residents of the District of Columbia. The District of Columbia had not had voting rights since it was carved out of portions of Virginia and Maryland in 1800. The amendment was consonant with the concurrent development of the "one man, one vote" idea.

— THOMAS ROBSON HAY AND HAROLD W. CHASE

TWENTY-FOURTH AMENDMENT

Proposed by Congress in 1962 and declared ratified on Feb. 4, 1964, the Twenty-fourth Amendment to the U.S. Constitution was passed to eliminate poll taxes in federal elections. Although there had been attempts to eliminate poll taxes in every Congress since 1939, five

The Twenty-fourth Amendment ended the use of the poll tax as a prerequisite for voting in all elections to public office.

states still required payment of poll taxes prior to passage of the amendment. When Virginia sought to retain the poll tax for state elections, a sharply divided Supreme Court declared the use of poll taxes in state elections a violation of the equal protection clause of the Fourteenth Amendment (*Harper* v. *Virginia Board of Elections*). The Twenty-fourth Amendment and the Supreme Court decision ended the use of the poll tax as a prerequisite for voting in all elections to public office.

BIBLIOGRAPHY

Harold W. Chase and Craig R. Ducat, *Corwin's Constitution and What It Means Today.*

— HAROLD W. CHASE

TWENTY-FIFTH AMENDMENT

Proposed in 1965 and ratified in 1967, the Twenty-fifth Amendment to the U.S. Constitution deals with one of the most troublesome problems of the American political system—presidential disability and succession. Sections 3 and 4 of the amendment set forth in detail what is to be done in the event that the president himself feels he is "unable to discharge the powers and duties of his office" or "Whenever the Vice-President and a majority of either the principal officers of the executive department or of such other body as Congress may by law provide . . . [find] that the President is unable to discharge the powers and duties of his office."

Ironically, the demise of President Richard M. Nixon and Vice-President Spiro T. Agnew gave more prominence to Section 2 of the amendment, which provides that "Whenever there is a vacancy in the office of the Vice-President, the President shall nominate a Vice-President who shall take office upon confirmation by a majority vote of both Houses of Congress." Agnew resigned as vice-president in October 1973, and the following month Rep. Gerald R. Ford was nominated and confirmed as vice-president. When Ford succeeded Nixon to the presidency, following Nixon's resignation in August 1974, and when Nelson A. Rockefeller was nominated by Ford and confirmed as vice-president, the United States for the first time in its history had an unelected president and vice-president. There were manifest concerns over that fact, and it has been suggested that in situations where an appointed vice-president succeeds to the presidency and there are several years left in the term, there should be a special election. Establishment of such a procedure would, of course, require further amendment of the Constitution.

BIBLIOGRAPHY

Harold W. Chase and Craig R. Ducat, *Corwin's Constitution and What It Means Today and Supplement.*

— HAROLD W. CHASE

TWENTY-SIXTH AMENDMENT

Proposed and ratified in 1971, the Twenty-sixth Amendment to the U.S. Constitution gives eighteen-year-olds the constitutional right to vote in both federal and state elections. Before enactment of the amendment, Congress had already lowered the voting age to eighteen in the Voting Rights Act of 1970, but the Supreme Court held that the law was constitutional and enforceable only in federal elections. This decision created confusion as to how the states should proceed and probably explains why the amendment was ratified so swiftly.

The successful drive to permit eighteen-year-olds to vote was a direct outcome of the political activism of young citizens in the 1960's whose desire to participate in the political process was manifest. Their "right" to do so was summed up in the Senate report that accompanied the proposal for the amendment: " . . . the Committee is convinced that the time has come to extend the vote to 18-year-olds in all elections: because they are mature enough in every way to exercise the franchise; they have earned the right to vote by bearing the responsibilities of citizenship; and because our society has much to gain by bringing the force of their idealism and concern and energy into the constructive mechanism of elective government."

BIBLIOGRAPHY

Harold W. Chase and Craig R. Ducat, *Corwin's Constitution and What It Means Today and Supplement.*

— HAROLD W. CHASE

TWO-PARTY SYSTEM

Although there have been minor political parties (third parties) throughout most of American history, the American party system has been dominated by two major, competitive parties. Beginning with the Federalists and the Antifederalists in the 1790's, only two political parties have usually had any substantial chance of victory in national elections. Indeed, since the Civil War the same two parties—the Democratic and Republican—have constituted the American two-party system.

Because of the two-party system all American presidents and almost all members of Congress elected since the Civil War have been either Democrats or Republicans. Furthermore, the competition of the two parties has been consistently close. From 1860 through 1972 only four presidents won more than 60 percent of the total popular vote: Warren G. Harding in 1920; Franklin D. Roosevelt in 1936; Lyndon B. Johnson in 1964; and Richard M. Nixon in 1972. And in the same period only one biennial election to the House of Representatives (that of 1920) saw a difference greater than 20 percent in the division of the total popular vote for the candidates of the two major parties.

While the two-party system has long characterized national politics, it has not invariably marked the politics of the states. In some measure, the national two-party system of the late 19th century was an aggregate of one-party states. The incidence of that statewide one-partyism has declined in the 20th century, but the Democrats maintained a one-party supremacy in the states of the Deep South from the Reconstruction period into the 1960's and in some cases into the 1970's. Occasionally, too, states have had three-party systems for short periods of time; the states of Wisconsin, North Dakota, and Minnesota all included a party from the

Progressive movement in their party systems in the 1930's and 1940's.

The American two-party system results in part from the relative absence of irreconcilable differences within the American electorate about basic social, economic, and political institutions and in part from the absence of electoral rewards for minor parties. The traditions of plurality elections from single-member constituencies and of a single elected executive give few chances of victory or reward to parties that cannot muster the plurality.

BIBLIOGRAPHY

Wilfred E. Binkley, *American Political Parties.*

V. O. Key, Jr., *Politics, Parties, and Pressure Groups.*

— FRANK J. SORAUF

TWO-THIRDS RULE

At the Democratic convention in Baltimore in May 1832, the committee on rules reported the following resolution:

> Resolved, that each state be entitled in the nomination to be made of a candidate for the vice-presidency, to a number of votes equal to the number to which they will be entitled in the electoral colleges, under the new apportionment, in voting for President and Vice-President; and that two thirds of the whole number of the votes in the convention shall be necessary to constitute a choice.

Thus originated the two-thirds rule, which was followed by all Democratic conventions in making nominations until the convention at Philadelphia in June 1936, when the rule was abolished and a majority vote substituted. Numerous attempts had been made to remove the rule, but it had always been strongly defended by the southern states, which, with the rule in effect, could control nominations. A fight on the question in the Philadelphia convention was avoided by the adoption of a resolution designed to secure a new method of apportioning delegates among the states that would take into account the Democratic strength within each state.

BIBLIOGRAPHY

E. Stanwood, *A History of the Presidency.*

— EDWARD B. LOGAN

U

"UNCLE SAM"

"Uncle Sam," a nickname of the U.S. government. First used during the War of 1812, the term was applied somewhat derisively to customhouse officers and to soldiers by those opposed to the war, but was avoided by the "war hawks." As contemporary newspapers show, the term was doubtless a jocular expansion of the letters "U.S." on uniforms and government property.

The name is also identified with Samuel Wilson of Troy, N.Y. (1766–1854), known as "Uncle Sam" Wilson, who supplied barrels of beef to the government. In 1961 Congress recognized Wilson as a namesake for America's symbol.

— ALBERT MATTHEWS

A famous World War I recruiting poster by James Montgomery Flagg shows "Uncle Sam," pointing his finger and declaring "I Want You. . . ." The popular character, an expansion of the letters "U. S.," was first used during the War of 1812. (Corbis-Bettmann)

UNCLE TOM'S CABIN, OR, LIFE AMONG THE LOWLY

Uncle Tom's Cabin; or, Life Among the Lowly, by Harriet Beecher Stowe, was published serially in the *Washington National Era* (June 5, 1851–Apr. 1, 1852) and appeared in book form Mar. 20, 1852. Mrs. Stowe was acquainted with the bitter criticism of the Fugitive Slave Law of 1850 in New England and was determined to write an account of slavery as she had known it in Cincinnati. She intended to condemn the system, not the slaveholder, and expected a favorable hearing in the South. Although based on fact, the book was not an accurate picture of the system, although it did show both the strength and weakness of southern society. The book had a popular reception never before accorded a novel. Three hundred thousand copies were sold the first year and more than one million by 1860. Dramatized and produced on the stage, it reached millions who never read the book. Northern people were incensed and aroused against the inhuman system. Many southerners read the book; some wrote ineffectual replies; others forbade its circulation. Measured by its emotional appeal and lasting influence, the book ranks high as reform propaganda. Most potent of all accounts of slavery, it lighted a torch in the North and was a contributing cause of the Civil War.

BIBLIOGRAPHY

Anne B. Stewart, *A Critique of Uncle Tom's Cabin.*
C. E. Stowe and L. B. Stowe, *Harriet Beecher Stowe.*

— FLETCHER M. GREEN

UNDERGROUND RAILROAD

Underground Railroad, the name used by both the abolitionists and the defenders of slavery to describe the informal network of sympathetic northerners that helped guide fugitive slaves through the free states to Canada in the years before the Civil War. The term dates from about 1830, when a slave-holder, after losing all trace of one of his slaves who had escaped in the vicinity of Ripley, Ohio, reportedly said that the slave "must have gone off on an underground road," Although George Washington had reported systematic efforts by Quakers to aid slaves as early as the 1780's, it was not until the 1830's that the idea of a deep-laid abolitionist scheme spread, and the term "Underground Railroad" gained currency. For the remainder of the antebellum period, southern efforts to obtain more rigid fugitive laws were based on the belief in the existence of highly coordinated efforts by the abolitionists to help slaves escape from the South. This view was affirmed by those abolitionists who took pride in the work of the "Liberty Line," as the Underground Railroad was also known, and counted its activities among the most important weapons in the war on the "peculiar institution." In the postwar years the legend of the Underground Railroad outstripped reality. The coordinated efforts of Quaker, Covenanter, and Methodist "conductors," secretly operating at night, to transport slaves from "station" to "station" along an intricate maze of routes through the northern states became a standard part of the romance of antebellum America. Yet as one historian noted early in the 20th century, the real Underground Railroad involved "much less system and much more spontaneity than has generally been supposed."

The number of slaves aided by the underground railroad has long been a matter of dispute and subject to widely varying estimates. On the eve of the Civil War a proslavery writer surmised that between 1810 and 1850 " 'underground railroads' and felonious abductions" had "plundered" the South of 100,000 slaves valued at $30 million. At the turn of the century historian Wilbur H. Siebert, basing his calculations on the fragmentary records of conductors, set the number of fugitives aided between 1830 and 1850 in Ohio alone at 40,000 and estimated that by the latter date the Underground Railroad as a whole had transported roughly 75,000 "passengers" to freedom. While this is modest compared to earlier estimates, it suggests greater numbers of escaped slaves than do the contemporary federal censuses. The 1850 census enumerated 1,011 fugitives for the previous year, and a decade later this figure had fallen to 803 for a similar period. Thus, rather than a flood of fugitive slaves portrayed by antebellum propagandists and later fiction writers, the actual numbers involved represented only a small fraction of those held in bondage.

The lot of the fugitive slave was extremely difficult, and a successful escape required not only extreme self-reliance and resourcefulness but also a good deal of luck. Although he might expect to receive some aid from sympathetic persons along the way, the fugitive was most often forced "to pilot his own canoe." In general if he had the good fortune to receive any aid from the Underground Railroad, this usually came after the most difficult part of his journey and most often represented simply a spontaneous individual response to the fugitive's plight. In the vicinity of Wilmington, Del., in southeastern Pennsylvania, and in parts of southern Ohio and Indiana, a number of dedicated persons gave a certain amount of coherence to Underground Railroad activities, but in general, according to one of its most famous conductors, the Underground Railroad "had no visible or real organization."

The most important group harboring escaped slaves and aiding their passage to freedom were the free blacks of the North, who most often acted with little or no support from white abolitionists. The stories of Josiah Henson and of Harriet Tubman—who reportedly made nineteen forays into the South to guide her fellow blacks out of bondage—are well known. Less spectacular, but more important, was the work of Robert Purvis and William Still in Philadelphia and the spontaneous action of unorganized blacks throughout the North, which proved to be the most important form of aid secured by the majority of fugitives. The vigilance committees of northern cities were often biracial, and a number of individual whites contributed in major ways to the activities of the Underground Railroad. Charles T. Torrey aided hundreds of slaves and was called the "father of the underground railroad"; he is credited with originating the idea that such activities should be organized and coordinated throughout the North. Thomas Garrett, a Quaker merchant of Wilmington, was reputed to have helped more than 2,700 slaves and served as the model for the fictional Simeon Halliday in Harriet Beecher Stowe's *Uncle Tom's Cabin* (1852). Another Quaker, Levi Coffin, who lived in Indiana but was a southerner by birth, was commonly referred to as the "president of the underground railroad" because of the open assistance he gave fugitives in southern Indiana and Ohio. These and many other lesser known persons—one historian compiled a list of over 3,200 conductors—violated the law to aid slaves fleeing their captivity.

BIBLIOGRAPHY

Larry Gara, *The Liberty Line: The Legend of the Underground Railroad.*

Wilbur H. Siebert, *The Underground Railroad From Slavery to Freedom.*

— WILLIAM G. SHADE

UNICAMERAL LEGISLATURES

With the exception of New Hampshire and South Carolina, the original colonies were governed by unicameral assemblies prior to the adoption of bicameralism. The early charters, which were derived from England's commercial policies rather than from its political policies, usually made no distinction between executive, legislative, and judicial powers. All of these powers were granted to a governor who was assisted by a council of counselors appointed by the crown, the proprietor, or the proprietary council, on the governor's recommendation. The council, drawn usually from the landed gentry or merchant class, had three distinct functions: it acted as an advisory cabinet for the governor, as a legislative chamber, and as a court of last resort. Deputies were added to the council as representatives of local interests, or freemen. There were clashes between the locally elected deputies on the one hand and the governor and counselors on the other, over issues of taxation, civil rights, and internal policy.

The transition from governor's council to senate and then to separate houses was the result of successive stages of development, including: (1) the introduction of the representative system; (2) the desire of the counselors to sit separately because the peoples' representatives eventually outnumbered them; and (3) the gradual separation of executive and judicial authority from the council, thus making it primarily a legislative body. When state governments were formulated during the revolutionary period, only Pennsylvania and Georgia adopted the unicameral legislative form. Georgia adopted bicameralism in 1789, after twelve years, and Pennsylvania in 1790, after fourteen years. Vermont provided for a unicameral legislature when it became an independent state in 1777—fourteen years before being admitted to the Union—and retained it until 1836 when the desire of the voters to conform with the U.S. Congress and other states prevailed.

A revival of interest in the unicameral form occurred during the period of progressive political thought during the period from 1910 to 1920. Although only Nebraska adopted the one-house legislature in 1934, the proposal received serious consideration in several of the states. Interest in unicameralism was revived yet again after the Supreme Court decision in *Reynolds* v. *Sims* (1964), which ruled that both houses must be apportioned on the basis of population.

— CALVIN B. T. LEE

UNION PACIFIC RAILROAD

Early in the railroad era visionaries like Asa Whitney dreamed of a transcontinental railroad that would span the continent from the Atlantic to the Pacific. Whitney petitioned Congress in 1845 for a charter and a grant of land sixty miles wide from the Great Lakes to the Pacific coast to aid in financing the project, but he only succeeded in obtaining publicity for it. The acquisition of California and Oregon brought the need for a Pacific railroad more sharply to public attention, and from 1850 to the outbreak of the Civil War it shared the spotlight with slavery, public land, and territorial questions. As few people thought that more than one trans-American railroad could ever be built, there was keen rivalry between the Old Northwest and the South, and between cities in each section, for the eastern terminus. This rivalry delayed federal assistance. Finally in 1862, with the South out of the Union, Congress incorporated the Union Pacific Railroad Company for the construction of a railroad by the central route from the western border of Iowa to the California-Nevada line, where it was to meet the Central Pacific Railroad and connect with San Francisco. For each mile of completed railroad Congress offered 6,400 acres of public lands and a loan of $16,000 to $48,000—depending on the terrain—which was to be a first mortgage on the railroad.

Despite the subsidy, the most liberal yet offered to a railroad, investors continued to regard the Union Pacific as a questionable speculation until 1864, when Congress doubled the land grant and made the financial subsidy a second lien on the property. The chances for profit making in the construction of the railroad, if not in its operation after completion, now seemed promising, capital was forthcoming, and construction work was pushed ahead under the forceful direction of Gen. Grenville M. Dodge. The Central Pacific was permitted by an act of 1864 to build 150 miles east of the California-Nevada line; in 1866 it was authorized to advance eastward until it met the westward moving Union Pacific. This led to the historic race between the two railroads that culminated in their dramatic union at Promontory, Utah, on May 10, 1869.

Charter restrictions and the continued difficulty of raising adequate capital induced the promoters of the Union Pacific to assign construction contracts at enormously inflated costs to the Crédit Mobilier—a railroad construction company that was controlled by Thomas C. Durant, Oakes Ames, and other insiders of the Union Pacific. To the Crédit Mobilier was transferred most of the liquid assets of the railroad, which were in turn paid out to the former's stockholders. Members of Congress and other influential people were assigned stock in the construction company, partly, it seems, to win their aid against the frequent attacks that were directed at the Union Pacific. In 1867, during Ulysses S. Grant's administration, the whole sordid story was unearthed by a congressional committee and many political reputations were blackened.

The Union Pacific Railroad was of great importance to the growth and development of such states as Nebraska, Colorado, Wyoming, Nevada, and California.

It brought immigrants to settle the railroad and public lands; it helped to end the migrations of the Plains Indians; it provided market facilities for the cattle, lumber, mining, and farming industries of the Great Plains and Interior Basin; and it brought the West Coast into closer political, economic, and social contact with the East.

Poor and costly construction, high rates, unfortunate financial management, and the other evils characteristic of railroad management in the late 19th century forced the Union Pacific into bankruptcy during the panic of 1893. Subsequently, Edward H. Harriman secured control of the railroad. He added many branch lines, rebuilt the roadbed, improved the rolling stock, and made of the Union Pacific one of America's premier railroads.

[See also Railroads, Sketches of Principal Lines.]

BIBLIOGRAPHY

J. P. Davis, *The Union Pacific Railway.*
J. R. Perkins, *Trails, Rails and War: The Life of Grenville Dodge.*
N. Trottman, *History of the Union Pacific.*

— PAUL W. GATES

UNION PARTY

After the Union defeat at the first Battle of Bull Run, July 21, 1861, many leaders urged that all Union men, regardless of party, stand together for the preservation of the Union. Consequently a Union party ticket, pledged to the prosecution of the war, appeared in most of the important state elections in the fall of 1861. In general the Union ticket represented a coalition of Republicans and Union, or War, Democrats. Separate Democratic tickets were common and in some states the Republicans also nominated candidates.

BIBLIOGRAPHY

J. B. McMaster, *A History of the People of the United States During Lincoln's Administration.*

— GLENN H. BENTON

UNITED MINE WORKERS OF AMERICA

United Mine Workers of America (UMWA), an industrial union representing workers in the bituminous and anthracite coal fields of the United States and Canada, founded in 1890. Despite the violent opposition of the mine operators it grew rapidly under the leadership of John Mitchell before World War I and had a membership of over 500,000 by 1920, when John L. Lewis became president of the union. One of the ablest leaders in American labor history, Lewis was nevertheless unable to overcome the industry depression and anti-unionism of the 1920's, and by 1930 he headed an organization of less than 100,000 working members. He capitalized on the legislation and spirit of the New Deal and rebuilt the UMWA into one of the most effective but imperially governed unions in the country. During World War II he led a number of unpopular strikes, but these and the postwar welfare fund strike brought labor-management contracts that made the American miner one of the best-paid and best-insured workers in the world. Lewis then took the lead in industry mechanization, which reduced the UMWA's membership by more than two-thirds but improved wages and the competitive position of the industry. He retired in 1960. The tenure of President W. A. Boyle was marked by incompetent autocracy, financial scandal, and the murder in 1969 of Boyle's opponent, Joseph A. Yablonski. In 1972 a reform slate led by Arnold Miller won an election supervised by federal authorities, and instituted a series of reforms to democratize the union and improve job security and safety in the mines.

BIBLIOGRAPHY

McAlister Coleman, *Men and Coal.*

— JOHN HUTCHINSON

UNITED NATIONS

The United States played a key role in the founding of the United Nations (UN) and maintained a strong if sometimes troubled relationship with the organization throughout the United Nations' first fifty years. The United Nations had its beginnings in a meeting between British Prime Minister Winston Churchill and President Franklin D. Roosevelt on Aug. 14, 1941, four months before U.S. entry into World War II. This meeting produced the Atlantic Charter, pledging "the final destruction of the Nazi tyranny" and proposed a postwar "establishment of a wider and permanent system of general security." In February 1945 Roosevelt met with Churchill and the Soviet leader Joseph Stalin at Yalta in the Soviet Crimea. There, even before the war's end, it was agreed to proceed with a United Nations Conference and draw up a UN Charter. Roosevelt believed that through the United Nations he could build a peaceful world and predicted that "the Crimean Conference . . . spells the end of the system of unilateral and exclusive alliances and spheres of influence and balances of power." He soon had misgivings about Stalin, however. On the day Roosevelt died, April 12, 1945, he asserted "that the spirit of Yalta was being betrayed by the Soviets." Thirteen days after Roosevelt's death the United Nations Conference convened in San Francisco. Two months later, on June 25, the delegates unanimously approved the UN Charter, and on July 28 the U.S. Senate ratified it by a vote of eighty-nine to two. The United Nations came into being on Oct. 24, 1945, with the approval of the required majority of the fifty-one participating nations.

An early concern was finding a permanent home for the new organization. The initial site of meetings was London, where the first General Assembly convened in January 1946. Several other European cities sought to have the UN headquarters, including Paris, Geneva, and The Hague. On Mar. 21, 1946, the Security Council moved into temporary quarters in the United States, the gymnasium on the Bronx Campus of Hunter College in New York City, while the search for a permanent home continued. When classroom space was needed by Hunter, the Security Council moved to the Sperry Gyroscope plant at Lake Success on Long Island and the General Assembly convened on the site of the 1939 New York City's World's Fair in Flushing Meadow, Queens. Then Robert Moses, New York's dynamic builder of bridges, tunnels, parks, and roads, suggested a permanent home in the Turtle Bay area of midtown Manhattan, six blocks of slaughterhouses and slums along the East River. The real estate entrepreneur William Zeckendorf put the parcels together, and on Dec. 11, 1946, John D. Rockefeller, Jr., offered to give $8.5 million to buy the site. The General Assembly accepted the offer by a vote of forty-six to seven. The UN complex, comprising a thirty-nine-story Secretariat building, a General Assembly hall, and a conference building for the Security Council on eighteen acres of land, was designed mainly by Wallace K. Harrison, one of the architects for Rockefeller Center. With the work completed in less than six years, the United Nations settled into its own complex in 1952, but a number of the specialized agencies occupied the old League of Nations sites in Geneva, with others in Vienna.

From the beginning, the UN atmosphere was quarrelsome because of the burgeoning cold war between the United States and the Soviet Union, both permanent members of the UN Security Council, which deliberates questions of peace and war. In 1946, only days after the election of the first UN Secretary-General, Trygve Lie of Norway, Stalin announced a new Five Year Plan for Soviet economic development that emphasized armaments rather than consumer goods. Stalin declared that the Soviet Union had to defend itself against "all kinds of eventualities" because "no peaceful international order is possible." Supreme Court Justice William O. Douglas described the speech as "the declaration of World War III." On Mar. 5, 1946, Winston Churchill, in company with President Harry S. Truman, delivered the address in which he described the Soviet takeover of Eastern Europe as an "iron curtain" that had descended across the Continent. Stalin declared the address "a call to war with the Soviet Union."

From its inception, the U.N. atmosphere was quarrelsome because of the burgeoning cold war between two prominent—and permanent—members of the Security Council.

In those early years the pattern was set for the next four decades. The General Assembly, to which all member nations belonged, had no authority other than to recommend. The authority of the Security Council, which held the powers of peace or war or other punitive measures, was consistently blocked by the Soviet Union, which had veto power by virtue of its being a permanent member of the Security Council. After the United States joined with eleven other nations to form the North Atlantic Treaty Organization (NATO) to deter communist aggression, in April 1949, NATO nations had to resort to Article 51 of the UN Charter, which sets forth "the inherent right of individual or collective self-defense," when they decided to intervene militarily.

The first real test of the United Nations came with the Korean conflict in 1950. In an emergency meeting, the Security Council granted President Truman the authority to conduct a "police action" to counter North Korea's attack on South Korea. This approval was possible only because of the absence of the Soviet Union, which at the time was boycotting the Security Council in an attempt to force it to seat the communist People's Republic of China. On July 7, 1950, the Security Council set up a unified UN command with soldiers from fifteen nations under General Douglas MacArthur. Through the persuasion of the U.S. ambassador to India, Chester Bowles, India introduced in the UN General Assembly a cease-fire resolution on Dec. 3, 1952, that was adopted by fifty-four nations. President-elect Dwight D. Eisenhower, en route to the United States from Korea, a few days later sent an open message heard around the world asking General MacArthur to meet him in New York City at the president's residence at Columbia University to plan a strategy to end the war. This psychological warfare strategy worked. Talks began between the UN Command and the North Koreans at Panmunjom at the thirty-eighth parallel on Apr. 27, 1953. So began the process that finally brought the armistice on July 27, 1953. Ironically, Secretary-General Lie was a victim of the armistice process when the Soviets charged that during the negotiations he had sided with the United States. The effectively ostracized Lie resigned in April 1953 and was succeeded by Dag Hammarskjöld, a member of the Swedish cabinet. Lie warned his successor that "the task of Secretary-General is the most impossible job on earth."

The Middle East was a concern of the United Nations from its inception. On Nov. 20, 1947, the UN General Assembly adopted a resolution that ended the British mandate in Palestine and, against Arab wishes, partitioned the country into an Arab state and a Jewish state. Jerusalem, in which the holy places of the three great religions were located, was to be under international administration. Immediately the Arab delegation marched out of the assembly and announced they would not be bound by this decision. Not dissuaded, the Provisional State Council in Tel Aviv proclaimed the birth of Israel at midnight, May 14, 1948. Within eleven minutes President Truman had announced recognition of Israel. The president's action cut off a UN move for a temporary trusteeship. Full-scale war, which immediately erupted between Israel and its Arab neighbors, was ended in January 1949 by a cease-fire negotiated by Dr. Ralph Bunche, a member of the UN Secretariat. Bunche returned to New York an international hero and became the first African American to be awarded the Nobel Peace Prize. In May 1949 Israel was admitted to the United Nations.

The United Nations emerged as a strong moral force during the Suez crisis of 1956, with the establishment of the use of UN peacekeepers. On July 26, 1956, Egypt seized the Suez Canal, which had been built by the French and was of great commercial importance to both France and Great Britain. Over the objections of the UN Security Council, those two countries, joined by Israel, launched an armed attack against Egypt. With the support of both the United States and the Soviet Union, the United Nations intervened by sending in a UN Emergency Force numbering 6,000 men, known as Blue Helmets, to supervise a cease-fire and the withdrawal of troops. In retrospect, this must be viewed as one of the most significant UN military interventions in its first half century.

The growth of Third World countries and their entry into the United Nations in large numbers after 1960 made it increasingly difficult for the United States to control votes in the General Assembly. (From 51 nations in 1945, UN membership grew to 185 by 1995.) These primarily poor nations paid an extremely small part of total UN operating costs, which bothered some Americans, even though the United States was often in arrears in its own dues payments. As the former British, French, Portuguese, German, Belgian, Dutch, and Italian colonies in Africa and elsewhere emerged as nations, many were taken over by regimes backed by the Soviets, thus increasing resistance in the UN General Assembly toward the U.S.-led Western alliance.

In 1961, Secretary-General Hammarskjöld personally led UN Swedish troops into the seceding Katanga portion of the Congo, with the full support of President John F. Kennedy, in an effort to stop the fighting. Hammarskjöld was killed in a plane crash during the operation and was posthumously awarded the Nobel Peace Prize for 1961. Despite the presence of 20,000 Blue Helmets, it took until 1964 to achieve a cease-fire. The United Nations did not intervene with a major military force again until the 1992 operation in Somalia.

During the 1960s the United Nations, led by Hammarskjöld's successor, U Thant of Burma, was ineffectual in dealing with the escalating conflict in Vietnam. U Thant did, however, succeed in sending the Blue Helmets to Cyprus to keep Greeks and Turks from conflict on that newly independent island. Another notable accomplishment was the General Assembly's 1968 approval of the Treaty on Nonproliferation of Nuclear Weapons.

The United Nations continued to play a role in events in the Middle East. Blue Helmets had occupied outposts between Egypt and Israel since the 1956 Suez emergency. In 1967, however, Egypt demanded their withdrawal. To the consternation of Great Britain and the United States, U Thant complied. A few weeks later the Six-Day War broke out between Israel and Arab forces (Egypt, Jordan, and Syria), and continued sporadic fighting led eventually to the Yom Kippur (or October) War of 1973. Cease-fire agreements in 1974 established a UN peacekeeping force and buffer zone between the two armies.

In December 1971, Kurt Waldheim of Austria succeeded U Thant as the fourth secretary-general of the United Nations; in 1982 Waldheim was forced to resign in the face of allegations that he had been a member of the Nazi party during the Third Reich. He was succeeded by Javier Pérez de Cuéllar of Peru, who presided over the General Assembly's 1987 adoption of a resolution with terms for ending the Iran-Iraq War, which had raged since 1980. In 1988 the Nobel Peace Prize was awarded to UN peacekeeping forces. By the end of 1991, the last day for Pérez de Cuéllar as secretary-general, peace was also coming to civil war-ravaged El Salvador, in part due to both U.S. and UN efforts.

When Iraq invaded Kuwait on Aug. 2, 1990, President George Bush, a former U.S. ambassador to the United Nations, immediately asked for UN action. For the first time Arab nations did not vote as a block and, with Russian and American support, the United

Nations authorized "all necessary means," which meant force to repel the invasion of Kuwait. UN forces led by the United States swiftly defeated the Iraqi army, and the now greatly enhanced Security Council appeared to have become what Roosevelt had envisioned—the heart of the United Nations. The Gulf War of 1991 was the third time the United Nations was an important instrument of the president of the United States during an international security crisis, just as it had been for Truman in 1950 and Eisenhower in 1956.

Boutros Boutros-Ghali, a former Egyptian diplomat and law professor, became the sixth secretary-general in 1991. Peacekeeping clearly had become the chief business of the United Nations in the post-cold war era. In its first four decades the Security Council had authorized only thirteen peacekeeping missions. In its fifth decade, 1985–1995, twenty were authorized. In 1995 alone the United Nations operated seventeen peacekeeping missions with 73,000 troops and police. During this era there were successful missions in Cambodia, Mozambique, and Haiti. A mission in December 1992 to end famine in Somalia was flawed, however, because it failed to impose political order despite the presence of 38,000 Blue Helmets, 25,000 of them from the United States. From March 1992 to October 1995, 20,000 UN peacekeepers also failed to stop the slaughter, known as ethnic cleansing, in the former Yugoslavia, the "safe areas" never being made safe. While the United States provided minimal air cover, it did not contribute ground soldiers to this effort.

The UN failure in Bosnia, combined with the desire of NATO to play a post-cold war role, set the stage for U.S. Secretary of State for European Affairs Richard Holbrooke to broker an agreement in Dayton, Ohio, among the Serbs, Croats, and the Bosnian government in October 1995. Signed in Paris in December 1995, the accord withdrew the UN from Bosnia and replaced them with a NATO-directed force of 60,000, including 20,000 Americans. (Russian personnel outside of NATO were also included.) In 1993 the United Nations established in The Hague an eleven-member war crimes tribunal; under the Dayton agreement the parties were to send indicted war criminals to The Hague for trial. The replacement of UN forces did not spell the end of peacekeeping as a basic mission of the United Nations but rather a failure in this instance without the dominant force of the United States.

From the beginning, UN policies were affected by the atrocities committed during World War II. It almost immediately appointed a human rights commission, which, under the leadership of Eleanor Roosevelt, issued the 1948 United Nations Universal Declaration of Human Rights. Since then the United Nations has endorsed other human rights treaties or covenants that the U.S. Senate has yet to ratify: the Convention on the Elimination of All Forms of Discrimination Against Women; the American Convention on Human Rights; the International Covenant on Economic, Social, and Cultural Rights; and the International Convention on the Elimination of All Forms of Racial Discrimination. The United Nations also sponsored four international conferences on women between the 1970s and 1995.

From the beginning, U.N. policies were affected by the atrocities committed during World War II.

Although the primary mission of the United Nations was to eliminate "the scourge of war," the preamble of its charter also states its purpose "to promote social progress and better standards of life in larger freedom" and "to employ international machinery for the promotion of the economic and social advancement of all people." On these grounds the UN specialized agencies were created. The International Labor Organization (ILO) of 1919 was revived. Added were the Food and Agriculture Organization (FAO), World Health Organization (WHO), and United Nations Educational, Scientific, and Cultural Organization (UNESCO). In all, by the 1990s there were nineteen specialized agencies with combined budgets far exceeding the operation of the United Nations itself (save for peacekeeping missions) and with more employees than the UN Secretariat. Clearly it had become a bureaucracy requiring reform. In the case of UNESCO, the United States withdrew from the organization in 1984 after a scathing critique of it by U.S. Ambassador Jeane Kirkpatrick. Still, there were some remarkable accomplishments among the specialized agencies. In 1980, for example, WHO announced global eradication of smallpox, and global eradication of polio was expected by the year 2000.

As leaders from 140 countries gathered in New York City in October 1995 to celebrate the fiftieth anniversary of the United Nations, there was a clear need for change and reform. The possible addition of states as permanent members of the Security Council remained a subject of dispute, as was the bloated UN bureaucracy. Yet for all its troubles, the world organization domiciled in New York proved its worth in its first fifty years; surely the world would have been a much more ugly, less satisfying place without it.

[See also Bosnia-Herzegovina; Gulf War of 1991; Middle East, Relations with; North Atlantic Treaty Organization; State, Department of.]

BIBLIOGRAPHY

Sidney D. Bailey, *The United Nations: A Concise Political Guide*, 3rd. ed. (Lanham, Md., 1995).
William Jacobs, *Search for Peace: The Story of the United Nations* (New York, 1994).
David Evan Trant Luard, *The United Nations: How It Works and What It Does* (New York, 1994).
Stanley Meisler, *United Nations: The First 50 Years* (New York, 1995).

— R. GORDON HOXIE

UNITED STATES OF AMERICA

United States of America was first used officially as a name for the thirteen colonies in the Declaration of Independence, where, however, it merely took the place of "United Colonies," hitherto employed in varying forms. The "United Colonies of New England" was the name of the New England Confederation, and it was therefore natural that "United Colonies" should be used to designate the new union. The earliest official use of the designation in the revolutionary period appears to have been in a communication of the Massachusetts Convention, May 16, 1775, in the *Journals of the Continental Congress* of June 2. The term was used by Congress itself in a resolution of June 7, 1775, again in a resolution of June 10, then definitely in George Washington's commission, June 17, and in his instructions, June 20. Thereupon, both officially and unofficially, "United Colonies," in variant forms, came into general use.

Among the earlier forms used were "all the English colonies on this continent" (the fast-day proclamation of June 12), "all the colonies from Nova Scotia to Georgia" (pledge of support to Washington, June 17), and "associated colonies" (committee report, June 19). In official documents thereafter, the name was usually the "United Colonies of America," or "of North America" (more often the latter), and frequently with "twelve" or "thirteen," as the case might be, prefixed, sometimes also preceded by the word "English." For instance, the imprint of the rules for the troops, June 30, 1775, names the governing authority as "the Twelve united English Colonies of North-America."

As the idea of independence grew and the term "colony" came to connote a status of dependence, writers more and more employed the term "states" to designate the American political entities. The term was accordingly used in the Virginia Resolutions of May 15, 1776, from which came the resolution proposed in Congress June 7, "That these United Colonies are, and of right ought to be, free and independent States." It was a matter of course that in the Declaration of Independence the name and variations of "United Colonies" should give way to "United States of America." From the Declaration of Independence the name was taken over into the Articles of Confederation (1777) and then into the Constitution (1787).

For a brief period the name the "United States of North America" was used. The prevailing inclination to use "North America" had found official expression in the Declaration on Taking Arms (July 6, 1775), and again (probably through Benjamin Franklin's preference for that form, as witness his proposed articles of confederation, July 21, 1775) in the treaty with France (Feb. 6, 1778), in which the name is set down as "the thirteen United States of North America." On May 19, 1778, Congress adopted "the Stile of the Treaties of Paris" (letters of the president of the Continental Congress, Henry Laurens, May 19, 20, 23); but on July 11 that action was rescinded, and the word "North" dropped from the name.

BIBLIOGRAPHY

Edmund C. Burnett, "The Name 'United States of America,'" *American Historical Review*, vol. 31.
John C. Fitzpatrick, "*The 'United States of America' and the 'U.S.A.,'*" *Daughters of the American Revolution Magazine*, vol. 54.

— EDMUND C. BURNETT

UNITED STATES V. *E. C. KNIGHT COMPANY*

United States v. *E. C. Knight Company*, 156 U.S. 1 (1895), was the first Supreme Court case involving the Sherman Antitrust Act (1890), which forbade combinations restraining interstate commerce. The American Sugar Refining Company purchased four independent concerns, giving it control of 98 percent of the country's output. The Court held that the acquisition of refineries and the business of sugar manufacturing within a state bore no direct relation to interstate commerce, and hence were not in violation of the act. The decision stimulated the formation of trusts.

BIBLIOGRAPHY

E. Jones, *The Trust Problem in the United States.*
A. H. Walker, *History of the Sherman Law.*

— RANSOM E. NOBLE, JR.

URBAN LIVING

Between 1970 and 1990 the urban population of the United States grew from 150 million to 187 million, or from 73.6 percent to 75.2 percent of the total. Major cities (more than 2.5 million people) slipped from 6.92 percent to 5.46 percent. Major metropolitan areas lost or gained slightly in population during the same years. Greater New York dropped 0.4 percent annually, while Chicago posted only a 0.4 percent annual gain; by contrast Los Angeles grew by 2.1 percent per year. The biggest increases occurred in such Sunbelt cities as Tampa-Saint Petersburg, Orlando, Miami, and Houston. Many urban dwellers left for the suburbs. Among the forty-four metropolitan areas in 1990 with more than I million residents, the suburbs of forty-two gained population; the central cities of eighteen lost, weakening the power of cities in state legislatures and Congress.

Cities have experienced revivals as highly educated, upwardly mobile young people, many attracted by inexpensive housing, flooded into their core areas.

Urban problems spiraled in the 1980s. Population losses translated into job flight to the suburbs, which captured more than 95 percent of new metropolitan manufacturing jobs from 1976 to 1980. One study of urban decline demonstrated that between 1960 and 1989, eighteen of the seventy-seven largest American cities lost employed residents. Pittsburgh, Newark, Saint Louis, Louisville, Buffalo, Cleveland, and Detroit lost more than one-fourth of employed residents. Lower-income people became increasingly concentrated in central cities. Because poverty begets social problems, the 1980s saw sharp increases in urban crime, drug use, unemployment, and births out of wedlock. Social plagues included severe illnesses such as AIDS. All these problems translated into higher costs for police and fire protection, judicial systems, jails, and public hospitals. Expenses translated into higher property and other taxes.

Cities remained centers for intellectual activities, cultural endeavors, and specialized retail facilities, including high-fashion stores, symphonies, medical centers, and institutions of higher learning. Cities still are the nodes for technology, transportation, and housing for low-income workers and newly arriving immigrants. Cities have experienced revivals as highly educated, upwardly mobile young people flooded into their core areas. Attracted by inexpensive housing and services, many such returned urbanites gentrified decaying neighborhoods with refurbished housing, restaurants, and stores. The economic uniformity of these "yuppies," as they were sometimes disparagingly called, also undercut the pluralism of cities. At worst, they forced long-term residents, especially the aged, from their homes and indirectly caused an increase in homelessness. Homosexuals have also concentrated in formerly decaying downtown areas; in addition to well-known gay neighborhoods like Greenwich Village in New York City and the Castro District in San Francisco, communities have arisen in Los Angeles, Houston, Seattle, Denver, Cincinnati, and Saint Louis.

[See also Crime; Demographic Changes; Housing; Poverty.]

BIBLIOGRAPHY

Anthony Downs, *New Visions for Metropolitan America* (Cambridge, Mass., 1994).

— GRAHAM RUSSELL HODGES

V

VAUDEVILLE

Vaudeville, live variety shows, extremely popular in the United States in the second half of the 19th and early 20th century. Singing, dancing, and acrobatic acts were seen in small concert halls and "museums" in the early 19th century. They grew in popularity and became known as "variety," and by 1860 there were theaters devoted to such programs in all the larger cities. Many noted legitimate actors first appeared in variety. It was late in the 19th century that the French word *vaudeville* came into use to describe these programs. B. F. Keith, who began managing a music hall in Boston in 1883, acquired a number of vaudeville theaters. Combining with a rival, F. F. Proctor, in 1906, he became the leading figure of the vaudeville world. Marcus Loew, Alexander Pantages, and the firm Sullivan and Considine and Orpheum were also operating large vaudeville circuits at that time. But between 1910 and 1930 motion pictures so supplanted stage shows in popular patronage that after 1930 vaudeville acts were rarely seen except as parts of the program at the larger motion picture theaters.

BIBLIOGRAPHY

M. B. Leavitt, *Fifty Years in Theatrical Management.*

— ALVIN F. HARLOW

VERACRUZ INCIDENT

When Victoriano Huerta seized the Mexican presidency in 1913, the United States refused to recognize him. Early in 1914, when Tampico was under martial law, some U.S. marines were arrested there, but they were quickly released and apologies made. Adm. Henry T. Mayo insisted that a salute of twenty-one guns to the American flag be fired, and he was supported in this demand by President Woodrow Wilson. When the salute was not forthcoming, Wilson ordered a fleet to Veracruz. Troops were landed on Apr. 21 and, aided by bombardment, they took the city with an American loss of seventeen killed and sixty-three wounded. Continued American political pressure forced Huerta out in July, and he fled to Jamaica.

U.S. sailors man an artillery piece in the streets of Vera Cruz, Mexico, in 1914. The city was taken and Victoriano Huerta was eventually forced out of the Mexican presidency. (Corbis-Bettmann)

BIBLIOGRAPHY

Robert E. Quirk, *An Affair of Honor: Woodrow Wilson and the Occupation of Veracruz.*

— ALVIN F. HARLOW

VERSAILLES, TREATY OF

Versailles, Treaty of, the comprehensive peace treaty between the Allies and Germany at the end of World War I. The treaty was signed on June 28, 1919, by the United States, Great Britain, France, Italy, Japan, and twenty-three other Allied and Associated Powers, and Germany. The treaty consisted of fifteen parts comprising 440 articles. Part I was the covenant of the League of Nations. Part II defined the boundaries of Germany in Europe: it lost the Alsace-Lorraine region to France, West Prussia and the province of Poznań to Poland, and three small areas to Belgium; it surrendered the Saar basin and the city of Danzig to the League of Nations and the city of Memel to the Allied Powers; and it agreed to plebiscites in North Schleswig, Allenstein and Marienwerder, and Upper Silesia.

In Part III Germany consented to the abrogation of the neutrality of Belgium and Luxembourg and to the exclusion of the latter from the German Customs Union. Germany acknowledged and promised to respect the independence of Austria; accepted the demilitarization of the Rhineland and of a zone extending 50 kilometers east of the Rhine; and ceded to France the coal mines of the Saar as compensation for the destruction of French mines during the war. Part IV deprived Germany of its overseas possessions, which were made mandated territories under the League of Nations, and of various rights and interests in China, Siam (now Thailand), Liberia, Morocco, Egypt, Turkey, and Bulgaria.

Part V provided for the disarmament of Germany, "in order to render possible the initiation of a general limitation of the armaments of all nations." Germany's army was limited to 100,000 men, recruited by long-term enlistment; the general staff was abolished; and all air forces were forbidden. The manufacture of munitions was limited and their import forbidden, and the maintenance of stocks of poisonous gases was also forbidden. The German navy was restricted to a small number of old ships. Inter-Allied commissions were established to supervise the execution of these clauses.

Part VI dealt with prisoners of war and graves. In Part VII, Wilhelm II, the former kaiser, was indicted for "a supreme offense against international morality and the sanctity of treaties," and he was to be tried by the five principal Allied Powers. (The trial never took place because the Netherlands, to which he fled after the war, refused to extradite him.) Germany also promised to deliver any of its nationals who might be accused by the Allies of having violated the laws and customs of war.

Part VIII dealt with reparation, beginning with the famous Article 231: "The Allied and Associated Governments affirm and Germany accepts the responsibility of Germany and her allies for causing all the loss and damage to which the Allied and Associated Governments and their nationals have been subjected as a consequence of the war imposed on them by the aggression of Germany and her allies." The purpose of this article was not to assess a moral judgment but to establish the legal liability of Germany for reparation, to which it had agreed in the armistice of Nov. 11, 1918. Under the terms of the armistice, Germany undertook to make compensation for "all damage done to the civilian population" of the Allies "by land, by sea and from the air." In the treaty, "damage" was defined broadly enough to include military pensions and separation allowances; Germany had furthermore to reimburse Belgium, with interest, for all sums that country borrowed from the Allies. A reparation commission was to determine, by May 1, 1921, the amount Germany should pay; in the meantime, Germany was to pay $5 billion in gold, commodities, ships, securities, or otherwise. Elaborate clauses provided in great detail for the delivery of goods in kind. The Allied Powers reserved the right to take whatever measures they deemed necessary in the event of "voluntary default" by Germany.

Part IX contained financial clauses. Part X dealt with tariffs, business contracts, and the like; in particular the Allies obtained the right to seize German private property in their territories to satisfy reparation debts. Many of these financial and economic clauses were of a temporary character. Part XI gave the Allies the right of unimpeded aerial navigation over Germany. In Part XII, which dealt with ports, waterways, and railways, international control of the Rhine, Oder, and Elbe rivers was established, in the interest of landlocked states. The Kiel Canal was opened to all nations. Part XIII established the International Labor Office as an autonomous branch of the League of Nations.

The Treaty of Versailles was regarded in Germany as a Diktat, *or dictated peace, and a violation of the Fourteen Points on whose basis Germany had surrendered.*

Part XIV provided for guarantees. The Allies were to occupy the Rhineland and its bridgeheads for fifteen years, although certain zones were to be evacuated at the end of five years and others at the end of ten. Article 430 empowered the Allies to reoccupy the region at any time if Germany defaulted on reparation payments.

Germany was to pay the cost of the armies of occupation. Part XV dealt with miscellaneous items.

By the Treaty of Versailles, Germany did not become a member of the League of Nations or the International Labor Office, although in time it could be eligible for membership in both. Germany lost more than 25,000 square miles of territory and some 6 million inhabitants in Europe, as well as many valuable resources abroad. The treaty was regarded in Germany as a *Diktat,* or dictated peace (no Allied-German negotiations preceded the presentation to Germany), and a violation of the Fourteen Points, on the basis of which Germany had surrendered and the Allies had promised to make peace. The harshness of the treaty, which both injured German pride and impeded Germany's economic recovery, is considered by many historians to have helped cause Adolf Hitler's rise to power and World War II.

In most Allied countries, the treaty was considered as just punishment to Germany for the war that Germany was deemed to have brought on the world in August 1914. In the United States, the treaty was received with mixed feelings. As bitterness against Germany decreased in some of the Allied countries in the 1920's, some provisions of the treaty were not fully enforced. Parts II, III, V, and XII were violated by Hitler in the 1930's.

The treaty was promptly ratified by Germany but more slowly by the Allied Powers. It came into force on Jan. 10, 1920, without having been ratified by the United States, and it was rejected by the U.S. Senate on Mar. 19, 1920. The war between the United States and Germany was formally ended in 1921 by the Treaty of Berlin.

BIBLIOGRAPHY

Frank S. Marston, *Peace Conference of 1919.*
Arno J. Mayer, *Politics of Peacemaking: Versailles, 1918–1919.*
H. W. V. Temperley and others, *History of the Peace Conference at Paris.*

— BERNADOTTE E. SCHMITT

VESEY REBELLION

Vesey Rebellion, a plot by South Carolina blacks in 1821–22 to annihilate completely the white population of Charleston. The leader of the conspiracy was Denmark (the name being a corruption of Telemaque) Vesey, who had been brought to Charleston in 1783. In 1800 he won $1,500 in the East Bay Street lottery in Charleston and with $600 purchased his freedom. The fact that his children, born of a slave mother, were the property of her master aroused his resentment. Sometime around Christmas 1821 the rebellion plot took concrete form. The participants, said by some accounts to include 2,000–3,000 slaves, planned to seize the arms and ammunition stored in the city and massacre the white population. The date for the attack was originally July 14, 1822, but was subsequently advanced to June 16. The plot was betrayed to the authorities, and Vesey and other principal conspirators were arrested, tried, and executed.

BIBLIOGRAPHY

A. H. Grimke, *Right on the Scaffold or Martyrs of 1822.*

— A. C. FLICK

VETERANS AFFAIRS, DEPARTMENT OF

In 1987 President Ronald Reagan threw his support behind a movement to raise the Veterans Administration, an independent government agency since its creation in 1930, to a cabinet-level department, and in 1988 he signed a bill creating the Department of Veterans Affairs (VA). In 1989 the secretary of veterans affairs became the fourteenth member of the president's cabinet. The VA is the second-largest cabinet-level department of the government; only the Department of Defense is larger. The VA is responsible for administering a wide variety of benefits for military veterans and their dependents. Within it are the Veterans Health Services and Research Administration, the Veterans Benefits Administration, and the National Cemetery System. Their heads and the general counsel for the VA are appointed by the president and confirmed by the Senate. Health benefits administered by the VA include hospitals, nursing homes, and outpatient medical and dental care. More than half the practicing physicians in the United States received part of their training within the health care system administered by the VA. There is a Prosthetics Assessment and Information Center, and programs include vocational as well as physical rehabilitation. The VA oversees military pensions, compensation for disabilities and death, and insurance and loans for veterans. The GI Bill of 1944 provided housing and educational benefits for World War II veterans, and benefits have been continued for veterans of the Korean and Vietnam Wars, all administered by the VA.

BIBLIOGRAPHY

Donald R. Whitnah, ed., *Government Agencies* (Westport, Conn., 1983).

— RICHARD W. MOODEY

VETO POWER OF THE PRESIDENT

The veto power of the president is one of his two constitutionally authorized instruments of legislative leadership, the complementary tool being the authority to send messages to Congress proposing legislation. The Constitution specifically provides for presidential participation in the legislative process. Within ten weekdays of the submission of a measure to him, the president may either (1) sign it into law; (2) disapprove it, returning it to the house of origin with his signature; or (3) do nothing, in which case the bill becomes law without his signature. If Congress adjourns within the ten weekdays, however, presidential failure to act kills the bill. This is referred to as a pocket veto. In the event that the president exercises his veto, Congress may pass the bill over the veto by a two-thirds vote in each house. All bills and joint resolutions are submitted to the president for approval or disapproval, with the exception of joint resolutions proposing constitutional amendments.

The framers of the Constitution apparently conceived of the presidential veto as one of the checks and balances designed to prevent legislative encroachments on the executive branch. It was employed sparingly by the first seven presidents. Andrew Jackson changed the nature of the veto power by using it to impose his policy views on Congress. His veto messages included social and economic policy considerations in addition to constitutional principles. Since that time presidents have used the veto as a means of shaping legislation. The threat of a veto can be a positive lever against congressional opposition to presidential objectives.

Until 1865 nine presidents had vetoed only thirty-six bills, with Jackson accounting for twelve. The veto has subsequently been used by all presidents except James A. Garfield, who had no opportunity to exercise it prior to his death. The most frequent users of the veto were Franklin D. Roosevelt (633), Grover Cleveland (413), Harry S. Truman (250), and Dwight D. Eisenhower (181). Usage under later presidents dropped sharply, with John F. Kennedy accounting for twenty-one vetoes, Lyndon B. Johnson thirty, Richard M. Nixon, forty-three, and Gerald R. Ford forty-four, through December 1975. The success of the veto is manifest in the low proportion (75 of 2,260) Congress managed to override between 1789 and 1972. Most of the overridden vetoes have been measures of considerable importance, such as the Taft-Hartley Labor Relations Act of 1947.

Some presidents, most notably Jackson, Franklin D. Roosevelt, Truman, and Eisenhower, have imparted an added dimension to the veto power by attaching qualifications to their approval of certain measures in the form of reservations and advance interpretations of specific provisions. Although such statements of qualified presidential approval of legislation are of doubtful validity and have never been tested in the courts, they have political value and significance.

After World War II, the presidential practice of impounding (that is, refusing to spend) appropriated funds has had the effect of giving the president a form of item veto over appropriations. Truman, Lyndon B. Johnson, and Nixon have withheld funds in response to statutory directive or on grounds of managerial prudence and efficiency. Because this practice is based on statutory rather than constitutional authority and involves an act of presidential discretion, it is highly controversial. There is no question that when it is employed, it expands the legislative powers of the president.

BIBLIOGRAPHY

Thomas E. Cronin, *The State of the Presidency.*

Louis Fisher, *President and Congress.*

Joseph E. Kallenbach, *The American Chief Executive: The Presidency and the Governorship.*

Charles F. Zinn, *The Veto Power of the President.*

— NORMAN C. THOMAS

VICE PRESIDENCY

The office of vice-president was established by the Constitution to provide a successor if the president should die, resign, or otherwise be unable to perform the duties of his office. In addition the vice-president was to be the presiding officer of the U.S. Senate, voting in case of a tie. Other functions performed by recent vice-presidents include ceremonial duties (often as a stand-in for the president), such as dedicating buildings and visiting foreign countries. Executive assignments, such as membership on various councils and commissions, have increased. Besides presiding over the Senate, some occupants of the office have attempted to exert behind-the-scenes influence in support of the president's legislative programs. Some recent vice-presidents also assumed various party and partisan activities, including campaigning for candidates and raising funds.

The office has a mixed historical record. In the early history of the republic it was held by such distinguished public figures as John Adams and Thomas Jefferson. In the 19th century it faded rather rapidly into obscurity, and the prominence of those selected for the office declined. In 1868 Gideon Welles, then secretary of the navy, suggested it was an office "without responsibility, patronage or any duty worthy of honorable aspiration." There was an occasional flurry of interest in the office, particularly when a president died, but it was usually short-lived. By 1975 eight vice-presidents had succeeded to the office on the death of the president, four of them in the 20th century; and one, Gerald R. Ford, had been appointed vice-president when the incumbent resigned and succeeded to the presidency when the president resigned.

The office has taken on a new look and importance since the 1950's, and presidents have made conscious effort to give additional duties to the vice-president. For example, during the presidency of Dwight D. Eisenhower, Richard M. Nixon was one of the most publicized vice-presidents in American history. He performed numerous political and ceremonial tasks, as well as assuming additional executive responsibilities. His successors, Lyndon B. Johnson, Hubert H. Humphrey, Spiro T. Agnew, and Ford, performed rather similar functions. Indeed, by the mid-1970's the office appeared to be achieving a status whereby the incumbent is one of the likely presidential nominees when the president does not run. Despite this increased status, the vice-president is in somewhat of a constitutional limbo between the executive and the legislature and depends a great deal on the good will and confidence of the president for his powers and functions.

Vice-presidential candidates are selected at the national party conventions. By custom, such a decision is made by the presidential candidate rather than by open convention decision. The main criterion in such a choice appears to be to choose someone who can bring support to the ticket from important electoral groups, whether sectional, economic, or religious. A vice-presidential candidate runs in tandem with the presidential candidate, so, at least since the ratification of the Twelfth Amendment (1804), both winners will be of the same political party.

Until the adoption of the Twenty-fifth Amendment (1967), there was no provision for filling the office of vice-president if a vacancy occurred. The most common cause of a vacancy was the succession of the vice-president to the presidency. The Twenty-fifth Amendment provides that if the office of vice-president becomes vacant, the president may nominate a successor, subject to confirmation by both houses of Congress by majority vote. Both Gerald R. Ford and Nelson A. Rockefeller assumed the office of vice-president by this method.

BIBLIOGRAPHY

Paul T. David, "The Vice-Presidency," *Journal of Politics* (1967).

Dale Vinyard, *The Presidency.*

Irving G. Williams, *The Rise of the Vice-Presidency.*

— DALE VINYARD

VICE PRESIDENCY AT THE END OF THE TWENTIETH CENTURY

The office of the vice president of the United States continued carrying a mixed legacy as the United States approached the end of the twentieth century. While the conception of its duties and its process of selection were flawed, the vice presidency has more or less performed the function the framers of the U.S. Constitution intended and has not—as some critics feared—led the nation into deep trouble. Choosing the vice-presidential candidate, and thus a vice president, remains above all an instrument for assisting in election of the president. The presidential candidate made the selection in every race between 1976 and 1992, as a rule picking someone with an appeal different from his. While traditional geographic and ideological "ticket balancing" remained alive–as in Jimmy Carter's selection of Walter Mondale in 1976—other considerations took on importance. Because Americans after the mid-1970s preferred presidential candidates (other than incumbents) from outside the ranks of national elective officeholders, running mates were insiders from Capitol Hill. Of the ten major party vice-presidential candidates between 1976 and 1992, all had served in Congress, seven of them in the Senate.

Recent years have seen innovations in the selection process. Mondale's choice in 1984 of the first woman, Geraldine Ferraro, acknowledged a changing political climate and created a new form of ticket balancing. George Bush's naming of Dan Quayle, a little-known senator with seemingly not much to offer the ticket or the nation, provoked much puzzlement, concern, and ridicule. Bill Clinton seemed to defy conventional logic in 1992, when he picked Senator Albert Gore, producing a ticket of two white males of similar age and ideology, both Baptist and both from southern states. Gore, however, enhanced an image that Clinton wished to project, and as a popular insider was strong in areas where Clinton was weak. None of these choices challenged the proposition that a vice-presidential candidate's responsibility was to help elect a president, nor did Ronald Reagan's selection in 1980 of Bush, a "moderate" balance to Reagan's conservatism and a candidate who could help the ticket in Texas, a critical state.

Despite the persistence of jokes about its impotence and irrelevance, the office of the vice president remains firmly established in U.S. government.

The people who have held the office—and who have run for it—since the 1970s generally have been capable, experienced individuals of sober judgment. The most apprehension arose from the candidacy of Quayle, who seemed ill-equipped and ill-prepared for the job despite several years in Congress. Recent presidents have made a point of having their vice presidents at important meetings and giving them special assignments. The issue of temporary succession came up twice during the presidency of Ronald Reagan, first when Reagan was shot on Mar. 30, 1981, and rushed into surgery, leaving it unclear as to who was in charge. When Reagan had surgery again in July 1985, he signed a transfer of power to the vice president for the period of his operation. For all the effort to promote the visibility of recent vice presidents, there is little to suggest they have had a major impact on policy. Indeed, Bush proudly asserted that he was not "in the loop" of decisions about the unpopular Iran-Contra episode. The most encouraging sign of change came with the Clinton administration in the mid-1990s. Clinton treated Gore as an equal partner during the election of 1992, and the two often campaigned together. Upon taking office Gore represented the new administration on environmental issues, operated behind the scenes in key congressional votes, and in 1993 presented the administration's case in a heralded debate with Ross Perot on the North American Free Trade Agreement. Projecting a refreshing self-confidence on most aspects of policy, Gore had a promising start.

Despite the persistence of jokes about its impotence and suggestions that it be changed, even abolished, the vice presidency remains firmly established in the U.S. government. Critics continue to insist that the vice president become more active and that the office serve as a training ground for the presidency. The process of selection, flawed—even risky—as it is, remains entrenched in party politics and is unlikely to change. The best the nation can hope for is that in choosing a running mate, the presidential nominee will give more heed to expertness in governance and less to politics, with the people making anyone pay who does not. Experience since the 1970s, and more broadly since 1945, has affirmed that in picking a running mate a presidential nominee probably is choosing a future presidential candidate. This proved true even of the most ridiculed of recent vice presidents, Quayle, whose national book tour in 1994 catapulted him into a potential presidential candidacy (before illness ruled it out).

[See also Presidency.]

BIBLIOGRAPHY

The Twentieth Century Fund, *A Heartbeat Away: Report of the Twentieth Century Task Force on the Vice Presidency* (New York, 1988).

Jules Witcover, *Crapshoot: Rolling the Dice on the Vice Presidency* (New York, 1992).

— ROSS GREGORY

VIETNAM WAR

Vietnam War, fought from 1957 until early 1975, started as a Communist insurgency supported by North Vietnam, and later involved direct North Vietnamese intervention supported by the Soviet Union and the People's Republic of China. The United States fought in conjunction with South Vietnam, with more assistance from other nations, including the Republic of Korea (South Korea), Australia, New Zealand, Thailand, and the Philippines, than was provided in the Korean War. There were 45,943 U.S. battle deaths, the fourth most costly American war in terms of loss of life. The Vietnam War followed the Indochina War of 1946–54 in which France sought to reestablish colonial control after challenged by Communist-dominated nationalists.

American involvement began in mid-1950 when President Harry S. Truman invoked the Mutual Defense Assistance Act of 1949 to provide aid to French forces in Vietnam, Laos, and Cambodia. Early U.S. aims were to halt the spread of communism and to encourage French participation in the international defense of Europe.

Through the Geneva Accords of 1954, ending the Indochina War, Vietnam was divided by the Demilitarized Zone (DMZ) at the seventeenth parallel. Designed for relocating opposing military forces, the division in effect created two nations: a Communist north (Democratic Republic of Vietnam) and a non-Communist south (Republic of Vietnam).

Following the accords, the United States through the Military Assistance Advisory Group (MAAG), Indochina, aided the South Vietnam government of President Ngo Dinh Diem under the Southeast Asia Treaty Organization (SEATO). With apparent settlement in Laos and Cambodia, the headquarters in 1955 became the MAAG, Vietnam, with 342 U.S. personnel. Upon French withdrawal in 1956, the United States doubled that number, maintaining that the additions conformed with limitations of the Geneva Accords in that they replaced French advisers. When Diem's government declined to sanction Vietnam-wide elections as provided by the accords, asserting that South Vietnam had not acceded to the treaty and that free elections were impossible in the north, the administration of U.S. President Dwight D. Eisenhower concurred.

In the months following the Geneva Accords, Diem established a surprisingly stable government, defeating powerful gangsters in the capital of Saigon, the Binh Xuyen, and autonomous armies of the Cao Dai and Hoa Hao religious sects. Anticipating control of South Vietnam through elections and preoccupied with internal problems, North Vietnam's charismatic leader, Ho

Chi Minh, provoked no interference until the election plan collapsed. Beginning in 1957, Communist guerrillas (Vietcong, or VC), who had gone underground after the accords, opened a terrorist revolt, which intensified as 65,000 Communists infiltrated from North Vietnam, where they had gone for insurgent training. The first American deaths occurred in July 1959, when two soldiers were killed during a VC attack on Bien Hoa, north of Saigon. North Vietnam in 1960 openly revealed complicity with the VC in creating a political arm, the National Front for the Liberation of South Vietnam, dedicated to overthrowing Diem and ousting the United States.

By mid-1961 the insurgency had so grown that President John F. Kennedy increased U.S. advisers to 16,000 and, the next year, to 23,000. American helicopter companies supported the ARVN (pronounced *Arvin*, for Army of the Republic of Vietnam). A joint (army, navy, air force) headquarters, Military Assistance Command, Vietnam (MACV), replaced the MAAG.

Yet the insurgency continued to increase through propaganda and terror, augmented supplies from North Vietnam, and Diem's autocratic methods, which fed popular discontent more than they inhibited the insurgents. Diem's assassination during a *coup d'état* on Nov. 1, 1963, led to a succession of unstable governments. A program to relocate the rural population in supposedly secure "strategic hamlets" collapsed. U.S. casualties increased: 45 killed in 1963, 118 in 1964. After two incidents in August 1964 involving U.S. destroyers and North Vietnamese patrol boats in the Gulf of Tonkin, American planes raided North Vietnam and Congress authorized President Lyndon B. Johnson to "repel any armed attack against the forces of the United States and to repel further aggression." That resolution served as a legal basis for subsequent increases in U.S. commitment, but after questions later arose as to whether the administration had misrepresented the incidents, Congress in 1970 repealed it.

Although slow to use the authority, Johnson was concerned as VC strength grew to 100,000, U.S. installations came under attack, and North Vietnamese army units headed south. The president at first authorized only limited covert operations by South Vietnamese in North Vietnam and U.S. bombing of North Vietnamese supply routes in Laos, known collectively as the Ho Chi Minh Trail.

When in February 1965 the VC killed thirty-one Americans at Pleiku and Qui Nhon, Johnson sanctioned retaliatory air strikes against North Vietnam. Soon afterward he sanctioned a sustained but carefully controlled aerial campaign beginning on Mar. 2. Hoping to convince the North Vietnamese to desist, he halted the bombing on occasion to await response, but without result. Johnson's basic aim was to halt communism's spread while assuring South Vietnam's independence, but also involved were U.S. credibility as an ally and a challenge to the Communist concept of "wars of national liberation."

When several North Vietnamese regiments were detected within South Vietnam, the MACV commander, Gen. William C. Westmoreland, requested U.S. troops to protect American installations. Five U.S. battalions and an airborne brigade arrived from March through May. In June, B-52 strategic bombers began raiding VC bases within South Vietnam, and the 173rd Airborne Brigade attacked an enemy sanctuary, War Zone D, the first American ground offensive of the war.

Advised by Westmoreland and others that only a major commitment of American troops could save South Vietnam, Johnson on July 28 announced deployments that by the end of 1965 brought U.S. strength to 180,000 and by 1969 reached a peak of 543,400. A stable government meanwhile emerged in Saigon under Nguyen Van Thieu.

Given South Vietnam's underdeveloped state, creating a logistical base was essential. Using troops and U.S. civilian engineering firms, MACV constructed or expanded ports at six sites, erected fortified camps for all American units, built vast depots, paved thousands of miles of roads, and created extensive airfields. Buying time for the logistical effort, Westmoreland employed early arriving combat units as fire brigades against major threats. The most notable success was against North Vietnamese in the Central Highlands, who apparently intended to cut South Vietnam in two. In the Battle of the Ia Drang Valley, the first U.S. airmobile unit, the First Cavalry Division, used helicopters expeditiously and drove a decimated North Vietnamese division into Cambodia.

That the enemy could retire with impunity into Cambodia and use the port of Sihanoukville (now Kompong Som) to offset the U.S. Navy's sealing of the South Vietnamese coast was frustrating; but in the hope of limiting the war, Johnson forbade cross-border operations except for bombing of the Ho Chi Minh Trail. This policy dictated for Westmoreland a strategic defensive aimed at enemy attrition. While some American units pursued large enemy formations and penetrated VC logistical bases, others worked with the ARVN to protect villages against local guerrillas, thereby supporting "pacification," a program conducted by the South Vietnamese government and U.S. civilian agencies to eliminate the Communist political cadre and to provide government services.

It was a checkerboard war without front lines in which units might move anywhere by helicopter. In some ways a primitive war, it nevertheless involved sophisticated weapons and equipment and required constant resort to ingenuity to root the enemy from jungle and verdant rice paddies. Fighting sometimes inevitably occurred among the population and produced civilian casualties, the latter as a result both of enemy terrorism and on one occasion, at My Lai in 1968, of a serious lapse of discipline in a U.S. unit.

In early 1967 North Vietnamese buildup within the DMZ prompted U.S. Army reinforcement of U.S. Marines in the north; and later that year North Vietnamese forays across Cambodian and Laotian frontiers produced sharp clashes and the siege of a marine base at Khe Sanh. These moves concealed a covert buildup around South Vietnam's cities, preliminary to an offensive aimed at generating a popular uprising and American ouster. Although U.S. intelligence gleaned something of the plan, the extent came as a surprise. On Jan. 30–31, 1968, during the Tet (lunar new year) holidays, 84,000 Communists attacked seventy-four towns and cities. Although the ARVN cleared most localities quickly, fighting in Saigon and Hue was protracted. Controlling Hue for almost a month, the enemy executed 3,000 civilians.

Despite 32,000 dead, the offensive produced no lasting Communist military advantage, but it made a sharp psychological impact on American public opinion, feeding already strident demands for withdrawal, which nurtured the Communist belief that victory lay, as with the French, in American disenchantment with the war. Although North Vietnam agreed to negotiate after Johnson halted most bombing of the north, the negotiations, opening in Paris in May, were unproductive for a long time.

The enemy's heavy losses nevertheless made possible gradual American withdrawal. A concerted program to upgrade the ARVN began in 1969 with the administration of President Richard M. Nixon, and the first American units withdrew that summer. Yet Nixon needed time if his program, called "Vietnamization," was to enable South Vietnam to stand alone. He gained some time when Ho Chi Minh died on Sept. 3, 1969, requiring North Vietnamese leadership adjustments. He gained more by American and South Vietnamese operations, which he sanctioned, in April-May 1970, to eliminate enemy sanctuaries in Cambodia and by an ARVN raid in February 1971 on the Ho Chi Minh Trail.

When North Vietnam during Easter 1972 attacked with twelve divisions spearheaded by Russian tanks, only a residual American ground force remained, but the U.S. Air Force and U.S. Navy provided critical support. The offensive scored sharp initial gains, including capture of South Vietnam's northernmost province, but the ARVN rebounded creditably. Nixon reacted by sealing the port of Haiphong and again bombing North Vietnam, this time with punishing technologically advanced bombs and B-52 bombers.

Stymied on the ground and hurt by the bombing and blockade, North Vietnam finally entered meaningful negotiations. Nixon's special adviser, Henry A. Kissinger, and North Vietnamese representative Le Duc Tho conducted months of secret discussions ending in a cease-fire effective Jan. 28, 1973. Under the agreement, prisoners of war were returned, all American troops withdrew, and a four-nation commission supervised the truce. The Communists retained control of the northern province, large tracts of sparsely populated mountain regions, and some enclaves in populated areas.

Because of the continued presence of North Vietnamese troops within South Vietnam, the position of the South Vietnamese was precarious, particularly after any possibility of American military intervention was eliminated when the U.S. Congress, apparently reflecting the tenor of American public opinion, passed an amendment to an appropriations bill prohibiting funds for all American combat action in Southeast Asia after Aug. 15, 1973. Through 1973–74 the North Vietnamese, in violation of the cease-fire agreement, massed more men and supplies inside South Vietnam and in January 1975 launched a major attack that ended in the capture of Phuoc Long province.

When that attack failed to produce any American reaction, the North Vietnamese in March opened an offensive in the Central Highlands and soon extended it to the northern provinces. Short of ammunition and other tools of war because of a sharp decrease in U.S. military assistance, the South Vietnamese attempted to withdraw and concentrate on the defense of the southern third of the country and of coastal enclaves in the north and center, but the withdrawal quickly turned into a rout. Successively the country's major cities fell, as much because of panic and the impact of thousands of terrified refugees as because of enemy pressure. The North Vietnamese quickly entered the cities and soon posed a major threat to Saigon.

With the eminent collapse of South Vietnam, President Thieu on Apr. 21 resigned in favor of his vice-president, who in turn resigned on Apr. 28 in favor of Gen. Duong van Minh, who was committed to negotiate with the Communists. The Minh government surrendered on Apr. 30, 1975, whereupon North Vietnamese and VC troops entered Saigon only hours after the U.S. completed an emergency airlift of embassy personnel and thousands of South Vietnamese who feared for their lives under the Communists.

It was the longest American war and in terms of money ($138.9 billion) only World War II cost more. In addition to U.S. combat deaths, 1,333 men were missing and 10,298 dead of noncombat causes, such as accidents. South Vietnam lost more than 166,000 military dead and about 415,000 civilians. The Communists lost at least 937,000 dead. The Communists gained control not only of South Vietnam but also of neighboring Cambodia, where the government surrendered to insurgent forces on Apr. 16, 1975, and Laos, where the Communists gradually assumed control.

BIBLIOGRAPHY

Joseph Buttinger, *Vietnam: A Political History.*
Frances Fitzgerald, *Fire in the Lake.*
David Halberstam, *The Best and the Brightest.*
S. L. A. Marshall, *Battles in the Monsoon.*
Don Oberdorfer, *Tet!.*
Walt W. Rostow, *The Diffusion of Power.*
William C. Westmoreland, *A Soldier Reports.*

— CHARLES B. MACDONALD

VIRGINIA AND KENTUCKY RESOLUTIONS

Virginia and Kentucky Resolutions were passed by the legislature of Virginia, Dec. 24, 1798, and of Kentucky, Nov. 16, 1798, and Nov. 22, 1799. The first two are those usually referred to and are the more important, although the word "nullification" first appears in the third. The Kentucky resolutions were written by Thomas Jefferson, although the authorship long remained unknown, and the Virginia one by James Madison. The immediate occasion was to protest against the passage of the Alien and Sedition Acts (1798) by the Federalist administration, but the problems considered were much wider in scope, having to do with the nature of the federal Union. Both sets of resolutions took the sound position that the federal government was one of limited and delegated powers only. But there was the further question as to who should judge whether the central government was overstepping its rightful powers or not.

Jefferson stated that the federal government could not be the final judge of its own powers, and that the states—perhaps even one state—should be. Madison's words were less emphatic, but all three resolutions, unless one is very careful to interpret political terms and philosophy in their contemporary significance, can easily be made to appear as advocating the doctrines of state sovereignty, nullification, and secession as those doctrines were later developed. The prevailing theory of divided sovereignty must be considered; and in 1828 when John C. Calhoun was preaching his versions of state sovereignty and nullification, Madison pointed out that the Union was a constitutional one, not a mere league, and that his Virginia resolution of 1798 could not be considered as affording a basis for Calhoun's interpretation. In the earlier year, the government was facing unsolved problems. If it appeared illogical that a central government of merely delegated powers should be the judge of whether it had overstepped them, the other horn of the dilemma, that of making the states judges, offered equal practical difficulties.

The resolutions, as passed in 1798 and 1799, were forwarded for comment to the legislatures of the other states, which proved cool to the suggestions made, and in a number of cases replied that states could not decide on the constitutionality of federal laws because that power belonged to the judiciary. There, in the course of U.S. development, it was finally to be lodged. But the resolutions may have helped by bringing the problem to a head and causing John Marshall to develop his theory of the functions of the Supreme Court. Later, the resolutions were used to buttress the doctrines of states' rights as promulgated particularly in the South, and their political influence was great. By many, the resolutions came to be considered as almost a part of the Constitution and to have a legal authority that in fact they never possessed.

BIBLIOGRAPHY

A. C. McLaughlin, *A Constitutional History of the U.S..*
E. D. Warfield, *The Kentucky Resolutions of 1798.*

— JAMES TRUSLOW ADAMS

VIRGINIA COMPANY OF LONDON

Virginia Company of London, one name for the commercial enterprise that was established in 1606 and that governed the colony of Virginia from 1609 to 1624. The Society of Adventurers (that is, investors) to trade in Virginia was organized by letters patent dated Apr. 10, 1606, and issued "to Sir Thomas Gates, Sir George Somers, and others, for two several Colonies and Plantations, to be made in Virginia, and other parts and Territories of America." Articles IV and V of the document specified that there were to be two colonies, called "the first Colony" and "the second Colony." The "first Colony" included "any place upon the said coast of Virginia or America" between thirty-four and forty degrees north latitude. The "second Colony," in which Thomas Hanham and others "of the town of Plimouth in the county of Devon or elsewhere" were allowed to begin a plantation, was to be between thirty-eight and forty degrees north latitude. Neither group of colonists was to "plant" itself within 100 miles of the other. Article VII provided that each colony was to be governed ultimately by a council in London and in day-to-day matters by a local council responsible to the body in London. To investors were left the tasks of raising funds, furnishing supplies, and sending out expeditions. However, the king retained authority over affairs in Virginia by making the governing council in England responsible to himself. (A modification of this council system government was later used when royal colonies replaced proprietary and corporate colonies throughout America.)

From 1606 to 1609 the private investors had little influence on affairs in Virginia, even in commercial matters. Business management was left to joint-stock companies, and the storehouse was controlled by a treasurer and two clerks elected by the president and council in the colony. The government of the colonies and of the territory of Virginia was reserved to the crown through the Council of Thirteen for Virginia, which was appointed by the king and resided in England. It recommended to the king persons to whom lands were to be granted, and it appointed the first council in Virginia.

The king retained authority over affairs in Virginia by making the governing council in England responsible to himself.

In 1609 a "Second Charter" was granted to the company, converting it into a corporation and body politic "for . . . enlargement . . . of the said Company and first Colony of Virginia." The organization was to be "called and incorporated by the name of, The Treasurer and Company of Adventurers and Planters of the City of London for the first Colony in Virginia." The limits of the colony were expressed in terms of distance from "Cape or Point Comfort": 200 miles to the north, 200 miles to the south, and from "sea to sea, west and northwest." The entrepreneurs, with Sir Thomas Smith as treasurer, became distinctly proprietary, retaining commercial responsibilities and also assuming governmental functions in place of the king. The investors had desired more authority, in part because they feared that either a desire to placate Spain or religious considerations might lead the crown to abandon the colonization scheme. Under the new charter, the company appointed a governor to run the colony (the council in Virginia became an advisory body). The council of the company in London, chosen by the investors, was to act as a standing committee for them and exercise controlling authority in place of the king.

Another charter, granted in 1612, strengthened the authority of the company, making it overlord of a proprietary province. Under this charter major decisions of the company were to be made in quarterly stockholder meetings called quarter courts. A system for joint management of land and an exemption from English customs duties, all to extend over a period of seven years, promised dividends to the investors and support to the planters.

In 1619 the Virginia Company adopted "Orders and Constitutions," which were intended to ensure legality of action and were read at one quarter court each year. The forms and usages followed in other commercial companies, in other corporate companies, and in Parliament greatly influenced the decisions of the company. Through reward or by purchase, an individual might own land without purchasing stock in the company, but he might obtain stock within three years by "planting" or peopling his land. Ownership of land and possession of an ownership interest in the company were not always coexistent. Each involved the possibility of the other. The company, headquartered at London, was thus a body of stockholders who had acquired stock in the company by paying money, rendering service, or settling on land in Virginia. The company was presided over by a treasurer, chosen by itself at will, and it conducted all of its business through its regularly elected officers of committees or through special committees. According to the "Orders and Constitutions," it kept a complete record of actions taken in the quarter courts and compelled its committees to maintain similar records.

Between 1619 and 1622 factions developed in the company as a result of the administration of Samuel Argall, deputy governor of the colony. Argall exploited the lands and trade of the company for his own benefit and that of his friends. This exploitation led to the formation of an administration under the Earl of Southampton, Lord Cavendish, Sir Edwin Sandys, John Ferrar, and Nicholas Ferrar. No radical alterations in policy were made, but certain changes gradually occurred. Emigration to Virginia by laborers, artisans, and apprentices was encouraged, to attain production of grain and to install industry.

An Indian massacre in 1622 added to the colony's problems. Also, political difficulties arose. The Sandys-Southampton party supported the parliamentary opposition in England, and the king and Sandys became bitter political enemies.

On Apr. 17, 1623, a committee headed by Lord Cavendish was summoned before the Privy Council to defend the company against the "grievances of Planters and Adventurers." As a result, the first blow was struck at the liberty of the company when the Privy Council announced that a commission had been appointed to inquire into the state of the Virginia and Somers Island plantation. On Nov. 4, 1623, a writ of quo warranto was issued by the Court of the Kings Bench. Judgment against the Virginia Company was rendered on May 24, 1624, and it was thereby dissolved. The patent roll, dated July 15, 1624, records the appointment of a "commission and certain others" to supplant the Virginia Company and establish the first royal province in America. The commission was composed of the lords of the Privy Council and "certain others," and the council register seems to indicate that it was usually the council that sat as the governing commission for Virginia. Papers, letters, instructions, and commissions to the councillors and to governors of the colony contained the privy seal and were engrossed on the patent roll, and the letters or papers from the colony were addressed to the council.

Although the advice of the company was sought by the king on questions affecting the government of the colony, Sandys was unsuccessful in his attempt to secure new letters patent. The *Discourse of the Old Company* was issued later in reply. A new charter for the company was never granted and its function as a trading organization ceased.

The company's records for the period from 1619 to 1624 are much greater in volume than those for the earlier years. The company's minutes comprise two volumes of the "court book" and fill 741 large manuscript pages. Between November 1623 and June 1624, Nicholas Ferrar was engaged in having these documents transcribed. The transcripts were obtained by Thomas Jefferson and were later deposited with the Library of Congress.

BIBLIOGRAPHY

W. F. Craven, *Virginia Company of London,* and *Dissolution of the Virginia Company.*

Susan M. Kingsbury, ed., *Records of the Virginia Company of London.*

— SUSAN MYRA KINGSBURY

VIRGINIA DECLARATION OF RIGHTS

Virginia Declaration of Rights was formulated by George Mason and adopted by the Virginia Convention on June 12, 1776, preceding by seventeen days the adoption of the constitution that made Virginia an independent state. It furnished a model for similar declarations in other state constitutions and also for the first ten amendments to the U.S. Constitution (the Bill of Rights).

BIBLIOGRAPHY

Robert A. Rutland, ed., *The Papers of George Mason: 1725–1792.*

— MATTHEW PAGE ANDREWS

VIRGINIA RESOLVES

Virginia Resolves were the first American protests against the Townshend Acts of 1767 and the treatment of Massachusetts for resenting these acts. The Virginia resolves were prepared by George Mason and introduced May 16, 1769, by George Washington in the House of Burgesses; they besought the king, "as the father of his people however remote from the seat of his empire," to quiet the minds of Virginians and avert from them threatened dangers to their lives and liberties. Among the burgesses approving these resolves were Patrick Henry, Thomas Jefferson, and Richard Henry Lee, each of whom sat for the first time. Adoption of the Virginia resolves led to similar adoptions by each of the other colonial assemblies.

BIBLIOGRAPHY

George E. Howard, *Preliminaries of the American Revolution.*

— C. H. AMBLER

VOLSTEAD ACT

The Eighteenth Amendment (ratified Jan. 29, 1919) needed a law to enforce it, and therefore the National Prohibition Act, introduced by Rep. Andrew J. Volstead of Minnesota, was passed by Congress in October 1919. It was vetoed by President Woodrow Wilson (Oct. 27), but repassed by the House the same day and by the Senate the following day. It construed intoxicating liquor as that containing as much as 0.5 percent alcohol by volume. It fixed penalties for liquor sales; provided for injunctions against—and the padlocking of—hotels, restaurants, and other such establishments found to be selling liquor; contained a search and seizure clause; and, oddly enough, continued the taxation of alcoholic beverages. It permitted the retention of private stocks of liquor bought before the act went into effect, and likewise the manufacture of beer by brewers, on condition that they reduce the alcoholic content to 0.5 percent before sale.

BIBLIOGRAPHY

J. A. Krout, *Origins of Prohibition.*

— ALVIN F. HARLOW

VOLUNTEERISM

Volunteerism, broadly defined as socially beneficiary activities by individuals and groups that are noncompulsory and not profit oriented, has become more significant since the 1970s, with increasing numbers of people contributing time and expertise to community organizations, mutual aid societies, and social welfare programs. As a national phenomenon volunteerism dates back to World War I, when Herbert Hoover and others encouraged individuals and especially businesses to cooperate in such wartime activities as food rationing and price controls. When volunteerism failed during the Great Depression its reputation diminished, only to be temporarily rescued during World War II. In addition to being associated with national cooperation efforts, volunteerism since the nineteenth century has denoted the unpaid philanthropic, social service, and political work of American women. The recession of the early 1970s and the subsequent ebbs and flows of the national economy led to an increasing reliance on technology, which resulted in a greater need for more highly trained workers. Unemployment plagued the economy, straining public assistance and social service programs. When the great numbers of children born in the decade following World War II entered the workforce in the 1970s, jobs were often unavailable for them. The jobs that were available often required training that traditional educational institutions could not provide.

As a national phenomenon, volunteerism dates back to World War I, when individuals and especially businesses were encouraged to cooperate in food rationing and price controls.

Volunteerism became one solution to these many social challenges. A few government programs supporting volunteer activity had been created in the 1960s, most notably the Peace Corps, Volunteers in Service to America (VISTA), the Foster Grandparents Program, and the Retired Senior Volunteer Program (RSVP). These programs set the stage for President Richard M. Nixon to inaugurate a major national volunteer force. In 1971 a new governmental agency, ACTION, was created to coordinate the existing programs and encourage participation on a national level. At the same time a nongovernment agency, the National Center for Voluntary Action, was created by Congress to centralize and promote volunteerism throughout the country. Older workers, who were increasingly encouraged to make way for younger employees by taking early retirement, were targeted as an important volunteer pool for community-based and public-sector social programs. Volunteerism by the young was emphasized as a solution to the need for both service to the community and specialized training not provided by the educational system. Since the 1970s "service learning" components have been incorporated into elementary, high school, and college curricula.

Aimed at decentralizing government welfare functions, the federalist policies of Presidents Ronald Reagan and George Bush in the 1980s continued the trend of the previous decade. Both administrations heralded community volunteerism as the ideal solution to social problems, and Reagan and Bush believed that cuts in government social services would stimulate voluntary community service. The leaders of many volunteer organizations, however, stated that voluntary efforts could not compensate for federal cuts. Volunteerism was also a significant concern of President Bill Clinton, who emphasized community service, the integration of education with labor needs, and grass-roots organizing against crime and other social problems. In 1993 Congress passed President Clinton's plan allowing students to repay federal college loans through community service. In the 1990s volunteer labor became an entrenched sector of the economy wherein volunteers engaged in "coproduction" along with traditional public- and private-sector providers.

[See also Peace Corps.]

BIBLIOGRAPHY

Susan J. Ellis and Katherine H. Noyes, *By the People: A History of American Volunteers* (San Francisco, 1990).

Jon Van Til, *Mapping the Third Sector: Voluntarism in a Changing Social Economy* (New York, 1998).

— JULIET NIEHAUS

VOTING

The election of public officials in America dates from the beginning of the colonial period. Originally, the practice of voting was an adaptation of the British practice of acclamation, raising of hands, or individual announcement. Most commonly the voter stood before the election officials and openly stated his preferences. Change began in 1634, when Massachusetts originated the use of the paper ballot. By 1800 almost all the states used paper ballots, although oral voting persisted in many areas; Kentucky, in 1890, was the last state to give up the practice. Paper ballots were unofficial; that is, each person supplied his own.

In the late 18th century political parties began supplying ballots, often printed on colored paper, identifying the party—which allowed the voter to hold up his ballot to show party officials that he was fulfilling promises to the party when he voted. By the Civil War election processes throughout the United States were marked by fraud. Violence, intimidation, and bribery were prevalent in most cities. Often voters were issued tissue-paper ballots, which enabled the party worker to see where a voter put his mark after the ballot was folded.

The major reform in voting was the introduction of the secret ballot, named the Australian ballot because it was first used in Queensland as early as 1857. Since the beginning of the 20th century all states have used the Australian ballot, printed at public expense by public authorities and listing all candidates for office on a single form. It is distributed only at polling places to bona fide voters, who then mark the ballot secretly, fold it, and deposit it in a ballot box. Although voting machines are now used in most voting districts, the basic protection of secrecy remains.

Voting in the United States has been limited by a minimum age; by the requirement of citizenship (in 1926 Arkansas was the last state to prohibit alien voting); poll taxes (invalidated by the Twenty-fourth Amendment in 1964); literacy tests; residence requirements; and disqualifications for criminal or mental incompetence. A special problem has faced black Americans, who have been blocked by the administration of election laws and by extralegal barriers, including physical intimidation. Voting by black Americans increased significantly under the protection of the Civil Rights Act of 1964 and the Voting Rights Act of 1965. Congress created the United States Commission on Civil Rights in 1957 to investigate and report discrimination against voters; the Justice Department has been given authority to supervise elections in many southern states; and local registrars now come under greater federal regulation and control.

BIBLIOGRAPHY

Kirk H. Porter, *A History of Suffrage in the United States.*
Constance E. Smith, *Voting and Election Laws.*

— DAVID C. SAFFELL

VOTING RIGHTS ACT OF 1965

Voting Rights Act of 1965 represents the utmost exertion of constitutional powers by Congress to eradicate all tactics used in some southern states to disfranchise black voters. The Civil Rights Act of 1957, with its 1960 and 1964 amendments, had proved ineffective in ending the literacy and other tests because its approach was through federal litigation on a case-by-case basis, which could reach only a small number of offending counties. The 1965 act provided for direct federal initiative to enable blacks to register and vote; it suspended literacy and other discriminatory voter registration tests in Alabama, Georgia, Louisiana, Mississippi, South Carolina, and Virginia, and in forty counties in North Carolina. It provided for the appointment of federal examiners empowered to list persons qualified to vote and to assign federal observers to monitor elections. By the Voting Rights Act amendments of 1970 the life of the 1965 act was extended from five to ten years, and in 1975 it was extended for an additional seven years.

The U.S. Supreme Court in upholding the constitutionality of the 1965 act the following year said, "Millions of non-white Americans will now be able to participate for the first time on an equal basis in the government under which they live" (*South Carolina* v. *Katzenbach*, 383 U.S. 301). In a 1969 case, the Supreme Court stated that the act had implemented the first intention of Congress "to rid the country of racial discrimination in voting" by providing "new remedies against those practices which had most frequently denied citizens the right to vote on the basis of their race" (*Allen* v. *State Board of Elections*, 393 U.S. 544).

The act was dramatically effective. Its most conspicuous effect was in Mississippi, where black registration went from 6.7 percent in 1965 to 59.8 in 1968. In Alabama the percentage went from 19.3 in 1965 to 51.6 in 1968; in Georgia, from 27.4 to 52.6; in Louisiana, from 31.6 to 58.9; and in South Carolina, from 37.3 to 51.2. In 1965 only 72 blacks held elective office in the South, but in 1974 Mississippi alone had 174 elected black officeholders; Alabama had 149. The total number of elected black officials in the South in 1974 was 1,307, marking an increase of about 1,800 percent in the first nine years after the passage of the act.

Black political power in the South does not, however, alone account for these changes. In Atlanta a black was elected mayor even though blacks constituted only 49 percent of the registered voters; in Raleigh, N.C., where 84.5 percent of the voters were white, a black was elected mayor; and in Greenville, Ga., a rural town whose population was 60 percent white, a black was elected mayor. It is not only the black's voting rights that have been enhanced; his entire political stance has been greatly altered in the direction of equality of political opportunities as well as political rights.

BIBLIOGRAPHY

V. O. Key, Jr., *Southern Politics.*
U.S. Commission on Civil Rights, *Political Participation.*
C. Vann Woodward, *Strange Career of Jim Crow.*

— MILTON R. KONVITZ

WACO SIEGE

Waco Siege (1993). The deaths of four federal agents and seventy-eight members of the Branch Davidian religious group during a fifty-one-day siege of their commune headquarters outside Waco, Texas, provoked widespread controversy over the use of force in dealing with dissident sects. A botched and bloody attempt on Feb. 28, 1993, to arrest the group's leader, David Koresh, on a weapons charge led to stalemate until U.S. Attorney General Janet Reno ordered the use of force on Apr. 19 to end the standoff. Fire engulfed "Ranch Apocalypse," killing seventy-two, including Koresh and seventeen children. Although some surviving members of the sect were tried for manslaughter and found not guilty, they were convicted of lesser charges and received extremely harsh sentences.

BIBLIOGRAPHY

Martin King and Marc Breault, *Preacher of Death: The Shocking Inside Story of David Koresh and the Waco Siege* (New York, 1993).

Dick J. Reavis, *The Ashes of Waco: An Investigation* (New York, 1996).

James D. Tabor and Eugene V. Gallagher, *Why Waco?: Cults and the Battle for Religious Freedom in America* (Berkeley, Calif., 1996).

— BRUCE J. EVENSON

WADE-DAVIS BILL

Wade-Davis Bill, passed by Congress July 2, 1864, provided that the government of a seceded state could be reorganized only after a majority of the white male citizens had taken the oath of allegiance to the United States and a constitution acceptable to the president and Congress was adopted. Rep. Henry W. Davis of Maryland and Sen. Benjamin F. Wade of Ohio, sponsors of the bill, believed along with other Radical Republicans that Reconstruction was the prerogative of Congress rather than of the president. Abraham Lincoln's pocket veto of this bill (July 4), which was the response of Congress to Lincoln's plan of Reconstruction, angered the radicals and presaged the contest over Reconstruction between President Andrew Johnson and Congress.

BIBLIOGRAPHY

Charles McCarthy, *Lincoln's Plan of Reconstruction.*

E. G. Scott, *Reconstruction During the Civil War in the United States.*

— WILLARD H. SMITH

WAGON TRAINS

For purposes of protection and efficiency, traders and emigrants of the trans-Mississippi West before 1880 customarily gathered their wagons into more or less organized caravans or trains.

There is some doubt as to who first used wagons of the prairie schooner or canvas-covered type over the tramontane trails to the Far West, but apparently William L. Sublette, one of the partners in the reorganized Rocky Mountain Fur Company, conducted a ten-wagon, mule-drawn train over the Oregon Trail from Saint Louis as far as the company's Wind River (Wyo.) rendezvous between Apr. 10 and July 16, 1830, arriving back at Saint Louis on Oct. 10. Capt. Benjamin L. E. Bonneville's fur-trading expedition is usually given the distinction of having first taken wagons through South Pass, when in July 1832 his twenty-wagon train, drawn by oxen and mules, reached the Green River by that route. It was not until 1843 that the celebrated "cow column" Oregon emigrant party of about 1,000 persons—under the leadership of Peter H. Burnett, Jesse Applegate, and Marcus Whitman—brought most of its 120 wagons over the trail to arrive near the Columbia River on Oct. 10, the first wagon train to reach Oregon. Separating from the main emigration of 1843 at Fort Hall, Joseph B. Chiles left Joseph R. Walker to guide a portion of his party with three wagons and reach California after abandoning their wagons just east of the Sierra Nevada at Owen's Lake. The so-called Stevens-Murphy-Townsend party of some fifty persons in October–December of the following year, with five of its original eleven ox-drawn vehicles, is claimed to have been the first group to bring wagons all the way from Missouri and through the Sierras by the California Trail, Donner Lake, and Truckee Pass; it was guided by Caleb Greenwood. William Becknell, a Missouri merchant, took the first wagon train, of three wagons, to Santa Fe in May–July 1822; and the first wagon trail from Santa Fe on to southern California seems to have been marked during the Mexican War by Lt. Col. Philip St. George Cooke with his Mormon Battalion (Oct. 19, 1846–Jan. 29, 1847), by way of Guadalupe Pass, the Gila River, and Colorado Desert to San Diego.

The eastern section of the Old Spanish Trail, from the Wasatch Mountains through Utah, Colorado, and New Mexico to Santa Fe, seems to have been seldom if ever traversed by wagons, although Mexican pack trains had used it at least as early as 1830. The western section of this trail, through southwestern Utah and across Nevada and California to the vicinity of Los Angeles, was used frequently during the gold rush days by wagon trains of emigrants turning southward from Salt Lake City. A number of well-marked wagon routes ran across Texas from its coast towns and from Louisiana, Arkansas, and the Indian Territory to El Paso or other points on the Rio Grande, from which connections could easily be made with the Gila Trail.

The number of wagons making the overland journey annually from 1843 to 1848 is difficult to determine with accuracy. But some idea of the increased emigration by wagon train, after the news of the California gold discovery was confirmed in the East, may be gathered from the report, dated June 23, 1849, that already that year 5,516 wagons had passed Fort Kearny on the Platte River, bound for California or the Columbia Valley. In 1865, when the prairie schooners were beginning to carry rather more freight than passengers, from thirty to fifty canvas-topped wagons, each capable of transporting from 4,000 to 7,000 pounds and drawn usually by five or six yoke of oxen, urged on by bullwhackers, were said to make up an ordinary train, and trains five miles in length were occasionally reported.

The organization and daily routine of a wagon train depended on the danger expected from Indians, the nature of the country to be traversed, and the number and character of the parties composing the train. Some trains, such as those of the Mormon migrations, had a semi-military formation, others were very loosely bound together. It was customary to elect a captain as central authority, and several lieutenants were put in charge of assigned sections of the train, their duties being chiefly to execute the commands of the captain, to keep order in their sections, and to place them properly in designated positions when the train paused for its encampments. One function of the captain was usually to select each night's camping site in accordance with the advice of a guide or the reports of horsemen sent out in advance during the day. At night the wagons were commonly drawn up in a circle or square, end to end, so as to form a corral for at least the more valuable horses, mules, and cattle, as well as a fortress for the passengers. Frequent reasons for these precautions were Indian thefts, buffalo herds, storms, and other alarms that might stampede the domestic draft animals. Horse- or mule-drawn wagons could make, as a rule, from ten to fifteen miles a day, the more dependable ox-drawn trains seldom more than ten, under average conditions of travel.

Westward pioneers break camp at daybreak in the Rocky Mountains, Colorado in an undated engraving. After the completion of the Union Pacific-Central Pacific railway in 1869, wagon trains were fewer and smaller. (Corbis-Bettmann)

After the completion of the Union Pacific-Central Pacific tramontane railway line in May 1869, wagon trains tended to decrease in size, save in the case of freighting lines. The establishment of stagecoach lines, the conquest of the Rocky Mountain and Great Plains Indians, the practical extermination of the buffalo, and the building of other far western railways in the 1880's, all combined to make the wagon train a means of freighting heavy goods rather than of carrying passengers, and it was increasingly safe for poorer emigrant families to make their way westward in a single covered wagon.

BIBLIOGRAPHY

H. H. Bancroft, *History of California*, vols. VI, VII, and *History of Oregon*, vol. II.

K. Coman, *Economic Beginnings of the Far West.*

O. C. Coy, *The Great Trek.*

R. L. Duffus, *The Santa Fé Trail.*

W. J. Ghent, *The Road to Oregon.*

L. W. Hastings, *The Emigrant's Guide to Oregon and California.*

— RUFUS KAY WYLLYS

WALL STREET

A stockade across lower Manhattan Island, built in 1653 to protect the little colony from marauders, gave its name to Wall Street, which over the years became the synonym for the financial interests of the United States. By the time American independence was achieved, Wall Street had become the location of the principal merchants of New York, of the Tontine Coffee House (an early type of life insurance association), and of Federal Hall, where President George Washington gave his inaugural address and the first Congress held its meetings. The buttonwood tree under which the brokers of the city are said to have met to agree on fees and terms of business was on Wall Street. When their organization was formalized in 1817 as the New York Stock Exchange, following the model set by Philadelphia in 1802, the location was still Wall Street. It remained there for a century until expanding business forced it to seek larger quarters around the corner on Broad Street. Other exchanges for coffee, cotton, produce, metals, and the like were attracted into this prestigious neighborhood; commercial banks, insurance companies, shipping agencies, and business corporations found it convenient to be nearby.

By 1810 New York City had outstripped its principal competitor, Philadelphia, in both population and foreign trade, and by 1825, with the opening of the Erie Canal, in domestic trade also. A firm foundation was laid for the preeminence of New York in finance. The first large offering of securities available to investors had been the obligations of the federal government created through the funding of the state debts under Alexander Hamilton, first secretary of the Treasury. These securities were enormously popular, since investors had previously found few outlets for their savings except land or a share in a ship, neither of which was readily negotiable. Gradually the bonds of the states, stock of banks and insurance companies, and issues of a few corporations chartered by special act of state legislatures for roads, canals, bridges, or water companies were added to the federal bonds. Subscriptions for such securities were usually made by signing a book open for the purpose in the office of a bank or broker on Wall Street. Many more issues appeared in the market when general incorporation laws were passed by the states, beginning with that of North Carolina in 1795. Industrial issues appeared during the 1830's and railroad stocks and bonds made up a large part of the trading list from the 1840's on. European investors found American securities attractive and very early bought large amounts of federal and state bonds, bank stock, and railroad bonds. Foreign bankers maintained branch offices on Wall Street, and American firms had similar offices on London's Lombard Street.

Because of the way security trading was financed in the United States, a close and not always healthy relationship developed between banks and brokers. Banks made call loans to brokers, often without adequate security, to provide the funds with which brokers paid for their own and their customers' purchases. This business was very profitable for the banks, and they competed for it by methods that were sometimes overzealous. Banks also made loans to the underwriters of new issues; if the market did not absorb the offering, the lending bank found itself with a heavy loss. Much of the unsavory reputation of Wall Street resulted from the crises associated with the manipulation of security prices by various methods associated with the names of such unscrupulous operators as John Jacob Astor, Daniel Drew, Jay Gould, Jim Fisk, and William Vanderbilt.

After 1900 the United States no longer needed foreign capital and began to make loans to other countries. World War I had stripped European nations of much of their wealth and financial power, and Wall Street institutions took over some of the business formerly done abroad. Foreign trade began to be financed in dollars instead of in English pounds, and long-term loans were made by American investment bankers to countries that were not always able to repay. The dramatic crash of stock prices in Wall Street in late 1929 and the ensuing depression of the 1930's brought about banking reform legislation and, in 1934, the establishment of the Securities and Exchange Commission, making illegal the former linkage of banks, investment banks, and brokers.

In 1946 the newly formed International Monetary Fund (IMF) and the International Bank for Reconstruction and Development located their head offices in the United States, confirming the prestige of the U.S. dollar. This favorable situation continued for two decades, until the enormous expenditures of the Vietnam War caused both a deficit in the U.S. balance of payments and inflation, which spread rapidly to other countries. In August 1971 the dollar was devalued, its redemption in gold terminated, and a system of flexible exchange rates instituted.

Special Drawing Rights (SDRs) were granted by the International Monetary Fund in order to aid member countries threatened by payments crises, but the position of the dollar worsened and another devaluation occurred in February 1973. The possibility of large withdrawals of dollar balances by the oil-exporting countries and the urgent demands for more and cheaper loans to the poorer members of the IMF forced a still more radical change in the charter of that institution in January 1976. The system established at Bretton Woods in 1945, based on the gold standard and fixed exchange rates, was abandoned, and in its place was authorized the use of flexible exchange rates and easier lending policies.

Although the dollar still remained the leading currency for international financial transactions, its position was relatively less secure than before these changes. As a result Wall Street had lost much of its original prestige and earlier glamour.

BIBLIOGRAPHY

Charles F. Adams and Henry Adams, *Chapters of Erie and Other Essays.*

Louis Brandeis, *Other Peoples' Money and How the Banks Use It.*

Margaret G. Myers, *History of the New York Money Market to 1913.*

Sereno S. Platt, *The Work of Wall Street.*

— MARGARET G. MYERS

WALL STREET SINCE THE 1970S

No other street or location in the United States evokes the idea of money, financial power, and capitalism as does Wall Street, the financial district of capitalism, and that was never more true than during the 1980s and early 1990s, when a series of "bull" markets sent stock and bond prices on an upward spiral, doubling or tripling prices and encouraging Americans to invest. Interestingly, however, by this time New York City's Wall Street no longer was the epicenter of the nation's finance; there were also financial markets in London, Frankfurt, Tokyo, and Sidney. Smaller exchanges appeared in Western and Eastern Europe and in Latin America, all attracting money away from Wall Street. Computers, fax machines, and electronic wire transfers made location largely irrelevant. In minutes, trades and deals could be executed and money moved anywhere. Because of world differences in time, it also became possible to trade around the clock. A sign that every street in the world was becoming a competitor to Wall Street was the loss of occupants in prestigious buildings on "the street"; office vacancies were said to amount to eight empty buildings as large as the Empire State Building.

All the while there were new kinds of investors, new products, and new rules. Perhaps the greatest factor in change was the tremendous influx and influence of institutional money in all its configurations—public and private pension funds, corporate treasuries, and mutual funds. The mutual funds took on strength during bull markets, profoundly changing investing while enriching millions of middle-class Americans who previously had shied away from taking market risks. Everything seemed to be changing. Consider what happened with mutual funds in the 1980s and early 1990s. First offered in Boston in 1924, such investments initially had attracted little investor interest because growth was hampered by a legality—the "prudent man" rule obligated investment managers to preserve capital and avoid risks. It was a play-it-safe approach in which investing was done with an eye to not losing money rather than to achieving growth. Quantitative economic research developed ideas about managing portfolios of risk. Investments could be grouped and managed so that losses in one investment likely would be offset by gains in others. This key development—assisted by the growing ability to number-crunch data—liberated money managers. Mutual funds offered a convenient way for middle-income investors to obtain part of the riches being generated in financial markets at home and abroad in emerging markets. For investments of as little as $50 or $100, investors could buy into diversified portfolios. As stocks soared, mutual funds swelled, with millions of Americans moving money out of passbook savings and certificates of deposits. More money meant more funds. In 1980 there were roughly 500 mutual funds, with a total asset value of $135 billion. By 1995 there were about 5,300 mutual funds with $2.2 trillion in assets. One-third of U.S. households owned part of at least one fund.

Although computers and electronic wire transfers have made location largely irrelevant, Wall Street still dominates the U.S. economy like no other force.

The funds of the Boston-based Fidelity Investments firm illustrates the vast growth of mutual funds. Founded in 1946, the firm grew into a financial powerhouse. By 1994 it managed assets of nearly $300 billion, making it comparable to some of the largest banks. Its Magellan Fund, managed by Peter Lynch, generated double-digit returns and grew into the nation's largest mutual fund. Lynch himself became a star, writing best-selling books on investing, making television appearances, and finding his opinions regularly quoted by financial writers. It was, of course, difficult for fund managers to outperform the market. Lynch's successes, as well as the even greater investing success of Warren Buffett, an Omaha investor who ran Berkshire Hathaway, called into question the prevailing academic theory about Wall Street, called the efficient market theory (EMT), which claimed that Lynch and Buffett's methods of examining company performance and prospects in hopes of finding an undervalued stock were worthless. EMT maintained that a stock could neither be overpriced nor underpriced; each day the market correctly set a stock's price because the price reflected all the information about a company known that day. A popular book by Burton Malkiel, *A Random Walk Down Wall Street*, introduced EMT to the general public in the early 1970s.

EMT became the accepted gospel as classic market economics regained exalted status in political, academic, social, and economic circles, but holes in EMT began to pop open. The *Wall Street Journal* ran a six-month contest comparing the performance of four stocks selected by investment professionals to four stocks—expected to represent EMT—selected by throwing darts at a stock table pinned to a dart board. The experts, however, beat the dart board, albeit by a narrow margin. Meanwhile, Lynch, Buffett, and other investment managers, such as John Neff and John Templeton, punched more holes in the EMT by repeatedly outperforming the market by large margins. Nonprofessionals also gave EMT fits. A group of sixteen Illinois women—ages forty-one to eighty-seven and known as the Beardstown Ladies—created an investment strategy that generated an annual return of 23 percent between 1983 and 1994, outperforming the Standard & Poor's 500 index for the same period.

The flow of money into mutual funds helped sustain a strong bull market that started in October 1990 and by spring 1995 had become the third longest such market in Wall Street history. It was exceeded only by the six-year bull market from 1924 to 1929 and the five-year market from August 1982 to August 1987. The market of the early 1990s pushed the Dow Jones Industrial Average (DJIA) ever upward. Quoted in points instead of dollars, the index reflects the closing stock prices of thirty widely held companies. The companies represented one-fifth of the New York Stock Exchange's total value. In November 1972 the Dow Jones broke the 1,000-point barrier, although it collapsed during the recession associated with the oil embargo imposed by the Organization of Petroleum Exporting Countries. It was not until 1987 that the DJIA broke 2,000. The 3,000 barrier was broken in 1991 and the 4,000 and 5,000 barriers in 1995.

Wall Street became populated by aggressive, take-no-prisoners business school graduates attracted by the prospect of getting rich. Much money was made in corporate takeovers in which bankers, accountants, attorneys, and management made big fees and substantial bonuses. Buffett regularly criticized chief executives who "possess an abundance of animal spirits and ego" that send them hunting for deals. "When such a CEO is encouraged by his advisers to make deals," Buffett said, "he responds much as would a teenage boy who is encouraged by his father to have a normal sex life." He added: "It's not a push he needs." Often the deals left companies awash with debt, forcing them to divest holdings, fire employees, or plunge into bankruptcy to protect themselves from creditors. James Grant, writer of an influential New York investment newsletter, noted at the time (like Buffett employing a sexual metaphor) that "the 1980s are to debt what the 1960s were to sex."

Unfortunately, the market craze had a darker side. The get-rich mentality of the 1980s led some Wall Streeters to engage in criminal practices such as insider trading. The scandals of the decade landed some of the nation's best-known financiers in jail, including Michael Milken, who had pioneered the use of junk bonds in corporate takeovers, and Ivan Boesky, who specialized in securities arbitrage. Prosecutors snared a *Wall Street Journal* reporter who was trading stocks based on information gathered from a broker who was a source for stories. The scandals provided grist for a movie, *Wall Street* (1987), directed by Oliver Stone, in which a character similar to Milken and Boesky proclaimed that "greed is good."

The stock market's upward climb was not without fast and dangerous falls. One of those was the Oct. 19, 1987, market crash, known as Black Monday. That day the exchanges almost broke under the trading volumes. The DJIA plunged a record 508 points—a 22.6 percent decline. It was the largest single-day decline in percentage terms in stock market history. The crash, which unregulated computer-directed sell orders helped accelerate, left investors wary, but they surprised observers of the market, who expected smaller investors to cash out. Instead, money was shifted into less aggressive stock investments, where the cash stayed while investors waited for the market to improve. Eventually the markets shrugged off the losses. Volume grew from 26.2 billion shares in 1982 to 103.4 billion shares in 1992. Much trading shifted from the New York Stock Exchange (NYSE) to the National Association of Securities Dealers Automated Quotations (NASDAQ). In 1983 the NYSE had 55 percent of the 39.5 billion shares traded on the U.S. exchanges, with NASDAQ responsible for 40 percent and the American Stock Exchange for 5 percent. By 1992 NASDAQ's share percentage had increased to nearly half. The tradition-bound NYSE found itself challenged by NASDAQ, which advertised itself as "the market for the next hundred years." Advertisements featured NASDAQ's stellar stocks, many of them high-technology companies that went public during the 1970s and 1980s, including Microsoft, the software corporation; Apple Computer, maker of the Macintosh computer; and Intel, whose microprocessors powered personal computers.

Throughout these years of change there was a dropping away of government and exchange rules, known as deregulation. The abolition of rules was international. In 1973 a nearly forty-year period of fixed rates for currency exchanges under the Bretton Woods Agreement of 1944 ended when major Western governments allowed currencies to be traded against each other. Supply and demand would determine the value of each currency. Freely traded currencies opened up a whole new arena for markets in which to speculate or protect against changes in currency values. Trading currencies—the U.S. dollar, Japanese yen, German mark, French franc, English pound—linked what previously were largely separate and isolated financial markets across the world. A second and this time internal U.S. deregulation occurred in 1975, when Congress forced the New York Stock Exchange to end its 183-year-old practice of fixed brokerage commissions, a reform that the Securities and Exchange Commission and others both inside and outside the exchange had pushed for years. Announced on May 1, the decision was dubbed Mayday—the international distress-call signal. For some brokerages it was just that, but others like the new brokerage house of Charles Schwab thrived. Schwab established a brokerage that offered no financial advice, merely trades at rock-bottom prices. Interestingly, the first office opened in San Francisco, not on Wall Street.

The 1980's and 1990's saw a constant expansion of new investments—some, like "derivatives," of dubious character.

A landmark in U.S. financial deregulation was the elimination in the early 1980s of Regulation Q, established by the Federal Reserve in 1933, which had limited the interest rates banks could pay on deposits. In 1966 the regulation had been extended to savings and loans. With its termination in 1982, banks and thrifts found they had to pay higher interest to attract depositors. Savers woke up to rates, looking harder at where they deposited money. Banks and thrifts had to compete for business—paying more for deposits and earning less.

The 1980s and early 1990s saw a constant expansion of new investments, and in the early 1990s a novelty known as derivatives began to raise questions. It was not easy to understand, even for professionals. In 1994 and 1995 professionals who invested heavily in derivatives, investment instruments tied to interest rates, incurred large losses when rates rose. Wealthy Orange County in southern California filed for protection from bankruptcy in 1994 because of $1.3 billion in losses in its investment in derivatives. A twenty-eight-year-old British trader in Singapore lost $1.5 billion in 1994, pushing the 233-year-old House of Baring Bank in London into bankruptcy. Also in 1994 a government bond trader at Kidder Peabody was accused of fabricating $350 million in phony profits to boost his year-end bonus; Kidder claimed it was unaware of what was going on, but was so damaged by the deals that it was sold to another brokerage. Losses resulted in calls for new regulations, although the general experience was that regulations never could keep abreast with innovations. Moreover, Wall Street regulations only encouraged trading in other markets, often those abroad.

[See also Banking and Finance.]

BIBLIOGRAPHY

Marshall E. Blume, Jeremy J. Siegel, and Dan Rottenberg, *Revolution on Wall Street: The Rise and Decline of the New York Stock Exchange* (New York, 1993).

Paul Gibson, *Bear Trap: Why Wall Street Doesn't Work* (New York, 1993).

Michael Lewis, *Liar's Poker: Rising Through the Wreckage on Wall Street* (New York, 1989)

Joseph Nocera, *A Piece of the Action: How the Middle Class Joined the Money Class (New York, 1994).*

— THOMAS G. GRESS AND BRENT SCHONDELMEYER

WAMPUM

The beads known as wampum were of great value to the American Indians, especially of the eastern Great Lakes area. The word is Algonkin, the concept appearing among the Algonkin-speakers of the Eastern Woodlands. Wampum was not a form of money, although it has sometimes been popularly and erroneously considered as such. The strings of wampum, smoothly polished tubular and disc beads of white, purple, and blue shells, with carefully woven threads, served as mnemonic devices for the recounting of events, messages, treaties, or for the correct rendition of a ritual. Among the Algonkin tribes that, under Iroquois influence in the Northeast, took on some sense of a political, fed-

erated organization, wampum served as the badge of chiefly rank. The Iroquois, in turn, borrowed the idea of wampum from their Algonkin neighbors. Related to wampum was the sacred pipestem, the calumet, which among the Algonkin and Iroquois alike was associated with the ratification of treaties and agreements. But the calumet had no mnemonic significance. Although the Algonkin tribes sometimes scratched reminders on birchbark, these too lacked the solemn symbolism of wampum. The value of wampum lay in its essentially historical quality. Solemn drama marked its display and the words associated with it.

BIBLIOGRAPHY

Ruth M. Underhill, *Red Man's America.*

— ROBERT F. SPENCER

WAPPINGER CONFEDERACY

Wappinger Confederacy, a confederation of nine Algonkin-speaking tribes that originally occupied the east bank of the Hudson River from Poughkeepsie to Manhattan Island, as well as the territory extending east to the lower Connecticut River valley. Between 1640 and 1645 they were involved in a war with the Dutch settlers, in which 1,600 Indians were killed, the principal sufferers being the Wappinger proper. As these Indians gradually dwindled in number, they sold their lands to the whites, and the survivors joined the Mahican and Nanticoke. They were finally merged with the Delaware.

BIBLIOGRAPHY

John R. Swanton, *The Indian Tribes of North America.*

— KENNETH M. STEWART

WAR CRIMES TRIALS

From November 1945 to October 1946, at Nuremberg, Germany, the surviving leaders of the Nazi regime were tried before an international tribunal (the United States, Great Britain, Russia, and France) as war criminals. They were charged with violations of international law, with having waged aggressive warfare, and in general with "crimes against humanity." Of twenty-two high officials brought to trial, nineteen were found guilty. Twelve, including Hermann Göring, Joachim von Ribbentrop, and Artur von Seyss-Inquart, were sentenced to death. Eight were eventually hanged. In addition a number of lesser officials were tried, most of whom were convicted.

Comparable trials of Japanese leaders were held at Tokyo, from May 1946 to November 1948, with similar results.

The trial of war criminals rested on the assumption that aggressive warfare was a crime, and on the still broader assumption that the principles of jurisprudence as developed in England and the United States applied to international relations as well. Yet many people objected that these principles were themselves disregarded in the trials. Thus it was charged that to try men for committing acts that were only later designated as crimes was to pass judgment *ex post facto.* The only answer to this was that the crimes of the Nazi leaders—the full magnitude of which became apparent only as the trials unfolded—were so horrible as to deserve, if not to demand, such punishment.

— CHRISTOPHER LASCH

WAR, DECLARATION OF

The power to declare war was unequivocally placed in the legislative branch of the government by the constitutional framers of 1789. But such modern apologists for asserted presidential authority as Leonard C. Meeker have invoked (inexplicably) the explicit Article I, Section 8, "Congress shall have Power . . . to declare War," as a partial basis for presidential power to initiate wars or military actions resembling wars. Under such claimed authority and, more importantly, under the power of the presidents as commanders in chief, the awesome power to initiate either general or limited wars has in actual practice become the prerogative of presidents. This transferal of power from the legislative branch to the chief executive did not result from formal interpretations of the federal courts, but evolved through the gradual acquiesence of the Congress to presidential assertions of power. Indeed, while a number of key issues involving the relations between the president and Congress regarding wars remained unresolved in the last quarter of the 20th century, early federal court decisions decisively supported congressional authority. In 1801 the Supreme Court, in *Talbot* v. *Seeman* (5 U.S. 1), flatly held that it was Congress's power to make war and that its authority embraced the power to specify the dimensions of such wars. That the president is constitutionally obligated to observe the limitations on war-making imposed by Congress is a doctrine laid down in 1804 in *Little* v. *Barreme* (6 U.S. 170). The issue raised frequently in the 20th century about the independent presidential initiation of hostilities in situations such as Vietnam was decided in 1806. Significantly the definitive decision (*United States* v. *Smith*, 27 Federal Cases 1192) was written by Supreme

Court Justice William Paterson, who had served as a delegate to the federal Convention of 1789, as a delegate to the New Jersey ratifying convention, and as a senator in the First Congress in 1789. Paterson's opinion, written while he presided in the middle circuit in New York, flatly rejected the notion that the president could legally authorize a military expedition against a nation with which the United States was at peace. Paterson stated: "That power is exclusively vested in Congress." He then asserted that "There is a manifest distinction between our going to war with a nation at peace, and a war made against us by an actual invasion, or a formal declaration. In the former case, it is the exclusive province of Congress to change a state of peace into a state of war." Paterson's conception stands in sharp contrast to the modern argument of former Secretary of State William Rogers that the presidential power to initiate hostilities was a necessary attribute of the chief executive's power to protect the nation's national security.

Controversy over the precise authority and intent of the Tonkin Gulf Resolution prompted congressional efforts to clarify the relative war powers of the executive and legislative branches.

Although Congress is granted the power to declare war, the president's dominant role in the shaping of foreign policy and in the determination of the positioning of the armed forces by virtue of his power as commander in chief has often resulted in *de facto* executive control. The last occasion in which Congress declared war (prior to actual hostilities) was the beginning of the war with Mexico in 1845. The constitutionality of President Abraham Lincoln's actions initiating military operations in the Civil War was tested in 1863 in the Prize Cases (2 Black 635). Lincoln's proclamation (April 1861) ordering the blockade of Confederate ports was held to be sufficient evidence that a state of war existed that necessitated such presidential initiative. The majority of the Court accepted the argument of one counsel, Richard Henry Dana, that "War is a state of things, and not an act of legislative will" since Lincoln felt impelled to act to save the Union despite the absence of a congressional declaration of war. In the two world wars of the 20th century the presidents in office, Woodrow Wilson and Franklin D. Roosevelt, requested Congress to recognize by a formal declaration the state of war initiated by hostilities of other nations. The controversy over Vietnam stimulated a strong Senate Foreign Relations Committee reaction to an assertion by Assistant Secretary of State Nicholas Katzenbach. In testifying on Aug. 18, 1967, Katzenbach argued that the Tonkin Gulf Resolution gave President Lyndon B. Johnson as much authority as a declaration of war. Controversy over this and other aspects of the Vietnam War ultimately brought congressional efforts to clarify the relative positions of the executive and legislative branches.

In November 1973 Congress passed, over the veto of President Richard M. Nixon, the War Powers Act, designed to restore congressional authority in an area long dominated by presidential assertions of initiatives. In its final form, the act provided that: (1) the president could commit U.S. armed forces to hostilities (or situations likely to lead to hostilities) pursuant to a declaration of war, specific statutory authorization, or a national emergency created by an attack; (2) the president should consult with Congress before committing U.S. forces; (3) the president must report in writing within forty-eight hours to the speaker of the House and president pro tempore of the Senate on combat commitments or enlargement thereof; (4) these legislative officers are authorized to reconvene Congress to consider such presidential reports; (5) troop commitments be terminated within sixty days of the president's initial report unless congressional authorization is given, war declared, or Congress is unable to convene; and (6) Congress by concurrent resolution could, in absence of a declaration of war, direct the president to disengage troops. The efficacy of this measure and Congress' support of it were challenged by Nixon's successor, Gerald R. Ford, and by Secretary of State Henry Kissinger in the mid-1970's.

BIBLIOGRAPHY

Richard A. Falk, ed., *The Vietnam War and International Law.*

Leonard Meeker, *The Legality of United States Participation in Defense of Vietnam,* bulletin of the Department of State.

William Rogers, "The President and the War Powers," *California Law Review,* vol. 59 (1971).

Francis D. Wormuth, "The Nixon Theory of the War Power: A Critique," *California Law Review,* vol. 60 (1972).

— JOHN R. SCHMIDHAUSER

WAR DEPARTMENT

War Department, the civilian agency created in 1789 to administer the field army under the president (as commander in chief) and the secretary of war. After the War of 1812 Secretary of War John C. Calhoun reorganized the department under a system of bureaus, whose chiefs held office for life, and a commanding general in the field, a position not authorized by Congress. The bureau chiefs acted as advisers to the secretary of war and at the same time commanded their own troops and field installations. Conflicts among the bureaus were frequent, but in disputes with the commanding general the secretary of war generally supported the bureaus. Congress regulated the affairs of the bureaus in minute detail, and their chiefs looked to that body for support.

The Spanish-American War demonstrated that more effective control over the department and bureaus was necessary. In 1903 Secretary Elihu Root sought to achieve this goal in a businesslike manner by appointing a chief of staff as general manager and a European-type general staff for planning. His successor, William Howard Taft, returned to the traditional secretary–bureau chief alliance, subordinating the chief of staff to the adjutant general, a powerful office since its creation in 1775.

In 1911 Secretary Henry L. Stimson and Maj. Gen. Leonard Wood, his chief of staff, sought to revive the Root reforms. The general staff assisted them in their efforts to rationalize the army's organization along modern lines and in supervising the bureaus. The bureau chiefs and Congress struck back and in the National Defense Act of 1916 reduced the size and functions of the general staff so much that few members remained when America entered World War I.

Secretary Newton D. Baker, supported by President Woodrow Wilson, opposed efforts to control the bureaus and war industry until competition for limited supplies almost paralyzed industry and transportation, especially in the North. Yielding to pressure from Congress and industry, Baker placed Benedict Crowell in charge of munitions and made Maj. Gen. George W. Goethals acting quartermaster general and Gen. Peyton C. March chief of staff. Assisted by industrial advisers, they reorganized the army's supply system and practically wiped out the bureaus as independent agencies. March reorganized the general staff along similar lines and gave it direct authority over departmental operations.

The bureaus regained their former independence from Congress after the war. Gen. John J. Pershing realigned the general staff on the pattern of his American Expeditionary Forces field headquarters. While the general staff had little effective control over the bureaus, the chiefs of staff gradually gained substantial authority over them by 1939, when Gen. George C. Marshall assumed that office.

Marshall's principal task was advising the president on military strategy; he had little time to act as general manager of the department. But the whole organization was poorly geared to direct the army in a global war, for authority and responsibility were still fragmented among many agencies, and the chief of staff was burdened with too many details. Marshall said it was a "poor command post" and, supported by Henry L. Stimson, who once again held the post of secretary of war, he reorganized it after Pearl Harbor under the War Powers Act. He created three new major commands to run the department's operations: the Army Ground Forces to train land troops; the Army Air Forces, which developed an independent air arm; and the Army Service Forces, which directed administrative and logistical operations. The Operations Division acted as Marshall's general planning staff.

After the war Marshall's organization was abandoned for the fragmented prewar pattern, while the independent services continually parried efforts to reestablish firm executive control over their operations. Under the National Security Act of 1947, as amended in 1949, the War Department became the Department of the Army within the Department of Defense and the secretary of the army an operating manager for the new secretary of defense.

BIBLIOGRAPHY

Ray S. Cline, *Washington Command Post: The Operations Division*, United States Army in World War II.

James E. Hewes, Jr., *From Root to McNamara: Army Organization and Administration, 1900–1963.*

Leonard D. White, *The Jeffersonians: A Study in Administrative History, 1801–1829.*

— JAMES E. HEWES, JR.

WAR FINANCE CORPORATION

War Finance Corporation was created by Congress on Apr. 5, 1918, to aid in the prosecution of World War I. Its chief purpose was to facilitate the extension of credit to vital war industries, primarily by making loans to financial institutions. During the six months of its wartime existence, it advanced $71,387,222. In 1919 it gave substantial financial assistance to the director general of railroads and to railroad companies, and until 1920 it served as the chief agency through which the Treasury purchased government obligations. With the return of peace, amendments to the corporation's charter greatly expanded its activities. In 1919 it became interested in financing American exports, particularly agricultural products, and in 1921 it initiated a nationwide system of loan agencies for the benefit of the agricultural and livestock industries. As a result of the passage of the Agricultural Credits Act in 1923, the active life of the corporation was terminated in 1924, after it had loaned $700 million. In many respects the corporation was the forerunner of the federal Intermediate Credit Bank and the Reconstruction Finance Corporation.

BIBLIOGRAPHY

Charles Gilbert, *American Financing of World War I.*

— CHARLES C. ABBOTT

WAR HAWKS

War Hawks was the term applied to those members of the Twelfth Congress (1811–13) whose advocacy of war with Great Britain brought on the War of 1812. Their leaders, among whom were Sen. Henry Clay and Rep. Richard M. Johnson of Kentucky, Rep. Peter B. Porter of western New York, Rep. Felix Grundy of Tennessee, and Rep. John C. Calhoun of South Carolina, came chiefly from the West and South, the regions least affected by British interference with "free trade and sailors' rights." Their enthusiasm for war may be attributed partly to their youthful exuberance—they were nearly all young men. But as spokesmen for their sections they envisioned concrete advantages as the fruit of war. Men of the Northwest commonly held the British responsible for their troubles with the Indians (exemplified in the activities of Tecumseh and the bloody encounter at Tippecanoe, Nov. 7, 1811) and expected to end these difficulties by driving the British from Canada. Southerners planned to wrest Florida from Spain, Great Britain's ally. Thus the war hawks represented the expansionist aims of the frontier.

BIBLIOGRAPHY

J. W. Pratt, *Expansionists of 1812.*

— JULIUS W. PRATT

WAR INDUSTRIES BOARD

War Industries Board, a wartime agency of 1917–18 that grew out of the efforts to coordinate American industry to war purposes. The Council of National Defense—composed of the secretaries of war, navy, agriculture, commerce, labor, and the interior—was set up in 1916 under the Army Appropriation Act. An advisory committee of seven members was also set up and included such men as Samuel Gompers and Bernard M. Baruch. The council and its advisory committee made a study of industrial and economic problems that would arise during wartime and set up agencies or boards to implement the shifting of the economy to wartime production. But the council itself enjoyed only advisory powers and could not compel any governmental or private agency to accept its advice. There were five procurement agencies in the War Department, and they frequently competed for the same materials and manufacturing facilities. The lack of planning in the program of war industries led to a serious congestion in the New England area, since the procurement agencies gave most of their contracts to firms in that area and had new factories built there. Shortages of transportation, labor, and material resulted in a serious slow-up of the war program in the winter of 1917–18.

The War Industries Board was formed in July 1917 out of the General Munitions Board of the Council of National Defense, but it was as powerless as the other agencies had been. When the extremely limited production of military equipment in the United States was discussed in Congress early in 1918, the aim of many leaders was the establishment of a munitions ministry on the English model. In order to forestall this thinly veiled censure of his administration, President Woodrow Wilson, on Mar. 4, 1918, appointed Baruch as chairman of the War Industries Board with greatly augmented powers based on an executive order. This grant of authority enabled the War Industries Board to utilize all the agencies of the Council of National Defense, to mobilize industry, and to force the adoption of its orders by the various procurement agencies of the War Department. This board had control of all available resources and manufacturing facilities. It fixed prices, raised the volume of munitions produced, and brought order out of industrial chaos. It was terminated by executive order on Jan. 1, 1919.

BIBLIOGRAPHY

Bernard M. Baruch, *American Industry in the War; A Report of the War Industries Board.*

Grosvenor B. Clarkson, *Industrial America in the War.*

— H. A. DEWEERD

WAR LABOR BOARD

War Labor Board (1918–19) consisted of joint chairmen representing the public, chosen respectively by national associations of employers and employees, and five representatives of each of these two groups. The members of the board were appointed by the secretary of labor. The creation of the board was approved and affirmed by President Woodrow Wilson in his proclamation of Apr. 8, 1918, in which he summarized its powers, functions, and duties. The function of the

John L. Lewis, president of the United Mine Workers of America, during a War Labor Board hearing. The function of the board was to secure voluntary, peaceful arbitration of industrial disputes. (UPI/Corbis-Bettmann)

board was to secure voluntary, peaceful arbitration of industrial disputes. Because the board was a nonstatutory body, its decisions were not enforceable by law; reliance for enforcement was placed principally on the patriotic cooperation of employers and employees and on public opinion. But because many of the large contracts for war supplies contained a clause requiring arbitration of disputes and adherence to awards, and because union recognition in a number of industries was established on the same grounds, an element of compulsion entered into the action of the board.

Among the major principles governing the board's adjustments were: abandonment of strikes and lockouts during the war, recognition of the right of collective bargaining, adjustment of disputes by conciliation and mediation, maintenance of maximum production, determination of wages and hours in accordance with prevailing local standards, and the recognition of the right to a living wage. By the middle of April 1919 the number of cases docketed aggregated 1,244, only 33 of which had not been disposed of.

BIBLIOGRAPHY

G. S. Watkins, *Labor Problems and Labor Administration in the United States During the World War.*

— GORDON S. WATKINS

WAR OF 1812

War of 1812 was provoked by Great Britain's maritime policy in its war with Napoleon and by its over-friendly relations with the Indian tribes of the American Northwest. The advent of the war was facilitated by the desire of the West and South to secure possession of Canada and Florida.

Neither England nor France, in their life-and-death struggle (1793–1802, 1803–15), paid much heed to the rights of neutrals. While Napoleon—through a series of decrees—sought to exclude neutral ships from all trade with Great Britain, British Orders in Council forbade neutral ships to trade with France or with French dependencies except after touching at English ports. Thus American ships conforming to the demands of one belligerent were subject to confiscation by the other. Meanwhile, Great Britain insisted on the right of its naval officers to "impress" from American ships on the high seas deserters from the Royal Navy or other British subjects liable to naval service, and bona fide American citizens were frequently the victims of this practice.

The dispute over British practices became acute in 1806 and reached a climax in 1807, when the British frigate *Leopard* fired on the U.S.S. *Chesapeake* and removed four sailors, three of them American citizens. Finding it impossible to adjust the disputes with the belligerents by negotiation, and unwilling to resort to war, President Thomas Jefferson experimented with a policy of "peaceful coercion." At his request Congress passed the Embargo Act of 1807, forbidding the departure from American ports of both American and foreign vessels, except those American ships engaged in the coastwise trade. When the embargo proved more injurious to the United States than to its intended victims, France and England, it was repealed (March 1809), and in its place the Nonintercourse Act merely forbade trade with the offending powers. This in turn gave way to Macon's Bill No. 2 (May 1810), which reopened trade with all the world, but promised that if either England or France would revoke its obnoxious measures, nonintercourse would be revived against the other.

Napoleon, through a pretended revocation of his Berlin and Milan decrees, inveigled President James

Madison into reinstituting nonintercourse against Great Britain (November 1810), and when the British government refused, until too late (June 1812, when the Orders in Council were in fact repealed), to modify its policy toward the United States, Madison called Congress a month ahead of time and on Nov. 5, 1811, recommended that that body prepare the country for hostilities.

The Twelfth Congress, which received Madison's bellicose message, proved to be dominated by the war hawks—a group of young men, chiefly from the West and South, who resented the injuries inflicted on the country by Great Britain and wished to avenge them. In their eyes, British crimes were not confined to the high seas. While western agriculture, like that of other sections, suffered from the British blockade of France, the West had peculiar grievances that were not felt along the seaboard. On the northwestern frontier, in Ohio and in the territories of Indiana, Illinois, and Michigan, the Indians, led by the enterprising Shawnee chief Tecumseh, were showing a new disposition to unite in opposition to further encroachments on their lands. It was no secret that British agents in Canada were sympathetic toward Tecumseh and his policy. It was known that the Indians received British arms and ammunition, and it was believed (somewhat unjustly) that the British were actively inciting the Indians to hostilities against American settlers. Even as Congress met, a western army under Gen. William Henry Harrison, governor of Indiana Territory, suffered severe losses in an attack by the Indians near the village of Tippecanoe (Nov. 7, 1811). Almost with one voice, the Northwest held England responsible for this bloodshed and demanded the expulsion of the British from Canada as the only remedy for Indian troubles.

It took a combination of the maritime and the frontier grievances to bring about the War of 1812 with Great Britain; neither set alone would have been sufficient.

The northwestern demand for Canada was balanced by a southwestern and southern demand for the conquest of East Florida and West Florida. These Spanish provinces were coveted because of their strategic position, their navigable rivers draining American territory, and the harborage that they gave to hostile Indians and runaway slaves. The United States had long claimed a portion of West Florida as part of the Louisiana Purchase, and had begun absorbing it piecemeal. The fact that Spain was an ally of Great Britain offered a plausible excuse for seizing the remainder of both provinces in the event of war.

These frontier grievances and ambitions occupied a prominent place in the war debates in Congress. It is impossible to disregard them in estimating the causes of the war. On the whole, it seems safe to say that it required a combination of the maritime and the frontier grievances to bring about war with Great Britain; that neither set alone would have been sufficient. Certain it is that it was the hope of the war hawks, as one of them phrased it, "not only to add the Floridas to the South, but the Canadas to the North of this empire."

On June 4, 1812, the House approved a declaration of war by a vote of seventy-nine to forty-nine. The Senate approved the declaration on June 17, by a nineteen-to-thirteen vote. Madison signed it the following day. Unfortunately, Congress had spent seven months in debating without making adequate military, naval, or financial preparation for war. The consequence of congressional trifling, of insufficient and ill-trained troops, of military incompetence in high command, and of defective strategy was a series of military disasters that, had not England's hands been tied in Europe, might have spelled national calamity. The first year of war witnessed the surrender of Gen. William Hull at Detroit (Aug. 16) and the failure of generals Stephen Van Rensselaer and Alexander Smyth on the Niagara River and of Gen. Henry Dearborn at the foot of Lake Champlain (November). The next year saw the recovery of Detroit and the defeat of the British at the Thames River (Oct. 5) by Harrison, but closed with the complete failure of Gen. James Wilkinson's campaign against Montreal (Nov. 11), the capture of Fort Niagara (Dec. 18), and the burning of Buffalo, N.Y., by the British (Dec. 29–30). By the summer of 1814, generals Jacob Brown and Winfield Scott had imbued the northern army with excellent discipline and a fighting spirit, but British veterans were now present in such force that the Americans could hope for nothing more than to hold their own. The hard fighting at Chippewa (July 5, 1814), Lundy's Lane (July 25), and Fort Erie (Aug. 2-Sept. 1) demonstrated the prowess of the U.S. Army but failed to conquer any territory.

Meanwhile, a British army landed on the shores of the Chesapeake Bay, burned Washington, D.C. (Aug. 24–25), but failed to take Baltimore (Sept. 12–14). Another, advancing from Montreal, reached Plattsburgh, N.Y., on Lake Champlain, but retreated hastily when the accompanying fleet was destroyed. At New Orleans on Jan. 8, 1815 (two weeks after the signing of the peace

treaty), Gen. Andrew Jackson inflicted on a British army under Gen. Edward Pakenham the most crushing military defeat of the war.

War in the West

When the War of 1812 was approaching, the Sioux of the Mississippi Valley, having long had their trade with the English, were strongly favorable to the English cause. The Sioux of the Missouri Valley having had American trade with Saint Louis favored the Americans. The Yanktonai, ranging from Big Stone Lake to the Missouri River, had been won to English support through the marriage of the sister of their chief to Robert Dixon, the British agent in the West. In 1811 Manuel Lisa was on the upper Missouri and, discovering the likelihood of an alliance of the Yanktonai, Hidatsa, and Mandan of North Dakota in opposition to the American interest, returned to Saint Louis to lay the matter before Capt. William Clark, then western commissioner of Indian affairs. Clark sent Lisa back to the upper Missouri with about 100 men, directing him to build a post at a point where the semihostile Indians could be best controlled. Lisa reached a point just below the forty-sixth parallel, where he built a post, strongly stockaded, which he had ready for occupation late in October 1812. From the first, the English Indians were unfriendly and difficult, and this situation became more and more critical until about Mar. 10, 1813, when the united enemy tribes fell on the fort, burned it, and killed fifteen of Lisa's men. Lisa escaped with the remnant of his men and some of his wares, and at Cedar Island, below the present Pierre, N.D., established a camp where he made an asylum for the old and destitute Sioux, taught them agriculture, purchased their furs, and kept the Sioux of the Missouri friendly and comfortable. Because the British had burned the files of the Indian office in Washington, this phase of the war was unknown to historians until the 20th century. In 1918 Stella Drumm of Saint Louis unearthed the diary of John Luttig, Lisa's chief clerk, which revealed the activities of Clark and Lisa on the Missouri.

Blockade of U.S. Seaboard

Meanwhile, the U.S. Navy had given a good account of itself. The victories on Lake Erie (September 1813) and Lake Champlain (September 1814) gave the United States control of those important waterways. The numerous single-ship actions on the high seas proved the mettle of the navy, but failed to diminish the overwhelming superiority of the British fleet, which gradually tightened its blockade on the American coast.

Although Congress declared that a state of war existed with Great Britain on June 18, 1812, the British government delayed giving orders for a blockade of the United States until November, when it instructed Adm. John B. Warren to blockade rigorously the Chesapeake and Delaware bays. The blockaded areas were gradually extended to include New York, Charleston, Port Royal, S.C., Savannah, and the mouth of the Mississippi in the spring of 1813; Long Island Sound in November 1813; and the entire eastern seaboard (including New England, previously exempt because of pro-British sentiment in that section) in May 1814.

To enforce the blockade, the British Admiralty maintained off the American coast at least ten ships of the line (necessitated by the superiority of the American 44-gun frigates over the British "thirty-eights") and a large number of frigates and sloops of war. So effective was their work that only rarely was a swift American vessel able to steal through, and maritime trade practically ceased. This was true of coastwise trade no less than of foreign trade; even the sounds and inland channels of the southern coast were penetrated by the ubiquitous blockading ships.

The effect was disastrous on both private business and government revenues. Only from Georgia, by way of Spanish Florida, and from New England up to the summer of 1814 could American produce be exported. Exports from Virginia fell from $4.8 million in 1811 to $17,581 in 1814. New York and Philadelphia suffered almost as heavily. The destruction of exports, ruinous to the farmer, forced the suspension of specie payments by all banks south of New England by the early fall of 1814. Imports, likewise, practically ceased, save through the favored New England ports; and import duties fell proportionately. Revenue from this source, more than $13 million in 1811, declined to less than $6 million in 1814, and from the ports south of New England fell close to the zero mark. Economic ruin and governmental bankruptcy were averted only by the timely termination of the war.

Peace

As an indirect result of an offer of mediation by the czar of Russia, American and British peace commissioners met at Ghent in Belgium in the summer of 1814. The Americans (Secretary of the Treasury Albert Gallatin; John Quincy Adams, American minister in Saint Petersburg; Speaker of the House Henry Clay; Sen. James A. Bayard of Delaware, a Federalist; and Jonathan Russell, former American chargé d'affaires in London) were in no position to ask for territory and soon found it necessary to drop even their demands for concessions in regard to neutral rights and impressments. The British commissioners, in their turn, abandoned their demands for boundary readjustments and for a permanent

Indian barrier state in the Northwest and at length accepted the American ultimatum of peace on the basis of the *status quo ante bellum* as to territory. The British right to navigate the Mississippi and the American right to engage in inshore fishing on the coasts of British North America, both provided in the Definitive Treaty of Peace (1783), were allowed to lapse. The fact was that both nations were war-weary, and the British government was advised by Arthur Wellesley, Duke of Wellington, that it could not hope for better terms without an expenditure of energy that it was unprepared to make.

The Treaty of Ghent, signed Dec. 24, 1814, although it gained not one of the ends for which the United States had gone to war, was joyously received in America and unanimously ratified by the Senate. It nipped in the bud a rising sectional opposition to government policy, which had appeared rather ominously in the Hartford Convention (1814–15).

The Treaty of Ghent (1814), although it gained not one of the ends for which the U.S. had gone to war, was joyously received in the States, and unanimously ratified by the Senate.

Although, measured by military achievement or by the terms of the treaty of peace, the war was a failure, it is not wholly correct to regard it as such. Through it the West and South, although indirectly, achieved their principal objectives. Canada was not conquered, but the war shattered British prestige among the Indians, ended British interference in their affairs, and left them powerless to check the American advance. In the South, although efforts to seize Florida were blocked by northern opposition, Jackson's campaign against the Creek (1813–14) opened for settlement an enormous area in Georgia and Alabama and started the train of events that ended with Spain's surrender of Florida by the Adams-Onís Treaty (1819). The cessation of impressments and of interference with neutral trade, although brought about almost entirely by the termination of the war in Europe, doubtless contributed to the feeling that the war, though ill-fought, had not been wholly devoid of profit.

BIBLIOGRAPHY

R. H. Brown, *The Republic in Peril: 1812.*

E. A. Cruikshank, ed., *The Documentary History of the Campaign Upon the Niagara Frontier, 1812–14.*

Reginald Horsman, *The Causes of the War of 1812.*

Bradford Perkins, *Prologue to War,* and *The First Rapprochement.*

Julius W. Pratt, *Expansionists of 1812.*

— JULIUS W. PRATT AND DOANE ROBINSON

WAR OPPOSITION ORGANIZATIONS

Antiwar sentiment has always been the attitude of a minority of Americans. It has a long history dating back to the colonial period, when it was especially notable among Quakers. The Society of Friends could be labeled an antiwar movement, given its organized and consistent adherence to pacifism since the 1750's, but peace was not its organizing principle. Not until the unpopular War of 1812 and its aftermath were groups formed solely on the basis of opposition to war; their makeup was middle class and their method was persuasion. In 1828 William Ladd created the American Peace Society (APS). It was political and propagandistic but, like contemporaneous reform movements, was sustained by persons whose ultimate commitment was to the abolition of slavery. Quaker abolitionists would not fight in the Civil War, but the APS supported the North. It continued its activities after the war, walking a line between the public's apathy and the radicals' dissatisfaction with its compromising tactics, a viewpoint that found expression in the Universal Peace Union (UPU). Led by Alfred Love, the UPU called for immediate disarmament, an international treaty substituting arbitration for war, and an end to imperialism; and it reached out to embrace the labor movement.

Toward the end of the 19th century, organized religion began to voice its opposition to war. The Women's Christian Temperance Union and advocates of woman's rights declared for peace. As conflict with Spain over Cuba increased, the APS felt that any attempt to resolve the crisis would be futile, while the UPU worked tirelessly to avert war. Peace found another ally in the Anti-Imperialist League, founded in 1898, which included some prominent American politicians and capitalists. In the years immediately preceding World War I over sixty peace societies were in existence. The American Society for the Judicial Settlement of International Disputes, the World Peace Foundation, the Carnegie Endowment for International Peace, and a series of peace congresses were paralleled by peace leagues and associations in the secondary schools and colleges and the expression of peace sentiments in the business world and by the American Federation of Labor. A peace bloc arose in Congress, and President Woodrow Wilson appointed a pacifist, William Jennings Bryan, as his secretary of state. War in Europe triggered the formation of the Woman's Peace Party, feminist led; the American Union

Against Militarism, antiinterventionist and antipreparedness; and the League to Enforce Peace, an international organization. But almost none of these groups could withstand the patriotic pressures of the war years. After the war blatant nationalism and militarism, abetted by the belief that World War I had been a tragic mistake, stimulated the peace movement once again. Out of the Woman's Party emerged the U.S. branch of the Women's International League for Peace and Freedom; the Quaker-influenced Fellowship of Reconciliation, created during the war, found a constituency in Protestant churches. The War Resisters' International, a secular development from the Fellowship for Reconciliation, focused on conscientious objectors. The National Council for the Prevention of War was especially effective in applying political pressure. It explicitly identified war with capitalism. College students made known their opposition to armed conflict (even forming, either fatalistically or facetiously, the Veterans of Future Wars). In 1933 thirty-seven peace organizations formed the National Peace Conference, but within two years the movements were dividing into isolationists and collective security advocates. After Pearl Harbor the movement collapsed. Because of the general popularity of World War II and the belief that pacifism in the 1930's had weakened the response to Axis aggression, the antiwar movement did not recover until the late 1950's, when the National Committee for a Sane Nuclear Policy arose to combat the horror of universal destruction and the civil rights movement showed the potential of passive resistance. But it was the war in Vietnam that brought the antiwar movement, now organized on college campuses, into the streets and made it, during the mid-1960's, a powerful political force. Although the termination of the war brought an end to the organized movement, its effect on American society was profound and pervasive.

BIBLIOGRAPHY

Joseph R. Conlin, *American Anti-War Movements.*

Merle Curti, *Peace or War: The American Struggle, 1636–1936.*

Lawrence S. Wittner, *Rebels Against War: The American Peace Movement, 1941–1960.*

— JOSEPH E. ILLICK

WAR POWERS ACT

War Powers Act (1973), officially the War Powers Resolution. According to the Constitution, the president as chief executive is also commander-in-chief of U.S. armed forces, but the Constitution explicitly assigns to Congress the authority to declare war. Rather than distinguishing clearly between the authority to initiate war and the authority to wage it, this effort to distribute war-making authority has fostered ambiguity and political controversy. In practice, chief executives have employed the U.S. military without congressional mandate virtually as a matter of routine throughout much of U.S. history, especially during the cold war. The purposes for which presidents have deployed U.S. forces range from a show of force to minor hostilities to large-scale warfare. Although such actions have not been uniformly popular, the existence of a consensus regarding U.S. foreign policy generally muted any complaint about presidents exceeding their constitutional prerogatives.

That consensus collapsed with the Vietnam War. Presidents Lyndon B. Johnson and Richard M. Nixon cited the Tonkin Gulf Resolution of August 1964 as congressional authorization for involvement in Vietnam and escalation of the U.S. role in the war. The conflict proceeded without benefit of any formal declaration of war, becoming increasingly unpopular as it dragged on. Within the federal government, opposition to the war was lodged in the Congress. Critics attributed the costly U.S. involvement in the Vietnam War to a failure to prevent successive presidents from usurping authority that rightly belonged to the legislative branch. This perception provoked calls for a reassertion of congressional prerogatives to check future presidential adventurism. Such thinking culminated in passage of the War Powers Resolution of November 1973, which was passed despite President Nixon's veto. The resolution directed the president to consult with Congress prior to introducing U.S. forces into hostilities; it required the president to report to Congress all nonroutine deployments of military forces within forty-eight hours of their occurrence; and it mandated that forces committed to actual or imminent hostilities by presidential order would be withdrawn within sixty days unless Congress declared war, passed legislation authorizing the use of U.S. forces, or extended the deadline. The sixty-day time limit could be extended to ninety days if the president certified that additional time was needed to complete the withdrawal of U.S. forces.

Heralded as a congressional triumph, the War Powers Resolution proved to be of limited use. Presidents continued to insist that the resolution was an unconstitutional infringement on executive authority. Time and again they circumvented or disregarded its provisions: Gerald Ford in 1975 at the time of the *Mayaguez* operation; Jimmy Carter in 1980 with the Desert One hostage rescue attempt; Ronald Reagan in 1983 with the intervention in Grenada and in 1986 with the air attack on Libya; and George Bush with the 1989 invasion of Panama. Even the U.S. military response to the Iraqi invasion of Kuwait in August 1990 was launched without benefit of congressional mandate. President Bush relied on executive authority in ordering the U.S. buildup of 500,000 troops in the Persian Gulf. When it came to legitimizing his action, the president showed more interest in securing the endorsement of the United Nations Security Council than of the U.S. Congress. It was only when U.S. forces were in place and the decision to use force had effectively been made that Bush consulted Congress, even then acting less for constitutional than for political reasons. On Jan. 12, 1991, Congress narrowly passed a resolution authorizing Bush to do what he clearly intended to do anyway—forcibly eject Iraqi troops from Kuwait. When four days later Operation Desert Storm began, the usefulness of the War Powers Resolution seemed more problematic than ever and the goal of restoring a division of war-making powers appeared ever more elusive.

[See also War, Declaration of; Grenada Invasion; Gulf War of 1991; Panama Invasion.]

— ANDREW J. BACEVICH

WARREN COMMISSION

On Nov. 29, 1963, President Lyndon B. Johnson appointed the U.S. Commission to Report Upon the Assassination of President John F. Kennedy and named Chief Justice Earl Warren to head it. Other members of the Warren Commission, as it is commonly known, were Sen. Richard B. Russell of Georgia; Sen. John Sherman Cooper of Kentucky; Rep. Hale Boggs of Louisiana; Rep. Gerald R. Ford of Michigan; Allen W. Dulles, former director of the Central Intelligence Agency (CIA); and John J. McCloy, former president of the World Bank and adviser to Kennedy. The commission and its staff (which included Lee J. Rankin, general counsel; Francis W. H. Adams; Joseph A. Ball; William T. Coleman; Albert E. Jenner; and Norman Redlich) reviewed reports by the Federal Bureau of Investigation (FBI) and other law enforcement agencies, and weighed the testimony of 552 witnesses, most of whom they questioned at private hearings from Feb. 3 to June 18, 1964.

In its final report, which was presented to Johnson on Sept. 24, 1964, the commission unanimously concluded that Lee Harvey Oswald alone assassinated Kennedy, that Jack Ruby alone murdered Oswald, and that neither man was part of any foreign or domestic conspiracy against the president. The report asserted that the commission had investigated and disproved twenty-two myths and rumors concerning such things as the number, origin, and direction of the shots; the number of assassins; and the possible connections between Oswald and the FBI, the CIA, and the Soviet and Cuban governments. The commission failed to identify Oswald's motive, but cited his overwhelming hostility to his environment as one of several contributing factors. The report criticized the FBI and the Secret Service for inadequately protecting the president and for poorly coordinating their information. The commission offered several recommendations for improving presidential security.

The Warren Report, the official title of which is *Report of the President's Commission on the Assassination of President John F. Kennedy*, was published and sold to the public, and aroused great controversy. Several books challenging its conclusions were published in 1966. Critics further charged that autopsy photographs and X rays, as well as motion pictures taken by eyewitness Abraham Zapruder, contradicted the commission's findings. The debate subsided, then revived again during Vice-President Nelson Rockefeller's post-Watergate investigation of the CIA in 1975. Information indicating that the CIA had plotted against Cuban Premier Fidel Castro's life led to the speculation that Kennedy might have been assassinated in retaliation. The Rockefeller Commission's Report, made public on June 10, 1975, maintained that there was no connection between any CIA activities and Kennedy's death.

BIBLIOGRAPHY

Mark Lane, *Rush to Judgment: A Critique of the Warren Commission's Inquiry Into the Murder of President John F. Kennedy, Officer J. D. Tippit, and Lee Harvey Oswald.*

William R. Manchester, *The Death of a President.*

— WILLIAM P. DUNKEL

WARSHIPS

Sailing Warships

On Oct. 13, 1775, the Continental Congress ordered the purchase of two merchantmen for conversion to fighting ships. Later, additional vessels were constructed and purchased, including frigates, brigs, sloops, and schooners. In 1777 the Continental Navy reached its peak strength with thirty-four ships and approximately 4,000 men. The navy guarded convoys to the West Indies and Europe, conducted commerce raiding, and fought several ship-to-ship actions, the most famous of which was the *Bonhomme Richard*, commanded by John Paul Jones, against the British *Serapis*.

After gaining its independence, the United States sold all its naval ships. In 1794, however, the depradations of Barbary pirates against American shipping led Congress to authorize the building of six frigates. In 1798–1800, during the Quasi-War with France, the superiority of American frigates was demonstrated by the victories of the *Constellation*, commanded by Commodore Thomas Truxtun, over the *Insurgente* (Feb. 9, 1799) and over the *Vengeance* (Feb. 1–2, 1800). In the Barbary Wars, 1801–05 and 1815, U.S. squadrons of fighting sail brought the rulers of these North African states to terms.

During the administration of Thomas Jefferson, the government, in order to cut defense costs, replaced large sailing warships with boats carrying one or two guns. These vessels were of little value.

At sea the War of 1812 was essentially a frigate war. When hostilities erupted the navy had seven of these large, swift, and heavily armed ships. The victories of such American frigates as the *Constitution* (Capt. Isaac Hull) over the *Guerrière* on Aug. 19, 1812, and the *United States* (Commodore Stephen Decatur) over the *Macedonian* on Oct. 25, 1812, shocked Britain and immediately caused the British navy to upgrade its frigate designs.

America possessed such outstanding shipbuilders as Joshua Humphreys, Josiah Fox, and William Doughty. During the period 1815–50, powerful American ships of the line, such as the 74-gunners *Washington* and *Ohio*, formed the backbone of the navy. These ships, unmatched in their class, served in the Mediterranean and the Orient guarding U.S. commerce and diplomatic interests.

Changes in naval technology made inevitable the demise of the sailing warship. In 1817 the navy listed 110 sailing ships and one steam vessel; by 1845, when the Mexican War began, the navy had 67 sailing ships and 9 steam-powered ships. The trend toward steam was clear. When the Civil War ended the navy had 681 ships, of which only 109 were sail. By the 1870's the era of the sailing warships was over.

— PAUL B. RYAN

Steam and Nuclear Warships

The first steam warship, the *Demologos* ("Voice of the People"), was designed by Robert Fulton for the defense of New York against the British in the War of 1812. Completed after the end of hostilities, it was destroyed by an accidental explosion in 1829. Except for the *Sea Gull*, a tiny steamer purchased in 1822 for service against the West Indian pirates, the *Demologos* had no successors until 1837, when the large steam frigate *Fulton* was launched in New York. By this time there were already several hundred successful commercial steamers in the United States, but American naval experts remained skeptical about the value of steam for warships. The large paddle wheels of the steamers presented vulnerable targets and limited the amount of space that could be devoted to broadside batteries.

These problems were largely solved with the adoption of the screw propeller to replace the paddle wheel. The American frigate *Princeton*, launched in 1843, was the first warship to be fitted with the new device. By the outbreak of the Civil War the United States possessed twenty wooden, screw-propelled men-of-war, such as the sloop-of-war *Hartford*, Adm. David G. Farragut's flagship at the Battle of New Orleans.

The Civil War marked the beginning of an era of intense experimentation and rapid innovation in naval warfare. The battle between the ironclads C.S.S. *Virginia* (actually the captured Union *Merrimack*) and the U.S.S. *Monitor* at Hampton Roads in 1862 ushered in the era of armored steam warships. The *Monitor* and the *Virginia* were not the first armored warships (there were nearly fifty completed or under construction in Europe at the time of the battle), but they were the first to fight another armored ship and the first to be powered entirely by steam. In the period 1860–90 armor improved in quality, guns increased in power, mines became more reliable, and the self-propelled torpedo, perfected around 1870, introduced a dangerous new factor into naval warfare.

The Civil War marked the beginning of an era of intense experimentation and rapid innovation in naval warfare.

For some years after 1865 the United States took little part in the frantic search for ever more powerful naval weapons. Although the American navy consisted mainly of old wooden cruisers and Civil War-type monitors armed with obsolete smoothbore cannon, Congress was reluctant to appropriate money for new warships until 1883, when approval was at last given for three modern steel cruisers, the *Atlanta, Boston*, and *Chicago*, and a dispatch boat, the *Dolphin*, which were to form the nucleus of the "New Navy" of the 1890's.

By the time of the Spanish-American War (1898) the United States possessed a respectable fleet, including four battleships, three other armored ships, and more than a score of cruisers, gunboats, and torpedo boats. The war with Spain gave added impetus to naval expansion, and by 1907 President Theodore Roosevelt was able to send a fleet of sixteen battleships on a goodwill cruise around the world. Yet all sixteen were by that time out-of-date, rendered obsolete by a new British battleship, the *Dreadnought*, which was faster and slightly larger than contemporary battleships and carried only guns of the largest caliber, with some light weapons to protect it against torpedo boats.

This combination of speed and firepower enabled the *Dreadnought* to outrange and outshoot any contemporary battleship. The first American all-big-gun ships, the *South Carolina* and *Michigan*, had actually been planned before the *Dreadnought* but were not completed until 1910.

With the introduction of the Dreadnought class, warships assumed the general characteristics they would retain for the next fifty years. Besides the battleship, there was the heavy cruiser, developed toward the end of World War I, a fast, lightly armored ship of about 10,000 tons, armed with 8-inch guns and used for scouting, patrolling, and raiding commerce; the light cruiser, usually smaller than the heavy cruiser and mounted with 6-inch guns; and the destroyer, a small, fast ship of 1,000 to 2,000 tons armed with torpedoes and a few 4- or 5-inch guns. Originally designed as a destroyer of torpedo boats, the destroyer soon usurped their function and also proved invaluable against submarines. The submarine itself grew from a small vessel of less than 200 tons to a formidable weapon of war that could threaten the survival of even the strongest seapower.

The most important new warship developed between the two world wars was the aircraft carrier. Unlike other warships, the aircraft carrier's principle weapon was not its own armament but the bombs and torpedoes of the planes that were able to take off and land at sea from its large flat deck. In World War II the aircraft carrier made possible naval battles between fleets hundreds of miles apart in which the opposing surface forces never sighted each other.

The most striking development in warship design after World War II was the use of nuclear power as a propulsion source, employed first in the submarine U.S.S. *Nautilus* in 1954. Besides giving warships greater speed and reliability, nuclear power made them virtually independent of their bases. The nuclear submarine *Triton*, for example, can operate for almost two years without refueling. The success of the *Nautilus* led the U.S. Navy to apply nuclear propulsion to surface ships; and in the early 1960's three nuclear-powered vessels—the U.S.S. *Enterprise*, a carrier, the *Long Beach*, a cruiser, and the *Bainbridge*, a frigate or super destroyer—were completed. All were considerably larger than their World War II counterparts. The *Bainbridge* at 8,580 tons was nearly as large as a conventional cruiser, while the *Enterprise* at 85,000 tons was more than twice the size of the World War II carrier.

Beginning in the late 1950's, missile weapons began to replace guns as the primary armament of the larger surface ships. A typical American warship of the 1970's carried antisubmarine and antiaircraft missiles of various types in addition to, or instead of, its gun armament. A ship-to-ship missile was also under development in the U.S. Navy and was already in use in some foreign fleets.

— RONALD SPECTOR

Battleships

By the time of the American Revolution ordinary ships were still being armed with cannon in rough-and-ready conversion to warships; a famous instance was the French East Indiaman that John Paul Jones named the *Bonhomme Richard.* But throughout the 18th century increases in the size and penetration power of cannon necessitated the thickening of a warship's hull, thus increasing its cost at least three times that for a merchantman of identical dimensions. As the *Bonhomme Richard* was actually sunk by the much stouter *Serapis*, combat between an extemporized and a true warship was generally fatal for the former. Yet, since only a nation could afford to build warships, especially the giants "fit to lie in the line of battle" (and hence originally called "ships of the line"), converted merchantmen were generally used for privateering or raiding. By 1900 "battleship" had its present meaning and was sometimes listed as a "capital ship." After 1928 capital ships included aircraft carriers.

Although the *South Carolina* and *Michigan* anticipated (on the drawing board) the definitive "all-big-gun, centerline turrets" design, the British *Dreadnought* was afloat before them in 1906 and its name became a synonym for battleship. The largest battleships ever were the World War II Japanese Yamato class of 63,000 tons, with nine 17.9-inch guns. The toughest battleship, perhaps, was the German *Bismarck*, 52,000 tons with eight 15-inch guns.

The 1921–22 Washington Naval Conference stemmed the battleship race. Although the United States had parity with Great Britain and was allowed fifteen modern vessels, it had only ten "treaty" battleships by World War II. It had scrapped an eleventh. Yet only the old *Arizona* and *Oklahoma* were destroyed at Pearl Harbor, chiefly because of the amazing new antiaircraft shell fuse and its close working relationship with aircraft carriers. All ten treaty ships had 16-inch main batteries. Six of the vessels displaced 35,000 tons: the 1940–41 *North Carolina, Washington, Alabama, Indiana, Massachusetts,* and *South Dakota*; and four others displaced 45,000 tons: *Iowa, Missouri, New Jersey,* and *Wisconsin.* Their collective durability was outstanding in a war in which the British lost five battleships, the French six, the Japanese eleven (their all), the Germans four (their all), and the Italians three. No conventional battleship was sunk after World War II, although American ships served during the Korean and Vietnam wars.

By 1975 the rocket had eclipsed the gun. Some authorities have claimed that future battleships will be modeled on either the U.S. frigates or the Russian *Variag,* which has two pairs of quadruple launching mounts for 33-foot missiles. It is estimated that these missiles can soar 300 miles at the speed of sound.

Cruisers

During the era of wooden ships, the term "cruiser" denoted a form of duty rather than a type of ship, namely, the task of sailing along trade routes either to attack or to defend merchantmen. Even ships of the line (the largest class of ships) might be so employed, as the British had done when they had more ships than any other nation. Frigates and smaller men-of-war, however, were the everyday cruisers. The duty of attacking commerce was always coveted because of the opportunities for prize money.

The introduction of steam, horizontal shellfire, and armor confused the matter with respect to size for a few decades; for example, the 776-ton *Monitor* could easily have destroyed the biggest unarmored ships afloat if any ventured within range of its two 11-inch guns. Thus the entire classification of naval vessels was jumbled. When it became apparent that speed was a good defense, the unarmored ship became popular; and the cruiser gradually evolved into the now familiar warship, rated just below the relatively ponderous battleship.

The first American cruisers by type were designed in 1882: the 4,500-ton *Chicago* and the 3,000-ton *Atlanta* and *Boston.* Heralded as the "cavalry of the seas" for their speed of 14 knots, the *Chicago,* bearing an 8-inch rifled main battery, and the other two, bearing 6-inch main batteries, could overtake most extant merchantmen and easily evade battleships with 12-inch guns. The *Chicago* was protected by a thin armor deck over its vitals because rifled projectiles had a trajectory at long ranges that made them plunge onto targets. This ship was a prototype of the heavy cruiser and was classed as "CA," or heavy cruiser, in the 1920's. Later CAs retained 8-inch guns but added belt armor to protect propulsion spaces, gun turrets, and control positions. The thickness of armor was calculated to stop 8-inch projectiles on the premise (carried over from sail-ship construction) that a vessel's side should stop the penetration of a shot identical to the size of its main battery. The light cruiser (CL) had 5- or 6-inch guns and equivalent armor.

Naval architects successfully sought greater speeds, the wisest defense against battleships and the best offense against commerce and weaker warships. The 1889 protected cruiser *Charleston* made 19 knots and the 1904 *Charleston* made 22; later cruisers reached a plateau of 33 knots with the 1942 *Rochester.* The speed of the nuclear-powered *Long Beach* has been kept secret. Light cruisers are generally a knot or two faster than heavy cruisers.

Naval architects successfully sought greater speeds, the wisest defense against battleships and the best offense against commerce and weaker warships.

Tonnage rose a little more quickly. The 1889 *Charleston* was 3,730 tons and the second *Charleston* was 9,700 tons. World War I classes leveled off at approximately 14,000 tons, including the mined *San Diego,* the largest vessel lost by the United States in that conflict. In World War II the 8-inch guns of America's thirty-two heavy cruisers were mainly used in shore bombardments. More frequently they used their secondary batteries for antiaircraft fire, as did most of the forty-two light cruisers. Indeed, the *Atlanta* and *Juneau* (five-inch, 38-gun light cruisers) were designed as antiaircraft vessels. Altogether, ten cruisers were lost during World War II.

In 1973 heavy cruisers were the largest gunships in commission and almost invariably were flagships.

Destroyers

The invention by Robert Whitehead of England of a self-propelled torpedo in 1868 instigated a race to build speedboats capable of using the new weapon. Some enthusiasts thought that these vessels would supersede all other kinds of warships. By 1884 Russia had 138 such speedboats, Britain 130, and France 107. The first speedboat in the United States, the *Cushing* (1890), so impressed Secretary of the Navy Benjamin F. Tracy that he requested 100 more. But Congress authorized only one, the *Ericsson.* Finally completed in 1897, its design was typical: three 18-inch torpedo tubes and four 1-pounder quick firers. Manned by a crew of 22, the vessel could travel at 24 knots and its hull measured 150 feet by 15.5 feet, drawing 4 feet 9 inches and displacing 120 tons.

Congressional reluctance was soon justified because a ship designed specifically as a torpedo-boat destroyer was proving far superior. The 1900 *Decatur,* for instance, had two 18-inch tubes, a pair of 3-inch guns, and a crew of 73 going 28 knots in a hull 250 feet long,

24 feet wide, and drawing 6.5 feet, displacing 450 tons. A second *Decatur*, used during World War II, had four 18-inch tubes, four 4-inch and two 3-inch guns, and 126 men, went 36 knots, was 314 feet long, and weighed 1,190 tons. This was the famous "four-piper" type, of which fifty were leased to Britain in 1940 after the Battle of Dunkirk. The 1956 *Decatur* had similar torpedo armament plus additional armament for anti-submarine attack, three 5-inch and four 3-inch guns, and 311 men, went 33 official knots, and displaced 3,800 tons. Experimentation in the 1970's with hydrofoils, "surface effects," and "captured air bubbles" and possibilities of speeds in excess of 100 knots may radically alter the form but not the multiple roles of future destroyers.

The United States had 267 destroyers in World War I and none were lost. Of the 459 destroyers used in World War II, 71 were lost, plus 11 of the 498 lesser version known as the destroyer escort.

Frigates

Among sailing vessels, the frigate was the intermediate man-of-war and was principally employed as a cruiser. Present at battles between ships of the line, frigates had the subordinate roles of repeating signals from the flagship, towing disabled ships, and rescuing survivors. Generally frigates never fired at ships of the line in single duel, except for token shots "for the honor of the flag." On its weatherdeck a heavy frigate carried from 38 to 44 long guns, usually 18- or 24-pounders. In addition, it could have as many as a dozen short-range guns called carronades, which fired up to 68-pounder shot, albeit these were uncounted in classifying a frigate's "rate" because their effective range was under 300 yards. A light frigate had from 24 to 36 long guns, 12- or 18-pounders. Rarely was a frigate exclusively armed with carronades, as was the ill-destined *Essex*, the adversaries of which bombarded it (beyond carronade range) into surrender. Even the first U.S. frigates were exceptionally sturdy compared to those of the British and were armed as heavily as practicable. Thus the stirring victories during the War of 1812. The most famous frigate was the 44-gun *Constitution* (which was still afloat in Boston in 1975, as was the 38-gun *Constellation* in Baltimore).

The advent of horizontally fireable shells—differing from the long-standing use of mortars or "bombs"—and steam propulsion confused the rating of warships. For instance, the 1854 steam frigate *Merrimack* could engage any man-of-war afloat even before its metamorphosis into the Confederate ironclad *Virginia*. By the 1870's the frigate was more commonly called the cruiser.

World War II and British usage revived the term "patrol frigate" to designate convoy escorts larger than destroyer escorts. The 100 patrol frigates built by the United States had an exceptionally long range: 17,000 miles at an economical 11 knots. Some 28 of these vessels were lend-leased to the Soviet Union to form the core of a Pacific fleet for service against Japan. After 1945 many of the frigates were sold or given to such friendly nations with small navies as Colombia and South Korea.

In 1975 an American frigate like the *Mitscher* had the displacement of a World War II light cruiser, might be nuclear powered, and was armed principally with missiles.

— R. W. DALY

BIBLIOGRAPHY

James P. Baxter III, *The Introduction of the Ironclad Warship.*
Frank M. Bennett, *The Steam Navy of the United States.*
Bernard Brodie, *Seapower in the Machine Age.*
Howard L. Chapelle, *The History of the American Sailing Navy.*
Philip Cowburn, *The Warship in History.*
Alexander Laing, *American Sail.*
Bjorn Landstrom, *The Ship.*
Harold and Margaret Sprout, *The Rise of American Naval Power, 1776–1918.*

WASHINGTON NAVAL CONFERENCE

Washington Naval Conference (1921–22), officially the International Conference on Naval Limitation, was called by the United States to deal with a naval armaments race and the problems of security in the Pacific. All the principal powers attended, with the exception of the Soviet Union, which government the major powers did not recognize, and Germany.

U.S. Secretary of State Charles Evans Hughes astonished the opening session with a proposal for the scrapping of 1,878,043 tons of capital ships (battleships and battle cruisers) by the United States, Great Britain, and Japan, and a ten-year holiday on their construction by these same powers as well as France and Italy.

Subsequently, nine treaties were drafted and signed by the participants. The four major treaties were (1) the Four-Power Treaty (Dec. 13, 1921), involving the United States, Great Britain, France, and Japan (the Big Four), in which the signatories promised to respect each others' rights over island possessions in the Pacific; (2) another Big Four treaty, in which each country agreed to consult the others in the event of "aggressive action" by another power; (3) the Five-Power Naval Treaty (Feb. 6, 1922), declaring a ten-year holiday on capital ship construction and fixing the ratio of capital ship tonnage between the United States, Great Britain, Japan, France, and Italy at 5:5:3:1.67:1.67; and (4) the Nine-Power Treaty (also signed Feb. 6) in which all of the conference participants (the Big Four, Italy, Portugal, China, Belgium, and the Netherlands) affirmed the Open Door principle for China and agreed to respect China's territorial integrity and independence. A fifth treaty restricted the use of submarines during war and outlawed poison gases. The four remaining treaties dealt with increased Chinese sovereignty and U.S. and Japanese cable rights in the Pacific.

The conference's accomplishments, although less than some contemporary leaders claimed, were substantial. The post-World War I capital ships arms race was halted by the first naval disarmament agreement among the major powers. China's integrity was maintained until the Japanese occupation of Manchuria in 1931. Finally, because of the extensive scrapping of naval tonnage by the United States, Great Britain, and Japan and the agreements between the Big Four on the Pacific, general security in the area was much enhanced.

BIBLIOGRAPHY

Thomas A. Bailey, *A Diplomatic History of the American People.*
Samuel Flagg Bemis, *A Diplomatic History of the United States.*
Thomas H. Buckley, *The United States and the Washington Conference.*

— JOHN R. PROBERT

WASHINGTON'S FAREWELL ADDRESS

Washington's Farewell Address, first published on Sept. 19, 1796, in the *Philadelphia Daily American Advertiser*, set forth George Washington's reasons for not running for a third term as president. He had hoped to evade his second election and had roughed out a declination at that time; but political pressure and the critical state of U.S. foreign relations forced a change of purpose. Reasons for the inclusion of other matters than a simple declination of candidacy are to be found in Washington's habit of mind and honest love of his country. The first part of the address gives his reasons for retiring; the second presents his reflections on the necessity of a strong union of the states and the principles upon which permanent domestic contentment could be maintained and foreign respect compelled; the third, and briefest part, justified his neutrality toward France and England. That justification was merged with the more important principles of the address, which flowered from his deeply rooted personal experiences in managing a revolutionary army for eight years of disheartening war and directing an untried form of republican government for eight years of difficult peace. The unselfish honesty of his hope that the address would be of some occasional good in moderating the fury of party spirit, warning against foreign intrigue, and guarding against the impostures of pretended patriotism does not entirely conceal the deep wound inflicted on his sensibilities by the malignant and unscrupulous political enemies of his administration. But the address is, nonetheless, one of the world's remarkable documents. After so many years it still remains a wholesome political guide to the people of the nation to whom it was addressed. It was never publicly read by Washington.

BIBLIOGRAPHY

Victor H. Paltsits, *Washington's Farewell Address.*

— JOHN C. FITZPATRICK

WATERGATE, AFTERMATH OF

The term "Watergate" has resonated in America's collective consciousness since the scandals and crimes committed during the 1972 presidential election campaign by members of President Richard M. Nixon's administration became public. The exposé published by the *Washington Post*, which revealed that the burglary of National Democratic Party headquarters on June 17, 1972, at the Watergate apartment-office complex in Washington, D.C., was committed by employees of the Committee to Reelect the President, arguably encouraged investigative journalism and accentuated the adversarial relationship between government and media. Congress acted quickly after the Senate Watergate hearings in 1973 by enacting laws limiting executive control over foreign policy, notably the War Powers Act of 1973, passed in November over President Richard M. Nixon's veto shortly after what came to be called the "Saturday Night Massacre," when Nixon fired Special Watergate Prosecutor Archibald Cox. Congress enacted campaign finance reforms, conflict-of-interest legislation, stronger freedom of information statutes, and protection of privacy laws. The Ethics in Government Act of 1978 provided for judicially appointed special independent prosecutors to investigate executive wrongdoings.

The Iran-Contra affair of 1985–1986 during President Ronald Reagan's administration—with a similar cast of characters, embattled presidential aides, televised congressional hearings and special prosecutor—evoked a sense of Watergate déjà vu, although this time Congress stopped short of impeaching a popular president. The suffix "-gate" became a descriptive label to denote political scandals: "Korea-gate" involved bribes of members of Congress by South Korean agents in 1976–1978; "Billygate" referred to President Jimmy Carter's brother Billy and his connection to the Libyan government; and "Iraq-gate" concerned secret and illegal loans to Iraq by the administrations of Reagan and George Bush before the Persian Gulf War of 1991. Other terms that emerged during the Watergate investigations and hearings—"smoking gun," "dirty tricks," "enemies list," and "stonewall"—have remained in political parlance.

Political analysts noted a "post-Watergate morality," a new set of expectations about the ethical behavior of public officials. Remembrance of past transgressions led to watchful surveillance. Law schools offered more courses on legal ethics. Public-interest organizations such as Common Cause tripled in membership. In 1977 the House and Senate passed new codes of conduct for its members on financial disclosure, imposed limits on outside income, and added new restrictions on campaign fund-raising. States passed similar laws. Private as well as public morality of government officials came under scrutiny, such as when a special prosecutor was appointed to investigate a presidential aide accused of cocaine use. As the media investigated the sexual behavior of presidential candidates and Supreme Court nominees, some people reportedly shunned public office lest they endure the media circus and public exposure mandated by post-Watergate reforms. Whether a healthy concern for public ethics had become an obsession, Watergate irrevocably changed political mores in the United States.

Debate continues over whether Watergate was a constitutional crisis or a personal aberration. Investigations in the aftermath of Watergate exposed assassination plots by the Central Intelligence Agency and other abuses of power by presidents before Nixon. Defenders of Nixon made it seem that his greatest crime was in getting caught. It became less clear which Watergate offenses Nixon alone had perpetrated (obstruction of justice) and which had become routine during an arrogant, imperial presidency. A conservative interpretation thus depicted Watergate as more scandal than crisis, a morality play in which Nixon's liberal enemies in the press and Congress harried the president from office over minor offenses. A British historian called Watergate "the first media Putsch in history, as ruthless and anti-democratic as any military coup by bemedaled generals with their sashes and sabers." The liberal interpretation downplayed the media story and depicted Watergate as raising "weighty questions of governance, especially concerning the role of the presidency and its relation to other institutions in the governmental apparatus." Liberals advocated a number of campaign financing reforms and limitations on presidential power, including a special prosecutor mechanism to prevent future Watergates, none of which has operated very effectively. Conservatives contended that the system worked without the need for additional safeguards. By contrast, radical historians characterized Nixon's 1974 resignation and subsequent pardon by President Gerald Ford as "an inexpensive expiation" that prevented a fundamental reevaluation of the American national security state and reinforced a two-tier system of justice that does not hold top U.S. politicians accountable for illegal or unconstitutional actions.

Debate continues over whether Watergate was a constitutional crisis or a personal aberration.

A 1987 Gallup Poll asked Americans what major events had most affected their thinking. Only 5.9 percent listed Watergate, placing it behind the Vietnam War, Ronald Reagan's presidency, and the Great Depression. Apparently, most Americans remember Watergate more as a frothy scandal than as a serious constitutional crisis. Nixon's later efforts at political rehabilitation reflected the continuing ambiguity of Watergate. In televised interviews in 1977, he claimed he "did not commit a crime, an impeachable offense," although "I did let down our system of government." His memoirs, published the following year, asked for public acceptance and public sympathy. Watergate, he predicted, would get only a footnote when future historians assessed his foreign policy triumphs. With more books on foreign affairs, international trips, op-ed pieces, the opening of the Nixon Library in 1990, his advice solicited by Presidents Reagan, Bush, and Bill Clinton, Nixon seemed to achieve the status of elder statesman before he died in 1994, but his Gallup Poll approval rating in 1990 had risen to only 38 percent (from 24 percent in 1974), indicating that Watergate remained "the spot that will not out." The eulogies at Nixon's funeral notwithstanding, the subsequent publication of diaries by key individuals involved in Watergate and documentaries commemorating the twentieth anniversary of Watergate reminded everyone that Nixon was the first president to resign because of a constitutional crisis.

[See also Iran-Contra Affair; Nixon, Resignation of.]

BIBLIOGRAPHY

Stephen E. Ambrose, *Nixon: Ruin and Recovery* (New York, 1991).
Katy Harriger, *Independent Justice* (Lawrence, Kans., 1991).
Godfrey Hodgson, *All Things to All Men: The False Promise of the Modern American Presidency* (New York, 1980).
Joan Hoff, *Nixon Reconsidered* (New York, 1994).

Stanley Kutler, *The Wars of Watergate: The Last Crisis of Richard Nixon* (New York, 1980).
Tom Wicker, *One of Us: Richard Nixon and the American Dream* (New York, 1991).

— J. GARRY CLIFFORD

WELFARE

Welfare in the United States generally refers to the complex of social insurance programs such as social security, disability insurance, Medicare, and public assistance programs of two varieties: in-kind programs, such as food stamps, the Special Supplemental Food Program for Women, Infants, and Children (WIC), and Medicaid; and income maintenance programs, such as Aid to Families with Dependent Children (AFDC), generally known as welfare, and General Assistance (GA), relief provided by the states. In the years since these programs came into being, social welfare policy has been constantly debated and adjusted. Public assistance of the 1990s had its roots in the Social Security Act of 1935. The Great Depression shattered many of the myths about the ability of the United States to provide full employment to all citizens, and the ability of people to "pull themselves up by their own bootstraps." Although private assistance was available from voluntary organizations and from churches, these services could not meet the great need in the 1930s. In the 1960s the Great Society programs of President Lyndon B. Johnson's administration were established. Welfare reform in these years consisted of extending AFDC to families with unemployed fathers, authorizing work training, and adding social services to move people off the welfare rolls. The trend of poverty and welfare programs also was to increase benefits to the elderly. There were new in-kind programs, such as housing subsidies, public housing units, and nutritional programs. In 1970 Congress made food stamps available at no cost to families below the poverty line, mostly welfare recipients, and at a small price to those just above the poverty line, the so-called working poor.

The Great Depression shattered confidence in the ability of the U.S. to provide full employment to all citizens and in people's ability to "pull themselves up by their own bootstraps."

Most of the increase in welfare spending during the last quarter of the twentieth century was in the AFDC program. In addition to loosened eligibility, participation rates among the eligible rose sharply. One reason for the increase was worsening economic conditions for black Americans due to the mechanization of southern agriculture, which pushed blacks northward into cities where automation and deindustrialization were greatly reducing the number of factory jobs. Another reason for higher participation rates was the "feminization of poverty," due to the increasing divorce rate, increased out-of-wedlock births, continuing gender discrimination in employment, and increased activity by welfare rights organizations. The overall poverty rates declined in 1960–1986. By some accounts white poverty decreased by 38 percent, black poverty by 26 percent. Child poverty, although dropping precipitously between 1960 and 1974 (from 27 percent to 15 percent), subsequently increased to 21 percent in 1986. The rise in female-headed households was largely responsible for this trend.

Although always controversial, welfare became a political target in the mid-1970s, when large-city and federal deficits increased tremendously. The "welfare state" was characterized as out of control. In many states General Assistance was the first program cut through "welfare reform," because it was the program whose recipients were most "employable." Young single people who were not parents, regardless of their skills or prospects for finding or holding a job providing a living wage, were cut from the GA rolls. Despite talk of job training or retraining, very few of these individuals went into the workforce. They were more likely to end up in homeless shelters, whose numbers were growing. Other public assistance benefits slipped between the mid-1970s and the mid-1980s. The maximum AFDC benefit dropped by one-third and the combined AFDC and food stamp benefits dropped by one-fifth.

In the 1980s major welfare cuts were enacted during the administration of President Ronald Reagan. Supplemental Security Income (SSI), granted to people of any age unable to work for at least one year because of disabilities since the 1960 and 1965 amendments to the Social Security Act, was withdrawn from 200,000 recipients. People with mental disabilities were particularly vulnerable to being ruled ineligible. AFDC sustained a large cut. By 1983, 408,000 people lost eligibility, and 299,000 lost their benefits. The average dollar loss to an AFDC family was $1,555 per year, and the savings to federal and state governments were $1.1 billion. Between 1982 and 1985 total funds spent on unemployment insurance went down 6.9 percent, food stamps went down 12.6 percent, child nutrition programs were cut 27.7 percent, housing assistance 4.4 percent, and low-income energy assistance 8.3 percent. Only WIC was increased.

Welfare policy was criticized by both political parties, by conservatives and liberals, and by other groups. One conservative argument is that welfare is antilibertarian. This criticism is based on the assumption that welfare redistributes income. Conservatives also state that welfare has failed to end poverty, crime, and lack of education. A third argument is that welfare costs too much, given the lack of significant results. Another is that the federal role in welfare programs is too great and constitutes "social engineering." Another argument is that welfare erodes family values. Liberal arguments against welfare claim that it has failed to reduce economic inequality, that welfare programs cannot counteract the distributive injustice resulting from a capitalist system, and that welfare does not promote collective responsibility, but provides scapegoats for workers who have been able to find employment.

A feminist criticism of welfare is that while gender has been a fundamental organizing principle of the welfare system, it has been largely invisible. When gender is brought into view, it becomes apparent that there is a double standard for men and women: welfare policy accepts the premise that women, particularly mothers, should be at home and supported by men. The alternatives offered to women are dependence on the state through AFDC or independence through work. Because programs to train and employ AFDC recipients have never been wholeheartedly supported by sufficient funding and private sector cooperation, and because backing in the larger society in the form of equal job opportunities for women, equal pay, and high-quality affordable day care have been slow in coming, it can be surmised that as a society, Americans prefer to keep women dependent. The stigmatizing of recipients makes welfare an unattractive alternative to being supported by men. Therefore, it can be argued, the welfare system in the United States functions to keep women dependent on men and men dependent on work.

In the public discourse on welfare, a distinction is made between the "deserving" and "undeserving" poor. Throughout welfare history there has always been a preoccupation with such groupings. The deserving poor are those who "through no fault of their own" have fallen from a higher economic level to a temporary and reluctant dependency on the state. The undeserving are characterized as dependent by nature, having different values and aspirations than productive Americans, and lacking morality, restraint, and decorum. There is also a racial element in these characterizations, with the undeserving poor most often assumed to be African American. There are still other presumed shortcomings of the welfare system. One is that public assistance grants are too small to permit a decent standard of living and do nothing to get recipients out of poverty. By design these programs do not allow recipients to build equity of any kind, and therefore it is extremely difficult for them to improve their situation. Public assistance recipients (less so for recipients of social insurance) are stigmatized in U.S. society. Prior to the passage of the Family Support Act of 1988, only twenty-eight states had AFDC-UP (Aid to Families with Dependent Children—Unemployed Parent [father]) programs. Elsewhere, families with two parents were ineligible for assistance, which encouraged fathers to desert wives and children so they could obtain assistance. Even three years after the passage of that act only 7.1 percent of AFDC recipients received benefits based on unemployment in a two-parent family. Another criticism is that AFDC and other public assistance programs are bureaucratized, overregulated, and hence inefficient. Further, there are loopholes in eligibility. It is possible to be very poor with no real prospect of work and still be ineligible for assistance. Potential recipients can be denied benefits in some states until the sixth month of pregnancy with their first child; if they are under eighteen and not in school; if their income has dropped within two months from a level at which they would be ineligible; or if there is a stepfather living in the home, regardless of his willingness to support the applicant child.

Although welfare is usually discussed in terms of the altruistic and moral purposes that this set of programs serves, or fails to serve, historical analysis shows the expansions and contractions of welfare benefits in functional terms. Some researchers assert that the two principal functions of welfare are maintaining civil order and enforcing work. The assistance programs begin or expand during times of widespread unemployment and civil unrest and decrease when order is restored to provide an incentive for work.

[See also Budget, Federal; Medicare and Medicaid; Poverty.]

BIBLIOGRAPHY

Linda Gordon, ed., *Women, the State, and Welfare* (Madison, Wis., 1990).

Michael B. Katz, *In the Shadow of the Poorhouse: A Social History of Welfare in America.* (New York, 1986), and *The Undeserving Poor: From the War on Poverty to the War on Welfare* (New York, 1989).

Frances Fox Piven and Richard A. Cloward, *Regulating the Poor: The Functions of Public Welfare* (New York, 1971).

William J. Wilson, *The Truly Disadvantaged: The Inner City, the Underclass, and Public Policy* (Chicago, 1987).

— ELLEN GRAY

WELLS, FARGO AND COMPANY

The founders of the American Express Company, Henry Wells, William G. Fargo, and associates, orga-

nized Wells, Fargo and Company in 1852 to function as a western ally of the American. The two companies were to divide the continent approximately at the Mississippi and Missouri rivers. Wells, Fargo and Company at once installed ocean service between New York and San Francisco via Panama, erected a fine office building in San Francisco, and began to operate, not only in the gold region of California, but over the entire Pacific coast. In less than ten years it had either bought out or eliminated nearly all competitors and become the most powerful company in the Far West. It was the chief vehicle of letter-carrying for citizens in remote mining camps where the mails had not yet penetrated; and, even after the mails came, was often preferred as being more dependable. It spread rapidly through the entire Rocky Mountain region. It carried more gold, silver, and bullion by many millions than any other agency. In 1861 it took over the famous Pony Express after the failure of the original projectors. It extended its operations to western Canada, Alaska, Mexico, the West Indies, Central America, and Hawaii, and for a short time even carried letters to China and Japan. Later, it pushed its service eastward to the Atlantic coast. The company's banking services were sold in 1905. Along with all the other expresses, Wells, Fargo and Company was merged with the American Railway Express Company in 1918, but as a separate corporation it continued to function for more than thirty years on 14,000 miles of railway in Mexico and in Cuba. As a subsidiary of American Express, Wells, Fargo became an armored-car service.

BIBLIOGRAPHY

Alvin F. Harlow, *Old Waybills.*

— ALVIN F. HARLOW

WESTERN EXPLORATION

The Spanish and French were well established west of the Mississippi in the 17th and 18th centuries and British fur traders had learned much about the Far Northwest; but the Louisiana Purchase of 1803 has always been a traditional starting point for the study of trans-Mississippi exploration.

The plans for the Lewis and Clark Expedition (1804–06) were already laid when the United States acquired the Louisiana Territory from France in 1803. President Thomas Jefferson sent Meriwether Lewis and William Clark up the Missouri River, despite protests from Spain and an abortive Spanish attempt to intercept the expedition. Lewis and Clark were instructed to seek a water route to the Pacific; to counsel with the Indians and summon certain important chiefs to Washington, D.C., for further parleys; and to make careful observations of the land and its resources. Leaving its base camp near Saint Louis in May 1804, the party wintered with the Mandan in present North Dakota. By November 1805 they had pushed on across the Rocky Mountains to the mouth of the Columbia River. The expedition returned to Saint Louis in September 1806 with extensive maps and journals, which later aroused intense public interest in the West.

While that exploring party was still out, young Zebulon Montgomery Pike was sent by Gen. James Wilkinson, then governor of Louisiana Territory, in 1805–06 to examine the upper Mississippi River and in 1806–07 to explore the region

FIVE HUNDRED DOLLARS

REWARD!

WELLS, FARGO & CO.

WILL PAY

FIVE HUNDRED DOLLARS,

For the arrest and conviction of the robber who stopped the Quincy Stage and demanded the Treasury Box, on Tuesday afternoon, August 17th, near the old Live Yankee Ranch, about 17 miles above Oroville. By order of

J. J. VALENTINE, Gen'l Supt.

Oroville, August 18, 1875. RIDEOUT, SMITH & CO., Agents.

An announcement posted by Wells, Fargo & Company, offering a $500 reward for the arrest and conviction of a robber who held up the Quincy Stagecoach on Tuesday, August 17, 1875. (Corbis-Bettmann) drained by the headwaters of the Red and Arkansas rivers. After sighting the peak that bears his name and spending a rigorous winter on the upper Arkansas with a misleading map and inadequate food and clothing, Pike strayed into Spanish territory by crossing the Rio Grande in the belief that it was the Red River. He was detained for a time by the Spanish, who lodged strong protests with President James Madison and who then conducted him back to U.S. territory. Pike's published report of 1810 turned public attention to the Spanish borderlands.

There were less extensive government explorations during the next three decades, including studies of the Ouachita and lower Red rivers, and a reconnaissance by Stephen H. Long in 1820 into Colorado and along the Arkansas and Canadian rivers, failing as did Pike to find the head of the Red River. By this time naturalists such as John Bradbury, Thomas Nuttall, and David Douglas were beginning to develop an interest in the West.

The early 19th century was noteworthy for the contribution of the fur trade to the advancement of geographical knowledge. Individual traders and organizations such as the Hudson's Bay Company and the American Fur Company were penetrating new areas. Manuel Lisa and Pierre Chouteau dominated trade on the upper Missouri. The Astorians, financed by John Jacob Astor, went by land and sea to the mouth of the Columbia in 1811–12. Joseph R. Walker and Jedediah S. Smith ranged the Great Basin, between the Wasatch Mountains and the Sierra Nevada, and journeyed to the Pacific coast. While most of the so-called mountain men did not make maps or keep journals, their detailed knowledge of the region was highly valuable to a generation of government explorers.

One man who relied heavily on experienced guides, and who never claimed to be the "pathfinder" his proponents called him, was John Charles Frémont. As a young officer in the Corps of Topographical Engineers, Frémont traveled in 1842 to South Pass and the western slopes of the Wind River Range in present Wyoming, accompanied by seasoned western men and a trained topographer. (Frémont himself was well schooled in the techniques of surveying and mapmaking.) A second expedition in 1843–44 took him once more to South Pass, then southwest to an examination of the Great Salt Lake, and on by way of the Oregon Trail to the Dalles of the Columbia. Descending through central Oregon and western Nevada, he crossed the Sierra Nevada, traveled in California as far south as the Tehachapi Mountains, and then returned east via the old Spanish Trail, Utah Lake, Colorado, and Kansas. His published accounts of these two expeditions comprise the first truly extensive reports of the West, complete with detailed and accurate maps, and did much to encourage migration to California, Utah, and Oregon. His description of the Great Basin, a large area of the West with no drainage to the Atlantic or Pacific, was the first account of this dominating feature of the West. Frémont's later expeditions were less productive, one involving him in the Bear Flag Revolt in California in 1846 and another leading him to a disastrous winter impasse in the San Juan Mountains of Colorado in 1848–49 as he attempted to prove the feasibility of a year-round rail route across the central part of the continent.

Contemporary with Frémont was the naval captain Charles Wilkes, who commanded a fleet of six ships and a party of scientists to the South Pacific, the Antarctic, and the Pacific Northwest. His charts of the Northwest coast, appearing in the 1840's, were soon combined with Frémont's maps of the interior to produce a much-needed picture of the Oregon Country.

The Mexican War and resulting acquisition of California produced further exploration, including a commission appointed to survey the boundary with Mexico. The rapid growth of a West Coast population, stimulated in part by the discovery of gold in 1848, brought public demands for wagon roads and railroads—and hence more surveys. By then it was common practice for surveying and reconnoitering parties to be accompanied by scientists and expert topographers.

The general anxiety of regional promoters over the location of railroads, and particularly the rivalry between North and South as tensions grew before the Civil War, induced the Department of War in 1853 to authorize the surveying of all feasible continental rail routes. Topographers, botanists, geologists, and zoologists probed the West from the thirty-second parallel to the forty-ninth parallel, producing several large volumes of *Pacific Railroad Reports* between 1855 and 1860. Although much was learned, the approaching Civil War diverted the nation from immediate implementation of the reports. Eventually they became the basis for the first rail route across the continent as well as later major routes.

After the Civil War the American people turned to the West with renewed vigor, and the government adopted a more sophisticated approach to exploration. Between 1867 and 1879, four great surveys were conducted by Clarence King, George M. Wheeler, Ferdinand V. Hayden, and John Wesley Powell, sponsored by the Department of War and the Department of the Interior. The vast areas examined by these men and their scientific corps produced thousands of pages of published data and hundreds of detailed maps, some of which are still definitive for isolated areas of the West.

Smaller explorations filled the gaps, often as byproducts of army activity during the Indian wars. For example, when Gen. George A. Custer led an expedition to the little-known Black Hills of Dakota Territory in 1874, ostensibly to examine the area for possible military posts, his entourage included an engineering detachment to map the route for publication, as well as a geologist, a botanist, a zoologist, and two practical miners to prospect for gold.

The establishment of the U.S. Geological Survey in 1879 marked the end of an age of exploration that had begun with Jefferson's preoccupation with the West and his role in the success of the Lewis and Clark Expedition.

BIBLIOGRAPHY

R. A. Bartlett, *Great Surveys of the American West.*
R. A. Billington, *Westward Expansion.*
W. H. Goetzmann, *Army Exploration in the American West,* and *Exploration and Empire.*

— DONALD JACKSON

WESTERN UNION TELEGRAPH COMPANY

Western Union Telegraph Company grew out of the New York and Mississippi Valley Printing Telegraph Company, which was organized in 1851 by Hiram Sibley and Samuel L. Seldon of Rochester, N.Y., to use Royal Earl House's recently invented printing telegraph.

In 1860 Western Union's telegraph lines reached from the Atlantic to the Mississippi; by 1900 it boasted more than a million miles of line and had laid two international cables.

Sibley saw opportunities for great expansion in the Middle West and, with Ezra Comell, reorganized the company as the Western Union in 1856. It absorbed smaller companies rapidly, and by 1860 its lines reached from the Atlantic to the Mississippi River, and from the Great Lakes to the Ohio River. By 1861 it had established the nation's first transcontinental telegraph line. The company enjoyed phenomenal growth during the next few years. Its capitalization rose from $385,700 in 1858 to $41 million in 1876. Then, top heavy with stock issues, it was also threatened by rival companies, among them the Atlantic and Pacific, of which Jay Gould obtained control in 1874. In 1881 Gould sold this and another company to Western Union on terms that raised the latter's capital stock to $80 million and gave him control of it.

Western Union was briefly involved in telephone communications, but withdrew from that field after losing a court battle with Bell Telephone in 1879. By 1900 the company had set up more than a million miles of telegraph lines and laid two international cables. The company continued to grow, acquiring more than 500 smaller competitors. Its position as the chief telegraph power on the continent was assured when, in 1943, it bought Postal Telegraph, Inc., its most serious rival.

During the 1960's and 1970's, as revenues from individual telegrams declined, Western Union became involved in a number of fields other than telegraphy, including satellite communications, computer systems, hotel reservation and money-order services, and teleprinters.

BIBLIOGRAPHY

Robert L. Thompson, *Wiring a Continent: The History of the Telegraph Industry in the United States, 1832–1866.*

— ALVIN F. HARLOW

WESTWARD MOVEMENT

The movement of people that resulted in the settlement of America constitutes one of the most fascinating and significant topics in the history of the United States. In character, volume, and rate of progress the westward movement in America is not fully paralleled elsewhere in world history. Invading armies have swept over many lands. There have been numerous colonial projects, fostered by governments and rulers. But nowhere else has an area of equal size been settled in so short a time almost entirely as a result of the initiative of individuals and small groups.

Treated fully, the history of the westward movement might well include the establishment of the English colonies in America. In general usage, the westward movement is considered to have begun with the first expansion from Atlantic tidewater settlements into the interior. In most respects the movement lost its typical characteristics around the closing years of the 19th century, when there could no longer be said to be a frontier line.

Thus limited, the story may well begin in 1635, when a group of Massachusetts Bay colonists, led by Roger Ludlow, moved westward into the Connecticut Valley. Windsor, Hartford, Wethersfield, and Springfield soon appeared, and thereafter settlers pushed up the Connecticut as far as Deerfield and Northfield. King Philip's War (1675–76) temporarily checked expansion, and during the series of struggles between the

French and the English the New England frontier settlements suffered from frequent Indian raids. It speaks volumes for the heartiness, courage, and persistent land hunger of the New England pioneers that by 1754 the frontier had been extended well into Vermont, New Hampshire, and Maine.

Nowhere but in America has an area of equal size been settled in so short a time almost entirely on the initiative of individuals and small groups.

The settlement of interior New York was long delayed, because of geographical obstacles, hostility of the Iroquois, exposure to French attack, and especially because of the unenlightened land policy of the colony. The only notable activity before the French and Indian War (1754–63) was that of German immigrants, fleeing from the desolation of the war-ridden Palatinate. Beginning in 1710 they settled on both banks of the Hudson River near Saugerties. A few years later some of these Germans made homes for themselves along the Schoharie River; and still later (1723–24) others went far up the Mohawk River and established the settlement known as the German Flats (opposite the present town of Herkimer).

Pennsylvania presented a striking contrast. The religious toleration, liberal land policy, and widespread advertising of that colony attracted a host of immigrants who rapidly moved into the interior. By 1750 the frontier settlements extended along the foot of the mountains from Easton southwestward to the Maryland line. This westward expansion was largely the work of Germans and Scotch-Irish, with a mingling of Swiss Mennonites, who began pouring into Pennsylvania by the thousands in the early decades of the 18th century.

South of Pennsylvania, frontier expansion was the achievement of two streams of settlers: one that pushed westward from the tidewater regions, and the other that flowed southward from Pennsylvania. Virginia was well occupied as far west as the fall line by 1700. During the first quarter of the 18th century the settlement of the country between the fall line and the Blue Ridge Mountains was in full swing, as small farmers were crowded out of the tidewater section by large plantation owners. The Shenandoah Valley received some settlers from eastern Virginia, but its settlement was accomplished mainly by Germans and Scotch-Irish moving southward from Pennsylvania between 1730 and 1750. The occupation of the piedmont and mountain regions in the Carolinas came a little later and in about the same manner, with Scotch-Irish, Germans, and others from the North pioneering the way in the upland backcountry.

Thus, by 1750 settlements extended far into the interior of New England; there were agricultural outposts up the Mohawk in New York; from Pennsylvania southward settlers were living close up against the Appalachian barrier; and there were scattered cabins on westward-flowing streams. There the advance was halted by the French and Indian War, and the frontier line even receded temporarily.

No sooner had Fort Duquesne and the other western posts of France been captured in 1758 and 1759 than the westward march was resumed, and the frontier crossed the mountains in complete disregard of the royal Proclamation of 1763. By Braddock's Road settlers from Maryland and Virginia moved inland as far as the Forks of the Ohio, where they were joined by others coming across Pennsylvania by Forbes Road. In Virginia, the Carolinas, and Georgia cabins appeared farther and farther up the streams flowing into the Atlantic and even in Powell's Valley and on such westward-flowing rivers as the Cheat, the Holston, the Clinch, and the French Broad. About 1769, pioneers from Virginia began to settle along the Watauga River, in what is now northeastern Tennessee, and after 1771 they were joined by discouraged Regulators from North Carolina. Before the beginning of the revolutionary war numerous settlements were made in West Florida. By this time also settlements had been established in central Kentucky around Boonesborough.

This was the situation at the close of the revolutionary war, when the new American nation came into existence. The small stream of settlers that had begun to trickle over the mountain passes now swelled to an ever-increasing torrent that spread with amazing rapidity over the great interior valley, and within scarcely more than half a century deposited outposts of settlement on the Pacific coast. The decennial reports of the federal census, beginning in 1790, are valuable sources for the study of this great westward movement of land-hungry settlers. The dates of the creation of territories and the admission of states are other indications of the volume and direction of the movement. A series of shaded maps, in the *Report of the Eleventh Census* (1890), showing population density and the spread of settlements by decades, tells the story even more graphically. But to gain an intimate, first-hand view of the process by which the United States was settled, one must go to the letters, diaries, journals of travel, newspapers, and other writings of those who witnessed the movement while it was in progress.

These sources tell of roads crowded year after year, from early spring to late fall, with settlers moving westward, singly, by families, or in groups. The typical migrating unit was the family, moving to a new home in the West with their belongings in a single covered wagon and with perhaps a cow or two. There is frequent mention of well-equipped cavalcades of well-to-do farmers or plantation owners. On the other hand, a two-wheeled cart, pulled by a horse or an ox, was the only vehicle of many, while others made the journey on horseback or on foot.

Thousands of settlers placed their possessions, often including livestock, on flatboats on the upper Ohio and floated down that river highway to their destination in the West, or on down the Mississippi River. Similarly the canal boats on the Erie Canal, after its completion in 1825, were often crowded with emigrants on their way to western New York or to Michigan and northern Ohio, Indiana, and Illinois. Steamboats later played a large role in transporting settlers upstream to lands along the Mississippi and the Missouri rivers.

The close of the revolutionary war was followed by a great outpouring of people, principally from Virginia and North Carolina, into central Kentucky and Tennessee. Across the Ohio River there also appeared the vanguard of the stream of emigrants who soon transformed that region into a land of homes, farms, and towns. The principal effects of the westward movement down to 1810 were seen in Ohio, Kentucky, and Tennessee. The next decade witnessed the so-called "Great Migration" following the War of 1812, when the entire frontier moved westward. So many settlers poured into the Old Southwest that Mississippi and Alabama were admitted into the Union before the close of the decade. The movement into the Old Northwest resulted in the creation of the states of Indiana and Illinois. Across the Mississippi the influx of settlers set the stage for the great struggle over the admission of Missouri. By 1830 not only had all the western states received large accessions of population, but the tide of settlers was moving into the territories of Michigan and Arkansas, and there were probably 20,000 Americans in Texas, which still belonged to Mexico.

During the decade of the 1830's the movement to Michigan and Arkansas, especially to the former, reached such large proportions that two new states were admitted. Illinois nearly tripled in population, and two new territories (Wisconsin and Iowa) were created. The "fabulous forties" were notable years in the history of the westward movement. Not only was the frontier expansion into Wisconsin and Iowa vigorous, but thriving American settlements appeared on the Pacific coast. Early in that decade there began the movement of pioneers over the long Oregon Trail to the Pacific Northwest. In 1846 and 1847 the Mormons made their famous hegira from Nauvoo, Ill., to their new home in Utah. Then just at the close of the decade came the mad rush of thousands of people of every description to the newly discovered gold fields in California.

During the decade of the 1850's migration to Oregon, California, and Texas continued unabated. New converts swelled the population of the Mormon colony in Utah, and the Territory of New Mexico attracted thousands of settlers. The struggle for Kansas brought streams of zealous emigrants from the North and the South into that turbulent territory, which had a population of more than 100,000 in 1860. But in many respects the most significant phase of the westward movement of that decade is to be found in the fact that the population of the eight states of the upper Mississippi Valley increased by more than 3.35 million, or more than 167 percent. This growth, attributable partly to natural increases but mainly to the westward migration of Americans and hosts of foreign immigrants, definitely established the numerical and economic superiority of the North and had profound political effects.

The Civil War naturally checked the westward movement. And yet, even during those troubled years, there was a surprisingly large migration to the Far West, for this was the period of constantly recurring gold and silver discoveries in Colorado, Nevada, Oregon, Idaho, and Montana. For instance, an observer writing in 1863 stated that the road at Omaha was "covered most of the time with the wagons of those bound for Colorado, California, and Oregon; one train of nine hundred wagons was noted, another of twelve hundred. On the Kansas route this year a traveler from Colorado, sixteen days on the road, met on an average five hundred wagons a day going to Colorado and California." After the close of the war the movement to the Far West was greatly augmented and was notable in the South as well as in the North, and particularly in the border states where large numbers of southern sympathizers left their homes for the West.

Even during the turbulent Civil War years there was a surprisingly large migration to the Far West—particularly toward gold and silver.

It was during the decades of the 1870's and the 1880's that the Great Plains—the last American frontier—received the greatest number of westward-moving settlers. This was the region long known as the Great American Desert. Then it became the scene of an extensive range-cattle industry. But steadily and inexorably the settlers moved westward, and the great cattle range disappeared. By 1890 Kansas and Nebraska were populous states, and the newly admitted states of North Dakota and South Dakota had substantial populations. Just at the close of the decade of the 1880's the dramatic rush to Oklahoma recalled scenes that had been witnessed many times when Indian lands were opened to settlement.

With the closing decade of the 19th century the story of the westward movement in America may well close. The farmers' frontier had advanced into some part of almost every section and region, and the pioneer phase of the occupation of the land within continental boundaries of the United States, excluding Alaska, was finished.

[See also Colonial Wars; Missouri Compromise.]

BIBLIOGRAPHY

Ray Allan Billington, *Westward Expansion: History of the American Frontier.*

John A. Hawgood, *America's Western Frontiers.*

Francis Philbrick, *The Rise of the West, 1754–1830.*

— DAN E. CLARK

WHEAT

Throughout the colonial and national periods of American history wheat has been the principal bread cereal. It was introduced by the first English colonists and early became the major cash crop of farmers on the westward-moving frontier. In colonial times its culture became concentrated in the middle colonies, which became known as the "bread colonies." In the mid-18th century, wheat culture spread to the tidewater of Maryland and Virginia, where George Washington became a prominent grower.

As the frontier crossed the Appalachian Mountains, so did wheat raising. The census of 1840 revealed Ohio as the premier wheat-producing state, but twenty years later Illinois took the lead; it retained the lead for three decades, until it was overtaken by Minnesota in 1889. Leadership moved with the farming frontier onto the Great Plains in the first years of the 20th century. The census takers in 1909 found North Dakota in the lead followed by Kansas, but between 1919 and 1975 the order was reversed, except in 1934 and 1954, when Oklahoma and then Montana moved into second place. In the meantime, the soils of the Columbia Valley became productive, the state of Washington ranking fourth in wheat production in 1959.

The majority of the farmers east of the Mississippi River preferred soft winter wheat varieties, such as the Mediterranean (introduced in 1819), but those who settled the Great Plains found those varieties ill-adapted to the climates of that area. Hard red spring wheats, such as Red Fife and bluestem, proved more suited to the northern Plains, while Turkey, a hard red winter wheat introduced into central Kansas by German Mennonite immigrants from Russia, became popular on the southern Plains. The introduction of these hard wheats provoked a major change in the grinding of wheat into flour, a shift from millstones to rollers.

Wheat breeders soon developed still more adapted varieties. Early maturing Marquis was introduced from Canada in 1912, and by 1929 it was planted on 87 percent of the hard spring wheat acreage. It proved susceptible to the black stem rust and after 1934 lost favor to Thatcher and in the late 1960's to Chris and Fortuna. On the southern Plains, Tenmarq, released by the Kansas Agricultural Experiment Station in 1932, superseded Turkey and was in turn replaced first by Pawnee and later by Triumph and Scout. In the 1960's the wheatgrowers of the Columbia Valley began to favor a new short-stemmed soft white winter wheat, known as Gaines, which doubled yields in that area within a four-year period.

Whatever the variety, wheat in the colonial and early national period was sown by broadcasting, reaped by sickles, and threshed by flails. In rapid succession in the 19th century, sowing with drills replaced broadcasting, cradles took the place of sickles, and the cradles in turn were replaced by reapers and binders. Steam-powered threshing machines superseded flails. In the 1930's the small combine combined reaping and threshing into one operation.

The marketing of wheat went through parallel changes. Initially the harvest was sacked, shipped, and stored in warehouses, but after the Civil War wheat began to flow first to the country elevators and from there to terminal elevators, from which it was sold through grain exchanges to flour millers and exporters. Farmers soon accused the elevator men of undergrading, shortweighting, and excessive dockage and sought control over marketing through the organization of co-operatives.

Since colonial times wheat growers have produced a surplus for export. Exports of wheat and flour varied from 868,500 bushels in 1814 to 223,811,000 in 1898, providing foreign exchange for the nation's industrialization. However, expansion of acreage during World War I and contraction of demand overseas after its termination created an accumulation of surpluses that could not be marketed. The resulting low prices prompted growers to seek government support of prices, first through the McNary-Haugen bills, which failed to become law, and later through the Agricultural Adjustment Act of 1933 and its many revisions. Increasing production, which reached a billion bushels in 1944, permitted an expansion of wheat and flour exports as part of the nation's foreign assistance programs. In fiscal year 1966 these exports amounted to 858,657,000 bushels, of which 571,154,000 were disposed of as food aid. A disastrous drought in the Soviet Union in 1972 led to the sale of 388,489,000 bushels to that country in one year and the conclusion in 1975 of an agreement to supply the Soviets with breadstuffs over a five-year period.

BIBLIOGRAPHY

Kirby Brumfield, *This Was Wheat Farming.*

Harry Fornari, *Bread Upon the Waters.*

Don F. Hadwiger, *Federal Wheat Commodity Programs.*

James C. Malin, *Winter Wheat in the Golden Belt of Kansas.*

K. S. Quisenberry and L. P. Reitz, "Turkey Wheat: The Cornerstone of an Empire," *Agricultural History,* vol. 48 (1974).

L. P. Reitz, "Wheat Breeding and Our Food Supply," *Economic Botany,* vol. 8 (1954).

— ROBERT G. DUNBAR

WHIG PARTY

Whig Party, a major political party formed in the early 1830's to challenge the policies of the Democratic party under Andrew Jackson. The Whig party's leaders, who charged "King Andrew" with executive tyranny, were mainly representatives of the vested property interests of the North and South. The term "Whig" was used in 1832 by the antitariff leaders of South Carolina, but it soon came to be applied to all elements that found themselves opposed to the Jacksonian Democratic party. Jackson's 1832 proclamation against nullification (of federal laws by state governments) resulted in Henry Clay's cooperation with the nullifiers and their sympathizers in enacting the so-called Compromise Tariff of 1833, which significantly lowered tariffs. Jackson's war on the Bank of the United States brought new recruits to the opposition, both from the South and from the North. His promotion in 1836 of Martin Van Buren as his successor in the presidency alienated another political group, the supporters of the aspirations of Judge Hugh L. White of Tennessee. Even before that controversy, most of the former National Republicans and the remnants of the Anti-Masonic party had joined the opposition. Van Buren's criticism of state banks during the panic of 1837 also hurt the Democrats, and Whig candidate William Henry Harrison's successful "log cabin" campaign for the presidency in 1840 gave the party important strength in the back-country, which had previously seen little attraction in Whiggery.

The Whig success of 1840 made it the temporarily dominant party, charged with the responsibilities of power. Clay promptly laid down a nationalistic program, to which the majority of the party rallied, despite the insistence of John Tyler (who became president when Harrison died shortly after his inauguration) on continuing what were to him the true Whig traditions of the 1830's. Read out of the party, Tyler watched in dismay the acceptance of the Clay formula by the vast body of Whigs. The issues of the annexation of Texas and of the extension of slavery into the territories in time proved a menace to the solidarity of the party. The election of 1844, in which Democrat James Polk defeated Clay, showed that the Whigs had lost the support of expansionist forces that had, in 1840, yielded to the lure of the Harrison campaign. The conservative property interests of leading Whigs made them opponents of the Mexican War and of expansion, and the "no territory" resolutions they supported were largely sponsored by their southern leaders. While some of the northern Whigs were antislavery people (Conscience Whigs), other party supporters were sufficiently proslavery to earn the label "Cotton Whigs." In the sectional disputes of 1850–51, southern Whigs were prominent among the Union forces that fought secession. By 1852 sectional allegiance had become so strong that the party began to disintegrate, and it suffered a defeat at the polls that marked the beginning of its demise.

[See also Compromise of 1850.]

BIBLIOGRAPHY

Lee Benson, *The Concept of Jacksonian Democracy: New York as a Test Case.*

Arthur C. Cole, *The Whig Party in the South.*

Richard P. McCormick, *The Second American Party System: Party Formation in the Jacksonian Era.*

— ARTHUR C. COLE

WHISKEY

Whiskey used in the earlier years of the colonies was imported from Great Britain. Among the early settlers were many from Ireland and Scotland who were acquainted with the art of distilling whiskey, principally from malt, although rye, wheat, and even potatoes were sometimes used in early American stills. Many of the Irish and Scottish immigrants settled in western Pennsylvania, which in the late 17th and early 18th centuries became a center of rye-whiskey making. Maryland began producing this liquor about the same time. Whiskey became the leading spirituous drink for the entire country outside of New England, where rum remained the favorite drink for more than a century. Appalling excesses in the use of whiskey and rum brought about the temperance movement. There was a still in Bourbon County, Ky., as early as 1789. Kentuckians discovered that whiskey could be produced from Indian corn, and this eventually became America's leading spirituous product, exceeding in volume the rye whiskeys of Maryland and Pennsylvania. In 1792 there were 2,579 small distilleries in the United States. By 1810 Kentucky alone had 2,000, some of which shipped whiskey to the East via New Orleans by flatboat down the rivers, and thence by ocean vessels. Some enormous distilling plants grew up in Kentucky, manufacturing sour mash, sweet mash, Bourbon—so called from the Kentucky county of that name—and a small percentage of rye. Other states in the corn belt, such as Ohio and Illinois, also developed large distilling industries. During the period from 1901 to 1919 there were withdrawn from bonded warehouses after payment of tax a yearly average of 60 million gallons of whiskey. The Prohibition era (1919–33) worked enormous changes in the business, destroying many long-established companies whose distilleries, if reopened at all after the repeal of the law, were in many cases under other ownership. In 1935 Kentucky produced 197 million gallons of whiskey. Producing a relatively low 104 million gallons in 1955, whiskey distillers in the United States put out 160 million gallons in 1970. By 1972 production had fallen again, to 126 million gallons.

BIBLIOGRAPHY

Gerald Carson, *Social History of Bourbon.*

Henry G. Crowgey, *Kentucky Bourbon: The Early Years of Whiskey Making.*

— ALVIN F. HARLOW

WHISKEY REBELLION

Whiskey Rebellion (1794). The American backcountry in the 1790's was intensely democratic in its views and resented the way in which Secretary of the Treasury Alexander Hamilton's fiscal policies concentrated power in the hands of the upper classes. Other grievances accentuated western resentment, notably the failure to open the Mississippi River to navigation, the dilatory conduct of the Indian wars, the speculative prices of land, arduous and ill-paid militia duty, scarcity of specie, and the creation of a salaried official class. The excise law of 1791, which taxed whiskey—the chief transportable and barterable western product—furnished a convenient peg on which to hang these grievances, and for three years the opposition to this measure increased.

Daniel Morgan (1736-1802) fought against the British during the American Revolution, then later led federal troops on orders to quell the Whiskey Rebellion of 1794 in Pennsylvania. (Library of Congress/Corbis)

The fact that noncomplying distillers from western Pennsylvania had to go to York or Philadelphia for trial (a procedure that would cost the value of the average western farm) formed so legitimate a grievance that in May and June 1794 Congress passed a measure making offenses against the excise law cognizable in state courts. While the bill was in Congress the U.S. District Court of Pennsylvania issued a series of processes returnable to Philadelphia. The fact that these processes were not served until July, six weeks after the easing measure was passed, angered the citizens of the southwestern counties. A federal marshal was attacked in Allegheny County while serving a process, and on July 17 several hundred men, led by members of a local "Democratic society," attacked and burned the home of Gen. John Neville, the regional inspector of the excise.

The attackers would probably have stopped with this action, but certain leaders robbed the mail and found in the stolen letters expressions that they used in stirring up the people to attack Pittsburgh. A muster of the southwestern militia was called at Braddock's Field for Aug. 1. The citizens of Pittsburgh were so alarmed that they exiled the odious townsmen, including Neville, and thus averted the wrath of the recalcitrants. The militia march on Pittsburgh on Aug. 2 was carried through without violence. Nevertheless, on Aug. 7 President George Washington issued a proclamation ordering the disaffected westerners to their homes, and calling up the militia from Maryland, Virginia, Pennsylvania, and New Jersey.

On Aug. 14–15 delegates from the Monongahela Valley met at Parkinson's Ferry, but were prevented from drastic measures by the parliamentary tactics of the moderates. A committee appointed by Washington met with a western committee and arranged that the sentiment of the people of the western counties concerning submission be taken on Sept. 11. The vote was unsatisfactory, and Washington set in motion the militia army that had meanwhile been gathering in the East. The western counties were occupied during November, and more than a score of prisoners were sent to Philadelphia. All of them were acquitted or pardoned, or the cases were dismissed for lack of evidence.

The result of the rebellion was simply to strengthen the political power of Hamilton and the Federalists, and circumstantial evidence seems to indicate that Hamilton promoted the original misunderstanding and sent the army west solely for that purpose. It is likely also that the defeat of the democrats encouraged investors to accelerate the economic development of the region that they had already begun.

BIBLIOGRAPHY

Leland D. Baldwin, *Whiskey Rebels.*
John C. Miller, *The Federalist Era, 1789–1801.*

— LELAND D. BALDWIN

WHITE HOUSE

White House, the residence of every president of the United States since John Adams became its first occupant on Nov. 1, 1800. The selection of a site for the president's house in the new federal city of the District of Columbia was made by President George Washington and Maj. Pierre Charles L'Enfant, the French planner of the city of Washington. In 1792 the commissioners of the federal city drew up a competition for the design of a house for the president. Among the persons entering the competition was an anonymous citizen who signed his entry "A. Z." and who was later revealed to be Thomas Jefferson. The winning design was the creation of James Hoban, an Irish-born architect who modeled his entry after Leinster House in Dublin, Ireland. Hoban's design remains the familiar view of the White House to the present day, built on 18 acres on the south side of Pennsylvania Avenue. In Jefferson's time (1807) the east and west terraces were added to the mansion; in 1824 the South Portico was completed, and in 1829 the North Portico. The terraces were the work of the architect Benjamin Latrobe, and the two porticoes incorporated the designs of both Latrobe and Hoban. In 1948 a balcony was added to the South Portico at the request of President Harry S. Truman. The West Wing of the White House, which contains the offices of the president and his staff, was built in 1902 as a temporary office building. It expanded over the years until it was double its original size. The East Wing was completed during World War II (1942) to provide further office space. Both wings were constructed at lower elevations than the residence.

Throughout its history, the White House has undergone extensive interior change and renovation. Only the exterior walls remained standing after the British set fire to the president's house on Aug. 24, 1814, and James Monroe did not move into the White House until December of 1817. In 1902 President Theodore Roosevelt commissioned a major refurbishing of the interior, and during the Truman administration (1948–52) the residence was completely renovated and made structurally sound. In 1961 Jacqueline Kennedy, wife of President John F. Kennedy, began an extensive program to acquire American antique furnishings and paintings for the White House. The project continued under Lady Bird (Claudia Alta) Johnson, wife of President Lyndon Johnson, and expanded under the guidance of Patricia R. Nixon, wife of President Richard M. Nixon; the White House soon had an outstanding collection of American furniture from the late 18th and early 19th centuries and American paintings from the late 18th century to the early 20th century. The White House has retained the classical elegance of an early 19th-century house and continues to serve as the home and office of the president of the United States and as a symbol of the government of the United States.

BIBLIOGRAPHY

Constance M. Green, *Washington: Capital City, 1879–1950,* and *Washington, Village and Capital, 1800–1878.*

White House Historical Association, *The White House: An Historic Guide.*

— CLEMENT E. CONGER

WHITE SUPREMACISTS

Since World War II the number of whites who profess belief in racial equality has steadily increased, but there continue to be many Americans who proudly proclaim their belief in white supremacy. White supremacist organizations in the United States tend to be short-lived, but new organizations always take the place of those that die. The best known of these groups is the Ku Klux Klan (KKK), a name that a number of organizations have used. A group of ex-Confederate soldiers, who were mainly interested in amusing themselves with pranks and practical jokes, started the first Klan in Pulaski, Tenn., in 1866. It grew rapidly in the former Confederate states, but was breaking up into separate groups

White supremacist groups in the U.S. tend to be short-lived, but new organizations always spring up to replace them.

by the time it was suppressed by the federal government under legislation passed in 1871. Since then there have been several periods when a number of new Klans sprung up, a large group after World War I and smaller ones in the 1960s during the civil rights movement and still again in the late 1970s and 1980s. In the 1990s there were numerous Klans active under a variety of names. A partial list of other white supremacist groups in the 1990s includes the American Nazi Party, Nazi Skinheads, Posse Comitatus, Aryan Nations, The Order, the National Alliance, Populist Party, Liberty Lobby, White Patriot Party, the John Birch Society, and the Church of Jesus Christ Christian. These groups varied in the degree to which they advocated armed violence as a means to realize their goals. Many white supremacists are Identity Christians, who believe that white "Aryans" are the only true descendants of the Israelites, God's chosen people.

[See also Ku Klux Klan.]

BIBLIOGRAPHY

Mark S. Hamm, *American Skinheads* (Westport, Conn., 1993).

James Ridgeway, *Blood in the Face: The Ku Klux Klan, Aryan Nations, Nazi Skinheads, and the Rise of a New White Culture* (New York, 1990).

— RICHARD W. MOODEY

"WIGWAM"

"Wigwam," the name given to the headquarters of Tammany societies, so called because of the pseudo-Indian organization of the society. The name was first used by the Tammany Hall organization in New York City. It was applied to the building erected opposite the City Hall in 1810. The most famous "wigwam" was that on Fourteenth Street, also in New York, where, between 1868 and 1928 (when a new building was completed on Union Square), ruled the famous succession of bosses: William Marcy Tweed, John Kelly, Richard Croker, and Charles F. Murphy.

BIBLIOGRAPHY

M. R. Werner, *Tammany Hall.*

— ALVIN F. HARLOW

WILDCAT MONEY

Wildcat money currency issued by wildcat banks. The name calls attention to the practice of wildcat banks of locating their main offices in remote places where it would be difficult for noteholders to present notes for payment. They flourished in the period 1830–60. Often they were started with specie borrowed only long enough to show the banking commissioners. They created a confusion in the currency and gave point to Secretary of the Treasury Salmon P. Chase's demand for a national bank currency (*see* Banking).

BIBLIOGRAPHY

H. White, *Money and Banking.*

— JAMES D. MAGEE

WILDCAT OIL DRILLING

Hardly had Edwin L. Drake completed his oil well on Oil Creek, Pa., late in August 1859, than others seeking similar good fortune set to drilling nearby with spring poles. Thus was born a romantic American figure, the wildcatter, who has fairly overshadowed the prospector in color, wild hopes, and rosy dreams of quick wealth. The wildcatter hazarded his all and often that of his supporters on the point of an ever-deepening drill. Frequently dry holes or a host of dupes were the only fruit of his gamble. By discovering oil in the most unexpected places, he made paupers into millionaires overnight. Proration checked him and conservation impeded his operations, but human nature being what it is, he and his hopes would not die. The early oil companies depended on his explorations, and to him in part, at least, must be credited the swift development of America's petroleum resources.

BIBLIOGRAPHY

C. G. Gilbert and J. E. Pogue, *America's Power Resources.*

— JOHN FRANCIS, JR.

WILDERNESS ROAD

Wilderness Road ran from eastern Virginia (where the Maryland and Pennsylvania roads from the north and the Carolina and east Tennessee roads from the south converged) through the mountain pass known as Cumberland Gap, to the interior of Kentucky and thence to the Ohio and beyond. A rudimentary route already existed when, in March 1775, Daniel Boone and a party of about thirty woodsmen undertook to clear and mark out a trail. They traveled from the Indian treaty-ground at Fort Watauga, in what is now east Tennessee, by way of the Cumberland Gap and through the rugged mountains and rolling canelands of Kentucky, to the mouth of Otter Creek, on the Kentucky River. They chose this last site for a fortified town, which they named Boonesborough (now Boonesboro). Later the road forked at the Hazel Patch, in Laurel County, one branch leading by the Crab Orchard and Danville to the Falls of the Ohio at Louisville.

This primitive road, made up in large part of a succession of irregular woodland paths trodden down and worn bare by wandering herds of buffalo and roving Indian hunters or war parties, was blazed by Boone at the instance of the Transylvania Company. Its total length was close to 300 miles; and fully two-thirds of the distance had to be opened and marked to guide an endless train of pioneers who followed in the wake of Boone and his fellow road builders. At first it was little more than a footpath or packhorse trail. Spasmodic but insufficient measures were taken by the Virginia government to enlarge and improve the crowded thoroughfare, but a score of years elapsed before it was passable by wagons. After Kentucky had become a separate state, renewed efforts to grade, widen, and reinforce the road were put forth. Sections of the road were leased to contractors who, in consideration of materials and labor furnished to maintain the road, were authorized to erect gates or turnpikes across it and collect tolls from travelers. In legislation on the subject, the road was generally called the "Wilderness Turnpike Road." Blockhouses were erected and manned at intervals along the way to protect travelers against marauding Indians and outlaws. For more than half a century after Boone blazed the way in 1775, the Wilderness Road was a principal avenue for the movement of immigrants and others to and from the early West. The Ohio River afforded the only alternative route; and over these converging highways to the great inland empire of the new nation thousands upon thousands of Americans of the pioneer period passed and repassed in a never-ending procession. The Wilderness Road is still an important interstate arterial roadway and constitutes a part of U.S. Route 25, known as the Dixie Highway.

BIBLIOGRAPHY

A. B. Hulbert, *Boone's Wilderness Road.*
W. A. Pusey, *The Wilderness Road to Kentucky.*
Thomas Speed, *The Wilderness Road.*

— SAMUEL M. WILSON

WILDLIFE PRESERVATION

Wildlife Preservation was not the highest priority of the earliest settlers. Nevertheless, the first game law, for the protection of deer, was passed by the town of Newport, in what is now Rhode Island, in 1639. Other colonies followed suit, and after independence state and local communities continued to pass laws regulating the taking of game, fish, and birds. The contradictory maze of early state, county, and local ordinances, with no machinery for centralized enforcement, provided typically for a closed season and fines for offenders—part of which (usually half) went to the informer and the rest to the treasury. These laws were almost universally ineffective and seemed to have no relation to the survival or extinction of a species. Although the passenger pigeon, once numerous beyond all reckoning, and the heath hen were both the objects of legal protection, neither escaped extermination; but other species, subject to the same depredations, survived. Trappers in pursuit of the beaver—a small, useful animal, whose misfortune it was to possess a highly desired pelt—opened up and explored much of the North American continent. But the beaver managed to survive, not through legislation but because of the change in men's fashion for silk hats.

The North American bison, or buffalo—once as abundant as the passenger pigeon—had no legal protection (except for unenforced laws that provided for closed seasons in Idaho, Kansas, and Colorado). Somehow they survived, although by 1875 they were largely gone from the Central Plains. After 1897, a small herd of several hundred head in Yellowstone National Park was all that remained in the wild of the great herds that once numbered in the tens of millions and that once ranged over most of North America, particularly the grasslands of the Great Plains. Although the park was patrolled and protected by the army, the remaining animals were steadily depleted by poachers, and only twenty-one remained by 1903. Determined and concerted effort saved the buffalo. Congressional funds were used to fence a buffalo ranch in Yellowstone Park, which was augmented by purchases of privately owned captive bison, and by 1927 the Yellowstone herd had grown to 1,000. Congress established the National Bison Range on the Flathead Indian Reservation in Montana in 1907, and other ranges were subsequently created. By the 1970's they were nearly all stocked to capacity, with the total number of wild bison stabilized at around 5,000. The physical survival of the bison was also assured by the discovery of remnants in Canada, which became the nucleus of the large herd of 40,000 head in Canada's Wood Buffalo Park.

During the last two decades of the 19th century the game enforcement machinery was dramatically improved on the state level. Agencies grew in size, complexity, and centralization. An important innovation, widely adopted, was a North Dakota law of 1895 requiring a hunting license, which for the first time provided a steady and dependable source of revenue. By 1904 most states had some kind of fish and game agency. The federal government took an important step in 1900 with the passage of the Lacey Act, which made it illegal to ship game killed in violation of state law across state lines. This law dealt a severe blow to market hunting, formerly an important industry. Yet all such efforts were concerned with the narrow enforcement of laws regulating the killing of game, and the problem of preserving a wild environment in which the living game could survive received little attention. Hunting for sport or profit unquestionably took its toll, but even greater threats arose from the political and economic uses of technology, and from the expanding human population. A swamp drained to make way for a subdivision destroyed the habitat of wildfowl and other creatures, and endangered their survival more surely than an army of determined hunters bent on extermination. Until this factor was considered, no effective long-range policy of preservation was possible.

The concept of refuges was crucial in the growth of concern for the wild habitat. It began with the creation of Yellowstone National Park in 1872, which became an inviolate game preserve. Later parks followed this pattern, and on Aug. 25, 1916, the National Park Service, a regulatory agency with power to formulate a park wildlife policy, was established. Meanwhile, the Bureau of Biological Survey had already acquired regulatory powers, along with the beginnings of a domain. Created by Congress in 1885 by a small appropriation for research in the Department of Agriculture, it was charged in 1900 with enforcement of the Lacey Act. An act of 1913 placed migratory and insectivorous birds under federal authority, and the 1916 treaty with Great Britain for the protection of migratory birds in the United States and Canada expanded this power to regulate. In 1903 the first wildlife sanctuary outside the park system, Pelican Island, off the east coast of Florida, was placed under its jurisdiction. The Biological Survey, which merged with the Bureau of Fisheries in 1940 to become the Fish and Wildlife Service, eventually presided over a vast network of such refuges—in 1971, a total of 29,284,761 acres in 329 areas. The final ingredient in the emergence of a diversified federal refuge system was the creation of breeding sanctuaries for game in the national forest reserves, under the jurisdiction of the Forest Service.

The concept of wildlife refuges began with the creation of Yellowstone National Park in 1872, which became an inviolate game preserve.

After the concept of a refuge system, the doctrine of the Forest Service was the most important element in the development of a wildlife policy. Basic forestry principle held that trees were an agricultural resource and that forests should be managed so as to produce a yield year after year. The doctrine of perpetual use through management was not at first applied to wildlife policy, which was dominated primarily by a concern for preservation of populations. But the 1920's famine among the Montana elk, and catastrophic destruction through starvation of all but a remnant of the giant deer herd of the Kaibab Plateau in Arizona, led to the gradual realization that concern for the range, and attention to the habitat in general, was essential. Significantly, it was a forester, Aldo Leopold, who did most to spread the new gospel that "game is a crop," a resource to be cultivated and periodically harvested like any other crop. The final stage in the institutionalization of this attitude was the emergence of the profession of wildlife management. In 1934 the Biological Survey set up research and training programs in ten land grant universities. From this beginning wildlife management grew to full professional status, and by the 1970's training through the doctorate was available in many universities.

The growth of a public wildlife policy was partly a response to pressures from organized groups. The Boone and Crockett Club, formed in 1887 by a group of socially prominent sportsmen, illustrates the influence such organizations exerted. It worked for game laws on the state level, watched over the development of Yellowstone as a game preserve, lobbied for the crea-

tion of more parks, and rallied support for bison protection. Among its members were President Theodore Roosevelt, Chief Forester Gifford Pinchot, Rep. John F. Lacey, who gave his name to the act ending market hunting, and George Bird Grinnell, the editor of *Field and Stream.* Other organizations and clubs—such as the Sierra Club, the New York Audubon Society, the American Game Conference (later North American Wildlife Conference), and the American Ornithological Union (which was mainly responsible for the creation of the first refuge at Pelican Island)—formed an expanding interlocking wildlife lobby on the national and state levels. These and numerous groups of sportsmen, scientists, and nature lovers of every description were supported and sometimes financed by economic interests such as firearms manufacturers, railroads, and automobile associations that hoped to profit from the recreation needs of burgeoning urban populations. Together they presided over the evolution of wildlife policy, sparked the passage of important legislation, and functioned both as defender and as clientele of public institutions.

BIBLIOGRAPHY

T. S. Palmer, *Chronology and Index of the More Important Events in American Game Protection, 1776–1911,* Biological Survey Bulletin, no. 41.

James B. Trefethen, *Crusade for Wildlife: Highlights in Conservation Progress.*

Robert Welker, *Birds and Men: American Birds in Science, Art, Literature and Conservation.*

— JAMES PENICK, JR.

WILMOT PROVISO

Soon after the Mexican War began, President James K. Polk requested $2 million from Congress with which to negotiate peace, it being understood that territory would be acquired from Mexico. On Aug. 8, 1846, a bill to appropriate the sum was moved in the House of Representatives. David Wilmot, a Democrat from Pennsylvania, hitherto identified with the administration, proposed the following amendment to the bill:

> Provided, That, as an express and fundamental condition to the acquisition of any territory from the Republic of Mexico by the United States, by virtue of any treaty which may be negotiated between them, and to the use by the Executive of the moneys herein appropriated, neither slavery nor involuntary servitude shall ever exist in any part of said territory.

This amendment became known as the Wilmot Proviso. It precipitated a bitter debate over the question of slavery in the territories.

An effort was made in the House to amend the Wilmot Proviso by limiting its application to the region north of the Missouri Compromise line, but this was defeated. The appropriation bill carrying the Wilmot Proviso was then passed by the House by a vote of eighty-seven to sixty-four. The bill as amended was then sent to the Senate; but the Senate adjourned (Aug. 10) for the session before a vote was taken.

In the next Congress, a bill to appropriate $3 million for peace negotiations was introduced in the House, and Wilmot again moved his proviso. The bill as amended was carried in the House, Feb. 15, 1847, by a vote of 115 to 106. The Senate refused to consider the amended bill, but passed one of its own appropriating the desired sum. After bitter debate the House concurred in the Senate bill, and the $3 million became available to Polk without Wilmot's conditions.

In the meantime debates over the proviso had aroused the country. State legislatures and other public bodies approved and condemned the principle incorporated in the proviso. Sectional animosity was heightened. The principle of the proviso, contained in other legislation, continued to provoke sectional debate. The modern Republican party was later founded on this principle, and Abraham Lincoln was elected on a platform pledged to carry it out.

Modern historical scholarship recognizes that more is involved in the Wilmot Proviso than meets the eye. Polk was unpopular with northern Democrats in 1846 because of his recent settlement of the Oregon question, the Walker Tariff of 1846, and his recent veto of a rivers and harbors bill. Votes for the Wilmot Proviso were calculated to embarrass the president. The motive of Wilmot, an administration Democrat, has been puzzling. The usual theory is that he merely served as an accommodating mouthpiece for an anti-administration Democrat, Rep. Jacob Brinkerhoff of Ohio. Some historians now maintain that Wilmot, not Brinkerhoff, was the real author of the plan, and that his motive was not unconnected with a desire to regain the support of his Pennsylvania constituency, alienated by his recent tariff vote.

BIBLIOGRAPHY

Chaplain W. Morrison, *Democratic Politics and Sectionalism: The Wilmot Proviso Controversy.*

— HAYWOOD J. PEARCE, JR.

WINNEBAGO

Winnebago, a tribe of American Indians, was originally located in east central Wisconsin from Green Bay westward to the Wisconsin River and southward to the Fox River. Known from roughly 1671, when they were nearly destroyed in a war with the Illinois, their population of that date is estimated at 3,800. The tribe spoke a Siouan language fairly closely related to Oto and Iowa. The Winnebago were well adapted to life in the central Wisconsin forests and remained in the area in the face of the movement of Algonkin-speaking peoples to the west as a result of Atlantic coastal and eastern population pressures. With the arrival and dispersion of the Chippewa, the Winnebago retained hold of their native area in the 18th and 19th centuries, remaining on fairly favorable terms with the invaders. Pushed west of the Mississippi by governmental decree in 1825 and 1832, the Winnebago settled in sections of Iowa and Minnesota. During the Civil War, white settlers, alarmed at the Dakota outbreak of 1862, forced the removal of many to Dakota Territory, and some continued southward to settle with the Omaha in Nebraska. Others managed to retain their Wisconsin and Iowa holdings. The tribe, as a result, is much fragmented.

Culturally, the Winnebago belong to the Woodlands configuration; they adapted to hunting, fishing, and trapping patterns. In their social life, they suggest their congeners, the Omaha, Iowa, and Osage, without, however, possessing the Plains quality characteristic of these peoples. Their forest life precluded bison hunting. While they stressed war, the vision quest, and the sacred bundles, these features of their culture were given a distinctive quality, characteristic of the Winnebago rather than of the Plains. Winnebago social organization and religion were remarkably complex. The group was divided into two paternal units, with twelve clans. The two paternal units, conceptualized as above and below, embraced the clan organizations, four clans being assigned to the upper moiety and eight to the lower. The clans had political, ritual, and ceremonial functions as well as purely social ones. Thus, the tightness of the social system effected a solidarity among the Winnebago, providing an example of the fact that social fabric may create a sense of nation, as was true of many American Indian tribes.

BIBLIOGRAPHY

Paul Radin, *The Winnebago Tribe.*

— ROBERT F. SPENCER

WITCHCRAFT

Witchcraft has been a pet delusion of mankind always, but the papal bull of Innocent VIII gave it the authority of the Catholic church in 1484, and the *Malleus Maleficarum* published in 1489 became the great textbook of its manifestations. The superstition spread over the Western world, and many thousands of victims were hanged and burned in Europe in the 16th and 17th centuries. The conduct of Sir Matthew Hale at the Suffolk Assizes in 1664 rather fixed the subsequent procedure for English courts.

Undoubtedly belief in witchcraft was universal and sincere, and came to America with the colonists. Margaret Jones was executed for witchcraft in Boston in 1648. Soon after, Mary Parsons of Springfield, Mass., was indicted for witchcraft, but actually executed for murdering her child. Ann Hibbins was hanged in Boston on June 19, 1656. Other accusations, some of them with fatal results, occurred in scattered points in New England and the other colonies. Even William Penn presided over the trial of two Swedish women for witchcraft. The execution of a woman named Goody Glover in Boston in 1688, largely on the evidence of Martha Goodwin (a child of thirteen) whose case was studied by Cotton Mather, most closely paralleled the Salem, Mass., hysteria. The latter probably made Mather the champion of the witchcraft persecution.

In February 1692 in Salem Village (now Danvers), a group of young women and girls, who had been amusing themselves during the long winter listening to the lurid tales of Tituba, an old slave of the Rev. Samuel Parris, showed signs of hysteria. These "afflicted children," including Parris' daughter and niece, presently began to accuse persons of bewitching them. They fell down in fits supposed to be caused by the alleged witches, who were also accused of pinching them and sticking pins into them. The local physician could not see that the children had any malady, so Parris called in other ministers to confer on the strange manifestations. A powerful and inflammatory sermon was preached at the village by a visiting clergyman against the machinations of the devil. The civil magistrates entered the case. A special court to try the cases was appointed by the governor, and between May and September 1692 several hundred persons were arrested; nineteen were hanged and many imprisoned. Bridget Bishop, a young tavern keeper, was the first to be tried (June 2) and convicted of witchcraft; she was hanged on June 10. The cases were tried in Salem in an atmosphere of terror and tense excitement. No one knew who would be accused next and condemned on charges by the "afflicted children." Resistance to the delusion, at first terrorized into silence, grew rapidly, and by October the people came to their senses. Many strong characters exhibited high courage in resisting the excitement at the risk of their lives. Early in the next year all those arrested had been released with or without trial, and the episode was over.

No person convicted of witchcraft was ever burned in Salem. Giles Corey, who was pressed to death, was so treated under an old English law for refusing to plead to the indictment, not for witchcraft. Nowhere except

An engraving by Howard Pyle depicts the accusation of a bedeviled girl during the Salem witch trials. The original caption reads: "There is a flock of yellow birds around her head." (Corbis-Bettmann)

in Massachusetts did the participants in such a delusion have the courage to publicly confess their errors. The general court passed a resolution to that effect Dec, 17, 1696. Judge Samuel Sewall handed to his minister a confession to be read in his meetinghouse while he stood in his pew, and the twelve jurymen signed a statement admitting their error and asking forgiveness.

While a few later cases of witchcraft occurred in Virginia in 1706, in North Carolina in 1712, and perhaps in Rhode Island in 1728, this outbreak at Salem Village practically ended prosecutions for witchcraft in America.

BIBLIOGRAPHY

John Demos, "Underlying Themes in the Witchcraft of Seventeenth Century New England," *American Historical Review*, vol. 85.

Chadwick Hansen, *Witchcraft at Salem.*

S. E. Morison, *The Intellectual Life of Colonial New England.*

— JAMES DUNCAN PHILLIPS

WOMAN'S CHRISTIAN TEMPERANCE UNION

Woman's Christian Temperance Union had its origin in the Woman's Temperance Crusade, which started in Fredonia, N.Y., and Hillsboro, Ohio, in December 1873. The crusade women marched to saloons singing hymns, praying, and pleading with liquor sellers to close their businesses. The spirit of the crusade spread, and saloons were closed in many towns across several states. But within six months some of the same saloons had reopened, and the women realized that they would have to organize in order to battle the liquor traffic. Thus, leading crusade women met in Chautauqua, N.Y., and issued a call for a national convention of temperance women to be held in Cleveland on Nov. 18–20, 1874. Delegates from seventeen states answered the call, and the National Woman's Christian Temperance Union (WCTU) was founded with Annie Wittenmyer as the first president.

Every state soon had a WCTU organization, and the impact of these organizations began to be felt in public affairs. They campaigned for state legislation requiring scientific temperance instruction in the public schools, which was accomplished by 1902. Many of the victories over the liquor traffic, including national prohibition, are attributable to voters who had learned in school the evil effects of alcoholic beverages.

The foresighted leaders of the WCTU, under the guidance of Frances Elizabeth C. Willard, established a wide-ranging program of reform, including woman suffrage, equal rights, child welfare, better home standards, prison reforms, moral education, purity standards, international arbitration, and world peace. It has also continually waged a major fight against the liquor traffic, narcotics and tobacco, child labor, juvenile delinquency, prostitution, and gambling.

The emblem of the WCTU is a white ribbon bow with the motto "For God and Home and Everyland." By 1975 it had organizations in more than seventy nations and approximately 250,000 members in the United States. The World's Woman's Christian Temperance Union was tentatively organized in 1883 with Margaret Lucas Bright of England as presiding officer. Miss Willard was elected the first president at the first world convention held in Boston in 1891.

BIBLIOGRAPHY

Elizabeth P. Gordon, *Women Torch Bearers.*

Agnes Dubbs Hays, *Heritage of Dedication.*

E. D. Stewart, *Memories of the Crusade.*

Helen E. Tyler, *Where Prayer and Purpose Meet.*

— EDITH KIRKENDALL STANLEY

WOMAN'S PARTY, NATIONAL

Inspired by her experience with English suffragettes, Alice Paul led a group of women out of the National American Woman Suffrage Association in 1914 to form a new organization, the Congressional Union, renamed the National Woman's Party in 1916. Its purpose was to put pressure on the Democratic party to secure the right of women to the suffrage.

Beginning on July 14, 1917 (the anniversary of the fall of the Bastille in France), women began picketing in Washington, D.C., under purple, white, and gold banners using such slogans as "Liberty, Equality, Fraternity" and "Kaiser Wilson, have you forgotten your sympathy with the poor Germans because they were not self-governing? Twenty million American women are not self-governing. Take the beam out of your own eye." Mobs attacked the women and destroyed their banners without interference from the police. Picketing continued through Oct. 6 of that year. Although the demonstrations were peaceful, many women were jailed and drew attention to their campaign through hunger strikes. This period was climaxed by the attempted burning in effigy of President Woodrow Wilson on New Year's Day, 1917.

Wilson did give official support to the Nineteenth Amendment, which was the object of the women's campaign, and eventually persuaded the one senator whose vote was needed to pass it (1920). Subsequently the activities of the Woman's Party were oriented toward passage of further legislation to end discrimination against women and toward ratification of enfranchisement by state legislators.

BIBLIOGRAPHY

Inez Haynes Irwin, *The Story of the Woman's Party.*
Maud Park, *Front Door Lobby.*
Doris Stevens, *Jailed for Freedom.*

— CAROL ANDREAS

WOMAN'S RIGHTS MOVEMENT

Pioneer women who came to America from Europe are remembered mainly in the biographies of men: "first wife died at twenty-four, leaving six children"; "eight children born within twelve years"; "first wife died at nineteen, leaving three children." Women were indispensable on the frontier and many were brought over as indentured servants, willingly or unwillingly. Some transcended their caste positions in the home by assuming the business interests of a husband after his death. A few women challenged male domination of religious life, but they were banished (such as Anne Hutchinson) or put to death as witches.

Women who were active in the fight against the crown organized to spur the boycott of British goods. During this time, prominent women, such as Abigail Adams, wrote and spoke privately about the need for the male leaders of the struggle for independence to rectify the inferior position of women, promising rebellion if their words were not heeded. But only in the 19th century, when large numbers of women left their homes—where they had been accepting piecework as weavers and garmentmakers—to assume factory jobs in the textile industry and teaching jobs in the grammar schools, did they begin to act politically in their own behalf.

On Jan. 1, 1808, the importation of slaves into the United States was outlawed. One-third of the imported slaves had been women. They were used primarily to increase the slave population and were not sold or exchanged as often as male slaves, but they were subject to the sexual advances of white men against whom they had no defense. Early organizers for woman's rights began by working with black women who had escaped slavery and wanted to learn how to read and write. Others organized against inhumane conditions in the factories. The women who first spoke in public on questions of slavery and female abuse were viciously attacked, and women who organized schools in the early 1800's were harassed incessantly. Several who attended an antislavery convention in London were refused seats. While in London they laid plans to launch a movement for woman's rights on their return to the United States.

Women across the country had already been corresponding with each other about their situations. Later they organized self-improvement clubs that quickly became consciousness-raising centers about issues that affected them directly as women. These clubs never bore titles that betrayed their real function. But they owed their existence in part to the work of the women who had met in London and who, in 1848, called a public convention at Seneca Falls, N.Y., to discuss the status of women. At this convention a declaration written by Elizabeth Cady Stanton, Lucretia Mott, and others laid the groundwork for a series of meetings and new associations, most of which existed with the support of at least some men.

Men abandoned the women's movement during the struggle for the emancipation of slaves. Before the Civil War, literary and social critics, black and white, male and female, had begun to live together in communes throughout New England and the Midwest and were engaged in a radical transformation of their lives, including in some cases the abolition of marriage, but these efforts collapsed under the pressure of the war.

Because many feminists were also Socialists, and because woman's inferior position made them easy prey for exploitation in factories, business interests opposed the women's movement solidly—the liquor industry most of all. Women had no legal redress against drinking husbands and could not divorce them. An alliance between the temperance campaign and the movement for suffrage began to replace the earlier alliance between abolitionists and feminists who were committed to more radical changes than securing the vote. A split in the movement developed in 1869, rival publications were launched, and women divided on many issues, not the least of which was the issue of religion. One group attacked organized religion openly and worked with immigrant groups who were organizing unions in industry. Another nominated Victoria Woodhull, an advocate of free love and socialism, for president of the United States in 1872.

After the turn of the century the Woman's Christian Temperance Union, the Young Women's Christian Association, and hundreds of other women's clubs centered mainly in the Midwest joined in a federation to secure the vote for women, and their more radical sisters joined with them in national organization toward that end. Black women's clubs, which had been organized mainly around problems of health and the proliferation of prostitution in the cities, also joined the federation, even though some of the member organizations were openly racist.

Women secured the vote only after a long struggle and after another split in the movement occurred between women who wanted to work legally state by state and women who organized ongoing militant actions in the nation's capital. Most feminists who advocated and fought for workers' control of the mines and factories never committed themselves to the suffrage cause, but less revolutionary professional and middle-class women who worked with poor women organizing settlement houses in the cities did gain much support for suffrage from working-class women.

After securing the vote through ratification of the Nineteenth Amendment in 1920, gaining improved working conditions in factories, and bettering the legal status of women in marriage and divorce, women retired temporarily from organized activity pertaining to woman's rights. During the depression of the 1930's usually only women who gave up the option of marriage and children could hope to advance themselves professionally, and many women did so, sometimes in special organizations or orders established for that purpose within churches. During World War II, women again assumed new work roles and new prerogatives by joining in the war effort, but when the war was over they were encouraged to return to domestic careers. Liberal arts schools that had been established by and for women in the 19th century began to emphasize "feminine" pursuits, day-care centers that had been established during the war were closed down, and books and articles stressing the need for women to realize themselves through service to men and children proliferated.

Political apathy in the 1950's was followed by a rebirth of feminist activity in the 1960's—sparked, as in the past, by the experience of women who were involved in other social causes along with men. On college campuses, where young people were engaged in antiwar and civil rights struggles, those who had long been articulating the frustrations of women were heard. In welfare rights organizations poor women asserted themselves to demand dignity and control over their own lives. Women united to demand the legalization of abortion, the allocation of public monies for child care, the freedom to pursue new life-styles, and more information on the history of women. They began to publish their own newspapers and journals and to reach out to apolitical women through the establishment of small discussion groups in towns and cities throughout the country. Other groups, such as the National Organization for Women (NOW), organized in 1966, joined the struggle at other levels, pushing for a series of legislative measures to equalize the opportunities of men and women. A debate centered around the drive to secure passage of the Equal Rights Amendment, first introduced in 1923, and presented to the states for ratification in 1972, which would help professional women by eliminating restrictions imposed on the advancement of women at work, but would not help most working women unless the protections previously afforded them as women were granted to men, especially the protection from compulsory overtime. Women eventually united in support of the amendment, but the required number of state ratifications had not been secured by 1976. Many states, however, had passed individual equal rights amendments. Debate also centered around the differing priorities of black women, other Third World women, and white women. Chicano women working along the Mexican frontier won a major victory in 1974 in a prolonged struggle for union recognition and gave impetus to further organizing drives in workplaces where women predominate. The Caucus of Labor Union Women (CLUW) was formed in 1973 and has active chapters across the United States. Both CLUW and NOW have experienced conflicts between reform positions, supported by the more privileged women, and leftist revolutionary positions, which have grown out of the struggles of working-class women. These conflicts renew the ideological debates experienced at the turn of the century, and that result from the multiclass nature of the women's movement. Most of those who were developing feminist awareness in the 1960's and 1970's believed that the possibilities for liberation under capitalism are limited, but they were not sure how much emphasis to place on mass organizing for revolutionary change and how much to place on the extension and transformation of families and personal relationships in a drive toward undermining existing power structures. A strong component of the movement of the 1970's was openly lesbian and developed a politics of its own.

Many local women's groups began working in ways that did not involve them immediately in national issues, attempting to provide alternatives to the usual mass media presentations of women, attempting to increase women's options in controlling impregnation and protecting health, and providing services and sharing skills with women who needed them in order to survive economically and psychologically without becoming subservient to men.

BIBLIOGRAPHY

Carol Andreas, *Sex and Caste in America.*

Eleanor Flexner, *Century of Struggle.*

Aileen S. Kraditor, ed., *Up From the Pedestal.*

Gerda Lerner, *Black Women and White America.*

Robin Morgan, ed., *Sisterhood Is Powerful.*

Andrew Sinclair, *The Emancipation of the American Woman.*

— CAROL ANDREAS

WOMEN'S MOVEMENT SINCE THE 1970S

The reemergence of the women's movement in the United States in the late 1960s is commonly referred to as the second wave of feminism, which serves to distinguish it from the period more than a century earlier when women first organized around demands for full citizenship. While this modern wave of feminism changed during its first three decades, the demand for greater equity and self-determination for women in the United States remained its core. Through its many struggles and achievements, the women's movement remained a salient force for social justice and equity in the 1990s. The roots of the second wave lay in large-scale structural changes that occurred in the United States after 1960. Demographic change, including a rapidly falling birth rate, increased longevity, a rising divorce rate, and an increase in the age at which people married, radicalized the expectations of girls and women. They flooded into the full-time labor force, stayed in school longer, secured college and postgraduate degrees in increasing numbers, and linked their newfound sexual freedom with the desire to control their own reproduction.

What women found as they emerged from the relative shelter of wife and mother roles, however, was a society reluctant to accept them as full and equal participants. This contradiction variously produced disappointment, outrage, anger, and finally a social movement determined to acquire for women full rights of citizenship. The earliest organized forms of second-wave feminism were modeled on the civil rights movement's successful challenge to racial injustice in the United States. Many early activists in the women's movement had participated in the civil rights and antiwar movements or in the New Left politics and counterculture of the 1960s. The organizing lessons learned and the contacts developed served as the basis for their own attempts at change.

The ideology of the movement was diverse from the beginning, but there were underlying themes common to all those who sought to improve women's status. One was that of sexism—the notion that there are political and social institutions as well as deep-seated cultural attitudes that discriminate against women, denying them the opportunity to reach their fullest potential. A second theme was the goal of individual self-determination—the claim that women should be free to choose their own paths in life, perhaps helped by but not constrained by men or other women. Finally, perhaps the most widely publicized theme was that the "personal is political," the conviction that the only way Many early activists in the "second wave" women's movement had participated in the civil rights and antiwar movements of the 1960's.to change women's individual problems in the form of battering, rape, low-paying jobs, unfair divorce laws, discriminatory education, or degrading notions of femininity is through political organizing and political struggle.

Many early activists in the "second wave" women's movement had participated in the civil rights and antiwar movements of the 1960's.

Organizations and small groups appeared in the late 1960s and the 1970s as feminists grappled with the difficult question of how to act on these themes and insights. The largest and most structured of the new feminist organizations, the National Organization for Women (NOW), founded in 1966, fought legal and legislative battles in an unsuccessful attempt to secure passage of the Equal Rights Amendment, intended to eliminate discrimination against women in education and the labor force and safeguard women's reproductive freedom. In contrast, the small, loosely organized consciousness-raising groups typical of the early women's liberation movement held intimate discussions in which women explored their struggles to become more assertive and to resist a socialization process that had taught them to be passive and self-denigrating.

Some feminists believed that street protests were the most effective way to communicate feminism's message to large numbers of people. Direct-action tactics included protests at the Miss America pageant in 1968; the hexing of the New York Stock Exchange by women dressed as witches; the Women's Strike for Equality on Aug. 26, 1970, involving more than 100,000 women throughout the country; and, later, huge demonstrations to assert women's right to abortion. Other activists worked for a feminist vision of change by organizing alternative institutions. Rape hot lines and battered women's shelters were established; women's health clinics, food stores, publishers, a symphony orchestra, art galleries, bookstores, banks, and bars provided outlets for creative energies and entrepreneurial skills. Although there was much disagreement within the movement about which of these disparate tactics was most effective, their combined effect was staggering. They touched the lives of millions of Americans and began to transform the ways people thought about and acted toward women.

In the 1990s the women's movement faced new challenges and problems. Despite substantial gains in many areas over thirty years, sexist attitudes and behavior endured. The gap between women's and men's incomes narrowed but persisted, with women earning approximately 25 percent less than men regardless of education. Abortion rights, while guaranteed, came under renewed attack and in some states were eroded. Sexual harassment was a recognized crime but continued to compromise women's full equality. More women were running for and winning elective office than ever before but in 1994 women constituted only 10 percent of the Congress. Many women earning their own incomes had to work a "second shift" because they remained responsible for most or all of their families' care, even in two-earner households. These and other concerns shaped the ideological debates within feminism at the end of the twentieth century. The women's movement continued to contain within itself a plethora of differing analyses and opinions concerning women and social change.

One such debate focused on the issue of sexual violence. Feminists were divided about the role of pornography in engendering and encouraging the sexual violence rampant in the United States. Many who believed that pornography was a major cause of woman-centered violence called for strict regulation or outlawing of pornography as a violation of women's civil rights. Other feminists were concerned about the difficulty of defining pornography, claiming that the real causes of violence against women are complex and rooted deep within our culture and social institutions. They argued that pornography is a form of free speech—however abhorrent—that must be tolerated in a democratic society. Disagreements were apparent as well on the question of how to define and punish such problems as sexual harassment, date rape, and marital rape. Some questioned the legitimacy of a "battered woman defense," giving women victims of systematic violence the right to strike back against their abusers. While all feminists agreed that gender-based crimes against women, including violent acts against lesbian women, were a virulent form of sexism that must be eradicated, they differed in their analyses of and remedies for these problems.

Another debate divided "difference" feminists from "equality" feminists. Difference feminists stressed that women resemble one another and differ from men in fundamental ways. They focused on the value of presumed feminine characteristics, claiming women's greater empathy, cooperation, intuition, and care and posited these as superior to those thought to characterize men. Although they frequently pointed to socialization rather than biology as the source of sex differences, these feminists believed women's characteristics are shared by all women and difficult if not impossible to alter. Equality feminism, in contrast, rejected the view that there are basic social and psychological differences between women and men. It focused on eliminating barriers to fulfilling individual potential. Equality feminism defined social justice in a gender-neutral fashion, anticipating a future that would provide women and men with opportunities to exercise individual choice on a wide range of issues, including reproduction, education, employment, legal rights, sexual orientation, and personal relationships. It rejected the traditional idea that women's differences from men are inherent or can ever be legitimately used to justify either sex's exclusion from any aspect of society or social life. The political ramifications of difference and equality feminism were many. They divided feminists who advocated special provisions for women in the labor force and the law from those who wanted equal treatment for women and men. One practical aspect of this debate concerned the appropriate remedy for the persistent disadvantages of women in the labor force. When compared to men, women earned less, were promoted less frequently, and continued to be segregated in "female" occupations. Most harmful of all was the pattern of interrupted work histories that characterized large numbers of women as they continued to drop out of the labor force in order to almost single-handedly rear children and care for their homes.

Insisting on preserving women's special relationship to home and children, difference feminists addressed women's disadvantaged position in the workforce with such solutions as the "mommy track." This special arrangement of part-time work enables female lawyers, for example, to spend more time at home without forgoing their law practices. Women retain their relationships with firms even though the ability to qualify as partners is delayed and salaries are considerably lower than are those of full-time lawyers. Equality feminists, however, rejected such special protections. Their search for remedies focused rather on finding ways to equalize men's and women's responsibilities for home and child care. Many equality feminists believed that parental leaves of absence from work when children are young or ill, expanded availability of low-cost and high-quality day care, and greater participation of men in fairly dividing responsibilities for housework and child rearing were the only real solutions to women's dual-workload problem. By the middle of the 1990s, however, neither difference nor equality feminists had been able to exercise the political power necessary to resolve women's continuing disadvantages in the labor force.

The ideologies of difference and equality separated feminists with respect to strategies for building the movement itself. Difference feminists tended to be wary of coalitions, especially those with men. They were generally pessimistic about the possibility of changing what they saw as men's essentially intractable sexist attitudes and behavior and frequently claimed that only women can understand and fight women's oppression. As a result, feminists influenced by a difference model tended to be separatist, inward looking, and focused on what they saw as women's inevitable victimization. Their activism often took the form of trying to shield women from sexism, especially by separating them from its sources. Thus, one of their primary goals was the creation of all-women environments that were considered safe spaces, such as those at women's music festivals or retreats.

The ideology of equality feminism, in contrast, concentrated on eradicating sexism by removing its causes. For many equality feminists this included working in coalition with men to change their attitudes and behavior toward women. They focused on issues that could unite women and men of different social classes and races, such as the disproportionate poverty of U.S. women and their children, federal funding for abortions, and the need for day care. Their goal was to change those aspects of the society that engender sexism. They fought for fair laws and nonsexist legislation and staged large demonstrations and protests to create a broad-based, diverse, and effective movement for ending sexism.

The establishment of women's studies courses and programs in virtually every university in the nation is one of the most significant achievements of the women's movement.

The difference and equality debate raged within academic institutions. The establishment of women's studies courses and programs in almost every institution of higher education in the country was unquestionably one of the women's movement's most significant achievements. These programs and the women's centers with which they were often associated on college campuses altered the way scholars and students thought about issues of gender. Reversing a situation in which women and their contributions to history, science, and society were almost entirely ignored, women's studies courses educated millions of young people about the importance of both women and men to our cultural heritage and contemporary world. Despite their success, women's studies programs faced an identity crisis in the 1990s. On one side, equality feminists argued that the subjects of women and gender should be integrated into the curriculum and not require separate courses or programs. To them the primary goal of women's studies programs was to facilitate that integration. In contrast, difference feminists claimed that only an independent women's studies curriculum could fulfill the continuing need for courses dedicated to women's unique place in and approach to the world. Thus, feminists celebrated the many accomplishments of women's studies programs even as they disagreed about the strategy that should be adopted by such programs.

The women's movement remained a forum for debate, with issues, strategies, and tactics subject to controversy. While such diversity may have confused a public looking for simple definitions or perplexed those who wanted to know, finally, "What do women want?"

its multifaceted nature was the movement's strength. The women's movement had room for everyone who agreed that sexism has no place in a society dedicated to social justice. The most important contribution of the women's movement of the late twentieth century was to improve women's lives by reducing obstacles to the full expression of their desires and choices. Feminists contributed to the wider society as well, because their activism was an important element in the continuing struggle for a more equitable and just society for all.

[See also Abortion; Affirmative Action; Contraception; Equal Rights Amendment; Family; Gay and Lesbian Movement; Marriage and Divorce.]

BIBLIOGRAPHY

Alice Echols, *Daring To Be Bad: Radical Feminism in America, 1967–1975* (Minneapolis, 1989).

Sara M. Evans, *Born for Liberty: A History of Women in America* (New York, 1989).

Jo Freeman, *The Politics of Women's Liberation* (New York, 1975).

Victor R. Fuchs, *Women's Quest for Economic Equality* (Cambridge, Mass., 1988).

Arlie Hochschild, *The Second Shift* (New York, 1989).

bell hooks, *Ain't I A Woman? Black Women and Feminism* (Boston, 1981).

Wendy Kaminer, *A Fearful Freedom: Women's Flight from Equality* (New York, 1990).

Kristin Luker, *Abortion and the Politics of Motherhood* (Berkeley, Calif., 1984).

Susan Schechter, *Women and Male Violence* (Boston, 1982).

Carol Tavris, *The Mismeasure of Woman* (New York, 1992).

— JOAN D. MANDLE

WOODSTOCK

Woodstock (1969 and 1994). Near the end of the 1960s, with the anti–Vietnam War and counterculture movements peaking in strength, a series of rock music festivals crisscrossed the United States, especially in 1969. The Woodstock Music and Art Fair was the high point of the festivals and, many would argue, of the decade as well. From 400,000 to 500,000 people crammed onto a farm in Bethel, N.Y., near Woodstock, to camp, listen to music, and commune with nature. The festival attracted many of the top musicians and bands of the 1960s, including Janis Joplin, Jimi Hendrix, Joan Baez, Santana, The Who, Joe Cocker, and Crosby, Stills, Nash, and Young. The festival also attracted many of the era's favorite recreational drugs, including marijuana and LSD, although the latter sometimes came laced with toxic substances. Added to the mix of music and drugs, heavy rains turned the farmland into acres of mud and led thousands to shed their clothes. A benevolent chaos and anarchy ruled the festival, with many attendees cutting down the gates surrounding the farm to avoid the eighteen-dollar ticket charge. For many in the counterculture and antiwar movement, Woodstock represented the best of the 1960s. Reality, however, tarnishes the myth. For all of its antiestablishment underpinnings, a corporate and government presence constantly hovered over the festival. Organizers later said that their main goal was to make money from the festival; Warner Brothers had cameras present and produced an Academy Award-winning movie, while Atlantic Records recorded the festival for a multi-record set. When food and water ran out, helicopters ferried in those supplies along with medicine—the same type of helicopters that ferried soldiers and munitions during the Vietnam War, the target of much of the counterculture's wrath.

Woodstock organizers staged a reunion concert in Saugerties, N.Y., in August 1994. This festival was openly corporate, with Pepsi, Häagen Dazs ice cream, and MCI among the sponsors. It was also expensive: advance tickets cost $135 each; those attending found a Häagen Dazs ice cream bar selling for $3 dollars and a cup of Pepsi for $2 while an official program cost $15. This second concert's music lineup was geared toward the tastes of baby boomers' children, with "alternative" rock and punk bands such as Green Day, Nine Inch Nails, and Porno for Pyros as the headliners. On the other hand Bob Dylan performed this time, while several Woodstock I performers showed up, including Cocker, Santana, and Crosby, Stills, and Nash. Moreover, two stalwarts of the original festival—drugs and mud—reappeared. Many concertgoers used marijuana and LSD, despite the efforts of a large security force to confiscate the contraband, but there was less drug use than in 1969. Heavy rains left the more than 300,000 people in attendance covered with muck.

[See also Music, Rock and Roll.]

BIBLIOGRAPHY

Joel Makower, *Woodstock: The Oral History* (New York, 1989).

Robert Stephen Spitz, *Barefoot in Babylon: The Creation of the Woodstock Music Festival, 1969* (New York, 1979).

— THOMAS G. GRESS

WORKS PROGRESS ADMINISTRATION

One of the first actions of the administration of President Franklin D. Roosevelt was to extend federal relief to the unemployed in 1933. Work relief was devised where possible, but many able-bodied unemployed were added to relief roles in the emergency. Yet Roosevelt shared President Herbert Hoover's aversion to the dole, calling it in 1935 "a narcotic, a subtle destroyer of the human spirit," and in the spring of that year he asked

Congress for $4.8 billion to put all able-bodied men to work, while turning the sick, aged, blind, and disabled over to the states with financial assistance promised under the Social Security program. Congress made the appropriation, and Roosevelt established the Works Progress Administration (WPA) by executive order on May 6, 1935, to organize "light" public works projects for those workers not employed by the "heavy" public works agencies, primarily the Public Works Administration (PWA) and the Tennessee Valley Authority (TVA). As it turned out, the WPA became the government's major public works effort, since director Harry L. Hopkins (1935–39) proved to be more energetic and innovative than Harold L. Ickes, the cautious head of PWA. In 1939 the WPA was renamed Works Projects Administration.

The WPA faced certain limits on its scope beyond the size of the initial appropriation. By its estimates, there were 3.5 million employable citizens looking for work in 1935 (actually, the number was at least twice that), and a decent level of relief for them required projects on which costs of materials were low. In order to minimize political difficulties, the government projects could not compete with private enterprise and had to have a persuasive social value. It was a formidable assignment to spend the money effectively, given these limits, the pressures of time, and the variety of skills among the unemployed.

Hopkins set up divisions in every state, sought local sponsors for the work, and began approving an impressive range of projects. Where people had useful skills, the WPA was eager to preserve them. Discovering that artists, musicians, and writers were hit hard by the Great Depression, the WPA organized projects to utilize their talents. The Federal Theatre Project, headed by Hallie Flanagan, reached an audience estimated at 30 million people with performances of Christopher Marlowe's *The Tragedy of Dr. Faustus*, Sinclair Lewis' *It Can't Happen Here*, and T. S. Eliot's *Murder in the Cathedral*; presented *Macbeth* by an all-black cast with Haitian stage settings; and invented a dramatic depiction of current events called *The Living Newspaper*. The Federal Arts Project employed artists to decorate public buildings with murals. The Federal Writers' Project turned out city, state, and territorial guides; regional and geographic studies; and histories of America's ethnic groups.

Since federal aid to the arts was unprecedented, WPA arts projects were the agency's most controversial programs. But WPA was no less inventive in conserving the skills of other citizens without jobs. WPA funds were used to pay unemployed dentists for repairing teeth, nurses for making home visits, taxidermists for stuffing birds, and biologists for planting oysters. But the main thrust of WPA projects was directed toward offering employment to semiskilled and unskilled citizens. This meant a major effort in the construction of public facilities. The American landscape at the end of the 1930's bore numerous marks of WPA effort—high-school stadiums, privies for rural schools, municipal auditoriums, airports, rural roads, improved parks and recreation areas, and reclaimed swamps. The WPA built 1,634 new school buildings, 105 airports, 3,000 tennis courts, 3,300 storage dams, 103 golf courses, and 5,800 mobile libraries. By 1941 the agency had spent $11.3 billion to provide work for 8 million victims of a decade of depression.

The WPA organized projects to employ the talents of jobless artists, musicians, and writers, resulting in public murals, city guides, ethnic histories, and rare folk music recordings.

The agency was popular in the country at large, particularly among low-income people for whom unemployment was either a threat or a reality. The "reliefers" themselves formed a union, the Workers' Alliance, to lobby for the extension of the WPA and for the improvement of its wages. Yet the program also generated criticism. The charge that WPA projects were too often frivolous seems narrow-minded today and forgetful of the pressures of emergency. Fears that the huge WPA work force was evolving into a permanent group that would give political support to any incumbent administration seem in retrospect more justified. Yet the Roosevelt administration actually held WPA back from attaining its full potential. With unemployment ranging from 8 to 15 million, WPA never employed more than 3.2 million people in any month (its low was 1.7 million in 1937), and its average monthly earnings were far below prevailing or even "security" wages. Historians have generally praised the agency for preserving the pride and enhancing the usefulness of millions of citizens at a paltry cost and have not been sympathetic with fears of the political impact of so many Americans going onto the federal payroll. In the 1930's the political effect of extended unemployment seemed more dangerous. World War II ended the argument between friends of WPA, who wished the government to become the employer of last resort permanently, and those who feared the erosion of citizen independence inherent in federal

employment. On June 30, 1943, with wartime production absorbing most of the unemployed, Roosevelt gave WPA its "honorable discharge," and in three months the agency mailed its last checks.

BIBLIOGRAPHY

Josephine C. Brown, *Public Relief, 1929–1939.*

Donald S. Howard, *The W.P.A. and Federal Relief Policy.*

William F. McDonald, *Federal Relief Administration and the Arts.*

— OTIS L. GRAHAM, JR.

WORLD WAR I

World War I (1914–18), overall the second most costly war in history, in which the United States became involved in 1917. When the June 1914 assassination of the heir to the Austro-Hungarian throne at Sarajevo (now part of Yugoslavia) propelled the European powers into war, President Woodrow Wilson urged Americans to remain "impartial in thought as well as action." Despite intense propaganda to the contrary, most Americans tried to conform until early in 1915, when Germany opened submarine warfare and in May sank the British liner *Lusitania*, with a loss of 1,198 lives, including 128 Americans. Although Britain too was violating freedom of the seas by blockading Germany and neutral European nations, loss of life in the submarine campaign turned opinion more against Germany. So vigorous was Wilson's diplomatic protest that his pacifist secretary of state, William Jennings Bryan, resigned.

Lacking enough submarines to achieve victory by that means, Germany, in September 1915, promised to warn passenger liners before sinking and safeguard passengers' lives. When, in March 1916, a submarine sank the French channel steamer *Sussex* with further loss of American lives, Germany responded to Wilson's protest by again promising safeguards. Meanwhile, Britain intensified the blockade, published a long list of contraband items, and blacklisted U.S. firms trading with the Central Powers. Believing a German victory would be calamitous, Wilson, while protesting vigorously, tolerated Britain's intransigence and blocked an attempt in Congress to embargo munitions, which would have been unfavorable to the Allies. In late 1915 Wilson repealed a ban on loans to belligerents, thereby further stimulating trade with the Allies.

While still championing neutrality and offering to mediate for the warring powers, Wilson was so disturbed by the submarine threat and the carnage in Europe that he advocated limited increases in American armed forces, but not enough to satisfy his secretary of war, Lindley M. Garrison, who resigned. Spurred by trouble along the Mexican border, Congress in May 1916 passed the National Defense Act, which projected ultimately an army of 223,000 and a National Guard of 450,000 and gave the president power to place defense orders and force industry to comply. Yet even at maximum strength the army would be far smaller than European armies.

Having lost appalling numbers of men in 1916 and with victory still elusive, Germany's military and naval leaders persuaded Kaiser Wilhelm II that France and Britain could be crushed by unrestricted submarine warfare before the United States could make its weight felt. On Jan. 31, 1917, Germany informed all neutrals that beginning immediately U-boats would sink all vessels, neutral and Allied alike, without warning.

In response, Wilson broke diplomatic relations with Germany, although he still hoped to avoid war. He demurred even when Britain on Feb. 23 revealed the contents of an intercepted telegram from the German foreign secretary, Arthur Zimmerman, to the German minister in Mexico proposing an alliance of Germany, Mexico, and Japan against the United States. In return, Mexico was to regain the territory of Texas, New Mexico, and Arizona. Wilson's only move was to ask Congress for authority to arm merchant ships; blocked by a filibuster by a small minority, he had to proceed under an old law.

In the next few weeks submarines sank four American ships at a cost of fifteen American lives. Convinced at last that American participation was inevitable, Wilson on Apr. 2 asked Congress for a declaration of war. The Senate approved, 82 to 6; the House, 373 to 50. Wilson signed the declaration on Apr. 6. By that time, keyed up by the submarine campaign, Allied propaganda rich with atrocity stories, and bumbling German espionage and sabotage in the United States, a majority of Americans supported the move.

As the United States entered the war, Allied fortunes were approaching the nadir. Russian military units riven by revolutionary cells had begun to collapse, opening the way for the Bolshevists to seize power in the October Revolution and sue for peace. Mutiny spread through fifty-four French divisions, and a British offensive—the Battle of Passchendaele—resulted in 245,000 casualties, twice those of the Germans. Before an Austrian offensive—the Battle of Caporetto—the Italian army lost 305,000 men and fell back a hundred miles in panic. Yet the most serious crisis of all was at sea, where in February alone submarines had sunk 781,000 tons of shipping; at such a rate Britain would soon have to give in.

Only the U.S. Navy was in a position to provide immediate help. An emissary from Washington, William S. Sims, convinced the British Admiralty to employ a system of convoys protected by warships. Although the system failed to defeat the submarines, it reduced losses sharply and ended the crisis.

The U.S. Army numbered only 307,000 men, it did not have a single unit of divisional size, and its arsenal was either bare or obsolete. Maj. Gen. (later General of the Armies) John J. Pershing nevertheless went to France in May at the head of an advance contingent of the American Expeditionary Forces. Deeming a boost to Allied morale essential, the U.S. Army created the First Division by culling men from various units. Pershing was in Paris on July 4, and a battalion of the division paraded to French cheers of near delirium. He participated in a ceremony at the tomb of the Marquis de Lafayette, where an officer in the Quartermaster Corps, Lt. Col. C. E. Stanton—not Pershing, as legend would long have it—uttered the words "Lafayette, we are here." Yet it was months before the First Division, or any other, was sufficiently trained to fight.

Meanwhile, on May 18, 1917, Congress passed the Selective Service Act, eventually enrolling 10 million men. Of close to 4 million who eventually served, 2.8 million were drafted. The army began feverishly to build vast cantonments to house the new troops.

Created by the National Defense Act of 1916, the Council of National Defense served as a central planning agency to mobilize industry. A subordinate agency, the War Industries Board, had broad powers to coordinate purchasing by the army and navy, to establish production priorities, to create new plants and convert existing ones to priority uses, and to coordinate various civilian war agencies. Herbert Hoover, as food administrator, stimulated food production dramatically. When the transportation system by autumn of 1917 appeared about to collapse, the U.S. Treasury took charge of all railroads. The powers of the U.S. Shipping Board, created in 1916, were expanded in 1917, and by the end of the war its Emergency Fleet Corporation had built up a fleet of 10 million tons. But not until 1918 was the National War Labor Board created to coordinate labor. The efforts of the Committee on Public Information to influence public opinion, begun in April 1917, were soon reinforced by the Espionage Act of 1917 and, later, by the Sedition Act of 1918, which sharply curtailed public expression of opinion. Stung by congressional criticism of delays in getting troops into action, Wilson promoted the Overman Act, passed on May 20, 1918, giving him almost unlimited power to reorganize, coordinate, and centralize governmental functions. About two-thirds of war expenses, including loans to the Allies, were met by bond issues widely oversubscribed.

So urgent was the need for weapons and equipment that industry was hard-pressed to meet it. Only the Springfield rifle was available in appreciable numbers, and its production could be augmented by plants that had been filling Allied orders for the British Lee-Enfield rifle. All American troops reaching France in 1917 had to use Allied machine guns and automatic rifles, although new and excellent U.S. Browning models became available in volume by mid-1918. Of some 2,250 artillery pieces used by U.S. forces, only 100 were of American manufacture. A small U.S. tank corps had to use French tanks throughout, and American aviators had to fly Allied planes despite an

Captain Edward Vernon Rickenbacker (1890-1973), American World War I aviator. By the end of the war, he had flown 134 missions and scored twenty-six victories, earning him the Medal of Honor in 1931. (Corbis-Bettmann)

ambitious airplane-building program involving hundreds of millions of dollars.

Soon after reaching France, Pershing recommended sending 1 million men by the end of 1918. The disasters that soon befell Allied forces prompted him and the president's personal envoy, Col. Edward M. House, to press for even more troops if a German victory were to be averted. Pershing eventually asked for 100 U.S. divisions. The army reached a strength of 3.7 million in 62 divisions, 42 of which went overseas.

Part of Pershing's charge was to cooperate with Allied forces but to maintain American forces as "a separate and distinct component of the combined forces." That prompted him to resist strong pressures from the British and French to feed the ill-trained, inexperienced American soldiers into Allied divisions as replacements so that, the Allies argued, their strength could be quickly brought to bear. Pershing instead set up an extensive training program for incoming American units. Not until January 1918 did he deem any division capable of moving even into a quiet sector, and not until the end of May were American forces to participate actively in the fighting. The American divisions contained 28,000 men, almost double the size of Allied and German divisions.

The first major action involving an American unit developed in a quiet sector in Lorraine where a German regiment, on Apr. 20, 1918, attacked units of the Twenty-sixth Division defending the village of Seicheprey. The Germans took the village but lost it to U.S. counterattack. The Germans left behind 160 dead but took 135 prisoners and inflicted 634 casualties. The first American offensive was by a regiment of the First Division, which on May 28 captured the village of Cantigny and held against powerful counterattacks. The Americans lost 1,607 men, including 199 killed.

Through the spring of 1918 the Germans launched a series of powerful offensives, culminating in an attack in late May against the Chemin des Dames, a commanding ridgeline covering Soissons and an important approach to Paris. Attacking on May 27, the Germans scored a quick success and in three days reached the Marne River at Château-Thierry, less than fifty miles from Paris, almost as close as in the opening drive of the war. Under pressure of the crisis, Pershing offered U.S. help. By the night of May 31 the Third Division was moving into defenses behind the Marne, and the next day the Second Division took up positions north of the river astride the main highway to Paris. Both divisions threw back every German thrust, and on June 6 the Second Division counterattacked through Belleau Wood and the villages of Bouresches and Vaux. It was a costly American debut—9,777 casualties, including 1,811 dead—but the moral effect on both sides was great. With 250,000 U.S. troops arriving every month and their abilities amply demonstrated along the Marne, the effect on Allied troops and the French population was electric.

In July, in what proved to be the final German offensive, the Third, Twenty-eighth, and Forty-second U.S. divisions bolstered French defenses along the Marne. In the French counterattack that followed, these and the Fourth, Twenty-sixth, Thirty-second, and Seventy-seventh divisions participated, along with two U.S. corps headquarters.

The fight through the Argonne Forest in 1918 was the greatest battle fought by American troops to that time: 1.25 million participated, incurring 120,000 casualties.

Pershing meanwhile pressed his case for a separate American force holding its own portion of the front. The overall Allied commander, Marshal Ferdinand Foch, designated a sector in Lorraine facing a salient near Saint-Mihiel. With Pershing as commander, headquarters of the U.S. First Army opened on Aug. 10. Some American units nevertheless continued to fight alongside the Allies. The II Corps with the Twenty-seventh and Thirtieth divisions fought throughout at the side of the British, and eight other divisions fought from time to time alongside the French. Only one, the Ninety-third, a black unit, was broken up and parceled out within a French division.

As Foch prepared a general offensive, the First Army attacked to reduce the Saint-Mihiel salient, employing a French corps and three American corps with nine divisions. Anticipating the attack, the Germans had begun to withdraw before the preliminary bombardment began, so that success was swift.

As part of the general offensive, the First Army attacked on Sept. 26 northward along the west bank of the Meuse River through the Argonne Forest in the direction of Sedan. The fight through mud, forest, and three successive German defense lines was grueling. Since American success would jeopardize the main lateral German railway, the German command committed twenty-seven reserve divisions in the sector. Not until the end of October was the third German line broken. It was the greatest battle fought by American troops to that time—1.25 million participated, incurring 120,000 casualties.

Despite this and other strong stands, the overall German position was becoming desperate. On Oct. 4 the German chancellor cabled Wilson, asking for an armistice in keeping with the Fourteen Points that Wilson had proposed early in the year; but the British and French objected on the basis that the Germans should be given no quarter. Wilson rejected the German request. The kaiser meanwhile had begun to listen to the voices of a disillusioned people, the noise of riots in the streets, and the rumblings of Marxist revolution. Bulgaria had left the war on Sept. 30, Turkey on Oct. 30, and Austria-Hungary on Nov. 3. As the Allies renewed their general offensive, the kaiser, on Nov. 8, sent delegates to France to discuss armistice terms. On Nov. 9 he abdicated and fled into exile. The fighting ended at 11 A.M., Nov. 11, 1918.

More than 8.5 million men died in the war among total casualties of 37.5 million. American casualties were 320,710, only a small part of the whole, but American involvement had provided the advantage that assured Allied victory.

BIBLIOGRAPHY

Edward M. Coffman, *The War to End All Wars.*

Harvey A. DeWeerd, *President Wilson Fights His War.*

S. L. A. Marshall and the editors of *American Heritage, The American Heritage History of World War I.*

— CHARLES B. MACDONALD

WORLD WAR II

By 1939 the international situation had become so delicate that isolationism was no longer gospel, except to a small segment who were pacifists or America First advocates. Militarist-dominated Japan was by then clearly embarked on the conquest and domination of eastern Asia. German Führer Adolf Hitler in Central Europe was recognized as a danger to the United States, as well as to his neighbors and to humanity at large. The invasion of Poland that year was the handwriting on the wall.

Background to Pearl Harbor

After its defeat and disarmament in World War I, Germany eventually fell into the hands of extreme nationalists. The National Socialists rearmed the nation, reentered the Rhineland (March 1936), forced a union with Austria (March 1938), seized Czechoslovakia with false promises (October 1938–March 1939), made a nonaggression pact with Russia to protect its eastern frontier (Aug. 23, 1939), and then overran Poland (Sept. 1–Oct. 6, 1939), bringing France and Great Britain into the war in consequence of their pledge to maintain Polish independence. In May 1940 a power thrust swept German troops forward through France, drove British forces back across the English Channel (June 4), and compelled France to surrender (June 22). An attack on England, aimed to deny use of Britain as a springboard for reconquest of the Continent, failed in the air and did not materialize on land. Open breach of the nonaggression treaty was followed by a German invasion of Russia in June 1941.

Meanwhile, Japan had been fortifying Pacific islands in secret violation of 1921 treaties, encroaching on China in Manchuria and Tientsin in 1931 and in Shanghai in 1932, starting open war at Peking in 1937, and thereafter, as Germany's ally, planning further conquests.

The United States opposed this Japanese expansion diplomatically by every means short of war, and military staff planning began as early as 1938 to consider that a two-ocean war was bound to come and to calculate that the issues in the Orient would have to be largely decided in Europe. It would be America's safest course in the long run, it was felt, to maintain the integrity of the Western Hemisphere by preventing the defeat of the British Commonwealth. Ever since the Russo-Japanese War of 1905, the U.S. Army had been convinced that America could not hold Manila. The U.S. government had agreed in 1921 not to fortify further there or on Guam. It was felt that America's eventual western defense line must run from Alaska through Hawaii to Panama.

Rearmament started at home, developing and producing new weapons and new planes, and speeding up motorization of U.S. land forces. The Uranium Committee was created in 1939, the National Defense Research Committee in 1940, and the Office of Scientific Research and Development in 1941 to develop radar and antisubmarine devices. Formation of the Council of National Defense to coordinate industry, finance, transportation, and labor in the event of open war, showed a high-level realization of the seriousness of impending events. Prior to America's formal entry into war, the United States assisted France and Britain by shipping tanks and weapons and by furnishing much material to help equip the British Home Guard. The United States turned over naval destroyers to Britain to hold down the submarine menace, and itself patrolled large areas of the Atlantic Ocean against the German U-boats, with which U.S. ships were involved in prewar shooting incidents. The United States also took over rights and responsibilities at defense bases on British possessions bordering the Atlantic.

In 1940 the U.S. course was mapped by rapidly passing events. The April and May invasions of Norway, Denmark, Holland, Belgium, Luxembourg, and France triggered American actions. In his Chicago speech of 1937, President Franklin D. Roosevelt had promised to quarantine aggressors. In his Charlottesville, Va., speech on June 10, 1940, he went further. He not only indicted Germany's new partner Italy, but also issued a public promise of help to "the opponents of force." In June also, he assured himself of bipartisan political support by appointing the Republicans Frank Knox and Henry L. Stimson to head the Navy and War departments. Military expansion began in earnest.

The Selective Service and Training Act of Sept. 16, 1940, instituted peacetime conscription for the first time in U.S. history, registering 16 million men in a month. Also—following Woodrow Wilson's technique of 1916—it brought the National Guard into active federal service to ready it for combat. In July 1940 the Export Embargo Act was passed, which was to be used as a war measure, followed by the Lend-Lease Act of March 1941 to help prospective allies and others in need of aid. U.S. military leaders strongly preferred to avoid a war with Japan, believing that America was not ready for it. In November 1940 Adm. Harold R. Stark and Gen. George C. Marshall jointly declared that America's major course of action for the time being would therefore be: (a) to rearm; (b) to avoid provoking attack; and (c) to restrict Pacific actions so as to permit major offensive action in the Atlantic theater should war actually come. In January 1941 in view of possible future developments, there were Anglo-American staff conferences in Washington, D.C. In August 1941 Roosevelt and Prime Minister Winston Churchill met at Argentia, Newfoundland, and formulated war aims, and with their staffs delved into overall strategy and war planning. For the first time in U.S. history the country was, for all practical purposes, militarily allied before war came. At this meeting was established the Atlantic Charter. In September 1941, with the signs clear as to the future, the draft act was extended beyond its previous limit of one year—even though by the slim margin of a single vote in Congress—and the full training, reorganization, and augmentation of U.S. forces began.

Organization, Preparation, and Strategy

On Dec. 7, 1941, a sneak attack by Japanese carrier-based planes surprised and severely crippled the U.S. fleet at Pearl Harbor, dooming American forces in the Philippines. Japan was now free to expand into Southeast Asia and the East Indies toward Australia. The very next day Congress declared war on Japan, and on Dec. 11 met declarations from Italy and Germany—allied to Japan by treaties—by similar declarations put through in a single day of legislative action in committees and on the floor of both houses of Congress. There was no choice. The United States had been attacked by one power and had war declared on it by two other powers.

Before the month of December was out, Churchill was again in Washington, bringing with him military and naval experts for what has been called the Arcadia conference (beginning Dec. 22); and within weeks there was created in Washington the Combined Chiefs of Staff, an international military, naval, and air body that was used throughout the war to (a) settle strategy; (b) establish unified interallied command in the separate theaters of war; and (c) issue strategic instructions to theater commanders. Allied to it were the Munitions Assignment Board to allocate materials to the different theaters and the Combined Raw Materials Board and Combined Shipping Assignment Board, neither of which played an extremely important role during the war.

The day after the attack on Pearl Harbor, Congress declared war on Japan; three days later, Germany and Italy declared war on the U.S.

Almost instantly on the declaration of war, under the first War Powers Act, there began a reorganization and expansion of the army and the navy, including the National Guard already in federal service. Increasing numbers of reservists were called to active duty, not as units but as individuals, to fill gaps in existing units, to officer the training centers, and to officer new units being formed. Additional divisions were created and put into training, bearing the numbers of World War I divisions in most cases, but with scarcely any relation to them in locality or in personnel of previously existing reserve divisions. Field artillery regiments were broken up, and greater flexibility was achieved with separate battalions. Cavalry units were transformed into armored forces. Antiaircraft units were improved and greatly increased in number, later to be armed with the new proximity fuse for their projectiles. New types of troops were formed: mountain units, armored divisions, and airborne divisions. The old square infantry divisions were altered to the new triangular division pattern for greater mobility and increased firepower. New activities were created for psychological warfare, and for civil affairs and military government in territories to be liberated or captured. The air force also underwent a great expansion, in personnel, in units, and in planes. Some units were assigned to coastal defense on the Atlantic and Pacific coasts, the latter then actually vulnerable to invasion. Others were sent to overseas stations. Notable was the creation and shipment to England of high-level, precision daylight bombing units, which worked with the British to rain tons of bombs on enemy centers. Later they assisted the invasions and major attacks. Increasingly by their bombing they disrupted German factories and rail lines and, weakening the entire economy of Germany, were extremely important in bringing Hitler to his downfall. Lighter units of fighter-bombers were trained to work closely with the U.S. front-line ground forces on critical occasions. The armed forces of the United States, in general, expanded their strength and put to use a host of details in tactics and in equipment that had been merely experimental in the economy years preceding. From new planes to new rifles, from motorization to emergency rations, from field radio telephones to long-range radar, progress was widespread.

The War Department was completely reorganized in March 1942. Combat branch chiefs were abolished and new broader agencies took over—the air forces, the ground forces, and the services of supply. A new and important operations division was created for strategic planning. The air forces were separated from the army for all practical purposes and were represented coequally with the army and navy in staff meetings.

To previous American concepts of war, not only had there been added new concepts of operation and new and improved mechanized matériel; there had also been added a reasoned and complete concept of an all-out popular effort, a greater national unity, a greater systematization of production, and, especially, a more intense emphasis on technology. The efforts of World War I were far surpassed. The U.S. effort would truly be, as Churchill predicted after the Dunkirk defeat, "the new world with all its power and might" stepping forth to "the rescue and liberation of the old." Quickly there came from Congress the first War Powers Act (Dec. 18, 1941) and the second War Powers Act (Mar. 27, 1942). Congress also passed the Emergency Price Control Act (Jan. 30, 1942), with its Office of Price Administration, and established the War Production Board (Jan. 13, 1942), the National War Labor Board (Jan. 12, 1942), the Office of War Information (June 13, 1942), and the Office of Economic Stabilization (filled Oct. 4, 1942). In many fields volunteer civilian assistants administered to the people the local details of contact and control. Critical items such as food, coffee, sugar, meat, butter, and canned goods were rationed for civilians, as were also heating fuels and gasoline. Rent control was established. Two-thirds of the planes of civilian airlines were taken over by the air force. Travel was subject to priorities for war purposes. There was also voluntary censorship of newspapers, under only general guidance from Washington.

There was special development and production of escort vessels for the navy; of landing craft—small and large—for beach invasions; a program of plane construction for the air force on a huge scale; of high octane gasoline; and of synthetic rubber. It was recognized and accepted that, as Stimson said, "in wartime the demands of the Army enter into every aspect of national life." Local draft boards had been given great leeway in drawing up their own standards of exemption and deferment from service and at first had favored agriculture over industry; but soon controls were established according to national needs. By 1945 the United States had engaged more than 16 million men under arms and still improved its economy. Production was needed to save the war, and indeed production would very nearly win the war, with its pipelines of supply bringing to the fronts a great mass of material that America's enemies could not match. It has been calculated that at one time it took half the total resources of the nation in materials and labor to support U.S. forces and to help U.S. allies. It was a war of "power and might," as Churchill had predicted.

Vitally important was the successful development of new air and sea methods of protecting the delivery of troops and munitions across the Pacific and especially across the submarine-infested Atlantic to beleaguered Britain. German submarines were active against all transocean shipping, and also along the eastern coast of the United States against oil shipments from the Caribbean and the Gulf of Mexico to Atlantic coastal ports. The challenge was severe, but it was met by inventiveness as well as by determination and organization, by air and sea action against enemy underwater craft, and by the construction of two great pipelines to bring oil overland from Texas fields to the eastern seaboard.

The grand strategy, from the beginning, was to defeat Germany while containing Japan, a strategy maintained and followed by the Combined Chiefs of Staff, closely coordinated with the thinking of Roosevelt and Churchill—except on one occasion when in the early summer of 1942 Adm. Ernest J. King (chief of naval operations) and Marshall (army chief of staff) met the news that there would be no attempt to create a beachhead in Europe that year by suggesting a shift of U.S. power to the Pacific. Roosevelt promptly overruled them.

Campaign in the Pacific

Almost immediately after the strike at Pearl Harbor, the Japanese invaded the Philippines and overran American garrisons on Guam and Wake in late December. They soon captured Manila, then conquered the U.S. forces on the Bataan peninsula by Apr. 8, 1942, and the last U.S. stronghold on Corregidor on May 6. Japan then feinted into the North Pacific, easily seizing Attu and Kiska in the Aleutian Islands in early June 1942. It continued to attract U.S. attention and some troops toward Alaska until its forces were withdrawn in March 1943.

Gen. Douglas MacArthur had been pulled out of the Philippines before the fall of Corregidor and sent to Australia to assume responsibility for protecting that continent against Japanese invasion, increasingly imminent since Singapore (Feb. 15, 1942) and Java (Mar. 9) had been taken. Limited numbers of troops were sent to him because in this area there was to be only a containing effort, and these troops had to come to him and be supplied over a long sea route protected only by the occupation of some intervening islands in the Pacific. With great skill, MacArthur used American and Australian forces to check Japanese inroads in New Guinea at Port Moresby and land and sea forces to push the Japanese back from spot to spot to take the villages of Buna and Sananda, although not until January 1943. To block a hostile thrust against MacArthur's communications through New Zealand back home, marine and infantry divisions landed in the Solomon Islands, where they took Guadalcanal by February 1943 after bitter touch-and-go land, sea, and air fighting. The push north continued to Bougainville in November 1943 and Green Islands in February 1944, leaving many hostile stations in the Solomons cut off from supply and destined to futility. Unwilling to perform merely containing operations, MacArthur then used air and sea power to leapfrog his ground units along the northern coast of New Guinea and west to Morotai by September 1944, employing to the full the new capabilities of modern planes and using amphibious assaults to capture Japanese airfields. In his forward movements he got excellent aid from the Australian airmen to cover his open left flank, to neutralize bypassed Japanese forces, and to assist in supporting landings on Tarakan and Borneo.

Previously and almost concurrently, the navy with marine and army troops was attacking selected Japanese bases in the Pacific, moving steadily westward and successfully hitting the Marshall Islands at Eniwetok and Kwajalein, the Gilberts at Makin and Tarawa, and—turning north—the Marianas at Guam and Saipan in June and July 1944, largely bypassing Truk and the Carolines and leaving them and many other individual spots to be mopped up at leisure. To assist the army's move on the Philippines, the navy and marines also struck westward at the Palau Islands in September 1944, and had them in hand within a month. American control of the approaches to the Philippines was now assured. Two years earlier, in the Coral Sea and also in the open spaces near Midway, in May and June 1942, respectively, the U.S. Navy had severely crippled the Japanese fleet. Air and submarine strikes closer in had a serious weakening effect. It was the result of these efforts, equally with the army advance in the New Guinea area, that enabled MacArthur's forces, supported by Adm. William F. Halsey and the Third Fleet, to return in October 1944 to the Philippines on the island of Leyte. Their initial success was endangered by a final, major Japanese naval effort there near Leyte, which was countered by a U.S. naval thrust that wiped much of the Japanese fleet from the waves. Army progress through the Philippines was thereafter steady. Manila and Corregidor were again under U.S. control in February 1945. Mindanao was cleared in March.

American land and sea forces were now in position to drive north directly toward Japan itself. Marines had landed on Iwo Jima on Feb. 19 and invaded Okinawa on Apr. 1, both within good flying distance of the main enemy islands. The Japanese navy and air force were so depleted that in July 1945 the U.S. fleet was steaming off the coast of Japan and bombarding almost with impunity. Between July 10 and Aug. 15, 1945, forces under Halsey destroyed or damaged 2,084 enemy planes, sank or damaged 148 Japanese combat ships, and sank or damaged 1,598 merchant vessels, in addition to administering heavy blows at industrial targets and war industries.

Until the island hopping brought swift successes in 1944, it had been expected that the United States would need the China mainland as a base for an attack on Japan. Japanese southward moves had dug into Burma and imperiled India. Gen. Joseph W. Stilwell had been sent: (a) to command American forces in China; (b) to serve Chiang Kai-shek as chief of staff; and (c) anomalously, to serve under the British commander of the Burma-India theater of operations. Efforts to reinforce the Chinese against the Japanese on the Asian mainland had not been fully successful. Cargo planes had tried to fly sufficient supplies over "the hump" from India and Burma. An attempt was made to build a road from Lashio in Burma over the mountains to K'un-ming and Chungking, but Japanese thrusts forced Stilwell out of China and Burma in disastrous retreat. Nevertheless, the sea and land successes of MacArthur and the navy admirals Chester W. Nimitz, Halsey, and Marc A. Mitscher had brought the United States to positions where in the spring of 1945 it was possible to think of an actual invasion of Japan without using China as a base at all. This situation had been achieved as a result of some factors that made for greater and swifter successes than had been planned for this containing operation in the Pacific. These factors were: (a) the new naval technique of employing the fleet as a set of floating air bases, as well as for holding the sea lanes open; (b) the augmentation and improvement of U.S. submarine service to a point where it was fatal to Japanese shipping, sinking more than 200 enemy combat vessels and more than 1,100 merchant ships, and thus seriously disrupting the desperately needed supply of Japanese troops on the many islands; and (c) MacArthur's leapfrogging tactics, letting many advanced Japanese bases simply die on the vine. Not to be overlooked was MacArthur's own energy and persuasive skill. He received more troops than had been originally calculated for him, and he and the navy received by 1944 as many beach landing craft as were assigned to all of Europe. The British had complained that the operations in the Pacific were too expansively progressive for the broad strategic plan that had been established. Not to be overlooked, either, was the monumental performance of the air force, bombing ahead of the army from spot to spot, smashing enemy airplanes and airfields, and crippling Japanese supply lines.

The Japanese navy and air force were so depleted by July 1945 that the U.S. fleet was steaming off the coast of Japan and bombarding almost with impunity.

These results had been accomplished with limited materials while the major national effort of the United States had been diverted toward Europe. Such results had demonstrated great skill in the coordination of air power with land and sea power, and the weight of even a restricted part of U.S. production. The Japanese had foolishly challenged the manpower and the industrial power and the skill and fighting spirit of the United States, and had been driven along the road to defeat by only that portion of American resources that could be spared for the Pacific area. And this had happened in spite of the initial, serious, and dangerous crippling of the U.S. naval concentration at Pearl Harbor. The United States was simply too strong to be beaten, even though it was at the same time fighting another war across the Atlantic.

Campaigns in Africa and Italy

In Europe the United States first participated in the war by furnishing materials to Britain, air bombardment units, and a small but steadily growing number of ground troops. Also, planes and tanks were sent to and around Africa to bolster the defense of Egypt, threatened by German successes in the Western Desert. Special facilities were set up in the Persian Gulf to furnish tanks and trucks through Iran to Russia, the other U.S. ally. The Office of Strategic Services (OSS) collected data from behind enemy lines and parachuted personnel into enemy-held territory to work with local resistance groups.

Pressures, notably from Russian leaders, early began building for an invasion of the European mainland on a second front. There not being sufficient buildup in England for a major attack across the Channel in 1942—even for a small preliminary beachhead—U.S. troops were moved, some from Britain with the British and some directly from America, to invade northwest Africa from Casablanca to Oran and Algiers on Nov. 8, 1942. The aim was to save that area for the French, and to seize Tunisia and block from the rear the German forces now retreating before a British drive from Cairo. After the long coastal strip had been seized and the temporarily resisting French brought to the side of the Allies, the Anglo-American forces pushed east. The Germans were reinforced and concentrated. Sharp and costly fighting by air, army, and armor attacks and counterattacks, notably in February 1943 at the Kasserine Pass, ended with the Allied conquest of Tunisia and a great German surrender at Tunis, Bizerte, and Cape Bon on May 12–13, 1943. The operation was conducted with Gen. Dwight D. Eisenhower in command, using a mixed Anglo-American staff. Shortly before this, at their conference in Casablanca in late January, Roosevelt and Churchill called for the "unconditional surrender" of the Axis powers. It would be a war to the finish, not a negotiated, temporary peace.

The next step was an Anglo-American invasion of Sicily, beginning July 9, 1943, using large-scale parachute drops and perfected beach-landing skills, as a step toward knocking Italy out of the war. On Sept. 3 Italy proper was invaded, the British crossing the Strait of Messina and the Americans landing at Salerno near Naples. Five days later Italy surrendered, but the Germans occupied Rome and took control of the Italian government. After a long check midway up the boot of Italy on a line through Cassino, a dangerous landing was made at Anzio, Jan. 22, 1944. Fierce German counterattacks there were stopped short of success, and a following breakthrough carried U.S. forces past Rome, which fell June 4, 1944, and the next month to the line of Florence and the Arno River, the British on the east and the Americans on the west. Thereafter, although some Anglo-American advances were made and a final offensive in April 1945 carried American troops to the Po Valley, Italy ceased to be the scene of major strategic efforts; the theater was drained to support the Normandy invasion by a landing in southern France.

Campaigns in France, Germany, and the Low Countries

For the principal invasion of France, an inter-Allied planning staff had been created in March 1943 in London. In May the first tentative attack date was set—early May of the following year—for what was called Operation Overlord. That same summer some U.S. troops from the Mediterranean theater began to be withdrawn and shipped to England. The buildup of units and supplies proceeded steadily for nearly a year, and was helped greatly by improved successes against German submarines aimed at seagoing convoys. There was a one-month delay in the target date for the invasion of France, to secure more landing craft and more troops to make a broader beach base for the initial thrust. Finally, after a day's further delay owing to bad weather conditions, on June 6, 1944, the greatest amphibious invasion in history was launched across the English Channel, involving more than 5,300 ships and landing craft. Minesweepers preceded. Naval ships assisted with gunfire from battleships, cruisers, and destroyers. Aerial bombers flew over to attack enemy fortifications. It was a huge, carefully and intricately coordinated land, sea, and air action, with a precisely scheduled flow of reinforcements and supplies. To hit from Dover, England, to Calais across the channel would have been shorter, but inland thence the terrain was cut by many water lines. Brittany was too far by water and by air. To land in Normandy would provide better flank protection by the Seine and Orne rivers, and ample space for maneuvering, and would be just within practicable air-fighter support. So it was on the Normandy coast, from the Cherbourg peninsula to the mouth of the Orne that the landings were made at selected beaches, the Second British Army and the First Canadian Army on the east and the American First Army on the west. All ground forces were under the command of British Gen. Bernard L. Montgomery, with Eisenhower as Supreme Allied Commander. The landing force was assisted and protected by costly but successful landing by parachute and glider of 12,000 British and American troops.

The battle on the Normandy beaches on June 6 was vicious, particularly on "Omaha Beach" in front of Calvados, where a reinforcing German division had just arrived; only raw courage and determination brought success. Yet the invaders moved inland in spite of losses and confusions. The buildup of reinforcements had been carefully planned and scheduled, as was the forwarding of supplies. Over the beaches the shallow-draft landing craft passed along a steady stream of men and materials, seriously interrupted only once, when a four-day storm starting June 19 prevented beach debarkations and destroyed a large but temporary pier on the American beach. As a result, the First Army was down to one day's supply of ammunition at one point. By that time, there were about 314,514 American troops ashore, and about the same number of British. All were reorganizing and pressing inland. The weather cleared; the Americans had a good foothold, as did the British on the American left; by June 27 Cherbourg had fallen; and the U.S. forces had a seaport and were ready to spin about and go south.

Finally, after a year's preparation, on June 6, 1944, the greatest amphibious invasion in history was launched across the English Channel.

The Germans had been reinforcing their positions, although badly hampered by aerial bombardments of road and rail lines and convoys in motion. There followed a month of almost pedestrian fighting through thick hedgerow country to establish a forward line through the road center at Saint-Lô. Then, late in July, with the British holding and drawing to their front by Caen a large proportion of the German forces—particularly much of their armor—the American infantry and tanks, aided by a massive air bombardment, pierced the enemy line near Saint-Lô and swung rapidly to the southwest toward Coutances, capturing outflanked German troops.

At this juncture Montgomery relinquished command of all ground troops and took over only the British Twenty-first Army Group, while Gen. Omar Bradley moved from command of the American First Army to that of the Twelfth Army Group, including both the First and Third armies.

The Germans reacted to this penetration by finally drawing their reserve Fifteenth Army out of the Calais area, where it had been held by an Allied ruse and the threat of a second beach landing there. They struck directly west across the American front to try to cut off the leading U.S. troops who had already begun entering Brittany. This German effort was blocked by Bradley's forces; the British pushed slowly but inexorably southwards; the American First and Third armies mostly abandoned the drive in Brittany and Brest and raced eastwards toward Paris. At the same time they circled northeast around Falaise, nineteen miles southeast of Caen, to pocket against the advancing British a large force of Germans who were killed and captured in vast numbers. German resistance in northern France now crumbled. On Aug. 25 Paris fell to American and French divisions with scarcely a battle.

The Germans retreated rapidly and skillfully for the distant frontier and their defense lines, except where they at points resisted the British in order to try and hold the seaports along the northern coast. There were some substantial captures, notably at a large pocket near Mons, but the German withdrawal was generally successful. In spite of the enormous American support buildup on the Normandy beaches, in spite of emergency supply by airplane, and in spite of immobilizing some units to use their trucks to carry food, ammunition, and gasoline to the most forward units, forward supply was seriously lacking to U.S. forces. Some troops actually at times had to subsist on captured German rations. It was not possible to hit the distant German frontier line soon or hard enough.

While these events were taking place, a landing had been made in southern France on Aug. 15, 1944, by a Franco-American force under American command. It swept from the Riviera up the Rhone Valley, made contact with the previously exposed right flank of the racing American Third Army, and then turned east and northeast to extend the front of the U.S. forces that had come east across northern France from Normandy. By September, Brest fell into U.S. hands, and a German army in southwest France had surrendered, completely cut off. Also by September the general American eastward advance was checked by well-fortified Germans at about the frontier line, largely because the U.S. forces had run ahead too fast for their supplies. German units halted the major Allied offensive (Sept. 17–25) to capture the Rhine bridges at Arnhem. But France was almost completely liberated from German occupation.

For more than two months, with the British moving up on the U.S. left and some French on the right, the American armies plugged through very difficult country against hard German resistance and at the cost of heavy casualties, all the while rebuilding forward supply and preparing to push into the Palatinate and on to the Rhineland plain toward Koblenz and Cologne. The overall strategic idea was to make the final major Allied effort over the Rhine north of Cologne and through the relatively open country north of the Ruhr. But the Americans were still miles from the Rhine. As infantry and tanks slugged forward aided by exceptional air support, Aachen fell in October and the line of the Ruhr River and the Eifel Mountains was reached. Applying pressure on their left, the Americans thinned their center. There the Germans struck hard on Dec. 16 in the wooded and hilly Ardennes, in their final bid with a newly trained and reorganized force. During five days of fierce fighting, the Americans held strongly on the shoulders of the penetration, which was aimed northwest at Liège and Antwerp; the U.S. First Army was regrouped to check the main drive to the northwest. The Americans threw in some divisions that had been out of line—either to exploit a possible success or to meet just such a threat as this—swung their Third Army to block from the south near Bastogne in southeast Belgium, and received reserves from the British. Split from the Third Army, the U.S. First Army was temporarily placed under Montgomery's command. Then, at the peak of the German penetration—not far from the Meuse River—leading German units, out of gasoline, were captured. American air bombardments, both close and deep, had seriously weakened German transportation, both rail and road. They could not get their motor fuel nor capture that of the Americans. On the U.S. side, losses had been serious; but by Jan. 1, every lost tank and artillery piece had been replaced from the American supply pipeline. Germany could not match the weight of U.S. industrial support. In bitter January weather, the Germans stubbornly resisted, but the U.S. troops dogged and chewed them up and slowly forced them back. The Battle of the Bulge was their final major effort. They had used up their last major resources and had failed.

By a phenomenon of large-scale production and mass transportation, the U.S. air forces in Europe had been built to high strength so that they could take severe losses and still beat the enemy down. From bases in Britain and from bases successively in North Africa and Italy, American bombers had struck at the heart of the German economy. By large-scale air raids, like those on Ploesti, Romania, a decisive proportion of German oil refinery production was knocked out. German planes and tanks faced being starved for fuel. German fighter planes, beaten back by the British in 1940, were later cut down by the Americans' heavily armed bombers and their long-range fighter escorts. Except for a short, sharp, and costly new campaign in the final month of 1944, German planes had ceased to be a serious major threat. At the same time, the U.S. fighter-bombers were taking the air under conditions over the Ardennes when they should not have flown at all and aiding the ground troops. German flying bombs (V-1) and rocket bombs (V-2) had continued to blast Britain until their installations were overrun in late March 1945, but they had no effect on ground operations or on air superiority as a whole.

In February 1945 the American armies struck out into the Palatinate and swept the German forces across the Rhine. The enemy destroyed bridges as they crossed—all but one. On Mar. 7 an advanced armored unit of the U.S. First Army approached the great railway bridge at Remagen, downstream from Koblenz, found it intact, dashed over it, tore the fuses from demolition charges, and drove local Germans back. Plans had not existed for a crossing here, but the opportunity was promptly exploited. Troops were hustled over the bridge for several days before it collapsed from damage, but by then pontoon bridges were in place. The U.S. east bank holdings were slowly expanded against the sharp German resistance attracted there, thus making easier the planned later crossing north of Cologne by the British and by the American Ninth Army. It also allowed troops of the Third Army to cross upriver with comparative ease, at one place without a defensive shot being fired against them.

Avoiding the heavily wooded Ruhr region in the center, the previously planned northern crossing of the Rhine was effected with navy, air, and parachute help on Mar. 2, 1945; all arms drove directly eastwards into Germany while the First and Third armies drove eastwards below the Ruhr, the first of these soon swinging north at the end of March through Giessen and Marburg to make contact at Paderborn and Lippstadt (Apr. 1) with the northern force. More than 300,000 Germans were thus enclosed in the Ruhr pocket.

Germany's military strength had now practically collapsed. The British on the American left raced toward Hamburg and the Baltic. The U.S. First Army pressed through to Leipzig (Apr. 20), and met the Russians on Apr. 25, 1945, at Torgau on the Elbe River, which had been established at the Yalta Conference as part of the post-hostilities boundary with the Russians. The U.S. Third Army dashed toward Bavaria to prevent possible German retreat to a last stand in the south. The southernmost flank of the American forces swung southwards toward Austria at Linz and toward Italy at the Brenner Pass. The U.S. Seventh Army on May 4 met the Fifth Army at the Brenner Pass, coming up out of Italy where German resistance had likewise collapsed. Germany asked for peace and signed it at Allied headquarters at Rheims on May 7, 1945.

Surrender of Japan

Progress in the Pacific theater by this time had been substantial. U.S. ships and planes dominated sea and air close to Japan. Troops were soon to be redeployed from the European theater. Protracted cleanup operations against now-isolated Japanese island garrisons were coming to a close. American planes were bombing Tokyo regularly. A single raid on that city on Mar. 9, 1945, had devastated 16 square miles, killed 80,000 persons, and left 1.5 million people homeless. But the Japanese were still unwilling to surrender. Approved by Roosevelt, scientists working under military direction had devised a devastating bomb based on atomic fission. A demand was made upon Japan on July 26 for surrender, threatening with repeated warnings the destruction of eleven Japanese cities in turn. The Japanese rulers scorned the threats. Then President Harry S. Truman gave his consent for the use of the atomic bomb, and on Aug. 6 Hiroshima was hit, with 75,000 people killed. There were more warnings, but still no surrender. On Aug. 9 Nagasaki was bombed. Two square miles were wiped out and 39,000 people killed. Five days later, on Aug. 14, the Japanese agreed to surrender. The official instrument of surrender was signed on Sept. 2, 1945, on board the battleship *Missouri* in Tokyo Bay.

A single raid on Tokyo on March 9, 1945, devastated 16 square miles, killed 80,000 persons, and left 1.5 million homeless, yet the Japanese would not surrender.

BIBLIOGRAPHY

A. Russell Buchanan, *The United States and World War II.*
Peter Calvocoressi and Guy Wint, *Total War: The Story of World War II.*
John Creswell, *Sea Warfare, 1939–1945.*
Kenneth S. Davis, *Experience of War: The United States in World War II.*
Basil H. Liddell Hart, *History of the Second World War.*
Samuel Eliot Morison, *The Two Ocean War: Short History of United States Navy in the Second World War.*
John Toland, *The Last Hundred Days.*

— ELBRIDGE COLBY

WORLD'S FAIRS

World's Fairs are one-time international expositions that feature exhibits showcasing developments in science, technology, industry, and the arts. Held in cities, they typically run for six months, from spring to fall. Exhibitors include governments, corporations, and large private organizations. The Crystal Palace Exhibition held in London in 1851 began the modern era of international expositions. Staged to demonstrate the superiority of British industry, it housed exhibits of machinery, art, and crafts and attracted more than 6 million visitors. Since the Crystal Palace world's fairs have become more than demonstrations of industrial progress and have acquired symbolic purposes. The Philadelphia Centennial Exposition of 1876 commemorated the anniversary of the Declaration of Independence. The 1893 World's Columbian Exposition at Chicago celebrated the anniversary of the discovery of America. In

1915 the San Francisco Panama-Pacific International Exposition honored the opening of the Panama Canal and the city's recovery from the earthquake of 1906.

Fairs held in the United States during the 1930s helped visitors cope with the Great Depression. In 1933–1934 Chicago's Century of Progress International Exhibition took shape around the theme of scientific and industrial progress since the city's founding. It marked the first time that such firms as General Motors constructed pavilions to display their products. The 1939–1940 New York World's Fair, billed as "The World of Tomorrow," drew more than 44 million visitors. It introduced television and promoted suburban living and pollution-free, automated factories. World War II and its aftermath precluded international expositions until the late 1950s. The United States did not host a postwar world's fair until the 1962 Century 21 Exposition in Seattle. The inspiration for this fair came in part from the cold war; after the Soviet Union launched *Sputnik* in 1957, U.S. leaders and scientists wanted to demonstrate the nation's scientific prowess. The Seattle fair featured the 605-foot Space Needle, a monorail, an amusement park, and many exhibits. In 1964–1965 the New York World's Fair drew more than 51 million visitors, offered striking pavilion architecture, and pioneered audiovisual display techniques. It included 200 buildings and the Unisphere, a 140-foot-high stainless steel globe signifying "Peace Through Understanding." In response to the ecological crisis of the 1970s the United States hosted three fairs dealing with energy conservation and the environment: Spokane (1974), Knoxville (1982), and New Orleans (1984). The Bureau of International Expositions, which since 1928 has overseen world's fairs, authorizing dates and enforcing exhibition standards, authorized three events through the year 2000: Expo 96 in Budapest, Hungary; Expo 98 in Lisbon, Portugal; and Expo 2000 in Hanover, Germany.

[See also Centennial Exposition.]

BIBLIOGRAPHY

John E. Findling and Kimberly D. Pelle, eds., *Historical Dictionary of World's Fairs and Expositions, 1851–1988* (Westport, Conn., 1987).

Robert W. Rydell, *World of Fairs: The Century-of-Progress Expositions* (Chicago, 1993).

— ANDREW FELDMAN

WRITS OF ASSISTANCE

Writs of Assistance were general search warrants issued to the customs officers by the superior courts of the various colonies. They were first issued in Massachusetts in 1751. Neither the issue nor the use of such writs seems to have excited controversy prior to 1761. In that year new writs were applied for as the old ones were expiring. These were opposed as unconstitutional by some merchants through their attorney, James Otis (February 1761). Otis gave an impassioned speech in which he insisted that if Parliament passed an act authorizing such writs, it would be void. Nevertheless, he lost the case. There was some delay but the writs were issued (1762) after instructions had been received from England supporting their legality. That closed the controversy in Massachusetts.

The Townshend Revenue Act (1767) authorized writs of assistance, but did not specify any form. A form was prepared by the customs officers similar to the one that had been granted in Massachusetts. Every customs officer in America was sent a copy of the desired writ and directed to request the attorney general of his colony to secure such writs from the superior court. This action made writs of assistance an issue in the superior court of every province in America. The form of the writ was novel to the judges and seemed to encroach on important rights of citizens.

The term "writ of assistance" as used in the law was a common legal expression used to designate a search warrant. But it was difficult to convince the judges that such words meant general search warrants. There was delay in most of the courts, and the issue dragged through 1768 to 1772. This resulted in a direct refusal by the courts of Connecticut, Rhode Island, New York, New Jersey, Pennsylvania, Maryland, Virginia, and North Carolina, although the judges offered to issue "writs of assistance," in particular cases, "as directed by law." In some cases the refusals stated that the forms presented to the judges were novel and unconstitutional.

Finally in 1772 the customs officers reported that they had secured writs in East Florida, West Florida, South Carolina, Bahama, Bermuda, New Hampshire, Nova Scotia, and Quebec. It is obvious that the controversy over writs of assistance was not a Massachusetts affair only, and it was not the speech of Otis that made their issue a cause of the Revolution, especially as his speech did not become generally known until long after the Revolution was over. It was the raising of the issue in every superior court in America, dragged through five years, that made writs a common grievance as stated in the Declaration of Independence.

BIBLIOGRAPHY

O. M. Dickerson, "Essay on Writs of Assistance," in R. B. Morris, ed., *The Era of the American Revolution.*

A. B. Hart, *American History Told by Contemporaries,* vol. II.

William Macdonald, *Select Charters.*

— O. M. DICKERSON

XYZ AFFAIR

XYZ Affair, the most dramatic incident in the bitter dispute between the French Directory and the United States. Incensed at the negotiation by the United States of Jay's Treaty with Great Britain in 1794, France issued decrees against American shipping and refused to receive Charles Cotesworth Pinckney, the newly appointed American minister. President John Adams held to a pacific course and sent a mission to Paris composed of Pinckney, then in Holland, John Marshall, and Elbridge Gerry.

The American ministers arrived on Oct. 4, 1797, just after their supporters in the French legislature had been destroyed by a coup d'état. The Directory's armies were victorious in Italy and the Rhineland, and Charles Maurice de Talleyrand-Périgord, the new foreign minister, thought he could take advantage of the bitter feud between Federalists and Democratic-Republicans in the United States and embarrass the Federalist administration without running any risk of war. Reports from the United States showed the Democratic-Republicans were gaining ground, and even Thomas Jefferson had suggested to the French consul general that France would profit by temporizing.

Talleyrand received the envoys unofficially on Oct. 8 and stated they would have an audience with the Directory as soon as a report could be prepared on American affairs. Weeks of official silence ensued. Meanwhile, three unofficial agents of the foreign minister—later referred to in dispatches as X, Y, and Z—called on the Americans suggesting a gratuity of $250,000 for Talleyrand, a loan to France, and an indemnity for Adams' criticism of France in a speech to Congress. The ministers were willing to consider a payment to Talleyrand after a treaty had been signed, and they even proposed that one of them return to confer with Adams regarding a loan, provided the Directory would cease its attacks on American shipping and negotiate with the two ministers who remained. Not even these concessions could secure the reception of the ministers by the Directory.

On Jan. 17, 1798, Pinckney, Marshall, and Gerry presented a dignified statement of the American position, defending Jay's Treaty, offering France the same privileges Britain enjoyed under that document, and demanding compensation for the losses of American shipping. Talleyrand deferred his reply until Mar. 18, when he made an insulting proposal to treat with Gerry alone, characterizing him as the only minister friendly to France. Although Gerry refused to negotiate with Talleyrand, he remained in Paris after the departure of his colleagues, in the honest but erroneous belief that his presence there prevented war.

The publication of its ministers' dispatches by the American government created such a stir in the country that the affair acquired a unique place in the popular mind. The incident was given a mysterious quality by the substitution of the letters X, Y, and Z for the names of Talleyrand's agents. The Federalists made political capital of the situation, and Congress abrogated the treaties of 1778, suspended commercial relations with France, authorized the seizure of armed French vessels, and strengthened the nation's naval and military forces. Talleyrand, thoroughly alarmed, sought to prevent a declaration of war. The wise policy he and Adams then pursued led to the Convention of Sept. 30, 1800, which ended the misunderstanding.

BIBLIOGRAPHY

Gerald H. Clarfield, *Timothy Pickering and American Diplomacy, 1795–1800.*

Alexander DeConde, *Quasi-War: The Politics and Diplomacy of the Undeclared War With France, 1797–1801.*

— E. WILSON LYON

Y

YALTA CONFERENCE

Yalta Conference of U.S. President Franklin D. Roosevelt, British Prime Minister Winston Churchill, and Soviet Marshal Joseph Stalin took place Feb. 4–11, 1945, at a turning point of World War II, when the imminent collapse of Germany made it necessary to make plans for administering Europe. In addition to this purpose Roosevelt had a desire for this personal meeting with Stalin as a means of winning the latter's confidence in American goodwill and thereby ensuring a peaceful postwar world.

After amicable discussions Roosevelt, Churchill, and Stalin announced publicly on Feb. 11 agreement on (1) the occupation of Germany by the United States, Great Britain, the Soviet Union, and France in four separate zones; (2) a conference of the signatories of the United Nations Declaration to open at San Francisco Apr. 25, 1945, for the purpose of establishing a world peace organization; (3) a (then secret) big-power voting formula in the new organization; (4) an eastern boundary of Poland mainly following the Curzon Line (which gave the Soviet Union about one-third of prewar Poland), for which Poland was to be compensated by unspecified German territory in the north and west, and a new, freely elected, democratic Polish government; and (5) freely elected democratic governments for other liberated European nations. A supplementary secret agreement provided for Soviet entry into the war with Japan in two or three months after Germany surrendered, and in return British and American acceptance of (1) the status quo of Outer Mongolia; (2) restoration to the Soviet Union of its position in Manchuria before the Russo-Japanese War (1904–05), with safeguarding of Soviet interests in Dairen, Port Arthur, and the Manchurian railways; and (3) the cession to the Soviet Union of the Kurile Islands and the southern half of Sakhalin Island.

In February 1945, the "Big Three"—British Prime Minister Winston Churchill, U. S. President Franklin D. Roosevelt, and Soviet Marshal Joseph Stalin—met at Yalta to discuss plans for adminstering the postwar world. (F. D. R. Library)

The conference has been harshly criticized, particularly on the grounds that the Americans and British betrayed Poland and that their concessions to the Soviet Union at the expense of Nationalist China were unnecessary since Japan collapsed before much Russian power was brought to bear against it.

— CHARLES S. CAMPBELL

YANKEE

Yankee, a famous privateer brig from Bristol, R.I., with eighteen guns and 120 officers and men. During the War of 1812, it cruised off Halifax, Nova Scotia, and in the south Atlantic and took eighteen prizes worth nearly $1 million. In two later voyages under Elisha Snow the *Yankee* cruised off Ireland and in the Atlantic with success, one prize (the *San Jose Indiano*) netting $500,000. In six voyages it captured British ships worth $5 million, $1 million of which actually reached Bristol.

BIBLIOGRAPHY

E. S. Maclay, *History of American Privateers.*

— WALTER B. NORRIS

"YELLOW-DOG" CONTRACT

"Yellow-Dog" Contract, an agreement signed by a worker in which he promises not to join a union while working for a company. Such agreements, often called ironclad documents in the late 19th century, were first used during the period of labor unrest of the 1870's. One of the first companies to make its workers pledge that they would not join a union was the Western Union Telegraph Company in 1870.

Companies used these agreements to prevent unions from securing a base in their firms. But there were those inside and outside the labor movement who wanted to protect the right of a worker to join a union, and by the 1890's fifteen states had enacted laws that prohibited "yellow-dog" contracts. In addition, Congress passed the Erdman Act in 1898, which outlawed the "yellow-dog" contract as a condition of employment on the railroads. But the U.S. Supreme Court in 1908 (*Adair* v. *United States*) declared unconstitutional the Erdman Act provisions dealing with the "yellow-dog" contract, while in 1915 (*Coppage* v. *Kansas*) it voided a similar state law.

As unions attempted to expand in the 20th century, use of the "yellow-dog" contract increased. Mine workers at the Hitchman Coal and Coke Company, for example, had to sign the following agreement if they wished to work:

> I [the worker] am employed by and work for the Hitchman Coal and Coke Company with the express understanding that I am not a member of the United Mine Workers of America and will not become so while an employee of the . . . Company; . . . and agree that while I am in the employ of that company I will not make any efforts amongst its employees to bring about the unionizing of that mine against the company's wish.

In 1917 a case involving this contract reached the Supreme Court (*Hitchman Coal and Coke Company* v. *Mitchell*), which again ruled that such agreements were voluntary acts and that unions should not try to convince workers to void such contracts by joining a union. Indeed, the Supreme Court declared that injunctions could be issued against a union that tried to organize these workers. The use of these agreements, which spread after the *Hitchman* decision, hampered the growth of unions in such industries as coal, shoe, glass, full-fashioned hosiery, clothing, metal trades, and commercial printing trades.

In the Norris—La Guardia Anti-injunction Act passed in 1932, Congress declared that "yellow-dog" contracts were in conflict with public policy and that therefore the courts could not enforce them. After the passage of the Wagner Act in 1935, the National Labor Relations Board ruled that an employer was engaging in an unfair labor practice if he demanded that workers sign such an agreement. As a result of these two actions, the "yellow-dog" contract disappeared from the labor scene.

BIBLIOGRAPHY

Joel I. Seidman, *The Yellow Dog Contract.*
Benjamin J. Taylor and Fred Witney, *Labor Relations Law.*

— ALBERT A. BLUM

YELLOW FEVER

In that indispensable sourcebook *The History of New England* (1647) by John Winthrop, then governor of Massachusetts, the first reference is found to yellow fever in America. The effort of the Massachusetts court on that occasion to exclude from Massachusetts the crew and the cargo of the ship that had brought the fever (Barbados distemper) from the West Indies to America was the colonies' initial enforcement of quarantine. British ships that had sailed from Boston in an unsuccessful effort to capture Martinique brought back an epidemic of yellow fever in 1694, and subsequently, despite its endemic focus on the African coast, yellow fever emerged as a peculiarly American disease ("the American plague"). It spread through America as the African slave trade increased and proliferated. With the single exception of smallpox, the most dreaded verdict on the lips of a colonial physician was "yellow fever." The summer or autumn that brought yellow fever heard the death carts roll through the streets and the cry of the gravediggers, "Bring out your dead!"

The worst American epidemic of yellow fever, in 1793, which doomed the supremacy of Philadelphia among American cities, was described by an eyewitness, the bookseller and publisher Mathew Carey:

> People uniformly and hastily shifted their course at the sight of a hearse coming towards them. Many never

> walked on the foot-path, but went into the middle of the street, to avoid being infected in passing houses wherein people had died. Acquaintances and friends avoided each other in the streets, and only signified their regard by a cold nod. The old custom of shaking hands fell into such general disuse that many shrunk back with affright at even the offer of a hand. A person with crape or any appearance of mourning was shunned like a leper. And many valued themselves highly on the skill and address with which they got to windward of every person whom they met.

The tragedy of this behavior was its utter uselessness; yellow fever is not contagious.

Benjamin Rush, the noted colonial physician, was relentless in his insistence on bloodletting and the use of calomel and jalap, but Rush's treatments did not stop the epidemic. After noting a meteor, a dead cat, and large numbers of mosquitoes ("the usual attendants of a sickly autumn"), Rush decided yellow fever was caused by spoiled coffee on a wharf.

In 1900 the U.S. Army Yellow Fever Commission, with Walter Reed, James Carroll, Jesse W. Lazear, and Aristides Agramonte, was sent to track the pestilence in Cuba. The group, working with the aid of Carlos J. Finlay, demonstrated Finlay's theory that the infection is transmitted by the bite of the female *Aëdes aegypti* mosquito. William Crawford Gorgas, chief sanitary officer of the Panama Canal Commission from 1904 until 1913, eliminated the mosquito in the region of the canal and made possible the building of the Panama Canal.

The last epidemic of yellow fever in the United States occurred in New Orleans in 1905. Vaccines against the disease were developed in the early 1940's and are required of anyone traveling to a hazardous area.

BIBLIOGRAPHY

Walter Reed and others, "The Etiology of Yellow Fever," *Philadelphia Medical Journal* (1900).

— VICTOR ROBINSON

YELLOW JOURNALISM

James Gordon Bennett, who founded the *New York Morning Herald* in 1835, was the first American publisher to introduce sensationalism in news stories, but not until the 1880's was the term "yellow journalism" applied to this kind of news presentation. In about 1870 the development of pulp paper and the increase in advertising made possible a general reduction in newspaper prices and a consequent increase in readership.

Advertising paid a large share of the publishing costs, and since space rates were based on distribution, there was constant pressure to increase the number of subscribers. After his purchase of the *New York World* in 1883, Joseph Pulitzer used high-pressure methods to accomplish this end. One of his innovations was a Sunday edition, carrying special articles and comic strips.

At the turn of the century the scare headline, the scandal section, the sob story, and elaborate Sunday features had become permanent elements of the sensational press.

One of the strips featured a character called the "Yellow Kid," and from this character the name "Yellow journalism" was derived. Sensationalism in newspaper reporting gained a new recruit in William Randolph Hearst, publisher of the *San Francisco Examiner.* In 1895 he acquired the *New York Morning Journal* and began a subscription war with the *World* that intensified the use of yellow journalism. The question of whether the United States should intervene in the Cuban rebellion against Spanish rule was made to order for the methods of the two publishers. They made substantial propagandistic capital favoring the rebels by their sensational reporting of Spanish concentration camps in Cuba; the anti-American content of a letter written by the Spanish minister to the United States, Enrique Dupuy de Lôme, in 1898; and the sinking of the U.S. battleship *Maine* in Havana harbor in the same year.

At the turn of the century the scare headline, the scandal section, the sob story, and elaborate Sunday features had become permanent elements of the sensational press. Some newspapers never adopted the extreme methods of yellow journalism, but a considerable number of metropolitan newspapers used some if not all the innovations that appeared in the newspapers of the late 19th century.

BIBLIOGRAPHY

W. G. Bleyer, *Main Currents in the History of American Journalism.*

— THEODORE G. GRONERT

YELLOWSTONE NATIONAL PARK

The world's first national park, Yellowstone is 3,468 square miles (2,219,823 acres) of scenic grandeur in Wyoming, Montana, and Idaho. Its establishment by act of Congress, signed Mar. 1, 1872, by President Ulysses S. Grant, marked the start of the national-park movement, which led to the establishment by more than 100 nations of some 1,200 national parks or preserves.

The national-park idea is one of the major, original contributions of the United States to world thought. Park historians H. M. Chittenden and Louis C. Cramton credit David E. Folsom, a Montana surveyor, and Cornelius Hedges, a Massachusetts-born Montana judge, with proposing Yellowstone as a national park. The Yellowstone National Park Act, both historians report, was drawn up by William H. Clagett, Jr., Montana territorial delegate, who wrote the legislation in his own handwriting and introduced it in Congress; Nathaniel Langford, territorial revenue collector and later first park superintendent; and Ferdinand V. Hayden, member of the U.S. Geological Survey, whose 1871 expedition showered Congress with Yellowstone photographs by W. H. Jackson.

Yellowstone was still the country's largest national park in 1975. Its 3,000 hot springs and 200 geysers, including the popular Old Faithful, are the world's largest concentration of thermal features. Its wildlife include grizzly and black bears, elk, bighorn mountain sheep, moose, antelope, coyotes, occasional wolves and mountain lions, the country's only continuously wild herd of buffalo, and the once nearly extinct trumpeter swan and 240 other species of birdlife. The park was administered by the U.S. Army from 1886 to 1918.

One of the highest national parks, Yellowstone contains large portions of the Gallatin and Absaroka ranges of the Rocky Mountains. Yellowstone Lake is the largest high-mountain lake in North America, covering 137 square miles at an elevation of 7,730 feet. There the Yellowstone River starts its 671-mile journey to the Missouri, bequeathing the park its 1,200-foot deep Grand Canyon of the Yellowstone and its Upper Falls and Lower Falls, the latter twice as high as Niagara. The park observed its centennial in 1972 as host to the Second World Conference on National Parks. Visits in 1975 totaled 2,246,132.

BIBLIOGRAPHY

Louis C. Cramton, *Early History of Yellowstone National Park and Its Relation to National Park Policies.*

H. M. Chittenden, *The Yellowstone National Park.*

Nathaniel Pitt Langford, *Diary of the Washburn Expedition to the Yellowstone and Firehole Rivers in the Year 1870.*

— JOHN VOSBURGH

YOSEMITE NATIONAL PARK

Yosemite National Park, called "the greatest marvel of the continent" by Horace Greeley, was also described by John Muir as having "the noblest forests . . . the deepest ice-sculptured canyons." Located in the California High Sierra country and consisting of 1,189 square miles (760,917 acres), Yosemite Valley was visited annually by hundreds of people several years before Congress authorized the first national park in 1872. The American artist George Catlin had envisioned "a nation's park" in 1832 while traveling in the West. William Cullen Bryant had advocated a public park for New York City, and Henry Thoreau had called for "national preserves" in 1858.

Capt. Joe Walker's trappers discovered much of the area around Yosemite in 1833, but there is no record of a white man entering Yosemite Valley until William Penn Abrams, a millwright, did so in 1849 while tracking a grizzly bear. State volunteers, under Maj. James D. Savage, explored and named the hidden vale in 1851. "Yosemite" is a derivation of "Uzumati," which is the name of the resident Indian tribe and its word for "grizzly bear." In 1864 President Abraham Lincoln signed an act of Congress granting Yosemite Valley and the Mariposa Grove of giant sequoia trees to California on condition that the areas "be held for public use, resort and recreation . . . inalienable for all time." The grant stimulated park action in other states.

In 1890 Congress authorized Yosemite National Park—about 2 million acres surrounding the Yosemite Valley state park. In 1905 California ceded Yosemite Valley to federal control, and boundary changes eventually reduced the park to its present size. From 1891 to 1916 the park was administered by the U.S. Army. From 1901 to 1913 Yosemite was the center of a bitter conservation controversy over San Francisco's attempts to build a dam in the park on the Tuolumne River for water and power. The dam, completed in 1913, destroyed the park's Hetch Hetchy Valley, similar in grandeur to Yosemite Valley and described by John Muir as "a mountain temple."

Yosemite has the three largest exposed granite monoliths in the world, the El Capitan rockface, rising 3,000 feet from the valley floor. Few countries can match the park's waterfalls. The 1,430-foot Upper Yosemite Falls is one of the world's five highest. Only four trees, also California giant sequoias, surpass Yosemite's 2,700-year-old Grizzly Giant in size. The Wawona Tunnel Tree, perhaps the most famous tree in the world, was felled by a winter storm in 1969. Yosemite has attracted more than 2 million visitors a year since 1965.

BIBLIOGRAPHY

Douglass H. Hubbard, *The Origin of the National Park Idea in America.*

Hans Huth, *Yosemite, The Story of an Idea.*

John Ise, *Our National Park Policy.*

— JOHN VOSBURGH

YUROK

A unique development of native American culture arose in northwestern California and adjacent coastal Oregon. The area had several tribal groups speaking different and unrelated languages but with remarkably similar life modes. These included the Yurok and Wiyot, Algonkin-speakers; the Karok, speaking Hokan; and the Hupa and Tolowa, Athapascan-speaking tribes. These tribes lived as small population enclaves—the Yurok with 2,500 in 1770—along the beaches and in the valleys fronting the northwestern California coast. Culturally, the groups may be classed as basically Californian, possessing the strong sense of separatism characteristic of the area, as well as acorn dependence and basketry elaboration. On the other hand, unlike tribes in the rest of California, the Yurok and their neighbors were influenced by the rich culture of the Northwest Coast. Modified plank houses and salmon dependence suggest regions farther north, as do a dependence and emphasis on wealth. But whereas the tribes of the Northwest Coast founded individual and social status on largess, on distributions of wealth, these northwestern Californian tribes built a social system in which wealth was valued for its possession. The unit of wealth, the dentalian shell, also reflects a departure from the Northwest Coast culture. The social system was integrated by the presence of men of wealth, each accorded a place based not only on what he had amassed but also on the wealth of previous generations. Quickly overcome by European-American settlers, these tribes had a minimal historical role. Interest in them is based on their intermediate cultural position.

Theodore Roosevelt with the naturalist John Muir atop a glacier point above Yosemite Valley, California. In 1872 Congress authorized the first national park encompassing the area. Undated photograph. (Corbis-Bettman)

BIBLIOGRAPHY

Alfred L. Kroeber, *Handbook of the Indians of California.*

— ROBERT F. SPENCER

Z

ZENGER TRIAL

From his arrival in 1732 William Cosby, colonial governor of New York, provoked controversy. His prosecution of the interim governor, Rip Van Dam, and his removal of Chief Justice Lewis Morris stirred up an opposition party. This group established John Peter Zenger as printer of the *New-York Weekly Journal*, first published Nov. 5, 1733, and the first newspaper in America to be the organ of a political faction. Strictures published in this paper led the governor to have Zenger arrested and put in jail. His cause became that of the people, and when the governor arbitrarily debarred his New York counsel, his case was taken by Andrew Hamilton of Philadelphia, the most distinguished advocate in the colonies. It was tried Aug. 4, 1735.

The printer was charged with seditious libel. Hamilton admitted the publication, but denied that it was a libel unless false and sought to prove the truth of the statements. The court held that the fact of publication was sufficient to convict and excluded the truth from evidence. Hamilton made an eloquent appeal to the jury to judge both the law and the fact, and the verdict was "not guilty." Zenger was released, and the Common Council voted Hamilton the "Freedom of the Corporation." It was a notable victory for the freedom of the press and set a precedent against judicial tyranny in libel suits.

BIBLIOGRAPHY

Livingston Rutherfurd, *John Peter Zenger.*

— MILTON W. HAMILTON

ZIMMERMAN TELEGRAM

Tensions between the United States and Germany, arising from German submarine action during World War I, resulted in U.S. severance of diplomatic relations with Germany on Feb. 3, 1917. On Feb. 24 the British delivered to the U.S. ambassador in London an intercepted German telegram, dated Jan. 19, declaring that unrestricted submarine warfare would begin on Feb. 1. The note, sent by German Foreign Secretary Arthur Zimmerman to the German minister in Mexico, expressed the fear that the United States would then not remain neutral and directed the minister to arrange an alliance between Mexico and Germany and to urge Japan to switch to the German side. Mexico was to attack the United States on its Southwestern border and recover Texas, New Mexico, and Arizona. The publication of the note on Mar. 1 caused popular indignation against Germany to mount and was an important factor in the affirmative response of the U.S. Congress to President Woodrow Wilson's Apr. 2 request for a declaration of war against Germany.

BIBLIOGRAPHY

Barbara W. Tuchman, *The Zimmerman Telegram.*

— RICHARD E. YATES

Index

B

F

G

I

J

L

O

S